HOOVER'S HANDBOOK

PROFILES OF OVER 500 MAJOR CORPORATIONS

EDITED BY

GARY HOOVER

ALTA CAMPBELL

PATRICK J. SPAIN

The financial data (How Much section and Where and What tables) in this book are from a variety of sources. Standard & Poor's Compustat, Inc., provided data for most of the US publicly traded companies, US private companies with public debt, and foreign companies with American Depository Receipts (ADRs). Some of the data for mutual life insurance companies are from *Fortune*'s annual Service 500 list. Information on the advertising industry and advertising expenditures by companies in this book is from *Advertising Age*. Data on the beverage and real estate industries are from *Beverage Industry* and *National Real Estate Investor* magazines, respectively. Some data for private companies are from the *Forbes* 400 US Private Companies list. Information on the legal, consulting, and accounting industries is from *The National Law Journal*, *Consultants News*, and *Public Accounting Report*, respectively. The Reference Press obtained other information directly from the enterprises profiled and from other public sources. The Reference Press, Inc., is solely responsible for the presentation of this data.

The Reference Press, Inc.

10 9 8 7 6 5 4 3 2 1

Publisher Cataloging-In-Publication Data

HOOVER'S HANDBOOK: Profiles of Over 500 Major Corporations. Edited by Gary Hoover, Alta Campbell, and Patrick J. Spain

Includes indexes.

1. Business enterprises—Directories. 2. Corporations — Directories.

HF3010 338.7

ISBN 1-878753-00-2

This book was produced in house by The Reference Press on Apple Macintosh computers using Aldus PageMaker 4.0 and Adobe fonts from the Clearface and Futura families. It was output to a Linotronic 300 imagesetter by RJL Graphics of Austin, Texas, and printed by Crest Litho Inc. at Watervliet, New York, on International Paper's Springhill paper (text 60 lb. offset, cover 10 point).

This book is distributed to the North American book trade exclusively by

PUBLISHERS GROUP WEST

4065 Hollis, Emeryville, California 94608 415-658-3453

HOOVER'S HANDBOOK is available at special discounts for bulk purchases for sales promotions, premiums, fund-raising, or educational use. Special editions or book excerpts can also be created to specification. For details, contact **The Reference Press, Inc.**, 6448 Highway 290 E., Suite E-104, Austin, Texas 78723 Phone: 512-454-7778 FAX: 512-454-9401

Contents

Companies Profiled

A PERSONAL NOTE FROM GARY HOOVER

I grew up in Anderson, Indiana, a General Motors factory town. I was amazed by the pervasive role of that enterprise in Anderson. Equally amazing, my friends and teachers seemed to know very little about GM. Bookstores were of no help either.

In the intervening 25 years, I have worked for three giant corporations and started two smaller ones, the most recent being The Reference Press, publisher of this book. My story, and that of The Reference Press, is told on page 457.

This book would not exist if I had not wanted it for myself, as I have ever since those years in Anderson. This book would not exist if I had not used much of my own money to fund the start-up of The Reference Press. Most important, this book would not exist were it not for people.

Enterprise — the act of getting people to try something new — is entirely a human endeavor. No enterprise — whether General Motors, the Red Cross, or The Reference Press — succeeds without the participation of individual men and women, sometimes hundreds of thousands of them. In the case of this book, about 60 people; they are named on the following page. I thank those people for making my ideal book a real book, and I dedicate it to them.

I finally have, in my hands, a book that tells the story of our major enterprises — from General Motors on down. I think it is a useful book and hope you will agree. Please use the postage-paid postcards in the back of the book to give us ideas that will make next year's edition even better.

Gary Hoover
Austin, Texas
October 1990

ACKNOWLEDGMENTS

Publisher and Senior Editor: Gary Hoover (GH)
Editor-in-Chief: Alta Campbell
Senior Editor: Patrick J. Spain (PJS)
Senior Writer: Alan Chai (AC)
Production Director: Holly Whitten
Desktop Publishing Director: Marcia Jenkins
Publishing Consultant: Ray Bard, Bard Productions
Office Manager: Tammy Fisher

Senior Writers
Cliff Avery (CA), Dale Ann Bean-Underwood (DAB), Scott A. Blech (SAB), John Mark Haney (JMH)

Contributing Writers
Sharon Adams (SA), John T. Cathey (JTC), Frank Arthur Dunaway (FAD), Paul A. Garlinghouse (PAG), Geri Hoekzema (GSH), Linda R. Kelly (LK), Tom Linehan (TL), Tom Logan (TWL), Glen F. Martin (GFM), Elloa M. Mathews (EMM), Todd Nichols (TN), Rebecca L. Salinger (RLS), David Henry Sanders (DHS), Polly Ragatz Huntsman Tagg (PRHT), Leslie Townsend (LT), Patrick J. Underwood (PJU), Trevor Zelman (TZ)

Financial Editor
Michael P. McNamara

Senior Editors
Cynthia G. Dooley, Lawrence A. Hagemann, Jeff Morris, Deborah Stratton

Contributing Editors
Kathy Bork, Jon Hockenyos, Allan L. Reagan

Senior Proofreaders and Fact Checkers
Peter A. Balderas, K. C. Francis, Susan K. Hausmann, Barbara E. Wand

Proofreaders and Fact Checkers
Kathryn A. Baker, Roxanne Bogucka (RB), Jane H. Chamberlain, Jacqueline Corcoran, Tara Ellis, Linda L. Gittins, Maria Veres Homic, Britton E. Jackson, Gene Krane, Kathleen A. Magor, Jeanne Minnich, Jim Patterson, Barbara M. Spain, Lori Vermaas

Senior Desktop Publishers
Scott T. Allen, Kristin M. Jackson, Lisa C. Norman

Desktop Publishers
Lana R. Castle, Patricia Gaddis, Marcille E. Godwin, Holly G. Hans, Karen J. Kezele, Fred A. Meredith, Mercedes Newman, Donna G. Rawls, Richard W. Shannon, Susan E. Weikum

Indexers
Alana Cash, Linda Webster

Other Contributors
Janet D. Dooley, Jeanine Gaddis, Barbara Jezek, Marsha F. Kearns, Pamela Kern, Mark Longley, Jack Moncure, Linda K. Oats, Daniel Quinn, Rennie M. Quinn, Deborah A. Uhlman

Note: At the bottom of each profile, we have placed the initials of the writer(s) responsible for that page.

TEST YOUR BUSINESS I.Q.

(Questions on the Back Cover)

Answers: The correct answer to all four questions is c.

The largest U.S. S&L, H. F. Ahmanson (see profile on page 60), is making $200 million a year and is fit as a fiddle.

The world's three biggest automakers are General Motors (page 255), Ford (page 243), and Toyota (page 537).

PepsiCo (page 430) operates or franchises over 18,000 fast-food restaurants under the names Kentucky Fried Chicken, Pizza Hut, and Taco Bell, making it the largest fast-food chain in the world.

Since its acquisition of SOHIO, British Petroleum (page 138) has become the largest oil producer in the 50 states, largely because of its presence on the Alaskan North Slope.

ABOUT *HOOVER'S HANDBOOK*

The core of this book is 542 one-page profiles of major enterprises, of all types, from around the world. These profiles are arranged alphabetically. They contain basic information on the nature of each enterprise, its history, the people who run it, the products or services it delivers, and its financial performance.

This information can be considered required reading for anyone interviewing for a job with, selling products or services to, buying from, competing with, or considering investing in one of these enterprises.

The profiles are preceded by two other types of information. First, immediately following this page, we have included some ideas about how to use and understand the information in the book. This section includes a basic explanation of corporations and the way they are measured, recommendations for further reading, and a glossary explaining the corporate takeover terms that are frequently encountered in the book. We have tried to explain business in plain English, assuming little or no prior knowledge. Second, we have included a number of lists of the largest companies, compiled from our own data and many other sources.

Following the profiles are four indexes: first, a list of broad industry groupings and the enterprises in each group; second, an index of the profiled enterprises by headquarters location; third, an index of people named in the profiles; and fourth, the main index of the book, which lists all enterprises and products named in the profiles. ♦

GETTING THE MOST OUT OF *HOOVER'S HANDBOOK*

Because of the pervasive nature of business corporations, we at The Reference Press believe we can all benefit from a better understanding of these giant enterprises. Certainly, if we are thinking about buying stock, we need to know what to look for, how to predict which businesses will be successful, and how to judge and measure the performance of a company. But it is becoming equally important to judge the performance of corporations as employers, suppliers, and customers. We can no longer assume that, just because a business is big, it is permanent, or that it is a secure place to work. Most of us were born into a world where "the Big Three" meant GM, Ford, and Chrysler; within 10 years, we may find that Asia and Europe each has one of "the Big Three," perhaps all three.

You will notice that we have included 29 selected nonprofit and governmental enterprises in this book. These enterprises, not unlike business corporations, hire and fire people; they must garner adequate capital to function; and they too must exercise vision if they are to prosper in a changing world. Whether you are thinking about working for one of them or donating money to them, it is equally important to have some idea of what they are about and how well they are run.

Thousands of business strategists, analysts, journalists, and managers spend their lifetimes trying to figure out what's important in business, what separates the winners from the losers. Thousands of books and articles have been written on topics from management methods to marketing tactics. While *HOOVER'S HANDBOOK* does not pretend to be a textbook, we believe the book will be most useful if you have a basic grasp of the key issues in business.

In the following pages, we've tried to concisely and clearly explain some of these key concepts. First, we address the big picture — the study of why businesses do the things they do. This approach is called strategic analysis or economic analysis.

Second, we look at financial analysis — the study of the financial performance of businesses. This section also touches on key concepts useful to investors.

We then describe how to use each profile and its components, and end with a brief section of recommendations for further reading and a glossary of takeover terms.

THE BIG PICTURE

ENTERPRISES

The 542 organizations profiled in this book are best described as enterprises. Some are large, with bold objectives: the best example is the United States of America. Most began with more humble goals. These enterprises deliver a variety of products and services, from ketchup to hammers, from Ph.D. degrees to surgery. To illustrate the diversity of enterprises at work in the world around us, we have included public companies and private companies, U.S. companies and foreign companies, and even several nonprofit and governmental entities.

Nevertheless, all can be called enterprises. Each began in the mind of one person or a small group of people. To have made it to the size and influence required to be included in this book, they must have enlisted more people over time. To one degree or another, these people must share the same underlying goals. For an enterprise, whether private or public, for profit or not, is simply a group of people who have joined together in pursuit of a common goal.

Business Enterprises

Most of the enterprises in this book are business enterprises. These differ primarily from nonbusiness organizations in the way they are financed. Whether General Motors or the Red Cross, enterprises need money. Governments usually get most of their funds from taxation. Universities and religious and service organizations generally rely on the charitable instincts of people who share their interests.

By definition, business enterprises are funded by private capital. These enterprises cannot rely on taxation or on charitable solicitation. Instead, they must find investors or lenders. The most fundamental source of financing for private enterprise is equity capital (selling stock), which is further described later in this section.

In order to persuade people or financial institutions to invest their savings in a business enterprise, that enterprise must offer the promise of a financial reward, or return. While this book is full of stories of successful enterprises, others here have not been good investments.

When industry began evolving from individual craftspeople and cottage industry, requiring larger groups of people to maximize the technology of the industrial revolution, business was usually financed by people who already had a great deal of capital: often those who had inherited land from their feudal ancestors.

As more and more individuals, such as small merchants and skilled craftspeople, began to prosper from this revolution, there was no way for them to readily participate in large business ventures, other than by working for a paycheck. This new middle class, with modest savings, could not become part owners of a major enterprise. While they were interested in participating in the profits of these enterprises, they could not afford to take the risks involved.

The most traditional forms of business enterprise are the sole proprietorship and the partnership. In a sole proprietorship, you put everything you own at risk. If your business goes broke or gets sued successfully, you can lose your house and all your other personal property. The same is true of partners in a general partnership. Even if you put up $5 and your partner $1,000,000, people owed money by the partnership could come after you for everything you've got. This high level of risk prevented small investors from sharing in the success of great enterprises.

The Corporation

It seems a natural evolution that society figured out a way around this. The idea of incorporation is that a business enterprise is an entity unto itself, that the individuals putting up the money are not personally liable for all the debts and problems of the enterprise. If you buy stock in a corporation, your risk or liability is limited to the amount you invest. In the U.S., we use the term "corporation"; in France, the equivalent of "anonymous society" (SA); and in the United Kingdom, "public limited company" (PLC), stressing the limited-liability aspect of the corporate entity.

When the concept of the corporation was first invented, it was considered revolutionary. Even economist Adam Smith thought the concept was a fad that would not last, one of his few obvious errors of prediction. Today, the corporation is taken for granted. Many of us who work for corporations underestimate the power of this invention.

The concept of incorporation, in whatever language, has allowed millions of people to share in the fruits of enterprise, whether their own enterprise or that of others. The corporate form of business organization has allowed massive projects to be undertaken and new ideas to be tried — ideas that would never have seen the light of day were they dependent on taxes, charity, or the willingness of sole proprietors and partners to risk everything they had.

The business corporation pervades our lives. Most of us work for one, be it large or small. Virtually everything we consume comes from one. And whether we buy stocks or bonds directly, put our money into mutual funds or pension programs, or loan it to banks or life insurance companies, much of our savings ends up financing business corporations.

THE ROLE OF DEMAND

Any understanding of a company must first start with a basic grasp of the industry that the company competes in. And that industry perspective starts with the demand for the products or services produced by the industry. In looking at any company, three questions must precede all others:

1. How much of the product or service do people (or other companies) buy?
2. How much of it do they buy from the enterprise under consideration, compared to what they buy from competitors (market share)?
3. How easily can customers substitute some other product?

All products, from diamonds to bread, have unique characteristics, but none are as important as these three. All companies have their own attributes, as discussed in the following pages, but none are as critical as these three.

The nature of the soap company, whose products almost everyone uses, is different from the jet engine maker who sells to a few. The maker of specialized orthopedic shoes looks at the world differently than the mass producer of sneakers; he or she faces a different world. If your company has a market share leader like Kodak film or Heinz ketchup, the challenges are vastly different from those for a new, young competitor. Most business enterprises have products that are well established as well as new, experimental products. The makers of slide rules found out the hard way that their product was replaceable when the more powerful but inexpensive pocket calculator came into being.

What answers should we look for to these three questions? While each case is unique, a company is generally in pretty good shape if everybody uses lots of the product, doesn't buy it from anybody else, and can't substitute anything for it. Aside from government-endorsed monopolies like electric utilities, we can't think of any case in this book in which a company can respond to all three questions with such strong answers.

That is what makes business such a challenge for the people who manage it.

Changing Demand

Of equal importance to the three answers is the trend in the answers: in other words, for each question, is the answer this year the same as the answer last year? Is the answer getting better or worse? A lot better or a little better? A lot worse or a little worse? To understand the direction of change over time (better or worse) and the rate of change over time (a lot or a little), we can rephrase the three questions:

1. Are people buying more or less of the product or service each year?
2. Is this firm's market share rising or falling?
3. Are people more often substituting other products, or is the product becoming more entrenched?

The direction of change (up or down) is the starting point here. A company with rising demand for its products (for example, VCRs) has a more promising future than the maker of black-and-white TV sets. The company with a rising market share (Toyota) is headed in a better direction than the firm that's losing share (General Motors). At one time the telegraph and the telephone were competitors; railroads and airlines fought over passengers. In each case, correctly picking the survivor paid off for investors and employees alike.

Any analysis of trends must also pay attention to the rate or relative size of change. For example, your company shipped 9,000 items last year and 10,000 this year and crows about the increase of 1,000 to all within earshot. But are you listening to the competitor who went from 1,000 to 2,000 in the same period of time? Next year, will they just gain 1,000 again, or will they double again, to 4,000? Any analysis of change must focus on the percentage rate of change, which was 11% (increased by 1/9) for your firm but 100% (doubled) for your smaller competitor.

The Customer

Whether we look at the absolute level (how much) or the rate of change (what percent), understanding demand is the starting point for understanding any enterprise. For those charged with the task of managing an enterprise, this means that nothing is more important than understanding the customer and the customer's needs.

We believe that the managers of the successful enterprises in this book generally follow three simple rules with regard to their customers:

1. These managers put themselves in the shoes of their customers and follow The Golden Rule. They treat their customers the way they would like to be treated. They use, and believe in, their own products. When Lee Iacocca starts driving a Toyota, it's time to sell your Chrysler stock.
2. These managers go out of their way to know the characteristics of their customers. Where do they live? How old are they? How much money do they make? How much schooling do they have? Are they single or do they have families? If customers are individuals or families, the answers to these demographic questions are discovered by market research (*e.g.*, surveys) and by studying the census. If customers are other businesses, many of the answers are in this book.
3. These managers do everything in their power to ensure that potential customers know that the company's products and services exist, and know where to find them.

Once we understand the demand for a company's products and whether the firm is gaining or losing market share (and at what rate), we can look at the other ways in which industries and companies differ.

COMPARING INDUSTRIES

Each industry has its own unique set of characteristics that go beyond basic demand and that affect every company in the industry.

Cyclicality versus stability

The home-building industry goes up and down with mortgage interest rates and other factors. Stockbrokers prosper in good markets and lose customers after crashes. On the other hand, the demand for toothpaste and shoes is pretty reliable. The cyclical company must be prepared for the natural cycles it will experience; on the other hand, Coke is more worried about market share and Pepsi than about year-to-year swings in total soft drink demand.

Business products and services versus consumer products and services

The skills required by Walt Disney are vastly different from those required by Caterpillar. Selling millions of $5 movie tickets or $30 videocassettes is a radically different proposition from selling bulldozers at $500,000 apiece. Cat requires fewer but longer sales calls; Disney announces its products with ads and opens the doors. Disney doesn't even know the names of all of its customers. Some companies with expertise in selling to businesses have tried and failed to sell to individual consumers, and vice versa.

Different Price Points

There is also a big difference between selling $10,000 cars and $50,000 cars and between selling $300 washing machines and rolls of toilet paper. Marketing skills demonstrated in one area may not be successful at different price points. Higher-priced items usually require more effort per sale on the part of both buyer and seller than small, inexpensive things.

Commodities versus differentiated products

When you buy gasoline, you know pretty much what you're getting. Commodities are simple products, often made in huge quantities by many firms. Usually, the most important factor in picking whom you'll buy from is price. Texaco couldn't sell gas at $5 a gallon next door to a Shell station selling it for $.50. At least Texaco wouldn't sell much. However, determining the difference between Giorgio perfume and Obsession is much trickier. Individual emotions and tastes come into play. The two products do not appear the same to the consumer. Novels by James Michener are not exact substitutes for those of Sidney Sheldon. Most companies in this book try to differentiate their products from those of the competition; some are successful and some are not.

There are many other ways that industries differ; the four listed above are among the most common. There is nothing inherently good or bad about a cyclical industry or a commodity-producing company. But a company's odds of prospering are greatest if demand is stable and growing and if that company has successfully differentiated its products or services from those of the competition.

COMPARING COMPANIES

Within any industry, each company may take any number of approaches. Which approaches it takes are what managers are paid to decide. The individual characteristics of a company include attributes relating to strategy, financing, and managing.

Comparing Companies: Strategy

Every company has a strategy, whether expressed or not. Those firms with no apparent strategy can be considered to have haphazardness as a strategy. Companies can also have the same strategy year after year or change strategies periodically, sometimes falling into haphazard phases. Perhaps more than any other aspect of a company, strategy is a direct reflection of the views of the people at the top.

Consistency

In general, the most successful companies in this book are those that have kept a clear vision in place for many years. McDonald's, while a relatively young company, has not diversified out of restaurants or even into coffee shops. For them, adding seats and adding breakfast were big changes.

At the same time, it is pointless to stick to strategies that time has passed by. When the railroads first lost their passenger business to airlines, and then most of their small freight business to truckers, they were forced to review their status. The successful ones have emerged as huge haulers of bulky commodities such as grain and coal and of heavy products like automobiles. Many of our older industries have had to develop creative strategies to adjust to changing times, new technologies, and foreign competition.

Diversification

Probably the single most common method of shifting strategy is to diversify. While this term generally connotes moving into whole new fields of endeavor, it can also take three other forms:

1. **Geographical diversification.** One of the most fundamental forms of growth is to take a good idea to new territory. Holiday Inns started in Memphis and worked outward; Wal-Mart began in Arkansas and is still in only 32 states. Coca-Cola early in its history began peddling its product in Mexico and Canada and now sells worldwide.
2. **Horizontal diversification.** This term, from economics, means to diversify by buying competitors or similar companies in other locations. The giant trusts of the late 19th and early 20th centuries (for example, U.S. Steel) were formed by combining most of the major companies in an industry. Our largest trash collectors, Browning-Ferris and Waste Management, were originally formed by buying up local and regional mom-and-pop operations.
3. **Vertical diversification, more commonly referred to as vertical integration.** This means buying up your customers and/or your suppliers. At one time, Henry Ford's River Rouge plant in Detroit made its own steel and glass, and finished Fords rolled off the other end of the production line. Integrated oil companies are those with wells, refineries, and filling stations.

Geographical, horizontal, and vertical diversification are all well-established strategies for increasing the size and competitiveness of a company. In the 1960s and 1970s, more companies began to diversify into vastly different fields.

The term *conglomerate* came into use in the 1960s to describe firms that operated in several unrelated industries. Managers of these firms came to believe they could manage anything, that the basics of running a steel mill were no different from those of running an airline. While managers undoubtedly will continue this debate, the companies in this book indicate that prosperity is easier to achieve when an enterprise is focused, or at least sticks to fields with something in common. While Sears retail stores seem different from Allstate car insurance, the company originally sold the insurance to its retail customers. Sears's later introduction of the Discover Credit Card was a natural outgrowth of its experiences with its own Sears credit operation.

This book contains only 27 enterprises that were so diversified that we could not assign them to some broad industry group. While almost all the firms have diversified to one degree or another, most have remained in fields that are in some way related, such as mass-marketed consumer products. Most of the diversified companies are in two or three industries. General Electric stands out as one company that is an industry leader in several businesses that are, at best, only vaguely related.

Technology and Innovation

Each company can also take any number of roads with regard to innovation. Fred Smith at Federal Express created a whole new industry. Some companies take a good idea and apply it in a different way: Home Depot is the application of the Toys "R" Us concept of giant, low-priced specialty stores to home-improvement retailing. Other companies are truly clones: Amdahl was founded to make copies of IBM mainframe computers for a lower price. Costco Wholesale applied the Price Company concept in another part of the U.S.

While successful innovators can reap substantial rewards, they also entail substantial risk. The first successful large computer was the UNIVAC, made by a predecessor of Unisys. A late entrant to the field, IBM, made more money from the idea. The large general merchandise discount store was created by small, entrepreneurial companies. But no one executed the idea as successfully as K mart, until the even later entry of Wal-Mart.

While innovation often comes from small, entrepreneurial enterprises, this is not always the case. Minnesota Mining and Manufacturing (3M) is an unusual company that seems to specialize in innovation, from Scotch tape to Post-it notes. This tradition continues even as 3M grows larger and larger.

Whether we look at technology in computers, in chicken growing, or in toy stores, the management of each company must decide whether it will be a leader or a follower, which technologies to bet on, and how much to bet.

This book includes successful companies that have taken many routes with regard to innovation. The one common denominator of the successful enterprises is that they make quality products, year after year after year.

Comparing Companies: Financing

Business corporations have a number of choices as to how they finance themselves. Their first choice is whether to sell shares of stock to raise money or to borrow the money. While all companies have stock, they can have no debt, some debt, or a great deal of debt. The companies in this book range from zero indebtedness to several billion dollars of debt. This debt can take many forms, including bank loans and direct loans from individual or corporate investors (*e.g.*, bonds, debentures, commercial paper, mortgages). The heavy use of debt (called leverage) can increase the returns to shareholders but also entails substantial risk. The distinctions between debt and equity and the risks of leverage are further examined in the financial analysis section, starting on page 18.

Another decision is whether to operate as a public or a private company. Most corporations are private, also called privately held or closely held corporations. Most, but not all, of the biggest corporations are public companies, or publicly held.

Private companies do not sell stock to the general public; while they may have thousands of shareholders, most are owned primarily by family members, managers, or employees. You cannot call a stockbroker and buy or sell shares. It is harder to get your money out of an investment in a private company (an "illiquid" investment). Private companies cannot raise money as easily as public companies, since they do not have access to the public stock markets. On the other hand, private companies are not required by law to reveal information about themselves, and some are indeed very secretive. This book includes more than 50 private companies.

Public companies, since their stock is available to anyone who calls a stockbroker, are required by the Securities and Exchange Commission (SEC) to report their sales and profits quarterly and to produce a full report to shareholders annually. When you call a broker and buy or sell stock in a public company, the transaction is normally executed in a matter of minutes; therefore, common stocks of public companies are "very liquid." Stocks can be traded on the New York Stock Exchange (NYSE, or Big Board), the American Stock Exchange, or the Over-the-Counter (OTC) market, the most important part of which is NASDAQ (National Association of Securities Dealers Automatic Quote system). Most of the largest U.S. companies are listed on the NYSE.

Most companies begin life as private companies; when and if they decide to sell stock, they are said to "go public" through an Initial Public Offering (IPO). At that time, the SEC requires that they publish a prospectus detailing virtually every aspect of their business and management. Because these documents are so revealing, smart potential investors pore over prospectuses.

Public companies can also "go private," a practice virtually unknown 15 years ago. This recent financing strategy most commonly occurs in the form of the leveraged buyout (LBO). In an LBO, a small group of investors borrows enough money to buy all the stock in a company on the stock market. This investor group usually includes an investment firm specializing in LBOs (for example, Kohlberg Kravis Roberts). The group often includes the management of the company being bought out. LBOs require huge amounts of debt — up to billions of dollars. Often, the debt is in the form of "junk bonds" sold directly to the public — a concept we will return to in the financial analysis section.

Because of the rise of LBOs, there are now several companies whose stock is privately held (by the investor group) but whose bonds (debt) are publicly held. RJR Nabisco is a good example of this. While technically not publicly held, such companies are required by the SEC to release substantial information because the public can loan money to these enterprises (that is, buy bonds issued by the companies).

Comparing Companies: Management

Perhaps the most important differences between the companies in this book are their management styles. While strategies and financing methods reflect management, there are also more direct ways to compare managers.

One of the most common ways of dividing managements is into centralized and decentralized management. The idea here is that, prior to Alfred P. Sloan's innovations at General Motors in the 1920s, most companies were run "from the top down," with all key decisions made by very few people at headquarters, often by one person. Sloan developed the idea of passing authority and responsibility "down the line." Heads of divisions and other operating units were considered closer to the customer and were entrusted with more power. Sloan's ideas were widely copied in organizations worldwide.

Today, the distinctions have become blurred: it is not uncommon for a company to have highly centralized financial controls, while production and other decisions are decentralized. Other companies change their approach periodically, and yet others give decentralization lip service without much reality behind it. Also, such questions of management structure are not readily discernible from annual reports and other company literature; you really have to talk to the people who work in the organization.

Another difference among these companies is their management style, or corporate culture. It has become very stylish to talk about corporate culture. This very broad subject can cover everything from dress (blue jeans or pinstripes) to reward systems (based on seniority or contribution to sales and profits). An enterprise's culture is usually a direct reflection of the personalities of its leaders.

An aspect of management that is less discussed is the profession of the people at the top. While, as top executives, they are defined as "management," these people worked their way up through more specific fields: finance, marketing, engineering, law, operations or production, etc. Years ago, people were classified in broad groups like doctors, lawyers, and businessmen. But to call a printer or a broadcaster or a carmaker a businessman or businesswoman is not very useful. These are very different professions. Companies that really understand their own strengths often have clear ideas about what skills are most important at the top. Pharmaceutical maker Merck is run by a man with a Ph.D. whose strength is research; Dow Jones is run by journalists; Disney is run by an entertainment professional; and Coke is run by a lifelong Coke marketer. We believe that much of the success of these companies flows from having the right type of people in the top jobs.

COMPLETING THE PICTURE

Before descending into the mathematical details of financial analysis, we believe there are two last viewpoints that are important to a broad understanding of business: the view that each enterprise evolves over time, and the view that enterprise is a human activity. While these two perspectives may seem obvious, it is not uncommon for analysts to financially analyze a company "six ways to Sunday" without having completed the big picture; these two brief sections put the final touches on that picture.

The Natural Evolution of Enterprises

As can be seen from the above comments, every enterprise is unique. And yet, they do share one process: like living organisms, they grow, evolve, and mature. Each enterprise begins as an idea, usually on the part of one person or a small group of people. This idea, or invention, can be a product or a way of doing things, from service to production. In order to succeed, it should represent a better or more efficient way; it should add value. This is often described as "finding a need and filling it."

Many of the companies in this book took roundabout routes to their "destinies" — Armstrong made bottle corks before floors; Cummins Engine was based on the tinkerings of a banker's chauffeur. Other creative products were discovered by accident. Once a company "hits stride," mass-producing a commercially viable product or service, early growth is usually rapid.

As an enterprise ages, this growth slows, eventually to very low growth (no higher than the growth of the overall economy). This fast growth–medium growth–slow growth cycle is called the S-curve, based on the shape shown here.

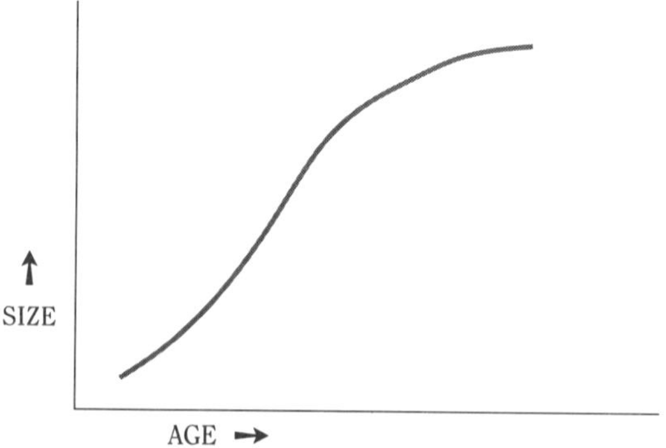

As companies evolve along this curve, they become more established, more structured, and usually more bureaucratic. As they grow, they can become more focused on protecting their assets than on inventing new products and services. In this way, they become vulnerable to the attacks of the next generation of entrepreneurs coming along, who have less to lose but more to gain through innovation.

While it has become all the vogue to praise the achievements of entrepreneurs, we often forget that managing a mature enterprise can be a very difficult challenge. At the same time that a company is at its wealthiest, with the largest number of jobs and lives depending on it, it is often also at its most vulnerable, and perhaps about to "die."

Death comes to enterprises differently than it does to living organisms. It often takes many years and is at first unrecognizable. Those closest to the company may refuse to face up to the realities. Companies with big bank accounts, many offices, and established reputations may rest on their laurels for many years before they are forced to admit that their time has come. Death, for a business enterprise, is more often a period of confusion, selling and closing facilities, and perhaps selling the whole company, rather than a sudden, single event. Even companies that have entered bankruptcy often reemerge, usually in a much smaller form.

The large corporation, unlike a living organism, can be reborn. The S. S. Kresge company of 1960 was a tired chain of variety stores, third in the industry after Woolworth and W. T. Grant. Sales and earnings were going nowhere. A manager named Harry Cunningham convinced top management to try a new concept: K mart. Thirty years later, Grant is gone (fatal bankruptcy) and Woolworth is a fraction of the size of the renamed K mart Corporation. Today, that enterprise must in turn react to relative newcomer Wal-Mart.

Sears, Roebuck was a mail-order giant selling to rural and small-town America. If they'd stayed like that, they'd be gone today. As an encore, they became a dominant retailer for America's suburbs. The icing on the cake was their successful entry into financial services, first by insuring cars. Today, Sears appears to be at another crossroads: their giant retail chain is losing market share to dozens of new competitors and struggling to find a role to play in the marketplace of the 1990s. Whether Sears will again revitalize itself is one of the many unfinished corporate life stories in this book.

No analysis of an enterprise is complete without a good grasp of whether that enterprise is a child, an adolescent, or in some later stage of life.

The Human Nature of Enterprise

It is easy to become overfocused on the strategies of businesses and on the ways we measure their performance. It is equally easy to forget that each enterprise is fundamentally a human endeavor. No computer can plan strategies, no computer can hire and fire people, no computer can motivate people. Balance sheets and profit and loss statements do not tell the underlying story of the people in an organization. Yet, each organization really consists only of people and tools for people to use.

As a successful enterprise evolves, more people must be attracted to "the cause." In order to maintain leadership, the corporation must attract and keep talented people. These people must remain creative and responsive to their ever-changing environment.

Whether Sears survives is up to the people of Sears. Whether 3M continues to develop innovative products depends on 3M's people. Every enterprise in this book reflects the people of that enterprise: the people of the past, the present, and the future. ♦

THE NUMBERS MADE SIMPLE

The preceding sections give us a grasp of a business — its industry, its strategies, its evolution, and its people. With this foundation in place, we can proceed to more detailed and quantitative financial analysis.

Organizations are expected to perform in a number of ways: serving customers well, creating jobs, providing secure jobs, etc. In general, the company that is performing well financially is better able to perform these other tasks well. The firm that is losing money or buried in debt is less likely to provide secure jobs or to serve customers well. Measures of financial performance are therefore key to anyone interested in the enterprise; they also tend to be more consistently applied and less subjective than most measures of product quality, job satisfaction, company reputation, etc.

If you are familiar with business accounting or have invested, you know there are a bewildering array of measures that can be used to judge the financial performance of companies. The most fundamental measure of any company's financial success, however, is return on investment (ROI).

RETURN ON INVESTMENT

ROI is best understood if we remember that business corporations are financed by people's savings, whether those savings are invested directly by individuals or via institutions like banks, insurance companies, mutual funds, and pension funds. When you invest your savings, you should earn a return on them. The first question to ask is, "How much return?"

When you loan money to anyone, you first give up the use of the money. Even if you trust your neighbor a great deal and know that she's going to take the $1,000 you loan her for a year and put it in a safe deposit box, she should pay you interest. For the next year, you will not have the use of the money; should you have an emergency, you cannot get it back. Maybe at the end of the year you plan on buying a $1,000 stereo with it; in the meantime, you could buy the stereo now and enjoy a year's use of it. The value of the temporary sacrifice of cash is called the time value of money, and it is the first reason we need to get interest, or a return, on our money. The time value of money alone may only justify a very small rate of return — perhaps as low as 1% per year.

The next reason we need to earn a return on our money is inflation. While history has had several periods of deflation (declining prices), the economic boom times of the late 19th century and the 20th century have been characterized by inflation, usually in the 2-5% per year range. So the $1,000 stereo you want to buy may cost 5% more, or $1,050, a year from now. If you think inflation will be higher, you (as an investor or lender) need to ask for a higher rate of interest.

The next layer of determining a fair rate of return is the level of risk involved. Your neighbor may lose the $1,000 you loan her or not be able to pay the money back for other reasons. While we can get lulled into believing that big companies are all secure, cases such as W. T. Grant, Penn Central, Continental Illinois Bank, and Drexel Burnham Lambert teach us otherwise. Every company has some degree of risk.

In developing anticipated rates of return, we start with the "risk-free" interest rate, for which we use the rate of interest paid by the United States government for short-term loans like Treasury Bills (T Bills). While the U.S. government is not really risk-free, it is as close as we can come. If the government did collapse, we'd probably all have a lot more to worry about than getting our loans repaid. Normally, the rate of interest paid by the government is slightly above anticipated inflation — enough to also cover the time value of money. As of September 1990, T Bills were paying about 7.5% a year in interest.

The "risk premium" — the amount of additional interest charged for riskier loans — varies with the risk. At the time that the government was paying 7.5%, General Motors Acceptance Corporation (GMAC), one of the biggest corporate borrowers, was paying about 7.9% when it borrowed from individual investors (through a security called commercial paper). Big corporations borrowing from banks or borrowing money for long time periods (bonds) were paying 9-10%. New start-up enterprises are much riskier than big, established ones, so the rates they pay must be higher to reflect the higher risk.

DEBT VERSUS EQUITY

Another fundamental concept in understanding corporate finance is that money can be invested in an enterprise in two different ways — by loaning money to a company (debt) or by buying part ownership in the company (equity). Bonds and debentures are debt; stocks represent equity. The fundamental differences between debt and equity are three:

1. Debts are intended to be repaid. If you borrow $50,000 you are expected to repay the $50,000 principal, as well as interest on the loan. When a company sells you a $50,000 bond, it is under the same obligations. On the other hand, when you buy $50,000 worth of stock, whether from the company itself or from another stockholder, the company does not plan ever to give you your $50,000 back. You can earn a return on stock only by selling it to someone else at a higher price or by receiving dividends from the company. Often, stockholders get both.
2. The interest payments on a debt are usually fixed and guaranteed. You know how much you'll receive and how often. Dividends on a stock, on the other hand, are strictly voluntary on the part of a company. The board of directors can reduce or delete them (or increase them) at any time. In reality, a company that goes broke usually defaults on debt payments, but this occurs after they've stopped paying dividends on stock.
3. If a company is dissolved or liquidated, debt-holders (creditors) have higher priority than stockholders: the debt-holders get their money first. In a bankruptcy, it is not unusual for debt-holders to get $.50 for every dollar owed them, while stockholders are wiped out. This is called "liquidation preference."

Taken together, these different characteristics of debt and equity mean that equity bears more risk but can carry higher rewards. Let's say your neighbor has a great new invention and needs $10,000. You have the $10,000 to spare. He says you can loan it to him or buy half-interest in the invention. If the idea fails, you may get the loan back, but the half-interest becomes worthless. If, however, he has another Xerox or IBM, the loan will only get back $10,000 plus interest — no more, no less. If you buy the half-interest, and the idea is a home run, there is no real limit on what your equity might be worth.

To use common business buzz words, debt has limited downside and limited upside. It does not share in the benefits of an enormously successful enterprise. On the other hand, equity has big downside and big upside — more to lose and more to gain.

FINANCIAL STATEMENTS

While most businesses pour forth a multitude of statements and reports, there are two that tell the financial story of an enterprise: the balance sheet and the profit and loss statement, or P&L. The balance sheet is simply a table of what a business owns and what it owes; it is calculated periodically (say monthly) and is a statement as of a certain time (*e.g.*, midnight on December 31). The P&L, on the other hand, is a report that tells what came in and what went out and covers a time span (*e.g.*, one minute after midnight on January 1 through midnight, January 31).

The easiest way to understand these is through an example. Perhaps the most basic business is the time-honored lemonade stand. Let's say Joey has $5 in savings from his allowance and wants to make some money for video games by running a lemonade stand one day. He borrows a pitcher from his mother but has to spend $2 on lemonade mix and $2 on paper cups. He plans to make change with the leftover $1. At the start of the day, his balance sheet is:

ASSETS	LIABILITIES
$1 Cash	$0 Debt
$2 Lemonade	
$2 Cups	**EQUITY**
	$5 Owner's Equity
$5 Total	$5 Total

Note that the total of the left side is $5, and the total of the right side is $5. A balance sheet must balance. Let's say Joey sells out of lemonade pretty fast — 20 cups at 50¢ each. His first day P&L looks like this:

Lemonade sales	$10.00
Lemonade costs	– 2.00
Cup costs	– 2.00
Profit	$ 6.00

For this example, we'll assume Joey evades his taxes. (We do not recommend you try this at home.) At the end of the day, Joey has a new balance sheet:

ASSETS	LIABILITIES
$11 Cash	$0 Debt
	EQUITY
	$11 Owner's Equity
$11 Total	$11 Total

The $11 cash represents his $1 change fund plus the $10 in sales he's taken in. Since Joey doesn't owe anybody anything, the $11 is all his — it is all equity. He can either pocket the money (pay himself a dividend) or leave it in the business (retained earnings) for future growth.

Joey is now so enthusiastic about more than doubling his money in one day that he gets more aggressive the second day. He borrows $15 from Mom, borrows three pitchers, and tells three kids they can have half of the sales if they run three lemonade stands for him. He starts day 2 with this balance sheet:

ASSETS	LIABILITIES
$10 Lemonade	$15 Borrowed from Mom
$10 Cups	
$ 6 Change	**EQUITY**
	$11 Owner's Equity
$26 Total	$26 Total

Joey has another bang-up day and sells all his lemonade; he even decides to pay Mom $1 in interest.

DAY 2 P&L	
Lemonade sales	$ 60
Commissions	- 30
Lemonade	- 10
Cups	- 10
Operating profit	10
Interest expense	- 1
Net profit	$ 9

Before Joey pays Mom her interest and principal, his balance sheet looks like this:

ASSETS	LIABILITIES
$36 Cash	$16 Owed to Mom
	EQUITY
	$20 Owner's Equity
$36 Total	$36 Total

Joey started the day with $6 in cash and added $60 in sales less $30 in commissions, ending up with $36. But he still owes Mom her $15 loan principal plus $1 in interest. After Joey pays Mom, the balance sheet looks like this:

ASSETS	LIABILITIES
$20 Cash	$0 Debt
	EQUITY
	$20 Owner's Equity
$20 Total	$20 Total

It is important to realize that the balance sheet and P&L are related: what happens to your P&L in a time period results in changes between your starting balance sheet and your ending balance sheet. Unless Joey takes out a dividend, his owner's equity is always the previous equity plus profits since then.

The left side (assets) of the balance sheet tells what the company owns — "current" assets such as cash, securities, inventories, and bills sent out but not yet paid (receivables) — as well as "fixed" assets like buildings, furniture, equipment, computers, etc. The right side of the balance sheet tells how the company is financed — how much is debt and how much is owner's equity. Debt is also broken into short-term (bills due, or payables, and loans due in the next year) and long-term (mortgages, bonds due over many years, etc.). The P&L tells whether the business is making money or not.

MEASURING RETURN ON INVESTMENT

The primary measures of return on investment are return on equity (ROE) and return on assets (ROA). ROE tells what kind of return Joey is getting on the money he has invested in the business — the return on his owner's equity. The first day, Joey put up $5 and made a profit of $6. This is an ROE of 120% (6/5). The second day, he had $11 of his money invested and made $9, for a return of 81% (9/11). For the real companies in this book, a return that is above interest rates (7-8% per year now) isn't too bad. An ROE of 15-20% is very good, and anything above that is exceptional.

Return on assets tells how a business is doing on the total amount invested — whether that investment be owner's equity or borrowed money (debt). The first day, Joey made $6 on a total investment of $5 (all equity), so his ROA was the same 120% as his ROE. However, since he used debt the second day, the ROE and ROA numbers start to differ. Before paying his mother the $1 in interest, Joey made $10 the second day, but he had $26 at work to do it ($11 of his own equity and $15 borrowed from Mom). His ROA was only 38% (10/26), still a good return. As long as his ROA is above interest rates (here, he paid Mom $1 to borrow $15, a 7% rate), he can afford to borrow and put the money to work in the business. This is called "using leverage" — he is using other people's money to "leverage" his own money.

This is best illustrated if we greatly expand Joey's business with debt.

DAY 3	
ASSETS	**LIABILITIES**
$1,000 Lemonade	$2,100 Loan from Neighbor
$1,000 Cups	
$ 120 Change fund	**EQUITY**
	$ 20 Owner's Equity
$2,120 Total	$2,120 Total

Joey is now "highly leveraged" — 99% (2,100/2,120) of his financing is in the form of debt. Let's say the neighbor charges 10% interest for the use of the money for a day (generally called loansharking). Let's also say Joey can maintain his 38% return on assets. On $2,120 of total assets, Joey would make $806 (.38 X $2,120) before paying interest of $210 (.1 X $2,100). After interest, Joey's profit would be $806 – $210 = $596, not a bad return on his $20 equity — in fact, a 2,980% return. If the lemonade stand business were really this profitable, Joey would probably have several competitors by now, unless he could get his dad, the mayor, to give him a monopoly.

As long as Joey's ROA is higher than his interest rate, he can afford to borrow money for the business. In the above example, a 38% ROA combined with an interest rate of only 10% to give Joey a phenomenal ROE of almost 3,000%. Joey gained from "the spread" — the difference between his profitability (ROA) and his cost of money (interest rate).

But leverage has its risks: say, instead of Joey making his 38% ROA on day 3 ($806 before interest), a storm comes up as soon as he starts selling lemonade. All the lemonade mix, paper cups, and money blow away. Joey is left with only $2,310 in debt and interest owed to his neighbor. If he had never gone into debt, Joey would just lose his $20 in equity. But, as things evolve, the neighbor threatens to break Dad's kneecaps, and Dad sells his golf cart to raise the $2,310 to pay off the debt. Joey decides to pursue another career.

OTHER MEASURES OF FINANCIAL PERFORMANCE

Return on Assets and Return on Equity can be used to measure any business. They can be used to compare a steel factory to an airline to a movie company, because they look only at how profitably a business puts money to work. There are many other widely used measures of business performance, but these are only meaningful when comparing similar businesses. A common example is Return on Sales (ROS), or profit as a percent of sales. This statistic would be a high percent (say 30%) for a good computer maker, but only 2% for a good supermarket. The reason is that the computer maker requires a lot more investment in assets (equipment, labs) than does a supermarket to generate the same sales. The supermarket, with a lower ROS, can have just as high an ROA, which is what really matters:

	COMPUTER MAKER	SUPERMARKET
Sales	$ 1,000,000	$ 1,000,000
Profits	$ 300,000	$ 20,000
ROS	30%	2%
Assets	$ 1,500,000	$ 100,000
ROA	20%	20%

However, within an industry or similar industries measures like ROS can be very helpful. Other common measures include:

Current Ratio. This is the ratio of current assets to current liabilities. If a company had to pay off all its bills tomorrow, would it have enough cash and things quickly convertible into cash (such as inventory) to cover the bills? If a company's current ratio is 1, it has just enough money. If the ratio is 2, it has twice what it needs; if the ratio is .5, it has only half of what it needs. Again, this measure is most useful in comparing similar companies.

Debt Ratio. This is the percent of long-term financing that is provided by debt. Ignoring short-term liabilities, such as bills due, the ratio focuses on long-term debt (bonds, debentures, mortgages) and equity. If a company is financed by $75,000 in debt and $25,000 in equity, the debt ratio is 75% ($75,000/($75,000 + $25,000)). This is a basic measure of how leveraged a business is. A predictable business like an electric utility can generally afford to carry more debt than a risky or fluctuating enterprise. On the other hand, even 50% debt might be too much for a movie company that has hits one year and flops the next. Before his business's collapse, Joey's debt ratio was 99%.

Productivity Measures. There are many ways to measure how productive an enterprise is, such as sales per employee, factory production as a percent of capacity, etc. Again, these are most useful when comparing two similar companies.

In addition to general measures like these, each industry has its own measures of performance — for example, load factor for airlines (how many of the seats are taken), occupancy for hotels (how many of the rooms are taken), ratings for TV networks (what share of viewers are tuned in), and sales per square foot for retail stores.

TREND ANALYSIS

An important part of evaluating any business is looking at the trends. Which of these companies would you rather invest in or go to work for?

ROE by Year

	1986	1987	1988	1989	1990
Joey's Hot Dogs	50%	40%	30%	20%	15%
Alice's Restaurant	11%	12%	13%	14%	15%

Whether one is studying market share, productivity measures, profitability measures, ROA, or ROE, the direction and rate of change is very important. The stock market also usually puts a premium on consistency and predictability, because there is less risk. In the group below, the market would probably value the third company the most highly, even though all three made the same amount of profit in the latest year.

Profits by Year

	1985	1986	1987	1988	1989	1990
First Co.	$100	$200	$ 50	$400	$ 0	$200
Second Co.	$450	$400	$350	$300	$250	$200
Third Co.	$ 25	$ 50	$ 75	$100	$150	$200

MEASURES OF SIZE

The companies in this book make it clear that big is not neccessarily successful. While all of these companies must have had some good years to get to be big, big companies can go broke just like small companies. Nevertheless, in understanding the companies, it is good to know who is big and who is less big, especially when comparing companies in one industry.

By far the most universal measure of size is sales (or revenues). The total amount of money an enterprise receives from its customers is the basis for most popular rankings, like the *Fortune* 500. When we say, "It's a $3 billion company," we usually mean sales.

In some industries, like banking and insurance, it has become common practice to rank firms by assets — the total amount of money and property under the company's control.

Another interesting measure, increasingly used and the basis of the *Business Week* rankings included in this book, is market value or market capitalization. This is what it would cost you to buy up all the stock in a company. At this writing, the most valuable companies in the United States are Exxon and IBM.

Note that market value is often much greater than the owners' (or stockholders') equity: this is because the value of a company's reputation and the talents of its people are not fully reflected on the balance sheet. The stock market makes its own decision as to the value of Coke's internationally known trademark and values the company way above what the balance sheet shows. This valuation results from thousands of individual and corporate investors buying stock when they think it is cheap (undervalued) and selling stock when they think it is expensive (overvalued).

Less frequently, companies are ranked by other measures such as number of employees and dollars of profits. We have included several size-based lists immediately preceding the profiles in this book.

FOUR KEY CONCEPTS FOR INVESTORS

When potential investors consider buying stock in a company, they first evaluate the balance sheet and P&L, with a clear focus on trends. In addition to the basics discussed in the preceding paragraphs, investors also need to understand four key concepts, examined below.

Shares of Stock

A company can have any number of shares of stock that it wants to have, from one share to billions. The number of shares is simply how many pieces the ownership is divided into. A stock split occurs when a company divides its stock into smaller pieces. Companies do this to make their price per share less, so more people can afford the shares.

3-for-1 Split

	Before Split	After Split
Number of Shares	1,000,000	3,000,000
Equity	$30,000,000	$30,000,000
Equity per share	$30	$10
Annual Profits (Earnings)	$3,000,000	$3,000,000
Earnings Per Share	$3.00	$1.00
Stock Price	$60.00	$20.00
Market Value	$60,000,000	$60,000,000
Shares I own:	100	300

Many of the concepts discussed above have parallel terms on a per-share basis, because that is the way most investors look at their investments:

	Total Company	Per-Share Basis
Owners' Equity	Shareholders' Equity	Book Value
Profits	Net Income or Earnings	Earnings Per Share (EPS)
Market Value	Market Value or Market Capitalization	Stock Price

Earnings Per Share (EPS), or the profits of the company divided by the number of shares, is perhaps the single most important term for investors in stock.

EPS Growth Rate

This is the compound annual growth rate for the Earnings Per Share of a company. Sometimes companies sell more stock over time to raise more money for the business without going into too much debt. In these cases, the number of shares increases over time and the old owners are "diluted" (their percentage of ownership of the business shrinks). Their best measure of profits is to look at their EPS. Here is a company that sold more stock, but still did a good job for investors, old and new:

	1988	1989	1990
Total Net Income	$100,000	$200,000	$300,000
Shares of Stock	100,000	150,000	200,000
EPS	$1.00	$1.33	$1.50
Growth in EPS		33%	13%

Depending on whether we are in boom times or a recession, our U.S. economy usually grows between 0% and 5% a year, excluding inflation. With inflation included, the growth runs 3% to 10% a year. All business combined will grow at about that rate. If you see a business in this book with compound sales or profit growth rates of 15% or 20%, that is pretty impressive, especially if they've done it year in and year out for 5, 10, or even 25 years.

Price/Earnings Ratio (P/E)

This is how many times profits a stock sells for. Since the owner of a share of stock is entitled to all the future profits on his or her share, stocks sell for several times last year's profits per share (EPS). A company earning $1 per share per year is worth some multiple (P/E) of that $1. The statistic is quoted daily in the *Wall Street Journal* for each stock. Look at these three companies:

Annual Earnings per Share	1987	1988	1989	1990
Company A	$1.00	$1.33	$1.50	$1.75
Company B	$1.00	$1.01	$1.02	$1.03
Company C	$.25	$2.50	$.65	$2.00

Company A would be considered a growth company, with consistent double-digit (over 10% a year) growth. This stock is probably worth the most money of the three. It might sell as high as 20 times earnings (P/E = 20). If so, the stock price would be $35 (20 X $1.75).

Company B is not even growing as fast as the economy as a whole. Unless it pays a big dividend (see below), its stock is not worth much, maybe 6 times earnings. This P/E of 6 would result in the stock selling for just over $6.

Company C is a cyclical company and probably the hardest to analyze. The stock market's valuation of the stock would depend on whether next year is going to be one of its good years or one of its bad years. The stock could sell for $5, or it could sell for $20 or more.

It is important to remember that there are many people trying to predict the stock market and the performance of each company. To these people, the future is much more important than the past. If company A announces a five-year delay in introducing its new computer, the stock will probably plummet. Past growth rates and financial performance are used more as a tool to guess the future than anything else.

To the experienced investor, the absolute price of a stock doesn't tell you whether the stock is really cheap or expensive. The P/E ratio tells you whether it is cheap or expensive.

	Cheap Stock	Expensive Stock
Last Year EPS	$5.00	$.50
This Year EPS	$5.10	$1.00
Projected EPS	$5.20	$2.00
Current Stock Price	$51.00	$20.00
P/E on This Year EPS	10	20

In the example above, two stocks (in two companies) are compared. While an inexperienced investor might think the stock priced at $51 per share is "more expensive" than the one selling for $20, this is misleading. Although the $51 stock sells for about 2 1/2 times the price of the $20 stock, the first company's profits (This Year EPS) are over five times as much ($5.10 versus $1.00).

Another way of looking at this: which is a "cheap" car — a Yugo for $12,000 or a new Mercedes for $15,000? The P/E ratio is the best measure of value. In general, the higher the growth rate of a company's EPS, the higher the P/E should be, because the P/E reflects the stock market's beliefs about the future EPS of the company. As a result, a high P/E stock may still be a better long-term investment than a low P/E stock.

Dividends

Like Joey in the example above, every company has two options as to what to do with its profits:

1. Put them back into the business as retained earnings.
2. Pay them out to shareholders as dividends. Most young, growing companies keep most or all of their profits, believing that their stockholders will benefit most if the company plows the money into new stores or new plants or whatever. To justify retaining most earnings, a company should have a high return on investment (higher than investors could earn on their own). On the other hand, more mature or stable enterprises may have trouble finding good investments for all the profits they are generating. These companies are more likely to pay out their earnings as dividends. If management believes investors are relying on dividends, they may continue paying dividends even when the company is losing money, at least as long as they can.

Young investors tend to invest for long-term price increases in stocks and are more interested in growth than dividends. Most older investors are ready to take some of their savings out now for living expenses, and many rely on these dividends.

The two key measures of dividends are:

Payout. The percentage of profits that a company pays out as dividends. For many growth companies, this is 0%. Some older companies pay out 70% or more.

Yield. This is the dividend per share divided by the current market price of the share. If you pay $20 for a stock that is paying a $1 annual dividend, you get a 5% (1/20) yield. For dividend-conscious investors, this is a key number. Also of interest is the trend in dividends over time. Has the dividend been steady over the years? Has it gone up? How fast?

This section has discussed the basic concepts of financial analysis and investing. In the next section, we touch on some of the tricky things in financial analysis that can be confusing or misleading.

SOME POTHOLES ON THE ROAD TO UNDERSTANDING

Incorporation and Corporate Names

In this book, we give the date and state of incorporation for each business. It is worth remembering that businesses reincorporate for any of a number of reasons, often just related to legal details. For that reason, the date of incorporation is often not the date of the initial incorporation and often not the date of founding. Additionally, a corporation can pick any state to incorporate in, again for legal reasons. Delaware, for example, is a very popular state because of the powers and protections its laws give to the managements of corporations. The state of incorporation has nothing to do with the headquarters or even office and plant locations of a corporation.

Companies are also free to change their names at will. Often they are reflecting a new direction in their business or dropping a name they perceive to be dated. A corporate name change often does not represent any real change in the business — it has the same history, the same officers, etc.

Mergers and Acquisitions

Companies also often buy and sell one another, or acquire and divest. As strategies shift, management decides to be or not to be in any given business. While acquisitions are often referred to as mergers in the press, we have usually used that word only in the case of the true merger of equals or near-equals. In reality, one of the two companies almost always ends up "on top" — with its management in charge of the combined enterprise and with its shareholders owning most of the company. We therefore prefer the terms *acquisition* or *purchase*, rather than *merger*.

When a company sells (divests) another business, they can give its shares out to their own shareholders, or they can sell it to another corporation or to management and employees. They can also sell the business directly to the public. These divestitures are sometimes called spinoffs. We have included a glossary of takeover terms at the end of this section, to help you understand this jargon-filled aspect of big business.

Divisions and Subsidiaries

These are legal terms for parts of a company; divisions are normally 100% owned by the parent company, whereas subsidiaries are technically separate corporations and can be partially owned. When the ownership is partial, we have pointed that out. We have treated companies as subsidiaries only when the parent company owns 51% or more.

Leveraged Buyouts (LBOs)

One way in which investors, employees, or managers can acquire a company is by way of a leveraged buyout. In effect, the investors put up a very small down payment (equity capital) and borrow a large amount of money to pay for the purchase. Often, the borrowed money is in the form of low-quality bonds (junk bonds) sold to individual or corporate investors. These bonds are considered low quality because they carry higher risk of default than normal corporate bonds and because they often pay off after other bonds in the event the company goes broke. Because of this higher risk, junk bonds normally pay a high yield (interest rate).

In order to complete an LBO, investors and lenders must be convinced that the business will generate enough cash to meet the interest and principal obligations. While there have been a number of cases in which the investors were wrong (for example, Campeau), there are others in which the forecasts of cash flow have been right — so far.

Accounting

In order to make it easy to compare different companies, the accounting industry and government regulators have developed a set of accounting standards for use by corporations. These standards have evolved over time and become fairly complex. Things to observe:

Accounting Results vs. Real, or Economic, Results

Most people do not realize that a company's profit and loss statement can be showing profits when the company is running out of cash. This can happen for several reasons: for example, the company is investing heavily in inventories or plants, or the company cannot collect money owed to it. When companies go broke, their financial statements occasionally look fine right up until the day they go under.

The study of accounting is a field unto itself, with hundreds of textbooks available. For the purposes of this book, it is probably sufficient to realize that a company's financial statements are really just best estimates of how the company is doing. In strong, well-financed, growing companies, these estimating procedures are accurate enough, and they're certainly the best we can do. Accounting data is presented in the How Much section of each profile.

Timing

The accrual system of accounting adopted by the corporate world revolves around a concept called "matching." This just means that expenses on the P&L must be shown at the same time that relevant revenues are booked. For example, if a retailer bought inventory in 1989 but did not sell it until 1990, the company could not show the expense for the inventory until 1990, even though cash had been spent the prior year.

Another example: your company buys a $500,000 computer that it will use for 5 years to help in the business. Under matching rules, the P&L may show an expense of $100,000 a year for each of the next 5 years, even though the company had to pay for the computer up front. There are numerous other cases like this, generally grouped under the headings "depreciation" and "amortization."

Calendars

Each company may have its year start and end on any date; this is called its fiscal year. While many companies have a fiscal year that matches the calendar year (ends on December 31), many have years that end on May 31, June 30, etc. Companies usually pick a fiscal year that reflects the seasonal nature of their business. For example, most big retailers have a fiscal year that ends on the Saturday closest to January 31. This is because they want to have a month to clean up their business after the big Christmas season (markdowns, inventory-taking, etc.), and they want to have a fiscal year that ties to their traditional Sunday-through-Saturday weekly cycle.

Investors usually look at stock price ranges on a calendar-year basis, even though the company's sales and earnings are reported on a fiscal year basis.

Tax vs. Book

Companies also maintain one set of books for the I.R.S. and one set for accounting and shareholder reporting purposes. This is all very legal — in fact, sometimes the accountants require a company to report data one way to shareholders, while the I.R.S. has contradictory rules. The amount shown in financial statements for "taxes" is rarely the amount of the check the company wrote to the I.R.S. Big companies have numerous people devoted to the task of minimizing the taxes they pay, while staying within the law. Since tax rules change every year, and since many tax rules are subject to various interpretations, tax accounting and tax law have become big businesses in themselves.

Changing Rules

Just as tax rules are always changing, the accounting-standards setters also change their rules frequently. Sometimes a company will restate prior years' results, so that the "last year" column on a financial statement does not match the "this year" column in last year's reports. Companies can also do unusual things with businesses they are getting out of (discontinued operations) and unusual one-time expenses or profits (extraordinary items). For this book, we have tried our best to adjust the information for each company so that the data is comparable. We have generally shown historical data as originally reported, not as restated. In some cases our numbers will not match those you find in other sources, including company annual reports, because of these factors.

Foreign Companies

As might be expected, every country has its own accounting and tax rules. It can be very hard to compare foreign companies with American ones. Many major foreign companies issue American Depository Receipts (ADRs), which means that you can buy their stock in the U.S., and they have to report information in U.S. dollars and under U.S. accounting rules. On the other hand, foreign companies without ADRs usually report sales and profits in their own currencies. You will see that, in most of these cases, we have presented data in the company's domestic currency.

USING THE PROFILES

Organization of the Profiles

The 542 profiles are presented in alphabetical order. This alphabetization is generally word by word, which means that America West Airlines precedes American Brands. We have shown the full name of the enterprise at the top of each page, unless it is too long, in which case you will find it above the address in the Where section of the profile. If a company name starts with a person's first name, like Arthur Andersen or Walt Disney, it will be alphabetized under the first name; if the company name starts with initials, like J. C. Penney or H. J. Heinz, look for it under the last name. All company names (past and present) used in the profiles are indexed in the last index in the book.

Certain pieces of basic data are listed at the top right of each profile: where the company's stock is traded if it is public, the stock ticker symbol used by the stock exchange, the most recent incorporation date and place, and the company's fiscal year-end.

The annual information contained in the profiles was current through fiscal year-end 1989 (including companies whose years ended as late as February 28, 1990). To the extent possible, we have also noted significant, more recent developments through September 1990.

Overview

In this section we have tried to give a thumbnail description of the company and what it does. We recommend that you read this section first to get a snapshot view of the company as it stands today.

When

This longer section reflects our belief that every enterprise is the sum of its history, and that you have to know where you came from in order to know where you are going. While some companies have very little historical awareness and were unable to help us much, and other companies are just plain boring, we think the vast majority of the enterprises in the book have colorful backgrounds. When we could find information, we tried to focus on the people who made the enterprise what it is today. We have found these histories to be full of twists and ironies; they can make for some fascinating quick reading.

Who

Here we list the names of the people that run the company, insofar as space allows. In the case of public companies, we have shown the ages and pay levels of key officers. In some cases, the published data are based on last year although the company has announced promotions or retirements since year end. We have tried to show current officers, with their pay for the latest year available, often prior to a promotion. These pay data represent cash compensation, including bonuses, but exclude stock option programs and retirement benefits. Such data is not usually available for foreign companies.

While companies are free to structure their management titles any way they please, most modern corporations follow standard practices. The ultimate power in any corporation lies with the shareholders, who elect a board of directors, usually including officers or "insiders" as well as individuals from outside the company. The chief officer, the person on whose desk the buck stops, is usually called the chief executive officer (CEO). Normally, he or she is also the chairman of the board. As corporate management has become more complex, it is common for the CEO to have a "right-hand man" who oversees the day-to-day operations of the company, allowing the CEO plenty of time to focus on strategy and long-term issues. This right-hand person is usually designated the chief operating officer (COO) and is often the president of the company. In other cases, one person is both chairman and president.

A multitude of other titles exist, including chief financial officer (CFO), chief administrative officer, and vice chairman (VC). Our best advice is that officers' pay levels are clear indicators of who the board of directors thinks are most important in the management team.

The people named in the profiles are indexed at the back of the book by their last names.

The Who section also includes the name of the company's auditing (accounting) firm and the number of employees. This last statistic can be viewed as a measure of the complexity of managing the enterprise, since most managing is managing people.

Where

Here we include the company's headquarters street address and phone and fax numbers as available. The back of the book includes an index of companies by headquarters locations. Telephone numbers of foreign companies are shown as they would be dialed from the U.S.

We have also included as much information as we could gather, and fit, with regard to the geographical distribution of the company's business, including sales and profit data. Note that these profit numbers, like those in the What section below, are usually operating profits rather than net profits. Operating profits are generally those before financing costs (interest payments) and before taxes, which are considered costs attributable to the whole company rather than to one division or part of the world. For this reason, the net income figures (in the How Much section) are usually much lower, since they are after interest and taxes. Pretax profits are after interest but before taxes.

What

This section lists as many of the company's products, services, brand names, and divisions as we could fit. We have tried to include all its major lines and all brand names with broad familiarity. The nature of this section varies by industry, company, and the amount of information available. When the company publishes sales and profit information by type of business, we have included it. The product, brand, and division names are included in the last index in the book, alongside past and present company names.

Rankings

Here we have included the rankings of the companies in the major lists published by the financial press. The best-known and oldest of these lists is the *Fortune 500*, which lists the 500 largest U.S. publicly held industrial (manufacturing) corporations. This list does not generally include banks, retailers, foreign companies, private companies, etc.

Fortune produces these other lists, which we have included in the Rankings section:

- 100 Largest US Banks
- 100 Largest Diversified US Service Companies
- 50 Largest Diversified US Financial Service Companies
- 50 Largest US Life Insurance Companies
- 50 Largest US Retailers
- 50 Largest US Transportation Companies
- 50 Largest US Utilities
- 50 Largest US Exporters (Manufacturers)
- 500 Largest World Industrial Companies (US and Foreign combined)
- 100 Largest Foreign Banks

These lists rank all companies by sales, except banks, savings and loans, financial service companies, insurance companies, and utilities, which are ranked by assets.

Forbes, a more recent participant in the "list game," puts all of the companies together in one list, ranked by sales as the *Forbes* Sales 500. We have also shown the rank of private companies in *Forbes*'s 400 Largest U.S. Private companies and have shown the ranks of foreign companies in that magazine's 100 Largest Foreign Investments in the U.S. *Forbes* also ranks companies by other measures; we have not included those rankings in this book. The magazine has made an art of estimating the wealth of rich people, both U.S. and foreign. While the resultant rankings are not included in our book, we recommend these lists as fascinating background reading.

Our final set of rankings comes from *Business Week*, the largest (in circulation) of the big three business magazines. The lists compare companies based on the market value of their stock, or market capitalization. They produce two lists: the 1,000 biggest U.S. companies by this measure and the 1,000 biggest in the world (U.S. and foreign combined). These lists include only public companies, but they include companies from all industries.

All of the above lists are published annually by these magazines.

Competition

In this section we have listed those other companies in the book that compete with the company on this page. This feature is included as a quick way to turn to similar companies and compare them. In the case of some highly diversified or always-changing companies, we didn't have enough room to list everybody and have referred you to broad industry groupings. All the companies in the book are listed by broad industry groups in the first index at the back of the book.

How Much

Here we have tried to present as much data about each enterprise's financial performance as we could compile in the allocated space. While the information varies somewhat from industry to industry, and is less complete in the case of private companies that do not release this data, the following information is generally present. (Most of the terms used below are more fully defined in the preceding section, The Numbers Made Simple.)

A ten-year table, with relevant nine-year (1980 through 1989) compound growth rates, covering:

- Fiscal year sales
- Fiscal year net income (before extraordinary items)

- Fiscal year income as a percent of sales (ROS)
- Fiscal year Earnings Per Share (EPS) (fully diluted unless italicized)
- Calendar year stock price high, low, and close
- Calendar year high and low Price/Earnings ratio (P/E)
- Fiscal year dividends per share
- Fiscal year-end book value (shareholders' equity per share)

For fiscal years ending between March 1, 1989, and February 28, 1990, we have called the year 1989.

Key year-end 1989 statistics that generally show the financial strength of the enterprise, including:

- Debt ratio (long-term debt as a percent of combined long-term debt and shareholders' equity)
- Return on Average Equity (average of beginning shareholders' equity and ending shareholders' equity) for the fiscal year
- Cash and marketable securities on hand at the end of fiscal 1989
- Current ratio at year-end fiscal 1989 (ratio of current assets to current liabilities)
- Total long-term debt at year-end fiscal 1989
- Number of shares of common stock outstanding at year-end fiscal 1989
- Dividend yield (fiscal year 1989 dividends per share divided by the year-end closing stock price)
- Dividend payout (fiscal year dividends divided by fiscal year Earnings Per Share for 1989)
- Market value at the end of 1989 (calendar year-end closing stock price multiplied by fiscal year-end number of shares outstanding)

Note that, throughout the How Much section, per-share data are based on common shares of stock, ignoring preferred stock. Historical per share data is adjusted for stock splits. The data for public U.S. companies (and selected others) has been provided to us by Standard & Poor's Compustat, a unit of McGraw-Hill and the nation's leading compiler of corporate share data. Compustat has gone to great lengths to make the data comparable between companies, sometimes producing numbers that will disagree with the numbers you may find in other sources. See the previous section, "Potholes on the Road to Understanding."

In the case of private companies, we usually did not have access to such standardized data. We have gathered estimates of sales and other statistics from numerous sources; among the most helpful were trade publications such as *Advertising Age*, and *Forbes*'s estimates of the largest private companies. We have also had to become creative in deciding which statistics to use for nonprofit and governmental entities.

In the case of foreign companies, we have shown data in U.S. dollars if available and unless otherwise noted. In the case of certain industries, we have substituted more relevant statistics for the above data. For example, the current ratio is not meaningful for financial service businesses, and for most of these we have shown total assets instead. ♦

BEYOND *HOOVER'S HANDBOOK*: FURTHER READING AND RESOURCES

The business periodical and reference publishing industry is large and growing. Because of the many ways to look at companies and the many measures used, it is often useful to compare several sources.

Basic Data

The two largest compilers of business reference books are Moody's and Standard & Poor's. These organizations produce a wide variety of books and loose-leaf binders. The annual set of *Moody's Manuals*, broken into volumes covering industry groups, are the definitive sources on histories of public companies, including the many thousands too small to be included in this book. Standard & Poor's Sheets, commonly found in stock brokerage offices, contain quick two-page synopses on most public companies and are updated frequently. The *Standard & Poor's Stock Guide* is an invaluable monthly booklet with one line on each major publicly held company, primarily containing information of interest to investors.

Dun & Bradstreet is the nation's largest provider of credit information on companies, including small and private ones. A D&B report is often the only available source of information on these enterprises.

One of the best sources of information on the larger companies is the *Value Line Investment Service*, a black binder which quarterly updates one-page reports on each of 1,700 publicly held companies. Unlike other services, Value Line gives specific stock recommendations and future performance projections. The service has established an excellent reputation among investors.

Information from the Companies

The primary data source for this book was contact with the companies themselves, either through their public relations departments or through their investor relations departments. Every publicly held company is required to produce quarterly and annual reports to its shareholders. While the Securities and Exchange Commission (SEC) and accounting-standards setters require certain basic data, companies often use these reports to espouse management philosophies, explain strategies, and examine product successes. Investors generally consider a company's annual report the single most important document they receive in any given year.

Companies also produce a report for investors called the "10-K," which is just a version of the annual report that meets specific SEC guidelines. These reports sometimes contain information not included in the regular annual report. Each year, each public company also holds an annual meeting of shareholders. Since most shareholders do not attend these, the company sends out a proxy statement which sets forth the issues to be voted on, including the election of the board of directors. These proxy statements include data on managers and directors, including pay data.

All of these documents are generally available free of charge from the company upon request. They are also maintained by a company named Disclosure, which makes them available in printed and electronic form.

Depending on the company's publicity consciousness or secrecy, most companies also produce a wealth of product information and sometimes histories and other information. Such supplementary company information can be most useful.

Analysts' Reports

Most stock brokerage firms maintain teams of securities analysts — professionals specializing in the study of one industry or a few related industries. These people are well paid to spend their full energies understanding the companies in an industry and predicting their futures. Some of the reports they write are widely circulated; others must be obtained from the brokerage firms.

Business Periodicals

The U.S. is blessed with a strong business press. For a general understanding of business, we believe the daily *Wall Street Journal* is without peer. In addition to being the basic daily news source about business, the *Journal* has become recognized as one of the best-written newspapers in the nation. The *Journal* increasingly covers international developments, marketing, and other aspects of the world that are of interest to the general public.

Forbes, *Fortune*, and *Business Week* are the country's leading business magazines. Each tries to "scoop" its competitors and provide more useful information. This intense competition has, we believe, led to high quality on the part of all three magazines. Each has its fans and its detractors: we suggest you read as much as you can get your hands on. Because *Forbes* takes substantial editorial risks, we believe that this magazine is both more often right and more often wrong than its competitors. We read it religiously, with skepticism.

America's interest in business has led to the creation of many other fine periodicals, including *Investors Daily, Inc.*, and *Financial World.* Every industry also has trade publications specializing in that industry. *Advertising Age*, *Chain Store Age*, and *Aviation Week* are good examples. Many of these trade publications compile annual lists comparing the companies in one industry.

We would be remiss to exclude the major national dailies: papers like the *New York Times*, the *Chicago Tribune*, the *Los Angeles Times*, and the *Dallas Morning News* are well known for their coverage of local, national, and international business developments. Most American cities also have a local business weekly or daily; this recent phenomenon has produced some very good papers.

Library References

In addition to the broad reference books discussed above, there are a multitude of business references on specific industries and topics; most of these books are fairly expensive, but most are available at a good library. These titles include *Best's* guides to insurance companies and *Ward's* lists of companies, the latter title distributed by Gale Research, a major library supplier. There are also several books covering foreign companies, usually a separate book for each country.

It is hard to beat a good library, whether for these references or for other books and periodicals. At The Reference Press, we have made extensive use of the Austin Pubic Library and the libraries of the Universities of Chicago, Texas, and California-Berkeley.

Electronic Sources

Those readers with access to computers with modems will find it useful to hook up to such information services as Dow Jones News Retrieval and CompuServe. These and other services make available literally thousands of sources, including indexes to periodicals, stock market data, etc.

Other Books

There have been books written about many of the more visible companies in this book: General Motors, Coca-Cola, IBM, Walt Disney, etc. While not as widely distributed, many less well-known companies have also been documented, sometimes in histories commissioned by the companies themselves.

While there are hundreds of books on management strategies, marketing methods, etc., there are not many widely available books about the history of business in general. The one we would cite in particular is Alfred Chandler's *The Visible Hand.* This and other books by Chandler give a sweeping view of how big business evolved, and we highly recommend them. The works of Peter Drucker are also consistently insightful with regard to the world of enterprise, and we think Alfred Sloan's *My Years with General Motors* is the best management book ever written.

The Real World

When studying companies, it is easy to forget that they are all around us. You probably buy products produced by, live near a plant or office of, or know someone who works for many of the enterprises in the book. Respected investor Peter Lynch has suggested that you buy stocks based on where you shop, what brands you like, what kinds of shoes your kids wear, etc. We agree: with access to our profiles, you can supplement what you already know about the businesses around you. ♦

Takeover Glossary

The mergers and acquisitions industry of the 1980s has spawned its own vocabulary to describe the behavior of its various players. *HOOVER'S HANDBOOK* uses some of this vocabulary for brevity. Some of the jargon is simply amusing. The following glossary is intended to assist, and perhaps entertain, the reader of this book.

Bear hug – an unnegotiated letter offer, made directly to the target company's board of directors, that is not very attractive but attractive enough to get shareholder protests if the board refuses it.

Black book – a defensive strategy to be implemented in the event of a hostile takeover.

Black knight – a party who makes a takeover offer that is hostile to the company's present management.

Creeping takeover – a takeover in which the acquirer gradually accumulates enough stock (bought in the open market) to control the company.

Crown jewel option – the strategy of selling or optioning a company's best assets to a third party so that it is a less attractive takeover prospect.

Drop-dead fee – a fee paid to lenders by potential acquirers when the proposal fails and lines of credit to finance the acquisition are not used.

Flip-over provision – a provision added to the charter of a target company allowing the conversion of preferred shares into common stock of the target company or acquiring company. This makes the takeover less attractive because it increases the number of shares that have to be bought.

Freeze-out – pressure on remaining minority stockholders to turn over their stock after a new owner has gained control of the company.

Godfather offer – a tender offer so generous that management of the target company is not in a position to refuse it.

Golden handcuffs – an employment agreement that makes it very costly for senior managers to leave the company.

Golden parachute – generous termination benefits approved for senior executives when someone else buys control of the company.

Gray knight – a potential acquirer whose intentions are not known; usually a third party who makes an offer to purchase a target after a black or white knight (or both) have done so.

Greenmail – the premium paid by the target company to buy back its shares from a potential acquirer so that the acquirer will abandon the takeover attempt.

Jonestown defense – defensive tactics so extreme as to seem suicidal.

Junk bond – a high-yield, high-risk debt frequently used to finance takeovers.

Killer bees – a team of specialists (lawyers, bankers, proxy solicitors) who are kept on retainer by a company in case they are needed to fight an unfriendly takeover.

Lady Macbeth strategy – a tactic in which a third party appears to be a white knight but then changes and supports the hostile acquirer.

LBO – (leveraged buyout) a method of taking control of a company using a high degree of debt in relation to equity.

Lockup agreement – an agreement between the target company and the acquirer that makes the target very unattractive to any other acquirer.

Lollipop tactic – a means of stopping a hostile takeover by allowing current shareholders to tender their shares at a premium price if an unfriendly bidder buys a certain number of shares.

MBO – (management buyout) the purchase of a company by its management.

Mezzanine financing – intermediate term funding (two to ten years) for LBOs; investors often receive equity in the form of stock options, warrants, or convertible debentures as part of the deal.

Nibble strategy – the purchase of a minority stock position in the target company followed by a tender offer for the remaining stock.

Pac-Man defense – a tactic in which the target company tries to purchase control of the hostile acquirer before the hostile acquirer gains control of it.

Poison pill – a tactic used by the target company to make the takeover more expensive. Frequently this involves issuing to common shareholders new preferred stock that they can profitably convert into common shares in the event of a takeover attempt.

Porcupine provisions – corporate charter or bylaw provisions intended to thwart takeover attempts.

Radar alert – close monitoring of a company's stock market activity to determine whether an outside party is accumulating stock prior to a hostile takeover attempt.

Raider – a hostile outside party seeking to take control of another company.

Recapitalization – the radical alteration of the capital structure, such as the payment of a large cash dividend to shareholders, to make the target company less attractive to a raider.

Saturday night special – a seven-day cash tender offer for a company's stock. It usually begins on a Saturday so that the target company has difficulty reaching its key advisers.

Scorched earth defense (or selling the crown jewels) – a tactic by the target company to discourage hostile acquirers by selling assets of the company, making it less attractive.

Shark repellent – antitakeover provisions in the company's charter to discourage a takeover (such as a poison pill).

Showstopper – litigation designed to stop a hostile takeover attempt.

Sleeping beauty – a takeover target company.

Takeover – the acquisition (friendly or unfriendly) of one company by another.

Target – a company that is the object of a takeover attempt.

Tender offer – an offer (made directly to shareholders) to purchase part or all of a company's outstanding shares of stock.

Tidal wave purchase – a raider's open market purchase of a company's stock in a short time period (the target company is overwhelmed).

Tin parachute – termination benefits approved for all employees in the event they lose their jobs following a takeover.

White knight – a friendly person or firm who saves a company from a hostile takeover by taking it over. ♦

A List-Lover's Compendium

Note: Data in these lists may not agree with data in the profiles because of different methods of compilation.

The 100 Largest Companies in *HOOVER'S HANDBOOK*

Rank	Company Name	1989 Sales ($ mil)
1	General Motors Corporation	124,993
2	Mitsubishi Group	108,778
3	Ford Motor Company	96,146
4	Exxon Corporation	86,656
5	Royal Dutch/Shell Group	85,412
6	International Business Machines Corp.	62,710
7	Toyota Motor Corporation	55,701
8	General Electric Company	53,884
9	Sears, Roebuck & Co.	53,794
10	American Telephone & Telegraph Company	50,976
11	Mobil Corporation	50,220
12	The British Petroleum Company PLC	48,611
13	Hitachi Ltd.	48,496
14	Daimler-Benz AG	45,202
15	Nippon Telegraph and Telephone Corp.	44,257
16	Cargill, Inc.	43,000
17	Matsushita Electric Industrial Co., Ltd.	41,699
18	Fiat	41,089
19	Philip Morris Companies, Inc.	39,011
20	Volkswagen AG	38,670
21	Salomon Inc	38,608
22	Citicorp	37,970
23	Siemens AG	36,170
24	E. I. du Pont de Nemours and Company	35,099
25	Chrysler Corporation	34,922
26	Unilever Group	34,434
27	Nissan Motor Co. Ltd.	33,417
28	Texaco Inc.	32,416
29	Nestlé SA	31,192
30	Renault	30,125
31	Philips NV	29,985
32	K mart Corporation	29,793
33	Chevron Corporation	29,443
34	BASF AG	28,176
35	Hoechst AG	27,159
36	Wal-Mart Stores, Inc.	25,811
37	Bayer AG	25,621
38	American Express Company	25,047
39	Amoco Corporation	23,966
40	Dai-Ichi Kangyo Bank, Ltd.	23,618
41	NEC Corporation	23,179
42	American Stores Company	22,004
43	The Procter & Gamble Company	21,398
44	ABB Asea Brown Boveri Ltd.	20,560
45	The Boeing Company	20,276
46	Occidental Petroleum Corporation	20,068
47	ITT Corporation	20,054
48	Aetna Life & Casualty Company	19,671
49	United Technologies Corporation	19,614
50	The Kroger Co.	19,104

Rank	Company Name	1989 Sales ($ mil)
51	Eastman Kodak Company	18,398
52	Robert Bosch GmbH	18,099
53	The Dow Chemical Company	17,600
54	USX Corporation	17,533
55	GTE Corporation	17,424
56	Deutsche Bank AG	17,381
57	Xerox Corporation	16,806
58	Sony Corporation	16,678
59	Fujitsu Ltd.	16,576
60	J. C. Penney Company, Inc.	16,405
61	CIGNA Corporation	15,654
62	Atlantic Richfield Company	15,351
63	B.A.T Industries PLC	15,281
64	PepsiCo, Inc.	15,242
65	Volvo Corporation	14,656
66	McDonnell Douglas Corporation	14,581
67	American International Group, Inc.	14,546
68	BCE Inc.	14,406
69	Safeway, Inc.	14,325
70	Tenneco, Inc.	14,083
71	BellSouth Corporation	13,996
72	The Chase Manhattan Corporation	13,904
73	Electrolux AB	13,697
74	Dayton Hudson Corporation	13,644
75	Thomson SA	13,273
76	NYNEX Corporation	13,211
77	Westinghouse Electric Corporation	12,844
78	RJR Nabisco, Inc.	12,764
79	Digital Equipment Corporation	12,742
80	Rhône-Poulenc SA	12,650
81	The Travelers Corporation	12,523
82	Rockwell International Corporation	12,518
83	United Parcel Service of America, Inc.	12,400
84	Phillips Petroleum Company	12,384
85	Fleming Companies, Inc.	12,045
86	Minnesota Mining and Manufacturing Co.	11,990
87	Allied-Signal Inc.	11,942
88	Hewlett-Packard Company	11,899
89	Bridgestone Corporation	11,729
90	Sara Lee Corporation	11,718
91	Federal National Mortgage Association	11,557
92	Bell Atlantic Corporation	11,449
93	BankAmerica Corporation	11,389
94	International Paper Company	11,378
95	ConAgra, Inc.	11,340
96	Merrill Lynch & Co., Inc.	11,335
97	Samsung Group	11,245
98	The Great Atlantic & Pacific Tea Company	11,148
99	Super Valu Stores, Inc.	11,136
100	Caterpillar, Inc.	11,126

Note: This list excludes mutual insurance companies.

The 100 Most Profitable Companies in *HOOVER'S HANDBOOK*

Rank	Company Name	1989 Net Income ($ mil)	Rank	Company Name	1989 Net Income ($ mil)
1	General Motors Corporation	4,224	51	Anglo-American Corp. of South Africa	1,037
2	Royal Dutch/Shell Group	4,125	52	BCE Inc.	1,037
3	General Electric Company	3,939	53	Daimler-Benz AG	1,006
4	Ford Motor Company	3,835	54	The Southern Company	969
5	International Business Machines Corp.	3,758	55	USX Corporation	965
6	Exxon Corporation	2,975	56	Aluminum Company of America	945
7	Philip Morris Companies, Inc.	2,946	57	Eli Lilly and Company	940
8	The British Petroleum Company PLC	2,860	58	ITT Corporation	922
9	American Telephone & Telegraph Company	2,697	59	Westinghouse Electric Corporation	922
10	Fiat	2,611	60	Loews Corporation	907
11	The Dow Chemical Company	2,487	61	Pacific Gas and Electric Company	901
12	E. I. du Pont de Nemours and Company	2,480	62	PepsiCo, Inc.	901
13	Texaco Inc.	2,413	63	Texas Utilities Company	888
14	Toyota Motor Corporation	2,403	64	Siemens AG	872
15	Nippon Telegraph and Telephone Corp.	1,997	65	International Paper Company	864
16	The Nomura Securities Company, Ltd.	1,986	66	Abbott Laboratories	860
17	Atlantic Richfield Company	1,953	67	Alcan Aluminium Ltd.	835
18	B.A.T Industries PLC	1,892	68	Hewlett-Packard Company	829
19	Mobil Corporation	1,809	69	Volvo Corporation	826
20	Grand Metropolitan PLC	1,719	70	SCECorp	823
21	BellSouth Corporation	1,695	71	BankAmerica Corporation	820
22	Unilever Group	1,687	72	NYNEX Corporation	808
23	Matsushita Electric Industrial Co., Ltd.	1,617	73	Federal National Mortgage Association	807
24	Amoco Corporation	1,610	74	J. C. Penney Company, Inc.	802
25	Renault	1,607	75	Nissan Motor Co. Ltd.	799
26	Nestlé SA	1,566	76	Broken Hill Proprietary Company Ltd.	779
27	Merck & Co., Inc.	1,495	77	Deutsche Bank AG	778
28	Sears, Roebuck & Co.	1,446	78	Anheuser-Busch Companies, Inc.	767
29	GTE Corporation	1,417	79	SmithKline Beecham PLC	766
30	Hitachi Ltd.	1,406	80	Bristol-Myers Squibb Company	747
31	Dai-Ichi Kangyo Bank, Ltd.	1,382	81	Security Pacific Corporation	741
32	American International Group, Inc.	1,367	82	Guinness PLC	736
33	Hanson PLC	1,309	83	Rockwell International Corporation	735
34	Minnesota Mining and Manufacturing Co.	1,244	84	McDonald's Corporation	727
35	Pacific Telesis Group	1,242	85	The Seagram Company Ltd.	711
36	American Information Technologies Corp.	1,238	86	Xerox Corporation	704
37	Bayer AG	1,233	87	The Walt Disney Company	703
38	The Procter & Gamble Company	1,206	88	United Technologies Corporation	702
39	The Coca-Cola Company	1,193	89	Commonwealth Edison Company	694
40	BASF AG	1,192	90	United Parcel Service of America, Inc.	693
41	American Express Company	1,157	91	American Electric Power Company, Inc.	692
42	Hoechst AG	1,141	92	Pfizer Inc.	681
43	U S West, Inc.	1,111	93	Monsanto Company	679
44	Glaxo Holdings PLC	1,108	94	The Boeing Company	675
45	American Home Products Corporation	1,102	95	Georgia-Pacific Corporation	661
46	Southwestern Bell Corporation	1,093	96	Tokio Marine & Fire	645
47	Johnson & Johnson	1,082	97	The Prudential Insurance Co. of America	644
48	Wal-Mart Stores, Inc.	1,076	98	Aetna Life & Casualty Company	639
49	Bell Atlantic Corporation	1,075	99	American Brands, Inc.	631
50	Digital Equipment Corporation	1,073	100	Telefónica de España, SA	629

The 100 Most Valuable Public Companies in *HOOVER'S HANDBOOK*

Rank	Company Name	1989 Market Value ($ mil)	Rank	Company Name	1989 Market Value ($ mil)
1	Nippon Telegraph & Telephone Corp.	161,417	51	American Home Products Corporation	16,799
2	Exxon Corporation	62,515	52	Sony Corporation	16,356
3	Dai-Ichi Kangyo Bank, Ltd.	59,052	53	Waste Management, Inc.	16,302
4	General Electric Company	58,358	54	Texaco Inc.	15,600
5	International Business Machines Corp.	54,094	55	The Walt Disney Company	15,154
6	Toyota Motor Corporation	50,394	56	Abbott Laboratories	15,044
7	American Telephone & Telegraph Company	48,949	57	U S West, Inc.	14,983
8	The Nomura Securities Company, Ltd.	46,699	58	American Express Company	14,575
9	Royal Dutch/Shell Group	41,546	59	Hanson PLC	14,318
10	Hitachi Ltd.	38,928	60	The Boeing Company	13,689
11	Philip Morris Companies, Inc.	38,650	61	Unilever Group	13,563
12	Matsushita Electric Industrial Co., Ltd.	38,647	62	Eastman Kodak Company	13,348
13	Merck & Co., Inc.	30,644	63	Sears, Roebuck & Co.	13,058
14	Bristol-Myers Squibb Company	29,419	64	McDonald's Corporation	12,489
15	The British Petroleum Company PLC	29,060	65	Bayer AG	11,948
16	E. I. du Pont de Nemours and Company	28,099	66	BCE Inc.	11,856
17	Amoco Corporation	27,942	67	Schlumberger NV	11,675
18	BellSouth Corporation	27,870	68	Pfizer Inc.	11,489
19	The Coca-Cola Company	26,034	69	Hewlett-Packard Company	11,229
20	General Motors Corporation	25,590	70	MCI Communications Corporation	11,000
21	Mobil Corporation	25,583	71	Anheuser-Busch Companies, Inc.	10,895
22	Wal-Mart Stores, Inc.	25,405	72	Westinghouse Electric Corporation	10,740
23	Nissan Motor Co. Ltd.	25,289	73	BASF AG	10,118
24	Siemens AG	24,442	74	Grand Metropolitan PLC	9,979
25	Chevron Corporation	24,053	75	Digital Equipment Corporation	9,966
26	NEC Corporation	23,444	76	Berkshire Hathaway, Inc.	9,942
27	GTE Corporation	23,121	77	Hoechst AG	9,932
28	Daimler-Benz AG	22,831	78	Capital Cities/ABC, Inc.	9,891
29	Roche Holding, Ltd.	22,796	79	CS Holding	9,860
30	The Procter & Gamble Company	22,760	80	Schering-Plough Corporation	9,673
31	Tokio Marine & Fire	22,218	81	Pacific Gas and Electric Company	9,438
32	Bell Atlantic Corporation	21,942	82	Glaxo Holdings PLC	9,414
33	Mitsubishi Group	21,564	83	Citicorp	9,377
34	Pacific Telesis Group	20,997	84	Loews Corporation	9,326
35	Ford Motor Company	20,626	85	The Southern Company	9,204
36	B.A.T Industries PLC	20,260	86	USX Corporation	9,137
37	Nestlé SA	19,845	87	Bridgestone Corporation	8,978
38	Deutsche Bank AG	19,833	88	J. C. Penney Company, Inc.	8,755
39	Fiat	19,783	89	The Seagram Company Ltd.	8,734
40	Johnson & Johnson	19,775	90	Emerson Electric Co.	8,691
41	The Dow Chemical Company	19,221	91	SCECorp	8,602
42	Southwestern Bell Corporation	19,200	92	The Dun & Bradstreet Corporation	8,518
43	Eli Lilly and Company	19,099	93	Kellogg Company	8,242
44	Fujitsu Ltd.	18,456	94	Federal National Mortgage Association	8,092
45	American Information Technologies Corp.	18,373	95	J.P. Morgan & Co. Inc.	8,084
46	Atlantic Richfield Company	18,286	96	Occidental Petroleum Corporation	8,006
47	NYNEX Corporation	18,005	97	Commonwealth Edison Company	7,970
48	Minnesota Mining and Manufacturing Co.	17,730	98	Broken Hill Proprietary Company Ltd.	7,927
49	American International Group, Inc.	16,941	99	United Telecommunications, Inc.	7,870
50	PepsiCo, Inc.	16,876	100	Tenneco, Inc.	7,840

The 100 Largest Employers in *HOOVER'S HANDBOOK*

Rank	Company Name	1989 Employees	Rank	Company Name	1989 Employees
1	General Motors Corporation	775,100	51	Michelin	124,408
2	Sears, Roebuck & Co.	500,000	52	Westinghouse Electric Corporation	122,000
3	International Business Machines Corp.	383,220	53	Chrysler Corporation	121,947
4	Daimler-Benz AG	368,226	54	BCE Inc.	120,000
5	Ford Motor Company	366,600	55	The British Petroleum Company PLC	119,850
6	K mart Corporation	365,000	56	ITT Corporation	119,000
7	Siemens AG	365,000	57	Nissan Motor Co. Ltd.	117,330
8	B.A.T Industries PLC	311,917	58	The May Department Stores Company	115,000
9	Anglo-American Corp. of South Africa	300,000	59	The Goodyear Tire & Rubber Company	111,469
10	Unilever Group	300,000	60	Xerox Corporation	111,400
11	General Electric Company	292,000	61	Safeway, Inc.	110,000
12	Hitachi Ltd.	290,811	62	Rockwell International Corporation	108,700
13	Philips NV	290,000	63	TW Holdings, Inc.	108,000
14	Fiat	286,294	64	American Express Company	107,542
15	American Telephone & Telegraph Company	283,500	65	Allied-Signal Inc.	107,100
16	Nippon Telegraph and Telephone Corp.	283,294	66	Fujitsu Ltd.	104,503
17	Wal-Mart Stores, Inc.	275,000	67	NEC Corporation	104,022
18	PepsiCo, Inc.	266,000	68	Exxon Corporation	104,000
19	Volkswagen AG	257,561	69	General Dynamics Corporation	102,200
20	United Parcel Service of America, Inc.	237,700	70	Motorola, Inc.	102,000
21	Marriott Corporation	230,000	71	Sara Lee Corporation	101,800
22	United Technologies Corporation	201,400	72	BellSouth Corporation	101,000
23	J. C. Penney Company, Inc.	198,000	73	Melville Corporation	100,541
24	Nestlé SA	196,940	74	Campeau Corporation	100,000
25	Matsushita Electric Industrial Co., Ltd.	193,088	75	Thomson SA	100,000
26	ABB Asea Brown Boveri Ltd.	189,493	76	NYNEX Corporation	95,400
27	Roman Catholic Church (US)	182,200	77	Hewlett-Packard Company	95,000
28	McDonald's Corporation	176,000	78	Jardine Matheson Holdings, Ltd.	94,000
29	Samsung Group	175,710	79	Winn-Dixie Stores, Inc.	94,000
30	Robert Bosch GmbH	174,742	80	Bridgestone Corporation	93,193
31	Renault	174,573	81	Citicorp	92,000
32	American Stores Company	170,400	82	Toyota Motor Corporation	91,790
33	Bayer AG	170,200	83	The Great Atlantic & Pacific Tea Company	91,000
34	The Kroger Co.	170,000	84	Bass PLC	90,138
35	Hoechst AG	169,295	85	Tenneco, Inc.	90,000
36	The Boeing Company	163,900	86	AMR Corporation	89,000
37	GTE Corporation	158,000	87	Hanson PLC	89,000
38	Philip Morris Companies, Inc.	157,000	88	Minnesota Mining and Manufacturing Co.	87,584
39	Electrolux AB	152,913	89	Rhône-Poulenc SA	85,629
40	Grand Metropolitan PLC	152,175	90	General Mills, Inc.	83,800
41	E. I. du Pont de Nemours and Company	145,787	91	Johnson & Johnson	83,100
42	Woolworth Corporation	138,000	92	Lockheed Corporation	82,500
43	Eastman Kodak Company	137,750	93	Unisys Corporation	82,300
44	BASF AG	136,990	94	Hyatt Corporation	80,000
45	Dayton Hudson Corporation	135,000	95	Bell Atlantic Corporation	79,100
46	Royal Dutch/Shell Group	135,000	96	The Procter & Gamble Company	79,000
47	Blue Cross and Blue Shield Association	128,729	97	Sony Corporation	78,900
48	McDonnell Douglas Corporation	127,926	98	Volvo Corporation	78,690
49	The ARA Group, Inc.	125,000	99	Federal Express Corporation	78,500
50	Digital Equipment Corporation	125,000	100	R. H. Macy & Co., Inc.	78,000

Note: This list excludes governmental entities.

Companies in *HOOVER'S HANDBOOK* by Metropolitan Area

Enterprises within each metropolitan area or town are listed in order of 1989 sales; companies for which sales were not available are grouped alphabetically at the bottom of each list.

	1989 Sales ($ mil)
Akron, OH	
The Goodyear Tire & Rubber Company	10,869
Roadway Services, Inc.	2,661
Ashland, KY	
Ashland Oil, Inc.	8,062
Atlanta, GA	
BellSouth Corporation	13,996
Georgia-Pacific Corporation	10,171
The Coca-Cola Company	8,966
Delta Air Lines, Inc.	8,089
The Southern Company	7,492
SunTrust Banks, Inc.	3,296
The Home Depot, Inc.	2,759
Cox Enterprises, Inc.	1,974
Turner Broadcasting System, Inc.	1,065
American Cancer Society	358
Austin, TX	
The University of Texas at Austin	619
The Reference Press, Inc.	0
Baltimore, MD	
USF&G Corporation	4,679
The Black & Decker Corporation	3,190
Bartlesville, OK	
Phillips Petroleum Company	12,384
Battle Creek, MI	
Kellogg Company	4,652
Benton Harbor, MI	
Whirlpool Corporation	6,289
Bentonville, AR	
Wal-Mart Stores, Inc.	25,811
Bethlehem, PA	
Union Pacific Corporation	6,492
Bethlehem Steel Corporation	5,251
Birmingham, AL	
Bruno's, Inc.	2,134
Vulcan Materials Company	1,076
Bloomington, IL	
State Farm	NA
Boise, ID	
Albertson's, Inc.	7,423
Boise Cascade Corporation	4,338
Boston, MA	
Digital Equipment Corporation	12,742
John Hancock Mutual Life Insurance Co.	9,451
Raytheon Company	8,796
Bank of Boston Corporation	6,844
The Stop & Shop Companies, Inc.	4,636
The Gillette Company	3,819
Bank of New England Corporation	3,478
Wang Laboratories, Inc.	2,869
General Cinema Corporation	1,914
Polaroid Corporation	1,905
Reebok International Ltd.	1,822
EG&G, Inc.	1,650
Prime Computer, Inc.	1,518
Data General Corporation	1,314
Harvard University	952
Lotus Development Corporation	556
Boston Celtics LP	27
Charlotte, NC	
NCNB Corporation	6,036
Duke Power Company	3,648
Springs Industries, Inc.	1,909

	1989 Sales ($ mil)
Chicago, IL	
Sears, Roebuck & Co.	53,794
Amoco Corporation	23,966
Sara Lee Corporation	11,718
American Information Technologies Corp.	10,211
UAL Corporation	9,794
Motorola, Inc.	9,620
Baxter International Inc.	7,399
McDonald's Corporation	6,065
Commonwealth Edison Company	5,751
The Quaker Oats Company	5,724
First Chicago Corporation	5,611
Walgreen Co.	5,380
Abbott Laboratories	5,380
Montgomery Ward & Co., Inc.	5,349
Waste Management, Inc.	4,459
Beatrice Companies, Inc.	4,262
Navistar International Corporation	4,241
Inland Steel Industries, Inc.	4,147
Whitman Corporation	3,986
Household International, Inc.	3,490
FMC Corporation	3,415
Arthur Andersen & Co.	3,382
Continental Bank Corporation	3,203
R. R. Donnelley & Sons Company	3,122
Santa Fe Pacific Corporation	2,978
Farley Industries	2,865
Brunswick Corporation	2,826
Kemper Corporation	2,774
Premark International, Inc.	2,592
Tribune Company	2,455
Hyatt Corporation	2,400
City of Chicago	2,366
Borg-Warner Corporation	2,216
USG Corporation	2,191
Bally Manufacturing Corporation	1,990
Square D Company	1,631
Zenith Electronics Corporation	1,549
Outboard Marine Corporation	1,464
Morton International, Inc.	1,407
Hartmarx Corporation	1,297
Wm. Wrigley Jr. Company	993
Chicago and North Western	955
Commerce Clearing House, Inc.	677
Midway Airlines, Inc.	494
The University of Chicago	362
Baker & McKenzie	341
Johnson Publishing Company, Inc.	241
Skidmore, Owings & Merrill	71
Johnson Products Company, Inc.	29
Blue Cross and Blue Shield Association	NA
Rotary International	NA
Cincinnati, OH	
The Procter & Gamble Company	21,398
The Kroger Co.	19,104
American Financial Corporation	7,177
Chiquita Brands International, Inc.	3,823
The United States Shoe Corporation	2,557
Mercantile Stores Company, Inc.	2,337
Cleveland, OH	
TRW Inc.	7,340
Eaton Corporation	3,671
The Sherwin-Williams Company	2,123
Reliance Electric Company	1,411
American Greetings Corporation	1,287
Columbus, IN	
Cummins Engine Company, Inc.	3,511

Companies in *HOOVER'S HANDBOOK* by Metropolitan Area (continued)

	1989 Sales ($ mil)
Columbus, OH	
American Electric Power Company, Inc.	5,140
The Limited, Inc.	4,648
Banc One Corporation	3,163
Wendy's International, Inc.	1,051
The Ohio State University	NA
Corning, NY	
Corning Inc.	2,439
Dallas-Fort Worth, TX	
J. C. Penney Company, Inc.	16,405
AMR Corporation	10,480
The Southland Corporation	8,352
Texas Instruments Inc.	6,522
The LTV Corporation	6,362
Kimberly-Clark Corporation	5,734
Halliburton Company	5,660
Burlington Northern Inc.	4,606
Texas Utilities Company	4,321
Tandy Corporation	4,181
Dresser Industries, Inc.	3,956
Trammell Crow Company	1,628
Southwest Airlines Company	1,015
Dr Pepper/Seven-Up Companies, Inc.	514
Dayton, OH	
NCR Corporation	5,956
The Mead Corporation	4,612
Decatur, IL	
Archer-Daniels-Midland Company	7,929
Denver, CO	
U S West, Inc.	9,691
Tele-Communications, Inc.	3,026
Rio Grande Industries, Inc.	2,702
Manville Corporation	2,192
Cyprus Minerals Company	1,790
Adolph Coors Company	1,764
Storage Technology Corporation	983
Detroit, MI	
General Motors Corporation	124,993
Ford Motor Company	96,146
Chrysler Corporation	34,922
K mart Corporation	29,793
Masco Corporation	3,151
Eden, NC	
Fieldcrest Cannon, Inc.	1,362
Fremont, MI	
Gerber Products Company	1,068
Grand Rapids, MI	
Amway Corporation	1,513
Green Bay, WI	
The Green Bay Packers, Inc.	30
Greensboro, NC	
Burlington Holdings, Inc.	2,181
Harrisburg, PA	
Rite Aid Corporation	3,173
AMP Inc.	2,797
Hershey Foods Corporation	2,421
Hartford, CT	
Aetna Life & Casualty Company	19,671
United Technologies Corporation	19,614
The Travelers Corporation	12,523
Honolulu, HI	
HAL, Inc.	349

	1989 Sales ($ mil)
Houston, TX	
Tenneco, Inc.	14,083
The Coastal Corporation	8,271
Sysco Corporation	6,851
Continental Airlines Holdings Inc.	6,685
Cooper Industries, Inc.	5,115
Compaq Computer Corporation	2,876
Panhandle Eastern Corporation	2,781
Browning Ferris Industries, Inc.	2,551
Baker Hughes Inc.	2,328
Pennzoil Company	1,985
Union Texas Petroleum Holdings, Inc.	981
King Ranch, Inc.	NA
Huntsville, AL	
SCI Systems, Inc.	987
Intergraph Corporation	860
Indianapolis, IN	
Eli Lilly and Company	4,176
Mayflower Group, Inc.	676
Jacksonville, FL	
Winn-Dixie Stores, Inc.	9,151
Barnett Banks, Inc.	3,038
Kalamazoo, MI	
The Upjohn Company	2,916
Kansas City, MO-KS	
United Telecommunications, Inc.	7,549
Hallmark Cards, Inc.	2,500
Yellow Freight System	2,220
Kenosha, WI	
Snap-on Tools Corporation	938
Lakeland, FL	
Publix Super Markets, Inc.	5,331
Lancaster, PA	
Armstrong World Industries, Inc.	2,513
Little Rock, AR	
Dillard Department Stores, Inc.	3,049
Los Angeles, CA	
Occidental Petroleum Corporation	20,068
Atlantic Richfield Company	15,351
Rockwell International Corporation	12,518
Unocal Corporation	10,056
Security Pacific Corporation	10,018
Lockheed Corporation	9,891
SCECorp	6,904
First Interstate Bancorp	6,535
Northrop Corporation	5,248
The Vons Companies, Inc.	5,221
Litton Industries, Inc.	5,023
The Walt Disney Company	4,594
H. F. Ahmanson & Company	4,378
Great Western Financial Corporation	3,881
National Medical Enterprises, Inc.	3,679
Teledyne, Inc.	3,531
The Times Mirror Company	3,475
MCA Inc.	3,272
Carter Hawley Hale Stores, Inc.	2,787
Castle & Cooke, Inc.	2,718
Fleetwood Enterprises, Inc.	1,619
Mattel, Inc.	1,237
First Executive Corporation	1,195
Hilton Hotels Corporation	954
Louisville, KY	
Humana Inc.	4,088
Brown-Forman Corporation	1,006

Companies in *HOOVER'S HANDBOOK* by Metropolitan Area (continued)

	1989 Sales ($ mil)
Melbourne, FL	
Harris Corporation	2,214
Memphis, TN	
Federal Express Corporation	5,167
Miami, FL	
Ryder System, Inc.	5,073
Knight-Ridder, Inc.	2,268
Midland, MI	
The Dow Chemical Company	17,600
Milwaukee, WI	
Northwestern Mutual	6,307
Johnson Controls, Inc.	3,684
Harley-Davidson, Inc.	791
Minneapolis, MN	
Cargill, Inc.	43,000
Dayton Hudson Corporation	13,644
Minnesota Mining and Manufacturing Co.	11,990
Super Valu Stores, Inc.	11,136
NWA, Inc.	6,554
Carlson Companies, Inc.	6,200
Honeywell Inc.	6,059
General Mills, Inc.	5,621
Control Data Corporation	2,935
Deluxe Corporation	1,316
Cray Research, Inc.	785
Modesto, CA	
E. & J. Gallo Winery	NA
Moline, IL	
Deere & Company	7,127
Nashville, TN	
Hospital Corporation of America	4,274
Service Merchandise Company, Inc.	3,307
New Orleans, LA	
Entergy Corporation	3,724
McDermott International, Inc.	2,423
New York, NY-CT-NJ	
Exxon Corporation	86,656
International Business Machines Corp.	62,710
General Electric Company	53,884
American Telephone & Telegraph Company	50,976
The Prudential Insurance Co. of America	43,034
Philip Morris Companies, Inc.	39,011
Salomon Inc	38,608
Citicorp	37,970
Texaco Inc.	32,416
American Express Company	25,047
ITT Corporation	20,054
GTE Corporation	17,424
Xerox Corporation	16,806
New York Life Insurance Company	15,297
PepsiCo, Inc.	15,242
American International Group, Inc.	14,546
The Chase Manhattan Corporation	13,904
NYNEX Corporation	13,211
Equitable	13,201
RJR Nabisco, Inc.	12,764
United Parcel Service of America, Inc.	12,400
Allied-Signal Inc.	11,942
International Paper Company	11,378
Merrill Lynch & Co., Inc.	11,335
The Great Atlantic & Pacific Tea Company	11,148
Loews Corporation	11,098
J.P. Morgan & Co. Inc.	10,394
Johnson & Johnson	9,757
Bristol-Myers Squibb Company	9,189
Woolworth Corporation	8,820

	1989 Sales ($ mil)
Union Carbide Corporation	8,744
Manufacturers Hanover Corporation	8,420
Chemical Banking Corporation	8,227
Time Warner Inc.	7,642
Borden, Inc.	7,593
Melville Corporation	7,554
American Brands, Inc.	7,265
Bankers Trust New York Corporation	7,258
R. H. Macy & Co., Inc.	6,974
American Home Products Corporation	6,747
Merck & Co., Inc.	6,551
Supermarkets General Holdings	6,299
W. R. Grace & Company	6,115
Morgan Stanley Group Inc.	5,831
Primerica Corporation	5,695
Pfizer Inc.	5,672
Consolidated Edison Co. of New York, Inc.	5,551
The Bank of New York Company, Inc.	5,497
The United Nations	5,443
MacAndrews & Forbes Holdings Inc.	5,325
Champion International Corporation	5,163
CPC International Inc.	5,103
Colgate-Palmolive Company	5,039
Capital Cities/ABC, Inc.	4,957
American Cyanamid Company	4,825
Public Service Enterprise Group Inc.	4,805
Ames Department Stores, Inc.	4,793
Toys "R" Us, Inc.	4,788
Schlumberger NV	4,686
Trans World Airlines, Inc.	4,507
The Dun & Bradstreet Corporation	4,322
Warner-Lambert Company	4,196
AMAX Inc.	3,892
Pan Am Corporation	3,561
Ingersoll-Rand Company	3,447
Paramount Communications Inc.	3,392
American Standard Inc.	3,334
Avon Products, Inc.	3,300
Schering-Plough Corporation	3,158
First Fidelity Bancorporation	3,028
CBS Inc.	2,962
Advance Publications, Inc.	2,882
Pitney Bowes, Inc.	2,876
General Re Corporation	2,771
Riklis Family Corporation	2,500
Marsh & McLennan Companies, Inc.	2,428
ASARCO Inc.	2,211
The Hertz Corporation	2,181
The Hearst Corporation	2,094
The Stanley Works	1,972
General Signal Corporation	1,918
Estee Lauder Inc.	1,900
The Reader's Digest Association, Inc.	1,832
Becton, Dickinson and Company	1,811
McGraw-Hill, Inc.	1,789
The New York Times Company	1,769
JWP, Inc.	1,742
Dow Jones & Company, Inc.	1,688
Automatic Data Processing, Inc.	1,678
Viacom Inc.	1,436
Liz Claiborne, Inc.	1,411
New York City Transit Authority	1,401
Helmsley Enterprises Inc.	1,400
Hillsborough Holdings Corporation	1,387
Ogden Corporation	1,369
TLC Beatrice International Holdings, Inc.	1,141
Computer Associates International, Inc.	1,030

Companies in *HOOVER'S HANDBOOK* by Metropolitan Area (continued)

	1989 Sales ($ mil)
New York, NY-CT-NJ (continued)	
International Flavors & Fragrances Inc.	870
Young & Rubicam Inc.	865
C. R. Bard, Inc.	778
McKinsey & Co.	635
New York Stock Exchange, Inc.	349
The Ford Foundation	307
The Rockefeller Foundation	305
The Goldman Sachs Group, LP	NA
Kohlberg Kravis Roberts & Co.	NA
Metropolitan Life Insurance Company	NA
Teachers Insurance	NA
Newton, IA	
Maytag Corporation	3,089
Norfolk, VA	
Norfolk Southern Corporation	4,536
North Wilkesboro, NC	
Lowe's Companies, Inc.	2,651
Oklahoma City, OK	
Fleming Companies, Inc.	12,045
Omaha, NE	
ConAgra, Inc.	11,340
Peter Kiewit Sons' Inc.	5,058
Berkshire Hathaway, Inc.	2,483
Peoria, IL	
Caterpillar Inc.	11,126
Philadelphia, PA	
CIGNA Corporation	15,654
Bell Atlantic Corporation	11,449
Unisys Corporation	10,097
Sun Company, Inc.	9,805
Campbell Soup Company	5,672
Scott Paper Company	5,066
The ARA Group, Inc.	4,244
Consolidated Rail Corporation	3,411
Commodore International Ltd.	940
Phoenix, AZ	
Greyhound Dial Corporation	3,537
The Circle K Corporation	3,493
Phelps Dodge Corporation	2,700
Pinnacle West Capital Corporation	1,508
America West Airlines, Inc.	993
Pittsburgh, PA	
USX Corporation	17,533
Westinghouse Electric Corporation	12,844
Aluminum Company of America	10,910
H. J. Heinz Company	5,801
PPG Industries, Inc.	5,734
PNC Financial Corp	4,645
Mellon Bank Corporation	3,607
Portland, OR	
Fred Meyer, Inc.	2,285
NIKE, Inc.	1,711
Portsmouth, NH	
The Henley Group, Inc.	1,566
Providence, RI	
Textron, Inc.	7,431
Hasbro, Inc.	1,410
Racine, WI	
S.C. Johnson & Son, Inc.	NA
Reading, PA	
V. F. Corporation	2,533

	1989 Sales ($ mil)
Richmond, VA	
CSX Corporation	7,745
Reynolds Metals Company	6,143
James River Corporation	5,872
Universal Corporation	2,920
Rochester, MN	
Mayo Foundation	1,058
Rochester, NY	
Eastman Kodak Company	18,398
Sacramento, CA	
State of California	NA
Salisbury, NC	
Food Lion, Inc.	4,717
Salt Lake City, UT	
American Stores Company	22,004
Thiokol Corporation	1,168
San Antonio, TX	
Associated Milk Producers, Inc.	2,987
San Diego, CA	
The Price Company	5,012
San Francisco, CA	
Chevron Corporation	29,443
Safeway, Inc.	14,325
Hewlett-Packard Company	11,899
BankAmerica Corporation	11,389
Pacific Telesis Group	9,593
Pacific Gas and Electric Company	8,588
McKesson Corporation	7,046
Transamerica Corporation	6,834
Wells Fargo & Company	5,649
Apple Computer, Inc.	5,284
Bechtel Group, Inc.	5,111
Consolidated Freightways, Inc.	3,760
Levi Strauss and Company	3,680
Intel Corporation	3,127
American President Companies, Ltd.	2,300
Longs Drug Stores Corporation	2,111
Amdahl Corporation	2,101
Sun Microsystems, Inc.	1,765
National Semiconductor Corporation	1,648
Tandem Computers Inc.	1,633
Seagate Technology, Inc.	1,372
The Clorox Company	1,356
The Charles Schwab Corporation	553
Atari Corporation	424
Genentech, Inc.	383
Stanford University	NA
Seattle-Tacoma, WA	
The Boeing Company	20,276
Weyerhaeuser Company	10,106
PACCAR Inc.	3,523
Costco Wholesale Corporation	3,000
Nordstrom, Inc.	2,671
Alaska Air Group, Inc.	917
Microsoft Corporation	804
McCaw Cellular Communications, Inc.	504
Spartanburg, SC	
TW Holdings, Inc.	3,485
Milliken & Co., Inc.	2,900
Springdale, AR	
Tyson Foods, Inc.	2,538
Springfield, MA	
Massachusetts Mutual Life Insurance Co.	10,226

Companies in *HOOVER'S HANDBOOK* by Metropolitan Area (continued)

	1989 Sales ($ mil)
St. Louis, MO	
McDonnell Douglas Corporation	14,581
General Dynamics Corporation	10,043
The May Department Stores Company	9,602
Anheuser-Busch Companies, Inc.	9,481
Southwestern Bell Corporation	8,730
Monsanto Company	8,681
Emerson Electric Co.	7,071
Ralston Purina Company	6,658
INTERCO Inc.	1,656
Tampa, FL	
Jack Eckerd Corporation	3,171
Toledo, OH	
Dana Corporation	5,157
Owens-Illinois, Inc.	3,605
Owens-Corning Fiberglas Corporation	3,000
Washington, DC-MD-VA	
Mobil Corporation	50,220
Federal National Mortgage Association	11,557
Mars, Inc.	8,541
Marriott Corporation	7,536
MCI Communications Corporation	6,471
USAir Group, Inc.	6,252
Martin Marietta Corporation	5,796
Gannett Co., Inc.	3,518
Giant Food, Inc.	3,249
GEICO Corporation	1,929
Teamsters	1,545
The Washington Post Company	1,444
National Geographic Society	426
American Association of Retired Persons	291
AFL-CIO	NA
Democratic Party	NA
National Organization for Women, Inc.	NA
National Park Service	NA
Republican Party	NA
Roman Catholic Church (US)	NA
United States of America	NA
United Way of America	NA
West Palm Beach, FL	
FPL Group, Inc.	6,180
Wilmington, DE	
E. I. du Pont de Nemours and Company	35,099
The Columbia Gas System, Inc.	3,204
Hercules, Inc.	3,092
The E.W. Scripps Company	1,266
Wooster, OH	
Rubbermaid Inc.	1,344
Youngstown, OH	
Edward J. DeBartolo Corporation	1,189

Foreign Companies in *HOOVER'S HANDBOOK* by Country

	1989 Sales ($ mil)
Australia	
Broken Hill Proprietary Company Ltd.	7,887
The News Corporation Ltd.	6,397
Canada	
BCE Inc.	14,406
Campeau Corporation	10,439
Canadian Pacific Ltd.	9,517
Alcan Aluminium Ltd.	8,839
The Seagram Company Ltd.	4,508
France	
Renault	30,125
Thomson SA	13,273
Rhône-Poulenc SA	12,650
Michelin	9,566
BSN SA	8,425
Germany	
Daimler-Benz AG	45,202
Volkswagen AG	38,670
Siemens AG	36,170
BASF AG	28,176
Hoechst AG	27,159
Bayer AG	25,621
Robert Bosch GmbH	18,099
Deutsche Bank AG	17,381
Bertelsmann AG	7,386
Hong Kong	
Hutchison Whampoa Ltd.	2,267
Jardine Matheson Holdings, Ltd.	1,931
Hongkong & Shanghai Banking Corp. Ltd.	NA
Italy	
Fiat SpA	41,089
Japan	
Mitsubishi Corporation	108,778
Toyota Motor Corporation	55,701
Hitachi Ltd.	48,496
Nippon Telegraph and Telephone Corp.	44,257
Matsushita Electric Industrial Co., Ltd.	41,699
Nissan Motor Co. Ltd.	33,417
Dai-Ichi Kangyo Bank, Ltd.	23,618
NEC Corporation	23,179
Sony Corporation	16,678
Fujitsu Ltd.	16,576
Bridgestone Corporation	11,729
The Nomura Securities Company, Ltd.	8,139
Honda Motor Co., Ltd.	3,489
Tokio Marine & Fire	NA
Korea	
Samsung Co., Ltd.	11,245
Hyundai Group	8,424
Netherlands	
Royal Dutch/Shell Group	85,412
Unilever Group	34,434
Philips NV	29,985
KPMG	4,300
KLM	2,787
South Africa	
Anglo-American Corp. of South Africa	NA
Soviet Union	
Soviet Union	NA
Spain	
Telefónica de España, SA	6,495

Foreign Companies in *HOOVER'S HANDBOOK* by Country (continued)

	1989 Sales ($ mil)
Sweden	
Volvo Corporation	14,656
Electrolux AB	13,697
Switzerland	
Nestlé SA	31,192
ABB Asea Brown Boveri Ltd.	20,560
Roche Holding, Ltd.	6,373
CS Holding	6,203
Arthur Andersen & Co.	3,382
The Red Cross	NA
United Kingdom	
Royal Dutch/Shell Group	85,412
The British Petroleum Company PLC	48,611
Unilever Group	34,434
B.A.T Industries PLC	15,281
Grand Metropolitan PLC	14,970
Hanson PLC	11,267
SmithKline Beecham PLC	7,884
Bass PLC	6,498
Guinness PLC	4,952
Cadbury Schweppes PLC	4,578
Glaxo Holdings PLC	4,138
Price Waterhouse & Co.	2,468
Pearson PLC	2,351
Maxwell Communications Corp., PLC	2,238
Reuters Holdings PLC	1,916
Saatchi & Saatchi Company PLC	1,572
Lloyd's of London	NA

20 Largest Airline Companies in the World

Rank	Company	Country	1989 Sales ($ mil)	1989 Passenger Miles (bil)
1	AMR	US	10,590	73.5
2	UAL	US	9,915	69.6
3	Japan	Japan	8,509	33.7
4	Delta	US	8,090	55.9
5	British Airways	Britain	7,529	35.9
6	Lufthansa	Germany	6,941	22.5
7	Continental	US	6,769	50.4
8	NWA	US	6,554	45.7
9	USAir	US	6,257	33.7
10	Air France	France	6,217	22.9
11	All Nippon Airways	Japan	4,858	16.1
12	Scandinavian Airlines System	*	4,567	9.5
13	TWA	US	4,507	35.0
14	Hanjin Group	South Korea	4,244	11.1
15	PanAm	US	3,794	28.9
16	Alitalia	Italy	3,734	12.9
17	Swissair	Switzerland	3,175	9.8
18	Air Canada	Canada	3,104	16.3
19	Iberia	Spain	3,016	13.1
20	KLM	Netherlands	2,939	14.9

* Sweden, Denmark, and Norway

Source: *Fortune*, September 24, 1990.

Leading Brands in the US by Category

Category	Brand	Company
Analgesics	Tylenol	Johnson & Johnson
Antacids	Maalox	Rhône-Poulenc
Apparel	Levi's, Dockers	Levi Strauss
Appliances (major)	General Electric	General Electric
Appliances (small)	Black & Decker	Black & Decker
Athletic shoes	NIKE	NIKE
Autos & trucks (Asian imports)	Toyota	Toyota
Autos & trucks (European imports)	Volkswagen	Volkswagen
Autos & trucks (US)	Ford	Ford
Bathroom tissue	Charmin	Procter & Gamble
Beer	Budweiser	Anheuser-Busch
Cereal	Cheerios	General Mills
Cigarettes	Marlboro	Philip Morris
Chocolate candy	M&Ms	Mars
Coffee	Folgers	Procter & Gamble
Consumer electronics	Panasonic	Matsushita
Cosmetics	Cover Girl	Procter & Gamble
Coughs/colds	Halls	Warner-Lambert
Deodorant	Secret	Procter & Gamble
Detergent	Tide	Procter & Gamble
Facial tissue	Kleenex	Kimberly-Clark
Frozen meals	Stouffer's	Nestlé
Fruit juices	Tropicana	Seagram
Hand soap	Dial	Greyhound Dial
Liquor	Bacardi	Bacardi
Paper towels	Bounty	Procter & Gamble
Shampoo	Pert Plus	Procter & Gamble
Soft drinks	Coca-Cola	Coca-Cola
Toothpaste	Crest	Procter & Gamble
Wine	Carlo Rossi	E. & J. Gallo

Source: *Superbrands 1990, Adweek Supplement*

30 YEARS OF CHANGE IN THE *FORTUNE* 500

The 25 Largest US Industrial Companies

Rank	1959	1969	1979	1989
1	General Motors	General Motors	Exxon	General Motors
2	Standard Oil (NJ)	Standard Oil (NJ)	General Motors	Ford
3	Ford	Ford	Mobil	Exxon
4	General Electric	General Electric	Ford	IBM
5	U. S. Steel	IBM	Texaco	General Electric
6	Socony Mobil Oil	Chrysler	Standard Oil (CA)	Mobil
7	Gulf Oil	Mobil	Gulf Oil	Philip Morris
8	Texaco	Texaco	IBM	Chrysler
9	Chrysler	ITT	General Electric	Du Pont
10	Swift	Gulf Oil	Standard Oil (IN)	Texaco
11	Western Electric	Western Electric	ITT	Chevron
12	Du Pont	U. S. Steel	Atlantic Richfield	Amoco
13	Bethlehem Steel	Standard Oil (CA)	Shell Oil	Shell Oil
14	Standard Oil (IN)	Ling-Temco-Vought	U. S. Steel	Procter & Gamble
15	Westinghouse Electric	Du Pont	Conoco	Boeing
16	Armour	Shell Oil	Du Pont	Occidental Petroleum
17	General Dynamics	Westinghouse Electric	Chrysler	United Technologies
18	Shell Oil	Standard Oil (IN)	Tenneco	Eastman Kodak
19	Boeing	General Telephone & Electronics	Western Electric	USX
20	National Dairy Products	Goodyear	Sun	Dow Chemical
21	Goodyear	RCA	Occidental Petroleum	Xerox
22	Standard Oil (CA)	Swift	Phillips Petroleum	Atlantic Richfield
23	Union Carbide	McDonnell Douglas	Procter & Gamble	PepsiCo
24	Radio Corporation of America	Union Carbide	Dow Chemical	RJR Nabisco
25	Procter & Gamble	Bethlehem Steel	Union Carbide	McDonnell Douglas

The 10 Largest US Retail Companies

Rank	1959	1969	1979	1989
1	Great Atlantic & Pacific Tea	Sears, Roebuck	Sears, Roebuck	Sears, Roebuck
2	Sears, Roebuck	Great Atlantic & Pacific Tea	Safeway Stores	K mart
3	Safeway Stores	Safeway Stores	K mart	Wal-Mart
4	Kroger	J. C. Penney	J. C. Penney	American Stores
5	J. C. Penney	Kroger	Kroger	Kroger
6	Montgomery Ward	Marcor	Great Atlantic & Pacific Tea	J. C. Penney
7	F. W. Woolworth	F. W. Woolworth	F. W. Woolworth	Safeway Stores
8	American Stores	S. S. Kresge	Lucky Stores	Dayton Hudson
9	National Tea	Federated Department Stores	Federated Department Stores	May Department Stores
10	Federated Department Stores	Food Fair Stores	Montgomery Ward	Great Atlantic & Pacific Tea

The 10 Largest US Transportation Companies

Rank	1959	1969	1979	1989
1	Pennsylvania Railroad	Penn Central	Trans World	United Parcel Service
2	Southern Pacific	UAL	UAL	AMR
3	New York Central Railroad	Southern Pacific	United Parcel Service	UAL
4	Atchison, Topeka & Santa Fe Rwy.	Trans World Airlines	American Airlines	Delta Air Lines
5	Union Pacific Railroad	Pan American World Airways	Burlington Northern	CSX
6	Baltimore & Ohio Railroad	American Airlines	Eastern Air Lines	Texas Air
7	American Airlines	Norfolk & Western Railway	Southern Pacific	Union Pacific
8	Pan American World Airways	Burlington Northern	Santa Fe Industries	NWA
9	Trans World Airlines	Chesapeake & Ohio	Pan American World Airways	USAir
10	Chesapeake & Ohio Railway	Eastern Air Lines	Delta Air Lines	Federal Express

Source: *Fortune* annual lists issues, 1960-1990

20 Largest US Advertisers

Rank	Company	1989 Ad Spending ($ mil)
1	Philip Morris	2,072
2	Procter & Gamble	1,779
3	Sears	1,432
4	General Motors	1,364
5	Grand Metropolitan	823
6	PepsiCo	786
7	McDonald's	774
8	Eastman Kodak	719
9	RJR Nabisco	704
10	Kellogg	612
11	Nestlé	608
12	Unilever	604
13	Ford	602
14	Anheuser-Busch	592
15	Warner-Lambert	586
16	AT&T	568
17	Time Warner	568
18	K mart	561
19	Chrysler	533
20	Johnson & Johnson	487

Source: *Advertising Age*, September 26, 1990, Crain Communications, Inc.

20 Most Powerful Brands in the US

Rank	Brand	Parent Company
1	Coca-Cola	Coca-Cola
2	Campbell's	Campbell Soup
3	Disney	Walt Disney
4	Pepsi-Cola	PepsiCo
5	Kodak	Eastman Kodak
6	NBC	General Electric
7	Black & Decker	Black & Decker
8	Kellogg	Kellogg
9	McDonald's	McDonald's
10	Hershey's	Hershey
11	Levi's	Levi Strauss
12	GE	General Electric
13	Sears	Sears
14	Hallmark	Hallmark
15	Johnson & Johnson	Johnson & Johnson
16	Betty Crocker	General Mills
17	Kraft	Philip Morris
18	Kleenex	Kimberly-Clark
19	Jell-O	Philip Morris
20	Tylenol	Johnson & Johnson

Source: Landor Associates' ImagePower Survey in *Superbrands 1990, Adweek Supplement*

20 Most Advertised US Brands, Products, and Services

Rank	Brand, Product or Service	Parent Company	1989 Measured Ad Spending ($ mil)
1	McDonald's restaurants	McDonald's	425
2	Kellogg cereals	Kellogg	373
3	Sears stores	Sears	364
4	AT&T	AT&T	314
5	Ford passenger cars	Ford	197
6	Budweiser beer	Anheuser-Busch	183
7	Chevrolet passenger cars	General Motors	181
8	Nissan passenger cars	Nissan	174
9	Burger King restaurants	Grand Metropolitan	170
10	Toyota passenger cars	Toyota	162
11	Miller beer	Philip Morris	147
12	Macy's stores	R. H. Macy	147
13	Oldsmobile passenger cars	General Motors	129
14	K mart stores	K mart	129
15	Mazda passenger cars	Mazda	126
16	American Express credit cards	American Express	124
17	Ford trucks & vans	Ford	121
18	Kentucky Fried Chicken	PepsiCo	119
19	Wrigley	Wrigley	113
20	Pontiac passenger cars	General Motors	112

Source: LNA/Arbitron Multi-Media Service; *Advertising Age*, May 21, 1990, Crain Communications, Inc.

20 Most Powerful Brands in the World

Rank	Brand	Parent Company
1	Coca-Cola	Coca-Cola
2	Sony	Sony
3	Mercedes-Benz	Daimler-Benz
4	Kodak	Eastman Kodak
5	Disney	Walt Disney
6	Nestlé	Nestlé
7	Toyota	Toyota
8	McDonald's	McDonald's
9	IBM	IBM
10	Pepsi-Cola	PepsiCo
11	Rolls-Royce	Rolls-Royce
12	Honda	Honda
13	Panasonic	Matsushita
14	Levi's	Levi Stauss
15	Kleenex	Kimberly-Clark
16	Ford	Ford
17	Volkswagen	Volkswagen
18	Kellogg	Kellogg
19	Porsche	Porsche AG
20	Polaroid	Polaroid

Source: Landor Associates' ImagePower Survey in *Superbrands 1990, Adweek Supplement*

10 Largest Soft Drink Companies in the US

Rank	Parent Company	1989 Market Share %
1	Coca-Cola	41.1
2	PepsiCo	31.1
3	Dr Pepper/7Up	10.1
4	Cadbury Beverages (Cadbury Schweppes)	3.2
5	Royal Crown	2.8
6	A&W Brands	2.3
7	National Beverage	1.6
8	Monarch	1.5
9	Barq's	0.4
10	Double-Cola	0.3
	Top ten total	94.4
	All others	5.6
	Total industry	100.0

Source: *Beverage World,* March 1990

8 Largest Beer Companies in the US

Rank	Company	1989 Market Share %
1	Anheuser-Busch	42.1
2	Miller (Philip Morris)	22.8
3	Stroh	10.1
4	Adolph Coors	9.4
5	Heileman	7.1
6	Pabst	3.6
7	Genesee	1.3
8	Latrobe	0.3
	Total	96.7
	All others	3.3
	Industry total	100.0

Source: *Beverage World,* March 1990

10 Largest Restaurant Sales in the US

Rank	Chain	1989 US Sales ($ mil)	Parent Company
1	McDonald's	12,012	McDonald's
2	Burger King	5,700	Grand Metropolitan
3	Pizza Hut	3,240	PepsiCo
4	Kentucky Fried Chicken	3,000	PepsiCo
5	Hardee's	2,980	Imasco
6	Wendy's	2,827	Wendy's International
7	Domino's Pizza	2,500	Domino's Pizza
8	Marriott	2,120	Marriott
9	Taco Bell	2,000	PepsiCo
10	Dairy Queen	1,938	American Dairy Queen

Source: NRN Research; *Nation's Restaurant News,* August 6, 1990
Note: Includes franchisees

10 Largest Restaurants in the US

Rank	Restaurant	1989 Total Sales ($ thou)
1	The Rainbow Room, New York, NY	26,700
2	Smith & Wollensky, New York, NY	18,000
3	Phillips Harborplace, Ocean City, MD	15,873
4	Spengers' Fish Grotto, Berkeley, CA	14,050
5	El Charro Avitia, Carson City, NV	14,000
6	Kapok Tree Restaurant, Clearwater, FL	13,922
7	Zehnders, Frankenmuth, MI	12,916
8	The Waterfront, Covington, KY	12,130
9	Frankenmuth Bavarian Inn, Frankenmuth, MI	11,410
10	Bob Chinn's Crabhouse Restaurant, Wheeling, IL	10,810

Source: *Restaurant Hospitality,* June 1990

20 Largest Retailers in the US

Rank	Company	1989 Sales ($ mil)
1	Sears	31,599
2	K mart	29,533
3	Wal-Mart	25,811
4	American Stores	22,004
5	Kroger	19,104
6	J. C. Penney	16,103
7	Safeway	14,325
8	Dayton Hudson	13,644
9	Great A&P	11,148
10	Campeau	10,440
11	May Department Stores	9,425
12	Winn-Dixie	9,151
13	Woolworth	8,820
14	Southland	8,275
15	Melville	7,554
16	Albertson's	7,423
17	R. H. Macy	6,974
18	Supermarkets General	6,299
19	Publix	5,386
20	Walgreen	5,380

Source: *Chain Store Age Executive,* August 1990
Note: Retail store sales only

20 Largest Advertising Agencies in the World

Rank	Agency	1989 Worldwide Sales ($ mil)
1	Dentsu Inc.	1,316
2	Saatchi & Saatchi Advertising Worldwide	890
3	Young & Rubicam	865
4	Backer Spielvogel Bates Worldwide	760
5	McCann-Erickson Worldwide	716
6	Ogilvy & Mather Worldwide	700
7	BBDO Worldwide	657
8	J. Walter Thompson Co.	626
9	Lintas: Worldwide	593
10	Hakuhodo Inc.	586
11	DDB Needham Worldwide	553
12	Foote, Cone & Belding Communications	511
13	Grey Advertising	499
14	Leo Burnett Co.	484
15	D'Arcy Masius Benton & Bowles	472
16	EWDB Worldwide	381
17	Publicis-FCB Communications B.V.	359
18	NW Ayer Inc.	211
19	Bozell Inc.	191
20	RSCG	175

Source: *Advertising Age*, March 26, 1990, Crain Communications, Inc.

20 Largest Advertising Agencies in the US

Rank	Agency	1989 US Sales ($ mil)
1	Young & Rubicam	410
2	Saatchi & Saatchi Worldwide	395
3	BBDO Worldwide	374
4	Backer Spielvogel Bates	311
5	Ogilvy & Mather Worldwide	305
6	DDB Needham Worldwide	303
7	Leo Burnett Co.	289
8	Foote, Cone & Belding	281
9	J. Walter Thompson Co.	267
10	Grey Advertising	241
11	D'Arcy Masius Benton & Bowles	232
12	Lintas: Worldwide	225
13	McCann-Erickson Worldwide	209
14	Bozell Inc.	155
15	Wells, Rich, Greene	133
16	NW Ayer Inc.	129
17	Ketchum Communications	113
18	Chiat/Day/Mojo	106
19	Ross Roy Group	98
20	Della Femina, McNamee EWDB	88

Source: *Advertising Age*, March 26, 1990, Crain Communications, Inc.

25 Largest Magazines in the US

Rank	Magazine	1989 Sales ($ mil)	1989 Paid Circulation (thou)	Parent Company
1	*TV Guide*	928	15,868	News Corp.
2	*Time*	637	4,339	Time Warner
3	*People*	606	3,271	Time Warner
4	*Sports Illustrated*	566	3,598	Time Warner
5	*Reader's Digest*	419	16,344	Reader's Digest
6	*Newsweek*	398	3,180	Washington Post
7	*Parade*	315	32,633	Advance Publications
8	*Business Week*	299	890	McGraw-Hill
9	*Better Homes & Gardens*	276	8,005	Meredith Corp.
10	*Family Circle*	249	5,462	New York Times
11	*Good Housekeeping*	245	5,152	Hearst
12	*U.S. News & World Report*	245	2,210	U.S. News & World Report
13	*National Geographic*	226	10,891	National Geographic Society
14	*National Enquirer*	220	4,101	Macfadden Holdings
15	*Woman's Day*	213	4,705	Hachette
16	*Ladies' Home Journal*	207	5,038	Meredith Corp.
17	*Cosmopolitan*	204	2,702	Hearst
18	*Fortune*	203	669	Time Warner
19	*Forbes*	195	744	Forbes Inc.
20	*PC Magazine*	183	732	Ziff Communications
21	*Star Magazine*	173	3,562	Macfadden Holdings
22	*McCall's*	168	5,089	New York Times
23	*Money*	143	1,835	Time Warner
24	*Glamour*	142	2,224	Advance Publications
25	*Vogue*	141	1,248	Advance Publications

Source: *Advertising Age*, June 18, 1990, Crain Communications, Inc.
Note: Excludes AARP publications

25 Largest Newspapers in the US

Rank	Newspaper	1989 Avg. Daily Circulation (thou)	Parent Company
1	*Wall Street Journal*	1,931	Dow Jones
2	*USA Today*	1,342	Gannett
3	*Daily News* (New York)	1,230	Tribune
4	*Los Angeles Times*	1,120	Times Mirror
5	*New York Times*	1,117	New York Times
6	*Washington Post*	812	Washington Post
7	*Chicago Tribune*	740	Media General
8	*Newsday*	698	Times Mirror
9	*Detroit News*	676	Gannett
10	*Detroit Free Press*	629	Knight-Ridder
11	*San Francisco Chronicle*	556	Chronicle Publishing
12	*Chicago Sun-Times*	555	Chicago Sun-Times
13	*New York Post*	535	Peter Kalikow
14	*Boston Globe*	510	Affiliated Publications
15	*Philadelphia Inquirer*	500	Knight-Ridder
16	*Star-Ledger* (Newark)	458	Newark Star Ledger
17	*Plain Dealer* (Cleveland)	448	Advance Publications
18	*Miami Herald*	443	Knight-Ridder
19	*Houston Chronicle*	428	Hearst
20	*Minneapolis Star Tribune*	403	Cowles Media
21	*St. Louis Post-Dispatch*	378	Pulitzer Publishing
22	*St. Petersburg Times*	376	Times Publishing
23	*Arizona Republic* (Phoenix)	372	Central Newspapers
24	*Rocky Mountain News* (Denver)	365	E.W. Scripps
25	*Boston Herald*	360	News Corp.

Source: The Audit Bureau of Circulations

40 Largest US Media Companies

Rank	Company	1989 Media Sales ($ mil)
1	Capital Cities/ABC	4,767
2	Time Warner	4,575
3	Gannett	3,518
4	General Electric	3,392
5	CBS	2,960
6	Advance Publications	2,882
7	Times Mirror	2,807
8	Tele-Communications	2,353
9	Knight-Ridder	2,262
10	News Corp.	2,203
11	Tribune	2,099
12	Hearst	2,095
13	New York Times	1,769
14	Cox	1,664
15	Washington Post	1,373
16	Thomson	1,328
17	Viacom	1,199
18	E.W. Scripps	1,180
19	Dow Jones	975
20	Continental Cablevision	780
21	Turner Broadcasting	729
22	Ingersoll Publications	670
23	Westinghouse	646
24	Advo-Systems	618
25	MediaNews Group	594
26	Reader's Digest	589
27	Reed Publishing	580
28	McGraw-Hill	557
29	Meredith	531
30	Valassis Inserts	525
31	SCI Holdings	516
32	Affiliated Publications	515
33	Comcast Corp.	502
34	United Artists Entertainment	501
35	Cablevision Systems Corp.	493
36	Media General	451
37	Freedom Newspapers	450
38	Harte-Hanks Communications	436
39	Central Newspapers	436
40	Chronicle Publishing	421

Source: *Advertising Age*, June 25, 1990, Crain Communications, Inc.

10 Largest US TV Broadcast Companies

Rank	Company	1989 TV Sales ($ mil)
1	General Electric	3,392
2	Capital Cities/ABC	3,371
3	CBS	2,779
4	News Corp.	700
5	Westinghouse	530
6	Tribune	419
7	Gillett Holdings	367
8	Gannett	319
9	Cox Enterprises	306
10	Chris-Craft Industries	247

Source: *Advertising Age*, June 25, 1990, Crain Communications, Inc.

10 Largest US Radio Broadcast Companies

Rank	Company	1989 Radio Sales ($ mil)
1	Capital Cities/ABC	214
2	CBS	181
3	Westinghouse	116
4	Cox	94
5	Gannett	89
6	Bonneville International	73
7	Great American Communications	68
8	Viacom	56
9	Tribune	49
10	Hearst	26

Source: *Advertising Age*, June 25, 1990, Crain Communications, Inc.

10 Largest US Newspaper Companies

Rank	Company	1989 Newspaper Sales ($ mil)
1	Gannett	2,852
2	Times Mirror	2,066
3	Knight-Ridder	1,988
4	Advance Publications	1,745
5	Tribune	1,631
6	New York Times	1,399
7	Dow Jones	941
8	E.W. Scripps	780
9	Cox	754
10	Washington Post	727

Source: *Advertising Age*, June 25, 1990, Crain Communications, Inc.

10 Largest US Magazine Companies

Rank	Company	1989 Magazine Sales ($ mil)
1	Time Warner	1,855
2	Hearst	993
3	Advance Publications	842
4	Thomson Corp.	733
5	News Corp.	713
6	Reader's Digest	589
7	Reed Publishing	580
8	McGraw-Hill	460
9	International Data Group	420
10	Meredith Corp.	417

Source: *Advertising Age*, June 25, 1990, Crain Communications, Inc.

40 Largest Electronics Companies in the US

Rank	Company	1989 Electronics Sales ($ mil)	1989 Total Sales ($ mil)	Electronics Sales as % of Total
1	IBM	62,710	62,710	100
2	AT&T	16,586	36,112	46
3	Digital Equipment	12,937	12,937	100
4	Xerox	12,431	12,431	100
5	Hewlett-Packard	12,345	12,345	100
6	GM Hughes Electronics	11,359	11,359	100
7	Unisys	10,097	10,097	100
8	Motorola	9,620	9,620	100
9	General Electric	8,920	54,574	16
10	Texas Instruments	6,522	6,522	100
11	Honeywell	6,059	6,059	100
12	NCR	5,956	5,956	100
13	Apple	5,372	5,372	100
14	Raytheon	5,333	8,796	61
15	Rockwell International	4,926	12,534	39
16	Tandy	4,284	4,284	100
17	Eastman Kodak	4,200	18,398	23
18	Lockheed	3,830	9,891	39
19	Ford	3,500	96,146	4
20	Litton	3,297	5,073	65
21	3M	3,297	11,990	27
22	Martin Marietta	3,188	5,796	55
23	Intel	3,127	3127	100
24	Control Data	2,935	2,935	100
25	Allied-Signal	2,900	11,942	24
26	ITT	2,888	20,054	14
27	Compaq	2,876	2,876	100
28	TRW	2,870	7,340	39
29	Westinghouse	2,783	12,844	22
30	Harris	2,776	2,776	100
31	Wang	2,697	2,697	100
32	Boeing	2,420	20,276	12
33	AMP	2,377	2,797	85
34	Du Pont	2,300	35,534	6
35	Emerson	2,190	6,998	31
36	GTE	2,140	17,424	12
37	Pitney Bowes	2,120	2,876	74
38	Amdahl	2,101	2,101	100
39	Sun Microsystems	2,062	2,062	100
40	Seagate	1,797	1,797	100

Source: *Electronic Business,* July 23, 1990

20 Largest Computer Companies in North America

Rank	Company	1989 Information Systems Sales ($ mil)	1989 Total Sales ($ mil)	Info. Systems Sales as % of Total
1	IBM	60,805	62,710	97
2	Digital Equipment	12,937	12,937	100
3	Unisys	9,390	10,097	93
4	Hewlett-Packard	7,800	11,899	66
5	Apple	5,372	5,372	100
6	NCR	5,319	5,956	89
7	Compaq	2,876	2,876	100
8	AT&T	2,865	36,112	8
9	Xerox	2,790	17,635	16
10	Wang	2,697	2,697	100
11	General Motors	2,478	5,467	45
12	Amdahl	2,101	2,101	100
13	Sun Microsystems	2,063	2,063	100
14	Tandy	1,892	4,286	44
15	Seagate	1,797	1,797	100
16	Control Data	1,691	2,935	58
17	ADP	1,690	1,690	100
18	Tandem	1,677	1,677	100
19	TRW	1,643	7,340	22
20	Prime	1,520	1,520	100

Source: *Datamation,* June 15, 1990

20 Largest Computer Companies in the World

Rank	Company	1989 Information Systems Sales ($ mil)	1989 Total Sales ($ mil)	Info. Systems Sales as % of Total
1	IBM	60,805	62,710	97
2	Digital Equipment	12,937	12,937	100
3	NEC	11,480	23,389	49
4	Fujitsu	11,379	18,074	63
5	Unisys	9,390	10,097	93
6	Hitachi	8,719	49,064	18
7	Hewlett-Packard	7,800	11,899	66
8	Groupe Bull	6,465	6,465	100
9	Siemens	6,011	32,515	18
10	Olivetti	5,573	6,584	85
11	Apple	5,372	5,372	100
12	NCR	5,319	5,956	89
13	Toshiba	4,595	28,897	16
14	Canon	3,783	9,791	39
15	Matsushita	3,664	40,877	9
16	Compaq	2,876	2,876	100
17	AT&T	2,865	36,112	8
18	Philips	2,815	26,981	10
19	Nixdorf	2,793	2,793	100
20	Xerox	2,790	17,635	16

Source: *Datamation,* June 15, 1990

20 Largest Management Consulting Firms in the US

Rank	Firm	1989 Sales ($ mil)
1	Andersen Consulting	1,442
2	Ernst & Young	814
3	Marsh & McLennan Cos.	800
4	KPMG Peat Marwick	650
5	McKinsey & Co.	635
6	Towers Perrin	621
7	Coopers & Lybrand	536
8	Deloitte & Touche	526
9	Price Waterhouse	508
10	Booz-Allen & Hamilton	453
11	Wyatt	396
12	CSC Consulting	287
13	Alexander Proudfoot	285
14	Hewitt Assoc.	248
15	Bain	242
16	Arthur D. Little	228
17	PA Consulting	217
18	Hay Group	210
19	Alexander Consulting Group	194
20	American Management Systems	190

Source: Kennedy Publications, September 26, 1990

20 Largest Law Firms in the US

Rank	Firm	1990 Number of Lawyers
1	Baker & McKenzie, Chicago	1,519
2	Jones, Day, Reavis & Pogue, Cleveland	1,202
3	Skadden, Arps, Slate, Meagher & Flom, New York	1,133
4	Gibson, Dunn & Crutcher, Los Angeles	738
5	Morgan, Lewis & Bockius, Philadelphia	672
6	Sidley & Austin, Chicago	707
7	Fulbright & Jaworski, Houston	685
8	Shearman & Sterling, New York	624
9	Morrison & Foerster, San Francisco	588
10	Latham & Watkins, Los Angeles	570
11	Mayer, Brown & Platt, Chicago	566
12	Weil, Gotshal & Manges, New York	552
13	O'Melveny & Meyers, Los Angeles	533
14	McDermott, Will & Emery, Chicago	520
15	Milbank, Tweed, Hadley & McCloy, New York	504
16	Baker & Hostetler, Cleveland	503
17	Vinson & Elkins, Houston	503
18	Akin, Gump, Strauss, Hauer & Feld, Dallas	435
19	Hunton & Williams, Richmond	471
20	White & Case, New York	462

Source: *The National Law Journal*, September 24, 1990

22 Largest Accounting Firms

Rank	Firm	1989 Sales ($ mil) World	US
Big Six			
1	KPMG	4,300	1,773
2	Ernst & Young	4,200	2,000
3	Deloitte & Touche	3,900	1,900
4	Arthur Andersen & Co.	3,382	1,994
5	Coopers & Lybrand	3,000	1,250
6	Price Waterhouse	2,500	1,100
Second Tier			
7	Laventhol & Horwath	685	345
8	Grant Thornton	771	205
9	BDO Seidman	842	175
10	McGladrey & Pullen	468	157
11	Kenneth Leventhal	335	141
12	Pannell Kerr Forster	381	98
13	Spicer & Oppeheim	75	75
Third Tier			
14	Baird, Kurtz & Dobson	49	49
15	Clifton, Gunderson & Co.	48	48
16	Crowe, Chizek & Co.	43	43
17	Altschuler, Melvoin and Glasser	42	42
18	Plante & Moran	40	40
19	Moss Adams	35	35
20	Richard A. Eisner & Co.	29	29
21	Cherry, Bekaert & Holland	28	28
22	Geo S. Olive & Co.	26	26

Source: *1990 Public Accounting Report*, Professional Publications

Distribution of Companies in *HOOVER'S HANDBOOK* by Auditor

Firm	Number of Companies	% of Total
Ernst & Young	98	18
Price Waterhouse	92	17
Deloitte & Touche	83	15
Arthur Andersen & Co.	82	15
KPMG	67	12
Coopers & Lybrand	58	11
Laventhol & Horwath	4	1
Others	24	5
Inapplicable or unknown	34	6
Total	**542**	**100**

10 Largest Investment Institutions in the US

Rank	Company	Year-end 1989 ($ mil)
1	Prudential	204,083
2	American Express	194,764
3	Metropolitan	126,524
4	Bankers Trust	121,080
5	Equitable	113,114
6	J.P. Morgan	101,889
7	Citicorp	97,713
8	Wells Fargo	94,501
9	Aetna	86,684
10	Mellon Bank	71,253

This table ranks the ten top institutions according to assets under management, when all assets are considered — the institutions' own as well as those of their clients. Total reflects investments in the securities and real estate markets but not commercial and personal loans.

Source: *Institutional Investor*, July 1990

20 Largest Brokerage Houses in the US

Rank	Company	1989 Total Consolidated Capital ($ mil)
1	Merrill Lynch	10,048
2	Shearson Lehman Hutton (American Express)	8,966
3	Salomon	5,757
4	Goldman, Sachs	4,018
5	Morgan Stanley	2,648
6	Prudential-Bache (Prudential Insurance Co.)	1,840
7	First Boston (CS Holding)	1,783
8	PaineWebber Group	1,523
9	Bear, Stearns & Co.	1,444
10	Dean Witter Reynolds (Sears)	1,429
11	Smith Barney, Harris Upham (Primerica Corp.)	927
12	Donaldson, Lufkin & Jenrette (Equitable)	900
13	Kidder, Peabody (General Electric)	728
14	Shelby Cullom Davis	551
15	BT Securities (Bankers Trust)	479
16	J.P. Morgan	469
17	Nomura	376
18	Charles Schwab	344
19	A.G. Edwards & Sons	304
20	UBS Securities (Union Bank of Switzerland)	293

Source: *Institutional Investor*, April 1990

10 Biggest Leveraged Buyouts of the 1980s

Rank	Date Announced	Acquired Company	Buyer	Price Paid ($ bil)
1	10/21/88	RJR Nabisco	Kohlberg Kravis Roberts	29.6
2	1/24/88	Federated Dept. Stores	Campeau	7.4
3	10/16/85	Beatrice	Kohlberg Kravis Roberts	6.2
4	7/27/86	Safeway	Acquisition group led by Kohlberg Kravis Roberts	5.7
5	7/3/87	Southland	Acquisition group	5.1
6	9/15/88	Hospital Corp.	Acquisition group led by management	4.9
7	4/12/87	Borg-Warner	Acquisition group led by Merrill Lynch	4.2
8	3/7/88	Montgomery Ward	Acquisition group	3.8
9	10/21/85	R. H. Macy	Acquisition group led by management	3.7
10	6/19/89	NWA	Wings Holdings Inc.	3.7

Source: I.D.D. Information Services, Inc.; *Wall Street Journal* 5/16/90

Profiles of 542 Major Enterprises

ABBOTT LABORATORIES

OVERVIEW

Abbott Labs is a major pharmaceutical company, but more than 1/2 its revenues come from nutritionals and diagnostic equipment, markets in which it has a leading share (54% of the US nutritionals market). The company also supplies hospitals worldwide with intravenous fluids, pumps, anesthetics, and critical care instruments. Blood banks rely on Abbott screening tests to detect the AIDS and hepatitis viruses. Abbott ranks 6th in sales in the US pharmaceutical industry, and 9th worldwide.

R&D expenditures have increased steadily in the 1980s and stand at 9.3% of sales in 1989. Abbott filed new US drug applications in 1989 for 2 antibiotics. FDA approval of a new drug for sleeping disorders is expected in 1990.

Abbott owns 1/2 of Takeda-Abbott Pharmaceuticals, a joint venture with a Japanese drug company, and is the major shareholder in Amgen, one of the larger biotechnology companies.

NYSE symbol: ABT
Incorporated: Illinois, 1900
Fiscal year ends: December 31

WHO

Chairman and CEO: Duane L. Burnham, age 48, $850,472 pay (prior to promotion)
President and COO: Thomas R. Hodgson, age 48, $681,515 pay (prior to promotion)
SVP and CFO: Gary P. Coughlan
Auditors: Arthur Andersen & Co.
Employees: 40,929

WHEN

Family physician Wallace Abbott founded the Abbott Alkaloidal Company in a Chicago suburb in 1888 to sell his improved form of the dosimetric granule (a pill that supplied uniform quantities of drugs). By 1900 sales were $125,000. The AMA criticized Dr. Abbott for his aggressive promotional style, but the doctor successfully defended himself, receiving support from much of the medical profession.

During WWI Abbott scientists discovered techniques for synthesizing anesthetics and sedatives previously available only from the more advanced German companies. In 1922 the company acquired a strong research department by buying Dermatological Research Laboratories. In 1928 Abbott acquired John T. Milliken and Company of St. Louis, which brought to Abbott a force of well-trained salesmen.

Abbott went public in 1929 and acquired Swan-Myers of Indianapolis (glass ampuls for injectable drugs). Flamboyant salesman DeWitt Clough became president in 1933; the Abbott magazine *What's New*, prepared by his promotional staff, was considered a significant new corporate marketing tool. The company began to operate internationally as early as the mid-1930s, opening branches in England, Mexico, Brazil, Argentina, and Cuba.

Abbott was one of several drug companies that stepped up production to make the penicillin needed during WWII. After the war the company introduced new products, including different forms of penicillin. Research toward other antibiotics yielded Erythrocin (1952), Abbott's form of the antibiotic erythromycin. After a period of slow growth in the early 1950s, sales improved as Erythrocin became more widely used. In the 1960s the company added consumer products (Selsun shampoo, Murine) and infant and nutritional formula (Similac), but drugs and hospital products remained its mainstay. The artificial sweetener Sucaryl (introduced 1950) was banned by the FDA in 1970 after tests indicated it might be carcinogenic. In 1971 millions of intravenous solutions had to be recalled following reports of contamination.

In the 1970s Abbott built its diagnostics division (early products included the Auscell hepatitis test and VP clinical analyzer) and in 1981 introduced a nutritional support service for hospitals. In the early 1980s the company expanded operations in Japan and obtained licenses to sell in the US pharmaceuticals developed by the Japanese. After 1979 when Robert Schoellhorn became CEO, Abbott had a steady increase in profits. Despite his successes Schoellhorn later came under criticism for trying to cut R&D funds and firing several top managers and in March 1990 was himself terminated. In August 1990 the company announced it had developed a compound that inhibited AIDS in test tube experiments.

WHERE

HQ: One Abbott Park Rd., Abbott Park, IL 60064
Phone: 708-937-6100
FAX: 708-937-1511

The company has 18 US plants, 26 foreign plants, and R&D facilities in 5 countries, and sells its products in 30 countries.

	1989 Sales		1989 Operating Income	
	$ mil	% of total	$ mil	% of total
US	3,542	66	1,019	77
Europe, Mideast & Africa	1,028	19	188	14
Other countries	810	15	119	9
Adjustments	—	—	(105)	—
Total	**5,380**	**100**	**1,221**	**100**

WHAT

	1989 Sales		1989 Operating Income	
	$ mil	% of total	$ mil	% of total
Hospital & lab prods.	2,595	48	484	38
Drugs & nutritional products	2,785	52	797	62
Adjustments	—	—	(60)	—
Total	**5,380**	**100**	**1,221**	**100**

Brand Names

Consumer Products
Faultless (rubber sundries)
Murine (eye and ear care products)
Selsun Blue (shampoo)

Nutritional Supplements
Ensure (adult nutrition)
Osmolite (adult nutrition)
Similac (infant formula)

Prescription Drugs
Abbokinase (blood clot dissolver)
Hytrin (blood pressure drug)
Lupron (prostate cancer drug)
Tranxene (anxiety drug)

Hospital Products
ADD-Vantage (IV equipment)
ADx (drug testing equipment)
Aminosyn (IV nutrition)
Opticath (cardiorespiratory monitor)
Pentothal (anesthetic)

RANKINGS

90th in *Fortune* 500 Industrial Cos.
245th in *Fortune* Global 500 Industrial Cos.
44th in *Fortune* 50 Exporters
162nd in *Forbes* Sales 500
36th in *Business Week* 1000
78th in *Business Week* Global 1000

COMPETITION

American Home Products
C. R. Bard
Baxter
Becton, Dickinson
Dow Chemical
Du Pont
Hoechst
Johnson & Johnson
Monsanto
Nestlé
Other pharmaceutical companies

HOW MUCH

	9 Yr. Growth	1980	1981	1982	1983	1984	1985	1986	1987	1988	1989
Sales ($ mil)	11.4%	2,038	2,343	2,602	2,928	3,104	3,360	3,808	4,388	4,937	5,380
Net income ($ mil)	16.7%	214	247	289	348	403	465	540	633	752	860
Income as % of sales	—	10.5%	10.6%	11.1%	11.9%	13.0%	13.8%	14.2%	14.4%	15.2%	16.0%
Earnings per share ($)	17.9%	0.43	0.50	0.59	0.72	0.83	0.96	1.15	1.37	1.65	1.90
Stock price – high ($)	—	7.13	8.06	10.31	13.34	12.19	18.00	27.50	33.50	26.19	35.19
Stock price – low ($)	—	4.27	5.91	6.34	9.03	9.19	9.97	15.84	20.00	21.44	23.13
Stock price – close ($)	19.1%	7.06	6.75	9.69	11.31	10.44	17.09	22.81	24.13	24.06	34.00
P/E – high	—	16	16	17	19	15	19	24	24	16	19
P/E – low	—	10	12	11	13	11	10	14	15	13	12
Dividends per share ($)	18.8%	0.14	0.17	0.20	0.24	0.29	0.34	0.40	0.48	0.58	0.68
Book value per share ($)	12.8%	2.08	2.35	2.68	2.93	3.33	3.91	3.89	4.62	5.48	6.16

1989 Year End:
Debt ratio: 5.1%
Return on equity: 32.6%
Cash (mil): $49
Current ratio: 1.52
Long-term debt (mil): $147
Number of shares (mil): 442
Dividends:
1989 average yield: 2.0%
1989 payout: 35.5%
Market value (mil): $15,044

Stock Price History high/low 1980-89

40 35 30 25 20 15 10 5 0

ADOLPH COORS COMPANY

OVERVIEW

Adolph Coors Company, America's 3rd largest brewer, realizes 70% of its total revenues from beer. Coors has been producing beer from a single facility in Golden, Colorado, since 1873. Coors is vertically integrated, with its own raw materials and its own packaging, labeling, transportation, distribution, and recycling operations. Coors also operates businesses engaged in energy exploration, biotechnology, and ceramics, which provide services and products to the brewery and to 3rd parties.

Coors grew from a regional favorite, promoted mostly by "word-of-mouth," into a major product line, marketed in most states and many foreign countries. Even so, increasingly competitive markets and higher expansion costs have depressed earnings since 1986. However, things seem to be looking up for Coors; sales in the first 1/2 of 1990 were up 16%; profits were up 172%; and Coors Light was on the verge of passing Bud Light as the #3 beer brand.

The Coors family owns 100% of Coors's voting stock and, along with management, 55% of the nonvoting stock.

WHEN

Adolph Coors landed in Baltimore in 1868, a 21-year-old stowaway fleeing Germany's military draft. He worked his way west to Denver, where he bought a bottling company in 1872 and became partners with Jacob Schueler, a local merchant, in 1873. The partners built a brewery in Golden, Colorado, a small town with many clear springs in the nearby Rocky Mountain foothills. In 1880 Coors became sole owner of the company. For most of the company's history, Coors confined sales to western states. The cost of nationwide distribution was prohibitive because Coors used a single brewery, natural brewing methods, and no preservatives; Coors beer was made, shipped, and stored under refrigeration, with a shelf life of only one month.

Coors survived Prohibition (1914-1933) by making near beer and malted milk and by entering cement and porcelain chemicalware production. By this time Coors's 3 sons worked in the business, which has been run by family men to the present day. After Repeal, beer output grew steadily in Coors's 11-state market. By the 1960s Coors had achieved national popularity, as thousands of loyal customers from outside the market area packed it home.

Between 1965 and 1969 Coors jumped from 12th to 4th place in American brewing, and by 1975 Coors beer was the top seller in 10 of its 11 state markets (Coors sometimes restricted distributors in these areas to selling its beer exclusively). But Coors's meteoric rise was blunted by a fall back to 5th place in 1976 and continuing sales declines through 1978, mainly due to campaigns for new "light" and "super-premium" beers introduced by Miller and Anheuser-Busch. Coors responded by opening a marketing department and introducing light and super-premium brands. As a result of its 1975 loss in a restraint of trade suit, the company removed distribution restrictions and expanded its market area from 11 to 16 states.

In the late 1970s and 1980s Coors began expanding nationwide at a rate of about 2 states per year while at the same time enduring boycotts and strikes due to alleged discriminatory labor practices. After years of protests from workers and federal agencies, Coors improved its minority employment policies. During the 1970s Joe Coors, a grandson of Adolph, financed and led many ultraconservative projects, expressing the Coors family's strong opposition to student radicalism and liberal media.

In 1989 Coors agreed to purchase Stroh Brewing, then the 3rd largest US brewer (Coors surpassed them in 1990). However, the deal fell apart in 1990, purportedly due to unresolved antitrust issues, but Coors did later buy Stroh's Memphis brewery in order to meet increasing demand for its beer.

HOW MUCH

	9 Yr. Growth	1980	1981	1982	1983	1984	1985	1986	1987	1988	1989
Sales ($ mil)	7.9%	888	930	915	1,110	1,133	1,281	1,315	1,351	1,522	1,764
Net income ($ mil)	(16.3%)	65	52	40	89	45	53	59	48	47	13
Income as % of sales	—	7.3%	5.6%	4.4%	8.0%	4.0%	4.2%	4.5%	3.6%	3.1%	0.7%
Earnings per share ($)	(16.7%)	1.86	1.48	1.15	2.55	1.28	1.52	1.65	1.32	1.28	0.36
Stock price – high ($)	—	20.38	16.50	15.00	29.13	21.63	22.25	31.63	30.00	21.00	24.38
Stock price – low ($)	—	9.50	10.13	9.88	11.88	12.00	14.50	20.38	16.25	16.88	17.38
Stock price – close ($)	2.5%	15.75	10.38	12.25	20.25	16.13	21.63	24.00	16.88	20.00	19.75
P/E – high	—	11	11	13	11	17	15	19	23	16	68
P/E – low	—	5	7	9	5	9	10	12	12	13	48
Dividends per share ($)	6.9%	0.28	0.30	0.30	0.35	0.40	0.40	0.50	0.50	0.50	0.50
Book value per share ($)	3.9%	20.34	21.52	22.37	24.57	25.45	26.46	27.41	28.19	28.96	28.75

1989 Year End:
Debt ratio: 0.0%
Return on equity: 1.2%
Cash (mil): $44
Current ratio: 1.74
Long-term debt (mil): $0
Number of shares (mil): 37
Dividends:
1989 average yield: 2.5%
1989 payout: 138.9%
Market value (mil): $729

Stock Price History high/low 1980-89

NASDAQ symbol: ACCOB
Incorporated: Colorado, 1913
Fiscal year ends: December 31

WHO

Chairman and President: William K. Coors, age 73, $391,329 pay
VC: Joseph Coors, age 72
Chairman, President, and CEO, Coors Brewing Company: Peter H. Coors, age 43, $496,021 pay
EVP Corporate Finance and Administration: Harold R. Smethills, age 41
Auditors: Price Waterhouse
Employees: 10,600

WHERE

HQ: Golden, CO 80401
Phone: 303-279-6565
FAX: 303-277-6564

Coors operates one brewery in Colorado, distributorships in 6 states, and other facilities in 13 states, Brazil, Scotland, and Switzerland. Coors markets its products in 49 states (all but Indiana), the District of Columbia, Bermuda, Canada, Japan, the Virgin Islands, and on US military bases worldwide.

WHAT

	1989 Sales		1989 Operating Income	
	$ mil	% of total	$ mil	% of total
Beer	1,367	70	71	148
Ceramics	167	9	12	24
Aluminum	167	9	9	20
Other	240	12	(44)	(92)
Adjustments	(177)	—	27	—
Total	**1,764**	**100**	**75**	**100**

Coors Brewing Co.
Coors
Coors Extra Gold
Coors Light
Coors Rocky Mountain Sparkling Water
George Killian's Irish Red
Keystone
Keystone Light
Winterfest

Coors Ceramics Co.
Alpha Optical Systems, Inc.
Alumina Ceramics, Inc.
Coors Ceramica Tecnica do Brasil, Ltda.
Coors Ceramicon Designs, Ltd.
Coors Ceramics Electronics, Ltd.
Coors Electronic Package Co.
MicroLithics Corp.
Wilbanks International, Inc.

Coors Technology Cos.
Coors BioTech, Inc.
Coors Energy Co.
Golden Aluminum Co.
Golden Technologies Co., Inc.
Graphic Packaging Corp.

RANKINGS

231st in *Fortune* 500 Industrial Cos.
432nd in *Forbes* Sales 500
681st in *Business Week* 1000

COMPETITION

Anheuser-Busch
Bass
BSN
Guinness
Philip Morris

ADVANCE PUBLICATIONS, INC.

OVERVIEW

Advance Publications, based in Staten Island, is the holding company for a media conglomerate built by Samuel Irving Newhouse. The company is the largest privately held media group in the US and ranks among the top 10 in all of its business segments: newspapers, magazines, books, and cable TV.

The heart of the business, Newhouse Newspapers, is the 3rd largest newpaper chain in the US. The Portland *Oregonian*, Cleveland *Plain Dealer*, *Newark Star-Ledger*, and New Orleans *Times-Picayune* are all the largest papers in their states; most of the company's papers have no competition in their markets. Condé Nast, publisher of *Vogue* and *Vanity Fair,* also publishes 28 magazines in Europe. Random House is America's largest trade (excluding texts) book publisher.

Barron's and *Fortune* have speculated that the Newhouse family is the wealthiest in the US, with a net worth approaching $10 billion. All of Advance Publications's voting stock is held in a trust managed by sons S. I. Newhouse, Jr., and Donald Newhouse and, afterward, their male heirs.

Private company
Founded: New York, 1922

WHO

Chairman: Samuel I. ("Si") Newhouse, Jr., age 61
President: Donald E. Newhouse, age 60
Controller: Arthur Silverstein
Employees: 19,000

WHERE

HQ: 950 Fingerboard Rd., Staten Island, NY 10305
Phone: 718-981-1234
FAX: 718-981-5679 (Staten Island *Advance*)

Advance Publications has 31 newspapers and 3 cable TV groups in the US and book and magazine operations in New York and Europe.

		1989 Newspaper Circulation	
		Daily	**Sunday**
Birmingham	*Birmingham News*	169,059	210,805
Huntsville	*Huntsville News*	14,207	12,719
	The Huntsville Times	58,313	76,123
Mobile	*The Mobile Press*	24,897	
	The Mobile Register	29,306	53,056
New Orleans	*The Times-Picayune*	278,248	278,248
Springfield, MA	*Union-News*	112,758	
	Sunday Republican		159,303
Pascagoula	*Mississippi Press*	22,345	
	Mississippi Press Register		23,681
Jersey City	*Jersey Journal*	59,193	
Newark	*Star-Ledger*	461,080	681,802
Trenton	*Times*	65,474	84,117
Staten Island	*Advance*	77,654	75,394
Syracuse	*Herald-American*		232,617
	The Post-Standard	84,877	
	Syracuse Herald-Journal	101,980	
Cleveland	*Plain Dealer*	452,343	552,481
Portland	*The Oregonian*	323,184	406,933
Harrisburg	*The News*	51,614	
	The Patriot	53,323	
	The Patriot-News		168,876
Booth Newspapers (MI)			
Ann Arbor	*The Ann Arbor News*	45,632	59,232
Bay City	*Times*	38,803	47,374
Flint	*The Flint Journal*	112,161	123,792
Grand Rapids	*The Grand Rapids Press*	136,511	182,388
Jackson	*Citizen Patriot*	38,187	42,330
Kalamazoo	*Kalamazoo Gazette*	63,416	75,945
Muskegon	*The Muskegon Chronicle*	47,611	
	The Sunday Chronicle		51,742
Saginaw	*The Saginaw News*	57,133	63,558
Total		**2,979,309**	**3,662,516**

WHEN

Samuel I. Newhouse dropped out of school at 13 due to family poverty. He went to work for a lawyer who received the *Bayonne* (New Jersey) *Times* as payment for a debt. The lawyer put Sam, age 16, in charge of the failing newspaper in 1911; Sam turned the company around. In 1922 he bought the Staten Island *Advance,* the core of Advance Publications's holdings.

Newhouse used profits from the *Advance* to buy newspapers throughout the New York area, operating out of a briefcase rather than a headquarters suite. He purchased the *Long Island Press* (1932), the Newark *Star-Ledger* (1933), the *Long Island Star-Journal* (1938), and the *Syracuse Journal* (1939). In the 1940s he maintained this pattern with the acquisitions of the *Syracuse Herald-Standard* (1941), the *Jersey Journal* (1945), and the Harrisburg *Patriot* (1948).

In 1955 Newhouse expanded into the South by buying the *Birmingham News* and the *Huntsville Times.* Newhouse purchased Condé Nast (*Vogue, Bride's, House & Garden*) as an anniversary gift for his wife Mitzi in 1959. Newhouse acquired the *New Orleans Times-Picayune* and *New Orleans States-Item* for $42 million (1962), a record price for a newspaper transaction that held until he broke it with the purchase of the Cleveland *Plain Dealer* for $54 million (1967). By 1967 Newhouse had also established NewChannels, which owned several cable systems, with 10,000 subscribers, primarily in cities where the family owned other media holdings. As the prices of newspapers continued to rise, Newhouse set yet another record by purchasing the Booth chain of 8 Michigan newspapers, including the *Grand Rapids Press,* for $304 million (1976).

Newhouse died in 1979, leaving his sons S.I., Jr., and Donald as trustees of the company's 10 shares of voting stock. The sons' IRS filing claimed that the estate was worth $181.9 million, taxable at $48.7 million. The IRS argued that the holdings were worth at least $1.2 billion and billed the Newhouses $658 million, plus a $305 million penalty for fraud. When the estate tax case — the largest ever — went to court in 1989, the Newhouses brought in a group of financial experts, including Rupert Murdoch (News Corporation), to testify on their behalf. In 1990 the case was decided against the IRS.

Meanwhile, the sons have continued to expand the properties of Advance Publications, buying Random House (1980) and Crown Publishing (1989). Also in 1980, the company sold 5 TV stations that Newhouse had bought in earlier years to Times Mirror for $82 million. Some of the money from the sale of the stations went to buy more cable systems. The company resurrected *Vanity Fair* (1983) and bought *The New Yorker* (1985). In 1990 a decision by the Newhouses to stem the losses at Pantheon Books by cutting titles led to the resignation of senior editors and a protest by authors and publishers.

HOW MUCH

	9 Yr. Growth	1980	1981	1982	1983	1984	1985	1986	1987	1988	1989
Total media sales ($ mil)	—	—	—	1,616	1,740	1,900	2,030	2,200	2,482	2,655	2,882
Cable TV revenues ($ mil)	—	—	—	—	—	—	—	186	203	229	295
Cable subscribers (thou)	—	—	518	596	703	850	917	1,027	1,098	1,078	1,147
Newspaper revenues ($ mil)	—	—	—	—	—	—	—	1,470	678	745	842
Newspapers	(1.2%)	29	28	27	27	26	26	27	26	36	26
Daily circulation (thou)	(0.8%)	3,256	3,167	3,156	3,203	2,943	2,933	3,035	3,018	3,018	2,979
Magazine revenues ($ mil)	—	—	—	—	—	—	—	544	678	745	842

Total Media Sales ($ mil) 1982-89

3000
2500
2000
1500
1000
500
0

WHAT

Magazines
Bride's
Details
Glamour
Gourmet
GQ
HG (House & Garden)
Mademoiselle
The New Yorker
Parade
Self
Traveler
Vanity Fair
Vogue
Woman

Book Publishing
Alfred A. Knopf
Ballantine
Crown
Del Rey
Fawcett
Modern Library
Outlet Books
Pantheon
Random House
Vintage

Cable Groups
NewChannels (Syracuse)
MetroVision (Atlanta)
Vision Cable (Paramus, NJ)

RANKINGS

41st in *Forbes* 400 US Private Cos.

COMPETITION

Book, newspaper, and magazine publishers

AETNA LIFE & CASUALTY COMPANY

OVERVIEW

Aetna is one of the world's major providers of insurance (life, health, and property-casualty) and financial services to corporations, public and private organizations, and individuals. With assets of $87.1 billion, the company is the largest stockholder-owned insurance organization in the US and one of the 15 largest US corporations, measured by assets.

The Hartford-based company, with more than 200 US branch and marketing offices, also provides insurance and financial services in the Pacific Basin, South America, Canada, and Europe. More than 95% of total revenues in 1989 were from US sources.

Aetna is the largest US stockholder-owned insurance company in underwriting and administering group insurance and managed health care products and services, based on 1989 premiums of $13 billion, and in managing group pension funds, based on assets of $45 billion. These group services currently generate 44% of Aetna's revenues.

The Commercial Insurance Division provides most kinds of property-casualty insurance: liability, workers' compensation, commercial automobile, and multi-peril coverage. This division currently generates 24% of revenues.

WHEN

Hartford businessman and judge Eliphalet Bulkeley started Connecticut Mutual Life Insurance Company, a mutual company owned by policyholders, in 1846. A year later he was ousted by agents who gained control of the company by obtaining proxies (votes) from policyholders.

In 1853 Bulkeley and a group of Hartford businessmen founded Aetna Life Insurance Company as a spin-off of Aetna Fire Insurance Company. Aetna's early growth is attributed to Dr. Thomas Lacey, a former Aetna medical examiner, who became known in the late 1800s as the "father" of Aetna's agency system for enlisting agents around the US to sell policies.

During the 1860s the company expanded by developing the participating life policy, which returns dividends to policyholders based on investment earnings. This policy, developed by Aetna's 2nd president Thomas Enders, allowed the company to compete with mutual life insurance companies. In 1868 Aetna was the first company to offer renewable term life policies.

Morgan Bulkeley, son of the founder, became president in 1879 and served 43 years. Aetna began to offer multiple lines by introducing accident insurance in 1891, health insurance in 1899, worker's compensation in 1902, and automobile and other property insurance in 1907. Bulkeley increased the company's visibility by serving as mayor of Hartford, as governor of Connecticut, and as a US senator, all while also serving as Aetna president.

By 1920 Aetna had added ocean marine and inland marine insurance and by 1922 was the largest multiple-line insurance group in the nation. Aetna's non–life insurance companies, particularly the automobile line, expanded too fast during the 1920s, thus threatening Aetna's financial solvency. By restricting underwriting and reestablishing sufficient reserves, the company was able to withstand the Depression.

After World War II the company expanded into group life, health, and accident insurance. In 1967 the company reorganized into a holding company, Aetna Life and Casualty, which owned the stock of each insurance line affiliate.

Since the 1960s the company has continued to expand its multiple lines of insurance while entering and leaving other businesses. In 1982 it bought Geosource Inc., an oil services firm, which it sold 2 years later at a loss. In 1989 Aetna sold Federated Investors (an institutional investment management firm bought in 1982) to a new company owned by Federated's management, for $350 million and an equity interest in the new company.

HOW MUCH

	9 Yr. Growth	1980	1981	1982	1983	1984	1985	1986	1987	1988	1989
Sales ($ mil)	4.6%	13,143	13,398	14,164	14,411	15,411	18,612	20,483	22,114	24,296	19,671*
Net income ($ mil)	2.6%	508	491	522	325	183	430	714	867	668	639
Income as % of sales	—	3.9%	3.7%	3.7%	2.3%	1.2%	2.3%	3.5%	3.9%	2.7%	3.3%
Earnings per share ($)	(1.1%)	6.30	6.11	5.80	3.06	1.59	3.84	6.18	7.48	5.85	5.69
Stock price – high ($)	—	40.13	47.63	48.25	43.50	39.00	53.50	66.25	68.25	52.50	62.50
Stock price – low ($)	—	29.88	30.00	32.88	32.88	27.25	36.13	52.25	43.75	39.50	46.63
Stock price – close ($)	5.3%	35.38	44.00	36.38	36.00	36.50	53.50	56.38	45.25	47.25	56.50
P/E – high	—	6	8	8	14	25	14	11	9	9	11
P/E – low	—	5	5	6	11	17	9	8	6	7	8
Dividends per share ($)	3.0%	2.12	2.32	2.52	2.64	2.64	1.98	2.64	2.73	2.76	2.76
Book value per share ($)	4.7%	40.79	42.90	44.04	41.40	38.74	41.52	49.14	53.56	58.11	61.94

1989 Year End:
Debt ratio: 12.8%
Return on equity: 9.5%
Cash (mil): $2,572
Assets (mil): $87,099
Long-term debt (mil): $1,016
Number of shares (mil): 112
Dividends:
1989 average yield: 4.9%
1989 payout: 48.5%
Market value (mil): $6,327

Stock Price History high/low 1980-89

* Decrease due to accounting rule change

NYSE symbol: AET
Incorporated: Connecticut, 1967
Fiscal year ends: December 31

WHO

Chairman and CEO: James T. Lynn, age 63, $1,051,538 pay
President: Ronald E. Compton, age 57, $747,885 pay
SVP: Philip R. Roberts, age 48, $449,615 pay
SVP: David A. Kocher, age 48, $445,192 pay
SVP Finance: Patrick W. Kenny, age 47
Auditors: KPMG Peat Marwick
Employees: 45,000

WHERE

HQ: 151 Farmington Ave., Hartford, CT 06156
Phone: 203-273-0123
FAX: 203-275-2677

Aetna operates throughout the US and in some foreign countries.

	1989 Sales		1989 Pretax Income	
	$ mil	% of total	$ mil	% of total
US	19,102	97	1,073	101
Foreign	569	3	(14)	(1)
Adjustments	—	—	(246)	—
Total	**19,671**	**100**	**813**	**100**

WHAT

	1989 Sales		1989 Pretax Income	
	$ mil	% of total	$ mil	% of total
Reinsurance	1,121	6	169	16
Life, health, & annuity	1,100	6	105	10
Personal property -casualty	3,071	16	(185)	(18)
Investment mgmt.	240	1	175	17
Insurance				
Commercial	4,796	24	265	25
International	569	3	(14)	(1)
Group	4,315	22	398	37
Pensions & related financial svcs.	4,459	22	146	14
Adjustments	—	—	(246)	—
Total	**19,671**	**100**	**813**	**100**

Product Lines
Annuities
Life, health, and disability insurance
Managed health care
Pension plan services
Property-casualty insurance

Subsidiary
American Re-Insurance Co.

RANKINGS

4th in *Fortune* 50 Life Insurance Cos.
24th in *Forbes* Sales 500
104th in *Business Week* 1000
303rd in *Business Week* Global 1000

COMPETITION

Blue Cross
CIGNA
Equitable
GEICO
ITT
John Hancock
Kemper
Loews
Massachusetts Mutual
Metropolitan
New York Life
Northwestern Mutual
Prudential
Transamerica
Travelers
USF&G
Other insurers

AFL-CIO

OVERVIEW

The American Federation of Labor and Congress of Industrial Organizations is a union of unions, representing over 14 million workers (about 83% of all unionized workers in the US) through 90 affiliated unions and their more than 60,000 locals.

The Executive Council (president, secretary-treasurer, and 33 VPs) oversees 50 state central bodies, local central bodies in 626 communities, and 8 trade and industrial departments (*e.g.,* building trades, public employees), and sets policy between the biennial conventions. The federation's revenues are derived from regular per-capita dues paid by affiliates on behalf of their members.

The AFL-CIO encourages its affiliates' autonomy (through voluntary membership and separate officers and policies) and conducts no independent bargaining. The federation does settle jurisdictional disputes, help with organizing drives, sponsor voter registration, and present a unified labor front before legislatures (seeking job retraining, health care, etc.).

WHEN

The American Federation of Labor (AFL) formed in 1886 in Columbus, Ohio, from the merger of a small federation of 6 craft unions and a renegade craft section of the Marxist-flavored Knights of Labor. Samuel Gompers, a New York cigar factory worker who headed the AFL until his death in 1924, initiated the AFL's pragmatic focus: to work within, not to overthrow, the economic system in order to increase wages, shorten hours (to an 8-hour workday), and improve working conditions (and abolish child labor).

Gompers's successes (the initial membership grew to 2 million by 1916) incensed employers, whose arsenal, supported by the US courts and public opinion, included court injunctions and government-backed police forces to crush strikes; "yellow dog" contracts, which pledged workers never to join a union; and the Sherman Anti-Trust Act, used to assail union monopoly powers.

WWI's production needs boosted AFL membership to 4 million (1919). Labor clashes with management were widespread in the 1920s amidst the fear of Bolsheviks; as part of open-shop drives, employers replaced strikers with southern blacks and Mexican peasants.

The Great Depression brought a more acquiescent public and various pro-labor laws: the Norris-Laguardia Act eliminated legal restrictions on strikes (1932); the National Industrial Recovery Act (NIRA) allowed union organizing and collective bargaining (1933), but was declared unconstitutional. The Wagner Act (1936) restated many of NIRA's provisions and established the legal basis for unions, which remains to the present.

Union power split in 1935 over the attempts of AFL coal miner John L. Lewis to organize the flood of unskilled mass production workers. Lewis and his rebels, expelled from the AFL, formed the Congress of Industrial Organizations (CIO, 1938) and enjoyed great success in unionizing the auto, steel, textile, and other industries. The protection of the Wagner Act had swelled the AFL's membership to 9 million by 1946 and the CIO's to 5 million.

Amidst postwar public concern over rising consumer prices and Communist infiltration and corruption of the unions, Congress passed the labor-regulating Taft-Hartley Act (1947). The hostility led the AFL (headed by plumber George Meany) and the CIO (headed by autoworker Walter Reuther) to merge in 1955. The AFL-CIO soon expelled the Teamsters and other corrupt unions.

During its zenith of power in the 1960s, the AFL-CIO supported equal pay for women and civil rights. Public union membership jumped after President Kennedy gave federal employees the right to unionize (1962); state, county, and municipal workers soon followed.

A decline, begun with the vast increase in imported manufactured goods in the 1970s, accelerated in the 1980s: union-heavy smokestack industries were dying from stiff foreign competition, and new technologies continued to eliminate traditional jobs. Lane Kirkland (president since 1979) launched a reunification effort that attracted the United Auto Workers (1981), the Teamsters (1987), and the United Mine Workers (1989). Union efforts now focus on white-collar professionals and the public sector.

HOW MUCH

	9 Yr. Growth	1980	1981	1982	1983**	1984	1985	1986	1987	1988	1989
Membership (mil)*	—	—	13.6	—	13.8	—	13.1	—	12.7	—	14.2
Total dues ($ mil)	—	28.4	30.1	35.9	60.9	43.5	46.9	47.1	47.0	54.0	—
All unionized workers as % of total labor force	—	23.0%	—	—	20.1%	18.8%	18.0%	17.5%	17.0%	16.8%	16.4%

All Unionized Workers as % of Total Labor Force 1980-89

25%
20%
15%
10%
5%
0%

*Membership figures only kept for odd years due to biennial convention periods
**Fiscal year switched from June 30 to December 31

Labor federation
Founded: Ohio, 1886
Fiscal year ends: December 31

WHO

President: Lane Kirkland, age 68, $175,000 pay
Secretary-Treasurer: Thomas R. Donahue, age 62, $150,000 pay
VP: Albert Shanker (Teachers)
VP: Gerald McEntee (Public Employees)
VP: John Sweeney (Service Employees)
VP: William Wynn (Food and Commercial Workers)
Auditors: KPMG Peat Marwick
Membership: 14,158,000 (1989)
Employees: 400

WHERE

HQ: American Federation of Labor and Congress of Industrial Organizations, 815 16th St. NW, Washington, DC 20006
Phone: 202-637-5010
FAX: 202-637-5058

The AFL-CIO represents 90 unions with more than 60,000 locals in the US, Canada, and Puerto Rico.

Largest Member Unions	1989 Members (thou)
International Brotherhood of Teamsters (IBT)	1,600
State, County, Municipal (AFSCME)	1,090
Food and Commercial Workers (UFCW)	999
Automobile, Aerospace, and Agriculture (UAW)	917
Service Employees (SEIU)	762
Electrical Workers (IBEW)	744
Carpenters (UBCJA)	613
Teachers (AFT)	544
Machinists and Aerospace (IAM)	517
Communication Workers (CWA)	492

WHAT

Standing Committees
Civil Rights
Community Services
Economic Policy
Education
Housing
International Affairs
Legislative
Organization and Field Services
Political Education
Public Relations
Research
Safety and Occupational Health
Social Security

Trades Represented
Building and Construction Trades
Food and Allied Service Trades
Industrial Union
Maritime Trades
Metal Trades
Professional Employees
Public Employees
Transportation Trades
Union Label and Service Trades

H. F. AHMANSON & COMPANY

OVERVIEW

H. F. Ahmanson, a Los Angeles–based holding company for Home Savings of America, is the largest US savings and loan organization, with $44.6 billion in assets, $33.1 billion in deposits, and $194 million in earnings in 1989. Ahmanson ranked #1 in new mortgage loans in 1989 with Citicorp and Great Western Financial, each with about $11 billion.

Home Savings, which represented 99% of Ahmanson's revenues and assets in 1989, has 331 branches in 9 states, plus 26 Bowery Savings branches in New York. Ahmanson also makes loans outside California through Home Savings's Ahmanson Mortgage and Bowery Mortgage.

Of Ahmanson's $38.4 billion in mortgage loans outstanding at year-end 1989, 93% were monthly adjustable rate mortgages (ARMs), compared to a 39% national average of ARMs for mortgage lenders. In 1989 all of the company's new mortgage loans were on residential real estate, with 92% being single-family homes.

WHEN

By 1889 Walter Bonynge, 35, already had made a fortune in silver in Nevada and started a fire insurance company in San Antonio when he organized Home Investment Building and Loan, a savings and loan, in Los Angeles. In the early 1900s the company served customers from several locations in downtown Los Angeles, making Bonynge a pioneer in establishing branch banking in the US. The company changed its name to Home Building and Loan Association in 1922. Bonynge remained as secretary and director until his death in 1924.

In 1947 Howard Ahmanson, a Los Angeles insurance man, bought the company, which then became a subsidiary of H. F. Ahmanson & Company (founded 1928). In 1950 Home Building purchased Long Beach Savings and Loan, with offices in Long Beach and Huntington Park. The company changed its name to Home Savings and Loan Association in 1951 and opened a Beverly Hills branch in 1953. By the end of the 1950s, the $700 million institution led the savings industry in total assets, deposits, customer base, and mortgage lending.

In 1961 Home Savings became the first savings and loan in the US to have $1 billion in assets. That same year the company was the first savings and loan in the country to have a celebrity spokesman, Harry von Zell of the "Burns and Allen" TV show. Ahmanson was chairman of the company until the late 1960s, and family members, as trustees of the Ahmanson Foundation, are still members of the company's board of directors in 1990.

During the 1970s Ahmanson's Home Savings grew to over 100 offices throughout California. Assets were $12 billion by 1980 compared to $2 billion in 1967. In the 1980s Home Savings implemented a long-range strategy by developing new products, including adjustable rate mortgages, interest checking, check guarantee cards, and overdraft protection.

With regulators approving expansion across state lines, Home Savings in a 4-week period in late 1981 moved into Florida, Missouri, Texas, and Illinois. The company became Home Savings of America and expanded into New York (1984), Arizona (1985), and Washington (1985). In 1988 Home Savings purchased The Bowery Savings Bank, one of New York's largest and oldest savings banks. Ahmanson maintained net income averaging over $200 million annually during the late 1980s when many savings institutions were in trouble. The company focused on single-family mortgages while other institutions made riskier commercial real estate and business loans.

HOW MUCH

	9 Yr. Growth	1980	1981	1982	1983	1984	1985	1986	1987	1988	1989
Sales ($ mil)	13.8%	1,371	1,525	2,015	2,214	2,714	3,058	3,038	2,652	3,515	4,378
Net income ($ mil)	16.8%	48	(62)	(45)	108	48	221	304	200	203	194
Income as % of sales	—	3.5%	(4.0%)	(2.2%)	4.9%	1.8%	7.2%	10.0%	7.5%	5.8%	4.4%
Earnings per share ($)	12.2%	0.69	*(0.86)*	*(0.63)*	1.34	0.58	2.63	3.22	2.03	2.05	1.95
Stock price – high ($)	—	8.33	7.00	11.04	13.50	11.50	16.33	28.75	26.88	18.63	25.00
Stock price – low ($)	—	5.00	4.71	2.67	7.50	5.25	8.13	15.79	13.00	13.75	15.75
Stock price – close ($)	12.7%	6.50	5.04	9.25	10.25	8.79	16.21	21.63	16.50	16.38	19.00
P/E – high	—	12	—	—	10	20	6	9	13	9	13
P/E – low	—	7	—	—	6	9	3	5	6	7	8
Dividends per share ($)	9.2%	0.40	0.40	0.25	0.25	0.40	0.40	0.45	0.88	0.88	0.88
Book value per share ($)	5.9%	12.06	10.90	10.00	11.04	11.23	13.43	17.14	18.28	19.11	20.22

1989 Year End:
Debt ratio: 75.6%
Return on equity: 9.9%
Cash (mil): $2,859
Assets (mil): $44,652
Long-term debt (mil): $6,186
Number of shares (mil): 99
Dividends:
1989 average yield: 4.6%
1989 payout: 45.1%
Market value (mil): $1,880

NYSE symbol: AHM
Incorporated: Delaware, 1985
Fiscal year ends: December 31

WHO

Chairman and CEO: Richard H. Deihl, age 61, $1,189,453 pay
VC: Robert M. De Kruif, age 71, $421,180 pay
President and COO: Charles R. Rinehart, age 43, $237,500 pay
EVP, General Counsel, and Secretary: George G. Gregory, age 57, $418,086 pay
EVP and CFO: Jack A. Frazee, age 46, $268,298 pay
Auditors: KPMG Peat Marwick
Employees: 10,819

WHERE

HQ: 660 S. Figueroa St., Los Angeles, CA 90017
Phone: 213-955-4200
FAX: 818-814-5659 (Public Relations)

H. F. Ahmanson has 104 loan office operations in 19 states.

WHAT

	1989 Sales		1989 Pretax Income	
	$ mil	% of total	$ mil	% of total
Savings & loan	4,329	99	310	90
Real estate	49	1	36	10
Adjustments	—	—	(6)	—
Total	**4,378**	**100**	**340**	**100**

Financial Services
Consumer deposit accounts
Mortgage-backed securities
Mortgage loan servicing
Mortgage loans
Secondary mortgage loan sales

Subsidiaries
Ahmanson Mortgage
Bowery Mortgage
Bowery Savings
Home Savings of America
Savings of America

RANKINGS

1st in *Fortune* 50 Savings Institutions
196th in *Forbes* Sales 500
336th in *Business Week* 1000
958th in *Business Week* Global 1000

COMPETITION

Bank of New York
BankAmerica
Barnett Banks
Chase Manhattan
Chemical Banking
Citicorp
First Chicago
First Interstate
Great Western
Manufacturers Hanover
NCNB
Security Pacific
SunTrust
Wells Fargo

ALASKA AIR GROUP, INC.

OVERVIEW

Alaska Air Group is a holding company for Alaska Airlines and Horizon Air Industries, 2 Seattle-based airlines serving the western US, Mexico, and Canada.

Since 1973 Alaska has carried more passengers between Alaska and the lower 48 states than any other airline (52% in 1989). Emphasizing service (Condé Nast's *Traveler* magazine named it the best US airline in 1989), Alaska spends about $7.50 per person on food, compared to the $4.25 industry average. Wine is free on all Alaska flights, and the planes have fewer seats, with more leg room, than any competitor's equivalent jet.

The airline's link to its heritage is illustrated by the Eskimo painted on the tail of every Alaska craft.

Horizon, the largest regional commuter airline in the Pacific Northwest, carried 1.6 million passengers in 1989. The airline also serves Vancouver and Victoria, British Columbia.

NYSE symbol: ALK
Incorporated: Delaware, 1985
Fiscal year ends: December 31

WHO

Chairman, CEO, and President: Bruce R. Kennedy, age 51, $468,668 pay
EVP and COO, Alaska Airlines: Raymond J. Vecci, age 47, $284,178 pay
VP Finance and CFO: J. Ray Vingo, age 51, $208,573 pay
Auditors: Arthur Andersen & Co.
Employees: 5,663

WHEN

Pilot Mac McGee pioneered air service between Anchorage and Bristol Bay, Alaska, in 1932, flying under the name of McGee Airways. He joined other local operators in 1937 to form Star Air Lines and began air mail service between Fairbanks and Bethel in 1938. Star bought 3 more airlines in 1943, including Lavery Airways, which had a mail route between Anchorage and Fairbanks. The company was listed on the American Stock Exchange in 1943 (changing to the NYSE in 1983).

Renamed Alaska Airlines (1944), the company bought 2 more local carriers and established freight service to Africa and Australia (1950). This growth, coupled with the seasonal nature of the airline's business, led to financial losses that continued through the early 1970s. Alaska gained a direct route between Seattle and Fairbanks in 1951 but lost it to Pan Am in 1965. In 1968 Alaska bought Cordova Airlines and Alaska Coastal Airways, thereby expanding operations in southeastern Alaska.

In 1969 Bruce Kennedy's real estate development company pledged $300,000 to guarantee Alaska's debt, taking over the financially ailing airline in 1972. The airline acquired several Alaskan hotel properties (1970-1972) and experienced the first of 17 consecutive years of profitability in 1973. However, the Civil Aeronautics Board forced the company to drop service to cities in northwestern Alaska, including Nome (1975). By 1978 the company served only 10 Alaskan cities and Seattle.

Kennedy became CEO in 1979, shortly after congressional approval of the 1978 Airline Deregulation Act. Deregulation allowed Alaska to extend operations into new areas and to regain routes it had previously lost. Kennedy began with service to California, then expanded operations in Alaska by reestablishing service to Nome and adding service to Prudhoe Bay, Barrow, Bethel, Kenai, and Kodiak, making Alaska Airlines the largest carrier operating between the US mainland and Alaska by 1982.

In 1986 the company acquired Jet America Airlines. Based in Long Beach, California, Jet America expanded Alaska's route network eastward, offering flights to Chicago, St. Louis, and Dallas. The company also bought Seattle-based Horizon Air Industries, a regional carrier serving 30 cities in the Northwest, in 1986. However, in 1987 competition in the East and Midwest resulted in a 35% reduction in profits. Kennedy shut down Jet America and concentrated on Alaska's and Horizon's operations along the Pacific coastline.

The airline began service to 2 Mexican resorts in 1988 and plans to expand its West Coast–Mexican operations in 1990. Alaska hopes to win DOT approval to offer flights from Anchorage to 3 Soviet cities in 1991. In 1990 International Lease Finance Corporation, a major financer of aircraft, purchased $62.5 million of convertible preferred stock in the airline.

WHERE

HQ: 19300 Pacific Hwy. South, Seattle, WA 98188
Phone: 206-431-7040
FAX: 206-433-3366

Alaska serves 32 cities in Alaska, Arizona, California, Idaho, Oregon, and Washington, and 5 cities in Mexico. Horizon serves 34 cities in Idaho, Montana, Oregon, Utah, Washington, and Canada.

Hub Locations

Alaska	Horizon
Anchorage, AL	Boise, ID
Portland, OR	Portland, OR
Seattle, WA	Seattle, WA
	Spokane, WA

WHAT

	1989 Sales	
	$ mil	% of total
Passenger service	834	91
Freight and mail	62	7
Contract service & other	21	2
Total	**917**	**100**

Operating Companies

Alaska Airlines, Inc.

Horizon Air Industries, Inc.

Regional Commuters
To 68 Alaskan communities through agreements with 5 local airlines

Flight Equipment	Owned	Leased	Total
Alaska			
Boeing 727	1	27	28
Boeing 737	3	4	7
MD-80	8	12	20
	12	43	55
Horizon			
Fairchild Metroliner	5	26	31
de Havilland Dash 8	–	13	13
Fokker F-28	–	2	2
	5	41	46
Total	**17**	**84**	**101**

RANKINGS

29th in *Fortune* 50 Transportation Cos.

COMPETITION

America West
AMR
Delta
NWA
UAL

HOW MUCH

	9 Yr. Growth	1980	1981	1982	1983	1984	1985	1986	1987	1988	1989
Sales ($ mil)	24.1%	131	182	235	281	362	433	468	710	814	917
Net income ($ mil)	26.6%	5	8	11	16	24	26	18	13	37	43
Income as % of sales	—	3.9%	4.2%	4.5%	5.6%	6.6%	6.0%	3.8%	1.9%	4.6%	4.7%
Earnings per share ($)	10.3%	1.04	0.97	1.15	1.44	1.93	1.85	1.30	0.87	2.30	2.51
Stock price – high ($)	—	5.10	8.33	14.38	18.63	17.25	26.38	22.75	27.88	22.50	30.50
Stock price – low ($)	—	3.06	3.69	4.63	10.38	9.25	14.25	14.25	12.25	13.50	19.88
Stock price – close ($)	20.2%	3.93	6.13	13.25	14.13	15.13	16.13	20.00	13.50	20.00	20.63
P/E – high	—	5	9	13	13	9	14	18	32	10	12
P/E – low	—	3	4	4	7	5	8	11	14	6	8
Dividends per share ($)	—	0.00	0.00	0.12	0.09	0.14	0.15	0.16	0.16	0.16	0.20
Book value per share ($)	22.2%	3.63	6.39	6.65	8.05	10.12	13.05	14.31	17.37	19.59	22.08

1989 Year End:
Debt ratio: 39.9%
Return on equity: 12.0%
Cash (mil): $111
Current ratio: 1.05
Long-term debt (mil): $227
Number of shares (mil): 15
Dividends:
1989 average yield: 1.0%
1989 payout: 8.0%
Market value (mil): $319

Stock Price History high/low 1980-89

ALBERTSON'S, INC.

OVERVIEW

Albertson's, America's 6th largest food retailer, is extremely profitable, ranking high among its major competitors in both net earnings ($197 million in 1989) and return on equity (22.7%). Based in Boise, the company operates grocery stores in western and southern states.

Part of the company's superior performance is due to efficient, modern distribution facilities strategically placed to allow servicing of Albertson's widely dispersed stores. Unlike other grocers who tend to cluster their stores, Albertson's operates only a few locations in each market. In addition, 80% of the company's square footage is in large, food/drug combination stores or superstores.

Albertson's is also highly regarded throughout the industry for its management. Warren McCain, who joined the company 39 years ago, has received numerous awards as top industry CEO. The company directs much attention to the morale of its employees, 49% of whom are unionized. Unlike its more weakly performing rivals, Albertson's managed to sidestep the corporate raiders in the 1980s and consequently is not burdened by high debt. Founder Joe Albertson and wife Kathryn continue to influence the company's activities as directors.

WHEN

J. A. "Joe" Albertson gave up a position as district manager for Safeway in 1939 and opened his first food store, Albertson's Food Center, in Boise, Idaho. The store differed from others of the time because it covered 10,000 square feet — 8 times the competitors' average — and had plenty of free parking, as well as an in-store butchery, bakery, and ice cream shop. With these innovations, Albertson was one of the key developers of the "supermarket" concept in food retailing.

In 1949 Albertson's extended its bakery and ice cream trademark brand, Dutch Girl, by opening the Dutch Girl Ice Cream Plant in Boise. Albertson's refined its supermarket concept further by opening its first combination food and drug store (1951), a 60,000-square-foot superstore, and by locating its new stores in growing suburban areas. Jonathan Scott, who became president of Albertson's in 1955, married Joe's daughter, Barbara; despite their later divorce, Joe retained Scott as president until 1975. Albertson's went public to raise expansion capital in 1959, and by 1960 the company had 62 stores in Idaho, Washington, Oregon, and Utah. Albertson's acquired Greater All American Markets (1964), a grocery chain based in Downey, California, and Semrau & Sons (1965) of Oakland, aiding the company's thrust into the California market.

Salt Lake City–based drugstore chain Skaggs (now part of American Stores) and Albertson's formed a partnership in 1969 to jointly operate large Skaggs Albertsons food and drug combination stores. In 1973 the company built its first full-line distribution facility in Brea, California, and opened an even larger facility in Salt Lake City in 1976. Albertson's and Skaggs dissolved their partnership in 1977, with each taking 1/2 of the units in the jointly owned chain. By 1985 the company had reached $5 billion in sales, a 5-fold increase over 1975. Albertson's added an additional distribution facility in Denver in 1982 and its first mechanized distribution center in Portland, Oregon, in 1988.

In 1989 Albertson's board of directors adopted a 5-year plan of expansion, remodeling, and modernization, aimed at giving Albertson's one of the most up-to-date facilities in the industry. The company opened 36 new stores in 1989, as well as new distribution facilities in Fort Worth and Sacramento. Present plans are to open 40-50 stores per year through 1994, especially in the fast-growing areas of the country: California, Texas, Florida, and Arizona.

HOW MUCH

	9 Yr. Growth	1980	1981	1982	1983	1984	1985	1986	1987	1988	1989
Sales ($ mil)	10.4%	3,039	3,481	3,940	4,279	4,736	5,060	5,380	5,869	6,773	7,423
Net income ($ mil)	18.8%	42	48	58	70	80	85	100	125	163	197
Income as % of sales	—	1.4%	1.4%	1.5%	1.6%	1.7%	1.7%	1.9%	2.1%	2.4%	2.6%
Earnings per share ($)	17.7%	0.68	0.79	0.95	1.08	1.21	1.29	1.50	1.88	2.44	2.93
Stock price – high ($)	—	6.22	7.41	12.38	15.13	14.75	16.63	24.75	34.00	38.75	60.25
Stock price – low ($)	—	4.13	4.88	6.03	9.88	11.25	13.19	15.25	20.25	24.00	36.63
Stock price – close ($)	30.5%	5.06	6.63	11.81	13.56	14.50	16.25	21.50	25.38	37.88	55.50
P/E – high	—	9	9	13	14	12	13	17	18	16	21
P/E – low	—	6	6	6	9	9	10	10	11	10	13
Dividends per share ($)	13.0%	0.20	0.17	0.31	0.30	0.26	0.37	0.41	0.47	0.68	0.60
Book value per share ($)	16.4%	3.52	4.01	5.22	5.97	6.87	7.80	8.90	10.02	11.96	13.88

1989 Year End:
Debt ratio: 19.0%
Return on equity: 22.7%
Cash (mil): $44
Current ratio: 1.2
Long-term debt (mil): $218
Number of shares (mil): 67
Dividends:
1989 average yield: 1.1%
1989 payout: 20.5%
Market value (mil): $3,716

Stock Price History high/low 1980-89

NYSE symbol: ABS
Incorporated: Delaware, 1969
Fiscal year ends: Thursday closest to January 31

WHO

Chairman and CEO: Warren E. McCain, age 64, $1,058,462 pay
VC and CFO: Gary G. Michael, age 49, $610,923 pay
President: John B. Carley, age 56, $610,923 pay
Auditors: Deloitte & Touche
Employees: 55,000

WHERE

HQ: 250 Parkcenter Blvd., PO Box 20, Boise, ID 83726
Phone: 208-385-6200
FAX: 208-385-6349

The company operates 523 stores in 17 western and southern states. Full-line distribution facilities are located in Brea, CA; Denver; Fort Worth; Portland, OR; and Salt Lake City.

	No. of Stores
California	122
Florida	68
Washington	64
Texas	59
Oregon	41
Colorado	40
Utah	31
Idaho	28
Nevada	18
New Mexico	15
Louisiana	9
Wyoming	8
Montana	7
Arizona	5
Nebraska	5
North Dakota	2
South Dakota	1
Total	**523**

WHAT

	No. of stores	Area (sq. ft. thou.)
Combination units	139	8,006
Superstores	195	8,149
Conventional stores	157	4,277
Warehouse stores	32	1,379
Total	**523**	**21,811**

Warehouse Stores
The Canned Food Store
The Grocery Warehouse
Maxx Warehouse Food and Drug
Monte Mart

RANKINGS

15th in *Fortune* 50 Retailing Cos.
111th in *Forbes* Sales 500
170th in *Business Week* 1000
422nd in *Business Week* Global 1000

COMPETITION

American Stores
Bruno's
Campeau
Food Lion
Fred Meyer
Great A&P
Kroger
Longs
Publix
Safeway
Vons
Winn-Dixie

ALCAN ALUMINIUM LTD.

OVERVIEW

Montreal-based Alcan is a Canadian company with a leading position in the international aluminum industry. The company's vertically integrated operations include mining and processing bauxite (an aluminum-bearing ore); refining bauxite into alumina; generating electricity for smelting aluminum; smelting, recycling, fabricating, marketing, and distributing aluminum; and producing and selling industrial chemicals.

The company derives approximately 83% of its sales from aluminum in ingot and fabricated form. Fabricated aluminum products (plate, sheet, foil, and extruded shapes), of which Alcan sold over 1.5 million tons in 1989, generate 66% of sales. Approximately half of the aluminum produced globally is converted into rolled products (aluminum plate, sheet, and foil).

Alcan operates a global network of facilities that help to provide and process its raw materials. The company also purchases scrap and used aluminum (791,450 tons in 1989) for reprocessing. The company's name and its symbol are registered trademarks in more than 100 countries.

NYSE symbol: AL
Incorporated: Canada, 1928
Fiscal year ends: December 31

WHO

Chairman and CEO: David Morton, age 60, $828,692 pay
President and COO: Jacques Bougie, age 42, $457,031 pay
VP and CFO: Allan A. Hodgson, age 52, $401,854 pay
Auditors: Price Waterhouse
Employees: 57,000

WHEN

In 1900 the Aluminum Company of America (Alcoa) established its first Canadian smelter at Shawinigan Falls, Quebec. In 1928 Alcoa organized its Canadian and all other foreign operations as a separate company (mandated by a US antitrust divestment order), which took the name Aluminium Limited (name changed to Alcan in 1966). Alcan retained close ties with Alcoa (the Mellon and Davis families held stock in both companies) and appointed Edward K. Davis (the brother of former Alcoa chairman Arthur Vining Davis) as its first president. At the time of its formation, Alcan existed primarily as a smelter for raw bauxite that came from a company-owned mine in British Guiana (which would become Guyana).

After narrowly surviving the Great Depression years of the early 1930s, Alcan established a global sales force and a number of overseas plants in Europe, Australia, India, China, and Japan. The company profited tremendously from WWII when the need for aluminum made it the world's largest smelter. At the end of the war, Alcan was 5 times larger than it had been in 1937.

In 1950 US courts, ruling on an earlier antitrust suit, ordered the Mellon and Davis families to end their joint ownership of Alcoa and Alcan. Both families opted to stay with Alcoa and sold most of their stock in Alcan. In 1954 Alcan opened its giant Kitimat-Kemano power complex in British Columbia.

During the 1960s and 1970s the company (which had previously supplied aluminum to other companies for fabrication) started fabricating and distributing it themselves. In 1961 the company started fabricating products in the USA in Oswego, New York.

In 1971 Alcan had to readjust its supply strategy when Guyana nationalized its raw resources. Six years later Jamaica (another major provider of bauxite) acquired 70% of all of Alcan's mining and refining assets, which resulted in the formation of a joint venture (Jamalcan).

In 1979 David Culver became CEO of the company (the first non–Davis family member to hold the position) and led Alcan through an early 1980s recession with a massive cost-cutting campaign. In 1988 the company achieved record profits ($931 million). In 1989 Alcan commissioned the world's largest aluminum beverage can recycling plant in Berea, Kentucky. That same year Culver stepped down as CEO and was replaced by David Morton.

During the 1990s Alcan will provide its Aluminum-Structured Vehicle Technology (ASVT) to Jaguar for the production of the Jaguar XJ220 (an energy-saving aluminum automobile). The company expects the cars to open a new market for aluminum.

WHERE

HQ: 1188 Sherbrooke St. West, Montreal, Quebec, Canada H3A 3G2
Phone: 514-848-8000
FAX: 514-848-8115

The company produces alumina in 9 countries and has bauxite holdings in 8, smelting operations in 7, and aluminum fabricating plants in 18.

	1989 Sales		1989 Net Income	
	$ mil	% of total	$ mil	% of total
Canada	1,265	14	368	44
US	3,073	35	15	2
Latin America	523	6	63	7
Europe	2,878	33	73	9
Pacific	989	11	243	29
All other	111	1	79	9
Adjustments	—	—	(6)	—
Total	**8,839**	**100**	**835**	**100**

WHAT

	1989 Sales	
	$ mil	% of total
Fabricated products	5,827	66
Ingot products	1,537	17
Other products	1,215	14
Other revenues	260	3
Total	**8,839**	**100**

Products

Aluminum
Alumina
Bauxite
Cathode blocks
Containers
Extruded shapes
- Airplane components
- Automotive bumpers
- Doors
- Truck chassis
- Windows

Foil
Ingot
Packaging
Petroleum coke
Plate
Sheet
Wire

Chemicals
Aluminum fluoride
Cryolite

RANKINGS

141st in *Fortune* Global 500 Industrial Cos.
364th in *Business Week* Global 1000

COMPETITION

Alcoa
AMAX
Reynolds Metals

HOW MUCH

	9 Yr. Growth	1980	1981	1982	1983	1984	1985	1986	1987	1988	1989
Sales ($ mil)	6.0%	5,215	4,978	4,644	5,208	5,467	5,718	5,956	6,797	8,529	8,839
Net income ($ mil)	4.9%	542	264	(58)	58	216	(216)	218	433	931	835
Income as % of sales	—	10.4%	5.3%	(1.2%)	1.1%	4.0%	(3.8%)	3.7%	6.4%	10.9%	9.4%
Earnings per share ($)	2.1%	2.98	1.44	(0.31)	0.28	0.98	(0.96)	0.97	1.68	3.85	3.58
Stock price – high ($)	—	17.28	17.78	12.61	18.50	18.33	13.89	15.39	25.25	22.25	25.13
Stock price – low ($)	—	10.06	8.72	7.06	11.44	10.44	10.11	12.28	12.61	15.67	20.17
Stock price – close ($)	5.0%	14.78	10.22	12.39	17.67	12.78	12.89	12.56	17.92	21.75	22.88
P/E – high	—	6	12	—	65	19	—	16	15	6	7
P/E – low	—	3	6	—	40	11	—	13	8	4	6
Dividends per share ($)	7.2%	0.60	0.80	0.60	0.40	0.53	0.49	0.36	0.39	0.59	1.12
Book value per share ($)	4.6%	13.53	14.15	13.10	12.83	13.08	12.23	13.18	15.04	18.06	20.30

1989 Year End:
Debt ratio: 18.3%
Return on equity: 18.7%
Cash (mil): $247
Current ratio: 1.66
Long-term debt (mil): $1,079
Number of shares (mil): 227
Dividends:
- 1989 average yield: 4.9%
- 1989 payout: 31.3%

Market value (mil): $5,194

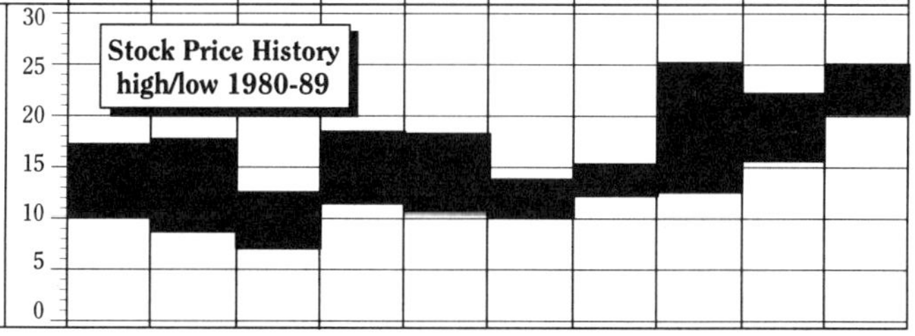

Stock Price History high/low 1980-89

ALLIED-SIGNAL INC.

OVERVIEW

Allied-Signal operates 43 businesses in the aerospace, automotive, and chemical industries. A leading manufacturer of turbine engines for under-20-passenger regional and executive jets, Allied-Signal Aerospace is also the world's largest maker of aircraft environmental control systems. The aerospace division produces technical systems for NASA as well as components for missiles and other defense mechanisms, but sales to the government (as a percent of revenues) have declined from 55% in 1986 to 44% in 1989.

Allied-Signal's automotive division produces a variety of automotive systems and components, boasting trade names such as Autolite, Bendix, Fram, and Garrett, and is the world's foremost maker of automotive braking systems. The company's chemical division is the 3rd largest manufacturer of nylon in the US and leads the world in the production of hydrofluoric acid (for refrigerants).

NYSE symbol: ALD
Incorporated: Delaware, 1985
Fiscal year ends: December 31

WHO

Chairman and CEO: Edward L. Hennessy, Jr., age 61, $1,675,000 pay
President and COO: Alan Belzer, age 57, $1,162,500 pay
SVP and CFO: John W. Barter, age 43
Auditors: Price Waterhouse
Employees: 107,100

WHEN

During WWI Germany controlled much of the world's chemical industry, causing shortages of such commodities as dyes and drugs. In response, *Washington Post* publisher Eugene Meyer and scientist William Nichols organized the Allied Chemical & Dye Corporation in 1920 from 5 existing companies.

In 1928 Allied opened a synthetic ammonia plant near Hopewell, Virginia, becoming the world's leading producer of ammonia. This represented the company's earliest venture into new markets. After WWII Allied began manufacturing other new products, including nylon 6 (for making everything from tires to clothes) and refrigerants. In 1958 it became Allied Chemical Corporation.

In 1962 Allied bought Union Texas Natural Gas, which owned oil and gas properties throughout the Americas. Allied regarded it mainly as a supplier of raw materials for its chemical products, but this changed in the early 1970s when CEO John Connor (former Secretary of Commerce under President Johnson) sold many of Allied's unprofitable businesses and invested in oil and gas exploration. By 1979 when Edward Hennessy, Jr., became CEO, Union Texas produced 80% of Allied's income.

Through purchases directed by Hennessy, Allied entered new fields, including electronics (Eltra Corporation, 1979; Bunker Ramo Corporation, 1981) and health and scientific products (Fisher Scientific Company, 1981). Renamed the Allied Corporation (1981), the company went on to buy the Bendix Corporation, an aerospace and automotive company, in 1983. By 1984 Bendix generated 50% of Allied's income while oil and gas generated 38%.

In 1985 Allied merged with The Signal Companies to form Allied-Signal. Founded by Sam Mosher in 1922 as The Signal Gasoline Company, Signal originally produced gasoline from natural gas. In 1928 the company changed its name to Signal Oil & Gas, entering into oil production the same year. Signal merged with the Garrett Corporation, a Los Angeles–based aerospace company, in 1964; acquired Mack Trucks in 1967 (spun off 1983); and in 1968 adopted The Signal Companies as its corporate name. Signal bought the Ampex Corporation in 1981.

The addition of Signal's Garrett division to Bendix made aerospace Allied-Signal's largest business sector. In 1985 the company sold 50% of Union Texas (by then America's largest independent oil producer) and in 1986 spun off 35 mostly unprofitable chemical and engineering businesses, collectively known as the Henley Group, to its stockholders. Hennessy sold 7 more businesses in 1987, leaving Allied-Signal with its current core segments: aerospace, automotives, and engineered materials (chemicals).

WHERE

HQ: Columbia Rd. and Park Ave., PO Box 4000R, Morristown, NJ 07962
Phone: 201-455-2000
FAX: 201-455-4807

Allied-Signal operates 500 facilities in the US and in 46 foreign countries.

	1989 Sales		1989 Net Income	
	$ mil	% of total	$ mil	% of total
US	9,339	78	391	74
Canada	382	3	21	4
Europe	1,663	14	88	17
Other	558	5	28	5
Total	**11,942**	**100**	**528**	**100**

WHAT

	1989 Sales		1989 Operating Income	
	$ mil	% of total	$ mil	% of total
Aerospace	5,079	43	514	44
Automotive	3,849	32	302	26
Engineered matls.	2,993	25	355	30
Adjustments	21	—	(225)	—
Total	**11,942**	**100**	**946**	**100**

Aerospace
AiResearch LA
Bendix
Bendix/King
Garrett

Products: Flight control systems, gyroscopes, sonars, torpedo propulsion, turbo engines, wheels and brakes

Automotive
Allied-Signal
Autolite
Bendix
Friction Materials
Garrett

Products: Brake components; braking systems; oil, air, and transmission filters; safety restraints and air bags; spark plugs, and turbochargers

Engineered Materials
Fibers
Fluorine Products
Norplex Oak
Plastics

Products: Nylon and polyester fibers, hydrofluoric acid, polyethylene, refrigerants and solvents, and tar products

RANKINGS

31st in *Fortune* 500 Industrial Cos.
87th in *Fortune* 500 Global Industrial Cos.
18th in *Fortune* 50 Exporters
52nd in *Forbes* Sales 500
115th in *Business Week* 1000
352nd in *Business Week* Global 1000

COMPETITION

BASF
Borg-Warner
Dana
Du Pont
Eaton
EG&G
Electrolux
Hoechst
Honeywell
Lockheed
Martin Marietta
Robert Bosch
Rockwell International
United Technologies
Other chemical, automotive, and aerospace companies

HOW MUCH

	9 Yr. Growth	1980	1981	1982	1983	1984	1985	1986	1987	1988	1989
Sales ($ mil)	9.0%	5,519	6,407	6,167	10,022	10,734	9,115	11,794	11,116	11,909	11,942
Net income ($ mil)	6.9%	289	348	272	450	487	(279)	605	515	463	528
Income as % of sales	—	5.2%	5.4%	4.4%	4.5%	4.5%	(3.1%)	5.1%	4.6%	3.9%	4.4%
Earnings per share ($)	(4.6%)	5.43	6.11	4.15	4.61	5.02	(3.28)	3.26	3.07	3.10	3.55
Stock price – high ($)	—	41.17	39.92	30.25	38.75	38.17	48.13	54.50	49.25	36.88	40.38
Stock price – low ($)	—	26.00	26.00	19.17	21.42	28.25	33.75	36.75	26.00	28.00	31.75
Stock price – close ($)	(0.3%)	35.67	29.25	21.58	37.17	34.50	46.75	40.13	28.25	32.50	34.88
P/E – high	—	8	7	7	8	8	—	17	16	12	11
P/E – low	—	5	4	5	5	6	—	11	8	9	9
Dividends per share ($)	2.6%	1.43	1.57	1.60	1.60	1.75	1.80	1.80	1.80	1.80	1.80
Book value per share ($)	(3.7%)	33.13	37.54	38.07	30.62	33.08	33.29	21.05	20.87	22.09	23.53

1989 Year End:
Debt ratio: 35.8%
Return on equity: 15.6%
Cash (mil): $525
Current ratio: 1.28
Long-term debt (mil): $1,903
Number of shares (mil): 145
Dividends:
1989 average yield: 5.2%
1989 payout: 50.7%
Market value (mil): $5,057

ALUMINUM COMPANY OF AMERICA

OVERVIEW

Now popularly known as Alcoa, the Pittsburgh-based Aluminum Company of America is the world's largest aluminum producer, serving the packaging, transportation, building, and industrial markets.

Alcoa accounts for about 17% of world aluminum production and derives its largest single block of revenue (89%) from aluminum-related sales. Aerospace and Industrial Products, Packaging Systems, and Materials Science make up the balance of the company's business.

The smelting process requires gigawatts of electricity, accounting for about 30% of production costs. Alcoa generates 43% of the power used at its smelters. The company claims about 36% of total US beverage can recycling, which takes 95% less electricity than producing aluminum from bauxite.

Alcoa's early 1980s reorganization reduced dependence on aluminum sales and expanded overseas earnings. Less than 50% of operating profits originated in the US in 1989; the Pacific share doubled to 48%. In 1989 sales rose 11% and earnings 10% over 1988 levels, both setting record volumes. Alcoa plans to produce more finished products, reducing reliance on primary aluminum sales to 50% by 1995.

WHEN

In 1886, 2 chemists, one in France and one in the US, simultaneously discovered an inexpensive process for aluminum production. The American, Charles Martin Hall, pursued commercial applications. In 1888, with an investor group led by Captain Alfred Hunt, Hall formed the Pittsburgh Reduction Company. The first salesman, Arthur Vining Davis, secured an initial order for 2,000 cooking pots.

In 1889 the Mellon Bank loaned the company $4,000. In 1891 Alcoa recapitalized as a million-dollar corporation, with the Mellon brothers holding 12% of the stock. By the 1920s the Mellons had increased their share to 33%.

Hunt died in 1899 and Hall in 1914. Davis led the company, which remained highly centralized, for 47 years until 1957. Alcoa, the first industrial user of Niagara Falls (1893), introduced aluminum foil (1910) and found applications for aluminum in emerging industries (*e.g.*, electric wire, airplanes, and automobiles). The present name was adopted in 1907.

By the end of WWI, Alcoa was integrated backward into bauxite mining and forward into end-use production. Alcoa transferred most foreign properties to Aluminium Ltd., a Canadian subsidiary, in 1928.

Patents for the smelting process expired in 1912, and the government brought charges of antitrust violations. In 1946 a federal appeals court found Alcoa guilty of conspiring to monopolize the aluminum industry. The ruling forced Alcoa to sell many operations built during WWII (when US smelting capacity doubled) as well as its Canadian subsidiary, today Alcan, its largest competitor.

In the more competitive aluminum industry of the 1960s, Alcoa relied on its laboratories (established 1919) and entrepreneurship. The company devised lower-cost production methods and gained greater market shares, especially in beverage cans. Alcoa reentered the international arena, establishing 23 locations in 13 countries between 1959 and 1965.

In the 1970s Alcoa recognized that diversification was necessary and focused on new products such as aerospace components and lithographic sheet. Since 1981 Alcoa has doubled R&D expenditures, spent $500 million on acquisitions, and invested heavily in joint ventures and plant modernization.

Sales and earnings set records in 1988 and 1989. Alcoa's future is in producing value-added, custom-made products from aluminum, ceramic, plastic, and various mixes.

HOW MUCH

	9 Yr. Growth	1980	1981	1982	1983	1984	1985	1986	1987	1988	1989
Sales ($ mil)	8.7%	5,148	4,978	4,648	5,263	5,751	5,163	4,667	7,767	9,795	10,910
Net income ($ mil)	8.1%	470	296	(9)	165	256	(17)	264	224	861	945
Income as % of sales	—	9.1%	6.0%	(0.2%)	3.1%	4.5%	(0.3%)	5.7%	2.9%	8.8%	8.7%
Earnings per share ($)	5.7%	6.29	3.93	(0.15)	2.03	3.13	(0.23)	3.08	2.48	9.50	10.36
Stock price – high ($)	—	38.19	37.50	32.75	47.75	48.63	40.75	46.38	64.75	57.38	79.63
Stock price – low ($)	—	26.13	22.63	21.88	29.25	30.75	29.75	32.63	33.75	38.63	55.25
Stock price – close ($)	10.8%	29.81	25.63	31.00	44.88	37.00	38.50	33.88	46.75	56.00	75.00
P/E – high	—	6	10	—	24	16	—	15	26	6	8
P/E – low	—	4	6	—	14	10	—	11	14	4	5
Dividends per share ($)	6.1%	1.60	1.80	1.65	1.20	1.20	1.20	1.20	1.20	1.30	2.72
Book value per share ($)	4.7%	39.25	41.24	38.60	39.06	40.39	39.84	41.99	43.62	51.76	59.41

1989 Year End:
Debt ratio: 20.0%
Return on equity: 18.6%
Cash (mil): $805
Current ratio: 1.74
Long-term debt (mil): $1,316
Number of shares (mil): 88
Dividends:
1989 average yield: 3.6%
1989 payout: 26.3%
Market value (mil): $6,566

Stock Price History high/low 1980-89

80 70 60 50 40 30 20 10 0

NYSE symbol: AA
Incorporated: Pennsylvania, 1888
Fiscal year ends: December 31

WHO

Chairman and CEO: Paul H. O'Neill, age 54, $1,306,843 pay
President and COO: C. Fred Fetterolf, age 61, $988,391 pay
SVP Corporate Development and General Counsel: Richard L. Fischer, age 53, $470,793 pay
SVP Employee Relations: Donald R. Whitlow, age 57
SVP Finance: James W. Wirth, age 57
Auditors: Coopers & Lybrand
Employees: 61,000

WHERE

HQ: 1501 Alcoa Bldg., Pittsburgh, PA 15219
Phone: 412-553-4545
FAX: 412-553-4498

Alcoa has 152 operating and sales locations in 20 countries.

	1989 Sales		1989 Operating Income	
	$ mil	% of total	$ mil	% of total
US	6,696	61	652	31
Other Americas	1,392	13	392	18
Pacific	2,040	19	1,018	48
Europe	782	7	62	3
Adjustments	—	—	(29)	—
Total	**10,910**	**100**	**2,095**	**100**

WHAT

	1989 Sales		1989 Operating Income	
	$ mil	% of total	$ mil	% of total
Alumina & chemicals	1,743	16	1,183	56
Aluminum processing	8,019	73	902	43
Nonaluminum products	1,148	11	33	1
Adjustments	—	—	(23)	—
Total	**10,910**	**100**	**2,095**	**100**

Operations & Products
Advanced electronic ceramics
Alumina-based industrial chemicals
Alumina refining
Aluminum and plastic bottle caps
Aluminum foil
Aluminum sheet for cans
Aluminum smelting
Bauxite mining
Can recycling
Fabricated aluminum products (*e.g.*, bar, extrusions)
Fiber optic cable
Finished aluminum products
Separation, purification, and filtration systems

RANKINGS

37th in *Fortune* 500 Industrial Cos.
101st in *Fortune* Global 500 Industrial Cos.
34th in *Fortune* 50 Exporters
63rd in *Forbes* Sales 500
100th in *Business Week* 1000
310th in *Business Week* Global 1000

COMPETITION

Alcan
AMAX
Reynolds Metals

AMAX INC.

OVERVIEW

AMAX, the 6th largest US metals company, oversees subsidiaries developing a wide range of natural resources. Wholly owned Alumax is the 3rd largest aluminum company in the US, after Alcoa and Reynolds, producing everything from aluminum ingot to building materials. Alumax operates more than 100 plants in 30 states, Canada, and Western Europe.

Amax Coal Industries is the 3rd largest US coal producer, with the bulk of its production in Wyoming. Amax Oil & Gas explores for and produces oil and natural gas in 22 states and the Gulf of Mexico.

AMAX owns 87% of Amax Gold, which produced 307,000 ounces of gold in 1989. The open-pit Sleeper mine in Nevada leads the company's production, but Amax Gold also operates another Nevada site and a New Zealand mine and plans a California project. Climax Metals is one of the world's largest producers of molybdenum, a metal used to harden steel.

AMAX Chairman Allen Born argues that the future belongs to the "low-cost producer" of commodities. Applying a "fix it, sell it, or shoot it" test to AMAX operations, he has streamlined the company to climb out of the $1.7 billion hole it dug for itself with losses from 1982 to 1986, generating almost $1.2 billion in income in the last 3 years.

NYSE symbol: AMX
Incorporated: New York, 1887
Fiscal year ends: December 31

WHO

Chairman, CEO, and President: Allen Born, age 56, $1,185,000 pay
President, Alumax Inc.: Paul E. Drack, age 61, $1,200,000 pay
SVP and CFO: Stephen C. Knup, age 47, $416,167 pay
EVP: Thomas A. McKeever, age 46, $557,117 pay
EVP and General Counsel: Malcolm B. Bayliss, age 62, $391,667 pay
Auditors: Coopers & Lybrand
Employees: 20,000

WHEN

In 1884 Berthold Hochschild arrived in New York from Frankfurt to trade in metals for a German banking firm. The firm had expanded beyond Hanover, into London, and hoped to profit with the opening of rich American copper deposits.

Hochschild's operation prospered and in 1887 became American Metal, Amco for short. The name proved prophetic when the company severed ties with Germany during WWI.

In 1916 Amco formed a syndicate to exploit Colorado deposits of molybdenum. Climax Molybdenum operated independently of Amco until their 1957 merger created American Metal Climax — informally known as AMAX until the company made it official in 1974.

Along with molybdenum, AMAX ventured into other mining operations, including Canadian tungsten (1961), Missouri lead (1963), and Australian iron (1963). Most important was AMAX's entry into aluminum with the purchase of Kawneer of Michigan and Apex Smelting of Chicago (1962). AMAX Chairman Walter Hochschild, son of the original Hanoverian representative, oversaw the move to aluminum. A new entity, AMAX Aluminum Group, was formed under Ian MacGregor, later AMAX chairman.

AMAX added to its aluminum holdings with the purchase of California-based Hunter Engineering (1963) and expansion to an international network of plants. It sold 50% of its aluminum holdings to Mitsui (which sold 5% to Nippon Steel) in 1974. The new, California-based aluminum venture was renamed Alumax.

In 1969 AMAX acquired Ayrshire Collieries, a midwestern coal producer. In the mid-1970s the company added mines in Wyoming and renewed petroleum exploration, begun and abandoned in the 1960s.

Ventures into copper and nickel in the early 1980s turned sour, and demand for other metals plummeted during a recession. AMAX chief Pierre Gousseland led opposition to 2 purchase offers, in 1981 and 1984, by Standard Oil of California (later Chevron).

In late 1985 AMAX's board replaced Gousseland with Allen Born, grandson of a Colorado miner. Born aggressively sold assets (phosphate and lead operations) and wrote off others (nickel and copper mining, copper refining) to return the company to record $741 million earnings (1988). He also repurchased the Japanese interest in Alumax (1986) and launched the company into open-pit Nevada gold mining (1986).

WHERE

HQ: 200 Park Ave., New York, NY 10166
Phone: 212-856-4200
FAX: 212-856-5986 (Investor Relations)

AMAX operates in the United States, Canada, Mexico, Australia, and Europe.

	1989 Sales		1989 Operating Income	
	$ mil	% of total	$ mil	% of total
US	3,258	83	504	85
Foreign	655	17	87	15
Adjustments	(21)	—	26	—
Total	**3,892**	**100**	**617**	**100**

WHAT

	1989 Sales		1989 Operating Income	
	$ mil	% of total	$ mil	% of total
Aluminum	2,531	65	480	74
Gold	123	3	46	7
Molybdenum	298	8	20	3
Other metals	264	7	4	1
Coal	614	15	88	13
Oil & gas	62	2	16	2
Adjustments	—	—	(37)	—
Total	**3,892**	**100**	**617**	**100**

Fabricated Aluminum
Building and construction
Consumer durables
Containers and packaging
Transportation

Energy
Coal
Oil and natural gas

Gold

Other Metals
Lead
Molybdenum
Potash
Potassium sulfate
Silver
Tungsten
Zinc

RANKINGS

120th in *Fortune* 500 Industrial Cos.
338th in *Fortune* Global 500 Industrial Cos.
214th in *Forbes* Sales 500
280th in *Business Week* 1000
943rd in *Business Week* Global 1000

COMPETITION

Alcan
Alcoa
Anglo American
ASARCO
Broken Hill
Cyprus Minerals
FMC
Hanson
Phelps Dodge
Reynolds Metals
Oil companies
Other mining companies

HOW MUCH

	9 Yr. Growth	1980	1981	1982	1983	1984	1985	1986	1987	1988	1989
Sales ($ mil)	3.1%	2,949	2,799	2,416	2,290	2,399	1,789	1,277	3,351	3,944	3,892
Net income ($ mil)	(2.9%)	470	231	(390)	(489)	(238)	(610)	(15)	77	741	360
Income as % of sales	—	16.0%	8.2%	(16.2%)	(21.4%)	(9.9%)	(34.1%)	(1.2%)	2.3%	18.8%	9.3%
Earnings per share ($)	(6.2%)	7.40	3.30	(6.53)	(7.74)	(3.86)	(9.18)	(0.35)	0.82	8.42	4.18
Stock price – high ($)	—	58.75	69.00	48.88	32.75	27.75	19.00	16.38	29.25	24.63	29.75
Stock price – low ($)	—	39.13	37.50	17.50	21.50	15.50	10.50	10.50	12.00	15.25	20.75
Stock price – close ($)	(6.3%)	41.25	47.25	21.75	23.75	16.25	13.63	12.13	20.00	22.63	23.00
P/E – high	—	8	21	—	—	—	—	—	36	3	7
P/E – low	—	5	11	—	—	—	—	—	15	2	5
Dividends per share ($)	(14.3%)	2.40	2.40	0.85	0.20	0.20	0.10	0.00	0.00	0.20	0.60
Book value per share ($)	(5.6%)	39.77	40.51	32.60	24.60	20.49	10.61	10.81	13.49	20.24	23.62

1989 Year End:
Debt ratio: 32.4%
Return on equity: 19.1%
Cash (mil): $106
Current ratio: 1.84
Long-term debt (mil): $976
Number of shares (mil): 86
Dividends:
1989 average yield: 2.6%
1989 payout: 14.4%
Market value (mil): $1,988

Stock Price History high/low 1980-89

AMDAHL CORPORATION

OVERVIEW

Amdahl is a $2.1 billion manufacturer of IBM-compatible mainframe computers and peripherals. Based in Sunnyvale, California, 20-year-old Amdahl was the first to successfully design and build mainframes to compete head-to-head with IBM computers. Peripheral products such as disk drives designed for IBM mainframes work with Amdahl's machines as easily as they do with IBM's.

Over the years Amdahl has distinguished itself from IBM by responding to IBM's product introductions with reliable, lower-cost compatible systems, often within months of IBM's product announcement. And in 1988 Amdahl beat IBM to the market with its 5990 mainframe, which was 50% faster than IBM's largest mainframe (the 3090). Amdahl has pioneered its own technologies, including air cooling for large-scale computers and the Multiple Domain Feature, a product that allows an Amdahl computer to run up to 4 operating systems simultaneously. In 1989, according to *Business Week*'s R&D Scoreboard, Amdahl spent more on R&D per employee than any other US computer company.

Japan's Fujitsu, a major manufacturer of computers and electronic equipment, owns 44% of Amdahl's stock and is Amdahl's primary supplier of technology, subassemblies, and components.

WHEN

In the 1960s Gene Amdahl worked for IBM, where he was the principal architect of IBM's popular family of mainframe computers, the System 360. After his idea for a more advanced computer was rejected, Amdahl quit IBM in 1970 to start his own company, Amdahl, manufacturing IBM-compatible mainframes.

Amdahl, unable to convince conventional money sources of a market for IBM-compatible computers, turned to foreign investors and succeeded in getting capital from Japan's Fujitsu. In 1975, with $47 million invested in R&D, Amdahl introduced its first computer, the 470V/6, a one-for-one compatible computer to IBM's largest 370 mainframe, the Model 168. IBM users could transfer to the less-expensive Amdahl V/6 and continue to use their existing software and peripherals.

Amdahl's strategy to build IBM clones with better performance for less money succeeded. Amdahl went public in 1976 and, by 1978, its sales had reached $321 million. Amdahl followed its 470V/6 with the V/7 in 1977 and a V/8 model in 1978. By using IBM's operating system and peripherals, Amdahl kept development costs low. It kept manufacturing costs down by relying on Fujitsu for its components.

In 1979 sales of IBM-compatible computers declined in anticipation of IBM's new 4300 series. The drop in Amdahl's cash flow forced it to sell more stock to Fujitsu to raise cash. By 1979 Fujitsu owned 34% of Amdahl's stock. That year Amdahl's stockholders voted to replace Gene Amdahl with Eugene White as president. Gene Amdahl resigned and started Trilogy Systems, Inc., a company set up to develop an advanced superchip. The project was subsequently abandoned because of its complexity.

In 1983 Amdahl Corporation's revenues shot up 68% from the previous year to $778 million following shipments of its new 5860 mainframe (to compete with IBM's 308X line) and diversification into disk drives (6000 series). Sales flattened in 1984, however, due to bugs in the new computer. Amdahl bounced back in 1985 with its 5890 family of computers (comparable to IBM's 3090 series), which increased sales to $1.5 billion (1987), $1.8 billion (1988), and $2.1 billion (1989).

In 1989 Amdahl responded to IBM's 1988 introduction of the new MVS/ESA operating system by providing support for it on Amdahl's 5890 and 5990 machines.

HOW MUCH

	9 Yr. Growth	1980	1981	1982	1983	1984	1985	1986	1987	1988	1989
Sales ($ mil)	20.4%	394	443	462	778	779	862	966	1,505	1,802	2,101
Net income ($ mil)	29.2%	15	27	5	43	36	24	39	142	214	153
Income as % of sales	—	3.9%	6.0%	1.1%	5.6%	4.7%	2.8%	4.1%	9.4%	11.9%	7.3%
Earnings per share ($)	24.0%	0.20	0.33	0.06	0.48	0.40	0.26	0.41	1.37	1.99	1.39
Stock price – high ($)	—	9.63	11.50	8.41	14.88	10.13	9.06	12.88	25.06	28.00	23.38
Stock price – low ($)	—	3.78	5.91	4.31	7.09	4.75	5.06	6.75	9.56	14.06	10.75
Stock price – close ($)	6.1%	8.44	7.38	7.44	9.19	6.69	7.31	11.69	17.63	20.25	14.38
P/E – high	—	48	35	140	31	25	36	32	18	14	17
P/E – low	—	19	18	72	15	12	20	17	7	7	8
Dividends per share ($)	0.0%	0.10	0.10	0.10	0.10	0.10	0.10	0.10	0.10	0.10	0.10
Book value per share ($)	13.2%	3.55	3.84	3.85	4.80	4.58	4.82	5.19	7.32	9.51	10.80

1989 Year End:
Debt ratio: 6.9%
Return on equity: 13.7%
Cash (mil): $563
Current ratio: 2.02
Long-term debt (mil): $87
Number of shares (mil): 109
Dividends:
1989 average yield: 0.7%
1989 payout: 7.2%
Market value (mil): $1,565

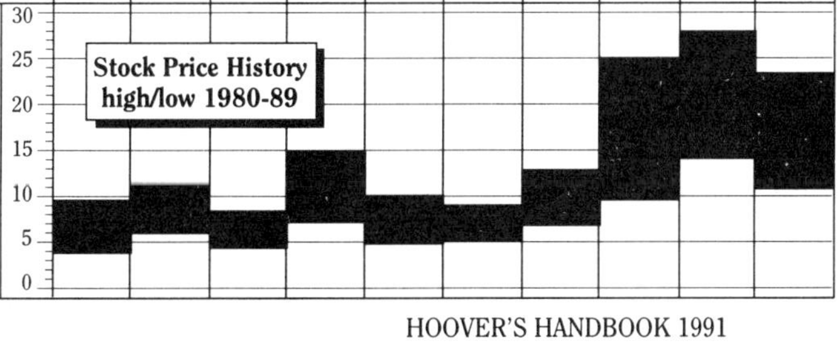

Stock Price History high/low 1980-89

ASE symbol: AMH
Incorporated: Delaware, 1972
Fiscal year ends: Last Friday in December

WHO

Chairman and CEO: John C. Lewis, age 54, $865,346 pay
President and COO: E. Joseph Zemke, age 49, $574,541 pay
VC: Eugene R. White, age 58, $171,281 pay
VP, CFO, and Secretary: Edward F. Thompson, age 51
Auditors: Arthur Andersen & Co.
Employees: 8,200

WHERE

HQ: 1250 E. Arques Ave., Sunnyvale, CA 94088
Phone: 408-746-6000
FAX: 408-746-6468

The company does business in 25 countries and has manufacturing facilities in Northern California; Dublin, Ireland; and Ontario, Canada.

	1989 Sales		1989 Operating Income	
	$ mil	% of total	$ mil	% of total
US	1,077	51	76	35
Europe	710	34	120	55
Canada	136	6	10	5
Pacific Basin & other	178	9	11	5
Adjustments	—	—	7	—
Total	**2,101**	**100**	**224**	**100**

WHAT

	1989 Sales	
	$ mil	% of total
Processors	1,457	70
Storage products	258	12
Communications products	72	3
Maintenance services	281	13
Software & education services	33	2
Total	**2,101**	**100**

Mainframe Computers
5890 series
5990 series
7300 series

Storage Products
6100 storage processor
6110 solid-state storage system
6380 series of magnetic-disk storage units

Communications Products
4745 communications processor
Network Processor Series/2700

Systems Software
UTS

RANKINGS

201st in *Fortune* 500 Industrial Cos.
385th in *Forbes* Sales 500
379th in *Business Week* 1000

COMPETITION

Control Data
Hitachi
IBM
NEC
Siemens
Storage Technology
Unisys

AMERICA WEST AIRLINES, INC.

OVERVIEW

America West flies to 59 cities in 21 states and Canada from its Phoenix and Las Vegas hubs. The airline dominates service from Phoenix with 181 daily departures and offers 122 daily departures from its hub at McCarran International Airport in Las Vegas.

The company accomplished an industry first early in 1990 by generating $1 billion in a one-year period after only 6 years of operations. America West's employees have the industry's highest productivity rating, the company has the industry's lowest per seat operating expense, and the airline has posted an outstanding on-time record since 1987.

America West attributes this performance to its employee ownership program; employees buy stock equal to 20% of their first year's salary, giving each employee a stake in the performance of the company. America West is nonunion, and 2 attempts to unionize in 1989 were voted down.

America West is the official airline of the Phoenix Cardinals and, through its charter service, transports 36 professional and college sports teams. The company agreed in 1989 to sponsor a new sports complex for the Phoenix Suns to be named the America West Arena.

WHEN

For years airline consultant Edward Beauvais had urged clients to build a Phoenix-based airline, linking cities in the Southwest to California. No one listened, so Beauvais took his own advice and in 1981 founded America West Airlines. His concept was simple: by offering low-fare flights with certain amenities such as free cocktails and newspapers, America West would attract business commuters, creating a niche for itself in a region largely ignored by the major airlines. Operations began in 1983.

Starting with 9 daily flights from Phoenix to Albuquerque, Des Moines, Oklahoma City (discontinued 1984), Tulsa (discontinued 1984), and San Diego in 1983, America West by 1986 served 34 cities, generating $329 million in revenues and a modest $2 million profit. That same year America West initiated Nite Flite service (late night flights) from Las Vegas to 7 cities.

The company doubled its operations in 1987, offering flights to Chicago, New York, and Baltimore. Beauvais established a 2nd hub at Las Vegas, but expansion-related costs and increased competition in Phoenix (with Southwest Airlines and USAir) contributed to losses of $15 million in the first half of 1987.

Industry analysts worried that America West's rapid rate of expansion would require additional capital and would result in a larger airline absorbing the company. Beauvais and President Michael Conway (formerly of Continental) responded by selling 20% of the company's stock to Australian-based Ansett Airlines, a company that had previously sold planes to America West, for $31.8 million. Combined with the 30% interest already owned by America West's employees, this put 50% of the company's stock in "friendly hands." Furthermore, employees were guaranteed up to 250% of their annual salaries in the event of a takeover. The company finished 1987 with a $46 million loss.

To reduce costs Beauvais and Conway sold several planes, furloughed 500 employees, and streamlined service, cutting flights 10% overall (25% to New York), resulting in planes filled to 58.4% capacity — nearly 2 points above breakeven (1988). The airline gained access to Washington, DC (by buying routes from bankrupt Eastern) and inaugurated service to Hawaii in 1989. By the end of 1989, America West was providing 43% of the flights out of Phoenix and 35% out of Las Vegas, offering 286 daily flights to 56 cities, including Honolulu, Seattle, and New York. In 1990 the airline added service to Boston, Houston, and San Francisco and awaits DOT approval for routes to Australia and Japan.

HOW MUCH

	6 Yr. Growth	1980	1981	1982	1983	1984	1985	1986	1987	1988	1989
Sales ($ mil)	—	—	—	—	18	123	241	329	575	776	993
Net income ($ mil)	—	—	—	—	(10)	(15)	6	2	(46)	(12)	13
Income as % of sales	—	—	—	—	(54.3%)	(12.6%)	2.5%	0.5%	(7.9%)	(1.6%)	1.3%
Earnings per share ($)	—	—	—	—	(3.07)	(3.26)	0.42	0.33	(1.35)	(0.18)	0.68
Stock price – high ($)	—	—	—	—	14.13	12.50	12.75	13.50	12.38	7.13	12.88
Stock price – low ($)	—	—	—	—	6.13	4.88	6.88	7.63	3.50	3.63	6.50
Stock price – close ($)	(2.4%)	—	—	—	11.75	7.88	10.75	9.75	3.75	6.50	10.13
P/E – high	—	—	—	—	—	—	30	41	—	—	19
P/E – low	—	—	—	—	—	—	16	23	—	—	10
Dividends per share ($)	—	—	—	—	0.00	0.00	0.00	0.00	0.00	0.00	0.00
Book value per share ($)	0.8%	—	—	—	4.69	4.82	6.46	5.53	3.15	3.74	4.91

1989 Year End:
Debt ratio: 84.5%
Return on equity: 15.7%
Cash (mil): $80
Current ratio: 0.91
Long-term debt (mil): $475
Number of shares (mil): 18
Dividends:
1989 average yield: 0.0%
1989 payout: 0.0%
Market value (mil): $179

Stock Price History high/low 1983-89

OTC symbol: AWAL
Incorporated: Delaware, 1981
Fiscal year ends: December 31

WHO

Chairman and CEO: Edward R. Beauvais, age 53, $642,932 pay
President and COO: Michael J. Conway, age 44, $530,457 pay
SVP Finance and CFO: Alphonse E. Frei, age 51, $210,221 pay
SVP Operations: Don Monteath, $209,530 pay
SVP Sales and Product Development: Mark J. Coleman, $191,479 pay
Auditors: KMPG Peat Marwick
Employees: 11,442

WHERE

HQ: 4000 E. Sky Harbor Blvd., Phoenix, AZ 85034
Phone: 602-894-0800
FAX: 602-693-5728 (Corporate Communications)

America West serves 59 cities in 21 states, the District of Columbia, and Canada.

Hub Locations
Phoenix, AZ
Las Vegas, NV

WHAT

	1989 Sales	
	$ mil	% of total
Passenger	934	94
Cargo	29	3
Other	30	3
Total	**993**	**100**

Services
Air Cargo
America West Express small package service
AmeriWest Vacations tour packages
Careliner Shuttle
Bus service to resort area at Scottsdale, AZ, from Phoenix Airport
Contract Services charter flights
FlightFund frequent flyer program
Las Vegas Nite Flite Service
Late night flights to Las Vegas and 36 other destinations
The Phoenix Club airport lounges
VUSA (Visit USA Program)
Special fares for international travelers in US

Flight Equipment	Owned	Leased	Total
Boeing 737	19	52	71
Boeing 747	2	2	4
Boeing 757	2	9	11
Boeing DHC-8	—	10	10
Total	**23**	**73**	**96**

RANKINGS

28th in *Fortune* 50 Transportation Cos.

COMPETITION

Alaska Air
AMR
Continental
Delta
Southwest
UAL

AMERICAN ASSOCIATION OF RETIRED PERSONS

OVERVIEW

The American Association of Retired Persons (AARP) is the nation's largest organization dedicated to protecting and increasing the rights of citizens over the age of 50. Its 32 million members (40% of them still working) receive services including group insurance rates, discounted pharmaceuticals, reduced car rental and hotel rates, an investment program, a travel service, subscriptions to *Modern Maturity* magazine and *AARP Bulletin*, and membership in the AARP credit union. Annual membership dues are $5.

AARP acts as a political advocate for its members, primarily focusing on 4 issues: health care, older workers' equity, women's initiatives, and minority affairs. It uses its well-organized mail network to solicit new members as they turn 50, advertise its services, and promote the organization's political agenda. AARP has more than 3,700 local chapters, and its paid staff of almost 1,500 is supplemented with more than 350,000 active volunteers.

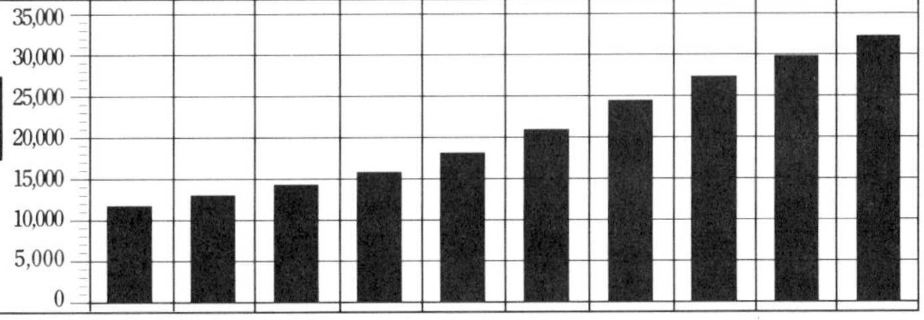

Nonprofit organization
Founded: California, 1958
Fiscal year ends: December 31
Motto: To serve, not be served

WHO

Executive Director: Horace B. Deets
President: Robert B. Maxwell
Principal Financial Officer: James A. Maigret
Principal Human Resources Officer: Angela Spicer
Auditors: Price Waterhouse
Employees: 1,491

WHEN

In 1958 Ethel Andrus, a retired Los Angeles high school principal and founder of the National Retired Teachers Association (NRTA, 1947), organized the American Association of Retired Persons (AARP) to "enhance the quality of life . . . promote independence . . . lead in determining the role in society . . . and improve the image of aging" for older Americans.

Andrus offered the new members the same attractive low rates for health and accident insurance that NRTA members enjoyed. Other services quickly followed, including a mail-order discount pharmacy and a travel service for older people. Andrus began publishing the organization's bimonthly magazine *Modern Maturity* in 1958, and AARP's first local chapter opened in Youngstown, Arizona in 1960.

Andrus led the organization in its increasingly influential role in legislation that concerned the elderly. She directed AARP until her death in 1967. In her honor, AARP and the University of Southern California built the Ethel Percy Andrus Gerontology Center (1973), a $4 million institute dedicated to the study of aging.

AARP (and NRTA, which eventually joined AARP in 1982) continued to expand in scope and size. Attractive new services included the popular auto club, financial services such as mutual funds and expanded insurance policies, and hotel and motel discounts. In 1983 it lowered the eligibility age from 55 to 50 and raised its annual dues from $3 to $5. AARP grew at a phenomenal rate to its 1990 membership of over 32 million. It currently adds approximately 8,000 new members a day.

AARP acts as an agent between its members and selected service providers: Prudential for health insurance; Hartford for auto and home insurance; Scudder, Stevens & Clark for mutual fund investment services; and Amoco for auto club services. *Modern Maturity* and the *AARP Bulletin,* sent to all AARP members, have the first and 2nd largest magazine circulation totals in the US.

A new AARP credit union, which began operations in 1988 with over $66 million in deposits, is predicted to become the nation's largest credit union.

AARP's influence and organizational skills have increased as its constituency has grown. Its numerous programs and services are generally focused on 4 priorities: health care (controlling health care costs and promoting healthy lifestyles); women's initiatives (emphasizing women's contributions and addressing concerns of middle-aged and older women); worker equity (protecting rights and security of older workers through preretirement and employment planning programs and litigation); and minority affairs (encouraging changes in thinking and actions in older minorities and society at large). The association publishes a variety of promotional and informational materials and sponsors many training and educational programs.

Steadfastly nonpartisan (the membership is 40% Democratic, 40% Republican, and 20% independent), AARP's main office in Washington, DC, is the center of its lobbying efforts. It has garnered the reputation for being well-informed, organized, tenacious, and often successful in its political activities.

One notable exception was AARP's support of the ill-fated Medicare Catastrophic Coverage Act (passed by Congress in 1988), which was designed to pay expenses for extensive hospital care. A surtax on Medicare premiums, targeted at eligible participants, was proposed to pay for the costly program. Vociferous opposition from middle-class and affluent older citizens, many of them AARP members, exerted enough pressure to have the act repealed in 1989.

WHERE

HQ: 1909 K St. NW, Washington, DC 20049
Phone: 202-872-4700
FAX: 202-659-1555 (Membership Development)

AARP has 32 million members worldwide.

WHAT

	1989 Operating Revenues	
	$ mil	% of total
Membership dues	96	33
Group insurance administrative allowances	80	27
Publication advertising	40	14
Income from other programs & royalties	27	9
Interest income	48	17
Total	**291**	**100**

Political Advocacy
Lobbying Congress and state legislatures
Educating voters
Working to increase older citizens' representation on local boards and commissions

Periodicals
AARP Bulletin
Modern Maturity

Social Services
Educational publications and audiovisual materials
Employment planning
Legal assistance
Medicare assistance
Retirement planning
Support groups
Volunteer organizing

Insurance Plans
Automobile (Hartford)
Health/Medigap (Prudential)
Homeowners (Hartford)

Financial Services
AARP Federal Credit Union
Credit cards (Bank One)
Mutual funds (Scudder, Stevens & Clark)

Travel Services
Auto club/road service (Amoco Motor Club)
Hotel, auto rental, and airline discounts (various providers)

Affiliated Entities
AARP Foundation
AARP Andrus Foundation

HOW MUCH

	9 Yr. Growth	1980	1981	1982	1983	1984	1985	1986	1987	1988	1989
Membership (thou)	11.9%	11,695	12,973	14,251	15,753	18,075	20,880	24,371	27,262	29,739	32,163

Membership (thou) 1980-89

35,000
30,000
25,000
20,000
15,000
10,000
5,000
0

AMERICAN BRANDS, INC.

OVERVIEW

American Brands, the nation's 5th largest cigarette manufacturer, is a diversified consumer products company operating mainly in the US and the UK with businesses in tobacco, insurance, golf products, liquor, office supplies, optical services, and hardware products. Its well-known cigarette brands in the US (Carlton, Tareyton, Pall Mall, and Lucky Strike) and the UK (Benson & Hedges, Silk Cut, and Berkeley, through subsidiary Gallaher) provided 65% ($907 million) of the company's 1989 operating income. Jim Beam, the world's leading bourbon, contributed to the company's robust 23% growth in total bourbon exports in 1989.

American Brands is one of the most diversified major tobacco companies. Served well by its core tobacco business with a 10% increase in operating income in 1989, American Brands also saw a healthy 10% revenue increase in its office products division. Sales of 120 million golf balls (Titleist) reflect an 8% increase from 1988. The optical goods and services group (Dollond & Aitchison) is the largest in Europe, with 775 branches in 5 countries.

NYSE symbol: AMB
Incorporated: Delaware, 1985
Fiscal year ends: December 31

WHO

Chairman and CEO: William J. Alley, age 60, $1,171,159 pay
President and COO: Thomas C. Hays, age 54, $687,575 pay
EVP Finance and CFO: Arnold Henson, age 58, $586,050 pay
Auditors: Coopers & Lybrand
Employees: 47,300

WHEN

American Brands began in 1864 as W. Duke and Sons, a small tobacco company started by Washington Duke, a North Carolina farmer. James Buchanan Duke joined his father's business at age 14 (1870) and by age 25 was its president. James Duke was the first to use the Bonsack cigarette rolling machine, which produced substantially cheaper cigarettes and allowed him to undercut competitors' prices. He advertised to expanding markets; bought rival cigarette, snuff, and plug tobacco firms; and by 1904 controlled the tobacco industry. That year he merged all the competitive groups into the American Tobacco Company.

In a 1911 antitrust suit the US Supreme Court dissolved American Tobacco into its original competitive firms, ordering them to operate independently.

Duke left American Tobacco in 1912. He remained president of British American Tobacco Company (now B.A.T, which he had founded in 1902) and continued his work with Southern Power Company, a North Carolina company he had started in 1905. He later merged that company with Duke Power and Light. Duke established a $100 million trust fund, composed mainly of holdings in Duke Power and Light, for the local Trinity College, which became Duke University in 1924.

American Tobacco merely drifted under Duke's successor Percival Hill, but it found a dynamic new leader in George Washington Hill, who succeeded his father as president in 1925. For the next 19 years until his death, Hill proved himself a consummate ad man, pushing Lucky Strikes, Pall Malls, and Tareyton cigarettes to top sales.

In 1953 research first linked cigarette smoking to lung cancer, and smokers switched to filter-tipped cigarettes in record numbers. American Tobacco, however, ignored the trend and continued to rely on its popular filterless brands until the mid-1960s.

American Tobacco remained solely in the tobacco business until 1966, when it purchased Sunshine Biscuits (sold in 1988) and Jim Beam Distillery. Later came Swingline (office supplies, 1970) and Master Lock (padlocks, 1970). Reflecting its increasing diversity, the company became American Brands in 1970.

Threatened by a takeover by E-II Holdings (a conglomerate of brands split from Beatrice), American Brands bought E-II for $1.1 billion in 1988. The company retained 5 of E-II's companies: Day-Timers (time management products), Aristokraft (cabinets), Waterloo (tool storage), Twentieth Century (plumbing supplies), and Vogel Peterson (office partitions). The balance (Culligan International and Samsonite) were sold to Riklis Family Corporation.

WHERE

HQ: 1700 E. Putnam Ave., Old Greenwich, CT 06870
Phone: 203-698-5000
FAX: 203-637-2580

Division	HQ Location
ACCO World Corp.	Deerfield, IL
Acushnet Co.	New Bedford, MA
The American Tobacco Co.	Stamford, CT
The Franklin Life Insurance Co.	Springfield, IL
Jim Beam Brands Co.	Deerfield, IL
MasterBrand Industries	Deerfield, IL

	1989 Sales		1989 Operating Income	
	$ mil	% of total	$ mil	% of total
US	4,522	38	880	63
Europe	7,263	61	504	36
Other	137	1	14	1
Adjustments	(4,657)	—	(68)	—
Total	**7,265**	**100**	**1,330**	**100**

WHAT

	1989 Sales		1989 Operating Income	
	$ mil	% of total	$ mil	% of total
Tobacco products	7,010	59	907	65
Distilled spirits	735	6	107	8
Specialty businesses	1,875	16	62	4
Life insurance	831	7	154	11
Hardware & home improvement prods.	503	4	70	5
Office products	968	8	97	7
Adjustments	(4,657)	—	(67)	—
Total	**7,265**	**100**	**1,330**	**100**

Representative Brand Names

Cigarettes
American
Benson & Hedges (UK)
Berkeley (UK)
Carlton
Lucky Strike
Pall Mall
Silk Cut (UK)
Tareyton

Distilled Spirits
DeKuyper
Gilbey's
Jim Beam
Kamchatka
Old Crow
Old Grand-Dad
Old Taylor
Whyte & MacKay
Windsor Canadian

Office Products
ACCO
Day-Timers
Swingline
Vogel Peterson
Wilson Jones

Other Products
Master Lock
Titleist

HOW MUCH

	9 Yr. Growth	1980	1981	1982	1983	1984	1985	1986	1987	1988	1989
Sales ($ mil)	6.1%	4,277	4,039	4,026	4,436	4,475	4,692	5,261	5,036	7,236	7,265
Net income ($ mil)	5.0%	405	386	381	390	414	421	365	503	541	631
Income as % of sales	—	9.5%	9.6%	9.5%	8.8%	9.3%	9.0%	6.9%	10.0%	7.5%	8.7%
Earnings per share ($)	6.9%	3.34	3.23	3.19	3.30	3.52	3.59	3.12	4.29	5.13	6.08
Stock price – high ($)	—	22.03	23.00	25.50	30.19	32.56	35.00	52.50	60.00	71.75	81.88
Stock price – low ($)	—	14.63	17.00	17.69	21.69	26.44	26.63	31.31	36.50	42.25	61.25
Stock price – close ($)	15.5%	19.38	18.38	22.94	29.63	32.13	32.94	42.50	44.50	65.50	71.00
P/E – high	—	7	7	8	9	9	10	17	14	14	13
P/E – low	—	4	5	6	7	8	7	10	9	8	10
Dividends per share ($)	6.1%	1.48	1.61	1.75	1.78	1.86	1.95	2.04	2.11	2.26	2.51
Book value per share ($)	7.7%	15.76	16.66	17.45	18.45	19.19	21.72	23.13	26.64	26.69	30.68

1989 Year End:
Debt ratio: 36.7%
Return on equity: 21.2%
Cash (mil): $149
Current ratio: —
Long-term debt (mil): $1,717
Number of shares (mil): 96
Dividends:
1989 average yield: 3.5%
1989 payout: 41.3%
Market value (mil): $6,800

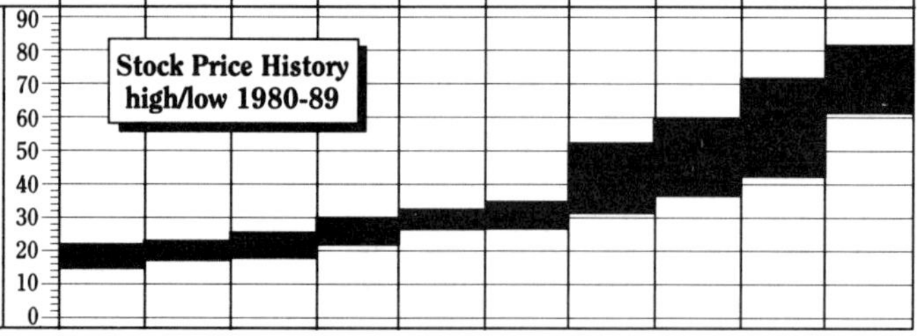

RANKINGS

64th in *Fortune* 500 Industrial Cos.
178th in *Fortune* Global 500 Industrial Cos.
115th in *Forbes* Sales 500
90th in *Business Week* 1000
284th in *Business Week* Global 1000

COMPETITION

B.A.T	Hanson	RJR Nabisco
Black & Decker	Ingersoll-Rand	Seagram
Brown-Forman	Loews	Life insurance companies
Grand Metropolitan	Philip Morris	
Guinness		

AMERICAN CANCER SOCIETY

OVERVIEW

The American Cancer Society is the largest nongovernmental source of funds for cancer research in the US. The society spends substantial amounts on public and professional education and patient and community services. The society gave 838 research grants and awards in 1989. The Nobel Prize has been given to 23 of the society's researchers.

Emphasis today is placed on prevention through eliminating possible environmental exposures to carcinogens and encouraging proper nutrition. The Cancer Prevention Study II, begun in 1982, has used 77,000 volunteers to collect information on 1.2 million Americans to help determine the causes of cancer.

Public education programs reach an estimated 55 million people, and the society's 2.3 million volunteers assist over 650,000 patients. The society's Great American Smokeout is in its 14th year.

Although cancer survival rates have increased since the 1940s (40% survive 5 years versus 25% then), the incidence of new melanomas and lung, prostate, and colorectal cancers has increased since the early 1970s.

Nonprofit organization
Founded: New York, 1913
Fiscal year ends: August 31

WHO

Chairman: John R. Seffrin
VC: Stanley Schmishkiss
President: Robert J. Schweitzer
VP: Gerald D. Dodd
EVP and CEO: William M. Tipping, $188,867 pay
SVP Finance and Administration: James T. Bell, $103,731 pay
Auditors: Arthur Andersen & Co.
Paid Employees: 4,806
Volunteers: 2,300,000

WHEN

Concerned over lack of progress in detecting and treating cancer, a group of 10 physicians and 5 laymen met in New York City in 1913 to form the American Society for the Control of Cancer. Cancer in those days was a dirty word, not discussed in public. The society's earliest goal was to educate the public about the need for early detection and reverse the notion that nothing could be done.

Early success in fund-raising and the establishment of a volunteer membership structure are credited to Elsie Mead, daughter of an ASCC founder. In its early years the society struggled with the dilemma of how to educate the public without also raising unnecessary fears. The society also faced the opposition of some physicians who preferred keeping knowledge of the disease from the lay public.

In the 1920s the society started sponsoring cancer clinics and began collecting statistics on the disease. By 1923 some states could report improvements in early diagnosis and faster treatment. In 1937 the society started its first nationwide public education program with the help of volunteers known as the Women's Field Army. President Roosevelt named April as National Cancer Control Month, a practice since followed by every president.

By 1944 some cancer rates were rising and the word cancer couldn't be mentioned on the radio. Mary Lasker, the wife of prominent advertising executive Albert Lasker, was instrumental in getting cancer messages broadcast, and, at her insistence, in 1945 the ACS (name changed in 1944) began donating at least 25% of its budget to research. The society raised $4 million in its first major national fund-raising campaign in 1945.

With the support of board member Elmer Bobst (Hoffmann-LaRoche president), Dr. Charles Cameron, ACS medical director, used society volunteers in the early 1950s to follow nearly 200,000 subjects in a study that first showed the link between smoking and lung cancer. That information became part of the Surgeon General's Report of 1964. In 1973 an ACS branch in Minnesota held the first Great American Smokeout, now a national event to encourage people to quit.

The ACS backed the 1971 congressional bill that inaugurated the "War on Cancer." The society was attacked in the 1970s for emphasizing cures rather than prevention because, critics claimed, research on prevention would reveal environmental causes from industrial products made by companies with connections to ACS directors. In the 1970s and 1980s the ACS backed tougher restrictions on tobacco and, in response to earlier criticism, directed research toward prevention as well as treatment. The society played a major role in the 1989 airline smoking ban.

WHERE

National Office: 1599 Clifton Rd. NE, Atlanta, GA 30329
Phone: 404-320-3333
Information about cancer: 1-800-ACS-2345
FAX: 404-325-0230

The society has 57 chartered divisions nationwide and 3,400 local units.

WHAT

1989 Sources of Revenue	$ mil	% of total
Public contributions	185	52
Legacies & bequests	90	25
Organization contributions	43	12
Investment income	38	11
Other	2	—
Total	**358**	**100**

1989 Expenses	$ mil	% of total
Research	89	28
Public education	61	18
Professional education	31	9
Patient services	47	14
Community services	23	7
Administration & fund-raising	80	24
Total	**331**	**100**

Research Grants & Awards

Public Education Programs
Great American Food Fight Against Cancer
Great American Smokeout
I Can Cope
Smart Move (stop smoking)
"Why Charlie Brown, Why?" (TV program)

Professional Education Programs
American Cancer Society Textbook of Clinical Oncology
Cancer Staging Awareness
Cancer Topics on Tape
Clinical News
Current Concepts in Head and Neck Cancer (textbook)
Medical Affairs (newsletter)
Primary Care Newsletter
Tobacco-Free Young America (program)

Patient Services Programs
Back to School: A Handbook for Parents of Children with Cancer
Back to School: A Handbook for Teachers of Children with Cancer
CanSurmount
Look Good... Feel Better Guide for ACS Volunteers
Reach to Recovery

HOW MUCH

All amounts in $ mil	9 Yr. Growth	1980	1981	1982	1983	1984	1985	1986	1987	1988	1989
Total revenue	7.9%	181	200	223	233	252	281	308	331	336	358
Public contributions	8.3%	155	170	183	203	221	243	271	304	301	318
Investment & other income	4.9%	26	30	40	30	31	38	37	27	35	40
Total expenses	8.3%	162	178	195	207	226	251	272	296	324	331
Research expenses	6.6%	50	54	57	58	64	69	77	83	89	89
Education expenses	8.8%	43	47	51	56	60	70	75	84	86	92
Patient & community svcs.	9.5%	31	34	39	41	46	50	54	59	63	70
Admin. & fund-raising exp.	8.6%	38	42	48	52	56	62	66	70	85	80
Admin. & fund-raising as a % of total expenses	—	23.5%	23.6%	24.6%	25.1%	24.8.%	24.7%	24.3%	23.6%	26.2%	24.2%

Total Revenue ($ mil) 1980-89

AMERICAN CYANAMID COMPANY

OVERVIEW

American Cyanamid is the leading US supplier of biologicals (vaccines), 2nd largest world manufacturer of surgical products, and a major US chemical company.

Originally a chemical company, Cyanamid derived 40% of its 1989 worldwide sales from its Medical Group that includes pharmaceuticals, biologicals, and medical devices and supplies. Centrum (mulitvitamin) and Pipracil (penicillin) are US market leaders. The company has been a leading US supplier of the DPT (diphtheria-pertussis-tetanus) vaccine for US children since the 1940s.

The Chemicals Group makes more than 2,000 chemicals, structural adhesives, and other materials for 14 major industries, including aerospace, automobile, paint, paper, and plastics. Herbicides, particularly Pursuit and Scepter, are major products of the Agricultural Group. American Cyanamid sells more than 3,000 products worldwide.

The company divested its consumer products operations in 1990. Pine-Sol (cleaner) and Combat (insecticide) were sold to Clorox, Old Spice to Procter & Gamble, and Breck hair care products to Greyhound Dial.

WHEN

Frank Washburn, a civil engineer seeking new uses for hydroelectric power, learned of a German process that extracted nitrogen, lime, and carbide to make cyanamid, a basic component of fertilizer. Washburn bought the North American rights to the process and founded American Cyanamid (Maine, 1907). Washburn then began producing calcium cyanamide, the world's first synthetic fertilizer, in a process powered by a dam he built.

In 1916 the company bought Amalgamated Phosphate as a source of phosphoric acid, another ingredient in fertilizer. Washburn died in 1922 and his assistant, William Bell, became president. The company began selling cyanide to the mining industry for extracting minerals from ore. The company diversified, buying American Powder (nitrocellulose for blasting powders, 1929), Calco Chemical (dyestuffs, chemicals, 1929), Selden (sulfuric acid, 1929) , Kalbfleisch (chemicals, acids, 1929), and Chemical Construction (design and construction of chemical plants, 1930).

In 1930 American Cyanamid bought Lederle Antitoxin Laboratories (antitoxins, vaccines, sulfa drugs, and veterinary products) and Davis & Geck (surgical sutures). During WWII the company supplied US troops with typhus vaccine, dried blood plasma, and surgical sutures. In 1948 Lederle became a major pharmaceutical business with its discovery of Aureomycin, an antibiotic used to treat human infections worldwide.

In 1956 American Cyanamid diversified into consumer-related businesses, buying Formica (major part sold to Formica's management and Shearson Lehman/American Express, 1985). In 1963 the company bought John H. Breck, Inc. (shampoo) and Dumas Milner Corporation (Pine-Sol cleaner). American Cyanamid's last purchase of a consumer company was Shulton (Pierre Cardin and Old Spice fragrances) in 1971.

American Cyanamid introduced Combat (roach control system) and Old Spice solid antiperspirant in 1985. In 1986 the company increased its interest in Applied Solar Energy to 75% (sold to McDonnell Douglas, 1989) and bought Acufex Microsurgical and Storz Instrument. In 1988 the company introduced Novantrone (anticancer drug) and bought Conap (adhesives, sealants). In 1989 the company bought Praxis Biologics (vaccines). American Cyanamid has decided to focus on its research-driven agricultural, medical, and chemical businesses. It left the dye business in 1989, selling its operations to BASF, and in 1990 began divesting its consumer products business.

HOW MUCH

	9 Yr. Growth	1980	1981	1982	1983	1984	1985	1986	1987	1988	1989
Sales ($ mil)	3.8%	3,454	3,649	3,454	3,536	3,857	3,536	3,816	4,166	4,592	4,825
Net income ($ mil)	7.0%	159	197	132	166	216	120	203	264	306	292
Income as % of sales	—	4.6%	5.4%	3.8%	4.7%	5.6%	3.4%	5.3%	6.3%	6.7%	6.1%
Earnings per share ($)	7.3%	1.66	2.06	1.37	1.71	2.21	1.25	2.18	2.89	3.41	3.12
Stock price – high ($)	—	19.00	18.25	18.75	29.50	26.56	29.63	44.94	57.00	56.00	60.38
Stock price – low ($)	—	10.31	12.25	12.19	16.81	21.06	24.00	27.13	29.00	41.88	45.63
Stock price – close ($)	14.1%	16.31	14.50	17.38	25.00	25.00	28.75	38.94	41.25	46.75	53.63
P/E – high	—	11	9	14	17	12	24	21	20	16	19
P/E – low	—	6	6	9	10	10	19	12	10	12	15
Dividends per share ($)	5.7%	0.80	0.84	0.88	0.88	0.93	0.95	0.95	1.03	1.16	1.31
Book value per share ($)	5.5%	14.97	15.94	15.91	16.37	17.13	17.53	18.71	20.85	23.02	24.30

1989 Year End:
Debt ratio: 16.5%
Return on equity: 13.2%
Cash (mil): $486
Current ratio: 1.37
Long-term debt (mil): $458
Number of shares (mil): 96
Dividends:
1989 average yield: 2.4%
1989 payout: 42.1%
Market value (mil): $5,122

Stock Price History high/low 1980-89

NYSE symbol: ACY
Incorporated: Maine, 1907
Fiscal year ends: December 31

WHO

Chairman, President, and CEO: George J. Sella, Jr., age 61, $1,062,814 pay
VC: William A. Liffers, age 61, $520,989 pay
VP and Principal Financial Officer: Richard L. Martino, age 59
Auditors: KPMG Peat Marwick
Employees: 35,394

WHERE

HQ: One Cyanamid Plaza, Wayne, NJ 07470
Phone: 201-831-2000
FAX: 201-831-3151

American Cyanamid's major manufacturing facilities are located in Louisiana, Missouri, New York, Great Britain, Italy, West Germany, India, Japan, and Taiwan.

	1989 Sales		1989 Operating Income	
	$ mil	% of total	$ mil	% of total
US	2,965	62	266	46
Other Western Hemisphere	537	11	65	11
Eastern Hemisphere	1,323	27	249	43
Adjustments	—	—	(77)	—
Total	**4,825**	**100**	**503**	**100**

WHAT

	1989 Sales		1989 Operating Income	
	$ mil	% of total	$ mil	% of total
Medical products	1,975	40	326	57
Agricultural chemicals	1,101	23	188	32
Chemicals	1,140	24	48	8
Consumer products	609	13	18	3
Adjustments	—	—	(77)	—
Total	**4,825**	**100**	**503**	**100**

Medical
Acufex Microsurgical, Inc. (instruments)
Davis & Geck (surgical products)
Lederle Labs (pharmaceuticals)
Lederle-Praxis Biologicals (vaccines)
Praxis Biologics, Inc. (vaccines)
Storz Instrument Co. (surgical products)

Agricultural Chemicals
Feed supplements
Herbicides
Insecticides
Plant growth regulant
Veterinary medicines

Chemicals
Acrylic fibers
Adhesives
Herbicides
Insecticides
Melamine
Urethane

Joint Venture
Criterion Catalyst Company L.P. (with Shell Oil to sell process catalysts)

RANKINGS

106th in *Fortune* 500 Industrial Cos.
274th in *Fortune* Global 500 Industrial Cos.
183rd in *Forbes* Sales 500
121st in *Business Week* 1000
350th in *Business Week* Global 1000

COMPETITION

C. R. Bard
Becton, Dickinson
Dow Chemical
Du Pont
FMC
W. R. Grace
Hercules
Monsanto
Rhône-Poulenc
Other pharmaceutical and chemical companies

AMERICAN ELECTRIC POWER COMPANY, INC.

OVERVIEW

American Electric Power (AEP) is an integrated electrical system, providing power to customers in parts of 7 midwestern and Appalachian states, through 8 operating utilities. The company ranks as America's 7th largest electric utility in terms of revenues, generating over $5.1 billion in 1989.

AEP sold 117.5 billion kilowatt-hours of electricity in 1989, a gain of 12.2% over sales in 1988. The company's 38 generating plants have a total capacity of nearly 24 million kilowatts.

AEP produces almost 90% of its electricity from coal and since 1976 has been working to develop cleaner and more efficient methods of using this resource. To this end the company, with the US Department of Energy and the State of Ohio's Coal Development Office, will begin operation of the first Pressurized Fluidized Bed Combustion (PFBC) unit in North America at AEP's Tidd Plant, near Brilliant, Ohio, in the fall of 1990. PFBC uses 10% less coal to generate the same amount of electricity produced by conventional steam plants and removes 90% of harmful emissions by burning dolomite, a type of limestone, with the coal. AEP hopes to make PFBC a viable option for commercial electric generation by the early years of the 21st century.

NYSE symbol: AEP
Incorporated: New York, 1925
Fiscal year ends: December 31

WHO

Chairman and CEO: Willis S. "Pete" White, Jr., age 63, $656,045 pay
President: Richard E. Disbrow, age 59, $430,065 pay
Treasurer and EVP Administration: Peter J. DeMaria, age 55, $225,835 pay
VP and Principal Financial Officer: Gerald P. Maloney, age 57
Auditors: Deloitte & Touche
Employees: 22,700

WHEN

In 1907 Richard Breed, Sidney Mitchell, and Henry Doherty consolidated various utilities into American Gas & Electric (AG&E). Based in New York, AG&E by 1926 was serving communities in Michigan, Indiana, Kentucky, West Virginia, Virginia, and Ohio. The company also served the areas around Atlantic City, New Jersey, and Scranton, Pennsylvania (these divisions were sold in 1935).

In 1918 George Tidd, an AG&E engineer (later the company's president), supervised construction of a generating plant near Wheeling, West Virginia. Although 55 miles from Canton (the area it was designed to serve), the plant was the first ever to be located near its fuel supply and connected to its service area by transmission lines, thus eliminating the need to build power plants within cities.

Philip Sporn, another AG&E engineer, pioneered research on the effects of lightning on power lines, leading to the development of his high-voltage, super-fast circuit breaker in 1935. Known as the Henry Ford of power, Sporn became AG&E's president in 1947 and started an ambitious building program that continued through the 1950s and 1960s. During this period, power plants designed by AG&E were among the world's most efficient, and electric rates stayed 25-38% below the national average.

The company changed its name to American Electric Power (AEP) in 1958 when it bought 23 utilities from the Philadelphia-based Electric Company of America.

Sporn retired in 1961, and Donald Cook took over as president. In the early 1970s Cook came under fire from environmentalists concerned about acid rain when he refused to attach scrubbers (devices used to decrease sulfur dioxide emissions) on the smokestacks of AEP's coal-fired plants. Believing that scrubbers were unnecessary, Cook chose instead to increase the height of the plants' chimneys to dilute the harmful emissions. Coal had long been AEP's primary fuel; a 1974 AEP ad claimed: "America has more coal than the Middle East has oil. Let's dig it!"

AEP's first nuclear facility, the Donald C. Cook Plant, went on-line in 1975. The company moved its headquarters from New York to Columbus, Ohio, in 1980 after buying the Columbus & Southern System (renamed Columbus Southern Power Company, 1987). In 1984 AEP began converting the Zimmer Plant (its 2nd nuclear facility) to a coal-fired plant after the Nuclear Regulatory Commission halted construction for failure to keep adequate construction records. This conversion is scheduled for completion in 1991.

WHERE

HQ: 1 Riverside Plaza, Columbus, OH 43215
Phone: 614-223-1000
FAX: 614-223-1823

AEP serves portions of Indiana, Kentucky, Michigan, Ohio, Tennessee, Virginia, and West Virginia.

Generating Facilities

Coal-Fired
Beckjord (OH)
Big Sandy (KY)
Breed (IN)
Cardinal (OH)
Clinch River (VA)
Conesville (OH)
Gen. James M. Gavin (OH)
Glen Lyn (VA)
John E. Amos (WV)
Kammer (WV)
Kanawha River (WV)
Mitchell (WV)
Mountaineer (WV)
Muskingum River (OH)
Philip Sporn (WV)
Picway (OH)
Rockport (IN)
J.M. Stuart (OH)
Tanners Creek (IN)

Gas Turbine
Fourth Street (IN)

Hydroelectric
Berrien Springs (MI)
Buchanan (MI)
Buck (VA)
Byllesby (VA)
Claytor (VA)
Constantine (MI)
Elkhart (IN)
Leesville (VA)
London (WV)
Marmet (WV)
Mottville (MI)
Niagara (VA)
Racine (OH)
Reusens (VA)
Smith Mountain (VA)
Twin Branch (IN)
Winfield (WV)

Nuclear
Donald C. Cook (MI)

WHAT

	1989 Sales	
	$ mil	% of total
Residential	1,574	31
Commercial	1,020	20
Industrial	1,438	28
Miscellaneous retail	72	1
For resale	976	19
Other	60	1
Total	**5,140**	**100**

Operating Companies
Appalachian Power Co.
Columbus Southern Power Co.
Indiana Michigan Power Co.
Kentucky Power Co.
Kingsport Power Co.
Michigan Power Co.
Ohio Power Co.
Wheeling Power Co.

RANKINGS

16th in *Fortune* 50 Utilities
174th in *Forbes* Sales 500
99th in *Business Week* 1000
322nd in *Business Week* Global 1000

HOW MUCH

	9 Yr. Growth	1980	1981	1982	1983	1984	1985	1986	1987	1988	1989
Sales ($ mil)	3.5%	3,756	4,193	4,180	4,368	4,952	4,848	4,843	4,788	4,841	5,140
Net income ($ mil)	5.6%	425	456	441	534	590	585	603	583	693	692
Income as % of sales	—	11.3%	10.9%	10.5%	12.2%	11.9%	12.1%	12.4%	12.2%	14.3%	13.5%
Earnings per share ($)	3.4%	2.41	2.37	2.03	2.44	2.65	2.54	2.62	2.60	3.24	3.25
Stock price – high ($)	—	19.75	18.38	19.75	20.13	21.38	24.88	31.50	31.63	29.75	33.38
Stock price – low ($)	—	15.25	15.38	15.38	16.88	15.13	19.88	22.75	23.13	25.88	25.75
Stock price – close ($)	7.7%	16.88	16.25	17.75	17.13	21.13	23.63	27.50	26.25	27.25	33.00
P/E – high	—	8	8	10	8	8	10	12	12	9	10
P/E – low	—	6	6	8	7	6	8	9	9	8	8
Dividends per share ($)	0.6%	2.23	2.26	2.26	2.26	2.34	2.26	2.26	2.34	2.34	2.36
Book value per share ($)	0.8%	21.07	20.61	20.15	20.24	20.39	20.35	20.71	20.94	21.84	22.71

1989 Year End:
Debt ratio: 48.9%
Return on equity: 14.6%
Cash (mil): $1,173
Current ratio: 1.09
Long-term debt (mil): $4,727
Number of shares (mil): 194
Dividends:
1989 average yield: 7.2%
1989 payout: 72.6%
Market value (mil): $6,387

Stock Price History high/low 1980-89

35
30
25
20
15
10
5
0

AMERICAN EXPRESS COMPANY

OVERVIEW

American Express is the largest US diversified financial services organization. The company is best known for its travel-related services, with more than 1,500 worldwide locations, and for its American Express and Optima cards and Travelers Cheques. American Express Travel Related Services currently generates 72% of company profits and includes the direct marketing of consumer products, life insurance, and investment products to 34 million American Express cardmembers.

The company's international activities include American Express Bank, with $18.4 billion in assets and 86 locations in 39 countries. American Express's securities business consists of Lehman Brothers investment banking and Shearson Lehman Brothers. The company's IDS Financial Services has more than 6,000 personal financial planners providing clients in the US with a wide range of savings, insurance, and investment services.

American Express's newest business, American Express Information Services, provides high-volume information processing and communications services. American Express is one of the world's largest 3rd-party processors of debit and credit card transactions, including those of Visa and MasterCard. The company also publishes several lifestyle and travel magazines.

WHEN

In 1850 Henry Wells combined his New York messenger delivery service (for carrying cash and valuables) with his 2 main competitors to form American Express. The company spread throughout the Midwest by acquiring other competitors. When American Express directors refused to expand to California in 1852, Wells and VP William Fargo, while remaining at American Express, started Wells Fargo.

American Express merged with Merchants Union Express, its main competitor, in 1868. To compete with the government's postal money order, the company developed its own money order. Fargo's difficulty in cashing letters of credit in Europe resulted in the company introducing Travelers Cheques, designed by Marcellus Berry, in 1891. Annual sales of Cheques exceeded $6 million by 1901.

In 1918, following a US government order, express companies consolidated into one company, American Railway Express. American Express received about $12 million in stock with a guaranteed dividend, but, without its original business, the company concentrated on selling travelers checks.

In 1958 the company introduced the popular American Express card (users had no credit limits and were required to pay off balances each month). In 1968 the company bought Fireman's Fund American Insurance Companies and Equitable Securities.

James D. Robinson III became CEO at age 41 in 1977 and led the company to become one of the US's largest financial services companies. In 1981 it bought Shearson Loeb Rhoades, a major national brokerage firm. The next year the company acquired Robinson-Humphrey, an Atlanta brokerage firm, and Balcor, a real estate investment company (the assets of which are now being sold). It purchased Lehman Brothers Kuhn Loeb and Investors Diversified Services (IDS) in 1984 and E.F. Hutton (brokerage firm) in 1987.

American Express sold portions of Fireman's Fund to the public in 1985 and 1986, retaining a minority interest that was exchanged in 1989 for Fireman's preferred stock. In 1986 the company also sold its half of Warner Amex, a struggling cable television operator, to partner Warner Communications.

In 1990 American Express, following several financial setbacks to Shearson Lehman Hutton, cut 2,000 employees, contributed more than $1 billion to Shearson, and acquired the remaining Shearson shares it did not own. The company then split Shearson into 2 major divisions, Lehman Brothers and Shearson Lehman Brothers.

HOW MUCH

	9 Yr. Growth	1980	1981	1982	1983	1984	1985	1986	1987	1988	1989
Sales ($ mil)	18.3%	5,504	7,211	8,093	9,770	12,895	12,944	16,746	17,531	22,934	25,047
Net income ($ mil)	13.3%	376	518	581	515	610	810	1,110	533	988	1,157
Income as % of sales	—	6.8%	7.2%	7.2%	5.3%	4.7%	6.3%	6.6%	3.0%	4.3%	4.6%
Earnings per share ($)	8.3%	1.31	1.39	1.50	1.26	1.37	1.74	2.43	1.20	2.29	2.67
Stock price – high ($)	—	10.09	13.59	17.69	24.79	19.50	27.50	35.06	40.63	30.38	39.38
Stock price – low ($)	—	6.13	9.38	8.81	14.00	12.50	17.94	25.25	20.75	22.88	26.38
Stock price – close ($)	14.8%	10.06	11.03	16.06	16.31	18.81	26.50	28.31	22.88	26.63	34.88
P/E – high	—	8	10	12	20	14	16	14	34	13	15
P/E – low	—	5	7	6	11	9	10	10	17	10	10
Dividends per share ($)	6.2%	0.50	0.38	0.55	0.78	0.64	0.66	0.69	0.57	0.97	0.86
Book value per share ($)	6.1%	7.58	7.15	7.96	9.47	10.10	11.41	12.60	10.11	11.39	12.90

1989 Year End:
Debt ratio: 67.4%
Return on equity: 22.0%
Cash (mil): $9,899
Assets (mil): $130,855
Long-term debt (mil): $11,774
Number of shares (mil): 418
Dividends:
1989 average yield: 2.5%
1989 payout: 32.2%
Market value (mil): $14,575

Stock Price History high/low 1980-89

45
40
35
30
25
20
15
10
5
0

NYSE symbol: AXP
Incorporated: New York, 1965
Fiscal year ends: December 31

WHO

Chairman, President, and CEO: James D. Robinson III, age 54, $2,600,000 pay
Chairman, American Express Travel Related Services: Aldo Papone, age 57, $1,375,000 pay
President and CEO, IDS Financial: Harvey Golub, age 50, $1,248,654 pay
President and CEO, TRS North America: Edwin M. Cooperman, age 46, $1,181,154 pay
President and CEO, American Express International: G. Richard Thoman, age 45, $1,159,615 pay
EVP and General Counsel: Gary A. Beller, age 51
EVP: Kenneth Roman, age 59
Acting CFO: Michael P. Monaco, age 42
Auditors: Ernst & Young
Employees: 107,542

WHERE

HQ: American Express Tower, World Financial Center, New York, NY 10285
Phone: 212-640-2000
FAX: 212-619-9802

American Express has offices throughout the US and in over 120 countries.

	1989 Sales		1989 Pretax Income	
	$ mil	% of total	$ mil	% of total
US	20,617	81	1,239	81
Europe	2,611	10	223	15
Asia/Pacific	1,338	5	181	12
All other	910	4	(116)	(8)
Adjustments	(429)	—	—	—
Total	**25,047**	**100**	**1,527**	**100**

WHAT

	1989 Sales		1989 Pretax Income	
	$ mil	% of total	$ mil	% of total
Intl. banking	2,100	8	10	1
Investment svcs.	12,501	49	104	6
Financial svcs.	1,934	8	229	14
Travel related svcs.	8,357	32	1,187	72
Information svcs.	660	3	118	7
Adjustments	(505)	—	(121)	—
Total	**25,047**	**100**	**1,527**	**100**

Financial Services
American Express Bank
American Express cards
American Express Information Services
American Express Travelers Cheques
AMEX Life Assurance
IDS Financial Services
Lehman Brothers
Optima card
Shearson Lehman Brothers

Magazines
Atlanta
Departures
D Magazine
Food & Wine
L.A. Style
New York Woman

RANKINGS

1st in *Fortune* 50 Diversified Financial Cos.
17th in *Forbes* Sales 500
41st in *Business Week* 1000
114th in *Business Week* Global 1000

COMPETITION

Banks
Credit card issuers
Insurance companies
Investment bankers
Magazine publishers
Securities brokers
Travel services
Travelers check issuers

AMERICAN FINANCIAL CORPORATION

OVERVIEW

American Financial is a Cincinnati-based holding company with affiliates operating in diverse industries. The company takes in large amounts of cash in the form of insurance premiums and annuity receipts, which need to be profitably invested; unlike most insurers, which invest in many small holdings, American Financial invests in relatively few companies and takes an active part in their management.

On the financial services side of its business, American Financial operates Hunter, one of the largest savings and loans in Ohio. Great American Insurance offers multiline coverage, while Great American Life Insurance sells tax-sheltered annuities, primarily to schoolteachers.

Other holdings include majority ownership of Chiquita Brands International, a $3.4 billion food company, and The Charter Company (oil); and minority holdings in Penn Central, a $1.7 billion diversified manufacturing company, and bankrupt Circle K. American Financial subsidiaries operate TV and radio stations in 13 of the top 50 US markets and produce and distribute programming.

All of American Financial's common stock is owned by the Lindner family. Carl Lindner and his 2 brothers, Robert and Richard, serve as directors of the company. Carl's sons, Carl III, Craig, and Keith, run the insurance, investment, and Chiquita operations, respectively. The company is said to be interested in disposing of several of its units to raise cash.

WHEN

Carl Lindner, who had built his family's dairy business into the 220-unit United Dairy Farmers ice cream store chain, purchased 3 savings and loan companies in 1959. Lindner changed the company's name from Henthy Realty to American Financial in 1960 and announced plans to create a new kind of company offering diversified financial services. American Financial bought out United Liberty Life Insurance Company (1963) and purchased Cincinnati's historic Provident Bank (1966).

After going public in 1968, American Financial diversified into several new areas. The company formed American Financial Leasing & Services Company (1968) to lease airplanes, computers, and other equipment to corporate customers. American Financial acquired Rubenstein Construction (1969), a large Phoenix developer, and renamed it American Continental. In 1971 American Financial bought several life, casualty, and mortgage insurance companies and entered publishing by purchasing a 95% stake in the *Cincinnati Enquirer*. In 1972 American Financial increased both its insurance and its publishing holdings by acquiring National General, which owned the Great American Insurance Group; paperback publisher Bantam Books; and hardback publisher Grosset & Dunlap.

American Financial suffered during the mid-1970s when inflation grew faster than regulated insurance rates. In addition to selling off its book publishers (1974), the company sold the *Enquirer* (to Combined Communications, owned by Karl Eller) and divested American Continental (1975), leaving American Financial primarily an insurance and financial services company. The insurance companies were consolidated under the Great American Insurance Company name in 1976. American Financial spun off Provident Bank as a special dividend to shareholders in 1980.

Lindner took American Financial private in 1981 by buying all of the company's outstanding stock. That year, the company's American Financial Enterprises subsidiary acquired a 20% interest in Penn Central, the former railroad that emerged from a 1970 bankruptcy as an industrial manufacturer. American Financial sold small convenience store chain UtoteM to Circle K, gaining a minority interest in Circle K. American Financial increased its holdings in United Brands, later named Chiquita Brands International, from 29% to 45% in 1984; Lindner installed himself as CEO of United Brands and reversed the company's losses. In 1987 American Financial reentered the media industry by purchasing Taft Broadcasting, renamed Great American Communications. Since 1988 Lindner has focused his attention on American Financial's internal growth and the financial problems at Circle K. The company is said to be negotiating to sell Hanna-Barbera to MCA, and to be considering the sale of its radio stations. In September 1990 the company announced that it was negotiating to merge its Hunter S&L unit with Provident Bancorp.

HOW MUCH

	9 Yr. Growth	1980	1981	1982	1983	1984	1985	1986	1987	1988	1989
Sales ($ mil)	20.6%	1,334	1,488	1,832	2,042	1,959	2,310	2,791	2,588	6,814	7,177
Net income ($ mil)	—	70	72	100	167	(40)	(23)	184	127	102	3
Income as % of sales	—	5.2%	4.8%	5.5%	8.2%	(2.0%)	(1.0%)	6.6%	4.9%	1.5%	0.0%

1989 Year End:
Debt ratio: 89.4%
Return on equity: —
Cash (mil): $894
Assets (mil): $11,969
Long-term debt (mil): $2,799

Net Income ($ mil) 1980-89

Private company
Incorporated: Ohio, 1955
Fiscal year ends: December 31

WHO

Chairman and CEO: Carl H. Lindner, age 70, $3,665,000 pay
President and COO: Ronald F. Walker, age 51, $2,853,000 pay
VC and SVP: Robert D. Lindner, age 69
VP and Tresurer: Fred J. Runk, age 47, $1,036,000 pay
Auditors: Ernst & Young
Employees: 53,000

WHERE

HQ: One E. Fourth St., Cincinnati, OH 45202
Phone: 513-579-2121
FAX: 513-579-2580

American Financial operates worldwide.

	1989 Sales	
	$ mil	% of total
US	6,157	86
Europe, Latin America & Far East	1,020	14
Total	**7,177**	**100**

WHAT

	1989 Sales		1989 Pretax Income	
	$ mil	% of total	$ mil	% of total
Property & casualty insurance	1,808	25	102	—
Annuities	315	4	16	—
Savings & loan	116	2	8	—
Food products	3,890	54	68	—
Broadcasting & entertainment	397	5	(116)	—
Petroleum marketing	661	9	6	—
Other	60	1	101	—
Adjustments	(70)	—	(182)	—
Total	**7,177**	**100**	**3**	**—**

Subsidiaries/Affiliates
The Charter Co. (51% owned)
Petroleum marketing
Chiquita Brands International, Inc. (81% owned)
Great American Communications Co. (65% owned)
5 TV, 11 FM, and 6 AM stations
Great American Insurance Co.
Personal property and casualty
Great American Life Insurance Co.
Tax-sheltered annuities
Hanna-Barbera Productions, Inc. (65% owned)
Animated film production
Hunter Savings Association
Kings Island Co.
Theme park

Other Holdings
The Circle K Corp. (15% owned)
The Penn Central Corp. (34% owned)
Spelling Entertainment Inc. (45% owned)
Sprague Technologies, Inc. (32% owned)

RANKINGS

8th in *Fortune* 100 Diversified Service Cos.
28th in *Forbes* 400 US Private Cos.

COMPETITION

Banks and savings and loans
Food and tobacco companies
Food retailers
Insurance companies
Media companies
Petroleum companies

AMERICAN GREETINGS CORPORATION

OVERVIEW

American Greetings creates and sells greeting cards, gift wrap, paper party supplies, gift items, frames, stationery, and card display cabinets; licenses characters such as Ziggy, the Care Bears, and Holly Hobbie; and manufactures and sells hair care products.

The company, which is the 2nd largest in the industry after Hallmark and the largest publicly held, sells its products in 50 countries through 90,000 retail outlets. Of $1.3 billion in revenue in its most recent fiscal year, 17% was derived from foreign markets. The company has Carlton Cards subsidiaries in England, France, and Canada, and a manufacturing subsidiary in Mexico.

American Greetings increased revenues in fiscal 1990 for the 84th consecutive year and is creating new card lines for older people and expanding alternative card lines.

WHEN

In 1906, 22-year-old Jacob Sapirstein, nicknamed "J. S.," began a card wholesaling business in his Cleveland home. J. S.'s sons joined the company (9-year-old Irving in 1918 and Morris in 1926) to sell cards for their dad. By 1932 J. S. began producing his own cards, and the company hired its first salesperson in 1934. A 3rd son, Harry, joined the family business (1935), and the company opened its first branch office in Detroit (1936). The name American Greetings Publishers was adopted in 1938. By 1940 the company's sales had topped $1 million.

During the 1940s the company opened an Ohio production plant (1946), signed its first licensing agreement (1949), and developed new card-sorting technology. The company established a color processing plant in 1951, and in 1952 American Greetings went public, selling stock to raise capital, and dropped Publishers from its name. Hi Brows, a line of funny studio cards, was introduced in 1956. In 1958 American Greetings added Carlton Cards, a Canadian subsidiary.

In 1960 Irving Stone (all 3 sons had changed their last name to Stone) was named president and J. S. became chairman. The next year the company opened a new plant in Arkansas. Its Ohio plant was expanded (1965), employment grew to over 6,000 (1966), and new plants were opened in Kentucky (1967, 1969). In 1967 Holly Hobbie made her first appearance on greeting cards; in 1968 sales exceeded $100 million, and the next year the company opened a manufacturing subsidiary in Mexico City.

In 1972 American Greetings introduced Ziggy. In 1978 the company bought Plus Mark, which made seasonal wrapping paper, boxed cards, and accessories; and Irving replaced his father as chairman. Morry Weiss, Irving's son-in-law, became president and COO. In 1979 American Greetings started its Amtoy subsidiary, making toys, novelties, and giftware.

The licensing of Holly Hobbie prompted American Greetings to create its own licensing division, Those Characters From Cleveland (1980). The company also acquired several European cardmakers. In 1981 American Greetings began advertising on TV and in 1982 started a joint venture with Christian Publishing, a South African card company operating in European countries. American Greetings made the *Fortune* 500 list (1982) and introduced the Care Bears, licensed characters that appeared in an animated film. The company bought Drawing Board Greeting Cards in 1985 and Acme Frame Products in 1986. Revenues topped $1 billion in 1985.

In 1987 J. S. died and Morry Weiss became CEO; American Greetings bought SMD Industries, a maker of paper products and frames. In 1988 the company sold Amtoy and its subsidiaries in Belgium, the Netherlands, and Luxembourg, and opened a new plant in Toronto. In 1989 the company bought Wilhold Hair Care Products.

HOW MUCH

	9 Yr. Growth	1980	1981	1982	1983	1984	1985	1986	1987	1988	1989
Sales ($ mil)	11.3%	489	606	722	817	919	1,012	1,103	1,175	1,253	1,287
Net income ($ mil)	11.8%	27	33	45	60	74	74	63	33	44	72
Income as % of sales	—	5.4%	5.4%	6.2%	7.3%	8.1%	7.4%	5.7%	2.8%	3.5%	5.6%
Earnings per share ($)	9.8%	0.97	1.20	1.54	1.91	2.35	2.32	1.97	1.04	1.38	2.25
Stock price – high ($)	—	6.94	10.38	21.63	29.25	34.25	37.50	42.00	31.63	22.38	37.13
Stock price – low ($)	—	4.75	5.31	9.00	17.31	21.50	26.75	24.00	13.00	13.38	20.38
Stock price – close ($)	22.3%	5.75	10.06	18.88	26.50	31.00	32.63	26.25	14.00	20.75	35.25
P/E – high	—	7	9	14	15	15	16	21	30	16	17
P/E – low	—	5	4	6	9	9	12	12	13	10	9
Dividends per share ($)	10.9%	0.26	0.27	0.31	0.40	0.54	0.62	0.66	0.66	0.66	0.66
Book value per share ($)	10.6%	7.61	8.31	10.18	11.62	13.35	15.01	16.55	17.02	17.55	18.89

1989 Year End:
Debt ratio: 28.0%
Return on equity: 12.3%
Cash (mil): $123
Current ratio: 3.39
Long-term debt (mil): $236
Number of shares (mil): 32
Dividends:
1989 average yield: 1.9%
1989 payout: 29.3%
Market value (mil): $1,128

Stock Price History high/low 1980-89

45 40 35 30 25 20 15 10 5 0

OTC symbol: AGREA
Incorporated: Ohio, 1944
Fiscal year ends: Last day in February

WHO

Chairman: Irving I. Stone, age 81, $264,046 pay
President and CEO: Morry Weiss, age 50, $555,000 pay
President, US Greeting Card Division: Edward Fruchtenbaum, age 42, $301,792 pay
SVP and CFO: Henry Lowenthal, age 58, $234,833 pay
Auditors: Ernst & Young
Employees: 20,750

WHERE

HQ: 10500 American Rd., Cleveland, OH 44144
Phone: 216-252-7300
FAX: 216-252-6519 (Corporate Communications)

American Greetings has 21 US offices and production facilities and 10 offices, production facilities, and distribution plants in England, Scotland, Mexico, Canada, and France.

	1989 Sales		1989 Operating Income	
	$ mil	% of total	$ mil	% of total
US	1,088	83	129	90
Foreign	221	17	15	10
Adjustments	(22)	—	(22)	—
Total	**1,287**	**100**	**122**	**100**

WHAT

	1990 Sales
	% of total
Everyday greeting cards	41
Holiday greeting cards	24
Gift wrap and party goods	17
Frames, candles, etc.	9
Stationery and miscellaneous	9
Total	**100**

Licensed Characters
Care Bears
Holly Hobbie
Strawberry Shortcake
Ziggy

Card Lines
78TH ST.
Cartoon Factory
Couples
Hi Brows
In Touch
Kid Zone
Soft Touch

Consumer Products
Acme Frame Products
Plus Mark (cards and gift wrap)
Wilhold Hair Care Products

Manufacturing
A.G. Industries (display fixtures)

RANKINGS

296th in *Fortune* 500 Industrial Cos.
510th in *Business Week* 1000

COMPETITION

Deluxe
Hallmark
United Nations

AMERICAN HOME PRODUCTS CORPORATION

OVERVIEW

American Home Products is the 8th largest pharmaceutical company in the world and 3rd largest based in the US. AHP sells several well-known, over-the-counter consumer health care items (Anacin, Advil), foods (Chef Boyardee, Maypo), and household products. Most household products (Black Flag, Easy-Off) were part of its Boyle-Midway division, sold in July 1990 to Reckitt & Colman PLC, a London-based consumer brands company.

AHP's R&D expenditures were below the industry average until 1989, when they were boosted to 10.5% of drug sales, compared to 5.5% in 1988. That amount will continue to increase in the 1990s as the company seeks FDA approval for new products. Approval is expected within 2 to 3 years for 6 new drugs, including an implantable contraceptive that can last for 5 years.

The company made 30% of its sales and 24% of its profit overseas in 1989. AHP is a major advertiser, spending $563 million in 1989; *Advertising Age* ranked it 27th among all advertisers in 1988. The company has not had a decrease in quarterly profits since 1952.

NYSE symbol: AHP
Incorporated: Delaware, 1926
Fiscal year ends: December 31

WHO

Chairman and CEO: John R. Stafford, age 52, $1,185,000 pay
President: Bernard Canavan, age 54, $600,000 pay (before promotion)
EVP and Principal Financial Officer: Robert G. Blount, age 51, $600,000 pay
Auditors: Arthur Andersen & Co.
Employees: 51,000

WHEN

Incorporated in 1926, American Home Products consolidated several small companies that made proprietary medicinals such as Hill's Cascara Quinine and St. Jacob's Oil. AHP's history is largely one of continuous acquisitions. One of its earliest, Wyeth Chemicals, came from Harvard University in 1932 (Stuart Wyeth, last heir to the company, had willed it to Harvard).

During the Great Depression AHP bought over 30 food and drug companies. A sunburn oil acquired in 1935 was transformed into the hemorrhoid treatment Preparation H, still a best-selling product. Other acquisitions in the 1930s included 3-in-One Oil, Anacin, Affiliated Products (Neet), and Black Flag. Chef Boyardee was added in 1946.

With the purchase of Canadian company Ayerst Laboratories in 1943 (cod liver oil; vitamins; and Premarin, estrogen from pregnant mares' urine), AHP completed the foundations of its prescription drug business, which today is consolidated into Wyeth-Ayerst. Ayerst made penicillin for the Canadian armed forces in WWII and later introduced Antabuse (alcohol deterrent, 1951), developed in alliance with British drug company Imperial Chemical Industries (ICI). From the research alliance with ICI, Ayerst also got Inderal (1968), the first of the beta-blocker class of antihypertensives.

William F. LaPorte, who became chairman and president in 1965, introduced a highly centralized management style, unusual for such a large company. In the early 1970s the company fought with the FTC over claims made for Preparation H, and later for Anacin, and eventually had to modify advertising copy. AHP has been a major advertiser but is virtually unknown to the average consumer, preferring to use divisional names such as Whitehall Labs (Advil, Anacin). Introduced in 1984, Advil, AHP's over-the-counter version of the analgesic ibuprofen, outsold the runner-up, Bristol-Myers's Nuprin, by more than three to one in 1989.

Recent acquisitions include Sherwood Medical Group (medical supplies, 1982) and Bristol-Myers's animal health division (1987). In 1988 AHP won a takeover battle against Rorer for A.H. Robins (Robitussin, Dimetapp), the company bankrupted by suits over the Dalkon Shield contraceptive device. AHP established a $2.3 billion fund to pay the damages and finally closed the transaction in December 1989. In the 1980s AHP sold its non–health care businesses, including Ekco (housewares, 1984), E. J. Brach (candies, 1986), Sergeant's pet care (1989), and all its South African interests (1989). In 1990 the company agreed to sell its Boyle-Midway household products subsidiary (Black Flag, Easy Off, Woolite) for $1.25 billion.

WHERE

HQ: 685 Third Ave., New York, NY 10017
Phone: 212-878-5000
FAX: 212-878-5771

The company has 32 manufacturing plants located in 19 states and in Puerto Rico.

	1989 Sales		1989 Pretax Income	
	$ mil	% of total	$ mil	% of total
US	4,755	70	1,068	76
Other Americas	607	9	126	9
Europe & Africa	1,058	16	174	12
Asia & Australia	327	5	46	3
Total	**6,747**	**100**	**1,414**	**100**

WHAT

	1989 Sales		1989 Operating Income	
	$ mil	% of total	$ mil	% of total
Food & household	1,484	22	208	14
Health care prods.	5,263	78	1,325	86
Adjustments	—	—	(21)	—
Total	**6,747**	**100**	**1,512**	**100**

Major Divisions & Subsidiaries
Corometrics Medical Systems (ultrasound)
Fort Dodge Laboratories (veterinary)
A.H. Robins (ethical pharmaceuticals)
Sherwood Medical (medical supplies)
Whitehall-Boyle (drugs, household products)
Whitehall Laboratories
Wyeth-Ayerst (ethical pharmaceuticals)

Brand Names

Advil	Dimetapp	Maypo
Anacin	Dristan	Preparation H
Chap Stick	Gulden's	Primatene
Chef Boyardee	Jiffy Pop	Robitussin

HOW MUCH

	9 Yr. Growth	1980	1981	1982	1983	1984	1985	1986	1987	1988	1989
Sales ($ mil)	6.6%	3,799	4,131	4,582	4,857	4,485	4,685	4,927	5,028	5,501	6,747
Net income ($ mil)	10.6%	446	497	560	627	656	717	779	845	932	1,102
Income as % of sales	—	11.7%	12.0%	12.2%	12.9%	14.6%	15.3%	15.8%	16.8%	16.9%	16.3%
Earnings per share ($)	10.7%	1.42	1.59	1.80	2.00	2.13	2.35	2.59	2.87	3.19	3.54
Stock price – high ($)	—	15.94	18.63	24.00	27.13	27.88	33.44	47.44	48.38	42.44	54.69
Stock price – low ($)	—	10.69	14.06	16.63	20.88	23.38	25.06	30.63	31.00	35.19	39.88
Stock price – close ($)	16.1%	14.06	18.25	22.38	24.81	25.25	31.44	38.44	36.38	41.63	53.75
P/E – high	—	11	12	13	14	13	14	18	17	13	15
P/E – low	—	8	9	9	10	11	11	12	11	11	11
Dividends per share ($)	9.7%	0.85	0.95	1.08	1.20	1.32	1.45	1.55	1.67	1.80	1.95
Book value per share ($)	3.2%	4.73	5.33	5.91	6.57	6.87	7.59	8.03	8.71	10.18	6.30

1989 Year End:
Debt ratio: 49.0%
Return on equity: 42.9%
Cash (mil): $1,208
Current ratio: 3.19
Long-term debt (mil): $1,896
Number of shares (mil): 313
Dividends:
1989 average yield: 3.6%
1989 payout: 55.2%
Market value (mil): $16,799

Stock Price History high/low 1980-89

60
50
40
30
20
10
0

RANKINGS

68th in *Fortune* 500 Industrial Cos.
190th in *Fortune* Global 500 Industrial Cos.
124th in *Forbes* Sales 500
32nd in *Business Week* 1000
79th in *Business Week* Global 1000

COMPETITION

Abbott Labs	Pfizer
C. R. Bard	Procter & Gamble
Baxter	Rhône-Poulenc
Bayer	Roche Holding
Bristol-Myers Squibb	Schering-Plough
Campbell Soup	Siemens
Eastman Kodak	SmithKline Beecham
Eli Lilly	Upjohn
General Electric	Warner-Lambert
Hoechst	Other drug companies
Johnson & Johnson	Other food products companies
Merck	Other medical supply companies

AMERICAN INFORMATION TECHNOLOGIES CORP.

OVERVIEW

AT&T spin-off Ameritech, the 5th largest US telephone holding company, provided telephone service via 15,899,000 lines as of year-end 1989, in a territory that serves 17% of the US population. Based in Chicago, Ameritech provided phone service through its Bell subsidiaries and grew 2.8% in terms of telephone lines that year — its highest rate since its 1984 beginnings. The company has led all of the Bell companies for 6 consecutive years in return on equity (now 15.9%).

Since 1989 Ameritech Information Systems has provided sales and sales support services to its regulated Bell subsidiaries for customer-owned equipment. Ameritech has more than 242,000 cellular telephone subscribers in 22 cities through its Ameritech Mobile subsidiary. Ameritech Publishing provides directory advertising and publishing services. Ameritech Credit arranges financing for customers who lease telecommunications products; it provided nearly $100 million of financing during 1989. Ameritech Enterprise is a holding company for information service businesses, primarily supplying voice mail and audiotex services in the US, the UK, and Japan.

WHEN

Ameritech began as an arm of AT&T. Illinois Bell, now Ameritech's largest operating company, was originally known as Chicago Telephone and operated between 1881 and 1920. From 1880 to 1885 the Bell System consolidated small, individual telephone companies such as Chicago's into larger telephone companies that, under franchise agreements, could construct long-distance lines to other Bell exchanges but not to non-Bell exchanges. Gradually the long-distance lines became AT&T Long Lines; local operations were retained by the Bell Operating Companies.

The E. T. Gilliland Company of Indianapolis, long part of Ameritech's Indiana Bell company, was vital to the Bell System in its early years. In the late 1870s Gilliland was considered Bell's most innovative manufacturer. In 1881 Gilliland sold a 61% stake in his operations to Western Electric, at that time controlled by Bell's chief rival, Western Union. The purchase could have destroyed Bell and changed the history of US telephony, but later the same year Bell regained Gilliland through an outside investor named Jay Gould, who bought shares quietly.

In 1983 AT&T spun off its local operating subsidiaries as part of its settlement of an antitrust suit. Ameritech incorporated that same year and began independent operations throughout the Great Lakes region in 1984. Ameritech received 5 of AT&T's 22 telephone subsidiaries, Ameritech Mobile Communications (cellular service provider), and a share in Bell Communications Research (R&D arm shared by the Bell companies).

In 1984 Ameritech formed several subsidiaries: Ameritech Information Systems (sales and service of phone system hardware to businesses); Ameritech Credit (equipment leasing and financing); Ameritech Development (new business development); Ameritech Publishing (directory publishing); Ameritech Applied Technologies (software development); and Ameritech Enterprise Holdings (holding company for information service acquisitions).

Since divestiture Ameritech has expanded paging services by purchasing existing operations. The company made an unsuccessful stab at the software market, purchasing Applied Data Research in 1986 and selling it in 1988 because it was unprofitable. In partnership with Bell Canada and Telenet, Ameritech started iNet (1987), an electronic mail and information services company. In 1988 the company invested in 2 companies to gain a presence in voice messaging and audiotex services. Ameritech is focusing current efforts upon increasing network usage in its Great Lakes region by developing information services. In 1990 Ameritech was chosen, along with Bell Atlantic, to purchase New Zealand's public phone system for about $2.5 billion.

HOW MUCH

	5 Yr. Growth	1980	1981	1982	1983	1984	1985	1986	1987	1988	1989
Sales ($ mil)	4.1%	—	—	—	—	8,347	9,021	9,362	9,536	9,903	10,211
Net income ($ mil)	4.6%	—	—	—	—	991	1,078	1,138	1,188	1,237	1,238
Income as % of sales	—	—	—	—	—	11.9%	11.9%	12.2%	12.5%	12.5%	12.1%
Earnings per share ($)	6.2%	—	—	—	—	3.39	3.67	3.94	4.24	4.54	4.58
Stock price – high ($)	—	—	—	—	—	26.00	35.50	50.75	49.94	48.94	68.25
Stock price – low ($)	—	—	—	—	—	20.79	24.83	32.67	37.00	41.00	46.88
Stock price – close ($)	21.6%	—	—	—	—	25.58	35.50	44.17	42.31	47.88	68.00
P/E – high	—	—	—	—	—	8	10	13	12	11	15
P/E – low	—	—	—	—	—	6	7	8	9	9	10
Dividends per share ($)	8.3%	—	—	—	—	2.00	2.20	2.40	2.55	2.76	2.98
Book value per share ($)	3.4%	—	—	—	—	24.08	25.51	26.61	27.71	29.14	28.45

1989 Year End:
Debt ratio: 39.7%
Return on equity: 15.9%
Cash (mil): $520
Current ratio: 0.86
Long-term debt (mil): $5,069
Number of shares (mil): 270
Dividends:
1989 average yield: 4.4%
1989 payout: 65.1%
Market value (mil): $18,373

NYSE symbol: AIT
Incorporated: Delaware, 1983
Fiscal year ends: December 31

WHO

Chairman and CEO: William L. Weiss, age 60, $1,305,000 pay
VC: Ormand J. Wade, age 50, $755,000 pay
VC and CFO: William H. Springer, age 60, $690,000 pay
President, Ameritech Bell Group: Robert L. Barnett, age 49, $668,400 pay
President, Ameritech Enterprise Group: William P. Vititoe, age 52, $582,000 pay
Auditors: Arthur Andersen & Co., Coopers & Lybrand (for some subsidiaries)
Employees: 77,326

WHERE

HQ: 30 S. Wacker Dr., Chicago, IL 60606
Phone: 312-750-5000
FAX: 312-207-1601

Ameritech's telephone companies operate in Illinois, Indiana, Michigan, Ohio, and Wisconsin.

WHAT

	1989 Sales	
	$ mil	% of total
Local service	4,679	46
Interstate access	1,941	19
Intrastate access	541	5
Long distance	1,259	12
Directory & other	1,791	18
Total	**10,211**	**100**

Telephone Companies
Illinois Bell Telephone Co.
Indiana Bell Telephone Co., Inc.
Michigan Bell Telephone Co.
The Ohio Bell Telephone Co.
Wisconsin Bell, Inc.

Wholly Owned Subsidiaries/Affiliates
Ameritech Applied Technologies, Inc.
Ameritech Audiotex Services
Ameritech Capital Funding Corp.
Ameritech Credit Corp.
Ameritech Development Corp.
Ameritech Enterprise Holdings, Inc.
Ameritech Information Systems, Inc.
Ameritech Mobile Communications
Ameritech Properties Corp.
Ameritech Publishing, Inc.
Ameritech Services, Inc.
Bell Communications Research, Inc. (14.28%)
The Tigon Corp.

RANKINGS

10th in *Fortune* 50 Utilities
67th in *Forbes* Sales 500
26th in *Business Week* 1000
73rd in *Business Week* Global 1000

COMPETITION

AT&T
Bell Atlantic
BellSouth
GTE
McCaw Cellular
MCI
NYNEX
Pacific Telesis
Southwestern Bell
United Telecommunications
U S West

AMERICAN INTERNATIONAL GROUP, INC.

OVERVIEW

AIG is the US's largest international insurer, the only US insurer founded overseas, the US's leading commercial and industrial insurer, and the largest foreign insurer in Japan. Through subsidiaries, AIG is the largest life insurer in southeast Asia, the Philippines, and the Middle East. AIG's joint venture with People's Insurance is the only such alliance China has made with a foreign insurer.

AIG's General Insurance Underwriting provides property-casualty insurance worldwide. The Domestic General–Broker Group conducts US property-casualty operations. This group is the leading provider of pollution liability protection; has the largest share of the environmental liability insurance market; and is the nation's largest provider of directors' and officers' insurance, malpractice coverage, and risk management services (*e.g.*, claims administration and loss control) to brokers and their customers.

AIG's Domestic General–Agency Group writes property-casualty insurance through independent agents. United Guaranty writes mortgage guaranty insurance. The Foreign General Group provides international underwriting. The Life Group (operating worldwide) has approximately 23,000 agents.

WHEN

Ice cream parlor proprietor Cornelius Starr founded casualty and property insurer C. V. Starr & Company in Shanghai in 1919. For many years, Starr merely passed business to other insurers. China remained Starr's operational base until WWII, when he relocated to the US.

In 1954 Starr began seeking multinational companies as clients. To do so, he developed an international benefits pool that provided disability, health, and life insurance, and pension plans that were transferable as employees moved from country to country. The strategy proved successful: today the company manages benefit pools for many of the *Fortune* 500.

In 1967 Starr handpicked his successor, attorney Maurice Greenberg; Starr died the following year. By 1972 CEO Greenberg had established American International Group as a holding company for the many insurance companies Starr operated worldwide. Greenberg is widely regarded as a brilliant insurance executive and the true genius behind AIG.

AIG takes risks that its competitors shun, such as insuring satellites. During the mid-1970s AIG insured offshore oil rigs when other insurers would not, charging annual premiums as high as 10% of value. Greenberg uses reinsurers around the world to help leverage otherwise risky ventures. AIG will accept larger single risks than any other insurer, making AIG the largest source of reinsurance in the US.

In 1975 the company became the first insurance company in the Western Hemisphere to be allowed to resume business operations in China. By then it was the largest foreign life insurer in Hong Kong, Japan, Malaysia, the Philippines, Singapore, and Taiwan, and the only insurer with sales and support facilities operating on a worldwide basis.

From 1979 to 1984 the property-casualty business suffered heavy price competition that cost the industry almost $21 billion in underwriting losses, but during this period AIG outperformed all rivals in terms of its combined ratio (expenses plus losses divided by premiums). In 1986 the company again leveraged its international presence by offering services to foreign manufacturers interested in the US market.

A large percentage (approximately 40%) of AIG stock is used as management incentive compensation. Upon death or resignation, an executive's stock shares must be sold back to an AIG holding company for recycling to other executives as bonuses or incentives.

HOW MUCH

	9 Yr. Growth	1980	1981	1982	1983	1984	1985	1986	1987	1988	1989
Sales ($ mil)	20.5%	2,709	3,155	3,563	3,996	4,282	5,815	8,844	11,385	13,815	14,546
Net income ($ mil)	19.2%	282	345	413	427	317	374	657	945	1,175	1,367
Income as % of sales	—	10.4%	10.9%	11.6%	10.7%	7.4%	6.4%	7.4%	8.3%	8.5%	9.4%
Earnings per share ($)	17.3%	1.98	2.40	2.79	2.86	2.13	2.45	4.04	5.74	7.14	8.29
Stock price – high ($)	—	21.33	27.70	33.40	38.88	36.50	55.00	71.75	83.75	68.75	112.00
Stock price – low ($)	—	13.00	19.47	22.00	26.15	25.44	32.50	52.00	53.50	49.00	66.25
Stock price – close ($)	20.0%	20.00	25.90	31.60	32.13	34.06	53.00	61.13	60.00	67.75	103.50
P/E – high	—	11	12	12	14	17	22	18	15	10	14
P/E – low	—	7	8	8	9	12	13	13	9	7	8
Dividends per share ($)	14.7%	0.13	0.15	0.18	0.21	0.22	0.22	0.23	0.26	0.35	0.44
Book value per share ($)	18.4%	11.23	13.66	16.01	18.28	19.35	24.15	29.83	35.27	42.84	51.35

1989 Year End:
Debt ratio: 33.6%
Return on equity: 17.6%
Cash (mil): $168
Assets (mil): $46,143
Long-term debt (mil): $4,257
Number of shares (mil): 164
Dividends:
1989 average yield: 0.4%
1989 payout: 5.3%
Market value (mil): $16,941

Stock Price History high/low 1980-89

120
100
80
60
40
20
0

NYSE symbol: AIG
Incorporated: Delaware, 1967
Fiscal year ends: December 31

WHO

Chairman, President, and CEO: Maurice R. (Hank) Greenberg, age 64, $1,570,000 pay
VC Finance: Edward E. Matthews, age 58, $440,000 pay
VC, Foreign General Insurance: Houghton Freeman, age 68, $410,700 pay
VC External Affairs: John J. Roberts, age 67, $310,000 pay
VC, Domestic General Insurance: Thomas R. Tizzio, age 52, $300,000 pay
Auditors: Coopers & Lybrand
Employees: 33,000

WHERE

HQ: 70 Pine St., New York, NY 10270
Phone: 212-770-7000
FAX: 212-770-7821

AIG and its member companies have 424 offices throughout the world and write insurance in more than 130 countries and jurisdictions.

	1989 Sales		1989 Pretax Income	
	$ mil	% of total	$ mil	% of total
US & Canada	8,718	62	861	49
Far East	3,521	25	626	36
Other foreign	1,911	13	267	15
Adjustments	396	—	(48)	—
Total	**14,546**	**100**	**1,706**	**100**

WHAT

	1989 Sales		1989 Pretax Income	
	$ mil	% of total	$ mil	% of total
General insurance	9,571	67	1,100	64
Life insurance	3,843	27	454	26
Agency & service fee income	215	2	34	2
Financial services	498	4	144	8
Adjustments	419	—	(26)	—
Total	**14,546**	**100**	**1,706**	**100**

Affiliated Companies
American Home Assurance Co.
American International Assurance Co., Ltd.
American International Reinsurance Co., Ltd.
American International Underwriters Overseas, Ltd.
American Life Insurance Co.
Delaware American Life Insurance Co.
Lexington Insurance Co.
Nan Shan Life Insurance Co., Ltd.
National Union Fire Insurance Co.
New Hampshire Insurance Co.
Pacific Union Assurance Co.
The Philippine American Life Insurance Co.
Ticino Societa d'Assicurazioni Sulla Vita
United Guaranty Residential Insurance Co.

RANKINGS

9th in *Fortune* 50 Diversified Financial Cos.
38th in *Forbes* 500 Sales
35th in *Business Week* 1000
77th in *Business Week* Global 1000

COMPETITION

Aetna
CIGNA
General Re
Lloyd's of London
Tokio Marine & Fire
Travelers
USF&G
Other insurance companies

AMERICAN PRESIDENT COMPANIES, LTD.

OVERVIEW

American President offers an integrated system of ocean, rail, and truck transportation between North America and Asia. With a fleet of 23 containerships (ships carrying intermodal containers), American President serves more than 3,500 delivery points on 5 continents. It has 12% of the transpacific market. Because the containers are intermodal, freight can be taken from shipboard, loaded on a truck or rail car, then sent onward in the same container.

US freight operations focus on double-stack rail cars. American President also operates a fleet of 574 trucks but is increasingly converting truck cargo to stacktrains.

Truck and rail operations are further integrated with Red Eagle Service — guaranteed on-time delivery using a combination of stacktrains and trucks. American President's critical delivery customers include Toyota and the Ford Motor Company.

American President provides customers access to information in its computer regarding the location of their shipments, through a sophisticated tracking system utilizing touch-tone telephones, personal computers, and facsimile machines.

Profits in 1989 declined precipitously due to higher operating expenses and lower rates per container shipped.

WHEN

New York merchant William Aspinwall founded the Pacific Mail Steamship Company in 1848, planning to launch the first shipping line between Panama and California. Later that year the company's first steamers sailed from New York shipyards to San Francisco Bay.

In the early 1860s Cornelius Vanderbilt (owner, Atlantic Mail Steamship Company) sent 4 ships to the Pacific, hoping to break Pacific Mail's West Coast monopoly, but sold his ships to Pacific Mail after a prolonged rate war. In 1866 Pacific Mail bought Atlantic Mail while Vanderbilt went on to take over the New York Central Railroad (1867). In 1867 Pacific Mail pioneered trade to the Orient.

During the depression of 1873, Pacific Mail narrowly averted bankruptcy brought on by an overambitious construction program. Jay Gould gained control of the company in 1874, and by 1885 Gould's Union Pacific Railroad completely owned Pacific Mail.

C. P. Huntington of the Central Pacific and Southern Pacific railroads bought Pacific Mail in 1893. Upon his death (1900), Southern Pacific bought the company. Edward Harriman took over Southern Pacific in 1902, operating it and Pacific Mail until his death in 1909. W. R. Grace bought Pacific Mail in 1915, then in 1926 it was acquired by the Dollar Steamship Company.

Founded by Robert Dollar, the Dollar Company had conducted transpacific trade since 1902. However, weakened by strikes, the company faced bankruptcy by the mid-1930s. In 1938 the Maritime Commission forced the Dollar family to transfer control of the company to the government, reorganizing it as The American President Lines, Ltd.

From 1946 to 1952 the Dollar family tried to regain the company which, by court order, was put up for sale. A venture capitalist group led by Ralph Davies (formerly of Standard Oil) bought American President in 1952. Davies's Natomas Company (offshore oil) bought the company in 1956. Bruce Seaton (SVP Finance, Natomas) became president of American President in 1976, emphasizing transpacific trade using intermodal containers.

After buying Natomas in 1983, Diamond Shamrock spun off American President as an independent company. In 1988 American President invested in Amtech (providing electronic tracking of intermodal containers) and added 5 new ships to its fleet. However, high operating costs and interest expenses led to an 86% decline in earnings between 1988 and 1989.

HOW MUCH

	9 Yr. Growth	1980	1981	1982	1983	1984	1985	1986	1987	1988	1989
Sales ($ mil)	16.5%	581	659	685	806	977	1,235	1,506	1,891	2,194	2,300
Net income ($ mil)	—	43	43	51	26	103	38	18	79	81	11
Income as % of sales	—	7.4%	6.5%	7.5%	3.3%	10.6%	3.1%	1.2%	4.2%	3.7%	0.5%
Earnings per share ($)	—	—	—	—	1.51	5.78	1.86	0.70	3.23	3.26	0.23
Stock price – high ($)	—	—	—	—	20.39	24.42	29.00	29.00	51.00	35.88	38.75
Stock price – low ($)	—	—	—	—	11.81	14.81	13.88	16.88	21.63	22.63	26.75
Stock price – close ($)	6.4%	—	—	—	19.34	21.83	18.88	26.13	29.50	34.00	28.13
P/E – high	—	—	—	—	14	4	16	41	16	11	168
P/E – low	—	—	—	—	8	3	7	24	7	7	116
Dividends per share ($)	—	—	—	—	0.00	0.00	0.38	0.50	0.50	0.55	0.58
Book value per share ($)	7.6%	—	—	—	19.21	24.54	25.87	25.96	28.87	30.52	29.73

1989 Year End:
Debt ratio: 46.2%
Return on equity: 0.8%
Cash (mil): $127
Current ratio: 1.34
Long-term debt (mil): $511
Number of shares (mil): 20
Dividends:
1989 average yield: 2.0%
1989 payout: 250.0%
Market value (mil): $562

Stock Price History high/low 1983-89

60
50
40
30
20
10
0

NYSE symbol: APS
Incorporated: Delaware, 1983
Fiscal year ends: Last Friday in December

WHO

Chairman, President, and CEO: W. Bruce Seaton, age 64, $587,500 pay
President and COO, American President Lines, Ltd.: Timothy J. Rhein, age 49, $269,693 pay
President and COO, American President Domestic Company, Ltd.: Donald C. Orris, age 48, $269,693 pay
SVP and CFO: Robert K. Dahl, age 49
Auditors: Arthur Andersen & Co.
Employees: 4,994

WHERE

HQ: 1800 Harrison St., Oakland, CA 94612
Phone: 415-272-8000
FAX: 415-272-7941

American President operates 159 offices in North America, Asia, the Middle East, Europe, Africa, and Australia. With 23 containerships and 105,000 containers, the company serves 39 ports in the Pacific and Indian oceans and the Arabian Gulf.

	1989 Sales	
	$ mil	% of total
Domestic	658	29
International	1,642	71
Total	**2,300**	**100**

WHAT

	1989 Sales		1989 Operating Income	
	$ mil	% of total	$ mil	% of total
Transportation	2,279	99	51	85
Real estate	21	1	9	15
Total	**2,300**	**100**	**60**	**100**

International Transportation Services
American Consolidation Services, Ltd.
Consolidation services in Asia for US importers
American President Lines, Ltd.
Eagle Marine Services, Ltd.
Stevedoring and terminal services

Domestic Transportation Services
American President Automotive Distribution Co., Ltd.
Automotive parts and components transport
American President Distribution Services, Ltd.
Domestic transportation brokerage
American President Intermodal Co., Ltd.
Rail car operations manager
American President Trucking Co., Ltd.
Red Eagle Service

Real Estate
American President Real Estate Co., Ltd.
387 acres in California

RANKINGS

20th in *Fortune* 50 Transportation Cos.
367th in *Forbes* Sales 500
800th in *Business Week* 1000

COMPETITION

Consolidated Freightways
CSX
Other trucking companies and railroads

AMERICAN STANDARD INC.

OVERVIEW

Based in New York City, privately owned American Standard is the world's largest producer of plumbing products and braking systems for heavy trucks and buses. In addition, the company is the 2nd largest global producer of air conditioning products, after the Carrier division of United Technologies.

American Standard's Plumbing Products segment is the only full-line producer of plumbing products operating on a global basis and is the leading producer of plumbing products in Canada and Europe, and in several other areas outside the US. The company generated 70% of its 1989 operating income abroad.

The plumbing operations produce mainly fixtures and fittings, primarily for the construction industry. Most of these products are sold through distributors and wholesalers.

The Transportation Products segment produces pneumatic, hydraulic, and electronic braking systems as well as components and control systems for heavy vehicles. Products in this segment are sold directly to the manufacturer under the WABCO (Westinghouse Air Brake Company) and Clayton Dewandre trademarks. Spare parts are primarily sold through dealers.

The Air Conditioning Products segment produces air conditioning systems, refrigerated display cases, and gas furnaces, primarily under the Trane name. Trane products are sold through company sales offices as well as through a network of about 5,000 independent dealers.

WHEN

In 1881 American Radiator was created in Buffalo to manufacture steam and hot water heating equipment. J. P. Morgan acquired the company and bought out almost every other US heating equipment company, consolidating them all under the American Radiator name in 1899.

That same year Louisville-based Ahrens & Ott joined with Pittsburgh-based Standard Manufacturing (both plumbing supply companies) to create Standard Sanitary. Standard Sanitary produced enameled cast iron plumbing parts and developed the one-piece lavatory, built-in bathtubs, and single taps for hot and cold running water.

Both American Radiator and Standard Sanitary grew through numerous acquisitions in the early decades of the 20th century. In 1929 the 2 companies merged to form American Radiator & Standard Sanitary Corporation, headquartered in New York City. Later that year they bought CF Church (toilet seats).

During the next 3 decades the company expanded its operations across North and South America and into Europe. By the 1960s American Radiator & Standard Sanitary was the largest manufacturer of plumbing fixtures in the world.

In 1967 the company changed its name to American Standard, then diversified beyond the bathroom, acquiring a number of companies, the most important of which was Westinghouse Air Brake (WABCO, 1968).

WABCO traces its history to Union Switch and Signal, begun in 1882. In 1917 Union Switch was acquired by Westinghouse Air Brake. George Westinghouse had invented the air brake before turning his attention to electricity. Union Switch merged with its parent company and adopted the WABCO name in 1951.

During the 1970s and 1980s American Standard consolidated its operations and sold off numerous businesses that were outside its traditional product line. It purchased Clayton Dewandre (truck brake manufacturing, 1977) and Queroy (faucets and fittings, 1982). In 1984 the company purchased Trane (air conditioners).

In 1988 American Standard fought off a hostile takeover attempt by Black & Decker. The company agreed to be purchased by ASI Holding Corporation (formed by the leveraged buyout firm Kelso & Company) for $3 billion and taken private. ASI acquired 95% of common stock.

The transaction left American Standard deeply in debt. The resulting increase in interest expense led to losses in 1988 and 1989. To raise cash the company sold its Manhattan headquarters in 1988 and sold its Steelcraft division (doors and windows) to Masco for $100 million in cash in 1989. In 1990 the company sold its railway brake products operations to a group led by Investment AB Cardo (Sweden) for $250 million.

HOW MUCH

	9 Yr. Growth	1980	1981	1982	1983	1984	1985	1986	1987	1988	1989
Sales ($ mil)	2.5%	2,674	2,471	2,125	2,182	3,215	2,912	2,998	3,400	3,716	3,334
Net income ($ mil)	—	157	111	36	63	117	(3)	110	133	(26)	(34)
Income as % of sales	—	5.9%	4.5%	1.7%	2.9%	3.6%	(0.1%)	3.7%	3.9%	(0.7%)	(1.0%)

1989 Year End:
Debt ratio: 97.9%
Return on equity: —
Cash (mil): $57
Current ratio: 1.57
Long-term debt (mil): $2,117

Net Income ($ mil) 1980-89

Private company
Incorporated: Delaware, 1929
Fiscal year ends: December 31

WHO

President and CEO: Emmanuel A. Kampouris, age 55, $981,667 pay
Chairman: William A. Marquard, age 70, $366,667 pay
SVP Transportation Products: Nicolas M. Georgitsis, age 55, $680,833 pay
Auditors: Ernst & Young
Employees: 33,300

WHERE

HQ: 1114 Ave. of the Americas, New York, NY 10036
Phone: 212-703-5100
FAX: 212-703-5177 (Main Office)

The company operates in 26 countries.

	1989 Sales		1989 Operating Income	
	$ mil	% of total	$ mil	% of total
US	1,774	52	94	30
Europe	1,209	36	175	56
Other	413	12	42	14
Adjustments	(62)	—	(32)	—
Total	**3,334**	**100**	**279**	**100**

WHAT

	1989 Sales		1989 Operating Income	
	$ mil	% of total	$ mil	% of total
Plumbing products	947	28	95	31
Transportation prods.	602	18	92	30
Air conditioning products	1,785	54	124	39
Adjustments	—	—	(32)	—
Total	**3,334**	**100**	**279**	**100**

Products

Plumbing
Acrylic tubs
Fittings
Fixtures
Vitreous china

Transportation
Braking systems
Heavy vehicle components

Air Conditioning
Air-handling products
Applied air conditioning systems
Commercial air conditioning products
Gas furnaces
Refrigerated display cases
Residential air conditioners

Brand Names

Plumbing
American-Standard
Ideal-Standard
Standard

Transportation
Clayton Dewandre
WABCO

Air Conditioning
American-Standard
Trane
Tyler

RANKINGS

26th in *Forbes* 400 US Private Cos.

COMPETITION

Allied-Signal
Black & Decker
Eaton
Electrolux
Masco
United Technologies

AMERICAN STORES COMPANY

OVERVIEW

American Stores, based in Salt Lake City, is the largest food retailer in the US and ranks 4th among all US retailers. It is the only company to have a major presence in both grocery and drugstore retailing.

Acquisitions have fueled the growth of American Stores. As a result the company operates stores under a variety of familiar names: Acme in the mid-Atlantic states, Jewel in the Midwest, Jewel Osco in Florida, Buttrey in Montana and surrounding states, Skaggs Alpha Beta in Texas and neighboring states, Alpha Beta in California, Sav-on mainly in California and Nevada, and Osco nearly everywhere. The company is currently engaged in a modernization effort. This program included the sale or closing of 87 unprofitable locations and the opening of 64 new stores in 1989.

The founding Skaggs family continues to play an important role in the development of American Stores. Community involvement tends to be focused at the local level; for example, the California stores raised $1.2 million to benefit earthquake victims in 1989.

WHEN

Leonard S. Skaggs, one of 6 sons of Safeway founder Marion Skaggs, bought Pay Less Drug Stores in Salt Lake City in 1939 with the proceeds from the sale of Safeway stock. Leonard Skaggs, Jr., the current chairman, took over after his father's death in 1950. In 1965, when the business had grown to 69 locations, it incorporated as Skaggs Drug Centers and sold stock to the public. In 1969 the company formed a joint venture with Albertson's, which operated grocery stores in several western states, to develop food/drug combination stores under the name Skaggs Albertsons.

Skaggs merged in 1979 with a larger company, American Stores of Philadelphia. American Stores had been formed in 1917 by the combination of 5 grocers, including Acme Tea company (founded 1885), and operated stores throughout the mid-Atlantic states. Skaggs then changed its name to American Stores and continued to operate as a holding company, with stores under the Acme, Skaggs, and other local names. In 1977 Skaggs and Albertson's dissolved their joint venture, with each receiving 1/2 of the jointly owned locations. After acquiring American Stores, which had owned the Alpha Beta stores in Southern California since the 1940s, the company renamed its 1/2 of the joint-venture stores Skaggs Alpha Beta.

American Stores sold the assets of its Alphy's Restaurants division to Denny's in 1983 and the next year sold several of its Arizona Alpha Beta food stores and Houston Sav-on drug stores, as well as another drug chain, Rea & Derick. Also in 1984 American acquired Chicago-based Jewel Companies. Jewel, originally the Jewel Tea Company, had begun in Chicago in 1899 as a route-delivery grocery operation in the pre-automobile days and had opened grocery stores in the 1930s. It operated stores under the names of Jewel in the Chicago area, Jewel Osco in Florida, Star Market in Massachusetts, Buttrey's in Montana and nearby states, and Osco Drug.

American Stores bought Lucky Stores, a major California-based chain, in 1988, bringing the company's total number of stores in that state to 710. A court order prevented the company from integrating the Southern California store operations of Lucky Stores and Alpha Beta on antitrust grounds. American Stores appealed, arguing that the California attorney general didn't have the authority to prevent the merger, but the US Supreme Court ruled in 1990 against the company.

Jonathan Scott, formerly president of A&P and Albertson's (and former son-in-law of Joe Albertson), became CEO of American Stores in 1989.

In 1990 the company agreed to sell its Buttrey Food & Drug stores for $184 million and announced that it intends to sell Alpha Beta.

HOW MUCH

	9 Yr. Growth	1980	1981	1982	1983	1984	1985	1986	1987	1988	1989
Sales ($ mil)	14.7%	6,420	7,097	7,508	7,984	12,119	13,890	14,021	14,272	18,478	22,004
Net income ($ mil)	9.7%	52	65	90	118	186	154	145	154	98	118
Income as % of sales	—	0.8%	0.9%	1.2%	1.5%	1.5%	1.1%	1.0%	1.1%	0.5%	0.5%
Earnings per share ($)	10.6%	1.37	1.81	2.69	3.61	5.71	4.11	3.79	4.19	2.51	3.40
Stock price – high ($)	—	10.17	9.92	23.33	44.00	41.13	68.25	71.25	86.25	66.50	72.50
Stock price – low ($)	—	6.71	6.92	8.42	19.25	26.50	38.75	51.63	41.50	47.63	53.00
Stock price – close ($)	25.9%	7.13	9.83	21.67	39.63	40.00	64.75	54.38	50.50	57.88	56.50
P/E – high	—	7	5	9	12	7	17	19	21	27	21
P/E – low	—	5	4	3	5	5	9	14	10	19	16
Dividends per share ($)	15.8%	0.27	0.27	0.33	0.44	0.64	0.69	0.84	0.84	0.93	1.00
Book value per share ($)	17.3%	8.28	9.80	12.15	15.26	21.40	24.44	26.96	29.38	30.51	34.86

1989 Year End:
Debt ratio: 73.9%
Return on equity: 10.4%
Cash (mil): $87
Current ratio: 1.01
Long-term debt (mil): $3,399
Number of shares (mil): 34
Dividends:
1989 average yield: 1.8%
1989 payout: 29.4%
Market value (mil): $1,948

Stock Price History high/low 1980-89

90
80
70
60
50
40
30
20
10
0

NYSE symbol: ASC
Incorporated: Delaware, 1965
Fiscal year ends: Saturday closest to January 31

WHO

Chairman: L. S. Skaggs, age 66, $914,642 pay
CEO: Jonathan L. Scott, age 60, $1,076,283 pay
President and COO: Alan D. Stewart, age 47, $618,295 pay
SVP Finance: Teresa Beck, age 35
Auditors: Ernst & Young
Employees: 170,400

WHERE

HQ: 5201 W. Amelia Earhart Dr., Salt Lake City, UT 84116
Phone: 801-539-0112
FAX: 801-531-0768 (Shareholder Relations)

The company operates 1,894 stores in 40 states.

WHAT

	1989 Stores
Alpha Beta	
Alpha Beta (Los Angeles) California	175
American Drug Stores	
Osco Drug (Chicago) 26 states	498
Sav-on (Chicago) California, Nevada, Utah	174
American Food and Drug	
Buttrey Food-Drug (Great Falls, MT) Idaho, Montana, North Dakota, Utah, Washington, Wyoming	48
Jewel Osco (Tampa, FL) Florida	3
Skaggs Alpha Beta (Dallas) Arkansas, New Mexico, Oklahoma, Texas	72
American Superstores	
Acme Markets (Philadelphia) Delaware, Maryland, New Jersey, New York, Pennsylvania, Virginia, West Virginia	285
Jewel Food Stores (Chicago) Illinois, Indiana, Iowa, Michigan	216
Star Market (Boston) Massachusetts, Rhode Island	33
Lucky Stores	
Lucky (Oakland) California, Nevada	390
Total	**1,894**

RANKINGS

4th in *Fortune* 50 Retailing Cos.
20th in *Forbes* Sales 500
289th in *Business Week* 1000
839th in *Business Week* Global 1000

COMPETITION

Albertson's
Campeau
Food Lion
Giant Food
Great A&P
Jack Eckerd
Kroger
Longs
Melville
Safeway
Stop & Shop
Supermarkets General
Vons
Walgreen

AMERICAN TELEPHONE & TELEGRAPH COMPANY

OVERVIEW

The kids may have left home, but Ma Bell is far from being an "empty nest" victim. She — AT&T — is not only the largest US telecommunications company, but also the largest US service company of any kind.

Most of AT&T's revenue (54%) comes from long-distance service, and AT&T retains about 70% of that market. AT&T has begun offering a combination credit card/calling card, and response has far exceeded company expectations.

Since the 1984 breakup of the Bell system, in which AT&T was separated from the local telephone operating companies, AT&T has reshuffled to compete. Chairman Robert Allen has cut levels of management, eliminated jobs, and divided the company into 19 operations.

In the computer arena, AT&T has scored successes by selling custom computer networks. The company also markets its increasingly popular UNIX operating system.

NYSE symbol: T
Incorporated: New York, 1885
Fiscal year ends: December 31

WHO

Chairman and CEO: Robert E. Allen, age 55, $1,743,700 pay
VC: Randall L. Tobias, age 47, $1,000,800 pay
VC and CFO: Morris Tanenbaum, age 61, $963,800 pay
Auditors: Coopers & Lybrand
Employees: 283,500

WHEN

"Mr. Watson. Come here. I want you."

Alexander Graham Bell's legendary summons, the first words on a telephone, came as he was perfecting his invention in 1876. As demand for the new device spread, Bell's backers, fathers of deaf students he was tutoring, organized Bell Telephone (1877) and New England Telephone (1878). The companies attracted funding from Boston financiers and were consolidated as National Bell Telephone in 1879.

After several years of litigation, National Bell barred rival Western Union from the telephone business in 1879. Western Union had tried to market Elisha Gray's competing patent, filed just hours after Bell's. By 1882 the Bell company had prospered enough to wrest control of Western Electric, the nation's largest electrical equipment manufacturer, from Western Union. Western Electric, founded in 1869 by Enos Barton and the same Elisha Gray from the patent fight, became prime manufacturer of Bell equipment.

Bell's patents expired in the 1890s, and independent phone companies raced into the market. Bell struggled to compete. After changing its name to American Telephone and Telegraph and relocating the headquarters from Boston to New York in 1899, AT&T shifted focus to swallowing smaller companies. AT&T also blocked independents from access to Bell System phone lines.

Banker J. P. Morgan and his allies gained control of AT&T and installed Theodore Vail as president in 1907. AT&T won control of Western Union in 1909. After complaints by independent phone companies, the Wilson administration threatened antitrust action against AT&T. In the 1913 Kingsbury Commitment, AT&T promised the government it would sell Western Union, buy no more independent phone companies without regulatory approval, and grant independents access to AT&T networks.

Bell Labs, the heralded research and development arm of AT&T, was formed in 1925. Bell Labs would later sponsor research that would win the Nobel Prize for invention of the transistor (1956), develop the first communications satellite (1961), and receive more than 25,000 patents.

In 1949 the Justice Department sued to force AT&T to sell Western Electric. The 1956 settlement allowed AT&T to keep Western Electric but prohibited it from entering nonregulated businesses. Federal Communications Commission rulings stripped AT&T of its monopoly on telephone equipment (1968) and permitted specialized carriers, such as MCI, to hook microwave-based communications to the phone network (1969), injecting competition into the long-distance arena.

The government's 1974 decision to sue to force the sale of AT&T's regional networks led to the 1982 settlement that, in 1984, spun off the 7 regional holding companies. AT&T kept the long-distance business, Western Electric, and Bell Labs.

WHERE

HQ: 550 Madison Ave., New York, NY 10022
Phone: 212-605-5500
FAX: 212-308-1820 (Communications Dept.)

AT&T markets its telecommunications services and products worldwide.

WHAT

	1989 Sales	
	$ mil	% of total
Telecommunications services	34,390	68
Business, data, & consumer products	7,638	15
Telecommunications network systems	6,782	13
Other	2,166	4
Total	**50,976**	**100**

Business Units

AT&T American Transtech (shareholder, employee services)
AT&T Computer Systems (PCs, minis)
AT&T Credit Corp. (leasing, financing)
AT&T Microelectronics (electronic components)
AT&T Paradyne (data communication)
Business Communications Services (custom long-distance services)
Business Communications Systems (larger systems)
Cellular Systems (telephone networks)
Consumer Communications Services (basic long distance)
Consumer Products (telephones, answering systems)
Federal Systems Advanced Technologies (US government)
General Business Systems (smaller systems)
International Communications Services (international long distance)
Network Cable Systems (fiber optic, cable)
Operations Systems (software and hardware support for networking)
Switching Systems (switching machines, software)
Synchronous Terminal Products (mainframe terminals and controllers)
Transmission Systems (communications systems)
UNIX Software Operation (operating software)

RANKINGS

1st in *Fortune* 100 Diversified Service Cos.
10th in *Forbes* Sales 500
4th in *Business Week* 1000
13th in *Business Week* Global 1000

COMPETITION

BCE	MCI
Fujitsu	NEC
GTE	Siemens
Hitachi	United Telecommunications
IBM	Computer manufacturers

HOW MUCH

	9 Yr. Growth	1980	1981	1982	1983	1984	1985	1986	1987	1988	1989
Sales ($ mil)	0.0%	50,791	58,214	65,093	69,403	53,821	56,431	53,680	51,209	51,974	50,976
Net income ($ mil)	(8.6%)	6,080	6,888	6,992	5,747	1,370	1,557	314	2,044	(1,669)	2,697
Income as % of sales	—	12.0%	11.8%	10.7%	8.3%	2.5%	2.8%	0.6%	4.0%	(3.2%)	5.3%
Earnings per share ($)	(12.4%)	8.19	8.55	8.06	6.00	1.25	1.37	0.21	1.88	(1.55)	2.50
Stock price – high ($)	—	56.13	61.50	64.63	70.25	20.25	27.88	27.88	35.88	30.38	47.38
Stock price – low ($)	—	45.00	47.50	49.88	59.00	14.88	19.00	20.50	22.25	24.13	28.13
Stock price – close ($)	(0.6%)	47.88	58.75	59.38	61.50	19.50	25.00	25.00	27.00	28.75	45.50
P/E – high	—	7	7	8	12	16	20	133	19	—	19
P/E – low	—	6	6	6	10	12	14	98	12	—	11
Dividends per share ($)	(14.7%)	5.00	5.40	5.40	5.85	1.20	1.20	1.20	1.20	1.20	1.20
Book value per share ($)	(17.3%)	65.51	67.52	69.07	62.92	13.26	13.68	12.64	13.46	10.68	11.84

1989 Year End:
Debt ratio: 39.0%
Return on equity: 22.2%
Cash (mil): $1,183
Current ratio: 1.25
Long-term debt (mil): $8,144
Number of shares (mil): 1,076
Dividends:
1989 average yield: 2.6%
1989 payout: 48.0%
Market value (mil): $48,949

Stock Price History high/low 1980-89

AMES DEPARTMENT STORES, INC.

OVERVIEW

Ames Department Stores operates 458 Ames stores (general merchandise discount stores), down from 690 stores in January 1990, and 15 Crafts & More stores (hobby and home crafts). The company also distributes wholesale sporting goods. Traditionally located in small towns in rural areas and now also in metropolitan areas, Ames stores mainly serve middle- to lower-income customers.

Ames was reasonably profitable until it acquired money-losing Zayre in October 1988 in a controversial transaction that split the board. The turnaround effort proved too much for Ames, causing massive losses in 1989. Ames filed for Chapter 11 bankruptcy in April 1990, and has since brought in new management and aggressively lowered costs by closing stores.

WHEN

Ames Department Stores began in 1958 in the former Ames Worsted Textile Company building in Southbridge, Massachusetts. Mortgaging the family farm for $30,000, founders Milton and Irving Gilman believed that discount retail stores would succeed in small towns. Ames produced $1 million in sales the first year.

The Gilmans, with brother Herb, opened additional stores in abandoned factory buildings in upstate New York and northern Vermont (1960). The company went public (1962), and by 1970 there were 23 Ames stores, with $50 million in sales.

In the 1970s and 1980s the company built new stores and bought other chains in the Northeast. As established retailers closed (*e.g.*,W.T. Grant), Ames moved in. Acquisitions included Joseph Leavitt and K&R Warehouse (1972), Davis Wholesale (1978), 23 Neisner Brothers' stores (1978), 42 King's stores (1984), 372 G.C. Murphy's stores (1985), and the Zayre Discount Division of Zayre Corporation (now TJX Companies), with 392 stores for $800 million (1988). Ames also opened the Crafts & More stores (1988).

As the Gilmans retired (Milton and Irving in 1981 and Herb in 1987), nonfamily members assumed company leadership. Peter Hollis, a former executive of Zayre (1969 to 1982), became president (1986) and CEO (1987) of Ames until resigning in April 1990.

Although the company initially closed 74 Zayre stores, conversion of the remaining stores to Ames's format was costly and slow. In addition, sales decreased at the converted Zayre stores, which lost traditional customers when management changed marketing strategy from periodic sales to an "everyday low prices" policy.

The company attempted to raise capital, completing an agreement in May 1989 with J. Baker to become the shoe licensee in the Zayre stores, raising $60 million. In September 1989 Ames sold 130 G.C. Murphy stores and 25 Bargain World stores to E-II Holdings, a subsidiary of the Riklis Family Corporation, for $77.6 million. The sale of convertible bonds in October 1989 raised an additional $155 million.

Efforts to trim costs included corporate restructuring (consolidation of merchandising and advertising of Zayre and Ames stores) and store closings (6 Office Shop Warehouse stores in December 1989). As the company's cash flow decreased, unpaid vendors refused to ship new merchandise in early 1990. Consequently, on April 25, 1990, Ames filed for Chapter 11 bankruptcy. Steven Pistner, former chief of Dayton Hudson's Target division and of Montgomery Ward, was hired as CEO in April 1990.

The company has since obtained $250 million in interim financing from Chemical Bank. In June 1990 Ames also announced closings of 221 stores (37 Ames and 184 former Zayre stores, with a total operating loss of $47.5 million in 1989) and 2 distribution centers and layoffs of 18,000 employees, mostly in Illinois, Indiana, Ohio, North Carolina, and Florida.

HOW MUCH

	9 Yr. Growth	1980	1981	1982	1983	1984	1985	1986	1987	1988	1989
Sales ($ mil)	35.7%	307	353	402	617	783	1,449	1,810	2,027	3,271	4,793
Net income ($ mil)	—	9	10	12	20	29	40	27	33	47	(220)
Income as % of sales	—	2.8%	2.8%	3.1%	3.2%	3.6%	2.8%	1.5%	1.6%	1.4%	(4.6%)
Earnings per share ($)	—	0.38	0.47	0.50	0.77	1.00	1.19	0.73	0.88	1.20	*(6.19)*
Stock price – high ($)	—	2.26	3.88	6.13	13.22	15.25	26.88	34.63	29.75	18.75	20.00
Stock price – low ($)	—	1.42	2.04	3.33	5.29	8.50	12.25	19.25	7.50	10.50	8.75
Stock price – close ($)	19.9%	2.03	3.48	5.58	11.88	13.44	25.38	23.63	10.38	14.00	10.38
P/E – high	—	6	8	12	17	15	23	47	34	16	—
P/E – low	—	4	4	7	7	9	10	26	9	9	—
Dividends per share ($)	8.0%	0.05	0.07	0.07	0.07	0.10	0.10	0.10	0.10	0.10	0.10
Book value per share ($)	11.6%	2.09	2.50	3.08	3.80	4.75	9.87	10.51	11.34	12.43	5.65

1989 Year End:
Debt ratio: 30.4%
Return on equity: —
Cash (mil): $37
Current ratio: 0.77
Long-term debt (mil): $156
Number of shares (mil): 38
Dividends:
1989 average yield: 1.0%
1989 payout: —
Market value (mil): $390

NYSE symbol: ADD
Incorporated: Delaware, 1962
Fiscal year ends: Last Saturday in January

WHO

Chairman: James A. Harmon, age 54
CEO: Steven L. Pistner, age 58
President and COO: George M. Granoff, age 43
EVP and CFO: Peter Thorner, age 46
EVP, Merchandising: Gerald L. Kanter, age 55
EVP, Stores: Jack E. Bush, age 55
Auditors: Coopers & Lybrand
Employees: 55,000 (before anticipated reductions)

WHERE

HQ: 2418 Main St., Rocky Hill, CT 06067
Phone: 203-563-8234
FAX: 203-257-7806 (Investor and Public Relations)

Ames operates 458 Ames discount stores in 17 eastern, southern, and midwestern states and in Washington, DC; 15 Crafts & More stores in 8 states; and a wholesale sporting goods company.

	Announced Fall 1990	
State	Ames discount stores	Crafts & More stores
Connecticut	18	1
Delaware	10	—
Dist. of Columbia	1	—
Indiana	15	—
Kentucky	2	—
Maine	29	1
Maryland	41	1
Massachusetts	42	—
Michigan	13	—
New Hampshire	23	—
New Jersey	8	—
New York	91	—
North Carolina	—	2
Ohio	38	2
Pennsylvania	61	2
Rhode Island	7	—
South Carolina	—	2
Vermont	13	—
Virginia	30	4
West Virginia	16	—
Total	**458**	**15**

WHAT

	Fall 1990	Jan. 27, 1990	Jan. 28,1989
Ames stores	458	690	678
Crafts & More	15	15	5
G.C. Murphy	—	—	135
Bargain World	—	—	25
Office Shop Warehouse	—	—	6
Total Stores	**473**	**705**	**849**

Other Companies
Mathews & Boucher (wholesale sporting goods)

RANKINGS

28th in *Fortune* 50 Retailing Cos.
166th in *Forbes* Sales 500

COMPETITION

Dayton Hudson
K mart
Price Co.
Riklis Family
Sears
Stop & Shop
Wal-Mart
Woolworth
Department and specialty stores

AMOCO CORPORATION

OVERVIEW

Chicago-based Amoco is the 2nd largest US natural gas producer, 7th largest US crude oil producer, 8th largest world petroleum company, and 9th largest US chemical exporter. Its 3 principal businesses are petroleum refining and marketing, oil and gas exploration and production, and chemical manufacturing. Amoco meets half of its crude and natural gas needs from domestic reserves, the remainder from its operations in over 40 countries.

The company's symbol, the familiar torch on a red, white, and blue oval background, accompanies Amoco's fuel and oil brand names: American, Amoco, Standard (in the Midwest), LDO, and Permalube. The company sells batteries and tires under the Atlas name. It also manufactures chemicals used in polyester fibers, plastics, and synthetic rubber.

WHEN

John D. Rockefeller organized the Standard Oil Trust in 1882. In 1886 he risked buying Lima (Ohio) crude oil and storing it, believing someone would develop a process to remove the sulphur from this high-sulphur crude ("skunk oil"). In 1889 Standard Oil organized Standard Oil of Indiana (Chicago) as its upper midwestern subsidiary, turning over its new Whiting, Indiana, refinery to the subsidiary. In 1887 Herman Frasch (chemist) patented a copper oxide process that removed sulphur from crude. Certain that the process would work on a commercial scale, Frasch persuaded the company to try it on the Lima crude, a success that assured Standard Oil (Indiana) a continued oil supply.

Standard (Indiana) built a strong retail marketing organization, including company-owned service stations, and set up a research laboratory at the refinery, both innovations in the industry. Research led to the patent (1913) of the (William) Burton process, producing gasoline from crude oil using high heat and pressure.

In 1911 the Supreme Court ordered Standard Oil to split up because of antitrust violations, creating 33 new independent oil companies. The decision left Standard (Indiana) with only 2 operations, oil refining and domestic marketing, and its exclusive right to the Standard name in the Midwest. The company purchased its crude oil and transportation from Prairie Oil & Gas and Prairie Pipe Line.

In 1917 Standard (Indiana) began buying crude oil production companies. In 1925 the company purchased a controlling interest (81% by 1929) in Pan American Petroleum and Transport, one of the world's largest crude producers, with production facilities in Mexico and Venezuela. In 1923 Pan American bought a 50% interest in American Oil, founded in 1922 by Louis Blaustein, who introduced the first antiknock gasoline, which he marketed under the name Amoco gas. Standard (Indiana), recognizing the additional value of oil converted to chemicals, began Amoco Chemicals in 1945.

In 1956 the company purchased Utah Oil Refining along with other refineries in the 1950s and 1960s. The supertanker Amoco Cadiz ran aground off the French coast in 1978, spilling 120,000 tons of oil (6 times more than the 1989 Exxon Valdez oil spill off the Alaskan coast), resulting in a $141 million settlement against the company in 1989. Standard (Indiana) bought Cyprus Mines (copper and industrial minerals) in 1979. The company exited the industrial minerals, metals, and coal businesses by spinning off the assets of Amoco Minerals (including Cyprus Mines) as Cyprus Minerals in 1985.

Standard (Indiana) changed its name to Amoco in 1985. In 1988 Amoco bought debt-ridden but resource-rich Dome Petroleum of Canada. In 1990 the company sold its life insurance operation.

HOW MUCH

	9 Yr. Growth	1980	1981	1982	1983	1984	1985	1986	1987	1988	1989
Sales ($ mil)	(1.0%)	26,133	29,947	28,073	27,635	26,949	26,922	18,281	20,174	21,150	23,966
Net income ($ mil)	(1.9%)	1,915	1,922	1,826	1,868	2,183	1,953	747	1,360	2,063	1,610
Income as % of sales	—	7.3%	6.4%	6.5%	6.8%	8.1%	7.3%	4.1%	6.7%	9.8%	6.7%
Earnings per share ($)	(0.5%)	3.27	3.28	3.13	3.20	3.85	3.71	1.46	2.66	4.00	3.12
Stock price – high ($)	—	49.75	40.00	28.13	27.50	30.31	35.13	36.06	45.13	40.13	55.75
Stock price – low ($)	—	19.00	23.63	16.75	19.13	24.06	25.13	26.56	28.50	33.81	36.81
Stock price – close ($)	3.5%	39.94	26.00	19.88	25.38	26.44	30.94	32.63	34.50	37.50	54.63
P/E – high	—	15	12	9	9	8	9	25	17	10	18
P/E – low	—	6	7	5	6	6	7	18	11	8	12
Dividends per share ($)	7.4%	1.00	1.30	1.40	1.40	1.50	1.65	1.65	1.65	1.75	1.90
Book value per share ($)	5.8%	16.05	18.06	19.55	21.29	23.07	22.39	22.14	23.50	25.80	26.75

1989 Year End:
Debt ratio: 29.3%
Return on equity: 11.9%
Cash (mil): $1,180
Current ratio: 1.09
Long-term debt (mil): $5,658
Number of shares (mil): 512
Dividends:
1989 average yield: 3.5%
1989 payout: 60.9%
Market value (mil): $27,942

Stock Price History high/low 1980-89

60 50 40 30 20 10 0

NYSE symbol: AN
Incorporated: Indiana, 1889
Fiscal year ends: December 31

WHO

Chairman and CEO: Richard M. Morrow, age 64, $1,558,627 pay
President: H. Laurance Fuller, age 51, $1,057,518 pay
EVP: Richard H. Leet, age 63, $716,476 pay
EVP: Lawrason D. Thomas, age 55, $630,699 pay
EVP and CFO: Frederick S. Addy, age 58
Auditors: Price Waterhouse
Employees: 53,653

WHERE

HQ: 200 E. Randolph Dr., Chicago, IL 60601
Phone: 312-856-6111
FAX: 312-856-2460 (Amoco FAX center)

Amoco sells gasoline through about 10,000 stations, primarily in the Midwest, East, and Southeast. It operates 60 chemical plants in 13 countries, and 8 refineries, including Texas City, TX; Whiting, IN; Mandan, ND; Yorktown, VA; Casper, WY; Salt Lake City, UT; Savannah, GA; and Milford Haven, Wales.

	1989 Sales		1989 Operating Income	
	$ mil	% of total	$ mil	% of total
US	19,724	73	2,308	67
Canada	2,541	10	225	7
Europe	2,000	8	244	7
Other foreign	2,279	9	667	19
Adjustments	(2,578)	—	(434)	—
Total	**23,966**	**100**	**3,010**	**100**

WHAT

	1989 Sales		1989 Operating Income	
	$ mil	% of total	$ mil	% of total
Chemicals	4,274	16	744	22
Exploration & production	3,399	13	1,695	49
Refining, mktg. & transportation	18,736	70	1,080	31
Other	135	1	(75)	(2)
Adjustments	(2,578)	—	(434)	—
Total	**23,966**	**100**	**3,010**	**100**

Lines of Business
Chemical manufacturing
Marketing of refined products and chemicals
Oil and gas exploration and production
Petroleum refining
Transportation of refined products

RANKINGS

12th in *Fortune* 500 Industrial Cos.
34th in *Fortune* Global 500 Industrial Cos.
45th in *Fortune* 50 Exporters
18th in *Forbes* Sales 500
9th in *Business Week* 1000
30th in *Business Week* Global 1000

COMPETITION

Ashland	Du Pont	Royal Dutch/Shell
Atlantic Richfield	Exxon	Sun
BASF	Mobil	Texaco
British Petroleum	Occidental	Union Texas
Chevron	Pennzoil	Unocal
Coastal	Phillips	USX

AMP INC.

OVERVIEW

AMP of Harrisburg, Pennsylvania, is the world's largest supplier of electrical and electronic connectors. It supplies more than 50,000 electrical and electronic equipment manufacturers with over 100,000 different types and sizes of terminals, splices, and connectors, as well as cable and panel assemblies, switches, and touch-screen data entry systems. *Fortune* called AMP one of the companies that competes the best in the highly competitive electrical/electronic connector market. AMP customers include Nissan, Honda, and Toyota.

AMP holds 10,000 patents worldwide and adds dozens more each year. The company spends a relatively large amount on R&D (9% of sales annually), which includes research for companies such as IBM and Digital Equipment. Almost 4,000 scientists and engineers work closely with manufacturers at every stage of product development. In the future AMP will incorporate fiber-optics devices, laser technology, and microminiaturized electronics into its product line.

WHEN

U. A. Whitaker founded Aircraft-Marine Products of Elizabeth, New Jersey, in 1941, just 2 months before the attack on Pearl Harbor. As a manufacturer of parts for aircraft, ships, and radios, AMP grew rapidly during WWII. In 1943 the company moved to Harrisburg, Pennsylvania. A preinsulated electrical terminal and a special crimping tool invented in 1943 would later become AMP's mainstay.

The company nearly failed in its transition to a peacetime economy, with profits dropping sharply in 1946. Focusing on commercial markets, primarily for its electrical terminal, the company was doing well again by the 1950s. In 1956 the company went public, shortening its name to AMP (pronounced as a single word).

AMP began international expansion in the 1950s, forming 10 subsidiaries in other countries, including Canada, Japan, France, and West Germany. AMP's success is partially attributed to a policy of rapidly building plants wherever it had a market for its products, using local labor even for top management, and carefully adapting to foreign requirements. When Fiat needed electrical connectors for its cars, the company built a plant in Italy in 1959. AMP entered the ranks of the *Fortune* 500 in 1966 with sales of $142 million.

In the 1970s and 1980s AMP developed new connecting devices for manufacturers of computers, telecommunications equipment, and home entertainment systems. AMP's electrical components were used in the high-speed French TGV railroad and the Washington Metro.

Expanding production in the early 1980s resulted in an excess of capacity, causing an earnings drop after the 1982 economic slowdown. The company invested in plant modernization in the mid-1980s and in the last 5 years has saved an estimated $60 million through additional quality-control measures.

AMP spent $100 million in the 1980s developing fiber-optics technology and now has several high-speed fiber-optics devices on the market. It also introduced new cable and data communication connectors, now standard on local area networks such as Ethernet and IBM's Token Ring. New products in the late 1980s were AMP's "smart" connectors — linking voice and data communications equipment — and undercarpet flat cables for offices.

Expansion into the Far East continued in 1987 with the opening of plants in Taiwan, South Korea, and Singapore. AMP has avoided diversification and has grown instead by inventing new devices. The company has recently entered several new connector markets through acquisitions (including Matrix Science, 1988; Garry Screw Machine, 1989; and Decolletage S.A. St-Maurice, 1989) and through a joint venture with Akzo (1990).

HOW MUCH

	9 Yr. Growth	1980	1981	1982	1983	1984	1985	1986	1987	1988	1989
Sales ($ mil)	10.3%	1,155	1,234	1,243	1,515	1,813	1,636	1,933	2,318	2,670	2,797
Net income ($ mil)	8.8%	131	135	119	163	201	108	164	250	319	281
Income as % of sales	—	11.4%	10.9%	9.6%	10.8%	11.1%	6.6%	8.5%	10.8%	12.0%	10.0%
Earnings per share ($)	8.9%	1.22	1.25	1.10	1.52	1.87	1.00	1.52	2.31	2.96	2.63
Stock price – high ($)	—	18.75	20.83	23.50	39.00	39.50	37.88	45.00	71.50	54.25	49.38
Stock price – low ($)	—	11.00	14.50	15.17	22.00	26.13	27.50	32.88	34.13	40.50	40.00
Stock price – close ($)	11.1%	17.29	16.96	22.71	38.13	33.38	36.00	36.13	46.75	44.50	44.50
P/E – high	—	15	17	21	26	21	38	30	31	18	19
P/E – low	—	9	12	14	15	14	28	22	15	14	15
Dividends per share ($)	15.3%	0.33	0.40	0.47	0.53	0.64	0.72	0.74	0.85	1.00	1.20
Book value per share ($)	12.3%	5.35	6.13	6.64	7.45	8.57	9.23	10.50	12.54	14.16	15.27

1989 Year End:
Debt ratio: 4.1%
Return on equity: 17.9%
Cash (mil): $334
Current ratio: 1.98
Long-term debt (mil): $70
Number of shares (mil): 106
Dividends:
1989 average yield: 2.7%
1989 payout: 45.6%
Market value (mil): $4,738

Stock Price History high/low 1980-89

NYSE symbol: AMP
Incorporated: Pennsylvania, 1989
Fiscal year ends: December 31

WHO

Chairman and CEO: Harold A. McInnes, age 62, $470,481 pay
President and COO: James E. Marley, age 54, $433,747 pay
EVP and CFO: Benjamin Savidge, age 60, $298,214 pay
Auditors: Arthur Andersen & Co.
Employees: 24,400

WHERE

HQ: 470 Friendship Rd., Harrisburg, PA 17111
Phone: 717-564-0100
FAX: 717-986-7605

AMP has over 160 office, warehouse, distribution, and manufacturing facilities in 28 countries.

	1989 Sales		1989 Net Income	
	$ mil	% of total	$ mil	% of total
US	1,282	46	125	43
Europe	864	31	107	37
Asia/Pacific	507	18	46	16
Other Americas	144	5	11	4
Adjustments	—	—	(8)	—
Total	**2,797**	**100**	**281**	**100**

WHAT

Products
Electrical/electronic connection devices
Machines for applying connectors
Printed circuit boards
Screw machines
Tools for applying connectors

Business Units
Aerospace/Government Systems
Automotive/Consumer
Capital Goods

Sales Units
AMP NETCON Division
Distributor Marketing Division
Industrial Division
Information Systems Division

Affiliated Manufacturing Co.
Pamcor, Inc. (Puerto Rico)

US Subsidiaries
AMP Packaging Systems, Inc. (panel assemblies, Austin, TX)
AMP Products Corp. (Valley Forge, PA)
Carroll Touch, Inc. (touch screen systems, Austin, TX)
Garry Screw Machine Corp. (small metal parts, New Brunswick, NJ)
Lytel Inc. (optoelectronic devices, Somerville, NJ)
Mark Eyelet Inc. (sockets, Wolcott, CT)
Matrix Science Corp. (aerospace and military connectors, Torrance, CA)

Joint Venture
AMP/AKZO, N.V.

RANKINGS

160th in *Fortune* 500 Industrial Cos.
447th in *Fortune* Global 500 Industrial Cos.
299th in *Forbes* Sales 500
113th in *Business Week* 1000
323rd in *Business Week* Global 1000

COMPETITION

Hitachi
Square D

AMR CORPORATION

OVERVIEW

AMR is the parent company of American Airlines. In 1989 American became the largest US airline in terms of passenger miles flown (almost 74 billion), taking the lead position from United. AMR has the highest revenues of any airline in the world.

American added new service to Australia, New Zealand, and Scotland in 1990 and has applied to the DOT for authority to fly from Chicago to Tokyo. Final approval (Chicago-Tokyo) is not expected until November 1990, and American faces stiff opposition from United Airlines, which has applied for the same route authority.

More travel agencies utilize American's SABRE computer reservations system than any other system. American also administers the industry's oldest and largest frequent flyer program (AAdvantage).

American Eagle, the company's group of commuter airlines, flies to 161 cities in 27 states, the District of Columbia, and 15 Caribbean and Bahamian islands.

AMR operates subsidiaries that serve the airline and 3rd parties. These subsidiaries include ground handling, information processing, telemarketing, leasing, and investment management services.

WHEN

In 1929 Sherman Fairchild's Fairchild Aviation Corporation created a New York City holding company called The Aviation Corporation (AVCO). By 1930 AVCO owned about 30 small aviation companies, thereby establishing an unconnected coast-to-coast network. Hoping to consolidate this route structure, AVCO created American Airways in 1930.

In 1934 AVCO decided to sell its airline interests in order to pursue its manufacturing concerns. American Airlines was formed and, through an exchange of stock, bought the assets of American Airways. Former AVCO manager C. R. Smith became president.

American's rise to its position as America's #1 airline in the late 1930s was due mostly to Smith's management. In 1934 he and Donald Douglas began discussing the development of the Douglas DC-3. Introduced into service by American in 1936, the fast, comfortable DC-3 was the first commercial airliner to pay its way on passenger revenues alone. Emphasizing American's safety record, Smith hoped to dispel the public's fear of flying with his forthright "Afraid to Fly" advertisement in 1937.

After WWII, American bought American Export Airlines (renamed American Overseas Airlines), with flights to northern Europe, but sold this division to Pan Am in 1950. American introduced SABRE, an automated reservations system, in 1964.

Smith retired in 1968. American bought Trans Caribbean Airlines in 1971, gaining routes to the Caribbean. In 1977 Americana Hotels (American's hotel subsidiary, established 1963) bought the Howard Corporation's hotel properties and by 1978 operated 21 hotels and resorts in the US, Latin America, and Korea. American had sold all of its hotels by 1987, except the Inn of the Six Flags at Arlington, Texas.

In 1979 American moved its headquarters from New York to Dallas/Fort Worth. Credited with updating American's SABRE system, former CFO Bob Crandall became president in 1980. Using SABRE to keep track of mileage, Crandall introduced the industry's first frequent flyer program in 1975. In 1982 American adopted AMR Corporation as its corporate name.

After acquiring Nashville Eagle (commuter airline) in 1987, American established AMR Eagle to operate commuter services, buying 4 new commuters in 1988 and 1989.

In 1989 American weathered an unsolicited takeover bid by Donald Trump and, through an agreement with Texas Air (now Continental Airlines Holdings), bought its Eastern Air Lines Latin American routes later that year.

HOW MUCH

	9 Yr. Growth	1980	1981	1982	1983	1984	1985	1986	1987	1988	1989
Sales ($ mil)	11.9%	3,821	4,109	4,177	4,763	5,354	6,131	6,018	7,198	8,824	10,480
Net income ($ mil)	—	(152)	17	(20)	228	234	346	279	198	477	455
Income as % of sales	—	(4.0%)	0.4%	(0.5%)	4.8%	4.4%	5.6%	4.6%	2.8%	5.4%	4.3%
Earnings per share ($)	—	*(5.70)*	0.26	*(1.00)*	4.48	4.16	5.88	4.63	3.28	7.66	7.15
Stock price – high ($)	—	11.38	21.63	25.75	39.13	41.25	50.75	62.13	65.50	55.00	107.50
Stock price – low ($)	—	6.75	8.63	9.00	18.50	24.25	33.50	39.25	26.75	32.63	52.13
Stock price – close ($)	23.0%	9.00	11.00	24.75	36.13	36.13	41.38	53.63	35.25	53.63	58.00
P/E – high	—	—	83	—	9	10	9	13	20	7	15
P/E – low	—	—	33	—	4	6	6	8	8	4	7
Dividends per share ($)	—	0.10	0.00	0.00	0.00	0.00	0.00	0.00	0.00	0.00	0.00
Book value per share ($)	10.7%	24.22	25.42	22.45	26.87	31.23	37.17	42.30	45.58	53.54	60.54

1989 Year End:
Debt ratio: 38.0%
Return on equity: 12.5%
Cash (mil): $601
Current ratio: 0.6
Long-term debt (mil): $2,306
Number of shares (mil): 62
Dividends:
1989 average yield: 0.0%
1989 payout: 0.0%
Market value (mil): $3,608

Stock Price History high/low 1980-89

120
100
80
60
40
20
0

NYSE symbol: AMR
Incorporated: Delaware, 1982
Fiscal year ends: December 31

WHO

Chairman, President, and CEO: Robert L. Crandall, age 54, $1,066,666 pay
EVP and CFO: Donald J. Carty, age 43, $613,917 pay
Auditors: Ernst & Young
Employees: 89,000

WHERE

HQ: 4200 American Blvd., Fort Worth, TX 76155
Phone: 817-967-1234
FAX: 817-967-9641 (Investor Relations)

American serves 162 airports in 41 states, the District of Columbia, and 16 foreign countries.

Hub Locations

Chicago	Raleigh/Durham
Dallas/Fort Worth	San Jose
Miami	San Juan
Nashville	

	1989 Sales	
	$ mil	% of total
US & Canadian	9,117	87
Latin American	524	5
European	734	7
Pacific	105	1
Total	**10,480**	**100**

WHAT

	1989 Sales	
	$ mil	% of total
Passenger service	9,327	89
Freight operations	419	4
Corporate/other	734	7
Total	**10,480**	**100**

American Airlines, Inc.

AMR Eagle, Inc. (commuter services)

Command Airways, Inc.	Simmons Airlines, Inc.
Executive Airlines, Inc.	West Wings Airlines, Inc.
Nashville Eagle, Inc.	

Flight Equipment	Owned	Leased	Total
American Airlines			
Airbus A300	—	25	25
BAe 146	—	6	6
Boeing 727	124	40	164
Boeing 737	1	10	11
Boeing 747	2	—	2
Boeing 757	—	8	8
Boeing 767	17	28	45
DC-10	46	13	59
MD-80	90	90	180
Total	**280**	**220**	**500**

RANKINGS

2nd in *Fortune* 50 Transportation Cos.
65th in *Forbes* Sales 500
152nd in *Business Week* 1000
486th in *Business Week* Global 1000

COMPETITION

Alaska Air	KLM	Southwest
America West	Midway	TWA
Continental	NWA	UAL
Delta	Pan Am	USAir
HAL		

AMWAY CORPORATION

OVERVIEW

Amway, headquartered in Ada, Michigan, a suburb of Grand Rapids, is privately owned and operated by founders Richard DeVos and Jay Van Andel. Amway sells its products through direct sales representatives (called distributors), who earn commissions not only on products but also on sponsoring new distributors. In 1989 Amway had almost one million distributorships worldwide, in more than 40 countries and territories. The company is famous for its employee and distributor motivation programs and rallies.

Products include household and laundry cleaners such as Liquid Organic Cleaner (LOC); nutritional supplements such as Nutrilite vitamins; personal care products such as the Artistry cosmetics line; Queen cookware; educational books for children; and a number of services, including access to Amway's Ultimate legal and travel networks.

Since the company's start, Amway has been environmentally conscious; LOC was biodegradable when it was introduced in 1959. Many of Amway's products are concentrated, and the company sends its excess paper and plastic to recyclers. Amway scientists were among those attending the 1989 Symposium on Global Warming, held in Utah.

The company also owns 2 resorts and a radio network.

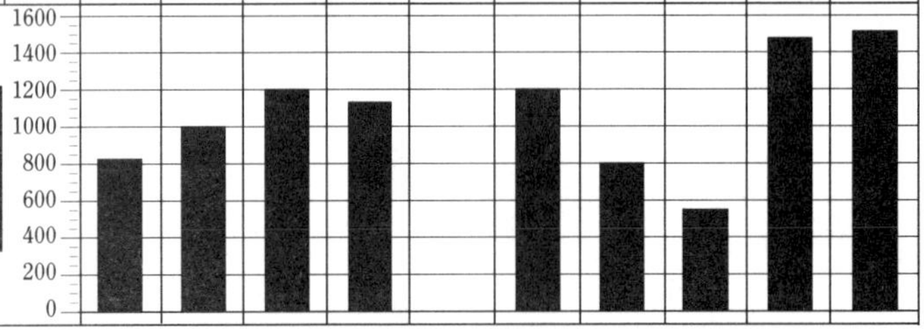

Private company
Founded: Michigan, 1959
Fiscal year ends: August 31

WHO

Chairman: Jay Van Andel
President: Richard M. DeVos
VP Finance: James Rosloniec
Employees: 7,000

WHERE

HQ: 7575 Fulton St. East, Ada, MI 49355
Phone: 616-676-6000
FAX: 616-676-5088

Amway operates in the following countries and regions:

Australia
Canada
The Caribbean
Guatemala
Hong Kong
Japan
Malaysia
New Zealand
Panama
Taiwan
Thailand
US
Western Europe

WHEN

Richard DeVos and Jay Van Andel founded Amway Corporation in the basement of Van Andel's Ada, Michigan, home in 1959. In the late 1950s DeVos and Van Andel were distributors for Nutrilite, a direct-sales vitamin company in California. Their business had been so successful that they branched out into other ventures, such as a health foods bakery. In 1958, when Nutrilite's leadership was failing, DeVos and Van Andel decided to develop their own product line.

Amway's first product was a multipurpose liquid cleaner originally called Frisk and later renamed LOC (Liquid Organic Cleaner). The company began making laundry detergent, other household cleaners, and personal grooming products soon afterwards. Amway estimated its retail sales at $500,000 in 1960; by 1977 sales had reached $375 million. Amway expanded its physical space as well, with 70 building projects, including factories and warehouses, between 1960 and 1978. Amway expanded to Australia in 1970, Europe in 1972, Hong Kong in 1974, Japan in 1979, and Taiwan in 1982.

Amway has often been a target of government investigations, but it denies that it is a pyramid company (a company whose salespeople make money primarily by signing on new salespeople rather than selling products).

When a distributor "sponsors" a new salesperson, he or she takes responsibility for the new worker, including training. Distributors earn award pins upon reaching consecutively higher sales levels. Amway is noted for its motivational rallies for employees and for its near-religious devotion to free enterprise.

In 1973 Amway opened its Center for Free Enterprise in Ada. The center includes various displays and an Amway museum. In the late 1970s Amway purchased the Mutual Broadcasting System (1977), with radio stations in Chicago and New York; the Pantlind Hotel (1978, Grand Rapids), which was renovated and renamed the Amway Grand Plaza; and a resort in the Virgin Islands (1978). In 1981 Amway had estimated revenues of $1 billion.

In 1982, after several years of investigation by Canadian authorities, Van Andel and DeVos were indicted on charges of defrauding the Canadian government of $22 million in import duties. Amway pleaded guilty and paid $20 million in fines. From 1984 to 1986 the company experienced a sales slump during which revenues dropped to about $800 million from $1.2 billion in 1982, and following several suits alleging abusive sales practices, Amway brought in William Nicholson, former appointments secretary for President Gerald Ford, as an outside advisor to help the company reorganize. Amway then shifted to emphasizing sales training rather than evangelism. Company revenues rebounded to an estimated $1.5 billion in 1989, according to *Forbes.*

Since beginning operations in Japan in 1979, Amway has had double-digit growth rates and is the 7th fastest-growing company (foreign or domestic) in Japan. In 1989 Amway, assisted by takeover specialist Irwin L. Jacobs, made a $2.1 billion buyout offer of Avon that the latter rejected. Prior to the offer Amway and Jacobs disclosed that they had bought 10.3% of Avon's stock.

WHAT

Products

House Care
- Air fresheners
- Bug spray
- Car care items
- Dish detergents
- Disinfectants
- Floor cleaners
- Furniture polish
- Laundry products
- Spot remover
- Vacuum cleaners

Health
- Diet products
- Vitamins

Personal Care
- Cologne
- Cosmetics
- Deodorant
- Hairspray
- Mouthwash
- Shampoo
- Sunscreens
- Toothpaste

Commercial Products
- Institutional laundry products
- Janitorial supplies

Catalog Merchandise
- Furniture
- Luggage
- Stereo systems
- Watches

Education
- Dictionaries
- *Encyclopedia Americana*
- *Grolier Atlas*
- *Harvard Classics*

Other
- Air purifiers
- Alarm systems
- Canister sets
- Cookware
- Plant pots
- Smoke detectors
- Thermostats
- Water purifiers

Hotels

Amway Grand Plaza Hotel (Grand Rapids, MI)
Peter Island Resort (British Virgin Islands)

Communications

Mutual Broadcasting System (radio network with approx. 800 affiliates nationwide)

RANKINGS

86th in *Forbes* 400 US Private Cos.

COMPETITION

Avon
Colgate-Palmolive
Corning
Estée Lauder
Johnson & Johnson
S.C. Johnson
Johnson Products
MacAndrews & Forbes
Procter & Gamble
Unilever

HOW MUCH

	9 Yr. Growth	1980	1981	1982	1983	1984	1985	1986	1987	1988	1989
Corporate revenues (est.)($ mil)	7.0%	825	1,000	1,200	1,130	—	1,200	800	550	1,477	1,513
Estimated retail sales ($ mil)	6.3%	1,100	1,400	1,500	—	1,200	1,200	1,300	1,500	1,800	1,900

Corporate Revenue Estimates ($ mil) 1980-89

1600
1400
1200
1000
800
600
400
200
0

ANGLO AMERICAN CORP. OF SOUTH AFRICA

OVERVIEW

Anglo American is the lead company in the largest industrial and finance group in South Africa, controlling 60% of the value of the Johannesburg Stock Exchange. Indeed, there are few areas of the economy of South Africa in which companies controlled by Anglo American are not active. The company is also the world leader in diamond, gold, and platinum production.

Anglo American controls its empire of over 600 affiliated companies both at home and abroad through minority stakes, holding companies, and a wilderness of cross-holdings of stock. For this reason, the company is sometimes referred to as the "octopus." A prominent example is De Beers Centenary, a newly formed marketing arm that owns 21% of Minorco, Anglo American's foreign investment company. De Beers Centenary is itself owned by De Beers, which in turn is 26% owned by Anglo American Investment Trust and 7% by Anglo American.

The international furor over South Africa's racial policies has both helped and harmed Anglo American. It has allowed the company to buy the assets of foreign firms exiting South Africa. Despite its stated goal of racial equality, the company was blocked by US courts from buying Britain's Consolidated Gold Fields in 1989, partly because of western attitudes toward apartheid and US fears over foreign control of strategic metals gold and platinum.

WHEN

In 1905 the Oppenheimers, a German family with major interest in the Premier Diamond Mining Company of South Africa, acquired control of Consolidated Mines Selection, one of the smaller South African gold mining companies, and used it to buy up some of the richest gold-producing land in South Africa by 1917. The family formed Anglo American that year to raise money from J. P. Morgan and other US banking and mining interests for mine development. The name was chosen to disguise the company's German background during WWI and because the original suggestion, African American, was rejected by the US investors.

Under chairman Ernest Oppenheimer, Anglo American acquired diamond fields in German Southwest Africa (now Namibia) in 1920, and from this position the company broke the De Beers hegemony in diamond production. De Beers Consolidated Mines had been formed by Cecil Rhodes in 1888 with the financial help of England's powerful Rothschild family and had since extended its control over the South African diamond industry. De Beers was able to reap large profits because of its monopoly position and cheap black labor, and had diversified into cattle ranching, agriculture, wine production, coal, railroads, explosives, and other basic industries. The diamond monopoly was reestablished, however, in 1929 when Anglo American took control of De Beers.

After WWII Anglo American and De Beers extended control over the gold industry, becoming the largest producers in South Africa by 1958. The companies were also major world producers of coal, uranium, and copper. In the 1960s and 1970s Anglo American expanded its influence on South African and worldwide business interests through mergers and cross-holdings in industrial and financial companies. With a 39% interest in Minorco, Anglo American expanded its interests overseas, becoming by 1980 the largest foreign investor in several countries, including the US (a position since lost). Other important holdings included 25% of Barlow Rand, a diversified conglomerate, then South Africa's 3rd largest industrial company (1971); and 50% of Freight Services Holdings, a dominant transport company (1975).

Anglo American came under intense scrutiny during the 1980s because of South Africa's racial policies. The Oppenheimers, who still hold an 8% stake in Anglo American, have long supported moderate opposition politicians and the formation of black labor unions. In 1985 former Anglo American chairman Gavin Relly met with leaders of the African National Congress, which was banned from the country. But in 1987, when black unions went on strike, Anglo American dismissed 60,000 workers and 7 men died in the ensuing violence.

HOW MUCH

$= R2.55 (Dec. 31, 1989)	9 Yr. Growth	1980	1981	1982	1983	1984	1985	1986	1987	1988	1989
Attributable earnings (R mil)	16.9%	307	527	503	507	556	601	806	1,031	1,037	1,254
Equity earnings (R mil)	19.7%	525	866	758	638	810	880	1,193	1,503	1,809	2,645
ADR price - high ($)	—	21.50	16.63	15.88	24.50	20.00	16.13	11.60	17.80	18.75	30.38
ADR price - low ($)	—	10.00	11.75	6.50	14.63	10.50	5.54	6.10	8.50	12.63	15.75
Dividends per ADR ($)	(6.2%)	0.75	1.08	0.86	0.84	0.66	0.48	0.59	0.90	0.80	0.42

1989 Year End:
Debt ratio: 16.7%
Return on equity: 9.3%
Cash (mil): R2,095
Current ratio: 2.53
Long-term debt (mil): R2,034
Number of shares (mil): 230

Stock Price History high/low 1980-89

OTC symbol: ANGLY (ADR)
Founded: South Africa, 1917
Fiscal year ends: March 31

WHO

Chairman of the Executive Committee: Julian Ogilvie Thompson
Chairman of the Administrative Committee: C. L. Sunter
Group Accountant: G. A. Chalmers
Auditors: Aiken & Peat; Pim Goldby
Employees: 300,000

WHERE

HQ: 44 Main St., Johannesburg 2001, South Africa
Phone: 011-27-638-9111
FAX: 011-27-638-3221

Anglo American's gold and diamond sales are carried out worldwide.

WHAT

	1989 Equity Accounted Earnings	
	R mil	% of total
Diamonds	679	25
Mining finance	604	23
Industry & commerce	498	19
Gold & uranium	391	15
Platinum & other mining	200	8
Banking, insurance & property	139	5
Coal	80	3
Prospecting	(139)	(5)
Other	193	7
Total	**2,645**	**100**

Affiliates

Anglo American Coal Corp. (51% owned)
Coal mining and export

Anglo American Corp. of South America (40% owned)
Mining and other investments in Brazil, Chile, and Argentina

Anglo American Farms (50% owned)
Grain, produce, meat, and wine production

Anglo American Industrial Corp. (45% owned)
Steel, autos, paper, and chemicals

Anglo American Investment Trust (52% owned) & Anglo American Gold Investment Co. (49% owned)
Investments in diamond and metals mining

Anglo American Properties (66% owned)
Real estate property management

De Beers Consolidated Mines (33% owned)
Diamond mining and marketing

Eastern Investments (40% owned)
Gold mining, financial services, and retailing

Minorco (39% owned)
Luxembourg-based holding company; owns 30% of Engelhard Corporation (US) and 36% of Charter Consolidated (UK)

RANKINGS

33rd in Forbes 100 Foreign Investments in the US

COMPETITION

AMAX
ASARCO
Broken Hill
Cyprus Minerals
FMC
Hanson
Phelps Dodge

ANHEUSER-BUSCH COMPANIES, INC.

OVERVIEW

Anheuser-Busch is the largest brewer in the world, with 12 US breweries and 6 foreign licensees. Despite diversification, the major focus remains beer. Over 90% of 1989 profits came from brewing. In 1989 Anheuser-Busch widened its lead, making over 80 million barrels and taking a 42% US market share. Three of the top 5 beers in America in 1989 were company brands: Budweiser, Bud Light, and Busch. Budweiser is the world's best-selling beer, with sales representing more than 1/2 of US premium-priced beer sales.

The driving force behind company dominance is a huge marketing effort. Hundreds of millions are spent each year on promotional campaigns and sporting event sponsorships. Anheuser-Busch acquired Sea World in late 1989 to become the nation's 2nd largest theme park operator, after Walt Disney.

Anheuser-Busch operates 10 can and lid plants and recycled 9 billion aluminum cans in 1989. The company also markets snack foods and bakery products through its Eagle Snacks and Campbell Taggart subsidiaries. Other subsidiaries involve the company in malt and rice production, real estate development, and transportation. The company has also taken an equity position in 16 of its wholesalers.

WHEN

Anheuser-Busch began in St. Louis in 1852 as The Bavarian Brewery, founded by George Schneider. In 1860 soap maker Eberhard Anheuser took over the failing brewery. His son-in-law Adolphus Busch joined the company in 1865 and in 1876 assisted restauranteur Carl Conrad in creating Budweiser, a light beer like those brewed in the Bohemian town of Budweis. The brewery's rapid growth was based in part on the popularity of Budweiser over heavier, darker beers. The company adopted Anheuser-Busch Brewing Association as its corporate name in 1879.

In 1901 Budweiser became the 2nd American brewer to sell one million barrels annually. When Adolphus died in 1913, his son August took over the company, which was renamed Anheuser-Busch, Inc., in 1919. As beer vats lay dry during Prohibition (1920 to 1933), August saved the company by selling yeast, refrigeration units, truck bodies, syrup, and soft drinks. When repeal came in 1933, Busch quickly resumed brewing, delivering a case of Budweiser to President Franklin Roosevelt in a carriage drawn by Clydesdale horses, which have since become the company's symbol. However, the tribulations of Prohibition had damaged August Busch's health, and he killed himself in 1934.

In 1957 Budweiser knocked Schlitz out of first place. In 1970 Miller held 7th place in the industry, but tobacco giant Philip Morris acquired it and began a long, fierce challenge to Budweiser's leadership. By 1978 Miller had passed Schlitz and Pabst to take 2nd place, but Anheuser-Busch triumphed, becoming the first brewer to sell 40 million barrels a year. By 1980 the 2 foes produced over 50% of the beer sold in America, largely at the expense of smaller, independent breweries.

For 130 years and 4 generations of Busch family control, the company's steady climb in industry ranks has resulted from skillful marketing and product innovation. Anheuser-Busch's beer line today includes 13 domestic and 3 imported brands. First brewed in 1896, Michelob fills the popular super-premium niche. The company introduced Natural Light in 1977 in response to Miller Lite's success.

Anheuser-Busch acquired the St. Louis Cardinals baseball team (1953) and Campbell Taggart (baked goods, 1982), and created Busch Entertainment (theme parks, 1959), Busch Creative Services (marketing services, 1980), and Eagle Snacks (snack foods, 1982). In 1990 the company mounted an unusual television advertising campaign to oppose proposed increases in the beer excise tax.

HOW MUCH

	9 Yr. Growth	1980	1981	1982	1983	1984	1985	1986	1987	1988	1989
Sales ($ mil)	12.5%	3,295	3,847	4,577	6,034	6,501	7,000	7,677	8,258	8,924	9,481
Net income ($ mil)	18.1%	172	217	287	348	392	444	518	615	716	767
Income as % of sales	—	5.2%	5.7%	6.3%	5.8%	6.0%	6.3%	6.7%	7.4%	8.0%	8.1%
Earnings per share ($)	17.4%	0.63	0.77	0.98	1.08	1.23	1.42	1.69	2.04	2.45	2.68
Stock price – high ($)	—	5.21	7.35	11.79	12.83	12.40	22.88	29.06	40.13	34.38	46.00
Stock price – low ($)	—	3.50	4.60	6.44	9.75	8.96	11.81	19.75	25.75	29.00	30.63
Stock price – close ($)	26.6%	4.63	6.85	10.75	10.42	12.08	21.13	26.13	33.38	31.50	38.50
P/E – high	—	8	10	12	12	10	16	17	20	14	17
P/E – low	—	6	6	7	9	7	8	12	13	12	11
Dividends per share ($)	19.2%	0.17	0.19	0.23	0.27	0.31	0.37	0.44	0.54	0.66	0.80
Book value per share ($)	12.4%	3.83	4.42	5.27	6.08	6.91	7.84	8.61	9.87	10.95	10.95

1989 Year End:
Debt ratio: 51.6%
Return on equity: 24.5%
Cash (mil): $36
Current ratio: 0.98
Long-term debt (mil): $3,307
Number of shares (mil): 283
Dividends:
1989 average yield: 2.1%
1989 payout: 29.9%
Market value (mil): $10,895

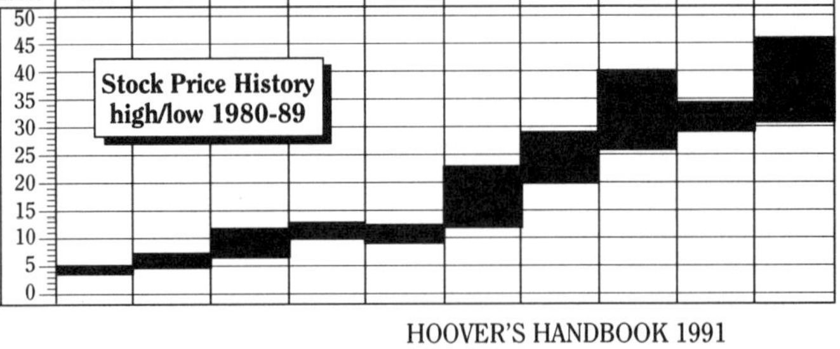

Stock Price History high/low 1980-89

50 45 40 35 30 25 20 15 10 5 0

NYSE symbol: BUD
Incorporated: Delaware, 1979
Fiscal year ends: December 31

WHO

Chairman, President, and CEO: August A. Busch III, age 52, $1,464,450 pay
Group Executive and Principal Financial Officer: Jerry E. Ritter, age 55, $767,000 pay
VP and Group Executive: Patrick T. Stokes, age 47, $542,008 pay
VP and Group Executive: Barry H. Beracha, age 48, $438,000 pay
Auditors: Price Waterhouse
Employees: 46,608

WHERE

HQ: One Busch Place, St. Louis, MO 63118
Phone: 314-577-3314
FAX: 314-577-2900

Anheuser-Busch has 12 breweries in the US and operations in Canada, Japan, Israel, the UK, Ireland, Denmark, Korea, Spain, and France. It exports to more than 40 other nations.

WHAT

	1989 Sales		1989 Operating Income	
	$ mil	% of total	$ mil	% of total
Beer & beer-related	7,406	78	1,245	94
Entertainment	286	3	27	2
Food products	1,803	19	57	4
Adjustments	(14)	—	—	—
Total	**9,481**	**100**	**1,329**	**100**

Brand Names

Beverages
Bud Light
Budweiser
Busch
Carlsberg
Elephant Malt Liquor
Master Cellars Wines
Michelob
Natural Light
O'Doul's

Food & Snacks
Campbell Taggart (baked goods)
Eagle Snacks (chips and nuts)
El Charrito (Mexican food)

Busch Entertainment Corporation
Busch Gardens/Sea World Theme Parks
St. Louis Cardinals Baseball Team

Other Services
Busch Agricultural Resources, Inc. (grain processing)
Busch Creative Services Corp. (communications)
Busch Properties, Inc. (real estate development)
Container Recovery Corp. (recycling)
Metal Container Corp. (beverage containers)
Metal Label Corp. (metalized and paper labels)
St. Louis Refrigerator Car Co. (railway cars)

RANKINGS

49th in *Fortune* 500 Industrial Cos.
131st in *Fortune* Global 500 Industrial Cos.
84th in *Forbes* Sales 500
45th in *Business Week* 1000
115th in *Business Week* Global 1000

COMPETITION

Adolph Coors
Bass
Borden
Brown-Forman
BSN
Campbell Soup
E. & J. Gallo
Grand Metropolitan
Guinness
MCA
PepsiCo
Philip Morris
Ralston Purina
RJR Nabisco
Tribune
Turner Broadcasting
Walt Disney
Whitman

APPLE COMPUTER, INC.

OVERVIEW

Based in Cupertino, California, Apple Computer popularized the personal computer with the introduction of the Apple I in 1976. By 1989 Apple Computer had become a $5.3 billion company.

Apple's Macintosh, launched in 1984 and noted for its more intuitive graphical user interface, offered a distinct alternative to the IBM personal computer. According to *Datamation*'s 1990 listing of the top 100 information technology companies, Apple is the 2nd largest PC maker in the world (based on % of total PC revenues). IBM is #1.

Macintosh applications range from word processing and spreadsheets to desktop publishing and 3-D design work. The company also develops interactive multimedia tools (text, video, animation, and sound) for educational purposes applicable to both school and business environments.

Education and business are Apple's principal markets. Apple dominates the elementary education market with the Apple II product family. A low-cost color Macintosh for the education market is scheduled to be out by 1991. With the increasing power and versatility of its product line — more networking options and business software — Apple is increasing its share in the business market, which currently represents 1/2 of its sales.

WHEN

Two college dropouts, Steven Jobs and Stephen Wozniak, founded Apple in 1976 in the Santa Clara Valley. The original plan to sell circuit boards for a $25 profit changed to selling fully assembled microcomputers after Jobs's first sales call resulted in an order for 50 units. They built the Apple I in Jobs's garage and sold it without a monitor, keyboard, or casing.

The initial demand for the Apple I made Jobs aware of the market for small computers. The choice of Apple as the company name (recalling the time Jobs spent on an Oregon farm) and the computer's "user-friendly" appearance set it apart from other companies' computers, making it appealing even to nontechnical buyers.

By 1977 Wozniak, who invented the Apple I, had substantially improved it by adding a keyboard, color monitor, and 8 slots for peripheral devices. This latter feature gave the new machine, the Apple II, considerable versatility and inspired numerous 3rd-party add-on devices and software programs.

By 1980 over 130,000 Apple II units had been sold. Revenues went from $7.8 million in 1978 to $117 million in 1980, and, when Apple went public (1980), it did so with one of the largest stock offerings in recent history.

By 1983 Wozniak had left and Jobs had hired John Sculley from Pepsi to succeed Mike Markkula, the company's president. In 1985 Jobs left after a tumultuous power struggle.

Following the failure of the Apple III and Lisa computers (1983), Apple roared back in 1984 with the revolutionary Macintosh. Its introduction was preceded by an intriguing commercial, aired during the Super Bowl, that challenged IBM, its chief rival. Advertised as the computer "For the Rest of Us," the uniquely designed machine incorporated a graphical approach to operating the computer, inspired by Xerox's Alto computer (now the subject of litigation with rivals Microsoft and Hewlett-Packard). In 1986 Apple moved into the office market with the Mac Plus and the Laserwriter printer, a combination that ushered in the desktop publishing revolution.

Today Apple is a $5.3 billion company. Sales growth slowed in 1989 due in part to slower industry growth. The 1990s began with the departure of 2 of Apple's top executives (Jean Louis Gassée and Allan Loren) and with Sculley taking charge of R&D. In July 1990, citing the strategic importance of software, Apple reversed its decision to spin off its software subsidiary Claris.

HOW MUCH

	9 Yr. Growth	1980	1981	1982	1983	1984	1985	1986	1987	1988	1989
Sales ($ mil)	52.7%	117	335	583	983	1,516	1,918	1,902	2,661	4,071	5,284
Net income ($ mil)	50.2%	12	39	61	77	64	61	154	218	400	454
Income as % of sales	—	10.0%	11.8%	10.5%	7.8%	4.2%	3.2%	8.1%	8.2%	9.8%	8.6%
Earnings per share ($)	45.6%	0.12	0.35	0.53	0.64	0.53	0.50	1.20	1.65	3.08	3.53
Stock price – high ($)	—	18.00	17.25	17.44	31.63	17.19	15.56	21.94	59.75	47.75	50.38
Stock price – low ($)	—	11.00	7.13	5.38	8.63	10.88	7.13	10.88	20.06	35.50	32.50
Stock price – close ($)	8.4%	17.06	11.06	14.94	12.19	14.56	11.00	20.25	42.00	40.25	35.25
P/E – high	—	150	49	33	49	33	31	18	36	16	14
P/E – low	—	92	20	10	13	21	14	9	12	12	9
Dividends per share ($)	—	0.00	0.00	0.00	0.00	0.00	0.00	0.00	0.12	0.32	0.40
Book value per share ($)	52.2%	0.27	1.60	2.25	3.19	3.84	4.45	5.54	6.63	8.17	11.77

1989 Year End:
Debt ratio: 0.0%
Return on equity: 35.4%
Cash (mil): $809
Current ratio: 2.56
Long-term debt (mil): $0
Number of shares (mil): 126
Dividends:
1989 average yield: 1.1%
1989 payout: 11.3%
Market value (mil): $4,451

OTC symbol: AAPL
Incorporated: California, 1977
Fiscal year ends: Last Friday in September

WHO

Chairman, President, and CEO: John Sculley, age 50, $2,251,175 pay
COO: Michael H. Spindler, age 47, $712,666 pay (prior to promotion)
SVP and CFO: Joseph A. Graziano, age 46
Auditors: Ernst & Young
Employees: 12,000 full-time and 2,500 temporary or part-time

WHERE

HQ: 20525 Mariani Ave., Cupertino, CA 95014
Phone: 408-996-1010
FAX: 408-996-0275

The company has 11 manufacturing facilities in California, Ireland, and Singapore. It does business in more than 120 countries and has 250 sales, distribution, and other offices worldwide.

	1989 Sales		1989 Operating Income	
	$ mil	% of total	$ mil	% of total
US	3,402	64	305	47
Europe	1,209	23	251	38
Other	673	13	101	15
Adjustments	—	—	(23)	—
Total	**5,284**	**100**	**634**	**100**

WHAT

Computers
Apple II
Macintosh II
Macintosh Plus
Macintosh Portable
Macintosh SE

Software
A/UX
HyperCard
Macintosh OS
Multifinder
ProDos

Peripheral Products
Disk drives (floppy, hard, CD-ROM)
Monitors (monochrome and color)
Printers (dot matrix and laser)
Scanner

Subsidiaries/Affiliates
Claris Corp. (software)
General Magic Corp.

Communication Products
File servers
Local and wide area networks
Modems

RANKINGS

96th in *Fortune* 500 Industrial Cos.
251st in *Fortune* Global 500 Industrial Cos.
163rd in *Forbes* Sales 500
120th in *Business Week* 1000
363rd in *Business Week* Global 1000

COMPETITION

Atari
Commodore
Compaq
Data General
Digital Equipment
Hewlett-Packard
Hyundai
IBM
Matsushita
Microsoft
NCR
NEC
Prime
Sun Microsystems
Tandy
Unisys
Wang

THE ARA GROUP, INC.

OVERVIEW

Privately owned ARA is a leading US diversified services company with emphasis on food services. ARA's businesses — food and refreshments, health and education services, uniform rental and maintenance, and publication distribution — operate in all 50 states and 5 foreign countries.

In various capacities, ARA serves food to most *Fortune* 500 companies, prisons, conference centers, airports, hospitals, campuses, parks, and stadiums in 400,000 locations worldwide. Clients include NASA's Johnson Space Center in Houston, Spectrum Stadium in Philadelphia, and the Olympic National Park Resort in Washington state. One subsidiary, ARA/CORY Refreshment Services, serves a billion cups of coffee and 6 million gallons of soda each year. Other services range from supplying "clean room" garments for the electronics industry to distribution of 500 million printed items to 20,000 retail locations in the US and to the military abroad each year. ARA is the largest contract food services company in Japan.

Private company
Incorporated: Delaware, 1959
Fiscal year ends: September 30

WHO

Chairman, President, and CEO: Joseph Neubauer, age 47, $869,200 pay
SVP and CFO: James E. Ksansnak, age 49, $341,200 pay
Auditors: Arthur Andersen & Co.
Employees: 125,000

WHERE

HQ: 1101 Market St., Philadelphia, PA 19107
Phone: 215-238-3000
FAX: 215-238-3333

ARA operates in all 50 states and in Belgium, Canada, Germany, Japan, and the UK.

WHEN

The ARA Group was incorporated in 1959 when Davidson Automatic Merchandising, owned by Davre Davidson and serving California, was merged with a midwestern vending company owned by William Fishman. Davidson became chairman and CEO, and Fishman was made president of the new company. Originally named Automatic Retailers of America, the company adopted its present name in 1969.

Like other vending services of its time, ARA serviced mainly candy, beverage, and cigarette machines. By 1961 ARA was operating in 38 states and ranked first in sales among vending companies. ARA moved into hot and cold food vending in the early 1960s, with clients such as the Southern Pacific Railway. Between 1959 and 1963 ARA acquired 150 local food service companies across the country, including Slater Systems in 1961, which gave ARA a top spot in operating cafeterias for institutions such as campuses, hospitals, and work sites. Davidson and Fishman eased ARA into manual vending because they recognized that, while profit margins were slimmer, the demands for capital were less. And while vending machine prices at the time could rise only in nickel increments, manual food service permitted cost increases to be passed on quickly by adding pennies to the price. Growth was so rapid the FTC stepped in, and ARA agreed to restrict future vending acquisitions.

In 1967 ARA began diversifying into other service businesses, such as publication distribution companies. In 1970 the company expanded into janitorial and maintenance services by buying Ground Services, which provides cleaning and loading services for airlines. In 1968 ARA stepped into the Olympic arena, providing food service at the Mexico City games. Since then the company has provided service and management at 13 Olympic events, most recently the Calgary Winter Games and the Summer Games in Seoul (1988). In 1973 ARA acquired National Living Centers, which under its present name of ARA Living Centers operates residential communities for the elderly. A 1976 joint venture with Mitsui & Company introduced ARA food services to Japan. ARA bought Work Wear, a uniform rental business, in 1977 and National Child Care Centers in 1980.

In 1984 a former director, William Siegel, and 2 Texas-based partners offered chairman Joseph Neubauer $722 million for the company. Neubauer refused and, to avoid a hostile takeover, took the company private in a $1.2 billion deal. Initially 70 senior managers owned 26% of the company. ARA gradually repurchased shares from other investors (investment banks and employee-benefit plans) to increase management's stake to more than 90%. By 1989 stock ownership had been offered to more than 900 managers. After the LBO, observers inside and outside the company hailed new enthusiasm among the ranks that allowed ARA to retain both clients and personnel. The company moved into new Philadelphia headquarters in 1986.

During the mid- to late-1980s, the company also made acquisitions in various service fields, including Szabo (correctional food services, 1986), Cory Food Services (1986), and Children's World Learning Centers (1987). In 1990 ARA began operating lodging and food services at Olympic National Park in Washington state.

WHAT

	1989 Sales		1989 Operating Income	
	$ mil	% of total	$ mil	% of total
Food & refreshments	2,500	60	124	47
Textile rental	584	14	64	24
Health & education	734	17	42	16
Distribution	376	9	33	13
Total	**4,244**	**100**	**263**	**100**

Food & Refreshment Services
ARA Business Dining Services
ARA Campus Dining Services
ARA Fine Dining
ARA Healthcare Nutrition Services
ARA Leisure Services Group (park concessions)
ARA School Nutrition Services
ARA/CORY Refreshment Services (coffee and soda services)
Conference Center Management
International Services
Szabo Correctional Food Service (prison meals)

Textile Rental & Maintenance
ARA Environmental Services, Inc. (janitorial)
ARA Ground Services, Inc. (airline meals)
ARATEX (uniform rental)
Encore Services (home repair)
GMARA Industrial Cleaning (joint venture with GM)

Health & Education
ARA Living Centers, Inc. (nursing homes)
Children's World Learning Centers, Inc. (day care)
Correctional Medical Systems, Inc. (prison health care)
Spectrum Emergency Care, Inc. (physician staffing)

Distribution Services
ARA Magazine & Book Division, Inc.

HOW MUCH

	9 Yr. Growth	1980	1981	1982	1983	1984	1985	1986	1987	1988	1989
Sales ($ mil)	4.7%	2,806	2,916	2,806	3,057	3,406	2,652*	3,749	4,019	3,917	4,244
Net income ($ mil)	(5.2%)	63	45	39	54	64	6	16	22	5	39
Income as % of sales	—	2.3%	1.5%	1.4%	1.8%	1.9%	0.2%	0.4%	0.5%	0.1%	0.9%

1989 Year End:
Debt ratio: 98.4%
Return on equity: —
Cash (mil): $28
Current ratio: 1.06
Long-term debt (mil): $1,151
Assets (mil): $3,542

* Nine-month period due to change in fiscal year end

RANKINGS

23rd in *Forbes* 400 US Private Cos.

COMPETITION

Berkshire Hathaway
Greyhound Dial
Marriott
MCA
Ogden
TW Holdings

ARCHER-DANIELS-MIDLAND COMPANY

OVERVIEW

Based in Decatur, Illinois, Archer-Daniels-Midland (ADM) is a major processor, transporter, and marketer of agricultural products. The company is a leading processor of oilseeds in the US and ranks among the nation's largest flour millers and corn refiners. Other operations include grain storage and marketing, peanut shelling, rice milling, biochemicals, sugar refining, commodity hedging services, a bank, and the production of food, feed, and malt products.

ADM's oilseed segment processes a number of seed types for the production of vegetable oil and high-grade food meals. The company sells its crude vegetable oil to other industries for the production of margarine, shortening, and other food and industrial products. ADM holds a trademark on textured vegetable protein (TVP) and produces a number of high-protein soy products.

The company's corn operations primarily produce corn syrup, starch, glucose, sweeteners, and ethanol (corn alcohol used to make gasohol).

ADM has taken an active role in environmental protection efforts with the development of biodegradable trashbags and with its continued production of ethanol, which produces lower emissions of carbon monoxide than traditional fossil fuels.

NYSE symbol: ADM
Incorporated: Delaware, 1923
Fiscal year ends: June 30

WHO

Chairman and CEO: Dwayne O. Andreas, age 71, $1,337,500 pay
President: James R. Randall, age 64, $891,662 pay
EVP: Michael D. Andreas, age 40, $512,500 pay
SVP: Martin L. Andreas, age 50
VP: G. Allen Andreas, age 46
VP, Controller, and CFO: Douglas J. Schmalz, age 43
Auditors: Ernst & Young
Employees: 10,214

WHEN

In 1878 John W. Daniels started crushing flaxseed to produce linseed oil and in 1902 formed Daniels Linseed Company in Minneapolis. George A. Archer, another experienced flaxseed crusher, joined the company in 1903.

In 1923 the company bought Midland Linseed Products and adopted the name Archer-Daniels-Midland. During the 1920s the company started to conduct research (an uncommon practice at the time) on the chemical composition of linseed oil and acquired several other linseed oil companies.

ADM entered the flour milling business in 1930 with the purchase of Commander-Larabee (then the 3rd-ranking flour miller in the US). In the 1930s the company's research division discovered a method for extracting lecithin (a food additive used in candy and other products) from soybean oil.

After WWII ADM went through a period of rapid growth. By 1949 the company was the leading processor of linseed oil and soybeans in the US and was 4th in flour milling. During the early 1950s the company entered a period of foreign expansion and bought the resin division of US Industrial Chemicals (1954).

ADM encountered financial difficulty in the early 1960s due to fluctuating commodities prices and losses in the chemical division. In 1966 the company's leadership passed to Dwayne O. Andreas, a former Cargill executive who purchased a block of Archer family stock (the Andreas family now owns some 8% of the company's stock). He sold the chemical division and bought Fleischmann Malting (malt for beer, etc.) in 1967.

Andreas, aware of the future potential of the soybean (which is about 50% protein once processed), prompted the company's effort to produce textured vegetable protein. In 1969 he established a plant in Decatur, Illinois, to produce edible soy protein.

Andreas's restructuring paved the way for productivity and expansion. In 1971 the company acquired Corn Sweeteners (glutens, high fructose syrups), which today also produces ethanol. Other acquisitions included Supreme Sugar (1973), Tabor (grain, 1975), and Columbian Peanut (1981); the latter made ADM the leading domestic sheller of peanuts.

In the late 1980s Andreas, who knows Gorbachev personally, planned a joint venture with a Soviet farm cooperative in which ADM would process Soviet wheat (Andreas had arranged a deal in 1954 to sell butter to the Soviets but was blocked by the US government).

WHERE

HQ: 4666 Faries Pkwy., Box 1470, Decatur, IL 62525
Phone: 217-424-5200
FAX: 217-424-5839 (Public Relations)

The company operates 118 processing plants in the US and 19 foreign plants.

WHAT

	1989 Sales % of total
Oilseed operations	53
Corn operations	27
Wheat flour operations	8
Other operations	12
Total	**100**

Divisions/Subsidiaries
ADM Corn Processing Division (corn products and ethanol)
ADM Europe B. V.
ADM Europoort B. V. (oilseed products)
ADM Feed Corp. (animal feeds and pet foods)
ADM Grain Co.
ADM/GROWMARK
ADM Investor Services, Inc. (commodity hedging)
ADM Milling Co. (wheat, corn, rice, oats, and barley)
ADM Olmuhlen GmBH (oilseed products)
ADM Processing Division (soybean products and canola)
ADM Protein Specialities Division
Agrinational Insurance Co.
American River Transportation Co. (barges and terminal facilities)
Archer-Daniels-Midland International, S. A. (commodities trading)
Archer-Daniels-Midland, S. A.
The British Arkady Co., Ltd. (vegetarian foods)
Fleischmann-Kurth Malting Co., Inc. (barley malts)
Gooch Foods, Inc. (pasta)
Hickory Point Bank & Trust (banking)
Krause Milling Co.
Smoot Grain Co.
Southern Cotton Oil Co.
Supreme Sugar Co., Inc. (sugar refining)
Tabor Grain Co.

HOW MUCH

	9 Yr. Growth	1980	1981	1982	1983	1984	1985	1986	1987	1988	1989
Sales ($ mil)	12.3%	2,802	3,647	3,713	4,292	4,907	4,739	5,336	5,775	6,798	7,929
Net income ($ mil)	15.5%	116	176	155	110	118	164	239	265	353	425
Income as % of sales	—	4.1%	4.8%	4.2%	2.6%	2.4%	3.5%	4.5%	4.6%	5.2%	5.4%
Earnings per share ($)	11.2%	0.58	0.77	0.64	0.45	0.43	0.59	0.86	0.93	1.24	1.51
Stock price – high ($)	—	8.26	7.07	6.87	8.37	7.79	9.87	13.46	16.78	14.06	23.50
Stock price – low ($)	—	4.09	4.06	3.69	6.00	5.10	6.40	8.96	10.08	11.27	13.02
Stock price – close ($)	14.0%	7.09	5.79	6.79	6.63	6.66	9.51	10.58	12.85	13.25	23.13
P/E – high	—	14	9	11	19	18	17	16	18	11	16
P/E – low	—	7	5	6	13	12	11	10	11	9	9
Dividends per share ($)	6.4%	0.04	0.04	0.04	0.04	0.05	0.05	0.05	0.06	0.06	0.06
Book value per share ($)	13.0%	3.59	4.38	4.98	5.52	5.96	6.50	7.33	8.29	9.41	10.79

1989 Year End:
Debt ratio: 18.5%
Return on equity: 15.0%
Cash (mil): $842
Current ratio: 3.4
Long-term debt (mil): $690
Number of shares (mil): 281
Dividends:
1989 average yield: 0.3%
1989 payout: 4.2%
Market value (mil): $6,501

Stock Price History high/low 1980-89

25
20
15
10
5
0

RANKINGS

57th in *Fortune* 500 Industrial Cos.
156th in *Fortune* Global 500 Industrial Cos.
100th in *Forbes* Sales 500
96th in *Business Week* 1000
232nd in *Business Week* Global 1000

COMPETITION

Borden	CSX
Cargill	Salomon
ConAgra	Other agribusinesses

ARMSTRONG WORLD INDUSTRIES, INC.

OVERVIEW

Armstrong World Industries is the largest domestic manufacturer and marketer of non-textile floor coverings (resilient flooring and ceramic tile) and is a leading manufacturer of other interior furnishings, including building products and furniture. The company also manufactures and markets specialty products for the automotive, textile, and other industries.

The company is divided into 4 primary operating segments: Floor Coverings, Building Products, Furniture, and Industrial Products. Floor Coverings is the largest segment, with 1989 sales of just over $1.4 billion. The Building Products division ($709 million) primarily produces ceiling materials, as well as acoustical wall tiles and architectural products. Furniture ($438 million), both residential and commercial, is manufactured through the company's Thomasville subsidiary. Industrial Products ($279 million) include such things as pipe insulation, gasket materials, adhesives, and textile mill supplies.

Home improvement and new residential construction are Armstrong's largest markets, together representing over 1/2 of the company's business. Sluggishness in the construction industry over the past year has reduced demand for a number of Armstrong's products.

WHEN

Thomas Armstrong and John Glass started the Armstrong Brothers cork cutting shop in Pittsburgh in 1860. Armstrong carved the corks by hand and made his first deliveries in a wheelbarrow.

During its early years the company struggled through the Civil War, financial panics, and factory fires. Thomas Armstrong overcame such obstacles through hard work and attention to quality. By 1864 he was stamping his name on each cork. Concerned with fairness to his customers, he rejected the maxim of *caveat emptor* (let the buyer beware) and put a written guarantee in each of his burlap sacks of corks before shipping them. By the mid-1890s Armstrong Brothers was the largest cork company in the world. In 1895 the company changed its name to Armstrong Cork.

To compensate for the decreasing cork markets near the turn of the century (due to the invention of screw-top mason jars and spring bottle stoppers), the company found new uses for its cork in insulated corkboard and brick. In 1906 Armstrong Cork turned its attention to linoleum (which then was made with cork powder) and started construction on a new factory in Lancaster, Pennsylvania. Thomas Armstrong died in 1908, a year before the company's linoleum hit the market.

Armstrong continued to produce mainly flooring and insulating materials through the 1950s while establishing foreign operations (primarily in Canada, Europe, and Australia). During the 1960s the company expanded its line to include home furnishings by purchasing E & B Carpet Mills (1967) and Thomasville Furniture Industries (1968). In 1969 the company sold its packaging materials operations.

In 1980 the company dropped cork from its name and changed to Armstrong World Industries (the only cork the company still produces comes from a small Spanish plant and is mainly for champagne bottles). During the 1980s the company went through a period of rapid expansion with numerous acquisitions, including Applied Color Systems (computerized color systems, 1981, sold in 1989), Chemline Industries (chemicals, 1985), the W.W. Henry Company (adhesives and powder products, 1986), and American Olean (ceramic tile, 1988). In 1989 Armstrong sold its carpet operations.

In 1989 affiliates of the Canadian Belzberg family announced that they had purchased 9.85% of the company's stock and were considering taking control of the company. Armstrong's board of directors is opposed to a Belzberg takeover or the sale of the company.

HOW MUCH

	9 Yr. Growth	1980	1981	1982	1983	1984	1985	1986	1987	1988	1989
Sales ($ mil)	7.4%	1,323	1,376	1,286	1,439	1,569	1,679	1,920	2,365	2,680	2,513
Net income ($ mil)	13.7%	49	47	20	63	92	101	122	150	163	154
Income as % of sales	—	3.7%	3.4%	1.5%	4.4%	5.9%	6.0%	6.4%	6.4%	6.1%	6.1%
Earnings per share ($)	13.5%	0.97	0.94	0.40	1.27	1.90	2.10	2.54	3.18	3.51	3.03
Stock price – high ($)	—	9.31	9.38	13.25	16.88	17.00	22.63	35.00	47.38	44.00	50.88
Stock price – low ($)	—	6.19	7.00	6.63	10.63	11.13	15.19	19.81	22.50	29.50	33.38
Stock price – close ($)	20.2%	7.13	8.38	12.38	13.81	16.81	22.31	29.88	32.25	35.00	37.25
P/E – high	—	10	10	34	13	9	11	14	15	13	17
P/E – low	—	6	7	17	8	6	7	8	7	8	11
Dividends per share ($)	7.4%	0.55	0.55	0.55	0.55	0.59	0.64	0.73	0.89	0.98	1.05
Book value per share ($)	4.1%	11.65	12.06	11.76	12.26	13.21	15.02	16.84	19.50	21.83	16.72

1989 Year End:
Debt ratio: 15.7%
Return on equity: 15.7%
Cash (mil): $17
Current ratio: 1.81
Long-term debt (mil): $181
Number of shares (mil): 42
Dividends:
1989 average yield: 2.8%
1989 payout: 34.5%
Market value (mil): $1,574

NYSE symbol: ACK
Incorporated: Pennsylvania, 1891
Fiscal year ends: December 31

WHO

Chairman and President: William W. Adams, age 55, $580,360 pay
EVP: E. Allen Deaver, age 54, $326,979 pay
EVP: George A. Lorch, age 48, $330,086 pay
SVP Finance: William J. Wimer, age 55
Auditors: KPMG Peat Marwick
Employees: 26,000

WHERE

HQ: PO Box 3001, Lancaster, PA 17604
Phone: 717-397-0611
FAX: 717-396-2787 (Public Relations)

The company operates 67 manufacturing facilities in the US and 19 in 10 other countries.

	1989 Sales		1989 Operating Income	
	$ mil	% of total	$ mil	% of total
US	2,239	78	268	77
Europe	426	15	61	17
Other foreign	193	7	20	6
Adjustments	(345)	—	(86)	—
Total	**2,513**	**100**	**263**	**100**

WHAT

	1989 Sales		1989 Operating Income	
	$ mil	% of total	$ mil	% of total
Floor coverings	1,432	50	155	44
Furniture	438	15	28	8
Industrial products & other	279	10	42	12
Building products	709	25	124	36
Adjustments	(345)	—	(86)	—
Total	**2,513**	**100**	**263**	**100**

Products

Floor Coverings
Ceramic tile
Coved risers
Marble aggregate
Resilient flooring
Rubber tile
Stair treads
Vinyl tile
Vinyl wall base

Building Products
Acoustical wall panels
Ceiling materials
Ceiling systems

Furniture
Imported furniture
Thomasville (wood furniture)
Upholstered furniture

Industrial Products
Adhesives
Flexible pipe insulation
Gasket materials
Specialty chemicals
Textile mill supplies

RANKINGS

158th in *Fortune* 500 Industrial Cos.
440th in *Fortune* Global 500 Industrial Cos.
327th in *Forbes* Sales 500
384th in *Business Week* 1000

COMPETITION

INTERCO
Masco
3M
Premark
USG

ARTHUR ANDERSEN & CO.

OVERVIEW

Geneva-based Arthur Andersen & Co., Societé Coopérative is the 3rd largest accounting firm in the world, after Ernst & Young and KPMG, and is the world's largest business consulting organization. Although the firm is increasing its international presence, it still derives 59% of its revenues from the US.

During the 1980s Andersen consulting grew from $192 million to $1.4 billion while its accounting business grew from $613 million to $1.9 billion. But this growth brought challenges: business regulatory bodies began to wonder if firms could work closely with companies as consultants and still audit them objectively. Also, in 1989 revenues per partner on the consulting side of the firm were $2.3 million, compared to $1.4 million on the accounting side, and some consultants resented sharing their earnings with the accountants.

In order to address this situation, the firm reorganized in 1989, establishing 2 distinct units: Arthur Andersen, providing auditing, business advisory services, tax services, and corporate specialty services; and Andersen Consulting, for systems integration and technology consulting. These units operate under the umbrella of the Arthur Andersen Worldwide Organization and are coordinated by a Swiss entity, Arthur Andersen & Co., S. C.

WHEN

Arthur Andersen, an orphan of Norwegian parents, worked in the Chicago office of Price Waterhouse in 1907. In 1908 at 23, after becoming the youngest CPA in Illinois, he began teaching accounting at Northwestern University. Following a brief period in 1911 as controller at Schlitz Brewing, Andersen became head of the accounting department at Northwestern. In 1913 at age 28, he formed a public accounting firm, Andersen, DeLany & Company, with Clarence DeLany.

Establishment of the Federal Reserve and implementation of the federal income tax in 1913 aided the firm's early growth by increasing the demand for accounting services. The firm opened a branch office in Milwaukee in 1915 and gained large clients, including ITT, Briggs & Stratton, Colgate-Palmolive, and Parker Pen, during the period between 1913 and 1920. After DeLany's departure in 1918, the firm adopted its present name.

Andersen grew rapidly during the 1920s and, to its list of services, added financial investigations, which formed the basis for its future strength in management consulting. The firm opened 6 offices in the 1920s, including New York (1921), Kansas City (1923), and Los Angeles (1926). When Samuel Insull's empire collapsed in 1932, Andersen was appointed as the bankers' representative and guarded the assets during the refinancing. During the post-Depression period, Andersen opened additional offices in Boston and Houston (1937) and in Atlanta and Minneapolis (1940).

Arthur Andersen's presence dominated the firm during his life. He established the company's original organizational structure and pattern for growth. Upon his death in 1947, the firm found new leadership in Leonard Spacek. Under Spacek's tenure, which continued until 1963, the firm opened 18 new US offices and began a period of foreign expansion with the establishment of an office in Mexico City (1955), followed by 25 more in other countries. Over the same period (1947–1963) revenues increased from $6.5 million to $51 million.

Andersen has been an innovator among the major accounting firms in many ways. The company opened Andersen University, its Center for Professional Development, in the early 1970s on a campus in St. Charles, Illinois, and was the first to provide a worldwide annual report in 1973. During the 1970s Andersen anticipated the growth in professional service, increasing its consulting business, which accounted for 21% of revenues by 1979; by 1988 consulting fees made up 40% of revenues, making Andersen the world's largest consulting firm.

In 1989 a rash of mega mergers among the so-called "Big 8" led Andersen and Price Waterhouse (PW) to discuss a merger. Before the year was out, however, Andersen and PW ended merger discussions because of unresolved business, legal, and stylistic issues.

HOW MUCH

	9 Yr. Growth	1980	1981	1982	1983	1984	1985	1986	1987	1988	1989
Revenues ($ mil)	17.3%	806	973	1,124	1,238	1,388	1,574	1,924	2,316	2,820	3,382
No. of countries	2.3%	44	43	42	45	45	49	50	49	49	54
No. of offices	5.4%	152	156	157	168	176	215	219	226	231	243
No. of partners	6.9%	1,170	1,274	1,388	1,477	1,528	1,630	1,847	1,957	2,016	2,134
No. of employees	11.3%	18,766	20,157	22,397	22,815	24,852	28,172	34,270	37,688	43,902	49,280

1989 profits per partner:
$1,584,800
No. of partners:
618 Consulting
1,371 Accounting

Revenues ($ mil) 1980-89

Private company
Founded: Illinois, 1913
Fiscal year ends: August 31

WHO

Chairman: Gerard Van Kemmel
Managing Partner-Chief Executive: Lawrence A. Weinbach, age 50
Managing Partner, Arthur Andersen: Richard L. Measelle
Managing Partner, Andersen Consulting: George T. Shaheen
CFO: John D. Lewis
Employees: 51,414 (including 2,134 partners)

WHERE

HQ: Arthur Andersen & Co., Société Coopérative, 18, quai Général-Guisan, 1211 Geneva 3, Switzerland
Phone: 011-41-22-214444
FAX: 011-41-22-224418
US HQ: 59 W. Washington St., Chicago, IL 60602
US Phone: 312-580-0069
US FAX: 312-507-6748

Arthur Andersen & Co. maintains 243 offices in 54 countries.

	1989 Revenues	
	$ mil	% of total
US	1,994	59
Europe, Africa & Middle East	977	29
Asia/Pacific	254	7
Other Americas	157	5
Total	**3,382**	**100**

WHAT

	1989 Revenues	
	$ mil	% of total
Arthur Andersen	1,940	57
Andersen Consulting	1,442	43
Total	**3,382**	**100**

Arthur Andersen
Auditing and business advisory
Corporate specialty services
Tax services

Andersen Consulting
Change management services
Management information systems consulting
Software consulting
Software sales
Systems integration

Center for Professional Education
Client services training
In-house technical training
Management training

RANKINGS

30th in *Forbes* 400 US Private Cos.

COMPETITION

General Motors
IBM
KPMG
Marsh & McLennan
McKinsey & Co.
Price Waterhouse
Saatchi & Saatchi

ASARCO INC.

OVERVIEW

New York–based ASARCO (formerly American Smelting and Refining Company) is the 4th largest US copper producer. ASARCO's primary businesses are mining, smelting, and refining metals (from its own mines and those of other companies), and manufacturing chemicals for finishing and processing metals. Its metals businesses include nonferrous (copper, lead, and zinc) and precious (silver and gold) metals.

ASARCO expanded its specialty chemicals business in the late 1980s to offset the fluctuations of the nonferrous metals market. At the same time ASARCO increased its mineral (limestone) operations in Tennessee and Virginia and began a hazardous waste facility for metals in Corpus Christi.

The company has spent the last 4 years cutting costs and acquiring mines in an effort to become an integrated metal producer that can be profitable even at the bottom of the metal market price cycle.

ASARCO's largest shareholder is M.I.M. Holdings (Australia), which owns 24.9% of the company.

WHEN

Henry Rogers, who had helped form Standard Oil Trust in 1882, joined with Leonard and Adolph Lewisohn (copper mine owners) and others in 1899 to consolidate the US lead–silver smelting (melting and then separating ores) and refining (purifying metals) industry. The major holdouts to the enterprise, M. Guggenheim's Sons, the smelting and refining business of the Guggenheim family of Colorado (later benefactors of Mount Sinai Hospital and the Guggenheim Museum in New York), rejected the $11 million offered for their US and Mexico lead and silver smelters and their US copper refinery.

The newly formed American Smelting and Refining Company (officially renamed ASARCO in 1975) began with 16 smelters, 18 refineries, and some mines. Strong competition from the Guggenheims along with labor strikes against ASARCO resulted in immediate financial troubles. In 1901 M. Guggenheim's Sons merged with ASARCO for $45.2 million in ASARCO stock. The Guggenheims and their allies accounted for 51% of the stock. Daniel Guggenheim became chairman (president in 1905), and 4 of his brothers sat on the board. After the panic of 1907, the Guggenheims sold all but 10% of their ASARCO stock to the public.

The company expanded, buying 5 mines in Mexico (1901), Federal Mining and Smelting in Idaho (1903), and a controlling interest in US Zinc (1903). Next ASARCO bought copper mining properties in the Silver Bell district of Arizona in 1910. It began the company's first open-pit copper mine there in 1954. The company entered manufacturing with an interest in Michigan Copper and Brass (later Revere Copper and Brass, makers of Revere Ware) in 1928 (sold 1982).

In 1919 Daniel retired, his brother Simon was elected president, and an independent report in 1920 showed that the Guggenheims had become rich at ASARCO's expense. Nevertheless, Simon, the last Guggenheim to run ASARCO, remained president until 1941.

The company started mining in Peru in 1921. In 1930 ASARCO invested in Mount Isa Mines (now M.I.M. Holdings), an Australian silver, lead, zinc, and copper mining company. ASARCO expanded into specialty chemicals in 1957 with the purchase of Enthone and began asbestos mining in Quebec in 1958. The company added coal to its mining operations in 1970 with the purchase of 4 mines in Illinois (sold 1990).

ASARCO bought OMI International (chemicals, 1988) and IMASA Group (chemicals, 1989) to augment its chemical subsidiary, Enthone. ASARCO exited asbestos mining in 1989.

HOW MUCH

	9 Yr. Growth	1980	1981	1982	1983	1984	1985	1986	1987	1988	1989
Sales ($ mil)	2.2%	1,817	1,532	1,351	1,512	1,325	1,167	1,057	1,355	1,988	2,211
Net income ($ mil)	0.7%	216	50	(39)	58	(306)	(62)	9	208	207	231
Income as % of sales	—	11.9%	3.3%	(2.9%)	3.9%	(23.1%)	(5.3%)	0.9%	15.4%	10.4%	10.5%
Earnings per share ($)	(3.3%)	7.31	1.54	(2.40)	1.54	(12.56)	(2.87)	(0.05)	4.88	4.78	5.40
Stock price – high ($)	—	58.50	48.50	31.00	44.25	34.50	27.75	22.88	34.25	29.50	35.88
Stock price – low ($)	—	25.50	24.75	17.25	25.63	18.50	15.75	10.00	14.88	19.38	26.13
Stock price – close ($)	(4.0%)	43.25	25.75	29.13	30.00	19.00	18.38	14.88	28.50	27.38	29.88
P/E – high	—	8	32	—	29	—	—	—	7	6	7
P/E – low	—	3	16	—	17	—	—	—	3	4	5
Dividends per share ($)	(2.3%)	1.85	1.40	0.50	0.40	0.30	0.00	0.00	0.10	0.70	1.50
Book value per share ($)	(2.7%)	44.37	42.46	38.77	39.63	26.73	23.33	23.09	28.49	31.67	34.56

1989 Year End:
Debt ratio: 18.9%
Return on equity: 16.3%
Cash (mil): $23
Current ratio: 1.71
Long-term debt (mil): $334
Number of shares (mil): 42
Dividends:
1989 average yield: 5.0%
1989 payout: 27.8%
Market value (mil): $1,243

Stock Price History high/low 1980-89

NYSE symbol: AR
Incorporated: New Jersey, 1899
Fiscal year ends: December 31

WHO

Chairman, President, and CEO: Richard de J. Osborne, age 55, $1,058,333 pay
EVP: Thomas C. Osborne, age 62, $402,416 pay
EVP: George W. Anderson, age 56, $390,000 pay
VP Finance and Administration: Francis R. McAllister, age 47, $440,749 pay
Auditors: Coopers & Lybrand
Employees: 9,000

WHERE

HQ: 180 Maiden Ln., New York, NY 10038
Phone: 212-510-2000
FAX: 212-510-2271

ASARCO's principal US mines are located in Arizona, Colorado, Idaho, Missouri, Montana, and Tennessee. Major foreign mines are located in Australia, Canada, Mexico, and Peru.

	1989 Sales	
	$ mil	% of total
Domestic	2,029	92
Foreign	182	8
Total	**2,211**	**100**

WHAT

	1989 Sales		1989 Operating Income	
	$ mil	% of total	$ mil	% of total
Minerals	33	1	5	2
Copper properties	1,259	57	206	88
Lead/zinc properties	222	10	51	22
Precious metals properties	324	15	7	3
Specialty chemicals	238	11	4	2
Other	135	6	(40)	(17)
Adjustments	0	—	33	—
Total	**2,211**	**100**	**266**	**100**

Mining/Smelting

Antimony	Gold	Platinum
Cadmium	Lead	Silver
Copper	Molybdenum	Zinc

Major Subsidiaries/Affiliates
American Limestone Co.
Capco Pipe Co. (PVC pipe)
Encycle, Inc. (recycling)
Enthone, Inc. (chemicals)
Imasa Group (chemicals)
Mexico Desarrollo Industrial Minero, SA de CV (mining, 34%)
M.I.M. Holdings Ltd. (mining, 18.7%)
OMI International (chemicals)
Southern Peru Copper Corp. (52.3%)

RANKINGS

370th in *Forbes* Sales 500
453rd in *Business Week* 1000

COMPETITION

AMAX	Hanson
Anglo American	Manville
Broken Hill	Phelps Dodge
Cyprus Minerals	Chemical companies
FMC	

ABB ASEA BROWN BOVERI LTD.

OVERVIEW

Asea Brown Boveri (ABB) is the 2nd largest company based in Switzerland (after Nestlé). It operates 1,150 companies, grouped into 8 business segments, around the world. To prevent confusion, all company correspondence is in English and the dollar is the company-wide measure of value.

ABB holds a commanding lead in its core businesses, electric power production and transmission equipment. These businesses include gas, nuclear, and clean-coal power plant construction and instrumentation, and cable and transformer production. The company is also a world leader in the design and production of mass-transit systems equipment, high-speed trains, robotics, and manufacturing process control systems. The 1989 acquisitions of America's Combustion Engineering and Westinghouse's power transmission and distribution business are projected by the company to increase ABB's North American sales from $3.2 billion to $6.5 billion.

It is impossible to buy stock directly in ABB since the company is owned 50-50 by ASEA and BBC Brown Boveri, which maintain separate stock market identities. ASEA, controlled by the wealthy Wallenberg family, is the largest company in Sweden in terms of market value and has substantial holdings in Electrolux and SAS Airlines. BBC Brown Boveri is the 9th largest Swiss company in market value and has 5 major subsidiaries in addition to its holdings in ABB.

WHEN

Asea Brown Boveri was formed in 1987 when 2 giants, ASEA of Sweden and BBC Brown Boveri of Switzerland, combined their electrical engineering and equipment businesses. Percy Barnevik, head of ASEA, became CEO of the new company, which set up headquarters in Oerlikon, outside Zurich.

ASEA was founded in Stockholm in 1883 as Electriska Aktiebolaget. The electrical equipment manufacturer changed its name to Allmänna Svenska Electriska Aktiebolaget (ASEA) in 1890. The company rapidly expanded into related areas, acquiring electrical generation and transmission equipment companies such as Skandinaviska Elektricitetsverk (1912) and Svenska Turbinfabriks (1916), a Swedish turbine maker. In the period following WWII, ASEA expanded both within the domestic market and into foreign markets. In 1962 the company bought 20% of electric appliance maker Electrolux and formed Scandinavian Glasfiber with Owens-Corning Fiberglas (US). Through the acquisitions of transportation equipment manufacturer Hagglund & Soner (1972) and BICC Capacitors (UK, 1984), the power plant equipment joint venture ASEA-ATOM (1982), and numerous other investments, ASEA became one of the world's largest companies in electrical production and transmission equipment, appliances, electronics, and transportation and industrial equipment.

BBC Brown Boveri was formed as a partnership, Brown, Boveri, and Company, by Charles Brown and Walter Boveri in Baden, Switzerland, in 1891 to produce electrical generation equipment. It produced the first steam turbines in Europe (1900). BBC established companies in Germany (1893), France (1894), and Italy (1903) to produce and distribute its steam and gas turbine equipment. After WWII the company diversified into nuclear power generating equipment. Electrical machinery production expanded with the purchase of Maschinenfabrik Oerlikon (1967), a Swiss company that manufactured electrical equipment in France and Spain. BBC's US operation increased in 1979 when the company formed a joint venture with Gould to produce electrical equipment. The company adopted its current name in 1987.

In an unusual form of merger, both ASEA and BBC withheld certain assets, such as ASEA's holdings in Electrolux, from the combination, and each company continues as a separate entity, sharing ownership in the new company 50-50. Asea Brown Boveri formed 2 joint ventures with Westinghouse in 1988, one to produce turbines and generators, the other to manufacture electrical transmission and distribution equipment. In 1989 ABB bought Westinghouse's half of the transmission and distribution joint venture. The company has been restructuring to strengthen its power generation business and exploit opportunities in mass transit, electronics, and manufacturing and environmental control systems for the paper and food processing industries.

HOW MUCH

	1 Yr. Growth	1980	1981	1982	1983	1984	1985	1986	1987	1988	1989
Sales ($ mil)	15.3%	—	—	—	—	—	—	—	—	17,832	20,560
Net income ($ mil)	52.6%	—	—	—	—	—	—	—	—	386	589
Income as % of sales	—	—	—	—	—	—	—	—	—	2.2%	2.9%

1989 Year End:
Debt ratio: 30.9%
Return on equity: 16.8%
Cash (mil): $4,332
Assets (mil): $24,156
Current ratio: 1.24
Long-term debt (mil): $1,746

Foreign company
Incorporated: Switzerland, 1987
Fiscal year ends: December 31

WHO

President and CEO: Percy Barnevik, age 49
Deputy CEO: Thomas Gasser, age 57
EVP, US Region: Gerhard Schulmeyer, age 52
Auditors: KPMG Klynveld Peat Marwick Goerdeler SA
Employees: 189,493

WHERE

HQ: P. O. B. 8131, CH-8050 Zurich, Switzerland
Phone: 011-41-1-31771-11
FAX: 011-41-1-31198-17
US HQ: 900 Long Ridge Rd., Stamford, CT 06904
US Phone: 203-329-8771
US FAX: 203-328-2263 (Public Relations)

ABB maintains headquarters in Switzerland but conducts business through 1,150 companies located worldwide.

	1989 Sales		1989 Employees	
	$ mil	% of total	no.	% of total
Western Europe – EC	6,573	32	64,746	34
Western Europe – Other	6,352	31	70,354	37
North America	3,251	16	17,121	9
Asia & Australasia	2,785	14	18,993	10
Other	1,599	7	18,279	10
Total	**20,560**	**100**	**189,493**	**100**

WHAT

	1989 Sales		1989 Operating Income	
	$ mil	% of total	$ mil	% of total
Power plants	2,795	12	219	16
Power transmission	4,775	21	288	21
Power distribution	2,516	11	140	10
Industry	2,019	9	131	9
Transportation	957	4	57	4
Environmental control	2,843	12	130	9
Financial services	1,446	6	95	7
Intragroup	(2,385)	—	(144)	—
Other	5,594	25	341	24
Total	**20,560**	**100**	**1,257**	**100**

Products
Fossil fuel and hydropower
Instrument, motors, robotics, and superchargers
Low- and medium-voltage systems
Mass transit rail systems
Production control systems
Reinsurance and leasing
Transformers and switches
Waste treatment and industry anti-pollution systems

Major US Holdings
AccuRay
Allen Bradley/Strömberg Inc.
Combustion Engineering Inc.
Industrial Ceramic Inc.

RANKINGS

43rd in *Fortune* 500 Industrial Cos.
11th in *Forbes* 100 Foreign Investments in the US
91st in *Business Week* Global 1000

COMPETITION

Bechtel
Cooper Industries
Daimler-Benz
Duke Power
General Electric
Halliburton
Hitachi
McDermott
Mitsubishi
Reliance Electric
Siemens
Square D
Westinghouse

ASHLAND OIL, INC.

OVERVIEW

Although its headquarters are tucked away in a small town in Kentucky (in Russell, not Ashland), Ashland Oil is the largest US independent petroleum refiner and marketer, and its operations extend around the world.

Ashland Exploration drills in the US (concentrating on natural gas) and in Nigeria (crude oil). Ashland Petroleum's 3 refineries sell much of their gasoline output to independent marketers. Ashland refineries also provide gasoline to the company's SuperAmerica convenience/gas stores, nearly 600 of them in 17 states.

Ashland owns Valvoline, which includes the well-known motor oil and other automotive products. Ashland Chemical is the leading US distributor of petrochemicals needed for fiberglass-reinforced plastics. Other products include resins, foundry chemicals, water-treatment chemicals, and chemicals for semiconductor production. Ashland Coal (46% owned) operates mines in West Virginia and Kentucky.

APAC, the company's construction group, operates a network of 167 asphalt plants and is a major supplier of construction services and materials. APAC also builds highways and other major projects in 15 Sunbelt states. Ashland is selling chunks of its troubled engineering consulting segment.

NYSE symbol: ASH
Incorporated: Kentucky, 1936
Fiscal year ends: September 30

WHO

Chairman and CEO: John R. Hall, age 57, $936,607 pay
President and COO: Charles J. Luellen, age 60, $668,108 pay
SVP and CFO: Paul W. Chellgren, age 46, $496,629 pay
SVP Human Resources and Law: Richard W. Spears, age 53, $479,511 pay
SVP and Group Operating Officer: John A. Brothers, age 49, $476,767 pay
Auditors: Ernst & Young
Employees: 37,800

WHEN

J. Fred Miles sold his Oklahoma oil drilling company in 1917 to wheel and deal in Kentucky. He attracted Chicago backers and prominent Kentuckians to invest in his Swiss Oil Company drilling venture.

In 1924 Swiss bought a troubled refinery in Catlettsburg, then a rough-and-tumble river town near the more sedate Ashland, and created the Ashland Refining subsidiary. Miles battled Swiss directors for control, lost, and resigned in 1927.

Swiss expanded by purchasing Tri-State Refining (1930) and Cumberland Pipeline's eastern Kentucky network (1931). Swiss changed its name to Ashland Oil and Refining in 1936.

Following WWII, CEO Paul Blazer spurred Ashland to acquire small independent oil firms (Allied Oil in 1948, Aetna Oil in 1950). When Ashland bought Freedom-Valvoline in 1950, it acquired the venerable Valvoline name. Ashland purchased Frontier Oil of Buffalo and National Refining of Cleveland in 1950.

Blazer passed the torch to Orin Atkins in 1965. Ashland formed its Ashland Chemical subsidiary in 1967 after acquiring Anderson-Prichard Oil (1958), United Carbon (1963), and ADM Chemical (1967). The company added its SuperAmerica retail marketing chain (1970) and began exploring Nigeria for oil (1973).

In 1975 Atkins admitted ordering Ashland executives to make illegal contributions to the Nixon campaign. Atkins was deposed in 1981 after Ashland made questionable payments to highly placed "consultants" with connections to oil-rich Middle Eastern governments. In one such payment, Ashland had bankrolled a consultant's scheme to manufacture reusable sausage casings.

Atkins was arrested in 1988 for attempting to fence purloined documents regarding litigation between Ashland and the National Iranian Oil Company. Ashland, which launched the federal investigation that led to Atkins's arrest, settled with NIOC for $325 million in 1989. Atkins pleaded guilty to charges related to the documents and, while he awaited sentencing in 1990, cooperated in the prosecution of a Florida lawyer on related charges. The Floridian was acquitted.

Even without Atkins as a lightning rod, Ashland faced challenges. Chairman John Hall had to fend off a hostile takeover by the Belzberg family of Canada (1986) by expanding an employee stock ownership plan. In the late 1980s Ashland refocused on refining and marketing.

WHERE

HQ: 1000 Ashland Dr., Russell, KY 41169
Phone: 606-329-3333
FAX: 606-329-5274

Ashland businesses operate worldwide.

WHAT

	1989 Sales		1989 Operating Income	
	$ mil	% of total	$ mil	% of total
Exploration	253	3	20	6
Chemical	2,230	23	128	39
Petroleum	3,177	33	142	43
Gasoline & mdse. stores	1,795	18	53	16
Motor oil	616	6	36	11
Construction	1,066	11	40	12
Engineering	601	6	(90)	(27)
Adjustments	(1,676)	—	(148)	—
Total	**8,062**	**100**	**181**	**100**

Businesses
APAC (construction)
Arch Mineral Corp. (coal, 50% owned)
Ashland Branded Marketing, Inc. (retailing)
Ashland Chemical, Inc. (chemicals)
Ashland Coal, Inc. (coal, 46% owned)
Ashland Exploration, Inc. (oil and gas production)
Ashland Petroleum (refining, transportation)
Ashland Technology Corp. (engineering)
Beaird Industries, Inc. (engineering)
Riley Consolidated, Inc. (engineering)
SuperAmerica Group, Inc. (retailing)
Valvoline, Inc. (automotive products)

Brand Names

Ashland	Payless	Save More
Bi-Lo	Pyroil	SoLo
Hi-Fy	Red Head	SuperAmerica
IG-LO	Rich Oil	TECTYL
Mac's	Save Mart	Valvoline

HOW MUCH

	9 Yr. Growth	1980	1981	1982	1983	1984	1985	1986	1987	1988	1989
Sales ($ mil)	(0.1%)	8,118	9,262	8,865	7,852	8,330	7,945	7,083	6,993	7,826	8,062
Net income ($ mil)	(9.2%)	205	90	181	97	(172)	147	209	133	184	86
Income as % of sales	—	2.5%	1.0%	2.0%	1.2%	(2.1%)	1.8%	2.9%	1.9%	2.3%	1.1%
Earnings per share ($)	(8.3%)	3.37	1.11	2.64	1.11	(4.46)	2.06	3.08	2.14	3.29	1.55
Stock price – high ($)	—	22.88	20.88	17.50	19.00	14.75	19.69	32.13	35.88	38.13	43.00
Stock price – low ($)	—	12.88	13.50	10.25	12.38	10.38	12.00	17.75	23.25	26.38	33.13
Stock price – close ($)	7.8%	20.31	15.63	14.50	14.25	12.00	18.69	28.00	28.88	33.50	40.00
P/E – high	—	7	19	7	17	—	10	10	17	12	28
P/E – low	—	4	12	4	11	—	6	6	11	8	21
Dividends per share ($)	(1.1%)	1.10	1.20	1.20	1.10	0.80	0.80	0.85	0.90	0.95	1.00
Book value per share ($)	1.4%	17.33	18.29	19.70	19.63	15.10	16.37	14.92	17.17	19.06	19.62

1989 Year End:
Debt ratio: 48.5%
Return on equity: 8.0%
Cash (mil): $70
Current ratio: 1.17
Long-term debt (mil): $1,074
Number of shares (mil): 58
Dividends:
1989 average yield: 2.5%
1989 payout: 64.5%
Market value (mil): $2,326

Stock Price History high/low 1980-89

RANKINGS

58th in *Fortune* 500 Industrial Cos.
158th in *Fortune* Global 500 Industrial Cos.
99th in *Forbes* Sales 500
295th in *Business Week* 1000
905th in *Business Week* Global 1000

COMPETITION

Amoco	Exxon	Sun
Atlantic Richfield	Mobil	Texaco
Bechtel	Occidental	Unocal
British Petroleum	Pennzoil	USX
Chevron	Phillips	Other chemical companies
Coastal	Royal Dutch/Shell	
Du Pont		

ASSOCIATED MILK PRODUCERS, INC.

OVERVIEW

San Antonio–based Associated Milk Producers, Inc. (AMPI) is the largest milk cooperative in the US, accounting for 12% of the country's milk supply and 25% of nonfat dry milk production. The association has over 19,400 members in 21 states, down from 23,500 in 1986 due to the continuing attrition of dairy farms.

The 3 operating regions of AMPI differ in their market focus. The North Central Region processes most of its milk production into cheese, nonfat dry milk, and canned sauces under the name State Brand. The Morning Glory Farms Region supplies milk to the Chicago market and manufactures cheese, sour cream, and frozen yogurt. The Southern Region concentrates on supplying Grade A milk to several markets but also operates 9 manufacturing plants.

Modern farm cooperatives are the descendants of thousands of cooperatives formed in the 1870s by a national farmers' organization called the Grange. Originally established to aid farmers with their purchasing, storage, and marketing needs, these cooperatives have consolidated over the last century and have extended the services they offer to their members to include credit, life insurance, and retirement programs.

Through C-TAPE, the largest agricultural PAC in the US, AMPI expects to contribute $1 million to political campaigns in 1990 in an effort to ensure that the 1990 Farm Bill increases price supports and that the international negotiations to liberalize trade, known as GATT, won't harm dairy interests. In 1988 AMPI formed TEX-TAPE to focus political efforts in the Texas legislature.

WHEN

In 1969, faced with declining dairy income and milk consumption by the public, about 100 dairy cooperatives in the Midwest and the South merged to form Associated Milk Producers, Inc. (AMPI). The membership elected John Butterbrodt, from a Wisconsin cooperative, as the first president and established headquarters in San Antonio, home of the largest of the predecessor cooperatives, Milk Producers Association. Cooperatives throughout the central US clamored to join, and mergers took place almost weekly, making AMPI the largest US dairy cooperative within 2 years of its formation.

Almost from the beginning, AMPI became embroiled in the 2 main controversies that have concerned dairy cooperatives: monopolistic practices and political contributions. In 1972 it was alleged by consumer advocate Ralph Nader that the 3 main dairy cooperatives — AMPI, Dairymen, and Mid-America Dairymen — had illegally contributed $422,000 to President Nixon's re-election campaign in an attempt to obtain higher price supports (enacted in 1971) and an agreement that the administration would drop its antitrust suits against the cooperatives. Watergate investigators subpoenaed Nixon's tapes, and AMPI was accused of bribery, destruction of evidence, and attempting to achieve "complete market dominance." In 1974 AMPI pleaded guilty to making illegal political contributions in 1968, 1970, and 1972. By 1975, 3 former AMPI employees had been convicted of various charges and Butterbrodt had resigned.

AMPI spent the last half of the 1970s quietly reorganizing, including establishing its current regional management structure. In 1982 another suit for monopolistic practices, originally filed in 1971 by the National Farmers' Organization (NFO), finally reached the federal courts. The case was decided in favor of AMPI and 2 other large cooperatives, but before the year was out an appeals court reversed the decision, saying AMPI and its codefendants had conspired to eliminate competitive sellers of milk. In 1983 Congress rejected a bill to cut price supports for dairy farmers and instead adopted a program to pay farmers not to produce milk. Industry critics charged that the 3 major milk cooperatives had bought the legislation through large political contributions.

AMPI extended its dominance of the industry in 1985 by merging its central region, then called the Mid-States Region, with 2,200 members of Shawano, Wisconsin–based Morning Glory Farms Cooperative to form the Morning Glory Farms Region. In 1989 the NFO antitrust case against the dairy cooperatives finally reached the US Supreme Court, which refused to alter the appeals court's ruling.

HOW MUCH

	9 Yr. Growth	1980	1981	1982	1983	1984	1985	1986	1987	1988	1989
Sales ($ mil)	2.6%	2,361	2,593	2,592	2,654	2,485	2,416	2,489	2,710	2,777	2,987
Net income + capital retains ($ mil)	4.8%	21	18	21	18	17	16	21	25	23	32
Member farms	(3.5%)	26,700	26,500	26,400	25,400	24,600	23,300	23,500	22,400	20,800	19,428
Milk deliveries (mil lbs.)	1.6%	15,000	15,560	15,730	16,400	15,050	15,700	15,900	17,200	17,700	17,300

1989 Year End:
Debt ratio: 51.1%
Cash (mil): $3
Current ratio: 1.45
Long-term debt (mil): $158
Members' equity(mil): $151

Sales ($ mil) 1980-89

3000
2500
2000
1500
1000
500
0

Mutual company
Incorporated: Kansas, 1969
Fiscal year ends: December 31

WHO

President: Irvin J. Elkin
General Manager: Ira E. Rutherford
Controller and CFO: Harry Pickens
Auditors: Deloitte & Touche
Employees: 4,200

WHERE

HQ: 6609 Blanco Rd., PO Box 790287, San Antonio, TX 78279
Phone: 512-340-9100
FAX: 512-340-9158

AMPI is divided into 3 regions. The North Central Region encompasses parts of Iowa, Michigan, Minnesota, Missouri, Nebraska, and North and South Dakota. The Morning Glory Farms Region includes parts of Illinois, Indiana, Iowa, Michigan, Ohio, and Wisconsin. The Southern Region serves Arkansas, New Mexico, Oklahoma, Texas, and parts of Colorado, Kansas, Kentucky, Mississippi, Missouri, Nebraska, and Tennessee.

	1989 Regional Membership	
	member farms	% of total
North Central Region	8,278	43
Morning Glory Farms Region	7,224	37
Southern Region	3,926	20
Total	**19,428**	**100**

WHAT

	1989 Production million pounds
Milk	17,300
American cheese	493
Butter	136
Nonfat dry milk	214
Dried whey	207

Dairy Activities
Grade A milk production

Production and packaging of dairy products, canned cheese sauces, and other milk-based goods under the State Brand, Morning Glory, and other labels

Northland Foods Cooperative (82%)
A subsidiary cooperative

Membership Services
AMPI Investment Corp.
Investment subsidiary of the Southern Region

Women and Young Cooperator programs, retirement plans, and member insurance

Political Activities
Committee for Thorough Agricultural Political Education (C-TAPE)

Texans for Thorough Agricultural Political Education (TEX-TAPE)

RANKINGS

34th in *Fortune* 100 Diversified Service Cos.

COMPETITION

Borden
Philip Morris
RJR Nabisco

ATARI CORPORATION

OVERVIEW

Atari Corporation, once America's premier video game producer, today is a major manufacturer of personal computers. The Sunnyvale, California, company continues to manufacture and develop game systems, but personal computers, ranging from laptops to powerful PC-compatibles to the Atari ST series, are Atari's primary product line (76% of net sales).

Atari's most recent introduction in the PC market is a "palmtop" computer, the Portfolio, which weighs less than a pound. It is small enough to fit in a coat pocket. The Portfolio runs on 3 AA batteries and comes with 5 built-in applications including a Lotus 1-2-3–compatible spreadsheet program.

Atari's 1989 introduction of its Lynx may revive its games segment. Initial sales of the full-color, hand-held video game have been brisk (Atari anticipates one million units will sell in 1990), but the recent introduction of comparable products from NEC and Sega is giving Lynx stiff competition.

Although overseas markets, principally Europe, represent 82% of Atari's sales, the company is launching a multimillion dollar advertising campaign in the US to boost sales. Atari's primary competitor in the game market is Nintendo, which commands 80% of the US market.

WHEN

Atari was established in Sunnyvale, California, in 1972 by Nolan Bushnell, an engineer, who produced his first video arcade game while tinkering with microcomputers at home. The game, Computer Space, developed in 1971, was a commercial flop, but Bushnell's 2nd game, Pong, became an overwhelming success. Atari sold 10,000 of its units in 1973 and 150,000 home versions in 1975.

Atari's success lured others into the industry, including Magnavox, Bally, Coleco, and RCA. With the added competition, prices dropped and the demand for new games increased. By 1976 the enthusiasm for home video games had waned, and Atari was in need of an infusion of capital. That year Bushnell sold Atari to Warner Communications for $28 million, of which Bushnell received $15 million. Bushnell left Atari 2 years later and went on to start Chuck E. Cheese pizza parlors, among other things.

In 1979 Atari sales picked up due to the popularity of its Video Computer System, a cartridge-loaded color graphics console that sold for $200 (introduced in 1977), and the success of its newer, more advanced video arcade games (Asteroids and Missile Command). In 1980 Atari sales reached $415 million, representing 1/3 of Warner's sales.

Atari introduced its first line of personal computers in 1980. Initial sales were disappointing, however, and the company took a loss of $10 million in computer sales its first year.

By 1982 the interest in video games had diminished. In 1983 Atari's competitors began dropping out of the market, and Atari lost $533 million. In 1984 Warner sold Atari to Jack Tramiel, former CEO of Commodore — Atari's prime competitor in home computers.

By 1986 Tramiel had Atari in the black, with net income of $25 million on revenues of $258 million. Contributing to the turnaround was Atari's successive introductions of low-cost personal computers (Atari ST line).

In 1988 Atari took a loss of $84.8 million due largely to discontinuation of certain operations of its electronics retail chain, Federated Group (acquired by Atari in 1987). In 1989 Atari placed Federated up for sale and in 1990 succeeded in selling 26 of its California stores to Silo and closed the rest. The company ended 1989 with a net income of $4 million on sales of $424 million.

HOW MUCH

	4 Yr. Growth	1980	1981	1982	1983	1984	1985	1986	1987	1988	1989
Sales ($ mil)	31.5%	—	—	—	—	—	142	258	493	452	424
Net income ($ mil)	—	—	—	—	—	—	(14)	25	44	39	4
Income as % of sales	—	—	—	—	—	—	(10.1%)	9.7%	9.0%	8.7%	0.9%
Earnings per share ($)	—	—	—	—	—	—	(0.31)	0.53	0.74	0.67	0.07
Stock price – high ($)	—	—	—	—	—	—	—	7.63	16.19	9.13	12.75
Stock price – low ($)	—	—	—	—	—	—	—	5.63	4.88	4.88	4.75
Stock price – close ($)	—	—	—	—	—	—	—	7.06	7.50	5.63	8.63
P/E – high	—	—	—	—	—	—	—	14	22	14	182
P/E – low	—	—	—	—	—	—	—	11	7	7	68
Dividends per share ($)	—	—	—	—	—	—	0.00	0.00	0.00	0.00	0.00
Book value per share ($)	—	—	—	—	—	—	(0.60)	1.82	2.91	1.44	1.49

1989 Year End:
Debt ratio: 47.4%
Return on equity: 4.8%
Cash (mil): $55
Current ratio: 1.83
Long-term debt (mil): $77
Number of shares (mil): 58
Dividends:
1989 average yield: 0.0%
1989 payout: 0.0%
Market value (mil): $498

Stock Price History high/low 1986-89

ASE symbol: ATC
Incorporated: Nevada, 1984
Fiscal year ends: Saturday closest to December 31

WHO

President, COO, and CEO: Sam Tramiel, age 39, $200,198 pay
Chairman: Jack Tramiel, age 60, $177,158 pay
VP: Taro Tokai, age 43, $183,055 pay
VP and CFO: Gregory A. Pratt, age 40, $150,204 pay
Auditors: Deloitte & Touche
Employees: 1,420

WHERE

HQ: 1196 Borregas Ave., Sunnyvale, CA 94086
Phone: 408-745-2000
FAX: 408-745-4306

The company has offices in the US and 19 foreign countries and a manufacturing facility in Taiwan.

	1989 Sales		1989 Operating Income	
	$ mil	% of total	$ mil	% of total
North America*	93	22	(2)	—
Europe	308	73	(2)	—
Other	23	5	8	—
Total	**424**	**100**	**4**	**—**

*including exports from North America

WHAT

	1989 Sales	
	$ mil	% of total
Computer products	322	76
Game products	102	24
Total	**424**	**100**

Portable Personal Computers
Atari Portfolio

Laptop
Stacy

Personal Computers
ABC386SX
Atari MEGA4
Atari PC4
Atari PC5
Atari ST
Atari STE
Atari Transputer Workstation
Atari TT030

Game Products
Atari 2600
Atari 7800
Atari Lynx
Video games

RANKINGS

946th in *Business Week* 1000

COMPETITION

Apple
Commodore
Hyundai
Mattel
NEC
Tandy
Makers of IBM-compatible personal computers

ATLANTIC RICHFIELD COMPANY

OVERVIEW

Los Angeles–based Atlantic Richfield (ARCO) is the largest US producer of low-sulfur coal, the 8th largest US petroleum refiner, and #1 in profit per barrel of oil and gas equivalent. After a record year, the 1989 ROE of 29.5% makes ARCO the most profitable major US integrated petroleum company. It produces 90% of its crude oil and natural gas liquids from US assets, including 60% from Alaska (425,000 barrels of oil a day).

ARCO left the East Coast gasoline market in 1985 and became the West Coast's largest seller of gasoline, bypassing leader Chevron in late 1986. ARCO operates its am/pm minimarkets (with and without accompanying gasoline pumps) in the same region and has licensed minimarkets in Japan and Taiwan. ARCO also runs the largest coal mine in the Western Hemisphere, Black Thunder, located in Wyoming's Powder River Basin.

WHEN

In 1866 Charles Lockhart and other pioneers in the Pennsylvania oil industry formed Atlantic Petroleum Storage in Philadelphia. In 1870 the company changed its name to Atlantic Refining after it bought a small refinery. Atlantic Refining became a secret affiliate of Standard Oil in 1874, and in 1911 the Supreme Court dissolved Standard Oil, spinning off Atlantic Refining with refining and marketing capabilities only.

In the 1920s Atlantic Refining explored for oil in Iraq and in the 1930s designed the first all-welded ship. Through the 1950s and 1960s Atlantic Refining bought oil and plastic companies. In 1963 it bought Hondo Oil & Gas (New Mexico) from independent oilman Robert Anderson. The company paid Anderson with shares of the company's stock, making him the largest shareholder. In 1965 the board elected Anderson chairman.

Under Anderson, Atlantic Refining grew from a small East Coast oil refiner to a large West Coast integrated oil leader. In 1966 Atlantic Refining formed a joint venture (Oxirane Chemical, fully acquired 1980) with Halcon International. Also in 1966 Atlantic Refining purchased Richfield Oil, founded as Rio Grande (California, 1905), and adopted Atlantic Richfield (ARCO) as its name. Richfield's assets included an exploration program on the North Slope of Alaska (at Prudhoe Bay).

In 1968 ARCO, exploring on the North Slope in partnership with Humble Oil (later Exxon), drilled into the largest oil deposit in North America. To transport the oil to the lower 48 states, 8 oil companies formed the Trans Alaska Pipeline System (TAPS). The primary owners of TAPS were Sohio (33%), ARCO (21%), Exxon (20%), and BP (17%). In 1977 the oil field began production, and the completed pipeline began transporting oil from Prudhoe Bay to the ice-free coastal waters of Valdez, 800 miles away.

In 1969 ARCO bought Sinclair Oil, a midwestern integrated oil company. ARCO moved its headquarters to Los Angeles in 1972. Diversifying into other natural resources, ARCO bought Anaconda (1977), a Montana copper and uranium mining company. Anderson, who had planned to lead only 3 years, stayed for 21, retiring in 1986.

In 1985 ARCO authorized the repurchase of up to $4 billion of its common stock to make itself a less appealing takeover target. The company sold or closed its weak, noncore businesses, including Anaconda operations, and buttressed its energy and chemical businesses. ARCO bought the California oil and gas properties of Tenneco in 1988 for $700 million. In 1989 ARCO spun off 50.1% of Houston-based Lyondell Petrochemical, a subsidiary created in 1988. Net proceeds of the stock sale were $1.2 billion, resulting in a $634 million pretax gain.

HOW MUCH

	9 Yr. Growth	1980	1981	1982	1983	1984	1985	1986	1987	1988	1989
Sales ($ mil)	(4.7%)	23,744	27,797	26,462	25,147	23,768	21,723	14,487	16,282	17,626	15,351
Net income ($ mil)	1.9%	1,651	1,671	1,676	1,548	1,129	333	615	1,224	1,583	1,953
Income as % of sales	—	7.0%	6.0%	6.3%	6.2%	4.8%	1.5%	4.2%	7.5%	9.0%	12.7%
Earnings per share ($)	6.0%	6.64	6.66	6.61	6.03	4.41	1.55	3.38	6.68	8.78	11.26
Stock price – high ($)	—	74.38	66.50	50.00	52.75	52.50	67.88	64.38	99.13	90.88	114.38
Stock price – low ($)	—	38.63	38.25	32.25	37.00	40.63	42.00	45.25	58.75	67.50	80.38
Stock price – close ($)	6.4%	63.63	46.88	42.00	43.25	44.13	63.75	60.00	69.00	80.63	111.38
P/E – high	—	11	10	8	9	12	44	19	15	10	10
P/E – low	—	6	6	5	6	9	27	13	9	8	7
Dividends per share ($)	10.7%	1.80	2.20	2.40	2.40	3.00	3.75	4.00	4.00	4.00	4.50
Book value per share ($)	2.8%	31.13	35.77	39.88	43.44	42.02	30.62	29.62	33.07	36.32	39.96

1989 Year End:
Debt ratio: 44.7%
Return on equity: 29.5%
Cash (mil): $3,009
Current ratio: 1.58
Long-term debt (mil): $5,313
Number of shares (mil): 164
Dividends:
1989 average yield: 4.0%
1989 payout: 40.0%
Market value (mil): $18,286

Stock Price History high/low 1980-89
120
100
80
60
40
20
0

NYSE symbol: ARC
Incorporated: Delaware, 1985
Fiscal year ends: December 31

WHO

Chairman and CEO: Lodwrick M. Cook, age 61, $1,930,346 pay
President and COO: Robert E. Wycoff, age 59, $1,248,146 pay
EVP: James S. Morrison, age 60, $1,002,425 pay
EVP: James A. Middleton, age 54, $958,672 pay
EVP and CFO: Ronald J. Arnault, age 46, $954,417 pay
Auditors: Coopers & Lybrand
Employees: 26,600

WHERE

HQ: 515 S. Flower St., Los Angeles, CA 90071
Phone: 213-486-3511
FAX: 213-486-2063

ARCO explores for and produces oil and gas in the US, the North Sea, and Indonesia. It has 2 West Coast refineries and chemical plants in 5 countries. It sells gasoline at 1,700 ARCO service stations in 5 West Coast states. ARCO also mines coal in Colorado, Utah, Wyoming, and Australia.

	1989 Sales	
	$ mil	% of total
US	12,419	81
Foreign	2,932	19
Total	**15,351**	**100**

WHAT

	1989 Sales		1989 Operating Income	
	$ mil	% of total	$ mil	% of total
Oil & gas	8,138	42	1,464	53
Coal	519	3	138	5
Refining & mktg.	6,789	36	484	17
Transportation	862	5	424	15
Intermediate chemicals & specialty prods.	2,663	14	596	21
Other	55	—	(317)	(11)
Adjustments	(3,675)	—	(580)	—
Total	**15,351**	**100**	**2,209**	**100**

Major Operations
Chemical manufacturing
Coal mining
Oil and gas exploration and production
Petroleum refining
Transportation of crude and refined products

RANKINGS

22nd in *Fortune* 500 Industrial Cos.
60th in *Fortune* Global 500 Industrial Cos.
34th in *Forbes* Sales 500
19th in *Business Week* 1000
33rd in *Business Week* Global 1000

COMPETITION

Amoco
Ashland
British Petroleum
Chevron
Coastal
Du Pont
Exxon
Mobil
Occidental
Pennzoil
Phillips
Royal Dutch/Shell
Sun
Texaco
Union Texas
Unocal
USX
Coal companies
Other chemical companies

AUTOMATIC DATA PROCESSING, INC.

OVERVIEW

Automatic Data Processing (ADP) is the largest independent information processing company in the US and sells payroll services to 200,000 employers that pay 11 million workers. Services include payroll tax calculation, check processing, and human resource record keeping. Employer Services provides 50% of the company's revenues, with processing centers located in the US, Canada, Brazil, and Western Europe.

The company offers on-line stock and commodity trading, quotation, and information services to stockbrokers in the US, Canada, Europe, and Hong Kong through 55,000 terminals. ADP also distributes corporate documents to stockholders.

ADP sells information services, including parts catalogs on computer disks, to over 6,500 vehicle and heavy-equipment dealers in the US. ADP recently introduced its new hand-held computer for insurance adjusters to use in outlying locations.

ADP also produces on-site accounting and inventory systems for manufacturers, distributors, and wholesalers and provides financing for its systems. The company ended 1989 with increases in earnings per share for the 28th consecutive year.

NYSE symbol: AUD
Incorporated: Delaware, 1961
Fiscal year ends: June 30

WHO

Chairman and CEO: Josh S. Weston, age 60, $669,487 pay
President and COO: William J. Turner, age 45, $472,998 pay
SVP Administration and Finance: Arthur F. Weinbach, age 46, $318,926 pay
SVP, Secretary, and Counsel to Board: Fred S. Lafer, age 60
Auditors: Deloitte & Touche
Employees: 21,000

WHEN

Henry Taub started Automatic Payrolls, a company that prepared payrolls manually for other firms, in 1949 in Paterson, New Jersey. Taub's business had 8 accounts creating gross revenues of around $2,000 in 1949. In 1952 Taub's brother Joe joined the company, as did a childhood friend, Frank R. Lautenberg, who became the company's first salesman. During the 1950s the company continued selling its payroll services to new clients and grew steadily.

In 1961 the company went public and changed its name to Automatic Data Processing (ADP). The next year ADP offered back-office services to brokerage houses and bought its first computer, beginning the automation of the company's manual accounting business. In 1962 ADP's revenues reached $1 million.

During the 1970s ADP bought more than 30 companies in the US, Brazil, and England, all involved in data and payroll processing, shareholder services, computer networks, inventory control, or automated banking. ADP stock began trading on the NYSE (1970), revenues reached $50 million (1971), and the company started data centers in Florida (1972) and Connecticut (1973). In 1975 Lautenberg became CEO.

ADP bought over 25 more businesses during the 1980s in the US, Canada, and Germany, mainly in data and information services. ADP's purchases of stock information providers GTE Telenet (1983) and Bunker Ramo's information system business (1986) brought the company 45,000 stock quote terminals in brokerages like E.F. Hutton, Dean Witter, and Prudential-Bache. When Frank Lautenberg resigned as CEO to become one of New Jersey's US senators in 1983, Josh Weston, who had joined ADP as VP of planning in 1970, replaced him.

By 1984 ADP revenues had climbed to $1 billion. In 1985, when founder Henry Taub retired as chairman, Weston was elected to replace him. In 1986 the company sold the German data processing firm it had bought in 1981, as well as the US banking operations ADP had bought earlier in 1986 as part of Bunker Ramo. ADP installed 15,000 computer workstations at brokerages in 1986, and in 1989 the company began installing more than 38,000 new integrated workstations at Merrill Lynch and Shearson Lehman Hutton. Also in 1989 ADP sold its automated teller, banking, and real estate services and its Canadian brokerage quotation businesses and bought a payroll processing company. In 1990 the company sold most of its Brazilian businesses.

WHERE

HQ: One ADP Blvd., Roseland, NJ 07068
Phone: 201-994-5000
FAX: 201-994-5387

The company has over 72 regional processing centers in the US, Canada, Brazil, and Western Europe, and back- and front-office brokerage service centers in New Jersey.

WHAT

	1989 Approximate % of Sales
Employer services	50
Brokerage services	20
Dealer services	10
Other	10
Total	**100**

Employer Services
Payroll processing
Payroll tax filing
Personnel record keeping and reporting
Unemployment compensation management

Brokerage Services
Brokerage processing
Cage management
On-line inquiry and data collection
On-line trading
Order matching
Portfolio reporting
Stock loan accounting

Dealer Services
Computer systems sales and maintenance
Software licensing and support

Other
Automatic claims services
Interactive business services
Leasing and financing services
Timeshared computing services

RANKINGS

62nd in *Fortune* 100 Diversified Service Cos.
447th in *Forbes* Sales 500
160th in *Business Week* 1000
439th in *Business Week* Global 1000

COMPETITION

Citicorp
Control Data
Dow Jones
Knight-Ridder
Reuters
Banks offering payroll services

HOW MUCH

	9 Yr. Growth	1980	1981	1982	1983	1984	1985	1986	1987	1988	1989
Sales ($ mil)	15.6%	455	558	669	753	889	1,030	1,204	1,384	1,549	1,678
Net income ($ mil)	18.7%	40	47	58	65	75	88	106	132	170	188
Income as % of sales	—	8.8%	8.5%	8.6%	8.6%	8.5%	8.5%	8.8%	9.5%	11.0%	11.2%
Earnings per share ($)	15.9%	0.65	0.76	0.86	0.93	1.07	1.24	1.40	1.68	2.14	2.46
Stock price – high ($)	—	13.25	15.88	19.00	22.25	20.13	30.00	38.75	54.50	47.25	50.75
Stock price – low ($)	—	8.13	11.69	10.31	16.44	14.75	17.63	28.00	27.75	34.63	35.75
Stock price – close ($)	16.5%	12.38	12.56	18.50	17.75	19.50	29.50	35.25	44.88	38.75	49.00
P/E – high	—	20	21	22	24	19	24	28	32	22	21
P/E – low	—	12	15	12	18	14	14	20	17	16	15
Dividends per share ($)	13.9%	0.17	0.20	0.23	0.26	0.29	0.32	0.35	0.40	0.46	0.54
Book value per share ($)	16.0%	3.42	4.67	5.33	6.02	6.75	7.77	9.05	11.29	12.71	13.05

1989 Year End:
Debt ratio: 21.5%
Return on equity: 19.1%
Cash (mil): $373
Current ratio: 1.93
Long-term debt (mil): $260
Number of shares (mil): 73
Dividends:
 1989 average yield: 1.1%
 1989 payout: 22.0%
Market value (mil): $3,565

Stock Price History high/low 1980-89

AVON PRODUCTS, INC.

OVERVIEW

Avon achieved household-word status in the US through the company's direct-sales method and advertising campaign "Avon calling." Avon is the #4 cosmetics company in the US, with US sales at $1.6 billion and foreign sales at $1.7 billion in 1989. Products include toiletries and cosmetics, costume jewelry, gift items, fashions, preschool educational toys, and fitness videos.

Avon's newest beauty products include Avon Color, color-coordinated makeup, and BioAdvance, skin products that Avon says repair aging skin. Avon's Giorgio Beverly Hills makes prestige fragrances Giorgio and Red, the nation's top-selling fragrances in 1989; newly launched Red's sales were $100 million.

The company credits direct selling for its initial success in the US and current top sales status in foreign countries. At the end of 1989, Avon's 1,455,000 active representatives (450,000 in the US) sold products at their workplaces, as a part-time job, and through personal contacts. Avon leads cosmetics sales in all the company's Latin American countries except Peru. In Taiwan and Malaysia profits before taxes more than doubled in 1989.

WHEN

In New York during the 1880s, book salesman David McConnell gave small bottles of perfume to housewives who listened to his sales pitch. The perfume was more popular than the books, so in 1886 McConnell created the California Perfume Company and hired women to sell door-to-door. The company was renamed Avon in 1950 after the Avon River in England.

From the 1960s until the mid-1980s, Avon was the world's largest cosmetic company, known for its appeal to middle-class homemakers, an image reinforced by pictures of impeccably made-up housewives.

Avon hit hard times in 1974. Recession made many of its products unaffordable for blue-collar customers. Women were leaving home to enter the workforce, making door-to-door sales less viable. Avon's traditional products had little appeal for younger women. In response to these trends, President David Mitchell directed Avon's attempts to diversify and overhaul its product line, introducing the Colorworks line for teenagers with the slogan "It's not your mother's makeup." It also updated its image through the campaign "You never looked so good," with ads picturing active young women.

In 1979 Avon acquired the Tiffany jewelry company to help improve the company's image, sold it in 1984, and decided to expand into the health care field. CEO Hicks Waldron oversaw the acquisitions of Mallinckrodt, Inc. (hospital supply and chemical company, 1982), Foster Medical (1984), and 60 other medical suppliers. The health care field soon proved unprofitable due to stricter reimbursement policies set by Medicare. In 1986 Avon sold Mallinckrodt and continued to sell off remaining health care companies through 1990.

To boost profits Avon entered the retail prestige fragrances business by launching a joint venture with Liz Claiborne (1985) and buying Giorgio (1987). When Avon bought Parfums Stern, a Claiborne competitor, in 1987 (since sold), Claiborne dissolved the joint venture. That same year Avon sold 40% of Avon Japan (started in 1969) for $218 million to the Japanese public.

In 1988 Avon introduced Avon Color cosmetics and in 1989 introduced sleepwear, preschool toys, and videos. In 1989 Amway and Irwin Jacobs made an unsuccessful attempt to buy Avon. In 1990 Avon sold its remaining 60% of Avon Japan to Friends of Freesia (Japan), for $338 million plus royalties from sales of Avon products. Avon also entered an agreement with the Chinese government, becoming the first company ever to do direct selling in mainland China.

HOW MUCH

	9 Yr. Growth	1980	1981	1982	1983	1984	1985	1986	1987	1988	1989
Sales ($ mil)	2.8%	2,569	2,614	3,001	3,000	3,141	2,470	2,883	2,763	3,063	3,300
Net income ($ mil)	(5.0%)	241	220	197	164	182	128	159	238	121	152
Income as % of sales	—	9.4%	8.4%	6.6%	5.5%	5.8%	5.2%	5.5%	8.6%	4.0%	4.6%
Earnings per share ($)	(6.9%)	4.01	3.66	2.75	2.21	2.16	1.60	2.18	3.35	1.70	2.11
Stock price – high ($)	—	40.75	42.38	30.50	36.88	26.00	29.00	36.38	38.63	28.38	41.25
Stock price – low ($)	—	31.13	29.13	19.38	21.25	19.25	17.88	25.00	19.25	18.63	19.50
Stock price – close ($)	0.9%	34.13	30.00	26.75	25.13	21.88	27.63	27.00	25.75	19.50	36.88
P/E – high	—	10	12	11	17	12	18	17	12	17	20
P/E – low	—	8	8	7	10	9	11	11	6	11	9
Dividends per share ($)	(11.3%)	2.95	3.00	2.50	2.00	2.00	2.00	2.00	2.00	1.50	1.00
Book value per share ($)	(14.5%)	15.31	15.51	16.40	16.16	14.47	11.69	9.76	10.66	4.11	3.72

1989 Year End:
Debt ratio: 74.7%
Return on equity: 53.9%
Cash (mil): $84
Current ratio: 1.06
Long-term debt (mil): $674
Number of shares (mil): 56
Dividends:
1989 average yield: 2.7%
1989 payout: 47.4%
Market value (mil): $2,083

Stock Price History high/low 1980-89

45 40 35 30 25 20 15 10 5 0

NYSE symbol: AVP
Incorporated: New York, 1916
Fiscal year ends: December 31

WHO

Chairman, President, and CEO: James E. Preston, age 56, $843,932 pay
EVP: Stuart Ochiltree, age 48, $459,218 pay
EVP: Robert W. Pratt, Jr., age 59
EVP and CFO: Edward J. Robinson, age 49, $436,974 pay
Auditors: KPMG Peat Marwick
Employees: 28,400

WHERE

HQ: 9 W. 57th St., New York, NY 10019
Phone: 212-546-6015
FAX: 212-546-6136

Avon has 3 manufacturing plants in the US, 5 in Europe, 6 elsewhere in the Americas, and 3 in the Pacific. It has 5 US distribution centers, 6 in Europe, 12 elsewhere in the Americas, and 8 in the Pacific.

	1989 Sales		1989 Operating Income	
	$ mil	% of total	$ mil	% of total
US	1,576	48	185	38
Europe	592	18	59	12
Other Americas	699	21	169	34
Pacific	433	13	78	16
Adjustments	—	—	(88)	—
Total	**3,300**	**100**	**403**	**100**

WHAT

	1989 Sales		1989 Operating Income	
	$ mil	% of total	$ mil	% of total
Direct selling	2,999	91	454	92
Retail sales	301	9	37	8
Adjustments	—	—	(88)	—
Total	**3,300**	**100**	**403**	**100**

Direct Sales
Costume jewelry
Fashions
Fragrances
Gift items
Makeup lines
Preschool educational toys
Skin care products
Videos

Retail Sales
Giorgio
Oscar de la Renta
Perry Ellis
Red by Giorgio
Uninhibited by Cher

RANKINGS

135th in *Fortune* 500 Industrial Cos.
253rd in *Forbes* Sales 500
322nd in *Business Week* 1000

COMPETITION

Amway
Colgate-Palmolive
Estée Lauder
Johnson Products
MacAndrews & Forbes
Procter & Gamble
Unilever

BAKER & MCKENZIE

OVERVIEW

Baker & McKenzie is the largest law firm in the world. Its practice includes virtually every field of law in the domestic and international arenas. As of June 1990 it has 1,521 lawyers (including 480 partners and 1,041 associate lawyers) in 48 offices in 30 countries. Over 50% of its lawyers are not US citizens. Baker & McKenzie is a prime example of the new generation of "megafirms" intended to meet the complete legal needs of their clients.

Its far-flung operations, growth through mergers with other law firms, and practice of employing local lawyers rather than American expatriates in its overseas offices have led some to call the firm a franchise and to compare it with fast-food chains. While separate partnerships exist in many countries to comply with local requirements, Baker & McKenzie operates as a single firm (an Illinois partnership) in which the governing principle is one vote per partner. Although a complex profit-sharing formula favors the offices and lawyers originating revenue, the firm is managed as a single business.

The firm seems likely to continue its rapid growth and commitment to the international practice of law. Its recruitment in early 1990 of David Ruder, former chairman of the SEC, and its agreement to provide him with whatever staff is necessary to meet the needs of any clients he may bring in, are indicative of the firm's commitment to being one of the foremost corporate law firms in the world.

WHEN

Russell Baker arrived in Chicago from his native New Mexico on a railroad freight car to attend law school. Upon graduation in 1925, he began the practice of law with his classmate Dana Simpson as the firm of Simpson & Baker. Inspired by Chicago's role as a manufacturing and agricultural center for the world and influenced by the strong international focus of his alma mater, the University of Chicago, Baker dreamed of developing an international law practice headquartered in Chicago.

In his first cases Baker represented members of Chicago's growing Mexican-American community in a variety of minor criminal and civil matters. Since he frequently dealt with Mexican lawyers and issues involving multiple jurisdictions and legal systems, Baker developed an expertise in international law, which brought in other clients. In 1934 Abbott Laboratories retained him to handle its worldwide legal affairs, and Baker was on his way to fulfilling his dream.

In 1949 Baker joined forces with Chicago litigator John McKenzie to form the law firm that bears their names. In 1955 Baker opened the firm's first foreign office in Caracas to meet the needs of his expanding US client base. During the next 10 years the firm opened offices in Amsterdam, Brussels, Zurich, São Paulo, Mexico City, London, Frankfurt, Milan, Tokyo, Toronto, Paris, Manila, Sydney, and Madrid. Growth continued with another 23 offices added in Europe, Asia, and the Americas between 1965 and 1990. Baker's death in 1979 did not slow the firm's growth nor change its international character.

To manage what had become the world's largest law firm, in 1984 Baker & McKenzie created the new position of chairman of the executive committee. Robert Cox has held this office since its creation. He has forsaken, for a time, the practice of law in order to guide the firm — a rare situation in large firms, where income is usually tied to the number of hours billed to clients. Cox's mandate is to maintain Baker & McKenzie as the strongest full-line international law firm in the world.

Baker & McKenzie was one of the first firms to begin practice in China following its opening to the West and now has 3 offices there. In the spirit of *glasnost*, the firm opened an office in Moscow in 1989.

HOW MUCH

	9 Yr. Growth	1980	1981	1982	1983	1984	1985	1986	1987	1988	1989
Total lawyers	10.5%	544	583	613	658	704	755	908	946	1179	1339
No. of partners	8.8%	203	222	236	256	276	287	333	338	404	432
No. of associates	11.5%	341	361	377	402	428	468	575	608	775	907
Associates per partner	—	1.68	1.63	1.60	1.57	1.55	1.63	1.73	1.80	1.92	2.10
No. of offices	7.5%	25	26	27	28	29	30	31	35	41	48

Starting Salaries for First Year Associates:

1980 — $32,000
1984 — $47,000
1986 — $65,000
1990 — $70,000

For the Fiscal Year Ending June 30, 1989

Gross revenues: $341,245,000

Profits per partner: $335,967

Total No. of Lawyers 1980-89

1,400
1,200
1,000
800
600
400
200
0

Private company
Founded: Illinois Partnership 1949
Fiscal Year Ends: June 30

WHO

Chairman of the Executive Committee: Robert Cox
Director of Hiring: Daniel J. Burns
CFO: Charles W. Kessler
Auditors: Arthur Andersen & Co.
Lawyers: 1,521

WHERE

HQ: One Prudential Plaza, 130 E. Randolph Dr., Chicago, IL 60601
Phone: 312-861-8000
FAX: 312-861-2898

Other Offices

Amsterdam	Juárez	San Diego
Bangkok	London	San Francisco
Barcelona	Los Angeles	São Paulo
Beijing	Madrid	Seoul
Bogotá	Manila	Shanghai
Brussels	Melbourne	Singapore
Budapest	Mexico City	Sydney
Buenos Aires	Miami	Taipei
Cairo	Milan	Tijuana
Caracas	Moscow	Tokyo
Dallas	New York	Toronto
Frankfurt	Palo Alto	Valencia
Geneva	Paris	Vienna
Guangzhou	Rio de Janeiro	Washington, DC
Hong Kong	Riyadh	Zurich
Jakarta	Rome	

WHAT

Areas of Practice

Admiralty	Corporate	Litigation
Antitrust	Criminal	Municipal
Banking	Employment	Patent
Bankruptcy	Environmental	Real estate
Civil rights	Estates	Securities
Commodities	Insurance	Taxation
Computer	International	Trademark
Copyright	Labor	

Representative Clients

Amdahl	Ford	Tandem
BASF	Harris	Tyson Foods
Brunswick	NCR	
R. R. Donnelley	Sun Microsystems	

Journals & Bulletins

Banking Law Reporter
Canadian Legal Report
China Law Quarterly
Colombian Newsletter
Computer & Software Update
EEC Competition Law Newsletter
Employee Benefits Update
European Benefits Update
European Legal Developments Bulletin
US Employment Law Update
Hazardous Waste Update
Newsletter from Spain
Pacific Basin Legal Developments Bulletin
Taiwan Newsletter

RANKINGS

1st in *National Law Journal* 250

BAKER HUGHES INC.

OVERVIEW

Baker Hughes provides products and services for the oil well and mining industries. The company has 20 divisions organized in 3 major operating groups — drilling equipment, production tools, and process equipment — and is a world leader in each of its industry segments. Baker Hughes is 6.9% owned by Borg-Warner Corporation.

The Drilling Equipment division (1989 operating income $49 million) produces drill bits and other equipment used in the oil and gas well drilling process. The Production Tools division (1989 operating income $83 million) produces equipment and provides services involved in the completion and rehabilitation of oil and gas wells. The Process Equipment division (1989 operating income $47 million) provides equipment used in wastewater processing in various industries, produces instruments used in the mining industry, and is an industry leader in production of mining drill bits. The company spun off 71% of BJ-Titan Services (pumping services) to the public in the summer of 1990.

WHEN

Howard R. Hughes, Sr., developed the first successful oil well drill bit for rock in 1909. Hughes and partner Walter Sharp opened a plant in Houston, and Sharp & Hughes soon had a near monopoly on rock bits. When Sharp died in 1912, Hughes bought his 1/2 of the company, incorporating as Hughes Tool Company. Hughes held 73 patents when he died in 1924 and the company passed to Howard R. Hughes, Jr.

It is estimated that the tool company, which has had a 45% market share for most of its life, provided Hughes, Jr., with $745 million in pretax profits between 1924 and 1972, which he used to diversify into movies (RKO), airlines (TWA), and Las Vegas casinos at various times. In 1972 Hughes sold the tool division of the Hughes Tool Company to the public for $150 million. After 1972 the company expanded into above-ground oil production tools.

In 1913 oil well drilling contractor Carl Baker organized the Baker Casing Shoe Company in California to manage the collection of royalties from companies licensed to manufacture his 3 oil tool inventions. In 1918 Baker began to manufacture his own products. In 1928 the company adopted the name Baker Oil Tools, Inc., to better reflect its full line of products. Baker expanded nationwide and began international sales during the 1920s. Sales increased sixfold between 1933 and 1941 despite a slump during the worst of the Great Depression. In the late 1940s and the 1950s, Baker grew with the boom in oil drilling.

During the 1960s Baker prospered despite fewer US well completions. Foreign sales increased from 19% to 33% of total revenues. The company bought Kobe (oil field pumping equipment) in 1963. Baker diversified into mining equipment with the purchase of Galigher (1969) and Ramsey Engineering (1974). The company bought Reed Tool (oil drill bits) in 1975. In 1979 revenues topped $1 billion for the first time.

Between 1982 and 1986 US expenditures for oil services fell from $40 billion to $9 billion. In 1987, when both Baker and Hughes were faced with declining revenues and Hughes had large debts from expansion, the 2 companies merged to form Baker Hughes. By consolidating, closing plants, and combining operations, the company cut annual expenses by $80 million and was profitable by the end of fiscal 1988. In 1989 Baker Hughes sold its mining equipment businesses and bought Eastman Christensen (world leader in directional and horizontal drilling equipment) from Norton for $550 million cash. The company also made several smaller acquisitions in 1989, including Bird Machine Company (process centrifuges), Vetco Services (drilling equipment), and EDECO Petroleum Services (pumps and liner hangers).

HOW MUCH

	9 Yr. Growth	1980	1981	1982	1983	1984	1985	1986	1987	1988	1989
Sales ($ mil)	4.6%	1,547	2,140	2,535	1,838	1,834	1,904	1,557	1,924	2,316	2,328
Net income ($ mil)	(5.6%)	139	225	249	(64)	71	88	(362)	(255)	59	83
Income as % of sales	—	9.0%	10.5%	9.8%	(3.5%)	3.9%	4.6%	(23.2%)	(13.2%)	2.6%	3.6%
Earnings per share ($)	(12.4%)	2.11	3.36	3.60	(0.91)	1.00	1.25	(5.15)	(2.22)	0.45	0.64
Stock price – high ($)	—	53.50	49.38	38.88	26.63	23.50	18.88	17.88	27.38	19.88	27.63
Stock price – low ($)	—	26.25	31.75	17.63	16.00	15.00	14.13	8.88	11.13	12.13	13.63
Stock price – close ($)	(6.9%)	48.63	38.00	22.50	19.25	16.63	17.88	11.88	13.63	14.00	25.50
P/E – high	—	25	15	11	—	24	15	—	—	44	43
P/E – low	—	12	9	5	—	15	11	—	—	27	21
Dividends per share ($)	3.1%	0.35	0.50	0.76	0.92	0.92	0.92	0.81	0.46	0.46	0.46
Book value per share ($)	(3.1%)	11.01	14.03	16.98	14.78	14.34	14.43	9.67	7.78	8.10	8.31

1989 Year End:
Debt ratio: 29.4%
Return on equity: 7.8%
Cash (mil): $116
Current ratio: 2.14
Long-term debt (mil): $417
Number of shares (mil): 120
Dividends:
1989 average yield: 1.8%
1989 payout: 71.9%
Market value (mil): $3,071

Stock Price History high/low 1980-89

NYSE symbol: BHI
Incorporated: Delaware, 1987
Fiscal year ends: September 30

WHO

Chairman, President, and CEO: James D. Woods, age 58, $1,107,808 pay
SVP; President, Baker Hughes Drilling Equipment: Joel V. Staff, age 45, $515,881 pay
SVP; President, Baker Hughes Production Tools: Max L. Lukens, age 41, $389,999 pay
SVP; President, Baker Hughes Process Equipment: Stephen T. Harcrow, age 43, $430,313 pay
SVP and CFO: Thomas W. Cason, age 46
Auditors: Deloitte & Touche
Employees: 20,400

WHERE

HQ: 3900 Essex Ln., Houston, TX 77027
Phone: 713-439-8600
FAX: 713-439-8699

Baker Hughes has 111 plants worldwide.

WHAT

	1989 Sales		1989 Operating Income	
	$ mil	% of total	$ mil	% of total
US	1,174	50	40	19
Europe	416	18	66	32
Other countries	738	32	100	49
Adjustments	—	—	(36)	—
Total	**2,328**	**100**	**170**	**100**

	1989 Sales		1989 Operating Income	
	$ mil	% of total	$ mil	% of total
Mining & process	625	27	47	23
Drilling	724	31	49	24
Production	663	28	83	40
Pumping services	316	14	27	13
Adjustments	—	—	(36)	—
Total	**2,328**	**100**	**170**	**100**

Business Operations
Downhole drilling motors
Drilling fluids
Fracturing materials
Liquids processing equipment
Mining drill bits
Oil production tools
Oil well drilling equipment
Surface and downhole data collection instruments

RANKINGS

191st in *Fortune* 500 Industrial Cos.
351st in *Forbes* Sales 500
172nd in *Business Week* 1000
558th in *Business Week* Global 1000

COMPETITION

Cooper Industries
Dresser
FMC
Halliburton
Ingersoll-Rand
LTV
Pearson
Schlumberger

BALLY MANUFACTURING CORPORATION

OVERVIEW

Bally operates in 3 industry segments: casino hotels, fitness centers, and gaming and fitness equipment. Bally is the largest operator of casino hotels in the world. The company owns 2 casino hotels in Atlantic City, one in Las Vegas, and one in Reno. The 4 properties include about 9 million square feet of space, including 268,000 square feet of casino space, 6,600 hotel rooms, and 21 restaurants.

Bally is also the largest operator of fitness centers in the US. Bally's Health and Tennis subsidiary operates 310 fitness centers under 10 different names in major cities throughout the US. The fitness centers operate on a membership basis and offer planned exercise programs, exercise equipment, steam rooms, whirlpools, and other services.

Bally's Scientific Games subsidiary designs, produces, and sells lottery equipment to 17 of the 33 jurisdictions currently operating lotteries in the US. Bally is also a leading manufacturer of slot machines and other gaming equipment. The company's Life Fitness subsidiary designs, manufactures, and sells fitness equipment such as stationary bicycles and rowing machines.

WHEN

Bally's predecessor, Lion Manufacturing of Chicago, produced its first pinball machine, called the Ballyhoo, in 1932 and its first slot machine in 1938. In 1963, after Lion's founder died, sales manager William O'Donnell gained control of the company by forming a partnership with a New Jersey distributor of Lion products. The company was renamed Bally in honor of its first pinball game. During the mid-1960s the market for slot machines grew worldwide; industry leader Bally's sales doubled between 1967 and 1969, to $12.1 million.

In 1969 Bally became a publicly owned company. The company expanded its plants in Chicago and Ireland and bought Midway Manufacturing (arcade games, 1969) and Gunter Wulff Appartebau (Germany, amusement games, 1972). Over the next 5 years, Bally bought its distributors in Belgium, Sweden, Germany, and Nevada.

Bally bought the Aladdin's Castle chain of amusement arcades in 1974 and formed its Bally's Park Place subsidiary in 1977 to purchase and operate a casino hotel in Atlantic City. The New Jersey Gaming Commission required Chairman and CEO O'Donnell to resign and place his company stock in a blind trust before it would issue a gaming license, because a portion of the money O'Donnell had borrowed to buy the company in 1963 had come from persons connected with organized crime. O'Donnell admitted that accepting the money had been a mistake but asserted that the company had no connection with organized crime. Bally's Park Place hotel opened in 1979 and had revenues of $210 million in 1980.

In 1979 the company's Midway division introduced a new generation of video arcade games, including Space Invaders (1979), Pac-Man (1980), and Ms. Pac-Man (1982). Bally's amusement game sales rose from $120 million in 1978 to $434 million in 1982, then dropped to $99 million in 1983 as the arcade game fad passed. In 1984 Bally took a $121 million write-off on its amusement game business.

During the 1980s Bally broadened its presence in the leisure industry, buying Six Flags Corporation (1982), Health and Tennis Corporation of America (1983), Great America Theme Park from Marriott (1984), Lifecycle (1984), MGM Grand Hotels in Las Vegas and Reno (1986), and the Golden Nugget Casino in Atlantic City (1987). Bally sold its theme park business in 1987, most of its amusement game business in 1988, and Aladdin's Castle in 1989, completing its evolution out of the amusement game business. In 1990 Bally agreed to buy the Clermont Club casino in London.

HOW MUCH

	9 Yr. Growth	1980	1981	1982	1983	1984	1985	1986	1987	1988	1989
Sales ($ mil)	12.7%	679	866	1,254	1,148	1,309	1,295	1,209	1,676	1,867	1,990
Net income ($ mil)	(7.8%)	53	82	91	5	(100)	26	17	(6)	38	26
Income as % of sales	—	7.9%	9.4%	7.3%	0.5%	(7.7%)	2.0%	1.4%	(0.4%)	2.0%	1.3%
Earnings per share ($)	(11.6%)	2.01	3.03	3.20	0.20	(3.86)	0.95	0.60	(0.60)	1.12	0.66
Stock price – high ($)	—	36.50	32.25	32.38	28.13	23.13	18.63	24.13	27.75	25.25	29.75
Stock price – low ($)	—	17.50	17.13	22.50	19.38	11.63	11.13	14.63	10.50	12.88	13.50
Stock price – close ($)	(4.6%)	23.00	29.13	23.38	19.63	11.63	16.50	19.75	12.88	22.13	15.13
P/E – high	—	18	11	10	141	—	20	40	—	23	45
P/E – low	—	9	6	7	97	—	12	24	—	12	20
Dividends per share ($)	12.3%	0.10	0.10	0.15	0.20	0.20	0.20	0.20	0.20	0.22	0.29
Book value per share ($)	6.3%	12.23	15.26	18.62	18.49	14.16	15.15	15.91	21.17	21.63	21.25

1989 Year End:
Debt ratio: 74.0%
Return on equity: 3.1%
Cash (mil): $75
Current ratio: 1.12
Long-term debt (mil): $1,701
Number of shares (mil): 28
Dividends:
1989 average yield: 1.9%
1989 payout: 43.2%
Market value (mil): $423

Stock Price History high/low 1980-89

40 35 30 25 20 15 10 5 0

NYSE symbol: BLY
Incorporated: Delaware, 1968
Fiscal year ends: December 31

WHO

Chairman and CEO: Robert E. Mullane, age 57, $1,680,000 pay
President and CEO, Bally's Park Place, Inc.: Richard Gillman, age 58, $4,000,000 pay
President and CEO, Bally's Health and Tennis: Donahue L. Wildman, age 57, $1,925,000 pay
President and COO: Roger N. Keesee, age 53, $862,596 pay
VP, Treasurer, and CFO: Paul J. Johnson, age 66, $340,000 pay
Auditors: Ernst & Young
Employees: 32,900

WHERE

HQ: 8700 W. Bryn Mawr Ave., Chicago, IL 60631
Phone: 312-399-1300
FAX: 312-693-2982

The company operates 2 casino hotels in Nevada, 2 casino hotels in New Jersey, and 310 fitness centers throughout the US; it has offices or manufacturing facilities in California, Georgia, Illinois, Iowa, Maine, Nevada, New Jersey, New York, West Virginia, Berlin, and Munich.

WHAT

	1989 Sales		1989 Operating Income	
	$ mil	% of total	$ mil	% of total
Casino hotels	948	46	142	—
Amusement games & services	35	2	59	—
Fitness centers	778	37	58	—
Products & services	320	15	30	—
Adjustments	(91)	—	(156)	—
Total	**1,990**	**100**	**133**	**—**

Principal Businesses

Casino Hotels
Bally's Grand
Bally's Las Vegas
Bally's Park Place
Bally's Reno

Fitness Centers
Chicago Health Clubs
Health and Racquet Clubs
Holiday Fitness and Racquet Clubs
Holiday Health
Holiday Spa
Jack LaLanne
President's First Lady
Scandinavian
The Vertical Club
Vic Tanny

Products
Fitness equipment
Gaming machines
Lottery equipment

RANKINGS

50th in *Fortune* 100 Diversified Service Cos.
389th in *Forbes* Sales 500

COMPETITION

Bass
Control Data
Hanson
Hilton
Premark

BANC ONE CORPORATION

OVERVIEW

Columbus, Ohio–based Banc One is a bank holding company with 52 banks and 670 branches in 6 states: Ohio, Indiana, Wisconsin, Michigan, Kentucky, and Texas. Through its conservative approach to lending and expansion, Banc One has managed to avoid the problems of most banks in recent years, delivering increases in earnings for 21 straight years.

Its $27 billion in assets ranks 26th among US banks. Its Texas holdings — failed MCorp banks and Bright Banc thrifts seized by federal regulators — are being purchased over time from the government. If its Texas assets were figured in (accounting rules forbid that until Banc One buys more equity), Banc One would rank 16th in the US in assets.

Banc One grew in the Midwest by adding smaller banks, consolidating some back-office operations, and mixing local control with regional marketing clout. Banc One stresses retail banking — loans for small businesses and consumers. It processes 8.6 million credit and debit card accounts, including 4.5 million for 1,500 other companies.

Banc One is known for early adoption of cutting-edge technology such as ATMs and computer-based home banking experiments.

NYSE symbol: ONE
Incorporated: Ohio, 1989
Fiscal year ends: December 31

WHO

Chairman: John B. McCoy, age 46, $1,076,109 pay
VC: Robert H. Potts, age 65, $479,295 pay (prior to reassignment to Texas)
EVP: Donald L. McWhorter, age 54, $417,045 pay
VP and CFO: John W. Westman, age 48
Auditors: Coopers & Lybrand
Employees: 23,000

WHERE

HQ: 100 E. Broad St., Columbus, OH 43271
Phone: 614-248-5944
FAX: 614-248-5624

Banc One operates retail banks in 6 states.

WHEN

Banc One began in 1868 when F. C. Session opened a banking house in Columbus, Ohio. He later combined his operations with those of J. A. Jeffrey and Orange Johnson to form Commercial Bank, later Commercial National.

In 1929 Commercial National and City National Bank of Commerce combined to form City National Bank and Trust. In 1935 John H. McCoy became the bank's president, beginning a dynasty that would eventually oversee a multistate bank holding company stretching from the Great Lakes to the Gulf of Mexico.

John G. McCoy succeeded his father in 1958, and in the 1960s City National began to break from tradition. The bank hired a housewife-turned-comedienne from Lima, Ohio, for radio and TV commercials. Both Phyllis Diller and City National were on their way.

In 1966 the upstart bank introduced the first VISA (then BankAmericard) credit card service outside California. McCoy formed the First Banc Group of Ohio in 1967, folding in City National. In its first foray outside Columbus, the company bought Farmers Savings and Trust of Mansfield, Ohio (1968), the first of 44 Ohio banks it would add by 1985.

While it grew through acquisitions, First Banc Group scored a coup in 1977 when Merrill Lynch hired it to handle its Cash Management Account. The breakthrough financial service package combined a retail brokerage account with a checking account and debit card.

In 1979 First Banc Group changed its name to Banc One, and all affiliated banks included Bank One — with a "k" — in their names. The holding company uses a "c" in its name because Ohio law restricts use of the term "bank." John B. McCoy, the 3rd generation of bankers, succeeded his father as CEO in 1984 as barriers to interstate banking were falling. Banc One expanded rapidly into Indiana (buying Indiana's 2nd largest bank, American Fletcher, in 1986), Kentucky, Michigan, and Wisconsin. In 1989 Banc One announced it was acquiring, with a large dose of federal aid, 20 failed MCorp banks in beleaguered Texas. Banc One paid $34 million for $11 billion in assets, including $2.5 billion in problem loans managed by Banc One but guaranteed by the government. Banc One will buy out the FDIC's 92.5% share over the next 5 years.

Banc One, hoping to convert the big Texas operation to its brand of retail banking, added failed Dallas-based Bright Banc Savings to its Texas holdings in 1990. It paid $45 million for 48 more branches, $2.7 billion in deposits, and $1 billion in consumer loans.

WHAT

	1989 Sales	
	$ mil	% of total
Loan and lease interest	2,167	69
US government interest	335	11
Local government interest	111	4
Other interest income	39	1
Fiduciary activities	80	2
Service charges	94	3
Card processing	203	6
Securities gains	(2)	—
Other	136	4
Total	**3,163**	**100**

Loans
Commercial loans
Credit card loans
Installment loans
Leases
Real estate loans
Tax-exempt loans

Deposit Accounts
Demand deposits
Money market accounts
Savings deposits
Time deposits

Financial Services
Consumer finance
Credit life insurance
Discount brokerage
Equipment leasing
Mortgage banking
Trust services

Affiliates
Banc One Indiana Corp.
Banc One Ohio Corp.
(Kentucky, Michigan, Ohio)
Banc One Wisconsin Corp.
Bank One, Texas, NA

Nonbank Affiliates
Banc One Financial Services, Inc.
Banc One Leasing Corp.
Banc One Mortgage Corp.
Banc One Services Corp.
Bonnet Resources Corp.

HOW MUCH

	9 Yr. Growth	1980	1981	1982	1983	1984	1985	1986	1987	1988	1989
Sales ($ mil)	30.0%	299	414	591	743	1,049	1,192	1,847	1,960	2,735	3,163
Net income ($ mil)	30.0%	33	39	58	83	108	130	200	209	340	348
Income as % of sale	—	11.0%	9.3%	9.7%	11.2%	10.3%	10.9%	10.8%	10.7%	12.4%	11.0%
Earnings per share ($)	11.9%	0.88	1.00	1.09	1.28	1.44	1.65	1.75	1.79	2.35	*2.41*
Stock price – high ($)	—	5.98	7.45	12.14	14.17	13.15	20.94	27.38	24.38	25.11	33.64
Stock price – low ($)	—	3.36	5.89	7.04	10.02	10.39	12.52	17.66	14.67	19.42	20.23
Stock price – close ($)	19.4%	5.98	7.18	11.69	11.73	12.84	19.35	18.91	19.83	20.23	29.43
P/E – high	—	7	7	11	11	9	13	16	14	11	14
P/E – low	—	4	6	6	8	7	8	10	8	8	8
Dividends per share ($)	13.5%	0.30	0.33	0.36	0.43	0.49	0.58	0.68	0.74	0.84	0.95
Book value per share ($)	12.4%	5.46	5.92	6.46	7.42	8.55	10.02	11.40	12.52	14.18	15.66

1989 Year End:
Debt ratio: 13.5%
Return on equity: —
Cash (mil): $1,904
Assets (mil): $26,552
Long-term debt (mil): $356
Number of shares (mil): 144
Dividends:
1989 average yield: 3.2%
1989 payout: —
Market value (mil): $4,238

Stock Price History high/low 1980-89

35
30
25
20
15
10
5
0

RANKINGS

26th in *Fortune* 100 Commercial Banking Cos.
261st in *Forbes* Sales 500
149th in *Business Week* 1000
412th in *Business Week* Global 1000

COMPETITION

American Financial
Chase Manhattan
Chemical Banking
First Interstate
NCNB
PNC Financial
Other multistate bank holding companies

BANK OF BOSTON CORPORATION

OVERVIEW

Bank of Boston, the 15th largest US banking organization, with $39 billion in assets at the end of 1989, owns First National Bank of Boston, New England's largest bank, and banks in Connecticut, Maine, Rhode Island, and Vermont.

About 85% of the company's total loans at the end of 1989 were to US borrowers and the balance to borrowers overseas. Of the domestic loans, some 65% were made in New England, through 250 branches.

Bank of Boston's national banking group provides credit, operating, investment, and merchant banking services outside New England to large and middle-market corporations, as well as to specialized industries, including high technology, transportation, energy, and media and entertainment.

The company's global banking group serves US multinational customers in Europe and elsewhere. Bank of Boston finances trade in the Asia/Pacific market, where it processed more than $4 billion of intra-Asian letters of credit in 1989. The company has been serving US customers in South America since 1917 and has the 3rd largest market share in Argentina. Unlike its US operations, the company's foreign operations are profitable.

NYSE symbol: BKB
Incorporated: Massachusetts, 1970
Fiscal year ends: December 31

WHO

Chairman and CEO: Ira Stepanian, age 53, $1,247,500 pay
President: Charles K. Gifford, age 47, $775,500 pay
EVP: Peter C. Read, age 53, $483,750 pay
EVP: T. Lincoln Morison, Jr., age 49
EVP: Kevin J. Mulvaney, age 41
EVP and CFO: Peter J. Manning, age 51
Auditors: Coopers & Lybrand
Employees: 18,800

WHEN

William Phillips and 5 other leading Boston merchants founded the Massachusetts Bank in 1784. Profitable from the beginning, the bank was known as very conservative, with strict credit requirements, a policy that both made enemies and encouraged competing banks to open. In 1865 the bank became Massachusetts National Bank, joining the National Bank System after other Boston banks.

Deposits of the bank grew from $1 million to over $6 million between 1900 and 1903, under President John Weeks. In 1903 Weeks and others purchased First National Bank of Boston (founded in 1859) and then combined it with Massachusetts National, adopting the purchased bank's name. Weeks selected Dan Wing, 32, as president of First National.

Under Wing the bank grew to become the 8th largest US bank in deposits in 1932. The bank expanded internationally, opening branches in Argentina (1917) and Cuba (1923). By 1927 the bank also had representative offices in Europe and was a leading US bank in financing foreign trade, serving New England companies.

In 1929 the bank acquired Old Colony Trust Company, a major Boston banking and trust organization. In 1934 the bank, complying with the Banking Act of 1933, spun off its investment banking business into a new corporation, The First Boston Corporation.

In 1945 the bank got approval to open a branch in Brazil. In the late 1940s Bank of Boston became the first US bank to offer a full factoring service (allowing a manufacturer to check the credit of a customer before shipping goods and taking the credit risk itself if the customer does not pay). This service began to produce substantial income during the 1950s. In the early 1960s the bank started Boston Overseas Financial for international factoring.

In 1970 the bank reorganized as a subsidiary of First National Boston Corporation, which changed its name to Bank of Boston Corporation in 1983. In the 1970s and 1980s the bank became the largest in New England, with purchases of banks in Massachusetts, Maine, Connecticut, Vermont, and Rhode Island. In 1989 Bank of Boston Corporation earned a net income of $70 million despite a $722 million provision for possible real estate and foreign loan losses to less developed countries. The company moved into the 1990s as a "superregional" banking organization, with the objective of investing its capital based on return on equity and the strategic value of a new business to the corporation's future.

WHERE

HQ: 100 Federal St., Boston, MA 02110
Phone: 617-434-2200
FAX: 617-434-8330

Bank of Boston has operations in 20 states in the US and 25 foreign countries.

	1989 Net Income	
	$ mil	% of total
US	(27)	(39)
Latin America	79	113
Europe	8	11
Asia/Pacific	4	6
Other	6	9
Total	**70**	**100**

WHAT

	1989 Sales	
	$ mil	% of total
Loan and lease interest	3,965	58
Other interest	1,985	29
Financial service fees	340	5
Trust & agency fees	154	2
Trading profits	16	—
Investment gains	16	—
Other noninterest	368	6
Total	**6,844**	**100**

Financial Services
Corporate lending
Correspondent banking
International banking
Investment banking
Leasing
Mortgage services
Real estate lending
Retail banking
Securities and payments services
Trust services

Major Bank Subsidiaries
Bank of Boston Connecticut
Bank of Vermont
Casco Northern Bank (Maine)
First National Bank of Boston
Rhode Island Hospital Trust National Bank

RANKINGS

15th in *Fortune* 100 Commercial Banking Cos.
120th in *Forbes* Sales 500
495th in *Business Week* 1000

COMPETITION

Bank of New England
Major money center banks
Mutual savings banks
Savings and loans

HOW MUCH

	9 Yr. Growth	1980	1981	1982	1983	1984	1985	1986	1987	1988	1989
Sales ($ mil)	12.7%	2,331	2,952	2,734	2,599	3,402	3,436	3,540	4,269	5,296	6,844
Net income ($ mil)	(4.0%)	102	119	124	136	164	174	233	20	322	70
Income as % of sales	—	4.4%	4.0%	4.6%	5.2%	4.8%	5.1%	6.6%	0.5%	6.1%	1.0%
Earnings per share ($)	(8.8%)	1.83	2.08	2.22	2.47	2.78	2.82	3.49	0.10	4.43	0.80
Stock price – high ($)	—	8.67	10.64	13.21	15.88	14.63	20.83	29.92	38.00	30.00	30.63
Stock price – low ($)	—	5.47	7.53	7.13	10.88	9.67	13.21	19.29	17.88	20.88	15.75
Stock price – close ($)	10.2%	7.92	10.14	11.25	13.50	13.25	20.83	26.58	22.50	23.63	19.00
P/E – high	—	5	5	6	6	5	7	9	380	7	38
P/E – low	—	3	4	3	4	3	5	6	179	5	20
Dividends per share ($)	10.5%	0.51	0.58	0.66	0.72	0.78	0.82	0.91	1.02	1.12	1.24
Book value per share ($)	8.3%	12.89	14.34	16.23	17.75	19.58	21.53	24.47	23.62	27.02	26.51

1989 Year End:
Debt ratio: 44.3%
Return on equity: 3.0%
Cash (mil): $5,985
Assets (mil): $39,178
Long-term debt (mil): $1,664
Number of shares (mil): 71
Dividends:
1989 average yield: 6.5%
1989 payout: 155.0%
Market value (mil): $1,353

Stock Price History high/low 1980-89

BANK OF NEW ENGLAND CORPORATION

OVERVIEW

Bank of New England, a Boston-based regional bank holding company, is the 21st largest commercial banking organization in the US (2nd in Massachusetts after the Bank of Boston), with $29.8 billion in assets at the end of 1989.

The company provides banking, trust, and other financial services through over 400 branches of 5 banks in Massachusetts, Connecticut, Rhode Island, and Maine. Bank of New England (Boston) and Connecticut Bank & Trust (Hartford) are its largest banks.

Bank of New England had a $1.1 billion loss in 1989, primarily from problem real estate loans. In 1990 the company, under federal banking regulatory orders, began selling $8 billion in loans and assets to improve capital and liquidity.

Battered by continuing weakness in the New England economy, the bank is struggling for survival. A new management team hopes to create a smaller, regional bank that provides consumer banking, trust and private banking, small and middle-market corporate banking, and real estate lending services.

WHEN

The Merchants Bank received its charter from Massachusetts in 1831 to become the 18th bank in Boston. In 1864 the bank received a national charter and became the largest bank in Boston.

In 1912 Merchants purchased State National Bank and the following year joined the Federal Reserve System. Other acquisitions soon followed: National Bank of Commerce (1914), Winthrop National (1915), and Old Boston National (1916). In 1922 Merchants started a trust department.

In 1942 the bank opened its first branch, at Copley Square. The bank continued to grow in the 1950s with the purchase of Day Trust Company in 1956 and Pilgrim Trust Company in 1958. In 1961 Merchants purchased The New England Trust Company, the oldest and 2nd largest trust company in Boston, and then changed its name to New England Merchants National Bank.

In 1970 the bank established and became owned by a holding company, New England Merchants Company, Inc. The bank purchased Barnstable County National Bank (1973), Fall River National Bank (1975), and Chatham Trust Company (1979). In 1980 it added Bay State National and Cape Ann Bank and Trust Company.

In 1981 New England Merchants purchased TNB Financial Corporation and 6 other banks. In 1982 the bank and holding company adopted the name of Bank of New England.

In 1985 the US Supreme Court upheld the regional interstate banking laws to permit the first regional interstate merger in the US, of Bank of New England and Hartford-based Connecticut Bank & Trust, a $6.9 billion banking company (founded 1792). The same year, Bank of New England bought Maine National (Portland) and Old Colony (Providence). In 1986 it purchased 6 more banks in Connecticut, Maine, and Massachusetts, creating a banking system of more than 450 offices in 4 states. The bank added The Conifer Group, a bank holding company in Worcester, Massachusetts, in 1987.

The bank had record earnings in 1988 but earnings suffered throughout 1989 due to bad loans, particularly in real estate. Quarterly losses occurred in the 4th quarter of 1989 and first quarter of 1990. In March 1990 the US comptroller of the currency ordered the bank to raise its equity/assets ratio to at least 3% by May 31 and to meet certain capital tests. By the end of the 2nd quarter of 1990, the company had not met the 3% requirement, as nonperforming assets increased to $2.78 billion from $2.2 billion at the end of 1989.

HOW MUCH

	9 Yr. Growth	1980	1981	1982	1983	1984	1985	1986	1987	1988	1989
Sales ($ mil)	28.9%	355	599	643	623	810	1,710	1,910	2,726	3,197	3,478
Net income ($ mil)	—	22	34	36	37	46	131	172	141	282	(1,113)
Income as % of sales	—	6.2%	5.6%	5.6%	5.9%	5.7%	7.7%	9.0%	5.2%	8.8%	(32.0%)
Earnings per share ($)	—	1.73	1.98	2.11	2.13	2.60	*3.11*	*3.52*	*2.04*	*4.06*	*(16.11)*
Stock price – high ($)	—	8.43	11.39	13.79	18.57	17.07	28.50	39.50	37.25	30.88	24.88
Stock price – low ($)	—	5.00	7.79	8.25	11.64	11.71	15.79	26.13	20.25	21.63	7.25
Stock price – close ($)	1.6%	8.14	9.86	12.71	13.14	16.64	26.75	29.75	25.00	22.00	9.38
P/E – high	—	5	6	7	9	7	9	11	18	8	—
P/E – low	—	3	4	4	5	5	5	7	10	5	—
Dividends per share ($)	7.4%	0.54	0.62	0.69	0.74	0.78	0.93	1.09	1.21	1.33	1.02
Book value per share ($)	(7.0%)	11.82	13.06	14.40	15.76	17.38	19.17	22.45	20.61	23.28	6.17

1989 Year End:
Debt ratio: 63.0%
Return on equity: —
Cash (mil): $2,180
Assets (mil): $29,773
Long-term debt (mil): $779
Number of shares (mil): 69
Dividends:
1989 average yield: 10.9%
1989 payout: —
Market value (mil): $650

NYSE symbol: NEB
Incorporated: Massachusetts, 1971
Fiscal year ends: December 31

WHO

Chairman and CEO: Lawrence K. Fish, age 45
President: Gordon I. Ulmer, age 57, $461,393 pay
CFO: Kent Price, age 46
General Counsel and Secretary: Edward Lane-Reticker, age 64
Auditors: Ernst & Young
Employees: 15,000

WHERE

HQ: 28 State St., Boston, MA 02109
Phone: 617-742-4000
FAX: 617-573-7798 (Public Relations)

Bank of New England has operations in the US, the Bahamas, and the UK.

WHAT

	1989 Sales	
	$ mil	% of total
Interest income		
Commercial loans	1,115	32
Mortgages	758	21
Consumer loans	444	13
Real estate loans	350	10
Lease financing	156	4
Foreign loans & leases	32	1
Other	366	10
Noninterest income		
Trust fees	102	3
Service fees	151	4
Other	163	5
Income (loss) from asset sales	(108)	(3)
Corporate adjustment	(51)	—
Total	**3,478**	**100**

Financial Services
Consumer branch banking
Middle-market and corporate banking
Mutual fund and payroll processing
Real estate lending
Small commercial and community banking
Trust and private banking

Banks
Bank of New England
Bank of New England–Old Colony
Bank of New England–West
The Connecticut Bank and Trust Company
Maine National Bank

Nonbank Subsidiaries
BancNew England Mortgage Co., Inc.
Bank of New England Trust Co.
BNE Asset Sales, Inc.
BNE Associates, Inc.
BNE Capital Markets, Inc.
BNE Information Services, Inc.
BNE Vehicle Leasing
Constitution Capital Management Co.
New England Capital Corp.

RANKINGS

21st in *Fortune* 100 Commercial Banking Cos.
242nd in *Forbes* Sales 500

COMPETITION

Bank of Boston
Other commercial banks in New England

THE BANK OF NEW YORK COMPANY, INC.

OVERVIEW

The Bank of New York is the 11th largest bank holding company in the US and focuses on 5 businesses: corporate banking, retail banking, securities processing, trust and investment management, and financial market services.

The bank serves the international banking needs of US companies in foreign trade financing as one of the industry's largest participants in issuance of letters of credit and international funds transfer systems. The bank added 50 branches with the 1988 acquisition of Irving Bank. The bank currently has the largest network of branches (229) in the suburbs of New York City. It provides custom banking at 13 locations in New York City for individuals with high net worth.

As the leading provider of securities processing services in the US, Bank of New York is custodian for $650 billion in securities; it is the largest bank lender of securities to other institutions. The bank also is #1 in providing securities clearing services to the government securities market. Its personal trust business is ranked 8th largest in the US in assets under management.

NYSE symbol: BK
Incorporated: New York, 1968
Fiscal year ends: December 31

WHO

Chairman and CEO: J. Carter Bacot, age 57, $1,223,718 pay
President: Peter Herrick, age 63, $779,454 pay
VC: Samuel F. Chevalier, age 55, $670,684 pay
SEVP (Principal Financial Officer): Deno D. Papageorge, age 51, $557,299 pay
Auditors: Deloitte & Touche
Employees: 17,766

WHEN

Alexander Hamilton and a group of influential New York merchants and lawyers founded New York City's first bank, the Bank of New York, in 1784. Attorney Hamilton at age 27 recognized the need to grant credit for the new nation's economy and to return credibility to the monetary system.

For 15 years the bank was the only commercial lending firm in the city. The Bank of New York, with the Bank of North America (created by the US Congress), became the depository for the first foreign loans granted by the US. The bank has paid dividends continuously since 1785.

Hamilton became US Secretary of the Treasury in 1789. He soon negotiated the new US government's first loan, issued by the Bank of New York for $200,000. The bank also assisted in financing the War of 1812 by offering subscription books for $16 million, and the Civil War by loaning the government $150 million. In 1878 the bank became a US Treasury depository for the sale of 4% government bonds, selling about $50 million worth the first 6 months.

Bank of New York emphasized commercial banking to select customers, and, because it did not compete for size with other banks, the bank was no longer one of the largest in the US by 1904. In 1922 the bank merged with New York Life Insurance and Trust Company to form Bank of New York and Trust Company. The bank began to develop trust and investment services, investing trust assets in common stocks, including IBM, after the 1929 Crash. In 1938 the bank changed its name to Bank of New York.

In 1948 Bank of New York acquired the Fifth Avenue Bank to get a mid-Manhattan location and expand trust services. In 1966 the bank acquired Empire Trust Company, which specialized in lending to developing industries. The Bank of New York Company, Inc., a new holding company created in 1968, expanded statewide by acquiring banks in White Plains, Endicott-Binghamton, Albany, Olean, Syracuse, and Buffalo. In 1980 the bank bought Empire National Bank (Newburgh), with 38 branches, the 2nd largest branch network in the state outside New York City.

The company acquired New York competitor Irving Bank in a 1988 hostile takeover for $1.4 billion in cash and equity securities to make it the 10th largest US banking company at the time. In 1989 the bank consolidated after the Irving acquisition by reducing staff by more than 3,000 and eliminating duplicative branches. Thus the bank entered 1990 with lower operating expenses.

WHERE

HQ: 48 Wall St., New York, NY 10286
Phone: 212-495-1784
FAX: 212-495-1239 (Public Relations)

Bank of New York has offices or affiliates in 11 states and 22 countries.

	1989 Sales		1989 Net Income	
	$ mil	% of total	$ mil	% of total
US	3,990	73	245	—
Europe	482	9	7	—
Asia	294	5	11	—
Other foreign	731	13	(212)	—
Total	**5,497**	**100**	**51**	—

WHAT

Banking Services

Corporate Banking
Accounts receivable factoring
Asset-based lending

International Banking
Foreign trade financing
Funds transfer
Letters of credit

Retail banking
Credit cards
Mortgage loans

Global Securities Processing
Mutual fund servicing
Securities custody
Securities lending
Stock transfer services

Trust & Investment Management

Financial Market Services

HOW MUCH

	9 Yr. Growth	1980	1981	1982	1983	1984	1985	1986	1987	1988	1989
Sales ($ mil)	19.6%	1,098	1,496	1,521	1,340	1,577	1,594	1,750	2,141	2,620	5,497
Net income ($ mil)	0.4%	49	58	73	91	108	130	155	103	213	51
Income as % of sales	—	4.4%	3.9%	4.8%	6.8%	6.8%	8.2%	8.9%	4.8%	8.1%	0.9%
Earnings per share ($)	(20.7%)	2.17	2.54	2.77	3.15	3.57	4.02	4.54	2.81	5.21	0.27
Stock price – high ($)	—	12.42	15.79	18.58	22.08	24.50	34.92	46.75	45.88	37.25	55.00
Stock price – low ($)	—	8.92	10.96	12.04	15.75	17.50	23.25	32.83	24.50	25.88	36.75
Stock price – close ($)	14.8%	11.58	14.29	16.58	21.83	23.67	34.25	38.88	25.75	37.00	40.25
P/E – high	—	6	6	7	7	7	9	10	16	7	204
P/E – low	—	4	4	4	5	5	6	7	9	5	136
Dividends per share ($)	8.7%	0.93	1.02	1.08	1.16	1.26	1.40	1.56	1.71	1.83	1.97
Book value per share ($)	6.6%	19.68	21.10	23.05	25.39	27.88	28.38	31.76	33.65	37.34	34.87

1989 Year End:
Debt ratio: 25.6%
Return on equity: 0.7%
Cash (mil): $3,530
Assets (mil): $48,856
Long-term debt (mil): $951
Number of shares (mil): 68
Dividends:
1989 average yield: 4.9%
1989 payout: 729.6%
Market value (mil): $2,733

Stock Price History high/low 1980-89

60
50
40
30
20
10
0

RANKINGS

11th in *Fortune* 100 Commercial Banking Cos.
97th in *Fortune* World's 100 Commercial Banks
161st in *Forbes* Sales 500
248th in *Business Week* 1000

COMPETITION

American Express
BankAmerica
Bankers Trust
Chase Manhattan
Chemical Banking
Citicorp
Dai-Ichi Kangyo
Deutsche Bank
First Chicago
Hongkong & Shanghai Banking
Manufacturers Hanover
J.P. Morgan
Security Pacific

BANKAMERICA CORPORATION

OVERVIEW

BankAmerica, the 3rd largest US bank holding company after Citicorp and Chase Manhattan, provides banking services through Bank of America and Seattle–First National in California, Washington, and Nevada. BankAmerica provides retail banking to consumers and small companies through 1,046 branches and 1,822 ATMs in those states. The bank is a major credit card issuer, with $6 billion in loans outstanding at the end of 1989. The San Francisco–based company also has lending and specialized financial services for corporations, government agencies, and institutions at 59 branches and offices worldwide.

The company's nonbank subsidiaries offer BankAmerica travelers checks, credit life and disability insurance, securities futures trading, and venture capital investment services.

BankAmerica at the end of 1989 had $75.9 billion in loans outstanding, evenly divided among 4 categories: commercial (25%), real estate (27%), consumer (25%), and international (23%). In 1989 it made a public commitment to lend at least $50 million annually for California low-income housing, creating the Bank of America Special Income Credit (BASIC) program, making consumer loans more available to lower-income Californians.

WHEN

Amadeo Giannini, son of Italian immigrants, founded the Bank of Italy in San Francisco in 1904. Two years later he saved the cash, gold, and notes from the bank before it was destroyed by the fire caused by the 1906 earthquake. Giannini opened for business in a temporary location on a pier and loaned money to finance the reconstruction.

Giannini circumvented a 1921 federal ruling prohibiting branching by acquiring the Bank of America of Los Angeles, which had 21 branches. In 1928 Giannini formed a holding company, Transamerica Corporation, to manage his banks and other financial services. By 1930 Bank of Italy and Bank of America were operating as Bank of America.

By the end of 1945 Bank of America had passed Chase Manhattan to be the largest US bank. The Bank Holding Company Act of 1956 forced the 1958 separation of Bank of America from the insurance and other services of Transamerica. Also in 1958 Bank of America introduced BankAmericard, the bank credit card that became VISA in 1977.

In the 1950s and 1960s the bank expanded internationally, and by 1970 it was one of the largest international lenders in the US, with offices throughout the world. The bank became the subsidiary of BankAmerica Corporation, a bank holding company formed in 1968.

A. W. Clausen became CEO in 1970, and the bank rapidly expanded in real estate and foreign loans. Earnings and assets quadrupled during the 1970s but decreased steadily in the early 1980s when the bank suffered loan losses. At the end of 1980, Citicorp had replaced BankAmerica as the largest US bank.

In 1981 Clausen became head of the World Bank and was replaced by Samuel Armacost. In 1983 the company acquired Seafirst (Seattle–First National Bank) and Charles Schwab (discount brokerage, sold back to Schwab in 1987). By 1985 loan losses had forced Armacost to lay off employees for the first time in company history. In 1986 BankAmerica's board of directors, after continued losses and pressure from regulators, forced Armacost to resign and reappointed Clausen as CEO.

After reducing costs and domestic problem loans, the bank became profitable again in 1988 after 3 years of losses. In 1989 the bank continued to improve its profitability, credit quality, and capital adequacy. In 1990 Clausen retired and President Richard M. Rosenberg became chairman and CEO. That same year BankAmerica won government approval to purchase Western Savings & Loan, Arizona's 2nd largest savings institution, for $80 million.

HOW MUCH

	9 Yr. Growth	1980	1981	1982	1983	1984	1985	1986	1987	1988	1989
Sales ($ mil)	(0.6%)	12,071	15,085	14,956	13,299	14,397	13,880	12,483	10,163	10,181	11,389
Net income ($ mil)	2.7%	643	445	390	390	346	(337)	(518)	(955)	547	820
Income as % of sales	—	5.3%	3.0%	2.6%	2.9%	2.4%	(2.4%)	(4.2%)	(9.4%)	5.4%	7.2%
Earnings per share ($)	(1.7%)	4.36	3.02	2.61	2.18	1.77	(2.68)	(3.74)	(6.43)	2.77	3.74
Stock price – high ($)	—	30.25	30.75	26.25	25.50	23.13	22.75	18.75	15.38	19.13	36.38
Stock price – low ($)	—	20.25	20.63	15.63	18.00	14.50	12.88	9.50	5.25	6.75	17.00
Stock price – close ($)	(1.4%)	30.25	21.25	20.13	20.88	18.13	15.63	14.63	6.88	17.63	26.75
P/E – high	—	7	10	10	12	13	—	—	—	7	10
P/E – low	—	5	7	6	8	8	—	—	—	2	5
Dividends per share ($)	(9.1%)	1.41	1.50	1.52	1.52	1.52	1.16	0.00	0.00	0.00	0.60
Book value per share ($)	(1.4%)	26.55	27.72	28.96	29.43	29.10	25.11	21.49	15.12	18.43	23.32

1989 Year End:
Debt ratio: 42.4%
Return on equity: 17.9%
Cash (mil): $10,316
Assets (mil): $98,764
Long-term debt (mil): $4,075
Number of shares (mil): 210
Dividends:
1989 average yield: 2.2%
1989 payout: 16.0%
Market value (mil): $5,626

NYSE symbol: BAC
Incorporated: Delaware, 1968
Fiscal year ends: December 31

WHO

Chairman and CEO: Richard M. Rosenberg, age 59, $1,250,000 pay (prior to promotion)
VC: Lewis W. Coleman, age 48, $866,667 pay
VC and CFO: Frank N. Newman, age 47, $845,833 pay
VC: Glenhall E. Taylor, Jr., age 64, $750,000 pay
Auditors: Ernst & Young
Employees: 63,075

WHERE

HQ: Bank of America Center, San Francisco, CA 94104
Phone: 415-622-2091
FAX: 415-622-2780

BankAmerica provides banking services in 3 western states of the US and has 59 offices worldwide.

	1989 Sales	
	$ mil	% of total
US	8,194	72
Europe, Middle East & Africa	1,108	10
Asia	898	8
Latin America & the Caribbean	1,035	9
Canada	154	1
Total	**11,389**	**100**

WHAT

	1989 Sales	
	$ mil	% of total
Loan interest	7,913	70
Other interest	1,646	14
Noninterest	1,830	16
Total	**11,389**	**100**

Financial Services
Bank credit cards
Capital market services
Consumer and real estate loans
Corporate lending
Credit-related insurance
Depository services
Employee benefit trusts
Investment banking
Money transfer services
Mortgage banking
Payment services
Travelers checks

RANKINGS

3rd in *Fortune* 100 Commercial Banking Cos.
45th in *Fortune* World's 100 Commercial Banks
56th in *Forbes* Sales 500
97th in *Business Week* 1000
282nd in *Business Week* Global 1000

COMPETITION

H. F. Ahmanson
American Express
Bank of New York
Bankers Trust
Chase Manhattan
Chemical Banking
Citicorp
CS Holding
Dai-Ichi Kangyo
First Interstate
Great Western
J.P. Morgan
Security Pacific
Wells Fargo
Other foreign banks

BANKERS TRUST NEW YORK CORPORATION

OVERVIEW

Bankers Trust New York Corporation owns Bankers Trust, one of the largest US banks, and provides corporate finance, money and securities market trading, and trust services.

Having sold its consumer banking business, Bankers provides wholesale (corporate) banking nationally and internationally. International operations, which accounted for 43% of the bank's revenue in 1989, incurred an almost $1.2 billion loss because of a $1.6 billion special provison for credit losses in less developed countries. The company is now in 40 financial markets worldwide, including the developed countries of Europe and Japan, growth economies of Asia, emerging third world markets, and Eastern Europe.

BT Securities, a Bankers subsidiary, is an underwriter and dealer in US Treasury and agency securities, municipal bonds, and other debt securities. BT Securities also offers investment and brokerage services, mergers and acquisitions advice, and other financial advisory services.

The PROFITCo division, which conducts trust and custodial services and securities processing, grew by 25% in 1989 in assets under management. Its international trust business, particularly in Japan, provides a major income growth area.

NYSE symbol: BT
Incorporated: New York, 1965
Fiscal year ends: December 31

WHO

Chairman: Charles S. Sanford, Jr., age 53, $1,500,000 pay
EVP: Edward A. Lesser, age 56, $1,200,000 pay
EVP: Ralph L. MacDonald, Jr., age 48, $1,200,000 pay
EVP: Eugene B. Shanks, Jr., age 42, $1,200,000 pay
EVP: George J. Vojta, age 54, $1,200,000 pay
EVP and CFO: William C. Jennings, age 50
Auditors: Ernst & Young
Employees: 13,230

WHEN

Henry Davison, a 35-year-old New York banker, and his young banker friends founded Bankers Trust Company in 1903 to handle trust business referred by commercial banks. The company raised capital with the sale of 10,000 shares of stock totaling $20 million in subscriptions.

In 1908 the company started a foreign department to handle transactions with correspondent banks abroad. Bankers Trust bought Mercantile Trust (1911), Manhattan Trust (1912), and Astor Trust (1917). Under the Federal Reserve Act of 1913, banks were allowed to offer trust services, eliminating Bankers Trust's competitive advantage. To be able to offer broader banking services, Bankers Trust became a member of the Federal Reserve System in 1917.

The bank's securities department, started in 1916, expanded in 1919 to include underwriting and distributing securities and in 1928 became a subsidiary; in 1931 it closed to comply with the Glass-Steagall Act (which required separation of investment banking from commercial banking).

In 1945 Bankers Trust opened a metropolitan division and for the first time offered savings accounts, checking accounts without minimum balances, home improvement loans, automobile loans, and unsecured business loans.

In 1950 the company bought Lawyers Trust, Title Guaranty & Trust's banking division, and Flushing National Bank. The company also added Commercial National (1951), Bayside National (1953), and Public National (1955). From 1955 through 1965 the company added 22 branches and bought South Shore Bank (Staten Island) and First National Bank (Long Island).

In 1965 Bankers Trust formed a holding company to own Bankers Trust Company and 3 other banks in upstate New York. By 1967 the holding company had 89 offices in New York and 2 in London. In the next 8 years the company grew to more than 200 offices. The company's international operations expanded in the 1970s to more than 30 countries, with a correspondent network of more than 1,200 banks in 123 countries.

In the early 1980s the company sold its consumer banking business to various financial institutions in order to focus on corporate services, particularly commercial and merchant banking in international markets.

WHERE

HQ: 280 Park Ave., New York, NY 10017
Phone: 212-250-2500
FAX: 212-850-1704 (Public Relations)

Bankers Trust has operations worldwide.

	1989 Sales		1989 Net Income	
	$ mil	% of total	$ mil	% of total
US	4,753	57	208	—
Asia & the Pacific	1,358	16	57	—
Western Hemisphere	633	7	(1,134)	—
Europe	646	8	(59)	—
UK	934	11	62	—
Middle East & Africa	86	1	(114)	—
Eliminations	(1,152)	—	—	—
Total	**7,258**	**100**	**(980)**	**—**

WHAT

	1989 Sales	
	$ mil	% of total
Interest	5,305	73
Noninterest	1,953	27
Total	**7,258**	**100**

Financial Services
Commercial banking services
Corporate finance
Fiduciary and securities services
Global operating and information services
International merchant banking
Investment management

RANKINGS

10th in *Fortune* 100 Commercial Banking Cos.
89th in *Fortune* World's 100 Commercial Banks
116th in *Forbes* Sales 500
196th in *Business Week* 1000
556th in *Business Week* Global 1000

COMPETITION

Bank of New York
BankAmerica
Chase Manhattan
Chemical Banking
Citicorp
Continental Bank
CS Holding
Dai-Ichi Kangyo
Deutsche Bank
First Chicago
Hongkong & Shanghai Banking
Manufacturers Hanover
J.P. Morgan
Security Pacific

HOW MUCH

	9 Yr. Growth	1980	1981	1982	1983	1984	1985	1986	1987	1988	1989
Sales ($ mil)	7.8%	3,693	4,651	4,611	3,858	4,834	4,699	4,923	5,693	5,851	7,258
Net income ($ mil)	—	214	188	223	257	307	371	428	1	648	(980)
Income as % of sales	—	5.8%	4.0%	4.8%	6.7%	6.3%	7.9%	8.7%	0.0%	11.1%	(13.5%)
Earnings per share ($)	—	4.32	3.45	3.88	4.20	4.76	5.39	6.01	0.02	8.09	(12.10)
Stock price – high ($)	—	15.94	18.94	22.75	24.75	29.13	37.81	52.50	55.25	41.25	58.25
Stock price – low ($)	—	8.97	13.44	12.63	17.81	18.88	26.81	32.88	26.25	29.63	34.50
Stock price – close ($)	11.6%	15.44	16.94	18.56	22.56	27.38	36.75	45.25	31.75	35.00	41.38
P/E – high	—	4	6	6	6	6	7	9	2,763	5	—
P/E – low	—	2	4	3	4	4	5	5	1,313	4	—
Dividends per share ($)	10.8%	0.85	0.95	1.05	1.15	1.26	1.38	1.53	1.71	1.92	2.14
Book value per share ($)	2.8%	20.48	22.54	24.93	27.65	30.51	34.32	38.78	37.39	43.14	26.29

1989 Year End:
Debt ratio: 50.5%
Return on equity: (34.9%)
Cash (mil): $9,154
Assets (mil):$55,658
Long-term debt (mil): $2,435
Number of shares (mil): 81
Dividends:
1989 average yield: 5.2%
1989 payout: (17.7%)
Market value (mil): $3,362

Stock Price History high/low 1980-89

60 50 40 30 20 10 0

C. R. BARD, INC.

OVERVIEW

Bard develops, manufactures, and distributes medical, surgical, diagnostic, and patient care devices to worldwide health care facilities. The company, known traditionally in the urological field for its Foley catheter, produces a wide variety of products for cardiovascular care (almost 50% of sales) as well as surgical products. Bard markets nearly 20,000 products through hundreds of distributors around the world. Bard is ranked 9th in its industry by *Business Week*.

Bard, which had experienced steady growth for 17 years, had a net income decrease of 17% in 1989, caused primarily by the company's recall of the New Probe angioplasty catheter from the US market at the direction of the FDA. This was followed by a voluntary withdrawal of the Sprint and Solo angioplasty catheters in March 1990 after a company investigation revealed improper labeling. Both of these recalls have resulted in Bard's temporary withdrawal from the US balloon angioplasty market.

Despite these problems, Bard still experienced a 3% growth in sales over 1988, largely due to an increase in international sales and sales of surgical products.

NYSE symbol: BCR
Incorporated: New Jersey, 1972
Fiscal year ends: December 31

WHO

Chairman: Robert H. McCaffrey, age 63, $408,000 pay
President and CEO: George T. Maloney, age 57, $420,000 pay
EVP and COO: William H. Longfield, age 51, $243,562 pay
EVP and CFO: George A. Davis, age 62, $204,000 pay
Auditors: Arthur Andersen & Co.
Employees: 8,300

WHEN

When visiting Europe at the turn of the century, silk importer Charles Russell Bard discovered that Gomenol, a mixture of olive oil with an extract distilled from eucalyptus, gave him relief from urinary problems caused by tuberculosis. He brought the "medicine" to America and began distributing it.

In 1907 Bard began selling a ureteral catheter developed by J. Eynard, a French firm. Bard incorporated in 1923 under the company's present name. In 1926, because of failing health, Charles Bard sold the company to John F. Willits, his sales manager, and Edson L. Outwin, his accountant. He stayed on as a consultant until 1932 and died in 1934. That year the company became the sole agent for Davol Rubber's newly developed Foley catheter. By 1948 sales had topped $1 million.

From 1950 to 1959 sales increased over 400% to $9 million. The company introduced its first presterilized packaged product in 1958 and began to expand its product line with disposable drainage tubes and an intravenous feeding device.

In 1963 Bard formed 2 joint ventures with Davol to manufacture and distribute hospital and surgical supplies internationally. The company began manufacturing plastic tubing in 1964 and by 1969 was manufacturing over 75% of the 6,000 products it distributed. During this period Bard acquired United States Catheter and Instrument (1966). Net sales had increased to $51 million by 1969.

The company bought over a dozen companies during the 1970s, diversifying into the cardiovascular, respiratory therapy, home-care product, and kidney dialysis fields. By 1976 Bard was offering 13,000 products.

In 1979 Bard introduced the first angioplasty catheter, a nonsurgical device to clear blocked arteries. Bard bought Automated Screening Devices (producers of a high-tech blood pressure monitor) in 1980. Also that year the company purchased Davol for $48 million, assuring Bard's supply of its #1-selling Foley catheters and more than doubling sales of surgical implants.

Bard increased its R&D budget throughout the 1980s, spending $36.2 million in 1989, but that year breakage problems caused the company to recall an angioplasty catheter. Net income dropped from $79 million in 1988 to $65 million in 1989. In March of 1990 the company recalled its angioplasty catheters from the US market because of improper labeling.

The company's new incontinence product, Contigen, could have a generous impact on sales once it is submitted to the FDA and subsequently approved.

WHERE

HQ: 730 Central Ave., Murray Hill, NJ 07974
Phone: 201-277-8000
FAX: 201-277-8240

Bard has manufacturing plants in 15 states and in France, Ireland, Malaysia, and the UK. Bard sells products worldwide; its biggest markets are the US, Canada, Europe, and Japan.

	1989 Sales		1989 Operating Income	
	$ mil	% of total	$ mil	% of total
US	606	78	88	71
Foreign	172	22	36	29
Adjustments	—	—	(8)	—
Total	**778**	**100**	**116**	**100**

WHAT

	1989 Sales	
	$ mil	% of total
Cardiovascular products	375	48
Urological products	166	21
Surgical products	170	22
General health products & services	67	9
Total	**778**	**100**

Products

Angiographic catheters
Blood oxygenators
Cardiopulmonary support systems
Cardiotomy reservoirs
Cardiovascular recanalization devices (balloon angioplasty catheters, laser devices)
Disposable obstetrical instruments
Drug infusion pumps
Electrophysiology products (pacing, diagnostic, and therapeutic electrodes; cardiac mapping)
Hemo-concentrators
Ostomy devices
Surgical products (wound drainage devices, vascular access catheters and ports)
Urological products (catheters, trays, collection systems)
Wound management and skin care products

HOW MUCH

	9 Yr. Growth	1980	1981	1982	1983	1984	1985	1986	1987	1988	1989
Sales ($ mil)	13.6%	247	330	343	397	417	465	548	641	758	778
Net income ($ mil)	16.5%	17	23	27	33	35	42	51	62	79	65
Income as % of sales	—	6.7%	6.8%	7.9%	8.4%	8.5%	9.0%	9.3%	9.7%	10.4%	8.4%
Earnings per share ($)	17.1%	0.29	0.38	0.46	0.56	0.58	0.70	0.86	1.07	1.38	1.18
Stock price – high ($)	—	4.06	5.48	8.75	11.69	9.44	11.00	20.19	25.13	24.63	26.50
Stock price – low ($)	—	1.73	3.29	4.58	6.88	4.75	5.41	9.38	12.50	16.88	18.75
Stock price – close ($)	23.1%	3.42	5.04	7.56	8.63	5.63	11.00	18.13	17.25	23.00	22.13
P/E – high	—	14	14	19	21	16	16	23	23	18	22
P/E – low	—	6	9	10	12	8	8	11	12	12	16
Dividends per share ($)	21.3%	0.06	0.08	0.09	0.10	0.11	0.13	0.17	0.22	0.28	0.36
Book value per share ($)	12.4%	2.14	2.45	2.81	3.22	3.66	4.25	4.56	5.23	5.83	6.12

1989 Year End:
Debt ratio: 17.4%
Return on equity: 19.7%
Cash (mil): $11
Current ratio: 2.48
Long-term debt (mil): $70
Number of shares (mil): 55
Dividends:
1989 average yield: 1.6%
1989 payout: 30.5%
Market value (mil): $1,206

Stock Price History high/low 1980-89

RANKINGS

393rd in *Fortune* 500 Industrial Cos.
591st in *Business Week* 1000

COMPETITION

Abbott Labs
American Cyanamid
American Home Products
Baxter
Becton, Dickinson
Eli Lilly
Johnson & Johnson
Pfizer

RNETT BANKS, INC.

OVERVIEW

Jacksonville-based Barnett is Florida's largest financial institution and the 8th largest banking organization in Georgia. The $29-billion-asset banking company has 563 offices, 521 in Florida and 42 in Georgia.

Barnett leads other Florida banks with a 22.5% share of bank deposits in the state (up from 18.2% in 1985), ranking it first, 2nd, or 3rd in 43 Florida counties. Having grown with the boom in Florida and the South, Barnett has 51% of its loans in real estate with more than half of those in mortgages.

The company's nonbank affiliates offer trust services, collection services, full-service securities brokerage, credit-related insurance, and credit card, mortgage, and consumer finance services.

Barnett is a decentralized operation, allowing affiliates to act autonomously in most day-to-day decisions. Early in 1990 Barnett announced the consolidation into regional structures of staff functions not directly related to customer service; this is intended to bring economies of scale while keeping local autonomy.

With the current slowdown of the Florida economy, Barnett is seeking increased market share in the Southeast, based on improved efficiency and customer service. The state's real estate problems have resulted in problem loans for Barnett, and the bank announced a $60 million charge to earnings in the first quarter of 1990.

WHEN

William Barnett, a Kansas banker, and his family moved to Jacksonville, Florida, in 1877 for his wife's health. The same year he started a family-owned company, The National Bank of Jacksonville.

In 1930 the Barnetts formed Barnett National Securities Corporation, a bank holding company, which soon acquired and reopened 3 banks that had failed after the 1929 stock market crash (in Cocoa, DeLand, and St. Augustine). The day before President Franklin Roosevelt's bank holiday during the Great Depression in 1933, Barnett opened every teller window and had tellers slowly count money for withdrawals using nothing larger than a $20 bill; the strategy prevented a run on the bank because many people in line were reassured and went home.

Jacksonville attorney Guy W. Botts, who joined the bank as president in 1963, had a vision for the bank to become a statewide banking institution and a leader in every market. In 1966 Barnett acquired First National Bank of Winter Park, and by 1969 the holding company had purchased 7 other banks throughout Florida. To clarify its identity, the company changed its name to Barnett Banks of Florida in 1969 (changed to Barnett Banks, Inc. in 1987).

During the 1970s Barnett established Florida's first credit card franchise, which resulted in Barnett's becoming a leader among the state's banks in the use of computers. Barnett also was the first southeastern bank holding company to be listed on the New York Stock Exchange.

The company continued to pay its quarterly dividends throughout the Florida real estate crash in the mid-1970s. In 1977 state law changed to allow banks to open branch office operations instead of having to establish full-service banks. The company opened 4 branches in 1977 and 9 more the following year. By the end of the decade, the company also had bought 29 more banks.

Positioning itself for the likelihood of regional interstate banking, Barnett continued to acquire banks (over 32) and add branches (230) in the 1980s in order to strengthen market share. Florida approved a regional interstate banking law in 1985, and the following year Barnett moved into Georgia by acquiring First National Bank of Cobb County. Barnett now operates in 13 counties in Georgia.

HOW MUCH

	9 Yr. Growth	1980	1981	1982	1983	1984	1985	1986	1987	1988	1989
Sales ($ mil)	24.1%	434	582	776	988	1,358	1,574	1,914	2,286	2,546	3,038
Net income ($ mil)	23.8%	38	41	57	82	103	128	162	196	226	257
Income as % of sales	—	8.7%	7.1%	7.3%	8.3%	7.6%	8.2%	8.5%	8.6%	8.9%	8.5%
Earnings per share ($)	14.0%	1.25	1.35	1.48	1.92	2.20	2.57	2.96	3.25	3.75	4.07
Stock price – high ($)	—	9.04	13.19	15.50	18.89	19.56	30.00	40.88	41.75	37.38	40.00
Stock price – low ($)	—	4.96	8.22	8.33	11.56	14.44	18.67	25.67	27.13	29.00	32.25
Stock price – close ($)	17.1%	8.74	10.11	12.00	17.33	19.50	29.83	31.25	28.38	34.00	36.13
P/E – high	—	7	10	11	10	9	12	14	13	10	10
P/E – low	—	4	6	6	6	7	7	9	8	8	8
Dividends per share ($)	14.6%	0.34	0.41	0.47	0.52	0.59	0.67	0.77	0.89	1.01	1.16
Book value per share ($)	13.7%	8.44	9.37	10.53	12.60	14.60	16.34	19.07	21.97	24.37	26.79

1989 Year End:
Debt ratio: 18.8%
Return on equity: 15.9%
Cash (mil): $1,583
Assets (mil): $29,007
Long-term debt (mil): $391
Number of shares (mil): 63
Dividends:
1989 average yield: 3.2%
1989 payout: 28.5%
Market value (mil): $2,279

Stock Price History high/low 1980-89

NYSE symbol: BBI
Incorporated: Florida, 1930
Fiscal year ends: December 31

WHO

Chairman and CEO: Charles E. Rice, age 54, $952,280 pay
President and COO: Albert D. Ernest, Jr., age 59, $546,537 pay
VC and Chief Banking Officer: Allen L. Lastinger, Jr., age 47, $500,248 pay
SEVP and CFO: Stephen A. Hansel, age 42, $388,306 pay
Auditors: Price Waterhouse
Employees: 18,983

WHERE

HQ: 100 Laura St., Jacksonville, FL 32202; PO Box 40789, Jacksonville, FL 32203
Phone: 904-791-7720
FAX: 904-791-7166

Barnett Banks has 563 offices in Florida and Georgia.

WHAT

	1989 Sales $ mil	1989 Sales % of total
Interest income		
Loans	2,337	77
Investment securities	280	9
Federal funds sold	12	1
Securities purchased under agreements to resell	16	1
Noninterest income		
Trust income	38	1
Service charges	121	4
Credit card fees	72	2
Other service charges, fees	88	3
Other income	74	2
Total	**3,038**	**100**

Banking Services
Cash management services
Consumer banking
Corporate banking
Credit card services
Equipment lease financing
Foreign trade financing
Real estate lending

Nonbanking Services
Accident and health insurance
Credit life insurance
Mortgage loan servicing
Securities brokerage
Trust services

RANKINGS

23rd in *Fortune* 100 Commercial Banking Cos.
274th in *Forbes* Sales 500
328th in *Business Week* 1000
906th in *Business Week* Global 1000

COMPETITION

H. F. Ahmanson
Great Western
NCNB
SunTrust
Other banks and real estate lenders in Florida and Georgia

BASF AG

OVERVIEW

Well known to US consumers for its recording tapes, BASF is one of the world's largest chemical manufacturers. An integrated chemical concern, the company produces oil and gas and operates its own refineries. BASF is headquartered within its immense facility in Ludwigshafen and derives approximately 1/3 of its sales from West Germany and 1/3 from the rest of Europe. Since 1978 BASF has rapidly increased its US presence through a series of acquisitions.

BASF remains sensitive to price swings in commodity chemicals despite increased emphasis on specialty products. The company is spending over $1 billion annually on R&D in such high-margin areas as crop protection, engineering plastics, high-performance composites, biotechnology, and pharmaceuticals. BASF intends to build a biotech research center in the Boston area.

In a European joint venture with Siemens, BASF sells IBM plug–compatible mainframe computers manufactured by Hitachi.

WHEN

Originally known as Badische Anilin & Soda-Fabrik, BASF was founded in Mannheim, Germany, by jeweler Frederick Englehorn in 1861. Unable to find enough land for expansion in Mannheim, BASF moved to nearby Ludwigshafen in 1865. The company was a pioneer in coal tar dyes, developing a very successful synthetic indigo in 1897. BASF's synthetic dyes rapidly replaced more expensive, inconvenient organic dyes.

BASF scientist Fritz Haber synthesized ammonia in 1909, paving the way for the company's entry into nitrogenous fertilizers in 1913. Haber received a Nobel prize for his work with ammonia in 1919, but later was charged with war crimes for his work with poison gases. BASF continued to grow and concentrated its production at a sprawling manufacturing complex in Ludwigshafen.

Managed by Carl Bosch, another Nobel prize-winner, BASF entered into the I.G. Farben cartel with Bayer, Hoechst, and others in 1925, creating a German chemical colossus. Within the cartel BASF developed polystyrene, PVC, and magnetic tape in the 1930s. Part of the Nazi war machine, I.G. Farben manufactured synthetic rubber, using labor from the Auschwitz concentration camp during WWII.

After the war I.G. Farben was dismantled, and in 1952 BASF regained its independence and began rebuilding its war-ravaged factories. Strong post-war domestic demand for basic chemicals aided BASF's recovery. In the late 1950s BASF began joint ventures abroad, including one in the US with Dow Chemical in 1958 (BASF bought out Dow's 1/2 in 1978). The company moved away from coal-based products and into petrochemicals, even acquiring German oil and gas producer Wintershall (1969), and became a leading plastic and synthetic fiber manufacturer.

Acquisitions figured prominently in BASF's global expansion and diversification into related businesses. In the US, the company purchased Wyandotte Chemicals (1969), Chemetron (pigments, 1979), Fritzsche, Dodge & Olcott (flavors, fragrances, 1980), and Inmont (paint, ink, 1985), among others. Despite its acquisitions and new product releases, BASF remains largely dependent on sales of basic chemicals. As with competitor Hoechst, the company's attempts to open a biotechnology plant in Germany have met with popular resistance.

In 1989 BASF settled an acrimonious labor dispute stemming from the company's request for wage concessions and subsequent 1984 lockout of chemical workers at a plant in Louisiana. After the lockout, union representatives charged BASF with unsafe practices in handling highly toxic chemicals. The company denied the charges. All workers have been allowed to return to their jobs.

HOW MUCH

$=DM1.69 (Dec. 31, 1989)	9 Yr. Growth	1980	1981	1982	1983	1984	1985	1986	1987	1988	1989
Sales (DM mil)	6.5%	26,985	30,865	32,486	35,111	40,400	44,377	40,471	40,238	43,868	47,617
Net income (DM mil)	21.1%	359	367	275	517	895	998	910	1,051	1,410	2,015
Income as % of sales	—	1.3%	1.2%	0.8%	1.5%	2.2%	2.2%	2.2%	2.6%	3.2%	4.2%
Earnings per share (DM)	16.3%	9	9	7	12	20	19	17	19	25	35
Stock price – high (DM)	—	151	149	138	176	186	275	332	347	287	315
Stock price – low (DM)	—	121	114	109	118	147	177	239	237	223	256
Stock price – close (DM)	10.4%	123	137	125	176	186	271	276	256	280	300
P/E – high	—	17	17	20	15	9	14	20	18	11	9
P/E – low	—	13	13	16	10	7	9	14	12	9	7
Dividends per share (DM)*	4.6%	8.0	7.0	7.0	5.0	7.0	9.0	10.0	10.0	10.0	12.0
Book value per share (DM)	4.1%	169	173	174	180	194	207	217	214	219	243

1989 Year End:
Debt ratio: 15.4%
Return on equity: 15.2%
Cash (mil): DM6,150
Debt (mil): DM2,534
Number of shares (mil): 57
Dividends:
1989 average yield: 4.0%
1989 payout: 34.3%
Market value (mil): $10,118
Sales (mil): $28,176

Stock Price History high/low 1980-89

350
300
250
200
150
100
50
0

* not including rights offerings

Principal stock exchange: Frankfurt
Incorporated: West Germany, 1952
Fiscal year ends: December 31

WHO

Chairman of the Supervisory Board: Matthias Seefelder
Chairman of the Board of Executive Directors: Jürgen Strube, age 50
Principal Financial Officer: Dietrich Kley
Chairman, President, and CEO, BASF Corp. (US): J. Dieter Stein
Auditors: Schitag Schwäbische Treuhand-Aktiengesellschaft; Deloitte Haskins + Sells GmbH
Employees: 136,990

WHERE

HQ: D-6700 Ludwigshafen, Germany
Phone: 011-49-621-601
US HQ (BASF Corp.): 8 Campus Dr., Parsippany, NJ 07054
US Phone: 201-397-2700
US FAX: 201-397-2737

BASF manufactures products in 35 countries and sells them in over 160 countries.

	1989 Sales	
	DM mil	% of total
West Germany	15,211	32
Other Europe	15,335	32
North America	10,477	22
Asia, Africa & Australia	4,167	9
Latin America	2,427	5
Total	**47,617**	**100**

WHAT

	1989 Sales	
	DM mil	% of total
Chemicals	9,729	21
Consumer products	9,676	20
Dyestuffs & finishing products	8,711	18
Plastics	8,645	18
Raw materials & energy	5,752	12
Agricultural chemicals	5,104	11
Total	**47,617**	**100**

Chemicals
Basic and industrial chemicals
Colorants and dyes
Fertilizers
Fibers
Flavors and fragrances
Herbicides
Intermediates

Consumer Products
Audio- and videotapes
Coatings and paints
Computer diskettes
Pharmaceuticals (Knoll)
Printing inks and plates

Other Products
Coal
Feed additives
Oil and gas (Wintershall)
Plastics
Potash

RANKINGS

31st in *Fortune* Global 500 Industrial Cos.
18th in *Forbes* 100 Foreign Investments in the US
158th in *Business Week* Global 1000

COMPETITION

Allied-Signal
American Cyanamid
Bayer
Dow Chemical
Du Pont
Eastman Kodak
FMC
W. R. Grace
Hercules
3M
Monsanto
Polaroid
Rhône-Poulenc
Union Carbide
Oil and other chemical and drug companies

PLC

RVIEW

ass is Britain's leading brewer, a large operator of pubs and restaurants in the UK, the owner of Holiday Inns, and a major UK soft drink bottler. It has the European and Hong Kong franchises for Carling Black Label, Britain's bestselling beer. Bass sells 39% of its beer through its network of 2,405 company-managed and 4,373 tenant-managed pubs. The company enjoys extraordinary worker loyalty and a reputation for a strong corporate culture.

Since 1969 Bass has diversified into hotels and leisure-related businesses. The company has used proceeds from sales of existing, appreciated hotel properties to lower acquisition-related debt.

Britain's Monopolies and Mergers Commission is investigating large soft drink bottlers, including Bass's Britvic, for muscling out smaller suppliers.

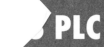

Principal stock exchange: London
Incorporated: England, 1967
Fiscal year ends: September 30

WHO

Chairman and CEO: Ian M. G. Prosser
Hotels Director: Bryan D. Langton
Brewing and Personnel Director: A. E. Robin Manners
Finance Director: David G. Inns
Auditors: Ernst & Young
Employees: 90,138 (prior to acquisition of US Holiday Inns)

WHEN

In 1777 William Bass decided to switch from transporting beer to brewing it in Burton-on-Trent in England. Burton's pure water supply allowed Bass to brew lighter ales than were being produced in London. In 1827, when Bass's grandson Michael took charge, the company produced 10,000 barrels. In 1876 Bass became the first company to gain trademark protection (for its red triangle) under the British Trademark Registration Act of 1875. By the time of Michael Bass's death in 1884, the 145-acre Bass brewery was the largest ale and bitter beer brewery in the world.

Most British brewers employed the tied-house system of brewer-controlled pubs, which limited the distribution of their products but assured them of a market for their beer. Bass used the free-trade system, selling its branded goods to independent and tied-house pubs through distributors. The temperance movement and WWI hurt all brewers, but, when rivals upgraded their tied-house pubs to compete with movies and other diversions, the independent pubs and Bass suffered. The company took its first step into tied-house pubs when it purchased neighboring brewer Worthington in 1926. Competing brewers then began forcing their tenant managers to emphasize their beers and sell less of the national brands. Bass failed to respond, instead purchasing several beer, wine, and spirit companies without integrating them with existing operations.

When Sir James Grigg, age 70, took over in 1959, he began looking for a merger partner. Bass merged with efficient regional brewer Mitchells & Butler in 1961 and gained expertise in streamlining its operations. Under Sir Alan Walker the company merged with Charrington United (Carling Black Label lager, pubs, 1967) to form a nationwide network of breweries and pubs. By 1970 Bass's British market share approached 25%. Led by lager, sales boomed.

When growth slowed in the 1980s, Bass sold its less profitable pubs and diversified. The rapid growth of the company's Crest Hotel chain (started in 1969) was augmented by the acquisition of Coral Leisure (hotels, gambling, 1980). Bass acquired Horizon Travel (packaged holidays) in 1987. The company bought the Holiday Inns chain in a series of steps beginning in 1987 and ending in 1990 with the $2.23 billion purchase of all North American and Mexican Holiday Inns.

Named after the Bing Crosby/Fred Astaire movie, Holiday Inns had been founded in Memphis in 1952 by Kemmons Wilson. Franchises rapidly emerged along US highways, creating one of the world's largest lodging chains. The company bought Harrah's (casinos, 1979) and Granada Royale Hometel (later renamed Embassy Suites, 1984) and started Homewood Suites (1988), all of which were spun off to the company's shareholders as Promus Companies when the Holiday Inns chain was sold to Bass.

WHERE

HQ: 66 Chiltern St., London W1M 1PR, England
Phone: 011-44-71-486-4440
FAX: 011-44-71-486-7190
US Address (Holiday Inns Worldwide): 3796 Lamar Ave., Memphis, TN 38195
US Phone: 901-362-4001
US FAX: 901-369-7172

Bass owns 13 breweries and 6,778 pubs throughout the UK. The company owns, manages, or franchises more than 1,600 hotels in 48 countries.

	1989 Sales		1989 Operating Income	
	£ mil	% of total	£ mil	% of total
UK	3,691	91	485	92
Europe	183	5	22	4
North America	109	3	18	3
Other countries	53	1	4	1
Total	**4,036**	**100**	**529**	**100**

WHAT

	1989 Sales		1989 Operating Income	
	£ mil	% of total	£ mil	% of total
Brewing & pubs	2,092	48	350	66
Hotels & restaurants	498	11	75	14
Leisure	869	20	54	10
Soft drinks & other	879	21	50	10
Adjustments	(302)	—	—	—
Total	**4,036**	**100**	**529**	**100**

Beer Brands
Barbican (nonalcoholic)
Bass
Carling Black Label
Stones
Tennent's
Worthington

Hotels & Restaurants
Holiday Inns
Toby Hotels
Toby Restaurants

Soft Drink Bottling (UK)
Britvic
Canada Dry
Pepsi
7-Up

Leisure
Betting (Coral Racing)
Bingo game promotion on US Indian reservations (British American Bingo)
Juke box and game-machine rental services for pubs and other outlets

Other
Alexis Lichine (wines)
Bass Developments Ltd (real estate)
Delta Biotechnology Ltd (81%)
Westbay Distributors (20%)

HOW MUCH

£=$1.61 (Dec. 31, 1989)	9 Yr. Growth	1980	1981	1982	1983	1984	1985	1986	1987	1988	1989
Sales (£ mil)	13.8%	1,263	1,713	1,861	1,988	2,252	2,411	2,710	3,213	3,734	4,036
Net income (£ mil)	19.5%	77	98	95	113	144	165	199	244	307	382
Income as % of sales	—	6.1%	5.7%	5.1%	5.7%	6.2%	6.8%	7.3%	9.0%	8.2%	9.5%
Earnings per share (p)	16.7%	27	31	29	35	44	50	60	72	88	108
Stock price – high (p)	—	243	251	302	346	483	692	840	1,050	867	1,155
Stock price – low (p)	—	188	182	196	287	300	472	625	579	733	793
Stock price – close (p)	19.8%	207	207	300	308	483	660	737	819	797	1,053
P/E – high	—	9	8	10	10	11	14	14	15	10	11
P/E – low	—	7	6	7	8	7	9	10	8	8	7
Dividends per share (p)	14.1%	8.6	9.5	10.1	11.4	12.9	14.7	17.0	19.5	23.5	28.2
Book value per share (p)	11.1%	307	317	334	354	381	419	438	721	733	792

1989 Year End:
Debt ratio: 22.0%
Return on equity: 14.2%
Cash (mil): £42
Long-term debt (mil): £770
Number of shares (mil): 344
Dividends:
1989 average yield: 2.7%
1989 payout: 26.0%
Market value (mil): $5,831
Sales (mil): $6,498

RANKINGS

238th in *Fortune* Global 500 Industrial Cos.
281st in *Business Week* Global 1000

COMPETITION

Adolph Coors
Anheuser-Busch
Bally
BSN
Cadbury Schweppes
Carlson
Coca-Cola
Dr Pepper/7Up
E. & J. Gallo
Grand Metropolitan
Guinness
Helmsley Enterprises
Hilton
Hyatt
Marriott

B.A.T INDUSTRIES PLC

OVERVIEW

Selling over 300 cigarette brands in 160 countries, B.A.T is the leader in cigarette sales outside the US. Major US brands include Kool and Capri. The company owns 40% of Imasco, the dominant Canadian cigarette manufacturer and operator of Shoppers Drug Mart (Canada's largest drugstore chain) and US-based Hardee's. Through its Farmers Group (US) and Allied Dunbar (UK) units, B.A.T has a major stake in the financial services industry.

Despite fending off a hostile takeover by Sir James Goldsmith, B.A.T is continuing to restructure. The company has sold its holdings in US retailers Marshall Field and Saks and has announced its intention to dispose of the rest of its retail operations and spin off its Wiggins Teape Appleton paper business, leaving it in 2 lines of business: tobacco and financial services.

WHEN

The British-American Tobacco Company was created to end a cigarette price war in Britain between Imperial Tobacco (UK) and American Tobacco. James Buchanan Duke, creator of American Tobacco and owner of exclusive rights to the best cigarette manufacturing technology of the times, had set his sights on the British market after attaining a 90% share in the US. After a year of vicious price cutting in Britain, Imperial counterattacked in America. The companies called a truce and created a cartel in 1902. The deal granted Imperial the British market, American the US market, and jointly-owned British-American the rest of the world, with rights to the brand names of its founders.

With Duke in control, British-American began spreading throughout the world. He had his greatest early success in China, where a massive billboard campaign in 1907 and the distribution of millions of free samples in 1909 generated annual sales of 25 billion cigarettes by 1920. When the Communist Revolution ended British-American's operations in China, the company lost over 25% of its sales.

A 1911 US antitrust action forced American to sell its interest in British-American and opened the US market to the company. The company purchased an American cigarette manufacturer, Brown & Williamson, in 1927 and continued to grow through geographical expansion until the 1960s. The 1902 agreement was terminated in Britain in 1972 with the advent of the EEC. British-American's subsequent attempts to penetrate the British market proved unsuccessful, and it withdrew from the market in 1984.

As public concern over smoking mounted, British-American acquired nontobacco businesses and changed its name to B.A.T Industries in 1976. Modest diversification efforts in the 1960s included packaging, paper, and cosmetics. Only the paper business remains unsold today. The company bought food retailers in the early 1970s but sold them in the 1980s.

The acquisitions of retailers Saks (1973), Argos (UK, 1979), Marshall Field (1982), and numerous others significantly diversified the company's sales base. B.A.T then developed a taste for insurance companies, acquiring Eagle Star (UK, 1984), Allied Dunbar (UK, 1985), and Farmers Group (US, 1988).

Responding to a 1989 hostile takeover bid from Sir James Goldsmith, B.A.T announced a restructuring plan calling for the spinoff of its British retailers and the sale of all other retail and paper operations, leaving the company with tobacco and financial services. In 1990, after California insurance regulators blocked Goldsmith's attempt to force B.A.T to sell Farmers Group to Axa-Midi (France), Goldsmith abandoned his bid. Meanwhile, B.A.T sold Marshall Field to Minneapolis-based Dayton Hudson for just over $1 billion and Saks to Investcorp, an Arabian partnership, for $1.5 billion.

HOW MUCH

	9 Yr. Growth	1980	1981	1982	1983	1984	1985	1986	1987	1988	1989
Sales ($ mil)	(1.8%)	17,936	17,409	18,313	11,574	11,798	12,926	13,580	14,409	14,508	15,281
Net income ($ mil)	14.5%	559	695	735	794	908	974	1,176	1,484	1,716	1,892
Income as % of sales	—	3.1%	4.0%	4.0%	6.9%	7.7%	7.5%	8.7%	10.3%	11.8%	12.4%
Earnings per share ($)	13.9%	0.39	0.48	0.51	0.55	0.62	0.66	0.79	1.00	1.14	1.24
Stock price – high ($)	—	1.84	1.84	2.72	2.75	4.25	4.63	7.00	11.56	8.81	15.25
Stock price – low ($)	—	1.25	1.50	1.63	2.00	2.50	3.56	4.19	6.69	6.75	8.00
Stock price – close ($)	28.7%	1.38	1.63	2.47	2.63	4.13	4.50	6.81	8.25	8.06	13.31
P/E – high	—	5	4	5	5	7	7	9	12	8	12
P/E – low	—	3	3	3	4	4	5	5	7	6	6
Dividends per share ($)	18.5%	0.14	0.13	0.12	0.13	0.14	0.19	0.24	0.33	0.41	0.66
Book value per share ($)	6.3%	2.87	2.92	3.03	3.15	3.37	3.59	4.15	4.97	4.28	4.97

1989 Year End:
Debt ratio: 33.9%
Return on equity: 26.8%
Cash (mil): $1,388
Current ratio: 1.26
Long-term debt (mil): $3,884
Number of shares (mil): 1,522
Dividends:
1989 average yield: 5.0%
1989 payout: 53.2%
Market value (mil): $20,260

Stock Price History high/low 1980-89

16 14 12 10 8 6 4 2 0

ASE symbol: BTI (ADR)
Incorporated: England, 1928
Fiscal year ends: December 31

WHO

Chairman: Patrick Sheehy, age 59, £601,813 pay
VC and Senior Finance Director: Brian P. Garraway, age 58
Auditors: Coopers & Lybrand Deloitte
Employees: 311,917

WHERE

HQ: Windsor House, 50 Victoria St., London SW1H 0NL, England
Phone: 011-44-71-222-7979
FAX: 011-44-71-222-0122
US Address (Brown & Williamson Tobacco Corp.): Brown & Williamson Tower, Suite 1500, Louisville, KY 40202
US Phone: 502-568-7000
US FAX: 502-568-7120 (Human Resources)

B.A.T and its subsidiaries conduct operations in over 80 countries.

	1989 Sales		1989 Operating Income	
	$ mil	% of total	$ mil	% of total
Europe	10,278	47	497	25
North America	6,984	32	1,106	56
Other countries	4,513	21	381	19
Adjustments	(6,494)	—	8	—
Total	**15,281**	**100**	**1,992**	**100**

WHAT

	1989 Sales		1989 Operating Income	
	$ mil	% of total	$ mil	% of total
Tobacco	11,471	37	1,342	41
Retailing	6,329	20	289	9
Paper	2,832	9	308	9
Other trading activities	1,143	4	45	1
Adjustments	(6,494)	—	8	—
Commercial activities	**15,281**	**70**	**1,992**	**60**
Financial Services	9,282	30	1,303	40
Total	**24,563**	**100**	**3,295**	**100**

Cigarettes (US Markets)
Barclay
Belair
Capri
Kool
Raleigh
Richland
Viceroy

Cigarettes (Non-US Markets)
Benson & Hedges
Kent
Lucky Strike
Pall Mall

Major Subsidiaries
Allied Dunbar (UK, insurance)
BAT Cigarettenfabriken (West Germany, tobacco)
British-American Tobacco (UK)
Brown & Williamson Tobacco Corp. (US)
Eagle Star (UK, insurance)
Farmers Group, Inc. (US, insurance)
Imasco (Canada; financial services, retailing, and tobacco; 40%)
Souza Cruz (Brazil, tobacco, 75%)
WD&HO Wills (Australia, tobacco, 67%)

RANKINGS

36th in *Fortune* Global 500 Industrial Cos.
4th in *Forbes* 100 Foreign Investments in the US
66th in *Business Week* Global 1000

COMPETITION

American Brands
Hanson
Loews
Philip Morris
RJR Nabisco
Insurance companies

BAXTER INTERNATIONAL INC.

OVERVIEW

Ranked 3rd in the medical products industry by *Business Week* (behind Johnson & Johnson and Abbott Laboratories), Baxter International develops, manufactures, and distributes products, systems, and services for the health care industry. The company manufactures products in 23 countries, operates more than 150 distribution centers in 26 countries, and sells in approximately 100 countries. These products are used by hospitals, laboratories, blood and dialysis centers, nursing homes, and doctors' offices, and in patients' homes. The company is the largest supplier of dialysis products in the world.

Baxter has a program that offers services and savings to hospitals, aimed at reducing costs and improving quality of patient care. In January 1990 Baxter signed purchase agreements with Hospital Corporation of America, HealthTrust, HCA Management, and Mercy National Purchasing. Baxter expects sales from these agreements to reach nearly $3 billion over the next 6 years. In 1989 sales under this program, called the Corporate Program, rose 13.5% over 1988.

The company has also begun a restructuring effort, hoping to save approximately $275 million in pretax dollars by 1993. This will include a reduction of its work force by 6,400, sale of some businesses, and closure of 21 plants.

NYSE symbol: BAX
Incorporated: Delaware, 1931
Fiscal year ends: December 31

WHO

Chairman and CEO: Vernon R. Loucks, Jr., age 55, $1,460,515 pay
President: Wilbur H. Gantz, age 52, $933,294 pay
EVP: C. A. (Lance) Piccolo, age 49, $563,612 pay
EVP: Robert J. Simmons, age 47
EVP: James R. Tobin, age 45, $533,715 pay
SVP and CFO: Robert J. Lambrix, age 50, $493,671 pay
Auditors: Price Waterhouse
Employees: 64,300

WHEN

Dr. Ralph Falk, an Idaho surgeon, his brother Harry, and Dr. Donald Baxter, a California physician, formed The Don Baxter Intravenous Products Corporation (1931) to distribute intravenous (IV) solutions manufactured by Dr. Baxter in Los Angeles. In 1933 the company opened its first manufacturing plant in Glenview, Illinois. Dr. Falk bought Dr. Baxter's interest in the company in 1935, and began in-house R&D efforts that led to the introduction of the first sterilized vacuum-type blood collection device (1939), which could store blood for 21 days instead of a few hours. Demand for medical supplies and growing acceptance of IV products during WWII spurred growth to more than $1.5 million in sales by 1945.

In 1949 the company started Travenol Laboratories to make and sell drugs. The company went public in 1951 and began an acquisition program in 1952. Failing health caused both Falks in 1953 to turn over control of the company to William Graham, manager since 1945. Graham continued the acquisition program that absorbed 5 US companies, including Hyland Laboratories (1952), Wallerstein Company (1957), Fenwal Laboratories and Flint, Eaton (1959), and Dayton Flexible Products (1967). Sales of $242 million put Baxter into the *Fortune* 500 in 1971.

Baxter moved to new headquarters in Deerfield, Illinois (1975). The company achieved $1 billion in sales in 1978, the same year it introduced the first portable dialysis machine. In 1985 Baxter acquired American Hospital Supply, a company founded by Foster McGaw in 1922 that had been a Baxter distributor from 1932 until 1962. American had 65% more sales than Baxter but had been more a distributor of lower-margin products than Baxter, which manufactured most of its own products. The merger made Baxter the world's largest hospital supply company.

Offering more than 120,000 products and an electronic order-entry system (ASAP) that connects customers with over 1,500 vendors, Baxter captured nearly 25% of the US hospital supply market in 1988. That same year the company changed its name from Baxter Travenol to Baxter International.

In recent years Baxter has begun to form alliances with such other large companies as Waste Management and Kraft to provide computerized services to hospitals relating to medical waste disposal and food services.

WHERE

HQ: One Baxter Pkwy., Deerfield, IL 60015
Phone: 708-948-2000
FAX: 312-948-3948

Baxter has manufacturing facilities in 23 countries and sells products in about 100 countries. The company also maintains 17 R&D centers in 5 countries and 310 service and distribution centers worldwide.

	1989 Sales		1989 Operating Income	
	$ mil	% of total	$ mil	% of total
US	5,776	78	553	60
Europe	835	11	185	20
Other countries	788	11	190	20
Adjustments	—	—	(162)	—
Total	**7,399**	**100**	**766**	**100**

WHAT

	1989 Sales		1989 Operating Income	
	$ mil	% of total	$ mil	% of total
Hospital products & services	3,824	52	377	40
Medical systems & specialties	1,667	22	220	24
Alternate site prods. & services	1,463	20	276	30
Industrial products	445	6	56	6
Adjustments	—	—	(163)	—
Total	**7,399**	**100**	**766**	**100**

Products
- Artificial heart valves
- Blood handling equipment
- Cardiac monitoring and bypass systems
- Diagnostic systems
- Gowns, gloves, and drapes
- Intravenous therapy products
- Laboratory apparatus and supplies
- Mail-order prescriptions
- Procedure trays and kits
- Respiratory and anesthesia products
- Surgical instruments and supplies

HOW MUCH

	9 Yr. Growth	1980	1981	1982	1983	1984	1985	1986	1987	1988	1989
Sales ($ mil)	20.6%	1,374	1,504	1,671	1,843	1,800	2,355	5,543	6,223	6,861	7,399
Net income ($ mil)	14.8%	128	151	187	218	29	137	181	323	388	446
Income as % of sales	—	9.3%	10.0%	11.2%	11.8%	1.6%	5.8%	3.3%	5.2%	5.7%	6.0%
Earnings per share ($)	6.4%	0.85	0.99	1.22	1.45	0.20	0.83	0.64	1.09	1.30	1.49
Stock price – high ($)	—	14.16	16.88	25.50	31.31	24.88	16.88	21.25	29.25	26.13	25.88
Stock price – low ($)	—	8.94	12.00	15.19	20.00	11.75	12.38	15.13	15.50	16.25	17.50
Stock price – close ($)	7.3%	13.22	16.75	24.19	23.25	13.13	15.75	19.25	22.75	17.63	25.00
P/E – high	—	17	17	21	22	124	20	33	27	20	17
P/E – low	—	11	12	12	14	59	15	24	14	13	12
Dividends per share ($)	14.9%	0.16	0.19	0.23	0.28	0.33	0.37	0.40	0.44	0.50	0.56
Book value per share ($)	9.2%	6.11	6.94	7.52	8.17	7.83	9.86	11.51	11.79	12.61	13.49

1989 Year End:
Debt ratio: 32.6%
Return on equity: 11.4%
Cash (mil): $67
Current ratio: 1.84
Long-term debt (mil): $2,052
Number of shares (mil): 249
Dividends:
1989 average yield: 2.2%
1989 payout: 37.6%
Market value (mil): $6,237

Stock Price History high/low 1980-89

RANKINGS

63rd in *Fortune* 500 Industrial Cos.
176th in *Fortune* Global 500 Industrial Cos.
112th in *Forbes* Sales 500
94th in *Business Week* 1000
307th in *Business Week* Global 1000

COMPETITION

Abbott Labs
American Home Products
C. R. Bard
Becton, Dickinson
Eli Lilly
Johnson & Johnson
Pfizer

BAYER AG

OVERVIEW

Bayer is one of the world's largest chemical producers, perennially vying for the top spot with fellow West German firms BASF and Hoechst. A diversified, research-driven chemical concern, Bayer manufactures basic chemicals, plastics, polyurethanes, pesticides, herbicides, coatings, drugs, photographic and imaging equipment, and consumer health care products. Better-known US brands include Alka-Seltzer, One-A-Day vitamins, and S.O.S. In WWI the company lost US rights to Bayer aspirin, now made and marketed in the US by Kodak's Sterling Drug unit.

Eighty percent of Bayer's sales are outside of Germany. The company has steadily added to its North American operations, which today include Mobay, Miles, and Agfa (the product of a merger of Agfa-Gevaert, Compugraphic, and Matrix Corporation). With the 1990 acquisition of the rubber division of Nova Corporation of Alberta, Bayer gained a foothold in the North American synthetic rubber market.

WHEN

Founded in Wuppertal-Barmen by Friedrich Bayer in 1863, Bayer was among the pioneers of the modern German chemical industry. The company's prolific research labs fueled Bayer's growth beyond its original synthetic dye business, leading to the introduction of such breakthrough compounds as Antinonin (first synthetic pesticide, 1892), aspirin (1899), and synthetic rubber (1915).

Bayer's German heritage figured prominently in its history. During WWI under Carl Duisberg, Bayer is said to have been the source of the first poison gas used by Germany. The US seized Bayer's American operations and trademark rights in 1917, selling them to Sterling Drug (US) in 1918.

Duisberg's desire to eliminate competition led to the merger of Bayer, BASF, Hoechst, and other German chemical concerns into the I.G. Farben Trust in 1925. Photography businesses of Bayer and the other I.G. Farben firms were combined, named Agfa, and folded into the trust. Between the wars Bayer's labs developed a treatment for African sleeping sickness (Germanin, 1921) and the first sulfa drug (Prontosil, 1935), while pioneering in the development of polyurethanes.

The outbreak of WWII found I.G. Farben solidly and profitably in the Nazi camp. The company took over chemical plants of Nazi-occupied countries and established factories near Auschwitz to take advantage of slave labor. I.G. Farben produced the deadly gas used in concentration camps. Twelve I.G. Farben executives were sentenced for war crimes at Nuremberg in 1948. At the end of the war, Bayer lost its 50% interest in Winthrop Laboratories (US) and Bayer of Canada, again to Sterling Drug. The Potsdam Agreement (1945) called for the breakup of I.G. Farben, and in 1951 Bayer emerged as an independent company consisting of many of its original operations, as well as Agfa.

After quickly rebuilding in Germany, Bayer entered into a US joint venture with Monsanto (Mobay, 1954) and later bought Monsanto's share (1967). Rapid postwar economic expansion in Germany and an expanding US economy bolstered Bayer's businesses. In the 1960s Bayer's labs continued to broaden the company's offerings in dyes, plastics, and polyurethanes, and the company built production facilities internationally. Agfa merged with Gevaert (photography, Belgium) in 1964. Bayer retained 60% ownership in Agfa-Gevaert.

Bayer acquired Cutter Labs (drugs, US, 1974), Metzeler (rubber, Germany, 1974), Miles Labs (Alka-Seltzer, Flintstones, One-A-Day vitamins, US, 1978), the rest of Agfa-Gevaert (1981), and Compugraphic and Matrix (electronic imaging, US, 1989). Bayer has continued its enviable record of product innovation in chemicals, pharmaceuticals, and imaging.

HOW MUCH

$=DM 1.69 (Dec. 31, 1989)	9 Yr. Growth	1980	1981	1982	1983	1984	1985	1986	1987	1988	1989
Sales (DM mil)	4.6%	28,825	33,742	34,834	37,336	43,032	45,926	38,284	37,143	40,468	43,299
Net income (DM mil)	13.9%	647	506	143	756	1,339	1,259	1,322	1,498	1,855	2,083
Income as % of sales	—	2.2%	1.5%	0.4%	2.0%	3.1%	2.7%	3.5%	4.0%	4.6%	4.8%
Earnings per share* (DM)	9.2%	15	20	3	15	26	27	24	24	29	33
Stock price – high (DM)	—	129	140	207	176	193	276	350	377	311	322
Stock price – low (DM)	—	106	108	104	112	152	185	263	247	237	275
Stock price – close (DM)	12.7%	108	115	114	176	193	276	317	264	307	316
P/E – high	—	9	7	69	12	7	10	15	16	11	10
P/E – low	—	7	5	35	7	6	7	11	10	8	8
Dividends per share** (DM)	6.2%	7.0	7.0	7.0	4.0	7.0	9.0	10.0	10.0	11.0	12.0
Book value per share (DM)	5.3%	153	144	139	143	161	191	214	219	233	244

1989 Year End:
Debt ratio: 11.0%
Return on equity: 13.8%
Cash (mil): DM4,006
Long-term debt (bil): DM1.8
Number of shares (mil): 63.9
Dividends:
1989 average yield: 3.8%
1989 payout: 36.4%
Market value (mil): $11,948
Sales (mil): $25,621

*not fully diluted **not including rights offerings

Principal foreign exchange: Frankfurt
Incorporated: Germany, 1952
Fiscal year ends: December 31

WHO

Chairman: Hermann J. Strenger, age 61
VC: Hermann Wunderlich
Chairman of the Committee of the Board for Finance: Helmut Loehr
Auditors: Treuhand-Vereinigung Aktiengesellschaft
Employees: 170,200

WHERE

HQ: 5090 Leverkusen, Bayerwerk, Germany
Phone: 011-49-2174-301
US HQ (Bayer USA Inc.): One Mellon Center, 500 Grant St., Pittsburgh, PA 15219
US Phone: 412-394-5500
US FAX: 412-394-5578 (Corporate Communications)

Bayer conducts operations in about 70 countries.

	1989 Sales		1989 Operating Income	
	DM mil	% of total	DM mil	% of total
Europe	25,477	59	3,040	71
North America	8,766	20	699	16
Asia	4,565	11	376	9
Latin America	2,567	6	118	3
Africa	1,924	4	57	1
Total	**43,299**	**100**	**4,290**	**100**

WHAT

	1989 Sales		1989 Operating Income	
	DM mil	% of total	DM mil	% of total
Industrial products	9,220	21	1,073	25
Health care	7,967	19	1,267	30
Imaging products	7,490	17	573	13
Polymers	7,109	16	249	6
Organic products	6,053	14	772	18
Agrochemicals	5,460	13	356	8
Total	**43,299**	**100**	**4,290**	**100**

US Consumer Brands
Alka-Seltzer (antacid)
Bactine (antiseptic)
Cutter (insect repellent)
Flintstones (vitamins)
One-A-Day (vitamins)
S.O.S. (soap pads)
Tuffy (scouring pads)

Other Products
Agricultural chemicals
Dyes
Flavors and food additives
Medical imaging equipment
Photographic films (Agfa)
Plastics
Polyurethanes
Rubber
Synthetic fibers
Typesetting and graphics equipment (Agfa, Compugraphic)
Veterinary products (Cutter, Diamond Scientific, Haver)

RANKINGS

38th in *Fortune* Global 500 Industrial Cos.
17th in *Forbes* 100 Foreign Investments in the US
132nd in *Business Week* Global 1000

COMPETITION

American Home Products
BASF
Becton, Dickinson
Bristol-Myers Squibb
Clorox
Dow Chemical
Du Pont
Eastman Kodak
General Electric
Hoechst
S.C. Johnson
3M
Polaroid
Rhône-Poulenc
Siemens
SmithKline Beecham
Other chemical and household goods companies

BCE INC.

OVERVIEW

BCE is the largest independent public company in Canada measured by revenues, 28% of which derive from US operations. Since its restructuring in 1983, the company has doubled its revenues.

The core of BCE's business is telecommunications. Its Bell Canada operation is the country's largest telephone company, serving nearly 7 million customers. Together with other BCE subsidiaries, Bell Canada provides local telephone service to 70% of Canada's population. BCE companies offer mobile telephone service, design and develop advanced telecommunications equipment, and perform consulting in a number of foreign countries. In 1989 the company acquired a minority interest in Videotron, which operates cable TV systems in the UK.

Northern Telecom, BCE's equipment manufacturing arm, is North America's 2nd largest telecommunications manufacturer behind AT&T. It plans to introduce new fiber optics telephone systems in the near future.

In 1989 BCE acquired Montreal Trustco Inc., one of Canada's oldest and most prestigious financial institutions, and now considers financial services one of its "core" businesses, along with telecommunications. However, it has withdrawn from its unsuccessful commercial real estate venture and in September 1990 announced its intention to sell its 49% stake in its TransCanada gas pipeline company in order to concentrate on expansion into overseas telecommunications markets.

NYSE symbol: BCE
Incorporated: Canada, 1983
Fiscal year ends: December 31

WHO

Chairman, President, and CEO: Joseph Victor Raymond Cyr, age 56, C$1,209,900 pay
EVP Finance: J. Stuart Spalding, age 55, C$508,400 pay
Auditors: Deloitte & Touche
Employees: 120,000

WHERE

HQ: 2000 McGill College Ave., Suite 2100, Montreal, Quebec H3A 3H7, Canada
Phone: 514-499-7000
FAX: 514-499-7098

BCE provides local phone service to most of Canada and sells in over 70 countries.

	1989 Sales		1989 Operating Income	
	$ mil	% of total	$ mil	% of total
Canada	10,078	70	2,575	73
US	3,983	28	937	27
Other countries	345	2	—	—
Adjustments	—	—	(520)	—
Total	**14,406**	**100**	**2,992**	**100**

WHEN

Bell Telephone Company of Canada was created by a Canadian Parliament act in 1880 to consolidate the operations of several smaller companies. Bell companies operating in the US originally owned part of the company, but AT&T, successor to the Bell companies, severed all ties in 1975. Bell Canada performed its role as a regional provider of telephone service for many years, but a series of mergers with smaller telephone exchanges beginning in 1954 gradually increased its presence in the national market.

Bell acquired a 90% interest in Northern Electric (small equipment, 1957) from the Western Electric subsidiary of AT&T, completing the buyout in 1964. As Canada's telecommunications needs grew and the technology became more complex, Bell branched out into related areas, including investment in a satellite joint venture (Telesat, 1970) and the formation of Bell Northern Research (1971) to direct the company's R&D. Tele-Direct, established in 1971, consolidated the company's directory publishing operations. Bell reduced its ownership in Northern Electric to 69% (1975) and changed the manufacturer's name to Northern Telecom (1976). Also in 1976 Bell formed BCI to provide international telecommunications consulting.

The Canadian government's commitment to affordable telephone service for all meant that Bell Canada's profitable telecommunications equipment operations subsidized the cost of local service. In response to proposed legislation to reduce local rates by further limiting Bell's allowable profit, the company in 1983 moved all of its assets into Bell Canada Enterprises (renamed BCE Inc., 1988), which acts as a holding company, separating the unregulated businesses from the local regulated carriers.

Freed from governmental restraint, BCE went on a diversification drive while continuing to build the communications side of its business. The company bought 42% of TransCanada PipeLines (natural gas, 1983) and branched into real estate with the purchase of a Toronto office building (1984) and 63% of Vancouver's Doan Development (1985; renamed BCE Development), all of which were discontinued or sold in 1990.

WHAT

	1989 Sales		1989 Operating Income	
	$ mil	% of total	$ mil	% of total
Telecommunications services	6,918	48	1,751	74
Telecommunications equip.	6,184	43	536	23
Financial services	851	6	50	2
Other operations	453	3	23	1
Adjustments	—	—	632	—
Total	**14,406**	**100**	**2,992**	**100**

Affiliates & Subsidiaries
BCE Information Services Inc. (directories)
BCE Mobile Communications Inc. (73%)
Bell Canada International Inc. (global telecommunications consulting)
Bell Canada and other local carriers
The Island Telephone Co. Ltd. (33.7%)
Maritime Telegraph and Telephone Co. (34%)
The New Brunswick Telephone Co. Ltd. (31.2%)
Newfoundland Telephone Co. Ltd. (56%)
Northern Telephone Ltd. (99.9%)
Northwestel Inc.
Télébec Ltée
Bell-Northern Research Ltd. (systems design and development)
Memotec Data, Inc. (30.8%; Teleglobe Canada) (overseas telecommunications and computers)
Montreal Trustco, Inc. (commercial and individual banking)
Northern Telecom (53.1%; telecommunications equipment)
Quebecor Inc. (21.2%; publishing)
STC (14.4%; communications)
Tele-Direct (Publications) Inc. (directories)
Telesat (24.6%; satellite services)
Videotron Corporation Ltd. (23.3%; cable TV in the UK)

HOW MUCH

	9 Yr. Growth	1980	1981	1982	1983	1984	1985	1986	1987	1988	1989
Sales ($ mil)	12.3%	5,053	6,230	6,838	7,135	8,008	9,479	10,116	11,267	12,788	14,406
Net income ($ mil)	14.6%	304	464	506	599	712	751	743	836	744	1,037
Income as % of sales	—	6.0%	7.5%	7.4%	8.4%	8.9%	7.9%	7.3%	7.4%	5.8%	7.2%
Earnings per share ($)	8.2%	1.66	2.44	2.46	2.71	2.97	2.95	2.74	2.96	2.59	3.38
Stock price – high ($)	—	18.38	17.13	19.75	27.13	27.13	33.00	30.00	33.38	32.63	39.38
Stock price – low ($)	—	14.50	14.13	13.25	18.13	22.38	26.00	24.88	23.50	28.13	30.50
Stock price – close ($)	9.9%	16.75	16.38	19.75	27.00	26.88	30.13	27.00	28.50	31.25	39.25
P/E – high	—	11	7	8	10	9	11	11	11	13	12
P/E – low	—	9	6	5	7	8	9	9	8	11	9
Dividends per share ($)	4.3%	1.44	1.54	1.61	1.71	1.70	1.66	1.70	1.82	2.00	2.10
Book value per share ($)	5.2%	17.33	18.33	18.43	19.84	20.48	21.24	22.90	25.34	27.09	27.30

1989 Year End:
Debt ratio: 53.4%
Return on equity: 12.4%
Cash (mil): $930
Current ratio: —
Long-term debt (mil): $10,313
Number of shares (mil): 302
Dividends:
1989 average yield: 5.3%
1989 payout: 62.1%
Market value (mil): $11,856

Stock Price History high/low 1980-89

All financial data is in US $ unless otherwise indicated.

RANKINGS

20th in *Forbes* 100 Foreign Investments in the US
152nd in *Business Week* Global 1000

COMPETITION

AT&T
Fujitsu
GTE
NEC
Siemens

BEATRICE COMPANIES, INC.

OVERVIEW

Privately owned Beatrice agreed to be acquired by ConAgra, Inc., in June 1990. A giant in the processed food industry, Beatrice produces and sells a wide range of food products for the consumer and wholesale markets. The company operates primarily through 3 subsidiaries: Beatrice/Hunt-Wesson, Swift-Eckrich, and Beatrice Cheese.

Beatrice/Hunt-Wesson commands a product line with such widely recognized brand names as Hunt's (tomato products), Manwich (sloppy joe sauce), Orville Redenbacher's (popcorn), Rosarita (refried beans), and La Choy (oriental foods), each of which holds the #1 position in its market.

Swift-Eckrich is a producer of refrigerated and frozen meat products. Its #1 product line includes Butterball (turkey brand), Swift Premium Brown 'N Serve (precooked breakfast sausage), Sizzlean (breakfast strip), and Eckrich (smoked sausage).

Beatrice Cheese is one of the largest US cheese producers. It sells its products under the brand names County Line, Treasure Cave (the #1 bleu cheese in the US), Pauly (food-service dairy products), and Reddi-Wip (the #1 aerosol dessert topping).

Since its LBO in 1986, Beatrice has sold off $7.7 billion in assets, shrinking to almost 1/3 its previous size.

Private company
Incorporated: Delaware, 1985
Fiscal year ends: Last day of February

WHO

President and CEO: Frederick B. Rentschler, age 50, $1,093,800 pay
SVP and CFO: William P. Carmichael, age 46, $424,373 pay
SVP and General Counsel: Karl M. Becker, age 46, $442,476 pay
SVP Human Resources and Corporate Relations: William L. Chambers, age 52, $424,326 pay
Auditors: Deloitte & Touche
Employees: 15,900

WHEN

In 1894 George Haskell and William Bosworth formed a partnership in Beatrice, Nebraska, to buy butter, poultry, eggs, and produce from local farmers. That same year they started churning butter themselves and delivered it in special packages to hotels, restaurants, and grocery stores. For efficiency, the men established skimming stations where the farmers could bring their milk. Their company, Beatrice Creamery, eventually distributed hand-controlled cream separators directly to the farmers for expediency. The partners consolidated the business in Lincoln and by 1898 had established 11 branches.

Around the turn of the century, Haskell traveled east to study dairy operations. When he returned, he built a modern creamery in Denver and in 1901 introduced the Meadow Gold brand. The company branched into ice cream in 1907 and in 1913 moved its headquarters to Chicago, acquiring several dairy operations in the next few decades.

The company took its first step outside the dairy business in 1943 with the purchase of La Choy (oriental food). William Karnes became CEO in 1952 and made Beatrice the most acquisitive firm at the time with such purchases as Thos. Richardson (candy, 1957), Bond Pickle (1957), Rosarita Mexican Foods (1961), and Fisher Nut (1962).

During the 1960s Beatrice launched a major international push and branched into chemicals, metals, and consumer products. The company's prolific acquisitions continued in the 1970s and included Peter Eckrich & Sons (meats, 1972), Samsonite (luggage, 1973), Martha White Foods (bakery products, 1975), Harman International (stereo equipment, 1977), Culligan (water softeners, 1978), and Tropicana (fruit juice, 1978).

During the early 1980s the company bought a number of Coca-Cola bottling operations. In 1984 Beatrice bought Chicago-based Esmark, a holding company that started as Swift Brothers (meat) in 1885. Swift Brothers (the inspiration for Upton Sinclair's novel *The Jungle*) grew from a meat industry behemoth to a holding company manufacturing everything from hi-fi products to women's swimwear. The acquisition brought Beatrice such major consumer product names as Butterball (turkeys), Danskin (swim- and dancewear), Peter Pan (peanut butter), and Playtex (the nation's largest producer of women's undergarments).

In 1986 a group of investors (including Esmark's ex-CEO Don Kelly) directed by Kohlberg Kravis Roberts (KKR) bought Beatrice for $6.2 billion and took it private in the largest LBO to date. Kelly became CEO of Beatrice and by mid-1987 had sold many of its business segments, covering the massive residual debt and giving back to KKR's limited partners the money they had invested. During the late 1980s Beatrice sold its Coca-Cola bottling operations (to Coca-Cola, $1 billion, 1986), Playtex (to a group of investors, $1.25 billion, 1986), Beatrice International Foods (to TLC Beatrice International Holdings, $985 million, 1987), and Tropicana (to Seagram, $1.2 billion, 1988).

In 1990 ConAgra agreed to acquire Beatrice from KKR for $1.34 billion, netting KKR about a 50% annualized return on its investment.

WHERE

HQ: Two N. LaSalle St., Chicago, IL 60602
Phone: 312-558-4000
FAX: 312-558-5472 (Public Relations)

The company owns 142 facilities (plants, warehouses, and distribution centers), most of which are located in the US.

WHAT

Brand Names

Butterball (turkey products)
County Line (cheese)
Eckrich (sausage and cold cuts)
Gebhardt (chili)
Hunt's (tomato products)
J. Hungerford Smith (dessert topping)
Jubilee (dessert topping)
La Choy (oriental foods)
Manwich (sloppy joe sauce)
Margharita (deli products)
Orville Redenbacher's (popcorn)
Pauly (food-service products)
Peter Pan (peanut butter)
Plume de Veau (veal)
Reddi-Wip (dessert topping)
Rosarita (refried beans)
Sizzlean (breakfast strip)
Slice 'N Serve (turkey)
Snack Pack (pudding)
Swift Premium (breakfast meat)
Swiss Miss (cocoa)
Treasure Cave (cheese)
Wesson (oils)

RANKINGS

25th in *Forbes* 400 US Private Cos.

COMPETITION

Anheuser-Busch
Borden
Chiquita Brands
ConAgra
CPC International
General Mills
Grand Metropolitan
Hershey
Nestlé
Philip Morris
Quaker Oats
Sara Lee
Tyson Foods
Whitman

HOW MUCH

	9 Yr. Growth	1980	1981	1982	1983	1984	1985	1986	1987	1988	1989
Sales ($ mil)	(7.7%)	8,773	9,024	9,188	9,327	12,595	11,396	8,926	4,012	4,066	4,262
Net income ($ mil)	(30.2%)	304	313	43	433	479	225	(79)	(105)	5	12
Income as % of sales	—	3.5%	3.5%	0.5%	4.6%	3.8%	2.0%	(0.9%)	(2.6%)	0.1%	0.3%

1989 Year End:
Debt ratio: 53.1%
Return on equity: 2.4%
Cash (mil): $107
Current ratio: 1.29
Long-term debt (mil): $987

Net Income 1980-89

BECHTEL GROUP, INC.

OVERVIEW

Privately owned, family-controlled Bechtel is one of the world's largest companies devoted solely to construction and engineering. Bechtel has worked on over 15,000 projects in over 135 countries on all 7 continents. Company projects include electric-power generation (nuclear, fossil, solar, hydro), environmental cleanups, oil and gas pipelines, chemical plants, transportation systems, mining, telecommunications, buildings, and infrastructure. The company has constructed over 1/2 of the US's nuclear power plants.

Bechtel is the US leader in design, design-construct, construction management, and hazardous waste treatment, and 2nd (after Fluor Daniels) in contract revenues and new work brought in. Bechtel also manages projects for others. The 20-year raising of industrial city Jubail, Saudi Arabia ($40 billion cost), is the world's biggest engineering project.

Bechtel's public reputation is that of a secret empire possessing access to the highest levels of government. George Schultz (secretary of the treasury under Nixon and state under Reagan) and Caspar Weinberger (secretary of defense under Reagan) were high-level Bechtel employees before their public service. Schultz returned to Bechtel's board of directors in 1989.

Following a recent downturn, Bechtel boasts the most first-time clients and the broadest mix of projects in its 92-year history.

Private company
Founded: 1898
Fiscal year ends: December 31

WHO

President and CEO: Riley P. Bechtel
Chairman Emeritus: Stephen D. Bechtel, Jr., age 66
EVP: Cordell W. Hull, age 58
EVP: John Neerhout, Jr., age 59
Auditors: Coopers & Lybrand
Employees: 27,800

WHERE

HQ: Fifty Beale St., San Francisco, CA 94105
Phone: 415-768-1234
FAX: 415-768-9038

Bechtel currently has projects in 77 countries with 9 major US offices and 13 major international field offices in Europe, the Middle East, Canada, South America, and Southeast Asia.

	1989 Sales	
	$ mil	% of total
US	3,424	67
Foreign	1,687	33
Total	**5,111**	**100**

WHEN

In 1898 26-year-old Warren A. Bechtel left his Kansas farm to grade railroads in the Oklahoma Indian territories, where he soon founded his namesake. After Bechtel settled in Oakland, California, his engineering and management skills led to large projects such as the Northern California Highway and Bowman Dam. By the time of its incorporation in 1925, Bechtel was the West's largest construction company.

Stephen Bechtel (president after his father's death in 1933) weathered the Great Depression with massive work projects such as the Hoover Dam (where Bechtel supervised 8 companies, including industrialist Henry Kaiser's) and the Oakland Bay Bridge. The rise of WWII meant full recovery, the many contracts including the construction of 570 ships in Bechtel-built yards in California.

In the postwar years Bechtel grew along with America's global presence, building pipelines (TransArabian, 1947; Canada's TransMountain, 1954; Australia's first, 1964) and numerous power projects, including one that doubled South Korea's energy output (1948). By the time Stephen Bechtel, Jr., became CEO in 1960 (when his father moved to chairman), the company was operating on 6 continents.

Bechtel built many nuclear power plants in the next 2 decades, including the world's first large one to be privately financed (Dresden, Illinois, opened 1960) and Canada's first (1962). Large transportation projects included San Francisco's Bay Area Rapid Transit system (BART, 1961-1974) and Washington, DC's subway system (early 1970s). Bechtel's Jubail project, begun in 1976, will raise from the desert a city of 275,000 (projected completion date 1996). Work on Canada's James Bay hydroelectric project was begun in 1972 (completed mid-1980s, supplying energy to 8 million people).

With the attractions of nuclear power fading in the wake of Three Mile Island (which Bechtel won the right to clean up, 1979-ongoing), Bechtel concentrated on less controversial markets like mining in New Guinea (gold and copper, 1981-1984) and China (coal, 1984).

Bechtel reeled under the general recession and rising third world debt of the early 1980s; revenues plummeted from 1983's record $14.1 billion to $8.6 billion a year later. The company cut its work force by 22,000 (almost 1/2 the total) and stemmed the losses by taking on small projects like plant modernizations.

Under 4th generation Riley Bechtel (CEO in 1990), the resurgent Bechtel (with 1989 new work awarded up 21% over last year) has won numerous contracts, including a $16 billion deal with Hong Kong for a new airport and transit system (by 1997), project management of the channel tunnel between Britain and France (1993), and a giant technology center outside of Moscow.

WHAT

Engineering, Construction & Management
Civil projects
- Airports
- Buildings and infrastructure
- Public transit systems, highways, tunnels, bridges, and ports
- Waste-to-energy conversion plants

Food-processing plants
Microelectronics plants
Mining and metals plants
Missile launch complexes
Petroleum and chemical plants
Pipelines
Power plants
- Fossil-fired plants
- Hydroelectric plants
- Nuclear plants

Pulp and paper mills
Weapons storage and security systems

Environmental
Environmental assessment
Hazardous waste cleanups (EPA Superfund sites, pesticide plants)
Regulatory compliance
Wastewater treatment

Operations
Nuclear and fossil fuel plants
Strategic petroleum reserves
Utilities

Major Projects
27 airport terminals (King Fahd and King Khaled International, Saudi Arabia)
300 fossil-fired power plants (Shoubrah El-Kheima plant, Egypt)
150 industrial manufacturing projects
62 marine terminals
31 modern rapid transit systems
80 nuclear generating units (Palo Verde Nuclear Generating Station, Arizona)
7 major telecommunications projects

Major Projects Under Way
Barcelona's 1992 Olympics
Boston Central Artery project
Costa del Sol theme park (Spain)
Eurotunnel (England/France)
Haneda International Airport (Tokyo)
San Francisco's Museum of Modern Art

HOW MUCH

	9 Yr. Growth	1980	1981	1982	1983	1984	1985	1986	1987	1988	1989
Sales ($ mil)	(4.3%)	7,600	11,400	13,600	14,100	8,600	6,891	6,679	4,501	4,472	5,111
Value of new projects ($ mil)	(7.9%)	11,300	10,600	5,700	13,000	5,000	4,982	3,675	3,537	4,486	5,427
Number of clients	—	—	550	—	—	—	750	—	800	900	950
Number of active projects	—	—	950	—	—	—	1,300	—	1,350	1,450	1,600

Sales ($ mil) 1980-89

16,000
14,000
12,000
10,000
8,000
6,000
4,000
2,000
0

RANKINGS

18th in *Forbes* 400 US Private Cos.

COMPETITION

Asea Brown Boveri
Ashland
Consolidated Rail
Duke Power
Halliburton
McDermott
Peter Kiewit Sons'
Raytheon
Union Pacific
Waste Management
Westinghouse

BECTON, DICKINSON AND COMPANY

OVERVIEW

Becton, Dickinson manufactures and sells a broad line of health care products worldwide to hospitals, doctors, laboratories, pharmaceutical companies, medical schools, and the general public. The company operates 2 business sectors: Medical (59% of 1989 revenues) and Diagnostic (41%). Leading the world in single-use medical devices, the company manufactures hypodermic needles and syringes, gloves, IV catheters, and insulin syringes. Becton, Dickinson produces more syringes than any other company in the world and has well over 50% of the US market. The company also produces thermometers, elastic support and suction products, and surgical blades.

The company has successfully met the challenge of a changing health care industry by providing cost-effective products, appealing to newly formed hospital buying groups, selling aggressively overseas, and developing new areas of technology (it is the world leader in microbiology, cellular analysis, and blood collection). In 1989 Becton, Dickinson experienced record sales of $1.8 billion (ranked 4th in the medical supply industry by *Business Week*).

WHEN

Maxwell Becton and Fairleigh Dickinson established a medical supply firm in New York in 1897. In 1907 the company moved into a new factory in East Rutherford, New Jersey, and became one of the first in the US to manufacture hypodermic needles.

During WWI Becton, Dickinson manufactured all-glass syringes and introduced a new product, the all cotton elastic (ACE) bandage. After the war, researchers Andrew Fleischer and Oscar Schwidetzky joined the firm. Fleischer designed an improved stethoscope, while Schwidetzky created specialized hypodermic needles.

During WWII the company received an award for excellence in medical equipment supplied to the armed forces, and Becton and Dickinson helped establish Fairleigh Dickinson Junior College (now Fairleigh Dickinson University). Becton, Dickinson continued to develop new products such as the VACUTAINER blood collection apparatus, the company's first medical laboratory aid.

After the deaths of Dickinson (1948) and Becton (1951), their sons Fairleigh Dickinson, Jr., and Henry Becton took over the company. Disposable hypodermic syringes developed by the company (1961) virtually replaced reusable syringes domestically, with disposables capturing almost the entire US syringe market by 1987. The company offered stock to the public (1963) to raise money for manufacturing, packaging, and distribution facilities for the new syringes. Becton, Dickinson opened a plant in Canada (1963) followed by plants in France, Ireland, and Brazil, and diversified into nonmedical businesses with purchases such as Edmont (industrial gloves, 1966) and Spear (computer systems, 1968).

Wesley J. Howe, successor to Dickinson, expanded the company's foreign sales from 19% of its 1974 volume to 40% by 1989. From 1976 to 1980 the company added new medical products through internal research and purchases such as Johnston Laboratories (automated bacteriology, 1979).

In 1978 the company thwarted a takeover bid by the Sun Company, which had purchased 32.5% of the company's stock. Howe began to sell the company's nonmedical businesses in 1983, ending with the 1989 sale of Edmont. The company acquired Deseret Medical (IV catheters, surgical gloves and masks) for $230 million in 1986.

In 1988 price competition from Japanese syringe maker Terumo (which aims to boost its market share from 5% to 20% in 3 years) threatened to erode the company's share of the US market, but the company has so far maintained its share and opened plants in Japan and Singapore.

HOW MUCH

	9 Yr. Growth	1980	1981	1982	1983	1984	1985	1986	1987	1988	1989
Sales ($ mil)	7.5%	942	1,066	1,114	1,120	1,127	1,144	1,312	1,582	1,709	1,811
Net income ($ mil)	10.4%	65	76	77	36	63	88	112	142	149	158
Income as % of sales	—	6.9%	7.1%	6.9%	3.2%	5.6%	7.7%	8.5%	9.0%	8.7%	8.7%
Earnings per share ($)	11.0%	1.57	1.81	1.82	0.86	1.52	2.10	2.62	3.42	3.69	4.00
Stock price – high ($)	—	26.31	27.25	25.19	26.75	20.63	33.00	61.25	69.00	62.13	62.25
Stock price – low ($)	—	13.13	18.56	18.00	17.00	15.38	19.75	30.94	42.25	46.50	48.38
Stock price – close ($)	10.1%	26.13	23.88	21.25	18.38	19.81	31.00	50.00	51.00	52.00	61.88
P/E – high	—	17	15	14	31	14	16	23	20	17	16
P/E – low	—	8	10	10	20	10	9	12	12	13	12
Dividends per share ($)	9.0%	0.46	0.50	0.55	0.58	0.58	0.60	0.66	0.74	0.86	1.00
Book value per share ($)	9.3%	12.55	14.01	14.21	14.40	15.03	16.82	19.62	21.62	24.33	27.99

1989 Year End:
Debt ratio: 32.5%
Return on equity: 15.3%
Cash (mil): $95
Current ratio: 1.53
Long-term debt (mil): $516
Number of shares (mil): 38
Dividends:
1989 average yield: 1.6%
1989 payout: 25.0%
Market value (mil): $2,371

Stock Price History high/low 1980-89

NYSE symbol: BDX
Incorporated: New Jersey, 1906
Fiscal year ends: September 30

WHO

President and CEO: Raymond V. Gilmartin, age 48, $584,986 pay
Sector President, Medical: Clateo Castellini, age 54, $294,046 pay
Sector President, Diagnostic: Walter M. Miller, age 46, $273,457 pay
VP Finance: Robert A. Reynolds, age 57
Auditors: Ernst & Young
Employees: 18,800

WHERE

HQ: One Becton Dr., Franklin Lakes, NJ 07417
Phone: 201-848-6800
FAX: 201-848-6475

The company has plants in 12 countries. Its principal markets are the US, Canada, Europe, Brazil, Mexico, and Japan.

	1989 Sales		1989 Operating Income	
	$ mil	% of total	$ mil	% of total
US	1,093	60	221	72
Europe	437	24	47	15
Other countries	281	16	41	13
Adjustments	—	—	(53)	—
Total	**1,811**	**100**	**256**	**100**

WHAT

	1989 Sales		1989 Operating Income	
	$ mil	% of total	$ mil	% of total
Medical	1,063	59	215	70
Diagnostic	748	41	94	30
Adjustments	—	—	(53)	—
Total	**1,811**	**100**	**256**	**100**

Medical
Disposable hypodermic products
Elastic support products
Examination gloves
Intravenous and cardiovascular catheters
Operating room products
Suction products
Surgical blades
Thermometers

Diagnostic
Blood collection products
Hematology instruments
Laboratory ware and supplies
Microbiology products
Other diagnostic systems

RANKINGS

220th in *Fortune* 500 Industrial Cos.
422nd in *Forbes* Sales 500
276th in *Business Week* 1000
776th in *Business Week* Global 1000

COMPETITION

Abbott Labs
American Cyanamid
American Home Products
C. R. Bard
Baxter
EG&G
Eli Lilly
Hewlett-Packard
Johnson & Johnson
Pfizer

BELL ATLANTIC CORPORATION

OVERVIEW

Bell Atlantic is the nation's 4th largest provider of local telephone services (with approximately 17 million lines), offered under the Bell name in New Jersey, Pennsylvania, Delaware, the District of Columbia, Maryland, Virginia, and West Virginia. Bell Atlantic provides cellular and paging services in the same region through Bell Atlantic Mobile Systems (BAMS), the nation's 6th largest cellular service provider. BAMS operates in 5 of the largest 15 markets. With the 1990 acquisition of Control Data's US and Canadian computer maintenance division, Bell Atlantic's Sorbus subsidiary is the leader in independent maintenance of both DEC and IBM hardware.

Bell Atlantic engages in equipment leasing (US, Canada, and Europe); directory publishing (in its region); telecommunications and computer hardware sales to both businesses and the consumer market (nationally); telecommunications consulting through Bell Atlantic International (outside the US); real estate services through Bell Atlantic Properties (in its region); and software and 3rd-party computer maintenance services (internationally). In 1989 Bell Atlantic invested $2.3 billion in its network, bringing to 414,000 its total miles of optical fiber (from 314,000 a year ago) and providing digital switching to 66% of its central offices.

NYSE symbol: BEL
Incorporated: Delaware, 1983
Fiscal year ends: December 31

WHO

Chairman and CEO: Raymond W. Smith, age 52, $1,233,800 pay
President: Anton J. Campanella, age 58, $354,439 pay
VC and CFO: Philip A. Campbell, age 53, $819,593 pay
EVP and General Counsel: Robert A. Levetown, age 54, $540,000 pay
VP Strategic Planning: William M. Newport, age 54, $352,200 pay
Auditors: Coopers & Lybrand
Employees: 79,100

WHEN

Bell Atlantic's mid-Atlantic telephone companies were rooted in the AT&T/Bell System, which began in the 1870s. For example, Bell Telephone of Pennsylvania was originally incorporated under the name Bell Telephone of Philadelphia in 1879. Local telephone traffic and service quality continued to grow from 1900 until the Depression, when demand for services declined. Since WWII, telephone traffic has steadily increased, and local telephone service is now a mature market, growing less than 4% annually.

In 1983 Bell Atlantic was split from AT&T in a now-historic antitrust settlement. Bell Atlantic was incorporated that year and began operations in 1984. The settlement gave Bell Atlantic local phone service rights in parts of 6 states and Washington, DC; Bell Atlantic Mobile Systems (cellular service); and 1/7th of an R&D arm, Bell Communications Research, Inc., shared by the Bell companies, formerly called the Central Services Organization.

Given the maturity of local telephone services, Bell Atlantic must look for growth in non-regulated services such as its cellular/paging operations, equipment leasing, electronic mail and other on-line services, voice messaging, directory publishing, and sales of computer and office supplies via catalog.

Bell Atlantic has invested heavily in data transport markets to supplement existing voice services. The company introduced a data network known as PDN (1986); began testing integrated voice/data network services known as ISDN (1987); acquired (1985) and divested (1988) CompuShop, a chain of retail computer stores; acquired 3 computer-maintenance vendors (by 1987); acquired ESS (1986), a computer parts sales and repair organization; and purchased computer parts distributor Camex (1987).

The company is reaching out internationally; for example, it helped modernize Spain's telephone network (1988 contract). Yet Bell Atlantic is not ignoring its mainstream revenue base. It introduced new custom-calling features to residences (1987) and plans to install optical fiber to residences beginning in 1991. Management believes fiber is required before residential customers subscribe to online information services.

In 1990 Bell Atlantic was chosen, along with Ameritech, to purchase New Zealand's public phone system for about $2.5 billion. It also entered into an agreement with the Korean Telecommunications Authority to explore areas of joint cooperation.

WHERE

HQ: 1600 Market St., Philadelphia, PA 19103
Phone: 215-963-6000
FAX: 215-466-2486

Bell Atlantic provides local telephone operations in 6 eastern states and Washington, DC. The company has cellular interests in 20 markets, all within the same territory as its local operations.

WHAT

	1989 Sales		1989 Operating Income	
	$ mil	% of total	$ mil	% of total
Communications	10,754	94	2,088	101
Financial & real estate services	695	6	(15)	(1)
Adjustments	—	—	363	—
Total	**11,449**	**100**	**2,436**	**100**

Telephone Subsidiaries
The Bell Telephone Co. of Pennsylvania
The Chesapeake and Potomac Telephone Co. (Washington, DC)
The Chesapeake and Potomac Telephone Co. of Maryland
The Chesapeake and Potomac Telephone Co. of Virginia
The Chesapeake and Potomac Telephone Co. of West Virginia
The Diamond State Telephone Co.
New Jersey Bell Telephone Co.

HOW MUCH

	5 Yr. Growth	1980	1981	1982	1983	1984	1985	1986	1987	1988	1989
Sales ($ mil)	7.2%	—	—	—	—	8,090	9,084	9,921	10,298	10,880	11,449
Net income ($ mil)	2.0%	—	—	—	—	973	1,093	1,167	1,240	1,317	1,075
Income as % of sales	—	—	—	—	—	12.0%	12.0%	11.8%	12.0%	12.1%	9.4%
Earnings per share ($)	1.8%	—	—	—	—	2.49	2.74	2.93	3.12	3.33	2.72
Stock price – high ($)	—	—	—	—	—	20.75	26.84	38.50	39.88	37.25	56.13
Stock price – low ($)	—	—	—	—	—	16.41	19.44	25.00	30.25	31.13	34.69
Stock price – close ($)	22.6%	—	—	—	—	20.09	26.63	33.75	32.50	35.56	55.63
P/E – high	—	—	—	—	—	8	10	13	13	11	21
P/E – low	—	—	—	—	—	7	7	9	10	9	13
Dividends per share ($)	0.6%	—	—	—	—	1.60	1.70	1.80	1.92	2.04	1.65
Book value per share ($)	2.9%	—	—	—	—	18.84	19.83	20.91	22.07	23.29	21.78

1989 Year End:
Debt ratio: 47.3%
Return on equity: 12.0%
Cash (mil): $443
Current ratio: 0.75
Long-term debt (mil): $7,721
Number of shares (mil): 394
Dividends:
1989 average yield: 3.0%
1989 payout: 60.8%
Market value (mil): $21,942

Stock Price History high/low 1984-89

60
50
40
30
20
10
0

RANKINGS

3rd in *Fortune* 50 Utilities
55th in *Forbes* Sales 500
24th in *Business Week* 1000
49th in *Business Week* Global 1000

COMPETITION

Ameritech
AT&T
BellSouth
GTE
McCaw Cellular
MCI
NYNEX
Pacific Telesis
Southwestern Bell
United Telecommunications
U S West

BELLSOUTH CORPORATION

OVERVIEW

BellSouth is the largest of 7 regional holding companies created in the AT&T breakup. It is the 2nd largest US utility, behind GTE, and the world's largest directory advertising and publishing business.

Chairman John Clendenin and BellSouth have aggressively pursued new technologies. BellSouth is among the largest cellular telephone operators in the nation and exports cellular service to Argentina. It operates an extensive mobile paging network and runs an electronic "gateway" to give computer users access to databanks.

The company wants the federal courts, still overseeing the AT&T case, to allow regional companies more freedom to offer new services. And BellSouth wants state regulators to permit incentive-based rates that, the company argues, would spur it to be even more profitable (it already makes more money than any other former Bell regional company) and more efficient.

NYSE symbol: BLS
Incorporated: Georgia, 1983
Fiscal year ends: December 31

WHO

Chairman, President, and CEO: John L. Clendenin, age 55, $1,285,000 pay
VC Finance and Administration: F. Duane Ackerman, age 47, $520,000 pay
EVP Governmental Affairs: Raymond L. McGuire, age 57, $410,500 pay
EVP and General Counsel: Walter H. Alford, age 51, $387,500 pay
EVP and CFO: Harvey R. Holding, age 55, $380,500 pay
SVP Corporate Human Resources: Roy B. Howard, age 61
Auditors: Coopers & Lybrand
Employees: 101,000

WHEN

Executives of Boston-based National Bell struggled at first as they tried to market Alexander Graham Bell's telephone throughout the nation. In 1878 general manager Theodore Vail recruited agent James Merrill Ormes, a former Union soldier, to head South.

Ormes created Bell exchanges throughout the region, but growth was hampered by competition with Western Union, then dominant in telecommunications. In 1879 Ormes, with approval of National Bell, hammered out an agreement with Western Union that ended telephone competition in the South and created Southern Bell Telephone and Telegraph. Western Union dropped its own telephone enterprise in exchange for a controlling interest in Southern Bell, and National Bell granted a license for the use of telephones. The agreement was the forerunner of a nationwide truce between National Bell and Western Union.

In the 1890s, after the Bell organization had acquired controlling interest in Southern Bell, another challenge arose. Bell's original telephone patents expired, and a slew of competitors entered the business. Southern Bell president Edward Hall forced his company to upgrade quality, undercut competition, and, when necessary, buy out rivals. Southern Bell had bought 23 of 52 competing telephone exchanges by 1909.

In 1912 the Atlanta-based company relinquished its Virginia and West Virginia territory, and AT&T arranged Southern Bell's merger with Cumberland Telephone and Telegraph, which served Kentucky, Louisiana, Mississippi, Tennessee, and parts of Illinois and Indiana. Illinois and Indiana franchises were later redistributed within the Bell system. Southern Bell hooked up its millionth customer in 1929, but revenues and subscribers dropped dramatically during the Great Depression. In the post-WWII boom, growth resumed.

In 1957 Southern Bell was structured into 2 divisions, a prelude to the 1968 split of the company into Birmingham-based South Central Bell (Alabama, Kentucky, Louisiana, Mississippi, and Tennessee) and Atlanta-based Southern Bell (Florida, Georgia, North Carolina, and South Carolina).

The division was short-lived. The 1982 settlement in a landmark federal antitrust case required AT&T to spin off 7 regional holding companies. BellSouth, reuniting Southern Bell and South Central Bell, was the largest of the 7.

BellSouth, bolstered by healthy local phone service profits, bought L. M. Berry, a directory publisher (1986), and MCCA, a paging and mobile communications firm (1986). Its bid for LIN Broadcasting, with extensive cellular telephone holdings, was thwarted in 1989, but BellSouth remains committed to cellular and other new technologies.

WHERE

HQ: 1155 Peachtree St. NE, Atlanta, GA 30367
Phone: 404-249-2000
FAX: 404-249-5599

BellSouth operates local phone service in 9 states through 2 subsidiaries. Directory and cellular firms operate throughout the US and overseas.

WHAT

	1989 Operating Revenues $ mil
Local service	5,479
Interstate access	2,801
Intrastate access	842
Toll	1,628
Other	3,244
Total	**13,996**

Subsidiaries

South Central Bell
Local phone service in Alabama, Kentucky, Louisiana, Mississippi, and Tennessee

Southern Bell
Local phone service in Florida, Georgia, North Carolina, and South Carolina

BellSouth Services
Staff support for regulated businesses

BellSouth Enterprises
Directory advertising
Mobile communications
Computer systems

Bell Communications Research, Inc. (14.3%)
Research and development
US government telecommunications

HOW MUCH

	5 Yr. Growth	1980	1981	1982	1983	1984	1985	1986	1987	1988	1989
Sales ($ mil)	8.0%	—	—	—	—	9,519	10,664	11,444	12,269	13,597	13,996
Net income ($ mil)	6.2%	—	—	—	—	1,257	1,418	1,589	1,665	1,666	1,695
Income as % of sales	—	—	—	—	—	13.2%	13.3%	13.9%	13.6%	12.3%	12.1%
Earnings per share ($)	4.5%	—	—	—	—	2.85	3.13	3.38	3.46	3.51	3.55
Stock price – high ($)	—	—	—	—	—	23.92	32.83	46.00	44.25	43.88	58.13
Stock price – low ($)	—	—	—	—	—	18.17	21.58	30.00	28.75	35.75	39.00
Stock price – close ($)	20.6%	—	—	—	—	22.67	32.67	38.50	36.38	39.88	57.88
P/E – high	—	—	—	—	—	8	11	14	13	13	16
P/E – low	—	—	—	—	—	6	7	9	8	10	11
Dividends per share ($)	7.5%	—	—	—	—	1.73	1.40	1.99	2.16	2.32	2.48
Book value per share ($)	5.3%	—	—	—	—	20.98	22.27	23.61	24.89	25.51	27.21

1989 Year End:
Debt ratio: 35.0%
Return on equity: 13.5%
Cash (mil): $500
Current ratio: 0.87
Long-term debt (mil): $7,055
Number of shares (mil): 482
Dividends:
1989 average yield: 4.3%
1989 payout: 69.9%
Market value (mil): $27,870

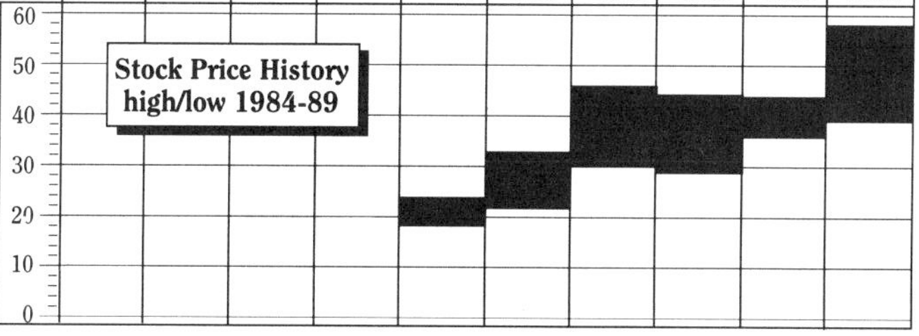

Stock Price History high/low 1984-89

60 50 40 30 20 10 0

RANKINGS

2nd in *Fortune* 50 Utilities
40th in *Forbes* Sales 500
12th in *Business Week* 1000
31st in *Business Week* Global 1000

COMPETITION

Ameritech
AT&T
Bell Atlantic
R. R. Donnelley
GTE
McCaw Cellular
MCI
NYNEX
Pacific Telesis
Southwestern Bell
United Telecommunications
U S West

BERKSHIRE HATHAWAY, INC.

OVERVIEW

Berkshire Hathaway is a holding company for a property/casualty insurance operation and 8 diverse businesses, including *World Book* encyclopedias and California's dominant producer/retailer of candy (See's Candies). Berkshire also makes significant equity investments in other public companies (*e.g.,* Coca-Cola, Capital Cities/ABC).

Berkshire's soul is Warren E. Buffett, one of the most successful investors ever. His closely read, chatty annual reports include such unique sections as "Mistakes of the First Twenty-five Years (A Condensed Version)."

The stock price has increased from $12 in 1965 to a high of $8,675 in 1989. Berkshire pays no dividends and shuns stock splits to discourage speculation and attract loyal, long-term stockholders. Buffett's 42% stake, worth an estimated $4.2 billion at the end of 1989, makes him the 2nd richest man in America (after John Kluge of Metromedia, according to *Forbes*). Virtually all will be left to charity.

WHEN

Superinvestor Warren Buffett began his career at age 11 (purchasing 3 shares of Cities Service). After graduating from the University of Nebraska in 1950, Buffett left for Columbia University to study under famed value investor Benjamin Graham. Buffett absorbed the master's teachings: employ strictly quantitative analysis to discover companies whose intrinsic worth (what a rational investor would pay) exceeds their stock price; value is paramount; popularity is irrelevant; and the market will eventually vindicate the patient investor.

Buffett returned to Omaha at age 25 to found Buffett Partnership, Ltd. (1956). The $105,000 in initial assets grew quickly from the start, allowing bargain purchases like Berkshire Hathaway (textiles, 1965) and National Indemnity (insurance, 1967). Feeling that stocks were overvalued, Buffett dissolved the partnership (1969); the initial value per share had grown 30-fold and net assets were over $100 million.

Buffett had become disenchanted with businesses having intrinsically poor economics (like enduring textile albatross Berkshire Hathaway, finally closed in 1985). After adopting the Berkshire name for his new investment firm, Buffett began searching for solid businesses with above-average returns on equity, low capital needs, high cash flows, and strong management. In 1972 Berkshire paid 3 times book value for See's Candies; its stake ($45 million) in GEICO insurance (accumulated 1976-1981) had increased to $1 billion by early 1990.

Buffett favorites were media-based companies that capital-intensive industries (*e.g.,* car or chemical manufacturers) need as advertising conduits. During the stock market slump of 1973 and 1974, Buffett obtained equity in advertising firms (Interpublic, 16%; Ogilvy & Mather, 8%) and newspapers (*Washington Post*; *Boston Globe*; Knight-Ridder Newspapers), followed by the *Buffalo News* (fully owned, 1977) and Capital Cities/ABC (1985).

In the 1980s Berkshire bought majority interests in Nebraska Furniture Mart (1983) and Fechheimer Brothers (uniform makers, 1986) and full ownership of Scott & Fetzer (which included the famous *World Book* encyclopedias and Kirby vacuum cleaners, 1986). In 1986 the company sold its interest in Affiliated Publications, the *Globe*'s parent. The company provided a haven for takeover targets, sinking $2 billion in high-yielding convertible preferreds into businesses offering strong franchises and generous dividends: Salomon (investment banking, 1987), Gillette (1989), USAir Group (1989), and Champion International (forest products, 1990).

Berkshire's recent long-term purchases exemplify Buffett's ideal companies: a stake in Coca-Cola (1988-1989) and Borsheim's jewelry store (1989).

HOW MUCH

	9 Yr. Growth	1980	1981	1982	1983	1984	1985	1986	1987	1988	1989
Sales ($ mil)	21.1%	444	422	421	534	640	826	2,049	2,158	2,317	2,483
Net income ($ mil)	29.7%	43	40	32	68	70	93	131	215	313	447
Income as % of sales	—	9.7%	9.4%	7.5%	12.8%	11.0%	11.3%	6.4%	10.0%	13.5%	18.0%
Earnings per share ($)	28.1%	42.07	40.27	31.93	63.93	61.21	81.04	114.62	187.24	273.37	390.01
Stock price – high ($)	—	470	590	775	1,385	1,360	2,730	3,250	4,270	5,000	8,875
Stock price – low ($)	—	245	425	430	755	1,220	1,275	2,220	2,635	3,000	4,625
Stock price – close ($)	39.8%	425	560	775	1,310	1,275	2,430	2,820	2,950	4,700	8,675
P/E – high	—	11	15	24	22	22	34	28	23	18	23
P/E – low	—	6	11	13	12	20	16	19	14	11	12
Dividends per share ($)	0.00%	0.00	0.00	0.00	0.00	0.00	0.00	0.00	0.00	0.00	0.00
Book value per share ($)	30.1%	401	526	738	976	1,109	1,644	2,073	2,477	2,976	4,298

1989 Year End:
Debt ratio: 16.8%
Return on equity: 10.7%
Cash (mil): $8,262
Current ratio: —
Long-term debt (mil): $996
Number of shares (mil): 1,146
Dividends:
1989 average yield: 0.0%
1989 payout: 0.0%
Market value (mil): $9,942

NYSE symbol: BRK
Incorporation: Delaware, 1973
Fiscal year ends: December 31

WHO

Chairman and CEO: Warren E. Buffett, age 59, $100,000 pay
VP; Chairman, Wesco: Charles T. Munger, age 66, $100,000 pay
VP, CFO, and Secretary: J. Verne McKenzie, age 61, $235,000 pay
Auditors: Deloitte & Touche
Employees: 20,000

WHERE

HQ: 1440 Kiewit Plaza, Omaha, NE 68131
Phone: 402-346-1400
FAX: 402-536-3030

Berkshire Hathaway's main plants are located in California, New York, Ohio, Texas, Arkansas, and Tennessee. The company operates 225 See's Candies in 12 western and midwestern states.

WHAT

	1989 Sales		1989 Operating Income	
	$ mil	% of total	$ mil	% of total
Insurance	865	36	440	65
Candy	186	7	33	5
Newspaper	136	5	45	7
Home furnishings — retail	157	6	17	2
Encyclopedias & reference materials	338	14	25	4
Home cleaning prods.	159	6	26	4
Uniform mfg. & distribution	94	4	12	2
Other	549	22	71	11
Adjustments	(1)	—	4	—
Total	**2,483**	**100**	**673**	**100**

Insurance
Columbia Insurance Co.
National Indemnity Co.

Noninsurance
Borsheim's (jewelry retailing, 80%)
Buffalo News (daily newspaper)
Fechheimer Brothers Co. (uniform manufacturing and distribution, 85%)
Kirby (home cleaning systems)
Nebraska Furniture Mart (80%)
Scott & Fetzer Co. (diverse manufacturing)
See's Candies
Wesco Financial Corp. (80.1%; includes Mutual Savings & Loan of California)
World Book encyclopedias

Equity Investments
Capital Cities/ABC (17%)
Champion International (9.25%)
Coca-Cola (6.3%)
Federal Home Loan Mortgage Corp. (4%)
GEICO (44%)
Gillette (11%)
Salomon (13%)
USAir Group (11%)
Washington Post Co. (16%)

RANKINGS

179th in *Fortune* 500 Industrial Cos.
332nd in *Forbes* Sales 500
61st in *Business Week* 1000
209th in *Business Week* Global 1000

COMPETITION

ARA
Cadbury Schweppes
Campbell Soup
Electrolux
Hanson
Hershey
Kohlberg Kravis Roberts
Mars
Maxwell
Maytag
V. F.
Whitman
Insurance companies
Investment funds

BERTELSMANN AG

OVERVIEW

Based in Gütersloh, West Germany, Bertelsmann is the world's largest publisher and one of the world's largest privately held businesses. The company has a reputation for exemplary personnel policies. Although Bertelsmann stock is not publicly traded, the company issues "profit sharing certificates," which are traded on German exchanges. Employees hold 40% of the certificates.

Through acquisitions Bertelsmann has gained a substantial foothold in the US book and music publishing market. Bantam (Stephen Hawking, Louis L'Amour), Doubleday (Leon Uris, Bill Cosby), and Dell (Danielle Steel, Irving Wallace) form the world's largest English-language trade book publishing group. Arista Records (Whitney Houston, The Grateful Dead) and RCA (Bruce Hornsby, Mr. Mister) together rank 3rd in record production, and Gruner + Jahr's *Parents* magazine has achieved over 1.7 million in circulation.

Bertelsmann is also the largest book club operator in the world, with 25 million members in 25 countries, but Doubleday's book clubs have lost money and members since Bertelsmann bought them. The company's other non-US operations include sheet music, map, and religious publishing in Europe. Gruner + Jahr publishes magazines in Germany (*Stern, Brigitte*), France (*Femme actuelle, Prima*), the UK (*best*), and Spain (*Mia*).

Private, foreign company
Founded: Gütersloh, Germany, 1835
Fiscal year ends: June 30

WHO

Chairman: Reinhard Mohn, age 70
President and CEO: Mark Wössner
CFO: Hermann Hoffmann
Auditors: TREUVERKEHR Aktiengesellschaft, Wirtschaftsprüfungsgesellschaft
Employees: 43,702

WHERE

HQ: Carl-Bertelsmann-Strasse 270, Postbox 55 55, D-4830 Gütersloh 100, Germany
Phone: 011-49-5241-801
FAX: 011-49-5241-75166
US HQ: 211 E. 43rd St., New York, NY 10017
US Phone: 212-687-1765
US FAX: 212-682-6699

	1989 Sales	
	DM mil	% of total
Germany	3,990	32
International	8,493	68
Total	**12,483**	**100**

WHEN

Carl Bertelsmann founded the company that bears his name in 1835 in Gütersloh, Germany. The company printed church hymnals but expanded into publishing in the 1850s. As WWII approached, Bertelsmann was still a small publisher of religious books; nevertheless, the Nazis closed it down.

Reinhard Mohn, whose grandfather had married Bertelsmann's granddaughter, was captured by the Allies while fighting for the Germans. He spent the remainder of the war in a Kansas POW camp, where he learned the workings of capitalism. He returned to Germany to find that Bertelsmann's assets had been destroyed and his 2 brothers killed. Mohn printed labels for a distillery in return for whiskey; he traded the whiskey for bricks and began rebuilding the family business.

In 1950 Bertelsmann started Lessering, the first book club in Germany. The club was such a success that the company founded other book clubs and by the late 1950s had started a record club. During the 1960s the company expanded its clubs into neighboring countries and increased its publishing and printing operations to supply their demand. Bertelsmann bought UFA, a major German TV and film production company in 1964. The company bought 25% of Gruner + Jahr, publisher of *Stern, Der Spiegel,* and several international magazines, in 1969 and acquired a controlling interest in 1973. Bertelsmann bought 51% of Bantam Books in 1977 (and the remaining stock in 1981) and Arista Records in 1979. In 1980 Bertelsmann used these companies to launch its US club, American Circle, which folded after 4 years of losses. Mohn retired as Bertelsmann's CEO when he reached age 60 in 1981, because that was the retirement age he himself had mandated for the position.

Bertelsmann increased its presence in the US publishing and music market in 1986 when it purchased RCA Records from General Electric and the Doubleday family's interest in Doubleday. Doubleday, founded in 1897 by Frank Doubleday, had grown to become one of the largest publishers in the US, due mainly to its strength in hardbacks, Dell paperbacks, and several successful book clubs. But Doubleday had struggled throughout the early 1980s because of poor quality, and Bertelsmann believed Doubleday's clubs would benefit from the company's management. Doubleday also owned the New York Mets, which the family, descendants of baseball inventor Abner Doubleday, had bought in 1980; Doubleday sold the team to a partnership partly owned by the family.

Bertelsmann did not enjoy as much success as hoped with its US operations in the late 1980s. The book clubs that had once provided Doubleday with 35% of its profits lost thousands of members, prompting Bertelsmann to state that it would develop new activities in the US through joint ventures rather than large acquisitions. Bertelsmann sold Doubleday Book Shops to B. Dalton in 1990. Mohn, whose family still owns 90% of the stock in Bertelsmann, announced in 1988 that he intends to leave his fortune to charity.

WHAT

	1989 Sales	
	DM mil	% of total
Book & record clubs	2,839	23
Gruner + Jahr magazines	2,963	23
Music & video	2,839	23
Printing & manufacturing	1,885	15
Publishing	1,719	14
Electronic media	238	2
Total	**12,483**	**100**

Book & Record Clubs
Bertelsmann Club (Germany)
Doubleday Book & Music Clubs (US)
The Leisure Circle (UK)

Publishing
Bantam Doubleday Dell
European Law Press
MMV Medizin Verlag

Printing & Manufacturing
Belser Offsetdruck (offset printing)
Bertelsmann Distribution
Bertelsmann Printing & Manufacturing (US)
Cartiere del Garda (paper production)

Music & Video
Arista Records
BMG Ariola
BMG Music Publishing
BMG Video

Electronic Media
Radio Hamburg
RTL plus (TV)
Ufa Filmproduktion

Gruner + Jahr Magazines
Estar Viva, Mia (Spain)
Femme actuelle, Prima (France)
Parents, YM (*Young Miss*), *Expecting* (US)
Prima, best (UK)
Stern, Der Spiegel (25% owned), *Geo* (Germany)

RANKINGS

191st in *Fortune* Global 500 Industrial Cos.
67th in *Forbes* 100 Foreign Investments in the US

COMPETITION

Advance Publications
Capital Cities/ABC
Commerce Clearing House
R. R. Donnelley
Hearst
Knight-Ridder
Maxwell
MCA
McGraw-Hill
News Corp.
Paramount
Pearson
Philips
Reader's Digest
Sony
Time Warner

HOW MUCH

$=DM 1.69 (Dec. 31, 1989)	9 Yr. Growth	1980	1981	1982	1983	1984	1985	1986	1987	1988	1989
Sales (DM mil)	11.2%	4,792	5,588	6,036	6,218	6,716	7,441	7,602	9,160	11,299	12,483
Net income (DM mil)	24.5%	56	63	105	159	289	337	329	207	362	402
Income as % of sales	—	1.2%	1.1%	1.7%	2.6%	4.3%	4.5%	4.3%	2.3%	3.2%	3.2%

1989 Year End:
Debt ratio: 33.6%
Return on equity: 24.3%
Cash (mil): DM126
Current ratio: 1.13
Long-term debt (mil): DM935
Sales ($ mil): $7,386

BETHLEHEM STEEL CORPORATION

OVERVIEW

Bethlehem, Pennsylvania, is home to Bethlehem Steel, the 3rd largest US steel producer (after USX and LTV). Bethlehem leads the US in the production of steel plates, structural shapes, and piling. The company produces 66% of its steel at 2 of its 5 steelmaking plants: Burns Harbor (Indiana) and Sparrows Point (Maryland).

In response to strong foreign steel competition in the 1980s, USX diversified, LTV filed for Chapter 11, and Bethlehem Steel sold many of its nonsteel assets to concentrate on basic steelmaking. To lower costs, Bethlehem has spent $4 billion since 1980 to modernize its steel plants. With the increased productivity possible in the modern mills, the company reduced its steel mill workforce by 62%, while annual production declined only 14% (to 9.5 million tons of steel shipped in 1989). Burns Harbor and Sparrows Point are 2 of the world's most efficient steel mills, able to produce a ton of steel in 3 and 4 labor hours, respectively.

NYSE symbol: BS
Incorporated: Delaware, 1919
Fiscal year ends: December 31

WHO

Chairman, CEO, and President: Walter F. Williams, age 61, $808,000 pay
SVP, General Counsel, and Secretary: Curtis H. Barnette, age 55, $479,000 pay
SVP and CFO: Gary L. Millenbruch, age 52, $419,000 pay
Auditors: Price Waterhouse
Employees: 30,500

WHEN

Bethlehem Steel began as Saucona Iron in South Bethlehem, Pennsylvania, in 1857, rolling iron railroad rails. In 1859 the company changed its name to Bethlehem Rolling Mills & Iron, then again in 1861 to Bethlehem Iron. In 1886 the US government urged Bethlehem to make armor plate and military items. The company settled on the name Bethlehem Steel in 1899.

The president of United States Steel, Charles Schwab, personally bought (1901), sold (1902), and again bought (1902) Bethlehem Steel. He then transferred Bethlehem to a new venture, United States Shipbuilding. This venture failed in 1903, spinning off Bethlehem Steel in 1904 with Schwab as president. Bethlehem's assets then included the steel plant in South Bethlehem, shipbuilding yards on both US coasts, and iron ore mines in Cuba.

Schwab saw the potential in Henry Grey's one-piece, wide-flange steel beams for building construction. Schwab built a structural mill at Saucon, Pennsylvania, and bought Grey's patents, and the resulting, successful Bethlehem section (1908) found a commercial market in the construction industry.

In 1912 Schwab bought the Tofo Iron Mines in Chile, a cheap source of superior-grade iron ore. Bethlehem grew with the purchases of Pennsylvania Steel and Maryland Steel in 1916. With shipbuilding facilities, steel manufacturing plants, and good sources of ore and coal, Bethlehem was well prepared for the steel and shipbuilding needs of WWI.

Bethlehem Steel continued to buy steel companies, including Lackawanna Steel (1922), Midvale Steel & Ordnance (1923), and Cambria Steel (1923). In 1930 the company bought Pacific Coast Steel and Southern California Iron & Steel. With the purchase of the fabricating business of McClintic-Marshall Construction (1931), Bethlehem entered bridge and building construction. Bethlehem made the steelwork for such structures as the Golden Gate bridge, Rockefeller Center, and the US Supreme Court building.

During WWII Bethlehem operated its steel plants above their rated capacity and built 1,121 ships. During the 1960s Bethlehem built research laboratories and developed such products as tin-free steel for cans.

In the 1970s and 1980s the US imported increased amounts of low-cost steel (26% of the US steel market in 1984 from less than 1% in the 1950s) from foreign producers. To face the import challenge, Bethlehem reduced production and sold some of its steel plants, shipyards, and mines. In 1981 the company initiated a major modernization of its steel plants, and in 1986 Bethlehem consolidated its primary business and began building new facilities. In 1989 Bethlehem bought an interest in Walbridge Coatings (electrogalvanized, corrosion-resistant steel sheets).

WHERE

HQ: 701 E. 3rd St., Bethlehem, PA 18016
Phone: 215-694-2424
FAX: 215-694-1509

Major Plants

Bethlehem, PA	Structural steel shapes, piling, foundry products
Burns Harbor, IN	Steel plate and sheet
Johnstown, PA	Steel bars, rods, wire
Sparrows Point, MD	Steel plate and sheet, tinplate, Galvalume sheet
Steelton, PA	Rail products, pipe

	1989 Pretax Income	
	$ mil	% of total
US	240	93
Foreign	18	7
Total	**258**	**100**

WHAT

	1989 Sales		1989 Operating Income	
	$ mil	% of total	$ mil	% of total
Basic steel operns.	4,907	93	405	152
Steel related operns.	344	7	(138)	(52)
Adjustments	—	—	105	—
Total	**5,251**	**100**	**372**	**100**

Products
Carbon and alloy bars
Coal mining and processing
Freight car manufacturing
Iron ore
Piling
Plates
Railroad rails, tie plates, joint bars, special trackwork
Rods, wire, pipe
Semifinished steel
Sheet and strip products
Structural shapes
Tin products

Major Markets
Appliance makers
Automotive industry
Construction industry
Container industry
Defense industry
Machinery industry
Oil and gas industry
Railroads
Service centers

RANKINGS

95th in *Fortune* 500 Industrial Cos.
250th in *Fortune* Global 500 Industrial Cos.
167th in *Forbes* Sales 500
395th in *Business Week* 1000

COMPETITION

Broken Hill
Cargill
Hyundai
Inland Steel
LTV
USX

HOW MUCH

	9 Yr. Growth	1980	1981	1982	1983	1984	1985	1986	1987	1988	1989
Sales ($ mil)	(2.7%)	6,743	7,298	5,260	4,898	5,392	5,118	4,333	4,621	5,489	5,251
Net income ($ mil)	8.2%	121	211	(1,470)	(314)	(132)	(196)	(153)	104	392	246
Income as % of sales	—	1.8%	2.9%	(27.9%)	(6.4%)	(2.4%)	(3.8%)	(3.5%)	2.2%	7.1%	4.7%
Earnings per share ($)	0.4%	2.77	4.83	(33.64)	(6.42)	*(3.32)*	*(4.37)*	*(3.37)*	1.48	4.77	2.86
Stock price – high ($)	—	28.75	32.00	23.50	28.50	29.50	21.13	22.00	19.75	25.50	28.50
Stock price – low ($)	—	19.00	19.75	14.50	19.00	14.25	12.50	4.63	6.38	15.25	15.25
Stock price – close ($)	(3.9%)	26.38	23.25	19.25	28.50	17.50	15.63	6.25	16.75	23.25	18.50
P/E – high	—	10	7	—	—	—	—	—	13	5	10
P/E – low	—	7	4	—	—	—	—	—	4	3	5
Dividends per share ($)	(20.6%)	1.60	1.60	1.30	0.60	0.60	0.30	0.00	0.00	0.00	0.20
Book value per share ($)	(10.4%)	60.03	63.26	28.31	23.53	20.02	15.13	11.98	14.74	19.59	22.37

1989 Year End:
Debt ratio: 24.7%
Return on equity: 13.6%
Cash (mil): $531
Current ratio: 1.71
Long-term debt (mil): $656
Number of shares (mil): 75
Dividends:
1989 average yield: 1.1%
1989 payout: 7.0%
Market value (mil): $1,392

Stock Price History high/low 1980-89

35
30
25
20
15
10
5
0

THE BLACK & DECKER CORPORATION

OVERVIEW

Black & Decker, the world's largest power tool and home improvement products company, is synonymous with convenient, innovative tools and appliances. The company manufactures, distributes, sells, and services its products to an international market. Continual introduction of new products (100 new and redesigned products and over 400 accessories in 1989) and emphasis on product quality and service contribute to its reputation for innovative, high-quality tools.

The 1989 purchase of Emhart Corporation (formerly American Hardware) broadened Black & Decker's product line for the do-it-yourself customer (with locks, faucets, and lawn and garden products) and the commercial contractor (with Molly bolts, POP rivets, and other mechanical fasteners). The purchase also burdened Black & Decker with $2.6 billion in debt, which the company is actively reducing by consolidating facilities and targeting Emhart components for sale.

WHEN

In 1910 when S. Duncan Black and Alonzo G. Decker opened the Black & Decker Manufacturing Company in Baltimore with a $1,200 investment, they began a partnership that would last over 40 years. Starting with milk-bottle-cap machines and candy dippers, the partners introduced their first major tool in 1916 — a portable 1/2" electric drill with patented pistol grip and trigger switch.

The company built its first manufacturing plant, which would become the company headquarters, in 1917 in rural Towson, Maryland. Sales passed $1 million in 1919 and the company added a 20,000-square-foot factory. Black & Decker quickly established itself in international markets. It had sales representatives in Russia, Japan, and Australia in 1918, and in 1922 Black & Decker Ltd., a Canadian subsidiary, opened as its first facility outside the US.

Black & Decker produced tools that defined the power tool industry — the first portable screwdriver (1922), the 1/2" BB special drill (1923), the first electric hammer (1936), portable electric drills for the do-it-yourself home consumer (1946), finishing sanders and jigsaws (1953), and the Dustbuster hand-held vacuum (1979). The original founders led Black & Decker until their deaths — Black in 1951 and Decker in 1956. Black's brother, Robert, was CEO until 1964; Alonzo G. Decker, Jr., then presided until 1975. Nolan Archibald is the 3rd CEO in the company's history who is not part of the Black or Decker family. He joined the company in 1985 and is currently chairman, president, and CEO.

In 1984 Black & Decker acquired the General Electric housewares operations, replacing the well-known GE brand with the Black & Decker hexagonal trademark on such items as toaster ovens, can openers, and irons.

While the company's brand maintained its strong reputation, by the mid-1980s it was rapidly losing market share. Administrative and production costs were high and product quality was suffering. Black & Decker's worldwide manufacturing network was inefficient, its management was fat, and customer service was faltering. In 1985 Black & Decker showed a $158 million loss on $1.7 billion in sales. A major restructuring, begun in 1985, closed 5 plants, streamlined distribution systems, consolidated overseas facilities, and cut employee count by 10%. By 1987 the company was showing steadily increasing net earnings — a 100% increase over 1986. Its 1989 earnings ($30 million) were down from the year before due to the expensive Emhart purchase. In October 1989 the company entered into an agreement to sell Emhart's Bastik adhesives group for $345 million and as of mid-1990 had sold 2 other smaller components of Emhart for $205 million.

HOW MUCH

	9 Yr. Growth	1980	1981	1982	1983	1984	1985	1986	1987	1988	1989
Sales ($ mil)	9.3%	1,438	1,431	1,160	1,168	1,533	1,732	1,791	1,935	2,281	3,190
Net income ($ mil)	(11.5%)	90	66	41	28	95	(158)	28	56	97	30
Income as % of sales	—	6.3%	4.6%	3.5%	2.4%	6.2%	(9.1%)	1.5%	2.9%	4.3%	0.9%
Earnings per share ($)	(14.7%)	2.13	1.56	0.97	0.65	1.95	(3.11)	0.49	0.95	1.65	0.51
Stock price – high ($)	—	23.75	21.88	19.50	27.25	28.63	26.88	25.25	26.50	24.75	25.25
Stock price – low ($)	—	16.75	14.25	12.00	17.88	17.25	17.25	14.50	13.00	17.13	18.13
Stock price – close ($)	0.7%	18.38	15.13	18.13	26.38	23.50	21.50	16.25	18.88	23.13	19.50
P/E – high	—	11	14	20	42	15	—	52	28	15	50
P/E – low	—	8	9	12	28	9	—	30	14	10	36
Dividends per share ($)	(6.6%)	0.74	0.76	0.76	0.52	0.58	0.64	0.58	0.40	0.40	0.40
Book value per share ($)	(1.2%)	13.64	14.44	10.70	11.79	13.58	9.94	10.61	11.12	12.38	12.24

1989 Year End:
Debt ratio: 78.5%
Return on equity: 4.1%
Cash (mil): $158
Current ratio: 1.28
Long-term debt (mil): $2,630
Number of shares (mil): 59
Dividends:
1989 average yield: 2.1%
1989 payout: 78.4%
Market value (mil): $1,149

30 25 20 15 10 5 0

Stock Price History high/low 1980-89

NYSE symbol: BDK
Incorporated: Maryland, 1910
Fiscal year ends: December 31

WHO

Chairman, President, and CEO: Nolan D. Archibald, age 46, $1,302,422 pay
EVP and CFO: Stephen F. Page, age 50
Auditors: Ernst & Young
Employees: 38,600

WHERE

HQ: 701 E. Joppa Rd., Towson, MD 21204
Phone: 301-583-3900
FAX: 301-583-2933

Black & Decker operates 108 manufacturing facilities, including 60 in the US and 48 in 17 foreign countries.

	1989 Sales		1989 Operating Income	
	$ mil	% of total	$ mil	% of total
US	1,734	55	118	44
Europe	936	29	94	35
Other countries	520	16	58	21
Total	**3,190**	**100**	**270**	**100**

WHAT

	1989 Sales	
	$ mil	% of total
Power tools	1,077	34
Household products	833	26
Outdoor products	301	9
Hardware, plumbing, other products	979	31
Total	**3,190**	**100**

Brand Names

Power Tools
Alligator (saws)
Black & Decker
DeWalt (stationary tools)
Kodiak (drills, screwdrivers)
Quattro (hammer drill)
ThunderVolt (cordless tools)
Univolt (charging system)
Wildcat (sander/grinder)
Workmate (work bench)

Appliances
Cup-At-A-Time (coffee maker)
Dustbuster (hand vacuum)
Spacemaker (under-the-cabinet appliances)
Toast-R-Oven

Lawn & Garden
GardenAmerica (watering, lighting systems)
Gard 'n' Grip (lawn tools)
SweepStick (cordless broom)
True Temper (lawn tools, golf club shafts)
YardCleaner (blowers)

Hardware
Corbin & Russwin (locks)
Kwikset (locks)
Molly (bolts)
POP (rivets)
Price Pfister (faucets)

RANKINGS

141st in *Fortune* 500 Industrial Cos.
396th in *Fortune* Global 500 Industrial Cos.
229th in *Forbes* Sales 500
503rd in *Business Week* 1000

COMPETITION

American Brands
American Standard
Deere
Electrolux
Emerson
Gillette
Honda
Ingersoll-Rand
Masco
Matsushita
Philips
Premark
Robert Bosch
Snap-on Tools
Stanley Works
Textron

BLUE CROSS AND BLUE SHIELD ASSOCIATION

OVERVIEW

The Blue Cross and Blue Shield Association is the national coordinating organization for the 74 autonomous Blue Cross and Blue Shield prepaid health care plans operating throughout the US. The "Blues," as they are called in the industry, are the oldest and largest health insurers in the country, serving over 100 million people and collecting approximately $56 billion in premiums in 1989. The Blues provide insurance plans for about 70% of the largest industrial firms in the US.

In recent years rising health care costs, competition from private insurers, and competition among the Blues for members have resulted in substantial losses and declining enrollment for the plans. The combined losses of the 74 plans in 1987 and 1988 were approximately $3 billion. To survive, some plans have had to abandon original precepts such as guaranteed enrollment; others have given up their nonprofit status to become mutual insurance companies. These actions together with expense cutting and rate increases have returned many of the Blues to profitability, estimated at $1 billion for all plans in 1989.

WHEN

Blue Cross prepaid hospital plans were developed to provide working people with a means of paying the high costs of private hospitalization and to ensure that hospitals were paid for their services. The first plans were sponsored by single hospitals in Texas, Iowa, and Illinois. The Dallas plan, begun in 1929, cost schoolteachers 50 cents per month and achieved 75% voluntary participation in the first year. Fundamental to the Blue Cross concept was its community rating system, in which premiums were calculated based on the claims experience of the subscriber's community, rather than on the individual subscriber's health or on the age, sex, or occupational makeup of the subscriber's group.

These early experiments were soon followed by larger plans in New Jersey, Cleveland, Chicago, and St. Paul, the last of which developed the Blue Cross name and symbol in 1934. By 1935 there were 15 Blue Cross plans in 11 states. In the late 1930s many states adopted legislation exempting plans from state insurance regulation and solidifying the nonprofit status of the proliferating plans. In 1936 the American Hospital Association (AHA) formed the Committee on Hospital Service (renamed the Blue Cross Association in 1948) as an umbrella for the plans.

Simultaneously with the rise of Blue Cross, state medical societies began to sponsor prepaid medical plans to cover physicians' fees. In 1946 they loosely banded together under the guidance of the AMA as the Associated Medical Care Plans (soon renamed Association of Blue Shield Plans).

In 1945 Blue Cross enrollment was 19 million, while that of Blue Shield stood at 3 million in 1946. To coordinate their efforts, in 1948 the Blues decided to merge, but last-minute opposition from the AMA killed the proposal. Blue Cross decided to form a nonprofit stock corporation to coordinate the activities of its various plans. Blue Shield did likewise. Despite the failure of formal union, the Blues cooperated with each other on public policy matters while competing vigorously for members.

The Blues enjoyed large enrollment gains in the late 1940s and 1950s, although their growth rate slowed due to increased competition from private insurers. In 1960 Blue Cross boasted almost 1/3 of the nation's population as members (56 million). The Blues became involved in administering federal health benefits (*e.g.,* Medicare) during the 1960s. Fifty percent of Blue Cross's 1970 premiums of $10 billion came from these government sources.

Rapidly rising medical costs in the 1970s required the Blues to adopt such cost control measures as utilization review of hospital admissions to stem increasing premiums; many plans even abandoned the community rating system. In the 1980s spiraling health costs began to undermine the financial health of the Blues (one plan lost $100 million in 2 years), which had finally joined forces in 1982. While many plans have managed to improve their financial performance in 1989 and 1990, it has sometimes come at the expense of the Blues' original goal of providing economical health care for all working people desiring it within a community.

HOW MUCH

	6 Yr. Growth	1980	1981	1982	1983	1984	1985	1986	1987	1988	1989
Pvt. subscribers (mil)	(1.5%)	86	85	80	80	80	78	77	76	74	73
Employees of plans (thou)	6.4%	—	—	—	89	89	98	110	118	125	129
HQ Budget ($ mil)	6.6%	—	—	71	71	85	87	98	95	97	104

Nonprofit organization
Incorporated: Illinois, 1948
Fiscal year ends: December 31

WHO

President and CEO: Bernard R. Tresnowski
SVP Finance and Management Services: Frederick C. Cue
SVP Legal and Corporate: Roger G. Wilson
SVP Business Support and Strategy: Preston Jordan
SVP Federal Programs: Harry P. Cain II
SVP National Marketing: Leonard Wood
SVP Representation and Public Affairs: Douglas S. Peters
Auditors: Coopers & Lybrand
Employees: 128,729 (all plans)

WHERE

HQ: 676 N. St. Clair St., Chicago, IL 60611
Phone: 312-440-6000
FAX: 312-440-6609

The association has offices in Chicago and Washington, DC; 74 licensees operating in 50 states, Canada, and Jamaica; and over 100 million private and Medicare subscribers.

WHAT

Policies/Programs
Group major medical insurance
Health maintenance programs
Individual major medical insurance
Medicare administration
Preferred-provider organizations

Organization Goals
Betterment of public health
Cooperation with federal, state, and local governments for provision of health services
Development and maintenance of membership standards
Protection of Blue Cross and Blue Shield service marks
Attainment of wide public acceptance of the principle of voluntary, nonprofit prepayment of health services

Publications
Inquiry (scholarly journal)
Your Healthy Best (health booklets)

COMPETITION

Aetna
CIGNA
John Hancock
Massachusetts Mutual
Metropolitan
Prudential
Travelers

THE BOEING COMPANY

OVERVIEW

Seattle-based Boeing is a diversified aerospace company that designs and manufactures commercial and military aircraft, missiles, helicopters, spare parts, and related products. The nation's largest exporter (54% of 1989 revenues were derived from exports), Boeing is also the largest commercial aircraft manufacturer in the world and has been the industry leader for over 30 years — since the 707 launched the jet age in 1958.

Boeing currently has record back orders totaling approximately $80 billion for its planes and has built over 60% of the commercial jets in service. The best-selling short-range jetliner in commercial aviation's history is Boeing's 737. Other commercial aircraft include the 757 standard-body and the 747 and 767 wide-body planes. The company participates in space projects and also provides on-line computer services. Boeing announced plans in 1989 to offer a new transport jet, designated the 777, which will carry 350 passengers and will be available by 1995.

WHEN

In 1915, 2 friends decided to build a plane for the fledgling aviation industry. Establishing an informal partnership in 1916, William Edward Boeing and Conrad Westervelt built a seaplane; later Boeing named their factory the Pacific Aero Products Company. Westervelt departed in 1916, but Boeing continued operations and incorporated. In 1919 he and a partner, Edward Hubbard, began airmail service between Seattle and Victoria (British Columbia). By 1934 Boeing had formed United Aircraft & Transport Corporation, which included Pratt & Whitney (engine manufacturer), Northrop (military airplane manufacturer), Sikorsky (amphibious vehicle manufacturer), United Air Lines (commercial airline service), and the Boeing airframe operation.

In 1934 new airmail regulations forced the company to sell off most of its constituent parts. Stripped down to aircraft manufacture, it was first named Boeing Airplane Company; not until 1961 did it become known officially as The Boeing Company.

Boeing continues to be best known for aircraft manufacture. Between 1935 and 1965 the company had many successful planes; among the more well known were the P-12 fighter planes; 4-engine Stratoliner; Clipper flying boats; B-17, B-29, B-47, and B-52 bombers; and 707 and 727 commercial jetliners. While military contracts helped secure its future during WWI and WWII, commercial airline sales have been a greater contributor to growth in subsequent decades.

Planning began in 1965 for one of Boeing's greatest commercial successes, the 747 — produced at the risk of bankruptcy. A cooperative effort between Boeing and Pan Am, the 747 required a $2 billion R&D budget. The giant plane would need to travel faster, use less fuel per passenger, fly higher, and carry more passengers than existing airplanes. The 747 became extremely popular and helped provide Boeing with the 60% worldwide commercial jet market share it now has.

Boeing continues to focus upon worldwide aerospace opportunities while reflecting an interest in acquiring high-technology companies. Boeing established Boeing Computer Services (1970), a data communications service provider; bought an equity interest in Carnegie Group (1984) for exploration of artificial intelligence in the aerospace industry; and purchased ARGOSystems (1987), a defense electronics company. Boeing has grown from a domestic leader to a worldwide one. Boeing's backlog, the largest in its history, both assures leadership into the 1990s and presents its biggest customer problem. For the first time in 20 years, Boeing is delivering planes behind schedule, and there has been speculation that key rival Airbus Industrie has benefited from Boeing's long delivery times.

HOW MUCH

	9 Yr. Growth	1980	1981	1982	1983	1984	1985	1986	1987	1988	1989
Sales ($ mil)	8.9%	9,426	9,788	9,035	11,129	10,354	13,636	16,341	15,355	16,962	20,276
Net income ($ mil)	1.3%	601	473	292	355	787	566	665	480	614	675
Income as % of sales	—	6.4%	4.8%	3.2%	3.2%	7.6%	4.2%	4.1%	3.1%	3.6%	3.3%
Earnings per share ($)	0.7%	1.85	1.45	0.89	1.09	2.29	1.64	1.90	1.38	1.79	1.96
Stock price – high ($)	—	13.61	13.11	10.52	14.30	17.63	23.44	28.83	24.33	30.06	41.25
Stock price – low ($)	—	9.33	6.52	4.44	9.44	10.56	16.07	20.33	15.11	16.61	25.72
Stock price – close ($)	13.1%	13.07	6.67	10.04	12.96	16.78	23.22	22.72	16.44	26.94	39.58
P/E – high	—	7	9	12	13	8	14	15	18	17	21
P/E – low	—	5	4	5	9	5	10	11	11	9	13
Dividends per share ($)	7.2%	0.41	0.41	0.41	0.41	0.41	0.46	0.53	0.62	0.69	0.78
Book value per share ($)	10.7%	7.12	8.15	8.63	9.28	11.26	12.50	13.83	14.56	15.67	17.73

1989 Year End:
Debt ratio: 4.3%
Return on equity: 11.7%
Cash (mil): $1,863
Current ratio: 1.3
Long-term debt (mil): $275
Number of shares (mil): 346
Dividends:
1989 average yield: 2.0%
1989 payout: 39.7%
Market value (mil): $13,689

Stock Price History high/low 1980-89

NYSE symbol: BA
Incorporated: Delaware, 1934
Fiscal year ends: December 31

WHO

Chairman and CEO: Frank A. Shrontz, age 58, $910,250 pay
VC: Malcolm T. Stamper, age 64, $642,606 pay
EVP and CFO: Harold W. Haynes, age 67, $641,782 pay
EVP; President, Boeing Commercial Airplane Group: D. D. Thornton, age 61, $502,492 pay
SVP and Secretary: Douglas P. Beighle, age 57, $402,971 pay
Auditors: Deloitte & Touche
Employees: 163,900

WHERE

HQ: 7755 E. Marginal Way South, Seattle, WA 98108
Phone: 206-655-2121
FAX: 206-655-7004 (Investor Relations)

Boeing operates in the US, Europe, Asia, Oceania, Africa, and throughout the Western Hemisphere.

	1989 Sales	
	$ mil	% of total
US	9,255	46
Europe	5,429	27
Asia & Oceania	4,377	21
Other countries	1,215	6
Total	**20,276**	**100**

WHAT

	1989 Sales		1989 Operating Income	
	$ mil	% of total	$ mil	% of total
Missiles & space	1,467	7	85	12
Commercial transportation	14,305	71	1,165	162
Military transportation	3,962	19	(559)	(78)
Other	542	3	26	4
Adjustments	—	—	(136)	—
Total	**20,276**	**100**	**581**	**100**

Jet Transports

Current Production	No Longer in Production
737	707
747	720
757	727
767	

Commuter Planes
Dash 8

RANKINGS

15th in *Fortune* 500 Industrial Cos.
1st in *Fortune* 50 Exporters
21st in *Forbes* Sales 500
27th in *Business Week* 1000
59th in *Business Week* Global 1000

COMPETITION

Daimler-Benz
General Dynamics
Lockheed
Martin Marietta
McDonnell Douglas
Northrop
Rockwell International
Textron
United Technologies

BOISE CASCADE CORPORATION

OVERVIEW

Boise Cascade is the 10th largest US forest products company, based on 1989 sales. The company is a producer of paper, paper products, and wood building supplies, and a wholesale distributor of office supplies.

Boise Cascade owns approximately 2.8 million acres of timberland in the US and Canada and leases another 3.4 million. The company plants 6 seedlings for each tree that is harvested and operates its own seed orchards and nurseries. Boise Cascade also buys logs and wood chips produced on both public and private lands, the former becoming more difficult due to citizen action against corporate access to public forests.

The company experienced financial difficulties during the early 1970s due to losses from real estate and bad acquisitions, but it recovered and focused on its original businesses — building materials and paper. In 1989 capital investment reached record levels and the company announced plans to invest $450 million to upgrade coated paper–producing facilities at its Rumford, Maine, mill, with construction to start in 1991.

NYSE symbol: BCC
Incorporated: Delaware, 1931
Fiscal year ends: December 31

WHO

Chairman and CEO: John B. Fery, age 60, $1,026,672 pay
President and COO: Jon H. Miller, age 52, $791,982 pay
EVP: Peter G. Danis, Jr., age 58, $499,632 pay
EVP and CFO: George J. Harad, age 45, $464,716 pay
Auditors: Arthur Andersen & Co.
Employees: 19,539

WHEN

Idaho's Boise Cascade Corporation was incorporated in 1931 as Boise Payette Lumber Company, a producer of lumber and building materials. In 1956 company leaders decided that Boise Payette needed to boost profits by diversifying into both fields that made broader use of timber and fields that had no visible connection to timber. The company brought in Robert Hansberger, a Harvard-educated manager (1957), to oversee diversification efforts. That year Boise Payette merged with Cascade Lumber Company of Yakima, Washington, and changed its name to Boise Cascade.

In 1969 Boise Cascade purchased Ebasco Industries, which had started out as a holding company (Electric Bond & Share) and expanded into a consulting, engineering, and construction firm. By 1970 Boise Cascade had become a conglomerate through more than 30 acquisitions in building materials, paper products, land, recreational vehicles, and publishing companies. Boise Cascade's management style gave managers much individual discretion and made the company an attractive place for young college graduates to work.

In the early 1970s Boise Cascade experienced a company timber scarcity. Unlike other major timber companies, Boise Cascade had continued to rely on its access to public timberlands instead of investing in a strong reforestation program. At the same time, Boise Cascade's plans to develop recreational communities in Hawaii, Washington, and California raised so much protest by environmentally conscious residents that the company scrapped all but 6 of the 29 projects. The remaining communities required far more money than originally allocated for sewage treatment and other facilities. By 1972 the company was $1 billion in debt; it recorded a loss of $171 million that year.

When John Fery became president in 1972, he tightened the company's management style by centralizing authority and sold off most of Hansberger's acquisitions; these included the recreational vehicle businesses (1972) and the assets of its publishing companies (1973), several of which were Communications/Research/Machines, George Macy Companies, and Ebasco.

Boise Cascade's focus during the last 5 years has been on manufacturing forest products and distributing building materials and office supplies. The company has dealt with its previous timber scarcity by acquiring more land; it now owns 46% of the timberland it uses. In 1989 Boise Cascade invested $602 million to upgrade 10 paper manufacturing facilities in the northwestern and midwestern US and in Canada.

WHERE

HQ: One Jefferson Sq., PO Box 50, Boise, ID 83728
Phone: 208-384-6161
FAX: 208-384-7298

Boise Cascade's 64 mills and plants are concentrated in the US and Canada but include 2 plants in Austria and one in Germany. The company's 9 wholesale building materials units are located in 6 states. The Mega office supply division has 34 distribution centers in 23 states.

	1989 Sales		1989 Operating Income	
	$ mil	% of total	$ mil	% of total
US	4,003	92	492	84
Canada	335	8	92	16
Adjustments	—	—	(73)	—
Total	**4,338**	**100**	**511**	**100**

WHAT

	1989 Sales		1989 Operating Income	
	$ mil	% of total	$ mil	% of total
Paper & paper prods.	2,380	55	405	69
Office products	1,012	23	67	11
Building products	936	22	107	18
Other	10	—	6	1
Adjustments	—	—	(74)	—
Total	**4,338**	**100**	**511**	**100**

Paper Products
Carbonless paper
Coated paper
Containerboard
Market pulp
Newsprint
Uncoated white paper

Building Products
Lumber
Particleboard
Plywood
Wholesale distribution of other building products from various manufacturers

Office Products
Retail and catalog distribution of 20,000 office products from various manufacturers (Mega)

RANKINGS

112th in *Fortune* 500 Industrial Cos.
306th in *Fortune* Global 500 Industrial Cos.
197th in *Forbes* Sales 500
376th in *Business Week* 1000

COMPETITION

Champion International
Georgia-Pacific
International Paper
James River
Kimberly-Clark
Manville
Mead
Scott
Weyerhaeuser

HOW MUCH

	9 Yr. Growth	1980	1981	1982	1983	1984	1985	1986	1987	1988	1989
Sales ($ mil)	4.1%	3,019	3,107	2,912	3,451	3,817	3,737	3,740	3,821	4,095	4,338
Net income ($ mil)	7.8%	136	120	7	60	70	104	102	183	289	268
Income as % of sales	—	4.5%	3.9%	0.2%	1.8%	1.8%	2.8%	2.7%	4.8%	7.1%	6.2%
Earnings per share ($)	7.1%	3.07	2.70	0.16	1.25	1.44	2.11	2.02	3.64	6.15	5.70
Stock price – high ($)	—	25.50	28.95	24.15	28.42	27.00	30.60	38.92	52.12	50.00	48.00
Stock price – low ($)	—	16.20	16.95	11.85	20.70	19.50	22.35	26.70	28.80	36.00	39.75
Stock price – close ($)	9.0%	20.47	20.55	23.40	26.25	24.37	28.20	35.85	40.80	41.25	44.38
P/E – high	—	8	11	155	23	19	14	19	14	8	8
P/E – low	—	5	6	76	17	14	11	13	8	6	7
Dividends per share ($)	3.5%	1.05	1.14	1.14	1.14	1.14	1.14	1.14	1.16	1.35	1.43
Book value per share ($)	1.7%	28.74	30.09	29.15	29.10	28.92	29.90	30.34	32.41	37.34	33.52

1989 Year End:
Debt ratio: 48.7%
Return on equity: 16.1%
Cash (mil): $25
Current ratio: 1.37
Long-term debt (mil): $1,498
Number of shares (mil): 38
Dividends:
1989 average yield: 3.2%
1989 payout: 25.1%
Market value (mil): $1,684

BORDEN, INC.

OVERVIEW

Borden, popularized by Elsie the cow, is the largest US dairy products manufacturer. Dairy operations account for $2.1 billion in revenues from milk, ice cream, frozen desserts, cottage cheese, yogurt, and sour cream. Borden was also the largest worldwide pasta producer in 1989 ($658 million), with 31% of the US retail market for dry pasta. Borden is the 2nd largest salty snacks maker in North America after Frito Lay (owned by PepsiCo) and the leading producer of sweet baked snacks in West Germany. The company is a leader in 26 niche grocery markets ($1.3 billion), with such products as caramel corn, bouillon, jellies, peanut butter, and coffee creamer.

Borden's nonfood group is the world's largest wallpaper producer and also makes glue. The films and adhesives component of this group has the largest share worldwide of vinyl foodwraps and wood adhesives.

After taking a $508 million restructuring charge, the company suffered a loss of $61 million in 1989 after 9 years of steady growth. Had the charge not been taken, operating income would have increased by just over 6%.

WHEN

Galveston resident Gail Borden, Jr., founded one of Texas's first newspapers (*Telegraph and Texas Register*, dissolved 1877) and in it headlined the phrase "Remember the Alamo." Over the years his inventions included a portable bathhouse, oar-driven steamboat, and nonperishable meat biscuit, created about 1850.

His meat biscuit led to the process for which he became famous. Returning from London (1851) after accepting an award for the biscuit, Borden witnessed infant deaths from putrefied milk and decided to make nonperishable milk. His process required condensation in a vacuum to preserve the milk. It took 4 efforts (1856) and a personal commendation from Sam Houston before the patent was approved.

In 1857 Borden located in Burrville, Connecticut, as Gail Borden, Jr., and Company; his first big break came with the Civil War when the US Army placed a 500-pound order for condensed milk. It was later carried on Peary's North Pole and Annapurna expeditions. By the time of his death (1874), Borden was the leading milk condenser in the US. Renamed New York Condensed Milk, the company sold condensed milk door to door in New York City and soon added fresh milk.

The company incorporated in 1899, gaining capital from 66 initial stockholders.

Between 1928 and 1929 Borden doubled in size through the purchase of more than 90 companies, gaining operations in ice cream, cheese, and powdered milk. By 1929 Borden was one of the nation's largest food companies, and had diversified into chemicals through the purchase of glue maker Casein.

By 1937 the company had expanded internationally and branched into synthetic adhesives. By the end of WWII, Borden was well positioned internationally and in the chemicals market. However, until 1956 upper management was still focused upon dairy operations. As part of a plan to reduce dependency upon dairy revenues, Augustine Marusi, as chemical division head and later president, expanded chemical operations by buying Columbus Coated Fabrics (plastic wall coverings, molded plastic consumer goods, 1961) and Smith-Douglass (agricultural chemicals, 1964).

Expansion into salted snacks began in 1964 with the purchase of Wise Foods and Cracker Jack. In 1979 Borden bought Buckeye and Guy's Food potato chip manufacturers. As part of a massive expansion effort (62 acquisitions over a 3-year period), Borden purchased Meadow Gold dairies in 1986. Borden is selling off 1/3 of its dairy operations but continues expansion in groceries. In 1989 it bought Moore's (snack foods), Pitch 'R Pak (dessert toppings), and Labatt (pasta).

HOW MUCH

	9 Yr. Growth	1980	1981	1982	1983	1984	1985	1986	1987	1988	1989
Sales ($ mil)	5.7%	4,596	4,415	4,111	4,265	4,568	4,716	5,002	6,514	7,244	7,593
Net income ($ mil)	—	148	160	166	189	191	194	223	267	312	(61)
Income as % of sales	—	3.2%	3.6%	4.0%	4.4%	4.2%	4.1%	4.5%	4.1%	4.3%	(0.8%)
Earnings per share ($)	—	0.76	0.87	0.94	1.08	1.19	1.25	1.50	1.81	2.11	(0.41)
Stock price – high ($)	—	4.65	5.00	8.75	10.17	10.83	17.83	26.25	31.94	30.56	38.63
Stock price – low ($)	—	3.27	4.17	4.48	7.54	8.31	10.54	15.88	15.00	23.56	27.69
Stock price – close ($)	26.0%	4.29	4.67	7.94	9.42	10.79	17.21	23.44	24.75	29.63	34.38
P/E – high	—	6	6	9	9	9	14	18	18	14	—
P/E – low	—	4	5	5	7	7	8	11	8	11	—
Dividends per share ($)	12.4%	0.31	0.34	0.36	0.40	0.44	0.49	0.55	0.62	0.75	0.90
Book value per share ($)	5.4%	6.93	7.50	7.84	8.28	8.77	9.14	9.77	11.26	12.51	11.12

1989 Year End:
Debt ratio: 46.7%
Return on equity: —
Cash (mil): $104
Current ratio: 1.31
Long-term debt (mil): $1,441
Number of shares (mil): 148
Dividends:
1989 average yield: 2.6%
1989 payout: —
Market value (mil): $5,086

Stock Price History high/low 1980-89

NYSE symbol: BN
Incorporated: New Jersey, 1899
Fiscal year ends: December 31

WHO

Chairman and CEO: R. J. Ventres, age 65, $1,490,500 pay
SVP and CFO: Lawrence O. Doza, age 51, $507,000 pay
Auditors: Price Waterhouse
Employees: 46,500

WHERE

HQ: 277 Park Ave., New York, NY 10172
Phone: 212-573-4000
FAX: 212-371-2659

Borden distributes throughout the US and in Brazil, Canada, Colombia, Ecuador, France, the UK, and Germany.

	1989 Sales	
	$ mil	% of total
US	5,770	76
Foreign	1,823	24
Total	**7,593**	**100**

WHAT

	1989 Sales		1989 Operating Income	
	$ mil	% of total	$ mil	% of total
Grocery and specialty products	1,999	26	336	45
Snacks and int'l consumer products	1,721	23	171	23
Dairy	2,126	28	79	10
Packaging and industrial products	1,747	23	163	22
Restructuring charge	—	—	(508)	—
Total	**7,593**	**100**	**241**	**100**

Dairy
Borden
Eagle Brand
Frostick
Glacier Bar
Lady Borden
Lite-line
Meadow Gold
Viva

Pasta
Catelli
Creamette
DeCecco
Luxury
Pennsylvania Dutch
Prince
Red Cross
Ronco
Silver Award

Snacks
Cheez Doodles
Jays
Krunchers!
La Famous
New York Deli
Ranch Fries
Seyfert's
Wise

Niche Grocery
Bennett's
Campfire
Classico
Cracker Jack
Cremora
Fisher
Harris
Hilton's
Kava
MacDonald's
MBT
None Such
Ocean Fresh
Orleans
ReaLemon
ReaLime
Snow's
Soup Starter
Wyler's

Nonfoods
Elmer's
Fill 'N Finish
Invisible Glove
Krazy Glue
Slide-All
Stix-All

RANKINGS

60th in *Fortune* 500 Industrial Cos.
169th in *Fortune* Global 500 Industrial Cos.
103rd in *Forbes* 500 Sales
133rd in *Business Week* 1000
360th in *Business Week* Global 1000

COMPETITION

Anheuser-Busch
Archer-Daniels-Midland
Associated Milk Producters
Beatrice
BSN
CPC International
General Mills
Grand Metropolitan
Hershey
Kellogg
Nestlé
PepsiCo
Philip Morris
Procter & Gamble
RJR Nabisco
TLC Beatrice
USG
Whitman

BORG-WARNER CORPORATION

OVERVIEW

Borg-Warner is a privately owned manufacturer of automobile parts and the leading provider of protective and security services. Merrill Lynch Capital Partners, a subsidiary of Merrill Lynch, now controls the company, having acquired 89% of company stock in a 1987 LBO.

The company's automotive segment produces a variety of drivetrain components for auto makers around the globe and is the international leader in the production of automotive chain. Since its inception, Borg-Warner has produced more than 50 million automatic and manual transmissions and overdrives. Approximately 30% of the company's 1989 sales were to Ford and General Motors. Borg-Warner is the sole supplier of transmissions to Ford.

Engineering, the heart of Borg-Warner's automotive operations, keeps the company at the forefront of technology. The company has been a sponsor of the Indianapolis 500 since 1936 and annually awards the coveted Borg-Warner trophy, a symbol of automotive excellence.

Borg-Warner's protective services subsidiary, Baker Industries (57% of sales), provides armored transportation, alarm systems, courier services, security guards, investigative services, and fire detection systems under the Wells Fargo, Burns, and Pony Express service marks.

Private company
Incorporated: Delaware, 1967
Fiscal year ends: December 31

WHO

Chairman and CEO: James F. Beré, age 67, $1,450,000 pay
VP Finance & Strategy: Donald C. Trauscht, age 56, $700,000 pay
Auditors: Deloitte & Touche
Employees: 70,000

WHERE

HQ: 200 S. Michigan Ave., Chicago, IL 60604
Phone: 312-322-8500
FAX: 312-322-8849 (main office)

The company's automotive segment maintains manufacturing, sales, and engineering operations in 9 countries. The protective services group operates in 5 countries.

	1989 Sales		1989 Operating Income	
	$ mil	% of total	$ mil	% of total
US	1,961	89	152	85
Europe	149	7	16	9
Canada	67	3	10	5
Other foreign	33	1	2	1
Adjustments	6	—	(30)	—
Total	**2,216**	**100**	**150**	**100**

WHAT

	1989 Sales		1989 Operating Income	
	$ mil	% of total	$ mil	% of total
Automotive	958	43	94	47
Protective services	1,252	57	86	43
Divested operations	6	—	21	10
Adjustments	—	—	(51)	—
Total	**2,216**	**100**	**150**	**100**

Automotive Products
Automatic transmissions
Automatic transmission components
- Actuators
- Bands
- Dampers
- Electronic sensors
- Engine control devices
- Engine timing systems
- Friction plates
- Solenoids
- Torque converters
- Transfer cases for four-wheel drive vehicles

Drive chains
Industrial transmissions
Manual transmissions
Marine transmissions

Protective Services
Burns
- Investigative services
- Security guards

Pony Express
- Courier services

Wells Fargo
- Alarm services
- Armored transport
- Investigative services
- Security guards
- Security systems

WHEN

Borg-Warner was formed in 1928 when 4 major auto parts companies (Borg & Beck, clutches; Warner Gear, transmissions; Mechanics Universal Joint; and Marvel Carburetor) merged in Chicago. In 1929 Borg-Warner acquired numerous other companies, including Ingersoll Steel & Disc (agricultural blades and discs) and Norge (refrigerators).

The Great Depression struck shortly after Borg-Warner's formation. The company weathered the crisis largely through the contributions of its Norge and Ingersoll divisions. In the late 1930s Borg-Warner purchased several companies including Calumet Steel (1935) and US Pressed Steel (1937).

In the early 1940s the company geared for wartime production and manufactured parts for planes, trucks, and tanks. In 1941 the company received a Navy contract to build amphibious tanks for use in the Pacific. Between 1942 and 1945 Borg-Warner produced more than 1.6 million automotive transmissions, leaving the company in a good position to manufacture transmissions for the growing automobile industry at the end of WWII. In 1948 Borg-Warner received a contract from Ford to build 1/2 of its transmissions. The contract resulted in massive growth for the company.

In 1950 Roy Ingersoll, president of the Ingersoll Steel & Disc division, assumed leadership of Borg-Warner and embarked on a major diversification program. In 1953 the company developed Cycolac, a thermoplastic resin with numerous consumer applications (including telephone casings, car interiors, aircraft fittings, and sporting goods). In 1956 Borg-Warner purchased several companies including York (air conditioning and refrigeration), Humphreys Manufacturing, Industrial Crane & Hoist, Dittmer Gear, and the Chemical Process Company.

Diversification continued into the 1960s and 1970s with several acquisitions that took Borg-Warner into foreign markets. In 1968 James Beré became president and continued to expand the company away from its core businesses. Key acquisitions during this time included Recold Corporation (refrigeration, 1966), Owens Plastics (1966), Precision Automotive Components (1966), E.W. Twitchell (fiber and paper products, 1967), H. Robert Industries (institutional products and furniture, 1970), and Unit Parts (auto parts, 1972). In 1978 the company bought Baker (fire-fighting equipment and protective services) for $123 million. Norge, which had added washers and dryers, was sold to Fedders Corporation for $20 million in 1968, and in 1980 the company sold its Ingersoll Products division to a group of investors led by Jack Maxwell.

In 1987 Borg-Warner was threatened by a takeover from Irwin Jacobs and Samuel Heyman until Merrill Lynch Capital Partners organized an LBO and took the company private, assuming $4.5 billion in debt. Following the LBO, the company sold many of its divisions to pay the newly acquired debt. The company sold its chemical group to General Electric for $2.3 billion in 1988 and its Chilton unit (credit information services) to TRW for $330 million in 1989.

HOW MUCH

	9 Yr. Growth	1980	1981	1982	1983	1984	1985	1986	1987	1988	1989
Sales ($ mil)	(2.1%)	2,673	2,761	3,195	3,542	3,916	3,330	3,379	2,957	2,145	2,216
Net income ($ mil)	(12.9%)	126	172	167	183	206	180	155	2	(3)	36
Income as % of sales	—	4.7%	6.2%	5.2%	5.2%	5.3%	5.4%	4.6%	0.1%	(0.2%)	1.6%

1989 Year End:
Debt ratio: 59.4%
Return on equity: —
Cash (mil): $20
Current ratio: 0.9
Long-term debt (mil): $926

RANKINGS

55th in *Forbes* 400 US Private Cos.

COMPETITION

Allied-Signal
Cooper Industries
Dana
Eaton
JWP

BOSTON CELTICS LP

OVERVIEW

Boston Celtics Limited Partnership operates what its fans hail as the most successful sports franchise ever. The team boasts 16 National Basketball Association titles, 17 Hall-of-Famers, and 15 Most Valuable Players.

The partnership consists of 3 men — Don Gaston, Alan Cohen, and Paul Dupee, Jr. — who own stock in a corporation that serves as the general partner, and approximately 60,000 public shareholders with about 44% of the partnership units.

The team generates its revenues through a combination of home game ticket sales; licensing of TV, cable, and radio rights; and the merchandising of the Celtics' name.

The Celtics play most of their home games in the historic 14,890-seat Boston Garden arena (the Garden) in downtown Boston, which the team rents from the New Boston Garden Corporation.

In Boston, where they must compete for attention with the Red Sox (baseball), Bruins (hockey), and Patriots (football), the Celtics maintain their hometown popularity with a winning tradition and by showcasing such basketball legends as Bill Russell and Larry Bird.

NYSE symbol: BOS
Incorporated: Delaware, 1986
Fiscal year ends: June 30

WHO

Chairman: Don F. Gaston, age 55
President: Arnold "Red" Auerbach, age 72, $290,000 pay
EVP and General Manager: Jan Volk, age 42, $233,000 pay
VP Finance: Joseph G. DiLorenzo, age 33, $73,000 pay
Head of Basketball Operations: Dave Gavitt, age 52
Head Coach: Chris Ford, age 41
Auditors: Ernst & Young
Employees: 39

WHEN

Walter Brown founded the Boston Celtics basketball team (so-named partially because of Brown's Irish background) in 1946. After 4 initial losing seasons, Brown hired Arnold "Red" Auerbach as head coach in 1950.

Auerbach quickly turned the Celtics into a competitive organization by acquiring such players as Bob Cousy, Chuck Cooper (the first black player in the NBA), Bill Sharman, and Frank Ramsey. Although the Celtics improved tremendously during Auerbach's first 6 years as head coach, the team was unable to win an NBA title.

The turning point came in 1956, when Auerbach traded 2 players to the St. Louis Hawks for a first-round draft pick that turned out to be Bill Russell. Around Russell's gifted play, Auerbach created the greatest dynasty in basketball history, winning 9 NBA championships (8 in a row) between 1956 and 1966. Auerbach stepped down as coach to become the team's general manager in 1966. Russell assumed coaching responsibilities (the first black NBA coach) and led the team to 2 additional titles in 1968 and 1969.

During the early 1970s, under new coach Tom Heinsohn, the team restructured and, with the talents of players like John Havlicek, Don Nelson, Jo Jo White, and Dave Cowens, took NBA titles in 1974 and 1976. By the late 1970s, however, the team had slipped into last place, and Brown sold his interest to Harry Mangurian.

During the 1979-1980 season the team registered another major turnaround, due largely to the efforts of 1978 draft choice Larry Bird. With the assistance of players like Kevin McHale and Robert Parish, the Celtics won their 14th title in 1981.

In 1983 Mangurian sold control of the team to a triumvirate consisting of Don Gaston, Paul Dupee, Jr., and Alan Cohen. K. C. Jones became head coach in 1983 and led the team to titles in 1984 and 1986.

In late 1986 the 3 owners established a limited partnership and offered 2.6 million shares of stock at $18 each to the public (a first for a pro franchise). Approximately 2/3 of the buyers were fans who purchased 10 or fewer shares. The offering yielded gains of over $100 million for the 3 principal shareholders.

In 1989 the Celtics purchased Boston-based station WFXT-TV (from Fox Television) and radio station WEEI (from Helen Broadcasting). In 1990, after a disappointing season, the Celtics fired coach Jim Rodgers. Rodgers's assistant, Chris Ford, was named coach.

WHERE

HQ: 150 Causeway St., Boston, MA 02114
Phone: 617-523-6050
FAX: 617-523-5949

The team plays the majority of its 41 regular-season home games at the Boston Garden arena in downtown Boston but also plays some games at the civic center in nearby Hartford, Connecticut.

WHAT

	1989 Sales	
	$ mil	% of total
Ticket sales	15	56
Television, cable & radio	11	41
Advertising, other	1	3
Total	**27**	**100**

	Scoring 1989		
	made	att'd	%
Field goals	3475	7183	.484
3-point field goals	133	459	.290
Free throws	1780	2294	.776

Rebounds (1989)
Offensive rebounds (1048)
Defensive rebounds (2222)
Total rebounds (3270)

Players
John Bagley (#5, Guard)
Scooter Barry (#12, Guard)
Larry Bird (#33, Forward)
Kevin Gamble (#34, Guard/Forward)
Dennis Johnson (#3, Guard)
Joe Kleine (#53, Center)
Reggie Lewis (#35, Guard/Forward)
Kevin McHale (#32, Forward/Center)
Robert Parish (#00, Center)
Jim Paxson (#4, Guard)
Ed Pinckney (#54, Forward)
Dave Popson (#42, Forward)
Charles Smith (#13, Guard)
Michael Smith (#11, Forward)
Kelvin Upshaw (#7, Guard)

The Celtics also operate television station WFXT-TV and radio station WEEI in Boston.

HOW MUCH

	3 Yr. Growth	1980	1981	1982	1983	1984	1985	1986	1987	1988	1989
Sales ($ mil)	7.1%	—	—	—	—	—	—	22	27	28	27
Net income ($ mil)	—	—	—	—	—	—	—	5	7	10	12
Income as % of sales	—	—	—	—	—	—	—	21.7%	26.6%	36.4%	44.6%
Earnings per share ($)	—	—	—	—	—	—	—	—	—	1.59	1.88
Stock price – high ($)	—	—	—	—	—	—	—	18.38	16.13	15.75	19.50
Stock price – low ($)	—	—	—	—	—	—	—	15.25	10.38	11.63	13.50
Stock price – close ($)	4.8%	—	—	—	—	—	—	15.75	11.50	13.75	18.13
P/E – high	—	—	—	—	—	—	—	—	—	10	10
P/E – low	—	—	—	—	—	—	—	—	—	7	7
Dividends per share ($)	—	—	—	—	—	—	—	0.00	0.70	1.60	1.60
Book value per share ($)	—	—	—	—	—	—	—	58.11	—	—	—

1989 Year End:
Debt ratio: 0.0%
Return on equity: —
Cash (mil): $8
Current ratio: 1.69
Long-term debt (mil): $0
Number of shares (mil): 6
Dividends:
1989 average yield: 8.8%
1989 payout: 85.1%
Market value (mil): $117

Stock Price History high/low 1986-89

RANKINGS

3rd in Eastern Conference, Atlantic Division

COMPETITION

Paramount
Turner Broadcasting

BRIDGESTONE CORPORATION

OVERVIEW

Bridgestone is the world's 2nd largest tire maker after Michelin and is #1 in Japan and #3 in the US. The company is also Japan's largest bicycle manufacturer and makes sporting goods, lithium batteries, weighing systems, and various rubber products. Bridgestone operates 1,550 MasterCare auto service centers in North America through its Firestone subsidiary. The company houses one of the world's largest private collections of Impressionist art in its Tokyo museum.

Bridgestone President Akira Yeiri has stated his belief that only 3 tire companies will survive in the world market. By buying Firestone, Bridgestone secured a large piece of the North American tire market and kept up with Michelin and Goodyear in global market share.

Bridgestone hopes to replicate the success of its LaVergne, Tennessee, plant by investing heavily in Firestone factories and involving employees in decision-making.

General Motors's decision to stop buying Firestone tires in 1991 poses a formidable challenge for Bridgestone in the US.

Principal stock exchange: Tokyo
Incorporated: Japan, 1931
Fiscal year ends: December 31

WHO

Chairman: Teiji Eguchi
President: Akira Yeiri, age 61
SVP Corporate Administration, Sports, and New Business: Takeshi Kakudo
VP Accounting, Treasury, Purchasing, and Information Systems: Akihiro Ono
Auditors: Asahi Shinwa & Co.
Employees: 93,193

WHEN

In 1906 on the southern Japanese island of Kyushu, Shojiro Ishibashi and his brother, Tokujiro Ishibashi, assumed control of their family's clothing business. They focused on making *tabi*, traditional Japanese footwear, and in 1923 they began working with rubber for soles. In 1931 Shojiro Ishibashi formed Bridgestone (Ishibashi means "stone bridge" in Japanese) to make tires. In the 1930s Bridgestone began producing auto tires, airplane tires, and golf balls. The company followed the Japanese military to occupied territories and built plants there. Ishibashi moved Bridgestone's headquarters to Tokyo in 1937.

Although Bridgestone lost all of its overseas factories in WWII, the Japanese plants escaped damage. The company began making bicycles (1946) and signed a technical assistance pact with Goodyear (1952), enabling Bridgestone to import badly needed technology. In the 1950s and 1960s Bridgestone started making nylon tires and radials and again set up facilities overseas, mostly in Asia. The company benefited from the rapid growth in Japanese auto sales in the 1970s. Shojiro Ishibashi died at age 87 in 1976.

In 1983 Bridgestone bought a plant in LaVergne, Tennessee, from the venerable US tiremaker Firestone. Harvey Firestone had founded his tire business in 1900 and expanded with the auto industry in the US. In the 1920s he leased one million acres in Liberia for rubber plantations and established a chain of auto supply and service outlets. After WWII Firestone started making synthetic rubber and various automotive components, expanded overseas, and acquired US tire producers Dayton Tire & Rubber and Seiberling. In the 1980s Firestone chairman John Nevin sought to maximize shareholder return by cutting costs, holding back on new investment in plants, and focusing on retail operations. The company began disposing of its inefficient production facilities.

Bridgestone had strong OEM sales to Japanese carmakers but little US retail exposure to the more lucrative aftermarket and no US production capacity prior to the purchase of the Firestone plant. In 1989 the 2 companies agreed to form a venture in which Bridgestone would be the majority owner of Firestone's tire manufacturing business. Soon after, Pirelli (tires, Italy) made a takeover bid for Firestone. Bridgestone topped the bid and bought Firestone for $2.6 billion, the most ever paid by a Japanese company for a US manufacturer. Simultaneously, General Motors announced that Firestone, then accounting for 21.5% of GM tire purchases, would be dropped as a supplier in 1991.

WHERE

HQ: 10-1, Kyobashi 1-chome, Chuo-ku, Tokyo 104, Japan
Phone: 011-81-3-567-0111
FAX: 011-81-3-535-2553
US HQ (Bridgestone USA, Inc.): One Bridgestone Park, PO Box 140991, Nashville, TN 37214
US Phone: 615-391-0088
US FAX: 615-872-2629

Bridgestone has manufacturing facilities on 6 continents and sells its products worldwide. US manufacturing plants are located in LaVergne and Morrison, TN; Decatur, IL; Wilson, NC; Des Moines, IA; Oklahoma City, OK; and Russellville, AR.

	1989 Sales	
	¥ bil	% of total
Japan	689	41
Other countries	1000	59
Total	**1,689**	**100**

WHAT

	1989 Sales	
	¥ bil	% of total
Tire operations	1,272	75
Other products	417	25
Total	**1,689**	**100**

Products

Batteries
Bicycles (Bridgestone)
Ceramic foam
Golf and tennis equip.
Industrial rubber prods.
- Belts and hoses
- Inflatable rubber dams
- Marine products
- Multi-rubber bearings
- Rubber crawlers
- Vibration-isolating and noise-insulating materials

Waterproofing materials
Polyurethane foam products
Roofing and flooring materials
Steel fiber for concrete reinforcement
Tires (Bridgestone, Firestone)
Water tanks
Weighing systems
Wheels

Retailing

MasterCare auto service centers

HOW MUCH

$ = ¥144 (Dec. 31,1989)	9 Yr. Growth	1980	1981	1982	1983	1984	1985	1986	1987	1988	1989
Sales (¥ bil)	10.6%	681	724	712	762	802	864	793	820	1,191	1,689
Net income (¥ mil)	(11.3%)	28,446	15,844	13,002	18,524	15,763	21,084	21,006	36,001	39,960	9,685
Income as % of sales	—	4.2%	2.2%	1.8%	2.4%	2.0%	2.4%	2.6%	4.4%	3.4%	0.6%
Earnings per share (¥)	(11.5%)	39	23	20	28	24	32	30	54	59	13
Stock price – high (¥)	—	408	473	411	530	544	484	646	1,318	1,436	2,070
Stock price – low (¥)	—	349	352	330	360	421	412	421	545	1,036	1,330
Stock price – close (¥)	18.7%	360	356	405	530	426	431	599	1,045	1,360	1,690
P/E – high	—	10	21	21	19	23	15	22	24	24	159
P/E – low	—	9	15	17	13	18	13	14	10	18	10
Dividends per share (¥)	6.5%	6.8	7.5	8.3	8.3	8.3	8.3	8.3	8.3	10.0	12.0
Book value per share (¥)	6.5%	325	343	360	381	394	417	440	482	527	574

1989 Year End:
Debt ratio: 29.6%
Return on equity: 2.4%
Cash (bil): ¥111
Long-term debt (bil): ¥185
Number of shares (bil): 765
Dividends:
1989 average yield: 0.7%
1989 payout: 92.3%
Market value (mil): $8,978
Sales (mil): $11,729

Stock Price History high/low 1980-89

2,500
2,000
1,500
1,000
500
0

RANKINGS

84th in *Fortune* Global 500 Industrial Cos.
30th in *Forbes* 100 Foreign Investments in the US
214th in *Business Week* Global 1000

COMPETITION

Goodyear
Michelin
Sears

BRISTOL-MYERS SQUIBB COMPANY

OVERVIEW

Bristol-Myers Squibb is the 2nd largest drug company in the world after Merck in terms of prescription drug sales. The company is first worldwide in anticancer drugs and treatments for high blood pressure. The blood pressure drug Capoten is one of 5 in the world with sales of over $1 billion annually. The company has a #1 brand (including Clairol, Windex, and Vanish) in 15 of 21 consumer categories in the US. Bufferin is #1 in Japan. The company is the largest maker of orthopedic implants and the 2nd largest producer of infant formula.

Bristol-Myers Squibb spent 8.6% of sales on R&D in 1989. The company is developing new treatments for hypertension, cancer, infections (including an AIDS vaccine), anxiety, depression, and skin diseases. It is also seeking FDA approval for drugs now sold overseas.

Under a special program approved by the FDA, the company provides Videx (DDI), currently undergoing clinical trials, to AIDS patients unresponsive to AZT.

NYSE symbol: BMY
Incorporated: Delaware, 1933
Fiscal year ends: December 31

WHO

Chairman and CEO: Richard L. Gelb, age 65, $1,687,700 pay
VC: William R. Miller, age 61, $989,200 pay
President: Richard M. Furlaud, age 66
EVP and CFO: Michael E. Autera, age 51, $648,100 pay
Auditors: Price Waterhouse
Employees: 54,100

WHEN

Competitors for many years, Bristol-Myers and Squibb both have origins in the 19th century. Squibb is one of the oldest American drug firms, founded by Edward Squibb in New York City in 1858. A navy doctor who developed his own techniques for making pure ether and chloroform, Squibb headed the business most of his life, turning it over to his sons in 1891. Theodore Weicker, one of Merck's founders, bought a major interest in Squibb in 1905.

Sales of $414,000 in 1904 grew to $13 million by 1928. Squibb was a major supplier of penicillin and morphine during WWII. By 1951 sales were $100 million. In 1952 the company was bought by Mathieson Chemical and then by Olin Industries in 1953 to form the Olin Mathieson Chemical Corporation.

In 1968 Squibb was spun off to shareholders, then merged with Beech-Nut (baby food, Life Savers candy); Squibb Beech-Nut bought Lanvin-Charles of the Ritz (cosmetics) in 1971 and changed the name to the Squibb Corporation. Other than pharmaceuticals, the most profitable product of the new company proved to be Life Savers. By 1975 sales had reached $1 billion. Capoten and Corgard, 2 major cardiovascular drugs, were introduced in the late 1970s. Capoten was the first drug developed by the method of "rational design" (*i.e.*, to attack a specific disease-causing mechanism), rather than by the traditional method of trial and error. In a restructuring, the company sold Lanvin-Charles of the Ritz to Yves Saint Laurent and Life Savers to Standard Brands in the 1980s. Squibb formed a joint venture with Denmark's Novo in 1982 to sell insulin.

Bristol-Myers originated as Clinton Pharmaceutical of Clinton, New York, founded by William Bristol and John Myers in 1887 (renamed Bristol-Myers in 1900). The company sold bulk pharmaceuticals to doctors and druggists. Bristol-Myers made tetracycline, penicillin, and other antibiotics after the 1943 purchase of Cheplin Biological Labs (renamed Bristol Labs).

The company began overseas expansion in the 1950s with the purchase of English and German drug and chemical companies. In 1959 Bristol-Myers bought Clairol. Subsequent acquisitions included Drackett (Windex, Drano, 1965), Mead Johnson (drugs, infant and nutritional formula, 1967), and Zimmer (orthopedic implants, 1972). Bufferin, Excedrin, Ban, and hair care products accounted for nearly 1/2 of Bristol-Myers's sales by the late 1970s. Bristol-Myers introduced new drugs for treating cancer (Platinol, 1978) and a new type of antianxiety drug (BuSpar, 1986). In 1986 the company acquired the biotech companies Oncogen and Genetic Systems. *Fortune* rated the October 1989 buyout of Squibb by Bristol-Myers for $12.7 billion as the 2nd biggest "Deal of the Year" for 1989 (after $25 billion RJR/Nabisco).

WHERE

HQ: 345 Park Ave., New York, NY 10154
Phone: 212-546-4000
FAX: 212-546-4020

Bristol-Myers Squibb has facilities in 12 countries and sells products globally.

	1989 Sales		1989 Operating Income	
	$ mil	% of total	$ mil	% of total
US	6,478	63	1,259	77
Other Western Hemisphere	769	8	119	7
Europe, Mid-East & Africa	2,127	21	228	14
Pacific	789	8	40	2
Adjustments	(974)	—	292	—
Total	**9,189**	**100**	**1,938**	**100**

WHAT

	1989 Sales		1989 Operating Income	
	$ mil	% of total	$ mil	% of total
Prescription drugs	4,442	48	703	45
Medical devices	1,227	14	282	18
Consumer health products	1,662	18	349	23
Toiletries, household prods.	1,858	20	215	14
Adjustments	—	—	389	—
Total	**9,189**	**100**	**1,938**	**100**

Pharmaceuticals
AIDS Test: GENIE HIV-1
Anti-AIDS
Antibiotics
Anticancer
Dry skin
High blood pressure
High cholesterol
Mental health

Nutritionals
Enfamil
Gerber
Isocál
Nutrament

Consumer Products
Ban
Drano
Miss Clairol
Renuzit
Theragran-M
Vanish
Vitalis
Windex

Nonprescription Drugs
Bufferin
Comtrex
Excedrin
Nuprin

HOW MUCH

	9 Yr. Growth	1980	1981	1982	1983	1984	1985	1986	1987	1988	1989
Sales ($ mil)	12.6%	3,158	3,497	3,600	3,917	4,189	4,444	4,836	5,401	5,973	9,189
Net income ($ mil)	11.9%	271	306	349	408	472	531	590	710	829	747
Income as % of sales	—	8.6%	8.7%	9.7%	10.4%	11.3%	12.0%	12.2%	13.1%	13.9%	8.1%
Earnings per share ($)	4.0%	1.00	1.12	1.27	1.48	1.70	1.90	2.03	2.43	2.85	1.41
Stock price – high ($)	—	13.00	14.69	18.50	23.94	26.31	34.25	44.25	55.81	46.50	58.00
Stock price – low ($)	—	7.63	11.44	12.69	15.59	20.50	24.50	30.13	28.25	38.13	44.00
Stock price – close ($)	18.0%	12.59	13.28	16.81	21.13	26.19	33.13	41.31	41.63	45.25	56.00
P/E – high	—	13	13	15	16	16	18	22	23	16	41
P/E – low	—	8	10	10	11	12	13	15	12	13	31
Dividends per share ($)	23.7%	0.30	0.45	0.51	0.73	0.80	0.94	1.18	1.05	2.18	2.03
Book value per share ($)	7.1%	5.23	5.88	6.34	7.00	7.82	8.88	9.91	11.23	12.33	9.68

1989 Year End:
Debt ratio: 4.5%
Return on equity: 12.8%
Cash (mil): $2,282
Current ratio: 2.09
Long-term debt (mil): $237
Number of shares (mil): 525
Dividends:
1989 average yield: 3.6%
1989 payout: 144.0%
Market value (mil): $29,419

Stock Price History high/low 1980-89

RANKINGS

50th in the *Fortune* 500 Industrial Cos.
132nd in *Fortune* Global 500 Industrial Cos.
85th in *Forbes* Sales 500
8th in *Business Week* 1000
21st in *Business Week* Global 1000

COMPETITION

American Cyanamid
American Home Products
Bayer
Clorox
Dow Chemical
Du Pont
Eastman Kodak
Eli Lilly
Genentech
Glaxo
Hoechst
Johnson & Johnson
Merck
Monsanto
Nestlé
Pfizer
Procter & Gamble
Rhône-Poulenc
Roche Holding
Schering-Plough
SmithKline Beecham
Upjohn
Warner-Lambert

THE BRITISH PETROLEUM COMPANY PLC

OVERVIEW

British Petroleum (BP) is the world's 4th largest international oil company after Exxon, Royal Dutch/Shell, and Mobil. The company leads the US and UK in oil production, deriving most of its output from holdings in Alaska and the North Sea. BP is a world leader in petrochemicals and animal feeds and owns 50% of the Trans Alaska Pipeline System.

BP markets products in over 50 countries and sells its gasoline through 22,000 service stations. The company's green and yellow logo will be increasingly evident in the US as BP America, formerly the Standard Oil Company of Ohio (SOHIO), continues to convert its 7,700 US service stations to the BP brand.

New BP chairman Robert Horton has slashed corporate staffing levels and announced his intention to focus on BP's core businesses, emphasize marketing and refining, and expand operations in Asia and Eastern Europe.

WHEN

After negotiating an extensive oil concession with the Grand Vizier in Persia, English adventurer William Knox D'Arcy began exploration in 1901. In 1908, with additional capital from Burmah Oil, D'Arcy's company became the first to strike oil in the Middle East. D'Arcy and Burmah Oil formed Anglo-Persian Oil Company in 1909 to exploit the enormous find. At Winston Churchill's urging, the British government purchased a 51% interest in cash-hungry Anglo-Persian in 1914.

Anglo-Persian had interests in the first major oil discoveries in Iraq (1927) and Kuwait (1938). In 1928, facing a potential oil glut, the company and its major competitors entered into a secret "As Is" agreement, fixing worldwide production and prices with some success for 2 decades.

While other oil companies were negotiating "50-50" deals with producer nations, Chairman Sir William Fraser refused to renegotiate the company's more lucrative concession with Iran. In 1951 its Iranian assets were seized. Following the 1953 coup that installed the Shah, an international consortium resumed business under a new concession in which the company was allowed a 40% interest. In 1954 the company changed its name to British Petroleum. The Khomeini regime ended foreign participation in Iranian oil production in 1979.

BP made major strikes in Prudhoe Bay, Alaska, in 1969 and in the North Sea in 1970. In 1970 BP swapped its Alaskan reserves for an eventual 55% interest in SOHIO. From 1979 to 1981 SOHIO invested its huge Alaskan oil profits in exploration and nonoil acquisitions, including Kennecott Copper (1981). Declining oil and copper prices in the mid-1980s, in addition to a large interest in a $1.7 billion dry hole in the Beaufort Sea, led to disappointing earnings. In 1986 BP appointed Robert Horton CEO of SOHIO. Horton ("the hatchet") cut SOHIO overhead and sold poorly performing units.

Britain acquired an additional 20.15% of BP in 1975, then reduced its holdings through public offerings in 1977 and 1979, finally selling its remaining shares in 1987.

Under the direction of Sir Peter Walters (knighted in 1984) from 1981 to 1990, BP purchased Purina Mills (1986), the remaining shares of SOHIO (1987), and Britoil (1988), a large North Sea oil and gas producer. BP sold most of its minerals businesses, including the remaining assets of Kennecott, to RTZ and $1.3 billion in oil properties to Oryx in 1989. In the same year, under pressure from the UK Monopolies and Mergers Commission, the Kuwaiti government reduced its holdings in BP from 21.6% to 9.9% of common stock, selling to the company shares acquired from the underwriters of the 1987 offering.

HOW MUCH

	9 Yr. Growth	1980	1981	1982	1983	1984	1985	1986	1987	1988	1989
Sales ($ mil)	(0.2%)	49,368	49,192	47,524	47,122	50,830	53,281	39,941	45,228	46,141	48,611
Net income ($ mil)	(2.0%)	3,430	2,047	1,160	1,257	1,878	2,077	1,201	2,281	2,154	2,860
Income as % of sales	—	6.9%	4.2%	2.4%	2.7%	3.7%	3.9%	3.0%	5.0%	4.7%	5.9%
Earnings per share ($)	(3.7%)	8.76	4.88	2.56	2.76	4.12	4.54	2.62	4.92	4.32	6.24
Stock price – high ($)	—	48.00	39.63	23.75	27.25	30.00	35.13	43.75	80.38	63.75	65.88
Stock price – low ($)	—	26.13	17.88	17.50	18.00	21.75	21.38	30.13	43.25	48.25	53.63
Stock price – close ($)	5.8%	39.25	23.75	18.88	23.63	22.63	32.38	43.50	55.88	53.75	65.38
P/E – high	—	5	8	9	10	7	8	17	16	15	11
P/E – low	—	3	4	7	7	5	5	12	9	11	9
Dividends per share ($)	10.9%	1.97	2.33	2.01	1.83	2.07	2.37	2.87	3.41	3.86	4.99
Book value per share ($)	1.0%	35.60	32.44	30.80	30.66	29.32	31.39	32.19	40.67	41.00	39.02

1989 Year End:
Debt ratio: 34.8%
Return on equity: 15.6%
Cash (mil): $675
Current ratio: 0.96
Long-term debt (mil): $9,271
Number of shares (mil): 445
Dividends:
1989 average yield: 7.6%
1989 payout: 79.9%
Market value (mil): $29,060

NYSE symbol: BP (ADR)
Incorporated: England, 1909
Fiscal year ends: December 31

WHO

Chairman and CEO: Robert B. Horton, age 50
Deputy Chairman, COO, and CFO: David A. G. Simon, age 50
Auditors: Ernst & Young
Employees: 119,850

WHERE

HQ: Britannic House, Moor Ln., London EC2Y 9BU, England
Phone: 011-44-71-920-8000
FAX: 011-44-71-920-2810 (Investor Relations)
US HQ (BP America Inc.): 200 Public Sq., Cleveland, OH 44114
US Phone: 216-586-4141
US FAX: 216-586-8066 (Investor Relations)

BP produces oil and gas in 13 countries and is engaged in exploration for reserves in more than 30 countries. The company's markets are worldwide.

	1989 Sales		1989 Net Income	
	$ mil	% of total	$ mil	% of total
UK	12,867	26	1,269	26
Europe	13,873	29	882	18
US	16,298	34	2,188	46
Other countries	5,573	11	477	10
Adjustments	—	—	(1,956)	—
Total	**48,611**	**100**	**2,860**	**100**

WHAT

	1989 Sales		1989 Operating Income	
	$ mil	% of total	$ mil	% of total
Coal	961	2	62	1
Nutrition	3,710	7	71	1
Refining & marketing	33,781	60	1,200	25
Exploration & production	11,242	20	2,581	54
Chemicals	5,745	10	886	18
Other & corporate	489	1	16	1
Adjustments	(7,317)	—	(1,317)	—
Total	**48,611**	**100**	**3,500**	**100**

Products and Services
Animal feeds
Chemicals and plastics
Coal mining
Crude oil and natural gas
Fueling services for the shipping and airline industries
Petroleum refining and marketing
Service stations, convenience stores

RANKINGS

10th in *Fortune* Global 500 Industrial Cos.
3rd in *Forbes* 100 Foreign Investments in the US
25th in *Business Week* Global 1000

COMPETITION

Amoco
Ashland
Atlantic Richfield
Chevron
Coastal
Du Pont
Exxon
Mobil
Occidental
Pennzoil
Phillips
Royal Dutch/Shell
Sun
Texaco
Unocal
Animal feed producers
Chemical and mining companies

BROKEN HILL PROPRIETARY COMPANY LTD.

OVERVIEW

Broken Hill Proprietary (BHP), Australia's largest public company, is an international resources concern with primary operations in steel, minerals, and petroleum.

With an annual production of 6.2 million metric tons, BHP generates over 80% of Australia's steel requirements. Twenty-two percent of steel revenues come from sales outside the country. BHP is a world leader in some of the high value-added steel products, including coated steels.

The company's Minerals Group is one of the largest and most successful global mining operations. Most of the production comes from the BHP-Utah Minerals International group which mines coal, iron ore, manganese, gold, copper, and other minerals, primarily in Australia (76%) and the US (10%).

BHP Petroleum explores for, produces, refines, and markets oil and natural gas in Australia's Bass Strait, Timor Sea, and North West Shelf; the US; and the North Sea. It claims reserves that rank it among the top 15 non–government-owned oil companies. Production of crude oil, propane, and dry gas totaled the equivalent of 308.1 million barrels in fiscal 1989.

NYSE symbol: BHP (ADR)
Incorporated: Victoria, Australia 1885
Fiscal year ends: May 31

WHO

Chairman: Sir Arvi Parbo, age 64
Deputy Chairman, Managing Director, and CEO: Brian T. Loton, age 61
Executive General Manager, Finance: G. E. Heeley, age 55
Auditors: Ernst & Young and Arthur Andersen & Co.
Employees: 49,000

WHERE

HQ: BHP House, 140 William St., Melbourne, Victoria 3000 Australia
Phone: 011-61-3-609-3333
FAX: 011-61-3-609-3015

The company has operations in more than 20 countries.

	1989 Sales	
	$ mil	% of total
Australia	4,647	53
North America	1,490	17
Japan	1,126	13
Other	1,569	17
Adjustment	(945)	—
Total	**7,887**	**100**

WHEN

In 1883 Charles Rasp, a boundary rider for the Mt. Gipps sheep station, discovered a massive lode of silver, lead, and zinc in the Broken Hill outcrop in New South Wales, Australia. The Broken Hill Proprietary Company was incorporated in 1885 to mine the ore, and 2 years later the company discovered iron ore deposits in southern Australia. By the early 1890s BHP was paying over £1 million a year in dividends.

Until 1915 the company mined, smelted, and refined iron ore, lead, silver, and zinc. That year BHP began producing steel at its Newcastle, Australia, plant. Aided by the steel demand caused by WWI, BHP soon became the largest steel producer in Australia and opened its own coal and iron ore mines to provide the necessary raw materials. By purchasing Australian Iron and Steel (1935) and a number of other steel companies, BHP gained a virtual monopoly on the Australian steel industry by 1939. The company closed its mine at Broken Hill in 1939 when reserves were exhausted.

In 1940 BHP established an operation to build deep-sea ships at Whyalla and later established its own fleet. During WWII the company produced munitions and led the syndicate that created Commonwealth Aircraft, a Melbourne-based manufacturer of fighters and training planes.

During the 1960s the company entered a partnership with Esso Standard Oil (Australia), subsidiary of Standard Oil of New Jersey, to explore for offshore oil and gas. In 1965 BHP and its partner found large quantities of natural gas and 2 years later discovered oil in the Bass Strait. The resulting Bass Strait oil and gas field would soon supply 70% of the nation's petroleum. In the 1960s and 1970s BHP started mining iron ore, manganese, and coal for export. In 1969 the company became joint owner of John Lysaght Ltd., a steel products manufacturer, and in 1979 became 100% owner.

In 1984 BHP bought Utah International's overseas assets from General Electric for $700 million; the acquisition allowed BHP to expand its mining operations in the US, South Africa, Canada, Chile, and Brazil. The company underwent a major reorganization between 1983 and 1987 to adapt to its new role as a global company. Acquisitions during the late 1980s included Energy Reserves Group (petroleum, 1985), Monsanto Oil (1986), Gulf Energy Development (1988), Aquila Steel (1988), and Hawaii-based Pacific Resources (crude oil, 1989). In 1990 BHP signed a letter of intent to buy a 70% interest in Mount Goldsworthy (iron ore); BHP already owned 30%.

WHAT

	1989 Sales		1989 Operating Income	
	$ mil	% of total	$ mil	% of total
Steel	4,071	46	339	42
Minerals	2,337	27	311	38
Petroleum	2,118	24	254	31
Other	305	3	(95)	(11)
Adjustments	(944)	—	—	—
Total	**7,887**	**100**	**809**	**100**

Products

Steel	**Minerals**	Monazite
Bar	Coking coal	Nickel
Coated products	Copper concentrate	Rutile
Plate	Energy coal	Zinc
Rail products	Ferro alloys	Zircon
Rod	Gold	
Rolled strip	Ilmenite	**Petroleum**
Slab	Iron ore	Crude oil
Structural products	Lead	Dry gas
Wire products	Manganese ore	Propane

HOW MUCH

	6 Yr. Growth	1980	1981	1982	1983	1984	1985	1986	1987	1988	1989
Sales ($ mil)	12.1%	—	—	—	3,973	4,848	4,710	6,078	6,240	7,877	7,887
Net income ($ mil)	23.8%	—	—	—	216	559	499	706	584	754	779
Income as % of sales	—	—	—	—	5.4%	11.5%	10.6%	11.6%	9.4%	9.6%	9.9%
Earnings per share ($)	23.8%	—	—	—	0.61	1.39	0.61	1.70	1.37	1.84	2.20
Stock price – high ($)	—	—	—	—	10.87	11.92	12.48	15.78	19.32	29.55	25.91
Stock price – low ($)	—	—	—	—	5.38	5.03	8.70	8.28	13.26	15.00	16.36
Stock price – close ($)	25.1%	—	—	—	5.73	11.81	9.26	14.99	17.61	18.64	21.93
P/E – high	—	—	—	—	18	9	21	9	14	16	12
P/E – low	—	—	—	—	9	4	14	5	10	8	7
Dividends per share ($)	16.7%	—	—	—	0.32	0.70	0.46	0.74	1.66	0.87	0.81
Book value per share ($)	4.8%	—	—	—	10.50	11.59	4.80	11.32	12.38	10.85	13.94

1989 Year End:
Debt ratio: 51.2%
Return on equity: 17.8%
Cash (mil): $453
Current ratio: 1.29
Long-term debt (mil): $5,275
Number of shares (mil): 361
Dividends:
1989 average yield: 3.7%
1989 payout: 36.9%
Market value (mil): $7,927

Stock Price History high/low 1983-89

30
25
20
15
10
5
0

RANKINGS

137th in *Fortune* Global 500 Industrial Cos.
149th in *Business Week* Global 1000

COMPETITION

AMAX	Inland Steel
Amoco	LTV
ASARCO	Mobil
Ashland	Pennzoil
Atlantic Richfield	Phelps Dodge
Bethlehem Steel	Phillips
British Petroleum	Royal Dutch/Shell
Chevron	Sun
Coastal	Texaco
Cyprus Minerals	Union Texas
Du Pont	Unocal
Exxon	USX

BROWN-FORMAN CORPORATION

OVERVIEW

Brown-Forman is a leading producer of spirits, wine, glassware, and luggage, including such names as Jack Daniel's Tennessee Whiskey, Canadian Mist Whiskey, Early Times Kentucky Whiskey, California Cooler, Southern Comfort liqueur, Korbel California Champagnes, Bolla Italian Wines, Hartmann luggage, and Lenox china, crystal, and giftware.

Brown-Forman's wine and spirits segment provides the lion's share (78%) of company sales. Operations include producing, bottling, importing, exporting, and marketing beverages.

Jack Daniel's ranks as the largest selling Tennessee whiskey in the US; Southern Comfort ranks as the #1 domestic proprietary liqueur; Korbel is the largest selling premium champagne; and Bolla is the leading premium imported table wine. Jack Daniel's and Southern Comfort are Brown-Forman's leading exports and are sold through an international network of distributors.

Brown-Forman's Consumer Durables segment is the largest domestic producer and marketer of fine china dinnerware and lead crystal stemware, as well as a leading producer of luggage. The company also operates retail and outlet stores through which it sells its products.

ASE symbol: BF.B
Incorporated: Delaware, 1933
Fiscal year ends: April 30

WHO

Chairman and CEO: W. L. Lyons Brown, Jr., age 53, $979,051 pay
President: Owsley Brown II, age 47, $873,468 pay
VC: Owsley Brown Frazier, age 54, $503,330 pay
VC: William M. Street, age 51, $618,902 pay
SVP and Director of Corporate Development: John P. Bridendall, age 40, $304,444 pay
SVP and Executive Director of Financial Operations: Clifford G. Rompf, Jr., age 59
Auditors: Coopers & Lybrand
Employees: 5,500

WHEN

In 1870 George G. Brown and John Forman opened the Brown-Forman Distillery in Louisville, Kentucky, to produce Old Forester brand bourbon. Old Forester sold well through the end of the century due in part to the company's innovative packaging of the product (safety seals and quality guarantees on the bottles). Forman sold his interest in the company to the Brown family (who still control Brown-Forman today) in 1902.

Old Forester continued to be successful under the Brown family, who advertised it as a healthy, life-prolonging product. The company went public just before Prohibition and obtained government approval to keep the distillery open to produce alcohol for medicinal purposes. The company reestablished the Old Forester image as an alcoholic beverage after Prohibition.

During WWII the government greatly curtailed alcoholic beverage production (alcohol was needed for the war effort). The company compensated by providing alcohol for wartime rubber and gunpowder production. In 1941 Brown-Forman correctly predicted that the war would be over by 1945 and subsequently started the 4-year aging process for its bourbon. As a result it dominated the bourbon market after the war.

In 1956 Brown-Forman expanded beyond Old Forester by purchasing Lynchburg, Tennessee–based Jack Daniel's (sour mash whiskey). The company retained the simple, black Jack Daniel's label and promoted the image of a small, Tennessee distillery. Today the brand sells 4 million cases a year and is known worldwide (Japanese executives pay upwards of $60 per bottle for it).

Brown-Forman continued to expand its alcohol line during the 1960s and 1970s, acquiring Korbel (champagne and brandy, 1965), Quality Importers (Ambassador Scotch, Ambassador Gin, and Old Bushmills Irish Whiskey, 1967), Bolla and Cella (wines, 1968), and Canadian Mist (blended whiskey, 1971). In 1979 Brown-Forman purchased Southern Comfort (a top-selling liqueur).

Brown-Forman acquired Lenox (the largest American producer of fine china, as well as crystal, gifts, and Hartmann luggage) in 1983 and California Cooler (wine coolers) in 1985. In 1989 Brown-Forman introduced Icy (Icelandic vodka).

Brown-Forman entered the 1990s with increasing sales in its china, crystal, and luggage divisions. The alcohol side of the business, stable in the US, continues to expand rapidly (30% annually) overseas.

WHERE

HQ: 850 Dixie Hwy., Louisville, KY 40210
Phone: 502-585-1100
FAX: 502-774-7164 (Public Relations)

The wines and spirits segment operates 10 facilities in the Tennessee-Kentucky area, 2 in Ontario, 2 in the US Virgin Islands, and 1 in Ireland. Consumer Durables operates 18 facilities in the US, 1 in El Salvador, and 13 domestic retail stores.

WHAT

	1989 Sales		1989 Operating Income	
	$ mil	% of total	$ mil	% of total
Wine & spirits	1,002	78	178	79
Consumer durables	285	22	48	21
Adjustments	(281)	—	(18)	—
Total	**1,006**	**100**	**208**	**100**

Brand Names

Spirits
Ambassador
Black Bush
Bols
Bushmills
Canadian Mist
Crystal Comfort
Earl Grey
Early Times
Gentleman Jack
Icy
Jack Daniel's
Old Forester
Pepe Lopez
Sempé
Southern Comfort
Usher's

Wine
Bolla
California Cooler
Cella
Fontana Candida
Korbel
Noilly Prat
Parducci

Consumer Durables
Athalon (luggage)
Hartmann (luggage)
Lenox (china and crystal)

HOW MUCH

	9 Yr. Growth	1980	1981	1982	1983	1984	1985	1986	1987	1988	1989
Sales ($ mil)	10.1%	423	500	578	605	864	928	995	1,098	1,067	1,006
Net income ($ mil)	12.4%	50	67	87	95	74	82	86	90	103	145
Income as % of sales	—	11.9%	13.4%	15.0%	15.7%	8.5%	8.8%	8.7%	8.2%	9.7%	14.4%
Earnings per share ($)	16.3%	1.32	1.77	2.29	2.51	1.93	2.29	2.68	2.78	3.25	5.15
Stock price – high ($)	—	13.42	19.33	24.08	30.08	26.00	21.92	32.00	43.00	55.38	58.00
Stock price – low ($)	—	10.33	11.46	17.33	18.75	18.33	15.50	20.42	29.83	26.63	33.88
Stock price – close ($)	17.7%	13.25	18.38	24.08	23.92	21.67	20.67	31.00	40.42	35.25	57.63
P/E – high	—	10	11	11	12	13	10	12	15	17	11
P/E – low	—	8	6	8	7	9	7	8	11	8	7
Dividends per share ($)	16.0%	0.40	0.45	0.51	0.59	0.59	0.59	0.67	0.90	1.24	1.52
Book value per share ($)	11.8%	7.11	8.42	10.20	12.07	13.42	14.11	16.10	18.01	15.82	19.44

1989 Year End:
Debt ratio: 17.2%
Return on equity: 29.2%
Cash (mil): $96
Current ratio: 2.53
Long-term debt (mil): $115
Number of shares (mil): 28
Dividends:
1989 average yield: 2.6%
1989 payout: 29.5%
Market value (mil): $1,612

RANKINGS

343rd in *Fortune* 500 Industrial Cos.
317th in *Business Week* 1000
960th in *Business Week* Global 1000

COMPETITION

American Brands
Anheuser-Busch
Colgate-Palmolive
Corning
E. & J. Gallo
Grand Metropolitan
Guinness
Nestlé
Owens-Illinois
Pearson
Riklis Family
Seagram

BROWNING-FERRIS INDUSTRIES, INC.

OVERVIEW

Houston-based Browning-Ferris Industries is the 2nd largest waste services company in the US (after Waste Management). Headed by William D. Ruckelshaus, former EPA director, the 23-year-old, $2.55 billion company collects, treats, and disposes of commercial, residential, and municipal solid waste. In 1990 the company announced it was withdrawing from the hazardous-waste portion of its business after 18 years of operation.

BFI, which started as a one-truck garbage collection business, today operates worldwide, with 410 locations serving 4.5 million residential accounts, 587 municipal contracts, and over 522,000 commercial accounts. The company has gone from a period of growth through acquisitions to one of expansion through internal growth and movement into foreign markets.

Public concerns about the environment have translated into business opportunities for BFI. In addition to solid-waste collection, the company handles medical waste, engages in asbestos abatement, and operates recycling programs. BFI is a joint partner with Air Products and Chemicals in American Ref-Fuel, a company that specializes in building and operating waste-to-energy plants.

NYSE symbol: BFI
Incorporated: Delaware, 1970
Fiscal year ends: September 30

WHO

Chairman and CEO: William D. Ruckelshaus, age 57, $1,166,100 pay
President and COO: John E. Drury, age 45, $615,700 pay
VC and Chief Marketing Officer: Norman A. Myers, age 53, $583,500 pay
EVP: Bruce E. Ranck, age 40
SVP and CFO: R. John Stanton, Jr., age 48
Auditors: Arthur Andersen & Co.
Employees: 25,400

WHEN

Accountant Tom Fatjo and Harvard MBA Louis Waters founded American Refuse Systems in 1967 with a single truck, providing garbage collection to a Houston neighborhood. They saw that the 1960s clean air laws created opportunities for large garbage businesses with the resources to comply with changing environmental regulations. In 1969 the company bought construction equipment distributor Browning-Ferris Machinery and changed its name to Browning-Ferris Industries. Subsequently BFI bought numerous waste disposal firms, acquiring a total of 157 subsidiaries by 1973.

Revenues fell 18% in 1975, and earnings dropped from $18 million to just under $5.3 million, due in part to decreased demand for waste paper, a business that had previously provided nearly 1/2 of revenues. BFI spun off its waste-paper subsidiary (Consolidated Fibers) in 1976. In late 1976 and again in 1977 BFI succeeded in hiking prices across its entire operation 5% to 5.5%, resulting in a 37% rise in earnings in 1977. That year Harry Phillips, who had joined BFI in 1970 when BFI acquired his 5 companies, became CEO, replacing Louis Waters, who became BFI's chairman. Tom Fatjo had left BFI in 1976 to run an investment company.

By 1980, with revenues of $553 million, BFI had become the 2nd largest US waste disposal company. Phillips continued to expand BFI, acquiring 508 companies from 1981 to 1988. The company bought hazardous-waste disposer CECOS International (1983), formed a joint venture to market trash-burning power plants (1984), and entered the medical-waste field by buying 2 small firms (1986).

BFI paid fines of $1.35 million after pleading guilty to price fixing in 1987, and $2.5 million in 1988 and $1.55 million in 1990 to settle suits arising from environmental violations at Louisiana hazardous-waste sites. The company has also appealed punitive damages of $6.1 million in an antitrust case for attempting to put a competitor out of business. Some of BFI's legal problems were the result of the actions of BFI's regional management and Phillips's "hands off" approach to managing its subsidiaries. Despite BFI's troubles, net income in 1989 was $263 million, up from $35 million in 1980.

After the EPA denied BFI permits to recommence operation of hazardous-waste facilities in Ohio and New York in 1990, the company discontinued hazardous-waste operations altogether.

WHERE

HQ: 757 N. Eldridge, Houston, TX 77079
Phone: 713-870-8100
FAX: 713-870-7844

BFI operates in 410 locations in the US (including Puerto Rico) and in Australia, Canada, Hong Kong, Italy, Kuwait, the Netherlands, New Zealand, Spain, the UK, and Venezuela.

	1989 Sales		1989 Operating Income	
	$ mil	% of total	$ mil	% of total
US & Puerto Rico	2,291	90	430	93
Foreign	260	10	35	7
Total	**2,551**	**100**	**465**	**100**

WHAT

	1989 Sales		1989 Operating Income	
	$ mil	% of total	$ mil	% of total
Solid waste	2,491	98	532	105
Chemical waste	60	2	(27)	(5)
Adjustments	—	—	(40)	—
Total	**2,551**	**100**	**465**	**100**

Solid-Waste Operations
Collection
Transportation
Treatment
Disposal
Recycling
Asbestos abatement
Medical-waste services (using incineration or autoclaving)
Portable-restroom services
Street and parking lot sweeping

Chemical-Waste Services
Chemical-waste treatment and processing
Wastewater processing

Subsidiaries/Affiliates
American Ecology (partial ownership)
American Ref-Fuel Co. (joint venture)
BFI Environmental Systems, Inc.
Browning-Ferris Industries, Europe Inc.
Browning-Ferris Overseas, Inc.
CECOS International, Inc.

HOW MUCH

	9 Yr. Growth	1980	1981	1982	1983	1984	1985	1986	1987	1988	1989
Sales ($ mil)	18.5%	553	661	715	844	1,001	1,145	1,328	1,657	2,067	2,551
Net income ($ mil)	25.3%	35	48	63	80	89	112	137	172	227	263
Income as % of sales	—	6.2%	7.3%	8.8%	9.4%	8.9%	9.8%	10.3%	10.4%	11.0%	10.3%
Earnings per share ($)	21.0%	0.31	0.41	0.52	0.60	0.65	0.80	0.95	1.15	1.51	1.74
Stock price – high ($)	—	4.75	6.23	9.21	11.91	11.13	16.00	23.69	35.75	29.25	42.75
Stock price – low ($)	—	2.04	3.81	4.08	8.19	6.63	9.16	15.13	17.50	20.88	26.88
Stock price – close ($)	29.0%	3.92	5.35	8.90	10.75	9.25	16.00	22.38	28.00	27.38	38.75
P/E – high	—	15	15	18	20	17	20	25	31	19	25
P/E – low	—	7	9	8	14	10	11	16	15	14	15
Dividends per share ($)	19.0%	0.12	0.14	0.17	0.20	0.24	0.27	0.32	0.40	0.48	0.56
Book value per share ($)	17.9%	1.88	2.37	1.82	2.99	3.39	3.95	5.11	5.93	7.05	8.33

1989 Year End:
Debt ratio: 43.2%
Return on equity: 22.6%
Cash (mil): $133
Current ratio: 1.01
Long-term debt (mil): $945
Number of shares (mil): 149
Dividends:
1989 average yield: 1.4%
1989 payout: 32.2%
Market value (mil): $5,779

RANKINGS

40th in *Fortune* 100 Diversified Service Cos.
310th in *Forbes* Sales 500
124th in *Business Week* 1000
286th in *Business Week* Global 1000

COMPETITION

Consolidated Rail
Ogden
Waste Management

BRUNO'S, INC.

OVERVIEW

Bruno's is a large supermarket chain in the Southeast with sales of $2.4 billion in 1990, up from 1989 sales of just over $2.1 billion. Headquartered in Birmingham, the company operates 230 stores in Alabama, Georgia, Mississippi, Florida, and Tennessee under several names — Bruno's Food & Pharmacy, Food World, Food Fair, Food Max, Bruno's Finer Foods, and Vincent's Market. The company also operates 76 Piggly Wiggly stores in central and southern Georgia through its subsidiary PWS Holding. Its 3 American Fare hypermarkets are a joint venture (49% owned by Bruno's) with K mart.

With an almost 25% market share in Alabama, Bruno's tailors store size, decor, and merchandise to a targeted clientele, allowing the company to operate several stores in the same market area. The company tightly controls operating costs through a lean management and high labor productivity and by buying large quantities of merchandise, often more than currently needed, at low prices. Bruno's competitive pricing and company growth has pushed up earnings 21% and sales almost 19% annually over the past 10 years.

The company owns 36 of its stores and 6 shopping centers and has interests in 14 of its store leases through PM Associates, a 50% joint venture with Metropolitan Life Insurance Company. The founding Bruno family still owns 26% of the company.

WHEN

Bruno's was founded in 1932 in Birmingham by brothers Joseph and Sam Bruno with $600 of their mother's savings. The 800-square-foot food store was a family operation run by their father, Vincent, a former steelworker, and their mother, Theresa, with the 8 children helping after school. A 2nd store opened in 1935.

Brothers Joseph, Sam, Lee, and Angelo Bruno incorporated as Bruno's, Inc., with 10 stores (1959). Bruno's opened Big B Discount Drug Stores in 1968, and later spun off the 70-store subsidiary in a stock distribution (1981). By 1970 there were 29 Bruno's Food Stores in Alabama. The company went public to develop discount food stores (1971) and began the Food World chain, opening large 40,000- to 48,000-square-foot discount supermarkets (1972).

The earlier Bruno's Food Stores were remodeled as Bruno's Food & Pharmacy (1983), combination supermarket and drug stores (52,000 to 60,000 square feet), located in suburban markets and featuring more extensive meat and seafood, produce, bakery, and delicatessen departments than conventional supermarkets. Bruno's Finer Foods (1983) are also combination stores. The Food Fair stores (1985) are small supermarkets (17,000 to 32,000 square feet) and offer competitive pricing in less-populated market areas unable to support a high-volume warehouse like Food World.

The company acquired the Megamarket stores in Birmingham (1985) and converted them to Food Max stores, large warehouse supermarkets (48,000 to 65,000 square feet). Vincent's Market in Birmingham (1988) targets an affluent clientele and offers gourmet foods and wines, an in-house chef, a 40-seat cafe, catering services, and home delivery.

In the 1970s Bruno's expanded into adjacent states. Recent acquisitions include 7 Albertson's (Alabama, 1985); Steven's Supermarket (Nashville, 1987); 82 Piggly Wiggly supermarkets (Georgia, 1988); and 7 BI-LO supermarkets (Macon, Georgia, 1988).

In 1989, as a joint venture, Bruno's and K mart opened American Fare, a 240,000-square-foot hypermarket, in Atlanta; Bruno's operates the supermarket section, while K mart operates the general merchandise areas. American Fare stores also opened in Charlotte, North Carolina, and Jackson, Mississippi (1990).

HOW MUCH

	9 Yr. Growth	1980	1981	1982	1983	1984	1985	1986	1987	1988	1989
Sales ($ mil)	18.6%	459	488	549	605	716	887	1,018	1,143	1,982	2,134
Net income ($ mil)	21.0%	9	9	12	15	19	25	30	31	43	48
Income as % of sales	—	1.9%	1.9%	2.3%	2.5%	2.6%	2.8%	3.0%	2.7%	2.2%	2.2%
Earnings per share ($)	18.6%	0.13	0.13	0.19	0.23	0.27	0.35	0.39	0.40	0.53	0.59
Stock price – high ($)	—	1.53	3.05	3.70	5.25	5.16	9.00	11.88	12.63	12.88	15.13
Stock price – low ($)	—	0.69	1.27	1.33	3.38	3.19	5.09	7.38	7.56	9.63	10.13
Stock price – close ($)	28.9%	1.50	1.28	3.48	3.69	5.13	8.75	7.56	10.38	10.25	14.75
P/E – high	—	12	23	20	23	19	26	31	32	24	26
P/E – low	—	5	9	7	15	12	15	19	19	18	17
Dividends per share ($)	16.8%	0.03	0.04	0.04	0.05	0.06	0.07	0.08	0.09	0.10	0.12
Book value per share ($)	24.3%	0.50	0.47	0.62	0.98	1.18	1.94	2.25	2.55	3.06	3.56

1989 Year End:
Debt ratio: 31.2%
Return on equity: 17.8%
Cash (mil): $23
Current ratio: 1.27
Long-term debt (mil): $132
Number of shares (mil): 82
Dividends:
1989 average yield: 0.8%
1989 payout: 20.3%
Market value (mil): $1,203

Stock Price History high/low 1980-89

NASDAQ symbol: BRNO
Incorporated: Alabama, 1959
Fiscal year ends: Saturday nearest June 30

WHO

Chairman Emeritus: Joseph S. Bruno, age 76, $250,000 pay
Chairman: Angelo J. Bruno, age 65, $325,000 pay
VC and SVP: Lee J. Bruno, age 69, $250,000 pay
President, CEO, and COO: Ronald G. Bruno, age 38, $240,000 pay (prior to promotion)
EVP; President, Piggly Wiggly Southern, Inc.: Paul F. Garrison, age 60, $225,000 pay
EVP, CFO, and Secretary: Glenn J. Griffin, age 51
Auditors: Arthur Andersen & Co.
Employees: 7,232 full time and 10,917 part time

WHERE

HQ: 300 Research Pkwy., Birmingham, AL 35211
Phone: 205-940-9400
FAX: 205-940-9534 (CFO)

Bruno's operates 230 supermarkets and combination food and drug stores in 5 southern states (Alabama, Florida, Georgia, Mississippi, and Tennessee).

Warehouses	Area (sq. ft.)
Birmingham, AL	986,000
Vidalia, GA	616,000
Total	**1,602,000**

WHAT

Stores (6/30/90)	No. of Stores
Food World (supermarkets)	74
Food Fair (supermarkets)	33
Food Max (warehouse supermarkets)	29
Bruno's Food & Pharmacy (combination stores)	10
Piggly Wiggly (supermarkets)	76
Bruno's Finer Foods (supermarkets)	7
Vincent's Market (supermarket)	1
Total	**230**

Subsidiaries

PWS Holding Corporation
Piggly Wiggly Southern, Inc.

Joint Ventures

American Fare hypermarkets (49% joint venture with K mart)

PM Associates (50% joint venture with Metropolitan Life Insurance Co.)

RANKINGS

48th in *Fortune* 50 Retailing Cos.
360th in *Forbes* Sales 500
488th in *Business Week* 1000

COMPETITION

Food Lion
Great A&P
Kroger
Winn-Dixie

BRUNSWICK CORPORATION

OVERVIEW

Brunswick is the world's largest producer of recreational marine engines and boats, which accounted for about 71% of 1989 total sales. Brunswick markets these products under several brand names, including Mercury, Mariner, Force, Bayliner, and Sea Ray.

Brunswick is perhaps best known for its bowling, billiards, fishing, and golf products, which comprise the Recreation segment (14% of sales). Brunswick is North America's largest bowling center chain operator and a US leader in the manufacture of bowling equipment and fishing reels.

Brunswick is selling most of its Technical segment but will retain the Defense Division, which manufactures an array of products — from robot arms to camouflage — for the DOD and its prime contractors.

Brunswick expects its marine business to return to growth in the 1990s. The company plans further expasion of international sales, which are presently growing in all divisions.

WHEN

Swiss immigrant woodworker John Brunswick built his first billiard table in 1845 in Cincinnati. In 1874 Brunswick formed a partnership with Julius Balke, and 10 years later they teamed with H. W. Collender, forming the Brunswick-Balke-Collender Company.

Following Brunswick's death, son-in-law Moses Bensinger became president and diversified into bowling equipment in the 1880s. His son B. E. followed as president (1904) and led the company into wood and rubber products, phonographs, and records. (Al Jolson recorded "Sonny Boy" on a Brunswick label.) Brunswick went public after WWI.

By 1930 Brunswick had sold many businesses to concentrate on bowling and billiards, sports which had acquired bad reputations during Prohibition and the Great Depression. When B. E. died in 1935, his son Bob became CEO and launched a massive promotional campaign, redesigned bowling alleys, and upgraded equipment lines to make the sports more respectable.

Bob Bensinger moved to chairman in 1954 and his brother Ted succeeded him as CEO. Rival A.M.F. introduced the first automatic pinsetter in 1952, and Brunswick followed in 1956. By 1958 Brunswick had captured the industry lead as bowling equipment sales rose 650% between 1956 and 1961. Under Ted, Brunswick diversified, adding MacGregor (sporting goods, 1958), Aloe (medical supplies, 1959), Mercury (marine products, 1961), and Zebco (fishing equipment, 1961). The company adopted its present name in 1960.

By 1963 bowling sales had dropped to $20 million, and in 1965 Brunswick lost $76.9 million. The company sold many unprofitable enterprises, intensified research on an automatic scorer and metal fiber technology (for industrial and defense applications), and emphasized health products through subsidiary Sherwood Medical Industries.

After discontinuing many of its receation lines, in 1978 Brunswick added Oxford Laboratories (medical diagnostics, $10 million) and the Vapor Corporation (energy and transportation products, $92 million). To foil a takeover by Whittaker Corporation in 1982, Brunswick sold Sherwood to American Home Products. CEO Jack Reichert, a former pin boy who became chairman in 1983, cut corporate staff 59% and emphasized the marine business.

In 1986 Brunswick sparked an industry-wide consolidation trend by spending $774 million to buy Bayliner and Ray Industries. Marine sales increased from 42% of 1982 total sales to 71% in 1989. Bowling and billiards now provide only a fraction of the Recreation segment's 14% of total sales.

A 1989 marine industry slump led to a $71.3 million loss. Brunswick has laid off 14% of its employees, closed or mothballed 7 boat plants, and announced plans to sell both its Technetics (aerospace products) and Industrial Products Divisions.

HOW MUCH

	9 Yr. Growth	1980	1981	1982	1983	1984	1985	1986	1987	1988	1989
Sales ($ mil)	10.0%	1,200	1,085	1,068	1,216	1,468	1,539	1,717	3,086	3,282	2,826
Net income ($ mil)	—	24	43	(20)	66	94	100	110	169	193	(71)
Income as % of sales	—	2.0%	3.9%	(1.9%)	5.4%	6.4%	6.5%	6.4%	5.5%	5.9%	(2.5%)
Earnings per share ($)	—	0.13	0.23	(0.17)	0.73	1.10	1.17	1.32	1.90	2.20	(0.81)
Stock price – high ($)	—	2.14	2.81	3.50	7.47	9.06	11.38	19.69	30.25	24.13	21.50
Stock price – low ($)	—	1.27	1.63	1.77	3.08	5.94	7.75	10.81	10.75	14.50	13.00
Stock price – close ($)	24.7%	1.94	2.33	3.13	7.22	8.47	10.91	16.94	14.75	16.88	14.13
P/E – high	—	17	12	—	10	8	10	15	16	11	—
P/E – low	—	10	7	—	4	5	7	8	6	7	—
Dividends per share ($)	16.7%	0.11	0.11	0.13	0.13	0.18	0.25	0.28	0.30	0.40	0.44
Book value per share ($)	13.7%	2.78	3.05	3.92	4.45	5.38	6.23	7.80	9.52	10.97	8.83

1989 Year End:
Debt ratio: 37.3%
Return on equity: —
Cash (mil): $22
Current ratio: 1.38
Long-term debt (mil): $462
Number of shares (mil): 88
Dividends:
1989 average yield: 3.1%
1989 payout: —
Market value (mil): $1,242

Stock Price History high/low 1980-89

NYSE symbol: BC
Incorporated: Delaware, 1907
Fiscal year ends: December 31

WHO

Chairman, President, and CEO: Jack F. Reichert, age 59, $762,350 pay
EVP: John M. Charvat, age 59, $441,493 pay
VP Finance: William R. McManaman, age 42
Auditors: Arthur Andersen & Co.
Employees: 25,700

WHERE

HQ: One Brunswick Plaza, Skokie, IL 60077
Phone: 708-470-4700
FAX: 708-470-4765

Brunswick operates approximately 57 US and 8 foreign manufacturing plants.

	1989 Sales		1989 Operating Income	
	$ mil	% of total	$ mil	% of total
US	2,474	88	(19)	(128)
Foreign	352	12	34	228
Adjustments	—	—	61	—
Total	**2,826**	**100**	**76**	**100**

WHAT

	1989 Sales		1989 Operating Income	
	$ mil	% of total	$ mil	% of total
Marine	2,001	71	(58)	(392)
Recreation	392	14	53	358
Technical	433	15	20	134
Adjustments	—	—	61	—
Total	**2,826**	**100**	**76**	**100**

Brand Names

Boats
Arriva
Astro
Bayliner
Cobra
Escort (trailers)
Fisher
Maxum
MonArk
Procraft
Quantum
Sea Ray
Ski Challenger
Spectrum
Starcraft

Boat Motors
Force
Mariner
MerCruiser
Mercury
Motor Guide
Quicksilver
U.S. Marine Power

Sporting Goods
Brunswick (billiards, bowling, golf)
Quantum, Zebco (fishing)

Bowling/Recreation Centers
125 Brunswick centers in the US, Canada, and Europe

Engineering/Industrial Products
Circle Seal
Cooper
ECS
Hydrosteam
RCS
Technetics
Texsteam
Vapor

RANKINGS

159th in *Fortune* 500 Industrial Cos.
445th in *Fortune* Global 500 Industrial Cos.
296th in *Forbes* Sales 500
442nd in *Business Week* 1000

COMPETITION

Honda
MacAndrews & Forbes
Outboard Marine
Reebok
Volvo
Defense contractors

BSN SA

OVERVIEW

Twenty years of acquisitions have transformed French glassmaker BSN into Europe's 4th largest packaged food concern. Although sales are concentrated in Europe, particularly in France, BSN products are sold worldwide. Such brands as Dannon, Gervais, and Evian contribute to the company's world leadership in dairy products and mineral water. In Europe, BSN is the largest biscuit and glass bottle producer and #2 in beer and pasta sales.

Under the leadership of Antoine Riboud, BSN has aggressively expanded in Europe in anticipation of 1992 market integration. Riboud's goal has been to establish and maintain #1 or #2 positions throughout Europe in all major BSN markets. The company recently announced its intention to sell its US cookie businesses (Mother's, Salerno) and concentrate on more rapidly growing Eastern European and Asian markets.

Riboud, now 71, has been the visionary and driving force behind BSN. He intends to lead the company until he is 80 and the question of succession has not yet been resolved.

WHEN

In 1965 Antoine Riboud replaced his uncle as chairman of family-run Souchon-Neuvesel, a Lyon-based glass bottle maker. Befitting a man whose brothers were Jean, then chairman of Schlumberger, and Marc, an internationally recognized photographer, he quickly made his mark on the company. Riboud's first move was to merge (1966) with Boussois, a major French flat-glass manufacturer, creating BSN. In an audacious attempt to expand the company's glass business, he made a bid in 1968 for Saint-Gobain, a diversified French glass manufacturer 3 times BSN's size. The attempt failed.

Undaunted, Riboud enlarged BSN's glass business and filled the company's bottles by acquiring well-established beverage and food concerns. In 1970 BSN purchased Brasseries Kronenbourg (France's largest brewer), Societe Europeenne de Brasseries (beer, France), and Evian (mineral water, France). The 1972 acquisition of Glaverbel (Belgium) gave BSN 50% of Europe's flat-glass market. A 1973 merger with Gervais Danone (yogurt, cheese, and Panzani pasta, France) put BSN into pan-European brand-name food products for the first time and raised sales to $1.7 billion.

In the 1970s increasing energy costs depressed flat-glass earnings. BSN elected to divest its flat-glass businesses, selling the last of them in 1982. In 1978 and 1979 the company acquired interests in brewers in Belgium, Spain, and Italy. BSN bought Dannon, the leading US yogurt maker, in 1981. The company became a major player in the French champagne industry, taking over Pommery and Lanson in 1984. BSN established a strong presence in the Italian pasta market by purchasing majority ownership of Ponte (1985) and a minority interest in Agnesi (1986).

In 1986 BSN purchased Generale Biscuit, the 3rd largest biscuit company in the world. In 1989 the company bought RJR Nabisco's European cookie and snack food business for $2.5 billion, quickly selling Walkers Crisps and Smiths Crisps (snack foods) to PepsiCo for $1.35 billion to help finance the acquisition.

In a series of acquisitions starting in 1986, BSN took over the largest mineral water companies in Italy and Spain, several European pasta makers, Sonnen-Bassermann (grocery products, West Germany, 1987), HP Foods (UK, 1988), Lea & Perrins (US, 1988), and La Familia (Spain, 1989), among others. The company has been active in strategic alliances, swapping 4.3% of its shares for 20% of IFIL Partecipazioni (investments and food, Italy, 1987) and taking a 20% stake in Birra Peroni (beer, Italy, 1988), a 50% interest in Alken-Maes (beer, Belgium, 1988), 50% in Guangzhou Dairy (yogurt, China, 1989), and minority interests in sauce and spice makers Star (Italy, 1989) and Starlux (Spain, 1989).

HOW MUCH

$ = FF5.78 (December 31,1989)	9 Yr. Growth	1980	1981	1982	1983	1984	1985	1986	1987	1988	1989
Sales (FF mil)	11.5%	18,233	19,256	21,890	24,889	27,293	28,475	33,623	37,156	42,177	48,669
Net income (FF mil)	26.3%	331	446	574	741	755	798	1,081	1,550	2,186	2,698
Income as % of sales	—	1.8%	2.3%	2.6%	3.0%	2.8%	2.8%	3.2%	4.2%	5.2%	5.5%
Earnings per share (FF)	16.6%	13	16	20	21	20	21	27	34	42	50
Stock price – high (FF)	—	116	125	156	273	289	276	475	542	650	780
Stock price – low (FF)	—	83	78	114	131	235	197	272	371	376	608
Stock price – close (FF)	25.0%	104	119	144	268	240	275	435	434	648	774
P/E – high	—	9	8	8	13	14	13	18	16	16	16
P/E – low	—	7	5	6	6	12	9	10	11	9	12
Dividends per share (FF)	12.5%	4.00	4.50	5.00	5.20	5.50	6.00	7.00	8.50	10.00	11.50
Book value per share (FF)	11.5%	132	151	172	171	189	196	221	267	303	351

1989 Year End
Debt ratio: 42.0%
Return on equity: 15.3%
Cash (mil): FF1,513
Term debt (mil): FF14,436
Number of shares (mil): 54
Dividends:
1989 average yield: 1.5%
1989 payout: 23.1%
Market value (mil): $7,231
Sales (mil): $8,425

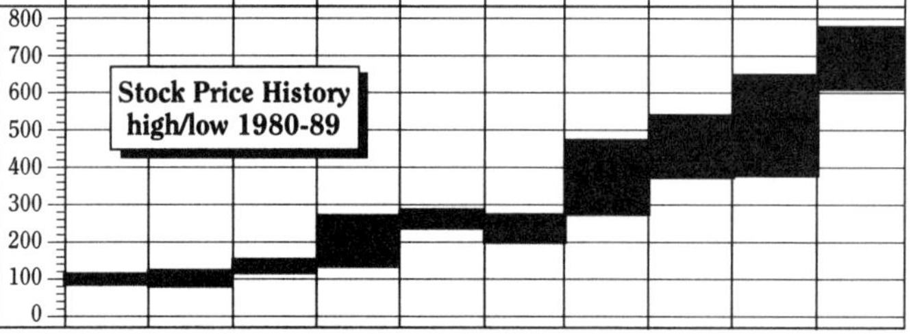

Principal Exchange: Paris
Incorporated: France, 1966
Fiscal Year Ends: December 31

WHO

Chairman: Antoine Riboud, age 71
VC and President: Georges Lecallier
SVP Finance: Christian Laubie
Auditors: Petiteau Scacchi et Associés (Price Waterhouse)
Employees: 49,693

WHERE

HQ: 7, rue de Téhéran - 75008 Paris, France
Phone: 011-33-1-44-35-20-70
FAX: 011-33-1-45-63-88-22
US HQ (The Dannon Company): 1111 Westchester Ave., White Plains, NY 10604
Phone: (914) 697-9700

	1989 Sales		1989 Operating Income	
	FF mil	% of total	FF mil	% of total
France	30,712	63	3,729	74
Rest of Europe	13,100	27	1,039	21
Outside Europe	4,857	10	246	5
Total	**48,669**	**100**	**5,014**	**100**

WHAT

	1989 Sales		1989 Operating Income	
	FF mil	% of total	FF mil	% of total
Dairy prods.	12,580	26	964	19
Grocery prods.	9,913	20	952	19
Biscuits	11,055	23	1,030	21
Beer	6,188	13	806	16
Champagne, mineral water	4,317	9	642	13
Containers	4,616	9	620	12
Total	**48,669**	**100**	**5,014**	**100**

Major Brand Names

Dairy Products
Dannon
Danone
Gervais

Grocery Products
Amora (condiments)
Blédina (baby food)
HP (sauces)
Lea & Perrins (Worcestershire sauce)
Liebig (soup and jam)
Panzani (pasta)
Ponte (pasta)
Sonnen-Bassermann (prepared food)

Biscuits
L'Alsacienne
Bakery Wagon
Belin
Jacob's
Lu
Mama's
Mother's
Saiwa
Salerno
Vandamme

Beer
Kanterbrau
Kronenbourg
Maes
Mahou

Champagne, Mineral Water
Badoit
Evian
Lanson
Pommery
Saratoga
Scharffenberger

RANKINGS

166th in *Fortune* Global 500 Industrial Cos.
204th in *Business Week* Global 1000

COMPETITION

Adolph Coors
Anheuser-Busch
Bass
General Mills
Grand Metropolitan
Guinness
H. J. Heinz
Nestlé
PepsiCo
Philip Morris
Ralston Purina
RJR Nabisco
TLC Beatrice
Unilever
Other food companies

BURLINGTON HOLDINGS, INC.

OVERVIEW

Burlington Holdings is the parent company of Burlington Industries and is owned by Burlington Industries Capital, which in turn is owned by Morgan Stanley and other investors. Burlington Industries, based in Greensboro, North Carolina, makes textiles for 2 applications: apparel and home furnishings. The company maintains production operations in the US and Mexico, as well as a separate merchandising headquarters at Burlington House in New York City.

The Products for Apparel segment is the world's largest producer of finished textiles for the apparel industry. The divisions produce yarns; cotton and cotton/polyester knitted fabrics; and worsted, denim, polyester, and various blends of woven fabrics. Major customers of the 5 apparel divisions include Levi Strauss and retailers who sell the products under their private labels.

The Home Furnishings segment is the world's largest manufacturer of decorative fabrics and prints for the home and is also a major producer of rugs and carpets. The 6 divisions that form this product group manufacture draperies, sheers, shades, and window top treatments; bedspreads and mattress tickings; upholstery fabrics; and carpets and bath and area rugs. Brand names include Burlington House, Lees Carpets, and Monticello Carpets. Retail stores form the primary customer base for this group's products.

Since taking the company private in an LBO in 1987, management has repaid $900 million of the $2.8 billion acquisition debt. The company has placed 16% of its stock in an employee stock ownership plan to encourage higher service and quality efforts.

WHEN

J. Spencer Love, who had entered the milling business after WWI, moved his North Carolina cotton mill from Gastonia to Burlington in 1923. In order to finance the new mill, he convinced the Chamber of Commerce of Burlington to help him sell stock in a new company, Burlington Mills. A year later the mill was struggling as the demand for its cotton products waned. Love switched from cotton milling to a new product, rayon, which was becoming popular, and sales increased. Burlington opened another mill in the city in 1926.

When textile prices dropped during the Great Depression, many mills went out of business, especially in the North, where labor was more expensive. Burlington continued to grow rapidly and bought several of these failed businesses. Corporate headquarters moved to Greensboro in 1935, and by 1936 the company had 22 plants in 9 towns. In 1940 the company started producing hosiery. In the 1950s Burlington expanded through acquisitions, buying Pacific Mills and Klopman Mills, and changed its name to Burlington Industries (1955).

Burlington further diversified into consumer products with the acquisitions of Charm Tred Mills (1959), a scatter rug manufacturer, and of Philadelphia carpet producer James Lees & Company (1960). The company bought Globe Furniture, based in High Point, North Carolina (1966), and made several other acquisitions in the furniture business through the 1970s. This strategy was partly a necessity, since a government order (1969) had prevented the company from acquiring additional textile companies. William Klopman, son of Klopman Mills's founder, became CEO in 1976 and focused on the renovation of plant facilities and the company's move into consumer products and clothing fabrics in response to increasing foreign competition in its traditional textiles markets.

By 1980 Burlington was by far the largest textile producer in the world, due largely to the company's rayon and other synthetic fiber products; however, most of the company's profits came from consumer products sold under private labels and Burlington's brand names: Anne Klein and Oleg Cassini (home products), Lees (carpets), and Monticello (linen). Several years of poor profits, due to the company's inability to move beyond the commodity textiles business, led to a takeover attempt by Montreal-based Dominion Textile, a former Burlington partner in the rayon business. Chairman Frank Greenberg, whose father had owned Charm Tred, led management in a buyout, taking the company private in 1987. Burlington has since sold off all of its foreign operations except those in Mexico and is focusing on repaying its acquisition debt.

HOW MUCH

	9 Yr. Growth	1980	1981	1982	1983	1984	1985	1986	1987	1988	1989
Sales ($ mil)	(3.1%)	2,901	3,263	2,876	2,990	3,169	2,802	2,778	3,279	2,452	2,181
Net income ($ mil)	—	81	115	52	88	62	13	57	22	(33)	(23)
Income as % of sales	—	2.8%	3.5%	1.8%	3.0%	2.0%	0.4%	2.0%	0.7%	(1.3%)	(1.1%)

1989 Year End:
Debt ratio: 101.0%
Return on equity: —
Cash (mil): $60
Current ratio: 2.15
Long-term debt (mil): $1,620

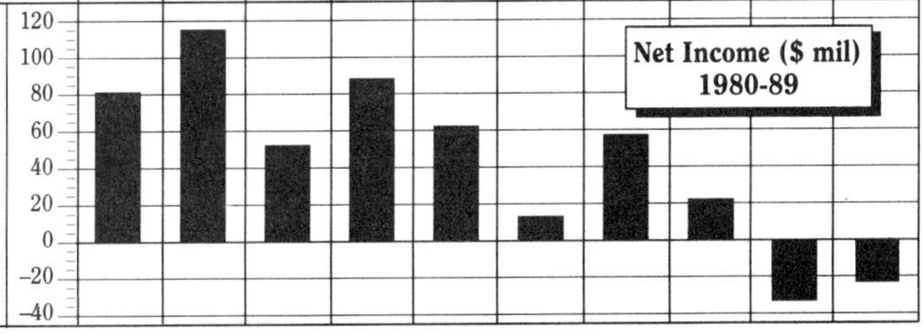

Private company
Founded: North Carolina, 1923
Fiscal year ends: Saturday closest to September 30

WHO

Chairman and President: Donald P. Brennan
Chairman and CEO of Burlington Industries: Frank S. Greenberg
EVP and CFO: Donald R. Hughes
Auditors: Ernst & Young
Employees: 27,500

WHERE

HQ: 3330 W. Friendly Ave., Greensboro, NC 27420
Phone: 919-379-2000
FAX: 919-379-4504

Burlington operates 44 plants in 7 states and 3 in Mexico.

	1989 Sales		1989 Operating Income	
	$ mil	% of total	$ mil	% of total
US	2,090	96	230	98
Mexico	91	4	4	2
Adjustments	—	—	(40)	—
Total	**2,181**	**100**	**194**	**100**

WHAT

	1989 Sales		1989 Operating Income	
	$ mil	% of total	$ mil	% of total
Apparel products	1,278	59	182	78
Home products	903	41	52	22
Adjustments	—	—	(40)	—
Total	**2,181**	**100**	**194**	**100**

Apparel Products

Products	Divisions
Knitted fabrics	Burlington Denim
Spun yarns	Burlington Knitted Fabrics
Textured yarns	Burlington Madison Yarn Co.
Woven fabrics	Burlington Menswear
	Klopman Fabrics

Home Furnishings Products

Products	Divisions
Area rugs	Burlington Decorative Prints
Bedspreads	Burlington House Area Rugs
Carpet tiles	Burlington House Decorative Fabrics
Carpets	Burlington House Draperies
Draperies and drapery fabrics	Lees Commercial Carpets
Mattress tickings	Lees Residential Carpets
Upholstery fabrics	

RANKINGS

53rd in *Forbes* 400 US Private Cos.

COMPETITION

Du Pont
Farley
Fieldcrest Cannon
Milliken
Springs Industries

BURLINGTON NORTHERN INC.

OVERVIEW

Burlington Northern (BN) operates the largest rail network in America, a 25,500-mile system spanning 25 states and 2 Canadian provinces. Since selling its trucking and natural resource operations in 1988, BN is strictly a railroading company.

With track stretching from Florida to Washington, Fort Worth–based BN controls a far-flung empire. The company hauls forest products from the Pacific Northwest, Midwest, and South; grain from the Midwest and Great Plains; and coal from Montana and Wyoming. BN also carries automotive, industrial, food, and consumer products, and offers "doublestack" intermodal (truck-to-train) services through its BN AMERICA program.

Coal transportation accounted for 33% of BN's revenues in 1989, with 91% of the coal coming from the Powder River Basin of Montana and Wyoming and the rest coming from mines in the South and Midwest. Most of the company's coal traffic terminated at electric generating plants in the North Central, South Central, Mountain, and Pacific regions of the US.

Subsidiary BN Leasing acquires rail cars for the railroad.

NYSE symbol: BNI
Incorporated: Delaware, 1981
Fiscal year ends: December 31

WHO

President and CEO; Chairman, President, and CEO, Burlington Northern Railroad Co.: Gerald Grinstein, age 57, $1,460,100 pay
Chairman: Richard M. Bressler, age 59
EVP and CFO: P. Jackson Bell, age 48, $468,750 pay
EVP Law: Edmund W. Burke, age 41, $455,585 pay
COO, Burlington Northern Railroad Co.: William E. Greenwood, age 51, $500,517 pay (prior to promotion)
Auditors: Coopers & Lybrand
Employees: 32,900

WHEN

Burlington Northern is largely the creation of James J. Hill, who began his railroad empire in 1878 by acquiring the St. Paul & Pacific Railroad in Minnesota. By 1893 Hill had completed the Great Northern Railway, which extended from St. Paul to Seattle. The following year he gained control of Northern Pacific (chartered in 1864), which had been constructed between Duluth, Minnesota and Tacoma, Washington, with extensions to Portland, Oregon and St. Paul. With the help of J. P. Morgan, in 1901 Hill acquired the Chicago, Burlington & Quincy (Burlington), whose routes included Chicago-St. Paul, Chicago-Denver, Omaha-Billings, and Billings-Denver-Fort Worth-Houston. To give Great Northern an entrance to Oregon, Hill in 1905 created the Spokane, Portland & Seattle Railway (SP&S), completed in 1908.

Hill intended to merge Great Northern, Northern Pacific, SP&S, and Burlington under his Morgan-backed Northern Securities Company, but in 1904 the Supreme Court found Northern Securities to be in violation of the Sherman Anti-Trust Act. Although the Court dissolved the holding company, Hill retained control of the individual railroads. He left the presidency of Great Northern to his son Louis in 1907 but remained a director until his death in 1916.

Meanwhile, Jim Hill's railroads produced some of America's best-known passenger trains. Great Northern's Empire Builder began service between Chicago and Seattle in 1929; it is operated today by Amtrak. The 1934 Burlington Zephyr was the nation's first streamlined passenger diesel.

After several years of deliberation by the Interstate Commerce Commission, Great Northern and Northern Pacific merged in 1970 along with jointly owned subsidiaries Burlington and SP&S. The new company, Burlington Northern Inc. (BN), acquired the St. Louis–San Francisco Railway (Frisco) in 1980. The Frisco, with lines stretching from St. Louis to such cities as Dallas, Oklahoma City, Kansas City, and Pensacola, added 4,653 miles to the BN rail network.

In 1985 the company formed Burlington Northern Motor Carriers (BNMC) by acquiring 5 trucking companies.

As part of its decision to focus only on railroads, in 1988 BN sold BNMC and spun off Burlington Resources Inc., an independent holding company for its nonrailroad businesses (primarily natural gas, oil, minerals, construction, and forest products, including 1.8 million acres of land), leaving Burlington Northern Railroad and BN Leasing as the remaining principal subsidiaries.

WHERE

HQ: 3800 Continental Plaza, 777 Main St., Fort Worth, TX 76102
Phone: 817-878-2000
FAX: 817-878-2314 (Finance)

Principal Cities Served by BN

Billings (MT)	Memphis
Birmingham	Minneapolis-St. Paul
Cheyenne	Mobile
Chicago	Omaha
Dallas	Pensacola
Denver	Portland
Des Moines	Seattle
Fargo-Moorhead (SD)	Spokane
Fort Worth	Springfield (MO)
Galveston	St. Louis
Houston	Tulsa
Kansas City	Wichita
Lincoln	

WHAT

Subsidiaries
BN Leasing Co.
Burlington Northern Railroad Co.

	1989 Sales	
Items Transported	$ mil	% of total
Coal	1,504	33
Agricultural commodities	718	16
Industrial products	682	15
Highway trailers/containers	649	14
Forest products	480	10
Food & consumer products	413	9
Automotive products	154	3
Other	6	—
Total	**4,606**	**100**

RANKINGS

12th in *Fortune* 50 Transportation Cos.
192nd in *Forbes* Sales 500
234th in *Business Week* 1000
704th in *Business Week* Global 1000

COMPETITION

Canadian Pacific
Chicago and North Western
Consolidated Freightways
Rio Grande Industries
Roadway
Santa Fe Pacific
Union Pacific
Yellow Freight

HOW MUCH

	9 Yr. Growth	1980	1981	1982	1983	1984	1985	1986	1987	1988	1989
Sales ($ mil)	1.7%	3,954	4,936	4,198	4,508	9,156	8,651	6,941	6,621	4,700	4,606
Net income ($ mil)	1.0%	223	272	178	413	579	633	(529)	367	207	243
Income as % of sales	—	5.6%	5.5%	4.2%	9.2%	6.3%	7.3%	(7.6%)	5.5%	4.4%	5.3%
Earnings per share ($)	(0.5%)	3.32	3.51	2.28	5.39	7.15	7.96	(7.53)	4.91	*2.76*	3.18
Stock price – high ($)	—	38.50	36.38	31.25	54.75	50.00	72.63	82.38	84.25	80.38	32.38
Stock price – low ($)	—	12.88	18.50	17.13	25.50	35.00	46.25	46.50	35.00	56.00	21.38
Stock price – close ($)	(0.2%)	32.19	26.81	26.56	49.50	47.00	68.25	53.25	62.75	79.00	31.50
P/E – high	—	12	10	14	10	7	9	—	17	29	10
P/E – low	—	4	5	8	5	5	6	—	7	20	7
Dividends per share ($)	8.5%	0.58	0.77	0.76	0.87	1.00	1.40	1.70	2.05	2.20	1.20
Book value per share ($)	(8.7%)	32.64	35.37	38.33	50.76	56.98	63.13	47.90	50.80	12.31	14.33

1989 Year End:
Debt ratio: 67.3%
Return on equity: 23.9%
Cash (mil): $83
Current ratio: 0.62
Long-term debt (mil): $2,220
Number of shares (mil): 75
Dividends:
1989 average yield: 3.8%
1989 payout: 37.7%
Market value (mil): $2,375

CADBURY SCHWEPPES PLC

OVERVIEW

With sales in over 110 countries, Cadbury Schweppes is a major international soft drink and candy maker. The company is #1 in the UK candy market, with a 26% market share. Its Wakefield, Great Britain, soft drink bottling plant is the largest in Europe. The company owns bottling facilities in many countries but uses 800 independent bottlers in the US.

Popular US brands include Orange Crush, Canada Dry, and Schweppes.

Cadbury Schweppes is expanding globally through acquisitions and international partnerships. Cadbury's US candy brands (Mounds, Almond Joy) are produced and marketed under license by Hershey. The company owns Crush International and 51% of highly successful UK bottler Coca-Cola Schweppes.

WHEN

Cadbury Schweppes is the product of a 1969 merger of 2 seasoned British firms. The world's first soft drink maker, Schweppes originated in 1783 London, where Swiss national Jacob Schweppe first sold his artificial mineral water. Schweppe returned to Switzerland in 1799, but the company continued its British operations, introducing a lemonade in 1835 and tonic water (containing antimalarial quinine) and ginger ale in the 1870s. Beginning in the 1880s Schweppes expanded worldwide, particularly in countries that would later form the Commonwealth. In the 1960s the company diversified into food products, acquiring, among others, Chivers (marmalade), Typhoo (tea), and Kenco (coffee).

John Cadbury began making cocoa in Birmingham, England, in 1831 and by 1841 was producing 15 varieties of chocolates. The Cadbury Dairy Milk bar, launched in 1905, soon became Britain's best-selling candy bar. In 1918 Cadbury bought Fry, a British candy producer. Cadbury established dominant market positions in the UK, Australia, South Africa, and India, building plants in Canada (1920), Australia (1922), and South Africa (1938).

Under the direction of CEO Dominic Cadbury, Cadbury Schweppes acquired Peter Paul (Mounds, Almond Joy) in 1978 to enhance its position in the vast US candy market. At the same time Schweppes was successfully increasing beverage sales on the Continent and in the Far East. The company's flagging share of the British chocolate market suddenly revived with the 1982 introduction of the Wispa bar. With the 1982 acquisition of Duffy-Mott, Cadbury Schweppes entered the US applesauce and juice market.

Through 1984 Cadbury Schweppes's businesses appeared to thrive, but by 1985 problems became apparent. British candy demand had stopped growing. US candy distributor stockpiling had accounted for much of Cadbury's perceived growth in sales. Schweppes tonic was losing share at home and in the US. The US Wispa introduction was a failure. Apple juice was found to be a low-margin business. Dominic Cadbury invoked what Cadbury Schweppes executives call "the R word" — restructuring.

In 1986 Cadbury Schweppes sold its noncandy, nonbeverage businesses, consolidated divisions, eliminated layers of management, and purchased Canada Dry, rights to Sunkist soda, and 34% of Dr Pepper (now 8.6% of Dr Pepper/Seven-Up). In 1987 Massachusetts-based General Cinema acquired 17% of Cadbury Schweppes stock, fueling rumors of a bid for the company. The company entered into a joint venture with Coca-Cola in the same year, creating a $1 billion UK bottling enterprise. In 1989 Cadbury Schweppes purchased Orange Crush from Procter & Gamble. Facing Mars's and Hershey's combined 70% share of US candy bar sales, Cadbury signed a $300 million licensing agreement with Hershey, ending direct involvement in the US candy market in 1988.

HOW MUCH

£ = $1.61 (Dec. 31, 1989)	9 Yr. Growth	1980	1981	1982	1983	1984	1985	1986	1987	1988	1989
Sales (£ mil)	11.3%	1,086	1,229	1,494	1,703	2,016	1,874	1,840	2,031	2,382	2,843
Net income (£ mil)	15.0%	46	47	49	61	73	48	76	109	141	162
Income as % of sales	—	4%	4%	3%	4%	4%	3%	4%	5%	6%	6%
Earnings per share (p)	8.2%	12.2	11.3	11.0	13.6	15.7	9.3	14.3	19.1	23.5	24.9
Stock price – high (p)	—	75	101	132	130	163	176	196	291	429	495
Stock price – low (p)	—	54	67	85	96	115	131	144	119	231	319
Stock price – close (p)	19.2%	71	86	117	117	163	158	187	231	338	346
P/E – high	—	6	9	12	10	10	19	14	15	18	20
P/E – low	—	4	6	8	7	7	9	10	6	10	13
Dividends per share (p)	11.2%	4.1	4.6	4.9	5.4	5.9	5.9	6.7	8.0	9.2	10.7
Book value per share (p)	1.4%	76	86	87	89	90	90	97	93	98	86

1989 Year End:
Sales (mil): $4,578
Debt ratio: 36.0%
Return on equity: 27.1%
Cash (mil): £91
Long-term debt (mil): £381
Number of shares (mil): 695
Dividends:
1989 average yield: 3.1%
1989 payout: 47.1%
Market value (mil): $3,872

NASDAQ symbol: CADBY (ADR)
Incorporated: England, 1897
Fiscal year ends: Saturday nearest December 31

WHO

Chairman: Sir Graham Day, age 56, £67,407 pay (prior to promotion)
CEO: N. Dominic Cadbury, age 49
Finance Director and Deputy Group CEO: Neville C. Bain, age 49
Auditors: Arthur Andersen & Co.; Coopers & Lybrand Deloitte
Employees: 34,982

WHERE

HQ: 1-4 Connaught Place, London W2 2EX, England
Phone: 011-44-71-262-1212
US HQ (Cadbury Schweppes Inc.): High Ridge Park, PO Box 3800, Stamford, CT 06905
US Phone: 203-329-0911
US FAX: 203-968-7854 (Communications and Public Affairs)

Cadbury Schweppes products are sold in more than 110 countries worldwide.

	1989 Sales		1989 Operating Income	
	£ mil	% of total	£ mil	% of total
UK	1,280	45	111	40
Europe	554	19	58	21
North America	364	13	39	14
Other countries	645	23	72	25
Total	**2,843**	**100**	**280**	**100**

WHAT

	1989 Sales		1989 Operating Income	
	£ mil	% of total	£ mil	% of total
Confectionery	1,145	40	132	47
Beverages	1,699	60	148	53
Total	**2,843**	**100**	**280**	**100**

Brand Names

(US Markets)

Soft Drinks
Canada Dry
Crush
Hires
Schweppes
Sun-drop
Sunkist

Other Products
Clamato (mixer)
Holland House (cocktail mixes, cooking wines)
Mott's (apple products)
Mr & Mrs "T" (cocktail mixes)
Red Cheek (apple juice)
Rose's (grenadine, lime juice)

(Foreign Markets)

Soft Drinks
Coca-Cola (UK bottling, 51% interest)
Gini
Schweppes
Solo
Trina

Confectionery
Cadbury
Fry's
Jamesons
Pascall
Poulain
Trebor
Wispa

RANKINGS

285th in *Fortune* Global 500 Industrial Cos.
457th in *Business Week* Global 1000

COMPETITION

Bass	Dr Pepper/7Up	Philip Morris
Berkshire Hathaway	Mars	RJR Nabisco
Campbell Soup	Nestlé	TLC Beatrice
Coca-Cola	PepsiCo	

STATE OF CALIFORNIA

OVERVIEW

California's diverse, $700 billion economy would be the world's 6th largest if it were a separate country. The state leads the US in microelectronics, biotechnology, aerospace, agriculture, entertainment, and foreign trade.

California is the US's leading exporter of agricultural and manufactured products. Its estimated 275 crops yield over 50% of the US's fruits, nuts, and vegetables. The state boasts high-tech meccas (such as Silicon Valley) and exceptional universities and draws over 40% of all new Japanese investment in the US.

The state's government is structured on the federal model (with executive, legislative, and judicial branches) but also includes a unique proposition process that allows voters to act directly on issues.

California (whose name derives from a fictional earthly paradise in 16th-century Spanish literature) has always been a frontier, an instigator of endless trends, and a lurer of generations of spiritual explorers, from Theosophists to Timothy Leary's space migrators. The US's most populous state, California gained 5.5 million people in the 1980s. Metropolitan Los Angeles is a magnet for immigrants; its Mexican, Vietnamese, Armenian, and Iranian populations (among others) are the largest outside their home countries.

Among the state's challenges in the 1990s are severe traffic congestion, water shortages, and environmental deterioration.

WHEN

Early European explorers of California, including Juan Rodriguez Cabrillo (Spain, 1542) and Sir Francis Drake (England, 1579) claimed the land for their native countries, but European interest remained low for nearly 2 centuries. In 1769, King Charles III of Spain extended his New Spain (Mexican) empire, securing California against imperial rivals England and Russia.

Father Junípero Serra and his Franciscan missionaries established 21 missions that became the centers of economic activity.

California became a province of Mexico following the latter's independence (1821); Americans, like Swiss-born John A. Sutter, slowly filtered westward and in 1846 revolted against Mexican rule. The US, victorious in its war with Mexico, absorbed the territory (1848).

Immigration following the discovery of gold at Sutter's mill (1848) pushed California's non-Indian population from 13,000 to 112,000 by 1850. Paper, flour, lumber, and textile mills, and iron works, shipyards, and banks sprouted. Supply centers San Francisco, Sacramento, and Stockton grew rapidly. Soon California had a constitution (1849), statehood (1850), and a state capital in Sacramento (1854).

The nation's first transcontinental railroad reduced shipping costs and isolation (1869). In the 1870s and 1880s the Southern Pacific and Santa Fe (and later the Panama Canal, 1914) opened huge new markets for crops and citrus fruits, launching a food processing industry and a Los Angeles real estate boom (1887). L.A.'s population expanded from 12,000 to 350,000 between 1880 and 1910. In 1906 San Francisco was decimated by an earthquake and 3-day fire.

California's climate drew filmmakers west; by 1913 Hollywood had become the world's film center. Shipbuilding, oil refining, and many new industries flourished during WWI.

The 1920s saw large oil discoveries and aviation pioneers (Donald Douglas, John Northrop, *et al.*) founding namesake firms. During the Great Depression the Golden Gate and Oakland Bay Bridges were built, and Dust Bowl refugees flooded the state.

During WWII California became a frontline staging area. The Korean and Vietnam conflicts created more defense jobs and fueled military industrialization in the early 1960s.

Stanford professor Frederick E. Terman helped create Silicon Valley in the 1970s when the personal computer and microprocessor were invented. In the 1980s old, heavy industries were replaced by new service and technical businesses.

HOW MUCH

	9 Yr. Growth	1980	1981	1982	1983	1984	1985	1986	1987	1988	1989
Population (mil)	2.3%	23.78	24.27	24.79	25.31	25.78	26.36	27.00	27.65	28.20	29.06
Gross state product (GSP) ($ bil)	8.5%	325.2	354.9	372.5	408.2	456.9	496.8	533.8	588.5	638.2	675.8
GSP per capita (const. $)	1.5%	20,353	20,137	19,143	20,290	20,952	21,994	22,332	22,928	23,880	23,310
GSP ($ bil, const. $)	3.7%	488	483	479	507	545	572	603	642	669	676
State revenues ($ bil)	8.7%	21.8	23.4	24.2	27.6	31.6	33.5	37.6	38.2	42.3	46.0
State expenditures ($ bil)	7.3%	24.4	24.8	24.9	26.4	30.4	34.0	37.1	39.6	43.5	46.1

GSP per capita ($ mil) 1980-89

25,000
20,000
15,000
10,000
5,000
0

Official name: State of California
Admitted as state: September 9, 1850
State capital: Sacramento
Motto: "Eureka"

WHO

Governor: George Deukmejian (R), $102,079 pay
Lieutenant Governor: Leo T. McCarthy (D), $87,068 pay
Secretary of State: March Fong Eu (D), $87,068 pay
Attorney General: John K. Van de Kamp (D), $93,073 pay
Controller: Gray Davis (D), $87,068 pay
Treasurer: Thomas Hayes (R), $87,068 pay
Senators: Pete Wilson (R), Alan Cranston (D)

WHERE

HQ: Office of the Governor, State Capitol, 1st Floor, Sacramento, CA 95814
Phone: 916-445-2841
FAX: 916-445-4633

California is the US's 3rd largest state, approximately the same size as Japan. The state has 58 counties. Total state land area is 158,692 square miles.

Largest Cities	1990 Population (thou)
Los Angeles–Long Beach	8,770
Riverside–San Bernardino	2,534
San Diego	2,510
Anaheim–Santa Ana	2,326
Oakland	2,069
San Francisco	1,605
Sacramento	1,467
San Jose	1,464
Oxnard–Ventura	669
Fresno	647

WHAT

1986 GSP Distribution	$ mil	% of total
Service	103,397	19
Manufacturing	97,680	18
Trade (wholesale & retail)	93,927	18
Finance, insurance & real estate	93,790	18
Government	62,029	12
Transportation & public utilities	41,928	8
Construction	23,855	4
Farms, forestry & fishing	11,282	2
Mining	5,927	1
Total	**533,816**	**100**

Imports	Exports
Clothing	Agricultural products
Computers	Aircraft
Home entertainment goods	Computers
Office machines	Electronic components
Passenger cars	Office machine components
Semiconductors	Semiconductors
Sporting goods	
Trucks	
Toys	

RANKINGS

6th in world GNP (including US)
1st in US agricultural output and exports
1st in US manufacturing output and exports
1st in US population

CAMPBELL SOUP COMPANY

OVERVIEW

Campbell Soup is the largest US maker of canned soups and a major producer of frozen dinners, pickles, and vegetable and tomato juices. Other products include frozen seafood, spaghetti sauces, baked goods, frozen prepared chicken, meat pies, sweet goods, and canned beans and pasta; soups make up less than 50% of Campbell's business. The 121-year-old company produces more than 3,000 items sold in the US and worldwide.

The company operates 4 divisions: Campbell U.S.A., Pepperidge Farm, Campbell Enterprises, and Campbell International.

Campbell's new president, former Gerber executive David Johnson, is selling unrewarding foreign operations; several North American businesses are also slated for sale. The moves are designed to improve Campbell's earnings growth and return on equity, which have been near industry lows over the last decade. Members of the Dorrance family, heirs of the founder, own about 58% of the company's stock.

NYSE symbol: CPB
Incorporated: New Jersey, 1922
Fiscal year ends: Sunday nearest August 1

WHO

President and CEO: David W. Johnson, age 57
Chairman: Robert J. Vlasic, age 64
SVP; President, Campbell U.S.A.: Herbert M. Baum, age 53, $512,736 pay
SVP; President, Campbell International: John W. Argabright, age 54, $308,480 pay
SVP Finance and CFO: Edwin L. Harper, age 48, $440,180 pay
Auditors: Price Waterhouse
Employees: 55,412

WHEN

Campbell Soup Company, one of America's oldest food retailers, began in Camden, New Jersey, in 1869 as a canning and preserving business. The company's founders, icebox maker Abram Anderson and fruit merchant Joseph Campbell, quickly established Campbell's enduring reputation for quality. Anderson left in 1876, and Arthur Dorrance took his place. Campbell retired in 1894, and the Dorrance family assumed control.

Arthur Dorrance's nephew, Dr. John Dorrance, joined Campbell in 1897. The talented chemist soon found a way to condense soup by removing most of its water, a discovery crucial to Campbell's subsequent success. Without the heavy bulk of water-filled cans, Campbell rapidly gained much wider, less costly distribution than its 2 major competitors, and its products soon spread across the country.

In 1904 the company introduced its Campbell Kids to help sell soup. Entering the California market in 1911, Campbell became one of the first American companies to achieve national distribution of a food brand. Campbell bought Franco-American, the first American soupmaker, in 1915.

Campbell's ubiquity in American kitchens made the Campbell soup can an American pop culture icon, as emphasized by Andy Warhol's 1960s print, and brought great wealth and social prestige to the Dorrance family. When Dorrance died in 1930 after 16 years as company president, he left the 3rd largest estate recorded at that time, $115 million. His son John Jr. became chairman in 1962 and, even after retirement, continued involvement with the company until he died in 1989.

Campbell built a reputation as a conservatively managed concern, more focused on food quality, operational efficiency, and production skills than on marketing hype. Campbell was similarly cautious in diversifying beyond soups. Campbell acquired V8 juice (1948), Swanson (1955), Vlasic pickles (1978), and Mrs. Paul's seafood (1982). Campbell formed Godiva Chocolatier (1966) to sell the chocolates in America. It introduced Prego spaghetti sauce and Le Menu frozen dinners in the early 1980s. The company has invested in almost every convenience food category and pushed into European markets.

In 1989 chairman Robert Vlasic touched off a family feud with "Project Toad," a bid to merge with Quaker Oats. The deal was scuttled, but 3 disenchanted Dorrance heirs, who control 17.4% of the company's stock, pressed for sale of the company. In 1990 the dissidents pledged to suspend their demands for a sale while new CEO David Johnson restructures the company for more profits.

WHERE

HQ: Campbell Place, Camden, NJ 08103
Phone: 609-342-4800
FAX: 609-342-3878

Campbell has operations in the US and in Argentina, Australia, Belgium, Canada, France, Germany, Hong Kong, Ireland, Italy, Japan, Mexico, the Netherlands, Spain, and the UK.

	1989 Sales		1989 Operating Income	
	$ mil	% of total	$ mil	% of total
US	4,233	74	295	138
Europe	984	17	(21)	(10)
Other foreign	543	9	(60)	(28)
Adjustments	(88)	—	322	—
Total	**5,672**	**100**	**536**	**100**

WHAT

	1989 Sales		1989 Operating Income	
	$ mil	% of total	$ mil	% of total
Campbell USA	2,777	49	175	82
Campbell Int'l	1,527	27	(81)	(38)
Pepperidge Farm	548	10	54	25
Vlasic Foods	441	8	39	18
Campbell Enterprises	327	6	27	13
Mrs. Paul's	140	2	—	—
Adjustment	(88)	(2)	322	—
Total	**5,672**	**100**	**536**	**100**

Brand Names

Bounty
Campbell
Franco-American
Godiva
Le Menu
Marie's
Mrs. Giles
Mrs. Kinser's
Mrs. Paul's
Open Pit
Pepperidge Farm
Prego
Swanson
Swift
V8
Vlasic
Win Schuler

HOW MUCH

	9 Yr. Growth	1980	1981	1982	1983	1984	1985	1986	1987	1988	1989
Sales ($ mil)	9.2%	2,561	2,798	2,945	3,292	3,657	3,989	4,379	4,490	4,869	5,672
Net income ($ mil)	(22.8%)	135	130	150	165	191	198	223	247	242	13
Income as % of sales	—	5.3%	4.6%	5.1%	5.0%	5.2%	5.0%	5.1%	5.5%	5.0%	0.2%
Earnings per share ($)	(22.7%)	1.02	1.00	1.16	1.28	1.48	1.53	1.73	1.91	1.87	0.10
Stock price – high ($)	—	8.22	8.47	12.44	16.03	18.03	29.06	34.25	35.38	35.25	60.63
Stock price – low ($)	—	6.31	6.56	7.00	10.69	13.56	15.09	22.00	22.75	23.88	30.50
Stock price – close ($)	25.2%	7.75	7.16	12.09	15.25	17.38	24.69	28.50	27.88	31.50	58.63
P/E – high	—	8	8	11	13	12	19	20	19	19	—
P/E – low	—	6	7	6	8	9	10	13	12	13	—
Dividends per share ($)	7.6%	0.47	0.51	0.53	0.54	0.57	0.61	0.65	0.71	0.81	0.90
Book value per share ($)	7.3%	7.28	7.76	8.19	8.91	9.76	10.69	11.86	13.35	14.69	13.72

1989 Year End:
Debt ratio: 26.1%
Return on equity: 0.7%
Cash (mil): $147
Current ratio: 1.3
Long-term debt (mil): $629
Number of shares (mil): 130
Dividends:
1989 average yield: 1.5%
1989 payout: —
Market value (mil): $7,597

Stock Price History high/low 1980-89

RANKINGS

88th in *Fortune* 500 Industrial Cos.
235th in *Fortune* Global 500 Industrial Cos.
145th in *Forbes* Sales 500
84th in *Business Week* 1000
254th in *Business Week* Global 1000

COMPETITION

American Home Products
Anheuser-Busch
Berkshire Hathaway
Cadbury Schweppes
ConAgra
CPC International
General Mills
H. J. Heinz
Hershey
Kellogg
Nestlé
Procter & Gamble
RJR Nabisco
Sara Lee
Unilever
Whitman

CAMPEAU CORPORATION

OVERVIEW

Toronto-based Campeau Corporation is one of the largest public companies in Canada, although 98% of its sales are in the US. In addition to its retail operations (Federated and Allied department stores and Ralphs supermarkets), Campeau owns or has joint ventures in US and Canadian shopping malls and office complexes, including Toronto's Scotia Plaza.

Through the purchase of Allied Stores in 1986 and Federated Department Stores in 1988, Campeau acquired some of the most prestigious names in retailing: Lazarus, Abraham & Straus, Burdines, Jordan Marsh, Rich's/Goldsmith's, The Bon Marché, and Bloomingdale's. Campeau also acquired Ralphs, a Southern California grocery chain, as part of the Federated buyout.

Poor earnings from the department stores, combined with high interest on the junk bond financing used to effect the acquisitions, resulted in huge losses for Campeau. Consequently, Federated and Allied both filed for bankruptcy in early 1990, and Campeau himself, although still a director, is no longer involved in the day-to-day management of the company.

WHEN

Robert Campeau got his start as a housing developer in Ottawa, Canada, after WWII. The homes he built had such a good reputation that "a Campeau-built home" indicated quality construction. He moved slowly into commercial and retail real estate development and in 1968 combined his 7 businesses to form Campeau Corporation. In 1969 he sold a majority interest in the company to raise capital but quickly regretted the move and borrowed the $38 million needed to regain a controlling stake.

In 1986 Campeau acquired Allied Stores Corporation, then the 6th largest department store operator in the US. Allied Stores had been founded in 1928 as Hahn Department Stores through the merger of 22 chains stretching from Jordan Marsh in Boston to The Bon Marché in Seattle to Maas Brothers in Tampa. The company changed its name to Allied Stores in 1935. Campeau bought the company for $3.6 billion and sold 17 of Allied's chains, including Ann Taylor, Brooks Brothers, Bonwit Teller, and Joske's, for $2.2 billion in order to reduce acquisition debt. Allied retained 4 chains: Bon Marché, Maas Brothers, Stern's, and Jordan Marsh.

Campeau bought the largest US department store operator, Federated Department Stores, in 1988 for $6.5 billion. Federated had been formed by 4 families in 1929 to spread their risk. These families owned Lazarus of Columbus, Shillito of Cincinatti, Bloomingdale's of New York, Abraham & Straus of Brooklyn, and Filene's of Boston. Federated had grown throughout its history to include some of the best-known department store chains in the US. Campeau sold the Bullock's/Bullock's-Wilshire and I. Magnin divisions to R. H. Macy and also sold Filene's, Gold Circle, Foley's, MainStreet, and The Children's Place. The company received $4.1 billion for these sales and kept only Abraham & Straus, Bloomingdale's, Burdines, Lazarus, and Rich's, which included Goldsmith's.

By 1989 Campeau had combined the headquarters operations of the 2 department store chains to increase efficiency, but the subsidiaries continued to lose money. Federated and Allied Stores filed for bankruptcy in 1990. The company closed several poorly performing stores and advanced a restructuring plan involving the liquidation of its real estate holdings. Later in 1990 the board removed Campeau from his position as chairman and CEO of the corporation.

HOW MUCH

	6 Yr. Growth	1980	1981	1982	1983	1984	1985	1986	1987	1988	1989
Sales ($ mil)	103.7%	—	—	—	146	160	156	982	3,530	8,668	10,439
Net income ($ mil)	—	—	—	—	17	21	24	62	(203)	(34)	(1,636)
Income as % of sales	—	—	—	—	11.6%	13.1%	15.4%	6.3%	(5.8%)	(0.4%)	(15.7%)
Earnings per share ($)	—	—	—	—	—	—	—	1.43	(5.21)	(1.04)	(37.25)
Stock price – high ($)	—	—	—	—	—	—	—	—	14.25	20.63	18.63
Stock price – low ($)	—	—	—	—	—	—	—	—	9.75	11.75	2.75
Stock price – close ($)	—	—	—	—	—	—	—	—	14.13	13.38	3.00
P/E – high	—	—	—	—	—	—	—	—	—	—	—
P/E – low	—	—	—	—	—	—	—	—	—	—	—
Dividends per share ($)	—	—	—	—	—	—	—	0.08	0.09	0.24	0.17
Book value per share ($)	—	—	—	—	—	—	—	3.65	(0.16)	(0.29)	(39.88)

1989 Year End:
Debt ratio: 222.4%
Return on equity: —
Cash (mil): $613
Current ratio: 1.41
Long-term debt (mil):$3,029
Number of shares (mil): 44
Dividends:
1989 average yield: 5.6%
1989 payout: —
Market value (mil): $133

Stock Price History high/low 1987-89

25
20
15
10
5
0

Principal stock exchange: Montreal
Incorporated: Ontario, 1978
Fiscal year ends: January 31

WHO

Interim Chairman: Robert Després
Interim Co-CEO: James D. Raymond
Interim Co-CEO: Gary M. Goodman
SVP Finance and Treasurer: David W. Beirnes
Auditors: Peat Marwick Thorne
Employees: 100,000

WHERE

HQ: 40 King St. West, Suite 5800, Toronto, Ontario, M5H 3Y8, Canada
Phone: 416-868-6460
FAX: 416-594-1888 (Public Relations)

Retail operations are conducted solely in the US. Real estate sales and rent revenues are derived from the US and Canada.

	1989 Sales		1989 Operating Income	
	$ mil	% of total	$ mil	% of total
Canada	202	2	119	13
US	10,237	98	778	87
Adjustments	—	—	(451)	—
Total	**10,439**	**100**	**446**	**100**

WHAT

	1989 Sales		1989 Operating Income	
	$ mil	% of total	$ mil	% of total
Department stores	7,574	73	595	66
Supermarkets	2,556	24	158	18
Rental	213	2	135	15
Real estate	96	1	9	1
Adjustments	—	—	(451)	—
Total	**10,439**	**100**	**446**	**100**

	1989 Retail Space	
	no. of stores	sq. ft. thou
Department Stores		
Federated Department Stores		
Abraham & Straus (NY & NJ)	15	5,651
Bloomingdale's (National)	17	4,514
Burdines (FL)	30	5,254
Lazarus (Midwest)	44	8,334
Rich's/Goldsmith's (Southeast)	26	6,216
Allied Stores		
The Bon Marché (Northwest)	40	4,645
Jordan Marsh (New England)	26	4,885
Maas Brothers (Southeast)	38	5,875
Stern's (NY, NJ & PA)	24	4,478
Supermarkets		
Ralphs (CA)	142	6,162
Total	**402**	**56,014**

RANKINGS

7th in *Forbes* 100 Foreign Investments in the US

COMPETITION

Albertson's
American Stores
Carter Hawley Hale
Dayton Hudson
Dillard
Edward J. DeBartolo
R. H. Macy
May Department Stores
Mercantile Stores
Montgomery Ward
Nordstrom
J. C. Penney
Sears
Trammell Crow
Vons

CANADIAN PACIFIC LTD.

OVERVIEW

Canada's 2nd largest independent company (after BCE), Canadian Pacific operates the 7th largest railway in North America (CP Rail), the largest hotel chain in Canada (Canadian Pacific Hotels), and several other successful ventures in transportation, energy, forest products, real estate, telecommunications, and manufacturing.

Montreal-based CP Rail provides freight rail and intermodal service (freight shipped by truck, train, or ship in the same container) to most of Canada's industrial centers. Canadian Pacific also owns the Minneapolis-based Soo Line, with freight rail operations in the midwestern US. Canadian Pacific is one of the world's largest newsprint and pulp producers, owning timberland in 4 provinces, and recently announced a major recycling program for 2 of its newsprint manufacturing plants. However, weak newsprint markets and lowered railroad freight traffic combined with the strengthened Canadian dollar to contribute to the company's 9% decline in earnings between 1988 and 1989.

NYSE symbol: CP
Incorporated: Canada, 1881
Fiscal year ends: December 31

WHO

Chairman and CEO: William W. Stinson, age 56, C$859,724 pay
President and COO: James F. Hankinson, age 46, C$482,676 pay (prior to promotion)
EVP and CFO: G. F. Michals, age 54, C$396,544 pay
EVP; Chairman, President, and CEO, CP Rail: I. B. Scott, age 60, C$386,993 pay
Auditors: Price Waterhouse
Employees: 75,600

WHEN

Realizing that Canada's future depended upon a railway linking the populous East with the western frontiers, bankers George Stephen and R. B. Angus joined James J. Hill (future president of Great Northern Railway) to found Canadian Pacific Railway Company (CP Rail) in 1881, with Stephen as president.

With a 25 million acre government land grant, the railroad was planned in 2 sections: one extending from Lake Nipissing to Lake Superior and the other crossing the Canadian prairies and mountains from Winnepeg to Kamloops Lake in British Columbia. William Cornelius Van Horne, CP Rail's general manager, started construction on the prairies in the spring of 1882, reached the summit of the Rockies in 1883, and saw the railroad completed at Eagle Pass in 1885, nearly 6 years ahead of schedule.

In 1886 a CP Rail passenger train made the first trans-Canadian rail crossing from Montreal to Port Moody — the world's longest scheduled train trip — in 139 hours. That same year CP Rail chartered ships to carry tea and silk from the Far East to the Canadian west coast, thereby laying the foundation for CP steamship services (later CP Ships). Hotel and telegraph services (later Canadian Pacific Hotels and CP Telecommunications) also developed along with the railroad, providing comfort and convenience for CP Rail's passengers and employees.

CP Rail expanded its service area by buying smaller railroads during the late 1800s and early 1900s and gained a major competitor in 1917 when the Canadian government combined several railroads to form Canadian National Railways (CN). In 1942 Canadian Pacific united 10 local airlines to form Canadian Pacific Air Lines, which pioneered the Vancouver-to-Amsterdam "polar route" in 1955. Both CP Rail and CN became all-freight railroads in 1979 after handing over passenger services to the government-operated VIA Rail Canada.

When William Stinson became CEO in 1985, Canadian Pacific operated a wide range of businesses, including Canadian Pacific Air Lines, the Minneapolis-based Soo Line Railroad, a hotel chain (Canadian Pacific Hotels), oil wells (PanCanadian Petroleum), pulp and paper manufacturing (Canadian Pacific Forest Products), a copper mine (Cominco), and a bone china maker (Syracuse China). Stinson sold the airline (to Pacific Western Airlines, 1986), Cominco (1986), and Syracuse China (1989) and to enhance Canadian Pacific's transportation and hotel interests bought 20% of Laidlaw (school bus operator, 1989) and 9 hotels, making Canadian Pacific Canada's largest hotel operator (1989).

WHERE

HQ: 910 Peel St., PO Box 6042, Station A, Montreal, Quebec H3C 3E4, Canada
Phone: 514-395-5151
FAX: 514-395-7306 (Investor Relations)

Canadian Pacific has operations throughout Canada, the US, and Europe.

	1989 Sales		1989 Net Income	
	$ mil	% of total	$ mil	% of total
Canada	7,183	75	519	95
US	1,793	19	(3)	(1)
Other countries	541	6	33	6
Adjustments	—	—	25	—
Total	**9,517**	**100**	**574**	**100**

WHAT

	1989 Sales		1989 Operating Income	
	$ mil	% of total	$ mil	% of total
Transportation	3,462	35	73	7
Forest products	2,487	25	332	31
Oil & gas, coal	987	10	252	24
Real estate, hotels	808	8	265	25
Manufacturing	1,587	16	93	9
Telecommun., other	549	6	46	4
Adjustments	(363)	—	213	—
Total	**9,517**	**100**	**1,274**	**100**

Transportation
CP Rail
CP Ships
CP Trucks
Soo Line Corp.

Forest Products
Canadian Pacific Forest Products Ltd. (80%)

Real Estate & Hotels
Canadian Pacific Hotels Corp.
Marathon Realty Co. Ltd.

Investments
Laidlaw (20%)

Oil & Gas, Coal
Fording Coal Ltd.
PanCanadian Petroleum Ltd. (87%)

Telecommunications & Manufacturing
AMCA International Ltd. (55%)
CP Telecommunications (60%)
Processed Minerals Inc.

RANKINGS

134th in *Fortune* Global 500 Industrial Cos.
82nd in *Forbes* 100 Foreign Investments in the US
299th in *Business Week* Global 1000

COMPETITION

American President
Burlington Northern

Other US railroads, trucking companies, hotel operators, petroleum and coal exploration companies, and newsprint and pulp manufacturers

HOW MUCH

	9 Yr. Growth	1980	1981	1982	1983	1984	1985	1986	1987	1988	1989
Sales ($ mil)	1.5%	8,357	10,399	9,991	10,258	11,079	10,754	9,058	8,978	9,314	9,517
Net income ($ mil)	1.8%	488	409	153	115	285	176	136	489	629	574
Income as % of sales	—	5.8%	3.9%	1.5%	1.1%	2.6%	1.6%	1.5%	5.4%	6.8%	6.0%
Earnings per share ($)	(2.5%)	2.26	1.90	0.70	0.53	1.32	0.79	0.46	1.62	2.03	1.80
Stock price – high ($)	—	15.00	14.75	11.75	14.29	14.33	15.75	14.63	22.88	20.13	24.38
Stock price – low ($)	—	9.50	10.33	6.42	9.50	9.38	11.63	10.00	12.75	15.88	18.00
Stock price – close ($)	7.0%	12.13	11.71	9.67	13.46	12.67	13.50	12.88	15.88	18.50	22.25
P/E – high	—	7	8	17	27	11	20	32	14	10	14
P/E – low	—	4	5	9	18	7	15	22	8	8	10
Dividends per share ($)	3.4%	0.53	0.53	0.44	0.38	0.36	0.35	0.35	0.41	0.56	0.71
Book value per share ($)	5.0%	13.58	15.28	14.98	15.05	15.84	14.76	13.98	16.37	19.28	21.12

1989 Year End:
Debt ratio: 33.3%
Return on equity: 8.9%
Cash (mil): $603
Current ratio: 1.09
Long-term debt (mil): $3,366
Number of shares (mil): 318
Dividends:
1989 average yield: 3.2%
1989 payout: 39.4%
Market value (mil): $7,080

Stock Price History high/low 1980-89

CAPITAL CITIES/ABC, INC.

OVERVIEW

Capital Cities/ABC operates the #2 network in the US — ABC — with 222 affiliates and owns 8 television stations, 5 in the nation's top 5 markets. The company also has radio stations (13 in the nation's top 10 markets) and the ABC Radio Networks, with 3,100 affiliates.

ABC's "World News Tonight" finished 1989 as the #1 early evening news program, a first in ABC's 37-year evening news history.

The company produces cable programming and owns part of several cable services, including ESPN, with the most subscribers (55.9 million).

Cap Cities/ABC, publishing daily and weekly newspapers mainly in the Northeast, ranks 14th among newspaper publishers. Cap Cities/ABC also publishes special-interest magazines and trade publications ranging from *Los Angeles* and *Institutional Investor* to *Hardware Age* and *Hog Farm Management*.

NYSE symbol: CCB
Incorporated: New York, 1946
Fiscal year ends: Sunday nearest December 31

WHO

Chairman: Thomas S. Murphy, age 65, $958,000 pay
President and CEO: Daniel B. Burke, age 61, $915,000 pay (prior to promotion)
SVP and CFO: Ronald J. Doerfler, age 48
Auditors: Ernst & Young
Employees: 19,860

WHERE

HQ: 77 W. 66th St., New York, NY 10023
Phone: 212-456-7777
FAX: 212-456-6850 (Public Relations)

Local Publishing & Broadcasting Activities

Daily newspapers	8 newspapers in CT, IL, MO, OR, PA, and TX
Weekly newspapers	77 newspapers in CT, IL, MA, MI, OR, and RI
Shopping guides & real estate magazines	39 publications in CA, CT, KS, MA, MI, MO, OR, PA, RI, and WA
TV stations	8 stations in CA, IL, NC, NY, PA, and TX
Radio stations	21 stations in CA, CO, DC, GA, IL, MI, MN, NY, RI, and TX

WHEN

Capital Cities/ABC resulted from the 1986 acquisition of the American Broadcasting Company by the much smaller Capital Cities Communications. ABC was started in 1926 by RCA's subsidiary, NBC, as a public service network. Less profitable than NBC's more commercial network, ABC (consisting of 3 radio stations and advertising airtime) was sold in 1943 to Edward J. Noble, Lifesavers candy promoter.

In the late 1940s and early 1950s, ABC was in 3rd place, with 5 TV stations and no daytime programming. Attempts to buy ABC by CBS and 20th Century Fox failed, but in 1953 the struggling network merged with United Paramount Theatres. United Paramount's Leonard Goldenson hired Disney Studios to produce a series for ABC's 1954-1955 season. Soon other movie studios, including Warner Brothers, were producing programming ("Ozzie and Harriet," "Wyatt Earp," "Cheyenne," 1955) for ABC.

About the same time (1954) Hudson Valley Broadcasting, owner of a struggling TV station in Albany, New York, hired Thomas Murphy to bail out the station. In 1957 Hudson Valley went public, becoming Capital Cities Television Corporation. While Cap Cities founder Frank Smith bought and sold TV and radio stations and publications, Murphy ran the company's operations. Smith died in 1966, and in 1968 Cap Cities, under Murphy's reign, bought Fairchild Publications, publisher of *Women's Wear Daily*, and continued throughout the 1970s buying and selling media companies.

Still in 3rd place in the 1960s, ABC fended off takeover attempts by Norton Simon, General Electric, and Howard Hughes. Programming whiz Fred Silverman defected from CBS, joining ABC in 1975. The next year ABC was the #1 network, and, with hits like "Love Boat" and "Happy Days," ABC stayed on top until 1979, the year after Silverman went to NBC. In 1979 ABC sold its records division and bought Chilton, a specialty publisher.

In the 1980s Cap Cities bought cable systems, and ABC produced programming for cable and bought ESPN in 1984. In 1986 Cap Cities, backed by Warren Buffett's Berkshire Hathaway, bought ABC for $3.5 billion, the largest purchase in media history. (Berkshire Hathaway now controls 18.7% of Cap Cities/ABC.) With the purchase Murphy became the chairman and CEO of the new company. In 1986 and 1987 Cap Cities/ABC sold its 53 cable systems to the Washington Post Company, formed a joint venture home video company, and bought radio stations.

In 1990 Cap Cities/ABC sold *Compute!* magazine, and Murphy, remaining as chairman, was replaced as CEO by Daniel Burke, president of Capital Cities since 1972.

WHAT

	1989 Sales		1989 Operating Income	
	$ mil	% of total	$ mil	% of total
Publishing	1,057	21	131	14
Broadcasting	3,900	79	836	86
Adjustments	—	—	(44)	—
Total	**4,957**	**100**	**923**	**100**

Broadcasting Networks
ABC Radio Networks
ABC Television Network
Satellite Music Network

Cable TV Networks
Arts & Entertainment (38% owned)
ESPN (80% owned)
Lifetime (33% owned)

Major TV Stations
KABC-TV (Los Angeles)
WABC-TV (New York)
WLS-TV (Chicago)

Major Newspapers
Fort Worth Star-Telegram
The Kansas City Star

Major Magazines
Institutional Investor
Los Angeles
M, The Civilized Man
McCall's Needlework & Crafts
W
Women's Wear Daily

Other Businesses
The Chilton Co. (auto guides)
NILS Publishing Co. (insurance law database)
Word, Inc. (religious books, music, and films)

HOW MUCH

	9 Yr. Growth	1980	1981	1982	1983	1984	1985	1986	1987	1988	1989
Sales ($ mil)	29.9%	472	574	664	762	940	1,021	4,124	4,440	4,773	4,957
Net income ($ mil)	23.9%	71	81	96	115	135	142	182	279	387	486
Income as % of sales	—	15.0%	14.0%	14.5%	15.0%	14.4%	13.9%	4.4%	6.3%	8.1%	9.8%
Earnings per share ($)	19.8%	5.38	6.12	7.25	8.53	10.40	10.87	11.20	16.46	22.31	27.25
Stock price – high ($)	—	72.00	80.50	136.75	157.50	174.50	229.00	279.75	450.00	369.75	568.00
Stock price – low ($)	—	40.00	56.50	64.38	114.75	123.50	152.25	208.25	268.00	297.00	353.00
Stock price – close ($)	28.6%	58.75	73.75	119.63	144.00	164.63	224.50	268.12	345.00	362.25	564.12
P/E – high	—	13	13	19	18	17	21	25	27	17	21
P/E – low	—	7	9	9	13	12	14	19	16	13	13
Dividends per share ($)	0.0%	0.20	0.20	0.20	0.20	0.20	0.20	0.20	0.20	0.20	0.20
Book value per share ($)	23.5%	27.96	34.07	41.30	47.72	57.08	68.42	120.84	137.40	168.09	187.74

1989 Year End:
Debt ratio: 34.0%
Return on equity: 15.3%
Cash (mil): $1,141
Current ratio: 3.17
Long-term debt (mil): $1,692
Number of shares (mil): 18
Dividends:
1989 average yield: 0.0%
1989 payout: 0.7%
Market value (mil): $9,891

Stock Price History high/low 1980-89

0 100 200 300 400 500 600

RANKINGS

17th in *Fortune* 100 Diversified Service Cos.
181st in *Forbes* Sales 500
50th in *Business Week* 1000
147th in *Business Week* Global 1000

COMPETITION

Bertelsmann
CBS
General Electric
News Corp.
Tele-Communications
Time Warner
Tribune
Turner Broadcasting
Viacom
Other media companies

CARGILL, INC.

OVERVIEW

With estimated revenues of $43 billion, Cargill is the largest privately owned company in the nation and ranks 8th among all US companies in terms of revenues. This 125-year-old food industry giant employs nearly 54,000 people and has operations that span the globe.

The root of Cargill's success has been the trading of a wide variety of commodities: grains and seed, sugar, coffee, orange juice, rubber, cocoa, molasses, precious and scrap metals, and petroleum products. The company buys, produces, transports, processes, and packages these goods and hedges its commodity prices through extensive futures trading. Cargill accounts for approximately 25% of the world's grain trade.

Cargill is also a major producer and trader of high-quality steel products (it operates the largest steel "minimill" in the US), animal feeds (Nutrena), and salt (Leslie). The company is one of the country's 3 largest meatpackers, with extensive feedlots, slaughterhouses, and pork and poultry operations. Cargill conducts its grain trading activity through Tradax International, a Panamanian company operating from Geneva, Switzerland.

The Cargill and MacMillan families still control 85% of Cargill's stock. Both of the families and the company have traditionally avoided publicity and are not well known even in Minneapolis, where Cargill is based.

WHEN

William Cargill, the son of a Scottish immigrant farmer, bought his first grain elevator in Conover, Iowa, shortly after the Civil War. By 1870 he and his brother Sam were buying grain elevators all along the Southern Minnesota Railroad, at a time when Minnesota was becoming an important shipping route for grain from the Upper Midwest destined for eastern and foreign locations, and the Pillsburys and others were establishing Minneapolis as a milling center. Sam and another brother, James, expanded the elevator operations while William worked with the railroads to monopolize the transport of grain to markets and coal back to the farmers. William moved to La Crosse, Wisconsin, in 1874 and worked from there to build his company.

Around the turn of the century, Cargill's son, also named William, invested in a Montana irrigation project and other ill-fated ventures. Cargill Sr. went to Montana to find that his name had been used to finance these undertakings and shortly afterward died of pneumonia. Cargill's creditors grew worried and started pressing for repayment, which threatened to bankrupt the company. John MacMillan, who had married William Sr.'s daughter Edna Cargill, wrested control after the founder's death and rebuilt Cargill. By the time the company recovered in 1916, it had been stripped of timber holdings and land in Mexico and Canada that William Sr. had collected. MacMillan opened offices in New York (1922) and Argentina (1929), expanding Cargill's grain trading and transport operations nationally and internationally.

During the Depression Cargill branched out from its grain business, building the river barges necessary to transport its products, and, when the grain fields turned into the Dust Bowl, Cargill bought up all the corn futures on the Chicago exchange, prompting the Board to kick Cargill's broker off the floor. During WWII Cargill built ships for the army and navy using its barge-building facilities.

After WWII North American wheat became an increasingly important product because of the ravages of war and a growing world population. In 1945 Cargill bought animal feed producer Nutrena Mills and also entered soybean processing; corn processing began a few years later and has grown along with the demand for corn sweeteners. In 1954 the US began lending money to third world countries to buy American grain, and Cargill was one of the main beneficiaries of the policy. The company's subsidiary Tradax, established in 1955, quickly became one of the largest grain traders in Europe. In 1965 Cargill entered sugar trading by buying sugar and molasses in the Philippines and selling it abroad.

As a requirement for an unsuccessful takeover bid of Missouri Portland Cement, Cargill first made its finances public in 1973, revealing it as one of America's largest companies ($5.2 billion sales), diversified into numerous commodities, farms, and food processing operations. In the 1970s the company expanded into coal, steel, and waste disposal, and throughout the 1980s developed these areas, becoming a major force in metals processing, beef, and salt production.

HOW MUCH

	9 Yr. Growth	1980	1981	1982	1983	1984	1985	1986	1987	1988	1989
US employees	4.7%	21,592	23,029	23,483	22,804	23,930	24,256	27,405	30,453	34,017	32,662
Foreign employees	5.3%	13,271	16,141	15,611	15,150	16,272	17,482	18,946	21,147	21,003	21,048
Total employees	4.9%	34,863	39,170	39,094	37,954	40,202	41,738	46,351	51,600	55,020	53,710

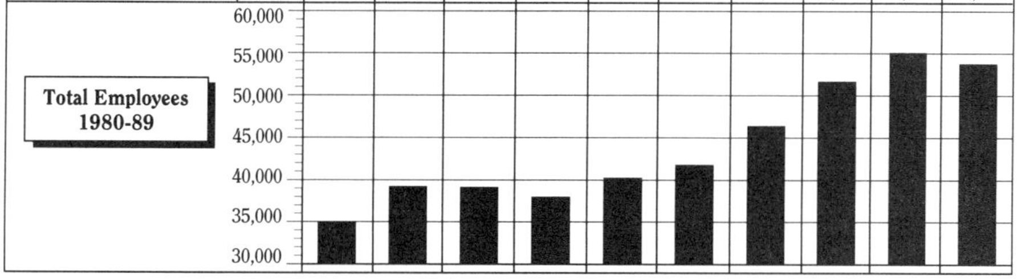

Total Employees 1980-89

60,000
55,000
50,000
45,000
40,000
35,000
30,000

Private company
Founded: 1865
Fiscal year ends: May 31

WHO

Chairman and CEO: Whitney MacMillan
President and COO: James R. Spicola
VP and CFO: Robert Lumpkins
Auditors: KPMG Peat Marwick
Employees: 53,710

WHERE

HQ: 15407 McGinty Rd., Minnetonka, MN 55343
Phone: 612-475-7575
FAX: 612-475-6208

Cargill, its subsidiaries, and affiliates have nearly 800 plants, 500 US offices, and 300 foreign offices in 60 countries. Its largest foreign operations are in Canada, Brazil, Argentina, and Europe.

WHAT

Commodities Trading & Transport
Barges and vessels (Cargo Carriers, Inc.)
Coffee and cocoa
Cotton (Hohenberg Bros)
Fertilizers
Grain and oilseeds
Iron and finished steel
Juice and fruit concentrates
Molasses and sugar
Oceangoing vessels
Petroleum products and petrochemicals
Rubber
Tallow

Industrial Products
Industrial chemicals
Scrap steel yards (Magnimet)
Steel and wire
Steel minimills (North Star)

Financial Operations
Equipment leasing
Futures trading and foreign exchange
Life insurance

Food Production & Processing
Animal byproducts
Beef, pork, and chicken processing and packaging
Bulk commodities
Corn syrup
Flour and corn milling
Salt

Agricultural Products
Animal feeds
Feed supplements
Seed and fertilizer

RANKINGS

1st in *Forbes* 400 US Private Cos.

COMPETITION

American President
Archer-Daniels-Midland
Bethlehem Steel
Chiquita Brands
ConAgra
CSX
General Mills
W. R. Grace
Inland Steel
LTV
Morton
Occidental
Ralston Purina
Salomon
Tyson Foods
USX
Chemical and food companies

CARLSON COMPANIES, INC.

OVERVIEW

Curtis L. Carlson, the founder, chairman, and CEO of Carlson Companies, has personally built his Minneapolis-based hotel/travel/marketing services company. The company is extremely goal oriented and does not encourage underperformers to stay on. Much emphasis is placed on developing "synergies" among the company's operations.

Carlson Companies is divided into 4 groups. Carlson Marketing Group is the largest motivation company in the world, providing sales and event promotion services and employee sales training and incentives programs. K-Promotions is the country's largest supplier of logo-identified promotional merchandise.

Carlson Hospitality Group operates and franchises 230 Radisson Hotels worldwide and 35 each of its Crest and Country Inn/Suites units. The group also oversees the company's resort operations, TGI Friday's restaurants, and Country Kitchens.

Most of the company's revenues come from the Carlson Travel Group, the largest travel organization in North America. The group includes Ask Mr. Foster, America's oldest and largest travel agency, and P. Lawson, the largest travel agency in Canada.

Carlson Investment Group develops commerical real estate throughout North America.

The company is a founding member of the Minnesota Keystone Club, whose members donate 5% of profits to charitable causes. The University of Minnesota renamed its business school in honor of Carlson after he had donated $25 million in 1986.

WHEN

Curtis Carlson, the son of Swedish immigrants, graduated from the University of Minnesota in 1937 and went to work as a Procter & Gamble soap salesman in the Minneapolis/St. Paul area. He noticed how incentives increased sales and put the observation to work by forming Gold Bond Stamp Company with a $50 loan in 1938 to sell trading stamps to grocery stores in his spare time. His wife, Arleen, dressed as a drum majorette and twirled a baton to promote the concept. By 1941 the company had 200 accounts. In 1952 a large local chain, Super Valu, started using the stamps, boosting Gold Bond's sales to $2.4 million. By 1960 the trading stamps were generating so much cash that Carlson began investing in other enterprises: Ardan catalog and jewelry showrooms, travel agencies, and business promotion and employee motivation programs.

In 1962 Carlson bought the Radisson Hotel in Minneapolis, originally opened in 1909, and he bought 7 more hotels throughout the state in the 1960s. In 1968 the Radisson chain expanded outside Minnesota, buying the future Radisson Denver from Hyatt. By 1976 the majority of Radisson rooms were outside Minnesota. Carlson diversified into restaurants with the purchase of the 11-unit TGI (Thank God It's) Friday's, a dining and singles bar chain. In 1977 he bought Country Kitchen International, a roadside restaurant chain.

Radisson, which by 1978 already had 19 hotel properties, including one in the West Indies, expanded into major markets that year with the addition of the Radisson Chicago and the reopening of Detroit's Cadillac Hotel as a Radisson. Many of the Radissons were older hotels remodeled by Contract Services Associates, another Carlson company. Radisson fought the image of look-alike hotel chains with its ad campaign, "A Collection, Not a Chain," introduced in 1978. In 1979 Carlson added to his hotel operations with Colony Resorts, a hotel/condominium management company operating mainly in Hawaii, which he purchased from its founder, baseball commissioner Peter Ueberroth.

Carlson Companies slowed the pace of its acquisitions in the 1980s, focusing instead on internal growth. Carlson took TGI Friday's public in 1983 (retaining 76% of the stock) to fund expansion of the chain, but reacquired all outstanding shares in 1990 for approximately $50 million. Carlson operates its companies by outlining 5-year plans and using employee motivation programs to ensure performance. The current plan, announced in 1987, calls for expanding the company's hospitality and travel-related businesses, including the new Country Inn roadside motel chain, and reaching a $9.2 billion sales goal by 1992.

HOW MUCH

	9 Yr. Growth	1980	1981	1982	1983	1984	1985	1986	1987	1988	1989
Sales ($ mil)	19.0%	1,300	1,600	2,000	2,300	2,600	3,100	3,600	4,300	5,300	6,200
Employees (thou)	13.2%	20	22	38	38	45	48	50	50	53	61
Owned hotels & motels	30.1%	21	23	25	39	55	75	135	160	195	225
Hotel rooms	23.1%	7,700	7,100	7,500	9,200	14,000	20,000	32,000	38,000	47,000	50,000

Hotel Rooms 1980-89

Private company
Incorporated: Minnesota, 1938
Fiscal year ends: December 31

WHO

Chairman and CEO: Curtis L. Carlson, age 76
President and COO: Edwin C. Gage, age 49
VP and CFO: Kenneth F. Gudorf
Auditors: Arthur Andersen & Co.
Employees: 61,000

WHERE

HQ: Carlson Pkwy., PO Box 59159, Minneapolis, MN 55459
Phone: 612-540-5452
FAX: 612-540-5832

The Marketing Group operates in 32 US cities and in over 20 countries. The Travel Group has 1,100 offices throughout the US and Canada.

WHAT

	1989 Sales	
	$ mil	% of total
Marketing group	600	10
Hospitality group	2,000	32
Travel group	3,600	58
Total	**6,200**	**100**

Carlson Marketing Group
Carlson International Division
- Carlson Marketing Group International (includes joint venture operating Kentucky Fried Chicken franchises in Japan)
- Carlson Marketing Group Ltd. (Canada)

Carlson Motivation Division
- E.F. MacDonald Motivation
- Performax Systems International

Carlson Promotion Division
- Jason/Empire (sports optics and leisure products)
- K-Promotions

Carlson Hospitality Group
Colony Hotels and Resorts
Country Hospitality
- Country Inn
- Country Kitchen
- Country Suites

Radisson Hotels International
TGI Friday's

Carlson Travel Group
Ask Mr. Foster (commercial and retail travel agents)
A.T. Mays Group (76%)
Neiman Marcus Travel
P. Lawson Travel (Canada)
Supercities and Great Escapes (vacation packages)

Carlson Investment Group
Carlson Center (Minneapolis)
Plaza VII (Minneapolis)
Office buildings, hotels, and shopping centers

RANKINGS

13th in *Forbes* 400 US Private Cos.

COMPETITION

American Express
Bass
Helmsley Enterprises
Hilton
Hyatt
ITT
Loews
Marriott
Nestlé
Saatchi & Saatchi
Young & Rubicam

CARTER HAWLEY HALE STORES, INC.

OVERVIEW

From its headquarters in Los Angeles, Carter Hawley Hale (CHH) operates 114 "traditional" department stores, Broadway, Emporium, Thalhimers, and Weinstocks. Although some CHH stores are in the Southeast and the West, the company derives 75% of its sales from California.

Carter Hawley Hale entered the 1980s with 3 specialty retail chains acquired in the late 1960s and 1970s: Contempo Casuals, Bergdorf Goodman, and Neiman-Marcus. When the takeover threats that characterized the retail industry in the 1980s reached CHH in 1987, management responded by spinning off these chains to its shareholders as a new company, The Neiman-Marcus Group, and paying common shareholders a special dividend of $346 million ($17/share).

Since the restructuring, the company's employee ownership plan has increased its ownership to 40% to reduce the likelihood of another takeover attempt. Long-term debt taken on during the restructuring has had a negative impact on profitability.

NYSE symbol: CHH
Incorporated: Delaware, 1984
Fiscal year ends: Saturday closest to July 31

WHO

Chairman and CEO: Philip M. Hawley, age 64, $707,500 pay
President and COO: Waldo H. Burnside, age 60, $567,505 pay
EVP and CFO: John M. Gailys, age 48, $422,500 pay
Auditors: Price Waterhouse
Employees: 37,000

WHEN

Arthur Letts opened the first Broadway Department Store on the corner of Fourth and Broadway in Los Angeles in 1896. Letts, an English immigrant, had failed with his first store in Seattle and started the Broadway on the site of another failed store.

The Broadway opened suburban stores in Hollywood (1931) and Pasadena (1940) but continued as a small, local retailer until 1947 when Edward Carter, a 34-year-old Harvard graduate, became president. Carter expanded the Broadway stores further into the Los Angeles suburbs and in 1951, after merging with Hale Brothers Stores of San Francisco, operator of Weinstocks department stores, he renamed the company Broadway-Hale.

In 1956 the company acquired Dohrmann Commercial Company, a Northern California hotel-supply business that owned 24% of Emporium Capwell Company. The Emporium, itself the result of an 1897 merger with San Francisco's even larger Golden Rule Bazaar, had acquired H. C. Capwell, an Oakland retailer, in 1927 and had grown to become the largest department store chain in the Bay Area. Broadway-Hale sold Dohrmann Commercial (1962) and continued to buy Emporium stock, merging the 2 companies in 1970.

Broadway-Hale acquired interests in Coulter's department store (1960, Los Angeles), Marston (1961, San Diego), and Korrick's (1962, Arizona). The company diversified in 1969 into mail-order through the purchase of Sunset House, and into bookselling through its acquisition of Walden Book Company (renamed Waldenbooks; sold 1984 to K mart). Also in 1969 it acquired Texas specialty retailer Neiman-Marcus. During 1970 the company joined with Ogden Development to build Broadway Plaza in downtown Los Angeles, consisting of the flagship Broadway store, a shopping center, a 500-room hotel, and 32 floors of office space.

Broadway-Hale bought Bergdorf Goodman, the exclusive New York store, in 1972. The company changed its name to Carter Hawley Hale in 1974 to incorporate the names of Carter and his heir apparent, Philip Hawley. The company purchased John Wanamaker (1978; sold 1986), the department store chain founded in Philadelphia in 1861; Thalhimer Brothers (1978), founded in Richmond, Virginia, in 1842; and specialty retailer Contempo Casuals (1979).

Facing a takeover bid by The Limited, the company restructured in 1987, spinning off its specialty retailers Contempo Casuals, Bergdorf Goodman, and Neiman-Marcus into The Neiman-Marcus Group, a public company in which General Cinema obtained a 60% interest in exchange for its preferred stock in CHH.

WHERE

HQ: 444 S. Flower St., Los Angeles, CA 90071
Phone: 213-620-0150
FAX: 213-620-0555

Carter Hawley Hale operates 114 department stores in 10 states.

	Stores		Area	
	no.	% of total	sq. ft. thou	% of total
California	73	64	14,060	73
Virginia	13	11	1,775	9
Arizona	7	6	1,137	6
North Carolina	10	8	735	4
Nevada	3	3	460	2
Utah	3	3	444	2
South Carolina	2	2	223	1
New Mexico	1	1	162	1
Colorado	1	1	135	1
Tennessee	1	1	134	1
Total	**114**	**100**	**19,265**	**100**

WHAT

Store Divisions	Area	
	sq. ft. thou	% of total
The Broadway — Southern California (Los Angeles) Southern California (43 stores)	7,459	39
The Broadway — Southwest (Phoenix) Arizona, Colorado, Nevada & New Mexico (11 stores)	1,744	9
Emporium (San Francisco) Bay Area (22 stores)	5,260	27
Thalhimers (Richmond) Virginia, North Carolina, South Carolina & Tennessee (26 stores)	2,867	15
Weinstocks (Sacramento) Northern California, Nevada & Utah (12 stores)	1,935	10
Total	**19,265**	**100**

RANKINGS

37th in *Fortune* 50 Retailing Cos.
295th in *Forbes* Sales 500

COMPETITION

Campeau
Dillard
R. H. Macy
May Department Stores
Mercantile Stores
Montgomery Ward
Nordstrom
J. C. Penney
Sears
Specialty and discount stores

HOW MUCH

	9 Yr. Growth	1980	1981	1982	1983	1984	1985	1986	1987*	1988	1989
Sales ($ mil)	0.6%	2,633	2,871	3,055	3,633	3,724	3,978	4,090	1,164	2,617	2,787
Net income ($ mil)	(20.4%)	58	45	49	67	27	48	48	—	9	7
Income as % of sales	—	2.2%	1.6%	1.6%	1.9%	0.7%	1.2%	1.2%	—	0.4%	0.3%
Earnings per share ($)	(17.9%)	2.00	1.51	1.53	1.90	0.83	1.50	1.45	—	0.33	0.34
Stock price – high ($)	—	23.00	20.88	17.25	24.75	32.25	31.25	57.50	78.00	12.50	14.63
Stock price – low ($)	—	14.88	14.25	10.50	15.13	18.25	22.63	26.50	6.50	7.75	7.00
Stock price – close ($)	(8.4%)	18.25	15.00	15.63	23.50	23.63	28.63	48.00	8.50	8.38	8.25
P/E – high	—	12	14	11	13	39	21	40	—	38	43
P/E – low	—	7	9	7	8	22	15	18	—	23	21
Dividends per share ($)	—	1.15	1.21	1.22	1.22	1.22	1.22	1.22	1.22	17.00	0.00
Book value per share ($)	—	23.24	22.22	21.60	22.07	18.26	18.37	16.18	7.16	(10.19)	(9.18)

1989 Year End:
Debt ratio: 115.1%
Return on equity: —
Cash (mil): $28
Current ratio: 2.77
Long-term debt (mil): $1,609
Number of shares (mil): 23
Dividends:
1989 average yield: 0.0%
1989 payout: —
Market value (mil): $190

Stock Price History high/low 1980-89

80
70
60
50
40
30
20
10
0

* 1987 fiscal year was only 26 weeks, ending August 1, 1987.

CASTLE & COOKE, INC.

OVERVIEW

Castle & Cooke is a food products and real estate development company with 94% of 1989 sales from its Dole food subsidiary, the largest producer and marketer of fruits and vegetables worldwide. Originally planning to spin off Dole into a new publicly traded company, Castle & Cooke now intends to look at a possible sale of the subsidiary, since financing concerns and tax questions have arisen.

Castle & Cooke's real estate business, operating mainly through Oceanic Properties, develops residential and commercial property in Hawaii and California. The company operates resorts on Lanai, Hawaii's 6th largest island, of which it has 98% ownership. With 129,100 acres, Castle & Cooke is Hawaii's 3rd largest private landowner. The company also owns about 10,500 acres in California and 9,135 acres in Arizona.

Dole's major products, pineapples and bananas, are grown on company-owned or -leased plantations in Hawaii, Central and South America, the Philippines, and Thailand. Dole distributes fresh produce with its 30 refrigerated vessels, including 2 of the world's largest refrigerated container ships. The company also has a line of packaged fruit-based food and nuts.

WHEN

Samuel Castle and Amos Cooke, missionaries to Hawaii, formed a partnership, Castle & Cooke, in 1851 to manage their church's failing depository, which supplied outlying mission posts with staple goods. Within a year they had added a store in Honolulu, selling goods to the general public.

In 1858 they entered the sugar business and within 10 years served as agents for several Hawaiian sugar plantations and the ships that carried their cargoes.

In 1907 C&C became agent and part owner of Matson Navigation, the largest shipping company operating between Hawaii and the mainland. C&C entered another major Hawaiian industry in 1932, buying 1/5 of the Hawaiian Pineapple Company, founded by James Dole in 1901. Extensive advertising made Dole pineapples a major product by 1936.

After WWII, labor unions successfully organized and wages improved, almost doubling payrolls at C&C's sugar plantations. The sugar and pineapple industries responded by increasing mechanization in their operations.

In the late 1950s and early 1960s C&C began the transition to a food and land business. It bought an Oregon seafood company (Bumble Bee brand, 1959) and completed the purchase of Dole Pineapple (including thousands of acres of Hawaiian land, 1961). In 1964 C&C became a banana importer with the purchase of Standard Fruit of New Orleans and sold its 24% stake in Matson Navigation. The company started pineapple and banana farms in the Philippines in the 1960s to supply the Far East markets.

In the early 1980s the company was heavily in debt and earnings were down. In 1985, following 2 takeover attempts, C&C agreed to merge with Flexi-Van, a container-leasing company headed by David Murdock, who became a 23% owner of C&C stock and took over operations. He brought in management talent and capital as well as Flexi-Van's fleet of ships to transport Dole produce. Murdock trimmed operations, selling off Bumble Bee (1986) and Flexi-Van's container leasing business (1987), leaving C&C with its fruit and real estate operations. In 1987 C&C bought the agricultural operations of Apache Corporation and Tenneco West and in 1988 the raisin operations of Bonner Packing. The company's sales increased significantly in 1988 and 1989 because its investments in new technologies and recent acquisitions enabled Dole to meet increased worldwide demand for fresh fruit products.

NYSE symbol: CKE
Incorporated: Hawaii, 1894
Fiscal year ends: Saturday nearest December 31

WHO

Chairman and CEO: David H. Murdock, age 66, $1,300,000 pay
EVP; President, Dole Food: David A. DeLorenzo, age 43, $485,577 pay (prior to promotion)
EVP: Alan B. Sellers, age 41, $410,577 pay (prior to promotion)
EVP: Raymond F. Henze III, age 37
VP; President and CEO, Oceanic Properties: Thomas C. Leppert, age 35, $422,702 pay
VP Finance: William J. Hain, Jr., age 54
Auditors: Arthur Andersen & Co.
Employees: 45,000

WHERE

HQ: 10900 Wilshire Blvd., Los Angeles, CA 90024
Phone: 213-824-1500
FAX: 213-824-9505

The company conducts business in 50 countries and has 36 selling offices in North America, Western Europe, and the Far East.

	1989 Sales		1989 Operating Income	
	$ mil	% of total	$ mil	% of total
North America	1,988	73	88	40
Latin America	234	9	40	18
Far East	284	10	78	35
Europe	212	8	16	7
Adjustments	—	—	(23)	—
Total	**2,718**	**100**	**199**	**100**

WHAT

	1989 Sales		1989 Operating Income	
	$ mil	% of total	$ mil	% of total
Food products	2,546	94	196	88
Real estate	172	6	26	12
Adjustments	—	—	(23)	—
Total	**2,718**	**100**	**199**	**100**

Food & Other Products
DOLE and BUD
- Apples
- Bananas
- Pears
- Pineapples
- Table grapes

Dole Dried Fruit & Nut
DOLE juices
DOLEWHIP
Fresh Lites
Fruit'N Juice bars
Pure & Light juices
SunTops

Real Estate
Commercial
Industrial
Residential
Resorts

RANKINGS

39th in *Fortune* 100 Diversified Service Cos.
307th in *Forbes* Sales 500
309th in *Business Week* 1000
997th in *Business Week* Global 1000

COMPETITION

Chiquita Brands
Coca-Cola

HOW MUCH

	9 Yr. Growth	1980	1981	1982	1983	1984	1985	1986	1987	1988	1989
Sales ($ mil)	5.1%	1,734	1,845	1,823	1,552	1,520	1,601	1,738	1,749	2,469	2,718
Net income ($ mil)	12.8%	32	42	10	(39)	1	(10)	76	89	112	95
Income as % of sales	—	1.9%	2.3%	0.5%	(2.5%)	0.1%	(0.6%)	4.4%	5.1%	4.5%	3.5%
Earnings per share ($)	5.4%	1.00	—	0.17	(1.52)	(0.30)	(0.71)	1.21	1.49	1.90	1.60
Stock price – high ($)	—	14.53	13.37	9.91	17.93	19.02	15.87	20.25	26.63	29.38	45.25
Stock price – low ($)	—	9.34	8.30	6.62	8.36	8.84	9.57	13.00	12.00	17.25	25.38
Stock price – close ($)	14.1%	10.61	9.45	8.60	17.20	12.48	13.00	19.25	18.50	28.25	34.75
P/E – high	—	15	—	58	—	—	—	17	18	15	28
P/E – low	—	9	—	39	—	—	—	11	8	9	16
Dividends per share ($)	(100%)	0.74	0.74	0.55	0.00	0.00	0.00	0.00	0.00	0.00	0.00
Book value per share ($)	(0.9%)	15.35	15.98	15.53	13.51	9.36	8.35	9.97	11.22	12.53	14.11

1989 Year End:
Debt ratio: 22.7%
Return on equity: 12.0%
Cash (mil): $44
Current ratio: 1.08
Long-term debt (mil): $245
Number of shares (mil): 59
Dividends:
1989 average yield: 0.0%
1989 payout: 0.0%
Market value (mil): $2,059

Stock Price History high/low 1980-89

50
45
40
35
30
25
20
15
10
5
0

CATERPILLAR INC.

OVERVIEW

Based in Peoria, Illinois, Caterpillar is the world's #1 producer of earthmoving equipment and a leading producer of engines. Caterpillar is known for the high quality and performance of its products. Earthmoving, construction, and materials-handling machinery accounts for 76% of sales; the remainder comes from the manufacture of engines and electric power generation systems.

Company products sell under the Caterpillar, Cat, and Solar nameplates through 1,368 outlets. Caterpillar is the 9th largest US exporter, with 1989 foreign sales totaling almost $5.8 billion and accounting for 52% of total sales.

The company rebounded from losses of $953 million between 1982 and 1984 to post 1989 profits of $497 million. Caterpillar beat back heavy competition from Japanese rival Komatsu by beginning the "Plant with a Future" (PWAF) program in 1985 to reduce costs, improve efficiency, and increase divisional responsibility.

Caterpillar believes PWAF savings will exceed start-up costs by late 1990 and expects new market opportunities in Eastern Europe and the global emphasis on the environment to boost demand for its products throughout the decade. In 1990 the company announced that earnings would be below 1989 due to poor economic conditions in Brazil.

NYSE symbol: CAT
Incorporated: Delaware, 1986
Fiscal year ends: December 31

WHO

Chairman and CEO: Donald V. Fites, age 55, $535,688 pay (prior to promotion)
VC: James W. Wogsland, age 58, $404,688 pay (prior to promotion)
Group President, Construction and Mining Products Division: Glen A. Barton, age 50
Group President: Gerald S. Flaherty, age 51
Group President: Pierre C. Guerindon, age 62
VP (Principal Financial Officer): Charles E. Rager, age 61
Auditors: Price Waterhouse
Employees: 60,784

WHEN

In 1904 in Stockton, California, combine-maker Benjamin Holt modified the farming tractor by substituting a gas engine for steam and replacing iron wheels with crawler tracks. This improved the tractor's mobility over dirt by making it lighter and distributing its weight more evenly.

In 1915 the British adapted the "caterpillar" (a company-given nickname) design to the armored tank. Following WWI the US Army donated tanks to local governments for use in construction work. The caterpillar's efficiency surprised Holt and spurred the development of earthmoving and construction equipment.

Holt merged with another California company, Best Tractor, in 1925. In 1928 the new organization, named Caterpillar, moved to its present Peoria, Illinois, headquarters.

In the 1930s Cat expanded into foreign markets, forming a worldwide dealer network, and phased out combine production to concentrate on construction and road equipment.

Sales volume more than tripled during WWII when Cat supplied the military with earthmoving equipment. Returning servicemen touted Cat's durability and quality, and the company enjoyed continued high demand during the postwar reconstruction effort. Cat emerged in solid first place in the industry, far ahead of 2nd place International Harvester.

In 1951 Cat established its first overseas plant in England. In 1963 the company entered one of the first 50-50 joint ventures in Japan with Mitsubishi.

Sales increased steadily, reaching almost $8.6 billion by 1980. Diesel engine sales to outside customers nearly doubled between 1977 and 1980, accounting for 25% of total sales. In 1981 Cat purchased Solar Turbines (gasoline engines) for $505 million. However, 50 consecutive years of profits ended when Cat ran up 3 consecutive loss years (1982-1984) as equipment demand fell and competition from foreign firms intensified.

Cat doubled its product line between 1984 and 1989. The PWAF program, introduced in 1985, shifted production toward smaller equipment and cut the work force by 33%. Cat applied modernization expenses to current revenue, lowering earnings but minimizing price increases, thus recouping market share lost to foreign firms (especially Komatsu).

Cat achieved record $616 million profits in 1988, but 1989 profits declined 19.3% despite record sales, due to increased costs from higher wages and inflation.

WHERE

HQ: 100 NE Adams St., Peoria, IL 61629
Phone: 309-675-1000
FAX: 309-675-5948

Caterpillar operates 19 US and 13 foreign plants.

	1989 Sales*		1989 Operating Income	
	$ mil	% of total	$ mil	% of total
US	7,889	73	871	90
Europe	1,892	17	17	2
All other	1,101	10	80	8
Adjustments	244	—	(142)	—
Total	**11,126**	**100**	**826**	**100**

*Based on location of manufacturing operations.

	1989 Sales*	
	$ mil	% of total
US	5,376	48
Europe	1,939	18
Asia/Pacific	1,472	13
Latin America	829	7
Canada	778	7
Africa/Middle East	732	7
Total	**11,126**	**100**

*Based on location of sale.

WHAT

	1989 Sales		1989 Operating Income	
	$ mil	% of total	$ mil	% of total
Machinery	8,478	76	733	66
Engines	2,404	22	235	21
Financial services	244	2	147	13
Adjustments	—	—	(289)	—
Total	**11,126**	**100**	**826**	**100**

Products
Dump trucks
Excavators
Industrial engines
Lift trucks
Loaders
Motor graders
Paving products
Pipelayers
Skidders
Tractors
Turbines

Brand Names
Cat
Caterpillar
Solar

RANKINGS

38th in *Fortune* 500 Industrial Cos.
102nd in *Fortune* Global 500 Industrial Cos.
9th in *Fortune* 50 Exporters
60th in *Forbes* Sales 500
91st in *Business Week* 1000
263rd in *Business Week* Global 1000

COMPETITION

Cummins Engine
Deere
Dresser
Fiat
Ford
Hitachi
Hyundai
Ingersoll-Rand
Mitsubishi
Navistar
Tenneco
Volvo

HOW MUCH

	9 Yr. Growth	1980	1981	1982	1983	1984	1985	1986	1987	1988	1989
Sales ($ mil)	2.9%	8,598	9,155	6,469	5,424	6,576	6,725	7,321	8,180	10,435	11,126
Net income ($ mil)	(1.4%)	565	579	(180)	(345)	(428)	198	76	319	616	497
Income as % of sales	—	6.6%	6.3%	(2.8%)	(6.4%)	(6.5%)	2.9%	1.0%	3.9%	5.9%	4.5%
Earnings per share ($)	(2.8%)	6.32	6.44	*(2.04)*	(3.74)	(4.47)	2.00	0.76	*3.20*	6.04	4.88
Stock price – high ($)	—	64.00	73.25	55.25	49.50	52.75	43.13	55.63	74.75	68.50	69.00
Stock price – low ($)	—	43.50	49.63	33.13	37.38	28.38	29.00	36.63	39.88	53.88	52.88
Stock price – close ($)	0.0%	58.00	55.50	40.13	47.25	31.00	42.00	40.13	62.00	63.63	57.88
P/E – high	—	10	11	—	—	—	22	73	23	11	14
P/E – low	—	7	8	—	—	—	15	48	12	9	11
Dividends per share ($)	(7.1%)	2.33	2.40	2.40	1.50	1.25	0.50	0.50	0.50	0.75	1.20
Book value per share ($)	1.2%	39.68	44.03	39.61	35.07	29.46	31.19	31.86	35.15	40.56	44.11

1989 Year End:
Debt ratio: 33.8%
Return on equity: 11.5%
Cash (mil): $148
Current ratio: 1.46
Long-term debt (mil): $2,288
Number of shares (mil): 101
Dividends:
1989 average yield: 2.1%
1989 payout: 24.6%
Market value (mil): $5,870

Stock Price History high/low 1980-89

80
70
60
50
40
30
20
10
0

CBS INC.

OVERVIEW

CBS, #3 among the television networks, produces and distributes news, public affairs, sports and entertainment programming, and feature films to 212 affiliate TV stations and 5 owned and operated stations. The company, through its radio networks, provides programming services to 574 independently owned radio stations as well as 19 stations owned by CBS.

The company also owns 50% of CBS/Fox, a film, television, and video production company, and CBS/MTM, a film studio, and has the exclusive broadcast rights to the 1992 Winter Olympics.

WHEN

Young William Paley (23) was an early radio advertiser (1925) on behalf of his father's Philadelphia-based La Palina cigars. Sensing a great opportunity, Paley in 1928 bought control of the fledgling Columbia Broadcasting System radio network, which had been incorporated in 1927 by radio pioneer Major J. Andrew White, concert master Arthur Judson, and promoter George Coats.

Paley, still chairman of CBS in 1990, changed the face of broadcasting and created industry standards. He promoted daytime dramas; attracted stars from NBC such as George Burns, Gracie Allen, and Jack Benny for evening programming; developed a strong news organization; and gave this programming package to local affiliates, which grew from 22 in 1928 to 97 in 1935. Edward R. Murrow, who served at CBS from 1930 to 1960, broke new ground in broadcasting news and was well known for his denunciation of Senator Joseph McCarthy.

In 1938 CBS bought American Recording, which became CBS Records in 1939. To develop emerging technology, CBS hired scientist Peter Carl Goldmark (1936), who invented the long-playing record in 1948 and worked on a color TV system into the 1950s. To CBS's disappointment, the FCC approved RCA/NBC's color system in 1953.

From 1955 to 1968 CBS was #1 in the entertainment ratings. CBS lost ratings and revenues in the early 1970s due to bans on cigarette advertising, a national economic downturn, and lack of programming geared to younger viewers. From the 1960s to the 1980s, CBS bought and sold such famous names as the New York Yankees, Fender guitars, Steinway pianos, *Family Weekly* and *Cuisine* magazines, and the Holt, Rinehart and Winston publishing company.

CBS purchased cable companies in the 1960s, only to be forced to divest them in 1970 (forming Viacom) due to new FCC regulations prohibiting major networks from owning cable companies. In 1982 CBS and Twentieth Century Fox-Video formed CBS/Fox, and in 1983 CBS, HBO, and CPI Film Holdings formed Tri-Star Pictures (sold in 1985).

During the mid-1980s, costly takeover attempts by Ted Turner and by Ivan Boesky, an ideological battle with Senator Jesse Helms, and falling ratings following the retirement of trusted and popular anchorman Walter Cronkite weakened CBS's financial position. Paley's inability to pick a successor (he passed over 5 presidents) left the company without strong leadership between 1971 and 1986. In 1985 Loews Corporation, led by billionaire Laurence Tisch, began buying CBS stock with the blessing of CBS, and Tisch joined its board that year. In 1986 CBS sold off 2 jets, Fawcett Books, and its St. Louis TV station and laid off 1,200 employees. CBS rejected an approach from Coca-Cola in 1986 and elected Tisch (then CBS's largest stockholder, with almost 25% of its shares) acting CEO, and Paley acting chairman. In 1987 they were elected permanently.

CBS sold its educational and professional publishing division (1986), its magazine division (1987), and CBS Records (to Sony, 1988). In 1989 CBS bought a Miami TV station and 2 Detroit radio stations and agreed to sell one of its Tampa radio stations to Cox Enterprises.

HOW MUCH

	9 Yr. Growth	1980	1981	1982	1983	1984	1985	1986	1987	1988	1989
Sales ($ mil)	(3.2%)	3,963	4,027	4,052	4,458	4,831	4,677	4,646	2,762	2,778	2,962
Net income ($ mil)	4.9%	193	190	150	187	245	203	190	136	283	297
Income as % of sales	—	4.9%	4.7%	3.7%	4.2%	5.1%	4.3%	4.1%	4.9%	10.2%	10.0%
Earnings per share ($)	6.0%	6.92	6.82	5.35	6.31	8.24	*7.27*	*7.54*	5.53	11.14	11.65
Stock price – high ($)	—	55.75	61.25	67.00	81.75	87.75	126.25	151.50	226.25	182.75	221.00
Stock price – low ($)	—	42.50	46.00	33.38	55.00	61.50	70.88	110.00	127.50	146.00	166.00
Stock price – close ($)	16.5%	47.63	47.38	59.75	66.25	72.38	115.88	127.00	157.00	170.50	188.00
P/E – high	—	8	9	13	13	11	17	20	41	16	19
P/E – low	—	6	7	6	9	7	10	15	23	13	14
Dividends per share ($)	5.2%	2.80	2.80	2.80	2.80	2.85	3.00	3.00	3.00	3.35	4.40
Book value per share ($)	10.1%	42.68	44.62	45.02	48.54	52.25	20.53	34.28	50.83	93.54	101.22

1989 Year End:
Debt ratio: 24.9%
Return on equity: 12.0%
Cash (mil): $1,078
Current ratio: 2.32
Long-term debt (mil): $796
Number of shares (mil): 24
Dividends:
1989 average yield: 2.3%
1989 payout: 37.8%
Market value (mil): $4,446

Stock Price History high/low 1980-89

250
200
150
100
50
0

NYSE symbol: CBS
Incorporated: New York, 1927
Fiscal year ends: December 31

WHO

Chairman: William S. Paley, age 88, $700,000 pay
President and CEO: Laurence A. Tisch, age 67, $1,325,866 pay
VP; President, CBS Broadcast Group: Howard Stringer, age 48, $875,769 pay
SVP Finance: Peter W. Keegan, age 45
Auditors: Coopers & Lybrand
Employees: 6,750

WHERE

HQ: 51 W. 52nd St., New York, NY 10019
Phone: 212-975-4321
FAX: 212-975-7133

CBS owns and operates TV stations in 5 states and radio stations in 9 states and Washington, DC. The company also owns 1/2 of a video company and 1/2 of a film studio in California.

WHAT

	1989 Sales		1989 Operating Income	
	$ mil	% of total	$ mil	% of total
Broadcasting	2,960	100	295	100
Other	2	—	—	—
Corporate	—	—	(31)	—
Total	**2,962**	**100**	**264**	**100**

CBS/Broadcast Group
CBS Affiliate Relations
CBS Enterprises
CBS Entertainment
CBS Marketing
CBS News
CBS Radio
CBS Sports
CBS Television Stations

Television Stations
KCBS-TV, Los Angeles
WBBM-TV, Chicago
WCAU-TV, Philadelphia
WCBS-TV, New York
WCIX-TV, Miami

Production Companies
The CBS/Fox Co. (50%)
The CBS/MTM Co. (50%)

Radio Stations
KCBS (AM)/KRQR (FM), San Francisco
KLTR (FM), Houston
KMOX (AM)/KLOU (FM), St. Louis
KNX (AM)/KODJ (FM), Los Angeles
KTXQ (FM), Dallas
WBBM (AM/FM), Chicago
WCAU (AM)/WOGL (FM), Philadelphia
WCBS (AM/FM), New York
WLTT (FM), Washington, DC
WODS (FM), Boston
WSUN (FM), Tampa
WWJ (AM)/WJOI (FM), Detroit

RANKINGS

36th in *Fortune* 100 Diversified Service Cos.
283rd in *Forbes* Sales 500
148th in *Business Week* 1000
388th in *Business Week* Global 1000

COMPETITION

Boston Celtics
Capital Cities/ABC
Cox
General Electric
Hearst
Johnson Publishing
News Corp.
Paramount
Tele-Communications
Time Warner
Turner Broadcasting
Viacom

CHAMPION INTERNATIONAL CORPORATION

OVERVIEW

Champion International is the 4th largest domestic paper producer, manufacturing products for business communications, printing, publications, and newspapers. The company leads the industry in the number of types of paper it produces and the number of different groups it produces for. In addition, the company maintains sizable operations in plywood and lumber production.

The printing and writing paper segment, Champion's largest with 49% of paper sales, has an annual mill production of 1.5 million tons of pulp and 1.7 million tons of papers and bleached paperboard. Other paper segments include lightweight publication papers (17% of paper sales), bleached kraft market pulp (10%), newsprint (9%), and smaller operations such as paperboard and milk cartons.

Champion's wood products division sells lumber, various types of plywood, and other wood products directly to wholesalers, dealers, and industrial users through 4 company sales offices. Lumber, the segment's primary product, generates 34% of division sales.

WHEN

Champion International was formed by the 1967 merger of US Plywood and Champion Paper & Fibre. US Plywood had been founded by Lawrence Ottinger in New York in 1919 to sell glue and WWI surplus plywood. By 1932 the company was manufacturing, and in 1937 it consolidated its New York and Delaware divisions with Aircraft Plywood.

Champion Paper & Fibre, the other party in the merger, was created when Reuben Robertson, who founded Champion Fibre in Ohio in 1906, married the daughter of the founder of similarly-named Champion Coated Paper, incorporated in Ohio in 1893.

The first years for US Plywood–Champion Paper, the name given the company resulting from the 1967 merger, were marked by internal quarrels between the paper and plywood divisions (over such issues as allocation of the company's timber resources). The company diversified, buying Drexel Enterprises (furniture, 1968, sold in 1977); Trend Industries (carpet, 1969, sold in 1978); Path Fork Harlan Coal (to power the company's pulp and paper mills, 1970); and AW Securities (carpets, 1974, sold in 1980). In 1972 the company adopted its current name.

In 1974 board member Karl Bendetson was instrumental in the removal of company CEO Thomas Willers (Bendetson disapproved of the direction the company was taking under Willers, namely, his plans to diversify into chemicals). Andrew Sigler replaced Willers and quickly turned the company's focus back to forest products by selling over a dozen nonforest businesses.

In 1977 Champion International acquired Hoerner Waldorf, the 4th largest national producer of paper packaging products such as grocery bags and cardboard boxes. Hoerner Waldorf traces its roots back to the 1966 merger of Hoerner Boxes (formed in Keokuk, Iowa, in 1920) and Waldorf Paper (originated in St. Paul as part of Baker-Collins in 1886).

In 1984 Champion bought St. Regis (paper) for $1.8 billion. With the St. Regis acquisition, Champion narrowed its attention to focus primarily on pulp and paper production. The company sold its office products operations (office furniture and supplies, 1984); 39 corrugated container plants, 13 packaging plants, and 3 paperboard mills (1986); its Pasadena, Texas, mill (1987); and its McKinney, Texas, coating and finishing plant and Columbus, Ohio, specialty paper plant (1988).

In 1989 Champion sold 300,000 shares of new stock to Berkshire Hathaway (an investment firm controlled by Warren Buffett) in what is viewed as an attempt to discourage hostile takeovers. In 1990 another investment firm, Loews, began buying the company's shares.

HOW MUCH

	9 Yr. Growth	1980	1981	1982	1983	1984	1985	1986	1987	1988	1989
Sales ($ mil)	3.6%	3,753	4,004	3,737	4,264	5,121	5,770	4,388	4,615	5,129	5,163
Net income ($ mil)	10.1%	182	120	40	82	(6)	163	201	382	456	432
Income as % of sales	—	4.9%	3.0%	1.1%	1.9%	(0.1%)	2.8%	4.6%	8.3%	8.9%	8.4%
Earnings per share ($)	3.7%	3.19	1.88	0.45	1.22	(0.36)	1.59	2.05	3.92	4.65	4.43
Stock price – high ($)	—	28.88	30.25	24.88	28.88	28.88	25.38	34.00	44.63	38.13	37.75
Stock price – low ($)	—	19.38	17.38	11.75	21.75	16.88	20.00	22.50	23.25	29.50	28.88
Stock price – close ($)	3.0%	24.50	19.75	23.75	28.88	22.25	24.88	30.75	34.50	32.13	32.00
P/E – high	—	9	16	55	24	—	16	17	11	8	9
P/E – low	—	6	9	26	18	—	13	11	6	6	7
Dividends per share ($)	(2.9%)	1.44	1.48	0.67	0.40	0.40	0.46	0.52	0.72	0.95	1.10
Book value per share ($)	3.1%	29.33	29.17	28.85	29.65	25.27	26.34	27.52	30.82	35.06	38.60

1989 Year End:
Debt ratio: 36.1%
Return on equity: 12.0%
Cash (mil): $56
Current ratio: 1.33
Long-term debt (mil): $2,025
Number of shares (mil): 93
Dividends:
1989 average yield: 3.4%
1989 payout: 24.8%
Market value (mil): $2,975

Stock Price History high/low 1980-89

45 40 35 30 25 20 15 10 5 0

NYSE symbol: CHA
Incorporated: New York, 1937
Fiscal year ends: December 31

WHO

Chairman and CEO: Andrew C. Sigler, age 58, $1,225,000 pay
President and COO: L. C. Heist, age 58, $750,000 pay
VC: Kenwood C. Nichols, age 50, $500,000 pay
EVP: Byron T. Edwards, age 52, $516,000 pay
EVP: William H. Burchfield, age 54, $500,000 pay
SVP Finance: Gerald J. Beiser, age 59
Auditors: Arthur Andersen & Co.
Employees: 29,500

WHERE

HQ: One Champion Plaza, Stamford, CT 06921
Phone: 203-358-7000
FAX: 203-358-2975

	1989 Sales		1989 Operating Income	
	$ mil	% of total	$ mil	% of total
US	4,256	82	604	75
Canada	596	12	89	11
Brazil	311	6	115	14
Adjustments	—	—	(39)	—
Total	**5,163**	**100**	**769**	**100**

Owned and Leased Timberland	Acres
Western US (CA, MT, OR, WA)	1,594,635
Southeastern US (northern AL, GA, eastern FL, MS, NC, SC, TN, VA)	1,680,052
Gulf US (southern AL, western FL, TX)	1,534,238
Northern US (MA, MI, NH, NY, VT)	1,622,978
Canada (Alberta)	2,461,000
Brazil	220,231
Total	**9,113,134**

WHAT

	1989 Sales		1989 Operating Income	
	$ mil	% of total	$ mil	% of total
Wood products	1,126	22	115	14
Paper	4,037	78	693	86
Adjustments	—	—	(39)	—
Total	**5,163**	**100**	**769**	**100**

Products

Paper
Bleached hardwood kraft pulp
Bleached paperboard
Bleached softwood kraft pulp
Directory paper
Linerboard
Milk and juice cartons
Newsprint
Ovenable packaging
Printing paper
Publication papers
Pulp
Writing paper
Xerographic paper

Wood
Hardboard
Logs
Lumber
Plywood
Sidings

RANKINGS

97th in *Fortune* 500 Industrial Cos.
171st in *Forbes* Sales 500
233rd in *Business Week* 1000

COMPETITION

Boise Cascade
Georgia-Pacific
International Paper
James River
Kimberly-Clark
Mead
Scott
Weyerhaeuser

THE CHARLES SCHWAB CORPORATION

OVERVIEW

Charles Schwab is the nation's largest discount brokerage service, with 1.3 million customer accounts representing 45% of the discount brokerage market. Schwab's customers are mostly individual investors who want stock-trading services but do not want to pay charges for research or portfolio management. Discount brokers can save the investor 40% to 70% per transaction. The company expects to gain more business in the next decade from baby boomers as they mature into their earnings and savings years.

The firm held about $10.7 billion in Schwab One cash-management accounts and $25.3 billion in total customer assets at year-end 1989.

Schwab will open 15 new branch offices in 1990 and 20 to 30 in 1991. The firm also plans to spend $13 million expanding and enhancing computer and telecommunications systems. A new service center can handle up to 2.7 million customer phone calls annually.

Schwab's employees and management own 53% of the company's stock; Charles R. Schwab is the beneficial owner of 28% of the stock.

NYSE symbol: SCH
Incorporated: Delaware, 1986
Fiscal year ends: December 31

WHO

Chairman and CEO: Charles R. Schwab, age 52, $1,133,168 pay
President and COO: Lawrence J. Stupski, age 44, $899,576 pay
EVP and CFO: A. John Gambs, age 44, $412,908 pay
Auditors: Deloitte & Touche
Employees: 2,700

WHERE

HQ: 101 Montgomery St., San Francisco, CA 94104
Phone: 415-627-7000
FAX: 415-627-8538 (Corporate Communications)

The firm has 111 branch offices throughout the US.

WHEN

After his graduation from Stanford, Charles Schwab managed personal investment portfolios, started a mutual fund, and published a newsletter in the 1960s for his California investment firm, named the First Commander Corporation. The firm became Charles Schwab & Company, Inc., in 1971.

Initially a full-service broker, Schwab put his idea for a discount brokerage service into effect in May 1975 following the repeal of rules requiring fixed commissions in the industry. Schwab cut its rates to about 1/2 of what most charged.

From 1977 to 1983, Schwab's revenues grew from $4.6 million to $126.5 million and the number of customer accounts from 20,000 to 648,000. This growth enabled the firm to automate its operations and develop systems that could provide cash-management accounts.

To gain additional capital necessary for growth, Schwab agreed to be bought by BankAmerica Corporation Holdings (BAC) for $55 million, effective in 1983. Schwab expanded its data processing capabilities, opened new offices, and added customers while a member of the BankAmerica family. However, Schwab couldn't offer mutual funds or add services like telephone trading, which would have violated federal banking regulations.

In a 1987 leveraged buyout Charles Schwab bought his company back for $280 million. In 1987 the company made its first public stock offering, raising $125 million to pay off the LBO debt and expand the company. The stock market crash in October of that year dropped Schwab's daily trading volume from a peak of 17,900 transactions to 8,800 in late 1988. Revenues declined to $392 million in 1988 from $465 million in 1987 but rebounded to $553 million in 1989, when individual investors returned to the stock market.

Recently the firm has begun to diversify its services to attract other kinds of customers. In the past 3 years professional financial advisors have used Schwab to broker about $3 billion for clients. Commissions on stock transactions, which accounted for 64% of revenues in 1987, were only about 42% of revenues in 1989. The company spent $10 million a year in the late 1980s on computer systems to automate trading and has reduced its break-even point to 10,000 trades per day (compared to 12,000 per day 3 years ago).

In 1989 Schwab bought Rose & Company (discount brokerage firm), introduced Schwab TeleBroker Services (to place orders electronically by touch-tone phone), and offered PC Broker (investment software that enters orders with Schwab in seconds).

WHAT

	1989 Sales	
	$ mil	% of total
Commission revenue	229	42
Interest revenue	273	49
Mutual fund service fees	29	5
Other revenue	22	4
Total	**553**	**100**

Accounts & Services
Charles Schwab Select Card (Visa and MasterCard)
Financial Advisors Service (management for fee-based investment advisors)
Option Finance Service (stock options)
Schwab 144 Stock Service (sale of restricted stock)
Schwab Brokerage Account
Schwab IRA/Keogh Accounts
Schwab MoneyLink Transfer Service (automatic funds transfer)
Schwab One Asset Management Account
Schwab TeleBroker Service (trading and information by telephone)

Investment Choices
Charles Schwab CD Service
Equities and Options
Fixed Income Investments
Money Market Funds
Mutual Fund Marketplace

Investor Information
The Equalizer (personal investment system software)
Investor Seminars
InvestorSource (catalog of investment products and information guides)
PC Broker software (on-line trading via modem)

RANKINGS

872nd in *Business Week* 1000

COMPETITION

American Express
Merrill Lynch
Primerica
Prudential
Sears
Other securities brokers

HOW MUCH

	9 Yr. Growth	1980	1981	1982	1983	1984	1985	1986	1987	1988	1989
Sales ($ mil)	39.3%	28	41	67	126	148	203	308	465	392	553
Net income ($ mil)	—	—	—	5	11	1	11	32	26	7	19
Income as % of sales	—	—	—	7.5%	8.7%	0.7%	5.4%	10.4%	5.5%	1.9%	3.4%
Earnings per share ($)	—	—	—	—	—	—	—	—	1.12	0.27	0.68
Stock price – high ($)	—	—	—	—	—	—	—	—	17.00	9.63	17.00
Stock price – low ($)	—	—	—	—	—	—	—	—	5.75	5.88	6.75
Stock price – close ($)	—	—	—	—	—	—	—	—	6.00	6.75	13.88
P/E – high	—	—	—	—	—	—	—	—	15	36	25
P/E – low	—	—	—	—	—	—	—	—	5	22	10
Dividends per share ($)	—	—	—	—	—	—	—	—	0.00	0.00	0.09
Book value per share ($)	—	—	—	—	—	—	—	—	5.89	6.26	6.78

1989 Year End:
Debt ratio: 42.2%
Return on equity: 10.4%
Cash (mil): $2,336
Assets (mil): $3,480
Long-term debt (mil): $125
Number of shares (mil): 25
Dividends:
1989 average yield: 0.6%
1989 payout: 13.2%
Market value (mil): $351

Stock Price History high/low 1987-89

THE CHASE MANHATTAN CORPORATION

OVERVIEW

Chase Manhattan is the 2nd largest US commercial banking concern, after Citicorp. The holding company's principal subsidiary is Chase Manhattan Bank.

Chase is reorganizing. CEO Willard Butcher announced his retirement in late 1990, and successor Thomas Labrecque was expected to slash expenses 8% after losses on real estate loans in Arizona and on loans to less-developed countries (LDCs). As part of the restructuring, Labrecque abandoned Chase's 3-pronged strategy (global, institutional, and individual banking). Ten business heads report directly to new president Arthur Ryan.

Chase subsidiaries offer equipment leasing, securities clearing, real estate financing, and investment management. Chase is the 2nd largest US issuer of credit cards, with balances of about $10 billion. Subsidiaries operate commercial banks and branches throughout New York City and in upstate New York, Arizona, Florida, Maryland, and Ohio.

WHEN

Chase Manhattan traces its roots to a water utility founded in 1799. The Manhattan Company was created by the New York legislature to bring pure water to the city, but investor Aaron Burr, later US vice president and the man who killed Alexander Hamilton in a duel, lobbied to allow the company to use surplus funds for other services. The Bank of the Manhattan Company was the result, and, after the water company was sold to the city in 1808, it survived as the Bank of Manhattan.

On the other side of the family tree, John Thompson formed Chase National Bank (1877), named in honor of Abraham Lincoln's secretary of the treasury, Salmon P. Chase. Chase National grew to prominence under Albert Wiggin, who became president in 1911.

Wiggin engineered Chase's merger with John D. Rockefeller, Jr.'s, Equitable Trust (1930), and Chase became the world's largest bank in assets. After retiring in 1932, Wiggin was implicated in a scandal involving speculation with bank funds.

In 1932 Rockefeller's brother-in-law, Winthrop Aldrich, stepped in to lead the bank. Aldrich secured international beachheads for Chase, including postwar Germany and Japan, and he recruited his eventual successor — nephew David Rockefeller. In 1955 Chase merged with the Bank of Manhattan, which had expanded to branches in all 5 boroughs.

David Rockefeller, the last Rockefeller to command center stage in business, became co–chief executive in 1960 and chairman in 1969. His globe-trotting brought prestige and controversy to the bank. Critics accused Rockefeller of tilting US foreign policy, most notably in Vietnam and Iran.

Rockefeller retired in 1981, leaving Willard Butcher to face (in 1982) assumption of liabilities from the failed Drysdale Government Securities and the collapse of Penn Square Bank, an Oklahoma City bank bloated by bad oil loans. Chase eventually charged off $161 million in Penn Square loans.

Chase formed a Delaware subsidiary in 1982 to market consumer credit instruments across state lines. In 1984 Chase purchased Lincoln First, with 135 bank branches in upstate New York. The bank also bought thrifts in Ohio, created a subsidiary in Maryland, and purchased a Phoenix bank.

In 1989, along with many other large US banks, Chase was forced to absorb special charges for third world and other loans totalling almost $1.3 billion.

There have been some potholes on the road to a nationwide banking operation: Chase, like many other major banks, stumbled on real estate loans. In the second quarter of 1990, past-due real estate loans and foreclosed properties rose 52%, and Chase issued a dour statement offering scant hope for a quick turnaround.

HOW MUCH

	9 Yr. Growth	1980	1981	1982	1983	1984	1985	1986	1987	1988	1989
Sales ($ mil)	6.4%	7,977	10,573	10,110	8,523	9,881	9,733	9,460	10,745	12,365	13,904
Net income ($ mil)	—	354	412	307	430	406	565	585	(895)	1,059	(665)
Income as % of sales	—	4.4%	3.9%	3.0%	5.0%	4.1%	5.8%	6.2%	(8.3%)	8.6%	(4.8%)
Earnings per share ($)	—	4.66	5.37	3.65	5.22	4.33	6.15	6.50	(11.56)	11.48	(7.94)
Stock price – high ($)	—	24.31	29.94	30.19	31.13	26.38	36.63	49.50	46.25	30.75	44.88
Stock price – low ($)	—	16.94	20.50	15.63	20.56	17.81	23.25	34.00	19.38	20.88	28.00
Stock price – close ($)	4.2%	24.06	26.94	24.50	22.75	23.88	36.31	35.63	22.13	28.63	34.75
P/E – high	—	5	6	8	6	6	6	8	—	3	—
P/E – low	—	4	4	4	4	4	4	5	—	2	—
Dividends per share ($)	6.0%	1.40	1.55	1.70	1.75	1.83	1.90	2.05	2.16	2.16	2.36
Book value per share ($)	0.4%	35.13	39.18	40.71	43.91	45.81	49.19	52.95	38.70	47.19	36.40

1989 Year End:
Debt ratio: 56.3%
Return on equity: —
Cash (mil): $12,006
Assets (mil): $107,369
Long-term debt (mil): $6,371
Number of shares (mil): 113
Dividends:
1989 average yield: 6.8%
1989 payout: —
Market value (mil): $3,916

Stock Price History high/low 1980-89

NYSE symbol: CMB
Incorporated: Delaware, 1969
Fiscal year ends: December 31

WHO

Chairman and CEO: Willard C. Butcher, age 63, $1,178,088 pay (to retire 10/31/90)
President and COO: Thomas G. Labrecque, age 51, $942,200 pay (Chairman-designate)
VC Individual Banking: Arthur F. Ryan, age 47, $744,300 pay (President-designate)
EVP and CFO: Michael P. Esposito, Jr., age 50
Auditors: Price Waterhouse
Employees: 41,610

WHERE

HQ: 1 Chase Manhattan Plaza, New York, NY 10081
Phone: 212-552-2222
FAX: 212-552-5005

Chase has operations in 56 countries.

	1989 Sales	
	$ mil	% of total
US	7,891	57
Asia	878	6
Western Hemisphere	3,557	26
Elsewhere	1,578	11
Total	**13,904**	**100**

WHAT

	1989 Sales	
	$ mil	% of total
Loan fees & interest	8,827	64
Interest on deposits	1,139	8
Investment interest	879	6
Other interest	1,114	8
Fees & commissions	1,377	10
Other	568	4
Total	**13,904**	**100**

Lines of Business

Individual Banking
Automobile loans
Consumer loans
Credit cards
Residential mortgages

Wholesale Banking
Cash management
Commercial real estate loans
Corporate finance activities
Foreign exchange services
Institutional trust services
Investment banking
Lease and commodities financing

RANKINGS

2nd in *Fortune* 100 Commercial Banking Cos.
38th in *Fortune* World's 100 Commercial Banks
204th in *Business Week* 1000
653rd in *Business Week* Global 1000

COMPETITION

H. F. Ahmanson
American Express
Bank of New York
BankAmerica
Bankers Trust
Chemical Banking
Citicorp
CS Holding
Dai-Ichi Kangyo
Deutsche Bank
First Chicago
First Interstate
Hongkong & Shanghai Banking
Manufacturers Hanover
J.P. Morgan
Security Pacific

CHEMICAL BANKING CORPORATION

OVERVIEW

New York–based Chemical is America's 6th largest banking organization, with a leading position in 3 states: Chemical Bank in New York, Texas Commerce Bancshares, and Chemical Bank New Jersey (formerly Horizon Bancorp).

Chemical dominates the 9-county New York City area in market share of middle-sized businesses, with 41% of that market. The company is one of the largest in the area in consumer banking, known for designing products for specific market segments. Its private banking group's personal trust business is the 3rd largest among US banks.

Chemical's Texas Commerce has the largest capital markets (securities trading) staff among major Texas banks. Texas Commerce also is the primary bank in Texas for 43% of the companies that have more than $250 million in sales. Following Chemical's lead, Texas Commerce has added more than 2,700 mid-sized companies as customers since 1987.

Chemical is recognized for investment banking, having originated or syndicated financings that raised more than $52 billion in 1989 for its corporate clients worldwide. The company also serves its institutional clients as custodian for more than $300 billion in global assets of corporations. Chemical also has a profitable transaction-processing business with the most widely used computerized cash management system in the world.

NYSE symbol: CHL
Incorporated: Delaware, 1968
Fiscal year ends: December 31

WHO

Chairman and CEO: Walter V. Shipley, age 54, $1,119,500 pay
President: Robert J. Callander, age 59, $633,500 pay
CFO: Joseph G. Sponholz, age 46
Auditors: Price Waterhouse
Employees: 29,139

WHEN

Balthazar P. Melick founded Chemical Bank as part of the New York Chemical Manufacturing Company in 1824. The bank was run by a small group of New York businessmen and operated separately from the manufacturing company. In 1844 the bank's directors liquidated the chemical firm and obtained a charter to operate only in banking.

The bank was a founding member (1853) of the New York Clearing House, an association formed to expedite the exchange and settlement of funds among New York City banks. In 1865 the bank took a national charter and started issuing national bank notes backed by government bonds. Building on a strong correspondent banking business (acting as agent for other banks), Chemical grew by 1900 to be one of the largest and strongest US banks.

In 1920 the bank acquired Citizens National Bank in the first of several mergers with New York institutions. Chemical opened its first branch in 1923 and its first foreign office in London in 1929. The same year, Chemical converted to a state charter in order to gain trust powers and to facilitate a merger with United States Mortgage & Trust.

The bank acquired another dozen banks in New York state, including, in 1954, Corn Exchange Bank Trust Company, a major branching system. Other major acquisitions were New York Trust, an extensive wholesale banking (corporate and institutional clients) and trust operation (1959), and Security National Bank (1975), with a Long Island branch system.

To allow acquisition of related businesses outside traditional banking, Chemical formed a bank holding company (1968). The bank acquired companies handling consumer loans, mortgage banking, and factoring. The 1960s also saw a vast expansion of Chemical's international business.

Chemical is known as a technological innovator. The bank introduced BankLink (1977), a computerized cash management system with more than 10,000 business customers, and Pronto, the first electronic home banking service in the US (1982).

Chemical's growth through mergers increased in the 1980s with the acquisition of Texas Commerce Bancshares (1987), one of the 4 largest Texas banking operations, and Horizon Bancorp (1989), the 5th largest bank holding company in New Jersey. Chemical's losses in 1987 and 1989 were due largely to nonperforming third world loans.

WHERE

HQ: 277 Park Ave., New York, NY 10172
Phone: 212-310-6161
FAX: 212-593-2194

Chemical has offices in 26 US states and operations in 19 foreign countries.

	1989 Sales		1989 Net Income	
	$ mil	% of total	$ mil	% of total
US	6,809	83	134	—
International:				
Europe	457	5	(25)	—
Latin America	622	8	(570)	—
Asia & Pacific	189	2	(38)	—
Middle East, Africa	58	1	(21)	—
North America	92	1	38	—
Total	**8,227**	**100**	**(482)**	—

WHAT

Financial Services
Cash management services
Commercial lending
Consumer banking
Consumer, personal, and mortgage loans
Corporate foreign exchange
Credit cards
Investment banking
Private placements
Securities services
Trust and investment services

Subsidiaries
Chemical Bank
Chemical Bank New Jersey
Chemical Financial Services
Texas Commerce Bancshares

RANKINGS

6th in *Fortune* 100 Commercial Banking Cos.
71st in *Fortune* World's 100 Commercial Banks
97th in *Forbes* Sales 500
303rd in *Business Week* 1000
916th in *Business Week* Global 1000

COMPETITION

H. F. Ahmanson
American Express
Bank of New York
BankAmerica
Bankers Trust
Chase Manhattan
Citicorp
CS Holding
Dai-Ichi Kangyo
Deutsche Bank
First Chicago
First Fidelity
Great Western
Hongkong & Shanghai Banking
Manufacturers Hanover
J.P. Morgan
NCNB
Security Pacific

HOW MUCH

	9 Yr. Growth	1980	1981	1982	1983	1984	1985	1986	1987	1988	1989
Sales ($ mil)	7.5%	4,295	5,636	5,445	4,903	5,857	5,651	5,488	6,755	7,644	8,227
Net income ($ mil)	—	173	205	241	306	341	390	402	(854)	754	(482)
Income as % of sales	—	4.0%	3.6%	4.4%	6.2%	5.8%	6.9%	7.3%	(12.6%)	9.9%	(5.9%)
Earnings per share ($)	—	4.28	4.88	5.12	6.02	6.26	7.15	7.42	(16.68)	12.02	(8.29)
Stock price – high ($)	—	19.94	28.00	31.58	37.50	35.88	46.25	56.25	49.50	33.88	41.13
Stock price – low ($)	—	14.78	18.67	17.67	25.67	23.50	33.13	40.75	20.25	20.00	28.50
Stock price – close ($)	5.2%	18.94	24.22	27.00	29.33	34.50	45.38	42.25	21.38	31.00	29.88
P/E – high	—	5	6	6	6	6	6	8	—	3	—
P/E – low	—	3	4	3	4	4	5	6	—	2	—
Dividends per share ($)	6.5%	1.55	1.71	1.92	2.16	2.36	2.48	2.60	2.72	2.72	2.72
Book value per share ($)	(0.6%)	35.78	38.98	41.70	43.74	46.86	51.17	56.14	41.14	47.07	34.00

1989 Year End:
Debt ratio: 44.5%
Return on equity: —
Cash (mil): $6,866
Assets (mil): $71,513
Long-term debt (mil): $2,970
Number of shares (mil): 82
Dividends:
1989 average yield: 9.1%
1989 payout: —
Market value (mil): $2,462

Stock Price History high/low 1980-89

60
50
40
30
20
10
0

CHEVRON CORPORATION

OVERVIEW

Chevron is the largest US industrial company headquartered west of the Mississippi. The company is the largest producer of natural gas in the US and the biggest combined oil and gas producer in the lower 48 states.

Chevron is a vertically integrated oil company (doing business from wellhead to filling station). It looks for and produces petroleum in 27 countries; refines and produces petrochemicals, primarily in the US, Japan, and France; and markets its products in more than 11,000 outlets worldwide (not including half-owned Caltex outlets in the Far East). Chevron has also taken the first steps toward a joint venture with the Soviets to develop a multi-billion-barrel oilfield in the Caspian Sea area.

In spite of its size, Chevron executives fear it may be a takeover candidate and are leery of Pennzoil's 8.9% stake. Chevron chairman Kenneth Derr is whittling the payroll, restructuring exploration and production operations, and selling marginal oil and gas properties.

WHEN

Thirty years after the California Gold Rush, a small company started selling a different product from the ground — oil. The crude came from wildcatter Frederick Taylor's well north of Los Angeles. In 1879 Taylor and other oil marketers in the area formed Pacific Coast Oil.

Pacific Coast's debut wasn't as earthshaking as Sutter's Mill's, but in time it attracted the attention of John D. Rockefeller's Standard Oil in California. Standard and Pacific Coast competed fiercely until Standard bought Pacific Coast in 1900.

When the Supreme Court ordered the breakup of Standard Oil in 1911, West Coast operations became the stand-alone Standard Oil Company (California), the only former subsidiary considered a truly integrated petroleum company — with production, refining, pipelines, and marketing. All its former Standard stablemates were running on fewer than those 4 legs.

The San Francisco–based company, nicknamed Socal and marketing products under the Chevron name, found itself at a different kind of golden gate when it won drilling concessions on the island of Bahrain and in Saudi Arabia in the 1930s.

The desert oil trove proved so vast that Socal summoned Texaco to help market the crude. They formed Caltex — the California Texas Oil Company — as equal partners. In 1948 Jersey Standard (later Exxon) and Socony (later Mobil) bought 40% of Caltex's Saudi operations, and the Saudi arm became Aramco (Arabian American Oil Company).

Socal exploration pushed into Louisiana and into the Gulf of Mexico in the 1940s. In 1961 Socal bought Standard Oil Company of Kentucky — Kyso — to acquire southern service stations.

Caltex suffered nationalization of some Arab holdings in the OPEC-spawned upheaval of the 1970s, and in 1980 Aramco became an arm of the Saudi Arabian government.

In 1984 Socal renamed itself Chevron, assuming its brand name. Also in 1984 Chevron purchased Gulf for a record $13.3 billion, serving as a white knight to ward off corporate raider T. Boone Pickens's overtures.

Gulf began in the 1901 Spindletop gusher in Texas as J.M. Guffey Petroleum, bankrolled by the Mellon family of Pittsburgh. Founder Guffey was unseated by William Larimer Mellon in 1902, and the company's name was changed to Gulf in 1907.

Gulf, spurred by strikes in Louisiana and Oklahoma, became an oil power developing Kuwaiti concessions. In the 1970s OPEC-inspired oil cutbacks in Kuwait and revelations of payoffs to officials at home and abroad hobbled Gulf.

The Gulf deal almost doubled Chevron's oil and gas reserves. As that indicator of an oil company's health began to sag in 1988, Chevron spent $2.5 billion for Tenneco wells in the Gulf of Mexico.

HOW MUCH

	9 Yr. Growth	1980	1981	1982	1983	1984	1985	1986	1987	1988	1989
Sales ($ mil)	(3.5%)	40,479	44,224	34,362	27,342	26,798	41,742	24,351	26,015	25,196	29,443
Net income ($ mil)	(22.2%)	2,401	2,380	1,377	1,590	1,534	1,547	715	1,007	1,768	251
Income as % of sales	—	5.9%	5.4%	4.0%	5.8%	5.7%	3.7%	2.9%	3.9%	7.0%	0.9%
Earnings per share ($)	(22.2%)	7.02	6.96	4.03	4.65	4.48	4.52	2.09	2.94	5.17	0.73
Stock price – high ($)	—	58.75	51.75	42.88	40.88	40.25	40.75	48.13	64.63	52.00	73.50
Stock price – low ($)	—	26.75	35.13	23.50	30.88	30.00	29.25	34.00	32.00	39.00	45.38
Stock price – close ($)	3.5%	49.75	42.88	32.00	34.63	31.25	38.13	45.38	39.63	45.75	67.75
P/E – high	—	8	7	11	9	9	9	23	22	10	101
P/E – low	—	4	5	6	7	7	6	16	11	8	62
Dividends per share ($)	5.0%	1.80	2.20	2.40	2.40	2.40	2.40	2.40	2.40	2.55	2.80
Book value per share ($)	2.2%	32.38	37.13	38.72	41.23	43.15	45.47	45.29	46.13	43.23	39.38

1989 Year End:
Debt ratio: 34.6%
Return on equity: 1.8%
Cash (mil): $1,628
Current ratio: 1.14
Long-term debt (mil): $7,390
Number of shares (mil): 355
Dividends:
1989 average yield: 4.1%
1989 payout: 383.6%
Market value (mil): $24,053

Stock Price History high/low 1980-89

80 70 60 50 40 30 20 10 0

NYSE symbol: CHV
Incorporated: Delaware, 1926
Fiscal year ends: December 31

WHO

Chairman and CEO: Kenneth T. Derr, age 53, $1,011,978 pay
VC: J. Dennis Bonney, age 59, $679,566 pay
VC: James N. Sullivan, age 52, $449,430 pay
VP Finance: Martin R. Klitten, age 45
VP; President, Chevron USA: Willis J. Price, age 58, $518,977 pay
Auditors: Price Waterhouse
Employees: 54,826

WHERE

HQ: 225 Bush St., San Francisco, CA 94104
Phone: 415-894-7700
FAX: 415-894-0855

Chevron conducts integrated petroleum operations in the US and 97 other countries, with chemical operations centered in the US, France, and Japan. The company also develops real estate, primarily in California.

	1989 Sales		1989 Operating Income	
	$ mil	% of total	$ mil	% of total
US	23,294	79	(20)	(1)
Canada	1,091	4	240	13
Other foreign	4,955	17	1,583	88
Adjustments	103	—	(718)	—
Total	**29,443**	**100**	**1,085**	**100**

WHAT

	1989 Sales		1989 Operating Income	
	$ mil	% of total	$ mil	% of total
Petroleum	25,822	88	1,259	70
Chemicals	3,048	10	532	29
Minerals	470	2	12	1
Adjustments	103	—	(718)	—
Total	**29,443**	**100**	**1,085**	**100**

Chevron has interests in 513 entities.
Major subsidiaries include:
Caltex (refining and marketing, 50% owned)
Chevron Chemical (industrial chemicals, consumer products)
Chevron International Oil (trading and marketing)
Chevron Pipe Line (petroleum products transportation)
Chevron Shipping (marine management)
Chevron Transport (marine transportation)
Chevron USA (integrated petroleum)

RANKINGS

11th in *Fortune* 500 Industrial Cos.
25th in *Fortune* Global 500 Industrial Cos.
15th in *Forbes* Sales 500
14th in *Business Week* 1000
36th in *Business Week* Global 1000

COMPETITION

Amoco
Ashland
Atlantic Richfield
British Petroleum
Coastal
Du Pont
Exxon
Mobil
Occidental
Pennzoil
Phillips
Royal Dutch/Shell
Sun
Texaco
Union Texas
Unocal
USX
Chemical companies

CITY OF CHICAGO

OVERVIEW

The "Second City" is the 3rd largest city in the US (after New York and Los Angeles). Its name is American Indian in origin and has been variously translated as "strong," "powerful," "skunk," and "wild onion." It occupies 228.2 square miles along 26 miles of the southwestern shoreline of Lake Michigan. The downtown and North Side are vibrant, bustling commercial areas surrounded by dozens of ethnic neighborhoods of varying economic vitality. Its South and West Sides are among the nation's worst examples of urban blight. The city remains the Midwest's commercial, financial, shipping, and industrial center, and the nation's rail, truck, and air hub. Blessed with a spectacular greenbelt of parks and harbors along its lakefront, numerous museums, and a world-renowned symphony, it is also home to many great educational institutions.

Plagued by an early reputation for vice, its gangster legacy, and its "second city" status, Chicago has spent much of its civic effort overcompensating. It claims the first skyscraper (Home Insurance Building); the world's tallest building (Sears Tower), busiest airport (O'Hare), largest commercial building (Merchandise Mart), and largest stock options and futures exchanges (Chicago Board Options Exchange and Chicago Board of Trade); and the self-proclaimed "world's greatest newspaper" (*Chicago Tribune*).

WHEN

Chicago was visited by French explorers Louis Joliet and Father Jacques Marquette in 1673. The city's first permanent settler was Jean Baptiste Point du Sable, a fur trader of African-French descent who arrived in 1779. In 1803 the US built Fort Dearborn. Most of its inhabitants were slain by Indians in 1812. The fort was rebuilt in 1816 and was occupied until the 1830s. In 1830, 48 blocks of what was to become Chicago were first platted. In 1833 its 200 inhabitants incorporated as a town, and in 1837 it incorporated as a city of 4,170.

From the 1830s to 1870 the city became a port for Great Lakes shipping and a terminus for more than 20 railroad lines. By 1865 its population was over 300,000, and by 1870 it had become the largest city in the Midwest.

In 1871 the Great Chicago Fire killed 250 people and leveled 17,450 buildings. Rising from the ashes, the city rebuilt rapidly and gloriously. Within 3 years virtually all traces of the fire were gone and by 1880 Chicago's population had ballooned to half a million.

The 1880s and 1890s found Chicago the focus of labor unrest. The Haymarket Riot of 1886, prompted by labor's demand for an 8-hour day, resulted in the death of 7 policemen and the probably wrongful execution of 4 anarchists. In 1894 Eugene Debs led the Pullman strike, halting national rail traffic.

The Columbian Exposition of 1892-1893, with its 686 acres, 27.5 million visitors, and total cost of about $40 million, allowed the city to flaunt its prosperity. During the 1890s and early 20th century, the city was home to such great architects as Dankmar Adler, Daniel Burnham, Louis Sullivan, and Frank Lloyd Wright. During the 1920s and 1930s it was also home to such infamous gangsters as Al Capone and John Dillinger.

Fueled by immigration from Europe (particularly Ireland and Poland) and migration of southern blacks, the city's population reached 3.4 million by 1940. Following WWII, urban decay and flight to the suburbs sapped the city's strength. Not until the election of Mayor Richard J. Daley in 1955 did the city's fortunes change. Daley ruled a coalition of labor and business for 21 years, backed by the awesome power of the last big-city political machine. His efforts and those of his successors (including the current mayor, his son Richard M. Daley), and the continued migration to the city of those seeking better lives (particularly Hispanic and Asian immigrants), have kept Chicago a vital center of commerce and cultural activity.

HOW MUCH

	9 Yr. Growth	1979	1980	1981	1982	1983	1984	1985	1986	1987	1988
Population (mil)	—	3.02	3.00	3.00	3.00	2.99	2.99	3.01	3.01	3.02	3.02
Households (mil)	0.1%	1.14	1.14	1.09	1.09	1.10	1.10	1.12	1.13	1.14	1.15
Employment (mil)	0.6%	1.17	1.24	1.19	1.12	1.08	1.14	1.18	1.20	1.25	1.24
Per capita income ($)	6.3%	6,725	7,160	7,297	7,612	7,994	8,956	9,788	10,315	11,092	11,619
Mkt. value of real estate ($ bil)	7.5%	35	45	47	47	48	50	51	58	60	67
New construction costs ($ mil)	7.2%	438	555	507	544	484	322	617	519	644	817
Retail sales ($ bil)	1.5%	12.8	12.2	12.5	12.4	12.6	14.4	14.5	14.7	14.8	14.6
City revenue ($ mil)	3.9%	1,672	1,645	—	1,999	2,035	2,051	2,076	2,126	2,388	2,366

Mkt. Value of Real Estate ($ bil) 1979-88

Incorporated: 1837
Form of government: Mayor/Council
Fiscal year ends: December 31
Motto: Urbs in Horto (City in a Garden)

WHO

Mayor: Richard M. Daley, $80,000 pay
City Treasurer: Walter S. Kozubowski, $60,000 pay
City Clerk: Miriam Santos, $60,000 pay
City Comptroller: Walter K. Knorr
City Council: 50 Aldermen, $40,000 pay each
Auditors: Deloitte & Touche
Employees: 38,500

WHERE

HQ: 121 N. LaSalle St., Chicago, IL 60602
Phone: 312-744-4000
FAX: 312-744-9538 (Mayor's office)
County: Cook
Altitude: 623 feet above sea level

WHAT

	1988 Revenues	
	$ mil	% of total
Property tax	497	21
Utility tax	267	11
Sales tax	270	11
Transportation tax	206	9
State income tax	159	7
Other taxes	207	9
Internal service	154	7
Licenses/permits	30	1
Fines	29	1
Interest	43	2
Charges–services	49	2
Government grants	438	18
Miscellaneous	17	1
Total	**2,366**	**100**

Vital Statistics	
Airports	3
Beaches	31
Colleges	95
Firefighters	4,622
Libraries	88
Manholes	146,000
Parks	560
Police officers	12,247
Population	3,021,912
Public school students	410,230
Square miles	228.2
TV stations	9

Sights/Institutions

Adler Planetarium
Art Institute
Chicago Historical Society
Chicago Symphony Orchestra
Comiskey Park
Field Museum of Natural History
Lincoln Park Zoo
Museum of Science & Industry
Newbery Library
Oriental Institute
Robie House
Shedd Aquarium
Soldier Field
University of Chicago
Wrigley Field

RANKINGS

3rd largest city in US
18th best place to live in America—*Places Rated Almanac*
30th best place to live—*Money* Magazine

COMPETITION

None

CHICAGO AND NORTH WESTERN

OVERVIEW

Chicago and North Western Holdings Corp. is a private holding company formed in the 1989 takeover of CNW Corporation by Blackstone Capital Partners LP. CNW operates a 5,800-mile railroad, the Chicago and North Western Transportation Company (the North Western), whose main east-west line lies between Chicago and terminals in Council Bluffs, Iowa, and Fremont, Nebraska. This line forms a central link between the Union Pacific Railroad and major railroads serving the East. The company transports coal, grain, automotive and steel products, bulk and consumer products, and intermodal (truck-to-train) freight. The North Western also operates a commuter rail system in Chicago and its suburbs through a contract with a regional transportation authority.

CNW's most profitable subsidiary, Western Railroad Properties, Inc., hauls low-sulfur coal from the Powder River Basin of Wyoming to electrical generating plants, primarily in the Midwest and Southwest. In 1989 the company signed contracts with other shippers to haul roughly 43 million tons of Powder River coal per year.

Blackstone Capital Partners, composed partly of CNW managers and the Union Pacific Railroad, acquired control of the company (ensuring Union Pacific's direct access to Chicago) after Japonica Partners made a hostile takeover bid for CNW in 1989.

Private company
Incorporated: Delaware, 1989
Fiscal year ends: December 31

WHO

Chairman, President, and CEO: Robert Schmiege, age 48, $539,583 pay
SVP Sales and Marketing, CNWT: Arthur W. Peters, age 47, $335,833 pay
SVP Operations, CNWT: Robert A. Jahnke, age 45, $308,333 pay
SVP, General Counsel, and Secretary: James P. Daley, age 62, $283,667 pay
SVP Administration: Jerome W. Conlon, age 50, $276,333 pay
SVP Finance and Accounting: Thomas A. Tingleff, age 43
Auditors: Arthur Andersen & Co.
Employees: 7,562

WHEN

William Ogden founded the Galena & Chicago Union Railroad (G&CU) in 1836 but did not begin its construction until 1848. The road eventually operated between the Chicago area and Fulton, Illinois. In 1855 the Chicago, St. Paul & Fond du Lac Railroad was founded to link Cary, Illinois; St. Paul, Minnesota; and the iron and copper mines of northern Wisconsin. In 1859 it was reorganized as the Chicago & North Western Railway (the North Western), which was consolidated with the G&CU (1864) and the Chicago, Milwaukee & North Western (1883).

In 1925 the company acquired the Chicago, St. Paul, Minneapolis & Omaha. By this time the North Western had trackage in Minnesota, Wisconsin, Illinois, Missouri, Wyoming, Nebraska, Iowa, and South Dakota. Ben Heineman became president of the North Western in 1956 and promptly became famous for, among other things, making the railroad's Chicago commuter trains run on time. The North Western gained a route into St. Louis with the 1958 merger of the Litchfield & Madison and also acquired the 1,500-mile Minneapolis & St. Louis (1960). Heineman intended to create a large midwestern railroad through the acquisition of 3 rival lines: the Chicago, Rock Island & Pacific (Rock Island); the Chicago, Milwaukee, St. Paul & Pacific (the Milwaukee Road); and the Chicago Great Western. Heineman succeeded only in purchasing the Chicago Great Western (1968), however, and in the meantime had turned his attention to diversification rather than further railroad acquisitions. In 1967 Heineman led the creation of Northwest Industries, a holding company for the railroad and its diversified interests, including the Velsicol Chemical and Michigan Chemical Corporations (both acquired in 1965).

The North Western's unstable earnings record, labor problems, and other handicaps led Heineman to put the railroad up for sale in 1969. The following year he offered the North Western to former acquisition target Milwaukee Road, which refused the deal. A group of North Western employees led by President Larry S. Provo expressed an interest, however, and in 1972 bought the railroad from Northwest Industries by assuming its $400 million debt load, making it the first employee-owned major railroad in America. In 1976 the company and Burlington Northern (BN) began construction of a 103-mile rail line serving Wyoming's Powder River Basin, a rich source of low-sulfur coal. The North Western dropped out of the project in 1979 because of a shortage of cash but won a court battle with BN to reacquire a 1/2 interest in the line for $76 million (1983). The railroad created a new holding company, CNW Corporation, in 1985.

In 1988 CNW began selling certain nonessential assets, such as snowplow manufacturer Douglas Dynamics (acquired 1986), to lower its high-interest-rate debt. The following year Blackstone Capital Partners bought CNW for $1.6 billion, in the process raising the company's debt from $536 million to over $1.3 billion.

WHERE

HQ: Chicago and North Western Holdings Corp., One North Western Center, Chicago, IL 60606
Phone: 312-559-7000
FAX: 312-559-7072

The railroad has 5,800 miles of track in 9 midwestern states.

Principal Cities Served

Casper, WY	Green Bay, WI
Cedar Rapids, IA	Kansas City, MO
Chicago, IL	Madison, WI
Council Bluffs, IA	Milwaukee, WI
Des Moines, IA	Peoria, IL
Duluth, MN	Rapid City, SD
Fremont, NE	Sioux City, IA
	St. Louis, MO

WHAT

	1989 Sales	
	$ mil	% of total
Railroad freight	843	88
Suburban & other	112	12
Total	**955**	**100**

	1989 Sales	
Business group	$ mil	% of total
Coal	247	24
Grain	187	18
Automotive & steel	165	16
Intermodal	96	9
Bulk & consumer products	243	23
Suburban & other	112	10
Allowances, absorptions & adjustments	(95)	—
Total	**955**	**100**

Operating Subsidiaries
Chicago and North Western Transportation Co.
CNW Realco, Inc.
Transportation Quality Systems
Western Railroad Properties, Inc.

RANKINGS

27th in *Fortune* 50 Transportation Cos.

COMPETITION

Burlington Northern
Trucking companies

HOW MUCH

	9 Yr. Growth	1980	1981	1982	1983	1984	1985	1986	1987	1988	1989
Sales ($ mil)	0.2%	936	982	804	860	882	898	959	957	995	955
Net income ($ mil)	—	39	45	(19)	34	21	(31)	43	30	69	(21)
Income as % of sales	—	4.2%	4.6%	(2.4%)	3.9%	2.4%	(3.4%)	4.5%	3.1%	7.0%	(2.2%)

1989 Year End:
Debt ratio: 84.7%
Cash (mil): $85
Current ratio: 0.9
Long-term debt (mil): $1,313
Assets (mil): $1,435

Net Income ($ mil) 1980-89

CHIQUITA BRANDS INTERNATIONAL, INC.

OVERVIEW

Chiquita Brands is the world's leading marketer of fresh fruits and vegetables. Chiquita Bananas, the company's flagship brand, is one of the great global product names. With 13 billion sold in 1989, Chiquita bananas contributed 36% of company sales.

Chiquita Brands is divided into 2 segments: Fresh Foods and Prepared Foods. The Fresh Foods segment, which accounts for 45% of total sales, includes bananas, pineapples, melons, vegetables, and various types of citrus and tropical fruits. The Prepared Foods segment, with 55% of total sales, produces fruit juices, puree, margarine, shortening, and various processed meats marketed under the John Morrell, Rath Black Hawk, and numerous regional brand names.

Although Chiquita Brands is a US company, the largest market for Chiquita Bananas is Europe, where 47% of the company's bananas are sold. The North American market generates 35% of banana sales, with the remainder going primarily to the Far East.

WHEN

In 1870 Lorenzo Baker, captain of the schooner *Telegraph*, sailed into Jersey City with 160 bunches of Jamaican bananas. Finding the new fruit profitable, Baker arranged to sell bananas through Boston produce agent Andrew Preston. With the support of Preston's partners, the 2 men formed the Boston Fruit Company in 1885.

In 1899 Boston Fruit merged with 3 other banana companies that had been importing produce and incorporated as United Fruit Company. Soon the company was importing bananas from numerous Central American plantations for expanded distribution in the US.

The company entered the Cuban sugar trade (Fidel Castro worked on a United Fruit sugar plantation) with the purchase of Nipe Bay (1907) and Saetia Sugar (1912). In 1930 the company bought Samuel Zemurray's Cuyamel Fruit Company, leaving Zemurray as the largest shareholder. Zemurray, who had masterminded the overthrow of the Honduran government in 1905 to establish a government favorable to his business, forcibly established himself as United Fruit's president in 1933. Because of its broad influence throughout Honduran politics and society, Hondurans came to call the company "Octopus."

In 1954, when leftist Guatemalan leader Jacobo Arbenz threatened to seize United Fruit holdings, the company convinced Congress and the American public that Arbenz was a Communist threat and provided its own ships to transport CIA-backed troops and ammunition for his ultimate overthrow. In 1961 United Fruit provided 2 ships for the unsuccessful Bay of Pigs invasion of Cuba. The term "banana republics" originates from United Fruit's involvement in establishing Central American regimes friendly to its operations.

During the 1950s the company introduced its catchy calypso-style Chiquita Banana ad campaign and in the 1960s diversified, buying A&W (restaurants and root beer, 1966) and Baskin-Robbins (ice cream, 1967).

Eli Black, founder of AMK (which included the Morrell meat company), bought United Fruit in 1970 and changed its name to United Brands. After hurricane Fifi destroyed much of the Honduran banana crop and the news leaked that he had bribed the Honduran president for lower export taxes, Black committed suicide in 1975.

During the 1970s and 1980s United Brands sold many of its previous acquisitions including Baskin-Robbins (1973), Foster Grant (sunglasses, 1974), and A&W (restaurants, 1982; soft drinks, 1987). Financier Carl Lindner's American Financial took over the controlling interest in United Brands in 1987 (it now owns over 65%). In 1990 the company changed its name to Chiquita Brands International.

HOW MUCH

	9 Yr. Growth	1980	1981	1982	1983	1984	1985	1986	1987	1988	1989
Sales ($ mil)	0.2%	3,763	4,058	2,406	3,360	3,220	2,288	3,307	3,268	3,503	3,823
Net income ($ mil)	9.1%	31	29	(167)	46	21	23	54	61	60	68
Income as % of sales	—	0.8%	0.7%	(7.0%)	1.4%	0.7%	1.0%	1.6%	1.9%	1.7%	1.8%
Earnings per share ($)	8.8%	0.78	0.76	(4.61)	1.05	0.46	0.46	1.09	1.30	1.45	1.67
Stock price – high ($)	—	5.58	5.79	3.88	9.04	7.25	9.29	12.33	16.67	19.88	17.63
Stock price – low ($)	—	3.25	3.13	2.17	2.58	3.42	3.50	7.38	9.33	13.75	12.88
Stock price – close ($)	13.5%	5.54	4.00	2.83	5.17	3.58	9.25	11.08	15.21	16.38	17.38
P/E – high	—	7	8	—	9	16	20	11	13	14	11
P/E – low	—	4	4	—	2	7	8	7	7	9	8
Dividends per share ($)	6.2%	0.12	0.17	0.05	0.00	0.00	0.02	0.02	0.15	0.20	0.20
Book value per share ($)	(3.1%)	15.83	16.97	5.09	6.90	7.21	7.70	8.82	9.69	10.38	11.94

1989 Year End:
Debt ratio: 47.3%
Return on equity: 15.0%
Cash (mil): $289
Current ratio: 1.84
Long-term debt (mil): $417
Number of shares (mil): 39
Dividends:
1989 average yield: 1.2%
1989 payout: 12.0%
Market value (mil): $675

Stock Price History high/low 1980-89

20 18 16 14 12 10 8 6 4 2 0

NYSE symbol: CQB
Incorporated: New Jersey, 1899
Fiscal year ends: December 31

WHO

Chairman and CEO: Carl H. Lindner, age 70, $400,000 pay
President and COO: Keith E. Lindner, age 30, $923,000 pay
VP and CFO: Fred J. Runk, age 47
Auditors: Ernst & Young
Employees: 44,000

WHERE

HQ: 250 E. 5th St., Cincinnati, OH 45202
Phone: 513-784-8011
FAX: 513-784-8030

The company owns approximately 100,000 acres of land in Central America. Most of its bananas are sold in Europe, North America, and the Far East.

	1989 Sales		1989 Operating Income	
	$ mil	% of total	$ mil	% of total
North America	2,798	73	12	8
Central & South America	186	5	34	24
Europe	647	17	65	46
Other	192	5	31	22
Adjustments	—	—	4	—
Total	**3,823**	**100**	**146**	**100**

WHAT

	1989 Sales		1989 Operating Income	
	$ mil	% of total	$ mil	% of total
Fresh foods	1,733	45	142	93
Prepared foods	2,090	55	10	7
Adjustments	—	—	(6)	—
Total	**3,823**	**100**	**146**	**100**

Brand Names

Bananas
Amigo
Bananos
Chico
Chiquita
Consul
Petite 150

Other Fruit and Vegetables
Chiquita Grapefruit
Chiquita Kiwi
Chiquita Melons
Chiquita Pineapples
Classic
Pascual
Premium

Meats
Bob Ostrow
Hunter
John Morrell
Krey
Mosey's
Nathan's Famous
Partridge
Peyton's
Rath Black Hawk
Rodeo
Scott Petersen
Solar AquaFarms
Tobin's First Prize

Prepared Foods
Chiquita Processed Foods (fruit juices)
Chiquita Caribbean Splash
Chiquita Orange Banana Juice
Chiquita Tropical Squeeze
Numar Processed Foods (vegetable oils)
Clover
Maravilla
Numar

RANKINGS

123rd in *Fortune* 500 Industrial Cos.
345th in *Fortune* Global 500 Industrial Cos.
217th in *Forbes* Sales 500
642nd in *Business Week* 1000

COMPETITION

Beatrice
Cargill
Castle & Cooke
ConAgra
Occidental
Philip Morris
Tyson Foods

CHRYSLER CORPORATION

OVERVIEW

Chrysler, the 3rd largest US automobile producer (behind GM and Ford) and the 6th largest in the world, produces and sells vehicles under the Chrysler, Dodge, Plymouth, Jeep/Eagle, and Lamborghini nameplates. In 1989 Chrysler generated 97% of its revenue in North America, holding 10.4% of the US car market and 19.4% of the truck market. Chrysler also operates the 4th largest nonbank finance company in the US, with revenues exceeding $4.1 billion; produces and sells automotive parts; and owns 3 car rental companies (Dollar, Snappy, and Thrifty).

A US network of 5,321 dealers averaged sales of 377 vehicles each in 1989. Chrysler purchases goods and services from 16,000 suppliers.

A restructuring to be completed in 1990 will cut excess capacity. Chrysler's new 5-year, $15 billion product plan includes the 10-cylinder Viper sports car introduction and the substitution of the new LH platform for the K platform in 1992. After disappointing financial results in 1989, CEO Iacocca has stated his intention to remain past his scheduled 1991 retirement and to make Chrysler "the low-cost, high-quality producer of cars and trucks in North America."

NYSE symbol: C
Incorporated: Delaware, 1986
Fiscal year ends: December 31

WHO

Chairman and CEO: Lee A. Iacocca, age 65, $889,151 pay
VC: Robert S. Miller, Jr., age 48, $502,995 pay
EVP and CFO: Jerome B. York, age 51
Auditors: Deloitte & Touche
Employees: 121,947

WHERE

HQ: 12000 Chrysler Dr., Highland Park, MI 48288
Phone: 313-956-5741
FAX: 313-956-3747

	1989 Sales		1989 Pretax Income	
	$ mil	% of total	$ mil	% of total
US	30,750	88	279	51
Canada	3,213	9	173	31
Other	959	3	100	18
Adjustments	—	—	—	—
Total	**34,922**	**100**	**552**	**100**

WHEN

When the Maxwell Motor Car Company entered receivership in 1920, a bankers' syndicate hired Walter Chrysler, former Buick president and GM VP, to reorganize it. Chrysler became president in 1923.

In 1924 he introduced his own car, the Chrysler. Offering the attractions of a high-performance model (*e.g.,* top speed 50 mph) at a mid-range price, the Chrysler borrowed from WWI aircraft in the design of its 6-cylinder, high-compression engine. In 1925 Chrysler took over Maxwell and renamed it after himself.

In 1928 Chrysler acquired Dodge and introduced the low-priced Plymouth and the luxurious DeSoto. The Chrysler R&D budget never decreased during the Great Depression, and innovations included overdrive and a 3-point engine suspension on rubber mountings. In 1933 Chrysler's sales surpassed Ford's. In 1935 Walter Chrysler retired.

To minimize costs Chrysler kept the same car models from 1942 until 1953, while other manufacturers were making yearly style modifications. Consequently, Chrysler lost market share and slipped to 3rd place by 1950.

Chrysler misjudged customer demands in the 1960s when it introduced small cars and in the 1970s when it maintained production of large cars. Steadily declining market share led to losses of over $1 billion in 1979 and 1980.

Lee Iacocca, former Ford president, became CEO in 1978. Iacocca became one of the most visible CEOs ever, appearing in TV commercials, publishing a best-selling autobiography, and making a public issue of Japanese trading practices.

Iacocca consolidated advertising under one agency; announced the 30-day money-back guarantee; and persuaded the government to cosign $1.5 billion in loans. Chrysler cut production costs by using the K-car chassis for several models and repaid all guaranteed loans by 1983, 7 years ahead of schedule. Chrysler's minivan (1984) created a new market.

Chrysler purchased Gulfstream Aerospace (corporate jets), E.F. Hutton Credit, and Finance America in 1985 for a total of $1.2 billion. In 1986 Chrysler began a joint venture with Mitsubishi (Diamond-Star) and in 1987 purchased American Motors.

In 1989 Chrysler acquired 2 car rental companies, Thrifty and Snappy, and agreed to purchase Dollar Rent-A-Car in 1990. A $931 million restructuring charge, year-end sales incentive rebates averaging $1,000 per car, and a glutted North American auto market combined to allow Chrysler disappointing 1989 profits. In 1990 Chrysler sold Gulfstream Aerospace for $825 million.

WHAT

	1989 Sales		1989 Operating Income	
	$ mil	% of total	$ mil	% of total
Cars & trucks	30,987	88	594	56
Financial services	4,079	12	460	44
Adjustments	(144)	—	2,771	—
Total	**34,922**	**100**	**3,825**	**100**

Chrysler
Imperial
LeBaron
New Yorker
Town & Country
Shadow
Spirit
Stealth

Dodge
Aries
Caravan
Dakota
Daytona
Dynasty
Monaco
Ram

Eagle
Premier
Summit
Talon
Vista

Jeep
Cherokee
Grand Wagoneer
Wrangler

Lamborghini
Countach
Diablo

Plymouth
Acclaim
Colt
Laser
Reliant
Sundance
Voyager

Major Subsidiaries
Chrysler Financial Corp.
Dollar Rent-A-Car Systems, Inc.
Snappy Car Rental
Thrifty Rent-A-Car Systems

Minority Holdings
Maserati (16%)
Mitsubishi (12%)

HOW MUCH

	9 Yr. Growth	1980	1981	1982	1983	1984	1985	1986	1987	1988	1989
Sales ($ mil)	15.9%	9,225	10,822	10,045	13,240	19,573	21,256	22,586	26,277	35,473	34,922
Net income ($ mil)	—	(1,710)	(476)	(69)	302	1,496	1,635	1,404	1,290	1,050	315
Income as % of sales	—	(18.5%)	(4.4%)	(0.7%)	2.3%	7.6%	7.7%	6.2%	4.9%	3.0%	0.9%
Earnings per share ($)	—	*(11.56)*	*(3.19)*	*(0.57)*	1.04	5.19	6.22	6.29	5.89	4.65	1.55
Stock price – high ($)	—	5.17	3.39	8.28	15.83	15.00	20.89	31.42	48.00	27.88	29.63
Stock price – low ($)	—	1.83	1.33	1.56	6.22	9.28	13.28	18.11	19.63	20.50	18.13
Stock price – close ($)	27.3%	2.17	1.50	7.89	12.28	14.22	20.72	24.67	22.13	25.75	19.00
P/E – high	—	—	—	—	15	3	3	5	8	6	22
P/E – low	—	—	—	—	6	2	2	3	3	4	13
Dividends per share ($)	—	0.00	0.00	0.00	0.00	0.38	0.44	0.80	1.00	1.00	1.20
Book value per share ($)	—	(0.69)	(3.28)	(1.84)	4.17	12.10	18.50	24.67	29.39	32.53	32.42

1989 Year End:
Debt ratio: 65.9%
Return on equity: 4.2%
Cash (mil): $1,269
Assets (mil): $51,038
Long-term debt (mil): $13,966
Number of shares (mil): 223
Dividends:
1989 average yield: 6.3%
1989 payout: 88.9%
Market value (mil): $4,239

Stock Price History high/low 1980-89

RANKINGS

8th in *Fortune* 500 Industrial Cos.
16th in *Fortune* Global 500 Industrial Cos.
7th in *Fortune* 50 Exporters
12th in *Forbes* Sales 500
150th in *Business Week* 1000
548th in *Business Week* Global 1000

COMPETITION

Daimler-Benz
Fiat
Ford
General Motors
Hertz
Honda
Hyundai
Mitsubishi
Nissan
Toyota
Volkswagen
Volvo

CIGNA CORPORATION

OVERVIEW

CIGNA was the 2nd largest US publicly-owned insurance company (behind Aetna), based on 1989 assets.

Focused on commercial markets since 1988, the Philadelphia-based company provides services in 4 areas. Through Connecticut General and Insurance Company of North America (INA) subsidiaries, CIGNA provides employee life and health, employee retirement and savings, individual financial services, and property and casualty. Individual financial services, which CIGNA said it may divest, include life and disability insurance and investment products for small business owners and affluent individuals.

CIGNA's group retirement programs provide pension and profit-sharing services to middle-sized companies, with plans from $500,000 to $50 million. CIGNA is one of the largest US providers of group life, health, and long-term disability insurance. With its 1990 acquisition of EQUICOR-Equitable HCA Corporation, CIGNA becomes the dominant stock insurance company in managed health care services. The property and casualty division provides commercial property and casualty insurance through independent agents and brokers. Property and casualty insurance accounted for 48% of 1989 revenues.

WHEN

In 1982 Connecticut General and INA merged to form CIGNA Corporation. INA, the older of the 2, formed as Insurance Company of North America by a group of Philadelphia businessmen in 1792, was the first stock insurance company as well as the first marine insurance company in the US. It insured the ship *America* and its cargo on a trip from Philadelphia.

In 1794 INA issued its first life insurance policy, became the first US issuer of fire insurance outside city limits, and was the first to insure building contents against fire. In 1808 INA appointed independent agents in 5 states, thus originating the American Agency System. In the late 1800s INA grew internationally, appointing an agent for marine insurance in Canada (1873) and adding agents in London and Vienna (1887) and in Shanghai (1897); INA was the first US company to write insurance in China.

In 1942 INA's Indemnity Insurance company wrote accident and health insurance for the US Army's 30 men working on the Manhattan Project, the effort to develop the atom bomb. In 1950 INA introduced the homeowners' policy, the first homeowner coverage with broad availability. In 1978 INA bought HMO International, the largest publicly owned prepaid health care provider in the US.

In 1865 Dr. Guy Phelps, one of the founders of Connecticut Mutual, helped organize Connecticut General as a life insurance company. In 1912 Connecticut General formed an accident department to offer health insurance. The company in 1913 wrote its first group insurance for the *Hartford Courant* newspaper. In 1926 Connecticut General wrote the first individual regular accident coverage for airline passengers.

In the late 1930s Connecticut General was an industry leader in developing group medical and surgical insurance. Connecticut General in 1952 offered the first group medical coverage for general use and in 1964 introduced group dental insurance.

After the merger of INA and Connecticut General in 1982, CIGNA purchased Crusader Insurance (UK, 1983) and AFIA (1984). CIGNA sold its individual insurance products division to InterContinental Life (Jackson, Mississippi; 1988) and its Horace Mann Companies (individual financial services) to an investor group (1989) in order to focus on commercial business. In early 1990 CIGNA agreed to acquire EQUICOR-Equitable HCA Corporation, a group insurance and managed health care organization with $2.5 billion in 1989 revenues.

HOW MUCH

	9 Yr. Growth	1980	1981	1982	1983	1984	1985	1986	1987	1988	1989
Sales ($ mil)	12.8%	5,279	5,649	11,787	12,564	14,775	16,197	17,064	16,909	17,889	15,654
Net income ($ mil)	4.2%	317	357	490	401	39	(855)	535	617	410	458
Income as % of sales	—	6.0%	6.3%	4.2%	3.2%	0.3%	(5.3%)	3.1%	3.6%	2.3%	2.9%
Earnings per share ($)	(3.5%)	7.66	8.65	6.38	5.22	0.11	(12.46)	6.26	7.14	4.88	5.58
Stock price – high ($)	—	50.50	58.25	55.38	51.50	45.50	64.25	77.25	69.50	55.38	66.75
Stock price – low ($)	—	29.25	41.75	31.00	37.63	27.00	43.50	51.13	41.25	42.75	45.88
Stock price – close ($)	2.8%	46.50	50.00	44.25	43.75	44.38	64.25	55.00	43.88	47.13	59.50
P/E – high	—	7	7	9	10	414	—	12	10	11	12
P/E – low	—	4	5	5	7	245	—	8	6	9	8
Dividends per share ($)	7.7%	1.52	1.76	2.24	2.48	2.60	2.60	2.60	2.80	2.96	2.96
Book value per share ($)	3.0%	54.06	60.41	62.71	66.74	62.79	51.84	58.83	63.52	66.64	70.59

1989 Year End:
Debt ratio: 10.4%
Return on equity: 8.1%
Cash (mil): $733
Assets (mil): $57,779
Long-term debt (mil): $640
Number of shares (mil): 78
Dividends:
1989 average yield: 5.0%
1989 payout: 53.0%
Market value (mil): $4,653

Stock Price History high/low 1980-89

NYSE symbol: CI
Incorporated: Delaware, 1981
Fiscal year ends: December 31

WHO

Chairman and CEO: Wilson H. Taylor, age 46, $1,103,000 pay
EVP: G. Robert O'Brien, age 53, $709,000 pay
EVP and CFO: James G. Stewart, age 47, $705,000 pay
Auditors: Price Waterhouse
Employees: 47,677

WHERE

HQ: One Liberty Place, Philadelphia, PA 19192
Phone: 215-523-4000
FAX: 215-523-7915

CIGNA serves customers in 69 countries through 164 offices and 3,000 independent agencies.

	1989 Sales		1989 Pretax Income	
	$ mil	% of total	$ mil	% of total
Domestic	13,327	85	637	108
Foreign	2,327	15	(45)	(8)
Total	**15,654**	**100**	**592**	**100**

WHAT

	1989 Sales		1989 Pretax Income	
	$ mil	% of total	$ mil	% of total
Employee retirement & savings	2,056	13	232	39
Property & casualty				
Commercial	6,157	40	(81)	(13)
Personal	541	3	(36)	(6)
Other	717	5	44	7
Employee life & health	4,998	32	337	57
Individual financial services	954	6	124	21
Other	231	1	(28)	(5)
Total	**15,654**	**100**	**592**	**100**

Financial Services
Group life, health, accident, and disability insurance
Health care services
Individual life and health insurance
Investment management
Pension and retirement services
Property and casualty insurance

RANKINGS

6th in *Fortune* 50 Diversified Financial Cos.
33rd in *Forbes* Sales 500
156th in *Business Week* 1000
470th in *Business Week* Global 1000

COMPETITION

Aetna
American Financial
AIG
Berkshire Hathaway
Blue Cross
Equitable
GEICO
General Re
ITT
John Hancock
Kemper
Lloyd's of London
Loews
Massachusetts Mutual
Metropolitan
New York Life
Northwestern Mutual
Primerica
Prudential
Sears
State Farm
Teachers Insurance
Tokio Marine & Fire
Transamerica
Travelers
USF&G
Xerox

THE CIRCLE K CORPORATION

OVERVIEW

After increasing sales six-fold in the course of a decade, Phoenix-based Circle K sought the protection of bankruptcy in 1990. The company is the 2nd largest convenience store operator in the country after Southland (7-Eleven). It also operates about 65 stores under the Charter name. Slow sales growth, large amounts of acquisition debt, and management shake-ups have placed Circle K's future in doubt.

Circle K grew from 1,221 stores in 1983 to 5,751 at the end of 1989, increasing its long-term debt from $40.5 million to $1.1 billion. Yet, despite sales almost 5 times the 1983 level, the company is producing the same net income, due in part to $96 million in annual interest payments. Also, the company had been charging higher prices than its competition and offering products that consumers did not want. In early 1990 prices were made more competitive and store managers were given more authority to purchase products desired by their customers, but it was too late to prevent Chapter 11 bankruptcy in May 1990.

Competition is likely to remain fierce among North America's 83,000 convenience stores. Cigarettes and beer, the stores' traditional high-volume sales categories, are less in demand, and gasoline companies have begun opening their own convenience store chains.

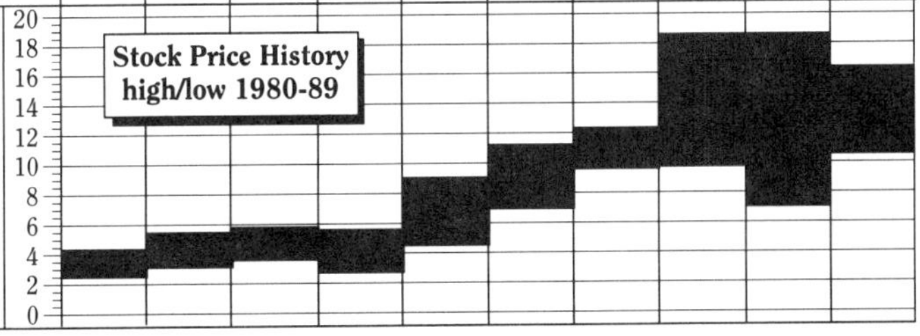

NYSE symbol: CKP
Incorporated: Texas, 1980
Fiscal year ends: April 30

WHO

Chairman and CEO: Bart A. Brown, Jr., age 58
President and COO: Robert A. Dearth, age 45
SVP Finance and CFO: Larry J. Zine, age 34, $156,000 pay
Auditors: Arthur Andersen & Co.
Employees: 27,264

WHERE

HQ: 1601 N. 7th St., PO Box 52084, Phoenix, AZ 85072
Phone: 602-253-9600
FAX: 602-257-4468

Circle K operates 4,685 convenience stores in 32 states, primarily in the Sunbelt, and 1,066 stores in 8 foreign countries.

	1989 Store Locations	
	# of stores	% of total
Florida	874	15
Texas	757	13
Arizona	679	12
California	578	10
Louisiana	317	6
Georgia	260	5
Other US	1,220	20
Total US	**4,685**	**81**
Japan	647	11
UK	245	4
Canada	87	2
Other foreign	87	2
Total	**5,751**	**100**

WHEN

Circle K Corporation was formed in Texas in 1951 by Fred Hervey, a 2-term mayor of El Paso. Hervey bought the 3 locations of Kay's Food Stores in El Paso that year and soon built the chain to 10 locations. In 1957, the year he expanded into Arizona, he changed the stores' name to Circle K and adopted the distinctive, western-style logo. Circle K went public in 1963. During the 1960s and 1970s the company expanded into New Mexico, California, Colorado, Montana, Idaho, and Oregon. In 1979 Circle K licensed UNY of Japan to operate Circle K stores there. UNY currently operates over 400 Circle K stores in Japan and Hong Kong.

The corporation changed to a holding company in 1980, operating its Circle K chain as a subsidiary, and began an expansion phase through acquisitions. In the same year, the company bought 13% of Nucorp Energy, an oil and gas development company. Nucorp filed for bankruptcy in 1982, and Circle K sold its remaining interest in 1983 at a large loss. Also in 1983, Circle K nearly doubled its size by acquiring the 960-store UtoteM chain from American Financial, headed by Cincinnati financier Carl Lindner. Hervey and Lindner chose their friend Karl Eller to be the chairman and CEO of Circle K.

Eller committed Circle K to an aggressive growth plan, aimed at increasing the number of stores almost 400% by 1990. The company made several acquisitions, including 435 Little General stores (1985) and the 449-store Shop & Go chain. Circle K bought its British licensee, Circle K UK, in 1986 and sold a half interest in 1987, as well as 186 stores from National Convenience Stores. In 1988 Circle K bought 473 of Southland's 7-Eleven stores, primarily in the Southeast, adding South Carolina to its territory. Later that year the company bought the 538 stores of Charter Company, also owned by Lindner, giving Circle K a foothold in several eastern states.

Circle K began having financial problems in 1989 and put itself up for sale, but no buyers emerged. Lindner, whose American Financial is not only Circle K's largest stockholder (15% of common stock plus preferred shares convertible to common) but also a major creditor, brought in Robert Dearth from his United Foods (Chiquita Brands) as Circle K's president and COO in 1990. Shortly afterward, Eller left the company "to pursue personal business opportunities" and Circle K filed for bankruptcy.

WHAT

	1989 Revenues	
	$ mil	% of total
Merchandise sales	1,962	56
Gasoline sales	1,479	42
Other revenues	52	2
Total	**3,493**	**100**

	1989 US Store Features
	# of stores
Gasoline pumps	3,693
Video rental	2,210
ATMs	1,146

RANKINGS

30th in *Fortune* 50 Retailers
222nd in *Forbes* Sales 500

COMPETITION

Atlantic Richfield
British Petroleum
Chevron
Coastal
Exxon
Kroger
Mobil
Royal Dutch/Shell
Southland
Texaco
Gasoline and grocery retailers

HOW MUCH

	9 Yr. Growth	1980	1981	1982	1983	1984	1985	1986	1987	1988	1989
Sales ($ mil)	23.2%	536	648	733	754	1,035	1,694	2,129	2,317	2,657	3,493
Net income ($ mil)	(1.0%)	17	14	(15)	15	22	33	40	49	55	15
Income as % of sales	—	3.2%	2.2%	(2.1%)	2.0%	2.1%	2.0%	1.9%	2.1%	2.1%	0.4%
Earnings per share ($)	(10.7%)	0.55	0.47	(0.47)	0.44	0.57	0.71	0.75	0.85	0.96	0.20
Stock price – high ($)	—	4.40	5.50	5.83	5.63	9.08	11.25	12.33	18.63	18.63	16.38
Stock price – low ($)	—	2.46	3.08	3.54	2.67	4.50	6.92	9.56	9.69	7.00	10.50
Stock price – close ($)	11.1%	4.40	3.83	3.92	4.79	8.50	10.54	10.31	16.13	10.63	11.38
P/E – high	—	8	12	—	13	16	16	16	22	19	82
P/E – low	—	4	7	—	6	8	10	13	11	7	53
Dividends per share ($)	4.1%	0.19	0.23	0.24	0.25	0.25	0.25	0.25	0.28	0.28	0.28
Book value per share ($)	13.1%	2.12	2.38	1.84	2.05	2.63	3.38	4.62	6.23	6.56	6.44

1989 Year End:
Debt ratio: 77.0%
Return on equity: 3.1%
Cash (mil): $38
Current ratio: 1.17
Long-term debt (mil): $1,104
Number of shares (mil): 44
Dividends:
1989 average yield: 2.5%
1989 payout: 140.0%
Market value (mil): $496

Stock Price History high/low 1980-89

20
18
16
14
12
10
8
6
4
2
0

CITICORP

OVERVIEW

New York–based Citicorp, with its primary operating company, Citibank, is the largest banking enterprise in the US (1989 year-end assets of $230.6 billion). The bank serves customers in over 3,300 locations in 43 states and Washington, DC, and in 89 other countries.

Citibank, the leading US international bank, operates in 23 of the 24 industrial nations that form the Organization for Economic Cooperation and Development. It ranks first worldwide in major industry surveys of foreign exchange providers, trading 90 different currencies in 50 locations.

The company's consumer businesses generated $842 million in revenues in 1989, with an average annual increase of 37% during the 1980s. The company is a market leader with 27 million credit cards in use by the end of 1989. Citicorp, H. F. Ahmanson, and Great Western were the largest residential mortgage lenders in 1989, each loaning about $11 billion. Citicorp expects that serving consumers worldwide will become an increasing portion of its total activity in the 1990s.

WHEN

Colonel Samuel Osgood, first commissioner of the US Treasury, founded City Bank of New York in 1812. City Bank initially served cotton, sugar, metal, and coal merchants. During the Civil War the bank changed its name to National City Bank of New York.

In the early 1900s the bank opened its first foreign (London, 1902) and first Latin American (Buenos Aires, 1914) branches. The bank expanded into retail (consumer) banking in the 1920s, opening branches for individuals (1921) and becoming the first commercial bank to make personal loans (1928). During the 1920s and 1930s the bank's international operations grew to 100 foreign offices by 1939.

James Stillman Rockefeller, who expanded the bank's retail banking in the late 1940s and early 1950s, became president in 1952. In 1955 the bank merged with First National (New York) to become First National City Bank. In 1961 the bank, under VP Walter Wriston, invented the certificate of deposit (CD), paying a higher interest rate on funds deposited for specified time periods. With CDs the bank could compete for funds with US government securities. Wriston served as president from 1967 to 1970 and chairman from 1970 to 1984, leading the bank to international prominence.

In 1968 the bank formed a bank holding company, First National City Corporation (renamed Citicorp in 1974), to offer nonbanking financial services. Other major banks soon formed holding companies. At the end of 1968, Citibank replaced Chase Manhattan as the largest New York City bank, with $19.4 billion in assets.

Citibank became a major issuer of Visa and MasterCard in the 1970s and acquired Carte Blanche (1978) and Diners Club (1981). In 1977 Citibank was the first bank to introduce Automated Teller Machines (ATMs) on a large scale, installing 500 in the New York City area alone. John Reed, who developed the ATM and consumer banking markets, became chairman when Wriston retired (1984).

At the end of 1980, the bank passed BankAmerica to become the largest US bank, with $114.9 billion in assets. In the 1980s Citibank's acquisitions included Fidelity Savings (California, 1982); First Federal of Chicago (1984); Biscayne Federal (Miami, 1984); and National Permanent Savings (Washington, DC, 1986).

The bank's loans to foreign countries became a problem in the late 1980s. Citicorp surprised competitors by reserving $3 billion in 1987 and $1 billion in 1989 against possible foreign losses. Nevertheless, the company was profitable for 1989.

HOW MUCH

	9 Yr. Growth	1980	1981	1982	1983	1984	1985	1986	1987	1988	1989
Sales ($ mil)	11.6%	14,197	18,232	17,768	17,037	20,494	22,504	23,496	27,988	32,024	37,970
Net income ($ mil)	0.0%	499	531	723	860	890	998	1,058	(1,138)	1,698	498
Income as % of sales	—	3.5%	2.9%	4.1%	5.0%	4.3%	4.4%	4.5%	(4.1%)	5.3%	1.3%
Earnings per share ($)	(5.4%)	1.92	2.01	2.67	3.08	3.18	3.56	3.57	*(4.26)*	4.87	1.16
Stock price – high ($)	—	13.13	15.19	20.00	23.06	20.25	25.88	31.88	34.19	27.00	35.50
Stock price – low ($)	—	8.50	10.44	10.75	15.25	13.69	18.44	23.44	15.88	18.00	24.63
Stock price – close ($)	10.1%	12.13	12.63	16.25	18.56	19.38	24.69	26.50	18.63	25.88	28.88
P/E – high	—	7	8	8	8	6	7	9	—	6	31
P/E – low	—	4	5	4	5	4	5	7	—	4	21
Dividends per share ($)	9.3%	0.71	0.78	0.86	0.94	1.03	1.13	0.92	1.32	1.45	1.59
Book value per share ($)	5.3%	15.86	17.08	18.92	21.00	22.91	25.31	27.96	22.83	25.93	25.36

1989 Year End:
Debt ratio: 70.4%
Return on equity: 4.5%
Cash (mil): $20,145
Assets (mil): $230,643
Long-term debt (mil): $23,950
Number of shares (mil): 325
Dividends:
1989 average yield: 5.5%
1989 payout: 136.6%
Market value (mil): $9,377

Stock Price History high/low 1980-89

NYSE symbol: CCI
Incorporated: Delaware, 1967
Fiscal year ends: December 31

WHO

Chairman: John S. Reed, age 51, $1,545,917 pay
President: Richard S. Braddock, age 48, $876,583 pay
VC: Lawrence M. Small, age 48, $876,583 pay
VC: Paul J. Collins, age 53, $741,447 pay
VC: James D. Farley, age 63, $663,183 pay
Sector Executive: Michael A. Callen, age 49, $802,917 pay
VP and Controller: Roger W. Trupin, age 48
Auditors: KPMG Peat Marwick
Employees: 92,000

WHERE

HQ: 399 Park Ave., New York, NY 10043
Phone: 212-559-1000
FAX: 212-291-6633

Citicorp operates in 90 countries.

	1989 Net Revenue*		1989 Net Income	
	$ mil	% of total	$ mil	% of total
North America	8,747	64	965	—
Other Americas	1,033	7	(712)	—
Europe, Middle East & Africa	2,495	18	(117)	—
Asia/Pacific	1,477	11	362	—
Total	**13,752**	**100**	**498**	**—**

*Sales less interest expense

WHAT

	1989 Net Income	
	$ mil	% of total
Global consumer	842	—
Global finance		
Developed economies	651	—
Developing economies	385	—
Information business	(178)	—
Cross-border refinancing	(1,151)	—
Corporate	(51)	—
Total	**498**	**—**

Services

Global Consumer	**Global Finance**
Checking and savings	Cash management
Consumer loans	Corporate banking
Credit cards	Corporate finance
Electronic banking	Foreign exchange
Investment accounts	Investment banking
	Securities trading

RANKINGS

1st in *Fortune* 100 Commercial Banking Cos.
11th in *Fortune* World's 100 Commercial Banks
9th in *Forbes* Sales 500
66th in *Business Week* 1000
235th in *Business Week* Global 1000

COMPETITION

ADP
H. F. Ahmanson
American Express
Bank of New York
BankAmerica
Bankers Trust
Barnett Banks
Chase Manhattan
Chemical Banking
CS Holding
Dai-Ichi Kangyo
Deutsche Bank
Dow Jones
First Chicago
First Interstate
Great Western
Hongkong & Shanghai Banking
Manufacturers Hanover
J.P. Morgan
Reuters
Security Pacific
SunTrust
Wells Fargo

THE CLOROX COMPANY

OVERVIEW

Clorox is the #1 US liquid bleach supplier, with over 50% of the US bleach market. Americans buy more than 1 million bottles of Clorox per day.

Clorox 2 is #1 among dry nonchlorine bleach brands and Soft Scrub is the most popular liquid cleanser. The company also develops, manufactures, and markets other major household products, including Formula 409, Liquid-plumr, and Kingsford charcoal. Household products are distributed to retail stores by a network of about 60 food brokers.

Clorox's best known food seasoning products are Hidden Valley Ranch dressings and K.C. Masterpiece barbecue sauce. Clorox is also in the water business, with Deer Park bottled water and Brita water filter systems.

New products and line extensions of mature products accounted for more than 69% of Clorox's sales growth from 1984 to 1989. The company has had an increase in its earnings per share every year since 1980. The company closed its 1990 fiscal year with record sales and earnings of almost $1.5 billion and $154 million, respectively.

NYSE symbol: CLX
Incorporated: Delaware, 1986
Fiscal year ends: June 30

WHO

Chairman and CEO: Charles R. Weaver, age 61, $735,900 pay
President and COO: Robert A. Bolingbroke, age 52, $313,614 pay (prior to promotion)
EVP Technology: Sheldon N. Lewis, age 56, $409,229 pay
VP and CFO: William F. Ausfahl, age 50, $307,280 pay
Group VP: G. Craig Sullivan, age 50
Group VP: Willard E. Lynn, age 46
Auditors: Deloitte & Touche
Employees: 5,300

WHEN

Known in its first few years as the Electro-Alkaline Company, Clorox was founded in 1913 by 5 Oakland investors to make bleach using water from salt ponds around San Francisco Bay. The next year the company registered the brand name Clorox and its diamond-shaped trademark; the name is believed to come from the product's 2 main ingredients, chlorine and sodium hydroxide. At first Clorox sold only industrial strength bleach, but in 1916 the company formulated a less concentrated household solution.

With the establishment of a Philadelphia distributor in 1921, Clorox began a national expansion. The company went public in 1928. In the late 1930s Clorox built 2 more plants, in Chicago and New Jersey; in the late 1940s and early 1950s it opened 9 more plants throughout the country. In 1957 Procter and Gamble (P&G) bought Clorox. Antitrust questions were raised by the FTC, and litigation ensued over the next decade. P&G was ordered to divest Clorox, and in 1969 Clorox again became an independent company.

Following its split with P&G, Clorox implemented plans to add new products, mostly household consumer goods and foods, acquiring the brands Liquid-plumr (drain opener, 1969), Formula 409 (spray cleaner, 1970), Litter Green (cat litter, 1971), and Hidden Valley Ranch (salad dressings, 1972). In 1970 the company introduced Clorox 2, a nonchlorine bleach to compete with new enzymatic cleaners. Clorox entered the specialty food products business by buying Grocery Store Products (Kitchen Bouquet, 1971), Martin-Brower (food products and restaurant equipment for the food service industry, 1972), and Kingsford (charcoal briquets, 1973). Sales of $412 million in 1973 put Clorox into the *Fortune* 500 for the first time.

In 1974 Henkel, a large West German maker of cleansers and detergents, purchased 15% of Clorox stock as part of an agreement to share research. The agreement was expanded in later years to include joint manufacturing and marketing. Beginning in 1977 Clorox sold off Country Kitchen Foods (1979) and other subsidiaries and brands to focus on household goods, particularly those sold through grocery stores. In 1977 Clorox introduced Soft Scrub, the first liquid cleanser in the US.

Introduced in 1980, Match Light, an instant-lighting charcoal briquet, was the first Clorox product developed internally by the company's Kingsford Division. Other new brands introduced in the 1980s included Tilex (stain remover, 1981) and Fresh Step (cat litter, 1984). In August 1990 Clorox bought American Cyanamid's household products group, which includes Pine Sol cleaner and Combat insecticide, for $465 million.

WHERE

HQ: 1221 Broadway, Oakland, CA 94612
Phone: 415-271-7000
FAX: 415-465-8875

Clorox sells products in 60 countries and produces them in more than 35 plants in 12 countries.

WHAT

Domestic Brands
BBQ Bag (single-use briquets)
Brita (water filter system)
Clorox (liquid bleach)
Clorox 2 (color-safe bleach)
Clorox Detergent
Clorox Pre-Wash (stain remover)
Combat (insecticide)
Control (cat litter)
Deer Park, Deep Rock (bottled water)
Formula 409 (spray cleaner)
Fresh Step (cat litter)
Hidden Valley Ranch (salad dressings)
K.C. Masterpiece (barbecue sauce)
Kingsford (charcoal briquets and lighter)
Kitchen Bouquet (seasoning sauce)
Liquid-plumr (drain opener)
Litter Green (cat litter)
Match Light (instant lighting briquets)
Moore's (onion rings)
Pine Sol (cleaner)
Salad Crispins (minicroutons)
Soft Scrub (liquid cleanser)
Tackle (household cleaner/disinfectant)
Tilex (mildew stain remover)

International Brands
Ayudin (liquid chlorine bleach)
Clorogar (bleach)
Sonic (bleach)

HOW MUCH

	9 Yr. Growth	1980	1981	1982	1983	1984	1985	1986	1987	1988	1989
Sales ($ mil)	8.8%	637	714	867	914	975	1,055	1,089	1,126	1,260	1,356
Net income ($ mil)	17.8%	33	38	45	66	80	86	96	105	133	146
Income as % of sales	—	5.2%	5.3%	5.2%	7.2%	8.2%	8.2%	8.8%	9.3%	10.5%	10.7%
Earnings per share ($)	15.5%	0.72	0.83	0.93	1.32	1.51	1.59	1.75	1.90	2.40	2.63
Stock price – high ($)	—	5.88	7.06	14.00	18.25	15.50	25.25	30.19	36.00	33.75	44.50
Stock price – low ($)	—	3.94	4.88	5.31	10.25	11.25	13.75	22.00	23.50	26.13	30.13
Stock price – close ($)	26.5%	5.06	5.63	12.38	13.25	14.38	23.81	25.31	27.75	31.00	42.00
P/E – high	—	8	9	15	14	10	16	17	19	14	17
P/E – low	—	5	6	6	8	7	9	13	12	11	11
Dividends per share ($)	12.3%	0.39	0.41	0.43	0.48	0.54	0.62	0.70	0.79	0.92	1.09
Book value per share ($)	12.2%	5.03	5.45	5.88	6.74	8.20	9.18	10.31	11.51	13.19	14.19

1989 Year End:
Debt ratio: 0.9%
Return on equity: 19.2%
Cash (mil): $233
Current ratio: 1.86
Long-term debt (mil): $7
Number of shares (mil): 55
Dividends:
1989 average yield: 2.6%
1989 payout: 41.4%
Market value (mil): $2,327

Stock Price History high/low 1980-89

RANKINGS

265th in *Fortune* 500 Industrial Cos.
302nd in *Business Week* 1000
852nd in *Business Week* Global 1000

COMPETITION

Amway
Bayer
Bristol-Myers Squibb
Colgate-Palmolive
Eastman Kodak
Greyhound Dial
H. J. Heinz
S.C. Johnson
Procter & Gamble
Unilever

THE COASTAL CORPORATION

OVERVIEW

Houston-based Coastal is the 12th largest energy company in the US. Its natural gas pipeline network, more than 19,000 miles long, is one of the US's 6 largest pipeline systems.

Coastal's pipeline systems purchase gas from producers, transport it, and sell it to end-users, utilities, or large industries. Chairman and founder Oscar Wyatt — even though he has stepped down from the CEO job — has drafted a $1+ billion plan to extend Coastal's pipelines into the lucrative northeastern US and Southern California markets. With a $581 million recapitalization ($381 million in a stock issuance and $200 million in debentures) under Coastal's belt, speculation about Coastal taking over companies already in those markets — a Wyatt specialty — has arisen.

Coastal subsidiaries operate 6 US refineries; a fleet of tugs, tankers, and barges; 14,000 trucks and tractor trailers; and 570 C-Mart convenience/gas stores. The company also mines coal in West Virginia, Kentucky, Virginia, and Utah. It drills for oil and gas in 15 states and in the Gulf of Mexico.

WHEN

After boyhood summers working in the oil fields, a stint as a bomber pilot in WWII, and a mechanical engineering degree from Texas A&M, Oscar Wyatt started a small natural gas gathering business in Corpus Christi, Texas. It was 1951.

In 1955 the company became Coastal States Gas Producing Company. It collected and distributed natural gas from South Texas oil fields. In 1962 Coastal purchased Sinclair Oil's Corpus Christi refinery and pipeline network.

Also in the early 1960s a Coastal subsidiary, Lo-Vaca Gathering, supplied natural gas to Texas cities and utilities. During the energy crisis of the early 1970s Lo-Vaca curtailed its natural gas supplies and then raised prices. Unhappy customers took Coastal to court, and regulators in 1977 ordered Lo-Vaca to refund $1.6 billion. To finance the settlement, Coastal spun off Lo-vaca as Valero Energy.

Meanwhile, the combative Wyatt, who would earn a reputation as one of the swashbuckling corporate raiders of the 1980s, had been expanding Coastal through a series of deals. Coastal sharpened its teeth by threatening a proxy fight to win Rio Grande Valley Gas, a small South Texas pipeline (1968), and then in 1973 mounted a successful $182 million hostile bid for Colorado Interstate Gas and changed its name to Coastal States Gas Corporation. With aggressive acquisitions, Coastal moved into low-sulfur Utah coal (Southern Utah Fuel, 1973), New England pipelines (Union Petroleum, 1973), California refining (Pacific Refining, 1976), and Florida petroleum marketing and transportation (Belcher Oil, 1977). In 1980 the company adopted its present name.

Wyatt tried to snare Texas Gas Resources (1983) and Houston Natural Gas (1984). Even though the bids were thwarted, when the companies had to buy back stock owned by Coastal to defend themselves, Coastal made money. Wyatt, a tenacious opponent, led the company in the courtroom as well as the boardroom. Among the lawsuits fought during his tenure was a libel action against a Houston newspaper that compared him to J. R. Ewing of TV's "Dallas." (The litigants settled out of court.)

In 1985 Coastal purchased Detroit-based American Natural Resources in a $2.45 billion hostile takeover. In 1989, just before Wyatt stepped down as CEO, Coastal bid $2.6 billion for Texas Eastern, but Texas Eastern sold to "white knight" Panhandle Eastern. Also in 1989 Coastal announced plans to sell its trucking operations. In the 1990s Coastal was racing crosstown rival Tenneco to expand into Southern California and has proposed a pipeline to transport Canadian gas into the northeastern US.

HOW MUCH

	9 Yr. Growth	1980	1981	1982	1983	1984	1985	1986	1987	1988	1989
Sales ($ mil)	5.5%	5,115	5,910	5,799	5,963	6,260	7,275	6,668	7,429	8,187	8,271
Net income ($ mil)	5.6%	110	(20)	66	94	102	142	72	113	157	178
Income as % of sales	—	2.1%	(0.3%)	1.1%	1.6%	1.6%	2.0%	1.1%	1.5%	1.9%	2.2%
Earnings per share ($)	5.0%	1.22	(0.37)	0.71	1.07	1.31	1.56	0.56	1.39	1.79	1.89
Stock price – high ($)	—	14.14	16.03	10.03	9.76	10.57	17.44	17.78	26.92	23.67	33.08
Stock price – low ($)	—	3.97	6.80	3.80	4.95	6.96	8.19	10.44	14.00	17.58	22.00
Stock price – close ($)	11.4%	12.49	9.53	5.29	9.02	8.37	17.39	15.56	17.33	22.83	33.08
P/E – high	—	12	—	14	9	8	11	32	19	13	17
P/E – low	—	3	—	5	5	5	5	19	10	10	12
Dividends per share ($)	9.3%	0.13	0.11	0.11	0.11	0.22	0.16	0.18	0.24	0.27	0.30
Book value per share ($)	10.0%	7.34	5.92	6.53	7.43	8.45	11.40	11.58	12.67	14.24	17.36

1989 Year End:
Debt ratio: 64.4%
Return on equity: 12.0%
Cash (mil): $149
Current ratio: 1.11
Long-term debt (mil): $3,248
Number of shares (mil): 103
Dividends:
1989 average yield: 0.9%
1989 payout: 15.8%
Market value (mil): $3,417

NYSE symbol: CGP
Incorporated: Delaware, 1972
Fiscal year ends: December 31

WHO

Chairman: Oscar S. Wyatt, Jr., age 65, $1,252,231 pay
President and CEO: James R. Paul, age 55, $957,767 pay
EVP and CFO: David A. Arledge, age 45, $512,088
Auditors: Deloitte & Touche
Employees: 13,100

WHERE

HQ: Nine Greenway Plaza, Houston, TX 77046
Phone: 713-877-1400
FAX: 713-877-6754

Coastal operates in 45 states and overseas.

WHAT

	1989 Sales $ mil	1989 Sales % of total	1989 Operating Income $ mil	1989 Operating Income % of total
Natural gas	2,254	27	424	58
Refining & Marketing	5,313	64	190	26
Exploration & Production	312	4	41	6
Coal	392	5	73	10
Adjustments	—	—	(60)	—
Total	**8,271**	**100**	**668**	**100**

Subsidiaries/Divisions

Exploration & Production
ANR Production
CIG Exploration
Coastal Javelina
Coastal Limited Ventures
Coastal Oil & Gas

Natural Gas
ANR Pipeline
Coastal Gas Marketing
Colorado Interstate Gas
Wyoming Interstate

Chemicals
Coastal Biotechnology
Coastal Chem

Refining & Marketing
Coastal Aruba Refining
Coastal Derby Refining
Coastal Eagle Point Oil
Coastal Fuels Marketing
Coastal Mart (C-Mart)
Coastal Mobile Refining
Coastal Oil New England
Coastal Oil New York

Coal
ANR Coal
Coastal Power Production
Coastal States Energy
Skyline Coal

RANKINGS

54th in *Fortune* 500 Industrial Cos.
150th in *Fortune* Global 500 Industrial Cos.
96th in *Forbes* Sales 500
218th in *Business Week* 1000
560th in *Business Week* Global 1000

COMPETITION

Amoco
Ashland
Atlantic Richfield
British Petroleum
Columbia Gas
Chevron
Du Pont
Exxon
Mobil
Occidental
Pennzoil
Panhandle Eastern
Phillips
Royal Dutch/Shell
Sun
Tenneco
Texaco
Union Texas
Unocal
USX

THE COCA-COLA COMPANY

OVERVIEW

Atlanta-based Coca-Cola is the world's largest soft drink producer. The Coke and Coca-Cola trademarks are the world's best known.

One of the South's great enterprises, Coke has also emerged as one of America's foremost global marketers. In 1989 over 1,000 independent bottlers produced more than 559 million servings daily in 160 countries.

Although the mature US market consumes 283 servings per person per year and the overseas market only 56, the overseas average is rising rapidly. Foreign operations currently generate 55% of sales and 76% of profits. Coke's market share of the global soft drink business is now 45%.

Coca-Cola uses a franchise system for distribution, with local bottlers purchasing syrup or concentrate from Coke. The largest US bottlers comprise a $4 billion public company, Coca-Cola Enterprises.

Though soft drinks exceed 80% of sales and 90% of profits, the company is also the leading US producer of citrus products (Minute Maid).

Coca-Cola has a long record of profitable growth and financial strength. It has also been an influential citizen of Atlanta: early leader Asa Candler gave land to Emory University and later chief Robert Woodruff gave Emory over $200 million.

WHEN

Atlanta pharmacist John S. Pemberton invented Coke in 1886. His bookkeeper Frank Robinson named the product after 2 ingredients, kola nuts and coca leaves (later cleaned of narcotics), and wrote the name in the now-familiar script. By 1891 Atlanta druggist Asa Candler had bought the company for $2,300. By 1895 the soda fountain drink was available in all states, entering Canada and Mexico by 1898.

Candler sold most US bottling rights in 1899 to Benjamin Thomas and John Whitehead of Chattanooga for $1.00. With the backing of John Lupton, these men developed the regional franchise bottling system, creating over 1,000 bottlers within 20 years. The bottlers used the contoured bottle designed by the C. J. Root Glass Company (Terre Haute, Indiana) in 1916.

In 1916 Candler retired to become Atlanta's mayor; his family sold the company to Atlanta banker Ernest Woodruff for $25 million in 1919, the same year Coca-Cola went public. In 1923 Woodruff appointed his son, Robert, president. Robert continued as chairman until 1942 and remained influential until his death in 1985 at age 95.

Robert Woodruff's contributions were in advertising and overseas expansion. He introduced "The Pause that Refreshes" (1929) and "It's the Real Thing" (1941), adding to the "Delicious and Refreshing" slogan used in the early days. During WWII Woodruff decreed that every soldier would have access to a 5-cent bottle of Coke. With government assistance Coca-Cola built 64 overseas bottling plants during WWII. Also during this period (1941) the company accepted "Coke" as an official name.

Coca-Cola bought Minute Maid in 1960 and introduced Sprite (now the world's #1 lemon-lime soft drink) in 1961, TAB in 1963, and Diet Coke in 1982. New Coke, introduced in 1985, was widely rejected, and the original formula soon returned as Coca-Cola Classic.

The company has entered and left several industries. The largest of these diversifications was the acquisition of Columbia Pictures in 1982, followed by other entertainment purchases (*e.g.,* Merv Griffin Enterprises), all sold to Sony in 1989.

In 1986 the company consolidated the US bottling operations it owned into Coca-Cola Enterprises and sold 51% of the new company, the largest US soft drink bottler, to the public. Other recent company changes include divesting South African operations, spinning off Canadian bottling operations, and consolidating UK bottlers with those of Cadbury Schweppes.

HOW MUCH

	9 Yr. Growth	1980	1981	1982	1983	1984	1985	1986	1987	1988	1989
Sales ($ mil)	4.7%	5,913	5,889	6,250	6,829	7,364	7,904	8,669	7,658	8,338	8,966
Net income ($ mil)	12.2%	422	447	512	558	629	678	934	916	1,045	1,193
Income as % of sales	—	7.1%	7.6%	8.2%	8.2%	8.5%	8.6%	10.8%	12.0%	12.5%	13.3%
Earnings per share ($)	12.9%	0.57	0.60	0.66	0.68	0.79	0.86	1.21	1.22	1.43	1.70
Stock price – high ($)	—	6.48	6.71	8.94	9.58	11.00	14.71	22.44	26.56	22.63	40.50
Stock price – low ($)	—	4.81	5.08	4.96	7.58	8.17	9.92	12.79	14.00	17.50	21.69
Stock price – close ($)	24.0%	5.56	5.79	8.67	8.92	10.40	14.08	18.88	19.06	22.31	38.63
P/E – high	—	11	11	14	14	14	17	19	22	16	24
P/E – low	—	8	8	8	11	10	12	11	12	12	13
Dividends per share ($)	7.3%	0.36	0.39	0.41	0.45	0.46	0.49	0.52	0.56	0.60	0.68
Book value per share ($)	6.0%	2.80	3.06	3.41	3.57	3.54	3.86	4.56	4.33	4.29	4.73

1989 Year End:
Debt ratio: 13.6%
Return on equity: 37.6%
Cash (mil): $1,182
Current ratio: 0.99
Long-term debt (mil): $549
Number of shares (mil): 674
Dividends:
1989 average yield: 1.8%
1989 payout: 40.1%
Market value (mil): $26,034

Stock Price History high/low 1980-89

45 40 35 30 25 20 15 10 5 0

NYSE symbol: KO
Incorporated: Delaware, 1919
Fiscal year ends: December 31

WHO

Chairman and CEO: Robert Goizueta, age 58, $2,541,500 pay
President and COO: Donald Keough, age 63, $1,865,025 pay
SVP and CFO: M. Douglas Ivester, age 43, $640,000 pay
VP Corporate Affairs: Carlton Curtis
Auditors: Ernst & Young
Employees: 19,000

WHERE

HQ: One Coca-Cola Plaza, NW, Atlanta, GA 30313
Phone: 404-676-2121
FAX: 404-676-6792

Soft drink products are sold in over 160 countries; syrup and/or concentrates are made at 44 plants worldwide.

	1989 Sales		1989 Operating Income	
	$ mil	% of total	$ mil	% of total
US	4,022	45	468	24
Latin America	646	7	227	11
European Community	1,855	21	541	27
Pacific & Canada	1,960	22	613	31
NE Europe & Africa	425	5	147	7
Adjustments	58	—	(270)	—
Total	**8,966**	**100**	**1,726**	**100**

WHAT

	1989 Sales		1989 Operating Income	
	$ mil	% of total	$ mil	% of total
Soft drinks	7,325	82	1,909	96
Foods	1,583	18	87	4
Adjustments	58	—	(270)	—
Total	**8,966**	**100**	**1,726**	**100**

Brand Names

Soft Drinks
Caffeine-free Coca-Cola
Caffeine-free Diet Coke
Caffeine-free TAB
Cherry Coke
Coca-Cola
Coca-Cola Classic
Coke
Diet Cherry Coke
Diet Coke
Diet Minute Maid
Diet Sprite
Fanta
Fresca
Hi-C
Mello Yello
Minute Maid
Mr. PiBB
Ramblin' Root Beer
Sprite
TAB

Juices & Foods
Bacardi Fruit Mixers
Belmont Springs Water
Bright & Early
Five Alive
Frogurt
Hi-C
Minute Maid
Shake Ups

RANKINGS

51st in *Fortune* 500 Industrial Cos.
136th in *Fortune* Global 500 Industrial Cos.
87th in *Forbes* Sales 500
15th in *Business Week* 1000
23rd in *Business Week* Global 1000

COMPETITION

Bass
Cadbury Schweppes
Castle & Cooke
Dr Pepper/7Up
PepsiCo
Seagram

COLGATE-PALMOLIVE COMPANY

OVERVIEW

Although headquartered in New York, Colgate is a true multinational, deriving 64% of its sales from abroad. The company is 3rd in domestic consumer products sales after Procter & Gamble and Unilever. The company sells such well-known brands as Fab and Dynamo (detergent), Irish Spring (soap), and Wash 'N Dri (towelettes).

Colgate toothpaste is the world's best-selling, with 42% of the global market (up from 37% in 1984). To promote its products and better oral care, Colgate mobile dental clinics provide free dental care in some countries. Colgate's Ajax brand is the #1 household cleaner in Europe and shares the lead with Fabuloso (another Colgate brand) in 25 countries worldwide. Colgate sells laundry products in 41 countries and, through a 1989 partnership, markets Clorox bleach in Mexico and the Pacific Basin. Colgate began marketing Hill's pet foods in Europe and Australia in 1989. Overall, Colgate introduced more than 200 new products worldwide in 1989, including 60 new personal care products.

NYSE symbol: CL
Incorporated: Delaware, 1923
Fiscal year ends: December 31

WHO

Chairman, President, and CEO: Reuben Mark, age 51, $1,406,550 pay
SEVP and COO: William S. Shanahan, age 49, $731,545 pay
SEVP: Roderick L. Turner, age 58, $595,651 pay
EVP and CFO: Robert M. Agate, age 54, $375,758 pay
Auditors: Arthur Andersen & Co.
Employees: 24,000

WHEN

William Colgate founded The Colgate Company, a soap- and candle-making business, in Manhattan in 1806, moving it to Jersey City in 1847. When William died (1857) his son Samuel took over and the firm changed its name to Colgate and Company. Colgate Dental Cream, introduced in 1877, became available in a tube in 1890. By 1906 Colgate was making 160 kinds of soap, 625 perfumes, and 2,000 other products. It went public in 1908.

In 1898 a Milwaukee soap maker, B. J. Johnson Soap Company (founded in 1864 by Caleb Johnson), introduced Palmolive, a soap made of palm and olive oils. The product became so popular that the firm changed its name to the Palmolive Company in 1917. In 1927 Palmolive merged with Peet Brothers Company of Kansas City (founded 1872), makers of fine soaps. Palmolive-Peet merged with Colgate in 1928, forming Colgate-Palmolive-Peet (shortened to Colgate-Palmolive, 1953). The stock market crash of 1929 prevented a planned merger of the company with Hershey and Kraft.

In the 1930s the company bought French and German soap makers and opened branches in Europe. After WWII, Palmolive, Colgate, and Ajax brand cleaning and personal hygiene products were outselling competitors in European markets. Beginning in the 1950s, the company opened plants in the Far East. In 1961 foreign sales were 52% of the total.

New products in the 1960s included Cold Power detergent (1965), Palmolive dishwashing liquid (1966), Ultra Brite toothpaste (1968), and Colgate with MFP (1968). In the 1960s and 1970s Colgate-Palmolive diversified, buying up to 70 other companies (including Helena Rubenstein, Ram Golf, Kendall, and Maui Divers). The strategy failed, however, and most were sold in the 1980s. In 1987 the company took a $145 million charge against earnings to cover reorganization and asset disposition costs. Princess House (crystal and giftware, 1978) and Hill's Pet Products (Science Diet, 1976) are among the only businesses still remaining with the company from its diversification attempt. Current chairman Reuben Mark (CEO since 1984) has focused on building Colgate's core businesses: personal care and household products. Recent product introductions are Palmolive Automatic dishwasher detergent (1986), Colgate Tartar Control toothpaste (1986), and Fab 1-Shot laundry detergent (1987). The company bought a French liquid bleach manufacturer in 1988 and is in the process of buying Javex, Canada's largest bleach business. Many new products have failed, keeping the company's profit margin low; however, Colgate's international operations have been strong enough to offset domestic performance.

WHERE

HQ: 300 Park Ave., New York, NY 10022
Phone: 212-310-2000
FAX: 212-310-3284

Colgate-Palmolive operates 162 facilities, 62 of them located in the US and 100 located in 41 foreign countries.

	1989 Sales		1989 Operating Income	
	$ mil	% of total	$ mil	% of total
US	1,828	36	180	37
Western Hemisphere	968	19	115	24
Europe	1,557	31	119	25
Far East & Africa	686	14	67	14
Adjustments	—	—	(55)	—
Total	**5,039**	**100**	**426**	**100**

WHAT

	1989 Sales		1989 Operating Income	
	$ mil	% of total	$ mil	% of total
Household & personal care	4,414	88	366	76
Specialty marketing	625	12	115	24
Adjustments	—	—	(55)	—
Total	**5,039**	**100**	**426**	**100**

Household Care
Ajax
Dermassage
HandiWipes
Palmolive
Stretch 'N Dust
Wash 'N Dri

Housewares & Gifts
Nouveau Cookware
Princess House Products (crystal and china)

Laundry Care
Ajax
Axion
Cold Power
Dynamo 2
Fab
Fresh Start

Personal Care
Cleopatra (soap, Europe)
Colgate
Dermassage (lotion)
Irish Spring (soap)
Palmolive
Respons (hair care, Europe)
Sesame Street (children's products)
Softsoap
Ultra Brite
Vel Beauty Bar
Village (bath products)
Wildroot (hair care)

Pet Care
Fresh Feliners (cat box liners)
Hill's (pet food)

HOW MUCH

	9 Yr. Growth	1980	1981	1982	1983	1984	1985	1986	1987	1988	1989
Sales ($ mil)	(0.2%)	5,130	5,261	4,888	4,865	4,910	4,524	4,985	4,366	4,734	5,039
Net income ($ mil)	4.0%	196	208	197	198	54	168	177	1	153	280
Income as % of sales	—	3.8%	4.0%	4.0%	4.1%	1.1%	3.7%	3.6%	0.0%	3.2%	5.6%
Earnings per share ($)	5.2%	2.40	2.55	2.41	2.42	0.64	2.11	2.50	0.01	2.21	3.80
Stock price – high ($)	—	17.63	18.38	22.63	25.38	26.50	33.38	47.00	52.63	49.50	64.88
Stock price – low ($)	—	11.00	13.88	16.00	19.00	20.50	22.63	30.38	28.00	38.50	44.13
Stock price – close ($)	17.7%	14.63	16.75	19.63	21.50	24.88	32.75	40.88	39.25	47.00	63.50
P/E – high	—	7	7	9	10	41	16	19	—	22	17
P/E – low	—	5	5	7	8	32	11	12	—	17	12
Dividends per share ($)	4.1%	1.09	1.14	1.20	1.26	1.28	1.30	1.36	1.39	1.58	1.56
Book value per share ($)	(4.1%)	15.40	15.69	15.97	16.21	14.69	12.66	13.81	13.54	16.48	10.59

1989 Year End:
Debt ratio: 48.5%
Return on equity: 28.1%
Cash (mil): $524
Current ratio: 1.92
Long-term debt (mil): $1,059
Number of shares (mil): 66
Dividends:
1989 average yield: 2.5%
1989 payout: 41.1%
Market value (mil): $4,197

Stock Price History high/low 1980-89

70
60
50
40
30
20
10
0

RANKINGS

103rd in *Fortune* 500 Industrial Cos.
265th in *Fortune* Global 500 Industrial Cos.
180th in *Forbes* Sales 500
155th in *Business Week* 1000
443rd in *Business Week* Global 1000

COMPETITION

Amway	Gillette	Pearson
Brown-Forman	S.C. Johnson	Procter & Gamble
Clorox	Mars	Unilever

Other household and personal care products companies

THE COLUMBIA GAS SYSTEM, INC.

OVERVIEW

Columbia Gas, one of America's largest integrated gas systems, operates 18,800 miles of natural gas pipeline linking oil and gas fields in the Gulf of Mexico, Texas, Louisiana, Appalachia, and Canada (3.2 million acres), with distributors in 14 states and the District of Columbia. In 1989 Columbia produced 78 billion cubic feet of gas and 1.9 million barrels of oil. Columbia's 6 distributors serve 1.8 million residential and industrial customers in Kentucky, Maryland, New York, Ohio, Pennsylvania, and Virginia. The company also serves 62,000 propane customers in 8 states.

Through a partnership with the Cogeneration Partners of America, Columbia's TriStar Ventures operates 4 gas-fired cogeneration facilities (producing both steam and electricity) and develops cogeneration plants throughout the US. Recently Columbia placed America's first natural gas–powered bus, "Columbia," (with lower exhaust emissions than diesel) into operation in Columbus, Ohio.

WHEN

In 1906, 4 eastern and midwestern businessmen founded Columbia Gas & Electric. Based in Huntington, West Virginia, Columbia managed about 232,000 acres of oil and gas fields in Kentucky and West Virginia and by 1909 operated a 180-mile pipeline carrying natural gas to 4 cities in Kentucky and Ohio. In 1926 Columbia merged with George Crawford's Ohio Fuel, which provided natural gas to parts of Ohio, Pennsylvania, and West Virginia. With Crawford as chairman and former Columbia chairman Philip Gossmer as president, the new Columbia moved to Wilmington, Delaware, and was listed on the NYSE in 1926. Purchases over the next 40 years expanded Columbia's service area to the District of Columbia, Maryland, and lower New York state.

In 1931 Columbia completed a 460-mile pipeline linking Washington with gas fields in Kentucky. The company became Columbia Gas System in 1948 and in 1958 bought Gulf Interstate Gas. Gulf operated an 845-mile pipeline linking Louisiana's gas fields to eastern Kentucky where the gas was distributed through the Columbia system. By 1972 Columbia was supplying about 1/10 of America's gas customers.

With fuel shortages predicted as early as 1970, Columbia explored for gas in Canada (Columbia Gas Development of Canada, 1971) and arranged for delivery of gas from Alaska's North Slope (Columbia Alaska Gas Transmission, 1974). Still, supplies ran short, forcing schools and factories to close throughout Columbia's territory during the winter of 1976-1977.

Hoping to assure future supplies, Columbia (with Consolidated System LNG) built a liquid natural gas plant at Cove Point, Maryland, in 1978. The plant closed in 1980 over price disputes with Algerian suppliers, and in 1988 Columbia sold 50% interest in the plant to Shell Oil. In 1981 Columbia bought Commonwealth Natural Resources, expanding its service area to central and eastern Virginia.

In another effort to secure future gas supplies, Columbia entered into several take-or-pay contracts between 1982 and 1984, agreeing to buy large amounts of gas at the seller's price. These contracts required Columbia to pay for the gas whether or not the company could resell it. Gas supplies rose in the mid-1980s while demand fell, and Columbia faced bankruptcy by 1985, mostly due to the take-or-pay contracts. CEO John Croom renegotiated the contracts (1985), and by 1989 Columbia was operating with some of the lowest costs and most competitive rates in the industry.

In August 1990 the company agreed to sell its Columbia Gas of New York to New York State Electric & Gas for $39 million.

HOW MUCH

	9 Yr. Growth	1980	1981	1982	1983	1984	1985	1986	1987	1988	1989
Sales ($ mil)	(1.4%)	3,637	4,426	5,071	5,078	4,593	4,053	3,370	2,798	3,129	3,204
Net income ($ mil)	(1.7%)	171	196	185	191	180	(94)	99	111	119	146
Income as % of sales	—	4.7%	4.4%	3.6%	3.8%	3.9%	(2.3%)	3.0%	4.0%	3.8%	4.6%
Earnings per share ($)	(4.9%)	5.02	5.50	5.10	4.87	4.22	(2.67)	2.12	2.29	2.46	3.19
Stock price – high ($)	—	47.00	41.50	33.88	35.50	37.50	40.00	46.00	56.50	44.75	52.75
Stock price – low ($)	—	33.75	27.88	26.88	27.88	27.00	26.75	34.75	35.50	26.88	33.75
Stock price – close ($)	2.9%	40.25	32.13	28.88	35.25	34.00	39.50	45.25	40.25	34.50	52.00
P/E – high	—	9	8	7	7	9	—	22	25	18	17
P/E – low	—	7	5	5	6	6	—	16	16	11	11
Dividends per share ($)	(2.7%)	2.56	2.70	2.86	3.02	3.18	3.18	3.18	3.18	2.30	2.00
Book value per share ($)	(0.1%)	35.96	38.50	40.73	41.16	41.22	35.10	34.06	34.08	34.18	35.50

1989 Year End:
Debt ratio: 42.5%
Return on equity: 9.2%
Cash (mil): $14
Current ratio: 0.87
Long-term debt (mil): $1,196
Number of shares (mil): 46
Dividends:
 1989 average yield: 3.8%
 1989 payout: 62.7%
Market value (mil): $2,373

60
50
40
30
20
10
0

Stock Price History high/low 1980-89

NYSE symbol: CG
Incorporated: Delaware, 1926
Fiscal year ends: December 31

WHO

Chairman, President, and CEO: John H. Croom, age 57, $735,800 pay
EVP and CFO: Robert A. Oswald, age 44, $341,167 pay (prior to promotion)
EVP: John D. Daly
Auditors: Arthur Andersen & Co.
Employees: 10,800

WHERE

HQ: 20 Montchanin Rd., Wilmington, DE 19807
Phone: 302-429-5000
FAX: 302-429-5461

Columbia Gas operates in Delaware, Kentucky, Louisiana, Maryland, Mississippi, New Jersey, New York, North Carolina, Ohio, Pennsylvania, Tennessee, Texas, Virginia, West Virginia, and the District of Columbia.

WHAT

	1989 Sales		1989 Operating Income	
	$ mil	% of total	$ mil	% of total
Gas transmission	1,290	40	195	52
Gas distribution	1,688	53	146	39
Oil & gas exploration & production	152	5	29	8
Other	74	2	3	1
Adjustments	—	—	(12)	—
Total	**3,204**	**100**	**361**	**100**

Transmission Companies (Gas Pipeline)
Columbia Gas Transmission Corp.
 18,800 miles through 14 states
Columbia Gulf Transmission Co.
 4,300 miles from Louisiana to Kentucky
Columbia LNG Corp.
 Liquid natural gas terminal at Cove Point, MD
Commonwealth Gas Pipeline Corp.
 600 miles in Virginia

Distribution Companies
Columbia Gas of Kentucky, Inc.
Columbia Gas of Maryland, Inc.
Columbia Gas of New York, Inc.
Columbia Gas of Ohio, Inc.
Columbia Gas of Pennsylvania, Inc.
Commonwealth Gas Services, Inc.

Oil & Gas Exploration
Columbia Gas Development Corp.
Columbia Gas Development of Canada, Ltd.
Columbia Natural Resources, Inc.

Other Energy Companies
Columbia Coal Gasification Corp. (coal reserves)
Columbia Propane Corp.
Commonwealth Propane, Inc.
The Inland Gas Co., Inc.
TriStar Ventures Corp. (cogeneration plants)

RANKINGS

40th in *Fortune* 50 Utilities
258th in *Forbes* Sales 500
287th in *Business Week* 1000
961st in *Business Week* Global 1000

COMPETITION

Coastal
Occidental
Panhandle Eastern
Tenneco

COMMERCE CLEARING HOUSE, INC.

OVERVIEW

Commerce Clearing House (CCH), a leading publisher of reports and books on tax and business law, also provides state-required legal representation and other services to corporations and processes income tax returns by computer.

Through Corporate Services, reports on stockholder meetings are also available, and several CCH subsidiaries provide federal and state government information retrieval and dissemination.

CCH publishes loose-leaf reports, available through subscription, that report administrative and legal rulings affecting taxes and business in the US, Australia, England, Mexico, New Zealand, Canada, and Singapore. The company also publishes tax and stock market manuals and has recently introduced an electronic research system for its publications.

Professional tax return preparers use CCH's computer processing services to prepare corporate, fiduciary, partnership, and individual tax returns.

The Thorne family owns 55% of the company's stock, insulating it from unwelcome takeover attempts.

OTC symbol: CCLR
Incorporated: Delaware, 1927
Fiscal year ends: December 31

WHO

Chairman: Oakleigh B. Thorne, age 57, $280,038 pay
President and CEO: Richard T. Merrill, age 61, $426,577 pay
EVP: Edward L. Massie, age 60, $319,731 pay
VP, Treasurer, and CFO: Bernard Elafros, age 63
Group VP: Oakleigh Thorne, age 32
Auditors: Deloitte & Touche
Employees: 7,782

WHEN

The Corporation Trust Company was formed in 1892 and began providing state-required legal representation to early customers such as US Steel, AT&T, and Prudential. When the Tariff Act of 1913 was introduced, the company began publishing *The Income Tax Reporter*, on this first federal income tax law, including the law's text, related administrative decisions, and other documents. The company began publications covering the new Federal Trade Commission and Federal Reserve Board in 1914, and subscriptions to the *Reporter* grew as tax laws were amended in 1916 and 1917.

By the late 1910s William KixMiller had started publishing import/export and income tax guides as Commerce Clearing House in Chicago. Both companies grew in the 1920s, reporting on the myriad new state, local, corporate, and inheritance tax laws. The 2 companies merged in 1927 as Commerce Clearing House (CCH), headquartered in Chicago.

CCH began buying independent state tax publications and utility and industrial indices and digests. In 1933 KixMiller sold his interest, and in the 1930s the company started new publications covering New Deal regulations and agencies. Tax increases brought on by WWII and reporting on war and labor law expanded CCH's publication list, and in 1945 CCH created a Canadian subsidiary.

The company published reports on the Defense Production Act (1950) after the outbreak of war in Korea, followed in the late 1950s by the *Corporation Law Guide* and the *New York Stock Exchange Guide*. CCH went public in 1961.

During the 1960s CCH started publications covering the European Common Market, taxes on interest and dividends, employment practices and accounting, British and Puerto Rican tax law and legislation, and education and environmental regulation. In 1965 CCH bought a Mexican tax and business law publisher, Facts on File, and formed Computax, a joint venture.

In the late 1960s CCH published reports on consumer credit, mutual funds, Medicare, and personnel issues. New publications in the early 1970s dealt with the Tax Reform Act of 1969, the IRS, and workplace and product safety regulations. CCH bought companies, including the Washington Service Bureau (1979), a software operation (1980), and Trademark Research Corporation (1983). In 1988 and 1989 CCH bought 4 companies involved in tax processing and financial and information services. Earnings decreased for CCH in 1989 due to development costs of its electronic publishing project and increased investments and acquisitions.

WHERE

HQ: 2700 Lake Cook Rd., Riverwoods, IL 60015
Phone: 708-940-4600
FAX: 708-940-0113

CCH operates in 50 states and 5 foreign countries.

	1989 Sales		1989 Operating Income	
	$ mil	% of total	$ mil	% of total
US	591	87	46	94
Other	86	13	3	6
Adjustments	—	—	1	—
Total	**677**	**100**	**50**	**100**

WHAT

	1989 Sales		1989 Operating Income	
	$ mil	% of total	$ mil	% of total
Publishing	374	55	41	84
Computer processing services	216	32	4	8
Corporate services	87	13	4	8
Adjustments	—	—	1	—
Total	**677**	**100**	**50**	**100**

Publications
CCH ACCESS (electronic publishing)
Commerce Clearing House (publications)
Facts on File (reference books)
LYF, S.A. de C.V. (49%) (Spanish language publications)

Tax Return Services
Accutax Systems
CCH Computax
Taxx, Inc.
TLS Co.

Other Services
CT Corporation System (representation)
CT Law Technology (law firm consulting)
McCord Co. (document distribution)
State Capital Information Service (information distribution)
Trademark Research Corp. (trademark research)
Washington Service Bureau (document distribution)

RANKINGS

425th in *Fortune* 500 Industrial Cos.
577th in *Business Week* 1000

COMPETITION

Dun & Bradstreet
Maxwell
McGraw-Hill
Mead

HOW MUCH

	9 Yr. Growth	1980	1981	1982	1983	1984	1985	1986	1987	1988	1989
Sales ($ mil)	11.5%	254	313	350	379	414	454	505	552	612	677
Net income ($ mil)	4.5%	23	29	32	25	40	45	48	53	49	34
Income as % of sales	—	9.1%	9.2%	9.0%	6.6%	9.7%	9.9%	9.4%	9.6%	8.1%	5.1%
Earnings per share ($)	4.6%	1.28	1.60	1.75	1.39	2.24	2.49	2.64	2.93	2.75	1.92
Stock price – high ($)	—	18.38	28.63	32.25	38.75	35.00	50.75	65.50	71.00	65.00	65.50
Stock price – low ($)	—	12.00	13.63	22.63	26.00	25.00	33.25	47.50	48.38	46.50	42.50
Stock price – close ($)	12.5%	14.88	28.63	31.00	30.00	33.25	49.25	61.00	61.50	47.50	43.00
P/E – high	—	14	18	18	28	16	20	25	24	24	34
P/E – low	—	9	9	13	19	11	13	18	17	17	22
Dividends per share ($)	11.6%	0.52	0.62	0.78	0.86	0.91	1.06	1.20	0.96	1.72	1.40
Book value per share ($)	19.6%	2.41	3.36	4.31	4.82	6.13	7.46	8.89	10.47	11.99	12.11

1989 Year End:
Debt ratio: 8.1%
Return on equity: 15.9%
Cash (mil): $96
Current ratio: 3.87
Long-term debt (mil): $19
Number of shares (mil): 18
Dividends:
1989 average yield: 3.3%
1989 payout: 72.9%
Market value (mil): $764

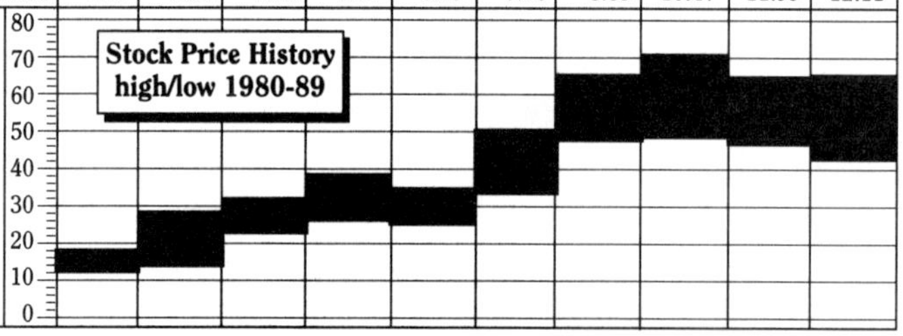

Stock Price History high/low 1980-89

COMMODORE INTERNATIONAL LTD.

OVERVIEW

Commodore International, based in West Chester, Pennsylvania, is a leading manufacturer of PCs for the home market and is fast becoming a contender in the professional PC market.

The Commodore 64C/128D computer, introduced in the mid-1980s, is an inexpensive entry-level color computer used for entertainment, educational, and home/office purposes. In 1989 the 64C/128D had an installed base of 10 million units.

The Amiga 2000 series (high-end computers with advanced graphics, audio, and desktop video capabilities) and MS-DOS PC-compatible computers constitute Commodore's professional PC products. Because of the Amiga's powerful color graphic capabilities, advertising agencies and graphics firms use it to design brochures, TV commercials, and magazine ads. Commodore's recently introduced Amiga 3000 is targeted for multimedia applications — eye-catching audiovisual programs used for training and sales presentations.

Europe is Commodore's strongest market, accounting for 69% of 1989 revenues. Fiscal 1990 sales ran slightly behind 1989, and profits were only $1.5 million, off 98% from the previous year due to the decline in sales of low-end products, increased marketing expenses, and the strength of the US dollar.

NYSE symbol: CBU
Incorporated: Bahamas, 1976
Fiscal year ends: June 30

WHO

Chairman and CEO: Irving Gould, age 70, $1,250,000 pay
President: Mehdi R. Ali, age 44, $1,380,769 pay
EVP and COO: Henri Rubin, age 62, $500,000 pay
Treasurer: Carden N. Welsh, age 36
Auditors: Arthur Andersen & Co.
Employees: 3,500

WHERE

HQ: 1200 Wilson Dr., West Chester, PA 19380
Phone: 215-431-9100
FAX: 215-431-9156

Commodore has offices and facilities in 19 countries, including manufacturing locations in the US, Germany, and Hong Kong.

	1989 Sales		1989 Operating Income	
	$ mil	% of total	$ mil	% of total
North America	224	24	(27)	(34)
Europe	650	69	103	130
Asia/Australia	66	7	3	4
Adjustments	—	—	9	—
Total	**940**	**100**	**88**	**100**

WHEN

Commodore, founded by Jack Tramiel, started as Commodore Portable Typewriter, a typewriter repair shop, in the Bronx in 1954. Tramiel relocated the business to Toronto in 1956, and, with financing from a Canadian company, Atlantic Acceptance, expanded into selling adding machines and typewriters.

Tramiel turned to another Canadian financier, Irving Gould, following the bankruptcy of Atlantic in 1965. Gould loaned Commodore $400,000, acquired controlling interest, and became chairman. In 1969 Commodore began producing low-priced pocket calculators and eventually became a major player in the business. In 1975 Texas Instruments, Commodore's microprocessor supplier, put Commodore out of the calculator business by introducing a pocket calculator priced at $49 — $1 cheaper than the microprocessor it sold to Commodore. That year Commodore lost $5 million on sales of $50 million.

Tramiel countered by buying one of its suppliers, MOS Technology, in 1976 for $800,000. MOS manufactured the 6502 chip, which Commodore sold to computer companies (Apple and Atari) and later used in its own computers.

In 1977 Commodore introduced its first computer, the PET. It quickly became a success, particularly in Europe, where there was less competition with Apple and Tandy's Radio Shack. Commodore followed with the VIC-20 and the Commodore 64 computers, both introduced in 1982. Sales of the 2 computers took Commodore's revenues over the $1 billion mark in 1984.

In 1984, after a falling out with Commodore chairman Gould, Tramiel resigned and resurfaced in 1985 as owner and CEO of Atari, Commodore's primary competitor.

From 1984 to 1987 Commodore's sales dropped 36%, from $1.27 billion to $807 million. In 1985 Commodore introduced the Amiga — a high-end home computer with superior color graphics — anticipating its sales would revive the company. But the Amiga was expensive for the home market and lacked the software and standard DOS operating system used in IBM PCs and compatibles for the business market. Commodore has since added a DOS PC-compatible to its Amiga line and is hoping recent introductions of the Amiga 2500 UX (1989), a UNIX-based machine, and Amiga 3000 (1990) will increase sales. In May 1990 Nolan Bushnell, founder of Atari, joined Commodore to assist in developing and launching a new interactive computer product.

WHAT

Commodore Amiga Computers
Amiga 500
Amiga 2000
Amiga 2000HD
Amiga 2500
Amiga 2500 UX
Amiga 3000

MS-DOS PC-Compatible Computers
Commodore PC Colt
Commodore PC 10 Series III
Commodore PC 20 Series III
Commodore PC-30 Series III
Commodore PC-40 Series III
Commodore PC 60

64C/128D Computers
Commodore 64C
Commodore 128D

Peripherals
Add-on memory boards
Application boards
Disk drives
Monitors
Printers

Semiconductor Integrated Circuits
Custom CMOS and NMOS Large Scale Integrated Circuit semiconductors
Logic circuits
Microprocessors
Read-Only Memory (ROM) chips

HOW MUCH

	9 Yr. Growth	1980	1981	1982	1983	1984	1985	1986	1987	1988	1989
Sales ($ mil)	25.1%	126	187	305	681	1,267	883	889	807	871	940
Net income ($ mil)	13.4%	16	25	41	88	144	(114)	(128)	23	48	50
Income as % of sales	—	12.9%	13.4%	13.3%	12.9%	11.3%	(12.9%)	(14.4%)	2.8%	5.5%	5.3%
Earnings per share ($)	12.9%	0.52	0.81	1.32	2.86	4.66	(3.66)	(4.08)	0.71	1.51	1.55
Stock price – high ($)	—	17.79	17.25	42.56	60.63	49.38	18.13	11.38	15.00	14.13	19.75
Stock price – low ($)	—	2.51	8.00	11.63	29.25	16.25	8.25	4.75	6.25	6.75	7.13
Stock price – close ($)	(4.7%)	16.58	15.33	33.13	41.50	16.38	10.63	8.88	7.50	14.00	10.75
P/E – high	—	34	21	32	21	11	—	—	21	9	13
P/E – low	—	5	10	9	10	3	—	—	9	4	5
Dividends per share ($)	0.0%	0.00	0.00	0.00	0.00	0.00	0.00	0.00	0.00	0.00	0.00
Book value per share ($)	22.7%	1.20	2.03	3.50	6.23	10.56	7.12	3.31	4.58	6.32	7.57

1989 Year End:
Debt ratio: 39.8%
Return on equity: 22.3%
Cash (mil): $114
Current ratio: 2.39
Long-term debt (mil): $159
Number of shares (mil): 32
Dividends:
1989 average yield: 0.0%
1989 payout: 0.0%
Market value (mil): $341

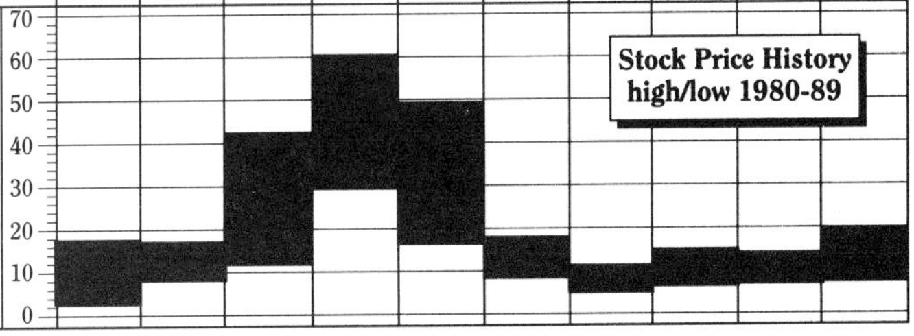

Stock Price History high/low 1980-89

COMPETITION

Apple
Atari
Compaq
Hyundai
IBM
NEC
Tandy
Makers of IBM-compatible personal computers

COMMONWEALTH EDISON COMPANY

OVERVIEW

With a service area covering 11,525 square miles in 25 Illinois counties, Commonwealth Edison (Comm Ed) provides electricity to about 8 million people — approximately 70% of the state's population. Although based in Chicago, the company derives 67% of its kilowatt sales and revenues from operations outside the city.

Comm Ed owns and operates the largest network of nuclear power plants in the US, with almost 83% of the electricity generated in 1989 coming from nuclear sources.

In 1989 the Illinois Supreme Court overturned a $480 million 2-step rate increase formerly approved by the Illinois Commerce Commission and ordered Comm Ed to refund $290 million in illegally high rates collected for electricity in 1989. The company is appealing a prior ruling in which it was ordered to refund $270 million to its customers.

The company's 42-year franchise agreement with the city of Chicago expires December 31, 1990. The city is currently weighing its options, including the possibility of buying Comm Ed's Chicago plants and facilities.

NYSE symbol: CWE
Incorporated: Illinois, 1913
Fiscal year ends: December 31

WHO

Chairman: James J. O'Connor, age 53, $727,443 pay
President: Bide L. Thomas, age 54, $367,337 pay
SVP: James W. Johnson, age 64, $263,863 pay
SVP: Cordell Reed, age 52
SVP and Principal Financial Officer: Ernest M. Roth, age 63, $243,405 pay
Auditors: Arthur Andersen & Co.
Employees: 17,850

WHEN

A group of Chicago businessmen formed Western Edison Light in 1882 to provide electricity to Chicago's residents. Reorganized in 1887 by its 39 shareholders, the company became Chicago Edison. Under the leadership of Samuel Insull, the company bought its main competitor, Chicago Arc Light & Power, in 1893, and in 1898 created Commonwealth Electric to buy other power companies in the Chicago area. In 1907 Commonwealth and Chicago Edison consolidated into Commonwealth Edison (Comm Ed).

The company finished its Northwest Station in 1912, the largest steam generator built to date, then surpassed its own technological achievement with the even more powerful Crawford Station in 1924. Comm Ed also continued to buy other utilities and by 1933 consisted of 77 separate companies.

Comm Ed bought the Public Service Company of Northern Illinois (1937) and Chicago District Electric Generating Corporation (1939), which, combined with Western United Gas & Electric and Illinois Northern Utility (both bought in 1950), created one unit providing power in northern Illinois (outside Chicago). Comm Ed solidified its position in Chicago through other purchases, including the Produce Terminal Corporation (1956) and Central Illinois Electric and Gas (1966).

In 1960 Comm Ed opened the world's first full-scale, privately owned nuclear facility (Dresden Station) and by 1974 had built 7 nuclear plants.

In 1974 the company bought the Cotter Corporation, a Colorado uranium mining company, to provide low-cost fuel for its nuclear plants. Later (1976) Comm Ed bought mining rights to 8,200 acres in Wyoming with extensive coal deposits and formed Edison Development Canada to explore uranium deposits in Newfoundland (1979).

In 1984 and 1985, 2 nuclear plants went on-line, but when construction costs skyrocketed in 1986, the Illinois Commerce Commission threatened to revoke licenses for 2 other nuclear plants (Byron 2 and Braidwood 1 & 2) still under construction. These went into service in 1987 and 1988. A decrease in tax credits related to the Byron and Braidwood construction, combined with higher operational and maintenance costs, contributed to a 36% decline in earnings from 1987 to 1989.

Even so, Comm Ed was touted as one of America's best-run nuclear utilities during the mid-1980s. In recent years, however, the company has drawn criticism from environmental and consumer groups for its heavy investment in nuclear construction, resulting in some of the highest utility bills in the US.

WHERE

HQ: 37th Floor, One First National Plaza, PO Box 767, Chicago, IL 60690
Phone: 312-294-4321
FAX: 312-294-3110

Commonwealth Edison operates in Chicago and approximately 400 other northern Illinois communities.

Generating Facilities

Fossil-Fueled
Collins (near Morris)
Crawford (Chicago)
Fisk (Chicago)
Joliet (near Joliet)
Kincaid (near Taylorville)
Powerton (near Pekin)
State Line (Hammond, IN)
Waukegan (Waukegan)
Will County (near Lockport)

Nuclear
Braidwood (near Braidwood)
Byron (near Byron)
Dresden (near Morris)
LaSalle County (near Seneca)
Quad-Cities (near Cordova)
Zion (Zion)

WHAT

	1989 Sales	
	$ mil	% of total
Residential	2,135	37
Commercial & industrial	3,064	53
Public authorities	427	7
Electric railroads	28	1
Sales for resale	82	2
Other	47	1
Provisions for refunds	(32)	(1)
Total	**5,751**	**100**

	1989 Fuel Sources	
	%	$ cost per mil Btu
Nuclear	83	0.63
Coal	17	2.65
Oil	—	3.45
Natural gas	—	3.55
Total	**100**	

RANKINGS

11th in *Fortune* 50 Utilities
149th in *Forbes* Sales 500
69th in *Business Week* 1000
270th in *Business Week* Global 1000

HOW MUCH

	9 Yr. Growth	1980	1981	1982	1983	1984	1985	1986	1987	1988	1989
Sales ($ mil)	6.3%	3,324	3,737	4,130	4,634	4,930	4,964	5,479	5,674	5,613	5,751
Net income ($ mil)	6.9%	382	450	607	802	875	956	1,050	1,086	738	694
Income as % of sales	—	11.5%	12.0%	14.7%	17.3%	17.8%	19.3%	19.2%	19.1%	13.1%	12.1%
Earnings per share ($)	(0.5%)	2.97	3.06	3.75	4.39	4.43	4.45	4.69	4.73	3.01	2.83
Stock price – high ($)	—	23.75	22.38	25.88	29.25	28.88	32.88	35.75	38.00	33.38	40.75
Stock price – low ($)	—	16.25	17.75	19.25	24.50	20.00	27.00	28.63	25.25	22.75	32.13
Stock price – close ($)	8.5%	18.13	19.88	25.25	26.00	27.88	29.38	33.88	27.50	33.00	37.63
P/E – high	—	8	7	7	7	7	7	8	8	11	14
P/E – low	—	5	6	5	6	5	6	6	5	8	11
Dividends per share ($)	1.6%	2.60	2.70	2.85	3.00	3.00	3.00	3.00	3.00	3.00	3.00
Book value per share ($)	2.2%	26.90	26.26	26.25	27.54	28.71	29.96	31.60	33.27	32.86	32.68

1989 Year End:
Debt ratio: 48.6%
Return on equity: 8.6%
Cash (mil): $286
Current ratio: 0.96
Long-term debt (mil): $6,964
Number of shares (mil): 212
Dividends:
1989 average yield: 8.0%
1989 payout: 106.0%
Market value (mil): $7,970

Stock Price History high/low 1980-89

COMPAQ COMPUTER CORPORATION

OVERVIEW

Houston's Compaq, the #1 maker of IBM-compatible computers, reached $1 billion in annual sales within 5 years, faster than any company in history. Unlike other IBM clone makers, the 8-year-old Compaq conducts its own R&D and engineers many of its products instead of assembling other manufacturers' components. Compaq has a long list of innovations. It was first to develop a fully compatible IBM portable, first to successfully integrate a hard disk drive into a portable, and first with a monitor that displays both graphics and high-resolution text.

Thirteen percent of Compaq's sales in 1989 were to Computerland. Compaq owns approximately 31% of hard disk manufacturer Conner Peripherals, from which it bought $204 million worth of products in 1989. At the end of 1989 Compaq's original $12 million investment in Conner had a market value of $150 million.

In 1990 Compaq delivered its first computer (DESKPRO 486/25) based on the Extended Industry Standard Architecture (EISA) championed by Compaq, an alternative to IBM's microchannel-based computers introduced in the PS/2 line. EISA computers offer greater computing power, yet, unlike IBM's PS/2, remain compatible with existing software programs and peripheral devices (*e.g.,* modems, enhanced graphic boards).

NYSE symbol: CPQ
Incorporated: Delaware, 1982
Fiscal year ends: December 31

WHO

Chairman: Benjamin M. Rosen, age 57
President and CEO: Joesph R. Canion, age 45, $2,114,955 pay
President, Europe and International: Eckhard Pfeiffer, age 48, $990,656 pay
President, North America: Michael S. Swavely, age 36, $756,464 pay
SVP Systems Engineering: Gary Stimac, age 38, $734,650 pay
SVP Engineering: James M. Harris, age 46, $733,000 pay
SVP Finance and CFO: Daryl J. White, age 42
Auditors: Price Waterhouse
Employees: 9,700

WHEN

Joseph R. (Rod) Canion and 2 other ex–Texas Instruments managers started Compaq in Houston in 1982 to manufacture and sell portable IBM-compatible computers. Compaq's first portable was developed from a prototype the 3 sketched on a paper placemat when they first discussed the product idea.

Compaq shipped its first computer in 1982 and in 1983 recorded sales of $111 million — unprecedented growth for a computer startup. The company went public in 1983. Sales continued to skyrocket in the following years, climbing to $329 million in 1984 and to $503 million in 1985. Compaq's success was due in part to its ability to hit the market with the right machine at the right time. In 1983 Compaq introduced a portable computer 18 months before IBM, and in 1986 it was first to market with a computer based on Intel's 386 chip.

However, introducing a product at the right time has not always meant being first to market. Compaq delayed introduction of its laptop until the prototype's display and battery technologies were satisfactorily developed. Although late in its introduction (1988), Compaq's SLT/286 laptop with its crisp display screen became an immediate success.

To sell its products, Compaq capitalized on the extensive base of dealers and suppliers built up around the IBM PC. Rather than establishing a large sales force, Compaq gave exclusive rights to dealers for sales and service of its products. By 1989 Compaq had a network of 3,000 retailers in 152 countries. The company's dealer channel has proven effective. In 1988 Compaq sales reached almost $2.1 billion, making it the first company to exceed the $2 billion mark in only 5 years from its first product introduction (1983-1988). Sales in 1989 climbed to $2.9 billion.

In 1989 the company dropped Businessland, its 2nd largest reseller, as an authorized dealer after Businessland demanded preferential discounts. Compaq reauthorized Businessland as a dealer in 1990 after it agreed to abide by Compaq's policies.

Compaq entered the 1990s with 3 introductions: a new laptop line (COMPAQ LTE), 2 new desktop models (DESKPRO) based on Intel's 386 and 486 microprocessors, and a PC system with the equivalent power of a minicomputer (COMPAQ SYSTEMPRO) — 3 products in the forefront of the industry's growing segments.

WHERE

HQ: 20555 SH 249, Houston, TX 77070
Phone: 713-370-0670
FAX: 713-374-1740

The company does business in 61 countries and has manufacturing facilities in Houston, Scotland, and Singapore.

	1989 Sales		1989 Operating Income	
	$ mil	% of total	$ mil	% of total
US & Canada	1,569	54	403	72
Europe	1,202	42	85	15
Other	105	4	72	13
Adjustments	—	—	(70)	—
Total	**2,876**	**100**	**490**	**100**

WHAT

Laptops
COMPAQ LTE
COMPAQ LTE/286
COMPAQ SLT/286

Portables
COMPAQ PORTABLE II
COMPAQ PORTABLE III
COMPAQ PORTABLE 386

Desktop PCs
COMPAQ DESKPRO 286
COMPAQ DESKPRO 286e
COMPAQ DESKPRO 386/33
COMPAQ DESKPRO 386s
COMPAQ DESKPRO 486/25

PC Systems
COMPAQ SYSTEMPRO

RANKINGS

157th in *Fortune* 500 Industrial Cos.
438th in *Fortune* Global 500 Industrial Cos.
293rd in *Forbes* Sales 500
164th in *Business Week* 1000
392nd in *Business Week* Global 1000

COMPETITION

Apple
Atari
Commodore
Data General
Digital Equipment
Hewlett-Packard
Hyundai
IBM
Matsushita
NCR
NEC
Sun Microsystems
Tandy

HOW MUCH

	6 Yr. Growth	1980	1981	1982	1983	1984	1985	1986	1987	1988	1989
Sales ($ mil)	72.0%	—	—	—	111	329	504	625	1,224	2,066	2,876
Net income ($ mil)	119.2%	—	—	—	3	13	27	43	136	255	333
Income as % of sales	—	—	—	—	2.3%	3.9%	5.3%	6.9%	11.1%	12.4%	11.6%
Earnings per share ($)	97.7%	—	—	—	0.13	0.47	0.90	1.33	3.57	6.27	7.76
Stock price – high ($)	—	—	—	—	12.50	14.63	14.25	21.63	78.50	65.75	112.50
Stock price – low ($)	—	—	—	—	11.00	3.50	6.13	11.63	19.25	42.00	59.25
Stock price – close ($)	36.1%	—	—	—	12.50	6.63	13.25	19.25	55.38	59.63	79.50
P/E – high	—	—	—	—	96	31	16	16	22	10	15
P/E – low	—	—	—	—	85	7	7	9	5	7	8
Dividends per share ($)	—	—	—	—	0.00	0.00	0.00	0.00	0.00	0.00	0.00
Book value per share ($)	42.5%	—	—	—	3.57	4.17	5.16	6.78	11.69	21.13	29.83

1989 Year End:
Debt ratio: 19.0%
Return on equity: 30.5%
Cash (mil): $161
Current ratio: 2.33
Long-term debt (mil): $274
Number of shares (mil): 39
Dividends:
1989 average yield: 0.0%
1989 payout: 0.0%
Market value (mil): $3,122

Stock Price History high/low 1983-89

120 100 80 60 40 20 0

COMPUTER ASSOCIATES INTERNATIONAL, INC.

OVERVIEW

Computer Associates is the world's largest independent firm engaged solely in the design of software; it is also one of the fastest-growing software firms, with an annual average growth of over 65% from 1981 through 1989.

The company is a leading supplier of mainframe computer software (systems, database management, and applications), with a presence in about 80% of the approximately 40,000 mainframe sites worldwide. Computer Associates is also a leader in software for PCs (spreadsheets, accounting, graphics) and Digital Equipment's VAX minicomputers.

Computer Associates' growth has been fueled primarily by its purchase of more than 30 software companies and products since 1982. The problems caused by the purchase in 1989 of database developer Cullinet (when Cullinet customers, unsure of continued support, froze buying decisions) contributed in part to the uncharacteristically flat fiscal 1990 revenues and earnings.

Overseas sales accounted for 41% of the 1989 total and 47% of the fiscal 1990 total; R&D remains high at 13% of revenues. In its first quarter of fiscal 1991, the company's sales declined 16% from the previous year's level, causing the stock to lose almost 40% of its value in one day.

NYSE symbol: CA
Incorporated: Delaware, 1974
Fiscal year ends: March 31

WHO

Chairman and CEO: Charles B. Wang, age 45, $1,956,512 pay
President and COO: Anthony W. Wang, age 47, $1,683,512 pay
EVP Research and Development: Russell M. Artzt, age 43, $531,918 pay
EVP Sales: Arnold S. Mazur, age 47, $667,961 pay
SVP Finance and CFO: Peter A. Schwartz, age 46
Auditors: Ernst & Young
Employees: 7,000

WHEN

Young Charles Wang and his family fled Communist China in 1952. After graduating from Queens College (New York), Wang in 1976 seized the opportunity to open a US subsidiary of Swiss-owned Computer Associates (CA) in Manhattan. Wang started with 4 employees and one product, a file organizer for IBM storage systems (CA-SORT); it was a great success.

Wang soon realized that a penetrating distribution and service network, fed by an ever-increasing number of products, would be the key to the software kingdom; acquiring existing software (and its customers) would reduce the risk of in-house development and move products to market sooner. CA's purchasing flurry (of mostly struggling software firms) produced the first independent software company to reach $1 billion in sales (1989); sales 5 years earlier had been $85 million.

Wang moved beyond mainframe utilities into microcomputer software, buying the popular SuperCalc spreadsheet (from Sorcim, 1984) and BPI (accounting software, 1987); data security software, including the Top Secret program (1985); and a string of applications vendors, including Software International (financial, 1986) and Integrated Software Systems (graphics, 1986).

CA's 1987 purchase of chief utilities rival UCCEL made CA the world's largest independent software supplier — and gave Swiss billionaire Walter Haefner 20% of CA. CA then had 64% of the tape/disk-management software market and strong presences in banking applications and data security.

CA also moved into database management systems, buying Applied Data Research from Ameritech (including the crucial Datacom/DB program, 1988); Cullinet (1989), for its large, high-profile user base and strong products (the IDMS database line, software for VAX computers, and banking applications); and DBMS, Inc. (1990).

CA's integration of its own software with that of acquired companies has produced the Masterpiece management system and CA90s (an umbrella environment that allows its customers to run CA software on computers from any vendor). The burgeoning network it feeds works well: Top Secret's annual sales jumped from $10 million outside the CA pipeline to $36 million inside.

Unencumbered by hardware ties (unlike prime competitor IBM), CA plans further cross-vendor solutions. Technical field support (up approximately 30% in fiscal 1990) remains a top priority.

WHERE

HQ: 711 Stewart Ave., Garden City, NY 11530
Phone: 516-227-3300
FAX: 516-227-3937

Computer Associates has offices in 22 countries.

	1989 Sales		1989 Pretax Income	
	$ mil	% of total	$ mil	% of total
US & Canada	609	59	208	78
Other	421	41	60	22
Total	**1,030**	**100**	**268**	**100**

WHAT

	1989 Sales	
	$ mil	% of total
Products	788	76
Maintenance	242	24
Total	**1,030**	**100**

Systems Management Software
Automated production control (CA-APCDOC)
Data center administration
Data center automation (CA-UNIPACK)
Performance measurement and accounting (CA-JARS)
Project estimation and planning
Security, control, and auditing (CA-TOP SECRET; CA-ACF2)
Storage and resource management

Information Management Software
Applications development
Information distribution
Programmer productivity (CA-LIBRARIAN)
Project management
Relational database management (CA-DATACOM/DB; CA-IDMS/DB)
Visual information systems

Applications Software
Banking and thrift institution
Business decision software (CA-SuperCalc spreadsheet)
Financial management (Masterpiece)
Specialized accounting

Micro Software
Accounting
Decision support (SuperCalc5 spreadsheet)
Micro-mainframe links

HOW MUCH

	8 Yr. Growth	1980	1981	1982	1983	1984	1985	1986	1987	1988	1989
Sales ($ mil)	65.8%	—	18	28	58	85	129	191	309	709	1,030
Net income ($ mil)	—	—	1	3	6	10	13	19	37	102	164
Income as % of sales	—	—	7.6%	9.1%	9.7%	11.2%	10.3%	9.7%	11.8%	14.4%	15.9%
Earnings per share ($)	54.6%	—	0.03	0.06	0.08	0.11	0.15	0.21	0.37	0.63	0.98
Stock price – high ($)	—	—	—	0.89	2.34	4.41	3.69	4.38	7.72	18.63	16.44
Stock price – low ($)	—	—	—	0.80	0.72	2.11	1.84	2.28	4.06	6.84	11.94
Stock price – close ($)	—	—	—	0.89	2.23	3.00	2.42	4.38	6.88	16.00	15.94
P/E – high	—	—	—	16	29	40	25	21	21	30	17
P/E – low	—	—	—	14	9	19	12	11	11	11	12
Dividends per share ($)	—	—	0.00	0.00	0.00	0.00	0.00	0.00	0.00	0.00	0.00
Book value per share ($)	80.3%	—	0.04	0.16	0.42	1.08	1.21	1.77	2.21	3.15	4.46

1989 Year End:
Debt ratio: 5.6%
Return on equity: 25.7%
Cash (mil): $53
Current ratio: 1.85
Long-term debt (mil): $44
Number of shares (mil): 168
Dividends:
1989 average yield: 0.0%
1989 payout: 0.0%
Market value (mil): $2,671

Stock Price History high/low 1982-89

20
18
16
14
12
10
8
6
4
2
0

RANKINGS

94th in *Fortune* 100 Diversified Service Cos.
226th in *Business Week* 1000
724th in *Business Week* Global 1000

COMPETITION

Dun & Bradstreet
IBM
Lotus
Microsoft
Other software companies

CONAGRA, INC.

OVERVIEW

ConAgra is a major diversified food company consisting of 4 segments: Agri-Products, Trading and Processing, Prepared Foods, and Finance Companies.

Agri-Products produces pesticides, fertilizer, feed, and feed additives, and operates 177 stores that sell home and garden products. Trading and Processing includes ConAgra's international and grain processing operations.

Prepared Foods produces red meat (Monfort, E. A. Miller), frozen foods (Banquet, Armour Classics, Morton, Patio, Chun King), poultry (Country Pride, Country Skillet), processed meats (Armour Golden Star, Decker, Webber), dairy foods, oil, deli products, and seafood. ConAgra also produces specialty products including jellies, peanut butter, gourmet foods, and pet products.

ConAgra's finance companies handle commodities brokerage and special financial services, including insurance, truck leasing, and short-term financing for ConAgra's other business groups.

Between 1980 and 1989, ConAgra grew from $843 million in sales to $11 billion. The 1990 acquisition of Beatrice (Hunt's, Wesson) made ConAgra one of the world's largest food producers.

WHEN

In 1919, 4 flour mills joined to form Nebraska Consolidated Mills and established headquarters in Omaha. The company operated only in Nebraska until the 1940s, when it expanded to other states.

During the 1950s the company developed Duncan Hines cake mix (later sold to Procter & Gamble) and in 1957 established a flour and feed mill in Puerto Rico. The company entered the poultry processing business in the 1960s while continuing to buy flour mills nationwide.

By 1970 the company had opened poultry processing plants in Alabama, Georgia, and Louisiana. In 1971 the company changed its name to ConAgra (which means "in partnership with the land" in Latin). During the 1970s the company expanded into the fertilizer, catfish, and pet accessory businesses. ConAgra was first listed on the NYSE in 1973.

Bad investments and commodity speculation caused ConAgra severe financial problems in 1974 when Charles M. "Mike" Harper, a former Pillsbury executive, took charge. Harper sold nonessential properties to reduce debt and had the company back on its feet by 1976. In 1977 ConAgra established large-scale grain and feed merchandising operations and in 1978 bought United Agri Products (agricultural chemicals).

Through a series of acquisitions in the 1980s, Harper transformed ConAgra into a diversified food giant. In 1980 the company bought Banquet (frozen food) from RCA and within 6 years had introduced almost 90 new products under the Banquet label. With the purchases of Singleton Seafood and Sea-Alaska products, ConAgra achieved $1 billion in sales for the first time in 1981. ConAgra bought Peavey (milling and specialty retailing) and Country Pride (chicken) in 1982 and in 1983 acquired Armour Food Company (meats, dairy products, and frozen food) from the Greyhound Corporation. By 1985 sales had reached nearly $5.5 billion.

In 1986 ConAgra bought RJR Nabisco's frozen food business, which included the Chun King, Morton, and Patio brands. The company became a major factor in the red meat market with the 1987 purchases of E. A. Miller (boxed beef), Monfort (beef and lamb), and Swift Independent Packing. Further acquisitions included O'Donnell-Usen (seafood, 1987), Blue Star (frozen food, 1988), Cook (ham, 1988), and Pillsbury's grain merchandising system (1989). ConAgra's 1988 purchase of International Multifood's flour mills increased its total number of nationwide flour mills to 28.

HOW MUCH

	9 Yr. Growth	1980	1981	1982	1983	1984	1985	1986	1987	1988	1989
Sales ($ mil)	33.5%	843	1,377	1,705	2,320	3,302	5,498	5,911	9,002	9,475	11,340
Net income ($ mil)	30.1%	19	27	33	48	65	92	105	149	155	198
Income as % of sales	—	2.2%	2.0%	1.9%	2.1%	2.0%	1.7%	1.8%	1.7%	1.6%	1.7%
Earnings per share ($)	19.2%	0.33	0.48	0.56	0.57	0.68	0.87	1.00	1.22	1.28	1.62
Stock price – high ($)	—	2.17	5.08	5.17	6.56	8.00	9.19	15.75	21.42	25.33	22.67
Stock price – low ($)	—	1.60	1.68	3.56	3.72	5.72	6.58	8.67	12.96	13.92	15.83
Stock price – close ($)	29.3%	1.92	5.06	3.86	6.22	7.61	9.13	14.17	19.08	16.92	19.33
P/E – high	—	6	11	9	12	12	11	16	18	20	14
P/E – low	—	5	4	6	7	8	8	9	11	11	10
Dividends per share ($)	15.2%	0.14	0.16	0.19	0.21	0.25	0.28	0.32	0.37	0.43	0.50
Book value per share ($)	17.0%	1.92	2.24	2.65	3.30	4.08	4.61	5.14	6.17	6.96	7.87

1989 Year End:
Debt ratio: 37.1%
Return on equity: 21.8%
Cash (mil): $607
Current ratio: 1.19
Long-term debt (mil): $560
Number of shares (mil): 121
Dividends:
1989 average yield: 2.6%
1989 payout: 30.7%
Market value (mil): $2,332

Stock Price History high/low 1980-89

NYSE symbol: CAG
Incorporated: Delaware, 1975
Fiscal year ends: May 28

WHO

Chairman and CEO: Charles M. Harper, age 61, $1,444,440 pay
President and COO: Philip B. Fletcher, age 56, $400,000 pay
VP Finance: L. B. Thomas, age 53
Auditors: Deloitte & Touche
Employees: 48,131

WHERE

HQ: ConAgra Center, One Central Park Plaza, Omaha, NE 68102
Phone: 402-978-4000
FAX: 402-978-4447 (Public Relations)

ConAgra produces agricultural products in the US and Canada. The company operates grain elevators at 100 locations in 18 states and 28 flour mills in 15 states. ConAgra International operates 54 global trading offices in 26 countries and processing facilities in Canada, Europe, Latin America, and the US.

WHAT

	1989 Sales		1989 Operating Income	
	$ mil	% of total	$ mil	% of total
Prepared foods	7,084	63	293	62
Agri-Products	2,243	20	82	18
Trading & processing	1,869	16	83	18
Finance companies	144	1	10	2
Adjustments	—	—	(24)	—
Total	**11,340**	**100**	**444**	**100**

Agri-Products
Animal feeds
Country General Stores (retail)
Crop protection chemicals
Feed additives
Fertilizer
Livestock health care

Trading & Processing
Corn meal and mixes
Feed ingredient merchandising
Flour, oat, and corn milling
Global commodity trading

Finance Companies
Commodity futures brokerage
Livestock financing
Truck financing

Prepared Foods
Armour (meat and poultry)
Armour Classics (frozen dinners)
Banquet (frozen dinners)
Chun King (Chinese food)
Cook Family Food (ham)
Country Pride (poultry)
Country Skillet (poultry)
Geisler/Snoopy (pet toys and feeds)
Healthy Choice (frozen food)
Home Brand (peanut butter)
Monfort (beef and lamb)
Morton (frozen dinners)
Patio (Mexican food)
Sergeant's (pet pest control products)
Taste O'Sea (seafood)
World's Fare (deli products)

RANKINGS

36th in *Fortune* 500 US Industrial Cos.
97th in *Fortune* Global 500 Industrial Cos.
37th in *Forbes* Sales 500
201st in *Business Week* 1000
522nd in *Business Week* Global 1000

COMPETITION

Anheuser-Busch
Archer-Daniels-Midland
Beatrice
Campbell Soup
Cargill
Chiquita Brands
CPC International
Nestlé
Occidental
RJR Nabisco
Sara Lee
Tyson Foods
Unilever
Whitman
Other food companies

CONSOLIDATED EDISON CO. OF NEW YORK, INC.

OVERVIEW

Consolidated Edison (Con Ed), in business since 1823, provides electric, gas, and steam power to about 8.1 million people. The company's service area covers 660 square miles of New York City and Westchester County. Con Ed generated more than $5.5 billion in revenues in 1989, making it America's 6th largest electric utility. Of the company's operating revenues in 1989, 82% came from electricity sales (2.9 million customers), 13% from gas sales (1 million customers), and 5% from steam sales (1,994 customers). Most of Con Ed's generators are fueled by oil, with about 90% originating from foreign suppliers.

Since 1971, when the company introduced its Save-A-Watt program, Con Ed has been an industry leader in conservation, promoting energy savings through programs designed to cut back usage during summer peak periods (Curtailable Electric Service Program) and to teach the public ways to save on residential energy costs.

NYSE symbol: ED
Incorporated: New York, 1884
Fiscal year ends: December 31

WHO

Chairman and CEO: Arthur Hauspurg, age 64, $808,246 pay
President and COO: Eugene R. McGrath, age 48, $440,977 pay
EVP and CFO: Raymond J. McCann, age 55, $381,687 pay
Auditors: Price Waterhouse
Employees: 19,798

WHEN

A group of New York professionals, led by Timothy Dewey, founded The New York Gas Light Company in 1823 to provide utility service to a limited area of Manhattan. Various companies served other areas of New York City, and in 1884, 5 of these joined with New York Gas Light to form The Consolidated Gas Company of New York.

This unification occurred on the heels of the introduction of Thomas Edison's incandescent lamp (1879). The Edison Electric Illuminating Company of New York was formed in 1880 to build the world's first commercial electric power station with the financial support of a group led by J. P. Morgan. Edison supervised this project, known as the Pearl Street Station, and in 1882 New York became the first major city to experience electric lighting.

Realizing that electric lighting would most certainly replace gas, Consolidated Gas started buying New York's electric companies, including Anthony Brady's New York Gas and Electric Light, Heat and Power Company (1900), which consolidated with Edison's Illuminating Company in 1901 to form the New York Edison Company. More than 170 other purchases followed, including the 1930 acquisition of The New York Steam Company (founded in 1882) to provide a cheap source of steam for the company's electric turbines. In 1936 this amalgamation of utilities unified as The Consolidated Edison Company of New York, furnishing power to all of New York City and Westchester County.

In 1962 Con Ed opened its first nuclear station at Indian Point. Environmentalists worried that Con Ed's proposed Cornwall pumped-storage plant to be built at the foot of Storm King Mountain would damage the local ecosystem and managed to delay construction throughout the 1960s and early 1970s. A federal court ordered Con Ed to cease construction of the plant in 1974. In the meantime Con Ed had trouble supplying enough power to meet demand. Inflation and the Arab oil embargo drove up the price of oil (Con Ed's main energy source), and in 1974 the company skipped a dividend for the first time since 1885. The New York State Power Authority bought 2 of Con Ed's unfinished power plants, saving the company about $200 million.

Con Ed started buying power from various suppliers, including Hydro-Quebec, and in 1984 agreed to a 2-year rate freeze, a boon to New Yorkers, whose electric bills were nearly twice as high as those of most other big city residents. Con Ed continues to contract for additional power and in 1990 agreed to buy up to 1,600 megawatts (780 from Hydro-Quebec) to be delivered during its peak demand period (April through October).

WHERE

HQ: 4 Irving Place, New York, NY 10003
Phone: 212-460-4600
FAX: 212-982-7816

Generating Facilities

Electric – Fossil-Fueled
Arthur Kill (Staten Island)
Astoria (Queens)
Bowline Point (Haverstraw, 66 2/3% owned)
East River (Manhattan)
Hudson Avenue (Brooklyn)
Ravenswood (Queens)
Roseton (Newburgh, 40% owned)
Waterside (Manhattan)
59th Street (Manhattan)
74th Street (Manhattan)

Electric – Gas Turbines
Gowanus (Brooklyn)
Indian Point (Buchanan)
Narrows (Brooklyn)

Electric – Nuclear
Indian Point (Buchanan)

Steam
East River (Manhattan)
Hudson Avenue (Brooklyn)
Ravenswood (Queens)
Waterside (Manhattan)
59th Street (Manhattan)
E. 60th Street (Manhattan)
74th Street (Manhattan)

HOW MUCH

	9 Yr. Growth	1980	1981	1982	1983	1984	1985	1986	1987	1988	1989
Sales ($ mil)	3.9%	3,947	4,866	5,067	5,516	5,729	5,498	5,198	5,094	5,109	5,551
Net income ($ mil)	6.8%	335	448	493	576	620	564	546	550	599	606
Income as % of sales	—	8.5%	9.2%	9.7%	10.4%	10.8%	10.3%	10.5%	10.8%	11.7%	10.9%
Earnings per share ($)	8.8%	1.17	1.61	1.78	2.08	2.24	2.13	2.13	2.21	2.47	2.49
Stock price – high ($)	—	6.63	8.41	10.56	12.94	15.63	19.81	26.44	26.00	23.75	29.88
Stock price – low ($)	—	4.91	5.66	7.72	9.50	11.31	14.69	18.81	18.75	20.44	22.19
Stock price – close ($)	18.7%	6.22	8.13	10.25	12.44	15.38	19.75	23.56	20.88	23.25	29.13
P/E – high	—	6	5	6	6	7	9	12	12	10	12
P/E – low	—	4	4	4	5	5	7	9	8	8	9
Dividends per share ($)	11.0%	0.67	0.74	0.84	0.94	1.06	1.20	1.34	1.48	1.60	1.72
Book value per share ($)	5.9%	11.44	12.28	13.16	14.27	15.44	16.35	17.03	17.59	18.44	19.21

1989 Year End:
Debt ratio: 38.8%
Return on equity: 13.2%
Cash (mil): $460
Current ratio: 1.46
Long-term debt (mil): $3,150
Number of shares (mil): 228
Dividends:
1989 average yield: 5.9%
1989 payout: 69.1%
Market value (mil): $6,645

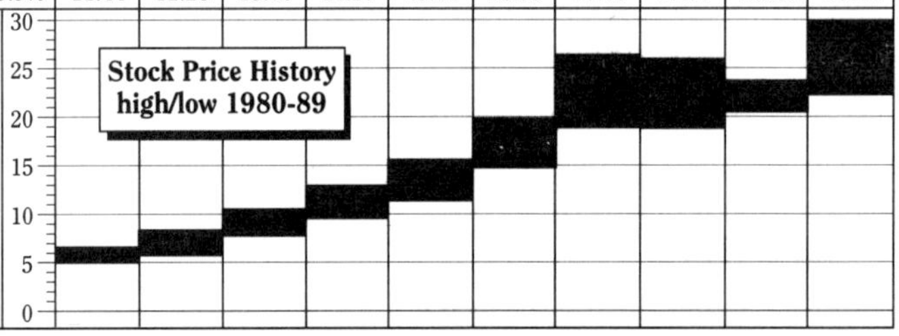

Stock Price History high/low 1980-89

WHAT

	1989 Sales	
	$ mil	% of total
Residential	1,747	31
Commercial & industrial	3,024	55
Sales to other utilities	147	3
Other	668	12
Adjustments	(35)	(1)
Total	**5,551**	**100**

	1989 Sales		1989 Operating Income	
	$ mil	% of total	$ mil	% of total
Electric	4,577	82	698	89
Gas	693	13	68	9
Steam	281	5	17	2
Total	**5,551**	**100**	**783**	**100**

RANKINGS

24th in *Fortune* 50 Utilities
160th in *Forbes* Sales 500
93rd in *Business Week* 1000
290th in *Business Week* Global 1000

CONSOLIDATED FREIGHTWAYS, INC.

OVERVIEW

Consolidated Freightways (CF), one of America's largest trucking companies, operates 4 long-haul trucking companies in the US, Canada, Puerto Rico, and the Caribbean, as well as 5 regional trucking companies, specializing in 2nd-day and overnight deliveries within 5 geographic areas of the US. CF has intermodal operations (freight shipped by truck, train, or ship in the same container) on both sea and rail. Its Emery Worldwide division (acquired 1989) provides express delivery in 90 countries.

CF experienced a 92% decline in profits from $113 million (1988) to $9 million (1989), resulting from higher fuel prices, rate wars, Emery's losses ($66 million on revenues of $1.2 billion, 1989), and one-time acquisition costs. However, Emery's global infrastructure has enhanced CF's existing network, making CF a full-service transportation company capable of delivering freight or packages to almost any address in the world by road, rail, sea, or air.

NYSE symbol: CNF
Incorporated: Delaware, 1958
Fiscal year ends: December 31

WHO

President and CEO: Lary R. Scott, age 53, $468,232 pay
SVP; President, Consolidated Freightways Corp. of Delaware: Robert H. Lawrence, age 52, $300,294 pay
SVP Finance: Norman R. Benke, age 58, $253,232 pay
Auditors: Arthur Andersen & Co.
Employees: 40,800

WHEN

Leland James, co-owner of a Portland, Oregon, bus company, founded Consolidated Truck Lines in 1929. Operating in the Pacific Northwest, the company offered heavy hauling, moving, and other transportation services. Operations extended to San Francisco and Idaho by 1934 and North Dakota by 1936. In 1939 the company adopted its present name.

James established Freightways Manufacturing in 1939, making CF the only trucking company to design and build its own trucks (Freightliners). Between 1940 and 1950 CF extended service (through acquisitions) to Chicago, Minneapolis, and Los Angeles and went public in 1951. By 1954 CF operated over 13,000 route miles in 11 western and midwestern states.

CF moved to Menlo Park, California, in 1956 and between 1955 and 1960 extended operations throughout the US and Canada through 52 purchases. A failed attempt to coordinate intermodal services with railroads and shipping lines in 1960 contributed to an after-tax loss of $2.7 million on $152 million in revenues. William White, formerly of the Delaware Lackawanna and Western Railroad, became president (1960), terminated intermodal operations, and decided to focus on less-than-truckload shipments (those weighing less than 10,000 pounds).

In 1969 CF bought Pacific Far East Lines, a San Francisco shipping line founded in 1946. CF still operates this company as CF Ocean Service, serving Europe, Australia, and the Pacific Rim. In 1970 CF formed CF AirFreight, offering air cargo services in the US and Canada. CF used the proceeds from the 1981 sale of Freightways Manufacturing (to Daimler-Benz) to establish regional trucking operations called Con-Way Transportation Services (1983).

In 1989 CF bought Wilton, Connecticut–based Emery Air Freight, an international air cargo service, operating it with CF AirFreight as Emery Worldwide. Founded in 1946 by ex-naval officer John Emery, Emery Air Freight expanded across America (and overseas, 1956) by utilizing extra cargo space on scheduled airlines (like Eastern and TWA). The company started chartering aircraft in the early 1970s and in 1979 bought its first plane. Emery established hubs at Dayton, Ohio (1981) and Maastricht, Holland (1985). After buying Purolator Courier in 1987, Emery faced unexpected problems merging Purolator's envelope delivery and its own air cargo businesses (1987 and 1988). It was further plagued by a takeover attempt by former Federal Express president Arthur Bass (1988), resulting in losses of almost $100 million in 1987 and 1988. CF's problems with Emery continue, although there are signs of improvement.

WHERE

HQ: 175 Linfield Dr., Menlo Park, CA 94025
Phone: 415-326-1700
FAX: 415-321-1741

Consolidated Freightways operates 11 businesses in 90 countries, with 667 freight terminals located throughout North America. The company owns more than 41,000 trucks, tractors, and trailers, and 98 aircraft.

	1989 Sales		1989 Operating Income	
	$ mil	% of total	$ mil	% of total
US	3,286	87	84	165
Foreign	474	13	(33)	(65)
Total	**3,760**	**100**	**51**	**100**

WHAT

	1989 Sales		1989 Operating Income	
	$ mil	% of total	$ mil	% of total
Long-haul trucking	1,996	53	108	212
Intermodal	559	15	40	79
Air freight	1,205	32	(97)	(191)
Total	**3,760**	**100**	**51**	**100**

Consolidated Freightways Corp. of Delaware
- Canadian Freightways
- CF Motor Freight
- Milne & Craighead Customs Brokers
- Road Systems, Inc. (trailer manufacturer)
- Willamette Sales Co. (equipment distributor)

Con-Way Transportation Services, Inc.
- CF Ocean Service, Inc. (intermodal)
- CF Truckload Service, Inc. (intermodal)
- Con-Way (regional trucking companies)
- Penn Yan Express, Inc.

Emery Worldwide
- EMCON (telecommunications)
- Emery Customs Brokers
- Emery Worldwide Airlines, Inc.

RANKINGS

15th in *Fortune* 50 Transportation Cos.
221st in *Forbes* Sales 500
703rd in *Business Week* 1000

COMPETITION

American President
Burlington Northern
Federal Express
Roadway
Union Pacific
UPS
Yellow Freight
Airlines

HOW MUCH

	9 Yr. Growth	1980	1981	1982	1983	1984	1985	1986	1987	1988	1989
Sales ($ mil)	9.6%	1,654	1,144	1,204	1,355	1,705	1,882	2,124	2,297	2,689	3,760
Net income ($ mil)	(16.1%)	42	64	55	65	74	79	89	75	113	9
Income as % of sales	—	2.5%	5.6%	4.6%	4.8%	4.4%	4.2%	4.2%	3.2%	4.2%	0.2%
Earnings per share ($)	(35.7%)	1.07	1.60	1.36	1.62	1.87	2.07	2.31	1.93	3.00	*0.02*
Stock price – high ($)	—	9.88	15.00	18.42	20.42	20.00	27.50	36.50	41.25	34.75	37.75
Stock price – low ($)	—	6.00	8.17	10.67	16.00	13.42	18.67	23.67	22.75	25.25	25.25
Stock price – close ($)	14.0%	8.17	13.17	16.67	20.08	19.17	26.50	30.00	27.50	33.00	26.50
P/E – high	—	9	9	14	13	11	13	16	21	12	—
P/E – low	—	6	5	8	10	7	9	10	12	8	—
Dividends per share ($)	9.5%	0.46	0.50	0.53	0.58	0.65	0.72	0.80	0.88	0.96	1.04
Book value per share ($)	8.6%	8.56	11.60	12.32	13.33	14.42	15.69	17.22	18.16	20.32	18.01

1989 Year End:
Debt ratio: 50.9%
Return on equity: —
Cash (mil): $111
Current ratio: 1.14
Long-term debt (mil): $652
Number of shares (mil): 35
Dividends:
1989 average yield: 3.9%
1989 payout: —
Market value (mil): $927

Stock Price History high/low 1980-89

CONSOLIDATED RAIL CORPORATION

OVERVIEW

Consolidated Rail Corporation (Conrail) is the dominant railroad in the populous and highly industrialized Northeast. Conceived in 1976 as a federally owned successor to Penn Central and 5 other bankrupt eastern railroads, Conrail was thought by many to be incapable of turning a profit (the Reagan administration considered liquidating the company's assets in 1981). Under the direction of CEO L. Stanley Crane (1981 to 1988), however, Conrail became a profitable railroad. The US government sold its 85% share in Conrail to the public in 1987 for $1.65 billion.

Today, the Philadelphia-based company operates 2,360 locomotives and nearly 71,000 freight cars over a 13,100-mile rail network. Conrail's tracks host the highest intermodal (truck-to-train) and automotive rail traffic in the US, with connections to the West Coast, Texas, and the South. In 1989 in its first step outside the railroad business the company announced a joint venture with OHM Corporation called Concord Resource Group to operate a network of solid and hazardous waste handling facilities.

NYSE symbol: CRR
Incorporated: Pennsylvania, 1976
Fiscal year ends: December 31

WHO

Chairman, President, and CEO: James A. Hagen, age 58, $450,000 pay
SVP Development: Charles N. Marshall, age 48, $218,097 pay (prior to promotion)
SVP Finance: H. William Brown, age 51, $205,538 pay
SVP Law: Bruce B. Wilson, age 54, $198,312 pay
SVP Operations: Donald A. Swanson, age 59
SVP Marketing and Sales: Gordon H. Kuhn, age 39
Auditors: Coopers & Lybrand
Employees: 31,574

WHEN

The Mohawk & Hudson (M&H) opened in 1831 between Albany and Schenectady, New York. In 1853 the M&H and 9 other railroads merged to form the New York Central (NYC) between Albany and Buffalo. In 1867 at the age of 73, Cornelius Vanderbilt (known as "Commodore" Vanderbilt for his earlier exploits in the ocean shipping trade) acquired NYC and merged it with other railroads 2 years later. By 1914 the railroad stretched from New York to Chicago and served a large portion of the Northeast and Midwest. In the 1950s Alfred E. Perlman (appointed president by chairman Robert R. Young) shifted the railroad's emphasis from passenger traffic to freight operations. He led the company to merge with the rival Pennsylvania Railroad (the "Pennsy") in 1968.

The Pennsy was chartered in 1846 to run from Harrisburg to Philadelphia. The line acquired other roads throughout the Northeast and Midwest, serving Washington, Baltimore, New York, and many of the major midwestern cities served by NYC. The Pennsy for many years led the industry in revenues and tonnage hauled and had an unequaled history of dividend payment until 1946. After WWII the company was burdened by an overbuilt system and declining traffic. In 1957 Pennsy chairman James M. Symes began planning a merger with NYC; the merger was completed 11 years later under his successor, Stuart T. Saunders. The new company was named Penn Central Transportation Company.

Penn Central, hurt by mismanagement and still-dwindling traffic, endured mounting losses for 2 years before declaring bankruptcy (one of the nation's largest) in 1970. After studying the chaotic state of the eastern rail system, in 1976 the US government created Consolidated Rail Corporation (Conrail) to assume the operations of Penn Central and 5 other failed railroads: Central of New Jersey, Erie Lackawanna, Lehigh & Hudson River, Lehigh Valley, and Reading (Penn Central survives as a diversified holding company). With federal financing of $2.1 billion, Conrail sold its intercity passenger operations to Amtrak, transferred commuter lines to regional authorities, and rebuilt its physical plant.

Conrail had lost $1.5 billion by 1981, when former Southern Railway chairman L. Stanley Crane became CEO. Crane, with the help of labor concessions and favorable federal legislation, engineered a dramatic turnaround that culminated in a 1984 net income of $472 million and the public sale of Conrail's government-held stock (1987). Conrail has continued to add railroad properties to its portfolio, upping its interest in the Monongahela Railway Company from 1/3 to 2/3 ownership in December 1989.

WHERE

HQ: Six Penn Center Plaza, Philadelphia, PA 19103
Phone: 215-977-4000
FAX: 215-977-5567

Conrail operates a 13,100-mile rail network in 14 northeastern and midwestern states, the District of Columbia, and Quebec.

Principal Cities Served

Albany, NY	Indianapolis, IN
Baltimore, MD	Louisville, KY
Boston, MA	Montreal, Quebec
Buffalo, NY	New York, NY
Charleston, WV	Newark, NJ
Chicago, IL	Philadelphia, PA
Cincinnati, OH	Pittsburgh, PA
Cleveland, OH	Syracuse, NY
Columbus, OH	Toledo, OH
Detroit, MI	Washington, DC
East St. Louis, IL	Wilmington, DE

WHAT

	1989 Revenues	
	$ mil	% of total
Chemical products	563	16
Intermodal	544	16
Automotive	514	15
Coal	495	14
Metal products	394	12
Food & grain	332	10
Forest products	303	9
Other	266	8
Total Freight Revenues	**3,411**	**100**

RANKINGS

16th in *Fortune* 50 Transportation Cos.
247th in *Forbes* Sales 500
282nd in *Business Week* 1000
646th in *Business Week* Global 1000

COMPETITION

Burlington Northern
CSX
Ryder
Waste Management
Other trucking companies

HOW MUCH

	9 Yr. Growth	1980	1981	1982	1983	1984	1985	1986	1987	1988	1989
Sales ($ mil)	(1.7)	3,982	4,201	3,617	3,076	3,379	3,208	3,144	3,247	3,490	3,411
Net income ($ mil)		(244)	39	174	298	472	361	316	267	306	148
Income as % of sales	—	—	0.9%	4.8%	9.7%	14.0%	11.3%	10.1%	8.2%	8.8%	4.3%
Earnings per share ($)		—	0.62	2.80	4.75	7.43	5.55	4.75	3.88	4.44	2.17
Stock price – high ($)	—	—	—	—	—	—	—	—	40.88	35.38	49.38
Stock price – low ($)	—	—	—	—	—	—	—	—	19.88	26.38	32.00
Stock price – close ($)	—	—	—	—	—	—	—	—	27.63	33.75	47.88
P/E – high	—	—	—	—	—	—	—	—	11	8	23
P/E – low	—	—	—	—	—	—	—	—	5	6	15
Dividends per share ($)	—	—	—	—	—	—	—	—	0.50	1.10	1.30
Book value per share ($)		—	2.46	5.38	10.65	18.56	25.99	26.54	55.52	59.00	60.24

1989 Year End:
Debt ratio: 17.5%
Return on equity: 3.6%
Cash (mil): $502
Current ratio: 1.14
Long-term debt (mil): $857
Number of shares (mil): 67
Dividends:
1989 average yield: 2.7%
1989 payout: 59.9%
Market value (mil): $3,214

Stock Price History high/low 1987-89

CONTINENTAL AIRLINES HOLDINGS INC.

OVERVIEW

Continental Airlines Holdings operates Continental Airlines, 3 commuter airlines, and, through a partnership with Electronic Data Systems Corporation (a GM subsidiary), the System One computer reservations system. The company also owns bankrupt Eastern Air Lines, but, in an unusual action, the bankruptcy court removed it from Eastern's management in April 1990.

Continental Airlines was America's 5th largest airline in 1989 (in terms of passenger miles flown). It is currently the dominant carrier at its Houston and Newark hubs and offers more flights to the New York City area than any other airline. Eastern, ranked 9th in terms of 1989 passenger miles, is now managed by former Continental Airlines president Martin R. Shugrue, Jr., a court-appointed trustee.

In a surprise move, Frank Lorenzo, Continental Airlines Holdings's chairman, president, and CEO, resigned in August 1990 after selling his stake in the company to Scandinavian Airlines System. SAS, which already owned 9.8% of the company, will raise its interest to 16.8% once the sale wins DOT approval.

ASE symbol: CTA
Incorporated: Delaware, 1980
Fiscal year ends: December 31

WHO

President and CEO: Hollis L. Harris, age 58
EVP, Treasurer, and Principal Financial Officer: Robert D. Snedeker, age 47, $345,837 pay
Auditors: Arthur Andersen & Co.
Employees: 31,400

WHEN

Trans Texas Airways, a Houston-based, local-service airline, began serving Texas communities in 1947. Becoming Texas International (1968), it was serving the West Coast and Mexico by 1970. However, the company was unable to compete with major airlines on interstate routes and commuter airlines in Texas and faced bankruptcy by 1972, when Frank Lorenzo and Robert Carney of Jet Capital Corporation gained control. By 1976, under Lorenzo's leadership, Texas International had netted over $3 million.

In 1980 Lorenzo and Carney organized Texas Air Corporation, a holding company for Texas International and New York Air (created by Texas Air to operate from New York to Washington, DC, 1980). Texas Air then bought controlling interest in Continental Airlines (1981). Founded as Varney Speed Lines (1934), Continental operated in the western US, the Pacific, and Mexico; however, competition resulting from deregulation had left it with $60 million in losses by 1982 when Texas Air bought the rest of the company. When contract negotiations failed in 1983, Continental's unions went on strike. Lorenzo took the airline into Chapter 11, thereby canceling all union contracts. Emerging from bankruptcy in 1986, the new, nonunion Continental emphasized low fares while operating with the industry's lowest labor costs.

Texas Air bought Eastern Air Lines in 1986. Founded as Pitcairn Aviation (1927), Eastern was the only airline operating from the Northeast to Florida from 1928 to 1944. WWI ace Eddie Rickenbacker ran the airline from 1935 until his 1963 retirement. Losses throughout the 1960s and 1970s, compounded by union disputes, forced CEO Frank Borman (ex-astronaut) to sell the airline. Texas Air also bought People Express Airlines and Frontier Airlines in 1986, making Texas Air America's #1 airline company in terms of passenger miles flown.

In 1988 Lorenzo sold Eastern's Air Shuttle to Donald Trump, but mounting losses and a machinists' strike forced Eastern into bankruptcy in 1989. In April 1990 the bankruptcy court took control of Eastern from Texas Air. In June Texas Air changed its name to Continental Airlines Holdings Inc. In August, Lorenzo resigned after selling his stake in the company to SAS for a substantial premium plus $19.7 million in salary and severance pay. Following Lorenzo's resignation, Hollis L. Harris, former president of Delta Air Lines, was named CEO.

While the company continued to lose money in early 1990, some analysts believe that, freed of Eastern and with one of the lowest cost structures in the industry, it will return to profitability later in the year.

WHERE

HQ: 333 Clay St., Suite 4040, Houston, TX 77002
Phone: 713-658-9588
FAX: 713-658-8337

Continental Airlines flies to 149 destinations in the US and 56 destinations in Europe, the Pacific, South America, the Caribbean, and Central America.

Hub Locations
Cleveland
Denver
Houston
Newark

WHAT

	1989 Sales	
	$ mil	% of total
Passenger	5,705	85
Cargo, mail & other	980	15
Total	**6,685**	**100**

Continental Airlines, Inc.

Eastern Air Lines, Inc.

Regional Commuters
Bar Harbor Airways, Inc.
Britt Airways, Inc.
Rocky Mountain Airways, Inc.

Flight Equipment	Owned	Leased	Total
Continental Airlines			
Airbus A300	2	10	12
Boeing 727	38	56	94
Boeing 737	32	62	94
Boeing 747	—	8	8
DC-9	6	35	41
DC-10	2	13	15
MD-80	11	54	65
Total	**91**	**238**	**329**

RANKINGS

6th in *Fortune* 50 Transportation Cos.
126th in *Forbes* Sales 500

COMPETITION

America West
AMR
Delta
HAL
KLM
Midway
NWA
Pan Am
Southwest
TWA
UAL
USAir

HOW MUCH

	9 Yr. Growth	1980	1981	1982	1983	1984	1985	1986	1987	1988	1989
Sales ($ mil)	41.6%	292	719	1,516	1,246	1,372	1,944	4,407	8,475	8,573	6,685
Net income ($ mil)	—	5	(47)	(49)	(180)	28	49	42	(466)	(719)	(886)
Income as % of sales	—	1.6%	(6.6%)	(3.2%)	(14.4%)	2.0%	2.5%	1.0%	(5.5%)	(8.4%)	(13.2%)
Earnings per share ($)	—	0.64	*(8.11)*	*(7.27)*	*(14.74)*	1.20	1.81	0.68	(12.58)	(18.88)	(22.71)
Stock price – high ($)	—	14.75	15.25	13.88	12.38	9.88	20.00	40.88	51.50	17.13	23.38
Stock price – low ($)	—	6.38	5.13	4.00	4.75	5.63	8.88	14.13	9.00	8.88	11.13
Stock price – close ($)	1.0%	10.50	5.63	10.75	6.63	9.13	15.00	33.75	10.88	11.88	11.50
P/E – high	—	23	—	—	—	8	11	60	—	—	—
P/E – low	—	10	—	—	—	5	5	21	—	—	—
Dividends per share ($)	—	0.16	0.16	0.16	0.08	0.00	0.00	0.00	0.00	0.00	0.00
Book value per share ($)	—	14.51	7.30	4.90	(8.88)	(5.24)	5.48	22	12.53	(5.47)	(26.80)

1989 Year End:
Debt ratio: 174.2%
Return on equity: 140.7%
Cash (mil): $1,271
Current ratio: 1.26
Long-term debt (mil): $2,596
Number of shares (mil): 41
Dividends:
1989 average yield: 0.0%
1989 payout: 0.0%
Market value (mil): $475

CONTINENTAL BANK CORPORATION

OVERVIEW

When Continental stumbled in 1984, it was the biggest banking collapse in US history: Continental was larger than all the banks that had failed during the Great Depression combined.

Even now Continental is the 22nd largest bank holding company in the nation. Its primary "holding" is the bank, Chicago's 2nd largest, all but indistinguishable from the corporate parent. All but 72 of Continental's more than 7,500 employees work for the bank.

Continental is attempting to recover with a new "business bank" orientation, the latest in a string of strategies since 1984. The bank is wooing corporate clients with services ranging from cash management to mergers and acquisitions. About one in 3 corporate customers is privately owned, and the bank serves well-to-do individuals with private banking services.

WHEN

Continental Bank, still struggling to climb out of its 1984 collapse and federal bailout, traces its modern history to another government rescue during the Great Depression.

In the 1920s Continental emerged from a series of Chicago bank mergers. Merchants' Loan and Trust, Illinois Trust and Savings, and Corn Exchange National Bank became Illinois Merchants' Trust in 1924. Illinois Merchants' Trust in turn joined with Continental and Commercial Banks in 1928 to become Continental Illinois Bank and Trust.

In 1932 the New Deal's Reconstruction Finance Corporation loaned $50 million to Depression-battered Continental. Walter Cummings, an official of the newly created FDIC, became chairman of the bank. His conservative leadership — investing in low-risk government securities and loaning to the most creditworthy of customers — retired the bank's debt to the government in 1939.

In 1959 Cummings retired, and successor David Kennedy, later to serve as Richard Nixon's first secretary of the treasury, loosened the purse strings for more aggressive lending. In the 1970s Continental surpassed archrival First Chicago, hobbled by loan problems of its own, as Chicago's largest bank. Continental eschewed gathering traditional deposits in favor of riskier, short-term transactions to raise money to lend.

Much of Continental's growth came from energy loans, some purchased from Penn Square, an oil-boom bank headquartered in an Oklahoma City shopping center. Penn Square's failure in 1982 left Continental with $1 billion in bad loans. That snowballed into a 1984 run on the bank by large depositors.

Federal officials and major banks shored up Continental with $4.5 billion in guarantees. The FDIC in effect nationalized the bank, taking 80% ownership. The government's stake was reduced to about 25% by 1989.

Federal officials recruited John Swearingen, Amoco's former chairman, to lead the bank. Continental bought 3 small suburban banks (1986) to boost retail deposits and purchased First Options, the nation's largest clearing firm for option traders (1986).

When Swearingen retired in 1987, Continental replaced him with Citicorp Vice Chairman Thomas Theobald. Theobald sold Continental's suburban holdings (1988) and Securities Settlement Corporation (1989) and announced its intention to sell First Options (1989) to reposition Continental to serve corporate customers. In 1988 Continental formally dropped "Illinois" from its name to stress its focus on nationwide banking.

Continental sold all retail accounts to First Chicago and lowered its exposure to bad international loans, but retooling to a business bank hasn't been easy. In 1990 the company cut 900 jobs from its trading and distribution payroll, an area it had beefed up only 2 years before.

The Tisch family believe the medicine may work; in August 1990 they announced their acquisition of 5.6% of Continental's stock.

HOW MUCH

	9 Yr. Growth	1980	1981	1982	1983	1984	1985	1986	1987	1988	1989
Sales ($ mil)	(4.2%)	4,719	6,276	5,890	4,381	4,091	2,880	2,566	2,788	3,060	3,203
Net income ($ mil)	2.7%	226	255	78	101	(1,087)	134	99	(610)	316	286
Income as % of sales	—	4.8%	4.1%	1.3%	2.3%	(26.6%)	4.7%	3.8%	(21.9%)	10.3%	8.9%
Earnings per share ($)	(16.3%)	23.00	25.76	7.80	9.84	(107.96)	1.68	1.16	(24.28)	5.19	4.64
Stock price – high ($)	—	131.50	171.00	146.00	103.50	91.00	40.50	41.00	24.50	23.50	26.63
Stock price – low ($)	—	84.50	123.50	60.50	74.00	11.00	23.00	20.00	9.00	11.00	18.50
Stock price – close ($)	(18.5%)	125.00	132.50	81.50	87.50	23.00	39.50	21.50	12.00	20.75	19.88
P/E – high	—	6	7	19	11	—	24	35	—	5	6
P/E – low	—	4	5	8	8	—	14	17	—	2	4
Dividends per share ($)	(20.6%)	6.80	7.60	8.00	8.00	2.00	0.00	0.08	0.32	0.44	0.85
Book value per share ($)	(18.5%)	155.06	172.79	171.23	172.55	56.41	64.06	42.92	17.48	23.60	24.51

1989 Year End:
Debt ratio: 39.6%
Return on equity: 19.3%
Cash (mil): $4,870
Assets (mil): $29,549
Long-term debt (mil): $1,103
Number of shares (mil): 50
Dividends:
  1989 average yield: 4.3%
  1989 payout: 18.3%
Market value (mil): $988

Stock Price History high/low 1980-89

NYSE symbol: CBK
Incorporated: Delaware, 1968
Fiscal year ends: December 31

WHO

Chairman and CEO: Thomas C. Theobald, age 52, $1,150,000 pay
VC: Richard L. Huber, age 53
VC: Garry J. Scheuring, age 50, $750,000 pay
VC: S. Waite Rawls III, age 41, $625,000 pay
CFO: Hollis W. Rademacher, age 54, $531,500 pay
General Counsel and Secretary: Richard S. Brennan, age 51
Auditors: Price Waterhouse
Employees: 7,560

WHERE

HQ: 231 S. LaSalle St., Chicago, IL 60697
Phone: 312-828-7450
FAX: 312-828-7150

Chicago-based Continental operates in 9 other US cities and 12 foreign countries: Argentina, Brazil, Chile, France, Germany, Hong Kong, Italy, Japan, Mexico, Singapore, the UK, and Venezuela.

	1989 Sales		1989 Operating Income	
	$ mil	% of total	$ mil	% of total
US	2,143	67	243	82
Europe	126	4	7	2
Latin America/ Caribbean	477	15	(5)	(2)
Asia/Pacific	171	5	9	3
UK	232	7	62	21
Other foreign	54	2	(20)	(6)
Total	**3,203**	**100**	**296**	**100**

WHAT

	1989 Sales	
	$ mil	% of total
Loan interest	1,776	56
Other interest	975	30
Fees & commissions	175	5
Trust income	72	2
Real estate gain	83	3
Other noninterest	122	4
Total	**3,203**	**100**

Corporate Finance
Distribution of loans
Loans to corporations
Syndication of loans

Market Making/Risk Management
Foreign exchange trading
Trading accounts
Venture capital

Specialized Financial Services
Cash management services
Personal trust services
Private banking services
Securities and clearing services

RANKINGS

22nd in *Fortune* 100 Commercial Banking Cos.
260th in *Forbes* Sales 500
543rd in *Business Week* 1000

COMPETITION

First Chicago
Other money-center and international banks

CONTROL DATA CORPORATION

OVERVIEW

Control Data Corporation (CDC) is a technology integrator: its 8 business units link computer systems with niche software and communications networks to provide specialized business services.

The service units (which now account for 43% of revenues) include the US's largest audience measurement service (Arbitron); systems management of 25% of the electricity transmitted in the US and 18% worldwide (Empros); a leader in trading-room systems (Micrognosis); and a large provider of credit card authorizations (TeleMoney). Computer products include high performance mainframes (CDC's original business) that are sold to the engineering and scientific community worldwide.

Founder William Norris's guiding vision of corporate philanthropy (*e.g.*, financing small farms, locating manufacturing plants in low-income areas) succumbed to losses of almost $1.5 billion between 1985 and 1989. After having sloughed off disk drives, supercomputers, and many employees, CDC's revenues are now 60% of 1984 levels.

NYSE symbol: CDA
Incorporated: Delaware, 1968
Fiscal year ends: December 31

WHO

President and CEO: Lawrence Perlman, age 51, $657,790 pay
EVP: David P. White, age 52, $319,559 pay
EVP: James E. Ousley, age 44
VP and Corporate Controller: John R. Eickhoff, age 49
Auditors: KPMG Peat Marwick
Employees: 18,000

WHERE

HQ: 8100 34th Ave. South, Box 0, Minneapolis, MN 55440
Phone: 612-853-8100
FAX: 612-853-7173

CDC's principal non-US offices are located in Canada, England, France, and Germany.

	1989 Sales		1989 Pretax Income	
	$ mil	% of total	$ mil	% of total
US	1,977	67	(618)	90
Foreign	958	33	(72)	10
Adjustments	—	—	23	—
Total	**2,935**	**100**	**(667)**	**100**

WHAT

	1989 Sales	
	$ mil	% of total
Sales & rentals	1,673	57
Services	1,262	43
Total	**2,935**	**100**

Businesses

The Arbitron Co. (radio and TV audience measurement, product tracking)
Automated Wagering (on-line lottery systems)
Business Management Services (payroll processing, payroll tax filing, accounting)
Computer Products (mainframes, minicomputers, workstations, networking software)
Data Services (credit union services, litigation support software, electronic data interchange network, credit card authorizations)
Empros Systems International (electric utility management)
Government Systems (computer systems for DOD, NASA)
Micrognosis Inc. (trading-room systems)

RANKINGS

153rd in *Fortune* 500 Industrial Cos.
286th in *Forbes* Sales 500
601st in *Business Week* 1000

COMPETITION

Amdahl
ADP
Bally
Data General
Digital Equipment
Dun & Bradstreet
Fujitsu
Hitachi
IBM
Intergraph
NEC
Prime
Reuters
Sun Microsystems
Unisys

WHEN

In 1957 William Norris founded Minneapolis-based Control Data Corporation (CDC) to challenge IBM in mainframe computers for scientific applications, the giant's weak side. Norris drew fellow engineers from Sperry Rand, where he had managed the Univac computer division. The gifted designer Seymour Cray helped create a stream of computers popular with the scientific community, starting with the 1604 mainframe (1958); Cray's genius also produced the advanced 6600 supercomputer (1963).

Booming computer sales allowed Norris to sponsor dearly loved social projects such as computer-based education (PLATO). CDC also diversified, buying Commercial Credit Company (1968) to provide financing for its customers' leasing needs. The company also entered joint ventures for tape and disk drive peripherals with several companies (including NCR, 1972, and Honeywell, 1975). CDC later formed the Imprimis peripherals division.

CDC's greatest coup was its settlement in 1973 of an antitrust suit against IBM, which allowed the company to purchase IBM's service bureau for far below market value. That service was the forerunner of several currently successful CDC businesses, including payroll processing and tax filing services.

In the early 1980s, CDC plunged into costly supercomputers (ETA Systems, discontinued in 1989) and semiconductors (VTC division, up for sale in 1990), which drained cash while remaining unprofitable. Meanwhile, CDC's Cyber mainframes and peripherals were suffering under intense Japanese competition. Losses in 1985 and 1986 totaling $800 million prompted Norris protégé Robert Price in 1986 to spin off Commercial Credit to its shareholders and sell PLATO to various buyers.

By the end of 1989, CDC had sold Imprimis (to Seagate, for cash and an 18% stake in Seagate), the 3rd-party maintenance service, and the rest of the education businesses; discontinued the supercomputer project; and put the semiconductor division up for sale. In 1989 alone losses were $680 million and the workforce fell from 33,500 to 18,000.

CDC has adopted industry standards such as the UNIX operating system (*e.g.*, in its Cyber 910 workstations, which are sold on an OEM basis to Silicon Graphics). CDC will again offer supercomputers through alliances with Convex Computer and Cray Research. Under new CEO Lawrence Perlman (1990), areas of focus will likely include the super-mainframe Cyber 2000, the Automated Wagering segment, and the company's Arbitron business. Both the Cyber 2000 and the Series 4000 workstation products are expected to be major contributors to profits after their introduction in the 2nd half of 1990.

HOW MUCH

	9 Yr. Growth	1980	1981	1982	1983	1984	1985	1986	1987	1988	1989
Sales ($ mil)	0.7%	2,766	3,101	4,292	4,583	5,027	3,680	3,347	3,367	3,628	2,935
Net income ($ mil)	—	148	170	155	162	5	(531)	(269)	25	2	(680)
Income as % of sales	—	5.3%	5.5%	3.6%	3.5%	0.1%	(14.4%)	(8.0%)	0.7%	0.0%	(23.2%)
Earnings per share ($)	—	*4.15*	*4.46*	4.04	4.19	0.12	(13.65)	(6.58)	0.59	0.03	(16.11)
Stock price – high ($)	—	38.81	42.13	42.75	64.38	48.50	38.75	28.75	38.25	30.50	24.00
Stock price – low ($)	—	21.50	29.81	21.13	35.50	24.38	15.13	18.75	17.63	16.38	16.25
Stock price – close ($)	(7.1%)	35.25	35.25	37.13	45.25	35.25	20.75	26.38	21.63	19.63	18.13
P/E – high	—	9	9	11	15	404	—	—	65	1,017	—
P/E – low	—	5	7	5	8	203	—	—	30	546	—
Dividends per share ($)	—	0.30	0.48	0.55	0.60	0.66	0.54	0.00	0.00	0.00	0.00
Book value per share ($)	(14.4%)	38.43	42.20	46.10	47.59	45.63	29.21	23.72	24.84	24.97	9.43

1989 Year End:
Debt ratio: 46.1%
Return on equity: (93.7%)
Cash (mil): $525
Current ratio: 1.51
Long-term debt (mil): $352
Number of shares (mil): 42
Dividends:
1989 average yield: 0.0%
1989 payout: 0.0%
Market value (mil): $770

COOPER INDUSTRIES, INC.

OVERVIEW

Cooper is one of the world's largest makers of electrical products and electrical power equipment. The company makes everything from power transformers that transmit electricity across large power grids to tiny fuses used on circuit boards. Cable TV signals are frequently transmitted over wire made by one of Cooper's many divisions.

CooperTools features 16 well-known brand names of do-it-yourself and professional tools, including Crescent wrenches and Xcelite screwdrivers. Cooper's Automotive Products division, bolstered by the 1989 purchase of Champion Spark Plug, also manufactures headlamps, windshield wipers, and brakes. Cooper makes Kirsch curtain rods and blinds. Cooper's original business, engines and compressors, now mostly serves the oil and gas industry with drilling and transmission equipment used in the world's oil fields. Cooper has finished 2 new tool projects in Germany and is building a plant expansion in Brazil and new electrical equipment plants in Wisconsin and Arkansas.

WHEN

In 1833 Charles Cooper sold a horse for $50 and borrowed money to open a foundry with his brother Elias in Mount Vernon, Ohio. Known as C. & E. Cooper, the company made plows, hog troughs, maple syrup kettles, stoves, and wagon boxes.

In the 1840s Cooper began making steam engines for use in mills and on farms, and later adapted the engines for wood-burning locomotives. In 1868 the company built its first Corliss steam engine, a significant improvement over earlier designs, and in 1875 introduced the first steam-powered farm tractor. By 1900 Cooper's steam engines were widely used and sold in the US and overseas, but steam was being replaced by the internal combustion engine. In 1909 Cooper introduced an internal combustion engine-compressor for natural gas pipelines; the company's last steam engine was shipped to Japan in 1920. The Cooper plant geared for war production in 1917, building artillery shells as well as engines and compressors during war years.

In the 1920s Cooper became the biggest seller of compression engines for oil and gas pipeline transmission. A 1929 merger with Bessemer (a maker of smaller gas and diesel engines) created Cooper-Bessemer. C-B diesel engines powered oil tankers, yachts, and other marine vessels. The company was hurt badly by the Depression; sales dropped 90% in 1931. The success of a new turbocharged diesel to power locomotives revived revenues. To make similar diesel engines for navy ships, Cooper-Bessemer was designated a defense plant in 1941.

Diversification began in the late 1950s with the purchase of Rotor Tools (1959). The company adopted its current name in 1965 and moved its headquarters to Houston in 1967. Cooper later acquired 20 other companies, including its "tool basket": Lufkin Rule (measuring tapes, 1967), Crescent (wrenches, 1968), and Weller (soldering tools, 1970).

The purchase of Gardner-Denver in 1979 doubled the company's size and gave it a strong position in petroleum drilling and mining equipment. The 1981 acquisition of electrical-equipment maker Crouse-Hinds (which included Belden) represented a significant diversification into a broad line of electrical construction materials. Another 1981 purchase was Kirsch, maker of drapery hardware.

The electrical power segment expanded further with the 1985 purchase of McGraw-Edison, manufacturer of consumer electrical products (Buss fuses) and of heavy transmission gear for electrical utilities. The acquisition nearly doubled Cooper's size again. Cooper added another maker of electrical equipment, RTE, in 1988. In 1989 Cooper bought Champion (spark plugs) and Cameron Iron Works (oil drilling equipment).

HOW MUCH

	9 Yr. Growth	1980	1981	1982	1983	1984	1985	1986	1987	1988	1989
Sales ($ mil)	12.1%	1,837	2,861	2,395	1,842	2,028	3,062	3,421	3,575	4,250	5,115
Net income ($ mil)	6.9%	147	241	135	71	107	135	148	174	224	268
Income as % of sales	—	8.0%	8.4%	5.6%	3.9%	5.3%	4.4%	4.3%	4.9%	5.3%	5.2%
Earnings per share ($)	2.4%	2.02	2.41	1.38	0.64	1.06	1.39	1.52	1.73	2.20	2.49
Stock price – high ($)	—	31.00	27.88	26.13	19.00	18.94	21.19	25.75	37.25	31.38	40.00
Stock price – low ($)	—	14.53	21.00	9.63	13.50	13.00	14.00	17.81	19.50	25.06	26.88
Stock price – close ($)	4.5%	26.88	25.75	14.31	17.38	14.19	21.00	20.69	27.75	27.00	40.00
P/E – high	—	15	12	19	30	18	15	17	22	14	16
P/E – low	—	7	9	7	21	12	10	12	11	11	11
Dividends per share ($)	7.1%	0.54	0.62	0.76	0.76	0.76	0.76	0.80	0.84	0.90	1.00
Book value per share ($)	6.8%	13.67	14.55	14.74	14.49	14.65	14.58	14.66	15.91	17.47	24.75

1989 Year End:
Debt ratio: 40.4%
Return on equity: 11.8%
Cash (mil): $29
Current ratio: 1.57
Long-term debt (mil): $1,829
Number of shares (mil): 109
Dividends:
1989 average yield: 2.5%
1989 payout: 40.2%
Market value (mil): $4,348

Stock Price History high/low 1980-89

NYSE symbol: CBE
Incorporated: Ohio, 1919
Fiscal year ends: December 31

WHO

Chairman, President, and CEO: Robert Cizik, age 59, $1,255,741 pay
SVP Finance: Dewain K. Cross, age 52, $419,664 pay
Auditors: Ernst & Young
Employees: 58,100

WHERE

HQ: First City Tower, Suite 4000, Houston, TX 77002
Phone: 713-739-5400
FAX: 713-739-5555

Cooper operates 185 plants in 38 countries.

	1989 Sales		1989 Operating Income	
	$ mil	% of total	$ mil	% of total
US	4,318	81	577	82
Europe	452	8	38	5
Canada	372	7	61	9
Other	215	4	28	4
Adjustments	(242)	—	(61)	—
Total	**5,115**	**100**	**643**	**100**

WHAT

	1989 Sales		1989 Operating Income	
	$ mil	% of total	$ mil	% of total
Petroleum & industrial equip.	1,083	21	107	15
Electrical products	1,585	31	281	40
Electrical power equipment	696	14	82	12
Tools & hardware	865	17	138	19
Automotive products	886	17	96	14
Adjustments	—	—	(61)	—
Total	**5,115**	**100**	**643**	**100**

Electrical Products
Belden electronic wire and cable
Buss fuses
Crouse-Hinds industrial lighting
Halo lighting

Electrical Power Equipment
McGraw-Edison transformers
RTE power system components

Tools & Hardware
Crescent wrenches
Kirsch drapery hardware
Wiss scissors and shears
Xcelite screwdrivers

Automotive Products
Anco windshield wipers
Champion spark plugs
Wagner brakes and lights

Petroleum, Industrial Equipment
Ajax engine-compressors
Gardner-Denver drilling equipment
Superior engines and compressors

RANKINGS

101st in *Fortune* 500 Industrial Cos.
175th in *Forbes* Sales 500
134th in *Business Week* 1000
547th in *Business Week* Global 1000

COMPETITION

Asea Brown Boveri
Baker Hughes
Borg-Warner
Dresser
Emerson
General Signal
Ingersoll-Rand
Robert Bosch
Siemens
Snap-on Tools
Square D
Stanley Works
Westinghouse

CORNING INC.

OVERVIEW

Corning is the leading worldwide specialty glass manufacturer, producing over 40,000 products used in all major world industries. Corning focuses glass production on 3 fields: Specialty Materials, Communications, and Consumer Products. Through its Laboratory Services group, Corning is also a leader in clinical and environmental testing and life-science research.

Corning's laboratory has been responsible for a flow of new products since its 1908 founding. Corning is involved in more than 20 joint ventures, which contributed almost 1/2 of 1989 net income.

The Houghton family, direct descendants of the founder, still manage the company and own a significant amount of its stock. Corning expects optical fibers, automotive emission-control substrates, video glass, and laboratory services to be the company's most dynamic sectors in the 1990s. Joint ventures and R&D will continue to be the cornerstone of the company's strategy.

NYSE symbol: GLW
Incorporated: New York, 1936
Fiscal year ends: Sunday nearest December 31

WHO

Chairman and CEO: James R. Houghton, age 53, $924,633 pay
VC and Principal Financial Officer: Van C. Campbell, age 51, $488,797 pay
Auditors: Price Waterhouse
Employees: 27,500

WHERE

HQ: Houghton Park, Corning, NY 14831
Phone: 607-974-9000
FAX: 607-974-8150

Corning operates 44 plants in 8 countries.

	1989 Sales		1989 Operating Income	
	$ mil	% of total	$ mil	% of total
US	2,047	84	189	93
Europe	300	12	19	9
Latin America, Asia-Pacific & Canada	92	4	(4)	(2)
Adjustments	—	—	33	—
Total	**2,439**	**100**	**237**	**100**

WHAT

	1989 Sales		1989 Operating Income	
	$ mil	% of total	$ mil	% of total
Consumer products	683	28	40	12
Communications	503	21	93	27
Specialty materials	672	27	111	32
Laboratory services	581	24	99	29
Adjustments	—	—	(106)	—
Total	**2,439**	**100**	**237**	**100**

Consumer Products
Corelle (dinnerware)
Corning Ware (cookware)
Pyrex (glassware)
Revere Ware (cookware)
Serengeti (sunglasses)
Steuben (crystal)
Visions (cookware)

Communications
Flat-panel displays
Optical fiber

Laboratory Services
Environmental testing
Pharmaceutical evaluation

Specialty Materials
Auto emission control substrates

Major Joint Venture Partners
Dow Chemical (Dow Corning)
IBM (PCO)
3M (Raycom Systems)
Mitsubishi (Cormetech)
PPG (Pittsburgh Corning)
Samsung (Samsung-Corning)
Siemens (Siecor)

WHEN

Amory Houghton started the Houghton Glass Company in Massachusetts in 1851 and moved to Corning, New York, in 1868. Renamed Corning Glass Works, by 1876 the company was already manufacturing several types of technical and pharmaceutical specialty glass and in 1880 supplied the glass for Thomas Edison's first light bulb.

Houghton's son, Amory Jr., enlisted the help of a Cornell University physicist in 1877 to develop an improved lens for railroad signal glasses. For the next 2 decades the railroads were Corning's main customers, and, by using red, yellow, and green lenses, the company contributed to the development of the current standard traffic signal color system.

In 1912 Corning improved the brakeman's lantern by using borosilicate glass (able to withstand sudden temperature changes), which was also used in 1915 to make the Pyrex brand of oven and laboratory ware.

Joint ventures have been crucial to Corning's success. The early ones included Pittsburgh Corning (Pittsburgh Plate Glass, 1937, glass blocks for construction industry), Owens-Corning (Owens-Illinois, 1938, fiberglass), and Dow Corning (Dow Chemical, 1943, silicones development).

By 1945 Corning's laboratories (established 1908) had given the company undisputed leadership in the specialty glass (*i.e.*, not flat glass or containers) market. Among the applications for Corning's glass technology are television tubes (which Corning was the first to mass produce), Pyroceram (able to go directly from the freezer to the oven), Corning Ware (as hard as steel and able to withstand up to 1,200 degrees F), and sealed-beam car headlights.

Between 1945 and 1963 sales increased at an annual rate of 10.5%. Consumer sales rose from 12% of total 1953 sales to 25% in 1963 as Corning emphasized products such as cookware. Corning expanded globally, nearly tripling foreign sales between 1966 and 1970. In the 1970s Corning pioneered the development of optical fiber and catalytic converter technology.

Recognizing maturing markets for 2 of its main products, light bulbs and television tubes, Corning worked in the 1980s to sharpen its focus in higher-growth areas. The acquisitions of MetPath (clinical testing, 1982) and Hazleton (life-science preclinical research, 1987) strengthened the company's position in laboratory services. Corning also pursued endeavors in fiber optics, biotechnology, emission control, and video displays. In 1988 Corning strengthened its consumer products line by purchasing Revere Ware (cookware).

Reflecting its new, broader orientation, Corning in 1989 dropped Glass Works from its name. Also in 1989 the company acquired Enseco (environmental laboratories) and G.H. Besselaar (clinical evaluation) in stock swaps.

HOW MUCH

	9 Yr. Growth	1980	1981	1982	1983	1984	1985	1986	1987	1988	1989
Sales ($ mil)	5.3%	1,530	1,599	1,579	1,589	1,733	1,691	1,856	2,084	2,122	2,439
Net income ($ mil)	9.5%	115	97	75	92	89	108	162	189	292	259
Income as % of sales	—	7.5%	6.1%	4.7%	5.8%	5.1%	6.4%	8.7%	9.1%	13.8%	10.6%
Earnings per share ($)	6.6%	1.57	1.33	0.88	1.10	1.06	1.27	1.85	2.05	3.25	2.79
Stock price – high ($)	—	18.94	18.81	17.00	22.56	18.56	31.44	40.75	38.50	34.94	43.38
Stock price – low ($)	—	11.38	12.50	9.81	16.25	14.88	17.06	23.31	17.38	22.38	32.00
Stock price – close ($)	12.5%	14.91	12.97	16.47	17.44	17.25	30.88	27.44	23.38	34.69	43.00
P/E – high	—	12	14	19	21	18	25	22	19	11	16
P/E – low	—	7	9	11	15	14	13	13	8	7	11
Dividends per share ($)	7.6%	0.54	0.58	0.58	0.58	0.60	0.66	0.70	0.71	0.96	1.05
Book value per share ($)	4.3%	12.46	13.21	11.99	12.25	12.60	13.82	15.20	17.05	17.56	18.16

1989 Year End:
Debt ratio: 26.7%
Return on equity: 15.6%
Cash (mil): $353
Current ratio: 1.71
Long-term debt (mil): $625
Number of shares (mil): 94
Dividends:
1989 average yield: 2.4%
1989 payout: 37.6%
Market value (mil): $4,051

Stock Price History high/low 1980-89

RANKINGS

181st in *Fortune* 500 Industrial Cos.
337th in *Forbes* Sales 500
147th in *Business Week* 1000
393rd in *Business Week* Global 1000

COMPETITION

Brown-Forman
Hanson
Owens-Illinois
Pearson
Roche Holding

COSTCO WHOLESALE CORPORATION

OVERVIEW

Costco Wholesale is the 2nd largest membership wholesale club in the US (behind Sam's, a division of Wal-Mart), with revenues of almost $3 billion in 1989, up 48% from 1988 sales of just over $2 billion. Costco's warehouse stores each averaged $57.3 million in sales in 1989.

In mid-1990 the company operated 62 stores in 9 western and southeastern states in the US and in 2 western Canadian provinces. These 100,000- to 125,000-square-foot stores contain a limited variety of low-priced, brand-name merchandise, including housewares, appliances, apparel, jewelry, office supplies and furniture, automotive supplies, and consumer electronics. New and remodeled stores have pharmacies, optical stores, and extensive fresh food departments, the latter a Costco innovation. The company also has a revolving credit plan.

Costco chooses markets where its stores can effectively achieve high turnover rates and sales volumes. The company sharply undercuts competitors' prices by ordering in large quantities, by shipping merchandise directly to stores, and by paying vendors early in exchange for favorable discounts. Small merchandise is usually sold by the case or carton or in multiple packages. Costco stores carry an average of 3,600 items of the fastest-selling products, compared to full-line discount chains, which average 40,000 to 60,000 items. Costco maintains low overhead costs in sparsely decorated, self-service warehouse stores by limiting hours, employees, and advertising.

Costco's 3 million members, paying annual fees of $25 (business members) or $30 (individual members), include small businesses, nonprofit organizations, and employees of government agencies, utilities, medical establishments, schools, financial institutions, airlines, and railroads.

WHEN

Costco Wholesale began as Cost Club, founded in Seattle by Jeffrey Brotman and James Sinegal (1983), who still run the company. The company soon incorporated as Costco Wholesale and opened the first warehouse stores in Seattle, Portland, and Spokane (1983).

During the past 5 years the company has primarily concentrated expansion in Washington, Oregon, California, and Florida. In 1984 Costco opened its first warehouse stores in Florida, Alaska, and Utah. The company went public and opened initial units in California, Nevada, British Columbia, and Alberta (1985). Costco briefly entered the Midwest with 3 stores in Minnesota and Wisconsin (opened 1986, 1987; closed 1988). Costco opened a unit in Honolulu, Hawaii, in 1988.

Costco grew steadily, with 7 stores added in fiscal 1984, followed by 8 in 1985, 7 in 1986, 17 in 1987, 4 in 1988, and 13 in 1989. The company recently closed 3 unprofitable units in western Florida (1990; opened 1984, 1987). By the 3rd quarter of fiscal 1990, Costco had opened 9 new warehouse stores, for a net gain of 6 units.

Recent sale of 3.2 million common shares (1989) garnered $95 million for expansion. With the new Boston office (opened 1989), Costco plans to enter the highly competitive Northeast, with a store opening in West Springfield, Massachusetts (late 1990) and with 3 more units in Connecticut, Massachusetts, and New York. The company plans a total of 10 to 14 additional stores in existing and new markets for fiscal 1991.

Carrefour, a large French hypermarket chain, currently owns about 20% of the company through an affiliate, Carrefour Nederland B.V., while the founders still own almost 10% of the company, worth about $100 million as of December, 1989.

HOW MUCH

	4 Yr. Growth	1980	1981	1982	1983	1984	1985	1986	1987	1988	1989
Sales ($ mil)	68.6%	—	—	—	—	—	371	762	1,401	2,030	3,000
Net income ($ mil)	—	—	—	—	—	—	(6)	3	4	12	27
Income as % of sales	—	—	—	—	—	—	(1.5%)	0.5%	0.3%	0.6%	0.9%
Earnings per share ($)	—	—	—	—	—	—	(0.51)	0.15	0.14	0.46	0.95
Stock price – high ($)	—	—	—	—	—	—	12.88	19.50	15.25	16.25	35.63
Stock price – low ($)	—	—	—	—	—	—	10.63	8.50	5.63	8.38	15.75
Stock price – close ($)	31.6%	—	—	—	—	—	11.75	13.38	8.25	15.88	35.25
P/E – high	—	—	—	—	—	—	—	130	109	35	38
P/E – low	—	—	—	—	—	—	—	57	40	18	17
Dividends per share ($)	—	—	—	—	—	—	0.00	0.00	0.00	0.00	0.00
Book value per share ($)	37.3%	—	—	—	—	—	2.20	3.41	3.65	4.32	7.82

1989 Year End:
Debt ratio: 35.5%
Return on equity: 15.7%
Cash (mil): $1
Current ratio: 1.1
Long-term debt (mil): $133
Number of shares (mil): 31
Dividends:
1989 average yield: —
1989 payout: —
Market value (mil): $1,094

Stock Price History high/low 1985-89

OTC symbol: COST
Incorporated: Washington, 1987
Fiscal year ends: Sunday nearest August 31

WHO

Chairman: Jeffrey H. Brotman, age 47, $339,217 pay
President, CEO, and COO: James D. Sinegal, age 53, $346,318 pay
EVP Operations: Richard D. DiCerchio, age 46, $208,695 pay
SVP, CFO, and Treasurer: Richard A. Galanti, age 33
Auditors: Arthur Andersen & Co.
Employees: 11,000

WHERE

HQ: 10809 120th Ave. NE, Kirkland, WA 98033
Phone: 206-828-8100
FAX: 206-828-8103

Costco operates 62 warehouse clubs with 3 million members in 9 states in the western, northwestern, and southeastern US and in 2 Canadian provinces.

State/Province	Warehouses(6/90)
Alaska	1
California	27
Florida	9
Hawaii	1
Idaho	1
Nevada	2
Oregon	5
Utah	1
Washington	9
Alberta	3
British Columbia	3
Total	**62**

WHAT

	1989 Sales	
	$ mil	% of total
Net sales	2,944	98
Membership fees	56	2
Total	**3,000**	**100**

Sales by Product Line (1989)	% of total
Food	30
Dry, fresh, and packaged foods	
Sundries	32
Snack foods; health and beauty aids; tobacco; soft drinks; cleaning supplies	
Hardlines	24
Appliances; electronics; tools; office supplies; automotive supplies	
Softlines	13
Apparel; linens; cameras; jewelry; housewares; books	
Other	1
Pharmacy; optical; tire shop	
Total	**100**

RANKINGS

34th in *Fortune* 50 Retailing Cos.
256th in *Forbes* Sales 500
474th in *Business Week* 1000

COMPETITION

Dayton Hudson
Fred Meyer
K mart
Price Co.
Wal-Mart
Other general merchandise retailers
Food retailers
Discount retailers

RLS

COX ENTERPRISES, INC.

OVERVIEW

Privately held Atlanta-based Cox Enterprises is a diversified publisher and broadcaster owned by the descendants of founder and one-time presidential candidate James M. Cox. Since 1980 the combined annual revenues of Cox Enterprises and its formerly publicly held sister company, Cox Communications, have nearly tripled. Currently Cox Newspapers accounts for over 30% of the company's revenues; Cox Cable and Cox Broadcasting each contributes about 25%.

Cox Newspapers is the 10th largest newspaper publisher in the nation, with *The Atlanta Journal* and *Constitution* ranked 13th nationally in circulation. The division publishes 18 daily newspapers and 10 weekly "shopper" publications. Trader Publications publishes 105 magazines, including *Auto Trader*.

Cox Cable is one of the 10 largest cable operators in the US, with over 24,000 miles of cable; the Cox-owned San Diego system is the 3rd largest in the country. The division owns interests in cable programmers The Discovery Channel (25%), Viewer's Choice (17%), and Movietime (11%). STOFA, a 50% joint venture, is the largest private cable operator in Denmark, and Cox owns 35 franchised Blockbuster Video stores.

Cox Broadcasting's Atlanta, Dayton, and Orlando TV stations, as well as the Charlotte radio stations, are #1 in their markets. Cox's Manheim Auctions group owns 4 of the 10 largest auto auctions in the nation. The auctions allow auto dealers and fleet operators to dispose of unwanted vehicles.

Private company
Founded: Ohio, 1898
Fiscal year ends: December 31

WHO

Chairman and CEO: James Cox Kennedy
VP and CFO: John R. Dillon
VP Human Resources: Timothy W. Hughes
Auditors: Deloitte & Touche
Employees: 25,000

WHERE

HQ: 1400 Lake Hearn Dr., Atlanta, GA 30319
Phone: 404-843-5000
FAX: 404-843-5777

Cox Enterprises operates businesses in 34 states.

WHEN

James Middleton Cox dropped out of school at 16 and worked as a teacher, reporter, and congressional secretary before buying the *Dayton Daily News* in 1898 at the age of 28. He acquired the nearby Springfield *Press-Republican* in 1905 and soon took an interest in politics. Cox served 2 terms in the US Congress (1909-1913) and 3 terms as governor of Ohio (1913-1915; 1917-1921). In 1920 Cox became the Democratic candidate for president, with Franklin D. Roosevelt as his running mate, but lost to rival Ohio publisher Warren G. Harding. Afterward Cox returned to his media interests, buying the Miami *Daily News* (1923) and forming WHIO-AM, Dayton's first radio station. In 1939 Cox bought Atlanta's WSB-AM, the first radio station in the South, which he expanded in 1948 by starting WSB-FM and WSB-TV, the South's first FM radio and TV stations. The following year Cox started WHIO-FM and WHIO-TV, the first FM radio and TV broadcasters in Dayton. The *Atlanta Constitution*, now the company's flagship paper, joined Cox's collection in 1950. When Cox died in 1957, his company owned 7 newspapers, 3 television stations, and several radio stations.

Cox Enterprises expanded its broadcasting interests with the acquisitions of WSOC-AM/FM/TV (Charlotte, 1959) and KTVU-TV (San Francisco–Oakland, 1963). The company became one of the first major broadcasting companies to enter cable TV when it purchased a small system in Lewistown, Pennsylvania (1962). In 1964 the company created publicly held Cox Broadcasting to consolidate the family's broadcasting interests, but the newspapers continued as privately held Cox Enterprises. Cox Broadcasting's cable holdings were split off as publicly held Cox Cable Communications in 1968, with 83,450 subscribers, and by 1969 the company was the 2nd largest cable operator in the US. The broadcasting arm diversified into auto auctions with the purchase of Manheim Services, the industry's largest operator (1968), and Kansas City Automobile Auction (1969).

During the 1970s Cox's many businesses flourished. Cox Broadcasting acquired TeleRep (1972), a TV industry advertising sales representation firm, and Christal (1973), which performs the same services for radio. Cox Cable had expanded into 9 states and served nearly 500,000 subscribers by 1977, when it merged back into Cox Broadcasting. The broadcasting company changed its name to Cox Communications in 1982; the increasing value of its holdings, especially its cable interests, led the family to take the company private again in 1985, combining it with Cox Enterprises. James Cox Kennedy, grandson of the founder, became chairman of the sprawling media empire in 1987.

WHAT

	Number
Auto auctions	25
Cable systems	23
Cable subscribers	1,555,213
Daily newspapers	18
Daily newspaper circulation	1,305,534
Radio & TV stations	19
Weekly newspapers	10
Weekly newspaper circulation	1,044,795

Major Cox Newpapers and Magazines
Arizona and *Florida Pennysaver* weeklies
The Atlanta Journal and *Constitution*
Austin American-Statesman
Auto Trader magazine
The Daily Sentinel (Grand Junction, CO)
Dayton Daily News
The Palm Beach Post and *Daily News* (FL)
Springfield News-Sun (OH)

Cox Broadcasting
Radio stations
KFI (AM) and KOST (FM) - Los Angeles
WCKG (FM) - Chicago
WHIO (AM) and WHKO (FM) - Dayton
WIOD (AM) and WGTR (FM) - Miami
WSB (AM and FM) - Atlanta
WSOC (AM and FM) - Charlotte
WWRM (FM) - Tampa/St. Petersburg
TeleRep sales representation firm
Television stations
KTVU - San Francisco
WFTV - Orlando
WHIO - Dayton
WKBD - Detroit
WPXI - Pittsburgh
WSB - Atlanta
WSOC - Charlotte

Other Activities
Manheim Auctions
25 auto auctions in the US and Canada
The Clipper and Stuffit direct mail services
Cox Cable
Cable systems in 18 states and holdings in Discovery Channel and other cable programmers
Cox Home Video
Franchisee of 35 Blockbuster Video locations
Southeast Paper Manufacturing
Newsprint production and recycling

RANKINGS

72nd in *Forbes* 400 US Private Cos.

COMPETITION

Advance Publications
CBS
Gannett
Hearst
News Corp.
E.W. Scripps
Tele-Communications
Time Warner
Tribune
Viacom

HOW MUCH

	9 Yr. Growth	1980	1981	1982	1983	1984	1985	1986	1987	1988	1989
Sales ($ mil)	12.6%	677	820	968	1,132	1,347	1,472	1,569	1,666	1,816	1,974
Cable subscribers (thou)	7.6%	805	1,020	1,132	1,348	1,494	1,511	1,372	1,442	1,442	1,555
Daily newspapers	1.3%	16	18	17	18	19	19	20	20	20	18
Daily circulation (thou)	1.4%	1,148	1,195	1,169	1,196	1,236	1,210	1,250	1,275	1,310	1,306

1989 Year End:
Sales (mil): $1,974
Capital expenditures:
Existing businesses (mil): $183
New businesses (mil): $48

Sales ($ mil) 1980-89

Note: Figures prior to 1985 are for the combined operations of the predecessor companies, Cox Enterprises and Cox Communications.

CPC INTERNATIONAL INC.

OVERVIEW

Beginning as a corn refinery, modern-day CPC, headquartered in Englewood Cliffs, New Jersey, generates nearly 80% of its sales from consumer products and is one of the 15 largest food processors in the US. CPC garnered 55% of its $5.1 billion 1989 revenues outside the US, a higher percentage than any other US-based food processor. Consumer food operations are divided into 4 geographic segments. Best Foods is responsible for North American operations; other divisions are located in Europe, Latin America, and Asia.

Consumer products include sauces, soups, and bouillons ($1.1 billion in 1989 revenues worldwide); mayonnaise and corn oils ($1 billion); peanut butter, margarine, jams, jellies, and cheeses ($330 million); bakery and pasta products ($610 million); and syrups, starches, desserts, seasonings, and household products (just over $1 billion).

The company's corn refining business produced worldwide sales in 1989 of just under $1.1 billion, with more than 50% derived from sales of sweeteners, including glucose, dextrose, and high fructose corn syrup. CPC has over 1,000 trademarks and 1,400 patents for its products.

NYSE symbol: CPC
Incorporated: Delaware, 1959
Fiscal year ends: December 31

WHO

Chairman and CEO: James R. Eiszner, age 62, $1,330,000 pay (deceased; no successor appointed)
VC: Richard W. Siebrasse, age 63, $576,667 pay
President: Charles R. Shoemate, age 50, $470,000 pay
VP; President, Best Foods Division: Robert J. Gillespie, age 47, $410,000 pay
VP Financial Planning: Konrad Schlatter, age 54
Auditors: KPMG Peat Marwick
Employees: 33,500

WHEN

In 1842 Thomas Kingsford developed a technique for separating starch from corn, and by 1890 the corn refining industry had emerged. Severe competition forced a group of 20 cornstarch and syrup manufacturers, known as National Starch Manufacturing, to band together. The group combined to establish production quotas and gained 70% of the cornstarch market, but their pool broke down and ruinous pricing competition resumed.

This pattern of collusion was typical of the highly unstable corn refining industry for the next decade. By 1906 price competition had forced Edward Bedford's New York Glucose to merge with Glucose Sugar Refining Company, of which National Starch was by then a part, forming Corn Products Refining Company. CPRC became the first stable corn refining company by improving refinery equipment and processes. That year CPRC controlled 64% of starch and 100% of glucose output in the US.

Between 1910 and 1916 CPRC dominated corn refining and faced antitrust action. In 1916 Judge Learned Hand forced CPRC's eventual sale of portions of its business.

In 1922 CPRC faced antitrust charges in connection with Karo syrup. CPRC guaranteed buyers that Karo's price would not decline; the charges were later dismissed. Between 1940 and 1942 the FTC filed antitrust charges against CPRC for "phantom freight" prices; CPRC, to control prices, charged for shipping from places other than actual point of origin. The elimination of phantom freight (1945) effectively retarded industry concentration; by 1954 CPRC had only a 46% share of corn-grinding capacity.

Although the company produced some branded products (Mazola, Karo, Argo, and Kingsford's), CPRC remained largely a corn refinery until 1958. That year the company merged with Best Foods, producers of Hellmann's, Best Foods, Skippy, and Rit brands, and bought C. H. Knorr (soups). During the 1960s CPRC bought 4 educational companies — the best known of these (MIND) made remedial training systems to improve workers' skills — but sold them all by 1980.

In 1969 the company was renamed CPC International to place emphasis upon international expansion. CPC bought S. B. Thomas (English muffins, 1969); C. F. Mueller (pasta, 1983); and Arnold Foods (Old London brand crackers, 1986). Since 1986 CPC has acquired 17 consumer food businesses (all foreign) and since 1987 introduced 70 to 80 new products each year. Acquisitions include Italy's leading jam and jelly producer, Santa Rosa.

WHERE

HQ: International Plaza, PO Box 8000, Englewood Cliffs, NJ 07632
Phone: 201-894-4000
FAX: 201-894-0297

Corn refineries operate in the US, Canada, and 9 countries in Latin America. Overall, CPC has 112 manufacturing plants in 47 countries.

	1989 Sales		1989 Operating Income	
	$ mil	% of total	$ mil	% of total
US	2,260	45	294	45
Europe	1,691	33	186	28
Latin America	760	15	120	18
Canada	222	4	24	4
Asia	170	3	33	5
Adjustments	—	—	(24)	—
Total	**5,103**	**100**	**633**	**100**

WHAT

	1989 Sales		1989 Operating Income	
	$ mil	% of total	$ mil	% of total
Consumer foods	4,049	79	506	77
Corn refining	1,054	21	151	23
Adjustments	—	—	(24)	—
Total	**5,103**	**100**	**633**	**100**

Brand Names

Mayonnaise
Best Foods
Goodall's
Hellmann's
Lady's Choice
Mazola

Corn Oil
Lady's Choice
Mazola

Soups, Spices
Goodall's
Knorr

Peanut Butter
Skippy

Margarines
Holiday
Royal

Baked Goods
Arnold
Old London
Thomas'

Cornstarches
Argo
Kingsford

Corn Syrups
Crown
Golden Griddle
Karo

Laundry Starches
Argo
Niagara

Pastas
Mueller's
Royal

Dyes
Rit

HOW MUCH

	9 Yr. Growth	1980	1981	1982	1983	1984	1985	1986	1987	1988	1989
Sales ($ mil)	2.4%	4,120	4,343	4,092	4,011	4,373	4,210	4,549	4,903	4,700	5,103
Net income ($ mil)	5.8%	197	218	232	136	193	142	219	355	289	328
Income as % of sales	—	4.8%	5.0%	5.7%	3.4%	4.4%	3.4%	4.8%	7.2%	6.2%	6.4%
Earnings per share ($)	8.2%	2.07	2.29	2.40	1.41	1.99	1.45	2.30	4.31	3.66	4.20
Stock price – high ($)	—	18.81	17.88	21.00	22.44	20.94	26.63	44.25	58.50	58.38	73.75
Stock price – low ($)	—	13.63	13.88	14.69	16.81	17.13	19.13	23.25	26.00	39.50	49.38
Stock price – close ($)	18.7%	15.75	17.75	20.81	19.25	20.00	25.50	39.63	40.50	51.88	73.75
P/E – high	—	9	8	9	16	11	18	19	14	16	18
P/E – low	—	7	6	6	12	9	13	10	6	11	12
Dividends per share ($)	8.4%	0.85	0.96	1.05	1.10	1.10	1.10	1.14	1.29	1.52	1.75
Book value per share ($)	1.7%	11.61	12.93	13.48	13.46	13.63	14.10	11.58	13.61	15.25	13.46

1989 Year End:
Debt ratio: 41.0%
Return on equity: 29.3%
Cash (mil): $107
Current ratio: 1.19
Long-term debt (mil): $845
Number of shares (mil): 76
Dividends:
1989 average yield: 2.4%
1989 payout: 41.7%
Market value (mil): $5,576

Stock Price History high/low 1980-89

80
70
60
50
40
30
20
10
0

RANKINGS

102nd in *Fortune* 500 Industrial Cos.
176th in *Forbes* Sales 500
122nd in *Business Week* 1000
305th in *Business Week* Global 1000

COMPETITION

Anheuser-Busch
Archer-Daniels-Midland
Beatrice
Borden
Campbell Soup
General Mills
Grand Metropolitan
H. J. Heinz
Hershey
Philip Morris
RJR Nabisco
Sara Lee
Unilever
Whitman

CRAY RESEARCH, INC.

OVERVIEW

Minneapolis-based Cray Research, the company that invented supercomputers, is the largest manufacturer of supercomputers in the world (80% of the supercomputer market). Cray's supercomputers can process in one minute what it takes a mainframe 3 hours to compute.

Cray's computers are used predominantly by scientists and engineers for modeling physical events. These computationally intensive simulations include weather forecasting, seismic analysis, and molecular modeling. While government (58% of sales) and universities (26% of sales) comprise the majority of Cray's installed base, commercial sales are on the rise. Aerospace and automobile manufacturers shorten their product development cycles by simulating their designs on a Cray.

With 18.3% of the company's revenues invested in research, Cray ranked #3 in R&D per employee of US computer companies in 1989.

List price for Cray's top-of-the-line Y-MP8/8128 is $22.9 million. In 1990 Cray introduced an entry-level Y-MP2E model priced at $2.2 million, much less expensive than its former entry-level Y model priced at $5 million.

NYSE symbol: CYR
Incorporated: Delaware, 1972
Fiscal year ends: December 31

WHO

Chairman, CEO, and President: John A. Rollwagen, age 49, $420,291 pay
EVP and CFO: John F. Carlson, age 51, $285,207 pay
VC and Counsel: Andrew Scott, age 61, $231,840 pay
Auditors: KPMG Peat Marwick
Employees: 4,708

WHERE

HQ: 608 Second Ave. South, Minneapolis, MN 55402
Phone: 612-333-5889
FAX: 612-334-6727 (Investor Relations)

The company has 2 manufacturing facilities; one software development, marketing, and administrative facility; and 29 sales and support offices in the US. It operates 19 subsidiary operations abroad.

	1989 Sales		1989 Operating Income	
	$ mil	% of total	$ mil	% of total
US	485	61	217	67
Western Europe	225	29	80	25
Other foreign	75	10	24	8
Adjustments	—	—	(156)	—
Total	**785**	**100**	**165**	**100**

WHEN

Cray Research was started in 1972 in Chippewa Falls, Wisconsin, by Seymour Cray after he left Control Data Corporation (CDC). While at CDC, Cray had developed the CDC 1604 computer in 1959 (one of the first to use transistors), the CDC 6600 in 1963 (fastest computer on the market), and the CDC 7600 in 1968. When Cray's planned 8600 was put on hold in 1972, he left CDC and set up Cray Research. Four years later (1976) Cray introduced the first supercomputer, the Cray-1, and took the company public.

The Cray-1, with its unusual design (from above, it looks like a "C"), was faster than any other mainframe (10 times faster than the CDC 7600). Cray recovered the $8.6 million investment in the Cray-1 with its first sale to the National Center for Atmospheric Research.

By 1980 Cray's annual revenues had grown to $61 million. In 1981 Seymour Cray turned over leadership of the company to John Rollwagen, freeing Cray to work on the Cray-2.

In 1982 Cray introduced the highly successful X-MP computer line, a project headed by Taiwanese computer whiz Steve Chen. The X-MP was 3 times faster than the Cray-1. The Cray-2 — 10 times faster than the Cray-1 — was introduced in 1985, and the current top-of-the-line Y-MP machine was released in 1987.

Cray Research began work on a 64-processor MP under the direction of Chen in 1986. However, in 1987, after realizing it would require double the $50 million originally budgeted and breakthroughs in 5 technologies, Rollwagen pulled the plug on the MP. Chen quit Cray to start Supercomputer Systems, which, with backing from IBM, is developing a computer targeted to be 100 times faster than existing Crays (due in 1995).

In 1989 Cray Research, realizing it could not devote the resources to 2 major development projects, spun off Cray Computer Corporation (CCC) to Cray shareholders. CCC, headed by 64-year-old Seymour Cray, will continue work on the Cray-3, now 2 years behind schedule, enabling Cray Research to focus on the C-90, a follow-on project to the Y-MP. Cray Research retained 10% interest in CCC.

Growing competition has put pressure on Cray Research to deliver a more powerful supercomputer. Cray's advantage, however, is its installed base and large software library.

In 1990, following flat revenue growth in 1989 and a restructuring process that resulted in an 800-person layoff, Cray expanded into the high-growth minisupercomputer (low-end supercomputer) market by acquiring Supertek Computers, a manufacturer of small, less expensive Cray-compatible supercomputers.

WHAT

	1989 Sales	
	$ mil	% of total
Sales (products)	575	73
Leased systems	72	9
Service fees	138	18
Total	**785**	**100**

Supercomputers
CRAY X-MP series
CRAY Y-MP8 (8-processor models)
CRAY Y-MP4 (4-processor models)
CRAY Y-MP2 (2-processor models)
CRAY-2 series

Solid State Storage Devices
SSD-3I
SSD-5I
SSD-5
SSD-6
SSD-7

Systems Software
COS
UNICOS (UNIX-based operating system)

HOW MUCH

	9 Yr. Growth	1980	1981	1982	1983	1984	1985	1986	1987	1988	1989
Sales ($ mil)	32.9%	61	102	141	170	229	380	597	687	756	785
Net income ($ mil)	26.3%	11	18	19	26	45	76	125	147	157	89
Income as % of sales	—	17.9%	17.9%	13.5%	15.4%	19.8%	19.9%	20.9%	21.4%	20.7%	11.3%
Earnings per share ($)	24.3%	0.43	0.66	0.69	0.89	1.53	2.47	3.99	4.65	4.99	3.02
Stock price – high ($)	—	24.25	24.19	22.88	28.56	29.69	70.75	99.63	135.75	88.50	65.88
Stock price – low ($)	—	6.33	14.00	10.00	18.19	19.25	24.94	57.25	47.00	52.63	30.50
Stock price – close ($)	5.4%	24.25	18.25	19.31	27.81	26.25	65.50	80.88	70.75	60.75	39.00
P/E – high	—	57	37	33	32	19	29	25	29	18	22
P/E – low	—	15	21	15	21	13	10	14	10	11	10
Dividends per share ($)	0.0%	0.00	0.00	0.00	0.00	0.00	0.00	0.00	0.00	0.00	0.00
Book value per share ($)	25.2%	2.79	3.48	4.98	5.91	7.51	10.23	14.59	19.85	23.14	21.11

1989 Year End:
Debt ratio: 19.5%
Return on equity: 13.7%
Cash (mil): $68
Current ratio: 2.11
Long-term debt (mil): $144
Number of shares (mil): 28
Dividends:
1989 average yield: 0.0%
1989 payout: 0.0%
Market value (mil): $1,098

Stock Price History high/low 1980-89

140
120
100
80
60
40
20
0

RANKINGS

391st in *Fortune* 500 Industrial Cos.
445th in *Business Week* 1000

COMPETITION

Fujitsu
Hitachi
IBM
NEC

CS HOLDING

OVERVIEW

CS Holding is the new name of the 134-year-old, Zurich-based Crédit Suisse Group. CS owns Crédit Suisse, Switzerland's 3rd largest bank after Union Bank of Switzerland and Swiss Bank Corporation, and holds interests in Bank Leu, Switzerland's 5th largest bank; CS First Boston, a leading investment banking concern; and Elektrowatt, a Swiss utility holding company. The company has paid a dividend in each year since its inception.

Although CS tries to limit its non-Swiss assets to 50% of its total, it has established a large international investment banking system in CS First Boston. Major markets are served by First Boston (New York), CSFB (London), and CS Pacific (Tokyo). CS chairman Rainer Gut hopes to create a global banking network capable of providing both commercial and investment banking services.

WHEN

Shortly after the creation of the Swiss federal government, Alfred Escher opened the doors of Crédit Suisse (CS) in Zurich in 1856. Initially, CS operated more as a venture capital company than as a lender. The bank helped start Swiss railroads and other industries while opening banks in Italy and Switzerland, including Swiss Bank Corporation. In 1867 CS suffered the only annual deficit in its history when a collapse in cotton prices following the American Civil War led to losses on cotton import financing.

CS shifted to conventional commercial banking in 1867 and sold most of its stock holdings. By 1871 CS was Switzerland's largest bank. Rapid Swiss industrialization and growth buoyed the bank's business in issuing securities. In 1895 CS helped create a hydroelectric business that was the predecessor of Swiss utility Elektrowatt. CS bought several Swiss and foreign banks prior to WWI and in 1905 opened its first branch in Basel, where dye and pharmaceutical firms were expanding.

WWI disrupted foreign operations, but Swiss neutrality minimized the war's effect on CS's domestic business. CS's foreign activity expanded rapidly in the 1920s. During the Great Depression a run on banks forced CS to sell assets at a loss and dip into its undisclosed reserves (profits from past years hidden on its balance sheet). CS helped finance rising Swiss government debt through the Depression and WWII. By 1944 debt of the Swiss government and municipalities made up 1/3 of CS's loans.

Swiss neutrality helped CS survive WWII, and the bank's international business took off as Switzerland emerged as a major banking center in the postwar period. Foreign exchange dealing and gold trading became important activities to CS. The bank purchased Valcambi (gold ingots and coins, 1966), Crédit Foncier Suisse (mortgage financing, 1976), and Alliance Credit (consumer credit, 1976). In 1977 CS announced that managers of its Chiasso branch had diverted funds to create their own holding company. CS was reported near collapse but again dug into its undisclosed reserves and took over the holding company's businesses, and soon reported that they were profitable.

Following Merrill Lynch's 1978 purchase of CS's former Euromarket partner, White Weld, the bank formed a new relationship with First Boston called Crédit Suisse First Boston (CSFB). CS owned 60% of CSFB, which owned a minority interest in First Boston. CSFB almost instantly became the largest Eurobond issuer and was quick to devise floating-rate, zero-coupon, and nondollar securities. Following management disputes and the rise of Nomura Securities (Japan) to the #1 position in the Eurobond market (1987), CS merged CSFB with troubled First Boston (1989) and took a 44.5% interest in the new company, CS First Boston. The bank created CS Holding as an umbrella organization for its operating units in 1989. In 1990 CS Holding gained control of 235-year-old Bank Leu (Switzerland).

HOW MUCH

$=SF 1.54 (Dec. 31, 1989)	9 Yr. Growth	1980	1981	1982	1983	1984	1985	1986	1987	1988	1989
Net revenue (SF mil)	—	4,881	6,453	6,622	5,486	6,360	6,347	6,365	6,894	8,594	11,640
Net income (SF mil)	—	281	276	303	352	417	507	566	550	634	783
Income as % of revenue	—	5.8%	4.3%	4.6%	6.4%	6.6%	8.0%	8.9%	8.0%	7.4%	6.7%
Earnings per share (SF)*	—	104	99	111	127	145	169	177	168	182	222
Stock price – high (SF)	—	2,426	2,617	2,236	2,236	2,308	3,581	3,910	3,840	2,930	3,020
Stock price – low (SF)	—	1,850	1,770	1,486	1,854	1,975	2,250	3,100	2,325	2,185	2,330
Stock price – close (SF)	1.0%	2,426	1,863	1,844	2,236	2,250	3,581	3,800	2,435	2,700	2,665
P/E – high	—	23	26	20	18	16	21	22	23	16	14
P/E – low	—	18	18	13	15	14	13	18	14	12	10
Dividends per share (SF)	3.7%	72.00	81.00	74.90	77.45	87.10	91.95	96.80	100.00	100.00	100.00
Book value per share (SF)	—	1,555	1,624	1,759	1,789	1,816	1,864	1,980	2,025	2,143	2,256

1989 Year End:
Debt ratio: 68.0%
Return on equity: 10.1%
Cash (mil): SF35,225
Long-term debt (mil): SF18,123
Number of shares (thou): 3,063
Dividends:
1989 average yield: 3.8%
1989 payout: 45.0%
Market value (mil): $9,860
Sales (mil): $6,203

Stock Price History high/low 1980-89

4,000
3,500
3,000
2,500
2,000
1,500
1,000
500
0

1980-87 results for Crédit Suisse only. All share data presented for bearer shares. *not fully diluted

Principal stock exchange: Zurich
Incorporated: Switzerland, 1856
Fiscal year ends: December 31

WHO

Chairman: Rainer E. Gut, age 57
President, Executive Board: Robert A. Jeker
Member of the Executive Board (Accounting): Hans Geiger
Auditors: Revisuisse Swiss Auditing Company
Employees: 17,539

WHERE

HQ: Paradeplatz 8, CH-8001 Zurich, Switzerland
Phone: 011-41-1-333-11-11
FAX: 011-41-1-332-55-55
US HQ (Crédit Suisse): 100 Wall St., New York, NY 10005
US Phone: 212-612-8000
US FAX: 212-612-8368

CS Holding and its subsidiaries have 311 offices in Switzerland and 73 offices in 30 other countries, including 8 locations in the US.

	Assets 12/31/89	
	SF mil	% of total
Switzerland	67,303	49
UK	15,662	11
US	11,490	8
Other industrialized countries	34,019	25
Financial centers not in industrialized countries	3,951	3
Other countries	5,099	4
Total	**137,524**	**100**

WHAT

	1989 Net Revenue	
	SF mil	% of total
Interest, discount income & dividends	9,290	80
Commissions	1,342	12
Foreign exchange, precious metals & securities	882	7
Other	126	1
Total	**11,640**	**100**

Major Holdings

Bank für Handel und Effekten (Switzerland, commercial banking)
Bank Hofmann Ltd. (Switzerland, investment banking)
Bank Leu (Switzerland, over 66%)
Bank Neumünster (Switzerland, commercial banking, 92.1%)
CS First Boston, Inc. (US, investment banking, 44.5%)
Elektrowatt Ltd. (Switzerland, utility, 45.3%)
Fides Holding Ltd. (Switzerland, trust company, 99.6%)
Gibraltar Trust Bank Ltd. (Gibraltar, 95%)
SKA (Deutschland) AG (West Germany, commercial banking)

RANKINGS

54th in *Fortune* World's 100 Commercial Banks
36th in *Forbes* 100 Foreign Investments in the US
245th in *Business Week* Global 1000

COMPETITION

American Express
Bank of New York
BankAmerica
Bankers Trust
Chase Manhattan
Chemical Banking
Citicorp
Dai-Ichi Kangyo
Deutsche Bank
First Chicago
Goldman Sachs
Hongkong & Shanghai Banking
Manufacturers Hanover
J.P. Morgan
Security Pacific
Other banks and investment banking companies

CSX CORPORATION

OVERVIEW

CSX Corporation provides a broad array of services, engaging in rail, intermodal (ship/truck/train), and ocean container shipping; trucking; inland barging; warehousing; and distribution. The company also operates resorts, develops real estate, and runs several communications and information processing services.

CSX operates a 19,700-mile rail system in the eastern and midwestern US and Ontario, Canada. The railroad, which provides roughly 2/3 of the company's revenues, hauls coal, chemicals, automobiles, food, forest products, metals, fertilizers, and intermodal freight.

CSX operates the nation's largest inland barge line, American Commercial Lines (which owns the WATERCOM marine phone system), as well as the largest US-flag container-shipping company, Sea-Land Service. Sea-Land serves 80 ports around the globe.

Other CSX activities include CSX Realty, CSX Technology (which provides information services to CSX and outside customers), and management of the Greenbrier and Grand Teton Lodge resorts.

WHEN

CSX Corporation was formed in 1980, when Chessie System and Seaboard Coast Line merged in an effort to reduce costs, attract new business, and improve the efficiency of their railroads.

Chessie System was a holding company for several railroads in the Northeast and Midwest. The oldest of these, the Baltimore & Ohio (B&O), was chartered in 1827 to help the port of Baltimore compete against Philadelphia and New York for freight traffic. By the late 1800s the railroad served Washington, New York, Cincinnati, Chicago, and St. Louis. During the tenure of Daniel Willard (president from 1910 to 1941), B&O modernized its tracks and equipment and gained a reputation for courteous service. The Chesapeake & Ohio (C&O) acquired B&O in 1962.

C&O originated in Virginia with the Louisa Railroad (1836). C&O gained access to Cincinnati, Washington, and Chicago, and by the mid-1900s had become one of the nation's major carriers of coal. In 1967, B&O and C&O acquired joint control of Baltimore-based Western Maryland Railway. The 3 railroads became subsidiaries of newly formed Chessie System in 1973.

Among the predecessors of Seaboard Coast Line, Seaboard Air Line Railroad (SAL) had its beginnings in the Virginia-based Portsmouth & Roanoke Rail Road of 1832. By 1875 the line was controlled (along with 2 other railroads) by John M. Robinson, who gave the SAL system its name. The railroad eventually acquired routes in Georgia, Florida, and Alabama.

Atlantic Coast Line Railroad (ACL) took shape between 1869 and 1893 as William T. Walters acquired a number of southern railroads. In 1902 ACL acquired the Plant System (several railroads in Georgia, Florida, and other southern states) and the Louisville & Nashville (a major north-south line connecting New Orleans, Nashville, St. Louis, Cincinnati, and Chicago), giving ACL the basic form it retained until 1967, when it merged with SAL to form Seaboard Coast Line (SCL). The merger enabled the railroads to eliminate their duplicate routes.

CSX inherited from Chessie System and SCL a combined rail network of over 27,000 route miles (later reduced to 19,700 miles). The company acquired a gas pipeline firm, Texas Gas Resources (1983), and that company's river barge subsidiary, American Commercial Lines (1984), as well as an ocean container-shipping company, Sea-Land Corporation (1986). In an effort to improve its market value the company sold its oil and gas properties, its communications holdings (LightNet), and most of its resort properties (Rockresorts) in 1988 and 1989.

HOW MUCH

	9 Yr. Growth	1980	1981	1982	1983	1984	1985	1986	1987	1988	1989
Sales ($ mil)	5.4%	4,841	5,432	4,909	5,787	7,934	7,320	6,345	8,043	7,592	7,745
Net income ($ mil)	4.7%	282	368	338	272	465	(118)	418	432	(38)	427
Income as % of sales	—	5.8%	6.8%	6.9%	4.7%	5.9%	(1.6%)	6.6%	5.4%	(0.5%)	5.5%
Earnings per share ($)	6.2%	2.38	2.97	2.70	2.07	3.15	(0.78)	2.73	2.78	(0.33)	4.09
Stock price – high ($)	—	16.46	20.17	19.75	27.50	26.25	31.88	37.50	41.75	32.50	38.63
Stock price – low ($)	—	6.32	13.67	12.08	15.42	18.38	22.38	25.63	22.13	24.38	29.75
Stock price – close ($)	9.5%	15.92	19.33	17.04	24.75	24.00	30.25	29.13	29.13	31.75	35.88
P/E – high	—	7	7	7	13	8	—	14	15	—	9
P/E – low	—	3	5	4	7	6	—	9	8	—	7
Dividends per share ($)	8.6%	0.61	0.90	0.95	0.99	1.04	1.13	1.16	1.18	1.29	1.28
Book value per share ($)	4.0%	23.44	25.31	26.83	31.00	32.82	30.15	31.64	31.25	30.39	33.24

1989 Year End:
Debt ratio: 44.5%
Return on equity: 12.9%
Cash (mil): $591
Current ratio: 0.73
Long-term debt (mil): $2,727
Number of shares (mil): 98
Dividends:
1989 average yield: 3.6%
1989 payout: 31.3%
Market value (mil): $3,505

Stock Price History high/low 1980-89

NYSE symbol: CSX
Incorporated: Virginia, 1980
Fiscal year ends: December 31

WHO

Chairman: Hays T. Watkins, age 64, $1,223,762 pay
President and CEO: John W. Snow, age 50, $888,812 pay
SVP Finance: James Ermer, age 47
Auditors: Ernst & Young
Employees: 53,000

WHERE

HQ: One James Center, Richmond, VA 23219
Phone: 804-782-1400
FAX: 804-782-1409

CSX Rail Transport serves 21 states in the East and Midwest, and Ontario, Canada.

WHAT

	1989 Sales		1989 Operating Income	
	$ mil	% of total	$ mil	% of total
Transportation	7,428	96	703	80
Properties	284	4	171	20
Technology	33	—	3	—
Adjustments	—	—	(8)	—
Total	**7,745**	**100**	**869**	**100**

Principal Subsidiaries
American Commercial Lines Inc. (inland barges)
CSX Realty Inc. (real estate development)
CSX Technology Inc. (electronic data interchange)
CSX Transportation Inc. (rail service)
Sea-Land Service Inc. (container shipping)
The Greenbrier Resort Management Co. (resort hotels)
Waterway Communications System Inc. (marine telephone service)

	1989 Sales	
	$ mil	% of total
Rail commodities		
Coal	1,568	20
Intermodal	590	7
Chemicals	565	7
Forest products	476	6
Automotive	355	4
Minerals	315	4
Agricultural products	284	4
Phosphates & fertilizer	267	3
Metals	237	3
Food & consumer products	198	3
Other	133	2
Container shipping	2,343	29
Barge	302	4
Nontransportation	317	4
Eliminations/other	(205)	—
Total	**7,745**	**100**

RANKINGS

5th in *Fortune* 50 Transportation Cos.
101st in *Forbes* Sales 500
190th in *Business Week* 1000
598th in *Business Week* Global 1000

COMPETITION

American President
Archer-Daniels-Midland
Consolidated Rail
Norfolk Southern
Other trucking companies

CUMMINS ENGINE COMPANY, INC.

OVERVIEW

Cummins, the world's largest diesel engine maker, designs and manufactures in-line and V-type engines of up to 2,000 horsepower. The company sells primarily to heavy-duty truck manufacturers but also to construction, mining, agricultural, and other industrial equipment manufacturers. Cummins also produces a range of engine-related parts (21% of sales) and power systems (15% of sales).

In 1989 Cummins captured over 50% of the heavy-duty engine market for the 9th straight year. All major North American truck manufacturers offer Cummins engines. The largest customer is Navistar, which accounts for 8.7% of sales.

Despite record sales in 1989, Cummins lost just over $6 million, due to a drop in heavy-truck demand and high warranty expenses in the 2nd half of the year. Having twice repelled unwelcome foreign suitors in 1989, Cummins entered a 1990 agreement to sell 27% of its stock, collectively, to Ford, Tenneco, and Japanese tractor maker Kubota for $250 million, a move that will allow the company to pay down debt and protect itself against future takeover bids.

NYSE symbol: CUM
Incorporated: Indiana, 1919
Fiscal year ends: December 31

WHO

Chairman and CEO: Henry B. Schacht, age 55, $528,254 pay
President and COO: James A. Henderson, age 55, $456,000 pay
VP and CFO: Peter B. Hamilton, age 43, $255,844 pay
VP Human Resources: Mark E. Chesnut, age 43
Auditors: Arthur Andersen & Co.
Employees: 25,100

WHEN

Chauffeur Clessie Cummins believed that Rudolph Diesel's cumbersome and smoky engine could be improved for use in transportation. Borrowing money and work space from his employer — Columbus, Indiana, banker W. G. Irwin — Cummins founded Cummins Engine in 1919.

Irwin eventually invested over $2.5 million in the business, and in the mid-1920s Cummins produced a fairly dependable mobile diesel engine. Truck manufacturers were reluctant to make the switch from gas to diesel, so Cummins advertised his engine with publicity stunts (including racing in the Indianapolis 500 and driving from New York to Los Angeles), and Irwin installed the engines in his California Purity Stores delivery truck fleet. The company earned its first profit in 1937, the year Irwin's grandnephew, J. Irwin Miller, began a 40-year term as company leader. During WWII the engine was used in trucks transporting large, heavy shipments.

Heavy postwar demand caused sales to jump from $20 million in 1946 to over $100 million by 1956. In the 1950s Cummins pioneered a line of 4-stroke diesel engines, started its first overseas plant in Scotland (1956), and purchased Atlas Crankshafts (1958). By 1967 Cummins had 50% of the diesel engine market. Two years later General Motors agreed to offer Cummins engines.

In 1970 Cummins acquired businesses not related to diesel engine production, including the K2 Ski Company (fiberglass skis) and Coot Industries (all-terrain vehicles), but sold them by 1976. In 1979 Cummins introduced a 10-liter engine to accompany its 14-liter model, long the company mainstay.

Henry Schacht, CEO since 1973, began a program to modernize company plants after touring Japanese factories. When he learned that some of his customers were testing engines from Japanese firms (*e.g.,* Komatsu and Nissan), he lowered Cummins prices 20% to 40%.

In the early 1980s Cummins introduced a line of midrange engines developed in a joint venture with Tenneco subsidiary J.I. Case. To remain competitive in manufacturing, Cummins cut costs 22%, which doubled productivity in its US and UK plants and spent $1.8 billion to update factories.

The strategy yielded mixed results. Though Cummins maintains its US market share of over 50%, profits have been erratic. Restructuring prevented the company from taking full advantage of an industry boom between 1987 and 1988. By the end of 1989, Cummins's stock price had dropped nearly 50% from its 1987 high, due to the company's combined 1988 and 1989 losses of $69 million.

WHERE

HQ: 500 Jackson St., Columbus, IN 47202
Phone: 812-377-5000
FAX: 812-377-3334

The company's principal US manufacturing facilities are located in Indiana, New York, and North Carolina. Other operations are located in Australia, Brazil, Canada, England, France, Scotland, and Spain.

	1989 Sales		1989 Operating Income	
	$ mil	% of total	$ mil	% of total
US	2,442	69	(15)	(27)
UK/Europe	763	22	49	89
All other	306	9	21	38
Total	**3,511**	**100**	**55**	**100**

WHAT

	1989 Sales	
	$ mil	% of total
Engines	2,456	64
Components	792	21
Power systems	575	15
Adjustments	(312)	—
Total	**3,511**	**100**

Products
Diesel engines
Engine components
Power systems

Principal Markets
Construction, mining, agricultural, and other industrial equipment manufacturers
Heavy-duty truck manufacturers

RANKINGS

132nd in *Fortune* 500 Industrial Cos.
368th in *Fortune* Global 500 Industrial Cos.
237th in *Forbes* Sales 500
889th in *Business Week* 1000

COMPETITION

Caterpillar
Fiat
Mitsubishi
Navistar
Volvo

HOW MUCH

	9 Yr. Growth	1980	1981	1982	1983	1984	1985	1986	1987	1988	1989
Sales ($ mil)	8.6%	1,667	1,962	1,587	1,605	2,326	2,146	2,304	2,767	3,310	3,511
Net income ($ mil)	—	(11)	100	8	5	188	50	(107)	14	(63)	(6)
Income as % of sales	—	(0.7%)	5.1%	0.5%	0.3%	8.1%	2.3%	(4.7%)	0.5%	(1.9%)	(0.2%)
Earnings per share ($)	—	*(1.31)*	11.16	0.21	0.36	19.38	5.22	(10.18)	1.14	(3.84)	0.68
Stock price – high ($)	—	36.75	58.75	49.25	81.50	88.25	88.50	78.75	94.75	68.00	72.25
Stock price – low ($)	—	25.88	30.00	26.00	47.63	61.25	58.25	51.25	40.75	43.13	48.00
Stock price – close ($)	5.9%	30.25	35.50	48.75	80.50	77.63	72.00	67.13	47.25	64.25	50.75
P/E – high	—	—	5	235	226	5	17	—	83	—	106
P/E – low	—	—	3	124	132	3	11	—	36	—	71
Dividends per share ($)	2.3%	1.80	1.85	2.00	2.00	2.05	2.20	2.20	2.20	2.20	2.20
Book value per share ($)	(3.3%)	53.84	65.31	58.18	53.38	68.62	74.29	61.89	64.99	55.03	39.78

1989 Year End:
Debt ratio: 42.1%
Return on equity: 1.4%
Cash (mil): $73
Current ratio: 1.3
Long-term debt (mil): $406
Number of shares (mil): 10
Dividends:
1989 average yield: 4.3%
1989 payout: 323.5%
Market value (mil): $519

Stock Price History high/low 1980-89

CYPRUS MINERALS COMPANY

OVERVIEW

Cyprus Minerals is a diversified mining company that is the world's largest producer of molybdenum and lithium. The company also ranks as the 2nd largest US copper producer (after Phelps Dodge), the largest US talc producer, and one of the 20 largest coal companies in the US.

Copper, molybdenum, and gold accounted for 67% of sales and 91% of company operating income in 1989. Gold production was 29% greater than in 1988.

Since being spun off by Amoco in 1985, Cyprus has broadened its mining operations and increased sales volume with more than 20 acquisitions. Increased sales and higher copper prices resulted in record profits in 1989.

In February 1990 Australian raider Robert Holmes à Court (deceased September 1990) filed with the SEC to purchase $15 million or more of Cyprus stock. The company responded by establishing a leveraged employee stock ownership plan and borrowing $150 million to buy nearly 11% of its stock, discouraging the takeover.

NYSE symbol: CYM
Incorporated: Delaware, 1985
Fiscal year ends: December 31

WHO

President and CEO: Kenneth J. Barr, age 63, $734,246 pay
EVP Operations: James C. Compton, age 64, $378,892 pay
SVP, Coal and Iron Ore: Chester B. Stone, Jr., age 54, $436,297 pay
SVP, Metals: Donald P. Bellum, age 57, $344,885 pay
SVP, Specialty Metals and Industrial Minerals: Thomas A. Williams, age 54, $321,690 pay
SVP and CFO: Gerald J. Malys, age 45
Auditors: Price Waterhouse
Employees: 8,500

WHEN

In 1912 prospector Charles Gunther persuaded Philip Wiseman and Seeley Mudd, both veteran managers of western copper mines, to back his exploration for mineral deposits, especially copper, in the countries along the Mediterranean Sea. In 1914 he found ores with as much as 5% copper (first grade) on Cyprus. Wiseman and Mudd, with offices in Los Angeles, formally founded Cyprus Mines in 1916.

The company encountered problems mining ore in Cyprus in the years that followed, including shortfalls of capital, the military and political turmoil of WWI, and the remote location. In the winter of 1919 the miners discovered "devil's mud," a slimy, corrosive material that contained gold and silver, which the company began to mine in 1932.

During the 1920s and 1930s the company continued exploring for minerals on Cyprus and eventually operated 6 mines there. In the early 1940s Cyprus Mines produced strategic minerals (copper and zinc) to help the US war effort.

In 1951 the company began diversifying, with interests in oil in Kansas, Texas, and Louisiana. Cyprus Mines entered joint ventures with Utah Construction in 1952 to mine iron ore on the Marcona Plateau in Peru and in 1954 to mine copper near Tucson, because the mines on Cyprus by then were nearing depletion. During the 1950s, 1960s, and 1970s, the company added other mining operations in the US, including lead, zinc, talc, calcium carbonate, and clay.

In 1979 Amoco Minerals (subsidiary of Amoco, an integrated petroleum company) bought Cyprus Mines. The operations of Amoco Minerals grew through additional purchases to include mining for coal and molybdenum. In 1985 Amoco spun off its unprofitable Amoco Minerals as an independent, publicly traded company, renaming it Cyprus Minerals. Amoco retained only its interest in a mining project in New Guinea.

Cyprus Minerals then went on a buying spree, purchasing coal mines in Utah (Plateau, 1985), Colorado (Yampa and Twentymile, 1985), and Wyoming (Shoshone, 1987) and copper mines in Arizona (Sierrita, 1986; Casa Grande, 1987) and New Mexico (Pinos Altos, 1987). Also in 1987 Cyprus Minerals began to mine for gold, both in Arizona (Copperstone) and in Australia (Gidgee).

Cyprus Minerals continued its rapid growth, buying Foote Mineral (lithium, 1988), Windsor Minerals (talc division of Johnson & Johnson, 1989), Sociedad Chilena (lithium, fully acquired 1989), Reserve Mining (iron ore, 1989), and Warrenton Refining (copper ingot, 1989). In early 1990 the company purchased MCR (copper rod, Chicago).

WHERE

HQ: 9100 E. Mineral Circle, Englewood, CO 80112
Phone: 303-643-5000
FAX: 303-643-5049

Cyprus has major operations in 24 states and 7 foreign countries.

Mines

Copper	**Zinc**	**Coal**
Arizona	New Mexico	Colorado
Illinois	Mexico	Kentucky
New Mexico		Pennsylvania
	Lithium	Utah
Molybdenum	Nevada	West Virginia
Arizona	Chile	Wyoming
Idaho		
Nevada	**Talc**	**Iron Ore**
	Alabama	Minnesota
Gold	California	
Arizona	Montana	
Australia	Vermont	
New Zealand	Spain	

WHAT

	1989 Sales		1989 Operating Income	
	$ mil	% of total	$ mil	% of total
Coal/iron ore	408	23	6	2
Copper/gold/ molybdenum	1,210	67	351	91
Lithium/talc	172	10	27	7
Adjustments	—	—	(51)	—
Total	**1,790**	**100**	**333**	**100**

RANKINGS

229th in *Fortune* 500 Industrial Cos.
427th in *Forbes* Sales 500
521st in *Business Week* 1000

COMPETITION

AMAX
Anglo American
ASARCO
Broken Hill
FMC
Hanson
Phelps Dodge

HOW MUCH

	4 Yr. Growth	1980	1981	1982	1983	1984	1985	1986	1987	1988	1989
Sales ($ mil)	26.2%	—	—	—	—	—	706	811	795	1,289	1,790
Net income ($ mil)	—	—	—	—	—	—	(429)	21	26	170	250
Income as % of sales	—	—	—	—	—	—	(60.8%)	2.6%	3.3%	13.2%	14.0%
Earnings per share ($)	—	—	—	—	—	—	—	0.54	0.68	3.98	5.30
Stock price – high ($)	—	—	—	—	—	—	11.75	16.58	20.00	24.00	33.00
Stock price – low ($)	—	—	—	—	—	—	7.33	9.58	9.33	13.17	21.33
Stock price – close ($)	24.4%	—	—	—	—	—	11.08	10.83	16.17	21.67	26.50
P/E – high	—	—	—	—	—	—	—	31	29	6	6
P/E – low	—	—	—	—	—	—	—	18	14	3	4
Dividends per share ($)	—	—	—	—	—	—	0.00	0.00	0.00	0.13	0.63
Book value per share ($)	10.8%	—	—	—	—	—	20.49	21.34	21.95	25.62	30.92

1989 Year End:
Debt ratio: 7.3%
Return on equity: 18.7%
Cash (mil): $44
Current ratio: 2
Long-term debt (mil): $108
Number of shares (mil): 38
Dividends:
1989 average yield: 2.4%
1989 payout: 12.0%
Market value (mil): $1,014

Stock Price History high/low 1985-89

DAI-ICHI KANGYO BANK, LTD.

OVERVIEW

Dai-Ichi Kangyo Bank (DKB) is the world's largest bank and the oldest bank in Japan. DKB is the premier source of yen-denominated financing. Business is concentrated in Japan, where the bank gathers deposits through the country's largest branch network. DKB owns 60% of New York–based CIT Group, a commercial lending company.

Reacting to recent international agreement on capital adequacy (equity-to-assets ratio) standards for banks, DKB has raised new equity capital and shifted its emphasis from size to profitability. Recent weakness in Japanese bond and equity markets has eroded DKB's substantial hidden reserves (unrealized appreciation on stock and real estate investments).

WHEN

When established in 1873, Dai-Ichi Kokuritsu (First National) Bank was the first to be organized under the Japanese National Bank Act of 1872. As such, Dai-Ichi was authorized to issue currency until the Bank of Japan took over that role in 1883. Founder Shibusawa Eiichi's beliefs in ethical business behavior and positive work attitudes have had a lasting effect on Japanese management practices. Wanting widespread ownership of the bank rather than the common *zaibatsu* (family-controlled conglomerate) affiliation, Shibusawa issued stock in Dai-Ichi. After a series of acquisitions between 1912 and 1964, Dai-Ichi merged with Nippon Kangyo Bank in 1971 to create Japan's largest bank, Dai-Ichi Kangyo.

The Japanese government had established Nippon Kangyo in 1897 as a financing institution for farmers and industry. From 1921 to 1944 Nippon Kangyo consolidated its operations with several similar organizations. The bank suffered terrible losses on its real estate–backed loan portfolio in WWII but emerged as a full-service commercial bank in 1950.

A merger agreement calling for a strict balance of power between Dai-Ichi and Kangyo executives created a bureaucratic morass and institutionalized a culture clash between the two banks. Although merger-induced inertia slowed DKB's expansion overseas, the bank's size and Japan's rapid economic expansion enabled it to prosper.

Like other Japanese banks, DKB benefited from the low cost of funds that resulted from the extraordinarily high Japanese savings rate (2 to 3 times the US rate). As government policies discouraged foreign investment and encouraged domestic savings, banks became the principal conduit of investment capital for Japan.

Although DKB still considers itself to be different from its *zaibatsu*-affiliated brethren, the bank organized the Sankin-Kai (3rd Friday group), leaders from 47 major Japanese firms, in 1978. The Sankin-Kai meets regularly, as do the leaders of former *zaibatsu* groups.

In the 1970s and 1980s DKB chose internal growth over acquisitions and called itself "the bank with heart," using pink heart emblems in its retail banking advertisements. By the late 1980s the bank had 375 Japanese branches (155 in Tokyo). Measured in assets, DKB became the world's largest privately owned bank in 1984, although the massive Japanese Post Office savings operation remained the world's biggest bank.

Japanese financial deregulation of the 1980s introduced foreign competition and facilitated the use of debt securities in place of bank loans. DKB has tried to offset lower profitability in lending to large corporations by emphasizing consumer credit and bolstering its US and middle market business with the 1989 purchase of 60% of the CIT Group from Manufacturers Hanover for $1.28 billion. New Jersey-based CIT engages in asset-based financing including leasing, factoring (purchasing receivables from companies at a discount, then collecting them), and LBO funding.

HOW MUCH

$=¥144 (Dec. 31, 1989)	9 Yr. Growth	1980	1981	1982	1983	1984	1985	1986	1987	1988	1989
Sales (¥ bil)	13.3%	1,109	1,552	1,938	1,900	1,827	2,282	2,120	2,102	2,568	3,401
Net income (¥ bil)	25.9%	25	28	36	38	57	59	63	102	152	199
Income as % of sales	—	2.3%	1.8%	1.9%	2.0%	3.1%	2.6%	3.0%	4.9%	5.9%	5.9%
Earnings per share (¥)	23.8%	11	11	14	15	22	23	25	40	59	75
Stock price – high (¥)	—	313	470	458	460	1,291	1,791	1,825	3,223	3,400	3,750
Stock price – low (¥)	—	275	304	439	453	456	1,244	1,367	1,796	2,590	3,120
Stock price – close (¥)	29.3%	313	470	458	460	1,291	1,527	1,777	2,730	3,380	3,160
P/E – high	—	28	42	33	31	59	78	73	81	58	50
P/E – low	—	25	28	31	30	21	54	55	45	44	42
Dividends per share (¥)	7.7%	3.85	3.85	4.71	5.18	5.66	6.13	6.6	6.8	7.5	7.5
Book value per share (¥)	15.9%	144	151	168	178	195	247	276	309	406	542

1989 Year End:
Assets (bil): ¥54,862
Return on equity: 15.8%
Cash (bil): ¥12,803
Long-term debt (¥ mil): —
Number of shares (mil): 2,691
Dividends:
1989 average yield: 0.2%
1989 payout: 100%
Market value (mil): $59,052
Sales (mil): $23,618

Stock Price History high/low 1980-89

4,000
3,500
3,000
2,500
2,000
1,500
1,000
500
0

Principal exchange: Tokyo
Incorporated: Japan, 1971
Fiscal year ends: March 31

WHO

Chairman: Ichiro Nakamura, age 65
President: Kuniji Miyazaki, age 59
Auditors: Century Audit Corporation
Employees: 18,411

WHERE

HQ: 1-5, Uchisaiwaicho 1-chome, Chiyoda-ku, Tokyo 100, Japan
Phone: 011-81-3-596-1111
New York branch: One World Trade Center, Suite 4911, New York, NY 10048
Phone: 212-466-5200
FAX: 212-524-0579

Dai-Ichi Kangyo has 375 branches in Japan and operates in 41 cities in 28 countries.

	1989 Sales % of total
Japan	67
Other Asia & Oceania	7
Europe	14
The Americas	12
Total	**100**

WHAT

	1989 Sales ¥ bil	% of total
Interest		
Loans & discounts	1,485	44
Securities	282	8
Deposit	663	19
Foreign exchange	426	13
Other	13	—
Fees & commissions	89	3
Gains on sales of securities	363	11
Other	80	2
Total	**3,401**	**100**

Operating Segments
Business Information
Capital Markets
Corporate Banking
International Banking
National Banking (Retail)

Major Subsidiaries
Chekiang First Bank
CIT Group (60%)
Dai-Ichi Kangyo Bank Nederland
Dai-Ichi Kangyo Bank (Schweiz)

RANKINGS

1st in *Fortune* World's 100 Commercial Banks
11th in *Business Week* Global 1000

COMPETITION

Bank of New York
BankAmerica
Bankers Trust
Chase Manhattan
Chemical Banking
Citicorp
CS Holding
Deutsche Bank
First Chicago
Ford
Hongkong & Shanghai Banking
Manufacturers Hanover
J.P. Morgan
Security Pacific
Other international banks

DAIMLER-BENZ AG

OVERVIEW

Stuttgart-based Daimler-Benz has diversified into electrical equipment and aerospace but continues to depend on its Mercedes-Benz car and truck unit for most of its sales and profit.

Measured by sales, Daimler-Benz is Germany's largest company and Europe's #2 heavy-truck maker after the new Volvo/Renault partnership. Daimler-Benz is Germany's leading aerospace company but is far smaller than European rivals British Aerospace and Aerospatiale (France). Deutsche Bank and the London-based Kuwait Investment Office own approximately 28% and 14%, respectively, of Daimler-Benz stock.

Daimler-Benz had just finished assembling a large arms business when the Berlin Wall began to fall and, with it, prospects for the defense industry. The company has entered into several partnerships in an effort to use some of its weapon-making capacity for commercial production. Daimler-Benz has begun discussions with the Mitsubishi Group (Japan) concerning ventures that would increase the access of each to the other's markets. The companies are also exploring joint development and production of vehicles, semiconductors, and aircraft.

WHEN

Daimler-Benz is the product of a merger between companies started by German automobile pioneers Gottlieb Daimler and Karl Benz. Daimler and Wilhelm Maybach set up an engine workshop near Stuttgart in 1882. In the 1880s they created the first motorcycle and sold their engines to French automakers Panhard, Levassor, and Peugeot. In 1890 they incorporated as Daimler Engine. Austro-Hungarian Emil Jellinek arranged to purchase 36 high-performance racing cars from Daimler in 1900, with the understanding that they would be named after his daughter Mercedes. The cars won a race in 1901, and Daimler registered the Mercedes mark the following year.

Benz & Companies was established in Mannheim in 1883 and by 1886 had patented a 3-wheel car. Despite crashing into a brick wall in the first public demonstration of his vehicle, Benz enjoyed quick success, and by 1899 his company was the world's largest automaker.

Ford's Model T and WWI hurt both Daimler and Benz. Sales remained sluggish, and the companies merged in 1926. Daimler-Benz recovered in the 1930s as Germany began building autobahns (highways). The company's factories turned out military vehicles and airplane engines during WWII. Most Daimler-Benz plants were destroyed by bombing near the end of the war.

In the 1950s Daimler-Benz bounced back as Germany's postwar recovery led to strong demand for cars and trucks. The company bought Auto Union (Audi) in 1958 and sold it to Volkswagen in 1966. Daimler-Benz acquisitions in the 1960s strengthened its positions in truck and engine markets.

Mercedes sales expanded worldwide in the 1970s. The high-quality luxury car appealed to the growing high end of the automobile market. The oil crisis did not affect the company severely because of the wealth of its car customers, its line of diesel-powered automobiles, and strong Arab demand for its trucks.

Fearing increased competition in the luxury car market, especially from the Japanese, vice-chairman Edzard Reuter and shareholder Deutsche Bank sought to diversify and acquire technology to make more sophisticated, "intelligent" cars. In 1985 Daimler-Benz bought 65.6% of Dornier; all of MTU; and 80% of AEG, all West German firms.

Chairman since 1987, Reuter engineered the acquisition of Messerschmitt-Bölkow-Blohm (defense, aerospace) in 1989. In 1990 he established an aircraft engine alliance with United Technologies (US).

HOW MUCH

$= DM1.69 (Dec. 31, 1989)	9 Yr. Growth	1980	1981	1982	1983	1984	1985	1986	1987	1988	1989
Sales (DM mil)	10.5%	31,054	36,661	38,905	40,005	43,505	52,409	65,498	67,475	73,495	76,392
Net income (DM mil)	15.1%	481	304	944	1,034	1,145	1,735	1,805	1,787	1,675	1,700
Income as % of sales	—	1.5%	0.8%	2.4%	2.6%	2.6%	3.3%	2.8%	2.6%	2.3%	2.2%
Earnings per share (DM)	13.0%	12	7	23	25	27	41	43	42	40	36
Stock price – high (DM)	—	188	240	290	524	517	1,041	1,256	1,220	772	831
Stock price – low (DM)	—	151	169	202	277	417	481	896	575	527	626
Stock price – close (DM)	18.8%	175	209	290	481	480	1,009	1,233	575	737	828
P/E – high	—	16	34	13	21	19	25	29	29	19	23
P/E – low	—	13	24	9	11	15	12	21	14	13	17
Dividends per share (DM)*	6.8%	6.66	7.32	7.35	8.45	8.51	8.51	11.75	12	12	12
Book value per share (DM)	11.9%	126	145	159	178	200	225	233	210	241	348

1989 Year End:
Debt ratio: 19.9%
Return on equity: 12.2%
Cash (mil): DM9,001
Long-term debt (mil): DM4,205
Number of shares (mil): 47
Dividends:
1989 average yield: 14%
1989 payout: 33.3%
Market value (mil): $22,831
Sales (mil): $45,202

Stock Price History high/low 1980-89

1,400
1,200
1,000
800
600
400
200
0

*Not including rights offerings

Principal exchange: Frankfurt
Incorporated: Germany, 1926
Fiscal year ends: December 31

WHO

Chairman, Board of Management: Edzard Reuter
Deputy Chairman, Board of Management: Dr. Werner Niefer
Board of Management – Finance and Materials: Dr. Gerhard Liener
Auditors: KPMG Deutsche Treuhand-Gesellschaft Aktiengesellschaft
Employees: 368,226

WHERE

HQ: Postfach 80 02 30, D-7000 Stuttgart 80, Germany
Phone: 011-49-7-11-1-79-22-87
FAX: 011-49-7-11-1-79-41-16
Mercedes-Benz of North America: One Mercedes Dr., Montvale, NJ 07645
Phone: 201-573-0600
FAX: 201-573-0117

Daimler-Benz has plants in Germany, Argentina, Brazil, South Africa, Spain, and the US.

	1989 Sales	
	DM mil	% of total
Germany	29,562	9
Other EC	16,912	22
Non-EC Europe	4,515	6
North America	13,032	17
Latin America	3,790	5
Other	8,581	11
Total	**76,392**	**100**

WHAT

	1989 Sales	
	DM mil	% of total
Mercedes-Benz	54,969	72
AEG	11,852	15
Deutsche Aerospace	7,489	10
Other	2,082	3
Total	**76,392**	**100**

Corporate Units & Divisions
AEG (electrical equipment and transit, 80%)
Deutsche Aerospace
- Dornier (aviation, space, defense)
- Messerschmitt-Bölkow-Blohm (aircraft, 50%)
- Motoren-und Turbinen-Union (propulsion systems)
- Telefunken Systemtechnik (defense electronics)

Mercedes-Benz
- Commercial Vehicle Division
- Passenger Cars Division

RANKINGS

13th in *Fortune* Global 500 Industrial Cos.
64th in *Forbes* 100 Foreign Investments in the US
42nd in *Business Week* Global 1000

COMPETITION

Fiat
Ford
General Dynamics
General Motors
Volkswagen
Volvo
Other auto, truck, and bus makers
Aerospace companies
Defense contractors
Electrical equipment manufacturers

DANA CORPORATION

OVERVIEW

Headquartered in Toledo, Dana's principal business ($3.7 billion in 1989 revenues) is the production of components for trucks and other vehicles, including drivetrain components, engine and chassis parts, and universal joints.

Dana's industrial segment ($1.1 billion) produces mechanical, fluid power, and electrical power transmission products. Diamond Financial Holdings ($250 million), which constitutes the remaining segment, includes an S&L and leasing, real estate, and management services.

The majority of Dana's sales (63%) are to OEMs. The remainder are to service parts businesses. Dana's largest customer is the Ford Motor Company (14.8% of 1989 sales).

Dana is modernizing manufacturing capabilities to lower production costs, due to increased competition from foreign producers. The company is continuing to reduce its dependence on cyclical OEM markets by emphasizing its global parts distribution business.

NYSE symbol: DCN
Incorporated: Virginia, 1916
Fiscal year ends: December 31

WHO

Chairman, CEO, President, and COO: Southwood J. Morcott, age 51, $747,999 pay (prior to promotion)

President, North American Operations and Haynes-Dana Inc.: John E. Doddridge, age 49

VP Finance, Treasurer, and CFO: James E. Ayers, age 57

Auditors: Price Waterhouse

Employees: 37,500

WHEN

Clarence Spicer began developing a universal joint and driveshaft for automobiles while studying at Cornell University. Leaving Cornell in 1904, he patented his design and founded Spicer Manufacturing in Plainfield, New Jersey. Spicer marketed the product himself, signing Mack Trucks in 1906 and International Harvester in 1914. Both have been continuous customers.

The company encountered financial trouble in 1913, and in 1914 New York attorney Charles Dana joined, advancing Spicer money to refinance.

Acquisitions after WWI strengthened Spicer's position in the growing truck industry: Chadwick Engine Works (U-joints), Parish Pressed Steel (vehicle frames), Brown-Lipe Gear Company (truck transmissions), and Salisbury (axles) and Sheldon (axles).

The company moved to Toledo in 1929 to be nearer the emerging Detroit automotive center. Sales increased 18.4% annually from 1930 to 1940, rising to $19 million. In 1946 the company was renamed in honor of Charles Dana, who became chairman 2 years later. In the 1950s sales topped $150 million.

In the 1960s Dana adopted a strategy of market penetration and product development, targeting the heavy truck and service industries. Dana entered a new market by purchasing 2 replacement-parts makers in 1963: Perfect Circle and Aluminum Industries. In 1966 Dana added Victor Manufacturing and Gasket. Dana also decentralized, giving divisional managers more responsibility. Charles Dana retired in 1966, after 50 years of service.

Dana continued to grow throughout the 1970s, adding the Weatherhead Company (1977, hoses, fittings, and couplings), the Wix Corporation (1979, filters), and Tyrone Hydraulics (1980, pumps and motors). By 1980 sales had exceeded $2.5 billion. In 1981 Dana purchased General Ohio S&L for $23 million.

Dana polished its production and sourcing methods during the 1980s. As a result, sales rose to $4.9 billion by 1989, while employment remained about even. Overall dependence on automotive original equipment decreased from nearly 60% of total sales to 50%. The company emerged as a leader in mobile fluid power (*e.g.*, pumps, motors, and hoses) and mechanical and electrical industrial equipment.

In 1989 Dana introduced a 9-speed, heavy-duty truck transmission (developed jointly with Navistar), the first all-new design of its type in over 25 years. A sluggish truck market during the last half of 1989 extending into 1990 caused sales to the highway vehicle segment to drop sharply, hurting Dana's earnings and forcing the company to lay off some employees.

WHERE

HQ: 4500 Dorr St., Toledo, OH 43615
Phone: 419-535-4500
FAX: 419-535-4643

Dana operates 132 manufacturing plants in North America and 78 overseas.

	1989 Sales		1989 Operating Income	
	$ mil	% of total	$ mil	% of total
US	3,835	75	251	63
Europe	570	11	37	9
Other international	702	14	110	28
Adjustments	50	—	119	—
Total	**5,157**	**100**	**517**	**100**

WHAT

	1989 Sales		1989 Operating Income	
	$ mil	% of total	$ mil	% of total
Vehicular	3,747	73	318	80
Industrial	1,110	22	70	18
Financial services	250	5	10	2
Adjustments	50	—	119	—
Total	**5,157**	**100**	**517**	**100**

Drivetrain Systems
Chelsea
Spicer

Engine Parts
Perfect Circle
Speedostat
Victor
Wix

Chassis Products
C&M
Parish
Perfect Circle
Spicer
Victor
Weatherhead

Fluid Power Systems
Boston
Chelsea
Everflex
Gresen
Hyco
Tyrone
Weatherhead

Industrial Power Transmission Products
Boston
Con-vel
Formsprag
Gerbing
Seco
Spicer
Warner Electric
Wichita

Financial Services Subsidiaries
Dana Commercial Credit
Diamond Savings and Loan
Shannon Properties

HOW MUCH

	9 Yr. Growth	1980	1981	1982	1983	1984	1985	1986	1987	1988	1989
Sales ($ mil)	8.3%	2,524	2,711	2,423	2,865	3,575	3,754	3,695	4,142	5,190	5,157
Net income ($ mil)	3.6%	96	116	52	109	191	165	86	141	162	132
Income as % of sales	—	3.8%	4.3%	2.1%	3.8%	5.4%	4.4%	2.3%	3.4%	3.1%	2.6%
Earnings per share ($)	5.9%	1.85	2.17	0.95	1.97	3.40	2.95	1.68	3.21	3.79	3.10
Stock price – high ($)	—	18.17	22.33	23.67	33.33	31.13	30.38	36.50	54.25	40.50	42.88
Stock price – low ($)	—	11.92	14.17	14.58	20.58	21.13	22.25	25.50	27.50	32.50	33.00
Stock price – close ($)	10.4%	14.25	19.67	23.17	28.00	26.63	27.25	34.88	34.13	38.88	34.63
P/E – high	—	10	10	25	17	9	10	22	17	11	14
P/E – low	—	6	7	15	10	6	8	15	9	9	11
Dividends per share ($)	4.8%	1.05	1.07	1.07	1.08	1.20	1.28	1.28	1.40	1.54	1.60
Book value per share ($)	3.4%	18.43	18.82	18.67	19.80	21.73	22.73	21.40	21.63	23.61	24.93

1989 Year End:
Debt ratio: 53.3%
Return on equity: 12.8%
Cash (mil): $71
Current ratio: —
Long-term debt (mil): $1,165
Number of shares (mil): 41
Dividends:
1989 average yield: 4.6%
1989 payout: 51.6%
Market value (mil): $1,416

Stock Price History high/low 1980-89

60
50
40
30
20
10
0

RANKINGS

99th in *Fortune* 500 Industrial Cos.
260th in *Fortune* Global 500 Industrial Cos.
172nd in *Forbes* Sales 500
409th in *Business Week* 1000

COMPETITION

Allied-Signal
Borg-Warner
Eaton
Emerson
General Electric
Reliance Electric
Robert Bosch
Rockwell International
Vehicle manufacturers

DATA GENERAL CORPORATION

OVERVIEW

Data General (DG), based in Westboro, Massachusetts, is a 22-year-old minicomputer manufacturer. The $1.3 billion company has an installed base of 275,000 computer systems.

Responding to a 4-year trend of declining earnings, DG adopted a strategy in 1988 to decrease its reliance on its proprietary ECLIPSE/MV minicomputer series by developing an open-system, industry-standard computer (the AViiON) and communications products to connect with other vendors' computers.

DG's AViiON, introduced in 1989, is a family of computers based on Motorola's 88000 RISC microprocessor that runs the widely used UNIX operating system. The entry-level $7,950 AViiON, priced the same as DG's first NOVA minicomputer (1969), is 170 times faster with 1,000 times the memory capacity. While DG will continue to support and enhance its core ECLIPSE/MV series, it is counting on the success of the AViiON and DG's communications products to spur growth. Despite these efforts, DG expects another loss year for 1990.

Foreign sales comprise 48% of DG's revenues. Service income (maintenance, software support, and training) represents 33%.

NYSE symbol: DGN
Incorporated: Delaware, 1968
Fiscal year ends: September 30

WHO

Chairman: Edson D. de Castro, age 51, $630,231 pay
President and CEO: Ronald L. Skates, age 48, $459,231 pay
VC: Herbert J. Richman, age 54, $494,539 pay
SVP: J. Thomas West, age 50, $289,654 pay
SVP: Colin Crook, age 47
CFO: Michael B. Evans, age 45
Auditors: Price Waterhouse
Employees: 12,000

WHEN

Edson de Castro and 2 other engineers left Digital Equipment Corporation (DEC) in 1968 to form Data General in Westboro, Massachusetts. Starting with $800,000, the company developed a minicomputer targeted at distributors who would add customized software and sell it to specialized markets such as manufacturers and hospitals.

Data General's first computer, the 16-bit NOVA minicomputer, quickly became a success by filling a gap in DEC's product line. The NOVA's simple design made use of the latest advances in chips and incorporated large-size printed circuit boards that reduced the computer's costs. With low overhead, an aggressive pricing strategy, and a brash marketing campaign, DG soon became a major contender in the minicomputer market. DG later began making computers ranging from microcomputers to its $600,000 ECLIPSE, all based on the NOVA architecture. In 10 years (1969-1979) DG sold over 70,000 computers. It made the *Fortune* 500 list in 1978.

By 1979, however, DG was slipping. Many of its rivals had already introduced 32-bit superminicomputers. In response DG introduced its version, called the MV8000, in 1980. The crash project to build the supermini was chronicled in Tracy Kidder's 1981 bestseller *The Soul of a New Machine*.

Between 1980 and 1984, DG's sales climbed following the introduction of new machines and the highly rated Comprehensive Electronic Office (CEO) software, an office automation product that included word processing, electronic mail, and a filing system. In 1984 gross revenues were up 40% from 1983.

Like its rivals in the minicomputer industry, however, DG's growth slowed after 1985 due to increased competition from the less expensive but powerful PCs. In response, between 1985 and the end of 1989, DG reduced its work force from 16,535 to 12,000 and closed several plants. Nevertheless DG's net income continued to drop. In 1989 the company lost $120 million.

In 1989 founder Edson de Castro stepped down as CEO and assumed the title of chairman. DG's earnings continued to decline in 1990, with 3 consecutive quarters of losses. The company announced another round of layoffs (2,000 employees, 17% of its work force) in its fiscal 4th quarter 1990. On the bright side, DG introduced 4 new AViiON family products, was awarded a $127 million contract with the US Department of the Interior for 6,000 AViiONs, and made an agreement to sell $60 million of its AViiONs to Resource Information Management Systems.

WHERE

HQ: 4400 Computer Dr., Westboro, MA 01580
Phone: 508-366-8911
FAX: 508-366-1319

The company has 27 subsidiaries and more than 300 sales and service offices in 60 countries.

	1989 Sales		1989 Operating Income	
	$ mil	% of total	$ mil	% of total
US	676	52	(109)	—
Europe	394	30	(24)	—
Far East	111	8	6	—
Other international	133	10	3	—
Adjustments	—	—	77	—
Total	**1,314**	**100**	**(47)**	**—**

WHAT

	1989 Sales	
	$ mil	% of total
Products	875	67
Services	439	33
Total	**1,314**	**100**

Computers
AViiON (workstations and multiuser systems)
DASHER (personal computers)
DATA GENERAL/One (laptops)
ECLIPSE/MV series
NOVA (16-bit computer systems)

Software
CEO (integrated office automation)
CEO Connection (communications)
CEO Object Office (PC graphics interface)
CEOwrite (word processing)

Peripheral Equipment
Communication controllers
Graphics workstations
Magnetic disc memories
Video display terminals

Operating Systems
AOS/VS
DG/UX
MV/UX

RANKINGS

290th in *Fortune* 500 Industrial Cos.

COMPETITION

Apple
Compaq
Control Data
Digital Equipment
Fujitsu
Hewlett-Packard
Hitachi
IBM
NCR
NEC
Prime
Sun Microsystems
Tandem
Unisys
Wang

HOW MUCH

	9 Yr. Growth	1980	1981	1982	1983	1984	1985	1986	1987	1988	1989
Sales ($ mil)	8.1%	654	737	806	829	1,161	1,239	1,268	1,274	1,365	1,314
Net income ($ mil)	—	55	41	20	23	80	24	6	(83)	(16)	(120)
Income as % of sales	—	8.4%	5.5%	2.5%	2.8%	6.9%	2.0%	0.5%	(6.5%)	(1.1%)	(9.1%)
Earnings per share ($)	—	2.60	1.93	0.92	0.94	3.07	0.92	0.21	(3.07)	(0.55)	(4.10)
Stock price – high ($)	—	43.88	34.19	27.31	41.38	59.75	76.00	48.50	38.75	28.13	19.50
Stock price – low ($)	—	26.38	20.25	10.13	19.19	38.00	31.00	25.00	16.00	16.75	11.75
Stock price – close ($)	(10.2%)	32.94	26.88	19.88	37.25	58.75	45.38	29.63	23.63	18.50	12.50
P/E – high	—	17	18	30	44	19	83	231	—	—	—
P/E – low	—	10	11	11	20	12	34	119	—	—	—
Dividends per share ($)	0.0%	0.00	0.00	0.00	0.00	0.00	0.00	0.00	0.00	0.00	0.00
Book value per share ($)	1.5%	15.50	18.21	19.56	20.71	24.32	25.84	25.76	21.32	21.51	17.68

1989 Year End:
Debt ratio: 11.9%
Return on equity: —
Cash (mil): $129
Current ratio: 1.6
Long-term debt (mil): $71
Number of shares (mil): 30
Dividends:
1989 average yield: 0.0%
1989 payout: 0.0%
Market value (mil): $369

Stock Price History high/low 1980-89

80
70
60
50
40
30
20
10
0

DAYTON HUDSON CORPORATION

OVERVIEW

Dayton Hudson operates in 3 areas of retailing: department stores, discount soft goods, and discount general merchandise. The high-end Dayton's, Hudson's, and Marshall Field's department stores dominate the markets in Minneapolis, Detroit, and Chicago, respectively. The company's Mervyn's discount soft-goods stores and Target general-merchandise discount stores generated 84% of Dayton Hudson's 1989 sales and income.

Dayton Hudson's 1990 acquisition of the Marshall Field's department stores marks a change in a company policy that has emphasized growth in the discount store area since the 1970s. While Dayton Hudson plans to continue expansion of its discount store chains, the addition of Marshall Field's should increase the company's higher-margin, high-end department store sales by about 60%. Dayton Hudson's board of directors is highly independent; 11 of the 13 members are from outside the corporation. Dayton Hudson has a long record of community involvement; in 1989 the corporation was awarded the America's Corporate Conscience Award by the Council on Economic Priorities.

WHEN

Dayton Hudson began as 2 great local department stores, Hudson's in Detroit and Dayton's in Minneapolis. The Panic of 1873 left Joseph Hudson bankrupt. He paid his debts at 60 cents on the dollar and worked for others until 1881, when he had saved enough to open a men's clothing store in Detroit. Among Hudson's innovations were merchandise return privileges and price marking in place of bargaining. By 1891 Hudson's was the largest retailer of men's clothing in America. Hudson repaid his creditors from 1873 in full with compound interest.

In 1902 former banker George Dayton established a dry-goods store in Minneapolis on the spot where he found the highest foot traffic. Like Hudson, Dayton offered return privileges as well as liberal credit. His store grew to a full-line department store 12 stories tall.

When Joseph Hudson died in 1912, his 4 nephews took over and expanded the business. In 1928 Hudson's built a new building in downtown Detroit that was to become the 2nd largest retail store building in the US, eventually growing to 25 stories with 49 acres of floor space.

After WWII the managers of both companies realized that the future lay in the suburbs. In 1954 Hudson's built Northland in Detroit, the largest US shopping center at the time. In 1956 Dayton's built the world's first fully enclosed shopping mall, Southdale, in Minneapolis.

In 1962 Dayton's management opened in St. Paul the first of more than 400 Target upscale discount stores. Dayton's followed Target with B. Dalton Booksellers, which grew to be one of the nation's 2 largest bookstore chains. In 1966 Dayton's went public; Hudson's was still family owned. In 1969 Dayton's bought Hudson's for stock to form Dayton Hudson.

During the 1970s and 1980s Dayton Hudson sold off its regional shopping centers (9 in 1978) and less profitable stores and concentrated on expanding its discount store chains. In 1978 the company acquired Mervyn's, a California-based chain of discount soft goods stores. Dayton Hudson sold its John A. Brown (Oklahoma) and Diamond's (Arizona) stores to Dillard in 1984. In 1986 the company shrank by 731 stores when it sold the B. Dalton chain to the owners of New York's Barnes and Noble. By 1988 over 75% of Dayton Hudson's profits came from Target and Mervyn's. In 1989 the company opened 8 new Mervyn's stores and 58 new Targets. In 1990 Dayton Hudson bought Chicago's Marshall Field's department store chain from B.A.T for $1.04 billion, adding 24 high-end department stores and making it the dominant Midwest department store operator.

HOW MUCH

	9 Yr. Growth	1980	1981	1982	1983	1984	1985	1986	1987	1988	1989
Sales ($ mil)	14.5%	4,034	4,943	5,661	6,963	8,009	8,793	9,259	10,677	12,204	13,644
Net income ($ mil)	12.8%	138	160	198	243	259	284	255	228	287	410
Income as % of sales	—	3.4%	3.2%	3.5%	3.5%	3.2%	3.2%	2.8%	2.1%	2.4%	3.0%
Earnings per share ($)	15.6%	1.45	1.67	2.06	2.50	2.67	2.91	2.61	2.40	3.44	5.35
Stock price – high ($)	—	13.56	15.69	32.13	40.63	37.25	48.75	58.50	63.00	45.50	67.00
Stock price – low ($)	—	9.13	10.88	13.19	25.00	26.13	29.38	40.00	21.50	28.25	38.75
Stock price – close ($)	21.6%	10.94	15.00	27.56	31.13	31.50	45.88	42.50	27.63	39.63	63.63
P/E – high	—	9	9	16	16	14	17	22	26	13	13
P/E – low	—	6	7	6	10	10	10	15	9	8	7
Dividends per share ($)	10.3%	0.46	0.51	0.56	0.61	0.67	0.76	0.84	0.92	1.02	1.12
Book value per share ($)	9.2%	11.16	12.42	13.98	15.91	17.90	20.04	22.38	23.15	23.97	24.73

1989 Year End:
Debt ratio: 58.9%
Return on equity: 22.0%
Cash (mil): $103
Current ratio: 1.42
Long-term debt (mil): $2,510
Number of shares (mil): 71
Dividends:
1989 average yield: 1.8%
1989 payout: 20.9%
Market value (mil): $4,509

Stock Price History high/low 1980-89

0 10 20 30 40 50 60 70

NYSE symbol: DH
Incorporated: Minnesota, 1902
Fiscal year ends: Saturday nearest January 31st

WHO

Chairman and CEO: Kenneth A. Macke, age 51, $1,446,533 pay
President: Stephen E. Watson, age 45, $708,595 pay
Chairman and CEO, Target: Robert J. Ulrich, age 46, $806,784
Chairman and CEO, Department Stores: Marvin W. Goldstein, age 45
Chairman and CEO, Mervyn's: Walter T. Rossi, age 47, $649,420 pay
SVP and CFO: Willard C. Shull III, age 49
Auditors: Ernst & Young
Employees: 135,000

WHERE

HQ: 777 Nicollet Mall, Minneapolis, MN 55402
Phone: 612-370-6948
FAX: 612-370-5502

Dayton Hudson operates 689 stores in the US.

Major Markets	No. of Targets	No. of Mervyn's
Atlanta	13	6
Dallas/Ft. Worth	15	12
Denver	12	—
Detroit	—	6
Houston	15	9
Los Angeles	41	22
Minneapolis/St. Paul	19	—
Phoenix	—	7
San Diego	12	—
San Francisco	13	27

Department Stores	Locations	No. of Stores
Dayton's	Minnesota	12
	North Dakota	3
	Other	2
Hudson's	Michigan	17
	Other	3
Marshall Field's	Illinois	15
	Texas	4
	Wisconsin	4
	Other	1

WHAT

	1989 Sales		1989 Operating Income	
	$ mil	% of total	$ mil	% of total
Target	7,519	56	449	46
Mervyn's	3,858	28	358	36
Department stores	1,801	13	179	18
Other	466	3	—	—
Adjustments	—	—	(41)	—
Total	**13,644**	**100**	**945**	**100**

RANKINGS

8th in *Fortune* 50 Retailing Cos.
42nd in *Forbes* Sales 500
130th in *Business Week* 1000
345th in *Business Week* Global 1000

COMPETITION

Ames
Campeau
Carter Hawley Hale
Costco
Dillard
K mart
R. H. Macy
May Department Stores
Mercantile Stores
Montgomery Ward
J. C. Penney
Price Co.
Sears
Wal-Mart

DEERE & COMPANY

OVERVIEW

Deere is the largest manufacturer of farm equipment in the world. Deere is also a leading manufacturer of industrial equipment, primarily for the construction and forestry industries, and lawn care equipment for the consumer. Deere finances purchases of other manufacturers' equipment as well as Deere products; finance and insurance contributed 24% of 1989 operating income.

The company counts its independent dealer network, numbering 3,340 in North America, as one of its greatest assets. Deere takes pride in its history and tradition, and claims to be guided by its founder's standards of product quality, superior value and service, honesty, and individual employee contribution.

Deere looks for increased worldwide demand for its products. The company expects that a strengthening North American agricultural economy and emerging markets in Europe will boost earnings and sales. Deere plans to continue expansion through joint ventures and carefully chosen acquisitions.

NYSE symbol: DE
Incorporated: Delaware, 1958
Fiscal year ends: October 31

WHO

Chairman: Robert A. Hanson, age 65, $905,659 pay
President and CEO: Hans W. Becherer, age 54, $557,943 pay
SVP Accounting-Control: Joseph W. England, age 49, $392,849 pay
Auditors: Deloitte & Touche
Employees: 38,950

WHEN

Vermont-born John Deere moved westward to Grand Detour, Illinois, in 1836 and set up a blacksmith shop. Deere and other pioneers had trouble with the black midwestern soil sticking to the iron plows designed for sandy eastern soils, and in 1837 Deere used a circular steel saw blade to fashion a self-scouring plow. Deere sold only 3 in 1838 but was making 25 a week by 1842.

Deere moved to Moline, Illinois, in 1847. His son Charles joined the firm in 1853, beginning a tradition of family management. All 5 presidents prior to 1982 were related by blood or marriage. Charles Deere set up a system of distribution to independent dealerships (today numbering over 3,000) and expanded the product line to include wagons, buggies, and corn planters.

Under Deere's son-in-law William Butterworth (1907-1928), the company bought other agricultural equipment manufacturers and developed harvesting equipment and tractors with internal combustion engines. Butterworth's nephew Charles Wiman, who became president in 1928, extended credit to farmers throughout the Great Depression, a policy that won long-term customer loyalty. In 1931 Deere opened its first foreign plant in Canada.

William Hewitt, Wiman's son-in-law, became CEO in 1955. In 1958 Deere passed International Harvester to become the largest US producer of agricultural equipment, and by 1963 it had become the largest in the world. Operations abroad expanded to include Mexico, Argentina, France, and Spain; today 20% of revenues come from sales in 110 countries and 7 foreign plants.

Deere used joint ventures (Yanmar, small tractors, 1977; Hitachi, excavators, 1983) and internal research to diversify in the 1970s and 1980s.

Despite an industry-wide sales slump culminating in losses totaling $328 million in 1986 and 1987, Deere was the only major agricultural equipment maker to neither change ownership nor close factories during the 1980s. Deere cut its work force 44% and improved efficiency, resulting in a manufacturing break-even point at 35% of capacity, down from 70%.

Robert Hanson became the first nonfamily CEO in 1982. He poured $2 billion into R&D during the 1980s, and in 1989 Deere introduced its largest new product offering, including the 9000 series of combines, which had taken 15 years to develop. Deere acquired Funk Manufacturing, a power-train components manufacturer, for $87 million in 1989. Deere credits its record 1989 income of $380 million to higher worldwide sales volume for its farm and industrial equipment and increased income from the financial services sector.

WHERE

HQ: John Deere Rd., Moline, IL 61265
Phone: 309-765-8000
FAX: 309-765-5772

The company sells its products worldwide. Deere operates 14 factories in the US and Canada and additional plants in West Germany, Spain, Argentina, Australia, France, South Africa, and Mexico.

	1989 Sales		1989 Operating Income	
	$ mil	% of total	$ mil	% of total
US & Canada	5,692	80	622	85
Overseas	1,421	20	111	15
Adjustments	14	—	120	—
Total	**7,127**	**100**	**853**	**100**

WHAT

	1989 Sales		1989 Operating Income	
	$ mil	% of total	$ mil	% of total
Farm equip.	4,924	70	454	62
Industrial equip.	1,310	18	103	14
Credit	460	6	116	16
Insurance & health care	419	6	60	8
Adjustments	14	—	120	—
Total	**7,127**	**100**	**853**	**100**

Agricultural Equipment
Balers
Combines
Planters
Tillage tools
Tractors

Lawn Care Equipment
Riding mowers
Small tractors
Walk-behind mowers

Industrial Equipment
Crawler dozers
Elevating scrapers
Excavators
Loaders
Log skidders
Motor graders
Powertrain components

Financial Services
Customer credit
Property and life insurance

Health Care Services
Heritage National Healthplan Services (HMO)

HOW MUCH

	9 Yr. Growth	1980	1981	1982	1983	1984	1985	1986	1987	1988	1989
Sales ($ mil)	3.0%	5,470	5,447	4,608	3,968	4,399	4,061	3,516	4,135	5,365	7,127
Net income ($ mil)	5.8%	228	251	53	23	105	31	(229)	(99)	287	380
Income as % of sales	—	4.2%	4.6%	1.1%	0.6%	2.4%	0.8%	(6.5%)	(2.4%)	5.3%	5.3%
Earnings per share ($)	3.9%	3.59	3.74	0.78	0.34	1.55	0.45	(3.38)	(1.46)	3.90	5.06
Stock price – high ($)	—	49.75	48.00	36.88	42.38	40.38	33.13	35.13	43.00	50.50	64.25
Stock price – low ($)	—	28.50	32.13	22.00	28.88	24.63	24.25	21.50	22.50	33.38	44.00
Stock price – close ($)	2.8%	48.00	35.50	29.50	38.50	29.75	28.75	22.88	34.75	48.00	61.50
P/E – high	—	14	13	47	125	26	74	—	—	13	13
P/E – low	—	8	9	28	85	16	54	—	—	9	9
Dividends per share ($)	(3.8%)	1.85	1.95	2.00	1.00	1.00	1.00	0.75	0.25	0.65	1.30
Book value per share ($)	0.8%	34.25	36.29	35.29	33.60	33.78	33.29	29.46	28.23	32.92	36.76

1989 Year End:
Debt ratio: 37.9%
Return on equity: 14.5%
Cash (mil): $929
Current ratio: —
Long-term debt (mil): $1,694
Number of shares (mil): 76
Dividends:
1989 average yield: 2.1%
1989 payout: 25.7%
Market value (mil): $4,651

Stock Price History high/low 1980-89

RANKINGS

66th in *Fortune* 500 Industrial Cos.
180th in *Fortune* Global 500 Industrial Cos.
41st in *Fortune* 50 Exporters
109th in *Forbes* Sales 500
106th in *Business Week* 1000
325th in *Business Week* Global 1000

COMPETITION

Black & Decker
Caterpillar
Dresser
Fiat
Ford
Hitachi
Honda
Hyundai
Ingersoll-Rand
Mitsubishi
Tenneco
Volvo

DELTA AIR LINES, INC.

OVERVIEW

With about 2,380 daily departures, Delta flies to 175 cities in 44 states, the District of Columbia, Puerto Rico, and 12 countries abroad. Every 36 seconds a Delta jet takes to the sky. Delta is the 3rd largest airline in the world based on passenger miles (after AMR and UAL)

Although originally a domestic airline, in recent years Delta has increased its international presence, adding flights to Hamburg and Taipei in 1989 and planning service to Amsterdam in mid-1990. The Delta Connection, independent regional airlines, gives more passengers access to Delta's domestic network through low fares and coordinated schedules.

In 1989 Delta, Swissair, and Singapore Airlines each bought about 5% of the others' common stock. The 3 airlines now have coordinated route schedules and offer joint fares.

Delta is the official airline of Walt Disney World (since 1987) and built the Dreamflight attraction that recently opened at the Orlando, Florida, theme park.

Only 13% of Delta's employees are represented by unions, and the airline has achieved recognition for its employee benefits plan.

WHEN

Delta might not exist today if in the 1920s the boll weevil had not ravaged southern cotton fields. The company started in Macon, Georgia, in 1924 as Huff-Daland Dusters, the world's first crop-dusting service, and moved to Monroe, Louisiana, in 1925. Field manager C. E. Woolman and 2 partners bought the company in 1928, forming Delta Air Service. The name *Delta,* alluding to the Mississippi Delta region served by the airline, was suggested by Catherine Fitzgerald, a secretary who later became Delta's treasurer.

In 1929 Delta pioneered a passenger route from Dallas to Jackson, Mississippi, operating without benefit of a government mail subsidy until 1934, when the US Postal Service awarded Delta a mail contract from Fort Worth to Charleston, South Carolina, via Atlanta.

The company moved to Atlanta in 1941, becoming Delta Air Lines in 1945, with Woolman as president. Woolman ran the company until his death in 1966.

Delta added flights to Cincinnati and New Orleans in 1943 and from Chicago to Miami in 1945. Its 1952 purchase of Chicago and Southern Airlines added a direct route from Chicago to New Orleans, making Delta the 5th largest US airline, with service to cities in the South, Midwest, Texas, and the Caribbean.

Recognized today for its in-flight hospitality, Delta introduced Royal Service in 1958, featuring complimentary champagne, a selection of mealtime entrees, reserved seating, and fast baggage handling at no extra charge. Delta offered its first transcontinental flight in 1961. In 1972 the company bought Northeast Airlines, thereby expanding service to New England and Canada, and then crossed the Atlantic in 1978 with service to London.

In 1982 Delta's employees pledged $30 million to buy a Boeing 767 jet. Christened *The Spirit of Delta,* this aircraft was a gesture of appreciation to the company from its employees. With a "cradle-to-grave" company-paid benefits plan, Delta is considered one of the best companies to work for in the US.

In 1983, however, Delta succumbed to the ailing US economy by offering too many discount flights with too few passengers and posted an annual loss of $87 million, its first in 36 years. Earnings rebounded to $259 million in 1985, and in 1986 Delta bought Los Angeles–based Western Air Lines.

Delta established service to the Far East in 1987, and by 1989 international routes provided 11% of the company's passenger revenues. In 1990 Delta, TWA, and Northwest formed a jointly owned computer reservation service called Worldspan.

HOW MUCH

	9 Yr. Growth	1980	1981	1982	1983	1984	1985	1986	1987	1988	1989
Sales ($ mil)	11.8%	2,957	3,533	3,618	3,616	4,264	4,684	4,460	5,318	6,915	8,089
Net income ($ mil)	19.4%	93	146	21	(87)	176	259	47	264	307	461
Income as % of sales	—	3.2%	4.1%	0.6%	(2.4%)	4.1%	5.5%	1.1%	5.0%	4.4%	5.7%
Earnings per share ($)	16.6%	2.35	3.69	0.52	(2.18)	4.42	6.50	1.18	5.90	6.27	9.34
Stock price – high ($)	—	29.88	41.38	47.00	51.00	45.88	52.75	51.88	67.13	55.13	85.75
Stock price – low ($)	—	15.56	23.69	22.63	29.00	27.00	36.13	37.75	32.00	36.00	48.75
Stock price – close ($)	9.8%	29.50	24.50	44.25	39.75	43.63	39.00	48.13	37.13	50.13	68.25
P/E – high	—	13	11	90	—	10	8	44	11	9	9
P/E – low	—	7	6	44	—	6	6	32	5	6	5
Dividends per share ($)	8.0%	0.60	0.70	0.95	1.00	0.60	0.70	1.00	1.00	1.20	1.20
Book value per share ($)	9.7%	23.19	26.17	25.75	22.56	26.38	32.21	32.45	39.84	44.99	53.17

1989 Year End:
Debt ratio: 21.2%
Return on equity: 19.0%
Cash (mil): $530
Current ratio: 0.84
Long-term debt (mil): $703
Number of shares (mil): 49
Dividends:
1989 average yield: 1.8%
1989 payout: 12.8%
Market value (mil): $3,362

Stock Price History high/low 1980-89

NYSE symbol: DAL
Incorporated: Delaware, 1967
Fiscal year ends: June 30

WHO

Chairman, President, and CEO: Ronald W. Allen, age 47, $672,352 pay
SVP Legal and Corporate Affairs and Secretary: James W. Callison, age 61, $302,623 pay
SVP Finance and CFO: Thomas J. Roeck, Jr., age 45
Auditors: Arthur Andersen & Co.
Employees: 58,784

WHERE

HQ: Hartsfield Atlanta International Airport, Atlanta, GA 30320
Phone: 404-765-2600
FAX: 404-765-2233

Delta serves 175 cities in the US, Puerto Rico, and 12 foreign countries.

Hub Locations

Atlanta	Los Angeles
Boston	Orlando
Cincinnati	Portland, OR
Dallas/Fort Worth	Salt Lake City

WHAT

	1989 Sales	
	$ mil	% of total
Passenger	7,579	94
Freight & express	274	3
Mail	120	2
Other	116	1
Total	**8,089**	**100**

Delta Air Lines, Inc.

The Delta Connection (commuters)
Atlantic Southeast Airlines
Business Express
COMAIR
SkyWest Airlines

Worldspan (reservation system, 40%)

Flight Equipment

Delta Air Lines	Owned	Leased	Total
Boeing 727	107	23	130
Boeing 737	1	73	74
Boeing 757	27	23	50
Boeing 767	15	15	30
DC-8	—	2	2
DC-9	31	5	36
L-1011	40	—	40
MD-88	15	25	40
Total	**236**	**166**	**402**

RANKINGS

4th in *Fortune* 50 Transportation Cos.
94th in *Forbes* Sales 500
175th in *Business Week* 1000
535th in *Business Week* Global 1000

COMPETITION

Alaska Air	NWA
America West	Pan Am
AMR	Southwest
Continental	TWA
HAL	UAL
KLM	USAir
Midway	

DELUXE CORPORATION

OVERVIEW

Deluxe Corporation is the nation's largest supplier of checks, deposit tickets, and other magnetic ink–encoded transaction forms, with over 50% of the market. Though primarily a check-printing company, Deluxe also provides electronic funds transfer software and processing services, ATM card services, new-account verification services, and sales development services to financial institutions.

The company, headquartered in St. Paul, Minnesota, has diversified in recent years to include 5 wholly owned subsidiaries: Chex Systems, the nation's largest new-account verification service; Colwell Systems, a supplier of business forms to medical institutions; Deluxe Sales Development Systems, a bank marketing consultant; Deluxe Data Systems, a supplier of software and processing services for ATMs and point-of-sale terminals; and Current, the nation's largest direct mail distributor of greeting cards and other products.

Deluxe Corporation had its 51st consecutive year of sales growth in 1989, with sales of $1.3 billion. An anticipated decrease in check printing caused by the growth in electronic banking has forced the company to develop a wider product base. The company has also begun to do business in Western Europe.

WHEN

The 75-year history of Deluxe Corporation is characterized by challenge, determination, opportunity, and pioneering. From the company's beginnings in 1915, newspaper-publisher-turned-chicken-farmer William R. Hotchkiss was determined to produce one product better, faster, and more economically than anyone else.

From his office in St. Paul, Minnesota, Hotchkiss set out to provide the banks of the Federal Reserve Ninth District with business checks, offering 48-hour delivery. Sales reached $4,173 at the end of 1916, tripled the next year, rose to $18,961 in 1918, and increased 106% to $39,163 in 1919. Deluxe became even more prosperous in the 1920s when Hotchkiss introduced the most successful product in Deluxe's history, the Long Handy, a small pocket check.

Because Deluxe Check Printing was a private company, it avoided some effects of the 1929 stock market crash, but the company suffered along with other businesses during the Great Depression. Although Deluxe cut employee hours and pay during this period, not a single employee lost his job.

George McSweeney, sales manager, became a driving force for the company. He created the Personalized Check Program in 1939. Then, after Hotchkiss relinquished his title as president in September 1941, McSweeney was elected president. During WWII he persuaded Washington to release its grip on Deluxe's paper supply and stabilized the company by printing ration forms for banks.

In the 1950s Deluxe entered the new era of automation as one of the first to implement the government's magnetic ink character recognition program. Because of its leadership, by 1960 Deluxe was selling its printing services to 99% of the nation's commercial banks.

Deluxe went public in 1965, introduced its new Fashion Chec covers that year, and brought out its Distinctive line of checks, featuring American scenic designs, in 1969. In 1971 sales surpassed $110 million; by 1979 the figure had risen to $366 million. Sales increased from $428 million in 1980 to $1.3 billion in 1989. Deluxe diversified by acquiring Chex Systems (new-account verification service) in 1984, Colwell Systems (business forms for medical markets) and John A. Pratt and Associates (renamed Deluxe Sales Development) in 1985, A. O. Smith Data Systems (now Deluxe Data Systems) in 1986, and Current (greeting cards and specialty products) in 1987. In 1988, the company adopted its present name.

HOW MUCH

	9 Yr. Growth	1980	1981	1982	1983	1984	1985	1986	1987	1988	1989
Sales ($ mil)	13.3%	428	504	550	620	683	764	867	948	1,196	1,316
Net income ($ mil)	14.7%	44	53	65	77	88	104	121	149	143	153
Income as % of sales	—	10.4%	10.6%	11.8%	12.4%	12.9%	13.6%	14.0%	15.7%	12.0%	11.6%
Earnings per share ($)	15.5%	0.49	0.58	0.71	0.84	1.01	1.22	1.42	1.74	1.68	1.79
Stock price – high ($)	—	6.88	7.88	10.13	11.94	14.50	24.81	38.00	42.25	28.38	35.75
Stock price – low ($)	—	4.09	6.00	4.63	8.69	8.88	13.63	21.56	20.00	21.00	24.00
Stock price – close ($)	20.0%	6.69	7.03	10.06	9.97	14.25	23.38	35.25	24.38	25.00	34.38
P/E – high	—	14	14	14	14	14	20	27	24	17	20
P/E – low	—	8	10	7	10	9	11	15	12	13	13
Dividends per share ($)	20.2%	0.19	0.22	0.27	0.31	0.39	0.49	0.58	0.76	0.86	0.98
Book value per share ($)	15.6%	2.01	2.38	2.81	3.18	3.48	4.14	4.85	5.77	6.65	7.40

1989 Year End:
Debt ratio: 1.6%
Return on equity: 25.5%
Cash (mil): $45
Current ratio: 1.57
Long-term debt (mil): $10
Number of shares (mil): 85
Dividends:
1989 average yield: 2.9%
1989 payout: 54.7%
Market value (mil): $2,929

NYSE Symbol: DLX
Incorporated: Minnesota, 1920
Fiscal year ends: December 31

WHO

Chairman: Eugene R. Olson, age 63
President and CEO: Harold V. Haverty, age 59, $674,001 pay
EVP: Jerry K. Twogood, age 49, $437,327 pay
SVP and CFO: Charles M. Osborne, $267,302 pay
Auditors: Deloitte & Touche
Employees: 17,000

WHERE

HQ: 1080 W. County Rd. F, St. Paul, MN 55126
Phone: 612-483-7111
FAX: 612-483-7821

Deluxe Corporation has 79 facilities located in 34 states. Deluxe also does business in Canada, the UK, and Western Europe.

WHAT

	1989 Sales		1989 Operating Income	
	$ mil	% of total	$ mil	% of total
Consumer specialty products	188	14	14	6
Payment & business systems	1,128	86	230	94
Total	**1,316**	**100**	**244**	**100**

Deluxe Check Printers
Checks
Deposit tickets
Transaction forms

Business Systems Division
Short-run business forms

Subsidiaries

Chex Systems, Inc.
New account verification

Colwell Systems, Inc.
Medical Forms

Current, Inc.
Gift wrap
Greeting cards
Stationery

Deluxe Data Systems, Inc.
ATM software
Electronic funds transfer software processing
Point-of-sale (POS) terminals

Deluxe Sales Development Systems, Inc.
Sales, marketing, and training services for banks

RANKINGS

293rd in *Fortune* 500 Industrial Cos.
247th in *Business Week* 1000

COMPETITION

American Greetings
Hallmark
NCR
United Nations

DEMOCRATIC PARTY

OVERVIEW

One of the oldest surviving political organizations in existence, the Democratic party is the majority party in America. Known as an "everyone party," the Democrats' support base is more diverse than that of the Republican Party; traditionally, urban dwellers, blacks, labor, immigrants, and southern whites have constituted the core of the party. The party's donkey symbol traces its origin to the Jacksonian era.

Although the party strengthened its lead in Congress following the 1988 election (it now holds 54 Senate and 258 House seats), it has lost 7 of the last 10 presidential elections and is losing the allegiance of many of its previous supporters.

Democratic National Committee (DNC) chairman Ronald Brown has made an effort to modernize the operation of the party, decrease the fighting within its ranks, and increase fundraising, which has suffered greatly due to the popularity of the Reagan and Bush administrations. In the first 15 months of the 1989-1990 election cycle, the Democrats raised only $24 million, while the Republicans raised $113 million.

WHEN

During the 1790s Antifederalists supporting popular government united their support behind Thomas Jefferson and took the name Republicans, creating a 2-party system: the Federalists and the Jeffersonian Republicans. In 1800 Jefferson narrowly won the presidential election over John Adams.

During the early 1800s the party broke into numerous factions and virtually collapsed. In the election of 1828, 3 major factions came together and carried Andrew Jackson into the White House. The Jacksonians reaffirmed the ideals of the Jeffersonians and, at the convention of 1840, adopted the name Democratic party.

Following Jackson's retirement in 1837, the Democrats dominated presidential contests for the next 2 decades with the elections of Martin Van Buren (1836), James Polk (1844), Franklin Pierce (1852), and James Buchanan (1856). During this time the party began to divide over the issues of slavery and westward expansion. The growing schism proved disastrous at the Charleston convention of 1860, when the northern and southern Democrats nominated separate candidates. The split allowed the newly formed Republicans to elect Lincoln, who would lead the nation during the Civil War.

After the Civil War, white Southerners (who associated the Republicans with the harsh Radical Reconstruction movement) became strongly Democratic (the "Solid South"), and the party became agrarian and conservative. Between 1860 and 1900 the Democrats held the White House for only 8 years, during the 2 terms of Grover Cleveland (1884, 1892).

The Democrats did not regain the presidency until 1912, when a split in the Republican party allowed them to elect Woodrow Wilson. Wilson was reelected in 1916, but the party lost control of Congress, a situation that would prove fatal to Wilson's League of Nations.

During the 1920s the Democrats again broke into factions, allowing the Republicans to dominate the decade. When the Great Depression hit, the nation turned to Democratic candidate Franklin D. Roosevelt, whose New Deal changed the party's direction and united a new generation of Democrats that included farmers, organized labor, minorities, and liberals. The Democrats regained control of Congress and kept the presidency until 1952, with Roosevelt (who was elected to a record 4 terms before his death in 1945) and Harry S Truman.

During the 1960s John F. Kennedy's "New Frontier" and Lyndon B. Johnson's "Great Society" were extensions of New Deal politics. Kennedy (assassinated in 1963) and Johnson, who actively supported civil rights and desegregation, lost the support of many southern Democrats. The war in Vietnam split the party further, and the Democrats' 1968 Chicago convention was marred by riots and internal strife. The Democratic candidate, Hubert Humphrey, was defeated by Richard Nixon, as was George McGovern in the 1972 election.

Jimmy Carter, the last Democratic president to date, lost his reelection to the Reagan-Bush ticket in a landslide in 1980. In 1984 the Democrats nominated the first female candidate from a major party (Geraldine Ferraro) to run for vice-president.

HOW MUCH

	8 Yr. Growth	1979-1980	1981-1982	1983-1984	1985-1986	1987-1988
Money raised ($ mil)	16.7%	37	39	99	65	128
Money spent ($ mil)	16.9%	35	40	97	66	122

Money Raised ($ mil) 1979-88

Political party
Founded: 1840 (the year the party adopted its name)

WHO

Chairman: Ronald H. Brown
Vice Chairpersons: Lynn Cutler, Jack Otero, Carmen Perez, James Ruvolo, Lottie Shackelford
Secretary: Dorothy V. Bush
Treasurer: Robert Farmer

WHERE

HQ: 430 S. Capitol St., Washington, DC 20003
Phone: 202-863-8000
FAX: 202-863-8028

WHAT

Net Revenues 1987-88 Election Cycle

	$ mil	% of total
DNC services	52	41
Senatorial	16	12
Congressional	12	9
Assn. of State Dem. Chair	10	8
Convention	10	8
State & local	28	22
Total	**128**	**100**

Party Presidential Voting 1860-1988

year	Democratic candidate	popular votes (mil)	electoral votes	won/ lost
1988	Michael S. Dukakis	41.8	111	L
1984	Walter F. Mondale	37.6	13	L
1980	Jimmy Carter	35.5	49	L
1976	Jimmy Carter	40.8	297	W
1972	George S. McGovern	29.2	17	L
1968	Hubert H. Humphrey	31.3	191	L
1964	Lyndon B. Johnson	43.1	486	W
1960	John F. Kennedy	34.2	303	W
1956	Adlai E. Stevenson	26.0	73	L
1952	Adlai E. Stevenson	27.3	89	L
1948	Harry S Truman	24.2	303	W
1944	Franklin D. Roosevelt	25.6	432	W
1940	Franklin D. Roosevelt	27.3	449	W
1936	Franklin D. Roosevelt	27.8	523	W
1932	Franklin D. Roosevelt	22.8	472	W
1928	Alfred E. Smith	15.0	87	L
1924	John W. Davis	8.4	136	L
1920	James M. Cox	9.1	127	L
1916	Woodrow Wilson	9.1	227	W
1912	Woodrow Wilson	6.3	435	W
1908	William J. Bryan	6.4	162	L
1904	Alton B. Parker	5.1	140	L
1900	William J. Bryan	6.4	155	L
1896	William J. Bryan	6.5	176	L
1892	Grover Cleveland	5.6	277	W
1888	Grover Cleveland	5.5	168	L
1884	Grover Cleveland	4.9	219	W
1880	Winfield S. Handcock	4.4	155	L
1876	Samuel J. Tilden	4.3	184	L
1872	Horace Greeley	2.8	—	L
1868	Horatio Seymour	2.7	80	L
1864	George McClellan	1.8	21	L
1860	Stephen A. Douglas	1.4	12	L
	John C. Breckenridge	.8	72	L

COMPETITION

The Republican party

DEUTSCHE BANK AG

OVERVIEW

Deutsche Bank is the largest bank in Germany, 18th largest in the world, and a leading Euromarket underwriter. Deutsche is active in commercial, retail, and investment banking and operates more than 1,700 offices internationally. Business is concentrated in Europe.

German banking regulations have allowed Deutsche to accumulate large equity interests in its clients, including 28.2% of Daimler-Benz and 10% of Europe's leading insurer, Allianz. The equity holdings, with an estimated market value of $12 billion, are included on the bank's balance sheet at cost and give Deutsche considerable influence in the German economy.

When deregulation increased competition among banks in Germany, Deutsche diversified into related financial services and expanded abroad. Deutsche is acquiring leading corporate banking firms in European markets in anticipation of 1992, when trade barriers are slated to drop. The bank has been quick to establish 140 branches in East Germany and offices in Poland and Hungary.

WHEN

In 1870, concurrent with German unification, Deutsche Bank opened its doors in Berlin under the leadership of Georg von Siemens. He quickly opened branches in Bremen and Hamburg and, with an eye on foreign trade, established branches overseas, the first in London (1873). The bank's foreign business allowed it to survive a German financial crisis (1873-1875) and buy other German banks, greatly increasing its size and importance.

In the late 1800s Deutsche helped finance the electrification of Germany and the construction of railroads, including the Baghdad Railway (Ottoman Empire) and the Northern Pacific Railway (US). Von Siemens managed the bank until his death in 1901.

In the face of extreme economic difficulty plaguing Germany following its defeat in WWI, Deutsche merged with its largest competitor, Disconto-Gesellschaft and survived the Depression. By purchasing government debt, Deutsche helped finance the Nazi war machine. After WWII, Allied investigators revealed the bank's links to Gestapo leader Himmler and its seizure of bank assets in occupied countries. In 1945 Allied authorities split the bank's West German operations into 10 separate institutions, closed its East German branches, and stripped it of its overseas operations. Deutsche Bank was reassembled from its West German parts in 1957.

Led by Hermann Abs, Deutsche rapidly regained international prominence. After concentrating on commercial banking for a relatively small group of West German companies in the 1940s and 1950s, the bank began offering a wide array of retail banking services in the 1960s. Between 1957 and 1970 the bank expanded from 345 to 1,100 branches. Eurochecks (personal checks accepted throughout Western Europe), conceived at Deutsche, were launched in 1969 to combat US banks' credit cards.

In the 1960s and 1970s Deutsche helped finance the West German export boom and became a major Euromarket dealer. The bank again expanded overseas, buying banks and opening branches abroad. At home, Deutsche acquired stakes in many large companies and by 1979 was represented on the boards of approximately 140 companies.

Until the 1987 stock market crash, Deutsche was active in public stock offerings, including Flick (industrial group, 1985). In the 1980s Deutsche diversified and bought banks, including Bank of America's Italian subsidiary (1986) and the large UK merchant bank, Morgan Grenfell (1989).

Deutsche Bank chairman Alfred Herrhausen, a symbol of German big business, was murdered by terrorists in 1989.

HOW MUCH

$= DM1.69 (Dec. 31, 1989)	9 Yr. Growth	1980	1981	1982	1983	1984**	1985	1986	1987	1988	1989
Sales (DM mil)	6.6%	16,478	20,501	19,890	18,574	18,890	19,943	20,665	20,692	23,360	29,374
Net income (DM mil)	—	—	397	328	635	662	854	1056	658	1183	1315
Income as % of sales	—	—	1.9%	1.6%	3.4%	3.5%	4.3%	5.1%	3.2%	5.1%	4.5%
Earnings per share (DM)	—	—	*16*	*12*	*23*	*23*	*27*	*33*	*19*	*33*	*33*
Stock price – high (DM)	—	301	297	288	352	385	935	920	817	569	843
Stock price – low (DM)	—	227	261	245	259	302	384	724	387	357	502
Stock price – close (DM)	13.0%	280	263	274	349	383	925	822	388	563	843
P/E – high	—	—	19	24	15	17	35	28	43	17	26
P/E – low	—	—	16	20	11	13	14	22	20	11	15
Dividends per share (DM)*	3.2%	9	10	10	11	12	12	12	12	12	12
Book value per share (DM)	4.2%	243	244	243	253	266	281	281	299	318	353

1989 Year End:
Debt ratio: —
Return on equity: 9.8%
Cash (mil): DM7,443
Long-term debt (mil): —
Number of shares (mil): 40
Dividends:
1989 average yield: 1.4%
1989 payout: 36.4%
Market value (mil): $19,833
Sales (mil): $17,381

*not including rights offerings **accounting change

Principal stock exchange: Frankfurt
Founded: Germany, 1870
Fiscal year ends: December 31

WHO

Speaker of the Board of Managing Directors: Hilmar Kopper
Member of the Board of Managing Directors for Accounting and Controlling: Jürgen Krumnow
Employees: 56,580

WHERE

HQ: Taunusanlage 12, PO Box 100601, D-6000 Frankfurt am Main, Germany
Phone: 011-49-69-71500
US HQ (Deutsche Bank AG, New York Branch): 31 W. 52nd St., New York, NY 10019
US Phone: 212-474-8000
US FAX: 212-355-5655

The Deutsche Bank Group has banking branches throughout Germany and in major cities around the world. Affiliated companies are located in 15 countries and Hong Kong.

WHAT

	1989 Sales	
	DM mil	% of total
Interest	24,947	85
Commission surplus	2,779	9
Leasing business	1,639	6
Life insurance business	9	—
Total	**29,374**	**100**

Major Subsidiaries & Affiliated Companies
BAI Leasing S.p.A. (Italy)
Bain & Company Ltd. (Australia, investment banking, 50%)
Banca d'America e d'Italia S.p.A. (Italy, commercial banking, 98.6%)
Banco Comercial Transatlántico, S.A. (Spain, commercial banking, 72.1%)
Banco de Montevideo (Uruguay, commercial banking, 95.4%)
DB Capital Markets (Asia) Ltd. (Hong Kong, Japan, investment banking, 60%)
Europäische Hypothekenbank der Deutschen Bank (Luxembourg, mortgage banking)
Frankfurter Hypothekenbank AG (Germany, mortgage banking, 93.1%)
H. Albert de Bary & Co. N.V. (Netherlands, commercial banking)
Lübecker Hypothekenbank AG (Germany, mortgage banking)
McLean McCarthy Ltd. (Canada, investment banking)
MDM Sociedade de Investimento, S.A. (Portugal, investment banking)
Morgan Grenfell Group plc (UK, investment banking, over 90%)
P.T. Euras Buana Leasing Indonesia (60%)
Schiffshypothekenbank zu Lübeck AG (Germany, mortgage banking)

RANKINGS

60th in *Business Week* Global 1000

COMPETITION

Bank of New York
BankAmerica
Bankers Trust
Chase Manhattan
Chemical Banking
Citicorp
CS Holding
Dai-Ichi Kangyo
First Chicago
Hongkong & Shanghai Banking
Manufacturers Hanover
Investment banking companies
Other international banks

DIGITAL EQUIPMENT CORPORATION

OVERVIEW

Digital is the US's 2nd largest information systems supplier (3rd, if the proposed Fujitsu-ICL merger occurs), a leader in networking and integrating computers, and the world's 3rd largest workstation manufacturer (after Sun and Hewlett-Packard). DEC has the world's largest private electronic mail network, with over 100,000 employee users.

Cofounder Kenneth H. Olsen, hailed as America's greatest entrepreneur (*Fortune*, 1986), built DEC without a single acquisition or merger. DEC derives 54% of its revenue (71% of operating income) abroad. Innovation remains sacred, with fiscal 1989 R&D exceeding $1.5 billion — the US's 5th highest.

After many years of success with hardware and operating systems software of its own design, DEC has been challenged by smaller rivals employing powerful, inexpensive desktop computers and industry standards such as DOS and UNIX. DEC has responded by launching DOS and UNIX workstations and by developing technology allowing existing DEC installations to be connected with industry standard systems.

NYSE symbol: DEC
Incorporated: Massachusetts, 1957
Fiscal year ends: Saturday nearest June 30

WHO

President: Kenneth H. Olsen, age 64, $949,592 pay
SVP: John F. Smith, age 55, $529,477 pay
SVP: Winston R. Hindle, Jr., age 60, $464,804 pay
VP Finance: James M. Osterhoff, age 54
Auditors: Coopers & Lybrand
Employees: 125,000

WHEN

Two young MIT engineers, Kenneth Olsen and Harlan Anderson, founded DEC in 1957 to pioneer beyond mainframes into smaller, less-expensive computers that were interactive. DEC's converted woolen mill near Boston soon produced innovations popular with engineers and scientists, including the PDP-1 (the first interactive computer, 1960) and the PDP-5 (dubbed the minicomputer, 1963). The PDP-8 (1965) and later the PDP-11 (1970) provided major number-crunching breakthroughs.

Olsen began minicomputer sales in the mid-1960s using the matrix management model (with individuals answerable to both functional and line managers) and sales to OEMs; revenue and profit growth averaged 30% per year for almost 2 decades.

DEC began its networking tradition in 1974, introducing the Digital network architecture (DNA) to link its PDP-11s to local- and wide-area networks (LANs and WANs); the result was DECnet Phase I. DEC engineering whiz Gordon Bell conceived the VAX line of computers, which allowed easy upgrades from PDPs and virtually unlimited memory; the VAX-11/780 appeared in 1977.

In 1979 Olsen pledged billions to an expanded VAX generation using all DEC-made components. Olsen dispensed with the matrix model and instituted unified marketing during the arduous 5-year undertaking. The company refocused the new VAXes (like the VAX 6000 mini, 1984) on the larger commercial market and extended its DECnet umbrella to provide global company/client/supplier connections. During the VAX glory days, between 1984 and 1988, sales doubled and earnings nearly quadrupled ($329 million to $1.3 billion).

By 1988 DEC was embracing open systems (which had left its proprietary VAX line isolated) and entering alliances to connect personal computers to VAXes (Apple, Compaq), to translate VAX software to ULTRIX (DEC's version of UNIX), and to bring popular software to the VAX line (Lotus 1-2-3, dBase). DEC also took a 5% stake in MIPS Computer (which provides the RISC chip for the RISC-based DECstation).

DEC has recently undertaken major restructuring (including worker redeployment to sales, software, and support) and workforce reductions (with severance pay — all voluntary). The company's Network Applications Support (NAS) was developed to link its VAX and RISC lines (as well as other vendors' machines). UNIX-based RISC software applications (already over 1,200) are growing at more than 100 per month. DEC is also reselling Tandy PCs and has introduced a mainframe (the VAX 9000, 1990) targeted directly at IBM's market.

WHERE

HQ: 146 Main St., Maynard, MA 01754
Phone: 508-493-5111
FAX: 508-493-8780

Digital does business in more than 70 countries.

	1989 Sales		1989 Operating Income	
	$ mil	% of total	$ mil	% of total
US	5,849	46	510	29
Europe	5,130	40	816	47
Canada/Far East/ Americas	1,763	14	411	24
Adjustments	—	—	(401)	—
Total	**12,742**	**100**	**1,336**	**100**

WHAT

	1989 Sales	
	$ mil	% of total
Products	8,190	64
Services & other	4,552	36
Total	**12,742**	**100**

Computers
Mainframes
- VAX 9000
- VAXclusters

Minicomputers
- DECstation series (RISC-based)
- MicroVAX series
- VAX 6000 series

Personal computers
- DECstation 210, 316, 320

Workstations
- DECstation 3100 (RISC-based)
- VAXstation 3100

Software
- ALL-IN-1 (networking)
- Business, engineering, and productivity applications
- DECnet (networking)
- ULTRIX (UNIX version)
- VMS (VAX operating system)

Peripherals
- Disk storage devices
- Displays
- Magnetic tape transports
- Printers
- Tape cassette devices
- Terminals

HOW MUCH

	9 Yr. Growth	1980	1981	1982	1983	1984	1985	1986	1987	1988	1989
Sales ($ mil)	20.6%	2,368	3,198	3,881	4,272	5,584	6,686	7,590	9,389	11,475	12,742
Net income ($ mil)	17.6%	250	343	417	284	329	447	617	1,137	1,306	1,073
Income as % of sales	—	10.6%	10.7%	10.8%	6.6%	5.9%	6.7%	8.1%	12.1%	11.4%	8.4%
Earnings per share ($)	13.4%	2.73	3.35	3.77	2.50	2.87	3.71	4.81	8.53	9.90	8.45
Stock price – high ($)	—	49.38	56.63	57.50	66.06	55.63	68.38	109.00	199.50	144.75	122.38
Stock price – low ($)	—	29.63	40.13	30.88	32.00	35.19	42.63	65.81	104.50	86.38	79.75
Stock price – close ($)	6.3%	47.50	43.25	49.75	36.00	55.38	66.25	104.75	135.00	98.38	82.00
P/E – high	—	18	17	15	26	19	18	23	23	15	14
P/E – low	—	11	12	8	13	12	11	14	12	9	9
Dividends per share ($)	0.0%	0.00	0.00	0.00	0.00	0.00	0.00	0.00	0.00	0.00	0.00
Book value per share ($)	15.4%	18.12	24.65	28.65	31.42	34.42	38.43	44.54	49.87	59.47	66.12

1989 Year End:
Debt ratio: 1.7%
Return on equity: 13.5%
Cash (mil): $1,655
Current ratio: 2.88
Long-term debt (mil): $136
Number of shares (mil): 122
Dividends:
1989 average yield: 0.0%
1989 payout: 0.0%
Market value (mil): $9,966

Stock Price History high/low 1980-89

RANKINGS

27th in *Fortune* 500 Industrial Cos.
78th in *Fortune* Global 500
16th in *Fortune* 50 Exporters
44th in *Forbes* Sales 500
47th in *Business Week* 1000
130th in *Business Week* Global 1000

COMPETITION

AT&T
Apple
Compaq
Control Data
Data General
Fujitsu
Hewlett-Packard
Hitachi
Intergraph
IBM
NCR
NEC
Prime
Siemens
Sun Microsystems
Tandem
Unisys
Wang

DILLARD DEPARTMENT STORES, INC.

OVERVIEW

Little Rock–based Dillard's is one of the largest department store chains in the US, operating 188 Dillard's stores and 13 Higbee's stores in 19 states from Arizona to Florida. Newly constructed mall stores average more than 150,000 square feet and carry middle- to upper middle-priced merchandise, primarily nationally recognized brand names in family apparel and home furnishings.

With 1989 sales of $3 billion and a 19% compound annual growth rate in the past 5 years, the company has grown as a result of shrewd management. Dillard's purchases underperforming department store companies with similar mixes of merchandise and customers in small markets. Within the retail industry, Dillard's is known for rapidly assimilating stores and making them profitable.

During the 1980s Dillard's maintained an average gross margin of 37% in spite of the depressed economy of the Southwest. To boost customer loyalty, the company maintains an everyday pricing strategy with few markdowns. Also, the company's computerized information system ("Quick Response"), with its hourly departmental inventory tracking and automatic reordering, allows close monitoring of sales in each store.

NYSE symbol: DDS
Incorporated: Delaware, 1964
Fiscal year ends: Saturday nearest January 31

WHO

Chairman and CEO: William Dillard, age 75, $1,618,995 pay
VC: E. Ray Kemp, age 65, $475,000 pay
President and COO: William Dillard II, age 45, $1,270,000 pay
EVP: Alex Dillard, age 40, $1,177,000 pay
EVP: Mike Dillard, age 38, $911,000 pay
VP and CFO: James I. Freeman, age 40
Auditors: Deloitte & Touche
Employees: 26,304

WHEN

At age 12 William Dillard began working in his father's general store in Mineral Springs, Arkansas. After graduation from Columbia University (1937), the 3rd generation retailer spent 7 months in the Sears, Roebuck manager training program in Tulsa.

With $8,000 borrowed from his father, Dillard opened his first department store in Nashville, Arkansas, in 1938. He sold the store in 1948 to finance a partnership in Wooten's Department Store in Texarkana, Arkansas, later buying out Wooten and establishing Dillard's, Inc., in 1949.

During the 1950s and 1960s the company became a strong regional retailer. Acquisitions included well-established downtown stores in small cities — Mayer & Schmidt (Tyler, Texas, 1956); Brown-Dunkin (Tulsa, 1960); Joseph Pfeifer (Little Rock, 1963); and Gus Blass (Little Rock, 1964). Dillard's moved its headquarters to Little Rock after the Pfeifer purchase. The company continued to add new stores, usually co-anchoring in suburban malls. When Dillard's went public in 1969, the chain had 15 stores in 3 states, with sales of $65.2 million.

During the early 1960s E. Ray Kemp, now vice-chairman, convinced Dillard to computerize operations, a decision that streamlined inventory and information management. In 1970 the company added computerized point-of-sale cash registers, which enabled management to get hourly departmental sales figures.

Dillard's acquisitions during the 1970s included 5 Fedways (Southwest, 1971); 5 Leonard's (Dallas–Fort Worth, 1974); and Alden's (Texarkana, 1978).

In 1978 Vendamerica B. V., a subsidiary of Vendex International N. V. (formerly Vroom en Dreesmann), a large retailer in the Netherlands, initially invested $24 million in Dillard's. The Dutch company now holds 35% of Class A shares and functions as a silent partner. Holding 99% of Class B stock, the Dillard family controls 9 of the 14 board positions.

Acquisitions in the 1980s included 12 Stix, Baer & Fuller stores (Kansas City, St. Louis, 1984); 12 Diamond's and 5 John A. Brown stores (Phoenix, Tucson, Las Vegas, 1984); 12 Macy stores (Kansas City, Topeka, Wichita, 1986); 27 Joske's (Texas, 1987); 4 Cain-Sloan stores (Nashville, Tennessee, 1987); 17 D. H. Holmes stores (New Orleans, 1989); and 23 J. B. Ivey stores (South Carolina, North Carolina, Florida, 1990). In a 1988 joint venture with Edward J. DeBartolo, Dillard's invested $30 million in a 50% interest in the 12 Higbee's stores in Cleveland, Akron, and Canton.

WHERE

HQ: 900 W. Capitol Ave., Little Rock, AR 72201
Phone: 501-376-5200
FAX: 501-376-5917

Dillard's operates 201 department stores in 19 midwestern and Sunbelt states.

	No. of stores	% of total
Alabama	1	1
Arizona	12	6
Arkansas	7	3
Florida	11	5
Illinois	1	1
Iowa	1	1
Kansas	10	5
Louisiana	19	10
Mississippi	2	1
Missouri	18	9
Nebraska	3	1
Nevada	3	1
New Mexico	4	2
North Carolina	11	5
Ohio (Higbee's)	13	7
Oklahoma	16	8
South Carolina	2	1
Tennessee	8	4
Texas	59	29
Total	**201**	**100**

Included above are 13 Higbee's stores in Ohio (50% interest with Edward J. DeBartolo).

WHAT

	1989 Sales % of total
Cosmetics	12
Clothing, accessories	64
Shoes	5
Housewares, furniture, appliances	16
Jewelry, other	3
Total	**100**

RANKINGS

33rd in *Fortune* 50 Retailing Cos.
273rd in *Forbes* Sales 500
253rd in *Business Week* 1000
603rd in *Business Week* Global 1000

COMPETITION

Campeau
Dayton Hudson
R. H. Macy
May Department Stores
Mercantile Stores
Montgomery Ward
J. C. Penney
Sears
Apparel retailers
Other department stores

HOW MUCH

	9 Yr. Growth	1980	1981	1982	1983	1984	1985	1986	1987	1988	1989
Sales ($ mil)	23.1%	471	593	711	847	1,277	1,601	1,851	2,206	2,558	3,049
Net income ($ mil)	37.4%	9	16	22	34	50	67	74	91	114	148
Income as % of sales	—	1.8%	2.7%	3.1%	4.0%	3.9%	4.2%	4.0%	4.1%	4.5%	4.9%
Earnings per share ($)	31.9%	0.36	0.69	0.93	1.38	1.82	2.29	2.35	2.83	3.53	4.36
Stock price – high ($)	—	2.02	3.11	6.95	15.69	20.94	38.50	45.75	57.50	46.50	74.25
Stock price – low ($)	—	1.50	1.58	2.75	5.66	10.81	18.13	32.00	24.00	25.13	41.00
Stock price – close ($)	51.4%	1.70	3.00	6.58	14.00	19.13	37.50	37.88	24.63	42.38	71.00
P/E – high	—	6	5	7	11	12	17	19	20	13	17
P/E – low	—	4	2	3	4	6	8	14	8	7	9
Dividends per share ($)	15.3%	0.05	0.05	0.05	0.08	0.09	0.11	0.12	0.14	0.16	0.18
Book value per share ($)	24.4%	4.30	4.94	5.81	7.36	10.24	12.42	17.31	20.00	23.39	30.68

1989 Year End:
Debt ratio: 41.4%
Return on equity: 16.1%
Cash (mil): $54
Current ratio: 2.86
Long-term debt (mil): $773
Number of shares (mil): 36
Dividends:
1989 average yield: 0.3%
1989 payout: 4.1%
Market value (mil): $2,533

Stock Price History high/low 1980-89

0, 10, 20, 30, 40, 50, 60, 70, 80

R. R. DONNELLEY & SONS COMPANY

OVERVIEW

Chicago-based R. R. Donnelley & Sons is North America's largest printer, churning out books, magazines, computer documentation, catalogs, and directories for more than 3,000 customers. With a 25% interest in AlphaGraphics, the company is involved in quick-printing services as well.

Through its Metromail subsidiary it handles mailing lists and databases for mail merchandisers. The company also provides editorial and design services, replicates computer disks, makes compact disks, and packages software.

Donnelley owns printing plants throughout the US, with its largest plants in Crawfordsville, Indiana; Lancaster, Pennsylvania; and Chicago. It owns 3 plants in the UK where it is also a major commercial printer and the largest printer of telephone directories.

As it enters the 1990s, Donnelley has expanded to Ireland and Japan. The company will enter new markets, producing books for professionals and for juvenile readers, with the construction of a maquiladora plant (uses duty free imported components to assemble products for export to the US) in Reynosa, Mexico. The company's goal is to become the leading global supplier of printing services, connecting its service centers through worldwide satellite links.

WHEN

R. R. Donnelley & Sons began in 1864 when printer Richard Robert Donnelley joined publishers Edward Goodman and Leroy Church of Chicago. Their partnership became Lakeside Publishing and Printing in 1870. The company was a major midwestern publishing house, producing a variety of periodicals and some of the first inexpensive paperback books. The Chicago Fire of 1871 destroyed the Lakeside building, but by 1873 the company was back in operation.

In 1877 Lakeside had fallen on hard times and closed its doors, but its paperback subsidiary survived as Donnelley, Loyd & Company. Richard R. Donnelley bought out his partners in 1879 and separated the firm's printing component (reorganized as R. R. Donnelley & Sons in 1882) from its publishing arm (Chicago Directory Company). Chicago Directory emerged as the Reuben H. Donnelley Corporation (1916), named for one of Richard Donnelley's sons. Reuben H. Donnelley Corporation was bought by Dun & Bradstreet (1961).

Before the turn of the century, R. R. Donnelley & Sons printed telephone books and the Montgomery Ward catalog. In 1910 it began printing the *Encyclopædia Britannica*. Capture of the printing contract for *Time* in 1927 propelled the company into the big leagues of printing. Donnelley's innovation in high-speed printing was a major factor in the decision to launch *Life* in 1936.

Donnelley has been a family business during most of its history. Donnelley descendants served as chairmen and as several of the company's presidents. An in-law, Charles Haffner, was chairman from 1952 to 1964, during which time the company's stock went public (1956). The first chairman from outside the family circle was Charles Lake in 1975.

During the late 1970s and the 1980s Donnelley expanded worldwide, acquiring printing companies in the UK (Ben Johnson, 1978; Index Press and Thompson Photo Litho, 1985), Japan (Dowa Insatsu, 1988), and Ireland (Irish Printers, 1989). In 1987 it bought Metromail, the largest US mailing list business.

Also during the 1980s Donnelley developed the Selectronic binding process that can tailor editions of magazines and catalogs to small target audiences. In 1989 Donnelley bought 25% of AlphaGraphics, the retail quick-print chain, and agreed to buy Meredith/Burda, a high-quality printer. The FTC balked at the combination, but the $487.5 million purchase cleared its first court hurdle in mid-1990.

HOW MUCH

	9 Yr. Growth	1980	1981	1982	1983	1984	1985	1986	1987	1988	1989
Sales ($ mil)	12.2%	1,111	1,244	1,404	1,546	1,814	2,038	2,234	2,483	2,878	3,122
Net income ($ mil)	13.9%	69	79	91	114	134	148	158	218	205	222
Income as % of sales	—	6.2%	6.4%	6.5%	7.4%	7.4%	7.3%	7.1%	8.8%	7.1%	7.1%
Earnings per share ($)	13.3%	0.93	1.05	1.20	1.50	1.75	1.94	2.03	2.80	2.64	2.85
Stock price – high ($)	—	9.56	10.75	16.84	24.00	24.63	32.19	40.00	45.38	38.75	51.25
Stock price – low ($)	—	5.94	7.53	8.94	14.59	16.00	23.00	29.44	25.50	29.88	34.25
Stock price – close ($)	21.6%	8.84	9.44	14.88	19.25	24.50	31.81	30.63	32.63	34.63	51.25
P/E – high	—	10	10	14	16	14	17	20	16	15	18
P/E – low	—	6	7	7	10	9	12	15	9	11	12
Dividends per share ($)	13.3%	0.29	0.32	0.36	0.41	0.50	0.58	0.64	0.70	0.78	0.88
Book value per share ($)	12.0%	6.68	7.42	8.21	9.25	10.44	11.73	12.90	14.91	16.69	18.56

1989 Year End:
Debt ratio: 4.1%
Return on equity: 16.2%
Cash (mil): $110
Assets (mil): $2,507
Long-term debt (mil): $63
Number of shares (mil): 78
Dividends:
1989 average yield: 1.7%
1989 payout: 30.9%
Market value (mil): $3,993

NYSE symbol: DNY
Incorporated: Delaware, 1956
Fiscal year ends: December 31

WHO

Chairman, President, and CEO: John R. Walter, age 43, $628,691 pay
EVP and CFO: Frank R. Jarc, age 47, $320,874 pay
Auditors: Arthur Andersen & Co.
Employees: 26,100

WHERE

HQ: 2223 Martin Luther King Dr., Chicago, IL 60616
Phone: 312-326-8000
FAX: 312-326-8543

The company owns 25 printing plants worldwide.

WHAT

	1989 Sales % of total
Catalogs	33
Magazines	20
Directories	18
Books	13
Documentation services	6
Other	10
Total	**100**

Book Group
Hardcover and softcover books

Catalog Group
Catalogs
Customized merchandising
Newspaper inserts

Documentation Services Group
Hardware documentation
Software documentation

Financial Group
Financial printing

Information Services Group
Creative services
Technical documentation

International Group
Far East operations
UK operations

Magazine Group
Newsweeklies
Special interest magazines
Sunday supplements

Metromail Corp.
Databases
Mail production
Mailing lists

Telecommunications Group
Directories

RANKINGS

143rd in *Fortune* 500 Industrial Cos.
267th in *Forbes* Sales 500
185th in *Business Week* 1000
570th in *Business Week* Global 1000

COMPETITION

Bertelsmann
Maxwell

JTC

THE DOW CHEMICAL COMPANY

OVERVIEW

Dow, America's 2nd largest chemical company (after Du Pont), produces chemicals used as raw materials for manufacturing in the food processing, personal care products, pharmaceuticals, pulp and paper, utilities, and other industries. More than 1/2 of Dow's business is conducted overseas through subsidiaries located in nearly every industrialized nation. Its CEO, Frank Popoff, has spent over a decade in overseas posts. Dow's recent successes in increasing sales, profits, and ROE earned it *Business Month*'s recognition as one of the 5 best-managed companies in 1989.

Dow's plastics are used in several markets, including automotive, electronics, packaging, and recreation. The company also makes several well-known consumer brands, including Dow bathroom cleaner, and through Marion Merrell Dow (67% owned) produces prescription drugs and over-the-counter health care items such as Cepacol mouthwash and Novahistine antihistamine. Dow owns 60% of DowElanco, which produces Gallant herbicide, Reldan insecticides, and other agricultural chemicals. Dow also has a 50% stake in silicone maker Dow Corning.

NYSE symbol: DOW
Incorporated: Delaware, 1947
Fiscal year ends: December 31

WHO

Chairman: Paul F. Oreffice, age 62
President and CEO: Frank P. Popoff, age 54, $962,747 pay
EVP: Joseph G. Temple, Jr., age 60, $505,089 pay
EVP; President, Dow Chemical USA: Keith R. McKennon, age 56, $682,886 pay
Financial VP: Enrique C. Falla, age 60, $445,655 pay
Auditors: Deloitte & Touche
Employees: 62,100

WHEN

Herbert Dow founded Dow Chemical in 1897 after developing a process that used electricity to extract bromides and chlorides from underground brine deposits around Midland, Michigan. The company's first product was chlorine bleach. Dow sold his products on the world market and eventually overcame British and German monopolies on bleach, bromides, and other chemicals.

In the mid-1920s the company rejected an attempt at takeover by the chemical giant Du Pont. By 1930, the year of Herbert Dow's death, sales had reached $15 million. Dow began building new plants around the country in the late 1930s. The Freeport, Texas, plant, completed in 1941 to supply magnesium and other products for the military, was the beginning of today's Texas Gulf Coast petrochemical complex.

Dow research yielded new plastics in the 1940s that became leaders in the industry by the 1950s. Saran Wrap (introduced 1953) was the company's first major consumer product. By 1957 plastics accounted for 32% of Dow's sales, compared to 2% in 1940. Consumer products became important after the 1957 merger with Cleveland-based Dobeckmun (plastics packaging). Plastics and silicone products helped boost sales through the 1950s and propelled Dow into the top ranks of US companies. In 1964 sales passed $1 billion. With the 1960 purchase of Allied Labs, Dow entered the pharmaceutical field.

Although Dow had exported chemicals for years (the diamond trademark on its indigo dyes was known in China before 1920), the company built its first plant outside North America in partnership with the Japanese in 1952 (Asahi-Dow) to make plastic nets for their fishing industry. In the 1960s the company built plants overseas, the largest at Terneuzen in Holland.

Despite increasing sales ($10.6 billion by 1980) Dow suffered earnings drops in the recession years of 1981 to 1983 due to drops in chemical prices. To limit the cyclical effect of chemicals on profits, Dow has continued to expand other business segments, notably pharmaceuticals (Merrell Drug, 1981) and consumer goods (Texize, household cleaners, 1984). Bulk chemicals accounted for less than 40% of sales in 1989, compared to 64% in 1982. In 1989, the company merged its pharmaceutical division, Merrell Dow, with the pharmaceutical company Marion Labs, creating Marion Merrell Dow (combined sales $2.3 billion). In a joint venture with Eli Lilly in 1989, Dow formed DowElanco, the 5th largest agricultural chemicals firm in the world.

WHERE

HQ: 2030 Willard H. Dow Center, Midland, MI 48674
Phone: 517-636-1000
FAX: 517-636-0922

Dow has 71 manufacturing plants in the US and 108 plants in 30 foreign countries.

	1989 Sales		1989 Operating Income	
	$ mil	% of total	$ mil	% of total
US	8,084	46	1,876	47
Europe	5,523	31	1,160	29
Other countries	3,993	23	974	24
Adjustments	—	—	(59)	—
Total	**17,600**	**100**	**3,951**	**100**

WHAT

	1989 Sales		1989 Operating Income	
	$ mil	% of total	$ mil	% of total
Consumer specialties	3,407	19	462	11
Chemicals & performance prods.	5,407	31	1,718	43
Plastic products	6,994	40	1,586	40
Hydrocarbons & energy	1,778	10	239	6
Other	14	—	5	—
Adjustments	—	—	(59)	—
Total	**17,600**	**100**	**3,951**	**100**

Chemicals & Performance Products
Antimicrobials (Dowicide and Dowicil)
Basic chemicals
Brake and de-icing fluids
Filmtec membrane systems

Plastic Products
Fabricated (Saranex, Styrofoam)
Thermoplastics and Thermosets

Major Consumer Brands
Cepacol
Fantastik
Gallant (herbicide)
Gaviscon (antacid)
Handi-Wrap
Nicorette
Perma Soft (hair care)
Saran Wrap
Spray 'n Wash

HOW MUCH

	9 Yr. Growth	1980	1981	1982	1983	1984	1985	1986	1987	1988	1989
Sales ($ mil)	5.8%	10,626	11,873	10,618	10,951	11,418	11,537	11,113	13,377	16,682	17,600
Net income ($ mil)	13.4%	805	564	342	293	549	58	741	1,245	2,410	2,487
Income as % of sales	—	7.6%	4.8%	3.2%	2.7%	4.8%	0.5%	6.7%	9.3%	14.4%	14.1%
Earnings per share ($)	13.5%	2.95	2.00	1.18	1.01	1.89	0.21	2.58	4.33	8.55	9.20
Stock price – high ($)	—	26.17	26.00	19.25	25.58	23.00	27.92	41.17	73.08	62.67	72.25
Stock price – low ($)	—	18.83	15.58	13.08	16.67	17.17	18.00	26.58	39.17	51.17	55.50
Stock price – close ($)	14.3%	21.42	17.50	17.25	22.25	18.33	27.33	39.00	60.00	58.50	71.38
P/E – high	—	9	13	16	25	12	135	16	17	7	8
P/E – low	—	6	8	11	17	9	87	10	9	6	6
Dividends per share ($)	8.9%	1.10	1.20	1.20	1.20	1.20	1.20	1.27	1.43	1.73	2.37
Book value per share ($)	6.9%	16.20	17.22	17.30	17.18	17.75	16.80	18.01	20.31	26.35	29.55

1989 Year End:
Debt ratio: 32.6%
Return on equity: 32.9%
Cash (mil): $289
Current ratio: 1.13
Long-term debt (mil): $3,855
Number of shares (mil): 269
Dividends:
1989 average yield: 3.3%
1989 payout: 25.7%
Market value (mil): $19,221

Stock Price History high/low 1980-89

RANKINGS

20th in *Fortune* 500 Industrial Cos.
53rd in *Fortune* Global 500 Industrial Cos.
25th in *Fortune* 50 Exporters
29th in *Forbes* Sales 500
23rd in *Business Week* 1000
75th in *Business Week* Global 1000

COMPETITION

BASF	Du Pont	Monsanto
Bayer	Hoechst	Union Carbide

Other chemical and household products manufacturers and petroleum and pharmaceutical companies.

DOW JONES & COMPANY, INC.

OVERVIEW

New York–based Dow Jones (DJ) is the leading provider of business and financial news in the US. The 108-year-old company is best known as publisher of *The Wall Street Journal*, the country's largest newspaper (1.95 million circulation). DJ also produces an Asian and European edition of the *Journal*, bringing worldwide circulation of the daily to over 2 million. The *Journal* celebrated its centennial year in 1989.

While DJ's business publication segment (*The Wall Street Journal, Barron's, National Business Employment Weekly*, etc.) is what DJ is best known for, it represents less than 1/2 of DJ's almost $1.7 billion in revenues. DJ's 2 other segments — Information Services and Community Newspapers — accounted for $935 million in 1989 revenues. Of that, DJ's wholly owned Telerate, an international supplier of real-time market data, accounted for $506 million. Also included in its Information Services segment is Dow Jones News/Retrieval, an on-line business and financial news service, and recently introduced JournalPhone, which provides access to business and financial updates by phone.

In 1990, for the 7th year in a row, DJ ranked #1 in its industry in quality of products and services in *Fortune* magazine's survey of corporate reputations.

WHEN

Charles Dow, Edward Jones, and Charles Bergstresser, 3 financial reporters, left their employer, The Kiernan News Agency, and began Dow Jones & Company (DJ) in 1882 working out of a humble office on Wall Street next door to the NYSE. The company sold handwritten bulletins with stock and bond trade information delivered to subscribers in New York's financial districts. In 1883 DJ printed the day's summary in the *Customers' Afternoon Letter* (annual subscription cost: $18.00), which evolved into *The Wall Street Journal* (1889). DJ offered more timely summary reports through its stock ticker service, acquired in 1897 from ex-employer Kiernan.

Jones sold out to his partners in 1899; in 1902 Dow and Bergstresser sold DJ to Clarence Barron, the company's Boston correspondent and owner of 2 other dailies (Dow died later in 1902). Circulation of the *Journal* grew from 7,000 in 1902 to over 50,000 in 1928, the year Barron died.

Until 1940 the *Journal* was primarily a financial newspaper. In 1941 the new managing editor, Bernard Kilgore, broadened its coverage to include summaries of major news events and more in-depth business articles. Kilgore became president of DJ in 1945. His leadership is credited with DJ's steady growth. By 1966, when Kilgore retired, the *Journal* had a circulation of 1 million. In 1962 DJ started the *National Observer*, a weekly general-interest newspaper; however, production of the *Observer* was stopped in 1977 due to accumulated losses of $16.2 million.

In 1975 DJ began to transmit the *Journal* via satellite to its regional plants around the country, enabling it to offer same-day service to all of its US readers.

By the end of 1989, DJ consisted of several financial and business news publications and an array of electronic news retrieval services, including Telerate, which DJ had begun acquiring through stock purchases in 1985 (acquisition completed in 1990).

Since the October 1987 stock market crash, ad sales have declined, as have subscriptions. Although circulation for DJ publications was up slightly in 1989, there is little anticipation of strong growth. DJ's best prospects for growth are in its information segment, which had a 13.5% increase in revenues in 1989, although costs relating to the Telerate purchase may temper earnings in 1990.

DJ is insulated from a hostile takeover, as 66% of its voting stock is owned by 3 of its directors (all cousins) and their relatives, heirs to Clarence Barron.

HOW MUCH

	9 Yr. Growth	1980	1981	1982	1983	1984	1985	1986	1987	1988	1989
Sales ($ mil)	13.7%	531	641	731	866	966	1,039	1,135	1,314	1,603	1,688
Net income ($ mil)	20.6%	59	71	88	114	129	139	183	203	228	317
Income as % of sales	—	11.1%	11.1%	12.1%	13.2%	13.4%	13.3%	16.2%	15.4%	14.2%	18.8%
Earnings per share ($)	19.6%	0.63	0.75	0.92	1.19	1.34	1.43	1.88	2.09	2.35	3.14
Stock price – high ($)	—	10.50	18.42	23.50	37.50	34.25	33.33	42.13	56.25	36.50	42.50
Stock price – low ($)	—	5.81	9.85	11.92	21.33	23.42	24.50	28.08	28.00	26.75	29.25
Stock price – close ($)	14.1%	10.17	16.50	21.92	32.42	27.83	31.50	39.00	29.88	29.50	33.25
P/E – high	—	17	24	26	32	26	23	22	27	16	14
P/E – low	—	9	13	13	18	17	17	15	13	11	9
Dividends per share ($)	11.7%	0.27	0.31	0.36	0.40	0.48	0.52	0.55	0.64	0.68	0.72
Book value per share ($)	21.7%	2.37	2.86	3.49	4.34	5.24	6.21	7.52	8.80	11.51	13.94

1989 Year End:
Debt ratio: 33.8%
Return on equity: 24.7%
Cash (mil): $46
Current ratio: 0.65
Long-term debt (mil): $719
Number of shares (mil): 101
Dividends:
1989 average yield: 2.2%
1989 payout: 22.9%
Market value (mil): $3,352

NYSE symbol: DJ
Incorporated: Delaware, 1949
Fiscal year ends: December 31

WHO

Chairman and CEO: Warren H. Phillips, age 63, $780,000 pay
President and COO: Peter R. Kann, age 47, $496,667 pay
SVP: James H. Ottaway, Jr., age 52, $372,000 pay
SVP: Kenneth L. Burenga, age 45, $371,000 pay
SVP: Carl M. Valenti, age 51, $317,417 pay
VP Finance and CFO: Kevin J. Roche, age 55
Auditors: Coopers & Lybrand
Employees: 9,818

WHERE

HQ: World Financial Center, 200 Liberty St., New York, NY 10281
Phone: 212-416-2000
FAX: 212-416-3299

Dow Jones business publications are circulated worldwide. Telerate has offices in 60 countries.

	1989 Sales		1989 Operating Income	
	$ mil	% of total	$ mil	% of total
US	1,338	79	263	74
Foreign	350	21	91	26
Adjustments	—	—	(18)	—
Total	**1,688**	**100**	**336**	**100**

WHAT

	1989 Sales		1989 Operating Income	
	$ mil	% of total	$ mil	% of total
Business publications	753	45	100	28
Information services	696	41	214	60
Community newspapers	239	14	40	11
Adjustments	—	—	(18)	—
Total	**1,688**	**100**	**336**	**100**

Information Services
AP-Dow Jones
Capital Markets Report
Dow Jones News Service
Dow Jones News/Retrieval
DowPhone
Federal Filings, Inc.
JournalFax
JournalPhone
Professional Investor Report
Telerate
"The Wall Street Journal Report" (radio & TV shows)
World Equities Report

Business Publications
AmericaEconomica
American Demographics
Asia Technology
Asian Wall Street Journal
Barron's
Far Eastern Economic Review
National Business Employment Weekly
The Wall Street Journal
The Wall Street Journal/Europe

Community Newspapers
Ottaway Newspapers, Inc. (operates daily newspapers in 23 communities nationwide)

RANKINGS

235th in *Fortune* 500 Industrial Cos.
448th in *Forbes* Sales 500
224th in *Business Week* 1000
711th in *Business Week* Global 1000

COMPETITION

ADP
Dun & Bradstreet
Gannett
Knight-Ridder
McGraw-Hill
Mead
New York Times
Pearson
Reuters
Time Warner

DR PEPPER/SEVEN-UP COMPANIES, INC.

OVERVIEW

A privately held, Dallas-based holding company, Dr Pepper/Seven-Up Companies, Inc., is the nation's 3rd largest soft drink manufacturer (after Coca-Cola and PepsiCo). The company manufactures and markets syrup for international Dr Pepper sales and Seven-Up sales in the US. The 2 subsidiaries are jointly managed but operate separate sales and marketing divisions within the parent company. The company's production facility in suburban St. Louis manufactures more than 200 brands of soft drink concentrate, many for contract customers.

The company's 1989 total sales were $514 million, with an operating income of $114 million. Seven-Up's dominant US market share of lemon-lime soda sales slipped from 46% in 1985 to 37% at the end of 1989. Competition from Coca-Cola's Sprite (with 42% of the market in 1989) has been particularly strong. The Dr Pepper brand, unique in its flavor category, is the nation's fastest growing noncola soft drink, with sales up 29% between 1987 and 1989.

WHEN

In 1988 a Dallas investment firm merged 2 of America's best-known soft drink companies into a private holding company — Dr Pepper/Seven-Up Companies, Inc.

The Dr Pepper brand was first sold in 1885 in Waco, Texas, at Morrison's Old Corner Drug Store. The pharmacist, Charles Alderton, concocted the unique syrup, and the store's owner, Wade Morrison, named the new drink after an acquaintance in his home state of Virginia. A Waco bottler, Robert Lazenby, began producing the syrup and bottling the drink at his Circle "A" Ginger Ale Bottling Works. Lazenby and Morrison formed a new company, the Artesian Manufacturing and Bottling Company, and in 1923 they moved its headquarters to Dallas. In 1924 the name was changed to the Dr Pepper Company. The drink's popularity continued to grow, and in 1946 the company's stock was listed on the NYSE. Dr Pepper remained a public company until 1984, when its shareholders voted to accept a $22-per-share bid by Forstmann Little & Company, which privatized the company.

Dr Pepper is distinguished by its noncola flavor and its memorable advertising slogans, including the 1930s motto "10, 2 and 4" (the times of day to drink Dr Pepper); the 1960s description as the most "misunderstood" soft drink; the "Be a Pepper" campaign in the 1980s; and the current "Just what the Dr ordered."

The 7-Up soft drink began in 1929 when C. L. Grigg, owner of The Howdy Company in St. Louis (home of Howdy Orange drink), introduced his new lemon-lime soda. The drink's success prompted Grigg to change his company's name to The Seven-Up Company in 1936, and by the late 1940s 7-Up was the world's 3rd best-selling soft drink. The company remained in family hands until it went public in 1967. Sales increased with the "Uncola" marketing campaign and the introduction of Diet 7-Up.

Philip Morris bought Seven-Up in 1978, but profits began to slide. By 1986 Philip Morris was negotiating to sell Seven-Up to PepsiCo. About the same time Coca-Cola was reaching an agreement to buy Dr Pepper. The FTC ruled that the sales were anticompetitive, and Hicks and Haas, a Dallas investment firm, stepped in to buy both companies in 1986. Dr Pepper sold for $416 million and Seven-Up sold for $240 million.

Hicks and Haas merged the 2 companies in 1988 to form Dr Pepper/Seven-Up Companies, Inc. The new company managers (many of them from Dr Pepper) consolidated plant operations at Seven-Up's St. Louis facility, selling other property and trimming Seven-Up staff. While sales for the Dr Pepper unit have grown since the company's merger, 7-Up sales have diminished, falling 7.2% in 1989 to $246.9 million.

HOW MUCH

	9 Yr. Growth	1980	1981	1982	1983	1984	1985	1986	1987	1988	1989
Sales ($ mil)	—	—	—	—	—	—	—	—	—	510	514
Net inc. ($ mil)	—	—	—	—	—	—	—	—	—	(68)	(42)
Dr Pepper sales ($ mil)	—	—	—	—	149	166	174	181	207	244	267
Dr Pepper net inc. ($ mil)	—	—	—	—	11	(24)	4	0	(2)	—	—
7-Up sales ($ mil)	—	—	—	—	275	301	291	272	297	266	247
7-Up net inc. ($ mil)	—	—	—	—	(5)	(3)	(4)	(7)	8	—	—
Dr Pepper cases sold (mil)	3.3%	311.1	298.6	288.4	284.4	301.5	320.5	323.6	355.6	399.5	416.8
Dr Pepper % of market	—	6.0	5.6	5.2	4.9	4.9	4.9	4.8	5.0	5.3	5.4
7-Up cases sold (mil)	(0.4%)	330.6	319.2	369.3	412.4	417.3	383.8	340.7	374.9	350.5	318.8
7-Up % of market	—	6.3	5.9	6.7	7.2	6.8	5.9	5.0	5.2	4.7	4.1
Total cases sold (mil)	1.5%	641.7	617.8	657.7	696.8	718.8	704.3	664.3	730.5	750.0	735.6

1989 Year End:
Debt ratio: 188.2%
Return on equity: 9.9%
Cash (mil): $5
Current ratio: 96%
Long-term debt (mil): $1,049

Total Cases Sold (mil) 1980-89

800
700
600
500
400
300
200
100
0

Private company
Incorporated: Delaware, 1988
Fiscal year ends: December 31

WHO

President and CEO: John Albers, age 58, $875,545 pay
EVP and CFO: Ira M. Rosenstein, age 50, $501,705 pay
SVP; EVP and COO, Dr Pepper: True Knowles, age 52, $327,969 pay
SVP; EVP and COO, Seven-Up: Dale Schaufel, age 47, $271,833 pay
SVP: Charles P. Grier, age 59, $228,006 pay
Auditors: KPMG Peat Marwick
Employees: 854

WHERE

HQ: 8144 Walnut Hill Ln., Dallas, TX 75231
Phone: 214-360-7000
FAX: 214-360-7981

Dr Pepper/Seven-Up Companies sell the 7-Up brands in the US only and the Dr Pepper brands throughout the US and in 15 countries.

Dr Pepper's Major World Markets
Canada
China
Japan
Middle East
Scandinavia
UK
West Africa
Western Europe

WHAT

	1989 Sales		1989 Operating Income	
	$ mil	% of total	$ mil	% of total
Dr Pepper	267	52	74	65
7-Up	247	48	40	35
Total	**514**	**100**	**114**	**100**

Brand Names
Dr Pepper
Diet Dr Pepper
Welch's (soft drinks only)
7-Up
Diet 7-Up
Cherry 7-Up
Like
IBC Root Beer
IBC Creme Soda

Contract Services
Beverage analysis
Concentrate production
Flavor formulation
Technical assistance for soft drink packaging, plant design, quality control, and marketing

RANKINGS

335th in *Forbes* 400 US Private Cos.

COMPETITION

Bass
Cadbury Schweppes
Coca-Cola
PepsiCo

DRESSER INDUSTRIES, INC.

OVERVIEW

Dallas-based Dresser Industries is a major world industrial equipment manufacturer. Since 1983 Dresser, under CEO Jack Murphy, has refocused its efforts on equipment for the petroleum industry.

Dresser's strategy is to manufacture equipment necessary all along the path, from wellhead to gas pump, reasoning that while one segment of the oil business suffers, another will thrive. Before the Iraqi invasion of Kuwait sent crude oil prices skyrocketing, that meant concentrating on "downstream" (refining and marketing) equipment while demand for "upstream" (exploration and production) products sagged.

Serving the upstream, Dresser's M-I Drilling Fluids (60% owned) is the industry leader in drilling fluids and is a joint effort with Halliburton. Dresser owns 30% of Western Atlas International (Litton owns the rest). Western Atlas is the leading firm offering seismic exploration and data processing services and core and fluid analysis.

Downstream, Dresser's engineering services unit — notably M. W. Kellogg — has grown rapidly, aided in part by a large Australian project. Dresser-Rand, a joint venture with Ingersoll-Rand, makes compressors and turbines.

Dresser continues to manufacture equipment for industries other than the petroleum business. Its Komatsu Dresser joint venture, a leader in heavy construction equipment, is the centerpiece.

WHEN

Solomon Dresser arrived in the oil boom town of Bradford, Pennsylvania, in 1878 with a consumptive wife and 4 children. He eked out a living in oil field jobs. He also tinkered with an invention, and in 1880 Dresser was granted a patent for a cap packer, a device that prevents crude oil from mixing with other fluids in a well. In the 1880s and 1890s he perfected a coupling that used fitted rubber to prevent leaks in pipeline connections.

As the natural gas industry grew, so did demand for the reliable Dresser coupling. The family firm prospered even after Solomon's death in 1911, but his heirs, anxious to pursue other interests and leery of the new, competing technology of welding, sold the company to W. A. Harriman & Company in 1928, and the investment banker took Dresser public.

Soon after, 3 Harriman executives — including Roland Harriman, son of the founder, and Prescott Bush, father of future US president George Bush — were discussing the vacant Dresser presidency. Just then, an old Yale friend, Neil Mallon, dropped by the office, and Harriman tapped Mallon for the top post.

During Mallon's 41-year career with Dresser, the company grew to an oil field conglomerate. Bryant Heating and Manufacturing was the first acquisition (bought in 1933 and sold in 1949). As Dresser tried to develop a high-speed compressor for gas pipelines, it purchased Clark Brothers, a compressor manufacturer (1937). It later abandoned its compressor research, but Olean, New York–based Clark became a cornerstone of the company.

The company moved its headquarters to Cleveland in 1945, then to Dallas in 1950. Dresser acquisitions ranged from International Stacey (construction and oil drilling equipment, 1944) to Magnet Cove (drilling "mud" lubricant for oil well holes, 1949) to Symington-Wayne (gasoline pumps, 1968).

In 1983, after an oil services boom had peaked, CEO Jack Murphy began refocusing the far-flung empire on the petroleum business, balancing upstream and downstream services and products. Dresser bought M. W. Kellogg Company (refinery engineering, 1988) just in time for a petrochemical boom but withdrew a 1989 bid for drill bit maker Smith International in the face of antitrust problems.

HOW MUCH

	9 Yr. Growth	1980	1981	1982	1983	1984	1985	1986	1987	1988	1989
Sales ($ mil)	*(0.2%)*	4,016	4,615	4,161	3,473	3,732	4,111	3,661	3,120	3,942	3,956
Net income ($ mil)	*(5.1%)*	261	317	172	5	97	*(196)*	1	16	123	163
Income as % of sales	—	6.5%	6.9%	4.1%	0.1%	2.6%	*(4.8%)*	0.0%	0.5%	3.1%	4.1%
Earnings per share ($)	*(3.5%)*	3.35	4.04	2.19	0.06	1.24	*(2.58)*	0.01	0.22	1.78	2.42
Stock price – high ($)	—	57.00	54.88	33.50	25.50	23.38	24.25	20.38	35.63	35.63	48.00
Stock price – low ($)	—	23.88	30.88	12.25	15.00	15.25	16.75	14.00	17.63	22.50	29.00
Stock price – close ($)	*(1.9%)*	53.50	33.25	19.75	20.75	18.25	18.13	19.38	26.25	29.38	44.88
P/E – high	—	17	14	15	425	19	—	—	162	20	20
P/E – low	—	7	8	6	250	12	—	—	80	13	12
Dividends per share ($)	5.4%	0.56	0.66	0.77	0.80	0.80	0.80	0.70	0.40	0.55	0.90
Book value per share ($)	1.3%	21.09	24.50	25.58	24.62	24.90	21.60	21.33	21.51	22.38	23.75

1989 Year End:
Debt ratio: 12.9%
Return on equity: 10.5%
Cash (mil): $455
Current ratio: 1.82
Long-term debt (mil): $238
Number of shares (mil): 68
Dividends:
1989 average yield: 2.0%
1989 payout: 37.2%
Market value (mil): $3,038

Stock Price History high/low 1980-89

60
50
40
30
20
10
0

NYSE symbol: DI
Incorporated: Delaware, 1956
Fiscal year ends: October 31

WHO

Chairman, President, and CEO: John J. Murphy, age 58, $993,900 pay
EVP Administration: Bill D. St. John, age 58, $550,220 pay
SVP Accounting and Tax: James J. Corboy, age 60
VP, General Counsel, and Secretary: M. Scott Nickson, Jr., age 55, $273,209 pay
Auditors: Price Waterhouse
Employees: 31,400

WHERE

HQ: 1600 Pacific Bldg., Dallas, TX 75201
Phone: 214-740-6000
FAX: 214-740-6584

Dresser manufactures in the US and 13 foreign countries.

	1989 Sales		1989 Operating Income	
	$ mil	% of total	$ mil	% of total
US	2,278	58	168	61
Canada	114	3	16	6
Europe	871	22	49	17
Other countries	693	17	44	16
Adjustments	—	—	(106)	—
Total	**3,956**	**100**	**171**	**100**

WHAT

	1989 Sales		1989 Operating Income	
	$ mil	% of total	$ mil	% of total
Mining & construction equip.	352	9	9	3
Oil field products & services	509	13	28	10
Energy processing & conversion equip.	1,463	37	134	48
Engineering services	1,234	31	37	14
General industry	412	10	69	25
Adjustments	(14)	—	(106)	—
Total	**3,956**	**100**	**171**	**100**

Oil Field Products & Services
Drill bits
Drilling fluid systems
Exploration services
Production tools
Rigs and equipment

Energy Processing Products
Compressors and turbines
Control products
Engineering services
Marketing systems (Wayne gas pumps)
Power systems
Pumps

Industrial Operations
Mining, construction equipment
Pneumatic tools
Refractory products
Specialty products

RANKINGS

119th in *Fortune* 500 Industrial Cos.
330th in *Fortune* Global 500 Industrial Cos.
211th in *Forbes* Sales 500
192nd in *Business Week* 1000
554th in *Business Week* Global 1000

COMPETITION

Baker Hughes
Caterpillar
Cooper Industries
Deere
FMC
Halliburton
Ingersoll-Rand
Schlumberger

E. I. DU PONT DE NEMOURS AND COMPANY

OVERVIEW

Du Pont is the largest chemical producer in the US. The Wilmington, Delaware–based company's products, however, go beyond chemicals, ranging from fibers to oil to firearms. With $35.1 billion in sales, 40% of which comes from overseas, Du Pont is the 7th largest exporter in the US.

Du Pont has 6 principal business segments industrial products (organic and inorganic chemicals); fibers (Dacron, Lycra, Orlon, etc.); polymers (nylon resins, acetyl resins, Teflon, etc.); petroleum (Conoco); coal (Consolidation Coal Company); and diversified businesses (agricultural products, electronics, imaging systems, pharmaceuticals, and sporting goods). Du Pont is the 11th largest natural gas producer in the world and the 2nd largest US coal producer after AMAX. It is also one of the world's largest producers of crop-protection products.

In 1989 Du Pont spent almost $1.4 billion on research, making it the 6th largest R&D spender in the US. Du Pont has pledged to reduce emission levels at its facilities 60% by 1993 (from 1987 levels). It has also committed to phase out chlorofluorocarbon (CFC) production before 2000. Du Pont also intends to continue its penetration of foreign markets.

Du Pont's largest shareholder is Seagram, which holds a 24% equity interest.

NYSE symbol: DD
Incorporated: Delaware, 1915
Fiscal year ends: December 31

WHO

Chairman and CEO: Edgar S. Woolard, Jr., age 55, $1,287,247 pay
VC: Elwood P. Blanchard, Jr., age 58, $969,320 pay
SVP Finance: John J. Quindlen, age 57
Auditors: Price Waterhouse
Employees: 145,787

WHERE

HQ: 1007 Market St., Wilmington, DE 19898
Phone: 302-774-1000
FAX: 302-774-7322

Du Pont conducts operations in 40 countries.

	1989 Sales		1989 Net Income	
	$ mil	% of total	$ mil	% of total
US	21,382*	60	1,985	69
Europe	10,329	29	777	27
Other countries	3,823	11	119	4
Adjustments	(435)	—	(401)	—
Total	**35,099**	**100**	**2,480**	**100**

*includes $4,844 million of export sales.

WHEN

Eleuthère Irénée du Pont de Nemours, a Frenchman who had studied gunpowder manufacture under chemist Antoine Lavoisier, fled to America in 1800 after the French Revolution. In 1802 with the help of French capital, he founded E. I. du Pont de Nemours and Company and set up a gunpowder plant on Delaware's Brandywine Creek.

Within a decade the plant grew to be the largest of its kind in the US and benefited greatly from government contracts in the War of 1812. After Irénée's death in 1834, his sons Alfred and Henry took over, buying out the other partners to ensure du Pont family control. Under their leadership the company profited from selling gunpowder to the US government in the Mexican-American War (1840s) and to both sides in the Crimean War (1850s). Du Pont added dynamite and nitroglycerine (1880) and introduced guncotton (1892) and smokeless powder (1894).

In 1902 du Pont cousins Pierre, Alfred, and Coleman bought Du Pont and in 1903 instituted a centralized structure with functionally organized departments, an innovation that big business widely adopted. By 1906 Du Pont controlled 70% of the American explosives market. A 1912 antitrust decision forced Du Pont to dispose of part of the powder business by forming Hercules and Atlas Powder Companies, but the outbreak of WWI in 1914 generated Du Pont $89 million in earnings to use in diversifying into paints, plastics, and dyes.

In 1917 Du Pont acquired an interest in General Motors that had increased to 37% by 1922. In 1962, after 13 years of litigation, the US Supreme Court ordered the Du Pont–GM connection broken for antitrust violations; Du Pont distributed its GM shares to Du Pont shareholders.

In the 1920s Du Pont bought and improved French cellophane technology and began production of rayon. Du Pont's list of inventions includes neoprene synthetic rubber (1931), Lucite (1937), nylon and Teflon (1938), Orlon, Dacron, and many others.

The last du Pont to head the company resigned as chairman in 1972, but du Pont family members still control about 22% of common stock.

In 1981 Du Pont acquired Conoco, formerly Continental Oil, for $7.6 billion — one of the largest US acquisitions as of that date — and added to its energy business in 1986 by purchasing 2 coal companies for $155 million. Petroleum and coal contributed 35% and 5% of 1989 sales.

WHAT

	1989 Sales		1989 Operating Income	
	$ mil	% of total	$ mil	% of total
Coal	1,818	5	294	6
Industrial products	3,702	10	960	20
Fibers	5,966	17	1,099	23
Polymers	5,581	16	710	14
Petroleum	12,314	35	1,315	27
Other businesses	6,153	17	477	10
Adjustments	(435)	—	(365)	—
Total	**35,09**	**100**	**4,490**	**100**

Energy Subsidiaries
Conoco (crude oil, natural gas production)
Consolidation Coal Co. (coal mining)

Consumer Product Materials
Antron
Dacron
Kevlar
Lucite
Lycra
Mylar
Orlon
Teflon

Other Products
Agricultural herbicides and insecticides
Firearms (Remington)
Imaging systems
Industrial chemicals (*e.g.*, titanium)
Integrated circuits
Pharmaceuticals

HOW MUCH

	9 Yr. Growth	1980	1981	1982	1983	1984	1985	1986	1987	1988	1989
Sales ($ mil)	11.1%	13,652	22,729	33,150	35,173	35,680	29,239	26,907	30,224	32,514	35,099
Net income ($ mil)	14.8%	716	1,081	894	1,127	1,431	1,118	1,538	1,786	2,190	2,480
Income as % of sales	—	5.2%	4.8%	2.7%	3.2%	4.0%	3.8%	5.7%	5.9%	6.7%	7.1%
Earnings per share ($)	9.1%	1.61	1.93	1.25	1.56	1.98	1.53	2.11	2.46	3.04	3.53
Stock price – high ($)	—	16.50	18.67	14.79	18.92	18.38	23.13	30.83	43.67	30.96	42.17
Stock price – low ($)	—	10.38	11.92	10.00	11.71	14.13	15.88	19.83	25.00	25.25	28.71
Stock price – close ($)	12.7%	14.00	12.42	11.96	17.33	16.50	22.63	28.00	29.13	29.42	41.00
P/E – high	—	10	10	12	12	9	15	15	18	10	12
P/E – low	—	6	6	8	7	7	10	9	10	8	8
Dividends per share ($)	5.2%	0.92	0.92	0.80	0.83	0.97	1.00	1.02	1.10	1.23	1.45
Book value per share ($)	6.9%	12.40	14.53	14.96	15.68	16.69	17.21	18.25	19.55	21.36	22.71

1989 Year End:
Debt ratio: 20.8%
Return on equity: 16.0%
Cash (mil): $692
Current ratio: 1.21
Long-term debt (mil): $4,149
Number of shares (mil): 685
Dividends:
1989 average yield: 3.5%
1989 payout: 41.1%
Market value (mil): $28,099

Stock Price History high/low 1980-89

RANKINGS

9th in *Fortune* 500 Industrial Cos.
19th in *Fortune* Global 500 Industrial Cos.
6th in *Fortune* 50 Exporters
11th in *Forbes* Sales 500
10th in *Business Week* 1000
29th in *Business Week* Global 1000

COMPETITION

Allied-Signal
American Cyanamid
BASF
Bayer
Burlington Holdings
Dow Chemical
Fieldcrest Cannon
FMC
W. R. Grace
Hercules
Hoechst
Monsanto
Occidental
Rhône-Poulenc
Union Carbide
Petroleum and drug companies
Other chemical and textile companies

DUKE POWER COMPANY

OVERVIEW

Duke, America's 7th largest public utility measured in kilowatt-hour sales, provides electricity and electric service to about 4.5 million people in a 20,000-square-mile service area covering 56 counties of North and South Carolina. The company is widely viewed as one of the best run utilities in the industry, ranking first in efficiency of its fossil fuel plants for 15 consecutive years. The company sold 67 billion kilowatt-hours of electricity in 1989, with electric revenues totaling $3.6 billion (70% from North Carolina, 30% from South Carolina).

Nantahala Power & Light provides electricity in 5 North Carolina counties.

Duke Engineering & Services provides engineering and technical expertise to various clients, and, through a partnership with the Fluor Corporation (Duke/Fluor Daniel), Duke designs, builds, and manages coal-fired plants nationwide. The company's Mill-Power Supply, currently for sale, sells industrial electrical equipment. Duke also owns 270,000 acres of Carolina timberland and engages in real estate development through Crescent Resources, Inc.

NYSE symbol: DUK
Incorporated: North Carolina, 1964
Fiscal year ends: December 31

WHO

Chairman and President: William S. Lee, age 60, $496,616 pay
VP Finance: Richard J. Osborne, age 38
Auditors: Deloitte & Touche
Employees: 20,000

WHERE

HQ: 422 S. Church St., Charlotte, NC 28242
Phone: 704-373-4011
FAX: 704-373-8038

Generating Facilities

Coal-Fired
Allen (NC)
Belews Creek (NC)
Buck (NC)
Cliffside (NC)
Dan River (NC)
Lee (SC)
Marshall (NC)
Riverbend (NC)

Hydroelectric
Boyds Mill (SC)
Bridgewater (NC)
Buzzard Roost (SC)
Cedar Creek (SC)
Cowans Ford (NC)
Dearborn (SC)
Fishing Creek (SC)
Gaston Shoals (SC)
Great Falls (SC)
Holliday's Bridge (SC)
Idols (NC)
Jocassee pumped storage (SC)
Keowee (SC)
Lookout Shoals (NC)
Mountain Island (NC)
Ninety-Nine Islands (SC)
Oxford (NC)
Rhodhiss (NC)
Rocky Creek (SC)
Saluda (SC)
Spencer Mountain (NC)
Stice Shoals (NC)
Turner (NC)
Tuxedo (NC)
Wateree (SC)
Wylie (SC)

Nuclear
Catawba (12 1/2%) (NC)
McGuire (NC)
Oconee (SC)

Oil & Gas
Buck (NC)
Buzzard Roost (SC)
Dan River (NC)
Lee (SC)
Riverbend (NC)

WHEN

In 1899 engineer-turned-surgeon Dr. W. Gill Wylie founded the Catawba Power Company, hiring engineer W. S. Lee to design the company's India Hook Shoals hydroelectric plant near Fort Mill, South Carolina. Operational by 1904, this plant set the standard for the company's future plants — each one designed by company engineers and after 1924 built by company construction teams.

In 1905 the Southern Power Company was formed out of the American Development Company, which had acquired all of Catawba Power's stock. Wylie was installed as president and Lee as chief engineer. James "Buck" Duke (founder of the American Tobacco Company and the W. Duke and Sons tobacco empire), instrumental in the formation of the power companies, became president in 1910 and organized Mill-Power Supply to sell heavy electric equipment to the region's textile mills. In 1913 Duke formed The Southern Public Utility Company (SPUC) to buy various Piedmont utilities (gas, water, and electric). By 1933 SPUC provided power to 195 North and South Carolina communities.

In 1917 Duke established Wateree Electric. Wateree became Duke Power Company in 1924 and by 1935 owned all of the properties formerly held by Southern Power. In 1924 Duke authorized construction of the company's first steam generating plant (completed 1926).

When Buck Duke died (1925), approximately 85% of Duke Power's stock was held by the Duke family, Doris Duke Trust, and Duke Endowment, a trust created in 1924 for Duke University (Trinity College, renamed in Buck Duke's honor, 1924) and other Piedmont area colleges. When the company's stock was first traded publicly (Curb Exchange, 1950), the Duke family, Endowment, and Trust still owned 67%. This was diluted to about 15% after the company was listed on the NYSE in 1961.

In the late 1950s Duke Power helped finance an experimental nuclear reactor at Parr Shoals, South Carolina. Oconee, the company's first nuclear plant, designed by Lee's grandson, W. S. Lee III, was operational by 1974. Duke also bought 3 Kentucky coal mining companies (1970) to provide fuel for its steam generators.

Duke Power bought the electrical systems at Duke University (1975) and at the University of North Carolina at Chapel Hill (1976). Its McGuire nuclear plant was operational by 1984, and a 3rd nuclear plant (Catawba) went on-line in 1986.

Duke began offering its engineering expertise to outside firms in 1982, forming Duke Engineering and Services in 1987. In 1988 the company organized the Duke Energy Corporation to develop and finance power projects outside the Piedmont area.

WHAT

	1989 Sales	
	$ mil	% of total
Residential	1,199	33
Commercial	851	23
Industrial	1,148	31
Wholesale & other energy sales	396	11
Other electric revenues	45	1
Adjustments	9	1
Total	**3,648**	**100**

Generation by Source	%
Coal	35
Nuclear	63
Hydroelectric	2
	100

Subsidiaries/Affiliates
Church Street Capital Corp.
Crescent Resources, Inc. (real estate)
Duke Energy Corp. (plant construction)
Duke Engineering & Services, Inc.
Duke/Fluor Daniel (partnership with Fluor Corp.)
Louisiana Energy Services (uranium enrichment)
Mill-Power Supply Co. (electrical equipment)
Nantahala Power and Light Co.

HOW MUCH

	9 Yr. Growth	1980	1981	1982	1983	1984	1985	1986	1987	1988	1989
Sales ($ mil)	8.9%	1,687	1,913	2,250	2,426	2,717	2,906	3,409	3,714	3,636	3,648
Net income ($ mil)	7.0%	311	336	350	431	461	438	468	500	448	572
Income as % of sales	—	18.4%	17.6%	15.6%	17.8%	17.0%	15.1%	13.7%	13.5%	12.3%	15.7%
Earnings per share ($)	5.8%	3.07	3.18	3.07	3.76	3.98	3.72	4.04	4.40	*3.90*	5.12
Stock price – high ($)	—	19.25	22.50	24.00	26.38	30.13	36.88	52.00	51.75	49.00	56.50
Stock price – low ($)	—	13.75	15.88	20.25	21.75	22.25	28.50	34.88	39.38	42.25	42.75
Stock price – close ($)	13.4%	18.13	20.63	23.25	25.13	29.00	35.38	45.25	42.88	46.25	56.13
P/E – high	—	6	7	8	7	8	10	13	12	13	11
P/E – low	—	4	5	7	6	6	8	9	9	11	8
Dividends per share ($)	5.1%	1.95	2.08	2.24	2.32	2.42	2.54	2.64	2.74	2.88	3.04
Book value per share ($)	5.2%	22.82	23.83	24.89	26.26	27.80	28.98	30.34	31.96	34.01	36.10

1989 Year End:
Debt ratio: 40.9%
Return on equity: 14.6%
Cash (mil): $72
Current ratio: 1.25
Long-term debt (mil): $2,822
Number of shares (mil): 101
Dividends:
1989 average yield: 5.4%
1989 payout: 59.4%
Market value (mil): $5,684

RANKINGS

26th in *Fortune* 50 Utilities
228th in *Forbes* Sales 500
102nd in *Business Week* 1000
327th in *Business Week* Global 1000

THE DUN & BRADSTREET CORPORATION

OVERVIEW

Dun & Bradstreet (D&B) is the largest purveyor of marketing and business information in the US. D&B offers over 3,000 products and services for a wide range of business activities.

Marketing information is D&B's biggest business. A.C. Nielsen measures television audiences and performs marketing research. Donnelley is the largest publisher of *Yellow Pages* telephone directories. D&B's commercial credit service has information on over 9 million US businesses and 7 million businesses in 26 foreign countries. Moody's Investors Service provides more than 15 million pieces of financial and corporate information annually.

Other divisions offer market information services to the food, tobacco, and health care industries. D&B announced plans in 1990 to sell Donnelley Marketing, a direct-mail distributor of grocery coupons; Datastream and Interactive Data, investment information services; and 3 other units.

Dun & Bradstreet's profits dropped the first 2 quarters of 1990 (22% and 18%), reflecting adverse publicity over sales practices in the company's credit services business.

NYSE symbol: DNB
Incorporated: Delaware, 1973
Fiscal year ends: December 31

WHO

Chairman and CEO: Charles W. Moritz, age 53, $1,271,739 pay
President and COO: Robert E. Weissman, age 49, $896,598 pay
EVP Finance and CFO: Edwin A. Bescherer, Jr., age 56
Auditors: Coopers & Lybrand
Employees: 71,500

WHEN

Dun & Bradstreet's origins were in Lewis Tappan's Mercantile Agency, established in 1841 in New York City. The Mercantile Agency was one of the first commercial credit reporting agencies created to supply wholesalers and importers with information on their customers. Tappan's credit reporters, who prepared written reports on companies, included 4 men who became US Presidents (Lincoln, Grant, Cleveland, and McKinley). In the 1840s Tappan opened offices in Boston, Philadelphia, and Baltimore and in 1857 established offices in Montreal and London. Two years later Robert Dun took over the agency, changing its name to R.G. Dun & Company. The first edition of *Dun's Reference Book* (1859) contained information on 20,268 businesses; by 1886 the number had risen to over one million. By 1869 Dun had a branch office in San Francisco. John M. Bradstreet, a rival company founded in Cincinnati in 1849, merged with Dun in 1933; the company adopted the Dun & Bradstreet name in 1939.

In 1961 Dun & Bradstreet bought Reuben H. Donnelley Corporation, publisher of the *Yellow Pages* (first published in 1886), 10 trade magazines, and a direct-mail advertising business. The following year Moody's Investors Service (founded 1900) and Official Airline Guide (guides first published 1929) became part of D&B.

D&B's records were first computerized in the 1960s and eventually became the largest private database in the world (2nd only to the government's). By 1975 D&B had a national electronic network with a centralized database. Able to create new products by repackaging information from its vast database (such as *Dun's Financial Profiles* in 1979), the company was able to double sales in 5 years to $1.4 billion by 1980.

Since the late 1970s the company has purchased National CSS (computer services company, 1979), McCormack & Dodge (software, 1983), and Technical Publishing (trade and professional publications, 1978). The addition of A.C. Nielsen (includes Nielsen TV ratings, 1984) and IMS International (pharmaceutical sales data, 1988) made D&B the largest marketing research company in the world. In 1988 D&B sold Official Airline Guide to Maxwell Communications for $750 million. In 1989 some customers complained that company sales representatives misled them to buy more services than they needed; D&B, without admitting wrongdoing, settled a class action lawsuit for $18 million and dozens of other suits for undisclosed sums, according to *Business Week*. D&B announced in August 1990 its intention to sell its IMS pharmaceutical market research unit.

WHERE

HQ: 299 Park Ave., New York, NY 10171
Phone: 212-593-6800
FAX: 212-593-8979

The company provides services in the US and 26 foreign countries.

	1989 Sales		1989 Operating Income	
	$ mil	% of total	$ mil	% of total
US	2,895	67	653	72
Europe	999	23	158	18
Other foreign	428	10	87	10
Adjustments	—	—	(32)	—
Total	**4,322**	**100**	**866**	**100**

WHAT

	1989 Sales		1989 Operating Income	
	$ mil	% of total	$ mil	% of total
Risk-management info. services	954	22	266	28
Directory info. svcs.	437	10	140	14
Marketing info. svcs.	1,715	39	355	37
Financial info. svcs.	325	8	109	11
Business services	891	21	101	10
Adjustments	—	—	(105)	—
Total	**4,322**	**100**	**866**	**100**

Business Groups
Business services
Directory information services
Financial information services
Marketing information services
Risk-management information services

Major Operating Companies
Dataquest
Dun & Bradstreet
McCormack & Dodge
Moody's Investors Service, Inc.
A. C. Nielsen Co.
The Reuben H. Donnelley Corp.

RANKINGS

21st in *Fortune* 100 Diversified Service Cos.
198th in *Forbes* Sales 500
55th in *Business Week* 1000
190th in *Business Week* Global 1000

COMPETITION

Commerce Clearing House
Computer Associates
Control Data
Dow Jones
Knight-Ridder
McGraw-Hill
Reuters
TRW
U S West

HOW MUCH

	9 Yr. Growth	1980	1981	1982	1983	1984	1985	1986	1987	1988	1989
Sales ($ mil)	15.6%	1,176	1,331	1,462	1,510	2,397	2,772	3,114	3,359	4,267	4,322
Net income ($ mil)	21.4%	103	121	142	142	253	295	340	393	499	586
Income as % of sales	—	8.7%	9.1%	9.7%	9.4%	10.5%	10.6%	10.9%	11.7%	11.7%	13.6%
Earnings per share ($)	14.7%	0.91	1.08	1.26	1.25	1.66	1.93	2.23	2.57	2.66	3.14
Stock price – high ($)	—	14.75	17.56	26.00	35.00	33.75	43.94	60.19	71.75	57.50	60.25
Stock price – low ($)	—	8.56	13.31	14.63	24.44	25.56	31.38	40.38	44.50	45.88	41.25
Stock price – close ($)	13.9%	14.25	15.75	24.63	31.00	32.81	41.88	52.63	54.75	53.63	46.00
P/E – high	—	16	16	21	28	20	23	27	28	22	19
P/E – low	—	9	12	12	20	15	16	18	17	17	13
Dividends per share ($)	16.4%	0.49	0.57	0.67	0.77	0.91	1.06	1.24	1.45	1.68	1.94
Book value per share ($)	14.6%	3.47	3.89	4.48	5.15	8.06	8.92	9.80	10.95	11.18	11.80

1989 Year End:
Debt ratio: 0.0%
Return on equity: 27.3%
Cash (mil): $760
Current ratio: 1.17
Long-term debt (mil): $0
Number of shares (mil): 185
Dividends:
1989 average yield: 4.2%
1989 payout: 61.6%
Market value (mil): $8,518

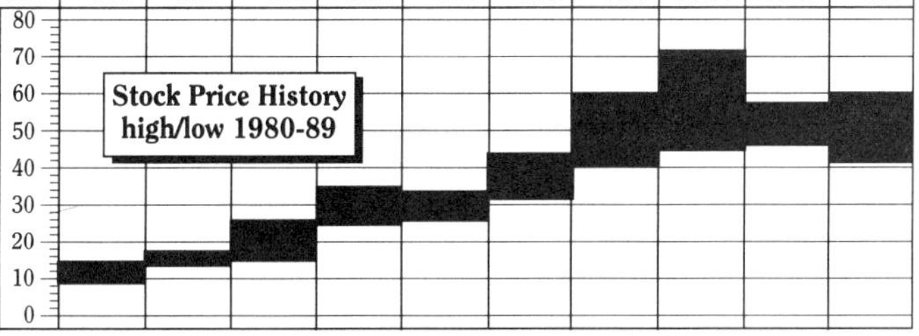

Stock Price History high/low 1980-89

EASTMAN KODAK COMPANY

OVERVIEW

Rochester, New York–based Eastman Kodak, long known as a market leader in the amateur photography business, is a major player in the imaging, chemical, health, and information industries. The familiar bright red-and-yellow Kodak logo is found all over the world on film, cameras, photographic paper and chemicals, X-ray machines, and color copiers. But many of Kodak's products — such as recyclable plastic bottles, synthetic fibers, and plastic food containers — do not bear the company's logo.

Having spent $1.25 billion on R&D in 1989, Kodak was the 9th largest R&D spender in the US. And with 41% of its revenues attributed to international sales, it was the 11th largest US exporter in 1989.

Kodak's imaging sector (cameras, films, batteries, audiovisual equipment, etc.) is the company's largest revenue producer with 1989 sales of $7 billion. Kodak is the market leader in film in the US and Europe. The information sector (copiers, computer storage disks, electronic publishing equipment, etc.) ranked 2nd in 1989 company sales ($4.2 billion), followed by health (Sterling Drugs and Lehn & Fink, $4 billion) and chemicals (Eastman Chemical, $3.2 billion).

WHEN

George Eastman, after developing a method for dry-plate photography, established The Eastman Dry Plate and Film Company in 1884 in Rochester, New York. The company went through a succession of name changes, settling on Kodak in 1892, after Eastman tried many combinations of letters starting and ending with "K," which he thought was a "strong, incisive sort of letter."

In 1888 the company introduced its first camera, a small, easy-to-use device that sold for $25, loaded with enough film for 100 pictures. To develop the film, owners mailed the camera to Kodak, which returned it with the pictures and more film. The very successful Brownie followed in 1900. In 1923 Kodak introduced a home-movie camera, projector, and film.

Ailing and concluding his work was done, Eastman shot and killed himself at the age of 77 (1932). Kodak continued to dominate the photography industry with the introduction of color film (Kodachrome, 1935) and the Brownie hand-held movie camera (1951). Kodak established manufacturing facilities in Tennessee (1920) and Texas (1950) to produce the chemicals, plastics, and fibers used in its film production.

The Instamatic, introduced in 1963, became Kodak's biggest success. The camera, with the film in a foolproof cartridge, eliminated the need for loading in the dark. By 1976 Kodak had sold an estimated 60 million Instamatics, 50 million more cameras than all its competitors combined. Subsequent introductions have included the Kodak instant camera (which caused Polaroid to wage a successful legal suit for patent infringement against the company) and the disc camera. Both products have since been discontinued, the instant camera because of the Polaroid suit and the disc camera because of inferior photo quality (too grainy).

In 1983, responding to lagging sales and growing competition, Kodak streamlined operations and began diversifying into electronic publishing, batteries, floppy disks (Verbatim, 1985, sold 1990), and, more recently, pharmaceuticals. In 1988 Kodak acquired Sterling Drug (Bayer aspirin and Lysol) for $5.1 billion, its largest acquisition ever. Paying off the debt for Sterling continues to burden Kodak, due in part to the sluggish performance of Sterling's products. At the beginning of 1990, Kodak was also grappling with stiffer competition in the photographic film and paper business from Fuji and Konica USA.

HOW MUCH

	9 Yr. Growth	1980	1981	1982	1983	1984	1985	1986	1987	1988	1989
Sales ($ mil)	7.3%	9,734	10,337	10,815	10,170	10,600	10,631	11,550	13,305	17,034	18,398
Net income ($ mil)	(8.3%)	1,154	1,239	1,162	565	923	332	374	1,178	1,397	529
Income as % of sales	—	11.9%	12.0%	10.7%	5.6%	8.7%	3.1%	3.2%	8.9%	8.2%	2.9%
Earnings per share ($)	(7.2%)	3.18	3.40	3.16	1.52	2.54	0.99	1.12	3.48	4.26	1.63
Stock price – high ($)	—	33.22	37.94	43.61	40.78	34.67	35.58	46.67	70.67	53.25	52.38
Stock price – low ($)	—	19.06	26.94	29.06	28.50	26.78	27.33	30.58	41.92	39.13	40.00
Stock price – close ($)	3.2%	31.00	31.61	38.22	33.83	31.94	33.75	45.75	49.00	45.13	41.13
P/E – high	—	10	11	14	27	14	36	42	20	13	32
P/E – low	—	6	8	9	19	11	28	27	12	9	25
Dividends per share ($)	3.9%	1.42	1.56	1.58	1.58	1.60	1.62	1.63	1.71	1.90	2.00
Book value per share ($)	2.4%	16.60	18.52	20.25	20.18	20.37	19.37	18.84	18.54	20.90	20.46

1989 Year End:
Debt ratio: 52.6%
Return on equity: 7.9%
Cash (mil): $1,279
Current ratio: 1.31
Long-term debt (mil): $7,376
Number of shares (mil): 325
Dividends:
1989 average yield: 4.9%
1989 payout: 122.7%
Market value (mil): $13,348

Stock Price History high/low 1980-89

NYSE symbol: EK
Incorporated: New Jersey, 1901
Fiscal year ends: December 31

WHO

Chairman, President and CEO: Kay R. Whitmore, age 57, $820,875 pay (prior to promotion)
SVP and Director of Finance and Administration: Paul L. Smith, age 54
Auditors: Price Waterhouse
Employees: 137,750

WHERE

HQ: 343 State St., Rochester, NY 14650
Phone: 716-724-4000
FAX: 716-724-0663

Eastman Kodak sells its products in 150 countries and has offices around the world.

	1989 Sales		1989 Operating Income	
	$ mil	% of total	$ mil	% of total
US	10,869	59	785	49
Latin America	1,339	7	239	15
Europe	4,556	25	470	30
Other countries	1,634	9	98	6
Adjustments	—	—	874	—
Total	**18,398**	**100**	**2,466**	**100**

WHAT

	1989 Sales		1989 Operating Income	
	$ mil	% of total	$ mil	% of total
Chemicals	3,204	17	643	40
Imaging	6,985	38	821	52
Health	4,009	22	487	31
Info. systems	4,200	23	(360)	(23)
Adjustments	—	—	875	—
Total	**18,398**	**100**	**2,466**	**100**

Chemicals
Kodel polyester
Plastics and adhesives
Polymers and resins

Health & Other
Bayer aspirin
Blood analyzers
Campho-Phenique
d-Con
Diaperene
Lysol
Midol
Minwax
Mop & Glo
Neo-Synephrine
pHiso Hex
Red Devil
Stridex
X-ray films

Imaging
Batteries
Cameras
Film and papers (Ektachrome and Kodachrome)

Information Systems
Atex (publishing)
Diconix printers
Optical disks
Photocopiers

RANKINGS

18th in *Fortune* 500 Industrial Cos.
50th in *Fortune* Global 500 Industrial Cos.
11th in *Fortune* 50 Exporters
27th in *Forbes* Sales 500
39th in *Business Week* 1000
103rd in *Business Week* Global 1000

COMPETITION

American Home Products
BASF
Bayer
Bristol-Myers Squibb
Clorox
Dow Chemical
Du Pont
General Electric
Johnson & Johnson
S.C. Johnson
3M
Polaroid
Procter & Gamble
Siemens
Xerox
Chemical, pharmaceutical, photo, and household products companies

EATON CORPORATION

OVERVIEW

Eaton, headquartered in Cleveland, is a leading manufacturer of automobile and truck components. The company manufactures more than 5,000 products, principally truck transmissions, axles, engine components, electrical equipment, and controls (for industrial, military, and appliance/automotive uses). Eaton's 2 groups, Vehicle Components and Controls, serve the transportation, industrial, aerospace, and military markets.

A high-technology company employing more than 2,000 engineers, scientists, and technicians, Eaton spent $123.3 million on R&D in 1989 (3.3% of sales). Its largest customer is Ford, whose purchases amounted to 24% of 1989 net sales. Since restructuring in 1982-1983, ROE has averaged 18%, the best in company history.

Eaton will continue investing heavily in R&D and capital equipment in order to maintain its crucial technological edge into the 1990s. The company plans to expand business in Europe and the Pacific Rim. Developing business with Japanese automobile companies manufacturing in the US is an important objective.

WHEN

In 1911 Joseph Eaton and Viggo Torbensen started the Torbensen Gear and Axle Company to manufacture an internal-gear rear axle for trucks patented by Torbensen in 1902. The company moved from Newark, New Jersey, to Cleveland in 1914. In 1917 Republic Motor Truck purchased Torbensen.

Eaton formed the Eaton Axle Company in 1919, repurchased Torbensen in 1922, and by 1931 had bought 11 more automotive parts companies (producing bumpers, springs, heaters, gasoline tank caps, and engine parts). In 1932 Eaton renamed the company Eaton Manufacturing.

The Great Depression reduced demand for automobiles and profits plummeted. Researchers produced the first heavy-duty, 2-speed axle in 1934. In 1937 Eaton opened its first foreign plant in Ontario. Heavy wartime demand helped Eaton recover, and in 1946 the company acquired Dynamatic (eddy-current drives). Joseph Eaton died in 1949.

The company built or renovated 11 plants during the 1950s. Attempting to diversify, Eaton acquired Fuller Manufacturing (truck transmissions, 1958), Cleveland Worm & Gear (worm gearing, 1959), Dole Valve (controls, valves, and beverage dispensers, 1963), and Yale & Towne Manufacturing (locks and fork-lift trucks, 1963). In 1966 the company changed its name to Eaton Yale & Towne.

The acquisitions augmented Eaton's international business, and foreign sales increased from virtually zero in 1961 to 20% of total sales by 1966. In 1971 Eaton adopted its present name.

In 1978 Eaton sold the lock and security business to Scovill Manufacturing and acquired Cutler-Hammer (industrial controls and defense electronics), Kenway (automated storage and retrieval systems), and Samuel Moore (plastics technology and fluid power). By 1980 Eaton was supplying the space shuttle's landing and communications system and traffic control systems for the air and waterways. In 1981 the US government awarded Eaton the $3 billion B-1B bomber defense avionics (radar-jamming) contract.

Downturns in the truck and automobile industries forced Eaton to close 30 plants and trim 23,000 employees between 1979 and 1983. In 1982 the company reported its first loss in 50 years, but a restructuring plan called "Operation Shrink" led Eaton to record profits and sales by 1984.

In 1987 Eaton announced plans to sell its defense electronics businesses (partially completed) and buy back about 27% of its stock. Vehicle components and controls now form the basis for Eaton's business.

HOW MUCH

	9 Yr. Growth	1980	1981	1982	1983	1984	1985	1986	1987	1988	1989
Sales ($ mil)	1.6%	3,176	3,165	2,453	2,674	3,510	3,675	3,812	3,138	3,469	3,671
Net income ($ mil)	6.8%	116	82	(71)	93	254	231	138	206	228	210
Income as % of sales	—	3.6%	2.6%	(2.9%)	3.5%	7.2%	6.3%	3.6%	6.6%	6.6%	5.7%
Earnings per share ($)	8.0%	2.79	1.95	(1.60)	1.97	5.00	4.48	2.78	4.79	6.11	5.59
Stock price – high ($)	—	23.25	27.67	23.92	37.00	37.67	43.25	53.25	71.83	57.33	67.50
Stock price – low ($)	—	13.50	17.67	15.17	19.08	25.17	33.00	42.00	37.00	44.67	53.00
Stock price – close ($)	13.0%	19.00	21.25	21.33	36.83	35.42	42.75	49.17	52.83	55.75	57.00
P/E – high	—	8	14	—	19	8	10	19	15	9	12
P/E – low	—	5	9	—	10	5	7	15	8	7	9
Dividends per share ($)	6.4%	1.15	1.15	1.15	0.53	0.73	0.90	1.07	1.27	1.67	2.00
Book value per share ($)	2.4%	25.04	24.77	18.57	20.55	24.58	28.33	28.63	28.51	31.24	31.01

1989 Year End:
Debt ratio: 42.2%
Return on equity: 18.0%
Cash (mil): $193
Current ratio: 2.1
Long-term debt (mil): $836
Number of shares (mil): 37
Dividends:
1989 average yield: 3.5%
1989 payout: 35.8%
Market value (mil): $2,104

Stock Price History high/low 1980-89

NYSE symbol: ETN
Incorporated: Ohio, 1916
Fiscal year ends: December 31

WHO

Chairman and CEO: James R. Stover, age 63, $1,149,715 pay
President and COO: William E. Butler, age 59, $689,747 pay
VC and Chief Financial and Administrative Officer: Stephen R. Hardis, age 54, $661,059 pay
President, Vehicle Components Group: Robert W. Gillison, age 54, $516,187 pay
President, Controls Group: Alexander M. Cutler, age 38, $401,313 pay
Auditors: Ernst & Young
Employees: 43,048

WHERE

HQ: Eaton Center, Cleveland, OH 44114
Phone: 216-523-5000
FAX: 216-523-4787

Eaton has 130 facilities in 20 countries.

	1989 Sales		1989 Operating Income	
	$ mil	% of total	$ mil	% of total
US	2,830	73	308	75
Canada	206	5	16	4
Europe	633	17	66	16
Other countries	190	5	20	5
Adjustments	(188)	—	(35)	—
Total	**3,671**	**100**	**375**	**100**

WHAT

	1989 Sales		1989 Operating Income	
	$ mil	% of total	$ mil	% of total
Vehicle components	2,105	57	255	62
Controls	1,566	43	155	38
Adjustments	—	—	(35)	—
Total	**3,671**	**100**	**375**	**100**

Vehicle Components
Axles
Brakes
Clutches
Engine valves
Fan drives
Hydraulic and hydrostatic equipment
Transmissions

Controls
Controllers
Distribution equipment
Electric drives
Materials-handling systems
Sensors
Starters
Switches
Timers

RANKINGS

115th in *Fortune* 500 Industrial Cos.
313th in *Fortune* Global 500 Industrial Cos.
226th in *Forbes* Sales 500
316th in *Business Week* 1000
888th in *Business Week* Global 1000

COMPETITION

Allied-Signal
American Standard
Borg-Warner
Dana
Raytheon
Reliance Electric
Robert Bosch
Rockwell International
Square D
Tenneco
Westinghouse
Vehicle manufacturers

EDWARD J. DEBARTOLO CORPORATION

OVERVIEW

Edward J. DeBartolo Corporation, based in the founder's hometown of Youngstown, Ohio, is a leading builder and operator of enclosed shopping malls in the US. It placed 2nd after Melvin Simon & Associates in 1989 retail development activity, with 11.8 million square feet under construction. DeBartolo had about $1.2 billion in 1989 revenues. The company's 70 million square feet of mall space makes up nearly 10% of all mall space in the country and is visited by approximately 40 million customers each week.

Although some of the malls are managed for others or operated as joint ventures, most of the sites are owned directly by the company. Recently built urban malls, such as New Orleans Centre and The Rivercenter in San Antonio, ride the trend toward downtown "urban centers." As of May 1990 the company had 10 malls under construction and 14 more planned. DeBartolo also owns and manages 18 smaller strip shopping centers, with more planned or under construction.

The company uses promotions and gimmicks to increase business in its malls. These include mall credit cards, frequent shopper prizes, shopper magazines, and an exercise program promoted by Richard Simmons.

DeBartolo also owns 50% of Cleveland's Higbee's department stores, in a joint venture with Dillard's. In addition, the company develops and operates office buildings, office parks, and hotels. DeBartolo's sports holdings include the 1990 Super Bowl champion San Francisco 49ers, the Pittsburgh Penguins hockey team, and the Remington Park horse racing track in Oklahoma City.

WHEN

Edward J. DeBartolo left his stepfather's paving business in 1948 to establish the company that bears his name. He built subsidized housing in Boardman, Ohio (near Youngstown) for young WWII veterans who were anxious to move to the suburbs. DeBartolo's foresight of the growth of the suburbs led him to build one of the first strip-style malls outside California in Boardman in 1950. Over the next 15 years the company built 45 more strip centers throughout the US.

DeBartolo also anticipated the real estate boom in Florida and bought large tracts of land there in the 1960s. Although the market developed later than DeBartolo had expected, the company had 1/3 of its holdings there when the boom did hit. Also in the 1960s DeBartolo became one of the first to develop large, covered regional malls in many parts of the nation.

DeBartolo opened Louisiana Downs, the first of his racetracks, in 1974; the track closed after 50 days of racing because it could not meet its payroll on time. With better economic times in the late 1970s, the track prospered. DeBartolo expanded his sports interests when he bought the San Francisco 49ers in 1977. The Pittsburgh Penguins came under DeBartolo ownership in 1978 when he received them as repayment for a debt.

In 1986 Allied Stores's management asked DeBartolo to help fend off a bid by Campeau. DeBartolo, recognizing that control of Allied's department store chains would complement his mall development activities by providing anchor stores, instead loaned Campeau $150 million for the takeover. In 1988 he stepped in with a $480 million loan to Campeau for its acquisition of Federated Department Stores. DeBartolo is now the largest creditor of the bankrupt Allied and Federated store chains.

Meanwhile, DeBartolo has continued to expand his other interests, opening the newest of its racetracks, Remington Park, in Oklahoma City in 1988. The $94 million racetrack's location was chosen because the company's research indicated that Oklahoma City had the highest number of horses per capita in the US (one horse for every 14 people); the research proved correct, with 11,000 people going to the track each race day. The Rivercenter (San Antonio) and Lakeland Square (Florida) malls also opened in 1988, with over one million square feet apiece; Chesapeake Square (Virginia) and Port Charlotte Town Center (Florida) opened in 1989.

DeBartolo's son Edward Jr. is the owner of the 49ers as well as president and COO of the company. DeBartolo's daughter Marie Denise York is credited with developing employee programs that have become models for the industry.

HOW MUCH

	3 Yr. Growth	1980	1981	1982	1983	1984	1985	1986	1987	1988	1989
Revenues ($ mil)	33.5%	—	—	—	—	—	—	500	650	1,066	1,189
No. of employees	10.9%	—	—	—	—	—	—	11,000	12,000	12,000	15,000
Total sq. ft. under construction (thou)	—	—	—	—	—	—	—	—	—	—	12,377

Revenues ($ mil) 1986-89

Private company
Incorporated: Ohio, 1948

WHO

Chairman and CEO: Edward J. DeBartolo, age 80
President and COO: Edward J. DeBartolo, Jr., age 43
EVP Personnel and Public Relations: Marie Denise DeBartolo York
SVP Corporate Planning and Finance and CFO: Anthony Liberati
Auditors: Deloitte & Touche
Employees: 15,000

WHERE

HQ: 7620 Market St., PO Box 3287, Youngstown, OH 44513
Phone: 216-758-7292
FAX: 216-758-3598

The company owns or manages 69 malls with over 70 million square feet in 20 states.

	1990 Retail Mall Space	
	square feet	% of total
Florida (23 malls)	25,654,785	37
Ohio (9 malls)	10,164,927	14
Indiana (5 malls)	5,602,075	8
Washington (4 malls)	4,339,792	6
New Jersey (4 malls)	4,108,784	6
Other states (24 malls)	20,557,695	29
Total (69 malls)	**70,428,058**	**100**

WHAT

Retail Stores
Higbee's, Cleveland (50% owned)

Major Malls
Aventura Mall, Miami
Castleton Square, Indianapolis
Century III Mall, Pittsburgh
Dadeland Mall, Miami
The Florida Mall, Orlando
Great Lakes Mall, Cleveland
Lafayette Square, Indianapolis
Northshore Shopping Center, Peabody, MA
Randall Park Mall, Cleveland

Office Projects & Hotels
(14 office projects and 3 hotels in 7 states)
Brickell Bay Office Tower, Miami
CNG Tower, New Orleans
DeBartolo Square, Pittsburgh (under development)
Sheraton Plaza Hotel at The Florida Mall, Orlando

Sports Enterprises & Complexes
(2 sports franchises, 3 horse racing tracks, and 3 sports/entertainment complexes)
Civic Arena, Pittsburgh
Pittsburgh Penguins (hockey)
Remington Park, Oklahoma City
San Francisco 49ers (football)

RANKINGS

119th in *Forbes* 400 US Private Cos.

COMPETITION

Campeau
Green Bay Packers
Helmsley Enterprises
Paramount
Sears
Trammell Crow
Other real estate development companies

EG&G, INC.

OVERVIEW

EG&G's 94 companies provide technologically advanced products and services in 6 business segments. The Instruments segment produces airport security and precision scientific instruments. The Components segment provides mechanical, optical, and electronic devices. The Technical Services segment conducts automotive product testing and provides support services for government agencies. The Aerospace segment provides products for the worldwide aviation industry. The Defense segment provides products and services for DOD. The DOE Support segment provides services, instruments, and components related to energy research.

EG&G derives the majority of its income from sales to and contracts with the US government. Under government contracts EG&G is active in engineering, developmental, and site-management programs related to national defense and security, physics and space research, and nuclear and non-nuclear energy research and development.

NYSE symbol: EGG
Incorporated: Massachusetts, 1947
Fiscal year ends: December 31

WHO

Chairman and CEO: John M. Kucharski, age 54, $455,822 pay
President: Donald M. Kerr, age 50, $306,040 pay
SVP and CFO: John R. Dolan, age 63
VP: James O. Zane, age 56, $298,559 pay
VP: Peter H. Zavattaro, age 52, $273,383 pay
VP: James R. Dubay, age 53, $272,277 pay
Auditors: Arthur Andersen & Co.
Employees: 30,000

WHEN

MIT professor Harold Edgerton invented the strobe light in 1931 while researching the operation of electric motors. Edgerton tried to sell the new device to General Electric. When it was not interested, Edgerton and former student Kenneth Germeshausen formed a consulting business using the strobe light and high-speed photography to help manufacturers solve industrial problems. As business picked up, they brought in another former student, Herbert Grier, and formed Edgerton, Germeshausen and Grier, Inc., in Massachusetts in 1947.

The company's first contract was to use its high-speed photographic techniques to record the explosions of nuclear weapons being tested by the government in Nevada. The company's original 1947 contract to monitor nuclear weapons tests has expanded in scope and continued without interruption to the present day.

In 1959 the company first sold shares to the public. In 1966 it adopted the name EG&G and began to move away from being a one-contract firm through a program of expansion and diversification involving internal growth and acquisition of existing companies. Over the past 24 years EG&G has bought over 70 companies involved in electronic instruments and components, biomedical services, energy research and development (nuclear, geothermal, coal, oil, and gas), nuclear weapons research and development, manufacture of seals and gaskets, automotive testing, and various aspects of the aerospace industry. Key acquisitions included Reynolds Electrical & Engineering (1967), which provides support services for the DOE and DOD, including the nuclear weapons testing program; Sealol, Inc. (1968), a worldwide manufacturer of seals for industrial applications; and Automotive Research Associates (1973).

In 1983 EG&G was awarded a contract to provide institutional management and technical support at the Kennedy Space center in Florida. In 1988 EG&G secured a contract to manage and operate the DOE's Mound facility in Miamisburg, Ohio, which is involved in R&D and production in the fields of components for nuclear weapons and nuclear electric generators for use in spacecraft. The company won another contract in 1988 to support Universities Research Association, Inc., in the development of the DOE's Superconducting Super Collider project in Texas. In 1989 the company bought Laboratorium Prof. Dr. Berthold of Germany (bioanalytical instruments), which had sales of over $45 million in 1989. In January 1990 company founder Edgerton died at age 86. In the same month EG&G took over operation of the DOE's Rocky Flats nuclear weapons components production facility near Golden, Colorado.

WHERE

HQ: 45 William St., Wellesley, MA 02181
Phone: 617-237-5100
FAX: 617-431-4115

Although EG&G operates worldwide, business is concentrated in the US.

	1989 Sales		1989 Operating Income	
	$ mil	% of total	$ mil	% of total
US	1,537	93	107	88
Foreign	113	7	14	12
Adjustments	—	—	(23)	—
Total	**1,650**	**100**	**98**	**100**

WHAT

	1989 Sales		1989 Operating Income	
	$ mil	% of total	$ mil	% of total
Instruments	165	10	12	10
DOE support	611	37	28	23
Components	231	14	22	18
Technical services	281	17	29	24
Aerospace	120	7	12	10
Defense	242	15	18	15
Adjustments	—	—	(23)	—
Total	**1,650**	**100**	**98**	**100**

Products
Aircraft components
Fans and heat sinks
Nuclear weapons components
Optoelectronic components
Seals and mechanical devices
Test and measurement systems

Services
Aeronautical ground support
Automotive testing
High energy physics consulting and support
Weapons testing and research

RANKINGS

245th in *Fortune* 500 Industrial Cos.
456th in *Forbes* Sales 500
484th in *Business Week* 1000

COMPETITION

Allied-Signal
Becton, Dickinson
Hewlett-Packard
Raytheon
Thiokol
Thomson

HOW MUCH

	9 Yr. Growth	1980	1981	1982	1983	1984	1985	1986	1987	1988	1989
Sales ($ mil)	11.6%	613	704	801	904	1,072	1,155	1,145	1,236	1,406	1,650
Net income ($ mil)	11.5%	26	34	40	47	54	56	45	55	69	70
Income as % of sales	—	4.3%	4.8%	5.0%	5.2%	5.0%	4.8%	3.9%	4.5%	4.9%	4.2%
Earnings per share ($)	11.2%	0.93	1.17	1.33	1.53	1.85	2.07	1.65	2.00	2.30	2.40
Stock price – high ($)	—	24.31	22.00	30.63	38.13	36.13	43.00	43.00	45.13	39.00	36.50
Stock price – low ($)	—	11.25	16.19	14.50	26.00	26.13	31.25	27.63	27.00	26.63	28.38
Stock price – close ($)	5.1%	21.81	19.75	28.25	32.50	31.63	38.38	28.25	33.25	28.75	34.00
P/E – high	—	26	19	23	25	20	21	26	23	17	15
P/E – low	—	12	14	11	17	14	15	17	14	12	12
Dividends per share ($)	14.6%	0.20	0.25	0.32	0.36	0.40	0.48	0.52	0.56	0.60	0.68
Book value per share ($)	13.1%	3.97	4.86	5.93	7.13	5.59	7.47	8.62	9.79	11.07	12.04

1989 Year End:
Debt ratio: 2.5%
Return on equity: 20.8%
Cash (mil): $29
Current ratio: 1.59
Long-term debt (mil): $9
Number of shares (mil): 29
Dividends:
1989 average yield: 2.0%
1989 payout: 28.3%
Market value (mil): $986

Stock Price History high/low 1980-89

50 45 40 35 30 25 20 15 10 5 0

ELECTROLUX AB

OVERVIEW

Electrolux is a global producer of appliances marketed under established brand names in the US and Europe. The Swedish company is the leading white goods (*e.g.*, washers, dryers, refrigerators) manufacturer in Europe and, through its Cleveland-based White Consolidated subsidiary, is #3 in the US. Electrolux is the world's largest producer of vacuum cleaners, industrial laundry equipment, and chainsaws, and Europe's leader in food service equipment and seat belts. Other activities include aluminum smelting and gardening equipment production. Well-known US brands include Tappan, Kelvinator, Frigidaire, and Eureka. Electrolux Corporation, an unrelated company, owns the US rights to the Electrolux mark. Sharp Corporation distributes Electrolux appliances in Japan.

After 2 decades of buying US and European market share, brand names, and production capacity, Electrolux expects to focus on marketing, product development, and production synergies among acquired companies.

WHEN

In 1910 Swedish salesman Axel Wenner-Gren saw an American-made vacuum cleaner in a Vienna store window and envisioned selling the cleaners door-to-door, a technique he had learned in the US. In 1912 he worked with fledgling Swedish vacuum cleaner makers AB Lux and Elektromekaniska to improve their existing designs. In 1919 the 2 companies merged to form Electrolux. When the board of the new company balked at Wenner-Gren's suggestion to mass-produce vacuum cleaners, he guaranteed Electrolux's sales through his own sales company.

In the 1920s the company used the "Every home — an Electrolux home" slogan as Wenner-Gren drove his sales force on and launched new sales companies in Europe, the US, and South America. Company lore has him paying a sales call on the pope in competition with 4 other vacuum cleaner salesmen. After the others had swept their preassigned portions of the carpet, Wenner-Gren pushed his Electrolux over the area cleaned by the competition, dumped out a large pile of dust, and won the order. He scored another publicity coup by securing the blessing of Pope Pius XI to vacuum the Vatican, gratis, for a year. By the end of the 1920s, Electrolux had purchased most of Wenner-Gren's sales companies (excluding Electrolux US) and had gambled on refrigerator technology and won. By buying vacuum cleaner maker Volta (Sweden, 1934), Electrolux gained retail distribution.

Despite the loss of East European subsidiaries in WWII, the company did well until the 1960s, when Electrolux backed an unpopular refrigeration technology. In 1964 Swedish electrical equipment giant ASEA, controlled by Marcus Wallenberg, bought a large stake in Electrolux. In 1967 Wallenberg installed Hans Werthén as chairman. Werthén slashed overhead and sold the company's minority stake in Electrolux US to Consolidated Foods (the US Electrolux business was taken private in 1987). He also bought troubled appliance companies, modernized their factories, and gained global component manufacturing efficiencies.

Since 1970 Electrolux has acquired over 200 companies, including National Union Electric (Eureka vacuum cleaners, US, 1974), Tappan (appliances, US, 1979), Granges (metals, Sweden, 1981), Zanussi (appliances, industrial products, Italy, 1984), White Consolidated (appliances, industrial products, US, 1986), and the garden products division of Roper (US, 1988), to become the world's largest white goods producer.

In 1990, reacting to sluggish demand for its products, Electrolux announced plans to eliminate 15,000 jobs by the end of 1991.

HOW MUCH

$= SEK 6.2 (Dec. 31, 1989)	9 Yr. Growth	1980	1981	1982	1983	1984	1985	1986	1987	1988	1989
Sales (SEK mil)	15.7%	22,874	26,595	31,661	32,146	34,547	39,688	53,090	67,430	73,960	84,919
Net income (SEK mil)	15.5%	704	750	304	1,036	1,418	1,997	1,790	2,116	2,375	2,582
Income as % of sales	—	3.1%	2.8%	1.0%	3.2%	4.1%	5.0%	3.4%	3.1%	3.2%	3.0%
Earnings per share (SEK)	10.6%	14.2	15.1	5.9	19.8	25.9	30.5	25.6	28.8	32.3	35.2
Stock price – high (SEK)	—	46	68	59	130	144	195	344	342	301	380
Stock price – low (SEK)	—	38	38	41	58	108	123	194	189	192	240
Stock price – close (SEK)	22.5%	45	110	59	119	121	194	311	193	293	280
P/E – high	—	3	5	10	7	6	6	13	12	9	11
P/E – low	—	3	3	7	3	4	4	8	7	6	7
Dividends per share (SEK)	13.3%	3.75	3.75	4.00	4.50	5.50	6.50	7.50	8.75	10.00	11.50
Book value per share (SEK)	14.2%	70	85	92	98	115	131	161	164	203	232

1989 Year End:
Debt ratio: 44.6%
Return on equity: 16.2%
Cash (mil): SEK 1,864
Long-term debt (mil): SEK 13,681
Number of shares (mil): 73
Dividends:
1989 average yield: 4.1%
1989 payout: 3.27%
Market value (mil):$3,297
Sales (mil): $13,697

OTC symbol: ELUXY (ADR)
Established: Sweden, 1919
Fiscal year ends: December 31

WHO

Chairman: Hans Werthén, age 71
President and CEO: Anders Scharp, age 56
SEVP and CFO: Lennart Ribohn, age 47
Auditors: Hagström & Olsson AB
Employees: 152,913

WHERE

HQ: Lilla Essingen, S-105 45 Stockholm, Sweden
Phone: 011-46-8-738-6000
FAX: 011-46-8-56-44-78
US HQ (White Consolidated Industries): 11770 Berea Rd., Cleveland, OH 44111
US Phone: 216-252-3700
US FAX: 216-252-8160

Electrolux conducts operations in approximately 50 countries. US employees constitute 21% of the company's work force.

	1989 Sales	
	SEK* mil	% of total
EEC	31,499	37
Other European countries	21,072	25
North America	25,874	30
Other countries	6,474	8
Total	**84,919**	**100**

WHAT

	1989 Sales		1989 Operating Income	
	SEK* mil	% of total	SEK* mil	% of total
Household appliances	43,682	51	2,005	42
Commercial appliances & services	11,552	14	807	17
Industrial products	16,890	20	1,059	22
Other products	12,795	15	906	19
Adjustments	—	—	504	—
Total	**84,919**	**100**	**5,281**	**100**

*Swedish kronor

Home Appliances (US)
Electrolux
Eureka
Frigidaire
Gibson
Kelvinator
Tappan
Viking
White
White-Westinghouse

Outdoor Products
American Yard Products
Paramount
Poulan/Weed Eater
Rally
Yardpro

Other Products
Home cabinetry (Diamond, J-Wood, Kemper, Quaker Maid, Richwood, Schrock)
Seat belts and other auto safety equipment (Electrolux Autoliv, Klippan)

RANKINGS

77th in *Fortune* Global 500 Industrial Cos.
26th in *Forbes* 100 Foreign Investments in the US
683rd in *Business Week* Global 1000

COMPETITION

Allied-Signal
Berkshire Hathaway
Black & Decker
General Electric
Masco
Maytag
Premark
Raytheon
Robert Bosch
Siemens
Textron
TRW
Whirlpool

ELI LILLY AND COMPANY

OVERVIEW

Indianapolis-based drug company Eli Lilly is a major supplier of several important antibiotics and has been known for decades to diabetics for its life-saving insulin. The 12th largest drug company in sales in the world and 8th in the US, Lilly's profits as a percentage of sales were 2nd highest in the 1989 *Fortune* 500, at 22.5%. The company's top products are the antidepressant Prozac, the antibiotic Ceclor, and Humulin insulin; 8 others also bring in over $100 million annually. The company also makes medical devices (including monitors and pacemakers), diagnostic products, and animal health products. Pregnancy and prostate cancer tests are key products of Lilly's Hybritech unit.

More than 1/2 of Lilly's sales force is employed overseas, where the company expects to expand in the 1990s. Foreign operations now account for 36% of sales.

R&D expenditures of 14.5% of sales are among the highest in the industry. Products in development include new types of antibiotics, anticancer agents, and drugs for treating nervous system diseases.

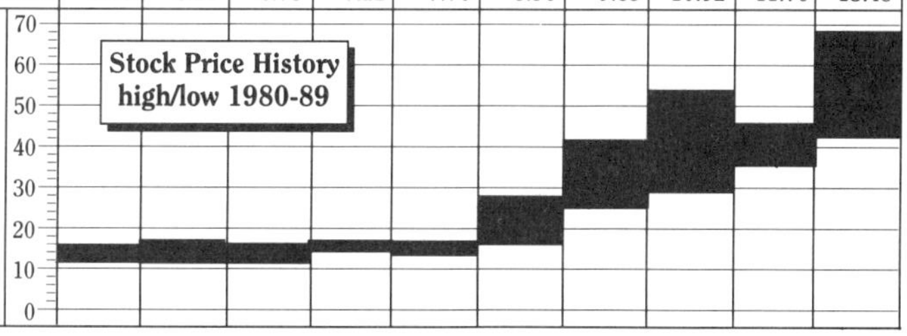

NYSE symbol: LLY
Incorporated: Indiana, 1901
Fiscal year ends: December 31

WHO

Chairman, President, and CEO: Richard D. Wood, age 63, $1,511,947 pay
VP Finance: James M. Cornelius, age 46
Auditors: Ernst & Young
Employees: 28,200

WHERE

HQ: Lilly Corporate Center, Indianapolis, IN 46285
Phone: 317-276-2000
FAX: 317-276-2095

The company has 40 plants in 9 countries and sells its products in 120 countries.

	1989 Sales		1989 Pretax Income	
	$ mil	% of total	$ mil	% of total
US	2,659	64	945	70
Japan, Middle East & Europe	1,151	27	304	23
Other countries	366	9	94	7
Adjustments	—	—	(13)	—
Total	**4,176**	**100**	**1,330**	**100**

WHEN

Colonel Eli Lilly, pharmacist and Union officer in the Civil War, opened Eli Lilly & Company in Indianapolis in 1876 with $1,300. By 1881 sales had reached $81,637. Colonel Lilly developed a process in 1879 for coating pills with gelatin, and later the company made gelatin capsules, which it continues to sell today. After Lilly died in 1898, his son and 2 grandsons successively headed the company until 1953.

Following an intensive research effort, Lilly introduced insulin in 1923. To extract one ounce of the substance in those days, the pancreas glands of 6,000 cattle or 24,000 hogs had to be processed. Other Lilly products created in the 1920s and 1930s included liver extracts (for pernicious anemia), digitalis preparations (for heart disease), Merthiolate (an antiseptic), and Seconal (a powerful sedative). Sales went from $13 million in 1932 to $72 million by the end of WWII. In 1952 Lilly researchers isolated the antibiotic erythromycin from a species of mold found in the Philippines. In the 1950s Lilly produced more than 60% of Salk vaccine supplies. In the 1950s and 1960s the company opened manufacturing plants overseas.

Diversification began in the 1970s with the purchase of Elizabeth Arden (cosmetics, 1971) and IVAC (medical instruments, 1977). Lilly's Darvon captured 80% of the prescription analgesic market. Increases in R&D spending resulted in new antibiotics, including Ceclor (1979). In the 1980s antibiotics accounted for about 1/3 of Lilly's sales.

Not all Lilly products have been wonder drugs. Since 1974 the company has been involved in litigation over DES (diethylstilbestrol; widely used until 1971, it may have caused cancer and other problems in children whose mothers took the drug) and lost a $6 million lawsuit in 1983 over a death caused by the arthritis drug Oraflex. The company halted distribution at one of its plants in 1989 for quality-control problems after an FDA investigation.

In 1982 Lilly became the first company to market a biotechnology product when it introduced Humulin (licensed from Genentech), a genetically engineered insulin identical to human insulin. In 1986 Lilly acquired Hybritech, a biotechnology company, for more than $300 million. In 1987 the company sold Elizabeth Arden to a subsidiary of Riklis Family Corporation.

In 1988 Lilly introduced Axid (antiulcer drug) and Prozac (best-selling antidepressant, with nearly 20% of the market in early 1990). A recent joint venture with Dow Chemical will combine plant sciences and pesticide operations into DowElanco, creating the largest such firm in North America.

WHAT

	1989 Sales	
	$ mil	% of total
Anti-infectives	1,447	34
Medical instruments	698	17
Central nervous system products	574	14
Diabetic care	489	12
Animal health products	337	8
Other products	631	15
Total	**4,176**	**100**

Pharmaceutical Products
Antiulcer agent (Axid)
Anti-infectives (Ceclor)
Cardiovascular therapy (Dobutrex)
Central nervous system agents (Prozac)
Diabetic care (Humulin)
Hormones (Humatrope)
Oncolytic agents (Oncovin)

Subsidiaries
Advanced Cardiovascular Systems, Inc. (balloon catheter systems)
Cardiac Pacemakers, Inc.
Devices for Vascular Intervention, Inc. (catheter systems)
Elanco Products Co. (animal health products)
Elco Diagnostics Co. (diagnostic products)
Hybritech, Inc. (immunodiagnostic products)
Ivac Corp. (patient-monitoring systems)
Physio-Control Corp. (cardiac monitors)

HOW MUCH

	9 Yr. Growth	1980	1981	1982	1983	1984	1985	1986	1987	1988	1989
Sales ($ mil)	5.6%	2,559	2,773	2,963	3,034	3,109	2,510	2,934	3,236	3,607	4,176
Net income ($ mil)	11.9%	342	374	412	457	490	518	558	643	761	940
Income as % of sales	—	13.4%	13.5%	13.9%	15.1%	15.8%	15.8%	15.0%	11.3%	18.7%	22.5%
Earnings per share ($)	12.4%	1.1	1.2	1.4	1.5	1.7	1.8	2.0	1.4	2.7	3.2
Stock price – high ($)	—	15.9	17.2	16.3	17.1	16.9	28.0	41.8	53.9	45.9	68.5
Stock price – low ($)	—	11.4	11.3	11.3	14.1	13.3	16.1	25.1	28.9	35.4	42.4
Stock price – close ($)	17.6%	15.9	14.0	14.4	14.5	16.5	27.9	37.1	39.0	42.8	68.5
P/E – high	—	14	14	12	11	10	15	21	38	17	21
P/E – low	—	10	9	8	9	8	9	13	20	13	13
Dividends per share ($)	10.5%	0.55	0.59	0.65	0.69	0.74	0.80	0.90	1.00	1.15	1.35
Book value per share ($)	10.0%	5.73	6.21	6.78	7.22	7.76	8.56	9.85	10.92	11.76	13.48

1989 Year End:
Debt ratio: 6.7%
Return on equity: 25.4%
Cash (mil): $652
Current ratio: 1.71
Long-term debt (mil): $270
Number of shares (mil): 279
Dividends:
1989 average yield: 2.0%
1989 payout: 42.2%
Market value (mil): $19,099

RANKINGS

116th in *Fortune* 500 Industrial Cos.
317th in *Fortune* Global 500 Industrial Cos.
25th in *Business Week* 1000
45th in *Business Week* Global 1000

COMPETITION

Abbott Labs
American Cyanamid
American Home Products
C. R. Bard
Baxter
Bayer
Becton, Dickinson
Bristol-Myers Squibb
Dow Chemical
Du Pont
Genentech
Glaxo
Hoechst
Johnson & Johnson
Merck
Monsanto
Pfizer
Procter & Gamble
Rhône-Poulenc
Roche Holding
Schering-Plough
SmithKline Beecham
Upjohn
Warner-Lambert

EMERSON ELECTRIC CO.

OVERVIEW

Emerson is the 7th largest maker of electrical and electronic products in the US, based on 1989 sales of $7.1 billion. The company had its 32nd consecutive year of increased earnings in 1989.

Emerson's 50-plus divisions supply industrial, commercial, government, and individual users. Products include electric motors; uninterruptible power supplies for computers; meters and instrumentation; switches and valves; and heating, ventilating, and air conditioning equipment, to name just a few. Consumer products include saws, drills, and sanders. For the DOD Emerson makes airborne radar systems, missile launching systems, and antisubmarine warfare equipment, among other products.

Emerson has a first- or 2nd-ranked product in 84% of its markets; some of the leaders include In-Sink-Erator (kitchen waste disposers) and Ridge Tool (commercial hand and power tools). *Fortune* calls Emerson one of the companies that competes the best.

Expanding international sales accounted for 23% of Emerson's business in 1989.

WHEN

Emerson was cofounded in St. Louis in 1890 by Alexander and Charles Meston, inventors of an alternating current electric motor based on the pioneering work of Nikola Tesla. The inventors were backed by venture capitalist (and former judge and US marshal) John Emerson. Their most widely recognized product was an adaptation of the electric motor — the electric fan, first introduced in 1892.

Fans and small motors were Emerson's mainstay for many years, but the company also put its motors to use in player pianos, hair dryers, sewing machines, and water pumps. In the 1910s the company played a part in developing the first forced-air circulating systems.

The Great Depression and labor problems in the 1930s nearly forced Emerson into bankruptcy. New developments, including a hermetic motor for refrigerators, pulled the company back from the brink. Emerson's electric motors were adapted to new uses during WWII, particularly in aircraft. Emerson also made the gun turret for the B-24 bomber.

The company, having grown dependent on defense business, suffered again in postwar years. A new president, Wallace Persons, took over in 1954; Persons retooled Emerson's plants to make new products and began turning Emerson into a major manufacturer of electrical products.

Beginning in the early 1960s Persons bought smaller companies, mostly makers of electronics products and small motors: White-Rodgers (1962, thermostats and gas controls); Ridge Tool (1966, commercial hand and power tools); In-Sink-Erator (1968, waste disposers); Browning (1969, power transmission products); Harris (1973, welding and cutting tools); and Louisville Ladder (1973). Persons retired in 1974; Emerson's sales had grown from $56 million when he became CEO in 1954 to $800 million in 1973.

Charles Knight, chairman and CEO since 1974, changed Emerson's character again, taking it into high-tech fields such as computer technology, process controls, and analytical instruments. Acquisitions included Varec (1975, chemical and petroleum measurement systems); Rosemount (1976, industrial measurement and control systems); Weed Eater (1977); Skil (1979, power tools); Western Forge (1981, Craftsman hand tools for Sears); Beckman Industrial (1984, analytical and electrical instruments); Hazeltine (1986, defense electronics); and Liebert (1987, computer support systems). In the mid-1980s Emerson moved 3,000 jobs overseas to lower costs and beat Asian competitors. In 1990 Emerson announced plans to spin off its defense-related subsidiaries (including Hazeltine) because of declining sales.

HOW MUCH

	9 Yr. Growth	1980	1981	1982	1983	1984	1985	1986	1987	1988	1989
Sales ($ mil)	9.7%	3,067	3,429	3,502	3,476	4,179	4,649	4,953	6,170	6,652	7,071
Net income ($ mil)	10.6%	238	273	300	303	349	401	409	467	529	588
Income as % of sales	—	7.8%	8.0%	8.6%	8.7%	8.4%	8.6%	8.3%	7.6%	8.0%	8.3%
Earnings per share ($)	8.7%	1.24	1.42	1.46	1.47	1.70	1.81	1.87	2.00	2.31	2.63
Stock price – high ($)	—	13.63	16.58	21.33	22.96	23.92	27.50	30.88	41.92	36.00	39.88
Stock price – low ($)	—	9.83	12.00	13.29	18.29	19.38	22.25	26.04	26.75	27.25	29.50
Stock price – close ($)	13.8%	12.17	15.13	20.17	22.17	23.17	27.08	27.92	34.63	30.38	39.00
P/E – high	—	11	12	15	16	14	15	16	21	16	15
P/E – low	—	8	8	9	12	11	12	14	13	12	11
Dividends per share ($)	8.6%	0.53	0.59	0.67	0.70	0.77	0.87	0.92	0.97	1.00	1.12
Book value per share ($)	8.8%	6.43	7.23	7.58	8.28	9.09	10.03	10.90	11.68	12.51	13.79

1989 Year End:
Debt ratio: 12.0%
Return on equity: 20.0%
Cash (mil): $113
Current ratio: 1.86
Long-term debt (mil): $419
Number of shares (mil): 223
Dividends:
1989 average yield: 2.9%
1989 payout: 42.6%
Market value (mil): $8,691

NYSE symbol: EMR
Incorporated: Missouri, 1890
Fiscal year ends: September 30

WHO

Chairman and CEO: Charles F. Knight, age 53, $1,776,523 pay
President and COO: A. E. Suter, age 54
VC and Chief Administrative Officer: R. W. Staley, age 54, $425,000 pay
EVP and CFO: W. C. Bousquette, age 53
Auditors: KPMG Peat Marwick
Employees: 72,600

WHERE

HQ: 8000 W. Florissant Ave., PO Box 4100, St. Louis, MO 63136
Phone: 314-553-2000
FAX: 314-553-3527

Emerson has 197 plants in 16 countries.

	1989 Sales		1989 Pretax Income	
	$ mil	% of total	$ mil	% of total
US	5,450	77	737	77
Europe	1,140	16	128	13
Other foreign	481	7	93	10
Adjustments	—	—	(4)	—
Total	**7,071**	**100**	**954**	**100**

WHAT

	1989 Sales		1989 Operating Income	
	$ mil	% of total	$ mil	% of total
Commercial & industrial prods.	5,129	72	717	74
Consumer products	1,266	18	227	23
Government & defense products	676	10	34	3
Adjustments	—	—	95	—
Total	**7,071**	**100**	**1,073**	**100**

Major Business Units
Branson (ultrasound equipment)
Computer support products (power supplies)
Emerson Motors
Hazeltine (defense electronics)
In-Sink-Erator (waste disposers)
Joucomatic (pneumatic and solenoid valves)
Kay-Ray (specialty level sensors)
Louisville Ladder
Ridge Tool (commercial power and hand tools)
Rosemount (industrial measurement and control systems)
Skil (power tools)
Western Forge (Sears Craftsman hand tools)
White-Rodgers (thermostats and gas controls)

RANKINGS

67th in *Fortune* 500 Industrial Cos.
185th in *Fortune* Global 500 Industrial Cos.
117th in *Forbes* Sales 500
51st in *Business Week* 1000
179th in *Business Week* Global 1000

COMPETITION

Black & Decker
Cooper Industries
Dana
General Electric
Honeywell
Litton
Raytheon
Reliance Electric
Robert Bosch
Snap-on Tools
Square D
Stanley Works
Teledyne
Texas Instruments
TRW
Other defense electronics companies

ENTERGY CORPORATION

OVERVIEW

For 41 years Entergy (formerly Middle South Utilities) has been the leading supplier of electricity along the lower reaches of the Mississippi River. The company provides electricity to 1.7 million customers in a 91,000-square-mile area of Arkansas, Louisiana, Mississippi, and southeastern Missouri through 4 operating utilities: Arkansas Power & Light (AP&L), Louisiana Power & Light (LP&L), Mississippi Power & Light (MP&L), and New Orleans Public Service, Inc. (NOPSI). Entergy also provides natural gas in New Orleans and certain parts of Arkansas and Missouri.

Entergy's System Fuels subsidiary buys up to 25,000 barrels of oil every day and buys, delivers, and stores the natural gas, coal, and nuclear fuels used to operate the company's generating plants.

In May 1990 the City of New Orleans rejected a proposed $700 million buyout of NOPSI. Entergy and the city had reached a tentative agreement in February, the result of the city's plan to municipalize NOPSI's electric and natural gas properties.

WHEN

Middle South Utilities was formed in 1949 as a New Orleans–based holding company for 4 public utilities serving Arkansas, Louisiana, and Mississippi. These companies, Arkansas Power & Light (AP&L), Louisiana Power & Light (LP&L), Mississippi Power & Light (MP&L), and New Orleans Public Service, Inc. (NOPSI), had developed independently from predecessors dating back to the mid-1920s.

AP&L, based in Little Rock, resulted from the consolidation of several Arkansas utilities in 1926. AP&L continued to buy (and sell) other electric, water, and gas companies until 1950, when it sold the last of its nonelectric holdings.

Soon after its founding in 1927, New Orleans–based LP&L bought 6 more Louisiana electric companies and continued to expand its service area through acquisitions made during the 1940s and 1950s.

Three Mississippi power companies consolidated in 1927 to form Jackson-based MP&L. The company operated gas, electric, water, and transportation companies until 1955, when it sold the last of its nonelectric properties.

NOPSI was created by the consolidation of 3 New Orleans electric companies in 1926.

Operating as Middle South Utilities (MSU), AP&L, LP&L, MP&L, and NOPSI joined 7 other companies in 1966 to exchange power on a seasonal-need basis with the Tennessee Valley Authority. Floyd Lewis, who had joined the corporate legal staff in 1949, became MSU's president in 1970. When he retired in 1985, former CFO Edwin Lupberger took over.

In 1971 MSU bought the Arkansas-Missouri Power Company and its affiliate, Associated Natural Gas, consolidating both with AP&L in 1981. The new AP&L system provided electricity to 78 counties and natural gas to 91 communities in Arkansas and Missouri.

MSU's first nuclear plant, near Russellville, Arkansas, went on-line in 1974. MSU formed Middle South Energy (later renamed System Energy Resources) that year to finance and construct the 2 units of its Grand Gulf nuclear plant. Grand Gulf 1 was completed 6 years behind schedule at a cost of $3.8 billion (1985). When MSU tried to pass on to its customers Grand Gulf 1 construction costs, rate disputes with state regulators and lawsuits followed. Construction on Grand Gulf 2 was halted (1985), and losses related to the unsettled rate issues took MSU to the brink of bankruptcy (1987). In 1989 MSU absorbed a $900 million loss on its $926 million investment in Grand Gulf 2 to help end the disputes and then, to distance itself from the controversy, adopted the name Entergy Corporation.

HOW MUCH

	9 Yr. Growth	1980	1981	1982	1983	1984	1985	1986	1987	1988	1989
Sales ($ mil)	5.3%	2,342	2,772	2,902	2,910	3,146	3,238	3,486	3,455	3,565	3,724
Net income ($ mil)	—	251	342	379	458	575	492	542	449	498	(397)
Income as % of sales	—	10.7%	12.3%	13.1%	15.7%	18.3%	15.2%	15.5%	13.0%	14.0%	(10.7%)
Earnings per share ($)	—	2.01	2.44	2.33	2.46	2.76	2.01	2.21	1.74	2.01	(2.31)
Stock price – high ($)	—	14.25	13.88	15.75	16.75	14.75	15.25	15.00	16.25	16.13	23.25
Stock price – low ($)	—	10.25	11.00	12.25	13.13	9.25	8.13	10.50	7.75	8.50	15.50
Stock price – close ($)	8.1%	11.50	12.63	14.88	13.38	13.75	10.63	13.13	8.25	16.00	23.25
P/E – high	—	7	6	7	7	5	8	7	9	8	—
P/E – low	—	5	5	5	5	3	4	5	4	4	—
Dividends per share ($)	(6.1%)	1.59	1.63	1.67	1.71	1.75	0.89	0.00	0.00	0.20	0.90
Book value per share ($)	1.7%	17.69	17.64	17.75	18.00	18.28	19.03	21.20	22.06	23.87	20.62

1989 Year End:
Debt ratio: 58.3%
Return on equity: —
Cash (mil): $953
Current ratio: 1.39
Long-term debt (mil): $6,347
Number of shares (mil): 204
Dividends:
1989 average yield: 3.9%
1989 payout: —
Market value (mil): $4,743

25
20
15
10
5
0

Stock Price History high/low 1980-89

NYSE symbol: ETR
Incorporated: Florida, 1949
Fiscal year ends: December 31

WHO

Chairman, President, and CEO: Edwin Lupberger, age 53, $691,066 pay
Chairman and CEO, AP&L and MP&L: Jerry L. Maulden, age 53, $501,094 pay
President and COO, LP&L and NOPSI: Donald E. Meiners, age 54, $309,347 pay (prior to promotion)
EVP Finance and External Affairs: Jerry D. Jackson, age 45
Auditors: Deloitte & Touche
Employees: 13,190

WHERE

HQ: 225 Baronne St., New Orleans, LA 70112
Phone: 504-529-5262
FAX: 504-569-4265 (Administrative Services)

Entergy serves Arkansas, Louisiana, Mississippi, and southeastern Missouri.

Generating Facilities

Coal
Independence (57%)
White Bluff (57%)

Hydroelectric
Carpenter (AP&L)
Remmel (AP&L)

Natural Gas & Oil
A. B. Paterson (NOPSI)
Baxter Wilson (MP&L)
Blytheville (AP&L)
Buras (LP&L)
Cecil Lynch (AP&L)
Delta (MP&L)
Gerald Andrus (MP&L)
Hamilton Moses (AP&L)
Harvey Couch (AP&L)
Lake Catherine (AP&L)
Little Gypsy (LP&L)
Lynch (AP&L)
Mabelvale (AP&L)
Market Street (NOPSI)
Michoud (NOPSI)
Natchez (MP&L)
Ninemile Point (LP&L)
Rex Brown (MP&L)
Richie (AP&L)
Robert E. Ritchie (AP&L)
Sterlington (LP&L)

Nuclear
Arkansas Nuclear One (AP&L)
Grand Gulf (System Energy Resources)
Waterford (LP&L)

WHAT

	1989 Sales	
	$ mil	% of total
Electricity		
Residential	1,331	36
Commercial	930	25
Industrial	1,022	27
Governmental	122	3
Municipals & co-ops	95	3
Adjoining utility systems	82	2
Other	52	2
Natural gas	90	2
Total	**3,724**	**100**

Utility Companies
Arkansas Power and Light Co.
Louisiana Power and Light Co.
Mississippi Power and Light Co.
New Orleans Public Service, Inc.

Other Subsidiaries
Electec, Inc. (nonutility operations)
Entergy Operations, Inc. (nuclear plant management)
Entergy Services, Inc. (technical support)
System Energy Resources, Inc. (owns Grand Gulf Nuclear Station)
System Fuels, Inc.

RANKINGS

15th in *Fortune* 50 Utilities
223rd in *Forbes* Sales 500
146th in *Business Week* 1000

EQUITABLE

OVERVIEW

Equitable is the 3rd largest life insurance company in the US based on assets, with over $258 billion of life insurance in force. It is also a major institutional investor, with $131 billion in assets under management.

Equitable specializes in individual life insurance, annuities, investment and advisory services, investment banking, pension fund management, agribusiness financing, and real estate investment management.

Equitable's core life insurance, annuity, and pension businesses generated $4.56 billion in 1989 premium income. The company also has a Japanese life insurance subsidiary, Equitable Seimei Hoken.

Donaldson, Lufkin & Jenrette, Equitable's investment banking subsidiary, is a leading equity securities research and block trading firm. Equitable's Alliance Capital Management is a leading US manager of tax-exempt and public retirement funds. Alliance, which also manages $12 billion in mutual funds, had $44 billion in assets under management at the end of 1989.

Equitable Agri-Business manages $2.3 billion in assets and is one of the largest US agricultural lenders and property managers. Equitable Real Estate Investment Management is #1 in *Pensions & Investment Age*'s ranking of equity real estate managers (for tax-exempt investors) in the US; total real estate assets under management currently exceed $35.4 billion.

WHEN

As a student in Catskill, New York, Henry Hyde was advised by his teacher, General John Johnston, who formed Northwestern Mutual Life Insurance Company in 1857, to pursue life insurance as a career. Hyde joined Mutual Life of New York and left in 1859 at the age of 25 to found The Equitable Life Assurance Society in New York as a mutual life insurance company (owned by policyholders).

Hyde named the company after the Equitable Life Assurance Society of London. In its early years Equitable grew faster than the overall insurance industry and by 1899 was the first company in the world to have $1 billion of life insurance in force.

Equitable was also the first insurance company to write group insurance when it insured Montgomery Ward employees in 1911. The company developed an experience rating system to determine how to apportion dividends to a particular group. This rating method was adopted by others in the industry.

Equitable began offering variable-premium life insurance (death benefit linked to investment performance) in 1972. The company first sold fixed-premium variable life in 1976 and universal life (flexible-premium payments as age and income change) in 1985.

The company formed a securities firm in 1971 to allow its agents who were registered representatives under securities laws to sell investment services. The company in 1985 acquired Alliance Capital Management, a leading investment manager of retirement funds, and Donaldson, Lufkin & Jenrette, a major investment banking firm (headed by Richard Jenrette). In 1986 Equitable and Hospital Corporation of America formed Equicor, a jointly run provider of healthcare and other employee benefit services, which CIGNA agreed to purchase in 1990.

In 1988 Equitable returned to profitability with a $63 million increase in surplus after losses of $57 million in 1987 attributed to guaranteed investment contracts (GICs). Equitable's surplus, however, increased only $15 million in 1989 due to continued losses from GICs and a one-time after-tax charge of $26.4 million for the decline in market value of Lomas Financial stock (received from 1987 sale of company's leasing business). In 1990 Chairman Richard Jenrette succeeded John B. Carter as CEO and announced that Equitable, which had reduced costs by $50 million during the 1988-1989 period, would have to cut another $50 million in 1990.

HOW MUCH

Life Insurance Only	9 Yr. Growth	1980	1981	1982	1983	1984	1985	1986	1987	1988	1989
Assets ($ mil)	6.6%	34,600	37,219	41,090	44,445	46,418	51,168	54,577	56,974	58,028	61,708
Premium & annuity income ($ mil)	2.3%	6,096	6,469	6,568	6,338	6,952	7,838	8,786	8,566	7,416	7,452
Net investment income ($ mil)	6.5%	2,447	2,926	3,172	3,440	3,649	3,778	3,867	3,954	4,543	4,312
Net income ($ mil)	—	—	—	—	—	—	—	—	(87.6)	190.1	126.1
Net income as % of assets	—	—	—	—	—	—	—	—	—	0.3%	0.2%
Life insurance in force ($ bil)	3.0%	198.4	227.3	234.1	252.4	278.3	321.5	187.2	213.7	236.3	258.2

1989 Company Totals:
Total assets (mil): $61,709
Revenue (mil): $13,201
Surplus (mil): $1,328
Premiums (mil): $6,361
Net investment income (mil): $4,312
Policyowner dividends (mil): $186
Total life insurance in force (mil): $258,187

Mutual company
Incorporated: New York, 1859
Fiscal year ends: December 31

WHO

Chairman, President, and CEO: Richard H. Jenrette, age 61
VC: Harry D. Garber, age 62
CFO: Thomas M. Kirwan
Auditors: Deloitte & Touche
Employees: 12,700

WHERE

HQ: The Equitable Life Assurance Society of the United States, 787 Seventh Ave., New York, NY 10019
Phone: 212-554-1234
FAX: 212-554-2320

The company is licensed in all 50 states, Puerto Rico, the District of Columbia, and the US Virgin Islands. It markets life insurance through a wholly owned subsidiary in Japan. Investment subsidiaries have offices in US and major foreign financial centers.

WHAT

	1989 Sales	
	$ mil	% of total
Premiums	6,361	48
Net investment income	4,312	33
Other income	2,528	19
Total	**13,201**	**100**

	12/31/89 Assets	
	$ mil	% of total
Bonds	21,123	34
Real estate & mortgage loans	20,656	33
Policyowner loans	2,845	5
Other assets	17,084	28
Total	**61,708**	**100**

Major Operations & Subsidiaries

Insurance Companies
Equico Securities, Inc.
The Equitable of Colorado, Inc.
Equitable Seimei Hoken
Equitable Variable Life Insurance Co.
Pension Financial Management Group
TRAEBCO

Equitable Investment Corp.
Alliance Capital Management Corp.
Donaldson, Lufkin & Jenrette, Inc.
Equico Capital Corp.
Equitable Agri-Business, Inc.
Equitable Capital Management Corp.
Equitable Real Estate Investment Management, Inc.

RANKINGS

3rd in *Fortune* 50 Life Insurance Cos.

COMPETITION

Aetna
AIG
CIGNA
First Executive
John Hancock
Kemper
Massachusetts Mutual
Metropolitan
New York Life
Northwestern Mutual
Primerica
Prudential
Sears
State Farm
Teachers Insurance
Transamerica
Travelers
USF&G

ESTÉE LAUDER INC.

OVERVIEW

Estée Lauder is the leading brand of cosmetics sold in department stores. Privately held by the Lauder family, the group of companies includes Aramis, Clinique Laboratories, Estée Lauder, Prescriptives, and Estée Lauder International. Each company has its own marketing and sales department. The company spends $62 million annually on advertising.

Estée Lauder has cultivated an image of aloof elegance. It restricts its products to upscale department stores (it's the #1 vendor at Bloomingdale's) and resists the temptation to dilute brand loyalty with new products. Estée Lauder trains employees in week-long sessions at Vassar College.

None of the major cosmetics companies in the US (Revlon, Elizabeth Arden, Max Factor) remained independent after the death or retirement of the founder. CEO Leonard Lauder, son of the founder, hopes the family's company will prove the exception.

WHEN

Estée Lauder (then Josephine Esther Mentzer) started her beauty career by selling skin care products formulated by a Hungarian uncle, John Schotz, during the 1930s. Eventually she packaged and peddled her own variations of her uncle's formulas, which included an all-purpose face cream and a cleansing oil.

With the help of her husband, Joseph Lauder, she set up her first office in New York City in 1944 and added lipstick, eye shadow, and face powder to her line. Joseph oversaw production, and Estée sold her wares to beauty salons and department stores, using samples and gifts to convince customers to buy her products. At one Manhattan beauty salon, Estée Lauder asked the owner about her blouse: Where had she bought it? The owner looked down her nose at the cosmetics saleswoman and scoffed that she didn't need to know, because she would never be able to afford it. Lauder has been driven ever since. Throughout the 1950s Lauder traveled cross-country, first to sell her line to high-profile department stores like Neiman-Marcus, I. Magnin, and Saks, later to train saleswomen in the same stores.

Estée Lauder created her first fragrance, a bath oil called Youth Dew, in 1953. In the late 1950s many of the large cosmetics houses in the US introduced "European" skin care lines, products that had scientific-sounding names and supposedly advanced skin repair properties. Estée Lauder's contribution was Re-Nutriv cream. It sold for $115 a pound in 1960, the same year the company hit the million-dollar profit mark. Re-Nutriv was expensive for the Lauder line, which has always been sold exclusively in department stores. The advertising campaign for the cream established the "Lauder look": aristocratic, sophisticated, and tastefully wealthy, an image that Estée Lauder herself cultivated.

In 1964 the company introduced Aramis, a fragrance for men, and in 1968, with the help of a *Vogue* editor, launched Clinique, one of the first hypoallergenic skin care lines. In 1972 Estée Lauder's son Leonard became president, although Estée remained CEO.

Much of her work was as a living symbol of the confident sophisticate, sharing meals with the rich and with royalty. When Princess Diana was to be fêted at a White House dinner, she commanded the presence of Bruce Springsteen, Robert Redford, and Estée Lauder.

By 1978 the Aramis line consisted of 40 products; Aramis cologne and aftershave accounted for 50-80% of men's fragrance sales in some department stores. Also in 1978 the company put out 2 fragrances for women, White Linen and Cinnabar. In 1979 Estée Lauder introduced Prescriptives, a skin care and makeup line targeted at young professional women.

Under Leonard Lauder, between 1978 and 1983, the R&D budget for skin care products was increased, resulting in Night Repair, one of the company's largest-selling formulas. The company also expanded international marketing. Leonard Lauder was named CEO in 1983; brother Ronald pursued a public service career, first in the Reagan administration, then as a candidate for New York City mayor.

By 1988 Estée Lauder had captured 33% of the US market in prestige cosmetics. Its $1.9 billion in revenues included $700 million from the international market. Its 1989 net sales were an estimated $650 million.

In 1990 the company recruited Robin Burns, 37, to head its domestic branch. Burns was the executive behind Calvin Klein Cosmetics Corporation's Obsession fragrance and the sultry ad campaign that sold it. Estée Lauder is also attempting to attract younger customers with model Paulina Porizkova.

HOW MUCH

	4 Yr. Growth	1980	1981	1982	1983	1984	1985	1986	1987	1988	1989
Sales ($ mil) est.	12.2%	—	—	—	—	—	1,200	1,200	1,350	1,600	1,900

Sales ($ mil) est. 1985-89

Private company
Incorporated: New York, 1958

WHO

Chairman: Estée Lauder, age 82
President and CEO: Leonard A. Lauder, age 58
SVP: Evelyn H. Lauder
SVP and CFO: Robert Aquilina
Employees: 10,000

WHERE

HQ: 767 5th Ave., New York, NY 10153
Phone: 212-572-4600
FAX: 212-572-3941

Estée Lauder's products are sold worldwide, exclusively in department stores.

Manufacturing Plants

Australia	England	Switzerland
Belgium	Mexico	US
Canada	Spain	Venezuela

	Estimated Sales	
	$ mil	% of total
US	1,200	63
Foreign	700	37
Total	**1,900**	**100**

WHAT

	Estimated US Sales	
	$ mil	% of total
Estée Lauder Brand	600	50
Clinique	475	40
Prescriptives	50	4
Aramis	75	6
US Total	**1,200**	**100**

Subsidiaries/Affiliates

Aramis Inc.
(Men's toiletries)
Aramis 900
Aramis Classic
Lab Series
New West
Tuscany

Clinique Laboratories Inc.
(Hypoallergenic skin care and makeup)
Clinique skin care
Precision makeup
Skin Supplies for Men

Estée Lauder Inc.
(Makeup and fragrances)
Beautiful
Cinnabar
Lauder for Men
White Linen

Estée Lauder International Inc.
(Marketing and sales abroad for Lauder companies)

Estée Lauder Realty Corp.
(Owns properties in Long Island, New York)

Len-Ron Manufacturing Co., Inc.
(Manufactures cosmetics)

Prescriptives, Inc.
(Makeup and skin care marketed to professional women)
Calyx (fragrance)
Custom-blended powder and foundation

RANKINGS

67th in *Forbes* 400 US Private Cos.

COMPETITION

Amway
Avon
MacAndrews & Forbes
Procter & Gamble
Unilever

EXXON CORPORATION

OVERVIEW

Exxon, the world's largest oil company, explores for and produces crude oil, natural gas, and natural gas liquids in 80 countries worldwide. The company owns 49.9 million acres of developed oil and gas properties and 198 million acres of undeveloped properties, chiefly in the US, Canada, Western Europe, Malaysia, and Yemen.

Exxon also manufactures and sells petrochemicals, explores for and mines coal and other minerals, and owns 60% of Castle Peak station in Hong Kong, the largest coal-fired electric generating plant in Asia.

In 1989, Exxon spent $4.1 billion to acquire Texaco Canada and its 1,500 retail outlets.

Lately, Exxon has drawn fire from environmentalists over the *Exxon Valdez* oil spill in Prince William Sound, Alaska (1989) and, more recently, a ruptured pipeline that sent heating oil into the Arthur Kill channel of New York harbor (1990). Excluding costs related to the *Valdez* cleanup, Exxon spent $1.2 billion on environmental conservation projects in 1989 and plans to spend another $2.8 billion total in 1990 and 1991.

NYSE symbol: XON
Incorporated: New Jersey, 1882
Fiscal year ends: December 31

WHO

Chairman and CEO: Lawrence G. Rawl, age 61, $1,384,952 pay
President: Lee R. Raymond, age 51, $909,056 pay
SVP: Jack G. Clarke, age 62, $844,504 pay
SVP: Donald K. McIvor, age 61, $781,461 pay
SVP: Charles R. Sitter, age 59, $752,283 pay
VP and Treasurer (Principal Financial Officer): E. A. Robinson, age 56
Auditors: Price Waterhouse
Employees: 104,000

WHEN

John D. Rockefeller, a commodity trader, started his first oil refinery in 1863 in Cleveland. Realizing that the price of oil at the well would shrink with each new strike, Rockefeller chose to monopolize oil refining and transportation. He raised $1 million in loans and investments and in 1870 formed the Standard Oil Company. In 1882 Rockefeller and his associates created the Standard Oil Trust, which allowed Rockefeller and 8 other trustees to dissolve existing Standard Oil affiliates and set up new, ostensibly independent companies in different states, including the Standard Oil Company of New Jersey (Jersey Standard).

Initially capitalized at $70 million, the Standard Oil Trust controlled 90% of the petroleum industry. In 1911, after 2 decades of political and legal wrangling, the Supreme Court disbanded the Trust into 34 companies, the largest of which was Jersey Standard. In this year John D. Archbold took over as president of Jersey Standard and commenced more active exploration efforts.

Walter Teagle took over the presidency in 1917, secretly bought half of Humble Oil of Texas (1919), and expanded into South America. In 1928 Jersey Standard joined in the Red Line Agreement, which reserved most Middle East oil for a handful of companies. Congressional investigation of a prewar research pact giving Farben of Germany patents for a lead essential to the development of aviation fuel in exchange for a formula for synthetic rubber (never received) led to Teagle's resignation in 1942.

The 1948 purchase of a 30% interest in Arabian American Oil Company for $74 million, combined with a 7% share of Iranian production acquired in 1954, facilitated Jersey Standard's rise to its position as the world's largest oil company.

Other US companies still using the Standard Oil name objected to Jersey Standard marketing in their territories as Esso (derived from the initials S.O. for Standard Oil). To end the confusion, Jersey Standard became Exxon in 1972. The name change cost $100 million.

In the 1970s nationalization of oil assets by producing countries reduced Exxon's access to oil. Despite increased exploration in the 1970s and 1980s, Exxon's reserves continued to shrink faster than new reserves could be found. However, new finds in the Gulf of Mexico, Louisiana, Alaska, and the North Sea in 1989 added about 1.5 billion barrels to Exxon's existing reserves.

After the *Exxon Valdez* oil spill in 1989, Exxon launched the largest shoreline cleanup operation in history, a project that has cost the company more than $1.7 billion.

WHERE

HQ: 1251 Ave. of the Americas, New York, NY 10020
Phone: 212-333-1000
FAX: 212-333-1348

Exxon conducts operations in the US and 79 foreign countries.

	1989 Sales		1989 Net Income	
	$ mil	% of total	$ mil	% of total
US	23,025	25	505	14
Other Western Hemisphere	16,271	17	366	10
Eastern Hemisphere	53,848	58	2,687	76
Adjustments	(6,488)	—	(583)	—
Total	**86,656**	**100**	**2,975**	**100**

WHAT

	1989 Sales		1989 Operating Income	
	$ mil	% of total	$ mil	% of total
Chemicals	9,210	10	1,609	20
Petroleum	83,934	90	6,350	80
Adjustments	(6,488)	—	5	—
Total	**86,656**	**100**	**7,964**	**100**

Energy/Minerals
Coal
Copper
Crude oil
Gasolines
Natural gas
Zinc

Fuel additives
Oil field chemicals
Petrochemicals
Plastics
Rubber
Solvents
Specialty resins

Chemicals
Aromatics
Fertilizers

Convenience Stores
Over 5,000 stores in the US and Europe

RANKINGS

3rd in *Fortune* 500 Industrial Cos.
3rd in *Fortune* Global 500 Industrial Cos.
32nd in *Fortune* 50 Exporters
3rd in *Forbes* Sales 500
2nd in *Business Week* 1000
6th in *Business Week* Global 1000

COMPETITION

Amoco
Ashland
Atlantic Richfield
British Petroleum
Chevron
Coastal
Du Pont
Mobil
Occidental
Pennzoil
Phillips
Royal Dutch/Shell
Sun
Texaco
Union Texas
Unocal
USX
Chemical and mining companies

HOW MUCH

	9 Yr. Growth	1980	1981	1982	1983	1984	1985	1986	1987	1988	1989
Sales ($ mil)	(1.9%)	103,142	108,107	97,173	88,561	90,854	86,673	69,888	76,416	79,557	86,656
Net income ($ mil)	(6.9%)	5,650	5,567	4,186	4,978	5,528	4,870	5,360	4,840	5,260	2,975
Income as % of sales	—	5.5%	5.2%	4.3%	5.6%	6.1%	5.6%	7.7%	6.3%	6.6%	3.4%
Earnings per share ($)	(3.7%)	3.25	3.22	2.41	2.89	3.39	3.23	3.71	3.43	3.95	2.32
Stock price – high ($)	—	22.19	20.50	16.13	19.88	22.75	27.94	37.06	50.38	47.75	51.63
Stock price – low ($)	—	13.00	14.75	12.44	14.25	18.06	22.06	24.19	30.88	32.00	40.50
Stock price – close ($)	10.6%	20.16	15.63	14.88	18.69	22.50	27.56	35.06	38.13	44.00	50.00
P/E – high	—	7	6	7	7	7	9	10	15	12	22
P/E – low	—	4	5	5	5	5	7	7	9	8	17
Dividends per share ($)	6.1%	1.35	1.50	1.50	1.55	1.68	1.73	1.80	1.90	2.15	2.30
Book value per share ($)	5.3%	14.70	16.42	16.42	17.40	18.42	19.90	22.29	24.38	24.64	23.38

1989 Year End:
Debt ratio: 23.5%
Return on equity: 9.7%
Cash (mil): $2,016
Current ratio: 0.75
Long-term debt (mil): $9,275
Number of shares (mil): 1,250
Dividends:
1989 average yield: 4.6%
1989 payout: 99.1%
Market value (mil): $62,515

Stock Price History high/low 1980-89

FARLEY INDUSTRIES

OVERVIEW

Farley Industries is the creation of William F. Farley. Its main component is a private, Chicago-based holding company, Farley, Inc. (7.7% owned by Farley himself). The company owns businesses involved in the footwear, motor vehicle parts, and other industries, including Acme Boots (western boots) and Magnus (railroad ball bearings), and has a controlling stake in 2 public companies: underwear maker Fruit of the Loom (20% owned) and sheet and towel maker West Point–Pepperell (95% owned).

Fruit of the Loom is America's leading maker of men's and boy's underwear. It generated $1.3 billion in sales in 1989, ranking 292nd in the *Fortune* 500. In August 1990 Farley Inc. sold $43 million of Fruit of the Loom stock to Land Free Investment Ltd., presumably to help pay off some of Farley Inc.'s LBO debt. The company had defaulted on interest payments to bondholders at about the time of the sale, causing its debt to be downgraded to a "D" rating. Farley himself has sold over 900,000 of his shares in Fruit of the Loom since March 1990.

Since the collapse of the junk bond market early in 1990, William Farley has not been able to secure the $83 million he needs to buy the remaining 5% of West Point–Pepperell. He had hoped to raise the cash by floating bonds through now-defunct Drexel Burnham Lambert. Pepperell ranked 172nd in the 1989 *Fortune* 500, with $2.6 billion in sales.

Private company
Founded: Chicago, 1977
Fiscal year ends: December 31

WHO

Chairman and CEO: William F. Farley, age 48
SEVP Corporate Development: Richard M. Cion, age 47
EVP Finance: Paul M. O'Hara
Auditors: Ernst & Young
Employees: 46,500

WHERE

HQ: Farley, Inc., 233 S. Wacker Dr., 6300 Sears Tower, Chicago, IL 60606
Phone: 312-876-1724
FAX: 312-993-1783

WHEN

In 1976 William Farley, a former door-to-door encyclopedia salesman-turned-entrepreneur, bought his first business, an Anaheim, California, citrus-processing plant called Anaheim Citrus Products. Farley, then 33, bought the company for $1.7 million through an LBO. His personal investment was $25,000. One year later he formed Farley Industries, a Chicago-based holding company that by the mid-1980s would be one of the largest privately owned US industrial corporations, with about $2 billion in annual sales.

Between 1977 and 1984 Farley made several acquisitions, including Baumfolder (paper folding machines) and Condec (defense and electrical equipment), but none compared to the $1.4 billion LBO of Ben Heineman's Northwest Industries in 1985, completed with the aid of LBO specialists Drexel Burnham Lambert. Northwest's Union Underwear Company marketed Fruit of the Loom brand men's and boy's briefs. The Northwest acquisition also brought Acme Boots, the world's leading manufacturer of western-style boots (Acme, Dingo, Dan Post, Lucchese), General Battery Corporation, and Velsicol Chemical under the Farley corporate umbrella. Farley spun off Northwest's Lone Star Steel Company (1985) and, to offset acquisition debt, sold Northwest's stake in 2 other businesses. Once it became a unit of Farley, Northwest changed its name to Farley/Northwest Industries (1985) and then to Fruit of the Loom (1987), selling, in the meantime, Velsicol's agrichemical division (1986) and General Battery (1987). In 1987 Farley made a 27-million-share offering of its Fruit of the Loom stock but retained control of the company. In the meantime, the highly visible William Farley toyed with the idea of running for president of the US.

In 1989 Farley (still aligned with Drexel) paid over $1.5 billion in an LBO of Georgia-based West Point–Pepperell. Fresh from acquiring J. P. Stevens & Company in 1988, Pepperell controlled 35% of the US sheet market and 22% of the towel market. Pepperell also owned Cluett, Peabody & Company (acquired 1986), makers of Arrow shirts and Gold Toe socks. Farley acquired 95% of Pepperell in 1989, agreeing to pay about 20 times the company's 1989 earnings, and to take on Pepperell's existing $1 billion debt. Farley then sold Cluett's Arrow, Gold Toe, and Schoeneman divisions to the US subsidiary of Bidermann in 1990 but, without full Pepperell ownership, could not use the $410 million proceeds to pay Farley's debt ($2.4 billion of which was related to the Pepperell acquisition). In March 1990 the unit Farley had established to buy Pepperell (West Point Acquisition Corporation) defaulted on $1.5 billion in bond payments and a $796 million bank loan.

Beleaguered by massive LBO debt and pretax losses of about $40 million (1989), Farley sold Doehler-Jarvis, its aluminum die-casting business, in July 1990 in an effort to raise cash.

WHAT

Apparel

Fruit of the Loom, Inc.	Major Brands
Union Underwear (20%)	BVD
Socks	Fruit of the Loom
Sweats	Screen Stars
T-shirts	
Underwear	

Automotive Parts & Accessories

Tool & Engineering
Prototype automotive body parts

Footwear

Acme Boot Co., Inc.	Major Brands
Lucchese Boot Co.	Acme
Nonathletic footwear	Dan Post
Western boots	Dingo
	Lucchese

Metal Parts & Fasteners

Magnus
Railroad ball bearings

Southern Fastening Systems
Precision metal fasteners

Textiles

West Point–Pepperell, Inc.	Major Brands
J. P. Stevens & Co., Inc. (95%)	Lady Pepperell
Blankets	Martex
Sheets	Vellux
Towels	
Other bed and bath accessories	

HOW MUCH

	5 Yr. Growth	1980	1981	1982	1983	1984	1985	1986	1987	1988	1989
Sales ($ mil)	32.6%	—	—	—	—	700	962	1,110	1,318	1,517	2,865
Net income ($ mil)	—	—	—	—	—	50	(73)	(17)	44	(29)	—
Income as % of sales	—	—	—	—	—	7.1%	(7.6%)	(1.5%)	3.3%	(1.9%)	—

Net Income ($ mil) 1984-88

RANKINGS

40th in *Forbes* 400 US Private Cos.

COMPETITION

Burlington Holdings
Fieldcrest Cannon
INTERCO
Milliken
Springs Industries

FEDERAL EXPRESS CORPORATION

OVERVIEW

Federal Express (FedEx), still run by founder Fred Smith, has become a $5.2 billion company in just 20 years, making it one of the greatest entrepreneurial success stories of our era. The company, with headquarters and distribution hub in Memphis, operates one of the largest expedited delivery services in the world and continues aggressive overseas expansion. The company also combines delivery with a logistics service called PartsBank, which allows customers to use FedEx-owned warehouses for inventory storage.

FedEx maintains a fleet of more than 350 aircraft, with daily airlift capacity of 7,000 tons; the company ships an average of more than 1 million express packages daily and delivers them with almost 29,000 vehicles. With the 1989 acquisition of Tiger International, the company also runs the world's largest full-service, all-cargo airline, with operations in 119 countries, and is authorized to serve more countries than any other US carrier.

Employee-oriented FedEx offers Guaranteed Fair Treatment, minority recruitment, and no-layoff policies and has high employee morale.

NYSE symbol: FDX
Incorporated: Delaware, 1971
Fiscal year ends: May 31

WHO

Chairman, President, and CEO: Frederick W. Smith, age 45, $879,895 pay
EVP and COO: James L. Barksdale, age 46, $674,659 pay
SVP and CFO: David C. Anderson, age 47, $404,793 pay
SVP, Domestic Ground Operations: Theodore L. Weise, age 45, $396,672 pay
SVP, Sales and Customer Service: Thomas R. Oliver, age 48, $387,564 pay
Auditors: Arthur Andersen & Co.
Employees: 58,000 full time and 20,500 part time

WHEN

FedEx was the inspiration of Fred Smith, who recognized in the late 1960s that the US was becoming a service-oriented economy with a need for reliable, overnight delivery services. Smith presented FedEx's business concept in a Yale term paper — his grade, a mere "C," now seems ironic. After 2 tours in Vietnam, Smith bought Arkansas Aviation, a small aviation maintenance company. In 1969 plans for FedEx began. Between 1969 and 1971 Smith found investors willing to contribute $40 million, used $8 million of family money, and eventually received sufficient bank financing to total $90 million, making FedEx the largest start-up ever funded by venture capital.

Smith incorporated FedEx in 1971 and began operations in 1973. Initial services included overnight and 2nd-day delivery services and a Courier Pak envelope for expediting documents at a cost of $5 per package. When operations began, service was available to 22 cities. Offering virtually the same services today, FedEx has spread to include delivery to any domestic destination and 119 countries.

Several factors contributed to the company's success. Air passenger traffic was growing rapidly so that parcel service became less important to commercial airlines; United Parcel Service union workers went on strike in 1974, disrupting customer service; and, finally, competitor REA Express went bankrupt. By fiscal year-end 1975, FedEx had lost $29.3 million; by 1976, only 3 years after beginning operations, FedEx was profitable — but owed creditors $49 million. It went public in 1978 and has had a steady history of strong earnings since that time.

FedEx had one significant fiasco. Believing hard-copy delivery services could be severely eroded by the burgeoning electronic mail market, the company invested heavily in ZapMail, a satellite-based network to provide 2-hour document delivery service. Failing to anticipate the impact of low-cost fax machines, FedEx lost over $300 million in 1986 alone on the now-disbanded ZapMail. Yet, it is to FedEx's credit that, even while sustaining heavy ZapMail losses, the company remained profitable.

FedEx has not diversified beyond delivery services and now focuses upon international expansion, some through acquisitions. The company bought Island Courier Companies and Cansica Inc. (1987), SAMIMA (Italy, 1988), and 3 Japanese freight carriers (1988). In 1989 the company purchased Tiger International (Flying Tigers cargo airline) for $880 million, as part of an effort to increase its share of larger cargo services.

WHERE

HQ: 2005 Corporate Ave., Memphis, TN 38132
Phone: 901-369-3600
FAX: 901-795-1027

Federal Express's US shipping hub is located in Memphis, with regional hubs in Newark, NJ, and Oakland, CA; European hub is in Brussels. FedEx delivers in over 36 countries; uses independent contractors in over 64 countries; and, with the addition of Flying Tigers, provides services to over 110 countries.

	1989 Sales		1989 Operating Income	
	$ mil	% of total	$ mil	% of total
US	4,145	80	467	110
Foreign	1,022	20	(43)	(10)
Total	**5,167**	**100**	**424**	**100**

WHAT

	1989 Sales	
	$ mil	% of total
Express		
FedEx Priority Overnight	2,874	55
FedEx Letter	975	19
FedEx Standard Overnight	30	1
Standard Air	622	12
Air Freight	363	7
Charter	85	2
Other	219	4
Total	**5,167**	**100**

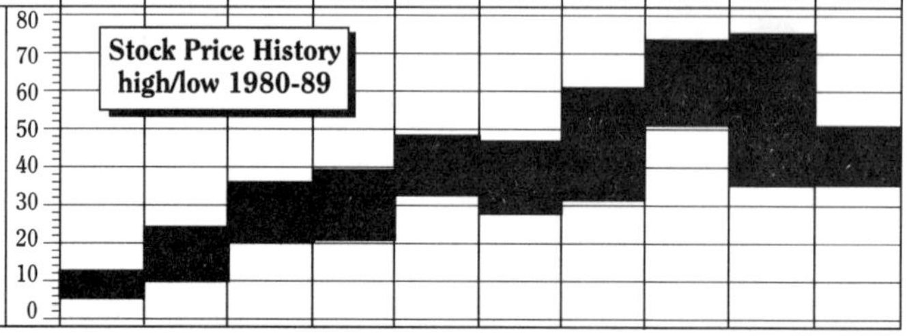

RANKINGS

10th in *Fortune* 50 Transportation Cos.
122nd in *Forbes* Sales 500
220th in *Business Week* 1000
826th in *Business Week* Global 1000

COMPETITION

Consolidated Freightways
Roadway
Union Pacific
UPS
Airline companies

HOW MUCH

	9 Yr. Growth	1980	1981	1982	1983	1984	1985	1986	1987	1988	1989
Sales ($ mil)	32.3%	415	590	804	1,008	1,436	2,031	2,606	3,178	3,883	5,167
Net income ($ mil)	17.6%	39	59	78	89	115	76	132	167	188	166
Income as % of sales	—	9.3%	10.1%	9.8%	8.8%	8.0%	3.7%	5.1%	5.3%	4.8%	3.2%
Earnings per share ($)	13.4%	1.03	1.45	1.85	2.04	2.52	1.61	2.64	3.21	3.56	3.18
Stock price – high ($)	—	12.75	24.38	36.13	39.38	48.50	47.00	61.00	73.75	75.50	51.00
Stock price – low ($)	—	5.25	9.72	20.25	20.75	32.56	27.75	31.38	51.00	35.25	35.38
Stock price – close ($)	17.7%	11.66	22.13	31.25	37.13	46.25	34.50	60.63	63.13	39.88	50.63
P/E – high	—	12	17	20	19	19	29	23	23	21	16
P/E – low	—	5	7	11	10	13	17	12	16	10	11
Dividends per share ($)	0.0%	0.00	0.00	0.00	0.00	0.00	0.00	0.00	0.00	0.00	0.00
Book value per share ($)	22.2%	4.70	6.99	8.44	11.47	15.47	17.27	21.49	20.90	25.17	28.59

1989 Year End:
Debt ratio: 58.9%
Return on equity: 11.8%
Cash (mil): $157
Current ratio: 1.01
Long-term debt (mil): $2,139
Number of shares (mil): 52
Dividends:
1989 average yield: 0.0%
1989 payout: 0.0%
Market value (mil): $2,644

Stock Price History high/low 1980-89

80 70 60 50 40 30 20 10 0

FEDERAL NATIONAL MORTGAGE ASSOCIATION

OVERVIEW

The Federal National Mortgage Association, better known as Fannie Mae, was created by the federal government to support the national goal of providing housing for low- and moderate-income families. Fannie Mae dominates the national secondary real estate market, buying mortgages (its 1990 mortgage size limit is $187,450) from loan originators (*e.g.*, banks, S&Ls) with money borrowed at favorable rates because of its government backing. This allows lenders to offer more loans, improving the flow and availability of credit to mortgage seekers. Fannie Mae's income results from the difference between mortgage interest rates and rates on borrowed money and from fees collected from lenders for making commitments to buy mortgages from them.

The company is a publicly owned, private corporation chartered by the US government. It operates for profit, pays federal corporate income taxes, and pays dividends to its stockholders. Fannie Mae is one of the largest corporations in the US, with assets of over $124 billion. Fannie Mae is also the largest private borrower in the country, 2nd only to the US Treasury.

Fannie Mae operates as a "corporate instrumentality" of the US government and enjoys exemption from state and local taxes and from the SEC's registration requirements. However, Fannie Mae is also subject to extra government regulation. The secretaries of HUD (Housing and Urban Develpment) and the Treasury have regulatory powers over the company in order to assure that it fulfills its charter.

NYSE symbol: FNM
Founded: 1938
Fiscal year ends: December 31

WHO

Chairman and CEO: David O. Maxwell, age 60, $1,317,661 pay
VC: James A. Johnson, age 46
President and COO: Roger E. Birk, age 59, $857,291 pay
EVP Operations and Systems: Samuel A. Alward, age 58, $460,953 pay
EVP and Chief Credit Officer: Michael A. Smilow, age 52, $444,659 pay
EVP, Secretary, and General Counsel: Caryl S. Bernstein, age 56
EVP and CFO: J. Timothy Howard, age 41
EVP Marketing: Dale P. Riordan, age 41, $367,818 pay
Auditors: KPMG Peat Marwick
Employees: 2,500

WHEN

Fannie Mae was created by President Franklin Roosevelt to buy FHA (Federal Housing Administration) loans in 1938 as part of the government-owned Reconstruction Finance Corporation. Fannie Mae began buying VA (Veterans Administration) mortgages in 1948. In 1954 it was rechartered as a partly private, partly governmental "mixed ownership corporation." The Housing Act of 1968 separated the corporation into 2 entities: the Government National Mortgage Association (Ginnie Mae) remained part of HUD, while Fannie Mae became privately owned, selling stock to the public. Fannie Mae retained its "Treasury Backstop Authority" whereby the secretary of the Treasury can purchase up to $2.24 billion of the company's obligations.

Fannie Mae introduced nationwide uniform conventional loan mortgage documents in 1970; began to purchase conventional, in addition to VA and FHA, mortgages in 1972; and began to purchase condominium and planned unit development mortgages in 1974. By 1976 Fannie Mae was purchasing more conventional loans than FHA and VA loans.

The 1980s were a decade of change for Fannie Mae and the US real estate market in general. In 1981 Fannie Mae was losing money at the rate of over $1 million each business day. In that year the company began to deal in mortgage-backed securities (MBSs) and introduced adjustable rate mortgages (ARMs) on a national basis. The company began to issue securities based on ARMs in 1982 and funded 14% of the home mortgages in the US.

In 1984 Fannie Mae began purchasing conventional multifamily and co-op housing loans and began borrowing money overseas. In 1985 Fannie Mae issued securities aimed at foreign investors, becoming the first US corporation to issue a yen-denominated security in the domestic market. The company issued its first real estate mortgage investment conduit (REMIC) securities (shares in mortgage pools of specific maturities and risk classes) and introduced a program to allow small lenders to pool loans with other lenders to create MBSs in 1987. By 1989 Fannie Mae's improved financial condition allowed it to earn net income of $807 million.

WHERE

HQ: 3900 Wisconsin Ave., NW, Washington, DC 20016
Phone: 202-752-7000
FAX: 202-752-6099

Fannie Mae operates throughout the US.

Regional Offices
Atlanta
Chicago
Dallas
Pasadena
Philadelphia

WHAT

	1989 Sales	
	$ mil	% of total
Mortgage interest	10,103	87
Investment interest	977	8
Guaranty fees	408	4
Sale of mortgages	9	—
Other income	60	1
Total	**11,557**	**100**

	1989 Mortgage Purchases	
	$ mil	% of total
Single family		
FHA/VA	940	4
Conventional		
30-year fixed-rate	11,813	52
Intermediate-term fixed-rate	3,306	15
ARMs	4,492	20
Second mortgages	406	2
Multifamily	1,561	7
Total	**22,518**	**100**

HOW MUCH

	9 Yr. Growth	1980	1981	1982	1983	1984	1985	1986	1987	1988	1989
Sales ($ mil)	9.3%	5,203	5,862	7,166	8,256	9,084	10,342	10,540	10,078	10,635	11,557
Net income ($ mil)	56.6%	14	(190)	(134)	76	(57)	37	183	376	507	807
Income as % of sales	—	0.3%	(3.2%)	(1.9%)	0.9%	(0.6%)	0.4%	1.7%	3.7%	4.8%	7.0%
Earnings per share ($)	50.8%	0.08	(1.07)	(0.73)	0.38	(0.29)	0.17	0.82	1.54	2.11	3.10
Stock price – high ($)	—	5.79	4.04	9.08	10.04	8.42	9.88	14.00	16.13	17.54	46.08
Stock price – low ($)	—	3.50	2.13	2.38	6.58	3.63	4.67	7.58	8.33	9.67	16.71
Stock price – close ($)	26.9%	3.96	2.83	8.17	7.67	5.13	8.63	13.58	10.17	16.92	33.88
P/E – high	—	76	—	—	27	—	57	17	10	8	15
P/E – low	—	46	—	—	17	—	27	9	5	5	5
Dividends per share ($)	1.7%	0.37	0.13	0.05	0.05	0.05	0.05	0.07	0.12	0.24	0.43
Book value per share ($)	4.8%	8.22	7.01	6.13	6.46	6.12	6.14	7.20	7.67	9.58	12.52

1989 Year End:
Debt ratio: 96.4%
Return on equity: 28.1%
Cash (mil): $11,870
Current ratio: —
Long-term debt (mil): $79,718
Number of shares (mil): 239
Dividends:
1989 average yield: 1.3%
1989 payout: 14.0%
Market value (mil): $8,092

Stock Price History high/low 1980-89

50
45
40
35
30
25
20
15
10
5
0

RANKINGS

2nd in *Fortune* 50 Diversified Financial Cos.
54th in *Forbes* Sales 500
57th in *Business Week* 1000
173rd in *Business Week* Global 1000

COMPETITION

Other financial institutions in the secondary mortgage market

FIAT

OVERVIEW

Fiat is Italy's biggest private-sector company and the world's 15th largest corporation. The company, 40% controlled by the Agnelli family, is a fully integrated automobile manufacturer and diversified industrial giant. In 10 years Managing Director Cesare Romiti engineered a stunning turnaround that made Fiat Europe's top automaker at the end of the 1980s and returned the company to financial health.

Steady productivity increases through factory automation have lowered break-even points in automaking, while diversification has broadened Fiat's sales base. The company has periodically considered mergers to gain global auto production capacity and market share. Fiat advocates EC restrictions on Japanese auto imports in conjunction with European market unification in 1992.

WHEN

Ex-cavalry officer Giovanni Agnelli founded Fabbrica Italiana di Automobili Torino (Fiat) in 1899. The Turin-based automaker soon expanded into trucks (1903), railcars (1906), aviation (1908), and tractors (1918). Protected by high import tariffs, Fiat became Italy's dominant auto company. Between WWI and WWII the low-end carmaker continuously reduced its dependence on foreign suppliers by manufacturing its own parts.

Mussolini's WWII modernization drive boosted Fiat's fortunes, but subsequent bombing damaged many of its plants. With US support Fiat rebuilt its facilities in the postwar period and survived weak domestic demand by exporting and by building assembly operations abroad. In 1950 Fiat licensed its know-how to Spain's SEAT, a state-owned automaker. As growth resumed in Italy, Fiat began making steel and construction equipment.

When the EC forced Italy to lower import tariffs in 1961, Fiat lost market share and responded with a new mid-range car and an import-bashing campaign in its *La Stampa* newspaper. Fiat's domestic woes were offset by success abroad. In 1965 Fiat agreed to build a USSR plant to produce 600,000 cars annually.

In 1966 Giovanni Agnelli II, the founder's grandson, became Fiat's chairman. Under Agnelli, Fiat bought high-end Italian carmakers Lancia and Ferrari (1969) and diversified into biotechnology and telecommunications. Allis Chalmers and Fiat merged their earthmoving equipment businesses in 1973.

Labor strife and the oil crisis hurt Fiat badly in the 1970s. By 1979, 27 company executives had been wounded by the leftist Red Brigade. Strapped for cash, the company sold a 10% interest to Libya in 1976.

In 1980 Cesare Romiti became Managing Director. Dubbed "Il duro" (the hard one), Romiti announced the elimination of 23,000 jobs. After a 5-week strike, 40,000 workers marched in support of Fiat management, crushing the strike and union influence at the company.

In the 1980s factory automation drastically improved Fiat's productivity, and its Comau machine tool unit became a leader in manufacturing technology. The Uno, a small car, was an instant success in 1983. The company ended its chronically unprofitable Fiat auto sales operations in the US (1983) and most of South America.

Merger talks with Ford collapsed in 1985, but Fiat's truck operations and Ford's British truck business were combined in 1986. In the same year Libya sold its holdings and Fiat outbid Ford for Alfa-Romeo, whose dealers accounted for 50% of Fiat's domestic sales. The company announced agreements with Chrysler (1988) to market Alfas in the US.

In 1989 and 1990 Fiat agreed to help build 600,000 additional cars annually in the USSR and 240,000 cars per year in Poland. In 1990 Fiat and Ford agreed to merge their farm and construction equipment businesses. Fiat will own 80% of the new firm.

HOW MUCH

$ = L1,266 (Dec. 31,1989)	9 Yr. Growth	1980	1981	1982	1983	1984	1985*	1986	1987	1988	1989
Sales (L bil)	12.4%	18,138	20,312	20,619	21,985	23,813	27,594	29,873	39,644	45,512	52,019
Net income (L bil)	—	—	90	137	253	627	1,326	2,162	2,373	3,026	3,306
Income as % of sales	—	—	0.4%	0.7%	1.2%	2.6%	4.8%	7.2%	6.0%	6.6%	6.4%
Earnings per share (L)	—	—	64	98	180	298	630	924	1,014	1,293	1,433
Stock price - high (L)	—	1,794	1,255	959	1,627	2,224	5,750	15,865	16,503	10,455	12,189
Stock price - low (L)	—	671	673	711	786	1,611	1,986	6,280	7,965	7,602	9,021
Stock price - close (L)	32.6%	880	786	808	1,627	2,067	5,721	13,817	8,220	9,813	11,131
P/E - high	—	—	20	10	9	7	9	17	16	8	9
P/E - low	—	—	11	7	4	5	3	7	8	6	6
Dividends per share (L)**	22.4%	60	67	77	87	106	144	212	270	320	370
Book value per share (L)	—	—	1,704	2,328	2,425	3,000	3,468	4,282	4,877	5,790	6,821

1989 Year End:
Debt ratio: 41.5%
Return on equity: 22.7%
Cash (bil): L10,189
Long-term debt (mil): L11,314
Number of shares (mil): 2,250
Dividends:
1989 average yield: 3.3%
1989 payout: 25.8%
Market value (mil): $19,783
Sales (mil): $41,089

Stock Price History high/low 1980-89 (in thousands)

18 16 14 12 10 8 6 4 2 0

*accounting change **not including rights offerings

NYSE symbol: FIA (ADR)
Incorporated: 1906
Fiscal year ends: December 31

WHO

Chairman: Giovanni Agnelli, age 69
Managing Director: Cesare Romiti, age 67
EVP Financing and Accounting: Francesco Paolo Mattioli, age 49
President, Fiat USA, Inc.: Vittorio Vellano
Auditors: Arthur Andersen & Co.
Employees: 286,294

WHERE

HQ: Fiat S.p.A., Corso Marconi 10-20, 10125 Turin, Italy
Phone: 011-39-11-65651
US HQ (Fiat USA, Inc.): 375 Park Ave., New York, NY 10152
US Phone: 212-355-2600
US FAX: 212-688-2848

Fiat conducts operations in 58 countries and owns 217 plants, principally in Italy, Brazil, Germany, France, Spain, and the UK.

	1989 Sales		1989 Operating Income	
	L bil	% of total	L bil	% of total
Italy	34,854	67	3,634	75
Other Europe	14,598	28	826	17
Other countries	2,567	5	377	8
Total	**52,019**	**100**	**4,837**	**100**

WHAT

	1989 Sales		1989 Operating Income	
	L bil	% of total	L bil	% of total
Automobiles	27,968	54	2,362	49
Commercial vehicles	7,704	15	624	13
Farm & construction equipment	2,876	5	186	4
Other	13,471	26	1,665	34
Total	**52,019**	**100**	**4,837**	**100**

Brand Names

Automobiles
Alfa Romeo
Ferrari
Fiat
Innocenti
Lancia-Autobianchi

Commercial Vehicles
Iveco (heavy trucks)

Farm & Construction Equipment
Fiatagri
FiatAllis
Hesston
Laverda
Woods

Major Subsidiaries

Comau Finanziaria S.p.A. (factory automation)
Fidis S.p.A. (financial services)
Gilardini S.p.A. (industrial components)
Magneti Marelli S.p.A. (automotive components)
Teksid S.p.A. (metallurgical products)

RANKINGS

15th in *Fortune* Global 500 Industrial Cos.
68th in *Business Week* Global 1000

COMPETITION

Caterpillar
Chrysler
Daimler-Benz
Deere
Dresser
Ford
General Motors
Hitachi
Honda
Hyundai
Ingersoll-Rand
Mitsubishi
Navistar
Nissan
PACCAR
Raytheon
Renault
Tenneco
Toyota
Volkswagen
Volvo

FIELDCREST CANNON, INC.

OVERVIEW

Headquartered in Eden, North Carolina, Fieldcrest Cannon is the 5th largest textile manufacturer in the US. The company designs and produces a broad spectrum of home textiles, including sheets, blankets, towels, and woven and tufted carpets. In the US, Fieldcrest Cannon has 48% of the electric blanket market, a 45% share of the towel market, and nearly 20% of the sheet market.

Although an unstable retail industry continues to affect the textile industry, major corporate restructuring, plant modernization, and product redirection in the last 2 years have reversed company losses. In 1989 the company made $23.4 million in profits on sales of nearly $1.4 billion after losing almost $4 million on revenues of $1.4 billion in 1987.

Fieldcrest Cannon is managed by Amoskeag Company, a Boston trust company and originally a New England textile manufacturer. Amoskeag holds 99% of Class B common stock (35% of total common stock) and controls nearly 84% of aggregate voting rights.

NYSE symbol: FLD
Incorporated: Delaware, 1953
Fiscal year ends: December 31

WHO

Chairman and CEO: Joseph B. Ely, II, age 51, $739,000 pay
VC: C. Edward Midgley, age 53, $663,000 pay
President: Charles G. Horn, age 50, $659,000 pay
EVP and CFO: W. Randle Mitchell, Jr., age 55, $281,125 pay
SVP: John J. Riley, $355,000 pay
SVP: K. William Fraser, Jr., age 52
Auditors: Ernst & Young
Employees: 20,416

WHEN

Fieldcrest's founder, industrialist Benjamin Franklin Mebane, built 6 mills between 1898 and 1905 in Eden, North Carolina. When Mebane was unable to repay loans from Marshall Field & Company, the Thread Mills Company, a subsidiary of the Chicago retailer, assumed mill operations (1910).

Thread Mills built the community of Fieldale, Virginia, and the Fieldale Mill (1916, renamed Dumaine Mill 1989), and began making huck and terry towels (1919). Royal Velvet towels (1954) are still manufactured there. The company also introduced Karastan, an oriental-design carpet (1928) and developed the patented Kara-loc carpet loom (1948).

In 1935 Marshall Field organized mills in North Carolina and Virginia as the Manufacturing Division to sell textile goods nationwide. It later changed the name of Thread Mills to Fieldcrest Mills (1947) to enhance brand name identity. Marshall Field sold Fieldcrest Mills to Amoskeag Company, a Boston investment trust (1953), to finance department store expansion in shopping centers. Fieldcrest went public in 1962.

Acquisitions included Muscogee Manufacturing (1963); North Carolina Finishing (1964); Winchester Spinning (1966, merged 1970); Morgan Carpet Mills Division (1967); Foremost Screen Print (merged 1969); and Swift Spinning Mills (1973; sold 1989 to Masaru Tsuzuki of Kitaura Spinning, Japan).

In January 1986 Fieldcrest paid $250 million to entrepreneur David Murdock for rival Cannon Mills's name and its sheet, towel, and rug plants (Murdock retained 2 manufacturing plants). Murdock had paid $413 million in 1982 for the ailing Cannon Mills of Kannapolis, North Carolina, originally founded by James Cannon (1888) to produce cotton fabric and, later, huck towels (1894) and terry towels (1898). The 2 companies merged as Fieldcrest Cannon, Inc. (June 1986) and quickly bought Bigelow-Sanford, a South Carolina carpet company (December 1986).

The company restructured (1988), establishing Fieldcrest, Cannon, and Karastan Bigelow as 3 divisions with separate corporate managements and sales forces to respond quickly to customer needs and changing markets, but with shared manufacturing facilities to lower production costs. Closing inefficient plants and shifting more automated plants to 24-hour operations, the company began a 5-year $250 million capital investment program to modernize towel manufacturing plants (1989). The company is completing construction of 2 new Axminster looms to boost Karastan production by 15% (1990) and plans to have all sheet printing facilities automated by 1992. A new computerized inventory system will track production and take orders directly from customers.

WHERE

HQ: 326 E. Stadium Dr., Eden, NC 27288
Phone: 919-627-3000
FAX: 919-627-3109 (Finance)

Fieldcrest Cannon manufactures home furnishing textiles, does custom finishing in 34 plants (primarily in the Southeast), and has 22 distribution facilities.

	No. of Manufacturing Plants
Alabama	2
Georgia	3
North Carolina	22
Pennsylvania	1
South Carolina	5
Virginia	1
Total	**34**

WHAT

	1989 Sales	
	$ mil	% of total
Bed & bath products	1,007	74
Carpets & rugs	326	24
Other products	29	2
Total	**1,362**	**100**

	1989 Sales
Home Furnishings	% of total
Brand names	91
Private labels	9
Total	**100**

Brand Names
Bed and bath products
- Cannon
- Charisma
- Fieldcrest
- Monticello
- Royal Family
- Royal Velvet
- St. Mary's

Carpets and rugs
- Bigelow
- Karastan

Private Labels
Bed and bath products
- Common Sense (Wal-Mart)
- Legacy (Federated)
- Martha Stewart (K mart)
- Royal Court (Sears)
- Whisper (Burdine's)

Subsidiaries
Cannon Mills International, Ltd. (UK)
Cannon Mills International Sales Corp.
Delaware Valley Wool Scouring Co.
Encee, Inc.
Fieldcrest Mills International, Inc.
St. Marys, Inc.

HOW MUCH

	9 Yr. Growth	1980	1981	1982	1983	1984	1985	1986	1987	1988	1989
Sales ($ mil)	11.1%	527	526	492	551	573	586	1,083	1,400	1,338	1,362
Net income ($ mil)	3.3%	17	10	10	15	4	13	17	(4)	11	23
Income as % of sales	—	3.3%	1.8%	2.1%	2.7%	0.7%	2.2%	1.6%	(0.3%)	0.8%	1.7%
Earnings per share ($)	(0.3%)	2.21	1.21	1.32	1.88	0.54	1.64	2.11	(0.36)	1.10	2.14
Stock price – high ($)	—	14.94	18.13	15.38	19.50	19.50	17.63	43.00	41.00	24.75	30.25
Stock price – low ($)	—	11.25	9.81	8.56	14.00	12.63	12.88	17.31	13.25	14.25	18.63
Stock price – close ($)	6.6%	12.63	11.19	14.50	18.38	15.50	17.44	33.50	14.38	19.88	22.50
P/E – high	—	7	15	12	10	36	11	20	—	23	14
P/E – low	—	5	8	6	7	24	8	8	—	13	9
Dividends per share ($)	(2.9%)	1.00	1.00	1.00	1.00	1.00	0.63	0.57	0.68	0.68	0.77
Book value per share ($)	2.7%	21.48	21.54	21.93	22.66	22.25	23.22	26.37	25.36	25.73	27.24

1989 Year End:
Debt ratio: 54.9%
Return on equity: 8.1%
Cash (mil): $7
Current ratio: 2.85
Long-term debt (mil): $342
Number of shares (mil): 10
Dividends:
  1989 average yield: 3.4%
  1989 payout: 36.0%
Market value (mil): $232

Stock Price History high/low 1980-89

COMPETITION

Burlington Holdings
Du Pont
Farley
Milliken
Springs Industries

FIRST CHICAGO CORPORATION

OVERVIEW

First Chicago is the 13th largest bank holding company in the nation. Its major asset, First National Bank of Chicago, is the 11th largest US bank. First Chicago, through its Delaware subsidiary, is the 3rd largest issuer of credit cards in the US, with more than 6 million accounts and more than $6 billion in outstanding balances.

The company's banking operations are divided into 2 major "bank" groups. The Global Corporate Bank (accounting for 59% of earnings and about 2/3 of assets) provides commercial and investment banking services to large international corporations, governments, and institutions. Along with its US and Canadian business, the bank operates 5 affiliates and 15 offices in 17 countries.

The Superregional Bank (41% of earnings, 1/3 of assets) provides Chicago-area individuals and middle-market businesses with traditional banking services (through subsidiary American National Bank), operates the bankcard business, and engages in local community retail banking. First Chicago oversees its subsidiaries from its distinctive 60-story building downtown.

NYSE symbol: FNB
Incorporated: Delaware, 1969
Fiscal year ends: December 31

WHO

Chairman and Principal Executive Officer: Barry F. Sullivan, age 59, $1,460,824 pay
President and Principal Financial Officer: Richard L. Thomas, age 59, $986,590 pay
Chairman, American National Corporation: Michael E. Tobin, age 64
Auditors: Arthur Andersen & Co.
Employees: 18,158

WHEN

In 1863 the US Comptroller of the Currency granted Charter #8 to the First National Bank of Chicago. First National, from its first office nestled on LaSalle Street, grew rapidly after the Civil War. When the Chicago Fire leveled much of the city, First National's "fireproof" building burned too. A cashier named Lyman Gage, later to become president of the bank and McKinley's secretary of the treasury, discovered that the bank's documents and money had survived in a vault, and the bank resumed operations quickly as the city rebuilt.

First National bought the Union National Bank in 1900 and Metropolitan National Bank in 1902, almost doubling in size in 2 years. First National launched a subsidiary called First Trust and Savings Bank in 1903, renamed First Union Trust and Savings Bank after the 1929 merger with Union Trust.

As the Great Depression settled in, First National took over troubled Foreman State banks (1931), weathered a run on the bank for $50 million (1933), and folded First Union Trust back into First National (1933). WWII spurred the bank's growth again, and in 1959 it stretched into the international marketplace, opening an office in London. It added a Tokyo office in 1962. A 1969 reorganization created First Chicago as the bank's holding corporation.

First Chicago grew rapidly — some said too rapidly — in the early 1970s under Chairman Gaylord Freeman. After Deputy Chairman Robert Abboud took over in 1975, the bank wrestled with $2 billion in problem loans, particularly in real estate, and with the threat of a shutdown by federal regulators. Abboud tempered the bank's growth and drew criticism from and, eventually, dismissal by the bank's board of directors in 1980.

Barry Sullivan replaced Abboud and resumed the bank's growth. First Chicago acquired credit card accounts from Bankers Trust New York (1982), Beneficial National Bank of Delaware (1987), and Society for Savings Bancorp (1989), to make it the 3rd largest credit card issuer in the nation.

Chief competitor Continental of Illinois stumbled in 1984 and required a federal bailout. First Chicago surged ahead of its rival, acquiring the $3 billion American National Corporation, holding company for American National Bank and Trust, Chicago's 5th largest bank. In the late 1980s First Chicago added more Chicagoland banking concerns — First United Financial Services (1987), Gary-Wheaton (1988), Bank of Ravenswood (1989), Winnetka Bank (1989), and a small Wisconsin bank (1990). It even bought 95,000 personal and small business accounts from beleaguered old foe Continental Bank.

WHERE

HQ: One First National Plaza, Chicago, IL 60670
Phone: 312-732-4000
FAX: 312-732-5976 (Corporate Affairs)

The bank operates in the US and 18 other countries.

	1989 Sales		1989 Net Income	
	$ mil	% of total	$ mil	% of total
Domestic operns.	4,483	80	461	128
Europe, Middle East & Africa	477	8	(21)	(6)
Latin America	143	3	(112)	(31)
North America & Caribbean	130	2	18	5
Asia & Pacific	378	7	13	4
Total	**5,611**	**100**	**359**	**100**

WHAT

	1989 Sales	
	$ mil	% of total
Loan interest	3,345	60
Other interest	1,130	20
Credit card income	326	6
Fees & commissions	280	5
Other noninterest	530	9
Total	**5,611**	**100**

Divisions

Global Corporate Bank
Capital Markets Group
Credit Products Group
Customer Service Group
International Banking Group
Merchant Banking Group
New Products Development Group
North American Banking Group
Service Products Group

Superregional Bank
American National Corp. (American National Bank)
Bankcard Group
Community Banking Group

HOW MUCH

	9 Yr. Growth	1980	1981	1982	1983	1984	1985	1986	1987	1988	1989
Sales ($ mil)	5.7%	3,408	4,319	4,388	3,675	4,526	4,370	4,083	4,255	4,816	5,611
Net income ($ mil)	21.3%	63	119	137	184	86	169	276	(571)	513	359
Income as % of sales	—	1.8%	2.7%	3.1%	5.0%	1.9%	3.9%	6.8%	(13.4%)	10.7%	6.4%
Earnings per share ($)	13.6%	1.59	2.98	3.33	3.92	1.19	2.84	4.70	(10.71)	7.92	4.99
Stock price – high ($)	—	16.63	20.75	23.13	28.00	27.00	30.13	34.88	34.00	35.25	49.63
Stock price – low ($)	—	10.75	15.13	13.50	17.13	18.63	20.13	26.38	16.63	18.75	29.25
Stock price – close ($)	10.1%	15.63	19.25	18.13	25.38	21.38	29.50	28.63	18.88	29.63	37.13
P/E – high	—	10	7	7	7	23	11	7	—	4	10
P/E – low	—	7	5	4	4	16	7	6	—	2	6
Dividends per share ($)	4.6%	1.20	1.20	1.20	1.26	1.32	1.32	1.32	1.50	1.50	1.80
Book value per share ($)	1.6%	30.26	31.87	33.55	35.80	34.12	34.10	36.91	24.21	31.29	34.82

1989 Year End:
Debt ratio: 33.4%
Return on equity: 15.1%
Cash (mil): $8,315
Assets (mil): $47,907
Long-term debt (mil): $1,351
Number of shares (mil): 65
Dividends:
1989 average yield: 4.8%
1989 payout: 36.1%
Market value (mil): $2,424

Stock Price History high/low 1980-89

RANKINGS

13th in *Fortune* 100 Commercial Banking Cos.
99th in *Fortune* World's 100 Commercial Banks
159th in *Forbes* Sales 500
305th in *Business Week* 1000
951st in *Business Week* Global 1000

COMPETITION

H. F. Ahmanson
American Express
BankAmerica
Bank of New York
Bankers Trust
Chase Manhattan
Chemical Banking
Citicorp
CS Holding
Dai-Ichi Kangyo
Deutsche Bank
Hongkong & Shanghai Banking
Manufacturers Hanover
J.P. Morgan
Security Pacific
Other money-center and international banks

FIRST EXECUTIVE CORPORATION

OVERVIEW

First Executive owns Executive Life, the 16th largest US life insurance company, which gets 51% of its life business from policyholders in California, Florida, Illinois, New York, and Texas. Annuities are the Los Angeles–based company's 2nd most important business. Nearly 1/2 of this business is conducted in 3 states — California, New York, and Texas.

The company offers group and individual whole life insurance (offering current market interest rates and permitting policy loans), universal life insurance (offering discretionary premium payment schedules), single-premium deferred annuities (offering guaranteed interest rates), single-premium immediate annuities (providing periodic payments for a fixed length of time or for life), and guaranteed investment contracts (GICs). In 1989 a decline in the value of the portfolio, coupled with major defaults in large holdings of junk bonds, forced the company to write off certain equity securities and to increase its allowance for securities losses. After the charges the company posted a net loss for the year of $776 million.

In 1990 the company experienced growing requests by customers for surrender of single-premium deferred annuities, high levels of policy borrowing, and an increasing rate of customers allowing their policies to lapse.

WHEN

Until 1974 First Executive was an obscure insurance company. In that year Fred Carr, a highly successful mutual fund manager during the 1960s, became CEO. Carr, who had taken a publicity beating in 1970 when his high-risk "go-go" fund plummeted, transformed the struggling First Executive from a $15 million a year company to a $1.6 billion a year company by 1982.

Carr sold annuities to raise cash. In response to soaring interest rates during the mid-1970s, insurance companies were bringing out new products with higher returns than traditional whole life and term policies. Carr recognized that First Executive was too small to compete in the life insurance market, which required large cash reserves. Instead he aggressively marketed a single-premium deferred annuity in which a prepaid lump sum earned tax-deferred interest. Using his investment skills he quickly became the industry leader in investment returns.

The annuities market took a precipitous decline in 1983; the 2 industry leaders, Baldwin-United and Charter, went bankrupt and exited the market, respectively, making First Executive the largest annuities seller. First Executive might have followed its rivals, but Carr was ready: he had increased subsidiary Executive Life's insurance policies in force from about $700 million (1975) to $7.5 billion (1983). The whole life policy, which he had introduced in 1979, was largely responsible. Geared toward professionals and executives and made feasible by Carr's high investment returns, the policy offered higher cash accumulation and lower premiums than traditional policies. He bought 2 insurance companies, Bay Colony Life (1982, renamed First Delaware Life) and Lincoln Liberty (1984).

While selling through independent agents, Carr established reinsurance companies and gave agents a stake in the business, providing First Executive with high policy renewal rates.

The firm is plagued with investigations into its investments. Its higher-than-average returns are attributable in part to heavy investments in junk bonds, which comprised more than 1/2 of the company's portfolio in late 1989. New York State has insisted that it limit junk bonds to 20% of investments. Congress is investigating Carr's role in the Pacific Lumber takeover, in which a PL employees' pension fund was raided to finance a buyout. Liquidity continues to be a problem as cash reserves are used for surrendering policyholders, inviting speculation that the company may go private.

HOW MUCH

	9 Yr. Growth	1980	1981	1982	1983	1984	1985	1986	1987	1988	1989
Sales ($ mil)	6.7%	666	1,376	1,759	1,342	935	1,365	2,218	2,294	2,138	1,195
Net income ($ mil)	—	9	17	27	44	73	93	104	125	175	(776)
Income as % of sales	—	1.4%	1.2%	1.5%	3.3%	7.8%	6.8%	4.7%	5.4%	8.2%	—
Assets ($ mil)	42.4%	798	1,876	3,451	4,810	6,547	9,040	14,716	16,903	18,782	19,256
Premium & annuity income ($ mil)	7.0%	494	1,109	1,374	862	290	457	979	655	234	258
Net investment income ($ mil)	48.2%	58	150	333	480	615	868	1,214	1,633	1,892	1,995
Net income as % of assets	—	2.4%	1.9%	1.6%	3.2%	1.1%	1.0%	0.7%	0.7%	0.9%	(4.0%)
Life insurance in force ($ mil)	42.9%	2,404	3,304	9,719	20,412	28,284	35,298	46,109	54,119	57,276	59,748

1989 Company Totals:
Total assets (mil): $19,256
Revenue (mil): $1,195
Surplus (mil): —
Premiums (mil) $258
Net investment income (mil): $1,995
Stock price – high: $17.13
Stock price – low: $7.88
Stock price – close: $9.25
Market value (mil): $815

Life Insurance in Force ($ mil) 1980-89

OTC symbol: FEXC
Incorporated: Delaware, 1969
Fiscal year ends: December 31

WHO

Chairman and CEO: Fred Carr, age 59, $604,734 pay
President and COO: Alan C. Snyder, age 44
VP, General Counsel, and Secretary: William J. Adams, age 61, $216,719 pay
VP: Allan L. Chapman, age 52, $171,838 pay
VP, CFO, and Treasurer: William L. Sanders, age 44
Auditors: Deloitte & Touche
Employees: 1,050

WHERE

HQ: 11444 W. Olympic Blvd., Los Angeles, CA 90064
Phone: 213-312-1000
FAX: 213-477-3279

First Executive serves customers in all 50 states; Washington, DC; Puerto Rico; Guam; and the US Virgin Islands through independent agents.

WHAT

	1989 Sales	
	$ mil	% of total
Premiums	258	22
Net investment income	1,995	167
Gains (losses) on investments	(1,058)	(89)
Total	**1,195**	**100**

	1989 Assets	
	$ mil	% of total
Investments	17,470	91
Cash	27	—
Investment income accrued	373	2
Deferred policy acquisition costs	1,212	6
Other assets	174	1
Total	**19,256**	**100**

Life Insurance Companies
Executive Life Insurance Co.
Executive Life Insurance Co. of New York
First Delaware Life Insurance Co.
Lincoln Liberty Life Insurance Co.

Other Services
Annuities
Guaranteed investment contracts

RANKINGS

16th in *Fortune* 50 Life Insurance Cos. (Executive Life)
358th in *Forbes* Sales 500

COMPETITION

Aetna
AIG
CIGNA
Equitable
John Hancock
Kemper
Massachusetts Mutual
Metropolitan
New York Life
Northwestern Mutual
Primerica
Prudential
Sears
State Farm
Teachers Insurance
Travelers
Transamerica
USF&G

FIRST FIDELITY BANCORPORATION

OVERVIEW

First Fidelity is the largest bank in New Jersey and the 20th largest US banking organization, serving New Jersey and Pennsylvania with almost 500 banking offices.

The Lawrenceville, New Jersey–based company's principal affiliates are 4 First Fidelity banks and Morris Savings Bank in New Jersey, and Fidelity Bank and 2 Merchants Banks in Pennsylvania. The company also has some nonbank subsidiaries that provide mortgage banking, commercial finance, and discount brokerage services.

First Fidelity's strength is in serving small, middle-market companies and consumers in its region. Almost 44% of First Fidelity's $20 billion in loans are made to commercial and financial clients. Corporate borrowers include businesses in service industries, manufacturing, finance and insurance, and wholesale and retail trade. About 34% of the portfolio, including 10% in mortgages, comprises consumer loans. The remaining loans are commercial mortgages (10%), construction loans (6%), and leasing (6%).

WHEN

The New Jersey legislature established the State Bank of Newark in 1812 with $400,000 in authorized stock, 1/2 of which was reserved for the state. Within a year the bank bought the state's rights to the stock and paid a dividend, the first in an uninterrupted series of regular dividend payments that continues today.

In 1865 the bank got a national charter and became the National State Bank of Newark. The bank grew to about $3.5 million in assets by 1900. As a result of business and industry growth in the Newark area, the bank's assets totaled $7 million in 1920. National State Bank got through the Great Depression on the strength of its 1920s growth. By 1940 the bank's assets were about $38 million.

In 1949 National State bought Merchants and Newark Trust Company. The following year the bank purchased Orange (New Jersey) First National Bank, giving it a presence in Newark's suburbs, and United States Trust Company ($40 million in assets). The bank continued expanding by opening an office at the Newark airport (1953) and by acquiring Newark-based Lincoln National Bank (1955) and Federal Trust Company in Newark (1958). The bank's total assets were more than $418 million after these acquisitions.

Having expanded outside Newark, the bank changed its name to First National State Bank of New Jersey in 1965. The bank formed First National State Bancorporation in 1969 and continued its expansion throughout New Jersey by purchasing another 15 banks during the 1970s.

In 1984 First National State, by then New Jersey's largest banking organization, acquired Fidelity Union Bancorporation, the #3 bank organization in the state, to form First Fidelity Bancorporation, a $10 billion banking organization. The acquisition brought together First National's corporate banking and financial services and Fidelity Union's personal banking services, resulting in a new organization with 288 offices in 21 New Jersey counties.

First Fidelity became a major regional bank in 1988 when it merged with Fidelcor, Inc., a $13 billion organization with 190 banking offices in eastern Pennsylvania. Fidelcor, founded in 1866 as a safe-deposit company, was a major banking institution centered on its largest bank, Fidelity Bank of Philadelphia. Fidelcor's loan quality problem depressed 1988 earnings.

In 1990 Anthony Terracciano, former president of Mellon Bank, became CEO of First Fidelity. He and his management team began moving the company to a more efficient, centralized management structure by announcing the elimination of 10% of the staff (1,400) and expense cuts, for a total of $95 million in expected cost savings in 1990 and $115 million in 1991.

HOW MUCH

	9 Yr. Growth	1980	1981	1982	1983	1984	1985	1986	1987	1988	1989
Sales ($ mil)	29.4%	298	456	465	526	1,065	1,056	1,210	2,414	2,805	3,028
Net income ($ mil)	25.3%	21	30	35	47	82	94	120	86	34	160
Income as % of sales	—	7.1%	6.6%	7.5%	9.0%	7.7%	8.9%	9.9%	3.6%	1.2%	5.3%
Earnings per share ($)	0.4%	2.42	2.83	3.30	3.48	3.18	3.42	3.95	1.37	0.50	2.52
Stock price – high ($)	—	11.79	12.14	17.00	21.13	23.44	31.81	42.50	46.50	40.88	34.00
Stock price – low ($)	—	7.98	9.52	10.69	14.06	15.63	22.75	28.38	27.00	25.25	21.38
Stock price – close ($)	10.2%	9.70	10.50	15.63	20.69	23.44	30.81	35.00	29.88	26.88	23.25
P/E – high	—	5	4	5	6	7	9	11	34	82	14
P/E – low	—	3	3	3	4	5	7	7	20	51	8
Dividends per share ($)	7.5%	1.05	1.06	1.15	1.26	1.38	1.50	1.62	1.76	1.92	2.00
Book value per share ($)	3.4%	17.79	19.60	21.11	23.32	24.59	26.42	29.31	25.80	23.52	24.07

1989 Year End:
Debt ratio: 33.3%
Return on equity: 10.6%
Cash (mil): $1,766
Assets (mil): $30,728
Long-term debt (mil): $780
Number of shares (mil): 59
Dividends:
1989 average yield: 8.6%
1989 payout: 79.4%
Market value (mil): $1,360

NYSE symbol: FFB
Incorporated: New Jersey, 1987
Fiscal year ends: December 31

WHO

Chairman, President, and CEO: Anthony P. Terracciano, age 51
VC and Chief Credit Officer: Peter C. Palmieri, age 55
VC and CFO: Wolfgang Schoellkopf, age 57
VC: Edward D. Knapp, age 55, $435,000 pay
SEVP: Leslie E. Goodman, age 46, $300,000 pay
Auditors: KPMG Peat Marwick
Employees: 13,500

WHERE

HQ: 1009 Lenox Dr., Lawrenceville, NJ 08648
Phone: 609-895-6800
FAX: 609-895-6863 (Investor Relations)

First Fidelity has offices in New Jersey, Pennsylvania, Delaware, Florida, and New York, and 6 overseas locations.

WHAT

	1989 Sales	
	$ mil	**% of total**
Interest income		
Loans	2,086	69
Investment securities	559	19
Federal funds sold	8	—
Bank deposits	13	—
Trading account securities	12	—
Noninterest income		
Trust income	78	3
Service charges	89	3
Other service charges, fees	92	3
Trading account gains, losses	9	—
Net securities transactions	18	1
Other income	64	2
Total	**3,028**	**100**

Financial Services

Commercial Lending
- Asset-based
- Equipment leasing
- Lines of credit
- Real estate
- Short- and medium-term

Consumer Banking
- Auto leasing
- Deposit accounts
- Personal and mortgage loans

Investment Services

Nonbank Subsidiaries

Fidelcor Business Credit Corp.
First Fidelity Brokers, Inc. (stock brokerage)
First Fidelity Community Development Corp.
First Fidelity Leasing Group, Inc.
Latimer & Buck, Inc. (mortgage banking)

RANKINGS

20th in *Fortune* 100 Commercial Banking Cos.
280th in *Forbes* Sales 500
438th in *Business Week* 1000

COMPETITION

Chemical Banking
Mellon Bank
PNC Financial

Other banks operating in New Jersey and Pennsylvania

FIRST INTERSTATE BANCORP

OVERVIEW

First Interstate Bancorp is the 9th largest US banking enterprise. First Interstate owns 28 subsidiary banks with 1,041 branches in 14 states. Five of the larger subsidiary banks conduct international banking.

The company also franchises its First Interstate name and logo and offers basic services to banks that do not belong to First Interstate. At the end of 1989, First Interstate was serving 39 franchise banks with 143 branches in 11 states, including 7 where First Interstate owned no subsidiaries.

First Interstate is reeling from bad loans in Texas and Arizona. Former chairman Joseph Pinola did not take advantage of the federal assistance that other multistate holding companies used to take over troubled Texas thrifts. First Interstate's once-lucrative Arizona portfolio stumbled, too, and the company posted a $152 million net loss in 1989 after providing reserves for shaky loans in those states.

NYSE symbol: I
Incorporated: Delaware, 1958
Fiscal year ends: December 31

WHO

Chairman and CEO: Edward M. Carson, age 60, $731,120 pay (prior to promotion)
President: William E. B. Siart, age 43, $615,200 pay (prior to promotion)
EVP and CFO: Thomas P. Marrie, age 51
Auditor: Ernst & Young
Employees: 36,000

WHERE

HQ: 707 Wilshire Blvd., Los Angeles, CA 90017
Phone: 213-614-3001
FAX: 213-614-5873

Subsidiary banks operate in 14 states and 19 countries.

	1989 Locations	
	number	% of total
California	329	31
Arizona	191	18
Oregon	175	17
Washington	105	10
Nevada	69	7
Texas	59	6
Other	113	11
Total	**1041**	**100**

	1989 Net Income
	$ mil
Retail branch banking	
California	203
Texas	(388)
Arizona	(154)
Oregon	91
Washington	49
Nevada	56
Rocky Mountain & other	60
Wholesale banking	61
Nonbank & consumer finance	78
Restructuring units	(93)
Parent corporation	(115)
Total	**(152)**

WHEN

First Interstate began as a gleam in the eye of Amadeo Peter Giannini, the son of an Italian immigrant. Giannini made enough money in his stepfather's produce firm to retire at age 31. Instead he began dabbling in real estate and banking. He launched the San Francisco–based Bank of Italy in a remodeled tavern in 1904.

Giannini dreamed of a nationwide bank chain and formed Transamerica in 1928 as the umbrella company over Bank of Italy and Bank of America. In 1930 Transamerica bought an Oregon bank and, over the next several years, acquired other non-California banks.

Under the mandates of the Bank Holding Company Act of 1956, Transamerica spun off 2 new entities — Bank of America, comprised of California banks, and Firstamerica, with 23 banks in 11 other western states. The 2 former siblings were destined to become arch-competitors.

Firstamerica bought California Bank (1959) and First Western Bank and Trust (1961). The 2 merged to become United California Bank, with 122 branches in 30 counties. In 1961 Firstamerica changed its name to Western Bancorporation.

In 1978 Joseph Pinola became chairman and CEO of Western. Pinola had spent 25 years rising through the ranks of Bank of America after answering a help wanted ad when he was discharged from the navy. At Western, the fiery Pinola centralized policymaking and launched an ambitious acquisition program, including an unsuccessful bid to purchase Bank of America and its parent company for $3.4 billion (1986).

In 1981 Western changed its name to First Interstate Bancorp. First Interstate began franchising its name, advertising, signs, products, and computer services to locally owned banks (1982). In 1985 the company divided its California banking operations into 2 sections, retail and wholesale (banking to other corporations). The wholesale arm used a London-based merchant bank bought from Continental Illinois.

First Interstate acquired retail banks in Denver (1983) and in Oklahoma (1986). Even Pinola acknowledged the mistake in First Interstate's purchase of Texas's troubled Allied Bancshares for $160 million (1988). In 1989 First Interstate announced it wanted to sell $400 million more stock to cover real estate loan losses. Stockholders, who saw their holdings diluted, lambasted the move. Pinola stepped down under fire in 1990.

First Interstate scaled down the offering to $276 million in 1990 and sold 40% of the new stock to Kohlberg Kravis Roberts, a firm known for its takeover triumphs. KKR agreed to limit its First Interstate holdings to 10% for 2 years and to give First Interstate a chance to buy the shares first if a hostile bidder tries to buy the company.

WHAT

	1989 Sales	
	$ mil	% of total
Loan interest	4,320	66
Other interest	1,056	16
Noninterest	1,159	18
Total	**6,535**	**100**

Loans
Commercial, agricultural, and financial
Installment
Real estate construction
Real estate mortgages

Services
Bank credit cards
Checking and NOW accounts
Savings accounts

RANKINGS

9th in *Fortune* 100 Commercial Banking Cos.
84th in *Fortune* World's 100 Commercial Banks
128th in *Forbes* Sales 500
351st in *Business Week* 1000
910th in *Business Week* Global 1000

COMPETITION

H.F. Ahmanson
Banc One
BankAmerica
Chase Manhattan
Chemical Banking
Citicorp
NCNB
Security Pacific
Wells Fargo
Other multistate bank holding companies

HOW MUCH

	9 Yr. Growth	1980	1981	1982	1983	1984	1985	1986	1987	1988	1989
Sales ($ mil)	8.0%	3,279	4,298	4,593	4,341	4,965	5,235	5,290	5,080	5,932	6,535
Net income ($ mil)	—	225	236	221	247	276	313	338	(556)	102	(152)
Income as % of sales	—	6.9%	5.5%	4.8%	5.7%	5.6%	6.0%	6.4%	(11.0%)	1.7%	(2.3%)
Earnings per share ($)	—	5.70	5.83	5.35	5.72	6.01	6.64	7.13	(11.99)	2.03	(3.89)
Stock price – high ($)	—	36.00	44.88	38.00	47.00	45.25	55.38	67.38	62.75	53.50	70.38
Stock price – low ($)	—	23.25	32.75	21.63	29.25	30.25	41.50	50.75	35.00	39.13	40.75
Stock price – close ($)	1.7%	36.00	35.75	31.38	41.63	43.00	52.88	52.00	39.25	43.38	41.88
P/E – high	—	6	8	7	8	8	8	9	—	26	—
P/E – low	—	4	6	4	5	5	6	7	—	19	—
Dividends per share ($)	5.8%	1.79	1.99	2.12	2.22	2.32	2.46	2.62	2.77	2.89	2.98
Book value per share ($)	(0.1%)	37.24	41.24	43.85	47.42	51.29	55.02	58.65	44.39	42.56	36.77

1989 Year End:
Debt ratio: 61.4%
Return on equity: —
Cash (mil): $8,119
Current ratio: —
Long-term debt (mil): $3,719
Number of shares (mil): 49
Dividends:
1989 average yield: 7.1%
1989 payout: —
Market value (mil): $2,043

FLEETWOOD ENTERPRISES, INC.

OVERVIEW

Headquartered in Riverside, California, Fleetwood Enterprises is the nation's largest producer of recreational vehicles (motor homes and travel trailers) and manufactured housing. Fleetwood commanded about 29% of the 1989 motor home market, producing the Jamboree, Pace Arrow, Southwind, Tioga, Limited, Bounder, Flair, and Cambria brands. Fleetwood also controlled about 30% of the travel trailer market, producing Avion, Prowler, Terry, and Wilderness.

Additionally, the company held 17% of the 1989 manufactured housing market, making it the nation's largest homebuilder for the 6th consecutive year. Fleetwood also owns a credit operation (financing customer recreational vehicle purchases — unique in the industry) and supply operations providing lumber, aluminum windows, fiberglass, and cabinet doors for its own operations and to other companies. The company produces manufactured housing only against firm orders from dealers.

Fleetwood plans to further its supply relationships with outside companies and to expand its recreational vehicle credit operations nationwide. The company will also look at expanding international sales, currently a negligible percentage of business.

WHEN

In 1950 John Crean started a business in California to assemble and sell venetian blinds to the motor home manufacturing industry. This small enterprise was the forerunner of Fleetwood, Crean's 1957 entry into the manufactured housing industry, headquartered in Riverside.

Fleetwood entered the recreational vehicle market in 1964 with the purchase of a small plant producing the Terry travel trailer. The following year Fleetwood went public; Crean currently holds 19% of the outstanding stock.

In 1969 Fleetwood acquired Pace Arrow, a motor home producer, expanding Fleetwood's offerings in the rapidly growing recreational vehicle market. Between 1968 and 1973 Fleetwood's sales grew at a nearly 55% annual rate.

An industry-wide recession caused by the 1970s oil shock and subsequent credit crunch dropped Fleetwood's stock from a 1972 high of $49.50 to $3.50 in 1974. Intensive cost cutting helped position Fleetwood for the eventual upturn, and in 1976 the company purchased Avion Coach Corporation, a manufacturer of luxury-class travel trailers and motor homes.

COO Glenn Kummer succeeded Crean as president in 1982, but Crean remains chairman and CEO. Strong recreational vehicle sales helped pull Fleetwood out of a mild recession in the mid-1980s, when the company's stock plummeted again, from a 1983 high of $42 to $14 in 1985.

In 1987 the company opened its first credit office in Southern California to finance customer purchases of recreational vehicles, avoiding riskier loans to manufactured housing buyers. Fleetwood Credit Corporation now has offices in California, Oregon, Indiana, Georgia, Massachusetts, and Texas.

Fleetwood added to its existing supply operations (fiberglass and lumber) with the purchase of a cabinet door manufacturer (1988) and an aluminum window maker (1989).

In 1989 Fleetwood became the first company to surpass the $1 billion annual sales mark in recreational vehicles, increasing market share during an industry slump. Total sales increased 15% to a company record $1.6 billion, while Fleetwood continued to steer clear of any long-term debt. The company added 2 new motor home models to its recreational vehicle line: the lower-priced Flair and the curved-wall Cambria.

In 1990 Fleetwood improved its product offering by acquiring Coleman's folding trailer business, the largest in the industry.

HOW MUCH

	9 Yr. Growth	1980	1981	1982	1983	1984	1985	1986	1987	1988	1989
Sales ($ mil)	14.7%	472	428	581	858	1,420	1,277	1,218	1,259	1,406	1,619
Net income ($ mil)	—	(8)	2	9	30	64	54	39	40	48	70
Income as % of sales	—	(1.8%)	0.6%	1.6%	3.5%	4.5%	4.2%	3.2%	3.2%	3.4%	4.4%
Earnings per share ($)	—	(0.38)	0.11	0.41	1.33	2.71	2.29	1.69	1.70	2.08	3.06
Stock price – high ($)	—	6.38	4.94	7.38	20.63	41.88	30.75	28.75	33.50	32.00	26.63
Stock price – low ($)	—	3.50	2.56	4.06	5.31	18.00	14.13	17.50	20.75	14.00	17.00
Stock price – close ($)	20.7%	4.63	4.38	6.44	20.44	26.63	26.38	24.38	25.38	17.38	25.13
P/E – high	—	—	45	18	16	15	13	17	20	15	9
P/E – low	—	—	23	10	4	7	6	10	12	7	6
Dividends per share ($)	10.5%	0.26	0.26	0.26	0.27	0.30	0.36	0.44	0.52	0.60	0.64
Book value per share ($)	15.1%	4.93	4.78	4.87	6.85	9.25	11.10	12.37	13.56	15.02	17.49

1989 Year End:
Debt ratio: 0.0%
Return on equity: 18.8%
Cash (mil): $25
Current ratio: 1.56
Long-term debt (mil): $0
Number of shares (mil): 23
Dividends:
1989 average yield: 2.5%
1989 payout: 20.9%
Market value (mil): $576

NYSE symbol: FLE
Incorporated: Delaware, 1977
Fiscal year ends: Last Sunday in April

WHO

Chairman and CEO: John C. Crean, age 65, $770,098 pay
President and COO: Glenn F. Kummer, age 56, $675,711 pay
Financial VP and CFO: Paul M. Bingham, age 48, $338,251 pay
Auditors: Arthur Andersen & Co.
Employees: 12,000

WHERE

HQ: 3125 Myers St., Riverside, CA 92523
Phone: 714-351-3500
FAX: 714-351-3690

Fleetwood operates 46 manufacturing plants in 16 states and in Canada. The company sells its products through independent dealers from 3,600 locations in 49 states and in Canada.

WHAT

	1989 Sales		1989 Operating Income	
	$ mil	% of total	$ mil	% of total
Manufactured housing	535	33	23	23
Supply operations	17	1	5	5
Recreational vehicles	1,055	64	81	81
Finance operations	15	1	3	3
Corporate & other	8	1	(12)	(12)
Adjustments	(11)	—	2	—
Total	**1,619**	**100**	**102**	**100**

Manufactured Housing

Recreational Vehicles
Avion
Bounder
Cambria
Coleman (folding trailers)
Flair
Jamboree
Limited
Pace Arrow
Prowler
Southwind
Terry
Tioga
Wilderness

Subsidiaries
C. V. Aluminum, Inc.
Continental Lumber Products, Inc.
FEI Corp.
Fleetwood Credit Corp.
Fleetwood Foreign Sales Corp.
Fleetwood Holidays, Inc.
Fleetwood Insurance Services, Inc.
Fleetwood International, Inc.
Flordevco, Inc.
Gibraltar Insurance Co., Ltd.
Gold Shield Fiberglass, Inc.
Gold Shield Fiberglass of Indiana, Inc.
GSF Installation Co.
Hauser Lake Lumber Operation, Inc.
Housing Supply, Inc.
Westfield Manufactured Homes, Inc.

RANKINGS

249th in *Fortune* 500 Industrial Cos.
480th in *Forbes* Sales 500
770th in *Business Week* 1000

COMPETITION

Harley-Davidson
Hillsborough
MacAndrews & Forbes

FLEMING COMPANIES, INC.

OVERVIEW

Fleming Companies of Oklahoma City is the largest wholesale food distributor in the US. With 1989 sales of more than $12 billion, up 15% over 1988, Fleming services over 5,000 retail food stores in 36 states with 38 distribution centers carrying a variety of groceries, produce, meats, dairy products, frozen foods, and general merchandise. Independent retailers represent 69% of sales volume, with corporate chains providing the balance.

The company maintains 24 additional cash/carry warehouses that serve small institutions and grocers. The company also operates 100 retail food stores in 8 midwestern and southern states under the names of Piggly Wiggly, Food 4 Less, Thriftway, and Sentry. In addition, the company provides support services to food retailers, including accounting, financing, data processing, advertising, insurance, and store design and engineering.

WHEN

Fleming Companies was incorporated in 1915 as Lux Mercantile, a Topeka, Kansas, wholesale grocery founded by O. A. Fleming, Gene Wilson, and Sam Lux. In 1918 the company became Fleming-Wilson Mercantile.

Facing stiff competition from chain stores, independent wholesalers and grocers formed the "voluntary group," a partnership developed to provide competitive mass merchandising, advertising, and efficient store operations. Fleming's son Ned helped establish the company as the first voluntary wholesaler west of the Mississippi (1927). The company was later renamed The Fleming Company, Inc. (1941), and Ned Fleming became president (1945-1964) and later chairman and CEO (1964-1981). The company went public in 1959, adopted its present name in 1972, and was reincorporated in Oklahoma (1981).

Since the 1930s the company has grown steadily by acquiring other companies, mostly wholesale food distributors and supermarkets. Acquisitions in the 1930s and 1940s included Hutchinson Wholesale Grocery (Kansas, 1935); Carroll, Brough & Robinson (Oklahoma City, 1941); Ryley-Wilson Grocery (Kansas City, Missouri, 1949); and Golden Wedding Coffee (Kansas City, Missouri, 1948; renamed Certified Brands, 1949). In the 1950s and 1960s Fleming bought Ruston Bakery (Wichita, Kansas, 1953; renamed Certified Bakers, products marketed under the label Magic Bake); Topeka Wholesale Drug (1958; renamed Drug Distributors); Grainger Brothers (Lincoln, Nebraska, 1962; renamed The Fleming Company of Nebraska); Inter-State Grocer (Joplin, Missouri, 1964); and Nelson Davis (Austin, Texas, 1964). Acquisitions in the 1970s included Kahan & Lessin (health food distributor, Los Angeles, 1972; sold 1983); Quality Oil (independent gasoline distributor in the Midwest, 1972; sold 1984); and Benson-Dixieland, with 44 supermarkets in the Southeast (1974). The most recent acquisitions include 27 A&P supermarkets in Kansas City (1982; resold to independent retailers); American-Strevell (Salt Lake City, Portland, 1983); 20 Alpha Beta stores and one distribution center (Northern California, 1985; stores resold to independent retailers); Associated Grocers of Arizona (1985); wholesale distribution center of Foodland Super Markets (Hawaii, 1986); and Godfrey, with 32 Sentry supermarkets and 4 Sun warehouse markets (Wisconsin, 1987).

The $600 million purchase of Tennessee-based Malone & Hyde (1988), the 6th largest wholesale food distributor in the US, made Fleming the largest food distributor in the US. In 1988 Fleming sold the Malone & Hyde subsidiary, M&H Drugs, a 99-store retail drugstore chain, for $55 million and White Swan (Austin, Texas, bought in 1982) for $217 million. The company closed the Fremont, California, distribution center (1990) when Albertson's completed its own warehouse and Alpha Beta merged with Lucky.

HOW MUCH

	9 Yr. Growth	1980	1981	1982	1983	1984	1985	1986	1987	1988	1989
Sales ($ mil)	17.5%	2,817	3,399	3,688	4,898	5,512	7,095	7,653	8,608	10,467	12,045
Net income ($ mil)	16.2%	21	26	29	42	50	60	36	49	65	80
Income as % of sales	—	0.7%	0.8%	0.8%	0.9%	0.9%	0.8%	0.5%	0.6%	0.6%	0.7%
Earnings per share ($)	5.1%	1.63	1.78	1.98	2.27	2.57	2.79	1.67	1.86	2.43	2.54
Stock price – high ($)	—	13.50	16.13	23.31	31.13	35.38	41.88	44.88	45.88	35.50	40.00
Stock price – low ($)	—	7.63	11.56	11.31	22.25	22.25	32.00	31.00	22.00	26.50	27.50
Stock price – close ($)	9.9%	12.88	13.00	22.75	28.88	34.13	38.88	34.63	27.25	35.00	30.13
P/E – high	—	8	9	12	14	14	15	27	25	15	16
P/E – low	—	5	7	6	10	9	11	19	12	11	11
Dividends per share ($)	7.3%	0.53	0.59	0.64	0.71	0.84	0.97	1.00	1.00	1.00	1.00
Book value per share ($)	10.2%	9.57	10.44	13.09	14.73	17.72	20.56	21.33	19.58	21.79	22.95

1989 Year End:
Debt ratio: 57.2%
Return on equity: 11.4%
Cash (mil): $37
Current ratio: 1.47
Long-term debt (mil): $991
Number of shares (mil): 30
Dividends:
1989 average yield: 3.3%
1989 payout: 39.4%
Market value (mil): $908

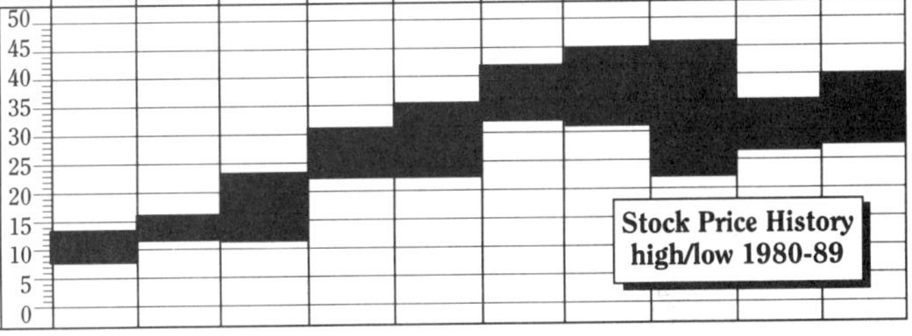

Stock Price History
high/low 1980-89

NYSE symbol: FLM
Incorporated: Oklahoma, 1981
Fiscal year ends: Last Saturday in December

WHO

Chairman and CEO: E. Dean Werries, age 60, $544,677 pay (prior to promotion)
President and COO: John E. Moll, age 55, $432,331 pay (prior to promotion)
EVP and CFO: R. Randolph Devening, age 48
EVP, Western Region: Gerald G. Austin, age 52, $265,129 pay
EVP, Distribution: E. Stephen Davis, age 49
EVP, Mid-America Region: Glenn E. Mealman, age 55
EVP, Southern Region: James E. Stuard, age 55, $271,729 pay
Auditors: Deloitte & Touche
Employees: 22,800

WHERE

HQ: 6301 Waterford Blvd., Oklahoma City, OK 73126
Phone: 405-840-7200
FAX: 405-841-8149

Fleming operates 38 wholesale food and general merchandise distribution centers totaling 19.1 million square feet and serving more than 5,000 stores in 36 states.

	1989 Sales % of total
Western US	26
Southern US	21
Central US	14
Eastern US	14
Malone & Hyde subsidiary	25
Total	**100**

WHAT

	1989 Sales % of total
Groceries	58
Perishables	37
General merchandise	5
Total	**100**

Volume by Customer Type (1989)	% of total
Independents	
Voluntary groups	49
Nonfranchised	20
Corporate chains	31
Total	**100**

Volume by Store Format (1989)	% of total
Conventional supermarkets	56
Combination stores	17
Superstores	13
Price impact stores	14
Total	**100**

RANKINGS

2nd in *Fortune* 100 Diversified Service Cos.
50th in *Forbes* Sales 500
544th in *Business Week* 1000

COMPETITION

McKesson
Super Valu

FMC CORPORATION

OVERVIEW

Chicago-based FMC is a diversified company whose largest businesses are industrial chemicals, defense systems, and machinery and equipment. Precious Metals, its gold and silver production business, supplied only 6% of FMC's revenues in 1989 but 25% of its profits. Performance Chemicals makes agricultural and pharmaceutical product ingredients.

FMC leads the world in the production of natural soda ash (used in chemicals and glass) and the seaweed product carrageenan (a food stabilizer); the West in the manufacture of tracked, armored personnel carriers; and North America in the production of hydrogen peroxide (a bleach alternative). FMC also manufactures the widely used insecticide Furadan, which the company has sold in the US (to use on corn), in China (rice), and in the USSR (sugar beets).

Sales outside the US (including the USSR and China) accounted for 18% of FMC's revenues in 1989. Almost 31% of the company's stock is owned by its employees (through FMC Employees' Thrift and Stock Purchase Plan), officers, and directors.

NYSE symbol: FMC
Incorporated: Delaware, 1928
Fiscal year ends: December 31

WHO

Chairman and CEO: Robert H. Malott, age 63, $1,089,602 pay
President: Robert N. Burt, age 52, $439,898 pay (prior to promotion)
EVP: Larry D. Brady, age 47
VP Finance: Arthur D. Lyons, age 53
Auditors: KPMG Peat Marwick
Employees: 24,110

WHEN

After retiring to California, inventor John Bean developed a pump to deliver a continuous spray of insecticide (1884). This invention led to the Bean Spray Pump Company (1904). In 1928 Bean Spray Pump went public and bought Anderson-Barngrover (food growing and processing equipment). The new company name, John Bean Manufacturing, gave way to Food Machinery Corporation in 1929. The company bought Peerless Pump (agricultural and industrial pumps) in 1933.

During WWII the company started manufacturing military equipment and entered the agricultural chemical field with the purchase of Niagara Sprayer & Chemical (1943). After the war, it bought Westvaco Chemical (industrial chemicals, 1948) and changed its name to Food Machinery & Chemical. The company extended its product line, buying such companies as Oil Center Tool (wellhead equipment, 1957), Sunland Industries (fertilizer, insecticides, and seeds; 1959), and Barrett Equipment (automotive brake equipment, 1961). The Bean family ran the company until 1956, when John Crummey, grandson of John Bean, retired as chairman.

In light of its growing diversification, the company changed its name to FMC in 1961. FMC's major purchases in the 1960s were American Viscose (rayon and cellophane, 1963) and Link-Belt (equipment for power transmission and for bulk-material handling, 1967).

To be more centrally located, FMC moved its headquarters from San Jose to Chicago in 1972. In 1976 it sold its pump division (which had been Peerless Pump), its fiber division, and its 50% interest in Ketchikan Pulp (part of the American Viscose purchase). FMC continued to sell its slow-growing businesses, including the Semiconductor Division (1979), the Industrial Packaging Division (1980), the Niagara Seed Operation (1980), and the Power Transmission Group (1981).

In 1979 FMC entered mining in a joint venture (30/70) with Freeport Minerals to continue developing a gold mine in Jerritt Canyon, Nevada (discovered 1973, mine in operation 1982). In the 1980s FMC found more gold near Gabbs, Nevada (Paradise Peak) and entered the lithium business with the purchase of Lithium Corporation of America (integrated lithium producer, 1985). To lessen the possibility of a takeover, FMC increased its debt in 1986 by financing a $2 billion recapitalization plan in which it gave shareholders $80 in cash plus one new share for each old share and exchanged employees' old shares for new shares on a basis of almost 6 to 1. In 1989 FMC bought the French company Mather et Platt (harvesters and food processing equipment).

WHERE

HQ: 200 E. Randolph Dr., Chicago, IL 60601
Phone: 312-861-6000
FAX: 312-861-6176

FMC conducts operations at 89 plants and mines in 24 states and 14 foreign countries.

	1989 Sales		1989 Pretax Income	
	$ mil	% of total	$ mil	% of total
US	2,875	82	348	84
Latin America, Canada	112	3	1	—
Europe	503	14	66	16
Other countries	29	1	1	—
Adjustments	(104)	—	(115)	—
Total	**3,415**	**100**	**301**	**100**

WHAT

	1989 Sales		1989 Pretax Income	
	$ mil	% of total	$ mil	% of total
Defense systems	900	26	47	12
Performance chemicals	566	16	83	21
Machinery & equip.	783	23	28	7
Industrial chemicals	976	29	138	35
Precious metals	190	6	101	25
Adjustments	—	—	(96)	—
Total	**3,415**	**100**	**301**	**100**

Industrial Chemicals
Hydrogen peroxide
Pesticides
Phosphates
Soda ash

Machinery
Airline machinery (*e.g.*, cargo loaders)
Auto repair equipment
Conveyors
Industrial food processing and packaging machinery
Oil field machinery
Street sweepers

Precious Metals
Gold
Lithium
Silver

Performance Chemicals
Food additives
Herbicides
Pharmaceutical ingredients

Defense Systems
Armored tanks and personnel carriers
Naval weapons

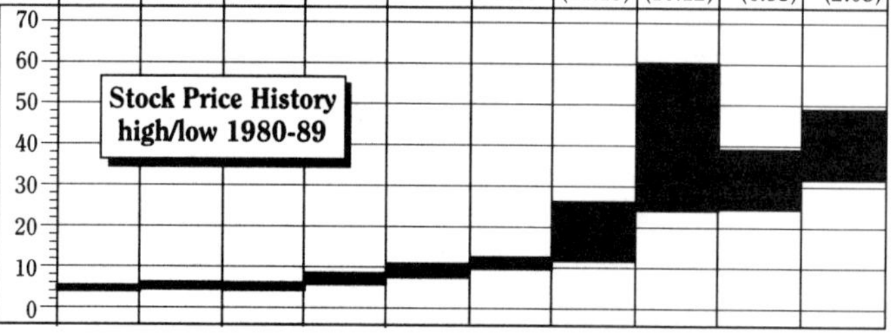

RANKINGS

133rd in *Fortune* 500 Industrial Cos.
374th in *Fortune* Global 500 Industrial Cos.
48th in *Fortune* 50 Exporters
246th in *Forbes* Sales 500
458th in *Business Week* 1000

COMPETITION

American Cyanamid
Baker Hughes
BASF
Cyprus Minerals
Dow Chemical
Dresser
Du Pont
Halliburton
Hanson
Hercules
Hoechst
Ingersoll-Rand
LTV
Monsanto
Pearson
Other chemical companies

HOW MUCH

	9 Yr. Growth	1980	1981	1982	1983	1984	1985	1986	1987	1988	1989
Sales ($ mil)	(0.2%)	3,482	3,367	3,499	3,498	3,338	3,261	3,003	3,139	3,287	3,415
Net income ($ mil)	1.0%	143	177	152	169	226	197	153	191	129	157
Income as % of sales	—	4.1%	5.2%	4.4%	4.8%	6.8%	6.0%	5.1%	6.1%	3.9%	4.6%
Earnings per share ($)	22.6%	0.69	0.86	0.75	0.83	1.27	1.30	1.62	4.52	3.60	4.34
Stock price – high ($)	—	5.51	6.31	6.18	8.60	10.94	12.71	26.38	60.38	39.13	49.00
Stock price – low ($)	—	3.82	4.28	4.08	5.56	7.32	9.48	11.50	24.00	24.38	31.63
Stock price – close ($)	23.2%	5.38	4.52	5.69	8.14	9.95	11.56	25.75	33.75	32.00	35.25
P/E – high	—	8	7	8	10	9	10	16	13	11	11
P/E – low	—	6	5	5	7	6	7	7	5	7	7
Dividends per share ($)	(100%)	0.26	0.28	0.29	0.32	0.34	0.39	0.10	0.00	0.00	0.00
Book value per share ($)	—	6.77	6.97	7.32	7.65	6.65	7.69	(11.25)	(10.12)	(6.53)	(2.05)

1989 Year End:
Debt ratio: 105.6%
Return on equity: —
Cash (mil): $95
Current ratio: 1.1
Long-term debt (mil): $1,326
Number of shares (mil): 35
Dividends:
1989 average yield: 0.0%
1989 payout: 0.0%
Market value (mil): $1,216

Stock Price History high/low 1980-89

FOOD LION, INC.

OVERVIEW

Salisbury, North Carolina–based Food Lion is one of the fastest-growing grocery chains in the US. It is also very profitable, with pretax margins nearly double the industry average. In the 1980s Food Lion increased its number of stores over 500% — from 106 to 663.

In 1989 Food Lion expanded into its 9th and 10th states, building stores in Kentucky and West Virginia, and opened a new distribution facility in Clinton, Tennessee, to aid its expansion into the eastern half of that state and into northern Georgia. The company also announced plans to enter the Pennsylvania market, with several stores and a warehouse in the Greencastle area and to build a 2nd distribution center in Florida.

Food Lion's expansion strategy follows an "ink blot" approach in which the company builds many relatively small stores (average size 24,700 square feet) in a new market, allowing it to increase the efficiency of its distribution facilities by serving as many locations as possible. This saturation policy, along with a nonunionized work force and an obsession with operating efficiencies, have enabled the company to sell at extremely low prices.

Food Lion plans to maintain its high growth rate by adding 110 new stores in 1990. Delhaize "Le Lion," Belgium's 3rd largest public company, controls 50% of the company's voting stock.

WHEN

Food Lion was formed in 1957 in Salisbury, North Carolina, by 3 former Winn-Dixie employees — Wilson Smith, Ralph Ketner, and his brother Brown Ketner. They named the market Food Town and peddled stock in the new company at $10 a share to anyone in Salisbury who would buy. Two of the new store's first employees were bagger Tom Smith (now CEO) and produce manager Jerry Helms (now COO), both hired in 1958.

The company struggled through its first 10 years and by the end of 1967, after the founders had opened 16 stores and closed 9, the company was foundering. Trading stamps, contests, and drawings had failed to attract customers. That year Ralph Ketner tried a new idea: he pored over 6 months of store receipts and determined that if Food Town lowered the prices on all 3,000 items and sales increased 50%, the company would survive. The gamble paid off and the company was reborn as a resolute cost-cutter. The company's slogan, LFPINC (Lowest Food Prices in North Carolina), soon appeared on bumper stickers throughout the state.

In 1974 a Belgian grocery company, Etablissements Delhaize Freres et Cie, "Le Lion" S.A., which used a lion as its symbol, began investing in Food Town, gradually raising its stake to 50% of voting stock by 1989. Food Town expanded to South Carolina in 1976, to Virginia in 1978, and into Georgia in 1981, always following the company's low-price, cost-cutting formula.

The company changed its name in 1983 to avoid confusion with another Food Town store in its growing market area. Ketner adopted the name Food Lion not only because of the lion symbol of Delhaize Freres, but also because he could save money by only replacing the *t* and the *w* at the company's stores.

Food Lion opened a distribution center in Virginia in 1983, which allowed it to expand into Maryland the following year, and opened another distribution center in South Carolina in 1984. In 1987 the company built a distribution center in North Carolina and opened its first stores in Florida and Delaware.

Food Lion has made its 100+ original shareholders (87% of whom still live in the Salisbury area) very rich; its phenomenal growth, from $5.8 million in 1967 to $4.72 billion in 1989, is reflected by the fact that a single share of stock bought for $10 in 1957 would have split into 12,960 shares, worth over $140,000 today.

HOW MUCH

	9 Yr. Growth	1980	1981	1982	1983	1984	1985	1986	1987	1988	1989
Sales ($ mil)	27.1%	544	667	947	1,172	1,470	1,866	2,407	2,954	3,815	4,717
Net income ($ mil)	27.9%	15	19	22	28	37	48	62	86	113	140
Income as % of sales	—	2.8%	2.9%	2.3%	2.4%	2.5%	2.6%	2.6%	2.9%	3.0%	3.0%
Earnings per share ($)	27.2%	0.05	0.06	0.07	0.09	0.12	0.15	0.20	0.27	0.35	0.43
Stock price – high ($)	—	0.67	1.08	2.27	2.48	2.42	3.71	7.31	13.69	12.88	12.50
Stock price – low ($)	—	0.44	0.62	0.86	1.67	1.42	2.21	3.33	5.50	9.00	9.00
Stock price – close ($)	37.7%	0.61	1.06	2.19	1.71	2.42	3.63	5.56	12.00	9.38	10.88
P/E – high	—	13	17	32	28	20	25	38	51	37	29
P/E – low	—	9	10	12	19	12	15	17	20	26	21
Dividends per share ($)	41.6%	0.00	0.01	0.01	0.01	0.01	0.01	0.02	0.05	0.07	0.10
Book value per share ($)	27.1%	0.19	0.25	0.31	0.39	0.51	0.65	0.83	1.05	1.34	1.67

1989 Year End:
Debt ratio: 26.6%
Return on equity: 28.6%
Cash (mil): $16
Current ratio: 1.31
Long-term debt (mil): $195
Number of shares (mil): 322
Dividends:
1989 average yield: 0.9%
1989 payout: 23.7%
Market value (mil): $3,502

Stock Price History high/low 1980-89

14
12
10
8
6
4
2
0

NASDAQ symbol: FDLNA and FDLNB
Incorporated: North Carolina, 1957
Fiscal year ends: Saturday nearest to December 31

WHO

Chairman: Ralph W. Ketner, age 69, $275,691 pay
President and CEO: Tom E. Smith, age 48, $580,573 pay
SVP and COO: Jerry W. Helms, age 49, $337,176 pay
VP Finance: Dan A. Boone, age 37
Auditors: Coopers & Lybrand
Employees: 20,252 full time; 20,484 part time

WHERE

HQ: 2110 Executive Dr., PO Box 1330, Salisbury, NC 28145
Phone: 704-633-8250
FAX: 704-636-5024

Food Lion operates 663 grocery stores in 10 states.

	1989 Store Locations	
	no. of stores	% of total
North Carolina	280	42
Virginia	157	24
South Carolina	81	12
Florida	57	9
Other states	88	13
Total	**663**	**100**

	1989 Warehouse Space	
	sq. ft. thou	% of total
Dunn, NC	1,226	21
Prince George County, VA	1,150	19
Elloree, SC	1,055	18
Salisbury, NC (2 sites)	1,055	18
Green Cove Springs, FL	730	12
Clinton, TN	726	12
Total	**5,942**	**100**

WHAT

	1989 Sales	
	$ mil	% of total
Existing stores	4,447	94
New stores	270	6
Total	**4,717**	**100**

	1989 Stores	
	no. of stores	% of total
Existing stores	567	86
New stores	96	14
Total	**663**	**100**

RANKINGS

25th in *Fortune* 50 Retailing Cos.
186th in *Forbes* Sales 500
25th in *Forbes* 100 Foreign Investments in the US
179th in *Business Week* 1000

COMPETITION

American Stores
Bruno's
Great A&P
Kroger
Publix
Safeway
Winn-Dixie

THE FORD FOUNDATION

OVERVIEW

The Ford Foundation is the largest philanthropic foundation in the US. Through 1989, $7 billion had been granted to over 9,000 organizations in all 50 states and more than 80 foreign countries.

Educational, research, and development grants (mainly to organizations) focus on urban and rural poverty, human rights, public policy, education, the creative and performing arts, and international affairs. Overseas grants target developing countries, which receive about 35% of the overall program budget.

A board of trustees sets broad policies (*e.g.*, affirmative action for both staff and grantees) and grants objectives; the program staff identifies and recommends worthy recipients. The foundation's headquarters, completed in 1967, is in New York and is noted for its award-winning architectural design.

The foundation no longer has stock in Ford Motor Company or ties to the Ford family. Funds are derived solely from an internal stock and bond portfolio; the 1980s bull market pushed the endowment to a record $5.6 billion (1989).

Nonprofit organization
Chartered: Michigan, 1936
Fiscal year ends: September 30

WHO

Chairman: Edson W. Spencer
President: Franklin A. Thomas
VP Program Division: Susan V. Berresford
VP and Chief Investment Officer: John W. English
VP, Legal, Financial, and Administrative Services and General Counsel: Barron M. Tenny
Auditors: Price Waterhouse
Employees: 568

WHEN

Henry Ford and his son Edsel established the Ford Foundation in Michigan in 1936 with an initial gift of $25,000, followed the next year by 250,000 shares of nonvoting stock in the Ford Motor Company. The foundation's activities were limited mainly to Michigan until the deaths of Edsel (1943) and Henry (1947) made the foundation the owner of 90% of the automaker's nonvoting stock (catapulting the endowment to $474 million, the US's largest).

In 1951 under a new mandate and president (Paul Hoffman, formerly head of the Marshall Plan), the foundation announced broad commitments to world peace, strengthening of democracy, and improved education. Early education program grants overseen by University of Chicago chancellor Robert Maynard Hutchins ($100 million in 1951-1953 alone) helped establish major international programs (*e.g.*, Harvard's Center for International Legal Studies) and the National Merit Scholarships.

Under McCarthyite criticism for its experimental education grants, the foundation in 1956 granted $550 million (after selling 22% of its Ford shares to the public) to non-controversial recipients: 600 liberal arts colleges, 3,500 nonprofit hospitals, and 44 private medical schools. Ford money set up the Radio and Television Workshop (1951). Public TV support (totaling some $293 million by 1977) became a foundation trademark.

Overseas work, begun in Asia and the Middle East (1950) and extended to Africa (1958) and Latin America (1959), focused on education and rural development; the foundation also supported the Population Council and research in high-yield agriculture with the Rockefeller Foundation. Other grants supported the arts and the upgrading of US engineering schools.

An emerging activism in the early 1960s (as the foundation spent $300 million a year and exceeded its income) targeted innovative approaches to employment, race relations, and minority voting rights. Grants to the arts included $80 million to numerous symphony orchestras. Assets were $3.7 billion by 1968.

McGeorge Bundy (1966, formerly President Kennedy's national security advisor) increased the activist trend with grants for direct voter registration; the NAACP and the Urban League; public interest law centers serving consumer, environmental, and minority causes; and housing for the poor.

The early 1970s saw support for black colleges and scholarships ($100 million) and women (child care, job training), but by 1974 inflation, weak stock prices, and overspending had seriously eroded assets. Programs, including support for public-interest law and public TV, were cut.

Under black lawyer Franklin Thomas (president in 1979) the foundation has kept expenditures in line with income. The resurgent assets in the 1980s have allowed the foundation to help the homeless and, in cooperation with companies and local charities, to revitalize poor neighborhoods. A new reorganization along program (rather than geographical) lines permits greater sharing of solutions within a field and between countries to address concerns such as global warming.

WHERE

HQ: 320 E. 43rd St., New York, NY 10017
Phone: 212-573-5000
FAX: 212-599-4584

The foundation has field and suboffices in Asia, Latin America, and Africa.

	1989 Program Expenditures	
	$ mil	% of total
US & international affairs programs	148	60
Developing country programs	70	29
Other	27	11
Total	**245**	**100**

WHAT

	1989 Program Expenditures	
	$ mil	% of total
Urban Poverty	40	16
Rural Poverty and Resources	27	11
Human Rights and Social Justice	32	13
Governance and Public Policy	38	16
Education and Culture	47	19
International Affairs	24	10
Other programs	10	4
Other	27	11
Total	**245**	**100**

Representative Programs

Urban Poverty
Economic development projects (Bedford Stuyvesant Restoration Corporation, Brooklyn, NY)
Policy research (RAND Corporation)

Rural Poverty and Resources
Agricultural productivity (government of Egypt)
Employment generation (Arkansas Enterprise Group, Arkadelphia, AR)
Land and water management (Designwrights Collaborative, Santa Fe, NM)

Human Rights and Social Justice
Access to social justice and legal services (Wider Opportunities for Women, Washington, DC; Howard University)
Refugees' and migrants' rights (ACLU, New York; Haitian Refugee Center, Miami, FL)

Governance and Public Policy
Government structures and functions (Urban Institute, Washington, DC)
Local initiatives (National AIDS Network, Washington, DC)

Education and Culture
Artistic creativity and resources (Studio Museum, Harlem, NY)
Curriculum development (Afro Charities, Baltimore)

International Affairs
International organizations and law (World Federation of United Nations Associations, Switzerland)
International studies (Radio Free Europe, Washington, DC)

HOW MUCH

	9 Yr. Growth	1980	1981	1982	1983	1984	1985	1986	1987	1988	1989
Assets ($ mil)	9.2%	2,518	2,401	2,701	3,388	3,322	3,748	4,535	5,225	4,856	5,582
Net investment income ($ mil)	7.1%	165	197	226	203	218	246	253	252	289	307
Program expenditures ($ mil)	10.1%	103	112	122	121	154	139	205	229	242	245

Assets ($ mil) 1980-89

FORD MOTOR COMPANY

OVERVIEW

Ford is the 2nd largest automobile producer in the world and the 2nd largest industrial corporation (after General Motors). Ford's principal business (86% of sales) is the manufacture, assembly, and sale of cars, trucks, and related parts and accessories. Ford manufactures models under the Ford, Lincoln, and Mercury nameplates.

Ford also provides financial services (Ford Motor Credit, First Nationwide Financial, United States Leasing International, and The Associates).

Ford spent $3.1 billion on R&D in 1989, the 3rd highest of any US company. In 1990 Ford launched the new Escort, Explorer, Tracer, and Lincoln Town Car. The company plans to increase international sales (33% of 1989 sales) and to enlarge the financial services share of earnings to 30%.

Weakness in US auto sales forced Ford to cut production in the first 9 months of 1990.

NYSE symbol: F
Incorporated: Delaware, 1919
Fiscal year ends: December 31

WHO

Chairman and CEO: Harold A. Poling, age 64, $1,188,594 pay
President and COO: Philip E. Benton, Jr., age 61, $719,455 pay
VP and CFO: Stanley A. Seneker, age 58
Auditors: Coopers & Lybrand
Employees: 366,600

WHEN

Henry Ford began the Ford Motor Company in 1903 in Flint, Michigan, hoping to design a simple, inexpensive car he could mass-produce. In 1908 Ford introduced the Model T, and in 1909 he dropped all other models.

His business manager, James Couzens, recommended he lower the selling price to $600, so Ford perfected the moving assembly line. Couzens and William Knudsen (later GM president) also created the first branch assembly plant system and a national dealer network. By 1916 the cars cost $360; by 1920 60% of all vehicles on the road were Fords.

In 1916 Ford omitted its customary extra dividend in order to retain earnings for reinvestment. Stockholders sued for payment, and in 1919 Ford purchased all outstanding shares for $100 million. It was 1956 before the Fords again allowed outside ownership, and the family still retains 40% voting power.

Ford purchased Lincoln in 1922 and discontinued the Model T in 1927. Its replacement, the Model A (1932), was the first low-priced car with a V-8 engine, triple the horsepower of the Model T's engine.

With Henry Ford's health deteriorating, his son Edsel became president in 1932. Despite the introduction of the Mercury (1938), market share slipped behind GM and Chrysler from 1933 to 1950.

Following Edsel's sudden death in 1943, the navy released his son, Henry II, to run the company. Henry the elder stepped in until 1945; he died in 1947. Henry II restructured the company — then losing $10 million a month — following the GM model of decentralization. In 1950 Ford recaptured 2nd place from Chrysler.

In the 1950s Ford expanded international operations (begun in England, 1911), created the Aerospace Division (1956), and introduced the Edsel (1958), its biggest flop. In 1963 the company launched the perennially popular Mustang, created by then Ford president Lee Iacocca. In 1979 Henry II retired.

Ford cut its work force by 33% and closed 15 manufacturing facilities during the 1980s. In 1986 Ford earned higher profits than GM (on 33% less revenue) for the first time since 1924. With the acquisition of New Holland (1986) and Versatile (1987), Ford became the world's 3rd largest agricultural equipment maker. Ford purchased First Nationwide in 1986, adding financial muscle. The 1988 introduction of the Taurus and Sable (both the inspiration of CEO Donald Petersen) spurred Ford to its largest US car market share (21.7%) in 10 years, surpassed in 1989 by a 22.3% share. In 1989 Ford bought The Associates from Paramount Communications ($3.35 billion), and Jaguar ($2.5 billion).

Harold Poling succeeded Petersen as CEO in 1990. The company has announced plans to sell its aerospace division and to merge its Ford New Holland agricultural equipment unit with Fiat.

WHERE

HQ: The American Rd., Dearborn, MI 48121
Phone: 313-322-3000
FAX: 313-322-7896

	1989 Sales		1989 Net Income	
	$ mil	% of total	$ mil	% of total
US	64,182	67	1,627	42
Europe	20,971	22	1,289	34
Canada	4,332	4	186	5
Other countries	6,661	7	733	19
Total	**96,146**	**100**	**3,835**	**100**

WHAT

	1989 Sales		1989 Pretax Income	
	$ mil	% of total	$ mil	% of total
Automotive mfg.	82,879	86	5,155	86
Financial services	13,267	14	874	14
Total	**96,146**	**100**	**6,029**	**100**

Ford
Aerostar
Bronco II
Econoline
Escort
Explorer
F-Series
Festiva
LTD Crown Victoria
Mustang
Probe
Ranger
Taurus
Tempo
Thunderbird

Jaguar
Sovereign
Vanden Plas
XJ-6
XJ-12

Lincoln
Continental
Mark VII
Town Car

Mercury
Capri
Cougar
Grand Marquis
Sable
Topaz
Tracer

Agricultural & Industrial Equipment
Ford New Holland

Financial Subsidiaries
The American Road Insurance Co.
Associates First Capital Corp.
First Nationwide Financial Corp.
Ford Motor Credit Co.
United States Leasing International, Inc.

Other Holdings
Autolatina (South American joint venture with Volkswagen [49%])
Mazda Motor Corp. (25%)

HOW MUCH

	9 Yr. Growth	1980	1981	1982	1983	1984	1985	1986	1987	1988	1989
Sales ($ mil)	11.2%	37,086	38,247	37,067	44,455	52,366	52,774	62,716	71,643	92,446	96,146
Net income ($ mil)	—	(1,543)	(1,060)	(658)	1,867	2,907	2,515	3,285	4,625	5,300	3,835
Income as % of sales	—	(4.2%)	(2.8%)	(1.8%)	4.2%	5.6%	4.8%	5.2%	6.5%	5.7%	4.0%
Earnings per share ($)	—	(2.63)	*(1.96)*	*(1.21)*	3.21	4.97	4.41	6.06	8.92	10.80	8.12
Stock price – high ($)	—	7.94	5.78	9.25	15.58	17.13	19.71	31.75	56.31	55.00	56.63
Stock price – low ($)	—	4.03	3.50	3.69	7.61	11.00	13.38	17.92	28.44	38.06	41.38
Stock price – close ($)	28.9%	4.44	3.72	8.64	14.13	15.21	19.33	28.13	37.69	50.50	43.63
P/E – high	—	—	—	—	5	3	4	5	6	5	7
P/E – low	—	—	—	—	2	2	3	3	3	4	5
Dividends per share ($)	20.1%	0.58	0.27	0.00	0.17	0.67	0.80	1.11	1.58	2.30	3.00
Book value per share ($)	13.2%	15.79	13.57	11.20	13.74	17.62	21.97	27.68	36.44	43.87	48.07

1989 Year End:
Debt ratio: 63.1%
Return on equity: 17.7%
Cash (mil): $11,932
Current ratio: —
Long-term debt (mil): $38,921
Number of shares (mil): 473
Dividends:
1989 average yield: 6.9%
1989 payout: 36.9%
Market value (mil): $20,626

Stock Price History high/low 1980-89

RANKINGS

2nd in *Fortune* 500 Industrial Cos.
2nd in *Fortune* Global 500 Industrial Cos.
3rd in *Fortune* 50 Exporters
2nd in *Forbes* Sales 500
16th in *Business Week* 1000
43rd in *Business Week* Global 1000

COMPETITION

Caterpillar
Chrysler
Daimler-Benz
Deere
Fiat
General Motors
Honda
Hyundai
Mitsubishi
Navistar
Nissan
PACCAR
Renault
Toyota
Volkswagen
Volvo
Financial companies
Savings and loans

FPL GROUP, INC.

OVERVIEW

FPL Group provides electricity to 3.1 million customers on Florida's east and lower west coasts, an area that includes 5 of the 6 fastest-growing metropolitan areas in the US. In 1989 it was America's 4th largest electric utility.

FPL operates several nonutility businesses under its FPL Group Capital umbrella. Its largest nonutility enterprise is Colonial Penn Group, Inc., a Philadelphia-based insurance company specializing in coverage for persons aged 50 and over. Early in 1990 FPL began investigating a possible spinoff or sale of Colonial Penn in the interest of concentrating more fully on its electric business. FPL has also reduced direct involvement with Telesat Cable, another Group subsidiary that offers cable television service in some Florida cities.

FPL plans to continue developing nonutility energy sources through ESI Energy, including solar and windpower facilities in California. FPL also plans to keep its businesses in Florida citrus and commercial real estate development.

WHEN

Florida experienced a land boom in 1923. New homes and businesses were built at an impressive rate; however, electric utilities were few and far between. No transmission lines linked one system to another. In 1925 American Power & Light Company (AP&L), a holding company already operating utilities throughout the Americas, set up Florida Power and Light (FPL) to buy and consolidate Florida's electric properties. AP&L built transmission lines from Miami to Stuart on the Atlantic Coast and from Arcadia to Punta Gorda on the Gulf Coast, linking 58 communities in the FPL power system. Besides electric generating and transmission facilities, FPL's holdings included ice, water, and cold storage companies; streetcar and telephone companies; a steam laundry; and a limestone quarry.

Other purchases in 1926 almost doubled FPL's electric properties. In 1927 the company bought 5 more electric companies and, using an electric pump, demonstrated how swamp lands could be drained and cultivated. In the 1940s and 1950s FPL sold its nonelectric properties. AP&L ceased operations in 1950 and, as part of its dissolution plan, spun off FPL to its stockholders. FPL was listed on the NYSE in 1950.

Marshall McDonald became president of FPL in 1971. FPL's first nuclear plant (Turkey Point), located on the mud flats south of Miami, went into operation in 1972. While the plant was under construction (1965-1972), FPL established youth camps, nature trails, shrimp ponds, and a US Air Force Sea Survival School at Turkey Point to illustrate the company's concern for the area's ecological balance.

In the 1970s and 1980s the company expanded beyond utility operations by forming Fuel Supply Service (1973, oil and uranium acquisition, later renamed Qualtec), W. Flagler Investment (1981, real estate development, later renamed Alandco), and ESI Energy (1985, nonutility fuel sources), and buying Telesat Cablevision (1985, cable television operator), Colonial Penn Group (1985, insurance), and Turner Foods Corporation (1988, citrus grower). FPL sold Praxis Group, Inc., a Colonial Penn subsidiary providing information services, in 1988.

In 1981 McDonald, then chairman, began a quality improvement program (QIP), using teams of employees and statistical methods to track and solve company problems. Received with little enthusiasm at first, McDonald's QIP eventually caught on with impressive results. In 1989 FPL became the first non-Japanese company to win the Deming Prize, Japan's prestigious international award for quality.

HOW MUCH

	9 Yr. Growth	1980	1981	1982	1983	1984	1985	1986	1987	1988	1989
Sales ($ mil)	11.4%	2,347	3,089	2,941	3,353	3,941	4,349	4,092	4,439	5,854	6,180
Net income ($ mil)	9.6%	198	224	267	314	349	419	413	451	493	454
Income as % of sales	—	8.4%	7.3%	9.1%	9.4%	8.9%	9.6%	10.1%	10.2%	8.4%	7.4%
Earnings per share ($)	5.2%	1.97	2.13	2.39	2.51	2.62	3.11	2.90	3.10	3.42	3.12
Stock price – high ($)	—	14.06	16.00	18.81	21.13	22.81	29.00	38.00	34.88	32.50	36.75
Stock price – low ($)	—	9.94	11.94	14.06	17.50	17.63	20.50	26.38	24.38	27.75	29.00
Stock price – close ($)	12.1%	13.06	14.69	18.13	20.13	22.38	28.25	31.63	28.63	31.13	36.38
P/E – high	—	7	8	8	8	9	9	13	11	10	12
P/E – low	—	5	6	6	7	7	7	9	8	8	9
Dividends per share ($)	6.2%	1.32	1.48	1.64	1.77	1.86	1.94	2.02	2.10	2.18	2.26
Book value per share ($)	4.5%	17.45	17.95	18.80	19.47	20.14	21.38	22.99	23.82	24.90	25.89

1989 Year End:
Debt ratio: 47.7%
Return on equity: 12.3%
Cash (mil): $61
Assets (mil): $12,325
Long-term debt (mil): $3,465
Number of shares (mil): 133
Dividends:
1989 average yield: 6.2%
1989 payout: 72.4%
Market value (mil): $4,850

Stock Price History high/low 1980-89

NYSE symbol: FPL
Incorporated: Florida, 1984
Fiscal year ends: December 31

WHO

President and CEO: James L. Broadhead, age 54, $792,742 pay
President and COO, Florida Power & Light: Robert E. Tallon, age 63, $475,470 pay
Chairman and CEO, Colonial Penn: Richard W. Ohman, age 49, $449,140 pay
VP and CFO: Joe L. Howard, age 48, $293,312 pay
Auditors: Deloitte & Touche
Employees: 19,000

WHERE

HQ: 11770 US Hwy. One, North Palm Beach, FL 33408
Phone: 407-694-6300
FAX: 407-694-6385

FPL Group's utility business is concentrated in Florida; however, nonutility operations extend throughout the US.

Generating Facilities

Coal
St. Johns River Power Park (Jacksonville)

Natural Gas and Oil
Cape Canaveral (Cocoa)
Cutler (Miami)
Fort Myers (Fort Myers)
Lauderdale (Dania)
Manatee (Parrish)
Martin (Indiantown)
Port Everglades (Port Everglades)
Putnam (Palatka)
Riviera (Riviera Beach)
Sanford (Lake Monroe)
Turkey Point (Florida City)

Nuclear
St. Lucie (Hutchinson Island)
Turkey Point (Florida City)

WHAT

	1989 Sales		1989 Operating Income	
	$ mil	% of total	$ mil	% of total
Utility operations	4,946	80	913	98
Insurance & financial services	1,234	20	14	2
Adjustments	—	—	(13)	—
Total	**6,180**	**100**	**914**	**100**

Florida Power & Light Co.

FPL Group Capital, Inc.
Alandco, Inc. (Florida real estate development)
Bay Loan (financial services)
Colonial Penn Group, Inc. (insurance)
ESI Energy, Inc. (energy projects)
Qualtec, Inc. (quality services)
Telesat Cablevision, Inc. (cable television operator)
Turner Foods Corp. (Florida citrus groves)

RANKINGS

18th in *Fortune* 50 Utilities
134th in *Forbes* Sales 500
140th in *Business Week* 1000
426th in *Business Week* Global 1000

COMPETITION

Other financial services and real estate companies

FRED MEYER, INC.

OVERVIEW

Portland-based Fred Meyer, Inc., is a $2.28 billion retail chain of 121 stores in 7 western states, primarily Oregon (48 stores) and Washington (39). Its 92 "multidepartment" hypermarkets, up to 200,000 square feet under one roof, feature as many as 220,000 items in 12 departments. The 29 specialty mall stores are smaller (15,000 to 39,000 square feet) and carry jewelry, health food, or apparel.

The 46th largest retailer in the US lost $6.8 million in 1989, primarily due to costs of remodeling and replacing older stores and to converting to a company-wide computer system capable of improved inventory tracking and information management. Strikes at the Seattle stores and a distribution center also negatively affected income.

The company also has a dairy; kitchen; bakery; photo-finishing lab; main distribution center in Clackamas, Oregon; and 2 smaller facilities in Salt Lake City. Total square footage is 3.1 million.

OTC symbol: MEYR
Incorporated: Delaware, 1981
Fiscal year ends: Saturday nearest January 31

WHO

Chairman and CEO: Frederick M. Stevens, age 53, $582,780 pay
VC: Jerome Kohlberg, Jr., age 64
President and COO: Cyril K. Green, age 58, $414,426 pay
SVP, CFO, and Secretary: Kenneth Thrasher, age 40
Auditors: Deloitte & Touche
Employees: 22,237

WHEN

Founder Fred G. Meyer (1886-1978) peddled coffee, tea, and spices door-to-door in Portland, Oregon (1909) and opened his first grocery and variety store in downtown Portland (1923). Meyer opened a branch store in Hollywood, a Portland suburb, after police banned downtown parking because customers' parked cars caused traffic problems (1931).

During the next 3 decades, the Fred Meyer Super Centers developed and spread throughout Oregon and southern Washington state. Meyer's innovations included free parking, fluorescent lights, prepackaged goods, cash-and-carry pricing, self-service, and one-stop shopping with separate departments under one roof.

In 1960 the 18-store chain went public, posting sales of $56 million. During the 1960s and 1970s the company expanded into Idaho, Alaska, and western Montana. Acquisitions included Marketime Drugs (Seattle,1960); Roundup (wholesale grocery, Spokane, 1964); Market Basket (supermarkets, Seattle, 1965; sold by 1970); Roundup Properties (1966); 5 Valu Mart stores (Oregon, 1973); 9 Weisfield (Leslie) stores and 3 Bazar stores (Washington and Alaska, 1975). The company added more services (*e.g.*, Ready Foods Service, prepared entrees and frozen foods, 1968), and home improvement and garden centers (late 1960s).

In 1974 Meyer personally purchased Fidelity Savings and Loan of Oregon, a one-branch savings and loan with deposits of $3.8 million. Opening an untapped savings market of blue-collar workers, the 17 Fred Meyer Savings and Loans with 15 branches located within the company stores made $500,000 in profit on $78 million in deposits by 1976. Anticipating electronic fund transfer systems, the S&Ls also issued "My Money" cards, which automatically debited customers' savings accounts on store purchases.

Kohlberg Kravis Roberts (KKR) took the company private in a $420 million management LBO (1981). The company bought the 30-store Grand Central chain based in Salt Lake City, retaining 21 stores in Utah and Idaho (1984). KKR took the company public (1986), selling a 35% stake and raising $63 million to reduce debt. During its 5 years as a private company, sales increased 53%, from $1.1 billion to $1.7 billion, and net income increased 340%, from $5.1 million to $22.5 million. KKR controls 65% of the voting stock.

The company installed point-of-sale registers with electronic scanning in the food departments in the mid-1980s and expects to convert all departments to electronic scanning by 1991. In 1989 a $49 million restructuring charge resulted from store closings and conversion of the existing company-wide Honeywell mainframe computer system to an IBM system. Company plans include 5 to 10 new 200,000-square-foot hypermarkets, including 2 to 3 in California, during 1990 and 1991.

WHERE

HQ: 3800 SE 22nd Ave., Portland, OR 97202
Phone: 503-232-8844
FAX: 503-233-4535 (Public Affairs)

Fred Meyer operates 92 multidepartment retail stores and 29 specialty stores in 7 western states.

State	No. of Stores (8/90)
Alaska	8
California	3
Idaho	8
Montana	2
Oregon	48
Utah	13
Washington	39
Total	**121**

WHAT

	1989 Sales	
Segment	**$ mil**	**% of total**
Nonfood sales	1,526	67
Food sales	759	33
Total	**2,285**	**100**

Store Types	No. of Stores (8/90)
Multidepartment stores	
With food	65
Without food	27
Specialty stores	
Grocery	2
Fine jewelry	18
Soft goods	3
Nutrition	4
General merchandise	2
Total	**121**

Limited Partnership
Fred Meyer Real Estate Properties, Ltd.

RANKINGS

46th in *Fortune* 50 Retailing Cos.
359th in *Forbes* Sales 500
955th in *Business Week* 1000

COMPETITION

Albertson's
Costco
K mart
Longs
Safeway

HOW MUCH

	4 Yr. Growth	1980	1981	1982	1983	1984	1985	1986	1987	1988	1989
Sales ($ mil)	9.6%	—	—	—	—	—	1,584	1,688	1,848	2,074	2,285
Net income ($ mil)	—	—	—	—	—	—	19	24	32	37	(7)
Income as % of sales	—	—	—	—	—	—	1.2%	1.4%	1.7%	1.8%	(0.3%)
Earnings per share ($)	—	—	—	—	—	—	1.06	1.15	1.31	1.50	(0.28)
Stock price – high ($)	—	—	—	—	—	—	—	14.63	17.88	17.25	23.00
Stock price – low ($)	—	—	—	—	—	—	—	12.63	9.50	10.75	15.75
Stock price – close ($)	—	—	—	—	—	—	—	13.13	10.63	16.13	18.50
P/E – high	—	—	—	—	—	—	—	13	14	12	—
P/E – low	—	—	—	—	—	—	—	11	7	7	—
Dividends per share ($)	—	—	—	—	—	—	0.00	0.00	0.00	0.00	0.00
Book value per share ($)	17.5%	—	—	—	—	—	5.87	8.61	9.88	11.53	11.18

1989 Year End:
Debt ratio: 45.1%
Return on equity: —
Cash (mil): $25
Current ratio: 1.61
Long-term debt (mil): $206
Number of shares (mil): 23
Dividends:
1989 average yield: 0.0%
1989 payout: 0.0%
Market value (mil): $416

Stock Price History high/low 1986-89

25
20
15
10
5
0

FUJITSU LTD.

OVERVIEW

Fujitsu is the #1 mainframe computer manufacturer in Japan, the only country in which IBM is not the leader. Amdahl and Siemens sell Fujitsu's IBM-plug-compatible mainframes in the US and Europe, respectively.

Originally a telephone manufacturer, Fujitsu continues to make telecommunications equipment. The company is also a world leader in DRAM production. Fujitsu and its original parent, Fuji Electric, are still related through cross-holdings of stock. Fujitsu owns controlling interests in Amdahl and the UK's International Computers Ltd. (ICL, 80% purchased 1990), and in Japanese companies Fanuc, Fujitsu General, and Fujitsu Business Systems.

Fujitsu is trying to expand in the supercomputer and PC markets and is stepping up spending on semiconductor production and development. The company spent 10.3% of sales on R&D in 1989. In 1990 Fujitsu announced a new line of powerful mainframes designed to compete with expected offerings from IBM and Hitachi and reverse a recent decline in domestic market share. The company also plans to sell fault-tolerant computers.

WHEN

In 1923 Siemens and Furukawa Electric created Fuji Electric to produce electrical equipment. Fuji spun off Fujitsu, its communications division, in 1935. Originally a manufacturer of telephone equipment, Fujitsu produced antiaircraft weapons in WWII. After the war Fujitsu returned to telecommunications, becoming one of 4 major suppliers to state-owned monopoly Nippon Telegraph and Telephone and benefiting from Japan's rapid economic recovery in the 1950s and 1960s.

With encouragement from Japan's Ministry of International Trade and Industry (MITI), Fujitsu entered the data processing industry by developing the country's first commercial computer in 1954. Starting in 1959 MITI erected trade barriers to protect Japan's new computer industry. In the early 1960s MITI sponsored the production of mainframe computers, directing Fujitsu to develop the central processing unit. The company expanded into the related areas of semiconductor production and factory automation in the late 1960s. Fujitsu's factory automation business was spun off as Fujitsu Fanuc in 1972. Now called Fanuc, the company has become an important manufacturer of industrial robots.

In the 1970s Fujitsu sought to gain market share by making IBM-plug-compatible computers that provided superior value to buyers. The company bought 30% (since raised to 44%) of plug-compatible manufacturer Amdahl (1972) and gained badly needed technical information. In 1974 Fujitsu introduced its first plug-compatible computer and the following year began supplying Amdahl with OEM mainframe subassemblies. In 1979 Fujitsu passed IBM-Japan to become Japan's largest computer manufacturer.

Fujitsu entered major markets through joint ventures. In Europe the company entered into computer marketing ventures with Siemens (1978) and ICL (1981). In the US Fujitsu teamed with TRW to sell point-of-sale systems in 1980 and assumed 100% control of the operation in 1983. The company released its first supercomputer in 1982. The company dropped its 1986 bid for Fairchild Semiconductor when the Reagan administration expressed concern over foreign ownership of the chipmaker.

In 1985 IBM accused Fujitsu of stealing proprietary operating system software technology. Fujitsu objected, citing a secret 1983 agreement under which Fujitsu had paid IBM for software information. In 1988 an arbitrator awarded IBM $237 million, plus between $25 million and $50 million annually for Fujitsu's rights to inspect certain IBM software for one decade. Fujitsu's rights do not extend to IBM's new Summit computers, expected in 1991.

HOW MUCH

$ = ¥144 (Dec. 31, 1989)	9 Yr. Growth	1980	1981	1982	1983	1984	1985	1986	1987	1988	1989
Sales (¥ bil)	18.9%	501	582	800	957	1,210	562	1,692	1,789	2,047	2,387
Net income (¥ mil)	18.1%	15,645	18,453	31,761	48,265	66,669	89,028	38,926	21,206	42,115	69,948
Income as % of sales	—	3.1%	3.2%	4.0%	5.0%	5.5%	5.7%	2.3%	1.2%	2.1%	2.9%
Earnings per share (¥)	11.4%	14	15	24	33	44	55	24	13	24	37
Stock price — high (¥)	—	407	666	758	1,125	1,313	1,187	1,250	1,610	1,930	1,690
Stock price — low (¥)	—	261	323	409	635	884	793	819	700	1,160	1,400
Stock price — close (¥)	17.0%	368	503	718	1,010	1,136	1,000	1,060	1,110	1,510	1,510
P/E — high	—	29	44	32	34	30	22	53	120	82	46
P/E — low	—	19	22	17	19	20	15	35	52	48	38
Dividends per share (¥)	8.7%	3.8	5.2	4.5	4.5	5.1	5.9	7.6	7.4	8.0	8.0
Book value per share (¥)	—	91	158	205	245	296	394	410	427	484	546

1989 Year End:
Debt ratio: 24.8%
Return on equity: 7.2%
Cash (bil): ¥156
Long-term debt (bil): ¥316
Number of shares (mil): 1,760
Dividends:
1989 average yield: 0.5%
1989 payout: 21.6%
Market value (mil):$18,456
Sales (mil): $16,576

2,000
1,800
1,600
1,400
1,200
1,000
800
600
400
200
0

Principal stock exchange: Tokyo
Established: Japan, 1935
Fiscal year ends: March 31

WHO

President: Takuma Yamamoto, age 64
EVP: Matami Yasufuku
Auditors: Showa Ota & Co.
Employees: 104,503

WHERE

HQ: 6-1, Marunouchi 1-chome, Chiyoda-ku, Tokyo 100, Japan
Phone: 011-81-3-216-3211
US HQ: 680 Fifth Ave., New York, NY 10019
US Phone: 212-265-5360
US FAX: 212-541-9071

Fujitsu manufactures its products at 15 plants in Japan and 15 plants in other countries.

	1989 Sales ¥ mil	% of total
Japan	1,859,129	78
Other countries	528,313	22
Total	**2,387,442**	**100**

WHAT

	1989 Sales ¥ mil	% of total
Computers & data processing systems	1,578,617	66
Communications systems	375,464	16
Electronic devices	334,316	14
Other operations	99,045	4
Total	**2,387,442**	**100**

Computer & Data Processing Systems
FAST Series (retail automation systems)
FENICS (value-added network [VAN] services)
FM R Series, FM TOWNS (personal computers)
Fujitsu S (engineering workstations)
K-600 and K-100 Series (small business computers)
M Series (mainframe computers)
MSP-EX (operating system)
VP-2000 (supercomputers)

Telecommunications Products
COINS (corporate information network systems)
FETEX and 3000A Series (digital switching and PBX systems)
Integrated services digital network (ISDN) systems

Other Products
Car audio equipment
Electronic components
Semiconductors

RANKINGS

49th in *Fortune* Global 500 Industrial Cos.
29th in *Forbes* 100 Foreign Investments in the US
71st in *Business Week* Global 1000

COMPETITION

AT&T
BCE
Compaq
Computer Associates
Control Data
Cray Research
Data General
Digital Equipment
GTE
Harris
Hewlett-Packard
Hitachi
Hyundai
IBM
ITT
Mitsubishi
Motorola
National Semiconductor
NCR
NEC
Philips
Prime
Seagate
Siemens
Sun Microsystems
Tandem
Texas Instruments
Unisys
Wang
Electronics companies
Telecommunications manufacturers

E. & J. GALLO WINERY

OVERVIEW

Gallo is the world's largest winemaker based on gallons shipped, with 40% of the total wine shipments in California. Gallo's Modesto winery produces about 250,000 cases a day.

The privately owned company's success is due to the unique partnership between brothers Ernest and Julio Gallo, who now rank among the world's billionaires. Ernest is the marketing genius; Julio runs the winery, applying scientific principles to the art of winemaking. Another brother, Joseph, a cheesemaker, has tried to capitalize on the Gallo name but has so far been thwarted by his brothers in court.

Gallo grows less than 5% of the grapes it uses. Most wines are made in stainless steel tanks (except the premium wines, which are aged in barrels of Yugoslavian and French oak). Gallo's storage tanks can hold about 300 million gallons of wine.

Fortune estimates Gallo's sales at over $1 billion, representing 43% of California and 30% of US wine sales. Gallo's Andre champagne is the leading US sparkling wine, with a 28% market share of sales volume in a shrinking market; US sparkling wine shipments decreased in 1989 for the 5th straight year because of health and drunk driving issues. E & J Brandy is a brand leader, and 5 Gallo blush table wines are in the top 20 in sales.

Gallo has also been facing a decline in sales of low-priced table wines, its area of leadership; its Carlo Rossi and Gallo generic wines are ranked #1 and #2 among California jug table wines. The company has relied on Bartles & Jaymes wine coolers, its best seller (2nd to Seagram's in US wine cooler sales) with 17 million cases sold in 1989, to replace some lost sales. It also introduced the Wm. Wycliffe varietal label wine to capture some sales at finer restaurants. Gallo is establishing over 600 acres of new vineyards in California's Sonoma Valley.

WHEN

At the end of Prohibition in 1933, the Gallo brothers, Ernest and Julio, began making wine with a $200 grape crusher and redwood casks in a rented warehouse in Modesto, California. Ernest sold their first product, 6,000 gallons of table wine, to Pacific Wine Company (Chicago distributor), which bottled the wine under several labels. The Gallos reported making a $34,000 profit their first year.

In 1938 the brothers built a bottling plant in Modesto and began selling their own bottled wine. Two years later they bought plants in Los Angeles and New Orleans. In 1942 the Gallos got their first trademark, "Jolly Old Gallo." In the late 1940s Julio began experimenting with over 100 grape varieties to find those best for the Northern California climate. The company later led the industry in applying new technologies to the art of making wine. In the 1950s the company built its own bottle-making plant, becoming the first winery to do so.

Thunderbird, a juice-flavored fortified wine introduced in 1957, was one of the company's first big successes (2.5 million bottles sold in one year), but the cheap wine image it gave the company has been difficult to shake. Gallo no longer sells a similar wine, Ripple, but still makes Thunderbird.

By the 1960s most small California vintners had folded or had been absorbed by larger wineries. Gallo grew by spending large amounts on advertising (nearly 1/2 that spent by the entire wine industry in 1963), keeping prices low, and securing long-term grape contracts. In 1964 Gallo introduced Hearty Burgundy, leading a trend in dry California jug wines. Even in the face of increasing European imports, Gallo was the #1 winemaker in the US at the end of the decade, annually producing 66 million gallons of wine.

Gallo introduced the carbonated, fruit-flavored Boone's Farm Apple Wine in 1969, creating an interest in "pop" wines that lasted for a few years. In the mid-1970s the company introduced its first premium varietal wines.

In the mid-1970s Gallo field workers switched unions, dropping the United Farm Workers. Repercussions included protests and boycotts, but sales were largely unaffected. From 1976 to 1982 Gallo was placed under an FTC order limiting its control over wholesalers (lifted after Gallo's market share declined). Gallo has, however, remained the country's top winemaker. Its latest moneymaker has been the wine cooler Bartles & Jaymes (introduced 1985), promoted by "Ed and Frank" in humorous TV ads. In 1988 Gallo began bottling Hearty Burgundy with a cork rather than a screw cap and started labeling all of its varietal wines with a vintage date.

HOW MUCH

	9 Yr. Growth	1980	1981	1982	1983	1984	1985	1986	1987	1988	1989
Wine shipments (mil of gals.)	3.7%	121.9	131.4	137.3	146.1	143.6	154.3	169.2	166.0	165.4	169.2

Private company
Founded: 1933
Fiscal year ends: December 31

WHO

Chairman: Ernest Gallo, age 81
President: Julio Gallo, age 80
VP Finance: Louis Freedman
President, Gallo Sales Co.: Joseph E. Gallo
President, Gallo Glass Co. and Fairbanks Trucking Inc.: Robert J. Gallo
President, Midcal Aluminum Inc.: James E. Coleman
Employees: 3,000

WHERE

HQ: PO Box 1130, Modesto, CA 95353
Phone: 209-579-3111
FAX: 209-579-4361 (Public Relations)

Vineyards in California (counties)

Fresno	Napa
Mendocino	San Luis Obispo
Merced	Sonoma
Monterey	Stanislaus

WHAT

Label Names
Andre
Ballatore
Bartles & Jaymes
Boone's
Carlo Rossi
E & J Brandy
Ernest & Julio Gallo
Gallo
Livingston Cellars
The Reserve Cellars of Ernest & Julio Gallo
Tott's
Wm. Wycliffe

Subsidiaries
E & J Gallo Winery Europe (wholesale distributor in Europe)
Fairbanks Trucking Inc. (long-distance trucking)
Frei Bros. Winery (Sonoma winery and vineyards)
Gallo Glass Co. (glass wine bottles)
Gallo Sales Co. (wholesale wine distributor)
Midcal Aluminum Inc. (metal bottle closures)
Mountain Wine Distributing Co. (Gallo wines distributor in Colorado)
San Joaquin Valley Express (partnership, agricultural trucking)
United Packing Co. (partnership, importer of wine bottle corks)
US Intermodal Services (partnership, freight brokerage)
Valley Vintners Wine Co. (wholesale distributor of Gallo wines in Southern California and Pacific Northwest)

RANKINGS

146th in *Forbes* 400 US Private Cos.

COMPETITION

Anheuser-Busch	Grand Metropolitan
Bass	Seagram
Brown-Forman	

GANNETT CO., INC.

OVERVIEW

Gannett is the largest newspaper group in the US. Headquartered in Arlington, Virginia, Gannett owns and operates 83 daily and 52 nondaily newspapers and is best known as publisher of *USA TODAY*. From the time Gannett went public in 1967 until 1990 it recorded 89 consecutive quarters of earnings gains. This uninterrupted streak — one of the longest in corporate history — was broken in the 2nd quarter of 1990 when it reported earnings of $105 million, 6% lower than 1989 2nd quarter earnings.

USA TODAY, the colorful national daily with a circulation of 1.76 million (2nd only to the *Wall Street Journal*), is in its 8th year of publication. It has yet to turn an annual profit.

Gannett owns 10 TV stations, 16 radio stations, and the largest outdoor advertising company in North America. Other ventures include Gannett News Services and the Louis Harris & Associates international opinion research company.

The Gannett Foundation, with 11% of the company's stock and assets of $650 million, is a significant contributor to charitable causes in communities served by Gannett. All of the company's Class A common stock was willed to the foundation by founder Frank Gannett, who died in 1957.

NYSE symbol: GCI
Incorporated: Delaware, 1972
Fiscal year ends: Last Sunday of the calendar year

WHO

Chairman, President, and CEO: John J. Curley, age 51, $1,281,250 pay
VC and CFO: Douglas H. McCorkindale, age 50, $1,020,000 pay
EVP Marketing; Publisher, *USA TODAY*: Cathleen P. Black, age 45, $600,000 pay
Auditors: Price Waterhouse
Employees: 36,650

WHEN

The Gannett Company started in 1906 in Elmira, New York, when Frank Gannett and his associates purchased a 1/2 interest in the *Elmira Gazette*. The small company expanded slowly, purchasing 2 additional small newspapers by 1912. In 1918 the company moved to Rochester, where it acquired 2 more newspapers, and in 1923 Frank Gannett, having bought out his associates' interests, formed the Gannett Company. In 1929 Frank Gannett co-invented the teletypesetter. Gannett continued to buy up small and medium-sized dailies in the Northeast, and by 1947 it operated 21 newspapers and 7 radio stations. At the time of his death in 1957, Frank Gannett had accumulated 30 newspapers.

During the 1960s Gannett continued its acquisition of local newspapers, expanding beyond a regional focus to become a national newspaper chain. It was not until 1966, however, that Gannett started its own newspaper, *TODAY,* in Cocoa Beach, Florida. Gannett went public in 1967.

Gannett went through its greatest expansion during the 1970s and 1980s under the direction of Allen Neuharth, who became CEO in 1973 and chairman in 1979. Gannett captured national attention in 1979 when it merged with Phoenix-based Combined Communications Corporation (CCC), another media conglomerate whose holdings included TV and radio stations, an outdoor advertising business (2nd largest in the US), the Louis Harris polling business, and the *Cincinnati Enquirer* and the *Oakland Tribune*. Gannett's revenues passed the $1 billion mark in 1979.

In 1982 Gannett started *USA TODAY,* a national newspaper whose splashy format and short articles made it an industry novelty. By 1989 circulation of *USA TODAY* had grown to 1.76 million, making it 2nd only to the *Wall Street Journal* in daily circulation.

Gannett's largest acquisition came in 1986 when it bought the Evening News Association for $717 million, giving Gannett 5 more newspapers, including the *Detroit News,* and 2 TV stations. In 1988 Gannett started the "USA Today on TV" program. The program was taken off the air in 1990 due to poor ratings and consistent losses.

Neuharth retired as chairman of Gannett in 1989. During his 16-year tenure as the company's leader, Neuharth spent approximately $1.5 billion on acquisitions and increased the combined circulation of Gannett's newspapers to 6.3 million.

WHERE

HQ: 1100 Wilson Blvd., Arlington, VA 22234
Phone: 703-284-6000
FAX: 703-243-0823

Gannett has facilities in 41 states, the District of Columbia, and 6 foreign countries.

	1989 Pretax Income	
	$ mil	% of total
US	629	97
Foreign	18	3
Total	**647**	**100**

WHAT

	1989 Sales		1989 Operating Income	
	$ mil	% of total	$ mil	% of total
Newspaper publishing	2,852	81	670	82
Broadcasting	408	12	111	14
Outdoor advertising	258	7	38	4
Adjustments	—	—	(62)	—
Total	**3,518**	**100**	**757**	**100**

Major Newspapers
Cincinnati Enquirer
Courier-Journal (Louisville, KY)
Des Moines Register
Detroit News
USA TODAY/USA WEEKEND

TV Stations
10 stations in 9 states and the District of Columbia

Radio Stations
16 FM and AM stations in 6 states

Other Businesses
Gannett Direct Marketing Services, Inc.
Gannett News Services
Gannett Outdoor division (billboards)
Gannett TeleMarketing, Inc.
Louis Harris & Associates (opinion research)
USA TODAY Update (electronic information)

HOW MUCH

	9 Yr. Growth	1980	1981	1982	1983	1984	1985	1986	1987	1988	1989
Sales ($ mil)	12.5%	1,215	1,367	1,520	1,704	1,960	2,209	2,802	3,079	3,314	3,518
Net income ($ mil)	11.3%	152	173	181	192	224	253	276	319	364	398
Income as % of sales	—	12.5%	12.6%	11.9%	11.3%	11.4%	11.5%	9.9%	10.4%	11.0%	11.3%
Earnings per share ($)	11.4%	0.94	1.06	1.13	1.20	1.40	1.58	1.71	1.98	2.26	2.47
Stock price – high ($)	—	12.89	15.33	22.00	24.00	25.38	33.06	43.56	56.25	39.88	49.88
Stock price – low ($)	—	8.67	11.17	9.83	17.13	16.69	23.50	29.63	26.00	29.25	34.50
Stock price – close ($)	15.1%	12.22	12.04	21.13	19.67	23.50	30.63	36.06	39.13	35.63	43.50
P/E – high	—	14	15	19	20	18	21	25	28	18	20
P/E – low	—	9	11	9	14	12	15	17	13	13	14
Dividends per share ($)	10.3%	0.46	0.52	0.58	0.61	0.67	0.77	0.86	0.94	1.02	1.11
Book value per share ($)	11.0%	4.83	5.26	5.82	6.39	7.12	7.94	8.88	9.94	11.09	12.40

1989 Year End:
Debt ratio: 31.6%
Return on equity: 21.0%
Cash (mil): $56
Current ratio: 1.4
Long-term debt (mil): $922
Number of shares (mil): 161
Dividends:
1989 average yield: 2.6%
1989 payout: 44.9%
Market value (mil): $7,002

RANKINGS

130th in *Fortune* 500 Industrial Cos.
365th in *Fortune* Global 500 Industrial Cos.
236th in *Forbes* Sales 500
82nd in *Business Week* 1000
272nd in *Business Week* Global 1000

COMPETITION

Advance Publications	Hearst	Times Mirror
Cox	Knight-Ridder	Tribune
Dow Jones	New York Times	Washington Post
	E.W. Scripps	

GEICO CORPORATION

OVERVIEW

GEICO is the holding company for Government Employees Insurance Company, which provides preferred-risk insurance of automobiles (8th largest in the US) and homeowners and other property and casualty insurance.

Auto insurance accounted for over 90% of GEICO's premium revenue in 1989. Other GEICO subsidiaries offer life insurance (Garden State Life and GEICO Annuity), higher risk classes of auto insurance (GEICO Indemnity and Criterion Casualty), and other financial services. The company has announced plans to sell Garden State Life and GEICO Annuity during 1990.

GEICO markets its insurance products primarily by direct marketing to preferred-risk government and military employees and drivers age 50 and over. This method saves the expense of commissioned agents. Almost 59% of new auto insurance business comes from customer referrals. GEICO also markets by mail directly to members of groups or associations who sponsor GEICO insurance programs. In addition, the company concentrates on retention of current policyholders; in 1989 more than 91% of auto policyholders who were offered renewals accepted.

GEICO enters the 1990s as a company known for strict underwriting guidelines, with a focus on personal property and casualty business.

NYSE symbol: GEC
Incorporated: Delaware, 1978
Fiscal year ends: December 31

WHO

Chairman and CEO: William B. Snyder, age 60, $700,000 pay
VC: Louis A. Simpson, age 53, $759,177 pay
President: Edward H. Utley, age 60, $186,223 pay
President, Government Employees Insurance: Olza M. Nicely, age 46, $196,379 pay
SVP and Principal Financial Officer: W. Alvon Sparks, Jr., age 54
SVP: Marion E. Byrd, age 53
SVP: Donald K. Smith, age 57
Auditors: Coopers & Lybrand
Employees: 6,435

WHEN

Leo Goodwin, an accountant for a San Antonio insurance company, thought of the simple concept of providing auto insurance at a significant savings directly to customers without going through a middleman. In 1936, at age 50, Goodwin founded Government Employees Insurance Company in Fort Worth with $25,000, plus $75,000 from Fort Worth banker Cleaves Rhea.

In the early years Leo and his wife Lillian worked 12 hours a day for a combined income of $250 a month. Using direct-mail marketing, they targeted government employees (good drivers with steady incomes). In 1937 the company moved to Washington, DC, where the most government workers were.

GEICO had $15,000 net income in 1940, the first of 35 consecutive profitable years. In 1941 a major hailstorm damaged cars in the Washington area, and Goodwin engaged auto repair shops to work 24 hours a day solely for GEICO policyholders. Because of this extraordinary service, his policyholders told friends about the company. GEICO participated in the post-WWII boom by insuring the new homes and autos of veterans.

GEICO's new premium income was $2.5 million in 1946, a 50% increase over 1945. In 1948 the Rhea family sold its 75% interest to the Graham-Newman Corporation which, later that year, following a stock split, distributed its shares to its stockholders, and the company became publicly owned. In 1949 GEICO exceeded $1 million in profits and formed life insurance and finance companies.

The company expanded its market to include state, county, and municipal employees in 1952 and nongovernmental professional, technical, and managerial employees in 1958. Goodwin retired in 1958 as president.

GEICO struggled in the early 1970s with federal wage and price controls and no-fault insurance. In 1975 these factors, combined with some bad management decisions, resulted in an $85 million loss, its first in 36 years, and GEICO was close to insolvency. In 1976 new CEO John Byrne increased rates, cut costs, reunderwrote all policies, and retained Salomon Brothers to underwrite a $76 million stock offering to raise capital. The plan worked and GEICO returned to profitability in 1977.

In 1982 GEICO bought GEICO General Insurance and Garden State Life Insurance. In 1988 GEICO decided to sell all its businesses other than personal property and casualty insurance.

WHERE

HQ: 5260 Western Ave., Chevy Chase, MD 20815
Phone: 301-986-3000
FAX: 301-986-2113

GEICO operates in all 50 states and Washington, DC.

WHAT

	1989 Sales		1989 Operating Income	
	$ mil	% of total	$ mil	% of total
Property & casualty insurance	1,812	94	270	101
Reinsurance	6	—	—	—
Life & health insurance	51	3	(3)	(1)
Finance	31	2	(1)	—
Other	16	1	1	—
Adjustments	13	—	(12)	—
Total	**1,929**	**100**	**255**	**100**

Insurance Services
Auto insurance
Homeowners and renters insurance
Life and health insurance
Personal liability insurance

Subsidiaries
Criterion Casualty
Garden State Life Insurance
GEICO Annuity and Insurance
GEICO Financial Services
GEICO General Insurance
GEICO Indemnity
GEICO Philanthropic Foundation
Government Employees Financial

RANKINGS

39th in *Fortune* 50 Diversified Financial Cos.
408th in *Forbes* Sales 500
285th in *Business Week* 1000
862nd in *Business Week* Global 1000

COMPETITION

Aetna
Berkshine Hathaway
CIGNA
ITT
Kemper
Metropolitan
Prudential
Sears
State Farm
Travelers
USF&G
Xerox

HOW MUCH

	9 Yr. Growth	1980	1981	1982	1983	1984	1985	1986	1987	1988	1989
Sales ($ mil)	11.4%	727	723	814	869	988	1,212	1,419	1,570	1,746	1,929
Net income ($ mil)	15.2%	60	64	77	95	100	78	119	150	134	213
Income as % of sales	—	8.2%	8.9%	9.5%	10.9%	10.2%	6.4%	8.4%	9.6%	7.7%	11.0%
Earnings per share ($)	20.4%	2.59	2.98	3.67	4.48	5.11	4.21	6.91	9.01	8.48	13.74
Stock price – high ($)	—	16.50	29.38	45.75	64.00	65.63	88.00	105.50	136.75	132.00	156.00
Stock price – low ($)	—	8.13	14.38	21.00	41.00	48.88	57.13	77.75	90.13	101.50	122.75
Stock price – close ($)	29.8%	14.63	27.75	43.00	58.13	58.00	87.00	98.50	110.50	124.00	152.50
P/E – high	—	6	10	12	14	13	21	15	15	16	11
P/E – low	—	3	5	6	9	10	14	11	10	12	9
Dividends per share ($)	17.2%	0.43	0.48	0.56	0.72	0.88	1.00	1.08	1.36	1.64	1.80
Book value per share ($)	22.8%	9.28	11.76	16.85	19.88	22.40	29.14	37.33	39.18	45.82	59.18

1989 Year End:
Debt ratio: 24.1%
Return on equity: 26.2%
Cash (mil): $23
Current ratio: —
Long-term debt (mil): $285
Number of shares (mil): 15
Dividends:
1989 average yield: 1.2%
1989 payout: 13.1%
Market value (mil): $2,314

Stock Price History high/low 1980-89

160
140
120
100
80
60
40
20
0

GENENTECH, INC.

OVERVIEW

Genentech is one of the largest and most profitable companies worldwide that make pharmaceuticals using biotechnology. It had only 2 approved products as of the end of 1989. Investor confidence in Genentech is evident in that it ranks 11th in market value among drug companies (most of whom have far greater sales) and it has one of the highest P/E ratios on the stock market.

The company has a subsidiary in Canada and a small research unit in Japan. Sales outside the US are made through foreign drug companies (Mitsubishi in Japan, Boehringer Ingelheim in Europe, among others), who pay royalties to Genentech. Genentech has agreed to sell 60% of itself to the Swiss drug giant Roche, which will have an option to buy the rest through 1995.

Genentech spends a huge proportion of sales on R&D — nearly 40% in 1989. It received 9 genetic engineering patents in 1989, the most of any company or other research entity in the US. In 1990 the FDA recommended approval of a new product, Actimmune, and allowed the company to sell Activase for treating blood clots in vessels to the lungs.

NYSE symbol: GNE
Incorporated: Delaware, 1987
Fiscal year ends: December 31

WHO

Chairman: Robert A. Swanson, age 42, $600,000 pay (before promotion)
President and CEO: G. Kirk Raab, age 54, $560,000 pay (before promotion)
SVP: James M. Gower, age 41, $345,000 pay
SVP: William D. Young, age 45, $300,000 pay
VP and CFO: Louis J. Lavigne, age 41, $275,000 pay
Auditors: Ernst & Young
Employees: 1,790

WHEN

Venture capitalist Robert Swanson and molecular biologist Herbert Boyer founded Genentech of South San Francisco in 1976 to commercialize products of the new science of genetic engineering. Boyer held a patent on techniques for splicing genes into microorganisms that could then be used as "microfactories" to produce large amounts of specific therapeutic substances. Genentech's first product was a bioengineered human form of insulin. Before any product reached the market, however, Genentech achieved fame when company stock went public in 1980. Its market value doubled on the first day of trading to $668 million but fell back closer to its issue level within a month. Boyer's initial investment of a few hundred dollars was briefly worth $80 million.

In 1982 Genentech's insulin became the first biotech product to be approved by the FDA. The company licensed it to Eli Lilly, who sold it by the trade name Humulin. Selling marketing rights to major firms in exchange for royalties allowed the company to focus on research, which could cost over $100 million per product. The company next developed the human immune system protein alpha interferon and licensed it to Hoffmann-La Roche, who sold it as Roferon-A (cancer treatment). The first product to bear the Genentech name was its human growth hormone, Protropin, approved by the FDA in 1985. An accounting charge for R&D expenses resulted in a significant drop in profits and the recording of a loss in 1986.

Genentech achieved the largest first-year sales of any new drug ($180 million in 1988) with Activase, a natural clot-dissolving substance (also known as t-PA) used to treat heart attacks, which was approved by the FDA in 1987. In 1988 and 1989 half of Genentech's sales came from Activase.

Genentech has fought competitors in court to protect its exclusive right to make and sell Activase as well as other genetically engineered products. In April 1990 it won a federal suit against 2 other makers of t-PA and may get exclusive marketing rights in the US. UK courts have invalidated Genentech's t-PA patent. Development of Activase required $200 million and 5 years. The company anticipated sales of $1 billion by 1990, but expectations have dropped since a March 1990 announcement that heart attack survival rates are no greater with Activase than with its rival, streptokinase, which costs 1/10 as much.

In April 1990 Genentech sold a 60% interest to Roche Holding, a Swiss drugmaker, for $2.1 billion. This development will allow Genentech to devote to R&D the funds needed to continue creating innovative products.

WHERE

HQ: 460 Point San Bruno Blvd., South San Francisco, CA 94080
Phone: 415-266-1000
FAX: 415-588-3255

Genentech manufactures and sells products in the US and Canada; the company licenses the rights to market its products internationally.

	1989 Sales	
	$ mil	% of total
US	357	93
Europe	18	5
Asia	3	1
Canada	5	1
Total	**383**	**100**

WHAT

	1989 Sales	
	$ mil	% of total
Product sales	319	83
Contract & other	64	17
Total	**383**	**100**

On the Market
Actimmune (gamma interferon; for infections associated with a rare immune disorder)
Activase (for dissolving clots in vessels to the heart and lungs)
Humulin (recombinant human insulin licensed to Eli Lilly)
Protropin (human growth hormone)
Roferon-A (alpha interferon cancer treatment)

Under Development
Activin/Inhibin (sickle-cell anemia)
Argatroban (anticoagulant)
CD4 (AIDS treatment)
HER-2 monoclonal antibody (cancer)
IGF-1 (nutritional support and wound healing)
Lung surfactant (premature infants)
Nerve growth factor (Alzheimer's disease)
Relaxin (to ease childbirth and reduce cesareans)
TGF-Beta (wound healing)

HOW MUCH

	9 Yr. Growth	1980	1981	1982	1983	1984	1985	1986	1987	1988	1989
Sales ($ mil)	57.3%	7	15	29	42	66	82	127	219	323	383
Net income ($ mil)	88.0%	0	0	1	1	3	6	(352)	42	21	44
Income as % of sales	—	2.3%	2.0%	2.2%	2.7%	4.1%	6.9%	(276.6%)	19.3%	6.4%	11.5%
Earnings per share ($)	67.2%	0.01	0.01	0.01	0.02	0.05	0.09	(5.08)	0.50	0.24	0.51
Stock price – high ($)	—	11.88	7.96	8.17	12.44	10.56	18.81	49.38	65.25	47.50	23.38
Stock price – low ($)	—	5.83	4.33	4.33	6.47	7.19	8.56	16.44	26.00	14.38	16.00
Stock price – close ($)	12.3%	7.33	6.04	6.96	8.63	8.56	17.44	42.50	42.00	16.00	20.75
P/E – high	—	2,375	1,194	613	622	222	209	—	131	198	46
P/E – low	—	1,167	650	325	323	151	95	—	52	60	31
Dividends per share ($)	0.0%	0.00	0.00	0.00	0.00	0.00	0.00	0.00	0.00	0.00	0.00
Book value per share ($)	20.7%	1.02	1.09	1.46	1.60	1.71	2.98	3.69	4.35	4.82	5.57

1989 Year End:
Debt ratio: 24.8%
Return on equity: 9.8%
Cash (mil): $205
Current ratio: 4.31
Long-term debt (mil): $154
Number of shares (mil): 84
Dividends:
1989 average yield: 0.0%
1989 payout: 0.0%
Market value (mil): $1,749

Stock Price History high/low 1980-89

70
60
50
40
30
20
10
0

RANKINGS

283rd in *Business Week* 1000
885th in *Business Week* Global 1000

COMPETITION

Abbott Labs	Du Pont	Pfizer
American Cyanamid	Eli Lilly	Procter & Gamble
American Home Products	Glaxo	Rhône-Poulenc
Bayer	Hoechst	Schering-Plough
Bristol-Myers Squibb	Johnson & Johnson	SmithKline Beecham
Dow Chemical	Merck	Upjohn
	Monsanto	Warner-Lambert

GENERAL CINEMA CORPORATION

OVERVIEW

General Cinema operates 1,488 movie screens in 32 states, making it America's 3rd largest movie theater operator, after United Artists Entertainment and American Multi-Cinema. Most of the company's theaters are multi-screen facilities located in or near major shopping centers, a strategy that reduces the risk of losses associated with any one film. More than 80 million people attended movies at General Cinema theaters in 1989.

In addition to movie theaters, General Cinema owns 60% of the Neiman Marcus Group, a public company comprised of Neiman Marcus, Bergdorf Goodman, and Contempo Casuals stores. The Group offers home shopping through Horchow Mail Order. General Cinema also owns 17% of Cadbury Schweppes, an international maker of soft drinks and confections.

General Cinema plans to use some of the proceeds from the $1.77 billion sale of its soft drink bottling operations (1989) to buy another line of business, related to its theater and retailing activities, that will contribute to the company's growth through the 1990s.

NYSE symbol: GCN
Incorporated: Delaware, 1950
Fiscal year ends: October 31

WHO

Chairman and CEO: Richard A. Smith, age 65, $1,051,250 pay
President and COO: Robert J. Tarr, Jr., age 46, $962,500 pay
VC and CFO: J. Atwood Ives, age 53, $739,063 pay
SVP, General Counsel, and Secretary: Samuel Frankenheim, age 57, $591,250 pay
Auditors: Deloitte & Touche
Employees: 24,200

WHEN

Philip Smith, a former salesman for Pathe films, first started to put together a chain of movie theaters in the 1920s. Before WWII he pioneered in building drive-in theaters and in 1950 founded a chain of drive-ins called Mid-West Drive-In Theaters. In 1951 Mid-West built the first theater located in a shopping center. In 1960 when the Boston-based company went public, it owned 20 outdoor theaters and 19 indoor theaters in several eastern and midwestern states under the corporate name General Drive-In Corporation.

When Smith died in 1961, his son Richard took over the company. General Drive-In opened its first 2-screen theater in 1963. By that time the company operated 72 theaters. It adopted its present name in 1964.

General Cinema bought Ohio and Florida Pepsi-Cola bottling plants in 1968, thereby entering the soft drink bottling business. By the mid-1970s it also owned 7UP and Dr Pepper bottlers. The Justice Department charged that the company's 1970 purchase of 15 Minneapolis theaters eliminated competition in the Minneapolis–St. Paul area among exhibitors bidding for films, and the company was ordered to sell 9 of its 21 area theaters. General Cinema entered broadcasting in 1972, buying control of a Miami television station, and subsequently bought radio stations in Chicago (1973) and Boston (1979). The company sold all of its stations between 1982 and 1986.

In 1973 General Cinema was the largest movie theater operator in the country, with 501 theaters and $118 million in sales. However, the rising costs of suburban land led to a phase-out of drive-ins and by 1978 the company operated only 10 outdoor theaters.

The company's soft drink bottling division continued to grow, and by 1981 General Cinema had become America's largest independent soft drink bottler. The company, which had introduced Sunkist Orange Soda in 1979, sold its Sunkist operations to R. J. Reynolds in 1984. Also in 1984 General Cinema bought 39% of Carter Hawley Hale, operator of the Broadway, Emporium, Bergdorf Goodman, and Neiman Marcus retail stores, increasing its stake in CHH to 49% in 1986. When CHH spun off its specialty stores as the Neiman Marcus Group in 1987, General Cinema exchanged its stake in CHH for 60% of the new company.

General Cinema bought an 8% interest in British candy and soft drink maker Cadbury Schweppes in 1987, increased its share in 1988, and currently owns 17%. In 1989 General Cinema sold its soft drink bottling operations to PepsiCo for $1.77 billion ($1.20 billion after tax).

WHERE

HQ: 27 Boylston St., Chestnut Hill, MA 02167
Phone: 617-232-8200
FAX: 617-738-4007 (Investor Relations)

The company operates 1,488 movie screens in 314 theaters in 32 states. Neiman Marcus, based in Dallas, has 23 stores in 10 states and the District of Columbia. Bergdorf Goodman operates at 2 locations in New York City. Contempo Casuals has 228 stores in 31 states.

WHAT

	1989 Sales		1989 Operating Income	
	$ mil	% of total	$ mil	% of total
Theaters	446	23	9	10
Specialty retailing	1,468	77	83	90
Adjustments	—	—	(30)	—
Total	**1,914**	**100**	**92**	**100**

	1989 Pretax Income	
	$ mil	% of total
Securities sales	85	40
Neiman Marcus	66	31
Dividend income	35	16
Bergdorf Goodman	23	11
Theaters	9	4
Contempo Casuals	3	2
Horchow Mail Order	(8)	(4)
Adjustments	(33)	—
Total	**180**	**100**

Motion Picture Theaters

Specialty Retailing (60% interest in Neiman Marcus Group, Inc.)
Bergdorf Goodman
Contempo Casuals
Horchow Mail Order
Neiman Marcus

Investments
Cadbury Schweppes p.l.c. (17% owned)

RANKINGS

400th in *Forbes* Sales 500
358th in *Business Week* 1000

COMPETITION

Campeau
Carter Hawley Hale
Dayton Hudson
Dillard
The Limited
R. H. Macy
May Department Stores
Nordstrom
Paramount
Tele-Communications
Woolworth

HOW MUCH

	9 Yr. Growth	1980	1981	1982	1983	1984	1985	1986	1987	1988	1989
Sales ($ mil)	10.8%	759	824	886	929	916	967	998	1,040	2,324	1,914
Net income ($ mil)	13.7%	33	44	48	99	74	88	90	87	83	106
Income as % of sales	—	4.4%	5.4%	5.4%	10.6%	8.0%	9.1%	9.0%	8.3%	3.6%	5.5%
Earnings per share ($)	15.9%	0.38	0.50	0.60	1.31	0.98	1.17	1.23	1.18	1.12	1.43
Stock price – high ($)	—	3.23	5.06	7.63	11.44	14.00	21.13	29.50	31.75	25.75	28.50
Stock price – low ($)	—	2.00	3.13	3.72	6.84	8.38	12.13	18.31	13.75	15.75	23.13
Stock price – close ($)	25.9%	3.23	4.56	7.28	11.25	13.38	19.31	22.13	19.38	25.50	25.75
P/E – high	—	9	10	13	9	14	18	24	27	23	20
P/E – low	—	5	6	6	5	9	10	15	12	14	16
Dividends per share ($)	18.5%	0.09	0.11	0.12	0.14	0.17	0.21	0.26	0.32	0.37	0.41
Book value per share ($)	31.3%	1.92	2.32	2.28	5.60	7.13	5.77	7.25	—	8.75	22.28

1989 Year End:
Debt ratio: 30.5%
Return on equity: 9.2%
Cash (mil): $1,688
Current ratio: 2.04
Long-term debt (mil): $680
Number of shares (mil): 69
Dividends:
1989 average yield: 1.6%
1989 payout: 28.7%
Market value (mil): $1,785

Stock Price History high/low 1980-89

GENERAL DYNAMICS CORPORATION

OVERVIEW

General Dynamics, the nation's 3rd largest defense supplier, produces a wide range of major weapons systems for all branches of the armed forces; 84% of its sales are to the US government. The company builds the F-16 fighter aircraft, Tomahawk cruise missile, Stinger antiaircraft system, Phalanx gun system, Trident and SSN 688 class submarines, M1 Main Battle Tank, and defense electronics such as the army's Single Channel Ground and Airborne Radio System.

General Dynamics sells Atlas and Centaur launch vehicles for both government and commercial space launches. Company subsidiary Cessna Aircraft is one of the world's top makers of business jets (with 50% of the market); another subsidiary, Material Service Corporation, sells building and highway construction materials, lime, and coal.

New or upcoming projects include the navy's A-12 attack aircraft (produced with McDonnell Douglas) and the Advanced Tactical Fighter (General Dynamics is one of 2 contractor teams competing to produce the aircraft). The company's Electric Boat division is one of 2 shipbuilders constructing the new Seawolf class attack submarine for the navy.

WHEN

The history of General Dynamics begins with the Electric Boat Company, a New Jersey ship and submarine builder founded by John Holland in 1899. Electric Boat produced large numbers of submarines, ships, and PT boats during WWII. Faced with dwindling orders after the war, the company, under the direction of John Jay Hopkins, began to diversify with the 1947 purchase of Canadian aircraft builder Canadair. Hopkins formed General Dynamics in 1952, merging Electric Boat and Canadair into the new company. General Dynamics bought California-based Consolidated Vultee Aircraft (Convair), a major producer of military and civilian aircraft, in 1954.

Electric Boat launched the first nuclear submarine, the *Nautilus*, in 1955; the following year, at the urging of Howard Hughes, Convair began designing its first commercial jetliners, the Convair 880 and 990. While nuclear subs became a mainstay for General Dynamics, the company gave up on its jetliners after losses on the aircraft reached $425 million (1961). Meanwhile, weakened by the cost of producing the 880 and 990, General Dynamics in 1959 had merged with profitable Chicago building materials supplier Material Service Corporation, whose owner, Colonel Henry Crown, received a 20% stake in General Dynamics.

During the 1960s General Dynamics developed the controversial F-111 fighter. Despite numerous problems, the aircraft proved financially and militarily successful (F-111s participated in the 1986 US bombing raid on Libya).

Backed by Crown (the company's largest stockholder), David Lewis became CEO in 1970. Under Lewis, General Dynamics won contracts for such items as the navy's 688 class attack submarine (1971), liquified natural gas tankers for Burmah Oil Company (1972), the Trident ballistic missile submarine (1974), and the F-16 lightweight fighter aircraft (1975). The company sold Canadair (1976) and bought Chrysler Defense, which already had a contract to build the army's new M-1 tank, in 1982. Lewis returned General Dynamics to profitability but retired in 1985 amid federal investigations of overcharges to the government. The new CEO, Stanley Pace, instituted tough ethics rules and cut costs. The company bought Cessna Aircraft, a large general aviation manufacturer (1986), and sold its Quincy shipyard in 1987. In 1989 General Dynamics received orders (along with Tenneco subsidiary Newport News Shipbuilding) for the Seawolf attack submarine. In 1990 Saudi Arabia ordered 315 M-1 tanks for delivery starting in 1993.

HOW MUCH

	9 Yr. Growth	1980	1981	1982	1983	1984	1985	1986	1987	1988	1989
Sales ($ mil)	8.7%	4,743	5,063	6,155	7,146	7,839	8,164	8,892	9,344	9,551	10,043
Net income ($ mil)	4.6%	195	124	161	287	382	373	(63)	437	379	293
Income as % of sales	—	4.1%	2.5%	2.6%	4.0%	4.9%	4.6%	(0.7%)	4.7%	4.0%	2.9%
Earnings per share ($)	7.9%	3.53	2.25	2.90	5.29	8.07	8.80	(1.46)	10.25	9.03	7.01
Stock price – high ($)	—	44.88	43.00	36.63	61.75	69.75	84.00	89.25	79.00	59.00	60.50
Stock price – low ($)	—	28.88	21.00	18.75	30.63	42.00	62.00	64.25	42.63	46.75	42.50
Stock price – close ($)	0.5%	42.75	24.50	33.00	58.13	69.50	68.75	67.75	48.75	50.75	44.88
P/E – high	—	13	19	13	12	9	10	—	8	7	9
P/E – low	—	8	9	6	6	5	7	—	4	5	6
Dividends per share ($)	5.3%	0.63	0.72	0.72	0.93	1.00	1.00	1.00	1.00	1.00	1.00
Book value per share ($)	11.9%	18.54	19.99	21.56	23.91	24.58	31.46	29.45	38.19	46.10	51.12

1989 Year End:
Debt ratio: 29.9%
Return on equity: 14.4%
Cash (mil): $14
Current ratio: 1.92
Long-term debt (mil): $906
Number of shares (mil): 42
Dividends:
1989 average yield: 2.2%
1989 payout: 14.3%
Market value (mil): $1,866

Stock Price History high/low 1980-89

NYSE symbol: GD
Incorporated: Delaware, 1952
Fiscal year ends: December 31

WHO

Chairman and CEO: Stanley C. Pace, age 68, $1,198,750 pay
VC: William A. Anders, age 56, $550,000 pay
President and COO: Herbert F. Rogers, age 65, $775,000 pay
EVP: James R. Mellor, age 59, $550,500 pay
EVP; Chairman, Material Service Corp.: Lester Crown, age 64, $507,000 pay
EVP; Chairman, Cessna Aircraft Co.: Russell W. Meyer, Jr., age 57, $464,250 pay
VP and CFO: James J. Cunnane, age 51
Auditors: Arthur Andersen & Co.
Employees: 102,200

WHERE

HQ: Pierre Laclede Center, St. Louis, MO 63105
Phone: 314-889-8200
FAX: 314-889-8839

	1989 Sales	
	$ mil	% of total
US	8,521	85
Foreign (through US government)	949	6
Foreign (direct)	573	9
Total	**10,043**	**100**

WHAT

	1989 Sales		1989 Operating Income	
	$ mil	% of total	$ mil	% of total
Government aerospace	6,029	60	386	66
Submarines	1,679	17	41	7
Land systems	989	10	71	12
General aviation	601	6	76	13
Material service & resources	414	4	27	5
Other	331	3	(17)	(3)
Total	**10,043**	**100**	**584**	**100**

Principal Operating Units
Military Aircraft (F-16, A-12)
Submarines (SSN 688, Trident, Seawolf)
Land Systems (M1 tank)
General Aviation (Cessna Citation, Caravan)
Material Service (sand, gravel, lime, coal)
Electronic Systems (SINCGARS, avionics)
Missile Systems (Tomahawk, Sparrow, Stinger)
Space Systems (Atlas, Centaur)

RANKINGS

44th in *Fortune* 500 Industrial Cos.
117th in *Fortune* Global 500 Industrial Cos.
21st in *Fortune* 50 Exporters
72nd in *Forbes* Sales 500
381st in *Business Week* 1000

COMPETITION

Boeing
Daimler-Benz
FMC
General Electric
General Motors
Litton
Lockheed
Martin Marietta
McDonnell Douglas
Northrop
Raytheon
Rockwell International
Tenneco
Textron
Thiokol
Thomson
United Technologies
Vulcan
Electronics companies

GENERAL ELECTRIC COMPANY

OVERVIEW

General Electric is a $53.9 billion conglomerate with roots to Thomas Edison's 1879 invention of the light bulb. GE's market value of $58 billion is 2nd only to Exxon in the US. Based on sales, GE is the 5th largest company in the US and the 7th largest in the world. GE's business segments range from financial services (GE Financial Services, GEFS) to aircraft engines to broadcasting (National Broadcasting Company).

GE's strategy for the 1980s was to retain only those businesses with the potential to become first or 2nd in the world market. GE enters the 1990s with a leading market position in each of its business segments and an overall ranking of 3rd most profitable company in the world in 1989. GE's top producer is GEFS (financing, insurance, brokerage [Kidder, Peabody], equipment leasing), with 1989 revenues of $12.9 billion. If it were a bank, GEFS would be the 4th largest (ranked by assets) in the US. In 1989 GE ranked 7th among US companies in total R&D spending.

GE's sophisticated management training institute in Crotonville, New York, has long been a model for American businesses. As a part of its recent restructuring, GE has developed a "Work-Out" program that brings together employees from all functions and levels to identify and cut bureaucratic impediments from the system and propose and implement faster, simpler processes.

NYSE symbol: GE
Incorporated: New York, 1892
Fiscal year ends: December 31

WHO

Chairman and CEO: John F. Welch, Jr., age 54, $2,648,700 pay
VC and Executive Officer: Lawrence A. Bossidy, age 55, $1,782,200 pay
VC and Executive Officer: Edward E. Hood, Jr., age 59, $1,437,900 pay
SVP Finance: Dennis D. Dammerman, age 44
Auditors: KPMG Peat Marwick
Employees: 292,000

WHEN

General Electric was established in 1892 in New York, the result of a merger between the Thomson-Houston Company and the Edison General Electric Company, with combined sales of $14 million. Charles Coffin was GE's first president and Thomas Edison one of its directors. Edison left the company in 1894.

GE's financial strength (backed by the Morgan banking house) and focus on research (it started one of the first corporate research laboratories in 1900) led to the company's success. Products included elevators (1885), trolleys, motors, toasters (1905), and other appliances under both the GE and Hotpoint label, and the light bulb. In the 1920s GE joined Westinghouse and AT&T in a joint venture, Radio Corporation of America (RCA), a radio broadcasting company. GE sold off its RCA holdings (1930) because of an antitrust ruling (one of 65 antitrust actions against GE between 1911 and 1967).

By 1940 GE had grown to a company of 86,000 employees and $456 million in sales. From 1940 to 1952 annual sales increased sixfold to $2.6 billion. GE entered the computer industry in 1956 (ranked 5th in computer sales by 1965) but abandoned the business in 1970 (sold to Honeywell) because of operating losses. By 1980 GE had achieved sales of $27 billion from products that included plastics, consumer electronics, diesel electric motors, nuclear reactors, and jet engines.

Since 1981 GE's strategy has been to retain and pursue only high-performance ventures. GE's targets have become medical equipment, financial services, and high-performance plastics and ceramics. GE bought Employers Reinsurance in 1984 ($1.1 billion); RCA, including National Broadcasting Company, in 1986 ($6.4 billion); 80% of the investment banking firm of Kidder, Peabody in 1986 for $600 million; and CGR medical equipment from Thomson of France in 1987. The latter was part of an exchange for GE's consumer-electronics division (radios, televisions, VCRs). During that same period GE shed its businesses in central air conditioning (1982), housewares (1984), mining (1984), and semiconductors (1988).

By 1989 GE had sold operations that comprised 25% of its 1980 sales and had embarked on a $10 billion share repurchase program. The strategy paid off. Between 1985 and 1989 GE increased revenues 91% and boosted its stock price 128%.

WHERE

HQ: 3135 Easton Turnpike, Fairfield, CT 06431
Phone: 203-373-2211
FAX: 203-373-3131

GE is a large, diversified company with operations all over the world.

	1989 Sales		1989 Operating Income	
	$ mil	% of total	$ mil	% of total
US	47,805	88	6,070	86
Foreign	6,769	12	974	14
Adjustments	(690)	—	(8)	—
Total	**53,884**	**100**	**7,036**	**100**

WHAT

	1989 Sales		1989 Operating Income	
	$ mil	% of total	$ mil	% of total
Aerospace	5,205	9	646	9
Aircraft engines	6,794	12	1,050	15
Broadcasting	3,391	6	603	9
Industrial products	6,358	12	847	12
Major appliances	5,620	10	399	6
Materials	4,896	9	1,057	15
Power systems	5,001	9	507	7
Technical products & services	4,351	8	589	8
Financing	7,333	14	1,152	17
Insurance	2,710	5	407	6
Securities	2,897	5	(53)	(1)
Other	324	1	(192)	(3)
Adjustments	(996)	—	24	—
Total	**53,884**	**100**	**7,036**	**100**

Products/Services
Aircraft engines
Appliances
Broadcasting
Electrical and electronic equipment
Electronics
Finance and insurance
Generators
Information services
Lighting products
Locomotives
Medical imaging equipment
Military vehicles
Plastics
Radar
Satellites
Spacecraft
Transformers
Turbines

HOW MUCH

	9 Yr. Growth	1980	1981	1982	1983	1984	1985	1986	1987	1988	1989
Sales ($ mil)	8.9%	24,959	27,240	26,500	26,797	27,947	28,285	35,211	39,315	49,414	53,884
Net income ($ mil)	11.2%	1,514	1,652	1,817	2,024	2,280	2,336	2,492	2,119	3,386	3,939
Income as % of sales	—	6.1%	6.1%	6.9%	7.6%	8.2%	8.3%	7.1%	5.4%	6.9%	7.3%
Earnings per share ($)	11.2%	1.66	1.82	2.00	2.23	2.52	2.57	2.73	2.33	3.73	4.32
Stock price – high ($)	—	15.75	17.47	25.00	29.44	29.69	36.94	44.38	66.38	47.88	64.75
Stock price – low ($)	—	11.00	12.78	13.75	22.69	24.13	27.81	33.25	38.75	38.38	43.50
Stock price – close ($)	17.3%	15.31	14.34	23.72	29.31	28.31	36.38	43.00	44.13	44.75	64.50
P/E – high	—	9	10	13	13	12	14	16	28	13	15
P/E – low	—	7	7	7	10	10	11	12	17	10	10
Dividends per share ($)	9.7%	0.74	0.79	0.84	0.94	1.03	1.12	1.19	1.33	1.46	1.70
Book value per share ($)	11.0%	9.00	10.02	11.19	12.39	13.82	15.25	16.57	18.25	20.47	23.09

1989 Year End:
Debt ratio: 43.5%
Return on equity: 19.8%
Cash (mil): $2,258
Assets (mil): $128,344
Long-term debt (mil): $16,110
Number of shares (mil): 905
Dividends:
1989 average yield: 2.6%
1989 payout: 39.4%
Market value (mil): $58,358

RANKINGS

5th in *Fortune* 500 Industrial Cos.
7th in *Fortune* Global 500 Industrial Cos.
4th in *Fortune* 50 Exporters
5th in *Forbes* Sales 500
3rd in *Business Week* 1000
5th in *Business Week* Global 1000

COMPETITION

Maytag
Philips
Siemens
United Technologies
Westinghouse
Whirlpool

GE also competes with dozens of other companies, from finance companies to broadcasters.

GENERAL MILLS, INC.

OVERVIEW

Minneapolis-based General Mills is the 2nd largest producer of breakfast cereals ($1.3 billion sales) after Kellogg and holds the first- or 2nd-place position in other food categories, including dessert mixes (#1, $420 million), flour and dry mixes (#1, $270 million), yogurt (#2, $200 million), frozen seafood (#1, $190 million), ready-to-make dinners (#1, $170 million), fruit snacks (#2, $100 million), and microwave popcorn (#2, $80 million). Consumer foods generated nearly $4 billion in sales in 1989.

General Mills's Red Lobster and The Olive Garden restaurants, with sales of $1.3 billion and $300 million, respectively, make the company the nation's 5th largest food-service company. International markets are served via subsidiaries in Canada, Holland, Spain, France, and Latin America.

In the realm of philanthropy, General Mills is the 3rd largest national contributor of food to the Second Harvest food bank, to which it donated nearly 7 million pounds in 1989.

WHEN

In 1866 Cadwallader Washburn founded the Washburn Crosby Company. After winning a gold medal for flour at an 1880 exhibition, the company introduced the Gold Medal Flour trademark. In 1921 advertising manager Sam Gale created fictional spokeswoman Betty Crocker so that correspondence to housewives could go out with her signature. The company introduced Wheaties ready-to-eat cereal in 1924. James F. Bell, made president of Washburn Crosby in 1925, consolidated the company with other mills around the country (including Red Star, Rocky Mountain Elevator, and Kalispell Flour) to form General Mills, the world's largest miller. Although the companies operated independently of one another, a corporate headquarters coordinated advertising and merchandising.

General Mills introduced convenience foods such as Bisquick (1930s) and Cheerios (1941) and supported these brands with radio and, later, television advertising. Along with flour these products generated sufficient sales to permit General Mills to keep paying dividends throughout the 1930s and 1940s. During WWII the company produced goods needed for the war, such as ordnance equipment, and developed chemical and electronics divisions.

When Edwin Rawlings became CEO in 1961, he closed down 1/2 the flour mills and divested such unprofitable lines as electronics. This cost $200 million in annual sales but freed resources for such acquisitions as the Tom Huston Peanut Company (snack foods, 1966), Kenner Products (toys, 1967), and Parker Brothers (board games, 1968). The Kenner and Parker purchases made General Mills the world's largest toy company. Other acquisitions included Gorton's (frozen seafood, 1968), Monet (jewelry, 1968), David Crystal (Izod sportswear, 1969), Red Lobster (restaurants,1970), Eddie Bauer (outerwear, 1971), and Talbots (women's clothing, 1973).

In 1977 the company sold the chemical division and bought Ship 'n Shore (blouses), Wallpapers to Go (interior decorating supplies), and the rights to Yoplait yogurt. The restaurant division started The Olive Garden restaurants (1983), which along with Red Lobster led the restaurant industry in sales growth in 1989.

When toy and fashion division profits fell more than 30% in 1984, the company spun off these groups as Kenner Parker Toys and Crystal Brands (1985). Reemphasizing food, General Mills sold Wallpapers to Go (1986) and Eddie Bauer and Talbots (1989) and entered a venture with Nestlé to market cereal in Europe (1989). Today General Mills focuses solely on 2 areas, consumer foods and chain restaurants — down from 13 distinct industries of the 1970s.

HOW MUCH

	9 Yr. Growth	1980	1981	1982	1983	1984	1985	1986	1987	1988	1989
Sales ($ mil)	3.4%	4,170	4,852	5,312	5,551	5,601	4,285	4,587	5,189	5,179	5,621
Net income ($ mil)	7.1%	170	197	226	245	233	115	184	222	265	315
Income as % of sales	—	4.1%	4.1%	4.2%	4.4%	4.2%	2.7%	4.0%	4.3%	5.1%	5.6%
Earnings per share ($)	9.6%	1.69	1.95	2.23	2.45	2.49	1.29	2.06	2.50	3.05	3.85
Stock price – high ($)	—	15.19	15.31	19.75	27.38	28.88	30.00	34.63	47.38	62.13	58.00
Stock price – low ($)	—	11.75	9.50	13.38	16.44	22.13	20.81	23.88	28.25	40.75	43.13
Stock price – close ($)	17.1%	12.50	13.50	17.94	24.38	26.13	25.44	30.56	43.13	49.63	51.88
P/E – high	—	9	8	9	11	12	23	17	19	20	15
P/E – low	—	7	5	6	7	9	16	12	11	13	11
Dividends per share ($)	12.7%	0.64	0.72	0.82	0.92	1.02	1.12	1.13	1.25	1.60	1.88
Book value per share ($)	(1.2%)	10.16	11.37	12.25	12.84	13.53	11.51	7.61	8.28	7.75	9.08

1989 Year End:
Debt ratio: 42.3%
Return on equity: 45.7%
Cash (mil): $11
Current ratio: 0.81
Long-term debt (mil): $536
Number of shares(mil): 81
Dividends:
1989 average yield: 3.6%
1989 payout: 48.8%
Market value (mil): $4,181

Stock Price History high/low 1980-89

NYSE symbol: GIS
Incorporated: Delaware, 1928
Fiscal year ends: Last Sunday in May

NYSE symbol: GIS

WHO

Chairman and CEO: H. Brewster Atwater, Jr., age 58, $1,431,382 pay
VC and Chief Financial and Administrative Officer: F. Caleb Blodgett, age 62, $1,069,402 pay
VC: Arthur R. Schulze, age 58, $764,673 pay (prior to promotion)
President and COO: Mark H. Willes, age 48, $997,290 pay
Auditors: KPMG Peat Marwick
Employees: 83,800

WHERE

HQ: 1 General Mills Blvd., PO Box 1113, Minneapolis, MN 55440
Phone: 612-540-2311
FAX: 612-540-4925

General Mills has plants and mills in 9 US states, Canada, and several foreign countries and exports its products worldwide. Its 2 restaurant chains operate 635 locations in 38 states and Canada.

WHAT

	1989 Sales		1989 Operating Income	
	$ mil	% of total	$ mil	% of total
Consumer foods	3,999	71	452	78
Restaurants	1,622	29	128	22
Adjustments	—	(35)	—	
Total	**5,621**	**100**	**545**	**100**

Brand Names

Cereals
Cheerios
Cinnamon Toast Crunch
Clusters
Cocoa Puffs
Crispy Wheats 'N Raisins
Fiber One
Golden Grahams
Kix
Lucky Charms
Oatmeal Raisin Crisp
Oatmeal Swirlers
Raisin Nut Bran
Total
Total Oatmeal
Total Raisin Bran
Trix
Wheaties

Other Foods
Bac*Os
Betty Crocker
Bisquick
Bugles
Creamy Deluxe
Fruit Roll-Ups
Fruit Wrinkles
Gold Medal
Gorton's
Hamburger Helper
MicroRave (popcorn)
Nature Valley
Oriental Classics
Pop Secret
Potato Buds
Suddenly Salad
Tuna Helper
Yoplait

Restaurants
The Olive Garden
Red Lobster

RANKINGS

85th in *Fortune* 500 Industrial Cos.
227th in *Fortune* Global 500 Industrial Cos.
135th in *Forbes* Sales 500
101st in *Business Week* 1000
271st in *Business Week* Global 1000

COMPETITION

Borden
BSN
Campbell Soup
Cargill
Grand Metropolitan
Kellogg
McDonald's
PepsiCo
Philip Morris
Quaker Oats
Ralston Purina
TW Holdings
Wendy's
Whitman
Other food and restaurant companies

GENERAL MOTORS CORPORATION

OVERVIEW

Detroit-based General Motors is the world's largest company (nearly $125 billion in 1989 sales), the biggest private employer, the biggest R&D spender ($5.2 billion in 1989), and the largest automaker, outselling Ford and Chrysler combined. Nearly 81% of GM sales comes from automotive products.

GM produces cars and trucks under the Chevrolet, Buick, Cadillac, Pontiac, Oldsmobile, and GMC nameplates in the US, leading the domestic car market with a 35% share. GM also provides financial and insurance services and, through its Electronic Data Systems and Hughes Aircraft units, manages information systems and manufactures weapon systems, locomotives, and commercial satellites.

Despite a declining US car market share, GM's profits rose from $1 billion in 1982 to $4.2 billion in 1989. New CEO Stempel's biggest challenge is to galvanize GM's giant organization to adapt to rapidly changing markets. GM plans European expansion (through ventures with Saab and Hungary's state-owned truck maker) and continued cost reduction and technological improvement.

WHEN

In its early years the automobile industry consisted of hundreds of firms, each producing a few models. William Durant, who bought and reorganized a failing Buick Motors in 1904, reasoned that if several makers united, each would be protected in an off year. After attempts to join with Ford and Maxwell failed, Durant formed the General Motors Company in Flint, Michigan, in 1908.

Durant had bought 17 companies (including Oldsmobile, Cadillac, and Pontiac) by 1910, the year a bankers' syndicate gained control and forced him to step down. In a 1915 stock swap, Durant regained control of GM through Chevrolet, a company he had formed in 1911 with race car driver Louis Chevrolet. In 1919 GM acquired Fisher Body and Frigidaire (sold 1979) and created the GM Acceptance Corporation (auto financing).

Du Pont, looking to invest company profits, began purchasing GM stock in 1917. Durant resigned in 1920 and sold his stock to Du Pont, bringing its total stake to 23%. Du Pont kept this share until a 1957 Supreme Court antitrust ruling forced it to divest.

Alfred Sloan, president from 1923 to 1937, implemented a decentralized management system, now emulated worldwide. Sloan remained chairman until 1956, and his 1963 book, *My Years with General Motors*, is considered a management classic.

GM competed by offering models ranging from luxury to economy, colors besides black, and yearly style modifications. By 1927 GM had become the industry sales leader. Later improvements included independent front-wheel suspension and automatic transmissions. Following WWII GM expanded globally.

The first US company to downsize its cars (1977) in response to Japanese imports, GM introduced a line of front-wheel drive compacts in 1979. A $70 billion, 10-year capital investment program (which modernized or built 40 plants) initiated in 1979 included a company-wide restructuring and cost-cutting program. Under Roger Smith, CEO from 1981 to 1990, GM laid off 40,000 workers, whose plight was depicted in the award-winning 1989 film *Roger and Me*.

GM bought Electronic Data Systems (1984) and Hughes Aircraft (1986) and entered into more than 50 joint ventures in the 1980s. Since 1985 GM has redesigned over 84% of its cars, and in 1988 Chevrolet launched the Geo line of compacts. Still, intense competition from imports and Ford dropped GM's market share from 47% in 1979 to 35% by 1989.

President and COO Robert Stempel became CEO in 1990. The Saturn Corporation, which will produce GM's first new nameplate since 1926, is scheduled to unveil its offering by the end of 1990.

HOW MUCH

	9 Yr. Growth	1980	1981	1982	1983	1984	1985	1986	1987	1988	1989
Sales ($ mil)	9.0%	57,729	62,699	60,026	74,582	83,890	96,372	102,813	101,781	121,816	124,993
Net income ($ mil)	—	(763)	333	963	3,730	4,517	3,999	2,945	3,551	4,632	4,224
Income as % of sales	—	(1.3%)	0.5%	1.6%	5.0%	5.4%	4.2%	2.9%	3.5%	3.8%	3.4%
Earnings per share ($)	—	(1.33)	0.54	1.55	5.92	7.11	6.14	4.11	5.03	*6.82*	6.17
Stock price – high ($)	—	29.44	29.00	32.25	40.00	41.38	42.50	44.31	47.06	44.06	50.50
Stock price – low ($)	—	19.75	16.94	17.00	28.00	30.50	32.13	32.94	25.00	30.00	39.13
Stock price – close ($)	7.3%	22.50	19.25	31.19	37.19	39.19	35.19	33.00	30.69	41.75	42.25
P/E – high	—	—	54	21	7	6	7	11	9	6	8
P/E – low	—	—	32	11	5	4	5	8	5	4	6
Dividends per share ($)	8.2%	1.48	1.20	1.20	1.40	2.38	2.50	2.50	2.50	2.50	3.00
Book value per share ($)	7.6%	29.61	28.72	28.87	32.52	37.97	46.29	47.99	53.13	57.81	57.37

1989 Year End:
Debt ratio: 61.3%
Return on equity: 10.7%
Cash (mil): $5,170
Current ratio: —
Long-term debt (mil): $55,333
Number of shares (mil): 606
Dividends:
1989 average yield: 7.1%
1989 payout: 48.6%
Market value (mil): $25,590

NYSE symbol: GM
Incorporated: Delaware, 1916
Fiscal year ends: December 31

WHO

Chairman and CEO: Robert C. Stempel, age 56, $725,000 pay (prior to promotion)
President: Lloyd E. Reuss, age 53, $567,000 pay (prior to promotion)
EVP and CFO: Robert T. O'Connell, age 51
Auditors: Deloitte & Touche
Employees: 775,100

WHERE

HQ: 3044 W. Grand Blvd., Detroit, MI 48202
Phone: 313-556-5000
FAX: 313-556-5108

GM has manufacturing and other facilities at 240 US locations and in 9 other countries. GM cars and trucks are sold by 15,400 dealerships.

	1989 Sales		1989 Net Income	
	$ mil	% of total	$ mil	% of total
US & Canada	100,985	80	1,567	37
Europe	19,345	15	1,830	43
Other countries	6,602	5	834	20
Adjustments	(1,939)	—	(7)	—
Total	**124,993**	**100**	**4,224**	**100**

WHAT

	1989 Sales		1989 Operating Income	
	$ mil	% of total	$ mil	% of total
Automotive prods.	99,106	81	5,131	90
Financing & insurance	11,254	9	—	—
Other products	12,852	10	580	10
Adjustments	1,781	—	7,564	—
Total	**124,993**	**100**	**13,275**	**100**

Cars & Trucks
Buick
Cadillac
Chevrolet
GMC
Lotus
Oldsmobile
Opel
Pontiac

Major Divisions & Subsidiaries
Allison Gas Turbine Division
Allison Transmission Division
Delco Electronics Corp.
Electro-Motive Division (locomotives)
Electronic Data Systems Corp.
General Motors Acceptance Corp. (GMAC)
GMAC Mortgage Corp.
GMFanuc Robotics Corp.
GM Hughes Electronics Corp.
Hughes Aircraft Co.
Motors Insurance Corp.
Power Products and Defense Operations

RANKINGS

1st in *Fortune* 500 Industrial Cos.
1st in *Fortune* Global 500 Industrial Cos.
2nd in *Fortune* 50 Exporters
1st in *Forbes* Sales 500
6th in *Business Week* 1000
26th in *Business Week* Global 1000

COMPETITION

Arthur Andersen
Chrysler
Daimler-Benz
Fiat
Ford
Honda
Hyundai
IBM
Mitsubishi
Navistar
Nissan
PACCAR
Renault
Toyota
Volkswagen
Volvo
Defense contractors
Electronics companies

GENERAL RE CORPORATION

OVERVIEW

General Re has consistently been the nation's largest reinsurer — a business that sells insurance for part or all of the risk of other insurance companies — since the 1940s (through subsidiary General Reinsurance) and is currently the 3rd largest reinsurer in the world. Most of General Re's business is written on an excess-of-loss basis, meaning that the company pays only after a primary insurer's losses exceed a specified sum.

The company provides property-casualty reinsurance in the US primarily through its General Reinsurance unit. General Re is consistently profitable: even while the insurance industry was exposed to unprecedented catastrophic losses amounting to nearly $8 billion in 1989 from the California earthquake, Hurricane Hugo, and other incidents, General Re's domestic property-casualty operations showed a profit. In 1989 the company handled more than 12,000 active and 10,000 potential insurance claims representing over $2 billion in reinsurance losses.

General Re also provides property-casualty reinsurance internationally in 7 countries (accounting for 5% of 1989 revenue).

WHEN

General Casualty and Surety Reinsurance Corporation was organized in 1921 with A. Duncan Reid as president. The New York–based company was a provider of reinsurance at a time when the field was virtually nonexistent in the US. By 1923 the company's name had changed to General Reinsurance Corporation; Carl Hansen, an underwriting expert, became VP and general manager. By 1925 Hansen and 2 partners controlled the company, and General Reinsurance began providing property and casualty reinsurance — its domain to this day.

Reinsurance was a small market, and business grew slowly until the 1940s. The company began to take off when, in 1945, the Mellon family united its privately owned Mellon Indemnity with General Re and took over operations. Edward Lowry, Jr., was brought in to head the company in 1946. At that time, reinsurers paid claims on losses but provided no other services. Lowry, recognizing that reinsurers were the first to know when a branch of the industry was at risk, began offering management consulting services, which have become important to General Re in customer retention.

As a result of the merger General Re held a near monopoly on reinsurance. From 1945 to 1980, General Re's policy was to charge the highest premiums in the business. Thus, the company was consistently the largest and most profitable reinsurance enterprise in the US.

Lowry retired from General Re in 1960. Successor James Cathcart began international expansion in 1962, starting Zurich-based International Reinsurance and buying Stockholm's Swedish Atlas Reinsurance and an interest in Reinsurance Company of Australasia. During the late 1960s and early 1970s General Re expanded its facultative group (companies that insure against specific risks such as earthquakes), started in 1954. Beginning from a negligible revenue base, the group contributed 1/2 of General Re's premium income by 1978. During the mid-1970s the company also began reinsuring against medical malpractice and equipment leasing losses.

By 1978 General Re had suffered stiff price competition from smaller start-ups; concurrently, approximately a dozen of the company's senior managers left, some to form competitor Trenwick Re. General Re invested in other insurers in the 1980s, buying British-based Trident Insurance Group (1980, sold in 1985) and Monarch Insurance Company of Ohio (1985). Now based in Stamford, Connecticut, General Re's goal is to be the #1 reinsurer worldwide.

HOW MUCH

	9 Yr. Growth	1980	1981	1982	1983	1984	1985	1986	1987	1988	1989
Sales ($ mil)	10.8%	1,104	1,423	1,498	1,659	1,842	2,123	3,175	3,448	2,729	2,771
Net income ($ mil)	16.2%	154	178	207	192	72	159	279	486	513	599
Income as % of sales	—	14.0%	12.5%	13.8%	11.6%	3.9%	7.5%	8.8%	14.1%	18.8%	21.6%
Earnings per share ($)	15.6%	1.77	2.03	2.33	2.13	0.80	1.69	2.74	4.79	5.39	6.52
Stock price – high ($)	—	15.31	21.88	32.25	36.50	34.13	53.13	69.50	68.88	59.38	96.25
Stock price – low ($)	—	9.38	12.84	16.94	26.00	23.13	30.19	49.25	46.00	45.50	54.38
Stock price – close ($)	23.1%	13.41	20.19	31.88	34.25	31.88	50.06	55.50	55.88	55.50	87.13
P/E – high	—	9	11	14	17	43	31	25	14	11	15
P/E – low	—	5	6	7	12	29	18	18	10	8	8
Dividends per share ($)	16.3%	0.35	0.44	0.54	0.64	0.72	0.78	0.88	1.00	1.20	1.36
Book value per share ($)	15.0%	9.70	11.11	12.64	14.60	15.16	18.50	23.47	26.21	29.04	34.31

1989 Year End:
Debt ratio: 8.3%
Return on equity: 20.6%
Cash (mil): $27
Assets (mil): $10,390
Long-term debt (mil): $278
Number of shares (mil): 90
Dividends:
1989 average yield: 1.6%
1989 payout: 20.9%
Market value (mil): $7,833

Stock Price History high/low 1980-89

NYSE symbol: GRN
Incorporated: Delaware, 1980
Fiscal year ends: December 31

WHO

Chairman, President, and CEO: Ronald E. Ferguson, age 48, $1,201,197 pay
VC: John C. Etling, age 54, $858,160 pay
VP, General Counsel, and Secretary: Edmond F. Rondepierre, age 60, $446,812 pay
VP Investments: Jerry S. Wilbourn, age 50, $386,000 pay
VP Finance: Ronald G. Anderson, age 41, $346,840 pay
Auditors: Coopers & Lybrand
Employees: 2,379

WHERE

HQ: 695 E. Main St., Stamford, CT 06904
Phone: 203-328-5000
FAX: 203-328-5329

General Re conducts business in the US and Canada and through 11 offices in Australia, Egypt, England, Switzerland, Japan, Spain, and New Zealand.

	1989 Sales		1989 Pretax Income	
	$ mil	% of total	$ mil	% of total
US/Canada	2,631	95	697	95
Foreign	140	5	36	5
Adjustments	—	—	3	—
Total	**2,771**	**100**	**736**	**100**

WHAT

Domestic Operations
General Reinsurance Corp.
General Re Services Corp.
General Star Indemnity Co.
General Star Management Co.
General Star National Insurance Co.
Genesis Underwriting Management Co.
Herbert Clough, Inc. (reinsurance intermediary)
North Star Reinsurance Corp.
United States Aviation Underwriters, Inc.

International Operations
General Re Correduría de Reaseguros, S.A. (Spain)
General Reinsurance Corp. (Europe)
General Reinsurance Ltd. (England)
Reinsurance Company of Australasia Ltd. (Australia/New Zealand)

RANKINGS

30th in *Fortune* 50 Diversified Financial Cos.
302nd in *Forbes* Sales 500
68th in *Business Week* 1000
215th in *Business Week* Global 1000

COMPETITION

Aetna
AIG
CIGNA
Kemper
Lloyd's of London
Metropolitan
Prudential
Tokio Marine & Fire
USF&G

GENERAL SIGNAL CORPORATION

OVERVIEW

General Signal, based in Stamford, Connecticut, is a leading supplier of equipment for the electrical, semiconductor, process control, and transportation industries. It is a diversified conglomerate with $1.9 billion in sales and products ranging from industrial valves to freight car braking equipment to advanced photolithography products for the semiconductor manufacturing industry.

Of General Signal's 4 primary business segments (process controls, technology industries, electrical controls, and transportation controls), process controls is its largest. This segment supplies mixing equipment, industrial valves and pumps, and control systems predominantly to the chemical, pulp and paper, and water and wastewater treatment industries.

General Signal's technology industries segment is working with the SEMATECH consortium to develop the next-generation manufacturing process for the semiconductor industry. The transportation segment supplies the rail industry with signaling, control, and braking systems, and the bus industry with electronic fareboxes. GS's electrical controls segment includes power protection equipment, uninterruptable power system products, and alarm systems.

WHEN

General Railway Signal Company, incorporated in 1904, set up in Rochester, New York, to manufacture railway safety equipment (railroad signals, crossing gates, automatic train controls, etc.) and grew to become the largest supplier in the US, with 50% of the market in 1930. Sales grew from $8.7 million in 1930 to $15.9 million in 1954 to $21.7 million in 1959.

There was little change in General Railway Signal's product line until 1960 when it acquired Regina (vacuum cleaners). Two years later, following the hiring of Nathan Owen (former partner in a venture capital firm, J.H. Whitney) as CEO, the company launched an aggressive diversification effort. Its present name was adopted in 1963.

GS's early acquisitions were specialty electronics and electrical equipment companies. Between 1961 and 1966 GS acquired 8 such companies. Owen's strategy to become a small General Electric changed with the acquisition of New York Air Brake (1967), a maker of air brakes and pneumatic and hydraulic control systems. The acquisition doubled the size of GS and put it on the *Fortune* 500 list in 1967 with sales of $169.5 million (ranked 410th). It also gave GS a foothold in the water and wastewater treatment business. By 1972 GS had acquired 5 more pollution control–related companies.

GS entered the energy control business by acquiring Sola Basic Industries (specialty products for utility companies, 1977) and Leeds & Northrup (devices for measuring and controlling temperature and pressure, 1978).

Between 1980 and 1985 GS ventured into the semiconductor and telecommunications equipment businesses. Acquisitions included Xynetics (semiconductor fabrication systems), Kayex (silicon crystal–growing furnaces), and Telecommunications Technology (electronic testing equipment for telecommunications systems). Of GS's 17 acquisitions between 1981 and 1985, 8 were in the semiconductor business and 4 were in the telecommunications market. GS sold Regina in 1984.

GS's earnings dropped from $109 million in 1984 to $49 million in 1985, caused in part by a slowdown in the semiconductor capital equipment market. Since the hiring of Chairman and CEO Edmund Carpenter (1988), GS has pared its operations, sold off units, sold assets to lower debt resulting from the company's buyback of 30% of its stock, and merged its 45 units into 28. In 1990 GS announced its intention to sell 3 of its semiconductor businesses.

HOW MUCH

	9 Yr. Growth	1980	1981	1982	1983	1984	1985	1986	1987	1988	1989
Sales ($ mil)	2.6%	1,522	1,702	1,622	1,575	1,787	1,801	1,583	1,603	1,760	1,918
Net income ($ mil)	(3.1%)	104	117	108	90	109	49	75	69	25	78
Income as % of sales	—	6.8%	6.9%	6.6%	5.7%	6.1%	2.7%	4.7%	4.3%	1.4%	4.1%
Earnings per share ($)	0.2%	4.01	4.18	3.81	3.12	3.75	1.71	2.58	2.45	0.91	4.09
Stock price – high ($)	—	54.25	51.38	47.00	52.38	54.00	53.88	54.25	61.25	56.50	57.88
Stock price – low ($)	—	28.25	33.38	28.00	40.50	39.63	37.00	39.25	33.25	40.00	45.75
Stock price – close ($)	0.8%	44.75	38.63	44.88	50.75	47.00	46.38	44.25	47.00	47.50	48.25
P/E – high	—	14	12	12	17	14	32	21	25	62	14
P/E – low	—	7	8	7	13	11	22	15	14	44	11
Dividends per share ($)	3.4%	1.33	1.51	1.62	1.68	1.74	1.80	1.80	1.80	1.80	1.80
Book value per share ($)	0.8%	24.78	27.17	28.66	29.66	31.53	31.47	32.33	33.02	24.19	26.50

1989 Year End:
Debt ratio: 39.6%
Return on equity: 16.1%
Cash (mil): $24
Current ratio: 1.74
Long-term debt (mil): $331
Number of shares (mil): 19
Dividends:
1989 average yield: 3.7%
1989 payout: 44.0%
Market value (mil): $921

70
60
50
40
30
20
10
0

Stock Price History
high/low 1980-89

PSE and NYSE symbol: GSX
Incorporated: New York, 1904
Fiscal year ends: December 31

WHO

Chairman and CEO: Edmund M. Carpenter, age 48, $1,052,408 pay
SVP Finance and CFO: Stephen W. Nagy, age 49, $355,200 pay
Auditors: KPMG Peat Marwick
Employees: 19,400

WHERE

HQ: 1 High Ridge Park, PO Box 10010, Stamford, CT 06904
Phone: 203-357-8800
FAX: 203-329-4159

The company does business worldwide. It has 94 plants in the US and abroad, and subsidiaries in Australia, Canada, England, France, Germany, Holland, Hong Kong, Italy, Japan, Mexico, the Netherlands, New Zealand, Singapore, and Spain.

	1989 Sales		1989 Operating Income	
	$ mil	% of total	$ mil	% of total
US	1,659	83	134	83
Foreign	351	17	27	17
Adjustments	(92)	—	(28)	—
Total	**1,918**	**100**	**133**	**100**

WHAT

	1989 Sales		1989 Operating Income	
	$ mil	% of total	$ mil	% of total
Electrical controls	421	22	49	30
Process controls	727	38	82	51
Technology ind.	453	24	8	5
Transportation controls	289	15	21	13
Dispositions	28	1	1	1
Adjustments	—	—	(28)	—
Total	**1,918**	**100**	**133**	**100**

Process Controls
Distributed control systems
Electronic measurement and control instrumentation
High-vacuum pumps
Industrial aerators
Industrial valves (DeZurik)
Mechanical mixers (Labmaster)
Supervisory control and data acquisition systems

Technology Industries
Crystal-growing furnaces
Diffusion/deposition systems
Photolithography wafer steppers and lenses
TV and FM stereo transmission line, filters, and antennas
Wafer saws and polishers

Electrical Controls
Electrical fittings
Fire alarm systems
Power conditioning equipment
Signaling devices
Transformers

Transportation Controls
Cab, wayside, and centralized traffic-control components and systems
Centralized fleet-control systems and electronic fareboxes (General Farebox)
Pneumatic and hydraulic braking systems and controls (New York Air Brake)

RANKINGS

219th in *Fortune* 500 Industrial Cos.
412th in *Forbes* Sales 500
527th in *Business Week* 1000

COMPETITION

Cooper Industries
General Electric
Honeywell
Square D

GEORGIA-PACIFIC CORPORATION

OVERVIEW

Georgia-Pacific Corporation is now the world's largest forest products company, having surpassed International Paper and Weyerhaeuser in early 1990. In the US it is the largest manufacturer and distributor of building materials and ranks 2nd in production of printing and writing papers. Georgia-Pacific manufactures lumber, structural wood panels, shingles, gypsum wallboard, corrugated packaging, paper, tissue, newsprint, linerboard, and market pulp. Brand names include Spectrum business papers, AngelSoft tissue, and Delta paper towels.

Georgia-Pacific owns 7.4 million acres of timberland in the US and Canada, most of which is located in the Pacific Northwest, Maine, and the Southeast, and has manufacturing plants, research facilities, or distribution centers in all 48 contiguous states, as well as in Canada, Brazil, and the UK. In addition, the company owns several gypsum mines. Georgia-Pacific's timber management program plants approximately 35 million seedlings every year.

Georgia-Pacific's dependence on pulp and paper increased when its 1990 acquisition of Great Northern Nekoosa raised pulp and paper sales to more than 50% of the company's total.

WHEN

Owen Cheatham founded the Georgia Hardwood Lumber Company in Augusta, Georgia, in 1927 to wholesale hardwood lumber (which he bought from others). By 1938 the company was operating 5 southern sawmills and a few years later became the largest lumber supplier to the US armed forces during WWII.

In 1947 the company bought a plywood mill in Bellingham, Washington. Recognizing the potential of plywood (which was gaining rapid acceptance in the construction field), Cheatham acquired several more plywood mills in the late 1940s.

In 1951 Cheatham began an aggressive land buying spree that would give the company its first timberlands. The company moved its headquarters to Oregon in 1954 and 3 years later adopted its present name. In 1957 Georgia-Pacific entered the pulp and paper business by establishing a new mill at Toledo, Oregon, and embarked on a period of explosive growth. By 1960 the company had one million acres of timberland.

During the 1960s the company acquired several competitors and built new facilities that allowed it to diversify into containers, paperboard, tissue, and chemicals, producing its own chemicals for paper, resin, plywood glue, and other products. By 1968 the company had reached $1 billion in sales.

In 1972 the FTC forced Georgia-Pacific to sell 20% of its assets to reduce its size (the spinoff became Louisiana-Pacific). The following year, the company purchased Boise Cascade's wood products operations at Fort Bragg, California, and in 1975 acquired Exchange Oil and Gas.

In 1976 Chairman Robert Flowerree continued the diversification into chemicals and cautiously introduced cheaper substitutes for plywood, like waferboard. Under Flowerree the company acquired timberland in the South and modernized existing paper mills. In 1979 Georgia-Pacific bought Hudson Pulp and Paper and reached $5 billion in sales.

The company returned to Georgia in 1982, and in 1984 decided to sell most chemical operations unrelated to forest products. During the 1980s, because of a slump in the home-building industry, the company emphasized selling materials for home remodeling rather than home building.

In 1988 Georgia-Pacific purchased Brunswick Pulp and Paper in Georgia, greatly increasing its southern timber holdings. The 1990 $3.8 billion takeover of Great Northern Nekoosa increased consolidated debt $5 billion, prompting a $1 billion asset sale program.

HOW MUCH

	9 Yr. Growth	1980	1981	1982	1983	1984	1985	1986	1987	1988	1989
Sales ($ mil)	8.2%	5,016	5,414	5,402	6,469	6,682	6,716	7,223	8,603	9,509	10,171
Net income ($ mil)	11.7%	244	160	52	105	253	207	296	458	467	661
Income as % of sales	—	4.9%	3.0%	1.0%	1.6%	3.8%	3.1%	4.1%	5.3%	4.9%	6.5%
Earnings per share ($)	13.9%	2.28	1.49	0.50	0.96	2.24	1.80	2.64	4.21	4.75	7.37
Stock price – high ($)	—	34.88	32.38	27.25	31.88	25.75	27.38	41.25	52.75	42.88	62.00
Stock price – low ($)	—	21.50	17.75	13.25	22.38	18.00	20.50	24.75	22.75	30.75	36.63
Stock price – close ($)	7.6%	25.00	20.13	26.25	24.75	25.00	26.50	37.00	34.50	36.88	48.50
P/E – high	—	15	22	55	33	12	15	16	13	9	8
P/E – low	—	9	12	27	23	8	11	9	5	6	5
Dividends per share ($)	2.1%	1.20	1.20	1.05	0.60	0.70	0.80	0.85	1.05	1.25	1.45
Book value per share ($)	5.5%	19.32	19.47	19.63	19.83	19.85	20.80	22.84	25.59	27.79	31.35

1989 Year End:
Debt ratio: 46.2%
Return on equity: 24.9%
Cash (mil): $23
Current ratio: 1.98
Long-term debt (mil): $2,336
Number of shares (mil): 87
Dividends:
1989 average yield: 3.0%
1989 payout: 19.7%
Market value (mil): $4,203

Stock Price History high/low 1980-89

70 60 50 40 30 20 10 0

NYSE symbol: GP
Incorporated: Georgia, 1927
Fiscal year ends: December 31

WHO

Chairman and CEO: T. Marshall Hahn, Jr., age 63, $1,769,666 pay
VC: Harold L. Airington, age 62, $1,110,286 pay
President and COO: Ronald P. Hogan, age 49, $925,018 pay
EVP and CFO: James C. Van Meter, age 51, $601,673 pay
Auditors: Arthur Andersen & Co.
Employees: 44,000

WHERE

HQ: 133 Peachtree St. NE, Atlanta, GA 30303
Phone: 404-521-4000
FAX: 404-521-4422

The company has over 250 manufacturing facilities in the US, Canada, the UK, and Brazil.

WHAT

	1989 Sales		1989 Operating Income	
	$ mil	% of total	$ mil	% of total
Building products	6,088	60	533	36
Pulp & paper	4,042	40	917	63
Other	41	—	15	1
Adjustments	—	—	(118)	—
Total	**10,171**	**100**	**1,347**	**100**

Building Products
Adhesives
Building product–related chemicals
Doors
Fiberboard
Gypsum
Hardboard
Insulation
Lumber
Metal construction products
Particleboard
Roofing
Siding
Specialty products
Structural wood panels

Pulp & Paper Products
Computer paper
Containers
Envelopes
Market pulp
Packaging materials
Paperboard
Printing paper
Tissue
Writing paper

Paper Products Brand Names
AngelSoft
Big 'n Pretty
Big 'n Soft
Big 'n Thirsty
Coronet
Delta
MD
Sparkle

RANKINGS

41st in *Fortune* 500 Industrial Cos.
113th in *Fortune* Global 500 Industrial Cos.
68th in *Forbes* Sales 500
158th in *Business Week* 1000
495th in *Business Week* Global 1000

COMPETITION

Boise Cascade
Champion International
International Paper
James River
Kimberly-Clark
Manville
Mead
Scott
USG
Weyerhaeuser

GERBER PRODUCTS COMPANY

OVERVIEW

Gerber Products, based in Fremont, Michigan, is the world's leading producer of processed baby foods. The company's growing market share of baby food is now about 72% in the US. The company's other operations include infant and children's apparel, child-care products (nursers, vaporizers, humidifiers, toys, and infant care items), and life and health insurance.

The company's 183 varieties of baby food (which include First Foods fruits and vegetables, strained, junior and toddler wet products, dry cereals, juice, and bakery products) account for just over half of the company's sales, with the balance coming from Gerber's merchandise and service sectors.

Gerber's Apparel Group is divided into 3 subsidiaries: Buster Brown Apparel, Weather Tamer, and Gerber Childrenswear. Gerber Life Insurance sells insurance via mail and agents in all 50 states.

Gerber has maintained a record of solid earnings growth. The company's sales passed the $1 billion mark for the first time in 1989.

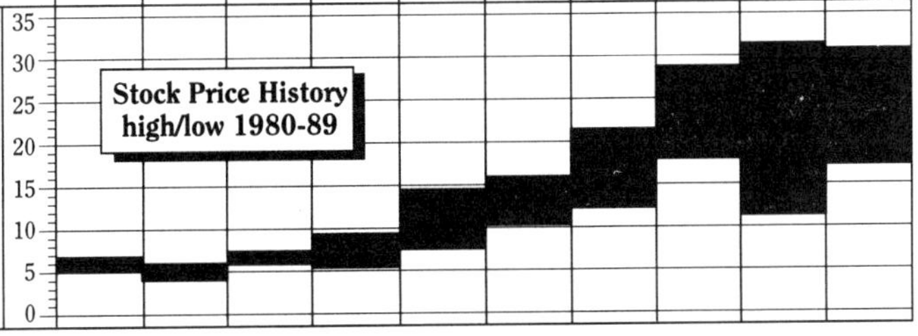

NYSE symbol: GEB
Incorporated: Michigan, 1901
Fiscal year ends: March 31

WHO

Chairman and CEO: David W. Johnson, age 56, $924,000 pay
President and COO: Alfred A. Piergallini, age 42
EVP; President, Gerber Products Division: Robert L. Johnston, age 57, $263,067 pay
EVP; General Manager, Apparel Group: Kenneth B. Peirce, age 46, $285,636 pay
EVP and CFO: Fred K. Schomer, age 50, $198,801 pay
Auditors: Ernst & Young
Employees: 14,691

WHEN

In 1901 Frank Gerber helped found and became president of the Fremont Canning Company, a small company established to provide a market for local produce in Fremont, Michigan. In 1920 Gerber's son Daniel joined the company and became assistant general manager in 1926.

By 1928 Daniel Gerber was married with a baby. At that time parents had to strain all of their babies' food by hand, and Daniel's wife Dorothy asked if he could do the straining at the cannery. This gave Daniel Gerber the idea for a line of commercially prepared baby food. Frank Gerber approved, and a series of marketing tests predicted success.

In late 1928 the company released its first line of Gerber strained baby foods (peas, carrots, spinach, prunes, and vegetable soup), which sold for 15¢ a can. The Gerbers began using a charcoal sketch of a baby by artist Dorothy Hope Smith in advertisements, putting it also on baby food labels in 1932. The Gerber baby became a successful trademark, and today Gerber keeps the original sketch under glass in the company vault.

Sales increased during the 1930s, which led the company to introduce new varieties. At the same time Gerber began issuing consumer information on such topics as nutrition, child care, and home economics.

In 1941 the company changed its name to the Gerber Products Company and 2 years later dropped all of its adult foods. Consumer demand led Gerber to open new plants in Oakland, California (1943); Rochester, New York (1950); and Niagara, Ontario (1950). Frank Gerber died in 1952.

During the 1960s Gerber expanded into a number of foreign countries while diversifying its product line to include toys, lotions, vaporizers, bibs, and vinyl baby pants (the last would become part of the Gerber Babywear line). The company began producing its own metal cans in 1962. In 1968 it organized Gerber Life Insurance and in 1970 entered the child-care business by acquiring Jack & Jill School of Villa Park, which it reorganized as Gerber Children's Centers (sold in 1989).

By 1973 Gerber was the world's largest supplier of baby foods. In 1982 the company created a children's furniture division (sold in 1988) and in 1986 introduced its First Foods line of baby food (single-serving fruits and vegetables). That same year the company's market share dropped from around 69% to 52% when a rumor started of broken glass in its baby food jars. Gerber reestablished its reputation and in 1989 entered into a joint baby formula venture with Bristol-Myers. The Gerber family still owns a significant portion of the company.

WHERE

HQ: 445 State St., Fremont, MI 49412
Phone: 616-928-2000
FAX: 616-928-2723 (Public Relations)

The company owns baby food plants in Fremont, MI; Fort Smith, AR; and Asheville, NC. Foreign subsidiaries own baby food plants in Canada and Costa Rica. Nonfood products are manufactured at 34 plants in the United States, one in Canada, and 2 in the Dominican Republic.

Gerber markets its products throughout the US and in more than 65 other countries.

Foreign assets and operations are less than 10% of corporate totals.

WHAT

	1989 Sales		1989 Pretax Income	
	$ mil	% of total	$ mil	% of total
Gerber Products Division	598	56	125	76
Apparel Group	353	33	28	17
Other	117	11	11	7
Corporate	—	—	(28)	—
Total	**1,068**	**100**	**136**	**100**

Subsidiaries

Gerber Products Division
Baby food — 183 varieties
- Junior and toddler wet products
- Dry cereals
- Juices

General merchandise
- Nursers, toys, vaporizers, humidifiers

Apparel Group
Buster Brown Apparel, Inc.
- Playwear and hosiery

Gerber Childrenswear, Inc.
- Playwear, sleepers, infantwear

Weather Tamer, Inc.
- Snowsuits, rainwear, jackets

Other
Gerber Life Insurance Company

HOW MUCH

	9 Yr. Growth	1980	1981	1982	1983	1984	1985	1986	1987	1988	1989
Sales ($ mil)	6.6%	602	631	703	719	805	929	968	917	943	1,068
Net income ($ mil)	12.4%	30	34	39	39	50	56	46	37	53	85
Income as % of sales	—	4.9%	5.5%	5.6%	5.4%	6.2%	6.1%	4.7%	4.1%	5.6%	8.0%
Earnings per share ($)	12.2%	0.77	0.86	0.98	0.97	1.24	1.39	1.12	0.93	1.33	2.17
Stock price – high ($)	—	6.86	6.03	7.44	9.42	14.58	16.00	21.50	28.81	31.50	30.81
Stock price – low ($)	—	5.11	3.97	5.78	5.33	7.42	10.25	12.19	17.88	11.25	17.13
Stock price – close ($)	21.1%	5.25	5.94	6.36	8.21	14.17	12.38	21.19	20.69	17.25	29.31
P/E – high	—	9	7	8	10	12	12	19	31	24	14
P/E – low	—	7	5	6	5	6	7	11	19	8	8
Dividends per share ($)	8.3%	0.36	0.39	0.42	0.45	0.49	0.58	0.66	0.66	0.66	0.74
Book value per share ($)	5.1%	5.52	5.91	6.51	7.04	7.86	8.62	9.10	8.35	8.24	8.68

1989 Year End:
Debt ratio: 30.7%
Return on equity: 25.6%
Cash (mil): $34
Current ratio: 2.28
Long-term debt (mil): $146
Number of shares (mil): 38
Dividends:
- 1989 average yield: 2.5%
- 1989 payout: 34.0%

Market value (mil): $1,116

Stock Price History high/low 1980-89

35 30 25 20 15 10 5 0

RANKINGS

312th in *Fortune* 500 Industrial Cos.
380th in *Business Week* 1000

COMPETITION

BSN	H. J. Heinz
Hasbro	Ralston Purina

GIANT FOOD, INC.

OVERVIEW

Landover, Maryland–based Giant Food operates 151 stores in the Baltimore-Washington-Richmond corridor. It is the #1 grocer in both the Washington, DC, market (where it has an almost 50% share) and the Baltimore market. Most of the stores are located in shopping centers, 11 of which the company owns.

Giant Food differs from other retailers by its extraordinary degree of vertical integration. Company subsidiaries perform site analysis, buy real estate, design and construct stores, and produce advertisements. The company also produces many of its own products and offers some of its services to other companies.

Giant Food's high concentration of stores in a relatively small area allows it to exploit efficiencies in the manufacture and distribution of food and in advertising. The company also relies on state-of-the-art scanning and ordering systems and highly automated warehouses to reduce costs. SUPERdeals, a program initiated in 1990, offers large-size and multi-pack items at steep discounts.

Giant Food maintains a slow but steady rate of growth, adding 5 stores each year, but enjoys sales of $22.1 million per store compared to nearby supermarket chain Food Lion's average of $7.1 million. Although Giant Food is a public company, all voting stock is held by Israel Cohen and other descendants of the founding partners. Cohen has said he won't retire until age 90.

AMSE symbol: GFSA
Incorporated: Delaware, 1935
Fiscal year ends: Last Saturday in February

WHO

Chairman, President, and CEO: Israel Cohen, age 77, $1,212,716 pay
SVP Finance: David B. Sykes, age 71, $547,433 pay
SVP Operations: Alvin Dobbin, age 58, $346,294 pay
SVP General Counsel: David W. Rutstein, age 45, $343,908 pay
SVP Labor Relations and Personnel: Roger D. Olsen, age 45
Auditors: Laventhol & Horwath
Employees: 26,500

WHEN

Nehemiah Cohen, who owned 3 groceries in Lancaster, Pennsylvania, and Jac Lehrman, a wholesale grocer in Harrisburg, formed Giant Food Shopping Center, Inc., in 1935. The pair opened their first store on Georgia Avenue in Washington, DC, the following year. A second store, opened in 1937, was outstanding for its design and beauty. Giant Food was the first to operate self-service grocery stores in Washington and one of the earliest builders of supermarkets on the East Coast.

Giant Food adopted its current name in 1957 and first sold stock to the public 2 years later. The company grew slowly, preferring to add locations through internal growth rather than through acquisitions and keeping an eye on service. Giant Food's policy of developing the services it needs in-house whenever possible led it to form Giant Construction in 1967 and its own advertising agency in 1972.

By the mid-1970s the company was 2nd in the Washington market and 4th in Baltimore. Also during the mid-1970s Giant Food diversified into other retailing ventures: discount department stores, optical stores, and apparel outlets. The last of these enterprises, The Pants Corral, was divested in 1985.

Cohen retired in 1979, when he was 90, leaving his son, Israel Cohen, in charge. Israel, who had started out by helping in his father's butcher shop when he was 12, had been running the company since 1964 and had become president in 1977. In 1979, Giant Food became the first food chain in the world to install laser scanners in all its stores, demonstrating the company's habit of quickly adapting new technologies to enhance its operations. The company opened a gourmet store, Someplace Special, in 1983, with heavy emphasis on service departments and specialty items such as llama steaks and triple cream cheese. Giant Construction built 22 new stores between 1986 and 1989; during the same period the company closed 9 stores, reflecting its desire to maintain modern, efficient locations.

In 1987 the company developed a consumer information program with the National Cancer Institute called Eat for Health, which used signs, brochures, and labeling to provide nutritional information to consumers. A "frequent buyer" program began testing in 1989 to increase consumer loyalty. Giant Food opened 4 new stores in 1989 and currently has plans for opening 16 more by 1995.

WHERE

HQ: 6300 Sheriff Rd., Landover, MD 20785
Phone: 301-341-4100
FAX: 301-341-4804

Giant Food operates 151 stores, principally in Washington, DC; Maryland; and Virginia. The company maintains distribution and manufacturing facilities in Landover, Jessup, and Silver Spring, Maryland.

	1989 Grocery Store Locations	
	# of stores	% of total
Washington, DC metro area	101	68
Baltimore metro area	40	27
Other Maryland & Virginia	7	5
Total	**148**	**100**

WHAT

	1989 Store Formats	
	# of stores	% of total
Supermarkets	148	98
Drugstores	2	1
Gourmet store	1	1
Total	**151**	**100**

	1989 Sources of Sales by %
Grocery & nonfood	66
Meat, seafood, dairy & deli	25
Fresh produce	9
Total	**100**

Food Processing
Baked goods
Bottled water
Frozen yogurt
Ice cubes
Milk and milk bottles
Orange juice
Soft drinks

Other Operations
Automated teller machines
Construction
Import-export
In-house advertising agency
Shopping centers
Trucking brokerage
Wholesale tobacco

Affiliate
Shaw Community Supermarket (85%)

RANKINGS

35th in *Fortune* 50 Retailing Cos.
257th in *Forbes* Sales 500
368th in *Business Week* 1000

COMPETITION

American Stores
Great A&P
Safeway

HOW MUCH

	9 Yr. Growth	1980	1981	1982	1983	1984	1985	1986	1987	1988	1989
Sales ($ mil)	9.1%	1,483	1,684	1,852	1,957	2,139	2,247	2,529	2,721	2,987	3,249
Net income ($ mil)	21.8%	18	17	37	41	45	57	46	76	98	108
Income as % of sales	—	1.2%	1.0%	2.0%	2.1%	2.1%	2.5%	1.8%	2.8%	3.3%	3.3%
Earnings per share ($)	21.4%	0.31	0.28	0.63	0.68	0.75	0.94	0.76	1.24	1.60	1.78
Stock price – high ($)	—	1.57	1.83	4.54	6.25	7.50	13.44	16.81	21.19	25.88	36.25
Stock price – low ($)	—	1.10	1.39	1.52	4.23	4.81	6.78	11.88	12.06	16.06	22.13
Stock price – close ($)	39.6%	1.42	1.63	4.22	5.66	7.13	13.25	12.50	17.44	24.25	28.50
P/E – high	—	5	6	7	9	10	14	22	17	16	20
P/E – low	—	4	5	2	6	6	7	16	10	10	12
Dividends per share ($)	20.7%	0.09	0.10	0.12	0.15	0.20	0.25	0.30	0.33	0.40	0.50
Book value per share ($)	16.6%	2.07	2.25	2.76	3.30	3.84	4.53	4.99	5.91	7.11	8.25

1989 Year End:
Debt ratio: 32.9%
Return on equity: 23.2%
Cash (mil): $182
Current ratio: 1.53
Long-term debt (mil): $242
Number of shares (mil): 60
Dividends:
1989 average yield: 1.8%
1989 payout: 28.1%
Market value (mil): $1,703

Stock Price History high/low 1980-89

THE GILLETTE COMPANY

OVERVIEW

Boston-based Gillette is a leading producer and developer of personal products, with profitable lines in razors and blades, toiletries and cosmetics, stationery products, electric shavers and household appliances (Braun), and dental products (Oral-B).

Gillette's razor and blades division (Trac II, Atra, Good News), which accounts for 33% of net sales, leads the market in North America as well as in most other areas of the world. Sensor, the company's newest razor (which took 10 years and $200 million to develop before its introduction in 1990), has already received favorable consumer and trade responses. With it the company hopes to shift its emphasis away from low-margin disposable razors.

The toiletries division holds a strong international position with such well-known names as Right Guard, Foamy, and Dry Idea. Gillette's stationery products division (Paper Mate, Waterman, Liquid Paper) is the world's leading seller of writing instruments and correction fluids, and its Oral-B division is the #1 seller of toothbrushes in the US.

WHEN

In 1895 King C. Gillette, a salesman for the Baltimore Seal Company, originated the idea of a disposable razor blade while shaving with a dull straight razor at his home in Brookline, Massachusetts. For the next 6 years Gillette developed his idea, yet could find neither investors nor toolmakers to back him. Finally in 1901 MIT machinist William Nickerson joined with Gillette and perfected the safety razor. With the financial support of some wealthy friends, the 2 men formed the American Safety Razor Company in Boston.

Gillette put his first safety razor on the market in 1903, selling only 51 razor sets the first year. Word of the new product spread quickly, and Gillette sold 90,844 sets the following year. In 1905 Gillette established his first overseas operation in London and 3 years later adopted the Gillette diamond trademark.

Gillette sold most of his interest in the business in 1910 (although he remained president of the company until 1931) to pursue his utopian corporate theories, which he had first published in his 1894 book *The Human Drift*.

During WWI the company created Service Set shaving kits for soldiers and sold 3.5 million of them to the US government. In the 1920s the company distributed free razors through such diverse mediums as banks (via the "Shave and Save" plan) and boxes of Wrigley's gum. The sales tactic brought millions of new customers who depended on Gillette for the blades.

During the difficult years of the 1930s, Gillette began its program of sponsoring major sporting events like bowl games and the World Series. The many sporting events that the company sponsored became known as Gillette's "Cavalcade of Sports" and carried its advertising worldwide.

In 1948 the company took its first step toward diversifying its product line by purchasing Toni (home permanent kits), which was renamed the Personal Care Division in 1971. During the 1950s Gillette adopted its present name, introduced Foamy (shaving cream, 1953), and purchased Paper Mate (pens, 1955).

During the 1960s and 1970s the company expanded its product line further by introducing Right Guard (aerosol spray deodorant, 1960), Trac II (twin-blade razors, 1971), Cricket (disposable lighters, 1972), Good News (disposable razors, 1975), and Erasermate (erasable pens, 1979), and acquiring Braun (electric shavers and appliances, 1967) and Liquid Paper (correction fluid, 1979).

In 1984 Gillette branched into dental products with the purchase of Oral-B and in 1990 released Sensor, a technologically advanced, spring-mounted twin blade.

HOW MUCH

	9 Yr. Growth	1980	1981	1982	1983	1984	1985	1986	1987	1988	1989
Sales ($ mil)	5.7%	2,315	2,334	2,239	2,183	2,289	2,400	2,818	3,167	3,581	3,819
Net income ($ mil)	9.7%	124	124	135	146	159	160	16	230	269	285
Income as % of sales	—	5.4%	5.3%	6.0%	6.7%	7.0%	6.7%	0.6%	7.3%	7.5%	7.5%
Earnings per share ($)	11.6%	1.00	1.00	1.08	1.15	1.24	1.23	0.13	1.97	2.44	2.68
Stock price – high ($)	—	7.75	8.91	12.25	12.88	14.63	18.00	34.44	45.88	49.00	49.75
Stock price – low ($)	—	4.41	6.75	7.66	10.22	10.66	13.28	17.19	17.63	29.13	33.00
Stock price – close ($)	24.2%	7.00	8.44	11.25	12.16	14.16	17.38	24.63	28.38	33.25	49.13
P/E – high	—	8	9	11	11	12	15	276	23	20	19
P/E – low	—	4	7	7	9	9	11	138	9	12	12
Dividends per share ($)	8.4%	0.45	0.50	0.55	0.58	0.61	0.65	0.67	0.74	0.86	0.94
Book value per share ($)	(20.8%)	5.93	5.95	5.93	6.16	6.42	7.26	4.01	5.20	(0.88)	0.72

1989 Year End:
Debt ratio: 93.7%
Return on equity: (3506.5%)
Cash (mil): $137
Current ratio: 1.75
Long-term debt (mil): $1,041
Number of shares (mil): 97
Dividends:
1989 average yield: 1.9%
1989 payout: 34.9%
Market value (mil): $4,758

Stock Price History high/low 1980-89

50 45 40 35 30 25 20 15 10 5 0

NYSE symbol: GS
Incorporated: Delaware, 1917
Fiscal year ends: December 31

WHO

Chairman and CEO: Colman M. Mockler, Jr., age 60, $1,121,250 pay
VC: Alfred M. Zeien, age 60, $708,717 pay
VC: Derwyn F. Phillips, age 59, $543,260 pay
SVP and CFO: Thomas F. Skelly, age 56
Auditors: KPMG Peat Marwick
Employees: 30,400

WHERE

HQ: Prudential Tower Bldg., Boston, MA 02199
Phone: 617-421-7000
FAX: 617-421-7123

Gillette sells its products in over 200 countries and manufactures at 54 locations in 26 countries.

	1989 Sales		1989 Operating Income	
	$ mil	% of total	$ mil	% of total
US	1,348	35	219	31
Europe	1,504	40	279	40
Latin America	422	11	110	16
Other	545	14	87	13
Adjustments	—	—	(31)	—
Total	**3,819**	**100**	**664**	**100**

WHAT

	1989 Sales		1989 Operating Income	
	$ mil	% of total	$ mil	% of total
Blades & razors	1,238	33	429	62
Toiletries & cosmetics	1,036	27	71	10
Stationery products	430	11	65	9
Appliances	892	23	106	16
Oral care	219	6	24	3
Other	4	—	—	—
Adjustments	—	—	(31)	—
Total	**3,819**	**100**	**664**	**100**

Brand Names

Razors & Blades
Atra Plus
Braun (shavers)
Daisy Plus
Good News
Sensor
Trac II

Stationery Products
Flair (pens)
Liquid Paper (correction fluid)
Paper Mate (pens)
Waterman (pens)

Small Appliances
Braun

Toiletries & Cosmetics
Aapri (skin care)
Antica Erboristeria (herbal toiletries)
Epic Waves (home permanents)
Foamy (shave cream)
Jafra (skin care)
Lustrasilk (hair care)
Right Guard (deodorant)
Silkience (hair care)
Soft & Dri (deodorant)
White Rain (hair care)

Dental Care
Oral-B

RANKINGS

124th in *Fortune* 500 Industrial Cos.
346th in *Fortune* Global 500 Industrial Cos.
218th in *Forbes* Sales 500
123rd in *Business Week* 1000
335th in *Business Week* Global 1000

COMPETITION

Black & Decker
Colgate-Palmolive
S.C. Johnson
Johnson & Johnson
Johnson Products
Johnson Publishing
Philips
Procter & Gamble
Unilever
Warner-Lambert

GLAXO HOLDINGS PLC

OVERVIEW

By virtue of its best-selling Zantac anti-ulcer drug, Glaxo is the 3rd largest pharmaceutical manufacturer in the world. Zantac sales account for approximately 50% of company revenue. Eschewing the pharmaceutical industry's recent passion for mergers, Glaxo is expanding through internal product development. R&D expenditures are running at a hefty 15% of sales. Promising drugs emerging from Glaxo's labs include Sumatriptan, a migraine headache medicine, and Ondansetron, a treatment for the side effects of chemotherapy, with possible applications for anxiety, schizophrenia, and nicotine and alcohol addiction.

A creative dealmaker, Glaxo recently swapped its over-the-counter version of Zantac for rights to a calcium channel blocker from Sandoz and agreed to sell 2 other heart drugs for Roche. By selling these drugs, Glaxo is preparing its salesforce for future, internally developed cardiovascular medications.

NYSE symbol: GLX (ADR)
Incorporated: England, 1972
Fiscal year ends: June 30

WHO

Chairman: Sir Paul Girolami, age 63, £598,081 pay
CEO: Dr. Ernest Mario, age 51
Finance Director: John M. Hignett, age 55
Auditors: Coopers & Lybrand Deloitte
Employees: 28,710

WHEN

Englishman Joseph Nathan started an import-export business in New Zealand in 1873. While on a buying trip in London, one of his sons encountered a process for drying milk. Intrigued, Nathan obtained the rights and began producing powdered milk in New Zealand. The product was most successful in its application as a baby food, sold under the Glaxo name.

Nathan's son Alec was dispatched to London to oversee sales of the baby food in Britain. He published the *Glaxo Baby Book*, a guide to child care, introducing the "Builds Bonnie Babies" slogan and leading to the rapid acceptance of Glaxo baby foods in the early 1900s. The company expanded in Britain and, shortly after WWI, began distribution in India and South America.

In the 1920s Glaxo acquired a license to process vitamin D and launched vitamin D–fortified formulations. The company entered the pharmaceutical business with its 1927 introduction of Ostelin, a liquid vitamin D concentrate, and continued to grow globally in the 1930s, introducing Ostermilk (vitamin-fortified milk), a successful retail product.

Glaxo produced penicillin and anesthetics during WWII. After the war the company stepped up penicillin production, isolated vitamin B12, and appointed its first female director. Following precipitous declines in antibiotic prices in the mid-1950s, Glaxo diversified, acquiring veterinary, medical instrument, and drug distribution firms.

Glaxo was the target of a hostile takeover attempt by Beecham in the 1970s. The company arranged a merger with drug manufacturer and retailer Boots to fend off Beecham's bid. The British Monopolies Commission quashed both transactions, claiming that increased size inhibited innovation.

Paul Girolami became CEO in 1980, as clinical trials of Zantac, an anti-ulcer drug, neared completion. At the time the company's sales in Nigeria exceeded those in the US. Armed with Zantac (deemed to have slightly fewer side effects than Tagamet, SmithKline's established blockbuster drug), Girolami mounted a marketing blitzkrieg on Tagamet's lucrative US market.

Negotiating the use of Hoffmann-La Roche's large, underutilized sales force, Girolami attained the US marketing clout he lacked. The 1983 Zantac sales assault stunned a complacent SmithKline, wrenching away leadership in US anti-ulcer drug sales and establishing a 53% share while reducing Tagamet's to 29%. Zantac's great success made Glaxo the world's 2nd largest pharmaceutical company in 1988, prior to recent industry consolidation.

In the 1980s Glaxo shed its nondrug operations and completed a $350 million research facility in North Carolina (1988). Knighted in 1987, Sir Paul Girolami turned over his post in 1989 to Glaxo's new CEO, American Ernest Mario.

WHERE

HQ: Clarges House, 6-12 Clarges St., London W1Y 8DH, England
Phone: 011-44-71-493-4060
FAX: 011-44-71-493-4809
US HQ: 5 Moore Dr., Research Triangle Park, NC 27709
US Phone: 919-248-2100
US FAX: 919-248-2381

Glaxo manufactures its products in 30 countries, principally the UK, Singapore, Italy, and the US, and sells them in 150 countries.

	1989 Sales	
	£ mil	% of total
North America	1,163	45
Europe	1,081	42
Southeast Asia & Far East	156	6
Other countries	170	7
Total	**2,570**	**100**

WHAT

	1989 Sales	
	£ mil	% of total
Anti-ulcerants	1,291	50
Respiratory drugs	585	23
Antibiotics	396	15
Other pharmaceuticals	285	11
Foods & animal health	13	1
Total	**2,570**	**100**

Brand Names (US Markets)

Anti-Ulcerant
Zantac

Antibiotics
Ceftin
Fortaz
Zinacef

Respiratory Drugs
Beclovent (anti-asthma)
Beconase (anti–hay fever)
Ventolin (anti-asthma)

HOW MUCH

£=$1.61 (Dec. 31, 1989)	9 Yr. Growth	1980	1981	1982	1983	1984	1985	1986	1987	1988	1989
Sales (£ mil)	17.2%	618	710	866	1,027	1,200	1,412	1,429	1,741	2,054	2,570
Net income (£ mil)	36.4%	42	61	80	109	169	277	400	496	571	688
Income as % of sales	—	6.8%	8.6%	9.2%	10.6%	14.1%	19.6%	28.0%	28.5%	27.7%	26.8%
Earnings per share (p)	35.0%	3.1	4.5	5.9	7.5	11.5	18.7	27.1	33.5	38.6	46.2
Stock price – high (p)	—	34	55	186	248	275	381	563	938	569	824
Stock price – low (p)	—	23	30	52	156	175	269	378	484	444	528
Stock price – close (p)	41.7%	34	53	156	176	275	378	525	491	534	785
P/E – high	—	11	12	32	33	24	20	21	28	14	18
P/E – low	—	7	7	9	21	15	14	14	14	12	11
Dividends per share (p)	34.7%	1.2	1.2	1.8	2.3	3.3	5.0	7.0	9.5	12.5	17.5
Book value per share (p)	21.9%	26	26	31	37	46	58	74	98	120	154

1989 Year End:
Debt ratio: 2.0%
Return on equity: 33.7%
Cash (mil): £1,294
Long-term debt (mil): £32
Number of shares (mil): 745
Dividends:
1989 average yield: 2.2%
1989 payout: 37.9%
Market value (mil): $9,414
Sales (mil): $4,138

Stock Price History high/low 1980-89

RANKINGS

303rd in *Fortune* Global 500 Industrial Cos.
90th in *Forbes* 100 Foreign Investments in the US
53rd in *Business Week* Global 1000

COMPETITION

Abbott Labs
American Cyanamid
American Home Products
Bayer
Bristol-Myers Squibb
Eli Lilly
Genentech
Hoechst
Johnson & Johnson
Merck
Monsanto
Pfizer
Procter & Gamble
Rhône-Poulenc
Roche Holding
Schering-Plough
SmithKline Beecham
Upjohn
Warner-Lambert

THE GOLDMAN SACHS GROUP, LP

OVERVIEW

Goldman Sachs is the 4th largest US investment banking organization based on total capital ($4.0 billion) and is the only private partnership among the major Wall Street investment bankers.

Goldman Sachs provides worldwide investment and financial services to institutional investors and wealthy individuals, rather than to the mass markets. In an investment banking industry often characterized by changes in ownership, strategy, and names, Goldman Sachs is distinguished by its stability.

In 1989 the firm was the #1 lead manager of international equity offerings; it led or co-managed 85 equity issues of $12.5 billion in 1989. And for the first time since 1980, Goldman Sachs was #1 in municipal bond underwriting, with $13.7 billion in new issues.

With an equity research staff following more than 1,200 companies in 65 industries worldwide, Goldman Sachs gained 16 first-team honors on the 1989 *Institutional Investor* "All-America Research Team," more than any other firm for the 3rd consecutive year.

Private company
Founded: New York, 1869
Fiscal year ends: Last Friday in November

WHO

Senior Partner and Co-Chairman of the Management Committee: Stephen Friedman, age 52
Senior Partner and Co-Chairman of the Management Committee: Robert E. Rubin, age 51
Auditors: Coopers & Lybrand
Employees: 6,400, including 128 general partners

WHEN

Philadelphia retailer Marcus Goldman moved to New York in 1869 to start a business of purchasing customers' promissory notes from jewelry merchants and reselling them to commercial banks for a small profit. The business, renamed M. Goldman and Sachs in 1882 when Samuel Sachs, Goldman's son-in-law, joined the firm, became Goldman, Sachs & Company in 1885.

In 1887 Goldman Sachs, through Kleinwort Sons, a British merchant banking firm, was able to offer its clients foreign exchange and currency arbitrage between the New York and London markets. To serve clients such as Sears, Roebuck, the firm expanded New York commercial paper operations to Chicago and St. Louis. In 1896 Goldman Sachs joined the NYSE.

In the late 1890s and early 1900s, Samuel Sachs established contacts in major European cities while Henry Goldman's efforts made the firm a major source of long-term financing for US industry. In 1906 Goldman Sachs co-managed its first public securities offering, a $4.5 million United Cigar Manufacturers (later General Cigar) preferred stock offering. By 1920 the firm had arranged for initial securities offerings of Sears, May Department Stores, Brown Shoe, Continental Can, Jewel Tea, B.F. Goodrich, and Merck.

Sidney Weinberg became a partner in 1927 at age 35 and was a leading force in the firm until he died in 1969. In the 1930s Goldman Sachs started an active securities dealer (rather than agent) operation and sales departments. Since WWII the firm has become a leader in nearly every investment banking activity. In the 1950s Goldman Sachs was instrumental in advising the Ford family on public ownership of the company and co-managed its first public offering (1956).

Under Gustave (Gus) Levy, who became senior partner in 1969, the firm was the first to handle big blocks of stock by buying them itself and then reselling. Under John L. Weinberg, senior partner from 1976 to 1990, Goldman Sachs expanded its international operations and was one of the leaders in merger and acquisitions during the 1980s. In 1982 Goldman led all firms by advising and negotiating $24.7 billion in mergers, including US Steel–Marathon Oil, Occidental Petroleum–Cities Service, and Connecticut General–INA. In 1989 a group of 8 major insurance companies made a $275 million fixed-return equity investment in the firm; at this time the firm formed a holding company called The Goldman Sachs Group, LP, a holding partnership for Goldman Sachs.

WHERE

HQ: 85 Broad St., New York, NY 10004
Phone: 212-902-1000
FAX: 212-902-3925

Goldman Sachs operates worldwide and has offices in these cities:

US
New York
Boston
Chicago
Dallas
Detroit
Houston
Los Angeles
Memphis
Miami
Philadelphia
San Francisco
Washington, DC

International
Hong Kong
London
Madrid
Montreal
Paris
Singapore
Sydney
Tokyo
Toronto
Zurich

HOW MUCH

	9 Yr. Growth	1980	1981	1982	1983	1984	1985	1986	1987	1988	1989
Total capital ($ mil)	38.2%	219	389	478	712	859	1,201	1,951	2,402	2,771	4,018
Equity capital ($ mil)	30.2%	200	272	363	502	585	868	1,529	1,656	1,876	2,145
Excess net capital ($ mil)	13.5%	218.5	266.2	443.6	528.9	539.9	699.7	1127.7	1107.0	1033.0	684.0
Employees	12.5%	2,217	2,527	3,145	3,251	3,903	4,516	6,049	6,087	6,500	6,400
Offices	3.2%	15	15	15	16	16	16	16	19	19	22
Registered representatives	12.3%	657	765	834	887	981	1,040	1,377	1,896	1,881	1,873
Corp. undrwrtg. ($ mil)*	26.2%	5,283	5,768	7,096	10,673	8,026	16,526	30,180	33,560	37,106	42,911
Muni. undrwrtg. ($ mil)*	13.8%	4,292	2,521	6,204	6,221	6,251	19,596	10,768	6,625	12,468	13,687
Intl. bond undrwrtg. ($ mil)*	18.8%	915	890	1,726	2,165	2,399	6,571	4,165	3,433	4,057	4,301

Debt ration: 47.6%
Cash (mil): $415
Long term debt (mil): $1,873

Total Capital ($ mil) 1980-89

4,500
4,000
3,500
3,000
2,500
2,000
1,500
1,000
500
0

*according to "full credit to lead manager" allocation method

WHAT

Commodity trading
Debt financing
Equity financing
Foreign exchange
Information technology
Investment research
Investment services
Mergers, acquisitions, and restructurings
Municipal finance
Real estate

RANKINGS

31st in *Forbes* 400 US Private Cos.

COMPETITION

CS Holding
Deutsche Bank
Merrill Lynch
Morgan Stanley
Nomura
Salomon
Travelers
Other investment banking firms

THE GOODYEAR TIRE & RUBBER COMPANY

OVERVIEW

Goodyear, headquartered in Akron, is the largest producer of rubber in the world. The last American-owned tire business, Goodyear leads the US market with a 16.9% share. Its distinctive blimps (*America, Columbia, Enterprise,* and *Spirit of Akron*) are some of the best-known advertising symbols in the US.

Goodyear became a giant by executing CEO Paul Litchfield's 1920s mandate of "making better tires cheaper and selling them harder." Tires and related products account for 82% of sales; chemicals, plastics, and rubber sales make up the remainder. The company has 86 plants in 26 countries and 6 rubber plantations.

Most tires are distributed through the more than 5,000 Goodyear dealers and through discount wholesalers under the Atlas and Kelly-Springfield names. Sales to automakers account for about 19% of total tire sales.

Goodyear accumulated $4.7 billion in debt and sold diversification ventures to fight a takeover bid in 1986. The company also owns an oil pipeline, constructed between 1984 and 1989 at a cost of $1 billion.

Plans are to continue the 1920s mandate, targeting Europe and the Pacific Rim. Goodyear plants, after a $3 billion makeover, are among the most modern in the industry.

NYSE symbol: GT
Incorporated: Ohio, 1898
Fiscal year ends: December 31

WHO

Chairman, President, and CEO: Tom H. Barrett, age 59, $954,814 pay
EVP; COO, Tires: Jacques R. Sardas, age 59, $542,214 pay
EVP and CFO: Oren G. Shaffer, age 47, $430,964 pay
EVP; COO, General Products: Hoyt M. Wells, age 63, $429,814 pay
EVP Research, Development, and Product Design: F. Vincent Prus, age 63, $373,544 pay
Auditors: Price Waterhouse
Employees: 111,469

WHEN

In 1898 in Akron, Frank and Charles Seiberling founded a tire and rubber company, naming it after Charles Goodyear (inventor of the vulcanization process, 1839). Initially producing bicycle and carriage tires, Goodyear soon targeted the fledgling automotive industry. The introduction of the Quick Detachable tire and the Universal Rim (1903) made Goodyear the world's largest tire manufacturer by 1916, the year it introduced the pneumatic truck tire.

The company is known for its marketing tactics. Frank Seiberling created the winged-foot emblem in 1900. In 1924 Goodyear acquired rights to manufacture zeppelins, and by the 1930s Goodyear blimps served as advertisements nationwide.

Goodyear began foreign manufacturing in Canada in 1910 and greatly expanded during the 1920s and 1930s (Australia, Argentina, Indonesia). The company established a sales office in England (1912) and began its own rubber plantations in Sumatra (1916). By 1926 Goodyear led the world in rubber production.

Financial troubles led to reorganization in 1921, and investment bankers Dillon, Read & Company forced out the Seiberlings. Succeeding a caretaker management team, Paul Litchfield, a Goodyear tire designer since 1900, began 3 decades as CEO (1926).

Goodyear opened company stores during the 1930s, acquired Kelly-Springfield in 1935, and began producing synthetic rubber tires in 1937. Following WWII the tire market boomed, and Goodyear led in implementing technological developments such as polyester tire cord (1962) and the bias-belted tire (1967). In 1971 Goodyear provided the tires used on the Apollo 14 lunar landing mission.

Michelin introduced the radial tire in the US in 1966. By 1976 radials accounted for 45% of tire sales and, with the introduction of the all-weather Tiempo and the Arriva (1980), Goodyear led the US market. Goodyear also introduced the Eagle, its most popular tire, in 1980.

Fending off Sir James Goldsmith's takeover attempt in 1986, CEO Robert Mercer raised $1.7 billion by selling nontire businesses (Motor Wheel, Goodyear Aerospace, and Celeron Oil) and by borrowing heavily, accumulating $4.7 billion of debt in a 47% stock buyback.

Goodyear sold its South African operations in 1989 for $41 million. Debt interest payments and expenses for its oil pipeline led to a 46% drop in 1989 profits.

Facing a declining share in the radial replacement market, in 1990 Goodyear initiated an aggressive advertising campaign. Goodyear may be near selling its oil pipeline.

WHERE

HQ: 1144 E. Market St., Akron, OH 44316
Phone: 216-796-2121
FAX: 216-796-2222

Goodyear operates 43 US plants in 21 states and 43 plants in 25 foreign countries.

	1989 Sales		1989 Operating Income	
	$ mil	% of total	$ mil	% of total
US	6,421	59	490	53
Europe	2,039	19	132	14
Latin America	1,180	11	245	27
Canada	602	5	10	1
Asia & Africa	627	6	49	5
Adjustments	—	—	(155)	—
Total	**10,869**	**100**	**771**	**100**

WHAT

	1989 Sales		1989 Operating Income	
	$ mil	% of total	$ mil	% of total
Tires & related	8,849	82	722	78
General products	2,008	18	261	28
Oil transportation	12	—	(57)	(6)
Adjustments	—	—	(155)	—
Total	**10,869**	**100**	**771**	**100**

Products
Auto body parts
Auto hoses, belts
Polyester resins
PVC films
Roofing systems
Rubber materials
Shoe soles
Tires
Vinyl laminates

Tire Brands
Arriva
Eagle
Invicta
Tiempo
Ultra Grip
Vector

Major Subsidiaries
Brad Ragan, Inc. (tire sales and service chain, 74.5%)
Celeron Corp. (oil pipelines)
All American Pipeline Co.
Celeron Gathering Corp.
Celeron Trading & Transportation Co.
Delta Tire
The Kelly-Springfield Tire Co.
Lee Tire & Rubber Co.
Reneer Films Corp. (vinyl laminates and films)
Wingfoot Corp. (stretch and shrink films for packaging and other uses)

HOW MUCH

	9 Yr. Growth	1980	1981	1982	1983	1984	1985	1986	1987	1988	1989
Sales ($ mil)	2.8%	8,444	9,153	8,689	9,736	10,241	9,585	9,103	9,905	10,810	10,869
Net income ($ mil)	(1.0%)	207	244	248	270	411	301	101	514	350	189
Income as % of sales	—	2.4%	2.7%	2.9%	2.8%	4.0%	3.1%	1.1%	5.2%	3.2%	1.7%
Earnings per share ($)	1.6%	2.85	3.36	3.35	2.71	3.87	2.81	0.94	8.49	6.05	*3.28*
Stock price – high ($)	—	18.38	20.25	36.88	36.38	31.50	31.25	50.00	76.50	67.88	59.75
Stock price – low ($)	—	10.75	15.88	17.88	27.00	23.00	25.13	29.00	35.00	47.00	42.13
Stock price – close ($)	11.8%	16.00	19.00	35.00	30.38	26.00	31.25	41.88	60.00	51.13	43.50
P/E – high	—	6	6	11	13	8	11	53	9	11	18
P/E – low	—	4	5	5	10	6	9	31	4	8	13
Dividends per share ($)	3.7%	1.30	1.30	1.40	1.40	1.50	1.60	1.60	1.60	1.70	1.80
Book value per share ($)	1.6%	32.09	32.96	33.14	28.61	29.78	32.44	30.93	32.19	35.30	37.09

1989 Year End:
Debt ratio: 58.0%
Return on equity: 91%
Cash (mil): $215
Current ratio: 1.49
Long-term debt (mil): $2,963
Number of shares (mil): 58
Dividends:
1989 average yield: 4.1%
1989 payout: —
Market value (mil): $2,515

Stock Price History high/low 1980-89

RANKINGS

39th in *Fortune* 500 Industrial Cos.
103rd in *Fortune* Global 500 Industrial Cos.
64th in *Forbes* Sales 500
288th in *Business Week* 1000
969th in *Business Week* Global 1000

COMPETITION

Bridgestone
Michelin
Sears

W. R. GRACE & COMPANY

OVERVIEW

New York–based W. R. Grace is an international specialty chemicals, specialty businesses, health care, and natural resources company.

The Specialty Chemicals Division accounts for 53% of company sales. Cryovac, a plastic film to protect fresh food products, has 50% of the US market and contributes 25% of Grace's chemical profits. Grace's Davison Division leads the world in producing fluid cracking catalysts (petroleum refining) and in supplying silica products (drying, free-flowing agents).

The company's specialty businesses include Grace Cocoa, a world leader in supplying cocoa and chocolate to the baking, candy, and dairy industries; and Baker & Taylor Books, the nation's leading supplier of books and audiocassettes to retailers and libraries.

Grace's Health Care Group includes (100% owned) National Medical Care, US leader in kidney dialysis services, and biotechnology research in diabetes and blood cholesterol.

Grace Energy (83.4% owned) is the largest US land-based contractor of drilling rigs, with 183 at year-end 1989. Grace Energy conducts oil and gas exploration, mines coal, and sells specialized services to the petroleum industry.

WHEN

W. R. Grace & Company grew from the Peruvian business activities of Irishman William R. Grace. Grace, who had left Ireland because of a potato famine, was in Peru in 1854 chartering ships to trade guano (bird dung), a natural fertilizer. In 1866 he moved his headquarters to New York and established 3-way shipping routes from New York to South America to Europe, trading fertilizer, agricultural products, and US manufactured goods.

W. R. Grace died in 1904. His brother Michael took over until 1907, when W. R.'s son Joseph became president. Under Joseph's direction the shipping business grew, powered first by sail, then by steam, and became known as the Grace Line. Joseph expanded the company's investments in South America, eventually owning cotton mills, sugar plantations, and sugar refineries in Peru and nitrate production facilities in Chile. In 1916 he established the W. R. Grace & Company's Bank (later the Grace National Bank). The company entered aviation in 1928 in a joint venture with Pan American Airlines, forming Pan American–Grace Airways, called Panagra, which served Latin America.

In 1945 J. Peter Grace, Joseph's son, took the helm at the age of 32. To capitalize his planned diversification of W. R. Grace, Peter took the company public in 1953. In 1954 Grace expanded into chemicals with the purchases of Davison Chemical (industrial and agricultural chemicals, silica gels) and Dewey & Almy Chemical (can sealants, batteries). To further fund the new direction of W. R. Grace, Peter sold Grace National Bank (1965), Panagra (to Braniff, 1967), and the Grace Line (1969), 3 of the oldest businesses of the company.

Purchases during the 1960s and 1970s further illustrated the changing nature of the company: American Breeders Service (1967); consumer goods companies such as Herman's (sporting goods stores, 56% interest, 1970) and Sheplers (western wear stores, 1976); El Torito-La Fiesta Restaurants (1976); and 2 home improvement stores, Handy City (1976) and Channel (1977). Internationally Grace was buying food companies and restaurants in Europe. The company bought Baker & Taylor book wholesalers in 1970. Peru nationalized Grace's paper and chemical enterprises in 1974.

In 1986 Grace sold virtually all of its full-service restaurants, Sheplers, and its 56% interest in Herman's Sporting Goods. In 1988 Grace sold its agricultural and fertilizer businesses to retire debt, to consolidate its business, and to focus on specialty (unique) chemicals.

HOW MUCH

	9 Yr. Growth	1980	1981	1982	1983	1984	1985	1986	1987	1988	1989
Sales ($ mil)	0.0%	6,101	6,521	6,128	6,220	6,728	5,193	3,726	4,515	5,786	6,115
Net income ($ mil)	(1.1%)	284	361	320	160	196	128	(375)	142	192	257
Income as % of sales	—	4.7%	5.5%	5.2%	2.6%	2.9%	2.5%	(10.1%)	3.1%	3.3%	4.2%
Earnings per share ($)	(0.4%)	2.96	3.72	3.27	1.63	2.01	1.23	(4.47)	1.67	2.19	2.86
Stock price – high ($)	—	31.75	29.81	23.13	25.19	23.44	24.75	30.38	37.31	29.88	39.13
Stock price – low ($)	—	16.31	19.25	14.25	19.13	18.25	17.75	22.63	19.13	23.50	25.13
Stock price – close ($)	1.2%	29.50	22.88	19.19	22.63	19.88	23.94	24.19	24.00	26.00	32.75
P/E – high	—	11	8	7	15	12	20	—	22	14	14
P/E – low	—	6	5	4	12	9	14	—	11	11	9
Dividends per share ($)	2.8%	1.09	1.23	1.35	1.40	1.40	1.40	1.40	1.40	1.40	1.40
Book value per share ($)	0.7%	18.97	21.51	22.71	22.40	22.53	21.70	15.41	17.31	18.18	20.16

1989 Year End:
Debt ratio: 48.6%
Return on equity: 14.9%
Cash (mil): $109
Current ratio: 1.36
Long-term debt (mil): $1,638
Number of shares (mil): 85
Dividends:
1989 average yield: 4.3%
1989 payout: 49.0%
Market value (mil): $2,799

NYSE symbol: GRA
Incorporated: New York, 1988
Fiscal year ends: December 31

WHO

Chairman and CEO: J. Peter Grace, age 76, $1,530,000 pay
President: Charles H. Erhart, Jr., age 64, $850,000 pay
Chairman of the Executive Committee: Paul D. Paganucci, age 58
EVP and CFO: Brian J. Smith, age 45
Auditors: Price Waterhouse
Employees: 49,700

WHERE

HQ: Grace Plaza, 1114 Ave. of the Americas, New York, NY 10036
Phone: 212-819-5500
FAX: 212-819-6876

Grace sells its products in over 45 countries throughout the world.

	1989 Sales		1989 Operating Income	
	$ mil	% of total	$ mil	% of total
US	3,986	65	342	55
Canada	140	2	11	2
Europe	1,577	26	154	25
Other	412	7	108	18
Adjustments	—	—	(240)	—
Total	**6,115**	**100**	**375**	**100**

WHAT

	1989 Sales		1989 Operating Income	
	$ mil	% of total	$ mil	% of total
Natural resources	448	7	39	6
Specialty chemicals	3,256	53	406	67
Specialty businesses	1,695	28	69	11
Health care	716	12	101	16
Adjustments	—	—	(240)	—
Total	**6,115**	**100**	**375**	**100**

Specialty Chemicals
90 product lines for construction, energy, water treatment, transportation, packaging, electronics, and graphic arts industries

Specialty Businesses
Agriculture (bull semen, livestock feed)
Book, videocassette, and software distribution
Cocoa and chocolate production
Textiles (mattress ticking, upholstery, fabrics)

Energy
Coal mining
Oil and gas exploration and production
Petroleum services and equipment

Health Care
Home infusion therapy
Kidney dialysis

RANKINGS

76th in *Fortune* 500 Industrial Cos.
207th in *Fortune* Global 500 Industrial Cos.
139th in *Forbes* Sales 500
244th in *Business Week* 1000
823rd in *Business Week* Global 1000

COMPETITION

Cargill
Oil, coal, and chemical companies

GRAND METROPOLITAN PLC

OVERVIEW

Once a major hotel operator, Grand Metropolitan has evolved into an important international food, liquor, and retailing concern. Measured by case volume, its International Distillers and Vintners unit is the world's largest wine and spirits company, led by such brands as J&B, Smirnoff, Baileys, and Almaden. Grand Met owns Pearle, the world's largest eye care retailer, and Burger King, the #2 hamburger chain. In the US the company's brands are leaders in refrigerated dough (Pillsbury), canned and frozen vegetables (Green Giant), and luxury ice cream (Häagen-Dazs).

Grand Met has been buying consumer goods and service companies whose products have international branding potential and complement each other. At recently acquired Pillsbury, Grand Met is trying to rebuild brand names and market shares by focusing resources on advertising and product development. The company views the upgrade of Burger King's operations and image as a long-term project.

WHEN

Maxwell Joseph dropped out of school in 1926 to work for a real estate agency in London. Five years later he set off on his own and began acquiring properties for resale. A weak British economy and WWII slowed his progress, but in 1946 he purchased a bomb-damaged hotel in London. Feeling that hotels were severely undervalued, he bought progressively larger and more prestigious hotels throughout the late 1950s and the 1960s, including the Mount Royal in London and the Hotel d'Angleterre in Copenhagen. Joseph's company, Grand Metropolitan, went public in 1961, just in advance of its acquisition of Grand Hotels (Mayfair) Ltd.

Diversification began in 1970 with the purchases of Express Dairy, Berni Inns (catering, restaurants), and Mecca (betting shops). In 1971, in what was the largest British takeover to date, Grand Met bought Truman Hanburg, a brewing concern, followed by Watney Mann in 1972. With Watney Mann's brewing operations came recently acquired International Distillers and Vintners, makers of J&B, Bombay Gin, and Baileys, as well as wine.

After pausing for a few years to sell unwanted assets and reduce debt, Grand Met returned to its acquisitive ways. Since it was under the scrutiny of the English Monopolies Commission, the company aimed its sights overseas. In a hotly contested 1980 transaction, it took over the Liggett Group, an American cigarette manufacturer whose Paddington subsidiary was the US distributor of J&B Scotch, Grand Met's leading brand. In his last major acquisition before his death, newly knighted Sir Maxwell engineered the 1981 buyout of Intercontinental Hotels from Pan Am.

After Sir Maxwell, Grand Met shifted focus. It bought Pearle Health Services (Pearle Vision Centers, US) in 1985 and sold the last of the Liggett tobacco businesses in 1986.

Under the leadership of Allen Sheppard, Grand Met acquired Heublein in 1987, picking up such brands as Smirnoff, Lancers, and Cuervo, and creating the world's largest wine and spirits company. Sheppard again changed the emphasis of the company, disposing of the Intercontinental chain in 1988 for 52 times earnings and acquiring the food giant Pillsbury (Burger King, Häagen-Dazs, Green Giant) in a 1989 hostile takeover. In the same year Grand Met sold several businesses because of the limited international appeal of their brands.

In early 1990 Grand Met announced its intention to sell its UK brewery operations (Watneys, Ruddles) to Elders IXL of Australia. Grand Met intends to use the proceeds of the sale to reduce debt incurred in the Pillsbury acquisition.

OTC symbol: GRMTY (ADR)
Incorporated: England, 1934
Fiscal year ends: September 30

WHO

Chairman and Group CEO: Allen J. G. Sheppard, age 57, £506,438 pay
Group Finance Director: David P. Nash, age 49
Auditors: KPMG Peat Marwick McLintock
Employees: 152,175

WHERE

HQ: 11-12 Hanover Sq., London W1A 1DP, England
Phone: 011-44-71-629-7488
US HQ (Grand Metropolitan, Inc.): 100 Paragon Dr., Montvale, NJ 07645
US Phone: 201-573-4000
US FAX: 201-573-9020

	1989 Sales		1989 Operating Income	
	£ mil	% of total	£ mil	% of total
UK, Ireland, Europe	5,139	55	490	51
North America	3,894	42	415	43
Other countries	265	3	62	6
Total	**9,298**	**100**	**967**	**100**

WHAT

	1989 Sales		1989 Operating Income	
	£ mil	% of total	£ mil	% of total
Food	2,872	31	245	25
Drinks	2,784	30	389	40
Retailing	2,040	22	230	24
Discontinued businesses	1,602	17	103	11
Total	**9,298**	**100**	**967**	**100**

Food
Erasco (Germany)
Express (UK)
Géant Vert (France)
Green Giant
Häagen-Dazs
Hungry Jack
Jeno's
Pillsbury
Totino's

Liquor
Baileys
Black Velvet
Bombay Gin
Gilbey's
Heublein
J&B
Metaxa
Popov
Sambuca Romana
Smirnoff

Pet Food
Alpo
Blue Mountain

Retailing
Burger King
Pearle Vision Centers
Peter Dominic (UK)
Texas State Optical
Wienerwald (Germany)

Wine
Almaden
Beaulieu Vineyards
Christian Brothers
Inglenook
Lancers

RANKINGS

73rd in *Fortune* Global 500 Industrial Cos.
5th in *Forbes* 100 Foreign Investments in the US
148th in *Business Week* Global 1000

COMPETITION

American Brands
Anheuser-Busch
Bass
Beatrice
Borden
Brown-Forman
BSN
ConAgra
CPC International
E. & J. Gallo
General Mills
Guinness
H. J. Heinz
Jack Eckerd
Mars
McDonald's
Nestlé
PepsiCo
Philip Morris
Procter & Gamble
Quaker Oats
Ralston Purina
RJR Nabisco
Sara Lee
Seagram
TLC Beatrice
TW Holdings
Unilever
United States Shoe
Wendy's
Whitman

HOW MUCH

£=$1.61 (Dec. 31, 1989)	9 Yr. Growth	1980	1981	1982	1983	1984	1985	1986	1987	1988	1989
Sales (£ mil)	15.3%	2,583	3,221	3,849	4,469	5,075	5,590	5,291	5,706	6,029	9,298
Net income (£ mil)	27.5%	120	137	151	201	235	272	261	461	702	1,068
Income as % of sales	—	4.6%	4.3%	3.9%	4.5%	4.6%	4.9%	4.9%	8.1%	11.6%	11.5%
Earnings per share (p)	12.6%	18.9	21.3	22.8	27.8	32.4	28.3	31.4	38.1	46.9	55.6
Stock price – high (p)	—	167	228	336	366	360	405	482	605	521	658
Stock price – low (p)	—	120	138	171	297	270	277	332	348	418	425
Stock price – close (p)	17.0%	153	188	334	350	315	398	457	449	430	628
P/E – high	—	9	11	16	13	11	14	15	16	11	12
P/E – low	—	6	6	8	11	8	10	11	9	9	8
Dividends per share (p)	11.6%	6.6	7.4	8.4	9.6	9.2	10.0	10.2	12.0	15.0	17.8
Book value per share (p)	—	—	—	—	—	—	—	—	—	—	—

1989 Year End:
Debt ratio: 57.0%
Return on equity: —
Cash (mil): £215
Long-term debt (mil): £3,725
Number of shares (mil): 987
Dividends:
1989 average yield: 2.8%
1989 payout: 32.0%
Market value (mil): $9,979
Sales (mil): $14,970

Stock Price History high/low 1980-89

700
600
500
400
300
200
100
0

THE GREAT ATLANTIC & PACIFIC TEA COMPANY

OVERVIEW

Montvale, New Jersey–based A&P, after struggling through the 1960s and 1970s, is on the rebound. The company is now the 4th largest food retailer in the US.

While most of its competitors have spent recent years fighting off takeover attempts and absorbing huge amounts of debt, A&P has slowly renovated its stores and bought strong, regional chains. Only 48% of the company's stores currently operate under the A&P banner.

This strategy has helped A&P increase its market presence. The company is now ranked first or 2nd in nearly all of its markets. It has the #1 position in New York City, where it operates A&P, Waldbaum's, and Food Emporium stores. The company's A&P and Dominion stores in Ontario also make it the market leader there.

A&P is 53% owned by Tenglemann, a German retailer, and itself owns 19.9% of Isosceles, which operates Gateway, the 3rd largest grocer in the UK. Profits have increased from a $232 million loss in 1981 to $147 million net income in 1989.

WHEN

Two partners, George Gilman and George H. Hartford, both of Augusta, Maine, set up shop in 1859 on the docks of New York City to sell tea at a 50% discount by eliminating middlemen. The company, The Great American Tea Company, advertised by using a red wagon drawn through the city's streets. By 1869 the company had 11 stores offering a variety of discounted items, and the name was changed to The Great Atlantic & Pacific Tea Company.

Gilman retired to luxury in 1878 and Hartford brought his sons George and John into the company. In 1912, when the company had 400 stores, John opened a new store on a low-price, cash-and-carry format, without customer credit or premiums. The format proved popular and when control of the company passed to the sons in 1916, A&P had over 1,000 cash-and-carry stores with identical layouts and had adopted a strategy of having "a store on every corner."

During the 1920s and 1930s when the company grew to over 15,000 stores throughout the US, there was a move by small retailers in the state and national legislatures aimed at restricting chain stores in general and A&P in particular. John Hartford initiated innovative marketing and customer service policies aimed at improving the company's image. A&P continued to grow in the 1940s by converting its stores to supermarkets. However, an antitrust suit in 1949 and the company's reluctance to expand the supermarket format to more nonfood items combined to push the company into decline. In a desperate bid to maintain operations, management shuttered stores in distant California and Washington to shore up the Northeastern stores.

In 1975, after a prolonged period of poor sales and failed discount format attempts, the board chose a new CEO: Jonathan Scott, former president of Albertson's (now CEO of American Stores). Under Scott, A&P closed stores and reduced the work force in an effort to cut costs, and the company established a Family Centers subsidiary in 1977. Scott's efforts to resuscitate the "Grandma" of grocery stores proved ineffective. The company's 1978 sales increases failed to keep ahead of inflation, and it posted a $52 million loss.

The Hartford Foundation sold its holdings in the company to the Tengelmann Group (1979), a German retailer, who appointed English-born James Wood as CEO (1980). A&P has since sold or remodeled most of its old stores and has acquired several store chains, including Super Fresh (1982), Kohl's (1983), Pantry Pride (1984), and Borman's (1989). The company is currently taking advantage of debt-weakened competitors by mounting an aggressive store-opening campaign.

HOW MUCH

	9 Yr. Growth	1980	1981	1982	1983	1984	1985	1986	1987	1988	1989
Sales ($ mil)	5.3%	6,990	6,227	4,608	5,222	5,878	6,615	7,835	9,532	10,068	11,148
Net income ($ mil)	—	(43)	(232)	21	31	51	56	69	103	128	147
Income as % of sales	—	(0.6%)	(3.7%)	0.5%	0.6%	0.9%	0.8%	0.9%	1.1%	1.3%	1.3%
Earnings per share ($)	—	(1.35)	(6.19)	0.57	0.84	1.35	1.48	1.82	2.71	3.34	3.84
Stock price – high ($)	—	8.63	6.63	9.38	14.25	18.00	22.00	27.75	46.88	48.13	65.38
Stock price – low ($)	—	4.50	3.50	3.75	8.00	11.63	14.38	19.25	23.63	31.88	44.25
Stock price – close ($)	30.8%	5.25	3.88	8.25	12.25	16.00	21.88	23.50	37.50	44.63	58.88
P/E – high	—	—	—	16	17	13	15	15	17	14	17
P/E – low	—	—	—	7	10	9	10	11	9	10	12
Dividends per share ($)	—	0.00	0.00	0.00	0.00	0.00	0.10	0.40	0.48	0.58	0.68
Book value per share ($)	11.3%	10.89	8.08	8.81	10.02	15.48	17.63	19.85	22.32	25.42	28.59

1989 Year End:
Debt ratio: 34.0%
Return on equity: 14.2%
Cash (mil): $35
Current ratio: 1.08
Long-term debt (mil): $563
Number of shares (mil): 38
Dividends:
1989 average yield: 1.1%
1989 payout: 17.6%
Market value (mil): $2,249

NYSE symbol: GAP
Incorporated: Maryland, 1925
Fiscal year ends: Last Saturday in February

WHO

Chairman, President, and CEO: James Wood, age 60, $3,421,442 pay
VC: Eckart C. Siess, age 53, $484,615 pay
EVP and CFO: Fred Corrado, age 49, $398,462 pay
Auditors: Deloitte & Touche
Employees: 91,000

WHERE

HQ: 2 Paragon Dr., Montvale, NJ 07645
Phone: 201-573-9700
FAX: 201-930-8106 (Investor Relations)

A&P operates 1,215 locations throughout most of the eastern 1/2 of the US and in the province of Ontario. The company also owns 3 bakeries, 2 coffee plants, and an ice cream plant.

	1989 Sales		1989 Pretax Income	
	$ mil	% of total	$ mil	% of total
US	9,197	83	195	78
Canada	1,951	17	56	22
Total	**11,148**	**100**	**251**	**100**

	1990 Store Locations	
	no. of stores	% of total
Mid Atlantic	465	38
South	245	20
Midwest	197	16
Ontario	194	16
New England	114	10
Total	**1,215**	**100**

WHAT

	1990 Store Names	
	no. of stores	% of total
A&P & related stores	609	50
Super Fresh	258	21
Waldbaum's	142	12
Farmer Jack	77	6
Kohl's	63	5
Dominion	36	3
Food Emporium	30	3
Total	**1,215**	**100**

A&P Related Store Names
A&P Futurestore
A&P Sav-A-Center
Dominion
Family Mart
Food Bazaar
Shopwell

RANKINGS

10th in *Fortune* 50 Retailing Cos.
59th in *Forbes* Sales 500
323rd in *Business Week* 1000
935th in *Business Week* Global 1000

COMPETITION

Albertson's
American Stores
Bruno's
Food Lion
Giant Food
Kroger
Publix
Safeway
Stop & Shop
Supermarkets General
Winn-Dixie

GREAT WESTERN FINANCIAL CORPORATION

OVERVIEW

Great Western is the holding company of the 2nd largest US thrift institution, Great Western Bank, with $37.2 billion in assets, behind H. F. Ahmanson. Beverly Hills–based Great Western, along with Citicorp and H. F. Ahmanson, was a 1989 national leader in new mortgage loans, originating $11 billion.

About 90% of the company's $32 billion real estate loan portfolio is home mortgages. Great Western, primarily through its Blazer Financial Services and City Finance affiliates, also has about $1.3 billion in consumer loans. The company became the first savings institution to offer its own group of mutual funds (Sierra) in 1989.

Great Western Bank, a federal savings bank, has more than 350 retail banking branches located statewide in California and in Arizona, Florida, New York, and Washington. With its recent CenTrust and Gibraltar purchases, the company became the largest savings and loan association in Florida, based on assets, deposits, and branches.

WHEN

Great Western began operations in California as a state-licensed savings and loan in 1919.

In 1955 Great Western became part of Great Western Financial Corporation, the holding company it formed. Within 5 years of its creation, Great Western Financial acquired Santa Ana Savings (1956), West Coast Savings (Sacramento, 1957), Guaranty Savings (San Jose, 1958), Central Savings (San Luis Obispo, 1959), and First Savings (Oakland, 1959). The company later bought Santa Rosa Savings (1968) and Safety Savings (Los Angeles, 1969).

In 1970 and 1971 Great Western continued its expansion throughout California by purchasing Belmont Savings, Citizen Savings (Santa Barbara), Victory Savings (North Hollywood), and Sentinel Savings (San Diego). In 1972 Great Western Financial combined its acquired subsidiary savings associations into Great Western Savings.

In 1974 the company was the first to offer variable-rate mortgages (interest rate changes according to lender's cost of funds), which by 1979 were 60% of the company's mortgage loans and accounted for about $20 million in annual revenues.

The company entered the 1980s with $9 billion in assets and began offering only adjustable-rate mortgages (ARMs) — tied to an index rate outside the lender's control — as soon as they were authorized by federal regulators in 1981. Under James F. Montgomery, CEO since 1979, the company has grown and diversified while building a strong capital position. Great Western expanded its consumer finance business in 1983 by buying Aristar and its Blazer Financial Services subsidiary. That year Great Western began mortgage lending in Florida by opening a real estate loan office in Boca Raton.

In 1984 the company became the first US savings institution to issue floating-rate notes in Europe. Its Florida expansion continued in 1986 with the purchase of Intercapital Savings (Jacksonville). By 1987, 75% of the company's fixed-rate and variable-rate mortgage loans were converted to ARMs. The company expanded its operations to Washington and Arizona and purchased City Finance (consumer finance, 1987).

Great Western almost eliminated commercial real estate lending by 1989 in order to focus on single-family mortgages and consumer loans. At year end the company added about $200 million to its loan reserves for commercial and multifamily real estate loans, resulting in net earnings of $100 million in 1989, compared to $248 million in 1988. In 1990 Great Western purchased 71 CenTrust Savings Bank branches and 18 Gibraltar Savings Bank branches in Florida from the Resolution Trust Company.

HOW MUCH

	9 Yr. Growth	1980	1981	1982	1983	1984	1985	1986	1987	1988	1989
Sales ($ mil)	16.3%	997	1,174	1,387	1,993	2,869	3,404	3,774	3,958	3,174	3,881
Net income ($ mil)	11.0%	39	(28)	(75)	74	94	202	301	210	248	100
Income as % of sales	—	3.9%	(2.4%)	(5.4%)	3.7%	3.3%	5.9%	8.0%	5.3%	7.8%	2.6%
Earnings per share ($)	1.3%	0.70	(0.50)	(1.07)	0.82	1.00	1.78	2.51	1.64	1.95	0.78
Stock price – high ($)	—	9.40	7.65	11.95	12.60	10.55	13.90	19.30	24.38	17.38	25.13
Stock price – low ($)	—	5.60	4.80	3.80	7.45	6.60	9.00	13.25	12.00	12.63	14.63
Stock price – close ($)	10.0%	7.45	5.80	10.95	8.80	10.15	13.85	18.60	15.25	15.00	17.50
P/E – high	—	14	—	—	15	11	8	8	15	9	32
P/E – low	—	8	—	—	9	7	5	5	7	6	19
Dividends per share ($)	9.4%	0.35	0.35	0.21	0.21	0.35	0.38	0.46	0.66	0.75	0.79
Book value per share ($)	3.2%	11.70	11.05	9.26	9.68	10.31	11.93	14.19	14.87	15.48	15.48

1989 Year End:
Debt ratio: 71.6%
Return on equity: 5.0%
Cash (mil): $1,890
Assets (mil): $37,176
Long-term debt (mil): $5,012
Number of shares (mil): 128
Dividends:
1989 average yield: 4.5%
1989 payout: 101.3%
Market value (mil): $2,248

Stock Price History high/low 1980-89

30
25
20
15
10
5
0

NYSE symbol: GWF
Incorporated: Delaware, 1955
Fiscal year ends: December 31

WHO

Chairman and CEO: James F. Montgomery, age 55, $1,298,248 pay
President and COO: John F. Maher, age 46, $873,103 pay
EVP and CFO: Carl F. Geuther, age 44
EVP Real Estate Services: Eugene A. Crane, age 52
EVP Retail Banking: Curtis J. Crivelli, age 47
President, Consumer Finance: Michael M. Pappas, age 56, $419,490 pay
Auditors: Price Waterhouse
Employees: 12,800

WHERE

HQ: 8484 Wilshire Blvd., Beverly Hills, CA 90211
Phone: 213-852-3411
FAX: 213-852-3799 (Corporate Communications)

Great Western has over 350 retail banking offices in 5 states; 198 real estate lending offices in 20 states; and 500 consumer finance offices in 25 states.

WHAT

	1989 Sales		1989 Pretax Income	
	$ mil	% of total	$ mil	% of total
Savings bank	3,529	92	155	72
Consumer finance	295	8	59	28
Adjustments	57	—	—	—
Total	**3,881**	**100**	**214**	**100**

	1989 Net Revenue	
	$ mil	% of total
Net interest income	956	86
Other income	157	14
Total	**1,113**	**100**

Financial Services
Adjustable rate mortgages
Installment loans
Real estate brokerage
Real estate lending and investing
Retail banking
Securities brokerage

Subsidiaries & Affiliates
Blazer Financial Services
City Finance Company
Great Western Bank
Great Western Financial Securities Corp.

RANKINGS

2nd in *Fortune* 50 Savings Institutions
216th in *Forbes* Sales 500
300th in *Business Week* 1000
835th in *Business Week* Global 1000

COMPETITION

H. F. Ahmanson
Bank of New York
BankAmerica
Barnett Banks
Citicorp
First Interstate
Ford
ITT
NCNB
Primerica
Security Pacific
SunTrust
Wells Fargo
Other major banks

THE GREEN BAY PACKERS, INC.

OVERVIEW

Eat your heart out, George Steinbrenner.

While some pro team owner-moguls grab the headlines, owners of the Green Bay Packers still remember the fans, mostly because they *are* the fans — 1,856 of them, at least.

That's how many shareholders own the 4,627 shares of The Green Bay Packers, Inc., a private, nonprofit corporation. Of course, a National Football League team can turn a buck or 2, between tickets and TV, but the Packers corporation pays no dividends. If the team is ever liquidated, proceeds will go to build a war memorial in Green Bay.

Green Bay Packers, Inc., is governed by 45 directors and a 7-person executive committee. The Packers didn't have a full-time CEO until 1982, but they've had 11 head coaches. The Packers have high hopes after Lindy Infante, coach #11, guided the Pack in 1989 to a 10-6 record, the best performance in years.

Private company
Incorporated: Wisconsin, 1922
Fiscal year ends: March 30

WHO

Chairman: Judge Robert J. Parins, age 72
President and CEO: Robert E. Harlan, age 53
EVP Football Operations: Tom Braatz, age 57
Controller: Richard Blasczyk, age 56
Head Coach: Lindy Infante, age 50
Employees: 93

WHEN

In 1919 Curly Lambeau and George Calhoun met in the newsroom of the *Green Bay Press-Gazette* to organize a football team. The pair later talked Lambeau's employer — Indian Packing — into buying equipment for the team; to honor the sponsor, the team became known as the Packers.

Fans passed the hat at games. Heartened by early gridiron successes, Lambeau and 2 businessmen in 1921 obtained a franchise from the National Football League. Packer receipts didn't cover expenses, and the franchise had to be forfeited at the end of the season.

Lambeau and other backers bought the franchise again in 1922, but the Packers ran afoul of bad weather. A game was rained out, and the team's insurance company wouldn't pay off on its rain-out policy because the rainfall was 1/100-inch less than the policy required. Later that year, a storm threatened to cancel another game and ruin the team's fiscal health, but A. B. Turnbull, an executive of the *Press-Gazette*, convinced merchants in Green Bay to underwrite the team, and the Packers became a corporation.

In 1934 a fan fell from the stands and successfully sued the Packers for $5,000. The club's insurance company went out of business, and the Packers were forced into receivership. Green Bay merchants raised $15,000 to revive the corporation.

With Lambeau as coach, Green Bay developed a reputation for hard-nosed football. Spurred by end Don Hutson, the Packers racked up championships in 1936, 1939, and 1944.

Even though pro football grew in popularity after WWII, Green Bay continued to suffer financially. A 1949 intrasquad game raised $50,000 to keep the team afloat, and a 1950 stock drive in the community raised another $118,000.

Lambeau resigned from the Packers in 1950 to coach the Chicago Cardinals (predecessor of the modern Phoenix team). Packer football fortunes dipped in the 1950s, but the team moved into an enlarged stadium called Lambeau Field (1957), and Dominic Olejniczak was named president of the corporation (1958). Coach Vince Lombardi arrived in 1959. The team immediately returned to winning, and Lombardi teams dominated the game, winning back-to-back Super Bowls (1967, 1968). Green Bay still boasts the most league championships (11).

Lombardi left coaching for the Packer front office in 1968, and the team struggled to regain its luster during dismal seasons in the 1970s and 1980s.

In 1982 Robert Parins became the team's first full-time chief executive. After a record loss during the 1982 strike-shortened season, Parins spurred the corporation to a record $3 million profit (1986). Parins assumed the chairmanship in 1989, and Robert Harlan, a former sports publicist, became president and CEO. The Packers posted a $1.3 million profit in 1988 but declined to just over $400,000 in 1989.

WHERE

HQ: 1265 Lombardi Ave., Green Bay, WI 54304
Phone: 414-496-5700
FAX: 414-496-5712

The Green Bay Packers, Inc. fields a football team. In the 1990-1991 season the Packers are scheduled to play 5 games in Green Bay, 3 in Milwaukee, and 1 each in (in order of occurrence) Detroit, Chicago, Tampa Bay, Los Angeles, Phoenix, Minneapolis, Philadelphia, and Denver.

	1989 Sales	
	$ mil	% of total
Home games	5.2	17
Out-of-town games	3.4	11
Other	21.5	72
Total	**30.1**	**100**

WHAT

	1989 Sales	
	$ mil	% of total
Regular season		
Net receipts from home games	5.2	17
Out-of-town games	3.4	12
TV, radio & programs	16.0	53
Preseason	1.5	5
Miscellaneous		
Allocation of NFL receipts	1.3	4
Private box income	.7	3
NFL properties	.6	2
Other	1.3	4
Total	**30.1**	**100**

Touchdowns (1989)
Passing (27)
Returns (2)
Rushing (13)

Defense (1989)
Interceptions (25)
Quarterback sacks (34)
Yards allowed
Rushing (2,008)
Passing (3,339)

RANKINGS

1989
2nd in NFC Central Division (10-6)
8th in NFL in points scored (tie)
19th in NFL in points allowed
19th in NFL in sacks for
23rd in NFL in sacks against

COMPETITION

Edward J. DeBartolo

HOW MUCH

	9 Yr. Growth	1980	1981	1982*	1983	1984	1985	1986	1987*	1988	1989
Sales ($ mil)	11.5%	11.3	11.7	12.3	20.2	22.8	24.4	27.4	23.7	28.0	30.1
Net income ($ mil)	—	1.3	.9	(1.7)	1.9	1.5	2.0	3.1	2.8	1.3	0.4
Attendance (thou)	—	943	919	460	847	874	821	865	697	811	876
Games won	—	5	8	5	8	8	8	4	5	4	10
Games lost	—	10	8	3	8	8	8	12	9	12	6
Games tied	—	1	0	1	0	0	0	0	1	0	0
Points for	—	231	324	226	429	390	337	254	255	240	362
Points against	—	371	361	169	439	309	355	418	300	315	356
Division finish	—	5	2	1	2	2	2	4	3	5	2
Winning percentage	—	31.3%	50.0%	55.6%	50.0%	50.0%	50.0%	25.0%	33.3%	25.0%	62.5%

Winning Percentage 1980-89

65%
60%
55%
50%
45%
40%
35%
30%
25%
20%

Note: All figures for regular season *strike-shortened season

GREYHOUND DIAL CORPORATION

OVERVIEW

Greyhound Dial makes and sells consumer goods, provides a panoply of services, manufactures buses, owns a piece of a Canadian bus line, and finances real estate and commercial activities.

The company sells a wide range of cleaning and personal hygiene products such as Dial, the nation's best-selling deodorant soap, and Brillo soap pads. The Consumer Products and Services divisions account for more than 75% of the company's operating income.

Greyhound Dial prepares food for companies and airlines; provides aircraft ground services; operates drug, gift, and duty-free shops; and runs resorts. The company also provides services to conventions and trade shows, has a temporary technical personnel service, sells money orders, and provides commercial financing in the US and abroad. The company no longer operates its US bus line, but it does own a cruise ship company.

WHEN

In 1914 Swedish immigrant Carl Eric Wickman used a 7-passenger car to run miners between Hibbing, Minnesota, and a nearby town with a saloon. Wickman's bus operations expanded and became Northland Transportation (1925). In 1928 Northland sold 80% of its stock for $240,000 to Great Northern Railroad. With the infusion of capital, Northland kept buying more bus lines, as many as 60 in 6 weeks, including some using Greyhound in their names. In 1930 Northland renamed itself The Greyhound Corporation and settled into new headquarters in Chicago.

During the Great Depression General Motors helped bail out its customer Greyhound by assuming $1 million of its debt. Another boon came when Clark Gable courted Claudette Colbert on a Greyhound bus in the 1934 film *It Happened One Night*. The company's business soared.

During WWII the company's crowded buses transported draftees to training centers under a military contract. In the postwar years it bought control in bus lines throughout the country. In the 1950s the company adopted its "Go Greyhound — and leave the driving to us" slogan. *Greyhound* became synonymous in America with *bus*.

In the 1960s Greyhound began to diversify away from buses. It bought an equipment leasing company (Boothe Leasing, 1962), a food service company (Prophet Company, 1964), and a money order business (Travelers Express, 1965).

In 1970 Greyhound stretched to purchase Armour & Company for $355 million. Armour, the meat-packing company begun in 1863, was annually selling $2.5 billion of products, from Dial soap to meat products. Greyhound, a new force in consumer products, moved its headquarters from Chicago to Phoenix (1971).

Airline and bus deregulation hurt Greyhound in the early 1980s. When Greyhound cut wages to stem losses, 12,700 workers staged a 7-week strike in 1983. Greyhound sold Armour Foods to ConAgra (1983) and established a cruise line (1984).

In 1987 it sold its US intercity bus business to a group of Dallas investors for $257 million. Greyhound, effectively removed from the US bus business that had made it famous, turned its attention to airports, purchasing Dobbs Houses, an airport and in-flight concessions company (1987).

Rather than running intercity buses in the US, it was building them through its Transportation Manufacturing Corporation subsidiary. In 1987 Greyhound added GM's bus manufacturing division to its holdings.

In 1990 the company changed its name to Greyhound Dial to highlight its consumer businesses and to distance itself from the Greyhound Lines it had sold.

HOW MUCH

	9 Yr. Growth	1980	1981	1982	1983	1984	1985	1986	1987	1988	1989
Sales ($ mil)	(3.3%)	4,766	4,699	4,526	2,131	2,201	2,562	2,584	2,259	3,305	3,537
Net income ($ mil)	(0.9%)	118	138	106	70	125	120	94	83	93	109
Income as % of sales	—	2.5%	2.9%	2.3%	3.3%	5.7%	4.7%	3.7%	3.7%	2.8%	3.1%
Earnings per share ($)	1.0%	2.50	2.89	2.29	1.43	2.52	2.44	2.07	2.09	2.41	2.74
Stock price – high ($)	—	18.63	20.25	19.00	28.00	26.25	34.50	38.00	46.00	36.88	37.75
Stock price – low ($)	—	12.50	13.25	12.63	17.13	18.63	23.88	27.13	19.25	25.38	28.75
Stock price – close ($)	9.7%	13.88	15.50	17.25	25.38	24.25	32.38	31.00	25.50	30.00	32.00
P/E – high	—	7	7	8	20	10	14	18	22	15	14
P/E – low	—	5	5	6	12	7	10	13	9	11	11
Dividends per share ($)	1.1%	1.20	1.20	1.20	1.20	1.20	1.26	1.32	1.32	1.32	1.32
Book value per share ($)	3.9%	19.14	20.90	22.06	22.86	24.07	24.99	26.72	24.80	26.32	27.00

1989 Year End:
Debt ratio: 62.6%
Return on equity: 10.3%
Cash (mil): $859
Current ratio: —
Long-term debt (mil): $1,797
Number of shares (mil): 40
Dividends:
1989 average yield: 4.1%
1989 payout: 48.2%
Market value (mil): $1,274

Stock Price History high/low 1980-89

50 45 40 35 30 25 20 15 10 5 0

NYSE symbol: G
Incorporated: Arizona, 1978
Fiscal year ends: December 31

WHO

Chairman, President, and CEO: John W. Teets, age 56, $1,927,095 pay
President and COO, The Dial Corp.: Andrew S. Patti, age 49, $518,177 pay
VP and Counsel: L. Gene Lemon, age 49, $504,611 pay
VP Finance: F. Edward Lake, age 55
President and CEO, Greyhound Financial Corp.: Samuel L. Eichenfield, age 53, $464,766 pay
Auditors: Deloitte & Touche
Employees: 37,000

WHERE

HQ: Greyhound Tower, Phoenix, AZ 85077
Phone: 602-248-4000
FAX: 602-248-5473

Greyhound Dial has 21 consumer product plants in the US and 7 offices in foreign countries. It has 318 offices, duty-free and gift shops, and construction and parts facilities in the US and foreign countries. It also operates 3 cruise ships and 453 food service centers. The company runs 550 bus stops, 9 garages, and 7 terminals (Canada), and manufactures buses at plants in the US and Canada.

	1989 Sales		1989 Operating Income	
	$ mil	% of total	$ mil	% of total
US	3,068	87	252	83
Foreign	469	13	53	17
Adjustments	—	—	131	—
Total	**3,537**	**100**	**436**	**100**

WHAT

	1989 Sales		1989 Operating Income	
	$ mil	% of total	$ mil	% of total
Consumer products	941	27	81	26
Transportation mfg.	565	16	50	16
Services	1,762	49	141	47
Financial	269	8	33	11
Adjustments	—	—	131	—
Total	**3,537**	**100**	**436**	**100**

Consumer Products
Armour Star canned meats
Lunch Bucket meals
Dial bar and liquid soaps
Dial deodorant
Tone soap
Borateem and Borax
Brillo
Purex bleach

Services
Dobbs Houses
Dobbs International Services
Greyhound Lines of Canada
Motor Coach Industries
Premier Cruise Lines
Republic Money Orders
Travelers Express Co.
26 other service companies

RANKINGS

29th in *Fortune* 100 Diversified Service Cos.
233rd in *Forbes* Sales 500
459th in *Business Week* 1000

COMPETITION

Financial services companies
Food manufacturers
Personal and household products manufacturers

GTE CORPORATION

OVERVIEW

GTE is swallowing Contel. Under a merger plan announced in mid-1990, GTE will become the largest US-based local telephone utility, with more lines and more assets than any of the former AT&T regional companies. GTE will also become the 2nd largest cellular telephone provider, behind McCaw Cellular.

Premerger GTE made 89% of its money in the telephone business, with more than 14 million customers in the US, Canada, and the Dominican Republic. GTE also produces phone directories and makes more than 6,000 types of Sylvania lamps and bulbs.

Other services are more futuristic. It experiments with credit card cellular phones in Hertz rental cars. Its Airfone provides ground-to-air phone service to 1,200 airliners. GTE's Spacenet provides satellite-based communications. In California it is testing the "network of the future": fiber optic–delivered telephone and 2-way television service.

NYSE symbol: GTE
Incorporated: New York, 1935
Fiscal year ends: December 31

WHO

Chairman and CEO: James L. Johnson, age 62, $1,410,503 pay
President and COO: Charles R. Lee, age 50, $934,035 pay
SVP External Affairs and General Counsel: Edward C. Schmults, age 59, $593,184 pay
SVP Finance: Nicholas L. Trivisonno, age 42, $565,054 pay
SVP Human Resources and Administration: Bruce Carswell, age 60, $559,923 pay
Auditors: Arthur Andersen & Co.
Employees: 158,000

WHEN

Two former staff members of the Wisconsin Railroad Commission — Sigurd Odegard and John O'Connell — formed Richland Center Telephone in Wisconsin dairy country in 1918.

On a vacation to California, Odegard came upon an independent telephone company for sale in Long Beach. With backing from a utilities executive and a Paine Webber partner, Odegard and O'Connell created Associated Telephone Utilities in 1926 to buy the Long Beach company. Associated Telephone grew rapidly, but the company ran afoul of the Great Depression. Lenders took control in 1932 and moved headquarters from Chicago to New York. Still beset by problems, Associated was forced into bankruptcy and emerged as General Telephone in 1935.

Attorney David Power, named CEO in 1951, guided post-WWII growth as General Telephone acquired Theodore Gary and Company (1955) and Sylvania (1959). The Gary acquisition included phone companies in Canada and the Dominican Republic, but the crown jewel was Automatic Electric, a manufacturer of telephone switching equipment. Automatic Electric traced its heritage to the 1889 invention of an automatic switch by Kansas City undertaker Almon Strowger. Strowger was convinced that he was losing business when the telephone company operators didn't handle calls properly. Even the Bell System bought from Automatic Electric while it was the only manufacturer of dial equipment.

The 1959 Sylvania purchase changed General Telephone's complexion and its name. It became a manufacturer and developer of lighting and electronics, and it became General Telephone and Electronics. Sylvania had begun in 1901 when Frank Poor invested in a Massachusetts company that refilled burned-out light bulbs. When absorbed into GTE, Sylvania had 45 plants, 22 laboratories, and annual sales exceeding $333 million.

The company, long the largest phone company independent of the Bell group, continued expansion with the purchase of phone companies, most notably in Florida (1957), the Southwest (1964), and Hawaii (1967). GTE sold its US consumer electronics to North American Philips in 1981, and GTE Mobilnet was formed in 1982 to provide cellular telephone service.

GTE, adopting its acronym for a name in 1982, spent the 1980s organizing its varied activities, from military hardware to phone books. Under Chairman James (Rocky) Johnson, it sold most of its US Sprint long-distance service, purchased in 1983 from Southern Pacific, to partner United Telecom in 1989. Concentrating again on its lucrative local phone businesses, GTE jettisoned Automatic Electric — as AG Communication Systems — creating a joint venture to be owned gradually by AT&T.

WHERE

HQ: One Stamford Forum, Stamford, CT 06904
Phone: 203-965-2000
FAX: 203-965-2277

In 1989 GTE had operations in 46 states and 41 foreign countries.

	1989 Sales		1989 Net Income	
	$ mil	% of total	$ mil	% of total
US	14,661	84	1,124	82
Foreign	2,763	16	246	18
Adjustments	—	—	(47)	—
Total	**17,424**	**100**	**1,417**	**100**

WHAT

	1989 Sales		1989 Operating Income	
	$ mil	% of total	$ mil	% of total
Telephone operns.	12,459	72	2,839	89
Electrical products	2,184	12	222	7
Telecommunications	2,838	16	128	4
Adjustments	(57)	—	(179)	—
Total	**17,424**	**100**	**3,010**	**100**

GTE Telephone Operations
Anglo-Canadian Telephone Co.
GTE California Inc.
GTE Florida Inc.
GTE Hawaiian Telephone Co.
GTE North Inc.
GTE Northwest Inc.
GTE South Inc.
GTE Southwest Inc.

GTE Telecommunications
AG Communications Systems
GTE Airfone
GTE Government Systems
GTE Information Services
GTE Mobile Communications
GTE Spacenet

GTE Electrical Products

GTE Laboratories

RANKINGS

1st in *Fortune* 50 Utilities
31st in *Forbes* Sales 500
18th in *Business Week* 1000
48th in *Business Week* Global 1000

COMPETITION

Ameritech
AT&T
BCE
Bell Atlantic
BellSouth
General Electric
IBM
ITT
McCaw Cellular
MCI
NYNEX
Pacific Telesis
Philips
Siemens
Southwestern Bell
United Telecommunications
U S West

Other telecommunications equipment manufacturers

HOW MUCH

	9 Yr. Growth	1980	1981	1982	1983	1984	1985	1986	1987	1988	1989
Sales ($ mil)	6.4%	9,979	11,026	12,066	12,944	14,547	15,732	15,112	15,421	16,460	17,424
Net income ($ mil)	9.6%	619	722	836	978	1,080	(161)	1,184	1,119	1,225	1,417
Income as % of sales	—	6.2%	6.5%	6.9%	7.6%	7.4%	(1.0%)	7.8%	7.3%	7.4%	8.1%
Earnings per share ($)	5.9%	2.46	2.75	3.03	3.29	3.45	*(0.63)*	3.44	3.22	3.53	4.11
Stock price – high ($)	—	20.00	22.83	30.42	32.25	29.25	30.92	42.58	44.75	45.88	71.13
Stock price – low ($)	—	14.75	16.33	17.58	25.75	23.25	25.42	30.17	29.38	33.75	42.88
Stock price – close ($)	16.2%	18.17	21.33	27.67	29.17	27.08	30.67	38.92	35.38	44.50	70.00
P/E – high	—	8	8	10	10	8	—	12	14	13	17
P/E – low	—	6	6	6	8	7	—	9	9	10	10
Dividends per share ($)	4.9%	1.81	1.85	1.92	1.97	2.03	2.08	2.20	2.48	2.60	2.80
Book value per share ($)	2.5%	19.30	19.87	21.01	22.59	24.07	21.49	23.28	23.83	24.91	24.02

1989 Year End:
Debt ratio: 56.5%
Return on equity: 16.8%
Cash (mil): $396
Current ratio: 0.98
Long-term debt (mil): $10,909
Number of shares (mil): 330
Dividends:
1989 average yield: 4.0%
1989 payout: 68.1%
Market value (mil): $23,121

Stock Price History high/low 1980-89

GUINNESS PLC

OVERVIEW

Although its name evokes images of dark, foamy stout, Guinness derives 80% of its operating profit from liquor sales. The company's beer and liquor brands include Guinness, Harp, Johnnie Walker (world's #1 scotch brand), Dewar's, I.W. Harper, Gordon's, and Tanqueray (best-selling imported gin in the US). Facing a continuing decline in worldwide hard liquor consumption, Guinness has successfully encouraged consumers to trade up to more expensive brands. Sales of Guinness's brewed products are concentrated in Ireland and Britain and growing rapidly in Southeast Asia.

In 1990 former Guinness CEO Ernest Saunders was found guilty of "dishonesty on a massive scale," according to UK trial judge Sir Denis Henry. Saunders had been accused of stock manipulation in connection with Guinness's 1986 takeover of Distillers Company.

WHEN

Arthur Guinness leased a small brewery in Dublin in 1759. The brewery, greatly updated and expanded, still exists today, its lease due to expire in the year 10759. At the brewery Guinness made ales (darker, more bitter beers) and porters (darker, heavier ales), which were at first sold only in Dublin. In 1799 Guinness began specializing in porters. In 1821 Extra Superior Porter, later named stout, represented 4% of Guinness's sales. In 1840 it represented 82% of sales and was spreading across Ireland to England. Sales growth was greatest in Ireland, which still consumes over 50% of Guinness's stout.

In 1886, managed by the 3rd generation of Guinnesses, the company went public. For many years Guinness was content to focus on stout, slowly extending its reach internationally and advertising the product's legendary health benefits. In the 1950s managing director Hugh E. C. Beaver persuaded company executives to launch Harp, a lager (lighter beer, served chilled), which today remains a leading brand in a highly fragmented British market. Beaver is also credited with conceiving of the remarkably successful *Guinness Book of World Records* in 1955.

In the 1970s Guinness embarked on an acquisition binge, buying over 200 unrelated companies, with disappointing results. In 1981 Guinness appointed Ernest Saunders CEO. He disposed of over 140 companies in 2 years, slashed overhead, and spent heavily on successful advertising of Guinness Stout. In 1984 Saunders began his own shopping spree, buying British newsstands, health spas, 7-Elevens, and Arthur Bell & Sons scotch. With earnings ascending, Saunders involved Guinness in a takeover battle against Argyll Group for control of Distillers Company (Johnnie Walker, Gordon's, Tanqueray). Saunders succeeded in acquiring Distillers for £2.5 billion.

In the months following the Distillers acquisition, the SEC investigation of Ivan Boesky's illegal trading activities uncovered records linking Saunders to a bold stock manipulation scheme. He is alleged to have promised illegal payments to financiers in exchange for their help in bidding up the price of Guinness stock prior to the Distillers acquisition. Such manipulation would have artificially increased the value of Guinness's stock-and-cash offer to Distiller shareholders. In January 1987 Saunders was fired.

Anthony Tennant, earlier passed over for the top job at Grand Metropolitan, became Guinness's chairman. He has focused Guinness on brewing, distilling, and controlling distribution, selling peripheral businesses and acquiring Schenley (Dewar's) in 1987.

In 1988 and 1989 Guinness bought 24% of French cognac, champagne, perfume, and leather goods maker Möet Hennessy Louis Vuitton (LVMH). LVMH then raised its stake in Guinness from 12% to 24% in 1990, encouraging takeover speculation. The 2 companies share sales companies in the US and Japan.

HOW MUCH

£=$1.61 (Dec. 31, 1989)	9 Yr. Growth	1980	1981	1982	1983	1984	1985	1986*	1987	1988	1989
Sales (£ mil)	16.4%	784	906	1,043	872	924	1,188	3,252	2,818	2,776	3,076
Net income (£ mil)	44.2%	17	23	23	30	38	54	241	274	342	457
Income as % of sales	—	2.2%	2.5%	2.2%	3.4%	4.1%	4.5%	7.4%	9.7%	12.3%	14.9%
Earnings per share (p)	15.5%	13.0	9.4	12.9	17.1	20.9	25.4	36.3	29.5	36.0	47.4
Stock price – high (p)	—	98	83	104	125	245	324	355	393	358	689
Stock price – low (p)	—	71	51	61	101	116	225	270	227	262	329
Stock price – close (p)	27.1%	79	63	103	116	244	320	313	291	334	686
P/E – high	—	8	9	8	7	12	13	—	15	10	15
P/E – low	—	5	5	5	6	6	9	—	9	7	7
Dividends per share (p)	13.5%	4.9	4.9	5.2	5.8	6.4	7.2	10.2	9.2	11.5	15.3
Book value per share (p)	11.1%	135	137	112	125	124	89	71	252	289	348

1989 Year End:
Debt ratio: 15.9%
Return on equity: 14.9%
Cash (mil): £224
Long-term debt (mil): £642
Number of shares (mil): 879
Dividends:
1989 average yield: 2.2%
1989 payout: 32.3%
Market value (mil): $3,745
Sales (mil): $4,952

Stock Price History high/low 1980-89

* 15-month accounting period

OTC symbol: GURSY (ADR)
Incorporated: England, 1986
Fiscal year ends: December 31

WHO

Chairman: Anthony Tennant, age 59, £495,000 pay
President: The Earl of Iveagh, age 52
Managing Director of Finance: Ian Duncan
Auditors: Price Waterhouse
Employees: 18,106

WHERE

HQ: 39 Portman Sq., London W1H 9HB, England
Phone: 011-44-71-486-0288
FAX: 011-44-71-486-4968
US HQ (Schenley Industries): 12770 Merit Dr., Dallas, TX 75251
Phone: 214-450-6400

Guinness has brewing interests in 30 countries and sells beer in 120 countries. The company's principal liquor operations are in Scotland, the US, Canada, Australia, New Zealand, Japan, and 8 European countries.

	1989 Sales		1989 Operating Profit	
	£ mil	% of total	£ mil	% of total
United Kingdom	1,024	33	124	18
Rest of Europe	824	27	147	22
North America	488	16	156	23
Asia/Pacific	492	16	130	19
Rest of the world	245	8	117	18
Discontinued operations	3	—	5	—
Total	**3,076**	**100**	**679**	**100**

WHAT

	1989 Sales		1989 Operating Profit	
	£ mil	% of total	£ mil	% of total
Liquor	1,938	63	542	80
Brewing	1,086	35	124	18
Enterprises	67	2	8	1
Discontinued operations	3	—	5	1
Total	**3,076**	**100**	**679**	**100**

Liquor
Bell's
Dewar's
Dimple/Pinch
Gordon's
I.W. Harper
Johnnie Walker
Old Parr
Tanqueray
White Horse

Brewed & Other Products
Budweiser (Ireland)
Carlsberg (Ireland)
Guinness
Guinness Book of World Records
Harp

Major Holdings
Guinness Anchor Berhad (Malaysia, 29%)
LVMH Moët Hennessy Louis Vuitton (France, 24%)
New Era Beverage Co. (US, 44.5%)

RANKINGS

370th in *Fortune* Global 500 Industrial Cos.
127th in *Business Week* Global 1000

COMPETITION

American Brands
Anheuser-Busch
Bass
Brown-Forman
BSN
Grand Metropolitan
Philip Morris
Seagram

HAL, INC.

OVERVIEW

HAL is the owner of Hawaiian Airlines and the West Maui Airport, an airport facility located at Mahinahina, Maui.

Based in Honolulu, Hawaiian flies passengers, mail, and cargo to 8 airports on the 6 major islands of Hawaii. Although it has shown only marginal profits for 3 of the past 9 years, the airline has maintained a slight lead over Aloha Airlines, its primary competitor for interisland traffic, carrying 51.7% of the passengers traveling between islands in 1989. The DOT granted temporary operating authority to a 3rd airline — Discovery Airways — in 1990 but revoked the license in July, when Discovery failed to abide by some of its conditions.

Hawaiian also flies to 7 cities in the South Pacific, including Sydney, Australia, and 4 cities in the western US, and offers worldwide charter services, with military charters accounting for about 55% of its charter revenues (1989). In February 1990 the DOD temporarily suspended use of Hawaiian for military charters pending an inquiry into record-keeping and maintenance practices.

AMEX symbol: HA
Incorporated: Hawaii, 1982
Fiscal year ends: December 31

WHO

Chairman and CEO: J. Thomas Talbot, age 54
President and COO: John A. Ueberroth, age 45
SVP Finance and CFO: Glen L. Stewart, age 47
Auditors: KPMG Peat Marwick
Employees: 3,075

WHERE

HQ: 1164 Bishop St., PO Box 30008, Honolulu, HI 96820
Phone: 808-835-3001
FAX: 808-835-3015 (Finance)

HAL flies to 6 Hawaiian islands, the West Coast, and the South Pacific. The company also provides worldwide charter services.

Hawaiian Destinations
Hilo and Kona, Hawaii
Honolulu, Oahu
Kahului and Mahinahina, Maui
Lanai, Lanai
Lihue, Kauai
Molokai, Molokai

Mainland Destinations
Las Vegas, NV
Los Angeles and San Francisco, CA
Seattle, WA

South Pacific Destinations
Agana, Guam
Apia, Western Samoa
Nuku´alofa, Tonga
Pago Pago, American Samoa
Papeete, Tahiti
Rarotonga, Cook Islands
Sydney, Australia

WHEN

In 1929 former WWI naval pilot Stanley Kennedy, then general manager of the Inter-Island Steam Navigation Company, persuaded the Inter-Island board to put up 76% equity financing to establish Inter-Island Airways, Ltd., a passenger line linking Honolulu (Oahu) with the islands of Hawaii, Maui, Kauai, Molokai, and Lanai. The company started airmail service from Honolulu to Hilo and Kauai in 1934.

The company was renamed Hawaiian Airlines, Ltd., in 1941. TWA bought 20% of the company in 1944 but sold it 4 years later. In 1946 the creation of Trans-Pacific Airlines (later Aloha Airlines) ended Hawaiian's 17-year service monopoly in Hawaii.

The 2 airlines operated almost identical routes, creating intense competition. Each struggled for technological superiority: Hawaiian introduced the Douglas DC-9 in 1966 and Aloha, the Boeing 737, in 1969. Rising costs were not matched by increased sales, however, and the airlines agreed to merge in 1970, with John Magoon, who had bought control of Hawaiian in 1964, as president. However, negotiations failed and merger plans were abandoned in 1971.

With the 1978 Airline Deregulation Act, Hawaiian, like other intrastate carriers, gained access to new markets. The company adopted HAL, Inc., as its corporate name in 1982 and by 1985 had expanded service to the West Coast (Los Angeles, San Francisco, Las Vegas, and Seattle) and the South Pacific (American Samoa and Tonga). While the airline was able to fill its planes to 65.2% capacity (the industry's highest), its yields per passenger were among the lowest because of fare discounts sparked by competition with United and Continental to the West Coast.

HAL built the $8.5 million West Maui Airport in 1987 but had to contend with increasing aircraft maintenance costs (up to $70 million in 1988 from $35 million in 1986) due to the corrosive salt air and stress from frequent short flights. Magoon decided to sell a 46.5% interest in the airline to a group of investors, which included long-time friend and ex–baseball commissioner Peter Ueberroth. The group, headed by Jet America Airlines's founder J. Thomas Talbot, bought HAL in 1989 for $37 million. Magoon remains a director of HAL, and Talbot, now chairman and CEO, plans to improve the company's on-time record and maintenance management. In 1990 the DOD suspension and competition from Discovery (which HAL sued in June) caused a small decline in first-half revenues and resulted in a loss for that period equal to the entire 1989 loss.

WHAT

Hawaiian Airlines, Inc.

West Maui Airport, Inc.

	1989 Sales $ mil	1989 Sales % of total
Passenger service	260	74
Charters	59	17
Cargo	20	6
Other	10	3
Total	**349**	**100**

Flight Equipment	Owned	Leased	Total
Lockheed L-1011	–	5	5
DC-8	–	6	6
DC-9	–	10	10
de Havilland DHC-7	2	6	8
Shorts SD3-30	–	3	3
Total	**2**	**30**	**32**

HOW MUCH

	9 Yr. Growth	1980	1981	1982	1983	1984	1985	1986	1987	1988	1989
Sales ($ mil)	14.3%	104	99	101	94	128	160	225	299	354	349
Net income ($ mil)	—	0	5	(17)	(6)	6	0	3	(9)	(9)	(47)
Income as % of sales	—	0.3%	5.4%	(16.7%)	(6.1%)	4.5%	(0.1%)	1.5%	(2.9%)	(2.5%)	(13.5%)
Earnings per share ($)	—	0.19	2.75	(8.79)	(3.01)	3.04	(0.10)	1.83	(4.57)	(4.48)	(24.00)
Stock price – high ($)	—	5.25	9.00	7.00	5.63	10.38	10.13	21.75	48.00	34.00	40.25
Stock price – low ($)	—	3.63	3.63	3.63	3.75	4.13	7.13	8.13	17.00	17.25	20.13
Stock price – close ($)	20.9%	3.75	4.25	4.88	4.63	7.50	9.00	21.75	17.75	23.25	20.63
P/E – high	—	28	3	—	—	3	—	12	—	—	—
P/E – low	—	19	1	—	—	1	—	4	—	—	—
Dividends per share ($)	0.0%	0.00	0.00	0.00	0.00	0.00	0.10	0.00	0.15	0.00	0.00
Book value per share ($)	(7.1%)	5.96	7.14	(1.65)	7.04	10.07	9.91	11.61	6.79	2.31	3.07

1989 Year End:
Debt ratio: 87.5%
Return on equity: —
Cash (mil): $26
Current ratio: 0.52
Long-term debt (mil): $46
Number of shares (mil): 2
Dividends:
1989 average yield: —
1989 payout: —
Market value (mil): $45

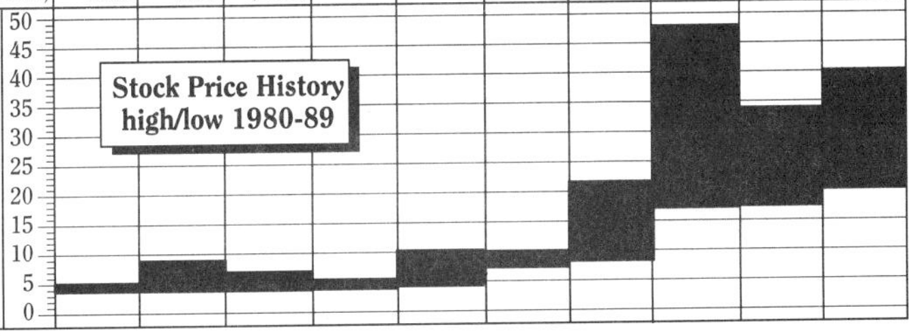

Stock Price History high/low 1980-89

0 5 10 15 20 25 30 35 40 45 50

RANKINGS

46th in *Fortune* 50 Transportation Cos.

COMPETITION

America West
AMR
Continental
Delta
NWA
Pan Am
TWA
UAL

HALLIBURTON COMPANY

OVERVIEW

Halliburton, a leading oil field engineering and construction services company, holds 60% of the worldwide market for oil well cementing and 50% for oil stimulation.

Its Brown & Root division is a leader in erecting offshore drilling platforms and laying underwater pipelines. Brown & Root is one of the US's largest nuclear power, chemical, and petrochemical plant builders.

Through recently acquired Gearhart Industries, the company has become a major player in wireline logging (a process for charting where oil and gas lie); newly acquired Geosource is a leading geophysical services company providing seismic data collection services.

Halliburton also provides property, casualty, and marine insurance, and health care cost-management services through Highlands Insurance and Health Economics companies. Already active in 112 foreign countries (50% of profits are derived from foreign operations), the company focused on international expansion in Eastern Europe in 1989 and continued investing in its oil and gas services business.

WHEN

Erle Halliburton began his oil career in 1916 when he went to work for Perkins Oil Well Cementing. Discharged for suggesting too many new ideas, Halliburton left for Burkburnett, Texas, in 1919 and started his Better Method Oil Well Cementing Company. Halliburton used cement to hold a steel pipe in a well, which kept oil out of the water table; although his contribution is widely recognized today, it was considered nonessential then. In 1921, the same year he moved to Duncan, Oklahoma, he recorded his first profit — of $0.50. In 1924 he incorporated as Halliburton Oil Well Cementing Company.

Between the 1950s and 1970s Halliburton built up its present-day, Dallas-based oil service business by buying companies with expertise throughout the oil and gas market. Halliburton acquired Welex, a well-logging company (1957), and Houston-based Brown & Root industrial/marine construction company (1966), which had expertise in offshore platforms. Halliburton formed Nova Pressure Service (1971), specializing in hydrostatic test operations. Halliburton bought Ebasco Services, an electric utility engineering company with expertise in nuclear plants (1973), but the Justice Department forced its sale (1976), fearing Halliburton's share of the utility engineering market (20%) would limit market competition.

The investments in Welex, Nova, and Brown & Root left Halliburton well positioned to benefit from the oil exploration boom of the 1970s. Later that decade, as drilling costs surged, Halliburton shifted focus and quickly became the leader in stimulating old and abandoned wells by developing new techniques for fracturing deep formations.

When the bottom fell out of the oil industry in 1982, Halliburton steered clear of further oil- and gas-related investments, instead cutting employment by more than 1/2, while rivals Schlumberger and Dresser were buying up distressed companies at bargain prices. Other Halliburton businesses were not faring well either. In 1985 Halliburton's largest division, Brown & Root, already suffering a scarcity of new construction projects, settled out of court for $750 million for mismanagement of the South Texas Nuclear Project.

In 1988 Halliburton began reinvesting in the oil and gas services market by buying Texas Instrument's Geophysical Services, the 2nd largest seismic service company in the US, and Geosource, another provider of geophysical services. That year Halliburton also purchased wireline services provider Gearhart Industries and merged it with Welex to form Halliburton Logging Services, and announced plans with Du Pont to enter the hazardous waste cleanup business.

HOW MUCH

	9 Yr. Growth	1980	1981	1982	1983	1984	1985	1986	1987	1988	1989
Sales ($ mil)	(4.2%)	8,327	8,435	7,282	5,511	5,428	4,781	3,527	3,836	4,826	5,660
Net income ($ mil)	(13.6%)	500	674	497	315	330	29	(515)	48	85	134
Income as % of sales	—	6.0%	8.0%	6.8%	5.7%	6.1%	0.6%	(14.6%)	1.3%	1.8%	2.4%
Earnings per share ($)	(12.6%)	4.25	5.72	4.21	2.66	2.87	0.27	(4.85)	0.45	0.81	1.26
Stock price – high ($)	—	86.44	84.50	52.75	47.25	44.00	33.88	28.00	43.13	36.50	44.50
Stock price – low ($)	—	41.00	44.13	21.00	29.25	27.13	24.50	17.38	20.13	24.38	27.50
Stock price – close ($)	(7.2%)	83.50	52.13	35.38	40.38	28.50	27.50	24.38	24.75	28.00	42.75
P/E – high	—	20	15	13	18	15	125	—	96	45	35
P/E – low	—	10	8	5	11	9	91	—	45	30	22
Dividends per share ($)	(0.5%)	1.05	1.30	1.60	1.65	1.80	1.80	1.20	1.00	1.00	1.00
Book value per share ($)	(1.3%)	22.39	26.85	29.49	30.18	31.19	26.30	20.30	19.76	19.80	19.90

1989 Year End:
Debt ratio: 8.5%
Return on equity: 6.3%
Cash (mil): $402
Assets (mil): $4,263
Long-term debt (mil): $198
Number of shares (mil): 107
Dividends:
1989 average yield: 2.3%
1989 payout: 79.4%
Market value (mil): $4,553

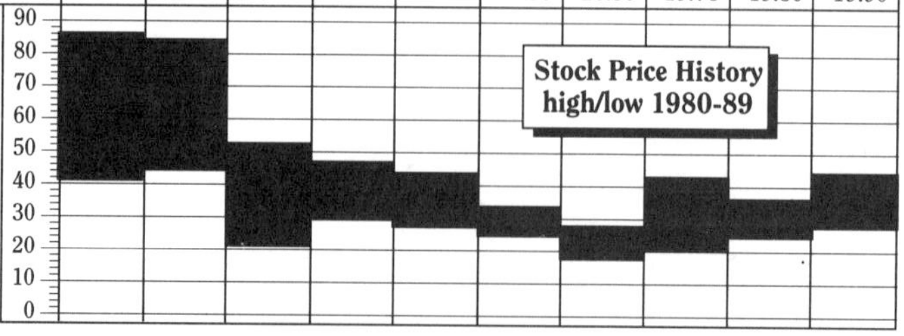

NYSE symbol: HAL
Incorporated: Delaware, 1924
Fiscal year ends: December 31

WHO

Chairman, CEO, and President: Thomas H. Cruikshank, age 58, $675,000 pay
Chairman and CEO, Brown & Root, Inc.: T. Louis Austin, Jr., age 71, $454,167 pay
President and EVP, Oil Field Services: Dale P. Jones, age 53, $362,500 pay
President, Halliburton Logging Services: James A. Dunlop, age 55, $300,000 pay
President, Oil Field Services Group; President, Halliburton Services Division: Alan A. Baker, age 57, $279,167 pay
EVP Finance and Corporate Development: Lester L. Coleman, age 47
Auditors: Arthur Andersen & Co.
Employees: 65,500

WHERE

HQ: 3600 Lincoln Plaza, Dallas, TX 75201
Phone: 214-978-2600
FAX: 214-978-2611

Halliburton conducts business in the US and in 112 foreign countries.

	1989 Sales		1989 Operating Income	
	$ mil	% of total	$ mil	% of total
US	3,928	70	128	50
Europe	696	12	14	5
Other foreign	1,038	18	117	45
Adjustments	(2)	—	(21)	—
Total	**5,660**	**100**	**238**	**100**

WHAT

	1989 Sales		1989 Operating Income	
	$ mil	% of total	$ mil	% of total
Oil field services	2,448	43	168	65
Insurance services	355	6	33	13
Engineering & construction	2,859	51	58	22
Adjustments	(2)	—	(21)	—
Total	**5,660**	**100**	**238**	**100**

Oil Field Services
Cementing and well stimulation
Industrial cleaning services
Jet perforating services
Logging equipment sales
Gas equipment leasing
Sales of seismic equipment
Sand and water control
Seismic data collection and data processing
Tubing-conveyed well completion systems
Wireline and mineral logging services

Engineering & Construction Services
Design and construction of utilities, chemical plants, mills, highways, and bridges
Environmental/waste management services
Marine services

Insurance Services
Health care cost containment
Property and casualty insurance

RANKINGS

14th in *Fortune* 100 Diversified Service Cos.
155th in *Forbes* Sales 500
131st in *Business Week* 1000
355th in *Business Week* Global 1000

COMPETITION

Baker Hughes
Bechtel
Dresser
FMC
General Electric
McDermott
Ogden
Peter Kiewit Sons'
Schlumberger
Siemens
Other oil service companies

HALLMARK CARDS, INC.

OVERVIEW

Privately owned Hallmark in Kansas City, Missouri, is a leading producer of greeting cards, ribbons and bows, gift wrap, crayons, candles, jigsaw puzzles, Christmas ornaments, wedding products, party goods, plush toys, and related gift items. Hallmark employs the world's largest creative staff, and its name is recognized by 99 out of 100 consumers.

Hallmark and its Ambassador division (which together own a 44% share of the greeting card market) publish over 11 million greeting cards and produce over 1.5 million other products each day. Hallmark produced enough ribbon in 1989 to circle the earth more than 17 times. Sales in 1989 were about $2.5 billion.

The company's greeting cards are published in over 20 languages and sold (through its Hallmark International division) in over 100 countries. Hallmark and Ambassador products are sold through 37,000 retail outlets, almost 11,000 of which are independently owned specialty shops. The company itself owns about 175 shops.

True to the ideals of the company's founder, Hallmark has developed a reputation for philanthropy, with over 500 charitable grants in 1989.

WHEN

Eighteen-year-old Joyce C. Hall started selling postcards from a rented room at the Kansas City, Missouri, YMCA in 1910. Hall's brother Rollie joined him in 1911 and the 2 added greeting cards (which were made by another company) to their product line in 1912. By the mid-teens the brothers had established Hall Brothers, a store which sold postcards, gifts, books, and stationery. After a 1915 fire destroyed their entire inventory (just before Valentine's Day), the brothers quickly regrouped, got a loan, bought an engraving company, and produced their first original greeting cards in time for Christmas. The company's first humorous greeting card depicted a small cartoon dog with the caption: "Not little like this tiny pup/But big just like a dog grown up! I'm wishing you a DOG-GONE MERRY CHRISTMAS."

During the 1920s a 3rd brother, William, joined the firm, and the company started stamping the back of its cards with the phrase "A Hallmark Card." By 1922 Hall Brothers had salesmen in all 48 states and for the first time expanded beyond greeting cards with the introduction of gift wrap. Joyce Hall placed the company's first national ad in the *Ladies Home Journal* in 1928.

In 1936 Hall Brothers introduced a display case fixture for greeting cards (which had previously been kept haphazardly under store counters) and sold it to retailers across the country. The company aired its first radio ad in 1938 and in 1944 adopted the slogan, "When You Care Enough to Send the Very Best," written by employee Ed Goodman. In 1942 Hall Brothers introduced a friendship card which showed a cart filled with flowers. The card would become the company's all-time best-seller, and is still sold today.

After WWII Hall Brothers grew tremendously as Joyce Hall strove to give his company's products a reputation for high quality. In 1950 the company opened its first greeting card retail store and in 1951 broadcast the first "Hallmark Hall of Fame" television production (a color version of *Amahl and the Night Visitors*). The critically acclaimed "Hallmark Hall of Fame" (with 61 Emmy awards to date) would become the longest-running dramatic television series in history. Hall Brothers changed its name to Hallmark in 1954 and 3 years later went international. In 1959 the company opened its Ambassador Cards division (greeting cards).

Hallmark introduced a line of paper party products and started putting "Peanuts" characters (Charlie Brown, Snoopy) on its cards in 1960. In 1968 the company started construction on Crown Center (a $500 million complex of offices, shops, and residences), which surrounds the company headquarters in Kansas City. Tragedy struck the complex in 1981 when a walkway collapsed at the Crown Hyatt Regency, killing 113. During the 1970s, Hallmark introduced Christmas ornaments to its product line.

In 1982 Joyce Hall died, and his son Donald became chairman of the board in 1983. The company acquired Binney & Smith (Crayola Crayons) in 1984 and Univision (Spanish-language TV network) in 1987. Hallmark celebrated its 75th anniversary in 1985 and opened its Hallmark Visitors Center, a museum which traces the history of the company. In 1990 Hallmark acquired Dakin (plush toys).

HOW MUCH

	9 Yr. Growth	1980	1981	1982	1983	1984	1985	1986	1987	1988	1989
Domestic employees*	3.1%	15,896	16,101	15,736	16,187	17,968	17,971	17,495	18,121	19,075	20,850
Sales ($ mil)	—	—	—	—	—	—	1,500	1,680	2,000	2,250	2,500

Domestic Employees 1980-89

25,000 · 20,000 · 15,000 · 10,000 · 5,000 · 0

*excludes Evenson's, Binney & Smith, and Univision, acquired in 1980, 1984, and 1987, respectively.

Private company
Founded: Missouri, 1910

WHO

Chairman: Donald J. Hall, age 61
VC: David H. Hughes, age 61
President and CEO: Irvine O. Hockaday, Jr., age 53
Employees: 21,500 full time and 12,000 part time

WHERE

HQ: 2501 McGee, PO Box 419580, Kansas City, MO 64141
Phone: 816-274-5111
FAX: 816-274-8513

Hallmark has production facilities in 4 cities in Kansas (Lawrence, Leavenworth, Osage City, and Topeka) and in Kansas City, MO. It also maintains distribution centers in Enfield, CT, and Liberty, MO.

Products are distributed in more than 100 countries.

WHAT

Products
Albums
Art supplies and crayons
Calendars
Candles
Christmas ornaments
Figurines
Gift wrap, ribbons, and bows
Gifts
Greeting cards
Home decorations
Jigsaw puzzles
Party goods
Plush toys
Wedding products
Writing papers and pens

Brand Names
Ambassador
Crayola (crayons)
Dakin (plush toys)
Hallmark
Liquitex (art supplies)
Springbok (jigsaw puzzles)

Subsidiaries
Binney & Smith, Easton, PA (crayons and art materials)
Crown Center Redevelopment Corp. (real estate complex in Kansas City, MO)
Graphics International Trading Co., Kansas City, MO (overseas supplies)
Hallmark Marketing, Kansas City, MO (sales)
Halls Merchandising, Inc., Kansas City, MO (3 clothing stores)
Heartline, Kansas City, MO (gifts)
Litho-Krome Co., Columbus, GA (lithography)
Univision Holdings, Inc., New York (Spanish-language TV)

RANKINGS

51st in *Forbes* 400 US Private Cos.

COMPETITION

American Greetings
Deluxe

HANSON PLC

OVERVIEW

Hanson PLC is both a management company and a trader in companies. Lord Hanson manages the British parent while Sir Gordon White directs Hanson Industries (US) from his New York office without ever visiting operating units. The company is an amalgam of low-tech enterprises in such diverse businesses as chemicals, shoes, tobacco, housewares, building products, and mining. Hanson-owned Gold Fields is the largest non–South African gold mining company, and Peabody Holdings is the largest coal mining organization in the US.

Hanson has grown by using bank debt to buy businesses with poor management or unrealized market value. Typically, Hanson quickly sells portions of purchased companies to help fund the acquisitions. The company slashes overhead and improves operations at remaining units and sells them if and when the price is right.

Both Lord Hanson and Sir Gordon are approaching retirement age, leading to speculation about a final, spectacular takeover or total divestiture of Hanson holdings.

WHEN

In the 1950s and 1960s James Hanson and Gordon White were British bon vivants. Hanson was once engaged to Audrey Hepburn and White enjoyed the company of Joan Collins. But since the mid-1960s they have become better known as sharp businessmen. Their earliest venture, Hanson-White Greeting Cards, was a success and was sold in 1963. When the buyer demanded £10,000 to sell back the right to use the Hanson-White name, White, displaying typical frugality, refused. After merging Wiles Group, a public fertilizer company, with the Hanson and White family businesses, they began hunting for bank-financed acquisitions in 1964 and changed the company name to Hanson Trust in 1965. From the beginning, Hanson and White sought poorly managed companies in mature industries at low prices. After almost 10 years of buying British firms and slashing costs, Hanson Trust consisted of 24 companies in such businesses as brickmaking, aggregates, and construction equipment, with sales in excess of $120 million.

Tired of antibusiness attitudes in England, White left for New York in 1973 to establish a subsidiary, Hanson Industries. Operating autonomously, White made his first American acquisition in 1974, buying Seacoast, an animal feed concern. He quickly followed with more acquisitions, including Hygrade (Ball Park Franks, 1976), Interstate United (food service, 1978), McDonough (tools, shoes, and shoe stores, 1981), and US Industries (conglomerate, 1984). Meanwhile, James Hanson picked up British EverReady (batteries, UK, 1981) and Allders (retail, UK, 1983).

In bitterly fought hostile takeovers on both sides of the Atlantic, Hanson acquired SCM (Smith-Corona office equipment, Glidden paints, Durkee's Famous Foods, SCM Chemicals) and Imperial Group (Britain's dominant cigarette company, John Courage beer, food, hotels, restaurants) in 1986. Within a year, sales of a few SCM units (including Glidden and Durkee) generated $960 million in cash, $30 million more than Hanson had paid. Sales of nontobacco Imperial assets (including Courage) covered 65% of its cost. Interstate United was sold in 1985 for over 3 times its cost.

In 1987 Hanson acquired Kaiser Cement for $250 million (later selling 6 plants for $283 million) and Kidde (security systems, fire protection, Jacuzzi) for $1.5 billion. In all acquired companies, corporate offices were a target of Hanson cost-cutting.

In 1989 Hanson acquired Consolidated Gold Fields (UK), and, with it, 49% of Newmont Mining (gold, US). It sold Gold Fields's South African investments, Kidde Systems, Allders, and Hygrade, and sold 52% of Smith-Corona to the public. The company acquired Peabody in 1990 from Boeing, Bechtel Investments, Eastern Enterprises, and Newmont.

HOW MUCH

£=$1.61 (Dec. 31,1989)	9 Yr. Growth	1980	1981	1982	1983	1984	1985	1986	1987	1988	1989
Sales (£ mil)	29.5%	684	856	1,148	1,484	2,382	2,674	4,312	6,682	7,396	6,998
Net income (£ mil)	13.5%	25	35	42	64	126	193	360	572	676	813
Income as % of sales	—	3.7%	4.1%	3.7%	4.3%	5.3%	7.2%	8.3%	8.6%	9.1%	11.6%
Earnings per share (p)	28.7%	1.9	2.5	2.8	3.5	5.7	7.9	10.7	14.0	15.9	18.4
Stock price – high (p)	—	17	24	45	65	123	129	161	194	157	243
Stock price – low (p)	—	10	16	23	42	58	98	106	116	124	154
Stock price – close (p)	33.3%	17	23	45	60	123	109	142	128	155	226
P/E – high	—	9	10	16	19	22	16	15	14	10	13
P/E – low	—	5	6	8	12	10	12	10	8	8	8
Dividends per share (p)	32.0%	0.7	0.8	1.0	1.2	1.8	2.4	3.2	4.4	6.8	8.5
Book value per share (p)	—	—	—	—	—	—	—	45	53	61	28

1989 Year End:
Debt ratio: 82.0%
Return on equity: 41.3%
Cash (mil): £5,266
Long-term debt (mil): £4,971
Number of shares (mil): 3,935
Dividends:
1989 average yield: 3.8%
1989 payout: 46.2%
Market value (mil): $14,318
Sales (mil): $11,267

Stock Price History high/low 1980-89

NYSE symbol: HAN (ADR)
Incorporated: England, 1950
Fiscal year ends: September 30

WHO

Chairman: Lord Hanson, age 68, £1,534,000 pay
Chairman, Hanson Industries: Sir Gordon White, age 67
VC: Martin G. Taylor, age 54
President and COO, Hanson Industries: David H. Clarke, age 48
Auditors: Ernst & Young
Employees: 89,000

WHERE

HQ: 1 Grosvenor Place, London SW1X 7JH, England
Phone: 011-44-71-245-1245
FAX: 011-44-71-235-3455
US HQ (Hanson Industries): 99 Wood Ave. South, Iselin, NJ 08830
US Phone: 201-603-6600
US FAX: 201-603-6878

	1989 Sales		1989 Pretax Income	
	£ mil	% of total	£ mil	% of total
UK	3,745	54	489	46
US	3,253	46	387	36
Interest/other	—	—	188	18
Total	**6,998**	**100**	**1,064**	**100**

WHAT

	1989 Sales		1989 Pretax Income	
	£ mil	% of total	£ mil	% of total
Consumer goods	3,898	56	347	32
Building products	1,194	17	193	18
Industrial operns.	1,906	27	336	32
Interest/other	—	—	188	18
Total	**6,998**	**100**	**1,064**	**100**

US Consumer Brands
Bear (archery equipment)
Ertl (toys, model kits)
Farberware (cookware)
Jacuzzi (spas)
Spartus (clocks)
Tommy Armour (golf supplies)
Universal (fitness equipment)

US Companies
Anderson Hickey (office furniture)
Endicott Johnson (shoes)
Gold Fields Mining
Grove Manufacturing (cranes)
Hanson Building Products
Hanson Lighting
Hanson Office Products (furniture)
International Proteins (49%)
Kaiser Cement
Newmont Mining (49%)
Peabody (coal mining)
SCM Chemicals (pigments)
Smith Corona (48%)

UK Companies
ARC (aggregates)
British EverReady (batteries)
Butterley Brick
Hanson Engineering
Imperial Tobacco
Lindustries (electrical and gas equipment)
London Brick

RANKINGS

79th in *Fortune* 500 Industrial Cos. (Hanson Industries)
91st in *Fortune* Global 500 Industrial Cos.
10th in *Forbes* 100 Foreign Investments in the US
55th in *Business Week* Global 1000

COMPETITION

Due to the broadly based and constantly shifting structure of Hanson PLC, the company faces innumerable and continually changing competitors in its product markets.

HARLEY-DAVIDSON, INC.

OVERVIEW

Harley-Davidson has over 45% of the US market for "heavyweight" motorcycles — those over 650cc engine size. The only US motorcycle maker today (its last competitor folded in 1953), Harley nearly went under itself trying to compete against the Japanese. Its comeback in the mid-1980s is one of the greatest successes of modern US business.

At its plants in Wisconsin and Pennsylvania, H-D turns out 270 motorcycles a day. It makes more than 30 models of touring and custom bikes, with retail prices ranging from $4,000 to $13,000. Increasing numbers are sold overseas, mostly in Canada, Japan, West Germany, and Austria. More are now sold in Japan than anywhere else overseas. About 110,000 members of H.O.G. (Harley Owners Group) receive the company's newsletter.

H-D also makes motor homes, travel trailers, and specialized commercial vehicles, as well as bomb casings and rocket, snow thrower, and marine engines.

The distinctive look of Harleys, an important element of the "mystique," is the creation of the vice president of styling, Willie G. Davidson, grandson of a company founder.

WHEN

William Harley and the Davidson brothers (Walter, William, and Arthur) of Milwaukee sold their first motorcycles in 1903. Essentially motor-assisted bicycles that required pedaling going uphill, they had 25-cubic-inch, 3-HP engines. Demand was high and most sold before they left the factory. In 1909 the company introduced a 2-cylinder, V-twin engine (an H-D trademark), and by 1914 introduced a step starter.

WWI put British cycle manufacturers out of the consumer cycle business and created a demand for American motorcycles overseas that made H-D's foreign sales important. In the 1920s H-D introduced new models with the "teardrop" gas tank that became part of the H-D look.

The Great Depression eliminated several H-D competitors (over 300 US motorcycle makers have existed at one time or another). Exports and sales to the police and military helped H-D survive. To improve sales, the company added styling features like art deco decals and 3-tone paint. The 1936 EL model with its "knucklehead" engine (so called because of its odd appearance) was a forerunner of today's models.

War again brought prosperity to H-D, with production elevated to record levels (90,000 cycles were built for the military). After WWII the company introduced new motorcycles: the K-model (1952), Sportster (1957), and Duo-Glide (1958). In 1960 H-D built a manufacturing plant in Italy and opened a branch in Switzerland. The company began making golf carts in the early 1960s.

In 1965 the company went public and in 1969 merged with American Machine and Foundry (AMF). By the late 1970s, certain that H-D would lose to Japanese bikes flooding the market, AMF put the company up for sale. Vaughn L. Beals and others from AMF's H-D division bought the company in 1981. Faced with decreased demand for big power bikes and competition from a Japanese product that was not only cheaper but better (circumstances that have broken other old-line US businesses), Beals fought back, updating manufacturing methods, improving quality, and expanding the model line. By 1987 H-D had gained 25% of the US "heavyweight" motorcycle market, up from 16% in 1985. H-D was doing well enough that in 1987 it asked for removal of a 5-year tariff on Japanese bikes a year ahead of schedule. H-D returned to public ownership in 1986 and by that year had also recovered enough to buy Holiday Rambler (recreational vehicles).

The company opened its first retail mall outlet, to sell Motor Clothes, in Kansas City in September 1990.

HOW MUCH

	4 Yr. Growth	1980	1981	1982	1983	1984	1985	1986	1987	1988	1989
Sales ($ mil)	28.8%	—	—	—	—	—	287	295	685	757	791
Net income ($ mil)	82.1%	—	—	—	—	—	3	4	18	27	33
Income as % of sales	—	—	—	—	—	—	0.9%	1.5%	2.6%	3.6%	4.1%
Earnings per share ($)	51.4%	—	—	—	—	—	0.36	0.41	1.36	1.71	1.89
Stock price – high ($)	—	—	—	—	—	—	—	6.94	13.25	14.94	21.50
Stock price – low ($)	—	—	—	—	—	—	—	3.63	4.63	5.94	12.19
Stock price – close ($)	—	—	—	—	—	—	—	5.25	6.50	12.69	19.63
P/E – high	—	—	—	—	—	—	—	17	10	9	11
P/E – low	—	—	—	—	—	—	—	9	3	3	6
Dividends per share ($)	—	—	—	—	—	—	0.00	0.00	0.00	0.00	0.00
Book value per share ($)	94.3%	—	—	—	—	—	0.63	2.30	4.55	7.04	8.97

1989 Year End:
Debt ratio: 32.4%
Return on equity: 23.6%
Cash (mil): $39
Current ratio: 1.38
Long-term debt (mil): $75
Number of shares (mil): 17
Dividends:
1989 average yield: 0.0%
1989 payout: 0.0%
Market value (mil): $342

NYSE symbol: HDI
Incorporated: Delaware, 1981
Fiscal year ends: December 31

WHO

Chairman: Vaughn L. Beals, Jr., age 62, $300,339 pay
President, CEO, and CFO: Richard F. Teerlink, age 53, $540,222 pay
VP, Continuous Improvement: Thomas A. Gelb, $274,205 pay
VP, Styling: William G. Davidson
VP; President and COO, Holiday Rambler Corp.: H. Wayne Dahl, age 50
President and COO, Motorcycle Division: James H. Paterson, $315,561 pay
Auditors: Ernst & Young
Employees: 5,000

WHERE

HQ: 3700 W. Juneau Ave., PO Box 653, Milwaukee, WI 53208
Phone: 414-342-4680
FAX: 414-935-4977

The company's motorcycles are sold in the US, Europe, and Japan by 708 independent dealers. Recreational vehicles are sold by 210 dealers in the US.

	1989 Sales		1989 Net Income	
	$ mil	% of total	$ mil	% of total
US	676	85	31	94
Foreign	115	15	2	6
Total	**791**	**100**	**33**	**100**

WHAT

	1989 Sales		1989 Operating Income	
	$ mil	% of total	$ mil	% of total
Motorcycles & related prods.	496	62	61	80
Defense & other	21	3	2	3
Transportation vehicles	274	35	13	17
Adjustments	—	—	(10)	—
Total	**791**	**100**	**66**	**100**

Motorcycles & Related Products
883cc Sportster
Eagle Iron (parts and accessories)
Fat Boy
FLTC and FLHTC Ultra Classics
FXR Super Glide
FXSTS Springer Softail
Harley-Davidson Motor Clothes
Leathers by Willie G.

Transportation Vehicles
Holiday Rambler Corp. (recreational)
Aluma-Lite Free Spirit
Imperial
Limited Crown Imperial
Utilimaster Corporation
Aeromate (walk-in van)
Parcel delivery vans

Defense (DOD) Products
Metal bomb casings and suspension systems
Rocket, snow thrower, and marine engines

RANKINGS

381st in *Fortune* 500 Industrial Cos.
973rd in *Business Week* 1000

COMPETITION

Fleetwood
Honda
Thiokol

HARRIS CORPORATION

OVERVIEW

Formerly a major manufacturer of printing equipment, Melbourne, Florida–based Harris has undergone a dramatic transformation since 1967 and now operates 4 electronics units, with 45% of sales made to the US government.

The Electronic Systems Sector (41% of sales) provides command, control, communication, and intelligence systems to the DOD and is expanding to provide products to state and local governments and businesses, both domestic and foreign.

The Semiconductor Sector (25% of revenues) supplies application-specific chips for signal processing and control, automotive devices, and smart cards; the acquisition of GE Solid State in 1988 made Harris the 6th ranked US supplier.

The Communications Sector (20% of sales) provides broadcast systems, terrestrial microwave and satellite communications, digital telephone switches, 2-way radios, and other communication products to businesses around the world. A recent focus is upon digital video transmission products.

The 4th sector, Lanier Worldwide (14% of sales), has one of the largest independent office-equipment distribution networks for copiers, FAX machines, and other products, and markets its products through 1,600 sales offices in more than 50 countries.

NYSE symbol: HRS
Incorporated: Delaware, 1926
Fiscal year ends: June 30

WHO

Chairman, President, and CEO: John T. Hartley, age 59, $842,600 pay
President, Semiconductor Sector: Jon E. Cornell, age 49, $387,463 pay
President, Electronic Systems Sector: Phillip W. Farmer, age 51, $351,779 pay
President, Communications Sector: Guy W. Numann, age 57, $347,462 pay
SVP Finance: Bryan R. Roub, age 48, $334,130 pay
Auditors: Ernst & Young
Employees: 35,100

WHEN

Harris was founded in Niles, Ohio, in 1895 by 2 brothers, Alfred and Charles Harris, both jewelers and inventors. Among their inventions was a printing press that became Harris Automatic Press Company's flagship product.

Harris remained a small, one-product company run by the Harris family until 1944, when engineer George Diveley was hired as general manager. Dively diversified into other areas of the printing field, and Harris began manufacturing bindery, typesetting, and paper converting equipment while remaining a leading supplier of printing presses. In 1957 Harris merged with Intertype, a typesetter manufacturer, and became known as Harris-Intertype Corporation. Harris-Intertype continued to expand its printing business through the purchase of bookbinder Sheridan (1964), printing equipment maker Scribner (1964), and paperboard equipment manufacturer and converter Langston (1966).

In 1967 Harris-Intertype bought electronics and data processing equipment manufacturer Radiation, a $50 million company heavily dependent upon government contracts. Harris relocated to Radiation's headquarters in Melbourne, Florida. Today Radiation operates as Harris Semiconductor Sector, the largest supplier of integrated circuits to the US government. The company also bought RF Communications (2-way radios, 1969), General Electric's television broadcast equipment line (1972), and UCC-Communications Systems (data processing equipment, 1972).

In 1974 the now-renamed Harris Corporation began moves toward general-purpose computing and communications and office information systems. In 1980 Harris bought Farinon, manufacturer of microwave radio systems and digital telephone switches, and Lanier Business Products (Atlanta), the leading manufacturer of dictating equipment. In 1983 Harris sold its printing equipment businesses, making its business 100% electronics.

In 1986 Harris formed a joint venture with 3M called Harris/3M Document Products, established to market copiers and fax machines worldwide, and in 1989 acquired the entire operation. In 1986 Harris acquired Scientific Calculations, a computer-aided design/manufacturing (CAD/CAM) software developer. In 1988 the company purchased General Electric's Solid State group, a semiconductor operation. Most recently Harris sold off its PC (1989) and information systems (1990) businesses and agreed to sell its data communications group (1990).

WHERE

HQ: 1025 W. NASA Blvd., Melbourne, FL 32919
Phone: 407-727-9100
FAX: 407-727-5118

Harris has 52 manufacturing and 663 other facilities in Asia, Australia, Europe, and Central, South, and North America.

	1989 Sales		1989 Pretax Income	
	$ mil	% of total	$ mil	% of total
US	1,954	88	125	75
International	260	12	42	25
Total	**2,214**	**100**	**167**	**100**

WHAT

	1989 Sales		1989 Operating Income	
	$ mil	% of total	$ mil	% of total
Semiconductors	542	25	54	24
Communications	442	20	41	19
Electronic systems	915	41	78	35
Office equipment	315	14	48	22
Adjustments	—	—	(56)	—
Total	**2,214**	**100**	**165**	**100**

Products/Services
Broadcast radio and television systems
Control systems for electric utilities and railroads
Digital telephone switches
Distributed data processing systems
Information systems for aircraft and spacecraft
Ground-based data collection systems
Land-based and satellite communications systems
Microwave and 2-way radios
Office equipment distribution
Standard, semicustom, and custom integrated circuits
Video teleconferencing systems
Wide- and local-area networks

HOW MUCH

	9 Yr. Growth	1980	1981	1982	1983	1984	1985	1986	1987	1988	1989
Sales ($ mil)	6.1%	1,301	1,552	1,719	1,424	1,996	2,281	2,217	2,079	2,063	2,214
Net income ($ mil)	4.3%	80	104	76	50	80	80	60	85	65	116
Income as % of sales	—	6.1%	6.7%	4.4%	3.5%	4.0%	3.5%	2.7%	4.1%	3.2%	5.2%
Earnings per share ($)	1.5%	2.59	3.33	2.40	1.58	2.01	1.99	1.47	2.03	1.63	2.97
Stock price – high ($)	—	55.75	60.25	41.13	51.88	42.63	35.00	36.88	42.75	33.25	39.50
Stock price – low ($)	—	26.75	37.50	20.38	33.25	22.75	22.25	25.50	22.00	24.25	26.38
Stock price – close ($)	(4.9%)	52.13	41.13	37.00	40.13	27.13	27.25	29.75	26.00	27.00	33.13
P/E – high	—	22	18	17	33	21	18	25	21	20	13
P/E – low	—	10	11	8	21	11	11	17	11	15	9
Dividends per share ($)	2.3%	0.72	0.80	0.88	0.88	0.88	0.88	0.88	0.88	0.88	0.88
Book value per share ($)	5.7%	14.89	17.81	19.05	20.12	20.48	21.56	22.37	23.64	24.94	24.45

1989 Year End:
Debt ratio: 24.9%
Return on equity: 12.0%
Cash (mil): $189
Current ratio: 1.24
Long-term debt (mil): $315
Number of shares (mil): 39
Dividends:
1989 average yield: 2.7%
1989 payout: 29.6%
Market value (mil): $1,283

Stock Price History high/low 1980-89

RANKINGS

180th in *Fortune* 500 Industrial Cos.
315th in *Forbes* Sales 500
436th in *Business Week* 1000

COMPETITION

Fujitsu
Hitachi
Hyundai
Intel
Motorola
National Semiconductor
NEC
Pitney Bowes
Raytheon
Rockwell International
Samsung
Siemens
Sony
Thomson
Xerox
Other electronics and defense companies

HARTMARX CORPORATION

OVERVIEW

Hartmarx Corporation, a leading name in the US in men's high quality suits, directs 43 manufacturers and over 500 retail stores that produce and sell men's and women's apparel. Its production facilities throughout the US make such brand-name clothes as Hart Schaffner and Marx (high quality men's suits, shirts, jackets); Hickey-Freeman (high quality men's suits); Country Miss (women's clothes); and Kuppenheimer (moderately priced men's clothes). Sales from these manufacturers to unaffiliated retailers produced 46% of Hartmarx's 1989 sales ($598 million).

Hartmarx's retail stores sell Hartmarx clothes (from 40% to 85% of their stock) and other brands. These retailers include Wallach's on the East Coast (33 stores); Silverwood's in California and Nevada (20 stores); and Jas. K. Wilson in Texas (13 stores). Retail sales from these stores produced 54% ($699 million) of 1989 sales.

Internationally, Hartmarx has licensed its products to 41 companies in 12 foreign countries. It plans to increase its exports and begin producing apparel outside the US for sale in world markets in 1990.

WHEN

Harry Hart (21) and his brother Max (18) began their Chicago men's clothing store, Harry Hart and Brother, in 1872. Additional partners, including Marcus Marx and Joseph Schaffner, provided several name changes until the company settled on Hart, Schaffner and Marx in 1887.

The young clothiers contracted with independent tailors on Chicago's West Side to produce suits for their new store. Recognizing the potential of the wholesale garment industry, they began selling to other merchants and sending salesmen with wardrobe trunks and fabric samples to potential buyers. In 1897 Hart, Schaffner and Marx launched an illustrated national ad campaign in leading magazines and newspapers.

In 1910 a walkout by 17 young women protesting low wages and poor working conditions in one of the company's 48 tailoring shops sparked a citywide garment workers' strike. Schaffner and Harry Hart negotiated a settlement (not honored by the other major Chicago companies) in January 1911, and their employees returned to work.

Hart, Schaffner and Marx maintained its Chicago retail stores and in 1935 began adding to its domain with the purchase of Wallach Brothers, a New York men's clothing chain. Active expansion followed with purchases of Hastings, a California clothier (1952); Hanny's in Arizona (1962); Hickey-Freeman, with stores in Chicago, New York and Detroit (1964); and Field Brothers in New York (1968).

A 1970 antitrust decree required that the company sell 30 of its 238 men's clothing stores and, for 10 years, refrain from further purchases without court approval. Despite this restriction, the company made approved purchases, including 49% of Roberts S.A., a Mexican clothing store chain (sold in 1990). In 1982 it bought its old rival Kuppenheimer's, a retail store founded in 1876.

In 1983 Hart, Schaffner and Marx changed its name to Hartmarx Corporation. A costly 1986 reorganization of the retail stores to automate, centralize buying, and consolidate credit, accounting, and distribution resulted in the termination of 800 employees; earnings that year fell 42%. In 1988 Hartmarx purchased the Raleigh clothing stores (Washington, DC) and in 1989 bought Biltwell Company, a Missouri manufacturer of slacks, suits, and coats.

While 1987 and 1988 showed good recovery, 1989 earnings were only $17.4 million, a 54% drop from the year before. The company cited an industry-wide decline in men's clothing sales and high wool prices as reasons for the slump. Nearly 65 stores are slated to be closed in 1990.

HOW MUCH

	9 Yr. Growth	1980	1981	1982	1983	1984	1985	1986	1987	1988	1989
Sales ($ mil)	7.5%	675	816	863	962	1,071	1,110	1,063	1,080	1,174	1,297
Net income ($ mil)	(2.8%)	23	27	32	38	42	43	25	41	38	17
Income as % of sales	—	3.3%	3.4%	3.7%	3.9%	3.9%	3.8%	2.3%	3.8%	3.2%	1.3%
Earnings per share ($)	(3.0%)	1.17	1.40	1.68	1.91	2.09	2.10	1.20	2.01	2.03	0.89
Stock price – high ($)	—	7.11	10.72	18.11	24.17	21.83	26.42	32.00	34.75	29.75	28.13
Stock price – low ($)	—	4.33	6.22	8.06	14.56	15.67	18.67	23.50	18.25	20.75	18.75
Stock price – close ($)	13.5%	6.33	10.22	16.44	21.58	19.00	26.33	27.00	23.50	24.25	19.75
P/E – high	—	6	8	11	13	10	13	27	17	15	32
P/E – low	—	4	4	5	8	7	9	20	9	10	21
Dividends per share ($)	11.8%	0.43	0.48	0.54	0.61	0.75	0.85	0.90	0.98	1.08	1.18
Book value per share ($)	4.9%	11.98	12.72	13.51	14.80	16.24	17.60	17.59	18.26	19.21	18.37

1989 Year End:
Debt ratio: 42.9%
Return on equity: 4.7%
Cash (mil): $3
Current ratio: 2.52
Long-term debt (mil): $271
Number of shares (mil): 20
Dividends:
1989 average yield: 6.0%
1989 payout: 132.0%
Market value (mil): $387

35
30
25
20
15
10
5
0

Stock Price History
high/low 1980-89

NYSE symbol: HMX
Incorporated: Delaware, 1983
Fiscal year ends: November 30

WHO

Chairman and CEO: Harvey A. Weinberg, age 52, $536,000 pay
President and COO: Elbert O. Hand, age 50, $466,000 pay
SVP and CFO: Jerome Dorf, age 53, $261,000 pay
VP, Secretary, and General Counsel: Carey M. Stein, age 42, $200,000 pay
Auditors: Price Waterhouse
Employees: 23,500

WHERE

HQ: 101 N. Wacker Dr., Chicago, IL 60606
Phone: 312-372-6300
FAX: 312-444-2710

Hartmarx has manufacturing facilities in 17 states. Its 502 clothing stores, operating under 41 different names, are located throughout the US.

WHAT

	1989 Sales		1989 Operating Income	
	$ mil	% of total	$ mil	% of total
Wholesale apparel	598	46	58	84
Retail apparel	699	54	11	16
Adjustments	—	—	(28)	—
Total	**1,297**	**100**	**41**	**100**

Brand Names

Men's Clothing
Allyn St. George
Austin Reed of Regent Street
Bannister & Beale
Bobby Jones
Briar
Christian Dior Monsieur
Confezioni Riserva Luciano Franzoni
Escadrille
Gieves & Hawkes
Gleneagles
Graham and Gunn
Hart Schaffner & Marx
Henry Grethel
Hickey-Freeman
J. G. Hook
Jack Nicklaus
John Alexander
Johnny Carson
Kuppenheimer
Nino Cerruti Rue Royale
Pierre Cardin
Racquet Club-Wimbledon
Sansabelt
Society Brand, Ltd.

Women's Clothing
Country Suburbans
Lady Sansabelt
Sterling & Hunt Womenswear
Weathervane

RANKINGS

294th in *Fortune* 500 Industrial Cos.

COMPETITION

Apparel manufacturers and department, specialty, and discount stores

HARVARD UNIVERSITY

OVERVIEW

Founded in 1636, Harvard University is the oldest and one of the most prestigious institutions of higher education in the US. The private, coeducational school, located across the Charles River from Boston, consists of Harvard College (the men's undergraduate college), Radcliffe (the women's undergraduate college), and 10 graduate schools. Harvard's endowment of approximately $4.2 billion is the nation's largest.

Only about 15% of freshmen applicants to Harvard are accepted. Beginning the sophomore year, all students live in one of 13 campus houses, each a self-sufficient community.

Harvard's outstanding campus resources include a computer center with 200 computers; the university museums; and a library system (led by the famous Widener Library) with 11 million bound volumes, 3 million microforms, and 100,000 periodical subscriptions.

Harvard's alumni list reads like a *Who's Who of American History*, including such notable figures as John Adams, John Quincy Adams, T. S. Eliot, Ralph Waldo Emerson, John Hancock, Rutherford B. Hayes, Oliver Wendell Holmes, Helen Keller, John F. Kennedy, Increase Mather, Franklin D. Roosevelt, Theodore Roosevelt, and Gertrude Stein. Additionally, 31 Nobel laureates and 30 Pulitzer Prize winners have been associated with the university.

WHEN

In 1636 the General Court of Massachusetts appropriated £400 for the establishment of a college. The first building (Old College) was completed at Cambridge in 1639 and was named for John Harvard, who had willed his collection of about 400 books and half of his land to the school. Henry Dunster, a master of Old Testament languages, became the school's first president (and faculty) in 1640. The first freshman class consisted of 4 students.

During its first century and a half, Harvard adhered closely to the educational standards of European schools, with heavy emphasis on classical literature and languages, logic, philosophy, and mathematics. Theology was studied only by graduate students (about half of Harvard's early graduates became ministers). The president and a small group of tutors (usually men who had just earned their BAs) taught all of the subjects. Harvard's early presidents included such notable figures as Increase Mather and John Leverett.

In 1721 Harvard established its first professorship (the Hollis Divinity Professorship), which was quickly followed by professorships in mathematics and natural philosophy. In 1780 Harvard became a university and in 1783 appointed its first professor of medicine.

Harvard went through a period of reform in the early 1800s after Edward Everett (a Greek literature professor) returned from studying abroad with reports of the modern teaching methods practiced at German universities. The school initiated an investigation and updated its curriculum. Harvard established a Divinity School in 1816, a Law School in 1817, and 2 schools of science in the 1840s.

In 1869 Charles W. Eliot became president of Harvard and engineered a period of growth that included the development of graduate programs in arts and sciences, engineering, and architecture. Eliot also raised the standards of the schools of medicine and law and laid the groundwork for the graduate School of Business Administration (there is no undergraduate business instruction at Harvard) and the School of Public Health. In addition, Eliot expanded the elective system to allow students to better design their own courses of study.

During the 20th century, Harvard experienced change as well as tremendous growth in its enrollment, faculty, and endowment. The Graduate School of Education was opened in 1920. Ten years later Harvard opened its first undergraduate residential house. In the 1930s and 1940s the school established a scholarship program as well as a General Education curriculum for undergraduates.

Since then the school has continued to grow, with new buildings, expanded programs, and a concerted effort to increase library holdings. In 1979, Harvard introduced its core curriculum, and in 1986 Harvard celebrated its 350th anniversary.

HOW MUCH

	9 Yr. Growth	1980	1981	1982	1983	1984	1985	1986	1987	1988	1989
Enrollment (degree candidates)	1.1%	16,132	16,053	16,027	16,566	16,781	16,871	17,298	17,419	17,454	17,762
Tuition ($)	10.2%	5,300	6,000	6,930	8,195	9,035	9,800	10,590	11,390	12,015	12,715
Additional fees ($)	7.6%	2,840	3,170	3,610	3,905	4,115	4,300	4,510	4,755	5,085	5,495
Endowment market value ($ mil)	13.6%	1,314	1,491	1,622	1,617	2,037	2,187	2,694	3,435	4,018	4,155

Annual Tuition ($) 1980-89

Private university
Founded: 1636
Fiscal year ends: June 30

WHO

President: Derek Bok, $138,027 pay in 1988
VP Finance: Robert H. Scott
Treasurer: D. Robert Daniel

WHERE

HQ: 1350 Massachusetts Ave., Cambridge, MA 02138
Phone: 617-495-1000
FAX: 617-495-0754

Harvard University is located on more than 380 acres (including Radcliffe College) in Cambridge, across the Charles River from Boston. The university owns more than 400 buildings in the Cambridge–Boston area.

Geographic Distribution of Freshman Class	% of total
Mid-Atlantic	31
New England	22
West	17
South	12
Midwest	12
Foreign	6
Total	**100**

WHAT

	1989 Revenues	
	$mil	% of total
Tuition & fees	304	32
Research	257	27
Endowment	181	19
Gifts	105	11
Other	105	11
Total	**952**	**100**

Academic Unit	1989 Enrollment	% of total
Harvard/Radcliffe	6,592	37
Graduate School of Arts and Sciences	2,934	16
Divinity School	450	3
Medical School	665	4
Dental School	140	1
School of Public Health	497	3
Law School	1,756	10
School of Design	465	3
School of Education	1,193	7
Kennedy School of Government	744	4
Business School	1,643	9
Extension	777	4
Less duplication	(94)	(1)
Total	**17,762**	**100**

Affiliated Institutions
Arnold Arboretum
Beth Israel Hospital
Center for Hellenic Studies
Children's Hospital
Dana-Farber Cancer Institute
Dumbarton Oaks Research Library
Harvard Art Museums
Harvard College Observatory
Harvard Forest
Harvard University Museums of Natural History
Harvard-Yenching Institute
John F. Kennedy School of Government
Joslin Diabetes Center
Loeb Drama Center
Semitic Museum
Villa I Tatti (Florence, Italy)

COMPETITION

Ohio State
Stanford
University of Chicago
University of Texas

HASBRO, INC.

OVERVIEW

Hasbro is the largest and most profitable toy company in the world. The company designs, produces, and markets a wide array of toys, games, puzzles, and infant products under such recognized names as Hasbro, Milton Bradley, and Playskool. Foreign operations represent 32% of sales; Toys "R" Us was the company's largest customer with 14% of sales.

Hasbro's toy line includes G.I. Joe (which accounted for 13% of revenues in 1989), My Little Pony, and Cabbage Patch Kids. Despite the strength of its existing toy line, the company continually emphasizes new product development. In 1989 Hasbro spent 4% of revenue on new product research and design.

The company's Milton Bradley division produces a broad line of board games, including Scrabble, Parcheesi, and Battleship. Playskool's toy line produces toys for preschool children, including such childhood standards as Lincoln Logs, Mr. Potato Head, and Raggedy Ann and Andy. The Playskool Baby line produces pacifiers, infant health care products, Tommee Tippee training cups, toys, and infant apparel.

Hasbro, 10% of which is still owned by the Hassenfeld family, engages in charitable activities aimed directly at children and their families. Through the Hasbro Charitable Trust and the Hasbro Children's Foundation, the company supports literacy programs, shelters for the homeless, and day-care centers, and donates toys to needy children.

WHEN

In 1923 Henry and Hillel Hassenfeld formed Hassenfeld Brothers in Pawtucket, Rhode Island, to distribute fabric remnants. By 1926 the company was manufacturing fabric-covered pencil boxes and shortly thereafter was making the pencils themselves.

Hassenfeld Brothers branched into the toy industry during the 1940s by introducing toy nurse and doctor kits. The company's toy division was the first to use TV to promote a toy product (Mr. Potato Head) in 1952.

The company continued to expand both its toy and pencil businesses. In the mid-1960s the company introduced G.I. Joe (an action doll for boys), which quickly became its primary toy line. Hassenfeld Brothers went public in 1968 and changed its name to Hasbro Industries. In 1969 Hasbro bought Romper Room (TV productions).

During the 1970s the toy and pencil divisions, managed by different members of the family, were in conflict over the company's finances, future direction, and leadership. The dispute caused the company (and the shareholders) to split in 1980. The toy division continued to operate under the Hasbro name; the pencil division (Empire Pencil Corporation in Shelbyville, Tennessee), led by Harold Hassenfeld, became a separate corporation.

Hasbro expanded rapidly in the 1980s under new CEO Stephen Hassenfeld, one of the third generation of family members to run the company. Hassenfeld reduced the number of products by 1/3 to concentrate on developing a stable line of toys aimed at specific markets.

During the 1980s Hasbro released a number of successful toys, including G.I. Joe (a newer and smaller version of the original, 1982), My Little Pony (a small horse with brushable hair, 1983), Transformers (small vehicles that "transform" into robots, 1984), and My Buddy (a large doll for boys, 1985).

In 1983 Hasbro acquired from Warner Bros. much of the inventory of Knickerbocker (plush toys). In 1984 the company bought Milton Bradley, a major producer of board games (Chutes and Ladders, Candy Land), puzzles, and preschool toys (Playskool). In 1989 Hasbro acquired certain items from Coleco (which went bankrupt in 1988), including Cabbage Patch Kids, Scrabble, and Parcheesi (board games). After Stephen Hassenfeld died in 1989, his brother Alan became CEO.

HOW MUCH

	9 Yr. Growth	1980	1981	1982	1983	1984	1985	1986	1987	1988	1989
Sales ($ mil)	33.9%	102	106	136	224	719	1,233	1,345	1,345	1,358	1,410
Net income ($ mil)	39.4%	5	4	7	15	52	99	99	48	72	92
Income as % of sales	—	4.5%	4.2%	5.2%	6.8%	7.3%	8.0%	7.4%	3.6%	5.3%	6.5%
Earnings per share ($)	31.1%	0.14	0.18	0.28	0.48	1.27	1.78	1.70	0.82	1.24	1.56
Stock price – high ($)	—	0.59	1.01	2.76	5.63	12.45	19.75	30.88	26.50	17.00	24.38
Stock price – low ($)	—	0.24	0.46	0.76	2.12	4.60	10.93	16.56	10.00	12.00	15.25
Stock price – close ($)	48.4%	0.54	0.84	2.16	5.40	10.85	17.38	19.50	13.25	15.63	18.75
P/E – high	—	4	6	10	12	10	11	18	32	14	16
P/E – low	—	2	3	3	4	4	6	10	12	10	10
Dividends per share ($)	—	0.00	0.01	0.02	0.04	0.05	0.08	0.08	0.09	0.11	0.15
Book value per share ($)	34.3%	0.96	1.12	1.37	2.27	6.21	8.59	10.95	12.07	13.19	13.67

1989 Year End:
Debt ratio: 6.7%
Return on equity: 11.6%
Cash (mil): $278
Current ratio: 2.1
Long-term debt (mil): $58
Number of shares (mil): 59
Dividends:
1989 average yield: 0.8%
1989 payout: 9.6%
Market value (mil): $1,101

Stock Price History high/low 1980-89

ASE symbol: HAS
Incorporated: Rhode Island, 1926
Fiscal year ends: December 31

WHO

Chairman and CEO: Alan G. Hassenfeld, age 41, $995,938 pay
Co-COO: Alfred J. Verrecchia, age 47, $426,275 pay
Co-COO: Barry J. Alperin, age 49, $410,509 pay
EVP and CFO: John T. O'Neill, age 45
Auditors: KPMG Peat Marwick
Employees: 8,200

WHERE

HQ: 1027 Newport Ave., Pawtucket, RI 02861
Phone: 401-431-8697
FAX: 401-727-5433

The company operates 46 facilities in the US and in 14 foreign countries.

	1989 Sales		1989 Operating Income	
	$ mil	% of total	$ mil	% of total
US	955	68	100	59
Foreign	455	32	70	41
Total	**1,410**	**100**	**170**	**100**

WHAT

	1989 Sales
	% of total
Playskool toys	25
Milton Bradley games	22
Hasbro toys & others	53
Total	**100**

Brand Names

Toys
Baby Uh-Oh
Busy Beads
Busy Toddler Playhouse
Cabbage Patch Kids
Dolly Surprise
G.I. Joe
Gloworm
Go-Go Gears
Goops
Lincoln Logs
Lite Bright
Little Walker
Mr. Potato Head
My Buddy
My Little Pony
New Kids on the Block dolls
Raggedy Ann and Andy
Record Breakers
Scribble Stix
Sounds Around
Steady Steps
Tiny Toons plush dolls
Tomy Wind-Ups
Transformers
WWF Action Figures

Games
Battleship
Candy Land
Chutes and Ladders
Connect Four
HeroQuest
Hungry Hungry Hippos
Life
Mousetrap
Nintendo Games
Operation
Parcheesi
A Question of Scruples
Scrabble
Shark Attack
Trouble
Twister
Win, Lose or Draw
Yahtzee

Infant Products
Hugger
Pur
Tommee Tippee

RANKINGS

277th in *Fortune* 500 Industrial Cos.
496th in *Business Week* 1000

COMPETITION

Mattel
Rubbermaid

THE HEARST CORPORATION

OVERVIEW

The privately held Hearst Corporation (100% of the stock is owned by the William Randolph Hearst Trust) is the world's 12th largest media company, with 1989 revenues of $2.1 billion, according to *Advertising Age*. Hearst's leading business, magazines (including *Good Housekeeping* and *Cosmopolitan*), ranks 2nd to Time Warner in revenues. Newspapers rank only 11th in revenues.

Hearst's King Features comics ("Blondie," "Beetle Bailey") and columns are distributed to 78 countries in 33 languages. Lifetime TV reaches 45 million households through 4,500 cable systems, and Arts & Entertainment reaches 41 million households through 4,300 cable systems. Hearst Magazines International distributes magazines in Europe, Latin America, and the Pacific Basin.

The sons of founder William Randolph Hearst, who beneficially own 40% of the company, are counted among the world's billionaires. While there are many Hearsts in management and on the board, the only family member in charge of a major operation is grandson William Randolph Hearst III, publisher of the *San Francisco Examiner*.

Private company
Founded: California, 1887

WHO

Chairman: Randolph A. Hearst, age 75
Chairman, Executive Committee: William R. Hearst, Jr., age 82
President and CEO: Frank A. Bennack, Jr., age 57
EVP: Gilbert C. Maurer, age 62
VP: George R. Hearst, Jr., age 63
VP and Controller: Peter J. DeMaria, age 51
VP and Treasurer: Edwin A. Lewis, age 48
Employees: 14,000

WHERE

HQ: 959 Eighth Ave., New York, NY 10019
Phone: 212-649-2000
FAX: 212-765-3528 (Corporate Communications)

Hearst licenses 65 magazine titles in 70 countries; the company has newspapers in 15 cities.

WHEN

William Randolph Hearst, son of a wealthy California mining magnate, began his career when he became editor of the family-owned *San Francisco Examiner* in 1887. The sensationalist style Hearst brought to the paper transformed it into a financial success. In 1895 he bought the *New York Morning Journal* and competed against the *New York World*, owned by Joseph Pulitzer, Hearst's first employer (Hearst worked as a reporter after being expelled from Harvard for playing jokes on his professors in 1884). The "yellow journalism" resulting from the rivalry of the 2 papers characterized American journalism at the turn of the century. Hearst was accused by some of causing the Spanish-American War in 1896 when he reportedly cabled artist Frederic Remington in Cuba, saying, "You furnish the pictures, and I'll furnish the war."

The growth of the Hearst empire continued with the establishment of 7 more daily papers by 1920. Hearst editorials initially supported public education, public ownership of utilities, and labor unions but later became known for communist-baiting and ultranationalism. In 1935 Hearst was at its peak with nearly 14% of total US daily and 24% of Sunday circulation, with newspapers in 19 cities; the largest syndicate (King Features); international news and photo services; 13 magazines; 8 radio stations; and 2 motion picture companies. Two years later the company began selling movie companies, radio stations, and magazines to lessen its large debt.

Hearst died in 1951 at the age of 88, leaving an estate estimated at $56 million. He left control of the corporation with trustees rather than risk a breakup of the company by his heirs; stock worth 1/3 of the company, which included the voting rights, was left in trust for his heirs, and the other 2/3 was left to 2 charitable foundations. Hearst had lived in style in San Simeon, his California estate, and had bought, among many other things, Tibetan yaks, Egyptian mummies, a Spanish abbey, and a castle in Wales. The controversial businessman inspired the famous 1941 Orson Welles film, *Citizen Kane*.

During the 1950s and early 1960s, Richard Berlin, in charge of the company since 1940, sold many failing papers and merged others to improve finances. Hearst's major magazines included *Good Housekeeping*, *Cosmopolitan*, and *Popular Mechanics*.

Since the late 1970s, Hearst has undergone a period of growth and tripled in size under Frank Bennack, Jr., president and CEO since 1979. Additions have included several publishing companies, notably William Morrow (1981); new magazines, including *Country Living* (1978), *Redbook* (1982), and *Esquire* (1986); and TV stations KMBC in Kansas City (1982) and WCVB in Boston (1986). In the 1980s Hearst introduced the Lifetime cable channel (in partnership with Capital Cities/ABC and Viacom) and the Arts & Entertainment channel (in partnership with Capital Cities/ABC and NBC [GE]).

WHAT

	1989 Sales	
	$ mil	% of total
Newspapers	700	34
Magazines	992	47
Broadcasting	270	13
Cable	21	1
Other	111	5
Total	**2,094**	**100**

US Magazines
Connoisseur
Cosmopolitan
Country Living
Esquire
Good Housekeeping
Harper's Bazaar
House Beautiful
Popular Mechanics
Redbook
Town & Country

Major Newspapers
Houston Chronicle
San Antonio Light
San Francisco Examiner
Seattle Post-Intelligencer

Broadcasting
KMBC-TV, Kansas City, MO
WAPA (AM), San Juan, PR
WBAL (AM), Baltimore
WBAL-TV, Baltimore
WCVB-TV, Boston
WDTN-TV, Dayton, OH
WHTX (FM), Pittsburgh
WISN (AM), Milwaukee
WISN-TV, Milwaukee
WIYY (FM), Baltimore
WLTQ (FM), Milwaukee
WTAE (AM), Pittsburgh
WTAE-TV, Pittsburgh

Book Publishers
Avon Books
Hearst
William Morrow

Business Publishing
American Druggist
Black Book series (auto guides)
Disneyland Official Guide
Motor Magazine
Walt Disney World Official Guide

Entertainment/ Syndication
Arts & Entertainment Cable Network (joint venture)
Cowles Syndicate
First DataBank (database)
King Features Syndicate
King Phoenix Entertainment
Lifetime Television (joint venture)
North America Syndicate

HOW MUCH

	8 Yr. Growth	1980	1981	1982	1983	1984	1985	1986	1987	1988	1989
Sales ($ mil)	7.2%	—	1,200	1,300	1,116	1,400	1,540	1,529	1,886	1,986	2,094
Newspaper revenue ($ mil)	—	—	—	—	—	—	—	390	650	689	700
Magazine revenue ($ mil)	—	—	—	—	—	—	—	780	873	919	992
Broadcast revenue ($ mil)	—	—	—	—	—	—	—	280	262	263	270
Cable TV revenue ($ mil)	—	—	—	—	—	—	—	9	11	15	21
Other media revenue ($ mil)	—	—	—	—	—	—	—	70	90	100	111

Total Sales ($ mil) 1981-89

2,500
2,000
1,500
1,000
500
0

RANKINGS

66th in *Forbes* 400 US Private Cos.

COMPETITION

Berkshire Hathaway
Bertelsmann
Capital Cities/ABC
CBS
Cox
Gannett
Knight-Ridder
McGraw-Hill
New York Times
News Corp.
Paramount
Reader's Digest
E.W. Scripps
Tele-Communications
Time Warner
Times Mirror
Tribune
Washington Post

H. J. HEINZ COMPANY

OVERVIEW

With over 3,000 products, Pittsburgh-based H. J. Heinz is one of the world's leading food processing companies. Heinz's products include ketchup, tuna, pet food, baby food, frozen potato products, soup, low-calorie frozen meals, beans, sauces and condiments, pickles, vinegar, frozen meat, rice cakes, and corn derivatives. Fifty-five percent of Heinz's international sales comes from products that hold the #1 brand position in their respective markets.

Heinz ketchup (the company's flagship brand) holds more than 50% of the US market. The company is the market leader in frozen entrees (Weight Watchers), canned cat food (9-Lives), and relish. Other high-share products include frozen potatoes (Ore-Ida, 48.2%) and tuna (Star-Kist, 37%).

In addition to domestic leadership, Heinz's products command a strong presence overseas and are sold in over 200 countries including Canada, the UK, Australia, Venezuela, and Japan.

The company (a significant portion of which is still owned by the Heinz family) has successfully maintained a reputation for high-quality products, good management, and generous social philanthropy.

NYSE symbol: HNZ
Incorporated: Pennsylvania, 1900
Fiscal year ends: April 30

WHO

Chairman, President, and CEO: Anthony J. F. O'Reilly, age 54, $2,756,545 pay
VC and SVP; Chairman, Star-Kist: Joseph J. Bogdanovich, age 78, $1,169,411 pay
SVP Corporate Development and CFO: R. Derek Finlay, age 58, $964,616 pay
Auditors: Coopers & Lybrand
Employees: 36,200

WHEN

In 1852 8-year-old Henry J. Heinz started selling produce from the family garden to his neighbors in Sharpsburg, Pennsylvania. In 1869 Heinz formed a partnership with his friend L. C. Noble to bottle horseradish sauce in Pittsburgh. After a period of prosperity, the business went bankrupt in 1875.

With the help of his brother John and his cousin Frederick, Heinz created F. & J. Heinz the following year. At his new company Heinz developed tomato ketchup (1876) and sweet pickles (1880). He gained financial control of the firm in 1888 and changed the name to the H. J. Heinz Company.

Heinz developed a reputation as an advertising and marketing genius. At the 1893 World's Fair in Chicago, he had the largest exhibit. Three years later he coined his "57 Varieties" slogan. In 1900, the year the company was incorporated, Heinz raised New York City's first large electric sign (which included a 40-foot green pickle) as an advertising gimmick.

By 1905 Heinz was manufacturing his food products in England. In America his Pittsburgh plants (complete with an indoor gym, swimming pool, hospital, and 3-story stable) became known as a "utopia for working men." While most of the food industry was opposed to the Pure Food Act in 1906, Heinz sent his son to Washington to campaign for the legislation. During the entire time that Heinz controlled his company, there was never a strike at his plants. Following the death of H. J. Heinz in 1919, the company, under the direction of Heinz's son and later his grandson (whose son, H. J. Heinz III, is now a US senator), continued to rely on its traditional product line for the next 4 decades. In 1969 R. Burt Gookin became CEO of the company (the first person not a member of the Heinz family to hold the position).

During the 1960s the company started a program of acquisition that would eventually include Star-Kist (1963), Ore-Ida (1965), Tuffy's (pet food, 1971), Weight Watchers (weight reduction programs and low-calorie frozen food products, 1978), and Chico-San (rice cakes, 1984).

Irishman Anthony J. F. O'Reilly became CEO in 1979 and set his sights on Europe. The company is also expanding its facilities in such developing countries as Zimbabwe, the People's Republic of China, and Thailand. In 1990 Heinz established a manufacturing facility in Kuwait.

WHERE

HQ: 600 Grant St., Pittsburgh, PA 15219
Phone: 412-456-5700
FAX: 412-237-5377 (Public Relations)

Heinz operates 70 food processing plants in 17 countries.

	1989 Sales		1989 Operating Income	
	$ mil	% of total	$ mil	% of total
US	3,473	61	467	58
Continental Europe	769	13	124	15
UK	770	13	105	13
Canada	375	6	46	6
Other	414	7	61	8
Total	**5,801**	**100**	**803**	**100**

WHAT

Brand Names

Sauces & Condiments
57 Sauce
Heinz barbecue sauce
Heinz ketchup
Heinz pickles
Heinz relish
Heinz tartar sauce
Heinz vinegar
HomeStyle Gravy

Food & Beverages
Alba (low-calorie beverage mixes)
Chico-San (rice cakes)
Heinz baby food
Heinz soups
Marie Elisabeth (sardines)
Near East (flavored rice products)
Ore-Ida (frozen potatoes)
Star-Kist (tuna)
Steak-umm (frozen meat products)
Weight Watchers (weight reduction programs and food products)

Pet Food
9-Lives
Amore
Jerky Treats
Kozy Kitten
Meaty Bones
Recipe

HOW MUCH

	9 Yr. Growth	1980	1981	1982	1983	1984	1985	1986	1987	1988	1989
Sales ($ mil)	7.9%	2,925	3,569	3,689	3,738	3,954	4,048	4,366	4,639	5,244	5,801
Net income ($ mil)	13.3%	143	167	193	214	238	266	302	339	386	440
Income as % of sales	—	4.9%	4.7%	5.2%	5.7%	6.0%	6.6%	6.9%	7.3%	7.4%	7.6%
Earnings per share ($)	14.2%	0.50	0.58	0.67	0.74	0.83	0.96	1.09	1.23	1.45	1.65
Stock price – high ($)	—	3.57	3.91	4.96	6.92	9.50	11.25	17.13	24.13	25.88	25.00
Stock price – low ($)	—	2.88	2.90	3.81	4.17	6.00	8.00	10.25	14.63	16.75	18.75
Stock price – close ($)	24.0%	3.38	3.88	4.67	6.73	9.50	10.75	16.19	20.25	20.19	23.38
P/E – high	—	7	7	7	9	11	12	16	20	18	15
P/E – low	—	6	5	6	6	7	8	9	12	12	11
Dividends per share ($)	16.3%	0.18	0.20	0.23	0.27	0.34	0.39	0.44	0.50	0.61	0.70
Book value per share ($)	9.1%	3.17	3.50	3.62	3.97	4.11	4.50	5.09	5.41	6.24	6.91

1989 Year End:
Debt ratio: 28.1%
Return on equity: 25.1%
Cash (mil): $238
Current ratio: 1.59
Long-term debt (mil): $693
Number of shares (mil): 257
Dividends:
1989 average yield: 3.0%
1989 payout: 42.1%
Market value (mil): $6,006

RANKINGS

82nd in *Fortune* 500 Industrial Cos.
144th in *Forbes* Sales 500
64th in *Business Week* 1000
194th in *Business Week* Global 1000

COMPETITION

BSN
Campbell Soup
Clorox
CPC International
General Mills
Gerber
Grand Metropolitan
Kellogg
Mars
Nestlé
Philip Morris
Quaker Oats
Ralston Purina
RJR Nabisco

HELMSLEY ENTERPRISES INC.

OVERVIEW

Helmsley is a holding company for real estate, hotel, shopping center, and related enterprises valued at $5 billion. The privately held company is owned by Harry and Leona Helmsley. Most of its properties are located in Manhattan; Harry is the 3rd largest individual owner of Manhattan property (Donald Trump is #1 and the deceased Sol Goldman's estate, which is being dissolved, is #2). He owns the deeds to an estimated 40 acres of Manhattan land.

In addition to owning properties, Helmsley also owns real estate and insurance broker Helmsley-Spear, which manages over 600 office and apartment buildings in New York, Florida, Texas, California, and elsewhere. Of these, the best known is the Empire State Building. The division's revenues are estimated at $1.1 billion annually.

Helmsley Hotels operates 6 luxury hotels, including the famed Helmsley Palace, in New York City, and the Harley Hotels. Although some Harleys have been sold recently, the chain still operates 17 hotels in 10 states. Subsidiaries include Deco Purchasing, the central purchasing arm for Helmsley Hotels, and Owners Maintenance, a cleaning services company that holds contracts with many Helmsley properties.

Leona Helmsley, spokeswoman and former "Queen" of the Helmsley Hotels in its advertising, was found guilty of tax evasion in 1989.

WHEN

Harry Helmsley began his career as a Manhattan rent collector in 1925. Rent collecting, then handled in person, gave Harry contact with building owners and an ability to evaluate a building. The real estate market crashed in 1929, allowing Harry to obtain property at a bargain price (1936). He paid $1,000 down for a building with a $100,000 mortgage and has quipped that he did so to provide employment for his father, whom he hired as superintendent. In 1946 he sold the building for $165,000 and used the funds to launch his enterprise.

In 1949 Harry teamed up with his lawyer Lawrence Wien, and the 2 became steadfast partners in their pursuit of Manhattan property. Helmsley located property; Wien found financing. The deal they made on the Empire State Building, purchased in 1961 after 3 years of negotiation, is typical of their tactics. They bought the building for $65 million and sold it to Prudential for $29 million, obtaining a 114-year leaseback. A public offering for the newly created Empire State Building Company made up the difference, and both men received stock for their efforts.

During the 1950s Harry bought into many noteworthy office buildings, including the Flatiron (1951), Berkeley (1953), and Equitable (1957). He bought the property management firm of Leon Spear in 1955. In the mid-1960s he began developing properties, beginning with a 52-story office tower on Broadway. By 1967 Harry was investing in shopping centers. In 1969 he bought the trust of Furman and Wolfson, which held about 30 buildings nationwide, for $165 million. To finance the trust, Harry borrowed $78 million in cash on his reputation — the largest unsecured signature loan ever.

Harry's association with Spear precipitated a meeting with successful real estate broker Leona Roberts, from whom Spear had purchased an apartment. Spear arranged for them to meet (1969); Helmsley hired Leona, promoted her to SVP, and later divorced his wife to marry her (1971).

Harry became interested in hotels in the 1970s, although the Manhattan market for luxury hotels was considered saturated. In 1974 he leased a historical building (now called the Helmsley Palace) from the Catholic church and began renovation; the Palace opened in 1980. Leona's extravagance cost Harry millions on the venture. Beginning in 1979 Harry invested in the booming Florida market, first building Miami Palace and, in a later project that went bankrupt, Helmsley Center.

During the 1980s Harry's empire began to crumble as Leona gained control. Numerous lawsuits, lackadaisical bookkeeping, shoddy building maintenance (a ceiling collapsed at the Helmsley Windsor, killing a guest), and extravagant spending culminated in indictments for tax evasion. Harry was declared mentally incompetent to stand trial, but in August 1989 Leona was convicted, fined $7.1 million, and sentenced to 4 years in jail. In August 1990 the Helmsleys put their Helmsley-Greenfield subsidiary up for sale.

HOW MUCH

	4 Yr. Growth	1980	1981	1982	1983	1984	1985	1986	1987	1988	1989
Est. sales ($ mil)	8.8%	—	—	—	—	—	1,000	1,000	1,700	1,430	1,400
Employees	6.8%	—	—	—	—	—	10,000	13,000	13,000	13,000	13,000

Private company
First investment: 1951

WHO

President: Harry Helmsley, age 80
President, Helmsley Hotels: Leona Helmsley, age 70
SVP: William Lubliner
VP and Assistant Secretary: Alvin Schwartz, age 69
VP and Assistant Secretary: Irving Schneider, age 71
Treasurer: Martin S. Stone
Employees: 13,000

WHERE

HQ: 60 E. 42nd St., New York, NY 10165
Phone: 212-687-6400
FAX: 212-687-6437

Helmsley Enterprises operates primarily in Manhattan but has holdings elsewhere in New York and in California, Florida, Illinois, and Texas.

WHAT

Real Estate Management & Sales
6th & 55th Corp.
36 Central Park South Corp.
77 Park Inc.
Basic Estates Inc.
Brown, Harris, Stevens, Inc.
California Jewelry Mart Realty Corp.
Charles F. Noyes Co. Inc.
Fifth-Central Park Corp.
Garden Bay Manor Associates
H 33 Manor Corp.
H 321 Cloister Corp.
Helmsley-Greenfield, Inc.
Helmsley-Noyes Co., Inc.
Helmsley-Spear Conversion Sales
Helmsley Spear Hospitality Services
Helmsley-Spear, Inc.
Investment Properties Associates
John J. Reynolds, Inc.
National Realty Corp.
Parkmerced Corp.
Willoughby Properties Inc.
York East Realty Corp.
York East Willoughby Properties Inc.

Hotels
Boardwalk & Missouri Corp.
Carlton House Hotel
Harley Hotels, Inc.
Helmsley Hotels, Inc. (The Helmsley Palace)
Hospitality Motor Inns (96.8%)
Moritz Inc. (Hotel St. Moritz)
Park Lane Hotel, Inc.

Other
Deco Purchasing Co. (purchasing agent)
Owners Maintenance Corp. (janitorial services)
Security Title & Guaranty Co. (title insurance)
Supervisory Management Corp. (management and public relations)

RANKINGS

94th in *Forbes* 400 US Private Cos.

COMPETITION

Bass	ITT
Carlson	Loews
Edward J. DeBartolo	Marriott
Hilton	Nestlé
Hyatt	Trammell Crow

THE HENLEY GROUP, INC.

OVERVIEW

The Henley Group's stated business objective is to enhance the value of its holdings for its stockholders. Consistent with this objective, Henley is not built around a core business but rather seeks to maximize the value of its assets through buying, developing, reorganizing, and selling businesses and operating segments as opportunities present themselves. The company has never made a profit, and each of its 3 business segments lost money in 1989.

Henley's holdings include 100% of Fisher Scientific Group (laboratory products and instruments for disease diagnosis); 100% of Pneumo Abex (aircraft landing gear, flight control systems, hydraulic pumps, braking materials, aircraft boarding bridges); 82% of Cape Horn Methanol (methanol production); 37% of Itel (transportation services, rail car leasing); 7% of Wheelabrator Technologies (trash-to-energy plants); and warrants for up to 15% of Henley Properties (real estate development). Henley's strategy is to break up and distribute its component parts to shareholders in the most tax-efficient manner.

OTC symbol: HENG
Incorporated: Delaware, 1989
Fiscal year ends: December 31

WHO

Chairman and CEO: Michael D. Dingman, age 58, $1,010,000 pay
President: Paul M. Montrone, age 48, $675,000 pay
Principal Financial Officer: Paul M. Meister, age 37
Auditors: Deloitte & Touche
Employees: 11,400

WHEN

The Henley Group was originally composed of 35 companies spun off from Allied-Signal in 1986. Henley's initial public stock offering of 60 million shares was priced at $21.25 per share or $1.28 billion, making it the largest initial stock offering in US history to that date. Soon after the stock was issued, Henley completed buying Imed (medical supplies) for $163 million. Henley has been active in corporate buying and selling ever since.

Henley's 1986 asset sales included its 10% share of Mack Truck for $37 million and 49% of its Wyoming soda ash operations for $100 million. During that year the company arranged a $3 billion revolving credit agreement with a consortium of 21 banks and bought Allied-Signal's remaining 15.6% share in Henley for $465 million.

During 1987 Henley pursued Santa Fe Southern Pacific, offering almost $10 billion. Henley purchased 16.9% of Santa Fe stock before giving up in 1988 and selling its interests in Santa Fe, along with its wholly owned Signal Capital and Equilease (railcars), to Itel for $827 million in cash and 18.7 million shares (40%) of Itel common stock. Also in 1987 Henley sold M. W. Kellogg Company (oil industry construction) to Dresser Industries, sold 17% of Wheelabrator Technologies stock to the public, and spun off Henley Manufacturing in a stock distribution to shareholders, with Henley retaining 55% ownership.

In 1988 the company was divided into The Wheelabrator Group, which owned 60% of The Wheelabrator Technologies, and The Henley Group in a spinoff of 19 million shares of new stock. The old Henley Group was renamed The Wheelabrator Group, and stock in the newly formed Henley Group was distributed to shareholders of old Henley. The new Henley Group owned 12% of The Wheelabrator Group, 81% of Fisher Group (medical and laboratory supplies), 100% of Signal Landmark Holdings (real estate), 82% of Cape Horn Methanol, 40% of Itel, and 50% of PA Holdings. PA Holdings, jointly owned by Henley and Wasserstein Perella & Company, bought Pneumo Abex (aerospace and defense technology) for $1.3 billion.

In 1989 Henley bought the remaining 50% of Pneumo Abex; the company's 55% interest in Henley Manufacturing was acquired by New Hampshire Oak, a company owned by Henley CEO Michael Dingman and president Paul Montrone; and Henley spun off Henley Properties (real estate) to its stockholders. In 1990 Henley announced plans to spin off to its shareholders its two largest operating companies, Fisher Scientific and Pneumo Abex, as separate companies, but when Itel agreed in August 1990 to buy back all shares of its stock owned by Henley, Henley announced that it would not spin off its Pneumo Abex holdings.

WHERE

HQ: Liberty Ln., Hampton, NH 03842
Phone: 603-926-5911
FAX: 603-926-2289

Henley has 35 US facilities and 18 facilities in 7 foreign countries.

	1989 Sales		1989 Net Income	
	$ mil	% of total	$ mil	% of total
North America	1,364	85	(218)	105
Europe & other	239	15	11	(5)
Adjustments	(37)	—	—	—
Total	**1,566**	**100**	**(207)**	**100**

WHAT

	1989 Sales		1989 Operating Income	
	$ mil	% of total	$ mil	% of total
Laboratory & Medical Prods.	978	62	(37)	—
Aerospace	369	24	(67)	—
Industrial Products	219	14	(50)	—
Adjustments	—	—	222	—
Total	**1,566**	**100**	**68**	**100**

Henley Business Segments
Laboratory and Medical Products
- Fisher Scientific (lab products)
- Instrumentation Laboratory (diagnostic instruments)

Aerospace Products and Services
- Abex Aerospace (pumps and motors)
- Cleveland Pneumatic (landing gear maintenance)
- NWL Control Systems (flight control systems)

Industrial Products
- Abex Friction Products (brake products)
- Cape Horn Methanol (82%)
- Jetway Systems (aircraft boarding bridges)

Other Interests
Henley Properties (15%)
Wheelabrator Technologies (7%)

HOW MUCH

	4 Yr. Growth	1980	1981	1982	1983	1984	1985	1986	1987	1988	1989
Sales ($ mil)	4.0%	—	—	—	—	—	1,845	3,172	3,516	1,036	1,566
Net income ($ mil)	33.6%	—	—	—	—	—	(65)	(426)	(278)	(271)	(207)
Income as % of sales	—	—	—	—	—	—	(3.5%)	(13.4%)	(7.9%)	(26.2%)	(13.2%)
Earnings per share ($)	—	—	—	—	—	—	—	(23.69)	(12.76)	(14.76)	(10.45)
Stock price – high ($)	—	—	—	—	—	—	—	112.22	136.67	116.11	74.25
Stock price – low ($)	—	—	—	—	—	—	—	76.67	80.00	83.33	50.50
Stock price – close ($)	—	—	—	—	—	—	—	100.56	86.11	96.11	54.25
P/E – high	—	—	—	—	—	—	—	—	—	—	—
P/E – low	—	—	—	—	—	—	—	—	—	—	—
Dividends per share ($)	—	—	—	—	—	—	0.00	0.00	0.00	0.00	0.00
Book value per share ($)	—	—	—	—	—	—	—	119.71	89.35	77.43	55.64

1989 Year End:
Debt ratio: 57.7%
Return on equity: —
Cash (mil): $147
Current ratio: 1.97
Long-term debt (mil): $1,592
Number of shares (mil): 21
Dividends:
1989 average yield: 0.0%
1989 payout: 0.0%
Market value (mil): $1,136

Stock Price History high/low 1986-89

140 120 100 80 60 40 20 0

RANKINGS

238th in *Fortune* 500 Industrial Cos.
476th in *Forbes* Sales 500
676th in *Business Week* 1000

COMPETITION

Allied-Signal
Becton, Dickinson
Eaton
General Electric
Hewlett-Packard
PPG
Robert Bosch
Ryder
Siemens

HERCULES, INC.

OVERVIEW

Hercules is a worldwide supplier of specialty chemicals and engineered polymers (absorbent and textile products and packaging films). The company also produces rocket boosters for US strategic missiles and space launch vehicles.

The specialty chemical sales segment is the company's sales leader, with 41% of sales. Hercules also makes resins used in rubber and plastics fabrication worldwide and markets fragrances and food gums to customers in over 80 countries. The company is a global leader in supplying chemicals to the paper-manufacturing industry.

Hercules manufactures polypropylene film, used in packaging consumer products such as fresh vegetables, candy, and snacks. The company's polymers are also used in disposable diapers. In the decorative fabrics and textiles market, Hercules is known for its Herculon olefin fiber. The Aqualon Group makes Hercules a leading worldwide manufacturer of water-soluble polymers, additives to foods and fluids.

Hercules's aerospace group makes solid rocket motor systems for Trident II missiles and Titan IV and Delta II space launch systems.

WHEN

A 1912 federal court decision forced Du Pont, which controlled 2/3 of US explosives production, to spin off 1/2 the business into 2 companies, Hercules Powder and Atlas Powder.

Hercules began operating explosives plants across the US in 1913. Russell Dunham, Hercules's first president, had expanded the company's operations by 1915 into Utah and Missouri. During WWI the company became the largest US producer of TNT, making 71 million pounds for the US military.

After WWI Hercules diversified into nonexplosive products, such as nitrocellulose for the manufacture of plastics, lacquers, and films. The 1920 purchase of Yaryan Rosin and Turpentine made Hercules the world's largest steam-distilled rosin and turpentine producer.

By the late 1920s the company's core business had changed from powders to chemicals, which would be its focus for the next 3 decades. Hercules expanded the marketing of its rosin products to dozens of industries, including the paper industry, the largest user. Hercules also became the largest US producer of nitrocellulose in 1930. In the 1940s the company developed water-soluble polymers.

In the early 1950s Hercules developed a new process for making phenol, used in plastics, paints, and pharmaceuticals. The company's explosives department made important contributions in rocketry, developing propellants for Nike rockets and making motors for Minuteman and Polaris missiles.

By the late 1950s Hercules was making chemical propellants, petrochemical plastics, synthetic fibers, agricultural and paper chemicals, and food additives. In the 1960s and early 1970s the company, renamed Hercules, Inc., in 1966, increased plastic resin and fabricated plastic production, opening 5 new plants.

Hercules also developed foreign markets, doubling export sales between 1962 and 1972. Following the energy crisis of the 1970s, CEO Alexander F. Giacco decided to reduce dependence on commodity petrochemicals and increase specialty chemical and defense-related rocket propulsion businesses. In 1987 it sold its interest in the polypropylene resins business (HIMONT) and in 1989 took full ownership of The Aqualon Group, which since 1987 had been a joint venture with Henkel KGaA of West Germany.

In 1989 Hercules had a $96 million loss, taking a $323 million charge to cover cost overruns on Titan IV, Delta II, and SRAM missile contracts. Technical problems and US defense budget uncertainties related to the Titan IV rocket system may cloud the company's outlook.

HOW MUCH

	9 Yr. Growth	1980	1981	1982	1983	1984	1985	1986	1987	1988	1989
Sales ($ mil)	2.5%	2,485	2,718	2,469	2,629	2,571	2,587	2,615	2,693	2,802	3,092
Net income ($ mil)	—	114	136	87	174	197	133	227	821	120	(96)
Income as % of sales	—	4.6%	5.0%	3.5%	6.6%	7.7%	5.1%	8.7%	30.5%	4.3%	(3.1%)
Earnings per share ($)	—	2.60	3.09	1.97	3.17	3.54	2.40	4.02	14.18	2.54	(2.09)
Stock price – high ($)	—	25.00	26.38	28.75	43.13	38.00	40.75	60.00	73.50	54.00	52.25
Stock price – low ($)	—	15.13	18.75	16.88	27.25	27.25	31.13	37.00	40.00	42.63	38.38
Stock price – close ($)	8.3%	19.00	22.63	27.63	35.75	33.88	39.38	50.63	47.00	44.50	39.00
P/E – high	—	10	9	15	14	11	17	15	5	21	—
P/E – low	—	6	6	9	9	8	13	9	3	17	—
Dividends per share ($)	7.2%	1.20	1.26	1.32	1.38	1.48	1.60	1.72	1.84	2.00	2.24
Book value per share ($)	6.2%	23.79	24.73	24.18	24.33	25.57	27.13	31.11	44.88	44.58	40.77

1989 Year End:
Debt ratio: 23.3%
Return on equity: —
Cash (mil): $70
Current ratio: 1.67
Long-term debt (mil): $576
Number of shares (mil): 47
Dividends:
1989 average yield: 5.7%
1989 payout: —
Market value (mil): $1,815

Stock Price History high/low 1980-89

NYSE symbol: HPC
Incorporated: Delaware, 1912
Fiscal year ends: December 31

WHO

Chairman and CEO: David S. Hollingsworth, age 62, $544,245 pay
President and COO: Fred L. Buckner, age 58, $388,500 pay
VC and CFO: Arden B. Engebretsen, age 58, $355,500 pay
Auditors: Coopers & Lybrand
Employees: 23,290

WHERE

HQ: Hercules Plaza, 1313 N. Market St., Wilmington, DE 19894
Phone: 302-594-5000
FAX: 302-594-5400

Hercules has nearly 100 production facilities worldwide, including subsidiaries and affiliates.

	1989 Sales		1989 Operating Income	
	$ mil	% of total	$ mil	% of total
US	2,306	74	(235)	—
Europe	605	20	101	—
Other	181	6	15	—
Adjustments	—	—	323	—
Total	**3,092**	**100**	**204**	**—**

WHAT

	1989 Sales		1989 Operating Income	
	$ mil	% of total	$ mil	% of total
Specialty chemicals	1,246	41	111	—
Engineered polymers	386	12	15	—
Aerospace	1,061	34	(243)	—
Other	399	13	(2)	—
Adjustments	—	—	323	—
Total	**3,092**	**100**	**204**	**—**

Specialty Chemicals
Aroma chemicals
Electronic chemicals
Fatty acids
Flavors and fragrances
Food gums
Paper chemicals
Resins
Rosin-based esters

Engineered Polymers
Polypropylene fibers
Polypropylene film
Synthetic paper pulp

Aerospace
Carbon fiber
Composite structures
Electromechanical and electronic equipment
Smokeless powders
Solid propellant rocket motors

RANKINGS

145th in *Fortune* 500 Industrial Cos.
407th in *Fortune* Global 500 Industrial Cos.
270th in *Forbes* Sales 500
362nd in *Business Week* 1000

COMPETITION

Allied-Signal
American Cyanamid
BASF
Bayer
Dow Chemical
Du Pont
FMC
W. R. Grace
Harley-Davidson
Hoechst
IFF
Monsanto
Rhône-Poulenc
Roche Holding
Thiokol
Union Carbide
Vulcan Materials

HERSHEY FOODS CORPORATION

OVERVIEW

The town of Hershey, Pennsylvania, is home to Hershey Foods, the #1 confectioner in North America.

The Hershey Chocolate U.S.A. division, the nation's largest chocolatier, holds approximately 44% of the US chocolate industry, making more than 55 brands of confectionery products. This division also makes cocoa, chocolate chips, baking bars, syrup, and flavored drink mixes. Hershey's chocolate milk is produced by approximately 30 independent dairies in the US.

Hershey Refrigerated Products sells ready-to-eat puddings in 4 candy bar flavors, the first product line to emerge from the company's effort to move into new areas.

Two international groups — Hershey Canada and Hershey International — manufacture and sell Hershey products, primarily confections, in Canada, the Far East, and Latin America.

Hershey Pasta Group, the 2nd largest pasta producer in the US, makes regionally distributed brands of pasta, including San Giorgio. Over 400,000 pounds of 65 different types of pasta are produced every day under the 75-year-old San Giorgio label.

NYSE symbol: HSY
Incorporated: Delaware, 1927
Fiscal year ends: December 31

WHO

Chairman and CEO: Richard A. Zimmerman, age 57, $805,209 pay
President and COO: Kenneth L. Wolfe, age 51, $571,411 pay
President, Hershey Chocolate U.S.A.: Joseph P. Viviano, age 51, $441,488 pay
SVP and CFO: Michael F. Pasquale, age 42, $290,902 pay
SVP: W. Lehr, Jr., age 49, $245,470 pay
Auditors: Arthur Andersen & Co.
Employees: 11,800

WHEN

Hershey is the legacy of Milton Hershey of Pennsylvania Dutch origin. Apprenticed in 1872 at age 15 to a candy maker, Hershey was a confectioner all his adult life and started Lancaster Caramel Company at age 30. During an 1893 visit to the Chicago Exposition, he noticed a new chocolate-making machine and, immediately interested, sold the caramel operations for $1 million in 1900 to start a chocolate factory.

The factory was completed in 1905 in Derry Church, Pennsylvania, renamed Hershey in 1906. In 1909 he founded the Milton Hershey School, an orphanage; in 1918 the company was donated to a trust and for years existed solely to fund the school. Although the company is now publicly traded, the school still retains majority stock control; former chairman William Dearden (1976-1984) was a graduate, as are many Hershey employees.

Hershey pioneered mass-production techniques for chocolates and developed much of the machinery for making and packaging its products. At one time the company supplied its own sugar cane from Cuba and enlarged the world's almond supply 6 times over through nut farm ownership. The Hershey bar has become Americana and is so universally recognized that it was used during WWII as currency.

Concerned more with benevolence than profits, Hershey put people to work during the Great Depression building a hotel, golf courses, a library, theaters, a museum, a stadium, and other facilities in Hershey.

One of Hershey's peculiarities was that he refused to advertise, believing quality would speak for itself. Even after his death in 1945, the company continued his policy. Then, in 1970, facing a sluggish candy market after failing to recognize a more diet-conscious public, Hershey lost share to Mars, and management relented. In 1989 advertising and promotion expenditures were 16% of net sales.

In the 1970s Hershey embarked on a diversification path to stabilize the effects of changing commodity prices. It brought out Big Block (large-sized) bars (1980), bought the Friendly Ice Cream chain (1979, sold in 1988), and ventured into pasta. The company continued to expand candy operations with the purchase of Cadbury's US candy business (1988). In 1990 Hershey formed a joint venture with Fujiya (Tokyo) to distribute Hershey confections and other products in Japan. Pasta, while accounting for less than 1/10th of sales, is also an area of expansion. The company purchased Ronzoni's pasta, cheese, and sauce operations in 1990.

WHERE

HQ: 100 Mansion Rd. East, Hershey, PA 17033
Phone: 717-534-4001
FAX: 717-534-4078

Hershey Foods manufactures its products in the US and Canada and internationally through joint ventures or licensing arrangements.

	1989 Sales		1989 Operating Income	
	$ mil	**% of total**	**$ mil**	**% of total**
US	2,236	92	306	99
Canada	185	8	4	1
Total	**2,421**	**100**	**310**	**100**

WHAT

Confections
Almond Joy
Bar None
Big Block
Cadbury's
Caramello
Golden Almond
Helps
Hershey's Kisses
Hershey's Miniatures
Kit Kat
Krackel
Luden's
Marabou
Mello Mint
Mounds
Mr. Goodbar
Oh Henry!
Queen Anne
Reese's
Rolo
RSVP
Skor
Special Dark
Symphony
Twizzlers
Whatchamacallit
Y&S Nibs
York
5th Avenue

Pasta
American Beauty
Delmonico
Light 'N Fluffy
P&R
Pastamania!
Perfection
Ronzoni
San Giorgio
Skinner

HOW MUCH

	9 Yr. Growth	1980	1981	1982	1983	1984	1985	1986	1987	1988	1989
Sales ($ mil)	6.8%	1,335	1,451	1,566	1,706	1,893	1,996	2,170	2,434	2,168	2,421
Net income ($ mil)	11.9%	62	80	94	100	109	121	133	148	145	171
Income as % of sales	—	4.6%	5.5%	6.0%	5.9%	5.7%	6.0%	6.1%	6.1%	6.7%	7.1%
Earnings per share ($)	11.2%	0.73	0.94	1.00	1.07	1.16	1.28	1.42	1.64	1.60	1.90
Stock price – high ($)	—	4.33	6.83	9.92	11.67	13.75	18.33	29.92	37.75	28.63	36.88
Stock price – low ($)	—	3.33	3.85	5.40	8.13	9.42	11.67	15.50	20.75	21.88	24.75
Stock price – close ($)	27.9%	3.92	6.00	9.40	10.54	12.88	17.17	24.63	24.50	26.00	35.88
P/E – high	—	6	7	10	11	12	14	21	23	18	19
P/E – low	—	5	4	5	8	8	9	11	13	14	13
Dividends per share ($)	12.8%	0.25	0.29	0.33	0.37	0.41	0.48	0.52	0.58	0.66	0.74
Book value per share ($)	12.6%	4.26	5.00	5.66	6.34	7.03	7.74	8.07	9.23	11.15	12.39

1989 Year End:
Debt ratio: 16.2%
Return on equity: 16.1%
Cash (mil): $52
Current ratio: 1.99
Long-term debt (mil): $216
Number of shares (mil): 90
Dividends:
1989 average yield: 2.1%
1989 payout: 38.9%
Market value (mil): $3,235

Stock Price History high/low 1980-89

40 35 30 25 20 15 10 5 0

RANKINGS

185th in *Fortune* 500 Industrial Cos.
345th in *Forbes* Sales 500
217th in *Business Week* 1000
626th in *Business Week* Global 1000

COMPETITION

Archer-Daniels-Midland
Berkshire Hathaway
Borden
Campbell Soup
CPC International
Mars
Nestlé
Philip Morris

THE HERTZ CORPORATION

OVERVIEW

Hertz is the world's largest car rental company. Hertz subsidiary Hertz Equipment Rental Corporation is the largest renter of construction and industrial equipment in the US. All of the company's stock is owned by Park Ridge Corporation, which is in turn owned 49% by Ford, 26% by Volvo North America, 20% by a Hertz management partnership, and 5% by Commerzbank Aktiengesellschaft. Hertz CEO Frank Olson is the sole voting member of the management partnership.

Hertz's centralized worldwide reservation center in Oklahoma City, the world's largest, handles approximately 20 million phone calls and delivers more than 12 million rentals worldwide each year. The Hertz #1 Club charge card for frequent travelers was the first in the industry and now is held by more than 9 million people.

The company operates a worldwide fleet of over 310,000 vehicles, with 180,000 in the US. Hertz is the world's largest private purchaser of vehicles, buying over $2.6 billion worth annually. The company makes about 70% of its vehicle purchases from Ford.

WHEN

In 1918, 22-year-old John Jacobs opened a car rental business in Chicago with 12 Model T Fords which he repaired himself. By 1923 the business was generating annual revenues of about $1 million. John Hertz, president of both Yellow Cab and Yellow Truck and Coach Manufacturing Company, bought Jacobs's car rental business that year. Jacobs continued as top operating and administrative executive of the company, renamed Hertz Drive-Ur-Self System. In 1925 General Motors acquired the rental business when it bought Yellow Truck from John Hertz and completed the company's coast-to-coast rental network. The company introduced the first car rental charge card in 1926 and the first one-way (rent-it-here/leave-it-there) plan in 1933.

In 1953 Omnibus bought Hertz from General Motors. Omnibus sold its bus interests and concentrated on car and truck leasing and renting. In 1954 Omnibus changed its name to The Hertz Corporation and was listed on the NYSE. Hertz bought pioneer New York City truck leasing firm Metropolitan Distributors in 1954. John Jacobs remained as president until he retired in 1960. In 1965 Hertz formed its Hertz Equipment Rental subsidiary to rent construction equipment worldwide. In 1967 Hertz was bought by RCA but maintained its own board of directors and management. In 1972 the company introduced the first frequent-traveler's club, the #1 Club, which allowed the rental location to prepare a rental agreement before the customer arrived at the counter. Hertz introduced nationwide emergency road service in 1978.

In 1980, the year Hertz introduced the industry's first express rental service, the company led the US market with a 40% share. In 1985 United Airlines bought Hertz from RCA as part of UAL's strategy to form a global travel service company. In 1987 UAL changed its plans and sold Hertz for $1.3 billion to Park Ridge, which had been formed by Hertz management and Ford specifically to acquire Hertz, Ford's largest customer. The company moved to new corporate headquarters in Park Ridge, New Jersey, in 1988. In the same year, Ford, which held 80% of Park Ridge, sold 20% to Volvo North America for $100 million. Although it maintained its #1 position, by 1988 the company's market share had declined to 31%.

In 1988 Hertz pleaded guilty to overcharging more than 100,000 customers between 1978 and 1985 for repairs on damaged rental vehicles. The company was fined $6.85 million, the largest criminal consumer fraud fine ever imposed on a corporation, and ordered to pay $13.7 million in restitution. Most of the restitution was made to insurance companies. Hertz had already returned $3 million voluntarily. The company fired 20 employees who had acted without authorization.

In 1988 Hertz sold its stock in the Hertz Penske truck leasing joint venture, which had operated a fleet of about 42,000 vehicles in 1987, for $85.5 million and issued Penske a license to use the Hertz name. In the same year Ford sold more Park Ridge shares to Volvo, reducing Ford's stake to 49% and upping Volvo's to 26%. In 1989 Hertz increased its share of Axus (car leasing; Belgium, Luxembourg, Holland, France, Italy, and Spain) from 25% to 79%, and introduced "#1 Club Gold Service" which allows members (who pay an annual fee) to rent a car without a counter rental transaction.

HOW MUCH

	9 Yr. Growth	1980	1981	1982	1983	1984	1985	1986	1987	1988	1989
Sales ($ mil)	6.2%	1,273	1,409	1,531	1,346	1,420	1,499	1,577	1,836	1,967	2,181
Net income ($ mil)	0.0%	65	19	40	41	50	31	48	54	80	65
Income as % of sales	—	5.1%	1.4%	2.6%	3.1%	3.5%	2.0%	3.0%	3.0%	4.1%	3.0%

1989 Year End:
Debt ratio: 66.8%
Return on equity: —
Cash (mil): $167
Current ratio: —
Long-term debt (mil): $1,396

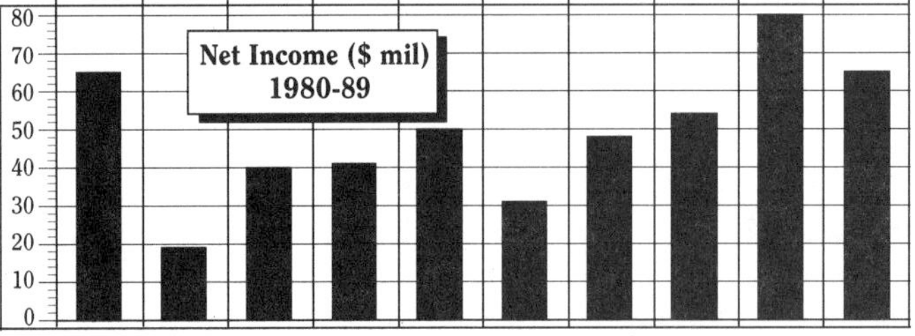

Net Income ($ mil) 1980-89

Private company
Incorporated: Delaware, 1967
Fiscal year ends: December 31

WHO

Chairman, CEO, and COO: Frank A. Olson, age 57, $657,692 pay
EVP; President, North America Rent A Car: Craig R. Koch, age 43, $316,800 pay
EVP International Operations: Fredy M. Dellis, age 44, $248,088 pay
EVP Sales and Marketing: Brian J. Kennedy, age 48
EVP; President, Hertz Equipment Rental: Daniel I. Kaplan, age 47, $269,908 pay
EVP and CFO: William Sider, age 56, $283,500 pay
SVP: Paul M. Tschirhart, age 49
SVP: Donald F. Steele, age 51
Auditors: Arthur Andersen & Co.
Employees: 18,000

WHERE

HQ: 225 Brae Blvd., Park Ridge, NJ 07656
Phone: 201-307-2000
FAX: 201-307-2644

Hertz rents 310,000 vehicles at its more than 5,000 locations in more than 120 countries worldwide. Hertz Equipment Rental has more than 100 branches in the US and Europe.

	1989 Sales		1989 Pretax Income	
	$ mil	% of total	$ mil	% of total
US	1,543	68	67	76
Foreign	710	32	21	24
Adjustments	(72)	—	—	—
Total	**2,181**	**100**	**88**	**100**

WHAT

	1989 Sales		1989 Operating Income	
	$ mil	% of total	$ mil	% of total
Car rental & leasing	1,990	91	225	82
Construction equip. rental & sale	191	9	49	18
Adjustments	—	—	(72)	—
Total	**2,181**	**100**	**202**	**100**

Subsidiaries
Axus, S.A. (79%; vehicle leasing in Europe)
Hertz System, Inc. (franchise licensing)
Hertz International, Ltd. (leasing)
Hertz Equipment Rental Corp. (construction equipment leasing)
HCM Claim Management Corp. (3rd party casualty and injury claim administration service)
Bierly & Associates, Inc. (worker's compensation claims service)

RANKINGS

45th in *Fortune* 100 Diversified Service Cos.

COMPETITION

Chrysler
Automakers' leasing units

HEWLETT-PACKARD COMPANY

OVERVIEW

Hewlett-Packard is the world's largest and most diversified manufacturer of electronic measurement and testing equipment and the world's 2nd largest workstation manufacturer (after Sun Microsystems), with over 26% of the market. HP is also a leader in factory automation and database management software.

Included in HP's over 10,000 product offerings are the broadest span of RISC chip–based machines on the market, the HP 3000 minicomputer line, medical electronic equipment, and chemical analysis systems. The company's laser printers are strong in the low and middle ends of the US market. HP is a leading practitioner of just-in-time manufacturing.

HP produced the world's first hand-held scientific calculator and the first desktop mainframe (workstation). HP Labs is one of the world's leading electronic research centers. R&D expenses are the 8th highest in the US ($1.3 billion or 11% of sales in 1989).

HP is often ranked by business leaders as one of America's most admired companies. The founders' nonhierarchical management style has been widely emulated within Silicon Valley. Generous benefits, valued employee input, consistently high quality, and internally financed growth are the HP way.

WHEN

In 1938, 2 young Stanford engineers named William Hewlett and David Packard, encouraged by their professor Frederick Terman (now known as the founder of Silicon Valley), founded their namesake in a Palo Alto, California, garage for a mere $538.

The demand for electronic testing instruments during WWII spurred sales growth from $34,000 (1940) to near $1 million (1943). In the 1950s HP expanded 50% to 100% yearly and opened European subsidiaries; later HP entered the fields of medicine (Sanborn Company, 1961) and analytical instrumentation (F&M Scientific Corporation, 1965).

HP's first computer (the HP2116A, 1966) gathered and analyzed data produced by HP instruments. In 1972 HP pioneered personal computing with the world's first hand-held scientific calculator and introduced the HP 3000 for business computing; by the late 1970s computers accounted for 1/2 of HP's revenues.

John Young, the founders' chosen successor (president in 1977, CEO in 1978), sponsored the first desktop mainframe (HP 9000, 1982), personal computers (HP-85, 1980; HP Vectra PC, 1985), and the LaserJet printer (HP's best-selling product ever, with over 2 million sold since 1985).

Young's 5-year, $250 million open systems effort (starting in the early 1980s) produced a high-performance RISC-based Spectrum line (1986) able to run the UNIX operating system. HP licensed its RISC chip to Hitachi and Samsung to increase the availability of Spectrum applications.

HP purchased workstation pioneer Apollo Computers in 1989. Differences between HP and Apollo technologies have led to difficulties in meshing their production lines. Recent joint ventures signal HP's new embrace of outside technology: networking with 3Com (including HP's taking a 5% stake in 3Com); manufacturing with Canon (laser printers) and Hitachi (next-generation RISC chip); and superconductivity research with Du Pont, Los Alamos Labs, and Conductus (HP has a 15% stake in the latter).

Recent introductions include New Wave software (the subject of litigation with Apple) to boost office productivity, and the advanced HP 3000 line, which launches HP into mainframe power. Future plans include a UNIX bridge to the HP 3000s and a melding of the HP and Apollo workstation lines using the advanced Motorola 68040 chip. Half HP's revenues now come from products introduced in the past 3 years.

HOW MUCH

	9 Yr. Growth	1980	1981	1982	1983	1984	1985	1986	1987	1988	1989
Sales ($ mil)	16.1%	3,099	3,578	4,254	4,710	6,044	6,505	7,102	8,090	9,831	11,899
Net income ($ mil)	13.3%	269	312	383	432	665	489	516	644	816	829
Income as % of sales	—	8.7%	8.7%	9.0%	9.2%	11.0%	7.5%	7.3%	8.0%	8.3%	7.0%
Earnings per share ($)	13.6%	1.12	1.28	1.53	1.69	2.59	1.91	2.02	2.50	3.36	3.52
Stock price – high ($)	—	24.25	26.94	41.25	48.25	45.50	38.88	49.63	73.63	65.50	61.50
Stock price – low ($)	—	12.81	19.19	18.00	34.25	31.13	28.75	35.75	35.75	43.75	40.25
Stock price – close ($)	8.7%	22.38	19.81	36.50	42.38	33.88	36.75	41.88	58.25	53.25	47.25
P/E – high	—	22	21	27	29	18	20	25	29	20	17
P/E – low	—	11	15	12	20	12	15	18	14	13	11
Dividends per share ($)	15.3%	0.10	0.11	0.12	0.16	0.19	0.22	0.22	0.23	0.28	0.36
Book value per share ($)	15.2%	6.42	7.83	9.37	11.33	13.82	15.50	17.08	19.52	19.35	22.92

1989 Year End:
Debt ratio: 8.0%
Return on equity: 16.7%
Cash (mil): $926
Current ratio: 1.53
Long-term debt (mil): $474
Number of shares (mil): 238
Dividends:
1989 average yield: 0.8%
1989 payout: 10.2%
Market value (mil): $11,229

Stock Price History high/low 1980-89

NYSE symbol: HWP
Incorporated: California, 1947
Fiscal year ends: October 31

WHO

Chairman: David Packard, age 77
VC, President, and CEO: John A. Young, age 57, $1,392,220 pay
EVP and COO: Dean O. Morton, age 57, $874,172 pay
SVP and CFO: Robert P. Wayman, age 44
Auditors: Price Waterhouse
Employees: 95,000

WHERE

HQ: 3000 Hanover St., Palo Alto, CA 94304
Phone: 415-857-1501
FAX: 415-857-7299

The company has 24 manufacturing plants in the US, 9 in Europe, and 12 elsewhere.

	1989 Sales		1989 Operating Income	
	$ mil	% of total	$ mil	% of total
US	5,561	46	881	54
Europe	4,131	35	359	22
Other	2,207	19	379	23
Adjustments	—	—	(424)	—
Total	**11,899**	**100**	**1,195**	**100**

WHAT

	1989 Sales	
	$ mil	% of total
Measurement, design, information, & manufacturing equipment	4,631	39
Peripherals & network products	3,486	29
Service for equipment & systems	2,157	18
Medical electronics	807	7
Analytical instrumentation & service	535	5
Electronic components	283	2
Total	**11,899**	**100**

Computer Products
Apollo (workstations)
HP 1000 (factory automation computers)
HP 3000 (commercial computers)
HP 9000 (UNIX-based workstations and multiuser computers)
HP Vectra (PCs)
LaserJet (laser printers)
OpenView (network management hardware and software)
ThinkJet, DeskJet, DeskWriter (ink jet printers)

Other Products
Electronic components
Hand-held calculators
Medical electronic equipment
Test and measurement systems

RANKINGS

33rd in *Fortune* 500 Industrial Cos.
89th in *Fortune* Global 500 Industrial Cos.
12th in *Fortune* 50 Exporters
49th in *Forbes* Sales 500
44th in *Business Week* 1000
128th in *Business Week* Global 1000

COMPETITION

Apple
C. R. Bard
Becton, Dickinson
Compaq
Data General
Digital Equipment
EG&G
IBM
NCR
Prime
Sun Microsystems
Tandem
Texas Instruments
Unisys
Wang
Electronic instrument manufacturers

HILLSBOROUGH HOLDINGS CORPORATION

OVERVIEW

Recently bankrupt Hillsborough Holdings was the nation's 4th largest home builder as late as 1987 and has built more than 270,000 homes since 1955. The company had become the largest producer of shell homes, which are unfinished inside, after establishing the market during the 1940s. The company had revenues of $1.4 billion in 1989.

Hillsborough also makes piping, which is sold for waste-water, pollution-control, high-rise, and other commercial and industrial applications. The company makes a variety of building materials, including aluminum coil and window screens. The company has diverse operations mostly related to its home construction business. Hillsborough has established insurance arms for its home buyers (Best); operates as a casualty reinsurer (Cardem), buying up policies of other insurers; arranges mortgage financing through Mid-State Homes, a former subsidiary; and has established a real estate brokerage (Jim Walter Homes). Hillsborough manufactures aluminum components (JW Aluminum) and weatherstripping for windows (JW Window Components).

Some operations are not directly related to construction. Hillsborough's Brookwood, Alabama–based operations mine coal, approximately 9 million tons annually; the company's De-Gas Division (Jim Walter Resources) produces gas through 223 wells, and the company engages in chemical manufacturing.

WHEN

Jim Walter was earning $50 a week as a Tampa truck driver in 1946 when he discovered an ad for an unfinished home. He bought the shell for $895 (largely borrowed from his father) and sold it 3 days later at a $300 profit. Walter, just out of the navy, thought other veterans would be interested in shell homes. He formed Walter Construction Company in 1946, changing the name to Jim Walter Corporation in 1955; by 1960, a shell-home industry had emerged, but most firms went broke or left the business in the 1961 building recession.

Walter began diversifying to stabilize his business. He sought related businesses, purchasing the First National Bank (St. Petersburg, Florida, 1959); Celotex (1964), a supplier of insulation, gypsum, roofing, and hardboard; Brentwood Financial Corporation (1966), owner of a Los Angeles–based savings and loan that would provide financing for his homes; Celotex's competitor, the Barrett division of Allied Chemical (1967); U.S. Pipe & Foundry (1969), a maker of valves and chemicals; and coal, oil, sugar, and jewelry businesses. By this time Walter had realized that his diverse business interests required greater management expertise, which he found in Harvard graduate and Celanese executive Frank Pizzitola, whom he hired as president. By 1972 the company was a major producer of building materials and was generating more than $1 billion in sales annually.

During the 1970s energy crisis, U.S. Pipe & Foundry's relatively unexplored coal reserves became a potential bonanza, and Pizzitola signed agreements with Japanese steel producers to sell them 3 million tons annually. The company had problems delivering, mainly due to a lack of experience in the field. Eventually, coal operations got going, and by 1986 the company was producing 8.1 million tons — just as energy prices began falling.

The company suffered other setbacks during the 1980s. Recession and high interest rates took a toll on its building business. Beginning in 1981 Celotex was hit with thousands of lawsuits by asbestos victims; by 1985 the division had paid out $3 million to $5 million annually in settlements. Joe Cordell replaced Walter as CEO in 1983 (Walter remains as chairman) and began selling minor operations and cutting overhead and production costs.

In 1987 LBO sponsor Kohlberg Kravis Roberts sold junk bonds to finance the $2 billion purchase of Jim Walter Corporation just prior to the stock market crash (purchase completed in 1988). Hillsborough Holdings Corporation was formed at the time of the LBO. Net sales and revenue for 1989 increased by 0.5% over the same 1988 period. Heavy debt service, continued weakness in its various operations, and difficulties relating to the Celotex asbestos litigation forced the company to file for Chapter 11 bankruptcy protection in 1989.

HOW MUCH

	9 Yr. Growth	1980	1981	1982	1983	1984	1985	1986	1987	1988*	1989
Revenues ($ mil)	—	1,916	1,972	1,955	2,054	2,288	2,292	2,368	2,429	1,050	1,387
Net income ($ mil)	—	84	23	6	71	97	112	139	166	(149)	(95)
Income as % of sales	—	4.4%	1.2%	0.3%	3.5%	4.2%	4.9%	5.9%	6.8%	(14.2%)	(6.8%)

1989 Year End:
Debt ratio: 107.1%
Return on equity: —
Cash (mil): $134
Current ratio: 4.07
Long-term debt (mil): $2,950
Number of shares (mil): 31

Net Income ($ mil) 1980-89

*Fiscal year change resulted in a 9-month period for which data are not directly comparable.

Private company
Incorporated: Originally incorporated as Jim Walter Corporation in Florida in 1955; taken private in 1988

WHO

Chairman, Walter Industries: James W. Walter, age 66, $934,061 pay
President and CEO, Walter Industries: Joe B. Cordell, age 61, $956,510 pay
SEVP and CFO, Walter Industries: Kenneth J. Matlock, age 61, $299,111 pay
SEVP and COO, Jim Walter Resources: William Carr, age 58, $244,476 pay
President and COO, U.S. Pipe: Henry C. Winsor, age 60, $200,100 pay
Auditors: Price Waterhouse
Employees: 9,000

WHERE

HQ: 9 W. 57th St., New York, NY 10019
Phone: 212-750-8300

Hillsborough's Jim Walter Homes subsidiary operates throughout the US, with 101 branch offices in 17 states.

WHAT

	1989 Sales $ mil
Homebuilding & related financing	159
Building materials	118
Industrial products	111
Water & wastewater transmission prods.	422
Natural resources	430
Other	147
Total	**1,387**

Subsidiaries in Reorganization
Best Insurors, Inc.
Best Insurors of Mississippi, Inc.
Coast to Coast Advertising, Inc.
Computer Holdings Corp.
Dixie Building Supplies, Inc.
Hamer Properties, Inc.
Homes Holdings Corp.
Jim Walter Computer Services, Inc.
Jim Walter Homes, Inc.
Jim Walter Insurance Services, Inc.
Jim Walter Resources, Inc.
Jim Walter Window Components, Inc.
JW Aluminum Co.
JW Resources Holdings Corp.
J.W.I. Holdings Corp.
J.W. Walter, Inc.
JW Window Components, Inc.
Land Holdings Corp.
Mid-State Holdings Corp.
Mid-State Homes, Inc.
Railroad Holdings Corp.
Sloss Industries Corp.
Southern Precision Corp.
United Land Corp.
United States Pipe & Foundry Co.
U.S. Pipe Realty, Inc.
Vestal Manufacturing Co.
Walter Home Improvement, Inc.
Walter Industries, Inc.
Walter Land Co.

Subsidiaries Not in Reorganization
Cardem Insurance Co., Ltd.
Jefferson Warrior Railroad Co.

RANKINGS

92nd in *Forbes* 400 US Private Cos.

COMPETITION

Manville
USG
Coal and gas companies

HILTON HOTELS CORPORATION

OVERVIEW

Hilton is one of the largest hotel operators in the US and has interests in approximately 95,000 rooms worldwide. Hilton owns or manages 43 US properties, franchises 214 properties (which are owned and operated by others), and owns 3 international hotels under the Hotel Conrad name in Dublin, Monte Carlo, and the French West Indies (3 more due in 1990 — Cancún, Hong Kong, and London).

The company has just opened the first of its CrestHil line, a moderately priced chain of country inns that will be operated under franchise agreements. Hilton has completed 3 of its new chain of Hilton Suites, each suite containing sleeping quarters and a parlor.

The company has 3 hotel/casinos in Nevada, an equity interest in a 4th in Australia, and 35% interest in a partially completed 575-room gaming operation in Istanbul; revenue from hotel/casinos accounted for 57% of sales and 44% of income in 1989.

Hotel design and furnishing services are provided through subsidiary Hilton Equipment. Hilton also owns 50% of Compass Computer, a computerized hotel reservation system. The remaining 50% is owned by Budget Rent-a-Car.

NYSE symbol: HLT
Incorporated: Delaware, 1946
Fiscal year ends: December 31

WHO

Chairman, President, and CEO: Barron Hilton, age 62, $967,274 pay
VC: Gregory R. Dillon, age 67, $407,341 pay
EVP Operations: Carl T. Mottek, age 61, $570,515 pay
EVP Nevada Gaming Operations: John V. Giovenco, age 53, $537,502 pay
SVP Finance: Maurice J. Scanlon, age 55, $392,995 pay
Auditors: Arthur Andersen & Co.
Employees: 39,000

WHEN

Conrad Hilton got his start in hotel management by renting rooms in his family's New Mexico home. He served as a state legislator and started a bank before leaving for Texas in 1919 with the intention of making his fortune in banking. There Hilton combined his $5,000 savings with a $20,000 loan and $15,000 from partners to buy his first hotel — in Cisco, Texas. Over the next decade he bought 7 more hotels, all in Texas. The Great Depression took a heavy toll on his business, and by 1934 he had only 5 hotels, but his business was saved, in part because he had leased land for his hotels instead of borrowing to buy it.

He began buying hotels again, moving into California (1938), New Mexico (1939), and Mexico (1942). In 1942 he met and married Zsa Zsa Gabor, whom he later divorced. He founded Hilton International to manage his foreign business (1948) and realized his ambition to run New York's Waldorf-Astoria (1949), which he called "the greatest of them all." Hilton's first European hotel opened in Madrid in 1953 and he bought the 10-hotel Statler chain ($111 million) in 1954 in the biggest transaction in hotel history to that date.

The company began franchising (1965) to capitalize on the best-known name in the hotel business and by 1987 had franchised 225 hotels. Conrad Hilton's son Barron became president (1966) and persuaded his father to sell the 38-chain Hilton International to TWA (1967) in exchange for TWA stock. Barron bought 2 hotels in Las Vegas (1970), creating a gaming division.

Upon Conrad's death in 1979, Barron became chairman and re-entered the international hotel business with Conrad International Hotels (1982), opening a gaming hotel in Australia (1985). The company spent $1.2 billion to refurbish and expand its 12 most glamorous hotels in the 1980s, including its 2 Las Vegas hotels (making them the 2 largest hotels in the world) and the Waldorf-Astoria.

Settlement of his father's will in 1988 gave Barron Hilton control of 25% of the company's stock. Hilton put the company up for sale in 1989, after high offers were made by foreign investors for other US hotels, but took it off the market after 9 months because bids did not meet his expectations.

In 1989 Hilton began to open Hilton Suites, hotels that provide only suites, and CrestHil, a chain of hotels that provides moderately priced lodging for the middle-market segment. In addition, Hilton plans to have 12 Conrad International hotels operating or under way by 1992.

WHERE

HQ: 9336 Civic Center Dr., Beverly Hills, CA 90209
Phone: 213-278-4321
FAX: 213-205-4599

Hilton owns, manages, or franchises hotels in 46 US states, Australia, the West Indies, Ireland, England, and Monaco.

WHAT

	1989 Sales	
	$ mil	% of total
Rooms	336	34
Food & beverage	217	22
Casino	311	31
Management & franchise fees	74	7
Other	59	6
Adjustments	(43)	—
Total	**954**	**100**

Owned Hotels
Atlanta Airport Hilton
Flamingo Hilton–Las Vegas (hotel/casino)
Flamingo Hilton–Reno (hotel/casino)
Hilton Suites (Brentwood, TN)
Hilton Suites (Orange, CA)
Las Vegas Hilton (hotel/casino)
New Orleans Airport Hilton
Palmer House (Chicago)
Portland Hilton
Waldorf-Astoria (New York)

Leased Hotels
Logan Airport Hilton (Boston)
Oakland Airport Hilton
Pittsburgh Hilton & Towers
San Diego Hilton
San Francisco Airport Hilton
Seattle Airport Hilton

Theme Casinos
O'Sheas (Las Vegas)
Paco's (Reno)

RANKINGS

97th in *Fortune* 100 Diversified Service Cos.
255th in *Business Week* 1000
760th in *Business Week* Global 1000

COMPETITION

Bally	ITT
Bass	Loews
Carlson	Marriott
Helmsley Enterprises	Nestlé
Hyatt	

HOW MUCH

	9 Yr. Growth	1980	1981	1982	1983	1984	1985	1986	1987	1988	1989
Sales ($ mil)	6.2%	554	571	600	649	647	684	719	815	915	954
Net income ($ mil)	0.4%	106	113	83	113	114	100	98	140	131	110
Income as % of sales	—	19.1%	19.7%	13.9%	17.3%	17.6%	14.6%	13.6%	17.2%	14.3%	11.5%
Earnings per share ($)	1.4%	2.00	2.11	1.56	2.10	2.17	2.02	1.96	2.80	2.72	2.27
Stock price – high ($)	—	24.31	26.13	26.00	30.13	29.00	36.75	40.13	45.88	55.25	115.50
Stock price – low ($)	—	12.75	16.63	13.81	20.06	22.75	27.88	30.25	27.50	34.00	48.38
Stock price – close ($)	16.3%	21.13	19.00	22.38	28.50	28.81	32.44	33.63	35.50	53.38	82.50
P/E – high	—	12	12	17	14	13	18	20	16	20	51
P/E – low	—	6	8	9	10	11	14	15	10	13	21
Dividends per share ($)	3.9%	0.71	0.83	0.90	0.90	0.90	0.90	0.90	0.90	0.98	1.00
Book value per share ($)	8.7%	8.70	9.99	10.65	11.87	12.00	13.14	14.23	15.79	17.03	18.40

1989 Year End:
Debt ratio: 35.6%
Return on equity: 12.8%
Cash (mil): $445
Current ratio: 1.04
Long-term debt (mil): $487
Number of shares (mil): 48
Dividends:
1989 average yield: 1.2%
1989 payout: 44.1%
Market value (mil): $3,960

HITACHI LTD.

OVERVIEW

Hitachi, meaning "rising sun" in Japanese, is Japan's 2nd largest industrial company after Toyota. Hitachi is a world leader in semiconductors and IBM-plug-compatible mainframe computers and is a major Japanese producer of industrial machinery, home electronics, and power systems. The company owns controlling stakes in several Japanese companies, including Hitachi Chemical, Hitachi Maxell, Hitachi Cable, and Hitachi Metals. Hitachi continues to invest substantial sums in semiconductor R&D and production facilities.

Hitachi's factories have been managed as independent profit centers where sales activities have sometimes been treated as unnecessary expense. As a result, Hitachi has a reputation as an excellent manufacturer but a less impressive marketer. The company is Japan's #2 VCR producer (after Matsushita) but, because most of Hitachi's VCRs are sold under other names (*e.g.*, RCA), brand recognition is low.

WHEN

Namihei Odaira, an employee of Kuhara Mining in the Japanese coastal city of Hitachi, wanted to prove that Japan did not have to depend on foreigners for technology. In 1910 he began building 5-hp electric motors in Kuhara's engineering and repair shop. Japanese power companies were forced to buy Odaira's generators when WWI made imports scarce. Impressed, they reordered, and in 1920 Hitachi became an independent company.

During the 1920s, acquisitions and growth turned Hitachi into a major manufacturer of electrical equipment and machinery. In the 1930s and 1940s Hitachi developed vacuum tubes and light bulbs and produced radar and sonar for the Japanese war effort. Postwar occupation forces removed Odaira and closed 19 Hitachi plants. Reeling from the plant closures, war damage, and labor strife, Hitachi was saved from bankruptcy by American military contracts during the Korean War.

In the 1950s Hitachi was designated a supplier to Nippon Telegraph and Telephone (NTT), the state-owned communications monopoly. Japan's economic recovery led to strong demand for the company's communications and electrical equipment. Hitachi began mass-producing home appliances, radios, TVs, and transistors. The company spun off Hitachi Metals and Hitachi Cable in 1956 and Hitachi Chemical in 1963.

With the help of NTT, the Ministry of International Trade and Industry (MITI), and computer technology licensed from RCA, Hitachi entered the data processing industry and produced its first computer in 1965. In the 1960s Hitachi began producing color TVs, built factories in Southeast Asia, and started manufacturing integrated circuits.

Hitachi launched an IBM-plug-compatible computer in 1974. The company sold its computers in the US through Itel until 1979, and afterwards through National Semiconductor's NAS unit. In the 1980s the company sold plug-compatibles in Europe through Olivetti (Italy) and BASF (West Germany). In a 1982 sting operation FBI agents caught Hitachi employees buying documents purportedly containing IBM software secrets. Hitachi settled a civil case with IBM for an estimated $300 to $500 million and $2 million to $3 million per month for 8 years as compensation for the use of IBM's software technology.

In the late 1980s the rising Japanese yen hurt exports. Hitachi responded by focusing on burgeoning domestic markets and investing heavily in factory automation. In 1988 the company and Texas Instruments agreed to join in the costly development and production of 16 megabyte DRAM. In 1989 Hitachi and Motorola became embroiled in a patent dispute that nearly halted sales of the Motorola microprocessor used in Apple's Macintosh. In the same year Hitachi bought 80% of NAS, giving the company direct control of its US distribution for the first time.

HOW MUCH

	9 Yr. Growth	1980	1981	1982	1983	1984	1985	1986	1987	1988	1989
Sales ($ mil)	15.4%	13,388	15,996	15,411	16,432	19,410	20,053	29,473	34,633	39,801	48,496
Net income ($ mil)	11.6%	524	615	571	627	743	841	884	705	1,094	1,406
Income as % of sales	—	3.9%	3.8%	3.7%	3.8%	3.8%	4.2%	3.0%	2.0%	2.8%	2.9%
Earnings per share ($)	9.9%	1.82	2.15	1.97	2.10	2.51	2.75	2.84	2.28	3.36	4.26
Stock price – high ($)	—	13.60	15.98	37.56	34.17	39.29	42.02	37.02	70.48	105.24	145.00
Stock price – low ($)	—	9.40	8.54	14.32	19.52	30.00	29.52	25.24	33.81	56.43	88.69
Stock price – close ($)	31.4%	10.54	15.42	28.81	34.05	34.29	32.74	36.90	65.71	86.43	122.86
P/E – high	—	7	7	19	16	16	15	13	31	31	34
P/E – low	—	5	4	7	9	12	11	9	15	17	21
Dividends per share ($)	11.0%	0.25	0.31	0.28	0.26	0.30	0.34	0.47	0.55	0.66	0.65
Book value per share ($)	16.2%	14.16	16.76	16.65	18.36	21.78	22.25	34.82	44.11	52.64	54.55

1989 Year End:
Debt ratio: 18.6%
Return on equity: 7.9%
Cash (mil): $15,329
Current ratio: 1.53
Long-term debt (mil): $3,946
Number of shares (mil): 317
Dividends:
1989 average yield: 0.5%
1989 payout: 15.2%
Market value (mil): $38,928

Stock Price History high/low 1980-89

160 140 120 100 80 60 40 20 0

NYSE symbol: **HIT (ADR)**
Incorporated: Japan, 1920
Fiscal year ends: March 31

WHO

President: Katsushige Mita, age 66
EVP: Shiro Kawada
Auditors: Peat Marwick Minato; Century Audit Corp.
Employees: 290,811

WHERE

HQ: 6, Kanda-Surugadai 4-chome, Chiyoda-ku, Tokyo 101, Japan
Phone: 011-81-3-258-1111
US HQ (Hitachi America, Ltd.): 50 Prospect Ave., Tarrytown, NY 10591
US Phone: 914-332-5800
US FAX: 914-332-5834

Hitachi manufactures its products in Japan and 10 other countries. US operations include 16 manufacturing subsidiaries and 28 sales and service subsidiaries.

	1990 Sales	
	$ mil	% of total
Japan	34,305	77
Other countries	10,492	23
Total	**44,797**	**100**

WHAT

	1990 Sales	
	$ mil	% of total
Power systems & equipment	6,257	14
Consumer products	6,332	14
Information systems & electronic devices	14,671	33
Industrial machinery & plants	7,643	17
Wire, chemicals & other	9,894	22
Total	**44,797**	**100**

Product Lines
Auto parts
Computers
Copper, iron, and steel products
Electrical controls
Electrical wire and cable
Elevators and escalators
Generators
Heavy machinery
Household appliances
Locomotives
Magnetic tape products (Maxell)
Power plants
Printed circuit boards
Robots
Semiconductors
Stereo/audio equipment
Synthetic resins
Telecommunications equipment
Turbines
Video equipment

RANKINGS

9th in *Fortune Global* 500 Industrial Cos.
17th in *Business Week* Global 1000

COMPETITION

Amdahl
AMP
Asea Brown Boveri
AT&T
BASF
Caterpillar
Deere
Commodore
Compaq
Control Data
Cray Research
Cummins Engine
Data General
Digital Equipment
Dresser
Eaton
Emerson
Fiat
Fujitsu
Harris
Hewlett-Packard
Hyundai
IBM
Ingersoll-Rand
3M
Mitsubishi
Motorola
NCR
NEC
Philips
Polaroid
Samsung
Seagate
Siemens
Sony
Sun Microsystems
Tenneco
Texas Instruments
Thomson
Unisys
Volvo
Wang
Xerox
Zenith

HOECHST AG

OVERVIEW

Hoechst (pronounced "Herxt") is one of the Big Three German companies that lead the world in chemical sales. The other 2 are Bayer and BASF. Hoechst is a diversified chemical producer, with substantial revenue from basic and agricultural chemicals, dyes, fibers, plastics, and pharmaceuticals. The company ranks 6th in the world in pharmaceutical sales and has one of Europe's largest drug sales forces. Hoechst does business in 140 countries and derives 3/4 of its revenue from outside West Germany. The London-based Kuwait Investment Office owns nearly 20% of Hoechst.

Chairman Wolfgang Hilger has shaken up the formerly staid Hoechst, steadily changing top management, defining corporate priorities, acquiring Celanese, and selling nonstrategic units such as Berger, Jenson & Nicholson paint company. R&D spending, (6% of sales in recent years), emphasizes pharmaceuticals and new specialty plastics, both high-margin businesses. Hoechst is investing heavily in engineering plastics production capacity.

Principal exchange: Frankfurt
Incorporated: 1952
Fiscal year ends: December 31

WHO

Chairman, Board of Management: Wolfgang Hilger, age 60
Deputy Chairman, Board of Management: Gunter Metz
Managing Director of Finance and Accounts: Jurgen Dorman
Auditors: Treuhand-Vereinigung Aktiengesellschaft
Employees: 169,295

WHEN

Chemist Eugene Lucius founded Hoechst in the German village of the same name in 1863 to make dyes. While successfully developing thousands of dyes, Hoechst chemists moved into the new field of pharmaceutical research, producing diphtheria vaccines and analgesics (1890s) and Salvarsan (syphilis cure, first man-made disease-specific medicine, 1910). In 1923 they isolated insulin. In the early 20th century, Hoechst acquired German dye and fertilizer producers.

In 1925 Hoechst joined with Bayer, BASF, and other German chemical firms to form the I.G. Farben cartel. The huge cartel was instrumental in supplying the Nazi war machine and was dismantled following WWII. Hoechst reemerged as an independent company in 1952, most of its plants having survived the war intact.

Expanding rapidly with the postwar boom in Germany, Hoechst moved into fibers, plastics, and petrochemicals in the 1950s. Most of the company's overseas expansion was accomplished by establishing foreign subsidiaries, until the 1970s when Hoechst acquired Berger, Jenson & Nicholson (Britain's largest paint producer), Hystron Fibers (US), and majority control of Roussel Uclaf (pharmaceuticals, perfume, France). The company enjoyed continued success in pharmaceuticals, particularly diuretics, diabetic medications, antibiotics, and polio vaccines.

In the 1980s Hoechst emphasized pharmaceuticals and US expansion. The company spent heavily on drug R&D and on enlarging its US sales force. Hoechst also invested in genetic engineering, establishing a joint venture with Massachusetts General Hospital. The company built a biotechnological manufacturing facility in Germany, but it has remained unopened for 5 years due to popular opposition to commercial production of genetically engineered products.

The company's $2.8 billion acquisition of Celanese made Hoechst the world's largest chemical concern in 1987. New York–based Celanese was founded in 1918 and through acquisitions had become a major diversified chemical company. The purchase gave Hoechst a major US presence in chemical production and marketing but countered the company's strategy of shifting away from low-margin commodity fibers and chemicals.

In 1990 the French government reduced its holdings in Roussel Uclaf to 1% when it gave 35% of the drug company, in which Hoechst owns a 54% stake, to Rhône-Poulenc. The transaction may presage collaborative drug development by Hoechst and Rhône-Poulenc. Roussel Uclaf is best known for its abortion pill, RU 486.

WHERE

HQ: Postfach 80 03 20, D-6230 Frankfurt am Main 80, Germany
Phone: 011-49-69-3050
US HQ, Hoechst Celanese: Route 202-206 N., Somerville, NJ 08876
Phone: 201-231-2000
FAX: 201-707-0684 (Corporate Communications)

	1989 Sales		1989 Operating Profit	
	DM mil	% of total	DM mil	% of total
EC	30,530	62	2,643	66
Other Europe	1,295	3	89	2
North America	11,496	24	974	24
Latin America	2,180	4	95	2
Africa, Asia, Australasia	3,507	7	240	6
Adjustments	(3,110)	—	—	—
Total	**45,898**	**100**	**4,041**	**100**

WHAT

	1989 Sales		1989 Operating Profit	
	DM mil	% of total	DM mil	% of total
Chemicals & Colors	11,640	25	1,161	29
Fibers & Film	9,013	20	555	14
Polymers	7,788	17	745	18
Health	8,292	18	947	23
Technology	6,515	14	489	12
Agriculture	2,650	6	144	4
Total	**45,898**	**100**	**4,041**	**100**

Chemicals & Colors
Chemicals
Dyes
Surfactants

Fibers & Film
Fibers and raw materials
Plastic films

Polymers
Paints and synthetic resins
Plastics and waxes

Health
Cosmetics
Pharmaceuticals

Technology
Industrial gases and welding
Plant engineering
Technical information systems

Major Holdings
Roussel Uclaf (54.5%)
Wacker-Chemie (50%)

HOW MUCH

$=DM1.69 (Dec. 31, 1989)	9 Yr. Growth	1980	1981	1982	1983	1984	1985	1986	1987	1988	1989
Sales (DM mil)	4.9%	29,915	34,435	34,986	37,189	41,457	42,722	33,231	36,956	40,964	45,898
Net income (DM mil)	11.9%	364	349	253	735	1,077	1,200	1,216	1,378	1,824	1,929
Income as % of sales	—	1.2%	1.0%	0.7%	2.0%	2.6%	2.8%	3.7%	3.7%	4.5%	4.2%
Earnings per share (DM)*	15.5%	9	8	5	16	21	23	22	25	32	33
Stock price – high (DM)	—	127	132	127	181	196	294	328	347	311	320
Stock price – low (DM)	—	107	111	104	109	156	183	239	227	237	259
Stock price – close (DM)	11.1%	113	121	113	181	191	294	269	251	305	291
P/E – high	—	14	17	25	11	9	13	15	14	10	10
P/E – low	—	12	14	21	7	7	8	11	9	7	8
Dividends per share (DM)**	6.2%	7.0	7.0	5.5	7.0	9.0	10.0	10.0	10.0	11.0	12.0
Book value per share (DM)	4.4%	133	134	130	139	157	158	190	155	179	196

1989 Year End:
Debt ratio: 24.6%
Return on equity: 17.6%
Cash (DM mil): 1,435
Long-term debt (DM bil): 4.4
Number of shares (mil): 58
Dividends:
1989 average yield: 4.1%
1989 payout: 36.4%
Market value (mil): $9,932
Sales (mil): $27,159

*not fully diluted **not including rights offering

RANKINGS

167th in *Fortune* Global 500 Industrial Cos.
14th in *Forbes* 100 Foreign Investments in the US
33rd in *Business Week* Global 1000

COMPETITION

Allied-Signal	Du Pont	Occidental
American Cyanamid	FMC	PPG
BASF	W. R. Grace	Rhône-Poulenc
Bayer	Hercules	Sherwin-Williams
Dow Chemical	Monsanto	

Other chemical and pharmaceutical companies

THE HOME DEPOT, INC.

OVERVIEW

Headquartered in Atlanta, Home Depot is the largest operator of home centers in the US, with 120 warehouse stores in 12 states and sales of $2.8 billion (1989), up 38% over 1988 sales of $2 billion.

Home Depot successfully exploits the do-it-yourself market by offering a wide variety of home improvement supplies, averaging 30,000 items per store, at low prices, usually 30% less than conventional hardware and building supply stores. The company's specialized customer service is an innovation in the building supply industry. Employees called "Homers," many professional craftsmen, not only aid customers in their purchases on a one-to-one basis, but also educate them through in-store clinics, thereby broadening the do-it-yourself customer base.

In an industry that relies mainly on part-timers, 95% of Home Depot's 18,000 employees work full time. The company requires that new employees initially receive 4 weeks of training as well as ongoing training, which can cost $400,000 per store annually.

Home Depot locates stores in suburban communities in or near metropolitan areas of the Sunbelt and the Northeast. Stores range from 67,000 to 140,000 square feet, with newer and remodeled stores averaging 100,000 to 140,000 square feet.

WHEN

Based on the idea of discounted building supplies, Home Depot was founded in Atlanta by Bernard Marcus, Arthur Blank, and Ronald Brill (1978). Targeting the do-it-yourself market, they opened 3 stores in the Atlanta area (1979), soon expanding to 4 stores (1980).

Home Depot went public, raising more than $4 million, opening 4 stores in southern Florida, and posting sales of $50 million (1981). With 2 more Florida stores and sales of $100 million (1982), the company was named Retailer of the Year in the home building supply industry.

The chain next entered Louisiana and Arizona, opening 5 stores, plus 4 more in Florida (1983). That year sales were more than $250 million. The company also began shifting from manual to computerized information management systems, installing computerized checkout systems. In 1984 inventory reordering was computerized.

Also in 1984 Home Depot was first listed on the NYSE, and the company acquired 9 Bowater Home Centers in Dallas, Shreveport, Mobile, and Baton Rouge. The company then entered the lucrative Southern California market, opening 6 stores and finishing the year with 50 stores and sales of $700 million (1985). The Bowater acquisition (at well over book value) and rapid internal expansion caused Home Depot to falter in 1985 and experience its only dip in earnings in its history.

Back on track in 1986, Home Depot opened 10 more stores (5 in California), and sales exceeded $1 billion in the 60 stores. The company initiated the current policy of "low day-in day-out pricing" (1987) and also began installing bar code scanning systems, completing conversion within 2 years.

With sales exceeding $2 billion in 96 stores (1988), Home Depot ranked 48th in retail sales in its first appearance on the *Fortune* 500 list, was selected for inclusion in the S&P 500, and was named Retailer of the Year for the 2nd time. Entering the competitive Northeast market, the company bought 3 Modell's Shoppers World stores on Long Island.

In 1989 the company added 22 stores, primarily in California (7), Florida (4), and New England (4). The company also installed a satellite communication network to enhance its continual-training policy.

In the next 5 years Home Depot intends to expand aggressively and projects nationwide growth to 350 stores and sales of $10 billion. Immediate expansion plans include 32 new stores in 1990 and 38 in 1991.

HOW MUCH

	9 Yr. Growth	1980	1981	1982	1983	1984	1985	1986	1987	1988	1989
Sales ($ mil)	70.8%	22	52	118	256	433	701	1,011	1,454	2,000	2,759
Net income ($ mil)	84.5%	0	1	5	10	14	8	24	54	77	112
Income as % of sales	—	2.0%	2.4%	4.5%	4.0%	3.3%	1.2%	2.4%	3.7%	3.8%	4.1%
Earnings per share ($)	74.3%	0.01	0.03	0.11	0.18	0.25	0.15	0.40	0.75	0.99	1.41
Stock price – high ($)	—	—	1.14	6.39	14.11	12.39	9.06	9.67	18.72	21.33	38.38
Stock price – low ($)	—	—	0.71	1.10	5.36	5.33	4.67	4.78	7.94	11.58	19.17
Stock price – close ($)	—	—	1.10	5.44	11.67	7.89	5.56	7.94	12.50	21.08	36.63
P/E – high	—	—	44	60	77	50	62	24	25	21	27
P/E – low	—	—	28	10	29	21	32	12	11	12	14
Dividends per share ($)	—	0.00	0.00	0.00	0.00	0.00	0.00	0.00	0.04	0.07	0.11
Book value per share ($)	—	(0.01)	0.12	0.36	1.17	1.42	1.57	2.55	4.33	5.08	6.67

1989 Year End:
Debt ratio: 37.2%
Return on equity: 24.0%
Cash (mil): $135
Current ratio: 1.94
Long-term debt (mil): $303
Number of shares (mil): 77
Dividends:
1989 average yield: 0.3%
1989 payout: 7.8%
Market value (mil): $2,812

Stock Price History high/low 1981-89

NYSE symbol: HD
Incorporated: Delaware, 1978
Fiscal year ends: Sunday nearest January 31

WHO

Chairman, CEO, and Secretary: Bernard Marcus, age 60, $1,585,892 pay
President and COO: Arthur M. Blank, age 47, $1,362,965 pay
EVP Merchandising: James W. Inglis, $356,667 pay
SVP and CFO: Ronald M. Brill, age 46, $369,492 pay
SVP Corporate Development: William E. Harris, $369,492 pay
SVP Merchandising: Bruce Berg
SVP Corporate Information Systems: W. Andrew McKenna
Auditors: KPMG Peat Marwick
Employees: 18,000

WHERE

HQ: 2727 Paces Ferry Rd., Atlanta, GA 30339
Phone: 404-433-8211
FAX: 404-431-2707

The Home Depot sells home improvement and building materials in 120 warehouse stores in the Sunbelt and Northeast.

	No. of stores	% of total
Alabama	2	2
Arizona	9	7
California	33	27
Connecticut	2	2
Florida	30	25
Georgia	13	11
Louisiana	5	4
New Jersey	2	2
New York	2	2
South Carolina	2	2
Tennessee	4	3
Texas	16	13
Total	**120**	**100**

WHAT

	1989 Sales % of total
Plumbing, heating & electrical supplies	30
Building materials, lumber, floor & wall coverings	31
Hardware & tools	12
Seasonal & specialty items	14
Paint & furniture	13
Total	**100**

RANKINGS

38th in *Fortune* 50 Retailing Cos.
304th in *Forbes* Sales 500
189th in *Business Week* 1000
395th in *Business Week* Global 1000

COMPETITION

K mart
Lowe's
Montgomery Ward
Sears
Sherwin-Williams
Supermarkets General

HONDA MOTOR CO., LTD.

OVERVIEW

Nobuhiko Kawamoto, Honda's president, has taken charge of the world's largest motorcycle producer and the manufacturer of the Accord, the best-selling car in the US. Sales are concentrated in the US market, where Honda and Toyota are closing on Chrysler for the #3 position in auto sales. The company has consistently received high marks in the US for the quality and design of its Honda and Acura cars. High real estate prices have slowed expansion of the company's dealership network in Japan.

Honda established global production capacity in a relatively low number of high-volume plants, including a large facility in Marysville, Ohio, a source of US-built auto exports to Japan. The company's 1990 purchase of 20% of the Rover Group (UK) paved the way for increased European production as 1992 market integration approaches.

WHEN

After 6 years as an apprentice at Art Shokai, a Tokyo auto service station, Honda Soichiro opened his own branch of the repair shop in Hamamatsu (1928). In addition to repairing autos, he raced cars and received a patent for metal spokes that replaced wood in wheels (1931). In a race in 1936, Honda set a long-standing Japanese speed record, then crashed at the finish line, but escaped critical injury.

In 1937 Honda started a new company, Tokai Seiki, to manufacture piston rings. The Sino-Japanese War and WWII increased demand for piston rings, and the company mass-produced metal propellers for Japanese bombers, replacing handmade wooden ones. When bombs and an earthquake destroyed most of Honda's factory, he sold it to Toyota (1945) for nearly $800,000. He took a year off, installed a large drum of alcohol in his home, drank, and entertained friends.

In 1946 Honda established the Honda Technical Research Institute to motorize bicycles with small, war-surplus engines. Running on Honda's blend of gasoline and turpentine, this inexpensive form of transportation proved popular amid the scarcity of postwar Japan, and Honda soon began manufacturing engines.

The company was renamed Honda Motor in 1948 and began producing motorcycles. To allow himself to focus on engineering, Honda hired Takeo Fujisawa (1949) to take on management tasks. Honda's innovative overhead valve design made the Dream Type E (1951) motorcycle an immediate runaway success. Fujisawa seized the opportunity to enlist 13,000 bicycle dealers to launch Honda's smaller F-type Cub (1952), which accounted for 70% of Japan's motorcycle production by the end of the year.

Funded by a public offering (1954) and heavy support from Mitsubishi Bank, Honda expanded capacity and began US and Southeast Asian exports in the 1950s. The versatile C100 Super Cub, released in 1958, became an international bestseller. American Honda Motor was formed in Los Angeles (1959), accompanied by the slogan "You meet the nicest people on a Honda," created to counter the stereotypical "biker" image. In the 1960s the company began producing lightweight trucks, sports cars, and minicars, despite initial resistance from the Japanese Ministry of International Trade and Industry (MITI), and added overseas factories.

In 1971, on the eve of the oil crisis, Honda introduced the economical Civic, emphasizing the US market and targeting Volkswagen buyers. Honda released the higher-priced Accord in 1976, as cumulative Civic sales surpassed one million cars. In 1982 Accord production started at Honda of America's Marysville, Ohio, plant. US production helped the company to avoid import quotas on Japanese cars. Honda successfully launched the mid- to upscale Acura line in the US in 1986.

HOW MUCH

$=144¥ (Dec. 31, 1989)	9 Yr. Growth	1980	1981	1982	1983	1984	1985	1986	1987	1988*	1989
Sales (¥ bil)	11.5%	1,308	1,676	1,883	2,230	2,374	2,740	3,009	2,961	3,499	3,489
Net income (¥ bil)	12.5%	28	93	66	72	96	129	147	84	108	81
Income as % of sales	—	2.1%	5.5%	3.5%	3.2%	4.0%	4.7%	4.9%	2.8%	3.1%	2.8%
Earnings per share (¥)	12.5%	34	105	74	77	104	138	149	85	107	98
Stock price – high (¥)	—	567	1,173	964	1,140	1,500	1,550	1,490	1,850	2,520	2,210
Stock price – low (¥)	—	454	460	528	682	985	1,090	981	1,120	1,230	1,780
Stock price – close (¥)	16.4%	468	725	936	1,110	1,210	1,200	1,380	1,300	2,030	1,830
P/E – high	—	17	11	13	15	14	11	10	22	—	23
P/E – low	—	13	4	7	9	9	8	7	13	—	18
Dividends per share (¥)	4.6%	8.2	9.1	9.1	10.0	11.0	11.0	12.0	12.0	13.0	12.0
Book value per share (¥)	14.9%	273	374	427	506	652	815	849	823	833	951

1989 Year End:
Debt ratio: 22.0%
Return on equity: 11.0%
Cash (bil): ¥247
Long-term debt (bil): ¥302
Number of shares (mil): 948
Dividends
1989 average yield: 0.7%
1989 payout: 12.2%
Market value (mil): $12,048
Sales (mil): $24,229

Stock Price History high/low 1980-89

3,000
2,500
2,000
1,500
1,000
500
0

*13-month accounting period

NYSE symbol: HMC (ADR)
Incorporated: Japan, 1948
Fiscal year ends: March 31

WHO

Chairman: Koichiro Yoshizawa, age 58
President: Nobuhiko Kawamoto, age 54
EVP Worldwide Production and R&D: Shoichiro Irimajiri
EVP North American Operations: Yoshihide Munekuni
Auditors: Peat Marwick Minato
Employees: 71,200

WHERE

HQ: No. 1-1, 2-chome, Minami-Aoyama, Minato-ku, Tokyo 107, Japan
Phone: 011-81-3-423-1111
FAX: 011-81-3-423-2442
US HQ (Honda North America, Inc.): 1290 Ave. of the Americas, Suite 3330, New York, NY 10104
US Phone: 212-765-3804
US FAX: 212-541-9855

Honda manufactures its products at 77 plants in 40 countries, including 3 plants in the US.

	1989 Sales	
	¥ bil	% of total
Japan	1,294	37
Other countries	2,195	63
Total	**3,489**	**100**

WHAT

	1989 Sales	
	¥ bil	% of total
Motorcycles	354	10
Automobiles	2,460	71
Power products	104	3
Parts & other	571	16
Total	**3,489**	**100**

Brand Names

Motorcycles
Cub
Elite (scooters)
FourTrax (all-terrain vehicles)
Gold Wing
Hawk
Pacific Coast
Rebel
Shadow
Transalp

Automobiles
Accord
Acura
Legend
Integra
NSX
Civic
CRX
Prelude

RANKINGS

30th in *Fortune* Global 500 Industrial Cos.
28th in *Forbes* 100 Foreign Investments in the US
126th in *Business Week* Global 1000

COMPETITION

Black & Decker
Brunswick
Chrysler
Daimler-Benz
Deere
Fiat
Ford
General Motors
Harley-Davidson
Hyundai
Mitsubishi
Nissan
Outboard Marine
Renault
Toyota
Volkswagen
Volvo

HONEYWELL INC.

OVERVIEW

Located in Minneapolis since its inception, Honeywell is the global leader in industrial control systems, providing components and systems through 3 divisions.

The Homes and Buildings division (contributing 34% of sales) provides energy management systems, fire and security alarms, thermostats, and other controls for small buildings and residences, protecting more than 65,000 homes with security systems.

The Industrial division (contributing 25% of sales) plays a similar role for large business customers; products include sensors, process controllers, recorders, and transmitters, as well as integrated control systems. This division has recently received contract awards in the USSR, Bulgaria, and Czechoslovakia.

The Space and Aviation division (contributing 33% of sales) supplies electronic control products — such as inertial guidance systems, radar altimeters, and flight management/display systems — and components for military and commercial aircraft, missiles, and other vehicles.

Other sales (8%) were contributed by non-US Defense and Marine Systems, Federal Systems, Inc. (markets and supports computer systems), Solid State Electronics Center (makes custom integrated circuits), and a real estate development unit.

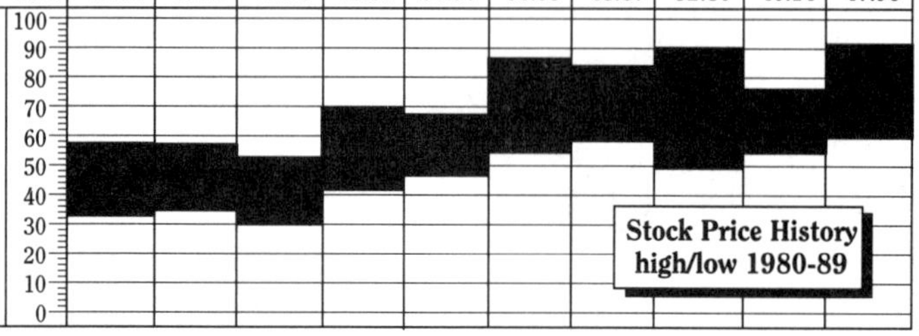

NYSE symbol: HON
Incorporated: Delaware, 1927
Fiscal year ends: December 31

WHO

Chairman and CEO: James J. Renier, age 60, $1,366,165 pay
President, International: Michael R. Bonsignore, age 48, $618,521 pay
President, Home and Building Automation and Control, Defense and Marine: Joseph E. Chenoweth, age 54, $565,228 pay
President, Industrial: Jerome J. Meyer, age 52, $536,013 pay
VP and CFO: Christopher J. Steffen, age 48, $486,737 pay
Auditors: Deloitte & Touche
Employees: 72,646

WHEN

An invention patented by Al Butz in 1885, the Damper Flapper, led to the building regulation equipment which Honeywell still provides. The Damper Flapper, forerunner of the thermostat, opened furnace vents automatically. Butz formed the Butz Thermo-Electric Regulator Company to market the product but sold patent rights to investor William Sweatt in 1893. Sweatt led the company for 4 decades. The company soon began producing a burner-control system for fire protection on oil and gas furnaces. Sweatt persuaded manufacturers to redesign furnaces to accommodate controls, establishing a new market.

In 1927 the company's primary competitor was the Mark Honeywell Heating Specialties Company (of Indiana), owned by Mark Honeywell. Honeywell used mercury to control heat and controlled patents that prevented Sweatt from using it for his furnaces. The companies merged (1927) as Minneapolis-Honeywell Regulator Company based in Minneapolis. Honeywell became president of the company and later served as chairman; Sweatt became vice-president. In 1964 the company adopted its present name.

Honeywell developed expertise in precision optics during WWII, when the US military sought Honeywell's assistance in developing instrumentation and control systems for long-range bombers, including B-17s and B-29s. The work led to achievements in laser inertial navigation systems, lightweight torpedoes, and a flight control system for the space shuttle.

In the 1950s Honeywell used computers in control and guidance systems. It formed Datamatic Corporation (1955) with Raytheon to develop and market data processors. Honeywell was up against IBM, already a formidable worldwide presence. In 1970 Honeywell purchased GE's computer division, receiving with it 66% interest in a French company, Machines Bull, giving the company 10% of the world market. Honeywell then bought Xerox's computer business in 1976 and merged its Machines Bull unit with a computer company owned by the French government, which purchased Honeywell's entire interest (after threatening to nationalize it) in 1982. In 1987 Honeywell renewed its ties with Bull, creating Honeywell Bull, Inc., owned 42.5% by Honeywell, 42.5% by Bull, and 15% by NEC. This unit is Honeywell's only remaining involvement in the computer business.

In 1990 Honeywell decided to sell its US defense segment in order to concentrate on commercial aircraft traffic alert, collision avoidance, and windshear detection systems.

WHERE

HQ: Honeywell Plaza, Minneapolis, MN 55408
Phone: 612-870-5200
FAX: 612-870-5780

Honeywell has a presence in 90 countries and operates facilities in the US, Australia, Belgium, Canada, France, Germany, the Netherlands, Singapore, Switzerland, and the UK.

	1989 Sales		1989 Operating Income	
	$ mil	% of total	$ mil	% of total
US	4,347	72	329	67
Europe	1,145	19	120	24
Other	567	9	44	9
Adjustments	—	—	(18)	—
Total	**6,059**	**100**	**475**	**100**

WHAT

	1989 Sales		1989 Operating Income	
	$ mil	% of total	$ mil	% of total
Homes & buildings	2,077	34	225	45
Industrial	1,492	25	137	28
Space & aviation	2,004	33	112	23
Other	486	8	21	4
Adjustments	—	—	(20)	—
Total	**6,059**	**100**	**475**	**100**

Products
Commercial avionics
Environmental controls
Industrial controls
Process controls
Security systems

Affiliates/Joint Ventures
Coeur d' Alene Development, Inc. (real estate)
Tetra Tech Data Systems, Inc. (fiber optics)
Honeywell Bull, Inc. (42.5%)
Yamatake-Honeywell Co. Ltd. (26.5%)

HOW MUCH

	9 Yr. Growth	1980	1981	1982	1983	1984	1985	1986	1987	1988	1989
Sales ($ mil)	2.3%	4,925	5,351	5,490	5,753	6,074	6,625	5,378	6,679	7,148	6,059
Net income ($ mil)	7.8%	281	256	271	231	335	275	13	254	(435)	550
Income as % of sales	—	5.7%	4.8%	4.9%	4.0%	5.5%	4.2%	0.2%	3.8%	(6.1%)	9.1%
Earnings per share ($)	8.5%	6.12	5.48	5.90	4.91	6.99	5.89	0.28	5.70	(10.22)	12.74
Stock price – high ($)	—	57.63	57.25	52.88	69.75	67.50	86.75	84.25	90.50	76.25	91.75
Stock price – low ($)	—	32.63	34.50	29.75	41.50	46.38	54.25	58.25	49.00	54.25	59.50
Stock price – close ($)	5.0%	55.88	34.94	42.69	65.00	63.25	74.13	59.13	53.88	59.75	86.75
P/E – high	—	9	10	9	14	10	15	301	16	—	7
P/E – low	—	5	6	5	8	7	9	208	9	—	5
Dividends per share ($)	5.5%	1.40	1.60	1.75	1.80	1.90	1.95	2.00	2.03	2.10	2.26
Book value per share ($)	1.5%	42.02	45.27	47.15	49.37	50.97	56.08	48.67	52.80	40.14	47.96

1989 Year End:
Debt ratio: 26.5%
Return on equity: 28.9%
Cash (mil): $254
Current ratio: 1.16
Long-term debt (mil): $693
Number of shares (mil): 40
Dividends:
1989 average yield: 2.6%
1989 payout: 17.8%
Market value (mil): $3,470

Stock Price History high/low 1980-89

RANKINGS

65th in *Fortune* 500 Industrial Cos.
143rd in *Forbes* Sales 500
184th in *Business Week* 1000
479th in *Business Week* Global 1000

COMPETITION

Allied-Signal
Emerson
General Signal
Johnson Controls
Rockwell International
Thomson
Other defense electronics companies

HONGKONG & SHANGHAI BANKING CORP. LTD.

OVERVIEW

Known in Hong Kong simply as "the Bank," Hongkong & Shanghai Banking is the world's 30th largest bank. The bank still plays a key economic role in Hong Kong, where it is the government's banker, even issuing bank notes.

The bank's Marine Midland unit is the largest foreign-owned bank in the US. The former money-center bank is retreating to become a northeastern regional bank after suffering large third world and real estate loan losses. In the UK, the Bank was once expected to buy the rest of 14.9%-owned Midland Bank, but continuing losses at Midland cast doubt on the transaction.

Because Hong Kong does not require full disclosure by banks, the bank maintains so-called inner reserves, profits that are hidden in good years and revealed in bad years to smooth earnings growth. After decades of good years the bank maintains inner reserves estimated to be US $1.3 billion to US $4 billion.

Principal stock exchange: Hong Kong
Incorporated: Hong Kong, 1865
Fiscal year ends: December 31

WHO

Chairman: William Purves, age 59
Deputy Chairman (Executive): F. R. Frame
Executive Director Merchant Banking; CEO, Wardley Holdings Ltd.: B. H. Asher
Executive Director Banking: John R. H. Bond
Executive Director Finance: John M. Gray
Auditors: Price Waterhouse; KPMG Peat Marwick
Employees: 53,375

WHEN

Founded by Scotsman Thomas Sutherland and a group of businessmen with Hong Kong interests, the Hongkong & Shanghai Bank opened its doors in Hong Kong in 1865. The bank initially financed and promoted British imperial trade in opium, silk, and tea in the East Asian region and quickly established a London office. Hongkong & Shanghai Bank created an international branch network emphasizing China and the Far East, where it claims to have been the first bank in Thailand (1888). After weathering a financial crisis in the mid-1870s, the bank rebounded and prospered. The bank issued most of China's government loans and became a powerful financial institution in the Far East.

War repeatedly disrupted the bank's operations, but it managed to survive. When chief manager Sir Vandeleur Grayborn died in a Japanese POW camp during WWII, the bank's headquarters was temporarily relocated to London. Except for a single office in Shanghai, the bank withdrew from China in 1955, following the Communist takeover. The bank played a key role in Hong Kong's explosive postwar growth by financing industrialists who fled there from China.

Hongkong & Shanghai Bank began expanding its Far East activities in the late 1950s and later executed a strategy of globalization. The bank acquired Mercantile Bank (India, Southeast Asia, 1959); 61.5% of Hang Seng, Hong Kong's 2nd largest bank (1965); a controlling interest in Marine Midland Bank (US, 1980); 51% of primary treasury security dealer Carroll McEntee & McGinley (US, 1983); major London stockbroker James Capel & Co. (1986); most of the assets and liabilities of the Bank of British Columbia (1986); and the rest of Marine Midland (1987), among many others. The bank established subsidiaries Wayfoong (mortgage and small business finance, Hong Kong, 1960), Wardley (investment banking, Hong Kong, 1972), Hongkong Bank of Canada (1981), and HongkongBank of Australia (1986). Results at many of the bank's newer acquisitions and subsidiaries have been disappointing.

Hongkong & Shanghai Bank's 1981 bid for the Royal Bank of Scotland failed when the British government stopped the transaction, citing the bank's international, rather than Scottish, orientation. Still seeking a European presence to complement its Asian and American operations, the bank bought 14.9% of Midland Bank (UK) in 1987 and agreed to refrain from purchasing additional shares until late 1990. The purchase led to speculation that the bank may relocate to London due to fears over the transfer of control of Hong Kong to China in 1997. Former bank chairman Michael Sandberg helped negotiate the transfer agreement with China.

WHERE

HQ: 1 Queen's Rd. Central, Hong Kong
Phone: 011-852-5-822-1111
US HQ: 5 World Trade Center, New York, NY 10048
US Phone: 212-839-5000
US FAX: 212-839-5024

The company and its subsidiaries conduct business at over 1,300 offices in about 50 countries.

	1989 Assets
Asia-Pacific	48%
Americas	30%
Middle East	4%
Europe	18%
Total	**100%**

WHAT

Principal Subsidiaries
The British Bank of the Middle East (UK)
Carlingford Insurance Co. Ltd. (Hong Kong)
Carroll McEntee & McGinley, Inc. (securities, US)
The Cyprus Popular Bank Ltd. (21.3%)
Equator Bank Ltd. (Bahamas, 83.3%)
Fort Hall Ltd. (investment holding, Hong Kong)
Gibbs Hartley Cooper Ltd. (insurance brokerage, UK)
Hang Seng Bank Ltd. (Hong Kong, 61.48%)
HongkongBank London Ltd.
HongkongBank of Australia Ltd.
Hongkong Bank of Canada
Hongkong Egyptian Bank SAE (40%)
HSBC Finance (Malaysia) Berhad
James Capel & Co. Ltd. (stockbrokerage, UK)
Marine Midland Bank, N.A. (US)
The Saudi British Bank (40%)
Wardley Ltd. (investment banking, Hong Kong)
Wayfoong Finance Ltd. (Hong Kong)
World Finance International Ltd. (Bermuda, 37.5%)
World Maritime Ltd. (Bermuda, 20%)
World Shipping and Investment Co. Ltd. (Cayman Islands, 20%)

HOW MUCH

$=HK$7.8 (Dec. 31, 1989)	9 Yr. Growth	1980	1981	1982	1983	1984	1985	1986	1987	1988	1989
Sales (HK$ mil)	—	—	—	—	—	—	—	—	—	—	—
Net income (HK$ mil)	13.5%	1,531	2,116	2,357	2,492	2,591	2,719	3,056	3,593	4,300	4,774
Income as % of sales	—	—	—	—	—	—	—	—	—	—	—
Earnings per share (HK$)	11.0%	0.32	0.42	0.45	0.47	0.49	0.52	0.58	0.65	0.75	0.82
Stock price – high (HK$)	—	4.83	5.25	4.28	3.84	4.35	4.73	6.69	8.02	6.86	7.60
Stock price – low (HK$)	—	2.36	3.21	2.53	1.37	2.85	4.13	4.52	5.33	5.36	4.95
Stock price – close (HK$)	5.4%	4.61	3.84	2.70	3.09	4.35	4.64	6.69	5.99	5.82	7.40
P/E – high	—	15	13	10	8	9	9	12	12	9	9
P/E – low	—	7	8	6	3	6	8	8	8	7	6
Dividends per share (HK$)	12.1%	0.15	0.20	0.22	0.24	0.25	0.27	0.30	0.32	0.36	0.42
Book value per share (HK$)	18.6%	1.95	2.39	2.63	3.75	4.00	4.19	5.08	5.82	6.23	9.06

1989 Year End:
Debt ratio: 28.2%
Return on equity: 10.7%
Cash (mil): HK$264,046
Long-term debt (mil): HK$20,690
Number of shares (mil): 5,816
Dividends:
1989 average yield: 5.7%
1989 payout: 51.2%
Market value (mil): $5,518

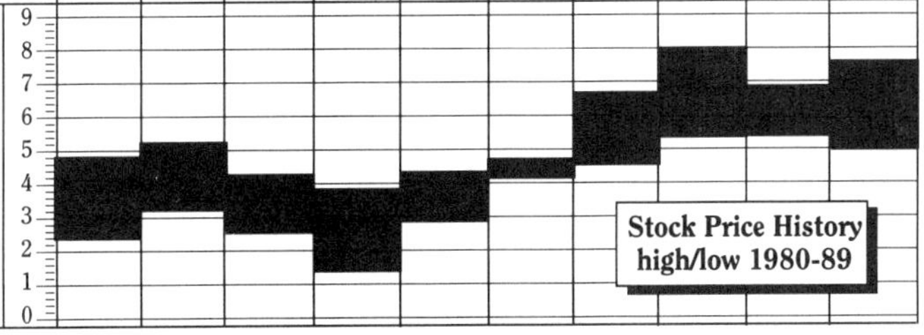

Stock Price History high/low 1980-89

RANKINGS

30th in *Fortune* World's 100 Commercial Banks
40th in *Forbes* 100 Foreign Investments in the US
378th in *Business Week* Global 1000

COMPETITION

Bank of New York
BankAmerica
Bankers Trust
Chase Manhattan
Citicorp
CS Holding
Dai-Ichi Kangyo
Deutsche Bank
First Chicago
Manufacturers Hanover
Other international money-center banks

HOSPITAL CORPORATION OF AMERICA

OVERVIEW

Privately owned Hospital Corporation of America was the largest for-profit owner and operator of medical/surgical and psychiatric hospitals in the US in 1989 measured by number of beds and hospitals owned. Of HCA's 77 medical/surgical facilities in 17 states, 70% are located in Florida, Georgia, Tennessee, Texas, and Virginia. The company also operates 55 psychiatric hospitals. Foreign investments include 15 hospitals in Australia and Brazil.

The company has been selling assets to repay a $1.3 billion bridge loan (due in 1991) undertaken as part of its March 1989 LBO. Sales of Allied Clinical Laboratories, HCA Management Company, the company's UK operations, and other assets have allowed the company to reduce the principal of the bridge loan. Agreements to sell its Australian operations and its 50% interest in Equicor have been reached as well. The company has also had its psychiatric hospital subsidiaries borrow money to pay down the bridge loan.

The company has budgeted $220 million for capital spending in 1990, down from $636 million in 1986. HCA's challenge for the 1990s is keeping its aging hospitals state-of-the-art while meeting its debt payments.

WHEN

Jack Massey, a one-time hospital supplier, druggist, and drugstore owner who spent 12 years building the Baptist Hospital in Nashville into one of the largest medical centers in the country (he also made a fortune with Kentucky Fried Chicken Corporation, which he founded), cofounded Hospital Corporation of America in 1968 with Dr. Thomas Frist and Frist's son, Thomas, Jr., also a physician. From a single 150-bed hospital in Nashville, they built HCA into the largest for-profit hospital company in the world.

In 1973 the company ran 50 hospitals and had 14 under construction, ranging from 50 to 300 beds. To economize HCA built all its hospitals to look alike. The company's concentration was the Southeast. Revenues reached $174 million with profits of $10 million. By 1977 the company owned 88 hospitals, which had increased to 148 in 1979. In 1981 the company acquired Hospital Affiliates International's 133 hospitals, a 65% increase in hospitals. By 1983 HCA owned and managed 376 hospitals (51,000 beds) in the US and 7 foreign countries. The next year the company earned $297 million on sales of $3.5 billion, but expansion expenses caused a debt amounting to 51% of capital.

Hoping to acquire capital for further expansion, HCA attempted in 1985 to merge with American Hospital Supply, the largest medical supply company in the country. Dr. Thomas Frist, Jr., then HCA's president and CEO, and AHS's chairman and CEO Karl Bays had thought to merge for several years. Their union would have created a company with a 1984 combined revenue total of $7.6 billion. The companies publicly announced the merger on March 31, 1985, but it fell through, and Baxter International bought AHS in July of that year.

Hospital occupancy rates had been falling since 1983, when the Health Care Financing Administration began reimbursing Medicare claims on a fixed schedule rather than on percentages of full cost. Many employers had also been switching to health maintenance organizations, which encourage preventive health care. By 1985 hospital occupancy reached a 40-year low, causing for-profit hospital chains to do poorly on Wall Street. To offset this slump, HCA launched its own HMO, Equicor, in 1986 (a venture with Equitable Life Assurance) to provide managed health care. In 1987 the company sold 104 hospitals to employees for $2.1 billion through a stock ownership plan. Then in 1989 Dr. Thomas Frist, Jr., now HCA's chairman, led a $4.5 billion LBO with an equity group that included the Rockefeller family, Goldman Sachs, Morgan Guaranty, and Texas financier Richard Rainwater.

The company went private in March 1989. To pay down debt from the LBO, Frist attempted to sell the company's 55 psychiatric hospitals through a $1.4 billion employee buyout plan, but the deal collapsed. In 1990 Equicor was sold to CIGNA Corporation for $777 million. In August 1990 the psychiatric division borrowed $515 million and transferred $500 million of it to the parent company to reduce the unpaid balance of its bridge loan to about $140 million.

As of September 1990 HCA has returned to its primary business of managing hospitals; it owns 130 facilities with over 24,000 beds in the US.

HOW MUCH

	9 Yr. Growth	1980	1981	1982	1983	1984	1985	1986	1987	1988	1989
Sales ($ mil)	14.8%	1,232	2,064	2,977	3,203	3,499	4,352	4,931	4,676	4,111	4,274
Net income ($ mil)	0.2%	81	111	172	243	297	284	175	(58)	259	83
Income as % of sales	—	6.6%	5.4%	5.8%	7.6%	8.5%	6.5%	3.5%	(1.2%)	6.3%	1.9%

1989 Year End:
Assets (mil): $6,880
Book value (mil): $564
Debt ratio: 88.6%
Cash (mil): $3
Current ratio: 1.03
Long-term debt (mil): $4,374

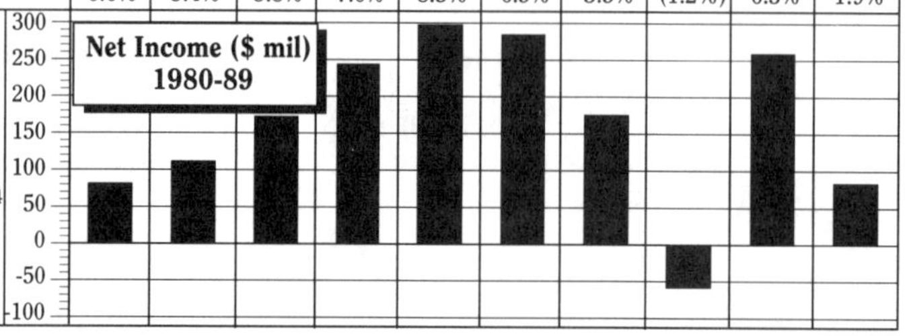

Private company
Incorporated: Tennessee, 1960
Fiscal year ends: December 31

WHO

Chairman, President, and CEO: Thomas F. Frist, Jr., age 51, $923,000 pay
EVP and CFO: Roger E. Mick, age 43, $418,750 pay
Auditors: Ernst & Young
Employees: 68,000

WHERE

HQ: One Park Plaza, Nashville, TN 37203
Phone: 615-327-9551
FAX: 615-320-2222 (Human Resources)

Location	No. of Medical/ Surgical Hospitals	No. of Psychiatric Hospitals
Arizona	—	1
Arkansas	1	—
California	2	3
Colorado	—	1
Delaware	—	1
Florida	18	6
Georgia	8	1
Illinois	—	2
Kansas	1	—
Kentucky	2	—
Louisiana	2	5
Missouri	—	1
Nevada	—	4
New Hampshire	2	1
New Mexico	3	1
North Carolina	2	1
Oklahoma	2	—
South Carolina	3	—
Tennessee	9	5
Texas	14	14
Utah	1	—
Virginia	5	4
West Virginia	2	1
Wisconsin	—	1
US subtotal	**77**	**53**
Australia	8	2
Brazil	5	—
Total	**90**	**55**

WHAT

	1989 Sales	
	$ mil	% of total
US medical/surgical hospitals	3,600	84
US psychiatric hospitals	537	13
Foreign hospitals	137	3
Total	**4,274**	**100**

	1989 Licensed Beds	
	no. of beds	% of total
US medical/surgical hospitals	18,434	71
US psychiatric hospitals	5,745	22
Foreign hospitals	1,851	7
Total	**26,030**	**100**

RANKINGS

22nd in *Fortune* 100 Diversified Service Cos.
24th in *Forbes* 400 US Private Cos.

COMPETITION

Humana
Mayo Foundation
National Medical

HOUSEHOLD INTERNATIONAL, INC.

OVERVIEW

Household International, the 17th largest diversified financial services company in the US, is expanding aggressively. Its goal, articulated in 1989, is to double its assets in 5 years.

One avenue of growth for the parent company is its consumer bank called Household Bank. Household hopes to expand by buying banks and thrifts in the area from Illinois to the East Coast. Household Bank targets customers who are more affluent than those served by Household Finance Corporation (HFC), the company's cornerstone. HFC, with more than 1.2 million accounts, provides consumer loans. The company is shifting HFC's back office operations to regional centers so it can focus on sales at its branch offices.

Household International, through its Household Retail Services subsidiary, handles credit card accounts for other businesses. It is the 2nd largest issuer of private label retail credit cards in the US, after GE Capital, with 3.2 million cardholders and $1.8 billion in receivables. The Alexander Hamilton Life Insurance subsidiary sells policies through independent agents and through its own sister companies.

Household Bank's performance and the parent company's loan portfolio have disappointed some skeptical analysts. Chairman Donald Clark defended his company, arguing that problem loans are only a small percentage of Household International's assets.

WHEN

"Never Borrow Money Needlessly..."

That radio jingle of the 1950s cheerfully admonished consumers about financial responsibility, a theme for Household Finance since its first stirrings in Minneapolis in 1878. Frank Mackey opened a finance company in the back of a jewelry store that year to loan cash to workers between paychecks.

In 1925 more than 30 such companies across the country, controlled by Mackey and operating under a variety of names, consolidated as Chicago-based Household Finance Corporation. The company went public in 1928.

In 1930, during the Great Depression, HFC set up a consumer education department — the Money Management Institute — to teach people how to handle credit. An early pamphlet illustrated how a family of 5 could live on $150 a month. After WWII the unleashed US demand for goods propelled HFC into the suburbs, and by 1960 it boasted 1,000 branch offices.

In the conglomerate-crazed 1960s, Household, viewing itself broadly as a retailer of money, began to diversify into other kinds of retailing — hardware stores (Coast-to-Coast, 1961), variety chains (Ben Franklin and TG&Y, 1965), vacuum jugs (King-Seeley Thermos, 1968), and car rental (National, 1969). Household also purchased a savings and loan, 4 banks, and Alexander Hamilton Life (1977).

The company adopted Household International as its corporate name in 1981. Later in the 1980s, as Wall Street turned sour on bric-a-brac conglomerates, Chairman Donald Clark refocused the company on financial services, particularly consumer banking. Amid the restructuring in 1984, Clark thwarted an $8 billion takeover by dissident shareholders. Household adopted a "poison pill" that, after a takeover, would have permitted stockholders to buy stock in the resulting company for 1/2 price.

Household sold its merchandising operations for more than $700 million in 1985 (to Foxmeyer Corp.; Donaldson, Lufkin & Jenrette Securities; and to former managers); National Car Rental in 1986 (to an investment group led by PaineWebber Capital); and most other nonfinancial operations. In 1989 Household announced the spin-off of 3 manufacturing units (Eljer Industries, Schwitzer, and Scotsman Industries).

HOW MUCH

	9 Yr. Growth	1980	1981	1982	1983	1984	1985	1986	1987	1988	1989
Sales ($ mil)	15.4%	960	7,280	7,768	7,912	8,322	3,383	2,741	3,441	2,637	3,490
Net income ($ mil)	5.0%	141	142	125	206	234	168	138	222	184	218
Income as % of sales	—	14.7%	2.0%	1.6%	2.6%	2.8%	5.0%	5.0%	6.4%	7.0%	6.3%
Earnings per share ($)	8.2%	2.75	2.56	2.01	3.50	3.95	2.82	2.85	5.32	4.78	5.60
Stock price – high ($)	—	19.75	19.25	26.13	34.00	34.38	43.38	52.50	62.50	61.00	65.50
Stock price – low ($)	—	13.63	14.25	14.75	19.00	24.00	32.25	39.13	32.50	39.50	46.38
Stock price – close ($)	13.8%	16.25	15.25	23.00	30.75	32.75	42.25	47.75	39.88	56.88	51.88
P/E – high	—	7	8	13	10	9	15	18	12	13	12
P/E – low	—	5	6	7	5	6	11	14	6	8	8
Dividends per share ($)	3.5%	1.58	1.63	1.65	1.68	1.73	1.78	1.84	1.93	2.07	2.14
Book value per share ($)	2.3%	27.46	28.08	27.59	28.92	30.28	31.70	28.57	28.96	33.59	33.82

1989 Year End:
Debt ratio: 84.2%
Return on equity: 16.6%
Cash (mil): $4,297
Current ratio: —
Long-term debt (mil): $6,776
Number of shares (mil): 35
Dividends:
1989 average yield: 4.1%
1989 payout: 38.2%
Market value (mil): $1,832

Stock Price History high/low 1980-89

70
60
50
40
30
20
10
0

NYSE symbol: HI
Incorporated: Delaware, 1981
Fiscal year ends: December 31

WHO

Chairman and CEO: Donald C. Clark, age 58, $1,160,000 pay
President and COO: Edwin P. Hoffman, age 47, $936,000 pay
Group VP and Chief Accounting Officer: Gaylen N. Larson, age 50
VP Human Resources: Colin P. Kelly, age 47
Auditors: Arthur Andersen & Co.
Employees: 14,510

WHERE

HQ: 2700 Sanders Rd., Prospect Heights, IL 60070
Phone: 708-564-5000
FAX: 708-205-7452

Household Bank has 116 branches in 8 states. HFC Bank PLC has 173 branches in the UK. The company's consumer finance subsidiaries (HFC) have 657 offices in the US, 126 in Canada, and 70 in Australia.

	1989 Sales		1989 Pretax Income	
	$ mil	% of total	$ mil	% of total
US	2,709	77	265	80
Canada	336	10	82	24
UK	344	10	(3)	(1)
Australia	101	3	(11)	(3)
Total	**3,490**	**100**	**333**	**100**

WHAT

	1989 Sales		1989 Pretax Income	
	$ mil	% of total	$ mil	% of total
Consumer financial services	2,658	76	298	78
Commercial financial services	447	13	55	14
Individual life insurance	385	11	30	8
Adjustments	—	—	(50)	—
Total	**3,490**	**100**	**333**	**100**

Major US Subsidiaries
Alexander Hamilton Life Insurance Co. of America
Household Bank, f.s.b. (full-service consumer banking)
Household Bank, N.A. (MasterCard and Visa accounts)
Household Commercial Financial Services, Inc.
Household Finance Corp. (consumer credit, home equity loans)
Household Mortgage Services (mortgage lending via Household Bank, f.s.b., and 4 loan origination offices)
Household Retail Services, Inc. (revolving credit administration for retailers)

RANKINGS

17th in *Fortune* 50 Diversified Financial Cos.
240th in *Forbes* Sales 500
353rd in *Business Week* 1000

COMPETITION

H. F. Ahmanson
Ford
General Electric
Great Western
ITT
Primerica
Textron
Transamerica
Banks
Life insurance companies
Savings and loan associations

HUMANA INC.

OVERVIEW

Headquartered in Louisville, Humana, the US's largest publicly-owned health care company and 2nd largest for-profit hospital system in the nation (after Hospital Corporation of America), owns 83 acute-care hospitals (17,421 beds) in 19 states, the UK, and Switzerland. All of these hospitals, except for one psychiatric hospital and 3 specialty hospitals, provide general medical and surgical care for patients.

Humana also provides health benefit plans for nearly one million people, either through health maintenance organizations and preferred provider organizations, which encourage the use of Humana hospitals, or indemnity plans, which offer financial incentives for the use of contracting hospitals. One such managed-care plan provides free care to Louisville's adult indigents.

In 1989 Humana experienced a 19% increase in revenues over 1988, from $3.4 billion to $4.1 billion. Occupancy at Humana hospitals increased 1.6% at a time when the nation's hospitals experienced an overall 1.5% decline. The company's health plans, which lost $37 million in 1988, showed a $4 million operating profit in 1989.

WHEN

In 1961 David Jones and Wendell Cherry, 2 Louisville lawyers, bought a nursing home as a real estate investment. Within 6 years their company, Extendicare, was the largest nursing-care chain in the US, with 8 homes.

Noticing that hospitals received nearly 7 times more money per patient per day than nursing homes and faced with a glutted market of over 80 nursing chains, the partners took their company public in 1968 to finance the buying of hospitals (one per month from 1968 to 1971). Gross sales revenues leaped from $7.7 million in 1968 to $106 million at the end of 1973, when the company decided to change its name to Humana.

Between 1972 and 1975 Humana constructed 27 hospitals in the South and Southwest. During this time the company sold its nursing homes. In 1978 Humana, then the 3rd largest for-profit hospital operator in the country, bought #2-ranked American Medicorp for $304 million, making the company the 2nd largest in America.

In marketing, operation, and location of its hospitals, Humana targeted young, privately insured patients because short hospital stays made the most money. The company kept its charity cases and bad-debt expenses to just 2.5% of revenues in 1980.

Humana experienced several problems between 1983 and 1987. In 1983 the government began reimbursing Medicare payments (40% of company revenues) on fixed rates rather than a percentage of full costs. Occupancy in hospitals dropped. Health insurance write-offs and several closed clinics amounted to a total of $130 million. The company's net income fell 75%, from $216 million in 1985 to $54 million in 1986.

The company solved its profitability problems by offering health insurance at low premiums to attract employers; policyholders paid no deductibles to use Humana hospitals. Humana drew attention by sponsoring a number of controversial operations (Dr. William DeVries performed the 2nd artificial-heart operation using the Jarvik heart device on William Schroeder in 1984 at one of Humana's Louisville hospitals). The company also began a humanitarian effort by contracting with local governments to treat all adult indigent patients at the University of Louisville School of Medicine for a fixed payment of public money. The plan has since spread to Florida and includes Medicare patients. Its efforts appear successful.

Humana's net income has increased steadily down this path, from $183 million (1987) to $256 million (1989), a trend which is continuing in 1990.

HOW MUCH

	9 Yr. Growth	1980	1981	1982	1983	1984	1985	1986	1987	1988	1989
Sales ($ mil)	15.5%	1,117	1,343	1,516	1,765	1,961	2,188	2,601	2,832	3,435	4,088
Net income ($ mil)	16.5%	65	93	127	161	193	216	54	183	227	256
Income as % of sales	—	5.8%	6.9%	8.4%	9.1%	9.9%	9.9%	2.1%	6.5%	6.6%	6.3%
Earnings per share ($)	16.8%	0.63	0.97	1.34	1.63	1.96	2.19	0.56	1.86	2.30	2.56
Stock price – high ($)	—	15.21	19.32	28.75	33.33	33.00	36.75	33.88	29.50	28.63	44.00
Stock price – low ($)	—	5.84	12.08	12.58	19.58	21.50	21.88	19.13	16.13	19.00	24.38
Stock price – close ($)	12.8%	14.87	14.58	28.13	21.88	23.50	31.25	19.13	19.25	25.38	44.00
P/E – high	—	24	20	22	20	17	17	61	16	12	17
P/E – low	—	9	12	9	12	11	10	34	9	8	10
Dividends per share ($)	23.1%	0.15	0.23	0.34	0.47	0.58	0.66	0.74	0.77	0.83	0.95
Book value per share ($)	20.6%	2.49	3.34	4.25	6.35	7.67	9.28	9.20	10.36	11.80	13.48

1989 Year End:
Debt ratio: 46.2%
Return on equity: 20.3%
Cash (mil): $184
Current ratio: 1.31
Long-term debt (mil): $1,140
Number of shares (mil): 98
Dividends:
1989 average yield: 2.2%
1989 payout: 37.1%
Market value (mil): $4,331

NYSE symbol: HUM
Incorporated: Delaware, 1961
Fiscal year ends: August 31

WHO

Chairman and CEO: David A. Jones, age 58, $1,037,717 pay
President and COO: Wendell Cherry, age 54, $754,719 pay
Senior EVP: Carl F. Pollard, age 51, $566,082 pay
EVP Finance and Administration: William C. Ballard, Jr., age 49, $471,721 pay
Auditors: Coopers & Lybrand
Employees: 55,100

WHERE

HQ: 500 W. Main St., Louisville, KY 40202
Phone: 502-580-1000
FAX: 502-580-3694 (Public Affairs Department)

	No. of Hospitals
Alabama	7
Arizona	2
California	5
Colorado	2
Florida	18
Georgia	4
Illinois	1
Indiana	1
Kansas	2
Kentucky	7
Louisiana	8
Tennessee	3
Texas	11
Virginia	3
West Virginia	2
Other states	4
Switzerland	1
UK	2
Total	**83**

WHAT

	1989 Sales		1989 Operating Income	
	$ mil	% of total	$ mil	% of total
Hospitals	3,000	73	588	99
Health plans	1,088	27	4	1
Adjustments	—	—	(115)	—
Total	**4,088**	**100**	**477**	**100**

Businesses
Health maintenance organizations
Hospitals
Indemnity insurance plans
Preferred provider organizations

	1989 Licensed Beds	
	no. of beds	% of total
Health Care Division	8,291	48
Hospital Division	8,647	50
Foreign Hospitals	483	2
Total	**17,421**	**100**

RANKINGS

24th in *Fortune* 100 Diversified Service Cos.
195th in *Forbes* Sales 500
162nd in *Business Week* 1000
420th in *Business Week* Global 1000

COMPETITION

Aetna
Blue Cross
CIGNA
Hospital Corp.
John Hancock
Massachusetts Mutual
Mayo Foundation
Metropolitan
National Medical
New York Life
Prudential
Other insurers

HUTCHISON WHAMPOA LTD.

OVERVIEW

Hutchison Whampoa is the first *hong* (colonial trading company) to pass from British to Chinese control. The company is a major property owner and container terminal operator in Hong Kong and is involved in retailing and telecommunications in the colony and abroad. Hutchison also owns stakes in Hongkong Electric (utility) and Husky Oil (Canada), the largest integrated oil company in Canada.

Hong Kong tycoon Li Ka-Shing controls 39.5% of Hutchison Whampoa stock through his Cheung Kong Holdings property company. Li, estimated by *Forbes* to be worth $1.2 billion, started a plastics manufacturing company and parlayed it into a real estate fortune.

Hutchison wants to reduce its total investment in Hong Kong from 80% to 50%. In 1990 the company sold its John D. Hutchison trading business.

WHEN

In 1977 Hong Kong companies Hutchison International and Hongkong and Whampoa Dock merged to form Hutchison Whampoa. Originally established in 1880 by John Hutchison, Hutchison International became a major Hong Kong consumer goods importer and wholesaler. Managed by Sir Douglas Clague, the company bought controlling interests in Hongkong and Whampoa Dock (dry docks) and A.S. Watson (drugstores, supermarkets, soft drinks) in the midst of a wild acquisition binge in the 1960s. The purchases were accomplished through a complex web of deals that fell apart in the mid-1970s. To save Hutchison International, the Hongkong & Shanghai Bank took a large stake in the company and replaced Clague with Australian turnaround specialist "Dollar" Bill Wyllie. Wyllie slashed expenses, sold 103 companies in 1976, and bought the rest of Hongkong and Whampoa Dock in 1977.

Hongkong and Whampoa Dock, the first registered company in Hongkong, was established in 1863. The company bought dry docks in Whampoa (port of Canton, China) following the kidnapping and disappearance of their owner, John Couper, during the 2nd Opium War. Hongkong docks were first purchased in 1865. Hongkong and Whampoa Dock operated shipyards and shipping container terminals at the time of the merger with Hutchison.

Hutchison Whampoa's finances improved vastly under Wyllie. In a surprise move, Hongkong sold its 22.8% stake in Hutchison to Li Ka-Shing's Cheung Kong Holdings in 1979 at a bargain price: 20% down with 2-year terms and at 50% of its estimated value. Bank chairman Michael Sandberg was thought to feel the need to increase the role of the Chinese in Hong Kong commerce in light of China's increasing scrutiny of the colony. Wyllie, believed to have been preparing his own bid for Hutchison, left in 1981.

In the 1980s Hutchison developed its former dockyard sites (now prime real estate). The company's International Terminals unit grew with Hong Kong's container traffic and became the world's largest privately owned container terminal operator. Following the appointment of former French foreign legion member Simon Murray as managing director in 1984, the company invested its substantial cash flow in large minority stakes in Hongkong Electric (utility, 1985), Cable and Wireless (telecommunications, UK, 1987), Husky Oil (Canada, 1987), and Cluff Resources (gold and minerals mining, UK, 1987). The company also purchased Australian paging and UK mobile telephone units (1988).

Hutchison backed out of a deal for the Hong Kong cable TV franchise in 1989, following the Tiananmen Square incident and the government's insistence on a larger financial commitment. Instead, the company proposed direct broadcasting from its 1/3-owned AsiaSat-I satellite and sold its stake in Cable and Wireless, newly appointed Hong Kong cable TV operator, in 1990.

HOW MUCH

$=HK$7.8 (Dec. 31, 1989)	9 Yr. Growth	1980	1981	1982	1983	1984	1985	1986	1987	1988	1989
Sales (HK$ mil)	20.9%	3,203	3,444	3,717	4,361	5,215	5,466	7,529	10,524	12,875	17,685
Net income (HK$ mil)	24.8%	412	791	952	1,171	1,029	1,194	1,630	1,864	2,340	3,031
Income as % of sales	—	12.9%	23.0%	25.6%	26.9%	19.7%	21.8%	21.6%	17.7%	18.2%	17.1%
Earnings per share (HK$)	22.6%	0.16	0.33	0.40	0.49	0.35	0.42	0.57	0.65	0.77	1.00
Stock price - high (HK$)	—	3.84	5.10	3.70	3.04	3.66	5.60	9.30	15.90	9.70	12.30
Stock price - low (HK$)	—	1.34	2.60	1.64	1.60	1.68	3.70	4.80	5.65	6.65	6.80
Stock price - close (HK$)	10.8%	3.50	3.50	1.89	2.90	3.64	5.50	9.25	7.05	8.60	8.80
P/E - high	—	24	15	9	6	10	13	16	24	13	12
P/E - low	—	8	8	4	3	5	9	8	9	9	7
Dividends per share (HK$)	27.7%	0.06	0.08	0.09	0.93	0.16	0.2	0.25	0.35	0.42	0.54
Book value per share (HK$)	21.3%	1.3	1.5	1.8	1.4	1.8	2.3	3.6	4.7	5.2	7.4

1989 Year End:
Debt ratio: 33.8%
Return on equity: 15.9%
Cash (mil): HK$7,558
Long-term debt (mil): HK$11,469
Number of shares (mil): 3,044
Dividends:
1989 average yield: 6.1%
1989 payout: 54.0%
Market value (mil): US$3,434
Sales (mil): US$2,267

Stock Price History high/low 1980-89

Principal stock exchange: Hong Kong
Incorporated: Hong Kong, 1977
Fiscal year ends: December 31

WHO

Chairman: Li Ka-Shing, age 62
Deputy Chairman: George C. Magnus
Group Managing Director: Simon Murray
Auditors: Price Waterhouse

WHERE

HQ: Hutchison House, 22nd Floor, Hong Kong
Phone: 011-852-523-0161
FAX: 011-852-5-810-0705

	1989 Sales		1989 Operating Income	
	HK$ mil	% of total	HK$ mil	% of total
Hong Kong	16,057	91	3,586	87
Asia	1,337	8	333	8
Europe	236	1	157	4
North America	55	—	29	1
Total	**17,685**	**100**	**4,105**	**100**

WHAT

	1989 Sales		1989 Operating Income	
	HK$ mil	% of total	HK$ mil	% of total
Property	4,821	27	2,128	45
Container terminals	1,704	10	1,094	23
Trading & other svcs.	10,089	57	1,050	22
Energy, finance & investment	1,071	6	423	10
Finance charges	—	—	(590)	—
Total	**17,685**	**100**	**4,105**	**100**

Property
Hutchison Whampoa Property Group (developing, managing, and investing in residential, commercial, industrial, and other real estate in Hong Kong and Australia)

Container Terminals
Hongkong International Terminals Ltd. (shipping services, 67%)
Hongkong United Dockyards Ltd. (ship repair and engineering, 50%)

Trading & Other Services
Hongkong Hilton Hotel (65%)
Hutchison China Trade Holdings Ltd. (trade activities with China)
Sheraton Hong Kong Hotel & Towers (39%)
A.S. Watson & Co. Ltd. (Park'N Shop supermarkets, Watson's personal care stores, Fortress appliance stores, Watson's bottled water, Mountain Cream ice cream)

Energy, Finance & Investment
Cluff Resources PLC (UK, mining, 21%)
Hongkong Electric Holdings Ltd. (utility, 34.6%)
Husky Oil Ltd. (Canada, 43%)

Telecommunications
Hutchison Paging Ltd. (70%)
Hutchison Satellite Systems Ltd. (33% ownership of AsiaSat-I telecommunications satellite)
Hutchison Telephone Co. Ltd. (70%)

RANKINGS

432nd in *Business Week* Global 1000

COMPETITION

Jardine Matheson

HYATT CORPORATION

OVERVIEW

Hyatt Corporation is the most well-known operation of Chicago's publicity-shy Pritzker family. Hyatt is a sister to the Pritzkers' mammoth Marmon Group, composed of some 60 industrial companies. The combined revenues of Hyatt and Marmon are estimated at almost $6 billion. Many of the firms are nuts-and-bolts concerns (railroad tank cars, casters), but with the Pritzker touch, they often make up in profits what they lack in glamour. A recent Pritzker acquisition is American Medical International, the country's 4th largest hospital company.

The hotel chain is known for its superlative service, and many of the amenities it introduced (complimentary shampoo, restricted-access floors) have been copied by other chains. In addition to managing hotels, Hyatt also owns a minority interest in many of its properties.

The company also operates Classic Residence by Hyatt (luxury retirement centers).

WHEN

Nicholas Pritzker came to Chicago from Kiev in 1881 to begin his family's ascent to a fortune now worth more than $4 billion.

Nicholas's son, A. N., left the family law practice in the 1930s and began investing in a variety of businesses. He turned one $25,000 investment (Cory Corporation) in 1942 into $23 million by 1967.

After WWII, A. N.'s son, Jay, followed in his father's wheeling-and-dealing footsteps. In 1953, with the help of his father's banking connections, Jay purchased Colson Company and recruited brother Bob, an industrial engineer, to restructure a company that made tricycles and navy rockets. By 1990 Jay and Bob had added 60 industrial companies, with annual sales exceeding $3 billion, to the entity they called the Marmon Group.

In 1957 Jay bought a hotel called Hyatt House, located near the Los Angeles airport, from Hyatt von Dehn. Jay had added 5 locations by 1961 and brought his gregarious youngest brother, Donald, to California to manage the company.

In 1967 the Pritzkers took the company public, but the move that opened new vistas for the hotel chain was the purchase of an 800-room hotel in Atlanta. Hilton and Marriott had turned down the deal. John Portman's innovative design, incorporating a 21-story atrium, a large fountain, and a revolving rooftop restaurant, became a Hyatt trademark. The Pritzkers formed Hyatt International in 1969 to operate hotels overseas, and the company grew rapidly during the 1970s, in the US and abroad. Donald Pritzker died in 1972, and his successor ran up some questionable expenses. This prompted the family to move corporate offices to Chicago (1977) and take the company and subsidiaries private (1979). In 1980 Hyatt introduced its first Park Hyatt, a European-style super-luxury hotel, near the Water Tower in Chicago. The Park Hyatt concept expanded slowly, and the company waited 6 years before it opened its next Park Hyatt, in Washington, DC.

Much of the growth in the 1970s came from contracts to manage, under the Hyatt banner, hotels built by other investors. In the 1980s Hyatt's cut on those contracts diminished, and it launched its own hotel and resort developments under Nick Pritzker, a cousin to Jay and Bob. In 1988, with US and Japanese partners, it built the $360 million Hyatt Regency Waikoloa on Hawaii's Big Island. The resort was, according to *Fortune*, the most expensive hotel ever built.

Through Hyatt subsidiaries, the Pritzkers purchased bedraggled Braniff Airlines in 1983 as it emerged from bankruptcy court. Braniff had been the carrier with many-colored planes but had fallen victim to airline deregulation. The Pritzkers made a bid for Pan Am in 1987 to combine operations, but Pan Am's unions refused wage concessions, and the deal fell apart. The Pritzkers sold Braniff in 1988 but kept some of its maintenance operations under the Dalfort name.

Using the real estate and hospitality skills from the Hyatt operations, the Pritzkers have branched out beyond innkeeping. Hyatt launched Classic Residence by Hyatt, an upscale retirement community (1989). To add to its arena-management activities from Long Island to Los Angeles and its computerized ticketing, the Pritzkers in 1990 applied for a hockey franchise in, of all places, Florida.

HOW MUCH

	9 Yr. Growth	1980	1981	1982	1983	1984	1985	1986	1987	1988	1989
Total hotels	8.9%	47	54	60	64	68	72	79	85	91	101
New hotels	—	5	7	6	4	4	4	7	6	6	10
Total rooms	7.2%	29,038	32,407	35,289	37,054	39,081	40,715	44,409	47,124	50,396	54,127
New rooms	—	4,009	3,369	2,882	1,765	2,027	1,634	3,694	2,715	3,272	3,731

Estimated 1989 Sales ($ mil)
Hyatt: $2,400
Marmon: $3,500

Total Rooms 1980-89

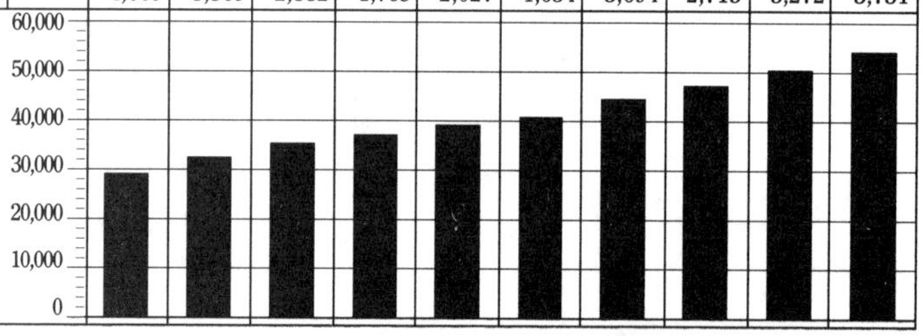

60,000
50,000
40,000
30,000
20,000
10,000
0

Private company
Founded: California, 1957

WHO

Chairman and CEO: Jay Pritzker, age 68
President; Chairman, Hyatt Hotels Corp.: Thomas V. Pritzker, age 40
SVP and CFO: Ken Posner
VP Marketing: Jim Evans
VP Human Resources: Myrna Hellerman
President, Hyatt Hotels Corp.: Darryl Hartley-Leonard
President, Classic Residence: Penny S. Pritzker, age 31
President, Marmon Group: Robert Pritzker, age 64
Auditors: KPMG Peat Marwick
Employees: 80,000

WHERE

HQ: 200 W. Madison, Chicago, IL 60606
Phone: 312-750-1234
FAX: 312-750-8550

As with many other Pritzker family enterprises, Hyatt operations are conducted worldwide.

	Hyatt Hotels - 1990	
	no. of hotels	% of total
US, Canada & Caribbean	116	68
Other countries	55	32
Total	**171**	**100**

WHAT

Subsidiaries
Hyatt Hotels Corp.
- Classic Residence by Hyatt (upscale retirement communities)
- Grand Hyatt
- Hyatt
- Hyatt Regency
- Park Hyatt

Hyatt Hotels International
Spectacor Management Group (arena development and management, 50%)

Related Pritzker Businesses
American Medical International (hospitals)
Conwood Co. (tobacco products)
Dalfort Corp. (aircraft maintenance)
Hawthorn Suites (lodging)
Marmon Group (60 industrial companies, annual sales)
Royal Caribbean Cruises Ltd. (cruise line, 50%)
Tampa Bay Hockey Group (applicant for National Hockey League Franchise)
Ticketmaster (event ticket sales)

RANKINGS

49th in *Forbes* 400 US Private Cos.

COMPETITION

American Express	ITT
Bass	Loews
Carlson	Marriott
Helmsley Enterprises	Nestlé
Hilton	Ogden

HYUNDAI GROUP

OVERVIEW

Hyundai is pronounced "hi-un-dye" everywhere except in the US, where American marketers preferred a pronunciation rhyming with Sunday. Hyundai is a *chaebol* (Korean family-owned conglomerate) consisting of 27 affiliated companies. The group is the 2nd largest *chaebol* in South Korea (behind Samsung) and an important force in the country's economy. Major group companies include Hyundai Corporation, Hyundai Engineering and Construction, Hyundai Heavy Industries, Hyundai Motor, and Hyundai Electronics.

Hyundai is continuing its quest for market share. Hyundai Motors is investing heavily to boost auto output and develop its own automotive technology. Booming domestic demand is picking up part of the increased production. Similarly, through strategic alliances, Hyundai Electronics is trying to acquire foreign technology and is investing in chipmaking capacity. The company hopes to be among the first to produce 16 megabyte computer memory chips.

WHEN

At the end of WWII, elementary school dropout Chung Ju-Yung went into business repairing trucks for US occupation forces in South Korea. In 1947 Chung established Hyundai Engineering and Construction, the first Korean contractor to win overseas construction projects. Chung's Hyundai Motor, formed in 1967, originally assembled Fords.

Chung repeatedly gambled on new businesses. When Hyundai won a $1 billion contract in the 1970s to build a port in Jubail, Saudi Arabia, Chung saved money by importing Korean parts and not insuring the shipments, risking ruin. The gamble paid off, and Hyundai became a major factor in Middle East construction.

In the 1970s Chung enjoyed the support of the Park government, and his Hyundai enterprises multiplied to create a *chaebol.* In 1973 he began building the world's largest shipyard (Hyundai Heavy Industries) despite having no experience in shipbuilding. He succeeded because of a combination of government backing, near-monopoly conditions, and an extremely hardworking Korean labor force. With help from 15% owner Mitsubishi Motors, Hyundai Motor built the first Korean automobile in 1975 — the popular Pony. Chung created Hyundai Corporation, the *chaebol's* trading arm, in 1976 and established the Ulsan Institute of Technology in 1977 to increase South Korea's pool of engineering talent.

The Hyundai *chaebol* continued to expand its scope in the 1980s, forming Hyundai Electronics Industries (1983) to produce semiconductors and microcomputer equipment despite a lack of experience in technology-based industries. Hyundai spent heavily on electronics but did not enjoy immediate success. In 1985 the company closed a plant in Santa Clara, California, when it found that Americans would not regularly work nights and weekends, as South Koreans will.

Hyundai took advantage of low labor costs to start an export drive in the 1980s, beginning shipments of the Pony to Canada (1984), where it became #4 in auto sales (1985). In the US, the company introduced Blue Chip brand IBM-compatible PCs (1986) and, in the most successful imported car launch in US history, inexpensive Excel subcompacts (1986).

In the late 1980s Hyundai suffered from a continued slump in worldwide shipbuilding, strikes (1987, 1989), slow progress in its electronics ventures, and the narrowing of its cost advantage as South Korean wages doubled in 3 years and the country's currency appreciated. In 1989 US sales of Hyundai cars nearly halved because of cost-induced price increases.

In 1990 Hyundai suffered strikes over the jailing of union leaders.

HOW MUCH

$=Won 677 (Dec. 31, 1989)	8 Yr. Growth	1980	1981	1982	1983	1984	1985	1986	1987	1988	1989
Sales (Won bil)	25.8%	—	908	1,057	1,547	1,550	2,853	3,876	5,254	5,622	5,703
Net income (Won bil)*	3.5%	—	3.5	4.2	5.4	3.2	4.5	4.9	3.7	8.6	4.6
Income as % of sales	—	—	0.4%	0.4%	0.3%	0.2%	0.2%	0.1%	0.1%	0.1%	0.1%
Earnings per share (Won)	—	—	—	—	—	1,005	1,394	1,530	761	1,798	966
Stock price – high (Won)	—	—	—	—	—	—	13,190	16,350	21,900	29,300	35,200
Stock price – low (Won)	—	—	—	—	—	—	8,590	9,210	12,800	17,500	22,700
Stock price – close (Won)	—	—	—	—	—	—	—	—	—	—	—
P/E – high	—	—	—	—	—	—	9	11	29	16	36
P/E – low	—	—	—	—	—	—	6	6	17	10	23
Dividends per share (Won)**	—	—	—	—	—	—	500	500	500	500	500
Book value per share (Won)	—	—	—	—	—	—	9,220	10,024	9,380	11,046	11,557

1989 Year End:
Debt ratio: —
Return on equity: 8.5%
Cash (mil): —
Long-term debt (mil): —
Number of shares (mil): 5
Dividends:
1989 average yield: —
1989 payout: 51.8%
Market value (mil): —
Sales (mil): $8,424

Stock Price History high/low 1985-89

40,000
35,000
30,000
25,000
20,000
15,000
10,000
5,000
0

*not including extraordinary items **not including rights offerings

Principal exchange: Seoul
Incorporated: South Korea, 1976
Fiscal year ends: December 31

WHO

Chairman: Lee Choon Lim
President: Eum Yong Ky
Auditors: Ernst & Young
Employees: 894

WHERE

HQ: 140-2, Kye-Dong, Chongro-Ku, Seoul, South Korea
Phone: 011-82-2-741-4141
FAX: 011-82-2-741-2341
US HQ (Hyundai Corporation U.S.A.): One Bridge Plaza North, Suite 600, 6th Floor, Fort Lee, NJ 07024
US Phone: 201-592-7766
US FAX: 201-585-5034

The company maintains 51 trading offices in 39 countries.

	1989 Sales % of total
Exports from South Korea	62
Imports into South Korea	38
Total	**100**

WHAT

	1989 Sales % of total
Machinery & transportation	38
Ships & industrial plants	17
Electronic & electrical equipment	28
Steel & metal	8
General merchandise	4
Resources & energy	5
Total	**100**

Major Affiliates
Aluminum of Korea
Hyundai Construction Equipment Industries
Hyundai Electronics Industries
Hyundai Engineering & Construction
Hyundai Heavy Industries
Hyundai Marine & Fire Insurance
Hyundai Merchant Marine
Hyundai Mipo Dockyard
Hyundai Motor
Hyundai Pipe
Hyundai Precision & Industry
Hyundai Robot Industry
Hyundai Wood Industries
Inchon Iron & Steel
Korea Kuwait Banking

RANKINGS

221st in *Fortune* Global 500 Industrial Cos. (Hyundai Motor)
300th in *Fortune* Global 500 Industrial Cos. (Hyundai Heavy Industries)

COMPETITION

Bethlehem Steel	General Motors	NEC
Broken Hill	Hitachi	Nissan
Caterpillar	Honda	Samsung
Chrysler	IBM	Siemens
Commodore	Inland Steel	Texas Instruments
Compaq	LTV	Toyota
Deere	Mitsubishi	USX
Fiat	Motorola	Volkswagen
Ford	National Semiconductor	Volvo
Fujitsu		

Information presented for Hyundai Corporation only.

INGERSOLL-RAND COMPANY

OVERVIEW

Ingersoll-Rand is a major international producer of industrial machinery and equipment. Global operations are divided into 3 segments: Standard Machinery, Engineered Equipment, and Bearings, Locks, and Tools.

The Standard Machinery segment (39% of sales) produces air compressors for industrial and home use, construction equipment, and mining machinery.

The Engineered Equipment segment (14% of sales) manufactures pumps and industrial process machinery (pulp and paper processing machinery, filters, aerators, etc.).

The Bearings, Locks, and Tools segment (47% of sales) produces bearings and components (sold primarily to the auto and aerospace industries), production equipment (air-powered equipment, waterjet cutting systems), and door hardware. The company is the largest domestic producer of a broad line of bearings.

Ingersoll-Rand's products are used worldwide, from drills in Soviet mines to pipeline pumps in Saudi Arabia to air compressors in the English Channel tunnel construction project. Customers outside of the US account for 34% of company sales.

NYSE symbol: IR
Incorporated: New Jersey, 1905
Fiscal year ends: December 31

WHO

Chairman, President, and CEO: Theodore H. Black, age 61, $1,103,183 pay
VC and CFO: Clyde H. Folley, age 62, $818,350 pay
Auditors: Price Waterhouse
Employees: 31,623

WHERE

HQ: 200 Chestnut Ridge Rd., Woodcliff Lake, NJ 07675
Phone: 201-573-0123
FAX: 201-573-3448

The company owns 78 plants worldwide.

	1989 Sales		1989 Operating Income	
	$ mil	% of total	$ mil	% of total
US	2,277	66	232	59
Europe	695	20	86	22
Other international	475	14	75	19
Adjustments	—	—	(32)	—
Total	**3,447**	**100**	**361**	**100**

WHEN

Simon Ingersoll invented the steam-driven rock drill in New York City in 1871. In 1874 he sold the patent to José Francisco de Navarro, who quickly financed the organization of the Ingersoll Rock Drill Company. Three years later the company merged with Sergeant Drill, a company formed by Navarro's former foreman, Henry Clark Sergeant.

In 1871, at the same time Ingersoll was inventing his drill, Albert, Jasper, and Addison Rand were forming the Rand Drill Company. Both companies continued to make drills and other equipment through the turn of the century. In 1905 they merged to become Ingersoll-Rand.

During the next several years Ingersoll-Rand started producing air compressors in addition to its basic line of rock drills. In 1912 the company added centrifugal compressors and turbo blowers to its product line. Further diversification occurred with the purchase of A. S. Cameron Steam Pump Works and Imperial Pneumatic Tool Company (portable air tools). For several decades the company continued to grow as a major manufacturer of compressed-air tools, sold mostly to the mining industry.

After WWII Ingersoll-Rand expanded its operations to Canada, Great Britain, Australia, South Africa, and several countries in Europe and South America. During the 1960s the company embarked on a series of acquisitions that would diversify it into new fields of specialized machinery. Acquisitions during this period included Aldrich Pump (high-pressure plunger pumps, 1961), Pendleton Tool (mechanics' service tools, 1964), and Torrington (antifriction bearings and textile machine needles, 1969).

Diversification continued during the 1970s and 1980s with the acquisitions of DAMCO (truck-mounted drilling rigs, 1973); Schlage Lock (lock and door hardware, 1974); California Pellet (1974); Western Land Roller (vertical water pumps for agriculture, 1977); the machinery division of Cabot (1980); and Fafnir Bearings, which made Ingersoll-Rand the largest bearing manufacturer in the US (1986).

During this time the company developed several new products, including small air compressors, high-speed pumps, hydraulic turbines for moderate-flow areas, and waterjet cutting systems capable of cutting through steel and concrete. In 1986 Ingersoll-Rand formed a partnership with Dresser Industries (Dresser-Rand) to produce gas turbines, compressors, and other similar equipment. In 1990 Ingersoll-Rand bought Aro (air-powered tools) from Todd Shipyards.

WHAT

	1989 Sales		1989 Operating Income	
	$ mil	% of total	$ mil	% of total
Standard machinery	1,328	39	156	40
Engineered equip.	485	14	32	8
Bearings, locks & tools	1,634	47	200	52
Adjustments	—	—	(27)	—
Total	**3,447**	**100**	**361**	**100**

Products/Services

Agricultural pumps
Air compressors
Air motor
Air tools
Aircraft support equipment
Asphalt paving equipment
Automated production systems
Automotive components
Ball bearings
Breathing air systems
Construction equipment
Door hardware
Electronic security systems
Engine starting systems
Fluid handling equipment
Food processing equipment
Generator sets
Hoists
Industrial pumps
Landfill compactors
Lubrication equipment
Material handling equipment
Mining machinery
Needle bearings
Pavement milling machines
Pneumatic valves
Pulp processing machinery
Road-building machinery
Rock drills
Roller bearings
Roller mills
Rough-terrain forklifts
Soil compactors
Spray coating systems
Waterjet cutting systems
Winches

HOW MUCH

	9 Yr. Growth	1980	1981	1982	1983	1984	1985	1986	1987	1988	1989
Sales ($ mil)	1.7%	2,971	3,378	2,775	2,274	2,478	2,637	2,799	2,648	3,021	3,447
Net income ($ mil)	2.6%	160	193	52	(112)	59	80	101	108	162	202
Income as % of sales	—	5.4%	5.7%	1.9%	(4.9%)	2.4%	3.0%	3.6%	4.1%	5.3%	5.9%
Earnings per share ($)	2.2%	3.08	3.70	0.94	(2.38)	1.08	1.51	1.90	1.94	2.99	3.76
Stock price – high ($)	—	32.00	32.00	23.30	23.10	22.30	22.70	27.55	45.75	44.63	50.25
Stock price – low ($)	—	18.35	21.10	14.20	15.50	14.20	17.70	20.35	22.50	31.00	33.63
Stock price – close ($)	5.9%	29.95	22.60	15.80	20.95	18.20	21.40	22.30	35.50	34.25	50.25
P/E – high	—	10	9	25	—	21	15	15	24	15	13
P/E – low	—	6	6	15	—	13	12	11	12	10	9
Dividends per share ($)	(1.5%)	1.33	1.36	1.33	1.04	1.04	1.04	1.04	1.04	1.04	1.16
Book value per share ($)	0.9%	24.57	25.93	24.63	20.88	20.44	21.22	22.09	21.96	24.26	26.73

1989 Year End:
Debt ratio: 16.9%
Return on equity: 14.7%
Cash (mil): $139
Current ratio: 2.37
Long-term debt (mil): $280
Number of shares (mil): 52
Dividends:
1989 average yield: 2.3%
1989 payout: 30.9%
Market value (mil): $2,667

Stock Price History high/low 1980-89

RANKINGS

134th in *Fortune* 500 Industrial Cos.
245th in *Forbes* Sales 500
214th in *Business Week* 1000
659th in *Business Week* Global 1000

COMPETITION

Baker Hughes
Black & Decker
Borg-Warner
Caterpillar
Cooper Industries
Deere
Farley
Fiat
FMC
General Signal
Masco
Raytheon
Stanley Works

INLAND STEEL INDUSTRIES, INC.

OVERVIEW

Inland Steel Industries, which ranks 4th in sales among US steel producers, is a fully integrated producer of steel, about 99% of which is carbon and high-strength, low-alloy steel. The company is divided into 2 segments: Integrated Steel and Steel Service Centers (customized steel products).

Integrated Steel Operations consists of Inland Steel Flat Products (steel strip, sheet, and plate) and Inland Bar and Structural (steel bars and structural shapes), both located at the company's Indiana Harbor Works. Total production for this segment in 1989 was 5.5 million tons, constituting 5.7% of the US steel industry.

Inland obtains its iron ore from fully and partially owned properties in the US and Canada. Raw materials are transported by the company's Great Lakes fleet and railroad hopper cars.

The Steel Service Center segment consists of Joseph T. Ryerson & Son (the largest steel service center organization in the US) and J. M. Tull Metals (one of the largest metal distributors in the southeastern US).

WHEN

In 1893 8 partners purchased 40 freight cars of used steel-making machinery from the bankrupt Chicago Steel Company and established Inland Steel in the Chicago Heights area. By 1894 the company was producing agricultural implements (plows, etc.).

In 1901 the Lake Michigan Land Company offered 50 acres of land at Indiana Harbor to any company that would spend $1 million to develop the land by building an open-hearth steel mill. Inland raised the money and built Indiana Harbor Works. In 1906 the company bought the Laura Ore iron mine in Minnesota.

Inland saw steady growth through the midteens. In 1916 the company began a program of rapid expansion to meet the need for steel caused by WWI. By 1920 Inland was producing 2% of the steel in the US. The company converted its mills back to peacetime production and in 1922 started producing rails.

During the difficult Great Depression years, Inland turned its production emphasis from heavy steel to the lighter steel (tinplate, sheets) needed for consumer goods. In 1931 the company, under Chairman L. E. Block, started construction on facilities to produce strip, sheet, and plate steel. Inland acquired Joseph T. Ryerson and Son (steel warehousing) in 1935 and Wilson & Bennett Manufacturing (later renamed Inland Steel Containers) in 1939. The company introduced Ledloy (a steel/lead alloy machining metal) in 1938.

Inland's attention was turned to wartime production again in the early 1940s. In 1947 the company expanded the capacity of its rolling mills. Inland introduced its line of galvanized steel sheets (marketed under the TI-CO trade name) in 1951. Inland expanded rapidly during the 1950s. In 1957 the company completed construction of its new skyscraper headquarters (one of the first to use external columns and stainless steel in its construction) in Chicago.

In the 1960s Inland started producing 76-inch steel sheets, which were soon adopted by the auto industry for the construction of the broader hoods and wider fenders typical of the newer automobiles. In 1966 Inland became a billion-dollar company. The 1970s brought a steel boom that Inland expected would continue. When the boom ended in the 1980s, Inland suffered big losses.

In 1986 Inland acquired J. M. Tull Metals from Bethlehem Steel. During the late 1980s Inland increasingly turned its attention to the production of custom work (such as painted steel for appliances). In 1987 and 1989 Inland entered into 2 joint ventures with Nippon Steel to build and operate cold rolling (I/N Tek) and coating (I/N Kote) facilities.

HOW MUCH

	9 Yr. Growth	1980	1981	1982	1983	1984	1985	1986	1987	1988	1989
Sales ($ mil)	2.7%	3,256	3,755	2,808	3,046	3,325	2,999	3,173	3,453	4,068	4,147
Net income ($ mil)	16.8%	30	57	(133)	(111)	(40)	(147)	35	112	249	120
Income as % of sales	—	0.9%	1.5%	(4.7%)	(3.6%)	(1.2%)	(4.9%)	1.1%	3.2%	6.1%	2.9%
Earnings per share ($)	9.3%	1.38	2.69	(6.27)	(4.51)	(1.93)	(6.14)	0.95	3.04	6.36	3.06
Stock price – high ($)	—	37.75	36.00	26.75	35.00	32.75	26.00	28.38	35.25	42.63	48.50
Stock price – low ($)	—	25.63	22.25	18.13	24.75	19.88	19.50	14.50	17.00	27.50	31.38
Stock price – close ($)	2.1%	27.88	23.38	26.00	31.00	23.25	22.63	18.88	30.38	41.50	33.75
P/E – high	—	27	13	—	—	—	—	30	12	7	16
P/E – low	—	19	8	—	—	—	—	15	6	4	10
Dividends per share ($)	(5.8%)	2.40	2.00	1.13	0.50	0.50	0.38	0.00	0.00	0.75	1.40
Book value per share ($)	(3.9%)	61.63	62.29	52.90	45.41	42.64	34.68	35.73	41.68	45.75	43.04

1989 Year End:
Debt ratio: 27.9%
Return on equity: 6.9%
Cash (mil): $237
Current ratio: 2.46
Long-term debt (mil): $578
Number of shares (mil): 35
Dividends:
1989 average yield: 4.1%
1989 payout: 45.8%
Market value (mil): $1,170

Stock Price History high/low 1980-89

NYSE symbol: IAD
Incorporated: Delaware, 1986
Fiscal year ends: December 31

WHO

Chairman and CEO: Frank W. Luerssen, age 62, $734,336 pay
President and COO: Robert J. Darnall, age 51, $520,900 pay
VP Corporate Planning: David B. Anderson, age 47, $294,720 pay
VP Finance: Paul M. Anderson, age 44
Auditors: Price Waterhouse
Employees: 20,715

WHERE

HQ: 30 W. Monroe St., Chicago, IL 60603
Phone: 312-346-0300
FAX: 312-899-3672

The company produces all of its raw steel products at Indiana Harbor Works in East Chicago, IN. Through its Ryerson and Tull segments, the company operates 44 steel service centers nationwide. In addition, the company operates a Great Lakes fleet of 3 ships, a fleet of 410 railroad hopper cars, and 3 iron ore mines.

WHAT

	1989 Sales		1989 Operating Income	
	$ mil	% of total	$ mil	% of total
Integrated Steel	2,183	53	175	73
Steel Service Centers	1,964	47	64	27
Adjustments	—	—	2	—
Total	**4,147**	**100**	**241**	**100**

Integrated Steel
Inland Steel Co.

Products
Bar steel
Coil
Expanded metal
Grating
Pipe
Plate
Raw steel
Rod
Semifinished products
Sheet
Strip
Structural steel
Tubing
Wire

Joint Ventures
I/N Kote (50%)
I/N Tek (60%)

Service Centers
Joseph T. Ryerson & Son, Inc.
J. M. Tull Metals Co., Inc.
AFCO Metals, Inc.
Southern Metals Corp.

RANKINGS

117th in *Fortune* 500 Industrial Cos.
320th in *Fortune* Global 500
206th in *Forbes* Sales 500
464th in *Business Week* 1000

COMPETITION

Bethlehem Steel
Broken Hill
Cargill
Hyundai
LTV
USX

INTEL CORPORATION

OVERVIEW

Intel is the 3rd largest US semiconductor manufacturer after Motorola and Texas Instruments. The company dominates the microprocessor business, its advanced metal oxide chips supplying the brains for a majority of all existing personal computers (PCs).

Intel also makes chips that control robots, run printers and communications systems, and store data in memory. Intel has recently begun producing computer systems (including PCs), all of which are sold under other manufacturers' names (*e.g.*, AT&T). The computer systems business accounted for almost 30% of fiscal 1989 sales. Add-on boards (which boost PC power, memory, etc.) are Intel's only retail products.

Intel changed the world with innovations such as the first DRAM (dynamic random access memory) and EPROM (erasable programmable read only memory) chips, and the first microprocessor — which in 1971 put the power of the 18,000 vacuum-tube ENIAC (the first electronic computer, 1946) on a silicon chip the size of a baby's thumbnail.

Intel maintains leadership in transistor density. R&D remains high at 12% of sales.

WHEN

In 1968, 3 PhD engineers from Fairchild Semiconductor created Intel in Mountain View, California, to realize the potential of large-scale integration (LSI) technology for silicon-based chips. Robert Noyce (co-inventor of the integrated circuit, 1957) and Gordon Moore handled long-range planning and the younger Andrew Grove oversaw manufacturing. Silicon Valley moneyman Arthur Rock, whose other ventures include Apple Computer and Teledyne, provided venture capital.

Intel started with 12 employees and first-year sales of $2,672, but soon mushroomed as a supplier of semiconductor memory for large computers (*e.g.*, DRAM chips, which replaced magnetic core memory storage with silicon wafers, 1970; and EPROM chips,which allowed memory to be erased and reused, 1971).

Memory chip success funded the logic chip designs of Ted Hoff, whose microprocessor (the 4004, 1971; and descendants 8008, 8080, and 8088) led to major transformations in electronic design; later, when IBM chose the 8088 chip for its 1981 IBM PC, Intel secured its place as the microcomputer standards supplier.

Noyce stepped down from top management in 1979, serving as a director and deputy chairman of the company's board until his death in June 1990.

Cutthroat pricing of DRAMs from 1985 to 1986 by Japanese competitors trying to capture US market share forced Grove (president and COO since 1979) to close plants, cut the work force by 30%, and withdraw from the DRAM market; 1984's $198 million profit became a $183 million loss by 1986.

Grove focused on proprietary PC chips such as the 80386 (1985). Intel has protected the popular 80386's technology, so far preventing it from being reverse engineered or cloned (unlike its earlier free sourcing of the 80286 chip, introduced 1982). In 1988 Grove also expanded Intel's systems division (started in 1975), noting the increasing value of microprocessors within the whole computer and the low value (but high margins) added after microprocessor insertion.

Intel countered competition from speedy RISC chips by introducing its own RISC versions: the i960 chips (1988), which are designed for specific applications (*e.g.*, to control robots, planes), and the i860 (1989), which powers a new supercomputer (iPSC/860). Digital video interactive (DVI) technology (purchased from GE, 1988; DVI chip due in 1990) will add full-motion video and stereo sounds to PCs.

The latest x86 member (i486, 1989), 4 years and $300 million in development, boosts Intel chips into mainframe power. Intel expects to introduce the 586 (1993), 686 (1996), and the Micro 2000 to open the new millenium.

HOW MUCH

	9 Yr. Growth	1980	1981	1982	1983	1984	1985	1986	1987	1988	1989
Sales ($ mil)	15.5%	855	789	900	1,122	1,629	1,365	1,265	1,907	2,875	3,127
Net income ($ mil)	16.8%	97	27	30	116	198	2	(183)	176	453	391
Income as % of sales	—	11.3%	3.5%	3.3%	10.4%	12.2%	0.1%	(14.5%)	9.2%	15.8%	12.5%
Earnings per share ($)	12.1%	0.74	0.20	0.22	0.70	1.13	0.01	(1.05)	0.98	2.51	2.06
Stock price – high ($)	—	16.50	13.92	13.83	33.00	29.00	21.67	21.50	41.83	37.25	36.00
Stock price – low ($)	—	9.17	7.50	6.92	12.33	16.50	13.83	10.92	13.83	19.25	22.88
Stock price – close ($)	11.1%	13.42	7.50	12.92	28.00	18.67	19.50	14.00	26.50	23.75	34.50
P/E – high	—	22	68	64	47	26	—	—	43	15	17
P/E – low	—	12	37	32	18	15	—	—	14	8	11
Dividends per share ($)	0.0%	0.00	0.00	0.00	0.00	0.00	0.00	0.00	0.00	0.00	0.00
Book value per share ($)	16.9%	3.38	3.72	4.06	6.69	7.97	8.16	7.22	7.76	11.52	13.81

1989 Year End:
Debt ratio: 13.9%
Return on equity: 16.3%
Cash (mil): $1,090
Current ratio: 2.35
Long-term debt (mil): $412
Number of shares (mil): 185
Dividends:
1989 average yield: 0.0%
1989 payout: 0.0%
Market value (mil): $6,366

Stock Price History high/low 1980-89

NYSE symbol: INTC
Incorporation: Delaware, 1989
Fiscal year ends: Last Saturday in December

WHO

President and CEO: Andrew S. Grove, age 53, $723,003 pay
Chairman: Gordon E. Moore, age 61, $665,533 pay
EVP: Craig R. Barrett, age 50, $492,363 pay
SVP and CFO: Robert W. Reed, age 43
Auditors: Ernst & Young
Employees: 21,700

Intel has 90 sales offices in 25 nations and sells through distributors in 34 countries; manufacturing plants are in the US, Israel, Malaysia, Singapore, and the Philippines.

WHERE

HQ: 3065 Bowers Ave., Santa Clara, CA 95052
Phone: 408-765-8080
FAX: 408-765-1402

	1989 Sales		1989 Operating Income	
	$ mil	% of total	$ mil	% of total
US	1,774	57	413	56
Europe	691	22	105	14
Japan	341	11	33	5
Asia, Pacific & other	321	10	180	25
Adjustments	—	—	(174)	—
Total	**3,127**	**100**	**557**	**100**

WHAT

Microprocessors
16-bit 8086
8088
80286
32-bit 386 DX
386 SX
i486
64-bit i860
Application-Specific Integrated Circuits (ASICs)
Board-level products
Microprocessor peripheral components

Memories
DRAM (reseller)
EPROM
Flash memories
SRAM

Embedded Control Products
8-bit 8048
16-bit 8096
32-bit i960

Computer Systems
Digital Video Interactive (DVI)
Microcomputers
Model 303
Model 302-20
Model 300-SX
Personal computer enhancement (add-in boards)
Networking products
Supercomputers
iPSC 860

Software
Developmental tools
High-level network systems
Microcomputer operating systems

RANKINGS

137th in *Fortune* 500 Industrial Cos.
388th in *Fortune* Global 500 Industrial Cos.
33rd in *Fortune* 50 Exporters
266th in *Forbes* Sales 500
65th in *Business Week* 1000
272nd in *Business Week* Global 1000

COMPETITION

Fujitsu
Harris
Hewlett-Packard
Hitachi
Hyundai
IBM
Motorola
National Semiconductor
NEC
Samsung
SCI Systems
Siemens
Sun Microsystems
Texas Instruments

INTERCO INC.

OVERVIEW

INTERCO, a major producer of furniture and footwear, consists of 4 core companies: Broyhill, Lane, Florsheim, and Converse.

INTERCO's furniture segment (Broyhill, Lane) generates 55% of sales. Broyhill, one of the industry's largest and best-known furniture companies, with a 3% market share, produces primarily wood, upholstered, and occasional furniture. Lane produces furniture through 8 independently operated companies and offers a product line of more than 5,000 items.

The company's shoe segment consists of Florsheim and Converse. Florsheim is the largest producer of men's quality footwear, with a 20% market share. Florsheim shoes are sold through about 450 company-owned Florsheim retail outlets and through approximately 5,000 independent dealers. Converse is a major producer of athletic footwear. Converse's strongest and most popular product line is its men's basketball shoes, which generates 42% of its revenues.

A recapitalization in 1988 permitted INTERCO to avoid a takeover, but left it burdened with $1.8 billion of debts. The company defaulted on interest payments due bond holders in mid-1990, its stock has sunk to historic lows, and it may have to seek chapter 11 protection.

NYSE symbol: ISS
Incorporated: Delaware, 1921
Fiscal year ends: Last Saturday in February

WHO

Chairman, President, and CEO: Richard B. Loynd, age 62, $678,816 pay
VP; Chairman, Lane Company: R. Stuart Moore, age 66, $469,815 pay
VP; President, Florsheim: Ronald J. Mueller, age 55, $298,978 pay
EVP and Principal Financial Officer: Eugene F. Smith, age 57
Auditors: KPMG Peat Marwick
Employees: 28,800

WHEN

In 1911 the Roberts, Johnson and Rand Shoe Company (founded 1898) and Peters Shoe Company (founded 1836) formed the International Shoe Company in St. Louis. The company existed for 4 decades as a successful US shoemaker. In 1953 International Shoe purchased Florsheim (a manufacturer and retailer of men's shoes) for $20.8 million, starting what would be a long history of acquisitions.

Despite the "International" in its name, the company did not expand out of the US until 1954 when it purchased Savage Shoes of Canada. In 1962 the company acquired a majority interest in Marlow Holding (men's shoes) in Melbourne, Australia, but by then was experiencing major difficulties with its retail shoe operations.

In 1962 Maurice Chambers, a former shoe salesman, became president of International Shoe. Chambers turned the company around by modernizing operations and trimming unprofitable stores and inventory. During Chambers's first decade as president, the company tripled its sales. In 1966 the company changed its name to INTERCO.

Chambers diversified during the 1960s and 1970s with a string of purchases, including Central Hardware Stores (1966); Campus Sweater & Sportswear (name changed to Megastar Apparel, 1968); Biltwell (men's pants, 1970); Golde's Department Stores (1971); Big Yank (leisure and work clothes, 1972); Devon Apparel (women's sportswear, 1974); Londontown (rainwear, 1976); and Stuffed Shirt/Stuffed Jeans (1976, the year Chambers stepped down as CEO). In 1986 INTERCO bought Converse (athletic shoes).

During the 1980s the company became a major force in the furniture industry with the purchases of Ethan Allen (for $151 million, 1980); Broyhill ($151 million, 1980); Highland House ($150 million, 1986); and Lane (for 11 million shares common stock, 1987).

In 1988 INTERCO, under CEO Harvey Saligman, repelled a takeover attempt by S. Rales and M. Rales by borrowing $1.8 billion to pay a special dividend of $76 per share. The company has not made money since. To reduce debt, INTERCO launched a restructuring effort and put 16 of its 20 operating units up for sale. In 1988 the company sold Londontown (to Londontown senior management, $178 million) and in 1989 sold Biltwell (to Hartmarx, $42 million), Central Hardware (to Handy Andy, $245 million), and Ethan Allen (to Green Mountain Holding, $388 million). The company intends to focus solely on the 4 core units now remaining.

WHERE

HQ: 101 S. Hanley Rd., St. Louis, MO 63105
Phone: 314-863-1100
FAX: 314-863-5306

The company's major plants, offices, and warehouses include 18 Broyhill, 5 Converse, 9 Florsheim, and 17 Lane facilities distributed throughout the US.

Florsheim has about 65 retail outlets outside of the US and operates subsidiaries in Australia and Canada. Converse products are sold in more than 90 countries.

WHAT

	1989 Sales		1989 Operating Income	
	$ mil	% of total	$ mil	% of total
Footware	746	45	49	32
Furniture	910	55	101	68
Adjustments	—	—	(17)	—
Total	**1,656**	**100**	**133**	**100**

Brand Names

Furniture
Broyhill
- Contract
- Highland House
- Premier
- Showcase Gallery
- Timbertown

Lane
- Hickory Chair
- James River Collection
- Mark Hampton Collection
- Weathermaster

Shoes
Converse
- All-Star
- American Sports Casuals
- Conasaurs
- Evolo
- Magic
- Small Stars

Florsheim
- ComforTech
- Designer Collection
- Idlers
- Imperial
- Outdoorsman
- Pro Action
- Ramblers
- Royal Imperial
- Sea Tracs
- Signature

HOW MUCH

	9 Yr. Growth	1980	1981	1982	1983	1984	1985	1986	1987	1988	1989
Sales ($ mil)	(3.9%)	2,368	2,674	2,567	2,679	2,626	2,511	2,614	3,341	2,012	1,656
Net income ($ mil)	—	124	119	86	116	72	92	99	145	(4)	(51)
Income as % of sales	—	5.3%	4.4%	3.3%	4.3%	2.7%	3.7%	3.8%	4.3%	(0.2%)	(3.1%)
Earnings per share ($)	—	3.81	3.62	2.61	3.51	2.23	2.92	3.13	3.50	(0.42)	(3.37)
Stock price – high ($)	—	26.81	28.63	30.88	42.50	34.00	36.81	47.63	54.00	73.63	3.88
Stock price – low ($)	—	18.06	22.75	17.75	29.00	27.50	29.63	33.50	29.50	3.13	0.19
Stock price – close ($)	(34.1%)	23.88	23.63	30.50	33.25	29.88	35.44	36.88	32.25	3.63	0.56
P/E – high	—	7	8	12	12	15	13	15	15	—	—
P/E – low	—	5	6	7	8	12	10	11	8	—	—
Dividends per share ($)	(100%)	1.32	1.44	1.44	1.44	1.52	1.54	1.57	1.60	39.49	0.00
Book value per share ($)	—	28.99	31.18	32.32	34.41	35.22	36.52	38.06	33.01	(26.70)	(25.08)

1989 Year End:
Debt ratio: —
Return on equity: —
Cash (mil): $48
Current ratio: 0.4
Long-term debt (mil): $1,493
Number of shares (mil): 39
Dividends:
1989 average yield: 0.0%
1989 payout: 0.0%
Market value (mil): $22

Stock Price History high/low 1980-89

RANKINGS

138th in *Fortune* 500 Industrial Cos.
389th in *Fortune* Global 500
433rd in *Forbes* Sales 500

COMPETITION

Armstrong World
Masco
May Department Stores
Melville
NIKE
Reebok
United States Shoe
Woolworth

INTERGRAPH CORPORATION

OVERVIEW

Intergraph is a leading producer of intelligent graphics/design computer systems. The company ranks first worldwide in architectural/engineering/construction (A/E/C) design software and mapping applications; 3rd in mechanical design software; 3rd in computer-aided design and manufacturing (CAD/CAM) software; and 4th in UNIX workstations. Intergraph is also a leading supplier of computer graphics to the US government.

Intergraph's computers incorporate or are compatible with industry-standard operating systems (*e.g.,* UNIX), networks (Ethernet), graphics (X Windows), and databases (SQL). Intergraph's more than 750 software applications help automate government agencies, discover oil and gas, manage utilities, and design virtually anything (from cars and ships to communities).

Much of Intergraph's business comes from industrial and military accounts, where the company is known for ably providing customized solutions. The company recently achieved a 94% customer satisfaction rating by Daratech market research. Intergraph is currently supplying a computer-integrated engineering system for NASA's Space Station Freedom program.

WHEN

James Meadlock, Terry Schantzman, and 3 other former IBM coworkers, all software developers for Saturn rockets at IBM's Federal Systems Division in Huntsville, Alabama, founded M&S Computing in 1969. The company's initial focus was consulting work. The first contract, a digital guidance system for the US Army Missile Command in Huntsville, used the real-time applications that later grew into Intergraph's core computer graphics business.

The first commercial graphics systems sale was for mapping applications (1973). Penetration of the key architectural, engineering, and construction (A/E/C) markets soon followed, with the introduction of a single graphics product, the Interactive Graphics Design System (IGDS). Meadlock packaged the graphics software with industry-accepted hardware such as the PDP-11 from Digital Equipment, while competitors stuck to more restricted proprietary versions.

In the late 1970s the company began making its own computers to produce customized solutions, compatibility across product lines, and larger profit margins. The company name was changed to Intergraph in 1980; the newly public Intergraph (1981) grew 40-60% yearly during the graphics boom of the early 1980s. In 1984 Intergraph introduced the competitive InterPro 32 workstation, followed by the first dual-screen workstation, Interact.

Intergraph supported open (freely communicating) systems by adopting the industry-standard UNIX operating system and networking Intergraph workstations on the Ethernet standard. The company powered the workstations with the speedy RISC microprocessor (in a variant called CLIPPER) and anticipated the demand for generic workstations unbundled from applications graphics software (introduced in 1987).

Intergraph also absorbed key technologies, buying its CLIPPER supplier (1987), scanning and plotting hardware (Optotronics, 1986; AnaTech, 1987), computer softwares (Tangent Systems, 50%, 1984; 82%, 1988), and software development tools (Quintus, 1989). Intergraph bought a 50% stake in Bentley Systems (creator of Intergraph's MicroStation software, 1987) and contracted with Cadence (in which it has a 5% interest from a 1989 swap of its Tangent shares) for its extensive electronic design software.

A 2nd-generation CLIPPER chip (the C300) fueled the 3000 workstation series (1988) and the successor 6000 series (1990). Future emphases include CLIPPER expansion with 2nd-source manufacturing by Samsung (Korea) and a new CLIPPER version (E100, 4 to 5 times faster than the C300); mapping and UNIX applications software; and sales to smaller A/E/C firms (90% of the market).

HOW MUCH

	9 Yr. Growth	1980	1981	1982	1983	1984	1985	1986	1987	1988	1989
Sales ($ mil)	35.3%	56	91	156	252	404	526	606	641	800	860
Net income ($ mil)	37.3%	5	8	13	29	63	68	70	70	88	80
Income as % of sales	—	8.1%	9.1%	8.4%	11.6%	15.6%	12.9%	11.6%	10.9%	11.0%	9.2%
Earnings per share ($)	31.6%	0.13	0.19	0.28	0.58	1.22	1.25	1.26	1.23	1.55	1.48
Stock price – high ($)	—	—	8.22	12.69	25.69	28.88	38.00	40.50	30.50	32.50	22.75
Stock price – low ($)	—	—	4.50	3.94	11.28	16.38	21.00	15.25	16.50	19.25	13.75
Stock price – close ($)	—	—	6.25	11.94	19.25	27.50	36.75	17.00	24.75	21.00	17.25
P/E – high	—	—	44	45	44	24	30	32	25	21	15
P/E – low	—	—	24	14	19	13	17	12	13	12	9
Dividends per share ($)	0.0%	0.00	0.00	0.00	0.00	0.00	0.00	0.00	0.00	0.00	0.00
Book value per share ($)	47.7%	0.37	1.10	1.41	3.17	4.52	7.28	8.80	10.06	11.72	12.58

1989 Year End:
Debt ratio: 1.1%
Return on equity: 12.2%
Cash (mil): $91
Current ratio: 3.6
Long-term debt (mil): $7
Number of shares (mil): 50
Dividends:
1989 average yield: 0.0%
1989 payout: 0.0%
Market value (mil): $863

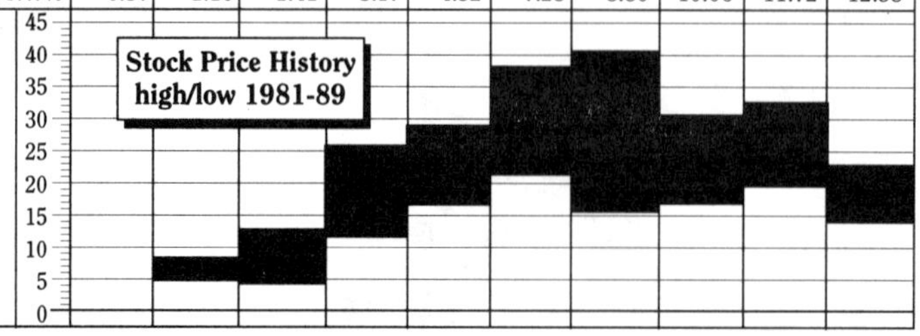

Stock Price History high/low 1981-89

OTC Symbol: INGR
Incorporated: Delaware, 1969
Fiscal year ends: December 31

WHO

Chairman and CEO: James W. Meadlock, age 56, $300,000 pay
President: Eliott D. James, age 49
EVP and CFO: Larry J. Laster, age 38
EVP: Richard H. Lussier, age 44, $224,775 pay
EVP: Maurice J. Romine, age 48, $157,725 pay
Auditors: Ernst & Young
Employees: 8,200

WHERE

HQ: Huntsville, AL 35894
Phone: 205-730-2000
FAX: 205-730-2164 (Investor Relations)

	1989 Sales		1989 Operating Income	
	$ mil	% of total	$ mil	% of total
US	495	57	84	85
Europe	281	33	11	11
Other foreign	84	10	4	4
Adjustments	—	—	(8)	—
Total	**860**	**100**	**91**	**100**

WHAT

	1989 Sales	
	$ mil	% of total
Systems	631	73
Service	229	27
Total	**860**	**100**

Intergraph Systems
Open network architecture
Peripherals (disk and tape drives, line printers, scanning hardware)
Printed circuit boards
Servers
6000 series (CLIPPER-based)
UNIX- and VAX-based software
Workstations
380 (VAX-based)
6000 series (CLIPPER-based)

Intergraph Systems Software
Data Management and Retrieval System (VAX-based)
Interactive Graphics Design System
MicroStation (for workstations, PCs)

Intergraph Applications
Architectural and engineering design
Civil engineering
Electrical design and engineering
Electronic publishing
Electronics design
Energy exploration and development
Geographic information systems
Mechanical design, engineering, and manufacturing
Plant design
Scanning and document management
Surveying and cartography
Utilities (gas and water)

RANKINGS

365th in *Fortune* 500 Industrial Cos.
486th in *Business Week* 1000

COMPETITION

AT&T
Apple
Compaq
Control Data
Data General
Digital Equipment
Hewlett-Packard
IBM
NCR
Prime
Sun Microsystems
Unisys
Wang

INTERNATIONAL BUSINESS MACHINES CORP.

OVERVIEW

IBM is the world's largest data processing firm, easily larger than its top 10 US competitors combined. IBM is a global leader in mainframe computers, PCs, systems software, service/maintenance, automated manufacturing, and semiconductors.

An exemplary multinational, IBM employs virtually all-native work forces in over 130 host countries; Europe alone has over 100,000 IBMers. Foreign sales, which have grown from 43% of total sales to 59% between 1985 and 1989, accounted for 100% of profits in 1989 (US operations lost $325 million).

The transforming innovations of Big Blue (as the company is unofficially, but widely, called) include the FORTRAN computer language, RISC semiconductors, and magnetic disk memory. IBM scientists won the Nobel Prize for Physics in 1986 and 1987; IBM patents exceed 10,000. R&D expenses top $5 billion a year (2nd highest in the US, after GM).

Unparalleled marketing and a no-layoff policy are IBM trademarks. Computer services and software (now a combined 24% of sales) are expected to overtake hardware sales (currently 64%) by 2000.

WHEN

In 1914 National Cash Register's star salesman, 40-year-old Thomas J. Watson, left to rescue the flagging Computing-Tabulating-Recording Company. Watson aggressively marketed C-T-R's Hollerith machine (a punch card tabulator) and supplied tabulators to the US government during WWI, tripling C-T-R's revenues to almost $15 million by 1920.

Watson then expanded operations to Europe, Latin America, and the Far East and in 1924 changed the company name to International Business Machines. IBM soon dominated the market for tabulators, time clocks, and electric typewriters (introduced in 1935), becoming the US's largest office machinery firm by 1940, with sales approaching $50 million. IBM supplied accounting machines during WWII, producing a further tripling in size.

IBM perfected electromechanical calculation (the Harvard Mark I, 1944) but initially dismissed the potential of computers. When Remington Rand's commercial computer (UNIVAC, 1951) began replacing IBM machines, IBM quickly recouped, using its superior R&D and marketing to build a market share near 80% in the 1960s and 1970s; competitors scattered to niches on the periphery.

Triumphs achieved under Thomas J. Watson, Jr. (president in 1952) included IBM's first computer (the 701, 1952), the STRETCH systems (which eliminated vacuum tubes, 1960), and the first compatible family of computers (System/360, 1964; System/370, 1970). Accompanying innovations included the FORTRAN programming language (1957) and floppy disk storage (1971).

IBM later moved into midrange systems (System/38, 1978; AS/400, 1988). The IBM PC (1981) spawned whole new PC-related industries. PC Jr. (1983) failed; the PC AT (1984) and PS/2 (1987) succeeded.

The industry shift to open, smaller systems has caused IBM wrenching change: US employment cuts of 37,000 (1985-1989) achieved through attrition and early retirement inducements, with 10,000 more scheduled for 1990; a 23% increase in customer support (1987-1989) and a 41% increase in software investments in 1989 alone; and R&D shifts to standards such as RISC chips (*e.g.,* the RISC System/6000 workstation series, 1990). IBM also sold many noncomputer businesses, like ROLM telecommunications (to Siemens, 1988) and the copier division (to Kodak, 1988). IBM is negotiating with Clayton & Dubilier to sell its typewriter and printer lines to that firm.

IBM's systems integration focus for the 1990s includes joint ventures (such as the Prodigy electronic information service with Sears) and numerous equity alliances (numbering 75 through 1989, including many software firms).

HOW MUCH

	9 Yr. Growth	1980	1981	1982	1983	1984	1985	1986	1987	1988	1989
Sales ($ mil)	10.2%	26,213	29,070	34,364	40,180	45,937	50,056	51,250	54,217	59,681	62,710
Net income ($ mil)	0.6%	3,562	3,308	4,409	5,485	6,582	6,555	4,789	5,258	5,491	3,758
Income as % of sales	—	13.6%	11.4%	12.8%	13.7%	14.3%	13.1%	9.3%	9.7%	9.2%	6.0%
Earnings per share ($)	0.7%	6.09	5.62	7.33	8.98	10.69	10.54	7.76	8.66	*9.27*	6.47
Stock price – high ($)	—	72.75	71.50	98.00	134.25	128.50	158.75	161.88	175.88	129.50	130.88
Stock price – low ($)	—	50.38	48.38	55.63	92.25	99.00	117.38	119.25	102.00	104.25	93.38
Stock price – close ($)	3.7%	67.88	56.88	96.25	122.00	123.13	155.50	120.00	115.50	121.88	94.13
P/E – high	—	12	13	13	15	12	15	21	20	14	20
P/E – low	—	8	9	8	10	9	11	15	12	11	14
Dividends per share ($)	3.6%	3.44	3.44	3.44	3.71	4.10	4.40	4.40	4.40	4.40	4.73
Book value per share ($)	10.1%	28.18	30.66	33.13	38.02	43.23	51.98	56.73	64.09	66.99	67.01

1989 Year End:
Debt ratio: 21.9%
Return on equity: 9.7%
Cash (mil): $4,961
Current ratio: 1.65
Long-term debt (mil): $10,825
Number of shares (mil): 575
Dividends:
1989 average yield: 5.0%
1989 payout: 73.1%
Market value (mil): $54,094

180
160
140
120
100
80
60
40
20
0

Stock Price History high/low 1980-89

NYSE symbol: IBM
Incorporated: New York, 1911
Fiscal year ends: December 31

WHO

Chairman: John F. Akers, age 55, $1,420,173 pay
President: Jack D. Kuehler, age 57, $918,190 pay
SVP; Chairman, IBM World Trade: C. Michael Armstrong, age 51, $680,300 pay
SVP; General Manager, IBM US: Terry R. Lautenbach, age 51, $680,300 pay
SVP Finance and Planning: Frank A. Metz, Jr., age 56, $677,775 pay
Auditors: Price Waterhouse
Employees: 383,220

WHERE

HQ: Old Orchard Rd., Armonk, NY 10504
Phone: 914-765-1900
FAX: 914-765-4190

	1989 Sales		1989 Net Income	
	$ mil	% of total	$ mil	% of total
US	25,745	41	(325)	(9)
Europe & other	23,170	37	2,676	70
Asia/Pacific	9,202	15	1,296	34
Americas	4,593	7	173	5
Adjustments	—	—	(62)	—
Total	**62,710**	**100**	**3,758**	**100**

WHAT

	1989 Sales	
	$ mil	% of total
Processors	16,087	27
Personal system workstations	8,242	13
Other workstations	4,019	6
Peripherals	11,021	18
Software	8,424	13
Maintenance services	7,070	11
Other information technology	5,841	9
Federal systems	2,006	3
Total	**62,710**	**100**

Brand Names (Current Offerings)
Application System/400
Disk Operating System 4.0
DisplayWrite 5
Enterprise System/3090
LaserPrinter
Micro Channel
Operating System/2
Personal System/1
Personal System/2
Portable 70
Proprinter
Quietwriter
RISC System/6000
Storyboard
System/390

RANKINGS

4th in *Fortune* 500 Industrial Cos.
5th in *Fortune* Global 500 Industrial Cos.
5th in *Fortune* 50 Exporters
4th in *Forbes* Sales 500
1st in *Business Week* 1000
2nd in *Business Week* Global 1000

COMPETITION

Amdahl
Apple
Arthur Andersen
AT&T
Compaq
Computer Associates
Control Data
Cray Research
Data General
Digital Equipment
Fujitsu
Hewlett-Packard
Hitachi
Honeywell
Hyundai
Matsushita
National Semiconductor
NCR
NEC
Siemens
Storage Technology
Sun Microsystems
Tandem
Tandy
Unisys
Wang
Other computer-related companies

INTERNATIONAL FLAVORS & FRAGRANCES INC.

OVERVIEW

New York–based International Flavors & Fragrances is the world's leading independent producer of synthetic tastes and smells. By one estimate IFF holds 13% of the world's market. The company states that it has over 80,000 recipes on file.

Most of IFF's fragrances are sold to makers of perfume, cosmetics, and household cleaners; famous clients include Procter & Gamble, Estée Lauder, Calvin Klein, and Halston. Most of the company's flavors are used in food, drugs, tobacco, and pet food.

In 1989 sales of fragrances increased most in Latin and North America, and both flavor and fragrance sales increased steadily in Pacific Rim countries. IFF hopes to expand sales into former communist bloc countries in the 1990s and, with 69% of its sales from overseas, the company is poised to take advantage of currency fluctuations that weaken the US dollar. With cash almost 30% of its $970 million in assets, it can pursue its capital spending without long-term debt.

IFF expected to spend a record $54 million on R&D in 1990. It researched olfactory neurons with Johns Hopkins Medical School and looked for ways to enhance flavor in microwaveable foods.

WHEN

International Flavors & Fragrances began when a Dutch immigrant and perfumer, A. L. van Ameringen, and William Haebler formed a fragrance company, van Ameringen-Haebler Inc., in New York (1909).

In 1953 the company produced the fragrance for Youth Dew, Estée Lauder's first big cosmetics hit. One biographer of Estée Lauder linked her romantically with van Ameringen after her 1939 divorce (she later remarried ex-husband Joseph before the end of WWII). The business association with van Ameringen's company endured, and by the late 1980s IFF had produced an estimated 90% of Lauder's fragrances.

In 1958 van Ameringen-Haebler bought Polak & Schwartz, a Dutch firm, and changed the name of the combined companies to International Flavors & Fragrances. The US market for fragrances grew as consumers bought items such as air fresheners and as manufacturers began adding fragrances to household items such as laundry detergent. IFF was a major supplier of scents.

In 1963 Henry Walter, the company's counsel, became CEO when van Ameringen retired. Walter expanded IFF's presence overseas, with highest sales in Europe and Latin America. Walter, once pictured in a national magazine riding his bicycle through Manhattan to work, boasted, "Most of the great soap fragrances have been ours," and so were many famous French perfumes. However, because most perfume companies wanted to retain product mystique, IFF often couldn't take credit for its scents.

While most of IFF's products were made for consumer goods manufacturers, under Walter's direction in the 1970s, IFF's R&D personnel experimented to find scents for museum exhibits and even participated in Masters & Johnson research on the connection between sex and smell. Said Walter, "Our business is sex and hunger."

During the early 1980s IFF conducted research into fragrances for relieving stress, lowering blood pressure, and alleviating depression. In 1982 IFF researchers developed a way to bind odors to plastic, a process that has been used by manufacturers of garbage bags and toys.

In 1985 Walter retired, and Eugene Grisanti became CEO. Grisanti reorganized the company's management structure, eliminating the COO position and giving the vice presidents more decision-making power. After a 3-year creative slump, IFF created fragrances for several prestige perfumes, such as Eternity (Calvin Klein) and Halston in 1988.

HOW MUCH

	9 Yr. Growth	1980	1981	1982	1983	1984	1985	1986	1987	1988	1989
Sales ($ mil)	7.6%	448	451	448	461	477	501	621	746	840	870
Net income ($ mil)	9.1%	63	66	63	68	69	70	86	107	129	139
Income as % of sales	—	14.1%	14.7%	14.1%	14.8%	14.5%	13.9%	13.8%	14.3%	15.3%	15.9%
Earnings per share ($)	8.7%	1.73	1.81	1.73	1.87	1.89	1.89	2.29	2.83	3.40	3.65
Stock price – high ($)	—	27.50	23.00	30.00	35.75	29.25	40.00	48.88	58.00	54.50	77.50
Stock price – low ($)	—	16.63	17.88	17.38	23.75	22.88	26.00	34.50	37.25	43.13	48.50
Stock price – close ($)	12.9%	22.75	19.50	27.63	27.25	28.00	40.00	37.25	44.38	49.38	67.75
P/E – high	—	16	13	17	19	15	21	21	21	16	21
P/E – low	—	10	10	10	13	12	14	15	13	13	13
Dividends per share ($)	9.3%	0.89	0.96	1.02	1.05	1.09	1.13	1.18	1.33	1.68	1.98
Book value per share ($)	9.9%	8.62	9.02	9.19	9.39	9.56	11.52	13.87	17.45	18.34	20.09

1989 Year End:
Debt ratio: 0.0%
Return on equity: 19.0%
Cash (mil): $289
Current ratio: 5.16
Long-term debt (mil): $0
Number of shares (mil): 38
Dividends:
1989 average yield: 2.9%
1989 payout: 54.2%
Market value (mil): $2,579

Stock Price History high/low 1980-89

NYSE symbol: IFF
Incorporated: New York, 1909
Fiscal year ends: December 31

WHO

Chairman and President: Eugene P. Grisanti, age 60, $660,000 pay
SVP; President, Fragrances: Ronald D. Anderson, age 57, $418,272 pay
SVP; President, Flavors: Hendrik C. van Baaren, age 50, $347,500 pay
VP Finance and Treasurer: John P. Winandy, age 63, $383,432 pay
Secretary and General Attorney: Wallace G. Dempsey, age 64
Controller: Thomas H. Hoppel, age 59
Auditors: Price Waterhouse
Employees: 4,217

WHERE

HQ: 521 W. 57th St., New York, NY 10019
Phone: 212-765-5500
FAX: 212-708-7132

The company operates 23 flavor and fragrance laboratories in 20 countries and maintains 46 sales offices in 34 countries.

	1989 Sales		1989 Operating Income	
	$ mil	% of total	$ mil	% of total
US	268	31	55	26
Western Europe	370	42	107	49
Other countries	232	27	54	25
Adjustments	—	—	(2)	—
Total	**870**	**100**	**214**	**100**

WHAT

	1989 Sales
	% of total
Fragrances	62
Flavors	38
Total	**100**

Flavors
Baked goods
Beverages
Candy
Convenience foods
Dairy products
Dental hygiene products
Desserts
Diet foods
Drink powders
Pet food
Pharmaceuticals
Tobacco

Fragrances
After-shave lotions
Air fresheners
Cosmetic creams
Deodorants
Detergents
Hair preparations
Household cleaners
Laundry soap
Lipsticks
Lotions and powders
Perfumes
Plastics
Soaps

RANKINGS

368th in *Fortune* 500 Industrial Cos.
279th in *Business Week* 1000
857th in *Business Week* Global 1000

COMPETITION

BASF
Bayer
Hercules
MacAndrews & Forbes
Roche Holding

INTERNATIONAL PAPER COMPANY

OVERVIEW

International Paper is the world's largest integrated paper manufacturer. It is the #1 producer of uncoated free-sheet paper (business needs), the #1 producer of bleached board (milk and food packaging), and the #2 producer of containerboard. International Paper controls about 6.4 million acres of US timberland. The company's products include Hammermill and Springhill (on which this book is printed) white paper and colored papers for the business market, coated papers for the magazine market, and Strathmore and Beckett papers for the fine stationery and art markets.

International Paper embarked on a major restructuring plan in the 1980s. It invested about $7 billion to improve its mills and change its business mix, and spent about $2.6 billion on strategic acquisitions. These activities plus strong demand for its products resulted in a doubling of sales and a tripling of earnings between 1986 and 1989.

WHEN

In 1898, 18 northeastern pulp and paper companies consolidated to lower operating costs. The resulting International Paper Company began with a total of 20 mills in 5 states: Maine, New Hampshire, Vermont, Massachusetts, and New York (including one at Ticonderoga, known for its Ticonderoga paper). Its 60% share of the US newsprint market in 1898 dropped to 26% by 1913 because the company's production did not keep up with demand in the growing US paper market.

These mills depended for wood pulp on the forests of the northeastern US and those in neighboring Canada. However, Canadian provinces were enacting legislation to prevent the export of pulpwood, wanting instead to export finished products. Thus in 1919 International Paper began its expansion into Canada, building a newsprint mill in Three Rivers, Quebec, and forming Canadian International Paper, which purchased the properties of Riordon (an integrated Canadian paper company) in 1925.

In the 1920s International Paper built a hydroelectric plant on the Hudson River, and between 1928 and 1941 the company called itself International Paper & Power. International Paper entered the *kraft* (German for strength) paper market (*e.g.,* paper sacks) in 1925 with the purchase of the Bastrop Pulp & Paper kraft paper mill in Bastrop, Louisiana. Mass production of paper was made possible by the Fourdrinier paper machine, which could make paper in a continuous sheet (invented in France by Nicholas Robert in 1799, improved upon and patented by Henry and Sealy Fourdrinier in England about 1807). International Paper first mass-produced kraft containerboard in 1931 using the Fourdrinier process at its new mill in Panama City, Florida. (The mill was sold in 1979.)

During the 1940s and 1950s International Paper bought Agar Manufacturing (shipping containers, 1940), Single Service Containers (Pure-Pak milk containers, 1946), and Lord Baltimore Press (folding cartons, 1958). The company diversified in the 1960s and 1970s, buying Davol (hospital products, 1968, sold to C. R. Bard in 1980), American Central (land development, 1968, assets sold to developers in 1974), and General Crude Oil (gas and oil, 1975, sold to Mobil Oil in 1979).

In the 1980s International Paper modernized its plants to change its business mix to less cyclical products and became the industry's low-cost producer. After selling Canadian International Paper (newsprint) in 1981, the company embarked on an ambitious acquisition program, buying Hammermill Paper (office paper) in 1986 for $1.1 billion and Masonite (composite wood products) in 1988 for $400 million. In 1987 it purchased privately owned Arvey (paper manufacturers and distributors) and in 1989 bought Aussedat Rey, the 2nd largest paper manufacturer in France, and Zanders, the largest coated-paper manufacturer in West Germany.

HOW MUCH

	9 Yr. Growth	1980	1981	1982	1983	1984	1985	1986	1987	1988	1989
Sales ($ mil)	9.5%	5,043	4,983	4,015	4,357	4,716	4,502	5,500	7,763	9,533	11,378
Net income ($ mil)	11.9%	314	525	161	255	120	131	305	407	754	864
Income as % of sales	—	6.2%	10.5%	4.0%	5.9%	2.5%	2.9%	5.5%	5.2%	7.9%	7.6%
Earnings per share ($)	10.8%	2.99	5.04	1.36	2.31	0.94	1.07	2.90	3.68	6.57	7.52
Stock price – high ($)	—	23.94	25.75	25.81	30.00	29.94	28.88	40.06	57.81	49.38	58.75
Stock price – low ($)	—	15.25	18.56	16.38	23.00	23.00	22.13	24.19	27.00	36.50	45.13
Stock price – close ($)	11.6%	21.00	19.56	24.19	29.50	26.94	25.38	37.56	42.25	46.38	56.50
P/E – high	—	8	5	19	13	32	27	14	16	8	8
P/E – low	—	5	4	12	10	24	21	8	7	6	6
Dividends per share ($)	2.7%	1.20	1.20	1.20	1.20	1.20	1.20	1.20	1.23	1.28	1.53
Book value per share ($)	5.8%	28.51	32.20	32.47	33.38	33.02	33.34	35.05	36.35	41.14	47.35

1989 Year End:
Debt ratio: 31.1%
Return on equity: 17.0%
Cash (mil): $102
Current ratio: 1.13
Long-term debt (mil): $2,324
Number of shares (mil): 109
Dividends:
1989 average yield: 2.7%
1989 payout: 20.3%
Market value (mil): $6,142

Stock Price History high/low 1980-89

60
50
40
30
20
10
0

NYSE symbol: IP
Incorporated: New York, 1941
Fiscal year ends: December 31

WHO

Chairman and CEO: John A. Georges, age 59, $1,310,833 pay
EVP, Timber and Specialty Products: David I. J. Wang, age 58, $558,250 pay
EVP, Packaging Businesses: John T. Dillon, age 51, $510,000 pay
EVP, Pulp and Paper Businesses: Dana G. Mead, age 54, $481,250 pay
SVP and CFO: Robert C. Butler, Jr., age 59
Auditors: Arthur Andersen & Co.
Employees: 63,500

WHERE

HQ: Two Manhattanville Rd., Purchase, NY 10577
Phone: 914-397-1500
FAX: 914-397-1596

International Paper manufactures products in 22 countries and distributes through 177 distribution branches worldwide.

	1989 Sales		1989 Operating Income	
	$ mil	% of total	$ mil	% of total
US	9,937	86	1,608	94
Europe	1,355	12	75	4
Other countries	235	2	29	2
Adjustments	(149)	—	(102)	—
Total	**11,378**	**100**	**1,610**	**100**

WHAT

	1989 Sales		1989 Operating Income	
	$ mil	% of total	$ mil	% of total
Pulp & paper	3,690	31	761	44
Paperboard & packaging	3,395	29	571	33
Wood products & timber	1,196	10	152	9
Specialty products	1,432	12	184	11
Distribution businesses	2,139	18	44	3
Adjustments	(474)	—	(102)	—
Total	**11,378**	**100**	**1,610**	**100**

Products

Bleached board
Coated and art papers
Composite wood products (Masonite)
Containerboard
Copy paper (Hammermill)
Decorative laminates
Folding cartons
Nonwoven products
Paper pulp
Photosensitive films and papers (Ilford)
Printing and writing papers
Pulpwood
Rosins and resins
Sawtimber

RANKINGS

35th in *Fortune* 500 Industrial Cos.
96th in *Fortune* Global 500 Industrial Cos.
27th in *Fortune* 50 Exporters
57th in *Forbes* Sales 500
105th in *Business Week* 1000
315th in *Business Week* Global 1000

COMPETITION

Boise Cascade
Champion International
Eastman Kodak
Georgia-Pacific
James River
Kimberly-Clark
Manville
Mead
Scott
Weyerhaeuser

ITT CORPORATION

OVERVIEW

ITT, one of America's largest widely diversified businesses, operates 9 businesses and has a 30% equity interest in Alcatel N.V. (Netherlands), the world's largest telecommunications equipment company.

ITT's automotive business is a large independent supplier of antilock brake (ITT Teves) and other electronic systems to automobile manufacturers in 12 countries. The company supplies electronic components and semiconductors to European satellite TV systems and electronic dashboard systems to automobile manufacturers. ITT Fluid Technology makes pumps, fluid controls, valves, and meters used in heating, cooling, water and wastewater, and industrial systems.

ITT designs and produces tactical military equipment, such as SINCGARS, the US Army's combat radio system. ITT Rayonier is the 26th largest US wood products manufacturer.

ITT services include ITT Hartford, the 9th largest US property/casualty insurer (based on new premiums written in 1989); ITT Financial, a large independent commercial and consumer finance company; ITT Sheraton, a 454-hotel network serving 25 million guests annually in 64 countries; and ITT World Directories, the leading publisher of Yellow Pages directories outside the US.

WHEN

Colonel Sosthenes Behn founded the International Telephone and Telegraph Corporation in 1920. The company initially managed Cuban and Puerto Rican telephone companies. By 1925 Behn had purchased 3 small Spanish telephone companies to form Compañía Telefónica Nacional de España (CTNE), comanaged with a government board.

In 1925 ITT purchased International Western Electric (renamed International Standard Electric) from AT&T, making ITT a major international phone equipment manufacturer. In the late 1920s the company bought United River Plate Telephone of Buenos Aires, the Mackay Companies (parent of Postal Telegraph and Commercial Cable), and Societatea Anonima Romana de Telefoane, from the Romanian government.

In the 1940s ITT sold Romana de Telefoane (1941), CTNE (1945), and River Plate (1946) to concentrate on equipment manufacturing rather than utilities. During the 1950s the company relied on its overseas operations for growth and financial strength. In 1959 Harold Geneen became CEO.

Geneen doubled company revenues and profits; 1962 revenues passed $1 billion for the first time. In 1964 the company formed ITT Financial Services by purchasing Aetna Finance, Kellogg Credit, and a 50% interest in Great International Life Insurance and by starting ITT Credit. This began a major shift by ITT to financial and consumer services.

The company added Avis car rental and a dozen other firms in 1965 and 1966. In 1968 ITT bought Continental Baking (Hostess and Wonder brands), Levitt & Sons (home construction), Sheraton hotels, and Rayonier (wood products). In 1969 it purchased Canteen Corporation (vending machines), Hartford Insurance, and Grinnell (fire-protection sprinkler systems).

In the early 1970s Geneen sold Avis, Levitt, and Canteen. But by 1979, ITT was only marginally profitable, posting earnings of just $382 million on sales of $22 billion.

After the Geneen era, Rand Araskog, CEO since 1979, sold all or part of 100 companies, leaving 9 basic businesses. In 1986 ITT spun off its European telecommunications operation into a joint venture, Alcatel N.V., run by a French company (Compagnie Générale d'Electricité). All told, between 1984 and 1987 the company's work force was slashed by about 2/3, leaving ITT today a leaner and more efficient conglomerate, capable of focusing on its strategic business segments.

HOW MUCH

	9 Yr. Growth	1980	1981	1982	1983	1984	1985	1986	1987	1988	1989
Sales ($ mil)	0.9%	21,996	23,197	21,921	20,249	19,553	20,007	17,437	19,525	19,355	20,054
Net income ($ mil)	0.3%	894	695	703	675	303	286	528	1,085	858	922
Income as % of sales	—	4.0%	3.0%	3.2%	3.3%	1.5%	1.4%	3.0%	5.6%	4.4%	4.6%
Earnings per share ($)	0.6%	5.95	4.63	4.68	4.44	2.00	1.83	3.45	7.13	5.97	6.30
Stock price – high ($)	—	33.88	35.63	34.38	47.75	47.38	38.88	59.50	66.38	54.88	64.50
Stock price – low ($)	—	22.88	25.13	22.38	30.00	20.63	28.38	35.38	41.75	43.25	49.75
Stock price – close ($)	7.8%	30.00	29.75	31.25	44.75	29.38	38.00	53.38	44.50	50.38	58.88
P/E – high	—	6	8	7	11	24	21	17	9	9	10
P/E – low	—	4	5	5	7	10	16	10	6	7	8
Dividends per share ($)	(5.2%)	2.45	2.62	2.70	2.76	1.88	1.00	1.00	1.06	1.31	1.51
Book value per share ($)	2.6%	45.58	43.16	42.67	41.81	40.87	43.75	48.28	55.52	58.05	57.67

1989 Year End:
Debt ratio: 46.0%
Return on equity: 10.9%
Cash (mil): $2,927
Assets (mil): $45,503
Long-term debt (mil): $6,875
Number of shares (mil): 123
Dividends:
1989 average yield: 2.6%
1989 payout: 24.0%
Market value (mil): $7,228

Stock Price History high/low 1980-89

70 60 50 40 30 20 10 0

NYSE symbol: ITT
Incorporated: Delaware, 1968
Fiscal year ends: December 31

WHO

Chairman and CEO: Rand V. Araskog, age 58, $2,387,562 pay
President and COO: DeRoy C. Thomas, age 64, $1,569,624 pay
VC and CFO: M. Cabell Woodward, Jr., age 61, $1,040,816 pay
EVP and General Counsel: Howard J. Aibel, $913,020 pay
Auditors: Arthur Andersen & Co.
Employees: 119,000

WHERE

HQ: 320 Park Ave., New York, NY 10022
Phone: 212-752-6000
FAX: 212-940-2243

ITT has operations in more than 80 countries.

	1989 Sales		1989 Operating Income	
	$ mil	% of total	$ mil	% of total
US	14,327	72	797	58
Western Europe	4,866	24	475	34
Canada & other	861	4	110	8
Adjustments	—	—	693	—
Total	**20,054**	**100**	**2,075**	**100**

WHAT

	1989 Sales		1989 Operating Income	
	$ mil	% of total	$ mil	% of total
Insurance	8,689	43	322	23
Auto products	2,852	14	211	15
Finance	1,806	9	195	14
Defense technology	1,580	8	82	6
Wood products	1,151	6	248	18
Electronic components	1,134	5	67	5
Fluid technology	960	5	102	8
Hotels	782	4	117	8
Information services	754	4	94	7
Other	346	2	(56)	(4)
Total	**20,054**	**100**	**2,075**	**100**

Major Subsidiaries/Affiliates
Alcatel, N.V. (37%)
Hartford Fire Insurance
ITT Cannon
ITT Rayonier
Sheraton Hotels

RANKINGS

10th in *Fortune* 50 Diversified Financial Cos.
23rd in *Forbes* Sales 500
81st in *Business Week* 1000
250th in *Business Week* Global 1000

COMPETITION

Automobile brake manufacturers
Communications equipment companies
Defense communications manufacturers
Electronic component manufacturers
Finance companies
Hotels
Insurance companies
Pulp and wood products companies
Water pump manufacturers

JACK ECKERD CORPORATION

OVERVIEW

Jack Eckerd, based in Clearwater, Florida, is the 3rd largest drugstore chain in the country, with 1,630 stores in 14 East Coast and southern states. The company has been privately held since management led a $1.2 billion LBO in 1986.

Eckerd drugstores rely heavily upon prescription sales, which account for 38% of company revenues. The company employs nearly 4,000 pharmacists who fill over 70 million prescriptions each year.

In 1989 the company acquired Insta-Care Pharmacy Services, a provider of prescription services to nursing homes and institutions in 6 states. Through this purchase and Eckerd's own store labs, the company has become one of the nation's largest institutional providers.

Jack Eckerd operates traditional drugstores, 189 of which include an Express Photo minilab.

The company also has 2 optical specialty store chains: Eckerd Optical provides traditional optical services, while the rapidly expanding Visionworks uses a "superstore" format with large selection, an on-site optometrist, and one-hour service.

WHEN

In 1898 Jack Eckerd's father, J. Milton Eckerd, started one of the first drugstore chains, in Erie, Pennsylvania. Jack worked for his father's company during the Great Depression but left to start his own chain of stores in Florida by buying 3 locations in Tampa and Clearwater in 1952. He fought the state's fair trade laws, which prevented him from underselling his competitors, in a case that went all the way to the Florida Supreme Court. He won the case.

Eckerd incorporated the company as publicly held Eckerd Drugs of Florida in 1961. The company began purchasing other companies, beginning with Old Dominion Candies in 1966 (sold 1972). In 1968 the company bought Jackson's/Byrons, renamed J. Byrons, a Miami junior department store chain. The company expanded into other areas in 1969 with its purchases of Gray Security Service and food service supplier Kurman Company, both sold in 1976.

Jack Eckerd began a political career in 1970 with an unsuccessful run for governor of Florida. He donated $10 million to Florida Presbyterian College, renamed Eckerd College, in 1971, and in 1974 he resumed his political ambitions by capturing the Republican nomination for the US Senate, but he didn't win the seat. He joined the Ford administration in 1975 as head of the General Services Administration, leaving the company in the hands of Stewart Turley, the current chairman.

Meanwhile, the company continued to expand its drugstores, buying Brown's Thrift City Wholesale Drugs and Mading-Dugan Drugs in 1970, then Ward Cut-Rate Drug and Eckerd Drugs Eastern in 1973. Finally, in 1977 Jack Eckerd Drugs bought Eckerd Drugs of Charlotte from Edward O' Herron, Jr., son-in-law of Milton Eckerd, bringing all the Eckerd stores under its control. Eckerd built up its Texas operations with the purchase of Abilene-based Sav-X drugstores (1980) and 40 Sommers Drug Stores from Malone & Hyde (1981). The company bought American Home Video (Video Concepts stores, an early video operation) in 1981, selling it and J. Byrons in 1985.

Eckerd's management turned to Merrill Lynch Capital Partners to handle a leveraged buyout of the company in 1986. The investor group included Merrill Lynch and members of Eckerd's management. The same year Eckerd closed 45 stores because of poor performance or potential, sold 11 stores in Tulsa, bought 32 Shoppers Drug Mart stores in Florida, and started 50 new stores. The company began remodeling stores, completing 250-300 units per year since the buyout at an annual cost of $20 million.

In 1987 the company's emphasis on health care resulted in 52% of store sales being prescription and over-the-counter drug sales; prescription sales approached $1 billion that year. Eckerd also opened 23 Visionworks stores and 79 Express Photo locations during the 1987-1989 period. Eckerd acquired 32 drugstores in 1989 and 220 stores from the bankrupt Ohio-based Revco chain in 1990.

HOW MUCH

	9 Yr. Growth	1980	1981	1982	1983	1984	1985	1986	1987	1988	1989
Sales ($ mil)	8.3%	1,548	1,753	2,080	2,325	2,622	2,509	1,912	2,727	2,876	3,171
Net income ($ mil)	—	69	79	71	72	85	58	(146)	(137)	(1)	(8)
Income as % of sales	—	4.5%	4.5%	3.4%	3.1%	3.3%	2.3%	(7.6%)	(5.0%)	0.0%	(0.3%)
Number of stores	4.1%	1,326	1,417	1,688	1,797	1,931	1,688	1,753	1,736	1,790	1,910

1989 Year End:
Debt ratio: 130.3%
Return on equity: —
Cash (mil): $10
Current ratio: 1.32
Long-term debt (mil): $896

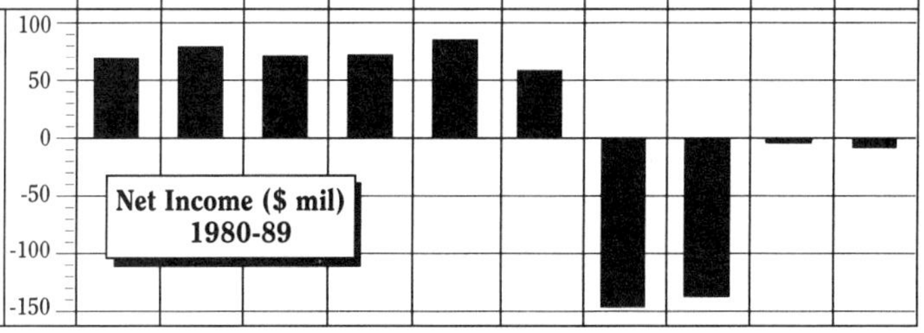

Private company
Incorporated: Florida, 1961
Fiscal year ends: Saturday closest to January 31

WHO

Chairman and President: Stewart Turley
President, Eckerd Drug Company: Harry W. Lambert
EVP, Eckerd Drug Company: Ronald D. Peterson
SVP Finance Administration: John W. Boyle
Auditors: KPMG Peat Marwick
Employees: 30,000

WHERE

HQ: 8333 Bryan Dairy Rd., PO Box 4689, Clearwater, FL 34618
Phone: 813-397-7461
FAX: 813-398-8369 (Public Affairs)

Jack Eckerd operates 1,630 drugstores (before the Revco purchase) in 14 states, with the highest concentration in Florida and Texas. The company also operates other specialty retail formats in 8 states.

	1989 Drugstores	
	# of locations	% of total
Florida	489	30
Texas	408	25
North Carolina	181	11
Georgia	164	10
Louisiana	114	7
South Carolina	80	5
Other	194	12
Total	**1,630**	**100**

WHAT

	1989 Store Formats	
	# of locations	% of total
Drugstores	1,630	85
Optical Centers	62	3
Visionworks	29	2
Express Photo	189	10
Total	**1,910**	**100**

Drugstores
Cosmetics
Health care advice
Over-the-counter drugs
Prescription drugs

Optical Centers

Visionworks
Contact lenses
Frames
One-hour service
Prescription lenses

Express Photo
One-hour minilabs
Photo finishing

RANKINGS

39th in *Forbes* 400 US Private Cos.

COMPETITION

American Stores
Grand Metropolitan
Melville
Rite Aid
Walgreen

JAMES RIVER CORPORATION

OVERVIEW

Richmond-based James River is a young company (founded 1969) and yet it is already #2 in the worldwide paper industry; only the much older International Paper (founded 1898) is larger. The buying fever of founders Halsey (CEO) and Williams (president) accounts for the tremendous growth of James River, from earnings of $166,000 in 1970 to $255 million in 1989.

James River is the largest US manufacturer of paper towel and tissue products and of paperboard and plastic beverage and food service products. It is the #1 world manufacturer of specialty papers for industry.

In August 1990 James River announced that it would sell 28 mills and close others due to poor results. This will result in a one-time charge to earnings of about $150 million and will lower the company's revenues by 25%. With the resulting capital it will reduce debt, buy back shares, and improve its operations.

NYSE symbol: JR
Incorporated: Virginia, 1969
Fiscal year ends: Last Sunday in April

WHO

Chairman and CEO: Brenton S. Halsey, age 62, $977,000 pay
President and COO: Robert C. Williams, age 59, $835,000 pay
SVP, CFO, and Group Executive: David J. McKittrick, age 43, $393,539 pay
Auditors: Coopers & Lybrand
Employees: 42,000

WHEN

In 1969 Ethyl Corporation (Richmond, Virginia) wanted to sell Albemarle Paper Company's Hollywood Mill, its small (100 employees), unprofitable paper manufacturing company. Ethyl executives Brenton Halsey and Robert Williams, some Albemarle employees, and a few investors joined forces to buy the Hollywood Mill, located on the James River in Richmond. Halsey became chairman and CEO, and Williams became president and COO of the resulting company, James River Paper. The company initially focused on new, special paper products, developing a new grade of oil filter paper for AC Spark Plug (division of General Motors) that same year. In 1973 the company went public and changed its name to James River Corporation of Virginia.

The company embarked on the course of buying paper and pulp enterprises from other companies rather than starting new ones. It purchased 80% of Pepperell Paper (packaging papers; East Pepperell, Massachusetts; 1971) from St. Regis Paper, and Weyerhaeuser Massachusetts (specialty papers; Fitchburg, Massachusetts; 1975) from Weyerhaeuser Co. In 1974 James River bought Peninsular Paper (Ypsilanti, Michigan) and in 1977 Curtis Paper (Newark, Delaware) and Rochester Paper (Rochester, Michigan). The company also purchased Riegel Products (packaging and electrical papers; Milford, New Jersey) from Southwest Forest Products in 1977.

James River entered the industrial film products market in 1978, buying Scott Graphics from Scott Paper, and the wood pulp business in 1980, buying Brown Paper from Gulf & Western. *Fortune* magazine first ranked James River in its top 500 companies in 1981, at 447. Net sales were then $561.3 million.

In 1982 the company bought Dixie/Northern paper and forest properties from American Can Company for $455 million, thereby becoming the maker of Dixie cups, Northern towels and tissues, and Marathon folding cartons. A year later James River purchased the pulp and papermaking facilities of Diamond International (Vanity Fair products).

James River expanded into Europe in 1984 (GB Papers, Scotland). In 1986 the company bought the pulp, papermaking, flexible packaging, and distribution businesses of Crown Zellerbach for $1.6 billion, then sold Crown's distribution concern for $250 million. Crown Zellerbach (San Francisco), founded about 1870, was one of the world's largest integrated paper companies, operating primarily in the western US. Crown had sales of $3.06 billion in 1985. The Crown assets, including brand names Nice'n Soft, Zee, and Spill Mate, brought James River to #2 in the US paper towel and tissue market.

James River bought 50% of Kaysersberg, France's leading manufacturer of paper towel and tissue products, in 1987. The company sold its Nonwovens Group in 1990.

WHERE

HQ: Tredegar St., Richmond, VA 23219
Phone: 804-644-5411
FAX: 804-649-4428

James River has 141 manufacturing plants (including those of its affiliates), of which 108 are located in the US, 24 in Europe, 7 in Canada, 1 in Mexico, and 1 in Turkey.

WHAT

	1989 Sales		1989 Operating Income	
	$ mil	% of total	$ mil	% of total
Paper & other products	4,009	68	485	74
Packaging & food service products	1,863	32	168	26
Adjustments	—	—	(72)	—
Total	**5,872**	**100**	**581**	**100**

	1989 Sales	
	$ mil	% of total
Hygienic paper products	1,563	27
Communications paper	1,332	23
Industrial packaging papers	849	14
Other paper	264	4
Food & consumer packaging	968	17
Food & beverage service products	896	15
Total	**5,872**	**100**

Product Lines
Baby wipes (Natural Touch)
Baking cups
Coated films and imaging materials
Coffee filters
Computer paper
Copy paper
Facial tissue (Zee)
Flexible multilayer packaging
Food wraps
High-volume forms bond
Institutional hygienic paper products
Laminated foam plates and bowls
Offset printing paper
Paper cups (Dixie), plates, and napkins
Paper napkins (Vanity Fair, Zee)
Paper towels (Brawny, Gala, Spill Mate)
Paperboard cartons
Plastic cups, plates, and utensils
Specialty industrial papers
Specialty packaging papers
Textured and colored printing media
Toilet paper (Northern, Nice'n Soft, Aurora)

RANKINGS

81st in *Fortune* 500 Industrial Cos.
220th in *Fortune* Global 500 Industrial Cos.
141st in *Forbes* Sales 500
325th in *Business Week* 1000
975th in *Business Week* Global 1000

COMPETITION

Boise Cascade
Champion International
Georgia-Pacific
International Paper
Kimberly-Clark
Mead
Mobil
Procter & Gamble
Reynolds Metals
Scott
Weyerhaeuser

HOW MUCH

	9 Yr. Growth	1980	1981	1982	1983	1984	1985	1986	1987	1988	1989
Sales ($ mil)	35.8%	374	561	773	1,656	2,301	2,492	2,607	4,479	5,098	5,872
Net income ($ mil)	35.4%	17	21	22	55	98	101	95	170	209	255
Income as % of sales	—	4.5%	3.8%	2.9%	3.3%	4.3%	4.1%	3.7%	3.8%	4.1%	4.3%
Earnings per share ($)	12.9%	0.96	0.98	0.85	1.48	1.97	1.93	1.73	2.03	2.36	2.87
Stock price – high ($)	—	7.78	7.56	10.37	16.94	28.17	23.92	26.42	35.00	43.75	29.75
Stock price – low ($)	—	4.25	4.26	6.56	5.89	15.44	15.67	15.83	22.00	18.50	21.13
Stock price – close ($)	19.6%	5.70	6.93	8.78	16.83	23.58	19.17	26.42	33.88	23.75	28.63
P/E – high	—	8	8	12	11	14	12	15	17	19	10
P/E – low	—	4	4	8	4	8	8	9	11	8	7
Dividends per share ($)	15.6%	0.13	0.14	0.18	0.18	0.27	0.37	0.37	0.40	0.40	0.48
Book value per share ($)	21.8%	4.26	5.30	6.01	9.32	11.75	13.35	14.40	21.22	23.12	25.24

1989 Year End:
Debt ratio: 45.0%
Return on equity: 11.9%
Cash (mil): $24
Current ratio: 1.98
Long-term debt (mil): $1,918
Number of shares (mil): 81
Dividends:
1989 average yield: 1.7%
1989 payout: 16.7%
Market value (mil): $2,320

Stock Price History high/low 1980-89

JARDINE MATHESON HOLDINGS, LTD.

OVERVIEW

Jardine Matheson is a holding company controlled by the Keswick family, descendants of one of its founders. Most of Jardine's investments are Hong Kong–based and include prime Hong Kong real estate, Mandarin Oriental hotels, Dairy Farm Supermarkets, Pizza Hut restaurants, trading companies, auto dealerships, stock brokerages, and insurance companies.

In light of the UK's agreement to transfer control of Hong Kong to China in 1997, Jardine has a stated goal of reducing its Hong Kong assets from 75% to 50% of the company's total. Jardine has reincorporated in Bermuda and lowered its stake in several of its Hong Kong–based holdings in recent years.

WHEN

Scotsmen William Jardine and James Matheson first met in Bombay in 1820. In 1832 they established Jardine, Matheson (Jardine) in Canton, the only city in which China, then a closed society, allowed foreigners to live. The trading company started shipping tea from China to Europe and smuggling opium from India to China. In 1839 Chinese authorities attempted to stop the drug trade, seizing 20,000 chests of opium, 7,000 of them Jardine's. Jardine convinced Britain to send gunboats to China, precipitating the First Opium War. China lost and signed an 1842 treaty opening 5 ports and ceding Hong Kong to Britain.

Jardine moved its headquarters to Hong Kong and resumed trading in opium. The Second Opium War resulted in Chinese concessions, including the opening of 11 more ports and the legalization of opium importation. Jardine flourished in China as it opened. The company left the politically dangerous opium business and entered brewing, silk trading, textiles, banking, insurance, and sugar; formed real estate company Hong Kong Land (HKL); introduced steamships to China; and built the country's first railroad. In 1930 employment reached 113,000.

The Sino-Japanese war and WWII shut down Jardine. In 1941 Tony Keswick, a Jardine relative and the company's *taipan* (big boss), was shot in Shanghai by a patriotic Japanese community leader.

In 1945 Jardine reopened in Hong Kong with an airline, a brewery, textile mills, and real estate operations. Attempts to reestablish operations in China ended in 1954 after the Communist takeover. Proceeds from Jardine's 1961 public offering (oversubscribed 56 to one) were used to expand into shipping.

In 1973 Jardine bought Reunion Properties (real estate, Britain) and Theo Davies (trading, sugar, Hawaii). In the 1970s local competition and the diminishing need for Hong Kong trading companies hurt the company. By 1980 Jardine was a takeover target. *Taipan* David Newbigging erected a defense by arranging for extensive crossholdings of Jardine and HKL stock. The heavy debt incurred pushed Jardine to the brink of bankruptcy, forcing the company to sell Reunion.

Tony Keswick's son Simon succeeded Newbigging in 1983 and in the next 2 years sold numerous businesses, including Jardine's sugar and shipping units, to lower debt. He invested in Mercedes Benz distributorships and fast food franchises, successfully turning Jardine around. In 1984, 9 months after the UK and China negotiated the 1997 transfer of Hong Kong to Chinese control, Keswick announced the relocation of Jardine's legal headquarters to Bermuda. In a 1986 antitakeover transaction, the company created Jardine Strategic Holdings to hold interests in HKL and its spin-offs.

In 1987 Jardine aborted its acquisition of 20% of Bear Stearns (stock brokerage, US) following the 1987 stock market crash, leading to litigation that continues as of this writing.

HOW MUCH

$=HK$7.8 (Dec. 31,1989)	9 Yr. Growth	1980	1981	1982	1983	1984	1985	1986	1987	1988	1989
Sales (HK$ mil)	8.1%	7,467	9,266	11,240	10,644	8,881	10,497	10,416	12,720	14,817	15,058
Net income (HK$ mil)	13.0%	525	723	708	139	80	157	499	785	1,113	1,577
Income as % of sales	—	7.0%	7.8%	6.3%	1.3%	0.9%	1.5%	4.6%	6.2%	7.5%	10.5%
Earnings per share (HK$)*	11.0%	*1.15*	*1.36*	*1.26*	*0.20*	*0.13*	*0.30*	*0.90*	*1.47*	*2.04*	*2.95*
Stock price – high (HK$)	—	26.07	19.79	13.29	11.50	10.29	9.86	16.86	28.40	14.90	25.50
Stock price – low (HK$)	—	8.39	8.79	8.07	5.64	3.93	5.75	7.86	8.50	9.90	14.30
Stock price – close (HK$)	3.3%	18.14	14.36	9.29	8.00	6.21	9.79	16.07	10.30	14.60	24.40
P/E – high	—	23	15	11	58	79	33	19	19	7	9
P/E – low	—	7	6	6	28	30	19	9	6	5	5
Dividends per share (HK$)	5.8%	0.57	0.57	0.57	0.29	0.07	0.07	0.29	0.48	0.65	0.95
Book value per share (HK$)	7.2%	9.67	11.91	11.06	9.18	7.32	8.26	8.67	10.02	15.83	18.13

1989 Year End:
Debt ratio: 10%
Return on equity: 8.7%
Cash (mil): HK$3,992
Long-term debt (mil): HK$1,232
Number of shares (mil): 627
Dividends:
1989 average yield: 3.9%
1989 payout: 32.2%
Market value (mil): $1,961
Sales (mil): $1,931

Stock Price History high/low 1980-89

30
25
20
15
10
5
0

*not fully diluted

Principal exchange: Hong Kong
Incorporated: Bermuda, 1984
Fiscal year ends: December 31

WHO

Chairman: Henry Keswick
Managing Director: Nigel Rich
Auditors: Price Waterhouse
Employees: 94,000

WHERE

HQ: Jardine House, Connaught Rd. Central, Hong Kong
Phone: 011-852-5-843-8388
FAX: 011-852-5-845-9005
US Subsidiary, Theo H. Davies & Co.: Davies Pacific Center, 841 Bishop St., Suite 2300, Honolulu, HI 96802
Phone: 808-531-8531
FAX: 808-521-7352

Jardine companies operate in 28 countries, primarily in the Asia-Pacific region.

	1989 Sales		1989 Net Income*	
	HK $ mil	% of total	HK $ mil	% of total
Hong Kong & China	6,089	40	855	54
Australasia	1,088	7	84	5
Europe	3,883	26	116	8
North America	2,291	15	126	8
Northeast Asia	580	4	251	16
Southeast Asia	1,127	8	145	9
Total	**15,058**	**100**	**1,577**	**100**

WHAT

	1989 Sales		1989 Net Income*	
	HK$ mil	% of total	HK$ mil	% of total
Marketing & distribution	9,223	61	585	37
Financial svcs.	2,277	15	426	27
Engineering & construction	2,553	17	90	6
Transport svcs.	858	6	195	12
Property	147	1	293	18
Corporate	—	—	(12)	—
Total	**15,058**	**100**	**1577**	**100**

* including profits in companies

Major Subsidiaries & Associated Companies
Jardine Fleming (50%)
Corporate banking
Investment management
Stock brokerage
Jardine Insurance Brokers
Jardine Pacific
Auto dealerships
Construction
Diverse services
Property
Trading and distribution
Jardine Strategic (54%)
Dairy Farm (supermarkets, restaurants, 45%)
Hong Kong Land (real estate, 33%)
Jardine Matheson Holdings (36%)
Mandarin Oriental (hotels, 48%)

RANKINGS

715th in *Business Week* Global 1000

COMPETITION

Hutchison Whampoa
Hyundai
Mitsubishi
Samsung
Financial services companies

JOHN HANCOCK MUTUAL LIFE INSURANCE CO.

OVERVIEW

Boston-based John Hancock is the 9th largest life insurance and 5th largest mutual life insurance company in the US, with $32.3 billion in assets at the end of 1989.

In addition to traditional life insurance and annuities, John Hancock offers ProtectCare, new long-term health protection against nursing and home health care costs. John Hancock provides group insurance services to 400 large multinational corporations and smaller companies.

The company's institutional and investment products currently have about 20% of assets under management in guaranteed investment contracts (guaranteed rate of return and fixed term) that are sold to pension plans. John Hancock Realty Services originated about $750 million in mortgage loans in 1989 for accounts it managed.

John Hancock sponsors running and fitness clinics in which world-class athletes have instructed 40,000 youngsters nationwide. The company also launched a pilot program to give Boston high school students the skills needed to get and keep jobs.

WHEN

Albert Murdock and other Boston businessmen founded John Hancock Mutual Life Insurance Company, named in honor of the signer of the Declaration of Independence, in 1862. Murdock became the company's first agent in Boston. In 1865 the company added agents in Pennsylvania, Illinois, Connecticut, and Missouri.

In 1866 the company began making an annual distribution (instead of every 5 years) of surplus to policyholders who had paid annual premiums. In 1879 John Hancock became the first US mutual life insurance company to offer industrial insurance (weekly premium life insurance in small amounts). The company also was a pioneer in granting dividends and cash surrender values (amount returned to policyholder when policy cancelled) with industrial insurance. In 1902 the company's weekly premium agencies began to sell annual premium insurance. By 1912, 50 years after its founding, the company had more than $600 million of insurance in force.

John Hancock began offering annuities in 1922, group insurance in 1924, and individual health insurance in 1957. In 1968 the company formed John Hancock Advisers (mutual funds) and John Hancock International Group Program (group health and life insurance to overseas divisions of US companies and to foreign companies). In 1969 the company bought Maritime Life Assurance (Canada). In the early 1970s the company started property and casualty insurance operations in partnership with Sentry Insurance.

In 1980 the company started an equipment-leasing company and introduced variable life insurance (death benefit linked to investment performance of its own investment account). Entry into the securities brokerage business came in 1982 when John Hancock bought Tucker Anthony & R. L. Day, a Boston-based regional firm with 36 offices. In the same year the company began offering mortgage banking services and tax-shelter investments. In 1983 the company introduced universal life (choice in amounts and timing of premium payments). John Hancock also bought Gabriele, Hueglin & Cashman, a New York fixed-income security and municipal bond firm, in 1985.

Under CEO E. James Morton, John Hancock entered the consumer banking business in 1985 to offer a complete line of financial services (forming First Signature Bank & Trust in New Hampshire). The company added Sutro & Co., a San Francisco investment firm with 12 California offices, in 1986. In 1986 and 1987 John Hancock started timber real estate funds for tax-exempt pension plans; by 1990 the company had more than $600 million of timber assets under management.

John Hancock also has been known in the 1980s for some nontraditional investments such as venture capital and agriculture.

HOW MUCH

Life Insurance Only	9 Yr. Growth	1980	1981	1982	1983	1984	1985	1986	1987	1988	1989
Assets ($ mil)	5.7%	18,761	19,937	21,710	23,459	24,671	26,256	27,213	27,355	28,315	30,925
Premium & annuity income ($ mil)	10.6%	2,436	2,426	2,533	2,397	2,348	2,351	4,174	4,403	4,866	6,018
Net investment income ($ mil)	7.1%	1,231	1,333	1,387	1,394	1,450	1,443	1,406	2,090	2,127	2,287
Net income ($ mil)	—	—	—	—	—	—	—	—	—	185	232
Net income as % of assets	—	—	—	—	—	—	—	—	—	0.7%	0.7%
Life insurance in force ($ bil)	4.5%	133.7	145.6	147.0	153.2	158.7	159.0	166.5	177.4	184.7	198.2

1989 Company Totals:
Total assets (mil): $32,344
Revenue (mil): $9,451
Surplus (mil): $1,234
Premiums (mil): $6,368
Net investment income (mil): $2,617
Policyowner dividends (mil): $391.7
Total life insurance in force (mil): $198,180

Mutual company
Incorporated: Massachusetts, 1862
Fiscal year ends: December 31

WHO

Chairman and CEO: E. James Morton, age 62
VC, President, and COO: Stephen L. Brown, age 52
CFO: William L. Boyan, age 52
General Counsel: Richard S. Scipione, age 51
Auditors: Ernst & Young
Employees: 15,655

WHERE

HQ: PO Box 111, Boston, MA 02117
Phone: 617-572-6000
FAX: 617-572-1899

John Hancock is licensed in all 50 states and the District of Columbia. It is also authorized in Puerto Rico, the US Virgin Islands, and Canada.

WHAT

	12/31/89 Assets $ mil	% of total
Bonds	10,962	34
Mortgage loans	10,604	33
Assets in separate accounts	4,244	13
Policyowner loans	2,086	6
Other assets	4,448	14
Total	**32,344**	**100**

	1989 Income (Before Expenses) $ mil	% of total
Premiums	6,368	67
Net investment income	2,617	28
Other income	466	5
Total	**9,451**	**100**

Financial Services
Group life, accident, and health insurance
Group retirement funds
Guaranteed investment contracts
John Hancock's First Signature Bank & Trust's credit cards
Life insurance and annuities
Long-term care insurance
Mortgage loans
Mutual funds
Property and casualty insurance
Securities brokerage and investment banking

RANKINGS

9th in *Fortune* 50 Life Insurance Cos.

COMPETITION

Aetna
American Express
AIG
Blue Cross
CIGNA
Equitable
First Executive
Kemper
Massachusetts Mutual
Metropolitan
New York Life
Northwestern Mutual
Prudential
Primerica
Sears
State Farm
Teachers Insurance
Transamerica
Travelers
USF&G
Mortage lenders
Other life insurance companies

JOHNSON & JOHNSON

OVERVIEW

Johnson & Johnson ranks first in total sales among world pharmaceutical companies, but more than 1/2 its business is in health products other than drugs — diagnostic equipment, orthopedic implants, infusion devices, monitors, and other medical equipment. An extensive line of consumer products includes such well-known names as Band-Aid and Tylenol.

Half of J&J's business is outside the US, with 42% of its profit coming from Europe through subsidiaries like Cilag and Janssen. J&J develops and markets new drugs in Japan through Janssen-Kyowa. In conjunction with the biotech firm Chiron, J&J developed the first screening test for hepatitis C, sold overseas and introduced in the US in 1990.

A major advertiser, J&J ranked 20th in the US in ad expenses in 1988, spending nearly $500 million. *Fortune* magazine in 1990 called J&J the most admired company in community and environmental responsibility.

WHEN

Brothers James Johnson and Edward Mead Johnson founded the medical products company that bears the family name in 1885 in New Brunswick, New Jersey. In 1886 Robert Johnson joined with his brothers to manufacture and sell an antiseptic surgical dressing he had developed after being inspired by surgeon Joseph Lister, who first advocated clean surgery. J&J became America's foremost supplier of individually wrapped sterile dressings.

In 1897 Edward Mead Johnson left to found the drug company Mead Johnson (now a part of Bristol-Myers Squibb). In 1916 J&J bought its first subsidiary, gauze-maker Chicopee Manufacturing. A by-product of Johnson's dressing, the Band-Aid, was introduced in 1921 along with Johnson's Baby Cream.

In 1932 Robert Johnson, Jr. became chairman and served until 1963. General Johnson (Army general in WWII) believed in decentralization; managers were given substantial freedom, a principle still in use today. Early product lines formed into business units like Ortho (birth control products) and Ethicon (sutures) in the 1940s. In the mid-1950s the company began to acquire other businesses, creating the divisions that today comprise J&J. In 1959 J&J bought McNeil Labs, which introduced Tylenol (acetaminophen) as an over-the-counter drug in 1960. Foreign acquisitions included Cilag-Chemie of Switzerland (1959) and Janssen of Belgium (1961).

J&J bought Iolab Corporation, a leader in the development of intraocular lenses used in cataract surgery (1980), and Lifescan, a maker of blood glucose monitoring systems for diabetics (1986). J&J's sales had grown to nearly $5 billion by 1980. But there have since been problems: the new drug Zomax (for arthritis pain) was linked to 5 deaths and had to be pulled in 1983; J&J quit selling disposable diapers in the US in 1981 after losing much of its market share to Procter & Gamble and Kimberly Clark. When someone laced Tylenol capsules with cyanide in 1982, killing 8 people, it cost J&J $240 million in recalls, advertising, and repackaging, and cut Tylenol's profits by nearly 50%. J&J's immediate recall of 31 million bottles and its openness in dealing with the problem saved the Tylenol brand. Now sold as tablets and caplets to prevent tampering, Tylenol has maintained its lead in the over-the-counter analgesic market.

New products in the 1980s included Acuvue, a disposable contact lens; Retin-A, the antiwrinkle cream; and Eprex, a bioengineered treatment for specific forms of anemia. In 1989 J&J bought L' Oreal's sanitary protection business in France, and Piz Buin (sun protection products). The joint venture Johnson & Johnson-Merck Consumer Pharmaceuticals, formed in 1989, sells Mylanta (antacid) and other nonprescription products bought from ICI Americas, the US branch of the British drug firm.

HOW MUCH

	9 Yr. Growth	1980	1981	1982	1983	1984	1985	1986	1987	1988	1989
Sales ($ mil)	8.1%	4,837	5,399	5,761	5,973	6,125	6,421	7,003	8,012	9,000	9,757
Net income ($ mil)	11.7%	401	468	523	489	515	614	330	833	974	1,082
Income as % of sales	—	8.3%	8.7%	9.1%	8.2%	8.4%	9.6%	4.7%	10.4%	10.8%	11.1%
Earnings per share ($)	12.9%	1.07	1.23	1.40	1.26	1.36	1.64	0.90	2.37	2.82	3.19
Stock price – high ($)	—	16.90	19.69	25.63	25.75	21.44	27.63	37.13	52.69	44.06	59.50
Stock price – low ($)	—	11.00	14.13	16.25	19.50	14.00	17.56	22.88	27.50	34.63	41.50
Stock price – close ($)	15.2%	16.63	18.56	24.81	20.44	18.06	26.31	32.81	37.44	42.56	59.38
P/E – high	—	16	16	18	20	16	17	41	22	16	19
P/E – low	—	10	11	12	15	10	11	25	12	12	13
Dividends per share ($)	13.1%	0.37	0.43	0.49	0.54	0.59	0.64	0.69	0.81	0.96	1.12
Book value per share ($)	8.2%	6.12	6.76	7.40	7.91	8.02	9.16	8.17	10.13	10.52	12.45

1989 Year End:
Debt ratio: 22.0%
Return on equity: 27.8%
Cash (mil): $583
Current ratio: 1.96
Long-term debt (mil): $1,170
Number of shares (mil): 333
Dividends:
1989 average yield: 1.9%
1989 payout: 35.1%
Market value (mil): $19,775

Stock Price History high/low 1980-89

NYSE symbol: JNJ
Incorporated: New Jersey, 1887
Fiscal year ends: January 1

WHO

Chairman and CEO: Ralph S. Larsen, age 51, $847,480 pay
VC: Robert E. Campbell, age 56, $782,600 pay
VC: Robert N. Wilson, age 49, $761,928 pay
VP Finance: Clark H. Johnson, age 54
Auditors: Coopers & Lybrand
Employees: 83,100

WHERE

HQ: One Johnson & Johnson Plaza, New Brunswick, NJ 08933
Phone: 201-524-0400
FAX: 201-214-0332

The company has manufacturing operations in 54 countries and sells products in nearly every country in the world.

	1989 Sales		1989 Operating Income	
	$ mil	% of total	$ mil	% of total
US	4,881	50	699	40
Europe	2,687	28	737	42
Other Americas	1,212	12	180	10
Africa, Asia, Pacific	977	10	142	8
Adjustments	—	—	(97)	—
Total	**9,757**	**100**	**1,661**	**100**

WHAT

	1989 Sales		1989 Operating Income	
	$ mil	% of total	$ mil	% of total
Consumer prods.	3,915	40	434	25
Professional prods.	3,190	33	441	25
Pharmaceuticals	2,652	27	883	50
Adjustments	—	—	(97)	—
Total	**9,757**	**100**	**1,661**	**100**

Consumer Products
Acuvue (contact lens)
Baby oil
Baby shampoo
Band-Aid
Glucoscan (blood monitor)
Imodium A-D (antidiarrheal)
Medipren (analgesic)
Modess (sanitary napkin)
Mylanta (antacid)
Piz Buin (sunscreen)
Reach (toothbrush)
Sesame Street (vitamins)
Sine-Aid (decongestant)
Stayfree (sanitary napkin)
Tylenol

Pharmaceuticals
Eprex (blood cell stimulant)
Ergamisol (cancer treatment)
Floxcin (antibiotic)
Hismanal (antihistamine)
Imodium (antidiarrheal)
Monistat (antifungal)
Orthoclone OKT3 (organ transplant antibody)
Ortho-Novum (birth control)
Prepulsid (digestive aid)
Retin-A (skin treatment)
Tolectin (antiarthritic))

Professional
Implants
IV devices
Surgical instruments
Surgical products

RANKINGS

47th in *Fortune* 500 Industrial Cos.
125th in *Fortune* Global 500 Industrial Cos.
78th in *Forbes* Sales 500
20th in *Business Week* 1000
47th in *Business Week* Global 1000

COMPETITION

Abbott Labs
American Cyanamid
American Home Products
Amway
C. R. Bard
Baxter
Becton, Dickinson
Dow Chemical
Procter & Gamble
Pharmaceutical and health care supply companies

S.C. JOHNSON & SON, INC.

OVERVIEW

S.C. Johnson & Son, Inc., headquartered in its Frank Lloyd Wright–designed building in Racine, Wisconsin, is one of the largest privately held consumer product companies in the US and the largest privately held company in Wisconsin.

With 1989 sales estimated by outside sources at $2 to $2.5 billion (60% overseas), the company is a leader and innovator in insect control (Raid and Off!), cleaning products (Pledge), and personal care products (Agree). Johnson Wax, as the company is called both within and outside its walls because of its well-known floor wax products, also has interests in real estate, recreational products, and venture capital financing.

The 5th generation of Johnsons is now working at this extremely paternalistic, employee-oriented, community-minded company, which operates a charitable foundation and is known for philanthropic civic contributions. It has never had a layoff or a strike and offers one of the most generous employee benefits packages in this or any other industry (*e.g.*, it runs a company store where employees can buy company products at deep discounts). Its employee turnover rate is one of the lowest of any company — less than 2% annually.

A recent joint venture in China and its 40% equity interest in Modern Home Care Products, an Indian company test-marketing floor cleaners, exemplify Johnson's belief that the future is in the international marketplace.

Private company
Incorporated: Wisconsin, 1932
Fiscal year ends: Friday nearest June 30

WHO

Chairman: Samuel C. Johnson, age 62
President and CEO: Richard M. Carpenter
President and COO, Worldwide Consumer Products: William D. George, Jr.
VP and CFO: David H. Cool
Auditors: Coopers & Lybrand
Employees: 13,000

Stockholder	Approx. % of total shares held
S.C. Johnson and immediate family	60
Henrietta Louis and immediate family	30
S.C. Johnson employees and directors	10
Total	**100**

WHEN

S.C. Johnson & Son, Inc., was founded in Racine, Wisconsin, in 1886 by Samuel C. Johnson, a carpenter whose customers were as interested in his floor wax product as in his parquet floors. Forsaking carpentry, Johnson began to manufacture floor care products. By the time his son and successor, Herbert Fiske Johnson, Sr., died in 1928, annual revenues were $5 million and the company had an international presence. A dispute over Herbert's intestate estate was settled after 10 years, with his son Herbert Jr. and his daughter Henrietta Louis receiving 60% and 40%, respectively, of the company.

In 1954 when annual sales of floor care products were $45 million, Herbert Jr.'s son, Samuel Curtis Johnson, joined the company. As new products director, Samuel turned his attention in 1955 to insect control products. In 1956 the company introduced Raid, the first indoor/outdoor insecticide, and soon thereafter an insect repellent, Off!, each of which now holds approximately 50% of its market. The 1950s and 1960s saw unsuccessful diversification efforts into the paint, chemical, and lawn care businesses. Home care products, however, prospered with the introduction of Pledge aerosol furniture polish and Glade aerosol air freshener.

Herbert Jr. suffered a stroke in 1965 and Samuel became president. Revenues reached $200 million that year. Herbert Jr. lived another 13 years, much of it spent ensuring continued family ownership of the business. Samuel, also determined to maintain family ownership, decided in 1965 to develop a recreational products business that could eventually be sold to pay estate taxes. This company, Johnson Diversified, acquired boating, fishing, and camping gear companies and a manufacturer of ink stamping equipment. When Samuel took the company public in 1987 as Johnson Worldwide Associates, Inc., the family retained a large ownership interest and effective voting control. Worldwide had 1989 sales of $232 million and earnings of $13.5 million.

In the 1970s successful product launches included Edge shaving gel and Agree shampoo and conditioner. The company also moved into real estate through Johnson Wax Development. In 1989 with a portfolio worth $600 million, Johnson announced that it would wind down Development and sell its portfolio.

S. Curtis Johnson, Samuel's son, joined Johnson in 1983 (all 4 of the chairman's children work there) and was instrumental in Johnson's becoming the largest investor in Wind Point Partners I, a $36 million venture capital fund, and, later, Wind Point Partners II through Johnson Venture Capital, Inc. In 1986 Johnson acquired Bugs Burger Bug Killers, Inc., to learn about the commercial pest control market.

In 1990 the company entered into an agreement with Mycogen Corporation for Mycogen to develop biological pesticides for household pests. Also in 1990 the company began marketing a new line of children's shampoos under the Fisher-Price (toy maker being spun off by Quaker Oats) label.

WHERE

HQ: 1525 Howe St., Racine, WI 53403
Phone: 414-631-2000
FAX: 414-631-2133

S.C. Johnson operates throughout the US and in 46 foreign countries; approximately 60% of sales are made overseas.

	No. of employees	% of total
US	3,300	25
Overseas	9,700	75
Total	**13,000**	**100**

WHAT

Principal US Subsidiaries

Johnson Venture Capital, Inc. (Racine, WI; major limited partner in venture capital fund Wind Point Partners LP)
Johnson Wax Development Corp. (Racine, WI; real estate development)
Micro-Gen Equipment Corp. (San Antonio, TX; pest control equipment and chemicals)
PRISM (Miami, FL; sanitation services for restaurants and hotels)

Brand Names

Home Care
Brite
Clean 'n Clear
Duster Plus
Favor
Fine Wood
Future
Glade
Glo-Coat
Glory
Jubilee
Klean 'n Shine
Klear
Pledge
Shout
Step Saver

Personal Care
Agree (hair care)
Aveeno (bath products)
Curél (lotion)
Edge (shaving products)
Fisher-Price (hair care)
Hälsa (hair care)
Soft Sense (lotion)

Insect Control
Off!
Raid

HOW MUCH

	9 Yr. Growth	1979	1980	1981	1982	1983	1984	1985	1986	1987	1988
Advertising expenditures ($ mil)	—	40.2	51.4	66.6	74.6	86.9	90.0	146.1	144.6	96.4	111.6

Advertising Expend. ($ mil) 1979-88

RANKINGS

64th in *Forbes* 400 US Private Cos.

COMPETITION

Amway
Clorox
Colgate-Palmolive
Dow Chemical
Eastman Kodak
Gillette
Greyhound Dial
Johnson & Johnson
Procter & Gamble
Unilever

JOHNSON CONTROLS, INC.

OVERVIEW

Milwaukee-based Johnson Controls is best known for systems and services that regulate energy use, lighting, security, fire alarms, and temperature, provided by its Controls segment (34% of sales).

Johnson's Automotive segment (32% of sales) is the largest independent supplier of seating for the North American automotive market; the group also manufactures window regulators, latches, locks, and components for automobiles and light trucks.

The Battery segment (18% of sales) is the largest manufacturer of automotive batteries for the US replacement market. Batteries are also sold to truck, boat, and construction markets and distributed primarily through private-label agreements such as that for the Sears DieHard.

The Plastics segment (16% of sales) is the largest producer of plastic soft drink bottles for the US market, is a leading producer of other plastic containers, and makes plastic automotive parts such as radiator caps and power steering reservoirs for OEMs. Johnson will become the first US plastic container manufacturer to open a plastics recycling plant.

NYSE symbol: JCI
Incorporated: Wisconsin, 1900
Fiscal year ends: September 30

WHO

President and CEO: James H. Keyes, age 49, $749,252 pay
VP, Controls Group: Joseph W. Lewis, age 54, $351,516 pay
VP, Automotive Systems Group: R. Eugene Goodson, age 54, $335,740 pay
VP, Battery Group: J. William Horton, age 51, $312,407 pay
VP, Plastics Technology Group: John M. Barth, age 43, $301,771 pay
VP and CFO: James M. Wade, age 46
Auditors: Price Waterhouse
Employees: 42,600

WHEN

Professor Warren Johnson developed the electric tele-thermoscope in 1880 so janitors at Whitewater, Wisconsin's State Normal School could regulate room temperature without disturbing classrooms. Johnson's device used mercury to move a heat element that opened and shut a circuit. Milwaukee hotelier William Plankinton, a believer in Johnson's invention, invested $150,000 for manufacture.

The men formed Johnson Electric Service Company in 1885; sold off marketing, installation, and service rights to the thermostat; and concentrated on manufacture. Johnson kept inventing other devices; in the 1890s he worked on the invention for which he is best remembered: tower clocks. Johnson also experimented with the telegraph, forming American Wireless Telegraph in 1900; this venture was abandoned when Johnson became intrigued with the automobile.

Johnson put his factory into steam-powered car production. He won the Post Office's first automotive delivery contract but never gained support for the steamers within his own company and continued to look elsewhere for financing until his death in 1911.

In 1912 the renamed Johnson Services regained full rights to its thermostats, and newly elected president Harry Ellis sold all other businesses. During the Great Depression the company brought out economy systems, which automatically lowered building temperature during off-peak periods, to keep the company going. During WWII Johnson Services diversified to aid the war effort — building devices to gather weather data, inspect barrage balloons, and test radar sets.

Beginning in 1960 Johnson Services established an international division and focused upon military and research facilities requiring highly reliable control systems. Meanwhile Johnson Services acquired Penn Controls (1968), a maker of water pump pressure controls. In the 1960s Johnson Services began R&D in electronics to develop centralized control systems, first introduced in 1967, for temperature, fire alarm, lighting, and security regulation.

In 1978 Johnson Controls (renamed in 1974) acquired automotive battery manufacturer Globe-Union. In 1985 the company bought auto seat and plastics manufacturer Hoover Universal; today automotive and plastics products contribute 48% of sales. It has continued expansion in the controls business through purchase of ITT's European controls group (1982) and Pan Am World Services (1989), a provider of facilities management to the government. In September 1990, the company announced it was considering selling its battery business.

WHERE

HQ: 5757 N. Green Bay Ave., PO Box 591, Milwaukee, WI 53201
Phone: 414-228-1200
FAX: 414-228-2302

Johnson Controls has 93 manufacturing plants and conducts business in approximately 40 countries.

	1989 Sales		1989 Operating Income	
	$ mil	% of total	$ mil	% of total
US	3,218	87	197	96
Foreign	466	13	8	4
Total	**3,684**	**100**	**205**	**100**

WHAT

	1989 Sales		1989 Operating Income	
	$ mil	% of total	$ mil	% of total
Batteries	659	18	34	17
Automotive	1,188	32	47	23
Plastics	585	16	58	28
Controls	1,252	34	66	32
Total	**3,684**	**100**	**205**	**100**

Automotive Systems Group Products
Latches
Locks
Seats and components
Window regulators

Battery Group Products
Automotive
Boat
Construction
Security
Telecommunications
Uninterruptible power supply

Controls Group Products
Building controls

Plastics Technology Group Products
Blowmolding machinery
Containers for beverages, food, and personal care items
Gears

HOW MUCH

	9 Yr. Growth	1980	1981	1982	1983	1984	1985	1986	1987	1988	1989
Sales ($ mil)	16.1%	965	1,128	1,252	1,323	1,425	1,787	2,639	2,677	3,100	3,684
Net income ($ mil)	12.4%	34	48	54	59	67	78	96	90	104	98
Income as % of sales	—	3.5%	4.3%	4.3%	4.5%	4.7%	4.4%	3.6%	3.3%	3.3%	2.6%
Earnings per share ($)	8.0%	1.22	1.72	1.92	2.09	2.36	2.40	2.36	2.20	2.71	2.42
Stock price – high ($)	—	16.50	17.13	19.38	24.38	24.69	25.31	36.00	40.00	38.50	46.75
Stock price – low ($)	—	9.00	11.13	8.75	17.00	18.75	19.44	23.88	20.50	24.75	27.88
Stock price – close ($)	8.9%	15.00	12.25	17.69	24.19	20.69	24.50	28.63	25.63	36.63	32.25
P/E – high	—	14	10	10	12	10	11	15	18	14	19
P/E – low	—	7	6	5	8	8	8	10	9	9	12
Dividends per share ($)	7.6%	0.60	0.65	0.70	0.75	0.83	0.93	1.00	1.06	1.10	1.16
Book value per share ($)	5.5%	12.59	13.64	14.53	15.75	16.32	20.41	21.89	20.88	23.42	20.38

1989 Year End:
Debt ratio: 31.3%
Return on equity: 11.1%
Cash (mil): $27
Current ratio: 1.31
Long-term debt (mil): $445
Number of shares (mil): 39
Dividends:
1989 average yield: 3.6%
1989 payout: 47.9%
Market value (mil): $1,271

Stock Price History high/low 1980-89

RANKINGS

126th in *Fortune* 500 Industrial Cos.
357th in *Fortune* Global 500 Industrial Cos.
213th in *Forbes* Sales 500
465th in *Business Week* 1000

COMPETITION

Eaton
General Motors
Honeywell
Owens-Illinois
Peter Kiewit Sons'
Reynolds Metals

JOHNSON PRODUCTS COMPANY, INC.

OVERVIEW

Johnson Products Co., based in Chicago, manufactures hair care products and cosmetics for black consumers. Its 200,000-square-foot manufacturing plant produces more than 100 products with a variety of brand names, including Ultra Sheen (hair relaxer), Soft Touch (conditioner), and Bantú (professional-label hair relaxer). Most of Johnson Products's sales are made through retail outlets — drug stores, grocery stores, and mass merchandising chains. Professional sales (through beauty salons and barber shops) account for 25% of the company's revenues.

Once the leader in the black hair care market, Johnson Products has been passed by other black-owned companies (such as Johnson Publishing, with its Fashion Fair and Supreme Beauty lines, and the very successful Soft Sheen company) and giant cosmetic firms such as Alberto Culver and Revlon. Its 1989 sales of $29 million put it in the 24th position in *Black Enterprise*'s list of top black companies.

WHEN

When George Johnson began Johnson Products Company with a $500 investment and Ultra Wave, a new hair relaxer for blacks, he started a company that would become an industry leader and a pioneer in the black business world. It was 1954 and Johnson was an assistant chemist and salesman for Fuller Products, a black cosmetics company in Chicago. With the help of Fuller's head chemist, Johnson developed Ultra Wave and traveled the roads between Chicago and New York City, selling the product to black barber shops and beauty salons.

In 1957 Johnson introduced Ultra Sheen, a gentle, long-lasting hair relaxer that could be applied at home. This alternative to the hot comb and grease treatment used in black beauty salons was a best seller. When the natural look became fashionable in the 1960's, Johnson Products responded with another hit product, Afro Sheen.

Johnson Products stock was offered on the ASE in 1971, becoming the first black-owned company ever offered for investment on a major exchange. It still remains as one of the few top black companies traded on a national exchange.

By 1974 Johnson Products had 50% of the black personal care market, with profits of $5 million. It was listed as #4 in *Black Enterprise*'s list of top black US companies. Its leading position was soon challenged by other black-owned companies and large established firms that moved into the lucrative market for black personal care products. When a 1976 government order required warning labels on hair products containing lye, Johnson complied while its competitors changed their formulas. By 1977 Johnson Products's market share had dropped to 32%. Current market leader Soft Sheen, another black-owned Chicago company, posted 1989 sales of $87.2 million and is listed #6 in *Black Enterprise*'s 1989 list.

In 1980 Johnson Products opened a manufacturing plant in Nigeria, where its products had been sold since the 1960s. It wrote down its investment in the plant in 1985 due to continued losses and the country's economic instability. It continues to distribute its products in some African countries, including Liberia, Zaire, and the Ivory Coast.

The company sold its chain of 13 beauty schools (Debbie's School of Beauty Culture) and its Ultra Precise Beauty Boutiques in 1986. In 1990 Johnson Products paid $2.5 million for 2 product lines (Sta-Sof-Fro and Curly-Perm) from M&M Products, an Atlanta black hair care product company.

George Johnson relinquished company control in 1989 as part of his divorce settlement. His ex-wife, Joan Johnson, and son Eric Johnson became chairperson and CEO, respectively. George Johnson continued to serve as a company consultant.

HOW MUCH

	9 Yr. Growth	1980	1981	1982	1983	1984	1985	1986	1987	1988	1989
Sales ($ mil)	(2.0%)	35	47	42	46	42	38	35	32	29	29
Net income ($ mil)	—	(2)	0	(4)	2	(4)	(5)	(2)	1	(2)	1
Income as % of sales	—	(6.8%)	0.8%	(8.5%)	3.6%	(9.8%)	(11.9%)	(5.7%)	1.8%	(8.5%)	4.3%
Earnings per share ($)	—	(0.60)	0.10	(0.91)	0.41	(1.03)	(1.13)	(0.50)	0.15	(0.62)	0.31
Stock price – high ($)	—	5.63	5.13	3.50	11.38	10.00	6.50	4.13	5.00	3.00	3.75
Stock price – low ($)	—	2.88	2.63	2.00	3.13	2.88	2.50	1.75	2.13	1.38	1.63
Stock price – close ($)	0.4%	3.13	3.13	3.25	9.13	4.00	3.25	4.00	2.63	1.88	3.25
P/E – high	—	—	51	—	28	—	—	—	33	—	12
P/E – low	—	—	26	—	8	—	—	—	14	—	5
Dividends per share ($)	—	0.27	—	—	—	—	—	—	—	—	—
Book value per share ($)	(8.4%)	5.86	5.96	5.05	5.46	4.43	3.29	2.80	3.10	2.16	2.66

1989 Year End:
Debt ratio: 0.0%
Return on equity: 12.9%
Cash (mil): $1
Current ratio: 1.51
Long-term debt (mil): —
Number of shares (mil): 4
Dividends:
1989 average yield: —
1989 payout: —
Market value (mil): $13

ASE symbol: JPC
Incorporated: Delaware, 1969
Fiscal year ends: August 31

WHO

Chairperson and Treasurer: Joan B. Johnson, age 60
President and CEO: Eric G. Johnson, age 38, $166,719 pay
VP Finance and CFO: Thomas P. Polke, age 27, $64,616 pay
Auditors: Arthur Andersen & Co.
Employees: 190

WHERE

HQ: 8522 S. Lafayette Ave., Chicago, IL 60620
Phone: 312-483-4100
FAX: 312-962-5741

Johnson Products sells hair care products and cosmetics throughout the US and overseas, with manufacturing facilities in Chicago and a distribution center in the UK.

The company's principal European markets are France, the UK, and West Germany.

WHAT

	1989 Sales % of total
Hair care products	96
Cosmetics & other products	4
Total	**100**

Subsidiaries
Mellow Touch Laboratories, Inc.
Celex Corporation (private-label personal care products)
Johnson Products of Nigeria (40%)

Brand Names

Hair Products
Afro Sheen
Bantú
Classy Curl
Gentle-Treatment
Precíse
Soft Touch
Ultra Sheen
Ultra Sheen Hair Food
Ultra Sheen Light
Ultra Sheen Supreme
Ultra Star

Cosmetics
Moisture Formula
Ultra Sheen

COMPETITION

Amway
Avon
Colgate-Palmolive
Estée Lauder
Gillette
Johnson Publishing
Procter & Gamble
Unilever

JOHNSON PUBLISHING COMPANY, INC.

OVERVIEW

Chicago-based Johnson Publishing is the world's largest black-owned publishing business and America's 2nd largest black-owned business of any type. Its premier publication, *Ebony*, is the most widely circulated black magazine, read by 8 million people worldwide. Advertising in *Ebony* and *Jet*, its 2nd biggest magazine, reaches over 1/2 of the adult blacks in the US.

Johnson Publishing is a family business, operated by its founder John Johnson since 1942. Johnson has no intention of letting the company go public; in line to succeed him as head of the company is his daughter, Linda Johnson Rice, who will become one of the few women to head a major corporation. Johnson's wife, Eunice, runs the Ebony Fashion Fair, the world's largest traveling fashion show.

Johnson Publishing's Book Division features the works of various black authors, including Lerone Bennett, Jr., an *Ebony* senior editor. In the 1990s Johnson plans to publish a series of books on black celebrities.

In 1987 *Black Enterprise* magazine selected Johnson as Entrepreneur of the Decade. Johnson has served on the advisory board of the Harvard Business School and is a major contributor to the United Negro College Fund and other black-oriented causes.

WHEN

John Johnson launched his publishing business in 1942 while still attending college in Chicago. The idea for a magazine oriented to blacks came to him while working part-time for a life insurance company where one of his jobs was to summarize news about the black community from magazines and newspapers. With $500 his mother raised by mortgaging family furniture, Johnson mailed a $2 charter subscription offer to potential subscribers. He got 3,000 replies and with that $6,000 printed the first issue of *Negro Digest*, a black-oriented magazine patterned after *Reader's Digest*. It was such a hit that within a year circulation had reached 50,000.

In 1945 Johnson started *Ebony* magazine, an immediate hit in the black community and still Johnson Publishing's premier publication. *Ebony* (similar to *Life*, but focusing on black culture and achievements) and *Jet* magazine (a shorter, celebrity-oriented magazine started in 1951) were the only black-oriented publications in the US for the next 20 years.

In the early days of *Ebony*, Johnson was unable to obtain advertising because of discrimination, so he formed his own mail order business called Beauty Star and advertised its products (dresses, wigs, hair care products, and vitamins) through his magazines. Even so, he realized he could not publish a magazine without outside advertisers and, through persistence, won his first major account, Zenith Radio, by 1947.

By the 1960s Johnson had become one of the most prominent black men in America. In 1963 he posed with John F. Kennedy to publicize a special issue of *Ebony* celebrating the Emancipation Proclamation. *Negro Digest*, renamed *Black World*, became an important information source for blacks, carrying some of the more provocative articles of the times. However, circulation (about 100,000 at its peak) dwindled to 15,000, and Johnson stopped publishing the magazine in 1975. In the meantime, in 1972 America's magazine publishers named Johnson Publisher of the Year — the magazine world's equivalent to the "Oscar."

Unable to find the proper makeup for his black *Ebony* models, Johnson founded his own cosmetics business, Fashion Fair Cosmetics, in 1973. Fashion Fair competed successfully against Revlon (who later introduced cosmetic lines for blacks) and another black cosmetics company, Johnson Products (unrelated) of Chicago. In 1982 sales for the Fashion Fair division alone were over $30 million. Customers bought Fashion Fair makeup not only in the US, Canada, and Great Britain, but also in the West Indies and Africa.

In 1973 Johnson also launched *Ebony Jr!*, a magazine for black preteens, the purpose of which, like many of Johnson Publishing's ventures, was to provide "positive black images." Johnson bought 2 radio stations in 1974 (WJPC in Chicago and WLOU in Louisville, Kentucky) and a 3rd radio station (WLNR in Lansing, Illinois) in the mid-1980s. WJPC, Chicago's first black-owned radio station, remains an important source of information and music for many blacks in Chicago today. In 1984 Johnson Publishing passed Motown Industries to become the largest black-owned business in America. Since 1987 it has been 2nd after TLC Beatrice.

HOW MUCH

	9 Yr. Growth	1980	1981	1982	1983	1984	1985	1986	1987	1988	1989
Sales ($ mil)	14.2%	73	81	103	118	139	155	174	202	217	241
Employees	16.3%	610	1,500	1,586	1,690	1,786	1,802	1,828	1,903	2,364	2,370

Sales ($ mil) 1980-89

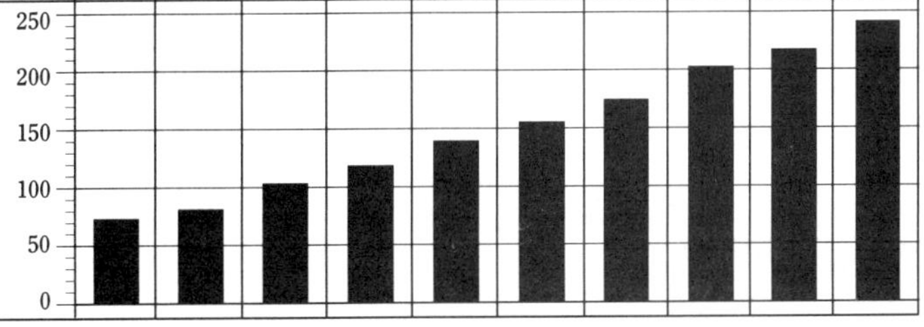

0
50
100
150
200
250

Private company
Founded: Illinois, 1942
Fiscal year ends: December 31

WHO

Chairman and CEO: John H. Johnson, age 72
President and COO: Linda Johnson Rice, age 32
Secretary/Treasurer: Eunice W. Johnson, age 69
Employees: 2,370

WHERE

HQ: 820 S. Michigan Ave., Chicago, IL 60605
Phone: 312-322-9200
FAX: 312-322-0918

WHAT

Beauty Aids
Fashion Fair Cosmetics
Supreme Beauty Products Co.
Duke (hair care for men)
Raveen (hair care for women)

Books
Johnson Publishing Co. Book Division

Fashion Shows
Ebony Fashion Fair

Magazines
Ebony
EM (Ebony Man)
Jet

Radio Stations
WJPC (AM), Chicago
WLNR (FM), Lansing, IL
WLOU (AM), Louisville

Television Productions
"American Black Achievement Awards"
"Ebony/Jet Showcase"

Subsidiaries
Johnson Communications, Inc.

RANKINGS

2nd in *Black Enterprise* 100 Industrial/Service Cos.

COMPETITION

Advance Publications
Amway
Avon
Colgate-Palmolive
Estée Lauder
Gillette
Johnson Products
MacAndrews & Forbes
Procter & Gamble
Time Warner
Unilever
Washington Post

JWP, INC.

OVERVIEW

JWP describes itself as the premier technical services company in the world specializing in facility and information systems and as an emerging leader in environmental systems. It is also the owner of the largest investor-owned water utility in New York state.

Its dozens of companies design, integrate, install, and maintain complex electrical, computer, communication, mechanical, and security systems throughout the US and in the UK. JWP is the largest specialty contractor in the US. It also owns companies that design, manufacture, and sell computer software and hardware.

JWP is a small but growing player in the environmental systems (*e.g.,* sludge processing) market. Its water utility generates 3% of revenues but 12% of its operating profits.

JWP's phenomenal growth through acquisitions placed it first in 1988 and 4th in 1989 on *Business Month*'s list of fastest-growing companies. It entered the *Fortune* diversified service 100 in 1989 for the first time at the rank of 55.

NYSE symbol: JWP
Incorporated: Delaware, 1987
Fiscal year ends: December 31

WHO

Chairman and President: Andrew T. Dwyer, age 41, $1,274,000 pay
EVP and CFO: Ernest W. Grendi, age 44, $753,875 pay
EVP and General Counsel: Sheldon I. Cammaker, age 50, $318,000 pay
SVP Corporate Marketing: Michael S. Battaglia, age 45, $205,000 pay
SVP Finance: John K. McQuade, age 48, $204,000 pay
Auditors: Ernst & Young
Employees: 16,000

WHEN

Jamaica Water Supply Company was incorporated in 1887 to supply water to some residents of Queens and Nassau counties in New York. In 1902 it made its first acquisition, absorbing the Jamaica Township Water Company. By 1906 it was generating $93,084 of revenue and making a healthy net operating profit of $25,158 (27%). By 1932 revenue reached $1,624,861, on which it made $324,594 net operating profit (20%). During the next 35 years the company grew as the population of its service area grew.

In 1966 the company was acquired by Jamaica Water and Utilities, a newly incorporated company, through an exchange of shares. That year it purchased Sea Cliff Water Company in another exchange of shares and 80% of Orbit International (San Juan, Puerto Rico), later selling its interest in Orbit but then reacquiring 51% of it in stages through 1979. In 1969 and 1970 the company acquired Welsbach (electrical contractors) and A to Z Equipment (construction trailer suppliers) and in 1974 briefly changed its name to Welsbach Corporation before becoming Jamaica Water Properties, Inc., in 1976.

Diversification proved unprofitable. In 1976 the company lost almost $2.5 million, and by 1979 it had lost $3.2 million on revenues of just over $40 million. In 1977 a major investor in the company, Martin Dwyer, and his son Andrew, a 29-year-old recent law school graduate, took over management control of the struggling company. By 1980 it was profitable. In 1983 the Dwyers began to diversify again.

Between 1983 and 1989 the Dwyers acquired more than 30 companies in the electrical and mechanical contracting, security systems, telecommunications, computer, and energy/environmental businesses. The company's revenues of $55 million (most of it from the water company) rose to over $1.7 billion (3% from the water company). In 1985 Andrew Dwyer became president and in 1986 the company changed its name to JWP, Inc., to reflect its increasing diversity.

Between 1986 and 1989 JWP acquired over a dozen companies, including Extel Corporation (1986, telecommunications), Gibson Electric (1987, electrical contracting), and Dynalectric (1988, specialty contracting).

In 1989 JWP purchased Drake & Scull, a British electrical contractor with revenues of $275 million, and in early 1990 it acquired NEECO, Inc., a reseller of computer systems, for stock worth approximately $100 million. In August 1990 the company reached an agreement to acquire another computer reseller, Compumat. The NEECO and Compumat acquisitions are part of JWP's strategy to make it a national computer systems integrator (computer related sales are now 25% of JWP's business).

WHERE

HQ: 2975 Westchester Ave., Purchase, NY 10577
Phone: 914-935-4000
Fax: 914-694-1215

The company operates 120 offices throughout the US and in the UK.

WHAT

	1989 Sales		1989 Operating Income	
	$ mil	% of total	$ mil	% of total
Water supply	53	3	12	12
Technical services	1,619	93	80	78
Energy & environmental	70	4	10	10
Adjustments	—	—	(9)	—
Total	**1,742**	**100**	**93**	**100**

Supply of Water
Water supply to several Long Island, NY communities

Energy & Environmental
Cogeneration facilities
Fluidized bed combustion and gasification systems
Regenerative fume oxidation systems
Sludge management
Wastewater treatment
Water and waste control systems
Trailer leasing

Technical Services
Communications terminals
Computer reselling
Control systems (security)
Electrical contracting services
Electronic data interchange software
Electronic security systems
Low electromagnetic emission (Tempest) computers
Information systems
Mechanical contracting services
Telecommunications systems

RANKINGS

55th in *Fortune* 100 Diversified Service Cos.

COMPETITION

Borg-Warner
Computer resellers
Electrical and mechanical contractors

HOW MUCH

	9 Yr. Growth	1980	1981	1982	1983	1984	1985	1986	1987	1988	1989
Sales ($ mil)	51.6%	41	42	51	55	90	132	379	637	925	1,742
Net income ($ mil)	—	(1)	2	2	3	3	5	14	22	28	39
Income as % of sales	—	(1.2%)	4.2%	4.6%	4.7%	3.8%	4.0%	3.6%	3.5%	3.0%	2.2%
Earnings per share ($)	—	(0.14)	0.20	0.25	0.25	0.26	0.37	0.80	1.20	1.48	1.90
Stock price – high ($)	—	2.33	3.08	4.67	8.25	9.25	8.42	18.33	22.00	18.00	31.50
Stock price – low ($)	—	1.08	1.42	2.25	3.83	4.25	5.17	6.75	7.83	9.25	16.17
Stock price – close ($)	34.2%	2.13	3.08	4.00	6.00	5.42	8.08	11.58	9.42	17.50	30.00
P/E – high	—	—	15	19	33	35	23	23	18	12	17
P/E – low	—	—	7	9	15	16	14	8	7	6	9
Dividends per share ($)	0.0%	0.00	0.00	0.00	0.00	0.00	0.00	0.00	0.00	0.00	0.00
Book value per share ($)	—	(0.09)	0.17	0.71	1.42	2.10	2.88	5.02	6.25	7.72	11.34

1989 Year End:
Debt ratio: 54.8%
Return on equity: 19.9%
Cash (mil): $37
Current ratio: 1.45
Long-term debt (mil): $301
Number of shares (mil): 22
Dividends:
1989 average yield: 0.0%
1989 payout: 0.0%
Market value (mil): $655

Stock Price History high/low 1980-89

K MART CORPORATION

OVERVIEW

Troy, Michigan–based K mart is the 2nd largest retailer in the world after Sears. While K mart may catch Sears in the near future, Wal-Mart is expected to pass both. Although the company diversified into other retail formats in the 1980s, K mart stores still account for 82% of the company's sales.

K mart's discount department stores have faced stiff competition in recent years, not only from rival discounter Wal-Mart, but also from steep-discount membership warehouses and superstores — specialty retailers like Toys "R" Us and Home Depot, which carry big selections at low prices.

K mart has responded by improving its stores and by acquiring membership warehouses and category killers of its own. It is pursuing an aggressive 5-year, $2.3 billion modernization effort and is integrating PACE, one of the largest membership warehouse chains, and Makro.

K mart also owns Waldenbooks (the nation's largest book chain) and Builders Square and is developing specialty discount chains Sports Authority and Office Square. In addition, K mart holds 21.4% of Coles Myer, the largest retailer in Australia.

WHEN

Sebastian S. Kresge and John McCrory opened five-and-dime stores in Memphis and Detroit in 1897. The partners split in 1899; Kresge got the Detroit store, and McCrory took the one in Memphis.

Kresge incorporated the S. S. Kresge Company in 1912 when it had grown into the 2nd largest dime store chain in the country. Kresge expanded rapidly, forming S. S. Kresge, Ltd., in 1929 to operate stores in Canada. During the late 1920s and 1930s the company began opening stores in suburban shopping centers. By the 1950s Kresge had grown to become one of the nation's largest general merchandise retailers.

In the middle of the 1950s Kresge's management re-evaluated the company's strategy. After a 1958 study, Harry Cunningham, a former newspaper reporter who later became chairman of the company, recommended that the company enter discount retailing. Three unprofitable locations were transformed to a discount format under the name Jupiter (1961). The company judged this a success and opened the first K mart discount store in Detroit (1962). Kresge formed a joint venture with G. J. Coles & Coy Ltd. (later Coles Myer Ltd., Australia's largest retailer) to operate K mart stores in Australia (1968).

The company built up the K mart format swiftly during the 1970s and adopted K mart for the corporate name in 1977. A program of diversification initiated in 1980 led to the purchase of Furr's Cafeterias (1980) and Bishop Buffets (1983), both of which were sold in 1986. In 1984 K mart acquired Walden Book Company and Builders Square, formerly Texas-based Home Centers of America.

In 1985 the company acquired Oregon-based Pay Less Drug Stores Northwest and Bargain Harold's Discount Outlets, a Canadian retailer, and in 1987 sold most of its remaining Kresge and Jupiter locations in the US to McCrory's, the chain that had been started by Sebastian Kresge's one-time partner.

Competition from Wal-Mart, Target (owned by Dayton-Hudson), and other discounters forced K mart to experiment with a more colorful and upscale format; to promote it the company hired former Charlie's Angel Jaclyn Smith as a spokesperson. The company also entered the warehouse club business, first buying Makro, a discount club (1988), and later merging it with the operations of Colorado-based PACE Club (1990). Also in 1988 K mart opened American Fare, its first hypermarket — a combination food and general merchandise store — in partnership with Alabama food retailer Bruno's.

HOW MUCH

	9 Yr. Growth	1980	1981	1982	1983	1984	1985	1986	1987	1988	1989
Sales ($ mil)	8.5%	14,343	16,679	16,942	18,789	21,303	22,645	24,046	25,864	27,550	29,793
Net income ($ mil)	2.4%	261	220	262	492	499	471	570	692	803	323
Income as % of sales	—	1.8%	1.3%	1.5%	2.6%	2.3%	2.1%	2.4%	2.7%	2.9%	1.1%
Earnings per share ($)	1.7%	1.38	1.17	1.37	2.53	2.56	2.42	2.84	3.40	4.00	1.61
Stock price – high ($)	—	17.67	15.92	18.17	26.17	25.08	27.67	38.25	48.38	39.75	44.88
Stock price – low ($)	—	10.08	10.25	10.33	14.50	17.83	20.42	22.42	21.63	29.00	32.50
Stock price – close ($)	12.7%	11.92	10.50	14.67	22.17	23.50	23.58	29.25	29.75	35.13	35.00
P/E – high	—	13	14	13	10	10	11	13	14	10	28
P/E – low	—	7	9	8	6	7	8	8	6	7	20
Dividends per share ($)	11.2%	0.60	0.63	0.66	0.71	0.80	0.91	0.97	1.12	1.28	1.56
Book value per share ($)	7.8%	12.66	13.20	13.93	15.57	17.24	17.32	19.66	22.08	25.12	24.90

1989 Year End:
Debt ratio: 37.9%
Return on equity: 6.4%
Cash (mil): $353
Current ratio: 1.86
Long-term debt (mil): $3,029
Number of shares (mil): 200
Dividends:
1989 average yield: 4.5%
1989 payout: 96.9%
Market value (mil): $6,989

Stock Price History high/low 1980-89

50 45 40 35 30 25 20 15 10 5 0

NYSE symbol: KM
Incorporated: Michigan, 1916
Fiscal year ends: Last Wednesday in January

WHO

Chairman, President, and CEO: Joseph E. Antonini, age 48, $898,928 pay
VP and CFO: Thomas F. Murasky, age 44
Auditors: Price Waterhouse
Employees: 365,000

WHERE

HQ: 3100 W. Big Beaver Rd., Troy, MI 48084
Phone: 313-643-1000
FAX: 313-643-5249

K mart operates 4,268 retail stores in all 50 states, Puerto Rico, and all provinces of Canada.

	1989 Sales		1989 Pretax Income	
	$ mil	% of total	$ mil	% of total
US	28,441	95	426	83
Foreign	1,092	4	89	17
Licensing	260	1	—	—
Total	**29,793**	**100**	**515**	**100**

WHAT

	1989 Sales		1989 Operating Income	
	$ mil	% of total	$ mil	% of total
Specialty retail	4,584	15	87	11
General merchandising	25,233	85	720	89
Adjustments	(24)	—	599	—
Total	**29,793**	**100**	**1,406**	**100**

General Merchandise Operations
American Fare (51%)
2 food/general merchandise hypermarkets
K mart
2,194 K mart discount department stores in the US and 157 K mart, Kresge, and Jupiter stores in Canada
PACE and Makro
47 PACE and 9 Makro discount warehouse stores

Specialty Retail Operations
Bargain Harold's Discount Outlets
155 limited-line discount stores in Canada
Builders Square
141 warehouse home improvement stores
Office Square
4 office supply warehouses
Pay Less Drug Stores Northwest
294 super drugstores in 9 western states
The Sports Authority and Sports Giant
10 warehouse sporting goods stores
Walden Book Co.
1,255 Waldenbooks stores

Other
Coles Myer Ltd. (21.4%)
1,652 stores in Australia and New Zealand
Meldisco (49%) operates footwear departments in K marts (51% owned by Melville)

RANKINGS

2nd in *Fortune* 50 Retailing Cos.
14th in *Forbes* Sales 500
76th in *Business Week* 1000

COMPETITION

Ames	Price Co.
Costco	Sears
Dayton Hudson	Stop & Shop
Howe Depot	Walgreens
Fred Meyer	Wal-Mart
Lowe's	Drug and other specialty retailers

KELLOGG COMPANY

OVERVIEW

Founded and still located in Battle Creek, Michigan, Kellogg produces breakfast cereals and other food products. Kellogg has 40% of the US cereal market and an even larger share of the foreign market — 52%. Kellogg produces 9 of the world's 10 best-selling cereals. Retail products under the Kellogg's brand name include All-Bran, Cocoa Krispies, Corn Flakes, Frosted Flakes, Rice Krispies, Special K, and other cereals, as well as croutons, granola bars, non-dairy creamers, toaster pastries, and stuffings.

Through its subsidiary Mrs. Smith, Kellogg makes Eggo waffles and has the largest share of the US frozen dessert pie market. Kellogg owns Salada Foods (tea and drink mixes); Fearn International (Fearn and LeGout brand soups, gelatins, pie fillings, and entrees for the wholesale market); and Whitney's Foods and LeShake (yogurts).

Recent product emphasis has been on high-fiber and oat bran products for older and health-conscious adults, including Müeslix, Heartwise, Common Sense, and Balance cereals. Earnings in 1989 declined from 1988 levels (for the first time in 37 years) due to strong consumer interest in oat bran products, for which Kellogg was not prepared.

NYSE symbol: K
Incorporated: Delaware, 1922
Fiscal year ends: December 31

WHO

Chairman, CEO, and President: William E. LaMothe, age 63, $1,070,000 pay
EVP; President, Kellogg International: Arnold G. Langbo, age 52, $471,000 pay
SVP, General Counsel, and Secretary: Richard M. Clark, age 52
EVP Administration and CFO: Charles W. Elliott, age 58, pay $372,000
EVP; President, US Food Products Division: Gary E. Costley, age 46, $332,400 pay
Auditors: Price Waterhouse
Employees: 17,268

WHEN

William Kellogg first discovered wheat flakes in 1894 while working for his brother, Dr. John Kellogg, at Battle Creek's famed homeopathic sanitarium. An experiment with grains (for patients' diets) was disrupted; by the time the men returned to the dough, the dough had absorbed water. They rolled it anyway, then toasted the result and accidentally created the first flaked cereal.

Dr. Kellogg sold the flakes via mail-order to former patients (1899) in a partnership that William managed. Later William started his own firm (1906) to produce corn flakes. As head of The Battle Creek Toasted Corn Flake Company, William competed against 42 cereal companies in Battle Creek (one run by ex-patient C. W. Post) and became the leader because of his innovative marketing ideas. A 1906 *Ladies Home Journal* ad helped to increase demand from 33 cases a day earlier that year to 2,900 a day by year-end. In 1907 he formed campaigns around his cereal's main ingredient, corn grit, termed "The Sweetheart of the Corn." Another ad, then considered risquê, offered a free box of cereal to every woman who winked at her grocer. In 1912 he used the world's largest sign (in Times Square) to advertise his logo. Kellogg was the first to use full-color magazine ads, test markets, and widespread consumer sampling.

William continued to introduce new products, such as Bran Flakes (1915), All-Bran (1916), and Rice Krispies (1928). Another innovation was the Waxtite inner lining to keep cereal fresh (1914). International expansion began in the same period and included Canada (1914), Australia (1924), and England (1938).

Concerned with nutrition, Kellogg pioneered nutrient labeling in the 1930s; produced the first combination grain product (1943) and first high-protein cereal (Special K, 1955); and became the first cereal company to label sugar (1977) and salt (1979) content.

Kellogg has diversified little beyond cereal and other breakfast products, but purchased Eggo waffles and Mrs. Smith's pies in the 1970s and developed Whitney's Foods, a yogurt maker, in 1982. In 1983 Kellogg's US market share hit a low of 36.7% due to aggressive competition by rival General Mills and others. The company targeted new cereals toward health-conscious adults and chose international growth over diversification. Today the company has 50% of the foreign cereal market.

Kellogg's newly constructed Memphis plant will increase the company's domestic capacity by 35% at a cost of $1.2 billion — the most expensive food-processing facility ever built.

WHERE

HQ: One Kellogg Square, Battle Creek, MI 49016
Phone: 616-961-2000
FAX: 616-961-2871

Kellogg manufactures its products in 16 countries and distributes them in 130 countries.

	1989 Sales		1989 Net Income	
	$ mil	% of total	$ mil	% of total
US	2,941	63	313	66
Europe	999	22	97	21
Other countries	712	15	61	13
Adjustments	—	—	(48)	—
Total	**4,652**	**100**	**422**	**100**

WHAT

Kellogg's Brand (Cereals)
All-Bran
Apple Jacks
Apple Raisin Crisp
Balance
Bran Buds
Cocoa Krispies
Common Sense
Cracklin' Oat Bran
Crispix
Froot Loops
Frosted Krispies
Frosted Mini-Wheats
Fruitful Bran
Fruity Marshmallow Krispies
Heartwise
Just Right
Kellogg's Bran Flakes
Kellogg's Corn Flakes
Kellogg's Frosted Flakes
Kellogg's Raisin Bran
Kellogg's Squares
Kenmei
Müeslix
Nut & Honey Crunch
Nutri-Grain
Oatbake
Pops
Product 19
Rice Krispies
Smacks
Special K

Other Brands
Croutettes (stuffing mix)
Culinary Classics (soups)
Eggo (frozen waffles)
Fearn (soups)
Gourmet Edge (bases)
LeGout (gravies, puddings, sauces)
LeShake (yogurt)
Mrs. Smith's (frozen desserts)
Pop-Tarts (toaster pastries)
Salada (tea and drink mixes)
Smart Start (cereal bars)
Whitney's Foods (yogurt)

HOW MUCH

	9 Yr. Growth	1980	1981	1982	1983	1984	1985	1986	1987	1988	1989
Sales ($ mil)	8.9%	2,151	2,321	2,367	2,381	2,602	2,930	3,341	3,793	4,349	4,652
Net income ($ mil)	9.6%	185	205	228	243	251	281	319	396	480	422
Income as % of sales	—	8.6%	8.8%	9.6%	10.2%	9.6%	9.6%	9.5%	10.4%	11.0%	9.1%
Earnings per share ($)	12.4%	1.21	1.35	1.49	1.59	1.68	2.28	2.58	3.20	3.90	3.46
Stock price – high ($)	—	10.88	12.50	15.56	16.50	21.38	36.00	58.75	68.75	68.50	81.63
Stock price – low ($)	—	7.81	8.69	10.88	12.56	13.50	19.25	31.50	37.88	49.00	57.75
Stock price – close ($)	23.5%	10.13	11.25	13.31	16.19	20.00	34.75	51.75	52.38	64.25	67.63
P/E – high	—	9	9	10	10	13	16	23	21	18	24
P/E – low	—	6	6	7	8	8	8	12	12	13	17
Dividends per share ($)	11.0%	0.67	0.71	0.76	0.81	0.85	0.90	1.02	1.29	1.52	1.72
Book value per share ($)	11.9%	4.86	5.30	5.79	6.39	3.96	5.54	7.27	9.82	12.07	13.41

1989 Year End:
Debt ratio: 18.5%
Return on equity: 27.2%
Cash (mil): $80
Current ratio: 0.87
Long-term debt (mil): $371
Number of shares (mil): 122
Dividends:
1989 average yield: 2.5%
1989 payout: 49.7%
Market value (mil): $8,242

Stock Price History high/low 1980-89

RANKINGS

108th in *Fortune* 500 Industrial Cos.
283rd in *Fortune* Global 500 Industrial Cos.
188th in *Forbes* Sales 500
71st in *Business Week* 1000
218th in *Business Week* Global 1000

COMPETITION

Borden
Campbell Soup
General Mills
Grand Metropolitan
H.J. Heinz
Nestlé
Quaker Oats
Ralston Purina
RJR Nabisco
Sara Lee
Whitman

KEMPER CORPORATION

OVERVIEW

Kemper Corporation is a financial services holding company offering products and services in life insurance, property-casualty insurance, reinsurance, asset management, and securities brokerage. Chicago area–based Kemper is the 25th largest diversified financial services company in the US.

The Insurance Services Group includes life insurance (Federated Kemper Life and Kemper Investors Life), which accounted for 27% of company revenue in 1989. Property-casualty (Economy Fire and Federal Kemper) represented 18% of revenues, and reinsurance operations added 14% of revenues.

Kemper's Investment Services Group, organized as Kemper Financial Companies, accounts for 38% of corporate revenues. Kemper employs more than 1,800 registered representatives (stockbrokers), making them collectively the 11th largest sales force in the US.

The company's money market funds had assets of $21.5 billion at the end of 1989, and 2 of the funds were among the 10 largest money funds in the US.

NYSE symbol: KEM
Incorporated: Delaware, 1967
Fiscal year ends: December 31

WHO

Chairman and CEO: Joseph E. Luecke, age 63, $650,590 pay
President and COO: David B. Mathis, age 52, $683,440 pay (prior to promotion)
EVP Investment Services: Thomas R. Anderson, age 52, $948,943 pay
SVP and CFO: John H. Fitzpatrick, age 33
Auditors: KPMG Peat Marwick
Employees: 10,000

WHEN

James Kemper founded Lumbermens Mutual Casualty Company, the predecessor of Kemper Corporation, in Illinois in 1912 to provide workers' compensation insurance for lumberyard owners. Within a few months the company was one of the first in the US to sell automobile insurance.

In 1913 Kemper started National Underwriters to provide additional fire insurance for lumber dealers. Lumbermens, with $1 million in assets in 1919, opened new offices in Philadelphia, Boston, and Syracuse. By 1921 the company had established its home office in Chicago, where a receptionist is believed to have begun answering the phone by saying "Kemper Insurance."

In 1926 Kemper founded American Motorists Insurance Company (AMICO), which writes personal and commercial insurance. During the early 1930s Kemper assumed management of Glen Cove Mutual Insurance (American Manufacturers Mutual Insurance) and also added boiler and machinery, surety bond, and inland marine insurance.

James Kemper and his brother Hathaway in 1936 helped found the Northwestern University Traffic Institute to promote safe driving and to provide scholarships for police officers. Following WWII Kemper founded the James S. Kemper Foundation to provide college students with scholarships and business experience. Kemper died in 1981 at the age of 94.

In 1957 Lumbermens began offering ocean marine coverage and began advertising on national television, sponsoring sports events. The Kemper Group of companies added Federal Kemper Life Assurance in 1961 and American Protection Insurance in 1962. In 1964 the company introduced Highly Protected Risk coverage in its commercial insurance.

Lumbermens formed Kemperco, Inc., a publicly owned holding company, now called Kemper Corporation, in 1967 to acquire 5 of the Kemper Group companies. The company's advertising program included the Kemper Open (golf), started in 1968.

In the 1980s the company purchased stock brokerage firms, including Loewi (1982), Prescott, Ball & Turben (1982), and Boettcher (1985). The company also added offices in West Germany, France, and Japan in 1985.

In 1989 Lumbermens purchased AMICO from Kemper Corporation for 9.6 million shares of Kemper stock and then authorized a reorganization of Kemper (approved by the stockholders in 1990) into Kemper Corporation and Kemper National Insurance Companies. Kemper Corporation now includes all the stockholder-owned companies, and Kemper National Insurance has all the mutual companies of the Kemper Group. Lumbermens still owns 38% of Kemper Corporation stock.

WHERE

HQ: Long Grove, Illinois 60049
Phone: 708-540-2000
FAX: 708-540-2494

Kemper provides financial services worldwide.

WHAT

	1989 Sales		1989 Pretax Income	
	$ mil	% of total	$ mil	% of total
Property-casualty insurance	498	18	50	16
Reinsurance	388	14	58	19
Life insurance	764	27	117	37
Investment services	1,090	38	72	23
Other	93	3	17	5
Adjustments	(59)	—	2	—
Total	**2,774**	**100**	**316**	**100**

Financial Services
Investment management and advisory services
Life insurance
Mutual funds
Property and casualty insurance
Reinsurance
Securities brokerage

Securities Brokerage Subsidiaries
Bateman Eichler, Hill Richards, Inc. (Los Angeles)
Blunt Ellis & Loewi, Inc. (Milwaukee)
Boettcher & Company, Inc. (Denver)
INVEST Financial Corp. (Tampa)
Kemper Capital Markets, Inc. (Chicago)
Kemper Clearing Corp. (Milwaukee)
Lovett Underwood Neuhaus & Webb, Inc. (Houston)
Prescott, Ball & Turben, Inc. (Cleveland)

RANKINGS

25th in *Fortune* 50 Diversified Financial Cos.
40th in *Fortune* 50 Life Insurance Cos. (Kemper Investors Life)
301st in *Forbes* Sales 500
333rd in *Business Week* 1000

COMPETITION

Aetna
American Express
AIG
CIGNA
Equitable
General Re
ITT
John Hancock
Lloyd's of London
Massachusetts Mutual
Merrill Lynch
Metropolitan
New York Life
Northwestern Mutual
Primerica
Prudential
Sears
Tokio Marine & Fire
Travelers
USF&G
Other insurers
Stockbrokers

HOW MUCH

	9 Yr. Growth	1980	1981	1982	1983	1984	1985	1986	1987	1988	1989
Sales ($ mil)	7.4%	1,460	2,076	1,985	2,222	2,302	2,882	3,330	3,669	3,488	2,774
Net income ($ mil)	12.0%	83	80	75	68	25	76	148	195	198	230
Income as % of sales	—	5.7%	3.9%	3.8%	3.1%	1.1%	2.6%	4.4%	5.3%	5.7%	8.3%
Earnings per share ($)	8.2%	2.19	2.03	1.77	1.56	0.57	1.54	2.51	3.19	3.37	4.44
Stock price – high ($)	—	12.17	12.50	14.67	17.21	15.42	24.33	35.50	38.75	27.50	51.88
Stock price – low ($)	—	6.96	10.00	7.67	12.04	9.75	14.67	23.00	19.25	20.75	22.75
Stock price – close ($)	17.6%	10.96	10.92	12.58	13.29	14.67	24.33	25.00	20.50	24.00	47.00
P/E – high	—	6	6	8	11	27	16	14	12	8	12
P/E – low	—	3	5	4	8	17	10	9	6	6	5
Dividends per share ($)	6.3%	0.47	0.53	0.60	0.60	0.60	0.60	0.60	0.60	0.72	0.81
Book value per share ($)	10.7%	14.12	15.02	16.27	18.32	17.51	19.18	23.48	26.50	29.97	35.25

1989 Year End:
Debt ratio: 10.8%
Return on equity: 13.6%
Cash (mil): $245
Assets (mil): $12,696
Long-term debt (mil): $208
Number of shares (mil): 49
Dividends:
1989 average yield: 1.7%
1989 payout: 18.2%
Market value (mil): $2,296

Stock Price History high/low 1980-89

SAB

KIMBERLY-CLARK CORPORATION

OVERVIEW

Kimberly-Clark makes paper and fiber products for personal care, health care, and industrial use but is best known for its Kleenex and Kotex brand consumer products, controlling about 45% of the facial tissue market and 30% of the feminine pad market in 1989. The company dominates the incontinence care market, controlling over 50% of the market share during the last 5 years. Kimberly-Clark also makes other household products, including disposable diapers and paper towels.

Kimberly-Clark ranks 5th in the US forest products industry in terms of 1989 sales.

Commercial products include barber towels, business paper, envelopes, cigarette and tea bag papers, and newsprint.

Kimberly-Clark's pioneering work in the development of nonwoven fabrics (with compressed rather than woven fibers) led to the manufacture of disposable surgical gowns, masks, and related products.

K-C Aviation, a Kimberly-Clark subsidiary, operates the company's Milwaukee-based commercial airline, Midwest Express, and aircraft maintenance facilities in Dallas and Milwaukee.

NYSE symbol: KMB
Incorporated: Delaware, 1928
Fiscal year ends: December 31

WHO

Chairman and CEO: Darwin E. Smith, age 64, $1,308,000 pay
President, North American Pulp and Paper: James G. Grosklaus, age 55, $559,440 pay
President, Personal Care: Wayne R. Sanders, age 42, $524,440 pay
SVP and Principal Financial Officer: Brendan M. O'Neill, age 51
Auditors: Deloitte & Touche
Employees: 39,664

WHEN

In 1872 Havilah Babcock, Charles Clark, John Kimberly, and Frank Shattuck founded Kimberly, Clark & Company in Neenah, Wisconsin, to manufacture newsprint from rags. Incorporated as Kimberly & Clark Company (1880), it went on to build a pulp and paper making plant on the Fox River in 1889, thereby creating Kimberly, Wisconsin.

In 1914 the company developed cellucotton, a cotton substitute used by the US army as surgical cotton during WWI. Army nurses discovered that cellucotton pads could be used as disposable sanitary napkins, and in 1920 the company introduced Kotex, the first disposable feminine hygiene product. The introduction of Kleenex, the first throw-away handkerchief, followed in 1924. Soon many Americans were referring to all sanitary napkins and paper tissues as Kotex and Kleenex.

In the 1920s the company built its first foreign pulp mill, in Ontario, and joined with the New York Times Company in 1926 to build a newsprint mill at the same location. The company adopted the name Kimberly-Clark Corporation in 1928, the same year it was listed on the NYSE.

Kimberly-Clark opened plants in Mexico, Germany, and the UK in the 1950s and expanded operations to 17 more foreign locations in the 1960s. The company continued to make newsprint and other types of paper and dominated the feminine hygiene products market until the 1960s, when Tampax tampons took over a large market share.

Before his retirement in 1971, Guy Minard (CEO since 1968) sold the 4 paper mills that handled Kimberly-Clark's unprofitable coated-paper business and entered the paper towel (Teri Towels) and disposable diaper markets. Minard's successor, Darwin Smith, introduced Kimbies diapers in 1968, but they leaked and were temporarily withdrawn from the market. Smith introduced an improved version of Kimbies in 1976, followed closely by the introduction of Huggies, a premium-priced diaper with elastic leg bands, in 1978.

The company formed Midwest Express Airlines, Inc., an airline tailored to the needs of business travelers, in 1984. Initially offering daily flights from Milwaukee to Boston and Dallas, Midwest Express added service to 6 other major cities by mid-1988.

Smith moved Kimberly-Clark's headquarters from Neenah to Dallas in 1985. From 1988 to 1989 he served as chairman and president of the King Ranch while still acting as chief executive of Kimberly-Clark.

Kimberly-Clark successfully introduced Huggies Pull-Ups, disposable training pants for toddlers, in 1989, and His/Hers Huggies, separate diapers for boys and girls, in 1990.

WHERE

HQ: PO Box 619100, DFW Airport Station, Dallas, TX 75261
Phone: 214-830-1200
FAX: 214-830-1289

Kimberly-Clark has manufacturing operations in 19 states and 17 foreign countries.

	1989 Sales		1989 Operating Income	
	$ mil	% of total	$ mil	% of total
US	4,064	69	485	70
Canada	780	13	86	12
Europe	741	12	61	9
Other countries	346	6	58	9
Adjustments	(197)	—	(17)	—
Total	**5,734**	**100**	**673**	**100**

WHAT

	1989 Sales		1989 Operating Income	
	$ mil	% of total	$ mil	% of total
Consumer & service products	4,481	77	535	77
Newsprint & paper	1,096	19	129	19
Air transportation	211	4	26	4
Adjustments	(54)	—	(17)	—
Total	**5,734**	**100**	**673**	**100**

Airlines
Midwest Express Airlines, Inc.

Consumer Brands
Delsey (bathroom tissue)
Depend (incontinence products)
Hi-Dri (paper towels)
Huggies (disposable diapers)
Huggies Pull-Ups (disposable training pants)
Kleenex (facial tissue, table napkins)
Kotex, Lightdays, New Freedom (feminine pads)

Industrial & Health Care Products
Cigarette, coated, and printing papers
Newsprint and pulp
Nonwoven surgical room materials
Physical therapy equipment

RANKINGS

86th in *Fortune* 500 Industrial Cos.
151st in *Forbes* Sales 500
116th in *Business Week* 1000
309th in *Business Week* Global 1000

COMPETITION

Boise Cascade
Champion International
Georgia-Pacific
International Paper
James River
Johnson & Johnson
Mead
Midway
Procter & Gamble
Scott
Southwest
Weyerhaeuser
Other paper companies

HOW MUCH

	9 Yr. Growth	1980	1981	1982	1983	1984	1985	1986	1987	1988	1989
Sales ($ mil)	9.2%	2,600	2,886	2,946	3,274	3,616	4,073	4,303	4,885	5,394	5,734
Net income ($ mil)	9.9%	182	205	197	189	218	267	269	325	379	424
Income as % of sales	—	7.0%	7.1%	6.7%	5.8%	6.0%	6.6%	6.3%	6.7%	7.0%	7.4%
Earnings per share ($)	11.6%	1.96	2.28	2.20	2.09	2.38	2.91	2.94	3.73	4.71	5.26
Stock price – high ($)	—	13.75	18.31	20.19	24.75	24.38	35.00	46.31	63.25	65.75	75.38
Stock price – low ($)	—	9.44	13.34	14.19	16.44	19.69	22.50	31.69	39.38	46.13	57.38
Stock price – close ($)	20.9%	13.31	16.44	18.47	23.00	23.81	33.50	39.94	50.00	58.25	73.50
P/E – high	—	7	8	9	12	10	12	16	17	14	14
P/E – low	—	5	6	6	8	8	8	11	11	10	11
Dividends per share ($)	14.0%	0.80	0.90	1.00	1.05	1.10	1.16	1.24	1.44	1.60	2.60
Book value per share ($)	6.8%	14.33	15.03	15.74	16.41	17.20	19.03	20.89	19.61	23.17	25.85

1989 Year End:
Debt ratio: 26.3%
Return on equity: 21.5%
Cash (mil): $164
Current ratio: 1.14
Long-term debt (mil): $745
Number of shares (mil): 81
Dividends:
1989 average yield: 3.5%
1989 payout: 49.4%
Market value (mil): $5,930

Stock Price History high/low 1980-89

KING RANCH, INC.

OVERVIEW

The King Ranch is the epitome of the Great Texas Ranching Empire. It inspired Edna Ferber's *Giant* and the Rock Hudson–Elizabeth Taylor–James Dean film that followed.

King Ranch's 825,000-acre expanse, larger than Rhode Island, sprawls across the southern tip of Texas. The ranch has, throughout its history, been the domain of one family — the heirs of the founder, Capt. Richard King. Three cousins — Ida Larkin Clement, Katherine Kleberg Yarborough, and Helen Kleberg Groves — now own the bulk of the stock, a family fortune said to exceed $1.3 billion. Oil and gas royalties on the South Texas ranch alone have surpassed $1 billion since WWII.

The ranch runs 60,000 head of Santa Gertrudis cattle, the breed that it developed. The ranch also breeds quarter horses and thoroughbreds. King Ranch owns overseas real estate and cultivates grain sorghum and cotton in Texas and sugarcane and sweet corn in Florida.

WHEN

Just as Texas was joining the Union in 1845, steamboat pilot Richard King arrived at the Rio Grande to ferry goods. After he had traveled through the vast plain between the river and Corpus Christi, he and a Texas Ranger friend began running cattle around Santa Gertrudis Creek in 1853.

The Ranger was later killed by a jealous husband, but King continued to build the ranch in the Wild Horse Desert, an area known for the mustangs that roamed free. In 1858 King and his wife, Henrietta, built their homestead at a site recommended by friend Robert E. Lee.

King relocated the residents of an entire drought-ravaged Mexican village to the ranch and employed them as ranch hands, known ever since as *Kineños* ("King's men"). King Ranch endured attacks from Union guerrillas during the Civil War and from Mexican bandits after the war. In 1867 the ranch used its famed Running W brand for the first time.

After King's death in 1885, a Corpus Christi attorney named Robert Kleberg married King's daughter Alice and managed the ranch for his mother-in-law.

Henrietta King died in 1925, and the Klebergs assembled land through inheritance or purchase from other heirs. Before his death in 1932, Kleberg passed control of the ranch to his sons, Richard Kleberg, Sr., and Bob Kleberg. In 1933 Bob Kleberg negotiated an exclusive and lucrative oil and gas lease, through the year 2013, with Humble Oil, later part of Exxon. The ranch was incorporated in 1935.

While Richard Kleberg, Sr., served in Congress, Bob Kleberg intensified crossbreeding of cattle. British breeds, imported to flesh out the stringy native longhorns, were not suited to dry, hot South Texas. From crossbreeding Indian Brahman cattle, the King Ranch developed the Santa Gertrudis breed, recognized by the US government in 1940 as the first beef breed ever created in America.

Bob Kleberg also made King Ranch a leader in breeding quarter horses, the stock used to work cattle. In thoroughbred breeding, Bob Kleberg bought Kentucky Derby winner Bold Venture (1938) and Idle Hour Stable, a noted Kentucky breeding farm (1946). In 1946 a King Ranch horse, Assault, won racing's Triple Crown.

Richard Kleberg, Sr., died in 1955, and, with Bob's death in 1974, the family turned to James Clement, husband of one of the founder's great-granddaughters, to become CEO. The corporation formed King Ranch Oil and Gas in 1980 to explore for and produce oil and gas in 5 states and the Gulf of Mexico.

When Clement retired in 1988, Darwin Smith became the first CEO not related by blood or marriage to founder Richard King; he moved company headquarters from Kingsville to Dallas. Smith doubled as CEO for Dallas-based Kimberly-Clark, and he returned full-time to Kimberly-Clark after only a year, passing the reins to Roger Jarvis, head of the Houston-based oil and gas operation. Corporate headquarters moved from Dallas to Houston, but Vice President Tio Kleberg, son of Richard Kleberg, Jr., remained in charge of the South Texas giant that his great-great-grandfather had carved out of the Wild Horse Desert.

HOW MUCH

	9 Yr. Growth	1981	1982	1983	1984	1985	1986	1987	1988	1989	1990
Taxable value ($ mil)											
Santa Gertrudis ISD	(16.8%)	1,133	1,086	1,070	997	1,078	593	336	243	197	216
Laureles ISD	(10.6%)	369	421	460	485	480	305	219	168	133	135
Total ($ mil)	(14.9%)	1,502	1,507	1,530	1,482	1,558	898	555	411	330	351

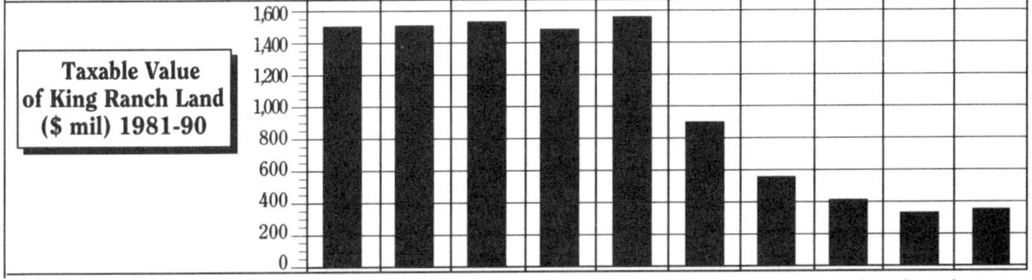

Taxable Value of King Ranch Land ($ mil) 1981-90

Note: The King Ranch comprises more than 90% of the property in 2 Texas school districts, Santa Gertrudis Independent School District (ISD) (197 sq. mi.) and Laureles ISD (360 sq. mi.)

Private company
Incorporated: Texas, 1935

WHO

Chairman: Leroy G. Denman, Jr.
President and CEO: Roger L. Jarvis, age 35
VP: Stephen J. "Tio" Kleberg, age 44
VP, Controller, and Assistant Secretary: James E. Savage
VP Audit: James B. Spear
VP, General Counsel, Secretary, and Assistant Treasurer: Larry L. Worden
Director: Thomas W. Keesee, Jr.
Director: Dr. Abraham Zaleznik
Employees: 400

WHERE

HQ: Two Greenspoint Plaza, 16825 Northchase, Suite 1450, Houston, TX 77060
Phone: 713-872-5566
FAX: 713-872-7209

King Ranch operates ranching and farming interests in South Texas, Florida, and Brazil. It breeds thoroughbred racehorses in Kentucky. King Ranch Oil and Gas, Inc., headquartered in Houston, explores for and produces oil and gas in Texas, Oklahoma, Mississippi, and the Gulf of Mexico.

US Ranching Operations
Big B Ranch (Belle Glade, FL)
Encino Ranch (Encino, TX)
Eslabon Feedyard (Kingsville, TX)
King Ranch Farm (Lexington, KY)
Laureles Ranch (Kingsville, TX)
Main Ranch (Kingsville, TX)
Norias Ranch (Kingsville, TX)

WHAT

Ranching Animals
Cattle
- Monkey (foundation sire of the Santa Gertrudis breed)
- Running W "A" herd

Quarter Horses
- Mr San Peppy
- Old Sorrel
- Peppy
- Peppy San Badger
- Wimpy

Thoroughbred Horses
- Assault (1946 Triple Crown winner)
- Bold Venture
- Chicaro
- Gallant Bloom
- High Gun
- Middleground

Farming
Cotton
Sod
Sugarcane
Sweet corn
Wheat

Oil & Gas Exploration & Production

Subsidiaries
Buck & Doe Run Valley Farms (cattle ranch)
King Ranch Oil & Gas I.C.
Kingsville Lumber (retails building material)
Kingsville Milling (owns commercial property)
Kingsville Publishing Co. (newspaper)
Robstown Hardware (farm equipment)

COMPETITION

Agricultural and oil companies

KLM

OVERVIEW

Amsterdam-based Koninklijke Luchtvaart Maatschappij (better known as KLM) is one of the world's most innovative and progressive airlines. The company is the only non-US airline to have its common stock traded on the NYSE. The Dutch government owns 38%.

Partly due to the small demand for air service to Amsterdam in comparison to other world capitals, KLM has developed into one of the most international of airlines. The company has fought for the liberalization of international restrictions on airline ownership and traffic and has made investments in British (Air UK), Belgian (Sabena), and US (Northwest) airlines. KLM has traditionally been among the first to adopt new airplane models.

KLM plans to meet the challenge of European economic liberalization in 1992 by building strategic alliances with other airlines to expand its reach and by continuing to modernize its fleet. The company is also expanding worker training, with an emphasis on quality service, and strengthening its maintenance operations at its Schiphol (Amsterdam's airport) hub to increase revenues from other airlines.

WHEN

KLM was founded in 1919 in The Hague by Albert Plesman, a young aviator, with the backing of several Dutch banking and business interests. The company's name, Koninklijke Luchtvaart Maatschappij, lent credibility to the venture because Koninklijke, meaning "royal," could be used only by permission of the Royal Dutch government. KLM's first flight was from London to Amsterdam (1920) and was so successful that flights from Amsterdam to Copenhagen also began that year. The company set up a separate department (1921) to conduct aerial survey and photography work, forming the basis for KLM Aerocarto (1954), now one of the leaders in the field. Service to Brussels (1922) and Paris (1923) added to KLM's growing list of destinations.

KLM's rapid expansion and quick adoption of new planes made by Dutch company Fokker earned it a wide reputation for efficiency and service in the late 1920s. The company initiated the longest air route in the world in 1927 (8,700 miles), from Amsterdam to Indonesia. KLM extended its European routes to Prague (1935), Vienna (1936), and Oslo (1939), but Hitler's invasion of the Netherlands shut down KLM's European operations. Plesman was arrested by the Germans while trying to negotiate peace between Germany and England but was released in 1942.

After WWII, Plesman quickly reestablished KLM service. The company had expanded to Africa and the Americas by 1948. After Plesman's death in 1954, the company suffered from low ridership, the expense of converting to jet aircraft, and nationalistic tendencies in the industry that prevented KLM, coming from a small country, from negotiating service to major ports. In 1966 the company established NLM Dutch Airlines (renamed NLM CityHopper, 1976) for commuter service within the country.

KLM addressed problems of overcapacity in the 1970s by converting the rear portions of its 747s to cargo storage (1975). In 1989 KLM became an investor in Wings Holdings, a company established to buy NWA (parent company of Northwest Airlines). In 1990 the DOT forced KLM to reduce its initial stake of $400 million (about 60% of the equity of NWA) to $150 million and only 5% of NWA's voting stock, partly due to a law preventing foreigners from owning more than 25% of a domestic carrier. Later in 1989 KLM completed negotiations allowing the company and British Airways to each acquire 20% of Sabena, the Belgian airline.

In 1990 the airline added more routes to Eastern Europe, reflecting the opening of those markets.

HOW MUCH

	9 Yr. Growth	1980	1981	1982	1983	1984	1985	1986	1987	1988	1989
Sales ($ mil)	6.8%	1,543	1,602	1,702	1,748	1,692	1,629	2,215	2,641	3,002	2,787
Net income ($ mil)	42.4%	7	5	12	15	35	84	118	148	169	175
Income as % of sales	—	0.5%	0.3%	0.7%	0.9%	2.1%	5.1%	5.3%	5.6%	5.6%	6.3%
Earnings per share ($)	36.6%	0.20	0.13	0.32	0.39	0.74	1.57	2.32	2.91	3.20	3.31
Stock price – high ($)	—	12.60	7.98	11.15	11.45	12.75	14.80	20.38	23.88	27.75	21.63
Stock price – low ($)	—	7.33	4.90	5.23	5.90	9.40	9.40	12.75	17.50	13.25	15.00
Stock price – close ($)	12.0%	7.60	5.23	7.50	10.85	12.50	12.88	18.75	18.13	15.75	21.00
P/E – high	—	63	61	34	29	17	9	9	8	9	7
P/E – low	—	37	38	16	15	13	6	6	6	4	5
Dividends per share ($)	0.7%	0.70	0.00	0.00	0.00	0.00	0.00	0.51	0.69	0.75	0.75
Book value per share ($)	5.7%	15.98	14.51	13.33	13.74	11.16	11.90	17.98	25.35	28.82	26.35

1989 Year End:
Debt ratio: 56.5%
Return on equity: 12.0%
Cash (mil): $920
Current ratio: 1.61
Long-term debt (mil): $1,929
Number of shares (mil): 53
Dividends:
1989 average yield: 3.6%
1989 payout: 22.5%
Market value (mil): $1,109

Stock Price History high/low 1980-89

NYSE symbol: KLM
Incorporated: Netherlands, 1919
Fiscal year ends: March 31

WHO

Chairman: M. Albrecht
President: Jan F. A. de Soet, age 64
SVP Finance and Holdings: P. C. W. Alberda van Ekenstein
Auditors: KPMG Klynveld Kraayenhof & Co.
Employees: 25,195

WHERE

HQ: Koninklijke Luchtvaart Maatschappij NV, Amsterdamseweg 55, Amstelveen, The Netherlands
Phone: 011-31-20-649-91-23
FAX: 011-31-20-412872
US HQ: 565 Taxter Rd., Elmsford, NY 10523
US Phone: 914-784-2000
US FAX: 914-784-2103

KLM's center of operations is Schiphol Airport, near Amsterdam. Routes cover 148 cities in 77 countries.

	1989 Sales	
	$ mil	% of total
North America	879	32
Far East	675	24
Europe	611	22
Central & South America	237	8
Africa	209	7
Near East	134	5
Charters	42	2
Total	**2,787**	**100**

WHAT

	1989 Sales	
	$ mil	% of total
Passengers & baggage	2,120	76
Freight	581	21
Mail	44	2
Charters	42	1
Total	**2,787**	**100**

Commuter Airlines
KLM Helicopters (helicopter charter services)
NetherLines (commuter service from Amsterdam to adjacent countries)
NLM CityHopper (regional airline service to north and central European destinations)

Other Airline Holdings
Air UK (15% owned)
Martinair Holland (30% owned)
NWA (US, 5% of voting stock owned)
Sabena (Belgium, 20% owned)
Transavia Holland (40% owned)

Other Activities
Covia Partnership (10% owned, Apollo airline reservation service)
Frans Maas Beheer (minority interest, truck company)
The Galileo Co., Ltd. (11% owned, automated distribution system)
Golden Tulip (hotel marketing and reservation service; KLM has an equity interest in 12 hotels)
KLM Aerocarto (60% owned, aerial photography and surveying)
Polygon Insurance Co., Ltd. (33% owned)
Service Q, General Service Co. (aircraft and building maintenance)

COMPETITION

AMR
Delta
NWA
Pan Am
TWA
UAL

KNIGHT-RIDDER, INC.

OVERVIEW

Based in Miami, Knight-Ridder, Inc., is an international information and communications company engaged in newspaper publishing; business news and information services; electronic retrieval services; news, graphics, and photo services; cable television; and newsprint manufacturing.

The company owns 29 daily newspapers in 26 cities in 16 states, including the *Miami Herald* (daily circulation: 424,563) and the *Detroit Free Press* (629,182).

Business Information Services (BIS) is the fastest-growing arm of Knight-Ridder, with 1989 revenues of $273 million. Within BIS is Dialog, the world's largest on-line, full-text information database, serving 102 countries; VU/TEXT, a computerized retrieval service; and The Financial Information Group (FIG).

Despite a weakening in advertising revenue, Knight-Ridder is optimistic about its growth in the 1990s as reflected in its winning the long-fought battle to create a joint operating agreement between the *Detroit Free Press* and the *Detroit News* in November 1989, and a $300 million expenditure to build a new production facility in Philadelphia.

WHEN

Knight-Ridder began as a 1974 merger between Knight Newspapers, the 2nd largest newspaper group by circulation, with 16 dailies, and Ridder Publications, the 3rd largest, with 19 dailies. Knight Newspapers swapped stock worth nearly $160 million for 77,000 shares of Ridder and dominated the new company's board of directors.

Knight Newspapers began in 1903 when Charles L. Knight, a lawyer-turned-editor, purchased the *Akron Beacon Journal* and became a publisher. Knight died in 1933, leaving the paper to his sons, Jack and Jim. With their guidance the company grew to include 16 metropolitan dailies, including the *Miami Herald* (1937), the *Detroit Free Press* (1940), and the *Philadelphia Inquirer* (1969). The company went public in 1969.

Ridder Publications began in 1892 when Herman Ridder bought a New York German-language newspaper, the *Staats-Zeitung*. He expanded in 1926 with the purchase of the *Journal of Commerce*, a New York shipping daily that is still operated by the company today. Over the next 5 decades the company grew to 19 dailies and 8 weeklies, mostly in the West. In 1969 Ridder became publicly owned. After the merger in 1974, Knight's Lee Hills became chairman and CEO and Ridder's Bernard H. Ridder, Jr., became vice-chairman. Knight's president, Alvah H. Chapman, became president of the new company until his promotion to CEO in 1976.

During the 1970s and 1980s Knight-Ridder expanded into television, radio, and book publishing. In 1978 the company purchased VHF stations in Rhode Island, New York, and Michigan. The company bought HP Books in 1979 and formed TKR Cable Company with Tele-Communications, Inc., in 1981. A year later Knight-Ridder launched VU/TEXT, an on-line library retrieval system, followed in 1983 with Viewtron, America's first full-scale consumer videotex system. In 1988 the company purchased Dialog, the world's largest on-line, full-text information system, from Lockheed for $353 million.

During the 1980s Knight-Ridder lost more than $90 million in Detroit because of fierce competition between the *Detroit News* (owned by Gannett Company) and the *Detroit Free Press*. Fearing the closing of the nation's 8th largest daily newspaper, the company sought a joint operating agreement with Gannett. After a 43-month battle in the federal courts over an antitrust issue, the 2 companies signed a 100-year joint operating agreement in November 1989, which will permit them to share the profits of both papers serving the nation's 5th largest market.

HOW MUCH

	9 Yr. Growth	1980	1981	1982	1983	1984	1985	1986	1987	1988	1989
Sales ($ mil)	8.4%	1,099	1,237	1,328	1,473	1,665	1,730	1,911	2,073	2,083	2,268
Net income ($ mil)	7.6%	93	100	103	119	141	133	140	155	147	180
Income as % of sales	—	8.5%	8.1%	7.8%	8.1%	8.5%	7.7%	7.3%	7.5%	7.0%	7.9%
Earnings per share ($)	10.1%	1.44	1.54	1.55	1.79	2.14	2.18	2.40	2.65	2.58	3.40
Stock price – high ($)	—	16.06	20.88	25.75	30.44	31.00	41.38	57.88	61.25	47.75	58.38
Stock price – low ($)	—	9.56	13.38	13.63	22.13	21.25	28.00	37.50	33.25	35.75	42.88
Stock price – close ($)	17.3%	13.94	15.13	24.75	26.50	29.25	39.88	46.88	40.13	45.38	58.38
P/E – high	—	11	14	17	17	14	19	24	23	19	17
P/E – low	—	7	9	9	12	10	13	16	13	14	13
Dividends per share ($)	14.3%	0.38	0.43	0.46	0.58	0.67	0.79	0.91	1.03	1.15	1.25
Book value per share ($)	7.4%	9.37	10.55	11.71	12.59	14.17	12.38	14.28	15.85	15.47	17.83

1989 Year End:
Debt ratio: 41.9%
Return on equity: 20.4%
Cash (mil): $61
Current ratio: 1.2
Long-term debt (mil): $661
Number of shares (mil): 51
Dividends:
1989 average yield: 2.1%
1989 payout: 36.6%
Market value (mil): $3,003

Stock Price History high/low 1980-89

70 60 50 40 30 20 10 0

NYSE symbol: KRI
Incorporated: Florida, 1976
Fiscal year ends: December 31

WHO

Chairman and CEO: James K. Batten, age 54, $677,992 pay
President: P. Anthony Ridder, age 49, $406,954 pay
SVP Finance: Robert F. Singleton, age 59
Auditors: Ernst & Young
Employees: 21,000

WHERE

HQ: One Herald Plaza, Miami, FL 33132
Phone: 305-376-3800
FAX: 305-376-3828

Knight-Ridder's media services reach audiences in 129 countries.

WHAT

	1989 Sales		1989 Operating Income	
	$ mil	% of total	$ mil	% of total
Newspapers	1,989	88	348	97
Business information svcs.	273	12	12	3
Other operations	6	—	—	—
Adjustments	—	—	(38)	—
Total	**2,268**	**100**	**322**	**100**

Major Newspapers	Daily Circulation (Average)
Akron Beacon Journal	155,958
The Charlotte Observer	233,585
Detroit Free Press	629,182
(Long Beach) *Press-Telegram*	130,907
Miami Herald	424,563
Philadelphia Daily News	236,445
The Philadelphia Inquirer	499,369
San Jose Mercury News	275,740
St. Paul Pioneer Press	192,124
The Wichita Eagle	119,542

Cable TV
SCI Holdings, Inc. (7.5% interest)
Tele-Communications, Inc.
TKR Cable Co. (joint venture)

Business Information Services
Dialog (database for scientific, medical, education, professional, and business clients)
Journal of Commerce
VU/TEXT (database for legal, corporate, and media clients)

Financial Information Group
Knight-Ridder Financial News
MoneyCenter, Tradecenter, American Quotation Systems, Commodity News Services (real-time news and pricing information for the securities and commodities exchange industries)

RANKINGS

189th in *Fortune* 500 Industrial Cos.
362nd in *Forbes* Sales 500
216th in *Business Week* 1000
748th in *Business Week* Global 1000

COMPETITION

Advance Publications
ADP
Bertelsmann
Capital Cities/ABC
Citicorp
Commerce Clearing House
Dow Jones
Dun & Bradstreet
Gannett
Hearst
McGraw-Hill
Reuters
Tele-Communications

KOHLBERG KRAVIS ROBERTS & CO.

OVERVIEW

To many, the name Kohlberg Kravis Roberts & Co. (KKR) is synonymous with the high-dollar LBOs of the 1980s. That's understandable: New York City–based KKR orchestrated 4 of the 10 largest buyouts of all time, including the granddaddy of them all, the $29.6 billion RJR Nabisco deal.

For the first 1/2 of the decade, KKR was the white knight, coming to the rescue of troubled companies. The firm arranged financing, cut the deal, and gave company managers a piece of the action. KKR's investors made millions, and the firm was praised for saving companies from unscrupulous raiders. Some investors were getting returns of 40% a year. Then, beginning in 1985, KKR changed to being an aggressive participant, initiating bids on unwilling targets. This new approach was apparently not consistent with partner Jerome Kohlberg, Jr.'s philosophy, so he left the firm in 1987.

KKR, like other LBO deal makers, raises money from pension funds, venture capital funds, and nonprofits (such as universities). These "blind" pools of funds then are leveraged by borrowing considerable amounts of money, frequently through junk bonds, in order for KKR and its partners to buy the company. KKR takes about a 1.5% management fee for each fund it manages, a transaction fee, and a 10% to 15% equity (ownership) in the company along with management of the company. Once management has been able to pay off the debt with cash flow and by selling assets, the company is sold.

With the collapse of the junk bond market in 1989, KKR's takeover activity has slowed, and the firm has turned to managing its huge holdings. These holdings, which KKR controls through partnerships with its investors, include companies with total revenues in excess of $40 billion.

WHEN

In 1976 Jerome Kohlberg left investment banker Bear Stearns, where he had been assisting corporate managements with leveraged buyouts for over a decade, to form his own firm. He brought with him Henry Kravis and Kravis's cousin, George Roberts. Together the 3 formed Kohlberg Kravis Roberts & Co., known throughout the industry as KKR.

KKR originally put together deals similar to those at Bear Stearns — friendly buyouts using equity contributed by a group of investors and a large amount of debt. The company assisted in the 1977 buyouts of brake-drum maker A. J. Industries ($23 million) and oil field equipment manufacturer L. B. Foster ($106 million). In 1979 KKR performed the first buyout of a major NYSE company, Houdaille Industries, a machine tool manufacturer, for $335 million. It was a sign of things to come in the 1980s.

KKR bought out the American Forest Products division of Bendix in 1981, but the deal went bad and investors lost all $93 million they had invested. By 1984 KKR had raised its 4th LBO fund, and in that year it performed the first $1 billion buyout, of Wometco Enterprises. The company also acquired Pace Industries (air conditioning) that year ($1.6 billion) and Amstar (sugar refiner), which was later sold for a $232 million profit.

In 1985 KKR raised its 5th LBO fund and put together the record-setting buyout of Beatrice ($6.2 billion). The Beatrice deal marked the first use of hostile tactics by KKR and depended heavily upon junk bond financing provided by Michael Milken of Drexel Burnham Lambert. This fund also financed the acquisitions of Safeway Stores ($5.7 billion) and Owens-Illinois ($3.6 billion) in 1986. KKR bought out Jim Walter Homes (now Hillsborough Holdings, $2.4 billion) in 1987 and Stop & Shop ($1.2 billion) in 1988.

In 1987 KKR held a majority stake in over 20 companies with combined sales of $38 billion, a total that (had it been eligible) would have placed KKR among *Fortune*'s 10 largest companies. That year Kohlberg, unhappy with the firm's hostile image, left to form Kohlberg & Company. KKR continued as a firm of 19 professionals and a receptionist who was an equity owner. Kravis continued to work in New York while Roberts and 2 other partners, Robert MacDonnell and Michael Michelson, operated out of San Francisco.

After raising a 6th LBO fund of $5.6 billion in 1988, KKR performed the largest buyout ever: the $29.6 billion acquisition of RJR Nabisco, bringing the sales of companies KKR controls to over $50 billion. KKR's LBO activity has slowed, although it looked at 50 different deals between early 1989 and mid-1990. The firm said there were few good opportunities, a lack of junk bonds and bank loans, and an expensive stock market.

HOW MUCH

	9 Yr. Growth	1980	1981	1982	1983	1984	1985	1986	1987	1988	1989
Value of major LBO deals ($ mil)	—	—	1,145	—	350	3,907	10,800	9,290	2,400	32,930	405
No. of major LBO deals	—	—	5	—	1	5	3	2	1	4	22

Value of Major LBO Deals ($ mil) 1980-89

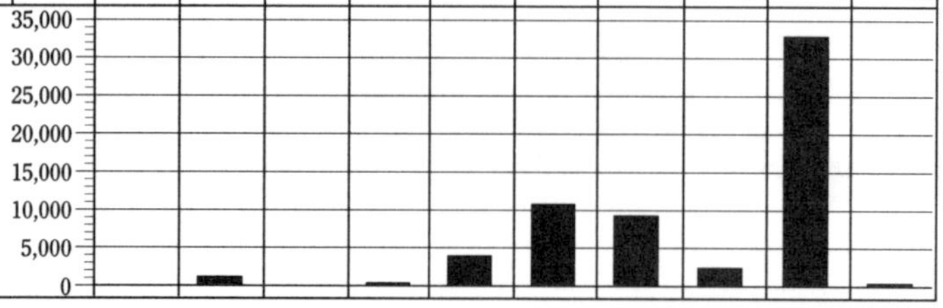

35,000
30,000
25,000
20,000
15,000
10,000
5,000
0

Partnership
Founded: New York, 1976

WHO

Founding Partner: Henry R. Kravis, age 46
Founding Partner: George R. Roberts, age 47
Employees: 20

WHERE

HQ: 9 W. 57th St., Suite 4200, New York, NY 10019
Phone: 212-750-8300
FAX: 212-593-2430 (public relations firm)

The companies controlled by KKR operate nationally and globally.

WHAT

Largest LBO Deals	$ bil
RJR Nabisco	29.6
Beatrice	6.2
Safeway	5.7
Owens-Illinois	3.6

Investment Holdings
Auto Zone automotive parts retailer
Beatrice (sale pending)
Duracell
First Interstate
Fred Meyer
Hillsborough Holdings
IDEX Corp.
K-III (formerly part of Macmillan Publishing)
Marley
Motel 6 (sale pending)
Owens-Illinois
PacTrust (Pacific Realty trust)
RJR Nabisco
Safeway
Seaman Furniture
The Stop & Shop Cos.
Union Texas Petroleum (sale pending)
World Color Press

Investors in KKR Partnerships
Insurance companies
- Equitable
- John Hancock
- Metropolitan

Nonprofit organizations
- Harvard
- MIT
- Salvation Army

State pension funds
- Michigan
- New York
- Oregon
- Washington

Bank venture capital firms
- BankAmerica
- Bankers Trust
- Continental Bank
- First Chicago
- Security Pacific

COMPETITION

Other firms active in buyouts include:
American Express
American Financial
Berkshire Hathaway
General Electric
Goldman Sachs
Hanson
Loews
McAndrews & Forbes
Merrill Lynch
Morgan Stanley
Prudential
Riklis Family
Salomon

KPMG

OVERVIEW

Klynveld Peat Marwick Goerdeler (KPMG) is the largest of the Big Six accounting firms, with total revenues of $4.3 billion. KPMG is owned by its 5,300 partners.

The firm has focused in recent years on increased international coverage, development of its consulting practice, and investment in technology. As a result, revenues in the Far and Middle East, Africa, and Australasia increased 56% from 1987 to 1989 and combined worldwide consulting fees grew 44% over the same period.

Another recent emphasis has been the development of a number of market specializations, including financial services, high technology, and media and entertainment. The firm has retained Lord Cockfield, an architect of the 1992 European market integration plan, as an adviser.

The firm expects recent mergers, such as the combination of Peat Marwick with Thorne Ernst & Whinney (Canada), Bohlins Revisionsbyrå (Sweden), and the Treuverkehr AG with Deutsche Treuhand (Germany), to increase worldwide revenues for 1990.

WHEN

KPMG was formed in 1987 when Peat, Marwick, Mitchell, & Copartners joined KMG, an international federation of accounting firms. The combined firms immediately jumped into first place in worldwide revenues.

Peat Marwick traces its roots back to 1911. In that year William Peat, who had established a respected accounting practice in London, met James Marwick on a westbound crossing of the Atlantic. Marwick and fellow University of Glasgow student S. Roger Mitchell had formed Marwick, Mitchell & Company in New York in 1897. Peat and Marwick agreed to join their firms, first under an agreement that terminated in 1919, and in 1925 through a permanent merger to form Peat, Marwick, Mitchell, & Copartners.

The firm grew slowly during the Great Depression and WWII despite the introduction of laws during 1933 and 1934 requiring publicly traded companies to undergo audits. In 1947 a partner named William Black became the senior partner of the firm, a position he held until 1965. In 1950 Peat Marwick merged with Barrow, Wade, Guthrie, the oldest and most prestigious firm in the US. Black also built up the firm's management consulting practice and acquired practices in Australia (1963). Peat Marwick restructured its international practice as PMM&Co. (International) in 1972 and reformed as Peat Marwick International in 1978.

In 1979 a group of European accounting firms led by the Netherlands' top-ranked Klynveld Kraayenhoff and Germany's 2nd-ranked Deutsche Treuhand discussed the formation of an international federation of accounting firms to aid in serving multinational companies. At that time 2 American firms that had been founded around the turn of the century, Main Lafrentz and Hurdman Cranstoun, agreed to merge in order to combat the growing reach of the "Big Eight." The Europeans needed an American member for their federation to succeed and had encouraged the formation of the new firm, Main Hurdman & Cranstoun. By the end of 1979 Main Hurdman joined the Europeans to form Klynveld Main Goerdeler (KMG), named after 2 of the member firms and the chairman of Deutsche Treuhand, Dr. Reinhard Goerdeler. Other members of the federation included C. Jespersen (Denmark), Thorne Riddel (Canada), Thomson McLintok (UK), and Fides Revision (Switzerland). KMG immediately became the 9th largest accounting firm in the US and 8th worldwide.

In 1987 Peat Marwick, then the 2nd largest firm, merged with KMG Main Hurdman to form Klynveld Peat Marwick Goerdeler (KPMG). Through the merger KPMG lost 10% of its business due to the departure of competing companies that had formerly been clients of Peat Marwick or KMG; but the firm nevertheless jumped into the #1 position worldwide, exceeding 2nd-ranked Arthur Andersen in total revenues in 1987.

HOW MUCH

	9 Yr. Growth	1980	1981	1982	1983	1984	1985	1986	1987	1988	1989
Revenues ($ mil)	20.3%	816	979	1,146	1,232	1,340	1,446	1,672	3,250	3,900	4,300
No. of countries	8.3%	57	66	71	79	82	89	88	115	—	117
No. of offices	11.2%	270	—	—	—	328	335	342	620	—	700
No. of partners	13.0%	1,769	1,931	2,015	2,242	2,326	2,507	2,726	5,150	5,050	5,300
No. of employees	14.0%	20,922	23,149	25,492	27,033	27,746	29,864	32,183	60,000	63,700	68,000

Revenues ($ mil) 1980-89

0
500
1,000
1,500
2,000
2,500
3,000
3,500
4,000
4,500

* Figures prior to 1987 are Peat Marwick only; 1987 through 1989 are total figures for KPMG Peat Marwick after 1987 merger.

Foreign partnership
Formed: 1987
Fiscal year ends: September 30

WHO

Chairman and CEO: Larry D. Horner, age 56
CFO: Robert Beecher
Personnel: 68,000

WHERE

HQ: Klynveld Peat Marwick Goerdeler, World Trade Center, Strawinskylaan 957, 1077 XX Amsterdam, The Netherlands
Phone: 011-31-20-75-0111
FAX: 011-31-20-71-1914
US HQ: 767 Fifth Ave., New York, NY 10153
US Phone: 212-909-5034
US FAX: 212-909-5299 (Communications)

KPMG maintains over 700 offices in 117 countries.

	1989 Revenues	
	$ mil	% of total
North & Latin America	2,020	47
Europe	1,890	44
Other	390	9
Total	**4,300**	**100**

WHAT

	1989 Revenues	
	$ mil	% of total
Auditing & accounting	2,800	65
Tax	850	20
Management consulting	650	15
Total	**4,300**	**100**

Areas of Specialization
Banking and financial services
Corporate recovery
Health care
High technology
Insurance
Media and entertainment
Mergers and acquisitions
Petroleum
Transportation

Representative Clients
Aetna
American Cyanamid
FMC
General Mills
Gillette
Hasbro
Kemper
Manufacturers Hanover
Melville
Motorola
Nestlé
PepsiCo
Philips
Polaroid
Security Pacific
Union Carbide

Major Member Firms
KPMG Deutsche Treuhand (Germany)
KPMG Klynveld Kraayenhoff (Netherlands)
KPMG Peat Marwick (US)
KPMG Peat Marwick McLintok (UK)
KPMG Peat Marwick Thorne (Canada)

RANKINGS

22nd in *Forbes* 400 US Private Cos.

COMPETITION

Arthur Andersen
Marsh & McLennan
McKinsey & Co.
Price Waterhouse
Saatchi & Saatchi

THE KROGER CO.

OVERVIEW

Cincinnati-based Kroger is the 2nd largest grocery chain in the US, behind American Stores. Kroger has been slimming down, putting about $333 million of assets on the block, to cope with $4.1 billion it borrowed to deflect unwelcome takeover overtures in 1988. Kroger lost $16 million in 1989, but, by cost-cutting and repackaging its debt, it was poised to make money again in 1990.

At the end of 1989, the company operated 1,234 food stores (1989 sales: $17.2 billion) under the Kroger, Dillon, and King Soopers banner, and it plans to add 40 new stores and remodel 100 each year into the mid-1990s. Kroger also operates 960 convenience stores (1989 sales: $783 million) under the names Kwik Shop, Turkey Hill Minit Market, and Time Savers Stores, among others.

Kroger makes many of the groceries it sells, operating 40 food processing plants, including dairies, bakeries, and ice cream plants.

NYSE symbol: KR
Incorporated: Ohio, 1902
Fiscal year ends: Saturday closest to December 31

WHO

Chairman: Lyle Everingham, age 63, $999,149 pay
President and CEO: Joseph A. Pichler, age 50, $701,789 pay
SVP and CFO: William J. Sinkula, $405,850 pay
Auditors: Coopers & Lybrand
Employees: 170,000

WHEN

Bernard Kroger was only 22 when he began the Great Western Tea Company in 1883 in Cincinnati. The son of German immigrant shopkeepers quickly turned a profit and added new stores. Kroger was the first grocer to use newspaper advertising for groceries, and, in another first, he introduced bakeries into stores.

In 1902 the company became Kroger Grocery and Baking Company, with 40 stores in Cincinnati and northern Kentucky. Two years later, Kroger became the first company to offer in-store butcher shops.

During his company's rise, Kroger developed a reputation as a demanding boss and a tough competitor, keeping overhead low and discounting prices. The company spread to St. Louis in 1912. Kroger sold his holdings in the company for $28 million in 1928, just before the stock market crash, and retired to Florida.

The company purchased other grocery companies in the late 1920s. Kroger bought units of the Piggly-Wiggly company in Ohio, Tennessee, Michigan, Kentucky, Missouri, and Oklahoma and acquired most of the stock of Piggly-Wiggly Corporation, which it held until the early 1940s.

In 1930 Kroger manager Michael Cullen suggested the idea of the supermarket, but Kroger executives demurred. Cullen left Kroger and began King Kullen supermarkets, still a chain in the Northeast.

Kroger continued to acquire companies in the 1950s, including stores in Texas, Georgia, and Washington, DC. With its 1960 purchase of Sav-on drug stores of New Jersey and its 1961 opening of the first SupeRx drug store in Ohio, Kroger broadened its sales beyond groceries.

In 1983 Kroger bought Kansas-based Dillon Food Stores. Also in 1983 it acquired Kwik Shop convenience stores.

In 1987 Kroger sold most of its interests in the Hook and SupeRx drug chains to private investors and focused on its combination food-and-drug stores. In 1988 Kroger faced take-over bids from the Herbert Haft family and from KKR, the LBO firm. Chairman and CEO Lyle Everingham and President Joseph Pichler warded off the raiders. They, in effect, launched an internal LBO; they borrowed $4.1 billion to pay a hefty dividend to shareholders and to purchase shares for an employee stock plan. Pichler was named CEO in 1990; Everingham remained chairman.

To reduce debt Kroger sold assets (most of its equity in Price Saver Membership Wholesale Clubs, 95 food stores, 29 liquor stores, and its Fry's California stores). The company also put 12 of its food processing plants up for sale. In 1990 it made its first major acquisition since the 1988 restructuring by buying 30 of 34 Meadowdale Food's Great Scott supermarkets in Detroit.

WHERE

HQ: 1014 Vine St., Cincinnati, OH 45202
Phone: 513-762-4000
FAX: 513-762-4454

Kroger operates 1,234 supermarkets in 32 midwestern and southern states. Of these, 246 are operated under other names in 10 states. The company also operates 960 convenience stores under various names in 16 states.

WHAT

	1989 Sales	
	$ mil	% of total
Food stores	17,161	90
Convenience stores	783	4
Other sales	888	5
Adjustments	272	1
Total	**19,104**	**100**

Grocery Stores
Circle Super Value (CO)
City Market (CO, NM, UT, and WY)
Dillon (KS)
Fry's Food Stores (AZ)
Gerbes (MO, OK, AR, and KS)
King Soopers (CO)
Kroger (Midwest and South)
M&M (GA)

Convenience Stores
Kwik Shop (KS, OK, IA, NE, and IL)
Loaf 'N Jug (CO, NM, and OK)
Mini Mart (CO, MT, ND, SD, WY, and NE)
Quik Stop Market (CA)
Time Savers Stores (LA)
Tom Thumb Food Stores (FL and AL)
Turkey Hill Minit Market (PA)

RANKINGS

5th in *Fortune* 50 Retailing Cos.
26th in *Forbes* Sales 500
508th in *Business Week* 1000

COMPETITION

Albertson's
American Stores
Ashland
Atlantic Richfield
Bruno's
Circle K
Coastal
Food Lion
Great A & P
Mobil
Safeway
Southland
Texaco
Winn-Dixie

HOW MUCH

	9 Yr. Growth	1980	1981	1982	1983	1984	1985	1986	1987	1988	1989
Sales ($ mil)	7.1%	10,317	11,267	11,902	15,236	15,923	17,124	17,123	17,660	19,053	19,104
Net income ($ mil)	—	103	129	144	127	157	181	56	183	35	(16)
Income as % of sales	—	1.0%	1.2%	1.2%	0.8%	1.0%	1.1%	0.3%	1.0%	0.2%	(0.1%)
Earnings per share ($)	—	*1.86*	2.22	2.32	1.38	1.73	2.03	0.60	2.18	0.23	(0.23)
Stock price – high ($)	—	11.88	13.94	23.63	21.44	19.75	30.81	35.00	41.50	59.00	19.75
Stock price – low ($)	—	7.00	9.63	11.69	16.88	14.56	18.94	21.38	23.38	8.38	8.38
Stock price – close ($)	3.4%	10.88	13.00	19.69	18.50	19.63	23.94	29.88	24.75	8.88	14.75
P/E – high	—	6	6	10	16	11	15	58	19	257	—
P/E – low	—	4	4	5	12	8	9	36	11	36	—
Dividends per share ($)	(100%)	0.70	0.79	0.88	0.96	1.00	1.00	1.03	1.05	40.82	0.00
Book value per share ($)	—	12.09	13.53	14.66	11.99	12.74	13.61	12.25	12.84	(36.20)	(35.42)

1989 Year End:
Debt ratio: 268.6%
Return on equity: 0.6%
Cash (mil): $115
Current ratio: 0.99
Long-term debt (mil): $4,724
Number of shares (mil): 84
Dividends:
1989 average yield: 0.0%
1989 payout: 0.0%
Market value (mil): $1,235

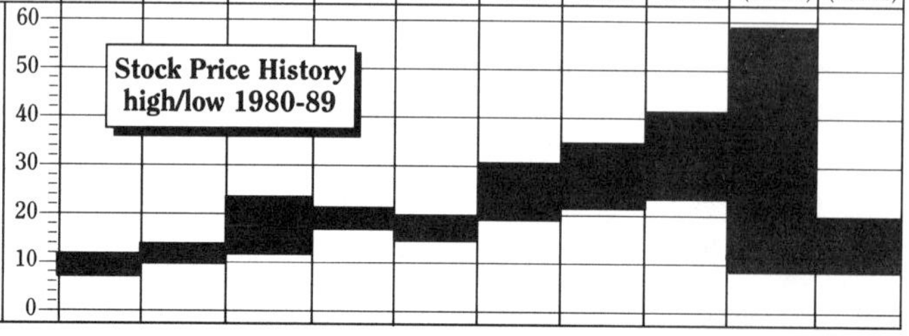

Stock Price History high/low 1980-89

LEVI STRAUSS AND COMPANY

OVERVIEW

With sales of $3.7 billion, privately owned Levi Strauss is the largest apparel manufacturer in the world and the 2nd largest jeans maker in the US after VF Corporation (Wrangler and Lee), and has the most internationally recognized apparel trademark. Aided by strong global demand (and the company's innovative advertising), Levi Strauss has sold over 2.5 billion pairs of Levi's jeans during its history.

The company's domestic operations consist of 6 marketing units: Men's Jeans, Youthwear, Womenswear, Menswear, Shirts, and Brittania Sportswear. Levi's branded products (which are usually made in the same region in which they are sold) are marketed through over 40,000 domestic retail outlets.

The company's International division is divided into 4 geographic areas (Europe, Canada, Latin America, and Asia/Pacific) and sells Levi's products in over 70 countries. Levi Strauss grants licenses to make and sell its products in countries where the company does not maintain manufacturing facilities.

Since its LBO in 1985, the company has greatly streamlined production. Levi Strauss's revolutionary new computer network (LeviLink) will connect the company with its fabric suppliers and will allow retailers to order and pay for new inventory electronically.

The company is committed to a program of social responsibility that includes a worldwide code of ethics and generous charitable contributions.

WHEN

Levi Strauss arrived in New York City from Bavaria in 1847 to join the dry goods business established by his 2 older brothers. In 1853 Strauss sailed to San Francisco to sell dry goods (particularly tent canvas) to the gold rush miners.

Shortly after Strauss arrived, a prospector informed him of the problem the miners were having finding pants that were rugged enough to last. Strauss fashioned a pair out of canvas for the old prospector, and word of the sturdy pants spread quickly.

Strauss made a few more pairs of canvas pants before switching to a durable French fabric called *serge de Nimes*, soon known as denim. Strauss began coloring the fabric with indigo dye and adopted the idea of Nevada tailor Jacob Davis of reinforcing the pants with copper rivets. In 1873 Strauss and Davis produced their first pair of Levi's Patent Riveted 501 (501 was the lot number) Waist High Overalls. The pants, which soon became the standard attire of lumberjacks, cowboys, railroad workers, oil drillers, and farmers, are the same today as they were in 1873 (minus the rivets on the crotch and back pockets). The 2-horse patch (on the back of every pair of pants) was introduced in 1886.

Strauss continued to build his lucrative pants and wholesaling business until his death in 1902 when the company passed to his 4 nephews, who continued to produce their uncle's bluejeans (the term *jeans* traces its roots to the cotton trousers worn by ancient Genoese sailors) for the next several decades, while maintaining the company's growing reputation for philanthropy.

After WWII Walter Haas, Jr., and Peter Haas (the 4th generation of the family) assumed leadership and in 1948 decided to discontinue the wholesaler segment (then the bulk of the company) and concentrate solely on manufacturing Levi's clothing.

Levi's bluejeans gained widespread popularity during the 1950s and were soon the accepted uniform of young people everywhere. Demand for the pants spurred more production plants in the South and East. During the 1960s the company introduced divisions for women's clothing and international sales.

In 1971 Levi Strauss went public and began diversifying its product line. The Haas family, concerned that the company was losing "important values and traditions" (such as philanthropy) to public ownership, regained control of Levi Strauss in 1985 and went private again.

In 1987 the company acquired Brittania and in 1988 restructured to operate more efficiently. In 1989 Levi Strauss made an initial public offering of Levi Strauss Japan K. K. (its Japanese subsidiary in Tokyo).

Today the company, under Robert Haas (great-great-grandnephew of Strauss), has sold its diversified apparel interests and is concentrating on the production of the traditional lines of pants and shirts that made the company famous.

HOW MUCH

	9 Yr. Growth	1980	1981	1982	1983	1984	1985	1986	1987	1988	1989
Sales ($ mil)	2.9%	2,841	2,851	2,572	2,731	2,514	2,600	2,750	2,870	3,120	3,680
Net income ($ mil)	0.1%	224	172	127	195	41	33	49	133	112	225
Employees	—	48,000	48,000	45,000	44,000	37,000	35,000	32,000	32,000	32,000	31,800

1989 Year End:
Debt ratio: 50.8%
Return on equity: 71.8%
Cash (mil): $49
Current ratio: 1.40
Long-term debt (mil): $407

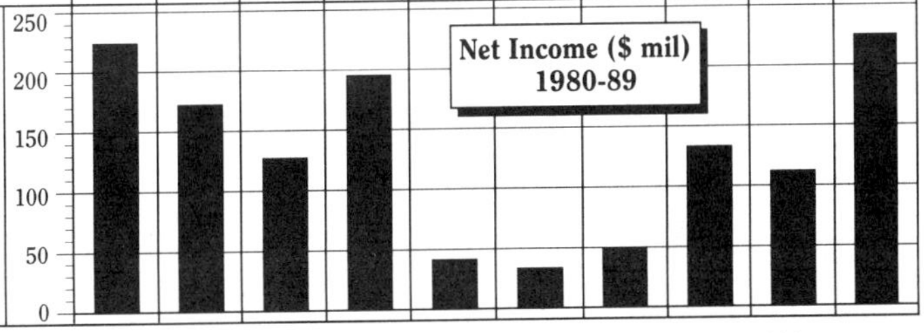

Net Income ($ mil)
1980-89

250
200
150
100
50
0

Private company
Incorporated: Delaware, 1985
Fiscal year ends: November 30

WHO

Chairman and CEO: Robert D. Haas, age 48, $1,255,976 pay
President and COO: Thomas W. Tusher, age 49, $887,332 pay
SVP and CFO: George B. James, age 52, $520,123 pay
Auditors: Arthur Andersen & Co.
Employees: 31,800

WHERE

HQ: 1155 Battery St., San Francisco, CA 94111
Phone: 415-544-6000
FAX: 415-544-3939

The company operates 30 production, 5 distribution, and 4 finishing facilities in the US. Foreign operations consist of 21 distribution, 11 production, and 4 finishing facilities.

	1989 Sales	
	$ mil	% of total
US	2,448	66
Europe	661	18
Asia/Pacific, Canada, Latin America	568	16
Other	3	—
Total	**3,680**	**100**

WHAT

	1989 Sales	
	$ mil	% of total
Men's Jeans	1,366	37
Menswear	400	11
Youthwear	345	9
Womenswear	147	4
Britannia	98	3
Shirts	92	3
Other/foreign	1,232	33
Total	**3,680**	**100**

Products
Jackets
Jeans
Shirts
Slacks
Sportswear
Tops

Brand Names
501 jeans
Bend Over
Brittania
Brittgear
Brittsport
Dockers
Levi's 900 Series
Levi's Action
Levi's for Men
Little Levi's
Silver Label
Sutter Creek

RANKINGS

33rd in *Forbes* 400 US Private Cos.

COMPETITION

Hartmarx
Liz Claiborne
V. F.

THE LIMITED, INC.

OVERVIEW

The Limited is one of the great success stories of modern retailing. From a single store in 1963, the company has grown to 3,168 stores in several divisions, with 1989 sales of $4.6 billion. The Limited's sales grew an average of 40% annually from 1984 to 1989, while it maintained an average ROE of 46% over the same period. It leads apparel retailers in ROE, profit margins, and sales growth.

The company's retail clothing store divisions include The Limited, Express (fashionable clothes for women and men), Victoria's Secret (the world leader in intimate apparel), Lerner (the largest US women's specialty apparel chain), and Lane Bryant (large-size fashions). The Limited also owns 4 large catalog operations.

The Limited acquires its goods through its contract manufacturing subsidiary, Mast Industries. The company operates a bank that issues credit cards and grants credit for each of the company divisions.

Atop all this is Leslie Wexner, a bachelor billionaire with a keen sense for women's fashion trends. His goals include more than doubling The Limited's sales and increasing after-tax profits to 10% within the next 5 years, and developing larger store formats.

NYSE symbol: LTD
Incorporated: Delaware, 1982
Fiscal year ends: Saturday closest to January 31

WHO

Chairman and President: Leslie H. Wexner, age 52, $1,654,921 pay
VC: Thomas G. Hopkins, age 57, $712,812 pay (prior to promotion)
President, Mast Industries: Martin Trust, age 55, $946,767 pay
EVP and CFO: Kenneth B. Gilman, age 43, $712,812 pay
President Store Planning: Charles W. Hinson, age 53, $510,202 pay
Auditors: Coopers & Lybrand
Employees: 63,000 (43,800 are part-time)

WHEN

Leslie Wexner, then 26, opened the first Limited store in 1963 in Columbus, Ohio, after a disagreement with his father over operations of the family store, Leslie's. The company, capitalized with $5,000 (borrowed from Wexner's aunt), sold moderately priced, high-fashion merchandise to teenagers and young women. By the time The Limited went public in 1969, the company still had only 5 locations, but the rapid development of large, covered malls spurred growth to 100 stores by 1976. The Limited acquired Mast Industries, an international apparel purchasing and importing company, in 1978. Two years later Wexner created Express, with a trendier format aimed at younger girls, which has since widened its product line.

The Limited made a number of acquisitions during 1982, beginning with Lane Bryant, founded by Lithuanian immigrant Lena Bryant in 1900, which specialized in "fashions for larger women." The Brylane fashion catalog division was formed when the company acquired Roaman's, a catalog merchandiser, that same year. Also in 1982 The Limited acquired Victoria's Secret, a chain of 4 stores and a catalog specializing in women's lingerie. The division has since surpassed Maidenform and Vanity Fair as the leading seller of lingerie in the US market. Meanwhile, at its Limited stores, a black-and-white decorating format and the introduction of the company's Forenza and Outback Red private-label merchandise helped increase sales.

The Limited sold the Coward Shoe division of Lane Bryant in 1983 and acquired Lerner Stores in 1985. It also bought Henri Bendel in 1985, a high fashion, eclectic apparel retailer. Beginning in 1984, Wexner made unsuccessful takeover bids for Carter Hawley Hale, Federated Department Stores, and R. H. Macy.

The Limited bought Abercrombie & Fitch (a well-known retailer of men's and women's sport fashions, founded in 1892) from Oshman's Sporting Goods in 1988. Since 1987 the company's Limited chain has emphasized the development of The Limited International fashion superstores, and has introduced several new shops including Cacique (French lingerie), Limited Too (children's fashions), Structure (men's clothes), and Victoria's Secret Bath Shops. In 1989 the company sold Lerner Woman and split the Brylane catalog divisions into 3 separate businesses. In June 1990 the company opened its 2nd Henri Bendel store in Columbus, Ohio.

WHERE

HQ: Two Limited Parkway, PO Box 16000, Columbus, OH 43216
Phone: 614-479-7000
FAX: 614-476-7226

The Limited operates the stores in its 7 divisions nationwide. Distribution centers are located in Columbus and Indianapolis. Mast Industries maintains buying offices in England, Hong Kong, Italy, Japan, Korea, Singapore, and Taiwan.

WHAT

	Stores open at year-end 1989
The Limited Stores (including The Limited, Limited International, Limited Too, Cacique)	766
Sportswear fashions for adults & children	
Express	469
European-style fashions for women & men	
Victoria's Secret	384
Intimate lingerie & gifts	
Lerner	802
Moderately priced women's fashions	
Lane Bryant	720
Large-size women's apparel	
Abercrombie & Fitch	26
Classic men's & women's sport fashions	
Henri Bendel	1
High fashion New York retailer	
Total	**3,168**

Other Operations
Brylane Catalog
Mast Industries, Inc.
Victoria's Secret Catalog
World Financial Network National Bank

HOW MUCH

	9 Yr. Growth	1980	1981	1982	1983	1984	1985	1986	1987	1988	1989
Sales ($ mil)	37.5%	265	365	721	1,086	1,343	2,387	3,143	3,528	4,071	4,648
Net income ($ mil)	51.3%	8	22	34	71	93	145	228	235	245	347
Income as % of sales	—	3.2%	6.1%	4.7%	6.5%	6.9%	6.1%	7.2%	6.7%	6.0%	7.5%
Earnings per share ($)	49.4%	0.05	0.13	0.19	0.39	0.51	0.80	1.21	1.25	1.36	1.92
Stock price – high ($)	—	1.14	1.41	4.08	10.33	9.33	21.25	34.50	52.88	27.88	39.88
Stock price – low ($)	—	0.45	0.90	1.14	3.77	5.08	8.67	20.50	15.88	16.38	25.25
Stock price – close ($)	49.7%	0.93	1.19	4.00	8.17	9.00	20.83	31.75	17.25	27.25	35.00
P/E – high	—	22	10	21	26	18	27	29	42	21	21
P/E – low	—	9	7	6	10	10	11	17	13	12	13
Dividends per share ($)	48.4%	0.01	0.01	0.02	0.04	0.08	0.11	0.16	0.24	0.24	0.32
Book value per share ($)	41.3%	0.31	0.50	0.70	1.08	1.54	2.25	4.14	4.08	5.28	6.90

1989 Year End:
Debt ratio: 26.4%
Return on equity: 31.5%
Cash (mil): $22
Current ratio: 2.43
Long-term debt (mil): $446
Number of shares (mil): 180
Dividends:
1989 average yield: 0.9%
1989 payout: 16.7%
Market value (mil): $6,295

Stock Price History high/low 1980-89

60, 50, 40, 30, 20, 10, 0

RANKINGS

26th in *Fortune* 50 Retailing Cos.
189th in *Forbes* Sales 500
72nd in *Business Week* 1000
185th in *Business Week* Global 1000

COMPETITION

General Cinema
Hartmarx
Melville
Nordstrom
United States Shoe
Department and discount stores

LITTON INDUSTRIES, INC.

OVERVIEW

Litton operates in 4 business segments: industrial automation, resource exploration, advanced electronics, and marine engineering. The industrial automation segment develops manufacturing systems for the automobile industry, automated material-handling systems, and document management systems. The resource exploration segment provides oil and other mineral exploration services and products. The advanced electronics segment produces and services inertial navigation systems; command, control, and communications systems; and electronic warfare systems, primarily for the US and Allied governments.

The marine engineering and production segment produces surface combatant ships, overhauls and modernizes ships, and conducts marine research studies, all primarily for the US Navy.

In fiscal 1989, 47% of Litton's sales and service revenue was from US government contracts. In the same period $7.5 billion of the company's $8.7 billion total backlog was for worldwide defense contracts. Due to the global political and economic changes of 1989 and 1990, Litton faces uncertainties in domestic oil exploration, defense contracts, and the automobile industry.

NYSE symbol: LIT
Incorporated: Delaware, 1953
Fiscal year ends: July 31

WHO

Chairman and CEO: Orion L. Hoch, age 60, $1,110,099 pay
VC and CFO: Joseph T. Casey, age 58, $713,156 pay
President and COO: Roland O. Peterson, age 57, $647,676 pay
EVP: Joseph F. Caligiuri, age 61, $549,544 pay
Auditors: Deloitte & Touche
Employees: 50,700

WHERE

HQ: 360 N. Crescent Dr., Beverly Hills, CA 90210
Phone: 213-859-5000
FAX: 213-859-5940

Litton maintains offices and plants at 52 locations in 24 states in the US and in Canada and Western Europe.

Company's Total US Plant & Office Space by State

California	18%	Illinois	5%
Mississippi	15%	Michigan	4%
Texas	15%	Virginia	3%
Pennsylvania	7%	Massachusetts	3%
Kentucky	6%	Maryland	3%
Connecticut	5%	Other states	16%

	1989 Sales		1989 Operating Income	
	$ mil	% of total	$ mil	% of total
US	3,683	74	349	77
Foreign	1,328	26	107	23
Adjustments	12	—	(61)	—
Total	**5,023**	**100**	**395**	**100**

WHEN

Charles "Tex" Thornton, head of the Statistical Control Department of the Army Air Force during WWII, was responsible for predicting manufacturing needs in the war effort. He foresaw a growing demand for new, technologically advanced military products in the postwar years. In 1953, after working for Ford and for Howard Hughes, he organized a company of his own (Electro Dynamics) to reap the benefits of this new market. Thornton began by borrowing $1.5 million and buying Litton Industries, which produced microwave tubes for the Navy. Thornton added 8 more smaller firms by the end of his company's first 9 months. Litton stock went public in 1954, and the cash generated was invested in R&D and expansion, which were to be the hallmarks of Litton for nearly 2 decades. In 1958 Litton bought privately owned Monroe Calculating Machine, and sales topped $100 million that year.

After 1959 Litton continued to expand both internally and by acquisition, buying over 50 companies during the next decade. These purchases included Svenska Dataregister A.B. (Sweden, cash registers, 1959), Western Geophysical (seismic oil exploration, 1960), Ingalls Shipbuilding, and Cole Steel Equipment (office furniture, 1961), Winchester Electronics (1963), and Fitchburg Paper (1964). With the acquisition of Royal McBee (typewriters) and Hewitt-Robbins (office equipment) in 1965, Litton's annual sales topped $1 billion. Litton continued to expand worldwide, acquiring Kester Solder, Rust Engineering, Business Equipment Holdings (Australia), Stouffer Foods, and Eureka X-Ray Tube in 1967; Landis Tool in 1968; and Triumph Werke Nürmburg (Germany, typewriters) in 1969. Litton's annual sales passed the $2 billion mark in 1968, but that year also saw the first quarterly decline in earnings in the company's history. Litton stock quickly dropped from over $120 to around $60.

During the 1970s and 1980s Litton management restructured the company. Although acquisitions continued, they were more strategic and were coupled with consolidations and major divestitures, including Rust Engineering (1972), Stouffer Foods food divisions (1973), and Triumph Werke Nürmburg (1980). During the 1970s Litton's sales and net earnings fluctuated as the company reorganized.

In the 1980s the company concentrated on its 4 core business segments, selling its unrelated and unprofitable businesses.

WHAT

	1989 Sales		1989 Operating Income	
	$ mil	% of total	$ mil	% of total
Marine engineering	1,049	21	127	28
Advanced electronics	2,131	42	185	40
Industrial automation exploration	1,834	37	147	32
Adjustments	9	—	(64)	—
Total	**5,023**	**100**	**395**	**100**

Products
Automated manufacturing systems
Inertial navigation and guidance systems, electronic warfare systems, electro-optical systems, and other advanced electronic systems
Material management and handling systems
Military and commercial ships

RANKINGS

100th in *Fortune* 500 Industrial Cos.
261st in *Fortune* Global 500 Industrial Cos.
178th in *Forbes* Sales 500
343rd in *Business Week* 1000
867th in *Business Week* Global 1000

COMPETITION

General Electric
Halliburton
Honeywell
Motorola
Raytheon
Robert Bosch
Schlumberger
Teledyne
Tenneco
Thomson
Westinghouse
Other defense companies

HOW MUCH

	9 Yr. Growth	1980	1981	1982	1983	1984	1985	1986	1987	1988	1989
Sales ($ mil)	1.9%	4,242	4,936	4,933	4,720	4,601	4,585	4,521	4,420	4,864	5,023
Net income ($ mil)	(5.3%)	291	312	315	232	277	299	71	138	167	178
Income as % of sales	—	6.9%	6.3%	6.4%	4.9%	6.0%	6.5%	1.6%	3.1%	3.4%	3.6%
Earnings per share ($)	0.4%	6.76	7.27	7.37	5.39	6.44	7.24	2.52	5.12	6.32	6.99
Stock price – high ($)	—	83.75	86.69	58.33	71.45	80.00	93.50	92.25	108.25	87.25	98.00
Stock price – low ($)	—	36.61	46.14	34.60	47.55	56.25	64.38	71.75	64.00	67.50	71.50
Stock price – close ($)	(0.9%)	83.75	54.19	49.14	70.63	64.88	83.75	74.00	72.13	71.88	77.25
P/E – high	—	12	12	8	13	12	13	37	21	14	14
P/E – low	—	5	6	5	9	9	9	28	13	11	10
Dividends per share ($)	(100%)	0.74	1.17	1.39	1.61	1.84	2.00	0.00	0.00	0.00	0.00
Book value per share ($)	6.8%	28.85	33.71	39.68	43.47	47.94	34.47	37.39	40.60	46.15	51.98

1989 Year End:
Debt ratio: 53.4%
Return on equity: 14.2%
Cash (mil): $1,069
Current ratio: 1.81
Long-term debt (mil): $1,454
Number of shares (mil): 24
Dividends:
1989 average yield: 0.0%
1989 payout: 0.0%
Market value (mil): $1,881

Stock Price History high/low 1980-89

LIZ CLAIBORNE, INC.

OVERVIEW

Liz Claiborne, Inc., with 1989 sales of $1.4 billion, is the largest US producer of clothing and accessories for the working woman. The company designs and markets popular sportswear; stylish professional suits, dresses, and tailored slacks; matched accessories; and fragrances for women under the labels Liz Claiborne, Elisabeth, Liz & Co., and Dana Buchman. It also produces a line of men's sportswear under the Claiborne label. The company introduced a new line of fragrances for men (1989) and its first collection of costume jewelry (1990).

Although Liz Claiborne products are considered "designer" items, prices tend to fall in the "better" apparel range, meaning that, compared to other designer lines, they are usually less expensive.

The company markets its products in the US and Canada in department stores, specialty shops, and 54 company-owned stores. It owns 7 shops that carry exclusively Liz Claiborne (women's) and Claiborne (men's) products and plans to open 7 additional Liz Claiborne stores in 1990. There are 22 Liz Claiborne outlet stores and 25 First Issue specialty stores.

WHEN

It was 1975. Liz Claiborne, a veteran New York dress designer in the Youth Guild division of Jonathan Logan, had a vision of stylish, sporty, and affordable clothes for America's working woman. Unable to sell the concept to her employer, Claiborne left the company and joined her husband Arthur Ortenberg and 2 other partners, Jerome Chazen and Leonard Boxer, to found Liz Claiborne, Inc., in 1976. With a starting investment of $250,000, the company was an immediate success. It showed a profit its first year and began its rise as the fastest-growing, most profitable US apparel company in the 1980s.

In 1981 Liz Claiborne offered stock to the public at $19 per share, raising $6.1 million. In 1986, after only 10 years, the company was on *Fortune*'s list of the 500 top industrial companies (revenues that year were over $800 million). Liz Claiborne's clothes bring in sales of $400 to $500 per square foot of retail space (about 3 times more than the average apparel supplier), and about 60% sell for full price (40% is the industry average).

The company is noted for its well-organized management, distribution, and sales teams. Until her retirement in 1989, Ms. Claiborne maintained close control over the design side of the business, overseeing and "editing" the work of the designers. The company's emphasis on detail, quality, and attention to consumer preferences has created a loyal customer base. It produces 6 new collections a year (holiday, spring I, spring II, summer, fall I, and fall II) which provide consumers with a new line of Claiborne styles every 2 months. These short cycles allow more frequent updates of new styles and put clothes on the racks in the appropriate season. An automated inventory network that gives each week's sales trends allows quick response to market demand.

Liz Claiborne expanded into men's clothing (Claiborne, 1985), cosmetics (Liz Claiborne, 1986), a clothing line for big and tall women (Elisabeth, 1989), and a line of knit sportswear (Liz & Co., 1989). A new label of higher-priced sportswear by in-house designer Dana Buchman was introduced in 1987.

The company moved into the retail apparel business in 1988 when it opened its first retail stores, offering the First Issue brand of casual sportswear. It expanded with Liz Claiborne and Claiborne stores in 1989. Liz Claiborne's "store-within-a-store" concept offers department store shoppers the recognizable Liz Claiborne image in a space of about 7000 square feet. These areas are jointly planned and managed by the stores and Liz Claiborne's staff.

Liz Claiborne and Arthur Ortenberg retired as chairman and vice-chairman in 1989. The company has announced plans to begin selling its products in the UK in 1991.

HOW MUCH

	9 Yr. Growth	1980	1981	1982	1983	1984	1985	1986	1987	1988	1989
Sales ($ mil)	31.9%	79	117	166	229	391	557	814	1,053	1,184	1,411
Net income ($ mil)	44.5%	6	10	14	22	42	61	86	114	110	165
Income as % of sales	—	7.8%	8.7%	8.5%	9.8%	10.7%	10.9%	10.6%	10.9%	9.3%	11.7%
Earnings per share ($)	—	—	0.13	0.17	0.27	0.50	0.71	1.00	1.32	1.26	1.87
Stock price – high ($)	—	—	1.29	2.56	4.69	6.63	12.38	24.25	39.13	20.00	27.75
Stock price – low ($)	—	—	0.86	0.99	2.00	3.09	5.88	11.88	12.25	12.75	16.50
Stock price – close ($)	—	—	1.22	2.33	4.25	6.38	12.13	21.38	16.50	17.25	24.00
P/E – high	—	—	10	15	18	13	17	24	30	16	15
P/E – low	—	—	7	6	8	6	8	12	9	10	9
Dividends per share ($)	—	—	0.00	0.00	0.00	0.05	0.08	0.12	0.16	0.17	0.19
Book value per share ($)	—	—	0.32	0.49	0.77	1.23	1.90	2.86	4.10	5.22	6.94

1989 Year End:
Debt ratio: 2.5%
Return on equity: 30.8%
Cash (mil): $373
Current ratio: 3.57
Long-term debt (mil): $16
Number of shares (mil): 88
Dividends:
1989 average yield: 0.8%
1989 payout: 10.4%
Market value (mil): $2,116

Stock Price History high/low 1981-89

40
35
30
25
20
15
10
5
0

OTC symbol: LIZC
Incorporated: Delaware, 1981
Fiscal year ends: Last Saturday in December

WHO

Chairman: Jerome A. Chazen, age 63, $800,000 pay
VC and President: Harvey L. Falk, age 55, $800,000 pay
VC; President, Women's Sportswear Group: Jay Margolis, age 41, $800,000 pay
SVP Finance: Samuel M. Miller, age 52
Auditors: Arthur Andersen & Co.
Employees: 5,400

WHERE

HQ: 1441 Broadway, New York, NY 10018
Phone: 212-354-4900
FAX: 212-719-9049

About 95 of Liz Claiborne's 320 independent suppliers are located in the US; the remainder are located principally in Hong Kong, South Korea, Taiwan, Singapore, the Philippines, and China. The company's products are sold by approximately 9,500 stores throughout North America.

WHAT

	1989 Sales	
	$ mil	% of total
Misses' sportswear	666	46
Petite women's sportswear	165	11
Accessories	163	11
Dresses	139	10
Men's sportswear	113	8
Cosmetics	60	4
Outlet stores	39	3
Retail specialty stores	33	2
Canada	27	2
Dana Buchman label	15	1
Elisabeth label	11	1
Men's furnishings	10	1
Liz & Co. label	8	—
Licensing	4	—
Intracompany	(42)	—
Total	**1,411**	**100**

Brand Names

Women's Apparel and Cosmetics
Collection
Dana Buchman
Elisabeth
First Issue
Liz & Co.
Liz Claiborne
Lizsport
Lizwear
Realities

Men's Clothing
Claiborne

RANKINGS

276th in *Fortune* 500 Industrial Cos.
299th in *Business Week* 1000
766th in *Business Week* Global 1000

COMPETITION

Hartmarx
Levi Strauss
V. F.

LLOYD'S OF LONDON

OVERVIEW

From its new landmark building on Lime Street in London, Lloyd's provides a physical, legal, and operational framework for the insurance of risks by individuals. The financial elite joining Lloyd's as insurers are called "Names." Names pool their resources by joining syndicates formed by underwriters, insurance experts who negotiate deals with Lloyd's brokers.

Although Lloyd's is best known and uniquely suited for insuring unusual risks, most of its business is mundane. Lloyd's has a 2% share of the worldwide insurance market (with 40% of its risks and 66% of its premiums in the US). It is still a major provider of marine insurance.

Names' profits have been declining due to natural disasters in Europe and the US, including Hurricane Hugo and the San Francisco earthquake in 1989; increasing environmental and asbestos claims; and changes in UK tax laws. Lloyd's has not kept up technologically — it uses an estimated 20 million computer punch cards annually — in upgrading its information systems.

Insurance society
Incorporated: England, 1871
Fiscal year ends: December 31

WHO

Chairman: Murray Lawrence
Deputy Chairman and CEO: Alan Lord
Deputy Chairman: Alan Jackson
Deputy Chairman: Colin Murray
Chairman, Finance and General Purposes Committee of the Council of Lloyd's: Stephen R. Merrett
Auditors: Ernst & Young
Employees: 2,157

WHEN

In the 2nd half of the 17th century, coffeehouses emerged in England as places to meet and do business. In 1688 Edward Lloyd opened Lloyd's Coffee House in London with an eye toward capturing a marine insurer clientele. Lloyd's provided brokers and individual underwriters with a central place to meet and agree to deals. Underwriters did not assume risks jointly; rather, each was liable for only his own portion of the deal. This enabled individuals to enter insurance syndicates knowing the maximum amount at risk.

Lloyd established a reputation for consistently obtaining accurate shipping news, an advantage that made Lloyd's the hub of London's maritime insurance industry. The coffeehouse pressed its advantage when it began publishing *Lloyd's List*, a shipping newspaper, in 1734.

Lloyd's attracted people who used insurance as a cover for gambling. In one instance, customers "insured" the gender of the Chevalier d'Eon, a transvestite. Serious insurers persuaded a Lloyd's waiter to open the New Lloyd's Coffee House nearby in 1769. By 1774 the brokers and underwriters needed more space and moved to the Royal Exchange, taking Lloyd's out of coffeehouses for good.

In the 1800s Lloyd's began regulating its membership. Parliament passed the Lloyd's Act in 1871 to establish Lloyd's as an incorporated society. In the 1880s Lloyd's branched out into nonmarine insurance. By the 1890s Lloyd's was writing 50% of the world's nonlife insurance.

Prompt settlement of claims related to the 1906 San Francisco earthquake boosted Lloyd's image in the US. Underwriters profited from war risk insurance in WWI. After the war, Lloyd's entered automobile, credit, and aviation insurance. In 1958 Lloyd's moved to its Lime Street headquarters.

Although Lloyd's continued to grow, it lost market share as automobile insurance, for which it was ill-suited, grew rapidly, and competition from private and state-owned institutions increased. Hurricane Betsy hit Florida in 1965, inflicting severe losses on Lloyd's underwriters and sharply reducing their capacity to take on subsequent risks.

Lloyd's has occasionally suffered scandals. In 1982 a Lloyd's broker admitted to funneling $40 million to offshore insurance companies in which he had an interest. In 1981 and 1982 a syndicate managed by Outhwaite, an underwriter, wrote so-called run-off contracts (accepted future liabilities of old insurance contracts with claims still pending, in exchange for premium income) that exposed Outhwaite Names to US asbestos-related claims — some from the 1940s — and potential losses of $480 million. Numerous questions about the transactions have been raised, most concerning the full disclosure required by Lloyd's when writing run-off policies.

In 1990 Lloyd's and Sun Alliance (UK) jointly formed Eurosure, an insurance venture, to pursue European business following market unification in 1992.

WHERE

HQ: One Lime St., London EC3M 7HA, England
Phone: 011-44-71-623-7100
FAX: 011-44-71-626-2389

Lloyd's underwriters accept business from all over the world. About 75% of this business originates overseas. Lloyd's has 28,770 participating Names (active underwriters).

WHAT

	1987* Net Premiums		1987* Net Income	
	£ mil	% of total	£ mil	% of total
Marine	1,467	35	292	33
Nonmarine	1,821	43	282	32
Aviation	428	10	246	28
Motor	479	12	61	7
Total	**4,195**	**100**	**881**	**100**

*Lloyd's has a 3-year accounting system; 1987 is the most recent year for which data are available.

Managing Agencies for Lloyd's Largest Underwriting Syndicates
Merrett Underwriting Agency Management Ltd. (syndicate Marine 418)
Murray Lawrence & Partners (syndicate Non-Marine 362)
R.W. Sturge & Co. (syndicates Marine 206 and Non-Marine 210)
Three Quays Underwriting Management Ltd. (syndicate Non-Marine 190)

Maritime & Legal Publications (Lloyd's of London Press Ltd.)
Legal textbooks and directories
Lloyd's Law Reports
Lloyd's List (insurance, transportation, freight, and other industrial news)
Lloyd's Loading List
Lloyd's Maritime and Commercial Law Quarterly
Lloyd's Monthly List of Laid up Vessels
Lloyd's Shipping Economist
Lloyd's Shipping Index
Lloyd's Voyage Record
Lloyd's Weekly Casualty Reports
Nautical Review
Product Liability International

HOW MUCH

£=$1.61 (Dec. 31, 1989)	9 Yr. Growth	1981	1982	1983	1984	1985	1986	1987	1988	1989	1990
Total Names	6.6%	19,137	20,145	21,601	23,438	26,050	28,597	31,484	33,532	34,218	34,146
UK Names	5.9%	16,669	17,393	18,588	19,986	21,941	24,032	25,855	27,417	27,940	27,820
US Names	9.6%	1,259	1,370	1,470	1,699	2,011	2,401	2,699	2,815	2,850	2,865
Participating Names	—	—	—	—	—	26,019	28,242	30,936	32,433	31,329	28,770
Underwriting capacity (£ bil)	13.3%	3.5	4.1	4.3	5.0	6.6	8.5	10.3	11.0	10.9	10.8
Net premiums (£ mil)	—	—	2,892	2,570	2,959	3,056	3,712	4,195	—	—	—
Profit to Names (£ mil)	—	—	—	—	290	196	649	509	—	—	—

Current Statistics
Average return on capacity (1987): 9.5%
No. of female Names (1990): 7,706

Total Names 1981-90

35,000
30,000
25,000
20,000
15,000
10,000
5,000
0

COMPETITION

Aetna
AIG
CIGNA
General Re
ITT
Kemper
Tokio Marine & Fire
Travelers
USF&G

LOCKHEED CORPORATION

OVERVIEW

Lockheed Corporation is the 2nd largest prime defense contractor, after McDonnell Douglas, and the largest defense research and development contractor in the US.

Approximately 85% of Lockheed's business involves sales to the US government. The company builds jet fighters, cargo transports, submarine-launched ballistic missiles, antisubmarine warfare systems, civilian space systems, and many other high-technology items. The company also offers services such as space shuttle processing, aircraft modification and maintenance, and data processing.

Lockheed is developing Milstar, a military communications satellite network, as well as the Trident II submarine-launched ballistic missile, hardware for the Strategic Defense Initiative, and systems for NASA's Space Station *Freedom*. The company is also developing (with Aerojet General) new space shuttle solid rocket motors and leads one of 2 industry teams competing to build the Air Force's new Advanced Tactical Fighter.

Lockheed wrote off $491 million in 1989 because of overruns on fixed-price defense contracts. The company is reducing its aerospace and electronics work force, selling most of its computer services companies, and entering new nondefense businesses such as airport development and operation.

WHEN

Brothers Allan and Malcolm Loughead (pronounced "Lockheed") of San Francisco formed the Alco Hydro-Aeroplane Company in 1912, producing their first airplane in 1913. After dissolving Alco in 1916, they moved to Santa Barbara and founded Loughead Aircraft Manufacturing, which went bankrupt in 1919. In 1926 the brothers teamed with Fred Keeler to form Lockheed Aircraft. John Northrop (later to found Northrop Corporation) designed Lockheed's first airplane, the famous Vega (flown by such pilots as Wiley Post and Amelia Earhart). Detroit Aircraft Company bought Lockheed in 1929 but went bankrupt in 1931.

Robert Gross, Carl Squier, and Lloyd Stearman purchased Lockheed in 1932. With designer Clarence "Kelly" Johnson, the company produced a long series of successes, including the Electra transport (1934); the P-38 Lightning fighter of WWII; the P-80 Shooting Star jet fighter (1944); the Constellation airliner (1945); the U-2 spyplane (1955); and the SR-71 Blackbird (on its retirement flight to the Smithsonian Institution in 1990, a 24-year-old SR-71 set 4 speed records, including a Los Angeles-to-Washington, DC, time of 64 minutes, 5 seconds). The company also produced submarine-launched ballistic missiles, beginning with the Polaris (1958); military transports such as the C-5 Galaxy (1968); and the L-1011 TriStar wide-body airliner (1970).

In the late 1960s and early 1970s the company suffered several setbacks, including the cancellation of its Cheyenne attack helicopter, the C-5A cost-overrun scandal, and financial problems with the L-1011. Government-sponsored loans saved the company from bankruptcy in 1971.

In the 1970s and 1980s, Lockheed developed the Space Shuttle's thermal insulation system, the Hubble Space Telescope, and the F-117A stealth fighter. The company acquired electronics maker Sanders Associates for $1.2 billion (1986), sold its DIALOG computer information system for $353 million to Knight-Ridder (1988), and sold 2 additional computer services companies, CADAM and Lockheed DataPlan (1989). Lockheed incurred large program losses on fixed-price contracts in 1989, primarily during development of the navy's P-7A patrol aircraft and in subcontract work for the Air Force's C-17 transport (now discontinued).

In 1990 the main aircraft plant in Burbank, California was closed, eliminating 5,500 jobs. Disappointing post-launch performance of the Hubble Telescope added to the company's woes.

HOW MUCH

	9 Yr. Growth	1980	1981	1982	1983	1984	1985	1986	1987	1988	1989
Sales ($ mil)	7.0%	5,396	5,176	5,613	6,490	8,113	9,535	10,273	11,321	10,590	9,891
Net income ($ mil)	(15.6%)	28	155	207	263	344	401	408	436	442	6
Income as % of sales	—	0.5%	3.0%	3.7%	4.1%	4.2%	4.2%	4.0%	3.9%	4.2%	0.1%
Earnings per share ($)	(16.4%)	0.50	2.96	3.59	4.14	5.26	6.09	6.17	6.63	7.34	0.10
Stock price – high ($)	—	16.08	16.67	28.17	47.50	48.75	58.00	60.25	61.50	48.00	54.75
Stock price – low ($)	—	7.38	8.50	14.46	24.17	30.13	40.75	43.00	28.75	34.75	35.75
Stock price – close ($)	14.9%	11.17	15.58	24.42	40.00	44.00	49.13	50.13	34.38	41.25	39.00
P/E – high	—	32	6	8	11	9	10	10	9	7	548
P/E – low	—	15	3	4	6	6	7	7	4	5	358
Dividends per share ($)	—	0.00	0.00	0.00	0.00	0.45	0.75	0.95	1.30	1.55	1.75
Book value per share ($)	16.0%	8.55	2.89	7.76	13.08	17.81	23.17	28.44	33.31	41.73	32.63

1989 Year End:
Debt ratio: 47.1%
Return on equity: 0.3%
Cash (mil): $86
Current ratio: 1.17
Long-term debt (mil): $1,835
Number of shares (mil): 63
Dividends:
1989 average yield: 4.5%
1989 payout: 1,750.0%
Market value (mil): $2,465

NYSE: LK
Incorporated: Delaware, 1986
Fiscal year ends: December 31

WHO

Chairman and CEO: Daniel M. Tellep, age 58, $763,943 pay
VC and COO: Robert A. Fuhrman, age 65, $433,519 pay
VC and CFO: Vincent N. Marafino, age 59, $663,348 pay
Auditors: Ernst & Young
Employees: 82,500

WHERE

HQ: 4500 Park Granada Blvd., Calabasas, CA 91399
Phone: 818-712-2000
FAX: 818-712-2329

	1989 Sales		1989 Operating Income	
	$ mil	% of total	$ mil	% of total
US	9,628	97	33	62
Foreign	263	3	20	38
Adjustments	—	—	400	—
Total	**9,891**	**100**	**453**	**100**

WHAT

	1989 Sales		1989 Operating Income	
	$ mil	% of total	$ mil	% of total
Missiles & space systems	4,780	48	368	—
Aeronautical systems	2,572	26	(377)	—
Technology services	1,432	14	36	—
Electronic systems	1,107	11	26	—
Adjustments	—	—	400	—
Total	**9,891**	**100**	**453**	**100**

	1989 Sales	
	$ mil	% of total
US government	8,407	85
Foreign governments	693	7
Commercial	791	8
	9,891	**100**

Principal Operating Units

Aeronautical Sytems (F-117A, F-22 Advanced Tactical Fighter prototype, C-130
Electronic Systems (ALQ-126B electronic warfare system)
Lockheed Missiles & Space (Hubble Space Telescope, Trident II submarine-launched ballistic missile, systems for Space Station Freedom, Milstar communications satellite)
Technology Services (space shuttle processing, International Airport, Toronto, Canada)

RANKINGS

45th in *Fortune* 500 Industrial Cos.
120th in *Fortune* Global 500 Industrial Cos.
39th in *Fortune* 50 Exporters
74th in *Forbes* Sales 500
281st in *Business Week* 1000
903rd in *Business Week* Global 1000

COMPETITION

Allied-Signal
Boeing
General Dynamics
General Electric
General Motors
Martin Marietta
McDonnell Douglas
Northrop
Raytheon
Rockwell International
Textron

LOEWS CORPORATION

OVERVIEW

Loews Corporation is a holding company that includes the US's 4th largest tobacco manufacturer, the US's 12th largest insurance firm, hotels worldwide, a watchmaker, and a controlling interest (nearly 25%) in CBS.

Lorillard's Newport cigarette brand (the 5th largest seller in the US) provides over 60% of Lorillard's profits. CNA insurance is the US leader in professional liability for architects and engineers and is 2nd in federal health insurance programs. Insurance represents 61% of the company's business. Loews puts its name on most of the 16 hotels it owns and/or operates; Loews Reservations International (LRI) services over 400 hotel properties worldwide.

The 2 founding Tisch brothers own 26% of Loews. Larry, an exceptional investor, handles the multibillion-dollar portfolio and is also president and CEO of CBS; Bob, who also served as Postmaster General in the mid-1980s, handles operations.

Together with 3 of their sons who are active in management, the brothers have given their shareholders an average growth of 17.9% over 10 years.

NYSE symbol: LTR
Incorporated: Delaware, 1969
Fiscal year ends: December 31

WHO

Chairman and Co-CEO: Laurence A. Tisch, age 67, $1,571,519 pay
President and Co-CEO: Preston Robert (Bob) Tisch, age 63, $994,254 pay
EVP: James S.Tisch, age 37
VP, Strategic Planning: Andrew H. Tisch, age 40
VP: Jonathan M. Tisch, age 36
SVP and CFO: Roy E. Posner, age 56
Auditors: Deloitte & Touche
Employees: 26,800

WHEN

In 1946 Larry Tisch, who had received an NYU business degree at age 18, dropped out of Harvard Law and with his younger brother Bob bought a Lakewood, New Jersey, resort hotel, with help from their parents.

Tisch Hotels, the new entity, purchased Atlantic City's Traymore and Ambassador Hotels in the early 1950s and 10 others by 1955. In the early 1960s the brothers erected 6 hotels simultaneously in New York City.

Moving beyond hotels, the brothers bought money-losing companies saddled with poor management; discarding the management along with underperforming divisions, they quickly tightened operational control and eliminated frills such as fancy offices, company planes, and even memos.

In 1960 Tisch Hotels gained control of MGM's ailing Loew's Theaters division following a 1959 antitrust ruling, and sold the prime real estate underneath many of the elegant one-screen theaters to developers. The company name became Loews in 1971; Loews sold its remaining theater operations in 1985.

In 1968 the company bought Lorillard, shed pet food and candy operations, and regained its slipping tobacco market share by introducing low-tar brands (Kent III, True). CNA Financial (1974) was next: the Tisch method turned losses of $208 million in 1974 to $110 million in profits the next year.

Bulova Watch (1979), guided by Larry's son Andrew, combated a nagging image problem with sleek new watch styles; profitability returned in 1984.

In 1985 Loews helped CBS fend off a takeover attempt by Ted Turner, and ended up with almost 25% of the company and Larry as president of CBS.

Loews's deep pockets allowed the purchase of 6 used tankers for $5.5 million apiece (average construction cost: $60 million) during a period of depressed prices for supertankers in the early 1980s. In 1990 Loews sold 3 of the Majestic supertankers for $133 million and exchanged the other 3 for 49% interest in the purchasing entity (Hellespont), for a pretax gain of $105 million. Loews bought offshore drilling rig operator Diamond M in 1989.

Loews's caution during the hotel overexpansion of the 1980s later enabled the company to purchase some bargains (*e.g.*, Loews Giorgio, Denver, 1989).

In 1989 Loews also entered a joint venture with Covia to create a new computer reservation service for hotels.

Despite heavy losses from Hurricane Hugo and the California earthquake, Loews's insurance operation remained profitable in 1989, leading the company to another year of record profits.

WHERE

HQ: 667 Madison Ave., New York, NY 10021
Phone: 212-545-2000
FAX: 212-545-2498

Loews operates throughout the US and has luxury, resort, and motor hotels in Monaco, France, and Canada.

WHAT

	1989 Sales		1989 Net Income	
	$ mil	% of total	$ mil	% of total
Property & casualty insurance	6,737	61	475	55
Life insurance	2,336	21	24	3
Cigarettes	1,447	13	355	41
Hotels	207	2	8	1
Watches & timers	174	2	(3)	—
Shipping	60	1	4	—
Offshore drilling	15	—	(5)	—
Adjustments	122	—	49	—
Total	**11,098**	**100**	**907**	**100**

CNA Financial (83%)
Insurance
Continental Casualty (property and casualty)
Continental Assurance (life, accident, and health)

Lorillard
Kent
Newport
Old Gold
Triumph
True

Loews Hotel
Loews Annapolis (Annapolis, MD)
Loews Giorgio (Denver, CO)
Loews Summit (NY)
Loews Vanderbilt Plaza (TN)

Bulova (97%)
Clocks
Mechanical time fuzes
Ultimé gold jewelry
Watch collections
Marine Star
Twentieth Century

CBS (24.8%)

Champion International (9%)
Paper products

Diamond M Holding
Offshore drilling rigs

Hellespont (49%)
Crude oil tankers

HOW MUCH

	9 Yr. Growth	1980	1981	1982	1983	1984	1985	1986	1987	1988	1989
Sales ($ mil)	11.0%	4,339	4,534	4,606	4,808	5,274	6,333	8,248	8,965	10,424	11,098
Net income ($ mil)	17.9%	206	257	216	266	329	503	546	656	890	907
Income as % of sales	—	4.8%	5.7%	4.7%	5.5%	6.2%	7.9%	6.6%	7.3%	8.5%	8.2%
Earnings per share ($)	23.1%	1.85	2.67	2.40	3.16	4.03	6.17	6.69	8.41	11.70	12.02
Stock price – high ($)	—	12.43	14.38	21.27	25.07	35.50	56.25	72.38	96.25	83.13	135.00
Stock price – low ($)	—	7.05	9.73	10.57	17.67	23.50	33.00	53.75	58.00	62.00	77.00
Stock price – close ($)	30.8%	11.05	11.87	19.13	24.87	35.00	54.50	58.25	66.63	78.88	124.25
P/E – high	—	7	5	9	8	9	9	11	11	7	11
P/E – low	—	4	4	4	6	6	5	8	7	5	6
Dividends per share ($)	22.6%	0.16	0.16	0.16	0.16	0.29	3.00	1.00	1.00	1.00	1.00
Book value per share ($)	20.4%	12.00	14.40	16.92	20.71	24.63	29.97	36.07	42.56	53.20	64.09

1989 Year End:
Debt ratio: 27.8%
Return on equity: 20.5%
Cash (mil): $3,738
Current ratio: —
Long-term debt (mil): $1,850
Number of shares (mil): 75
Dividends:
1989 average yield: 0.8%
1989 payout: 8.3%
Market value (mil): $9,326

Stock Price History high/low 1980-89

RANKINGS

14th in *Fortune* 50 Diversified Financial Cos.
28th in *Fortune* 50 Life Insurance Cos. (CNA)
61st in *Forbes* Sales 500
62nd in *Business Week* 1000
201st in *Business Week* Global 1000

COMPETITION

American Brands
B.A.T
Bass
Canadian Pacific
CSX
Helmsley Enterprises
Hilton
Hyatt
Marriott
Philip Morris
RJR Nabisco
Insurance companies

LONGS DRUG STORES CORPORATION

OVERVIEW

Walnut Creek, California–based Longs Drug Stores operates 248 drugstores in 6 western states. Of the company's locations 85% are in California where Longs holds a 20% market share.

Two things distinguish Longs from its competitors. First, the company gives store managers extraordinary independence in running their stores and ties managers' salaries to each location's performance. Consequently, store managers are able to tailor their stores to local preferences and are highly motivated to do so. This practice breeds management loyalty, which is further strengthened by the company's policy of promoting from within.

Second, the company's stores (averaging 24,000 square feet) are larger than the industry average. This allows each location to offer a greater selection of high-margin general merchandise. These 2 factors have allowed Longs to achieve the highest sales per employee and sales per store ($8.3 million in 1989) in the industry.

Longs has always been conservatively managed and employee-oriented, adding locations steadily and maintaining high profitability. Stock repurchases in recent years have left a smaller share of ownership in public hands: 45% of common stock is held either by the Long family or by employee benefit plans. The company has demonstrated consistent year-to-year growth and has no long-term debt. Its balance sheet remains one of the healthiest in the chain drug industry.

NYSE symbol: LDG
Incorporated: Maryland, 1984
Fiscal year ends: Last Thursday in January

WHO

Chairman: J. M. Long, age 77
President and CEO: Robert M. Long, age 51, $411,827 pay
EVP: S. D. Roath, age 49, $306,061 pay
SVP: R. A. Plomgren, age 56, $237,552 pay
SVP: Bill M. Brandon, age 51, $201,562 pay
SVP: O. D. Jones, age 51, $184,445 pay
VP Administration, Treasurer, and Principal Financial Officer: W. G. Combs, age 59
Auditors: Deloitte & Touche
Employees: 14,200

WHEN

Joseph Long, son-in-law of Safeway founder Marion Skaggs, and his brother Thomas opened their first store, Longs Self-Service Drug Store, in Oakland, California, in 1938 and their 2nd store in nearby Alameda in 1939. The brothers believed that the manager of each store should make the decisions regarding its operation. The stores offered the lowest prices in their neighborhoods.

By 1950 the company had 6 stores in the Oakland area and one in Fresno. Longs opened 10 more stores during the 1950s in California and Hawaii. In the late 1970s they expanded into Oregon, Alaska, Arizona, and Nevada.

Longs continued its decentralized philosophy in the late 1980s despite its growing number of locations. Unlike most chain stores, where stocking and operations decisions are made at headquarters, Robert Long, president since his father Joseph retired in 1975, has given each store manager extraordinary freedom in price setting, inventory selection, and sales promotion.

In 1987 the company departed from its habit of growing through new openings by acquiring one Osco Drug store in Denver and 11 in California from American Stores, increasing its market share in California to 20%. At the same time it sold all 15 locations in Arizona to Osco. The company has been repurchasing its own stock and reselling to its employee profit-sharing plan in order to increase employee participation in the company.

The company is also trying to position itself for the growth in the industry that it foresees as the elderly population increases. Part of this strategy has been to offer free blood pressure and cholesterol screenings and to promote its pharmacists as health care advisors through informational advertising. Pharmacy sales alone grew by over 20% in 1989. The company plans to continue its slow-growth pattern, opening 10 to 15 stores per year for the near future.

The pharmacy of each store remains the focal point of Longs. In late 1989 a pharmacy distribution center was opened in Southern California. And to speed up prescription dispensing, some high-volume stores have been upgraded to "super pharmacy" status. The company recently began experimenting with in-store photofinishing labs in 9 locations.

WHERE

HQ: 141 N. Civic Dr., Walnut Creek, CA 94596
Phone: 415-937-1170
FAX: 415-944-6657

Longs operates drugstores in 6 western states, primarily in California. The company also operates a pharmacy distribution center in Southern California.

	No. of Stores	% of Total
California	211	85
Hawaii	21	9
Nevada	6	2
Colorado	6	2
Arizona	2	1
Alaska	2	1
Total	**248**	**100**

WHAT

Estimated Product Mix	% of Total
Prescription drugs	18
Cosmetics	10
Housewares & appliances	9
Candy	7
Liquor, wine & beer	7
Nonprescription drugs	6
Food	6
Household supplies	6
Photofinishing & equipment	6
Stationery & greeting cards	5
Related drug items	4
Sporting goods & toys	3
Toiletries	2
Tobacco & magazines	2
Miscellaneous	9
Total	**100**

RANKINGS

49th in *Fortune* 50 Retailing Cos.
383rd in *Forbes* Sales 500
580th in *Business Week* 1000

COMPETITION

Albertson's
American Stores
Fred Meyer
K mart
Walgreen
Other supermarket companies

HOW MUCH

	9 Yr. Growth	1980	1981	1982	1983	1984	1985	1986	1987	1988	1989
Sales ($ mil)	10.0%	893	1,005	1,123	1,214	1,376	1,481	1,635	1,772	1,925	2,111
Net income ($ mil)	10.1%	26	30	31	36	40	38	39	49	56	61
Income as % of sales	—	2.9%	3.0%	2.8%	3.0%	2.9%	2.5%	2.4%	2.8%	2.9%	2.9%
Earnings per share ($)	10.6%	1.22	1.43	1.45	1.70	1.86	1.72	1.76	2.31	2.75	3.01
Stock price – high ($)	—	17.50	18.44	23.50	25.06	24.88	31.75	38.75	41.00	37.38	48.50
Stock price – low ($)	—	11.13	12.75	12.38	16.88	17.00	21.63	26.63	25.13	29.38	34.50
Stock price – close ($)	12.3%	15.75	14.44	17.81	24.31	22.13	30.63	29.50	30.38	35.50	44.63
P/E – high	—	14	13	16	15	13	18	22	18	14	16
P/E – low	—	9	9	9	10	9	13	15	11	11	11
Dividends per share ($)	9.7%	0.41	0.45	0.51	0.55	0.62	0.70	0.75	0.79	0.86	0.94
Book value per share ($)	9.4%	7.44	8.42	9.38	10.57	12.23	13.33	13.74	14.59	15.46	16.68

1989 Year End:
Debt ratio: 6.3%
Return on equity: 18.7%
Cash (mil): $25
Current ratio: 1.54
Long-term debt (mil): $ —
Number of shares (mil): 20
Dividends:
1989 average yield: 2.1%
1989 payout: 31.2%
Market value (mil): $898

Stock Price History high/low 1980-89

50
45
40
35
30
25
20
15
10
5
0

LOTUS DEVELOPMENT CORPORATION

OVERVIEW

Lotus dominates the spreadsheet market for IBM-compatible PCs (with an estimated 80% share) and is the 2nd largest independent maker of PC software (after Microsoft).

The phenomenally successful Lotus 1-2-3 is the de facto spreadsheet standard for PCs. Translated into 9 languages, including a top-selling Japanese version, it has sold over 6 million units. Lotus 1-2-3 and its sister, Symphony, still account for 60% of revenues.

Lotus has recently broadened its line, extending 1-2-3 to Sun workstations, DEC minicomputers, and IBM mainframes. Other products include CD-ROM–based financial information products (Lotus One Source), of which Lotus is a leading supplier; groupware (the $62,500 Notes product), which allows PC users to share creation of and access to information when using a local or wide area network; personal information manager (Agenda); and a hard disk utility (Magellan), which allows PC users to find information on their hard disks.

Founder Mitch Kapor served as guru to the nascent PC software industry; he left Lotus in 1986 to found ON Technology. Lotus looks to the foreign market (37% in 1989) eventually to provide 50% of its revenues.

OTC symbol: LOTS
Incorporated: Delaware, 1982
Fiscal year ends: December 31

WHO

Chairman and President: Jim P. Manzi, age 38, $991,358 pay
SVP Worldwide Sales and Service: Stephen J. Crummey, age 45, $440,000 pay
SVP Finance and Operations: Robert P. Schechter, age 41, $440,000 pay
SVP Software Products Group: W. Frank King III, age 50, $440,000 pay
Auditors: Coopers & Lybrand
Employees: 2,800

WHEN

When the IBM PC was introduced in 1981, Mitch Kapor quickly saw the light and designed an electronic spreadsheet for it. He called it Lotus 1-2-3 (after the Hindu symbol of enlightenment), and soon the former Transcendental Meditation teacher saw his Cambridge-based company blossom. One year after the 1982 founding, sales were $53 million; by 1985, $226 million.

Kapor brought to Lotus the values of his late 1960s Yale undergraduate days; consensus, jeans, and t-shirts were staples. Unwieldy growth, however, prompted the structure-shy Kapor to boost star marketer Jim Manzi to president in 1984. Manzi transformed Lotus into a market-driven company and injected a management team drawn from mainframe vendor ranks after Kapor left in 1986.

When the highly touted Symphony spreadsheet and Jazz (for Macintosh computers) drew muted responses, Manzi focused on 1-2-3. Lotus acquired a number of smaller companies offering 1-2-3 enhancements and developed foreign language versions for Europe, the Middle East, and Japan. In 1985 and 1986 Manzi began broadening beyond 1-2-3, purchasing Dataspeed, Inc. (Signal and Quotrek stock quote services), ISYS Corp. (developer of the One Source CD/ROM), and Graphics Communications (graphics software).

When competing spreadsheets threatened market share, Lotus undertook an arduous 3-year development of 1-2-3 Release 3.0, which doubled the work force and brought order to programming chaos with progress reports and shared standards. Release 3.0 (featuring 3-D graphics) and, for less powerful PCs, Release 2.2 (with spreadsheet publishing strength) finally appeared in 1989; customers seeking the attributes of both had to wait for Release 3.1 (1990).

In 1989 the company took a 15% equity position in Sybase, Inc., a database management software developer. In 1990 it agreed to acquire networking software leader Novell, but the deal collapsed before it was completed.

The new decade saw Lotus emerge leaner (stock-quote services Signal and Quotrek were shed in 1989) and focused on broadening 1-2-3's scope, releasing 1-2-3 for Sun workstations, IBM mainframes, and DEC minicomputers; 1-2-3 for Apple Macintoshes is planned for 1991 release.

Lotus has countered the current software glut by directly selling to and servicing their new high-end customers. Lotus has strong continuing interests in CD-ROM products, for which it seeks more mass-market appeal with CD/Marketplace (1990, direct mail use on the Macintosh).

WHERE

HQ: 55 Cambridge Pkwy., Cambridge, MA 02142
Phone: 617-577-8500
FAX: 617-225-1213

Lotus Development has locations in 16 foreign countries and conducts manufacturing and distribution operations in the US, Puerto Rico, and Ireland.

	1989 Sales		1989 Operating Income	
	$ mil	% of total	$ mil	% of total
North America	356	63	18	20
Foreign	204	37	70	80
Adjustments	(4)	—	(14)	—
Total	**556**	**100**	**74**	**100**

WHAT

Spreadsheets
1-2-3 enhancement products
  Datalens Developer Toolkit
  Add-in Toolkit
1-2-3/G (graphical user interface)
1-2-3 Release 2.0
1-2-3 Release 2.2
1-2-3 Release 3.0
1-2-3 Release 3.1
1-2-3 versions for DEC, IBM, Sun
Symphony
Symphony 2.0 Plus

Database Management
Lotus/DBMS

Graphics
Allways
Freelance Plus Release 3.01
Freelance Release 3J

Information Management
Lotus Agenda
Lotus Magellan
Lotus Notes

Information Services
Lotus One Source
  CD/Banking
  CD/Corporate
  CD/International
CD/Investment
CD/M&A
CD/Marketplace
CD/Private+

Investments
Sybase, Inc. (15%, relational database management)

HOW MUCH

	6 Yr. Growth	1980	1981	1982	1983	1984	1985	1986	1987	1988	1989
Sales ($ mil)	48.0%	—	—	—	53	157	226	283	396	469	556
Net income ($ mil)	30.1%	—	—	—	14	36	38	48	72	59	68
Income as % of sales	—	—	—	—	25.9%	23.0%	16.9%	17.1%	18.2%	12.6%	12.2%
Earnings per share ($)	29.8%	—	—	—	0.33	0.75	0.77	1.03	1.57	1.29	1.58
Stock price – high ($)	—	—	—	—	10.33	13.25	11.25	19.33	38.50	34.25	33.50
Stock price – low ($)	—	—	—	—	7.42	5.08	5.08	6.71	16.33	14.75	18.00
Stock price – close ($)	20.1%	—	—	—	10.33	8.00	8.33	17.25	30.75	18.25	31.00
P/E – high	—	—	—	—	32	18	15	19	25	27	21
P/E – low	—	—	—	—	23	7	7	7	10	11	11
Dividends per share ($)	—	—	—	—	0.00	0.00	0.00	0.00	0.00	0.00	0.00
Book value per share ($)	32.3%	—	—	—	1.25	2.02	2.85	2.72	4.60	5.57	6.69

1989 Year End:
Debt ratio: 42.1%
Return on equity: 25.8%
Cash (mil): $275
Current ratio: 3.73
Long-term debt (mil): $202
Number of shares (mil): 42
Dividends:
  1989 average yield: 0.0%
  1989 payout: 0.0%
Market value (mil): $1,290

Stock Price History high/low 1983-89

RANKINGS

394th in *Business Week* 1000

COMPETITION

Apple
Computer Associates
Microsoft
Other software companies

LOWE'S COMPANIES, INC.

OVERVIEW

Lowe's Companies, based in North Wilkesboro, North Carolina, since its founding in 1921, sells hardware and building materials through over 300 stores in 20 states, from Pennsylvania to Missouri and from Florida to Texas. Most of the stores are located in small cities, such as Tyler, Texas, and York, Pennsylvania, where the company can avoid the level of competition found in large urban centers. The company is #2 in the building supply/home center chain industry after Home Depot.

Since 1984 Lowe's has been shifting emphasis away from the highly cyclical building market toward the home improvement do-it-yourselfer. To this end the company has enlarged and relocated its stores to better accommodate do-it-yourself customers and plans to continue this through 1991. Sales to do-it-yourselfers are up from 52% of the company total in 1984 to 62% in 1989.

About 6% of Lowe's stock is owned by its officers and directors. Lowe's Companies Employee Stock Ownership Trust owns 24%. Chiefly because of its generous employee stock ownership plan, Lowe's has been honored as one of the 100 best companies to work for in the US.

NYSE symbol: LOW
Incorporated: North Carolina, 1952
Fiscal year ends: January 31

WHO

Chairman: Robert L. Strickland, age 59, $463,265 pay
President and CEO: Leonard G. Herring, age 62, $487,030 pay
EVP Sales/Store Operations: Wendell R. Emerine, age 51, $329,423 pay
SVP, Treasurer, and CFO: Harry Underwood II, age 47
Auditors: Deloitte & Touche
Employees: 15,271

WHEN

Lowe's was founded in 1921 as Mr. I. S. Lowe's North Wilkesboro Hardware in North Wilkesboro, North Carolina, where its corporate headquarters remains today. A family operation by 1945, Mr. Lowe's store was run by his son Jim and son-in-law Carl Buchan. Jim and Buchan opened a 2nd store in Sparta, North Carolina (about 40 miles from North Wilkesboro), in 1949. Buchan bought Jim Lowe's share in the company in 1952. Incorporating as Lowe's North Wilkesboro Hardware, Buchan kept Lowe's as part of the company name because he liked the slogan "Lowe's Low Prices." Sales in 1952 were $4 million. Buchan had 15 stores in North Carolina, Virginia, Tennessee, and South Carolina and sales of $31 million in 1960.

Buchan had been planning to create a profit-sharing plan on behalf of Lowe's employees, but he died of a heart attack in 1960. In 1961 a Lowe's management team and the executors of Buchan's estate established the Lowe's Employees Profit Sharing and Trust, which bought Buchan's 89% of the company (subsequently renamed Lowe's Companies) and financed the transaction through a public offering (1961). Lowe's was listed on the NYSE in 1979.

Harvard MBA Robert Strickland, who joined the company directly out of business school in 1957, became chairman in 1978. Revenues increased from $170 million in 1971 to more than $900 million, with net income of $25 million, in 1979. Traditionally, over 1/2 of Lowe's business was in sales to professional home builders, but in 1980 housing starts fell to 1.3 million and Lowe's net income dropped 24%.

Strickland rethought his store layout with the help of consultants and from 1979 to 1982 redesigned 1/2 of the 229 stores to be more oriented toward do-it-yourself consumers, a more stable market than the cyclical new construction market. The new stores featured softer lighting and displays of entire room layouts, features aimed especially at women, who made up over 1/2 of all do-it-yourself customers. In 1982 Lowe's made more than 50% of its sales to consumers for the first time in its history, and sales topped the $1 billion mark.

In 1984 Lowe's announced that it would increase its total store floor space from 2.5 million square feet to 5 million square feet by 1988 through new store construction and relocation. This accomplished, the company plans to add another 1.8 million square feet of floor space by 1991.

WHERE

HQ: PO Box 1111, North Wilkesboro, NC 28656
Phone: 919-651-4000
FAX: 919-651-4766

	No. of Stores
Alabama	14
Arkansas	7
Delaware	3
Florida	19
Georgia	25
Illinois	1
Indiana	5
Kentucky	18
Louisiana	12
Maryland	8
Mississippi	7
Missouri	1
North Carolina	69
Ohio	6
Pennsylvania	7
South Carolina	23
Tennessee	25
Texas	8
Virginia	34
West Virginia	14
Total	**306**

WHAT

	1989 Sales	
	$ mil	% of total
Building commodities, lumber	1,216	46
Home decorating, lighting	346	13
Yard, patio & garden products	261	10
Kitchen, bathroom & laundry products	237	9
Other products	591	22
Total	**2,651**	**100**

Principal Sales Segments
Building commodities
Heating, cooling, and water systems
Home decorating and lighting products
Home entertainment products
Kitchen, bathroom, and laundry fixtures
Millwork
Structural lumber
Tools
Yard, patio, and garden products

RANKINGS

43rd in *Fortune* 50 Retailing Cos.
318th in *Forbes* Sales 500
472nd in *Business Week* 1000

COMPETITION

Home Depot
K mart
Montgomery Ward
Sears
Shermin-Williams
Wal-Mart

HOW MUCH

	9 Yr. Growth	1980	1981	1982	1983	1984	1985	1986	1987	1988	1989
Sales ($ mil)	13.0%	884	888	1,034	1,431	1,689	2,073	2,283	2,442	2,517	2,651
Net income ($ mil)	16.5%	19	18	25	51	61	60	55	56	69	75
Income as % of sales	—	2.1%	2.0%	2.4%	3.5%	3.6%	2.9%	2.4%	2.3%	2.8%	2.8%
Earnings per share ($)	14.8%	0.58	0.55	0.76	1.40	1.70	1.64	1.41	1.41	1.83	2.01
Stock price – high ($)	—	9.95	11.35	22.35	32.75	25.13	31.13	41.50	32.75	24.38	32.13
Stock price – low ($)	—	5.35	6.30	7.13	17.33	16.25	20.75	22.50	15.25	16.25	20.75
Stock price – close ($)	16.3%	7.55	7.65	20.78	22.38	24.75	25.88	26.00	16.13	21.00	29.50
P/E – high	—	17	21	30	23	15	19	29	23	13	16
P/E – low	—	9	12	9	12	10	13	16	11	9	10
Dividends per share ($)	8.3%	0.24	0.29	0.29	0.32	0.32	0.36	0.40	0.43	0.46	0.49
Book value per share ($)	14.2%	5.23	5.45	5.96	8.04	9.42	10.99	13.64	14.75	15.80	17.33

1989 Year End:
Debt ratio: 20.6%
Return on equity: 12.1%
Cash (mil): $56
Current ratio: 1.94
Long-term debt (mil): $168
Number of shares (mil): 37
Dividends:
1989 average yield: 1.7%
1989 payout: 24.4%
Market value (mil): $1,099

THE LTV CORPORATION

OVERVIEW

The LTV Corporation, a Dallas-based conglomerate, began 1990 in its 4th year of Chapter 11 bankruptcy. LTV's restructuring has involved shutting down plants, modernizing existing ones, refocusing its product segments, and reducing its work force (from 56,800 in 1985 to 38,000 in 1989).

LTV's 4 business groups include Steel, Missiles and Electronics, Aircraft Products, and Energy Products. While LTV Steel is the most profitable and 3rd largest steel manufacturer in the US, demand for steel in 1989 was soft. Federal budget tightening in the defense industry and cost increases hurt its missiles and aircraft products industries, and the depressed oil and gas prices of the late 1980s have kept LTV's energy product revenues relatively flat.

A 1990 Supreme Court ruling requiring LTV to take back its underfunded pension plans (an estimated $3.3 billion liability) will likely delay LTV's emergence from bankruptcy. The court determined that LTV can correct its underfunding. The plans were taken over by the federal Pension Benefit Guaranty Corporation, which insures workers' pensions, in 1987 after LTV had filed for bankruptcy.

WHEN

LTV was established in Dallas in 1961, the result of a series of mergers and acquisitions orchestrated by James Ling. Ling had taken his company (Ling Electric) public in 1955, aggressively marketing his stock, even distributing its prospectus at the Texas State Fair. LTV's formation began with the acquisition of L. M. Electronics by Ling Electric in 1956. The company acquired Altec Electronics in 1959, and in 1960 merged with Temco (an electronics and missile company). In 1961 Ling-Temco acquired Dallas-based Chance Vought — a well-known manufacturer of navy planes — to become Ling-Temco-Vought (LTV).

In 1964 Ling was able to increase the value of LTV's assets by making it a holding company and breaking out its operations into 3 public companies: LTV Aerospace, LTV Ling Altec, and LTV Electrosystems. LTV maintained majority interest in all 3. This "redeployment" strategy drove up the price of each subsidiary's stock and subsequently raised the value of LTV's assets. LTV then used its shares in the 3 companies as collateral for further acquisitions.

With borrowed funds LTV continued its acquisition campaign — applying the redeployment strategy where profitable — beginning with Okonite (1965), a copper wire and cable manufacturer; Wilson (1967), the nation's 3rd largest meat packer with divisions in sporting goods and pharmaceuticals; Greatamerica (1968), parent company of Braniff and National Car Rental; and Jones & Laughlin Steel (1968).

In 1969 LTV's financial health began to deteriorate, made worse by a declining stock market. That year LTV reported a net loss of $38.1 million and was forced to sell off divisions to pay its debt. In 1970, having lost confidence in Ling as chairman, the LTV board demoted him to president. James Ling quit 6 weeks later at the age of 47. In 1971 LTV sold Okonite and Braniff as part of an antitrust settlement. The antitrust suit was a consequence of LTV's numerous acquisitions.

In 1977 LTV purchased Lykes, a petroleum equipment company, and Youngstown Sheet & Tube (steel). LTV sold off Wilson in 1981 and was left with LTV Steel, LTV Aerospace & Defense, and LTV Energy Products. In 1984, in an attempt to strengthen its position in steel, LTV acquired Republic Steel for $770 million. But by 1986, with steel and petroleum prices low and with 5 years of losses, LTV was forced into Chapter 11 bankruptcy — the largest industrial filing as of that date.

HOW MUCH

	9 Yr. Growth	1980	1981	1982	1983	1984	1985	1986	1987	1988	1989
Sales ($ mil)	(2.5%)	8,010	7,511	4,777	4,578	7,046	8,199	7,271	7,582	7,325	6,362
Net income ($ mil)	8.4%	128	405	(163)	(238)	(378)	(772)	(3,252)	503	(891)	265
Income as % of sales	—	1.6%	5.4%	(3.4%)	(5.2%)	(5.4%)	(9.4%)	(44.7%)	6.6%	(12.2%)	4.2%
Earnings per share ($)	(5.3%)	2.96	7.97	*(3.36)*	(4.79)	(5.84)	(9.50)	(35.41)	3.67	(8.97)	1.82
Stock price – high ($)	—	20.75	26.13	17.75	19.13	19.88	13.25	9.88	5.88	3.88	2.50
Stock price – low ($)	—	7.75	12.63	8.13	11.63	8.88	5.25	1.13	1.50	2.13	1.13
Stock price – close ($)	(27.5%)	20.25	16.38	11.38	18.38	9.88	6.75	1.63	2.50	2.25	1.13
P/E – high	—	7	3	—	—	—	—	—	2	—	1
P/E – low	—	3	2	—	—	—	—	—	0	—	1
Dividends per share ($)	0.0%	0.00	0.00	0.44	0.25	0.19	0.00	0.00	0.00	0.00	0.00
Book value per share ($)	—	22.20	26.12	22.38	20.50	16.21	7.19	(26.99)	(20.37)	(49.59)	(45.38)

1989 Year End:
Debt ratio: —
Return on equity: —
Cash (mil): $1,019
Current ratio: 2.62
Long-term debt (mil): $17
Number of shares (mil): 109
Dividends:
1989 average yield: 0.0%
1989 payout: 0.0%
Market value (mil): $122

Stock Price History high/low 1980-89

0 5 10 15 20 25 30

NYSE symbol: LTV
Incorporated: Delaware, 1958
Fiscal year ends: December 31

WHO

Chairman, CEO, President, and COO: Raymond A. Hay, age 61, $938,070 pay
President and CEO of LTV Steel: David H. Hoag, age 50, $571,416 pay
SVP and CFO: James F. Powers, age 51, $534,349 pay
Auditors: Ernst & Young
Employees: 38,000

WHERE

HQ: PO Box 655003, 2001 Ross Ave., Dallas, TX 75265
Phone: 214-979-7711
FAX: 214-979-7946

LTV offices and facilities are in the US and Canada.

WHAT

	1989 Sales		1989 Operating Income	
	$ mil	% of total	$ mil	% of total
Steel	4,086	64	310	134
Energy products	267	4	5	2
Aircraft products	653	10	(100)	(43)
Missiles & electronics	1,356	22	15	7
Adjustments	—	—	(34)	—
Total	**6,362**	**100**	**196**	**100**

LTV Steel
Galvanized products
Rolled sheet
Tin mill products
Tubular products

Aircraft Products
Production of military and commercial aircraft components; modernization and support programs
- A-7 aircraft program
- Advanced Technology Bomber (B-2) program
- Boeing 747 program
- Boeing 757 program
- Boeing 767 program
- Canadair program
- McDonnell Douglas C-17A program
- McDonnell Douglas DC-10 program

Missiles & Electronics
Antiradiation missile decoy systems
Army Tactical Missiles System
Computerized flight inspection systems
Military wheeled vehicles (the Hummer)
Multiple Launch Rocket System
Stationkeeping equipment
VT-1 Missile

Energy Products
Drilling, production, and other equipment
Oilfield supplies
Tubular products (casing, tubing, and drill pipe)

RANKINGS

72nd in *Fortune* 500 Industrial Cos.
205th in *Fortune* Global 500 Industrial Cos.
132nd in *Forbes* Sales 500

COMPETITION

Bethlehem Steel
Broken Hill
Cargill
Daimler-Benz
FMC
General Dynamics
Hyundai
Inland Steel
McDonnell Douglas
Northrop
Thomson
USX
Other defense companies

MACANDREWS & FORBES HOLDINGS INC.

OVERVIEW

MacAndrews & Forbes Holdings is Ron Perelman's conglomerate. It owns an eclectic group of businesses in industries ranging from beauty products to banking, including MacAndrews & Forbes, a maker of licorice extract used in flavorings; Coleman Company, a maker of camping and recreational products; and First Gibraltar, a group of Texas S&Ls. MacAndrews & Forbes Holdings also owns 57% of Beverly Hills–based Andrews Group, a public company that owns Marvel Entertainment Group (comic book publisher) and New World Entertainment, which produces such television shows as "Tour of Duty" and "The Wonder Years."

But the star of MacAndrews & Forbes Holdings is Revlon, the New York–based beauty business started by Charles Revson in 1932. With over $2.7 billion in sales for 1989, Revlon is America's 2nd largest cosmetics company (after Avon).

Perelman, the man who assembled the MacAndrews & Forbes empire by acquiring companies, was reading a stack of annual reports after school every day while still in his early teens. Today he uses his knowledge to choose acquisitions that are reliable moneymakers in industries which, for the most part, are not affected by seasonal sales fluctuations. After buying a company, he sells off unprofitable subsidiaries and invests heavily in what remains. This technique, adopted from his youth when he worked for his father, has proven successful; *Forbes* lists Perelman as one of the 400 wealthiest Americans, with an estimated worth of $2.75 billion (1989).

WHEN

Ron Perelman grew up in his father's Philadelphia-based conglomerate, Belmont Industries, but left it behind at the age of 35 to seek his fortune in New York. In 1978 he bought 40% of jewelry store operator Cohen-Hatfield Industries. Cohen-Hatfield bought a minority interest in MacAndrews & Forbes (licorice flavoring, 1979; acquired the rest of the company, 1980) and subsequently adopted MacAndrews & Forbes Group as its corporate name (1980).

In 1982 the company bought an 82% stake in Technicolor, a motion picture processor (sold in 1988). Perelman took MacAndrews & Forbes Group private in 1983. The company subsequently acquired control of video production company Compact Video (1983).

In 1984 MacAndrews & Forbes Group became a unit of new holding company, MacAndrews & Forbes Holdings. In effect, the Group owned MacAndrews & Forbes (licorice maker) and Technicolor, while the holding company (which was owned by Perelman) owned the Group. That same year MacAndrews & Forbes Holdings bought 80% of cigar maker Consolidated Cigar Holdings (sold in 1988).

MacAndrews & Forbes Holdings acquired control of Pantry Pride, a Florida-based supermarket chain, in 1985. Later that year Pantry Pride (by that time a corporate shell manipulated by Perelman) announced a $1.8 billion hostile takeover bid for Revlon.

Revlon was America's #1 cosmetics company until 1975, when founder Charles Revson died. His successor, Michel Bergerac, cut R&D spending on cosmetics and used beauty division earnings to buy health care and pharmaceutical companies. Perelman sold Revlon's health care businesses, except for National Health Laboratories (medical testing), and during the late 1980s bought several cosmetics companies (Max Factor, Germaine Monteil, Yves Saint Laurent's fragrance and cosmetic lines). MacAndrews & Forbes took Revlon private in 1987.

In 1988 MacAndrews & Forbes Holdings invested $315 million in 5 failing Texas S&Ls, which Perelman combined and named First Gibraltar. The company also bought the Coleman Company, a producer of camping equipment (1989).

The company's latest venture, the Andrews Group, started out as Compact Video, which was a dumping ground for Perelman's less profitable businesses for several years. Perelman plans to transform the recently renamed company into an entertainment conglomerate. Andrews Group owns television and movie producer Four Star International (and other entertainment companies) and bought controlling interest in Marvel Entertainment Group (publishers of *The Amazing Spider-Man* and *The Incredible Hulk*) from New World Entertainment in 1988, agreeing to buy the rest of New World in 1989.

HOW MUCH

	2 Yr. Growth	1980	1981	1982	1983	1984	1985	1986	1987	1988	1989
Sales ($ mil)	47.7%	—	—	—	—	—	—	—	2,440	2,500	5,325
Employees	—	—	—	—	—	—	—	—	28,000	24,582	44,000

Sales ($ mil) 1987-89

6,000 · 5,000 · 4,000 · 3,000 · 2,000 · 1,000 · 0

Private company
Incorporated: Delaware, 1983
Fiscal year ends: December 31

WHO

Chairman & CEO: Ronald O. Perelman, age 47
VC: Howard Gittis, age 56
VC: Donald G. Drapkin
President: Bruce Slovin, age 55
EVP: Meyer Laskin
EVP and CFO: Fred L. Tepperman
Auditors: KPMG Peat Marwick
Employees: 44,000

WHERE

HQ: 36 E. 63rd St., New York, NY 10021
Phone: 212-572-5980
FAX: 212-572-5022

MacAndrews & Forbes has facilities in 16 states, Puerto Rico, and 11 foreign countries.

WHAT

Subsidiaries

Andrews Group, Inc. (57%)
Four Star International, Inc. (television and film production)
Marvel Entertainment Group (comic book publishing)
New World Entertainment, Ltd. (television and film production)
Vid America, Inc. (motion picture and videocassette distribution)

Coleman Co., Inc.
Camping Trailer Division (campers and trailers)
Coleman Co., Inc. New Braunfels (plastics)
Coleman Faulkner, Inc. (trim for recreational vehicles)
Crosman Airguns Co. (small arms and small arms ammunition)
Master Craft Boat Co. (motorboats)
Skeeter Products, Inc. (boats)

First Gibraltar (savings and loan institutions)

MacAndrews & Forbes Group, Inc.
Boam Chemicals Co. (chemicals)
MacAndrews & Forbes Co. (flavorings)
M. F. Neal & Co. (flavorings)

Revlon Group, Inc.
Almay, Inc. (cosmetics)
Charles of the Ritz Group Ltd. (cosmetics and fragrances)
Germaine Monteil Cosmetiques (cosmetics)
Max Factor & Co. (cosmetics)
National Health Laboratories (80% medical testing services)
Prestige Fragrance & Cosmetics
The Princess Marcella Borghese, Inc. (cosmetics)
Revlon, Inc. (cosmetics and fragrances)

RANKINGS

12th in *Forbes* 400 US Private Cos.

COMPETITION

Amway
Avon
Brunswick
Estée Lauder
Fleetwood
IFF
Johnson Publishing
Outboard Marine
Proctor & Gamble
Roche Holding
Time Warner
Unilever
Other entertainment companies

R. H. MACY & CO., INC.

OVERVIEW

New York City–based R. H. Macy is one of the world's most recognized names in retailing. Since going private in 1986 in the decade's 3rd largest management-led LBO, Macy's has faced huge losses, and its suppliers have become increasingly nervous. However, sales have consistently grown in the last 5 years at an average annual rate in excess of 12% (1989 sales were $6.9 billion).

The company's flagship store is the Macy's in Herald Square in midtown Manhattan. At 2.15 million square feet of retail space, it is rightly billed as "the world's largest store," and since 1924 it has been associated with some of New York's grandest traditions: Macy's Thanksgiving Day Parade, Santaland, and 4th of July fireworks. The store draws tourists from the world over for its wide selection of fashionable merchandise and claims, "If you haven't seen Macy's, you haven't seen New York!"

Edward S. Finkelstein and other Macy executives hold 64% of the company's stock, with the rest held by other investors. A general weakening of retail climate coupled with the decline in the store's bonds have caused some Macy vendors to become increasingly concerned about the financial condition of the retail giant — a condition that was aggravated by a $39 million loss during the last Christmas season (2nd quarter).

WHEN

Rowland H. Macy, a Nantucket Quaker and whaling captain, opened a small store under his name in Manhattan in 1858. His policies of selling for cash only, setting fixed prices, advertising heavily, and underselling the competition were uncommon at the time and quickly gained him customers. He added new lines constantly, expanding whenever space became available in adjoining shops, and gained a reputation for selling everything the housewife might need.

Macy hired a woman, Margaret La Forge, as the store's superintendent in 1866, a first in the industry. La Forge, who was Macy's distant relative, had started as his bookkeeper in 1860. Upon Macy's death in Paris in 1877, La Forge and her husband Abiel became co-owners of the store with Robert Macy Valentine, the founder's nephew. After the death of Abiel La Forge, Valentine bought Margaret out and brought in a new partner, Charles Webster, who was a relative and Macy's employee. Valentine died shortly thereafter. His widow married Webster, who invited Isidor and Nathan Straus to become partners with him in 1887. The Straus family, New York china merchants, ran Macy's in partnership with Webster and finally bought him out in 1896. Macy's outgrew its site at 6th Avenue and 14th Street and moved to the Herald Square location at 34th and Broadway in 1902, becoming the world's largest department store.

The Strauses expanded the company outside New York by buying Lasalle & Koch, a Toledo retailer (1923) and Davison-Paxon-Stokes of Atlanta (1925). In 1929 the company bought New Jersey–based L. Bamberger and in 1945 O'Connor, Moffatt & Company, a San Francisco department store, which became the company's first West Coast location.

Meanwhile, the company continued to build its reputation as a New York institution. Macy's sponsored the first Thanksgiving Day Parade (1924), which has since announced the arrival of Santa Claus to Herald Square each year. Customers were encouraged to work around Macy's no-credit policy by depositing money with the company, against which they could charge purchases, and the company set up Macy's Bank in 1939 to manage these funds. In 1961 the company formed Macy's Credit in response to customers' growing needs to finance larger purchases.

The Straus family continued to run Macy's into the 3rd and 4th generations. By 1986 the only Straus still in Macy's management was board member Kenneth Straus, a retired chairman of the Buying Division. That year Chairman Edward Finkelstein and senior management led a buyout of the company. Macy's made a bid for Federated Department Stores in 1988, which it lost to Campeau, but was able to purchase the California-based I. Magnin and Bullock's units of Federated.

Macy's converted the Bullock's-Wilshire stores bought from Campeau to I. Magnins in 1990. Current plans call for opening a store in Springfield, Virginia, in 1991 and in Minnesota's Mall of America in 1992. The company also expects to open at least 20 new specialty stores a year through 1992.

HOW MUCH

	9 Yr. Growth	1980	1981	1982	1983	1984	1985	1986	1987	1988	1989
Sales ($ mil)	12.7%	2,374	2,657	2,979	3,468	4,065	4,368	4,653	5,210	5,729	6,974
Net income ($ mil)	—	103	120	136	187	222	189	221	(14)	(134)	(63)
Income as % of sales	—	4.3%	4.5%	4.6%	5.4%	5.5%	4.3%	4.7%	(0.3%)	(2.3%)	(0.9%)
Number of stores	6.9%	82	88	91	92	94	95	87	90	149	149

1989 Year End:
Debt ratio: 107.5%
Return on equity: 4.0%
Cash (mil): $47
Current ratio: 1.99
Long-term debt (mil): $4,661

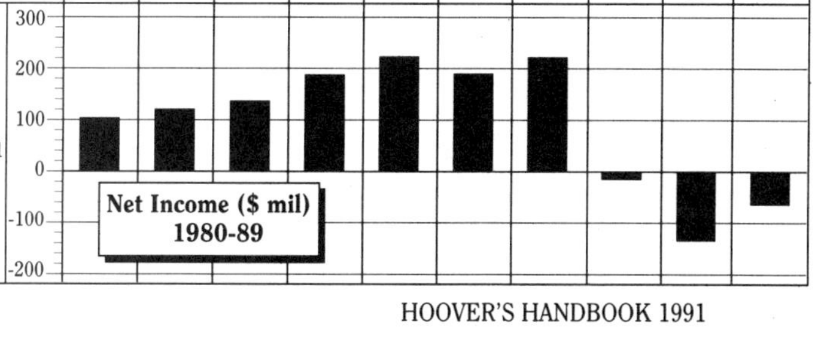

Private company
Incorporated: Delaware, 1985
Fiscal year ends: Saturday nearest July 31

WHO

Chairman and CEO: Edward S. Finkelstein, age 64, $1,135,824 pay
President and COO: Mark S. Handler, age 56, $851,531 pay
EVP and Principal Financial Officer: Myron E. Ullman III, age 42
SVP Personnel and Labor Relations: A. David Brown, age 47
Auditors: Deloitte & Touche
Employees: 78,000

WHERE

HQ: 151 W. 34th St., New York, NY 10001
Phone: 212-560-4249
FAX: 212-629-6814 (Public Relations)

Macy's operates 149 department stores in 18 states, under 4 names (the Bullock's-Wilshire stores were converted to I. Magnins in 1990).

WHAT

Store Divisions	Area sq. ft. thou	% of total
Macy's Northeast		
46 Macy's in Connecticut, Delaware, Maryland, New Jersey, New York, Pennsylvania & Virginia	14,587	45
Macy's South/Bullock's		
26 Macy's in Alabama, Florida, Georgia, Louisiana, South Carolina & Texas	5,743	17
22 Bullock's in Arizona, California & Nevada	4,395	13
Macy's California		
25 Macy's in California	5,846	18
I. Magnin–Bullock's-Wilshire		
23 I. Magnins in Arizona, California, Illinois, Maryland & Washington	1,735	5
7 Bullock's-Wilshire in California	634	2
Total	**32,940**	**100**

Macy's Specialty Stores operates 61 stores principally located in suburban malls under the names Aeropostale, Charter Club, and Fantasies by Morgan Taylor.

RANKINGS

16th in *Fortune* 50 Retailing Cos.
9th in *Forbes* 400 US Private Cos.

COMPETITION

Campeau
Carter Hawley Hale
Dayton Hudson
Dillard
May Department Stores
Nordstrom
J. C. Penney
Discount and specialty stores

MANUFACTURERS HANOVER CORPORATION

OVERVIEW

Manufacturers Hanover Corporation is a bank holding company that owns Manufacturers Hanover Trust Company, the 8th largest bank in the US and 5th largest in New York (with 221 branches). The bank has operations in 40 countries.

Manufacturers's regional banking serves consumers and small- and medium-sized businesses. The bank ranks first in market share among small- and mid-sized firms in metropolitan New York.

Corporate banking operations (commercial and investment banking) include GEOSERVE, an information and transactional service for cash management, funds transfer, and corporate trust, with more than $400 million in annual revenues. Manufacturers is one of the US's largest correspondent banks, offering check clearing, global custody and safekeeping of securities, funds transfer, loan syndication, and other services to 3,000 banking institutions. The bank's loan syndication expertise is one of the reasons it led an $11 billion financing for the 1989 merger of Time and Warner Communications.

WHEN

Manufacturers Hanover Corporation is the result of the 1961 merger of Manufacturers Trust Company and Hanover Bank, 2 banks started in the 1800s.

Manufacturers Trust Company started in Brooklyn in 1853 as Manufacturers National Bank and grew by purchasing 13 additional banks by 1930. In 1931 Harvey Gibson and a group of associates bought enough Manufacturers stock to make Gibson president. Within a year Manufacturers bought Chatham and Phenix National Bank of New York. Manufacturers continued to purchase banks, the largest being Brooklyn Trust Company (1950), with 26 branches.

The Hanover Bank opened in 1851 in Hanover Square, center of New York City's wholesale dry goods trade. In 1876 James Woodward began a 34-year term as president of Hanover. During his presidency the bank sought the business of country banks, which was the beginning of the bank's extensive correspondent banking business today. In 1901 Hanover made its first purchase, Continental Bank (Manhattan).

In 1929 Hanover merged with Central Union Trust to form Central Hanover Bank and Trust. Central Union Trust already had opened 5 overseas offices in the 1920s. In 1938 Central Hanover opened its first full-service foreign branch. Central Hanover changed its name back to Hanover Bank in 1951.

Less than 2 hours after the 1961 merger to form Manufacturers Hanover, the US Department of Justice filed an antitrust injunction, which left the new bank's fate in doubt for 5 years. The merger was regarded as an excellent combination of Manufacturers's large retail branch system and Hanover's wholesale, trust, and correspondent banking. In late 1965 the US Congress amended the Banking Act of 1960, allowing this merger and many others to be free of antitrust claims.

In 1969 the bank formed Manufacturers Hanover Corporation, a holding company. That same year the company became the first US bank to start a merchant bank in London. In the early 1970s the bank diversified, acquiring mortgage and consumer finance businesses and forming a leasing company. Manufacturers bought CIT Financial from RCA for $1.51 billion (1984) and then sold 60% of CIT to Dai-Ichi Kangyo Bank, for $1.28 billion (1989). That year Manufacturers also issued $750 million in new common stock in order to increase capital. Manufacturers Hanover incurred losses in 1987 and 1989, after increasing reserves against Latin American loans by $1.7 billion (1987) and $1.1 billion (1989).

NYSE symbol: MHC
Incorporated: Delaware, 1968
Fiscal year ends: December 31

WHO

Chairman and CEO: John F. McGillicuddy, age 59, $1,680,323 pay
VC: Edward D. Miller, age 49, $799,834 pay
President: Thomas S. Johnson, age 49, $650,000 pay
Sector EVP Investment Banking: Douglas E. Ebert, age 44, $625,913 pay
Sector EVP Banking and International: Donald G. McCouch, age 47
Sector EVP Corporate Banking: Donald H. McCree, Jr., age 53
EVP and Chief Credit Officer: William C. Langley, age 51
Auditors: KPMG Peat Marwick
Employees: 20,034

WHERE

HQ: 270 Park Ave., New York, NY 10017
Phone: 212-270-6000
FAX: 212-682-3761 (Communications)

Manufacturers Hanover has 221 branches in New York and operations in 40 countries.

	1989 Sales		1989 Net Income	
	$ mil	% of total	$ mil	% of total
US	5,424	64	401	—
Europe	1,273	15	(17)	—
Latin America, the Caribbean	1,011	12	(838)	—
Asia Pacific, the	480	6	(2)	—
Other foreign	232	3	(62)	—
Adjustments	—	—	(70)	—
Total	**8,420**	**100**	**(588)**	**—**

WHAT

	$ mil	% of total
Loan interest revenue	5,198	62
Other interest revenue	1,690	20
Noninterest revenue	1,532	18
Total	**8,420**	**100**

Financial Services

Commercial banking
- Cash management
- Credit
- Equipment/real estate loans

Correspondent banking
- Check clearing
- Funds transfer
- Global securities custody

Investment banking
- Foreign exchange
- Mergers and acquisitions
- Trade finance

Retail banking
- Credit cards
- Deposit services
- Personal/mortgage loans

Trust and investment services

RANKINGS

8th in *Fortune* 100 Commercial Banking Cos.
82nd in *Fortune* World's 100 Commercial Banks
95th in *Forbes* Sales 500
259th in *Business Week* 1000
780th in *Business Week* Global 1000

COMPETITION

American Express
Bank of New York
BankAmerica
Bankers Trust
Chase Manhattan
Chemical Banking
Citicorp
CS Holding
Dai-Ichi Kangyo
Deutsche Bank
Goldman Sachs
Hongkong & Shanghai Banking
Household International
ITT
J.P. Morgan
Other banks

HOW MUCH

	9 Yr. Growth	1980	1981	1982	1983	1984	1985	1986	1987	1988	1989
Sales ($ mil)	5.5%	5,184	7,465	7,638	6,596	8,315	8,385	7,965	7,757	8,545	8,420
Net income ($ mil)	—	229	252	295	337	353	407	411	(1,140)	752	(588)
Income as % of sales	—	4.4%	3.4%	3.9%	5.1%	4.2%	4.9%	5.2%	(14.7%)	8.8%	(7.0%)
Earnings per share ($)	—	6.87	7.48	7.78	8.37	7.12	8.38	8.80	(27.04)	14.25	(11.49)
Stock price – high ($)	—	35.50	40.25	45.00	51.00	41.50	47.38	57.75	49.13	31.63	44.75
Stock price – low ($)	—	26.50	30.50	26.00	34.75	22.50	33.88	41.13	21.13	18.75	27.75
Stock price – close ($)	0.1%	32.75	35.63	41.63	38.00	36.63	47.13	45.13	21.50	28.38	33.13
P/E – high	—	5	5	6	6	6	6	7	—	2	—
P/E – low	—	4	4	3	4	3	4	5	—	1	—
Dividends per share ($)	2.7%	2.57	2.77	2.95	3.07	3.17	3.21	3.25	3.28	3.28	3.28
Book value per share ($)	(2.2%)	50.89	55.02	59.34	64.27	64.94	70.08	74.32	42.01	55.88	41.50

1989 Year End:
Debt ratio: 50.1%
Return on equity: —
Cash (mil): $5,862
Assets (mil): $60,479
Long-term debt (mil): $3,400
Number of shares (mil): 70
Dividends:
1989 average yield: 9.9%
1989 payout: —
Market value (mil): $2,317

Stock Price History high/low 1980-89

MANVILLE CORPORATION

OVERVIEW

Headquartered in Denver, Manville is a leading fiberglass producer. It also produces forest products (*e.g.*, lumber, beverage containers, folding cartons, and plywood) and owns over 776,000 acres of timberland and 4 mines (producing diatomite, perlite, and platinum).

Manville was in Chapter 11 bankruptcy from 1982 until 1988, seeking protection from the large number of claims filed against the company in asbestos-related cases.

Since its Chapter 11 reorganization, a controlling interest in Manville has been held by a trust benefiting asbestos victims. Further, Manville is barred from paying common stock dividends through at least 1996.

After record 1989 earnings of $173 million (up 94% over 1988), Manville expects a slowing US economy to hurt nearly all of its businesses in 1990. Manville plans to use its $327 million of cash on hand to expand, concentrating on the forest products segment.

WHEN

In 1858 H. W. Johns founded a roofing materials business in Brooklyn. Experimenting with fire-retardant asbestos, in 1868 Johns obtained a patent for a materials coatings line. In 1901 the company merged with Manville Covering Company (begun 1886 in Milwaukee to produce pipe coverings and insulation materials).

Thomas Manville headed the new company, named Johns-Manville, until his 1925 death. His brother Hiram purchased most of the stock and in 1927 sold 53% of the company to J.P. Morgan & Company for about $20 million. Under Morgan the company focused on building materials, moving away from earlier diversification ventures such as automobile horns, fire extinguishers, spark plugs, and other items. By prohibiting commercial banks from underwriting corporate securities, the 1933 Banking Act forced Morgan to transfer its Johns-Manville holdings to the newly formed Morgan Stanley & Company.

In 1958 Johns-Manville acquired LOF Glass Fibers Company. Sales increased only 4% annually between 1950 and 1970, when the company began emphasizing building insulation through acquisitions and capital expenditures. Johns-Manville had completed its move to Colorado by 1973 and in 1979 acquired Olinkraft, a paper producer. The company adopted its present name in 1981.

In 1974, 448 WWII shipyard workers filed the first major asbestos health suit against Manville. Throughout the 1970s the number of cases multiplied. By 1982 Manville had settled over 4,100 suits yet faced a backlog of nearly 17,000. Bankruptcy followed.

While in Chapter 11, Manville closed its plastic pipe and residential roofing operations and terminated all activities related to asbestos. In 1985 the company acquired Eastex Packaging (forest products).

The reorganization plan finalized in 1988 created 2 separate trust funds and is designed to bar any party from taking future asbestos-related action directly against Manville. The personal injury trust, which has faced liquidity problems since 1989, owns 50% of the company's common stock, with options to increase it to 80%. Manville will pay this trust $75 million annually for 24 years beginning in 1991 and up to 20% of the company's earnings beginning in 1992.

Manville emerged from bankruptcy focusing on forest products, fiberglass, and mining. In 1988 Manville made the first platinum sale from its Montana mine (a joint venture with Chevron and Lac Minerals of Toronto), the first platinum mine outside of South Africa. In 1989 the company sold its Holophane lighting business for $125 million and purchased oil and gas reserves for $70 million.

Manville initiated a capital spending and R&D campaign in 1989. The company purchased DRG Cartons, the 3rd largest British folding carton company, in 1990.

HOW MUCH

	9 Yr. Growth	1980	1981	1982	1983	1984	1985	1986	1987	1988	1989
Sales ($ mil)	(0.4%)	2,267	2,186	1,772	1,729	1,814	1,880	1,920	2,063	2,062	2,192
Net income ($ mil)	8.8%	81	60	(88)	60	77	(45)	81	164	89	173
Income as % of sales	—	3.6%	2.8%	(4.9%)	3.5%	4.3%	(2.4%)	4.2%	8.0%	4.3%	7.9%
Earnings per share ($)	(7.6%)	2.47	1.53	(4.73)	1.47	2.18	(2.92)	2.34	5.79	0.73	1.21
Stock price – high ($)	—	31.38	26.50	16.50	16.63	13.63	8.63	8.88	5.38	8.00	10.50
Stock price – low ($)	—	18.25	13.75	4.25	9.88	5.63	5.13	1.63	1.75	1.25	6.88
Stock price – close ($)	(10.5%)	24.75	14.88	10.25	11.00	5.88	6.00	1.88	2.25	7.13	9.13
P/E – high	—	13	17	—	11	6	—	4	1	11	9
P/E – low	—	7	9	—	7	3	—	1	0	2	6
Dividends per share ($)	—	1.92	1.92	0.68	0.00	0.00	0.00	0.00	0.00	0.00	0.00
Book value per share ($)	(14.5%)	40.29	38.36	31.90	34.62	37.33	36.59	40.58	44.59	7.39	9.87

1989 Year End:
Debt ratio: 44.7%
Return on equity: 14.0%
Cash (mil): $327
Current ratio: 1.5
Long-term debt (mil): $802
Number of shares (mil): 48
Dividends:
1989 average yield: —
1989 payout: —
Market value (mil): $437

Stock Price History high/low 1980-89

NYSE symbol: MVL
Incorporated: Delaware, 1981
Fiscal year ends: December 31

WHO

Chairman: George C. Dillon, age 67, $300,000 pay
President and CEO: W. Thomas Stephens, age 47, $1,391,576 pay
VC: Will M. Storey, age 58, $483,923 pay
EVP; President, Manville Sales Corp.: John D. C. Roach, age 46, $751,040 pay
VP and Controller: Frank R. McCauley, age 40
Auditors: Coopers & Lybrand
Employees: 17,000

WHERE

HQ: 717 17th St., Denver, CO 80202
Phone: 303-978-2000
FAX: 303-978-2363

Manville has 56 plants in the US and 10 foreign countries; mines in California, Montana, New Mexico, France, and Spain; and timberlands in Arkansas, Louisiana, Texas, and Brazil.

	1989 Sales		1989 Operating Income	
	$ mil	% of total	$ mil	% of total
US	1,794	81	214	66
Foreign	419	19	111	34
Adjustments	21	—	(25)	—
Total	**2,192**	**100**	**300**	**100**

WHAT

	1989 Sales		1989 Operating Income	
	$ mil	% of total	$ mil	% of total
Fiberglass products	901	41	96	31
Forest products	776	35	170	56
Specialty products	515	24	38	13
Adjustments	—	—	(4)	—
Total	**2,192**	**100**	**300**	**100**

Fiberglass
Air duct materials
Automotive parts
Insulation

Mining
Diatomite
Perlite
Platinum

Forest Products
Beverage cartons
Containers and containerboard
Lumber
Paper coatings

Other Products
Calcium silicate insulation
Diatomite products
Perlite products
Roofing systems

RANKINGS

197th in *Fortune* 500 Industrial Cos.
372nd in *Forbes* Sales 500
896th in *Business Week* 1000

COMPETITION

ASARCO
Boise Cascade
Champion International
Georgia-Pacific
International Paper
James River
Mead
Owens-Corning Fiberglass
PPG
Weyerhaeuser
Other natural resource companies

MARRIOTT CORPORATION

OVERVIEW

Washington, DC–based Marriott is the largest hotel operator in the world. In 1989 the company had 7% of the US hotel market and nearly 3% of the world market. Through direct ownership or management, leases, or franchise agreements, Marriott operated 539 hotels containing over 134,000 rooms. The company develops more than $1 billion of real estate each year. The Lodging group also has entered the vacation timeshare market.

Marriott's Contract Services group is the world's largest provider of food and services management to the business, health care, and education industries; provides more food, beverages, and merchandise to airport and turnpike travelers than any other company through Howard Johnson, Big Boy, Burger King, and Host; and is the 2nd largest provider of facilities management services in the US.

Reducing hotel construction spending because of low occupancy rates industry-wide, Marriott is positioning itself for leadership in the US senior living services market. In 1989 the company operated 13 retirement communities. Marriott plans to develop 150 more retirement communities in the next 5 years. Marriott also has an interest in an employer-sponsored day care chain.

NYSE symbol: MHS
Incorporated: Delaware, 1929
Fiscal year ends: Friday nearest December 31

WHO

Chairman, President, and CEO: J. W. "Bill" Marriott, Jr., age 58, $1,012,500 pay
VC and EVP: Richard E. Marriott, age 51
EVP; President, Marriott Service Group: Francis W. Cash, age 47, $735,000 pay
EVP and CFO: William J. Shaw, age 44, $520,000 pay
EVP; President, Marriott Hotels and Resorts: William R. Tiefel, age 55, $416,169 pay
Auditors: Arthur Andersen & Co.
Employees: 230,000

WHEN

In 1927 John Marriott was living in the Mormon settlement of Marriott, Utah, founded by his grandparents. That year he moved to Washington, DC, to open an A&W root beer stand. In order to attract customers in the winter, Marriott converted the stand into a Hot Shoppe, selling tamales and chili con carne. Over the next 10 years Marriott built a chain of Hot Shoppes in and around Washington.

The company entered the airline food service business with a contract from Eastern Air Lines in 1937 and opened its first hotel in Arlington, Virginia, in 1957. When Marriott's son Bill became president (1964), the company had sales of $85 million from 4 hotels, 45 Hot Shoppes, and airline catering.

From 1964 to 1971 Marriott added 10 hotels; expanded in-flight services into Europe and South America (1964); bought Bob's Big Boy chain (California coffee shops, 1967); started Roy Rogers (roast beef restaurants, 1968); bought an Athens cruise line (Oceanic) and a 45% interest in another (Sun, 1971); and acquired Farrell's (ice cream parlors, 1972).

Bill Marriott became CEO in 1972 and opened 2 Great America theme parks near Chicago and San Francisco (1976, cost $155 million). The parks never made enough money; the company sold one and discontinued the other (1984).

By 1977 sales had topped $1 billion and Marriott operated 1,335 restaurants, 34 full-service hotels, and 14 franchised inns. As part of a plan to manage rather than own, Marriott sold 8 hotels to Equitable Life Assurance for $92 million (1978). The company originated moderately priced (then $49- to $72-a-night) Courtyard hotels (1983), which numbered 140 by 1989. In 1985 Marriott bought competitor Howard Johnson (sold manufacturing operations in 1986) for $531 million and in 1986 bought Saga (contract food service and restaurants) for $694 million.

In 1987 Marriott entered 3 new market segments: full-service suites (Marriott Suites), moderately priced suites (Residence Inn, acquired for $260 million), and $30- to $40-a-night economy hotels (Fairfield Inns) and sold its cruise ships. In 1988 Marriott began developing "life-care" communities, which provide apartments, meals, and limited nursing care to the elderly. In 1989 Marriott sold its airline catering businesses to Caterair Holdings (a management group) because of the lack of sufficient long-term growth potential. In 1989 it also decided to leave the fast food and family restaurant business, selling Roy Rogers to Hardee's in 1990.

WHERE

HQ: 10400 Fernwood Rd., Bethesda, MD 20058
Phone: 301-380-9000
FAX: 301-897-9014 (Public Relations)

Marriott lodging facilities are located in 50 states; Washington, DC; and 17 foreign countries. The company provides food and facilities management in the US, Canada, the Caribbean, and New Zealand and operates retirement communities in several states.

	1989 Sales		1989 Pretax Income	
	$ mil	% of total	$ mil	% of total
US	6,935	92	199	76
Foreign	601	8	62	24
Adjustments	—	—	37	—
Total	**7,536**	**100**	**298**	**100**

WHAT

	1989 Sales		1989 Operating Income	
	$ mil	% of total	$ mil	% of total
Lodging	3,546	47	132	43
Contract Services	3,990	53	172	57
Adjustments	—	—	149	—
Total	**7,536**	**100**	**453**	**100**

Lodging Services
Courtyard by Marriott
Fairfield Inns
Marriott hotels and resorts
Marriott Suites
Residence Inn by Marriott
Vacation ownership resorts

Contract Services
Food catering (business, industry, health care facilities, schools)
Host (airport concessions)
Marriott Travel Plazas

Retirement Communities
Brighton Gardens
Stratford Court

RANKINGS

5th in *Fortune* 100 Diversified Service Cos.
107th in *Forbes* Sales 500
229th in *Business Week* 1000
793rd in *Business Week* Global 1000

COMPETITION

ARA
Bass
Canadian Pacific
Carlson
Helmsley Enterprises
Hilton
Hyatt
ITT
Loews
Nestlé
Ogden
Owens-Illinois
TW Holdings

HOW MUCH

	9 Yr. Growth	1980	1981	1982	1983	1984	1985	1986	1987	1988	1989
Sales ($ mil)	17.9%	1,719	2,000	2,541	3,037	3,525	4,242	5,267	6,522	7,370	7,536
Net income ($ mil)	10.8%	72	86	94	115	135	167	192	223	232	181
Income as % of sales	—	4.2%	4.3%	3.7%	3.8%	3.8%	3.9%	3.6%	3.4%	3.1%	2.4%
Earnings per share ($)	13.5%	0.52	0.64	0.69	0.83	1.00	1.24	1.40	1.67	1.95	1.62
Stock price – high ($)	—	7.40	9.40	12.38	16.20	16.05	23.30	38.20	43.75	33.38	41.25
Stock price – low ($)	—	3.28	5.95	6.40	10.05	11.70	14.68	20.63	24.00	26.25	29.75
Stock price – close ($)	19.8%	6.55	7.18	11.70	14.25	15.15	21.80	29.00	30.00	31.63	33.38
P/E – high	—	14	15	18	20	16	19	27	26	17	25
P/E – low	—	6	9	9	12	12	12	15	14	13	18
Dividends per share ($)	21.9%	0.04	0.05	0.06	0.08	0.09	0.11	0.14	0.17	0.21	0.25
Book value per share ($)	10.5%	2.49	3.22	3.89	4.67	5.24	6.48	7.59	6.83	6.53	6.11

1989 Year End:
Debt ratio: 84.0%
Return on equity: 25.6%
Cash (mil): $100
Current ratio: 0.83
Long-term debt (mil): $3,286
Number of shares (mil): 103
Dividends:
1989 average yield: 0.8%
1989 payout: 15.4%
Market value (mil): $3,431

Stock Price History high/low 1980-89

MARS, INC.

OVERVIEW

Mars is the world's 2nd largest candy maker (after Hershey), is a major pet food producer, and was the US's 7th largest privately held company in 1989. It operates more than 50 businesses around the world.

The Mars family and the Mars Foundation own all of the company's stock. The family is one of the US's wealthiest, with net worth estimated at $12.5 billion by *Fortune*. They desire privacy to such an extent that very little is known about the company's history or operations. Executives are forbidden to be photographed or interviewed; publicity-shy Mars even refused to allow M&Ms to appear in the very successful movie *E.T. The Extra-Terrestrial*— an opportunity from which rival Hershey's Reese's Pieces benefited.

In 1988 Mars produced 4 of the US's top 10 candies, including the #1 candy (Snickers), and has 17% of the candy market in Europe. Candy generated $3.8 billion in 1988 revenues, according to a *Fortune* estimate.

Mars sells pet food under the Kal Kan, Pedigree, and Whiskas labels. Pedigree and Whiskas were Europe's 2 leading pet food brands in 1988. A substantial portion of Mars's total sales (perhaps a majority) comes from Europe.

The company produces Uncle Ben's rice, Dove ice cream bars, Snackmaster brand salty snacks, and Kudos granola bars. The electronics group produces coin changers and hand-held scanners.

Fortune estimated that the company had profits of $780 million in 1989.

WHEN

Frank Mars, inventor of the Milky Way candy bar (1923), hired his son Forrest after the latter's Yale graduation to work at his candy operation. After arguments between the 2 men, Forrest moved to England and started his own Mars company in the 1930s. The candy bars quickly became popular. Forrest also began making pet food and at one point controlled 55% of the British pet food market.

During WWII, Forrest returned to the US and introduced Uncle Ben's rice and M&Ms. The idea for M&Ms was borrowed from British Smarties, for which Mars obtained rights (from Rowntree Mackintosh) by relinquishing similar rights for its Snickers bar in some foreign markets. The ad slogan "Melts in your mouth, not in your hand" elevated Mars to industry leader.

Little is known about Mars between the mid-1940s and 1964, when Forrest merged his operations with his deceased father's company after bitter family quarrels. In 1968 Mars bought Kal Kan and followed with Puppy Palace pet shops in 1969 (sold in 1976). During the 1970s Mars produced 5 of the country's top 10 candy bars, including Snickers, which ranked first.

Mars refuses to discuss whether Forrest (born 1904) is alive; likened to the late Howard Hughes, he may be living as a recluse in Las Vegas, having delegated responsibility to his sons, Forrest E. and John F. Mars, in 1973. The men share the presidency and allegedly are engaged in a power struggle to control the company.

By 1978 the brothers, looking for snacks to replace dwindling candy revenues from a more diet-conscious America, brought out Twix, a chocolate covered cookie. In 1987 they bought Dove Bar International, an ice cream bar manufacturer that had been started by Greek immigrant Leo Stefanos in his Chicago candy store in 1939 (to keep his children from buying ice cream bars from the passing ice cream trucks) and had grown to production of 40,000 per day by 1985.

Around 1988 Forrest and John Mars purchased Ethel M Chocolates, producer of liqueur-flavored chocolates, a business their father began in his retirement. Ethel M Chocolates are made in Henderson, Nevada, 13 miles southeast of Las Vegas. Unlike the other secretive Mars plants, Ethel M is open to the public for conducted tours of its facilities.

Mars attempted to purchase Dutch candy maker Tonnema in 1988, but withdrew temporarily after dissent within the family-owned Tonnema erupted in lawsuits, and was eventually outbid by a European concern. Hershey's passed Mars as the US's largest candy maker in 1988 when it acquired Cadbury Schweppes US division (Mounds and Almond Joy). In 1989 Mars introduced Bounty Bars, PB Max, and Suissande Fine Chocolates.

Mars's success can be attributed to advertising and product quality. Consistently a leading ad spender, Mars also spends at least 45% of candy revenues on the highest quality candy ingredients available and was the first to date-code its products for freshness.

HOW MUCH

	9 Yr. Growth	1980	1981	1982	1983	1984	1985	1986	1987	1988	1989
Sales ($ mil)	—	—	4,000	—	—	—	5,300	7,000	7,700	8,000	8,541
Estimated ad spending ($ mil)	—	84	78	120	120	139	276	313	379	340	293

Private company
Incorporated: Delaware, 1952

WHO

CEO and Co-President: Forrest E. Mars, Jr., age 59
Co-President: John F. Mars, age 54
EVP: Michael Stefanos, age 37
Employees: 24,000

WHERE

HQ: 1651-T Old Meadow Rd., McLean, VA 22102
Phone: 703-821-4900
FAX: 703-448-9678

Mars owns candy plants in Hackettstown, NJ; Chicago, IL; Albany, GA; Waco, TX; Henderson, NV; and Cleveland, TN. It also owns a pet food plant in Vernon, CA, and a rice plant in Houston, TX.

Products are sold in over 25 countries.

WHAT

Estimated Sources of Revenue	
Candy	50%
Pet food	40%
Food	7%
Electronics	3%
Total	**100%**

Brand Names

Candy
3 Musketeers
Balisto
Bounty
M&Ms Peanut
M&Ms Plain
Mars
Milky Way
PB Max
Skittles
Snickers
Starburst
Suissande Fine Chocolates

Ice Cream Products
3 Musketeers
Dove
Rondos

Pet Food
Crave
Kal Kan
Mealtime
Pedigree
Sheba
Whiskas

Other
Kudos
Snackmaster
Twix

Rice
Uncle Ben's
Uncle Ben's Aromatica
Uncle Ben's Country Inn

Electronic Products
Coin changers
Hand-held scanning devices

RANKINGS

7th in *Forbes* 400 US Private Cos.

COMPETITION

Archer-Daniels-Midland
Berkshire Hathaway
Cadbury Schweppes
Campbell Soup
Grand Metropolitan
H. J. Heinz
Hershey
NCR
Nestlé
PepsiCo
Philip Morris
Quaker Oats
Ralston Purina
RJR Nabisco
Whitman

MARSH & MCLENNAN COMPANIES, INC.

OVERVIEW

Marsh & McLennan is the world's largest insurance broker. The New York–based company had $2.4 billion in 1989 revenues coming from its 3 principal services: insurance (58%), consulting (31%), and investment management (11%).

Marsh & McLennan, Inc. provides insurance brokerage services and advises corporate clients and others worldwide. The company's Guy Carpenter & Company and C. T. Bowring Reinsurance provide worldwide reinsurance (an insurer transfers risk to another insurer) advice and services.

William M. Mercer is a leading employee benefits consulting firm, providing services to companies in 20 countries. The company's other major consulting firm is Temple, Barker & Sloane/Strategic Planning Associates, an international, general management consulting firm. The company also has several other specialized consulting subsidiaries.

Marsh & McLennan's Putnam Companies is a major US investment firm, managing more than 50 mutual funds and 200 separate pension funds totaling $43 billion in assets under management at the end of 1989.

NYSE symbol: MMC
Incorporated: Delaware, 1969
Fiscal year ends: December 31

WHO

Chairman and CEO: Frank J. Tasco, age 62, $1,425,000 pay
VC, Marsh & McLennan, Inc.: Robert J. Newhouse, Jr., $942,500 pay
President: A. J. C. Smith, age 55, $1,145,000 pay
Chairman, Marsh & McLennan, Inc.: Robert Clements, age 57, $755,000 pay
SVP and CFO: Frank J. Borelli, age 54
Auditors: Deloitte & Touche
Employees: 23,600

WHEN

By 1905 Henry Marsh was sole owner of a Chicago insurance agency (Marsh, Ullmann) and had pioneered the broker concept, buying insurance from several underwriters to meet the client's needs. In the late 1890s Donald McLennan was with a Duluth, Minnesota, insurance agency that in 1900 became the Manley-McLennan agency, specializing in insuring railroads. In 1904 McLennan opened a small office in Chicago.

Promised the Burlington railroad account by one of its directors, Marsh and insurance agent Daniel Burrows retained McLennan as a railroad insurance expert. In 1904 they formed Burrows, Marsh & McLennan, whose clients soon included all the major midwestern railroads.

In 1906 Burrows retired and Marsh and McLennan bought his interest, renaming the firm Marsh & McLennan. The firm moved into marine insurance by arranging to insure 2 large freighters built by James Hill, builder of the Great Northern Railway.

In the early 1900s the firm added property owner clients by successfully negotiating their fire insurance premium rates with the insurance rating bureaus established by the major insurance companies. In 1910 Marsh got AT&T as an account by booking a reservation on the same ocean liner to England and back that AT&T President Theodore Vail was on and convincing Vail of his interest in AT&T. Vail then called Marsh in New York and appointed Marsh & McLennan as AT&T's broker and consultant.

In 1914 the firm became broker for the Canadian Pacific Railway, opened Marsh & McLennan, Ltd. of Canada, and later became broker for Canadian Pacific's marine business. In 1923 Marsh & McLennan invested in Guy Carpenter & Company, which became a subsidiary.

Marsh retired as chairman of the firm in 1935. McLennan remained as chief executive until 1944 when Charles Ward Seabury became chairman and CEO. In 1945 the firm began selling insurance to banks on installment loans, primarily for cars and appliances. Ford Motor selected the firm in 1947 to handle all insurance except employee benefits.

Marsh & McLennan bought Cosgrove (largest Pacific Coast regional broker, 1957); William M. Mercer (employee benefit plan consulting, 1959); Putnam (investments, 1970) through an exchange of stock; C. T. Bowring (international reinsurance, 1980); and National Economic Research Associates (research and analysis, 1983). The company acquired 2 other management consulting firms, Temple, Barker & Sloane (1987) and Strategic Planning Associates (1990).

WHERE

HQ: 1221 Ave. of the Americas, New York, NY 10020
Phone: 212-345-3000
FAX: 212-345-4838 (Public Affairs)

Marsh & McLennan operates in 80 countries.

	1989 Sales		1989 Operating Income	
	$ mil	% of total	$ mil	% of total
US	1,732	71	395	72
UK	374	15	87	16
Canada	167	7	37	7
Other countries	155	7	28	5
Adjustments	—	—	(37)	—
Total	**2,428**	**100**	**510**	**100**

WHAT

	1989 Sales		1989 Operating Income	
	$ mil	% of total	$ mil	% of total
Insurance services	1,401	58	348	64
Investment mgmt.	273	11	90	16
Consulting	754	31	109	20
Adjustments	—	—	(37)	—
Total	**2,428**	**100**	**510**	**100**

Subsidiaries
Clayton Environmental Consultants, Inc. (business research)
Guy Carpenter & Co., Inc. and C. T. Bowring Reinsurance Ltd. (reinsurance)
Lippincott & Margulies, Inc. (identity and image consulting)
Marsh & McLennan Group Associates, Inc. (program management)
Marsh & McLennan, Inc. (insurance brokerage)
National Economic Research Associates, Inc. (business and public policy research)
The Putnam Cos., Inc. (investment management)
Temple, Barker & Sloane, Inc./Strategic Planning Associates, Inc. (management consulting)
William M. Mercer Cos., Inc. (employee benefits consulting)

HOW MUCH

	9 Yr. Growth	1980	1981	1982	1983	1984	1985	1986	1987	1988	1989
Sales ($ mil)	15.2%	677	847	924	960	1,101	1,368	1,804	2,147	2,272	2,428
Net income ($ mil)	12.7%	101	120	120	94	59	163	243	302	296	295
Income as % of sales	—	14.9%	14.2%	13.0%	9.8%	5.3%	11.9%	13.5%	14.1%	13.0%	12.1%
Earnings per share ($)	11.3%	1.56	1.64	1.68	1.33	0.81	2.23	3.30	4.06	4.09	4.10
Stock price – high ($)	—	17.69	21.25	22.25	25.38	29.69	41.75	76.75	72.00	59.75	89.75
Stock price – low ($)	—	13.31	14.81	14.81	18.31	17.88	28.25	40.63	43.75	45.25	55.13
Stock price – close ($)	18.3%	17.19	16.50	20.63	24.88	29.50	40.75	60.75	49.50	56.25	78.00
P/E – high	—	11	13	13	19	37	19	23	18	15	22
P/E – low	—	9	9	9	14	22	13	12	11	11	13
Dividends per share ($)	12.0%	0.90	1.00	1.05	1.10	1.43	1.28	1.70	1.68	2.43	2.50
Book value per share ($)	5.3%	7.58	7.66	6.54	6.33	5.10	7.02	8.65	10.72	10.56	12.05

1989 Year End:
Debt ratio: 26.8%
Return on equity: 36.3%
Cash (mil): $293
Current ratio: 1.46
Long-term debt (mil): $319
Number of shares (mil): 72
Dividends:
1989 average yield: 3.2%
1989 payout: 61.0%
Market value (mil): $5,649

Stock Price History high/low 1980-89

RANKINGS

49th in *Fortune* 50 Diversified Financial Cos.
341st in *Forbes* Sales 500
119th in *Business Week* 1000
309th in *Business Week* Global 1000

COMPETITION

American Express
Arthur Andersen
General Re
KPMG
McKinsey & Co.
Merrill Lynch
Price Waterhouse
Prudential
USF&G
Money management firms

MARTIN MARIETTA CORPORATION

OVERVIEW

Martin Marietta's diverse operations include aerospace, information technologies, construction materials, and specialty chemical products. The company is the 6th largest defense contractor in the US.

Martin Marietta builds the space shuttle's giant external fuel tank as well as the Titan family of expendable launch vehicles and is developing the Flight Telerobotic Servicer, which will be used in construction and maintenance of the US Space Station *Freedom*. The *Magellan* spacecraft, launched in early 1989, began mapping the surface of Venus in 1990.

The company is a leading contractor for the Peacekeeper (MX) missile and produces a number of other military systems, including the LANTIRN airborne night vision system, the ADATS mobile air defense system, and shipboard missile launchers. The company also develops computer systems for air traffic control, data processing, military applications, and advanced computer simulations. Oak Ridge National Laboratory and other government nuclear facilities are managed by Martin Marietta Energy Systems.

The Materials Group supplies construction aggregates (crushed stone, sand, and gravel), magnesium products (used in the production of steel), and, through a joint venture with NKK Corporation of Japan, light metal components for aircraft.

NYSE symbol: ML
Incorporated: Maryland, 1961
Fiscal year ends: December 31

WHO

Chairman and CEO: Norman R. Augustine, age 54, $1,033,470 pay
President and COO: A. Thomas Young, age 51, $510,631 pay
SVP and CFO: Marcus C. Bennett, age 54
Auditors: Ernst & Young
Employees: 65,500

WHERE

HQ: 6801 Rockledge Dr., Bethesda, MD 20817
Phone: 301-897-6000
FAX: 301-897-6704

	1989 Sales	
	$ mil	**% of total**
US government	5,079	88
Other	717	12
Total	**5,796**	**100**

WHAT

	1989 Sales		1989 Operating Income	
	$ mil	**% of total**	**$ mil**	**% of total**
Astronautics	2,754	47	197	40
Electronics & Missiles	2,117	36	195	39
Information Systems	502	9	21	4
Materials	384	7	71	14
Other	39	1	15	3
Adjustments	—	—	(34)	—
Total	**5,796**	**100**	**465**	**100**

Principal Operating Units

Astronautics (Titan II, III, and IV, Commercial Titan, Space Shuttle External Tank, *Magellan* spacecraft, Flight Telerobotic Servicer, Peacekeeper/MX, Small ICBM)
Electronics and Missiles (Patriot, Optimized Hellfire, ADATS air defense, LANTIRN airborne night vision system, MK 41 Vertical Launching System)
Information Systems (All-Source Analysis System, engineering and systems integration for the National Airspace System Plan)
Materials (crushed stone, sand, gravel, magnesium oxide products, fabricated metal components)

WHEN

In 1917 Glenn Martin, a barnstormer and aircraft designer, founded the Glenn L. Martin Company in Cleveland, Ohio. The company moved to Baltimore in 1929. Martin produced America's first bombers (Donald Douglas, a founder of McDonnell Douglas, was chief designer until 1920) as well as military and commercial flying boats, including the M-130, the famous Pan Am "Clipper" that made transpacific air service practical (1935). Martin also designed the WWII-era B-26 Marauder bomber.

After the war Martin made an unsuccessful attempt to enter the commercial transport market with the M-202 airliner. Development costs of the new aircraft finally resulted in a 1951 loss of $22 million, after which George Bunker replaced Glenn Martin as chairman. Under Bunker the company began decreasing aircraft production in favor of missiles, electronics, and nuclear systems. In 1953 the company began designing the Titan, an intercontinental ballistic missile that later evolved into a versatile space launch vehicle. Martin produced its last airplane in 1960.

In 1961 Bunker consolidated Martin with the American-Marietta Company, a supplier of construction materials and chemical products. Formed in 1913 as American Asphalt Paint Company, American-Marietta had made dozens of acquisitions over the years to become a $368 million corporation with over 360 plants in the US and Canada. Bunker, now president of Martin Marietta Corporation, sold off many of the company's less-profitable holdings during the 1960s but made an important acquisition in 1968 with the purchase of Harvey Aluminum.

With a mix of aerospace, chemicals, electronics, building materials, and aluminum production, Martin Marietta began a period of growth in the 1970s. The company received government contracts for the Viking Mars landers (1969), the space shuttle's external fuel tank (1973), and the MX missile (1979).

Martin Marietta defeated a hostile takeover bid by Bendix in 1982. To reduce the $1.34 billion debt incurred during the takeover battle, the company, led by CEO Thomas Pownall, sold many of its businesses, including cement, chemical, and aluminum operations. By 1989 a brisk defense electronics business and accelerating orders for Titan launchers, space shuttle external tanks, and other space vehicles had helped push the company's sales to a record $5.8 billion.

HOW MUCH

	9 Yr. Growth	1980	1981	1982	1983	1984	1985	1986	1987	1988	1989
Sales ($ mil)	9.2%	2,619	3,294	3,527	3,899	3,920	4,410	4,753	5,165	5,727	5,796
Net income ($ mil)	5.6%	188	200	92	141	176	249	202	231	320	307
Income as % of sales	—	7.2%	6.1%	2.6%	3.6%	4.5%	5.7%	4.3%	4.5%	5.6%	5.3%
Earnings per share ($)	11.2%	2.24	2.40	1.30	2.70	3.02	4.36	3.67	4.25	6.02	5.82
Stock price – high ($)	—	21.59	22.74	20.94	28.78	30.92	44.38	48.50	56.50	48.25	53.50
Stock price – low ($)	—	11.93	12.63	9.89	16.72	20.17	27.42	32.25	35.00	38.25	37.75
Stock price – close ($)	8.4%	21.52	16.00	19.44	23.83	29.67	35.50	38.63	42.00	40.50	44.38
P/E – high	—	10	10	16	11	10	10	13	13	8	9
P/E – low	—	5	5	8	6	7	6	9	8	6	6
Dividends per share ($)	6.6%	0.69	0.80	0.85	0.86	0.89	0.97	1.00	1.05	1.10	1.23
Book value per share ($)	8.2%	13.10	14.71	8.45	14.17	9.64	12.83	15.35	17.16	22.73	26.67

1989 Year End:
Debt ratio: 26.1%
Return on equity: 23.6%
Cash (mil): $68
Current ratio: 1.56
Long-term debt (mil): $478
Number of shares (mil): 51
Dividends:
1989 average yield: 2.8%
1989 payout: 21.0%
Market value (mil): $2,255

Stock Price History high/low 1980-89

RANKINGS

84th in *Fortune* 500 Industrial Cos.
226th in *Fortune* Global 500 Industrial Cos.
148th in *Forbes* Sales 500
296th in *Business Week* 1000
930th in *Business Week* Global 1000

COMPETITION

Allied-Signal	Raytheon
Boeing	Rockwell International
General Dynamics	Textron
General Electric	TRW
General Motors	United Technologies
Lockheed	Vulcan Materials
McDonnell Douglas	Westinghouse
Northrop	

MASCO CORPORATION

OVERVIEW

The Masco Corporation is a leading US producer of home furnishings, faucets, plumbing supplies, home improvement products, and cabinets for the kitchen and bath. In 1989 most of Masco's $3 billion sales were generated by leading brands such as Delta (faucets); Henredon, Drexel Heritage, and Lexington (furniture); Merillat (cabinets); and Brass-Craft (plumbing fixtures).

In 1989 Masco's home furnishings products contributed 46% of the company's sales. Other contributors to the 1989 sales total were faucets, 14%; cabinets, 11%; other kitchen and bath products, 17%; and building and home improvement products, 12%.

Under the leadership of the founding Manoogian family, Masco owns or has partial ownership in more than 50 subsidiaries. This Masco Group, which includes more than 330 manufacturing plants around the world, posted 1989 sales of $6 billion.

WHEN

The history of Masco Corporation is a classic American success story. Alex Manoogian, Masco's founder, was a 19-year-old Armenian immigrant when he passed through Ellis Island in 1920.

A series of jobs in Detroit machine shops gave him enough experience by 1929 to start the Masco Screw Products Company with 2 partners, less than $5,000, and several used screw machines. "Masco" was an acronym for the founders' last names. The 2 other partners withdrew from the company within the year.

Largely dependent on Detroit's auto industry, Masco grew slowly in its first years, producing custom parts for Chrysler, Ford, Hudson Motor Company, and Spicer Manufacturing. By 1937, with sales of over $200,000, it offered shares to the public and was listed on the Detroit Stock Exchange. With the advent of WWII, Masco devoted its production to defense, and in 1942 sales topped $1 million. A new manufacturing plant, opened in 1948 in Dearborn, Michigan, expanded production space to nearly 100,000 square feet. Masco resumed peacetime business, primarily with the auto industry, although the Korean War prompted a return to some military production.

In 1954 Masco began producing and marketing Manoogian's version of a single-handle kitchen faucet, under the Delta brand. The faucet was efficient and popular. Delta sales had exceeded $1 million by 1958, and Masco opened a new faucet plant in Greensburg, Indiana.

Under the leadership of Alex Manoogian's son, Richard, the company (renamed Masco Corporation in 1961) diversified its product line and began buying other companies. In 1962 it was listed on the ASE.

Since 1964 Masco has acquired more than 50 companies, concentrating on tool and metal casting, energy exploration, and other industrial products such as pumping equipment and air compressors. The company continued to focus on both industrial and consumer products until 1984, when it underwent a major corporate restructuring that split it into 2 entities. Masco Corporation pursued the course set by its successful faucet sales, expanding its interests in home improvement and home furnishings companies. The company spun off its industrial products business into a separate public corporation, Masco Industries, in which it maintains a 49% interest.

Masco Corporation became the nation's largest furniture manufacturer in the mid-1980s by purchasing several leading North Carolina furniture makers, including Henredon and Drexel Heritage (1986), Hickorycraft and Lexington Furniture (1987), and Universal Furniture (1989).

Alex Manoogian is still serving as the company's chairman emeritus as of late 1990. Richard is chairman of the board.

HOW MUCH

	9 Yr. Growth	1980	1981	1982	1983	1984	1985	1986	1987	1988	1989
Sales ($ mil)	17.0%	766	877	856	1,059	1,020	1,154	1,452	2,023	2,439	3,151
Net income ($ mil)	12.4%	77	88	78	107	116	164	203	219	288	221
Income as % of sales	—	10.1%	10.1%	9.1%	10.1%	11.4%	14.3%	14.0%	10.8%	11.8%	7.0%
Earnings per share ($)	7.1%	0.76	0.87	*0.75*	0.96	1.00	1.26	1.54	1.61	2.06	1.41
Stock price – high ($)	—	8.63	10.56	14.25	18.50	16.94	21.19	34.50	40.88	30.38	31.13
Stock price – low ($)	—	4.94	7.00	6.72	12.38	11.25	13.00	19.50	18.75	22.00	23.75
Stock price – close ($)	13.8%	7.59	9.25	14.19	16.88	14.00	20.13	29.00	21.63	25.38	24.38
P/E – high	—	11	12	19	19	17	17	22	25	15	22
P/E – low	—	7	8	9	13	11	10	13	12	11	17
Dividends per share ($)	13.5%	0.16	0.18	0.20	0.22	0.25	0.29	0.34	0.38	0.44	0.50
Book value per share ($)	12.5%	4.12	4.89	5.49	6.47	6.60	7.60	8.84	10.34	11.30	11.94

1989 Year End:
Debt ratio: 38.3%
Return on equity: 12.1%
Cash (mil): $113
Current ratio: 2.58
Long-term debt (mil): $1,153
Number of shares (mil): 156
Dividends:
1989 average yield: 2.1%
1989 payout: 35.5%
Market value (mil): $3,793

Stock Price History high/low 1980-89

NYSE symbol: MAS
Incorporated: Delaware, 1968
Fiscal year ends: December 31

WHO

Chairman and CEO: Richard A. Manoogian, age 53, $1,055,700 pay
President and COO: Wayne B. Lyon, age 57, $791,900 pay
SVP Finance: Richard G. Mosteller, age 57, $526,800 pay
VP Human Resources: David G. Wesenberg, age 59
Auditors: Coopers & Lybrand
Employees: 42,000

WHERE

HQ: 21001 Van Born Rd., Taylor, MI 48180
Phone: 313-274-7400
FAX: 313-563-5975

Masco has approximately 140 manufacturing plants in 26 states and 16 countries.

	1989 Sales		1989 Operating Income	
	$ mil	% of total	$ mil	% of total
US	2,732	87	384	83
Foreign	418	13	78	17
Adjustments	1	—	(57)	—
Total	**3,151**	**100**	**405**	**100**

WHAT

	1989 Sales		1989 Operating Income	
	$ mil	% of total	$ mil	% of total
Building & home improvement products	1,690	54	307	66
Home furnishings	1,460	46	155	34
Adjustments	1	—	(57)	—
Total	**3,151**	**100**	**405**	**100**

Brand Names

Furniture
Dixie
Drexel Heritage
Frederick Edward
Henredon
Henry Link
Hickorycraft
La Barge
Lexington
Link-Taylor
Maitland-Smith
Marbro
Marge Carson
Robert Allen
Universal
Young-Hinkle

Plumbing Products
Alsons
American Bath
Aqua Glass
Artistic Brass
Brass-Craft
Damixa
Delex
Delta
Epic
Hot Spring Spa
Hueppe Duscha
Jung
Mariani
Peerless
Plumb Shop
The Plumber's Faucet
Sherle Wagner

Cabinets
Fieldstone
Merillat
StarMark

Hardware
Baldwin
Gibraltar
Saflok
Weiser

Appliances
Thermador
WasteKing

RANKINGS

142nd in *Fortune* 500 Industrial Cos.
401st in *Fortune* Global 500 Industrial Cos.
264th in *Forbes* Sales 500
161st in *Business Week* 1000
500th in *Business Week* Global 1000

COMPETITION

American Standard
Armstrong World
Black & Decker
Electrolux
General Electric
Hanson
Ingersoll-Rand
INTERCO
Stanley Works

MASSACHUSETTS MUTUAL LIFE INSURANCE CO.

OVERVIEW

MassMutual, headquartered in Springfield, Massachusetts, is the nation's 11th largest insurance company, with 1.4 million insurance policies, representing $106 billion in force at the end of 1989 and generating nearly $5 billion in annual revenues. MassMutual's Insurance and Financial Management division is among the nation's largest life insurers, with $12.5 billion in assets ($743 million in sales in 1989) and a policy lapse rate of 5.9%, among the industry's lowest.

The Life and Health Benefits Management division provides health coverage to more than 335,000 people and in 1989 generated an annual in-force premium of $1.4 billion ($325.2 million in new premium sales for the year).

MassMutual's Pension Management group ranks among the top 50 US pension managers, with assets of $12.5 billion under management ($1.6 billion in sales in 1989).

The Investment Management group invests premiums from other areas of the company and provides investment services to outside clients. The group's mortgage loan portfolio of more than $5 billion has enjoyed a very low default and foreclosure rate. Investment Management became a key player in private placement financing in 1989, providing $1.8 billion of financing.

Mutual company
Organized as mutual: Massachusetts, 1867
Fiscal year ends: December 31

WHEN

Springfield-based Massachusetts Mutual started providing whole life insurance in 1851. It was formed by George Rice, an insurance agent who wanted to form a company owned by policyholders (a mutual). Initially the company issued stock to investors, but in 1867 the company repurchased the stock, creating a mutual insurer. By 1868 MassMutual had spread to San Francisco — transcontinental before the railroads.

WWI required new sales strategies; to compensate for claims, the company adopted higher premiums on new policies. Ironically, a 1918 flu epidemic was more costly to the company than WWI. During the Great Depression MassMutual lent policyholders millions of dollars at low interest rates, through policy-backed loans and financing of premiums.

MassMutual's most important breakthrough occurred in 1946 when it wrote its first group policy for Brown-Forman Distillers (Louisville), makers of Jack Daniels. By 1950 MassMutual had over 200 people employed in its group insurance sector and had diversified into medical insurance.

MassMutual began investing in stocks in the 1950s, switching over from reliance upon bonds and mortgages. Concurrently shifting focus to technology, the company bought its first computer in the early 1950s and began automating its operations in 1961. By 1970 MassMutual had installed a computer network linking independent agents.

The company is conservative in product planning. By the 1980s competitors were offering universal life, which had an investment side fund: the customer did not have to pay insurance premiums as long as there was money in the investment fund to cover premiums. Unlike competitors, MassMutual offered only traditional whole life. An upgrade program, however, was embraced by nearly 3/4 million policyholders which offered them a higher dividend schedule akin to the universal life rates of the competition. In the 1980s the competition began diversifying into financial services; MassMutual elected to stick to its core business.

MassMutual, historically a "buy and hold" investor, became an active trader in 1986, reducing long-term commitments, segmenting investment portfolios for specific purposes, and using new investment vehicles such as zero-coupon and extendable bonds, so that stocks were only 5% of total investments. The new strategy paid off: the company emerged virtually unscathed from Black Monday, the stock market crash of 1987. The company has continually received the highest ratings possible from A. M. Best, Standard & Poor's, and Moody's Investor Service.

WHO

President and CEO: Thomas B. Wheeler
EVP and Chief Investment Officer: Richard G. Dooley
EVP, Insurance and Financial Management: Kenneth L. Fry, Jr.
EVP, Life and Health Benefits Management: James E. Miller
EVP and CFO: James L. Wertheimer
Auditors: Coopers & Lybrand
Employees: 11,500

WHERE

HQ: 1295 State St., Springfield, MA 01111
Phone: 413-788-8411
FAX: 413-730-6003

Massachusetts Mutual writes approximately 40% of its premiums in New York, California, Texas, Massachusetts, and Illinois and the remaining 60% in other states and in Puerto Rico and Canada.

WHAT

	1989 Divestment Portfolio % of total
Marketable bonds	33
Mortgage loans	29
Private placement	20
Common & preferred stock	8
Cash & short-term investments	6
Real estate equities	3
Other	1
Total	**100**

Services
Disability income protection
Health insurance
Investment management
Life insurance
Pension management

Subsidiaries
Mass Life Insurance Co. of New York
MML Bay State Life Insurance Co.
MML Life Insurance Co.
MML Pension Insurance Co.

RANKINGS

11th in *Fortune* 50 Life Insurance Cos.

COMPETITION

Aetna
AIG
Blue Cross
CIGNA
Equitable
First Executive
John Hancock
Kemper
Metropolitan
New York Life
Northwestern Mutual
Primerica
Prudential
Sears
State Farm
Teachers Insurance
Transamerica
Travelers
USF&G

HOW MUCH

Life Insurance Only	9 Yr. Growth	1980	1981	1982	1983	1984	1985	1986	1987	1988	1989
Assets ($ mil)	11.7%	9,145	10,022	11,152	12,173	13,449	15,579	18,028	19,879	22,404	24,842
Premium & annuity income ($ mil)	10.0%	1,240	1,225	1,388	1,307	1,603	2,421	2,488	2,510	2,826	2,930
Net investment income ($ mil)	13.1%	615	669	770	871	1,064	1,253	1,338	1,483	1,648	1,867
Net income ($ mil)	9.1%	65	78	121	73	59	80	56	22	46	142
Net income as % of assets	—	0.7%	0.8%	1.0%	0.6%	0.4%	0.5%	0.3%	0.1%	0.2%	0.6%
Life insurance in force ($ bil)	8.5%	51	56	57	62	65	69	77	86	95	106

Life Insurance in Force 1980-89

MATSUSHITA ELECTRIC INDUSTRIAL CO., LTD.

OVERVIEW

Matsushita is the world's largest consumer electronics manufacturer and the leader in VCR production. A significant part of the company's business is done through majority-owned, publicly held subsidiaries, including Victor Company of Japan (JVC), Matsushita Communications Industrial, and Matsushita-Kotobuki Electronics. The company derives 42% of its sales overseas. US consumer brands include Panasonic, JVC, and Technics. In addition to VCRs, televisions, stereo equipment, and appliances, Matsushita makes fax and telecommunications equipment, semiconductors, personal computers, and robots.

Traditionally a mass-producer of low-cost consumer electronics goods, Matsushita is transferring its renowned production skills to industrial electronics. To counter high production costs in Japan and local-content concerns abroad, the company is moving production near overseas markets, often involving local partners. Matsushita is increasing its influence over its highly autonomous and sometimes uncooperative subsidiaries.

WHEN

Grade school dropout Konosuke Matsushita started with $50 and built the largest consumer electronics company in the world. From the earliest days Matsushita imbued his employees with his philosophy that the company's mission was to promote peace, prosperity, and the well-being of mankind by providing the world with lots of low-priced, high-quality products. Revered as "Japan's God of management," he remained the company's spiritual leader until his death at age 94 in 1989.

Matsushita was founded in Osaka in 1918 to manufacture electrical sockets. Buoyed by the electrification of Japan, Matsushita grew by developing inexpensive lamps, batteries, radios, and motors in the 1920s and 1930s and registered the National name in 1925. WWII interrupted expansion as the Japanese government ordered the company to build wood-laminate products for the military. Postwar occupation forces prevented Matsushita from working at his company for 4 years.

Matsushita returned to his company just in time for Japan's postwar boom. In one of several deals to import technology to Japan, Matsushita entered into a joint venture, Matsushita Electronics, with Philips (Netherlands) in 1952. In the next year the company began producing televisions, refrigerators, and washing machines, and in the 1960s became Japan's largest home appliance maker. In 1954 Matsushita acquired a majority stake in Victor Company of Japan (JVC), originally established by RCA Victor. The 1959 opening of a subsidiary in New York began Matsushita's drive overseas.

By 1960 Matsushita had introduced vacuum cleaners, tape recorders, stereos, and color televisions. Marketed under the National, Panasonic, and Technics names, the company's products were usually not cutting-edge but were always made efficiently in enormous quantities and sold at low prices. In the 1960s and 1970s Matsushita continued to broaden its product lines, introducing air conditioners, microwave ovens, stereo components, and VCRs. The VHS format for VCRs was developed by JVC. In 1974 the company acquired Motorola's US television plants, adding Quasar to its brand name roster.

Having achieved a dominant worldwide position in consumer electronics, Matsushita began to grow more slowly in the early 1980s. Managed by Akio Tanii since 1986, the company has stepped up R&D spending and expanded its semiconductor, office and factory automation, automobile electronics, audio-visual, housing, and air conditioning product offerings. In 1988 the company acquired the remaining stock of its majority-owned export subsidiary, Matsushita Electric Trading Co. In 1990 Matsushita announced it would begin making supercomputers.

HOW MUCH

	9 Yr. Growth	1980	1981	1982	1983	1984	1985	1986	1987	1988	1989
Sales ($ mil)	17.7%	9,643	13,690	15,617	14,037	16,901	19,347	24,890	28,067	38,552	41,699
Net income ($ mil)	16.7%	401	585	709	604	774	977	1,214	1,004	1,303	1,617
Income as % of sales	—	4.2%	4.3%	4.5%	4.3%	4.6%	5.1%	4.9%	3.6%	3.4%	3.9%
Earnings per share ($)	13.7%	2.38	3.31	3.85	3.26	4.17	5.16	6.31	*5.25*	6.41	7.57
Stock price – high ($)	—	26.65	34.44	64.94	53.46	74.57	76.73	64.29	129.05	186.43	219.05
Stock price – low ($)	—	19.95	18.43	30.70	31.17	40.91	49.35	46.19	57.14	88.81	159.29
Stock price – close ($)	28.0%	21.47	33.16	46.75	52.81	74.57	58.57	61.31	120.71	160.36	197.62
P/E – high	—	11	10	17	16	18	15	10	25	29	29
P/E – low	—	8	6	8	10	10	10	7	11	14	21
Dividends per share ($)	12.9%	0.31	0.35	0.33	0.34	0.45	0.34	0.46	0.62	0.72	0.92
Book value per share ($)	19.1%	22.99	29.53	32.24	30.65	37.15	40.83	54.27	70.86	101.38	111.04

1989 Year End:
Debt ratio: 17.8%
Return on equity: 7.1%
Cash (mil): $12,516
Current ratio: 1.65
Long-term debt (mil): $4,711
Number of shares (mil): 196
Dividends:
1989 average yield: 0.5%
1989 payout: 12.2%
Market value (mil): $38,647

Stock Price History high/low 1980-89

250
200
150
100
50
0

NYSE symbol: MC (ADR)
Incorporated: Japan, 1935
Fiscal year ends: March 31

WHO

Chairman: Masaharu Matsushita
President: Akio Tanii, age 62
EVP: Shoji Sakuma
EVP: Masahiko Hirata
Auditors: Peat Marwick Minato
Employees: 193,088

WHERE

HQ: 1006, Oaza Kadoma, Kadoma City, Osaka 571, Japan
Phone: 011-81-6-908-1121
FAX: 011-81-6-909-5787
US HQ (Matsushita Electric Corp. of America): One Panasonic Way, Secaucus, NJ 07094
US Phone: 201-348-7000
US FAX: 201-348-8378 (Personnel)

Matsushita operates 69 manufacturing plants in 28 countries and sells its products in more than 130 countries.

	1989 Sales	
	$ mil	% of total
Japan	24,296	58
Other countries	17,403	42
Total	**41,699**	**100**

WHAT

	1989 Sales	
	$ mil	% of total
Video & audio equipment	15,784	38
Home appliances	5,885	14
Communication & industrial equipment	8,367	20
Energy & kitchen-related products	2,144	5
Electronic components, other	9,519	23
Total	**41,699**	**100**

Products
Answering machines
Batteries
Broadcasting equipment
Camcorders
Cameras
Cellular mobile telephones
Compact disc players
Copiers
Electronic keyboards
FAX machines
Industrial robots
Microwave ovens
Personal computers
Stereo equipment
Telephones
Televisions
Typewriters
Videocassette recorders

Brand Names
JVC
National
Panasonic
Quasar
Technics
Victor

RANKINGS

12th in *Fortune* Global 500 Industrial Cos.
24th in *Business Week* Global 1000

COMPETITION

Compaq
Electrolux
Hitachi
Maytag
Mitsubishi
Motorola
NEC
Philips
Samsung
Sony
Thomson
Xerox
Zenith
Computer manufacturers
Telecommunications equipment manufacturers

MATTEL, INC.

OVERVIEW

Mattel, Inc., seller of 14% of the world's toys, is the 3rd largest US toy producer, after Hasbro and Fisher-Price (owned by Quaker Oats but being spun off). With 1989 earnings of $80 million on sales of $1.2 billion, the company sells toys in over 100 nations and has offices in 19 foreign countries. International markets accounted for 47% of the company's 1989 sales.

Following a slump in the mid-1980s, new management redirected Mattel to focus on proven winners. The company's increased promotion of its most popular toy, the Barbie doll (adding a selection of military uniforms to her wardrobe), has proven particularly successful. In 1989 the doll's sales were $600 million, and Mattel estimates that 90% of young American girls own at least one Barbie doll.

The company's products include Hot Wheels miniature cars, the See 'N Say "talking" toy, and Masters of the Universe action dolls.

A Mattel/Disney line of infant and preschool toys was introduced in 1988, and in 1990 Mattel announced that it had acquired the toy-licensing rights to the popular TV cartoon program "The Simpsons."

NYSE symbol: MAT
Incorporated: Delaware, 1968
Fiscal year ends: Last Saturday in December

WHO

Chairman and CEO: John W. Amerman, age 58, $1,102,000 pay
President, Mattel USA Group: Robert Sansone, age 48, $630,693 pay
President, Mattel International: Lindsey F. Williams, age 53, $473,154 pay
EVP and CFO: James A. Eskridge, age 47
Auditors: Price Waterhouse
Employees: 11,000

WHERE

HQ: 5150 Rosecrans Ave., Hawthorne, CA 90250
Phone: 213-978-6100
FAX: 213-978-5913

Mattel conducts its manufacturing operations principally in China, Malaysia, Mexico, and Italy. Independent contractors make Mattel products in the Far East, Australia, and Spain.

	1989 Sales		1989 Operating Income	
	$ mil	% of total	$ mil	% of total
US	651	53	93	50
Canada & Western Europe	480	39	55	29
Far East & Latin America	106	8	40	21
Adjustments	—	—	(25)	—
Total	**1,237**	**100**	**163**	**100**

WHEN

In 1945 Mattel, Inc., began as a small California toy manufacturer operating out of a converted garage and producing toy furniture. Harold Matson and Elliot Handler named their new company Mattel, using letters from their last and first names. Matson soon sold his share to Handler and his wife, Ruth, who incorporated the business in 1948 with headquarters in Culver City, California.

By 1952 the company's toy line had expanded to include burp guns and musical toys, and sales exceeded $5 million. Sponsorship of Walt Disney's Mickey Mouse Club (1955), a first in toy advertising, was a shrewd marketing step for Mattel, providing direct, year-round access to millions of young potential customers.

In 1959 Mattel introduced the Barbie doll, named after the Handlers' daughter, Barbara, and later introduced Ken, named after their son. The doll, with her fashionable wardrobe and extensive accessories, was an immediate hit, and in the past 30 years it has become the most successful brand-name toy ever sold.

Mattel became a public company in 1960, with sales of $25 million, and within 2 years sales had jumped to $75 million. The company began its purchases of smaller toy companies and nontoy businesses, such as the Dee & Cee Toy Company (1962), the A&A Die Casting Company (1968), Western Printing (1979), and the Ringling Brothers-Barnum & Bailey Combined Shows circus (1979).

The Handlers were ousted from management in 1974 after an investigation by the SEC found irregularities in their reporting of the company's profits. The company was ordered to restructure its board and the Handlers, with 29% of the company's stock, could no longer direct Mattel's activities.

By the 1980s Mattel was a high-volume business with heavy overhead expenses and high development costs. In an effort to recapitalize, Mattel sold all its nontoy assets by 1983. In 1987 sales were over $1 billion, but Mattel showed a $93 million net loss. In that year John Amerman, the newly-appointed board chairman, closed down 40% of Mattel's manufacturing capacity, fired 22% of the headquarters staff, and reduced by 25% the number of toys produced. The results were positive. The next year Mattel posted a $36 million net income and in 1989 it showed an $80 million profit.

While Mattel is still introducing new toys (Nintendo Power Glove and Computer Warriors in 1989, The Simpsons in 1990), it will continue its focus on the promotion of its proven core products.

WHAT

Brand Names

Infant/Preschool Toys
Disney Action Blocks
Disney Dreamtime Carousel
Disney Ride-On Mickey
See 'N Say

Dolls
Barbie
Ken
Li'l Miss Dress Up
Li'l Miss Magic Hair
Li'l Miss Makeup
Magic Nursery
Nia
P.J. Sparkles

Action Toys
Convertables
He-Man
Hot Wheels
Light-Speeders
Skeletor

Video Games/Accessories
Computer Warriors
Power Glove
Super Glove Ball

HOW MUCH

	9 Yr. Growth	1980	1981	1982	1983	1984	1985	1986	1987	1988	1989
Sales ($ mil)	3.4%	916	1,134	1,342	633	881	1,051	1,059	1,020	990	1,237
Net income ($ mil)	29.3%	8	39	42	17	45	58	(1)	(93)	36	80
Income as % of sales	—	0.9%	3.4%	3.2%	2.7%	5.1%	5.5%	(0.1%)	(9.1%)	3.6%	6.4%
Earnings per share ($)	33.4%	0.12	1.55	1.66	*0.57*	1.17	1.00	(0.20)	(2.26)	0.75	1.60
Stock price – high ($)	—	16.75	12.50	31.50	16.88	13.63	17.13	15.50	15.88	10.75	20.88
Stock price – low ($)	—	6.38	6.00	10.13	4.88	4.88	9.88	7.75	6.38	6.13	9.38
Stock price – close ($)	7.0%	10.75	11.00	16.63	5.00	10.25	12.25	8.25	6.88	9.50	19.75
P/E – high	—	140	8	19	30	12	17	—	—	14	13
P/E – low	—	53	4	6	9	4	10	—	—	8	6
Dividends per share ($)	—	0.30	0.30	0.30	0.15	0.00	0.00	0.00	0.00	0.00	0.00
Book value per share ($)	(10.9%)	12.44	14.12	14.86	(7.55)	4.12	5.59	3.98	2.19	2.73	4.41

1989 Year End:
Debt ratio: 45.4%
Return on equity: 44.8%
Cash (mil): $220
Current ratio: 1.79
Long-term debt (mil): $178
Number of shares (mil): 49
Dividends:
1989 average yield: 0.0%
1989 payout: 0.0%
Market value (mil): $958

Stock Price History high/low 1980-89

RANKINGS

302nd in *Fortune* 500 Industrial Cos.
536th in *Business Week* 1000

COMPETITION

Atari
Hasbro
Rubbermaid

MAXWELL COMMUNICATIONS CORP., PLC

OVERVIEW

London-based Maxwell Communications is one of the foremost diversified media companies in the world. The company is led by colorful and charismatic Robert Maxwell, a former British MP known in the UK for his tough fights with unions and in the US for his rivalry with publisher Rupert Murdoch.

With its recent purchases of Macmillan (US) and Official Airline Guides for a combined $3.4 billion, Maxwell expects about 80% of future sales and profits to come from the US. Maxwell is also looking into acquisitions in East European and East Asian countries.

Maxwell's many subsidiaries produce a great range of material, from school textbooks (Macmillan/McGraw-Hill) and scientific journals to encyclopedias (*Collier's*), foreign language guides (*Berlitz*), computer manuals and computer trade books (Que), and databases (Maxwell Online). The company has also agreed to buy 3 major US supermarket tabloids (*Globe, National Examiner,* and *Sun*), which will make it a heavyweight in the tabloid business.

The company is currently restructuring and divesting "nonstrategic" assets, positioning itself for additional acquisition activity.

WHEN

Robert Maxwell, who was born Jan Ludwig Hoch in Czechoslovakia, fled to Britain to avoid Nazi persecution in 1940. He served in the British army with distinction for the rest of WWII and adopted the name Ian Robert Maxwell in 1945. In 1948 he began importing scientific journals from Germany for a London-based joint venture of German and British publishing interests. He bought the joint venture in 1951 and renamed it Pergamon Press, Limited.

Throughout the 1950s Maxwell built Pergamon by recruiting authors and editors who were expert in their fields. In 1956, with the backing of the US government, he established what later became the Pergamon Institute for the translation of Russian scientific literature. Maxwell took Pergamon public in 1964, the same year he was elected to Parliament for the Labour party. Leasco, a computer leasing company based in Los Angeles, bought Pergamon in 1969 and ousted Maxwell from his position as chairman. For several years Maxwell fought lawsuits arising from the Leasco takeover and his refusal to relinquish control of Pergamon's US operations. He lost his parliamentary seat in 1970 and was almost bankrupt when he launched his own takeover of Pergamon in 1974. His bid was successful and he retook control of the company.

Maxwell bought British Printing Company, renamed British Printing & Communications, in 1981 and entered newspaper publishing in 1984 when he purchased Mirror Group, publisher of the *Daily Mirror* and other prominent British newspapers. Both of these companies were failing when Maxwell purchased them, due mainly to overstaffing. After battling the companies' labor unions, he trimmed the labor force by almost 50%. The 2 companies were sold in 1989 in separate deals.

Maxwell began investing large sums in the US in 1988. After buying Alco Gravure (renamed Maxwell Graphics, sold in 1990), Maxwell became the largest media printer in the country. With his purchase of 98-year-old Macmillan the same year, Maxwell became a major publisher of foreign language instruction materials (*Berlitz*), encyclopedias (*Collier's*), computer manuals (Que), and electronic information (BRS). Other acquisitions included Science Research Associates (1988), London House (1988), a majority interest in Panini (sticker albums, 1988), BRS Europe (databases, 1989), Merrill Publishing (educational books, 1989), and from Paramount, the Prentice Hall tax and legal information business (1989). The acquisition of these companies further enhances the Maxwell core company holdings. The management talent resident in these acquisitions will support the growing global presence of the company.

Maxwell has recently turned his attention to the development of a weekly pan-European paper, the *European* (introduced May 1990), and to investments in publishing houses in East European countries.

In mid-1990 the Maxwell family added to its investment in the company, bringing its direct and indirect holdings to a 26% level.

HOW MUCH

£=$1.61 (Dec. 31, 1989)	8 Yr. Growth	1980	1981	1982	1983	1984	1985	1986	1987	1988	1989*
Sales (£mil)	—	—	198	193	231	267	265	462	884	—	1,390
Net income (£mil)	—	—	(14)	12	10	40	20	60	132	—	190
Income as % of sales	—	—	7.1%	6.2%	4.3%	15.0%	7.5%	13.0%	14.9%	—	13.7%
Earnings per share (p)	—	—	1.4	10.5	15	27.2	17	23.2	26.7	—	24
Dividends per share (p)	—	—	Nil	Nil	6	11	12	14	14	—	18

1989 Year End:
Debt ratio: 58.6%
Return on equity: 18.6%
Cash (mil): £ 61
Current ratio. 1.15
Long-term debt (mil): £1,445
Number of shares (mil) 622
Dividends:
1989 average yield: 12.7%
1989 payout: 75.0%

Sales (£ mil) 1981-89

*15-month fiscal year

Principal stock exchange: London
Founded: England, 1951
Fiscal year ends: March 31

WHO

Chairman and CEO: Robert Maxwell, age 67, £337,000 pay
Deputy Managing Director: Richard Baker
Finance Director: Reg Mogg
Auditors: Coopers & Lybrand
Employees: 20,375

WHERE

HQ: Headington Hill Hall, Oxford OX3 0BW, England
US HQ: 866 3rd Ave., New York, NY 10022
US Phone: 212-702-2000
US FAX: 212-702-9538

	1989 Sales		1989 Operating Income	
	£ mil	% of total	£ mil	% of total
UK	591	43	123	64
USA & Canada	646	46	68	35
Continental Europe	101	7	2	1
Other countries	52	4	(1)	—
Total*	**1,390**	**100**	**192**	**100**

*15-month fiscal year

WHAT

	1989 Sales		1989 Operating Income	
	£ mil	% of total	£ mil	% of total
Communications & publishing	413	30	74	38
Printing	929	67	107	56
Other	48	3	11	6
Total*	**1,390**	**100**	**192**	**100**

*15-month fiscal year

Maxwell Macmillan Pergamon Publishing
Information services and electronic publishing
- Official Airline Guides
- BRS and Maxwell Online
- Prentice Hall
- Satellite communication

Science, technology, and medicine
- Pergamon Press
- Macmillan Healthcare Information

Maxwell magazines and exhibitions
- *Insurance Age, Media Week,* and other business publications

Language instruction
- *Berlitz* language guides

Encyclopedia publishing
- *Collier's* and *Caxton's* encyclopedias

Macmillan Educational Publishing
- Elementary/high school and college textbook publishing

Macmillan Publishing
- Charles Scribner's Sons
- Que computer manuals

Printing
Printing operations in France, Belgium, Kenya, Thailand, and the US

RANKINGS

65th in *Forbes* 100 Foreign Investments in the US
896th in *Business Week* Global 1000

COMPETITION

Advance Publications
Berkshire Hathaway
Bertelsmann
R. R. Donnelley
McGraw-Hill
News Corporation
Paramount
Pearson

THE MAY DEPARTMENT STORES COMPANY

OVERVIEW

The May Department Stores Company, based in St. Louis, is today the largest operator of "conventional" department stores in the US. Each store division maintains a separate identity, such as Lord & Taylor or May Company, and has separate management (including merchandise buying).

In an industry characterized in the 1980s by slower expansion and heavy debt (R. H. Macy, Campeau), May has maintained its independence and financial strength. This environment has allowed May to acquire good operations from other companies.

May ventured into upscale discount stores (Venture), but has since left this field and has reduced its role in shopping mall development and management. The company does remain the largest factor in discount shoe selling.

The company ranks 9th in *Fortune*'s top retailers list, and has developed a reputation as an excellent training ground for merchants. The company has paid a dividend every quarter since December 1911.

WHEN

David May, age 15, arrived in New York from his native Germany in 1863. After several jobs in the Midwest, he tried (unsuccessfully) mining in Colorado. He finally tried retailing, opening a clothing store in Leadville in 1877 and expanding to Denver in 1888. In 1892 he and 3 brothers-in-law (the Schoenbergs) bought the Famous in St. Louis, and in 1898 they bought a Cleveland store.

Having moved headquarters to St. Louis in 1905, the partners bought competitor Barr's in 1911 when that store's owners ran out of money trying to build the Railway Exchange Building. The building still serves as May's headquarters and is the site of the flagship Famous-Barr store.

The company continued to buy others throughout the 20th century, including O'Neil's (Akron, 1912); Hamburger & Sons (Los Angeles, 1923); Bernheimer-Leader (Baltimore, 1927); Kaufmann's (Pittsburgh, 1946); Daniels & Fischer (Denver, 1957); Hecht's (Washington, 1959); G. Fox (Hartford, 1965); and Meier & Frank (Portland, Oregon, 1966).

Meanwhile, 2 other companies, the Associated Merchants Company and the United Dry Goods Companies, had reorganized in 1916 to form Associated Dry Goods. Their core business was Lord & Taylor in New York, Hahne's in Newark, and Hengerer's in Buffalo. This company also bought out numerous family-owned stores: J. W. Robinson (Los Angeles, 1955); Sibley's (Rochester, 1957); Pogue's (Cincinnati, 1961); Goldwater's (Phoenix, 1962); Stix, Baer (St. Louis, 1963); Denver Dry Goods (1965); Horne's (Pittsburgh, 1966); and Ayres (Indianapolis, 1972). Associated also created Robinson's of Florida in the 1970s.

Like other department store companies, both companies entered the discount store business, May with Venture Stores and Associated with Loehmann's and Caldor. May became heavily involved in the development and management of regional mall shopping centers (now joint-ventured with Melvin Simon and Prudential Insurance) and in 1979 acquired the Volume Shoe Corporation (Payless ShoeSource), the nation's largest operator of discount shoe stores.

The corporate restructuring that swept America in the 1980s affected the big retailers as well; in late 1986 May bought Associated for 70 million shares of stock. In 1988 May also bought Foley's (Houston) and Filene's (Boston) for $1.5 billion from Federated Department Stores (as it was being acquired by Campeau). Since then May has consolidated some operations, closed others, and announced its intention to sell yet others (Caldor, Loehmann's, and Venture). At the same time, where there are appropriate opportunities, May continues to build new stores: from 1990 through 1994, the company expects to open almost 100 new department stores and about 1,250 additional shoe stores.

HOW MUCH

	9 Yr. Growth	1980	1981	1982	1983	1984	1985	1986	1987	1988	1989
Sales ($ mil)	13.1%	3,173	3,413	3,670	4,229	4,762	5,080	10,376	10,581	11,742	9,602
Net income ($ mil)	17.9%	117	126	142	187	214	235	381	444	503	515
Income as % of sales	—	3.7%	3.7%	3.9%	4.4%	4.5%	4.6%	3.7%	4.2%	4.3%	5.4%
Earnings per share ($)	11.8%	1.34	1.44	1.62	2.16	2.48	2.69	2.44	2.90	3.41	3.64
Stock price – high ($)	—	9.33	10.67	16.42	21.00	21.56	32.50	44.13	50.88	40.00	52.63
Stock price – low ($)	—	6.00	7.75	7.67	13.33	15.17	19.06	30.00	22.25	28.75	34.63
Stock price – close ($)	20.7%	8.83	8.33	15.71	17.92	19.06	31.25	35.50	29.13	36.25	47.88
P/E – high	—	7	7	10	10	9	12	18	18	12	14
P/E – low	—	4	5	5	6	6	7	12	8	8	10
Dividends per share ($)	11.9%	0.50	0.55	0.60	0.65	0.78	0.92	1.02	1.12	1.25	1.39
Book value per share ($)	7.1%	10.08	10.97	11.94	13.39	14.99	16.58	17.01	18.26	20.45	18.65

1989 Year End:
Debt ratio: 56.4%
Return on equity: 18.6%
Cash (mil): $92
Current ratio: 2.03
Long-term debt (mil): $3,003
Number of shares (mil): 124
Dividends:
1989 average yield: 2.9%
1989 payout: 38.1%
Market value (mil): $5,953

NYSE symbol: MA
Incorporated: New York, 1910
Fiscal year ends: Saturday nearest January 31

WHO

Chairman and CEO: David C. Farrell, age 56, $1,530,628 pay
President: Thomas A. Hays, age 57, $1,224,502 pay
VC: Richard L. Battram, age 55, $850,073 pay
VC and CFO: Jerome T. Loeb, age 49, $835,796 pay
VC: Lawrence E. Honig, age 42, $767,166 pay
SVP Human Resources: Douglas J. Giles
Auditors: Arthur Andersen & Co.
Employees: 115,000

WHERE

HQ: 611 Olive St., St. Louis, MO 63101
Phone: 314-342-6300
FAX: 314-342-6584

May operates 13 department store divisions with stores in 29 states and Washington, DC. The Volume Shoe Corporation subsidiary has stores in 44 states and Washington, DC.

May Merchandising Corporation, based in New York, maintains buying offices around the world.

WHAT

Division, HQ	1989 Sales $ mil	No. of Stores
Foley's, Houston	1,121	35
Lord & Taylor, New York	1,034	47
May Company, Los Angeles	954	35
Hecht's, Washington, DC	829	22
Robinson's, Los Angeles	753	29
Kaufmann's, Pittsburgh	753	23
Famous-Barr, St. Louis	508	17
Filene's, Boston	484	18
May Company, Cleveland	436	16
G. Fox, Hartford	426	11
L.S. Ayres, Indianapolis	328	14
May D&F, Denver	297	13
Meier & Frank, Portland, OR	274	8
Total department stores	8,197	288
Volume Shoe Corp., Topeka	1,228	2,746
Total	**9,425**	**3,034**

1989 sales are shown here on a 52-week basis, as opposed to the 53-week year used for financial reporting purposes in 1989.

RANKINGS

9th in *Fortune* 50 Retailing Cos.
81st in *Forbes* Sales 500
92nd in *Business Week* 1000
243rd in *Business Week* Global 1000

COMPETITION

Campeau	Mercantile Stores
Carter Hawley Hale	J. C. Penney
Dayton Hudson	United States Shoe
Dillard	Woolworth
R. H. Macy	Specialty and discount retailers
Melville	

MAYFLOWER GROUP, INC.

OVERVIEW

Mayflower, a privately held company since 1986, provides moving and other transportation services through 2 operating units: Transit and Contract Services.

America's 4th largest mover in terms of 1989 operating revenues, Mayflower Transit offers household moving and storage services, specialized handling of electronic and other high-tech equipment, and international freight forwarding services, which accounts for 3% of sales. Mayflower Transit also sells tractors and trailers, group casualty and liability insurance, and moving supplies and uniforms to its agents and owner-operators.

Mayflower Contract Services operates school buses in 200 districts in 21 states, a school bus dealership, and year-round public bus services in 10 major American cities.

In April 1990 CEO Michael Smith announced that, in an effort to reduce its $213 million long-term debt, Mayflower may split its 2 operating units into separate companies. Contract Services would be sold in a public stock offering, and Mayflower managers and employees would be invited to buy Mayflower Transit. No action will be taken until December 1991, however, when the company will have retired its outstanding public debt.

WHEN

In 1927, 2 Indiana truck drivers, Conrad Gentry and Don Kenworthy, founded Mayflower Transit Company, an Indianapolis-based household mover named after the ship used by the Pilgrims in their historic transatlantic voyage. Shortly thereafter the company was reincorporated as Aero Mayflower Transit Company (1928). Within 3 years the company had appointed independent agents to operate Aero Mayflower moving vans and storage facilities in key metropolitan areas.

Aero Mayflower established America's first school for professional movers in 1934. In 1940 the company was first to receive Interstate Commerce Commission approval to operate nationwide household moving services. It expanded to Mexico and Canada in 1948 and Europe in 1956.

Aero Mayflower improved customer service by equipping its vans with Air-Ride suspension to provide a smoother ride (1960) and installing a computerized management system in its dispatch facilities to more efficiently track equipment and orders (1967). The Mayflower Corporation was formed in 1973 and, through an exchange of stock, it acquired Aero Mayflower. That same year the company opened a new headquarters facility in Carmel, Indiana. Mayflower made its first public stock offering in 1976.

Planning to expand service beyond household moving, Mayflower established Air Mayflower, an air freight forwarder, in 1976. Although Air Mayflower offered customers an alternative to highway transport, it did not compete effectively with established air freight forwarders such as Emery and Airborne Express and had ceased operations by 1983.

Other plans to diversify were more satisfactory. In 1979 Mayflower formed the Gentry Insurance Agency to provide limited insurance to its operators and agents. In 1981 Mayflower bought a 90% stake in ADI Appliances, a Midwest wholesaler of household appliances (Whirlpool and Litton) and home video equipment (RCA). By the end of 1981, Mayflower also offered Atari and Texas Instruments brand products through its ADI (Consumer Products) division. It sold this division in 1987.

In 1984 the company started offering school bus transportation services by purchasing R. W. Harmon & Sons, a school bus company, and 3 more school bus companies the following year. Mayflower's fleet of 4,500 buses was one of America's largest, 2nd only to Canada's Laidlaw Transportation. In 1986 Laidlaw offered $29.25 per share to gain control of Mayflower. Mayflower's managers, led by John B. Smith (Mayflower's chairman, president, and CEO), responded by taking the company private in a $259 million LBO, financed by several New York investment firms, including Smith Barney.

Over the next 2 years Mayflower's LBO-related debt contributed to losses of $6 million on revenues of $585 million (1987) and $9 million on revenues of $612 million (1988). In 1989 an attempted buyout led by former Mayflower Transit president Richard Russell failed when managers were unable to secure financing. Smith, who had backed the buyout plan, stepped down as chief executive. He continues to serve as Mayflower's chairman, while former Contract Services president Michael L. Smith (no family relationship to John Smith) serves as president and CEO.

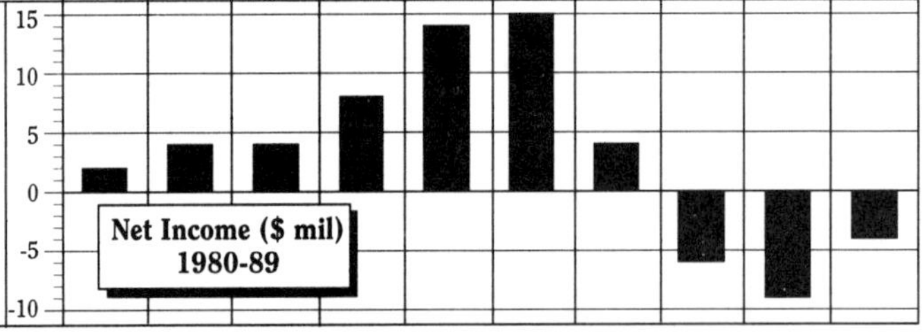

Private company
Incorporated: Indiana, 1986
Fiscal year ends: December 31

WHO

Chairman: John B. Smith, age 58, $501,525 pay
President and CEO: Michael L. Smith, age 41, $351,500 pay
SVP and CFO: Patrick F. Carr, age 38, $218,883 pay
SVP, Secretary, and General Counsel: Robert H. Irvin, age 38
Auditors: Ernst & Young
Employees: 2,900 full-time; 8,500 part-time

WHERE

HQ: 9998 N. Michigan Rd., Carmel, IN 46032
Phone: 317-875-1000
FAX: 317-875-2214

Mayflower owns and operates 32 moving and storage agencies in the US in addition to its network of 670 independent agents and 1,000 independent owner-operators throughout the US and Canada. The company owns 146 tractors, 1,618 trailers, and 4,755 school buses. Mayflower offers passenger transportation services in 22 states. The company also provides international freight forwarding services through 100 agents in 30 countries.

WHAT

	1989 Sales	
	$ mil	% of total
Transit		
Accessorial services	102	15
Electronic & Trade Show	83	12
Household Goods	205	31
International	20	3
Moving & Storage/other	96	14
Contract Services		
Bus sales	14	2
Public transportation	27	4
Student transportation	129	19
Total	**676**	**100**

Mayflower Transit, Inc.
Electronic and Trade Show (special handling and other services)
Household Goods (household moving services)
International (freight forwarding)
Moving and Storage (32 company-owned agencies)
Other Transportation Operations
Group insurance agency
Moving supplies and equipment sales
Road equipment maintenance
Tractor and trailer sales

Mayflower Contract Services, Inc.
Allied Bus Sales, Inc.
Public transportation (city bus operations)
Student transportation (school bus operations)

RANKINGS

34th in *Fortune* 50 Transportation Cos.
279th in *Forbes* 400 US Private Cos.

COMPETITION

Norfolk Southern
Ryder

HOW MUCH

	9 Yr. Growth	1980	1981	1982	1983	1984	1985	1986	1987	1988	1989
Sales ($ mil)	10.7%	271	330	341	379	481	619	706	585	612	676
Net income ($ mil)	—	2	4	4	8	14	15	4	(6)	(9)	(4)
Income as % of sales	—	0.7%	1.3%	1.3%	2.0%	2.9%	2.4%	0.5%	(1.1%)	(1.5%)	(0.5%)

1989 Year End:
Debt ratio: 95.6%
Return on equity: —
Cash (mil): $15
Current ratio: 0.84
Long-term debt (mil): $213

MAYO FOUNDATION

OVERVIEW

The Mayo Foundation is the governing body for the largest private medical center in the world (the Mayo Clinic in Rochester, Minnesota), with additional outpatient facilities in Jacksonville, Florida, and Scottsdale, Arizona. The Mayo Clinic in Rochester works in association with its 2 local hospitals (Saint Marys and Rochester Methodist). With over $1 billion in revenues in 1989, the foundation devoted over 8% of its budget to R&D.

Intertwined with the clinical practice are extensive programs in medical education and research. Since the clinic started keeping records in 1907, it has served over 4 million patients from more than 150 countries.

Medical education is conducted by the Mayo Graduate School of Medicine (one of the largest medical programs in the country), Mayo Medical School, and the Mayo School of Health-Related Sciences.

The Mayo Clinic is known for its integrated approach to health care. The clinic's team of more than 900 physicians and scientists work together to provide some of the most comprehensive health care possible.

The foundation also runs a number of enterprises complementary to its medical operations, including its *Health Letter* ($7 million of revenues), Mayo Medical Ventures to commercialize its research, and a testing laboratory. Mayo is also publishing a book on family health care and, through a subsidiary, runs the Rochester airport, 40% of whose passengers are connected to the clinic.

Nonprofit organization
Incorporated: Minnesota, 1915
Fiscal year ends: December 31

WHO

Chairman: Samuel C. Johnson
President and CEO: Robert R. Waller, $289,285 pay in 1988
Treasurer and CFO: John H. Herrell, $163,278 pay in 1988
Director for Education and Dean, Mayo Medical School: Franklyn G. Knox
Auditors: Deloitte & Touche
Employees: 16,506

WHERE

HQ: Mayo Clinic, Rochester, MN 55905
Phone: 507-284-2511
FAX: 507-284-8713 (Communications)

The Mayo Foundation is based in Rochester, Minnesota. The Rochester complex consists of 43 buildings with 8.7 million square feet of space. Mayo Clinic outpatient facilities exist in Rochester; Jacksonville, Florida; and Scottsdale, Arizona. Foundation hospitals are Saint Marys in Rochester, Rochester Methodist Hospital, and St. Luke's Hospital in Jacksonville.

	1989 Revenues	
	$ mil	% of total
Mayo Clinic, Rochester	518	49
Rochester hospitals	233	22
St. Luke's Hospital	74	7
Research	53	5
Reference laboratories	53	5
Mayo Clinic, Scottsdale	32	3
Mayo Clinic, Jacksonville	32	3
Other	63	6
Total	**1,058**	**100**

WHEN

William W. Mayo emigrated to the US from England in 1845. After studying medicine at Indiana Medical College, Mayo practiced medicine in Indiana and Minnesota until finally settling in Rochester, Minnesota, in 1863. Twenty years later a tornado struck the town, and Mayo was assigned to take charge of a makeshift hospital. Following the disaster, the Sisters of St. Francis (a Roman Catholic order) arranged for the construction of a permanent hospital and asked Mayo to assume leadership of the medical staff. Mayo reluctantly agreed (at that time hospitals were associated with the poor and the insane) and took charge when Saint Marys Hospital opened in 1889.

Mayo's 2 sons, William and Charles, had already joined their father's practice when Saint Marys opened, and they served with their father as the hospital's medical staff. After the elder Mayo retired, the sons ran the hospital by themselves, assisted only by a small group of Catholic sisters. The brothers accepted all medical cases, regardless of the patient's ability to pay, yet they were still able to make the hospital self-sufficient. Under the brothers' direction, Saint Marys was the first hospital in the US to implement the antiseptic surgical techniques developed by Joseph Lister.

By the turn of the century, the Mayos' expanding practice had helped thousands of patients. Physicians were added to the staff and a new wing was opened in 1905, at about the same time the present name was adopted (Saint Marys would remain one of the facilities under the Mayo umbrella). In 1914 a new clinic building was opened, and the following year the brothers established the Mayo Graduate School of Medicine in academic affiliation with the University of Minnesota. During WWI the brothers served as the head surgical consultants to the US Army.

In 1919 the brothers organized the Mayo Properties Association, a self-perpetuating charity, to assume ownership of the clinic and carry on its work after their deaths. Ten years later a new clinic building, with modern waiting rooms, laboratories, a library, and administrative offices, was opened. In 1933 the Clinic established the first blood bank in the US and in 1938 saw its millionth patient. Both of the brothers died in 1939.

In 1950 scientists at the clinic won a Nobel Prize for their discovery of the drug cortisone. The clinic continued to grow during the 1960s when it moved Rochester Methodist Hospital to a new building (1966) and completed a 10-story addition to the Mayo Building (1969).

In 1972 the Mayo Medical School (its 2nd medical school) was opened. The clinic's reputation for medical research and practice continued to grow, and it established satellite facilities in Jacksonville, Florida (1986), and Scottsdale, Arizona (1987). In 1985 the clinic started its liver transplant program and 3 years later performed its first coronary atherectomy (a new procedure to open clogged arteries).

WHAT

	Sources of Gifts	
	$ thou	% of total
Estates	12,479	41
Individuals	9,863	32
Personal/family foundations	3,037	10
Corporations	1,609	5
Philanthropic foundations	1,515	5
Alumni	902	3
Memorials	414	1
Other	941	3
Total	**30,760**	**100**

	1989 Revenues	
	$ mil	% of total
Medical services	932	88
Grants & contracts	54	5
Auxiliary & other	41	4
Investment return	31	3
Total	**1,058**	**100**

Mayo Services 1989	
Clinic patient registrations	328,341
Diagnostic X-ray procedures	975,432
Laboratory tests	6,720,240
Total surgical cases	65,189
Hospital beds licensed	2,249
Hospital occupancy %	57
Hospital admissions	60,089
Hospital days of patient care	467,415

HOW MUCH

	9 Yr. Growth	1980	1981	1982	1983	1984	1985	1986	1987	1988	1989
Revenues ($ mil)	—	—	—	—	—	—	—	—	—	965	1,058
Net Operating Inc.($ mil)	—	—	—	—	—	—	—	—	—	38	42
Patient Regs. (thou)	2.2%	270	273	272	277	280	282	283	303	320	328
Donations ($ mil)	8.6%	15	18	12	15	15	18	25	27	32	31

Patient Registration (thou) 1980-89

340, 320, 300, 280, 260, 240, 220, 200

COMPETITION

Hospital Corp.
Humana
National Medical

MAYTAG CORPORATION

OVERVIEW

Maytag manufactures and distributes a broad line of home appliances and a line of vending machines worldwide through its 12 business units. In an industry characterized by corporate acquisitions and mergers over the past decade, Maytag has emerged as the 4th largest appliance manufacturing firm in the US after General Electric, White Consolidated Industries (Electrolux), and Whirlpool.

Maytag has built its reputation on the quality and durability of its products, emphasizing this theme in its long-running "lonely repairman" advertising campaign. The company has maintained the emphasis on quality by manufacturing a high percentage of its own parts and by testing every machine it makes. In 1989 Maytag redesigned its washing machine transmission, long the industry standard, for the first time in 35 years in order to make it even more reliable.

Maytag's 1989 purchase of Chicago Pacific, whose Hoover unit manufactures a full line of home appliances overseas in addition to vacuum cleaners, has given the company increased access to markets in Europe and Australia, which are expected to expand more rapidly than the US market in the future.

WHEN

In 1893 F. L. Maytag and 3 associates formed the Parsons Bandcutter and Self Feeder Company in Newton, Iowa, to manufacture feeder attachments for grain threshing machines. In 1903 the firm changed its name to the Maytag Company. In 1907 Maytag produced its first washing machine, a hand-cranked wooden tub model. At about the same time F. L. Maytag became sole owner of the firm. The company introduced a washer with an electric motor in 1911, brought out a gasoline-powered washer in 1914, and in 1919 cast the first aluminum washer tub. L. B. Maytag, son of F. L. and president of the company from 1920 to 1926, along with Howard Snyder, head of Maytag's development department, designed and produced the first vaned agitator washer in 1922. The agitator washer was very successful, and Maytag concentrated on washing machine production, producing one million by 1927.

In 1925 the company's stock began trading on the NYSE. In 1929 Maytag's earnings reached a prewar high of $6.8 million on sales of $25.6 million. The company survived the Great Depression without a loss. During the war years, 1941 to 1945, Maytag suspended production of washers and made components for military airplanes. In 1949 the company built a 2nd plant to produce a new line of automatic washing machines. During the Korean War, Maytag built tank parts and other military hardware while continuing production of washers. Clothes dryers went into production in 1953. In the late 1950s Maytag began to make products for the commercial laundry field. In 1966 the company entered the kitchen appliance field, introducing a line of dishwashers and, in 1968, food waste disposers.

Maytag began growing by acquisition in 1981, entering the field of cooking appliances with the purchase of Hardwick Stove and Jenn-Air. In 1986 Maytag more than doubled its size by buying the Magic Chef group of companies, including Magic Chef, Toastmaster, and Admiral. The company sold Toastmaster in 1987 and in 1988 consolidated Admiral into the company's other divisions. Maytag sold Magic Chef air conditioning in 1988 and in 1989 bought Chicago Pacific (furniture manufacturing and Hoover appliances) for $960 million, doubling Maytag's debt. The company sold Chicago Pacific's 6 furniture manufacturing companies to Ladd Furniture for $213.4 million in 1989, retaining the Hoover unit. Hoover gives Maytag a significant presence in the European and Australian appliance markets as well as a 32% share of the US vacuum cleaner market. In 1989 the company introduced its first line of Maytag brand refrigerators.

HOW MUCH

	9 Yr. Growth	1980	1981	1982	1983	1984	1985	1986	1987	1988	1989
Sales ($ mil)	27.4%	349	409	441	597	643	684	1,724	1,909	1,886	3,089
Net income ($ mil)	15.7%	36	37	37	61	63	72	119	153	136	131
Income as % of sales	—	10.2%	9.2%	8.4%	10.2%	9.8%	10.5%	6.9%	8.0%	7.2%	4.3%
Earnings per share ($)	7.4%	0.67	0.66	0.67	1.09	1.16	1.33	1.38	1.91	1.77	1.27
Stock price – high ($)	—	7.38	7.50	9.75	14.19	13.75	19.94	27.44	32.31	27.63	26.75
Stock price – low ($)	—	5.38	5.97	5.56	9.16	9.06	10.88	18.00	17.00	18.88	18.88
Stock price – close ($)	13.9%	6.06	6.38	9.41	12.81	11.19	19.47	23.63	22.38	19.38	19.50
P/E – high	—	11	11	15	13	12	15	20	17	16	21
P/E – low	—	8	9	8	8	8	8	13	9	11	15
Dividends per share ($)	6.8%	0.53	0.54	0.54	0.68	0.75	0.83	0.85	0.95	0.98	0.95
Book value per share ($)	11.2%	3.42	3.43	3.58	4.00	4.22	4.72	6.53	5.43	6.55	8.89

1989 Year End:
Debt ratio: 48.3%
Return on equity: 16.5%
Cash (mil): $39
Current ratio: 2.33
Long-term debt (mil): $877
Number of shares (mil): 106
Dividends:
1989 average yield: 4.9%
1989 payout: 74.8%
Market value (mil): $2,059

Stock Price History
high/low 1980-89

35
30
25
20
15
10
5
0

NYSE symbol: MYG
Incorporated: Delaware, 1925
Fiscal year ends: December 31

WHO

Chairman and CEO: Daniel J. Krumm, age 63, $1,239,066 pay
EVP; President, Hoover Group: Frank E. Vaughn, age 60, $574,546 pay
EVP; President, Appliance Group: Leonard A. Hadley, age 55, $510,292 pay
EVP and CFO: Jerry A. Shiller, age 57, $467,155 pay
Secretary and General Counsel: Donald C. Byers, age 64, $305,421 pay
Auditors: Ernst & Young
Employees: 26,019

WHERE

HQ: 403 W. Fourth St. North, Newton, IA 50208
Phone: 515-792-8000
FAX: 515-792-8395

Maytag has 26 plants in 8 countries.

	1989 Sales		1989 Operating Income	
	$ mil	% of total	$ mil	% of total
North America	2,545	82	312	100
Other	544	18	1	—
Adjustments	—	—	(33)	—
Total	**3,089**	**100**	**280**	**100**

WHAT

	1989 Sales		1989 Operating Income	
	$ mil	% of total	$ mil	% of total
Home appliances	2,856	92	263	84
Vending equipment	233	8	50	16
Adjustments	—	—	(33)	—
Total	**3,089**	**100**	**280**	**100**

Business Units
Admiral, Galesburg, IL
Dixie-Narco, Ranson, WV
Domicor, Chicago, IL
Hoover Australia, Sydney
Hoover North America, North Canton, OH
Hoover plc, Merthyr Tydfil, South Wales
Hoover Trading, Dijon, France
Jenn-Air, Indianapolis, IN
Magic Chef, Cleveland, TN
Maycor Appliance Parts & Service Co., Cleveland, TN
Maytag Co., Newton, IA
Maytag Financial Services, Newton, IA

Appliance Brand Names
Admiral
Hardwick
Hoover
Jenn-Air
Magic Chef
Maytag
Norge

RANKINGS

146th in *Fortune* 500 Industrial Cos.
412th in *Fortune* Global 500 Industrial Cos.
271st in *Forbes* Sales 500
337th in *Business Week* 1000
767th in *Business Week* Global 1000

COMPETITION

Electrolux
General Electric
Raytheon
Whirlpool

MCA INC.

OVERVIEW

Headquartered in Universal City, California, MCA, Inc., produces and distributes film and music entertainment, operates a tour of Universal Studios Hollywood, and owns amphitheaters in Denver, Dallas, and Atlanta. The company manufactures entertainment and sports apparel and owns retail and mail order operations. Under the Putnam Berkley Group, MCA publishes adult, young adult, and children's books and mass market reprints of hardcover and paperback originals. The company operates WWOR-TV in Secaucus, New Jersey, and owns a 50% interest (with Paramount Communications) in USA Network. It also owns 50% of Cineplex Odeon, one of the largest movie theater chains in North America.

MCA experienced the most successful year in its history in 1989. Box office hits included *Back to the Future II*, *Do the Right Thing*, and *Sea of Love*. Universal Studios Hollywood, observing its 25th anniversary, had a record 5 million visitors.

The company opened Universal Studios Florida (owned jointly with Britain's Rank Organisation) in the 2nd quarter of 1990 and released several movies, including *Back to the Future III* and *The Jetsons*.

WHEN

In the early 1920s Jules Stein earned his way through Rush Medical College in Chicago by organizing bands to play one-night stands. A year after becoming an ophthalmologist, he formed the Music Corporation of America (MCA), and by 1927 his sideline had become so big that Stein left his practice for the company. MCA grew into the biggest agency of bands in the US. Stein expanded by signing up singers, dancers, and comedians and selling whole "packages" of groups. Later he further expanded to include radio, motion pictures, and television.

MCA moved to Hollywood in 1937 and began buying out other talent agencies, acquiring such famous clients as Betty Grable, Greta Garbo, Henry Fonda, Jimmy Stewart, and Ronald Reagan. MCA did a better job than the competition, broke the old studio contract system, and invented the percentage deal by which the company and client received a percentage of the profits of a picture. Eventually MCA handled 60% of all Hollywood talent.

Stein retired from active control in 1946, becoming chairman of the board and promoting Lew Wasserman, then 33, to president and CEO. In 1952 the company began producing television films. The Screen Actors Guild didn't like the idea of a talent agency producing its own films because it would be negotiating contracts between its clients and itself; however, MCA negotiated with the Guild for a waiver to produce TV programs.

In 1959 MCA bought Universal's 410-acre film lot in the San Fernando Valley for $11.3 million to provide room for its television production. The company absorbed Decca Records, which owned nearly 90% of Universal Pictures, in 1961. The studio, which had been producing movies as Universal-International since 1946, reverted to its original name in 1962. A year later came the first film released under MCA's ownership: Alfred Hitchcock's *The Birds*. In 1964 Universal Studios Hollywood opened, becoming the nation's 3rd largest theme park.

Today, filmed entertainment continues to be MCA's biggest business, contributing more than 50% of revenues in 1989. Of the 30 all-time most commercially successful movies, 9 are Universal's: *E. T.* (highest grossing in movie history and winner of 4 Academy Awards), *Jaws*, *The Sting* (7 Academy Awards), *Animal House*, *On Golden Pond* (3 Academy Awards), *American Graffiti*, *Smokey and the Bandit*, *Twins*, and *Back to the Future*.

In fall 1990 Japan's Matsushita Electric engaged MCA in acquisition discussions.

HOW MUCH

	9 Yr. Growth	1980	1981	1982	1983	1984	1985	1986	1987	1988	1989
Sales ($ mil)	10.8%	1,297	1,329	1,588	1,585	1,651	2,099	2,441	2,590	3,024	3,272
Net income ($ mil)	7.7%	125	90	176	147	95	150	155	137	165	245
Income as % of sales	—	9.7%	6.8%	11.1%	9.3%	5.8%	7.1%	6.4%	5.3%	5.5%	7.5%
Earnings per share ($)	7.3%	1.77	1.26	2.46	2.04	1.31	2.02	2.02	1.82	2.26	3.34
Stock price – high ($)	—	19.25	19.67	26.00	28.67	30.92	54.88	56.50	64.50	50.13	71.38
Stock price – low ($)	—	14.71	12.88	12.67	21.83	22.92	25.50	37.88	30.00	34.63	45.38
Stock price – close ($)	16.3%	15.96	13.79	23.63	28.33	26.42	49.25	38.38	34.50	45.38	62.25
P/E – high	—	11	16	11	14	24	27	28	35	22	21
P/E – low	—	8	10	5	11	18	13	19	16	15	14
Dividends per share ($)	3.5%	0.50	0.50	0.52	0.59	0.59	0.61	0.68	0.68	0.68	0.68
Book value per share ($)	7.8%	12.91	13.01	14.29	15.91	16.74	18.69	20.88	21.42	23.17	25.33

1989 Year End:
Debt ratio: 37.8%
Return on equity: 13.8%
Cash (mil): $114
Current ratio: 2.03
Long-term debt (mil): $1,132
Number of shares (mil): 73
Dividends:
1989 average yield: 1.1%
1989 payout: 20.4%
Market value (mil): $4,573

Stock Price History high/low 1980-89

NYSE symbol: MCA
Incorporated: Delaware, 1958
Fiscal year ends: December 31

WHO

Chairman and CEO: Lew R. Wasserman, age 76, $559,000 pay
President and COO: Sidney Jay Sheinberg, age 54, $729,000 pay
VP, Treasurer, and CFO: Harold M. Haas, age 64
Auditors: Price Waterhouse
Employees: 17,000

WHERE

HQ: 100 Universal City Plaza, Universal City, CA 91608
Phone: 818-777-1000
FAX: 818-777-6431

The company has facilities throughout the US and in Canada.

	1989 Sales		1989 Operating Income	
	$ mil	% of total	$ mil	% of total
US	3,331	99	405	83
Foreign	51	1	85	17
Adjustments	(110)	—	(140)	—
Total	**3,272**	**100**	**350**	**100**

WHAT

	1989 Sales		1989 Operating Income	
	$ mil	% of total	$ mil	% of total
Films	1,738	51	246	50
Music	765	23	57	12
Retail & mail order	275	8	6	1
Book publishing	189	6	24	5
Other	243	7	126	26
Broadcasting & cable	172	5	31	6
Adjustments	(110)	—	(140)	—
Total	**3,272**	**100**	**350**	**100**

Book Publishing
Coward-McCann
Grosset & Dunlap
Perigee Books
Philomel
Playland Books
Putnam
Tuffy Books

Broadcasting
USA Network (50%)
WWOR-TV, Secaucus, NJ

Motion Picture Film Production
MCA TV Entertainment
Universal Pictures Production

Filmed Entertainment Distribution
Cinema International (49%)
MCA Home Video
MCA TV International
United International Pictures (33%)
Universal Pay Television
Universal Pictures Distribution

Music
MCA Concerts
MCA Distributing
MCA Music Publishing
MCA Records
Universal Amphitheatre

RANKINGS

31st in *Fortune* 100 Diversified Service Cos.
249th in *Forbes* Sales 500
166th in *Business Week* 1000
419th in *Business Week* Global 1000

COMPETITION

Advance Publications
Anheuser-Busch
ARA
Bertelsmann
Capital Cities/ABC
General Cinema
News Corp.
Ogden
Paramount
Philips
Sony
Tele-Communications
Time Warner
Turner
TW Holdings
Walt Disney

MCCAW CELLULAR COMMUNICATIONS, INC.

OVERVIEW

McCaw Cellular is the largest cellular telephone company in the US, based on the number of subscribers (over 853,000) and potential users (about 59 million).

Nationwide in scope, McCaw follows a clustering strategy that targets dense population corridors to produce seamless service. Approximately 80% of McCaw's potential market lies in the nation's 30 most populous areas, including the key cities of New York, Los Angeles, Dallas, and Philadelphia; major regional systems include California, Florida, the Pacific Northwest, and Texas. McCaw is the chief operator under the Cellular One trademark.

McCaw is also the 6th largest radio common carrier (including radio paging) in the US, with more than 265,000 subscribers, over 90% of whom are in McCaw's cellular territory.

Aggressive license purchasing and heavy infrastructure costs have left McCaw heavily in debt and unprofitable; the buoyant stock price reflects projected increases in cash flow and efficiency. McCaw aims to create a single nationwide cellular network that would yield royalties to the company on every call made.

OTC symbol: MCAWA
Incorporated: Delaware, 1987
Fiscal year ends: December 31

WHO

Chairman and CEO: Craig O. McCaw, age 40, $288,756 pay
VC: Wayne M. Perry, age 40, $274,024 pay
President: Harold S. Eastman, age 51, $731,332 pay
EVP Acquisitions: John E. McCaw, Jr., age 39, $283,076 pay
CFO: Peter L. S. Currie, age 34
Auditors: Laventhol & Horwath
Employees: 3,400

WHEN

Seattle's radio-and-TV pioneer John Elroy McCaw started Centralia, Washington's first radio station (1937), was one of the first cable television operators (1952), and was among the first to air rock 'n' roll (New York City's WINS, 1950s). After Elroy's sudden death in 1969, his widow and 4 sons were forced to winnow the scattered, debt-ridden empire back to a sole, small cable system in Centralia.

While a student at Stanford, Elroy's son Craig took over McCaw Communications and adopted his father's strategy of securing loans against the Centralia business to buy cable companies; he then slashed costs, improved programming, and raised subscription rates. McCaw also moved into radio common carrier services (1974) and later formed a partnership in 1981 with Affiliated Publications (owners of the *Boston Globe*) to purchase cable systems before their prices skyrocketed. Affiliated's $12 million stake was eventually raised to $85 million (or 43% of McCaw).

But cellular technology soon attracted McCaw, who in the early 1980s got several of the first FCC-granted franchises. As late as 1984, McCaw paid a mere $5 per potential subscriber; by 1989 McCaw would ante up $350 per subscriber. Sagging under cable debt, McCaw wavered briefly in the face of uncertain demand (with phones costing over $2,000 apiece) but soon, with Affiliated's nod, began devouring licenses using junk-bond financing.

The purchasing pace accelerated after AT&T extended 100% financing for costly network switching equipment in 1985. McCaw's 1986 buys alone included major licenses from MCI, Maxcell Telecom Plus, and Charisma Communications.

McCaw tempered the rocketing debt in 1987 by selling the cable business (to Jack Kent Cooke) and offering to the public 12% of McCaw Cellular (into which the old McCaw Communications was merged). A subsequent buying spree included stakes in Metro Mobile CTS and Graphics Scanning and the purchase of Washington Post's Florida licenses.

In 1989 Affiliated spun off the stake in McCaw (then worth about $1.5 billion) to its shareholders. In 1989, as its $1.8 billion debt approached 87% of capital, McCaw sold a 22% stake to British Telecom PLC and sold its southeastern cellular systems to Contel.

McCaw's purchase of a 51.9% stake in LIN Broadcasting (which pushed debt to $3.6 billion) yielded major markets such as New York, Los Angeles, and Dallas. The alliance, crucial in weaving a nationwide blanket from McCaw's scattered properties, also potentially enables McCaw to dictate standards and obtain national accounts.

WHERE

HQ: 5400 Carillon Point, Kirkland, WA 98033
Phone: 206-827-4500
FAX: 206-828-8616

McCaw Cellular operates in 132 markets in 26 states; its services are available to about 48% of the US population residing in the top 305 metropolitan areas; McCaw has over 275,000 pagers in service.

WHAT

	1989 Sales		1989 Operating Income	
	$ mil	% of total	$ mil	% of total
Cellular telephone service	446	89	(140)	—
Radio paging service	58	11	(11)	—
Total	**504**	**100**	**(151)**	**—**

Cellular Operations
Cellular One telephone service
Cellular telephone sales and service
- Car-mounted
- Fully portable
- Transportable

Radio Common Carrier Operations
Paging services
Telephone answering
2-way mobile phone service

LIN Broadcasting (51.9%)
Cellular telephone systems
Specialty publishing (GuestInformant)
TV stations
- KXAN, Austin, TX
- KXAS, Dallas/Ft. Worth, TX
- WAND, Champaign, IL
- WANE, Fort Wayne, IN
- WAVY, Norfolk, VA
- WISH, Indianapolis, IN
- WOTV, Grand Rapids, MI

RANKINGS

88th in *Business Week* 1000
520th in *Business Week* Global 1000

COMPETITION

Ameritech
Bell Atlantic
BellSouth
GTE
NYNEX
Pacific Telesis
Southwestern Bell
U S West

HOW MUCH

	3 Yr. Growth	1980	1981	1982	1983	1984	1985	1986	1987	1988	1989
Sales ($ mil)	203.7%	—	—	—	—	—	—	18	150	311	504
Net income ($ mil)	—	—	—	—	—	—	—	(39)	(134)	(297)	(289)
Income as % of sales	—	—	—	—	—	—	—	(215.9)	(89.3%)	(95.6%)	(57.2%)
Earnings per share ($)	—	—	—	—	—	—	—	(0.40)	(1.31)	(2.39)	(1.95)
Stock price – high ($)	—	—	—	—	—	—	—	—	26.00	28.13	47.25
Stock price – low ($)	—	—	—	—	—	—	—	—	11.00	16.25	25.75
Stock price – close ($)	—	—	—	—	—	—	—	—	16.13	27.00	38.25
P/E – high	—	—	—	—	—	—	—	—	—	—	—
P/E – low	—	—	—	—	—	—	—	—	—	—	—
Dividends per share ($)	—	—	—	—	—	—	—	0.00	0.00	0.00	0.00
Book value per share ($)	—	—	—	—	—	—	—	(0.66)	1.04	(0.08)	6.13

1989 Year End:
Debt ratio: 63.4%
Return on equity: —
Cash (mil): $898
Current ratio: 4.48
Long-term debt (mil): $1,739
Number of shares (mil): 164
Dividends:
1989 average yield: 0.0%
1989 payout: 0.0%
Market value (mil): $6,260

MCDERMOTT INTERNATIONAL, INC.

OVERVIEW

Operating worldwide, McDermott is best known as a provider of energy services. The Marine Construction Segment provides technical services to the oil and natural gas market, including engineering, fabrication, and installation of offshore platforms, pipelines, and other facilities; this group has built the largest number of offshore structures in the world and provides similar services for shoreline and wetland production. The Marine Construction Segment is a technological innovator in offshore production, focusing recently on floating systems, tension-leg platforms, and deep-water structures. Marine Construction operates a shipyard for construction and maintenance of ships for company use and external markets.

McDermott's Power Generation Group (which includes Babcock & Wilcox) provides construction of power-generating facilities for the utility industry, focusing on upgrading aging generating plants in the US. This group is the US market leader for industrial and municipal boilers and provides construction services, pollution control systems, and other equipment and services to the pulp and paper industry and to fossil and nuclear utility power plants internationally.

WHEN

In 1923 R. Thomas McDermott won a contract to supply drilling rigs to a Texas wildcatter. Thomas financed the company, persuaded his father to supervise construction, and named the company after his father — J. Ray McDermott & Company. During the 1930s the oil industry expanded to Louisiana and the McDermotts followed, making New Orleans their headquarters. By 1946 when the company was incorporated, it was supplying services for marshland oil and natural gas production.

After WWII McDermott began exploring construction of offshore drilling platforms and is now a pioneer in this field. McDermott built the majority of the world's offshore oil structures, laid the deepest pipeline on the Gulf Coast, and erected an offshore structure taller than the Empire State Building. The company utilizes a fleet of 200 vessels in construction activities. In addition to the oil industry, the company sells to US Navy, salvage, and subsea markets.

In 1978 McDermott was heavily dependent upon marine construction, which generated 86% of 1978 revenues; in that year McDermott made its most significant acquisition in Babcock and Wilcox, now a division that is responsible for approximately 2/3 of the company's staff and revenues. B&W dates to 1856 when Stephen Wilcox developed his first water-tube boiler. In 1867 he and partner George Babcock patented an improved boiler and went into business. B&W manufactured boilers that powered the nation's first 2 electrical stations. They incorporated in 1881 and began exploring international markets that same year.

In 1889 B&W began building marine boilers. B&W sold more than 1,500 boilers to the navy by WWI; during WWII 75% of major US military vessels were powered by B&W boilers. After WWII the company focused on nuclear energy to produce steam and built the reactor for the first nuclear-powered merchant ship. During the 1950s B&W made significant contributions to the navy's nuclear program; today it supplies fuel and services to nuclear power plants. B&W also diversified into waste-disposal and emission-control systems.

In 1978 McDermott installed the first structure in 1,000 feet of water. By 1980 the company had fabricated and launched single-piece platforms. McDermott introduced a 13,000-ton-capacity barge (1986) and a 5,000-ton-capacity crane (1988) to install such platforms and is designing offshore structures for 2,000-foot depths. McDermott is now pursuing opportunities in the Soviet market.

HOW MUCH

	9 Yr. Growth	1980	1981	1982	1983	1984	1985	1986	1987	1988	1989
Sales ($ mil)	(3.3%)	3,283	3,600	4,843	3,708	3,089	3,234	3,257	3,289	2,352	2,423
Net income ($ mil)	—	88	107	213	51	121	19	56	87	(231)	(115)
Income as % of sales	—	2.7%	3.0%	4.4%	1.4%	3.9%	0.6%	1.7%	2.7%	(9.8%)	(4.7%)
Earnings per share ($)	—	1.76	2.07	4.56	1.37	2.95	0.51	1.52	2.31	(6.23)	(3.09)
Stock price – high ($)	—	26.13	46.63	41.88	38.13	26.38	31.63	30.13	23.38	33.13	21.50
Stock price – low ($)	—	15.88	19.13	27.13	14.75	17.13	23.75	16.38	13.63	13.00	13.75
Stock price – close ($)	(5.7%)	25.00	41.00	38.00	20.50	24.88	24.38	18.25	21.75	14.75	14.75
P/E – high	—	15	23	9	28	9	62	20	10	—	—
P/E – low	—	9	9	6	11	6	47	11	6	—	—
Dividends per share ($)	1.3%	1.25	1.45	1.65	1.80	1.80	1.80	1.80	1.80	1.80	1.40
Book value per share ($)	(6.0%)	27.90	28.51	31.92	33.13	33.92	32.57	32.57	27.94	19.95	16.00

1989 Year End:
Debt ratio: 61.0%
Return on equity: —
Cash (mil): $104
Current ratio: 0.89
Long-term debt (mil): $933
Number of shares (mil): 37
Dividends:
1989 average yield: 9.5%
1989 payout: —
Market value (mil): $550

Stock Price History high/low 1980-89

50
45
40
35
30
25
20
15
10
5
0

NYSE symbol: MDR
Incorporated: Panama, 1959
Fiscal year ends: March 31

WHO

Chairman and CEO: Robert E. Howson, age 58, $547,605 pay
EVP and CFO: John A. Lynott, age 54, $364,662 pay
SVP; Group Executive, Power Generation Group of Babcock & Wilcox: Joe J. Stewart, $211,386 pay
SVP; Group Executive, McDermott Marine Construction: William L. Higgins III, $192,799 pay
Auditors: Ernst & Young
Employees: 28,000

WHERE

HQ: 1010 Common St., New Orleans, LA 70112
Phone: 504-587-5400
FAX: 504-587-6433

McDermott's power generation equipment is sold throughout the US; marine services are provided worldwide.

	1989 Sales		1989 Operating Income	
	$ mil	% of total	$ mil	% of total
US	1,872	78	25	—
Europe & West Africa	128	5	(22)	—
Other foreign	423	17	(2)	—
Adjustments	—	—	(45)	—
Total	**2,423**	**100**	**(44)**	—

WHAT

	1989 Sales		1989 Operating Income	
	$ mil	% of total	$ mil	% of total
Marine construction services	590	24	(61)	—
Power generation systems & equipment	1,833	76	62	—
Adjustments	—	—	(45)	—
Total	**2,423**	**100**	**(44)**	—

Power Generation Equipment/Services
Air-cooled heat exchangers
Pollution control systems
Process recovery boilers
Utility plant repair and construction

Marine Construction Services
Construction of petrochemical plants
Engineering services
Marine pipelines
Offshore platforms
Shipyard operation
Vessel chartering operations

RANKINGS

205th in *Fortune* 500 Industrial Cos.
498th in *Fortune* Global 500 Industrial Cos.
537th in *Business Week* 1000

COMPETITION

Asea Brown Boveri
Bechtel
General Electric
Halliburton
Schlumberger
Westinghouse
Other power equipment companies

MCDONALD'S CORPORATION

OVERVIEW

The McDonald's Corporation is the largest food service organization in the world and has sold an estimated 75 billion hamburgers. McDonald's, under the leadership of founder Ray Kroc, pioneered the fast-food restaurant market with innovative marketing and operational techniques and an insistence on quality and uniformity throughout the system. McDonald's is the most highly advertised brand in the world, with $1.1 billion spent on advertising and promotion in 1989.

McDonald's owns 60% of its restaurant sites and holds leases on virtually all the rest. Sites are either used for company-operated restaurants, about 25% of the total, or leased/subleased to a franchisee who agrees to quality standards and operating procedures and returns a percentage of sales to the company. McDonald's restaurants are serviced by independent suppliers.

McDonald's is the largest employer of minority youth in the US. About 60% of franchisees who trained to become owner/operators in 1989 were minorities or women as the result of an affirmative-action program. McDonald's has the largest stock-option program in the history of US business and has a generous profit-sharing program. Ray Kroc's widow, Joan, owns more than 23 million McDonald's shares (6.5%).

NYSE symbol: MCD
Incorporated: Delaware, 1965
Fiscal year ends: December 31

WHO

Senior Chairman: Fred Turner, age 57, $1,359,286 pay
Chairman and CEO: Michael R. Quinlan, age 45, $900,935 pay
COO; President and COO, McDonald's USA: Edward H. Rensi, age 45, $632,075 pay
President, McDonald's International: James R. Cantalupo, age 46, $551,411 pay
SEVP and CFO: Jack M. Greenberg, age 47
Auditors: Ernst & Young
Employees: 176,000

WHEN

Corporate founder Ray Kroc was a 52-year-old malt machine salesman when he returned to Illinois with a contract to franchise the McDonald brothers' San Bernardino hamburger restaurant in 1954. The restaurant had been designed by the McDonalds to be fast, efficient, and inexpensive. In 1955 Kroc built his first restaurant in Des Plaines, Illinois. Kroc hired Tastee Freeze VP Harry Sonneborn, who developed McDonald's system of franchising and became CEO in 1959 when he arranged a $1.5 million loan on Kroc's net worth of $90,000. Kroc remained chairman and majority stockholder.

In 1961 the company borrowed $2.7 million to buy the rights to the name and operational techniques from the McDonald brothers. By 1964 sales were over $129 million, and the system had expanded to 637 units. McDonald's went public in 1965 and began to advertise on national television in 1966. By 1967, the year hamburgers went from 15 to 18 cents, Kroc and Sonneborn were deeply divided. Sonneborn favored tighter corporate control and a real-estate orientation, while Kroc favored decentralized authority and a hamburger orientation. Sonneborn resigned and Kroc became CEO. The year 1968 saw the opening of the system's 1,000th store and the appointment of longtime operations chief and Kroc protegé Fred Turner as CEO. Ray Kroc remained in overall control as chairman. McDonald's international expansion began under Turner in 1969, the year that women restaurant personnel were first hired.

During the 1970s the company grew at the rate of about 500 outlets per year. By 1972 the system comprised 2,000 restaurants and was worth $1 billion. In 1974 the first Ronald McDonald House (residence for families of hospitalized children) opened. In 1975, the year the drive-thru appeared, McDonald's formed the National Operators Advisory Board in response to a group of operators unhappy with the franchising system. The NOAB gave some power back to the franchisees. By 1978 McDonald's had more than 5,000 restaurants, with sales of over $3 billion worldwide.

During the 1980s McDonald's faced stiff competition in the domestic market as the system's US sales growth slowed from over 20% per year in the 1970s to just over 10% in the 1980s. International sales continued to grow at over 20% per year. In 1984 founder Ray Kroc died at age 81. The system continued to expand in the US and overseas throughout the 1980s, opening a restaurant in Moscow in 1990.

WHERE

HQ: McDonald's Plaza, Oak Brook, IL 60521
Phone: 708-575-3000
FAX: 708-575-6590

McDonald's operates or franchises 11,162 restaurants in 51 countries.

	No. of Restaurants
US	8,270
Japan	704
Canada	606
England	319
Germany	319
Australia	243
Other foreign	701
Total	**11,162**

	1989 Sales		1989 Operating Income	
	$ mil	% of total	$ mil	% of total
US	3,923	64	995	68
Canada	621	10	118	8
Europe	1,168	19	203	14
Other	430	7	143	10
Adjustments	(77)	—	(77)	—
Total	**6,065**	**100**	**1,382**	**100**

WHAT

	Restaurants	
	$ mil	% of total
Operated by the company	2,691	24
Operated by franchisees	7,573	68
Operated by affiliates	898	8
	11,162	**100**

	1989 Sales	
	$ mil	% of total
Company restaurants	4,601	76
Fees from franchised restaurants	1,464	24
	6,065	**100**

Products

Big Breakfast
Big Mac
Chicken McNuggets
Egg McMuffin
Filet-o-Fish
Happy Meal
McChicken Sandwich
McD.L.T.
McRib Sandwich
Quarter Pounder

RANKINGS

18th in *Fortune* 50 Retailing Cos.
42nd in *Business Week* 1000
127th in *Business Week* Global 1000

COMPETITION

General Mills
Grand Metropolitan
PepsiCo
TW Holdings
Wendy's

HOW MUCH

	9 Yr. Growth	1980	1981	1982	1983	1984	1985	1986	1987	1988	1989
Sales ($ mil)	12.0%	2,184	2,477	2,715	3,001	3,366	3,695	4,144	4,853	5,521	6,065
Net income ($ mil)	14.2%	221	265	301	343	389	433	480	549	646	727
Income as % of sales	—	10.1%	10.7%	11.1%	11.4%	11.6%	11.7%	11.6%	11.3%	11.7%	12.0%
Earnings per share ($)	15.0%	0.54	0.65	0.74	0.85	0.98	1.09	1.23	1.42	1.70	1.91
Stock price – high ($)	—	5.14	7.20	9.72	11.04	12.42	18.17	25.58	30.56	25.50	34.88
Stock price – low ($)	—	3.58	4.78	5.73	8.13	9.07	11.36	16.22	15.69	20.38	23.00
Stock price – close ($)	24.5%	4.81	6.46	8.94	10.44	11.47	17.97	20.29	22.00	24.06	34.50
P/E – high	—	9	11	13	13	13	17	21	22	15	18
P/E – low	—	7	7	8	10	9	10	13	11	12	12
Dividends per share ($)	17.1%	0.07	0.09	0.12	0.14	0.17	0.20	0.22	0.24	0.28	0.30
Book value per share ($)	14.2%	2.81	3.37	3.78	4.38	4.94	5.67	6.45	7.72	9.09	9.25

1989 Year End:
Debt ratio: 52.4%
Return on equity: 20.8%
Cash (mil): $137
Current ratio: 0.49
Long-term debt (mil): $3,901
Number of shares (mil): 362
Dividends:
1989 average yield: 0.9%
1989 payout: 15.8%
Market value (mil): $12,489

Stock Price History high/low 1980-89

MCDONNELL DOUGLAS CORPORATION

OVERVIEW

McDonnell Douglas Corporation (MDC) is the largest US defense contractor (66% of its sales are to the US government), the West's leading builder of combat aircraft, and the 3rd largest maker of commercial transports (after Boeing and Airbus Industrie).

MDC produces fighter aircraft (F-15, F/A-18, and AV-8B) as well as trainers (T-45) and flight simulators. Commercial transports include the medium-range MD-80 (143 passengers), the long-range MD-11 (323 passengers), and the MD-90 (153 passengers), an MD-80 derivative in development. During the past 5 years the company has received 29% of all orders for commercial aircraft (Boeing got 51%). The company builds commercial and military helicopters (such as the AH-64 attack helicopter), missiles, lasers, defense electronics systems, and many other aerospace and defense products.

MDC markets the Delta booster for space launches and is a prime contractor for Space Station Freedom. Military products in development include the C-17 airlifter, systems for the Strategic Defense Initiative, and the navy's A-12 attack aircraft (with General Dynamics).

WHEN

Donald Douglas started the Davis-Douglas Company in the back of a Los Angeles barbershop in 1920 and built the Cloudster biplane for David Davis, who intended to fly it in the first nonstop transcontinental flight in 1921. When the attempt failed, Davis left the firm, which then became the Douglas Company. Many records were set in Douglas airplanes, including the first round-the-world flight (completed in 1924 by the US Army). The company was renamed Douglas Aircraft in 1928.

In 1935 Douglas introduced the twin-engined DC-3 airliner. Fast, rugged, and economical, the legendary DC-3 revolutionized air travel, and the company built over 10,000 as military transports during WWII. Douglas also constructed attack aircraft, such as the Dauntless dive bomber. In the decade after the war the company produced the Skyraider, Skyhawk, and Skywarrior attack bombers.

The DC-3 and its descendants enabled Douglas to dominate the airliner market until the advent of the Boeing 707 jetliner in the late 1950s. The DC-8 (1958) proved unable to compete with the 707, but the smaller DC-9 (1965) became Douglas's best seller and one of the world's most popular airliners.

Despite its success, the DC-9's development costs and slow sales of the DC-8 resulted in losses (1966), leading Douglas to invite merger proposals from financially healthier companies. McDonnell Aircraft made the winning offer of $68.7 million in 1967.

James McDonnell had started his St. Louis–based company in 1939 mainly as a supplier of aircraft parts. A series of fighters included the navy's first jet, the FH-1 (1945), and culminated in the famous F-4 Phantom II (1958). Like Douglas, which produced an upper stage for the Saturn moon rocket (1961) as well as the Delta expendable launch vehicle (1960), McDonnell also built missiles and spacecraft, including the Mercury and Gemini capsules of the early 1960s.

After the merger, the new McDonnell Douglas Corporation produced the DC-10 widebody airliner (1970), the Skylab space station (1973), and several fighter/attack aircraft (F-15, 1972; F/A-18, 1978; AV-8B, 1978). With the 1984 purchase of Hughes Helicopter, the company inherited production of a number of "choppers," including the AH-64 Apache attack helicopter.

Although orders for airliners reached record levels in 1988 and 1989, the transport segment of McDonnell Douglas endured a $222 million operating loss in 1989 due to a reorganization and a rapid production buildup for the MD-80 (developed from the DC-9) and the MD-11 (a descendant of the DC-10).

HOW MUCH

	9 Yr. Growth	1980	1981	1982	1983	1984	1985	1986	1987	1988	1989
Sales ($ mil)	10.1%	6,125	7,454	7,412	8,242	9,819	11,618	12,772	13,289	15,069	14,581
Net income ($ mil)	—	145	177	215	275	325	346	278	313	350	(37)
Income as % of sales	—	2.4%	2.4%	2.9%	3.3%	3.3%	3.0%	2.2%	2.4%	2.3%	(0.3%)
Earnings per share ($)	—	3.65	4.44	5.44	6.91	8.07	8.60	6.86	7.75	9.13	(0.97)
Stock price – high ($)	—	52.88	49.63	44.50	62.75	73.75	87.00	91.13	87.50	79.38	94.50
Stock price – low ($)	—	25.25	22.50	28.63	39.75	47.63	64.25	71.00	54.50	59.00	59.63
Stock price – close ($)	2.4%	49.38	29.75	42.00	59.25	72.25	74.25	71.25	59.50	75.25	61.25
P/E – high	—	14	11	8	9	9	10	13	11	9	—
P/E – low	—	7	5	5	6	6	7	10	7	6	—
Dividends per share ($)	13.5%	0.9	1.06	1.24	1.42	1.62	1.84	2.08	2.32	2.56	2.82
Book value per share ($)	9.0%	39.5	42.93	47.24	52.39	58.55	65.34	70.12	76.71	83.40	85.82

1989 Year End:
Debt ratio: 44.7%
Return on equity: —
Cash (mil): $119
Current ratio: —
Long-term debt (mil): $2,654
Number of shares (mil): 38
Dividends:
1989 average yield: 4.6%
1989 payout: —
Market value (mil): $2,346

Stock Price History high/low 1980-89

NYSE symbol: MD
Incorporated: Maryland, 1939
Fiscal year ends: December 31

WHO

Chairman and CEO: John F. McDonnell, age 51, $634,438 pay
President: Gerald A. Johnston, age 58, $345,316 pay
President, McDonnell Douglas Space Systems Company: C. James Dorrenbacher, age 62, $370,655 pay
President, McDonnell Aircraft Company: William S. Ross, age 64, $227,819 pay
SVP Finance: Herbert J. Lanese, age 44
Auditors: Ernst & Young
Employees: 127,926

WHERE

HQ: PO Box 516, St. Louis, MO 63166
Phone: 314-232-0232
FAX: 314-777-1739 (Personnel)

	1989 Sales	
	$ mil	% of total
US government	9,669	66
Other	4,912	34
Total	**14,581**	**100**

WHAT

	1989 Sales		1989 Operating Income	
	$ mil	% of total	$ mil	% of total
Combat aircraft	5,919	40	268	107
Transport aircraft	4,741	33	(222)	(89)
Missiles, space & electronic systems	2,736	19	110	44
Financial services	497	3	77	31
Other	688	5	17	7
Adjustments	—	—	186	—
Total	**14,581**	**100**	**436**	**100**

Principal Operating Units

McDonnell Aircraft (F-15, F/A-18, AV-8B fighters, T-45 military trainer)
McDonnell Douglas Helicopter (AH-64 attack helicopter)
Douglas Aircraft (MD-80, MD-90, MD-11 commercial transports, C-17 military transport)
McDonnell Douglas Missile Systems (Harpoon antiship missile, Standoff Land Attack Missile, Tomahawk cruise missile)
McDonnell Douglas Space Systems (Delta II launch vehicle, Payload Assist Module, systems for Space Station Freedom)
McDonnell Douglas Electronics Systems (defense electronics, simulators, lasers)

RANKINGS

25th in *Fortune* 500 Industrial Cos.
68th in *Fortune* Global 500 Industrial Cos.
10th in *Fortune* 50 Exporters
36th in *Forbes* Sales 500
286th in *Business Week* 1000

COMPETITION

Allied-Signal
Boeing
Daimler-Benz
General Dynamics
General Electric
General Motors
Lockheed
Martin Marietta
Northrop
Raytheon
Rockwell International
Textron
Thomson
United Technologies

MCGRAW-HILL, INC.

OVERVIEW

New York–based McGraw-Hill is a diversified multimedia publishing and information services company. Services provided by the $1.8 billion company range from textbook and magazine publishing (*Business Week*, *BYTE*, etc.) to financial services (Standard & Poor's Ratings) to TV broadcasting.

The company's 60-year-old *Business Week* magazine carried more ad pages in 1989 than any other in the US. It was also the first magazine to include a "talking chip ad" developed by Texas Instruments to promote TI's integrated circuit. The company's joint venture company, the Macmillan/McGraw-Hill School Publishing Company, is the 2nd largest US textbook publisher, following Harcourt Brace Jovanovich.

McGraw-Hill prides itself on using the latest in technology to disseminate information. It was the first to produce compact discs with financial data on 12,000 public companies. It also produced (in partnership with Kodak and R. R. Donnelley) the first computerized college textbook that allows instructors to customize textbooks. Through its Compustat division, McGraw-Hill maintains an in-depth database of company financial information. (Many of the financial tables in this book were provided by Compustat.)

The McGraw family still owns over 5% of the company; members of it sit on the board and are active in management.

WHEN

Magazine publishers James McGraw (*Street Railway Journal*) and John Hill (*American Machinist* and *Locomotive Engineer*) formed the McGraw-Hill Book Company in 1909 in New York to publish scientific and technical books. Initially the 2 kept their magazines apart, but following Hill's death in 1916 the magazine segments were merged with McGraw-Hill. The company started its first year with a list of 200 titles; by 1919 it had grown to over 1,000, with McGraw-Hill well established in the higher education market.

In the 1920s McGraw-Hill expanded its offerings beyond purely technical books and pioneered the risky but successful "send-no-money" plan, giving customers a free 10-day examination of its books. In 1929, 2 months before the stock market crash, McGraw-Hill started *Business Week* magazine, in which it expressed concerns about the economy's health — a view contrary to general opinion.

During the 1930s and 1940s McGraw-Hill continued to expand as a publisher of trade journals and college textbooks. It entered the trade publishing business in 1930 under the Whittlesey House name (changed to McGraw-Hill in 1950), but it was not until the 1950s that the trade division earned some distinction. Its biggest commercial success was *Betty Crocker's Picture Cook Book* (1947), which sold 2.3 million copies the first 2 years.

McGraw-Hill continued to grow in the 1960s and 1970s, acquiring Standard & Poor's, a business investment information service (1966); 4 TV stations from Time (1972); Datapro Research Corporation, a product information service (1976); and Data Resources Inc. (DRI), an economic forecasting service (1979). In 1979 McGraw-Hill successfully fended off a hotly contested takeover attempt by American Express, which offered $830 million for the company.

In the 1980s McGraw-Hill focused on expansion of its electronic information services and acquisition of small, industry-specific publishing and information service companies. McGraw-Hill sold its 59-year-old trade books division in 1989. Also in 1989 Standard & Poor's downgraded its parent company's common stock rating to an A- from an A+ after McGraw-Hill took a $152 million loss in charges associated with a company reorganization and streamlining process.

HOW MUCH

	9 Yr. Growth	1980	1981	1982	1983	1984	1985	1986	1987	1988	1989
Sales ($ mil)	6.7%	1,000	1,110	1,194	1,295	1,402	1,491	1,577	1,751	1,818	1,789
Net income ($ mil)	(8.3%)	86	98	110	126	144	147	154	165	186	40
Income as % of sales	—	8.6%	8.8%	9.2%	9.8%	10.3%	9.9%	9.8%	9.4%	10.2%	2.2%
Earnings per share ($)	(8.0%)	1.74	1.97	2.20	2.52	2.86	2.92	3.04	3.27	3.83	0.82
Stock price – high ($)	—	23.13	28.00	40.50	53.88	48.75	52.00	64.00	84.50	76.00	86.13
Stock price – low ($)	—	12.13	19.69	22.44	35.00	34.00	39.75	46.50	43.00	46.75	53.50
Stock price – close ($)	10.5%	23.13	25.88	37.63	42.25	42.75	48.00	54.63	48.25	62.25	56.75
P/E – high	—	13	14	18	21	17	18	21	26	20	105
P/E – low	—	7	10	10	14	12	14	15	13	12	65
Dividends per share ($)	11.7%	0.76	0.84	0.94	1.08	1.24	1.40	1.52	1.68	1.84	2.05
Book value per share ($)	8.3%	8.84	9.97	10.86	12.29	13.87	15.40	17.04	17.11	19.01	18.08

1989 Year End:
Debt ratio: 30.0%
Return on equity: 4.4%
Cash (mil): $35
Current ratio: 1.06
Long-term debt (mil): $378
Number of shares (mil): 49
Dividends:
1989 average yield: 3.6%
1989 payout: 250.0%
Market value (mil): $2,763

NYSE symbol: MHP
Incorporated: New York, 1925
Fiscal year ends: December 31

WHO

Chairman, President, and CEO: Joseph L. Dionne, age 56, $971,210 pay
Chairman Emeritus: Harold W. McGraw, Jr.
EVP Operations: Harold W. McGraw, III, age 41
EVP and CFO: Robert J. Bahash, age 44, $345,138 pay
Auditors: Ernst & Young
Employees: 14,461

WHERE

HQ: 1221 Ave. of the Americas, New York, NY 10020
Phone: 212-512-2000
FAX: 212-512-4871

WHAT

	1989 Sales		1989 Operating Income	
	$ mil	% of total	$ mil	% of total
Information svcs.	733	41	134	78
Publishing	500	28	16	9
Financial services	459	26	(8)	(5)
Broadcasting	97	5	32	18
Adjustments	—	—	99	—
Total	**1,789**	**100**	**273**	**100**

Information Services
Aerospace and Defense (*Aviation Week & Space Technology* and Aviation/Aerospace Online)
Business Week
Computers and Communications (*UnixWorld*, *BYTE*, *LAN Times*, and Datapro Research)
Construction (Dodge Reports and *Architectural Record*)
Energy and Process Industries (*Modern Plastics* and *Chemical Engineering*)

Publishing
Education (college textbooks)
Legal (Shepard's legal citations)
Professional Publishing (international publishing, professional and reference books, and Osborne Books)

Financial Services
DRI/McGraw-Hill (business and information services)
J.J. Kenny Co. (municipal securities market information)
Tower (customs broker and freight forwarding)
S&P Information (Compustat, Retail Investor Services, Securities Information Services, and S&V Securities Trading Inc.)
Standard & Poor's Ratings

Broadcasting
KERO-TV (Bakersfield, CA)
KGTV (San Diego)
KMGH-TV (Denver)
WRTV (Indianapolis)

Joint Venture
Macmillan/McGraw-Hill School Publishing Co. (50%)

RANKINGS

230th in *Fortune* 500 Industrial Cos.
428th in *Forbes* Sales 500
245th in *Business Week* 1000
751st in *Business Week* Global 1000

COMPETITION

Bertelsmann
Commerce Clearing House
Dow Jones
Dun & Bradstreet
Hearst
Knight-Ridder
Maxwell
Mead
News Corp.
Paramount
Pearson
Reuters
Time Warner

MCI COMMUNICATIONS CORPORATION

OVERVIEW

MCI, headquartered in the nation's capital, is the US's 2nd largest long-distance telephone company; it processed 7.5 billion calls in 1989 (up 39% from 5.4 billion in 1988) via a network representing a $6.9 billion capital investment. In addition to the 50 states, MCI's long-distance services extend from the US to Puerto Rico and 165 countries.

MCI offers international telex and cablegram communications through its Western Union International and RCA Global Communications subsidiaries. Other services include the MCI Card for pay phone users; 800 and other services for large-volume business subscribers; 900 service; Vnet, a software-defined network with custom management features; private lines; and electronic mail under the name MCI Mail.

The company relies primarily upon its coast-to-coast optical fiber and microwave radio facilities to carry traffic; international traffic is carried by satellite and submarine cable, including the first fiber optic cable in the Atlantic, co-owned with other carriers.

WHEN

MCI's history is tied to a series of legal actions against AT&T. In 1963 John Goeken submitted a request to construct a microwave radio system between St. Louis and Chicago on behalf of his mobile radio company, Microwave Communications, Inc. At that time AT&T was acting as a monopoly. The monopoly had not been explicitly granted, but FCC authorization was required for MCI to compete with AT&T. Further, MCI would have to win the right to connect to AT&T's Bell companies.

In 1966 the FCC ruled that MCI was qualified to provide services. William McGowan, a consultant looking for new business opportunities, obtained new financing for the company in 1968. He served as chairman of newly named MCI Communications while Goeken independently went on to found Airfone, which provides air-to-ground service. In 1969 the FCC ruled that MCI could operate, with no assurances that it could expand its network or obtain interconnection to the Bell companies. After appealing, AT&T withdrew its arguments, and MCI began service in 1972.

By 1973 MCI's network reached over 40 cities but could not provide switched services, which required connection to the Bell system. MCI instead provided dedicated services between user-owned switches. In 1973 MCI won interconnection rights at AT&T facilities, prompting a new MCI switched service known as Execunet. Finally, in 1976, MCI won interconnection rights at its own facilities.

In response to Execunet, AT&T filed interconnection tariffs, which eliminated the cost savings MCI had provided to its customers. In 1978 MCI was forced to fight AT&T on antitrust grounds. This battle continued until 1983, when the US Court of Appeals overturned a $1.8 billion settlement in MCI's favor, concluding that AT&T had not engaged in predatory pricing.

MCI has been the 2nd largest long-distance provider since it began offering service and has continually introduced services that compete directly with AT&T. Major acquisitions include Western Union International (1982), a telex provider; Satellite Business Systems (1986), a satellite-based long-distance carrier; and RCA Global Communications (1988), a data communications service provider.

From 1986 to 1988, a period marked by high replacement of telephone facilities, MCI invested over $2.5 billion in digital upgrades to its network, largely in optical fiber. In 1990 the company purchased 25% of INFONET, a data network, from Computer Sciences Corporation and reached an agreement to purchase Telecom*USA, which has slightly more than 1% of the long-distance market. Following a 1987 heart transplant, McGowan returned to full-time duties as chairman.

HOW MUCH

	9 Yr. Growth	1980	1981	1982	1983	1984	1985	1986	1987	1988	1989
Sales ($ mil)	44.6%	234	506	1,073	1,665	1,959	2,542	3,592	3,939	5,137	6,471
Net income ($ mil)	47.1%	19	86	171	156	59	140	(431)	85	356	603
Income as % of sales	—	8.0%	17.1%	15.9%	9.4%	3.0%	5.5%	(12.0%)	2.2%	6.9%	9.3%
Earnings per share ($)	55.5%	0.04	0.43	0.82	0.67	0.25	0.59	(1.57)	0.30	1.26	2.26
Stock price – high ($)	—	3.56	9.03	22.88	28.44	16.25	11.38	13.25	12.13	24.50	48.50
Stock price – low ($)	—	1.13	2.72	6.53	12.63	6.00	7.38	6.00	5.00	9.38	21.63
Stock price – close ($)	33.3%	3.31	8.50	18.19	14.38	7.50	11.25	6.25	9.38	22.63	44.00
P/E – high	—	84	21	28	42	65	19	—	40	19	21
P/E – low	—	26	6	8	19	24	13	—	17	7	10
Dividends per share ($)	0.0%	0.00	0.00	0.00	0.00	0.00	0.00	0.00	0.00	0.00	0.00
Book value per share ($)	26.1%	0.99	1.25	3.31	4.87	5.11	5.59	4.43	4.73	5.59	7.98

1989 Year End:
Debt ratio: 52.9%
Return on equity: 33.3%
Cash (mil): $197
Current ratio: 0.83
Long-term debt (mil): $2,241
Number of shares (mil): 250
Dividends:
1989 average yield: 0.0%
1989 payout: 0.0%
Market value (mil): $11,000

Stock Price History high/low 1980-89

OTC symbol: MCIC
Incorporated: Delaware, 1968
Fiscal year ends: December 31

WHO

Chairman and Member of the Office of Chief Executive: William G. McGowan, age 62, $1,325,000 pay
VC and Member of the Office of Chief Executive: V. Orville Wright, age 69, $1,097,626 pay
President and COO: Bert C. Roberts, Jr., age 47, $932,626 pay
EVP and CFO: O. Gene Gabbard
EVP: Richard T. Liebhaber, age 54, $488,649 pay
EVP: Eugene Eidenberg, age 50
EVP: Kevin W. Sharer, age 41
EVP: H. Brian Thompson, age 50
Auditors: Price Waterhouse
Employees: 19,198

WHERE

HQ: 1133 Nineteenth St. NW, Washington, DC 20036
Phone: 202-872-1600
FAX: 202-887-2154

MCI operates throughout the US and through offices in London, Tokyo, Geneva, and 40 other locations serving 165 countries.

WHAT

Services
Corporate Account Service PLUS (call accounting service)
Fax Dispatch (exchange between fax and electronic mail)
Long distance service
MCI 800 Service (inbound WATS-like service)
MCI 900 Service (caller paid service)
MCI Card (provides long distance billing while traveling)
MCI Commerical Affinity Group Billing Arrangement (discounts to organizations that market MCI services)
MCI Corporate Account Service (call accounting service)
MCI Data Network Services
MCI fax (dedicated fax network)
MCI Hotel WATS
MCI Integrated Network Management Services
MCI Intelsat Business Services (digital private line service)
MCI Mail (electronic mail)
MCI PRISM (WATS-like service)
MCI PRISM PLUS (discount plan for volume usage)
MCI Telex
MCI University WATS
MCI View (interface to IBM's network management systems)
MCI Voice Grade Private Line (dedicated lines)
MCI WATS
Operator services
Prime Calling Option (discount pricing plan)
Switched 56 Kilobit Data Service (high-speed service)
Vnet (software-defined network)

RANKINGS

11th in *Fortune* 100 Diversified Service Cos.
131st in *Forbes* Sales 500
52nd in *Business Week* 1000
143rd in *Business Week* Global 1000

COMPETITION

AT&T
GTE
United Telecommunications
Other long-distance companies

MCKESSON CORPORATION

OVERVIEW

San Francisco–based McKesson Corporation is the nation's largest distributor of drugs and health and beauty aids, from which it derives 94% of its revenues. The company is also the leader in automotive care products and prescription drug claims and payments processing for 3rd parties. The company has approximately 20% of the US market for 5-gallon-size bottled water.

McKesson's drug distribution business supplies drugstores, discount department stores, and hospitals. The company's service merchandising division distributes health and beauty aids, specialty foods, and general merchandise to grocery stores and discount stores. The drug distribution business was strengthened in 1989 when it won the contract to supply the nearly 1,000 Wal-Mart stores and in 1990 when McKesson acquired 50% of Medis, a leading Canadian drug distributor.

WHEN

In Manhattan in 1833 (Andrew Jackson was President at the time), John McKesson formed a company that in 1853 he renamed McKesson-Robins to recognize the contributions of assistant Daniel Robbins. Having initially opened a drugstore, the company successfully expanded into chemicals and drug manufacturing. Differences between the descendants of both McKesson and Robbins could not be resolved, and the company was sold to F. Donald Coster in 1926.

Coster was actually twice-convicted felon Philip Musica. He purchased McKesson-Robbins using fraudulently obtained bank loans. For over a decade he was able to keep his real identity a secret — from all but a single blackmailer who knew of his previous convictions for bribery and record falsification.

By 1930 McKesson-Robbins had wholesale drug operations in 33 states, employing over 6,000 people. Serving over 15,000 retail druggists, the company appeared to be growing. But a sharp-eyed treasurer discovered a Musica-orchestrated accounting scam and a cash shortfall of $3 million, some of which was used to placate the blackmailer. Faced with certain exposure, Musica committed suicide in 1939. Bankruptcy followed.

McKesson & Robbins emerged from bankruptcy in 1941 and by the early 1960s was acquiring more drug suppliers. In a 1967 hostile takeover, San Francisco–based Foremost Dairies bought McKesson & Robbins to form Foremost-McKesson. Over the next 20 years, the company bought wholesalers in several industries, including "21" Brands (liquor, 1970), Moreland Chemical (1978), and now-defunct SKU (computer software, 1984). The company also bought several bottled water companies, entered and exited homebuilding, and sold Foremost Dairies (1983) in order to focus on distribution businesses.

The company, renamed McKesson in 1984, continued to build its drug wholesaling business through acquisitions. By 1985 McKesson was the US's largest distributor of drug and medical equipment, wine and liquor, bottled water, and car waxes and polishes.

In a 1988 antitrust action, the FTC blocked McKesson's proposed acquisition of drug and consumer goods wholesaler Alco Health Services, claiming that combined companies would control 90% of the drug distribution business in some states.

After becoming CEO in 1986, Thomas Field sold McKesson's liquor and chemical distribution operations to narrow the company's focus. Field resigned in 1989, following a dispute between McKesson's drug distribution customers (pharmacies) and its PCS prescription claim processing unit. PCS had yielded to pressure from insurance companies to cut costs by squeezing reimbursements to pharmacies. McKesson created a 2-man Office of the Chief Executive and named Alan Seelenfreund and Rex Malson to replace Field.

HOW MUCH

	9 Yr. Growth	1980	1981	1982	1983	1984	1985	1986	1987	1988	1989
Sales ($ mil)	7.5%	3,662	4,133	4,493	4,054	4,260	4,887	6,264	6,672	7,283	7,046
Net income ($ mil)	5.5%	58	69	69	63	63	64	78	94	95	94
Income as % of sales	—	1.6%	1.7%	1.5%	1.6%	1.5%	1.3%	1.2%	1.4%	1.3%	1.3%
Earnings per share ($)	2.9%	1.66	1.93	1.94	1.72	1.63	1.67	1.85	2.04	2.14	2.14
Stock price – high ($)	—	15.44	17.50	20.19	22.63	25.50	22.13	26.75	35.25	40.13	35.88
Stock price – low ($)	—	8.94	10.25	15.69	14.50	18.75	16.19	18.50	24.75	23.25	25.75
Stock price – close ($)	10.3%	12.88	15.75	18.38	20.13	19.94	19.13	26.19	31.75	26.50	31.13
P/E – high	—	9	9	10	13	16	13	15	17	19	17
P/E – low	—	5	5	8	8	12	10	10	12	11	12
Dividends per share ($)	6.2%	0.84	1.00	1.12	1.20	1.20	1.20	1.20	1.26	1.28	1.44
Book value per share ($)	3.0%	13.05	14.18	14.50	14.85	15.13	15.20	16.74	17.73	16.75	17.01

1989 Year End:
Debt ratio: 37.4%
Return on equity: 12.7%
Cash (mil): $48
Current ratio: 1.32
Long-term debt (mil): $414
Number of shares (mil): 40
Dividends:
1989 average yield: 4.6%
1989 payout: 67.3%
Market value (mil): $1,254

NYSE symbol: MCK
Incorporated: Delaware, 1987
Fiscal year ends: March 31

WHO

Chairman and CEO: Alan Seelenfreund, age 53, $657,363 pay
President and COO: Rex R. Malson, age 58, $718,300 pay
VP Finance: Garret A. Scholz, age 50
VP Finance: Thomas B. Simone, age 48
Auditors: Deloitte & Touche
Employees: 13,800

WHERE

HQ: McKesson Plaza, One Post St., San Francisco, CA 94104
Phone: 415-983-8300
FAX: 415-983-7160

McKesson and its subsidiaries operate throughout the US. Medis distributes drugs throughout Canada.

WHAT

	1989 Sales		1989 Operating Income	
	$ mil	% of total	$ mil	% of total
Drug distribution	5,761	82	134	56
Prescription claims processing	91	1	18	7
Service merchandising	811	12	4	2
Appearance-protection products	163	2	46	19
Water	213	3	38	16
Adjustments	7	—	(26)	—
Total	**7,046**	**100**	**214**	**100**

Major Brand Names & Service Marks

Drug Distribution
Economost (inventory management and ordering system)
Great Valu$ (special promotions)
Medalist (health and beauty aids)
SunMark (home health care products)
3PM (pharmacy computer systems)
Valu-Rite (cooperative marketing)

Service Merchandising
Bright Idea (kitchenware)
Valu-Star (health and beauty aids)

Water
Alhambra
Aqua-Vend
Crystal
Sparkletts

Appearance-Protection Products
Armor All (car cleaner, wax, and protectant)
No. 7 (engine appearance and maintenance)
Rain Dance (car wax)
Rally (car wax)

Prescription Claims Processing
Recap (electronic drug claims processing system)

RANKINGS

7th in *Fortune* 100 Diversified Service Cos.
104th in *Forbes* Sales 500
405th in *Business Week* 1000

COMPETITION

BSN
Fleming
Super Valu

MCKINSEY & CO.

OVERVIEW

Of the world's largest independent management consulting firm one partner is quoted as saying, "There are only three great institutions left in the world: the Marines, the Catholic Church and McKinsey."

McKinsey & Co., whose name is virtually synonymous with management consulting, practically invented the profession as it is practiced today. It is the oldest consulting firm in the US. The firm's meticulous approach to information gathering, its well-known discretion, and its cultivated mystique have given it a reputation as the ultimate source of reliable, objective advice.

It has worked for over 150 of the largest 500 companies in America, and its 2,300 alumni are woven into the fabric of American business life. Tom Peters, author of *In Search of Excellence* and other popular management books, was with McKinsey until 1981. The head of its Tokyo office, Kenichi Ohmae, is one of the best-known and most widely published commentators on world economic and business trends. McKinsey also has a reputation for generosity in its *pro bono* work, which reaps added benefits in the form of low-key marketing and relationship-building.

One of the earliest consulting firms to recognize the globalization of the economy (57% of its revenue is foreign), McKinsey has survived challenges to its dominance (several of the consulting arms of the Big Six accounting firms generate higher revenues) to retain its claim as the consummate management consulting firm.

The ownership and management of McKinsey reside with 391 active directors, principals, and administrators elected by the firm's associates (who make up the majority of its consulting staff).

WHEN

McKinsey & Co. was founded in Chicago in 1926 by University of Chicago accounting professor James O. McKinsey as a vehicle for his management consulting practice. The firm developed a reputation for collecting and analyzing data to provide its clients with advice on the overall structure and operation of their companies. After McKinsey's death in the 1930s, the firm moved to New York.

In 1950, with billings at $2 million, Marvin Bower became managing partner; he was to revolutionize the firm and the consulting industry. He emphasized the "big picture" rather than specific operating problems. He began hiring staff straight out of the nation's most prestigious business schools, a recruiting model still followed today by McKinsey and other consulting firms. Bower also implemented the "up or out" policy that requires employees who are not continuously promoted to leave the firm. Although fewer than one in 11 of all starting consultants become partners, the system has created a vast network of alumni who send business to the firm.

By 1959 Bower had expanded the firm to 5 US offices and opened the first overseas office in London, soon followed by others in Europe, all opened by Americans but staffed by locals. When Bower retired as managing partner in 1967, firm sales had reached $20 million, and McKinsey had become the preeminent management consulting firm in the world.

Throughout the late 1960s and 1970s the firm continued to expand its offices internationally. In 1976 Ronald Daniel became managing director and immediately faced the task of defending the firm's turf from several rapidly growing competitors that had begun attracting McKinsey's clients and, more importantly, the best business school graduates. Daniel responded by creating specialty practices to complement the firm's traditional emphasis on business generalism and by using McKinsey's established presence overseas to expand its foreign revenue base. He also changed the secretive attitude of the firm about its work and encouraged publication of books and articles by staff members. When Daniel retired in 1988, McKinsey's consulting staff had grown to 1,800; revenues had increased to $620 million; and 50% of billings came from overseas offices (which outnumbered US offices 2 to one).

In 1988 Fredrick W. Gluck, a graduate of Manhattan College and New York University with 2 engineering degrees (and no MBA), became managing director. Gluck, the Brooklyn-born son of a nightclub dancer, broke a longstanding tradition of blue-blooded Harvard MBAs heading McKinsey. He has concentrated on improving internal communication among the firm's 2,300 consultants and business analysts by using bulletins and computer-based systems to keep track of the firm's hundreds of ongoing projects.

HOW MUCH

	7 Yr. Growth	1980	1981	1982	1983	1984	1985	1986	1987	1988	1989
Estimated Sales ($ mil)	23.5%	—	—	145	—	—	350	400	510	620	635

Estimated Sales ($ mil) 1982-89

Private company
Founded: Chicago, 1926
Fiscal year ends: December 31

WHO

Managing Director: Frederick W. Gluck, age 54
CFO: James Rogers
Employees: 4,000

WHERE

HQ: 55 E. 52nd St., New York, NY 10022
Phone: 212-446-7000
FAX: 212-446-8575

McKinsey has 44 offices in 22 countries.

	1989 Estimated Sales	
	$ mil	% of total
US	273	43
Foreign	362	57
Total	**635**	**100**

WHAT

Areas of Practice
Cost reduction and profit improvement
Electronic data processing
Management controls
Manufacturing and operations management
Marketing
Operations research
Organizational change
Strategic planning

Representative Clients
Alcoa
American Express
AT&T
Citicorp
Deutsche Bank
First Interstate Bank
Ford
General Electric
General Motors
Hewlett-Packard
Levi Strauss
Merrill Lynch
Mobil
New York City Transit Authority
Nissan
Pacific Gas & Electric
PepsiCo
Royal Dutch/Shell
Wells Fargo Bank

***Pro Bono* Clients**
Golden Gate National Park Association
Greater Cleveland Regional Transit Authority
San Francisco Symphony

RANKINGS

291st in *Forbes* 400 US Private Cos.

COMPETITION

Arthur Andersen
KPMG
Marsh & McLennan
Price Waterhouse
Saatchi & Saatchi

THE MEAD CORPORATION

OVERVIEW

Mead is one of the world's largest paper manufacturers. At mills throughout the US and in several locations overseas, Mead produces 1.2 million tons of wood pulp annually for specialty and writing paper, coated paperboard, packaging materials, and office supplies.

The company owns or controls 1.3 million acres of timberland, mostly in Michigan and the South. Through its Zellerbach division, Mead distributes paper products in 73 cities. The company is the leading manufacturer of paper-based school and office supplies (Mead, Cambridge, and Ampad).

Mead is also an electronic publisher through its Mead Data Central division, which has agents in 7 other countries and has issued over 1 million user IDs. Its legal database LEXIS and its companion news database NEXIS are widely used by lawyers and other professionals for full-text, on-line research.

Mead's Cycolor products are used in color copiers and slide printers of leading manufacturers.

NYSE symbol: MEA
Incorporated: Ohio, 1930
Fiscal year ends: December 31

WHO

Chairman and CEO: Burnell R. Roberts, age 62, $917,504 pay
President and COO: Steven C. Mason, age 54, $651,252 pay
SVP and CFO: William A. Enouen, age 61, $397,283 pay
Auditors: Deloitte & Touche
Employees: 22,850

WHEN

Mead Paper came into existence in 1882 when Daniel Mead became the sole owner of a small Dayton, Ohio, paper mill (he had shared ownership since 1846). The company faltered after his death in 1891 until a grandson, George Mead, took over in 1905. To raise money for growth, Mead Pulp and Paper Company issued the company's first public stock the following year, and by 1915 George Mead had the company operating in the black. Over the next 40 years Mead expanded, buying and building pulp and paper mills in several eastern and southern states. By the 1930s several Mead Corporation plants were making cardboard from wood chips by a company-developed process.

After WWII Mead continued to grow, acquiring other paper companies and packaging firms both in the US and Europe. Jackson Box of Cincinnati (1955) was the beginning of Mead's container division; Atlanta Paper (1957) began the packaging division, which originated the 6-pack carrier. Mead began diversifying in the 1960s, eventually buying steel and rubber products, coal, furniture, and fabric companies. The 1966 purchase of Westab of Dayton, Ohio, began the school and office supply division. In 1968 Mead bought a small data processing company, Data Corporation, that became Mead Data Central, now the company's electronic publishing division. In the mid-1970s Mead Data Central introduced LEXIS, the largest legal research database, and NEXIS, the largest full-text database of news and business information.

Mead avoided a takeover attempt by Occidental Petroleum in the late 1970s that involved a protracted public battle for control. In the early 1980s the recession caused a slump in demand for paper products, and Mead suffered a loss of $62 million in 1982, its first loss in 44 years. An improved economy boosted demand, and its paper divisions (upgraded and expanded in the late 1970s) have since recovered.

In 1982 and 1983 Mead shed many divisions to better focus on forest products and electronic publishing. Mead school products were top sellers in the 1980s, those marked with the Smurfs and Garfield the Cat accounting for about 30% of the division's earnings in 1983. Acquisitions in recent years were Micromedex (medical database, 1985), Ampad (office supplies, 1986), Dataline (financial information, 1987), Zellerbach (paper distribution, 1988), and Michie (legal publishing, 1989). In 1988 the company introduced Cycolor, a copier paper that reproduces color by an inexpensive technique, and has entered joint ventures with others, including Seiko of Japan, to produce color copiers and printers.

WHERE

HQ: Mead World Headquarters, Courthouse Plaza NE, Dayton, OH 45463
Phone: 513-495-6323
FAX: 513-461-2424

Mead sells products worldwide.

WHAT

	1989 Sales		1989 Operating Income	
	$ mil	% of total	$ mil	% of total
Packaging & paperboard	850	18	94	22
Distrib. & school & office prods.	2,158	47	67	15
Electronic publishing	401	9	37	8
Paper	1,199	26	241	55
Corporate & other	4	—	(163)	—
Adjustments	—	—	24	—
Total	**4,612**	**100**	**300**	**100**

Distribution & School & Office Products
Ampad and Cambridge office products
Looney Tunes and Trapper Keeper binders
Safari school supplies
Zellerbach (distributor of papers, packaging)

Mead Data Central (Electronic Publishing)
Jurisoft (legal computer software)
LEXIS/NEXIS (on-line databases)
The Michie Co. (legal references)

Mead Imaging
Cycolor desktop copier and slide printer

Packaging & Paperboard
Coated Natural Kraft packaging board
Corrugated shipping containers

Paper
Offset printing paper
Premium text and cover papers
Security paper (checks, stock certificates)

Pulp & Wood Products
Lumber, plywood, waferboard
Northwood Forest Industries Ltd. (pulp) (50% owned)

Timberlands (1.3 million acres)

HOW MUCH

	9 Yr. Growth	1980	1981	1982	1983	1984	1985	1986	1987	1988	1989
Sales ($ mil)	6.1%	2,707	2,900	2,667	2,367	2,720	2,740	3,218	4,209	4,464	4,612
Net income ($ mil)	5.9%	129	107	(62)	30	139	94	109	218	364	216
Income as % of sales	—	4.8%	3.7%	(2.3%)	1.3%	5.1%	3.4%	3.4%	5.2%	8.2%	4.7%
Earnings per share ($)	3.9%	2.36	1.96	(1.19)	0.52	2.27	1.51	*1.75*	*3.47*	*5.54*	3.33
Stock price – high ($)	—	15.19	16.38	11.63	21.00	20.63	22.44	30.44	48.38	49.50	46.63
Stock price – low ($)	—	9.81	10.50	6.75	9.38	13.56	16.81	21.25	21.00	29.00	34.25
Stock price – close ($)	12.2%	13.00	11.50	9.38	19.38	17.13	22.19	27.31	33.88	39.00	36.75
P/E – high	—	6	8	—	41	9	15	17	14	9	14
P/E – low	—	4	5	—	18	6	11	12	6	5	10
Dividends per share ($)	(0.8%)	0.91	0.96	0.88	0.50	0.53	0.60	0.60	0.65	0.74	0.85
Book value per share ($)	5.6%	16.26	16.84	14.15	14.30	15.72	16.63	16.91	19.85	23.95	26.55

1989 Year End:
Debt ratio: 36.1%
Return on equity: 13.2%
Cash (mil): $21
Current ratio: 1.41
Long-term debt (mil): $950
Number of shares (mil): 63
Dividends:
1989 average yield: 2.3%
1989 payout: 25.5%
Market value (mil): $2,326

Stock Price History high/low 1980-89
50 45 40 35 30 25 20 15 10 5 0

RANKINGS

110th in *Fortune* 500 Industrial Cos.
286th in *Fortune* Global 500 Industrial Cos.
191st in *Forbes* Sales 500
315th in *Business Week* 1000
966th in *Business Week* Global 1000

COMPETITION

Boise Cascade
Champion International
Commerce Clearing House
Dow Jones
Georgia-Pacific
International Paper
James River
Kimberly-Clark
Knight-Ridder
McGraw-Hill
Paramount
Reuters
Scott
Weyerhaeuser

MELLON BANK CORPORATION

OVERVIEW

Mellon Bank is the 18th largest US (2nd in Pennsylvania) commercial banking organization, with assets of $31.5 billion. Mellon has 334 domestic banking branches.

Mellon strives for balance in 3 basic lines of business: wholesale and middle-market banking, retail banking, and service products. Geographically, its retail and middle-market business is strong in Pennsylvania, Delaware, and Maryland, and its wholesale and service businesses are primarily national with some international business.

Wholesale and middle-market banking, with $83 million in 1989 revenues, focuses on serving selected industries (government and health care). Retail banking, with $106 million in revenues, includes banking and credit card services for consumers and small businesses.

The 3rd sector, service products, contributed $151 million to revenues and includes trust and investment services and a leading cash management service.

The Mellon family, who control 12% of the bank's stock, are major philanthropists. The bank, too, is generous, contributing $7 million to community and charitable activities in 1989. Mellon employees also contributed nearly $5 million in money and time to charitable efforts.

NYSE symbol: MEL
Incorporated: Pennsylvania, 1971
Fiscal year ends: December 31

WHO

Chairman, President, and CEO: Frank V. Cahouet, age 57, $1,119,545 pay
VC Service Products: W. Keith Smith, age 55, $457,930 pay
VC and Chief Credit Officer: Richard H. Daniel, age 62, $381,850 pay
VC Middle Market Banking: Thomas F. Donovan, age 56, $375,000 pay
VC Credit Policy: David L. Eyles, age 50
VC Retail Banking: Richard A. Gaugh, age 49
VC Administration: Martin G. McGuinn, age 47
VC Wholesale Banking: Jeffrey L. Morby, age 52
EVP and CFO: Steven G. Elliott, age 43
Auditors: KPMG Peat Marwick
Employees: 16,500

WHEN

Judge Thomas Mellon founded T. Mellon and Sons in 1869. In 1882 at age 69, the judge turned over control of the bank to his son, Andrew, who 5 years later gave half of it to his brother Richard B. In 1902 T. Mellon and Sons became a national bank named Mellon National Bank.

Under Andrew Mellon the bank was instrumental in financing Pittsburgh businesses. Mellon investments by Andrew and Richard included Alcoa, Westinghouse, Bethlehem Steel, Pullman, Pittsburgh Coal, Pittsburgh Plate Glass, Koppers, and Carborundum. The bank's most successful investment was in an oil company that became Gulf Oil.

In 1921 Andrew went to Washington to serve as Secretary of Treasury under Presidents Harding, Coolidge, and Hoover. Richard B. assumed the presidency of Mellon National Bank. About a year before Andrew left, Richard B.'s son Richard K. Mellon had joined the bank as a messenger.

In anticipation of branch banking becoming federal law, Richard B. in 1929 formed Mellbank, a holding company of various banks in which the Mellons had a stake. Richard K. was assigned to manage Mellbank.

Richard B. died at the age of 75, and a few months later in 1934 Richard K. was elected president of Mellon National Bank. In 1946 Mellon merged with Union Trust Company to form Mellon National Bank & Trust. In 1967 Richard K. became honorary chairman, ending the Mellon family's near-century-long management of the bank. In 1972 the bank created a holding company, Mellon National Corporation (current name adopted 1984).

In 1983 under CEO J. David Barnes, the bank acquired Girard Bank and renamed the Philadelphia bank Mellon Bank East. Mellon, set back by loans to oil companies, the third world, and real estate developers, reported the first loss in its history, $60 million for the first quarter of 1987. Barnes followed this by announcing a dividend cut. The board and the Mellon family, who still owned 13.6% of the stock, forced his resignation. Two months later Frank V. Cahouet became CEO.

Cahouet is credited with turning the bank around. He froze wages and increased loan-loss reserves. In 1988 Cahouet spun off the worst of the real estate loans into a new affiliate, Grant Street National Bank. In 1989 Mellon Bank in Philadelphia bought 54 branches of PSFS, a savings institution. Returning to its local and regional focus, Mellon Bank enters the 1990s stronger financially than in 1987.

WHERE

HQ: One Mellon Bank Center, Pittsburgh, PA 15258
Phone: 412-787-5534
FAX: 412-234-6265

Mellon has operations in 20 states and 8 foreign countries.

WHAT

	1989 Net Income	
	$ mil	% of total
Wholesale banking	83	46
Retail banking	106	59
Service products	151	83
Real estate banking	(96)	(53)
LDC debt	(90)	(50)
Other	27	15
Total	**181**	**100**

Financial Services
Capital markets products
Corporate banking
Credit cards
Data processing services
Deposit accounts
Leasing
Money market accounts
Money transfer
Real estate loans
Trust and investment management

HOW MUCH

	9 Yr. Growth	1980	1981	1982	1983	1984	1985	1986	1987	1988	1989
Sales ($ mil)	9.5%	1,589	2,227	2,340	2,520	3,062	3,222	3,457	3,321	3,269	3,607
Net income ($ mil)	5.4%	112	116	134	184	159	202	183	(844)	(65)	181
Income as % of sales	—	7.1%	5.2%	5.7%	7.3%	5.2%	6.3%	5.3%	(25.4%)	(2.0%)	5.0%
Earnings per share ($)	(5.9%)	5.73	5.88	6.83	7.44	5.64	7.13	6.14	(31.19)	(3.65)	3.33
Stock price – high ($)	—	32.25	40.00	44.75	56.50	52.00	56.50	72.50	58.00	33.25	38.13
Stock price – low ($)	—	22.00	30.88	27.50	36.75	33.50	44.50	51.88	25.13	22.75	25.00
Stock price – close ($)	(1.1%)	31.75	36.75	37.88	51.00	46.75	52.13	55.38	27.00	25.00	28.63
P/E – high	—	6	7	7	8	9	8	12	—	—	11
P/E – low	—	4	5	4	5	6	6	8	—	—	8
Dividends per share ($)	(3.3%)	1.89	2.09	2.24	2.44	2.60	2.68	2.76	1.74	1.40	1.40
Book value per share ($)	(3.5%)	45.94	49.69	54.19	53.62	56.21	60.39	63.68	30.57	30.14	33.47

1989 Year End:
Debt ratio: 57.8%
Return on equity: 10.5%
Cash (mil): $4,908
Assets (mil): $31,467
Long-term debt (mil): $1,799
Number of shares (mil): 36
Dividends:
1989 average yield: 4.9%
1989 payout: 42.0%
Market value (mil): $1,044

Stock Price History high/low 1980-89

RANKINGS

18th in *Fortune* 100 Commercial Banking Cos.
230th in *Forbes* Sales 500
564th in *Business Week* 1000

COMPETITION

Bank of Boston	Citicorp
Bank of New England	First Chicago
Bank of New York	First Fidelity
BankAmerica	Manufacturers Hanover
Bankers Trust	J.P. Morgan
Chase Manhattan	PNC Financial
Chemical Banking	Other money center banks

MELVILLE CORPORATION

OVERVIEW

The Melville Corporation operates 15 chains of specialty retail stores and is one of the few major American retailers to operate stores profitably in diverse product lines, including apparel, footwear, prescription drugs, toys, and household furnishings. The company has started new chains from scratch and bought small chains with national potential, usually keeping and supporting acquired management talent. Melville leases store space primarily in regional malls and strip shopping centers. The company manufactures men's shoes in one factory and furniture in 5 factories.

Melville has a compounded annual growth rate of 16% in sales over the past 25 years. The company has accomplished its growth while maintaining a strong financial position, with long-term debt accounting for only 19% of capitalization. Dividends have been declared for 74 consecutive years. Melville adopted an employee stock ownership plan in 1989, which has put about 6% of the company's stock into the hands of its employees.

NYSE symbol: MES
Incorporated: New York, 1914
Fiscal year ends: December 31

WHO

Chairman, President, and CEO: Stanley P. Goldstein, age 55, $1,189,300 pay
EVP: Michael A. Friedheim, age 46, $722,500 pay
EVP and CFO: Robert D. Huth, age 44, $619,300 pay
VP: Jerald S. Politzer, $424,500 pay
Auditors: KPMG Peat Marwick
Employees: 100,541

WHEN

In 1892 shoe supplier Frank Melville took over 3 New York shoe stores when their owner left town owing him money, forming Melville Shoe. During WWI Ward Melville, Frank's son and vice-president of the firm, served in the Quartermaster Corps' shoe and leather division under shoe manufacturer J. Frank McElwain. The 2 men devised the merchandising scheme of mass-producing shoes for distribution through a chain of low-price stores. Melville opened the first of its Thom McAn (from the name of a Scottish professional golfer) stores, for which McElwain provided the shoes, in New York in 1922. There were 370 stores in the chain by 1927.

By 1931 Melville operated 476 shoe stores under the names John Ward, Thom McAn, Rival, and Courdaye and had income of $1.2 million on sales of over $26 million. In 1939 Melville bought the McElwain factory, consolidating production and distribution into one corporation. By 1958 Melville was operating 1,034 stores, 796 of them Thom McAn stores, but profits were declining because of changes in customer tastes and shifting populations.

Melville met the challenge of change, moving stores from urban areas to the suburbs and adding more fashionable merchandise to existing lines. The company's Meldisco division began leasing space for shoe sales operations in S.S. Kresge's K mart discount department stores in 1961. In 1968 the company launched its Chess King (young men's apparel) and Foxwood (young women's apparel) stores. Melville bought the Consumer Value Stores chain (CVS; drugstores) in 1969.

In 1975 S.S. Kresge demanded a 49% equity interest in all Meldisco subsidiaries operating in K mart stores. Melville accepted the terms of the new agreement rather than lose one of its largest divisions. The company purchased Marshalls, Inc. (discount department stores, 1976), Mack Drug (1977), Kay-Bee Toy and Hobby Shops (1981), Wilsons House of Suede (1982), Freddy's (deep-discount drugstores, 1984), Prints Plus (1985), This End Up Furniture (1985) and Accessory Lady (1987) and sold Foxmoor (1985).

Chairman and CEO Francis Rooney was succeeded by Stanley Goldstein in 1987. Shortly thereafter the Meldisco division signed an agreement (1988) to operate shoe outlets in Payless drugstores.

In 1990 Melville acquired the 490-store Peoples Drug chain, making Melville the 5th largest drugstore operator in the US.

The recent acquisition of Circus World mall-based toy stores makes Melville one of the largest toy retailers in the US.

WHERE

HQ: One Theall Rd., Rye, NY 10580
Phone: 914-925-4000
FAX: 914-925-4026

Melville has stores in all 50 states, the District of Columbia, Puerto Rico, and the US Virgin Islands.

WHAT

	1989 Sales		1989 Operating Income	
	$ mil	% of total	$ mil	% of total
Footwear	1,698	22	148	22
Drugstores	2,111	28	166	24
Apparel	2,713	36	265	39
Toys & household furnishings	1,032	14	100	15
Adjustments	—	—	(27)	—
Total	**7,554**	**100**	**652**	**100**

	No. of Stores
Apparel	
Accessory Lady	74
Chess King	546
Marshalls	347
Wilsons	503
Drugstores	
CVS	789
Freddy's	25
Peoples	490
Footwear	
Fan Club	77
Meldisco	2,441
Thom McAn	913
Toys & Household Furnishings	
Circus World	330
Kay-Bee	777
Linens 'n Things	126
Prints Plus	79
This End Up	233
Total	**7,750**

RANKINGS

14th in *Fortune* 50 Retailing Cos.
105th in *Forbes* Sales 500
126th in *Business Week* 1000
342nd in *Business Week* Global 1000

COMPETITION

American Stores
Dayton Hudson
General Cinema
INTERCO
Jack Eckerd
The Limited
Longs
May Department Stores
Rite Aid
Toys "R" Us
United States Shoe
Walgreen
Woolworth
Discount and department stores

HOW MUCH

	9 Yr. Growth	1980	1981	1982	1983	1984	1985	1986	1987	1988	1989
Sales ($ mil)	14.0%	2,332	2,761	3,262	3,923	4,423	4,775	5,262	5,930	6,780	7,554
Net income ($ mil)	14.8%	115	136	142	176	190	220	238	285	355	398
Income as % of sales	—	4.9%	4.9%	4.4%	4.5%	4.3%	4.6%	4.5%	4.8%	5.2%	5.3%
Earnings per share ($)	13.4%	1.14	1.32	1.37	1.68	1.80	2.04	2.20	2.63	3.26	3.52
Stock price – high ($)	—	10.47	12.00	19.13	23.81	22.75	26.44	36.88	42.00	38.31	53.63
Stock price – low ($)	—	5.88	8.78	9.22	15.19	15.38	17.63	24.63	22.13	26.63	36.88
Stock price – close ($)	19.9%	8.69	9.44	17.69	17.44	18.63	25.25	27.00	26.50	37.19	44.63
P/E – high	—	9	9	14	14	13	13	17	16	12	15
P/E – low	—	5	7	7	9	9	9	11	8	8	10
Dividends per share ($)	14.0%	0.40	0.45	0.51	0.55	0.66	0.72	0.78	0.88	1.05	1.30
Book value per share ($)	10.5%	5.02	5.87	6.73	7.89	9.03	10.20	11.64	13.41	15.65	12.28

1989 Year End:
Debt ratio: 19.4%
Return on equity: 25.2%
Cash (mil): $369
Current ratio: 2.19
Long-term debt (mil): $390
Number of shares (mil): 103
Dividends:
1989 average yield: 2.9%
1989 payout: 36.9%
Market value (mil): $4,582

Stock Price History high/low 1980-89

MERCANTILE STORES COMPANY, INC.

OVERVIEW

With annual sales of over $2 billion, Mercantile Stores is one of the nation's most consistently profitable and least well-known major retailers. The company operates 12 regional department store chains from its headquarters outside Cincinnati, recently relocated from New York. The best-known and largest of these chains include McAlpin's in Cincinnati, The Jones Store in Kansas City, Joslin's in Denver, and Gayfer's in the South. Most of the company's other stores are in smaller cities.

While other major department store organizations have either gone on acquisition sprees (May Department Stores, Dillard's) or been burdened by heavy debt (Campeau, Macy's), Mercantile has not made an acquisition since 1955 and operates with very little debt.

The company has prospered as the result of a unique merchandising strategy and extremely stable management and control. It has been effectively controlled by South Carolina's textile-producing Milliken family since after WWI; today, they control almost 44% of the stock. They have supported a stable management, encouraged by bonuses and stock options.

Mercantile enters the 1990s with its strategies well established, seemingly oblivious to the turmoil in the retail industry. The company plans to continue to build 2 to 3 new stores a year for its existing chains.

WHEN

H. B. Claflin Company, a large New York dry goods wholesaler, expanded into retailing around the turn of the century with the acquisitions of such major names as Lord & Taylor of New York and Hahne's of Newark. In 1914 the company collapsed into bankruptcy and eventually emerged as 2 creditor-controlled firms: Associated Dry Goods got Lord & Taylor and other premier, primarily northeastern names, while Mercantile Stores got the smaller and less attractive names. Mercantile's lead creditor was Milliken & Company, the textile giant. While Associated became part of May Department Stores Company in 1986, Mercantile has remained an independent public company under Milliken control.

With weak positions in their markets, the company's divisions barely survived the Great Depression. The chief executive ordered them to sell off inventory to raise cash but did it in person because he didn't trust the telephone. After WWII, management adopted a 2-part merchandising strategy. First, local buyers selected fashion merchandise to remain in tune with local markets, as did other department stores. Second, centralized buyers in New York bought commodity items such as sheets and socks to minimize costs and passed savings on to the customer (a strategy similar to that of Sears and Penney). The company also established a tradition of excellent expense control. These traditions remain in place at Mercantile today.

Mercantile acquired the Glass Block in Duluth (1944) and de Lendrecie's in Fargo (1955), the company's most recent acquisitions.

In the 1980s Mercantile's sales doubled and earnings tripled. The company has consistently been in or near the top of the industry in sales per square foot and profit margin. In conjunction with Milliken, Mercantile is experimenting with quick-response inventory replenishment, in which sales data are sent immediately and directly to manufacturers.

The company prides itself on employee longevity; few key people are lost to competitors and even fewer are hired from outside the company. Mercantile has recently witnessed intensified competition from Dillard's, which seems to buy Mercantile's competitors after Mercantile has taken away much of their business. Nevertheless, nothing in the company's past indicates that Mercantile will depart from one of the most consistent long-term strategies in retailing.

HOW MUCH

	9 Yr. Growth	1980	1981	1982	1983	1984	1985	1986	1987	1988	1989
Sales ($ mil)	8.6%	1,112	1,276	1,434	1,628	1,711	1,883	2,032	2,175	2,286	2,337
Net income ($ mil)	13.3%	42	58	70	83	85	102	111	130	144	130
Income as % of sales	—	3.8%	4.5%	4.9%	5.1%	5.0%	5.4%	5.5%	6.0%	6.3%	5.6%
Earnings per share ($)	13.3%	1.15	1.57	1.90	2.26	2.30	2.78	3.02	3.52	3.92	3.54
Stock price – high ($)	—	6.52	9.12	19.52	30.20	23.60	31.25	46.80	53.38	46.50	50.50
Stock price – low ($)	—	4.92	5.48	8.56	15.84	16.10	21.80	29.10	30.63	34.75	37.50
Stock price – close ($)	24.5%	5.44	8.94	18.52	22.00	22.60	31.25	38.30	37.00	42.75	39.13
P/E – high	—	6	6	10	13	10	11	16	15	12	14
P/E – low	—	4	3	5	7	7	8	10	9	9	11
Dividends per share ($)	16.2%	0.23	0.23	0.32	0.40	0.46	0.51	0.58	0.68	0.78	0.89
Book value per share ($)	13.2%	9.56	10.77	12.43	14.29	16.13	18.40	20.84	23.68	26.62	29.24

1989 Year End:
Debt ratio: 15.6%
Return on equity: 12.7%
Cash (mil): $71
Current ratio: 4.65
Long-term debt (mil): $199
Number of shares (mil): 37
Dividends:
1989 average yield: 2.3%
1989 payout: 25.1%
Market value (mil): $1,442

NYSE symbol: MST
Incorporated: Delaware, 1919
Fiscal year ends: January 31

WHO

Chairman and CEO: David R. Huhn, age 52, $575,207 pay
VC: James C. Lovell, age 63, $702,000 pay
President and COO: Roger D. Ciskie, age 49, $348,634 pay
VP, Treasurer, and CFO: David L. Nichols, age 48, $276,455 pay
Auditors: Arthur Andersen & Co.
Employees: 21,000

WHERE

HQ: 9450 Seward Rd., Fairfield, OH 45014
Phone: 513-860-8000
FAX: 513-860-8060

Mercantile operates 78 department stores and 2 specialty stores under 12 different chain names in 16 states. A buying office is maintained in New York City.

WHAT

Department Store Chains
Bacons
  Kentucky and Indiana
Castner Knott
  Tennessee, Kentucky, and Alabama
de Lendrecie's
  North Dakota
Gayfer's
  Alabama, Florida, Mississippi, and Georgia
Glass Block
  Minnesota
Hennessys
  Montana
J.B. White
  Georgia and South Carolina
The Jones Store Co.
  Missouri and Kansas
Joslin's
  Colorado and Wyoming
Lion
  Ohio
McAlpin's
  Ohio and Kentucky
Root's
  Indiana

Mercantile also operates 14 freestanding beauty salons.

RANKINGS

45th in *Fortune* 50 Retailing Cos.
356th in *Forbes* Sales 500
417th in *Business Week* 1000

COMPETITION

Campeau
Carter Hawley Hale
Dayton Hudson
Dillard
May Department Stores
J. C. Penney
Discount and specialty stores

MERCK & CO., INC.

OVERVIEW

Merck is the world leader in prescription drug sales, with almost 5% of the market. The company has 18 products that annually yield over $100 million each.

Merck also makes animal health products, pesticides, and specialty chemicals and owns a poultry breeding operation. The company's proportion of foreign sales (46%) is one of the highest of US drug firms.

Merck's R&D expenditures are the highest in the industry, totaling $4.5 billion in the last 10 years (more than 11% of sales in 1989). Products under development include the first chicken pox vaccine and drugs to treat AIDS, prostate problems, and asthma, and to reduce the complications of diabetes. Merck's AIDS research includes work on a vaccine with the biotech firm Repligen.

A 1990 *Fortune* survey rated Merck as the most admired company in the US, and *Business Week* called Merck one of the best managed and most innovative. Mevacor, Merck's cholesterol-lowering drug, was selected as top product of 1989 by *Medical Advertising News*.

NYSE symbol: MRK
Incorporated: New Jersey, 1927
Fiscal year ends: December 31

WHO

Chairman, President, and CEO: P. Roy Vagelos, age 60, $2,340,383 pay
VC: John E. Lyons, age 63, $1,377,452 pay
SVP: Abraham E. Cohen, age 53, $932,200 pay
SVP: Douglas J. MacMaster, age 59, $879,153 pay
SVP and CFO: Francis H. Spiegel, Jr., age 54
Auditors: Arthur Andersen & Co.
Employees: 34,400

WHEN

Merck was started in 1887 when chemist Theodore Weicker came to the US from Germany to set up an American branch of E. Merck AG of Germany. George Merck (grandson of the German company's founder) came in 1891 and entered into a partnership with Weicker. At first the firm imported and sold drugs and chemicals from Germany, but in 1903 it opened a plant in Rahway, New Jersey, to manufacture alkaloids. Weicker sold out to Merck in 1904 and bought a controlling interest in competitor Squibb. During WWI Merck gave the US government the 80% of company stock owned by family in Germany (George kept his shares). After the war the stock was sold to the public.

The company merged in 1927 with Powers-Weightman-Rosengarten of Philadelphia (major product, the antimalarial quinine). At its first research laboratory, established in 1933, Merck scientists did pioneering work on vitamin B-12 and developed the first steroid (cortisone, 1944). Five Merck scientists received Nobel prizes in the 1940s and 1950s. Unfortunately the company was also a major producer of DES (diethylstilbestrol, widely used until 1971, suspected of causing cancer in children of women who used it during pregnancy) and is still involved in lawsuits over the drug. In 1953 Merck merged with Sharp & Dohme of Philadelphia, bringing together complementary lines of pharmaceuticals and Sharp & Dohme's strong sales force.

Merck introduced Diuril (antihypertensive) in 1958 and other drugs in the early 1960s (Indocin, Aldomet), but for nearly 10 years there were few new drugs. John Horan, who took over in 1976, accelerated R&D in an effort to create new products. By the late 1970s the company had produced Clinoril (antiarthritic), Flexeril (muscle relaxant), and Timoptic (for glaucoma).

Biochemist Roy Vagelos, current chairman, who joined Merck in 1976 as head of research and became CEO in 1985, has continued the commitment to R&D. The company introduced 10 major new drugs in the 1980s, including Mevacor for treating high cholesterol and Vasotec for high blood pressure. In 1983 Merck bought half of the Japanese drug company Banyu.

To gain access to new markets, the company has formed alliances with other drug companies. In January 1990 Merck bought the nonprescription drug segment of ICI Americas (includes Mylanta) and will market the products in a joint venture with Johnson & Johnson. Also Merck and Du Pont formed a joint venture to market all of Du Pont's drugs worldwide and some of Merck's drugs overseas.

WHERE

HQ: PO Box 2000, Rahway, NJ 07065
Phone: 201-594-4000
FAX: 201-594-4662

Merck has 46 manufacturing plants in 18 countries, 17 research labs in 7 countries, and 10 experimental farms in 6 countries.

	1989 Sales		1989 Operating Income	
	$ mil	% of total	$ mil	% of total
US	3,488	54	1,558	69
OECD	2,901	44	722	32
Other foreign	162	2	(13)	(1)
Adjustments	—	—	(31)	—
Total	**6,551**	**100**	**2,236**	**100**

WHAT

	1989 Sales		1989 Operating Income	
	$ mil	% of total	$ mil	% of total
Human & animal health	6,059	92	2,156	97
Specialty chemicals	492	8	59	3
Adjustments	—	—	21	—
Total	**6,551**	**100**	**2,236**	**100**

Major Pharmaceuticals
Analgesic (Clinoril, Indocin)
Animal medicines (Ivomec, Heartgard-30)
Antibiotics (Primaxin, Mefoxin)
Antiglaucoma (Timoptic)
Anti-Parkinson (Sinemet)
Antiulcer (Pepcid)
Cardiovascular (Mevacor, Vasotec)
Muscle relaxant (Flexeril)
Vaccines (M-M-R II, Recombivax HB)

HOW MUCH

	9 Yr. Growth	1980	1981	1982	1983	1984	1985	1986	1987	1988	1989
Sales ($ mil)	10.2%	2,734	2,929	3,063	3,246	3,560	3,548	4,129	5,061	5,940	6,551
Net income ($ mil)	15.3%	415	398	415	451	493	540	676	906	1,207	1,495
Income as % of sales	—	15.2%	13.6%	13.6%	13.9%	13.8%	15.2%	16.4%	17.9%	20.3%	22.8%
Earnings per share ($)	16.8%	0.92	0.89	0.94	1.02	1.12	1.26	1.62	2.19	3.02	3.74
Stock price – high ($)	—	14.33	17.17	14.71	17.44	16.25	22.96	43.17	74.33	59.63	80.75
Stock price – low ($)	—	9.71	12.71	10.67	13.63	13.04	15.04	22.38	40.67	48.00	56.25
Stock price – close ($)	20.8%	14.13	14.13	14.10	15.06	15.67	22.83	41.29	52.83	57.75	77.50
P/E – high	—	16	19	16	17	15	18	27	34	20	22
P/E – low	—	11	14	11	13	12	12	14	19	16	15
Dividends per share ($)	17.7%	0.40	0.44	0.47	0.48	0.51	0.55	0.67	0.90	1.38	1.72
Book value per share ($)	8.8%	4.16	4.51	4.97	5.49	5.88	6.26	6.28	5.37	7.20	8.90

1989 Year End:
Debt ratio: 3.2%
Return on equity: 46.5%
Cash (mil): $1,144
Current ratio: 1.79
Long-term debt (mil): $118
Number of shares (mil): 395
Dividends:
1989 average yield: 2.2%
1989 payout: 46.0%
Market value (mil): $30,644

Stock Price History high/low 1980-89

RANKINGS

70th in *Fortune* 500 Industrial Cos.
193rd in *Fortune* Global 500 Industrial Cos.
30th in *Fortune* 50 Exporters
127th in *Forbes* Sales 500
7th in *Business Week* 1000
18th in *Business Week* Global 1000

COMPETITION

Abbott Labs
American Cyanamid
American Home Products
Bayer
Bristol-Myers Squibb
Dow Chemical
Eli Lilly
Genentech
Glaxo
Hoechst
Johnson & Johnson
Monsanto
Pfizer
Procter & Gamble
Rhône-Poulenc
Roche Holding
Schering-Plough
SmithKline Beecham
Upjohn
Warner-Lambert

MERRILL LYNCH & CO., INC.

OVERVIEW

Merrill Lynch & Co., Inc., is the holding company for the world's largest securities brokerage firm, Merrill Lynch, Pierce, Fenner & Smith, with more than 10,000 brokers. Merrill's 470 branch offices had more than 7.5 million customer accounts at the end of 1989.

Merrill Lynch, with $334 billion in assets at the end of 1989, is the largest US securities firm in consumer (retail) markets. This includes Merrill Lynch mutual funds, with $97 billion in assets. The firm's 1.3 million Cash Management Accounts totaled more than $214 billion at the end of 1989.

In capital markets the company is the world leader in total debt (bonds) and equity (stocks) underwritings. In 1989 Merrill Lynch was an advisor or financier in 147 merger and acquisition transactions valued at more than $88 billion, including Kohlberg Kravis Roberts's purchase of RJR Nabisco.

In 1989 *Institutional Investor* ranked Merrill Lynch's securities research department as the #1 "All-America Research Team" in its annual survey of investment professionals; the company also suffered its first loss year in more than a decade, largely as the result of restructuring charges.

NYSE symbol: MER
Incorporated: Delaware, 1973
Fiscal year ends: Last Friday in December

WHO

Chairman and CEO: William A. Schreyer, age 62, $1,550,000 pay
President and COO: Daniel P. Tully, age 58, $1,315,000 pay
EVP: Jerome P. Kenney, age 48, $1,100,000 pay
EVP: John L. Steffens, age 48, $1,100,000 pay
EVP and General Counsel: Stephen L. Hammerman, age 51, $725,000 pay
EVP and CFO: Thomas H. Patrick, age 46
Auditors: Deloitte & Touche
Employees: 40,000

WHEN

Wall Street bond salesman Charles Merrill opened his own underwriting firm in 1914 and within 6 months took on Edmund Lynch as a partner. In the 1920s Merrill profited from selling stock for new grocery companies, including Safeway. Merrill retired in 1930 and sold the business to E. A. Pierce, the largest stockbroker on Wall Street. In 1940 Merrill returned to the firm, and the next year it acquired Fenner & Beane (New Orleans), adopting the name Merrill Lynch, Pierce, Fenner & Beane.

In the post-WWII years Merrill Lynch focused on small individual investors as clients. The firm introduced the idea of stockbrokers being paid a salary so investors would not think the broker was only interested in trading stocks to earn commissions.

Winthrop Smith, a partner who ran the firm after Merrill's death in 1956, had his name added to the firm in 1958. That same year the partnership became a corporation (Merrill Lynch, Pierce, Fenner & Smith). Merrill Lynch expanded nationwide, following the individual investors as the US population expanded to the South and the West.

In the late 1960s Merrill Lynch continued to make a profit while more than 100 stock brokerage firms went out of business. Donald Regan, who later served as President Ronald Reagan's treasury secretary and chief of staff, became chairman in 1971. Merrill Lynch became part of Merrill Lynch & Co., Inc., a holding company, in 1973.

In 1977 under Regan, Merrill Lynch introduced an innovative product for which it received a patent, the Cash Management Account (CMA), which combines a money-market fund account with check writing and a Visa card provided by Merrill Lynch Bank & Trust and Banc One.

While keeping its strong individual customer base in the 1980s, the company also became #1 in global underwriting of stocks and debt securities. Credited with the company's growth in investment banking is William Schreyer, chairman since 1985, who expanded the firm's activities in trading, underwriting, and advising corporations in mergers and acquisitions.

Schreyer had to restructure the firm in the late 1980s because of poor earnings. In the 4th quarter of 1989, the company took a $470 million restructuring charge to pay for consolidating office space, shutting down some less profitable operations, and laying off employees (1,000 in 1989); it expects to lay off another 2,000 in 1990. Because of the restructuring charge, Merrill Lynch had a $217 million loss in 1989 despite record revenues of $11.3 billion.

WHERE

HQ: World Financial Center, North Tower, 250 Vesey St., New York, NY 10281
Phone: 212-449-1000
FAX: 212-608-1245

Merrill Lynch operates in the US and in 32 foreign countries.

	1989 Sales		1989 Pretax Income	
	$ mil	% of total	$ mil	% of total
US	9,685	85	(131)	—
Foreign	1,650	15	(27)	—
Total	**11,335**	**100**	**(158)**	**—**

WHAT

	1989 Sales		1989 Pretax Income	
	$ mil	% of total	$ mil	% of total
Insurance	554	5	55	—
Investment & financing svcs.	10,781	95	(213)	—
Total	**11,335**	**100**	**(158)**	**—**

Financial Services
Capital Builder Accounts
Cash Management Accounts
Commodity futures
Government and municipal securities
Investment banking and underwriting
Mutual funds
Securities and economic research
Securities brokerage

HOW MUCH

	9 Yr. Growth	1980	1981	1982	1983	1984	1985	1986	1987	1988	1989
Sales ($ mil)	15.8%	3,022	4,038	5,026	5,687	5,911	7,117	9,475	11,036	10,547	11,335
Net income ($ mil)	—	203	203	309	230	95	224	469	391	463	(217)
Income as % of sales	—	6.7%	5.0%	6.1%	4.0%	1.6%	3.2%	5.0%	3.5%	4.4%	(1.9%)
Earnings per share ($)	—	2.75	2.57	3.74	2.59	1.03	2.21	4.28	3.51	4.21	(2.35)
Stock price – high ($)	—	19.63	22.13	35.63	56.50	36.38	36.75	43.75	46.75	28.38	36.75
Stock price – low ($)	—	7.75	14.31	10.50	27.50	22.00	25.50	32.38	19.50	22.13	23.50
Stock price – close ($)	3.9%	18.56	16.56	30.00	32.00	27.00	34.38	36.50	22.38	24.00	26.25
P/E – high	—	7	9	10	22	35	17	10	13	7	—
P/E – low	—	3	6	3	11	21	12	8	6	5	—
Dividends per share ($)	7.5%	0.52	0.60	0.66	0.78	0.80	0.80	0.80	0.95	1.00	1.00
Book value per share ($)	8.9%	13.02	15.04	18.36	21.09	21.64	22.98	26.56	32.54	35.31	28.13

1989 Year End:
Debt ratio: 63.1%
Return on equity: (7.4%)
Cash (mil): $4,360
Assets (mil): $63,942
Long-term debt (mil): $5,400
Number of shares (mil): 112
Dividends:
1989 average yield: 3.8%
1989 payout: (42.6%)
Market value (mil): $2,940

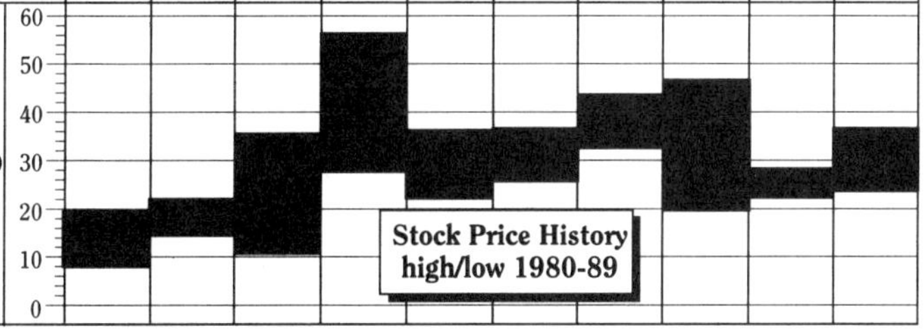

Stock Price History high/low 1980-89

60
50
40
30
20
10
0

RANKINGS

5th in *Fortune* 50 Diversified Financial Cos.
58th in *Forbes* Sales 500
272nd in *Business Week* 1000
822nd in *Business Week* Global 1000

COMPETITION

American Express
Charles Schwab
CS Holding
Deutsche Bank
Goldman Sachs
Kemper
Morgan Stanley
Nomura
Primerica
Prudential
Salomon
Sears
Travelers
Other insurance and financial services companies

METROPOLITAN LIFE INSURANCE COMPANY

OVERVIEW

Metropolitan Life surged ahead of rival Prudential in 1989. Prudential is still larger on the basis of assets, but Metropolitan Life (#2 in assets) had more life insurance in force (total face value of policies) than any other US company. Part of that is the result of record-breaking insurance sales in 1989.

Metropolitan is more than an insurance company, though. It invests in real estate, and its Century 21 subsidiary is the largest real estate franchise sales organization in the world. It operates real estate leasing, appraising, and mortgage banking subsidiaries. In addition it franchises and develops hotels in the Doubletree and Compri chains.

Other subsidiaries, led by State Street Research & Management, offer financing and investment services. International operations account for 12% of total assets.

WHEN

Metropolitan Life's blimp may brandish Snoopy as a WWI flying ace, but the company's origin goes back to another conflict — the Civil War.

Simeon Draper, a New York merchant with political connections, attempted to form National Union Life and Limb Insurance to insure Yankee soldiers, but investors were scared off by reports of heavy battlefield losses. The company stumbled after the war, undergoing a succession of reorganizations and name changes, and emerged in 1868 as Metropolitan Life Insurance.

Sustained in the early years by business from mutual assistance societies for German immigrants, Metropolitan followed upstart Prudential into industrial insurance — policies that paid workers' burial costs. Metropolitan agents combed working-class neighborhoods, collecting small premiums. Until much-needed reform in 1900, if a worker missed a payment, the company pocketed previous premiums and owed the policyholder nothing.

Aggressive sales became a Metropolitan hallmark, and the company imported seasoned British insurance salesmen when it found few prospects at home. The company's success was measured by the growth of the landmark New York City headquarters. The tower at One Madison Avenue was completed in 1909, and its beacon became an advertising symbol: "The Light That Never Fails."

In 1909 the company launched a health education effort, issuing booklets and offering a visiting nurse service for policyholders. Metropolitan became a mutual company, owned by policyholders, in 1915, and in 1917 it offered group insurance. Metropolitan expanded to Canada in 1924.

Led by the conservative Eckers, Frederick Sr. and Jr., from 1929 to 1963, Metropolitan began to change when it dropped industrial insurance in 1964, the year both men died. In 1974 Metropolitan began offering automobile and homeowner insurance.

Under President and CEO John Creedon, Metropolitan flexed its huge financial muscles in the 1980s. It bought Manhattan's Pan Am Building (1981) and State Street Research & Management (1983), founder of the first US mutual fund. Metropolitan bought Century 21 Real Estate (1985) and London-based Albany Life Assurance (1985). Metropolitan also expanded with a joint venture in Spain and a branch in Taiwan (1988). It purchased Allstate's group life and health business (1988).

In 1989, a record year for many of its operations, Metropolitan grew by 4 million policyholders. It purchased the property and casualty insurance portfolio of J. C. Penney Casualty Insurance; United Resources Insurance Services, a provider of retirement and financial programs; and Texas Life Insurance.

Also in 1989 Metropolitan launched a "Family Reunion" program to contact holders of those old industrial insurance policies. Several million of them remain in force, unbeknownst to some policyholders.

Creedon stepped down in 1989, and Chairman Robert Schwartz became CEO, promising to continue diversification and, with a contract that runs until 1995, to keep using Snoopy and the Peanuts gang for commercials.

HOW MUCH

	9 Yr. Growth	1980	1981	1982	1983	1984	1985	1986	1987	1988	1989
Assets ($ bil)	11.2%	49.5	53.3	57.5	74.7	80.6	94.1	105.0	114.2	120.4	128.4
Sales of insurance ($ bil)	22.4%	1.9	2.9	3.1	4.4	6.8	7.4	8.0	9.0	10.8	11.7
Net investment income ($ bil)	9.1%	3.6	4.0	4.5	5.0	5.7	6.8	7.2	7.4	7.7	7.9
Income before benefits, expenses & deductions	13.7%	10.3	10.9	16.3	17.9	21.7	25.8	28.	27.9	30.8	32.6
Insurance in force ($ bil)	9.6%	349.2	393.6	426.6	452.7	475.5	508.8	558.6	622.3	710.2	799.3
Surplus ($ bil)	6.8%	2.1	2.1	2.5	2.5	2.6	2.7	2.8	3.0	3.5	3.8

1989 Company Totals:
Premiums (mil): $15,193
Policyowner dividends (mil): $1,758

Insurance in Force ($ bil) 1980-89

800
700
600
500
400
300
200
100
0

Mutual company
Incorporated: New York, 1868
Fiscal year ends: December 31

WHO

Chairman, President, and CEO: Robert G. Schwartz, age 62
VC: Philip Briggs, age 62
SEVP: Stewart G. Nagler, age 47
SEVP: Robert E. Chappell, Jr., age 53
EVP and General Counsel: Harry P. Kamen, age 57
Auditors: Deloitte & Touche
Employees: 65,000

WHERE

HQ: One Madison Ave., New York, NY 10010
Phone: 212-578-2211
FAX: 212-685-1224 (Human Resources)

Metropolitan Life and its affiliated companies operate in the US, Canada, Europe, Australia, New Zealand, and Asia.

WHAT

US Affiliates

Insurance
MetLife Security Insurance Cos.
Metropolitan Insurance and Annuity Co.
Metropolitan Property and Casualty Insurance Co.
Metropolitan Reinsurance Co.
Metropolitan Tower Life Insurance Co.
Texas Life Insurance Co.

Financing & Investment
MetLife Capital Corp.
MetLife Capital Credit Corp.
MetLife Funding, Inc.
MetLife Securities, Inc.
MetLife-State Street Investment Services, Inc.
State Street Research & Management Co.

Real Estate
Century 21 Real Estate Corp.
Cross & Brown Co.
Farmers National Co.
Metmor Financial, Inc.

Health Care
Corporate Health Strategies, Inc.
MetLife HealthCare Management Corp.

Hotels
MetHotels, Inc. (Compri, Doubletree)

RANKINGS

2nd in *Fortune* 50 Life Insurance Cos.

COMPETITION

Aetna
AIG
Blue Cross
GEICO
General RE
ITT
John Hancock
Kemper
Lloyd's of London
Loews
Massachusetts Mutual
New York Life
Northwestern Mutual
Prudential
Sears
State Farm
Tokio Marine & Fire
Travelers
Other insurance companies
Other investment management companies
Real estate companies
Hotel companies

MICHELIN

OVERVIEW

With the 1989 purchase of Uniroyal Goodrich, Michelin claimed the #1 position in the world tire market. The French tiremaker has plants in Europe, North and South America, Africa, and Asia and produces natural rubber in Africa and Brazil. The company is organized as a *société en commandité par actions*, a French partnership allowing outside shareholdings. The Michelin family controls the company, permitting management to forfeit short-term profit in favor of long-term investment.

Michelin has announced its expectation of 3 to 4 difficult years resulting from intense competition, aggressive expansion plans, and the $1.5 billion Uniroyal Goodrich acquisition. The Uniroyal purchase gives Michelin an important position in the US aftermarket, ties to General Motors, and added US production capacity. However, Uniroyal's recent past has been troubled, and Michelin incurred substantial debt in connection with the acquisition.

WHEN

After dabbling in the manufacture of rubber balls, Edouard Daubrée and Aristide Barbier formed a partnership in Clermont-Ferrand, France, in 1863 and entered the rubber business in earnest. Both founders died shortly afterward and the company struggled. In 1866 the Barbier family asked André Michelin, a successful businessman who had married into the family, to take over. Unable to devote full time to the venture, André persuaded his brother, Edouard, a Paris artist, to run the company, renamed Michelin in 1889.

In 1889 Edouard noticed the riding comfort afforded by pneumatic (air-filled) tires. The tires were experimental at the time, glued to the rims, and required several hours to replace. In 1891 Edouard made a bicycle tire with a detachable bolt that allowed replacement in 15 minutes.

The Michelin brothers promoted their removable tires by persuading cyclists to use them in long-distance races in which punctures were likely. They once threw nails on the route to prove their point. The brothers demonstrated that pneumatic tires could work on cars in an auto race in 1895. In 1898 André commented that a stack of tires would look like a man if it had arms, a notion that led to "Bib," the Michelin Man. André also launched the Michelin Guide for auto tourists in 1900.

Michelin opened a sales office in London (1905) and began production in Italy (1906) and Milltown, New Jersey (1908). The company made airplanes during WWI. Michelin inventions included detachable rims and, consequently, spare tires (1906), tubeless tires (1930), treads (1934), and low-profile (squat, like today's) tires (1937). During the Great Depression Michelin closed the Milltown plant and accepted a stake in Citroen, later converted into a 6.1% interest in Peugeot, in lieu of payment for tires. André Michelin died in 1931, Edouard in 1940.

Michelin received a patent for radial tires in 1946. Expansion was largely confined to Europe in the 1950s. Michelin grew internationally in the 1960s, unchallenged in radials. In 1966 the company's US position was enhanced by Ford's decision to put Michelin radials on its 1968 Lincoln Continental MKIII and Sears's decision to sell Michelins. By 1970 Michelin was the world's #4 tiremaker.

Michelin enjoyed worldwide growth in radial sales in the 1970s. The company spent heavily on global expansion and started production in Greenville, South Carolina, in 1975. Michelin was the #2 tiremaker by 1980, but recession and expansion-related debt service induced losses of $1.5 billion between 1980 and 1984. Michelin rebounded and opened plants and sales companies in Asia. In 1989 the company bought Uniroyal Goodrich, the product of a merger of 2 US tire companies founded in the late 1800s.

HOW MUCH

$=FF5.78 (Dec. 31, 1989)	9 Yr. Growth	1980	1981	1982	1983	1984	1985	1986	1987	1988	1989
Sales (FF mil)	7.1%	29,802	33,653	36,610	41,084	44,382	46,641	46,328	46,936	51,280	55,256
Net income (FF mil)**	14.0%	815	(290)	(4,165)	(2,145)	(2,242)	1,040	1,908	2,647	3,591	2,653
Income as % of sales	—	2.7%	(0.9%)	(11.4%)	(5.2%)	(5.1%)	2.2%	4.1%	5.6%	5.0%	4.8%
Earnings per share (FF)***	1.6%	19	(9)	(101)	(52)	(55)	19	28	34	29	22
Stock price – high (FF)*	—	93	87	84	98	108	165	357	384	226	212
Stock price – low (FF)*	—	65	61	58	71	73	74	173	169	136	152
Stock price – close (FF)*	10.9%	66	62	63	80	75	165	255	178	197	168
P/E – high*	—	5	—	—	—	—	9	13	11	8	10
P/E – low*	—	3	—	—	—	—	4	6	5	5	7
Dividends per share (FF)*	3.5%	3.10	3.35	1.68	—	—	—	1.80	2.00	2.20	2.25
Book value per share (FF)	(5.9%)	290	319	324	267	187	140	138	165	173	168

1989 Year End:
Debt ratio: 54.0%
Return on equity: 12.9%
Cash (mil): FF10,796
Long-term debt (mil): FF20,008
Number of shares (mil): 103
Dividends:
1989 average yield: 1.3%
1989 payout: 13.8%
Market value (mil): $2,996
Sales (mil): $9,566

Stock Price History high/low 1980-89

400 350 300 250 200 150 100 50 0

*for refinance **for earnings per share ***"B" shares

Principal exchange: Paris
Incorporated: France, 1863
Fiscal year ends: December 31

WHO

Chairman, Managing Partner: François Michelin
Managing Partner: François Rollier
Managing Partner: René Zingraff
Auditors: Paul-Carlos Mulquin and Gonzague Lauras, Compagnie Régionale de Paris
Employees: 124,408

WHERE

HQ: Compagnie Générale des Etablissements Michelin, 23 Place des Carmes, 63040 Clermont-Ferrand Cedex, France
Phone: 011-33-73-30-42-21
FAX: 011-33-73-30-22-02
US HQ (Michelin Tire Corp.): PO Box 19001, Greenville, SC 29602
US Phone: 803-458-5000

Michelin operates 71 plants, primarily in Europe, and rubber plantations in Brazil, the Ivory Coast, and Nigeria. The company's products are sold in 140 countries.

	1989 Sales % of total
France	21
Western Europe, excluding France	47
Americas	25
Other countries	7
Total	**100**

WHAT

	1989 Sales % of total
Tires & wheels	96
General rubber goods, maps, guides & sundries	4
Total	**100**

Major subsidiaries
Compagnie Financière Michelin (holding company, 93%)
Companhia Brasileira de Pneumaticos Michelin Industriae Comercio (Brazil)
Nihon Michelin Tire Co. Ltd. (sales company, Japan)
Michelin Tire Corp. (US)
Michelin Tires (Canada) Ltd.
Manufacture Française des Pneumatiques Michelin (French operations, 99%)
Pneu Laurent (retreading)
Pneumatiques Kléber (tires)
Société Wolber (bicycle tires)
Michelin Korea Tire Co. Ltd. (47%)
Uniroyal Goodrich Tire Co.

RANKINGS

148th in *Fortune* Global 500 Industrial Cos.
851st in *Business Week* Global 1000

COMPETITION

Bridgestone
Goodyear
Sears

MICROSOFT CORPORATION

OVERVIEW

Microsoft is the leading developer of PC systems and applications software in the world. Based in Redmond, Washington, the 15-year-old company is headed by William Gates III, who, at age 19, cofounded the company. In fiscal year 1990, Microsoft reported revenues of $1.18 billion, making it the first PC software company to record revenues over $1 billion.

Microsoft's operating system software, MS-DOS, introduced with the IBM PC in 1981, today runs on over 30 million IBM PC and compatible computers.

Microsoft's offerings include systems software (MS-DOS, Microsoft OS/2, and Microsoft XENIX), operating environment software (Windows), applications software (word processing, spreadsheet, presentation graphics, etc.), computer reference books (Microsoft Press), and CD-ROM products.

In 1989 Microsoft formed a division to develop multimedia applications (ones that combine text, audio, and visual elements). The new division is also marketing CD-ROM products loaded with volumes of business, statistical, and programming reference materials. In 1990 Microsoft launched Windows 3.0 with great fanfare. Windows is an easy-to-use (Macintosh-like) interface for PCs that also allows more than one application to run simultaneously. Microsoft anticipates it will sell 2 million copies of Windows in calendar year 1990.

OTC symbol: MSFT
Incorporated: Delaware, 1986
Fiscal year ends: June 30

WHO

Chairman and CEO: William H. Gates III, age 34, $191,314 pay
President and COO: Jon A. Shirley, age 51, $315,084 pay
SVP: Steven A. Ballmer, age 33, $190,267 pay
VP: Michael J. Maples, age 47, $261,780 pay
SVP Finance and Administration: Francis J. Gaudette, age 53, $173,019 pay
Auditors: Deloitte & Touche
Employees: 4,037

WHEN

Microsoft started in 1975 after 19-year-old William Gates dropped out of Harvard and teamed up with high school friend Paul Allen to sell a condensed version of the programming language BASIC. While Gates was at Harvard, the 2 had written the language for the Altair, the first commercially available microcomputer (sold by MITS, an Albuquerque-based maker of electronic kits). Gates and Allen moved to Albuquerque and set up Microsoft in a hotel room to produce the program for MITS. Although MITS later folded (1979), Microsoft continued to grow by modifying its BASIC program for other computers.

Microsoft moved to the Seattle area (Bellevue) in 1977, where it developed software that enabled others to write programs for PCs. Microsoft's big break came in 1980 when it was chosen by IBM to write the critical operating system (software that controls the computer's basic functions and runs applications software such as word processing) for IBM's new PC. Given the complexity of the task and the time constraints, Microsoft bought the rights to an operating system for $50,000 from a Seattle programmer, Tim Paterson, and converted it to Microsoft Disk Operating System (MS-DOS).

The popularity of IBM's PC made MS-DOS a huge success. And because other PC makers wanted to be compatible with IBM, MS-DOS was licensed to over 100 companies, making it the standard PC operating system in the 1980s. By 1984 Microsoft sales had exceeded $100 million. Paul Allen, ill from Hodgkin's disease, left Microsoft in 1983. When he had recovered, he started his own software company, Asymetrix. Microsoft went on to develop other application programs for IBM, Apple, and Radio Shack computers.

Microsoft went public in 1986, raising over $61 million. Gates retained 45% of the shares, making him the PC industry's first billionaire in 1987. In 1990 his paper value surpassed $2 billion.

Most recently Microsoft has focused on developing easier-to-use graphic user interfaces (GUIs) for its operating systems. The company makes 2 GUIs for IBM-compatible PCs: Windows (MS-DOS) and Presentation Manager (OS/2), which runs on IBM's new PS/2. Microsoft is also working on a version of UNIX (an operating system originally developed by AT&T), with plans to bring graphics applications such as Presentation Manager to the UNIX environment.

WHERE

HQ: One Microsoft Way, Redmond, WA 98052
Phone: 206-882-8080
FAX: 206-883-8101

The company has 2 manufacturing facilities, in the US and Ireland. In addition it has subsidiaries in Australia, Brazil, Canada, England, France, Italy, Japan, Korea, Mexico, the Netherlands, Spain, Sweden, Switzerland, Taiwan, and Germany.

	1989 Sales		1989 Operating Income	
	$ mil	% of total	$ mil	% of total
US	519	65	153	64
Europe	212	26	73	30
Other international	73	9	13	6
Adjustments	—	—	(5)	—
Total	**804**	**100**	**234**	**100**

WHAT

Operating Systems
MS-DOS
Microsoft OS/2
Microsoft XENIX

Business Application Software
Microsoft Chart
Microsoft Excel
Microsoft File
Microsoft Learning DOS
Microsoft Mail
Microsoft Multiplan
The Microsoft Office
Microsoft PowerPoint
Microsoft Project
Microsoft Word
Microsoft Works
Microsoft Write

Systems/Languages Software
Microsoft BASIC
Microsoft C
Microsoft COBOL
Microsoft FORTRAN
Microsoft Pascal
Microsoft Macro Assembler
Microsoft Quick BASIC
Microsoft QuickC Compiler with Quick Assembler
Microsoft QuickPascal
Microsoft Windows/286
Microsoft Windows/386

Hardware, Recreation & CD-ROM
Microsoft Bookshelf (CD-ROM)
Microsoft Flight Simulator
Microsoft Mouse
Microsoft Programmer's Library (CD-ROM)
Microsoft Small Business Consultant (CD-ROM)
Microsoft Stat Pack (CD-ROM)

Microsoft Press Books
Microsoft Press publishes more than 100 titles on software, computers, and science and technology, under both the Microsoft Press and Tempus imprints.

HOW MUCH

	4 Yr. Growth	1980	1981	1982	1983	1984	1985	1986	1987	1988	1989
Sales ($ mil)	54.8%	—	—	—	—	—	140	198	346	591	804
Net income ($ mil)	63.4%	—	—	—	—	—	24	39	72	124	171
Income as % of sales	—	—	—	—	—	—	17.2%	19.9%	20.8%	21.0%	21.2%
Earnings per share ($)	55.5%	—	—	—	—	—	0.26	0.39	0.65	1.11	1.52
Stock price – high ($)	—	—	—	—	—	—	—	12.81	39.63	35.25	44.63
Stock price – low ($)	—	—	—	—	—	—	—	5.25	11.88	22.63	22.88
Stock price – close ($)	—	—	—	—	—	—	—	12.06	27.13	26.63	43.50
P/E – high	—	—	—	—	—	—	—	33	61	32	29
P/E – low	—	—	—	—	—	—	—	13	18	20	15
Dividends per share ($)	—	—	—	—	—	—	0.00	0.00	0.00	0.00	0.00
Book value per share ($)	69.1%	—	—	—	—	—	0.63	1.37	2.27	3.50	5.15

1989 Year End:
Debt ratio: 0.0%
Return on equity: 35.1%
Cash (mil): $301
Current ratio: 2.95
Long-term debt (mil): $0
Number of shares (mil): 109
Dividends:
1989 average yield: 0.0%
1989 payout: 0.0%
Market value (mil): $4,749

Stock Price History high/low 1986-89

45
40
35
30
25
20
15
10
5
0

RANKINGS

85th in *Business Week* 1000
213th in *Business Week* Global 1000

COMPETITION

AT&T
Apple
Computer Associates
Lotus

MIDWAY AIRLINES, INC.

OVERVIEW

Midway is the primary airline operating from Chicago's Midway Airport. Although more convenient and less congested than giant O'Hare, Midway offers fewer parking facilities and limited access to public transportation — shortcomings addressed by the City of Chicago's modernization plans for the airport. In 1989 Midway boarded about 70% of the passengers flying out of Midway Airport and, in the interest of future growth, added a 2nd hub in Philadelphia that year. Costs related to the new hub partially explain the airline's 1989 losses of $21 million on $494 million in revenues.

Midway inaugurated service to Montreal and Toronto in 1989, the first international flights offered from Midway Airport in 30 years. Midway's commuter service, Midway Commuter, links Midway Airport with 18 cities in 4 midwestern states.

Midway Aircraft Engineering, based at Miami International Airport, performs aircraft inspections and maintenence for Midway, Midway Commuter, and 3rd parties on a contract basis.

NYSE symbol: MDW
Incorporated: Delaware, 1976
Fiscal year ends: December 31

WHO

Chairman and CEO: David R. Hinson, age 57, $351,029 pay
SVP Airline Operations: Clyde R. Kizer, age 51
VP Finance and CFO: Alfred S. Altschul, age 50, $127,871 pay
VP Legal Affairs and Secretary: David B. Armstrong, age 50, $127,871 pay
Auditors: Ernst & Young
Employees: 5,250 full-time and 1,127 part-time

WHEN

In 1976 Irv Tague left his position as COO of Hughes' Airwest to establish an airline at Chicago's Midway Airport. Midway, once the world's busiest airport, was practically abandoned when most airline traffic was diverted to O'Hare in 1962, but Tague saw opportunity in the empty terminals. Planning to operate a no-frills, low-fare, low-cost airline, he raised $5.7 million from venture capitalists and in 1979 began operations from Chicago-Midway to Kansas City, Cleveland, and Detroit. By 1981 Midway (named after its home port) had added 7 more cities, including Omaha, St. Louis, Washington, and New York, and reported its first profit ($4 million on $74 million in revenues).

However, the airline was caught in fare wars with United, American, and Northwest, which caused it to barely break even in 1982. That year Tague left the company, and Arthur Bass, former president of Federal Express, became CEO.

Recognizing that Midway served important eastern and midwestern commercial centers, Bass upgraded the airline to appeal to business travelers by creating new business-class (Metrolink) flights that offered more spacious seating (due to fewer seats), complimentary cocktails, and gourmet snacks. Midway introduced Metrolink service between Chicago and New York in 1983. However, with fewer seats at fares below standard coach, the airline incurred losses of $23 million in 1984. Bass resigned (1985) and David Hinson, one of Midway's original investors, became CEO.

In the meantime Midway bought Miami-based Air Florida, operating it as Midway Express (1985). Hinson streamlined Express operations, retaining service within Florida and to the Virgin Islands, and phased out Metrolink flights. By the end of 1986, Midway experienced an 82% increase in passenger traffic, posting its first profit in 3 years ($5 million on $261 million in revenues).

Midway served 26 cities by 1987, dominating over 1/2 of Chicago-Midway's gates even though traffic overflows at O'Hare had brought competitors to the airport, including archrival Southwest. Profits rose to $11 million (1987). The airline offered flights to 8 additional cities (1988), but profits were down almost 64% from 1987 due to competition and lower earnings on the new routes.

In 1989 Midway established a 2nd hub at Philadelphia by purchasing boarding facilities at the Philadelphia Airport from Eastern Airlines. This transaction, which, among other assets, included Eastern's routes to Montreal and Toronto, cost Midway about $213 million.

WHERE

HQ: 5959 S. Cicero Ave., Chicago, IL 60638
Phone: 312-838-0001
FAX: 312-284-6439

Midway provides scheduled air service to 59 airports in 24 states, the District of Columbia, the Bahamas, the US Virgin Islands, and Canada. It also provides charter service in the US and between the US and Canada.

Hub Locations
Chicago
Philadelphia

WHAT

	1989 Revenues	
	$ mil	% of total
Passenger	472	96
Other	22	4
Total	**494**	**100**

Flight Equipment	Owned	Leased	Total
DC9-15	1	8	9
DC9-30 Series	17	18	35
MD-87	—	7	7
B737-200	2	8	10
Dornier 228	—	21	21
Total	**20**	**62**	**82**

Subsidiaries
Midway Aircraft Engineering, Inc.
Midway Airlines, Inc.
Midway Commuter

HOW MUCH

	9 Yr. Growth	1980	1981	1982	1983	1984	1985	1986	1987	1988	1989
Sales ($ mil)	39.3%	25	74	95	104	149	181	261	347	412	494
Net income ($ mil)	—	(5)	4	0	(15)	(23)	(4)	5	11	4	(21)
Income as % of sales	—	(19.7%)	5.9%	0.4%	(14.4%)	(15.5%)	(2.0%)	1.8%	3.3%	1.0%	(4.2%)
Earnings per share ($)	—	(5.80)	1.18	0.09	(2.52)	(3.15)	(0.50)	0.33	*0.99*	0.36	*(2.17)*
Stock price – high ($)	—	13.00	22.63	17.88	22.38	12.25	9.75	14.88	18.13	17.00	21.75
Stock price – low ($)	—	8.50	8.38	7.38	10.75	3.38	3.00	6.25	8.75	9.25	12.13
Stock price – close ($)	2.8%	9.75	12.25	16.75	11.75	4.00	6.88	13.13	11.00	12.25	12.50
P/E – high	—	—	19	199	—	—	—	45	18	47	—
P/E – low	—	—	7	82	—	—	—	19	9	26	—
Dividends per share ($)	0.0%	0.00	0.00	0.00	0.00	0.00	0.00	0.00	0.00	0.00	0.00
Book value per share ($)	6.4%	3.10	6.61	7.21	6.34	3.46	5.91	7.17	7.32	7.95	5.41

1989 Year End:
Debt ratio: 71.9%
Return on equity: —
Cash (mil): $22
Current ratio: 0.64
Long-term debt (mil): $142
Number of shares (mil): 10
Dividends:
1989 average yield: 0.0%
1989 payout: —
Market value (mil): $125

Stock Price History high/low 1980-89

RANKINGS

43rd in *Fortune* 50 Transportation Cos.

COMPETITION

America West
AMR
Continental
Delta
Kimberly-Clark
NWA
Pan Am
Southwest
TWA
UAL
USAir

MILLIKEN & CO., INC.

OVERVIEW

Milliken & Company, with headquarters in Spartanburg, South Carolina, and New York City, is the world's largest private textile company and the largest textile company in the US, with sales of approximately $2.9 billion.

Milliken produces finished fabrics that its customers make into a variety of products. Apparel fabrics are used by producers such as Haggar Apparel, and Milliken makes the cloth that becomes uniforms for McDonald's, Burger King, and other companies. The company makes stretch fabrics, used for swimsuits and sportswear, with Du Pont's Lycra fibers. Milliken owns more than 1,200 patents, including the one for Visa, a stain-resistant finish, which it has promoted aggressively. The company makes carpets and area rugs, which it sells under the Milliken and Callaway names.

Roger Milliken, who, along with brother Gerrish and cousin Minot, controls more than 50% of the company's stock, supports conservative political causes and has lobbied vigorously for legislation to protect the US textile industry from international trade. The company blamed foreign imports for the closing of one plant and production cutbacks at another in 1990.

WHEN

Seth Milliken and William Deering formed a company in 1865 to become selling agents for textile mills in New England and the South. Deering left the partnership and founded Deering Harvester (later folded into International Harvester, now Navistar) in 1869.

Milliken moved his operations to New York before the turn of the century, began buying the accounts receivable of cash-short textile mill operators, and invested in some of the companies. He also allied himself with leaders in the Spartanburg, South Carolina, area. Milliken and a Spartanburg associate tried to stem the power of the white labor unions by experimenting with black labor at the Vesta Cotton Mill. The venture failed in 1901 after Milliken withdrew his support.

In his position as agent and financier, Milliken was able to spot failing mills. He bought out the distressed owners at a discount and soon became a major mill owner himself. In 1905 Milliken and allies waged a bitter proxy fight and court case to win control of 2 mills, earning Milliken a fearsome reputation.

H. B. Claflin Co., a New York dry goods wholesaler who began operating retail stores, owed money to Milliken. After Claflin went bankrupt in 1914, Milliken won stores in the settlement. They became Mercantile Stores, and the Milliken family retains about 44% of the stock of the publicly traded department store chain (80 stores; 1989 sales: $2.3 billion).

Roger Milliken, grandson of the founder, became the president of the company in 1947 and ruled with a firm hand. He fired his brother-in-law W. B. Dixon Stroud in 1955, and none of Milliken's children, nephews, or nieces have ever been allowed to work for the company. In 1956 the workers at Milliken's Darlington, South Carolina, mill voted to unionize. The next day Milliken closed the plant. That began 24 years of litigation that ended at the US Supreme Court. Milliken settled with the workers for $5 million.

In the 1960s the company introduced Visa, a fabric finish for easy-care fabrics, and has since expanded its production of synthetics and finished fabrics.

Milliken launched its Pursuit of Excellence program in 1981. The program stressed self-managed teams of employees and has since eliminated 700 management positions. Roger Milliken also emphasized research, training, and new technology. The company adapted quickly to automation, sometimes buying all the latest equipment a manufacturer could make, and competitors were left out in the cold.

The company's quality record — some clients are so confident about Milliken goods they don't even inspect for defects — earned a highly coveted Malcolm Baldridge National Quality Award in 1989.

Away from that limelight, Milliken has always been a secretive, closely held business. In 1989 that secrecy and family control were threatened when members of the Stroud branch of the family sold stock to a group that includes executives of Milliken competitor Delta Woodside.

The Strouds have announced that they plan to sell all their Milliken stock, about 15% of the company. The Delta Woodside executives, who said they hope to buy more Stroud stock, sued Milliken to win the right to inspect its records and share the information with potential backers.

HOW MUCH

	4 Yr. Growth	1980	1981	1982	1983	1984	1985	1986	1987	1988	1989
Sales ($ mil)	9.7%	—	—	—	—	—	2,000	2,200	2,400	2,400	2,900

1989 Estimates
Income as % of sales: 8.0%
Dividend payout: 5.0%

Sales ($ mil) 1985-89

Private company
Founded: Maine, 1865
Fiscal year ends: November 30

WHO

Chairman: Roger Milliken, age 75
President and COO: Thomas J. Malone
VP and CFO: Minot K. Milliken
Auditors: Arthur Andersen & Co.
Employees: 14,300

WHERE

Manufacturing HQ: PO Box 1926, Spartanburg, SC 29304
Phone: 803-573-2020
FAX: 803-573-1998 (Executive Offices)
Merchandising HQ: 1045 Ave. of the Americas, New York, NY 10018
Phone: 212-819-4200

Milliken operates 47 manufacturing plants in the US and 8 plants in France, Belgium, and the UK.

WHAT

Milliken has 28 businesses that produce 48,000 different products.

	1989 Estimated Sales $ mil
Broadwoven fabric — cotton	2,131
Broadwoven fabric — synthetic	79
Knit underwear	44
Weft knit fabric	29
Knitting	39
Finishing — cotton	22
Carpets & rugs	35
Throwing & winding	78
Automotive & apparel trimmings	7
Other/Adjustments	436
Total	**2,900**

Lines of Business

Textiles
Apparel fabrics
Area rugs
Automotive upholstery
Carpet and carpet tiles
Lining fabrics
Shop towels
Stretch fabrics
Textured yarns
Uniform fabrics

Industrial Chemicals
The company makes chemicals that are used in several industries:
Oil industry
Paint industry
Paper industry
Plastics industry
Textile industry

RANKINGS

38th in *Forbes* 400 US Private Cos.

COMPETITION

Burlington Holdings
Du Pont
Farley
Fieldcrest Cannon
Springs Industries
Other chemical companies

MINNESOTA MINING AND MANUFACTURING CO.

OVERVIEW

Although 3M started slowly, with sandpaper as its only product, the corporation today is 32nd on the *Fortune* 500 list.

Encouraging engineers and technical people to be inventive has paid off for CEO Allen Jacobson. The company gives technical people time and money to perform research, encouraging them to spend 15% of their time pursuing ideas for future products or services. To generate and refine ideas, 3M conducts forums for scientists and other employees to share information. The 1989 R&D budget, $784 million (6.5% of sales), is about twice the average for US industry.

The company has 4 business segments: Industrial and Electronic, Information and Imaging Technologies, Life Sciences, and Commercial and Consumer. Sales are about 50% to service-related businesses, 40% to industry, and 10% to consumers.

International sales accounted for 46% of total sales in 1989 and may represent the majority of 1990 sales. 3M has targeted international markets because of their higher growth rates and larger size; in 1989 it opened an operation in India and generated sales of almost $1 billion in Japan alone.

NYSE symbol: MMM
Incorporated: Delaware, 1929
Fiscal year ends: December 31

WHO

Chairman and CEO: Allen F. Jacobson, age 63, $1,178,660 pay
SVP Finance: Roger W. Roberts, age 58
Auditors: Coopers & Lybrand
Employees: 87,584

WHERE

HQ: 3M Center, St. Paul, MN 55144
Phone: 612-733-1110
FAX: 612-736-8261

3M has manufacturing facilities in 26 US states and 41 foreign countries. It sells its products throughout the US and in 51 foreign countries.

	1989 Sales		1989 Operating Income	
	$ mil	% of total	$ mil	% of total
US	6,601	56	1,222	57
Europe	3,023	25	452	21
Asia/Pacific/Canada	1,834	15	347	16
Other areas	532	4	129	6
Total	**11,990**	**100**	**2,150**	**100**

WHEN

In 1902 Minnesota Mining and Manufacturing Company was started by 5 businessmen in Two Harbors, Minnesota, to sell corundum for grinding wheels to manufacturers in the East.

When they made only one sale, one of the founders, John Dwan, wrote to his friend Edgar Ober and asked him to furnish working capital in exchange for 60% of 3M's stock. Ober believed there was a need for a company to make sandpaper and abrasive wheels, but he didn't have the money. He convinced Lucius Ordway, vice-president of a St. Paul plumbing company, to underwrite 3M. At the 3rd annual meeting in May 1905, Ober and Ordway took over the company.

They moved 3M to Duluth and converted an old flour mill to a sandpaper factory. Orders began coming in by January 1906, but expenses exceeded sales, and Ordway's investment reached $200,000. In 1910 the plant moved to St. Paul to escape high humidity in Duluth.

Problems with inconsistent quality plagued 3M until it abandoned corundum and began using aluminum oxide. Three-M-Ite and Wetordry sandpapers began a profitable future.

In 2 years sales doubled, and the board of directors declared a dividend to stockholders in the last quarter of 1916. The company has not missed a quarterly dividend since.

The next 2 products 3M developed — Scotch brand masking tape (1925) and Scotch brand cellophane tape (1930) — assured 3M's future. From adhesive tape, 3M progressed to its 1947 introduction of the first commercially acceptable magnetic recording tape. In 1950, after a decade of work and $1 million, Carl Miller of 3M invented Thermo-Fax copying machines.

During the 1950s, 3M concentrated on reflective products, printing products, copying products, fluorochemicals, electrical tapes, and magnetic tapes.

The copying machine was the beginning of 3M's Duplicating Division, a group that produced image-related products such as microfilm, overhead-projection transparencies, carbonless papers, and FAX transmission and word processing equipment. From that division came the Graphic Systems Group and a nationwide sales and service organization, 3M Business Products Sales, Inc.

The company developed Post-it notes (1980) when a company scientist wanted to attach page markers to his church hymnal. Recalling that a colleague had developed an adhesive that wasn't very sticky, he brushed some on paper and began a new 3M product line.

WHAT

	1989 Sales		1989 Operating Income	
	$ mil	% of total	$ mil	% of total
Life Sciences	2,542	21	535	24
Industrial & Electronic	4,337	36	830	38
Information & Imaging Technologies	3,420	29	454	20
Commercial & Consumer	1,669	14	403	18
Adjustments	22	—	(72)	—
Total	**11,990**	**100**	**2,150**	**100**

Industrial & Electronic Products
Abrasives
Adhesives
Coatings
Connectors
Emblems
Fasteners
Fluorochemicals
Roofing granules
Shielding
Tape

Information & Imaging Technologies
Computer tapes
Digital imaging systems
Lithographic plates
Photographic film (Scotch)
Video and audio tape (Scotch)
X-ray films and screens

Life Sciences
Blood-gas monitors
Diaper closures
IV systems
Oxygenators
Stethoscopes

Commercial & Consumer Products
Carbonless papers
Masking tape
Self-stick notes (Post-it)
Tape (Scotch)
Cleaning pads (Scotch-Brite)

HOW MUCH

	9 Yr. Growth	1980	1981	1982	1983	1984	1985	1986	1987	1988	1989
Sales ($ mil)	7.8%	6,080	6,508	6,601	7,039	7,705	7,846	8,602	9,429	10,581	11,990
Net income ($ mil)	7.0%	678	673	631	667	733	664	779	918	1,154	1,244
Income as % of sales	—	11.2%	10.3%	9.6%	9.5%	9.5%	8.5%	9.1%	9.7%	10.9%	10.4%
Earnings per share ($)	7.5%	2.89	2.87	2.69	2.84	3.14	2.89	3.40	4.02	5.06	5.55
Stock price – high ($)	—	31.44	32.50	39.69	45.25	42.75	45.81	59.44	83.50	67.50	81.88
Stock price – low ($)	—	22.94	24.00	24.38	36.31	34.63	36.81	43.00	45.00	55.25	60.13
Stock price – close ($)	11.7%	29.50	27.25	37.50	41.25	39.31	44.88	58.31	64.38	62.00	79.63
P/E – high	—	11	11	15	16	14	16	17	21	13	15
P/E – low	—	8	8	9	13	11	13	13	11	11	11
Dividends per share ($)	7.1%	1.40	1.50	1.60	1.65	1.70	1.75	1.80	1.86	2.12	2.60
Book value per share ($)	6.2%	14.04	14.68	15.05	15.77	16.40	17.49	19.53	22.24	24.58	24.15

1989 Year End:
Debt ratio: 14.1%
Return on equity: 22.8%
Cash (mil): $887
Current ratio: 1.98
Long-term debt (mil): $885
Number of shares (mil): 223
Dividends:
1989 average yield: 3.3%
1989 payout: 46.8%
Market value (mil): $17,730

Stock Price History high/low 1980-89

RANKINGS

32nd in *Fortune* 500 Industrial Cos.
88th in *Fortune* Global 500 Industrial Cos.
31st in *Fortune* 50 Exporters
51st in *Forbes* Sales 500
21st in *Business Week* 1000
65th in *Business Week* Global 1000

COMPETITION

BASF
Bayer
Eastman Kodak
Hitachi
Polariod
PPG
Sony
USG
Xerox
Medical equipment

MITSUBISHI GROUP

OVERVIEW

Consisting of approximately 160 companies with interlocking stockholdings, the Mitsubishi Group is the largest *keiretsu* (industrial group) in Japan. The 3 core companies of the group are Mitsubishi Bank, Mitsubishi Corporation (trading), and Mitsubishi Heavy Industries (heavy machinery, Japan's biggest arms maker). Other important group companies include Mitsubishi Electric, known in the US for its large-screen Diamond Vision TVs (Mitsubishi means "3 diamonds" in Japanese), and Mitsubishi Motors, which has long supplied Chrysler with such cars as the Colt and the Horizon.

Activities of the group's companies are often coordinated. A Mitsubishi consortium launched its own communications satellite in 1989. Leaders of the 29 most important companies meet monthly in Tokyo to exchange information and discuss business and joint projects.

In 1990 Mitsubishi Group companies joined in talks with Daimler-Benz (autos, defense, Germany) concerning cooperative ventures, including some that would increase Mitsubishi's access to European markets. In the same year, Mitsubishi Corporation bought 74% of Pittsburgh-based Aristech Chemical.

WHEN

Yataro Iwasaki's close ties to the Japanese government ensured the early success of his shipping and trading company, Mitsubishi. Founded in 1870, Mitsubishi soon diversified into mining (1873), banking (1885), and shipbuilding (1887) and began its withdrawal from shipping in the 1880s. In the 1890s the company became a major investor in Japanese railroads and real estate.

In 1918 the Mitsubishi *zaibatsu* (family-controlled conglomerate) spun off its trading businesses to form Mitsubishi Trading, its purchasing, sales, and central management arm. By WWII the Mitsubishi *zaibatsu* had become an enormous amalgam of divisions and public companies. During WWII the group manufactured warplanes, ships, and explosives for the Japanese military.

US postwar occupation forces ordered *zaibatsu* families to sell their stock and in 1946 split Mitsubishi into 139 separate entities. In 1954, after occupation ended, Mitsubishi Trading regrouped with the merger of 4 of its old trading companies and regained its position as the trading arm and lead firm in the Mitsubishi constellation of companies.

In 1954 Mitubishi Trading established Mitsubishi International (New York), a trading subsidiary that has become a leading exporter of a broad assortment of US goods. In the 1960s and 1970s Mitsubishi Trading exploited Japan's increasing need for raw materials by importing minerals and fuels. Renamed Mitsubishi Corporation in 1971, the company was at the forefront of the Japanese government's export drive.

Many Mitsubishi companies have become huge. Mitsubishi Kasei (chemicals), separated from its Asahi Glass (now the largest glass maker in Japan) and Mitsubishi Rayon (fibers) divisions by Allied forces, spun off Mitsubishi Metal (aluminum, 1976) and grew to become Japan's largest chemical concern. Kirin is Japan's largest brewer. Mitsubishi Bank, the world's 4th largest, purchased the Bank of California in 1983. Mitsubishi Estate (real estate) purchased 51% of the Rockefeller Group (New York, 1989), owner of Rockefeller Center. Mitsubishi Electric became one of Japan's leading electrical equipment and electronics manufacturers.

The 1964 merger of 3 Mitsubishi companies created Mitsubishi Heavy Industries. The company became Japan's leading producer of ships, power plants, heavy machinery, and aircraft. Chrysler bought 15% of Mitsubishi Motors (1971), originally a Mitsubishi Heavy Industries subsidiary. Mitsubishi Motors and Chrysler formed Diamond Star Motor to make cars in Normal, Illinois (1985).

HOW MUCH

$=¥144 (Dec. 31, 1989)	9 Yr. Growth	1980	1981	1982	1983	1984	1985	1986	1987	1988	1989
Sales (¥ bil)	2.4%	12,675	14,834	15,635	15,683	15,815	17,221	17,095	12,660	13,365	15,644
Net income (¥ bil)	1.0%	42	45	34	25	27	32	32	27	31	46
Income as % of sales	—	0.3%	0.3%	0.2%	0.2%	0.2%	0.2%	0.2%	0.2%	0.2%	0.3%
Earnings per share (¥)	(1.1%)	32	32	24	18	19	23	23	18	20	29
Stock price – high (¥)	—	668	626	582	531	594	720	1,500	1,660	1,380	2,010
Stock price – low (¥)	—	501	455	427	455	500	510	582	941	959	1,350
Stock price – close (¥)	15.2%	562	582	495	494	555	624	990	989	1,330	2,010
P/E – high	—	21	20	24	30	31	31	65	92	69	69
P/E – low	—	16	14	18	25	26	22	25	36	48	47
Dividends per share (¥)	2.1%	5.79	5.79	6.06	6.36	6.36	6.68	7.00	7.00	7.00	7.00
Book value per share (¥)	2.9%	276	262	290	297	303	322	287	301	324	358

1989 Year End:
Debt ratio: 82.0%
Return on equity: 13.5%
Cash (bil): ¥3,230
Long-term debt (bil): ¥2,594
Number of shares (mil): 1,545
Dividends:
1989 average yield: 0.3%
1989 payout: 24.1%
Market value (mil): $21,564
Sales (mil): $108,778

Stock Price History high/low 1980-89

2,500
2,000
1,500
1,000
500
0

Principal stock exchange: Tokyo
Incorporated: Japan, 1918
Fiscal year ends: March 31

WHO

Chairman: Yohei Mimura, age 73
President: Shinroku Morohashi
Auditors: Deloitte Haskins & Sells; Tohmatsu Awoki & Sanwa
Employees: 13,529

WHERE

HQ: 6-3, Marunouchi 2-chome, Chiyoda-ku, Tokyo 100-86, Japan
Phone: 011-81-3-210-2121
US HQ (Mitsubishi International Corp.): 520 Madison Ave., New York, NY 10022
US Phone: 212-605-2000
US FAX: 212-605-2597

Mitsubishi Corp. has 57 offices in Japan and 105 in other countries. Its subsidiaries have offices in 69 locations outside Japan.

WHAT

	1989 Sales	
	¥ bil	% of total
Fuels	2,205	14
Metals	4,561	29
Machines/information systems & services	4,110	26
Foods	2,088	14
Chemicals	1,412	9
Textiles & general merchandise	1,268	8
Total	**15,644**	**100**

Major Affiliated Companies
Asahi Glass Co., Ltd.
Kirin Brewery
The Meiji Mutual Life Insurance Co.
Mitsubishi Aluminum Co., Ltd.
The Mitsubishi Bank, Ltd.
Mitsubishi Cable Industries, Ltd.
Mitsubishi Construction Co., Ltd.
Mitsubishi Electric Corp.
Mitsubishi Estate Co., Ltd.
Mitsubishi Gas Chemical Co., Inc.
Mitsubishi Heavy Industries, Ltd.
Mitsubishi Kakoki Kaisha, Ltd. (chemical-processing equipment)
Mitsubishi Kasei Corp. (chemicals)
Mitsubishi Metal Corp.
Mitsubishi Mining & Cement Co., Ltd.
Mitsubishi Motors Corp.
Mitsubishi Oil Co., Ltd.
Mitsubishi Paper Mills, Ltd.
Mitsubishi Petrochemical Co., Ltd.
Mitsubishi Plastics Industries, Ltd.
Mitsubishi Rayon Co., Ltd.
Mitsubishi Steel Manufacturing Co., Ltd.
The Mitsubishi Trust and Banking Corp.
Mitsubishi Warehouse & Transportation Co., Ltd.
Nikon Corp. (cameras)
Nippon Yusen Kabushiki Kaisha (NYK Line, marine transportation)
The Tokio Marine and Fire Insurance Co., Ltd.

RANKINGS

76th in *Business Week* Global 1000

Information presented for Mitsubishi Corp. only.

MOBIL CORPORATION

OVERVIEW

Mobil is the 3rd largest petroleum company in the world, behind Exxon and Royal Dutch/Shell, and one of the most active US companies in overseas trade.

It explores for and produces oil and natural gas in 25 countries, with major foreign operations in the North Sea, Nigeria, and Indonesia. Even before the Iraqi invasion of Kuwait pushed crude prices higher, Mobil planned to boost capital spending for exploration and production. The company owns all or part of 27 refineries worldwide, owns 34 oil tankers, and markets its petroleum products in more than 100 countries.

At the end of 1989, Mobil had 22,681 retail outlets, 58% outside the US. It planned to add to that figure with the 1990 purchase of 300 service stations and refinery support from Exxon's Australian subsidiary.

In the US, 85% of Mobil's retail gasoline sales comes from 14 states, mostly in the East, Midwest, and Florida. Mobil Chemical makes Hefty brand garbage bags, Baggies, and other plastic items.

WHEN

Mobil is yet another of the companies flung into orbit after the Big Bang breakup of John D. Rockefeller's Standard Oil universe. The pieces that would eventually form Mobil's cosmos were Rochester, New York–based Vacuum Oil and Standard Oil of New York. Vacuum, under founders Hiram Bond Everest and Mathew Ewing, had developed a way to make kerosene by distilling crude oil in a vacuum. Rockefeller bought 75% of Vacuum in 1879. The Standard Oil Company of New York was founded in 1882 and nicknamed Socony. Vacuum and Socony were 2 of the 33 subsidiaries cut loose when the US Supreme Court ordered the Standard Oil of New Jersey holding company dissolved in 1911.

After the breakup, Socony, which had depended on its sisters in the Standard Oil household for oil to sell in New York, New England, and overseas, quickly cast about for supplies of its own. The company bought control of Texas-based Magnolia Petroleum (1918) and acquired California-based General Petroleum (1926).

Vacuum, which had grown to 1,500 service stations in the Midwest, and Socony reunited in 1931 as Socony-Vacuum. Shortly after the new company emerged, it adopted the Flying Red Horse (Pegasus) as a trademark. The symbol (representing speed and power) was first used by company operations in South Africa and colored red by operations in Japan.

Socony-Vacuum still needed crude and, in a deal patterned after Caltex (the partnership of Standard Oil of California and Texaco in the Middle East), joined with Standard Oil (New Jersey) to form Stanvac in 1933 for drilling in the Far East. Socony-Vacuum added crude supplies when it bought a 10% stake in Aramco (Arabian American Oil Company) in 1948.

The company changed its name to Socony Mobil Oil, adopting its trade name, in 1955. That was shortened to Mobil Oil in 1966.

In 1974 it gained control of Marcor, Chicago-based parent of retailing chain Montgomery Ward & Company and of Container Corporation of America, the giant maker of paper packaging. While it dropped the "oil" from its name in 1976, Mobil continued as an outspoken defender of the petroleum industry, purchasing editorial-type advertising in major publications.

In 1984 Mobil bought Superior Oil, at the time the largest independent producer of crude and natural gas, for $5.7 billion. To reduce debt from the Superior deal and to refocus on energy, Mobil has sold $6 billion in assets, including Container Corporation of America (1986) and Montgomery Ward (1988).

The company is literally on the move: it is transferring headquarters from New York to Fairfax, Virginia.

HOW MUCH

	9 Yr. Growth	1980	1981	1982	1983	1984	1985	1986	1987	1988	1989
Sales ($ mil)	(1.9%)	59,510	64,488	59,946	54,607	56,047	55,960	44,866	51,223	48,198	50,220
Net income ($ mil)	(4.8%)	2,813	2,433	1,380	1,503	1,268	1,040	1,407	1,258	2,031	1,809
Income as % of sales	—	4.7%	3.8%	2.3%	2.8%	2.3%	1.9%	3.1%	2.5%	4.2%	3.6%
Earnings per share ($)	(4.4%)	6.62	5.72	3.31	3.70	3.11	2.55	3.45	3.06	4.93	4.40
Stock price – high ($)	—	44.75	41.19	28.63	34.63	32.13	34.38	40.88	55.00	49.13	63.25
Stock price – low ($)	—	24.88	24.13	19.50	24.25	23.13	25.50	26.25	32.00	38.63	45.25
Stock price – close ($)	5.0%	40.38	24.13	25.13	28.75	27.13	30.25	40.13	39.13	45.50	62.63
P/E – high	—	7	7	9	9	10	13	12	18	10	14
P/E – low	—	4	4	6	7	7	10	8	10	8	10
Dividends per share ($)	4.4%	1.73	2.00	2.00	2.00	2.20	2.20	2.20	2.20	2.35	2.55
Book value per share ($)	2.3%	30.74	34.45	36.30	34.30	33.42	34.50	37.28	40.80	38.19	37.88

1989 Year End:
Debt ratio: 24.6%
Return on equity: 11.6%
Cash (mil): $1,541
Current ratio: 1.06
Long-term debt (mil): $5,317
Number of shares (mil): 409
Dividends:
1989 average yield: 4.1%
1989 payout: 58.0%
Market value (mil): $25,583

70
60
50
40
30
20
10
0

Stock Price History high/low 1980-89

NYSE symbol: MOB
Incorporated: Delaware, 1976
Fiscal year ends: December 31

WHO

Chairman, President, CEO, and COO; Chairman and CEO, Mobil Oil Corp.: Allen E. Murray, age 60, $1,675,239 pay
VC; President and COO, Mobil Oil Corp.: Richard F. Tucker, age 63, $1,230,325 pay
VP and CFO: Lucio A. Noto, age 51
Auditors: Ernst & Young
Employees: 67,900

WHERE

HQ: 3225 Gallows Rd., Fairfax, VA 22037
Phone: 703-849-3000
FAX: 703-846-4669

Mobil conducts petroleum exploration and production in 25 countries and sells its products in more than 100 countries.

	1989 Sales		1989 Net Income	
	$ mil	% of total	$ mil	% of total
US	19,028	34	809	33
Canada	993	2	95	4
Other foreign	35,457	64	1,519	63
Adjustments	(5,258)	—	(614)	—
Total	**50,220**	**100**	**1,809**	**100**

WHAT

	1989 Sales		1989 Operating Income	
	$ mil	% of total	$ mil	% of total
Chemical	4,039	7	774	17
Exploration & production	4,824	9	2,703	58
Marketing & refining	46,615	84	1,130	25
Adjustments	(5,258)	—	(838)	—
Total	**50,220**	**100**	**3,769**	**100**

Principal Products & Activities
Coal mining
Crude oil and natural gas production
Petrochemicals and plastics
Petroleum pipelining, refining, and marketing
Phosphate rock mining
Plastic film and other packaging materials
Real estate development
Solar energy development
Specialty and synthetic lubricants

Brand Names
Baggies (plastic food storage bags)
Hefty (plastic bags, housewares)
Kordite (plastic garbage bags)

RANKINGS

6th in *Fortune* 500 Industrial Cos.
8th in *Fortune* Global 500 Industrial Cos.
7th in *Forbes* Sales 500
13th in *Business Week* 1000
34th in *Business Week* Global 1000

COMPETITION

Amoco
Ashland
Atlantic Richfield
British Petroleum
Chevron
Coastal
Du Pont
Exxon
Occidental
Pennzoil
Phillips
Royal Dutch/Shell
Sun
Texaco
Unocal
USX
Chemical and mining companies
Other petroluem companies

MONSANTO COMPANY

OVERVIEW

St. Louis–based Monsanto, the 4th largest US chemical company, operates worldwide with 36% of its total sales outside the US.

Monsanto's chemicals unit (46% of sales) makes nylon carpet fiber, Saflex (plastic interlayer), high-performance plastics, detergents, and other chemicals. Crop chemicals include Roundup and Lasso herbicides. Monsanto's Searle makes Calan SR, an antihypertensive drug that is one of the top 15 in US pharmaceutical sales. Half of Monsanto's NutraSweet sweetener sales are to the carbonated diet beverage market. Monsanto's NutraSweet subsidiary was the first company to introduce a fat substitute, Simplesse, in an ice cream–like product.

The company's Fisher Controls unit is a leading worldwide manufacturer of process control equipment, including valves and regulators. In the animal sciences business, Monsanto produces Alimet animal feed supplement.

Monsanto had record sales in 1988 and 1989, as the company continued to position itself away from the commodity chemical market and toward the pharmaceutical and biotechnology market.

WHEN

John Queeny, buyer for a St. Louis drug company, had only one source for saccharin in 1900: Germany. He believed that this sweetener (derived from coal tar) had a growing market in the US. Thus in 1901 in St. Louis, with $5,000 and using his wife's maiden name of Monsanto, Queeny founded Monsanto Chemical Works to manufacture saccharin. The German competition cut prices to drive Monsanto from the marketplace, but failed. Monsanto soon diversified with caffeine (1904), vanillin (1905), phenol (antiseptic used in WWI, 1916), and aspirin, when Bayer's German patent expired (1917). Monsanto Chemical went public in 1927.

In 1928 Edgar Monsanto Queeny, only son of the founder, became president. Edgar recognized the potential of rubber additives, buying Rubber Service Laboratories (Akron, Ohio, 1929), and plastics, buying Fiberloid (Springfield, Massachusetts, 1938). In 1943 Monsanto began production of styrene monomer (used in synthetic rubber) for the army's first synthetic tire in WWII.

Monsanto entered the synthetic fiber market (1949) in a joint venture with American Viscose, forming Chemstrand (bought Chemstrand, 1961); it developed Acrilan fibers (1952) and the synthetic surface AstroTurf (first used commercially in the Houston Astrodome, 1966). In 1952 Monsanto marketed "all" (detergent) but in 1957 disbanded its Consumer Products Division and sold "all" to Unilever.

In 1954 Monsanto and Bayer (Germany) entered into a joint venture (Mobay Chemical) for the R&D of urethane foams. Bayer bought Mobay in 1967.

In 1960 Edgar resigned as chairman. In 1964 the company changed its name to Monsanto Company to emphasize its diversity. Monsanto continued to introduce new products, including the herbicides Lasso (1969) and Roundup (1973). In 1969 Monsanto bought 67% of Fisher Governor (valves and control systems, Marshalltown, Iowa), changing its name to Fisher Controls (bought remaining 33%, 1983). In 1972 Monsanto stopped making saccharin due to price and process competition from Japan.

In 1985 Monsanto acquired G. D. Searle (pharmaceuticals, founded 1868) and, consequently, the lawsuits resulting from Searle's Copper-7 intrauterine contraceptive device (introduced in 1974). Through Searle, Monsanto also bought the licensing rights to manufacture NutraSweet (artificial sweetener) and formed a wholly owned subsidiary, NutraSweet. In 1990 Monsanto brought Simplesse to market.

HOW MUCH

	9 Yr. Growth	1980	1981	1982	1983	1984	1985	1986	1987	1988	1989
Sales ($ mil)	3.1%	6,574	6,948	6,325	6,299	6,691	6,747	6,879	7,639	8,293	8,681
Net income ($ mil)	18.4%	149	445	329	369	439	(128)	433	436	591	679
Income as % of sales	—	2.3%	6.4%	5.2%	5.9%	6.6%	(1.9%)	6.3%	5.7%	7.1%	7.8%
Earnings per share ($)	19.4%	1.02	2.86	2.05	2.24	2.71	(0.84)	2.78	2.82	4.14	5.02
Stock price – high ($)	—	17.56	21.88	22.25	29.09	26.94	27.69	40.75	50.13	46.19	62.13
Stock price – low ($)	—	10.56	14.88	14.16	18.56	20.31	20.31	22.38	28.50	36.75	40.25
Stock price – close ($)	14.4%	17.16	17.53	19.06	26.31	22.00	23.88	38.25	41.50	40.88	57.69
P/E – high	—	17	8	11	13	10	—	15	18	11	12
P/E – low	—	10	5	7	8	8	—	8	10	9	8
Dividends per share ($)	7.1%	0.89	0.94	0.99	1.04	1.13	1.23	1.29	1.38	1.48	1.65
Book value per share ($)	4.9%	19.41	21.09	21.49	22.40	23.21	22.19	24.34	26.32	27.60	29.79

1989 Year End:
Debt ratio: 27.2%
Return on equity: 17.5%
Cash (mil): $253
Current ratio: 1.69
Long-term debt (mil): $1,471
Number of shares (mil): 132
Dividends:
1989 average yield: 2.9%
1989 payout: 32.9%
Market value (mil): $7,632

NYSE symbol: MTC
Incorporated: Delaware, 1933
Fiscal year ends: December 31

WHO

Chairman and CEO: Richard J. Mahoney, age 56, $1,316,667 pay
President and COO: Earle H. Harbison, Jr., age 61, $900,000 pay
EVP: Nicholas L. Reding, age 55, $578,250 pay
SVP and CFO: Francis A. Stroble, age 59
Auditors: Deloitte & Touche
Employees: 42,200

WHERE

HQ: 800 N. Lindbergh Blvd., St. Louis, MO 63167
Phone: 314-694-1000
FAX: 314-694-7625

Monsanto produces and sells its products throughout the US and worldwide.

	1989 Sales		1989 Operating Income	
	$ mil	% of total	$ mil	% of total
US	5,590	64	721	64
Europe & Africa	1,800	21	282	25
Canada	430	5	50	4
Latin America	315	4	23	2
Asia/Pacific	546	6	60	5
Adjustments	—	—	(58)	—
Total	**8,681**	**100**	**1,078**	**100**

WHAT

	1989 Sales		1989 Operating Income	
	$ mil	% of total	$ mil	% of total
Crop chemicals	1,558	18	474	42
Chemicals	4,065	46	497	43
Process controls	852	10	64	6
Animal sciences	159	2	(42)	(4)
Pharmaceuticals	1,178	14	6	1
Low-calorie sweetener	869	10	180	16
Biotechnology R&D	—	—	(47)	(4)
Adjustments	—	—	(54)	—
Total	**8,681**	**100**	**1,078**	**100**

Major Products
Animal feed supplements
Herbicides
Industrial chemicals
Industrial process control equipment
Low-calorie sweeteners (NutraSweet, Equal)
Synthetic fibers and plastics
Prescription pharmaceuticals

RANKINGS

55th in *Fortune* 500 Industrial Cos.
146th in *Fortune* Global 500 Industrial Cos.
28th in *Fortune* 50 Exporters
92nd in *Forbes* Sales 500
75th in *Business Week* 1000
268th in *Business Week* Global 1000

COMPETITION

Allied-Signal
American Cyanamid
BASF
Bayer
Dow Chemical
Du Pont
FMC
W. R. Grace
Hercules
Hoechst
Occidental
Rhône-Poulenc
Union Carbide
Other drug companies

MONTGOMERY WARD & CO., INC.

OVERVIEW

For most of the 20th century, Montgomery Ward has suffered from sluggish sales growth, weak management, and a dowdy image. Following the 1988 management-led buyout, Chairman Bernard F. Brennan has refocused Montgomery Ward, the 9th largest US retailer.

Brennan's strategy for rebuilding the 335-store chain consisted of discontinuing the Jefferson-Ward discount chain and 113-year-old catalog operations. The company is shifting from private-label to name-brand merchandising, and in 1988 was the largest retailer of General Electric, Sony, and Maytag products. The brand-name approach has since been adopted by Sears, whose chairman is Brennan's brother Edward.

Another part of the company's strategy is the remodeling of each location into 4 distinct "specialty stores," often with separate entrances. These divisions represent the focus of Montgomery Ward's remaining product lines. Montgomery Ward has now had 4 years of record earnings and has reduced its debt to under $900 million. In 1990 the company began a stock incentive and bonus program for its employees.

Private company
Founded: Illinois, 1872
Fiscal year ends: December 31

WHO

Chairman, President, and CEO: Bernard F. Brennan, age 51
President Apparel Group: Daniel H. Levy
President Hardlines Merchandising and Financial Services: Dominic Mangone
President Marketing: Bernard W. Andrews
President Store Operations: Richard Bergel
Employees: 67,200

WHEN

Aaron Montgomery Ward started the company that bears his name in Chicago in 1872. The company was the world's first general merchandise mail-order concern. Prior to this time farmers purchased goods from the general store or peddlers. Ward provided them with an inexpensive way to shop, by mail-order catalog. In 1873 Ward took as a partner brother-in-law George Thorne. In 1875 the company pioneered the "Satisfaction Guaranteed or Your Money Back" policy.

In 1893 Thorne bought a controlling interest in the company. By 1900 Ward's sales had fallen behind flamboyant Chicago rival Sears (founded in 1893). In 1904 Ward introduced its first employee magazine, which is believed to be the first company magazine edited by employees without policy dictated by the company. Profits surpassed $1 million for the first time in 1909, and the following year George Thorne retired, leaving son Charles and 4 other sons in control of the company. In 1913 Ward died and Charles Thorne became president. Three years later Charles Thorne became chairman and his brother Robert became president. In 1919 Ward became a public corporation and General Robert Wood became general merchandise manager. The following year Ward suffered its first loss despite over $100 million in sales, and the Thornes were forced to raise capital by selling a new issue of stock.

From 1920 to 1924 Ward's sales grew by 47.5%, compared to Sears's 15.9% decrease. Because Wood wanted Ward to develop retail stores and the company wanted to remain in the mail-order business, Wood left Ward in 1924 and went to work for Sears. Two years later Ward opened its first retail store in Plymouth, Indiana. By the end of 1928 the company had 244 retail stores.

In 1931 Sewell Avery became CEO, and under his leadership Ward ended 4 years of losses and was profitable in 1934. Avery refused to turn over the company to federal control during a WWII labor dispute, and President Franklin Roosevelt had National Guardsmen carry Avery out of his office. Avery, who had correctly predicted the Great Depression, also was convinced there would be a recession after WWII and canceled expansion plans, missing out on the postwar boom and losing market share.

After Avery's departure (1955), Ward started a new expansion program, including adding stores for the first time in Alaska and opening its first major retail stores distribution center (1958). In 1968 the company merged with Container Corporation of America to form Marcor. In 1974 Mobil Oil bought $200 million in shares of preferred stock; with other stock bought previously and through a tender offer, Mobil had 54% control of Ward and completed the acquisition in 1976. Mobil made huge loans to the company in hopes of Ward's becoming profitable.

In 1985 Mobil, declaring that it had had enough, put Ward up for sale and brought in Bernard Brennan to lead Ward after jettisoning money-losing operations. Brennan and other senior management of the company led an investor group that bought Ward in a $3.8 billion LBO in 1988. Brennan then sold Ward's credit card business to General Electric Capital for about $1 billion in cash and the assumption of $1.7 billion in debt; this left Ward with only $812 million in debt at the end of 1989.

WHERE

HQ: Montgomery Ward Plaza, Chicago, IL 60671
Phone: 312-467-2000
FAX: 312-467-7158

Montgomery Ward operates 334 locations in 39 states. In addition, the company operates 23 liquidation stores, 24 distribution facilities, and 129 service centers. Buying offices are maintained in 4 foreign countries.

WHAT

	1989 Sales		1989 Operating Income	
	$ mil	% of total	$ mil	% of total
Retail merchandising	5,028	94	205	75
Direct marketing	295	6	70	25
Adjustments	26	—	7	—
Total	**5,349**	**100**	**282**	**100**

Retail Specialties
The Apparel Store
  Includes The Kids Store and Gold 'N Gems fine jewelry
Auto Express
  Auto parts and service
Electric Avenue
  Home electronics and appliances
Home Ideas
  Home furnishings and accessories

Subsidiaries
The Signature Group
  Montgomery Ward Auto Club, insurance, and direct-mail marketing
Standard T Chemical
  Paints and detergents

RANKINGS

16th in *Forbes* 400 US Private Cos.

COMPETITION

Ames
Campeau
Carter Hawley Hale
Costco
Dayton Hudson
Dillard
K mart
R. H. Macy
May Department Stores
Mercantile Stores
J. C. Penney
Price Co.
Sears
Wal-Mart

HOW MUCH

	9 Yr. Growth	1980	1981	1982	1983	1984	1985	1986	1987	1988	1989
Sales ($ mil)	(0.3%)	5,497	5,742	5,570	6,003	6,486	5,388	4,870	5,024	5,403	5,349
Net income ($ mil)	—	(137)	(124)	(75)	54	68	(298)	110	130	139	151
Income as % of sales	—	(2.5%)	(2.2%)	(1.3%)	0.9%	1.0%	(5.5%)	2.3%	2.6%	2.6%	2.8%

1989 Year End:
Debt ratio: 73.9%
Return on equity: 62.3%
Cash (mil): $631
Current ratio: –
Long-term debt (mil): $812

Net Income ($ mil) 1980-89

J.P. MORGAN & CO. INC.

OVERVIEW

J.P. Morgan is a holding company that traditionally specialized in "relationship banking" — arrangement of large-scale financing to governments, large corporations, and wealthy individuals. Its primary subsidiary is Morgan Guaranty Trust, the 4th largest US bank. The company operates one of the largest trust departments in the US.

Morgan is a major dealer in government securities, foreign currencies, and precious metals. The company operates a clearance system for internationally traded securities, handling transactions worth $3.4 trillion in 1989.

J.P. Morgan's foreign-related revenues made up 47% of its $10.4 billion total in 1989, but the company took a $2 billion charge to cover losses from loans to developing countries. It ended the year $1.275 billion in the red, the first loss for the company since 1940.

Morgan's hopes of returning to its glory days as a dealmaker were boosted in 1990, when the Federal Reserve Board approved the company's reentry into stock underwriting.

WHEN

J.P. Morgan & Co. was born into international capitalism and has lived there ever since. Junius Spencer Morgan became, in 1854, a partner in London-based financier George Peabody's banking house. Morgan assumed control and renamed the firm J. S. Morgan and Company when Peabody retired in the early 1860s.

Morgan's son began his own firm, J. Pierpont Morgan and Company, in New York in 1862. J. P. Morgan took partners — Charles Dabney (1864) and, after Dabney's retirement in 1871, the Drexel house of Philadelphia. Connections on both sides of the Atlantic led to profitability and power as the firm funneled European capital into the US economy.

Early in its career, the Morgan firm came to the rescue of the US government. In 1877, when Congress bickered over the Hayes-Tilden election and didn't get around to paying the army, a Morgan affiliate came up with the funds until Congress reconvened.

After Junius's death in 1890, his son reorganized his businesses in London and New York as J.P. Morgan & Co. The firm had already financed and restructured much of the American railroad network, and J. P. Morgan, who became the personification of Wall Street, helped devise the deals that created U.S. Steel, General Electric, and International Harvester.

In 1907 J.P. Morgan served as the country's *de facto* central bank when it led a group of bankers who rallied to stop a financial panic. The firm's influence was pervasive. In 1912 a congressional panel investigating collusion among big business discovered that Morgan partners held 72 directorships in 47 corporations with total resources of $10 billion.

Morgan's son, J. P. Morgan, Jr., became senior partner of the firm upon his father's death in 1913. Morgan yielded day-to-day control to partner Thomas Lamont, who tried in 1929, just as J. P., Sr., had in 1907, to stem national financial collapse; however, the stock crash overwhelmed the effort.

In 1933, following Glass-Steagall Act reform of American banking, the company split its activities. Morgan remained a commercial banking firm, and a spin-off entity — Morgan Stanley — became the underwriter for securities. In 1940 Morgan changed from a partnership to a corporation.

In 1959 Morgan merged with Morgan Guaranty Trust and in 1969 became a bank holding company. In the 1960s the company became the most active trader in government securities, and the firm intensified its international efforts. After a 1987 restructuring, Morgan pushed into merger-and-acquisitions services.

HOW MUCH

	9 Yr. Growth	1980	1981	1982	1983	1984	1985	1986	1987	1988	1989
Sales ($ mil)	8.2%	5,111	6,719	6,767	5,764	6,562	6,575	6,672	6,834	7,839	10,394
Net income ($ mil)	—	342	348	394	460	538	705	873	83	1,002	(1,275)
Income as % of sales	—	6.7%	5.2%	5.8%	8.0%	8.2%	10.7%	13.1%	1.2%	12.8%	(12.3%)
Earnings per share ($)	—	2.08	2.11	2.38	2.63	3.04	3.91	4.74	0.39	5.38	(7.04)
Stock price – high ($)	—	14.41	15.97	18.00	21.56	20.19	33.00	48.00	53.63	40.25	48.13
Stock price – low ($)	—	9.94	12.28	11.38	15.63	14.13	19.13	29.50	27.00	30.75	34.00
Stock price – close ($)	14.6%	12.91	13.44	16.88	16.84	19.63	32.06	41.25	36.25	34.88	44.00
P/E – high	—	7	8	8	8	7	8	10	138	7	—
P/E – low	—	5	6	5	6	5	5	6	69	6	—
Dividends per share ($)	10.0%	0.72	0.79	0.87	0.94	1.03	1.13	1.26	1.40	1.54	1.70
Book value per share ($)	4.9%	14.09	15.52	17.11	18.85	21.03	23.70	27.42	26.57	30.52	21.78

1989 Year End:
Debt ratio: 51.1%
Return on equity: —
Cash (mil): $12,980
Current ratio: —
Long-term debt (mil): $4,690
Number of shares (mil): 184
Dividends:
1989 average yield: 3.9%
1989 payout: —
Market value (mil): $8,084

Stock Price History high/low 1980-89

60
50
40
30
20
10
0

NYSE symbol: JPM
Incorporated: Delaware, 1968
Fiscal year ends: December 31

WHO

Chairman and CEO: Dennis Weatherstone, age 59, $1,450,000 pay (prior to promotion)
President: Douglas A. Warner III, age 43, $1,150,000 pay (prior to promotion)
VC: Roberto G. Mendoza, age 44, $2,000,000 pay (prior to promotion)
VC: John F. Ruffle, age 52, $1,150,000 pay
VC: Kurt F. Viermetz, age 50, $1,300,000 pay (prior to promotion)
SVP (Principal Financial Officer): Thomas H. Fox, age 47
Auditors: Price Waterhouse
Employees: 14,207

WHERE

HQ: 60 Wall St., New York, NY 10260
Phone: 212-483-2323
FAX: 212-422-5183

J.P. Morgan recently moved to 60 Wall Street from its stately old headquarters nestled between the New York Stock Exchange and Federal Hall. It oversees offices in 7 US cities and in 26 other cities around the world.

	1989 Revenues		1989 Pretax Income	
	$ mil	% of total	$ mil	% of total
US	5,506	53	400	—
Europe, Middle East & Africa	3,435	33	255	—
Western Hemisphere, excluding US	801	8	(1,703)	—
Asia & Pacific	652	6	(52)	—
Total	**10,394**	**100**	**(1,100)**	—

WHAT

Services to Clients
Financing
Investments
Long-term advisory relationships
Risk management
Strategic advice

RANKINGS

4th in *Fortune* 100 Commercial Banking Cos.
55th in *Fortune* World's 100 Commercial Banks
66th in *Forbes* Sales 500
83rd in *Business Week* 1000
256th in *Business Week* Global 1000

COMPETITION

Bank of New York
BankAmerica
Bankers Trust
Chase Manhattan
Citicorp
Continental Bank
Chemical Banking
CS Holding
Dai-Ichi Kangyo
Deutsche Bank
First Chicago
Hong Kong & Shanghai Banking
Manufacturers Hanover
Security Pacific
Other money center banks
Investment banking firms
Securities brokerage firms

MORGAN STANLEY GROUP INC.

OVERVIEW

Morgan Stanley, the 8th largest US diversified financial company, with $53.3 billion in assets, is a major international securities firm.

Morgan Stanley serves institutional and individual clients worldwide through 10 foreign offices in Canada, Europe, Hong Kong, Japan, and Australia. The firm is a leading underwriter of common and preferred stock and taxable fixed-income securities in the US market, and taxable fixed income and equity securities in international markets. Morgan Stanley advised clients in completed mergers and acquisitions valued at $130 billion in 1989; more than 1/3 of the value of these transactions involved a non-US corporation.

In merchant banking the firm invests its own capital, along with funds it manages for others, in acquisitions, restructurings, and high-yield financings. At the end of 1989, the firm had investments of $254 million in 41 companies.

Morgan Stanley provides sales, trading, and research services to clients worldwide. Recognized for its planning, Morgan Stanley became an industry pioneer in 1980 by designing a common database to be used to trade and settle securities transactions in any market in the world.

The firm announced that S. Parker Gilbert plans to retire as chairman at the end of 1990, and President Richard B. Fisher will become chairman and Robert F. Greenhill, president.

NYSE symbol: MS
Incorporated: Delaware, 1975
Fiscal year ends: December 31

WHO

Chairman: S. Parker Gilbert, age 56, $5,475,000 pay
President: Richard B. Fisher, age 53, $5,475,000 pay
VC: Robert F. Greenhill, age 53, $5,475,000 pay
Auditors: Ernst & Young
Employees: 6,600

WHERE

HQ: 1251 Ave. of the Americas, New York, NY 10020
Phone: 212-703-4000
FAX: 212-703-6503

Morgan Stanley operates from its headquarters, 3 US regional offices, and 10 foreign offices.

	1989 Sales $ mil	1989 Sales % of total
US	5,096	87
Foreign	735	13
Total	**5,831**	**100**

WHEN

The stock market crash of 1929 raised concerns in the US Congress about banks issuing stock to raise funds for their clients. In 1934 the Glass-Steagall Act required banks to separate commercial banking (deposit-taking and lending) from investment banking (issuing and trading securities) activities.

The prestigious J.P. Morgan decided to stay in commercial banking. In 1935 some of its partners, led by Henry Morgan and Harold Stanley, resigned and established Morgan Stanley as an investment banking firm. Capitalizing on its old ties to major corporations, the company handled $1 billion in issues during its first year.

In 1941 Morgan Stanley became a partnership so it could join the New York Stock Exchange. By this time the firm already had managed 25% of all bond issues underwritten since the Glass-Steagall Act.

In the 1950s Morgan Stanley was known as a well-managed firm that handled issues by itself and rarely participated with other firms. Despite having only $3 million in capital, the partnership was the investment bank for major US corporations including General Motors, US Steel, General Electric, and Du Pont.

Morgan Stanley chose not to help finance the merger wave of the 1960s (when conglomerates purchased unrelated companies), since Morgan Stanley's blue-chip clients were not involved. In the early 1970s it entered the mergers and acquisitions world by forming Wall Street's first M&A department. In 1974 Morgan Stanley handled its first hostile takeover, International Nickel's unsolicited takeover of ESB, the world's largest manufacturer of batteries. Competing investment banking firms then became involved in hostile takeovers.

In 1986 Morgan Stanley became a publicly owned corporation, with its managing directors and principals retaining 81% of the stock. The firm became a major investor in US companies in the late 1980s. By combining its own money with funds from pension plans and other institutions, Morgan led the investment banking industry. In 1989 Morgan Stanley exceeded $100 million in pretax profits derived from the sale of selected equity investments.

In 1989 foreign operations were 13% of the firm's revenues. Morgan Stanley enters the 1990s with a new international securities custody and clearing operation that it hopes will be as profitable as investment management.

WHAT

	1989 Sales $ mil	1989 Sales % of total
Investment banking	947	16
Trading, as principal	742	13
Investments, as principal	246	4
Commissions	250	4
Interest & dividends	3,518	61
Asset management	112	2
Other	16	—
Total	**5,831**	**100**

Financial Services
Asset management
Corporate finance
Futures, options, foreign exchange, and commodities trading
Merchant banking
Securities custody, clearance, and lending
Securities distribution and trading
Securities underwriting
Stock brokerage and research

HOW MUCH

	4 Yr. Growth	1980	1981	1982	1983	1984	1985	1986	1987	1988	1989
Sales ($ mil)	34.3%	—	—	—	—	—	1,795	2,463	3,148	4,109	5,831
Net income ($ mil)	43.0%	—	—	—	—	—	106	201	231	395	443
Income as % of sales	—	—	—	—	—	—	5.9%	8.2%	7.3%	9.6%	7.6%
Earnings per share ($)	—	—	—	—	—	—	—	5.57	5.95	10.12	11.21
Stock price – high ($)	—	—	—	—	—	—	—	54.67	57.25	56.58	79.50
Stock price – low ($)	—	—	—	—	—	—	—	40.92	25.50	31.17	54.83
Stock price – close ($)	—	—	—	—	—	—	—	43.25	34.17	55.33	64.63
P/E – high	—	—	—	—	—	—	—	10	10	6	7
P/E – low	—	—	—	—	—	—	—	7	4	3	5
Dividends per share ($)	—	—	—	—	—	—	0.00	0.23	0.53	0.63	1.00
Book value per share ($)	47.1%	—	—	—	—	—	10.22	21.05	26.96	38.17	47.85

1989 Year End:
Debt ratio: 23.7%
Return on equity: 26.1%
Cash (mil): $872
Assets (mil): $53,276
Long-term debt (mil): $627
Number of shares (mil): 37
Dividends:
1989 average yield: 1.5%
1989 payout: 8.9%
Market value (mil): $2,392

Stock Price History high/low 1986-89

RANKINGS

8th in *Fortune* 50 Diversified Financial Cos.
147th in *Forbes* Sales 500
267th in *Business Week* 1000
774th in *Business Week* Global 1000

COMPETITION

American Express
CS Holding
Deutsche Bank
Goldman Sachs
Merrill Lynch
Nomura
Prudential
Salomon
Major investment bankers
Major investment managers

MORTON INTERNATIONAL, INC.

OVERVIEW

Morton International is a Chicago-based manufacturer of specialty chemicals, salt, and automobile air bags.

Specialty chemicals account for 66% of Morton's sales and include adhesives and coatings for food packaging and liquid plastic coatings for automobiles. Morton also makes electronic materials used in printed circuit boards and semiconductor wafers and is a leading provider of dyes used for leak detection and for coloring petroleum products, plastics, food, and cosmetics. The company has chemical operations in the US and through 14 foreign subsidiaries and 3 foreign joint ventures.

Morton salt, accounting for 30% of sales, is the US market leader, and Morton's Windsor Salt leads in Canada. About 25% of the salt business comes from ice control and another 25% from water conditioning salt pellets.

Morton's air bag business (inflators and driver modules) accounts for only 4% of sales but is growing fast, with 50% of the worldwide market.

WHEN

Alonzo Richmond started Richmond & Company, agents for Onondaga Salt, in Chicago in 1848. During the first year Richmond received 36,656 barrels of salt for packing from Onondaga Lake near Syracuse.

In 1867 the company became Haskins, Martin & Wheeler, and the salt supply came by boat from lumber towns in northern Michigan. In 1886 Joy Morton became the controlling owner of Haskins, Martin & Wheeler (renamed Joy Morton & Company). The company remained a sales agency until 1890, when it built its first salt evaporation plant in Wyandotte, Michigan.

In 1910 the company was renamed Morton Salt Company. In 1914, after 3 years of advertisements featuring the Morton Salt girl holding an umbrella, the company added its well-known salt slogan: "When it rains it pours."

Morton introduced iodized salt for the prevention of goiter in 1924 and bought a salt plant in Michigan in 1931 to develop bromides for photography and pharmaceuticals. Morton expanded nationwide with 8 production centers in the 1940s. It also bought a Louisiana salt plant (1947) for salt cake (paper making) and muriatic acid (steel production).

In 1951 the company purchased Edwal Laboratories, an Illinois manufacturer of photographic chemicals, and introduced Morton Pellets, salt for recharging home water softeners. In 1954 Morton purchased The Canadian Salt Company Ltd.

In the 1960s Morton diversified by purchasing Adcote Chemicals (1964, commercial adhesives), Simoniz (1965, waxes), and Williams Hounslow (1967, food and cosmetic dyes). In 1969 privately owned Morton merged with Norwich Pharmacal, maker of drugs (Pepto-Bismol, Chloraseptic) and household cleaners (Fantastik, Spray 'n Wash), to form Morton-Norwich Products, Inc.

During the 1970s, CEO John W. Simmons organized the company in 4 divisions: salts, pharmaceuticals, household products, and specialty chemicals. In 1982 the company sold its Norwich-Eaton Pharmaceuticals division to Procter & Gamble for $371 million. Later that year Morton-Norwich bought Thiokol, Inc., a rocket and chemical manufacturer, to form Morton Thiokol, Inc.

The company successfully applied Thiokol's propulsion knowledge to develop automobile air bags (used by Mercedes, Chrysler, and Saab). However, CEO Charles S. Locke was concerned that aerospace represented about 45% of sales but only 28% of profits in 1987. By 1989 salt and specialty chemicals outperformed aerospace by an even wider margin, and the company spun off aerospace into a new company, Thiokol Corporation. Morton International retained the salt, chemical, and air bag businesses.

HOW MUCH

	5 Yr. Growth	1980	1981	1982	1983	1984	1985	1986	1987	1988	1989
Sales ($ mil)	7.0%	—	—	—	—	1,001	970	1,023	1,094	1,248	1,407
Net income ($ mil)	4.2%	—	—	—	—	79	157	90	105	116	97
Income as % of sales	—	—	—	—	—	7.9%	16.2%	8.8%	9.6%	9.3%	6.9%
Earnings per share ($)	—	—	—	—	—	—	—	—	—	2.43	2.03
Stock price – high ($)	—	—	—	—	—	—	—	—	—	—	41.88
Stock price – low ($)	—	—	—	—	—	—	—	—	—	—	31.50
Stock price – close ($)	—	—	—	—	—	—	—	—	—	—	35.88
P/E – high	—	—	—	—	—	—	—	—	—	—	21
P/E – low	—	—	—	—	—	—	—	—	—	—	16
Dividends per share ($)	—	—	—	—	—	—	—	—	—	—	0.00
Book value per share ($)	—	—	—	—	—	—	—	—	—	—	18.80

1989 Year End:
Debt ratio: 4.6%
Return on equity: —
Cash (mil): $53
Long-term debt (mil): $44
Number of shares (mil): 48
Dividends:
1989 average yield: 0.0%
1989 payout: 0.0%
Market value (mil): $1,718

Stock Price high/low 1989

45
40
35
30
25
20
15
10
5
0

NYSE symbol: MII
Incorporated: Indiana, 1989
Fiscal year ends: June 30

WHO

Chairman and CEO: Charles S. Locke, age 61, $659,333 pay (prior to Thiokol spin-off)
President and COO: S. Jay Stewart, age 51, $358,312 pay (prior to Thiokol spin-off)
Group VP, Salt: William E. Johnston, Jr., age 49, $355,742 pay (prior to Thiokol spin-off)
Group VP, Specialty Chemicals: Robert B. Covalt, age 58, $272,007 pay (prior to Thiokol spin-off)
VP Finance: John R. Bowen, age 56, $215,625 pay (prior to Thiokol spin-off)
Auditors: Ernst & Young
Employees: 8,400

WHERE

HQ: 110 N. Wacker Dr., Chicago, IL 60606
Phone: 312-807-2000
FAX: 312-807-2241

Morton has operations throughout the US and in 7 foreign countries.

	1989 Sales		1989 Operating Income	
	$ mil	% of total	$ mil	% of total
US	968	69	127	61
Canada & Bahamas	157	11	32	15
Europe	261	19	45	22
Other	21	1	3	2
Adjustments	—	—	(25)	—
Total	**1,407**	**100**	**182**	**100**

WHAT

	1989 Sales		1989 Operating Income	
	$ mil	% of total	$ mil	% of total
Specialty chemicals	936	66	144	69
Salt	421	30	68	33
Inflatable restraint systems	50	4	(5)	(2)
Adjustments	—	—	(25)	—
Total	**1,407**	**100**	**182**	**100**

Products

Auto air bag systems
Salt
- Morton and Windsor table salts
- Private label table salts
- Salt for ice melting
- Salt pellets (water conditioning)

Specialty chemicals
- Adhesives and coatings
- Dry film photoresists (for circuit boards)
- Specialty dyes and colors
- Specialty polymers

RANKINGS

194th in *Fortune* 500 Industrial Cos. (Morton Thiokol)
488th in *Forbes* Sales 500
352nd in *Business Week* 1000
977th in *Business Week* Global 1000

COMPETITION

Allied-Signal
American Cyanamid
Bayer
BASF
Cargill
Du Pont
FMC
W. R. Grace
Hercules
Hoechst
Rhône-Poulenc
TRW
Union Carbide
Specialty chemical manufacturers

MOTOROLA, INC.

OVERVIEW

Motorola is the leading US supplier in 2 major product categories — mobile radio and semiconductors — and ranks high in each worldwide (first in mobile radio and 4th in semiconductors).

Motorola is the largest worldwide supplier of cellular telephone systems, 2-way radio systems, paging systems, and pagers. The Communications Sector and the General Systems Sector accounted for 54% of sales. Motorola has aggressively pursued business overseas and is the only non-Japanese supplier of car telephones to Nippon Telegraph & Telephone.

Motorola's Semiconductor Products Sector makes over 50,000 products. Since 1979 the company has sold more than 30 million microprocessors, which are used primarily in telephone switches, laser printers, microcomputers, and factory automation systems. It is the only manufacturer of the 68030 chip used in the Apple Macintosh and Hewlett-Packard microcomputers, but this business is clouded by a court loss to Hitachi for patent infringement.

Motorola's Information Systems Group produces data communications hardware; the Government Electronics Group pursues defense contracts; and the Automotive and Industrial Electronics Group makes instrumentation and sensors for automobiles.

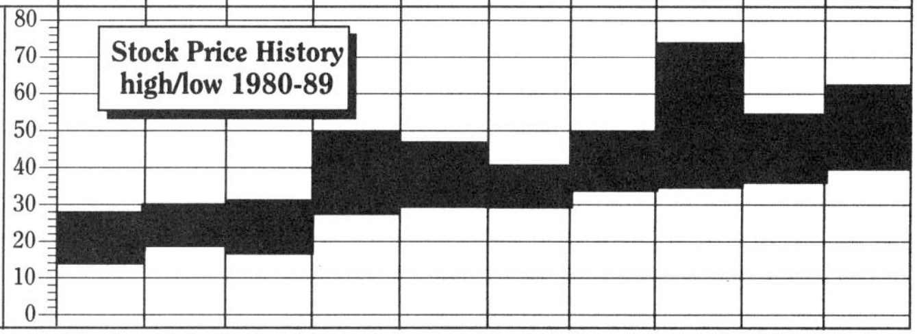

NYSE symbol: MOT
Incorporated: Delaware, 1973
Fiscal year ends: December 31

WHO

Chairman and CEO: George M. C. Fisher, age 49, $776,999 pay (before promotion)
VC: John F. Mitchell, age 61, $769,939 pay
President and COO: Gary L. Tooker, age 50, $668,315 pay (before promotion)
SEVP: Christopher B. Galvin, age 39
EVP and CFO: Donald R. Jones, age 59
Auditors: KPMG Peat Marwick
Employees: 102,000

WHERE

HQ: 1303 E. Algonquin Rd., Schaumburg, IL 60196
Phone: 708-576-5000
FAX: 708-576-8003

Motorola has major facilities in 11 states, Puerto Rico, Asia, Australia, Canada, Mexico, Europe, and the Middle East.

	1989 Sales		1989 Operating Income	
	$ mil	% of total	$ mil	% of total
US	8,123	62	623	67
Other nations	4,910	38	313	33
Adjustments	(3,413)	—	(140)	—
Total	**9,620**	**100**	**796**	**100**

WHEN

Two individuals share primary responsibility for shaping Motorola. The first, Paul Galvin, founded Galvin Manufacturing in 1928. Based in Chicago, Galvin began producing car radio receivers in 1929 and began speculating whether he could make a mobile radio for police. He met with Daniel Noble, a professor working on mobile design, and persuaded him to join the company. Noble influenced Galvin's first portable radio design and eventually led the company into TV and electronics.

In 1947 Galvin renamed the company Motorola, after its car radios. That same year Noble established an Arizona research laboratory for the pursuit of defense contracts for radio communications. Radios and TVs required vacuum tubes, which Motorola purchased from key competitor RCA. Noble convinced Galvin to invest R&D dollars in solid-state devices, and in the mid-1950s Noble went on to develop germanium transistors. In the late 1950s he turned to semiconductor development. Since then Motorola has manufactured integrated circuits and microprocessors; each allowed the company to market outside of its long-time mainstay, the automotive industry. In 1959 Galvin died and his son Robert became CEO. Noble continued as chairman of the science committee.

Motorola changed focus in the 1970s, selling its TV business to Matsushita (Japan, 1974) and investing in the data communications market for hardware such as modems, through acquisition of Codex (1977) and Universal Data Systems (1978). Motorola has recently invested more heavily in data communications: Codex increased its stake in StrataCom (1989), a manufacturer of multiplexers; Motorola acquired Mobile Data International (1988), a vendor of mobile data terminals; and the company is constructing mobile data networks.

New product development is key to Motorola's survival; in 1989 the company spent $784 million on R&D, 8% of revenues. Motorola touts its 1992 "Six Sigma" goal — to manufacture all products with only 3.4 defects per million parts. The company has become a leader in electronics markets otherwise dominated by Japan. Galvin's chosen successor, George Fisher, took over in 1990; his son, Christopher Galvin, is widely expected to become Fisher's successor. Motorola announced plans for a $2.3 billion global satellite system to connect cellular systems in 1990.

WHAT

	1989 Sales		1989 Operating Income	
	$ mil	% of total	$ mil	% of total
Government electronics	698	7	46	5
Communications	3,310	34	302	34
Information systems	552	6	18	2
Semiconductors	2,654	28	189	21
General systems	1,902	20	340	38
Other	490	5	4	—
Adjustments	14	—	(103)	—
Total	**9,620**	**100**	**796**	**100**

Products
Automotive electronics
Cellular telephone systems & telephones
Government electronic systems
Modems
Paging systems & pagers
Semiconductors
Two-way radios

Data Communications Hardware Brands
Codex
Universal Data Systems

HOW MUCH

	9 Yr. Growth	1980	1981	1982	1983	1984	1985	1986	1987	1988	1989
Sales ($ mil)	13.4%	3,099	3,336	3,786	4,328	5,534	5,443	5,888	6,707	8,250	9,620
Net income ($ mil)	11.6%	186	175	170	244	387	72	194	308	445	498
Income as % of sales	—	6.0%	5.2%	4.5%	5.6%	7.0%	1.3%	3.3%	4.6%	5.4%	5.2%
Earnings per share ($)	7.9%	1.94	1.85	1.55	2.09	3.27	0.61	1.53	2.39	3.43	3.83
Stock price – high ($)	—	28.00	30.17	31.17	50.00	46.92	40.75	50.00	74.00	54.63	62.50
Stock price – low ($)	—	13.71	18.58	16.42	27.33	29.25	29.13	33.63	34.50	35.88	39.50
Stock price – close ($)	10.2%	24.33	19.25	29.00	45.42	33.75	38.88	35.63	49.75	42.00	58.38
P/E – high	—	14	16	20	24	14	67	33	31	16	16
P/E – low	—	7	10	11	13	9	48	22	14	10	10
Dividends per share ($)	5.2%	0.48	0.53	0.53	0.53	0.61	0.64	0.64	0.64	0.67	0.76
Book value per share ($)	10.1%	12.25	13.60	14.80	16.49	19.18	19.15	21.48	23.26	26.02	29.16

1989 Year End:
Debt ratio: 16.6%
Return on equity: 13.9%
Cash (mil): $433
Current ratio: 1.42
Long-term debt (mil): $755
Number of shares (mil): 130
Dividends:
 1989 average yield: 1.3%
 1989 payout: 19.8%
Market value (mil): $7,612

Stock Price History high/low 1980-89

80
70
60
50
40
30
20
10
0

RANKINGS

48th in *Fortune* 500 Industrial Cos.
128th in *Fortune* Global 500 Industrial Cos.
14th in *Fortune* 50 Exporters
80th in *Forbes* Sales 500
54th in *Business Week* 1000
138th in *Business Week* Global 1000

COMPETITION

Fujitsu
Harris
Hitachi
Hyundai
Intel
Matsushita
Mitsubishi
National Semiconductor
NEC
Robert Bosche
Samsung
Siemens
Texas Instruments

NATIONAL GEOGRAPHIC SOCIETY

OVERVIEW

The National Geographic Society defines its primary purpose as "the increase and diffusion of geographic knowledge." Recent articles in the society's monthly magazine have covered the Alaska oil spill, culture in Austin, Texas, parks in the Himalayas, global warming, and new forest preserves in Mayan areas of Central America.

Since 1890 the Society has supported over 3,700 exploration and research projects ranging from Robert E. Peary's expedition to the North Pole to the exploration of the sunken *Titanic*. It now has 10.9 million members and an estimated 30 million to 50 million readers. The Society also publishes an array of maps, atlases, and books and makes its popular TV documentaries available on videotape.

The Society's educational programs received $2.8 million in 1989 from government and industry to promote better science education. Its Summer Geography Institute graduates trained 53,000 other teachers over the 1989-1990 school year. Educational media developed by the society include laser videodisc and interactive computer software to teach children about the world.

WHEN

On January 13, 1888, a group of prominent scientists and explorers gathered at Washington, DC's Cosmos Club, across from the White House, to form the National Geographic Society. Gardiner Hubbard was elected as its first president. The Society mailed the first edition of its magazine, dated October 1888, to 165 members. The magazine was clothed in a dull terra-cotta cover and contained a few esoteric articles (such as "The Classification of Geographic Forms by Genesis"). Regular monthly issues didn't appear until after the January 1896 issue, which was sold on newsstands in an attempt to boost sales.

In 1898, following Hubbard's death, his son-in-law, inventor Alexander Graham Bell, became president. Bell wanted to make the magazine as popular as *Harper's Weekly* and *McClure's*. To do the job, he hired Gilbert Grosvenor, who started as assistant editor in 1899 and became managing editor in 1900. Grosvenor later married Bell's daughter. Grosvenor turned the magazine from a dry, technical publication to one of more general interest. It was Bell's idea to send the magazine to "members only," a unique marketing concept still in use today.

Grosvenor accepted only accurate, first-hand accounts for Society magazine articles. The magazine pioneered the use of photography, including the first hand-tinted colored photographs in a 1910 edition. Rare photographs of remote Tibet were published in 1905, and the first bare-breasted native woman appeared in a photograph of "a Zulu bride and bridegroom" in the November 1896 issue. The Society sponsored Robert Peary's conquest of the North Pole in 1909 and Hiram Bingham's 1912 exploration of Machu Picchu in Peru. Members raised $100,000 in 1915 to save what is now Sequoia National Park in California. The 1900 circulation of 2,200 rose to 1.2 million in 1930. Grosvenor's policy of printing only "what is of a kindly nature . . . about any country or people" resulted in 2 articles that were sharply criticized for their kindly portrayal of prewar Nazi Germany (one picture showed children with the caption, "Green as Goslings now, but practice makes the goose step perfect"). That policy eased over the years, and in 1961 an article by Peter White and Wilbur Garrett was one of the first to describe the growing US involvement in Vietnam.

Gilbert Grosvenor retired in 1954 after serving the society for 55 years as editor (including 34 years as president). Circulation in that year was 2.1 million. His son, Melville Bell Grosvenor, who ran the magazine until 1967, accelerated book publishing (over 50 titles since 1957) and created a film and TV department that broadcast its first documentary, *Americans on Everest*, in 1965. Circulation hit 10 million in 1983, 3rd after *Reader's Digest* and *TV Guide*. A 3rd generation Grosvenor, Gilbert Melville, took over in 1970 (editor from 1970 to 1980; president since 1980). Since that time the magazine has increasingly covered important social and political events as well as scientific and environmental subjects, and continued its tradition of photographic innovation, printing a hologram in 1984. Threatened by an aging membership, geographic illiteracy, and the lure of alternative media (TV), the society has had to cut staff and tighten expense controls in recent years.

HOW MUCH

	9 Yr. Growth	1980	1981	1982	1983	1984	1985	1986	1987	1988	1989
Cumulative no. of projects supported	—	1,896	2,000	2,200	2,350	2,600	2,800	3,100	3,300	3,400	3,700
Magazine circulation (thou)	0.2%	10,712	10,861	10,614	10,626	10,393	10,549	10,765	10,499	10,575	10,891

Cumulative Number of Exploration and Research Projects Supported 1980-89

Nonprofit organization
Founded: Washington, D.C., 1888
Fiscal year ends: December 31

WHO

President and Chairman: Gilbert M. Grosvenor, age 59
Editor: William Graves, age 63
EVP: Owen R. Anderson
SVP and Treasurer: Alfred J. Hayre
SVP: Raymond T. McElligott, Jr.
SVP: Robert B. Sims
Employees: 2,400

WHERE

HQ: 1600 M St. NW, Washington, DC 20036
Phone: 202-857-7000
FAX: 202-828-6679

The Society has 10.9 million members worldwide.

WHAT

	1989 Sales $ mil	1989 Sales % of total
Membership dues & magazine subscriptions	214	50
Journal subscriptions	28	7
Advertising sales	37	9
Publications sales	112	26
TV and audiovisual receipts	32	7
Other	3	1
Total	**426**	**100**

Publications
Images of the World
Journey into China
Living Tribes
Lost Empires
National Geographic Atlas of the World
National Geographic Magazine
National Geographic Research
National Geographic Traveler
National Geographic World
Peoples and Places of the Past
The Adventure of Archaeology
We Americans

TV Documentaries
"Dr. Leakey and the Dawn of Man"
"Journey to the Outer Limits"
"Rain Forest"
"The World of Jacques-Yves Cousteau"

Educational Programs
GTV American history program
National Geographic Kids Network
National Geography Bee
The Jason Project
The Weather Machine software

People
Dr. Robert D. Ballard (discovery of the Titanic)
Dr. George F. Bass (underwater archaeology)
Jacques-Yves Cousteau (oceanography)
Drs. John and Frank Craighead (bioecology)
Dr. Harold E. Edgerton (strobe photography)
Dr. Kenan T. Erim (archaeology aphrodisias)
Dr. Jane Goodall (primatology)
Sir Edmund Hillary (mountaineer-Everest)
Drs. Richard and Mary Leakey (anthropology)
Thayer Soule (travel lectures)
Barbara and Bradford Washburn (cartography)

NATIONAL MEDICAL ENTERPRISES, INC.

OVERVIEW

National Medical Enterprises owns or operates acute, rehabilitative, psychiatric, substance abuse, and long-term care facilities in the US and overseas. The company's operations are divided into major areas: specialty hospitals and general hospitals. The company is the 3rd largest for-profit health care company in the nation after Hospital Corporation of America and Humana.

NME's Specialty Hospital Group operates 67 psychiatric hospitals in 23 states through Psychiatric Institutes of America (PIA). Through Recovery Centers of America (RCA), the group operates 13 freestanding recovery units in 9 states. Through Rehab Hospital Services Corporation (RHSC), the company operates 27 rehabilitation hospitals in 10 states. The group also manages psychiatric, chemical abuse, and rehabilitation units in acute-care hospitals.

Under its General Hospital Group, NME operates 37 fully equipped general hospitals in 6 states and 3 in Malaysia and Singapore. NME's Westminster Health Care Limited operates 19 long-term care facilities in the UK.

NYSE symbol: NME
Incorporated: Nevada, 1975
Fiscal year ends: May 31

WHO

Chairman and CEO: Richard K. Eamer, age 62, $1,879,109 pay
President and COO: Leonard Cohen, age 65, $1,407,708 pay
SEVP: John C. Bedrosian, age 55, $933,665 pay
President and CEO, General Hospital Group: Michael H. Focht, Sr., age 47, $723,636 pay
President and CEO, Specialty Hospital Group: Norman A. Zober, age 47, $710,170 pay
EVP and CFO: Taylor R. Jenson, age 51
Auditors: KPMG Peat Marwick
Employees: 45,300

WHEN

Hospital attorney and financial consultant Richard Eamer founded National Medical Enterprises in 1969. With $23 million from the sale of public stock in May 1969, the company bought 4 general hospitals, 3 nursing homes, an office building, and 3 potential hospital sites, all in California. Within 6 years the company owned, operated, and managed 23 hospitals, owned a home health care business, sold medical equipment, provided training for vocational nurses, and distributed bottled oxygen.

The company bought Stolte, a hospital construction company (1977), and Medfield's 5 Florida hospitals (1979). In 1980 the company expanded into long-term care with the acquisition of The Hillhaven Corporation, expanding services to 33 states.

NME signed a 5-year, billion-dollar health care contract with Saudi Arabia in 1980 and by 1981 had become the 3rd largest health care company in the US, owning or managing 193 hospitals and nursing homes (24,000 beds). Total revenues exceeded $1 billion for the first time in 1982.

During the first 1/2 of the 1980s, NME continued to expand, buying National Health Enterprises' 66 long-term homes (1982); Psychiatric Institutes of America (PIA), operator of 21 mental health centers (1983); and Rehabilitation Hospital Services Corporation (RHSC), which owned 5 specialized facilities (1985). In 1983 the company formed Recovery Centers of America (RCA), opening 8 substance abuse treatment programs (by 1989 this had grown to 48). By 1985 the company had become the 2nd largest publicly owned health care company in an industry 2nd only to food and agriculture as the largest in the nation. Before the end of the 1980s, NME's Specialty Hospital Group (PIA, RCA, and RHSC) was bringing in more than 50% of the company's net operating revenues.

In January 1990 NME spun off most of its long-term care businesses (including 345 long-term care facilities, 120 Medi-$ave Pharmacies, and 24 retirement homes) to its shareholders as The Hillhaven Corporation. NME kept 14% of the Hillhaven stock and about 1/3 of the nursing home real estate, which it leases to Hillhaven. NME kept the 19 long-term care facilities operated in the UK by its Westminster Health Care Limited subsidiary.

NME plans to continue expanding through its specialty hospital group and its general hospital group to meet increasing demand for intensive care beds and outpatient surgery.

WHERE

HQ: 2700 Colorado Ave., Santa Monica, CA 90404
Phone: 213-315-8000
FAX: 213-315-8329

Location	Specialty Hospitals	General Hospitals
California	13	18
Florida	16	5
Louisiana	5	4
Maryland	6	
Missouri	2	2
Pennsylvania	9	
Tennessee	1	3
Texas	17	5
Virginia	5	
Colorado, Georgia, New Jersey, Wisconsin (3 each)	12	
Arkansas, Illinois, Indiana, New Hampshire, North Carolina, Utah (2 each)	12	
Alabama, Arizona, Connecticut, District of Columbia, Michigan, Minnesota, New Mexico, Oklahoma, South Carolina (1 each)	9	
Total	**107**	**37**

WHAT

	1989 Sales		1989 Operating Income	
	$ mil	% of total	$ mil	% of total
Specialty hospitals	1,142	31	224	51
General hospitals	1,473	40	167	39
Long-term care	1,061	29	42	10
Adjustments	3	—	(4)	—
Total	**3,679**	**100**	**429**	**100**

1989 Licensed Beds	No. of Beds	% of Total
Specialty hospitals	7,669	13
General hospitals	6,726	12
Long-term care	43,162	75
Total	**57,557**	**100**

RANKINGS

28th in *Fortune* 100 Diversified Service Cos.
212th in *Forbes* Sales 500
241st in *Business Week* 1000
705th in *Business Week* Global 1000

COMPETITION

Hospital Corp.
Humana
Mayo Foundation

HOW MUCH

	9 Yr. Growth	1980	1981	1982	1983	1984	1985	1986	1987	1988	1989
Sales ($ mil)	22.1%	609	881	1,139	1,747	2,065	2,530	2,947	2,870	3,199	3,679
Net income ($ mil)	23.1%	30	52	75	93	121	149	118	140	170	192
Income as % of sales	—	4.8%	5.9%	6.6%	5.3%	5.9%	5.9%	4.0%	4.9%	5.3%	5.2%
Earnings per share ($)	13.7%	0.73	0.99	1.28	1.47	1.74	1.98	1.48	1.68	2.09	2.32
Stock price – high ($)	—	7.53	15.20	23.00	23.80	32.38	25.63	32.88	26.75	30.88	24.75
Stock price – low ($)	—	3.33	6.47	12.50	9.80	20.13	17.63	18.75	19.25	16.13	17.63
Stock price – close ($)	12.5%	7.43	14.80	13.90	23.20	23.00	23.38	22.38	22.50	18.88	21.50
P/E – high	—	10	15	18	16	19	13	22	16	15	11
P/E – low	—	5	7	10	7	12	9	13	11	8	8
Dividends per share ($)	17.2%	0.16	0.24	0.31	0.38	0.43	0.50	0.55	0.59	0.63	0.68
Book value per share ($)	14.5%	4.38	6.72	7.70	9.95	11.03	12.36	12.83	12.47	13.11	14.80

1989 Year End:
Debt ratio: 60.3%
Return on equity: 16.6%
Cash (mil): $109
Current ratio: 1.81
Long-term debt (mil): $1,671
Number of shares (mil): 74
Dividends:
1989 average yield: 3.2%
1989 payout: 29.3%
Market value (mil): $1,599

Stock Price History high/low 1980-89

NATIONAL ORGANIZATION FOR WOMEN, INC.

OVERVIEW

The National Organization for Women (NOW) is the nation's largest women's rights group, with over 250,000 female and male members (up from 140,000 in 1987) and an annual budget of over $10 million. The organization's broad goal is equality for women in American society. Specific activities include lobbying, litigation, educational programs, and political organizing involving such issues as economic equality; the Equal Rights Amendment; reproductive rights; lesbian/gay rights; elimination of racism; equal opportunities for women and girls in educational and sports activities; and economic protection for older women and for women in general who, with their children, are the fastest growing group in poverty.

NOW is governed by 4 national salaried officers and a board of directors and has several national issues committees. Local chapters of 10 or more members and state chapters (which help coordinate local chapters and lobby in state legislatures) are chartered by the national organization; each belongs to one of 9 regions.

WHEN

NOW, the National Organization for Women, began in June 1966 at a Washington, DC, conference on the status of women. The founding group of 28 feminists, headed by author Betty Friedan (*The Feminine Mystique*), held its first national conference, with more than 300 delegates, in October of that year.

Officially incorporated in 1967, NOW addressed a wide range of inequities toward American women in the law, employment, media, education, and economics. Its strategies to achieve its goal of bringing "women into full participation in the mainstream of American society" included mass mailings, lobbying, lectures, and demonstrations. From its beginning NOW promoted the development of local chapters, viewing their grassroots activities as the "focus of feminist action."

Conflict within NOW between various factions marked its development. In 1968 its early support of the Equal Rights Amendment (ERA) caused a split with members of the UAW union, an important group within the ranks of the newly founded NOW. The union reversed its position and supported the ERA in 1970. Disagreements among members concerning a woman's right to abortion and support for lesbian rights, differences between radical and moderate factions, and conflicting views of NOW's focus all resulted in a heady mix of impassioned arguments, changes, and compromises for the young organization. NOW activists broke off to form other more narrowly focused groups, such as the National Women's Political Caucus (NWPC), the Women's Equity Action League (WEAL), and the Older Women's League (OWL).

The feminist movement expanded rapidly during the early 1970s. A NOW-sponsored demonstration, the Women's Strike for Equality, on August 26, 1970, brought 10,000 women and men to New York City in a visible show of support. In 1972 Congress approved the ERA (a major part of NOW's social agenda), sending it to state legislatures for ratification. More traditional groups such as the League of Women Voters and the Young Women's Christian Association (YWCA) gave their support to many of NOW's causes. In 1975 NOW stated that endorsement of national and local candidates would be part of its official agenda, and in 1977 it focused its work on ratification of the ERA.

By June 30, 1982, even with a 3-year extension and the public support of over 75% of the population, only 35 of the required 38 states had ratified the ERA, and the amendment failed. The ERA was reintroduced on July 14, 1982, and ratification remains one of NOW's top priorities.

Despite this substantial setback, NOW remains the largest and best-known feminist organization in the US. It has continued to focus on political activism, with recent emphasis on the continuing controversy of reproductive rights. While membership declined from 1983 to 1985, it resurged with the massive East Coast/West Coast Abortion Rights demonstration in 1986 and then mushroomed in 1989 with the Supreme Court's decision in the *Webster* case. By 1990 NOW's paid membership had risen to 250,000. A 1989 march and rally for abortion rights organized by NOW drew 600,000 to Washington, DC. At its 1989 national conference, NOW, under the leadership of President Molly Yard, decided to explore the establishment of a new national political party and/or electoral reforms to "open up our representative democracy to women, minorities, and young people, who are nearly invisible in the policy-making bodies of this country."

HOW MUCH

	9 Yr. Growth	1981	1982	1983	1984	1985	1986	1987	1988	1989	1990
Membership (thou)	5.0%	162	199	176	141	115	127	139	135	205	252

Membership (thou) 1981-90

Nonprofit organization
Founded: Washington, DC, 1966
Fiscal year ends: December 31

WHO

President: Molly Yard
EVP: Patricia Ireland
VP, Action: Rosemary Dempsey
Secretary: Kim Gandy
Members: 252,000

NOW membership is available to women and men who support the organization's goals.

WHERE

HQ: 1000 16th St. NW, Suite 700, Washington, DC 20036
Phone: 202-331-0066
FAX: 202-785-8576

Regions	Areas Served
Northeast	Maine, New Hampshire, Vermont , New York, Rhode Island, Massachusetts, Connecticut
Mid-Atlantic	New Jersey, Pennsylvania, West Virginia, Virginia, Delaware, District of Columbia, Maryland
Southeast	North Carolina, South Carolina, Georgia, Florida, Puerto Rico, Virgin Islands
Mid-South	Tennessee, Alabama, Mississippi, Louisiana, Arkansas
South Central	Texas, Oklahoma, New Mexico, Kansas, Colorado
Great Lakes	Michigan, Wisconsin, Ohio, Indiana, Illinois, Kentucky
Prairie States	Minnesota, Missouri, Iowa, North Dakota, South Dakota, Nebraska
Northwest	Washington, Alaska, Oregon, Montana, Idaho, Wyoming
Southwest	California, Nevada, Utah, Arizona, Hawaii, Guam, American Samoa, Trust Territory of the Pacific Islands

WHAT

Political Advocacy
Campus organizing
Educational programs and materials
Litigation
Lobbying
National and regional conferences
Public demonstrations

Insurance Plans
NOWlife term life
NOWmed comprehensive medical
NOW Medicare supplement

Periodicals
NOW Times
State and chapter publications

Targeted Areas for Activity
Early childhood education
Economic rights for women
Education discrimination
Eliminating racism
Equal Rights Amendment
Homemakers' rights
Lesbian/gay rights
Older women's rights
Reproductive rights
Violence against women

RANKINGS

1st in membership among women's rights organizations

NATIONAL PARK SERVICE

OVERVIEW

The National Park Service, created in 1916 as a part of the Interior Department, manages 355 national parks, monuments, historic sites, and recreation areas in the US, Puerto Rico, the Virgin Islands, and Guam. With about 80 million total acres, America's national park system represents the largest public land holding in the world, including areas of spectacular beauty as well as points of scientific and historical interest.

The Park Service classifies areas by size and number of resources preserved; for instance, a national park is characterized by large water or land areas and a variety of flora, fauna, and topography (*e.g.*, Grand Canyon National Park), while a national monument is usually smaller and preserves at least one significant resource (*e.g.*, Statue of Liberty). Wrangell–St. Elias National Park and Preserve, the Park Service's largest area, encompasses more than 13 million acres in Alaska. The smallest area, Philadelphia's Thaddeus Kosciuszko National Memorial, covers less than 1,000 square feet.

The Park Service offers tours, films, and other guidance to more than 200 million park visitors every year. Campgrounds, lodging, food, and transportation services are also available at many of the sites.

WHEN

Yellowstone, the world's first national park, was created by an Act of Congress in 1872. Signed into law by President Grant, the act provided for the protection and preservation of the area "for the benefit and enjoyment of the people." Management of Yellowstone was entrusted to the secretary of the interior.

The Lacey Antiquities Act of 1906 gave the president authority to establish national monuments. That year, Teddy Roosevelt proclaimed Devil's Tower, a Wyoming stone formation, the first national monument. In 1910, with the number of national parks and monuments increasing, President Taft urged Congress to create a national park bureau, but no action was taken until 1915, when Secretary of the Interior Franklin Lane, with former University of California classmate Steven Mather and attorney Horace Albright as his assistants, promoted legislation that created the National Park Service in 1916 to conserve and provide for the enjoyment of the scenery, historic objects, and wildlife within the park areas. Mather became the Park Service's first director, followed by Albright in 1929. When Albright resigned in 1933, the Park Service was managing 128 units, compared to only 39 when it was established.

Mather's and Albright's legacy includes park recreational facilities and the educational services provided by rangers to teach visitors about each area's geology, history, and wildlife.

Between 1940 and 1955 the Park Service gained only 20 new areas, but visitors increased from fewer than 17 million to 56 million per year. The Park Service enjoyed one of its greatest periods of growth under the directorship of George Hartzog (1964-1972), gaining about 100 new areas for a total of 297 in 1972. By 1985, when William Penn Mott took over as the Park Service director and outlined his 12-point plan to protect the parks' natural resources, the number of visitors to the nation's 337 parks and monuments had grown to more than 200 million every year. The Park Service gained 3 new areas in 1989.

Smokey the Bear, the familiar spokesman for fire prevention, went into semiretirement in 1972 when the Park Service began its current policy of fire management. Lightning-caused blazes are regarded as a part of the forest ecocycle, cleaning out dead trees and debris and making room for new growth. These are allowed to burn naturally as long as there is no danger to people or private property. Human-caused fires are put out immediately. This policy came under public scrutiny in 1988 when extensive fires in Yellowstone Park threatened millions of acres, but the Park Service has been vindicated by the public's fascination with the regeneration of the burned areas.

HOW MUCH

	9 Yr. Growth	1980	1981	1982	1983	1984	1985	1986	1987	1988	1989
Total appropriations ($ mil)	8.2%	391	475	522	605	616	636	611	704	754	792
Number of areas	0.7%	333	334	334	335	334	337	338	343	354	355
Land (thou acres)	1.4%	70,936	73,665	74,800	74,846	74,913	75,749	75,863	75,970	76,176	80,105
Visits (mil)	—	—	239	244	244	249	263	281	287	283	269
Appropriations per visit ($)	—	—	1.99	2.14	2.48	2.47	2.42	2.17	2.45	2.66	2.94
Overnight stays (mil)	—	—	16	16	16	16	16	16	17	17	—

Visits (mil) 1981-89

290 280 270 260 250 240 230 220 210 200

Government agency
Established: 1916, Department of Interior
Fiscal year ends: September 30

WHO

Secretary of Interior: Manuel Lujan, Jr., age 62, $99,500 pay
Director National Park Service: James M. Ridenour, age 48, $80,700 pay
Associate Director Budget and Administration: Edward L. Davis, age 57, $78,600 pay
Employees: 12,614 full-time; 3,306 part-time, temporary, or seasonal; 53,600 volunteers

WHERE

HQ: 1800 C St. NW, Washington, DC 20240
Phone: 202-208-4990
FAX: 202-208-5977

The National Park Service administers 355 parks and national monuments in the District of Columbia, Puerto Rico, the Virgin Islands, Saipan, American Samoa, Guam, and every state except Delaware.

Classification	Acreage	No.	% of total
International Historic Site	35	1	—
National Battlefield	12,772	11	3
National Battlefield Park	8,767	3	1
National Battlefield Site	1	1	—
National Capital Park	6,469	1	—
National Historic Park	151,633	29	8
National Historic Site	18,477	69	20
National Lakeshore	227,244	4	1
National Mall	146	1	—
National Memorial	7,949	23	7
National Military Park	34,047	9	3
National Monument	4,844,610	79	22
National Park	47,319,321	50	14
National Parkway	168,618	4	1
National Preserve	22,155,498	14	4
National Recreation Area	3,686,923	18	5
National River	5,360,630	5	1
National Scenic Trail	3,172,203	3	1
National Seashore	597,097	10	3
National Wild and Scenic River and Riverway	292,597	9	3
Park (other)	40,121	10	3
White House	18	1	—
Total	**80,105,176**	**355**	**100**

WHAT

	1989 Sources of Revenues	
	$ mil	% of total
Appropriations	792	94
Revenues from operations	50	6
Total	**842**	**100**

Big Bend National Park (Texas)
Death Valley National Monument (California)
Everglades National Park (Florida)
Gettysburg National Park (Pennsylvania)
Glacier National Park (Montana)
Grand Canyon National Park (Arizona)
Lincoln Memorial (Washington, DC)
Mount Rushmore National Memorial (South Dakota)
Thomas Jefferson Memorial (Washington, DC)
Washington Monument (Washington, DC)
Yellowstone National Park (Wyoming)
Yosemite National Park (California)

COMPETITION

No other organization in this book competes with the National Park Service.

NATIONAL SEMICONDUCTOR CORPORATION

OVERVIEW

National Semiconductor is the 4th largest semiconductor manufacturer in the US. It is the world leader in Ethernet chips for local area networks (LANs) and one of the largest suppliers of semiconductors to the US military.

National offers more than 5,000 different semiconductor products (integrated circuits and discrete devices). The majority have been standard, commodity products, with a concentration in analog and digital devices.

Emphasis has recently shifted to more application-specific products to serve laser printer, PC, and disk drive markets.

To find the lowest costs, National assembles most of its products offshore; non-US employees account for 60% of the total. The company, with a reputation for high quality and service, frequently enjoys preferred-vendor status. R&D expenditure remains exceptionally high at over 16% of revenues.

WHEN

National Semiconductor, founded in 1959 as a transistor company in Danbury, Connecticut, was by 1967 struggling on only $7 million in sales. Peter Sprague, heir to the Sprague electric fortune, rescued the company (1967) and lured a manufacturing expert named Charles Sporck and a crew of talented linear circuit engineers from Fairchild Semiconductor

Sporck transferred operations to Santa Clara, California, halved the transistor work force, and plowed the savings into promising linear chips and, later, digital logic chips (in the early 1970s); both efforts were successful. Sporck's prescient move into metal oxide devices (1978) made National an industry leader in MOS technology within 2 years.

The chip successes pushed National by 1981 to over $1 billion in sales (a first for Silicon Valley chipmakers). It then purchased National Advanced Systems (a distributor/servicer of Hitachi mainframes, 1979) and Data Terminal Systems (point-of-sale terminals, 1983).

When Japanese manufacturers dumped digital memory chips on the market in 1984 and 1985, National pulled out of the memory business. Its logic chips also suffered price squeezes, and in 1986 the company lost $148 million.

Sporck's new strategy was to transform his low-cost commodity chipmaker into a higher-margin supplier of niche products. National bought most assets of troubled Fairchild Semiconductor for a mere 24% of its annual revenues (1987) to obtain superior BiCMOS logic chips (used in large computers) and custom linear circuits for the US military; National sold Fairchild's Clipper chip division to Intergraph (1987).

Sluggish mainframe demand, coupled with mounting mainframe competition from IBM and Amdahl, prompted National in 1989 to sell NAS for $386 million (to a Hitachi/Electronic Data Systems joint venture) and Datachecker for $126 million (to ICL, Inc.), consolidate plants, and lay off 5% of its work force.

In 1989 National reorganized and created the VLSI (Very Large Scale Integration) division, headed by Vice President Raymond Farnham. With 3 groups aligned along market (rather than product) lines, the VLSI division, the centerpiece of National's recovery strategy, is geared to offer a range of proprietary chip solutions to the customer.

Signaling the niche approach are National's numerous joint ventures, providing chips for emerging Integrated Services Digital Network applications (with SGS-Thomson Microelectronics, Northern Telecom); office imaging peripherals (with Canon, printers; Xerox, copiers); personal computer enhancements (with Acer Group of Taiwan, Dove Computer); and Ethernet LANs (with Hewlett-Packard, Cabletron Systems). Other emphases include National's new 32000 family of microprocessors (used in faxes and printers) and LAN support (Xicom, purchased in 1989).

HOW MUCH

	9 Yr. Growth	1980	1981	1982	1983	1984	1985	1986	1987	1988	1989
Sales ($ mil)	5.9%	980	1,110	1,104	1,211	1,655	1,788	1,478	1,868	2,470	1,648
Net income ($ mil)	—	52	53	(11)	(14)	56	34	(148)	(29)	63	(206)
Income as % of sales	—	5.3%	4.8%	(1.0%)	(1.2%)	3.4%	1.9%	(10.0%)	(1.5%)	2.5%	(12.5%)
Earnings per share ($)	—	0.85	0.80	(0.16)	(0.20)	0.66	0.38	*(1.73)*	*(0.42)*	0.53	(1.83)
Stock price – high ($)	—	8.14	17.17	13.96	8.75	20.00	19.25	15.13	15.63	22.25	15.00
Stock price – low ($)	—	4.11	5.54	5.83	4.38	7.17	9.50	10.13	8.25	9.75	8.13
Stock price – close ($)	2.7%	7.69	13.42	6.38	7.33	15.63	11.88	12.50	10.63	12.00	9.75
P/E – high	—	10	21	—	—	30	51	—	—	42	—
P/E – low	—	5	7	—	—	11	25	—	—	18	—
Dividends per share ($)	0.0%	0.00	0.00	0.00	0.00	0.00	0.00	0.00	0.00	0.00	0.00
Book value per share ($)	9.2%	3.74	4.94	4.83	4.68	7.12	7.64	7.91	8.69	9.41	8.28

1989 Year End:
Debt ratio: 5.8%
Return on equity: —
Cash (mil): $228
Current ratio: 1.51
Long-term debt (mil): $52
Number of shares (mil): 103
Dividends:
1989 average yield: 0.0%
1989 payout: 0.0%
Market value (mil): $999

NYSE symbol: NSM
Incorporated: Delaware, 1959
Fiscal year ends: Last Sunday in May

WHO

Chairman: Peter J. Sprague, age 51
President, CEO, and COO: Charles E. Sporck, age 62, $492,540 pay
VP Finance (acting): John G. Webb, age 46
VP: Edgar R. Parker, age 50, $187,970 pay
VP: Clements E. Pausa, age 59, $209,330 pay
VP: Kirk P. Pond, age 46, $218,514 pay
Auditors: KPMG Peat Marwick
Employees: 32,200

WHERE

HQ: 2900 Semiconductor Dr., PO Box 58090, Santa Clara, CA 95052
Phone: 408-721-5000
FAX: 408-739-9803

Wafer fabrication plants are located in the US, Israel, and Scotland; assembly plants are in Brazil, Hong Kong, Malaysia, the Philippines, Singapore, Thailand, Scotland, and the US; sales offices are in the US, Canada, Europe, Asia, Australia, and Latin America.

	1989 Sales	
	$ mil	% of total
Americas	908	55
Europe	371	23
Asia	369	22
Total	**1,648**	**100**

WHAT

Integrated Circuits (ICs)
Application-specific integrated circuits (ASICs)
- Customized ICs for computation, telecommunications, and military applications

Digital
- Memory
- Microprocessors
- Standard logic

Linear (analog)
- Audio amplifiers
- Automotive circuits
- Comparators
- Timers
- Voltage regulators

VLSI Division
- ICs for floppy and hard disks, laser printers, and computer terminals

Discrete devices
- Transistors

RANKINGS

187th in *Fortune* 500 Industrial Cos.
459th in *Forbes* Sales 500
599th in *Business Week* 1000

COMPETITION

Fujitsu
Harris
Hitachi
Hyundai
IBM
Intel
Motorola
NEC
Philips
Siemens
Texas Instruments

NAVISTAR INTERNATIONAL CORPORATION

OVERVIEW

Navistar, the successor of International Harvester, has led the US in combined medium and heavy truck production since 1980 (27.5% of the 1989 market). The company is also a leading producer of OEM diesel truck engines (principally to Ford) and school bus chassis, and it makes replacement parts.

Due to financial problems, Navistar sold its agricultural equipment (1982) and construction machinery (1983) manufacturing operations. The company has not paid dividends on its common stock since 1981. Navistar markets its trucks through the US's largest truck dealer network.

With new truck models and new technology, Navistar is looking for logical extensions of its truck business that can contribute to less cyclical earnings. Joint ventures with suppliers (such as those existing with Dana and Nissan) will continue to be important.

WHEN

Cyrus McCormick, the Virginia-born inventor who perfected the reaper in 1831, moved west and set up his first factory in Chicago in 1846. To compete with other manufacturers, McCormick offered such innovations as the installment plan, a written guarantee, and factory-trained repairmen. In 1886 a strike at the Chicago works in favor of the 8-hour workday led to the infamous Haymarket Square riot. In 1902, with the backing of J. P. Morgan, McCormick merged with Deering and several smaller firms to form International Harvester (IH). The new enterprise controlled 85% of US harvester production.

IH set up its first overseas factory in 1905 in Sweden. In 1906 Harvester entered the tractor industry and in 1907 began production of the Auto Buggy, forerunner of the truck. By 1910 the firm was annually producing 1,300 trucks and 1,400 tractors and had reached over $100 million in sales.

In 1913, Cyrus Jr. (Sr. had died in 1884) borrowed $5 million from John D. Rockefeller and gained control of the company. The new general manager, Alexander Legge (also president from 1922 to 1929) introduced the Farmall, the first all-purpose tractor, in 1924. In 1928 IH began production of a heavy truck with a 4-cylinder engine and by 1937 was the top US producer of medium and heavy trucks.

In the post-WWII industry boom, IH's neglect of product development and capital improvement, combined with the effects of overdiversification, caused market share to decline for most of its products. The company sold more trucks than agricultural equipment for the first time in 1955. IH lost its lead in agricultural equipment to John Deere in 1958. During the 1960s, IH lost its medium industry sales leadership to Ford, and the company's construction equipment business, although buoyed by the 1952 acquisition of the Payloader, consistently lost market share.

The 1980s recession, combined with a 6-month strike by the UAW (1980), sent IH to the edge of bankruptcy. Between 1980 and 1982 the company lost $2.3 billion. Restructuring, IH sold the construction equipment division to Dresser Industries in 1982. In 1985 Tenneco bought the agricultural equipment business and the International Harvester name. By 1986 the number of employees had dropped 85%, and plants had decreased from 48 worldwide to 6 in North America.

Renamed Navistar in 1986, the company has redesigned 85% of its truck line since 1987. In 1989 Navistar introduced 27 new truck models, plus a 9-speed heavy truck transmission (developed jointly with Dana), the first all-new design of its kind in more than 25 years. Navistar also introduced the Smokeless Diesel engine, which meets stricter emissions standards scheduled to take effect in 1994. Earnings in 1989 declined 66% due to new product start-up costs and a weak US truck market, which continues into 1990.

HOW MUCH

	9 Yr. Growth	1980	1981	1982	1983	1984	1985	1986	1987	1988	1989
Sales ($ mil)	(4.3%)	6,312	7,041	4,292	3,601	4,802	3,508	3,357	3,530	4,080	4,241
Net income ($ mil)	—	(370)	(636)	(1,266)	(533)	(61)	113	(2)	146	259	87
Income as % of sales	—	(5.9%)	(9.0%)	(29.5%)	(14.8%)	(1.3%)	3.2%	(0.1%)	4.1%	6.3%	2.1%
Earnings per share ($)	—	*(12.02)*	(17.70)	(34.36)	(9.42)	(0.50)	0.85	0.02	0.60	0.98	0.33
Stock price – high ($)	—	39.38	26.13	8.50	14.75	13.63	11.25	11.63	8.75	7.38	7.00
Stock price – low ($)	—	22.13	6.25	2.75	4.00	5.13	6.38	4.13	3.50	3.13	3.25
Stock price – close ($)	(18.9%)	25.63	7.13	4.25	11.50	8.13	8.50	4.75	4.25	5.38	3.88
P/E – high	—	—	—	—	—	—	13	—	15	8	21
P/E – low	—	—	—	—	—	—	8	—	6	3	10
Dividends per share ($)	(100%)	2.50	0.30	0.00	0.00	0.00	0.00	0.00	0.00	0.00	0.00
Book value per share ($)	(28.4%)	53.30	39.76	—	—	(10.76)	(13.81)	(2.78)	1.50	2.41	2.64

1989 Year End:
Debt ratio: 35.2%
Return on equity: 13.1%
Cash (mil): $674
Total assets (mil): $3,609
Long-term debt (mil): $496
Number of shares (mil): 251
Dividends:
1989 average yield: 0.0%
1989 payout: 0.0%
Market value (mil): $974

Stock Price History high/low 1980-89

0
5
10
15
20
25
30
35
40

NYSE symbol: NAV
Incorporated: Delaware, 1965
Fiscal year ends: October 31

WHO

Chairman, President, and CEO: James C. Cotting, age 56, $450,000 pay
VP; General Manager, Truck Operations: Roy S. Roberts, $250,000 pay
VP; General Manager, Engine and Foundry Operations: John R. Horne, $235,000 pay
VP; General Manager, Parts Operations: Gary E. Dewel, $200,000 pay
VP; General Manager, Financial Services: John J. Bongiorno
VP and Controller: Robert I. Morrison, age 51
SVP Employee Relations and Administration: John M. Sheahin, age 47
Auditors: Deloitte & Touche
Employees: 14,237

WHERE

HQ: 455 N. Cityfront Plaza Dr., Chicago, IL 60611
Phone: 312-836-2000
FAX: 312-836-2192

Navistar has 7 manufacturing and assembly plants in the US and one in Canada. The company sells its products through 896 dealers in North America.

	1989 Sales	
	$ mil	% of total
US	3,820	90
Canada	421	10
Total	**4,241**	**100**

WHAT

	1989 Sales		1989 Pretax Income	
	$ mil	% of total	$ mil	% of total
Truck mfg.	4,023	95	28	30
Financial services	218	5	66	70
Total	**4,241**	**100**	**94**	**100**

Transportation Products	1989 Sales
	% of total
Heavy trucks	40
Medium trucks	37
Replacement parts	13
Engines	10
Total	**100**

Products & Services
Customer financing
Diesel engines
International diesel trucks
Replacement parts
School buses
Used truck sales

RANKINGS

113th in *Fortune* 500 Industrial Cos.
309th in *Fortune* Global 500 Industrial Cos.
207th in *Forbes* Sales 500
498th in *Business Week* 1000

COMPETITION

Caterpillar
Cummins Engine
Daimler-Benz
Fiat
Ford
General Motors
PACCAR
Renault
Volvo

NCNB CORPORATION

OVERVIEW

NCNB Corporation is the largest banking company in the Southeast and the 7th-largest in the US, with $66 billion in assets (1989 year-end) and 800 banking offices in 7 states.

Charlotte-based NCNB owns statewide banks in North Carolina, Florida, South Carolina, and Texas, and banks in Atlanta, Baltimore, and northern Virginia. NCNB ranked first in Texas, 2nd in North Carolina, 3rd in South Carolina, and 5th in Florida by total deposits at year-end 1989.

In addition to providing lending and depository services to individuals and businesses, NCNB has trust investment management, securities trading, and investment banking services. NCNB Securities offers discount and full-service securities brokerage in 20 cities, and NCNB Mortgage originated $1.7 billion in new home mortgage loans in 1989. NCNB is one of the largest lenders to the cable television industry, with loan commitments of about $2.7 billion.

In response to Hurricane Hugo, in 1989 the company established NCNB Heart, which provided victims with an 800 number to call for financial help, and a $1.35 billion financing program.

NYSE symbol: NCB
Incorporated: North Carolina, 1968
Fiscal year ends: December 31

WHO

Chairman and CEO: Hugh L. McColl, Jr., age 54, $1,500,000 pay
VC: Timothy P. Hartman, age 51, $800,000 pay
VC: James W. Thompson, age 50, $800,000 pay
Corporate EVP: James M. Berry, age 59, $580,000 pay
EVP and CFO: James H. Hance, Jr., age 45
Auditors: Price Waterhouse
Employees: 27,000

WHEN

NCNB was formed from 3 North Carolina banks. In 1874 several prominent citizens of Charlotte organized Commercial National Bank, and in 1901 George Stephens and Word Wood of Charlotte started Southern States Trust Company, which was renamed American Trust Company in 1907.

In 1957 Commercial National and American Trust merged to become American Commercial Bank and 2 years later merged with First National of Raleigh to begin forming a statewide banking system. In 1960 American Commercial merged with Security National (founded Greensboro, 1933) to form North Carolina National Bank, with 40 offices in 20 North Carolina cities.

In the 1960s the bank expanded by buying 9 banks and formed NCNB Corporation, a holding company, in 1968. By 1970 NCNB had 91 offices in 27 North Carolina cities. In 1979 mergers with the Bank of Asheville and Carolina First (Lincolnton) helped make NCNB the largest bank in North Carolina.

In 1982 NCNB became the first non-Florida bank to expand its retail banking into Florida by buying First National Bank of Lake City. From 1982 to 1984 the company bought banks in Boca Raton, Tampa, Miami, and Bradenton. In 1985 NCNB bought Pan American, a $2 billion Miami bank with 51 offices. By 1988 NCNB was the 4th-largest bank in Florida, with 200 offices.

NCNB entered 2 more states by purchasing Southern National Bankshares, Inc., of Atlanta (1985) and Bankers Trust of South Carolina (122 branches statewide, 1986). It added Prince William Bank of Dumfries, Virginia (1986), to become the first banking organization in the South to operate in 5 states. In 1987 it bought CentraBank of Baltimore, adding a 6th state.

The company, under Hugh L. McColl, Jr., chairman since 1983, almost doubled its assets to $55 billion by forming NCNB Texas in 1988, when the FDIC chose NCNB to manage the restructured banks of First RepublicBank Corporation (closed by the FDIC earlier in 1988), the largest Texas bank. NCNB paid $210 million in 1988 for a 20% share in the bank and $1.11 billion in 1989 for the remainder. First RepublicBank, with 130 banking locations, was a company formed in 1987 by the merger of InterFirst and Republic, 2 large, struggling banking organizations. NCNB also bought University Federal Savings in Texas in 1989, to increase its Texas branch network to 232. In 1989 NCNB bought Florida-based Freedom Savings and Loan Association from the Resolution Trust Corporation.

WHERE

HQ: One NCNB Plaza, Charlotte, NC 28255
Phone: 704-374-5000
FAX: 704-339-6655

NCNB has operations in 12 states and 10 foreign countries.

WHAT

	1989 Sales $ mil	1989 Sales % of total
Interest income		
Loans	3,776	63
Taxable investment securities	988	16
Time deposits placed	200	3
Federal funds sold	123	2
Nontaxable investment securities	71	1
Other securities	102	2
Lease financing	31	—
Noninterest income		
Service charges	217	3
Trust fees	169	3
Bank card fees	79	1
Other service fees	78	1
Investment securities gains	121	2
Other income	197	3
FDIC interest in earnings	(116)	—
Total	**6,036**	**100**

Financial Services
Consumer banking
Corporate banking
Investment banking
Real estate loans
Securities brokerage
Trust and investment management

HOW MUCH

	9 Yr. Growth	1980	1981	1982	1983	1984	1985	1986	1987	1988	1989
Sales ($ mil)	26.2%	742	970	1,071	1,252	1,643	1,936	2,295	2,461	2,834	6,036
Net income ($ mil)	28.3%	48	55	76	92	119	164	199	167	252	447
Income as % of sales	—	6.4%	5.7%	7.1%	7.4%	7.3%	8.5%	8.7%	6.8%	8.9%	7.4%
Earnings per share ($)	14.6%	1.30	1.33	1.59	1.84	2.04	2.28	2.51	2.01	2.87	4.44
Stock price – high ($)	—	8.31	9.00	10.31	14.94	18.25	23.56	27.75	29.13	29.13	55.00
Stock price – low ($)	—	5.00	6.50	5.88	9.25	11.50	16.94	20.00	15.50	17.50	27.00
Stock price – close ($)	23.8%	6.75	7.44	9.38	13.69	17.94	22.63	21.50	17.25	27.25	46.25
P/E – high	—	6	7	6	8	9	10	11	15	10	12
P/E – low	—	4	5	4	5	6	7	8	8	6	6
Dividends per share ($)	12.5%	0.38	0.41	0.46	0.52	0.59	0.69	0.78	0.86	0.94	1.10
Book value per share ($)	13.8%	9.10	9.90	10.98	11.78	13.13	14.23	16.42	17.87	22.43	29.21

1989 Year End:
Debt ratio: 33.1%
Return on equity: 17.2%
Cash (mil): $7,077
Assets (mil): $66,191
Long-term debt (mil): $1,466
Number of shares (mil): 101
Dividends:
1989 average yield: 2.4%
1989 payout: 24.8%
Market value (mil): $4,682

Stock Price History high/low 1980-89

RANKINGS

7th in *Fortune* 100 Commercial Banking Cos.
78th in *Fortune* World's 100 Commercial Banks
136th in *Forbes* Sales 500
154th in *Business Week* 1000
496th in *Business Week* Global 1000

COMPETITION

H. F. Ahmanson
Banc One
Bank of New York
BankAmerica
Bankers Trust
Barnett Banks
Chase Manhattan
Chemical Banking
Citicorp
Continental Bank
First Chicago
First Interstate
Great Western
Manufacturers Hanover
J.P. Morgan
Security Pacific
SunTrust

NCR CORPORATION

OVERVIEW

NCR, based in Dayton since its 1884 founding, is the 2nd largest manufacturer of ATMs in the US (after Diebold) and has the largest share of the worldwide market. The company is also prominent in retail cash register systems, has moved to the #2 position in communication processors, and is #5 among US computer manufacturers in 1989 revenues.

The company is a minor but growing player in microcomputers and was an early implementer of the UNIX operating system. In 1989 NCR signed an international distribution agreement with Businessland stores for its microcomputers after Compaq broke off relations (since restored). NCR produces minicomputers, business forms, semiconductors, and components, and is a worldwide provider of 3rd-party computer maintenance services for over 120 computer manufacturers. The company's technological strategy is to base products on as few parts as possible, adopt industry standards wherever possible, and emphasize integration.

While NCR projects only single-digit growth this year, *Financial World* named it one of "The Great Companies of the 90s"; like IBM and Unisys, NCR provides hardware, software, applications, and service.

NYSE symbol: NCR
Incorporated: Maryland, 1926
Fiscal year ends: December 31

WHO

Chairman and CEO: Charles E. Exley, Jr., age 60, $1,166,000 pay
President: Gilbert P. Williamson, age 52, $571,374 pay
EVP: R. Elton White, age 47, $377,612 pay
VP, Secretary, and General Counsel: Charles P. Russ III, age 45, $307,256 pay
VP Finance and Administration and CFO: J. L. Giering, age 45
Auditors: Price Waterhouse
Employees: 56,000

WHEN

John Patterson founded National Cash Register in 1882, buying control of a Dayton cash register factory. By 1910 Patterson had created a market for cash registers. He rapidly gained a 90% share, drawing Justice Department attention. In 1913 he was fined for anticompetitive violations — which included tampering with products, spying, and bribing competitors — and sentenced to jail. A heavy flood hit Dayton that year; Patterson turned NCR's energies to rescue operations. Dayton officials commended his actions, and he stayed out of jail.

In 1899 Colonel Edward Deeds, later chairman, joined NCR. In 1904 he hired Dayton inventor Charles Kettering to develop an electric cash register. The 2 men also developed an electric automobile ignition system and left to start DELCO (purchased by General Motors in 1929).

Accounting machines, which prepared vouchers and audit sheets, were introduced in the early 1920s and became almost as important as cash registers to NCR. Patterson did not live to see business plunge in 1929 and NCR's stock drop from $154 to $6.87. By 1936 the company had recovered fully.

During the postwar period NCR faced competition from data processing. The company focused R&D efforts on computing (1945); acquired Computer Research for computer development (1952); opened data processing centers and introduced mainframes (1960); established microelectronics research facilities (1963); and introduced disk-based computers (1968). Yet NCR failed to anticipate how rapidly computers were evolving and their impact upon its products — still primarily cash registers and accounting machines; in 1969 the company had record profits of $50 million, but by 1971 they had plunged to $2 million.

In 1972 William Anderson became president and is credited with saving the company. Anderson reduced NCR's Dayton work force by 75%, reorganized, established NCR's presence in computing with retail scanners and ATMs, and, in 1974, gave the company its current name. By 1981 NCR again faced potential obsolescence due to the proprietary technology of its products in the face of a market moving toward standardization. To counter, NCR adopted widely used Unix and IBM-endorsed MS-DOS operating systems for its computers and introduced networking equipment.

Anderson retired in 1984. Now chaired by Charles Exley, NCR has become a market leader in ATMs and retail checkout scanners. R&D spending, up from 5.7% of revenue in 1979 to 7.5% in 1989, reflects increasing emphasis on change.

WHERE

HQ: 1700 S. Patterson Blvd., Dayton, OH 45479
Phone: 513-445-5000
FAX: 513-445-1238

NCR's products are sold in the US, Europe, Australasia, the Far East, Canada, Latin and South America, the Middle East, and Africa. The company maintains more than 340 domestic facilities and more than 640 international facilities in over 120 countries.

	1989 Sales		1989 Operating Income	
	$ mil	% of total	$ mil	% of total
US	2,442	41	327	46
Europe	1,908	32	211	29
Pacific & Canada	1,235	21	173	24
Latin America, Middle East & Africa	371	6	10	1
Adjustments	—	—	(25)	—
Total	**5,956**	**100**	**696**	**100**

WHAT

	1989 Sales	
	$ mil	% of total
Equipment & software	3,262	55
Media & business forms	495	8
Semiconductors & components	116	2
Services	2,083	35
Total	**5,956**	**100**

Products
Automated teller machines
Bank automation products
Data collection terminals
Microchips
Minicomputers
Networking software
Personal computers
Point-of-sale terminals and systems
Retailing and banking software
Self-service terminals

RANKINGS

78th in *Fortune* 500 Industrial Cos.
146th in *Forbes* Sales 500
129th in *Business Week* 1000
377th in *Business Week* Global 1000

COMPETITION

AT&T
Apple
Compaq
Data General
Deluxe
Digital Equipment
Fujitsu
Hewlett-Packard
IBM
Unisys
Wang

HOW MUCH

	9 Yr. Growth	1980	1981	1982	1983	1984	1985	1986	1987	1988	1989
Sales ($ mil)	6.7%	3,322	3,433	3,526	3,731	4,074	4,317	4,882	5,641	5,990	5,956
Net income ($ mil)	5.5%	255	208	234	288	343	315	337	419	439	412
Income as % of sales	—	7.7%	6.1%	6.6%	7.7%	8.4%	7.3%	6.9%	7.4%	7.3%	6.9%
Earnings per share ($)	9.5%	2.38	1.93	2.17	2.64	3.30	3.15	3.42	4.51	5.33	5.38
Stock price – high ($)	—	20.25	18.88	24.34	34.19	33.03	42.50	57.00	87.25	69.88	66.63
Stock price – low ($)	—	12.94	9.81	9.69	20.50	20.63	24.88	38.63	44.13	51.38	52.50
Stock price – close ($)	13.6%	18.75	10.91	21.50	32.00	26.63	40.25	44.13	63.25	53.38	58.88
P/E – high	—	9	10	11	13	10	14	17	19	13	12
P/E – low	—	5	5	4	8	6	8	11	10	10	10
Dividends per share ($)	11.2%	0.50	0.55	0.60	0.65	0.80	0.88	0.92	1.00	0.93	1.30
Book value per share ($)	6.5%	15.99	17.41	18.10	19.34	20.84	23.68	25.50	25.73	28.20	28.12

1989 Year End:
Debt ratio: 10.5%
Return on equity: 19.1%
Cash (mil): $784
Current ratio: 1.49
Long-term debt (mil): $233
Number of shares (mil): 71
Dividends:
1989 average yield: 2.2%
1989 payout: 24.2%
Market value (mil): $4,156

Stock Price History high/low 1980-89

90
80
70
60
50
40
30
20
10
0

NEC CORPORATION

OVERVIEW

NEC is a global supplier of computers, telecommunications, and semiconductors. Smaller operations include video products and on-line services. The company is the world leader in semiconductor production, 2nd to Fujitsu in Japanese computer revenue, and #1 in Japan in PC sales. Nippon Telegraph and Telephone remains NEC's biggest customer.

NEC has sacrificed short-term profit in favor of sales volume and development of technology to realize Chairman Emeritus Koji Kobayashi's vision of integrated computers and communication devices. The company has invested heavily in DRAM production and research and will need to spend much more to begin production of 16- and 64-megabyte DRAM chips in the 1990s.

Operating 79 plants in 13 countries, NEC is realigning international production. In the past the company simply produced goods near the markets in which they were sold. NEC is trying to integrate production across borders to take advantage of global cost differentials and specialized factories.

WHEN

A group of Japanese investors led by Kunihiko Iwadare formed Nippon Electric Company (NEC) in a joint venture with Western Electric (US) in 1899. Starting as an importer of telephone equipment, NEC soon became a manufacturer and major supplier to Japan's Communications Ministry. Western Electric sold its stake in NEC in 1925, and ITT (US) began accumulating shares (ITT's holdings reached 59% before they were sold in the 1960s). NEC became affiliated with the Sumitomo *zaibatsu* (conglomerate) in the 1930s.

When Nippon Telegraph and Telephone (NTT) was formed in 1952, it was modeled after AT&T — except for its equipment supply system. Rather than buying from a single manufacturer, NTT would buy from competing Japanese suppliers. Among the 4 companies chosen as lead suppliers, NEC was most favored.

The postwar need to repair Japan's telephone systems and the country's rapid economic recovery resulted in strong demand from NTT. In the 1950s and 1960s NTT business represented over 50% of NEC's sales, despite overseas expansion, diversification into home appliances, and a computer alliance with Honeywell (US). In 1968 NTT began working with NEC, Hitachi, and Fujitsu to develop computers for use in telecommunications.

In the 1970s Honeywell's lagging position in computers hurt NEC, but the company was able to recover through in-house development efforts and a mainframe venture with Toshiba. In 1977 CEO Koji Kobayashi articulated his C&C (computers and communications) vision of NEC's future as an integrator of computers and communications through semiconductor technology. While generally accepted today, Kobayashi's thoughts on such integration were outside the mainstream at the time.

A joint effort between the Japanese government and private industry to develop VLSI chips took place in NEC's labs in the 1970s. NEC invested heavily in R&D and capacity expansion and became the world's largest independent semiconductor manufacturer in 1985. The company produced the world's first prototype of a 4-megabyte DRAM chip in 1986.

The company enjoyed great success in the Japanese personal computer market, garnering over 50% of the market in the 1980s despite a proprietary operating system. NEC's portable IBM clones were also well received internationally. In 1986 the company entered into a mainframe computer partnership with Honeywell and Bull (France). NEC passed IBM to become Japan's 2nd largest computer maker, after Fujitsu, in 1986.

NEC is leaving the low-end consumer electronics market segment, instead focusing on higher-margin areas including HDTV.

HOW MUCH

	9 Yr. Growth	1980	1981	1982	1983	1984	1985	1986	1987	1988	1989
Sales ($ mil)	21.7%	3,954	4,711	4,872	6,013	7,830	8,998	13,116	16,779	21,893	23,179
Net income ($ mil)	22.4%	67	99	109	138	198	267	153	103	205	412
Income as % of sales	—	1.7%	2.1%	2.2%	2.3%	2.5%	3.0%	1.2%	0.6%	0.9%	1.8%
Earnings per share ($)	17.8%	0.30	0.43	0.46	0.54	0.74	0.93	0.54	0.37	0.70	1.32
Stock price – high ($)	—	7.50	11.75	16.14	17.86	28.86	29.66	33.63	79.00	90.00	91.88
Stock price – low ($)	—	5.57	6.14	10.31	11.23	15.80	18.98	18.63	30.25	45.00	67.50
Stock price – close ($)	30.4%	7.19	11.21	15.05	17.86	28.41	24.25	32.88	63.88	73.50	78.50
P/E – high	—	25	27	35	33	39	32	62	214	129	70
P/E – low	—	18	14	22	21	21	20	35	82	64	51
Dividends per share ($)	13.5%	0.11	0.12	0.13	0.11	0.15	0.16	0.25	0.29	0.35	0.34
Book value per share ($)	22.7%	2.75	3.34	3.41	4.89	6.65	6.92	10.09	12.51	16.29	17.36

1989 Year End:
Debt ratio: 46.3%
Return on equity: 7.8%
Cash (mil): $3,896
Current ratio: 1.21
Long-term debt (mil): $4,463
Number of shares (mil): 299
Dividends:
1989 average yield: 0.4%
1989 payout: 25.5%
Market value (mil): $23,444

Stock Price History high/low 1980-89

100 90 80 70 60 50 40 30 20 10 0

OTC symbol: NIPNY (ADR)
Established: Japan, 1899
Fiscal year ends: March 31

WHO

Chairman: Atsuyoshi Ouchi
President: Tadahiro Sekimoto
Auditors: Price Waterhouse
Employees: 104,022

WHERE

HQ: 7-1, Shiba 5-chome, Minato-ku, Tokyo 108, Japan
Phone: 011-81-3-454-1111
FAX: 011-81-3-798-1510
US HQ (NEC America, Inc.): 8 Old Sod Farm Rd., Melville, NY 11747
US Phone: 516-753-7000
US FAX: 516-753-7041

NEC operates 54 manufacturing plants in Japan and 25 plants in the US and 11 other countries.

	1989 Sales	
	$ mil	% of total
Japan	17,335	75
Other countries	5,844	25
Total	**23,179**	**100**

WHAT

	1989 Sales	
	$ mil	% of total
Telecommunications systems & equipment	6,033	26
Computers & industrial electronic systems	10,022	43
Semiconductors & electronic components	4,256	19
Home electronics products	1,696	7
Other operations	1,172	5
Total	**23,179**	**100**

Telecommunications Systems & Equipment
Direct broadcast satellite receiver systems
Fiber optic and radio transmission systems
Mobile and other telephones
Telecommunications networks

Computers & Industrial Electronics Systems
Automation systems for buildings
Computers (PCs to supercomputers) and peripheral equipment
Mail-processing systems

Semiconductors & Electronic Components

Home Electronics Products
Home automation systems
Kitchen appliances and air conditioners
TV sets, VCRs, and other video equipment

Other Operations
Electrical connectors
Measuring and testing systems
Subscription computer services (VANs)

RANKINGS

32nd in *Fortune* Global 500 Industrial Cos.
50th in *Business Week* Global 1000

COMPETITION

Amdahl
AT&T
AMP
Apple
Atari
BCE
Compaq
Control Data
Cray Research
Data General
Fujitsu
Harris
Hewlett-Packard
Hitachi
Honeywell
IBM
Mitsubishi
Motorola
Pitney Bowes
Raytheon
Siemens
Tandy
Texas Instruments
TRW
Unisys

NESTLÉ SA

OVERVIEW

Nestlé is the world's largest packaged food manufacturer, coffee roaster, and chocolate maker. The company's global candy aspirations have led to the purchase of several chocolate businesses, most recently the Curtiss division of RJR Nabisco.

Nestlé is the largest company in Switzerland but derives less than 2% of its revenue from its home country. Major US product lines and brand names include drinks (Nescafé, Taster's Choice, Quik), chocolate and candy (Crunch, Toll House Morsels), culinary products (Contadina), dairy products (Carnation), and frozen foods (Lean Cuisine). The company owns a minority interest in French cosmetics giant L'Oréal.

A Nestlé/General Mills breakfast cereal joint venture became the UK's #3 cereal maker when it bought the cereal business of Ranks Hovis McDougall in 1990.

Principal stock exchange: Zurich
Incorporated: Switzerland, 1866
Fiscal year ends: December 31

WHO

Chairman: Paul R. Jolles
Managing Director: Helmut Maucher
General Manager Finance, Control, Legal, Taxes, Administration: Reto F. Domeniconi
Auditors: KPMG Peat Marwick McLintock
Employees: 196,940

WHEN

In 1866 Americans Charles and George Page founded the Anglo-Swiss Condensed Milk Company in central Switzerland. Importing canned milk technology from the US, the brothers began production in 1867. In the same year, 120 miles away in Vevey, Switzerland, amid growing concern about infant mortality, Henri Nestlé tested his new concoction of concentrated milk, sugar, and cereal on a baby who refused his mother's milk. Six months later the healthy boy was still consuming the formula. Nestlé introduced his product, Farine Lactée, commercially in 1867.

By 1874 both firms were prospering, and Nestlé, age 61, was looking for a buyer. He sold his company, then doing business in 16 countries, to 3 local businessmen for one million francs in 1875. Until 1878 Nestlé and Anglo-Swiss were content to build capacity to meet skyrocketing demand for their products. Then Anglo-Swiss launched a milk-based infant food product. Nestlé's new owners responded by introducing a condensed milk product, beginning a battle that lasted until the companies merged in 1905 under the Nestlé name.

Aided by Swiss neutrality, Nestlé continued its worldwide expansion throughout WWI. In 1904 the company began selling chocolate under the Nestlé name. In 1929 Nestlé acquired Cailler, the first company to mass-produce chocolate bars, and Swiss General, inventor of milk chocolate.

Nestlé's 1920s investment in a Brazilian milk condensery paid an unexpected dividend. In 1930 Brazilian coffee growers suggested that Nestlé develop a water-soluble "coffee cube." Nescafé instant coffee was released in 1938 and received a boost when the US Army distributed it to troops in WWII.

Nestlé continued its global expansion, entering new product categories through acquisition and internal product development. Major purchases included Alimenta (first dehydrated soup, seasonings, Switzerland, 1947); Crosse & Blackwell (packaged foods, marmalade, UK, 1960); Findus International (frozen foods, Sweden, 1962); Beringer Brothers (wine, US, 1971); Stouffer (hotels, restaurants, frozen foods, US, 1973); 25% of L'Oréal (perfumes, cosmetics, hair products, France, 1974); Libby, McNeill & Libby (canned foods, US, 1976); Beech-Nut (baby food, US, 1979); Carnation (US, 1985); Hills Brothers and MJB (coffee, US, 1985); 52% of Vittel (mineral water, France, 1987); Buitoni (pasta, chocolate, Italy, 1988); and Rowntree (candy, UK, 1988). Among Nestlé's important product introductions were its Crunch bar (1938), Quik drink mix (1948), and Taster's Choice coffee (1966).

Since 1977 Nestlé has been boycotted internationally over the marketing of its infant formula in the Third World. In 1989, a year after Beech-Nut executives had been indicted for adulterating apple juice, Nestlé agreed to sell Beech-Nut to Ralston Purina.

WHERE

HQ: Ave. Nestlé 55, CH-1800 Vevey, Switzerland
Phone: 011-41-21-924-2111
US HQ (Nestlé Foods Corp.): 100 Manhattanville Rd., Purchase, NY 10577
US Phone: 914-251-3000
US FAX: 914-251-2961

Nestlé operates 421 factories worldwide, including 67 in the US.

	1989 Sales	
	SF mil	% of total
Europe	21,931	46
North America	12,791	26
Latin America & Caribbean	5,365	11
Other countries	7,949	17
Total	**48,036**	**100**

WHAT

	1989 Sales	
	SF mil	% of total
Drinks	11,864	25
Confections	7,333	15
Foods/culinary products	24,815	52
Pet foods	2,105	4
Drugs, cosmetics	1,346	3
Hotels, restaurants, other	573	1
Total	**48,036**	**100**

Brand Names (US Markets)

Drinks
Beringer (wines)
Hills Bros. (coffee)
Kern's (nectars)
Nescafé
Nestea
Quik
Taster's Choice

Confections
After Eight
Chunky
Crunch
Oh Henry!
Perugina
Raisinets

Foods
Carnation
Contadina
Lean Cuisine
Libby
Stouffer's
Toll House

Drugs, Cosmetics
Alcon (optical goods)
L'Oréal (25% owned)
Biotherm
Guy Laroche
Lancôme

Pet Foods
Chef's Blend
Fancy Feast
Friskies
Grand Gourmet
Mighty Dog

HOW MUCH

$ = SF1.54 (Dec. 31, 1989)	9 Yr. Growth	1980	1981	1982	1983	1984	1985	1986	1987	1988	1989
Sales (SF mil)	7.8%	24,479	27,734	27,664	27,943	31,141	42,225	36,909	34,183	39,502	48,036
Net income (SF mil)	15.0%	683	964	1,098	1,261	1,487	1,750	1,843	1,879	2,058	2,412
Income as % of sales	—	2.8%	3.5%	4.0%	4.5%	4.8%	4.1%	5.0%	5.5%	5.2%	5.0%
Earnings per share (SF)	12.4%	230	323	368	422	471	506	532	543	577	656
Stock price – high (SF)	—	3,440	3,125	3,688	4,801	5,499	9,034	9,697	11,244	8,863	8,930
Stock price – low (SF)	—	2,866	2,695	2,915	3,630	4,443	5,499	7,193	7,070	6,236	6,925
Stock price – close (SF)	12.2%	3,140	3,160	3,870	4,980	5,600	8,925	9,775	8,025	7,240	8,820
P/E – high	—	15	10	10	11	12	18	18	21	15	14
P/E – low	—	12	8	8	9	9	11	14	13	11	11
Dividends per share (SF)	9.9%	85.26	96.18	107.49	121.35	133.36	142.39	142.39	147.30	171.85	200.00
Book value per share (SF)	3.0%	2,903	3,004	3,379	3,728	4,168	3,370	4,564	4,600	3,193	3,793

1989 Year End:
Debt ratio: 32.8%
Return on equity: 17.3%
Cash (mil): SF4,231
Long-term debt (mil): SF6,798
Number of shares (thou): 3,465
Dividends:
1989 average yield: 2.6%
1989 payout: 30.5%
Sales (mil): $31,192

Note: All data pertains to bearer shares.

RANKINGS

26th in *Fortune* Global 500 Industrial Cos.
9th in *Forbes* 100 Foreign Investments in the US
41st in *Business Week* Global 1000

COMPETITION

Borden
Bristol-Myers Squibb
BSN
Cadbury Schweppes
Campbell Soup
ConAgra
General Mills
Grand Metropolitan
H. J. Heinz
Hershey
Mars
Philip Morris
Procter & Gamble
Ralston Purina
RJR Nabisco
Sara Lee
TLC Beatrice
Unilever
Whitman

NEW YORK CITY TRANSIT AUTHORITY

OVERVIEW

The New York City Transit Authority (NYCTA) is the government agency which operates all subways in 4 New York City boroughs, buses in all 5 boroughs, and the Staten Island Rapid Transit Operating Authority. It is the largest subway-bus system in the world. The NYCTA is part of the Metropolitan Transportation Authority, the regional agency responsible for all public transit in the New York City metropolitan area. It carried over 1.5 billion passengers in 1989 and has a 1990 operating budget of $3.6 billion.

Plagued by crime, vandalism, panhandlers, and the city's homeless, the system has a reputation as an unpleasant and unsafe means of getting around. In recent years, massive infusions of capital, a concerted fight against graffiti and crime, and changes in union work rules undertaken by former chairman David Gunn improved NYTC'S operations. During the 1980s, ridership, which had been declining for 40 years, began to increase. However, in 1990 ridership again began to decline.

WHEN

Mass passenger transit in New York City is said to have originated in 1746, when ox carts began carrying customers up Broadway from the Battery. Early in the 19th century, a number of private companies running omnibuses (horse-drawn multipassenger carriages) proliferated. By 1832 a horse-drawn car set on rails began operating on Fourth Avenue. Several years later this line was converted to steam power, but horse-drawn rail cars continued to prosper.

In 1864 local papers reported that cars and buses were overcrowded and drivers were intolerably rude to passengers. Construction of an underground railway was proposed, but the project died when authorizing legislation failed. In 1868 the legislature authorized an underground pneumatic subway in which a 22-passenger vehicle was shot through a 312-foot-long tube under Broadway. While novel when it was opened to the public in 1870, it never developed beyond the amusement stage. Companies were granted authority to build elevated train lines into the city during the next several years, but no progress was made in building a subway system.

In 1894 legislation was finally passed authorizing construction of underground rail lines and vesting ownership with public rather than private interests. Construction of the first line was completed in 1904. It was operated for the city by the Interborough Rapid Transit Company (IRT), which had the previous year leased the primary elevated train line for 999 years and enjoyed effective operating control of most of the rail transit in Manhattan and the Bronx. In 1905 the IRT merged with Metropolitan Street Railway, which controlled almost all surface rail operations in Manhattan, giving the combined company almost absolute control of rapid transit in the city. Public outrage over this private monopoly over public transit caused the city to grant licenses to operate rail lines to the Brooklyn Rapid Transit Company (later to be called the BMT), creating the Dual System. The 2 rail companies quickly covered most of the city.

By the 1920s the transit system was again in crisis, largely because the 2 lines were unable to raise the 5-cent fare which they had agreed to maintain for the life of their contract with the city — 49 years. In 1932 both the IRT and the BMT were in receivership; the city decided not only to own but to operate a part of the rail system and organized the Independent (IND) rail line. Pressure for public ownership and operation of the transit system resulted in the city's purchase of all assets of the IRT and BMT in 1940 for $326 million. The 3 lines were overseen by the Transit Commission of the New York State Department of Public Service.

In 1953 the legislature created the New York City Transit Authority (NYCTA), to which the city leased all transit facilities, creating the first truly unified system. During the 1950s ridership and revenue declined as people moved to the suburbs. The Metropolitan Transportation Authority (MTA) was created in 1968 to coordinate NYCTA's activities with other commuter services.

The 1970s and 1980s saw the NYCTA's infrastructure, service, and sanitary conditions deteriorate and crime, accidents, graffiti, and fares rise. In 1990 Alan Kiepper succeeded David Gunn as head of the NYCTA. Gunn, who had been responsible for some improvements in the system in the late 1980s, is reported to have said that he intended to go cut wood in Nova Scotia.

HOW MUCH

	9 Yr. Growth	1980	1981	1982	1983	1984	1985	1986	1987	1988	1989
Revenues ($ mil)	6.6%	79	949	1,034	1,056	1,231	1,228	1,372	1,401	1,411	1,401
Ridership (mil)	0.1%	1,555	1,525	1,501	1,529	1,488	1,512	1,524	1,547	1,568	1,559
Fare ($)	—	0.50	0.60	0.75	0.75	0.90	0.90	1.00	1.00	1.00	1.00

Ridership (mil) 1980-89

1,600
1,400
1,200
1,000
800
600
400
200
0

Government agency
Established: New York, 1953
Fiscal year ends: December 31

WHO

President: Alan F. Kiepper, age 61, $149,500 pay
EVP: David Winfield, age 45, $125,000 pay
SVP Operations: Lawrence G. Reuter, $130,000 pay
VP and CFO: Edward G. Towle, $107,000 pay
VP and General Counsel: Albert Cosenza, $109,500 pay
Auditors: Ernst & Young
Employees: 51,726

WHERE

HQ: 370 Jay St., Brooklyn, NY 11201
Phone: 718-330-3000
FAX: 718-852-6858

The NYCTA operates buses and subways in the Manhattan, Brooklyn, Bronx, Queens, and Staten Island boroughs of New York City.

	1989 Ridership	
	no. (mil)	% of total
Bronx	209	13
Brooklyn	379	24
Manhattan	726	47
Queens	218	14
Staten Island	27	2
Total	**1,559**	**100**

WHAT

	1989 Ridership	
	no. (mil)	% of total
Buses	486	31
Subways	1,073	69
Total	**1,559**	**100**

	1989 Train Route Miles	
	no.	% of total
Subway	137	59
Elevated	95	41
Total	**232**	**100**

	1989 Employees	
	no.	% of total
Operations	46,336	90
Engineering	1,379	3
Police	4,011	7
Total	**51,726**	**100**

Affiliates
Manhattan and Bronx Surface Transit Operating Authority
South Brooklyn Railroad
Staten Island Rapid Transit Operating Authority
Transit Authority Citizen's Advisory Council

RANKINGS

New York's subway system is the largest in the US and 5th largest in the world based on ridership.

COMPETITION

No other companies in this book compete with the New York City Transit Authority.

NEW YORK LIFE INSURANCE COMPANY

OVERVIEW

New York Life is the 6th largest life insurance company in the US, with assets of $46.6 billion and life insurance in force topping $300 billion. It was one of the first mutual life insurance companies in the US and has insured the lives of 11 US presidents.

New York Life offers life, health, and disability insurance; annuities; MainStay mutual funds; and other investments.

With the highest ratings for financial position and claims-paying ability by Moody's, Standard & Poor's, and Best's Insurance Reports, New York Life is recognized for its strong market position and solid capital structure. New York Life does business in all 50 states, the District of Columbia, Puerto Rico, Canada, and Hong Kong.

The company has assisted in AIDS research by making investments of $8.3 million in IDEC Pharmaceuticals in 1988 and $20 million in Biogen, Inc., in 1989.

WHEN

In 1841 actuary Pliny Freeman and 56 prominent New York businessmen invested $50,000 to found Nautilus Insurance Company as a mutual company, owned by its policyholders. The company began operating in 1845 and adopted its present name in 1849.

In 1846 New York Life had the first life insurance agent west of the Mississippi River, in Little Rock, Arkansas. By 1865 the company had assets of about $4 million, and by 1887 it had developed the branch office system that later was adopted throughout the industry.

By 1900 the company had established the Nylic Plan for compensating agents, which features a lifetime income after 20 years of active service. This plan was unique in the industry and is still being used today.

Much of the company's growth and new product development has occurred in recent years. In the early 1950s during Devereux Josephs's presidency, the company simplified insurance policy forms, slashed premium rates, and replaced mortality rates of the 1860s with a current table. These steps resulted in new company sales records and were widely copied by competitors. In 1956 the company was the first life insurance firm to use large-scale data processing equipment.

In 1968 New York Life was instrumental in developing variable life insurance, a new industry product with variable benefits and level premiums. Also that year the company entered the variable annuity field. In 1981 the company first offered single- and flexible-premium deferred annuities and in 1982 introduced a universal life product. New York Life also formed New York Life and Health Insurance Company in 1982 and New York Life Insurance Company of Canada in 1984.

To broaden financial products offered to its clients, the company in 1984 acquired MacKay-Shields Financial Corporation, which oversees its MainStay mutual funds. NYLIFE Realty, another wholly owned subsidiary, offered the company's first real estate limited partnership in 1987.

Donald K. Ross, president (1981-1990), continued the company's expansion in 1987 by purchasing control of Hillhouse Associates Insurance, a 3rd-party administrator of insurance plans, and Madison Benefits Administrators, which administers group insurance programs. In 1987 New York Life acquired Sanus Corporation Health Systems, the largest privately held manager of health care programs in the United States. A recent technological advancement is the New York Life Television Network, a satellite network started in 1988 to communicate to agency offices.

With the new "The Company You Keep" advertising campaign, New York Life enters the 1990s guided by its 1982 mission statement of using trained field representatives and new technologies to gain profitable, prudent growth.

HOW MUCH

Life Insurance Only	9 Yr. Growth	1980	1981	1982	1983	1984	1985	1986	1987	1988	1989
Assets ($ mil)	7.3%	19,725	21,041	22,549	24,228	25,600	27,978	29,794	31,844	35,154	37,302
Premium & annuity income ($ mil)	10.2%	2,682	2,637	3,070	3,554	1,083	3,830	3,477	5,596	6,929	6,428
Net investment income ($ mil)	9.1%	1,346	1,504	1,643	1,811	2,007	2,237	2,413	2,475	2,758	2,949
Net income ($ mil)	—	—	—	—	—	—	—	—	—	256	213
Net income as % of assets	—	—	—	—	—	—	—	—	—	0.7%	0.6%
Individual life insurance in force ($ bil)	8.4%	123	138	151	172	179	179	187	210	234	253

1989 Company Totals
Total assets: (mil): $46,648
Revenues (mil): $15,297
Surplus (mil): $2,115
Premiums (mil): $7,598
Net investment income (mil): $3,795
Policyowner dividends (mil): $1,073
Total life insurance in force (mil) $300,768

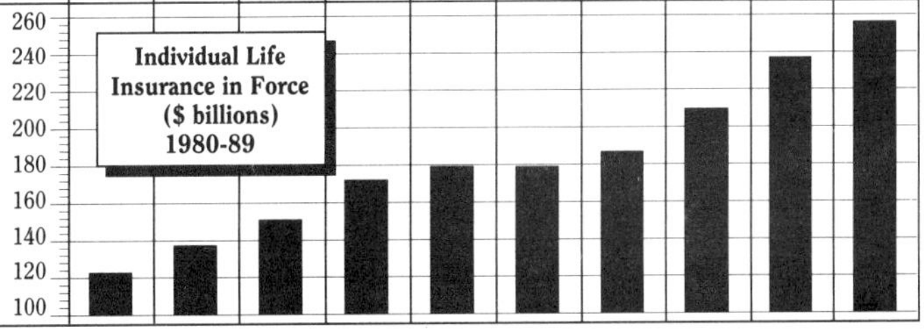

Mutual company
Incorporated: New York, 1893
Fiscal year ends: December 31

WHO

Chairman and CEO: Harry G. Hohn, age 58
President: George A. W. Bundschuh, age 56
VP and Treasurer: Bruce J. Davey, age 63
Auditors: Price Waterhouse
Employees: 19,438

WHERE

HQ: 51 Madison Ave., New York, NY 10010
Phone: 212-576-7000
FAX: 212-576-6794

Operations are conducted in all 50 states, the District of Columbia, Puerto Rico, all 10 provinces of Canada, and Hong Kong.

Largest underwritings by state are: California (14.4%), New York (9.4%), Illinois (4.5%), Texas (4.2%), and Florida (4.1%).

WHAT

	1989 Sales	
	$ mil	% of total
Premiums	7,598	50
Net investment income	3,795	25
Funds left with the company	224	1
Other income	3,680	24
Total	**15,297**	**100**

	12/31/89 Assets	
	$ mil	% of total
Bonds	27,798	59
Real estate & mortgage loans	7,739	17
Policyowner loans	4,971	11
Other assets	6,140	13
Total	**46,648**	**100**

Product Lines

New York Life Insurance Co.
Disability income insurance
Group life and health insurance
Guaranteed investment contracts
Pension fund investment accounts
Target life insurance
Term life insurance
Whole life insurance

New York Life Insurance and Annuity Co.
Deferred annuities
Immediate annuities
Variable annuities

MainStay (mutual funds)

New York Life (real estate, oil and gas limited partnerships)

RANKINGS

6th in *Fortune* 50 Life Insurance Cos.

COMPETITION

Aetna
CIGNA
Equitable
First Executive
John Hancock
Kemper
Massachusetts Mutual
Metropolitan
Northwestern Mutual
Primerica
Prudential
Sears
State Farm
Teachers Insurance
Transamerica
Travelers
USF&G

NEW YORK STOCK EXCHANGE, INC.

OVERVIEW

The New York Stock Exchange (NYSE) is the oldest and largest stock exchange in the US, with 1,366 seats held by 535 member firms and 1,720 listed companies, including 87 non-US companies. Among investors, it also is known as the Big Board.

The Big Board, which is an organized market for trading securities, had 41.7 billion shares traded in 1989. Initial public stock offerings on the NYSE in 1989 raised $11.3 billion for US companies. Trades are executed by NYSE-assigned dealers who are specialists, matching offers to buy with offers to sell. Securities trades are made and communicated to the participating parties within seconds by SuperDot, a computerized system.

Participants in the NYSE market include listed companies, individual and institutional investors, and securities firms and dealers. The NYSE Board of Directors includes representatives from the public and from the NYSE-member organizations (stockbrokers and securities firms).

The Exchange's market operates under rules approved by the SEC. The NYSE monitors sales practices and regulates the financial operation of its member firms with a computerized surveillance system.

WHEN

To prevent a monopoly on sales by securities auctioneers, 24 New York stockbrokers and businessmen made an agreement in 1792 to avoid "public auctions," to earn a commission on sales of stock, and to "give preference to each other" in their transactions. The historic Buttonwood Agreement, named after a tree on Wall Street under which they met, established the first organized stock market in New York.

The Stock Market was strong enough in 1817 for brokers to create the New York Stock & Exchange Board, a stock market with regular meeting times. In 1853 the NYS&EB first required companies to qualify for trading (listing) by furnishing statements of capital and number of shares. In 1863 the Board changed its name to the New York Stock Exchange.

Stock tickers replaced messenger boys as a faster and more accurate way to record securities trades in 1867. Two years later the Exchange consolidated with its strongest competitors, the Open Board of Brokers and the Government Bond Department (a market for trading bonds used to pay for defense of the Union).

During the 1920s the Exchange installed a centralized stock quotation service. The stock market crashed October 29, 1929, and a record total of more than 16 million shares were traded. The Exchange registered with the SEC as a national securities exchange in 1934. Four years later, following a period of increased federal government regulation of the securities industry, the NYSE reorganized with a board of directors representing member firms, nonmember broker firms, and the public. Also it hired its first full-time president, William McChesney Martin, Jr., a member of the Exchange.

In the 1960s NYSE introduced electronic trading, with stock quotation devices attached to ticker circuits. In 1968 the Exchange set a new one-day trading volume record, breaking the 1929 mark.

In 1971 the Exchange first incorporated as a not-for-profit corporation and member corporations began listing their stocks on the Exchange. The Exchange began in 1979 a long-term plan to upgrade capabilities to handle trading days of more than 150 million shares and sustained periods of high volume. In 1982 the Exchange reached 149 million shares traded in a day and a 2-week period when one billion shares were traded. Even before the 600-million-share days of the October 1987 crash, the NYSE had begun to invest in new technology to further expand trading capacity. Also the Exchange in 1990 announced plans to phase in computerized after-hours trading, which could result in 24-hour trading by the year 2000.

HOW MUCH

	9 Yr. Growth	1980	1981	1982	1983	1984	1985	1986	1987	1988	1989
Sales	11.3%	133	153	169	217	223	258	296	349	324	349
Net income (mil)	(0.1)	16	6	9	17	10	18	22	34	10	6
Income as % of sales	—	12.0	3.9	5.3	7.8	4.9	7.0	7.4	9.7	3.1	1.7
Reported share volume (mil)	15.6%	11,352	11,854	16,458	21,590	23,071	27,511	35,680	47,801	40,849	41,699
Daily average share volume (mil)	15.6%	44.8	46.9	65.1	85.3	91.2	109.2	141.0	188.9	161.5	165.5
No. of member organizations	(0.7%)	570	604	617	639	628	599	611	596	555	535
No. of listed companies	1.0%	1,570	1,565	1,526	1,550	1,543	1,541	1,575	1,647	1,681	1,720
Total shares listed (mil)	10.5%	33,709	38,298	39,516	45,118	49,092	52,427	59,620	71,802	76,175	82,972

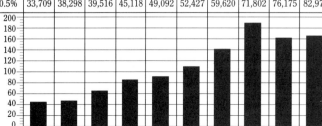

Daily Average Share Volume (mil) 1980-89

200 180 160 140 120 100 80 60 40 20 0

Not-for-profit corporation
Incorporated: New York, 1971
Fiscal year ends: December 31

WHO

Chairman and CEO: William H. Donaldson, age 59
President and COO: Richard A. Grasso, age 44
EVC: Richard R. Shinn
EVP Equity Marketing and NYFE: Lewis J. Horowitz, $550,000 pay
EVP Regional Firms Liaison and International Regulatory: David Marcus
EVP and General Counsel: Henry P. Poole
EVP Fixed Income, Options, and Administration: Donald J. Solodar
SVP Finance: David L. Domijan
Auditors: Price Waterhouse
Employees: Not available

WHERE

HQ: 11 Wall St., New York, NY 10005
Phone: 212-656-3000
FAX: 212-269-4830 (Communications)

The New York Stock Exchange has market operations in New York City. It has a service office in London to assist European companies. Some 87 foreign companies list their shares on the Exchange.

1989 US Stock Trades	%
NYSE	68
Other Exchanges	32
Total	**100**

WHAT

	1989 Sales	
	$ mil	% of total
Listing fees	108	31
Trading fees	80	23
Market data fees	55	16
Regulatory fees	39	11
Facility & equipment fees	37	11
Membership fees	8	2
Investment & other income	22	6
Total	**349**	**100**

Services
Market regulation
Member regulation
Securities clearing
Securities depository
Securities information
Securities trading

Subsidiaries/Affiliates
Depository Trust Company (33%)
National Securities Clearing Corporation (33%)
New York Futures Exchange, Inc.
Options Clearing Corporation (minority)
Securities Industry Automation Corporation (67%)

RANKINGS

Largest stock exchange in US
Largest centralized bond market of any exchange

COMPETITION

Reuters

SAB

THE NEW YORK TIMES COMPANY

OVERVIEW

The New York Times Company publishes newspapers and magazines, operates broadcast and information services, and produces newsprint.

The *New York Times* is circulated nationally and internationally, with an average daily circulation of almost 1.1 million (Sundays over 1.6 million), making the *Times* the nation's most-read Sunday paper (#5 weekdays). The company also owns 26 daily and 9 weekly and semi-weekly newspapers, mainly in the South, and a 1/3 interest in the *International Herald Tribune*, an international English language newspaper, in partnership with the Washington Post Company and the IHT Corporation.

The company owns several magazines, 2 classical radio stations in New York City, and 5 network-affiliated TV stations in 5 states. It also provides information services to others, including photographs, graphics, articles, databases, and the *New York Times* on microfilm. The company began testing TimesFax, article abstracts delivered via FAX, in Tokyo in 1990.

The company also owns interests in 3 newsprint mills in Canada and a magazine paper mill in Maine.

ASE symbol: NYTA
Incorporated: New York, 1896
Fiscal year ends: December 31

WHO

Chairman and CEO: Arthur Ochs Sulzberger, age 64, $867,387 pay
President and COO: Walter E. Mattson, age 57, $679,255 pay
SVP: Michael E. Ryan, age 51, $452,547 pay
SVP, CFO, and Treasurer: David L. Gorham, age 57, $412,291 pay
Auditors: Deloitte & Touche
Employees: 10,600

WHERE

HQ: 229 W. 43rd St., New York, NY 10036
Phone: 212-556-1234
FAX: 212-556-4607

The company owns 36 newspapers in 12 states. The *New York Times* is sold throughout the US and in 72 foreign countries. The company publishes magazines in the US, the UK, and Sweden. It owns 5 TV stations in as many states and 2 radio stations in New York City.

WHEN

The *New York Times* was founded in 1851 by George Jones and Henry J. Raymond, 2 former staffers on the *New York Tribune*, one of the first penny papers. The *Times* began a long tradition of political coverage during the Civil War and investigative reporting with the Tammany Hall scandals, but by the late 1800s it had lost popularity to the yellow journalism style of the Hearst and Pulitzer papers.

In 1896 Adolph Ochs, a newspaperman from Chattanooga, bought the *Times*. Choosing to continue covering hard news and business stories, Ochs added the slogan that still molds the paper's news content today, "All the news that's fit to print." Ochs's son-in-law Arthur Sulzberger and Sulzberger's son-in-law Orvil Dryfoos ran the paper from 1935 to 1963, when Dryfoos died, leaving Adolph's grandson, Arthur "Punch" Ochs Sulzberger, in charge.

In the 1960s declining ad revenues from Manhattan stores and a newspaper strike (1962–1963) sent the company into the red. To regain strength Punch began building what became the largest news-gathering staff of any newspaper. The *Times's* coverage of the Vietnam War changed public sentiment, and the newspaper won a Pulitzer Prize in 1972 for publishing the Pentagon Papers.

Punch began turning the company into a diverse media corporation in the 1970s. It bought magazines (*Golf Digest*, 1969; *Family Circle*, 1971; *Child*, 1987), publishing houses, television stations, smaller newspapers, and cable television systems and began copublishing the *International Herald Tribune*. It also published a wide range of books and educational materials, such as the *New York Times Index*. The *Times* started a wire service that is today received by more than 500 news organizations worldwide.

To contain costs the company bought controlling interests in several pulp and paper companies in Canada and in 1980 joined a partnership in a Maine paper mill.

In the 1980s the *Times* added feature sections on subjects from home decorating to science in order to compete with suburban papers. In 1989 the company bought *McCall's* magazine and sold its cable television systems. In 1990 the *Times* won its 61st Pulitzer Prize, an award that it has won more often than any other news organization.

In 1990, with Punch still at the helm, the company began nationwide distribution of an enhanced version of the *Times National Edition*, with a new lifestyle section that was introduced on the West Coast in 1988.

WHAT

	1989 Sales		1989 Operating Income	
	$ mil	% of total	$ mil	% of total
Magazines	296	17	(12)	(7)
Newspapers	1,398	79	182	100
Broadcasting/ information svcs.	75	4	13	7
Adjustments	—	—	(14)	—
Total	**1,769**	**100**	**169**	**100**

Newspapers
The New York Times
26 daily newspapers
9 nondaily newspapers
1/3 interest in *International Herald Tribune*

Broadcasting
KFSM-TV, Fort Smith, AR
WHNT-TV, Huntsville, AL
WNEP-TV, Wilkes-Barre, PA
WQAD-TV, Moline, IL
WQXR (AM/FM), New York
WREG-TV, Memphis, TN

Information Services
The New York Times Index
The New York Times Index Operations
The New York Times News Service
The New York Times Syndication Sales Corp.
Special Features (supplemental news and graphics)
Times On-Line Services, Inc.
TimesFax

Magazines
Child
Cruising World
Decorating Remodeling
Family Circle
Golf Digest
McCall's
Sailing World
Snow Country
Tennis

Forest Products
Donahue Malbaie, Inc.
Gaspesia Pulp & Paper Co. Ltd.
Madison Paper Industries
Spruce Falls Power & Paper

RANKINGS

227th in *Fortune* 500 Industrial Cos.
431st in *Forbes* Sales 500
332nd in *Business Week* 1000

COMPETITION

Advance Publications
Dow Jones
Gannett
Hearst
E.W. Scripps
Times Mirror
Time Warner
Tribune
Washington Post

HOW MUCH

	9 Yr. Growth	1980	1981	1982	1983	1984	1985	1986	1987	1988	1989
Sales ($ mil)	10.3%	731	840	925	1,091	1,230	1,394	1,565	1,690	1,700	1,769
Net income ($ mil)	5.9%	41	50	54	79	100	116	132	160	161	68
Income as % of sales	—	5.6%	6.0%	5.9%	7.2%	8.1%	8.3%	8.5%	9.5%	9.5%	3.9%
Earnings per share ($)	5.0%	0.56	0.67	0.72	1.01	1.27	1.45	1.63	1.96	2.00	0.87
Stock price – high ($)	—	6.33	6.42	9.54	15.29	19.50	25.44	42.00	49.63	32.75	34.75
Stock price – low ($)	—	3.00	4.42	5.48	9.00	10.94	17.50	23.31	24.75	24.38	24.50
Stock price – close ($)	18.7%	5.67	6.42	9.54	14.00	19.19	24.50	35.50	31.00	26.88	26.50
P/E – high	—	11	10	13	15	15	18	26	25	16	40
P/E – low	—	5	7	8	9	9	12	14	13	12	28
Dividends per share ($)	13.6%	0.16	0.18	0.19	0.22	0.25	0.29	0.33	0.40	0.46	0.50
Book value per share ($)	16.5%	3.44	3.91	4.38	5.17	6.09	7.24	8.59	10.04	11.02	13.63

1989 Year End:
Debt ratio: 24.0%
Return on equity: 7.1%
Cash (mil): $76
Current ratio: 0.86
Long-term debt (mil): $337
Number of shares (mil): 78
Dividends:
1989 average yield: 1.9%
1989 payout: 57.5%
Market value (mil): $2,069

Stock Price History high/low 1980-89

THE NEWS CORPORATION LTD.

OVERVIEW

The News Corporation, probably best known for its controversial founder Rupert Murdoch, is a global media giant. Although based in Australia, it derives 48% of its sales from the US and 22% from the UK.

The News Corporation publishes the *Australian* and the *Times* (UK). In the US, after buying and selling papers in Chicago (*Sun-Times*) and New York (*Post*), the company retains the *San Antonio Express-News* and the *Boston Herald*.

The company also publishes magazines, including *TV Guide*, the most widely distributed general circulation magazine in the US, reaching almost 48 million readers; *Seventeen*; *Soap Opera Digest*; and US, UK, and Australian versions of *New Woman*. Harper & Collins, with Harper & Row in the US and William Collins in the UK, forms the company's book-publishing division.

The company has expanded recently into the television and film fields. The News Corporation owns Twentieth Century Fox (*Die Hard*, "L.A. Law"), Fox Broadcasting ("Cops," "The Simpsons"), and Sky Television (UK). The company also owns 7 television stations in major US markets and runs a large printing operation.

WHEN

Rupert Murdoch graduated from Oxford in 1953, having inherited the *Adelaide News* (Australia) in 1952 after his father's death. To build circulation of the paper, Murdoch used sensationalist headlines, a technique he employed often over the years.

He gradually acquired other newspapers and TV stations in Australia and launched the *Australian*, the country's first national daily. Murdoch first expanded abroad in 1968 with the purchase of *News of the World*, a London Sunday paper. His gradually increasing foreign holdings prompted Murdoch's move to New York in 1974.

The company bought a 40% stake in Collins Publishers (1981), a large London book publisher that was being run by the Collins family at the time. The News Corporation added to its US newspaper holdings, which included the lowbrow *New York Post* (One headline: "Headless Body Found in Topless Bar"), with the purchase of the *Chicago Sun-Times* in 1983 (sold 1986).

A series of large acquisitions began in 1985. Murdoch bought Twentieth Century Fox, including a large film library, from Denver billionaire Marvin Davis for $575 million. He also acquired 13 travel, hotel, and aviation trade magazines from Ziff-Davis for $350 million. A year later, after he became a US citizen to comply with FCC rules on broadcast ownership, he purchased 6 Metromedia TV stations for $1.5 billion. He bought the Herald & Weekly Times group, Australia's largest media company, for $1.6 billion.

Murdoch's acquisition binge continued in 1987 with the purchase of Harper & Row, then the 5th largest book publisher in the US. He also launched Fox Broadcasting in 1986, the first new TV network in the US since 1948. It served as a profitable outlet for Twentieth Century Fox's film library, but the network's own programming attracted viewers with the animated hit "The Simpsons" in 1989.

In 1988 The News Corporation paid $3.2 billion for Walter Annenberg's Triangle Publications, publisher of *Seventeen* and *TV Guide*. That same year the company purchased Zondervan, a US religious publisher, and in 1989 started Sky Television, a British TV network broadcast via satellite. In 1990 Murdoch announced he was suspending large acquisitions for at least 2 years, concentrating instead on building his TV holdings and repaying The News Corporation's $6 billion debt. The company agreed to sell its supermarket tabloid, the *Star*, to G.P. Group, publisher of the competing *National Enquirer*, for $400 million.

HOW MUCH

	3 Yr. Growth	1980	1981	1982	1983	1984	1985	1986	1987	1988	1989
Sales ($ mil)	35.4%	—	—	—	—	—	—	2,575	3,503	4,355	6,397
Net income ($ mil)	35.2%	—	—	—	—	—	—	163	241	336	403
Income as % of sales	—	—	—	—	—	—	—	6.3%	6.9%	7.7%	6.3%
Earnings per share ($)	28.9%	—	—	—	—	—	—	1.2	1.68	2.17	2.57
Stock price – high ($)	—	—	—	—	—	—	—	—	35.75	21.88	27.13
Stock price – low ($)	—	—	—	—	—	—	—	—	12.25	14.88	16.63
Stock price – close ($)	—	—	—	—	—	—	—	—	16.88	16.50	22.25
P/E – high	—	—	—	—	—	—	—	—	21	10	11
P/E – low	—	—	—	—	—	—	—	—	7	7	6
Dividends per share ($)	38.7%	—	—	—	—	—	—	0.06	0.07	0.12	0.16
Book value per share ($)	51.4%	—	—	—	—	—	—	7.94	19.46	23.43	27.55

1989 Year End:
Debt ratio: 63.8%
Return on equity: 10.1%
Cash (mil): $121
Current ratio: 0.97
Long-term debt (mil): $6,504
Number of shares (mil): 134
Dividends:
1989 average yield: 0.7%
1989 payout: 6.3%
Market value (mil): $2,987

Stock Price History high/low 1987-89

40 35 30 25 20 15 10 5 0

NYSE: NWS (ADR)
Founded: Australia, 1953
Fiscal year ends: June 30

WHO

Chairman: Richard Henry Searby, age 58
Managing Director and CEO: Keith Rupert Murdoch, age 58
Finance Director: Richard Allen Sarazen, age 56
Auditors: Pannell Kerr Forster
Employees: 30,908

WHERE

HQ: 2 Holt St., Sydney, N.S.W. 2010, Australia
Phone: 011-61-2-288-3000
US HQ (News America Publishing Inc.): 10 E. 53rd St., New York, NY 10022
US Phone: 212-852-7000
US Fax: 212-852-7145 (Investor Relations)

The company operates worldwide.

	1989 Sales		1989 Operating Income	
	$ mil	% of total	$ mil	% of total
US	3,055	48	494	42
UK	1,386	22	328	28
Australia & Pacific Basin	1,956	30	357	30
Total	**6,397**	**100**	**1,179**	**100**

WHAT

	1989 Sales		1989 Operating Income	
	$ mil	% of total	$ mil	% of total
Newspapers	2,358	37	557	48
Magazines	951	15	224	19
Television	605	9	82	7
Films	981	15	98	8
Commercial printing	384	6	40	3
Other	1,118	18	178	15
Total	**6,397**	**100**	**1,179**	**100**

Newspapers
The Australian
The Boston Herald
Daily Racing Form
San Antonio Express-News
South China Morning Post
The Times (UK)

Magazines
New Woman
Seventeen
Soap Opera Digest
TV Guide (US, UK)
TV Week (Australia)

Television & Film
Fox Broadcasting (US)
Fox Television Stations (US)
Sky Television (UK)
Twentieth Century Fox (US)

Books
Harper & Collins (50%)
John Bartholomew & Sons (UK)

TV Broadcasting
KDAF, Dallas
KRIV, Houston
KTTV, Los Angeles
WFLD, Chicago
WFXT, Boston
WNYW, New York
WTTG, Washington

Other
Ansett Transport (airline; 50%)
Etak (electronic maps)
Pearson plc (17.4%)
World Printing

RANKINGS

202nd in *Fortune* Global 500 Industrial Cos.
43rd in *Forbes* 100 Foreign Investments in the US
964th in *Business Week* Global 1000

COMPETITION

Advance Publications
Bertelsmann
Capital Cities/ABC
CBS
Cox
General Electric
Hearst
Maxwell
MCA
McGraw-Hill
Paramount
Pearson
Time Warner
Turner Broadcasting
Walt Disney

NIKE, INC.

OVERVIEW

NIKE is a major designer, producer, and international distributor of high-quality athletic and leisure footwear. The NIKE and "swoosh" trademarks are recognized worldwide and are registered in over 100 countries. In addition to its shoes, NIKE offers its own apparel line, which includes fitness and sporting wear, athletic bags, and accessories.

NIKE leads the domestic athletic shoe market with a 24.8% market share. Domestic sales account for 80% of company revenues. NIKE sells its products to about 16,800 domestic retail outlets. Shoes for basketball, fitness, and running are its top-selling products. NIKE maintains an aggressive commitment to researching and developing high-tech footwear.

NIKE produces almost all of its shoes and about 52% of its apparel overseas through independent contractors. South Korea produces 58% of company footwear and Taiwan produces 18%. The company's products are sold in over 60 countries, with foreign sales accounting for 20% of total revenues.

OTC symbol: NIKE
Incorporated: Oregon, 1968
Fiscal year ends: May 31

WHO

Chairman and CEO: Philip H. Knight, age 52, $542,758 pay
President and COO: Richard K. Donohue, age 63
Deputy Chairman and SVP: William J. Bowerman, age 79
EVP: Delbert J. Hayes, age 55
VP Finance: George E. Porter, age 59
Auditors: Price Waterhouse
Employees: 4,070

WHEN

In 1958 Phil Knight, an undergraduate business student at the University of Oregon and a good miler, often spoke with his coach Bill Bowerman about the lack of a good American running shoe. Bowerman, resolving to create a better shoe, sent an original design to several leading sporting goods companies. Turned down by all of them, Bowerman made the shoes himself, using grocery bags for patterns.

In 1964 Knight and Bowerman joined to form their own athletic shoe company, named Blue Ribbon Sports. Knight arranged with Onitsuka Tiger, a Japanese shoe manufacturer, to produce the new shoes, which he and Bowerman, the only distributors, then sold in the United States. Knight and Bowerman put up $500 each for the first order of 300 pairs of shoes, which they stored in the basement of Knight's father's house. The men sold the shoes out of cars at track meets, at first only in western states.

In 1968 the 2 men formed NIKE, Inc., named for the Greek word for "victory," allegedly the last word spoken by the legendary runner from Marathon. In 1972 they broke with Onitsuka due to a dispute over distribution rights. The NIKE "swoosh" logo was designed by a graduate student named Carolyn Davidson, who was paid $35 for her work.

At the 1972 Olympic Trials in nearby Eugene, Oregon, Knight and Bowerman persuaded some of the marathoners to wear NIKE shoes. When a few of these runners placed, the 2 men quickly advertised that NIKEs were on the feet of "four of the top seven finishers."

In 1975 Bowerman conceived the idea for a new shoe sole, which he tested by stuffing a piece of rubber into a waffle iron. The result was the waffle sole, which NIKE promptly put on its running shoes. When running became popular in the 1970s, NIKE was quick to respond by constantly improving its line of running shoes to appeal to the new market. By 1982 company sales had reached almost $700 million annually.

When enthusiasm for running faded, NIKE responded with shoes for a variety of other sports, including football, basketball, baseball, volleyball, hiking, wrestling, and soccer. In 1988 the company purchased Cole Haan (dress shoes). NIKE introduced Air Jordan (a popular basketball shoe named for Chicago Bulls star Michael Jordan) in 1985, the Cross Trainer in 1987, the "Just Do It" slogan in 1988, Air Pressure (basketball shoes with inflatable soles) in 1989, and Aqua Sock (water shoes) in 1990.

In 1990 black civil rights group Operation PUSH (15% to 30% of NIKE's sales customers are black) announced a boycott of NIKE, which had refused to discuss PUSH's demands for investments in black communities. The boycott did not greatly affect sales and was criticized by some other civil rights groups.

WHERE

HQ: 3900 SW Murray Blvd., Beaverton, OR 97005
Phone: 503-641-6453
FAX: 503-626-7252 (Public Relations)

The company sells its products in over 60 countries and maintains administrative offices in the US, Europe, Asia, and Canada.

	1989 Sales		1989 Operating Income	
	$ mil	% of total	$ mil	% of total
US	1,362	80	230	78
Europe	241	14	35	12
Other foreign	108	6	30	10
Adjustments	—	—	(25)	—
Total	**1,711**	**100**	**270**	**100**

WHAT

	1989 US Sales	
	$ mil	% of total
Basketball	415	31
Fitness	238	18
Running	203	15
Racquet	58	4
Other	153	11
Nonathletic	87	6
Apparel	208	15
Total (US sales only)	**1,362**	**100**

Aerobics Shoes
Elite

Basketball Shoes
Air Jordan
Air Pressure
Flight
Force

Cross-Training Shoes
Air Trainer SC
All Conditions Gear

Running Shoes
Air Flow
Air Max Light
Air Pegasus
Air Stab
NIKE International

Tennis Shoes
Air Challenge Court
Air Tech Challenge
Challenge Court

Water Sports Shoes
Aqua Sock

Dress Shoes
Cole Haan

Apparel Products
Accessories
Athletic bags
Bicycling clothing
Fitness wear
Running clothes
Shirts
Shorts
Socks

HOW MUCH

	9 Yr. Growth	1980	1981	1982	1983	1984	1985	1986	1987	1988	1989
Sales ($ mil)	22.8%	270	458	694	867	920	946	1,069	877	1,203	1,711
Net income ($ mil)	33.4%	13	26	49	57	41	10	59	36	102	167
Income as % of sales	—	4.6%	5.7%	7.1%	6.6%	4.4%	1.1%	5.5%	4.1%	8.5%	9.8%
Earnings per share ($)	31.3%	0.39	0.76	1.37	1.53	1.07	0.27	1.55	0.93	2.70	4.45
Stock price – high ($)	—	—	11.63	14.25	28.00	23.75	16.38	14.75	20.50	24.75	34.38
Stock price – low ($)	—	—	9.00	8.63	12.44	14.38	6.63	7.88	10.38	11.50	17.25
Stock price – close ($)	—	—	10.50	14.13	22.56	14.50	7.88	14.13	11.75	19.50	26.50
P/E – high	—	—	15	10	18	22	61	10	22	9	8
P/E – low	—	—	12	6	8	13	25	5	11	4	4
Dividends per share ($)	—	0.00	0.00	0.00	0.00	0.20	0.40	0.40	0.30	0.40	0.50
Book value per share ($)	36.9%	0.89	2.37	3.76	6.46	7.37	7.27	8.39	8.91	11.10	15.06

1989 Year End:
Debt ratio: 5.7%
Return on equity: 34.0%
Cash (mil): $86
Current ratio: 2.96
Long-term debt (mil): $34
Number of shares (mil): 37
Dividends:
1989 average yield: 1.9%
1989 payout: 11.2%
Market value (mil): $988

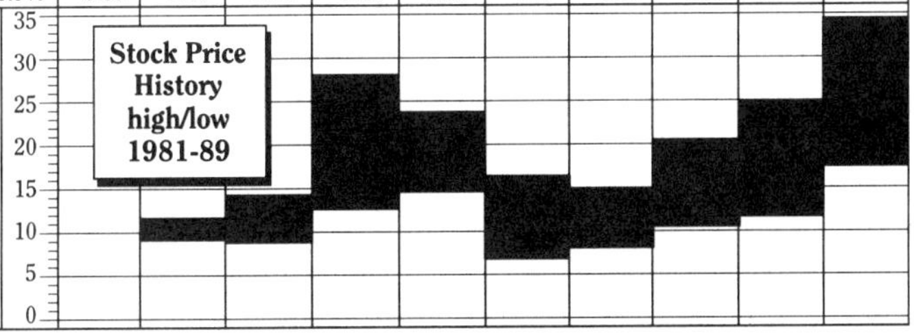

RANKINGS

59th in *Fortune* 100 Diversified Service Cos.
393rd in *Forbes* Sales 500
266th in *Business Week* 1000
673rd in *Business Week* Global 1000

COMPETITION

INTERCO	V. F.
Levi Strauss	United States Shoe
Reebok	Manufacturers of shoes and apparel

NIPPON TELEGRAPH AND TELEPHONE CORP.

OVERVIEW

Measured by stock market capitalization, Nippon Telegraph and Telephone (NTT) is the world's most valuable company. The telecommunications utility is Japan's largest employer. Telephone services account for 79% of company sales. Other activities include data communications and videotex services. The Japanese government owns 66.8% of the company's stock.

The Japanese government has been debating proposals to split the company along regional lines or into long-distance and local carriers, but NTT has successfully delayed further discussion of a breakup until 1995.

By 1995 NTT expects to have completed the upgrading of Japan's trunk lines to optical fiber, a prerequisite for digital networks. Other development areas include voice dialing and 2-way visual communications.

NTT gradually continues to increase its overseas purchases. Fiscal 1990 purchases from foreign suppliers totaled $334 million, 4% of the company's total. All of the company's US offices are for procurement only.

WHEN

The Japanese Ministry of Communications began telephone service in 1889 and operated as a monopoly after 1900. After WWII the ministry reorganized and, in 1952, formed Nippon Telegraph and Telephone Public Corporation (NTT). Regulated by the Ministry of Posts and Telecommunications, NTT was charged with rebuilding and operating Japan's war-ravaged telephone system. The ministry created a separate company (KDD) to handle international telephone service in 1953.

Japanese authorities created NTT in the image of AT&T but prohibited NTT from manufacturing, preferring to encourage competition among equipment suppliers. NTT bought most of its equipment from favored Japanese vendors. Four companies benefited most from this arrangement: NEC (the most favored), Hitachi, Fujitsu, and Oki Electric.

NTT expanded rapidly during the 1960s as Japan's economy surged. In the late 1960s NTT was installing 3 million lines per year. In 1968 NTT enlisted Hitachi, Fujitsu, and NEC to design and build computers for NTT's use, subsidizing critical R&D for Japan's future computer giants.

By the 1970s NTT had become a large, bureaucratic utility, and public suspicions of inefficiency and corruption led to political pressure to reform. In the late 1970s US trade representatives called for NTT to purchase non-Japanese equipment and were stunned when NTT president Tokuji Akikusa told them that the only items it would consider buying overseas were telephone poles and mops.

Change came to NTT in the 1980s. The company entered into an agreement in 1981 to open procurement to US companies. After Akikusa resigned following an expense-account scandal in 1981, Prime Minister Suzuki appointed free-market advocate Hisashi Shinto as president to reorganize and streamline the company. NTT inaugurated a public FAX network in 1981 and a videotex service in 1984. The company spent heavily in the 1980s on the nationwide installation of optical fiber for integrated systems digital networks (ISDN) capable of high-volume, high-speed data transmission.

In 1985 Japanese authorities began deregulating the telecommunications industry, opening NTT markets to competition (while maintaining price regulation), and selling NTT shares to the public. NTT became the world's most valuable public company upon its initial public offering. The Japanese government sold additional NTT shares to the public in 1987 and again in 1988, at 130 times earnings.

Shinto resigned and was arrested in 1988 for his alleged involvement in the Recruit stock and influence-peddling scandal. In 1990 NTT selected AT&T, Motorola, and Ericsson (Sweden) to help develop a digital mobile telephone system.

HOW MUCH

	9 Yr. Growth	1980	1981	1982	1983	1984	1985	1986	1987	1988	1989
Sales ($ mil)	12.7%	15,086	18,645	16,544	17,861	19,961	18,425	28,286	36,668	45,296	44,257
Net income ($ mil)	1.1%	1,814	1,839	1,443	1,544	1,709	1,298	1,032	1,320	2,137	1,997
Income as % of sales	—	12.0%	9.9%	8.7%	8.6%	8.6%	7.0%	3.6%	3.6%	4.7%	4.5%
Earnings per share ($)	—	—	—	—	—	—	—	—	85	137	128
Stock price – high ($)	—	—	—	—	—	—	—	—	—	—	—
Stock price – low ($)	—	—	—	—	—	—	—	—	—	—	—
Stock price – close ($)	—	—	—	—	—	—	—	—	—	—	—
P/E – high	—	—	—	—	—	—	—	—	—	—	—
P/E – low	—	—	—	—	—	—	—	—	—	—	—
Dividends per share ($)	—	—	—	—	—	—	—	—	—	—	0.00
Book value per share ($)	—	—	—	—	—	—	—	250.64	575.06	936.73	924.17

1989 Year End:
Debt ratio: 50.5%
Return on equity: 6.6%
Cash (mil): $3,442
Current ratio: 0.75
Long-term debt (mil): $30,653
Number of shares (mil): 16
Dividends:
1989 average yield: —
1989 payout: 0.0%
Market value (mil): —

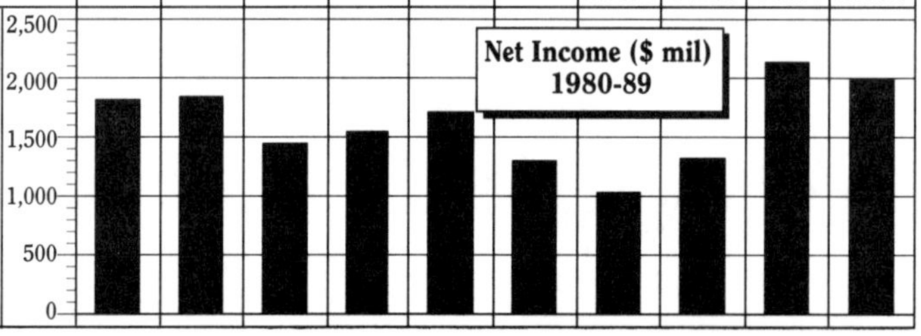

Net Income ($ mil) 1980-89

Principal stock exchange: Tokyo
Incorporated: Japan, 1985
Fiscal year ends: March 31

WHO

President and CEO: Haruo Yamaguchi
SEVP: Masashi Kojima
SEVP: Koichiro Kamo
SEVP: Tadasu Murakami
SEVP: Katsumi Iida
Auditors: Price Waterhouse
Employees: 283,294

WHERE

HQ: 1-6, Uchisaiwaicho 1-chome, Chiyoda-ku, Tokyo 100, Japan
Phone: 011-81-3-509-3101
FAX: 011-81-3-580-9104
US HQ (NTT America, Inc.): Room 2905, Pan American Bldg., 200 Park Ave., New York, NY 10166
US Phone: 212-867-1511
US FAX: 212-286-8970

NTT operates principally in Japan but provides telecommunications consulting services worldwide.

WHAT

	1989 Sales	
	$ mil	% of total
Telephone services	35,020	79
Telegraph services	405	1
Leased circuit services	2,533	6
Data communications facility services	1,409	3
Digital data exchange services	252	1
Pocket pager services	716	1
Other telecommunications services	1,180	3
Terminal equipment sales, consulting services & other businesses	2,742	6
Total	**44,257**	**100**

Services

Leased Circuit Services
High-speed digital circuit services
Satellite communications
Standard circuit services
Video and record communications

Data Communications Facility Services
ANSER (Automatic Answer Network System for Electrical Request) Response Service
Credit information systems
Public and private data communications facility services

Digital Data Exchange Services
Circuit-switching services
Packet-switching services

Other Telecommunications Services
FAX network services
Videoconference services
Videotex services

RANKINGS

1st in *Business Week* Global 1000

COMPETITION

No other companies in this book compete with NTT.

NISSAN MOTOR CO. LTD.

OVERVIEW

Tokyo-based Nissan is the world's 5th largest automobile manufacturer. Although exports account for 39% of the company's new vehicle registrations, Nissan is rapidly building production capacity in overseas markets, making substantial investments in the US, Mexico, and the UK.

Yutaka Kume, Nissan's president since 1985, has reformed the company's notoriously unresponsive management style. Highly automated, flexible production systems are expected to help Nissan quickly adapt models to local tastes.

The #2 automaker in Japan, Nissan has chipped away at Toyota's market share lead in recent years. Nissan's success in the Japanese luxury car market has not been matched in the US, where sales are slow for the company's new Infiniti line. Nissan trails Toyota and Honda in US sales of Japanese cars.

WHEN

In 1911 US-trained Hashimoto Masujiro established Tokyo-based Kwaishinsha Motor Car Works to repair, import, and produce automobiles. Using DAT ("fast rabbit" in Japanese) as its logo, Kwaishinsha made its first car in 1913. Called DAT Motors since 1925 and suffering from a strong domestic preference for American cars, the company consolidated its operations with ailing Jitsuyo Motors in 1926. In 1931 DAT introduced the son of DAT, the Datsun minicar (son means damage or loss in Japanese, hence the change in spelling).

Tobata Casting, a cast iron and auto parts maker, acquired the Datsun production facilities in 1933. Tobata was part of a new *zaibatsu* (conglomerate) controlled by Aikawa Yoshisuke, who believed that a niche existed for small cars that did not compete head-on with large US imports. Tobata's automotive operations were spun off as Nissan Motors in 1933. Aikawa imported American machinery and engineers in the 1930s. In 1936 he imported all the production equipment in a US plant owned by financially troubled Graham-Paige, the 14th largest US car maker, creating Japan's first mass-producer of automobiles.

In WWII the Japanese government forced Nissan to build trucks and airplane engines and to stop producing cars, leaving its dealers with little to sell. The resulting dealer defections gave Toyota a postwar marketing advantage over Nissan. During the occupation, Nissan survived in part on US Army business.

Nissan's 1952 licensing agreement with Austin Motor (UK) put the company back in the small-car business. Adhering to quality-control statistician William E. Deming's teachings, Nissan began mass-producing reliable, inexpensive autos in the 1950s. A 40% value-added tax on imports allowed the company to compete in Japan despite higher production costs than foreign manufacturers.

Nissan elected to enter the US market in 1958 using the Datsun name and established Nissan Motor Corporation in Los Angeles in 1960. The company built an assembly plant in Mexico (1961) and introduced the popular Sunny in Japan (1966) and the 240Z in the US (1969). Exports rose during the 1960s as quality increased and unit costs declined as a result of just-in-time inventory management, factory automation, and higher production volume.

In the 1970s, the decade of the oil crisis, Nissan rapidly expanded exports of fuel-efficient cars, such as the Datsun B210, and diversified into rockets and motorboats.

In the 1980s the company built facilities throughout the world, including a pickup truck plant in Smyrna, Tennessee, and an R&D center in Ann Arbor, Michigan. The US name change from Datsun to Nissan confused customers and took 6 years to complete (1981 to 1987). Nissan's high-end Infiniti line was launched in the US in 1989.

HOW MUCH

$ = ¥144 (Dec. 31, 1989)	9 Yr. Growth	1980	1981	1982	1983	1984	1985	1986	1987	1988	1989
Sales (¥ bil)	4.3%	3,304	3,649	3,901	4,071	4,308	4,626	4,628	4,273	4,244	4,812
Net income (¥ bil)	0.4%	106	107	102	105	74	82	36	20	65	115
Income as % of sales	—	3.2%	2.9%	2.6%	2.6%	1.7%	1.8%	0.8%	0.5%	1.5%	2.4%
Earnings per share (¥)	(1.9%)	57	55	41	46	36	39	16	9	29	48
Stock price – high (¥)	—	611	1,025	723	698	695	668	717	875	1,380	1,650
Stock price – low (¥)	—	508	572	576	538	575	569	529	550	705	1,250
Stock price – close (¥)	10.7%	589	690	690	686	625	570	550	725	1,200	1,470
P/E – high	—	11	19	18	15	19	17	45	97	48	34
P/E – low	—	9	10	14	12	16	15	33	61	24	26
Dividends per share (¥)	3.9%	9.9	9.9	10.7	11.6	12.7	12.7	14.0	14.0	14.0	14.0
Book value per share (¥)	5.5%	412	460	423	459	526	629	627	616	628	666

1989 Year End:
Debt ratio: 28.0%
Return on equity: 7.4%
Cash (bil): ¥899
Long-term debt (bil): ¥643
Number of shares (mil): 2,477
Dividends:
1989 average yield: 1.0%
1989 payout: 29.2%
Market value (mil): $25,289
Sales (mil): $33,417

Stock Price History high/low 1980-89

1,800 1,600 1,400 1,200 1,000 800 600 400 200 0

OTC symbol: NSANY (ADR)
Incorporated: Japan, 1933
Fiscal year ends: March 31

WHO

Chairman: Takashi Ishihara
President: Yutaka Kume
EVP Overseas Operations: Tetsuo Arakawa
EVP Manufacturing: Takuro Endo
EVP Finance: Atsushi Muramatsu
Auditors: Showa Ota & Co.
Employees: 117,330

WHERE

HQ: 17-1, Ginza 6-chome, Chuo-ku, Tokyo 104-23, Japan
Phone: 011-81-3-543-5523
US HQ (Nissan Motor Corp. in U.S.A.): 18501 S. Figueroa St., Carson, CA 90248
US Phone: 213-532-3111
US FAX: 213-719-5825 (Public Relations)

Nissan operates assembly and production facilities in Japan and 21 other countries.

	1989 Sales
Japan	47%
Other countries	53%
Total	**100%**

	1989 Unit Sales	
	no. of vehicles	% of total
Japan	1,155,981	41
North America	693,925	25
Europe	521,130	19
Latin America & Caribbean	117,860	4
Oceania	101,381	4
Southeast Asia	88,309	3
Africa	56,906	2
Middle East	49,601	2
Other countries	4,248	—
Total	**2,789,341**	**100**

WHAT

	1989 Sales	
	¥ bil	% of total
Vehicles	3,743	78
Automotive parts & others	956	20
Industrial machinery & marine equipment	45	1
Production parts & components	33	1
Aerospace equipment	24	—
Textile machinery	11	—
Total	**4,812**	**100**

Vehicle Models (US Markets)

Nissan
Maxima
Pathfinder
Pulsar
Sentra
Stanza
300ZX
240SX

Infiniti
M30
Q45

RANKINGS

17th in *Fortune* Global 500 Industrial Cos.
71st in *Forbes* 100 Foreign Investments in the US
51st in *Business Week* Global 1000

COMPETITION

Chrysler
Daimler-Benz
Fiat
Ford
General Motors
Honda
Hyundai
Mitsubishi
Renault
Toyota
Volkswagen
Volvo

THE NOMURA SECURITIES CO., LTD.

OVERVIEW

Measured by assets, Tokyo-based Nomura Securities was the world's largest financial institution in 1989. Aided by Japanese government restrictions on foreign investment houses and a fixed commission system, the company has been consistently among the most profitable of the world's financial services organizations. Tokyo stock market capitalization is the highest of any in the world, and Nomura dominates the Japanese securities industry. The company is also the leading Euromarket underwriter.

Nomura has made significant progress overseas, but the company's main business remains Japanese stock brokerage. The Japanese character for Nomura may also be read as "too tired," a pun used by the company's relentlessly driven telemarketing staff of 3,000.

WHEN

Nomura Tokushichi started a currency exchange business in Osaka under the Nomura Shoten name in 1872. As money changing subsided with Japanese monetary reform, Nomura entered stock dealing. His business prospered and was taken over by his son, Tokushichi II, prior to the senior Nomura's death in 1907. In 1910 Tokushichi II formed Nomura's first syndicate to underwrite a portion of a government bond issue. As business grew, Nomura established the Osaka Nomura Bank (1918). The bond department became independent in 1925 and was named Nomura Securities.

Nomura Securities survived the Great Depression by underwriting bond issues for public works projects. The company opened a New York office (1927), entered stock brokerage (1938), and introduced its enormously successful stock investment trusts (1941). Nomura lost 1/2 of its Japanese staff and offices in WWII. Nomura Tokushichi II died in 1945.

Nomura rebuilt and aggressively expanded retail operations after the war. The company encouraged stock market investing by promoting "million ryo [an old form of currency] savings chests," small boxes in which people were encouraged to save cash. When savings reached 5,000 yen, savers, usually women, would bring their boxes to Nomura and buy into investment trusts. Employing women to collect cash and sell securities, Nomura distributed over one million chests in 10 years.

The Japanese economy recovered during the Korean War, and Nomura looked overseas for investment capital, helping to underwrite a US issue of Sony stock (1961) and opening a London office (1962). The company emerged as Japan's leading securities firm after a 1965 stock market crash left rival Yamaichi Securities near bankruptcy. Nomura initiated the "stock of the week" program of touting and hard-selling stocks to the public. When trade surpluses encouraged the Ministry of Finance to allow public ownership of foreign securities in 1971, Nomura began offering *samurai* (yen-denominated foreign) bonds. The company grew rapidly in the 1970s as it ushered investment capital in and out of Japan and encroached on bank lending by issuing corporate debt securities.

Nomura expanded worldwide in the 1970s and 1980s, attained NYSE membership (1981), became a primary US Treasury dealer (1986), secured a seat on the London Stock Exchange (1986), opened Nomura Bank International in London (1986), became the world leader in Eurobonds (1987), and paid $100 million for 20% of merger and acquisition advisor Wasserstein Perella (1988). Nomura continued its aggressive pursuit of retail business, conducting Tupperware-style investment parties in Japan.

In 1989 Nomura tapped former Kidder, Peabody president Max Chapman to head US operations and reconcile culture clashes plaguing the company's US retail activities.

HOW MUCH

	9 Yr. Growth	1980	1981	1982	1983	1984	1985	1986	1987	1988	1989*
Sales (¥ bil)	19.2%	242	308	268	367	437	590	942	1,073	960	1,172
Net income (¥ bil)	25.2%	36	50	42	69	73	111	221	268	214	286
Income as % of sales	—	14.9%	16.2%	15.7%	18.8%	16.7%	18.8%	23.5%	25.0%	22.3%	24.4%
Earnings per share (¥)	24.9%	20	28	22	37	39	59	118	142	112	148
Stock price – high (¥)	—	345	637	551	690	853	1,287	3,612	5,816	4,185	4,100
Stock price – low (¥)	—	285	297	319	511	533	793	934	2,402	2,402	3,060
Stock price – close (¥)	31.5%	293	499	550	645	809	980	2,835	2,583	3,750	3,440
P/E – high	—	17	23	25	19	22	22	31	41	37	28
P/E – low	—	14	13	15	14	14	13	8	17	21	21
Dividends per share (¥)	—	4.65	5.69	5.86	6.04	6.67	7.25	9.71	12.14	13.11	7.25
Book value per share (¥)	19.9%	172	208	214	239	274	325	412	582	685	882

1989 Year End:
Debt ratio: —
Return on equity: 18.9%
Cash (bil): ¥1,232
Long-term debt (bil): —
Number of shares (mil): 1,954
Dividends:
1989 average yield: —
1989 payout: —
Market value (mil): $46,699
Sales (mil): $8,139

Stock Price History high/low 1980-89

*Fiscal year change—1989 accounting data include 6 months of fiscal 1989 and 6 months of fiscal 1990.

OTC symbol: NMRJY (ADR)
Principal stock exchange: Tokyo
Incorporated: Japan, 1925
Fiscal year ends: March 31

WHO

Chairman: Setsuya Tabuchi
President and CEO: Yoshihisa Tabuchi, age 56
EVP: Yoshiji Fukushima
EVP: Hideo Sakamaki
EVP: Masaki Yoshida
EVP: Masashi Suzuki
Auditors: Price Waterhouse
Employees: 10,643 (parent company only)

WHERE

HQ: 1-9-1, Nihonbashi, Chuo-ku, Tokyo 103, Japan
Phone: 011-81-3-211-1811
FAX: 011-81-3-278-0420
US HQ (Nomura Securities International, Inc.): The Continental Center, 180 Maiden Ln., New York, NY 10038
US Phone: 212-208-9300
US FAX: 212-509-8907

Nomura has 146 offices in Japan and 51 offices in 23 other countries.

	1989* Sales	
	¥ bil	% of total
Commissions	507	43
Underwriting & distribution	200	17
Net gain on trading	217	19
Interest & dividends	242	21
Other	6	—
Total	**1,172**	**100**

*Fiscal year change. Data presented for 1989 include 6 months of fiscal 1989 and 6 months of fiscal 1990.

WHAT

Lines of Business
Securities
- Brokerage
- Dealing
- Distribution
- Underwriting

Financial consulting
- Asset management
- Banking
- Leveraged leasing
- Mergers and acquisitions
- Real estate

Affiliated Companies (Minority Holdings)
Associated Japanese Bank (International) Ltd. (London)
Babcock & Brown, Inc. (San Francisco)
China International Finance Co. Ltd. (Shenzhen, China)
Eastdil Realty (New York)
International Union Leasing Co., Ltd. (Beijing, China)
N.N. Investment Ltd. (Hong Kong)
P.T. Finconesia (Indonesia)
Wasserstein Perella Group, Inc. (New York, 20%)

RANKINGS

19th in *Business Week* Global 1000

COMPETITION

CS Holding
Dai-Ichi Kangyo
Deutsche Bank
Goldman Sachs
Merrill Lynch
Other brokerage and investment banking firms

NORDSTROM, INC.

OVERVIEW

Specialty retailer Nordstrom has received a lot of attention in recent years for its superior customer service. The Seattle-based company, 40%-owned by the Nordstrom family, has increased sales more than 600% since 1980 but now faces challenges that threaten its uniqueness.

Some Nordstrom amenities are easily duplicated: a no-questions-asked return policy, oversized dressing rooms, and abundant inventories aimed to ensure that the right sizes and colors are in stock. But what has set the company apart from other retailers is the personal service provided to customers by commissioned salespeople. Stories of employees warming up customers' cars in winter, delivering packages on their way home, and writing thank you notes have enhanced Nordstrom's reputation as a special place to shop.

Recently Nordstrom's competitors have taken notice, placing their sales clerks on commission and even redesigning their stores in what has been called the "Nordstromization" of retailing. A more serious challenge is the state of Washington's 1990 decision that Nordstrom's after-hours requirements of its employees violate labor laws. Class-action lawsuits now pending as a result of the decision could cost the company substantial back wages.

WHEN

In 1901 John W. Nordstrom, a gold miner and lumberjack from Sweden, opened Wallin & Nordstrom shoe store in Seattle with shoemaker Carl F. Wallin. Nordstrom retired in 1928, selling his 1/2 of the business, which by then had opened a 2nd store, to his sons Everett and Elmer. Wallin sold out to the Nordstroms in 1929 and a 3rd Nordstrom son, Lloyd, joined in 1933. The shoe chain thrived and incorporated in 1946 as Nordstrom's, Inc.

By 1963 Nordstrom's was the largest independent shoe chain in the country. The company decided to expand into apparel retailing and that year acquired Best Apparel, which had a store in Seattle and another in Portland. In 1966 Nordstrom's bought Portland's Nicholas Ungar, a fashion retailer that it merged with a Portland Nordstrom's shoe store under the name Nordstrom Best.

The company, also renamed Nordstrom Best in 1966, went public in 1971; in 1973 the name changed simply to Nordstrom, Inc. Lloyd Nordstrom organized a group of investors to buy the Seattle Seahawks for $16 million in 1975. The family, a 51% owner of the team, considered selling its interest when the team's player representative was cut in 1984, causing many Seattle residents to protest in front of the downtown store and destroy their Nordstrom credit cards. The family later bought out the remaining investors and sold the franchise in 1988.

Meanwhile the company continued to expand the retail stores. In 1976 Nordstrom started Place Two, featuring apparel and shoes in smaller stores than the traditional Nordstrom. Expansion into Southern California began with the opening of a store in Orange County (1978). Nordstrom also had stores in Washington, Oregon, Alaska, and Utah when in 1988 the company opened its first store on the East Coast in Tysons Corner, in an affluent Virginia suburb of Washington, DC. This opening had the highest first-day sales in the company's history — $1 million — until a San Francisco opening later in the year eclipsed it with a $1.7 million first-day sales record.

Nordstrom has since opened stores in Sacramento and near the Pentagon in Virginia in 1989, and in Pleasanton, California, and metropolitan New York in 1990. The company built a large distribution center in Maryland, and new stores are being built or have been announced for Maryland, New Jersey, Connecticut, and Massachusetts. In addition, a thrust into the Midwest is planned for Illinois, Indiana, and Minnesota.

HOW MUCH

	9 Yr. Growth	1980	1981	1982	1983	1984	1985	1986	1987	1988	1989
Sales ($ mil)	23.2%	408	522	613	788	981	1,302	1,630	1,920	2,328	2,671
Net income ($ mil)	21.7%	20	25	27	40	41	50	73	93	123	115
Income as % of sales	—	4.8%	4.7%	4.4%	5.1%	4.1%	3.8%	4.5%	4.8%	5.3%	4.3%
Earnings per share ($)	19.2%	0.29	0.35	0.38	0.54	0.55	0.65	0.91	1.13	1.51	1.41
Stock price – high ($)	—	3.06	4.72	6.31	11.56	9.63	13.19	25.63	40.75	34.00	42.50
Stock price – low ($)	—	1.84	2.47	3.34	5.75	6.63	7.06	11.88	15.75	19.75	29.75
Stock price – close ($)	33.3%	2.81	3.94	6.06	8.94	7.75	11.94	20.88	19.75	30.25	37.25
P/E – high	—	11	13	17	22	18	20	28	36	23	30
P/E – low	—	6	7	9	11	12	11	13	14	13	21
Dividends per share ($)	22.5%	0.05	0.06	0.06	0.07	0.10	0.11	0.13	0.18	0.22	0.28
Book value per share ($)	18.5%	1.94	2.27	2.73	3.21	3.65	4.22	5.57	6.55	7.86	8.99

1989 Year End:
Debt ratio: 37.5%
Return on equity: 16.7%
Cash (mil): $33
Current ratio: 2.06
Long-term debt (mil): $441
Number of shares (mil): 82
Dividends:
1989 average yield: 0.8%
1989 payout: 19.9%
Market value (mil): $3,039

NASDAQ symbol: NOBE
Incorporated: Washington, 1946
Fiscal year ends: January 31

WHO

Co-Chairman: Bruce A. Nordstrom, age 56, $300,000 pay
Co-Chairman: John N. Nordstrom, age 53, $300,000 pay
Co-Chairman: James F. Nordstrom , age 50, $300,000 pay
President: John A. McMillan, age 58, $300,000 pay
SVP and Treasurer: John A. Goesling, age 44
Auditors: Deloitte & Touche
Employees: 28,000

WHERE

HQ: 1501 Fifth Ave., Seattle, WA 98101
Phone: 206-628-2111
FAX: 206-628-1289

Most Nordstrom stores are in West Coast states and in Utah; 2 are currently operating on the East Coast. Place Two stores are all in Washington and Oregon.

	1989 Retail Locations	
	sq. ft. thou.	% of total
California	3,900	56
Washington	1,318	19
Oregon	664	10
Washington, DC area	479	7
Other	537	8
Total	**6,898**	**100**

WHAT

	1989 Retail Sales
	% of total
Women's apparel	39
Women's accessories	20
Shoes	18
Men's apparel & furnishings	17
Children's apparel & other	6
Total	**100**

Retail Stores
Nordstrom
43 specialty stores in 6 states selling apparel, shoes, and accessories

Place Two
6 small specialty apparel stores

Other Operations
Nordstrom Rack
10 discount apparel stores in 3 states

Leased shoe departments
Shoe departments leased in 11 department stores in Hawaii

RANKINGS

42nd in *Fortune* 50 Retailing Cos.
311th in *Forbes* Sales 500
252nd in *Business Week* 1000

COMPETITION

Campeau
Carter Hawley Hale
General Cinema
Hartmarx
The Limited
R. H. Macy
May Department Stores
Melville
United States Shoe

NORFOLK SOUTHERN CORPORATION

OVERVIEW

Norfolk Southern Corporation owns 2 railroads, Norfolk & Western Railway and Southern Railway, which together make up the 4th largest railroad system in the US. Operating over 15,900 miles of track in the Midwest, Southeast, and Ontario, Canada, Norfolk Southern hauls coal, coke, iron ore, chemicals, automobiles, and many other commodities. The company also conducts a growing business in international trade, principally coal exports. Pocahontas Land Corporation (a subsidiary) has access to almost 2 billion tons of coal reserves.

Norfolk Southern has launched several intermodal programs (freight transported in the same container by train, truck, or ship) in recent years, including Triple Crown Services, which employs Roadrailers, freight containers that can be converted quickly from railcars (with undercarriages) to trailers (with truck wheels).

North American Van Lines (purchased in 1985) moves household goods, general merchandise, and specialized shipments by truck and forwards international freight traffic by sea and air.

WHEN

Norfolk Southern Corporation is the result of the 1982 merger of 2 major US railroads: Norfolk & Western Railway Company (N&W) and Southern Railway Company.

N&W dates to 1838, when a single track first connected Petersburg, Virginia, to City Point (now Hopewell). This 8-mile stretch became part of the Atlantic, Mississippi & Ohio (AM&O), which was created by the consolidation of 3 Virginia railways in 1870. In 1881 the Philadelphia banking firm of E. W. Clark and Company bought the AM&O, renamed it the Norfolk & Western, and established headquarters at Roanoke, Virginia. N&W rolled into Ohio by purchasing 2 other railroads (1892, 1901) and took over the Virginian Railway, a coal carrier with trackage paralleling much of its own (1959). In 1964 N&W acquired the New York, Chicago & St. Louis Railroad (a fast freight line nicknamed the Nickel Plate Road); the Akron, Canton & Youngstown; and Pennsylvania Railroad's line between Columbus and Sandusky, Ohio. Also in 1964 N&W leased the Wabash Railroad, gaining lines from Detroit and Chicago to Kansas City and St. Louis.

The Southern Railway can be traced back to the South Carolina Canal & Rail Road (SCC&RR), a 9-mile line chartered in 1827 and built by Horatio Allen to win trade for the port of Charleston. SCC&RR later became the longest railway in the world when it opened a 136-mile line to Hamburg, South Carolina (1833). Soon other railroads sprang up throughout the South, including the Richmond & Danville (Virginia, 1847) and the East Tennessee, Virginia & Georgia (1869), which were combined to form the Southern Railway System (Southern) in 1894. Southern eventually gained control of more than 100 railroads, forging a system that extended from Washington, DC, to St. Louis and New Orleans.

The 1982 merger of Southern and N&W created an extensive rail system operating throughout the East, South, and Midwest. Norfolk Southern bought North American Van Lines (1985) and attempted (unsuccessfully) to buy Consolidated Rail (1986). Triple Crown Services, the company's intermodal subsidiary, began operations in 1986. The company attempted to take over Piedmont Aviation in 1987 but sold its 17% stake when Piedmont agreed to merge with USAir. In 1988 under Arnold McKinnon (chairman and CEO since 1986) the company continued a cost-cutting program and reported record earnings of $635 million. A slow economy and higher costs resulted in slightly lower earnings ($606 million) for 1989.

HOW MUCH

	9 Yr. Growth	1980	1981	1982	1983	1984	1985	1986	1987	1988	1989
Sales ($ mil)	12.5%	1,576	1,802	3,359	3,148	3,525	3,825	4,076	4,113	4,462	4,536
Net income ($ mil)	11.2%	232	291	411	356	482	500	519	172	635	606
Income as % of sales	—	14.7%	16.2%	12.2%	11.3%	13.7%	13.1%	12.7%	4.2%	14.2%	13.4%
Earnings per share ($)	7.6%	2.33	2.90	2.19	1.89	2.55	2.65	2.74	0.91	3.51	4.49
Stock price – high ($)	—	15.46	18.42	21.67	23.54	21.42	27.08	33.08	38.25	32.88	41.25
Stock price – low ($)	—	8.04	13.13	13.42	17.13	16.17	19.25	24.63	21.00	24.50	30.25
Stock price – close ($)	12.9%	13.58	17.29	18.25	21.04	19.54	27.08	28.17	26.25	31.38	40.50
P/E – high	—	7	6	10	12	8	10	12	42	9	9
P/E – low	—	3	5	6	9	6	7	9	23	7	7
Dividends per share ($)	7.3%	0.73	0.87	0.90	0.93	1.07	1.13	1.13	1.20	1.26	1.38
Book value per share ($)	7.1%	16.40	18.46	18.48	22.11	23.69	25.20	26.78	26.48	28.74	30.44

1989 Year End:
Debt ratio: 11.8%
Return on equity: 15.2%
Cash (mil): $581
Current ratio: 1.42
Long-term debt (mil): $694
Number of shares (mil): 170
Dividends:
1989 average yield: 3.4%
1989 payout: 30.7%
Market value (mil): $6,877

Stock Price History high/low 1980-89

NYSE symbol: NSC
Incorporated: Virginia, 1980
Fiscal year ends: December 31

WHO

Chairman, President, and CEO: Arnold B. McKinnon, age 62, $1,229,260 pay
EVP Operations: Paul R. Rudder, age 57
EVP Finance: John R. Turbyfill, age 58, $673,458 pay
EVP Law: John S. Shannon, age 59, $581,774 pay
EVP Marketing: D. Henry Watts, age 58, $562,600 pay
Auditors: KPMG Peat Marwick
Employees: 33,274

WHERE

HQ: Three Commercial Place, Norfolk, VA 23510
Phone: 804-629-2680
FAX: 804-629-2777

Norfolk Southern currently operates a 15,985-mile rail system in 20 states, mainly in the Midwest and Southeast, and in Ontario, Canada. The company also offers trucking services throughout the US and Canada.

WHAT

	1989 Sales	
	$ mil	% of total
Railway operations		
Agricultural products	212	5
Automotive	383	8
Chemicals	428	9
Coal, coke & iron ore	1,299	28
Construction materials	229	5
Intermodal	351	8
Metals	151	3
Paper	404	9
Other commodities	123	3
Other sales	114	3
Motor carrier operations	842	19
Total	**4,536**	**100**

Railroads
Norfolk & Western Railway Company
Southern Railway Company

Motor Carriers
North American Van Lines, Inc.
Commercial Transport Division (truck freight shipments)
High Value Products Division (business and industrial moving, trade show and specialty transport)
Relocation Services Division (household moving)

Intermodal Carriers
Triple Crown Services, Inc.

Other Subsidiaries
Pocahontas Land Corporation

RANKINGS

11th in *Fortune* 50 Transportation Cos.
193rd in *Forbes* Sales 500
86th in *Business Week* 1000
253rd in *Business Week* Global 1000

COMPETITION

CSX
Mayflower
Ryder
Other trucking companies

NORTHROP CORPORATION

OVERVIEW

Northrop Corporation of Los Angeles is one of America's largest aerospace manufacturers. The company's principal product is the B-2 Stealth bomber, one of the most sophisticated (and most visually distinctive) aircraft ever produced. The B-2 accounts for about 1/2 of Northrop's revenues.

Northrop also builds fuselage sections for the Boeing 747 jetliner; 40% of the airframe for the F/A-18 fighter; and the Tacit Rainbow antiradar missile. The company produces advanced electronic systems (including the guidance system for the MX missile) and unmanned vehicles such as target drones.

Northrop and McDonnell Douglas are competing as a team for the $45 billion Advanced Tactical Fighter, the air force's next generation of aircraft.

Sales to the US government account for 89% of the company's business. Northrop, its future uncertain as diminished East-West tensions decrease demand for its products, has been facing legal problems, including federal investigations into foreign payoffs. The company pleaded guilty to 34 counts related to falsifying test results on some government projects. Chairman Thomas Jones, 70, CEO for 30 years, retired in fall 1990.

NYSE symbol: NOC
Incorporated: Delaware, 1985
Fiscal year ends: December 31

WHO

Chairman, President, and CEO: Kent Kresa, age 52, $412,916 pay (prior to promotion)
SVP Finance: John B. Campbell, age 66, $261,218 pay
SVP Electronics: David N. Ferguson, age 64, $260,833 pay
Auditors: Deloitte & Touche
Employees: 41,000

WHERE

HQ: 1840 Century Park East, Los Angeles, CA 90067
Phone: 213-553-6262
FAX: 213-553-2076

Northrop operates 6 US regional offices and has facilities in 9 states.

WHEN

John K. "Jack" Northrop, cofounder of Lockheed Aircraft (1927) and designer of that company's record-setting Vega monoplane, founded Northrop Aircraft Corporation in California in 1939. Northrop had previously established 2 other companies, Avion Corporation (formed in 1928 and bought by United Aircraft and Transportation) and Northrop Corporation (formed in 1932 in cooperation with Douglas Aircraft, which absorbed it in 1938).

During WWII California-based Northrop produced the P-61 fighter and provided airframes and parts for other manufacturers. The company also built the famous Flying Wing bombers, which advanced the state of aeronautical engineering but failed to win a production contract.

In the 1950s Northrop's income depended heavily on the F-89 fighter and the Snark missile, items which made Northrop sensitive to fluctuations in government funding. However, Thomas Jones introduced a new strategy when he succeeded Jack Northrop as president in 1959. By avoiding risky prime contracts in favor of numerous subcontracts and by diversifying the company with the purchase of a telecommunications firm (Page Communications Engineers, 1959) and an electronics company (Hallicrafters, 1966), Jones increased Northrop's profits and lessened its dependence on government contracts. He also tirelessly promoted the company's small, inexpensive F-5 fighter for export to developing countries and the T-38 trainer. F-5/T-38 production did not cease until 1989, when the 3,806th aircraft was completed.

Northrop was hit with a bribery scandal and the disclosure of illegal payments to Richard Nixon's 1972 campaign fund. In 1975 the company lost an air force fighter competition to General Dynamics's F-16, but the navy ordered a modified version of Northrop's aircraft (the F-18 Hornet). McDonnell Douglas won the role of prime contractor for the F-18, with Northrop getting 40% of the work.

Another major Northrop project initiated in the 1970s was the company-financed F-20 fighter. Jones championed the F-20 overseas, but none were sold. Northrop ceased marketing the airplane in 1986, but federal investigations into questionable payments to South Korean officials continued into 1990.

In 1981 Northrop won the contract to develop the B-2 Stealth bomber. The B-2 has proven to be extremely costly (estimates range from $500 million to $2.6 billion per plane) and faces an uncertain future. When Jones retired as chairman in 1990, President Kent Kresa succeeded him.

WHAT

	1989 Sales		1989 Operating Income	
	$ mil	% of total	$ mil	% of total
Aircraft	4,006	76	283	—
Electronics	780	15	(11)	—
Missiles & unmanned vehicle systems	305	6	(142)	—
Services	157	3	5	—
Adjustments	—	—	(112)	—
Total	**5,248**	**100**	**23**	**—**

Aircraft Division
Aircraft maintenance
Aircraft subassemblies
Base support services
Military and commercial aircraft R&D and manufacturing
Missile and unmanned vehicle R&D and manufacturing

B-2 Division
Aircraft R&D and manufacturing
B-2 Stealth bomber

Defense Systems Division
Military electronic countermeasure systems (ECM) (radar jamming)

Electronic Systems Division
Automated test equipment
Electronic sensor and tracking systems
Strategic guidance and navigation

Precision Products Division
Accelerometers
Gyroscopes
Inertial guidance and control systems

Northrop Research and Technology Center
Technology research programs

HOW MUCH

	9 Yr. Growth	1980	1981	1982	1983	1984	1985	1986	1987	1988	1989
Sales ($ mil)	13.7%	1,655	1,991	2,473	3,261	3,688	5,057	5,608	6,053	5,797	5,248
Net income ($ mil)	—	86	48	5	101	167	214	41	94	(31)	(81)
Income as % of sales	—	5.2%	2.4%	0.2%	3.1%	4.5%	4.2%	0.7%	1.6%	(0.5%)	(1.5%)
Earnings per share ($)	—	2.01	1.10	0.12	2.21	3.63	4.63	0.89	2.01	(0.65)	(1.71)
Stock price – high ($)	—	20.58	21.00	25.92	32.75	39.50	56.63	51.63	52.63	35.88	29.75
Stock price – low ($)	—	12.38	11.00	13.08	21.92	23.67	31.63	36.88	24.75	25.13	16.00
Stock price – close ($)	(1.6%)	20.17	17.46	25.13	28.75	35.25	44.13	39.25	25.50	27.75	17.50
P/E – high	—	10	19	216	15	11	12	58	26	—	—
P/E – low	—	6	10	109	10	7	7	41	12	—	—
Dividends per share ($)	8.0%	0.60	0.60	0.60	0.60	0.90	1.20	1.20	1.20	1.20	1.20
Book value per share ($)	5.8%	11.27	11.32	10.87	12.64	15.72	19.42	19.29	20.23	21.40	18.65

1989 Year End:
Debt ratio: 38.6%
Return on equity: (8.5%)
Cash (mil): $5
Current ratio: 1.06
Long-term debt (mil): $551
Number of shares (mil): 47
Dividends:
1989 average yield: 6.9%
1989 payout: —
Market value (mil): $821

Stock Price History high/low 1980-89

RANKINGS

98th in *Fortune* 500 Industrial Cos.
256th in *Fortune* Global 500 Industrial Cos.
168th in *Forbes* Sales 500
619th in *Business Week* 1000

COMPETITION

Allied-Signal
Boeing
General Dynamics
General Electric
General Motors
Lockheed
Martin Marietta
McDonnell Douglas
Rockwell International
Textron
United Technologies
Other aerospace companies

NORTHWESTERN MUTUAL

OVERVIEW

Northwestern Mutual is the 10th largest life insurance company in the US, with assets of $28.5 billion. The Milwaukee-based company has more than 2 million policyholders of life and disability insurance and annuities. Northwestern has 3.5 million policies, with over $200 billion of insurance in force.

Northwestern is the largest mutual company in sales of noncancelable individual disability insurance; the policies totaled $41.8 million in premium income in 1989.

Northwestern markets its services through a nationwide network of 7,000 exclusive agents. The company's sales force was ranked #1 in all 7 categories of *Sales & Marketing Management*'s 1989 life insurance industry sales survey of customers and peers.

In 1990 *Fortune* ranked the company as "the most admired" among the 10 largest life insurance companies; it has received the top ranking in all 8 years of the survey and is one of only 7 companies to attain the top ranking in its industry. In the last 50 years Northwestern has been first in dividend performance more times than any other company.

Mutual company
Incorporated: Wisconsin, 1857
Fiscal year ends: December 31

WHO

Chairman and CEO: Donald J. Schuenke, age 61
President: James D. Ericson, age 55
EVP Agencies and Marketing: Robert E. Carlson
SVP Human Resources and Administration: James W. Ehrenstrom, age 54
SVP Insurance Operations: Peter W. Bruce, age 45
SVP Investments: Edward J. Zore, age 45
SVP Planning and Finance: Walt J. Wojcik, age 50
Auditors: Price Waterhouse
Employees: 8,750

WHEN

In 1854 John Johnston, a successful New York insurance agent, moved to Wisconsin at age 72 to become a farmer. Three years later Johnston returned to the insurance business when he and 36 leading Wisconsin citizens founded Mutual Life Insurance Company.

The company changed its name to Northwestern Mutual Life Insurance Company in 1865. By then it was already the 14th largest company in total amount of insurance in force. By the 1880s the company had made clear its purpose to be first in benefits to policyholders rather than first in size.

In 1907 Northwestern appointed policyholders to evaluate the entire company's operations. This 5-person committee, whose members change every year, still operates, and a summary of their report is published in the company's annual report.

The company continued to offer level-premium life insurance in the 1920s while competitors offered new types of products. As a result of its conservatism, the company's rank by insurance in force fell from 6th in 1918 to 8th in 1946.

The company began to develop the industry's most comprehensive computer system in the late 1950s. One result was the 1962 introduction of the Insurance Service Account (ISA), in which all policies owned by a family or business could be combined into one premium with monthly payments by preauthorized checks. The ISA set the standard for the industry.

Northwestern was one of the first major companies, beginning in 1959, to give women a lower premium rate than men because of economic and health gains by females.

Northwestern in 1968 introduced Extra Ordinary Life (EOL), which combined whole life with term insurance, using dividends to convert term to paid-up whole life each year. In less than a year, EOL became the company's most popular policy.

Northwestern became a major advertiser in 1972 by spending $1.4 million on ABC's coverage of the summer Olympics to introduce "The Quiet Company" campaign. The result was a jump from 34th to 3rd place in public awareness of Northwestern.

In the 1980s Northwestern began financing leveraged buyouts (loaning money to a group of investors to acquire control of a company). In return Northwestern gained an ownership share and stock options in addition to loan payments. The company and other insurers bought a 2/3 interest in Congoleum, a flooring manufacturer.

The company bought a majority interest in Robert W. Baird, a Milwaukee securities firm (1982), and in Mortgage Guaranty Insurance (1985).

WHERE

HQ: The Northwestern Mutual Life Insurance Co., 720 E. Wisconsin Ave., Milwaukee, WI 53202
Phone: 414-271-1444
FAX: 414-226-7022

Northwestern Mutual operates in all 50 US states and the District of Columbia, with more than 100 general agency offices.

WHAT

	1989 Sales	
	$ mil	% of total
Premiums	3,737	59
Net investment income	2,133	34
Other income	437	7
Total	**6,307**	**100**

	12/31/89 Assets	
	$ mil	% of total
Bonds	11,251	39
Stocks	1,803	6
Mortgage loans	5,056	18
Real estate	893	3
Policyowner loans	4,982	18
Other assets	4,530	16
Total	**28,515**	**100**

Insurance Products
Annuities
Disability insurance
Mortgage insurance
Permanent and term life insurance
Securities brokerage

HOW MUCH

	9 Yr. Growth	1980	1981	1982	1983	1984	1985	1986	1987	1988	1989
Assets ($ mil)	10.8%	11,351	12,154	13,253	14,481	15,896	17,898	20,187	22,603	25,349	28,515
Premium & annuity income ($ mil)	13.6%	1,193	1,244	1,397	2,013	2,143	2,417	2,934	3,626	3,542	3,737
Net investment income ($ mil)	11.6%	790	841	921	1,006	1,172	1,321	1,439	1,555	1,829	2,133
Net income ($ mil)	—	—	—	—	—	—	—	—	—	118	372
Net income as % of assets	—	—	—	—	—	—	—	—	—	0.5%	1.3%
Life insurance in force ($ bil)	14.1%	61.3	70.1	79.3	92.6	107.6	121.0	137.1	157.6	178.8	200.5

1989 Company Totals:
Total assets (mil): $28,515
Revenue (mil): $6,307
Surplus (mil): $2,075
Premiums (mil): $3,737
Net investment income (mil): $2,133
Policyowner dividends (mil): $1,421
Total life insurance in force (mil): $200,539

Life Insurance in Force ($ billions) 1980-89

250
200
150
100
50
0

RANKINGS

10th in *Fortune* 50 Life Insurance Cos.

COMPETITION

Aetna	Primerica
AIG	Prudential
American Express	Sears
CIGNA	State Farm
Equitable	Transamerica
John Hancock	Travelers
Kemper	Other individual life insurance companies
Kohlberg Kravis Roberts	Other securities brokerage firms
Massachusetts Mutual	Mortgage insurance companies
Merrill Lynch	
Metropolitan	
Morgan Stanley	
New York Life	

NWA, INC.

OVERVIEW

NWA is the parent company of Northwest Airlines, America's leading airline to the North Pacific and 4th largest airline in terms of 1989 sales. Northwest serves 41 states in the US and 19 foreign countries and added flights to Paris, Singapore, and Saipan in 1989.

NWA's top management (former Marriott executive Alfred Checchi and former Beatrice CEO Frederick Rentschler) has almost no previous airline experience. However, since taking the company private in August 1989, Chairman Checchi has refinanced about $1.2 billion of NWA's $4.3 billion debt, raising part of the capital through mortgages on NWA's Japanese landholdings and by selling and then leasing back 12 of Northwest's jets. Checchi is exploring the possibility of buying Pan Am's transatlantic routes and some of Eastern Airlines's remaining assets, including gates in Atlanta, maintenance facilities in Miami and Atlanta, and planes. Management also plans to spend $422 million over the next 5 years improving Northwest's image by upgrading the quality of food, sprucing up aircraft interiors, and training employees.

WHEN

A group of Detroit and Minneapolis–St. Paul businessmen led by Colonel Louis Brittin founded Northwest Airways in 1926 to provide air mail service between Minneapolis and Chicago. Passenger service began in 1927. In 1928 Northwest was the first US airline to coordinate airline and railroad service, connecting with railroads serving both the East and West Coasts.

The company became Northwest Airlines in 1934, expanding its air routes west to Seattle. In 1945 service to New York completed the airline's transcontinental route.

Northwest pioneered a Great Circle route to the Orient in 1947, flying over Alaska and the Aleutians to the Far East; offered flights from Seattle to Honolulu in 1948; and still dominates US service to the Pacific.

Former Civil Aeronautics Board chairman Donald Nyrop became Northwest's president in 1954. Famous for his thrift, Nyrop held debt to 10% of the airline's capital, the lowest proportion in the industry. When Nyrop retired in 1978, his successor, Joseph Lapensky, continued this policy, making Northwest one of 2 consistently profitable airlines since the 1978 industry deregulation (Southwest is the other).

Northwest formed NWA, a holding company, in 1984, and in 1986 Steve Rothmeier, formerly VP of finance, became NWA's chairman and CEO. Rothmeier bought Mainline Travel, a national travel service, to help generate passengers and negotiated agreements with 4 regional airlines, providing commuter service to feed Northwest's routes. Northwest bought a 50% interest in PARS, TWA's computer reservations system (1986), becoming the last major airline to offer automated reservations and advance seat selection. Its 1986 purchase of Republic Airlines made Northwest America's 5th largest airline, dominating Minneapolis and establishing new hubs at Memphis and Detroit. Republic was the result of the 1980 merger of North Central Airlines, Southern Airways, and Hughes Air West.

Unfortunately, Rothmeier's failure in negotiations with Northwest's unions after the Republic acquisition led to low employee morale. Northwest's pilots still had no contract in 1989 when Wings Holdings, led by ex-Marriott executive Alfred Checchi, bought NWA for $3.65 billion and took the company private. Both Los Angeles financier Marvin Davis and Pan Am also bid for the airline.

When Rothmeier resigned, Checchi became NWA's chairman, making his first goal improved management-employee relations. Checchi also plans to develop a worldwide route system for Northwest and KLM Royal Dutch Airlines, a member of the Wings investment group.

HOW MUCH

	9 Yr. Growth	1980	1981	1982	1983	1984	1985	1986	1987	1988	1989
Sales ($ mil)	16.6%	1,639	1,854	1,878	2,196	2,445	2,655	3,589	5,142	5,650	6,554
Net income ($ mil)	54.7%	7	11	5	50	56	73	77	103	135	355
Income as % of sales		0.4%	0.6%	0.3%	2.3%	2.3%	2.7%	2.1%	2.0%	2.4%	5.4%
Passengers (thou)	14.3%	11,501	11,145	11,356	12,718	13,216	14,539	23,167	37,247	35,784	38,338
Revenue passenger miles (mil)	14.2%	13,811	14,252	15,675	17,712	19,772	22,341	28,815	39,550	40,148	45,663
Available seat miles (mil)	12.2%	24,904	24,815	26,257	29,511	32,664	37,149	48,408	61,421	61,275	70,213
Passenger load factor		55.5%	57.4%	59.7%	60.0%	60.5%	60.1%	58.5%	64.4%	65.5%	65.0%
Size of operating fleet	12.0%	117	111	113	117	120	130	312	316	321	324
Average age of fleet (yrs)		8.2	9.1	10.4	11.1	9.8	10.6	13.7	14.4	13.5	15.2
Employees	13.3%	12,748	13,096	13,754	14,187	15,185	16,864	33,427	33,724	35,532	39,323

1989 Year End:
Assets (mil): $5,374
Stockholders' equity (mil): $2,453

Net Income ($ mil) 1980-89

400
350
300
250
200
150
100
50
0

Private company
Incorporated: Delaware, 1984
Fiscal year ends: December 31

WHO

Chairman: Alfred A. Checchi, age 42
President and CEO: Frederick B. Rentschler, age 50
EVP Finance and Administration and CFO: John Dasburg
Auditors: Ernst & Young
Employees: 39,323

WHERE

HQ: Minneapolis/St. Paul International Airport, St. Paul, MN 55111
Phone: 612-726-2111
FAX: 612-726-3942 (Corporate Communications)

NWA, Inc., serves 220 cities in 20 countries in North America, Europe, and Asia. The company flies to 41 states in the US.

Hub Locations
Detroit, MI
Memphis, TN
Milwaukee, WI
Minneapolis/St. Paul, MN
Seoul, South Korea
Toyko, Japan

WHAT

Northwest Airlines, Inc.

Northwest Airlink (commuter services)

Subsidiaries
MLT Vacations, Inc. (wholesale travel and tour programs)
Northwest Aerospace Training Corp. (pilot training)
Northwest Aircraft, Inc. (acquires new and markets used aircraft)
PARS (50% owned computer reservations system)

Flight Equipment	Owned	Leased	Total
Airbus A320	7	—	7
Boeing 727	40	26	66
Boeing 747	32	14	46
Boeing 757	14	24	38
DC-9	105	34	139
DC-10	19	1	20
MD-80	6	2	8
Total	**223**	**101**	**324**

RANKINGS

8th in *Fortune* 50 Transportation Cos.
11th in *Forbes* 400 US Private Cos.

COMPETITION

Alaska Air
America West
AMR
Continental
Delta
KLM
Midway
Pan Am
Southwest
TWA
UAL
USAir

NYNEX CORPORATION

OVERVIEW

NYNEX, the US's 3rd largest provider of local telephone service, serves 7 northeastern states through subsidiaries New York Telephone and New England Telephone. Telephone revenues accounted for 84% of 1989 revenues.

NYNEX Mobile provides cellular services to 213,000 customers and plans to be the first cellular company to install digital technology in the US (1992). NYNEX Credit, which provides asset-based financing/leasing, had a 1989 asset base of $550 million and participated in transactions totaling $1 billion. NYNEX Properties acquires and manages real estate for NYNEX companies and its own investment portfolio. NYNEX Information Resources publishes Yellow Pages, distributing more than 30 million copies in 1989 and generating sales of $818 million. NYNEX Business Centers (Atlanta) is the nation's 3rd largest nonfranchised computer reseller, with 78 branches in 28 states. NYNEX Information Solutions Group provides — through 7 companies — software, systems, and network integration. NYNEX International, with agreements in Korea, the Philippines, Australia, and the USSR, markets NYNEX products and services overseas.

Although NYNEX retains 1/7th ownership of Bellcore, the shared research arm of the Bell operating company, the company has opened its own R&D facility employing more than 200 scientists and researchers.

WHEN

NYNEX's 2 telephone divisions, New York Telephone and New England Telephone, began as arms of AT&T. NYNEX's largest telephone company, New York Telephone, was incorporated in 1896 and grew out of 2 small, independent telephone companies, Metropolitan Telephone & Telegraph and Westchester Telephone. Gardiner Hubbard, Alexander Bell's father-in-law, formed New England Telephone Company in 1878 with a plan to offer switching hardware. Half interest was later sold to a group that included Colonel William Forbes, who merged New England Telephone into the Bell system.

In 1983 AT&T and the Bell companies were split up as part of the AT&T antitrust suit settlement. NYNEX incorporated that same year and began separate operations in 1984. NYNEX also received cellular service operations for the same territory (now called NYNEX Mobile Communications) and a 1/7th share in Bell Communications Research (R&D arm shared by the Bell companies).

Since divestiture it has formed other subsidiaries including NYNEX Information Resources (directory publishing); NYNEX Business Information Systems (computer reseller); NYNEX Information Solutions Group (data communications); NYNEX Materiel Enterprises (purchasing agent); NYNEX Properties (real estate); NYNEX International (international marketing arm); NYNEX Service (product development); NYNEX Systems Marketing (major account sales); and NYNEX Credit (equipment lessor).

NYNEX has invested in software development for banks and financial institutions through acquisition of Business Intelligence Services Limited (1987) and AGS Computers Inc. (1988). The company attempted to enter the market for international long-distance service between 1986 and 1988 but failed to receive the necessary approvals. NYNEX continues to form alliances with overseas telecommunications entities; it is developing a telemarketing center for France Telecom and a network management system for British Telecom.

NYNEX has suffered several setbacks recently. Over 60,000 union workers went on strike (1989); the company was fined $1.4 million and ordered to refund more than $35 million overcharged to ratepayers (1990); and, in the first criminal charge made against a Bell company for violation of the AT&T divestiture accord, NYNEX was accused of contempt because a subsidiary allowed MCI access to its computers (1990).

HOW MUCH

	5 Yr. Growth	1980	1981	1982	1983	1984	1985	1986	1987	1988	1989
Sales ($ mil)	6.8%	—	—	—	—	9,507	10,314	11,342	12,084	12,661	13,211
Net income ($ mil)	(3.9%)	—	—	—	—	986	1,095	1,215	1,277	1,315	808
Income as % of sales	—	—	—	—	—	10.4%	10.6%	10.7%	10.6%	10.4%	6.1%
Earnings per share ($)	(4.1%)	—	—	—	—	5.05	5.43	6.00	6.25	6.63	4.10
Stock price – high ($)	—	—	—	—	—	37.94	49.25	73.25	78.38	70.88	92.00
Stock price – low ($)	—	—	—	—	—	29.31	36.44	46.44	58.00	60.88	65.25
Stock price – close ($)	19.7%	—	—	—	—	37.13	48.88	64.13	64.25	66.00	91.38
P/E – high	—	—	—	—	—	8	9	12	13	11	22
P/E – low	—	—	—	—	—	6	7	8	9	9	16
Dividends per share ($)	7.8%	—	—	—	—	3.00	3.20	3.48	3.80	4.04	4.36
Book value per share ($)	4.0%	—	—	—	—	39.08	41.29	43.75	45.65	47.83	47.55

1989 Year End:
Debt ratio: 40.8%
Return on equity: 8.6%
Cash (mil): $155
Current ratio: 0.81
Long-term debt (mil): $6,465
Number of shares (mil): 197
Dividends:
1989 average yield: 4.8%
1989 payout: 106.3%
Market value (mil): $18,005

Stock Price History high/low 1984-89

NYSE symbol: NYN
Incorporated: Delaware, 1983
Fiscal year ends: December 31

WHO

Chairman and CEO: William C. Ferguson, age 59, $743,500 pay
VC and Principal Financial Officer: Robert J. Eckenrode, age 59, $503,700 pay
EVP: James E. Hennessy, age 56, $465,600 pay
EVP and General Counsel: Raymond F. Burke, age 56, $412,300 pay
Auditors: Coopers & Lybrand
Employees: 95,400

WHERE

HQ: 335 Madison Ave., New York, NY 10017
Phone: 212-370-7400
FAX: 212-682-1324 (Investor Relations)

NYNEX offers telecommunications services in Maine, Massachusetts, New Hampshire, Rhode Island, Vermont, New York, and Connecticut and mobile services in 18 metropolitan areas in the same territory. The company has overseas offices in Geneva, Frankfurt, London, and Hong Kong.

WHAT

	1989 Sales		1989 Operating Income	
	$ mil	% of total	$ mil	% of total
Telecommunications	11,040	84	1,936	95
Cellular	240	2	48	2
Publishing	818	6	115	6
Financial/real estate	57	—	51	3
Other	1,056	8	(121)	(6)
Adjustments	—	—	(272)	—
Total	**13,211**	**100**	**1,757**	**100**

Companies
New England Telephone
New York Telephone
NYNEX Business Information Systems Co.
NYNEX Business Centers
NYNEX Credit Co.
NYNEX Government Affairs
NYNEX Information Resources Co.
United Publishers Corp.
NYNEX Information Solutions Group, Inc.
AGS Computers, Inc.
The BIS Group Ltd.
The DATA Group Corp.
NYNEX Complex Systems Integration Group
NYNEX Computer Services
NYNEX Development
Telco Research Corp.
NYNEX International Co.
NYNEX Materiel Enterprises Co.
NYNEX Mobile Communications Co.
NYNEX Properties Co.
NYNEX Service Co.
NYNEX Systems Marketing Co.

RANKINGS

4th in *Fortune* 50 Utilities
43rd in *Forbes* Sales 500
28th in *Business Week* 1000
72nd in *Business Week* Global 1000

COMPETITION

Ameritech
AT&T
Bell Atlantic
BellSouth
GTE
McCaw Cellular
MCI
Pacific Telesis
Southwestern Bell
United Telecommunications
U S West

OCCIDENTAL PETROLEUM CORPORATION

OVERVIEW

Occidental Petroleum ("Oxy") is a diversified company consisting of a top-10 oil company; the 6th largest US chemical company; a 51% stake in the world's largest producer of fresh beef and pork (with a 24% and 12% market share, respectively); and US natural gas transmission and coal mining businesses.

Dr. Armand Hammer, at 91, controls Occidental despite stock holdings of under 1%. The company explores for, develops, and markets crude oil worldwide (stressing Latin America and the North Sea). Successful drillings (at the lowest cost) are a company trademark. Oxy's record profits during the oil boom in 1981 and 1982 succumbed to plummeting oil prices after 1985 (with oil and gas then 44% of Oxy's revenues).

The highly integrated chemical operation Occidental Chemical is now Oxy's most profitable segment (76% of 1989 profits) and leads worldwide in potassium hydroxide and phenolic molding materials and, domestically, in polyvinyl chloride (PVC) and chloralkali.

WHEN

The charmed life of Occidental CEO Dr. Armand Hammer has included friendships with several American and Soviet presidents (including Lenin, for whom he ran a pencil factory) and fortunes in Russian art, cattle breeding, and whiskey distilling, among others.

The Occidental Petroleum Corporation was founded in 1920 but remained small until 1956, when Dr. Hammer, seeking a tax shelter, sank $100,000 into the company (whose net worth was $34,000). Both wells drilled with the investment came in.

Occidental's discovery of California's 2nd largest gas field (1959) and listing on the NYSE (1964) were followed by the company's biggest coup: a concession from Libya's King Idris (1966) and the subsequent discovery of a billion-barrel Libyan oil field. In 1968 Oxy purchased Signal Oil's European refining and marketing organization to assure markets for the Libyan crude, and diversified, buying Island Creek Coal and Hooker Chemical. Oxy inherited the notorious Niagara Falls Love Canal, a toxic waste disposal site Hooker had sold to a school district years earlier for one dollar.

In 1969 Oxy sold — under duress — 51% of its Libyan production to the Libyan government (after Colonel Qaddafi ousted Idris). Oxy started oil exploration in Latin America (1971) and the North Sea (1972-1973) — where it discovered the lucrative Piper field. Other projects included a 20-year fertilizer-for-ammonia trade agreement with the USSR (1974) and a 30-year coal joint venture with China (final signing, 1985)

In the 1980s Oxy opted for safer domestic shores by purchasing Cities Service for almost $4 billion (US oil and gas exploration, 1982) and Midcon for $2.6 billion (US natural gas pipelines, 1986) and selling portions of its Colombian, Libyan, Gulf of Mexico, and North Sea operations (1984 and 1985). Oxy also bought Iowa Beef Processors (IBP) for stock worth $750 million (1981); the company resold 49% of IBP to the public in 1987 for $960 million. In 1988 Oxy's North Sea Piper platform exploded, claiming 167 lives.

In 1983 Hammer hired Ray Irani to revive Oxy's ailing chemical business (losses that year: $38 million). Irani integrated operations to ensure high operating rates during industry downturns, purchasing Diamond Shamrock Chemicals for $850 million (1986), Shell's vinyl chloride monomer business (1987), a Du Pont chloralkali facility (1987), and Cain Chemical (1988). Oxychem's profits reached $1.05 billion by 1989.

Oxy renewed its international focus in 1989 in response to high US drilling costs and a tough regulatory environment (after the *Exxon Valdez* spill); 900 domestic jobs were cut. Oxy plans 35 exploratory wells worldwide in 1990.

HOW MUCH

	9 Yr. Growth	1980	1981	1982	1983	1984	1985	1986	1987	1988	1989
Sales ($ mil)	5.4%	12,476	14,708	18,212	19,116	15,586	14,534	15,344	17,096	19,417	20,068
Net income ($ mil)	(10.7%)	711	722	156	480	569	455	172	184	313	256
Income as % of sales	—	5.7%	4.9%	0.9%	2.5%	3.6%	3.1%	1.1%	1.1%	1.6%	1.3%
Earnings per share ($)	(21.7%)	8.31	7.55	0.70	1.15	3.05	2.20	0.66	0.78	1.26	0.92
Stock price – high ($)	—	39.13	34.88	24.75	27.00	35.75	36.75	31.25	39.63	29.00	31.00
Stock price – low ($)	—	19.00	21.63	17.00	18.00	24.38	23.13	22.63	22.25	23.50	25.13
Stock price – close ($)	(1.7%)	34.63	24.00	19.75	24.88	28.00	31.00	27.50	24.38	25.38	29.63
P/E – high	—	5	5	35	23	12	17	47	51	23	34
P/E – low	—	2	3	24	16	8	11	34	29	19	27
Dividends per share ($)	2.9%	1.93	2.43	2.50	2.50	2.50	2.50	2.50	2.50	2.50	2.50
Book value per share ($)	(1.4%)	24.50	29.41	27.50	26.90	26.77	26.59	24.14	23.98	23.08	21.68

1989 Year End:
Debt ratio: 58.2%
Return on equity: 4.1%
Cash (mil): $303
Current ratio: 1.1
Long-term debt (mil): $8,217
Number of shares (mil): 270
Dividends:
1989 average yield: 8.4%
1989 payout: 271.7%
Market value (mil): $8,006

NYSE symbol: OXY
Incorporated: Delaware, 1986
Fiscal year ends: December 31

WHO

Chairman and CEO: Armand Hammer, age 91, $2,334,332 pay
President and COO: Ray R. Irani, age 55, $1,920,028 pay
EVP Finance and CFO: John J. Dorgan, age 66
Auditors: Arthur Andersen & Co.
Employees: 53,500

WHERE

HQ: 10889 Wilshire Blvd., Los Angeles, CA 90024
Phone: 213-879-1700
FAX: 213-824-2372

WHAT

	1989 Sales		1989 Operating Income	
	$ mil	% of total	$ mil	% of total
US	19,114	93	1,331	86
Europe	144	1	(7)	—
Other countries	1,143	6	234	14
Adjustments	(333)	—	(377)	—
Total	**20,068**	**100**	**1,171**	**100**

	1989 Sales		1989 Operating Income	
	$ mil	% of total	$ mil	% of total
Coal	671	3	8	1
Chemicals	5,203	26	1,056	76
Agribusiness	9,131	45	79	6
Oil & gas	2,902	14	91	6
Pipelining	2,494	12	154	11
Adjustments	(333)	—	(217)	—
Total	**20,068**	**100**	**1,171**	**100**

Oil & Gas
Occidental Crude Sales, Inc. (Houston)
Occidental International (Bakersfield, CA)
Occidental Oil and Gas Corp. (Tulsa, OK)
OXY USA, Inc. (Tulsa, OK)

Natural Gas Transmission
MidCon Corp. (Lombard, IL)

Chemicals
Occidental Chemical Corp. (Dallas)
Oxy Petrochemicals Inc. (Houston)

Agribusiness
IBP, inc. (Dakota City, NE)

Coal
Island Creek Corp. (Lexington, KY)

RANKINGS

16th in *Fortune* 500 Industrial Cos.
46th in *Fortune* Global 500 Industrial Cos.
17th in *Fortune* 50 Exporters
22nd in *Forbes* Sales 500
70th in *Business Week* 1000
217th in *Business Week* Global 1000

COMPETITION

American Cyanamid
Amoco
Ashland
Atlantic Richfield
BASF
Bayer
British Petroleum
Cargill
Chevron
Coastal
ConAgra
Dow Chemical
Du Pont
Exxon
Hoechst
Mobil
Monsanto
Pennzoil
Phillips
Royal Dutch/Shell
Sun
Texaco
Tyson Foods
Unocal
USX
Other chemical and oil companies
Pipeline and mining companies

OGDEN CORPORATION

OVERVIEW

Ogden is a diverse service management company, with $1.4 billion in sales in 1989.

Ogden Allied Services contributes 76% of corporate revenues and supplies catering at over 200 oil-drilling platforms in the Gulf of Mexico; promotes over 300 entertainment events, from the Rolling Stones to the Harlem Globetrotters; handles concession stands for professional sports teams; and serves over 35 million in-flight meals for the airline industry (1989). Since 1984 the building services operation, one of the largest US contractors, has cleaned and maintained buildings like New York's World Trade Center, which alone has 10 million square feet and 43,000 windows .

Ogden Projects, majority-owned by Ogden, operates 20% of the large-scale waste-to-energy facilities in operation or under construction in the US. The facilities currently operated or planned have a combined capacity of 27,000 tons per day to serve 13 million residents in more than 300 communities.

WHEN

Ogden Corporation started in Delaware in 1939 as a public utilities holding company, a successor in the reorganization of Utilities Power & Light Corporation.

Ogden liquidated its utility holdings in the late 1940s. The company then began buying and selling companies. Two important purchases were Luria Brothers (scrap metal dealer, 1955) and Avondale Shipyards (New Orleans shipbuilding, 1959).

Ralph E. Ablon, formerly Luria's president, became president of Ogden in 1962 and diversified the company through acquisitions, including International Terminal Operating (1962) and Better Built Machinery (industrial washers and dryers, 1965). The company entered the food products business by buying food processors Tillie Lewis Foods (1966), International Products (1967), and Wilson Foods (1967). It then added ABC Consolidated (food and beverage sales, 1967) and Chef's Orchid (airline food services, 1968).

To its scrap metal business the company added Mayville (Wisconsin) Metal Products and Wabash Alloys in 1968. Ogden expanded its shipyard and terminal operation with the 1969 purchase of Ogden Marine, a bulk carrier and tanker fleet operation. In 1969 the company also bought Ortner Freight Car, Waterford Park racetracks, Doggie Diner restaurants (Oakland), and Schreibers Catering (Cleveland).

In his first 10 years at Ogden, Ablon produced impressive results. Ogden led all major companies from 1962 through 1972 in earnings per share growth, at an annual compounded rate of more than 60%. Earnings continued to increase until 1982, when Ablon began restructuring the company.

In 1982 Ogden purchased Allied Maintenance (janitorial and maintenance services), a major step toward Ablon's plan to make Ogden a service company. The following year Ogden obtained the US rights to a waste-to-energy conversion process developed by Martin GmbH of West Germany; in 1984 the company established Ogden Projects, a subsidiary, to develop the waste-to-energy business. That year Ogden spun off Ogden Marine to Ogden shareholders and in 1985 sold its shipbuilding and industrial companies to an employee-owned company, Avondale Industries.

In 1986 Ogden sold Ogden Food Products Corporation to IC Industries for $320 million in cash. By the end of 1987 Ogden had become a 100% service company. The company sold about 14% of Ogden Projects, Inc., in 1989 public offerings. In 1990 Ogden Corporation bought ERC International to provide its customers with high-technology services in defense, energy, environmental services, and facilities management.

In May 1990 Ogden named Ralph Ablon's son, Richard, CEO.

HOW MUCH

	9 Yr. Growth	1980	1981	1982	1983	1984	1985	1986	1987	1988	1989
Sales ($ mil)	(5.1%)	2,187	2,324	2,202	1,728	2,137	1,026	800	858	1,088	1,369
Net income ($ mil)	1.6%	58	65	58	52	40	21	39	54	58	67
Income as % of sales	—	2.7%	2.8%	2.7%	3.0%	1.9%	2.1%	4.8%	6.3%	5.3%	4.9%
Earnings per share ($)	(2.0%)	2.00	2.25	1.51	1.32	1.00	0.54	0.97	1.32	1.41	1.66
Stock price – high ($)	—	16.67	19.94	14.38	17.19	15.25	17.31	24.00	44.63	32.38	34.75
Stock price – low ($)	—	9.13	12.38	8.75	12.63	12.06	13.25	13.75	17.50	25.13	25.50
Stock price – close ($)	8.4%	15.44	13.06	14.00	15.06	14.13	16.56	20.00	27.75	29.38	31.88
P/E – high	—	8	9	10	13	15	32	25	34	23	21
P/E – low	—	5	6	6	10	12	25	14	13	18	15
Dividends per share ($)	6.7%	0.70	0.85	0.90	0.90	0.90	0.90	0.90	1.00	1.10	1.25
Book value per share ($)	(4.4%)	16.48	16.84	14.28	9.43	9.48	8.00	10.25	10.63	10.74	11.00

1989 Year End:
Debt ratio: 79.2%
Return on equity: 15.3%
Cash (mil): $130
Current ratio: —
Long-term debt (mil): $1,681
Number of shares (mil): 40
Dividends:
1989 average yield: 3.9%
1989 payout: 75.3%
Market value (mil): $1,278

Stock Price History high/low 1980-89

NYSE symbol: OG
Incorporated: Delaware, 1939
Fiscal year ends: December 31

WHO

Chairman: Ralph E. Ablon, age 73, $2,284,240 pay
President and CEO: R. Richard Ablon, age 40, $788,793 pay (prior to promotion)
President and COO, Project Services: David L. Sokol, age 33, $786,709 pay
CFO; President and COO, Financial Services: Maria P. Monet, age 40, $733,617 pay
Auditors: Deloitte & Touche
Employees: 45,000

WHERE

HQ: Two Pennsylvania Plaza, New York, NY 10121
Phone: 212-868-6100
FAX: 212-868-4578

Ogden performs services for clients located throughout the US, in Canada, and at 11 European airports.

WHAT

	1989 Sales		1989 Operating Income	
	$ mil	% of total	$ mil	% of total
Operating services	1,039	76	46	60
Waste-to-energy	330	24	31	40
Adjustments	—	—	35	—
Total	**1,369**	**100**	**112**	**100**

Operating Services (Ogden Allied Services Corp.)
Asbestos clean-up
Catering and other support services for oil-drilling, mining, and construction workers
Child care services for corporate employees' children (Supertots subsidiary)
Contract services for airlines (*e.g.*, fueling, security, in-flight catering)
ERC International (environmental and energy services)
Industrial services (*e.g.*, warehousing and trucking)
International Terminal Operating Co., Inc. (50%; stevedoring services)
Logistical and operating services for federal agencies (*e.g.*, NASA flight centers)
Office building janitorial services
Sports and entertainment promotion
Stadium management and concession services

Project Services (Ogden Projects, Inc., 86%)
Ogden Martin Systems, Inc., waste-to-energy facilities for mass-burning solid waste to produce steam and electricity

Ogden Financial Services, Inc.
Financing for Ogden's services

RANKINGS

74th in *Fortune* 100 Diversified Service Cos.
487th in *Business Week* 1000

COMPETITION

ARA
Browning-Ferris
Greyhound Dial
Halliburton
MCA
TW Holdings
Union Pacific
Waste Management

THE OHIO STATE UNIVERSITY

OVERVIEW

With 52,895 students, Ohio State University in Columbus is the largest university in the country. The state school's 3,297-acre red-brick campus is a city within itself, with 380 buildings, a 500-acre airport, an 18-hole golf course, and housing for 9,610 students (about 500 of whom live in the football stadium).

OSU offers a staggering 8,500 courses with 219 programs leading to a bachelor's degree, 125 programs leading to a master's, and 94 leading to a doctorate. Students come to OSU from every state and over 100 foreign countries.

The school's modern library system consists of the William Oxley Thompson main and 28 other libraries with 4.1 million volumes, 2.8 million microforms, and 31,762 periodical subscriptions. The university also houses the only collection of medieval Slavic manuscripts in the nation.

OSU's 31 varsity teams make it the largest athletic program in the Big 10. A traditional powerhouse, OSU's football team (the Buckeyes) has produced 5 Heisman Trophy winners and 105 All-Americans, and has captured 4 national championships.

WHEN

In 1870 the Ohio legislature, prompted by governor Rutherford B. Hayes, agreed to establish the Ohio Agricultural and Mechanical College in Columbus as the state's land-grant college on property provided by the Morrill Act of 1862 (which provided land to states and territories for the establishment of colleges). The college opened in 1873 and admitted its first class of 24 students under president Edward Orton. Two years later the school appointed its first woman faculty member and in 1879 graduated its first female student. The school had changed its name to Ohio State University in 1878.

Under the administration of president William H. Scott (1883-1895), Ohio State grew dramatically, adding schools of veterinary medicine (1885), pharmacy (1885), law (1891), and dairy (1895). OSU awarded its first MA in 1886.

The university continued to grow in the early 20th century under president William Oxley Thompson. Enrollment surpassed 3,000 for the first time in 1908 and by 1923 had reached 10,000. New schools were added in education (1907), medicine and dentistry (1913), and commerce and journalism (1923). During WWI Ohio State designated part of its campus as training grounds and established the only college schools in the nation for airplane and balloon squadrons. OSU's stadium was dedicated in 1922.

In 1930 the university established departments of phonetics, medical and surgical research, photography, and adult education. During the difficult Great Depression years, Ohio State was forced to cut back salaries and course offerings. In the 1940s (under president Howard L. Bevis) the school geared for war once again by establishing radiation and war research laboratories as well as special programs and services for students who were drafted. OSU captured its first national football championship in 1942.

The 1950s ushered in the era of now-legendary OSU football coach Woody Hayes. Hayes led his beloved Buckeyes to 3 national championships and 9 Rose Bowl appearances before he was discharged for striking a Clemson player in 1978.

Novice G. Fawcett assumed leadership of the university in 1956 and began to restructure its various schools. During Fawcett's presidency OSU established 4 regional campuses.

In the early 1960s the university was engaged in internal free speech battles. By the end of the 1960s enrollment had surpassed 50,000. In 1970 the school library implemented a computerized control system to keep track of its extensive holdings. OSU opened its School of Social Work in 1976.

During the 1980s the Ohio State University Hospital performed revolutionary bone transplants for cancer patients. In 1986 OSU and hated rival Michigan shared the school's most recent Big 10 football conference title.

HOW MUCH

	9 Yr. Growth	1980	1981	1982	1983	1984	1985	1986	1987	1988	1989
Enrollment (Columbus campus)	(0.3%)	54,462	52,682	53,438	53,757	52,434	53,199	53,880	53,115	53,669	52,895
Tuition per quarter – resident undergrad ($)	7.8%	370	460	486	519	547	568	568	630	680	730
Tuition per quarter – nonresident undergrad ($)	10.9%	825	1,170	1,242	1,328	1,417	1,472	1,472	1,660	1,876	2,093
Endowment market value ($ mil)	15.9%	76	85	94	122	121	167	207	242	248	287

Public university
Founded: 1870
Fiscal year ends: June 30

WHO

Chief Executive: Edward Jennings
VP Business Affairs: Richard Jackson
Director of Admissions: James J. Mager
University Registrar: R. Eugene Schuster

WHERE

HQ: 1800 Cannon Dr., Columbus, OH 43210
Phone: 614-292-8500
FAX: 614-292-7199

Ohio State's 3,297-acre main campus is located in the state capital city of Columbus. The Ohio State system maintains additional campuses at Lima, Mansfield, Marion, Newark, and Wooster.

Geographic Distribution of Freshman Class	% of Total
Ohio	95
Other US	4
Foreign	1
Total	**100**

WHAT

Academic Unit	1989 Enrollment (Columbus Campus)	% of Total
Agriculture	1,219	2
Allied Medical Professions	595	1
Architecture	495	1
Arts and Sciences	9,395	18
Business	3,207	6
Continuing Education	1,876	4
Dental Hygiene	95	—
Education	1,507	3
Engineering	3,956	7
Home Economics	1,074	2
Natural Resources	292	1
Nursing	499	1
Pharmacy	475	1
Social Work	172	—
University College	15,265	29
Postbaccalaureate professional	2,708	5
Graduate (master's)	4,818	9
Graduate (post-master's)	5,247	10
Total	**52,895**	**100**

Affiliated Institutions
Bio-Medical Engineering Center
Center for Human Resources Research
Center for Medieval and Renaissance Studies
Comprehensive Cancer Research Center
ERIC Information Analysis Center
Institute for Polar Studies
Institute for Research in Vision
Lake Erie Area Research Center
Mershon Center for Public Policy
National Center for Research in Vocational Education
National Regulatory Research Institute
Nisonger Center for Mental Retardation

COMPETITION

Harvard
Stanford
University of Chicago
University of Texas

OUTBOARD MARINE CORPORATION

OVERVIEW

Outboard Marine Corporation (OMC), the world's largest producer of outboard motors, makes the well-known Evinrude and Johnson brands. The company is also the world's 2nd largest manufacturer of stern drive engines. OMC's motors range in size from 1.5 to 300 horsepower.

The company is the 2nd largest publicly held producer of powerboats for consumer use in the US (after Brunswick) with Chris-Craft, Donzi, Four Winns, and 9 other boat brands. The company's boats range in size from the 10-foot Sea Nymph to 50-foot Chris-Craft cruisers. The company is the world's largest manufacturer of fiberglass bass and aluminum boats. US sales totaled $1.1 billion in 1989. OMC sells boats and motors overseas through subsidiaries, which generated $340 million in revenue in 1989.

OMC distributes through the world's largest marine products network. The company's OMC Finance group offers extended payment plans to consumers. Its 65 Club Nautico centers rent OMC boats. The company's Top of the Dock retail outlets sell nautical apparel, boats, and boating accessories.

WHEN

In 1903 Ole Evinrude helped design Harley-Davidson's first carburetor. His outboard motor design provided the basis for his own company, Evinrude Motor Company, formed in Milwaukee in 1907. Evinrude sold the company to Chris Meyer (1914) and in 1921 formed ELTO Outboard Motor Company, producing a motor 33% lighter than the Evinrude.

In 1926 gasoline engine pioneer Briggs & Stratton purchased Evinrude Motor but sold it in 1929 to Briggs's cofounder Stephen Briggs, who formed a syndicate with Ole Evinrude called the Outboard Motors Corporation. OMC introduced electric starting outboards in 1930 and fully enclosed engines (for greater safety and noise reduction) in 1934. In 1935 OMC purchased Johnson Motors, makers of Sea Horse outboards.

After WWII OMC discontinued the ELTO line. In 1952 OMC purchased RPM Manufacturing of Lamar, Missouri, makers of power mowers. OMC renamed the mowers Lawn-Boy, and by 1957 Lawn-Boy led the nation in power mower sales.

Foreign sales, an important revenue source from early on, tripled between 1949 and 1956, the year the company adopted its present name. Between 1956 and 1958 OMC purchased Industrial Engineering, Canada's largest chain saw manufacturer (renamed Pioneer Chain Saw, sold to Electrolux in 1977); acquired Cushman Motor Works, makers of lightweight vehicles such as golf carts; and introduced the first mass-produced, die-cast, aluminum V-engine (a V-4).

In the 1960s OMC entered new product fields, most importantly stern drive marine engines. In 1967 the company introduced an all-electronic outboard ignition, now the industry standard. Additionally, OMC acquired Trade Winds (marine products) and Ryan Equipment (turf care equipment).

OMC expanded its marine business in the 1980s. In 1985 the company introduced the first V-8 outboard engine. Between 1986 and 1989 OMC spent approximately $230 million acquiring 10 boat manufacturers (including Chris-Craft and Donzi). In 1989 OMC sold both Cushman (to Ransomes America, $150 million) and Lawn-Boy (to Toro, $85 million).

The boating industry boomed between 1982 and June 1989, carrying OMC to record profits in 1988. Since then consumer demand for boats has declined, and in the first 3 quarters of 1990 OMC suffered a record loss of $1.76 per share.

OMC plans to use its status as an integrated manufacturer to strengthen sales of factory rigged and powered boats.

HOW MUCH

	9 Yr. Growth	1980	1981	1982	1983	1984	1985	1986	1987	1988	1989
Sales ($ mil)	8.8%	687	796	778	789	922	880	972	1,289	1,605	1,464
Net income ($ mil)	27.6%	2	27	34	39	53	29	11	47	72	21
Income as % of sales	—	0.3%	3.4%	4.4%	5.0%	5.7%	3.3%	1.1%	3.6%	4.5%	1.4%
Earnings per share ($)	25.6%	0.14	1.61	2.02	2.26	3.02	1.74	0.66	2.56	3.74	1.09
Stock price – high ($)	—	8.38	11.25	16.06	26.00	29.63	31.50	38.50	38.00	35.50	46.00
Stock price – low ($)	—	4.44	5.94	9.31	13.50	18.38	19.63	23.88	16.25	21.88	25.00
Stock price – close ($)	18.0%	5.88	10.00	14.44	24.88	28.50	28.00	27.00	21.88	31.00	26.00
P/E – high	—	60	7	8	12	10	18	58	15	10	42
P/E – low	—	32	4	5	6	6	11	36	6	6	23
Dividends per share ($)	9.6%	0.35	0.36	0.41	0.47	0.58	0.64	0.64	0.64	0.70	0.80
Book value per share ($)	8.2%	16.36	17.57	18.23	19.71	21.79	22.77	23.06	26.67	30.09	33.30

1989 Year End:
Debt ratio: 26.6%
Return on equity: 3.4%
Cash (mil): $20
Current ratio: 2.67
Long-term debt (mil): $233
Number of shares (mil): 19
Dividends:
1989 average yield: 3.1%
1989 payout: 73.4%
Market value (mil): $502

Stock Price History high/low 1980-89

NYSE symbol: OM
Incorporated: Delaware, 1936
Fiscal year ends: September 30

WHO

Chairman: Charles D. Strang, age 68, $1,174,631 pay
President and CEO: James C. Chapman, age 58, $630,466 pay (prior to promotion)
SVP Administration: Thomas J. Beeler, age 56, $408,383 pay
VP; President, Four Winns Boat Division: John A. Winn, age 42, $415,783 pay
VP Finance: Samuel J. Winett, age 55, $356,832 pay
VP Employee Relations: F. James Short, age 62
Auditors: Arthur Andersen & Co.
Employees: 14,000

WHERE

HQ: 100 Sea-Horse Dr., Waukegan, IL 60085
Phone: 708-689-6200
FAX: 708-689-5555

Outboard Marine operates 27 US plants in 12 states and 6 plants in Canada, Mexico, Belgium, Australia, Hong Kong, and Brazil.

	1989 Sales		1989 Operating Income	
	$ mil	% of total	$ mil	% of total
US	1,124	77	88	82
Europe	166	11	2	2
Other countries	174	12	18	16
Adjustments	—	—	(38)	—
Total	**1,464**	**100**	**70**	**100**

WHAT

Brand Names

Boats
Chris-Craft
Donzi
Four Winns
Hydra-Sports
Javelin
Lowe
Ryds
Sea Nymph
Seaswirl
Stratos
Sunbird
Suncruiser

Marine Power Systems
Evinrude
Johnson
OMC Cobra
OMC Sea Drive

Retailing
Club Nautico (boat rentals)
Top of the Dock (boat products)

Principal US Subsidiaries
Adventurent, Inc. – Ft. Lauderdale, FL
Bramco, Inc. – Culver, OR
Carl A. Lowe Industries, Inc. – Lebanon, MO
Donzi Marine Corp. – Tallevast, FL
Four Winns, Inc. – Cadillac, MI
Hydra-Sports, Inc. – Nashville, TN
OMCCC Inc. (Chris-Craft) – Bradenton, FL
Sea Nymph, Inc. – Syracuse, IN
Stratos Boats, Inc. – Nashville, TN
Sunbird Boat Co., Inc. – Columbia, SC

RANKINGS

242nd in *Fortune* 500 Industrial Cos.
797th in *Business Week* 1000

COMPETITION

Brunswick
Honda
MacAndrews & Forbes
Reebok
Volvo

OWENS-CORNING FIBERGLAS CORPORATION

OVERVIEW

Owens-Corning is the world's largest manufacturer of glass fiber materials (sold under the Fiberglas trademark) and a leading supplier of polyester resins. Glass fiber products are manufactured in 2 basic forms — as a wool-like material for construction products, and in textile filaments such as yarns, mats, and strands, for industrial products.

The Construction Products Group ($2 billion in sales) makes thermal and acoustical insulation products for buildings, mobile homes, and appliances; is the primary supplier of glass fibers to automobile manufacturers for exterior body panels; manufactures roofing products, including shingles, built-up roofing products (roofing membranes and insulation), and the industrial asphalts used to make and install roofing systems; and makes corrosion-resistant, fiber-reinforced polyester tanks used for underground storage of petroleum products.

The Industrial Materials Group ($1 billion in sales) makes glass fibers in several raw forms for sale directly or through distributors. These materials substitute for wood, steel, and other materials in marine, appliance, and consumer markets.

In 1989 the company spent $143 million, or nearly 5% of revenues, on quality control and productivity enhancements to its manufacturing system.

WHEN

In the 1930s Corning Glass Works and Owens-Illinois independently discovered desirable properties of strength and resilience in glass fibers. The 2 companies believed a large market would result and in 1938 formed Owens-Corning Fiberglas Corporation as a joint venture.

Harold Boeschenstein, VP and general manager of Owens-Illinois, was hired as CEO. The company rapidly expanded in the 1940s and 1950s, establishing numerous plants around the US and one in Ontario. Products included fine fibers, thermal wool, textiles, and continuous filaments.

In 1949 a US antitrust decree denied the 2 founding firms any control over Owens-Corning or claim to its earnings. Soon after (1952) Owens-Corning went public; the 2 founding companies retained 1/3 ownership each, which they later reduced.

During the 1950s the company developed new uses for glass fibers in automobile bodies, roofing shingles, and insulation, which helped increase sales 20% annually. The company expanded overseas in the 1960s. Uses for glass fibers continued to multiply, as applications developed in aerospace, tires, and noncorrosive underground storage tanks. In 1967 Boeschenstein retired and his son William became president and CEO in 1972.

In 1977 Owens-Corning bought Lloyd Fry (roofing and asphalt) for $108 million. By 1980 Owens-Corning had invested over $700 million in acquisitions and internal development to strengthen the company's position in roofing materials and introduced the Pink Panther in its ad campaigns to establish brand identification for its products. Owens-Corning introduced a rolled insulation in 1982.

A takeover attempt by Wickes Companies in 1986 was successfully fended off, but the effort necessitated a $2.6 billion debt burden and forced Owens-Corning to redirect its strategy. It sold 10 noncore businesses, halved its research budget, laid off or lost to divestitures 46% of its total work force, and mothballed 14% of productive capacity by 1987.

Debt reduction was ahead of schedule in 1989, and Owens-Corning completed full purchase of Fiberglas Canada, Canada's largest manufacturer of glass fiber insulation, for $195 million. Maximizing cash flow for debt reduction remains a top priority.

HOW MUCH

	9 Yr. Growth	1980	1981	1982	1983	1984	1985	1986	1987	1988	1989
Sales ($ mil)	3.1%	2,285	2,375	2,373	2,753	3,021	3,305	3,644	2,891	2,831	3,000
Net income ($ mil)	13.7%	54	50	30	80	114	131	16	220	197	172
Income as % of sales	—	2.4%	2.1%	1.3%	2.9%	3.8%	4.0%	0.4%	7.6%	7.0%	5.7%
Earnings per share ($)	9.7%	1.78	1.63	0.98	2.77	3.87	4.42	0.49	5.30	4.71	4.08
Stock price – high ($)	—	32.13	31.00	37.88	46.88	38.88	38.75	82.50	32.38	26.50	36.88
Stock price – low ($)	—	22.25	21.50	15.38	30.25	25.13	30.50	8.88	9.00	15.88	22.25
Stock price – close ($)	(0.7%)	26.75	22.50	37.50	36.50	32.00	37.50	13.75	16.38	22.25	25.13
P/E – high	—	18	19	39	17	10	9	168	6	6	9
P/E – low	—	13	13	16	11	7	7	18	2	3	5
Dividends per share ($)	—	1.20	1.20	1.20	1.20	1.30	1.40	53.05	0.00	0.00	0.00
Book value per share ($)	—	24.81	25.24	23.67	26.09	28.48	31.70	(25.93)	(20.23)	(15.18)	(10.78)

1989 Year End:
Debt ratio: 156.8%
Return on equity: —
Cash (mil): $29
Current ratio: 1.03
Long-term debt (mil): $1,201
Number of shares (mil): 40
Dividends:
1989 average yield: 0.0%
1989 payout: 0.0%
Market value (mil): $1,014

Stock Price History high/low 1980-89

NYSE symbol: OCF
Incorporated: Delaware, 1938
Fiscal year ends: December 31

WHO

Chairman and CEO: William W. Boeschenstein, age 64, $947,236 pay
President and COO: Max O. Weber, age 60, $452,160 pay
SVP and Principal Financial Officer: Paul V. Daverio, age 51, $356,573 pay
SVP Law: William W. Colville, age 55, $358,715 pay
SVP; President, Industrial Materials Group: Charles H. Dana, age 50
SVP; President, Construction Products Group: Larry T. Solari, age 47
Auditors: Arthur Andersen & Co.
Employees: 18,600

WHERE

HQ: Fiberglas Tower, Toledo, OH 43659
Phone: 419-248-8000
FAX: 419-248-5337 (Public Relations)

Owens-Corning operates manufacturing plants at 37 US and 17 foreign locations.

	1989 Sales		1989 Operating Income	
	$ mil	% of total	$ mil	% of total
US	2,306	77	298	65
Canada	141	5	11	2
Other	553	18	151	33
Total	**3,000**	**100**	**460**	**100**

WHAT

	Sales		Operating Income	
	$ mil	% of total	$ mil	% of total
Construction prods.	1,954	65	183	40
Industrial materials	1,046	35	277	60
Total	**3,000**	**100**	**460**	**100**

Construction Products
Asphalt materials for roofing, industrial uses, and paving
Built-up roofing products
Calcium silicate insulation
Glass fiber roofing shingles
Glass fiber–reinforced underground fuel storage tanks
Modified bitumen roofing membranes
Thermal and acoustical insulation for constructed and manufactured buildings, appliances, and air-handling duct systems

Industrial Materials
Chopped glass fiber strands
Gelcoats
Glass fiber mats
Glass fiber reinforcements for auto body panels
Glass fiber textile yarns (for, *e.g.*, reinforcements in paper and tape products)
Polyester resins

RANKINGS

149th in *Fortune* 500 Industrial Cos.
422nd in *Fortune* Global 500 Industrial Cos.
279th in *Forbes* Sales 500
568th in *Business Week* 1000

COMPETITION

Corning	Monsanto
Georgia-Pacific	PPG
Manville	USG

OWENS-ILLINOIS, INC.

OVERVIEW

With nearly $3.6 billion in sales, privately owned Owens-Illinois is one of the world's leading producers of glass and plastic packaging products. In addition, the company is the 6th largest operator of investor-owned US nursing and retirement homes, and ranks 3rd in sales among US skilled nursing care facilities.

Owens-Illinois's glass container division (its oldest and primary business) generates approximately 60% of sales and is a model of modern glass technology. The company is the world's largest producer of glass containers and owns about 40% of the US market. Primary customers for this segment include brewers, soft drink bottlers, and food producers.

Specialty glass products (12% of sales) include Libbey Glass (the leading producer of glass tableware), Kimble Glass (pharmaceutical packaging and laboratory ware), and a 50% interest in OI-NEG TV Products (glass TV parts).

Plastic packaging operations (20% of sales) produce a wide range of plastic containers, closures, and related items. The company's Owens-Brockway subsidiary is the leading producer and decorator of custom plastic containers (everything from shampoo bottles to chemical containers) in the US.

The Health Care and Retirement Corporation (HCR) subsidiary (8% of sales) operates over 130 long-term care facilities (including nursing homes, retirement centers, and assisted-living facilities) with about 16,000 beds.

WHEN

The Owens Bottle Machine Corporation was incorporated in Toledo in 1907 as the successor to a New Jersey company of the same name established in 1903. During the next 2 decades the company grew by acquiring several other small glass companies. In 1929 Owens bought The Illinois Glass Company (medical and pharmaceutical glass) and renamed itself Owens-Illinois Glass.

During the 1930s the company purchased Libbey-Glass (tableware, 1935) and started conducting research into the uses of glass fibers. In 1938 Owens-Illinois and Corning Glass, which had been conducting similar research, established a joint venture (Owens-Corning Fiberglas). With a clear lead in fiberglass technology, Owens-Corning gained a virtual monopoly on the industry and now ranks 149th on the *Fortune* 500.

After WWII Owens-Illinois started to diversify beyond glass. In 1956 the company bought National Container, then the 3rd largest producer of cardboard boxes. During the 1950s Owens-Illinois also turned its attention to plastic and created a semirigid plastic container that was adopted by several bleach and laundry detergent companies in 1958.

The 1960s were a period of tremendous growth and overseas expansion for the company. In 1960 Owens-Illinois, through a joint venture with National Distillers and Chemicals, established National Petro Chemicals to supply the company's plastic operations. The decade also gave new life to the glass industry with the introduction of the nonreturnable bottle. The thinner new bottles gave the company fresh fuel for the struggle against aluminum cans. During the late 1960s Owens-Illinois bought Lily Tulip Cups (paper products, 1968; sold to KKR in 1981) and entered such diverse ventures as Bahamas sugar cane farming and Florida phosphate mining.

In the 1970s Owens-Illinois modernized its production facilities to compensate for a worldwide recession in the container industry and started producing specialty optical and TV glass. During this time the company also adopted a strong environmental stance and was cited by Ralph Nader as the company with the best record on environmental issues.

While much of the glass industry was floundering at the beginning of the 1980s, Owens-Illinois invested over $600 million to realign and modernize its glass operations. In 1981 the company entered the health care field with a minority interest in Health Group, Inc. Three years later Owens-Illinois purchased the Health Care and Retirement Corporation.

In 1986 Kohlberg Kravis Roberts (KKR) offered to purchase the company. Owens-Illinois initially refused the offer but was forced to deal when the offer was raised to $60 per share. In 1987 KKR acquired the company for $3.6 billion and took it private. The following year the company acquired Brockway (glass and plastic containers).

Private company
Incorporated: Ohio, 1907
Fiscal year ends: December 31

WHO

Chairman and CEO: Robert J. Lanigan, age 61, $1,470,227 pay
President and COO: Joseph H. Lemieux, age 58, $960,759 pay
SVP and CFO: Lee A. Wesselmann, age 53, $346,003 pay
Auditors: Ernst & Young
Employees: 46,000

WHERE

HQ: One SeaGate, Toledo, OH 43666
Phone: 419-247-5000
FAX: 419-247-2839 (Main Office)

The company has over 70 plants in the United States and operations in 13 foreign countries. In addition, the company operates 130 long-term health care facilities in 19 states.

	1989 Sales		1989 Operating Income	
	$ mil	% of total	$ mil	% of total
US	3,265	90	371	81
Other Western Hemisphere	271	8	66	15
Europe	69	2	16	4
Adjustments	—	—	(8)	—
Total	**3,605**	**100**	**445**	**100**

WHAT

	1989 Sales		1989 Operating Income	
	$ mil	% of total	$ mil	% of total
Glass containers	2,152	60	228	50
Health care	303	8	26	6
Plastics & closures	719	20	119	26
Specialized glass	430	12	79	18
Adjustments	1	—	(7)	—
Total	**3,605**	**100**	**445**	**100**

Glass Products
Containers
Decorative glassware
Kimble laboratory ware
Libbey stemware
Prescription products
Television parts
Tumblers

Plastic Products
Carriers (for beverage containers)
Closures
Containers
Plastic drums
Plastic foam labels
Prescription products

Health Care Facilities
Assisted-living facilities
Nursing homes
Retirement centers

RANKINGS

27th in *Forbes* 400 US Private Cos.

COMPETITION

Brown-Forman
Corning
Johnson Controls
Marriott
Peter Kiewit Sons'
Reynolds Metals

HOW MUCH

	9 Yr. Growth	1980	1981	1982	1983	1984	1985	1986	1987	1988	1989
Sales ($ mil)	(0.9%)	3,906	3,943	3,553	3,422	3,510	3,674	3,642	3,098	3,572	3,605
Net income ($ mil)	—	149	154	40	69	136	156	179	(39)	(59)	(68)
Income as % of sales	—	3.8%	3.9%	1.1%	2.0%	3.9%	4.3%	4.9%	(1.3%)	(1.7%)	(1.9%)

1989 Year End:
Debt ratio: 102.6%
Return on equity: —
Cash (mil): $129
Current ratio: 1.38
Long-term debt (mil): $3,833

Net Income ($ mil) 1980-89

200
150
100
50
0
-50
-100

PACCAR INC.

OVERVIEW

Headquartered in Bellevue, Washington, PACCAR derives 83% of all revenues from the sale of trucks manufactured under the Peterbilt, Kenworth, and Foden (UK) nameplates. In 1989 PACCAR became the industry heavy truck leader, upping US market share from 23% to 24.5%.

PACCAR also provides financing and leasing services to support truck sales, markets medium-sized trucks made in Brazil by Volkswagen, manufactures oilfield extraction pumps and industrial winches (the world's largest full-line manufacturer), and sells automotive components through its 134 Al's Auto Supply and Grand Auto retailers.

PACCAR assembles major components (purchased mostly from outside suppliers); its trucks are customized products with a high-quality reputation. The company markets its trucks through 316 independent dealers.

Due to the soft truck market, PACCAR forecasts lower 1990 demand and has cut back production. The company is committed to increasing US medium truck market share (7.5% in 1989) and to becoming more competitive globally.

OTC symbol: PCAR
Incorporated: Delaware, 1971
Fiscal year ends: December 31

WHO

Chairman and CEO: Charles M. Pigott, age 60, $981,558 pay
President: Joseph M. Dunn, age 63, $669,877 pay
EVP: David J. Hovind, age 49, $434,018 pay
EVP and CFO: William E. Boisvert, age 47, $306,977 pay
SVP: Leonard A. Haba, age 58, $331,835 pay
SVP: Mark C. Pigott, age 35, $207,636
Auditors: Ernst & Young
Employees: 13,077

WHEN

William Pigott founded the Seattle Car Manufacturing Company in 1905 to produce railroad cars for timber transport. Meeting with immediate success, Pigott expanded production to other rail cars in 1906. The Seattle plant burned in 1907, and the company moved to near Renton, Washington. In 1911 Pigott renamed the company Seattle Car & Foundry.

Following a 1917 merger with the Twohy Brothers of Portland, the new company, Pacific Car & Foundry, was sold to American Car & Foundry in 1924. Under the new owners Pacific Car diversified into bus manufacturing, structural steel fabrications, and metal technology. A company metallurgist developed a strong, lightweight steel called Carcometal that was used to design tractor equipment and winches.

With the company in decline, in 1934 the founder's son, Paul Pigott, purchased Pacific Car. The company has remained under family management since. Pigott added Hofius Steel and Equipment, and Tricoach, a bus manufacturer, in 1936.

The company entered the growing truck manufacturing industry with the 1945 purchase of Seattle-based Kenworth. In the 1950s Pacific Car became the industry leader in mechanical refrigerator car production; began producing off-road, heavy trucks; and acquired Peterbilt Trucks of Oakland (1958). Paul Pigott died in 1961.

To augment its winch business, Pacific Car purchased Gearmatic, a Canadian company, in 1963. The company moved its headquarters to Bellevue in 1969 and changed its name to PACCAR in 1971. Acquisitions in the 1970s included Wagner Mining Equipment (1973); the largest US caboose producer, International Car (1975); and Braden Winch (1977). In 1980 PACCAR acquired Foden trucks of Britain.

A shift in customer demand toward smaller trucks caused industry heavy truck sales to decline 35% between 1979 and 1986, leading PACCAR to close 2 factories, the first closures in 41 years. In 1987 PACCAR introduced its first medium truck, bought Trico Industries (oil drilling equipment), and entered the auto parts sales market.

In 1989 PACCAR became the industry leader in heavy truck sales (surpassing Navistar), as market share rose to 24.5%. PACCAR also introduced more medium truck models and sold Wagner Mining Equipment.

Direct descendants of the founder, CEO Charles Pigott and his son Mark are company officers and Charles's brother James is a board member. Family members own over 12% of the company's stock.

WHERE

HQ: 777 106th Ave. NE, Bellevue, WA 98004
Phone: 206-455-7400
FAX: 206-453-4900

PACCAR has manufacturing plants in 8 US states, Canada, Australia, Mexico, and the UK. Exports are marketed through more than 50 dealerships in over 40 countries. Its 2 auto supply houses operate in over 134 locations in California, Nevada, Washington, and Alaska.

	1989 Sales		1989 Pretax Income	
	$ mil	% of total	$ mil	% of total
US	2,954	84	229	80
Canada	317	9	23	8
Other countries	262	7	33	12
Adjustments	(10)	—	80	—
Total	**3,523**	**100**	**365**	**100**

WHAT

	1989 Sales		1989 Pretax Income	
	$ mil	% of total	$ mil	% of total
Trucks	2,931	83	252	88
Other products	410	12	—	—
Financial services	192	5	33	12
Adjustments	(10)	—	80	—
Total	**3,523**	**100**	**365**	**100**

Product lines
Auto supply retailing
- Al's Auto Supply
- Grand Auto

Financing and leasing programs for trucks
Heavy trucks
- Foden
- Kenworth
- Peterbilt

Industrial winches
Medium trucks
Oilfield extraction pumps
Truck parts

HOW MUCH

	9 Yr. Growth	1980	1981	1982	1983	1984	1985	1986	1987	1988	1989
Sales ($ mil)	8.6%	1,674	1,735	1,230	1,412	2,249	1,893	1,796	2,424	3,267	3,523
Net income ($ mil)	12.9%	81	85	37	37	125	73	54	112	176	242
Income as % of sales	—	4.8%	4.9%	3.0%	2.7%	5.6%	3.9%	3.0%	4.6%	5.4%	6.9%
Earnings per share ($)	13.3%	2.23	2.35	1.03	1.04	3.46	2.01	1.51	3.13	4.90	6.90
Stock price – high ($)	—	16.88	19.83	22.38	29.50	29.75	26.63	29.13	39.13	44.00	52.50
Stock price – low ($)	—	9.43	13.58	13.13	20.25	19.25	19.88	20.50	21.75	27.00	37.75
Stock price – close ($)	11.5%	16.08	18.41	20.56	28.88	22.31	23.25	23.38	28.50	41.00	42.75
P/E – high	—	8	8	22	29	9	13	19	13	9	8
P/E – low	—	4	6	13	20	6	10	14	7	6	5
Dividends per share ($)	16.2%	0.65	0.66	0.50	0.53	1.10	1.10	0.70	1.60	2.40	2.50
Book value per share ($)	7.6%	14.90	16.58	16.11	16.66	18.88	19.70	20.27	22.33	25.18	28.87

1989 Year End:
Debt ratio: 32.5%
Return on equity: 25.5%
Cash (mil): $555
Total assets (mil): $3,067
Long-term debt (mil):$485
Number of shares (mil): 35
Dividends:
1989 average yield: 5.8%
1989 payout: 36.2%
Market value (mil): $1,492

RANKINGS

136th in *Fortune* 500 Industrial Cos.
383rd in *Fortune* Global 500 Industrial Cos.
250th in *Forbes* Sales 500
377th in *Business Week* 1000

COMPETITION

Daimler-Benz	Navistar
Fiat	Renault
Ford	Sears
General Motors	Volvo

PACIFIC GAS AND ELECTRIC COMPANY

OVERVIEW

Pacific Gas & Electric (PG&E), America's largest electric and natural gas utility in terms of 1989 sales, serves approximately 7.5 million customers in northern and central California. In 1989 its Diablo Canyon Nuclear Power Plant generated 15.8 billion kilowatt hours of electricity and $1.4 billion in revenues — about 16% of PG&E's revenues for that year. PG&E Enterprises, a subsidiary, manages nonutility projects, including ownership and operation of 8 power plants nationwide (PG&E-Bechtel Generating Company). PG&E Properties, the company's real estate development subsidiary, has completed 5 projects in California, including an apartment complex and an office building.

In an effort to help reduce air pollution, PG&E is investigating the potential of electric-powered and compressed natural gas (CNG)–powered vehicles and plans to open the nation's first CNG service station soon.

The company won the US Department of Labor's prestigious Opportunity 2000 Award in 1989 for its programs to advance equal opportunities for women and minorities and support of community job training programs.

WHEN

Peter Donahue founded the first gas company in the western US, San Francisco Gas, in 1852. This company became San Francisco Gas & Electric (SFG&E) in 1896 after merging with Edison Light & Power.

In the meantime in San Francisco, money broker George Roe and other investors founded California Electric Light (1879), the first electric utility in the US, predating Edison's New York Pearl Street Station by 3 years. California Electric and SFG&E consolidated in 1905 to form Pacific Gas & Electric (PG&E).

In 1928 PG&E discovered natural gas reserves in California's Kings County and, in 1930, began converting more than 2.5 million appliances to burn this fuel — the largest conversion in history. The company began exploring for out-of-state gas supplies in the 1950s, first in Texas and New Mexico and then in western Canada.

PG&E operated the world's first private atomic power plant (Vallecitos) in 1957, and developed the first geothermal plant (The Geysers) to operate in North America in 1960. PG&E's Humboldt Bay facility (completed in 1963) was one of the world's first nuclear plants to produce electricity at a cost commensurable to conventional steam plants.

From its inception through the late 1970s PG&E bought about 500 utilities (water, gas, and electric) and by 1978 was serving about 9 million customers. The company sold the last of its water systems by 1985, the same year Unit 1 of the Diablo Canyon nuclear facility went on line. Diablo Canyon, begun in 1968, had been plagued by delays and cost overruns (a design problem discovered in 1981 resulted in a 15-month review of construction plans and methods). Unit 2 was in operation by 1986. In 1988, instead of utilizing traditional rate structures, PG&E started basing revenues chiefly on how much electricity Diablo Canyon generates, creating a direct relationship between the plant's performance and the company's earnings. Settlement of the Diablo Canyon rate issues in 1988 and an unscheduled refueling outage resulted in negative earnings for that year.

Under natural gas deregulation, customers began to bypass PG&E in the mid-1980s (finding it cheaper to generate their own electricity or buy gas directly from suppliers); therefore, the company eliminated about 2,500 jobs (1987) and announced a 3-year phase-out of about 300 management positions (1990). PG&E is also negotiating special rate agreements with some industrial customers, formulated to compete with the costs of customer-owned generators.

HOW MUCH

	9 Yr. Growth	1980	1981	1982	1983	1984	1985	1986	1987	1988	1989
Sales ($ mil)	5.6%	5,259	6,195	6,785	6,647	7,830	8,431	7,817	7,186	7,646	8,588
Net income ($ mil)	6.2%	525	565	810	788	975	1,031	1,081	597	62	901
Income as % of sales	—	10.0%	9.1%	11.9%	11.9%	12.5%	12.2%	13.8%	8.3%	0.8%	10.5%
Earnings per share ($)	0.6%	1.80	1.71	2.46	2.15	2.62	2.65	2.60	1.29	(0.10)	1.90
Stock price – high ($)	—	12.38	12.06	14.38	16.75	17.25	20.38	27.50	27.88	18.38	22.00
Stock price – low ($)	—	9.63	9.75	10.13	13.94	12.00	16.00	18.75	15.00	14.00	17.25
Stock price – close ($)	8.9%	10.25	10.50	14.06	14.88	16.38	20.00	24.25	16.25	17.50	22.00
P/E – high	—	7	7	6	8	7	8	11	22	—	12
P/E – low	—	5	6	4	6	5	6	7	12	—	9
Dividends per share ($)	0.8%	1.30	1.36	1.47	1.58	1.69	1.81	1.90	1.92	1.66	1.40
Book value per share ($)	1.6%	15.05	15.15	15.87	16.39	17.18	18.05	19.06	18.68	16.79	17.38

1989 Year End:
Debt ratio: 48.0%
Return on equity: 11.1%
Cash (mil): $67
Current ratio: 1.27
Long-term debt (mil): $7,824
Number of shares (mil): 429
Dividends:
1989 average yield: 6.4%
1989 payout: 73.7%
Market value (mil): $9,438

Stock Price History high/low 1980-89

NYSE symbol: PCG
Incorporated: California, 1905
Fiscal year ends: December 31

WHO

Chairman and CEO: Richard A. Clarke, age 59, $695,281 pay
VC and Principal Financial Officer: Stanley T. Skinner, age 52, $476,299
President: George A. Maneatis, age 63, $470,189 pay
Chairman, President, and CEO, PG&E Enterprises: Mason Willrich, age 56, $325,833 pay
Auditors: Arthur Andersen & Co.
Employees: 26,200

WHERE

HQ: 77 Beale St., San Francisco, CA 94106
Phone: 415-972-7000
FAX: 415-543-7813

Pacific Gas & Electric supplies electric and natural gas service in northern and central California.

Generating Facilities

Fossil-Fueled
Contra Costa (Contra Costa County)
Humboldt Bay (Humboldt County)
Hunters Point (San Francisco County)
Kern (Kern County)
Mobile Turbines (Contra Costa and Humboldt Counties)
Morro Bay (San Luis Obispo County)
Moss Landing (Monterey County)
Oakland (Alameda County)
Pittsburg (Contra Costa County)
Potrero (San Francisco County)

Geothermal
The Geysers (Sonoma and Lake Counties)

Hydroelectric
Conventional (16 counties)
Helms Pumped Storage Plant (Fresno County)

Nuclear
Diablo Canyon (San Luis Obispo County)

WHAT

PG&E derives 100% of its revenue from US operations.

	1989 Sales		1989 Operating Income	
	$ mil	% of total	$ mil	% of total
Electricity	6,216	72	2,100	89
Gas	2,372	28	247	11
Total	**8,588**	**100**	**2,347**	**100**

Natural Gas Transmission & Supply
Alberta and Southern Gas Co. Ltd. (Canadian-based supplier)
Pacific Gas Transmission Co.

PG&E Enterprises
PG&E Operating Services Co. (technical support)
PG&E Properties (real estate development)
PG&E Resources Co. (natural gas and oil development)
PG&E-Bechtel Generating Co.

RANKINGS

6th in *Fortune* 50 Utilities
93rd in *Forbes* Sales 500
49th in *Business Week* 1000
161st in *Business Week* Global 1000

PACIFIC TELESIS GROUP

OVERVIEW

Pacific Telesis is the 7th largest US telephone company and, through the California market, serves an area that is growing in population at nearly twice the rate of the rest of the nation. The company provides local telephone service and access to long-distance services for approximately 13.8 million lines in California and Nevada.

Subsidiary PacTel Cellular provides cellular phone service to 381,000 customers in 33 markets (owning majority interests in 5 of the US's top 20 markets) and in 1989 showed a 255% net income growth over 1988. Pacific Telesis owns the US's 4th largest paging company, PacTel Paging, offering services in more than 30 markets. Pacific Telesis also engages in directory publishing through Pacific Bell Directory, which had revenues of $867 million in 1989.

Pacific Telesis has invested in several Far Eastern ventures, including Thai paging operations, a Pacific undersea fiber optic cable linking Japan to 14 countries, and a Korean credit card authorization system. It has also entered European markets, providing a German cellular system and cable TV and mobile phone services in the UK.

NYSE symbol: PAC
Incorporated: Nevada, 1983
Fiscal year ends: December 31

WHO

Chairman, President, and CEO: Sam Ginn, age 52, $919,908 pay
VC and CFO: John E. Hulse, age 56, $607,067 pay
Group President, PacTel Companies: C. Lee Cox, age 48, $539,858 pay
Group President, Bell Operating Companies: Philip J. Quigley, age 47, $534,233 pay
Auditors: Coopers & Lybrand
Employees: 68,452

WHEN

The Pacific and Nevada Bell companies owned by Pacific Telesis were formerly 2 of AT&T's 22 operating companies. California's first exchange was opened in 1878 in San Francisco, the city that was later one end (with New York) of the first coast-to-coast telephone call (1915).

By 1980 AT&T was rumored to be considering Pacific Bell's sale. Pacific Bell's battles with the California Public Utilities Commission (CPUC) had soured relations with AT&T, to the point that it claimed AT&T had denied it equity capital. But during 1980-1981, instead of selling, AT&T hired a new management team for the company. Donald Guinn, CEO of Pacific Bell (and chairman and CEO of Pacific Telesis from 1984 to 1988), and new CFO John Hulse took steps to cut spending and improve relations with the CPUC.

Pacific Bell was folded into parent Pacific Telesis Group in 1984, after divestiture from AT&T. Pacific Telesis gained California and Nevada phone territories; 1/7th interest in Bell Communications Research (R&D arm shared by the Bell companies); and PacTel Cellular.

In 1986 the CPUC ordered Pacific Bell to refund subscribers for fees derived from deceptive marketing practices (combining optional features with basic service and charging for both) and ordered a rate refund instead of the requested hike. But unregulated enterprises began to fuel Pacific Telesis's growth. The 1986 purchase of Communications Industries made Pacific Telesis a top player in cellular radio and paging, giving it 5 cellular and 14 paging operations outside of its territory. In 1988 Guinn retired.

In 1989 Pacific Telesis purchased a minority interest (8.5%) in International Digital Company, formed with several Japanese companies that are constructing a transpacific fiber optic cable. Pacific Telesis owns 26% of a group recently licensed (1989) to supply Germany with its first privately owned cellular phone system. The company agreed to buy an option for 68% of a Chicago cable TV franchise and ventured into the UK cable market. PacTel introduced voice mail, electronic mail, and 800 and 900 services. Pacific Telesis has also gained ground with the CPUC, which has allowed it greater pricing flexibility. In 1990 the company agreed to combine its Ohio and Michigan cellular operations with those of Cellular Communications, Inc. (CCI), gaining the option to acquire CCI over the next 8 years.

Investors who bought Pacific Telesis stock at its initial offering in 1983 have earned, through 1989, a higher return than if they had invested in any of the other 6 Bell companies.

WHERE

HQ: 130 Kearny St., San Francisco, CA 94108
Phone: 415-394-3000
FAX: 415-362-2913 (External Affairs)

Pacific Telesis provides telephone service and publishes directories in California and Nevada and has unregulated operations throughout the US and in Germany, Japan, South Korea, Thailand, and the UK.

	1989 Lines in Service	
	no. (thou)	% of total
California	13,446	98
Nevada	216	2
Total	**13,662**	**100**

WHAT

	1989 Sales	
	$ mil	% of total
Local service	3,130	33
Network access-interstate	1,630	17
Network access-intrastate	780	8
Toll service	2,194	23
Other	1,859	19
Total	**9,593**	**100**

Telephone Companies
Nevada Bell
Pacific Bell

Unregulated Operations
Bell Communications Research (14.28%)
Location Technologies (vehicle radiolocation services)
Pacific Bell Directory (directory publishing)
Pacific Telesis International (international operations)
PacTel Business Systems (communications equipment sales, service, and financing)
PacTel Cellular (cellular telephone service)
PacTel Paging (paging service)
PacTel Properties (real estate development)

HOW MUCH

	5 Yr. Growth	1980	1981	1982	1983	1984	1985	1986	1987	1988	1989
Sales ($ mil)	4.2%	—	—	—	—	7,824	8,499	8,977	9,131	9,483	9,593
Net income ($ mil)	8.2%	—	—	—	—	829	929	1,079	950	1,188	1,242
Income as % of sales	—	—	—	—	—	10.6%	10.9%	12.0%	10.4%	12.5%	12.9%
Earnings per share ($)	7.2%	—	—	—	—	2.12	2.27	2.51	2.21	2.81	3.00
Stock price – high ($)	—	—	—	—	—	17.78	21.47	31.13	34.50	32.50	51.13
Stock price – low ($)	—	—	—	—	—	13.13	16.66	19.38	22.50	24.88	30.38
Stock price – close ($)	23.9%	—	—	—	—	17.22	21.16	26.63	26.63	30.88	50.38
P/E – high	—	—	—	—	—	8	9	12	16	12	17
P/E – low	—	—	—	—	—	6	7	8	10	9	10
Dividends per share ($)	6.8%	—	—	—	—	1.35	1.43	1.52	1.64	1.76	1.88
Book value per share ($)	3.2%	—	—	—	—	16.20	17.04	18.01	18.47	19.30	18.92

1989 Year End:
Debt ratio: 40.3%
Return on equity: 15.7%
Cash (mil): $0
Current ratio: 0.75
Long-term debt (mil): $5,325
Number of shares (mil): 417
Dividends:
1989 average yield: 3.7%
1989 payout: 62.7%
Market value (mil): $20,997

Stock Price History high/low 1984-89

RANKINGS

7th in *Fortune* 50 Largest Utilities
82nd in *Forbes* Sales 500
22nd in *Business Week* 1000
58th in *Business Week* Global 1000

COMPETITION

Ameritech
AT&T
Bell Atlantic
BellSouth
GTE
McCaw Cellular
MCI
NYNEX
Southwestern Bell
United Telecommunications
U S West

PAN AM CORPORATION

OVERVIEW

Pan Am Corporation is the parent company of Pan American World Airways, Pan Am Express, and Pan Am Shuttle.

Pan American offers flights to 40 European destinations—more than all other US airlines combined—and plans to add nonstop flights to Helsinki and Berlin in 1990. Pan Am Express, Pan Am's Philadelphia-based regional airline (purchased 1986), serves 32 cities in the US and Europe.

In the days of Juan Trippe's flying clippers, Pan Am was considered America's unofficial flagship abroad. Now ranked 8th among US airlines, the company has lost money in 8 of the past 10 years, with net losses for the 1980s exceeding $2 billion. In an effort to bolster Pan American's operations, Pan Am announced in May 1990 that its East Coast commuter, Pan Am Shuttle, is for sale. Pan Am also hopes to foster expansion plans and reduce financial problems by becoming a part of a stronger airline or acquiring another airline (its 1989 bid for NWA failed).

WHEN

Army captain J. K. Montgomery founded Pan American Airways in 1927 to fly mail from Key West to Havana. Short of cash and equipment, the airline merged with Florida Airways and Juan Trippe's Aviation Company of America (1927). Under Trippe's leadership, Pan Am had extended operations throughout the Caribbean and Central America by 1929. Further expansion was temporarily stymied by W. R. Grace and Company, which had shipping operations along the South American west coast, but in 1929 the companies formed Pan American-Grace Airways (Panagra), with operations from Panama to Chile and across the Andes to Buenos Aires. By 1930 Pan Am was operating on South America's East Coast also.

In 1935 Pan Am's *China Clipper* made the world's first commercial transpacific flight (Honolulu-Manila). Pan Am launched the *Yankee Clipper* across the Atlantic (New York-Marseilles) in 1939.

After WWII Pan Am faced growing competition as more countries developed airlines and TWA and Northwest began flying overseas. Pan Am opened its chain of Intercontinental Hotels (1946), bought American Airline's European routes (1950), and inaugurated the world's first transatlantic jet service (1958). Juan Trippe retired in 1968. In the meantime Pan Am had been losing passengers to its competitors. TWA replaced it as America's #1 airline to Europe in 1969. In 1975, when Congress denied its request for a subsidy, Pan Am pared its routes, sold some planes, and in 1977 reported a profit. However, federal deregulation of the airline industry (1978) created new problems by allowing Pan Am's domestic competitors easier access to foreign routes. These airlines, with their extensive operations in the US, had a built-in system for channeling passengers into international routes. Pan Am, on the other hand, had no domestic operations. To remedy this the company bought Miami-based National Airlines (1980), gaining connections along the Eastern Seaboard and to the West Coast, but in a bidding war with Texas Air (now Continental Airlines Holdings) paid a hefty price.

To offset losses Pan Am sold its hotels to Grand Metropolitan of London (1981) and its Pacific division to UAL (1986). In 1986 Pan Am purchased Philadelphia-based regional air carrier Ransome Airlines, changing its name to Pan Am Express. The same year it made arrangements with Texas Air's Eastern to take over its Boston–New York and New York–Washington shuttles. The terrorist bombing of Flight 103 over Lockerbie, Scotland in 1988 dramatically reduced transatlantic revenues and contributed heavily to Pan Am's $452 million loss in 1989. Pan Am sold its World Services division (airport and space facilities management) to Johnson Controls in 1989.

HOW MUCH

	9 Yr. Growth	1980	1981	1982	1983	1984	1985	1986	1987	1988	1989
Sales ($ mil)	(1.3%)	4,016	3,797	3,716	3,789	3,685	3,484	3,039	3,593	3,569	3,561
Net income ($ mil)	—	80	(260)	(485)	(60)	(207)	49	(463)	(265)	(97)	(452)
Income as % of sales	—	2.0%	(6.8%)	(13.1%)	(1.6%)	(5.6%)	1.4%	(15.2%)	(7.4%)	(2.7%)	(12.7%)
Earnings per share ($)	—	1.01	(2.53)	(4.61)	*(0.68)*	(1.06)	*0.42*	(2.45)	(1.28)	(0.33)	(2.32)
Stock price – high ($)	—	6.13	6.00	4.25	9.00	9.25	9.00	9.50	6.38	3.38	5.13
Stock price – low ($)	—	3.75	2.38	2.50	3.50	4.00	4.00	4.00	2.63	2.25	2.25
Stock price – close ($)	(5.2%)	4.25	2.75	3.63	8.13	4.63	7.75	4.25	2.75	2.25	2.63
P/E – high	—	6	—	—	—	—	21	—	—	—	—
P/E – low	—	4	—	—	—	—	10	—	—	—	—
Dividends per share ($)	0.0%	0.00	0.00	0.00	0.00	0.00	0.00	0.00	0.00	0.00	0.00
Book value per share ($)	—	11.32	11.05	4.11	4.19	2.17	3.36	0.06	(1.75)	(2.12)	(4.26)

1989 Year End:
Debt ratio: 272.9%
Return on equity: 72.7%
Cash (mil): $4,239
Current ratio: 0.66
Long-term debt (mil): $4,994
Number of shares (mil): 148
Dividends:
1989 average yield: 0.0%
1989 payout: 0.0%
Market value (mil): $4,388

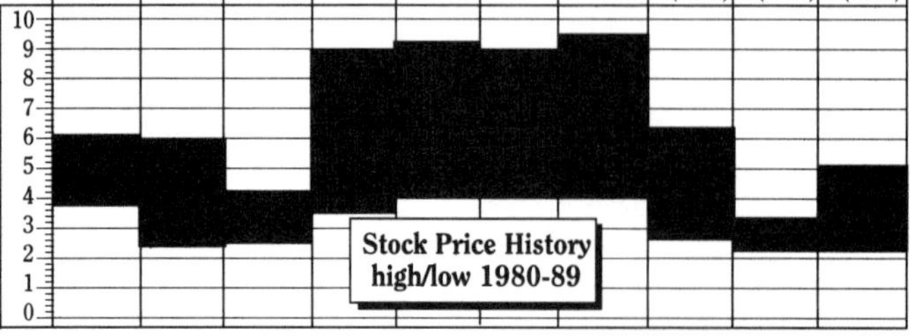

Stock Price History high/low 1980-89

NYSE symbol: PN
Incorporated: Delaware, 1984
Fiscal year ends: December 31

WHO

Chairman, President, and CEO: Thomas G. Plaskett, age 46, $500,000 pay
SVP and CFO: Richard H. Francis, age 57, $230,000 pay
Auditors: Ernst & Young
Employees: 28,750

WHERE

HQ: Pan Am Building, 200 Park Ave., New York, NY 10166
Phone: 212-880-1234
FAX: 212-880-1782

Pan Am serves 31 American cities and 68 destinations around the world.

Hub Locations

Berlin, Frankfurt, London, Miami, New York, Paris

	1989 Sales		1989 Operating Income	
	$ mil	% of total	$ mil	% of total
US	1,002	28	(147)	48
Latin America	724	20	102	(33)
Europe	1,835	52	(261)	85
Total	**3,561**	**100**	**(306)**	**100**

WHAT

	1989 Sales	
	$ mil	% of total
Passenger	3,105	87
Freight & mail	260	7
Charter & other	197	6
Total	**3,561**	**100**

	1989 Sales		1989 Operating Income	
	$ mil	% of total	$ mil	% of total
Pan Am	3,284	91	(328)	—
Express & shuttle	310	9	21	—
Adjustments	(33)	—	—	—
Total	**3,561**	**100**	**(307)**	**100**

Subsidiaries

Pan American World Airways, Inc.
Pan Am Express, Inc. (regional services)
Pan Am Shuttle, Inc. (commuter services)

Pan American World Airways	Flight Equipment		
Type	Owned	Leased	Total
Airbus A300	—	13	13
Airbus A310	3	16	19
Boeing 727	20	70	90
Boeing 747	9	26	35
Total	**32**	**125**	**157**

RANKINGS

14th in *Fortune* 50 Transportation Cos.
232nd in *Forbes* Sales 500
863rd in *Business Week* 1000

COMPETITION

Alaska Air
AMR
Continental
Delta
HAL
KLM
NWA
Southwest
TWA
UAL
USAir

PANHANDLE EASTERN CORPORATION

OVERVIEW

Houston-based Panhandle Eastern operates one of the largest integrated natural gas pipelines in America. The company's 27,500-mile pipeline system delivers natural gas from producing areas, primarily in the Southwest and Canada, to midwestern, mid-Atlantic, and New England states. In 1989 Panhandle Eastern's 4 transmission companies delivered 1.84 trillion cubic feet of natural gas, roughly 10% of America's gas consumption.

Panhandle Eastern plans 2 new links to its pipeline system, including the Indiana-Ohio pipeline, moving about 240 million cubic feet of gas per day starting late in 1990, and a 352-mile extension from the Arkhoma Basin in Oklahoma to Independence, Mississippi, to be completed in 1991 or 1992.

Through Trunkline LNG, Panhandle Eastern imports and regasifies Algerian liquid natural gas for sale in the US. The company's Source Cogeneration subsidiary has a 14.3% interest in the Source Midland Limited Partnership cogeneration project (producing steam and electricity).

NYSE symbol: PEL
Incorporated: Delaware, 1981
Fiscal year ends: December 31

WHO

Chairman: Robert D. Hunsacker, age 65, $658,285 pay
President and CEO: Philip J. Burguieres, age 47
Group VP and CFO: Charles E. Lasseter, age 58, $258,068 pay
Group VP: George L. Mazanec, age 54
Group VP: Dennis A. Staley, age 55, $217,322 pay
Auditors: KPMG Peat Marwick
Employees: 6,100

WHEN

Panhandle Eastern first appeared in 1929 as Interstate Pipe Line Company. Renamed Panhandle Eastern Pipe Line Company (1930), it completed its first pipeline in 1931, which extended 2,100 miles from the Texas Panhandle to eastern Illinois by the end of 1939.

In the 1940s Panhandle Eastern's 2nd major pipeline extended service into Ohio and Michigan. In the 1950s the company built Trunkline Gas Company's first pipeline, from the Gulf Coast to Panhandle Eastern's system in Illinois.

In 1959 Panhandle Eastern acquired Anadarko Production Company, an oil and gas exploration firm. Panhandle Eastern and National Distillers and Chemical Corporation formed National Helium Corporation in 1961, which built a helium extraction plant near Liberal, Kansas (1963).

In the meantime, Trunkline extended its system to the Indiana-Michigan border through 2 more pipelines. By the end of 1969, the combined Panhandle-Trunkline system supplied natural gas to 12 states and Canada.

Panhandle Eastern entered a 20-year contract for liquified natural gas (LNG) with Algerian supplier Sonatrach in 1975, hoping to reduce the effects of gas shortages. The company also bought a coal mining firm (Youghiogheny and Ohio Coal, 1976) and an oil drilling firm (Dixilyn Corporation, 1977), which owned 1/3 of an offshore contractor, Dixilyn Godager Company (renamed Dixilyn-Field Godager, 1979). Panhandle Eastern completed its acquisition of Dixilyn-Field in 1980.

The company adopted the name Panhandle Eastern Corporation in 1981 and, in response to falling gas prices, suspended its Algerian LNG contract in 1983. Sonatrach subsequently filed for international arbitration.

In 1986, after rejecting an unsolicited takeover bid from Wagner and Brown, a Midland, Texas–based oil and gas firm, the company spun off Anadarko to its stockholders. In 1987 Panhandle Eastern charged $460 million against earnings as part of its settlement with Sonatrach and shut down both Dixilyn-Field and Youghiogheny and Ohio Coal (sold 1990).

In 1989, when Texas Eastern Corporation (another Houston-based pipeline company) faced a hostile takeover by Coastal Corporation, Panhandle Eastern agreed to buy the company for $3.2 billion. Founded in 1947, Texas Eastern operated a gas pipeline extending from the Gulf Coast to the Eastern Seaboard which, in combination with Panhandle Eastern's transmission lines, created a 27,500-mile system.

After a second quarter operating loss was announced in 1990, the company cut its dividend 60%.

WHERE

HQ: 5400 Westheimer Ct., PO Box 1642, Houston, TX 77251
Phone: 713-627-5400
FAX: 713-627-4145

Panhandle Eastern operates a 27,500-mile natural gas pipeline system between producing regions in the Southwest and Canada and markets throughout the Northeast and Midwest.

WHAT

	1989 Sales	
	$ mil	% of total
Natural gas sales	1,830	66
Natural gas transportation	400	14
Petroleum products	109	4
Natural gas liquids	68	2
Other	374	14
Total	**2,781**	**100**

Gas Transmission
Algonquin Gas Transmission Co.
Northern Border Pipeline Co. (22.75%)
Panhandle Eastern Pipeline Co.
Texas Eastern Transmission Corp.
Trunkline Gas Co.

Liquid Natural Gas
Pan National Gas Sales, Inc.
Trunkline LNG Co.

Related Activities
Centana Energy Corp. (gas gathering system in Kansas)
National Helium Corp. (extraction and marketing of liquid petroleum products)
Panhandle Trading Co. (nonregulated natural gas sales)
Source Cogeneration Co., Inc.
Source Midland Limited Partnership (14.3%)
TEPPCO Partners (transportation and storage of petroleum products)

HOW MUCH

	9 Yr. Growth	1980	1981	1982	1983	1984	1985	1986	1987	1988	1989
Sales ($ mil)	1.3%	2,472	3,266	3,391	3,405	3,212	2,889	2,250	1,563	1,262	2,781
Net income ($ mil)	(10.2%)	184	262	220	152	166	125	(404)	110	(172)	70
Income as % of sales	—	7.4%	8.0%	6.5%	4.5%	5.2%	4.3%	(17.9%)	7.0%	(13.6%)	2.5%
Earnings per share ($)	(16.4%)	4.86	6.52	5.36	3.64	3.88	2.83	(8.23)	2.07	(3.13)	0.97
Stock price – high ($)	—	52.25	46.75	37.00	39.00	40.00	41.50	50.25	34.75	27.38	30.75
Stock price – low ($)	—	28.38	30.38	20.50	23.88	31.00	32.38	24.25	18.25	21	20.5
Stock price – close ($)	(4.4%)	44.88	36.75	26.25	36.13	37.25	38.00	27.75	20.75	25.63	29.88
P/E – high	—	11	7	7	11	10	15	—	17	—	32
P/E – low	—	6	5	4	7	8	11	—	9	—	21
Dividends per share ($)	1.6%	1.74	2.00	2.30	2.30	2.30	2.30	2.23	2.00	2.00	2.00
Book value per share ($)	(5.3%)	26.37	31.85	34.8	36.04	37.53	37.89	18.92	19.15	14.06	16.21

1989 Year End:
Debt ratio: 66.1%
Return on equity: 6.4%
Cash (mil): $237
Current ratio: 0.69
Long-term debt (mil): $2,754
Number of shares (mil): 87
Dividends:
1989 average yield: 6.7%
1989 payout: 206.2%
Market value (mil): $2,608

Stock Price History high/low 1980-89

RANKINGS

38th in *Fortune* 50 Utilities
300th in *Forbes* Sales 500
263rd in *Business Week* 1000
894th in *Business Week* Global 1000

COMPETITION

Coastal
Columbia Gas
Occidental
Tenneco

PARAMOUNT COMMUNICATIONS INC.

OVERVIEW

From a one-time auto parts distribution business called Gulf+Western, Paramount Communications has become a leading giant in entertainment and publishing. Paramount produces, finances, and distributes motion pictures (*Raiders of the Lost Ark, Beverly Hills Cop*), TV programs ("Cheers," "Family Ties"), and TV videocassettes.

The company owns (either wholly or through joint ventures) motion picture theaters (1,100 screens) throughout the US and 11 foreign countries. Paramount's Famous Players is one of the 2 largest theater chains in Canada. Paramount also owns and operates the 20,000-seat Madison Square Garden, which includes the New York Rangers (hockey) and New York Knicks (basketball) teams.

In a joint venture with MCA, Paramount owns one of the top basic cable television networks, USA Network, which supplies entertainment to more than 50 million households in the US. Paramount also owns the world's largest book publisher, Simon & Schuster.

Paramount Communications enters the 1990s with an extensive international distribution system for its movies, home videos, and TV programs, and over $2.5 billion in cash.

NYSE symbol: PCI
Incorporated: Delaware, 1967
Fiscal year ends: October 31

WHO

Chairman and CEO: Martin S. Davis, age 62, $4,094,900 pay
EVP and Chief Administrative Officer: Donald Oresman, age 64, $1,313,000 pay
SVP and CFO: Ronald L. Nelson, $818,300 pay
Auditors: Ernst & Young
Employees: 12,000

WHERE

HQ: 15 Columbus Cir., New York, NY 10023
Phone: 212-373-8000
FAX: 212-373-8558 (Corporate Communications)

Paramount operates in the US and Canada and sells its products and services worldwide.

WHEN

Paramount Communications (formerly Gulf+Western) was founded by Charles G. Bluhdorn, an Austrian immigrant who escaped the German invasion of Austria and the bombings of London to arrive in the US at age 16 in 1942.

Bluhdorn started his first job at $15 a week and then spent some time in the import-export business. In 1956 he bought Michigan Plating and Stamping Co. (which made the rear bumper for the Studebaker) for about $1 million. Two years later he merged the company with Beard & Stone Electric Co. (a Houston auto parts warehouse) with the idea of supplying auto replacement parts for the growing automobile industry. A year later, after buying another warehouse in El Paso, the company adopted the name Gulf+Western Industries.

By 1965 Gulf+Western had 27 regional warehouses and had reached $182 million in sales. Within the next 3 years the company acquired such companies as New Jersey Zinc, South Puerto Rico Sugar, E. W. Bliss (industrial products), Consolidated Cigar, Universal American (industrial equipment), Brown Company (paper and building products), and Associates Investment (auto loans). In 1966 Gulf+Western bought struggling Paramount Pictures because Bluhdorn saw an opportunity to turn it around.

Paramount had started in 1912 when Adolph Zukor bought the US rights to a French film starring Sarah Bernhardt. Zukor's company became Paramount Pictures after merging with a company formed by Jesse L. Lasky, Samuel Goldwyn, and Cecil B. DeMille. Paramount had converted from silent movies to talkies in 1928. In the 1940s the government forced Paramount to divest its theater holdings. All efforts to fight the newly emerging television industry failed to keep movie attendance from slipping in the 1950s. Gulf+Western bought Simon & Schuster in 1975 and Madison Square Garden in 1977. Bluhdorn died in 1983 and his successor, Martin Davis, dismantled the conglomerate, selling every business except Associates, Paramount, and Simon & Schuster. In 1984 the company bought Prentice-Hall, Inc., adding to its publishing business.

In addition to publishing, the company developed its motion picture, television, and home video production business in the 1980s. In 1989 it sold The Associates to Ford for $3.35 billion and changed the company name to Paramount Communications.

WHAT

	1989 Sales		1989 Operating Income	
	$ mil	% of total	$ mil	% of total
Entertainment	2,072	61	252	99
Publishing	1,320	39	2	1
Adjustments	—	—	(61)	—
Total	**3,392**	**100**	**193**	**100**

Paramount Pictures
Home video distribution
Movie production and distribution
Television programming and distribution
Cable TV programming (USA Network, 50%)

Theaters
Cinamerica (50%)
Cinema International Corporation (51%)
Famous Players (Canada)
United Cinemas International (25%)

Television Broadcasting
KRRT-TV, San Antonio
KXTA-TV, Dallas
KXTH-TV, Houston
WDCA-TV, Washington, DC
WLFL-TV, Raleigh/Durham
WTXF-TV, Philadelphia

Madison Square Garden
Arena
Miss Universe Pageant (65%)
NY Knicks (basketball)
NY Rangers (hockey)
Television programming

Publishing
Linden Press
Pocket Books
Poseidon Press
Prentice Hall
Simon & Schuster

HOW MUCH

	9 Yr. Growth	1980	1981	1982	1983	1984	1985	1986	1987	1988	1989
Sales ($ mil)	(4.9%)	5,338	5,702	5,331	3,993	4,182	1,677	2,094	2,904	3,056	3,392
Net income ($ mil)	(29.1%)	255	291	199	260	263	130	229	356	385	12
Income as % of sales	—	4.8%	5.1%	3.7%	6.5%	6.3%	7.7%	10.9%	12.3%	12.6%	0.3%
Earnings per share ($)	(27.2%)	1.56	1.74	1.22	1.63	1.80	0.92	1.83	2.88	3.21	0.09
Stock price – high ($)	—	10.44	11.06	9.38	15.75	17.50	25.44	36.25	46.75	45.75	66.38
Stock price – low ($)	—	5.55	7.00	5.63	8.00	12.56	13.88	23.88	29.81	34.06	39.50
Stock price – close ($)	22.8%	7.94	7.94	8.38	15.06	14.19	24.88	31.69	35.56	40.63	50.50
P/E – high	—	7	6	8	10	10	28	20	16	14	738
P/E – low	—	4	4	5	5	7	15	13	10	11	439
Dividends per share ($)	9.1%	0.32	0.38	0.38	0.38	0.45	0.45	0.45	0.56	0.68	0.70
Book value per share ($)	8.7%	14.67	14.35	14.67	12.26	13.11	14.57	15.42	17.52	19.50	30.98

1989 Year End:
Debt ratio: 16.3%
Return on equity: 0.4%
Cash (mil): $2,597
Current ratio: 2.47
Long-term debt (mil): $724
Number of shares (mil): 120
Dividends:
1989 average yield: 1.4%
1989 payout: 777.8%
Market value (mil): $6,060

Stock Price History high/low 1980-89

RANKINGS

13th in *Fortune* 100 Diversified Service Cos.
244th in *Forbes* Sales 500
114th in *Business Week* 1000
300th in *Business Week* Global 1000

COMPETITION

Advance Publications	Hearst	Tele-Communications
Bertelsmann	Maxwell	Time Warner
Boston Celtics	MCA	Turner Broadcasting
CBS	McGraw-Hill	Viacom
Edward J. DeBartolo	News Corp.	Walt Disney
General Cinema	Pearson	
	Sony	

PEARSON PLC

OVERVIEW

Pearson is primarily a publisher but has interests in such diverse businesses as wax museums (Madame Tussaud's), fine china (Royal Doulton), and investment banking (Lazard Brothers). Major publishing operations include the *Financial Times*, Addison-Wesley, Penguin, and Longman.

The founder's heirs have managed the company since 1927 and control about 20% of the stock. The News Corporation preferred stock is convertible into the 17% stake in Pearson held by the Murdoch-controlled firm. Pearson affiliate Lazard Frères controls another 9%, as does Netherlands-based Elsevier. Pearson's plans to acquire the Dutch publisher were shelved because of recent weakness in Pearson stock and tax considerations.

Pearson intends to add to its 14% stake in British Satellite Broadcasting (BSB). In 1990 BSB began competing directly with The News Corporation's Sky TV. BSB expects to lose £1 billion before turning profitable in 1993.

WHEN

Samuel and George Pearson founded S. Pearson & Son in 1856, the year in which George's son, Weetman, was born. The Yorkshire-based construction firm won its first London contract in 1882, 3 years after Weetman took over the firm. S. Pearson & Son enjoyed extraordinary success in Britain and abroad, winning numerous contracts, including one to build the first tunnel under New York's Hudson River for the Pennsylvania Railroad and another to construct the main drainage system in Mexico City. By the 1890s, S. Pearson & Son was the world's largest contractor. Weetman Pearson was knighted in 1894 and later received the titles of baron (1910) and viscount (1917).

In 1901 Weetman Pearson missed a railroad connection in Laredo, Texas, and, during his 9-hour wait, heard about the nearby Spindletop oil gusher. Recalling reports of oil seepages in Mexico, he bought drilling rights on huge tracts of Mexican land. Pearson sank $25 million into his Mexican Eagle Oil Company but profited nicely when he sold it to Shell Oil (1919) after repeatedly striking oil.

In 1919 Pearson, by then Lord Cowdray, restructured S. Pearson & Son as a holding company separate from the construction business. In the 1920s the company bought a stake in Lazard Brothers, engaged in oil exploration (including the start-up and sale of US-based Amerada), and bought newspapers. Cowdray died in 1927 and, without him, so did the construction business. His heirs took over S. Pearson & Son and added unrelated businesses to a company that has been called "a collection of rich men's toys."

In 1935 Pearson helped form British Airways and sold it to the British government in 1940. In 1957 the company bought control (it now owns all) of the *Financial Times* (FT) business newspaper and, with it, 50% of *The Economist* magazine. Pearson bought 54% of Château Latour (wine, 1963), 64% of Longman Press (1968), and, after going public (1969), Penguin Books (1971), Royal Doulton (1971), Madame Tussaud's (1978), the rest of Longman (1982), and Camco (oil services, 1987).

Hutchison Whampoa (Hong Kong) bought 4.9% of Pearson in 1986, fueling takeover speculation. Pearson's Lazard Frères affiliate bought a block of Pearson stock, discouraging the would-be suitor. In 1987 Murdoch's News Corporation bought a 20% stake in Pearson, rekindling rumors of a takeover or major restructuring.

Although Murdoch never took control, Pearson improved profitability and restructured modestly in 1988 and 1989, shedding Château Latour and its oil production businesses while buying publisher Addison-Wesley (US), *Les Echos* (financial newspaper, France), and Elsevier (22%, Netherlands), and adding the Reda Pump division of TRW to its oil services operations.

HOW MUCH

£ = $1.61 (Dec. 31, 1989)	9 Yr. Growth	1980	1981	1982	1983	1984	1985	1986	1987	1988	1989
Sales (£ mil)	10.6%	591	702	719	730	843	970	953	952	1,195	1,460
Net income (£ mil)	23.4%	26	37	31	42	54	58	74	98	127	172
Income as % of sales	—	4.4%	5.3%	4.3%	5.8%	6.4%	6.0%	7.8%	10.3%	10.6%	11.8%
Earnings per share (p)	15.7%	18	23	17	23	29	30	37	47	56	67
Stock price – high (p)	—	127	121	146	205	295	433	617	1,013	796	829
Stock price – low (p)	—	95	93	202	135	202	288	393	525	620	620
Stock price – close (p)	25.4%	100	105	135	204	291	425	616	684	646	769
P/E – high	—	7	5	9	9	10	14	17	22	14	12
P/E – low	—	5	4	12	6	7	10	11	11	11	9
Dividends per share (p)	15.3%	5.0	5.0	5.6	5.6	7.0	8.5	10.0	12.0	15.0	18.0
Book value per share (p)	4.6%	167	190	172	179	211	198	216	246	192	250

1989 Year End:
Debt ratio: 37.8%
Return on equity: 30.3%
Cash (mil): £61
Long-term debt (mil): £395
Number of shares (mil): 259
Dividends:
1989 average yield: 2.3%
1989 payout: 26.9%
Market value (mil): $3,207
Sales (mil): $2,351

Stock Price History high/low 1980-89

1,200
1,000
800
600
400
200
0

Principal stock exchange: London
Incorporated: England, 1897
Fiscal year ends: December 31

WHO

Chairman and CEO: Viscount Michael Blakenham, age 52, £465,000 pay
Managing Director and COO: Frank Barlow, age 60
Finance Director: James Joll, age 53
President, Pearson Inc.; Chairman, Camco: David Veit, age 51
Auditors: Coopers & Lybrand Deloitte
Employees: 27,915

WHERE

HQ: Milbank Tower, Millbank, London SW1P 4QZ, England
Phone: 011-44-71-828-9020
FAX: 011-44-71-828-3342
US HQ (Pearson, Inc.): One Rockefeller Plaza, New York, NY 10020
US Phone: 212-713-1919
US FAX: 212-247-4616

	1989 Sales		1989 Operating Income	
	£ mil	% of total	£ mil	% of total
UK	512	35	120	44
Europe	144	10	60	22
North America	573	39	54	20
Other countries	231	16	38	14
Total	**1,460**	**100**	**272**	**100**

WHAT

	1989 Sales		1989 Operating Income	
	£ mil	% of total	£ mil	% of total
Publishing & entertainment	991	68	157	62
Oil services	262	18	27	11
Fine china	201	14	23	9
Investment banking	—	—	45	18
Adjustments	6	—	20	—
Total	**1,460**	**100**	**272**	**100**

Periodicals
The Economist (50%)
Financial Times
Les Echos
Regional UK newspapers (Westminster Press)

Book Publishers
Addison-Wesley (textbooks)
Elsevier (22.3%, business and professional books)
Longman Group (study aids, reference books)
Penguin

Entertainment
Tussauds Group (tourist attractions, wax exhibitions)

Oil Services
Camco (well completion equipment)
Reda (pumps for offshore wells)
Reed Tool (drill bits)

Fine China
Minton
Royal Crown Derby
Royal Doulton

Investment Banking
Lazard Brothers (50%, UK)
Lazard Frères (10%, US and France)

RANKINGS

585th in *Business Week* Global 1000

COMPETITION

Advance Publications
Bertelsmann
Brown-Forman
Colgate-Palmolive
Dow Jones
FMC
Maxwell
McGraw-Hill
News Corp.
Paramount
Time Warner
Investment banking companies
Oil tool companies

J. C. PENNEY COMPANY, INC.

OVERVIEW

J. C. Penney, the 6th largest retailer in the US, operates more than 2,000 drugstores (Thrift Drug, Treasury Drug), general merchandise stores, and catalog stores throughout the US and Puerto Rico. The $16.4 billion company is changing its traditional image as an inexpensive department store to that of a more fashionable store by emphasizing higher-priced, brand-name soft goods (apparel and home fashions). Catalog operations (20% of sales) still carry hard goods (consumer electronics, appliances, photography equipment, etc.).

Insurance, banking, and real estate operations generate most nonretail revenue ($302 million, 1989). The telemarketing division also serves hotel, airline, and specialty catalog companies, and the JCPenney Television Shopping Channel reaches 12.5 million homes. Subsidiary JCP Realty has interests in more than 80 projects (primarily regional shopping malls).

WHEN

In 1902 James C. Penney (1875-1971) and 2 former employers opened The Golden Rule, a dry goods store, in Kemmerer, Wyoming. Buying out his partners (1907), Penney opened stores in small communities and sold high-demand soft goods. He based customer service policy on his Baptist heritage, holding employees, called "associates," to a high moral code. Managers, usually former sales clerks, were offered 1/3 partnerships in the stores.

The company incorporated in Utah (1913) as the J. C. Penney Company, with headquarters in Salt Lake City, but moved to New York City (1914) to aid buying and financial operations. During the 1920s the company expanded rapidly to nearly 1,400 stores and publicly offered stock in 1929. By 1951 sales had surpassed $1 billion in more than 1,600 stores.

A company study of consumer trends (1957) led the chain to introduce credit plans (1958; in all stores, 1962) and hard goods (1963; appliances, furniture, and automotive parts and services).

Through the purchase of General Merchandise Company (1962, Milwaukee, mail order catalog and Treasure Island discount stores, renamed The Treasury; sold 1981), the company established a catalog service (1963). JCPenney Financial Services started from insurance companies bought in the mid-1960s. Thrift Drug (bought 1969) now has 471 stores and 4 mail order pharmacies.

The company operated food stores (bought Supermarkets Interstate, 1970; closed 1977) and expanded overseas, buying Sarma, a retail and supermarket chain in Belgium (1968, sold 1987), and starting a chain of retail stores in Italy (1969, sold 1977).

The company bought First National Bank (Harrington, Delaware, 1983), renamed JCPenney National Bank (1984). In the 1980s the company discontinued automotive services and hard goods in stores, although hard goods are still available through the catalog, and closed many downtown locations or moved them to suburban malls. Stores were classified as metropolitan (urban) or geographic (small towns or cities). New and remodeled stores emphasized higher-priced apparel and home furnishings.

The company entered the cable television shopping market (1987) through Telaction, an interactive home shopping program, later discontinued (1989). The company also established a joint venture with Shop Television Network (1987; purchased and renamed JCPenney Television Network, 1989). In 1988 the company started JCPenney Telemarketing to take catalog phone orders and provide telemarketing services for other companies.

To cut expenses the company sold the 45-story headquarters in New York City for $350 million and moved to Dallas (1988). The company is building new headquarters on a 429-acre site in Plano, Texas.

HOW MUCH

	9 Yr. Growth	1980	1981	1982	1983	1984	1985	1986	1987	1988	1989
Sales ($ mil)	4.2%	11,353	11,860	11,414	12,078	13,451	13,747	14,740	15,332	15,296	16,405
Net income ($ mil)	13.0%	268	387	430	467	435	397	530	608	807	802
Income as % of sales	—	2.4%	3.3%	3.8%	3.9%	3.2%	2.9%	3.6%	4.0%	5.3%	4.9%
Earnings per share ($)	13.2%	1.92	2.75	2.94	3.13	2.91	2.66	3.53	4.11	5.92	5.86
Stock price – high ($)	—	14.50	18.25	29.00	33.94	28.56	28.88	44.19	66.00	55.75	73.25
Stock price – low ($)	—	9.81	10.75	13.63	20.88	23.00	22.31	26.31	35.63	38.00	50.38
Stock price – close ($)	22.5%	11.75	14.31	24.19	28.31	23.19	27.75	36.13	43.38	50.63	72.75
P/E – high	—	8	7	10	11	10	11	13	16	9	13
P/E – low	—	5	4	5	7	8	8	7	9	6	9
Dividends per share ($)	10.4%	0.92	0.92	1.00	1.08	1.18	1.18	1.24	1.48	2.00	2.24
Book value per share ($)	5.4%	18.83	20.41	21.97	23.97	25.63	27.16	29.00	30.15	26.47	30.32

1989 Year End:
Debt ratio: 38.8%
Return on equity: 20.6%
Cash (mil): $408
Current ratio: 2.22
Long-term debt (mil): $2,755
Number of shares (mil): 120
Dividends:
1989 average yield: 3.1%
1989 payout: 38.2%
Market value (mil): $8,755

Stock Price History high/low 1980-89

NYSE symbol: JCP
Incorporated: Delaware, 1924
Fiscal year ends: Last Saturday in January

WHO

Chairman and CEO: William R. Howell, age 54, $1,411,423 pay
VC; COO, J. C. Penney Stores and Catalog Division: Robert B. Gill, age 58, $944,210 pay (prior to promotion)
EVP; Director, J. C. Penney Stores: James E. Oesterreicher, age 48
EVP and CFO: Robert E. Northam, age 59, $546,681 pay (prior to promotion)
President, Catalog Division: Rodney M. Birkins, age 59
Auditors: KPMG Peat Marwick
Employees: 198,000

WHERE

HQ: 14841 N. Dallas Pkwy., Dallas, TX 75240
Phone: 214-591-1000
FAX: 214-591-1315

J. C. Penney operates 1,328 J. C. Penney retail stores, 471 Thrift and Treasury drugstores, 276 freestanding catalog stores, and 6 catalog distribution centers throughout the US and Puerto Rico.

WHAT

	1989 Sales	
	$ mil	% of total
Stores & catalogs	15,116	92
Drugstores	987	6
Insurance & investment income	197	1
Bank interest & fees	105	1
Total	**16,405**	**100**

	No. of Stores	% of Total
Metropolitan market stores	693	33
Geographic (outside large metropolitan areas) market stores	635	31
Drugstores	471	23
Freestanding catalog stores	276	13
Total	**2,075**	**100**

Subsidiaries/Operations
J. C. Penney Funding Corp.
J. C. Penney Global Finance N.V.
J. C. Penney Life Insurance Co., Inc.
JCPenney National Bank (Visa and MasterCard)
J. C. Penney Overseas Finance N.V.
J. C. Penney Properties, Inc.
JCP Realty, Inc. (shopping center ventures)
Thrift Drug
Treasury Drug

RANKINGS

6th in *Fortune* 50 Retailing Cos.
32nd in *Forbes* Sales 500
60th in *Business Week* 1000
212th in *Business Week* Global 1000

COMPETITION

Campeau
Carter Hawley Hale
Dayton Hudson
Dillard
May Department Stores
R. H. Macy
Mercantile Stores
Montgomery Ward
Nordstrom
Sears
Drugstore chains
Discount and specialty stores

PENNZOIL COMPANY

OVERVIEW

Pennzoil, best known for its motor oil, is the 18th largest US oil company, an umbrella for 4 wholly owned subsidiaries in the petroleum and minerals businesses.

Pennzoil Exploration and Production (PEPCO) searches for oil in Texas, Arkansas, New Mexico, North Dakota, Minnesota, and the Gulf of Mexico. It has just begun to explore in Indonesia.

Pennzoil Products manufactures the nation's best-selling motor oil, with about 20% of the market. Golfer Arnold Palmer is the longtime spokesman in the company's commercials. Pennzoil also owns 80% of Jiffy Lube International, the largest franchiser of quick-lube operations, with more than 1,000 independently owned outlets. Pennzoil is selling its Purolator automotive products business.

Pennzoil Sulphur extracts sulphur in far West Texas, mostly to make fertilizer. Another subsidiary, Richland Development, oversees real estate and mineral rights, including a gold and silver deposit in Borneo.

NYSE symbol: PZL
Incorporated: Delaware, 1968
Fiscal year ends: December 31

WHO

Chairman: J. Hugh Liedtke, age 68
President and CEO: James L. Pate, age 54, $269,200 pay (prior to promotion)
Group VP, Oil and Gas: William H. Schell, age 63
Group VP, Sulphur: Robert Semrad, age 63, $288,900 pay
Group VP, Motor Oil and Automotive Products: Richard A. Valentine, age 64, $219,200 pay
SVP Finance and Principal Financial Officer: David P. Alderson II, age 40
Auditors: Arthur Andersen & Co.
Employees: 10,700

WHEN

The post-WWII oil boom in West Texas attracted brothers J. Hugh and Bill Liedtke and a Connecticut scion named George Bush. Anxious to make their fortunes, they formed Zapata Petroleum. Zapata hit big with more than 120 producing wells in the Jameson Field in Coke County.

Zapata expanded with a subsidiary that drilled in the Gulf of Mexico. In 1959 Bush bought out the subsidiary and moved to Houston where he later embarked on a political career that continues in the White House. The Liedtkes set their sights on South Penn Oil of Oil City, Pennsylvania — a rusty relic from the 1911 dissolution of Standard Oil. Enlisting the support of oilman J. Paul Getty, the Liedtkes took control of South Penn in 1963, merged it with Zapata, renamed it Pennzoil in honor of the lubricant it sold, and moved the headquarters to Houston.

In 1965 J. Hugh Liedtke engineered the historic takeover of Shreveport-based United Gas Pipeline, 5 times the size of Pennzoil. Blessed with a large pipeline system and vast mineral interests, United Gas was beset with lethargic management.

Using a takeover tactic that would break ground for a generation of corporate raiding, Liedtke launched a hostile cash tender offer. Pennzoil invited United Gas shareholders to sell their shares at a price higher than the market price.

Shareholders tendered 5 times the number of shares that Pennzoil wanted to buy. Undaunted, the Liedtkes raised the additional funds to buy 42% of United Gas stock. Pennzoil spun off a scaled-down United in 1974.

In the late 1960s Pennzoil pioneered financing of oil exploration with the use of subsidiaries (with colorful acronyms like POGO and PLATO) that raised money for speculative drilling by selling stock directly to the public. Shareholders in the subsidiaries were given some security with rights to Pennzoil stock if the risky drilling proved unsuccessful.

In 1983 J. Hugh Liedtke hoped to purchase Getty Oil, the company begun by his old benefactor, and thought he had a deal. Texaco bought Getty instead. Pennzoil sued, and in 1985 a Texas jury awarded a record $10.53 billion in damages. Texaco sought refuge in bankruptcy court, emerging only after it had settled with Pennzoil for $3 billion.

Liedtke stepped down as CEO in 1988 but remained chairman as Pennzoil determined how to spend its booty. In 1989 Pennzoil spent $2.1 billion for 8.8% of Chevron, but Liedtke denied that his company had a takeover in mind. With Liedtke's swashbuckling history at Pennzoil, Chevron wasn't convinced and filed suit in 1989 to keep him at bay. Much of the suit was dismissed in 1990, and in July of that year Pennzoil announced that it intended to buy more of Chevron.

WHERE

HQ: Pennzoil Place, PO Box 2967, Houston, TX 77252
Phone: 713-546-4000
FAX: 713-546-7591

Exploration and Production: Drilling in 13 states and offshore, and in 4 foreign countries.

Products: 3 refineries — Rouseville, PA; Shreveport, LA; and Roosevelt, UT. Pennzoil motor oil sold internationally.

Sulphur: Mining in Culberson County, TX; processing in Galveston, TX, and in Antwerp, Belgium.

Richland Development: Acreage in Pennsylvania, West Virginia, Louisiana, and New Mexico; gold and silver deposits in Borneo.

WHAT

	1989 Sales		1989 Operating Income	
	$ mil	% of total	$ mil	% of total
Oil & gas	348	15	97	17
Automotive prods.	1,391	60	80	14
Sulphur	274	12	76	14
Other	317	13	309	55
Adjustments	(345)	—	(407)	—
Total	**1,985**	**100**	**155**	**100**

Brand Names
Gumout carburetor cleaner and automotive products
Jiffy Lube quick lubrication shops
Pennzoil gasoline (East Coast and upper Midwest)
Pennzoil motor oils, lubricants
Wolf's Head lubricants and related products

HOW MUCH

	9 Yr. Growth	1980	1981	1982	1983	1984	1985	1986	1987	1988	1989
Sales ($ mil)	(2.5%)	2,483	2,682	2,269	2,317	2,349	2,239	1,908	1,809	2,124	1,985
Net income ($ mil)	(3.0%)	309	222	189	164	214	188	69	46	(187)	236
Income as % of sales	—	12.4%	8.3%	8.3%	7.1%	9.1%	8.4%	3.6%	2.5%	(8.8%)	11.9%
Earnings per share ($)	0.4%	5.84	4.23	3.60	3.03	3.89	3.96	1.28	0.72	(5.22)	6.06
Stock price – high ($)	—	62.50	58.25	50.25	42.50	45.38	72.00	91.00	95.00	79.13	88.88
Stock price – low ($)	—	30.00	35.25	23.63	31.25	30.75	40.50	48.13	38.50	65.25	71.63
Stock price – close ($)	6.5%	50.38	48.00	35.13	34.00	44.50	64.00	67.00	71.00	71.75	88.63
P/E – high	—	11	14	14	14	12	18	71	132	—	15
P/E – low	—	5	8	7	10	8	10	38	53	—	12
Dividends per share ($)	4.6%	2.00	2.20	2.20	2.20	2.20	2.20	2.20	2.20	2.60	3.00
Book value per share ($)	6.6%	19.88	21.55	22.99	23.88	21.38	18.23	16.79	7.67	35.67	35.23

1989 Year End:
Debt ratio: 58.2%
Return on equity: 17.1%
Cash (mil): $469
Current ratio: 2.62
Long-term debt (mil): $1,786
Number of shares (mil): 36
Dividends:
1989 average yield: 3.4%
1989 payout: 49.5%
Market value (mil): $3,225

Stock Price History high/low 1980-89

100 90 80 70 60 50 40 30 20 10 0

RANKINGS

163rd in *Fortune* 500 Industrial Cos.
459th in *Fortune* Global 500 Industrial Cos.
352nd in *Forbes* Sales 500
213th in *Business Week* 1000
740th in *Business Week* Global 1000

COMPETITION

Amoco	Du Pont	Sun
Ashland	Exxon	Texaco
Atlantic Richfield	Mobil	Unocal
British Petroleum	Occidental	USX
Chevron	Phillips	
Coastal	Royal Dutch/Shell	

PEPSICO, INC.

OVERVIEW

PepsiCo is a major force in 3 different markets: soft drinks, fast-food restaurants, and snack foods. The company's respected and internationally known products generate retail sales of $41 billion.

Soft drinks are PepsiCo's leading segment, with 38% of sales and 36% of profits. The company's soft drinks, including Pepsi, Diet Pepsi, Mountain Dew, Slice, and 7UP (outside the US), command approximately 33% of the US market and 15% of the international market.

PepsiCo's restaurant segment, with 34% of sales and 22% of profits, has more units (18,483) than any other restaurant system in the world. The segment consists of Pizza Hut (the world's leading pizza chain), Kentucky Fried Chicken (the world's leading chicken chain), and Taco Bell (the leading US Mexican-food chain).

PepsiCo's snack food segment (Frito-Lay), generating 28% of company sales and 42% of profits, accounts for almost 13% of the total US snack industry. Frito-Lay dominates the US snack chip market with such respected names as Fritos, Lay's, Ruffles, and Doritos, and is more than 4 times the size of its nearest competitor.

NYSE symbol: PEP
Incorporated: North Carolina, 1986
Fiscal year ends: December 30

WHO

Chairman and CEO: D. Wayne Calloway, age 54, $1,505,096 pay
President, Worldwide Foods: Michael H. Jordan, age 52, $892,131 pay
President, Worldwide Beverages: Roger A. Enrico, age 45, $821,133 pay
EVP and CFO: Robert G. Dettmer, age 58, $587,582 pay
Auditors: KPMG Peat Marwick
Employees: 266,000

WHEN

In New Bern, North Carolina, pharmacist Caleb D. Bradham invented Pepsi in 1898. Bradham named his new drink Pepsi-Cola (he claimed it cured dyspepsia) and registered his trademark in 1903.

Following Coca-Cola's example, Bradham developed a system of bottling franchises. By WWI 300 bottlers had signed agreements with Pepsi-Cola. After the war Bradham stockpiled sugar as a safeguard against rising costs. The price of sugar plunged in 1920, and Bradham was forced to sell the company in 1923.

Pepsi existed on the brink of ruin under various owners for the next decade, until the Loft candy company bought Pepsi in 1931. The company's fortunes took a turn for the better in 1934 when, in the midst of the Depression, it doubled the size of its bottles to 12 ounces without raising the 5¢ price. In 1939 Pepsi introduced the world's first radio jingle. In 1941 Loft merged with its Pepsi subsidiary and became the Pepsi-Cola Company.

Pepsi started to produce drinks in cans in 1948. Two years later former Coca-Cola executive Alfred N. Steele became president of the company. Steele introduced the slogan "Be Sociable, Have a Pepsi" and in 1954 put his new wife, actress Joan Crawford, to work as a Pepsi spokesperson.

Donald M. Kendall, who became president of Pepsi in 1963, contributed his skills in efficient management and advertising. Kendall, a close friend of Richard Nixon, persuaded Soviet premier Nikita Khrushchev to down a Pepsi for the cameras at the Moscow Trade Fair and turned Pepsi's attention to young people ("The Pepsi Generation").

In 1965 Pepsi acquired Frito-Lay and became PepsiCo. Dallas-based Frito-Lay was created when Elmer Doolin (who had discovered Fritos at a cafe near the Mexican border in 1932) and Herman Lay (HW Lay & Company) joined efforts in 1960.

During the early 1970s Kendall broke into the Soviet market by agreeing to distribute Stolichnaya vodka in the US in exchange for Pepsi in the USSR. With the purchase of Pizza Hut (1977), Taco Bell (1978), and Kentucky Fried Chicken (1986), PepsiCo built a system of over 18,000 restaurants, the world's largest group and a major new market for Pepsi-Cola.

When Coca-Cola changed its formula in 1985, Pepsi stepped up the competition with its longtime archrival, claiming victory in the cola wars. In the 1990s PepsiCo hopes to penetrate the vast European snack food market while increasing its share of the international soft drink and restaurant markets.

WHERE

HQ: Purchase, NY 10577
Phone: 914-253-2000
FAX: 914-253-2070

PespiCo's soft drinks are sold in almost 150 countries. The company directly operates 6,383 restaurants in the US and 1,285 abroad.

	1989 Sales		1989 Operating Income	
	$ mil	% of total	$ mil	% of total
US	12,519	82	1,617	84
Western Europe	739	5	56	3
Canada, Mexico	899	6	126	6
Other countries	1,085	7	133	7
Adjustments	—	—	(153)	—
Total	**15,242**	**100**	**1,779**	**100**

WHAT

	1989 Sales		1989 Operating Income	
	$ mil	% of total	$ mil	% of total
Soft drinks	5,776	38	690	36
Snack foods	4,215	28	821	42
Restaurants	5,251	34	421	22
Adjustments	—	—	(154)	—
Total	**15,242**	**100**	**1,779**	**100**

Brand Names

Soft Drinks
Diet Mountain Dew
Diet Mug
Diet Pepsi
Diet Slice
H2Oh!
Miranda
Mountain Dew
Mountain Dew Sport
Mug
Pepsi A.M.
Pepsi-Cola
7UP (outside US)
Slice

Snack Foods
Chee•Tos
Doritos
Fritos
Grandma's
Lay's
Ruffles
Sabritas
Santitas
Smartfood
Smiths
Sunchips
Tostitos
Walkers

Restaurants
Kentucky Fried Chicken
Pizza Hut
Taco Bell

HOW MUCH

	9 Yr. Growth	1980	1981	1982	1983	1984	1985	1986	1987	1988	1989
Sales ($ mil)	11.0%	5,975	7,027	7,499	7,896	7,699	8,057	9,291	11,485	13,007	15,242
Net income ($ mil)	13.4%	292	333	224	284	207	420	458	605	762	901
Income as % of sales	—	4.9%	4.7%	3.0%	3.6%	2.7%	5.2%	4.9%	5.3%	5.9%	5.9%
Earnings per share ($)	13.8%	1.06	1.20	0.80	1.00	0.73	1.50	1.74	2.30	2.89	3.39
Stock price – high ($)	—	9.50	13.08	16.67	13.42	15.25	25.13	35.63	42.25	43.63	65.88
Stock price – low ($)	—	6.67	9.00	10.38	10.88	11.50	13.54	22.00	25.50	30.00	37.75
Stock price – close ($)	24.2%	9.08	12.13	11.92	12.75	14.29	24.25	26.00	33.38	39.50	64.00
P/E – high	—	9	11	21	13	21	17	20	18	15	19
P/E – low	—	6	8	13	11	16	9	13	11	10	11
Dividends per share ($)	9.6%	0.42	0.47	0.53	0.54	0.56	0.59	0.63	0.67	0.80	0.96
Book value per share ($)	12.2%	5.22	5.97	5.89	6.39	6.58	6.98	7.91	9.63	12.03	14.76

1989 Year End:
Debt ratio: 61.0%
Return on equity: 25.3%
Cash (mil): $1,534
Current ratio: 0.96
Long-term debt (mil): $6,077
Number of shares (mil): 264
Dividends:
1989 average yield: 1.5%
1989 payout: 28.3%
Market value (mil): $16,876

Stock Price History high/low 1980-89

RANKINGS

23rd in *Fortune* 500 Industrial Cos.
35th in *Forbes* Sales 500
63rd in *Fortune* Global 500 Industrial Cos.
29th in *Business Week* 1000
54th in *Business Week* Global 1000

COMPETITION

Anheuser-Busch
Borden
Coca-Cola
Dr Pepper/7Up
General Mills
Grand Metropolitan
McDonald's
Seagram
Wendy's

PETER KIEWIT SONS' INC.

OVERVIEW

Omaha-based Peter Kiewit Sons' is one of the largest US heavy-construction contractors, and its Continental Can operation is one of the largest producers of paper and plastic packaging products. Since the death of the founder's son Peter Kiewit in 1979, the company has been owned by its employees.

Kiewit Construction, the company's original business, acts as general contractor on many projects, 70% of which are public. Transportation accounts for 46% of Kiewit's contracts. Other projects include dams and water treatment plants. Digital networks installed by Metropolitan Fiber Systems (80% owned by Kiewit Construction) allow central business district customers to bypass local Bell monopolies.

Continental Can makes plastic containers for detergents and chemicals and containers for drinks, foods, and tennis balls. It also makes a wide range of disposable cups (CONOCUP) and plates and is the world leader in closures (White Cap) for glass and plastic food containers.

Kiewit also mines coal in 3 states and manages timberland in the southeastern US.

WHEN

Peter Kiewit, the son of Dutch immigrants, founded a masonry business in 1884 in Omaha, Nebraska. By 1912 several of the founder's 6 children were working at the company, and the name was changed to Peter Kiewit & Sons. One of the sons, Peter, started working at the company as a bricklayer at 19. He went to Dartmouth for a year, but grew bored and came back to work at the company full-time. He changed the company name to Peter Kiewit Sons' in honor of his father in 1931, after the rest of the family had left.

During the Depression, Peter Kiewit Sons' worked on huge public works projects initiated by the Roosevelt administration to put unemployed people back to work. In the 1940s the company focused on defense wartime emergency projects, including 1,500 buildings at Fort Lewis (built in 90 days) and the Martin Bomber Plant in Omaha (built in 6 months in 1941).

One of the company's most difficult projects was the construction of Thule Air Force Base in Greenland, above the Arctic Circle, where 5,000 men worked 12 hours a day and 7 days a week for more than 2 years beginning in 1951. During the 1950s and 1960s Kiewit took on bigger and bigger projects. The company was a contractor for the interstate highway system and in 1952 was awarded the largest contract ever in the US, a $1.2 billion gas diffusion plant in Portsmouth, Ohio.

In the 1970s the company faced charges of overruns and bid-rigging and was fined $5 million for rigging bids on Army Corps of Engineers projects in 1970 and 1976.

Peter Kiewit died in 1979, leaving instructions that the company, which was already largely employee-owned, should remain under employee control and that no one employee could own more than 10% of the company. Kiewit's stock, when contributed back to the company, increased the value of all the other employees' holdings, making many of them millionaires.

Under Walter Scott, who became chairman, president, and CEO in 1979, Peter Kiewit has continued to grow. In 1984 British takeover artist Sir James Goldsmith made a bid for the Continental Group, a diversified company that made cans and boxes, ran timber operations, and owned gas and oil operations. Peter Kiewit Sons' intervened to purchase the company with the help of developer David Murdoch (whom Kiewit later bought out). Kiewit sold off many of Continental's businesses, keeping the packaging and timber operations.

In 1990 Kiewit decided to dispose of the remainder of Continental's canning operations, selling its US and Canadian food and beverage metal can divisions to Crown Cork & Seal for $636 million and selling its European packaging operations (primarily metal cans) to Ball Corporation for just over $1 billion.

With these sales the only remaining parts of Continental's core packaging business retained by Kiewit are the plastic container, disposable paper container, bottle closure, and plastic bottle businesses.

HOW MUCH

	5 Yr. Growth	1980	1981	1982	1983	1984	1985	1986	1987	1988	1989
Sales ($ mil)	21.3%	—	—	—	—	1,926	4,377	4,661	4,682	4,820	5,058
Net income ($ mil)	(0.4%)	—	—	—	—	143	101	156	124	240	140
Income as % of sales	—	—	—	—	—	7.4%	2.3%	3.3%	2.6%	5.0%	2.8%

1990 Year End:
Debt ratio: 20.9%
Return on equity: 13.0%
Cash (mil): $885
Current ratio: 1.78
Long-term debt (mil): $302

Sales ($ mil) 1984-89

0
1,000
2,000
3,000
4,000
5,000
6,000

Private company
Incorporated: Delaware, 1941
Fiscal year ends: Last Saturday in December

WHO

Chairman and President: Walter Scott, Jr., age 58, $928,125 pay
VC: Donald L. Sturm, age 58, $755,223 pay
VC: William L. Grewcock, age 64, $520,770 pay
VP and CFO: Robert E. Julian, age 50
Auditors: Coopers & Lybrand
Employees: 28,000

WHERE

HQ: 1000 Kiewit Plaza, Omaha, NE 68131
Phone: 402-342-2052
FAX: 402-271-2829

Kiewit Construction performs work in the US, Canada, and Denmark. Mining is carried out in Montana, Texas, and Wyoming; timber operations are centered in the southeastern US. Continental Can has plants and sales worldwide.

	1989 Sales		1989 Operating Income	
	$ mil	% of total	$ mil	% of total
US	3,506	69	207	72
Europe	1,375	27	57	20
Canada	177	4	5	2
Other	—	—	16	6
Adjustments	—	—	(136)	—
Total	**5,058**	**100**	**149**	**100**

WHAT

	1989 Sales		1989 Operating Income	
	$ mil	% of total	$ mil	% of total
Packaging	3,357	67	111	39
Construction	1,491	29	80	28
Coal mining	205	4	72	25
Timberlands	5	—	22	8
Adjustments	—	—	(136)	—
Total	**5,058**	**100**	**149**	**100**

Subsidiaries

Kiewit Construction Group, Inc.
General contractor on highway, airport, mass-transit, and other public and private sector projects

Kiewit Mining Group, Inc.
Operates strip mines in 3 states

Continental Can, Inc.
Produces paper and plastic containers and sells packaging equipment and systems

Metropolitan Fiber Systems, Inc. (80%)
Installs and operates fiber-optic networks in major US cities

Kiewit Continental, Inc.
Peter Kiewit Sons' manages 103,000 acres of forest in the Southeast.

RANKINGS

14th in *Forbes* 400 US Private Cos.

COMPETITION

Bechtel
Dresser
Halliburton
Johnson Controls
Owens-Illinois
Reynolds Metals
Other coal mining companies

PFIZER INC.

OVERVIEW

New York City–based Pfizer is a major drug producer (ranking 5th in sales in the US and 7th worldwide). Its top-selling products in 1989 were the arthritis pain reliever Feldene ($612 million) and antihypertensive Procardia ($420 million).

Pfizer's health care products (64% of 1989 sales) include prescription drugs as well as medical devices such as heart valves, catheters, and blood oxygenators. Other company businesses include consumer products (*e.g.*, Visine, Ben-Gay), veterinary drugs, specialty minerals, and chemicals (such as the bulking agent polydextrose, used in dietetic foods).

Foreign sales are 45% of the total; Pfizer's largest market outside the US is Japan.

Pfizer had 2 new products approved by the FDA in early 1990: the antifungal Diflucan and Procardia XL, a longer-acting version of Procardia. Products for septic shock, allergies, and an antidepressant that may be useful in weight control are under FDA review. Pfizer spent 9.4% of sales on R&D in 1989. In July, 1990 Pfizer announced the sale of its citric acid business to Archer-Daniels-Midland.

NYSE symbol: PFE
Incorporated: Delaware, 1942
Fiscal year ends: December 31

WHO

Chairman and CEO: Edmund T. Pratt, Jr., age 63, $1,435,200 pay
President: Gerald D. Laubach, age 64, $1,076,400 pay
SVP Finance: Jean-Paul Vallès, age 53, $559,000 pay
Auditors: KPMG Peat Marwick
Employees: 42,100

WHEN

Charles Pfizer and his cousin, confectioner Charles Erhart, started to manufacture chemicals in Brooklyn in 1849. For the next 90 years Pfizer's products included camphor, citric acid (business sold in 1990), and santonin (an early antiparasitic). The company was incorporated in 1900 as Chas. Pfizer & Co. Pfizer was propelled into the modern drug business when the company was asked in 1941 to adapt its fermentation technology to mass-produce penicillin for the war effort.

After WWII Pfizer continued to make penicillin as well as streptomycin, most of which it sold to other pharmaceutical houses. The first Pfizer label appeared on penicillin and streptomycin exported to Europe in the late 1940s. Pfizer researchers discovered Terramycin, which the company introduced in 1950 and sold through a small but aggressive sales force. The sales campaign included expensive ads in medical journals; Terramycin was one of the first drugs promoted in that fashion.

Pfizer bought the drug firm Roerig in 1953, its first major acquisition. In the early 1950s the company opened its first overseas branches (Canada, Mexico, Cuba, the UK, and Belgium), and began manufacturing in Europe, Japan, and South America. By the mid-1960s Pfizer had worldwide sales of over $200 million in 100 countries.

Beginning in the late 1950s Pfizer made Salk and Sabin polio vaccines and began adding new pharmaceuticals, including Diabinese (antidiabetic, 1958) and Vibramycin (antibiotic, 1967). Pfizer acquired 14 other companies in the early 1960s, including makers of specialty metals, consumer products (Ben-Gay, Desitin), and cosmetics (Coty). The company bought its first hospital products company, Howmedica, in 1972 and heart valve maker Shiley in 1979. Failures of Shiley valves have subjected Pfizer to lawsuits in 1990.

Growth slowed during the 1970s, although sales had reached $2 billion by 1977. A new chairman, Edmund Pratt, increased R&D expenditures, resulting in the development of several new drugs, including Minipress (antihypertensive, 1975), Feldene (arthritis pain, 1982), and Glucotrol (antidiabetic, 1984). Licensing agreements with foreign drug companies allowed Pfizer to sell Procardia (for angina and hypertension, developed by Bayer in Germany) and Cefobid (antibiotic, from Japan). In the 1980s Pfizer expanded its hospital products division, buying 18 product lines or companies. The company bought Plax (mouthwash) in 1988 and has since introduced its oral care products in 14 countries. Led by Plax, foreign consumer product sales increased 53% in 1989.

WHERE

HQ: 235 E. 42nd St., New York, NY 10017
Phone: 212-573-2323
FAX: 212-573-7851

	1989 Sales		1989 Operating Income	
	$ mil	% of total	$ mil	% of total
US	3,097	55	565	60
Europe	1,190	21	239	25
Asia	876	15	83	9
Other countries	509	9	61	6
Adjustments	—	—	4	—
Total	**5,672**	**100**	**952**	**100**

WHAT

	1989 Sales		1989 Operating Income	
	$ mil	% of total	$ mil	% of total
Health care	3,629	64	826	87
Animal health	489	9	57	6
Chemicals	510	9	39	4
Consumer products	628	11	67	7
Minerals	416	7	(37)	(4)
Total	**5,672**	**100**	**952**	**100**

Prescription Drugs
Cardura
Cefobid
Feldene
Glucotrol
Minipress
Procardia
Terramycin
Unasyn
Vibramycin

Medical Devices
American Medical Systems
Deknatel
Howmedica
Infusaid
Schneider
Shiley
Valleylab

Consumer Products
Barbasol
Ben-Gay
Coty
Desitin
Plax
Unisom
Visine

HOW MUCH

	9 Yr. Growth	1980	1981	1982	1983	1984	1985	1986	1987	1988	1989
Sales ($ mil)	7.2%	3,029	3,250	3,454	3,750	3,855	4,025	4,476	4,920	5,385	5,672
Net income ($ mil)	11.5%	255	274	333	447	508	580	660	690	791	681
Income as % of sales	—	8.4%	8.4%	9.6%	11.9%	13.2%	14.4%	14.7%	14.0%	14.7%	12.0%
Earnings per share ($)	10.1%	1.70	1.79	2.11	2.72	3.07	3.43	3.89	4.07	4.70	4.03
Stock price – high ($)	—	26.88	27.44	40.31	44.75	42.38	56.25	72.88	77.00	60.25	75.75
Stock price – low ($)	—	16.00	20.00	24.94	33.56	29.38	37.63	46.25	41.25	47.38	54.00
Stock price – close ($)	11.2%	26.75	26.63	34.44	35.75	42.25	50.63	61.00	46.63	58.00	69.50
P/E – high	—	16	15	19	16	14	16	19	19	13	19
P/E – low	—	9	11	12	12	10	11	12	10	10	13
Dividends per share ($)	13.2%	0.72	0.80	0.92	1.16	1.32	1.48	1.64	1.80	2.00	2.20
Book value per share ($)	11.0%	10.70	11.32	12.82	13.67	15.45	17.87	20.70	23.60	26.00	27.44

1989 Year End:
Debt ratio: 4.0%
Return on equity: 15.1%
Cash (mil): $1,058
Current ratio: 1.55
Long-term debt (mil): $191
Number of shares (mil): 165
Dividends:
1989 average yield: 3.2%
1989 payout: 54.6%
Market value (mil): $11,489

Stock Price History high/low 1980-89

80
70
60
50
40
30
20
10
0

RANKINGS

80th in *Fortune* 500 Industrial Cos.
219th in *Fortune* Global 500 Industrial Cos.
154th in *Forbes* Sales 500
46th in *Business Week* 1000
136th in *Business Week* Global 1000

COMPETITION

Abbott Labs
American Cyanamid
American Home Products
C. R. Bard
Baxter
Bayer
Becton, Dickinson
Bristol-Myers Squibb
Dow Chemical
Du Pont
Eli Lilly
Glaxo
Hoechst
Johnson & Johnson
Merck
Monsanto
Rhône-Poulenc
Roche Holding
Schering-Plough
SmithKline Beecham
Upjohn
Warner-Lambert

PHELPS DODGE CORPORATION

OVERVIEW

Phoenix-based Phelps Dodge, the largest copper producer in North America, made a company record of one billion pounds of copper in 1989, accounting for approximately 35% of copper mined in the US. The company leads the world in the production of copper rod (used for electrical wire and cable) and is a major supplier of sulfuric acid, and copper in concentrate form. In addition, Phelps produces gold, silver, molybdenum, fluorspar, lead, and zinc from its mines in 23 countries.

During the past few years, the company has made an effort to reduce its production costs. In 1989 Phelps produced about 24% of its copper from the solvent extraction/electrowinning "SX/EW" process, which is substantially less expensive than the traditional mining techniques.

In the late 1980s Phelps added less cyclical businesses to its core mining business. Its resulting Industries segment includes Accuride, North America's largest steel rim and wheel manufacturer; Columbian Chemicals, the world's 2nd largest producer of carbon black (used to strengthen rubber); and Hudson Conductors, the world's leading specialty high-temperature conductors and alloys manufacturer.

NYSE symbol: PD
Incorporated: New York, 1885
Fiscal year ends: December 31

WHO

Chairman and CEO: Douglas C. Yearley, age 54, $1,111,236 pay
President and COO: Leonard R. Judd, age 50, $990,978 pay
SVP and CFO: Thomas M. St. Clair, age 54
SVP: Bernard G. Rethore, age 48
SVP: Patrick J. Ryan, age 53, $651,900 pay
Auditors: Price Waterhouse
Employees: 13,288

WHEN

In 1821, Anson Greene Phelps established a trading business between New York and England, exporting cotton and importing metals (particularly tin). In 1834 Phelps formed a partnership with sons-in-law William Dodge and Daniel James (James took charge of the England office), founding the firm Phelps Dodge & Company. In the 1830s Phelps Dodge invested in coal, iron, and timber in Pennsylvania. It established 2 metal manufacturing companies in Connecticut in the early 1840s: Ansonia Brass & Battery and Ansonia Manufacturing. Their products included the soft copper wire used for the first transcontinental telegraph (1861). Anson Phelps died in 1853.

Although still principally an East Coast mercantile business, Phelps Dodge bought 2 copper mines near Bisbee, Arizona: the Atlanta (1881) and the Copper Queen (1885). The company expanded its mining operations into the northern Sonora region of Mexico (founding Moctezuma Copper, 1895), the Morenci area of eastern Arizona (purchasing Detroit Copper Mining, 1897), and the Dawson, New Mexico area (buying coal miner Stag Canon Fuel).

In 1901 Phelps Dodge built a copper smelter near Bisbee, and the town of Douglas (named for a company geologist) grew up around the site. The company also built railroad connections to transport its copper, including the El Paso and Southwestern (1903). Copper mining was so successful that Phelps Dodge closed its original East Coast businesses in 1906.

In 1921 the company purchased the properties of Arizona Copper and in 1930 bought Nichols Copper, which had a modern refinery in El Paso. To increase its ore reserves, the company purchased Calumet & Arizona Mining (with properties in Bisbee and Ajo, Arizona, 1931) and mines in the Rio Verde Valley near Jerome, Arizona. In the 1950s the company expanded into other countries. In 1971 Phelps Dodge bought Western Nuclear (uranium mining) and a 40% interest in Consolidated Aluminum.

From 1982 to 1984 Phelps Dodge suffered its only losses in recent years because of the depressed metals market. To reduce costs, the company moved its headquarters from New York to Phoenix, and to lessen its dependence on copper, diversified, purchasing Columbian Chemicals (carbon black, 1986), Accuride (truck wheels and rims, 1988), and Hudson International Conductors (specialty wire and cable conductors, 1989).

WHERE

HQ: 2600 N. Central Ave., Phoenix, AZ 85004
Phone: 602-234-8100
FAX: 602-234-8337

Phelps Dodge operates mines and manufacturing plants in 23 countries.

	1989 Sales	
	$ mil	% of total
US	2,189	81
Foreign	511	19
Total	**2,700**	**100**

WHAT

	1989 Sales		1989 Operating Income	
	$ mil	% of total	$ mil	% of total
Mining	1,519	56	282	68
Manufacturing & chemicals	1,181	44	131	32
Adjustments	—	—	343	—
Total	**2,700**	**100**	**756**	**100**

Phelps Dodge Mining Company
Copper mining, smelting, and refining
Copper rod production
Silver, gold, molybdenum, and sulfuric acid (as by-products of copper operations)
Fluorspar, gold, silver, lead, zinc, and copper (from foreign mines)
Exploration for metals and minerals

Phelps Dodge Industries
Accuride Corp.
Truck wheels and rims
Columbian Chemicals Company
Carbon black
Synthetic iron oxide
Phelps Dodge Magnet Wire Company
Copper and aluminum wire
Hudson International Conductors
Specialty wire and cable conductors
Phelps Dodge International Corporation
Interests in foreign wire and cable producers

HOW MUCH

	9 Yr. Growth	1980	1981	1982	1983	1984	1985	1986	1987	1988	1989
Sales ($ mil)	7.2%	1,440	1,439	958	977	910	887	846	1,612	2,320	2,700
Net income ($ mil)	12.7%	91	59	(74)	(64)	(207)	19	42	151	420	267
Income as % of sales	—	6.3%	4.1%	(7.8%)	(6.5%)	(22.8%)	2.1%	4.9%	9.3%	18.1%	9.9%
Earnings per share ($)	6.6%	4.20	2.61	(3.59)	(2.76)	(8.81)	0.21	1.06	4.17	11.28	7.46
Stock price – high ($)	—	48.25	48.50	34.00	34.00	27.88	24.00	32.50	56.00	53.75	78.63
Stock price – low ($)	—	25.00	31.13	18.25	22.50	12.88	13.50	16.00	20.63	32.50	51.38
Stock price – close ($)	5.2%	37.63	33.63	28.13	25.25	13.88	23.00	20.75	47.00	53.00	59.13
P/E – high	—	11	19	—	—	—	114	31	13	5	11
P/E – low	—	6	12	—	—	—	64	15	5	3	7
Dividends per share ($)	26.5%	1.55	1.60	0.30	0.00	0.00	0.00	0.00	0.15	0.95	12.85
Book value per share ($)	(2.6%)	49.30	50.09	44.94	39.81	29.16	28.78	30.36	35.37	47.10	39.00

1989 Year End:
Debt ratio: 24.2%
Return on equity: 17.3%
Cash (mil): $13
Current ratio: 1.44
Long-term debt (mil): $432
Number of shares (mil): 35
Dividends:
1989 average yield: 21.7%
1989 payout: 172.3%
Market value (mil): $2,047

RANKINGS

165th in *Fortune* 500 Industrial Cos.
462nd in *Fortune* Global 500 Industrial Cos.
309th in *Forbes* Sales 500
290th in *Business Week* 1000
978th in *Business Week* Global 1000

COMPETITION

AMAX	Broken Hill
ASARCO	Cyprus Minerals
Anglo American	FMC

PHILIP MORRIS COMPANIES, INC.

OVERVIEW

Philip Morris Companies is a holding company that operates consumer product powerhouses Philip Morris, General Foods, Kraft, Oscar Mayer, and Miller Brewing. With revenues of $39 billion and net earnings of almost $3 billion in 1989, Philip Morris is the largest consumer packaged-goods company and the largest cigarette company in the world.

Tobacco products, Philip Morris's traditional business, account for 40% of revenues and 72% of operating income. Marlboro, the company's flagship brand, is the world's best-selling consumer packaged product and is the best-selling cigarette brand domestically, with over a 26% market share.

Food products generate 51% of revenues and 23% of operating profit. General Foods produces a prolific line of packaged products and is the largest coffee processor and marketer in the US. Kraft produces dairy and related products, and Oscar Mayer produces specialty meats.

Miller Brewing (8% of revenues and 3% of profits) is the 2nd largest brewing company in the world after Anheuser-Busch, with 23% of the US market in 1989. Miller Lite is the leading US low-calorie beer.

The remainder of the company's revenues and profits stem from its financial services and its Mission Viejo real estate operations.

WHEN

In 1847 Philip Morris opened a London tobacco store. By 1854 he was making his own cigarettes, and in 1870 he established the Oxford Blue, Cambridge, and Oval brands. When Morris died in 1873, the company passed to his brother and widow, who sold it to William Curtis Thomson in 1894.

A royal decree in 1901 made Philip Morris tobacconist for King Edward VII. In 1902 Thomson introduced his company's cigarettes to the United States. American investors purchased the rights to the Philip Morris name in 1919 and 10 years later began manufacturing cigarettes from their newly acquired Richmond, Virginia, factory.

When the original members of the old Tobacco Trust (broken up by the federal government in 1911) raised their prices in 1930, Philip Morris countered by introducing the Philip Morris economy brand cigarette. The success of the inexpensive cigarettes, popular with Depression-weary consumers, was further guaranteed by a popular ad campaign in 1933 featuring bellhop Johnny Roventini chanting the slogan, "Call for Philip Morris."

In 1954 Philip Morris acquired Benson & Hedges and its president Joseph Cullman III. Cullman, assigned to market the filtered Marlboro brand, enlisted the help of advertiser Leo Burnett, who created a simple red-and-white box, the slogan, "flavor, filter, fliptop box," and the hugely successful Marlboro Man. In 1968 the company introduced Virginia Slims, a cigarette designed for women. Under Cullman, Philip Morris experienced tremendous overseas expansion.

In 1970 Philip Morris purchased Miller Brewing Company (formed in 1855 by Frederic Miller), with aggressive marketing vaulting it from the #7 world position in beer to the #2 position by 1980. In 1978 it acquired Seven-Up Company (sold 1986).

In 1985 Philip Morris spent $5.6 billion to purchase food and coffee giant General Foods, which traces its origins to cereal developer C. W. Post. In 1925 Post's cereal company started a series of acquisitions that would become General Foods by 1929: Jell-O (1925), Birds Eye (frozen food, 1929), Kool-Aid (1953), and Oscar Mayer (meats, 1981), to name a few.

In 1988 Philip Morris spent $12.9 billion to purchase Kraft, which was created in 1930 when Thomas McInnerney's National Dairy Products bought Kraft-Phenix (formed in 1903 by cheese wholesaler James Kraft). With the 2 major acquisitions, Philip Morris is increasingly turning its attention to food. In 1990 it bought Swiss candymaker Jacobs Suchard.

HOW MUCH

	9 Yr. Growth	1980	1981	1982	1983	1984	1985	1986	1987	1988	1989
Sales ($ mil)	20.4%	7,328	8,307	9,102	9,466	10,138	12,149	20,681	22,279	25,860	39,011
Net income ($ mil)	19.9%	577	676	782	904	889	1,255	1,478	1,842	2,064	2,946
Income as % of sales	—	7.9%	8.1%	8.6%	9.5%	8.8%	10.3%	7.1%	8.3%	8.0%	7.6%
Earnings per share ($)	20.8%	0.58	0.68	0.78	0.90	0.91	1.31	1.55	1.94	2.22	3.18
Stock price – high ($)	—	6.06	6.89	8.47	9.05	10.41	11.89	19.50	31.13	25.50	45.75
Stock price – low ($)	—	3.64	5.25	5.52	6.75	7.77	9.00	10.98	18.16	20.13	25.00
Stock price – close ($)	25.5%	5.41	6.09	7.50	8.97	10.08	11.05	17.97	21.34	25.47	41.63
P/E – high	—	10	10	11	10	12	9	13	16	12	14
P/E – low	—	6	8	7	8	9	7	7	9	9	8
Dividends per share ($)	22.6%	0.20	0.25	0.30	0.36	0.43	0.50	0.62	0.79	1.01	1.25
Book value per share ($)	15.3%	2.86	3.29	3.64	4.03	4.21	4.96	5.94	7.21	8.31	10.31

1989 Year End:
Debt ratio: 60.5%
Return on equity: 34.2%
Cash (mil): $118
Current ratio: —
Long-term debt (mil): $14,685
Number of shares (mil): 929
Dividends:
1989 average yield: 3.0%
1989 payout: 39.3%
Market value (mil): $38,650

Stock Price History high/low 1980-89

NYSE symbol: MO
Incorporated: Virginia, 1985
Fiscal year ends: December 31

WHO

Chairman and CEO: Hamish Maxwell, age 63, $1,877,376 pay
VC; Chairman and CEO, Kraft General Foods: Michael A. Miles, age 50, $1,333,071 pay
President: John A. Murphy, age 60, $1,269,530 pay
SVP and CFO: Hans G. Storr, age 58
Auditors: Coopers & Lybrand
Employees: 157,000

WHERE

HQ: 120 Park Ave., New York, NY 10017
Phone: 212-880-5000
FAX: 212-878-2165

The company operates cigarette plants in 22 countries and food plants in 19 countries.

	1989 Sales		1989 Operating Income	
	$ mil	% of total	$ mil	% of total
US	31,233	73	6,061	86
Europe	8,424	20	692	10
Other countries	2,814	7	288	4
Adjustments	(3,460)	—	(252)	—
Total	**39,011**	**100**	**6,789**	**100**

WHAT

	1989 Sales		1989 Operating Income	
	$ mil	% of total	$ mil	% of total
Beer	3,435	8	226	3
Tobacco	17,864	40	5,063	72
Food	22,933	51	1,580	23
Finance/real estate	527	1	172	2
Adjustments	(5,748)	—	(252)	—
Total	**39,011**	**100**	**6,789**	**100**

Philip Morris
Alpine
Benson & Hedges
Cambridge
Chesterfield
Lark
Marlboro
Merit
Parliament
Virginia Slims

Kraft
Breakstone's
Breyers
Budget Gourmet
Bull's-Eye
Cheez Whiz
Chiffon
Cool Whip
Cracker Barrel
Light n' Lively
Miracle Whip
Parkay
Philadelphia
Sealtest
Seven Seas
Tombstone
Velveeta

General Foods
Brim
Country Time
Dream Whip
Jell-O
Kool-Aid
Log Cabin
Maxwell House
Post
Sanka
Shake 'n Bake
Stove Top
Tang

Oscar Mayer Foods
Claussen
Louis Kemp
Louis Rich
Lunchables
Oscar Mayer

Miller
Lite
Löwenbräu
Meister Bräu
Miller Genuine Draft
Milwaukee's Best
Sharp's

RANKINGS

7th in *Fortune* 500 Industrials Cos.
14th in *Fortune* Global 500 Industrial Cos.
15th in *Fortune* 50 Exporters
8th in *Forbes* Sales 500
5th in *Business Week* 1000
16th in *Business Week* Global 1000

COMPETITION

Adolph Coors
American Brands
Anheuser-Busch
Beatrice
General Mills
Kellogg
Nestlé
Procter & Gamble
RJR Nabisco
Unilever
Whitman
Other food, beer, and tobacco companies

PHILIPS NV

OVERVIEW

Selling its products under such well-known names as Norelco, Sylvania, Philips, and Magnavox, Philips is the world's 2nd largest consumer electronics company after Matsushita. The Dutch electronics giant also makes semiconductors, appliances, minicomputers, and PCs and is the world's largest light bulb maker. For inventing the digital audio technology used in CD players, Philips and Sony receive royalties on each one sold. Philips owns 80% of Polygram (recordings), 35% of Matsushita Electronics (component venture with Matsushita), and 32% of Grundig (electronics, Germany).

After closing 75 plants in 5 years, Philips continues to consolidate its sprawling international production capacity, while abandoning industry segments in which it is not a leader. Philips has established partnerships with Thomson-CSF (high-definition television), Whirlpool (appliances), and SGS-Thomson and Siemens (semiconductors), among others.

Jan Timmer replaced Cornelis van der Klugt as Philips's chairman after an early 1990 profit decline. Timmer, nicknamed "Hurricane Gilbert," has announced that Philips will lay off 10,000 workers and reduce its involvement in memory chip development.

WHEN

In 1891 the spread of electricity through Europe and improvements in incandescent lighting encouraged Gerard Philips (later joined by brother Anton) to start Philips Gloeilampenfabrieken (light bulb factory) in Eindhoven, Holland. Surviving an industry shakeout, Philips prospered as a result of Gerard's engineering and Anton's foreign sales efforts to become Europe's 3rd largest light bulb maker by the turn of the century.

Dutch neutrality during WWI allowed Philips to expand and integrate into glass manufacturing (1915) and X-ray and radio tubes (1918). The company set up sales offices abroad, beginning in Belgium (1919). In the 1930s Philips began building plants abroad to avoid trade barriers and tariffs.

During WWII Philips hedged its bets by creating US and British trusts to hold majority interests in North American Philips (NAP) and Philips's British operations. The British businesses were repurchased by Philips in 1955, while NAP operated as an independent company until it was reacquired in 1987. Philips expanded internationally after WWII, establishing hundreds of largely autonomous subsidiaries worldwide.

Philips began making televisions and appliances in the 1940s and 1950s. The company established a reputation for product innovation and acquired a stake in Matsushita Electronics through a technology-licensing agreement in 1952. Philips's ventures in the computer and office equipment markets in the 1960s failed to match its success in consumer electronics. In the 1960s Philips invented audiocassette, VCR, and laser disc technology.

Despite its development of new technologies, Philips was unable to maintain market share against an onslaught of inexpensive goods from Japan in the 1970s. NAP's rejection of Philips's Video 2000 VCR format in favor of Matsushita's VHS technology was a blow to the parent company. NAP acquired Magnavox (consumer electronics, US) in 1974. Philips's 1970s acquisitions included Signetics (semiconductors, US, 1975) and a minority interest in Grundig (1979).

Philips's 1980 European introduction of its Video 2000 system followed previous VHS and Beta (Sony) entries and failed to capture a major share of the VCR market. In 1983 the company began licensing VHS technology from Matsushita.

NAP purchased GTE Television (Sylvania, US, 1981) and Westinghouse's lighting business (1983). Philips's successful Polygram unit issued 20% of its stock to the public and acquired A&M and Island (recordings, US) in 1989 and 1990, respectively.

NYSE symbol: PHG (ADR)
Established: The Netherlands, 1920
Fiscal year ends: December 31

WHO

Chairman Board of Management: Jan D. Timmer, age 57
Group Finance Director: J. H. Goris
Auditors: KPMG Klynveld Kraayenhof & Co.
Employees: 290,000

WHERE

HQ: Groenewoudseweg 1, 5621 BA Eindhoven, The Netherlands
Phone: 011-31-40-791111
US HQ (North American Philips Corp.): 100 E. 42nd St., New York, NY 10017
US Phone: 212-850-5000
US FAX: 212-850-7314

Philips has subsidiaries in more than 60 countries.

	1989 Sales		1989 Operating Income	
	$ mil	% of total	$ mil	% of total
Netherlands	9,216	22	83	7
Other Europe	17,595	42	826	69
US & Canada	7,593	18	(188)	(15)
Asia	4,647	11	197	16
Other countries	2,962	7	275	23
Adjustments	(12,028)	—	8	—
Total	**29,985**	**100**	**1,201**	**100**

WHAT

	1989 Sales		1989 Operating Income	
	$ mil	% of total	$ mil	% of total
Lighting	3,965	12	399	39
Consumer prods.	12,480	39	579	57
Professional prods. & systems	8,487	26	21	2
Components	6,351	20	(65)	(6)
Miscellaneous	1,066	3	85	8
Adjustments	(2,364)	—	182	—
Total	**29,985**	**100**	**1,201**	**100**

Consumer Brands
Genie
JetVac
Magnavox
Norelco
Philco
Philips
Schick (electric shavers)
Sylvania

Products
Audio and video equip.
Banking automation systems
Batteries
Computers
Lighting
Medical electronics
Semiconductors
Telecommunications prods.

Subsidiaries/Affiliates
Airpax (electronic components)
AT&T Network Systems International (15%)
Grundig (32%)
Matsushita Electronics (35%)
North American Philips
Philips and Du Pont Optical (50%)
Polygram (80%)
A&M
Island
Signetics
Whirlpool International (47%)

RANKINGS

29th in *Fortune* Global 500 Industrial Cos.
13th in *Forbes* 100 Foreign Investments in the US
371st in *Business Week* Global 1000

COMPETITION

Electronics, computer, semiconductor, lighting, music, and consumer products companies

HOW MUCH

	9 Yr. Growth	1980	1981	1982	1983	1984	1985	1986	1987	1988	1989
Sales ($ mil)	6.5%	16,993	17,274	16,380	15,102	15,167	21,802	25,334	29,831	28,011	29,985
Net income ($ mil)	6.5%	236	131	165	212	314	356	441	458	265	415
Income as % of sales	—	1.4%	0.8%	1.0%	1.4%	2.1%	1.6%	1.7%	1.5%	0.9%	1.4%
Earnings per share ($)	2.5%	1.25	0.65	0.83	1.03	1.40	*1.65*	*1.91*	*1.87*	*1.03*	*1.56*
Stock price – high ($)	—	9.89	8.47	9.77	17.73	17.38	22.50	25.88	27.38	17.75	25.25
Stock price – low ($)	—	6.08	6.25	7.27	9.55	12.05	14.25	18.63	13.75	12.63	16.38
Stock price – close ($)	16.3%	6.42	7.39	9.43	13.07	15.63	22.38	19.88	14.50	17.13	25.00
P/E – high	—	8	13	12	17	12	14	14	15	17	16
P/E – low	—	5	10	9	9	9	9	10	7	12	11
Dividends per share ($)	2.1%	0.80	0.65	0.63	0.57	0.53	0.62	0.83	1.00	1.04	0.96
Book value per share ($)	0.0%	32.05	25.67	23.94	21.37	22.43	25.89	31.39	34.39	31.79	32.00

1989 Year End:
Debt ratio: 37.1%
Return on equity: —
Cash (mil): $809
Long-term debt (mil): $5,230
Number of shares (mil): 277
Dividends:
1989 average yield: 3.8%
1989 payout: —
Market value (mil): $6,913

Stock Price History high/low 1980-89

PHILLIPS PETROLEUM COMPANY

OVERVIEW

Phillips Petroleum is the 9th largest integrated petroleum company in the US.

The company's Exploration and Production group produced an average 218,000 barrels of crude oil, 164,000 barrels of natural gas liquids, and 1.2 billion cubic feet of natural gas each day in 1989.

Its Gas and Gas Liquids group owns interests in 49 US plants that remove gas liquids from natural gas for further processing. Phillips is the largest US producer of natural gas liquids, processing 152,000 barrels a day.

Its Downstream group runs 3 US refineries and can use 80% of its refining capacity on high-margin, high-sulfur crude. Phillips is racing to rebuild its Chemicals segment's polyethylene capacity after a 1989 explosion at the company's Houston complex.

Phillips's emphasis on chemicals and plastics relies heavily on research. It holds 4,331 active US patents, more than any other oil company. The company accomplishes this from its headquarters in Bartlesville, Oklahoma, a city of 35,000 that catches cold whenever Phillips sneezes.

WHEN

Frank Phillips was a prosperous Iowa barber who, after marrying a banker's daughter in 1897, turned to selling bonds. He met a Methodist missionary assigned to Indians in Oklahoma, and the missionary regaled him with stories of opportunities in the oil patch.

Phillips migrated to Bartlesville, Oklahoma, and established Anchor Oil (1903). Anchor's first 2 wells were dry holes, but the next one — the Anna Anderson No. 1 — began a string of 81 producing wells. Phillips and his brother, L. E., who doubled as bankers in Bartlesville, transformed Anchor into Phillips Petroleum (1917).

With continued success, particularly on Indian lands in Oklahoma, Phillips branched out to refining and marketing. In 1927 the company opened its first filling station in Wichita, Kansas. The Phillips 66 name for the company's gasoline was a salute to Route 66 (hence the highway-sign shape of the company's logo) and to the speed reached during a test drive using the gasoline.

Frank Phillips retired after WWII and was succeeded as chairman by William Keeler, a Cherokee called Tsula Westa Nehi (worker who doesn't sit down) by his tribesmen.

In 1951, 2 Phillips chemists stumbled onto a petrochemical compound. The chemical, eventually marketed as Marlex, became the building block for many modern plastic products. The hula hoop fad of the 1950s spurred demand for Marlex, saving the new substance from a rocky debut and earning a place for the toy in the Phillips president's office.

In the 1970s Phillips was rocked by disclosure of illegal campaign contributions. Settlement of the resulting stockholder-initiated suit required the company to name 6 new directors from outside the cloistered executive suite.

Phillips was besieged by corporate raiders T. Boone Pickens (1984) and Carl Icahn (1985) in separate takeover attempts. Phillips ran its debt up to $9 billion to repurchase stock and fend off the raiders. At one point it spent more on interest than it did on exploring for oil. The company beefed up the employee stock ownership plan, cut 8,300 employees from the payroll, and sold billions of dollars of assets.

Leaner after the takeover tries, the company's stock price and profits rebounded, but Phillips suffered another blow when its Houston Chemical Complex exploded and burned in 1989, killing 23 people and shutting down domestic polyethylene production.

Even with these woes, Phillips may face yet another takeover bid, but it has stocked up on poison pills. One would require a raider to buy the house of any employee he fires.

HOW MUCH

	9 Yr. Growth	1980	1981	1982	1983	1984	1985	1986	1987	1988	1989
Sales ($ mil)	(0.9%)	13,377	15,966	15,698	15,249	15,537	15,636	9,786	10,721	11,304	12,384
Net income ($ mil)	(16.2%)	1,070	879	646	721	810	596	234	35	650	219
Income as % of sales	—	8.0%	5.5%	4.1%	4.7%	5.2%	3.8%	2.4%	0.3%	5.8%	1.8%
Earnings per share ($)	(10.1%)	2.34	1.93	1.41	1.57	1.75	2.07	0.91	0.06	2.72	0.90
Stock price – high ($)	—	20.96	19.83	13.58	12.96	18.75	17.17	12.75	18.75	22.38	30.13
Stock price – low ($)	—	12.54	11.33	7.83	9.79	11.13	11.00	8.25	10.00	12.13	19.13
Stock price – close ($)	2.9%	19.58	13.50	10.88	11.50	14.92	12.13	11.75	14.00	19.50	25.25
P/E – high	—	9	10	10	8	11	8	14	313	8	33
P/E – low	—	5	6	6	6	6	5	9	167	4	21
Dividends per share ($)	6.1%	0.60	0.73	0.73	0.73	0.78	0.95	0.70	0.60	0.66	1.02
Book value per share ($)	(2.3%)	10.81	12.01	12.57	13.38	14.28	7.24	7.55	7.08	8.69	8.74

1989 Year End:
Debt ratio: 64.9%
Return on equity: 10.3%
Cash (mil): $708
Current ratio: 1.06
Long-term debt (mil): $3,939
Number of shares (mil): 244
Dividends:
1989 average yield: 4.1%
1989 payout: 113.7%
Market value (mil): $6,158

Stock Price History high/low 1980-89

NYSE symbol: P
Incorporated: Delaware, 1917
Fiscal year ends: December 31

WHO

Chairman and CEO: C. J. Silas, age 57, $1,239,880 pay
President and COO: Glenn A. Cox, age 60, $866,280 pay
EVP: Bill M. Thompson, age 57, $455,410 pay
SVP and General Counsel: William G. Paul, age 59, $494,150 pay
VP, Treasurer, and CFO: James J. Mulva, age 43
Auditors: Ernst & Young
Employees: 21,800

WHERE

HQ: Phillips Bldg., Bartlesville, OK 74004
Phone: 918-661-6600
FAX: 918-661-7636

Phillips owns properties for oil and gas exploration in Africa, Australia, the Norwegian North Sea, the Netherlands, New Guinea, Pakistan, the UK's North Sea, and the US.

	1989 Sales		1989 Operating Income	
	$ mil	% of total	$ mil	% of total
US	10,549	85	798	57
Norway	528	4	345	25
UK	732	6	89	7
Africa & other areas	575	5	159	11
Adjustments	—	—	(318)	—
Total	**12,384**	**100**	**1,073**	**100**

WHAT

	1989 Sales		1989 Operating Income	
	$ mil	% of total	$ mil	% of total
Exploration & production	1,284	10	395	28
Gas & gas liquids	789	7	82	6
Petroleum prods.	7,855	63	260	19
Chemicals	2,449	20	652	47
Corporate	7	—	2	—
Adjustments	—	—	(318)	—
Total	**12,384**	**100**	**1,073**	**100**

Operating Groups
Exploration and Production
Gas and Gas Liquids
Downstream Operations (petroleum products and chemicals)

RANKINGS

30th in *Fortune* 500 Industrial Cos.
82nd in *Fortune* Global 500 Industrial Cos.
48th in *Forbes* Sales 500
89th in *Business Week* 1000
276th in *Business Week* Global 1000

COMPETITION

Amoco
Ashland
Atlantic Richfield
British Petroleum
Chevron
Coastal
Du Pont
Exxon
Mobil
Occidental
Pennzoil
Royal Dutch/Shell
Sun
Texaco
Unocal
USX

PINNACLE WEST CAPITAL CORPORATION

NYSE symbol: PNW
Incorporated: Arizona, 1985
Fiscal year ends: December 31

OVERVIEW

Pinnacle West is a Phoenix-based holding company with subsidiaries involved in the utility, real estate, and financial services industries.

Arizona Public Service (APS), the state's largest electric utility, provides electricity to about 1.6 million people in 11 of Arizona's 15 counties and generated about 96% of Pinnacle West's revenues in 1989. SunCor, Pinnacle West's real estate development company, owns undeveloped properties in Tempe, northeast Phoenix, Glendale, and the Litchfield Park resort area. Through El Dorado, a venture capital firm, Pinnacle West has invested in more than 60 companies, including the Phoenix Suns basketball team.

Beginning in November 1989 Pinnacle West rejected a series of takeover bids from PacifiCorp, an Oregon-based utility. At the end of August 1990, a mutually beneficial agreement was reached. Although falling short of a merger, the deal gives both parties access to much needed seasonal power sharing.

WHEN

In 1906, 3 Phoenix businessmen organized the Pacific Gas & Electric Company (PG&E, no relationship to the California utility), which served the city's electric power needs until 1920 when Central Arizona Light & Power Company (Calapco) was formed to assume its operations. In 1924 Calapco became a subsidiary of American Power & Light and by 1926 had expanded westward beyond Phoenix to Buckeye. When Phoenix businessmen expressed interest in buying Calapco's stock, American Power & Light offered it to the public in 1945.

In 1949 Calapco expanded into northern Arizona by purchasing Northern Arizona Light & Power, which was founded as Prescott Gas & Electric in the late 1890s. In 1951 Calapco merged with Arizona Edison (formed in the 1920s by the consolidation of several central and south Arizona utilities) to form the Arizona Public Service Company (APS).

In the 1950s, when Arizona began experiencing unprecedented population growth, the demand for power was greater than ever. Between 1955 and 1960, APS built 3 gas-fired plants, then decided to develop coal as its major source of fuel. The Cholla Power Plant, near Joseph City, completed in 1962, was the company's first coal-burning power station.

Under CEO Keith Turley, APS was reorganized as a subsidiary of AZP Group, a holding company, in 1985. This signaled the beginning of a diversification plan, which included the purchase of MeraBank, a Phoenix-based S&L, an investment in undeveloped real estate through Suncor, and the purchase of Mobil Oil's Wyoming uranium mines in 1986. AZP also invested $115 million in venture capital, building a portfolio that includes a chain of nursing homes and the Phoenix Suns basketball team. In 1987 AZP adopted the name Pinnacle West Capital Corporation.

MeraBank bought 3 Texas S&Ls in 1988 to loosen Pinnacle West's financial dependence on Arizona, which was experiencing an economic downturn. Early in 1989 Pinnacle West had to cover about $100 million worth of bad real estate loans made by MeraBank. The thrift was taken over by federal regulators in January 1990. Pinnacle West was released from further obligation in the S&L's failure in March, after a $465 million capital infusion.

Turley, who had suspended dividends in 1989, retired in 1990 and was replaced by former Ramada executive Richard Snell. In July 1990 Pinnacle West sold its uranium mining firm (Malapai Resources Company) to Fuel International Trading Company, a US affiliate of Electricité de France, for $38 million in cash.

HOW MUCH

	9 Yr. Growth	1980	1981	1982	1983	1984	1985	1986	1987	1988	1989
Sales ($ mil)	7.8%	766	882	1,064	1,074	995	1,175	1,250	1,313	1,442	1,508
Net income ($ mil)	1.0%	143	197	231	265	298	324	273	301	38	157
Income as % of sales	—	18.7%	22.4%	21.7%	24.7%	29.9%	27.6%	21.9%	22.9%	2.6%	10.4%
Earnings per share ($)	(6.9%)	2.75	3.26	3.30	3.46	3.65	3.88	3.04	*3.21*	*0.05*	*1.44*
Stock price – high ($)	—	19.63	19.63	25.13	26.50	22.63	28.13	32.00	32.75	29.75	16.38
Stock price – low ($)	—	14.63	15.13	18.00	17.75	14.50	20.63	26.00	26.38	15.00	5.00
Stock price – close ($)	(5.0%)	17.63	19.38	24.38	19.38	22.00	27.25	28.38	27.75	15.75	11.13
P/E – high	—	7	6	8	8	6	7	11	10	595	11
P/E – low	—	5	5	5	5	4	5	9	8	300	3
Dividends per share ($)	(5.8%)	2.06	2.20	2.40	2.56	2.60	2.69	2.72	2.78	2.80	1.20
Book value per share ($)	(3.3%)	21.97	22.13	22.94	23.78	24.18	25.36	25.84	26.62	23.46	16.31

1989 Year End:
Debt ratio: 68.4%
Return on equity: —
Cash (mil): $130
Current ratio: 0.69
Long-term debt (mil): $3,424
Number of shares (mil): 87
Dividends:
1989 average yield: 10.8%
1989 payout: —
Market value (mil): $965

Stock Price History high/low 1980-89

0 5 10 15 20 25 30 35

WHO

Chairman, President, and CEO, Pinnacle West; Chairman, Arizona Public Service: Richard Snell, age 59
EVP and CFO: Henry B. Sargent, Jr., age 55, $323,345 pay
VP and Treasurer: Donald C. Heppermann, age 46, $128,389 pay
VP Corporate Planning and Development: Arlyn J. Larson, age 55, $104,772 pay
VP Corporate Relations and Administration and Secretary: Faye Widenmann, age 41, $82,889 pay
Auditors: Deloitte & Touche
Employees: 9,000

WHERE

HQ: 2828 N. Central Ave., Suite 800, Phoenix, AZ 85004
Phone: 602-234-1142
FAX: 602-234-3252

Pinnacle West's utility business is concentrated in 11 of Arizona's 15 counties. The company also owns real estate developments in Tempe, Glendale, Phoenix, and Litchfield Park, Arizona.

Major Generating Facilities

Coal-Fired
Cholla (Joseph City, AZ)
Four Corners, Units 1, 2, and 3 (near Farmington, NM)
Four Corners, Units 4 and 5 (15% owned, near Farmington, NM)
Navajo (14% owned, near Page, AZ)

Natural Gas & Oil
Ocotillo (Tempe, AZ)
Yucca (near Yuma, AZ)

Nuclear
Palo Verde (29% owned, west of Phoenix, AZ)

WHAT

Pinnacle West derives 100% of its revenues from US operations.

	1989 Sales	
	$ mil	% of total
Electricity	1,447	96
Real estate	61	4
Total	**1,508**	**100**

Subsidiaries
Arizona Public Service Co.
El Dorado Investment Co.
SunCor Development Co.

	1989 Generating Fuels
	% of total
Coal	75
Gas	11
Nuclear	13
Other	1
Total	**100**

RANKINGS

34th in *Fortune* 50 Utilities
486th in *Forbes* Sales 500
451st in *Business Week* 1000

PITNEY BOWES, INC.

OVERVIEW

Pitney Bowes is a leading manufacturer and marketer of business equipment, including mailing systems, copying systems, facsimile machines, voice-processing systems, and product-marking systems. The company's mailing products dominate the worldwide market and include postage meters, parcel registers, mailing machines, and other mailroom supplies and equipment.

Pitney Bowes produces a line of copiers for medium-volume business users and is a leading supplier of facsimile machines to large businesses. The company's Dictaphone subsidiary is the worldwide leader in dictation equipment. It also produces voice recorders and telephone answering systems. The Monarch Marking Systems subsidiary is a market leader in North America in equipment used to mark, encode, and track price and other retail merchandise information.

Pitney Bowes also provides reprographic and mailroom management services. The company's Financial Services division provides lease financing for its products as well as other financial services.

WHEN

In 1912 English-born addressing machine salesman Walter Bowes obtained control of the Universal Stamping Machine Company of Stamford, Connecticut. The company became a major producer of post office stamp cancelling machines. In 1920 Bowes formed a partnership with Arthur Pitney, who had been developing a postage-metering machine for 14 years. In 1921 Pitney received his final patent, congressional legislation authorizing the use of Pitney's invention was passed, and the Pitney-Bowes Postage Meter Company began leasing its new machines to customers.

By 1925 the company had leased 1,802 postage meters. In 1929 Pitney Bowes purchased a controlling interest in Universal Postal Frankers Limited of England, entering the international market. By 1932 the company had revenues of almost $1.5 million, with about half from rentals on 7,570 postage meters and the remainder from manufacture of stamping machines and other postal equipment. In 1945 the company adopted its current name. Pitney Bowes continued to grow in the postage meter and letter-handling business throughout the 1940s and 1950s.

In the 1960s the company undertook a program to accelerate its growth and reduce its vulnerability as a one-product company through a program of internal growth, acquisition, and diversification. In 1967 the company formed a copier products division to market a new line of internally produced copiers. In 1968 Pitney Bowes bought Monarch Marking Systems (retail price marking and inventory control products) and Malco Plastics (credit and ID cards).

In 1973 the company wrote off its 4-year-old point-of-sale terminal joint venture with Alpex for its first loss in 54 years. Despite this setback Pitney Bowes continued to grow during the 1970s. In 1979 the company bought Dictaphone Corporation, including subsidiaries Data Documents (computer supplies) and Grayarc (office supplies), for $124 million.

In 1980 the company bought Artec International (word-processing equipment) and merged it with Dictaphone. The company bought The Drawing Board (office supply catalog) in 1980 and in 1981 consolidated The Drawing Board and Grayarc into a new entity, The Wheeler Group. In 1982 Pitney Bowes entered the facsimile market, selling products provided by outside suppliers. The company sold Data Documents for $93 million and bought Baldwin Cooke Company (pocket and desk calendars) in 1988. In 1989 the company took a $110 million charge to earnings in transition costs related to reduction in the number of employees, establishment of a dedicated copier division, and administrative streamlining.

HOW MUCH

	9 Yr. Growth	1980	1981	1982	1983	1984	1985	1986	1987	1988	1989
Sales ($ mil)	9.6%	1,257	1,414	1,455	1,606	1,732	1,832	1,987	2,251	2,650	2,876
Net income ($ mil)	10.2%	75	70	83	118	138	145	166	199	237	180
Income as % of sales	—	6.0%	4.9%	5.7%	7.3%	8.0%	7.9%	8.4%	8.9%	8.9%	6.3%
Earnings per share ($)	8.7%	1.07	0.94	1.08	1.50	1.76	1.83	2.10	2.52	3.00	2.27
Stock price – high ($)	—	10.09	8.78	12.06	18.25	18.13	24.94	38.25	50.25	47.50	54.75
Stock price – low ($)	—	7.03	5.50	5.38	10.50	13.25	16.81	22.75	29.63	33.75	40.88
Stock price – close ($)	21.1%	8.50	6.25	11.44	16.31	17.75	24.25	36.63	38.25	42.75	47.50
P/E – high	—	9	9	11	12	10	14	18	20	16	24
P/E – low	—	7	6	5	7	8	9	11	12	11	18
Dividends per share ($)	12.4%	0.36	0.40	0.40	0.45	0.52	0.60	0.66	0.76	0.92	1.04
Book value per share ($)	13.0%	6.05	6.55	7.19	7.86	9.05	10.35	11.70	13.47	16.16	18.15

1989 Year End:
Debt ratio: 49.7%
Return on equity: 13.2%
Cash (mil): $61
Current ratio: 0.75
Long-term debt (mil): $1,411
Number of shares (mil): 78
Dividends:
1989 average yield: 2.2%
1989 payout: 45.8%
Market value (mil): $3,722

NYSE symbol: PBI
Incorporated: Delaware, 1920
Fiscal year ends: December 31

WHO

Chairman, President, and CEO: George B. Harvey, age 58, $862,688 pay
President, Dictaphone Corporation: Marc C. Breslawsky, age 47, $445,300
President, Business Systems International: Hiro R. Hiranandani, age 52, $403,129 pay
President, Pitney Bowes Business Systems: James L. Bast, age 53, $379,231 pay
President, Pitney Bowes Business Supplies and Services: Carole F. St. Mark, age 47, $376,946 pay
VP Finance and Administration and Treasurer: Carmine F. Adimando, age 45, $376,946 pay
Auditors: Price Waterhouse
Employees: 31,404

WHERE

HQ: Pitney Bowes, Inc., Stamford, CT 06926
Phone: 203-356-5000
FAX: 203-351-6158

Pitney Bowes products are sold in 116 countries.

Manufacturing Facilities

US
Australia
Canada
Mexico
Singapore
Switzerland
United Kingdom

	1989 Sales		1989 Operating Income	
	$ mil	% of total	$ mil	% of total
US	2,212	77	263	74
Europe	345	12	44	12
Canada, other	319	11	51	14
Adjustments	—	—	242	—
Total	**2,876**	**100**	**600**	**100**

WHAT

	1989 Sales		1989 Operating Income	
	$ mil	% of total	$ mil	% of total
Business equip.	2,120	74	181	51
Business supplies & services	301	10	44	12
Financial services	455	16	131	37
Adjustments	—	—	244	—
Total	**2,876**	**100**	**600**	**100**

Business Equipment
Business supplies and services
Copying systems
Facsimile systems
Financial services
Mailing systems
Mailroom and reprographics services
Merchandise identification equipment
Voice-processing systems

RANKINGS

152nd in *Fortune* 500 Industrial Cos.
428th in *Fortune* Global 500 Industrial Cos.
294th in *Forbes* Sales 500
177th in *Business Week* 1000
520th in *Business Week* Global 1000

COMPETITION

Harris
Hitachi
IBM
Matsushita
Xerox

PNC FINANCIAL CORP

OVERVIEW

Pittsburgh-based PNC Financial is the 14th largest banking company in the US and the largest in Pennsylvania, ranked by assets.

Through Pittsburgh National, Provident (Philadelphia), and 9 other major banking affiliates, PNC provides services at 529 locations in a 6-state region. PNC is known for decentralized management, with acquired banks keeping their autonomy.

Corporate banking, which provided 27% of PNC's net income in 1989, includes relationships with 300 of the *Fortune* 500 companies and 1/3 of the 9,000 middle-market companies in the region. More than 2 million households and 18,000 small businesses are served by PNC's retail banking network (35% of net income). Foreign operations accounted for 5% of total revenue.

The company is one of the 5 largest US banks in trust and money management, with $94.4 billion in assets. PNC's Provident Institutional Management manages $21 billion in mutual funds.

PNC's investment and merchant banking operations serve the middle- and upper-middle-market companies, primarily structuring corporate finance transactions in the $25 million to $50 million range.

WHEN

In 1863 First National Bank of Pittsburgh, chartered under the National Bank Act, began its operations. Ten years later it had $2 million in deposits.

First National and Second National Bank of Pittsburgh, chartered in 1864, consolidated their operations as First-Second National in 1913. The bank changed its name to First National in Pittsburgh in 1918 and, 3 years later, bought Peoples National (Pittsburgh).

In the 1940s First National purchased Peoples-Pittsburgh Trust (1946), Sewickley Valley Trust (1947), and Monongahela Trust (1947). The bank acquired 12 other Pennsylvania banks during the 1950s, including Fidelity Trust (1959). First National then changed its name to Pittsburgh National.

Pittsburgh National entered the bank credit card business in 1965 and joined the BankAmericard program 4 years later. The bank formed Pittsburgh National Corporation, a holding company, in 1968.

In the 1970s Pittsburgh National Corporation diversified by establishing new operations in commercial paper financing (Pittsburgh National Discount, 1972); insurance on consumer loans (PINACO, 1972); lease financing (Pittsburgh National Leasing, 1979); and credit life, health, and accident reinsurance (Pittsburgh National Life, 1979).

In 1983 Pittsburgh National merged with Provident National of Philadelphia to form PNC Corporation. Provident was a holding company that owned Provident National Bank, which had started as Provident Life & Trust in 1865. The merger, made possible by the easing of Pennsylvania's banking rules in 1982, combined Pittsburgh National's corporate lending strength with Provident's expertise in money management and trust operations.

The PNC network expanded by buying banks across Pennsylvania, including Marine (1984), Northeastern (1985), and Hershey (1986). Much of this growth and the interstate expansion that followed were directed by Thomas H. O'Brien, CEO since 1985. PNC purchased Citizen's Fidelity of Louisville (1987) and Central Bancorporation (Cincinnati, 1988). In 1987 PNC, with $37 billion in assets, passed Mellon as Pennsylvania's largest bank. That year PNC led the 15 largest US banking companies in return on assets and return on equity.

PNC continued to expand in 1988 by starting PNC National of Cherry Hill (New Jersey). In 1989 PNC moved into Delaware with the acquisition of Bank of Delaware and reached agreement to purchase Pittsburgh's First Federal Savings ($3 billion in assets).

HOW MUCH

	9 Yr. Growth	1980	1981	1982	1983	1984	1985	1986	1987	1988	1989
Sales ($ mil)	25.1%	618	854	856	1,218	1,499	1,790	2,392	3,153	3,827	4,645
Net income ($ mil)	25.7%	48	57	62	117	143	188	286	256	443	377
Income as % of sales	—	7.8%	6.7%	7.2%	9.6%	9.5%	10.5%	12.0%	8.1%	11.6%	8.1%
Earnings per share ($)	8.1%	1.94	2.32	2.49	2.75	3.10	3.64	4.19	2.93	4.95	3.91
Stock price – high ($)	—	11.81	14.13	18.88	23.13	23.44	35.63	51.00	51.00	46.50	49.00
Stock price – low ($)	—	8.25	11.06	11.44	15.75	18.06	22.81	34.88	33.25	36.50	38.50
Stock price – close ($)	15.8%	11.13	13.63	16.00	21.44	23.13	35.00	41.25	37.25	39.75	41.63
P/E – high	—	6	6	8	8	8	10	12	17	9	13
P/E – low	—	4	5	5	6	6	6	8	11	7	10
Dividends per share ($)	12.5%	0.71	0.81	0.91	1.01	1.11	1.28	1.47	1.64	1.83	2.06
Book value per share ($)	8.7%	14.21	15.69	17.26	18.45	21.22	24.47	25.68	25.60	28.83	30.16

1989 Year End:
Debt ratio: 20.2%
Return on equity: 13.3%
Cash (mil): $2,938
Assets (mil): $45,661
Long-term debt (mil): $715
Number of shares (mil): 94
Dividends:
  1989 average yield: 4.9%
  1989 payout: 52.7%
Market value (mil): $3,902

Stock Price History high/low 1980-89

NYSE symbol: PNC
Incorporated: Pennsylvania, 1983
Fiscal year ends: December 31

WHO

Chairman, President, and CEO: Thomas H. O'Brien, age 53, $1,090,072 pay
VC: Daniel C. Ulmer, Jr., age 57, $470,903 pay
VC: Robert E. Chappell, age 45, $416,214 pay
VC: James E. Rohr, age 41, $346,339 pay (prior to promotion)
VC: Edward P. Junker III, age 53
VC: Gary N. Kocher, age 42
VC: David L. Tressler, Sr., age 53
EVP Finance and Administration: Walter E. Gregg, Jr., age 48
Auditors: Ernst & Young
Employees: 15,600

WHERE

HQ: 5th Ave. and Wood St., Pittsburgh, PA 15222
Phone: 412-762-2666
FAX: 412-762-6238

PNC has operations in 17 states, the District of Columbia, and 7 foreign countries.

WHAT

	1989 Sales $ mil	% of total
Interest income		
Loans	2,954	64
Investment securities	934	20
Deposits with banks	142	3
Other income	34	—
Noninterest income		
Service charges	306	7
Trust fees	197	4
Other income	78	2
Total	**4,645**	**100**

Financial Services
Corporate banking
- Cash management services
- Corporate loans
- Depository accounts

Investment banking
- Corporate finance
- Public finance

Retail banking
- Consumer loans
- Credit cards
- Depository accounts
- Mortgage loans

Trust and money management
- Custodial services
- Securities processing

RANKINGS

14th in *Fortune* 100 Commercial Banking Cos.
190th in *Forbes* Sales 500
169th in *Business Week* 1000
610th in *Business Week* Global 1000

COMPETITION

Banc One
First Fidelity
Mellon Bank
Insurance companies
Investment banking firms
Other money center banks

POLAROID CORPORATION

OVERVIEW

The Polaroid Corporation holds more than 2,000 patents, which secure the company's place as the undisputed world leader in the field of instant image recording technology. Polaroid designs, manufactures, and markets a wide variety of products in this area, including instant cameras and films, electronic recording imaging devices, conventional film, videotape, floppy disks, polarizing filters, and polarizing lenses. The company spends heavily on R&D ($137 million, or 7% of sales, in 1989).

Polaroid is a significant presence in the Boston-Cambridge area, with the majority of its 57 buildings located in eastern Massachusetts. The company has budgeted 8% of its 1990 capital spending for environmental improvement projects and has earned a reputation as a good corporate citizen in the Boston area, contributing to scores of community projects. Polaroid provides many employee benefits, including subsidized day care and tuition for job-related education.

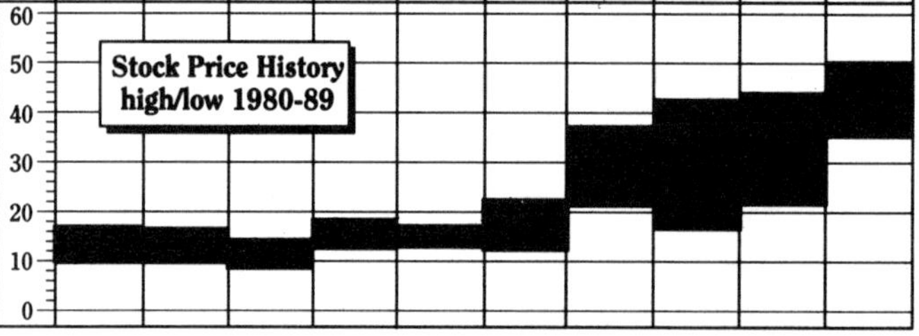

NYSE symbol: PRD
Incorporated: Delaware, 1937
Fiscal year ends: December 31

WHO

Chairman: William J. McCune, Jr., $311,199 pay
President and CEO: I. MacAllister Booth, age 58, $436,164 pay
EVP: Sheldon A. Buckler, age 58, $284,091 pay
SVP: Milton S. Dietz, age 58
SVP: Peter O. Kliem, age 51, $240,628 pay
VP and CFO: Bruce B. Henry, age 50
Auditors: KPMG Peat Marwick
Employees: 11,441

WHEN

Seventeen-year-old Edwin Land took a leave of absence from Harvard University in 1926. After 3 years of independent study and 3 more years of research in a lab back at Harvard, he produced the world's first synthetic material for polarizing light. Land, without graduating, formed a company to exploit the possible uses of the new material, dubbed Polaroid, in 1932. During the 1930s the company licensed the use of Polaroid material, using the cash to fund further research and development. The company went public in 1937 under the name Polaroid, with Land as president, chairman, and director of research.

Polaroid prospered during WWII, developing a number of military uses for its basic product. The company's sales rose from $1 million in 1941 to over $15 million by 1945. Although 1947 sales dropped back to about $1.5 million, in that year Land unveiled his instant-picture camera, and the course of the company was set. During the 1950s Polaroid became one of the first network TV sponsors, with Steve Allen demonstrating the camera live on his "Tonight Show." In 1956 the company sold its millionth camera.

By 1960, the year it unveiled instant color film, Polaroid was in 45 countries and was the 2nd largest producer of photographic equipment and film in the US. In 1964 Polaroid's revenues were higher in film than in cameras, spurring the introduction of the $14 Swinger in 1965, which sold 7 million by 1968.

In 1972, after $600 million in R&D, Polaroid introduced the SX-70 camera and film that eliminated the need to separate negative and positive prints. With the SX-70, Polaroid began manufacturing its own cameras, having contracted for production of its previous products. SX-70 sales grew slowly and Polaroid's net income foundered until 1975, when the company introduced the inexpensive Pronto, setting an annual sales record of 6 million cameras. In the same year Kodak introduced a line of instant cameras, and Polaroid promptly sued for patent infringement. Polaroid won on 7 of 12 counts in a case that still has not seen a damage settlement. Polavision, an instant movie format introduced in 1977, did not sell well and resulted in a $68 million write-off.

Edwin Land retired in 1982 as company management sought to diversify. Introduction of the new, high-quality Spectra camera and film in 1986 revived sales after 6 years of decline, but Polaroid spent most of the 1980s restructuring, creating new operating units and trimming management staff, in pursuit of profits and in the face of a hostile takeover bid (1988-1989) by Shamrock Holdings.

Polaroid introduced conventional film in 1989.

WHERE

HQ: 549 Technology Sq., Cambridge, MA 02139
Phone: 617-577-2000
FAX: 617-494-0249

Polaroid sells its products in 118 countries.

Polaroid owns or leases 57 buildings, primarily in eastern Massachusetts, which are used for manufacturing, office, and warehouse space.

	1989 Sales		1989 Operating Income	
	$ mil	% of total	$ mil	% of total
US	1,092	57	150	51
Europe	505	27	115	39
Other countries	308	16	31	10
Adjustments	—	—	8	—
Total	**1,905**	**100**	**304**	**100**

WHAT

Products
Camera backs
Film holders
Floppy disks
Instant and conventional films
Instant cameras
- One Step
- Spectra
- Studio Express (document cameras)
- SX-70

Instruments
Medical imaging systems
Overhead enlargers
Photo identification systems
Slide makers
Specialized photographic equipment
Videotapes

RANKINGS

218th in *Fortune* 500 Industrial Cos.
415th in *Forbes* Sales 500
257th in *Business Week* 1000
912th in *Business Week* Global 1000

COMPETITION

BASF
Bayer
Eastman Kodak
Hitachi
3M
Mitsubishi
Sony

HOW MUCH

	9 Yr. Growth	1980	1981	1982	1983	1984	1985	1986	1987	1988	1989
Sales ($ mil)	3.1%	1,451	1,420	1,294	1,255	1,272	1,295	1,629	1,764	1,863	1,905
Net income ($ mil)	6.1%	85	31	24	50	26	37	104	116	(23)	145
Income as % of sales	—	5.9%	2.2%	1.8%	4.0%	2.0%	2.8%	6.4%	6.6%	(1.2%)	7.6%
Earnings per share ($)	6.2%	1.30	0.48	0.37	0.81	0.42	0.60	1.67	1.88	(0.34)	2.23
Stock price – high ($)	—	17.13	16.75	14.50	18.63	17.38	22.63	37.38	42.75	44.13	50.38
Stock price – low ($)	—	9.50	9.50	8.38	12.38	12.69	12.13	21.13	16.50	21.50	35.13
Stock price – close ($)	15.5%	12.50	10.25	12.63	16.75	13.88	21.63	33.25	23.63	36.88	45.75
P/E – high	—	13	35	40	23	42	38	22	23	—	23
P/E – low	—	7	20	23	15	31	20	13	9	—	16
Dividends per share ($)	2.0%	0.50	0.50	0.50	0.50	0.50	0.50	0.50	0.60	0.60	0.60
Book value per share ($)	(16.7%)	14.77	14.58	14.58	14.88	14.80	14.89	16.06	17.34	14.12	2.86

1989 Year End:
Debt ratio: 80.2%
Return on equity: 26.3%
Cash (mil): $279
Current ratio: 1.91
Long-term debt (mil): $602
Number of shares (mil): 52
Dividends:
- 1989 average yield: 1.3%
- 1989 payout: 26.9%

Market value (mil): $2,384

Stock Price History high/low 1980-89

0 10 20 30 40 50 60

PPG INDUSTRIES, INC.

OVERVIEW

PPG is the world's largest automotive and industrial finishes supplier, the 3rd largest in flat glass, 2nd in fiberglass, 3rd in chlorine and caustic soda, and largest in optical resins.

Glass (40% of 1989 sales) is sold primarily to the automotive, commercial construction, and aircraft industries. Coatings and resins (36%) are sold to industrial, trade paints, and printing inks markets. Chemicals (21%) and biomedical systems (less than 3%) make up the remaining parts of PPG's business.

General Motors is a major PPG customer, accounting for 9% of total 1989 sales. Known for its high quality, PPG supplies paint to every Japanese automobile manufacturer located in the US.

By 1994 PPG plans to derive 40% (up from the earlier target of 33%) of both sales and earnings abroad by targeting Europe and Asia for global expansion.

WHEN

After the failure of 2 previous plants, John Ford convinced former railroad superintendent John Pitcairn to invest $200,000 in a 3rd plate glass factory in 1883 in Creighton, Pennsylvania. Named Pittsburgh Plate Glass, the enterprise became the first commercially successful US plate glass factory.

Ford left in 1896 when Pitcairn pushed through a plan to set up a company distribution system, replacing glass jobbers. Ford went on to found a predecessor of competitor Libbey-Owens-Ford, now owned by Pilkington (UK). Expanding the existing business, Pitcairn built a soda ash plant in 1899, bought a Milwaukee paint company in 1900, and began producing window glass in 1908.

Strong automobile and construction markets in the early part of the century increased demand for the company's products. Pitcairn died in 1916 and left his stock (31% of the total) to his sons. In 1924 PPG revolutionized the glass production process with the introduction of a straight-line conveyor manufacturing method. In the 1930s and 1940s PPG successfully promoted structural glass for use in the commercial construction industry.

PPG was listed on the NYSE in 1945. Soon after, researchers from Johns Hopkins helped show that schoolhouse color schemes could enhance student performance; the company called the system Color Dynamics. In 1952 PPG began making fiberglass. In 1968 the company adopted its present name.

Vincent Sarni, CEO since 1984, recognized that PPG's markets (85% of sales were to the construction and automobile industries) were maturing. Sarni wrote a document, entitled *Blueprint for the Decade, 1985-1994,* which spelled out his vision for the company. Principal among the goals were global expansion and an ROE of 18%.

In 1986 PPG spent $154 million on acquisitions, the most important of which were the worldwide medical electronics units of Litton Industries and Honeywell, which gave PPG its first entry into the high-technology instrumentation business. PPG spent another $100 million on acquisitions in 1987, acquiring the medical technology business of Allegheny International.

At its halfway point, Sarni judges the *Blueprint* a success. ROE has met the targeted 18% mark. In 1989 the company purchased Casco Nobel, a coatings distributor, and the Olympic and Lucite paint lines from Clorox for $134 million. PPG also received the Philip Crosby Quality Fanatic Award.

Despite sluggish automobile and construction markets, PPG achieved record sales and profits in the first half of 1990. The company has announced the acquisition of a Dutch fiberglass producer.

HOW MUCH

	9 Yr. Growth	1980	1981	1982	1983	1984	1985	1986	1987	1988	1989
Sales ($ mil)	6.9%	3,158	3,354	3,296	3,682	4,242	4,346	4,687	5,183	5,617	5,734
Net income ($ mil)	9.3%	209	211	155	233	303	303	316	377	468	465
Income as % of sales	—	6.6%	6.3%	4.7%	6.3%	7.1%	7.0%	6.8%	7.3%	8.3%	8.1%
Earnings per share ($)	11.4%	1.58	1.56	1.13	1.67	2.16	2.26	2.65	3.17	4.24	4.16
Stock price – high ($)	—	10.19	14.56	13.41	18.63	19.00	25.69	38.81	53.50	46.88	46.00
Stock price – low ($)	—	6.53	8.88	7.25	12.56	12.38	16.44	22.50	27.50	31.25	37.00
Stock price – close ($)	16.3%	10.19	9.44	12.94	17.44	16.44	25.50	36.44	33.13	40.38	39.75
P/E – high	—	6	9	12	11	9	11	15	17	11	11
P/E – low	—	4	6	6	8	6	7	9	9	7	9
Dividends per share ($)	12.1%	0.53	0.58	0.59	0.62	0.70	0.82	0.94	1.11	1.33	1.48
Book value per share ($)	7.2%	11.24	11.97	12.27	13.21	14.40	14.39	16.56	18.43	20.48	20.98

1989 Year End:
Debt ratio: 34.0%
Return on equity: 20.1%
Cash (mil): $65
Current ratio: 1.54
Long-term debt (mil): $1,178
Number of shares (mil): 109
Dividends:
1989 average yield: 3.7%
1989 payout: 35.6%
Market value (mil): $4,325

NYSE symbol: PPG
Incorporated: Pennsylvania, 1883
Fiscal year ends: December 31

WHO

Chairman and CEO: Vincent A. Sarni, age 61, $1,095,000 pay
Group VP, Coatings and Resins: Eugene B. Mosier, age 50, $473,800 pay
Group VP, Glass: Robert D. Duncan, age 50, $430,508 pay
Group VP, Chemicals: Richard M. Rompala, age 43, $421,422 pay
VP Finance: Raymond W. LeBoeuf, age 43, $331,633 pay
Auditors: Deloitte & Touche
Employees: 35,500

WHERE

HQ: One PPG Place, Pittsburgh, PA 15272
Phone: 412-434-3131
FAX: 412-434-2448

PPG has 75 major manufacturing plants in the US, Canada, Mexico, France, Italy, Spain, Taiwan, the UK, and Germany.

	1989 Sales		1989 Operating Income	
	$ mil	% of total	$ mil	% of total
US	3,963	69	612	73
Canada	418	7	44	5
Europe	1,237	22	150	18
Other countries	116	2	38	4
Adjustments	—	—	(8)	—
Total	**5,734**	**100**	**836**	**100**

WHAT

	1989 Sales		1989 Operating Income	
	$ mil	% of total	$ mil	% of total
Chemicals	1,175	21	257	31
Coatings & resins	2,070	36	287	34
Glass	2,312	40	315	37
Other	177	3	(15)	(2)
Adjustments	—	—	(8)	—
Total	**5,734**	**100**	**836**	**100**

Coatings & Resins
Adhesives
Automotive coatings
Consumer paints and stains (Olympic, Lucite, Pittsburgh)
Industrial coatings
Printing inks
Sealants

Glass
Fiberglass
Flat glass

Biomedical Systems
Medical electronic equipment

Chemicals
Industrial
Ophthalmic products
Paper milling
Personal care products
Soap and detergent manufacturing
Water treatment

RANKINGS

83rd in *Fortune* 500 Industrial Cos.
223rd in *Fortune* Global 500 Industrial Cos.
150th in *Forbes* Sales 500
135th in *Business Week* 1000
341st in *Business Week* Global 1000

COMPETITION

BASF
Du Pont
Hoechst
Manville
Owens-Corning Fiberglas
Sherwin-Williams
USG
Other chemical companies and medical electronics companies

PREMARK INTERNATIONAL, INC.

OVERVIEW

Premark, a Deerfield, Illinois–based spinoff of the former Dart & Kraft, holds 2/3 of the US market and is the worldwide leader for plastic storage and serving containers.

Premark's Tupperware Group ($1.03 billion sales in 1989) makes over 200 products, including plastic toys, plastic personal care items, and plastic home products (approximately 2/3 of sales are generated outside the US).

Premark's Food Equipment Group ($932 million sales) is a leading manufacturer of food preparation, cooking, storage, and cleaning equipment for restaurants and commercial food preparation facilities.

The Consumer and Decorative Products Group ($635 million sales) has 45% of the US market for decorative laminates, which are used on cabinetry, countertops, vanities, store fixtures, and furniture. It is also the leading US manufacturer of decorative laminates through its Ralph Wilson Plastics subsidiary and a leader in prefinished hardwood flooring through its Tibbals Flooring subsidiary. It manufactures small electric appliances such as woks, electric skillets, corn poppers, and slow cookers in 12 countries under 14 brand names, including West Bend, and makes Precor fitness equipment, sold through fitness specialty shops.

WHEN

The story of Premark begins with Justin Dart. A native of Illinois, Dart played football for Northwestern University in the 1920s and was elected president of his senior class. After college, he married (and subsequently divorced) the daughter of Walgreen Company's founder Charles Walgreen. When Walgreen died in 1939, Dart took over the company but left in 1941 to join United Drugs, a Boston-based drug company started in 1903. Dart took control of United Drugs in 1943, moving its headquarters from Boston to Los Angeles in 1945.

Boasting Rexall as a major brand, the company adopted the name Rexall Drug in 1947. Dart led Rexall through a series of acquisitions, including Tupper Corporation, former Du Pont chemist Earl Tupper's plastic container company (Tupperware, 1958); Ralph Wilson Plastics, a decorative laminated plastics manufacturer (Wilsonart, 1966); and West Bend, a cookware maker (1968). The company adopted the name Dart Industries in 1969.

Dart sold its Rexall division, the last vestige of the original drug company, in 1977 and bought P. R. Mallory and Company, maker of Duracell batteries, in 1978.

In 1980 the company merged with Kraft, the Chicago food conglomerate, to form Dart & Kraft. Founded in 1903 by cheese wholesaler James Kraft, Kraft merged with rival cheesemaker Phenix Cheese in 1928 to form Kraft-Phenix. In 1930 the company was acquired by National Dairy Products Corporation, which adopted the name Kraftco (1969) and then Kraft, Inc. (1976) to take advantage of the name value of its best-known products. After the Dart-Kraft merger, John Richman, chief executive of Kraft since 1979, became chairman and CEO of Dart & Kraft. Justin Dart acted as an advisor to the company until his death in 1984.

Warren Batts, former CEO of Mead Corporation, became president and COO of Dart & Kraft in 1981. That year the company bought Hobart Corporation, maker of commercial kitchen equipment, including KitchenAid appliances. The KitchenAid division was sold in 1986. Other purchases included Precor (fitness equipment, 1984) and Vulcan-Hart (gas stoves, 1986).

In 1986 the company decided to split its food and nonfood divisions. As a result, Tupperware, Hobart, Vulcan-Hart, Ralph Wilson Plastics, and West Bend were spun off into Premark International, a new company headed by Batts. Kraft kept all of its pre-1980 assets and Duracell batteries. Premark has since acquired several businesses, including oak flooring maker Tibbals (1988).

HOW MUCH

	4 Yr. Growth	1980	1981	1982	1983	1984	1985	1986	1987	1988	1989
Sales ($ mil)	10.1%	—	—	—	—	—	1,763	1,959	2,197	2,397	2,592
Net income ($ mil)	2.7%	—	—	—	—	—	70	(98)	72	121	78
Income as % of sales	—	—	—	—	—	—	4.0%	(5.0%)	3.3%	5.1%	3.0%
Earnings per share ($)	—	—	—	—	—	—	—	(2.87)	2.08	3.50	2.24
Stock price – high ($)	—	—	—	—	—	—	—	21.50	31.75	36.25	42.00
Stock price – low ($)	—	—	—	—	—	—	—	17.50	18.50	22.13	29.38
Stock price – close ($)	—	—	—	—	—	—	—	19.63	22.38	31.50	30.75
P/E – high	—	—	—	—	—	—	—	—	15	10	19
P/E – low	—	—	—	—	—	—	—	—	9	6	13
Dividends per share ($)	—	—	—	—	—	—	0.00	0.05	0.29	0.53	0.78
Book value per share ($)	—	—	—	—	—	—	—	16.84	19.68	22.27	23.53

1989 Year End:
Debt ratio: 24.1%
Return on equity: 9.8%
Cash (mil): $97
Current ratio: 1.73
Long-term debt (mil): $254
Number of shares (mil): 34
Dividends:
1989 average yield: 2.5%
1989 payout: 34.8%
Market value (mil): $1,046

Stock Price History high/low 1986-89

0 5 10 15 20 25 30 35 40 45

NYSE symbol: PMI
Incorporated: Delaware, 1986
Fiscal year ends: Last Saturday of December

WHO

Chairman and CEO: Warren L. Batts, age 57, $695,000 pay
EVP: James M. Ringler, age 44
VP Treasury and Information Systems (Principal Financial Officer): David S. Simon, age 49
Auditors: Price Waterhouse
Employees: 25,000

WHERE

HQ: 1717 Deerfield Rd., Deerfield, IL 60015
Phone: 708-405-6000
FAX: 708-405-6013

Premark operates 35 US and 24 foreign manufacturing plants.

	1989 Sales		1989 Operating Income	
	$ mil	% of total	$ mil	% of total
US	1,538	59	95	51
Europe	628	24	39	21
Pacific	210	8	28	15
Latin America & Canada	216	9	23	13
Adjustments	—	—	(26)	—
Total	**2,592**	**100**	**159**	**100**

WHAT

	1989 Sales		1989 Operating Income	
	$ mil	% of total	$ mil	% of total
Tupperware	1,025	40	104	56
Food equipment	932	36	22	12
Other	635	24	59	32
Adjustments	—	—	(26)	—
Total	**2,592**	**100**	**159**	**100**

Principal Subsidiaries
Dart Industries, Inc. (Tupperware)
Hobart Corp.
Precor, Inc.
Ralph Wilson Plastics Co.
Tibbals Flooring Co.
Vulcan-Hart Corp.
The West Bend Co.

Consumer Products
Precor (fitness equipment)
Tupperware (plastic products)
West Bend (appliances)

Decorative Products
Hartco (flooring installation and care products)
Tibbals (flooring)
Wilsonart (laminates)

Commercial Food Equipment
Adamatic
Hobart
Regethermic
Stero
Vulcan
Wolf

RANKINGS

170th in *Fortune* 500 Industrial Cos.
480th in *Fortune* Global 500 Industrial Cos.
321st in *Forbes* Sales 500
555th in *Business Week* 1000

COMPETITION

Armstrong World
Bally
Black & Decker
Electrolux
Hanson
Rubbermaid

THE PRICE COMPANY

OVERVIEW

The Price Company, based in San Diego, operates 47 Price Clubs, principally in the western and mid-Atlantic regions. Price Club Canada, operated by a joint venture, operates 6 locations; the company plans to buy the 50% interest that it does not own. Price Club members, who pay a $25 fee to join, spend more than $125 per visit, a figure well above the average at most other general merchandise stores.

Price Club's 100,000 square foot, warehouse-style discount stores average nearly $100 million in sales per location, making them more productive than most wholesale clubs. The company has 2.6 million members, mainly small businesses, union members, and government employees. In addition to groceries and appliances, the company operates in-store photo-processing, pharmacy, and optical departments, and is experimenting with furniture discounting.

As the first developer of large discount clubs, Price earned a reputation for efficiency and profitability; but imitators like Costco and Sam's Wholesale Clubs (operated by Wal-Mart) are gaining momentum through aggressive expansion.

Price, the 22nd largest publicly owned US retail company, has consistently demonstrated a high return on equity over the last 10 years.

OTC symbol: PCLB
Incorporated: California, 1976
Fiscal year ends: Sunday closest to August 31

WHO

Chairman, President, and CEO: Robert E. Price, age 47, $248,692 pay
VC and EVP: Giles Bateman, age 45, $246,346 pay (prior to promotion)
EVP and CFO: F. Anthony Kurtz, age 48
Auditors: Ernst & Young
Employees: 5,718 full time, 6,827 part time

WHEN

Sol Price, who from 1954 to 1974 built Fedmart into a $300 million chain selling general merchandise at a discount to government employees, sold that company to West German Hugo Mann in 1975. With son Robert, Rick Libenson, and Giles Bateman, Price opened the first Price Club warehouse in San Diego in 1976 to sell in volume to small businesses at steep discounts. Former Fedmart employees who joined the company added $500,000 to Sol's $800,000 to help get the venture going.

The company posted a large loss its first year, prompting the decision to expand membership to include government, utility, and hospital employees, as well as credit union members. In 1978 Price Club opened a 2nd store, in Phoenix. Laurence Price, Sol's other son, who had declined to join the startup company, started a chain of tire-mounting stores with the help of his father. The stores, located adjacent to Price Club locations on land leased from the company, mounted tires sold by the Price Clubs.

Price Company went public in 1980 with 4 stores in California and Arizona (Sol Price currently owns about 10% of the stock). Price Clubs expanded into Albuquerque and Richmond, Virginia, the first East Coast location (1984), and Glen Burnie, Maryland (1985). Steinberg, Inc., a Canadian retailer, and Price formed a joint venture in 1986 to operate stores in Canada. The first Canadian warehouse opened that year in Montreal.

In 1986 a quarrel between Sol and Laurence led Price Company to cancel the leases for the son's business. Laurence won a $3.7 million arbitration award but has since hired famed divorce lawyer Marvin Mitchelson to sue the company for $100 million in damages. In 1987 the company expanded to the East Coast, with stores in New York, Connecticut, and New Jersey.

Price acquired A. M. Lewis, a wholesale grocery distributor operating in Southern California and Arizona (1988), for Lewis's real estate. The company started a delivery service in 1989 to better serve its 1 million small business customers and opened Price Club Furnishings, a home and office furniture extension of the company's discount format, at 2 locations. Price has announced plans to open 19 more stores in 1990-1991, mainly on the East Coast. The company has set up a separate support operation for the eastern region in order to develop that market as it has the western US.

WHERE

HQ: 2657 Ariane Dr., San Diego, CA 92117
Phone: 619-581-4600
FAX: 619-581-4773

The Price Company operates 47 Price Clubs in 8 states and is 50% owner in a joint venture that operates 6 Price Club locations in Quebec and Ontario.

	Stores	% of Total
California	28	52
Arizona	7	13
Virginia	4	8
Maryland	3	6
New Mexico	1	2
New York	2	4
New Jersey	1	2
Connecticut	1	2
Price Club Canada	6	11
Total	**53**	**100**

WHAT

	1989 Merchandise Sales* % of total
Appliances & housewares	19
Food	26
Hardlines	11
Liquor	4
Soft goods	8
Sundries	32
Total	**100**

*excluding gasoline, photo, and other services

Membership
Business — 1 million
Gold Star — 1.6 million

Operations
Automotive centers
Club distribution
Meat processing
Photo processing
Price Club
Price Club Canada
Price Club Furnishings
Price Club Optical
Price Club Packaging
Price Club Pharmacy

RANKINGS

22nd in *Fortune* 50 Retailing Cos.
173rd in *Forbes* Sales 500
313th in *Business Week* 1000

COMPETITION

Ames
Costco
Dayton Hudson
K mart
Wal-Mart
Food retailers
Other general merchandise retailers
Specialty retailers

HOW MUCH

	8 Yr. Growth	1980	1981	1982	1983	1984	1985	1986	1987	1988	1989
Sales ($ mil)	47.0%	—	230	370	641	1,158	1,871	2,649	3,306	4,140	5,012
Net income ($ mil)	48.3%	—	5	8	15	29	46	59	73	95	117
Income as % of sales	—	—	2.2%	2.1%	2.3%	2.5%	2.5%	2.2%	2.2%	2.3%	2.3%
Earnings per share ($)	43.2%	—	0.13	0.20	0.34	0.64	1.02	1.25	1.50	1.93	2.30
Stock price – high ($)	—	—	—	12.00	20.69	24.38	36.13	55.75	52.50	42.25	49.50
Stock price – low ($)	—	—	—	3.06	9.56	11.88	20.38	28.25	23.50	31.00	34.75
Stock price – close ($)	—	—	—	12.00	16.19	20.88	35.00	32.75	32.75	37.50	46.25
P/E – high	—	—	—	61	61	38	36	45	35	22	22
P/E – low	—	—	—	16	28	19	20	23	16	16	15
Dividends per share ($)	—	—	0.00	0.00	0.00	0.00	0.00	0.00	0.00	0.00	1.50
Book value per share ($)	56.4%	—	0.30	0.51	1.55	2.25	3.53	6.18	7.74	9.73	10.75

1989 Year End:
Debt ratio: 28.6%
Return on equity: 22.5%
Cash (mil): $142
Current ratio: 1.22
Long-term debt (mil): $215
Number of shares (mil): 50
Dividends:
1989 average yield: 3.2%
1989 payout: 65.2%
Market value (mil): $2,303

PRICE WATERHOUSE & CO.

OVERVIEW

For decades London-based Price Waterhouse was one of the top 3 accounting firms in the US and the world. The firm earned a reputation as the "Rolls Royce" of auditors, due primarily to its impressive list of blue-chip clients, but slow growth and recent mergers among accounting firms have placed Price Waterhouse last among the Big Six.

Price Waterhouse responded to these changes by developing a 3-part strategy in 1988. First, the firm intends to focus on improving its client service and is dedicated to developing a high level of client responsiveness. The 2nd part of the firm's strategy is to improve its recruitment and training of young college graduates. To this end Price Waterhouse adopted the first performance-based compensation package in the industry for its professional staff. The firm also plans to establish a permanent training center in the US.

The final part of Price Waterhouse's strategy is to concentrate on selected types of clients. Unlike most accounting firms, which are broadening their services to include more industries and specializations, Price Waterhouse intends to focus on multinational companies, financial institutions, and information technology services. To support this objective the firm recently established its own R&D facility, The Technology Centre, in Menlo Park, California.

WHEN

In 1860 S. H. Price and Edwin Waterhouse, both chartered accountants, founded Price Waterhouse in England. The firm quickly attracted several important accounts and a group of prestigious partners that included 4 Knights of the British Empire. Aided by the explosive industrial growth of Britain and the rest of the world, Price Waterhouse expanded rapidly (as did the accounting industry as a whole), and by the late 1900s had established itself as the most prestigious accounting firm, providing its services in accounting, auditing, and business consulting.

Price Waterhouse resisted the establishment of offices outside of London, acting instead through field agents. By 1889 the firm's dealings in America had grown sufficiently to warrant permanent representation, so Lewis Jones and William Caesar were sent to open offices in New York City (1890) and Chicago (1891). Around the turn of the century they formed Jones, Caesar & Co. to undertake work for the Price Waterhouse account. In 1902 United States Steel chose the firm as its auditors.

The firm finally adopted the Price Waterhouse name for all its offices in 1907. Throughout the next several decades, Price Waterhouse's London office initiated tremendous expansion into other countries. By the 1930s, 57 Price Waterhouse offices boasting 2,500 employees were operating globally. Of these, the New York office grew to be the largest.

The growth of Price Waterhouse in New York was largely due to the Herculean efforts of partner Joseph Sterrett. During his tenure at Price Waterhouse, Sterrett participated in a US government–sanctioned investigation of the Mexican national economy, helped create the Reparation Commission in 1919, served the Treasury Department as an advisor, and received several distinguished awards including the Order of Leopold of Belgium and the Crown of Italy. The firm's reputation was enhanced further in 1935 when it was chosen to handle the Academy Awards balloting (which it still does today).

The firm's prestigious reputation attracted several important clients, notably large oil and steel interests. These clients in turn attracted additional prime accounts to Price Waterhouse's portfolio.

After WWII Price Waterhouse began the consolidation of various firms in all parts of the world that were then using the Price Waterhouse & Co. name. The firm lost its dominance in the 1960s, although by 1970 it still retained 100 of the *Fortune* 500 as clients. The company came to be viewed as the most traditional and formal of the major firms. Price Waterhouse has tried to change its image in the 1980s to show more aggressiveness.

In 1989 the firm announced plans to merge with Arthur Andersen, but the 2 managements were unable to agree on terms and style and the merger was called off. In 1989 it was 2nd among the Big Six in the number of *Fortune* 500 clients it audited (95), after Ernst & Young (116).

Following the failed merger the firm began expanding internationally, merging with Swiss firm Revisuisse and opening an office in Budapest (1989).

HOW MUCH

	9 Yr. Growth	1980	1981	1982	1983	1984	1985	1986	1987	1988	1989
Total revenues ($ mil)	14.1%	752	850	946	1,013	1,082	1,170	1,411	1,691	2,097	2,468
US revenues ($ mil)	14.1%	335	392	458	502	568	645	742	848	960	1,098

Foreign partnership
Founded: England, 1860
Fiscal year ends: June 30

WHO

Co-Chairman: Jeffery H. Bowman
Co-Chairman: Shaun F. O'Malley
CFO: Thomas H. Chamberlain
Employees: 40,770

WHERE

HQ: Southwark Towers, 32 London Bridge St., London SE1 9SY, England
Phone: 011-44-71-939-3000
FAX: 011-44-71-378-0647
US HQ: 1251 Ave. of the Americas, New York, NY 10020
US Phone: 212-489-8900
US FAX: 212-790-6620

Price Waterhouse maintains 420 offices in 103 countries.

	1989 Revenues $ mil	% of total
US	1,098	44
Foreign	1,370	56
Total	**2,468**	**100**

WHAT

	1989 Revenues % of total
Auditing and accounting services	56
Tax	24
Management consulting services	20
Total	**100**

Services

Audit & Business Advisory Services
CPS — Services for Growing and Middle-Market Companies
Government Services
International Business Development Services
International Trade Services
Inventory Services
Investment Management and Securities Operations Consulting
Management Consulting Services
Merger and Acquisition Services
Partnership Services
Personal Financial Services
Litigation and Reorganization Consulting
Tax Services
Valuation Services

Representative Clients

Anheuser-Busch
Barnett Banks
Baxter International
Campbell Soup
Chase Manhattan
Chemical Banking
CIGNA
Compaq
Du Pont
Exxon
Gannett
W. R. Grace
IBM
K mart
NIKE
Phelps Dodge
Royal Dutch/Shell
Scott
Warner-Lambert
Washington Post

RANKINGS

46th in *Forbes* 400 US Private Cos.

COMPETITION

Arthur Andersen
KPMG
Marsh & McLennan
McKinsey & Co.
Saatchi & Saatchi

PRIME COMPUTER, INC.

OVERVIEW

Prime Computer is the world's 2nd largest supplier of computer-aided design and computer-aided manufacturing (CAD/CAM) software (34% of revenues); the leader in the automotive, industrial equipment, and aerospace design software markets; and a major manufacturer of commercial superminicomputers (26% of revenues). The company derives 40% of its sales from service.

Prime bundles its superminicomputers into packages, which can include some of its over 2,500 applications software programs (like CAD/CAM), widely accepted operating systems, and networking products.

Prime targets the high-growth markets of engineering/science (its leading manufacturing, plant design, and data management software automates product creation) and commercial data processing (*e.g.*, finance, office automation); each represents about 50% of revenues. Prime derives approximately 60% of its revenue from outside the US.

In 1989 a takeover attempt by MAI Basic Four caused Prime to turn to investment firm J.H. Whitney (which formed DR Holdings to contain Prime). CAD/CAM, computer-integrated manufacturing (CIM), and commercial data processing remain Prime's focus.

Private company
Incorporated: Delaware, 1972
Fiscal year ends: December 31

WHO

Chairman: Russell E. Planitzer, age 46
VC and CEO: James F. McDonald, age 50, $461,538 pay
President and COO: John J. Shields, age 51
President and General Manager, Computervision Unit: Robert A. Fischer, age 53, $323,352 pay
President and General Manager, International Business Unit: Michael H. Forster, age 47, $265,801 pay
VP and CFO: Harvey A. Wagner, age 49
Auditors: Arthur Andersen & Co.
Employees: 9,100

WHEN

Seven ex-Honeywell engineers founded Prime Computer in Natick, Massachusetts, in 1972 to develop powerful 32-bit superminicomputers. Older manufacturers were loath to supersede their profitable 16-bit lines; unencumbered by such ties, Prime introduced its 200 model with full software support. The 200 was an instant success with technical users.

Kenneth Fisher, president in 1975, transformed Prime from a tiny R&D outfit into a hot growth company by sponsoring fully compatible product lines (like the 50 series of general-purpose minis, 1979), networking software (PRIMENET, RINGNET), and subsidiary expansion in Europe. Sales in Fisher's 6 years at Prime jumped from $11 million to $365 million; Prime became the youngest-ever NYSE-listed company in 1978.

IBM alumnus Joe Henson (president in 1982) centralized planning, expanded to the Far East, and began a growth-by-acquisition strategy that by 1988 had catapulted Prime to revenues of $1.59 billion.

Henson targeted CAD/CAM software companies, buying Compeda (1982), VersaCAD (1987), and Computervision (1988); Computervision alone raised Prime's CAD/CAM market share from 3.5% to 17%, with its popular CADDS and MEDUSA products. Prime purchased the CALMA mechanical design product from GE in 1988.

Prime also moved beyond superminis to provide platforms for its burgeoning CAD/CAM line. New computer platforms included supermicros (the EXL Series, 1987) and, in a series of joint ventures, workstations (with Sun Microsystems, the CADDStation and WS3600, 1987); mainframes (with Sequent Computers, the EXL 1200 series, 1989); and minisupers (with Cydrome, the MXCL 5, 1989). All use the open UNIX operating system.

Prime also extended its networking capabilities by developing PRIMELINK (for PC communications, 1986) and linking its PRIMENET with communications standards Ethernet and X.25.

In 1989 a hostile takeover attempt burdened Prime with heavy legal fees; net losses totaled $278 million. After J.H. Whitney, a New York investment firm, purchased Prime (transaction completed January 1990), new CEO James McDonald laid off 20% of the work force and decentralized the company into 5 new product-based divisions.

Plans include further software bridges between Prime's 50 series and UNIX-based computers, and emphasis on high-growth CAD/CAM areas like geographic information systems (GIS) and systems integration.

WHERE

HQ: Prime Park, Natick, MA 01760
Phone: 508-655-8000
FAX: 508-655-8000, ext. 5090

Prime has over 180 service locations in more than 60 countries.

	1989 Sales		1989 Operating Loss	
	$ mil	% of total	$ mil	% of total
US	657	43	(60)	—
Europe	662	44	(110)	—
Other	199	13	(33)	—
Adjustments	—	—	(3)	—
Total	**1,518**	**100**	**(206)**	**—**

WHAT

	1989 Sales	
	$ mil	%of total
Products	914	60
Service & other	604	40
Total	**1,518**	**100**

Business Units
Computervision
Design software
CADDS
CALMA
MEDUSA
Personal Designer
VersaCAD
Geographic information systems
System 9

Minicomputer
CADDstation (workstations)
50 series (minicomputers)
PRIME EXL series (supermicrocomputers to mainframes)
Prime INFORMATION (database management software)
PRIMELINK, PRIMENET (communications software)

International
Design software
Minicomputers

New Systems Integration
Custom information systems

Service
Field service support

HOW MUCH

	9 Yr. Growth	1980	1981	1982	1983	1984	1985	1986	1987	1988	1989
Sales ($ mil)	21.3%	268	365	436	517	643	770	860	961	1,595	1,518
Net income ($ mil)	—	31	38	45	33	60	58	47	65	13	(278)
Income as % of sales	—	11.7%	10.3%	10.3%	6.3%	9.3%	7.5%	5.5%	6.7%	0.8%	(18.3%)
Earnings per share ($)	—	0.71	0.83	0.99	0.68	1.25	1.20	0.97	1.23	0.27	—
Stock price – high ($)	—	27.58	32.83	25.83	30.25	21.50	23.88	28.00	31.00	18.75	21.00
Stock price – low ($)	—	5.96	11.50	10.42	13.25	11.75	14.50	15.63	12.13	11.88	6.00
Stock price – close ($)	(15.0%)	27.50	15.75	23.08	17.63	18.00	21.63	16.38	15.50	17.50	6.38
P/E – high	—	39	39	26	44	17	20	29	25	69	—
P/E – low	—	8	14	11	19	9	12	16	10	44	—
Dividends per share ($)	0.0%	0.00	0.00	0.00	0.00	0.00	0.00	0.00	0.00	0.00	0.00
Book value per share ($)	—	2.25	3.20	4.86	5.63	6.80	8.06	9.08	10.54	11.06	(5.07)

1989 Year End:
Debt ratio: 107.4%
Return on equity: —
Cash (mil): $67
Current ratio: 1.18
Long-term debt (mil): $1,106
Number of shares (mil): 32
Dividends:
1989 average yield: 0.0%
1989 payout: —
Market value (mil): $202

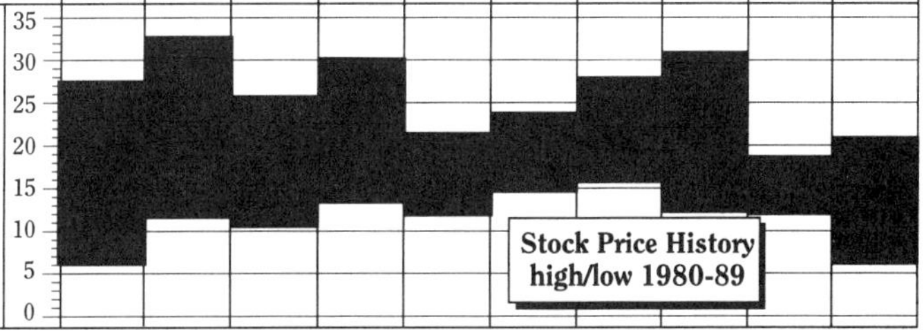

35
30
25
20
15
10
5
0

Stock Price History high/low 1980-89

RANKINGS

259th in *Fortune* 500 Industrial Cos.

COMPETITION

Control Data
Data General
Digital Equipment
Hewlett-Packard
IBM
Intergraph
NCR
Sun Microsystems
Tandem
Unisys
Wang

PRIMERICA CORPORATION

OVERVIEW

Primerica, the 20th largest US diversified financial services company, offers consumer finance, insurance, investment, and specialty retail services.

The consumer services group (32% of sales in 1989) includes Commercial Credit, which serves over 600,000 customers in 29 states, and Fingerhut. With the 1990 addition of BarclaysAmerican/Financial's offices in 7 additional states, Commercial Credit is now national in scope. Fingerhut, the 4th largest US direct mail marketer (consumer merchandise), filled more than 16 million orders in 1989.

A.L. Williams, which sells only term life insurance, heads the insurance services group (37% of Primerica 1989 sales). A.L. Williams sold 660,000 new policies in 1989. Other Primerica subsidiaries offer accident, health, and property/casualty insurance.

Investment services (31% of sales in 1989) include Smith Barney investment banking and securities brokerage services and American Capital Management, manager of $13.4 billion in 37 mutual funds.

WHEN

Primerica is a combination of the former American Can Company and Commercial Credit Company. American Can started in 1901 in New Jersey as an amalgam of 123 small canning and can manufacturing firms and became an industry leader in the 1920s and 1930s.

Commercial Credit, started in 1912 by Alexander Duncan and others, initially bought acceptances (negotiable bank time drafts) and receivables from manufacturers and financed motor vehicles and equipment.

Beginning in the 1950s American Can diversified into secondary tin and aluminum recovery and processing, paper products, and printing. In 1977 the company shifted its focus again, buying Pickwick International, the world's largest record distributor, and its retail subsidiary Musicland. The following year it purchased Fingerhut, a direct mail marketer of general merchandise.

In 1981, under chairman William Woodside, American Can purchased Associated Madison, a life insurance company headed by Gerald Tsai, Jr. As a result, Tsai became American Can's largest individual stockholder (3.4%) and was named EVP for financial services. In 1986 American Can sold its container business to Triangle Industries for $450 million in cash and 17% ownership of Triangle's stock. American Can, now primarily a financial services and specialty retail company, changed its name to Primerica in 1987 and purchased Smith Barney, Inc. (securities) for $750 million.

In 1986 Commercial Credit and its principal stockholder, Control Data Corporation, completed an initial public offering of 41.8 million shares of the company's stock, reducing Control Data's ownership to 18.4%. At that time Sanford I. Weill, former president of American Express, became chairman and CEO of Commercial Credit. In 1987 Commercial Credit purchased Control Data's remaining interest for $313 million.

In 1988 Commercial Credit purchased Primerica in a $1.54 billion stock-plus-cash transaction and assumed the name of the acquired firm, Primerica. Primerica shareholders received the same number of shares in the new Primerica as they owned in old Primerica. Weill remained as CEO of Primerica after the acquisition. In 1988 Primerica also sold Musicland to investors for $330 million and sold its interest in Triangle to CJI Industries for $124 million.

In 1989 Primerica increased its ownership of A.L. Williams (life insurance) from 69.8% to 100%, and in 1990 the company bought BarclaysAmerican/Financial, the US consumer lending unit of Barclays Bank, for $1.37 billion.

HOW MUCH

	9 Yr. Growth	1980	1981	1982	1983	1984	1985	1986	1987	1988	1989
Sales ($ mil)	21.1%	1,018	1,088	1,143	1,284	1,340	1,139	1,113	910	944	5,695
Net income ($ mil)	19.9%	57	50	42	30	66	32	38	102	162	289
Income as % of sales	—	5.6%	4.6%	3.6%	2.3%	4.9%	2.8%	3.4%	11.2%	17.1%	5.1%
Earnings per share ($)	—	—	—	—	—	—	—	0.95	2.00	3.61	2.87
Stock price – high ($)	—	—	—	—	—	—	—	22.75	34.63	29.00	30.00
Stock price – low ($)	—	—	—	—	—	—	—	19.75	17.00	20.50	20.25
Stock price – close ($)	—	—	—	—	—	—	—	20.50	22.38	21.75	28.50
P/E – high	—	—	—	—	—	—	—	24	17	8	10
P/E – low	—	—	—	—	—	—	—	21	9	6	7
Dividends per share ($)	—	0.00	0.00	0.00	0.00	0.00	0.00	0.06	0.24	0.27	0.29
Book value per share ($)	(16.1%)	113.81	199.75	799.81	699.75	700.00	200.00	18.38	15.33	20.28	23.52

1989 Year End:
Debt ratio: 55.3%
Return on equity: 13.1%
Cash (mil): $198
Assets: $17,955
Long-term debt (mil): $3,218
Number of shares (mil): 111
Dividends:
1989 average yield: 1.0%
1989 payout: 10.1%
Market value (mil): $3,153

Stock Price History high/low 1986-89

35 30 25 20 15 10 5 0

NYSE symbol: PA
Incorporated: Delaware, 1968
Fiscal year ends: December 31

WHO

Chairman, President, and CEO: Sanford I. Weill, age 56, $1,536,318 pay
Chairman, President, and CEO, Smith Barney: Frank G. Zarb, age 55, $1,587,500 pay
EVP and CFO: James Dimon, age 33, $660,000 pay
Auditors: KPMG Peat Marwick
Employees: 22,800

WHERE

HQ: 65 E. 55th St., New York, NY 10022
Phone: 212-891-8900
FAX: 212-891-8910 (Corporate Communications)

Primerica has 642 consumer finance offices in 36 states. Brokerage services are offered by 2,700 brokers in 96 US and 9 foreign offices. Insurance products are sold by 190,000 agents.

WHAT

	1989 Sales		1989 Pretax Income	
	$ mil	% of total	$ mil	% of total
Consumer services	1,812	32	251	33
Insurance	2,107	37	386	50
Investment svcs.	1,738	31	134	17
Adjustments	38	—	(258)	—
Total	**5,695**	**100**	**513**	**100**

Consumer Services
American Health & Life (credit-related insurance)
BarclaysAmerican/Financial (consumer loans)
Commercial Credit (consumer loans)
Fingerhut (direct marketing)
Primerica Bank (credit cards)

Insurance Services
A.L. Williams (life)
Gulf (property and casualty)

Investment Services
American Capital Management & Research (mutual funds)
Margaretten (home mortgages)
RCM Capital (investment management)
Smith Barney (securities brokerage and investment banking)

RANKINGS

20th in *Fortune* 50 Diversified Financial Cos.
153rd in *Forbes* Sales 500
198th in *Business Week* 1000
549th in *Business Week* Global 1000

COMPETITION

Aetna
H. F. Ahmanson
American Express
BankAmerica
Charles Schwab
CIGNA
Citicorp
Dai-Ichi Kangyo
Equitable
Ford
General Electric
Goldman Sachs
Great Western
Household International
ITT
John Hancock
Kemper
Massachusetts Mutual
Merrill Lynch
Metropolitan
Morgan Stanley
New York Life
Northwestern Mutual
J. C. Penney
Prudential
Salomon
Sears
Transamerica
USF&G
Stockbrokers
Other insurance companies
Other commercial banks

THE PROCTER & GAMBLE COMPANY

OVERVIEW

Cincinnati-based Procter & Gamble sells many of the most recognized brand names found on grocery store shelves in America and throughout the world. P&G's 130+ products include cleansers for home and laundry, personal care items, foods and beverages, and a growing list of beauty and health care products.

The company's products lead its competitors' in the US and are near the top in several foreign markets. P&G has a #1 item in 22 of 39 product categories. Among these are Crisco, Tide, Bounty, Charmin, Ultra Pampers, NyQuil, Metamucil, and Oil of Olay. The biggest US advertiser for many years, P&G is now the 2nd largest after Philip Morris, spending $1.66 billion in 1989.

P&G has become a major seller of nonprescription drugs in recent years. In ventures with drug companies, P&G is pursuing FDA approval of over-the-counter status for several prescription drugs it intends to market. Awaiting FDA approval is the fat substitute Olestra, which has the potential for huge sales. In 1990 P&G bought Hawaiian Punch, and Old Spice from American Cyanamid.

WHEN

Procter & Gamble came into existence in 1837 in Cincinnati when candlemaker William Procter and soapmaker James Gamble merged their small businesses. By 1859 they had become one of the largest companies in Cincinnati, with sales of $1 million. In 1879 the company introduced Ivory, a floating soap. The campaign for the product, a forerunner of P&G's advertising of later years, was one of the first to advertise directly to the consumer using billboards and printed media. P&G introduced its next major product, Crisco shortening, in 1911.

Family members headed the company until 1930, when William Deupree became president. In the 29 years that Deupree served as president and then chairman, P&G became the largest seller of packaged consumer goods in the US. P&G advertising innovations included the sponsorship of daytime dramas, the first being "The Puddle Family," a 1932 radio show. P&G introduced Tide detergent in 1947 after years of research to determine how to make a cleanser work well in hard water.

Acquisitions over the years included Spic and Span (1945), Duncan Hines (1956), Charmin Paper Mills (1957), Clorox (1957), and Folgers Coffee (1963). Following an antitrust action, P&G sold Clorox in 1968. Introduced in 1955, Crest was the first anticavity toothpaste with fluoride that was endorsed by the American Dental Association. Pampers disposable diapers and Head & Shoulders shampoo, introduced in 1961, eventually became major products worldwide.

A few brands haven't fared so well: P&G bought Crush soft drinks in 1980 and sold it in 1989; Duncan Hines lost out to Nabisco in the "cookie wars" of the early 1980s; Rely tampons had to be removed from the market in 1980 when investigators linked them to toxic shock syndrome. Several P&G products had lost market share by the mid-1980s.

In 1985 the company suffered its first decline in profits in 33 years. Under CEO John Smale, P&G improved existing products to make them more competitive and introduced new ones. The improved Ultra Pampers is now the #1 disposable diaper in markets worldwide. International operations, under the leadership of Edwin Artzt, rose from 29% of company sales in 1986 to 39% in 1989. In 1990 Artzt was appointed CEO.

Major acquisitions in the 1980s included moves into health care: Norwich-Eaton (1982, pharmaceuticals); the nonprescription drug division of G. D. Searle (1985, Metamucil); and Richardson-Vicks (1985, NyQuil, Formula 44). In 1990 P&G bought the rights from Rorer to sell Maalox. The purchase of Noxell (Cover Girl, Noxzema) in 1989 made P&G the biggest cosmetics company in America.

HOW MUCH

	9 Yr. Growth	1980	1981	1982	1983	1984	1985	1986	1987	1988	1989
Sales ($ mil)	7.9%	10,772	11,416	11,994	12,452	12,946	13,552	15,439	17,000	19,336	21,398
Net income ($ mil)	7.2%	643	668	777	866	890	635	709	327	1,020	1,206
Income as % of sales	—	6.0%	5.9%	6.5%	7.0%	6.9%	4.7%	4.6%	1.9%	5.3%	5.6%
Earnings per share ($)	6.6%	1.95	2.02	2.35	2.61	2.67	1.89	2.08	0.93	2.96	3.47
Stock price – high ($)	—	20.69	20.22	30.75	31.63	29.94	35.88	41.25	51.75	44.00	70.38
Stock price – low ($)	—	15.69	16.28	19.44	25.25	22.81	25.19	31.88	30.00	35.38	42.13
Stock price – close ($)	16.9%	17.22	20.09	29.56	28.44	28.50	34.88	38.19	42.69	43.50	70.25
P/E – high	—	11	10	13	12	11	19	20	56	15	20
P/E – low	—	8	8	8	10	9	13	15	32	12	12
Dividends per share ($)	6.5%	0.85	0.95	1.03	1.13	1.20	1.30	1.31	1.35	1.38	1.50
Book value per share ($)	4.4%	10.89	11.67	12.59	13.88	15.21	15.74	16.95	16.98	18.71	16.10

1989 Year End:
Debt ratio: 37.3%
Return on equity: 19.9%
Cash (mil): $1,587
Current ratio: 1.41
Long-term debt (mil): $3,698
Number of shares (mil): 324
Dividends:
1989 average yield: 2.1%
1989 payout: 43.2%
Market value (mil): $22,760

Stock Price History high/low 1980-89

80
70
60
50
40
30
20
10
0

NYSE symbol: PG
Incorporated: Ohio, 1905
Fiscal year ends: June 30

WHO

Chairman and CEO: Edwin L. Artzt, age 60, $1,436,359 pay
President: John E. Pepper, age 52, $1,250,218 pay
SVP and CFO: James W. Nethercott, age 62
Auditors: Deloitte & Touche
Employees: 79,000

WHERE

HQ: One Procter & Gamble Plaza, Cincinnati, OH 45202
Phone: 513-983-1100
FAX: 513-562-2062

P&G has operations in 47 countries.

	1989 Sales		1989 Net Income	
	$ mil	% of total	$ mil	% of total
US	13,312	61	927	69
Foreign	8,529	39	417	31
Adjustments	(443)	—	(138)	—
Total	**21,398**	**100**	**1,206**	**100**

WHAT

	1989 Sales		1989 Pretax Income	
	$ mil	% of total	$ mil	% of total
Laundry & cleaning	7,138	33	754	36
Personal care	10,032	47	1,031	48
Food & beverage	3,029	14	(14)	(1)
Pulp & chemicals	1,199	6	362	17
Adjustments	—	—	(94)	—
Total	**21,398**	**100**	**2,039**	**100**

Brand Names

Laundry & Cleaning
Bold
Bounce
Bounty
Cascade
Cheer
Comet
Dawn
Downy
Joy
Lestoil
Mr. Clean
Oxydol
Spic and Span
Tide

Food & Beverage
Citrus Hill
Crisco
Duncan Hines
Folgers
Hawaiian Punch
Jif
Maryland Club
Pringles

Personal Care
Bain de Soleil
Camay
Charmin
Clearasil
Coast
Cover Girl
Crest
Dramamine
Fixodent
Formula 44
Head & Shoulders
Ivory
Lava
Metamucil
Noxzema
NyQuil
Oil of Olay
Old Spice
Pampers
Pepto-Bismol
Puffs
Safeguard
Secret
Scope
VapoRub
Vidal Sassoon
Zest

RANKINGS

14th in *Fortune* 500 Industrial Cos.
41st in *Fortune* Global 500 Industrial Cos.
14th in *Forbes* Sales 500
17th in *Business Week* 1000
32nd in *Business Week* Global 1000

COMPETITION

Amway
Clorox
Colgate-Palmolive
Unilever
Drug, household goods, personal care, and food companies

THE PRUDENTIAL INSURANCE CO. OF AMERICA

OVERVIEW

Prudential is the largest insurance company in the US. The Prudential "rock" is one of the most widely recognized corporate symbols.

A mutual insurance company owned by its policyholders, Prudential had $299 billion in individual life insurance in force at the end of 1989. The company's 1989 revenues of $43 billion were primarily from investment income (34%), individual insurance (18%), group life and health insurance (18%), and group annuities (18%).

Prudential is a huge investor, with over $241 billion in assets under management. This figure includes $99 billion Prudential manages for others and $48 billion worth of real estate. Prudential-Bache Securities alone has 2 million customers holding over $92 billion in their accounts. The company's mutual fund (Prudential Mutual Fund Management, Inc.) is America's 10th largest.

Prudential is the largest commercial health insurer in the US, with the American Association of Retired Persons as its largest group-health client. In 1989 Prudential had $2 billion in group life and health insurance sales.

WHEN

In 1873 John Fairfield Dryden founded the Widows and Orphans Friendly Society in New Jersey to sell workers industrial insurance (life insurance with small face values and premiums paid weekly). In 1875 he changed the name to the Prudential Friendly Society, naming it after the successful Prudential Assurance Company of England. The following year Dryden visited the English company and copied some of its methods, such as recruiting agents from neighborhoods where insurance was to be sold. In 1877 the company adopted its current name.

In 1886 the company began issuing ordinary life insurance (term or whole life) in addition to industrial insurance, and by the end of 1890 it was selling more than 2,000 ordinary life policies a year. By this time the company had 3,000 field agents in 8 states. In 1896 Dryden commissioned the J. Walter Thompson advertising agency to design a company trademark, the Rock of Gibraltar.

In 1928 Prudential introduced 3 new insurance policies. An Intermediate Monthly Premium Plan combined some features of the industrial and ordinary life policies. The Modified 3 policy was a whole-life policy with a rate change after 3 years. The Accidental Death Benefit feature was added to weekly premium policies, resulting in beneficiaries receiving an extra $3 million in the next year alone.

In the late 1920s the company was the first to establish procedures in which an employer as client of the insurance company kept the records for group life insurance, instead of Prudential. Prudential issued its first group life insurance policy in 1916, and it became a leading group carrier in the mid-1940s.

In 1943 the company became a mutual insurance company owned by the policyholders. In the 1940s President Carroll Shanks implemented a program to decentralize the company's operations by establishing 7 regional home offices. Other companies copied Prudential after the system proved successful. The company introduced a Property Investment Separate Account (PRISA), which gave pension plans a real estate investment option. In 1974 the company, group pension leader in the life insurance industry, reported that 20 of the country's largest 100 corporations were PRISA contract holders.

In 1981 Prudential acquired the Bache Group, Inc. (now called Prudential-Bache Securities), a securities brokerage firm. Prudential-Bache increased its sales force by 30% with the 1989 purchase of Thompson McKinnon Securities. Other subsidiaries include Prudential Property and Casualty Insurance Company, a major issuer of homeowner's and automobile insurance, and Prudential Reinsurance Company.

HOW MUCH

Life Insurance Only	9 Yr. Growth	1980	1981	1982	1983	1984	1985	1986	1987	1988	1989
Assets ($ bil)	8.9%	59.8	62.5	66.7	72.2	78.9	91.1	103.3	108.8	116.2	129.1
Premium & annuity income ($ mil)	10.6%	8,669	9,935	9,698	9,515	15,082	14,332	17,380	14,049	14,397	21,535
Net investment income ($ mil)	9.5%	3,562	3,745	3,818	4,265	4,898	5,575	6,222	6,806	7,437	8,078
Net income ($ mil)	—	—	—	—	—	—	—	—	—	877	644
Net income as % of assets	—	—	—	—	—	—	—	—	—	0.8%	0.5%
Life insurance in force ($ bil)	6.6%	406.6	456.2	487.3	510.0	533.0	560.9	602.4	644.9	691.5	727.4

1989 Company Totals:
Total assets (mil): $163,967
Revenue (mil): $43,034
Surplus (mil): $4,780
Premiums (mil): $13,215
Net investment income (mil): $10,772
Policyowner dividends (mil): $2,460
Total life insurance in force: $727,400

Life Insurance in Force ($ billion) 1980-89

Mutual company
Incorporated: New Jersey, 1873
Fiscal year ends: December 31

WHO

Chairman and CEO: Robert C. Winters, age 59
President: Joseph C. Melone, age 59
VP and Comptroller: Eugene M. O'Hara, age 53
Auditors: Deloitte & Touche
Employees: 69,551

WHERE

HQ: 751 Broad St., Newark, NJ 07102
Phone: 201-802-6000
FAX: 201-802-6092 (Human Resources)

Prudential operates in all 50 states, the District of Columbia, the US Virgin Islands, Puerto Rico, Guam, Canada, Hong Kong, Taiwan, Korea, Japan, Spain, and Italy.

WHAT

	1989 Revenue $ mil	% of total
Premiums & annuities	25,094	58
Broker-dealer revenue	3,451	8
Investment & other	14,489	34
Total	**43,034**	**100**

	12/31/89 Assets $ mil	% of total
Fixed maturities	61,577	38
Mortgage loans	26,905	16
Separate account assets	26,840	16
Trading account securities	6,749	4
Other	41,896	26
Total	**163,967**	**100**

Product Lines
Annuities
Asset management
Credit card services
Deposit accounts
Estate and financial planning
Life, health, and property insurance
Residential real estate services
Reinsurance

Major Subsidiaries
The Prudential Asset Management Co., Inc.
Prudential-Bache Securities, Inc.
Prudential Capital and Investment Services, Inc.
Prudential Capital Corp.
The Prudential Investment Corp.
Prudential Property and Casualty Insurance Co.
The Prudential Real Estate Affiliates, Inc.
Prudential Reinsurance Co.
Prudential Relocation Management
Prudential Venture Capital Management, Inc.

RANKINGS

1st in *Fortune* 50 Life Insurance Cos.
259th in *Business Week* Global 1000

COMPETITION

Aetna
American Express
Blue Cross
CIGNA
Equitable
First Executive
John Hancock
Massachusetts Mutual
Metropolitan
New York Life
Northwestern Mutual
Sears
State Farm
Teachers Insurance
Travelers
Investment bankers
Real estate brokers
Stockbrokers
Other insurance companies

PUBLIC SERVICE ENTERPRISE GROUP INC.

OVERVIEW

Public Service Enterprise Group is the parent company of Public Service Electric and Gas Company (PSE&G), America's 8th largest electric and natural gas utility in terms of 1989 sales. With a service area covering the most populous region of New Jersey, PSE&G served 1.8 million electric and 1.4 million gas customers in 1989, representing about 70% of the state's population.

About 35% of the company's electric power is generated by its nuclear facilities, located in New Jersey and Pennsylvania. Units 2 and 3 of the Peach Bottom plant, shut down by the Nuclear Regulatory Commission in 1987 for safety violations, are back on-line, while a lawsuit filed by PSE&G against the plant's operator (Philadelphia Electric) is pending.

PSE Group is planning to spend about $1.8 billion on its nonutility businesses (Enterprise Diversified Holdings) over the next 4 years, mainly oil and gas exploration, cogeneration (production of steam and electricity), small power plants, and commercial real estate development in Florida, New Jersey, Pennsylvania, and Virginia.

NYSE symbol: PEG
Incorporated: New Jersey, 1985
Fiscal year ends: December 31

WHO

Chairman, President, and CEO: E. James Ferland, age 48, $501,022 pay
VP and Principal Financial Officer: Everett L. Morris, age 61, $316,709 pay
Treasurer: Francis J. Riepl, age 55
Secretary: Robert S. Smith, age 53
Auditors: Deloitte & Touche
Employees: 13,216

WHEN

Newark, New Jersey, was the scene of a tragedy in 1903 when a trolley full of high school students collided with a Delaware, Lackawanna and Western train. While investigating the accident, state attorney general Thomas McCarter discovered the basic financial weakness of the trolley company as well as of many of New Jersey's other transportation, gas, and electric companies. With the intention of buying and consolidating these companies under one management, McCarter resigned as attorney general. He and several colleagues then established the Public Service Corporation (1903).

The company originally formed separate divisions for gas utilities, trolley and other transportation companies, and electric utilities. Management spent most of its energies on the trolley company, rationalizing that these operations would be most profitable. Indeed, during its first full year of operation the trolley company generated $8.4 million in revenues, followed by $5.4 million from the gas company and $3.5 million from the electric company.

When trolleys gave way to buses in the early 1920s, a new company formed to operate bus lines (1924). This company merged with the trolley company in 1928 to form Public Service Coordinated Transport (later Transport of New Jersey). In the meantime the gas and electric companies consolidated as Public Service Electric & Gas (PSE&G, 1924).

PSE&G signed interconnection agreements with 2 Pennsylvania electric companies in 1928 to form the world's first integrated power pool — later known as the Pennsylvania–New Jersey–Maryland (PJM) Interconnection when Baltimore Gas & Electric joined in 1956. Four more companies joined in 1965.

PSE&G began exploring new gas fields in Texas and Louisiana in response to the 1972 Arab oil embargo and formed a research subsidiary in 1977 to develop solar and other non–fossil fuel energy sources.

The state of New Jersey, which had been subsidizing Transport of New Jersey, bought it from PSE&G in 1980. Public Service Enterprise Group (PSE Group), a holding company, was formed in 1985 to allow PSE&G to diversify into nonregulated and nonutility enterprises. Enterprise Diversified Holdings, a new subsidiary, was formed in 1989 to handle these activities, which include commercial real estate development. Meanwhile, the utility company bought 94 oil- and gas-producing properties in West Texas and the Gulf of Mexico (1988) and paid Houston-based Southdown, Inc., $320 million for Pelto Oil Company (1989).

WHERE

HQ: 80 Park Plaza, PO Box 1171, Newark, NJ 07101
Phone: 201-430-7000
FAX: 201-430-5983

The PSE Group operates in New Jersey.

Generating Facilities (% Ownership)

Combustion
Bayonne (NJ)
Bergen (NJ)
Burlington (NJ)
Conemaugh (PA, 23%)
Edison (NJ)
Essex (NJ)
Hudson (NJ)
Kearny (NJ)
Keystone (PA, 23%)
Linden (NJ)
Mercer (NJ)
National Park (NJ)
Salem (NJ, 43%)
Sewaren (NJ)

Nuclear
Hope Creek (NJ, 95%)
Peach Bottom (PA, 43%)
Salem (NJ, 43%)

Pumped Storage
Yard Creek (NJ, 50%)

Steam
Bergen (NJ)
Burlington (NJ)
Conemaugh (PA, 23%)
Hudson (NJ)
Kearny (NJ)
Keystone (PA, 23%)
Linden (NJ)

WHAT

	1989 Sales		1989 Operating Income	
	$ mil	% of total	$ mil	% of total
Electric	3,281	69	925	80
Gas	1,362	28	123	11
Other	162	3	103	9
Adjustments	—	—	(3)	—
Total	**4,805**	**100**	**1,148**	**100**

Public Service Electric & Gas Co.

Enterprise Diversified Holdings, Inc.
Community Energy Alternatives, Inc. (23 cogeneration and small power plants)
Energy Development Corp. (oil and gas exploration and development)
Gasdel Pipeline System, Inc. (gas pipeline)
Pelto Oil Co. International (foreign oil and gas exploration)
Producers Services, Inc. (25%, joint venture in Michigan pipeline)
Enterprise Capital Funding Corp. (financing for nonutility operations)
Enterprise Group Development Corp. (commercial real estate development)
Public Service Enterprise Group Capital Corp. (financing for nonutility operations)
Public Service Resources Corp. (outside investments)

RANKINGS

16th in *Fortune* 50 Utilities
184th in *Forbes* Sales 500
107th in *Business Week* 1000
318th in *Business Week* Global 1000

HOW MUCH

	9 Yr. Growth	1980	1981	1982	1983	1984	1985	1986	1987	1988	1989
Sales ($ mil)	5.4%	2,994	3,472	3,874	3,963	4,196	4,409	4,498	4,211	4,395	4,805
Net income ($ mil)	8.4%	275	264	343	390	490	545	430	559	560	571
Income as % of sales	—	9.2%	7.6%	8.9%	9.8%	11.7%	12.4%	9.6%	13.3%	12.7%	11.9%
Earnings per share ($)	2.6%	2.09	1.75	2.16	2.27	2.63	2.64	1.89	2.55	2.57	2.62
Stock price – high ($)	—	14.00	13.42	15.83	17.67	18.08	22.08	32.17	30.58	26.88	29.38
Stock price – low ($)	—	10.33	11.00	11.83	14.17	13.42	16.92	20.50	20.00	22.00	23.00
Stock price – close ($)	11.1%	11.33	12.00	15.50	15.17	17.83	21.08	26.83	23.88	24.50	29.25
P/E – high	—	7	8	7	8	7	8	17	12	10	11
P/E – low	—	5	6	5	6	5	6	11	8	9	9
Dividends per share ($)	3.3%	1.53	1.63	1.69	1.75	1.80	1.87	1.95	1.99	2.01	2.05
Book value per share ($)	1.0%	18.20	17.64	17.75	18.04	18.54	19.08	17.92	18.54	19.11	19.85

1989 Year End:
Debt ratio: 48.5%
Return on equity: 13.4%
Cash (mil): $83
Current ratio: 0.71
Long-term debt (mil): $4,348
Number of shares (mil): 211
Dividends:
1989 average yield: 7.0%
1989 payout: 78.2%
Market value (mil): $6,175

Stock Price History high/low 1980-89
35
30
25
20
15
10
5
0

PUBLIX SUPER MARKETS, INC.

OVERVIEW

Lakeland, Florida–based Publix is the largest grocery chain in that state, the 8th largest grocery chain in the US, and is one of the largest employee-owned companies in the US.

Unlike some regional grocery chains that have been tempted to expand into unfamiliar markets, Publix has continued to focus exclusively on Florida. The chain has saturated the most populous areas of the state, allowing Publix to serve a relatively high number of stores from just 6 distribution centers and to advertise effectively through fewer media.

The philosophy of founder George Jenkins was that Publix stores should be places "where customers find it a pleasure to shop and employees find it a pleasure to work." The company added "Singles Nights" to woo younger shoppers. At the same time, as its labor pool has grown smaller, it has recruited from Florida's senior citizens for jobs such as carry-out. About 5,000 of its 64,000+ employees are senior citizens.

Publix faces tough competition in the 1990s, however. Competitors such as Safeway, American Stores, and Pueblo International (the leading chain in Puerto Rico and the Virgin Islands) are making inroads in Florida.

WHEN

In 1930 George Jenkins, sporting a moustache to look older than his 20 years, left his position as manager of a Piggly Wiggly grocery store in Winter Haven, Florida. He took the money he had been saving to buy a car and instead opened his own grocery store, the first Publix, next door to his old employer. Despite the Depression the small store prospered, and in 1935 Jenkins opened another Publix in Winter Haven.

Jenkins studied stores across the country that used the new supermarket format, and in 1940 he closed his 2 smaller locations and opened a new Publix Market, a modern marble, tile, and stucco edifice. It boasted pastel colors and electric-eye doors. The store was the first in the nation to feature air-conditioning.

In 1944 Publix purchased All-American, a 19-unit chain of food stores based in Lakeland, Florida. Corporate headquarters also moved to Lakeland, and Publix built a warehouse there (1950) to serve its stores. Publix began offering S&H Green Stamps (1953) and replaced its original Winter Haven supermarket with a mall featuring an enlarged Publix, a Green Stamp redemption center, and other retailers (1956). The company expanded to populous southeastern Florida, first opening a Publix in Miami and then buying and converting 7 former Grand Union stores (1959).

As the population of Florida swelled, Publix continued to expand and opened its 100th store in 1964. The company expanded into Florida's Panhandle with the opening of a Publix in Tallahassee. In 1970 the company launched a discount chain under the Food World banner. Publix retreated from the discount market in the mid-1980s.

Publix was the first grocery chain in Florida to use bar code scanners at checkout lines and completed installing scanners in all of the company's 244 locations by the end of 1980. The company beat Florida banks to the punch installing ATMs, and during the 1980s began using debit card stations.

In 1980 Publix opened a dairy plant and bottling facility at the Lakeland complex to process its own milk, ice cream, and juices. In addition, the company operated 139 bakeries and was positioned to serve all parts of the state.

Publix continued to grow throughout the 1980s, unthreatened by the takeover activity that characterized much of the grocery business, because Publix has always been owned by employee-stockholders. In 1988 the company purchased additional locations from takeover-refugee Kroger. That same year, Publix installed the first automated checkout systems in South Florida, affording customers a checkout lane that is always open. The company's revenues climbed 16% in 1988, 11% in 1989.

The company completed its withdrawal from offering Green Stamps in 1989, and most of the $19 million decrease in Publix advertising expenditures was attributed to the end of the 36-year promotion. "Mr. George" — as visionary founder Jenkins is known — stepped down as chairman in favor of his son Howard (1989), after presiding (and bagging groceries) at scores of store openings over almost 60 years.

Private company
Incorporated: Florida, 1930
Fiscal year ends: Last Saturday in December

WHO

Chairman: Howard M. Jenkins, age 39
President: Mark C. Hollis, age 55
EVP: Charles H. Jenkins, Jr., age 46
EVP: Hoyt R. Barnett, age 46
VP and Treasurer: William H. Vass, age 40
Auditors: KPMG Peat Marwick
Employees: 64,037

WHERE

HQ: 1936 George Jenkins Blvd., Lakeland, FL 33801
Phone: 813-688-1188
FAX: 813-680-5257 (Public Relations)

Publix Super Markets operates 367 grocery stores, all located in Florida. The company also operates dairy processing plants at Deerfield Beach and Lakeland, a bakery at Lakeland, and distribution centers in Boynton Beach, Deerfield Beach, Jacksonville, Lakeland, North Miami, and Sarasota.

	1989 Store Locations	
	no. of locations	% of total
Broward County	44	12
Dade County	39	11
Palm Beach County	35	10
Pinellas County	30	8
Other counties	219	59
Total	**367**	**100**

WHAT

	1989 Sales	
	$ mil	% of total
Existing stores	5,000	94
New/closed stores	331	6
Total	**5,331**	**100**

Lines of Business
Food/drug supermarkets
Food processing plants
Dairy
Baking (Danish Bakery brand)
Bottling
Delicatessen
Supermarkets

Private Label Goods
Publix (outside manufacturers)

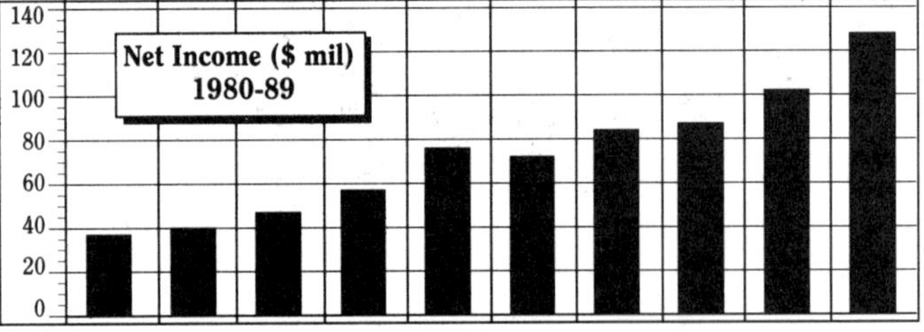

RANKINGS

20th in *Fortune* 50 Retailing Cos.
15th in *Forbes* 400 US Private Cos.

COMPETITION

Albertson's
Food Lion
Great A&P
Winn-Dixie

HOW MUCH

	9 Yr. Growth	1980	1981	1982	1983	1984	1985	1986	1987	1988	1989
Sales ($ mil)	10.6%	2,159	2,376	2,507	2,835	3,206	3,446	3,760	4,152	4,804	5,331
Net income ($ mil)	14.8%	37	40	47	57	76	72	84	87	102	128
Income as % of sales	—	1.7%	1.7%	1.9%	2.0%	2.4%	2.1%	2.2%	2.1%	2.1%	2.4%

1989 Year End:
Debt ratio: 1.8%
Return on equity: 16.1%
Cash (mil): $133
Current ratio: 1.27
Long-term debt (mil): $15

Net Income ($ mil) 1980-89

THE QUAKER OATS COMPANY

OVERVIEW

Best known for its cereal products, Quaker Oats is a diverse international food, pet food, and toy company. Three corporate groups manage its various enterprises: US and Canadian Grocery Products (which provided 57% of 1989's operating income), International Grocery Products (21%), and Fisher-Price toys (22%).

Quaker Oats brands hold the top share (64%) of the US hot cereal market. Its Aunt Jemima brand is also the leader (25% market share) in breakfast syrups, and its Van Camp's canned beans are #1. Gatorade is Quaker Oats's single largest-selling brand, with sales of over $625 million in 1989.

The past 10 years have seen growth and diversification for the company — 55% of its 1989 sales came from new brands acquired or developed since 1981. The company has particularly focused product development on cereals, pet foods, toys, convenience foods, and microwave items. The company's 1990 decision to spin off its Fisher-Price toy company emphasizes its focus on food brands.

WHEN

The familiar, friendly Quaker Man of the Quaker Oats Company was first used as a trademark in 1877 by Henry P. Crowell at his Quaker Mill in Ravenna, Ohio. Crowell was one of 7 prominent millers who formed the American Cereal Company of Chicago in 1891. This powerful consolidation (some called it the "oatmeal trust") changed its name to the Quaker Oats Company in 1901 and adopted Crowell's Quaker Man as its logo.

The company was an immediate success. Crowell's creative marketing practices and powerful sales staff covered the nation with the innovative image. The Quaker Man was everywhere — on billboards, in magazines, in newspapers, on cards on subways and streetcars, and in coupon promotions and miniature samples left on doorsteps — extolling the healthful virtues of oatmeal. Crowell spent nearly $500,000 on advertising in 1899, an enormous outlay for the time.

Robert Stuart, another founder, served as the company's first secretary-treasurer from 1891 to 1897. Stuart consolidated mill operations to 2 locations — a large mill in Akron, Ohio, and his Cedar Rapids mill, which he modernized and expanded. With streamlined facilities and the attraction of oatmeal as a cheap, nutritious food, Quaker Oats prospered during the difficult 1890s.

By 1911 the company was diversifying its product line with such purchases as animal feed and grocery items. Sales reached $123 million in 1918. In 1925 Quaker Oats bought Aunt Jemima pancake flour, one of its most successful brands. In 1969 Fisher-Price toys, then the world's largest maker of toys for preschool children, became a major addition to Quaker Oats.

Since 1981 the company has purchased companies with top-selling products. It bought Stokely-Van Camp in 1983 for $238 million and kept its top brands of canned beans and Gatorade beverage. In 1986 Quaker Oats paid $801 million for Anderson, Clayton & Company, a Houston food products company with such brands as Seven Seas salad dressings, Chiffon margarine, Igloo ice chests, and Gaines dog food (purchased from General Foods in 1984). Quaker subsequently sold all Anderson Clayton businesses except Gaines. In 1990 Quaker Oats announced that it would spin off its Fisher-Price toy company to its shareholders. Fisher-Price, which showed an 11% drop in operating income for 1989, is scheduled to become an independent public company in 1991.

Recent medical reports concerning the healthful benefits of oats, particularly oat bran, have helped boost cereal sales. A recent Quaker Oats ad campaign recalls the slogans of Crowell's sales force: "Quaker Oats...It's the Right Thing to Do."

HOW MUCH

	9 Yr. Growth	1980	1981	1982	1983	1984	1985	1986	1987	1988	1989
Sales ($ mil)	10.1%	2,405	2,600	2,712	2,611	3,344	3,520	3,671	4,421	5,330	5,724
Net income ($ mil)	8.6%	96	105	121	119	139	157	174	186	256	203
Income as % of sales	—	4.0%	4.0%	4.4%	4.6%	4.1%	4.4%	4.7%	4.2%	4.8%	3.5%
Earnings per share ($)	9.4%	1.14	1.25	1.50	1.46	1.68	1.88	2.18	2.36	3.20	2.56
Stock price – high ($)	—	8.94	9.44	12.16	15.97	19.06	31.50	44.88	57.63	61.50	68.88
Stock price – low ($)	—	6.03	7.50	8.00	10.19	13.66	16.50	27.38	31.75	38.50	49.63
Stock price – close ($)	25.2%	7.63	8.94	10.72	14.75	19.06	28.63	40.00	41.63	53.13	57.75
P/E – high	—	8	8	8	11	11	17	21	24	19	27
P/E – low	—	5	6	5	7	8	9	13	13	12	19
Dividends per share ($)	14.7%	0.35	0.40	0.45	0.50	0.55	0.62	0.70	0.80	1.00	1.20
Book value per share ($)	8.0%	7.21	8.00	8.04	8.02	8.89	9.76	10.65	13.68	15.76	14.44

1989 Year End:
Debt ratio: 40.3%
Return on equity: 17.0%
Cash (mil): $24
Current ratio: 1.77
Long-term debt (mil): $767
Number of shares (mil): 79
Dividends:
1989 average yield: 2.1%
1989 payout: 46.9%
Market value (mil): $4,549

Stock Price History high/low 1980-89

70 60 50 40 30 20 10 0

NYSE symbol: OAT
Incorporated: New Jersey, 1901
Fiscal year ends: June 30

WHO

Chairman and CEO: William D. Smithburg, age 51, $1,282,000 pay
President and COO: Frank J. Morgan, age 64, $885,750 pay
SVP Finance: Paul E. Price, age 55, $537,000 pay
SVP Human Resources: Lawrence M. Baytos, age 52
Auditors: Arthur Andersen & Co.
Employees: 31,700

WHERE

HQ: Quaker Tower, 321 N. Clark St., Chicago, IL 60610
Phone: 312-222-7111
FAX: 312-222-8304

Quaker has 70 manufacturing plants in 17 states and 13 foreign countries.

	1989 Sales		1989 Operating Income	
	$ mil	% of total	$ mil	% of total
US	4,074	71	304	68
Canada	284	5	24	6
Europe	1,085	19	68	15
Other countries	281	5	50	11
Adjustments	—	—	93	—
Total	**5,724**	**100**	**539**	**100**

WHAT

	1989 Sales		1989 Operating Income	
	$ mil	% of total	$ mil	% of total
Toys	845	15	97	22
Foods (US & Canada)	3,630	63	256	57
Foods (international)	1,249	22	93	21
Adjustments	—	—	93	—
Total	**5,724**	**100**	**539**	**100**

Brand Names

Cereals
Cap'n Crunch
Instant Quaker Oatmeal
Life
Oh!s
Quaker Oat Bran
Quaker Oat Squares
Quaker Oats
Granola Dipps
Quaker Rice Cakes
Rice-A-Roni
Van Camp's (pork & beans)
Wolf (chili)

Other Food Products
Aunt Jemima
Celeste (pizza)
Gatorade

Pet Food
Gaines Cycle
Ken-L-Ration
Kibbles 'n Bits
King Kuts
Puss 'n Boots

RANKINGS

87th in *Fortune* 500 Industrial Cos.
233rd in *Fortune* Global 500 Industrial Cos.
152nd in *Forbes* Sales 500
178th in *Business Week* 1000
485th in *Business Week* Global 1000

COMPETITION

Beatrice
General Mills
Grand Metropolitan
H. J. Heinz
Kellogg
Mars
Nestlé
Philip Morris
Ralston Purina
RJR Nabisco

RALSTON PURINA COMPANY

OVERVIEW

The well-known checkerboard packages of Ralston Purina cereals and pet foods represent a company that is the world-leading producer of dry dog foods, dry and moist cat foods, and dry-cell battery products. The 86-year-old St. Louis company owns the US's largest wholesale baker (Continental Baking Company, with Wonder Bread and Hostess baked goods), and its Beech-Nut baby food business is the 2nd largest brand (after Gerber) in the US.

Ventures into the restaurant business (including the Jack-in-the-Box fast food chain) and the seafood industry (Chicken of the Sea brand tuna) have been sold. Ralston Purina also sold its domestic livestock feed business, the core of the original enterprise, to concentrate on consumer goods such as cereals, baked goods, and pet foods. It continues to expand its worldwide leadership position in the consumer dry-cell battery industry.

WHEN

Ralston Purina began in 1894 as a small St. Louis feed company, the Robinson-Danforth Commission Company, founded by entrepreneur William Danforth. The company's slogan, "Where Purity is Paramount," inspired Danforth to name a new whole-wheat cereal product Purina (1898). The popularity of Danforth's cereal was enhanced by the endorsement of Everett Ralston, a well-known advocate of whole grain foods. In return, Ralston's name was included and the cereal became Ralston health breakfast food. Trading on the cereal's popularity, Danforth renamed his company Ralston Purina in 1902.

Danforth proved to be a skillful marketer, introducing slogans, trademarks, and logos which would support Ralston Purina's image and products for many years. In 1900 he introduced the distinctive checkerboard design used on Ralston packages, grain elevators, and delivery trucks. The pattern was based on his childhood memory of a neighboring family who dressed in red and white checks. He changed the word "feed" to "chow" in the company's brands after returning from the front lines of WWI, where he noted the soldiers' eager response to each evening's "chow call." Ralston's animal foods have used the word "chow" ever since.

Danforth retired in 1932 and devoted his next 20 years to a variety of philanthropic activities. His book, *I Dare You*, sets forth his life philosophy of enthusiasm, hard work, and optimism.

The modern Ralston Purina Company includes a diverse collection of well-known brand products. Purina Dog Chow, introduced in 1957, quickly became the nation's leading brand of dry dog food. Its pet foods business now produces a diverse group of dry and moist foods and treats for dogs and cats. Ralston's cereal brands (which provided 6.2% of 1989 sales), include the Chex line, whole grain/fiber products, and children's cereals (Teenage Mutant Ninja Turtles and Batman brands).

Ralston bought the Van Camp Seafood Company, with its Chicken of the Sea brands, in 1963 and sold it in 1988. The company purchased Foodmaker, Inc. (1968), which included Jack-in-the-Box hamburger restaurants (sold in 1985). In 1984 the company purchased Continental Baking Company from ITT for approximately $475 million. Continental is the nation's largest baker (Wonder Bread and Hostess Twinkies, Cupcakes, and Ding Dongs). In 1986 Ralston bought Union Carbide's line of Eveready and Energizer batteries.

Ralston sold its domestic livestock feed business, Purina Mills, Inc., to British Petroleum in 1986. Its international feed business was not affected by this sale. In 1989 Ralston bought Beech-Nut baby foods from Nestlé, and Ralston Energy Systems (Eveready's European division) acquired the battery brands Wonder and Mazda, giving it the largest market share in France. In that same year it bought the remaining interest in Eveready to complete its holdings in New Zealand and Australia.

HOW MUCH

	9 Yr. Growth	1980	1981	1982	1983	1984	1985	1986	1987	1988	1989
Sales ($ mil)	3.5%	4,886	5,225	4,803	4,872	4,980	5,864	5,515	5,868	5,876	6,658
Net income ($ mil)	8.9%	163	184	91	256	243	256	264	526	363	351
Income as % of sales	—	3.3%	3.5%	1.9%	5.3%	4.9%	4.4%	4.8%	9.0%	6.2%	5.3%
Earnings per share ($)	14.8%	1.45	1.63	0.84	2.51	2.61	3.08	3.37	7.15	5.22	5.04
Stock price – high ($)	—	13.38	14.63	18.88	30.00	36.13	50.63	77.00	94.00	88.38	101.50
Stock price – low ($)	—	9.25	10.00	10.88	17.13	25.00	33.75	43.75	57.63	63.75	78.75
Stock price – close ($)	25.8%	10.50	12.00	17.50	27.75	35.75	47.00	70.75	63.88	81.88	83.00
P/E – high	—	9	9	22	12	14	16	23	13	17	20
P/E – low	—	6	6	13	7	10	11	13	8	12	16
Dividends per share ($)	11.1%	0.63	0.70	0.77	0.83	0.90	0.98	1.08	1.21	1.44	1.61
Book value per share ($)	2.8%	10.49	11.39	10.84	11.61	11.55	11.53	13.10	13.70	15.75	13.50

1989 Year End:
Debt ratio: 68.3%
Return on equity: 34.5%
Cash (mil): $381
Current ratio: 1.38
Long-term debt (mil): $1,791
Number of shares (mil): 62
Dividends:
1989 average yield: 1.9%
1989 payout: 32.0%
Market value (mil): $5,113

Stock Price History high/low 1980-89

120
100
80
60
40
20
0

NYSE symbol: RAL
Incorporated: Missouri, 1894
Fiscal year ends: September 30

WHO

Chairman, CEO, and President: William P. Stiritz, age 55, $1,064,082 pay
VP; Chairman and CEO, Continental Baking: Jay W. Brown, age 44, $379,344 pay
VP and CFO: James R. Elsesser, age 45
Auditors: Price Waterhouse
Employees: 56,219

WHERE

HQ: Checkerboard Sq., St. Louis, MO 63164
Phone: 314-982-1000
FAX: 314-982-1211

The company has 175 production facilities in 34 countries and territories.

	1989 Sales		1989 Operating Income	
	$ mil	% of total	$ mil	% of total
US	4,826	72	645	82
Foreign	1,832	28	146	18
Total	**6,658**	**100**	**791**	**100**

WHAT

	1989 Sales		1989 Operating Income	
	$ mil	% of total	$ mil	% of total
Human & pet foods	4,132	62	579	72
Batteries, other	1,573	24	177	22
Agricultural prods.	953	14	53	6
Adjustments	—	—	(18)	—
Total	**6,658**	**100**	**791**	**100**

Brand Names

Pet Foods
Alley Cat
Cat Menu
Chuck Wagon
Fit & Trim
Lucky Dog
Meow Mix
Purina Cat Chow
Purina Dog Chow
Tender Vittles
Thrive

Pet Treats
Bonz
Hearty Chews
Purina Biscuits
Whisker Lickin's

Baby Food
Beech-Nut

Cereals
Almond Delight
Chex
Cookie Crisp
Oat Bran Options
Sun Flakes

Baked Products
Home Pride
Hostess Ding Dongs
Hostess Ho Hos
Hostess Sno Balls
Hostess Suzy Q's
Hostess Twinkies
Rykrisp
Wonder

Batteries
Energizer
Eveready

RANKINGS

69th in *Fortune* 500 Industrial Cos.
192nd in *Fortune* Global 500 Industrial Cos.
119th in *Forbes* Sales 500
117th in *Business Week* 1000
333rd in *Business Week* Global 1000

COMPETITION

Anheuser-Busch
General Mills
Gerber
Grand Metropolitan
Kellogg
Mars
Nestlé
Philip Morris
Quaker Oats
Whitman

RAYTHEON COMPANY

OVERVIEW

Raytheon produces electronic systems and equipment for the government and commercial customers. Sales to the government (mainly the DOD) accounted for 55% of the company's revenues in 1989. Raytheon's Patriot missile, scheduled to remain in production until 1992, has helped maintain the company's government-related earnings in a period marked by defense cutbacks.

Raytheon also makes Amana, Caloric, and Speed Queen appliances, as well as Beech aircraft; engages in geophysical exploration for the petrochemical industry (Seismograph); and builds chemical and power plants (Badger, United Engineers). Through D.C. Heath, Raytheon publishes textbooks.

Committed to education, especially in the sciences and mathematics, Raytheon sponsors programs such as the Academic Decathlon and Earthwatch Teacher Fellowships. The Lexington, Massachusetts–based company donated $250,000 in 1989 to support a partnership between Boston University and the city of Chelsea, Massachusetts, to improve learning programs at Chelsea schools.

WHEN

Raytheon started out as the American Appliance Company in 1922. Financed by several men, including Laurence Marshall, the company initially formed to manufacture C. G. Smith's new home refrigerator. Although it worked on paper, Smith's invention failed in practice, and Marshall turned to producing radio tubes. In 1925 the company renamed itself Raytheon, Inc., after the radio tube it produced.

Raytheon acquired the radio division of Chicago's Q. R. S. Company in 1928 and became Raytheon Manufacturing Company with Marshall as president. In 1929 Raytheon formed the Raytheon Production Company with the makers of the Eveready battery (National Carbon Company) to market Eveready Raytheon tubes. National Carbon withdrew from the venture in 1933.

During WWII Raytheon was the first company to produce magnetrons (tubes used in both radar and microwave ovens) and enjoyed a period of unprecedented growth throughout the war years, but by 1947 sales were down to $66 million from a wartime peak of $173 million. Amidst rumors of bankruptcy, Charles Francis Adams (still a director in 1990) became Raytheon's president. Adams sold the company's unprofitable radio and television business to the Admiral Corporation in 1956. The company adopted its present name in 1959.

Military orders stemming from the Korean conflict boosted sales in the mid-1950s. In the early 1960's Adams, then chairman, named Thomas Phillips, a Raytheon missile engineer since 1948, EVP (1962) and then president (1964). Phillips presided over a series of acquisitions designed to raise Raytheon's earnings in the commercial sector to an equal footing with the defense sector, beginning with Amana Refrigeration in 1965. Raytheon added D.C. Heath and Company (textbook publishing, 1966), the Caloric Corporation (stoves, 1967), and 3 companies involved in petrochemical construction and exploration (1966, 1968, 1969). In the meantime Raytheon built the on-board computers for the Apollo command and landing spacecraft.

In 1971 Raytheon started making computer terminals but could not compete with giants like IBM and ceased production in 1984. Raytheon began manufacturing single- and twin-engine planes in 1980 through the purchase of Beech Aircraft Corporation.

In spite of its diversification efforts, Raytheon still depended on missiles, radar, and communications systems for 90% of its earnings in 1987. A 1990 government investigation revealed that Raytheon and other defense contractors had been trading in Pentagon secrets. After pleading guilty, Raytheon agreed to pay a $1 million fine.

HOW MUCH

	9 Yr. Growth	1980	1981	1982	1983	1984	1985	1986	1987	1988	1989
Sales ($ mil)	6.5%	5,002	5,636	5,513	5,937	5,996	6,409	7,308	7,659	8,192	8,796
Net income ($ mil)	7.2%	282	324	319	300	340	376	393	445	490	529
Income as % of sales	—	5.6%	5.8%	5.8%	5.1%	5.7%	5.9%	5.4%	5.8%	6.0%	6.0%
Earnings per share ($)	10.1%	3.36	3.84	3.77	3.53	4.02	4.57	5.06	6.06	7.31	7.96
Stock price – high ($)	—	55.63	54.88	49.88	57.50	48.88	55.63	71.75	84.88	73.88	85.00
Stock price – low ($)	—	31.63	34.00	28.25	41.38	34.75	39.38	52.38	57.25	61.00	64.63
Stock price – close ($)	2.6%	55.00	37.38	44.75	43.13	40.13	53.63	67.25	66.63	67.00	69.50
P/E – high	—	17	14	13	16	12	12	14	14	10	11
P/E – low	—	9	9	8	12	9	9	10	9	8	8
Dividends per share ($)	9.2%	1.00	1.20	1.40	1.75	1.05	1.60	1.70	1.80	2.50	2.20
Book value per share ($)	10.0%	15.64	18.25	20.28	22.30	23.46	24.84	26.39	27.31	31.96	36.97

1989 Year End:
Debt ratio: 1.9%
Return on equity: 23.1%
Cash (mil): $99
Current ratio: 1.1
Long-term debt (mil): $46
Number of shares (mil): 66
Dividends:
1989 average yield: 3.2%
1989 payout: 27.6%
Market value (mil): $4,561

Stock Price History high/low 1980-89

90 80 70 60 50 40 30 20 10 0

NYSE symbol: RTN
Incorporated: Delaware, 1928
Fiscal year ends: December 31

WHO

Chairman and CEO: Thomas L. Phillips, age 65, $1,215,004 pay
President: Dennis J. Picard, age 57, $745,002 pay (prior to promotion)
SVP and Treasurer: Herbert Deitcher, age 56
Auditors: Coopers & Lybrand
Employees: 77,600

WHERE

HQ: 141 Spring St., Lexington, MA 02173
Phone: 617-862-6600
FAX: 617-860-2172

Raytheon has operations in 23 states and 6 foreign countries.

	1989 Sales		1989 Net Income	
	$ mil	% of total	$ mil	% of total
US	8,215	93	521	98
Foreign	581	7	8	2
Total	**8,796**	**100**	**529**	**100**

WHAT

	1989 Sales		1989 Operating Income	
	$ mil	% of total	$ mil	% of total
Electronics	5,333	61	707	76
Energy services	870	10	40	4
Appliances	1,070	12	53	6
Aircraft	915	10	75	8
Other	608	7	58	6
Adjustments	—	—	(187)	—
Total	**8,796**	**100**	**746**	**100**

Electronics
Air traffic control
Terminal Doppler Weather Radar
Military computers
Shipboard systems
Aegis radar and fire control equipment, Trident missile guidance systems
Submarine systems
Surveillance radars
Tactical missiles
Patriot, Hawk air-defense systems, Tacit Rainbow

Other
Cedarapids (road paving equipment)
D.C. Heath (textbook publisher)
Raytheon Service Co. (technical services)

Aircraft Products
Beech 1300 and 1900
Beech Bonanza
King Air
Starship I

Appliances
Amana
Caloric
Speed Queen

Energy Services
The Badger Co. (process industry engineering and construction)
GeoQuest Systems (geophysical and geological software)
Seismograph Service Corp.
United Engineers & Constructors

RANKINGS

52nd in *Fortune* 500 Industrial Cos.
22nd in *Fortune* 50 Exporters
89th in *Forbes* Sales 500
151st in *Business Week* 1000
459th in *Business Week* Global 1000

COMPETITION

Allied-Signal
Bechtel
Electrolux
General Dynamics
General Electric
Martin Marietta
Maytag
Rockwell International
Textron
Whirlpool
Other aerospace, defense, and electronics companies

THE READER'S DIGEST ASSOCIATION, INC.

OVERVIEW

Reader's Digest publishes and markets (via direct mail) books, magazines, and home entertainment products, including recorded music and videocassettes.

Reader's Digest, the "world's most widely read magazine," according to its cover, has an estimated readership of 100 million each month. Worldwide circulation is about 28 million; US circulation exceeds 16 million — the 3rd largest after *Modern Maturity* and the *NRTA/AARP News Bulletin.*

Each year the company's book and home entertainment segment sells over 21 million condensed books; 17 million how-to, cooking, travel, and other reference books; 4 million books in series (*Today's Best Nonfiction, World's Best Reading*); 5 million music collections; and 600,000 videos. Reader's Digest also publishes 3 special-interest magazines for home handypersons, travelers, and retirees. QSP, a subsidiary, is one of the largest organizations in the US assisting schools and youth groups in fund-raising efforts.

In February 1990 the company made its first public stock offering, a block of nonvoting shares that represent 21% of the total.

NYSE symbol: RDA
Incorporated: Delaware, 1951
Fiscal year ends: June 30

WHO

Chairman, President, COO, and CEO: George V. Grune, age 60, $1,010,707 pay
Editor-in-Chief: Kenneth O. Gilmore, age 59, $517,267 pay
VP and CFO: Anthony W. Ruggiero
Auditors: KPMG Peat Marwick
Employees: 7,400

WHERE

HQ: Pleasantville, NY 10570
Phone: 914-238-1000
FAX: 914-238-4559

Reader's Digest is published in 39 editions in 15 languages. US circulation is about 16 million, while foreign circulation is about 12 million.

	1989 Sales		1989 Operating Income	
	$ mil	% of total	$ mil	% of total
United States	856	47	121	48
Europe	725	40	97	38
Other	251	13	35	14
Adjustments	—	—	(46)	—
Total	**1,832**	**100**	**207**	**100**

WHEN

The first edition of DeWitt and Lila Wallace's monthly *Reader's Digest* appeared in 1922 and was an immediate success. Within 3 years circulation had almost quintupled, and the Wallaces moved from New York City to Pleasantville, New York. The idea of condensing material from other magazines into a compact, readable form proved to be very popular, and the magazine grew enormously in the 1920s and 1930s, reaching a circulation of one million by 1935. In 1939 the company moved its headquarters to Chappaqua, New York, but kept Pleasantville, the company's home since 1924, as a mailing address.

In the 1940s the *Digest* expanded internationally (the first overseas edition started in England in 1938), opening offices on 5 continents and providing foreign-language translations. Total circulation went from almost 3 million in 1939 to 9 million in 1946. During the 1940s DeWitt Wallace began to write his own articles (partly because some magazines had stopped allowing him reprint rights), giving the publication the conservative, optimistic style that has since characterized it.

In 1950 the company published the first of the Reader's Digest Condensed Books series. In 1955 the *Digest* accepted its first advertising but did not carry liquor ads until 1978 and has never carried cigarette ads. *Reader's Digest* published articles in the mid-1950s examining the link between smoking and cancer.

The company added the Recorded Music Division in 1959 and the General Books Division in 1963. The company was the first to use direct mail advertising with "personalized" letters to promote these products. Its huge mailing list was later used for promotions like the *Reader's Digest* Sweepstakes.

The Wallaces continued to manage the company until 1973. DeWitt died at age 91 in 1981; Lila died at age 94 three years later. Since the Wallaces had no children, their voting stock in the company passed to The DeWitt and Lila Wallace Trust, and about 6 million nonvoting shares were divided among 10 charities, including the Metropolitan Museum of Art, Lincoln Center, the New York Zoological Society, Macalester College (St. Paul, Minnesota), and the Sloan-Kettering Cancer Center.

Ex-marine George Grune took over as chairman and CEO in 1984. He cut costs by reducing staff by 20% and disposing of unprofitable subsidiaries, which ushered in an era of increased profitability for the company. Reader's Digest added a line of specialty magazines by purchasing *Travel-Holiday* in 1986 (the company's first acquisition of another US magazine), *Family Handyman* in 1988, *50 Plus* (renamed *New Choices for the Best Years*) in 1988, and *American Health* magazine in 1990. The company bought 50% of British publisher Dorling Kindersley in 1987.

The company announced plans to go public in 1989 and made an initial stock offering in February 1990. Since then, the company has endured unprecedented public scrutiny. Morale is low because many employees view the company as a public trust, with loftier goals than the bottom line of profit and loss. Reader's Digest has recently lost several top executives, including its president, general counsel, and CFO.

WHAT

	1989 Sales		1989 Operating Income	
	$ mil	% of total	$ mil	% of total
Reader's Digest	590	32	62	24
Books, records, video	1,086	59	192	76
Special-interest magazines	47	3	(17)	(7)
Other	109	6	16	7
Adjustments	—	—	(46)	—
Total	**1,832**	**100**	**207**	**100**

Products and Services

Magazines
American Health
The Family Handyman
New Choices for the Best Years
Reader's Digest
Travel-Holiday

Books, Records, Video
Anthology series (*e.g., World's Best Reading*)
General/reference books
Reader's Digest Condensed Books
Recorded music packages
Videocassette packages

Other Operations
Direct mail promotions
Fund-raising products and services for community groups (QSP, Inc.)
Sweepstakes

RANKINGS

225th in *Fortune* 500 Industrial Cos.
416th in *Forbes* Sales 500
221st in *Business Week* 1000
638th in *Business Week* Global 1000

COMPETITION

Advance Publications
Bertelsmann
Hearst
News Corp.
Paramount
Time Warner

HOW MUCH

	5 Yr. Growth	1980	1981	1982	1983	1984	1985	1986	1987	1988	1989
Sales ($ mil)	7.0%	—	—	—	—	1,304	1,217	1,255	1,420	1,712	1,832
Net income ($ mil)	48.6%	—	—	—	—	21	52	73	95	142	152
Income as % of sales	—	—	—	—	—	1.6%	4.3%	5.8%	6.7%	8.3%	8.3%

1989 Year End:
Debt ratio: 2.4%
Return on equity: 38.1%
Cash (mil): $331
Current ratio: 2.48
Long-term debt (mil): $11

THE RED CROSS

OVERVIEW

The International Red Cross and Red Crescent Movement is an international humanitarian effort to alleviate all forms of human suffering. The International Red Cross and Red Crescent Movement consists of 3 major components: the International Committee of the Red Cross (ICRC), the Red Cross's founding body, which is based in Geneva; the League of Red Cross and Red Crescent Societies, a federation of the national societies; and the 149 recognized national Red Cross and Red Crescent societies.

Completely neutral in its orientation, the Red Cross and Red Crescent Movement operates under the principles established by the Geneva Conventions. The Movement indiscriminately provides aid to victims of countless international conflicts and internal disturbances, often under fire from parties who disregard the Red Cross and Red Crescent emblems.

In 1989 the Red Cross/Red Crescent distributed 34,000 tons of food and material in 33 countries, visited prisoners of war (as well as civilian internees and security detainees) in 839 locations in 45 countries, and through its Central Tracing Agency forwarded 1.4 million family messages and registered about 660,000 pieces of information regarding persons reported missing or in captivity.

In 1989 the American Red Cross fielded over 1.1 million volunteers, raised $807 million, collected over 6 million pints of blood, and educated almost 10 million people through its health and safety courses.

WHEN

In 1859 Jean-Henri Dunant, a Swiss businessman who was traveling in northern Italy, witnessed the aftermath of the battle of Solferino, one of the century's bloodiest battles, in which more than 40,000 French, Italian, and Austrian troops were killed or wounded. Horrified by the countless wounded men left on the battlefield (as was the custom of the day), Dunant began organizing relief efforts in a nearby village.

Three years later Dunant published a pamphlet (*Un Souvenir de Solferino*) in which he called for the formation of international volunteer societies to aid wounded soldiers. In 1863 the Societe d'Utilite Publique (a public welfare organization) in Geneva set up a 5-person committee (which included Dunant) to explore his proposal. The 5 men formed the International Committee of the Red Cross (ICRC) and called a conference that was attended by delegates of 16 countries. The conference resulted in the formation of national Red Cross societies across Europe. A red cross on a white background (the reverse of the Swiss flag) was chosen as the organization's symbol.

In 1864 the ICRC principles were codified into international law through the Geneva Convention (the first of 4), which was initially signed by 12 nations. The ICRC's first major relief effort occurred during the Franco-Prussian War (1870) when the organization cared for 510,000 sick and wounded. The ICRC continued to draw new member nations during the latter half of the 19th century. By 1900 national Red Cross societies existed in almost 30 countries.

The American Red Cross was founded in 1882 by Clara Barton, who had become famous for her aid to soldiers on both sides in the US Civil War (1861-1865) and had subsequently assisted the International Red Cross in the Franco-Prussian War. Barton's contribution to the International Red Cross movement was her expansion of Red Cross aid to victims of natural disasters (fires, floods, etc.).

During WWI Red Cross workers from several nations served beside the armed forces on the battlefields of Europe. The horrors of WWI led the ICRC to recommend bans on chemical and biological weapons and to extend protection to prisoners of war. In 1919 Henry P. Davison, chairman of the Red Cross War Council, led the formation of the League of Red Cross Societies to establish a peacetime program of international assistance and development.

The International Red Cross mobilized massive relief efforts during WWII and again served beside the armed forces. Since then the Red Cross and Red Crescent (national organizations in Muslim countries) have developed humanitarian programs while providing assistance in hundreds of international conflicts, natural disasters, and areas of political turmoil. In 1977 the most recent additions to the Geneva Convention were adopted. Today the ICRC's 149 member societies are active worldwide, from Central America to the Israeli-occupied territories.

HOW MUCH

$= SF 1.54 (Dec. 31, 1989)	9 Yr. Growth	1979	1980	1981	1982	1983	1984	1985	1986	1987	1988
Total assets (SF mil)	13.4%	37	40	53	64	92	116	94	108	111	114
Total expenditures (SF mil)	—	—	—	—	—	224	305	475	248	264	349

Total Assets (SF mil) 1979-88

Nonprofit organization
Founded: 1863
Fiscal year ends: December 31

WHO

President of the ICRC: Cornelio Sommaruga
Director of Operations: Andre Pasquier
Head of Finance and Administration: Jacques Hertzschuch
Head of Human Resources: Philippe Dind
Head of Operational Support: Michel Convers
Head of Communication: Alain Modoux
Auditors: ATAG Fiduciaire Générale SA
Employees: 4,339

WHERE

HQ: The International Committee of the Red Cross, Geneva, Switzerland
American Red Cross HQ: 17th and D Sts. NW, Washington, DC 20006
Phone: 202-737-8300

The ICRC maintains 48 global delegations in Africa, Asia, Europe, North America, Latin America, and the Middle East.

In 1989 there were 149 national Red Cross and Red Crescent societies worldwide.

	1988 Expenditures by Region	
	SF thou	% of total
Africa	149,490	43
Asia & the Pacific	56,252	16
Middle East & N. Africa	40,224	12
Latin America	28,865	8
Europe & N. America	3,398	1
General activities	70,769	20
Total	**348,998**	**100**
Staff	**No.**	**% of total**
Headquarters staff	658	15
Field staff	3,681	85
Total	**4,339**	**100**

WHAT

	1988 Expenditures by Type of Activity	
	SF thou	% of total
Material assistance	115,656	33
Protection	60,306	17
Medical assistance	51,899	15
Operational support	28,544	8
Promotion of international humanitarian law	26,058	8
Support activities	20,896	6
Central Tracing Agency	13,759	4
Management activities	11,907	3
Extra-budgetary expenses	10,199	3
Aid to national societies	9,774	3
Total	**348,998**	**100**

Activities
Aid to prisoners of war and security detainees
Blood donations and tissue transplants
Health education
Medical and material relief to victims of war and disaster
Refugee aid
Tracing of victims of armed conflicts

Basic Principles
Humanity
Impartiality
Independence
Neutrality
Unity
Universality
Voluntary Service

REEBOK INTERNATIONAL LTD.

OVERVIEW

With a 23.7% market share, Reebok is the 2nd largest domestic producer of athletic shoes (after NIKE). The company's well-known shoe brand names include Reebok, Weebok, Rockport, Avia, and Ellesse. In addition the company produces a wide line of apparel. Reebok's Boston Whaler Division is a leading producer of fiberglass recreational boats.

Aerobic shoes (which generate 19.2% of revenues) continue as Reebok's strongest product line. Other major shoe categories include tennis (14.2%), basketball (12.2%), and cross-training (10.7%). Reebok remains at the forefront of athletic shoe technology with such innovations as THE PUMP, Energy Return System (ERS), Hexalite, and Energaire.

The company produces most of its shoes overseas. South Korea and Taiwan produce 61% and 16%, respectively, of company footwear. Reebok sells about 15 million pairs of shoes outside the US and is the leading brand in Australia, Canada, Hong Kong, New Zealand, and Singapore.

Through its Reebok Foundation, the company supports a wide range of philanthropic causes, with special emphasis on minority groups and human rights awareness.

WHEN

English runner Joseph W. Foster invented a spiked running shoe in 1894. Other runners liked the shoe so much that Foster started his own shoe company (JW Foster and Sons). In 1924 Foster supplied the shoes for the British Olympic team (of *Chariots of Fire* fame). Two of Foster's grandsons formed a companion company, Reebok (named for a speedy African antelope), in 1958 that eventually absorbed JW Foster & Sons.

Reebok remained a small British shoe company until 1979 when Paul Fireman, a distributor of fishing and camping supplies, noticed the shoes at a Chicago international trade show. Fireman quickly acquired the exclusive North American license to sell Reebok shoes. Pentland Industries, another British company, agreed to finance Fireman for 55.5% ownership of Reebok USA. Fireman acquired 40% of the new venture with the remainder going to a group of American investors. Reebok established its American headquarters in Avon, Massachusetts, and set up production facilities in Korea.

Sales executives at Reebok USA realized the difficulty the company would have competing with the running shoes of established competitors NIKE and Adidas; therefore, they looked to the aerobic shoe market. In 1982 Reebok introduced Freestyle, a women's sneaker with a terrycloth lining which resembled the type of shoes worn by chorus-line dancers. In 1983 Reebok followed with a line of men's fitness shoes.

Reebok's new aerobic shoe line coincided with a rise in the popularity of aerobics and Reebok's fashionable Freestyle became the largest selling shoe in history. Sales went from $3.5 million in 1982 to $800 million in 1986, enough to vault Reebok past NIKE as the leader in the athletic shoe industry.

In 1985 Reebok USA acquired full control of the British parent company. Later that year Reebok went public. Reebok acquired Rockport (walking and casual shoes) in 1986, Avia (athletic shoes) and Frye (boots) in 1987, and Boston Whaler (recreational boats) in 1989. It sold Frye in 1989.

Reebok introduced Weeboks (a line of children's shoes) in 1987. In 1988 the company sponsored Amnesty International's "Human Rights Now!" rock tour. Reebok adopted the slogan "the Physics Behind the Physiques" in 1989 and that same year introduced THE PUMP (a $170 inflatable basketball shoe).

Reebok (in second place for the first time since 1985 with 23.7% market share as opposed to NIKE's 24.8% market share) plans to explore the emerging Eastern European market during the 1990s.

HOW MUCH

	5 Yr. Growth	1980	1981	1982	1983	1984	1985	1986	1987	1988	1989
Sales ($ mil)	94.2%	—	—	—	—	66	307	919	1,389	1,786	1,822
Net income ($ mil)	96.3%	—	—	—	—	6	39	132	165	137	175
Income as % of sales	—	—	—	—	—	9.3%	12.7%	14.4%	11.9%	7.7%	9.6%
Earnings per share ($)	80.4%	—	—	—	—	0.08	0.45	1.28	1.49	1.20	1.53
Stock price – high ($)	—	—	—	—	—	—	4.96	17.63	25.19	18.38	19.63
Stock price – low ($)	—	—	—	—	—	—	3.29	4.19	7.00	9.50	11.13
Stock price – close ($)	—	—	—	—	—	—	4.67	11.69	10.63	12.25	19.00
P/E – high	—	—	—	—	—	—	11	14	17	15	13
P/E – low	—	—	—	—	—	—	7	3	5	8	7
Dividends per share ($)	—	—	—	—	—	0.00	0.00	0.00	0.20	0.30	0.30
Book value per share ($)	141.7%	—	—	—	—	0.09	0.93	2.82	5.20	6.12	7.42

1989 Year End:
Debt ratio: 11.6%
Return on equity: 22.6%
Cash (mil): $171
Current ratio: 3.86
Long-term debt (mil): $110
Number of shares (mil): 114
Dividends:
1989 average yield: 1.6%
1989 payout: 19.6%
Market value (mil): $2,163

Stock Price History high/low 1985-89

30
25
20
15
10
5
0

NYSE symbol: RBK
Incorporated: Massachusetts, 1985
Fiscal year ends: December 31

WHO

Chairman, President, and CEO: Paul B. Fireman, age 46, $14,606,200 pay
EVP and CFO: Paul R. Duncan, age 49, $598,558 pay
Auditors: Laventhol & Horwath
Employees: 3,000

WHERE

HQ: 100 Technology Center Dr., Stoughton, MA 02072
Phone: 617-341-5000
FAX: 617-341-5087

The company sells its products in 45 countries, with 80% of international revenues coming from the UK, Australia, France, Spain, Germany, Italy, and Japan. In 1989 Reebok introduced its products to the Soviet Union.

	1989 Sales		1989 Net Income	
	$ mil	% of total	$ mil	% of total
US	1,584	87	114	65
Europe	117	6	52	30
Other countries	121	7	9	5
Total	**1,822**	**100**	**175**	**100**

WHAT

	1989 Sales	
	$ mil	% of total
Reebok	1,365	75
Rockport	192	11
Avia	196	11
Apparel	42	2
Ellesse	21	1
Boston Whaler	6	—
Total	**1,822**	**100**

Shoes
Avia
Cantilever
Ellesse
Reebok
AXT
CXT
Dance Reebok
ERS
Freestyle
Metaphors
SXT
THE PUMP
Weebok
Rockport
Boating shoes
DresSports
Signature Collection
Walking Pump

Apparel
Aerobics outfits
Golf wear
Running clothes
Shirts
Shorts
Socks
Tennis wear

Recreational Boats
Boston Whaler

RANKINGS

423rd in *Forbes* Sales 500
306th in *Business Week* 1000

COMPETITION

Brunswick
INTERCO
Levi Strauss
MacAndrews & Forbes
NIKE
Outboard Marine
United States Shoe
V. F.
Other apparel manufacturers

THE REFERENCE PRESS, INC.

OVERVIEW

The Reference Press is the sole start-up venture in this book. As such, it is both the youngest company (founded February 1990) and the smallest (zero revenues as of this writing). It is also the publisher of this book, its initial product.

The Reference Press was created to distill business and economic information and deliver that information to a very broad audience. While there are many providers of business data, most of them sell their services by mail or subscription, and most of them are expensive. All Reference Press books will be available in bookstores and mass merchandise retail outlets at an affordable price.

As a pure reference book publisher, the company limits its present scope to the writing and presentation of information. The Reference Press does not intend to establish a sales force, printing plant, or warehouse; the company has retained experienced professionals to perform these tasks.

As a new entrepreneurial venture, the company has great aspirations. The many writers, fact-checkers, proofreaders, editors, desktop publishers, and others involved in *HOOVER'S HANDBOOK* hope you find the book useful.

WHEN

The Reference Press was founded in February 1990 by Gary Hoover to produce economic and business reference books.

While we often read of overnight successes in business, many of the companies in this book took some time to get off the ground. That is a good omen for the Reference Press, because *HOOVER'S HANDBOOK* reflects an idea that is over 20 years old. That idea began in the head of an unusual fellow named Gary Hoover.

Hoover developed several interests early in life: by the age of 9, he was collecting *World Almanacs* and *World Atlases*; by the age of 12, he was subscribing to *Fortune* (1963). At school, he learned reading and 'rithmetic, science and history. But outside of school in his hometown (Anderson, Indiana), the world seemed to revolve around something called General Motors, the largest employer in town.

The teenage Hoover would ask his teachers many questions; they had answers about everything but GM. What was it? Who started it? How did it work? Even the *World Book* and *Webster's* seemed to think GM didn't exist, although it had all the characteristics of being real, perhaps even evolving like a living thing.

The ensuing 25 years were probably better to Hoover than they were to General Motors. He studied economics at the University of Chicago, worked as a stock analyst for Citibank, and spent 7 years in the department store industry (having developed an interest in retailing). In 1982 he founded a bookstore chain (BOOKSTOP & BOOKSTAR) that he helped build into the nation's 4th largest seller of books before it was sold to B. Dalton in 1989. Throughout this period he collected more books, especially reference books.

He found books on blimps and bats, cacti and cars, movies and music, and travel and tetracycline, but few books about companies. Yet the headlines were full of economic news, of LBOs and mergers, and of stock markets around the world.

Finally, Hoover and a group of friends decided they had waited long enough. Hoover's idea of providing answers to people's questions about businesses became a reality on February 8, 1990, when Hoover's lawyers incorporated the company. By mid-March, 20 full-time and freelance people were on board and the project was underway.

Once 542 enterprises were selected to be in the book, based on their influence in our lives, each was contacted for information. Writers searched libraries for books, periodicals, and databases for more insights. Standard & Poor's Compustat provided data for most of the How Much sections. Each one-page profile was edited, cross-checked, and proofed. The investment made by Hoover and his friends rapidly approached $1,000,000. By September the number of full-time and part-time employees had grown to almost 60.

The book you hold in your hands represents 7 months of frenzied activity on the part of this small group of people. Let's hope *HOOVER'S HANDBOOK* is worth the long wait. At the least, Gary Hoover's reference shelf will finally contain a reference book that covers General Motors. Some things you just have to do for yourself.

HOW MUCH

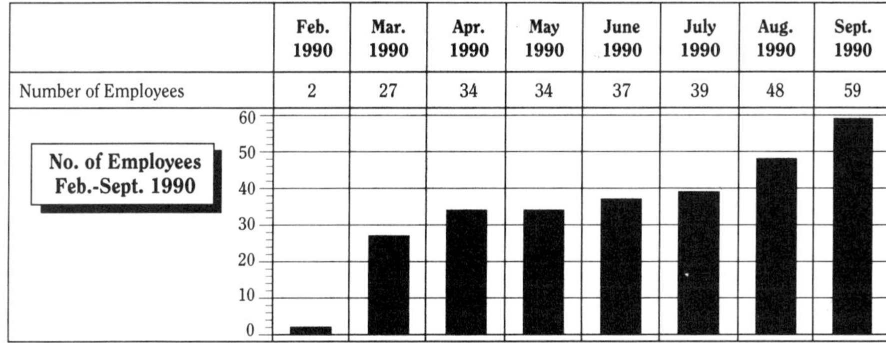

	Feb. 1990	Mar. 1990	Apr. 1990	May 1990	June 1990	July 1990	Aug. 1990	Sept. 1990
Number of Employees	2	27	34	34	37	39	48	59

Private company
Incorporated: Delaware, 1990
Fiscal year ends: March 31

WHO

Chairman, Publisher, and CEO: Gary Hoover, age 39, $36,000 pay
SVP and Editor-in-Chief: Alta Campbell, age 41
VP, Acting CFO, and Senior Writer: Alan Chai, age 38
VP and Editor: Patrick J. Spain, age 38
Auditors: Price Waterhouse
Employees: 7 full-time and more than 50 temporary and part-time; for a complete list of contributors, see Acknowledgments.

WHERE

HQ: 6448 Hwy. 290 E., Suite E-104, Austin, TX 78723
Phone: 512-454-7778
FAX: 512-454-9401

WHAT

Suppliers
Acorn Press (Austin)
Austin Coca-Cola Bottling Co. (Austin)
Best Printing (Austin)
Bizmart (Austin)
Classic Design Cabinets (Elgin, TX)
ComputerCraft (Austin)
Crest Litho, Inc. (Watervliet, NY)
Davis Group (Austin)
Disclosure Inc. (Dallas)
Dow Jones News Retrieval (Princeton, NJ)
Federal Express Corp. (Memphis)
Fitch, Even, Tabin & Flannery (Chicago)
Hixo, Inc. (Austin)
Mr. Gatti's Pizza (Austin)
Office Furniture Distributors (Austin)
Paychex, Inc. (Austin)
PR/Texas (Dallas)
R & B Corporate Park–La Costa (Austin)
Shapiro, Edens & Cook (Austin)
Standard & Poor's Compustat Services, Inc. (Englewood, CO)
Texas Commerce Bank (Austin)
Tracor Publications (Austin)
Tramex Travel (Austin)

The Reference Press Mission Statement

1. To produce business and economic reference books of the highest quality, accuracy, and readability
2. To make those books widely available through mass distribution at an affordable price
3. To make sure people are aware of our product through publicity, advertising, and shelf exposure
4. To create interesting, worthwhile jobs
5. To reward our employees creatively and fairly, without prejudice
6. To allow our key people to participate in the fruits of their labor through an incentive stock option program
7. To hold to the highest ethical business standards, including complete honesty and openness in all our dealings, erring on the side of generosity when in doubt
8. To enhance the wealth of our suppliers, from distributors and printers to landlords
9. To continually expand our product line
10. To enhance the wealth of our shareholders by creating an enterprise of lasting value

RELIANCE ELECTRIC COMPANY

OVERVIEW

Reliance Electric operates in 3 industry segments: telecommunications products, mechanical power transmission products, and electric motors and motor controls. The company is capable of providing complete plant automation in the manufacturing and materials handling industries.

Reliance's telecommunications business, Comm/Tec, manufactures and markets transmission, protection, and connection devices, power supplies, and related equipment. Sales are made to all US telephone companies.

The company's mechanical power transmission products are used to transmit power from the shaft of an electric motor or other power source to various types of driven machinery. Products include mounted bearings, speed reducers, conveyor belt components, transmissions, brakes and clutches, mechanical products used in bulk and unit material handling, food processing, and general industrial applications.

Electrical products include motors and motor controls, distributed control equipment, and power transformers. These products are sold to the metals and mining, forest products, petrochemical, petroleum refining, automotive, printing, machine tool, textile, and utility industries.

Once an Exxon subsidiary, Reliance is now owned primarily by company management, Citicorp, and Prudential-Bache.

WHEN

Reliance Electric was founded in Cleveland in 1907 as Lincoln Motor Works. The company changed its name to Reliance Electric and Engineering Company in 1909. Soon after WWI, Reliance produced a newly designed electric motor based on a year of customer research. The new product was very successful and established the company's position as a supplier of high-quality motors.

After this early success Reliance continued to make high-quality products but eventually lost touch with the demands of its marketplace. In the late 1950s Reliance designed a futuristic motor control unit that used a complex series of vacuum tubes. But customers found the drive too complicated and delicate, and it was a commercial failure. By the mid-1960s Reliance's annual growth rate was down to around 4% per year, far below more innovative competitors such as General Electric.

In 1967, following several years of self-examination, the company began to reorganize at the corporate level and to diversify in order to bring its production in line with market demands. The company's new corporate structure reflected the markets served rather than production operations. The company focused on production of industrial automation systems, which are used to cut costs, and, therefore, are not as cyclical as sales of electric motors, which are used to increase capacity. The company bought Dodge Manufacturing (mechanical power transmission products, 1967), Toledo Scale (weighing equipment, bulk material handling equipment, and elevators, 1967), and Applied Dynamics (analog computers, 1969). By 1970 the company was in a position to sell a full line of automation equipment, which provided over 80% of sales in that year.

Reliance entered the telecommunications field in the 1970s with the purchases of Lorain (power supplies, 1973), a unit of Continental Telephone (local transmission equipment, 1976), and Reliable Electric (wire and splicing equipment, 1977). Reliance also expanded overseas during this period, with international profits quadrupling between 1970 and 1974.

In 1979 Reliance announced plans to sell Haughton Elevator to Schindler Holdings of Switzerland for $40 million and bought Federal Pacific Electric (FPE, circuit breakers) for $345 million. In the same year Exxon bought Reliance for $1.2 billion, paying $72 per share for stock that had recently traded at $34, a premium of about $600 million. Exxon was looking for a manufacturer to produce a new alternating current synthesizer motor control that Exxon executives believed would revolutionize the industry. The device turned out to be impractical to produce. Reliance continued as a subsidiary of Exxon until 1987, when Reliance's top management, Citicorp, and Prudential-Bache paid $1.35 billion for the company in an LBO.

In 1989 Reliance sold Toledo Scale to a subsidiary of Ciba-Geigy of Switzerland for $210 million. The company used proceeds from the sale, as well as from earnings, to reduce its long-term debt from $800 million on December 31, 1988 to $630 million by March 31, 1990.

HOW MUCH

	2 Yr. Growth	1980	1981	1982	1983	1984	1985	1986	1987	1988	1989
Sales ($ mil)	0.1%	—	—	—	—	—	—	—	1,408	1,303	1,411
Net income ($ mil)	—	—	—	—	—	—	—	—	(5)	27	33
Income as % of sales	—	—	—	—	—	—	—	—	(0.4%)	2.1%	2.3%

1989 Year End:
Debt ratio: 98.3%
Return on equity: —
Cash (mil): $46
Current ratio: 2.27
Long-term debt (mil): $649
Total assets (mil) $1,140

Net Income ($ mil) 1987-89

35 30 25 20 15 10 5 0 -5

Private company
Incorporated: Delaware, 1986
Fiscal year ends: December 31

WHO

Chairman: H. Virgil Sherrill
President and CEO: John C. Morley
EVP: L. J. Hendrix, Jr.
CFO, VP, Controller, and Treasurer: Keith C. Moore, Jr.
VP; President, Reliance Comm/Tec: Dudley P. Sheffler
VP Employee and Community Relations: E. Scott Dalton
VP, General Counsel, and Secretary: John H. Portwood
VP Technology and Corporate Development: Peter J. Tsivitse
Auditors: Price Waterhouse
Employees: 13,000

WHERE

HQ: 6065 Parkland Blvd., Cleveland, OH 44124
Phone: 216-266-5800
FAX: 216-266-7666

Reliance operates 43 factories in Australia, Brazil, Canada, France, Germany, Italy, Japan, Mexico, Spain, Switzerland, the UK, and the US.

	1989 Sales		1989 Operating Income	
	$ mil	% of total	$ mil	% of total
US	1,285	90	184	94
Foreign	148	10	11	6
Adjustments	(22)	—	(8)	—
Total	**1,411**	**100**	**187**	**100**

WHAT

	1989 Sales		1989 Operating Income	
	$ mil	% of total	$ mil	% of total
Industrial products	1,042	74	161	83
Telecommunications	371	26	34	17
Adjustments	(2)	—	(8)	—
Total	**1,411**	**100**	**187**	**100**

Trademarks

Electrical Products
Programmable control products for manufacturing processes
A-C motors and generators
Low voltage D-C motors
Power utility transformers

Mechanical Products
English and metric bearings and mountings
Adjustable speed drives
Shaft mounted gear reducers

Telecommunications
Digital Subscriber Carrier Systems
Uninterruptible power supplies
Fiber optic monitoring test equipment

RANKINGS

275th in *Fortune* 500 Industrial Cos.
103rd in *Forbes* 400 US Private Cos.

COMPETITION

AT&T
Dana
Eaton
Emerson
General Electric
Siemens
Square D
Westinghouse

RENAULT

OVERVIEW

French government-controlled Renault is Europe's #6 carmaker. Renault and Volvo (Sweden) have agreed to cross-ownership of the companies' automobile and truck divisions. The alliance with Volvo gives Renault a badly needed infusion of cash, a boost in the luxury car arena, and potential cost efficiencies. On a combined basis, the Renault/Volvo truck business would be the largest in the world. Renault owns 40% of Mack Trucks, a US company suffering from profitability and labor problems, and has agreed to buy the rest.

Selling most of its cars in France and other protected markets, Renault is vulnerable to the opening of European markets in 1992 and an expected increase in Japanese competition. The company's ability to cut costs has been restricted by its status as a quasi-government agency and by strong Communist unions.

In 1990 an EC commission ordered Renault to repay over $1 billion in subsidies received from the French government in 1988, claiming the transaction distorted competition.

WHEN

In the Paris suburb of Billancourt in 1898, 21-year-old Louis Renault assembled a motorized vehicle with a transmission box of his own design. Louis and his brothers, Marcel and Fernand, established Renault Freres and produced the world's first sedan in 1899. Louis took sole possession of the company and renamed it Societe Louis Renault after Marcel died in a racing accident (1903) and Fernand left the business (1908).

Taxis soon became Renault's best-selling products. In 1914 a fleet of 600 Paris taxis shuttled French troops to fight off the Germans in the Battle of the Marne. Renault also contributed to the war effort by building light tanks and airplane engines.

Between the wars Renault became increasingly self-sufficient, producing its own components and building foundries. The company expanded into trucks and tractors and became a major aircraft engine maker. Renault sustained heavy damage in WWII, but Louis Renault operated the remaining Paris facilities for the Germans during their occupation of France. After the liberation of Paris, he was accused of collaboration with the enemy and died in prison, awaiting trial, in 1944.
De Gaulle nationalized Renault in 1945 and gave it its present name.

Worldwide economic growth aided Renault's postwar comeback in France and abroad. The company achieved its greatest success in high-volume, low-cost cars such as the 4 CV in the late 1940s and 1950s, the Renault 4 in the 1960s and 1970s, and the Renault 5 in the 1970s and 1980s.

In 1979 Renault acquired 42%, later raised to 45%, of Mack Trucks (US) and 46% of American Motors Corporation (AMC), expecting the purchase to help the company gain US market share. In the early 1980s AMC fared poorly, and Renault sales suffered from a worldwide slump in auto sales, an aging product line, and stiff competition from Japanese carmakers in the US. Decreasing sales revealed the company's unwieldy bureaucracy, low productivity, and above-average payscales. In 1984 Renault lost over $1.5 billion.

Georges Besse took over management of Renault in 1985, trimmed employment by 20,000, and tried to reinstill the profit motive in the government-owned firm. When Besse was assassinated by terrorists in 1986, Raymond Lévy assumed his role and continued his policies, laying off 30,000 more workers and selling AMC to Chrysler (1987). Renault returned to profitability, aided by a booming car market and strong protectionist policies against Japanese carmakers in France, Italy, and Spain. France restricts imports of Japanese origin to a maximum of 3% of the total market.

Renault and Volvo agreed to extensive cross-ownership and cooperation in international auto and truck operations in 1990.

HOW MUCH

$=FF5.78 (Dec. 31, 1989)	9 Yr. Growth	1980	1981	1982	1983	1984	1985	1986	1987	1988	1989
Sales (FF bil)	9.0%	80	82	97	102	107	111	122	148	161	174
Net income (FF mil)	—	—	(579)	(1,420)	(1,803)	(12,721)	(10,897)	(5,874)	3,256	8,834	9,289
Income as % of sales	—	—	(0.7%)	(1.5%)	(1.8%)	(11.9%)	(9.8%)	(4.8%)	2.2%	5.5%	5.3%
Personnel (thou)*	(4.3%)	105	104	104	103	98	86	79	76	72	71
Capital contributions by French Govt. (FF mil)	—	2,025	1,725	2,745	2,745	4,661	3,030	8,030	0	12,028	0
Book value per share (FF mil)	—	—	11,203	10,699	10,164	(234)	(9,450)	(11,433)	(7,811)	14,012	22,466

1989 Year End:
Debt ratio: 53%
Return on equity: 50.9%
Cash (mil): FF4,238
Current ratio: 0.886
Long-term debt (mil): FF25,336
Number of shares (mil): —
Dividends:
1989 average yield: —
1989 payout: —
Sales (mil): $30,125

Sales (FF bil) 1980-89

*parent company only

Government-owned company
Incorporated: France, 1945
Fiscal year ends: December 31

WHO

President and Director General: Raymond H. Lévy, age 63
Adjunct Director General: Philippe Gras
Adjunct Director General and Financial and Planning Director: Louis Schweitzer
Auditors: La Villeguerin Audit; Michel Poisson; HSD/Ernst & Young International
Employees: 174,573

WHERE

HQ: Régie Nationale des Usines Renault, 34, quai du Point du Jour, B.P. 103-92109 Boulogne-Billancourt Cedex, France
Phone: 011-33-1-46-09-15-30

Renault does business in over 100 countries.

	1989 Sales	
	FF mil	% of total
France	85,841	49
Other EC	60,457	35
Other Western Europe	3,687	2
Eastern Europe	1,837	1
Africa	3,215	2
US & Canada	12,519	7
Latin America	3,591	2
Near East	1,260	1
Far East & Oceania	2,070	1
Total	**174,477**	**100**

WHAT

	1989 Sales		1989 Pretax Income	
	FF mil	% of total	FF mil	% of total
Automobiles	135,717	78	8,167	84
Industrial vehicles	33,525	19	(476)	(5)
Other industrial prods.	5,235	3	224	2
Financial services	—	—	1,810	19
Total	**174,477**	**100**	**9,725**	**100**

US Affiliate
Mack Trucks, Inc.

Joint Venture Partners
DAF (small utility vehicles)
Matra (auto production)
Peugeot (motors, vehicle assembly)
Toyota (assembly of 4x4 vehicles)
Volvo (see table below)

	Cross-Holdings of Renault & Volvo	
	% owned by Renault	% owned by Volvo
Renault (parent company and auto div.)	—	20
Renault (truck division)	55	45
Volvo (parent company)	10	—
Volvo (auto division)	25	75
Volvo (truck division)	45	55

RANKINGS

27th in *Fortune* Global 500 Industrial Cos.
79th in *Forbes* 100 Foreign Investments in the US

COMPETITION

Fiat
Navistar
PACCAR

REPUBLICAN PARTY

OVERVIEW

The Republican party, often called the "Grand Old Party" (GOP), is the minority of the 2 major American political parties. More conservative than that of the Democratic party, Republican support consists largely of corporate, financial, and farming interests. Politically the party favors free enterprise, laissez-faire (government noninterference), and opposition to the welfare state. The party's symbol (the elephant) was invented by political cartoonist Thomas Nast.

Major party concerns claimed by President George Bush (elected in 1988) include maintaining a strong economy, not raising taxes, combating drugs, cleaning up the environment, and reforming education.

The Republican party has launched a major effort to regain majority party status by the year 2000. It hopes to broaden its support base by attracting groups (primarily minorities) that have historically voted for Democratic candidates.

In addition, the party hopes to regain control of the House and Senate, where they are outnumbered by the Democrats 258 to 176 and 54 to 45, respectively.

WHEN

In 1854 widespread opposition to the Kansas-Nebraska Act (which opened both territories to slavery) resulted in the formation of a new political party, named Republican after the party of the same name formed by Thomas Jefferson. The party grew quickly, absorbing many Whigs, Free Soilers, and Northern Democrats. After overcoming the rival American (Know-Nothing) party, the Republicans became the political power of the North.

The election of Abraham Lincoln (the first Republican president) in 1860 set the solidly Democratic South on the road toward secession, giving the Republicans control of the federal government. During the ensuing Civil War the Republican party split into Conservative and Radical factions. Following Lincoln's assassination in 1865, the Radical faction gained the upper hand in the Reconstruction process and passed the Fourteenth Amendment (civil rights) in 1868.

With the war over and the slaves freed, the Republicans lacked a central doctrine. Nevertheless, the Republican party dominated presidential elections for the next 2 decades with the victories of Ulysses S. Grant (1868,1872), Rutherford B. Hayes (1876), James A. Garfield (1880, assassinated in 1881), and Benjamin Harrison (1888).

In 1896 the Republicans committed themselves to the gold standard and, after defeating opposing candidate William Jennings Bryan, put William McKinley in the White House. The election was a turning point for the party because it gave the Republicans control of both houses of Congress and established them as the majority party (at which time they adopted the GOP nickname). McKinley was reelected in 1900, followed by Republicans Theodore Roosevelt (1904) and William H. Taft (1908).

The Republican party was divided in 1912 between Taft and Roosevelt (who split off the Bull Moose party) when both men sought the Republican nomination for the presidential race. The divided Republicans lost the election to Woodrow Wilson.

The Republicans regained the White House during the 1920s with the elections of Warren G. Harding (1920), during whose administration the infamous Teapot Dome scandal occured; Calvin Coolidge (1924); and Herbert Hoover (who was president when the stock market collapsed in 1929). The Great Depression crumbled Republican fortunes, and both its majority party position and control of Congress passed to the Democrats.

The Republicans would not elect another president until 1952, when WWII general Dwight D. Eisenhower (a moderate who defeated the conservative Taft for the nomination) took office. During his presidency the Republicans were caught up in the Communist witch-hunt concocted by Senator Joseph McCarthy (R-WI).

After Eisenhower the Republican party continued its movement to the political right, represented by such figures as Barry Goldwater (whose landslide presidential defeat in 1964 was the party's worst since 1932), Richard Nixon (lost the 1960 election; elected president 1968, 1972; resigned in 1974 following the Watergate scandal), Gerald Ford (who took Nixon's place in 1974 but lost the election in 1976), Ronald Reagan (1980, 1984), and George Bush (1988).

HOW MUCH

	8 Yr. Growth	1979-1980	1981-1982	1983-1984	1985-1986	1987-1988
Money raised ($ mil)	5.0%	170	215	298	255	263
Money spent ($ mil)	6.0%	162	214	301	259	257

Money Raised ($ mil) 1979-88

Political party
Founded: 1854

WHO

Chairman: Lee Atwater
Co-Chairman: Jeanie Austin
Vice Chairmen: Bernard M. Shanley, Shelia Roberge, Jack Londen, Martha Moore, Peter Secchia, Nelda Barton, Ernest Angelo, Jr., Kay Riddle, Elsie Vartanian
Secretary: Kit Mehrtens
Treasurer: William J. McManus

WHERE

HQ: 310 First St., SE, Washington, DC 20003
Phone: 202-863-8500
FAX: 202-863-8820

WHAT

Net Receipts for the 1987-88 Election Cycle

	$ mil	% of total
RNC	91	35
Senatorial	66	25
Congressional	34	13
Other natl. Republican	—	—
Convention	10	4
State and local	62	23
Total	**263**	**100**

Party Presidential Voting 1860-1988

Year	Repub. Candidate	Popular Votes (mil)	Electoral Votes	Won/ Lost
1988	George Bush	48.9	426	W
1984	Ronald Reagan	54.3	525	W
1980	Ronald Reagan	43.9	489	W
1976	Gerald R. Ford	39.1	240	L
1972	Richard M. Nixon	47.2	520	W
1968	Richard M. Nixon	31.8	301	W
1964	Barry M. Goldwater	27.2	52	L
1960	Richard M. Nixon	34.1	219	L
1956	Dwight D. Eisenhower	35.6	457	W
1952	Dwight D. Eisenhower	33.9	442	W
1948	Thomas E. Dewey	22.0	189	L
1944	Thomas E. Dewey	22.0	99	L
1940	Wendell Willkie	22.3	82	L
1936	Alfred M. Landon	16.7	8	L
1932	Herbert C. Hoover	15.8	59	L
1928	Herbert C. Hoover	21.4	444	W
1924	Calvin Coolidge	15.7	382	W
1920	Warren G. Harding	16.2	404	W
1916	Charles E. Hughes	8.5	254	L
1912	Theodore Roosevelt	4.2	88	L
	William H. Taft	3.5	8	L
1908	William H. Taft	7.7	321	W
1904	Theodore Roosevelt	7.6	336	W
1900	William McKinley	7.2	292	W
1896	William McKinley	7.0	271	W
1892	Benjamin Harrison	5.2	145	L
1888	Benjamin Harrison	5.4	233	W
1884	James G. Blaine	4.8	182	L
1880	James A. Garfield	4.4	214	W
1876	Rutherford B. Hayes	4.0	185	W
1872	Ulysses S. Grant	3.6	286	W
1868	Ulysses S. Grant	3.0	214	W
1864	Abraham Lincoln	2.2	212	W
1860	Abraham Lincoln	1.9	180	W

COMPETITION

The Democratic party

REUTERS HOLDINGS PLC

OVERVIEW

With 194,000 terminals installed in 127 countries, Reuters is the world's leading distributor of computerized information. Although Reuters may be best known for its general news wire, 65% of its sales comes from providing real-time financial news and market data.

On-line trading services are growing in importance to Reuters. Reuter Monitor Dealing 2000, the company's new currency trading service, includes an automated order matching system. The company's Instinet system is an electronic, off-exchange stock trading service. Similar electronic transaction services in the works include Globex, an international after-hours futures exchange being developed with the Chicago Mercantile Exchange, and an after-hours stock and options trading system to be developed with the Chicago Board of Options Exchange, the ASE, and the Cincinnati Stock Exchange.

Newspaper publishers owning Reuters stock since the 1940s collectively control a "golden share" enabling them to veto any transaction deemed to threaten Reuters's independence as a news source. Major shareholders include the Abu Dhabi Investment Authority (8.1%), the Daily Mail Trust (7.1%), and News Corporation (5.0%).

WHEN

In 1849 Berlin bookseller Paul Julius Reuter noticed delays in the flow of financial information between Paris and Berlin caused by a gap in a new telegraph system. Using carrier pigeons to bridge the gap between Aachen, Germany, and Brussels, Belgium, Reuter created a business that was successful until the telegraph system was completed.

Moving to London in 1851, just as the first cable under the English Channel was completed, Reuter began transmitting stock quotes between Paris and London and selling the information to financial institutions. He soon set up overseas agencies and broadened coverage to include general news sold to newspapers. The Duke of Saxe-Coburg-Gotha (Germany) conferred the title of baron upon Reuter in 1871.

Following Baron Reuter's death in 1899, his son Herbert managed the company. He made a financially disastrous decision to establish Reuters Bank (1913). After Herbert Reuter's suicide in 1915, the company was purchased by Roderick Jones. Under Jones, Reuters sold the bank (1917) and started using radio technology (1923) and teleprinters (1927). In 1941 Reuters again faced ruin as its far-flung correspondent network strained company finances. Winston Churchill saw the advantage of having a news gathering and disseminating organization based in London and persuaded British newspapers to buy Reuters. In 1947 Australian and New Zealand news publishers also bought in.

Responding to technical developments in the US, Reuters gained the non-US rights to Ultronic Systems Corporation's Stockmaster, an electronic stock price look-up system that eliminated the need to pore over ticker tapes for current quotes. Australian Glen Renfrew administered the successful launch of the system in 1964. When currency exchange rates began to float freely, Fred Taylor, a Reuters clerk, proposed electronically collecting and distributing real-time foreign exchange quotations entered into the system by market participants themselves. Reuters gambled on Taylor's idea, launching its extremely successful Monitor electronic marketplace in 1973. Monitor Dealing, introduced in 1981, enabled dealers to trade currencies on-line.

With Reuters's computer-based businesses dominating its general news services, Glen Renfrew took over as managing director in 1981. Since then, Reuters has gone public (1984); acquired Rich, Inc. (financial computer systems, US, 1985) and Instinet (off-exchange stock trading, US, 1987); and introduced a host of upgraded and new on-line financial news and quotation services.

HOW MUCH

	6 Yr. Growth	1980	1981	1982	1983	1984	1985	1986	1987	1988	1989
Sales ($ mil)	32.6%	—	—	—	352	363	629	921	1,635	1,814	1,916
Net income ($ mil)	36.6%	—	—	—	45	48	79	119	205	241	292
Income as % of sales	—	—	—	—	12.9%	13.2%	12.5%	12.9%	12.6%	13.3%	15.2%
Earnings per share ($)	—	—	—	—	—	0.38	0.58	0.87	1.47	1.74	2.11
Stock price – high ($)	—	—	—	—	—	10.63	16.38	25.50	45.69	31.25	53.63
Stock price – low ($)	—	—	—	—	—	8.44	9.94	15.06	20.25	22.88	28.13
Stock price – close ($)	—	—	—	—	—	10.13	16.19	24.94	27.69	28.38	49.63
P/E – high	—	—	—	—	—	28	28	29	31	18	25
P/E – low	—	—	—	—	—	22	17	17	14	13	13
Dividends per share ($)	—	—	—	—	0.00	0.05	0.15	0.24	0.41	0.56	0.64
Book value per share ($)	—	—	—	—	—	1.29	1.93	1.93	2.93	3.63	4.75

1989 Year End:
Debt ratio: 4.9%
Return on equity: 50.4%
Cash (mil): $408
Long-term debt (mil): $34
Number of shares (mil): 139
Dividends:
1989 average yield: 1.3%
1989 payout: 30.4%
Market value (mil): $6,886

NYSE symbol: RTRSY (ADR)
Incorporated: England, 1984
Fiscal year ends: December 31

WHO

CEO: Glen Renfrew, age 61
Chairman: Sir Christopher Anthony Hogg
Editor-in-Chief: Mark Wood, age 38
Financial Director: Nigel Judah, age 59
Auditors: Price Waterhouse
Employees: 10,071

WHERE

HQ: 85 Fleet St., London EC4P 4AJ, England
Phone: 011-44-71-250-1122
FAX: 011-44-71-353-1379
US HQ: 40 E. 52nd St., New York, NY 10022
US Phone: 212-593-5500
US FAX: 212-593-5591

Reuters has installed 194,750 video terminals in 127 countries.

	1989 Sales	
	$ mil	% of total
Europe, Middle East & Africa	1,168	60
Asia	403	21
America	379	19
Adjustments	(34)	—
Total	**1,916**	**100**

WHAT

	1989 Sales
	% of total
Real-time information	65
Transaction products	13
Trading room systems	11
Media products	7
Historical information	4
Total	**100**

Real-Time Information Services
Commodities 2000
Energy 2000
Money 2000
Monitor Capital Markets
Monitor Money Rates
Monitor Shipping

Transaction Products
Dealing 2000 (currencies)
Globex (futures)
Instinet (stocks)
Monitor Bonds Dealing

Other
Company Newsfile Service (news database)
Country Reports Service (text database)
News Picture Service
Reuters News Services
I. P. Sharp Associates (numeric databases)
Textline Service (text database)
Triarch 2000 (trading room systems)
Visnews (88.8%, TV news clips)

RANKINGS

192nd in *Business Week* Global 1000

COMPETITION

ADP
Citicorp
Control Data
Dow Jones
Dun & Bradstreet
Knight-Ridder
McGraw-Hill
Mead
New York Stock Exchange

REYNOLDS METALS COMPANY

OVERVIEW

Richmond-based Reynolds Metals is the 2nd largest US producer of aluminum (after Alcoa) and a major manufacturer of aluminum cans. It leads the world in the manufacture of aluminum foil and makes the #1 US household foil: Reynolds Wrap. The company, with its focus on consumer goods and gold, has enjoyed 4 consecutive years of increasing profits, with more than $500 million in profits in 1989. Reynolds is a mining company and a plastics and aluminum products manufacturer, distributor, and recycler. Its foreign endeavors include mining gold in Australia and marketing its aluminum cans in Europe, South America, and Japan.

David Reynolds (son of the founder) retired as chairman in 1988. David (now chairman emeritus) and his nephew Randolph (a vice-president) own a total of only 3.5% of the company's stock.

WHEN

Richard S. Reynolds began his business career in the tutelage of his uncle R. J. Reynolds, of tobacco industry fame and fortune. In 1912 Richard Reynolds returned to Bristol, Tennessee, to run his father's Reynolds Company (silica-based cleansers). The company relocated to Louisville, Kentucky, after a factory fire. Near the end of WWI, the company changed from producing cleansers to manufacturing waterproof gunpowder canisters (from tin, asphalt, and asphalt felt paper) for the military. After the armistice was signed (1918), the company needed a peacetime product. In 1919 Reynolds entered a joint venture with R. J. Reynolds Tobacco, forming United States Foil Company to roll tinfoil for cigarette packaging. Reynolds Tobacco sold its shares of US Foil to outsiders in 1924. US Foil then bought the company that made Eskimo Pies, the ice cream product wrapped in foil.

During 1928 Reynolds bought Robertshaw Thermostat, Fulton Sylphon, and part of Beechnut Foil. He added these companies to US Foil to form Reynolds Metals (1928). By the late 1920s Reynolds Metals was using both tin and the lighter-weight aluminum in its metal business. In the late 1930s Reynolds foresaw that the US need for aluminum would dramatically increase if it became involved in WWII. In 1940 the company began mining bauxite (aluminum ore) in Arkansas. In early 1941 Reynolds Metals built its first aluminum plant (near Sheffield, Alabama). The company quickly built other plants in Alabama and Washington.

In 1946 the US government forced Alcoa (ruled a monopoly by the Supreme Court in 1945) to give the government the patent rights to its process of obtaining aluminum from bauxite. Thus Reynolds Metals received this process gratis when it bought 6 surplus government aluminum plants (which used Alcoa's patented process) after WWII. Reynolds Metals developed many of the innovative uses of aluminum, including aluminum siding (1945) and Reynolds Wrap aluminum foil (1947). It sold Robertshaw Controls (the previous Robertshaw Thermostat and Fulton Sylphon companies) in 1947. The company began to search for bauxite in Jamaica (1949) and British Guyana (1952, mines nationalized 1975). In 1959 the company bought British Aluminum jointly with Tube Investments (sold to Tube, 1978). Reynolds Metals developed the aluminum beverage can (1963) and began the recycling of it (1968). The company bought Industrial Metals (1969) and May Aluminum (1971).

In 1982 the company introduced Reynolds Plastic Wrap (available in 4 colors in 1989). In 1986 the company began mining gold in Australia, and made a major strike in 1987. In 1988 it bought Presto Products (plastic bags, food wrap). In 1989 Reynolds Metals developed aluminum cans for the non-carbonated juice products of Welch's, Ocean Spray, and Campbell Soup companies.

HOW MUCH

	9 Yr. Growth	1980	1981	1982	1983	1984	1985	1986	1987	1988	1989
Sales ($ mil)	5.9%	3,653	3,481	2,981	3,341	3,728	3,416	3,639	4,284	5,567	6,143
Net income ($ mil)	12.8%	180	87	(24)	(91)	131	(298)	102	201	482	533
Income as % of sales	—	4.9%	2.5%	(0.8%)	(2.7%)	3.5%	(8.7%)	2.8%	4.7%	8.7%	8.7%
Earnings per share ($)	9.0%	4.16	2.04	(0.49)	(1.93)	2.85	(6.05)	1.94	3.67	8.35	9.06
Stock price – high ($)	—	20.44	19.88	13.69	20.69	20.81	20.63	26.38	61.75	58.00	62.75
Stock price – low ($)	—	13.63	11.56	9.38	12.44	13.00	15.13	18.19	20.19	34.00	49.00
Stock price – close ($)	13.2%	17.63	12.00	12.69	19.75	16.75	18.88	20.00	47.63	53.75	53.63
P/E – high	—	5	10	—	—	7	—	14	17	7	7
P/E – low	—	3	6	—	—	5	—	9	6	4	5
Dividends per share ($)	4.7%	1.13	1.20	0.88	0.50	0.50	0.50	0.50	0.58	0.90	1.70
Book value per share ($)	3.2%	34.08	34.38	33.11	28.09	30.45	22.92	27.05	29.69	37.77	45.24

1989 Year End:
Debt ratio: 30.3%
Return on equity: 21.8%
Cash (mil): $71
Current ratio: 1.8
Long-term debt (mil): $1,166
Number of shares (mil): 59
Dividends:
1989 average yield: 3.2%
1989 payout: 18.8%
Market value (mil): $3,182

Stock Price History high/low 1980-89

70 60 50 40 30 20 10 0

NYSE symbol: RLM
Incorporated: Delaware, 1928
Fiscal year ends: December 31

WHO

Chairman and CEO: William O. Bourke, age 62, $1,775,000 pay
President and COO: Richard G. Holder, age 58, $1,160,000 pay
EVP and CFO: R. Bern Crowl, age 58, $945,000 pay
EVP Fabricating Operations: Yale M. Brandt, age 59, $737,500 pay
Auditors: Ernst & Young
Employees: 30,800

WHERE

HQ: 6601 W. Broad St., PO Box 27003, Richmond, VA 23261
Phone: 804-281-2000
FAX: 804-281-4160 (Public Relations)

Reynolds has interests, operations, or key offices in 23 countries.

	1989 Sales		1989 Operating Income	
	$ mil	% of total	$ mil	% of total
US	4,834	79	430	54
Canada	321	5	179	22
Other foreign	988	16	194	24
Total	**6,143**	**100**	**803**	**100**

WHAT

	1989 Sales		1989 Operating Income	
	$ mil	% of total	$ mil	% of total
Aluminum production & processing	3,595	59	687	86
Finished products & other	2,548	41	111	14
Adjustments	—	—	5	—
Total	**6,143**	**100**	**803**	**100**

Major Products
Aluminum cans and containers
Aluminum foil (Reynolds Wrap)
Aluminum wire and cable
Baking cups (Baker's Choice)
Building products
Flat rolled aluminum
Plastic bags (Sure Seal)
Plastic containers and lids
Plastic film (Reynolds Plastic Wrap)
Semifinished aluminum
Wax paper (Cut-Rite)

Gold Mines
Boddington (Australia, 40%)
Mt. Gibson (Australia, 50%)

RANKINGS

75th in *Fortune* 500 Industrial Cos.
214th in *Fortune* Global 500 Industrial Cos.
138th in *Forbes* Sales 500
191st in *Business Week* 1000
566th in *Business Week* Global 1000

COMPETITION

Alcan
Alcoa
AMAX
Dow Chemical
Johnson Controls
Owens-Illinois
Peter Kiewit Sons'

RHÔNE-POULENC SA

OVERVIEW

Rhône-Poulenc, the largest chemical company in France and 9th largest in the world, is controlled by the French government. Major businesses include basic and agricultural chemicals, pharmaceuticals, and fibers. Half of Rhône-Poulenc's production is within France. Rhône-Poulenc owns 68% of Rhône-Poulenc Rorer, the product of a merger of Rhône-Poulenc's drug businesses with Rorer.

French government appointees have turned around an ailing Rhône-Poulenc. They have closed unprofitable plants and are reducing dependence on cyclical textile and fertilizer revenue by acquiring specialty chemical companies. Management is trying to expand Rhône-Poulenc to compete globally.

As a nationalized company, Rhône-Poulenc cannot issue common stock to the public to raise capital. Instead, it has issued unusual, stock-like securities, including nonvoting preferred investment certificates (CIPs), paying the same dividend as common shares owned by the government, plus 5 francs annually. The company has also issued capital equity notes (a debt-like security with no maturity date).

NYSE symbol: RPPRC (ADR)
Incorporated: France, 1961
Fiscal year ends: December 31

WHO

Chairman and CEO: Jean-René Fourtou, age 50
President; Chairman and CEO, Rhône-Poulenc Chimie: Jean-Marc Bruel, age 53
EVP; Chairman and CEO, Rhône-Poulenc Agrochimie and Rhône-Poulenc Inc. (US): Philippe Desmarescaux, age 51
Auditors: Coopers & Lybrand
Employees: 85,629

WHERE

HQ: 25, Quai Paul Doumer, 92408 Courbevoie Cedex, France
Phone: 011-33-1-47-68-12-34
US HQ (Rhône-Poulenc Inc.): PO Box 125, Black Horse Ln., Monmouth Junction, NJ 08852
US Phone: 201-297-0100
US FAX: 201-297-1597

Rhône-Poulenc operates 144 production facilities in Europe, 76 in North America, 20 in Latin America (principally Brazil), and 18 in other countries.

	1989 Sales*		1989 Operating Income*	
	FF mil	% of total	FF mil	% of total
France	42,569	48	4,322	62
Other Europe	25,016	28	1,001	14
US	10,498	12	936	13
Brazil	7,854	9	650	9
Other countries	2,627	3	98	2
Eliminations	(15,496)	—	56	—
Total	**73,068**	**100**	**7,063**	**100**

*by area of production

WHEN

The product of a merger between Société Chimiques des Usines du Rhône and Poulenc Frères, Rhône-Poulenc has continued to expand through mergers and acquisitions.

Etienne Poulenc, a pharmacist, had bought a Parisian apothecary in 1858. Poulenc began making pharmaceuticals and performed collaborative research with drug company Comptoir des Textiles Artificielles (CTA).

Société Chimique des Usines du Rhône was formed in Lyon in 1895 to produce dyes. Unable to survive German competition, the company switched to the manufacture of specialty chemicals. The company merged with CTA in 1922 and with Poulenc in 1928.

Rhône-Poulenc developed new drugs, including antibiotics and antihistamines, and increased fiber production until WWII. Growth resumed after the war, and the company acquired Theraplix (drugs, France, 1956), 50% of Institut Mérieux (drugs, France, 1968), and Progil and Pechiney–St. Gobain (basic and agricultural chemicals, France, 1969) in a government-orchestrated transaction. By 1970 Rhône-Poulenc dominated the French chemical industry and was the 3rd largest chemical company in Europe.

In the 1970s profits eroded as protectionist tariffs were lowered by the Common Market, exposing Rhône-Poulenc to international competition in its home market. By licensing the US marketing rights of Thorazine, a tranquilizer, to SmithKline, the company failed to fully capitalize on the drug's success. Between 1980 and 1982, Rhône-Poulenc lost over FF 3.1 billion. In 1982 the Mitterrand government nationalized the company.

The government selected Loïk Le Floch-Prigent, a 39-year-old civil servant, to restructure Rhône-Poulenc. Changing top management, eliminating unprofitable operations, cutting employment, and expanding abroad, Le Floch returned Rhône-Poulenc to profitability.

In 1986 Jean-René Fourtou took over from Le Floch. In his first 3 years, Fourtou sold 20 businesses and bought over 30, including Union Carbide's agricultural chemical operations (1986) and Stauffer's industrial chemical business (1987). In 1989 he acquired 20 more, including RTZ's chemical operations and a specialty chemical unit of GAF. Institut Mérieux bought Connaught BioSciences (vaccines, Canada, 1989).

In 1990 Rhône-Poulenc merged its drug businesses with Rorer (pharmaceuticals, US). In the same year the French government transferred to Rhône-Poulenc 35% of Roussel-Uclaf, France's 3rd largest drug producer. Hoechst is 54% owner of Roussel.

WHAT

	1989 Sales		1989 Operating Income	
	FF mil	% of total	FF mil	% of total
Chemicals	36,781	47	4,116	59
Health	17,766	23	1,874	27
Agricultural chemicals	10,527	14	1,202	17
Fibers	11,159	14	261	4
Other products	1,631	2	(477)	(7)
Eliminations	(4,796)	—	87	—
Total	**73,068**	**100**	**7,063**	**100**

Chemicals
Agricultural chemicals
Chemical and organic intermediates
Coatings
Industrial chemicals
Metals and minerals
Specialty chemicals

Health
Animal feed supplements
Pharmaceuticals
Vaccines and human proteins
Veterinary pharmaceuticals

Fibers
Industrial fibers and yarns
Nylon
Polyester

HOW MUCH

$=FF5.78 (Dec. 31, 1989)	9 Yr. Growth	1980	1981	1982	1983	1984	1985	1986	1987	1988	1989
Sales (FF mil)	10.3%	30,199	31,515	37,196	43,117	51,207	56,102	52,694	56,160	65,334	73,068
Net income (FF mil)	—	(1,947)	(335)	(844)	98	1,755	2,058	1,912	2,193	2,878	3,016
Income as % of sales	—	(6.4%)	(1.1%)	(2.3%)	—	3.4%	3.7%	3.6%	3.9%	4.4%	4.1%
Earnings per share (FF)	—	(85)	(15)	(26)	2	51	55	47	45	62	61
Stock price - high (FF)*	—	—	—	—	—	—	—	—	471	540	618
Stock price - low (FF)*	—	—	—	—	—	—	—	—	280	254	449
Stock price - close (FF)*	—	—	—	—	—	—	—	—	340	520	460
P/E - high	—	—	—	—	—	—	—	—	—	—	—
P/E - low	—	—	—	—	—	—	—	—	—	—	—
Dividends per share (FF)*	—	—	—	—	—	—	—	—	14.66	16.50	20.00
Book value per share (FF)	—	—	—	—	—	—	—	—	—	—	—

1989 Year End:
Debt ratio: 46.0%
Return on equity: 10.2%
Cash (mil): FF4,650
Current ratio: 1.18
Long-term debt (mil): FF20,467
Number of shares (mil)**: 48
Dividends:
1989 average yield: 4.3%
1989 payout: 26.0%
Sales (mil): $12,650

Sales (FF mil) 1980-89

*preferred investment certificates **common and preferred investment certificates

RANKINGS

95th in *Fortune* Global 500 Industrial Cos.
54th in *Forbes* 100 Foreign Investments in the US
506th in *Business Week* Global 1000

COMPETITION

American Cyanamid
BASF
Bayer
Dow Chemical
Du Pont
W. R. Grace
Hercules
Hoechst
Monsanto
Pharmaceutical companies
Other chemical companies

RIKLIS FAMILY CORPORATION

OVERVIEW

Its subsidiaries may make luggage and operate variety stores, but Riklis Family Corporation is best known for its deals. New York City–based Riklis Family Corporation is the holding company for Meshulam Ricklis's diversified and highly leveraged interests.

Riklis Family Corporation is private, but E-II Holdings, Inc., the largest part of the Riklis empire, has publicly traded debt. After the dust settled in the Riklis Family Corporation's acquisition of E-II and the sale of personal care manufacturer Fabergé, E-II included Ricklis's retail store chains (Bargain Time, J. J. Newberry, McCrory, S. H. Kress, T. G. & Y., and others), McGregor (apparel), Samsonite (luggage), and Culligan (water treatment). Since selling Fabergé, E-II has been buying back its own debt at substantial discounts from face value.

Meshulam Riklis and his wife, actress-turned-singer Pia Zadora, own Pickfair, the Los Angeles mansion once owned by Douglas Fairbanks, Jr., and Mary Pickford.

WHEN

Meshulam Riklis emigrated from Tel Aviv in 1947, graduated from Ohio State University with a degree in mathematics in 1950, and began working at the Minneapolis brokerage house of Piper, Jaffray, and Hopwood in 1951. With a pool of funds he coaxed from clients, he bought control of Rapid-American, an office machine and greeting card company, in 1957.

In the late 1950s Riklis used high-yield bonds and stock swaps to gain control of several firms, including clothing manufacturers and packaging companies. In 1960 Rapid bought McCrory's, a chain of variety stores. But poor earnings forced Riklis to sell all his holdings except a majority stake in the chain by 1963.

Riklis rebuilt Rapid, which bought Glen Alden Corporation and, with it, liquor distributor Schenley Industries (1972). But, squeezed by recession and tight credit, Rapid sold off holdings again in 1974. The companies sold included Lerner Shops, the women's clothing retailer, and undergarment companies Playtex and BVD; proceeds were used to reduce debt. Riklis took Rapid private in 1981. At this time, Rapid consisted of the McCrory chain, Family Bargain Centers, Schenley, and McGregor.

Rapid bought Fabergé and Elizabeth Arden in 1984. In 1986 Riklis transferred the assets of Fabergé to his Riklis Family Corporation, leaving Rapid's bondholders with nonvoting Fabergé preferred stock.

Riklis drew criticism for his role in the 1986 Guinness takeover of liquor producer Distillers Company. Riklis, Ivan Boesky, and others bought Guinness stock, raising the price, just as it was being used to acquire Distillers. Riklis's Schenley unit depended on continued US distribution rights of Dewar's, a Distillers brand, after the takeover. Amid the ensuing stock manipulation lawsuits, Guinness chief Ernest Saunders resigned, but Riklis escaped legal entanglement after selling Schenley to Guinness in 1987 at a loss.

A classic example of a Riklis deal was Riklis Family Corporation's acquisition of E-II. E-II Holdings began in 1987 as a debt-laden spin-off of Beatrice Company's nonfood businesses following the 1986 LBO of Beatrice by Kohlberg Kravis Roberts. E-II tried to raid cash-rich American Brands. In a "PacMan" takeover defense, American Brands turned on its predator and bought E-II.

After taking the E-II units it wanted (including Day-Timers, Inc.), American Brands sold E-II to Riklis for $1.2 billion in 1988. E-II owned Samsonite, Culligan, and Lowrey's Meat Specialties and had $1.5 billion in cash.

The day after the acquisition, Riklis drained $925 million in cash from E-II by selling it Fabergé. E-II bondholders sued over the transaction. The complaint was dismissed when, after a series of on-again, off-again negotiations, E-II sold Fabergé/Elizabeth Arden to Unilever in 1989 for $1.55 billion.

E-II sold Lowrey's in 1988 and Riklis transferred all the assets of Rapid to E-II in 1989. Other transactions in 1989 included the sale of Samsonite Furniture to Ditri Associates; the sale of Culligan's Arrowhead Industrial Water subsidiary to B.F. Goodrich; the sale of Martha White Foods, Inc., and Frozen Specialties, Inc., to Windmill Corp.; and the purchase of 130 GC Murphy stores and 25 Bargain World stores from Ames Department Stores.

Private company
Incorporated (E-II): Delaware, 1987
Fiscal year ends: January 31

WHO

Chairman; Chairman, President, and CEO, E-II: Meshulam Riklis, age 66, $2,836,097 pay
VC, E-II: Harold S. Divine, age 68, $957,193 pay
VC, E-II: Daniel J. Manella, age 64
VP Finance, E-II: Andrew Gregor, age 41
Auditors: Deloitte & Touche
Employees: 43,000

WHERE

HQ: 725 Fifth Avenue, New York, NY 10022
Phone: 212-735-9500
FAX: 212-735-9515

The company operates 1,193 variety and specialty stores and 281 discount stores throughout the US and maintains 19 US and 11 foreign plants and distribution centers.

	1989 Sales		1989 Operating Income	
	$ mil	% of total	$ mil	% of total
US	1,665	86	(78)	(162)
Canada	29	2	3	6
Europe	233	12	26	54
Other	3	—	1	2
Total	**1,930**	**100**	**(48)**	**100**

E-II Holdings only

WHAT

	1989 Sales		1989 Operating Income	
	$ mil	% of total	$ mil	% of total
Retail merchandising	996	51	(30)	(62)
Discount retailing	111	6	(72)	(150)
Manufacturing & distribution	823	43	54	112
Total	**1,930**	**100**	**(48)**	**100**

E-II Holdings only

Variety Stores
McCrory Stores
McCrory
McLellan
H. L Green
T. G. & Y.
J. J. Newberry
S. H. Kress
GC Murphy

Distribution
Gault Brothers (Canada)

Discount Retailing
Bargain Time
Bargain World

Manufacturing
McGregor apparel
McGregor
Botany 500
Anvil
Samsonite luggage
Samsonite
Lark
Culligan water treatment
Culligan
Everpure

Pet Specialties
ANF pet food

RANKINGS

47th in *Forbes* 400 US Private Cos.

COMPETITION

Ames
Brown-Forman
Hartmarx
K mart
V. F.
Wal-Mart
Woolworth

HOW MUCH

	4 Yr. Growth	1980	1981	1982	1983	1984	1985	1986	1987	1988	1989
Sales ($ mil)	8.3%	—	—	—	—	—	1,816	1,898	1,894	2,931	2,500

Sales ($ mil) 1985-89

RIO GRANDE INDUSTRIES, INC.

OVERVIEW

Rio Grande Industries (RGI) operates an integrated transportation system through 3 railroad subsidiaries: the Denver & Rio Grande Western Railroad (Rio Grande), Southern Pacific Transportation Company, and SPCSL Corporation, which operates an integrated rail line with Southern Pacific and Rio Grande from the Gulf Coast and Chicago.

Southern Pacific operates freight rail and intermodal (truck-to-train) services in 14 states, hauling a wide range of commodities such as chemicals, metals and ores, and lumber products. With 1989 sales exceeding $2.3 billion, it was the 19th largest transportation concern in the US. The company also operates nationwide trucking services and owns real estate in several major cities.

The Rio Grande is mainly a coal-hauling road but also handles other commodities, including transportation equipment and lumber products, over a central corridor route in the western US.

RGI is a private company, 75% owned by the Anschutz Corporation, a Denver-based holding company owned by billionaire Philip Anschutz. Anschutz is an extremely private individual with a personal fortune of about $1.3 billion, according to *Forbes*.

WHEN

Southern Pacific dates back to 1861, when 4 Sacramento merchants, later known as "The Big Four," founded the Central Pacific Railroad. Construction began in 1863 at Sacramento, and in 1869 the Central Pacific reached Promontory, Utah, where its rails were spiked to those of the Union Pacific (which had built westward from Omaha, Nebraska), thus completing the first transcontinental railway.

Central Pacific then expanded throughout California (1884) and to Texas (1881) and Oregon (1887) by constructing new trackage and buying other railroads, including the Southern Pacific (1868), a San Francisco–to–San Jose line founded in 1865. A Central Pacific/Southern Pacific headquarters was established in San Francisco (1873), and the 2 railroads officially merged in 1885 under a holding company called Southern Pacific Company.

Union Pacific bought control of Southern Pacific in 1901 but was later ordered to sell its stake on antitrust grounds (1913). In 1932 Southern Pacific bought control of the St. Louis Southwestern Railway (Cotton Belt), gaining an entrance to St. Louis.

Facing intense competition from Union Pacific and Burlington Northern (both of which had merged with other railroads to create enormous systems), Southern Pacific merged with competitor Atchison, Topeka & Santa Fe Railway in 1983 to form Santa Fe Southern Pacific Corporation. In 1987 the ICC deemed the merger "anticompetitive," and in 1988 Santa Fe Southern Pacific sold Southern Pacific to RGI — a holding company for the Rio Grande railroad — which was controlled by Anschutz Corporation.

The Rio Grande was founded as the Denver & Rio Grande in 1871 by General William Jackson Palmer to build a line from Denver to Mexico City. The company entered Salt Lake City in 1882, but an attempt to build on to San Francisco resulted in bankruptcy. Renamed the Denver & Rio Grande Western, the railroad emerged from receivership in 1924 and opened the Dotsero Cutoff in 1934, finally placing Denver on a transcontinental main line. Anschutz bought the Rio Grande in 1984.

The combined Southern Pacific and Rio Grande gained access to Chicago in 1989, when SPCSL Corporation (a new subsidiary of RGI) bought 282 miles of track between East St. Louis and Chicago from the trustees of bankrupt Chicago, Missouri & Western Railway Company.

HOW MUCH

	9 Yr. Growth	1980	1981	1982	1983	1984	1985	1986	1987	1988	1989
Rio Grande Industries											
Sales ($ mil)	—	—	—	—	—	—	—	—	—	—	2,702
Net income ($ mil)	—	—	—	—	—	—	—	—	—	—	14
Income as % of sales	—	—	—	—	—	—	—	—	—	—	0.5%
Southern Pacific Trans.											
Sales ($ mil)	(0.7%)	2,533	2,832	2,482	2,430	2,714	2,546	2,362	2,395	2,412	2,372
Net income ($ mil)	4.1%	68	81	9	32	141	118	(253)	143	219	98
Income as % of sales	—	2.7%	2.9%	0.4%	1.3%	5.2%	4.6%	(10.7%)	6.0%	9.1%	4.1%
Rio Grande Holdings											
Sales ($ mil)	—	—	363	304	314	*313	**252	309	257	276	***456
Net income ($ mil)	—	—	46	30	33	*67	**2	10	19	(4)	***12
Income as % of sales	—	—	12.7%	9.9%	10.5%	21.4%	0.8%	3.2%	7.4%	(1.4%)	26.0%

Southern Pacific Transportation Company Net Income ($ mil) 1980-89

300 200 100 0 -100 -200 -300

* 10 months ended 10/31/84 ** 9 months ended 7/31/85 *** 17 months ended 12/31/89

Private company
Incorporated: Delaware, 1988
Fiscal year end: December 31

WHO

Chairman, President, and CEO: Philip F. Anschutz, age 50
Chairman, President, and CEO, Rio Grande Holding, Inc.: W. J. Holtman, age 68
VC; Chairman and President, Southern Pacific Transportation Co.: D. K. McNear, age 64
VC and VP: D. L. Polson, age 47
VP; VC Southern Pacific Transportation Co.: R. F. Starzel, age 49
VP Finance: L. C. Yarberry, age 47
Auditors: KPMG Peat Marwick
Employees: 24,775

WHERE

Southern Pacific Transportation Co.: Southern Pacific Bldg., 1 Market Plaza, San Francisco, CA 94105
Phone: 415-541-1000
FAX: 415-541-1256
Rio Grande Holding, Inc.: 1515 Arapahoe St., Denver, CO 80202
Phone: 303-595-2254
FAX: 303-595-2562

Southern Pacific operates 20,000 miles of track in 14 western and southwestern states. Rio Grande operates 3,400 miles of track in 4 western states. SPCSL owns 282 miles of track between Chicago and St. Louis.

WHAT

	1989 Sales	
	$ mil	% of total
Railroad	2,671	99
Trucking	31	1
Total	**2,702**	**100**

Rio Grande Holding, Inc.
Denver & Rio Grande Western Railway Co.

SPTC Holding, Inc.
Southern Pacific Transportation Co.
Northwestern Pacific Railroad Co.
Southern Pacific Trucking Co.
SPT Real Estate
St. Louis Southwestern Railway Co. ("Cotton Belt," 99.9% owned)

SPCSL Corp.
Track between Chicago and St. Louis

COMPETITION

Burlington Northern
Santa Fe Pacific
Union Pacific
Trucking companies

RITE AID CORPORATION

OVERVIEW

Rite Aid Corporation operates 2,352 discount drugstores in 22 states east of the Mississippi River, making it the biggest drug chain, in number of stores, in the US. The drugstores are comparatively small, averaging 6,700 square feet, and feature over 1,000 private-label, as well as national brand, health and beauty aids, along with pharmaceuticals. Prescription sales account for 43% of drugstore revenues.

Rite Aid has shown an ability to buy drugstores that lost money for others and make them profitable. Purchased stores are converted to the standard Rite Aid format. Product mix, pricing, and display of merchandise are all controlled by the corporate administration.

Rite Aid also operates 75 auto parts stores under the names American Discount Auto Parts, ADAP, and Auto Palace; 49 Encore discount bookstores; 169 Concord Custom Cleaners locations; and 26 Sera-Tec Biologicals centers, which provide the pharmaceutical industry with plasma used in diagnostic and therapeutic products. Drugstore operations account for 95% of company sales.

NYSE symbol: RAD
Incorporated: Delaware, 1968
Fiscal year ends: Saturday nearest February 29 or March 1

WHO

Chairman and CEO: Alex Grass, age 62, $712,500 pay
President and COO: Martin Grass, age 36, $265,000 pay
SVP and Chief Accounting and Financial Officer: Frank Bergonzi, age 44
Auditors: KPMG Peat Marwick
Employees: 29,532

WHEN

In 1958 wholesale grocer Alex Grass incorporated Harrisburg, Pennsylvania–based Rack Rite Distributors to provide health and beauty aids and other nonfood products to grocery stores. Grass offered these same products at his first discount drugstore, Thrif D Discount Center, opened in 1962 in Scranton, Pennsylvania. By 1965 the company owned 25 stores in Pennsylvania, New York, New Jersey, Virginia, and Connecticut. In 1966 the first Rite Aid pharmacy opened, and the company counted 36 stores.

In 1968 Rite Aid adopted its current name and went public. In 1969 the company bought the 47 stores of Daw Drug, Blue Ridge Nursing Homes, and plasma suppliers Immuno Serums and Sero Genics.

The company bought Sera-Tec Biologicals of New Jersey (blood plasma), the 40 stores of Cohen Drug of Charleston, West Virginia, and 50% of Superdrug Stores, Ltd., a UK-based health and beauty aids chain, in 1971. Rite Aid filled over 5 million prescriptions that year. The company bought 2 Philadelphia-area chains, 50-store Warner and 49-store Thomas Holmes, in 1973 and bought the 52-store Keystone Centers in 1976. In 1977 the company bought the Read chain, adding 99 Baltimore drugstores. In that year its 836 private-label items made up 8% of total sales. The company sold its nursing homes in 1978.

By 1981 additional acquisitions had made Rite Aid the 3rd largest drugstore chain, and sales had exceeded $1 billion. In 1983 the company began to install point-of-sale and pharmacy computer systems in its stores. The company bought American Discount Auto Parts's 32-store chain and Encore Books's 19-store discount chain in 1984. In the same year the company spun off its wholesale grocery operation as Super Rite, retaining a 47% interest.

Rite Aid began renting videotapes in over 160 of its stores in 1985. The company bought 113 SupeRx drugstores in Florida, Georgia, and Alabama and 94 Gray Drug Fair stores and sold its share in Superdrug to Woolworth Holdings, netting about $68 million, in 1987. The company bought the rest of the 356-store Gray Drug Fair operation in 1988. The costs associated with rapid expansion eroded Rite Aid's profit margins from 4.4% in 1986 to 2.6% in 1989.

In 1989 the company stopped renting videos, sold its Super Rite interest to an investment group headed by CEO Alex Grass, and finished equipping all its stores with computers. In 1990 a trial judge tossed out a bribery case against Rite Aid and its president, Martin Grass. Both had been indicted for bribing a member of the Pharmacy Board of Ohio.

WHERE

HQ: Trindle Rd. and Railroad Ave., Shiremanstown, PA 17011
Phone: 717-761-2633
FAX: 717-975-5871

Rite Aid operates in the eastern US.

State	Drugstores
Alabama	4
Connecticut	39
Delaware	22
District of Columbia	4
Florida	199
Georgia	53
Indiana	7
Kentucky	79
Maryland	184
Massachusetts	39
Michigan	89
New Hampshire	12
New Jersey	161
New York	252
North Carolina	121
Ohio	355
Pennsylvania	326
Rhode Island	14
South Carolina	84
Tennessee	29
Vermont	7
Virginia	169
West Virginia	103
Total	**2,352**

HOW MUCH

	9 Yr. Growth	1980	1981	1982	1983	1984	1985	1986	1987	1988	1989
Sales ($ mil)	14.4%	944	1,066	1,295	1,223	1,446	1,564	1,757	2,486	2,868	3,173
Net income ($ mil)	9.6%	36	40	55	74	70	68	78	94	95	82
Income as % of sales	—	3.8%	3.7%	4.2%	6.1%	4.8%	4.3%	4.4%	3.8%	3.3%	2.6%
Earnings per share ($)	9.7%	0.85	0.95	1.31	1.76	1.69	1.65	1.89	2.27	2.30	1.97
Stock price – high ($)	—	8.44	12.08	17.83	23.44	27.25	33.50	35.50	46.25	40.88	41.13
Stock price – low ($)	—	4.88	7.75	9.00	14.08	17.50	21.50	24.25	28.50	29.13	29.50
Stock price – close ($)	16.8%	8.22	9.54	15.42	22.25	25.38	25.88	29.50	36.00	32.63	33.38
P/E – high	—	10	13	14	13	16	20	19	20	18	21
P/E – low	—	6	8	7	8	10	13	13	13	13	15
Dividends per share ($)	17.6%	0.20	0.23	0.28	0.34	0.43	0.52	0.60	0.68	0.76	0.84
Book value per share ($)	15.9%	4.51	5.17	6.19	7.68	8.58	9.65	10.96	13.81	15.35	16.98

1989 Year End:
Debt ratio: 43.5%
Return on equity: 12.2%
Cash (mil): $15
Current ratio: 3.93
Long-term debt (mil): $542
Number of shares (mil): 42
Dividends:
1989 average yield: 2.5%
1989 payout: 42.6%
Market value (mil):$1,385

WHAT

	1989 Sales		1989 Operating Income	
	$ mil	% of total	$ mil	% of total
Retail drug	3,011	95	200	95
Specialty retailing	123	4	6	3
Medical services	39	1	5	2
Total	**3,173**	**100**	**211**	**100**

Operating Units
ADAP (auto parts stores)
Auto Palace (auto parts stores)
Concord Custom Cleaners
Encore Books
Rite Aid (drugstores)
Sera-Tec Biologicals (plasma laboratories)

RANKINGS

36th in *Fortune* 50 Retailing Cos.
265th in *Forbes* Sales 500
421st in *Business Week* 1000

COMPETITION

Jack Eckerd
Melville
Supermarkets General
Walgreen

RJR NABISCO, INC.

OVERVIEW

Privately owned RJR Nabisco is one of the largest tobacco and food operations in the world, with a portfolio of strong brand names.

R.J. Reynolds, the company's tobacco division, is the 2nd largest producer of cigarettes in the US (after Philip Morris), with such popular brands as Camel (the first nationally branded cigarette), Winston, and Salem (the world's largest-selling menthol cigarette). The company's share of US cigarette sales is estimated at 31.5%.

RJR Nabisco's food operations consist primarily of Nabisco (the largest US producer of cookies and crackers) and Planters LifeSavers (the leader in packaged nuts and roll candy). Brand names that command the #1 positions in their respective US markets include Ritz crackers, Oreo cookies (almost one in 10 cookies bought in the US is an Oreo), and Milk Bone dog biscuits.

Tobacco International, the company's global division, sells over 55 brands of cigarettes in the international market. Camel is the segment's leading brand and is sold in 135 countries.

RJR Nabisco's $29.6 billion LBO was the biggest in history, and the company is selling assets to pay down its massive debt.

Private company
Incorporated: Delaware, 1970
Fiscal year ends: December 31

WHO

Chairman, President, and CEO: Louis V. Gerstner, Jr., age 48, $2,775,000 pay
EVP and CFO: Karl M. von der Heyden, age 53, $700,000 pay
Auditors: Deloitte & Touche
Employees: 48,000

WHERE

HQ: 1301 Ave. of the Americas, New York, NY 10019
Phone: 212-258-5600
FAX: 212-969-9173

R.J. Reynolds Tobacco's manufacturing plants are located in or near Winston-Salem, NC; the Tobacco International subsidiary has facilities in 11 foreign countries. The company's food and candy-processing plants are located throughout the US, Canada, and Puerto Rico.

	1989 Sales		1989 Operating Income	
	$ mil	% of total	$ mil	% of total
US	10,892	85	1,981	90
Canada	890	7	86	4
Europe	710	6	88	4
Other foreign	272	2	36	2
Adjustments	—	—	(138)	—
Total	**12,764**	**100**	**2,053**	**100**

WHEN

In 1875 R. J. Reynolds formed the R.J. Reynolds Tobacco Company in Winston, North Carolina, to produce chewing tobacco. During the late 1890s Reynolds was forced to sell his company to James Duke of the American Tobacco trust for $3 million (Duke threatened to break Reynolds with his Battle Ax brand cigarette if he did not sell). Reynolds regained his company in 1911 (after the Supreme Court dismantled the trust), turned his attention to cigarettes, and in 1913 introduced Camel, which became the company's best-selling cigarette. After Reynolds's death in 1918, company leadership passed to Bowman Gray, whose family would successfully run the company for the next 50 years.

With the success of Camel, R.J. Reynolds became the largest domestic cigarette company. During the 1930s and 1940s Camel was locked in a seesawing struggle for the #1 cigarette position with American Tobacco's Lucky Strike brand.

In the mid-1950s, in response to growing health concerns, the company introduced Winston (the first filtered cigarette, 1954) and Salem (the first filter-tipped menthol cigarette, 1956).

Antismoking sentiment led the company to embark on a diversification program during the 1960s and 1970s that included Chun King (Chinese food, 1966), Patio Foods (1967), McLean Industries (which owned the Sea-Land shipping company, 1969; sold in 1984), American Independent Oil (1970, sold in 1984), and Del Monte (fruits and other foods, 1979). In 1970 the company changed its name to R.J. Reynolds Industries.

Heublein, Inc., was acquired in 1982. Its Kentucky Fried Chicken chain was sold to PepsiCo in 1986. Grand Metropolitan bought the Heublein liquor business in 1987.

In 1985 the company bought Nabisco Brands for $4.9 billion. The National Biscuit Company was formed by the 1898 consolidation of several baking companies. Adolphus Green (Nabisco's first president) transformed the company from a loose network of regional bakeries to a uniform system producing the same powerhouse products (including Fig Newtons, Oreo, and Premium Saltines). Nabisco acquired Shredded Wheat (1929), Milk-Bone (1931), Dromedary (1954), Cream of Wheat (1961), James Welch (candy, 1963), and Standard Brands (Planters nuts, Blue Bonnet margarine, beer, wine, 1981). Standard Brands's CEO Ross Johnson emerged as CEO of Nabisco after the acquisition and later landed the top spot when R.J. Reynolds bought Nabisco (after which he moved company headquarters to Atlanta).

In 1987 Johnson tried to take advantage of falling stock prices by organizing an LBO. The plan backfired when Kohlberg Kravis Roberts (KKR) outbid Johnson and acquired the company for $29.6 billion and took it private in 1989. Johnson was replaced by former American Express president Louis Gerstner.

To reduce the tremendous debt incurred from the LBO ($22 billion), the company has sold many of its holdings, including Nabisco's European food business to BSN (France; $2.5 billion, 1989), Chun King ($52 million, 1989), and Del Monte's processed-food operations ($1.5 billion, 1990).

WHAT

	1989 Sales		1989 Operating Income	
	$ mil	% of total	$ mil	% of total
Tobacco	6,981	55	1,648	75
Food	5,783	45	543	25
Adjustments	—	—	(138)	—
Total	**12,764**	**100**	**2,053**	**100**

Brand Names

Cigarettes
Camel
Doral
More
Now
Salem
Vantage
Winston

Candy & Gum
Beech-Nut
Bubble Yum
Care*Free
Life Savers

Nabisco Cookies, Crackers & Cereals
Chips Ahoy!
Cream of Wheat
Fig Newtons
Honey Maid
Mallomars
Mister Salty
Oreo
Premium Saltines
Ritz
Shredded Wheat
Teddy Grahams
Triscuit
Wheat Thins

Other Products
A.1. Sauce
Blue Bonnet
Fleischmann's
Grey Poupon
Milk-Bone
Ortega
Planters
Vermont Maid

HOW MUCH

	9 Yr. Growth	1980	1981	1982	1983	1984	1985	1986	1987	1988	1989
Sales ($ mil)	4.7%	8,449	9,766	10,906	10,371	9,915	13,533	15,978	15,766	16,956	12,764
Net income ($ mil)	—	670	768	870	835	843	1,001	1,080	1,081	1,393	(1,172)
Income as % of sales	—	7.9%	7.9%	8.0%	8.1%	8.5%	7.4%	6.8%	6.9%	8.2%	(9.2%)

1989 Year End:
Debt ratio: 94.7
Return on equity: —
Cash (mil): $142
Current ratio: 1.02
Long-term debt (mil): $21,948

Net Income ($ mil) 1980-89

1,500
1,000
500
0
-500
-1,000
-1,500

RANKINGS

24th in *Fortune* 500 Industrial Cos.
66th in *Fortune* Global 500 Industrial Cos.
3rd in *Forbes* 400 US Private Cos.

COMPETITION

American Brands
Anheuser-Busch
B.A.T
Borden
BSN
Cadbury Schweppes
Campbell Soup
ConAgra
CPC International
General Mills
H. J. Heinz
Hershey
Kellogg
Loews
Mars
Philip Morris
Procter & Gamble
Quaker Oats
Ralston Purina
Unilever
Whitman
Wrigley

ROADWAY SERVICES, INC.

OVERVIEW

Roadway Services is a holding company specializing in the transportation of freight and packages on a regional and national scale. Roadway Express, the company's main operating subsidiary, specializes in less-than-truckload (LTL) freight shipments (those weighing less than 10,000 pounds) throughout the US, Mexico, and Canada. LTL shipments accounted for about 99% of the shipments and 89% of the revenues generated by Roadway Express in 1989. Other subsidiaries operated by Roadway Services include Spartan, which provides LTL service in the South and central US; Viking Freight, the leading regional carrier in the West; and Roberts Express, which offers expedited delivery of fragile, high security, and hazardous shipments throughout North America and Europe (as of March 1990).

Roadway Package System (RPS) offers small package pickup and delivery to businesses in 42 states. RPS has exceeded management's expectations in both revenues and earnings and is expected to grow both geographically (to Hawaii and Canada) and financially in 1990.

OTC symbol: ROAD
Incorporated: Ohio, 1982
Fiscal year ends: December 31

WHO

Chairman and President: Joseph M. Clapp, age 53, $590,629 pay
Group VP: William W. Blodgett, age 48, $352,091 pay
VP Finance and Secretary: D. A. Wilson, age 45, $287,737 pay
VP Properties and Materials Management: William F. Klug, age 50, $230,190 pay
President, Roadway Express: J. T. Topping, age 55, $266,398 pay
Auditors: Ernst & Young
Employees: 34,500

WHEN

Brothers Galen and Carroll Roush founded Roadway Express in 1930. Based in Akron, Ohio, the company started with 10 owner-operated trucks and terminals in Chicago, Houston, and Kansas City. By 1935 Roadway was moving freight over an extensive network in 20 eastern states.

In 1945 the company began converting from owner-operators to a company-owned fleet. This process, completed in 1956, coincided with the Roush brothers' decision (1950) to specialize in less-than-truckload (LTL) shipments. Although LTLs cost more to operate than full truckloads (since one truck carried multiple shipments to and from various destinations), rates were proportionately higher. By 1956 Roadway Express had 60 terminals to support its LTL route network.

The Roush brothers split in 1956. Carroll sold his half of the company to the public and went on to buy ONC Fast Freight (later part of ROCOR). Galen Roush remained Roadway's chairman until his retirement in 1974. By 1975 Roadway was operating 300 terminals in 40 states, with coast-to-coast operations by 1977.

During the recession of the mid-1970s, Roadway fared better than most trucking companies by cutting labor costs (which accounted for 60% of its operating expenses), thereby sustaining profits even though tonnage dropped 15% between 1974 and 1975. The company was also (and remains) debt-free.

In the early 1980s Roadway expanded its network in the West, concentrating on the Pacific Northwest (traditionally dominated by Consolidated Freightways), and established service to Alaska, Hawaii, Canada, Mexico, and Puerto Rico. Roadway bought 2 regional trucking companies to consolidate its transcontinental network: Spartan Express, based in Greer, South Carolina, which enhanced operations in the South (1984); and San Jose, California–based Viking Freight, which served 10 western states and Guam (1988). Roadway also acquired Roberts Express (1984), which specialized in direct (from shipper to consignee) express delivery.

However, increased competition in the LTL market made diversification necessary. In 1985 Roadway Express fell from its position as America's leading freight carrier, to #3 (behind Yellow Freight and Consolidated Freightways). The company entered the small package shipping market in 1985 by establishing Roadway Package System (RPS), which utilized owner-operated trucks to deliver packages weighing up to 100 pounds. RPS made its first profit in 1989, after only 4 years of service.

WHERE

HQ: 1077 Gorge Blvd., PO Box 88, Akron, OH 44309
Phone: 216-384-8184
FAX: 216-258-6599 (Corporate Planning)

Roadway has operations throughout North America. The company operates 838 terminals (424 owned, 414 leased) and 35,668 tractors, trailers, and trucks.

WHAT

Roadway Express (Akron, OH)
602 terminals in US, Canada, Mexico, Puerto Rico
E•Z Rate (simplified rate system)
E•Z Bill (computerized billing)
QUIKTRAK (shipment tracking)

Spartan Express (Greer, SC)
52 service centers in 16 central and southern states

Viking Freight (San Jose, CA)
37 terminals in 10 western states
Easy Rate (rating disk for IBM computer)
VFS Transportation (nationwide truckload)
Viking Freight System

Roberts Express (Akron, OH)
CarVan (automotive components)
Customer Link (satellite communications)
MediQuik (deliveries to hospitals)
Roberts Express, B.V. (European division)
"White Glove" (special handling)

Roadway Package System (Pittsburgh, PA)
147 terminals in 42 states (small package shipping)

Roadway Logistics Systems (Akron, OH)
(integrated logistics support)

HOW MUCH

	9 Yr. Growth	1980	1981	1982	1983	1984	1985	1986	1987	1988	1989
Sales ($ mil)	9.7%	1,155	1,130	1,147	1,253	1,462	1,580	1,717	1,909	2,185	2,661
Net income ($ mil)	3.6%	70	72	76	99	100	76	76	51	80	96
Income as % of sales	—	6.0%	6.4%	6.6%	7.9%	6.8%	4.8%	4.5%	2.6%	3.7%	3.6%
Earnings per share ($)	3.6%	1.78	1.82	1.92	2.47	2.49	1.90	1.91	1.26	2.00	2.44
Stock price – high ($)	—	19.88	25.13	31.50	37.38	35.25	35.75	45.75	43.00	35.00	43.25
Stock price – low ($)	—	11.00	16.38	15.25	28.50	23.50	24.75	30.75	23.25	26.75	27.75
Stock price – close ($)	10.2%	17.63	19.13	28.63	34.38	30.50	34.75	34.50	32.00	30.75	42.25
P/E – high	—	11	14	16	15	14	19	24	34	18	18
P/E – low	—	6	9	8	12	9	13	16	18	13	11
Dividends per share ($)	9.8%	0.48	0.63	0.70	0.83	0.98	1.00	1.10	1.10	1.10	1.10
Book value per share ($)	8.9%	8.50	10.10	11.37	13.12	14.49	15.37	16.28	16.45	17.06	18.35

1989 Year End:
Debt ratio: 0.0%
Return on equity: 13.8%
Cash (mil): $150
Current ratio: 1.04
Long-term debt (mil): $0
Number of shares (mil): 39
Dividends:
1989 average yield: 2.6%
1989 payout: 45.1%
Market value (mil): $1,654

Stock Price History high/low 1980-89

RANKINGS

18th in *Fortune* 50 Transportation Cos.
313th in *Forbes* Sales 500
390th in *Business Week* 1000

COMPETITION

Burlington Northern
Consolidated Freightways
Federal Express
Union Pacific
UPS
Yellow Freight
Other railroads

ROBERT BOSCH GMBH

OVERVIEW

Robert Bosch is the world's #1 electronic automobile equipment manufacturer and owns 6% of #2, Nippondenso (Japan). The company is the inventor and leading producer of fuel injection and antilock braking systems. The company's Blaupunkt unit is a major car audio manufacturer, and 50%-owned Bosch-Siemens Hausgeräte is a European appliance leader. Bosch continues to invest heavily in product development to maintain its reputation for innovation and quality, employing 12,000 R&D personnel.

Bosch is 90% owned by the Robert Bosch Foundation, a charitable organization whose shares have no voting rights. Control of the business rests with Robert Bosch Industrietreuhand, a partnership effectively controlled by the company's chief executive.

Bosch is reputed to be a paternalistic employer. Rising labor costs in West Germany, home of 2/3 of the company's work force, have increased costs of Bosch products. The company is moving production to lower-cost countries and is thought to be eyeing East Germany for future factory sites.

WHEN

Self-taught electrical engineer Robert Bosch opened a Stuttgart workshop in 1886 and, in the next year, produced the world's first alternator for a stationary engine. In 1897 his company produced the world's first automobile alternator, beginning a series of electrical automotive product launches, including spark plugs (1902), starters (1912), and regulators (1913). Bosch believed in treating employees well and shortened their workday to 8 hours (extraordinary for 1906). US operations started in 1909 were confiscated in WWI as part of a trade embargo against Germany. Bosch survived the German depression of the 1920s, introduced power tools (1928) and appliances (1933), and bought Blaupunkt (car radios, 1933). Growth in German industrial and military demand for the company's products continued from the 1930s until WWII. Robert Bosch died in 1942, leaving 90% of his company to charity.

Bosch suffered severe damage in WWII, and its US operations were again confiscated. The company rebuilt its plants and enjoyed growing demand for its appliances and automotive products as postwar incomes increased worldwide. In 1963 Hans Merkle took control at Bosch. Because Merkle believed fuel efficiency and pollution control would be important issues in the future, Bosch invested large sums to develop electronic automotive components that raised gas mileage and lowered emissions. Bosch made the world's first electronic fuel injection system in 1967, equipping Volkswagen Beetles to satisfy California's new, stringent emission standards. In the same year Bosch and Siemens (West Germany) formed Bosch-Siemens Hausgeräte, an appliance manufacturer.

The oil crisis of the 1970s increased awareness of fuel efficiency, benefiting sales of Bosch's electronic fuel injection systems. In 1974 Bosch reentered the US, buying a plant in Charleston, South Carolina, to make fuel injection systems. In the same year Bosch launched the first electronic ignition. The company introduced the first antilock braking system (ABS) in 1978.

A 1984 strike against Bosch in Germany disrupted automobile production throughout Europe and resulted in 38.5-hour work weeks for Bosch employees. By the end of the 1980s, electronic fuel injection was found in most new cars, and ABS was standard in most luxury cars. Bosch had a 50% share of each market. In 1989 the average US car was estimated to contain $1,400 worth of electronics, 3 times the 1984 level and 60 times the 1970 level. Throughout the 1980s Bosch acquired telecommunications companies making such products as cellular telephones and PBX systems. In the late 1980s the company developed a technology for multiplexing (employing one wire to replace many by using semiconductor controllers) in automobiles, established it as an industry standard, and licensed it to chipmakers Intel (US), Philips (Netherlands), and Motorola (US).

HOW MUCH

$= DM1.69 (Dec. 31, 1989)	9 Yr. Growth	1980	1981	1982	1983	1984	1985	1986	1987	1988	1989
Sales (DM mil)	11.2%	11,809	12,950	13,812	16,126	18,373	21,223	23,807	25,365	27,675	30,588
Net income (DM mil)*	15.1%	176	181	181	242	446	402	454	825	554	626
Income as % of sales	—	1.5%	1.4%	1.3%	1.5%	2.4%	2.0%	1.9%	3.3%	2.0%	2.0%
R&D expense (DM mil)	12.2%	639	681	753	883	977	1,097	1,262	1,425	1,640	1,803
Employees (thou)	4.1%	122	116	112	128	132	140	158	161	166	175
Equity (DM mil)	11.0%	2,615	2,888	3,228	3,725	4,377	4,664	5,177	5,623	6,174	6,668

1989 Year End:
Debt ratio: 21.1%
Return on equity: 9.7%
Cash (mil): DM5,157
Long-term debt (mil): DM1,780
Sales (mil): $18,099

Sales (DM mil) 1980-89

35,000
30,000
25,000
20,000
15,000
10,000
5,000
0

*includes minority interests

Private company
Incorporated: Germany, 1937
Fiscal year ends: December 31

WHO

Chairman: Marcus Bierich, age 63
Chairman and CEO, Robert Bosch Corp.: Hermann Scholl
Auditors: Schitag, Schwäbische Treuhand Aktiengesellschaft
Employees: 174,742

WHERE

HQ: Robert Bosch Platz 1, Postfach 10 60 50, D-7000 Stuttgart 10, Germany
Phone: 011-49-711-811-0
FAX: 011-49-711-811-6630
US HQ (Robert Bosch Corp.): 2800 S. 25th Ave., Broadview, IL 60153
US Phone: 708-865-5200
US FAX: 708-865-5203

Bosch has 110 plants operating in 18 countries and sales and service operations in 130 countries.

	1989 Sales	
	DM mil	% of total
Europe	25,041	82
US	3,642	12
Asia, Africa, Australia	1,905	6
Total	**30,588**	**100**

WHAT

	1989 Sales	
	DM mil	% of total
Automotive equipment	15,858	52
Communications technology	6,885	23
Consumer goods	5,870	19
Capital goods	1,975	6
Total	**30,588**	**100**

Major Products
Antilock braking systems
Broadcast TV Systems (BTS, 50%)
Electronic fuel injection systems
Entertainment electronics and mobile communications (Blaupunkt)
Factory automation (Weldun)
Heating technology (Junkers)
Household appliances (Bosch–Siemens Hausgeräte, 50%)
Hydraulics and pneumatics (Racine Fluid Power)
Industrial electronics
Medical electronics
Packaging machinery
Power tools
Safety equipment
Spark plugs
Telecommunications equipment (Telenorma, ANT, Teldix)
Traction control systems

RANKINGS

59th in *Fortune* Global 500 Industrial Cos.

COMPETITION

Allied-Signal
Black & Decker
Cooper Industries
Dana
Eaton
Electrolux
Emerson
Fiat
General Motors
ITT
Litton
Motorola
Philips
Siemens
Stanley Works
Whirlpool
Factory automation and telecommunications manufacturers

ROCHE HOLDING, LTD.

OVERVIEW

Through its F. Hoffmann–La Roche subsidiary, Roche is a major pharmaceutical manufacturer. The company's Rocephin is the US's most widely used antibiotic. Basel, Switzerland–based Roche is also the largest producer of vitamins and a supplier of fragrances to perfume houses. It owns 60% of Genentech, a leading US genetic engineering firm.

Roche has sought new drugs by investing in R&D (14.5% of sales in 1989), buying several companies, and entering into biotechnology partnerships. The company is providing Genentech with much-needed funding in exchange for access to a potentially prolific product pipeline. Roche has an option to buy the rest of Genentech at escalating prices in the future.

Roche was created in 1989 as a holding company for F. Hoffman–La Roche and Sapac, which had been separate but linked companies. The founder's descendants control Roche through its voting stock.

Primary stock exchanges: Basel, Zurich, Geneva
Incorporated: Switzerland, 1989
Fiscal year ends: December 31

WHO

Chairman and CEO: Fritz Gerber
COO: Armin M. Kessler
Executive Committee, Finance and Accounting: Henri B. Meier
Auditors: Allgemeine Treuhand AG (Ernst & Young International)
Employees: 50,203

WHEN

Backed by his family's wealth, Fritz Hoffmann–La Roche began making pharmaceuticals in a small lab in Basel, Switzerland, in 1894. At the time, drug compounds were mixed at pharmacies, resulting in a lack of uniformity. Hoffmann was not a chemist but was committed to the concept of standardization of pharmaceutical content and packaging. He recognized the potential for mass-produced, branded drugs with a reputation for quality.

Immediately prior to WWI, after years of financial difficulty, Hoffmann was selling Thiocal (cough medicine), Digalen (digitalis extract), and other products on 4 continents under the Roche name. During WWI the presence of a Roche factory in nearby Grenzach, Germany, engendered Allied speculation that the company was supporting the German war effort. Concurrently, the Germans suspected the company of supplying the French and began a boycott. The Bolsheviks seized Roche's St. Petersburg facility. Devastated by the war, Hoffmann–La Roche sold shares outside the family for the first time in 1919.

Between the wars Roche expanded its scope, synthesizing vitamins C, A, and E, and eventually became the world's leading vitamin manufacturer. As volume grew, the company built plants and research centers internationally, including a facility in Nutley, New Jersey (1928). Expecting war, Hoffmann–La Roche had split in two in 1926, transferring its more distant operations, including its American ones, into Sapac, a holding company.

Roche continued to develop successful drugs, including blockbuster tranquilizers Librium (1960) and Valium (1963). Valium was the world's best-selling drug until 1981, when SmithKline's Tagamet took the lead.

In the 1970s Roche was accused by several governments of Librium and Valium price gouging. After years of legal proceedings, Roche agreed to voluntary price restraints. In 1976 the company was found guilty of vitamin price fixing. In the same year a dioxin cloud escaped from a company-owned factory in Italy, killing tens of thousands of animals and forcing the evacuation of hundreds of families. Roche was criticized for its failure to respond quickly and accept the magnitude of the accident. Adolf Jann, Hoffmann–La Roche chairman, was quoted as saying, "Capitalism means progress and progress may occasionally bring some inconvenience."

Valium went off-patent in the US in 1985, and Roche's sales suffered for a few years. The company was able to maintain its large US sales force by agreeing in 1983 to sell Glaxo's Zantac. During the latter 1980s Roche spent heavily on R&D and, after losing a bid for Sterling Drug (US) to Eastman Kodak in 1988, purchased a controlling interest in Genentech, a leading US biotechnology firm (1990).

WHERE

HQ: POB CH-4002, Basel, Switzerland
Phone: 011-41-61-271122
US HQ (Hoffmann–La Roche, Inc.): 340 Kingsland St., Nutley, NJ 07110
Phone: 201-235-5000

Roche owns interests in operations in 52 countries.

	1989 Sales		1989 Employees	
	SF mil	% of total	no.	% of total
Switzerland	301	3	10,914	22
EC	3,201	33	11,768	23
Rest of Europe	535	5	827	2
North America	3,550	36	17,088	34
Latin America	707	7	4,130	8
Asia	1,161	12	4,397	9
Other	359	4	1,079	2
Total	**9,814**	**100**	**50,203**	**100**

WHAT

	1989 Sales	
	SF mil	% of total
Pharmaceuticals	4,375	45
Vitamins & fine chemicals	2,498	26
Diagnostics	1,405	14
Fragrances & flavors	1,098	11
Plant protection	378	4
Instruments	33	—
Other	27	—
Total	**9,814**	**100**

Pharmaceuticals
Anesthetics
Anticancer agents
Antidepressants
Anti-infectives
Anti-inflammatory agents
Antiviral drugs
Cardiovascular medicines
Dermatological preparations

Vitamins & Fine Chemicals
Animal feeds
Animal health products
Vitamin fortification products

Diagnostics
Drug abuse testing systems
Reagents and analytical systems

Fragrances & Flavors
Consumer and industrial goods fragrances
Flavorings
Perfumes (Givaudan)

RANKINGS

204th in *Fortune* Global 500 Industrial Cos.
77th in *Forbes* 100 Foreign Investments in the US
94th in *Business Week* Global 1000

COMPETITION

Agricultural chemical companies
Fragrance and flavorings companies
Pharmaceutical companies

HOW MUCH

$ = SF 1.54 (Dec. 31, 1989)	9 Yr. Growth	1980	1981	1982	1983	1984	1985	1986	1987	1988	1989
Sales (SF mil)	5.9%	5,856	6,775	7,103	7,510	8,267	8,940	7,822	7,705	8,690	9,814
Net income (SF mil)	15.6%	232	253	281	328	380	452	416	482	642	852
Income as % of sales	—	4.0%	3.7%	4.0%	4.4%	4.6%	5.1%	5.3%	6.3%	7.4%	8.7%
Earnings per share (SF)	15.1%	58	63	70	82	95	113	104	120	160	206
Stock price – high (SF)*	—	1,535	1,750	1,570	2,198	2,255	2,385	2,820	3,105	2,590	4,245
Stock price – low (SF)*	—	1,020	1,220	1,075	1,445	1,700	1,670	1,890	1,680	1,775	2,545
Stock price – close (SF)*	10.7%	1,440	1,275	1,560	2,170	1,700	2,385	2,250	1,840	2,545	3,590
P/E – high	—	26	28	22	27	24	21	27	26	16	21
P/E – low	—	18	19	15	18	18	15	18	14	11	16
Dividends per share (SF)	4.8%	20.00	20.00	20.46	20.90	21.82	24.50	25.70	25.70	26.40	30.50
Book value per share (SF)	6.0%	1,670	1,714	1,764	1,825	1,898	1,986	2,078	2,174	2,516	2,814

1989 Year End:
Debt ratio: 33.0%
Return on equity: 7.3%
Cash (mil): SF8,190
Long-term debt (mil): SF5,656
Number of shares (mil): 4,130
Dividends:
1989 average yield: 0.5%
1989 payout: 14.8%
Market value (mil): $22,796
Sales (mil): $6,373

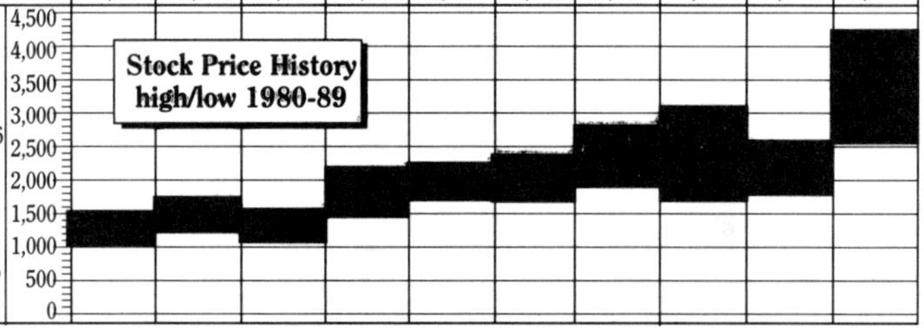

Stock Price History high/low 1980-89

4,500 4,000 3,500 3,000 2,500 2,000 1,500 1,000 500 0

*Participation certificates

THE ROCKEFELLER FOUNDATION

OVERVIEW

The Rockefeller Foundation is one of the US's oldest philanthropic organizations and currently among the 10 largest foundations by assets (with an endowment of $2.2 billion).

The foundation's non-US giving represents about 60% of total grants and fellowships (highest among major US foundations) and emphasizes the agricultural, population, and health sciences. Within the US, the foundation sponsors equal opportunity and the arts and humanities. Smaller grant programs include the global environment, school reform, and international security.

The foundation's scientific approach combats human suffering at its sources, supporting basic research and teaching/training programs. Once a strong research organization in its own right, the foundation is credited with discovering the cure for numerous diseases (*e.g.*, yellow fever).

Today, the foundation maintains no ties to the Rockefeller family or its other philanthropies and holds no original Rockefeller oil stock. An independent board of trustees sets program guidelines and approves all expenditures. Three of the foundation's presidents (John Foster Dulles, Dean Rusk, and Cyrus Vance) have gone on to become US secretary of state.

WHEN

Oil baron John D. Rockefeller, one of America's most criticized capitalists, was also one of its pioneer philanthropists. Before founding the Rockefeller Foundation in 1913, he funded the creation of the University of Chicago (with $36 million over a quarter century) and formed organizations for medical research (1901), the education of southern blacks (1903), and hookworm eradication in the southern US.

Rockefeller's faith in science's ability to cure all human ills was reflected in the foundation's early global campaigns to combat hookworm, malaria, and yellow fever (using his initial $35 million endowment); hookworm control alone spread to 62 countries on 6 continents. To ensure lasting effects on public health, Rockefeller gave another $50 million (1919) to strengthen medical schools in Europe, Canada, and Southeast Asia.

In the mid-1920s, the foundation started conducting basic medical research. In 1928 the foundation absorbed several other Rockefeller philanthropies, thus adding programs in the natural and social sciences and the arts and humanities.

During the 1930s the foundation developed the first effective yellow fever vaccine (1935), continued its worldwide battles against disease, and supported pioneering research in the field of biology. Other grants supported the performing arts in the US and social science research at various US research institutes.

During WWII the foundation supplied major funding for nuclear science, created new research tools (spectroscopy, X-ray diffraction), and stifled typhus epidemics.

After the war, with an increasing number of large public ventures modeled after the foundation (*e.g.*, the UN's World Health Organization) taking over its traditional physical/natural sciences territory, the foundation dissolved its famed biology division in 1951.

Emphasis swung to agricultural studies under chairman John D. Rockefeller III (1952). The foundation took wheat seeds developed at its Mexican food project (begun in 1942) to Colombia (1950), Chile (1955), and India (1956); a rice institute in the Philippines followed (1960). The resulting Green Revolution sprouted 12 more developing world institutes.

In the 1960s the foundation began dispatching expertise to African and Latin American universities in an effort to raise the level of training at those institutions.

The long bear market of the 1970s caused the foundation's assets to drop to a low of $732 million (1977).

President Peter Goldmark is trying to revive a faded star: $50 million over 5 years will be devoted to global environmental issues, and education reform efforts at home will target poor children.

HOW MUCH

	9 Yr. Growth	1980	1981	1982	1983	1984	1985	1986	1987	1988	1989
Assets ($ mil)	8.9%	1,001	883	1,014	1,119	1,109	1,354	1,615	1,676	1,845	2,152
Net investment income ($ mil)*	19.8%	60	67	64	51	59	206	367	288	157	305
Program expenditures ($ mil)	6.7%	42	43	40	37	38	43	48	71	65	75

Assets ($ mil) 1980-89

*Includes realized gains on sale of securities of $149 mil (1985); $304 mil (1986); $205 mil (1987); $67 mil (1988); and $216 mil (1989).

Nonprofit organization
Chartered: New York, 1913
Fiscal year ends: December 31

WHO

Chairman: John R. Evans
President: Peter C. Goldmark, Jr.
SVP: Kenneth Prewitt
VP: Hugh B. Price
Treasurer (acting): Webb Trammell
Auditors: Ernst & Young
Employees: 160

WHERE

HQ: 1133 Ave. of the Americas, New York, NY 10036
Phone: 212-869-8500
FAX: 212-764-3468

The foundation has field offices in India, Kenya, Malawi, and the Philippines, and maintains the Bellagio Study and Conference Center in Italy.

WHAT

	1989 Program Expenditures	
	$ mil	% of total
Agricultural sciences	14	19
Arts & humanities	14	19
Equal opportunity	14	19
Health sciences	10	13
Population sciences	9	12
Special programming	4	5
School reform	2	3
Special interests & explorations	4	5
Other	1	1
Interprogram	3	4
Total	**75**	**100**

Representative Programs

Agricultural Sciences
Genetically improved foodstuffs (International Rice Research Institute, Manila, the Philippines)
Biotechnology transfer (Kasetsart University, Bangkok, Thailand)
Improved food production systems in Africa (maize research, Malawi)

Health Sciences
Population-based health care (International Clinical Epidemiology Network — INCLEN)
Disease prevention through vaccinology and pharmacology (World Health Organization [WHO], Geneva, Switzerland)

Population Sciences
Contraception development and application (Chinese Academy of Medical Sciences, Beijing, China)
Cooperative initiatives in health (AIDS initiatives in Africa)

Global Environmental Program
Global warming and climate change research (Worldwatch Institute, Washington, DC)

Special Programming
Cross-specialty studies in agriculture, education, health, and population (Aga Khan Foundation, Transafrica Forum, The World Bank, Washington, DC)

Arts & Humanities
Cross-culture artistic experimentation (Dance Theatre Workshop, New York Shakespeare Festival, New York, NY)

Equal Opportunity
Combating urban poverty (Children's Defense Fund, Washington, DC;

School Reform
Improved public education for the poor (National Urban League, New York, NY)

International Security
Nuclear weapons delimitation, environmental discussion (Parliamentarians Global Action for Disarmament, Development, and World Reform, New York, NY)

ROCKWELL INTERNATIONAL CORPORATION

OVERVIEW

Most people think of the Space Shuttle and the B-1B bomber when they think of Rockwell International, but the El Segundo, California–based corporation is also a leading producer of heavy-duty automotive parts, newspaper presses, and electronics. With sales of over $12.5 billion in 1989, Rockwell is America's 7th largest defense supplier.

Rockwell produces industrial automation technologies, defense electronics, and telecommunications systems. The company builds 65% of the modems used in fax machines and holds a commanding market share in the field of avionics (aircraft electronic systems). Rockwell's rocket engines power the Space Shuttle, Atlas, and Delta launchers, and the company is building the new shuttle, *Endeavour*, as well as the power system for Space Station *Freedom*. Rockwell supplies a broad international market with axles, brakes, clutches, transmissions, and other components for vehicles ranging from small cars to heavy-duty trucks.

The Graphics segment achieved its first $1 billion sales year in 1989 with the success of its Goss Colorliner newspaper press.

WHEN

Rockwell International is the legacy of two early 20th-century entrepreneurs: Willard Rockwell and Clement Melville Keys.

Willard Rockwell gained control of Wisconsin Parts Company, an Oshkosh maker of automotive axles, in 1919. He went on to acquire a number of industrial manufacturers, merging them in 1953 to create Rockwell Spring & Axle. Renamed Rockwell-Standard (1958), by 1967 this company led the world in the production of mechanical automotive parts.

In 1928 Keys founded North American Aviation (NAA) as a holding company for his aviation interests. General Motors bought North American in 1934 and installed James Kindelberger as the company's president. Over the next 3 decades, Kindelberger and chief engineer Lee Atwood would build North American into an industry giant.

In 1935 the company moved from Dundalk, Maryland, to Inglewood, California, where it built military training planes. North American built over 15,000 AT-6 trainers during WWII and produced the B-25 bomber (1940) and the P-51 fighter (1940). By the end of WWII the company had built nearly 43,000 aircraft, more than any other US manufacturer. Sales peaked at $700 million in 1944.

North American's sales plunged at the end of WWII. In 1948 GM took its subsidiary public; Kindelberger revitalized the company, opening new factories in Downey, California (1948), and Columbus, Ohio (1950). Major products included the F-86 (1948), a highly successful jet fighter of the Korean War, and its successor the F-100 (1953), America's first production supersonic aircraft. The company also produced the X-15 rocket plane (1959) and the XB-70 bomber (1964).

In the 1960s NAA built rocket engines and spacecraft for the Apollo program. In 1967 the company merged with Rockwell Standard, creating North American Rockwell (which became Rockwell International in 1973).

The government awarded Rockwell the prime contracts for the B-1 bomber (1970) and the Space Shuttle Orbiter (1972). In 1973 Rockwell acquired Collins Radio, which would form the backbone of its avionics segment. The company ventured into consumer goods briefly, buying Admiral (1974) and selling it (1979).

Rockwell invested its B-1 proceeds in industrial electronics, acquiring Allen-Bradley for $1.7 billion in 1985. Facing decline in its defense-related revenues as B-1 production ended, chief Don Beall funneled billions into plant modernization and R&D for Rockwell's electronics and graphics segments. In 1989 Rockwell sold its Measurement & Flow Control Division and purchased Baker Perkins, a printing machinery company.

HOW MUCH

	9 Yr. Growth	1980	1981	1982	1983	1984	1985	1986	1987	1988	1989
Sales ($ mil)	6.8%	6,907	7,040	7,395	8,098	9,322	11,338	12,296	12,123	11,946	12,518
Net income ($ mil)	11.3%	280	292	332	389	497	595	611	635	812	735
Income as % of sales	—	4.1%	4.1%	4.5%	4.8%	5.3%	5.3%	5.0%	5.2%	6.8%	5.9%
Earnings per share ($)	13.7%	0.90	0.93	1.06	1.23	1.60	1.96	2.03	2.23	3.01	2.84
Stock price – high ($)	—	11.34	11.19	11.75	17.75	16.81	20.88	24.44	30.94	23.50	27.13
Stock price – low ($)	—	5.50	5.91	6.28	10.56	11.50	14.94	15.69	14.25	16.13	19.75
Stock price – close ($)	8.7%	11.25	8.19	10.63	16.50	15.19	17.88	22.69	19.00	21.75	23.75
P/E – high	—	13	12	11	14	11	11	12	14	8	10
P/E – low	—	6	6	6	9	7	8	8	6	5	7
Dividends per share ($)	9.3%	0.34	0.36	0.39	0.42	0.47	0.53	0.58	0.65	0.71	0.75
Book value per share ($)	11.9%	5.79	6.38	6.85	7.65	8.47	9.87	10.98	12.04	14.14	15.91

1989 Year End:
Debt ratio: 12.2%
Return on equity: 18.9%
Cash (mil): $332
Current ratio: 1.25
Long-term debt (mil): $552
Number of shares (mil): 250
Dividends:
1989 average yield: 3.2%
payout: 26.4%
Market value (mil): $5,933

NYSE symbol: ROK
Incorporated: Delaware, 1928
Fiscal year ends: September 30

WHO

Chairman and CEO: Donald R. Beall, age 52, $1,361,471 pay
EVP and COO: J. Tracy O'Rourke, age 55, $880,501 pay
EVP and COO: Kent M. Black, age 51, $596,890 pay
EVP and COO: Sam F. Iacobellis, age 61, $596,859 pay
SVP, Finance & Planning and CFO: Robert A. dePalma, age 55, $555,058 pay
Auditors: Deloitte & Touche
Employees: 108,700

WHERE

HQ: 2230 E. Imperial Hwy., El Segundo, CA 90245
Phone: 213-647-5000
FAX: 213-647-5524

Rockwell International operates in the US and 24 foreign countries.

	1989 Sales		1989 Operating Income	
	$ mil	% of total	$ mil	% of total
US	10,310	83	1,112	81
Canada	407	3	88	6
Europe	1,254	10	103	7
Other	547	4	87	6
Adjustments	—	—	(331)	—
Total	**12,518**	**100**	**1,059**	**100**

WHAT

	1989 Sales		1989 Operating Income	
	$ mil	% of total	$ mil	% of total
Electronics	4,914	40	488	35
Aerospace	3,909	31	418	30
Automotive	2,424	19	180	13
Graphics	1,110	9	129	9
Divested businesses	161	1	175	13
Adjustments	—	—	(331)	—
Total	**12,518**	**100**	**1,059**	**100**

Electronics
Allen-Bradley industrial automation
Avionics (aircraft electronics)
Defense electronics
Telecommunications

Graphics
Goss newspaper and commercial presses

Aerospace
B-1B support
NAVSTAR satellites
Rocketdyne rocket engines
Space Shuttle Orbiter

Automotive
Heavy vehicles systems/components
Light vehicles systems/components

RANKINGS

29th in *Fortune* 500 Industrial Cos.
80th in *Fortune* Global 500 Industrial Cos.
36th in *Fortune* 50 Exporters
46th in *Forbes* Sales 500
108th in *Business Week* 1000
266th in *Business Week* Global 1000

COMPETITION

Allied-Signal
Boeing
Dana
Eaton
General Dynamics
Harris
Lockheed
Martin Marietta
McDonnell Douglas
Northrop
Raytheon
Square D
Textron
United Technologies
Westinghouse
Other electronics and aerospace companies

ROMAN CATHOLIC CHURCH (US)

OVERVIEW

With over 20% of the population, the Roman Catholic Church is the largest religious denomination in the US. One of its principal achievements is the creation and operation of the largest private educational system in the world. Roman Catholics were traditionally lower- and middle-class, urban-dwelling immigrants who voted Democratic, but are increasingly geographically, economically, and politically indistinguishable from American society as a whole.

The church is a supporter of separation of church and state. However, like many religious organizations in the US, it has involved itself in the political arena in a number of instances, *e.g.*, support for federal aid to parochial schools and opposition to abortion. It supports missionary efforts abroad and since WWII has actively taken a leading role in the struggle for social and economic justice for the underprivileged.

One of the greatest challenges facing the US Catholic church today is the decline in the number of priests and nuns, and the not-unrelated pressure to abolish priestly celibacy and admit women to the priesthood.

WHEN

Tracing its foundation to AD 33 in Jerusalem by Jesus of Nazareth, Catholicism probably first came to North America with Norse traders in the 12th and 13th centuries. The next Catholics came in 1492 — Christopher Columbus and his crew.

There are some records of a bishop being appointed to the territory of Florida as early as 1528, but the first Catholic settlement in what is now the US was the Spanish colony of St. Augustine, founded in 1565. Missionary efforts were begun by the Spanish in New Mexico in 1582 and California in 1601 and by the French in 1613 in the northern and central US.

The history of the church in the British colonies began in 1634 when George Calvert founded the Maryland colony, the only English colony at the time to tolerate Catholics. Catholicism in the colonies remained confined largely to Maryland and tolerant Quaker Pennsylvania until well after the Revolutionary War. The first diocese in the new country was established at Baltimore in 1789 and encompassed the entire country. John Carroll, the first bishop, had 25 priests in his charge and a flock numbering 25,000 to 35,000, under 1% of the US population.

The first US Catholic school was probably the one set up by the monks at St. Augustine in 1606. Periodic attempts to start schools in New York (1634) and Maryland (1640 and 1673) were short-lived, as colonial authorities opposed them. The Church's first permanent schools, Georgetown Visitation (a secondary school for girls, established in Washington, DC, 1799) and one at Emmitsburg, Maryland (1810, generally considered the model for the parochial school system), were followed quickly by many others.

Immigration from Germany and Ireland and the annexation of French and Spanish territories caused the Catholic population in the US to grow to 200,000 in 1820 and 3 million by 1860, making it the largest Christian denomination in the US. Anti-Catholic sentiment continued into the 19th century with frequent attacks against "popery" by the Know-Nothing party in the 1850s and the American Protective Association in the 1880s.

By 1908 the Pope had removed the American Catholic church's mission status. The Catholic population rose from 10 million in 1890 to over 20 million by 1929. During this period Catholics began to take a more active role in political life. Alfred Smith was elected governor of New York, though anti-Catholic sentiment contributed to his defeat in the 1928 presidential election. In 1960, however, John F. Kennedy was elected president.

When the Second Vatican Council convened in 1962, the American hierarchy was the 2nd largest delegation. As a product of a pluralistic American society, the delegation was instrumental in updating liturgical practice (*e.g.*, by eliminating Latin as its primary language), giving lay persons (nonpriests) a greater voice in church affairs, and opening doctrinal matters to discussion.

Recently the US Catholic church has experienced several heated internal debates, most notably where modern lifestyle and church doctrine collided (*e.g.*, use of birth control).

HOW MUCH

	9 Yr. Growth	1980	1981	1982	1983	1984	1985	1986	1987	1988	1989
Members (mil)	1.1%	49.8	50.5	51.2	52.1	52.4	52.3	52.7	52.9	53.5	55.0
Priests	(1.1%)	58,621	58,398	58,085	57,870	57,891	57,317	57,183	53,382	53,522	52,948
Deacons	9.2%	4,093	4,725	5,471	6,066	6,702	7,204	7,562	7,981	8,512	9,065
Brothers	(1.4%)	7,941	7,966	7,880	7,658	7,596	7,544	7,429	7,418	7,069	6,977
Sisters	(2.1%)	126,517	122,653	121,370	120,699	118,027	115,386	113,658	112,489	106,912	104,419
Parishes	0.5%	18,794	18,829	18,903	19,039	19,118	19,244	19,313	19,546	19,596	19,705

Membership (mil) 1980-89

Religious denomination
Founded: AD 33
Fiscal year ends: December 31

WHO

His Holiness the Pope, Bishop of Rome, Vicar of Jesus Christ, Supreme Pontiff of the Catholic Church: Pope John Paul II (Karol Wojtyla), age 70
Apostolic Pro-Nuncio to the US: Archbishop Agostino Cacciavillan
President, National Conference of Catholic Bishops: Archbishop Daniel Pilarczyk
Treasurer, National Conference of Bishops: Archbishop Daniel Kucera
Auditors: Coopers & Lybrand
Employees: 182,200

WHERE

US HQ: 1312 Massachusetts Ave., NW, Washington, DC 20005
Phone: 202-541-3000
Fax: 202-541-3129 (Media Relations)

The church operates worldwide, serving its nearly 900 million members through 212,409 parishes and almost 2.3 million clerical and lay personnel. The US church operates through its 399 bishops, 185 dioceses, and 19,705 parishes in all 50 states.

	Members		Priests	
	mil	% of total	no.	% of total
New England	5.6	10	5,662	11
Mid-Atlantic	13.6	25	13,027	25
South Atlantic	3.4	6	4,381	8
Midwest	10.2	19	10,830	21
South Central	.7	1	1,300	2
North Central	3.5	6	5,267	10
Southwest	5.1	9	3,619	7
Mountain	2.0	4	1,965	4
Pacific	8.0	15	5,410	10
Other	.6	1	702	1
Military	2.3	4	785	1
Total	**55.0**	**100**	**52,948**	**100**

WHAT

Official Units
Campaign for Human Development
Canon Law Society of America
Catholic Charities
Catholic Relief Services
Conference of Major Religious Superiors of Men
Leadership Conference of Women Religious
National Catholic Education Association
National Conference of Catholic Bishops
National Council of Catholic Laity
National Council of Catholic Women
National Office for Black Catholics
The United States Catholic Conference
US Catholic Bishops' Advisory Council
Word of God Institute

Other Influential Organizations
Catholic Youth Organization
Confraternity of Christian Doctrine
Knights of Columbus
Opus Dei
Society of Jesus (Jesuits)
Sovereign Military Order (Knights) of Malta

ROTARY INTERNATIONAL

OVERVIEW

Rotary International is the oldest and most international service organization in the world. It has more than 1 million members forming almost 25,000 clubs in 167 countries. Many other service clubs, including the Kiwanis and Lions clubs, have patterned themselves after the Rotary.

The organization's motto, "Service Above Self," exemplifies the organization's dedication to its "four avenues" of club, vocational, community, and international service. The organization is devoted to promoting high ethical standards in business and international understanding, goodwill, and peace. Rotary's scholarship, immunization, and nutritional programs have helped hundreds of thousands of people throughout the world. It operates the world's largest privately sponsored scholarship program through the Rotary Foundation.

Rotary International has raised almost 1/4 billion dollars toward its goal of eradicating polio by the end of the century. Its Interact and Rotaract clubs for teens and young adults and its Youth Exchange program promote Rotarian values to young people.

WHEN

Conceived on the night of February 23, 1905, at Madame Galli's restaurant in Chicago by a shy, 37-year-old bachelor attorney, Paul Percy Harris, and 3 business acquaintances, the "Conspirators," as the club was first called, was to be an organization dedicated to fellowship and the mutual business advantage of its members (no 2 of whom were to be from the same profession or business). The club very early on assumed the additional objective of service, which has come to dominate its activities.

Rotary's first foray into community service occurred when it waged a successful 2-year campaign to bring the first public lavatory to Chicago in the face of opposition from tavern and department store owners who used their lavatory facilities to draw customers. The name Rotary was derived from the organization's early propensity to meet at different hotels and offices.

Initially Harris assumed no office in the Rotary Club of Chicago, the organization's first official name, waiting until 1907 to serve as its president. At this time, as its name suggested, the club still focused its activities on the Chicago area. Harris, wanting to spread the organization's ideals more widely, opened the 2nd club in San Francisco in 1908. Once started, expansion occurred rapidly. By 1910 there were 16 clubs (including the first international club in Winnipeg) and 1,500 Rotarians, and, to reflect its broader geographical base, the organization changed its name to the National Association of Rotary Clubs. By 1912 there were 50 clubs, including 3 outside the US, prompting yet another name change to the International Association of Rotary Clubs.

Chesley Perry succeeded Harris as president in 1911, holding that position for the next 32 years. Under him the Rotary continued to expand its membership and refine its concept of service. It adopted its present name in 1922.

The Rotary Foundation was established in 1917 to advance the cause of international understanding. The Foundation has since provided millions of dollars for scholarships, the prevention of polio, and other worthy causes. During WWI and WWII the Rotary was instrumental in assisting the victims of war and played an important role in the establishment of UNESCO in 1945. Rotary lost a number of clubs in Eastern Europe during and after WWII.

Growth in membership continued, rising to 682,183 in 1970 and 875,949 by 1980. In 1986 Rotary established the Village Corps to promote self-help community service projects among members. With the admission of women to the US clubs in May 1987, following a US Supreme Court decision upholding a California law prohibiting Rotary's ban of women members (extended worldwide in July 1989), membership again grew. In 1988 Rotary established the Peace Forum in an effort to enhance and formalize its well-known peacemaking efforts.

In 1989 the new political order in Eastern Europe prompted Rotarians to reestablish clubs abolished after WWII in Warsaw and Budapest and to begin exploratory discussions with representatives from the USSR to establish clubs, which culminated in the inauguration of the Moscow club on June 5, 1990.

HOW MUCH

	9 Yr. Growth	1980	1981	1982	1983	1984	1985	1986	1987	1988	1989
Membership (thou)	2.3%	876	896	908	926	961	991	1,013	1,039	1,057	1,077
Clubs	2.9%	18,827	19,339	19,786	20,187	20,838	21,662	22,365	23,095	23,679	24,408
Countries	0.9%	154	156	157	157	159	159	160	160	162	167

Membership (thou) 1980-89

Service organization
Founded: Chicago, 1905
Fiscal year ends: June 30

WHO

General Secretary: Spencer Robinson, Jr.
President: Paulo V.C. Costa (1990-1991 year)
Finance Officer: James Fallen
Auditors: Coopers & Lybrand
Employees: 487

WHERE

HQ: One Rotary Center, 1560 Sherman Ave., Evanston, IL 60201
Phone: 708-866-3000
FAX: 708-328-8554

Rotary International has 24,408 clubs in 167 countries.

WHAT

1989 Organization/Program	Membership
Rotary	1,076,913
Interact	140,932
Rotaract	103,845
Village Corps	2,631
Youth Exchange	7,800
Total	**1,332,121**

	1989 Foundation Budget	
	$ mil	% of total
Scholarships	17	30
Group Study Exchange	4	7
Health, Hunger & Humanity	3	5
Other general	5	9
Teacher & special grants	1	2
PolioPlus	26	45
Other programs	1	2
Total	**57**	**100**

Prominent Members

US Presidents
Dwight Eisenhower
Warren Harding
Herbert Hoover
John Kennedy
Richard Nixon
Franklin Roosevelt
Harry Truman
Woodrow Wilson

Politicians
Winston Churchill
J. William Fulbright
Mark Hatfield
Wayne Morse
Adlai Stevenson
Earl Warren

Literary Figures
Thomas Mann
Norman Vincent Peale
James Whitcomb Riley
Albert Schweitzer

Business Leaders
Frank Borman
Raymond Firestone
Connie Mack
Charles Walgreen

Royalty
King Baudouin I (Belgium)
Prince Bernhard (Netherlands)
King Carl VI Gustav (Sweden)
King Hassan II (Morocco)
Prince Philip (England)
Prince Rainier (Monaco)

Others
Neil Armstrong
Admiral Richard Byrd
Gordon Cooper
Alan Shepard
Orville Wright

ROYAL DUTCH/SHELL GROUP

OVERVIEW

The Royal Dutch/Shell Group handles 10% of the world's oil and gas. Ranked by sales, the company is the world's 2nd largest international oil concern, after Exxon, and the largest petrochemical producer. Its Houston-based Shell Oil unit alone ranks 13th in the *Fortune* 500.

Each operating unit is owned 60% by Royal Dutch Petroleum (Netherlands) and 40% by Shell Transport and Trading (UK). These dual parent companies maintain headquarters in The Hague and London. Group leadership alternates between the 2.

The well-known scallop shell logo stands over 50,000 gas stations around the globe. A truly international organization, Shell tries to adopt the local character of each of the 100+ countries in which it operates.

Because Shell's forecast calls for low inflation of oil prices into the mid-1990s, the company continues to emphasize refining and marketing over reserve accumulation. Should the forecast change, Shell has $6.5 billion in cash and securities available to acquire reserves.

WHEN

In 1870 Marcus Samuel inherited an interest in his father's London-based company, a trading business specializing in seashells from the Far East. Samuel expanded the business and, after securing a contract for Russian oil, began selling oil products in the Far East.

Standard Oil engaged in severe price-cutting to defend its Asian markets. Samuel secretly prepared his response and in 1892 unveiled the first of a fleet of tankers, all named after seashells. Specially designed to transport kerosene in bulk (Standard's was in cans), the ships pumped their cargo into storage tanks he had built at key ports. Samuel's transportation cost advantage allowed him to compete with Standard while competitors went bankrupt. Rejecting acquisition overtures from Standard, Samuel created Shell Transport and Trading in 1897.

Concurrently, a Dutchman, Aeilko Zijlker, struck oil in Sumatra and formed Royal Dutch in 1890 to exploit the oil field. Young, financially astute Henri Deterding joined Royal Dutch in 1896 and established a Far Eastern sales organization.

Deterding became president of Royal Dutch in 1900 amid the battle for Asian market dominance. In 1903 Deterding, Samuel, and the Rothschilds created Asiatic Petroleum, an oil marketing alliance in the Far East. In 1907, when Shell's non-Asian business was eroding, Deterding engineered a merger between Royal Dutch and Shell. The deal stipulated 60% control of the combined companies by Royal Dutch shareholders, 40% by owners of Shell Transport and Trading stock.

Controlling a transportation and marketing powerhouse, Deterding sought reserves, buying oil fields around the globe. Following the 1911 breakup of Standard Oil, Deterding entered the American market, building refineries and acquiring producers in the US. Shell products were available in every state by 1929. Royal Dutch joined the 1928 "As Is" cartel that divided world oil markets among participating producers and fixed prices for most of 2 decades.

Disturbed by Deterding's pro-Nazi sentiments, Shell management persuaded him to step down in 1936. At the time Shell was producing 10% of the world's oil.

In its post-Deterding years, Shell emphasized refining and marketing rather than accumulation of reserves and profited from tremendous worldwide growth in consumption of oil-based products. It acquired 100% control of its subsidiary, Shell Oil (US), in 1985.

In recent years Shell has been the target of antiapartheid demonstrations over its continued operations in South Africa.

HOW MUCH

	9 Yr. Growth	1980	1981	1982	1983	1984	1985	1986	1987	1988	1989
Sales ($ mil)	0.9%	78,920	77,550	83,785	80,417	84,790	81,562	64,761	78,312	78,394	85,412
Net income ($ mil)	3.7%	2,972	2,197	2,156	2,555	3,004	2,450	2,396	3,017	3,325	4,125
Income as % of sales	—	6.3%	4.7%	4.3%	5.3%	5.9%	5.0%	6.2%	6.4%	7.1%	8.1%
Earnings per share ($)	3.5%	5.55	4.10	3.97	4.80	5.57	4.57	4.33	5.66	6.27	7.58
Stock price – high ($)	—	28.06	24.69	18.56	25.06	27.31	32.56	48.00	70.50	62.13	77.63
Stock price – low ($)	—	16.63	13.50	14.06	16.75	20.63	24.19	29.88	47.19	52.19	56.88
Stock price – close ($)	13.7%	24.38	17.44	17.31	22.50	24.69	31.50	47.75	55.94	57.00	77.50
P/E – high	—	5	6	5	5	5	7	11	12	10	10
P/E – low	—	3	3	4	4	4	5	7	8	8	8
Dividends per share ($)	8.4%	1.63	1.31	1.46	1.41	1.44	1.65	2.64	3.16	3.62	3.36
Book value per share ($)	5.8%	32.14	28.29	30.56	31.82	33.08	37.77	41.42	48.08	50.67	53.58

1989 Year End:
Debt ratio: 8.5%
Return on equity: 14.5%
Cash (mil): $6,500
Current ratio: 1.35
Long-term debt (mil): $2,674
Number of shares (mil): 536
Dividends:
1989 average yield: 4.3%
1989 payout: 44.4%
Market value (mil): $41,546

Stock Price History high/low 1980-89

Note: Sales and cash are stated for Group. All other figures are stated for Royal Dutch only.

NYSE symbols: RD (Royal Dutch); SC (Shell) (ADR)
Incorporated: Netherlands, 1890; UK, 1897
Fiscal year ends: December 31

WHO

Group Chairman; President, Royal Dutch: L. C. van Wachem, age 59
Group VC; Chairman, Shell Transport: Sir Peter Holmes, age 58
President and CEO, Shell Oil Co. (US): Frank H. Richardson
VP Environmental and External Affairs, Shell Oil Co. (US): M. K. Seggerman
Auditors: KPMG Klynveld Kraayenhof & Co. (Netherlands); Ernst & Young (UK); Price Waterhouse (US)
Employees: 135,000

WHERE

HQ: Royal Dutch Petroleum Company, 30 Carel van Bylandtlaan, 2596 HR The Hague, The Netherlands
Phone: 011-31-70-377-4540
HQ: The "Shell" Transport and Trading Company, PLC, Shell Centre, London SE1 7NA, England
Phone: 011-44-71-934-3856
US HQ: Shell Oil Company, One Shell Plaza, PO Box 2463, Houston, TX 77252
US Phone: 713-241-6161
US FAX: 713-241-6781 (Communications)

Royal Dutch/Shell has operations in over 100 countries; more than 50 refineries in over 30 countries; and over 50 chemical plants, mostly in North America and Western Europe.

	1989 Sales	
	$ mil	% of total
Europe	44,721	49
Other Eastern Hemisphere	16,211	17
US	21,805	23
Other Western Hemisphere	10,204	11
Adjustments	(7,529)	—
Total	**85,412**	**100**

WHAT

	1989 Sales		1989 Operating Income	
	$ mil	% of total	$ mil	% of total
Oil & gas	90,035	85	4,340	69
Chemicals	11,956	11	1,615	26
Coal	1,301	1	124	2
Metals	2,724	3	276	4
Other	74	—	(40)	(1)
Less: sales tax	(20,678)	—	—	—
Total	**85,412**	**100**	**6,315**	**100**

RANKINGS

4th in *Fortune* Global 500 Industrial Cos.
2nd in *Forbes* 100 Foreign Investments in the US
4th in *Business Week* Global 1000

COMPETITION

Amoco
Ashland
Atlantic Richfield
British Petroleum
Chevron
Coastal
Du Pont
Exxon
Mobil
Occidental
Pennzoil
Phillips
Sun
Texaco
Unocal
USX
Chemical companies

RUBBERMAID INC.

OVERVIEW

Rubbermaid is a major producer of rubber and plastic products for the consumer and institutional markets. The company primarily manufactures housewares, decorative coverings, cookware, toys, and industrial maintenance goods, and products for leisure, office, and garden. Consumer products account for 79% of sales.

The company consists of several key operating divisions, including Housewares (the largest unit), Specialty Products, Little Tikes (toys), Commercial Products, Office Products, and Rubbermaid-Allibert, a joint venture with Allibert of Paris (resin furniture).

Rubbermaid maintained strong growth in sales and earnings during the 1980s, with 36 consecutive record quarters, and has successfully predicted new markets, with 30% of sales coming from products introduced over the past 5 years.

The company's recent joint venture with the Curver Group of the Dutch chemical concern DSM will make Curver-Rubbermaid the largest housewares operation in the European Economic Community. Foreign operations presently account for approximately 13% of sales.

Rubbermaid was ranked in the top 10 of *Fortune*'s "America's Most Admired Corporations" for the 5th consecutive year and was listed by *Industry Week* as one of the nation's best-managed companies.

NYSE symbol: RBD
Incorporated: Ohio, 1920
Fiscal year ends: December 31

WHO

Chairman and CEO: Stanley C. Gault, age 64, $889,329 pay
President and COO: Walter W. Williams, age 55, $684,981 pay
EVP; President, Housewares Division: Wolfgang R. Schmitt, age 45, $426,087 pay
SVP and CFO: Joseph G. Meehan, age 58, $327,605 pay
Auditors: KPMG Peat Marwick
Employees: 8,409

WHERE

HQ: 1147 Akron Rd., Wooster, OH 44691
Phone: 216-264-6464
FAX: 216-264-5206 (Public Relations)

The company operates manufacturing and/or warehousing facilities in 12 US states as well as Ireland and Canada.

	1989 Sales		1989 Operating Income	
	$ mil	% of total	$ mil	% of total
US	1,171	87	187	92
Foreign	173	13	16	8
Total	**1,344**	**100**	**203**	**100**

WHEN

In 1920, 5 local businessmen formed The Wooster Rubber Company in a rented building in Wooster, Ohio, to manufacture the Sunshine brand toy balloon. Horatio B. Ebert and Errett M. Grable purchased the company in the mid-1920s.

In the early 1930s, while at a department store, Ebert noticed a line of housewares products that had been developed by James R. Caldwell. Caldwell's product line (which he gave the brand name Rubbermaid) included rubber dustpans, drainboard mats, soap dishes, and sink stoppers. Ebert contacted Caldwell, and the 2 men agreed to join their businesses. In 1934 Wooster Rubber began producing Rubbermaid brand housewares products.

In 1942 the government froze civilian use of rubber due to WWII. The Wooster Rubber Company was forced to halt its production of housewares but was able to survive the war by producing self-sealing fuel tanks, life jackets, and tourniquets for the government.

At the end of WWII, Wooster Rubber resumed production of housewares products. In 1950 the company established a Canadian manufacturing facility. During the mid-1950s the company produced its first plastic product (a dishpan) and introduced a line of commercial goods for hotels, motels, restaurants, and institutions. In 1955 the company made its first public stock offering and 2 years later changed its name to Rubbermaid Inc. Caldwell stepped down as president in 1958, and Donald E. Noble became CEO in 1959.

When Noble retired in 1980, Rubbermaid acquired General Electric executive Stanley C. Gault, the son of one of the 5 founders, as its new chairman and CEO. Gault immediately restructured the company and led Rubbermaid through a decade of phenomenal growth: sales quadrupled from just over $300 million to over $1.3 billion, and manufacturing and distribution locations increased from 7 to 31.

Rubbermaid acquired Con-Tact (decorative coverings) in 1981, Little Tikes (plastic toys) in 1984, Gott (leisure and recreational products) in 1985, SECO (floor products) and MicroComputer Accessories in 1986, and Viking Brush (cleaning supplies) in 1987.

In 1990 Rubbermaid entered a joint venture with the Curver group of the Dutch chemical company DSM to market housewares in Europe, North Africa, and the Middle East.

WHAT

Products

Housewares
Bathware
Casual dinnerware
Decorative coverings
Food utensils
Laundry baskets
Microwave cookware
Rubber gloves
Trash containers
Vacuum cleaner bags
Workshop organizers

Little Tikes (toys)

Commercial Products
Ash/trash receptacles
Cleaning products
Recycling containers
Serving trays

Office Products
Floormats
Furniture

Specialty Products
Bird feeders
Blue Ice refreezable ice substitute
Horticulture products
Insulated chests
Outdoor resin furniture
Planters

HOW MUCH

	9 Yr. Growth	1980	1981	1982	1983	1984	1985	1986	1987	1988	1989
Sales ($ mil)	17.7%	309	357	376	436	566	671	795	1,015	1,194	1,344
Net income ($ mil)	21.6%	20	26	28	36	47	57	70	85	99	116
Income as % of sales	—	6.5%	7.2%	7.3%	8.2%	8.3%	8.5%	8.8%	8.3%	8.3%	8.7%
Earnings per share ($)	19.2%	0.33	0.41	0.45	0.58	0.69	0.79	0.96	1.15	1.35	1.58
Stock price – high ($)	—	3.75	5.06	8.00	12.50	11.31	17.44	28.50	35.00	27.00	37.75
Stock price – low ($)	—	2.50	2.92	4.36	7.31	8.16	10.94	16.63	19.00	21.00	25.00
Stock price – close ($)	31.8%	3.06	4.61	7.50	9.78	11.13	17.25	24.25	24.88	25.13	36.75
P/E – high	—	12	12	18	22	16	22	30	30	20	24
P/E – low	—	8	7	10	13	12	14	17	17	16	16
Dividends per share ($)	16.1%	0.12	0.14	0.16	0.18	0.20	0.23	0.26	0.32	0.38	0.46
Book value per share ($)	15.3%	2.25	2.51	2.77	3.18	3.53	4.16	4.91	5.94	6.95	8.12

1989 Year End:
Debt ratio: 7.8%
Return on equity: 21.0%
Cash (mil): $97
Current ratio: 2.55
Long-term debt (mil): $50
Number of shares (mil): 74
Dividends:
1989 average yield: 1.3%
1989 payout: 29.1%
Market value (mil): $2,707

Stock Price History high/low 1980-89

40
35
30
25
20
15
10
5
0

RANKINGS

285th in *Fortune* 500 Industrial Cos.
240th in *Business Week* 1000
681st in *Business Week* Global 1000

COMPETITION

Hasbro
Mattel
Premark

RYDER SYSTEM, INC.

OVERVIEW

Ryder System, best known for its bright yellow One-Way rental trucks, is the leading supplier of 3rd party transportation services in the world. It owns 151,000 vehicles and 47 commercial aircraft.

The leader in full-service truck leasing, Ryder provides clients such as Borden and GM with everything from custom vehicles, fuel, and maintenance to safety training and insurance. Ryder One-Way, comprised of 5,400 independent dealers in the US, Canada, and Great Britain, leases 35,000 trucks designed with the self-mover in mind.

Ryder transports 39% of all the new cars and light trucks sold in North America (more than 6.3 million vehicles in 1989) and hauls materials under contract for corporations such as Montgomery Ward, Xerox, and Toyota. Every school day Ryder carries 410,000 students, with more than 6,800 buses operating in 15 states.

Aviall and Caledonian Airmotive maintain jet engines for USAir, British Airways, and other airlines from bases in Texas, California, and Scotland. Ryder also leases aircraft and sells new and used aviation parts. Recent estimates of Ryder's break-up value ($35 to $40 per share) have fueled takeover rumors on Wall Street.

NYSE symbol: R
Incorporated: Florida, 1955
Fiscal year ends: December 31

WHO

Chairman, President, and CEO: M. Anthony Burns, age 47, $743,583 pay
SEVP and President, Vehicle Leasing and Service Division: David R. Parker, age 46, $509,889 pay
SEVP and CFO: Edwin A. Huston, age 51, $403,458 pay
SEVP, Aviation: Robert G. Lambert, age 59, $438,454 pay
SEVP, Government and Industry Relations: Donald W. Estes, age 59, $367,889 pay
Auditors: KPMG Peat Marwick
Employees: 42,210

WHEN

Miami-based Ryder Truck Rental, founded by 21-year old Jim Ryder in 1934, was America's first truck leasing firm. The company offered both long- and short-term truck rentals in 4 southern states until 1952 when it bought Great Southern Trucking, a southeastern freight hauling company. This doubled Ryder's size, and the company went public that year.

The company, known as Ryder System, bought Carolina Fleets, a South Carolina trucking company, and Yellow Rental, a northeastern leasing service, in 1955. More purchases over the next decade extended rental services (Ryder Truck Rentals) across the US and into Canada.

Meanwhile, the freight hauling division, consolidated as Ryder Truck Lines (1964), expanded throughout the South, East, and Midwest and in 1965 was sold to International Utilities.

Ryder established One-Way truck rental services for self-movers in 1968 and between 1968 and 1974 entered several new markets, including new automobile transport (1968), truck driver and heavy equipment training (1969), temporary services (1969), insurance (1970), truck stops (1971), and oil refining (1974). Profits reached $20 million in 1973, but the company's debt ($500 million), mostly in high-interest loans, cost Ryder $20 million in losses when interest rates soared in 1974.

Jim Ryder resigned (later founded Jartran, 1978), and Leslie Barnes, former president of Allegheny Airlines (later USAir), became CEO (1975). By selling the oil refinery and other assets, Barnes had Ryder in the black by the end of 1975.

Ryder operated Jack Rabbit Express, a small-package delivery service, from 1978 to 1982. When Barnes retired in 1983, 40-year-old Anthony Burns, Ryder's president since 1979, became CEO. He sold Ryder's truck stops (1984) and, through 65 acquisitions (1983-1987), reentered freight hauling (1983), moving and storage (1983), aircraft leasing (1984), aircraft engine overhauling (1985), and school busing (1985). By 1987 Ryder had become America's leader in truck leasing and automobile hauling, the world's largest nonairline provider of aviation maintenance and parts, and 2nd only to Canada's Laidlaw in the management of school bus fleets. The company's One-Way fleet surpassed U-Haul as America's leader in one-way moving services (1987).

In 1989 Ryder announced plans to sell Ryder Freight System (its full truckload freight hauling division) and its insurance interests.

WHERE

HQ: 3600 N.W. 82 Ave., Miami, FL 33166
Phone: 305-593-3726
FAX: 305-593-4129

Ryder offers truck rentals through 5,400 independent dealers at 949 locations in North America and Europe. The company operates aircraft engine overhaul facilities in Dallas, TX; Burbank, CA; and Prestwick, Scotland. Through its aviation subsidiaries, Ryder sells aircraft parts on 4 continents.

	1989 Sales	
	$ mil	% of total
US	4,581	90
Foreign	492	10
Total	**5,073**	**100**

WHAT

	1989 Sales		1989 Operating Income	
	$ mil	% of total	$ mil	% of total
Automotive carriers	716	14	18	5
Aviation services	1,184	23	75	22
Other	45	1	8	2
Vehicle leasing & services	3,155	62	235	71
Adjustments	(27)	—	61	—
Total	**5,073**	**100**	**397**	**100**

Highway Transportation Services
Automotive carriers
Commercial truck rental
Consumer truck rental
Dedicated contract carriage
Full-service truck leasing
Student transportation

Aviation Services
Aircraft leasing and services
Aircraft parts
Jet engine repair and maintenance

HOW MUCH

	9 Yr. Growth	1980	1981	1982	1983	1984	1985	1986	1987	1988	1989
Sales ($ mil)	13.0%	1,694	1,946	2,076	2,384	2,486	2,905	3,768	4,609	5,030	5,073
Net income ($ mil)	(0.9%)	57	74	83	101	118	125	161	187	135	52
Income as % of sales	—	3.3%	3.8%	4.0%	4.2%	4.7%	4.3%	4.3%	4.1%	2.7%	1.0%
Earnings per share ($)	(5.7%)	0.98	1.17	1.21	1.43	1.65	1.73	2.09	2.29	1.61	0.58
Stock price – high ($)	—	9.44	12.35	16.65	19.86	19.05	24.67	35.50	43.00	32.50	31.13
Stock price – low ($)	—	4.60	7.96	7.09	14.26	12.71	14.67	21.50	15.00	22.63	19.75
Stock price – close ($)	10.9%	8.03	8.96	15.79	18.85	16.21	22.25	33.38	26.50	26.00	20.38
P/E – high	—	10	11	14	14	12	14	17	19	20	54
P/E – low	—	5	7	6	10	8	8	10	7	14	34
Dividends per share ($)	7.6%	0.31	0.32	0.34	0.34	0.35	0.40	0.44	0.52	0.56	0.60
Book value per share ($)	12.8%	6.18	7.42	8.19	9.32	10.84	12.20	14.72	16.75	18.71	18.24

1989 Year End:
Debt ratio: 59.6%
Return on equity: 3.1%
Cash (mil): $104
Current ratio: 0.96
Long-term debt (mil): $2,193
Number of shares (mil): 76
Dividends:
1989 average yield: 2.9%
1989 payout: 103.4%
Market value (mil): $1,551

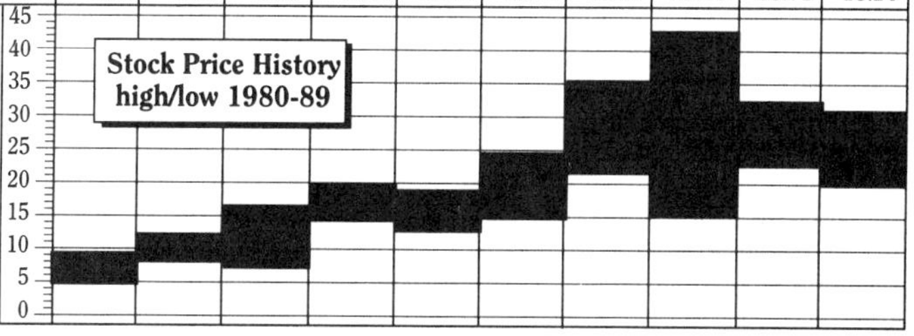

Stock Price History high/low 1980-89

RANKINGS

16th in *Fortune* 100 Diversified Service Cos.
177th in *Forbes* Sales 500
393rd in *Business Week* 1000

COMPETITION

Consolidated Rail
Hertz
Mayflower
Norfolk Southern
UPS
Other trucking companies

SAATCHI & SAATCHI COMPANY PLC

OVERVIEW

London-based Saatchi & Saatchi, once the largest advertising agency in the world, had fallen to 2nd by 1989 and appears headed further down. Its effort to create an interconnected supermarket of advertising (Backer Spielvogel Bates), consulting (Yankelovich), marketing (Marlboro), public relations (Rowland), and research and design services (Siegel & Gale) to meet the needs of a global marketplace has foundered on the seas of inopportune acquisitions and high debt. The company was one of the most creative agencies of the 1970s and 1980s, partly because its reclusive principals, Charles and Maurice Saatchi, were always able to keep the agency in the limelight. It did work for some of Britain's premier institutions, including the Health Council (ads featuring a man saying "Would you be more careful if it was you that got pregnant?") and the Conservative party ("Labour isn't working"). Losses of key personnel and clients — and widespread publication of the firm's problems — have made the job of revitalizing the firm a challenge for new CEO Robert Louis-Dreyfus.

WHEN

In 1947 Nathan Saatchi, a prosperous Jewish merchant, emigrated from Iraq to London with his wife and 3 sons, David, Charles, and Maurice. Charles left school at 17 and held a series of jobs before becoming a junior copywriter at an advertising agency. Feeling creatively confined, he moved to another agency in 1967 and from there briefly to yet another small advertising firm before opening his own consultancy in 1967. During this period his younger brother, Maurice, finished university and went to work for a publishing firm that wrote about the advertising industry.

By 1970 Charles wanted to start his own ad agency and recruited the financially oriented Maurice. The agency opened in 1971 with a flashy campaign of self-promotion. The agency prospered and, in 1973, showing a profit of £90,000, it began to make acquisitions; one of the first failed when its liabilities turned out higher — and assets lower — than expected. Despite this setback and an industry recession, profits rose steadily, reaching £400,000 in 1975. In that year the Saatchis completed the takeover of the much larger, publicly held Compton UK Partners, rising from 13th to 5th in size in the UK. Acquisitions and internal growth made Saatchi & Saatchi the largest agency in the UK by 1979.

Setting their sights on the US, in 1982 the Saatchis undertook another takeover of a much larger company — this time of Compton Advertising in New York, making Saatchi & Saatchi the 9th largest agency in the world. In 1985 the Saatchis acquired the Hay Group, an American consulting firm, for $125 million and the Howard Marlboro sales promotion company for $414 million. In 1986, the company bought the respected Ted Bates Worldwide ad agency for $450 million, vaulting the Saatchis to #1 in the world. The Bates acquisition caused several key clients to withdraw (taking away over $250 million in billings because of perceived client conflicts among the agencies now under the Saatchi umbrella).

Beginning in 1987 high debt and the lower-than-expected profitability of many of the consulting groups acquired by the Saatchis caused financial problems from which the agency has yet to recover. In 1989 the agency laid off 800 people.

Robert Louis-Dreyfus (nicknamed "Jaws"), named CEO in 1990, has sought to stem the financial hemorrhage and refocus the agency on advertising and has agreed to sell the Gartner, Hay and Peterson consulting groups. These sales were not as profitable as hoped, and in September 1990 Saatchi announced that it would not issue its October dividend, causing its already depressed stock to tumble another 17%.

HOW MUCH

	6 Yr. Growth	1980	1981	1982	1983	1984	1985	1986	1987	1988	1989
Sales ($ mil)	47.6%	—	—	—	152	181	425	642	1,257	1,458	1,572
Net income ($ mil)	—	—	—	—	9	14	34	63	123	142	(30)
Income as % of sales	—	—	—	—	5.9%	7.7%	8.0%	9.8%	9.8%	9.7%	(1.9%)
Earnings per share ($)	—	—	—	—	0.63	0.88	1.42	1.61	2.14	2.26	(1.12)
Stock price – high ($)	—	—	—	—	12.31	18.42	26.81	33.38	34.38	25.25	22.50
Stock price – low ($)	0.6%	—	—	—	11.81	12.09	15.68	18.38	16.50	17.00	11.25
Stock price – close ($)	—	—	—	—	12.31	17.79	26.81	24.28	23.25	17.88	12.75
P/E – high	—	—	—	—	20	21	19	21	16	11	—
P/E – low	—	—	—	—	19	14	11	11	8	8	—
Dividends per share ($)	—	—	—	—	0.00	0.17	1.01	2.37	0.87	1.21	1.06
Book value per share ($)	—	—	—	—	4.00	4.87	9.20	(0.34)	(1.85)	(5.70)	(11.11)

1989 Year End:
Debt ratio: —
Return on equity: 13.3%
Cash (mil): $135
Current ratio: 0.91
Long-term debt (mil): $211
Number of shares (mil): 53
Dividends:
1989 average yield: 8.3%
1989 payout: —
Market value (mil): $674

Stock Price History high/low 1983-89

35 30 25 20 15 10 5 0

NYSE symbol: SAA (ADR)
Incorporated: England, 1977
Fiscal year ends: September 30

WHO

Chairman: Maurice Saatchi, age 43, £625,000 pay
CEO: Robert L. M. Louis-Dreyfus, age 43
President: J. Kenneth Gill, age 69
Deputy Chairman: Jeremy T. Sinclair, age 43
Finance Director: Charles T. Scott, age 41
Auditors: KPMG Peat Marwick McLintock
Employees: 18,336

WHERE

HQ: Berkeley Sq., London W1X 5DH, England
Phone: 011-44-71-495-5000
US HQ (Saatchi & Saatchi Advertising Worldwide): 375 Hudson St., New York, NY 10014
US Phone: 212-463-2000
US FAX: 212-463-9855

At the end of fiscal 1989, the company operated 135 subsidiaries in 34 countries and numerous affiliates in 21 other countries.

	1989 Net Revenues		1989 Operating Income	
	$ mil	% of total	$ mil	% of total
UK	276	18	26	19
US	833	53	61	45
Other	463	29	48	36
Total	**1,572**	**100**	**135**	**100**

WHAT

	1989 Net Revenues		1989 Operating Income	
	$ mil	% of total	$ mil	% of total
Communications	1,171	74	112	83
Consulting	401	26	23	17
Total	**1,572**	**100**	**135**	**100**

US Groups

Communications
AC&R Advertising, Inc.
Backer Spielvogel Bates Worldwide, Inc.
Campbell-Mithun-Esty, Inc.
Conill Advertising, Inc.
Klemtner Advertising, Inc.
Kobs & Draft Advertising, Inc.
Marlboro Marketing, Inc.
Rowland Worldwide, Inc.
Rumrill-Hoyt, Inc.
Saatchi & Saatchi Advertising, Inc.
Saatchi & Saatchi Direct, Inc.
Siegel & Gale, Inc.

Consulting
Clancy, Shulman & Associates, Inc.
CPC Corporate Planners & Coordinators, Inc.
Litigation Sciences, Inc.
McBer & Company, Inc.
MSL International Consultants, Inc.
The National Research Group, Inc.
Syllogistics, Inc.
Yankelovich, Skelly & White, Inc.

COMPETITION

Arthur Andersen
McKinsey & Co.
KPMG
Price Waterhouse
Young & Rubicam

SAFEWAY, INC.

OVERVIEW

Oakland-based Safeway underwent a radical transformation in the late 1980s, symbolizing to many people both the virtues and the vices of LBOs. The world's largest grocer, long known for job security, emerged from the 1986 buyout — orchestrated by Kohlberg Kravis Roberts — 1,130 stores and 63,000 employees lighter.

Operations sold in the restructuring included those in Texas, Oklahoma, and Southern California, areas where the company's labor costs were higher than its competitors'. Although some of these locations continue to be operated by their buyers (Vons, Appletree), many were eventually closed. Safeway's prized 132-store UK holdings were also sacrificed to pay down acquisition debt.

As a result of the disposals and subsequent store openings, 44% of Safeway's 1,117 remaining US and Canadian locations are superstores averaging 43,000 square feet, compared to 31% before the buyout. Openings and modernizations focus on the company's "marketplace" format, emphasizing specialty departments in a boutique atmosphere.

Safeway went public again in 1990, but KKR still controls more than 75% of the stock. Peter Magowan, whose family has run the company since the 1950s, continues as chairman. The company's earnings before interest in 1989 were almost as much as in 1985, despite $5.3 billion lower sales.

NYSE symbol: SWY
Incorporated: Delaware, 1986
Fiscal year ends: Saturday closest to December 31

WHO

Chairman, President, and CEO: Peter A. Magowan, age 47, $1,213,000 pay
VC: Harry D. Sunderland, age 54, $595,000 pay
EVP and CFO: Michael M. Pharr, age 49
EVP: John N. Bell, age 64, $541,000 pay
EVP: E. Richard Jones, age 45, $534,000 pay
Auditors: Deloitte & Touche
Employees: 110,000

WHERE

HQ: 4th and Jackson Sts., Oakland, CA 94660
Phone: 415-891-3000
FAX: 415-444-5135

Safeway operates 1,117 stores in the western and mid-Atlantic US and in Canada. US stores are organized into 6 geographic divisions. In addition, the company owns 35% of Vons, which operates in Southern California.

	1989 Sales		1989 Operating Income	
	$ mil	% of total	$ mil	% of total
US	10,779	75	340	74
Canada	3,546	25	122	26
Total	**14,325**	**100**	**462**	**100**

	1990 Store Locations	
	no. of stores	% of total
Northern California, Nevada, & Hawaii	246	22
Western Canada	235	21
Washington state & parts of Idaho, Montana, & Wyoming	179	16
Maryland, Virginia, & Washington, DC	150	13
Colorado & parts of New Mexico, Wyoming, Kansas, Nebraska, & South Dakota	121	11
Oregon	101	9
Arizona	85	8
Total	**1,117**	**100**

WHEN

Marion Skaggs bought a grocery from his father in American Falls, Idaho, in 1915 and started Skaggs United Stores. Unlike other stores of the day, where merchandise was kept in barrels or stacked on tables, Skaggs installed shelves and made goods easy to reach. In 1926 Safeway, a 338-unit California and Hawaii grocer that had started as the Sam Seelig Company but changed its name in a contest, merged with the 428 Skaggs stores to form Safeway Stores in a deal put together by Charles Merrill (cofounder of Merrill Lynch). M. B. Skaggs, son of the founder, became president of the new company and his brother L. S. Skaggs (founder of what is now American Stores) became VP.

Safeway bought Arizona Grocery, Piggly Wiggly Pacific, and Eastern Stores in 1928 and Piggly Wiggly Western States, a grocer operating in California, Texas, and Nevada, in 1929. Since that time the company has made numerous acquisitions, expanding its reach nationwide. In 1931 the company had its greatest number of stores (3,527), but this number was reduced as Safeway eliminated smaller stores and adopted the supermarket format throughout the company.

In addition the company expanded internationally, into western Canada, the UK, and Australia. Safeway Food Stores, Ltd., a UK subsidiary, bought John Gardner Supermarkets and Prideaux in 1962. Australian Safeway, Pty., acquired Pratts Supermarkets and Chelsea Supermarkets in 1963. However, the company has drawn back from foreign markets in recent years, selling both its Australian and German operations in 1985.

The Magowan family has been important to the history of Safeway. Through Merrill's influence, Robert Magowan, a former Macy's executive who married Merrill's daughter, rose to become chairman of Safeway in the 1950s. After Robert's death in 1985, the Magowans continued to manage Safeway through his son Peter, the current chairman.

In 1986 Safeway received an unsolicited buyout bid from the Dart Group, controlled by the Haft family of Washington, DC. In response, Peter Magowan and takeover specialists Kohlberg Kravis Roberts took Safeway private in a leveraged deal, paying Dart $159 million profit on its shares. The company sold some 1,200 of its locations in Utah, Oklahoma, Kansas, Arkansas, and the UK in 1987 and in Texas in 1988. Safeway sold additional stores in Southern California to the Vons Companies for 35% of Vons's stock. While Safeway had a reputation for fairness to its workers, the LBO was marred by reports of suicide and illness afflicting some of the displaced employees. Management countered that employees were generally satisfied.

In 1990 Safeway reemerged as a public company by selling 10% of its stock. The proceeds are earmarked for store expansion and remodeling.

WHAT

Safeway operates stores under 2 different formats: the conventional store and the larger superstore.

	1990 Store Formats		
	no. of stores	% of total	average sq. ft.
Conventional format	624	56	25,800
Superstore format	493	44	43,300
Total	**1,117**	**100**	

Safeway also operates a number of plants that supply its stores with dairy products (Lucerne), soft drinks (Cragmont), baked goods, and other private-label items.

HOW MUCH

	9 Yr. Growth	1980	1981	1982	1983	1984	1985	1986	1987	1988	1989
Sales ($ mil)	(0.6%)	15,103	16,580	17,633	18,585	19,642	19,651	20,311	18,301	13,612	14,325
Net income ($ mil)	(34.9%)	119	115	160	183	185	231	(14)	(112)	(17)	3
Income as % of sales	—	0.8%	0.7%	0.9%	1.0%	0.9%	1.2%	(0.1%)	(0.6%)	(0.1%)	0.0%

1989 Year End:
Debt ratio: 116.8%
Return on equity: —
Cash (mil): $123
Current ratio: 0.87
Long-term debt (mil): $2,699
Assets (mil): $4,538
Interest payments (mil): $383

RANKINGS

7th in *Fortune* 50 Retailing Cos.
4th in *Forbes* 400 US Private Cos. (prior to 1990 public offering)

COMPETITION

Albertson's
American Stores
Food Lion
Fred Meyer
Giant Food
Great A&P
Kroger
Winn-Dixie

SALOMON INC

OVERVIEW

Salomon is an international investment banking firm recognized as a preeminent trader and market-maker in financial instruments as well as an oil and commodities leader. New York–based Salomon is the 3rd largest diversified financial company in the US, with assets of $118 billion.

The company's Salomon Brothers, the largest US securities firm in terms of assets, at $118 billion, had pretax earnings of $490 million, 66% of the firm's 1989 total. Salomon is currently the largest foreign securities firm in Japan and the 5th largest in the country, behind only the 4 largest Japanese firms. Salomon's Phibro Energy, which made $367 million in 1989 pretax earnings, is a leading global trader of crude oil and is the 4th largest independent oil refiner in the US. Salomon's Philipp Brothers is a New York–based commodities trader and was the only losing segment of the company in 1989.

NYSE symbol: SB
Incorporated: Delaware, 1960
Fiscal year ends: December 31

WHO

Chairman, President, and CEO: John H. Gutfreund, age 60, $3,500,000 pay
VC: Thomas W. Strauss, age 47, $3,000,000 pay
EVP: James L. Massey, age 47, $2,500,000 pay
EVP; Chairman and CEO, Phibro Energy: Ernst Weil, age 60, $6,400,000 pay
EVP and CFO: Donald S. Howard, age 61
Auditors: Arthur Andersen & Co.
Employees: 8,900

WHEN

Arthur, Herbert, and Percy Salomon founded Salomon Brothers as a money brokerage firm in 1910. In 1917 the company became an authorized US government securities dealer, recognized for its ability to buy and sell large blocks of those securities. Growth until the 1960s came primarily from a successful corporate and government bond trading operation.

In the late 1950s and early 1960s, Salomon expanded its research and trading departments. The firm started a bond research department in 1961, and the following year renowned economist Henry Kaufman joined Salomon.

Salomon entered the stock underwriting business in the 1960s by convincing clients that its bond trading expertise meant it could distribute new issues of stock. Salomon added corporate finance as a new department with international sales, bond analysis, and stock research in the late 1960s. In 1970 Salomon opened branches in London and Tokyo.

In 1978 John Gutfreund, who had headed corporate finance, was named managing partner. In the early 1980s large trading positions put the firm's capital at risk, and competition grew with major mergers in the industry. In 1981 Gutfreund's search for more capital resulted in the merger with Phibro Corporation, a leader in international oil and commodities trading, with annual revenues of $23.7 billion. Salomon Brothers remained autonomous under a holding company arrangement, and Gutfreund and Philbro's John Tendler became co-CEOs.

During the next few years Salomon's earnings grew much faster than Phibro's, enabling Gutfreund to become sole CEO over Phibro-Salomon in 1984. With the tremendous growth in the global capital markets, Salomon increased staff by 40% in 1986 alone, trying to keep pace.

In 1987 the company suffered significant losses in both its mortgage-backed securities business, which had in recent years accounted for as much as 40% of Salomon's earnings, and in its government bond trading operation. In 1987 the company suddenly withdrew from the municipal bond and commercial paper business. This was followed by resignations and terminations of key managers as Gutfreund reduced the firm's involvement in its historical strength of trading securities.

Salomon rebounded in 1988 with $280 million in net income compared to $142 million the prior year. Much of this was attributable to Phibro Energy's record earnings of $245 million. The company's emphasis the past 2 years has been on international investment banking and merchant banking, to augment a more conservative securities trading practice.

WHERE

HQ: One New York Plaza, New York, NY 10004
Phone: 212-747-7000
FAX: 212-422-3417

Salomon provides financial services worldwide through 35 domestic and foreign offices.

	1989 Pretax Income	
	$ mil	% of total
North America	65	9
Europe	548	74
Asia & other	127	17
Total	**740**	**100**

WHAT

	1989 Sales		1989 Pretax Income	
	$ mil	% of total	$ mil	% of total
Securities	8,282	21	490	66
Energy	21,285	56	367	50
Commodities	8,979	23	(117)	(16)
Adjustments	62	—	—	—
Total	**38,608**	**100**	**740**	**100**

Financial Services (Salomon Brothers)
Institutional money management
Investment banking
Merchant banking
Research and advisory services
Securities and foreign currency trading
Securities underwriting

Energy (Phibro Energy)
Crude oil trading
Energy-related commodities trading
Oil refining (Phibro Refining and Hill Petroleum)

Commodities (Philipp Brothers)
Agricultural products trading
Metals trading
Nonenergy-related commodities trading

HOW MUCH

	9 Yr. Growth	1980	1981	1982	1983	1984	1985	1986	1987	1988	1989
Sales ($ mil)	4.2%	26,570	25,098	26,703	29,757	28,911	27,896	22,789	25,103	28,808	38,608
Net income ($ mil)	(1.4%)	533	289	337	470	212	557	516	142	280	470
Income as % of sales	—	2.0%	1.2%	1.3%	1.6%	0.7%	2.0%	2.3%	0.6%	1.0%	1.2%
Earnings per share ($)	(2.1%)	3.88	2.06	2.27	3.10	1.41	3.60	3.32	0.86	1.63	3.20
Stock price – high ($)	—	32.19	27.88	30.44	40.63	34.75	46.75	59.38	44.50	28.38	29.38
Stock price – low ($)	—	10.06	11.25	10.06	23.69	20.75	30.00	37.38	16.63	19.38	20.50
Stock price – close ($)	(1.8%)	27.56	13.00	24.75	31.88	32.00	43.50	38.38	19.63	24.13	23.38
P/E – high	—	8	14	13	13	25	13	18	52	17	9
P/E – low	—	3	5	4	8	15	8	11	19	12	6
Dividends per share ($)	1.6%	0.56	0.50	0.47	0.52	0.54	0.54	0.64	0.64	0.64	0.64
Book value per share ($)	8.4%	11.69	10.85	12.84	15.73	16.62	19.93	22.72	21.15	21.82	24.08

1989 Year End:
Debt ratio: 75.0%
Return on equity: 13.9%
Cash (mil): $371
Assets (mil): $118,250
Long-term debt (mil): $8,595
Number of shares (mil): 119
Dividends:
1989 average yield: 2.7%
1989 payout: 20.0%
Market value (mil): $2,781

Stock Price History high/low 1980-89

RANKINGS

3rd in *Fortune* 50 Diversified Financial Cos.
86th in *Forbes* Sales 500
236th in *Business Week* 1000
647th in *Business Week* Global 1000

COMPETITION

American Express
Archer-Daniels-Midland
Cargill
Goldman Sachs
Merrill Lynch
Morgan Stanley
Prudential
Travelers
Oil refiners
Other investment banking firms

SAMSUNG GROUP

OVERVIEW

Consisting of 23 publicly and privately owned firms, Samsung is South Korea's leading *chaebol* (family-run conglomerate). The Lee family controls the group through interlocking ownership of the component companies. Samsung Company is the parent of the *chaebol* and a major South Korean import-export organization. Samsung Electronics is South Korea's largest semiconductor manufacturer. Other activities include electronics, shipbuilding, and food processing. Samsung management is highly regarded.

Samsung continues to emulate Japanese business strategies and corporate structures. The group has maintained a low-price, high-volume orientation and a willingness to take a long-term view to investing. Samsung Electronics is spending extremely heavily on R&D to establish itself as a world-class chipmaker. Importing technology has been a problem, and the company has suffered intellectual property lawsuits. Samsung and other South Korean companies are sharing the cost of developing 4 and 16 megabyte DRAM chips.

Rising South Korean wages are hurting Samsung's exports but helping imports. Aggressively anti-union Samsung has experienced labor unrest in recent years.

WHEN

Japan-educated Lee Byung-Chull began operating a rice mill in Korea, then under Japanese rule (1936). By 1938 Lee had begun trading in dried fish and had incorporated as Samsung (Korean for "Three Star"). WWII did not inflict widespread destruction in Korea, and, by the end of the war, Samsung had established transportation and real estate businesses.

The Korean War destroyed nearly all Samsung assets. Using the profits from a surviving brewery and importing goods for UN personnel, Lee reconstructed Samsung in South Korea. In 1953 he formed the Cheil Sugar Company. As the only South Korean sugar refiner at the time, Cheil was highly profitable. Later in the 1950s Samsung established Cheil Wool Textile (1954) and entered banking and insurance, forming a *chaebol.*

When a 1961 coup brought Park Chung Hee to power in South Korea, Lee, well known for his wealth and ties to the former government, was accused of illegal profiteering, and a 1966 smuggling scandal involving one of Lee's sons led to another investigation. The government dropped the charges when Lee agreed to give it an immense fertilizer plant he was building. Despite the setback Samsung continued to grow and diversify in the 1960s, expanding into paper, department stores, and newspaper publishing, and establishing Samsung Electronics with help from Sanyo in 1969. Samsung Electronics grew rapidly as a result of the South Korean government's export drive and low wage rates. The company gained engineering know-how by disassembling Western-designed electronic goods and producing inexpensive, private-label, black-and-white televisions and, later, color televisions, VCRs, and microwave ovens for General Electric, J. C. Penney, and Sears, among others.

In concert with the South Korean government's industrialization push, the *chaebol* established Samsung Shipbuilding (1974), Samsung Petrochemical (1977), and Samsung Precision Industries (aircraft engines and maintenance, 1977). A government-inspired export drive and a higher domestic standard of living helped group sales to reach $3 billion in 1979. The company entered radio and television broadcasting, but, following the assassination of President Park, the new Chun regime took over all Samsung's broadcast properties.

In the 1980s Samsung began exporting electronic goods under its own name in an effort to increase margins. Success in low-end products encouraged Samsung to export upmarket items. Recognizing its late start in technology, Samsung has set up 12 research centers in Korea and 2 in the US. Since Lee

HOW MUCH

$=Won 677 (Dec. 31, 1989)	6 Yr. Growth	1980	1981	1982	1983	1984	1985	1986	1987	1988	1989
Sales (Won bil)	24.7%	—	—	—	2,029	2,568	3,802	4,275	5,670	6,811	7,613
Net income (Won mil)	5.5%	—	—	—	8,000	7,000	6,100	6,908	8,455	10,855	11,055
Income as % of sales	—	—	—	—	—	—	—	0.2%	0.1%	0.2%	0.1%
Earnings per share (Won)	—	—	—	—	—	—	—	1,079	1,321	1,467	1,069
Stock price – high (Won)	—	—	—	—	—	—	—	15,480	18,300	32,400	36,300
Stock price – low (Won)	—	—	—	—	—	—	—	6,800	10,200	16,900	23,400
P/E – high	—	—	—	—	—	—	—	14	14	22	34
P/E – low	—	—	—	—	—	—	—	6	8	12	22
Dividends per share (Won)*	—	—	—	—	—	—	—	500	600	600	600

1989 Year End:
Debt ratio: —
Return on equity: —
Cash (mil): —
Long-term debt (mil): —
Number of shares (mil): 10
Dividends:
1989 average yield: —
1989 payout: 56.1%
Market value (mil): —
Sales (mil): US$11,245

Stock Price History high/low 1986-89

40,000
35,000
30,000
25,000
20,000
15,000
10,000
5,000
0

Note: Above figures for Samsung Co., Ltd. only *not including rights issues

Stock exchange: Seoul
Incorporated: Korea, 1952
Fiscal year ends: December 31

WHO

Chairman: Lee Kun-Hee
President: Rhee Pil-Gon
Auditors: Samil Accounting Corp.
Employees: 175,710 (1988)

WHERE

HQ (Samsung Co., Ltd.): 250, 2-ga, Taepyung-ro, Chung-gu, Seoul, South Korea
Phone: 011-82-2-751-2114
FAX: 011-82-2-752-7926
US HQ (Samsung Electronics America Inc.): 301 Mayhill St., Saddlebrook, NJ 07662
US Phone: 201-587-9600
US FAX: 201-587-9178

The Samsung Group's principal companies operate 159 branch offices in 46 countries.

WHAT

	1988 Sales	
	Won bil	% of total
Trade	6,811	34
Service	4,782	24
Electronics	4,252	21
Heavy industry & chemicals	1,570	8
Cultural & social welfare	1,146	6
Food processing & textiles	1,275	6
Precision products	287	1
Total	**20,123**	**100%**

Major Group Companies

Trade
Samsung Co., Ltd.

Service
Ankuk Fire & Marine Insurance Co., Ltd.
Hotel Shilla Co., Ltd.
Shinsegae Department Store Co., Ltd.

Electronics
Samsung Corning Co., Ltd.
Samsung Electronics Co., Ltd.
Samsung Semiconductor & Telecommunications Co., Ltd.

Heavy Industry & Chemicals
Chonju Paper Manufacturing Co., Ltd.
Korea Engineering Co., Ltd.
Samsung Construction Co., Ltd.
Samsung Shipbuilding & Heavy Industries Co., Ltd.

Cultural & Social Welfare
The Joong-ang Daily Newspaper Co., Ltd.
Joong-ang Development Co., Ltd.

Food Processing & Textiles
Cheil Industries, Inc.
Cheil Sugar & Co., Ltd.

Precision Products
Samsung Aerospace Industries, Ltd.
Samsung Watch Co., Ltd.

RANKINGS

20th in *Fortune* Global 500 Industrial Cos.

COMPETITION

Hyundai
Jardine Matheson
Mitsubishi
Other electronics companies

SANTA FE PACIFIC CORPORATION

OVERVIEW

Through its subsidiaries, Santa Fe Pacific (SFP) operates a petroleum pipeline; owns coal mines, gold mines, and oil and gas reserves; and develops real estate, but the company is known best for its 131-year-old railroad, the Atchison, Topeka & Santa Fe. In 1989 the Santa Fe hauled nearly 1.6 million carloads of freight, primarily of merchandise, vehicles and parts, food products, and chemicals, over 11,266 route-miles of railway serving the western US.

Santa Fe Pipelines, SFP's petroleum transmission subsidiary, owns 44% of Santa Fe Pipeline Partners, a publicly traded limited partnership that operates the largest refined petroleum products pipeline system in the western US. Another SFP subsidiary, Santa Fe Pacific Minerals, conducts mining operations in the Southwest. SFP's oil and gas wells and reserves are managed by Santa Fe Energy Resources and the 88%-owned limited partnership, Santa Fe Energy Partners. Santa Fe Realty currently owns valuable undeveloped property in 13 states, much of which is located in major cities. In April 1990 SFP announced that it would spin off Energy Resources and Santa Fe Realty, its real estate subsidiary, to its stockholders before the end of the year.

WHEN

Cyrus Kurtz Holliday founded the Santa Fe Railway in 1859 as the Atchison and Topeka Railroad Company to build a line from Atchison to Topeka, Kansas. Corporate offices were established in Topeka, and the company subsequently renamed itself the Atchison, Topeka & Santa Fe Railroad (1863). The Civil War and cash shortages delayed construction until 1868. Then, instead of Atchison, construction commenced from Topeka, both to the east (toward Atchison) and to the west. The railroad reached Albuquerque in 1880 and Los Angeles in 1887. The company also bought several other railroads, including the Gulf, Colorado & Santa Fe (Galveston to Fort Worth, 1886).

By 1890 the railroad had grown into a 9,000-mile giant under the guidance of President William B. Strong. But the depression of 1893 left "the Atchison," like many other railroads, in bankruptcy, and, when the company reorganized in 1895, it did so minus much of its mileage. The new Atchison, Topeka & Santa Fe Railway Company grew quickly and by 1929 had built or acquired over 13,000 miles of track throughout the Southwest. Guided by a succession of strong leaders and a conservative financial policy, the Santa Fe prospered into the 1960s. Santa Fe Industries was created in 1968 as a holding company for the Santa Fe Railway and its subsidiaries.

In 1983 Santa Fe Industries agreed to merge with competitor Southern Pacific to create Santa Fe Southern Pacific Corporation. The combined company, with more than 38,000 miles of track stretching from the West Coast to the Gulf Coast and Midwest, would have been the 2nd largest railroad in America (after Burlington Northern). However, CEO John Schmidt failed to propose an acceptable merger plan, and in 1988 the ICC ruled that the merger was "anticompetitive," ordering the company to sell one of its railway holdings. The company sold Southern Pacific to Rio Grande Industries (1988) and then adopted its present name (1989).

In the meantime (1987), the company fought off a takeover attempt by The Henley Group, a La Jolla, California–based conglomerate spun off from Allied-Signal in 1986. The target of the takeover appears to have been the company's prime real estate holdings (3 million acres in 14 states).

In 1990 the company, based in Chicago since 1904, announced plans to move its headquarters from the city to the western suburb of Schaumburg as part of a cost-cutting program that includes a planned 5% work force reduction by the end of 1992.

HOW MUCH

	9 Yr. Growth	1980	1981	1982	1983	1984	1985	1986	1987	1988	1989
Sales ($ mil)	0.5%	2,860	3,272	3,104	5,976	6,662	6,438	5,631	5,448	3,144	2,978
Net income ($ mil)	—	156	168	125	333	491	470	(269)	346	147	(195)
Income as % of sales	—	5.5%	5.1%	4.0%	5.6%	7.4%	7.3%	(4.8%)	6.3%	4.7%	(6.6%)
Earnings per share ($)	—	1.87	2.00	1.46	1.77	2.61	2.67	(1.63)	2.19	0.93	(1.23)
Stock price – high ($)	—	15.47	17.82	13.69	29.00	26.63	37.13	39.63	65.00	47.88	25.75
Stock price – low ($)	—	9.76	10.94	8.02	11.67	20.25	24.50	26.25	29.63	14.25	16.75
Stock price – close ($)	3.8%	13.25	13.20	11.75	26.25	25.75	34.88	29.63	46.00	17.25	18.50
P/E – high	—	8	9	9	16	10	14	—	30	51	—
P/E – low	—	5	5	6	7	8	9	—	14	15	—
Dividends per share ($)	(21.1%)	0.84	0.84	0.84	0.94	1.00	1.00	1.00	1.00	25.00	0.10
Book value per share ($)	(16.0%)	26.04	26.84	27.13	30.21	32.20	33.97	32.11	33.39	3.07	5.39

1989 Year End:
Debt ratio: 76.4%
Return on equity: —
Cash (mil): $285
Current ratio: 0.58
Long-term debt (mil): $2,763
Number of shares (mil): 158
Dividends:
1989 average yield: 0.5%
1989 payout: —
Market value (mil): $2,921

Stock Price History high/low 1980-89

70
60
50
40
30
20
10
0

NYSE symbol: SFX
Incorporated: Delaware, 1983
Fiscal year ends: December 31

WHO

Chairman, President, and CEO; Chairman and CEO, Santa Fe Railway: Robert D. Krebs, age 47, $913,860 pay

President, Santa Fe Energy Resources: James L. Payne, age 53, $483,459 pay (prior to promotion)

President and CEO, Santa Fe Pacific Realty: Vernon B. Schwartz, age 39, $702,100 pay

President and COO, Santa Fe Railway: Michael R. Haverty, age 45

SVP and CFO: Orval M. Adam, age 59, $558,000 pay

Auditors: Price Waterhouse

Employees: 19,076

WHERE

HQ: 224 S. Michigan Ave., Chicago, IL 60604
Phone: 312-786-6000
FAX: 312-786-6118

Santa Fe Pacific operates 11,266 route-miles of railroad in 12 states, linking Chicago with the West Coast and the Gulf of Mexico. The company's other subsidiaries operate mainly in the western US.

WHAT

	1989 Sales		1989 Operating Income	
	$ mil	% of total	$ mil	% of total
Transportation	2,227	75	253	47
Natural resources	453	15	107	20
Real estate	298	10	175	33
Adjustments	—	—	(35)	—
Total	**2,978**	**100**	**500**	**100**

Transportation

Santa Fe Pacific Pipelines, Inc. (refined petroleum products pipelines in 6 western and southwestern states)

Santa Fe Pacific Pipeline Partners, L.P. (44%-owned limited partnership)

The Atchison, Topeka and Santa Fe Railway Co.

Natural Resources

Santa Fe Energy Resources, Inc. (management and development of oil and gas reserves)

Santa Fe Energy Partners, L.P. (88%-owned limited partnership)

Santa Fe Pacific Minerals Corp. (hard mineral exploration in the Southwest)

Real Estate

Santa Fe Pacific Realty Corp. (real estate development and ownership in 13 western, southwestern, and midwestern states)

RANKINGS

17th in *Fortune* 50 Transportation Cos.
282nd in *Forbes* Sales 500
197th in *Business Week* 1000
494th in *Business Week* Global 1000

COMPETITION

Burlington Northern
Rio Grande Industries
Union Pacific
Mineral and pipeline companies

SARA LEE CORPORATION

OVERVIEW

Sara Lee Corporation is an international food (ranked 8th among food companies) and consumer goods company, with 1989 sales of over $11 billion. In addition to its well-known frozen baked goods brand (which leads the 1989 US market with a 30% share), Sara Lee sells other brand names, including Hanes and L'eggs hosiery (with 47% of the 1989 US market), Jimmy Dean breakfast sausage, Hillshire Farm smoked sausage, Ball Park hotdogs, Champion knitwear, and Douwe Egberts coffee. It manufactures and markets underwear, household, and personal care items and provides food service to restaurants.

The Chicago company has operations in more than 30 countries, with 27% of its sales from international markets, primarily Europe. Sara Lee's future plans are reflected in its international efforts. The company spent $1.4 billion on European acquisitions and capital expenditures from 1984 to 1989. It continues to buy and consolidate European brands in preparation for the unification of European markets in 1992.

NYSE symbol: SLE
Incorporated: Maryland, 1941
Fiscal year ends: Saturday nearest June 30

WHO

Chairman and CEO: John H. Bryan, age 53, $1,392,010 pay
President: Paul Fulton, age 55, $910,750 pay
EVP and CFO: Michael E. Murphy, age 53, $735,510 pay
Auditors: Arthur Andersen & Co.
Employees: 101,800

WHEN

Sara Lee Corporation began in 1939 when Nathan Cummings, a Canadian-born Chicago businessman, bought the C. D. Kenny Company, a small Baltimore wholesaler of coffee, tea, and sugar. Cummings soon purchased several grocery firms and subsequently changed the company's name to Consolidated Grocers (1945). In 1946 the company's stock was first listed on the New York Stock Exchange. In 1954 stockholders voted to rename the company Consolidated Foods Corporation (CFC).

Cummings served as company president until 1970. Focusing primarily on food and grocery concerns, he broadened his initial investments by buying and selling a diverse collection of food companies, grocery stores, and producers of personal care and consumer products. These included Piggly Wiggly Midwest supermarkets (bought in 1956) and Eagle Food Centers (bought in 1961). The company's Eagle Complex, which included Piggly Wiggly and Eagle stores, drug stores, and photo supply stores, was sold in 1968. The company also bought Shasta Water Company in 1960 (sold in 1985), Chicken Delight food franchises (bought in 1965, sold in 1979), and Electrolux Corporation (bought in 1968, sold in 1987).

In 1956 CFC purchased the Kitchens of Sara Lee, a Chicago bakery founded by Charles Lubin in 1951. Lubin had introduced Sara Lee cheesecake (named after his daughter) in 1949, and it became his most popular product. He remained with Consolidated Foods, successfully building the frozen desserts market under the Sara Lee brand.

The company has continued to buy and sell a long list of businesses in the US and Europe — over 150 separate acquisitions since 1960. Its operations have included foods, beverages, grocery stores, apparel, appliances, food services, and chemicals. In 1962 Consolidated Foods made its first European acquisition and began to build its international markets. Some of its major international purchases included Douwe Egberts (coffee, tea, and tobacco, Holland, 1978), Nicholas Kiwi (shoe polish and pharmaceuticals, Australia, 1984), Akzo Consumenten Produkten (food, household, and personal care products; Holland, 1987), and Dim (hosiery and underwear, France, 1989).

Some major US company purchases were Hanes Corporation (1979), Jimmy Dean Meat Company (1984), and Champion Products (athletic knitwear, 1989). Sales topped $1 billion in 1967, $5 billion in 1980, and $10 billion in 1988.

Consolidated Foods changed its name to Sara Lee Corporation in 1985, using one of its most respected brandnames to enhance the public's awareness of the company.

WHERE

HQ: Three First National Plaza, Chicago, IL 60602
Phone: 312-726-2600
FAX: 312-726-3712

Sara Lee conducts operations in more than 30 countries and sells its products worldwide.

	1989 Sales		1989 Operating Income	
	$ mil	% of total	$ mil	% of total
US	8,539	73	544	64
Canada	158	1	16	2
Europe	2,728	23	237	28
Other	315	3	50	6
Adjustments	(22)	—	(106)	—
Total	**11,718**	**100**	**741**	**100**

WHAT

	1989 Sales		1989 Operating Income	
	$ mil	% of total	$ mil	% of total
Food service	2,607	22	61	7
Packaged meats & bakery	3,440	29	216	25
Coffee & grocery	1,816	15	150	18
Personal products	2,873	24	305	36
Household & personal care	1,127	10	115	14
Adjustments	(145)	—	(106)	—
Total	**11,718**	**100**	**741**	**100**

Brand Names

Foods
Ball Park
Bryan
Chef Pierre
Douwe Egberts
Droste
Hillshire Farm
Hygrade
Jimmy Dean
Kahn's
Mr. Turkey
Rudy's Farm
Sara Lee
State Fair
Sweet Sue

Clothing
Aris
Bali
Champion
Dim
Hanes
Isotoner
L'eggs

Shoe Care
Kiwi
Tana

Home Care
Biotex
Bloo
Fuller Brush
Ty-D-bol

Leather Goods
Coach

HOW MUCH

	9 Yr. Growth	1980	1981	1982	1983	1984	1985	1986	1987	1988	1989
Sales ($ mil)	9.1%	5,343	5,614	6,039	6,572	7,000	8,117	7,938	9,155	10,424	11,718
Net income ($ mil)	13.9%	128	140	157	171	188	206	223	267	325	411
Income as % of sales	—	2.4%	2.5%	2.6%	2.6%	2.7%	2.5%	2.8%	2.9%	3.1%	3.5%
Earnings per share ($)	15.2%	0.49	0.55	0.65	0.71	0.81	0.90	1.01	1.18	1.42	1.75
Stock price – high ($)	—	3.41	4.31	5.94	6.81	8.72	13.00	18.41	24.56	25.75	33.75
Stock price – low ($)	—	2.47	2.92	3.72	4.77	6.25	7.78	11.78	13.25	16.44	21.44
Stock price – close ($)	30.7%	3.00	3.94	5.64	6.50	7.94	12.72	16.94	17.63	21.00	33.50
P/E – high	—	7	8	9	10	11	14	18	21	18	19
P/E – low	—	5	5	6	7	8	9	12	11	12	12
Dividends per share ($)	13.8%	0.22	0.23	0.26	0.28	0.32	0.35	0.39	0.48	0.58	0.69
Book value per share ($)	9.9%	3.60	3.92	3.97	4.05	4.33	4.63	5.41	6.39	7.12	8.42

1989 Year End:
Debt ratio: 43.7%
Return on equity: 22.5%
Cash (mil): $118
Current ratio: 1.1
Long-term debt (mil): $1,488
Number of shares (mil): 227
Dividends:
1989 average yield: 2.1%
1989 payout: 39.4%
Market value (mil): $7,616

Stock Price History high/low 1980-89

RANKINGS

34th in *Fortune* 500 Industrial Cos.
93rd in *Fortune* Global 500 Industrial Cos.
53rd in *Forbes* Sales 500
80th in *Business Week* 1000
264th in *Business Week* Global 1000

COMPETITION

Beatrice	Kellogg	TLC Beatrice
Campbell Soup	Nestlé	Tyson Foods
ConAgra	Philip Morris	Unilever
CPC International	Procter & Gamble	V. F.
Grand Metropolitan	Sysco	Whitman

SCECORP

OVERVIEW

SCECorp is the parent company of Southern California Edison, the 3rd largest electric utility in the US in terms of 1989 sales, after Pacific Gas & Electric and the Southern Company. Edison provides electricity to about 3.9 million customers in a 50,000-square-mile area of central and southern California. A proposed merger of Edison and San Diego Gas & Electric Company, now pending California regulatory approval, would add about one million customers and 4,100 square miles of service area to Edison's system.

Edison uses 9 different resources to obtain electricity — more than any other utility in the world. These include fossil fuels (coal, oil, natural gas) and several less frequently used resources such as the sun, wind, and geothermal energy. Nuclear power accounts for 16.5% of Edison's generating capability, and the company buys 38.2% of its power from other producers.

SCECorp is also involved in other, nonutility businesses related to its expertise in the energy field, including the engineering and construction of generating plants and transmission systems, and real estate development.

NYSE symbol: SCE
Incorporated: California, 1987
Fiscal year ends: December 31

WHO

Chairman and CEO: John E. Bryson, age 47, $418,500 pay (prior to promotion)
President: Michael R. Peevey, age 51, $406,900 pay (prior to promotion)
EVP: David J. Fogarty, age 62, $465,000 pay
EVP, Treasurer, and CFO: Michael L. Nael, age 48
Auditors: Arthur Andersen & Co.
Employees: 17,010

WHERE

HQ: 2244 Walnut Grove Ave., Rosemead, CA 91770
Phone: 818-302-1297
FAX: 818-302-4815 (Shareholder Services)

SCECorp operates a public utility company in central and southern California and nonutility businesses in 13 states, Great Britain, and Canada.

Generating Facilities

Coal-fired
Four Corners Units 4 and 5 (48%, NM)
Mohave (56%, NV)

Hydroelectric
Bishop hydro division (CA)
Northern hydro division (CA)
Southern hydro division (CA)

Nuclear
Palo Verde (16%, AZ)
San Onofre (80%, CA)

Oil and Gas
Alamitos (CA)
Axis (CA)
Cool Water (CA)
El Segundo (CA)
Etiwanda (CA)
Highgrove (CA)
Huntington Beach (CA)
Long Beach (CA)
Mandalay (CA)
Ormond Beach (CA)
Pebbly Beach (CA)
Redondo (CA)
San Bernardino (CA)

WHEN

In 1896 Elmer Peck, Walter Wright, William Staats, and George Barker organized the West Side Lighting Company to provide electricity to the growing number of Los Angeles residents. Barker (of Barker Brothers furniture stores) became the company's first president.

In 1897 West Side Lighting agreed to merge with the Edison Electric Company of Los Angeles, which owned the rights to use Thomas Edison's name and patents in Los Angeles and the surrounding area. Barker continued as president of the resulting company (which kept the Edison company's name), overseeing the installation of the first underground electrical conduits in the Southwest.

John Barnes Miller became president in 1901. Known as the "Great Amalgamator," Miller bought numerous utilities throughout Southern California and constructed several generating facilities, including 3 hydroelectric plants on the Kern River. By 1909, when the company adopted the name Southern California Edison, it served 5 counties from Santa Barbara to Redlands.

In 1917 Henry Huntington (founder of Pacific Light & Power) sold his Southern California electrical interests, including Mount Whitney Power and Electric Company in the San Joaquin Valley and the Big Creek generating complex, to Edison, doubling the company's assets. However, in 1912 the city of Los Angeles decided to develop its own power distribution system, and by 1922 Edison's authority inside the city had ended.

A 1925 earthquake destroyed the company's Santa Barbara station, and the 1928 collapse of the St. Francis Dam washed out substations in the Santa Clara river valley and caused extensive damage throughout the Los Angeles area.

Edison's merger with California Electric Power in 1964 consolidated its service area throughout Southern California.

Although the company built 11 oil-and-gas fueled power stations (1948-1973), it also diversified beyond the burning of fossil fuels. In 1963 Edison started construction of the San Onofre nuclear plant with San Diego Gas & Electric Company. In the late 1970s Edison began to build less conventional power plants, including solar, geothermal, and wind generators. In 1987 SCECorp was formed as a holding company for Edison and a group of nonutility subsidiaries collectively named The Mission Group.

In 1988 Edison agreed to buy San Diego Gas & Electric, a purchase which, if approved by California regulators, will create America's largest electric utility.

WHAT

	1989 Sales	
	$ mil	% of total
Electricity		
Residential	2,155	31
Commercial	2,356	34
Industrial	1,170	17
Agricultural	106	2
Public authorities	559	8
Resale & other	178	3
Investment & other	380	5
Total	**6,904**	**100**

Southern California Edison Co.

The Mission Group
Mission Energy Co. (cogeneration, geothermal, and other energy-related projects)
Mission First Financial (project financing, cash management, and venture capital)
Mission Land Co. (real estate development in California, Arizona, Indiana, and Illinois)
Mission Power Engineering Co. (energy-related engineering and construction for 3rd parties)

RANKINGS

13th in *Fortune* 50 Utilities
118th in *Forbes* Sales 500
58th in *Business Week* 1000
197th in *Business Week* Global 1000

HOW MUCH

	9 Yr. Growth	1980	1981	1982	1983	1984	1985	1986	1987	1988	1989
Sales ($ mil)	7.3%	3,662	4,055	4,304	4,466	4,901	5,171	5,313	5,494	6,253	6,904
Net income ($ mil)	11.2%	318	490	556	691	732	774	769	721	809	823
Income as % of sales	—	8.7%	12.1%	12.9%	15.5%	14.9%	15.0%	14.5%	13.1%	12.9%	11.9%
Earnings per share ($)	8.3%	1.74	2.46	2.55	3.08	3.15	3.22	3.27	3.08	3.49	3.56
Stock price – high ($)	—	13.88	15.31	18.56	21.38	24.38	28.50	38.75	37.00	37.25	41.00
Stock price – low ($)	—	10.00	11.44	14.00	17.19	17.13	22.13	24.75	27.63	29.13	31.25
Stock price – close ($)	13.3%	12.81	14.38	17.56	19.88	22.75	26.63	33.88	30.50	32.38	39.38
P/E – high	—	8	6	7	7	8	9	12	12	11	12
P/E – low	—	6	5	6	6	5	7	8	9	8	9
Dividends per share ($)	6.7%	1.42	1.55	1.69	1.83	2.01	2.13	2.25	2.36	2.46	2.54
Book value per share ($)	4.2%	16.67	16.94	17.54	18.83	19.96	21.12	22.10	23.13	23.18	24.21

1989 Year End:
Debt ratio: 48.3%
Return on equity: 15.0%
Cash (mil): $151
Current ratio: 0.61
Long-term debt (mil): $5,283
Number of shares (mil): 218
Dividends:
1989 average yield: 6.5%
1989 payout: 71.3%
Market value (mil): $8,602

Stock Price History high/low 1980-89

SCHERING-PLOUGH CORPORATION

OVERVIEW

Schering-Plough is the 9th largest pharmaceutical company in the US and 15th in the world. The company makes both prescription drugs and consumer products. Top-selling products are treatments for allergy and asthma, including the antiasthmatic Proventil and the allergy drug Chlor-Trimeton. A major product in foreign markets is Clariten, a nonsedating antihistamine taken once daily (FDA approval expected in 1990). A once-daily treatment for asthma, Uni-Dur, may also be approved in 1990. About 36% of the company's sales come from foreign markets today.

Schering-Plough spends about 10% of sales on R&D, focusing mostly on treatments for asthma and allergies, skin disorders, cancer and infectious diseases, and high blood pressure. About 25% of research money is spent on biotechnology to develop medicines that act on the immune system. A new research facility under construction in Kenilworth, New Jersey, will be completed in 1992.

WHEN

Schering takes its name from Ernst Schering, a Berlin chemist who formed the company in 1864 to sell chemicals to local apothecary shops. By 1880 the German company was exporting pharmaceuticals to the US. An American subsidiary was established in 1928 and during the 1930s developed processes for the mass production of sex hormones. At the outbreak of WWII the US government seized the US subsidiary and appointed government attorney Francis Brown director. Brown put together a research team whose efforts led to new drugs in the postwar years, including Chlor-Trimeton, one of the first antihistamines, and the cold medicine Coricidin in 1949.

In 1952 the government sold Schering to Merrill Lynch, which took it public. Brown became the company's first president. Its most profitable products in the 1950s were new steroids, including Meticorten (prednisone). Sales were over $80 million in 1957, the same year that Schering bought White Labs. In the 1960s the company introduced Tinactin (antifungal, 1965), Garamycin (antibiotic, 1964), and Afrin (decongestant, 1967).

The 1971 merger with Plough, Inc., expanded the product line to include cosmetics and consumer items like Coppertone and Di-Gel. Plough had originated in Memphis, Tennessee, in 1908. Abe Plough, its founder, borrowed $125 from his father to create an "antiseptic healing oil" consisting of cottonseed oil, carbolic acid, and camphor. Plough sold his concoction door-to-door, expanded his inventory, and went on to acquire 28 companies. After the merger he served as chairman of the board until 1976. Known for his philanthropy in Memphis, Plough died in 1984 at the age of 92.

Schering-Plough has introduced various new products since the merger, including Lotrimin (antifungal, 1975), Drixoral (cold remedy, made nonprescription in 1982), and the anti-asthmatics Vanceril (1976) and Proventil (1981). When Garamycin's patent expired in 1980, the company introduced a similar antibiotic, Netromycin. Schering-Plough was one of the first of the drug giants to make significant investments in biotechnology: it owns a portion of Biogen of Cambridge, Massachusetts, and acquired DNAX Research Institute of Palo Alto, California, in 1982. From Biogen it licenses Intron A (alpha interferon), the first biotech medicine for treating cancer (also FDA advisory panel–approved in 1990 as a treatment for hepatitis.)

The company has made several acquisitions since the late 1970s, including Scholl (footcare products, 1979), Key Pharmaceuticals (cardiovascular drugs, 1986), and Cooper Companies (eye care, 1988). Maybelline cosmetics, originally a Plough subsidiary, did well in the early 1980s, but lower sales in recent years led the company to sell it in 1990 for $300 million to the owners of Playtex.

HOW MUCH

	9 Yr. Growth	1980	1981	1982	1983	1984	1985	1986	1987	1988	1989
Sales ($ mil)	6.8%	1,740	1,809	1,818	1,809	1,874	1,927	2,399	2,699	2,969	3,158
Net income ($ mil)	7.8%	239	179	184	179	177	193	266	316	390	471
Income as % of sales	—	13.8%	9.9%	10.1%	9.9%	9.5%	10.0%	11.1%	11.7%	13.1%	14.9%
Earnings per share ($)	7.1%	1.11	0.83	0.85	0.84	0.87	0.92	1.07	1.35	1.72	2.06
Stock price – high ($)	—	11.41	10.63	10.94	12.03	10.00	16.63	22.00	27.63	29.69	43.00
Stock price – low ($)	—	7.28	6.22	6.56	9.19	8.25	8.81	14.00	15.63	22.63	27.69
Stock price – close ($)	17.4%	10.13	7.00	9.84	9.31	9.00	14.53	19.75	23.50	28.38	42.75
P/E – high	—	10	13	13	14	12	18	21	21	17	21
P/E – low	—	7	8	8	11	10	10	13	12	13	13
Dividends per share ($)	9.6%	0.39	0.42	0.42	0.42	0.42	0.42	0.45	0.51	0.70	0.89
Book value per share ($)	4.7%	5.71	6.05	6.23	6.28	6.49	7.15	6.24	6.45	7.46	8.64

1989 Year End:
Debt ratio: 8.7%
Return on equity: 25.6%
Cash (mil): $935
Current ratio: 1.69
Long-term debt (mil): $186
Number of shares (mil): 226
Dividends:
1989 average yield: 2.1%
1989 payout: 43.1%
Market value (mil): $9,673

Stock Price History high/low 1980-89

45 40 35 30 25 20 15 10 5 0

NYSE symbol: SGP
Incorporated: New Jersey, 1970
Fiscal year ends: December 31

WHO

Chairman and CEO: Robert P. Luciano, age 56, $1,514,550 pay
President and COO: Richard J. Kogan, age 48, $984,340 pay
EVP Finance: Harold R. Hiser, Jr., age 58
Auditors: Deloitte & Touche
Employees: 21,300

WHERE

HQ: One Giralda Farms, Madison, NJ 07940
Phone: 201-822-7000
FAX: 201-822-7447

	1989 Sales		1989 Operating Income	
	$ mil	% of total	$ mil	% of total
US	1,987	64	538	73
Europe, Middle East & Africa	562	18	98	14
Latin America	170	6	26	4
Canada, Pacific	378	12	63	9
Adjustments	61	—	(57)	—
Total	**3,158**	**100**	**668**	**100**

WHAT

	1989 Sales		1989 Operating Income	
	$ mil	% of total	$ mil	% of total
Pharmaceuticals	2,432	77	628	86
Consumer products	664	21	97	13
Divested businesses	62	2	4	1
Adjustments	—	—	(61)	—
Total	**3,158**	**100**	**668**	**100**

Pharmaceuticals
Elocon (topical anti-inflammatory)
Eulexin (for prostate cancer)
Garamycin (antibiotic)
Gyne-Lotrimin (antifungal)
Intron A (for cancer, hepatitis)
K-Dur (potassium supplement)
Netromycin (antibiotic)
Nitro-Dur (antianginal)
Normodyne (antihypertensive)
Proventil (antiasthma)
Theo-Dur (antiasthma)
Vancenase AQ (antiallergy)

Consumer Health Care
Afrin (decongestant)
Aftate (antifungal)
Aquaflex (contact lens)
Chlor-Trimeton (allergy drug)
Coppertone (sunscreen)
Coricidin (cold medicine)
Correctol (laxative)
Di-Gel (antacid)
Dr. Scholl's (foot care)
Drixoral (cold medicine)
Feen-a-mint (laxative)
Lotrimin AF (antifungal)
Saint Joseph (aspirin)
Solarcaine (sunburn pain)
Tinactin (antifungal)

RANKINGS

139th in *Fortune* 500 Industrial Cos.
394th in *Fortune* Global 500 Industrial Cos.
263rd in *Forbes* Sales 500
53rd in *Business Week* 1000
202nd in *Business Week* Global 1000

COMPETITION

Abbott Labs
American Home Products
Bayer
Bristol-Myers Squibb
Eli Lilly
Glaxo
Hoechst
Johnson & Johnson
Merck
Pfizer
Procter & Gamble
Rhône-Poulenc
Roche Holding
SmithKline Beecham
Upjohn
Warner-Lambert

SCHLUMBERGER NV

OVERVIEW

New York–based Schlumberger is the worldwide leader in wireline logging (a process used to chart where oil and gas lie in a well) and petroleum exploration services. Subsidiary GECO provides seismic surveys.

Schlumberger's Sedco Forex divisions operated 73 drilling rigs, 39 offshore and 34 on land, in 1989. The company consistently has spent more on wireline research than all its competitors combined.

Originally French, $4.7 billion Schlumberger, now incorporated in Curaçao (in the Netherlands Antilles), conducts business in more than 100 countries. Schlumberger makes utility meters in 11 countries. The company is the leading manufacturer of smart cards (which resemble credit cards and contain microchips for conducting financial transactions) through its Schlumberger Industries division.

Schlumberger's Technologies group utilizes VLSI (Very Large Scale Integration) technology in the manufacture of computer-aided design and manufacturing equipment, which is used by automotive, aviation, and electronic designers.

NYSE symbol: SLB
Incorporated: Curaçao, Netherlands Antilles, 1956
Fiscal year ends: December 31

WHO

Chairman, President, and CEO: D. Euan Baird, age 52, $1,140,000 pay
VC: Roland Génin, age 62, $780,000 pay
EVP Finance and CFO: Arthur Lindenauer, age 52, $510,000 pay
EVP: Victor E. Grijalva, age 51, $453,600 pay
EVP: Ian Strecker, age 50, $450,000 pay
Auditors: Price Waterhouse
Employees: 46,000

WHEN

Conrad and Marcel Schlumberger were Alsatian scientists who believed that electrical resistance could be used to measure the earth's subsurface. Paul Schlumberger, their father and fellow scientist, thought a business would follow and offered capital for the venture (1919), and the brothers' Paris home became the site of Schlumberger.

Their theories were proven by the mid-1920s, but no application developed until 1927, when Pechelbronn Oil became interested in using their technique to search for oil. Conrad asked his son-in-law, Henri Doll, to design a tool for the purpose, and the process of wireline logging, akin to an X-ray for charting where oil and gas lie in a well, was born. Doll turned out to be a tremendous asset — upon his 1967 retirement, one analyst estimated that 40% of Schlumberger revenues stemmed from his inventions. By 1938 Schlumberger was operating worldwide.

Conrad died in 1936, leaving Marcel in charge until 1953; Marcel's death resulted in factionalism. Separate family members controlled the 4 divisions (North American, South American/Middle Eastern, European, and Doll's US technical development), creating disorganization. Marcel's son Pierre took the company public, merged foreign operations with North American headquarters in Houston, and restructured the company in 1956 as Schlumberger Ltd, incorporated in the Netherlands Antilles. In 1965 Pierre ended nepotism, giving leadership of Schlumberger to another Frenchman, Jean Riboud. That year Riboud moved headquarters to New York, where it remains today.

Riboud began a series of acquisitions, including the Compagnie des Compteurs, a French electric-meter manufacturer (1970). He saw Schlumberger as an information vendor rather than an oil-services company and purchased Fairchild Camera & Instrument in 1979, believing that semiconductors would play an important future role. Today the Technologies Division, of which semiconductors are a part, accounts for only 6% of assets. Riboud bought Applicon, a producer of computer-aided design and manufacturing software, in 1982. Today 42% of revenues are derived from non–oil field products and services.

Schlumberger has invested through a series of acquisitions in artificial intelligence technology, which it introduced in oil fields in 1982. Known for providing state-of-the-art equipment to the oil industry, Schlumberger bought GECO (1986), a Norwegian geophysical company noted for marine seismic analysis. In 1989 Schlumberger expressed interest in pursuing markets in the USSR, the world's largest oil producer, where opportunities have developed due to the changing political climate.

WHERE

HQ: 277 Park Ave., New York, NY 10172
Phone: 212-350-9400
FAX: 212-350-9564

Schlumberger has 79 plants in 17 countries, operating in North America, Latin America, Europe, Africa, and Asia.

	1989 Sales		1989 Operating Income	
	$ mil	% of total	$ mil	% of total
US	1,276	28	11	2
Other Western Hemisphere	444	9	67	13
France	638	14	77	15
Other European	1,136	24	102	19
Other Eastern Hemisphere	1,192	25	264	51
Adjustments	—	—	(52)	—
Total	**4,686**	**100**	**469**	**100**

WHAT

	1989 Sales		1989 Operating Income	
	$ mil	% of total	$ mil	% of total
Oil field services	2,696	58	340	69
Measurement & systems	1,990	42	154	31
Adjustments	—	—	(25)	—
Total	**4,686**	**100**	**469**	**100**

Oil & Gas Operations
Cementing
Land-based well drilling
Offshore well drilling
Seismic surveys
Well evaluation
Well stimulation services
Wireline measurements

Other Operations
Electric utility load and rate management systems
Electronic payment terminals
Fuel-dispensing systems
Parking terminals
Signal processing systems
Smart cards
Utility meters for electricity, water, and gas

RANKINGS

273rd in *Fortune* Global 500 Industrial Cos.
40th in *Business Week* 1000
98th in *Business Week* Global 1000

COMPETITION

Baker Hughes
Dresser
Halliburton
Litton
McDermott

HOW MUCH

	9 Yr. Growth	1980	1981	1982	1983	1984	1985	1986	1987	1988	1989
Sales ($ mil)	(0.5%)	4,884	5,783	6,025	5,513	5,979	6,119	4,568	4,402	4,925	4,686
Net income ($ mil)	(9.1%)	994	1,266	1,348	1,084	1,182	351	(1,655)	503	454	420
Income as % of sales	—	20.4%	21.9%	22.4%	19.7%	19.8%	5.7%	(36.2%)	11.4%	9.2%	9.0%
Earnings per share ($)	(7.2%)	3.47	4.37	4.60	3.73	4.10	1.17	(5.76)	1.81	1.72	1.77
Stock price – high ($)	—	87.17	78.50	55.88	62.63	55.00	43.88	37.75	51.00	38.75	50.50
Stock price – low ($)	—	39.22	49.13	30.00	38.25	35.88	32.38	27.25	26.00	28.50	32.00
Stock price – close ($)	(5.0%)	78.00	55.88	46.63	50.00	38.13	36.50	31.75	28.75	32.63	49.13
P/E – high	—	25	18	12	17	13	38	—	28	23	29
P/E – low	—	11	11	7	10	9	28	—	14	17	18
Dividends per share ($)	7.5%	0.63	0.77	0.92	1.00	1.12	1.20	1.20	1.20	1.20	1.20
Book value per share ($)	0.9%	11.23	14.64	17.89	20.09	23.25	23.24	14.67	14.09	11.59	12.19

1989 Year End:
Debt ratio: 9.2%
Return on equity: 14.9%
Cash (mil): $1,353
Current ratio: 1.41
Long-term debt (mil): $292
Number of shares (mil): 238
Dividends:
1989 average yield: 2.4%
1989 payout: 67.8%
Market value (mil): $11,675

Stock Price History high/low 1980-89

SCI SYSTEMS, INC.

OVERVIEW

SCI Systems, based in Huntsville, Alabama, is the leading subcontractor to the computer and electronics industries. The $987 million company is also a major supplier of instrumentation, computers, and communications systems for government aerospace and defense programs.

At the end of 1989, with 68 surface-mount technology (SMT) production lines, it is estimated to be the 4th largest SMT production facility in the world. SMT involves gluing components to circuit boards instead of attaching them with wires (pin-in-hole method). The technology enables the same number of components to fit on a smaller board and increases reliability. In the first 1/2 of 1990, SCI added new circuit board production capacity at the rate of one assembly line per week.

During the 1980s IBM was by far SCI's biggest customer (63% of net sales in 1987). However, the company has made considerable progress in its diversification efforts, expanding both its customer and product bases. In 1989 IBM represented only 27% of sales. Two other major customers of SCI include Imprimis, now owned by Seagate, and Apple Computers. Combined, the 3 companies accounted for 50% of SCI's sales in 1989.

WHEN

Olin King, a former employee of Wernher von Braun's army rocket center, and 2 friends started SCI Systems in 1961 in Huntsville, Alabama. The 3 men combined their $21,000 in savings with $300,000 in venture capital and started SCI as a contract engineering firm to NASA.

SCI specialized initially in building electronics systems for the Saturn rocket and later for other NASA and military missile and satellite programs. Its product line expanded to include subsystems for military aircraft (*e.g.*, cockpit controls for the F-15 fighter plane) and military surface systems.

SCI's major breakthrough came in 1976 with a contract from IBM to produce subassemblies for IBM terminals. Subsequently, when IBM went to work on its personal computer (PC), introduced in 1981, it turned to SCI with a $30 million contract for the PC's first batch of circuit boards. IBM shipped 100,000 PCs in 1981. In 1984 that number had grown to 2.3 million — all outfitted with SCI boards. SCI's contracts with IBM, which extended to other parts and subassemblies for the PC, accelerated SCI's sales. The company was ranked as the 8th fastest-growing electronics company in the US in 1985 based on its sales growth between 1981 and 1985. SCI's 1985 sales totaled $538 million.

In an attempt to reduce its reliance on IBM contracts, which accounted for 60% of SCI's sales (1982-1983), SCI expanded into making entire microcomputers (1984) and selling them to companies like Kodak, which resold them under its label. However, microcomputer sales could not compensate for SCI's loss when IBM cut its orders for circuit boards in 1985. SCI's sales dropped 12% in 1986.

The company's sales bounced back in 1987 after SCI negotiated a new contract with IBM for circuit boards for IBM's PS/2 computers, but the experience of losing IBM's business sent SCI looking for new customers.

SCI built additional facilities in the US and overseas and moved quickly into surface-mount technology. Because of the high cost of surface-mount production, companies rely on subcontractors like SCI to supply surface-mount boards. Since 1987 SCI has become a leader in surface-mount technology. Consequently, its sales have gone from $553 million (1987) to $987 million (1989).

In 1989 the company set up a Tape Automated Bonding (TAB) development laboratory to prepare for what it anticipates will be the next evolution in electronics packaging.

HOW MUCH

	9 Yr. Growth	1980	1981	1982	1983	1984	1985	1986	1987	1988	1989
Sales ($ mil)	40.3%	47	59	90	183	437	538	470	553	774	987
Net income ($ mil)	28.9%	2	3	4	7	12	14	14	16	19	21
Income as % of sales	—	4.5%	5.2%	4.6%	3.6%	2.6%	2.6%	2.9%	2.9%	2.5%	2.1%
Earnings per share ($)	24.2%	0.14	0.21	0.25	0.38	0.61	0.67	0.67	0.77	0.91	1.00
Stock price – high ($)	—	3.56	5.89	10.17	20.33	17.00	10.50	14.25	23.13	15.25	16.00
Stock price – low ($)	—	1.39	2.78	3.50	9.50	7.17	6.92	9.00	11.13	10.63	7.63
Stock price – close ($)	10.7%	3.46	4.72	9.92	15.00	9.33	10.08	11.75	13.25	15.00	8.63
P/E – high	—	25	28	40	54	28	16	21	30	17	16
P/E – low	—	10	13	14	25	12	10	14	14	12	8
Dividends per share ($)	0.0%	0.00	0.00	0.00	0.00	0.00	0.00	0.00	0.00	0.00	0.00
Book value per share ($)	23.4%	1.22	1.43	1.98	2.50	3.97	4.78	5.53	6.39	7.27	8.11

1989 Year End:
Debt ratio: 62.1%
Return on equity: 13.0%
Cash (mil): $32
Current ratio: 2.84
Long-term debt (mil): $278
Number of shares (mil): 21
Dividends:
1989 average yield: 0.0%
1989 payout: 0.0%
Market value (mil): $180

25
20
15
10
5
0

Stock Price History
high/low 1980-89

OTC symbol: SCIS
Incorporated: Delaware, 1961
Fiscal year ends: June 30

WHO

Chairman and CEO: Olin B. King, age 55, $459,440 pay
President and COO: A. Eugene Sapp, Jr., age 52, $365,443 pay
Treasurer and CFO: James R. Daniel, age 42, $140,577 pay
Auditors: Ernst & Young
Employees: 8,578

WHERE

HQ: 2109 W. Clinton Ave., Huntsville, AL 35805
Phone: 205-882-4800
FAX: 205-882-4804

The company has 22 plants throughout the US and in Scotland, Singapore, Thailand, Ireland, Canada, Hong Kong, and Mexico.

	1989 Sales		1989 Operating Income	
	$ mil	% of total	$ mil	% of total
US	668	68	5	11
Foreign	319	32	37	89
Total	**987**	**100**	**42**	**100**

WHAT

	1989 Sales	
Customers	$ mil	% of total
IBM	270	27
Imprimis	120	12
Apple	103	11
All other	494	50
Total	**987**	**100**

Divisions

Manufacturing
Electronic and mechanical components and products
Full-service contract manufacturing to the electronic equipment industry

Government Aerospace & Defense Programs
Aircraft flight test instrumentation systems
Cockpit controls
Core Avionics Processor (for F-16)
Data management systems
Voice warning systems

Computers
OEM system blocks based on:
80286 microprocessor
80386 microprocessor
80386SX microprocessor
Peripherals (printers, communications controllers, storage devices)

RANKINGS

351st in *Fortune* 500 Industrial Cos.

COMPETITION

Intel

SCOTT PAPER COMPANY

OVERVIEW

Scott Paper Company is the world's leading manufacturer of tissue products, such as toilet paper and paper towels, and of coated printing and publishing papers, made by the company's S. D. Warren division.

Scott sells its paper and nonwoven fiber products in over 60 countries, and most of the company's foreign operations are at least 50% locally owned. Scott has 2.8 million acres of timberland in the US and Canada. The company's food service business includes paper napkins, plates, and cups sold to consumers and commercial food service companies.

Scott is best known for its tissue products for personal care; the company was the first in the US to market toilet paper. However, Scott also has substantial sales in the commercial sector, with items such as cloth replacement wipes and cleaners. The company's health care products include ProCare and Sani-Fresh soap-dispensing systems.

In 1989 Scott achieved record sales for the 7th consecutive year; however, the company did not bring in expected earnings, due partly to production difficulties at some of the Warren plants.

NYSE symbol: SPP
Incorporated: Pennsylvania, 1922
Fiscal year ends: Last Saturday in December

WHO

Chairman and CEO: Philip E. Lippincott, age 54, $755,805 pay
EVP; President, Scott Worldwide: J. Richard Leaman, Jr., age 55, $502,772 pay
EVP; President, S. D. Warren Co.: Robert E. McAvoy, age 61, $368,448 pay
VC: J. Lawrence Shane, age 55, $350,674 pay
SVP and CFO: Ashok N. Bakhru, age 47
Auditors: Price Waterhouse
Employees: 29,400

WHEN

The Scott Paper Company was founded in Pennsylvania in 1879 by brothers Irvin and Clarence Scott, who were the first to market rolls of tissue specifically for use as toilet paper. That year they began buying rolls of paper and converting it for use in the new indoor bathrooms. Arthur Scott, Irvin's son, adopted the advertising slogan "Soft as old linen." In 1907 Scott Paper introduced paper towels. The company went public in 1915 and ran its first ad in a national magazine shortly thereafter. One caption read, "They have a pretty house, Mother, but their bathroom paper hurts." Arthur Scott was president until 1927 and was succeeded by Thomas McCabe.

In the period prior to WWII Scott expanded its export business, using a network of sales agents overseas. The company credits its international success with its 50-50 formula; Scott would own up to 50% of a foreign venture, and a local company would own 50% or more. Sanyo Scott produced Japan's top paper towel brand during the 1970s. Other joint ventures included Spain's Gureola-Scott, Australia's Bowater-Scott, and Italy's Burgo-Scott.

Until the 1960s Scott was the leader in the "Great Toilet Paper War," as the industry called it. But in 1957 Procter & Gamble introduced Charmin toilet tissue, which soon surpassed Scott's sales. Between 1960 and 1971 Scott's share of consumer paper products sales dropped from 45% to 33%. In 1967 the company diversified by buying S. D. Warren (printing and publishing papers) and Plastic Coating Corporation. At the same time Scott introduced babyScott disposable diapers to compete with Procter & Gamble's Pampers, but babyScott didn't sell well.

Under new CEO Charles Dickey, Jr. (1971-1979), the company made major changes, including reducing administrative expenses by about 20%, restructuring marketing and research efforts, and withdrawing unsuccessful items from the consumer market in order to concentrate on household and industrial paper products such as towels, napkins, cups, and plates. In 1976 Scott introduced Cottonelle to compete with Charmin. Cottonelle captured approximately 35% of the 4-roll-pack market within several months of its introduction.

Scott began a 5-year, $1.6 billion US plant upgrade (1981), a 3-year $250 million European plant upgrade (1988), and a $475 million upgrade to 3 S. D. Warren plants (1988). In 1989 the company began operating a rebuilt paper machine in Taiwan and paper converting plants in France and Italy, and bought the White Swan Tissue Division (sanitary products) of E. B. Eddy Forest Products (Canada). It also sold 194,000 acres of timberland in the Pacific Northwest for a gain of $209 million.

WHERE

HQ: Scott Plaza, Philadelphia, PA 19113
Phone: 215-522-5000
FAX: 215-522-5129

Scott and S. D. Warren operate more than 60 manufacturing plants in the US and 21 foreign countries, and have 2.8 million acres of timberland in Alabama, Mississippi, Washington, Maine, and Nova Scotia.

	1989 Sales		1989 Operating Income	
	$ mil	% of total	$ mil	% of total
US	3,718	73	408	85
Europe	1,153	23	55	11
Pacific	169	3	17	4
Latin America	26	1	0	0
Adjustments	—	—	(11)	—
Total	**5,066**	**100**	**469**	**100**

WHAT

	1989 Sales		1989 Operating Income	
	$ mil	% of total	$ mil	% of total
Printing & publishing papers	1,282	25	212	44
Personal care & cleaning	3,784	75	268	56
Adjustments	—	—	(11)	—
Total	**5,066**	**100**	**469**	**100**

Consumer Products
Baby Fresh
Cottonelle
Family Scott
Scotties
ScotTissue
ScotTowels
Soft-Weve
Viva
Waldorf

Commercial Products
Durafab industrial garments
JRT jumbo roll tissue
Printing paper
ProCare
Sani-Fresh
Scottcloth
Viva napkins
WypAll

HOW MUCH

	9 Yr. Growth	1980	1981	1982	1983	1984	1985	1986	1987	1988	1989
Sales ($ mil)	10.4%	2,083	2,309	2,293	2,465	2,847	3,050	3,437	4,122	4,726	5,066
Net income ($ mil)	12.2%	134	133	74	124	187	201	187	234	401	376
Income as % of sales	—	6.4%	5.8%	3.2%	5.0%	6.6%	6.6%	5.4%	5.7%	8.5%	7.4%
Earnings per share ($)	12.9%	1.72	1.61	0.81	1.29	1.92	2.26	2.47	3.06	5.21	5.11
Stock price – high ($)	—	11.75	14.25	10.56	16.13	17.44	26.13	33.31	43.50	42.75	52.50
Stock price – low ($)	—	6.88	7.50	6.81	9.31	12.63	16.69	24.00	27.50	32.38	38.38
Stock price – close ($)	18.6%	10.38	8.00	10.13	15.81	17.31	25.31	31.38	35.25	39.25	48.13
P/E – high	—	7	9	13	13	9	12	14	14	8	10
P/E – low	—	4	5	8	7	7	7	10	9	6	8
Dividends per share ($)	5.4%	0.50	0.50	0.50	0.50	0.56	0.61	0.64	0.68	0.76	0.80
Book value per share ($)	7.7%	14.31	15.01	15.04	15.03	16.23	16.30	18.57	21.44	26.54	28.02

1989 Year End:
Debt ratio: 44.8%
Return on equity: 18.7%
Cash (mil): $49
Current ratio: 1.08
Long-term debt (mil): $1,678
Number of shares (mil): 74
Dividends:
1989 average yield: 1.7%
1989 payout: 15.7%
Market value (mil): $3,539

Stock Price History high/low 1980-89

60
50
40
30
20
10
0

RANKINGS

104th in *Fortune* 500 Industrial Cos.
267th in *Fortune* Global 500 Industrial Cos.
179th in *Forbes* Sales 500
193rd in *Business Week* 1000
613th in *Business Week* Global 1000

COMPETITION

Boise Cascade
Champion International
Georgia-Pacific
International Paper
James River
Kimberly-Clark
Mead
Procter & Gamble
Weyerhaeuser

THE E.W. SCRIPPS COMPANY

OVERVIEW

E.W. Scripps is the 9th largest US newspaper publisher, with 19 metropolitan and suburban papers. The largest daily, the *Rocky Mountain News* (Denver), has a circulation of 345,943; the largest Sunday paper, the *Pittsburgh Press*, prints 552,479. Other properties include several small circulation papers scattered across the country, from the *Naples Daily News* in Florida to the *Bremerton Sun* in Washington state. Scripps papers have received 33 Pulitzer Prizes for outstanding journalism.

Seven papers operate under joint operating agreements with erstwhile competing papers, sharing printing facilities and combining advertising and circulation operations.

The United Media division distributes syndicated columns, cartoons, and other features and has offices in Europe and Japan. The Pharos book division offers 54 titles, including *The World Almanac*. Scripps Howard Broadcasting (80.4% owned) operates 9 TV stations and 5 radio stations. Scripps cable TV operation, the 19th largest in the nation, passes one million homes in 10 states and has 558,000 basic cable subscribers.

OTC symbol: EWSCA
Incorporated: Delaware, 1987
Fiscal year ends: December 31

WHO

Chairman: Charles E. Scripps, age 70, $350,000 pay
President and CEO: Lawrence A. Leser, age 54, $881,000 pay
EVP: William R. Burleigh, age 54, $450,000 pay
SVP Finance and Administration: Daniel J. Castellini, age 50, $392,000 pay
Auditors: Deloitte & Touche
Employees: 9,900

WHERE

HQ: 1409 Foulk Rd., Suite 102, Wilmington, DE 19803
Phone: 302-478-4141
FAX: 303-892-5499 (*Rocky Mountain News*)

Scripps operates 9 TV stations, 5 radio stations, 19 daily newspapers, and 35 cable TV systems in 22 states and in Puerto Rico. The company's comics and other features are syndicated and licensed worldwide.

WHEN

With the launch of the *Cleveland Press* (1878) and the *Cincinnati Post* (1883), Edward Wyllis Scripps started the first newspaper chain in the US. In 1889 Scripps and business manager Milton McRae formed the Scripps-McRae League which, by WWI, consisted of 30 papers in 15 states.

Scripps conducted business from his California ranch, Miramar, where he moved in 1890 at the age of 36. At his death in 1926 he was worth $50 million. Scripps was one of the pioneers of the "people's papers," which he described as "schoolrooms" for the barely educated working classes of the day.

In 1907 the company combined 3 of its small wire services to form United Press, later headed by Roy Howard, a Scripps newspaper executive. Howard took over business management of the newspaper chain in 1922, operating the papers under the Scripps Howard trade name. The United Feature Service, an offshoot of United Press, was incorporated in 1923 to provide feature material to newspapers.

E. W. Scripps died in 1926, and most of the company's stock was assembled into a trust for his heirs. His son Robert gradually ceded editorial control of the company to Howard and his conservative bent.

In 1931 the company bought the *New York World* and merged it to create the *New York World-Telegram*. The paper later became the *World-Telegram and Sun* and then the *World Journal Tribune* before it fell prey to competition and closed in 1967.

War correspondent Ernie Pyle, who died on the battlefield in WWII, was a Scripps Howard reporter. United Press correspondents included Walter Cronkite, assigned to London during the war, and Merriman Smith, dean of White House correspondents for 30 years, whose "Thank you, Mr. President" close became a tradition.

In 1958 Scripps absorbed Hearst's International News Service into UP to form United Press International. It sold the wire service in 1982 to Media News Corporation.

In recent years, Scripps folded the *Cleveland Press* in 1982 and the Memphis *Press-Scimitar* in 1983. In 1986 and 1987 Scripps bought television stations and cable systems and sold nondaily papers, business journals, and magazines. Cable's growth has fueled increases in cash flow and operating income.

In 1986 Scripps completed purchase of 7 newspapers developed independently by John P. Scripps, grandson of the founder. In 1988 the company went public for the first time, but much of the stock (81%) remains in the hands of the Scripps and Howard family trusts.

WHAT

	1989 Sales		1989 Operating Income	
	$ mil	% of total	$ mil	% of total
Publishing	850	67	146	63
Broadcasting	223	18	58	26
Cable television	177	14	22	10
Other	16	1	2	1
Adjustments	—	—	(15)	—
Total	**1,266**	**100**	**214**	**100**

Major Newspapers
The Cincinnati Post
The Commercial Appeal (Memphis)
The Pittsburgh Press
Rocky Mountain News (Denver)

Pharos Books
The Kids' World Almanac
The New Kinsey Institute Report on Sex
The World Almanac

Licensing & Syndication
Columns
Jack Anderson
"Miss Manners"
Comic strips
"Garfield"
"Marmaduke"
"Nancy"
"Peanuts"
T-V Data (TV listings)
United Feature Syndicate

Major TV Stations
WCPO (Cincinnati)
WEWS (Cleveland)
WMC (Memphis)
WXYZ (Detroit)

Radio Stations
KUPL (Portland)
WBSB (Baltimore)
WMC-AM, WMC-FM (Memphis)

RANKINGS

298th in *Fortune* 500 Industrial Cos.
375th in *Business Week* 1000

COMPETITION

Cox
Gannett
Hearst
New York Times
Washington Post

HOW MUCH

	2 Yr. Growth	1980	1981	1982	1983	1984	1985	1986	1987	1988	1989
Sales ($ mil)	5.1%	—	—	—	—	—	—	—	1,147	1,214	1,266
Net income ($ mil)	40.6%	—	—	—	—	—	—	—	45	70	89
Income as % of sales	—	—	—	—	—	—	—	—	3.9%	5.8%	7.1%
Earnings per share ($)	35.6%	—	—	—	—	—	—	—	0.62	0.93	1.14
Stock price – high ($)	—	—	—	—	—	—	—	—	—	18.13	27.00
Stock price – low ($)	—	—	—	—	—	—	—	—	—	14.50	16.88
Stock price – close ($)	—	—	—	—	—	—	—	—	—	17.13	24.00
P/E – high	—	—	—	—	—	—	—	—	—	19	24
P/E – low	—	—	—	—	—	—	—	—	—	16	15
Dividends per share ($)	—	—	—	—	—	—	—	—	0.00	0.15	0.35
Book value per share ($)	12.0%	—	—	—	—	—	—	—	6.72	7.98	8.43

1989 Year End:
Debt ratio: 39.5%
Return on equity: 13.9%
Cash (mil): $19
Current ratio: 1.5
Long-term debt (mil): $421
Number of shares (mil): 76
Dividends:
1989 average yield: 1.4%
1989 payout: 30.3%
Market value (mil): $1,834

SEAGATE TECHNOLOGY, INC.

OVERVIEW

Seagate is the world's leading independent supplier of rigid disk drives and related products for storage (auxiliary memory) and components, offering the largest selection of products for a broad range of computers from personal to mainframe.

Far East production and strong vertical integration permit Seagate to offer price-performing, high-quality products. The company is the world's largest manufacturer of thin-film magnetic media. Domestic sales outperform international by a small margin. More than 5 million drives were shipped in 1989.

Seagate pioneered 5-1/4" disk drives for small computers and has been a consistent leader in reducing average data access time (now down to 10 milliseconds) and increasing memory densities.

In 1989 Seagate purchased Imprimis Technology, Inc. (the disk drive subsidiary of Control Data) for cash and stock that gave CDC an 18% stake in Seagate. This acquisition nearly doubled Seagate's size and gave it new expertise in component manufacturing for further vertical integration, thus positioning the company for even greater-capacity products.

OTC symbol: SGAT
Incorporated: Delaware, 1986
Fiscal year ends: June 30

WHO

Chairman and CEO: Alan F. Shugart, age 58, $762,924 pay
President and COO: David T. Mitchell, age 47, $874,193 pay
SVP and Chief Technical Officer: Douglas K. Mahon, age 48, $800,754 pay
SVP and CFO: Donald L. Waite, age 56, $475,560 pay
Auditors: Ernst & Young
Employees: 29,000

WHEN

In 1979 Seagate Technology was founded in Scotts Valley, California, by Alan Shugart, an 18-year IBMer who had made floppy disks standard on microcomputers at Shugart Associates; manufacturing expert Tom Mitchell, formerly of Commodore and Memorex; and design engineer Douglas Mahon. Seagate pioneered the downsizing of mainframe hard disk drives for PCs; the result was 30 times more storage than floppy disks, faster access times, and much higher long-term reliability.

Seagate's first product, the ST506 (a 5-1/4" hard disk, 1980), sold briskly. As IBM's memory choice for its new PCs, Seagate rose to $40 million in sales by 1982, with 1/2 of the market for small disk drives; by 1984, sales had reached $344 million. Soon, though, Seagate's heavy dependence on IBM showed its double edge as eroding IBM PC demand prompted them to cut orders. Sales in 1985 dropped to $215 million and profits to $1 million (from $42 million the year before).

Having distinguished itself through high-volume, low-cost, reliable manufacturing, Seagate now hastened the transfer of manufacturing to Singapore (and later Thailand); the California work force was halved.

The company also accelerated its vertical integration to ensure availability of critical components and reduce time to market.

Seagate purchased Grenex (thin-film magnetic media, 1984), Aeon (aluminum substrates, 1987), and Integrated Power Systems (custom semiconductors, 1987). Seagate also lured back IBM, which had turned to an alternate supplier in the interim.

With revenues more than doubling in 1986 and again in 1987 (to $958 million), Seagate spent $290 million and doubled the work force to 30,000 to increase 5-1/4" production while ignoring signs of a coming 3-1/2" standard for hard disk drives. The strong market in 1988 for 3-1/2" drives, coupled with IBM's decision to produce more drives in-house, prompted Seagate to reduce its work force by almost 4,000 and shift quickly to 3-1/2" production.

Seagate purchased Imprimis from Control Data (October 1989), thus creating the world's premier independent drive maker with 12% of the market (41% of 5-1/4" and 3-1/2" rigid disk drive market). Imprimis's strengths in R&D and high-capacity drives for large computers (sold to OEMs), combined with Seagate manufacturing talent, should provide the strength necessary to combat the onslaught of Asian competition and meet the demand for smaller, cheaper, high-quality recording capabilities. So far the strategy is working; Seagate closed out its fiscal year in June 1990 with sales of over $2.4 billion (up over 70%) and profits of $117 million.

WHERE

HQ: 920 Disc Drive, Scotts Valley, CA 95066
Phone: 408-438-6550
FAX: 408-438-6172

Seagate has sales and support offices in the US and 17 other countries around the world; primary manufacturing facilities are located in Singapore and Bangkok. The Imprimis division has manufacturing facilities in the US, Portugal, Malaysia, and Singapore.

	1989 Facilities	
	sq. ft. thou.	% of total
California	1,225	41
Florida	77	3
The Netherlands	27	1
Ohio	56	2
Scotland	74	2
Singapore	815	28
Thailand	633	21
Other	57	2
Total	**2,964**	**100**

	1989 Sales		1989 Operating Income	
	$ mil	% of total	$ mil	% of total
US	711	52	(95)	—
Far East	661	48	92	—
Adjustments	—	—	16	—
Total	**1,372**	**100**	**13**	**—**

WHAT

Rigid Disk Drives
3-1/2"
20 to 210 megabytes (MB) of memory
5-1/4"
20 MB to 1 gigabyte (GB)
8"(Sabre series)
386 MB to 2-1/2 GB
9" (fixed and removable)
14" (XMD series)
Up to 1.3 GB
14" (SMD)
80 to 300 MB

Subsidiaries
Seagate Microelectronics Ltd.
Seagate Substrates

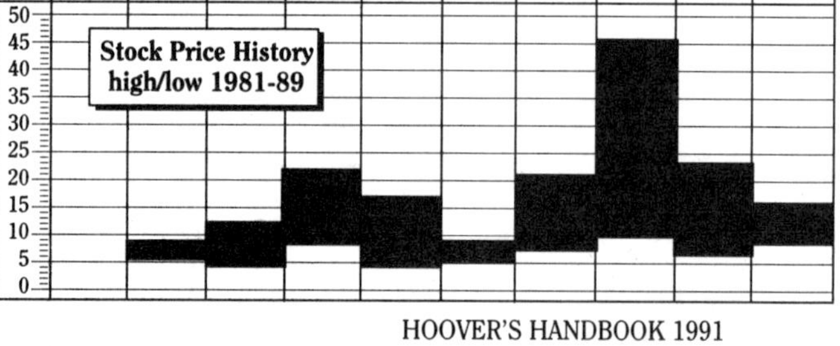

RANKINGS

281st in *Fortune* 500 Industrial Cos.
426th in *Forbes* Sales 500
480th in *Business Week* 1000

COMPETITION

Fujitsu
Hitachi
Mitsubishi

HOW MUCH

	8 Yr. Growth	1980	1981	1982	1983	1984	1985	1986	1987	1988	1989
Sales ($ mil)	85.0%	—	10	40	110	344	215	460	958	1,266	1,372
Net income ($ mil)	—	—	2	7	13	42	1	35	140	77	0
Income as % of sales	—	—	17.2%	17.2%	11.9%	12.2%	0.5%	7.5%	14.6%	6.1%	0.0%
Earnings per share ($)	17.6%	—	0.06	0.20	0.33	0.95	0.02	0.72	2.81	1.57	0.22
Stock price – high ($)	—	—	8.88	12.44	22.13	17.00	8.75	21.00	45.75	23.38	16.13
Stock price – low ($)	—	—	5.38	4.31	8.25	4.00	4.75	7.13	9.75	6.50	8.50
Stock price – close ($)	9.5%	—	7.25	10.50	13.88	5.00	7.25	19.13	14.88	8.63	15.00
P/E – high	—	—	161	64	67	18	438	29	16	15	73
P/E – low	—	—	98	22	25	4	238	10	3	4	39
Dividends per share ($)	—	—	0.00	0.00	0.00	0.00	0.00	0.00	0.00	0.00	0.00
Book value per share ($)	77.5%	—	0.09	0.96	2.77	3.74	3.66	4.41	7.36	8.89	8.85

1989 Year End:
Debt ratio: 40.8%
Return on equity: 2.5%
Cash (mil): $190
Current ratio: 2.46
Long-term debt (mil): $305
Number of shares (mil): 50
Dividends:
1989 average yield: 0.0%
1989 payout: 0.0%
Market value (mil): $750

Stock Price History high/low 1981-89

THE SEAGRAM COMPANY LTD.

OVERVIEW

Montreal-based Seagram is a leading producer and distributor of spirits, wine, wine coolers, fruit juices, and soft drinks, with such widely recognized names as 7 Crown, Crown Royal, and V.O. whiskeys, Chivas Regal scotch, Myers's rum, Martell cognac, Tropicana fruit juices, and Soho soft drinks. In addition, the company owns approximately 24.2% of Du Pont. Although Seagram is headquartered in Quebec, almost half of company sales come from the US.

Seagram operates distilleries and bottling operations in 22 countries, producing over 275 spirit brands. The company maintains a total daily capacity of 351,000 gallons (distilleries) and 368,000 standard cases (bottlers).

Seagram's wine operations (with an inventory of approximately 54 million gallons) produce and market over 400 brands. Tropicana, which is produced by the company's fruit juice segment, is the leading nonconcentrate orange juice in the US.

The Bronfman family (descendants of Samuel Bronfman, the company's founder) collectively own approximately 37% of the total outstanding shares.

NYSE symbol: VO
Incorporated: Canada, 1928
Fiscal year ends: January 31

WHO

Chairman and CEO: Edgar M. Bronfman, age 60, $1,616,170 pay
Co-Chairman: Charles R. Bronfman, age 58, $870,000 pay
President and COO: Edgar Bronfman, Jr., age 34, $1,038,435 pay
EVP Finance: Richard K. Goeltz, age 47
Auditors: Price Waterhouse
Employees: 17,600

WHEN

In 1916 Sam Bronfman bought the Bonaventure Liquor Store Company in Montreal and started selling liquor by mail order (the only legal way during Canadian Prohibition, which lasted from 1918 until the early 1920s). In 1924, with the help of his brother Allan, Bronfman opened the first family distillery in neighboring La Salle and took the name Distillers Corporation. Bronfman, who would come to be known as "Mr. Sam," purchased the larger Joseph Seagram & Sons in 1928, went public, and changed his company name to Distillers Corporation–Seagrams.

During the 1920s Bronfman established a lucrative bootlegging operation that smuggled whiskey by land and sea into the "dry" United States. The company may have accounted for half of the illegal liquor crossing the border.

In 1928 Bronfman, expecting the end of Prohibition in the US, began stockpiling whiskey. When Prohibition ended in 1933, Bronfman had the world's largest supply of aged rye and sour mash whiskeys.

Bootlegging had given whiskey a harsh image, which Bronfman sought to change by introducing his smooth, blended Seagram's 7 Crown in 1934. In 1939, after blending over 600 whiskey samples, Bronfman created Crown Royal in honor of the visit of King George VI and Queen Elizabeth to Canada.

During the 1940s Seagram expanded its liquor line. In 1942 Seagram formed a partnership with Fromm and Sichel to buy Paul Masson (sold in 1987) and shortly thereafter purchased distilleries in the West Indies that would later produce the Captain Morgan and Myers's brand rums. After WWII it acquired Mumm's and Perrier-Jouët (champagne), Barton & Guestier and Augier Frères (wine), and Chivas Brothers (scotch).

Edgar Bronfman succeeded his father as company president in 1957, expanding the Company's wine and spirits lines substantially.

Throughout this period the Bronfman family accumulated substantial cash and diversified into everything from Israeli supermarkets to Texas gas fields. The company adopted its present name in 1975 and in 1980 acquired a major interest (now 24.2%) in Du Pont (currently amounting to about 70% of Seagram's earnings). Seagram introduced its Golden Wine Cooler in 1986 and 2 years later acquired Martell SA (cognac) and Tropicana (fruit juices). In 1989 the company bought American Natural Beverages (Soho Natural Soda).

During the 1990s Seagram plans to discontinue many of its lesser-known brands and concentrate on marketing its higher-priced premium brands.

WHERE

HQ: 1430 Peel St., Montreal, Quebec, Canada H3A 1S9
Phone: 514-849-5271
FAX: 514-933-5390 (Public Relations)

The company has affiliates in 28 countries and sells its products in over 150 countries.

	1989 Sales		1989 Operating Income	
	$ mil	% of total	$ mil	% of total
Canada	205	4	121	21
Europe	1,863	33	290	50
Asia-Pacific & Latin America	772	14	113	20
US	2,742	49	50	9
Other	(1,074)	—	3	—
Total	**4,508**	**100**	**577**	**100**

WHAT

	1989 Sales		1989 Operating Income	
	$ mil	% of total	$ mil	% of total
Spirits & wines	3,457	77	502	85
Juices & sodas	1,051	23	86	15
Other	—	—	(11)	—
Total	**4,508**	**100**	**577**	**100**

Brand Names

Whiskeys
Calvert Extra
Chivas Regal
Crown Royal
Glen Grant
Glenlivet
Kessler
Lord Calvert
Passport
Royal Salute
Seagram's 7 Crown
Seagram's "83"
Seagram's V.O.

Other Spirits
Boodles (gin)
Captain Morgan (rum)
Janneau (armagnacs)
Leroux (cordials)
Martell (cognacs)
Myers's (rum)
Seagram's Extra Dry (gin)
Wolfschmidt (vodka)

Wines & Champagnes
Barton & Guestier
Charles Krug Winery
Heidsieck-Monopole
Matheus Müller
C.K. Mondavi
Mumm
Perrier-Jouët
Saltram
Sandeman
Sterling
Seagram's Wine Coolers

Fruit Juices & Sodas
Soho Natural Soda
Tropicana

HOW MUCH

	9 Yr. Growth	1980	1981	1982	1983	1984	1985	1986	1987	1988	1989
Sales ($ mil)	12.3%	1,588	1,790	1,916	1,781	2,006	2,114	2,412	2,799	3,935	4,508
Net income ($ mil)	31.4%	61	330	279	318	384	319	423	521	589	711
Income as % of sales	—	3.8%	18.5%	14.6%	17.8%	19.1%	15.1%	17.6%	18.6%	15.0%	15.8%
Earnings per share ($)	32.7%	0.58	3.14	2.95	3.53	4.05	3.34	4.30	5.26	6.12	7.37
Stock price – high ($)	—	21.75	20.50	24.92	40.00	40.38	48.75	65.13	82.38	61.88	91.50
Stock price – low ($)	—	11.00	15.08	14.54	24.04	30.00	37.38	42.75	49.00	50.00	60.25
Stock price – close ($)	18.7%	19.58	19.21	24.58	36.25	40.25	48.00	60.75	54.50	61.38	91.50
P/E – high	—	38	7	8	11	10	15	15	16	10	12
P/E – low	—	19	5	5	7	7	11	10	9	8	8
Dividends per share ($)	16.5%	0.36	0.44	0.60	0.68	0.80	0.80	0.95	1.05	1.18	1.40
Book value per share ($)	18.5%	12.21	26.59	27.94	30.96	33.50	37.31	41.42	47.03	50.65	56.12

1989 Year End:
Debt ratio: 27.3%
Return on equity: 13.8%
Cash (mil): $138
Current ratio: 1.32
Long-term debt (mil): $2,011
Number of shares (mil): 95
Dividends:
1989 average yield: 1.5%
1989 payout: 19.0%
Market value (mil): $8,734

Stock Price History high/low 1980-89

RANKINGS

337th in *Fortune* Global 500 Industrial Cos.
1st in *Forbes* 100 Foreign Investments in the US
210th in *Business Week* Global 1000

COMPETITION

American Brands
Brown-Forman
Coca-Cola
E. & J. Gallo
Grand Metropolitan
Guinness
PepsiCo
Procter & Gamble

SEARS, ROEBUCK & CO.

OVERVIEW

Sears, based in the Sears Tower in Chicago, is the largest retailer in the world, the 2nd largest property-liability insurer in the US, and a major force in financial services and real estate. Sears maintains a business relationship with 70% of US households and is able to build sales through cross-referencing its customers to other subsidiaries.

Sears's retail operations (847 department stores and 884 specialty stores) have declined in recent years as discounters and malls have drawn customers away. Sears has responded by adopting a strategy of developing "power formats" such as Brand Central, refurbishing its dowdy women's apparel departments, and shunning the nonstop cycle of advertised specials in favor of "everyday low pricing."

Meanwhile, Sears's other businesses continue to improve. Coldwell Banker has increased its share of the residential real estate market from 2% to 11% since 1982; Dean Witter is the most profitable of the 5 large retail brokerages; and Discover Card now has 32.7 million cardmembers.

Chairman Edward Brennan has personally taken charge of retail operations in an effort to control costs and hasten implementation of the power format strategy.

WHEN

In 1886 Richard W. Sears, a railway agent in Minnesota, purchased a shipment of watches being returned to the manufacturer. He started the R. W. Sears Watch Company 6 months later, relocated to Chicago, and in 1887 hired Indiana watchmaker Alvah C. Roebuck. Sears sold the watch business in 1889, and 2 years later formed another mail order business that adopted the name Sears, Roebuck, and Company in 1893. The company published its first general catalog in 1896, offering low prices and money-back guarantees to the rural farmers who were Sears's principal customers.

Roebuck left the young company in 1895 and Sears found 2 new partners: Aaron Nussbaum, who left in 1901, and Julius Rosenwald. In 1906 Sears went public to raise money for expansion. Differences soon arose between Sears and Rosenwald; Sears departed in 1908 and Rosenwald became president. Following WWI Rosenwald committed the bulk of his fortune to ensure the company's survival and in 1924 hired a new VP, General Robert Wood, a veteran of the Panama Canal, WWI, and Montgomery Ward.

Wood anticipated the changes that the automobile was having upon rural life during the 1920s and 1930s. He established Sears's first retail store so that farmers could drive to town to buy merchandise and in 1925 established a line of Sears tires under the name "Allstate." Sears eventually expanded Allstate into auto insurance (1931), life insurance (1957), and an auto club (1961). Wood, who had become president in 1928 and chairman in 1939, retired in 1954.

The company branched into other areas, including *Encyclopædia Britannica* (1920; donated to the University of Chicago in 1943), Homart Development (shopping centers, 1959), and several savings and loans. The Sears Tower — the world's tallest building — opened in 1973 as the company's headquarters. In 1981 Sears acquired Coldwell Banker (real estate sales and development) and Dean Witter (stock brokerage). The services of both companies were offered in 1982 through the newly established Sears Financial Network Centers, which subsequently embraced both the Allstate Insurance products and the Discover Card. In 1989 Sears sold the commercial brokerage operations of Coldwell Banker.

In reaction to declining market share in the 1980s, Sears initiated a restructuring of its merchandising division, acquiring the 405-store Western Auto chain (1988), introducing an "everyday low pricing" policy in early 1989 and announcing its relocation from the Sears Tower to a northwestern suburb starting 1992.

HOW MUCH

	9 Yr. Growth	1980	1981	1982	1983	1984	1985	1986	1987	1988	1989
Sales ($ mil)	8.8%	25,195	27,357	30,020	35,883	38,828	40,715	44,282	48,440	50,251	53,794
Net income ($ mil)	10.1%	606	650	861	1,342	1,455	1,303	1,351	1,649	1,032	1,446
Income as % of sales	—	2.4%	2.4%	2.9%	3.7%	3.7%	3.2%	3.1%	3.4%	2.1%	2.7%
Earnings per share ($)	8.8%	*1.92*	2.06	2.43	3.75	3.98	3.51	3.60	4.32	2.71	4.10
Stock price – high ($)	—	19.63	20.88	32.00	45.13	40.38	41.13	50.38	59.50	46.25	48.13
Stock price – low ($)	—	14.38	14.88	15.75	27.00	29.50	30.88	35.88	26.00	32.25	36.50
Stock price – close ($)	10.7%	15.25	16.13	30.13	37.13	31.75	39.00	39.75	33.50	40.88	38.13
P/E – high	—	10	10	13	12	10	12	14	14	17	12
P/E – low	—	7	7	6	7	7	9	10	6	12	9
Dividends per share ($)	4.4%	1.36	1.36	1.36	1.52	1.76	1.76	1.76	2.00	2.00	2.00
Book value per share ($)	5.6%	24.38	23.77	25.08	27.60	29.48	31.70	33.98	35.89	37.75	39.77

1989 Year End:
Debt ratio: 40.6%
Return on equity: 10.6%
Cash (mil): $2,314
Current ratio: —
Long-term debt (mil): $9,293
Number of shares (mil): 343
Dividends:
1989 average yield: 5.2%
1989 payout: 48.8%
Market value (mil): $13,058

60
50
40
30
20
10
0

Stock Price History high/low 1980-89

NYSE symbol: S
Incorporated: New York, 1906
Fiscal year ends: December 31

WHO

Chairman, President, and CEO: Edward A. Brennan, age 56, $1,593,211 pay
SVP and CFO: James M. Denny, age 57
SVP Administration: Charles F. Moran, age 60, $749,000 pay
Auditors: Deloitte & Touche
Employees: 500,000

WHERE

HQ: Sears Tower, Chicago, IL 60684
Phone: 312-875-2500
FAX: 312-875-8351

Sears operates throughout the US and in Mexico, Canada, and several other countries.

	1989 Sales		1989 Pretax Income	
	$ mil	% of total	$ mil	% of total
US	49,780	92	2,037	92
Canada & Mexico	4,135	8	189	8
Adjustments	(121)	—	(427)	—
Total	**53,794**	**100**	**1,799**	**100**

WHAT

	1989 Sales		1989 Pretax Income	
	$ mil	% of total	$ mil	% of total
Merchandise	31,599	58	1,136	51
Insurance	16,803	31	685	31
Financial services	4,065	8	297	13
Real estate	1,448	3	108	5
Adjustments	(121)	—	(427)	—
Total	**53,794**	**100**	**1,799**	**100**

Merchandising
Eye Care Centers of America
Pinstripes Petites
Prodigy Services (joint venture)
Sears Business Systems Centers
Sears catalogs
Sears stores
Western Auto stores

Insurance
Allstate
Auto
Business
Homeowners
Life

Lending
Consumer financing
Discover Card
Home mortgages
Sears Charge

Asset Management
Dean Witter
Annuities
Investment banking
Mutual funds
Portfolio management

Real Estate
Coldwell Banker & Homart
Office buildings
Residential brokerage
Shopping centers

RANKINGS

20th in *Fortune* 50 Life Insurance Cos.
1st in *Fortune* 50 Retailing Cos.
6th in *Forbes* Sales 500
37th in *Business Week* 1000

COMPETITION

Montgomery Ward
Department stores
Discount and specialty retailers
Diversified financial services companies
Insurance companies
Real estate companies

SECURITY PACIFIC CORPORATION

OVERVIEW

Los Angeles–based Security Pacific, with $84 billion in assets, is the 5th largest banking company in the US (2nd in California after BankAmerica). It also ranked 2nd in earnings in the US in 1989 after BankAmerica, with $741 million.

Security Pacific is the holding company for Security Pacific National Bank (Los Angeles); an interstate banking network (Alaska, Arizona, Nevada, Oregon, and Washington); and nonbanking financial services, such as consumer finance (400 offices nationwide), equipment leasing, and insurance (US, Europe, and the Far East).

Security Pacific's Retail Bank operates 557 branches in California and in 1989 was the first California bank to offer consumers a phone service to open accounts 7 days a week. The corporation's residential real estate mortgage loan services had $4 billion of originations in 1989.

The company's Business Bank serves major businesses in California. Security Pacific's Merchant Bank offers underwriting and trading services to corporate and institutional clients in the major financial and capital markets worldwide.

NYSE symbol: SPC
Incorporated: Delaware, 1971
Fiscal year ends: December 31

WHO

Chairman: Richard J. Flamson III, age 61, $1,514,300 pay
President and CEO: Robert H. Smith, age 54, $1,027,900 pay (prior to promotion)
Chairman of the Executive Committee: George F. Moody, age 59, $1,030,400 pay
VC and COO: John P. Singleton, age 53
VC and CFO: John F. Kooken, age 38
Auditors: KPMG Peat Marwick
Employees: 41,100

WHEN

Security Pacific had its origin with the founding of several banks that later merged. Isaias Hellman and John Downey founded the first, Farmers & Merchants, in 1871. In 1875 Los Angeles entrepreneur Hiram Mabury founded First National Bank of Los Angeles.

In 1889 attorney Joseph Sartori founded Security Savings Bank and Trust Company, which expanded rapidly within the growing Los Angeles area. Two more banks that would later join the Security Pacific system were Security Trust and Savings Bank of San Diego (founded in 1893 as Blochman Banking Company) and Citizens National Trust and Savings Bank of Riverside (1903).

In 1929 Sartori merged Security Trust with Los Angeles-First National to form Security-First National, one of the nation's 10 largest banks, with 142 branches and more than $600 million in assets.

Security merged with Farmers and Merchants (1956), Security Trust and Savings of San Diego (1957), and Citizens Bank of Riverside (1957) to establish the Security First National banking system, extending throughout Southern California and the southern San Joaquin Valley.

In 1968 Security made 3 significant strategic decisions: (1) to offer corporate banking to the Midwest and eastern US; (2) to expand internationally to assist its multinational customers; and (3) to become a statewide bank with expansion in Northern California. That same year the bank merged with Pacific National Bank of San Francisco, the largest one-office bank in the West, to form Security Pacific National Bank, the name in use today. Security Pacific Corporation, a holding company, was formed in 1971. Other banks in Northern California were acquired in the 1970s.

The holding company continued to make significant acquisitions in the 1980s, including Arizona Bancwest (1986), Seattle-based Rainier Bancorporation (1987), Oregon BanCorp (1987), San Francisco-based Hibernia (1988), Nevada National (1989), and Southwest of San Diego (1989).

The company's 1987 earnings dropped to $16 million after reserving $1.3 billion for potential loan losses. Robert Smith, CEO of the bank since 1987, made dramatic changes to improve the bank's competitiveness, including reducing staff by 30%, closing branch offices, centralizing operations, and setting a goal of establishing a sales mentality among branch office personnel. After record profits in 1988 and 1989, Security Pacific experienced problems in 1990 with bad loans in Australia, the UK, and Arizona.

WHERE

HQ: 333 S. Hope St., Los Angeles, CA 90071
Phone: 213-345-4540
FAX: 213-345-5598 (Public Affairs)

Security Pacific operates through 1,500 branches and offices in 45 states and 27 countries.

WHAT

	1989 Net Income	
	$ mil	% of total
Retail Bank	345	47
Business Bank	140	19
Merchant Bank	146	19
Financial Services System	174	23
Interstate Banking Network	(59)	(8)
Other	(5)	—
Total	**741**	**100**

Financial Services
Commercial loans
Consumer finance
Consumer loans
Credit cards
Equipment leasing
Information systems
Insurance
Investment banking
Mortgage loans
Securities processing
Trust and investment management

HOW MUCH

	9 Yr. Growth	1980	1981	1982	1983	1984	1985	1986	1987	1988	1989
Sales ($ mil)	13.9%	3,115	4,217	4,491	4,323	5,249	5,537	5,977	7,618	8,483	10,018
Net income ($ mil)	16.9%	181	206	234	264	291	323	386	16	639	741
Income as % of sales	—	5.8%	4.9%	5.2%	6.1%	5.5%	5.8%	6.5%	0.2%	7.5%	7.4%
Earnings per share ($)	9.6%	2.73	2.94	3.27	3.62	3.96	4.35	4.86	0.01	5.56	6.21
Stock price – high ($)	—	14.32	18.13	18.75	27.69	26.88	32.00	40.25	43.88	41.50	54.88
Stock price – low ($)	—	9.22	14.22	10.21	14.90	19.00	24.88	27.13	20.50	25.38	35.50
Stock price – close ($)	12.3%	14.32	16.98	15.42	25.50	25.75	31.88	34.63	25.38	36.13	40.63
P/E – high	—	5	6	6	8	7	7	8	4,388	7	9
P/E – low	—	3	5	3	4	5	6	6	2,050	5	6
Dividends per share ($)	11.7%	0.81	0.90	0.98	1.09	1.20	1.31	1.45	1.72	1.92	2.20
Book value per share ($)	8.1%	17.61	19.78	22.12	24.19	26.87	29.90	33.25	28.00	31.52	35.50

1989 Year End:
Debt ratio: 63.4%
Return on equity: 18.5%
Cash (mil): $10,562
Assets (mil): $83,943
Long-term debt (mil): $8,045
Number of shares (mil): 116
Dividends:
1989 average yield: 5.4%
1989 payout: 35.4%
Market value (mil): $4,705

Stock Price History high/low 1980-89

RANKINGS

5th in *Fortune* 100 Commercial Banking Cos.
62nd in *Fortune* World's 100 Commercial Banks
73rd in *Forbes* Sales 500
138th in *Business Week* 1000
406th in *Business Week* Global 1000

COMPETITION

H. F. Ahmanson
American Express
Bank of New York
BankAmerica
Bankers Trust
Chase Manhattan
Chemical Banking
Citicorp
First Chicago
First Interstate
Great Western
Manufacturers Hanover
J.P. Morgan
Wells Fargo

SERVICE MERCHANDISE COMPANY, INC.

OVERVIEW

Service Merchandise, based in the Nashville suburb of Brentwood, is the largest catalog store in the US. The company primarily sells hard goods, such as jewelry, cameras, and toys, through a chain of catalog showrooms where customers select merchandise by viewing samples.

Customers can preshop with the company's catalog — which lists products and prices, along with the suggested retail price — or order by mail; however, in recent years Wal-Mart, Target, and discount warehouses have raided the cataloger's market, and customers sometimes use the catalog merely to compare prices between retailers.

Service Merchandise also operates 5 Service Jewelry stores, featuring the company's jewelry and gemstones only. The company imported $211 million worth of gems and other goods in 1989.

Following the 1988 LBO of competitor Best Products, Service Merchandise leveraged itself in order to pay a special dividend and concentrated on expanding its catalog showrooms. Still, the company is dependent on jewelry sales and Christmas buying, and some analysts believe that the catalog showroom form of retailing has lost its competitive advantage.

WHEN

Harry and Mary K. Zimmerman and their son Raymond started Service Merchandise in 1960. Until 1967 they operated one Service Merchandise catalog showroom, located in Nashville, Tennessee. The idea was simple: the Zimmermans displayed samples of merchandise such as jewelry, toys, and appliances (almost no soft goods) on the showroom floor, from which customers made their selection and then ordered, paid, and waited while their merchandise was brought in from the adjoining warehouse. Service Merchandise went public in 1971, operating 5 showrooms in Nashville, Memphis, and Chattanooga by 1972. Raymond Zimmerman became president in 1973.

In 1974 the company acquired the catalog showroom operations of Malone & Hyde, which operated stores in Arkansas, Missouri, and Tennessee. By the end of the 1970s, Service Merchandise was a leader in the increasingly popular catalog showroom shopping business. Harry and Mary K. Zimmerman retired as chairman and secretary in 1980, leaving the operation of the company to Raymond, who began expanding into other formats to complement Service Merchandise's main business. The company opened Toy Store units — large discount stores stocking children's games, toys, and furniture — in Nashville and Louisville (1980) but abandoned the concept within a few years.

Service Merchandise bought Sam Solomon Company, a catalog showroom operator based in Charleston, South Carolina (1982); the Computer Shoppe, a computer retailer (1983); and Florida-based Home Owners Warehouse (1983). The company renamed Home Owners Warehouse Mr. HOW and tried to market it as a do-it-yourself discount home improvement center. The company disposed of the 22 Mr. HOW stores in 1986 after 3 years of poor sales.

Service Merchandise expanded its catalog merchandising business in 1985 with the purchase of Ellman's (Atlanta) and H. J. Wilson (Baton Rouge), catalog retailers that together added 87 stores to the chain. The absorption of these units depressed earnings through 1987. In 1988 the company's largest catalog competitor, Best Products, was bought by New York investment firm Adler and Shaykin. In order to discourage any potential takeovers, Service Merchandise took on close to $1 billion of debt in 1989, using part of the borrowed funds to pay stockholders a special dividend of $10 per share.

HOW MUCH

	9 Yr. Growth	1980	1981	1982	1983	1984	1985	1986	1987	1988	1989
Sales ($ mil)	16.1%	865	1,027	1,195	1,458	1,657	2,526	2,527	2,719	3,093	3,307
Net income ($ mil)	15.0%	20	23	32	45	45	11	(17)	25	76	72
Income as % of sales	—	2.4%	2.2%	2.6%	3.1%	2.7%	0.4%	(0.7%)	0.9%	2.5%	2.2%
Earnings per share ($)	11.1%	0.54	0.61	0.77	0.92	0.91	0.21	(0.34)	0.50	1.50	1.38
Stock price – high ($)	—	5.67	4.88	9.42	18.00	11.08	10.92	10.08	6.33	12.50	22.38
Stock price – low ($)	—	2.50	3.46	3.17	8.75	7.08	7.33	4.92	2.00	2.33	7.63
Stock price – close ($)	11.6%	3.50	3.92	9.33	10.75	7.92	8.25	5.17	2.33	11.92	9.38
P/E – high	—	11	8	12	20	12	51	—	13	8	16
P/E – low	—	5	6	4	10	8	34	—	4	2	6
Dividends per share ($)	81.6%	0.05	0.05	0.05	0.05	0.05	0.05	0.05	0.05	0.05	10.03
Book value per share ($)	—	3.18	3.74	4.72	5.58	6.42	6.57	5.57	6.14	7.62	(0.80)

1989 Year End:
Debt ratio: 104.7%
Return on equity: 40.5%
Cash (mil): $198
Current ratio: 1.39
Long-term debt (mil): $930
Number of shares (mil): 52
Dividends:
1989 average yield: 107.0%
1989 payout: 726.8%
Market value (mil): $491

Stock Price History high/low 1980-89

NYSE symbol: SME
Incorporated: Tennessee, 1970
Fiscal year end: Saturday nearest December 31

WHO

Chairman, President, and CEO: Raymond Zimmerman, age 57, $780,278 pay
VP and CFO: S. P. Braud, III, age 59, $364,824 pay
VP and General Counsel: Glen A. Bodzy, age 37
Auditors: Deloitte & Touche
Employees: 20,184

WHERE

HQ: 2968 Foster Creighton Dr., Nashville, TN 37204
Phone: 615-251-6666
FAX: 615-251-6329

Service Merchandise operates 334 catalog stores in 37 states throughout the East, Midwest, South, and Southwest. It also operates Service Jewelry stores in Nashville, Dallas, and Ft. Worth.

	1989 Store Locations	
	no. of locations	% of total
Alabama	8	2
Arkansas	4	1
California	12	4
Colorado	8	2
Connecticut	4	1
Florida	39	12
Georgia	16	5
Illinois	23	7
Indiana	15	5
Kansas	4	1
Kentucky	8	2
Louisiana	14	4
Maine	6	2
Massachusetts	10	3
Michigan	10	3
Mississippi	6	2
Missouri	7	2
New Hampshire	5	1
New Jersey	4	1
New York	20	6
North Carolina	5	1
Ohio	12	4
Oklahoma	8	2
Pennsylvania	9	3
South Carolina	6	2
Tennessee	18	5
Texas	34	10
Virginia	4	2
Other states	15	5
Total	**334**	**100**

WHAT

Retail catalog showrooms
Service Jewelry stores

RANKINGS

32nd in *Fortune* 50 Retailing Cos.
252nd in *Forbes* Sales 500
974th in *Business Week* 1000

COMPETITION

Ames
Costco
Dayton Hudson
K mart
Montgomery Ward
Price Co.
Sears
Wal-Mart
Department & specialty stores

THE SHERWIN-WILLIAMS COMPANY

OVERVIEW

Sherwin-Williams is the world's largest manufacturer (and a leading distributor) of paint and varnishes. The company makes coatings for consumer, automotive, industrial, and architectural markets under a variety of brand names, including Sherwin-Williams, Dutch Boy, Kem-Tone, and Krylon. Sherwin-Williams also manufactures application materials.

Sherwin-Williams brand products are exclusively marketed through more than 1,900 Sherwin-Williams stores. The stores also offer other home decorating materials. Over 70% of the stores' sales is wholesale business; the remainder is direct to consumers.

The company distributes its other brands through various dealers, including Sears, Wal-Mart, Home Depot, and many regionally based retailers. Sherwin-Williams also manufactures paint for sale under private labels (*i.e.,* K mart brand paint).

Sherwin-Williams plans to open 48 new stores (net of closings) in 1990 and to complete the installation of a point-of-sale system in all stores. The company also plans to expand sales in the Chemical Coatings Division.

WHEN

In 1870 Henry Sherwin bought out paint materials distributor Truman Dunham and joined with Edward Williams and A. T. Osborn to form Sherwin-Williams & Company, located in Cleveland, to manufacture and sell paint. Sherwin improved the paint-grinding mill and introduced a line of liquid paints in 1876. In 1877 Sherwin obtained a patent on a reclosable can and, in 1880, he introduced an improved liquid paint, which made Sherwin-Williams the industry leader.

In 1874 Sherwin-Williams introduced a special paint for carriages, beginning the concept of specific-purpose paint. By 1900 the company had paints for floors, roofs, barns, metal bridges, railroad cars, and automobiles. In 1891 the company established a dealership in Massachusetts, forerunner of the company-operated retail stores, now numbering nearly 1,900. In 1895 Sherwin Williams obtained its "Cover the Earth" trademark.

Before the Great Depression, Sherwin-Williams acquired a number of smaller paint manufacturers: Detroit White Lead (1910), Martin-Senour (1917), Acme White Lead & Color (1920), and The Lowe Brothers (1929). Responding to wartime government restrictions, Sherwin-Williams developed a new type of paint, fast drying and water reducible, called Kem-Tone, and a new paint applicator, the Roller-Koater, forerunner of the paint roller.

Company sales doubled during the 1960s as the company made several acquisitions, including a chemical company and Sprayon (aerosol paint, 1966), but earnings remained flat due to rising expenses. In 1972 the company expanded its stores to include carpeting, draperies, wallpaper, and other interior decorating items. But long-term debt ballooned from $80 million in 1974 to $196 million by 1977, when the company lost $8.2 million, causing a suspension of dividends for the first time since 1885.

Present CEO John Breen joined Sherwin-Williams in 1979, reinstated the dividend, purged over 1/2 of the top 100 management positions, and closed inefficient plants. Breen concentrated company stores' products on paint and wallpaper and purchased Dutch Boy (1980). Company stores' sales have increased from 46% of 1980 sales to 63% of 1989 sales.

In 1983 Sherwin-Williams sold its container business to a group of private investors and in 1985 sold most of the chemical business to PMC Specialties Group. Company sales almost doubled and earnings more than quadrupled from 1980 to 1989.

During 1990 Sherwin-Williams began selling Dutch Boy in all Sears stores and Kem-Tone in 400 Wal-Mart stores and acquired the Krylon aerosol business from Borden.

HOW MUCH

	9 Yr. Growth	1980	1981	1982	1983	1984	1985	1986	1987	1988	1989
Sales ($ mil)	5.9%	1,264	1,537	1,852	1,973	2,075	2,195	1,553	1,793	1,950	2,123
Net income ($ mil)	17.8%	25	31	43	55	65	75	96	94	101	109
Income as % of sales	—	2.0%	2.0%	2.3%	2.8%	3.1%	3.4%	6.2%	5.2%	5.2%	5.1%
Earnings per share ($)	18.9%	0.53	0.68	0.89	1.13	1.40	1.60	2.09	2.09	2.30	2.52
Stock price – high ($)	—	5.05	5.94	12.47	15.88	16.19	23.50	32.25	38.50	31.63	35.75
Stock price – low ($)	—	2.91	4.03	4.53	9.13	11.13	13.94	21.31	20.13	24.00	25.00
Stock price – close ($)	25.5%	4.44	5.50	11.00	13.13	14.00	22.13	27.63	24.38	25.38	34.38
P/E – high	—	10	9	14	14	12	15	15	18	14	14
P/E – low	—	5	6	5	8	8	9	10	10	10	10
Dividends per share ($)	18.7%	0.15	0.20	0.25	0.30	0.38	0.46	0.50	0.56	0.64	0.70
Book value per share ($)	9.1%	7.08	7.51	7.82	8.13	8.97	10.10	11.15	12.57	13.97	15.48

1989 Year End:
Debt ratio: 13.6%
Return on equity: 17.1%
Cash (mil): $202
Current ratio: 1.95
Long-term debt (mil): $105
Number of shares (mil): 43
Dividends:
1989 average yield: 2.0%
1989 payout: 27.8%
Market value (mil): $1,483

Stock Price History high/low 1980-89

40
35
30
25
20
15
10
5
0

NYSE symbol: SHW
Incorporated: Ohio, 1884
Fiscal year ends: December 31

WHO

Chairman and CEO: John G. Breen, age 55, $982,643 pay
President and COO: Thomas A. Commes, age 47, $581,216 pay
SVP Finance and CFO: Thomas R. Miklich, age 42, $348,717 pay
VP Human Resources: Thomas Kroeger, age 41
Auditors: Ernst & Young
Employees: 16,726

WHERE

HQ: 101 Prospect Ave. NW, Cleveland, OH 44115
Phone: 216-566-2000
FAX: 216-566-3310

Sherwin-Williams operates plants in 11 states and in Brazil, Canada, Ireland, Jamaica, Mexico, Panama, Saudi Arabia, and Trinidad. The company operates 1,896 Sherwin-Williams paint stores in 48 states.

	1989 Stores	
	no.	% of total
Midwest	507	27
Southeast	465	24
East	370	20
South-central	369	19
West	185	10
Total	**1,896**	**100**

	1989 Pretax Income	
	$ mil	% of total
US	159	94
Foreign	11	6
Total	**170**	**100**

WHAT

	1989 Sales		1989 Operating Income	
	$ mil	% of total	$ mil	% of total
Paint stores	1,346	63	91	44
Coatings	764	36	120	57
Real estate	13	1	(3)	(1)
Adjustments	—	—	(45)	—
Total	**2,123**	**100**	**163**	**100**

Brand Names

Paints & Coatings
Acme
Dupli-Color
Dutch Boy
Glas-Clad
Kem-Tone
Krylon
Martin-Senour
Perma-Clad
ProMar 200
Rogers
Sherwin-Williams
Sprayon
SuperPaint
Western Automotive Paint

Paint Brushes & Applicators
Rubberset
Sherwin-Williams

RANKINGS

203rd in *Fortune* 500 Industrial Cos.
380th in *Forbes* Sales 500
396th in *Business Week* 1000

COMPETITION

BASF
Du Pont
Hoechst
Home Depot
Lowe's
PPG
USG

SIEMENS AG

OVERVIEW

Munich-based Siemens is a European leader in electronics and electrical engineering. Businesses include communications, factory automation, power generation, medical electronics, auto electronics, semiconductors, and lighting products. Siemens owns Rolm, 50% of Bosch-Siemens Hausgeräte, and 6.8% of Fuji Electric. Despite spending heavily on R&D (11.2% of sales) and acquisitions, Siemens retains over $12 billion in cash and securities.

Siemens views semiconductor technology as critical to its future and is investing heavily to catch up with chip-making competitors. In 1990 Siemens announced joint development of 64-megabyte DRAM with IBM. Deregulation of the West German telephone equipment market is expected to end Siemens's near-monopoly status as the government's supplier in 1991.

WHEN

In 1847 Werner von Siemens, an electrical engineer, teamed with a craftsman, Johann Halske, to make telegraphs as Siemens & Halske in Germany. Although Halske left the firm 20 years later, the company name was not shortened to Siemens until 1966. The firm's first major project linked Berlin and Frankfurt with the first long-distance telegraph system in Europe (1848). Siemens continued to string telegraph wires across Europe and in 1870 completed the 6,600-mile India Line running from London to Calcutta. The company manufactured the first transatlantic cable that connected Ireland to the US in 1874.

Siemens built Europe's first electric power transmission system (1876), the world's first electrified railway (1879), and one of the first elevators (1880). As a result of Werner von Siemens's discussions with Thomas Edison (1881), the company received a license to manufacture incandescent lights. Disagreement between the 2 inventors contributed to the different electrical voltage standards employed by North America (110 volts) and Europe (220 volts). In 1896 the company patented the world's first X-ray tube and completed the first European subway in Budapest.

On the eve of WWI, Siemens was doing business in 49 countries and had 80,000 employees. Despite heavy losses in the war, the company rebounded and in 1919 formed OSRAM, a German light bulb cartel with AEG and Auer. In 1923 Siemens entered into a venture with Furukawa Electric called Fuji Electric, in which it still retains a 7% interest. Innovation continued to foster growth as Siemens developed radios and traffic lights in the 1920s, and in 1939 began production of electron microscopes.

Siemens suffered devastating losses in WWII and was stripped of its patent rights following the war. The company staged a quick recovery, developing silicates for semiconductors, data processing equipment, and the world's first implantable pacemaker in the 1950s. Siemens formed joint ventures with Bosch (Bosch-Siemens Hausgeräte, appliances, 1967) and AEG (Kraftwerk Union, nuclear power, 1969), among others. The company profited greatly from Germany's protectionist telecommunications policies, but its computer ventures with RCA and Philips in the 1960s and 1970s were disappointing.

In 1981 Karlheinz Kaske became the company's first CEO from outside the Siemens family. Under his direction Siemens entered into collaborative ventures with Philips (DRAM), Intel (computers), and Advanced Micro Devices (telecommunication chips) to gain access to advanced technologies. Siemens bought Bendix Electronics (US, 1988) and bolstered its telecommunications businesses by acquiring Rolm (PBXs, US, 1989) and the telecommunications business of Plessey (UK, 1989). In 1990 Siemens purchased ailing German computer maker Nixdorf.

HOW MUCH

$= DM1.69 (Dec. 31, 1989)	9 Yr. Growth	1980	1981	1982	1983	1984	1985	1986	1987	1988	1989
Sales (DM mil)	7.5%	31,960	34,561	40,106	39,471	45,819	54,616	47,023	51,431	59,374	61,128
Net income (DM mil)	10.7%	592	449	662	743	1,049	1,502	1,455	1,217	1,317	1,473
Income as % of sales	—	1.9%	1.3%	1.7%	1.9%	2.3%	2.8%	3.1%	2.4%	2.2%	4.7%
Earnings per share (DM)*	8.0%	15	11	17	17	24	32	31	25	27	30
Stock price - high (DM)	—	301	297	288	352	385	935	920	790	569	843
Stock price - low (DM)	—	227	251	245	259	302	384	724	387	357	502
Stock price - close (DM)	13.0%	280	263	274	349	383	925	822	388	563	843
P/E - high	—	20	27	17	21	16	29	30	32	21	28
P/E - low	—	12	23	14	15	13	12	23	15	13	17
Dividends per share (DM)**	3.6%	8	8	8	8	8	10	12	12	11	11
Book value per share (DM)	5.6%	219	221	241	244	263	280	317	324	344	358

1989 Year End:
Debt ratio: 9.0%
Return on equity: 8.5%
Cash (mil): DM21,240
Long-term debt (mil): DM1,743
Number of shares (mil): 49
Dividends:
1989 average yield: 0.2%
1989 payout: 36.7%
Market value (mil): $24,442
Sales (mil): $36,170

*not fully diluted **not including rights offering

Principal stock exchange: Frankfurt
Incorporated: 1897
Fiscal year ends: September 30

WHO

Chairman: Heribald Närger
President and CEO: Karlheinz Kaske
Corporate Finance: Karl-Hermann Baumann
Auditors: KPMG Deutsche Treuhand-Gesellschaft AG
Employees: 365,000

WHERE

HQ: Siemens AG Wittelsbacherplatz 2, D-8000 Munich 2, Germany
Phone: 011-49-89-2340
FAX: 011-49-89-234-4242
US HQ (Siemens Corp.): 1301 Ave. of the Americas, New York, NY 10019
US Phone: 212-258-4000
US FAX: 212-258-4370 (Corporate Communications)

Siemens operates in more than 120 countries.

	1989 Sales	
	DM mil	% of total
Germany	43,945	60
Other Europe	17,630	24
North America	7,345	10
Other countries	4,423	6
Adjustments	(12,215)	—
Total	**61,128**	**100**

WHAT

	1989 Sales	
	DM mil	% of total
Energy & Automation	14,147	22
Telecommunications & Security	10,951	17
Communication & Information	10,867	17
Power Generation	9,323	14
Medical Engineering	6,185	10
Electrical & Automotive	5,666	9
Semiconductors	2,257	3
Other products & services	5,608	8
Adjustments	(3,876)	—
Total	**61,128**	**100**

Major Product Areas & Subsidiaries
Appliances (Bosch-Siemens Hausgeräte, 50%)
Automotive electronics
Electrical motors and automation
Electronic components and semiconductors
Fiber optics (Siecor, 50% with Corning)
Imaging (Rudolf Hell)
Information processing (Nixdorf)
Lighting (OSRAM, 50%)
Medical instrumentation
Nuclear and non-nuclear power (KWU)
Power transmission
Telecommunications (Rolm, Tel Plus)

RANKINGS

22nd in *Fortune* Global 500 Industrial Cos.
37th in *Forbes* 100 Foreign Investments in the US
46th in *Business Week* Global 1000

COMPETITION

Amdahl
AT&T
Asea Brown Boveri
Bayer
BCE
Cooper Industries
Corning
Fujitsu
General Electric
Matsushita
NEC
Philips
Samsung

Other telecommunications, electronics, computer, and power products companies

SKIDMORE, OWINGS & MERRILL

OVERVIEW

Skidmore, Owings & Merrill (SOM) is the world's largest architectural/engineering firm. Its early development of a coherent body of work, emphasizing a functional, modernistic look, has made it perhaps the most pervasive influence on US commercial and public architecture in the latter 1/2 of the 20th century.

The firm has designed buildings in more than 40 countries and has won more than 500 awards for excellence. In addition to the office buildings and other corporate structures for which it is so well known, SOM has designed campuses, museums, airports, hospitals, religious structures, railway stations, hotels, retail centers, residential facilities, and even cities.

Each of SOM's 6 main offices functions independently but is able to draw on the collective resources of the firm through its computer-aided design facility, which functions as the nervous system of the firm.

SOM has, more than other modern architectural firms, allowed its architects (*e.g.*, recently deceased Gordon Bunshaft) to receive individual recognition for their work.

WHEN

In 1929, while attending school and working in Paris, Louis Skidmore met and, upon his return to the US in 1930, married Eloise Owings. In Paris Skidmore had become acquainted with 2 architects involved in planning the 1933-1934 Century of Progress Exposition in Chicago and arranged to be appointed chief designer for it. He asked his brother-in-law Nathaniel Owings to assist him with the work on the Exposition, thus beginning their professional association.

After the close of the Exposition in 1934, Skidmore and Owings pursued separate paths, only to come together again in 1936 to found a small design firm in Chicago bearing their names. Trading on corporate relationships developed at the Exposition, the firm soon had enough work for 3 draftsmen.

The following year Skidmore decided to open a New York office to serve one of its corporate clients, American Radiator Company. The New York presence and their previous experience at the 1933-1934 Exposition made Skidmore & Owings a logical choice to participate in the design of the New York World's Fair of 1939-1940. Gordon Bunshaft, who was to stay with the firm for 42 years and become its most famous and one of its most influential architects, joined the company in 1937. By 1939, when architectural engineer John Merrill joined the firm, it had already developed a reputation for clean, functional design for large corporate and institutional clients.

In 1940 the firm won the contract that would bring it to national prominence when it was selected to design the defense community of Oak Ridge, Tennessee, home of part of the Manhattan (atomic bomb) project.

During the period following WWII the firm enjoyed tremendous growth as it was selected to design a number of large institutional and corporate facilities, including Mount Zion Hospital in San Francisco, Fort Hamilton VA Hospital in Brooklyn, Lever House in New York City, and the H. J. Heinz vinegar plant in Pittsburgh, among others. In 1950 the SOM modernistic look had become so distinctive that it was the first architectural firm to be granted an exhibition at the New York Museum of Modern Art.

By 1958 SOM had grown to 14 partners and 1,000 employees working at 4 offices (San Francisco opened in 1946 and Portland, Oregon, in 1952). The 1960s saw more corporate (*e.g.*, IBM headquarters in Armonk, New York) and institutional (*e.g.*, University of Illinois at Chicago Circle campus) commissions, and in 1962 SOM received the American Institute of Architects' first firm award for architectural excellence.

In the 1970s the firm's influence was felt most profoundly in Chicago, where it designed the John Hancock building, the Sears Tower (the world's tallest building), Northwestern University's library, and Baxter Travenol's headquarters.

Beginning in the 1970s and continuing into the 1980s, the firm began to obtain more and more commissions outside the US. By the mid-1980s it had 47 partners and 1,400 other employees in 9 offices. In 1986 it opened its first foreign office in London. During the 1980s the firm's design approach became less monolithic, and individual designers were encouraged to express a more diverse range of styles.

Current major projects include Canary Wharf in London and Cityfront Center in Chicago.

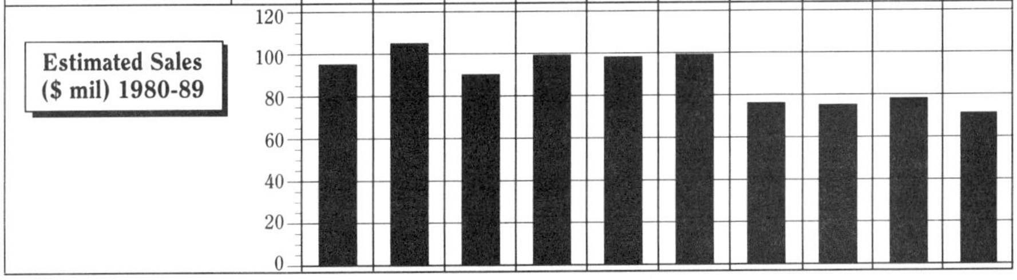

Private company
Founded: Chicago, 1936
Fiscal year ends: September 30

WHO

Managing Partner: Thomas J. Eyerman
Auditors: Arthur Andersen & Co.
Employees: 1,600

WHERE

HQ: 33 W. Monroe, Chicago, IL 60603
Phone: 312-641-5959
FAX: 312-332-5632

SOM has handled projects in the US and in more than 40 other countries.

	Staff	
Office Locations	no.	% of total
Chicago	616	38
London	301	19
Los Angeles	58	4
New York	300	19
San Francisco	220	14
Washington, DC	71	4
Other	34	2
Total	**1,600**	**100**

Sources of Revenue	
Illinois	20%
Other US	65%
Foreign	15%
Total	**100%**

WHAT

Types of Projects	
Commercial	45%
Housing	15%
Industrial	10%
Planning	10%
Educational	5%
Medical	5%
Other	10%
Total	**100%**

Functional Disciplines

Architecture
Building services engineering
Civil engineering
Environmental analysis
Equipment planning
Landscape architecture
Site planning
Space planning
Structural engineering
Urban estimating

Notable Projects

Bank of America (San Francisco, 1971)
Chase Manhattan Bank (New York, 1961)
Exchange House (London, 1990)
Haj Terminal at international airport (Jeddah, Saudi Arabia, 1982)
Hirshhorn Museum and Sculpture Garden (Washington, DC, 1974)
John Hancock building (Chicago, 1970)
LBJ Library (University of Texas, Austin)
Lever House (New York, 1952)
Library at Northwestern University (Evanston, IL, 1971)
Lincoln Center for the Performing Arts—Library-Museum (New York)
McCormick Place addition (Chicago)
New York City Building—1939 World's Fair
Oak Ridge, TN (1942-1946)
Sears Roebuck Tower (Chicago, 1974)
University of Illinois at Chicago Circle (1965)
US Air Force Academy (Colorado Springs, CO, 1962)
USG Building (Chicago)
Weyerhaeuser Headquarters (Tacoma, 1971)

HOW MUCH

	9 Yr. Growth	1980	1981	1982	1983	1984	1985	1986	1987	1988	1989
Estimated sales ($ mil)	(3.2%)	95	105	90	99	98	99	76	75	78	71

Estimated Sales ($ mil) 1980-89

SMITHKLINE BEECHAM PLC

OVERVIEW

The product of a 1989 merger between Beecham and SmithKline Beckman, UK-based SmithKline Beecham is a major health care company, selling goods and services in 130 countries. Ranking 5th in the world in pharmaceutical sales, SmithKline Beecham sells such products as Tagamet, an antiulcer drug with sales over $1 billion. Over-the-counter drugs and consumer products known in the US include Contac, Tums, Geritol, Sucrets, and Aquafresh. The company spent about 9% of 1989 sales on R&D.

The merger created one of the world's largest pharmaceutical sales forces. To keep its salesmen busy, SmithKline Beecham wants to gain approval for 2 of its drugs annually, a very aggressive rate by industry standards, and plans to increase penetration of Asian markets.

NYSE symbol: SBH (ADR)
Incorporated: England, 1989
Fiscal year ends: December 31

WHO

Chairman: Henry Wendt, age 56, £1,164,000 pay
CEO: Robert P. Bauman, age 58
Group Finance Director: Hugh R. Collum, age 49
Auditors: Price Waterhouse; Coopers & Lybrand Deloitte
Employees: 55,000

WHEN

Thomas Beecham established an apothecary in England in 1847 and began newspaper advertising for Beecham's Pills, a laxative, in 1859. He believed in the efficacy of advertising. At one point in the late 1800s, 14,000 newspapers carried advertisements for Beecham's Pills. Sales soared in the UK and the US, where pill production had begun in 1888, and the company's pill output surpassed one million per day in the early 1900s.

In 1924 after the death of Thomas's son Joseph, land developer Philip Hill purchased the Beecham estate and, with it, the pill business. He registered the enterprise as Beecham's Pills Ltd. in 1928 and began acquiring other consumer product lines including Macleans (toothpaste, US, 1938), Eno Fruit Salt (laxatives, UK, 1938), and Brylcreem (men's hair care, UK, 1939).

Beecham's 1940s and 1950s investment in pharmaceutical R&D paid off in 1959, when the company introduced the world's first partly synthetic penicillin, and in 1961, with the development of the first broad-spectrum antibiotic. Beecham's Amoxil became the most widely prescribed antibiotic in the US, and a derivative (Augmentin, 1985) is building on the success.

Beecham sought consumer goods companies with strong positions in markets outside the UK and acquired a diverse group of firms, including Margarete Astor (cosmetics, West Germany, 1967), Massengill (drugs, personal products, US, 1971), Calgon consumer products (bath products, US, 1977), Jovan (fragrances, US, 1979), Bovril (foods, UK, 1980), J.B. Williams (Aqua Velva, Sominex, Geritol, US, 1982), Germaine Monteil (Yardley, cosmetics, UK, 1984), and Norcliff Thayer (Tums, medications, US, 1985).

After years of lackluster earnings, Beecham changed strategy and CEOs in 1986, selling several of its smaller businesses and assigning American Robert Bauman the task of restructuring the company. Bauman sold Germaine Monteil, Yardley, and Bovril, among others, between 1987 and 1990. His most important move was merging Beecham with troubled SmithKline Beckman.

Starting in 1830 as a small Philadelphia apothecary, SmithKline became a major pharmaceutical company, developing the Benzedrine Inhaler (1936), Dexedrine (1944), and Tagamet (1976) and marketing Thorazine (1954) in the US. SmithKline's Contac cold medicine was a hit, but Tagamet, an antiulcer drug, transformed the company, becoming the world's best-selling drug in 1981. Led by CEO Henry Wendt since 1976, SmithKline diversified and invested heavily in R&D. Poor diversification results, low R&D productivity, and underestimation of Glaxo's Zantac, a Tagamet competitor, reversed the company's fortunes. With Zantac outselling Tagamet 2 to one, earnings in retreat, and few new products in the pipeline, SmithKline agreed to merge with Beecham in 1989.

WHERE

HQ: SB House, Great West Rd., Brentford, Middlesex TW8 9BD, England
Phone: 011-44-81-560-5151
FAX: 011-44-81-847-0830
US HQ: One Franklin Plaza, Philadelphia, PA 19101
US Phone: 215-751-4000
US FAX: 215-751-7655

SmithKline Beecham sells its products in more than 130 countries.

	1989 Sales		1989 Operating Income	
	£ mil	% of total	£ mil	% of total
UK	878	17	100	12
Europe	2,007	31	352	34
US	1,598	38	274	43
Other countries	757	14	92	11
Adjustments	(344)	—	—	—
Total	**4,897**	**100**	**818**	**100**

WHAT

	1989 Sales		1989 Operating Income	
	£ mil	% of total	£ mil	% of total
Pharmaceuticals	2,238	46	458	56
Consumer brands	1,216	25	185	23
Discontinued operns.	621	12	80	10
Animal health	337	7	50	6
Clinical laboratories	485	10	45	5
Total	**4,897**	**100**	**818**	**100**

Brand Names (US Markets)

Prescription Drugs
Amoxil (antibiotic)
Compazine (nausea drug)
Dyazide (blood pressure drug)
Eminase (blood clot dissolver)
Ornade (cold treatment)
Stelazine (antidepressant)
Tagamet (ulcer drug)
Thorazine (anxiety drug)

Consumer Products
Aquafresh
Brylcreem
Contac
Geritol
Massengill
Oxy (acne treatment)
Sominex
Sucrets
Tums

HOW MUCH

£=$1.61 (Dec. 31, 1989)	9 Yr. Growth	1980	1981	1982	1983	1984	1985	1986	1987	1988	1989*
Sales (£ mil)	—	1,028	1,195	1,407	1,702	1,944	2,289	2,603	2,730	2,480	4,897
Net income (£ mil)	—	81	88	120	152	162	167	174	200	239	476
Income as % of sales	—	7.9%	7.4%	8.5%	8.9%	8.3%	7.3%	6.7%	7.3%	9.6%	9.7%
Earnings per share (p)	—	14	15	21	26	26	26	26	31	36	37
Stock price – high (p)	—	204	263	461	468	444	444	505	671	566	631
Stock price – low (p)	—	123	181	244	342	324	322	364	393	501	495
Stock price – close (p)	12.9%	204	250	387	347	442	411	504	501	529	609
P/E – high	—	15	18	22	18	17	117	19	22	16	17
P/E – low	—	8	12	12	13	12	12	14	13	14	13
Dividends per share (p)**	—	7.0	7.6	9.1	10.4	11.6	12.9	13.7	14.8	16.3	204.4

1989 Year End:
Debt ratio: —
Return on equity: —
Cash (mil): £233
Current ratio: 0.87
Long-term debt (mil): £1,487
Sales (mil): $7,884

Stock Price History high/low 1980-89
700 600 500 400 300 200 100 0

Note: All 1980 through 1988 data is for Beecham only. *fiscal year change **includes 1989 distribution of Smithkline Beecham preferred stock at nominal value

RANKINGS

157th in *Fortune* Global 500 Industrial Cos.
39th in *Forbes* 100 Foreign Investments in the US
121st in *Business Week* Global 1000

COMPETITION

Abbott Labs
American Cyanamid
American Home Products
Bayer
Bristol-Myers Squibb
Colgate-Palmolive
Eli Lilly
Genentech
Glaxo
Hoechst
Johnson & Johnson
Merck
Monsanto
Pfizer
Procter & Gamble
Rhône-Poulenc
Roche Holding
Schering-Plough
Unilever
Upjohn
Warner-Lambert

SNAP-ON TOOLS CORPORATION

OVERVIEW

Based in Kenosha, Wisconsin, Snap-on Tools Corporation makes and distributes quality tools and equipment to 5,133 independent dealers in the US and abroad. Dealers, who are given established territories, sell the company's products out of van-type vehicles directly to mechanics at their shops. The dealers are given financial assistance and are supported by a network of branch offices, repair facilities, and distribution centers.

Snap-on's products are divided into 2 groups: hand tools and other equipment. Hand tools (which accounted for 77% of sales in 1989) include such things as wrenches, hammers, screwdrivers, chisels, automotive tools, aircraft tools, and drills. Other equipment (23% of sales) includes tool chests, roll cabinets, and automotive diagnostic equipment. The company's tools are used primarily for automotive service, manufacturing, repair, and maintenance.

Snap-on is constantly developing new tools to augment its 12,000-item product line. In 1989 the company spent over $15 million on new product research and development.

NYSE symbol: SNA
Incorporated: Delaware, 1930
Fiscal year ends: Saturday nearest December 31

WHO

Chairman, President, and CEO: Marion F. Gregory, age 56, $548,123 pay
SVP Administration: Harry W. Fry, age 58, $260,496 pay
SVP Sales: Daniel J. Riordan, age 46, $277,324 pay
SVP Manufacturing and Research and Engineering: Jay H. Schnabel, age 47
SVP Finance: Michael F. Montemurro, age 41
Auditors: Arthur Andersen & Co.
Employees: 7,400

WHEN

Joe Johnson's boss at American Grinder Manufacturing rejected Joe's idea of interchangeable wrench handles and sockets in 1919, and Snap-on Tools was born. Joe and coworker William Seidemann did not have the money to support his idea, but they made a sample set of 5 handles and 10 sockets, and 2 Wisconsin salesmen sold over 500 orders. Snap-on Wrench Company was incorporated in 1920.

Stanton Palmer and Newton Tarble, both salesmen, developed a distribution business demonstrating tool sets at customer sites, forming Motor Tool Specialty Company in 1920. The next year Palmer and Tarble bought out Johnson's original financial supporters, became partners, and elected Palmer president.

Snap-on's first catalog was published in 1923 with almost 50 items. In 1925 Snap-on had salesmen working out of 17 branches; by 1929 it had about 300 salesmen and 26 branches.

In 1930 the company reincorporated as Snap-on Tools, Inc., adopting its present name in 1937. In 1931 Palmer died, and Snap-on opened its first foreign subsidiary in Canada. Strapped from impending expansion and the Great Depression, Snap-on went to Forged Steel Products for help. Forged Steel rescued Snap-on, and William Myers, its owner, became the new president of the company. Sales grew as Snap-on extended credit to Depression-battered mechanics. Myers died in 1939, leaving Johnson as president.

By 1940 Snap-on had 556 salesmen and was making hand tools for military use. Due to tool shortages in the civilian arena during WWII, salesmen began carrying excess stock in their trucks and station wagons, and by 1945 walk-in vans loaded with tools were commonplace. Salesmen retailing to mechanics became independent dealers with their own regions.

In 1952 Snap-on opened a Mexican subsidiary. Seidemann retired in 1954 and 5 years later Johnson became chairman. In the 1960s Snap-on began buying branch outlets to give the company complete command over distribution and marketing. In 1965 Snap-on opened a branch in the UK and patented its Flank Drive wrench (which had superior gripping ability over its predecessors).

R&D during the 1960s produced pneumatic, hydraulic, and electric tools. A branch opened in West Germany (1977) and Snap-on was listed on the NYSE (1978).

By 1985 Snap-on had 4,000 dealers and salesmen. During the 1980s, Snap-on became a supplier of tools to NASA for the space shuttles and fought 35 lawsuits from 115 former dealers alleging that Snap-on had misrepresented their potential earnings.

WHERE

HQ: 2801 80th St., Kenosha, WI 53141
Phone: 414-656-5200
FAX: 414-656-5123

Snap-on has 10 manufacturing locations in the US and 2 in Canada, as well as 5 distribution centers in the US and one in Canada. The company sells in Australia, Belgium, Canada, France, Germany, Japan, Mexico, the Netherlands, the UK, and the US.

	1989 Sales		1989 Operating Income	
	$ mil	% of total	$ mil	% of total
US	751	84	146	86
Foreign	140	16	23	14
Adjustments	47	—	(2)	—
Total	**938**	**100**	**167**	**100**

WHAT

1989 Sales by Source	% of total
Dealers & distributors	80
Specialized industrial representatives	17
Foreign sales corporation	3
Total	**100**

1989 Sales of Products by Type	% of total
Hand tools	77
Equipment, cabinets & chests	23
Total	**100**

Hand Tools
Aircraft tools
Auto body tools
Chisels
Hammers
Pliers
Pneumatic impact wrenches
Power-assisted drills
Punches
Screwdrivers
Sockets
Wheel-balancing and -aligning equipment
Wrenches

Other Products
Electronic automotive diagnostic equipment
Roll cabinets
Tool chests

US Subsidiaries
ATI Industries, Inc.
American Assembly Tools, Inc.

HOW MUCH

	9 Yr. Growth	1980	1981	1982	1983	1984	1985	1986	1987	1988	1989
Sales ($ mil)	9.4%	416	457	450	477	566	623	696	785	893	938
Net income ($ mil)	11.8%	38	40	37	43	60	60	66	89	113	105
Income as % of sales	—	9.2%	8.8%	8.3%	9.0%	10.5%	9.6%	9.4%	11.3%	12.7%	11.2%
Earnings per share ($)	11.5%	0.96	0.99	0.92	1.06	1.47	1.46	1.59	2.13	2.72	2.55
Stock price – high ($)	—	14.38	15.13	14.75	17.13	18.75	21.19	32.13	46.50	44.88	41.88
Stock price – low ($)	—	9.25	9.00	8.25	12.25	13.50	16.00	20.38	24.25	32.63	28.88
Stock price – close ($)	14.1%	9.94	10.56	13.50	15.38	17.38	20.94	25.63	34.75	35.00	32.50
P/E – high	—	15	15	16	16	13	15	20	22	17	16
P/E – low	—	10	9	9	12	9	11	13	11	12	11
Dividends per share ($)	10.7%	0.42	0.42	0.42	0.43	0.47	0.58	0.61	0.70	0.88	1.04
Book value per share ($)	12.7%	4.76	5.28	5.75	6.38	7.33	8.24	9.28	10.97	12.35	13.93

1989 Year End:
Debt ratio: 1.3%
Return on equity: 19.4%
Cash (mil): $5
Current ratio: 3.15
Long-term debt (mil): $8
Number of shares (mil): 41
Dividends:
1989 average yield: 3.2%
1989 payout: 40.8%
Market value (mil): $1,336

Stock Price History high/low 1980-89

RANKINGS

363rd in *Fortune* 500 Industrial Cos.
432nd in *Business Week* 1000

COMPETITION

Black & Decker
Cooper Industries
Emerson
Stanley Works
Textron

SONY CORPORATION

OVERVIEW

The name Sony is derived from *sonus*, the Latin word for sound, symbolic of the company's early successes and Chairman Akio Morita's affinity for music. Sony is a world leader in consumer electronics, video technology, recordings, and films. The company generates 66% of its sales outside of Japan. Sony owns 52.5% of audio equipment manufacturer Aiwa.

Spending over $1 billion on R&D, Sony has traditionally sold innovative products at high prices rather than compete on price with commodity products. However, after consistently losing market leadership to price and cost-cutting rivals, Sony has become more price conscious. The company has also moved into less intensely competitive industrial markets.

The purchases of CBS Records and Columbia Pictures could enable Sony to quickly provide entertainment software in formats suitable for Sony's new hardware technologies, such as high-definition television, digital audio tape players, and 8mm video.

Chairman Morita's sterling US image was tarnished by the 1989 release of an America-bashing book he coauthored.

WHEN

Akio Morita, Masaru Ibuka, and Tamon Maeda, Ibuka's father-in-law, established Tokyo Telecommunications Engineering in 1946 with funding from Morita's father's sake business. Determined to innovate and create new markets, the company produced the first Japanese tape recorder (1950).

In 1953 Morita traveled to New York, purchased transistor technology licenses from Western Electric for $25,000, and returned to Japan to begin a revolution in consumer electronics. In 1955, one year after beginning transistor production, the company launched one of the world's first transistor radios. In 1957 the company introduced the first Sony-trademarked product, a pocket-sized radio (the company changed its name to Sony in 1958), followed by the first transistor TV (1959) and the first solid-state video tape recorder (1961). Sony preempted the competition and assumed leadership in these newly emerging markets.

Morita moved to New York in 1960 to oversee US expansion. Developing breakthrough products, Sony launched the first electronic desktop calculator (1964), video recorder (1964), solid-state condenser microphone (1965), and integrated circuit–based radio (1966). Sony's 1968 introduction of the Trinitron color TV tube began another decade of explosive growth. Its Betamax VCR (1976) was defeated in the marketplace by products employing VHS technology developed by Matsushita. The Walkman (1979), in all its forms, was another Sony success.

By 1980 Sony faced an appreciating yen and intense price and quality competition, especially from developing Far Eastern countries. The company began to use its technology base to diversify outside of consumer electronics and to move production to other countries to reduce the effects of currency fluctuations. In the 1980s Sony introduced Japan's first 32-bit workstation and became a major producer and marketer of semiconductors, audio/video chips and components, and floppy disk drives. The company remained active in the consumer market, introducing the Watchman and an 8mm camcorder, developing CD technology with Philips, and becoming the market leader in CD players. Sony made large investments in digital audiotape (DAT) technology and high-definition television.

Sony acquired CBS Records from CBS for $2 billion in 1988 and Columbia Pictures from Coca-Cola in 1989 for $4.9 billion. The purchases made Sony a major force in the rapidly growing entertainment industry and gave the company control of a large library of films, television programs, and recordings. Sony is spending heavily on film production and marketing.

HOW MUCH

	9 Yr. Growth	1980	1981	1982	1983	1984	1985	1986	1987	1988	1989
Sales ($ mil)	22.5%	2,683	4,266	4,863	4,578	4,804	5,211	6,788	8,309	11,450	16,678
Net income ($ mil)	25.1%	73	325	307	186	127	292	344	259	294	549
Income as % of sales	—	2.7%	7.6%	6.3%	4.1%	2.7%	5.6%	5.1%	3.1%	2.6%	3.3%
Earnings per share ($)	20.5%	0.34	1.51	1.34	0.81	0.55	1.18	1.38	1.04	1.15	1.82
Stock price – high ($)	—	10.75	16.75	26.13	18.00	16.75	17.38	21.38	23.50	40.25	58.50
Stock price – low ($)	—	6.63	6.00	14.50	11.00	12.63	12.75	13.50	18.13	18.25	35.38
Stock price – close ($)	25.3%	7.63	15.50	17.50	15.25	15.63	14.00	20.38	20.50	37.75	57.88
P/E – high	—	32	11	20	22	30	15	15	23	35	32
P/E – low	—	19	4	11	14	23	11	10	17	16	19
Dividends per share ($)	13.6%	0.11	0.14	0.15	0.18	0.18	0.18	0.20	0.28	0.33	0.34
Book value per share ($)	19.1%	5.05	7.15	8.47	8.36	8.85	9.58	12.23	16.19	21.79	24.44

1989 Year End:
Debt ratio: 19.5%
Return on equity: 7.9%
Cash (mil): $3,202
Current ratio: 1.28
Long-term debt (mil): $1,673
Number of shares (mil): 283
Dividends:
1989 average yield: 0.6%
1989 payout: 18.7%
Market value (mil): $16,356

Stock Price History high/low 1980-89

60
50
40
30
20
10
0

NYSE symbol: SNE (ADR)
Incorporated: Japan, 1946
Fiscal year ends: March 31

WHO

Chairman: Akio Morita, age 69
President and CEO: Norio Ohga
Auditors: Price Waterhouse
Employees: 78,900

WHERE

HQ: 7-35, Kitashinagawa 6-chome, Shinagawa-Ku, Tokyo 141, Japan
Phone: 011-81-3-448-2111
US Address (Sony Corp. of America): 9 W. 57th St., New York, NY 10019
US Phone: 212-371-5800
US FAX: 212-421-1674

Although Sony's production is primarily concentrated in Japan, the company operates 5 plants in the US, 8 in Europe, and 16 in other areas.

	1989 Sales	
	$ mil	% of total
Japan	5,540	34
US	4,441	27
Europe	3,772	23
Other countries	2,499	16
Adjustments	426	—
Total	**16,678**	**100**

WHAT

	1989 Sales	
	$ mil	% of total
Video equipment & TVs	6,934	43
Audio equipment	4,248	26
Records	2,577	16
Other products	2,493	15
Adjustments	426	—
Total	**16,678**	**100**

Consumer Brands
Betamax
Discman
Sony
Trinitron
Walkman
Watchman

Commercial & Industrial Products
Commercial display systems
Computer disks and drives
PCs and workstations
Semiconductors

Entertainment Subsidiaries
CBS Records
CBS Video Club
Columbia House Record and Tape Club
Columbia Pictures Entertainment
Tree Publishing Co.

RANKINGS

57th in *Fortune* Global 500 Industrial Cos.
15th in *Forbes* 100 Foreign Investments in the US
61st in *Business Week* Global 1000

COMPETITION

BASF
Bertelsmann
Hitachi
Matsushita
MCA
3M
Motorola
NEC
Paramount
Philips
Polaroid
Samsung
Thomson
Time Warner
Walt Disney
Zenith
Other electronics companies

THE SOUTHERN COMPANY

OVERVIEW

The Southern Company provides electricity to more than 3 million customers in 4 southern and southeastern states through 5 utilities: Alabama Power Company, Georgia Power Company, Gulf Power Company, Mississippi Power Company, and Savannah Electric & Power Company. SEGCO (Southern Electric Generating Company) operates electric generating plants on the Coosa River (Alabama), with Alabama and Georgia Power each entitled to 50% of the power SEGCO generates.

In 1989 Southern brought 2 coal-fired plants and one nuclear unit (Plant Vogtle unit 2) into service. The company's primary fuel is coal, which generated 76% of its total kilowatt hours in 1989. Nuclear sources generated about 17% of the company's kilowatt hour output.

Southern is the 2nd largest electric utility in the US after Pacific Gas & Electric, with 1989 sales exceeding $7.4 billion. The company's stock is among the 20 most widely held in America, and 53% of Southern's investors have held their shares for more than a decade.

NYSE symbol: SO
Incorporated: Delaware, 1945
Fiscal year ends: December 31

WHO

President and CEO: Edward L. Addison, age 59, $787,460 pay
EVP Nuclear: Joseph F. Farley, age 62, $596,453 pay
Financial VP: W. L. Westbrook, age 50
Auditors: Arthur Andersen & Co.
Employees: 30,530

WHERE

HQ: 64 Perimeter Center East, Atlanta, GA 30346
Phone: 404-393-0650
FAX: 404-668-3559

The Southern Company operates in Alabama, Georgia, northwestern Florida, and southeastern Mississippi.

Generating Facilities

Fossil Fueled
Barry (APC)
Bowen (GPC)
Crist (Gulf)
Daniel (50% Gulf, 50% MPC)
Eaton (MPC)
Gaston (SEGCO)
Gaston #5 (APC)
Gorgas (APC)
Hammond (GPC)
Harlee Branch (GPC)
Miller (APC)
Standard Oil Generating Station (MPC)
Sweatt (MPC)
Wansley (GPC)
Watson (MPC)
Yates (GPC)

Hydroelectric
Bartletts Ferry (GPC)
H. Neely Henry Dam (APC)
Harris Dam (APC)
Jordan Dam (APC)
L. Smith Dam (APC)
Lay Dam (APC)
Logan Martin Dam (APC)
Martin Dam (APC)
Tallulah Falls (GPC)
Wallace Dam (GPC)
Walter Bouldin Dam (APC)
Weiss Dam (APC)

Nuclear
Farley (APC)
Hatch (50%, GPC)
Vogtle (46%, GPC)

WHEN

Steamboat captain W. P. Lay founded the Alabama Power Company in 1906 to develop electric power on the Coosa River. James Mitchell, whose ties with the London investment firm of Sperling & Company later helped finance several hydroelectric dams in Alabama, took over Alabama Power in 1912, moving its headquarters from Montgomery to Birmingham. From 1912 until his death in 1920, Mitchell bought a number of Alabama's utilities, consolidating them with Alabama Power under his Canadian holding company Alabama Traction Light & Power (ATL&P).

Tom Martin, Alabama Power's legal counsel, became president in 1920 and reorganized ATL&P into Southeastern Power & Light. Southeastern formed Mississippi Power Company to take over electric utilities in Mississippi (1924) and Gulf Power Company to do the same in northern Florida (1925). In 1926 Southeastern bought Georgia Railway & Power Company and the electric utilities in several Georgia communities, including Athens and Macon. These companies consolidated as Georgia Power Company in 1927, with a service area covering about 1/2 the state.

In 1929 B. C. Cobb, CEO of Consumers Power Company of Michigan, acquired Southeastern, combining its properties with those of Penn-Ohio Edison to form the Commonwealth & Southern Corporation, a New York–based holding company that owned about 165 utilities. Martin served as president of Commonwealth & Southern until 1933 and was replaced by Wendell Willkie, who became the Republican nominee for president in 1940.

In 1942 Commonwealth & Southern was dissolved by the SEC. In 1949, 4 of its southern holdings (Alabama Power, Georgia Power, Gulf Power, and Mississippi Power) were placed under the authority of a newly created holding company named the Southern Company.

During the energy shortages of the 1970s, both Alabama and Georgia Power faced an anti-utility political environment, spearheaded by Governor George Wallace of Alabama. In late 1974 and early 1975 Georgia Power approached bankruptcy. Alabama Power suspended its $700 million construction program and laid off 4,000 employees in 1978. Wallace left office that year, and, without his constant pressure, state regulators allowed much-needed rate relief, ushering in a period of moderate growth for the Southern Company as a whole. Between 1980 and 1989 retail energy sales increased 40%, and the number of customers increased 25%. In 1988 Southern added Savannah, Georgia–based Savannah Electric & Power to its electric power system.

WHAT

	1989 Revenues	
	$ mil	% of total
Electricity		
Residential	2,194	29
Commercial	1,965	26
Industrial	2,011	27
Sales for resale	401	5
Nonterritorial & other	861	12
Other	60	1
Total	**7,492**	**100**

System Companies
Alabama Power Co.
Georgia Power Co.
Gulf Power Co.
Mississippi Power Co.
Savannah Electric & Power Co.
Southern Electric Generating Co. (supplies power to APC and GPC)

Engineering and Technical Services
Southern Company Services
Southern Electric International

Financial Services
The Southern Investment Group

RANKINGS

9th in *Fortune* 50 Utilities
108th in *Forbes* Sales 500
59th in *Business Week* 1000
180th in *Business Week* Global 1000

HOW MUCH

	9 Yr. Growth	1980	1981	1982	1983	1984	1985	1986	1987	1988	1989
Sales ($ mil)	8.0%	3,763	4,256	4,927	5,418	6,124	6,814	6,847	7,010	7,235	7,492
Net income ($ mil)	9.7%	422	413	545	699	828	947	1,003	678	966	969
Income as % of sales	—	11.2%	9.7%	11.1%	12.9%	13.5%	13.9%	14.6%	9.7%	13.4%	12.9%
Earnings per share ($)	2.1%	2.23	1.81	2.26	2.72	3.00	3.20	3.17	1.92	2.72	2.68
Stock price – high ($)	—	14.13	12.88	15.88	17.75	18.88	23.75	27.25	29.00	24.25	29.75
Stock price – low ($)	—	10.25	10.88	11.00	14.50	14.38	17.88	20.38	17.88	20.38	22.00
Stock price – close ($)	10.1%	12.25	12.00	15.63	16.38	18.88	22.25	25.38	22.38	22.38	29.13
P/E – high	—	6	7	7	7	6	7	9	15	9	11
P/E – low	—	5	6	5	5	5	6	6	9	8	8
Dividends per share ($)	3.6%	1.56	1.62	1.66	1.73	1.83	1.95	2.07	2.14	2.14	2.14
Book value per share ($)	2.9%	16.80	16.35	16.78	17.60	18.55	19.83	21.09	20.89	21.20	21.71

1989 Year End:
Debt ratio: 51.5%
Return on equity: 12.5%
Cash (mil): $230
Current ratio: 1.28
Long-term debt (mil): $8,575
Number of shares (mil): 316
Dividends:
1989 average yield: 7.3%
1989 payout: 79.9%
Market value (mil): $9,204

30
25
20
15
10
5
0

Stock Price History high/low 1980-89

THE SOUTHLAND CORPORATION

OVERVIEW

The Southland Corporation, under the 7-Eleven banner is the world's largest operator of convenience stores. Southland is struggling to cope with its 1987 $4.9 billion LBO. Unable to meet its debt obligations even after it sold more than 1,000 stores and a 50% interest in its Citgo Petroleum subsidiary, the company has labored to persuade holders of its junk bonds to allow the company to restructure its debts. If Southland can coax agreement from enough bondholders, its Japanese partner, Ito-Yokado, will buy 70% of the company for $400 million; if not, it may be forced to seek refuge in bankruptcy court.

The stakes for Southland are high. The company currently has 6,632 7-Eleven stores in the US and Canada, with nearly 13,000 company-operated, franchised, or operated under license worldwide, including 388 High's, Quik Marts, and Super-7s. Southland estimates that 7 million customers shop at 7-Eleven stores in the US and Canada daily, and 7-Eleven stores are the nation's largest seller of lottery tickets and the 2nd largest seller of money orders, after the US Postal Service.

WHEN

Claude Dawley, son of an ice company pioneer, formed the Southland Ice Company in Dallas in 1927 to buy 4 other Texas ice plant operations. Ice was both a rare commodity and a basic necessity during Texas summers for storing and transporting food and, especially, beer. Dawley was backed in his bid by Chicago utility magnate Martin Insull.

One of the ice operations Dawley bought was Consumers Ice, where a young employee, Joe C. Thompson, Jr., had made the firm some money with the suggestion of selling chilled watermelons off the truck docks.

After the Dawley enterprise was under way, an ice dock manager in Dallas, John Green, began stocking a few food items for customers. He demonstrated the idea to Thompson, who ran the ice operations, and the practice was adopted at all company locations.

Thompson promoted the grocery operations by calling them Tote'm Stores and erecting Alaska-made totem poles by the docks. In 1928 he arranged for the construction of gas stations at some stores.

Insull bought out Dawley in 1930, and Thompson became president and expanded Southland's operations even as the Depression-hurt company operated briefly under the direction of the bankruptcy court (1932-1934). The company began a dairy, Oak Farms, to meet its needs as the largest dairy retailer in the Dallas–Fort Worth area (1936). By 1946 the company had bought other ice-retail operations in Texas, changed its name to the Southland Corporation, and adopted the name 7-Eleven, a reference to the store hours, for its stores.

When Thompson died in 1961, his eldest son, John, became president and expanded the company into more states. New stores were opened in Colorado, New Jersey, and Arizona in 1962, and in Utah, California, and Missouri in 1963. The company purchased Gristede Brothers (1968), a New York grocer; Baricini Stores (1969), a candy chain; and Hudgins Truck Rental (1971, sold in 1980).

Southland franchised the 7-Eleven format in the United Kingdom (1971) and in Japan (1973) through one of that country's largest retailers, Ito-Yokado. In 1983 the company purchased Citgo, a gasoline refining and marketing business, later selling 50% of the company to Petroleos de Venezuela, a Venezuelan oil company (1986).

In 1988 John Thompson and his 2 brothers borrowed heavily to buy 70% of Southland's stock in an LBO. The company defaulted on $1.8 billion in publicly traded debt in mid-1990. Southland hoped to persuade bondholders to restructure the debt and take 25% of the company stock. That would clear the way for the purchase of 70% of Southland by its Japanese partner, Ito-Yokado.

Ito-Yokado ($12 billion in 1989 sales) was founded in 1913 and grew to include a group of 29 companies, 4 of which are traded on the Tokyo Stock Exchange. Ito-Yokado operates superstores, supermarkets (York-Benimaru, York Mart), department stores (Robinson's), specialty stores (Oshman's, Japan), discount stores, restaurants (Denny's, Japan), food processing and real estate operations, and 3,653 Japanese 7-Eleven stores.

HOW MUCH

	9 Yr. Growth	1980	1981	1982	1983	1984	1985	1986	1987	1988	1989
Sales ($ mil)	6.4%	4,759	5,694	6,757	8,772	12,035	12,719	8,578	8,125	7,991	8,352
Net income ($ mil)	—	78	94	106	132	160	213	112	(60)	(216)	(1,307)
Income as % of sales	—	1.6%	1.7%	1.6%	1.5%	1.3%	1.7%	1.3%	(0.7)	(2.7)	(15.6)

1989 Year End:
Debt ratio: —
Return on equity: —
Cash (mil): $8
Current ratio: 0.68
Long-term debt (mil): $3,457
No. of shares (mil): 205

Sales ($ mil) 1980-89

14,000
12,000
10,000
8,000
6,000
4,000

Private company
Incorporated: Texas, 1961
Fiscal year ends: December 31

WHO

Chairman: John P. Thompson, age 64, $779,642 pay
President and CEO: Jere W. Thompson, age 58, $779,642 pay
EVP and CFO: Clark J. Matthews II, age 53, $457,033 pay
EVP; COO, 7-Eleven Stores: S. R. Dole, age 52, $428,242 pay
SVP, General Counsel, and Secretary: John H. Rodgers, age 46, $257,653 pay
Auditors: Deloitte & Touche
Employees: 48,114

WHERE

HQ: 2711 N. Haskell Ave., Dallas, TX 75204
Phone: 214-828-7011
FAX: 214-828-7848

Southland operates 7-Eleven stores in 44 states, the District of Columbia, Canada, Mexico, and Sweden. Stores operated by others under license are located in 19 additional foreign countries.

	No. of Stores	% of Total
California	1,285	19
Virginia	674	10
Florida	621	9
Texas	604	9
Maryland	320	5
Other states	2,603	40
Canada	525	8
Total	**6,632**	**100**

WHAT

	1989 Sales	
	$ mil	% of total
Convenience stores	7,600	91
Other operations	675	8
Royalties & capital gains	77	1
Total	**8,352**	**100**

Convenience Stores
7-Eleven
High's Dairy Stores
Quik Mart
Super-7
Super Siete (Mexico)
Svenska/7-Eleven AB (Sweden)

Other Holdings
Citgo Petroleum (50%)
Citijet (aviation services)
Cityplace (Dallas real estate)
Rainbow Ticketmaster
Southland Foods (food supplier)

Brand Names
Aunt Bea's
Big Bite
Big Gulp
Casa Buena
Deli Shoppe
Hot-to-Go
Italini
Slurpee
Smileys
Sonritos
Super-7

RANKINGS

13th in *Fortune* 50 Retailing Cos.
8th in *Forbes* 400 US Private Cos.

COMPETITION

Amoco	Coastal	Phillips
Atlantic Richfield	Exxon	Royal Dutch/Shell
Chevron	Kroger	Texaco
Circle K	Mobil	Grocery retailers

SOUTHWEST AIRLINES COMPANY

OVERVIEW

Southwest, America's 8th largest airline (in terms of passengers carried), achieved over $1 billion in sales for the first time in 1989. Profitable since 1972, Southwest boasts one of the healthiest balance sheets in the industry. Specializing in single-class, frequent, low-fare flights, Southwest serves 29 cities in 14 southwestern and midwestern states. Schedules are geared toward city to city (as opposed to hub-and-spoke) flights. Trips average an hour or less, no meals are served, and between flights Southwest's planes spend less than 15 minutes on the ground—one of the fastest turnaround times in the industry. The company emphasizes excellence in customer service and is the only airline that has won the DOT Triple Crown on 3 separate occasions (March 1988, September 1989, and February 1990) for Best Ontime Record, Best Baggage Handling, and Fewest Customer Complaints in a single month.

WHEN

Texas businessman Rollin King and lawyer Herb Kelleher founded Air Southwest Company in 1967 as an intrastate airline, linking Dallas, Houston, and San Antonio. Braniff and Texas International immediately sued the fledgling company, questioning whether the region needed another airline, but the Texas Supreme Court ruled in Southwest's favor. In 1971 the company (renamed Southwest Airlines) made its first scheduled flight from Dallas Love Field to San Antonio.

Capitalizing on its home base at Love Field, Southwest adopted love as the theme of its early ad campaigns, complete with stewardesses wearing hot pants and serving love potions (drinks) and love bites (peanuts). When other airlines relocated to the Dallas–Fort Worth (D-FW) airport in 1974, Southwest stayed at Love Field, contributing to the company's virtual monopoly at the airfield. This monopoly proved to be limiting, however, when the Wright Amendment became law in 1979, preventing companies operating out of Love Field from providing direct service to states except those neighboring Texas. Southwest's customers could fly from Love Field to Louisiana, Arkansas, Oklahoma, and New Mexico, but had to buy new tickets and board different flights to points beyond.

When Lamar Muse, Southwest's president, resigned due to differences with King, Kelleher became president (1978). In 1985 Muse took over his son Michael's nearly bankrupt airline, Muse Air Corporation, selling it to Southwest. Kelleher operated the Houston-based airline as TranStar but liquidated it in 1987 when Southwest's total profits fell 60% below those of 1986, primarily due to increased competition from another Houston-based airline, Continental.

Kelleher then devoted his full energies to making Southwest the industry leader in low fares. He introduced advance purchase "Fun Fares" (1986) and a frequent flyer program based on the number of flights rather than mileage (1987). Hardly the typical airline executive, Kelleher seems to thrive on zaniness and has often starred in Southwest's whimsical television commercials.

When Southwest became the official airline of Sea World (Texas) in 1988, Kelleher painted a 737-300 to resemble Shamu, the park's killer whale. By 1989 Southwest was operating the industry's youngest all-jet fleet, with an average plane age of 5.8 years. It anticipates delivery of 12 new Boeing jets by the end of 1990.

Early in 1990 Southwest established an additional operating base at Phoenix Sky Harbor Airport and began head-to-head competition with rival America West. The company continued to develop its route structure through 1989 and 1990, adding flights to Oakland (1989), Indianapolis (1989), and Burbank (1990). Competition could heat up at Love Field in coming months, however, as Congress considers either modifying or repealing the Wright Amendment.

HOW MUCH

	9 Yr. Growth	1980	1981	1982	1983	1984	1985	1986	1987	1988	1989
Sales ($ mil)	18.9%	213	270	331	448	536	680	769	778	860	1,015
Net income ($ mil)	10.8%	28	34	34	41	50	47	50	20	58	72
Income as % of sales	—	13.4%	12.6%	10.3%	9.1%	9.3%	7.0%	6.5%	2.6%	6.7%	7.1%
Earnings per share ($)	6.8%	1.30	1.35	1.26	1.38	1.64	1.51	1.55	0.63	1.84	2.35
Stock price – high ($)	—	11.84	19.36	25.50	35.20	29.40	31.00	27.50	25.25	20.88	30.75
Stock price – low ($)	—	3.73	9.44	11.00	20.00	14.75	21.25	18.25	11.75	13.13	19.63
Stock price – close ($)	8.5%	11.52	11.55	21.30	27.20	22.00	26.88	20.63	13.38	20.25	24.00
P/E – high	—	9	14	20	25	18	21	18	40	11	13
P/E – low	—	3	7	9	14	9	14	12	19	7	8
Dividends per share ($)	5.7%	0.09	0.11	0.13	0.13	0.13	0.13	0.13	0.13	0.13	0.14
Book value per share ($)	18.0%	4.52	6.78	8.61	10.68	12.25	14.45	15.87	16.43	18.15	20.10

1989 Year End:
Debt ratio: 37.6%
Return on equity: 12.3%
Cash (mil): $146
Current ratio: 1.04
Long-term debt (mil): $354
Number of shares (mil): 29
Dividends:
1989 average yield: 0.6%
1989 payout: 6.0%
Market value (mil): $701

Stock Price History high/low 1980-89

NYSE symbol: LUV
Incorporated: Texas, 1971
Fiscal year ends: December 31

WHO

Chairman, President, and CEO: Herbert D. Kelleher, age 58, $460,631 pay
EVP and COO: Gary A. Barron, age 45, $175,961 pay
EVP Corporate Services: John G. Denison, age 45, $157,437 pay
VP Flight Operations: Paul E. Sterbenz, age 51, $163,179 pay
VP Finance and CFO: Gary C. Kelly, age 34
Auditors: Ernst & Young
Employees: 7,760

WHERE

HQ: PO Box 36611, Love Field, Dallas, TX 75235
Phone: 214-904-4000
FAX: 214-904-4022 (Finance)

Southwest flies to 29 cities in 14 states and Canada.

Cities Served

Albuquerque, NM	Los Angeles, CA
Amarillo, TX	Lubbock, TX
Austin, TX	Midland, TX
Birmingham, AL	Nashville, TN
Chicago, IL	New Orleans, LA
Corpus Christi, TX	Oakland, CA
Dallas, TX	Oklahoma City, OK
Detroit, MI	Ontario, Canada
El Paso, TX	Phoenix, AZ
Harlingen, TX	San Antonio, TX
Houston, TX	San Diego, CA
Indianapolis, IN	San Francisco, CA
Kansas City, MO	St. Louis, MO
Las Vegas, NE	Tulsa, OK
Little Rock, AR	

WHAT

	1989 Sales	
	$ mil	% of total
Passenger services	973	96
Freight operations	19	2
Other	23	2
Total	**1,015**	**100**

Services
Quick ticketing and boarding procedures
In-flight beverage services
Company Club
Frequent flyer program based on trips rather than mileage

Flight Equipment	Owned	Leased	Total
Boeing 737	62	22	94
Total	**62**	**22**	**94**

RANKINGS

25th in *Fortune* 50 Transportation Cos.
664th in *Business Week* 1000

COMPETITION

America West	NWA
AMR	Pan Am
Continental	TWA
Delta	UAL
Midway	USAir

SOUTHWESTERN BELL CORPORATION

OVERVIEW

St. Louis–based Southwestern Bell Corporation, a spinoff of the Bell system, provides telephone exchange services to over 9 million subscribers in 5 central and southwestern states. During 1989 the company provided over 34 billion minutes of network usage and connected almost one billion long-distance calls.

Southwestern Bell Mobile Systems provides service to 382,000 cellular subscribers in 24 markets (including 6 of the largest 15). Subsidiary Metromedia Paging, based in Secaucus, New Jersey, provides paging services to 809,000 paging subscribers in 32 markets (including 9 of the 10 largest US markets). Southwestern Bell Telecom markets communications equipment through its Business Systems (business market) and Freedom Phone (residential market) divisions and its Southwestern Bell Telecom (UK), Ltd., subsidiary in all 50 states, the UK, Canada, and New Zealand.

Southwestern Bell Publications publishes more than 450 phone directories in its region and 600 other products, and markets 6,000 directories worldwide. The directories are printed by Gulf Printing, which also provides full-service commercial printing services.

WHEN

Southwestern Bell was once an arm of AT&T, providing local communications services in its present region. Telephone service first arrived in Southwestern Bell territory in 1878, just 2 years after the telephone was invented. One man responsible for early growth of telephony in this region was George Durant, who located 12 customers for St. Louis's first telephone exchange. This grew into Bell Telephone Company of Missouri.

Meanwhile, the Missouri and Kansas Telephone Company had also been established. The first president of Southwestern Bell, Eugene Nims, negotiated the merger of Missouri and Kansas and Southwestern Bell into the Southwestern Telephone System around 1912. Southwestern Bell became part of AT&T in 1917; Nims served as president from 1919 to 1929. After WWII, demand for new telephone lines grew rapidly. By 1945 Southwestern Bell was providing service to one million telephones; by the 1980s this number had grown nearly ten-fold.

In 1983 AT&T was split from the Bell Operating Companies and Southwestern Bell became a separate legal entity; it began operations in 1984. At the time of the breakup, Southwestern Bell received local phone service rights in 5 states; Southwestern Bell Mobile Systems (cellular service provider); the directory advertising business; and a 1/7th share in Bell Communications Research, the R&D arm shared by the Bell companies. The company set up its telecommunications and publishing groups later.

Southwestern Bell has concentrated much of its diversification effort in mobile communications. The company purchased operations from Metromedia, Inc. (1987), which included paging in 21 cities and 6 major cellular franchises. Southwestern Bell also bought paging company Omni Communications (1988).

By 1988 Southwestern Bell had deployed more lines than any other company for an integrated voice and data phone service. That year the company began testing residential fiber-optic service in Kansas. The company also is expanding its publishing activities to include telephone directories outside of Southwestern Bell's region domestically and related activities in Sweden, Australia, and South Korea. Southwestern Bell sought permission to provide electronic directory services and has begun to provide voice messaging services, electronic mail, and videotex services.

HOW MUCH

	5 Yr. Growth	1980	1981	1982	1983	1984	1985	1986	1987	1988	1989
Sales ($ mil)	4.0%	—	—	—	—	7,191	7,925	7,902	8,003	8,453	8,730
Net income ($ mil)	4.4%	—	—	—	—	883	996	1,023	1,047	1,060	1,093
Income as % of sales	—	—	—	—	—	12.3%	12.6%	12.9%	13.1%	12.5%	12.5%
Earnings per share ($)	3.9%	—	—	—	—	3.01	3.33	3.42	3.48	3.53	3.64
Stock price – high ($)	—	—	—	—	—	23.83	29.50	38.79	45.50	42.63	64.38
Stock price – low ($)	—	—	—	—	—	18.33	22.79	26.33	28.25	33.00	38.88
Stock price – close ($)	22.1%	—	—	—	—	23.58	28.50	37.42	34.38	40.38	63.88
P/E – high	—	—	—	—	—	8	9	11	13	12	18
P/E – low	—	—	—	—	—	6	7	8	8	9	11
Dividends per share ($)	12.9%	—	—	—	—	1.40	1.97	2.10	2.27	2.44	2.57
Book value per share ($)	3.5%	—	—	—	—	23.43	24.75	26.07	27.26	28.31	27.83

1989 Year End:
Debt ratio: 39.5%
Return on equity: 13.0%
Cash (mil): $263
Current ratio: 0.88
Long-term debt (mil): $5,456
Number of shares (mil): 301
Dividends:
1989 average yield: 4.0%
1989 payout: 70.6%
Market value (mil): $19,200

Stock Price History high/low 1984-89

70 60 50 40 30 20 10 0

NYSE symbol: SBC
Incorporated: Delaware, 1983
Fiscal year ends: December 31

WHO

Chairman and CEO: Edward E. Whitacre, Jr., age 48, $1,064,900 pay (before promotion)
VC and CFO: Robert G. Pope, age 54, $881,100 pay
VC: Gerald D. Blatherwick, age 53, $859,800 pay
Senior EVP and General Counsel: James D. Ellis, age 46, $437,700 pay
SVP Corporate Development: Royce S. Caldwell, age 51
SVP Finance and Treasurer: Cassandra C. Carr, age 45
SVP Strategic Planning: Robert H. Glaser, age 50
SVP Corporate Communications: Gray Kerrick, age 47
SVP Human Resources: Guy E. Miller, Jr., age 58
Auditors: Ernst & Young
Employees: 66,200

WHERE

HQ: 1010 Pine St., St. Louis, MO 63101
Phone: 314-235-9800
FAX: 314-235-4687

Southwestern Bell Telephone provides telephone services in Texas, Kansas, Oklahoma, Arkansas, and Missouri. Other divisions operate nationally or internationally.

WHAT

	1989 Sales	
	$ mil	% of total
Local telephone service	3,325	39
Network access	2,658	30
Long-distance service	1,052	12
Directory advertising	732	8
Other	963	11
Total	**8,730**	**100**

Subsidiaries/Affiliates
Bell Communications Research (14%)
Gulf Printing Co.
Metromedia Paging Services
Southwestern Bell Mobile Systems
Southwestern Bell Publications
Southwestern Bell Telecom
Southwestern Bell Telephone Co.
Southwestern Bell Yellow Pages

RANKINGS

8th in *Fortune* 50 Utilities
91st in *Forbes* Sales 500
30th in *Business Week* 1000
69th in *Business Week* Global 1000

COMPETITION

Ameritech
AT&T
Bell Atlantic
BellSouth
Dun & Bradstreet
GTE
McCaw Cellular
MCI
NYNEX
Pacific Telesis
United Telecommunications
U S West

SOVIET UNION

OVERVIEW

The Union of Soviet Socialist Republics (USSR) is the largest country in the world in area. It is divided into 15 republics, with the national capital at Moscow.

The Soviet government is divided into the Council of Ministers (executive), the Congress of People's Deputies and the Supreme Soviet (legislative), and the Supreme Court of the USSR (judicial). The government of each republic is structured after the central government model. Historically, the heart of the Soviet political system has been the Communist Party of the Soviet Union.

The economy of the USSR has stagnated in recent years due to an inefficient, highly centralized bureaucracy. President Mikhail Gorbachev's policies of *perestroika* (restructuring) and *glasnost* (openness), introduced in 1987, are an attempt to move the economy towards greater decentralization and private enterprise and the political system toward more freedom and diversity.

For over 70 years the Soviets have seen themselves as the vanguard of a worldwide socialist revolution. But the domestic failure of socialist economics and the recent collapse of Communist party control in Eastern Europe have sharpened doubts as never before about the most fundamental tenets of Soviet society. Threatened by economic stagnation, ethnic strife, and resurgent internal nationalism, the Soviets face an uncertain future.

WHEN

As it entered the 20th century, Russia was still a nearly feudal monarchy. In 1917 a riot in Petrograd, caused mainly by discontent resulting from WWI, forced the abdication of Tsar Nicholas II and resulted in the establishment of a moderate provisional government, which was in turn overthrown by left-wing Bolsheviks under Vladimir Lenin. Lenin's rise to power was followed by a fierce civil war between the Bolsheviks (Reds) and opposing groups (Whites), which the Reds won in 1920.

When Lenin died in 1924, a power struggle ensued between Joseph Stalin and Leon Trotsky, both lieutenants of Lenin. Stalin prevailed (Trotsky was axe-murdered in exile in Mexico) and implemented a series of Five-Year Plans (the first in 1929) to industrialize the country. Stalin's power became absolute after his great purge of 1935-1938 (in which millions were killed or internally exiled).

In 1939 Stalin signed a nonaggression pact with Adolf Hitler. Hitler broke the agreement with a full-scale invasion of Russia in 1941. The Soviets joined the Allies and helped defeat Germany in 1945.

After WWII the USSR and the West entered a period of tension and mistrust (the Cold War). The Soviets quickly established control over much of Eastern Europe.

After a brief interregnum following Stalin's death in 1953, Nikita Khrushchev assumed leadership in 1955. The Soviets violently quelled a revolution in Hungary the following year. In 1957 the USSR launched Sputnik and 4 years later put the first man in space.

In 1961 the Soviets built the Berlin Wall to stem the tide of East German migration to the West. The Cuban Missile Crisis of 1962 occurred when the USSR attempted to deliver nuclear missiles to Cuba. Khrushchev was deposed in 1964 (due in part to economic failures) and was replaced by Leonid Brezhnev. East-West conflict intensified when the US and USSR took opposing sides in the civil war in Vietnam. In 1968 the USSR invaded Czechoslovakia to repress the progressive regime of Alexander Dubcek. The USSR engaged in arms limitation talks with the US during the 1970s and 1980s. In 1979 the USSR invaded Afghanistan, again worsening superpower relations.

Soviet history took an unexpected radical turn after the ascension of Mikhail Gorbachev to General Secretary of the Communist Party in 1985. The USSR announced its withdrawal from Afghanistan in 1988. In 1989 it allowed the Berlin Wall to be dismantled and released its hold on Eastern Europe. In an unprecedented display of cooperation with the United States and other Western nations, the Soviet Union, once Iraq's primary arms supplier, joined in the United Nations's condemnation of Saddam Hussein's military occupation of Kuwait in 1990.

HOW MUCH

	9 Yr. Growth	1979	1980	1981	1982	1983	1984	1985	1986	1987	1988
Population (mil)	0.9%	263	266	269	271	274	276	279	282	284	286
GNP ($ bil, constant $)	1.9%	2,145	2,181	2,209	2,257	2,318	2,348	2,369	2,450	2,492	2,535
GNP per cap. (const. $)	0.9%	8,143	8,188	8,217	8,326	8,473	8,497	8,492	8,702	8,773	8,852
Imports ($ mil)	7.1%	57,966	68,473	73,194	77,846	80,445	80,409	83,315	88,874	95,970	107,316
Exports ($ mil)	6.1%	64,912	76,437	79,380	87,168	91,652	91,495	87,196	97,053	107,664	110,740
Hard currency imports ($ mil)	3.2%	21,435	26,060	27,778	27,507	27,717	27,446	25,881	23,098	22,928	28,518

GNP per capita in constant dollars 1979-88

9,000
8,000
7,000
6,000
5,000
4,000
3,000
2,000
1,000
0

Official name: Union of Soviet Socialist Republics

WHO

President: Mikhail S. Gorbachev, age 59, 48,000 rubles (approx. $77,000) pay
Chairman of the Council of Ministers: Nikolai I. Ryzhkov
Minister of Finance: Boris I. Gostev
Auditors: Central Auditory Commission
Party Members: 19,412,153

WHERE

HQ: USSR Council of Ministers, The Kremlin, Moscow, USSR
US HQ: Embassy of the USSR, 1124 16th St., NW, Washington, DC 20036
Phone: 202-628-7551

The Soviet Union borders 12 other countries and spans 11 time zones.

It comprises 15 union republics:

Union Republic	Area (thou sq mi)	1989 Population (thou)	Capital
Armenian SSR	11.5	3,283	Yerevan
Azerbaidzhan SSR	33.4	7,029	Baku
Byelorussian SSR	80.2	10,200	Minsk
Estonian SSR	17.4	1,573	Tallinn
Georgian SSR	26.9	5,449	Tbilisi
Kazakh SSR	1,049.2	16,538	Alma-Ata
Kirghiz SSR	76.6	4,291	Frunze
Latvian SSR	24.9	2,681	Riga
Lithuanian SSR	25.2	3,690	Vilnius
Moldavian SSR	13.0	4,341	Kishinev
Russian SFSR	6,592.8	147,386	Moscow
Tadzhik SSR	55.3	5,112	Dushanbe
Turkmen SSR	188.5	3,534	Ashkhabad
Ukrainian SSR	233.1	51,704	Kiev
Uzbek SSR	172.7	19,906	Tashkent
	8,600.7		
Inland Water	49.1		
Total	**8,649.8**	**286,717**	

Largest Cities	1989 Population (thou)
Moscow	8,967
Leningrad	5,020
Kiev	2,587
Tashkent	2,073
Baku	1,757
Kharkov	1,611
Minsk	1,589
Gorky	1,438

WHAT

GNP (1988): $2.5 trillion
Currency: 1 Ruble = 100 kopeks

Imports	Exports
Grain and other agricultural products	Petroleum
Machinery and equipment	Natural gas
Steel products	Metals
Consumer goods	Wood
	Agricultural products

RANKINGS

1st in area
3rd in population (after China and India)
3rd in GNP (after US and Japan)

SPRINGS INDUSTRIES, INC.

OVERVIEW

Springs Industries is the 3rd largest public textile maufacturer in the US after Milliken and Burlington Industries. Headquartered for over a century in Fort Mill, South Carolina, the $1.9 billion company operates 45 plants in 10 states in the US (24 in South Carolina), Belgium, and England, and has a minority interest in a Japanese textile plant.

The company, the largest industrial employer in South Carolina, operates in 3 industry segments — home furnishings, finished fabrics, and industrial fabrics. Home furnishing products include sheets and bedding accessories, bathroom textiles, window shades, and blinds. The finished fabrics segment includes textiles for the home sewing market and for manufacturers of furniture, drapes, and clothing. Springs is the world's largest producer of woven fiberglass fabrics for industrial use (in printed circuit boards, electrical insulation, and aircraft parts). Specialty fabric using Du Pont's Kevlar is woven for sails and bulletproof vests.

The Close family, descendants of the founders, retains voting control of the company.

WHEN

Springs Industries of Fort Mill, South Carolina, began in 1887 as Fort Mill Manufacturing Company, organized by Samuel Elliott White and 15 others, including Leroy Springs, his future son-in-law. Springs, a self-made millionaire (cotton exporter and retail merchant), and other investors also started the Lancaster Cotton Mills in nearby Lancaster, South Carolina (1895). In the late 1890s Springs obtained control of Fort Mill Manufacturing.

In 1931 Elliott Springs, Leroy's only son, became president of the company when his father died, leaving massive debts and decaying plants. During the 1930s Elliott saved the company by modernizing mill equipment, acquiring 2 additional mills, and consolidating the plants into The Springs Cotton Mills (1933). During WWII the company's 7 mills made fabric for military use (up to 6 million yards a week).

In 1945 Springs began construction on the Grace Bleachery (named after Elliott's late mother) to finish (bleach, dye, print, and sew) raw cloth. That year he also started the Springmaid line of bedding and fabrics and bought a New York City building for national sales headquarters. Elliott Springs's satiric, risqué, but effective ads (beginning in 1948) helped the company become the world's biggest producer of sheets, with sales of $163 million by 1958.

In 1959 Elliott Springs died and his son-in-law H. William Close became president. Close oversaw construction of the Springs Building, current New York sales headquarters (1962), and a $200 million program to expand product lines and modernize plants. With profits sharply declining, the company went public as Springs Mills, Inc. (1966).

In 1969 the first nonfamily member, Peter G. Scotese from Federated Department Stores, was hired as president. Springs diversified into synthetic fabrics, buying a minority interest in a Japanese textile plant to distribute Ultrasuede (apparel fabric and car upholstery, 1971), and into frozen foods, buying Seabrook Foods (1973, sold 1981). The company ceased domestic knitting operations in 1978.

Recent acquisitions and mergers reflect Springs's focus on home furnishing and industrial textiles — Lawtex Industries (bedspreads, draperies, 1979); Graber Industries (window decorating products, 1979); M. Lowenstein (apparel, home furnishing, and industrial textiles, 1985); Clark-Schwebel Fiber Glass (industrial fabrics, 1985); Uniglass Division of United Merchants and Manufacturers (industrial fabrics, 1988); and Carey-McFall (Bali blinds, 1989).

In 1982 the company became Springs Industries.

HOW MUCH

	9 Yr. Growth	1980	1981	1982	1983	1984	1985	1986	1987	1988	1989
Sales ($ mil)	10.2%	794	917	875	894	945	1,014	1,505	1,661	1,825	1,909
Net income ($ mil)	8.1%	32	40	37	37	36	13	33	56	53	65
Income as % of sales	—	4.0%	4.4%	4.3%	4.1%	3.8%	1.3%	2.2%	3.4%	2.9%	3.4%
Earnings per share ($)	8.0%	1.82	2.25	2.11	2.08	2.03	0.75	1.83	3.13	2.98	3.64
Stock price – high ($)	—	9.38	13.38	20.13	22.50	20.13	23.00	28.44	38.25	38.75	45.25
Stock price – low ($)	—	6.38	8.13	10.00	17.06	15.25	15.63	20.50	20.75	27.00	30.50
Stock price – close ($)	17.9%	8.69	11.75	19.63	19.88	16.88	22.00	24.94	30.25	31.50	38.25
P/E – high	—	5	6	10	11	10	31	16	12	13	12
P/E – low	—	4	4	5	8	8	21	11	7	9	8
Dividends per share ($)	8.0%	0.60	0.68	0.72	0.76	0.76	0.76	0.76	0.82	1.01	1.20
Book value per share ($)	6.2%	19.24	20.76	22.47	23.74	25.04	25.03	26.24	28.64	30.67	33.08

1989 Year End:
Debt ratio: 28.0%
Return on equity: 11.4%
Cash (mil): $6
Current ratio: 2.41
Long-term debt (mil): $228
Number of shares (mil): 18
Dividends:
1989 average yield: 3.1%
1989 payout: 33.0%
Market value (mil): $677

NYSE symbol: SMI
Incorporated: South Carolina, 1966
Fiscal year ends: Saturday nearest December 31

WHO

Chairman, CEO, and President: Walter Y. Elisha, age 57, $764,400 pay (prior to promotion to president)
EVP; President, Home Furnishings Group: Julius Lasnick, age 60, $436,500 pay
EVP and CFO: A. Ward Peacock, age 60, $284,100 pay
EVP; President, Finished Fabrics Group: Robert W. Moser, age 51
President and CEO, Clark-Schwebel: Jack P. Schwebel, $339,330 pay
Auditors: Deloitte & Touche
Employees: 23,600

WHERE

HQ: 205 N. White St., Fort Mill, SC 29715
Phone: 803-547-3650
FAX: 803-547-3805

Springs operates 45 manufacturing plants (including 26 textile plants), located primarily in the southeastern US, with some in Belgium and England.

	1989 Sales	
	$ mil	% of total
US	1,775	93
Foreign	134	7
	1,909	**100**

WHAT

	1989 Sales		1989 Operating Income	
	$ mil	% of total	$ mil	% of total
Finished fabrics	565	30	6	5
Home furnishings	919	48	81	66
Industrial fabrics	425	22	35	29
Total	**1,909**	**100**	**122**	**100**

Home Furnishings
Bed and bath products
- Custom Designs
- Pacific
- Performance
- Springmaid
- Supercale
- Wamsutta
- Wondercale

Blinds, shades, draperies
- Bali
- FashionPleat
- Graber

Specialty products
- Pacific Silvercloth (antitarnish fabric)

Finished Fabrics
- Skinner
- Springmaid
- Ultrasuede
- Wamsutta

Industrial Fabrics
- Kevlar fabrics

RANKINGS

222nd in *Fortune* 500 Industrial Cos.
414th in *Forbes* Sales 500
706th in *Business Week* 1000

COMPETITION

Burlington Holdings
Farley
Fieldcrest Cannon
Milliken

SQUARE D COMPANY

OVERVIEW

The Square D Company manufactures a wide variety of electrical and electronic products in 2 industry segments: Electrical Distribution Products, Systems, and Services; and Industrial Control Products, Systems, and Services.

Electrical distribution products, used in the control and distribution of electricity, include transformers, busways, circuit breakers, and connectors. The company's industrial control products include switches, relays, automation products, semiconductor products, infrared measurement devices, and power protection systems.

Square D has implemented the self-directed work force concept in some of its factories, allowing employees to handle time and attendance scheduling, recordkeeping, and hiring. Under this system the employee-supervisor ratio in the company's central distribution facility has grown from 11:1 to 48:1 and productivity has posted double-digit gains.

Square D operates 35 plants in the US and 20 plants in 11 foreign countries. The company has paid dividends each of the 52 years it has been listed on the NYSE.

WHEN

In 1902 Bryson Horton and James McCarthy founded the McBride Manufacturing Company in Detroit to manufacture cartridge-type electrical fuses. The company was incorporated in 1903 with Horton as president. In 1905 the company introduced the "Arkless" enclosed fuse, invented by Horton.

In 1908 the company changed its name to Detroit Fuse and Manufacturing and bought the rights to an English invention, the Berry enclosed safety switch. In 1915 the company marketed a new sheet metal version of the safety switch with a "D" in a square embossed on the cover. It became known in the industry as the "square D" switch. The switch was very successful, and the company sold its fuse business and changed its name to Square D in 1917. In 1919 sales first exceeded $1 million.

In the 1920s Square D expanded into other electrical product lines, buying several companies, including Industrial Controller Company in 1929. The company obtained a license to manufacture and sell Westinghouse circuit breakers in 1929 and had sales of $4.5 million.

During the Great Depression, in 1932, Square D reported the 2nd of only 2 annual losses in its history. The company made a small profit in 1933 and by 1937 had increased net profits to over $1 million on sales of over $7.7 million. In 1939 the company entered the aircraft instrumentation field, buying Kollsman Instrument. Demand for the company's products rose as the US entered WWII, and at the end of 1941 defense work accounted for 90% of the company's production.

After the war, use of electricity increased in all areas of life, and Square D's sales rose rapidly, doubling the war years' peak by 1951. Throughout the 1950s and 1960s the company continued to broaden its line of products, expanding internally and through acquisition. Square D moved its headquarters to Park Ridge, Illinois, in 1960.

During the 1970s the company added millions of square feet to its existing operations while also growing through acquisitions, including Anderson Electric (connectors, 1970), Starkstrom Gummersbach (West Germany, industrial control products, 1978), and Commercial y Fabril Aper (Spain, motor control equipment, 1979). During this period Square D expanded its overseas markets, opening sales offices in Latin America and Asia.

Square D moved into the emerging digital electronics field in the early 1980s, buying several small companies. In 1984 the company began to implement programs to cut costs and boost productivity in response to intensifying global competition. By 1988 the work force had been reduced by 14% and 80 of the top 120 managers had been replaced.

HOW MUCH

	9 Yr. Growth	1980	1981	1982	1983	1984	1985	1986	1987	1988	1989
Sales ($ mil)	5.6%	999	1,144	1,057	1,144	1,366	1,348	1,403	1,484	1,657	1,631
Net income ($ mil)	2.5%	83	103	72	63	106	102	99	110	119	104
Income as % of sales	—	8.3%	9.0%	6.8%	5.5%	7.8%	7.6%	7.0%	7.4%	7.2%	6.4%
Earnings per share ($)	1.8%	3.41	3.82	2.61	2.22	3.71	3.52	3.40	3.79	4.42	3.99
Stock price – high ($)	—	33.50	37.38	34.75	41.25	41.50	43.63	50.00	65.50	55.75	62.75
Stock price – low ($)	—	17.63	24.38	21.75	30.38	31.13	35.13	39.25	43.00	45.38	47.50
Stock price – close ($)	7.0%	29.00	28.88	34.25	40.00	39.38	42.75	46.38	52.25	48.00	53.38
P/E – high	—	10	10	13	19	11	12	15	17	13	16
P/E – low	—	5	6	8	14	8	10	12	11	10	12
Dividends per share ($)	2.3%	1.63	1.74	1.84	1.84	1.84	1.84	1.84	1.86	2.04	2.00
Book value per share ($)	4.5%	15.99	17.50	17.32	17.70	19.17	21.00	23.16	24.57	24.76	23.68

1989 Year End:
Debt ratio: 18.3%
Return on equity: 16.5%
Cash (mil): $71
Current ratio: 1.41
Long-term debt (mil): $124
Number of shares (mil): 23
Dividends:
1989 average yield: 3.7%
1989 payout: 50.1%
Market value (mil): $1,254

Stock Price History high/low 1980-89

70
60
50
40
30
20
10
0

NYSE symbol: SQD
Incorporated: Delaware, 1989
Fiscal year ends: December 31

WHO

Chairman, President, and CEO: Jerre L. Stead, age 46, $628,550 pay
EVP, Electrical Distribution Sector: Charles W. Denny, age 54, $374,882 pay
EVP and CFO: Thomas L. Bindley, age 46, $314,437 pay
EVP, Industrial Control Sector: Juris Vikmanis, age 52, $294,215 pay
EVP, International Sector: Donald E. Marquart
Auditors: Deloitte & Touche
Employees: 19,300

WHERE

HQ: 1415 S. Roselle, Palatine, IL 60067
Phone: 708-397-2600
FAX: 708-397-8814

Square D operates 35 plants in the US and 20 plants in 11 foreign countries.

	1989 Sales		1989 Operating Income	
	$ mil	% of total	$ mil	% of total
US	1,343	82	151	85
Europe	127	8	10	6
Latin America	68	4	14	8
Other	93	6	2	1
Adjustments	—	—	27	—
Total	**1,631**	**100**	**204**	**100**

WHAT

	1989 Sales		1989 Operating Income	
	$ mil	% of total	$ mil	% of total
Electrical distrib.	1,118	69	142	80
Industrial controls	513	31	35	20
Adjustments	—	—	27	—
Total	**1,631**	**100**	**204**	**100**

Electrical Distribution Sector
Connectors
Distribution equipment
Power equipment

Industrial Control Sector
Automation products
Control products
Engineered systems
Infrared measurement devices
Power protection systems
Semiconductors
Technical services

RANKINGS

234th in *Fortune* 500 Industrial Cos.
463rd in *Forbes* Sales 500
370th in *Business Week* 1000

COMPETITION

AMP
Asea Brown Boveri
Cooper Industries
Daimler-Benz
Emerson
General Electric
General Signal
Mitsubishi
Reliance Electric
Rockwell International
Siemens
Teledyne
Thomson
Westinghouse

STANFORD UNIVERSITY

OVERVIEW

Stanford University, a private, coed institution located 30 miles south of San Francisco near Palo Alto, is widely regarded as one of the nation's finest schools. Enrollment at Stanford totals 13,354 students with a faculty of 1,325 (97% of whom have doctoral degrees).

Stanford's athletic program is a member of the NCAA (Division 1) and, unlike its Ivy League colleagues, is nationally competitive.

Admission to Stanford is competitive as well: 83% of undergraduate applications for the 1988-1989 school year were rejected. Approximately 40% of the students participate in overseas studies.

The school library system consists of 27 on-campus libraries with 5.1 million bound volumes, 2.6 million microforms, 49,300 periodical subscriptions, and 200,000 records and tapes. The Green Library (the main campus library) holds original works of such famous names as Martin Luther, Sir Isaac Newton, John Steinbeck, and William Butler Yeats.

The Stanford faculty includes 10 Nobel laureates and 5 Pulitzer Prize holders. Notable alumni include Herbert Hoover, William Rehnquist, Anthony Kennedy, Sandra Day O'Connor, John Elway, Sally Ride, Ted Koppel, and Derek Bok (Harvard's president).

WHEN

In 1885 Senator Leland Stanford, a wealthy California railroad magnate (he built the Central Pacific Railroad) and former governor, and his wife Jane established Leland Stanford Junior University in Palo Alto in memory of their recently deceased son. The Stanfords provided land from their own estate and established an endowment of more than $20 million for the new school.

Although the buildings were still under construction, the university opened its doors in 1891 to a freshman class of 559 students, one of whom was future president Herbert Hoover. Dr. David Starr Jordan, the former president of Indiana University, became Stanford's first president.

Leland Stanford died in 1893, but the Stanford family continued to oversee the school's development until 1903 when Jane Stanford turned the university over to the Board of Trustees. In 1906 an earthquake in nearby San Francisco killed 2 people on the Stanford campus and destroyed the library and gymnasium. The university rebuilt and in 1909 affiliated itself with the Cooper School of Medicine (changed to Stanford College of Medicine in 1912). In 1912 Herbert Hoover was elected to the Board of Trustees, where he would sit for almost 50 years.

During WWI the university mobilized 1/2 of its students into the Students' Army Training Corps. In 1917 the School of Education was founded, and the Hoover War Collection (which would become the Hoover Institution on War, Revolution, and Peace) was established in 1919. In 1921 Stanford established its Food Research Institute and in 1925 opened its School of Engineering and its Graduate School of Business.

After WWII J. E. Wallace Sterling became president of the university and started the transformation of Stanford from an average California school to a world-class institution. Sterling worked to develop Stanford's reputation for teaching and research. In 1947 the School of Mineral Sciences was opened. Under Sterling, the university started leasing some of its nearby land holdings to electronics companies. This policy augmented Stanford's revenues and resulted in the formation of Silicon Valley, the nation's preeminent high-tech center, which is still closely associated with the school. William Hewlett and David Packard, 2 students at this time, formed their electronics company (Hewlett-Packard), with a $538 Stanford grant, and have since become major contributors to the university.

In 1958 Stanford opened its first overseas campus (near Stuttgart, Germany) and in 1959 completed the Stanford Medical Center.

In 1980 Donald Kennedy became president of Stanford. Kennedy launched a major fund-raising effort in the late 1980s to establish more facilities, student financial aid, and faculty positions. During the 1980s Stanford experienced internal quarrels over the predominance of classes focused on Western civilization in the curriculum and the role of the Hoover Institution (which is dedicated to opposing Marxism).

HOW MUCH

	9 Yr. Growth	1980	1981	1982	1983	1984	1985	1986	1987	1988	1989
Enrollment	0.5%	12,618	12,866	12,870	13,075	13,217	13,261	13,079	13,272	13,292	13,224
Faculty	1.0%	1,209	1,230	1,260	1,266	1,292	1,292	1,295	1,315	1,335	1,325
Student/faculty ratio	—	10.4	10.5	10.2	10.3	10.2	10.3	10.1	10.1	10.0	10.0
Tuition	9.4%	5,595	6,285	7,140	8,220	9,027	9,705	10,476	11,208	11,880	12,564
Endowment market value ($ mil)	14.3%	958	673	738	935	1,038	1,199	1,503	1,741	1,637	2,088

Annual Tuition 1980-89

14,000
12,000
10,000
8,000
6,000
4,000
2,000
0

Private university
Founded: 1885 (opened 1891)
Fiscal year ends: August 31

WHO

President: Donald Kennedy, $182,917 pay in 1988
Dean of Admissions: Jean H. Fetter
Director of Financial Aid: Robert P. Huff
VP Finance: William F. Massy
Employees: 7,473

WHERE

HQ: Office of Admissions, Old Union, Leland Stanford, Jr., University, Stanford, CA 94305
Phone: 415-723-2300
FAX: 415-321-1324 (News Service)

Stanford University's 8,500-acre campus is adjacent to the suburban communities of Palo Alto and Menlo Park. The school operates study centers in France, Germany, Italy, Poland, and the UK.

Geographic Distribution of Freshman Class	% of Total
California	39
Other US	58
Foreign	3
Total	**100**

WHAT

	1989 Revenues % of total
Tuition & fees	39
Gifts & nongovernment grants	23
Income from prior gifts	21
Conferences, special programs & nonstudent fees	14
Federal support	4
Total	**100**

Academic Unit	1990 Enrollment	% of total
Graduate School of Business	782	6
School of Earth Sciences	203	1
Graduate School of Education	343	3
School of Engineering	3,032	23
School of Humanities and Sciences	4,125	31
School of Law	518	4
School of Medicine	596	4
Undeclared	3,755	28
Total	**13,354**	**100**

Affiliated Institutions
Environmental and Water Quality Laboratory
Frederick E. Terman Engineering Center
Hoover Institution on War, Revolution, and Peace
Hopkin's Marine Station
Institute for Electronics in Medicine
Institute for Energy Studies
Institute for Plasma Research
Jasper Ridge Biological Preserve
John C. Blume Earthquake Engineering Center
Joint Institute for Aeronautics and Acoustics
Leland Stanford, Jr. Museum
Radio Astronomy Institute
Remote Sensing Laboratory
Stanford Linear Accelerator Center
Stanford Medical Center
Thomas Welton Stanford Art Gallery

COMPETITION

Harvard
Ohio State
University of Chicago
University of Texas

THE STANLEY WORKS

OVERVIEW

Stanley Works, a hardware manufacturer based in New Britain, Connecticut, is the world's leading producer of hand tools. The company's operations are divided into 2 industry segments: home improvement and consumer products (hand tools, hardware, and residential door systems), which accounts for 53% of sales and of profits; and industrial and professional products (industrial and hydraulic tools, power-operated doors and gates, and high-density industrial storage and retrieval systems).

The company has remained devoted to its core tool business and its reputation for quality. Aside from hand tools, Stanley claims a leadership position in hinges, pedestrian-powered doors, air-powered tools, fasteners, industrial storage and retrieval systems, and mounted and portable hydraulic tools.

Stanley has consolidated its market position through an aggressive acquisition policy. During the 1980s the company bought 20 new businesses, which currently account for approximately 1/2 of the company's sales.

The company is currently developing its markets across the globe with increasing operations in Europe, the Far East, and Latin America. Foreign sales represent 29% of the company's total.

NYSE symbol: SWK
Incorporated: Connecticut, 1852
Fiscal year ends: December 30

WHO

Chairman, President, and CEO: Richard H. Ayers, age 47, $792,731 pay
VP Finance and CFO: R. Alan Hunter, age 43, $340,320 pay
Group VP: David M. Hadlow, age 61, $393,324 pay
Group VP: Robert G. Widham, age 54, $398,802 pay
Auditors: Ernst & Young
Employees: 18,464

WHERE

HQ: 1000 Stanley Dr., PO Box 7000, New Britain, CT 06050
Phone: 203-225-5111
FAX: 203-827-3901

The company operates manufacturing facilities in 18 states and 11 foreign countries.

	1989 Sales		1989 Operating Income	
	$ mil	% of total	$ mil	% of total
US	1,403	71	171	68
Europe	292	15	42	17
Other	277	14	36	15
Adjustments	—	—	(13)	—
Total	**1,972**	**100**	**236**	**100**

WHEN

In 1843 Frederick T. Stanley opened a bolt shop in a converted War of 1812–era armory in New Britain, Connecticut. With the first steam engine used in New Britain industry, Stanley produced bolts and house trimmings. In 1852 Stanley teamed with his brother and 5 friends to form The Stanley Works to cast, form, and manufacture various types of metal.

The business prospered during the 1860s when the Civil War and westward migration created a need for hardware and tools. When Stanley started to devote less time to the business to concentrate on political and civic affairs, management of the company fell to William H. Hart.

Hart quickly demonstrated his competitive business ability. He expanded the company, engaging in a "knuckles-bared" fight with Stanley's 4 leading (and larger) competitors. Through a combination of innovation, efficiency, quality, and marketing, Hart emerged as the sole survivor. He led the company into steel strapping production, which would become a major element in Stanley's operations. He was named president in 1884.

Stanley entered a period of rapid expansion in the early 20th century. During WWI the company produced belt buckles and rifle and gas mask parts. In addition to numerous domestic acquisitions, the company established operations in Canada (1914) and Germany (1926). In 1920 the company merged with Stanley Rule and Level (a local tool company formed in 1857 by a cousin of Frederick Stanley) and in 1925 opened a new hydroelectric plant near Windsor to provide power for all its operations. In 1929 Stanley organized its electric tool division.

After a difficult decade caused by the Great Depression, Stanley geared up production in the early 1940s for the war effort and was awarded numerous military "E" pennants. Following WWII the company embarked on a massive period of expansion which lasted 4 decades. Staying within its traditional product line, Stanley acquired a myriad of companies which strengthened and consolidated its position in the hardware industry, including Berry Industries (garage doors, 1965), Ackley Manufacturing and Sales (hydraulic tools, 1972), Mac Tools (1980), and National Hand Tool Corporation (1986).

Following difficult years caused by the recession of the early 1980s, Stanley continued to expand and modernize its operations. In the late 1980s the company took increased steps to becoming a global operation by establishing high-tech plants in Europe and the Far East.

WHAT

	1989 Sales		1989 Operating Income	
	$ mil	% of total	$ mil	% of total
Home improvement & consumer products	1,039	53	133	53
Industrial & professional products	933	47	117	47
Adjustments	—	—	(14)	—
Total	**1,972**	**100**	**236**	**100**

Products
Air tools
Automatic parking gates
Bolts and brackets
Boring tools
Chisels
Closet organizers
Door hardware
Electronic controls
Fasteners
Garage doors and openers
Hammers
Hasps
Hinges
Hydraulic tools
Industrial storage systems
Knives
Levels
Planes
Power-operated doors
Rules
Saws
Screwdrivers
Shelving
Sockets
Squares
Wrenches

Brand Names
Bostitch
Lightmaker
MAC mechanic's tools
Powerlock
Stanley
Stanley-Proto
U-install

HOW MUCH

	9 Yr. Growth	1980	1981	1982	1983	1984	1985	1986	1987	1988	1989
Sales ($ mil)	8.6%	940	1,009	963	984	1,158	1,208	1,371	1,763	1,909	1,972
Net income ($ mil)	9.9%	50	55	38	53	72	78	78	96	103	118
Income as % of sales	—	5.4%	5.5%	3.9%	5.4%	6.2%	6.5%	5.7%	5.5%	5.4%	6.0%
Earnings per share ($)	8.6%	1.28	1.39	0.93	1.27	1.73	1.89	1.84	2.22	2.39	2.70
Stock price – high ($)	—	14.33	14.42	18.00	19.00	19.67	22.50	30.83	36.63	31.75	39.25
Stock price – low ($)	—	9.00	10.42	8.50	13.50	13.00	16.33	20.50	21.25	23.63	27.50
Stock price – close ($)	14.4%	11.67	11.67	16.33	18.17	17.25	21.33	25.50	25.88	28.50	39.00
P/E – high	—	11	10	19	15	11	12	17	17	13	15
P/E – low	—	7	7	9	11	8	9	11	10	10	10
Dividends per share ($)	9.7%	0.44	0.48	0.51	0.52	0.60	0.67	0.73	0.82	0.92	1.02
Book value per share ($)	6.1%	9.19	9.66	9.66	10.35	11.00	12.03	13.05	14.59	16.31	15.67

1989 Year End:
Debt ratio: 38.2%
Return on equity: 16.9%
Cash (mil): $55
Current ratio: 2.68
Long-term debt (mil): $416
Number of shares (mil): 43
Dividends:
1989 average yield: 2.6%
1989 payout: 37.8%
Market value (mil): $1,678

Stock Price History high/low 1980-89

40
35
30
25
20
15
10
5
0

RANKINGS

212th in *Fortune* 500 Industrial Cos.
402nd in *Forbes* Sales 500
383rd in *Business Week* 1000

COMPETITION

Black & Decker
Cooper Industries
Emerson
Ingersoll-Rand
Masco
Robert Bosch
Snap-on Tools
Textron

STATE FARM

OVERVIEW

State Farm is the largest auto and homeowners' insurance underwriter in the US. With $22.2 billion in new property and casualty premiums written in 1989, State Farm was the industry leader, about $9 billion ahead of Allstate (Sears).

State Farm Mutual Automobile Insurance, a mutual company owned by policyholders, owns the subsidiary companies that provide property and life insurance.

The company has 33 million customers served by 17,000 State Farm agents who follow the company's small-town approach of being "Like a Good Neighbor," as seen in its TV advertising. Agents target the average consumer, who typically lives near their neighborhood offices.

State Farm Mutual maintains 900 offices for billing, policy renewals, and claims settlement in the US and Canada. The company has been able to maintain steady, profitable growth and low-cost insurance to policyholders.

WHEN

Retired farmer George Mecherle founded State Farm Mutual Automobile Insurance Company in Bloomington, Illinois, in 1922.

Endorsed by the Illinois State Association of Mutual Insurance Companies, State Farm trained secretaries of the association's member organizations to sell its policies. State Farm restricted membership, primarily to members of farm bureaus and farm mutual insurance companies, and charged a one-time membership fee and a premium to protect an automobile against loss or damage by fire, theft, or collision.

From the beginning State Farm, unlike most of its competitors, offered semiannual premium payments, which were easier to sell because customers only had to pay 6 months instead of a year in advance. State Farm also billed and collected renewal premiums from its home office, relieving the agent of the task. Another State Farm feature was a simplified system of classifying all automobiles into 7 classes, A to G, instead of charging separate rates for each auto model, as most stock (nonmutual) companies did.

Before the end of the first year, State Farm had placed policies in 46 rural counties of Illinois through 90 mutual company salesmen. In order to insure autos of nonfarmers, the company in 1926 started City and Village Mutual Automobile Insurance Company, which became part of State Farm the following year. Between 1927 and 1931 State Farm introduced wind coverage, borrowed-car protection, and insurance for buses or cars used in transporting children to school.

State Farm opened a branch office in Berkeley, California, in 1928 and started State Farm Life Insurance Company, a wholly owned subsidiary, in 1929. In 1935 the company established State Farm Fire Insurance Company. President George Mecherle became chairman in 1937, and his son Ramond assumed the presidency. George Mecherle remained active in the company, challenging company agents to write "A Million or More (policies) by '44." State Farm passed the one million mark in 5 1/2 years, with a 110% increase in policies.

In the 1940s State Farm began to concentrate more on metropolitan areas after most of the farm bureaus canceled their contracts with State Farm in order to form their own companies. By 1941 State Farm had become the largest insurance company in total automobile premiums written. In the late 1940s and 1950s, the company moved to a full-time agency force.

The company continued through 1989 to be the largest automobile insurer, with 20% of the market. In 1989, however, State Farm Mutual Auto had the highest claim payments for disasters (Hurricane Hugo and others) in its history, resulting in a 42% decline in earnings to $419 million. State Farm's fire companies had a record $1.1 billion in underwriting losses in 1989, compared with a $297 million underwriting gain in 1988.

HOW MUCH

Life Insurance Only	9 Yr. Growth	1980	1981	1982	1983	1984	1985	1986	1987	1988	1989
Assets ($ mil)	14.0%	3,330	3,760	4,293	4,980	5,669	6,588	7,485	8,454	9,590	10,839
Premium & annuity income ($ mil)	12.2%	536	597	637	944	1,035	1,156	1,225	1,349	1,438	1,563
Net investment income ($ mil)	16.4%	238	284	335	385	478	576	657	740	828	932
Net income ($ mil)	—	—	—	—	—	—	—	—	—	138	149
Net income as % of assets	—	—	—	—	—	—	—	—	—	1.4%	1.4%
Life insurance in force ($ bil)	13.3%	51.0	58.5	64.5	73.7	82.9	92.8	106.0	120.0	137.1	156.3

Life Insurance in Force ($ bil) 1980-89

Mutual company
Incorporated: Illinois, 1922
Fiscal year ends: December 31

WHO

Chairman, President, and CEO: Edward B. Rust, Jr., age 40
VC, Financial VP, and Chief Investment Officer: Rex J. Bates, age 67
EVP and Chief Administrative Officer: Vincent J. Trosino, age 50
SVP and Treasurer: Roger S. Joslin, age 54
Senior Agency VP: Don D. Rood, age 60
Auditors: Coopers & Lybrand
Employees: 41,000

WHERE

HQ: State Farm Mutual Automobile Insurance Company, One State Farm Plaza, Bloomington, IL 61710
Phone: 309-766-2311
FAX: 309-766-1181 (Public Relations)

State Farm has operations in all 50 states, the District of Columbia, and Canada.

WHAT

	1989 Net Income	
	$ mil	% of total
State Farm Mutual auto	419	98
State Farm fire companies	(142)	(33)
State Farm life companies	149	35
State Farm County Mutual (TX)	1	—
Total	**427**	**100**

Financial Services
Automobile insurance
Fire insurance
Homeowners insurance
Inland marine insurance
Life insurance

Affiliates
State Farm Annuity and Life Insurance Co.
State Farm County Mutual Insurance Co. of Texas
State Farm Fire and Casualty Co.
State Farm General Insurance Co.
State Farm Life and Accident Assurance Co.
State Farm Life Insurance Co.
State Farm Lloyds

RANKINGS

22nd in *Fortune* 50 Life Insurance Cos.

COMPETITION

Aetna
American Financial
AIG
Berkshire Hathaway
CIGNA
Equitable
First Executive
GEICO
General Re
ITT
John Hancock
Kemper
Loews
Massachusetts Mutual
Metropolitan
New York Life
Northwestern Mutual
Primerica
Prudential
Sears
Teachers Insurance
Transamerica
Travelers
USF&G

THE STOP & SHOP COMPANIES, INC.

OVERVIEW

Stop & Shop, based near Boston, is one of the largest private companies in New England. It operates 117 Stop & Shop supermarkets and 131 Bradlees discount department stores in the eastern US.

Stop & Shop is getting its house in order after the 1988 LBO that, with the assistance of takeover maven Kohlberg Kravis Roberts, took the company private. Chairman Avram Goldberg and his wife, President Carol Goldberg, daughter of the founding Rabb family, quit abruptly in 1989 over differences with KKR, and Lewis Schaeneman succeeded Avram Goldberg as CEO. Schaeneman is carrying another title in 1990, having named himself president of the beleaguered Bradlees chain after the sudden departure of George Granoff to Ames. Bradlees is struggling after a 35% decrease in operating profits in 1989 on a 17% drop in sales from the previous year.

Stop & Shop is highly leveraged. Some Bradlees stores have been sold to reduce debt.

Private company
Founded: Massachusetts, 1914

WHO

Chairman and CEO; President, Chairman, and CEO, Bradlees Discount Department Store Co.: Lewis G. Schaeneman, Jr.
SVP, General Counsel, Clerk, and Secretary: Samuel W. W. Mandell
SVP: Donald J. Comeau
SVP and CFO: Joseph D. McGlinchey
President and COO, Stop & Shop Supermarket Co.: Robert G. Tobin
SVP Merchandising and Marketing, Bradlees Discount Department Store: Barry Berman
Auditors: KPMG Peat Marwick
Employees: 42,000

WHEN

Stop and Shop was originally formed as the Economy Grocery Stores chain by the Rabinovitz family in Boston in 1914. By 1925, the year that guiding force Sidney Rabinovitz (later shortened to Rabb) became chairman, the company had 262 stores in the Boston area. Through the purchase of additional locations from Rood & Woodbury (1929) and United-Gray Stores (1932), the company grew to more than 400 stores. During the Great Depression, Economy Grocery Stores opened a massive store at the site of a former Ford assembly plant which was to be one of the earliest supermarkets in the US. The larger stores were dubbed Stop & Shop Supermarkets.

By 1945 the company operated 120 stores in Massachusetts and Vermont, 79 of which were operating under the Stop & Shop name. Stop & Shop was adopted as the corporate name in 1946.

The company expanded into discount department store retailing in 1961 with the purchase of the 7-store Bradlees chain and entered the discount drugstore market by launching Medi Mart (1968). Stop & Shop acquired Charles B. Perkins Tobacco Shops, an eastern New England chain, which it proceeded to develop as Hallmark Cards gift shops (1969).

A 1969 fire at the Readville, Massachuestts food distribution center hobbled supermarket operations for a time, and Rabb pushed to diversify by adding new Bradlees, Medi Mart, and Perkins locations.

In 1978 the company started Raxton Corporation, which operated women's clothing stores under the names Off the Rax and Raxton, Ltd., but Stop & Shop sold the company to Dress Barn in 1984. It continued to add stores, expanding its grocery and discount drug chains along the Eastern Seaboard. In the mid-1980s, the department store segment grew through the purchase of 19 Almy Stores (New York and New England) and 18 Jefferson Ward stores, acquired from Montgomery Ward (Philadelphia and Delaware), reaching 171 locations by the end of 1987. But the expanded Bradlees operations struggled against strong competitors such as Caldor. Bradlees, which accounted for almost 1/2 of Stop & Shop's revenues, had positioned itself at the upscale end of the discount store market, a limb that was sawed off when customers went looking for lower prices.

In 1985 Rabb died, and son-in-law Avram Goldberg, who had been CEO since 1979, was named chairman. His wife (Rabb's daughter), Carol Goldberg, was named president.

In 1986 Stop & Shop put its Medi Mart and Perkins chains up for sale in order to focus on its grocery and department stores. The 67 Medi Mart stores were sold to Walgreen and the Perkins chain was divided among 3 purchasers. In 1988 the Haft family's Dart Group made a hostile takeover bid. The Goldbergs turned to Kohlberg Kravis Roberts, which staged a $1.3 billion LBO and took the company private. To reduce Stop & Shop's debt, the company sold 70 locations of the Bradlees chain and trimmed 450 employees from the headquarters payroll.

The Goldbergs, who reportedly made $22 million from the LBO, resigned unexpectedly after 30 years of service in 1989, and Lewis Schaeneman, Jr., was named chairman and CEO.

WHERE

HQ: 1 Bradlees Circle, Braintree, MA 02184
Phone: 617-380-8000
FAX: 617-770-5440

Stop & Shop operates 117 supermarkets in Massachusetts, New York, Connecticut, and Rhode Island. The Bradlees Discount Department Store Company has 131 locations in Massachusetts, New York, Connecticut, New Hampshire, Pennsylvania, and Virginia.

WHAT

	1989 Sales		1989 Operating Income	
	$ mil	% of total	$ mil	% of total
Supermarkets	2,885	62	97	64
Department stores	1,751	38	55	36
Adjustments	—	—	(2)	—
Total	**4,636**	**100**	**150**	**100**

Stop & Shop Supermarkets

Stop & Shop Manufacturing
Bakery operations
Carbonated beverage processing
Commissaries
Cooked meat processing
Dairy operations
Household chemical manufacturing
Photo processing
Recycling operations
Salad processing
Seafood processing

Bradlees Discount Stores
General merchandise

RANKINGS

27th in *Fortune* 50 Retailing Cos.
17th in *Forbes* 400 US Private Cos.

COMPETITION

American Stores
Ames
Great A&P
K mart
Price Co.
Supermarkets General
Other general merchandise and specialty retailers

HOW MUCH

	9 Yr. Growth	1980	1981	1982	1983	1984	1985	1986	1987	1988	1989
Sales ($ mil)	9.4%	2,059	2,168	2,342	2,791	3,247	3,689	3,872	4,343	4,624	4,636
Net income ($ mil)	—	16	25	35	51	55	30	44	56	(22)	(23)
Income as % of sales	—	0.8%	1.1%	1.5%	1.8%	1.7%	0.8%	1.1%	1.3%	(0.5%)	(0.5%)

1989 Year End:
Debt ratio: 93.2%
Return on equity: —
Cash (mil): $18
Current ratio: 0.95
Long-term debt (mil): $1,275

Net Income ($ mil) 1980-89

STORAGE TECHNOLOGY CORPORATION

OVERVIEW

Storage Technology is a worldwide leader in the computer data storage and retrieval industry, ranking first in tape drives (which store data not needed instantaneously) and 4th in disk drives (which store data for immediate access).

Most of StorageTek's products are designed to work with IBM mid-range and mainframe computers and their clones. Besting its prime competitor, IBM, StorageTek brought out the first solid-state disk drives (fast, high-density) and the first product to successfully automate massive tape storage (the Automated Cartridge System, or ACS).

StorageTek's tape products have the highest reliability statistics in the industry and account for 63% of the firm's revenues. Other products include printers and specialized software for efficient data storage management.

The company's recent turnaround after bankruptcy (StorageTek's was one of the largest and quickest reorganizations in bankruptcy history) was fueled by booming demand for the ACS. StorageTek hopes to ride the ACS product to $2 billion in sales by 1995, but its outlook is clouded by lower than expected demand in the US and the uncertainty of what new products IBM might introduce.

NYSE symbol: STK
Incorporated: Delaware, 1969
Fiscal year ends: Last Friday in December

WHO

Chairman, CEO, and President: Ryal R. Poppa, age 56, $925,632 pay
EVP Finance and Administration: Harris Ravine, age 47, $500,537 pay
EVP Worldwide Field Operations: James M. MacGuire, age 58, $396,336 pay
EVP Operations: Lowell Thomas Gooch, age 45, $313,762 pay
Auditors: Price Waterhouse
Employees: 9,300

WHEN

A group of 4 former IBM engineers founded Storage Technology in Colorado in 1969 to fill a niche in tape drives for IBM-compatible mainframe computers. One of the founders, a Palestinian refugee named Jesse Aweida, led the company (dubbed StorageTek) to the top of its industry.

Heady growth inspired StorageTek to become a full-line supplier of computer peripherals. Acquisitions included Promodata (1973), Disk Systems (1974), Microtechnology (1979), and Documation (high-speed printers, 1980). The company also began developing an IBM-compatible mainframe computer and optical laser disk.

The Aweida whirlwind swept StorageTek's sales from $4 million to $922 million between 1971 and 1981, creating the world's leading supplier of tape drives (55% market share for IBM-compatible tape drives) and disk drives (35%) and the 9th largest company in the computer industry.

In 1982, however, delayed expansion projects ate capital while providing no return. In addition, malfunctions on disk drives installed earlier caused costly replacements and damage to the company's reputation. Aweida's termination of several product lines could not prevent a cash flow crisis, and in late 1984 StorageTek filed for bankruptcy under Chapter 11.

Aweida stepped down, and turnaround artist Ryal Poppa (CEO in 1985) sliced $85 million from the operating budget by eliminating 2 layers of management, 5,000 workers (down to 9,000), and the mainframe and optical disk projects.

Although awash in red ink, Poppa was able to convince creditors to fund his vision of automated tape storage at a fraction of disk drive prices. The resulting 4400 ACS (1987) was instrumental to the company's profitability following its emergence from bankruptcy in July 1987. The company's Library Server software has allowed StorageTek to adapt the ACS for Bull HN, Unisys, Control Data Corporation, Fujitsu, Siemens, and Cray computers, thus reducing StorageTek's dependence on IBM machines.

In 1989 the company purchased Aspen Peripherals to enter the mid-range tape market. Aspen president Jesse Aweida did not rejoin the company he helped found. An advanced, fault-tolerant disk-drive line using the inexpensive disks of personal computers is planned for 1991.

WHERE

HQ: 2270 S. 88th St., Louisville, CO 80028
Phone: 303-673-5151
FAX: 303-673-5019

StorageTek has 130 sales and service locations on 6 continents. Manufacturing facilities are located in the US, Puerto Rico, and the UK.

	1989 Sales		1989 Operating Income	
	$ mil	% of total	$ mil	% of total
US	682	70	62	92
Europe	198	20	7	10
Other	103	10	(1)	(2)
Adjustments	—	—	(12)	—
Total	**983**	**100**	**56**	**100**

WHAT

	1989 Sales	
	$ mil	% of total
Sales	691	70
Rental & service	292	30
Total	**983**	**100**

	1989 Sales	
	$ mil	% of total
Tape systems	623	63
Disk systems	226	23
Printer subsystems	134	14
Total	**983**	**100**

Disk Systems
Disk controllers
Rotating magnetic
8380 family
Solid state
4080
4305

Tape Systems
4400 ACS library
4480 18-track cartridge
4980 18-track
9914/13 9-track
Summit 4180 18-track
Summit 4280 18-track

Printers
5000 series impact
6024 nonimpact
6060 nonimpact
6100 series nonimpact

Software
Data management
Interfaces between disk and central processing unit
Library Server (for ACS) for Cray, Unisys, Control Data

RANKINGS

342nd in *Fortune* 500 Industrial Cos.
796th in *Business Week* 1000

COMPETITION

Amdahl
Fujitsu
Hitachi
IBM
Siemens

HOW MUCH

	9 Yr. Growth	1980	1981	1982	1983	1984	1985	1986	1987	1988	1989
Sales ($ mil)	5.6%	604	922	1,079	887	809	673	696	750	874	983
Net income ($ mil)	(2.4%)	45	82	63	(9)	(505)	(44)	17	19	44	36
Income as % of sales	—	7.5%	8.9%	5.9%	(1.1%)	(62.5%)	(6.5%)	2.4%	2.5%	5.1%	3.7%
Earnings per share ($)	(24.3%)	17.20	25.00	18.40	(2.80)	(146.20)	(12.60)	4.80	0.80	1.90	1.40
Stock price – high ($)	—	260.00	403.75	361.25	250.00	146.25	38.75	73.75	50.00	36.25	22.50
Stock price – low ($)	—	118.75	177.50	162.50	135.00	20.00	10.00	17.50	11.25	12.50	9.25
Stock price – close ($)	(28.0%)	226.25	350.00	212.50	136.25	22.50	17.50	35.00	18.75	17.50	11.75
P/E – high	—	15	16	20	—	—	—	15	63	19	16
P/E – low	—	7	7	9	—	—	—	4	14	7	7
Dividends per share ($)	—	0.00	0.00	0.00	0.00	0.00	0.00	0.00	0.00	0.00	0.00
Book value per share ($)	(19.3%)	90.73	139.70	159.21	147.03	0.81	(15.69)	(5.20)	10.23	12.46	13.12

1989 Year End:
Debt ratio: 51.6%
Return on equity: 10.9%
Cash (mil): $61
Current ratio: 1.73
Long-term debt (mil): $360
Number of shares (mil): 26
Dividends:
1989 average yield: 0.0%
1989 payout: 0.0%
Market value (mil): $302

Stock Price History high/low 1980-89

450
400
350
300
250
200
150
100
50
0

SUN COMPANY, INC.

OVERVIEW

Sun is the 11th largest petroleum refiner in the US. The company spun off its domestic production as independent Oryx Energy in 1988 but continues to drill for and produce oil and natural gas internationally, mostly in the North Sea.

Still, 90% of Sun's 1989 sales came from refining and marketing. Sun's refining and marketing group operates 5 US refineries that can process 595,000 barrels of crude oil a day. Sun owns 5 ocean tankers and has interests in 10,553 miles of US pipeline. Sun has the 2nd largest capacity in the US for manufacturing lubricating oils and waxes. In 23 eastern states, the company sells gasoline in 6,445 Sunoco and Atlantic service stations.

Sun owns 75% of Suncor, an integrated petroleum company (from drilling to refining to marketing) in Canada. Sun also owns coal mines, develops real estate, and leases capital equipment.

NYSE symbol: SUN
Incorporated: Pennsylvania, 1971
Fiscal year ends: December 31

WHO

Chairman, CEO, and President: Robert McClements, Jr., age 61, $938,360 pay
EVP and Principal Financial Officer: John P. Neafsey, age 50, $462,632 pay
EVP: Robert H. Campbell, age 52, $461,956 pay
EVP: Richard W. Ince, age 52
Auditors: Coopers & Lybrand
Employees: 21,600

WHEN

Joseph Newton Pew began his energy career in 1876 in a Pennsylvania natural gas pipeline partnership. One arm of his enterprise supplied Pittsburgh with the first-ever natural gas system for a major city's home and industrial use.

When oil discoveries in northwest Ohio sparked an 1886 boom, Pew organized Sun Oil Line, consolidated in 1890 as Sun Oil (Ohio). In an 1894 transaction, Sun created Diamond Oil to purchase a Toledo refinery; Sun traces its trademark diamond pierced by an arrow to that short-lived Diamond subsidiary.

With the 1901 Spindletop gusher, Pew dispatched nephew J. Edgar Pew to Texas where he bought land for a storage terminal and in 1902 won an auction for oil-rich properties of a bankrupt firm. Back East, the elder Pew bought Delaware River acreage in Pennsylvania for a shipping terminal and refinery to process Texas crude into Red Stock. The lubricating oil carved Sun a place in the Standard Oil–dominated petroleum industry.

Joseph Newton Pew died in 1912 and was succeeded by sons J. Howard, 30, and Joseph Newton, Jr., 26. The young Pews launched the company into shipbuilding (1916) and opened gasoline stations (1920). The company's gasoline was dyed blue (legend says it matched a Chinese tile chip Joe Pew and his wife had received on their honeymoon) and sold as Blue Sunoco.

When Howard Pew retired in 1947, brother Joe became chairman and Robert Dunlop became the first non-Pew president of Sun. Dunlop led the company to the first major foreign oil strike, in Venezuela's Lake Maracaibo in 1957.

In 1967, Dunlop's chance meeting with a Sunray DX executive in Midland, Texas, led Sun to acquire Sunray DX the next year. The addition of Sunray DX diluted the Pew family's stake in the company. In the 1970s President Robert Sharbaugh diversified the company away from its energy roots. The company dropped "oil" from its name in 1976. Sharbaugh left in 1978 after Sun's foray into the medical supply business.

To refocus on the oil business, the company purchased Seagram's Texas Pacific Oil for $2.3 billion in 1980, sold its venerable shipbuilding arm in 1982, and sold the medical supply business in 1985. In 1988 Sun acquired Atlantic Petroleum and its more than 1,000 service stations. Sun decided to forsake drilling in the US when, in 1988, it spun off its domestic oil and gas properties, first called Sun Exploration and Production and renamed Oryx Energy in 1989. Sun retained its international exploration and production business.

Ironically, Oryx purchased $1.1 billion of British Petroleum oil and gas properties in 1990 to compete with its former parent in the international arena.

WHERE

HQ: 100 Matsonford Rd., Radnor, PA 19087
Phone: 215-293-6000
FAX: 215-293-6204

Sun operates in the US, Canada, and 11 other foreign countries.

	1989 Sales		1989 Operating Income	
	$ mil	% of total	$ mil	% of total
US	8,957	80	158	82
Canada	1,345	12	49	26
Other	866	8	(15)	(8)
Adjustments	(1,363)	—	94	—
Total	**9,805**	**100**	**286**	**100**

WHAT

	1989 Sales		1989 Operating Income	
	$ mil	% of total	$ mil	% of total
Exploration & production	359	3	53	15
Refining & mktg.	10,099	90	300	84
Mining	403	4	(39)	(11)
Real estate & leasing	307	3	44	12
Adjustments	(1,363)	—	(72)	—
Total	**9,805**	**100**	**286**	**100**

Subsidiaries

Sun International E&P
Exploration and production outside the US
Sun Refining and Marketing Co.
Sun Coal Co.
Coal mining in Kentucky, Utah, Virginia, West Virginia, Wyoming
Suncor Inc.
Canadian petroleum exploration, production, marketing; mining, synthetic crude oil production
Radnor Corp.
Real estate development
Helios Capital Corp.
Equipment leasing
Secured lending
Sunoco Credit Corp.
Commercial paper

HOW MUCH

	9 Yr. Growth	1980	1981	1982	1983	1984	1985	1986	1987	1988	1989
Sales ($ mil)	(3.0%)	12,945	15,012	15,519	14,730	14,466	13,769	9,376	8,691	8,612	9,805
Net income ($ mil)	(19.9%)	723	1,076	537	453	538	527	385	348	7	98
Income as % of sales	—	5.6%	7.2%	3.5%	3.1%	3.7%	3.8%	4.1%	4.0%	0.1%	1.0%
Earnings per share ($)	(18.4%)	5.71	8.59	4.40	3.78	4.59	4.65	3.51	3.18	0.06	0.92
Stock price – high ($)	—	59.63	49.38	45.75	46.50	59.50	56.25	59.50	73.13	61.75	43.25
Stock price – low ($)	—	30.69	29.00	26.75	30.25	43.38	43.63	42.25	36.00	28.00	31.38
Stock price – close ($)	(1.9%)	48.75	45.50	31.38	43.75	46.13	51.75	54.25	51.38	32.13	40.88
P/E – high	—	10	6	10	12	13	12	17	23	1,029	47
P/E – low	—	5	3	6	8	9	9	12	11	467	34
Dividends per share ($)	0.5%	1.73	2.03	2.25	2.30	2.30	2.30	3.00	3.00	2.70	1.80
Book value per share ($)	(1.6%)	35.26	41.87	43.95	45.08	46.80	48.71	49.03	49.36	31.24	30.50

1989 Year End:
Debt ratio: 29.7%
Return on equity: 3.0%
Cash (mil): $416
Current ratio: 0.97
Long-term debt (mil): $1,377
Number of shares (mil): 107
Dividends:
1989 average yield: 4.4%
1989 payout: 195.7%
Market value (mil): $4,361

Stock Price History high/low 1980-89

RANKINGS

46th in *Fortune* 500 Industrial Cos.
122nd in *Fortune* Global 500 Industrial Cos.
76th in *Forbes* Sales 500
157th in *Business Week* 1000
440th in *Business Week* Global 1000

COMPETITION

Amoco	Du Pont	Royal Dutch/Shell
Ashland	Exxon	Texaco
Atlantic Richfield	Mobil	Unocal
British Petroleum	Occidental	USX
Chevron	Pennzoil	Convenience store operators
Coastal	Phillips	

SUN MICROSYSTEMS, INC.

OVERVIEW

Sun Microsystems is the world's leading supplier of workstations (powerful, high-resolution color graphics computers), with almost 29% of the market. The *wünderkind* Sun had entered the *Fortune* 500 and exceeded $1 billion in sales by its 6th year. Sun is now the 2nd-fastest-growing company in the computer industry.

Sun believes in open systems (where computers of different vendors communicate freely). The company was a pioneer in supporting the UNIX open operating system and the widespread licensing of its UNIX-friendly SPARC microprocessors and workstation connectivity software.

Workstations are the computer industry's fastest-growing segment, with 30% yearly growth expected over the next 5 years. Sun has shipped 270,000 computers since its birth in 1982. All products are adaptable to future hardware advances.

SPARC-based workstations and servers (which delegate data flow) now account for 90% of hardware revenues. Engineering clients (design, manufacturing) still predominate; commercial buyers (electronic publishing, financial services) are increasing.

OTC symbol: SUNW
Incorporated: Delaware, 1987
Fiscal year ends: June 30

WHO

Chairman, President, and CEO: Scott G. McNealy, age 34, $781,377 pay
VP Worldwide Field Operations: Dennis M. Ohryn, age 49, $352,645 pay
VP Operations Group: Robert A. Garrow, age 46, $291,973 pay
VP Research and Development: William N. Joy, age 34, $261,926 pay
VP Corporate Planning and Development and CFO: William J. Raduchel, age 43
Auditors: Ernst & Young
Employees: 10,200

WHEN

The 4 27-year-olds who founded Sun Microsystems in 1982 saw great market potential for workstations able to share data using the UNIX operating system so popular with scientists and engineers.

German-born Andreas Bechtolsheim, a Stanford engineering graduate student, had built a workstation from spare parts for his numerical problems. Two Stanford MBA graduates, Scott McNealy and India-born Vinod Khosla, liked Bechtolsheim's creation, and they tapped Berkeley's UNIX guru William Joy to supply the software.

By adopting AT&T's UNIX operating system, Sun's workstations, unlike the workstations of industry pioneer Apollo, from the outset networked easily with the hardware and software of other vendors. Sun, with lower prices afforded by existing technologies, zoomed to $500 million in sales in just 5 years, with only one major ad campaign.

The engineering market devoured such Sun offerings as the Sun-3 family (1985) and the 386i (1987). Sun hooked its workstations into networks with its NFS (a file access system widely adopted by others), SunNet, and SunLINK.

In 1987 Sun signed with AT&T to develop an enhanced UNIX operating system; AT&T took a 20% equity investment in Sun the following year. The product that emerged in late 1989 established a de facto high-end UNIX standard (System V, Release 4.0). Sun's development of the fast and highly adaptable SPARC microprocessor (using a simplified RISC design) gave its SPARCstation 1 (1989) minicomputer power.

Sun licensed SPARC to stimulate low-cost, high-volume production of SPARC systems and thus increase the number of 3rd-party applications available. Licensees included chipmakers Fujitsu, Philips, and Cypress and hardware vendors AT&T, Prime, Toshiba, and Taiwan's DataTech and Tatung.

Recent SPARCware support, such as Lotus 1-2-3 and Ashton-Tate's dBase IV for Sun systems, has broadened Sun's commercial market. In 1990 Sun signed with IBM for worldwide, nonexclusive cross-licensing, covering patents filed before mid-1995.

With workstations now so clonable, Sun maintains short product life cycles (average 12 months) and high R&D (about 13% of revenues). Gross margins on Sun workstations have fallen from 49% to 43% in the last 3 years. Culminating with its SPARCstation SLC (1990), Sun in the past 5 years has taken computing cost per million instructions per second (MIPS) from $46,500 to $399.

WHERE

HQ: 2550 Garcia Ave., Mountain View, CA 94043
Phone: 415-960-1300
FAX: 415-969-9131

Sun products are distributed through 98 domestic and 59 foreign sales and service offices.

	1989 Sales		1989 Operating Income	
	$ mil	% of total	$ mil	% of total
US	1,021	58	99	88
Europe	427	24	15	13
Pacific Rim	317	18	(1)	(1)
Adjustments	—	—	(25)	—
Total	**1,765**	**100**	**88**	**100**

WHAT

SPARC-Based Family
SPARCserver 300 series
SPARCstation 1
SPARCstation 330 series
SPARCstation 370 series

Family
Sun-3/80 (entry-level workstations based on Motorola chips)
Sun-3/400 (workstations and servers based on Motorola chips)

Sun386i Family
Workstations (based on the Intel 80386 chip)

Software
Development tools for computer-aided design, manufacturing, and engineering
Network File System
Open Network Computing
Open systems
System V Release 4 (UNIX)
OpenWindows
OPEN LOOK (graphical interface)
OpenWindows DeskSet (personal productivity tools)
Xtoolkit
SunLink (wide-area networking)

Other Products
Board-level central processing units
Specialized processors and peripherals (laser printers, mass storage devices)

HOW MUCH

	4 Yr. Growth	1980	1981	1982	1983	1984	1985	1986	1987	1988	1989
Sales ($ mil)	97.9%	—	—	—	—	—	115	210	538	1,052	1,765
Net income ($ mil)	61.4%	—	—	—	—	—	9	12	36	66	61
Income as % of sales	—	—	—	—	—	—	7.4%	5.7%	6.8%	6.3%	3.4%
Earnings per share ($)	43.3%	—	—	—	—	—	0.18	0.23	0.55	0.90	0.76
Stock price – high ($)	—	—	—	—	—	—	—	12.19	22.88	20.38	23.00
Stock price – low ($)	—	—	—	—	—	—	—	5.63	11.00	13.00	13.38
Stock price – close ($)	—	—	—	—	—	—	—	12.00	16.75	16.63	17.25
P/E – high	—	—	—	—	—	—	—	53	42	23	30
P/E – low	—	—	—	—	—	—	—	24	20	15	18
Dividends per share ($)	—	—	—	—	—	—	0.00	0.00	0.00	0.00	0.00
Book value per share ($)	81.9%	—	—	—	—	—	0.72	2.00	3.58	5.11	7.88

1989 Year End:
Debt ratio: 17.7%
Return on equity: 11.7%
Cash (mil): $54
Current ratio: 1.9
Long-term debt (mil): $143
Number of shares (mil): 84
Dividends:
1989 average yield: 0.0%
1989 payout: 0.0%
Market value (mil): $1,448

Stock Price History high/low 1986-89

25
20
15
10
5
0

RANKINGS

46th in *Fortune* 500 Industrial Cos.
390th in *Forbes* Sales 500
294th in *Business Week* 1000

COMPETITION

Apple
Compaq
Control Data
Data General
Digital Equipment
Hewlett-Packard
Intergraph
IBM
Prime
Wang

SUNTRUST BANKS, INC.

OVERVIEW

Atlanta-based SunTrust is the 19th largest publicly traded banking concern in the US. It oversees state holding companies in Georgia, Florida, and Tennessee.

SunTrust's book value per share would be 22% higher if it figured the appreciation of its 6 million shares of Coca-Cola stock. The stock has been held since the old Trust Company of Georgia received stock for helping with the initial underwriting of Coca-Cola in 1919. Ever since, SunTrust has carried the stock on its books at $110,000. At the end of 1989, the Coke stock would have sold for $466.1 million.

SunTrust operates the largest trust and investment management businesses in its 3 states, holding $39.4 billion in assets in its trust departments at the end of 1989. The Factoring Division of SunTrust's Atlanta bank is the US's 9th largest factor (*i.e.*, a firm that purchases and resells businesses' accounts receivable).

Once enjoying the boom of the Sunbelt, SunTrust has been burned a bit by bad real estate loans in Tennessee, and some analysts worry about its exposure to loans in Florida.

NYSE symbol: STI
Incorporated: Georgia, 1984
Fiscal year ends: December 31

WHO

Chairman: Joel R. Wells, Jr., age 61, $512,143 pay (prior to promotion)
President and CEO: James B. Williams, age 56, $471,375 pay (prior to promotion)
SEVP: L. Phillip Humann, age 44, $258,195 pay (prior to promotion)
EVP: George A. Snelling, age 60, $254,944 pay
EVP and CFO: John W. Spiegel, age 48
Auditors: Arthur Andersen & Co.
Employees: 20,023

WHEN

SunTrust was formed by the union of old-money Georgia and new-money Florida. Founded in 1891 as the Commercial Traveler's Savings Bank, the Trust Company of Georgia had served Atlanta's oldest and richest institutions. It helped underwrite Coca-Cola's first public stock sale in 1919, and the only written copy of the Coke formula rests in a Trust vault.

Beginning in 1933 Trust acquired controlling interests in 5 other Georgia banks. As regulation of multibank ownership relaxed in the 1970s, Trust acquired the remaining interests in its original banks and bought 25 more. At the height of the Sunbelt boom in 1984, Trust was the most profitable bank in the nation, with a low ratio of nonperforming assets — 0.9% of total loans.

Sun Banks began in 1934 as the First National Bank at Orlando. It grew into a holding company in 1967, and the Sun name was adopted in 1973. In the early 1970s the bank helped assemble the land for Orlando's Walt Disney World. It is the official bank of the Magic Kingdom.

Under Joel Wells, then president and CEO, Sun Banks acquired Florida's Century Banks ($1.2 billion in assets, 1982) and the Flagship Banks group ($3.3 billion in assets, 1984). Sun Banks grew from $1.9 billion to $9 billion in assets in only 8 years (1976-1984) and increased the number of its branches more than fivefold (51 to 274).

After a lingering courtship, Sun and Trust executives agreed in 1984 to wed the 2 companies, forming a super–holding company over the 2 organizations. The union followed state legislation in Georgia and Florida that permitted multistate bank holding companies, and, when the marriage was consummated in 1985, Sun brought a dowry of $9.4 billion in assets, and Trust contributed $6.2 billion. Bob Strickland, Trust's chairman, became chairman and CEO for the new Atlanta-based SunTrust, and Wells became president.

In 1986 SunTrust bought Nashville-based Third National Bank, the 2nd largest bank holding company in Tennessee, with assets of $5 billion. But problems with Tennessee real estate loans increasingly plagued SunTrust. In 1990 it increased the amount of loans it wrote off, and a credit rating service lowered SunTrust's ratings in light of nonperforming loans for properties in overbuilt Florida.

Strickland stepped down as chairman and CEO in 1990 but remained as chairman of the board's executive committee. Wells became chairman, and James Williams, a conservative banker who instilled strict fiscal management in Trust's Georgia banks, became president and CEO.

WHERE

HQ: 25 Park Place, NE, Atlanta, GA 30303
Phone: 404-588-7711
FAX: 404-827-6001

SunTrust owns 53 banks with 320 offices in Florida, 184 in Georgia, and 113 in Tennessee.

	1989 Net Income	
	$ mil	% of total
Banking subsidiaries		
Florida	162	48
Georgia	163	48
Tennessee	47	14
Nonbanking net income (expense)		
Mortgage banking	3	1
Other operating nonbanks	3	1
Parent company, debt service & other supporting operations	(41)	(12)
Total	**337**	**100**

WHAT

Corporate Banking
Cash management
Corporate finance
Credit products
Investment services
Trust services

Community Banking
Commercial loans
Deposit accounts
Individual loans
Small business loans

Trust & Investment Management
Equity funds
Trust services

Mortgage Banking

Insurance
Customer reinsurance

Data Systems
Processing for correspondent banks in 6 states

HOW MUCH

	9 Yr. Growth	1980	1981	1982	1983	1984	1985	1986	1987	1988	1989
Sales ($ mil)	29.6%	320	419	520	594	1,040	1,819	2,463	2,561	2,889	3,296
Net income ($ mil)	32.2%	27	27	34	46	65	167	245	283	309	337
Income as % of sales	—	8.5%	6.4%	6.6%	7.8%	6.2%	9.2%	10.0%	11.0%	10.7%	10.2%
Earnings per share ($)	9.0%	1.20	1.18	1.28	1.53	1.47	1.65	1.85	2.17	2.38	2.61
Stock price – high ($)	—	8.44	12.44	12.19	14.75	15.19	20.31	27.25	27.75	24.50	26.88
Stock price – low ($)	—	5.38	8.38	7.50	10.00	10.88	13.63	17.31	17.00	18.50	19.75
Stock price – close ($)	11.8%	8.38	9.25	11.06	13.25	15.19	19.13	20.00	18.25	19.88	22.88
P/E – high	—	7	11	10	10	10	12	15	13	10	10
P/E – low	—	4	7	6	7	7	8	9	8	8	8
Dividends per share ($)	7.4%	0.41	0.46	0.51	0.56	0.60	0.60	0.61	0.65	0.70	0.78
Book value per share ($)	6.9%	8.91	9.65	10.00	11.68	12.60	10.72	11.59	12.92	14.57	16.32

1989 Year End:
Debt ratio: 18.9%
Return on equity: 16.9%
Cash (mil): $2,897
Total assets (mil): $29,650
Long-term debt (mil): $485
Number of shares (mil): 128
Dividends:
1989 average yield: 3.4%
1989 payout: 29.9%
Market value (mil): $2,928

Stock Price History
high/low 1980-89

RANKINGS

19th in *Fortune* 100 Commercial Banking Cos.
254th in *Forbes* Sales 500
237th in *Business Week* 1000
655th in *Business Week* Global 1000

COMPETITION

H. F. Ahmanson
Barnett Banks
Chase Manhattan
Citicorp
NCNB
Other multistate bank holding companies

SUPER VALU STORES, INC.

OVERVIEW

Super Valu distinguishes itself from other food wholesalers by calling itself "The Retail Support Company." This support stretches across the nation to about 2,800 independent grocers, most of whom own fewer than 4 locations.

The company helps independent grocers compete against large supermarket chains by providing services in all phases of store operations, including store location, management and employee training, accounting, marketing, modernization, and insurance. Super Valu wholesales goods to the grocers at razor-thin margins, allowing them to buy as cheaply as the chain stores. Occasionally, Super Valu develops new store formats (Cub, Twin Valu). It currently operates 72 of its own grocery stores and the 98-store ShopKo general merchandise chain.

With revenues of $11.1 billion in 1989, Super Valu ranks as the 3rd largest diversified service company in the US, right behind AT&T and rival distributor Fleming. The company is held in high regard throughout the industry for its level of service and attention to customer needs.

NYSE symbol: SVU
Incorporated: Delaware, 1925
Fiscal year ends: Last Saturday in February

WHO

Chairman, President, and CEO: Michael W. Wright, age 51, $641,460 pay
SVP; President, ShopKo Stores: William J. Tyrrell, $269,123 pay
SVP: Laurence L. Anderson, $291,192 pay
SVP: Phillip A. Dabill, $314,461 pay
Treasurer: David Cairns
Auditors: Deloitte & Touche
Employees: 38,600

WHEN

Super Valu was formed as Winston & Newell of Minneapolis in 1926, through the combination of the 2 largest grocery distributors in the Midwest: Winston, Harper, Fisher and George R. Newell, both of Minneapolis and both founded in the 1870s. The purpose of the publicly held company was to help independent grocers compete with the new chain stores then becoming prevalent.

The company adopted its present name in 1954 and began a period of expansion, acquiring Joannes Brothers of Green Bay (1955) and Piggly-Wiggly Midland of La Crosse, Wisconsin (1958). Super Valu gradually extended its reach through the later acquisitions of J. M. Jones, a Champaign, Illinois, wholesaler (1963), and Lewis Grocer, based in Indianola, Missouri (1965).

In 1971 Super Valu entered nonfood retailing by acquiring ShopKo, a discount department store operator in Minnesota, Michigan, and Wisconsin. The ShopKo chain has since expanded to 98 stores and maintains distribution centers in Green Bay, Wisconsin; Omaha, Nebraska; and Boise, Idaho. Super Valu added a new format to its food operations with the 1980 purchase of Cub Stores of Stillwater, Minnesota, a family-owned, warehouse-style grocery operation founded in 1876. Cub Stores in Denver and Nashville have continually lost money, prompting the sale of the 2 Nashville locations in 1989. Super Valu combined its Cub Stores and ShopKo retail formats by opening a combination hypermarket in Cleveland called Twin Valu (1989).

Meanwhile the company has continued to build its wholesale distribution and services businesses. It formed SUVACO, a Bermuda-based reinsurance company, in 1979 to provide insurance, through its subsidiaries, to hundreds of independent grocers. Super Valu acquired West Coast Grocery Company, a large distributor in Oregon and Washington (1985), and West Coast Fruit & Produce (1986). In 1986 the company bought assets of Southern Supermarket Services of Louisiana and acquired Food Giant, a large Atlanta grocery chain, from Delhaize Frères, the Belgian owner of Food Lion. Super Valu had either closed all its Food Giant locations, reopened them as new businesses, or sold them to independent grocers by the end of 1989.

Super Valu's acquisitions and internal growth have almost tripled sales levels in the last decade from $4.2 billion in 1980 to $11.1 billion by 1990. The company has kept long-term debt low and plans to continue looking for acquisitions in markets that it currently does not serve.

WHERE

HQ: 11840 Valley View Rd., Eden Prairie, MN 55344
Phone: 612-828-4000
FAX: 612-828-8998

The 18 retail support divisions serve 2,800 stores in 33 states. Ninety-eight ShopKo stores are located in 13 states, primarily in the Midwest and Northwest. The company also exports fresh produce and meats to 35 countries.

WHAT

	1989 Sales		1989 Operating Income	
	$ mil	% of total	$ mil	% of total
Retail general merchandise	1,556	14	86	28
Retail support	7,950	71	225	71
Retail food	1,630	15	2	1
Adjustments	—	—	(16)	—
Total	**11,136**	**100**	**297**	**100**

Services Offered
Advertising and sales promotion
Commercial and group insurance
Consumer research
Labor management
Merchandising consulting
New store development and design
Retail accounting and tax services
Retail data systems
Super Valu University
Wholesaling

Stores Served
Bigg's
Byerly's
County Market
Cub Foods (some company-owned)
Dierberg's
Haggen's
IGA
NewMarket
Niemann's
QFC
Shop 'n Save
Sunflower
Super Valu
Twin Valu (company-owned)

Other Operations
Food processing and packaging under "R" BRANDS, SUPER VALU, FLAV-O-RITE, and other private labels
ShopKo discount stores

RANKINGS

3rd in *Fortune* 100 Diversified Service Cos.
62nd in *Forbes* Sales 500
329th in *Business Week* 1000

COMPETITION

Fleming
K mart
Wal-Mart
Grocery retailers

HOW MUCH

	9 Yr. Growth	1980	1981	1982	1983	1984	1985	1986	1987	1988	1989
Sales ($ mil)	11.4%	4,204	4,622	5,197	5,923	6,548	7,905	9,066	9,372	10,296	11,136
Net income ($ mil)	11.5%	56	65	68	77	83	91	89	112	135	148
Income as % of sales	—	1.3%	1.4%	1.3%	1.3%	1.3%	1.2%	1.0%	1.2%	1.3%	1.3%
Earnings per share ($)	11.1%	0.76	0.89	0.93	1.04	1.13	1.23	1.20	1.50	1.81	1.97
Stock price – high ($)	—	8.97	10.06	14.06	18.50	16.88	23.88	27.88	30.38	26.38	30.13
Stock price – low ($)	—	4.50	7.13	7.75	12.75	11.75	15.13	19.75	16.00	17.00	22.63
Stock price – close ($)	16.5%	7.34	9.81	12.94	14.63	15.81	22.38	24.50	17.88	24.50	29.00
P/E – high	—	12	11	15	18	15	19	23	20	15	15
P/E – low	—	6	8	8	12	10	12	16	11	9	11
Dividends per share ($)	13.2%	0.19	0.23	0.27	0.30	0.33	0.37	0.41	0.44	0.49	0.59
Book value per share ($)	15.5%	3.17	3.79	4.45	5.21	6.33	7.20	8.00	9.07	10.39	11.59

1989 Year End:
Debt ratio: 39.2%
Return on equity: 17.9%
Cash (mil): $2
Current ratio: 1.14
Long-term debt (mil): $561
Number of shares (mil): 75
Dividends:
1989 average yield: 2.0%
1989 payout: 29.7%
Market value (mil): $2,177

Stock Price History high/low 1980-89

SUPERMARKETS GENERAL HOLDINGS

OVERVIEW

Woodbridge, New Jersey–based Supermarkets General is deeply in debt and losing market share. The company spent 1989 dealing with management shake-ups and with stronger rivals eating away at its customer base.

During the first half of the 1980s, Supermarkets General, with stores under its Pathmark banner, was a high flier in the food retailing industry. The company had an average 33.6% return on equity during the 10 years leading up to 1987. It was the first to build mammoth (over 45,000 square feet) supermarkets on the East Coast, and it extended its reach into New England through acquisitions in the mid-1980s.

Dodging a Dart Group takeover, Supermarkets General went private and into debt with a 1987 buyout. Its Pathmark grocery chain has fallen from first to 3rd in the New York metropolitan market, behind faster-growing Great A&P and the Shop-Rite cooperative.

The company has a new CEO, pharmacist Jack Futterman, and the management of the company's Rickel home centers has been replaced after the chain lost $32 million in 1989.

WHEN

After WWII, supermarket operators in New York and New Jersey banded together to form a cooperative to combat chain grocers, and the Wakefern Cooperative was born. Members enjoyed enhanced buying power and, with some stores sharing the name Shop-Rite, extended advertising reach.

Three participants in the cooperative — Alex Aidekman, Herbert Brody, and Milton Perlmutter — combined in a smaller group to form Supermarkets Operating Company, precursor of Supermarkets General, in 1956. Supermarkets Operating's stores continued to use the Shop-Rite name and the Wakefern Cooperative's services.

In 1966, Supermarkets Operating merged with General Super Markets, an operator of 28 stores established in 1959, to become Supermarkets General Corporation. Supermarkets General was the largest member of the Wakefern organization.

Supermarkets General broke from Wakefern in 1968 and gave its stores the Pathmark name. The company branched into small-town department stores with the purchase of Genung's, which operated chains under the names Steinbach (New Jersey) and Howland (New York and New England). In 1969 the company added to its department store holdings with the purchase of Baltimore retailer Hochschild, Kohn & Co., and entered the home improvement market by purchasing the 6-store Rickel chain. On this basis the company grew steadily through the 1970s, pioneering the large supermarket and grocery/drug combinations in densely populated areas of the Tri-State (New York, New Jersey, and Connecticut) area. Supermarkets General's aggressive discounting and experimentation gave it not only profitability but also the reputation as one of the best-run supermarket chains in the US. The company became one of the largest grocers in the competitive New York metropolitan market.

Value House, a catalog showroom outgrowth of Supermarkets General's department store business, grew to 20 locations and was sold in 1978. Supermarkets General acquired Boston's Purity Supreme, operator of Purity Supreme and Heartland grocery stores and Li'l Peach convenience stores, for $80 million (1984). In 1985 the company opened Super Stores under both the Pathmark and Purity Supreme names, launching a drive to offer a greater variety of merchandise. Supermarkets General boosted its market share in the New England market with the purchase of Angelo's Supermarkets in 1986. The company sold its department store operations in 1986, and Aidekman stepped down as chairman in 1986. Leonard Lieberman, CEO since 1983, succeeded the last of the founders active in the business.

Supermarkets General's expansion plans were slowed when the Haft family's Dart Group made a $1.62 billion raid on the company in 1987. Merrill Lynch Capital Partners stepped in to assist the company's defense with an LBO, retaining control of Supermarkets General after the company was taken private. CEO Kenneth Peskin, who replaced Lieberman, resigned and was replaced in 1989 by Jack Futterman. Faced with high interest payments on junk bonds, management has been unable to build on its market base. The company has been squeezed in its markets by Great A&P and its former colleagues, the Shop-Rite stores of the Wakefern Cooperative.

HOW MUCH

	9 Yr. Growth	1980	1981	1982	1983	1984	1985	1986	1987	1988	1989
Sales ($ mil)	10.2%	2,629	2,999	3,247	3,518	4,347	5,123	5,508	5,767	5,962	6,299
Net income ($ mil)	—	26	30	38	41	52	64	63	(66)	(59)	(77)
Income as % of sales	—	1.0%	1.0%	1.2%	1.2%	1.2%	1.2%	1.1%	(1.1%)	(1.0%)	(1.2%)

1989 Year End:
Debt ratio: 107.6%
Return on equity: 112.1%
Cash (mil): $5
Current ratio: 0.81
Long-term debt (mil): $1,654

Private company
Incorporated: Delaware, 1987
Fiscal year ends: Saturday closest to January 31

WHO

Chairman, President, and CEO: Jack Futterman, age 56, $591,705 pay
SVP, Treasurer, and CFO: Jeffrey C. Girard, age 42, $384,990 pay
SVP Finance and Administration: Jerome F. Katcher, age 57, $256,952 pay
VP and Controller: Joseph W. Adelhardt, age 43
Secretary and General Counsel: Marc A. Strassler, age 41
Auditors: Deloitte & Touche
Employees: 19,000 full-time; 32,000 part-time

WHERE

HQ: 301 Blair Rd., Woodbridge, NJ 07095
Phone: 201-499-3000
FAX: 201-499-3072

The company operates 144 Pathmark supermarkets, 33 drugstores, and 44 Rickel home centers (New Jersey, New York, Pennsylvania, Connecticut, and Delaware). The company also operates 66 Purity Supreme, Heartland, and Angelo's supermarkets (Massachusetts, New Hampshire, and Connecticut). The 64 Li'l Peach convenience stores operate exclusively in Massachusetts.

WHAT

	1989 Sales		1989 Operating Income	
	$ mil	% of total	$ mil	% of total
Supermarkets & drugstores	5,821	92	203	119
Home centers	478	8	(33)	(19)
Adjustments	—	—	15	—
Total	**6,299**	**100**	**185**	**100**

Supermarkets & Drugstores
Pathmark
- Drugstores (33)
- Super Centers (130)
- Supermarkets (14)

Purity Supreme
- Super Stores (22)
- Supermarkets (44)
  - Angelo's
  - Heartland
  - Purity Supreme

Convenience Stores
Li'l Peach (64)

Home Centers
HOM store (1)
Rickel (44)

RANKINGS

17th in *Fortune* 50 Retailing Cos.
10th in *Forbes* 400 US Private Cos.

COMPETITION

American Stores
Great A&P
Home Depot
Rite Aid
Stop & Shop

SYSCO CORPORATION

OVERVIEW

Houston-based SYSCO is the nation's largest distributor of food products to the food service industry. The company's operations, in more than 150 US cities, serve approximately 225,000 restaurants, hotels, schools, hospitals, and fast-food outlets.

In an industry composed of more than 3,500 small, local distributors, SYSCO is a giant; although it serves only 7% of the market, the company has double the sales of its nearest competitor. With its 1988 acquisition of CFS Continental, SYSCO extended its reach into all parts of the country, building its market position in West Coast states and British Columbia.

SYSCO buys goods from more than 2,700 sources in over 30 countries. The company processes and repackages many of the 150,000 products it sells. In order to better serve small restaurants and fast-food outlets, SYSCO often partially prepares the food products or packages them in "customer-sized" units.

SYSCO plans to continue expanding by buying smaller competitors.

WHEN

SYSCO was founded in 1969 when John Baugh, a Houston wholesale foods distributor, convinced the owners of 8 other US wholesalers that they should combine and form a national distribution company. Joining Baugh's Zero Foods of Houston to form SYSCO were Frost-Pack Distributing (Grand Rapids, Michigan), Louisville Grocery (Louisville, Kentucky), Plantation Foods (Miami), Thomas Foods and its Justrite subsidiary (Cincinnati), Wicker (Dallas), and Texas Wholesale Grocery (Dallas). SYSCO, which derives its name from Systems and Services Company, benefited from Baugh's recognition of the trend toward dining out in American society. Until SYSCO was formed, food distribution to restaurants, hotels, and other nongrocers was provided by thousands of small, independent, regional operators.

During the 2 decades since its inception, SYSCO has grown to 25 times its original size, mostly through the acquisition of strong local distributors. The company has ensured the success of its acquisitions through buyout agreements requiring the seller to continue managing the company and earn a portion of the sale price with future profits. The company's major acquisitions in the 1970s were Albany Frosted Foods (New York, 1970), Arrow Food Distributors (Louisiana, 1970), Robert Orr & Co. (Nashville, 1972), and Hardin's (Memphis, 1972). Later purchases included Swan Food Sales (Augusta, Georgia, 1974), Marietta Institutional Wholesalers (Georgia, 1975), Glen-Webb (Maywood, California, 1978), and Select-Union (Hayward, California, 1979).

SYSCO's first major acquisition during the 1980s was Nobel, a large distributor operating in both Denver and Albuquerque (1982). In 1984 the company purchased Pelger & Company of Lincoln, Nebraska, and Bell Distributing, based in Asheville, North Carolina. The company made several large buys in 1985, including DiPaolo Food Distributors in Columbus, New York Tea Company in St. Paul, and the Texas assets of PYA/Monarch, the distribution unit of Sara Lee, which included distributors in Amarillo, Austin, and Beaumont.

In 1988, when SYSCO was already the largest food service distributor, it purchased Olewine's, a Harrisburg, Pennsylvania, distributor. It also acquired, for $800 million, CFS Continental, the food distribution unit of Staley Continental and the 3rd largest food distributor at the time. The acquisition of CFS added several warehouses and a large truck fleet and increased the company's penetration along the West Coast of the US and Canada.

HOW MUCH

	9 Yr. Growth	1980	1981	1982	1983	1984	1985	1986	1987	1988	1989
Sales ($ mil)	21.4%	1,193	1,376	1,700	1,950	2,312	2,628	3,172	3,656	4,385	6,851
Net income ($ mil)	20.3%	20	27	34	40	45	50	58	62	80	108
Income as % of sales	—	1.7%	1.9%	2.0%	2.1%	2.0%	1.9%	1.8%	1.7%	1.8%	1.6%
Earnings per share ($)	17.7%	0.27	0.35	0.43	0.49	0.54	0.59	0.67	0.70	0.90	1.19
Stock price – high ($)	—	3.44	5.28	10.47	11.13	9.59	11.63	16.94	20.75	19.44	32.00
Stock price – low ($)	—	1.65	3.34	4.64	7.81	6.44	7.94	11.19	11.25	13.00	18.31
Stock price – close ($)	28.5%	3.31	4.94	9.81	9.13	8.44	11.19	15.00	13.56	19.25	31.63
P/E – high	—	13	15	24	23	18	20	25	30	22	27
P/E – low	—	6	9	11	16	12	14	17	16	15	15
Dividends per share ($)	18.9%	0.04	0.05	0.06	0.08	0.09	0.10	0.11	0.13	0.15	0.17
Book value per share ($)	17.2%	1.69	1.99	2.50	2.89	3.42	3.93	4.50	5.10	6.02	7.07

1989 Year End:
Debt ratio: 49.1%
Return on equity: 18.2%
Cash (mil): $55
Current ratio: 1.8
Long-term debt (mil): $620
Number of shares (mil): 91
Dividends:
1989 average yield: 0.5%
1989 payout: 14.3%
Market value (mil): $2,874

Stock Price History high/low 1980-89

35
30
25
20
15
10
5
0

NYSE symbol: SYY
Incorporated: Delaware, 1969
Fiscal year ends: Saturday closest to June 30

WHO

Chairman and CEO: John F. Woodhouse, age 58, $825,654 pay
President and COO: Bill M. Lindig, age 52, $701,410 pay
EVP Finance and Administration (CFO): E. James Lowrey, age 61, $534,745 pay
EVP Foodservice Operations: Charles H. Cotros, age 52, $531,955 pay
EVP Procurement: James A. Schlindwein, age 60, $534,745 pay
Auditors: Arthur Andersen & Co. (as of fiscal 1990)
Employees: 19,000

WHERE

HQ: 1390 Enclave Pkwy., Houston, TX 77077
Phone: 713-584-1390
FAX: 713-584-1188

SYSCO serves approximately 225,000 food service establishments in the 48 contiguous states. The company maintains 82 distribution facilities in 35 states and a facility in western Canada.

WHAT

Customers	1989 Sales % of Total
Hospitals and nursing homes	14
Hotels and motels	7
Restaurants	57
Schools and colleges	9
Other	13
Total	**100**

Products	1989 Sales % of Total
Beverage products	3
Canned and dry products	27
Consumer-sized frozen products	5
Dairy products	7
Equipment and smallwares	3
Fresh & frozen meats	16
Fresh produce	4
Janitorial products	2
Other frozen products	15
Paper & disposable products	8
Poultry	5
Seafoods	5
Total	**100**

RANKINGS

9th in *Fortune* 100 Diversified Service Cos.
114th in *Forbes* Sales 500
246th in *Business Week* 1000

COMPETITION

Sara Lee

TANDEM COMPUTERS INC.

OVERVIEW

Cupertino, California–based Tandem Computers is a leading manufacturer of fault-tolerant computers. Used around the world for varied applications, the computers process thousands of transactions a second without interruption.

The finance industry — banks, stock exchanges, brokerage firms, insurance companies — is Tandem's largest market (41%), followed by manufacturers (14%). Tandem computers are used in banks' ATM networks. Its largest installation — the Securities Industry Automation Corporation — is responsible for the automation of the American and New York stock exchanges.

The $1.6 billion company is the 8th largest midrange computer manufacturer in the world according to the 1990 Datamation 100. International sales account for 50% of Tandem's revenues.

The core of Tandem's product line is the NonStop system family — computers ranging in size from the CLX minicomputer to the recently introduced NonStop Cyclone (Tandem's first mainframe model). In 1990 Tandem introduced the Integrity S2, a UNIX-based fault-tolerant computer based on RISC (Reduced Instruction Set Computing) technology. If a processor in the S2 fails, the computer takes it off-line, notifies the system operator, and reports the failure to a Tandem support center — all without interruption to the tasks in process.

NYSE symbol: TDM
Incorporated: Delaware, 1980
Fiscal year ends: September 30

WHO

Chairman: Thomas J. Perkins, age 57
President and CEO: James G. Treybig, age 49, $478,502 pay
SVP and COO: Robert C. Marshall, age 58, $337,853 pay
SVP and CFO: David J. Rynne, age 49, $305,565 pay
Auditors: Ernst & Young
Employees: 9,548

WHERE

HQ: 19333 Vallco Pkwy., Cupertino, CA 95014
Phone: 408-725-6000
FAX: 408-865-4545

The company and its subsidiaries manufacture products in the US, Germany, and Mexico, and support customers from more than 150 locations around the world.

	1989 Sales		1989 Pretax Income	
	$ mil	% of total	$ mil	% of total
US	818	50	123	63
Europe	530	33	55	27
Other	285	17	21	10
Adjustments	—	—	(13)	—
Total	**1,633**	**100**	**186**	**100**

WHEN

Tandem Computers was started in Cupertino, California, in 1974 by James Treybig, a former marketing manager at Hewlett-Packard and limited partner in venture capital firm Kleiner, Perkins, Caufield & Byers (KPC&B). Along with 2 computer engineers, and with initial funding from KPC&B, Treybig pioneered a way to link computers to work in tandem so that if one failed, another would take over without interruption. Tandem introduced its first fail-safe minicomputer, the NonStop16, in 1976.

Tandem's computers quickly became a success. Revenues doubled every year from 1976 to 1981. Designed to process on-line transactions quickly, the computers were popular with banks, brokerage firms, manufacturers, and hospitals. By 1987 Tandem was a $1 billion company with 130 offices worldwide.

Although Tandem dominated the fail-safe computer market in the 1970s, it faced stiff competition in the early 1980s from companies like Stratus Computer. From 1982 to 1985 Tandem's earnings were flat. Tandem, long noted for its unorthodox, people-oriented management, was forced to reassess both its product line and its business methods in 1984. It tightened its management control and broadened its array of hardware and software offerings. By 1987 Tandem had substantially revamped and expanded its product line.

The strategy worked. In 1987 revenues grew 35%. Contributing to the rise in sales were Tandem's 1987 introduction of a smaller CLX minicomputer and announcement of a new database software product (NonStop SQL) that offered greater versatility. While the initial sales of the CLX took off, Tandem missed the delivery date of its database software, slowing revenue growth to 27% in 1988.

In developing a more diversified product line, Tandem expanded into complementary specialty areas through acquisition of Atalla (1987, data security products), Integrated Technology (1988, telecommunications software), and Ungermann-Bass (1988, network specialists). Tandem has also established alliances with Apple, Motorola, AST Research, and AT&T to expand the capabilities and compatibility of its hardware and software. The 1989 introduction of the NonStop Cyclone moved Tandem into the mainframe market, competing head-on with IBM's comparable machine at 1/3 the cost.

WHAT

Computer Systems
Integrity S2
NonStop CLX
NonStop Cyclone
NonStop VLX

System Software
Guardian Operating System
NonStop SQL Software
NonStop-UX Operating System

Networking
Distributed Systems Management
Network security products offered through Tandem's subsidiary Atalla Corporation
Various networking products offered through Tandem's subsidiary Ungermann-Bass, Inc.

Storage Products
V80 disk storage
XL80 disk storage
4210/4220 disk subsystem
5200 optical storage facility

HOW MUCH

	9 Yr. Growth	1980	1981	1982	1983	1984	1985	1986	1987	1988	1989
Sales ($ mil)	35.1%	109	208	312	418	533	624	768	1,036	1,315	1,633
Net income ($ mil)	30.6%	11	27	30	31	43	34	64	106	94	118
Income as % of sales	—	9.8%	12.7%	9.6%	7.4%	8.1%	5.5%	8.3%	10.2%	7.2%	7.2%
Earnings per share ($)	23.4%	0.18	0.36	0.38	0.38	0.52	0.41	0.72	1.08	0.96	1.17
Stock price – high ($)	—	12.67	17.29	16.38	19.75	20.13	14.31	19.75	37.63	29.50	26.38
Stock price – low ($)	—	3.08	10.21	7.25	11.81	6.50	6.44	9.75	17.19	12.38	14.75
Stock price – close ($)	6.9%	12.67	13.88	12.69	17.56	9.75	11.13	17.13	27.50	16.88	23.00
P/E – high	—	72	48	43	52	39	35	27	35	31	23
P/E – low	—	17	28	19	31	13	16	14	16	13	13
Dividends per share ($)	0.0%	0.00	0.00	0.00	0.00	0.00	0.00	0.00	0.00	0.00	0.00
Book value per share ($)	26.6%	1.17	2.81	3.33	3.93	4.62	5.08	6.09	7.74	8.92	9.82

1989 Year End:
Debt ratio: 9.7%
Return on equity: 12.5%
Cash (mil): $197
Current ratio: 1.96
Long-term debt (mil): $107
Number of shares (mil): 101
Dividends:
1989 average yield: 0.0%
1989 payout: 0.0%
Market value (mil): $2,318

Stock Price History high/low 1980-89

RANKINGS

246th in *Fortune* 500 Industrial Cos.
450th in *Forbes* Sales 500
212th in *Business Week* 1000
691st in *Business Week* Global 1000

COMPETITION

Data General
Digital Equipment
Fujitsu
Hewlett-Packard
Hitachi
IBM
Prime
Unisys
Wang

TANDY CORPORATION

OVERVIEW

Tandy Corporation is the largest retailer of consumer electronics in the world, with sales of almost $4.2 billion in 1989. As of the fiscal year-end 1989, Tandy had 7,337 retail outlets: 4,812 company-owned Radio Shack stores, 2,233 dealer/franchise Radio Shacks, and 292 Tandy Name Brand Retail stores (McDuff and VideoConcepts).

The Tandy Marketing Companies division markets products produced by its subsidiaries Memtek Products (Memorex magnetic tape), O'Sullivan Industries (cabinets), Lika Corporation (printed circuits), and GRiD Systems (laptop and business computers). In 1989 Tandy transferred its business computer marketing from Radio Shack computer centers to GRiD Systems.

In addition to its retailing operations, Tandy is a billion-dollar manufacturer of computers and consumer electronic products. Tandy factories produce about 50% of the electronics sold in its Radio Shack stores, as well as OEM microcomputer products marketed by Digital Equipment Corporation and Panasonic (Matsushita).

WHEN

During the 1950s Charles Tandy expanded his family's small Fort Worth leather business, dating back to 1919, into a nationwide chain of leathercraft and hobby stores. By 1960 Tandy Corporation stock was being traded on the NYSE. In the early 1960s Tandy began to expand into other retail areas, buying a Fort Worth department store, Leonard's.

In 1963 Tandy purchased Radio Shack, a nearly bankrupt electronic parts supplier with a mail-order business and 9 retail stores in the Boston area. Tandy collected part of the $800,000 owed the company and began expansion, stocking the stores with quick turnover items and putting 8-9% of sales revenue into advertising. Between 1961 and 1969 Tandy sales grew from $16 to $180 million, and earnings rose from $720,000 to $7.7 million, with the bulk of the growth due to the expansion of Radio Shack. Between 1968 and 1973 Tandy expanded from 172 to 2,294 stores, with Radio Shack contributing over 50% of Tandy's net sales and 80% of earnings in 1973.

In 1974 the company sold its department store operations to Dillard. In 1975 Tandy spun off to shareholders its leather products business as Tandy Brands and its hobby and handicraft business as Tandycrafts, focusing Tandy Corporation on the consumer electronics business. During 1976 the boom in CB radio sales pushed income up 125% as Tandy opened 1,200 stores. The company then operated 18 factories in 4 countries, producing almost 40% of its products. In 1977 Tandy introduced the first mass-marketed personal computer, the TRS-80, which soon became the #1 personal computer on the market. In 1979, the year after Charles Tandy died, there were 5,530 McDonald's, 6,805 7-Elevens, and 7,353 Radio Shacks.

Tandy sales passed the $2 billion mark in 1982. In 1984 the company introduced the Tandy 1000 personal computer, the first IBM-compatible personal computer priced under $1,000, and the #1 seller in its first year, but income was up only 1%, due to heavy competition and shortages of semiconductors. Since 1984 Tandy has expanded primarily through the purchase of existing companies — Scott/McDuff and VideoConcepts in 1985 and GRiD Systems in 1988. In 1987 Tandy spun off to shareholders its foreign retail operations as InterTAN. In 1988 and 1989 the company's sales growth came primarily from its marketing and name brand retail companies, with the number of Radio Shack and name brand retail outlets remaining almost constant.

Fiscal year 1990 sales increased 8% to $4.5 billion, while profits fell to $290 million. In August 1990 Tandy announced a new laptop computer retailing for $1,999 to compete with Compaq's laptop.

HOW MUCH

	9 Yr. Growth	1980	1981	1982	1983	1984	1985	1986	1987	1988	1989
Sales ($ mil)	13.1%	1,385	1,691	2,033	2,475	2,737	2,841	3,036	3,452	3,794	4,181
Net income ($ mil)	12.5%	112	170	224	279	282	189	198	242	316	324
Income as % of sales	—	8.1%	10.0%	11.0%	11.3%	10.3%	6.7%	6.5%	7.0%	8.3%	7.7%
Earnings per share ($)	14.0%	1.12	1.65	2.17	2.67	2.75	2.11	2.22	2.70	3.54	3.64
Stock price – high ($)	—	25.56	39.13	60.75	64.50	43.38	42.13	45.00	56.50	48.63	48.75
Stock price – low ($)	—	7.06	20.06	22.75	33.25	23.25	24.00	30.50	28.00	31.50	37.00
Stock price – close ($)	5.3%	24.69	33.75	50.75	43.38	24.25	40.75	42.50	33.00	41.00	39.13
P/E – high	—	23	24	28	24	16	20	20	21	14	13
P/E – low	—	6	12	10	12	8	11	14	10	9	10
Dividends per share ($)	—	0.00	0.00	0.00	0.00	0.00	0.00	0.00	0.38	0.58	0.60
Book value per share ($)	23.0%	3.21	5.56	7.83	10.71	10.64	12.00	14.57	15.38	18.10	20.65

1989 Year End:
Debt ratio: 7.3%
Return on equity: 18.8%
Cash (mil): $58
Current ratio: 3.41
Long-term debt (mil): $141
Number of shares (mil): 86
Dividends:
1989 average yield: 1.5%
1989 payout: 16.5%
Market value (mil): $3,378

Stock Price History high/low 1980-89

NYSE symbol: TAN
Incorporated: Delaware, 1967
Fiscal year ends: June 30

WHO

Chairman, CEO, and President: John V. Roach, age 50, $970,710 pay
President, Radio Shack Division: Bernard S. Appel, age 57, $596,791 pay
President, Tandy Electronics Division: Robert M. McClure, age 53, $335,248 pay
SVP and Secretary: Herschel C. Winn, age 57, $326,976 pay
Acting Principal Financial Officer: Dwain H. Hughes, age 41
Auditors: Price Waterhouse
Employees: 38,000

WHERE

HQ: 1800 One Tandy Center, Fort Worth, TX 76102
Phone: 817-390-3700
FAX: 817-390-2774

Tandy has retail outlets throughout the US and 27 manufacturing plants in Korea, the US, and the People's Republic of China.

	1989 Sales		1989 Operating Income	
	$ mil	% of total	$ mil	% of total
US	4,041	97	531	101
Foreign	140	3	(6)	(1)
Adjustments	—	—	(10)	—
Total	**4,181**	**100**	**515**	**100**

WHAT

	1989 Sales	
	$ mil	% of total
Radio Shack-US	2,992	71
Tandy Name Brand Retail	365	9
Tandy Marketing	498	12
Outside sales	326	8
Total	**4,181**	**100**

Retail Outlets
McDuff Electronics
Radio Shack
VideoConcepts

Nonretail Subsidiaries & Divisions
A&A International
GRiD Systems
Lika Corporation
Memtek Products
O'Sullivan Industries
Personal Computer Division
Tandy Electronics Azle
Tandy Electronics Packaging
Tandy Molded Products
Tandy Wire and Cable
Tool Engineering Division

RANKINGS

29th in *Fortune* 50 Retailing Cos.
200th in *Forbes* Sales 500
223rd in *Business Week* 1000
622nd in *Business Week* Global 1000

COMPETITION

Apple
Atari
Commodore
Compaq
IBM
JWP
NEC
Specialty and general merchandise retailers

TEACHERS INSURANCE

OVERVIEW

Teachers Insurance and Annuity Association (TIAA) and College Retirement Equities Fund (CREF) provide nonprofit educational institutions in North America with an employee pension and insurance program that is fully funded, immediately vested, and portable.

Predating the Social Security system by 20 years, TIAA was organized as a charitable trust, exempt from security laws. It offers numerous life and health insurance programs to over 1.3 million members in 4,400 institutions. TIAA is unique in that it uses no agents to write policies. Trustees are selected educators and administrators from member organizations. TIAA's stable and conservative investment program (assets of $44 billion) has the A. M. Best Superior or A+ rating.

CREF, a separate but comanaged organization, was created in 1952 to provide investment vehicles that could protect members from the impact of inflation on their retirement benefits. With over $38 billion invested, members have a variety of investment alternatives ranging from money-market accounts, stocks and bonds, and annuities to its innovative Social Choice account, which invests only in companies that are not involved with weapons, alcohol, tobacco, South Africa, or Northern Ireland. The CREF portfolio showed a 28% rate of return in 1989.

WHEN

The Carnegie Foundation for the Advancement of Teaching established New York City–based TIAA in 1918 to provide retirement benefits and other forms of financial security to employees of nonprofit educational and research organizations. TIAA, now the major pension system of higher education in the US, was the first truly portable pension plan, allowing participants to move between institutions without losing retirement benefits.

During the 1950s TIAA led the fight to gain Social Security benefits for university employees and later that decade began offering group disability (1957) and group life insurance (1958).

In 1952 CEO William Greenough established the College Retirement Equities Fund (CREF), a companion organization to TIAA. CREF offered the nation's first variable annuity. Designed to supplement TIAA's fixed-dollar annuity, CREF invested part of the premiums paid to TIAA in common stocks for retirement purposes. CREF, like sister TIAA, is subject to New York insurance regulation.

In the 1970s TIAA established The Common Fund to help colleges boost investment returns from their endowments; TIAA went on to help manage endowments. TIAA-CREF also established, along with several colleges, the Investor Responsibility Research Center to provide information to enable investors to make socially responsible investment decisions.

For 70 years TIAA/CREF members had no way to exit the system other than retirement. In addition, members had only 2 investment choices — stocks through CREF or a transfer into TIAA's long-term bond, real estate, and mortgage fund. By 1987 the organization had 3,800 institutions as participants, one million members, and more than $63 billion in assets. After disgruntled university staffs intervened, the organization began offering a wider variety of investments and providing a means to transfer the pensions into other investment vehicles. That year TIAA/CREF introduced a money market fund and 6 mutual funds.

In 1988 TIAA announced its joint purchase with shopping center developer Rouse Company of McCormick Properties, which includes 90 buildings totaling approximately 6.1 million square feet of commercial building space and 470 acres of land. The association is focusing on adding more investment options: in 1989 it introduced the TIAA Interest Payment Retirement Option and announced new CREF accounts for 1990. Numerous states are now setting up optional retirement programs (ORPs) as alternatives or supplements to their regular public employee retirement plan. TIAA-CREF is now a carrier in 37 states (and Washington, DC) to provide ORPs.

HOW MUCH

	9 Yr. Growth	1980	1981	1982	1983	1984	1985	1986	1987	1988	1989
Assets ($ mil)	18.3%	9,748	11,439	13,520	16,144	19,205	23,159	27,887	33,210	38,631	44,374
Premium & annuity income ($ mil)	10.4%	1,316	1,792	1,296	1,642	1,752	2,240	2,655	3,060	3,065	3,198
Net investment income ($ mil)	19.3%	812	1,017	1,267	1,551	1,918	2,328	2,778	3,134	3,641	3,979
Net income ($ mil)	21.8%	69	5	5	38	160	118	182	206	418	406
Net income as % of assets	—	0.7%	0.0%	0.0%	0.2%	0.8%	0.5%	0.7%	0.6%	1.1%	0.9%
Life insurance in force ($ mil)	13.7%	7,587	9,072	10,902	12,544	13,660	15,272	17,266	19,218	21,538	24,033

Life Insurance in Force ($ mil) 1980-89

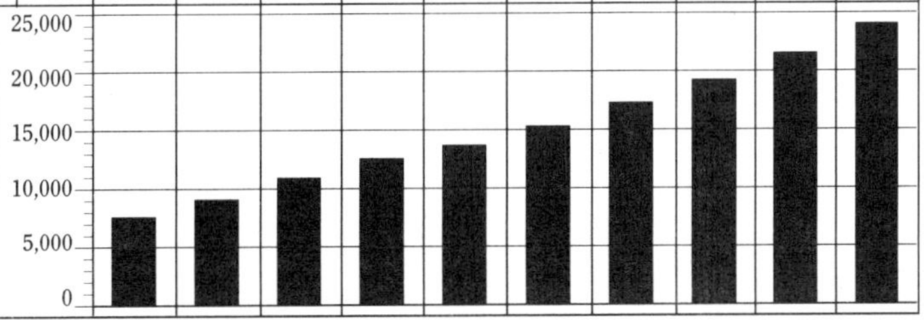

25,000
20,000
15,000
10,000
5,000
0

Nonprofit organizations
TIAA founded: 1918
Fiscal year ends: December 31

WHO

Chairman and CEO: Clifton R. Wharton, Jr.
President: John H. Biggs
EVP, Finance and Planning: Thomas W. Jones
EVP: Russell E. Bone
Auditors: Ernst & Young
Employees: 3,500

WHERE

HQ: Teachers Insurance and Annuity Association and College Retirement Equities Fund, 730 Third Ave., New York, NY 10017
Phone: 212-490-9000
FAX: 212-775-8424

TIAA/CREF is licensed in 37 states, Washington, DC, 9 Canadian provinces, and other states by correspondence.

WHAT

TIAA Asset Allocation ($44 billion assets)
46% Commercial loans
43% Mortgage loans
9% Commercial real estate
2% Short-term investments

CREF Asset Allocation ($38 billion assets)
66% US stocks
17% Stocks with above average growth patterns
13% Foreign stocks
4% Cash

TIAA Investment Vehicles
Cost-of-living life insurance
Group life insurance
Health insurance
Individual life insurance
Interest Payment Retirement Option
Retirement and Group Retirement Annuities

CREF Investment Vehicles
Bond Market Account
Money Market Account
Social Choice Account
Stock Account
Variable annuity

RANKINGS

5th in *Fortune* 50 Life Insurance Cos.

COMPETITION

Aetna
American Express
CIGNA
Equitable
First Executive
John Hancock
Kemper
Massachusetts Mutual
Metropolitan
New York Life
Northwestern Mutual
Primerica
Prudential
Sears
State Farm
Transamerica
Travelers
USF&G
Major banks
Investment managers

TEAMSTERS

OVERVIEW

The International Brotherhood of Teamsters is the US's largest and most diverse union. Its over 1.7 million members include freight trucking/warehousing workers (still dominant with 35% of total membership); cab drivers; airline employees; and factory, hospital, and sanitation workers.

Some members of the Teamsters' leadership have been alleged to have connections with organized crime. Several have been convicted of crimes themselves, including Jimmy Hoffa (jury tampering) and Roy Lee Williams (conspiracy to bribe a US senator). The federal government has prosecuted over 100 local Teamster leaders and has had court-appointed trustees actually take over several local unions.

The 742 local Teamster unions — some based on craft (specific jobs), some on industry (*e.g.*, all automotive jobs) — elect their own officers, employ their own full-time staff, and vote on their own contracts. Representatives of the locals elect the national leadership at the Teamster convention.

The locals' dues support the executive (president, secretary-treasurer, and 16 VPs); 10 state and 5 area conferences (which coordinate contracts and organize strike drives at their respective levels); and 11 trade divisions and 4 area trade conferences that cut across the geographically based structures.

As the result of a civil RICO (racketeering) suit brought by the federal government and settled by the Teamsters in 1989, the union will conduct its first-ever secret ballot, direct election of executive officers of the national organization, in 1991. This election is to be supervised by officials appointed by the federal courts.

WHEN

In 1903, 2 rival team-driver unions, the Drivers International Union and the Teamsters National Union, merged to form the International Brotherhood of Teamsters. Led by Cornelius Shea, the Teamsters established headquarters in Indianapolis.

Daniel Tobin (president for 45 years from 1907) demanded that union locals obtain executive approval before striking. Membership expanded from the team-driver base, prompting the union to add Chauffeurs, Stablemen, and Helpers to its name (1909).

Following the first transcontinental delivery by motor truck (1912), the Teamster deliverymen abandoned their horses for trucks. The union then began recruiting food processing, brewery, farm, and other workers to augment Teamster effectiveness during strikes; jurisdictional disputes with other unions soon became a Teamster trademark. In 1920 the Teamsters joined the AF of L.

Until the Depression era, the Teamsters were still a relatively small union (about 100,000 members) of predominantly in-city deliverymen. Then a Teamster Trotskyite from Minneapolis (Farrell Dobbs) organized the famous Minneapolis strikes in 1934 to protest local management's refusal to allow the workers to unionize. The militant workers clashed with police and National Guard units for 11 days before the management conceded to the workers' demands. The strikes demonstrated the potential strength of unions, and Teamsters membership swelled.

Union power was greatly curtailed during WWII when union officials were assigned positions on production committees. Nevertheless, the Teamsters continued to grow and in 1953 moved the organization's headquarters to Washington, DC.

The AFL-CIO expelled the Teamsters in 1957 when its ties to "the mob" became public during a US Senate investigation. New Teamster boss Jimmy Hoffa eluded indictment and took advantage of America's growing dependence on trucking to negotiate the powerful National Master Freight Agreement (1964). Hoffa also organized industrial workers and added enticements like medical programs and a strong political voice (DRIVE, 1963).

Hoffa also used the Teamsters' Central States Pension Fund to make mob-connected loans. Hoffa was later convicted of jury tampering and sent to prison. After his release, Hoffa disappeared outside of a Detroit restaurant in 1975. Although the case has never been closed, he was presumed murdered by mob elements within the Teamsters hierarchy.

In 1987 the Teamsters rejoined the AFL-CIO. In 1988 the government sued the Teamsters, who settled the suit in 1989 by agreeing to allow government-appointed officials to discipline corrupt union leaders, help run the union, and supervise its elections.

HOW MUCH

	9 Yr. Growth	1980	1981	1982	1983	1984	1985	1986	1987	1988	1989
Net assets ($ mil)	3.4%	142.1	149.7	155.3	176.0	193.7	198.6	198.6	198.0	193.8	191.6
Total receipts ($ mil)	30.9%	137.1	137.4	242.9	255.5	215.2	445.0	831.7	1,716.2	1,939.7	1,544.7
Total disbursements ($ mil)	30.7%	138.1	130.8	263.6	257.7	206.2	438.9	438.9	1,720.7	1,928.4	1,540.4

Total Receipts ($ mil) 1980-89

2,000
1,800
1,600
1,400
1,200
1,000
800
600
400
200
0

Labor union
Founded: Indiana, 1903
Fiscal year ends: December 31

WHO

General President: William J. McCarthy, $270,653 pay
General Secretary-Treasurer: Weldon L. Mathis, $240,848 pay
First VP, Conference Director, and International Representative: Joseph Trerotola, $150,374 pay
Auditors: Thomas Havey & Co.

WHERE

HQ: International Brotherhood of Teamsters, Chauffeurs, Warehousemen and Helpers of America, 25 Louisiana Ave., NW, Washington, DC 20001
Phone: 202-624-6800
FAX: 202-624-6918

The Teamsters have 742 local unions in the US and Canada.

WHAT

	1989 Cash Receipts	
	$ mil	% of total
Member dues & fees	74	83
Interest & dividends	14	16
Other sources	1	1
Total	**89**	**100**

	1989 Cash Disbursements	
	$ mil	% of total
Out-of-work benefits	4	4
Teamster Affiliates Pension	12	13
Affiliation fees	6	7
Organizing campaign expenses	5	6
Administrative, office & general	22	25
Magazine, education & communications	10	11
Legal fees & civil RICO expenses & settlements	8	9
Divisional & departmental	17	19
National headquarters building	4	4
Other	2	2
Total	**90**	**100**

Teamster Philosophy

Teamsters have more to offer — more in terms of protection and assistance — more in terms of economic strength.
When the chips are down, true collective bargaining can only take place when the employer and the union respect each other's economic strength.
Teamsters deliver the goods.
What we want we try to get; what we have we keep.
It is of benefit to nobody to perform a hysterectomy on the goose that lays the golden egg.
Job security is our most important product.
Bargain hard, bargain fair.
A free and strong labor movement means a free and strong America.
Our word is our bond.
Teamsters are good citizens.
We are not the best because we are the largest but the largest because we are the best.
A fair day's pay for a fair day's work.
In unity there is strength.
Our labor is our stock-in-trade.
A well-informed membership is our best security.
Equal pay for equal work.

TELE-COMMUNICATIONS, INC.

OVERVIEW

From its Denver headquarters, Tele-Communications, Inc., and its affiliates are wired into 10 million US homes, about one in 4 US cable television subscribers. It is the nation's largest cable company.

Through a complex transaction in 1989, TCI orchestrated the merger of United Cable and United Artists Communications under a venture, mostly owned by TCI, called United Artists Entertainment. UAE is the nation's largest motion picture theater operator, with 2,695 screens, and the 3rd largest cable operator. TCI owns a 42.5% indirect interest in SCI Holdings, the 4th largest US cable operator (Time Warner is #2).

TCI has invested in several cable programmers, including Turner Broadcasting Systems. It also has substantial investments in regional sports programming services.

The company frets over reregulation of the cable industry and is trying to allay fears about its power and size. It also is hedging its bets by participating, through its WestMarc subsidiary and through a joint venture with other cable operators, in new technology — direct broadcast of television signals from space.

OTC symbols: TCOMA, TCOMB
Incorporated: Delaware, 1968
Fiscal year ends: December 31

WHO

Chairman: Bob Magness, age 66, $402,807 pay
President and CEO: John C. Malone, age 49, $404,629 pay
SVP and Treasurer: Donne F. Fisher, age 52, $303,781 pay
EVP (Principal Operating Officer): J. C. Sparkman, age 58, $301,778 pay
Auditors: KPMG Peat Marwick
Employees: 34,000

WHEN

Tele-Communications, Inc., began in 1956 when rancher Bob Magness sold some cattle to raise money to build his first cable system in the Texas Panhandle hamlet of Memphis. In 1965 Magness moved the company to Denver to serve small Rocky Mountain towns.

TCI went public in 1970 just as the capital-intensive cable TV industry was taking its first steps. Magness hired 32-year-old John Malone from General Instrument Corporation in 1973. The deal-making Malone became known as the "godfather" of cable because he stabilized the company and extended its reach.

Malone's first battle was with the city council of Vail, Colorado, over cable services and rates. At the height of the argument, Malone showed nothing on the cable system for an entire weekend but the names and phone numbers of city officials. The city backed down.

In 1977 Malone restructured TCI's debt. He sat out the bidding for big-city franchises, instead buying them at hefty discounts after bigger competitors stumbled.

Congress deregulated the cable industry in 1984, and TCI aggressively bought new systems. In 1986 it won control of United Artists Communications, the largest operator of movie theaters as well as the 11th largest cable operator. TCI purchased Heritage Communications, including its Dallas system, in 1987 for $1.3 billion. In the late 1980s TCI spent nearly $3 billion for more than 150 cable companies, often in joint ventures with other multisystem operators. The debt TCI ran up led to losses in 1989 and early 1990.

Its size gave TCI clout with cable programmers, who kept their prices low to curry favor. Malone, recognizing that his systems would need a variety of programming to attract viewers, financed nascent channels in exchange for stock. Malone led a group of cable operators who chipped in to save Ted Turner's debt-plagued TBS in 1987; TCI came away with 21% of TBS stock and spearheaded the launch of TBS's TNT channel. The TBS stock was added to TCI investments in Black Entertainment Television (added in 1979), Discovery Channel (1986), Think Entertainment (1987), and American Movie Classics (1987). TCI agreed to buy 50% of Showtime Networks (Showtime and the Movie Channel) from Viacom in 1989, prompting an FTC review that continued into 1990.

In 1990, to forestall fears that it is too powerful and requires reregulation, TCI is considering a spin-off to create a separate company — to be called Liberty Media — consisting of much of its programming holdings and some cable systems.

WHERE

HQ: 4643 S. Ulster St., Denver, CO 80237
Phone: 303-721-5500
FAX: 303-779-1228

TCI and its affiliates operate cable television and movie theaters throughout the continental US and Hawaii.

Locations of Largest Cable Systems
Wayne, NJ
Hartford/Plainville/Vernon, CT
Louisville/Jefferson, KY
Chicago
Tulsa, OK
San Jose/Campbell, CA

WHAT

	1989 Sales		1989 Operating Income	
	$ mil	% of total	$ mil	% of total
Cable TV	2,353	78	501	88
Movie theaters	673	22	68	12
Total	**3,026**	**100**	**569**	**100**

Cable Programming Service
Affiliated Regional Communications (sports programming)
KBL Sports Network
TCI Utah Sports
TCI Northwest Cable Sports
TCI Bay Area Sports
American Movie Classics (50%)
Black Entertainment Television
Discovery Channel (34%)
Shopping channels
Showtime Networks (50%)
Think Entertainment
Turner Broadcasting System (21%)
X*Press Information Services (computer data via cable)

Cable Systems
Heritage
TCI
UAE
WestMarc

Publications
TV Entertainment (cable guide)

UA Theaters
2,695 in the US, Hong Kong, Puerto Rico, and the UK

HOW MUCH

	9 Yr. Growth	1980	1981	1982	1983	1984	1985	1986	1987	1988	1989
Sales ($ mil)	42.6%	124	181	283	347	449	577	646	1,709	2,282	3,026
Net income ($ mil)	—	8	13	10	16	17	10	72	6	56	(257)
Income as % of sales	—	6.6%	7.1%	3.7%	4.6%	3.8%	1.8%	11.2%	0.3%	2.5%	(8.5%)
Earnings per share ($)	—	0.03	0.04	0.04	0.06	0.06	0.04	0.24	0.02	0.16	(0.73)
Stock price – high ($)	—	2.48	2.65	2.39	3.71	4.13	6.50	9.71	15.13	14.00	21.63
Stock price – low ($)	—	0.61	1.39	1.06	1.98	2.58	3.75	5.85	7.63	10.19	12.63
Stock price – close ($)	24.7%	2.46	1.53	2.31	3.38	3.88	6.1	7.63	11.81	13.06	17.88
P/E – high	—	88	66	62	62	65	177	40	756	90	—
P/E – low	—	22	35	28	33	41	102	24	381	66	—
Dividends per share ($)	0.0%	0.00	0.00	0.00	0.00	0.00	0.00	0.00	0.00	0.00	0.00
Book value per share ($)	21.1%	0.46	0.75	0.86	0.93	0.91	1.31	2.44	2.60	3.41	2.57

1989 Year End:
Debt ratio: 89.0%
Return on equity: —
Cash (mil): $19
Current ratio: 0.23
Long-term debt (mil): $7,356
Number of shares (mil): 353
Dividends:
1989 average yield: 0.0%
1989 payout: 0.0%
Market value (mil): $6,311

Stock Price History high/low 1980-89

25
20
15
10
5
0

RANKINGS

22nd in *Fortune* 50 Utilities
276th in *Forbes* Sales 500
125th in *Business Week* 1000
356th in *Business Week* Global 1000

COMPETITION

Advance Publications
Capital Cities/ABC
CBS
Cox
General Cinema
General Electric
Hearst
Knight-Ridder
MCA
Paramount
Time Warner
Turner Broadcasting
Walt Disney
Washington Post

TELEDYNE, INC.

OVERVIEW

Teledyne, founded in 1960, is a conglomerate of over 100 different businesses. About 35% of its business is with the federal government, providing $1 billion in revenues to Teledyne's largest segment, Aviation and Electronics.

Its most profitable segment processes specialty metals like zirconium and titanium into alloys and end products. Probably its most well-known product, in its consumer products segment, is the Water-Pik.

Teledyne, slimmed down after spinning off its finance and insurance subsidiaries as Unitrin, may be too thin: Standard & Poor's lowered the company's credit rating because the departing Unitrin was fat with reserves and stock.

Chairman Henry Singleton, who owns 13.1% of Teledyne stock, has the reputation of keeping shareholders happy. In its 30 years Teledyne has never lost money. Singleton, 73, in preparation for retirement, has turned over day-to-day management to vice-chairman and CEO George Roberts, Singleton's former roommate at the US Naval Academy, and new president and heir-apparent William Rutledge. But rumors persist that Singleton will try to increase stock value by selling off pieces of Teledyne.

WHEN

Teledyne is the creation of Henry Singleton. The son of a well-to-do Texas rancher, Singleton earned a PhD in electrical engineering from MIT and learned business management while working for Hughes Aircraft, North American Aviation, and Litton Industries in the 1950s.

Singleton and another Litton executive, George Kozmetsky, invested $225,000 each and founded Teledyne in 1960 to make electronic components for aircraft manufacturers. The company grew from $4.5 million in sales its first year to nearly $90 million in 4 years. It beat out IBM and Texas Instruments to win the contract for an avionics system for a navy helicopter in 1965, and sales jumped to $250 million in 1966. Kozmetsky, laden with Teledyne stock, left in 1966 to become dean of the University of Texas Business School and, later, to found a think tank, the Institute for Constructive Capitalism, at UT.

Teledyne grew into a conglomerate, buying over 100 companies in a variety of mostly high-tech, defense-related businesses, including engines, unmanned aircraft, specialty metals, computers, and semiconductors. The company also moved into offshore oil drilling equipment, insurance and finance, and the Water-Pik line of bathroom hardware.

By 1969, as sales passed $1 billion, Singleton had realized a boyhood goal of creating a giant corporation. But in 1970 Singleton stopped buying companies, and Teledyne lost favor with investors. Earnings flattened, then dropped in 1974, when one of its insurance divisions lost money writing malpractice insurance for physicians.

In an unusual and now widely admired masterstroke, Singleton bought Teledyne shares back from stockholders between 1972 and 1976, when they sold as low as 7-7/8 a share. Yet the company continued to grow from within. Sales of $1.2 billion in 1970 reached $2.7 billion in 1979, and profits increased 315% from 1969 to 1978. Earnings per share skyrocketed 1,226%. When Wall Street rediscovered the company, happy shareholders enjoyed the appreciation. By 1979 Teledyne stock sold for well over $100 a share.

In 1986 Teledyne spun off its Argonaut Insurance unit and left the insurance business entirely with its 1990 spinoff of Unitrin, which owns 25% of the company stock of Litton Industries and 44% of Curtiss-Wright Corporation. Teledyne's defense businesses suffered a setback in 1989 when caught in an FBI investigation of fraud by defense contractors (Operation Ill Wind). The company paid $4.4 million in restitution.

HOW MUCH

	9 Yr. Growth	1980	1981	1982	1983	1984	1985	1986	1987	1988	1989
Sales ($ mil)	2.1%	2,926	3,238	2,864	2,979	3,494	3,256	3,241	3,217	4,523	3,531
Net income ($ mil)	(8.8%)	344	412	261	305	574	546	238	377	392	150
Income as % of sales	—	11.7%	12.7%	9.1%	10.2%	16.4%	16.8%	7.4%	11.7%	8.7%	4.3%
Earnings per share ($)	(1.3%)	3.05	3.99	2.52	2.97	7.54	9.33	4.07	6.45	6.81	2.71
Stock price – high ($)	—	30.60	34.95	28.75	34.70	60.48	67.60	73.55	78.00	69.70	76.15
Stock price – low ($)	—	12.13	23.60	13.90	24.60	29.45	45.40	58.20	48.40	58.05	63.50
Stock price – close ($)	10.1%	28.80	27.70	25.88	33.45	49.20	66.08	60.30	60.80	66.45	68.65
P/E – high	—	10	9	11	12	8	7	18	12	10	28
P/E – low	—	4	6	6	8	4	5	14	8	9	23
Dividends per share ($)	—	0.00	0.00	0.00	0.00	0.00	0.00	0.00	0.80	0.80	0.80
Book value per share ($)	13.4%	13.56	16.52	20.20	25.93	19.80	26.94	27.95	33.87	38.22	41.99

1989 Year End:
Debt ratio: 19.7%
Return on equity: 6.8%
Cash (mil): $236
Current ratio: 2.29
Long-term debt (mil): $571
Number of shares (mil): 55
Dividends:
1989 average yield: 1.2%
1989 payout: 29.5%
Market value (mil): $3,804

NYSE symbol: TDY
Incorporated: Delaware, 1960
Fiscal year ends: December 31

WHO

Chairman: Henry E. Singleton, age 73, $562,992 pay
VC and CEO: George A. Roberts, age 71, $819,225 pay
President: William P. Rutledge, age 48, $491,179 pay (prior to promotion)
Treasurer and CFO: Douglas Grant, age 39
Auditors: Arthur Andersen & Co.
Employees: 35,100

WHERE

HQ: 1901 Ave. of the Stars, Los Angeles, CA 90067
Phone: 213-277-3311
FAX: 213-551-4365

Teledyne operates in the US.

WHAT

	1989 Sales		1989 Operating Income	
	$ mil	% of total	$ mil	% of total
Industrial products	809	23	78	24
Aviation & electronics	1,466	42	92	28
Specialty metals	923	26	123	37
Consumer products	333	9	35	11
Adjustments	—	—	(53)	—
Total	**3,531**	**100**	**275**	**100**

Aviation & Electronics
Aviation piston engines
Doppler radars
Electronic navigation systems
Microcircuitry
Onboard computers for Viking Mars mission
Remotely piloted aircraft
Systems engineering for military, space shuttle

Specialty Metals
Molybdenum
Tantalum
Titanium
Tungsten
Vanadium
Zirconium

Industrial Products
Analytical instruments for pollution control, medical uses, deep-sea diving
Automated bakery production lines
Diesel engines for military tanks
Machine tools, dies
Mixing and processing equipment for chemical, food, and pharmaceutical products
Welding equipment

Commercial & Consumer Products
Instapure water and air filters
Laars swimming pool and spa heaters
Water-Pik oral hygiene products
Water-Pik Shower Massage

RANKINGS

109th in *Fortune* 500 US Industrial Cos.
234th in *Forbes* Sales 500
167th in *Business Week* 1000

COMPETITION

Emerson
General Electric
Honeywell
Litton
Raytheon
Texas Instruments
Textron
TRW
Other defense electronics companies

TELEFÓNICA DE ESPAÑA, SA

OVERVIEW

Spanish telephone monopoly Telefónica operates the world's 9th largest telephone system and owns 21.1% of Spain's telecommunications equipment leader, Alcatel Standard Eléctrica. The Kingdom of Spain and state-owned Banco de Espagne together own 33% of Telefónica. The company is subject to government regulation.

Despite heavy investment in modernization and expansion, Telefónica has not yet satisfied the booming domestic demand for telephone service resulting from Spain's rapid economic development. The company's 1989 installation backlog of 503,000 translated into a 6-month wait — but it was an improvement over 1988. The company will be further challenged by increased demand relating to the 1992 Barcelona Olympics.

Aiming to be a global concern, Telefónica has acquired significant stakes in South American telephone networks and has expressed interest in Mexico's system. The company is investing substantial sums to establish such services as paging and data transmission.

NYSE symbol: TEF (ADR)
Incorporated: Spain, 1924
Fiscal year ends: December 31

WHO

Chairman: Cándido Velázquez-Gaztelu Ruiz, age 54
Managing Director: Germán Ancochea Soto, age 46
Deputy General Manager Finance: Ignacio María Santillana del Barrio
Auditors: Price Waterhouse Auditores, S.A.
Employees: 71,155

WHEN

When a 1923 military coup brought General Miguel Primo de Rivera to power in Spain, the government-run telephone system was a shambles. Over 1/2 of the country's 90,000 lines did not work. With little cash in the government coffers, Primo de Rivera sought foreign assistance in running the Spanish telephone network. Several European telephone equipment manufacturers expressed interest, as did US-based telephone service company International Telephone and Telegraph (ITT).

Supported financially by National City Bank (now Citicorp), ITT bought 3 private Spanish telephone companies, later combining them to form Compañía Telefónica Nacional de España (Telefónica). After placing several influential Spaniards on Telefónica's board and getting help from the US ambassador to Spain, the ITT unit gained the telephone concession in 1924. ITT retained a controlling interest in Telefónica, and the government agreed not to try to reclaim the system for 20 years.

ITT purchased AT&T's European telephone equipment businesses and began operating a Spanish manufacturing subsidiary, the predecessor of Alcatel Standard Eléctrica. Modernization and expansion of the telephone network quickly followed. By the mid-1930s Telefónica accounted for 1/2 of ITT's worldwide phone installations.

When Franco came to power in 1939 he was thought to want to reward his German backers with the telephone franchise. US State Department pressure helped prevent expropriation, but Franco froze Telefónica's earnings and assets. ITT tried to sell Telefónica to German buyers in 1941 but backed out of the deal when the State Department objected. By 1944 Telefónica operated 400,000 lines.

In 1945 Spain bought ITT's share of Telefónica. Telefónica grew with the Spanish economy, introducing long-distance direct dialing in 1960, satellite communications in 1967, and international direct dialing in 1971.

In the 1980s Telefónica joined in several electronics and telecommunications partnerships with such companies as AT&T, Fiat, Fujitsu, and Electronic Data Systems. In 1988 Telefónica affiliate Amper (8% owned) entered into a manufacturing venture with the USSR that is expected to produce one million Soviet telephones annually. Spain's 1986 entry into the EC led to an explosion in demand for telephone services. Telefónica was unprepared, and complaints rose.

In 1990 Telefónica purchased a 43.7% stake in Compañía de Teléfonos de Chile from Australian Alan Bond. In the same year a Telefónica-led consortium that included Citicorp won a bid to manage (with 60% control) the southern 1/2 of Argentina's formerly state-run telephone system.

WHERE

HQ: Gran Vía, 28, 28013 Madrid, Spain
Phone: 011-34-1-584-7010 (Financial Department)
US HQ (Telefónica – USA, Inc.): 535 Madison Ave., 35th Floor, New York, NY 10022
US Phone: 212-221-5991
US FAX: 212-759-3084

Telefónica's domestic telephone network extends throughout mainland Spain and to the Balearic and Canary Islands and the North African cities of Ceuta and Melilla.

WHAT

	1989 Sales	
	$ mil	% of total
Subscriber service charges	1,677	26
Data & image transmission	631	10
Domestic automatic service	2,871	44
Trunk calls through operator	9	—
International service	883	14
Mobile land & maritime services	42	—
Directories & yearbooks	67	1
Connection fees & other	300	5
Adjustments	15	—
Total	**6,495**	**100**

Subsidiaries, Associated Companies & Investments
Alcatel Standard Eléctrica S.A. (telecommunications equipment, 21.1%)
Amper S.A. (electronic components, 7.6%)
ATT Microelectrónica (integrated circuits, 20%)
Compañía de Teléfonos de Chile (Chile, domestic telecommunications, 43.7%)
ENTEL (Chile, long-distance telecommunications, 20%)
European Silicon Structures (integrated circuits, 3.4%)
Fujitsu España S.A. (data processing, 40%)
Hispasat S.A. (telecommunications satellite, 25%)
Industria Electrónica de Comunicaciones S.A. (portable and mobile communications equipment, 30%)
Sistemas Técnicos de Loterías del Estado S.A. (lottery systems, 49%)
Telettra S.p.A., Telettra Española S.A. (European telecommunications projects, 10% each)
Torre de Collserola S.A. (communications tower, 35%)

RANKINGS

241st in *Business Week* Global 1000

COMPETITION

No other companies in this book compete with Telefónica.

HOW MUCH

	3 Yr. Growth	1980	1981	1982	1983	1984	1985	1986	1987	1988	1989
Sales ($ mil)	20.8%	—	—	—	—	—	—	3,688	4,955	5,406	6,495
Net income ($ mil)	20.8%	—	—	—	—	—	—	357	488	555	629
Income as % of sales	—	—	—	—	—	—	—	9.7%	9.8%	10.3%	9.7%
Earnings per share ($)	15.3%	—	—	—	—	—	—	1.33	1.76	1.87	2.04
Stock price – high ($)	—	—	—	—	—	—	—	—	29.50	26.25	27.88
Stock price – low ($)	—	—	—	—	—	—	—	—	16.00	21.38	22.63
Stock price – close ($)	—	—	—	—	—	—	—	—	22.38	23.63	24.63
P/E – high	—	—	—	—	—	—	—	—	17	14	14
P/E – low	—	—	—	—	—	—	—	—	9	11	11
Dividends per share ($)	—	—	—	—	—	—	—	0.00	0.70	1.39	1.40
Book value per share ($)	7.9%	—	—	—	—	—	—	30.45	39.17	36.40	38.26

1989 Year End:
Debt ratio: 39.8%
Return on equity: 5.5%
Cash (mil): $9
Current ratio: 0.42
Long-term debt (mil): $7,796
Number of shares (mil): 308
Dividends:
1989 average yield: 5.7%
1989 payout: 68.6%
Market value (mil): $7,592

TENNECO, INC.

OVERVIEW

Although Tenneco generates more revenues from its farm and construction equipment division than any other, it is most noted for its profit-leading natural gas operations. Running from Texas to Massachusetts, 18,000 miles of pipeline delivered 2 trillion cubic feet of natural gas (or 12% of US consumption) and generated revenues of $2.6 billion in 1989.

Subsidiary J. I. Case, the world's 2nd largest agricultural equipment manufacturer after Deere, provides farm and construction equipment through more than 3,800 dealers worldwide ($5.1 billion). Tenneco also sells automotive exhaust systems, emission control devices, shock absorbers, and brakes to OEM and replacement markets ($1.8 billion) through its automotive division.

Tenneco's Newport News Shipbuilding and Dry Dock Company is the largest shipbuilder in the US, selling nuclear-powered submarines and aircraft carriers to the navy ($1.9 billion).

Packaging Corporation of America supplies paperboard, shipping, and disposable plastic and aluminum containers ($1.3 billion). Tenneco sells phosphorus chemicals, bleaches, and surfactants ($1.2 billion) through Albright & Wilson, the 2nd largest specialty chemical producer headquartered in the UK. Other operations include financing services and land management of Tenneco's 97,000 acres ($91 million).

NYSE symbol: TGT
Incorporated: Delaware, 1954
Fiscal year ends: December 31

WHO

Chairman and CEO: J. L. Ketelsen, age 59, $1,636,136 pay
SVP and CFO: Robert T. Blakely, age 48, $557,602 pay
EVP: Allen T. McInnes, age 52, $775,033 pay
EVP: K. W. Reese, age 59, $1,023,372 pay
Auditors: Arthur Andersen & Co.
Employees: 90,000

WHERE

HQ: Tenneco Bldg., Houston, TX 77002
Phone: 713-757-2131
FAX: 713-757-1410

The company operates worldwide.

	1989 Sales		1989 Operating Income	
	$ mil	% of total	$ mil	% of total
US	9,798	69	1,021	73
Canada	853	6	90	6
Europe	2,793	20	174	13
Other foreign	639	5	107	8
Adjustments	—	—	(140)	—
Total	**14,083**	**100**	**1,252**	**100**

WHEN

Tennessee Gas and Transmission began in 1943 as a division of The Chicago Corporation, headed by Gardiner Symonds and authorized to construct a 1,265-mile pipeline between the Gulf of Mexico and West Virginia. As the nation faced WWII fuel shortages,the fledgling group completed the project in a record 11 months, obtaining rights-of-way from thousands of landowners and crossing 67 rivers.

Just after WWII, Tennessee Gas went public; Symonds became president. While expanding the pipeline, the company merged its oil and gas exploration interests into Tennessee Production Company (1954), which, with Bay Petroleum (bought 1955), formed subsidiary Tenneco Oil (1961). Symonds entered the chemical industry by acquiring 50% of Petro-Tex Chemical (1955), now Tenneco Chemicals.

In 1963 Tennessee Gas moved to its present Houston headquarters and in 1966 adopted the Tenneco name. In 1967 Tenneco purchased Kern County Land Company, which owned 2.5 million acres of California farmland and mineral rights. The purchase thrust Tenneco into the farming business; by 1984 Tenneco was the US's largest grower/shipper of table grapes and 2nd largest almond processor. The Kern purchase also included 2 Racine, Wisconsin–based manufacturers: J. I. Case is known for tractors and construction digging equipment; Walker Manufacturing entered the automotive field in 1912 producing jacks.

Symonds purchased Evanston, Illinois–based Packaging Corporation of America in 1965, maker of shipping containers, pulp, and paperboard products. In 1968 he acquired Newport News Shipbuilding, founded by Collis Huntington in 1886. Newport News built 710 ships in its first 100 years and began building submarines and nuclear-powered aircraft carriers in the 1960s.

Following Symonds's death in 1971 Tenneco bought shock absorber manufacturer Monroe of Monroe, Michigan (1977) and Philadelphia Life Insurance Company (1977); Philadelphia Life was sold to ICH Corporation in 1986. In 1985 Case bought major competitor International Harvester's agricultural equipment operations.

Tenneco will begin construction on a California pipeline in 1990. Newport News has the industry's largest order backlog and is expected to fare well in spite of proposed defense cutbacks.

WHAT

	1989 Sales		1989 Operating Income	
	$ mil	% of total	$ mil	% of total
Pipelines	2,638	19	341	24
Shipbuilding	1,949	14	211	15
Automotive parts	1,779	13	225	16
Packaging	1,336	9	206	15
Chemicals & minerals	1,224	9	119	9
Farm/construction equipment	5,066	35	247	18
Other	91	1	43	3
Adjustments	—	—	(140)	—
Total	**14,083**	**100**	**1,252**	**100**

Pipeline Operations
Channel Industries Gas
Creole Gas Pipeline
East Tennessee Natural Gas
Midwestern Gas Transmission
State Gas Pipeline
Tennessee Gas Pipeline
THC Pipeline
Viking Gas Transmission

Packaging Products
Packaging Corp. of America

Manufacturing Companies
Albright & Wilson Ltd. (chemicals)
J. I. Case Co. (farm equipment)
Monroe Auto Equipment Co. (automotive parts)
Newport News Shipbuilding and Dry Dock Co.
Walker Manufacturing Co. (automotive parts)

HOW MUCH

	9 Yr. Growth	1980	1981	1982	1983	1984	1985	1986	1987	1988	1989
Sales ($ mil)	0.7%	13,226	15,462	14,979	14,449	14,890	15,270	14,529	14,790	13,234	14,083
Net income ($ mil)	(2.4%)	726	813	840	716	631	431	139	(132)	(1)	584
Income as % of sales	—	5.5%	5.3%	5.6%	5.0%	4.2%	2.8%	1.0%	(0.9%)	0.0%	4.1%
Earnings per share ($)	(3.1%)	5.94	5.99	5.89	4.74	4.00	2.52	0.50	(1.22)	(0.18)	4.46
Stock price – high ($)	—	58.38	51.88	36.50	42.38	44.75	45.25	43.13	62.50	51.00	64.25
Stock price – low ($)	—	31.25	29.88	22.88	31.88	32.38	36.50	34.50	36.13	38.25	46.88
Stock price – close ($)	2.1%	51.63	33.50	32.38	41.00	37.88	39.75	38.25	39.75	48.88	62.25
P/E – high	—	10	9	6	9	11	18	86	—	—	14
P/E – low	—	5	5	4	7	8	14	69	—	—	11
Dividends per share ($)	2.4%	2.45	2.60	2.63	2.74	2.83	2.95	3.04	3.04	3.04	3.04
Book value per share ($)	(3.4%)	35.42	39.05	40.14	41.75	42.24	40.20	30.02	25.66	24.93	26.02

1989 Year End:
Debt ratio: 63.0%
Return on equity: 17.5%
Cash (mil): $276
Current ratio: 1.21
Long-term debt (mil): $5,573
Number of shares (mil): 126
Dividends:
1989 average yield: 4.9%
1989 payout: 68.2%
Market value (mil): $7,840

Stock Price History high/low 1980-89

RANKINGS

26th in *Fortune* 500 Industrial Cos.
46th in *Fortune* 50 Exporters
39th in *Forbes* Sales 500
56th in *Business Week* 1000
208th in *Business Week* Global 1000

COMPETITION

Caterpillar
Coastal
Deere
Fiat
Litton
Automotive parts manufacturers
Chemical companies
Other farm and construction equipment manufacturers
Other natural gas pipeline companies
Packaging companies
Shipbuilders

TEXACO INC.

OVERVIEW

Texaco is the 3rd largest integrated oil company in the US, behind Exxon and Mobil. With its famous and costly legal battle with Pennzoil concluded, it has scaled down into one of the most productive (in sales per employee) companies as well.

In "upstream" (exploration and production) activities, Texaco has focused on finding oil in existing fields where the risk is low. It has also used its financial muscle to buy new properties. In "downstream" (refining and marketing) operations, it has squeezed more bucks for the barrel at the refinery. It has added convenience food marts/gas stations, known as Star Marts (harking back to Texaco's well-known logo), to the landscape.

Overseas, its 50% stake in Caltex (along with Chevron) gives Texaco high visibility in 55 nations in Asia and the Pacific Rim. Caltex sells nearly 18% of the fuels and lubricants used there.

WHEN

"Buckskin Joe" Cullinan came to Texas in 1897 and, relying on sales to old friends from his days as a Standard Oil worker in Pennsylvania, began his own oil company.

When the Spindletop gusher hit in 1901, some 200 "oil companies" swarmed onto the scene. Cullinan surveyed the chaos around Beaumont and decided the way to make money was to sell oil other people had found. He enlisted the support of Arnold Schlaet, who managed investments for 2 New York leather merchants. Cullinan and the Schlaet interests formed Texas Fuel in 1902. In a few months, they changed the name to The Texas Company, selling under the Texaco brand.

The colorful Cullinan was deposed in a 1916 fight with New York executives. From its New York base The Texas Company quickly expanded across the globe. When Standard of California's discoveries in Saudi Arabia proved more than it could handle, it summoned Texaco, and the 2 companies spawned Caltex for overseas marketing in 1936. Again, Texaco was selling oil someone else had found.

Also in the 1930s, Texaco, partly through a company controlled by political boss Huey Long's family, leased a million acres of state-owned, oil-rich marshland in Louisiana. With such resources Texaco became the only oil company with service stations in all states. In the 1940s it began sponsoring radio opera and Milton Berle's TV show. Its ads urged that "You can trust your car to the man who wears the star," a reference to the company logo.

But Texaco, which took its trade name as its corporate name in 1959, fell from atop the oil industry in the 1960s and 1970s. US wells dried up. The company passed up drilling in Alaska's Prudhoe Bay. Texaco lost crude supplies when third world governments nationalized them.

Texaco thought it had found a source of oil in the $8.6 billion purchase of Getty Oil in 1983. But Getty had already agreed to be acquired by Pennzoil. A Texas court ordered Texaco to pay Pennzoil $10.53 billion in damages, and Texaco sought bankruptcy protection in 1987. As it settled with Pennzoil for $3 billion later that year, Texaco emerged from bankruptcy — just in time to fend off raider Carl Icahn.

After the Pennzoil and Icahn battles, Texaco trimmed down and raised about $7 billion, partly by selling Texaco Canada and its West German subsidiary (1988). The company rid itself of 2,500 unprofitable gasoline stations and pulled out of 11 states.

In 1989 Texaco launched a joint venture — Star Enterprise — with Saudi Arabia. Texaco put in 60% of its US refining and marketing operations, and the Saudis chipped in $812 million cash and a steady flow of crude. Again Texaco is selling someone else's oil.

HOW MUCH

	9 Yr. Growth	1980	1981	1982	1983	1984	1985	1986	1987	1988	1989
Sales ($ mil)	(5.0%)	51,196	57,628	46,986	40,068	47,334	46,297	31,613	34,372	33,544	32,416
Net income ($ mil)	0.8%	2,240	2,310	1,281	1,233	306	1,233	725	(4,407)	1,304	2,413
Income as % of sales	—	4.4%	4.0%	2.7%	3.1%	0.6%	2.7%	2.3%	(12.8%)	3.9%	7.4%
Earnings per share ($)	0.6%	8.31	8.75	4.92	4.80	1.03	4.84	3.00	(18.15)	5.19	8.74
Stock price – high ($)	—	54.38	49.13	34.88	39.13	48.38	40.88	37.13	47.50	52.50	59.00
Stock price – low ($)	—	27.50	31.50	26.00	30.50	31.50	27.00	26.00	23.50	35.63	48.50
Stock price – close ($)	2.3%	48.00	33.00	31.13	35.88	34.13	30.00	35.88	37.25	51.13	58.88
P/E – high	—	7	6	7	8	47	8	12	—	10	7
P/E – low	—	3	4	5	6	31	6	9	—	7	6
Dividends per share ($)	17.0%	2.45	2.80	3.00	3.00	3.00	3.00	3.00	0.75	2.25	10.10
Book value per share ($)	(4.7%)	46.64	53.11	55.12	56.86	55.15	57.04	56.71	37.76	31.13	30.31

1989 Year End:
Debt ratio: 33.9%
Return on equity: 28.5%
Cash (mil): $2,320
Current ratio: 1.21
Long-term debt (mil): $4,714
Number of shares (mil): 265
Dividends:
1989 average yield: 17.2%
1989 payout: 115.6%
Market value (mil): $15,600

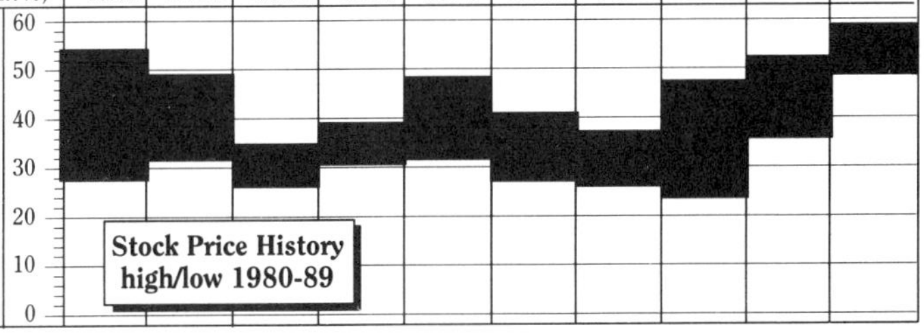

Stock Price History high/low 1980-89

NYSE symbol: TX
Incorporated: Delaware, 1926
Fiscal year ends: December 31

WHO

President and CEO: James W. Kinnear, age 61, $1,793,298 pay
Chairman: Alfred C. DeCrane, age 58, $1,464,857 pay
SVP and CFO: Allen J. Krowe, age 57, $810,360 pay
SVP and President, Texaco USA: James L. Dunlap, age 52, $625,918 pay
SVP and General Counsel: Stephen M. Turner, age 50
Auditor: Arthur Andersen & Co.
Employees: 37,067

WHERE

HQ: 2000 Westchester Ave., White Plains, NY 10650
Phone: 914-253-4000
FAX: 914-253-7753

Texaco is engaged in worldwide operations, from drilling in Indonesia and off the Chinese coast, to refining in Rotterdam, to marketing with Chevron in Asia and the Pacific Rim and with the Saudis on the US East Coast.

	1989 Sales		1989 Operating Income	
	$ mil	% of total	$ mil	% of total
US	18,706	58	735	29
Other Americas	3,730	11	1,389	56
Eastern Hemisphere	9,980	31	368	15
Adjustments	—	—	(1,581)	—
Total	**32,416**	**100**	**911**	**100**

WHAT

	1989 Sales		1989 Operating Income	
	$ mil	% of total	$ mil	% of total
Petroleum, natural gas & other	30,843	95	3,049	88
Petrochemical	1,573	5	399	12
Adjustments	—	—	(2,537)	—
Total	**32,416**	**100**	**911**	**100**

Brand Names
Havoline – motor oils introduced in 1934
Star Enterprise – the joint refining-and-marketing venture with the Saudis that is the US's 6th largest gasoline seller. It sells Texaco-branded products in 10,700 retail outlets in 26 states.
Star Mart – convenience/gas stores
System[3] – gasolines introduced in 1989; touted through national advertising campaign as engine-cleansing. Successor to Texaco Fire Chief gasoline (introduced in 1932) and Sky Chief (1938).

RANKINGS

10th in *Fortune* 500 Industrial Cos.
23rd in *Fortune* Global 500 Industrial Cos.
13th in *Forbes* Sales 500
34th in *Business Week* 1000
82nd in *Business Week* Global 1000

COMPETITION

Amoco
Ashland
Atlantic Richfield
British Petroleum
Chevron
Coastal
Du Pont
Exxon
Mobil
Occidental
Pennzoil
Phillips
Royal Dutch/Shell
Sun
Unocal
USX

TEXAS INSTRUMENTS INC.

OVERVIEW

Texas Instruments develops, manufactures, and markets electronics products, including semiconductors, computing equipment (digital products), defense systems, and metallurgical materials.

TI's business is based mainly on its broad semiconductor technology and derivative applications. TI owns many patents in the US and abroad relating to basic integrated circuit design (the "Kilby patent") and applications in memory chips and microprocessors. From 1987 to 1989 TI collected $539 million in patent royalties. In December 1989 the Kilby patent was upheld in Japan, potentially yielding an additional $100 to $650 million in annual royalties.

TI plans to revamp its semiconductor operation and reduce dependence on aging product lines by spending $1.2 billion on new plants and improvements (principally submicron CMOS wafer fabrication) over the next 3 years.

The digital products segment has posted losses for 3 consecutive years. Renamed the Information Technology Group, it seeks new revenues from custom software applications in areas such as operations management, factory automation, and programming productivity.

WHEN

In 1930 "Doc" Karcher and Eugene McDermott founded Geophysical Service Inc. (GSI) in Newark, New Jersey. The company specialized in reflective seismology, a new technology used to explore for oil and gas deposits. In 1934 the company moved its headquarters to Dallas.

GSI started making defense electronic equipment during WWII, when it made submarine detectors for the US Navy, and established a defense electronics manufacturing division in 1946. The company changed its name to Texas Instruments in 1951 and was listed on the NYSE in 1953.

TI started manufacturing transistors in 1952, after buying a license from Western Electric. Former Bell Laboratories scientist Dr. Gordon Teal handled research for TI, and the company invested about $2 million in efforts to reduce the price of the germanium transistor, which expanded the market for its uses and made possible the pocket transistor radio (1954). TI produced the first commercial silicon transistor in 1954 and invented the integrated circuit in 1958. By 1959 TI's semiconductor manufacturing division, which produced magnetics, sonar, radar, and related accessories, accounted for 1/2 of the company's total sales.

TI's technological know-how led to other firsts in microelectronics, including terrain-following airborne radar (1958), forward-looking infrared (FLIR) systems (1964), hand-held calculators (1967), single-chip microcomputers (1971), and the LISP chip, a 32-bit microcomputer for artificial intelligence applications (1987). GSI, TI's petroleum exploration subsidiary, introduced equipment capable of digitally recording seismic data in 1961.

During the 1960s TI concentrated on building its defense-related and semiconductor business. It moved into consumer products in the 1970s with hand-held calculators and digital watches. TI manufactured its products less expensively than its competitors by using automated assembly techniques and keeping salaries and wages low. In recent years TI has de-emphasized consumer products (although it still makes calculators) and concentrated on semiconductors, defense electronics, and materials and controls. It has also increased R&D to stimulate growth.

In 1988 TI sold 60% of GSI to Halliburton Company. This reduced TI's exposure to fluctuations in the petroleum industry; however, the company remains vulnerable to cuts in the defense budget.

HOW MUCH

	9 Yr. Growth	1980	1981	1982	1983	1984	1985	1986	1987	1988	1989
Sales ($ mil)	5.4%	4,075	4,206	4,327	4,580	5,742	4,925	4,974	5,595	6,295	6,522
Net income ($ mil)	3.6%	212	109	144	(145)	316	(119)	40	257	366	292
Income as % of sales	—	5.2%	2.6%	3.3%	(3.2%)	5.5%	(2.4%)	0.8%	4.6%	5.8%	4.5%
Earnings per share ($)	0.1%	3.01	1.54	2.01	(2.01)	4.32	(1.58)	0.38	2.95	4.05	3.04
Stock price – high ($)	—	50.25	42.08	50.83	58.67	49.83	43.92	49.42	80.25	60.00	46.75
Stock price – low ($)	—	26.21	25.00	23.50	33.67	37.25	28.75	34.25	36.25	34.50	28.13
Stock price – close ($)	(1.3%)	40.25	26.83	44.88	46.21	39.83	35.17	39.38	55.75	41.00	35.88
P/E – high	—	17	27	25	—	12	—	130	27	15	15
P/E – low	—	9	16	12	—	9	—	90	12	9	9
Dividends per share ($)	0.9%	0.67	0.67	0.67	0.67	0.67	0.67	0.67	0.71	0.72	0.72
Book value per share ($)	4.2%	16.69	17.81	19.18	16.69	20.86	18.91	22.51	21.95	21.36	24.10

1989 Year End:
Debt ratio: 19.9%
Return on equity: 13.4%
Cash (mil): $637
Current ratio: 1.88
Long-term debt (mil): $618
Number of shares (mil): 82
Dividends:
1989 average yield: 2.0%
1989 payout: 23.7%
Market value (mil): $2,924

Stock Price History high/low 1980-89

NYSE symbol: TXN
Incorporated: Delaware, 1938
Fiscal year ends: December 31

WHO

Chairman, President, and CEO: Jerry R. Junkins, age 52, $701,620 pay
EVP: William P. Weber, age 49, $428,500 pay
EVP: William B. Mitchell, age 54, $384,300 pay
EVP: William I. George, age 58, $320,800 pay
SVP, Treasurer, and CFO: William A. Aylesworth, age 47, $322,100 pay
Auditors: Ernst & Young
Employees: 73,854

WHERE

HQ: 13500 N. Central Expressway, PO Box 655474, Dallas, TX 75265
Phone: 214-995-2551
FAX: 214-995-4360

TI has 57 plants in 18 countries.

	1989 Sales		1989 Operating Income	
	$ mil	% of total	$ mil	% of total
US	4,475	69	355	86
Europe	969	15	(30)	(7)
East Asia	972	15	83	20
Other	106	2	6	1
Adjustments	—	—	(95)	—
Total	**6,522**	**100**	**319**	**100**

WHAT

	1989 Sales		1989 Operating Income	
	$ mil	% of total	$ mil	% of total
Components	3,211	49	276	66
Digital products	1,000	15	(68)	(16)
Defense electronics	2,148	33	196	47
Metallurgical matls.	165	3	12	3
Adjustments	(2)	—	(97)	—
Total	**6,522**	**100**	**319**	**100**

Products

Clad metals
Electrical and electronic control devices
Electronic calculators and learning aids
Electronic data terminals and printers
Electronic warfare systems
Missile guidance and control systems
Multiuser minicomputers
Personal computers and workstations
Radar and infrared surveillance systems
Semiconductors
Software development tools

RANKINGS

71st in *Fortune* 500 Industrial Cos.
197th in *Fortune* Global 500 Industrial Cos.
129th in *Forbes* Sales 500
208th in *Business Week* 1000
580th in *Business Week* Global 1000

COMPETITION

Emerson
Fujitsu
General Dynamics
Harris
Hewlett-Packard
Hitachi
Honeywell
Hyundai
Intel
Motorola
National Semiconductor
NEC
Rockwell International
Sun Microsystems
Teledyne
Other electronics companies

TEXAS UTILITIES COMPANY

OVERVIEW

Texas Utilities (TU) operates an electric utility system in north-central, east, and west Texas. TU has about 2.1 million customers in 371 cities, including the Dallas–Fort Worth Metroplex. Texas Utilities Electric Company (TU Electric), the company's principal subsidiary, is engaged in the generation, transmission, purchase, and sale of electricity. TU Electric operates 1 nuclear, 4 lignite, and 19 gas/oil generating plants and is building a 2nd reactor at its nuclear plant. The system can produce about 20.5 million kilowatts of electricity.

Texas Utilities Fuel Company owns a natural gas pipeline system and is involved in the delivery of natural gas and fuel oil to the TU Electric plants. Texas Utilities Mining Company mines lignite coal for the company's generating plants. Texas Utilities Services Company furnishes administrative services to the other companies in the system.

Texas Utilities has paid dividends every year since its incorporation in 1945 and has increased its dividend every year since 1948.

WHEN

The first electric power company in north Texas was founded in Dallas in 1883. Another was built in 1885 in Fort Worth. From these and other small power plants grew 3 companies that developed to serve the north-central, western and eastern regions of the state: Texas Power and Light (1912), Dallas Power and Light (1917), and Texas Electric Service Company (1929). By 1932 a network of transmission lines connecting these 3 utilities was virtually complete. Texas Utilities Company was formed in 1945 as a holding company for the 3 utilities, to provide an attractive common stock to raise capital and to obtain construction financing at lower cost.

Beginning in the 1940s the company moved away from strict dependence on natural gas, which was cheap and abundant at that time, and began to lease large lignite coal reserves. In 1952 the company formed Industrial Generating Company to mine lignite and operate an early coal-fired generating plant. The utility pioneered new lignite coal–burning technology during the 1960s, building larger boilers than had ever been used in the US. In 1971 the first of 9 large lignite plants went into use. In 1974 the company began construction of the Comanche Peak nuclear plant, 45 miles southwest of Fort Worth. In 1975 the cost of natural gas tripled relative to lignite.

In 1984 Dallas Power and Light, Texas Electric Service, Texas Power and Light, and Industrial Generating were combined as Texas Utilities Electric. All generating facilities were combined in the Generating Division of the new company. The mining facilities corporation was renamed Texas Utilities Mining.

In 1985 the Nuclear Regulatory Commission suspended licensing of the Comanche Peak nuclear plant due to allegations of improper construction and design. Agreements negotiated with the NRC and the intervening citizens' group resulted in the granting of a license to operate at 5% of capacity in 1990, with commercial operation expected by summer of that year. In the interim TU lost its 3 construction partners over the issue of multibillion dollar cost overruns and bought their interests for a total of $984.5 million.

In 1990 Santa Fe Pacific Corporation agreed to settle an antitrust suit brought by TU in 1981 over a 1977 lease agreement granting TU the right to mine about 228 million tons of coal owned by Santa Fe. TU, the 4th largest coal producer in the US in 1988, won substantial royalty and lease agreement concessions from Santa Fe in a new agreement, running from 1990 through 2017.

HOW MUCH

	9 Yr. Growth	1980	1981	1982	1983	1984	1985	1986	1987	1988	1989
Sales ($ mil)	7.9%	2,175	2,738	3,238	3,488	3,932	4,170	3,932	4,083	4,154	4,321
Net income ($ mil)	11.2%	341	406	475	513	587	654	705	769	738	888
Income as % of sales	—	15.7%	14.8%	14.7%	14.7%	14.9%	15.7%	17.9%	18.8%	17.8%	20.5%
Earnings per share ($)	3.8%	3.18	3.51	3.85	3.90	4.15	4.35	4.45	4.55	4.00	4.44
Stock price – high ($)	—	19.38	22.13	25.75	27.38	28.13	31.88	37.50	36.63	30.63	37.50
Stock price – low ($)	—	14.88	16.25	19.13	22.25	20.75	25.13	29.50	25.50	24.63	27.75
Stock price – close ($)	7.3%	18.63	19.63	23.50	23.25	26.38	29.88	31.50	27.00	28.13	35.13
P/E – high	—	6	6	7	7	7	7	8	8	8	8
P/E – low	—	5	5	5	6	5	6	7	6	6	6
Dividends per share ($)	5.8%	1.76	1.88	2.04	2.20	2.36	2.52	2.68	2.80	2.88	2.92
Book value per share ($)	5.3%	21.76	23.01	24.61	26.16	27.79	29.46	31.24	33.02	33.38	34.56

1989 Year End:
Debt ratio: 46.7%
Return on equity: 13.1%
Cash (mil): $64
Current ratio: 0.43
Long-term debt (mil): $6,417
Number of shares (mil): 183
Dividends:
1989 average yield: 8.3%
1989 payout: 65.8%
Market value (mil): $6,435

Stock Price History high/low 1980-89

NYSE symbol: TXU
Incorporated: Texas, 1945
Fiscal year ends: December 31

WHO

Chairman and CEO: Jerry S. Farrington, age 55, $500,000 pay
President: Erle Nye, age 52, $375,000 pay
President, Generating Division: Michael D. Spence, $272,667 pay
VP and Principal Financial Officer: T. L. Baker, age 44, $187,000 pay
SVP, TU Electric: E. L. Watson, $187,000 pay
Auditors: Deloitte & Touche
Employees: 15,248

WHERE

HQ: 2001 Bryan Tower, Dallas, TX 75201
Phone: 214-812-4600
FAX: 214-812-4079

Texas Utilities serves north-central, east, and west Texas.

Cities Served

Arlington	Odessa
Dallas	Plano
Fort Worth	Richardson
Irving	Tyler
Killeen	Waco
Midland	Wichita Falls

WHAT

	1989 Sales	
	$ mil	% of total
Residential	1,746	40
Commercial	1,292	30
Industrial	855	20
Government & municipal	158	3
Other utilities	246	6
Other	24	1
Total	**4,321**	**100**

	1989 Energy Generation
	% of total
19 gas/oil plants	41
4 lignite plants	45
Purchased power	14
Total	**100**

Subsidiaries
Basic Resources (resource development)
Chaco Energy Company (coal)
Texas Utilities Electric Co.
Texas Utilities Fuel Co. (pipeline, storage)
Texas Utilities Mining Co.
Texas Utilities Services (accounting and administrative services

RANKINGS

12th in *Fortune* 50 Utilities
199th in *Forbes* Sales 500
87th in *Business Week* 1000
255th in *Business Week* Global 1000

TEXTRON, INC.

OVERVIEW

Textron, one of the oldest US conglomerates, operates 4 business units: aerospace/defense, commercial products, financial services, and insurance.

Textron's Aerospace Technology divisions produce aircraft wings; engines for military aircraft, tanks, and business jets; and other aerospace systems and components. The company's contract to make engines and turret controls for the army's M-1 tank ends in 1992. Sales to the government have declined (from $2.6 billion in 1987 to $1.7 billion in 1989), reflecting lowered defense spending and Textron's efforts to capture more of the commercial aviation market.

Textron's Consumer Products sector manufactures products ranging from specialty fasteners to fashion jewelry to lawn care products. Sales to the automotive industry totaled $777 million in 1989, or $62 for every North American–built car and light truck.

Textron provides loans and credit-related insurance to businesses and consumers through its Avco financial subsidiaries. Paul Revere Insurance Group, Textron's insurance subsidiary, offers a full line of insurance products, including life, health, and disability.

WHEN

Pioneer conglomerate builder Royal Little founded Special Yarns Corporation, a Boston textile business, in 1923. To save the company from bankruptcy, he merged it with the Franklin Rayon Dyeing Company in 1928. The resulting company, Franklin Rayon Corporation, moved its headquarters to Providence, Rhode Island, in 1930 and changed its name to Atlantic Rayon in 1938.

The company expanded during WWII to keep up with government orders for parachutes and in 1944 adopted the name Textron (connoting "textile products made from synthetics"). But Textron failed in its postwar efforts to distribute Textron-brand cousumer products. In 1952 Little convinced Textron's shareholders to allow the company to diversify beyond the textile industry and between 1953 and 1960 bought more than 40 different companies, including Randall (auto parts, 1959) and E-Z-Go (golf carts, 1960). Before turning over the company to banker Rupert ("Rupe") Thompson in 1960, Little bought Bell Helicopter. Within 6 years, defense-related sales accounted for 41% of Textron's revenues.

Under Thompson, businesses deemed incapable of earning a 20% ROE were sold, including Amerotron, Textron's last textile business (1963). Known on Wall Street as "Miscellaneous, Inc.," Textron bought 20 companies between 1960 and 1965, mostly to enhance its existing business divisions. By 1968, when former Wall Street attorney G. William Miller stepped up to replace Thompson as CEO, Textron made products ranging from Homelite chain saws (acquired 1955) to Speidel watchbands (acquired 1964).

Miller tried unsuccessfully to make several large acquisitions, including Lockheed (1974). He sold several companies and bought Jacobsen Manufacturers (lawn care equipment, 1978). Miller left Textron in 1978 to head the Federal Reserve Board and became Treasury Secretary under President Carter. B. F. Dolan, who became president in 1980, sold Textron's least-profitable businesses, including its zipper and snowmobile makers (1980) and machine tool manufacturer Jones & Lamson (1985).

Textron bought Avco Corporation (aerospace and financial services, 1985) and Ex-Cell-O (defense and auto parts, 1986), financing these acquisitions by selling nondefense companies and increasing debt.

In 1989 Textron spent $250 million to buy British-based Avdel (metal fastening systems), but the FTC challenged the acquisition as anticompetitive. Textron still had not completed the acquisition by mid-1990.

HOW MUCH

	9 Yr. Growth	1980	1981	1982	1983	1984	1985	1986	1987	1988	1989
Sales ($ mil)	9.2%	3,377	3,328	2,936	2,980	3,221	4,039	5,023	5,388	7,279	7,431
Net income ($ mil)	5.3%	169	146	84	89	114	180	242	261	272	269
Income as % of sales	—	5.0%	4.4%	2.9%	3.0%	3.5%	4.5%	4.8%	4.8%	3.7%	3.6%
Earnings per share ($)	3.3%	2.26	1.95	1.15	1.20	1.56	2.42	2.93	2.97	3.10	3.02
Stock price – high ($)	—	16.19	19.25	14.06	18.44	21.75	29.88	35.00	39.75	30.00	29.38
Stock price – low ($)	—	10.31	12.25	8.63	11.75	12.94	16.19	24.31	17.25	20.63	22.63
Stock price – close ($)	5.7%	14.94	13.31	11.88	16.31	16.94	24.50	31.50	22.63	23.75	24.63
P/E – high	—	7	10	12	15	14	12	12	13	10	10
P/E – low	—	5	6	8	10	8	7	8	6	7	8
Dividends per share ($)	1.2%	0.90	0.90	0.90	0.90	0.90	0.90	0.90	0.98	1.00	1.00
Book value per share ($)	—	16.01	17.19	—	—	—	—	—	—	—	—

1989 Year End:
Debt ratio: 70.0%
Return on equity: —
Cash (mil): $29
Current ratio: —
Long-term debt (mil): $5,942
Number of shares (mil): 89
Dividends:
1989 average yield: 4.1%
1989 payout: 33.1%
Market value (mil): $2,190

Stock Price History high/low 1980-89

0 5 10 15 20 25 30 35 40

NYSE symbol: TXT
Incorporated: Delaware, 1967
Fiscal year ends: December 30

WHO

Chairman and CEO: B. F. Dolan, age 62, $2,316,875 pay
President and COO: James F. Hardymon, age 55
EVP and CFO: Dennis G. Little, age 54, $818,740 pay
Auditors: Ernst & Young
Employees: 58,000

WHERE

HQ: 40 Westminster St., Providence, RI 02903
Phone: 401-421-2800
FAX: 401-421-2878

Textron operates 154 plants in North America, Asia/Pacific, and Western Europe.

	1989 Sales		1989 Operating Income	
	$ mil	% of total	$ mil	% of total
US	6,551	88	628	86
Canada	577	8	62	8
Other	304	4	42	6
Total	**7,431**	**100**	**1,134**	**100**

WHAT

	1989 Sales		1989 Operating Income	
	$ mil	% of total	$ mil	% of total
Aerospace/defense	3,318	46	309	42
Commercial prods.	1,892	25	164	23
Financial svcs.	1,174	16	169	23
Other insurance	984	13	91	12
Adjustments	—	—	401	—
Total	**7,431**	**100**	**1,134**	**100**

Aerospace/Defense
Airfoil (blades and vanes)
Bell Aerospace (aircraft wings and systems)
Bell Helicopter
Cadillac Gage (armored vehicles)
Textron Lycoming (aircraft engines)

Commercial Products
Automotive trim and electromechanical parts
Chain saws (Homelite)
Fasteners and fastener systems
Golf carts (E-Z-Go)
Hand tools, power tools, machine tools
Lawn care equipment (Jacobsen)
Watches and fashion jewelry (Speidel)

Finance & Insurance
Consumer loans (Avco)
Credit-related insurance
Life, medical, and disability insurance (Paul Revere)

RANKINGS

61st in *Fortune* 500 Industrial Cos.
172nd in *Fortune* Global 500 Industrial Cos.
23rd in *Fortune* 50 Exporters
110th in *Forbes* Sales 500
297th in *Business Week* 1000
924th in *Business Week* Global 1000

COMPETITION

Allied-Signal	Electrolux	Snap-on Tools
Black & Decker	General Dynamics	Stanley Works
Boeing		United Technologies

Other aerospace, finance, and insurance companies; power and machine tool makers; lawn care equipment makers; automotive trim makers.

THIOKOL CORPORATION

OVERVIEW

Utah-based Thiokol is an aerospace and defense business. Thiokol is the largest US producer of solid fuel systems for rockets and makes the rocket motors for NASA's space shuttle. The company derives 98% of its sales from US government contracts.

Space Operations, the company's largest business (about 50% of sales), is benefiting from the space shuttle program's recovery from the 1986 Challenger disaster (caused by failure of the Thiokol-manufactured O rings for the solid-fuel booster rockets). Thiokol also provides solid motor propulsion systems for the Delta, Scout, and other launch vehicles and communications satellite placement motors.

Thiokol's Tactical Operations works on various military missile programs (surface-to-air, air-to-surface, and air-to-air). Strategic Operations manufactures systems for Peacekeeper, Trident II, and Midgetman ICBM missiles. Ordnance Operations manages US Army ammunition plants (Louisiana and Texas), which have had lower production levels in the past year due to reduced DOD budgets.

WHEN

Joseph Patrick, a chemist conducting a laboratory experiment in Kansas City to develop a cheap antifreeze, instead discovered synthetic rubber. As a result Thiokol (Greek for sulfur glue) Chemical Company started in 1929.

In the 1930s Thiokol's synthetic rubber was used in making gaskets and hoses. In 1943 the company developed a liquid polysulfide polymer, a nearly indestructible sealant for airplane fuel tanks, gun turrets, and seams of aircraft carriers.

Scientists at the Jet Propulsion Laboratory of the California Institute of Technology discovered in the late 1940s that liquid polymer was the best solid propellant fuel binder. Thiokol immediately started rocket operations in Elkton, Maryland, with a US Army contract. The company in 1949 also opened facilities at the army's Redstone Arsenal in Huntsville, Alabama.

In 1951 Thiokol opened a 2nd plant (Moss Point, Mississippi) to make liquid polymer as a sealant. The following year the company built a rocket R&D facility in Maryland. In 1958 Thiokol got a US Air Force contract to build the first stage of the Minuteman missile, the largest solid rocket motor built at that time, at its new $3 million plant in northern Utah.

Thiokol joined an air force research program for giant solid rocket motors in 1963. The Peacekeeper missile and space shuttle boosters were ultimate products of this research. The company at the same time entered into a joint venture with Hercules to develop a propulsion system for the navy's Poseidon submarine–launched missile. The joint venture also developed the Trident I and Trident II programs.

In 1972 the company formed its Utah division, where it manufactured illuminating flares. Thiokol's Louisiana division, formed in 1975, operated an army ammunition plant and became a major supplier of projectiles and explosive devices.

Thiokol diversified into specialty chemicals in 1974 by purchasing Dynachem, a leading world supplier of photopolymers and finishing compounds for printed circuits. In 1976 Thiokol purchased Ventron Corporation, a producer of sodium borohydride for pharmaceuticals and fine chemicals.

In 1982 the company underwent a major change when it merged with Morton International to become Morton Thiokol, a specialty chemicals, solid propulsion, and salt company. Only 4 years later, Morton Thiokol was under intense scrutiny after the explosion of the Challenger space shuttle, caused by failure inside the company's booster rockets.

To recover from the nationally televised disaster, the company acquired 3 chemical companies and developed its automobile air bag business. The bags are hidden inside a car until an accident occurs, when they inflate automatically to cushion passengers. The bags use the same technology Thiokol developed to propel torpedoes from navy submarines.

In 1989 the limited growth in aerospace prompted a division into Thiokol Corporation (aerospace) and Morton International (specialty chemicals, salt, and automobile air bags), both publicly held companies.

Morton Thiokol shareholders got one share of stock in Morton. After those shares were distributed, Thiokol adopted its present name and declared a 2-for-5 reverse stock split.

HOW MUCH

	4 Yr. Growth	1980	1981	1982	1983	1984	1985	1986	1987	1988	1989
Sales ($ mil)	7.9%	—	—	—	—	—	863	927	893	1,068	1,168
Net income ($ mil)	(18.6%)	—	—	—	—	—	41	43	33	33	18
Income as % of sales	—	—	—	—	—	—	4.8%	4.6%	3.7%	3.1%	1.5%

Net income ($ mil) 1985-89

0 5 10 15 20 25 30 35 40 45

NYSE symbol: TKC
Incorporated: Delaware, 1969
Fiscal year ends: June 30

WHO

Chairman: Robert T. Marsh, age 64
President and CEO: U. Edwin Garrison, age 62, $298,376 pay
SVP Space Operations: Robert E. Lindstrom, age 60, $225,000 pay
VP Tactical Operations: Luther C. Johnson, age 49, $195,323 pay
VP Strategic Planning: Philip R. Dykstra, age 59, $183,813 pay
VP Strategic Operations: Hugh B. Chare, age 40, $130,591 pay
VP and CFO: James R. Wilson, age 48
VP Human Resources: James F. McNulty, age 45
Auditors: Ernst & Young
Employees: 11,500

WHERE

HQ: 2475 Washington Blvd., Ogden, UT 84401
Phone: 801-629-2000
FAX: 801-629-2420

Thiokol has operations in Alabama, Louisiana, Maryland, Nevada, Texas, and Utah.

WHAT

	1989 Sales		1989 Operating Income	
	$ mil	% of total	$ mil	% of total
Space	508	44	28	36
Strategic	236	20	14	18
Tactical	224	19	28	36
Ordnance	200	17	7	10
Total	**1,168**	**100**	**77**	**100**

Products
Explosive devices
Flares
Infrared decoys
Missile launching systems
Mortar rounds
Munitions
Rocket propellant
Satellite positioning motors
Space shuttle booster motors

Subsidiary
Omneco, Inc.

COMPETITION

Allied-Signal
EG&G
General Dynamics
Hercules
Martin Marietta
McDonnell Douglas
Northrop
Raytheon
Rockwell International
Textron
United Technologies

THOMSON SA

OVERVIEW

French government–owned Thomson is the world's 4th largest consumer electronics company, and its 60%-owned Thomson-CSF subsidiary is a major defense electronics firm. The company leads in US TV sales and is 2nd to Philips in Europe. Thomson's US brands include RCA, General Electric (consumer electronics only), and Wilcox. European consumer brands include Thomson and Telefunken.

Thomson is an active participant in the research and development of high-definition TV in both the US and Europe.

In 1989 the French government extended CEO Alain Gomez's tenure for another 3 years despite a flap over Thomson's loss on a loan to an insolvent Saudi bank. In 1990 Thomson CSF merged its finance unit into Altus Finance, a partnership with French bank Crédit Lyonnais.

Under Gomez, Thomson has restructured and concentrated on consumer and defense electronics while seeking partners for its semiconductor business, SGS-Thomson (50% owned by Thomson-CSF).

WHEN

In 1892 a group of French businessmen bargained with Connecticut-based Thomson Houston Electric (later bought by General Electric) for access to the US company's patents. They created Compagnie Francaise Thomson-Houston (CFTH) in 1893 to make power generation equipment. CFTH soon diversified into electric railways and light bulbs. Through acquisitions in the 1920s and 1930s, the company started producing appliances, radios, broadcast equipment, X-ray equipment, and electrical cable. By WWII CFTH was a widely diversified electric concern.

CFTH's consumer goods businesses prospered in the postwar period. In the 1960s the company acquired electronics businesses. Following the purchase of Hotchkiss-Brandt (appliances, defense, automobiles, postal equipment, 1966), CFTH changed its name to Thomson-Brandt. The company merged its professional electronics businesses with Compagnie de Telegraphie Sans Fil (electronic components and equipment, communications) to form majority-owned Thomson-CSF in 1968. The next year Thomson-Brandt transferred its heavy equipment business to Compagnie Générale d'Electricité (CGE). In exchange, CGE ceded the French appliance and data processing markets to Thomson-Brandt. In the 1970s the company continued acquiring and diversifying, but profits began to erode as "les barons," Thomson senior executives, established fiefdoms, and financial controls broke down. In 1982 the technically bankrupt company lost $355 million and was nationalized by the Mitterand government.

The government selected Alain Gomez to run Thomson-Brandt. The new CEO discovered that the sprawling company had no treasury function. After requesting a financial report on Thomson-CSF, he was given one page of figures. He immediately hired Jean-Francois Henin as treasurer. Gomez cut costs and staffing and focused Thomson-Brandt on consumer electronics and Thomson-CSF on defense electronics, fields in which he felt the company could attain sufficient volume to compete globally.

In 1983 Gomez formed Thomson SA as a holding company for the firm's operating units and swapped the company's civil telecommunications business for CGE's military and consumer electronics units. Thomson-CSF won large contracts from Saudi Arabia (1984) and the US Army (1985); bought most of the assets of Mostek (semiconductors, US, 1986); and merged its chipmaking businesses with SGS Microelectronica (semiconductors, Italy, 1987) to create a chipmaker (SGS-Thomson) capable of global competion. Gomez traded Thomson's medical division and $800 million for General Electric's GE and RCA consumer electronics businesses in 1987. In 1988 Thomson bought Fergeson (consumer electronics, UK), and SGS purchased Inmos in 1989 (microprocessors, UK) and joined with Siemens and Philips in JESSI, a chip development project. In 1990 Thomson-CSF bought Philips's defense businesses and agreed to a joint venture with British Aerospace. Philips and Thomson also agreed to a $3.6 billion joint development effort in European high-definition TV.

HOW MUCH

$=FF5.78 (Dec. 31, 1989)	9 Yr. Growth	1980	1981	1982	1983	1984	1985	1986	1987	1988	1989
Sales (FF mil)	8.6%	36,540	43,657	47,031	49,448	57,895	59,883	62,650	60,182	74,834	76,663
Net income (FF mil)	—	—	—	(895)	(1,073)	(21)	126	882	1,063	1,197	497
Income as % of sales	—	—	—	(1.9%)	(2.2%)	—	0.2%	1.4%	1.8%	1.6%	0.6%
Earnings per share (FF)	—	—	—	(112)	(105)	(2)	9	51	56	63	24
Dividends per share (FF)	—	13.00	7.87	—	—	—	—	—	8.44	7.20	—
Book value per share (FF)	—	431	490	337	196	275	291	366	335	421	425

1989 Year End:
Debt ratio: 59.3%
Return on equity: 5.7%
Cash (mil): FF4,626
Long-term debt (mil):FF28,934
Number of shares (mil): 21
Dividends:
1989 average yield: —
1989 payout: 35.7%
Sales (mil): $13,273

Net Income ($ mil) 1980-89

1500
1000
500
0
-500
-1000
-1500

Government-owned company
Founded: France, 1893
Fiscal year ends: December 31

WHO

Chairman and CEO: Alain Gomez, age 51
EVP; CEO, Thomson Consumer Electronics: Pierre Garcin
SVP and General Counsel: Pierre Cabanes
SVP Finance: Alain Hagelauer
Auditors: Guy Barbier et Associés; Arthur Andersen & Co.
Employees: 100,000

WHERE

HQ: Cedex 67, 92045 Paris La Défense, France
Phone: 011-33-1-49-07-80-00
FAX: 011-33-1-49-07-83-00
US HQ (Thomson Consumer Electronics, Inc.): 600 N. Sherman Dr., Indianapolis, IN 46201
US Phone: 317-267-5000
US FAX: 317-231-4056

Thomson has commercial and industrial facilities in more than 50 countries.

	1989 Sales	
	FF mil	% of total
France	21,547	28
North America	21,349	28
Western Europe	15,915	21
Middle East	12,216	16
Far East	1,884	3
North Africa	1,108	1
Latin America	1,064	1
Other countries	1,580	2
Total	**76,663**	**100**

WHAT

	1989 Sales		1989 Operating Income	
	FF mil	% of total	FF mil	% of total
Electronic & defense systems	32,454	42	2,210	87
Consumer electronics	41,100	54	1,278	50
Corporate & other	3,109	4	(955)	(37)
Total	**76,663**	**100**	**2,533**	**100**

Consumer Brands (US Markets)

General Electric
- Clock radios
- Stereo equipment
- Telephones
- TV sets and VCRs

RCA
- Camcorders
- TV sets and VCRs

Major Holdings

Altus Finance (joint venture with Crédit Lyonnais)
Sextant Avionique (flight electronics, joint venture with Aerospatiale)
SGS-Thomson (semiconductors, joint venture with IRI/Finmeccanica)
Thomson-CSF (60% defense and professional)

RANKINGS

86th in *Fortune* Global 500 Industrial Cos.
49th in *Forbes* 100 Foreign Investments in the US

COMPETITION

EG&G
General Dynamics
Matsushita
Philips
Raytheon
Rockwell International
Samsung
Siemens
Sony
Zenith
Other consumer, semiconductor, and defense electronics companies

TIME WARNER INC.

OVERVIEW

The merger of Warner Communications and Time Inc. on Jan. 10, 1990, created the world's largest media and entertainment company, Time Warner Inc. The 6 divisions of the company publish books and magazines; produce TV programming, films, and music; and operate cable television networks and systems.

Time Warner Inc. is the nation's largest and most profitable magazine publisher, with major titles including *Time, Sports Illustrated, People, Fortune, Money*, and *Life*. In motion pictures, the company was ranked #1 in film rentals for 1989. *Batman* was the highest-grossing film of 1989 and *Driving Miss Daisy* won 4 Academy Awards. Warner Home Video is the world's largest home video operation.

Time Warner Inc. also boasts the world's largest distribution of television programs (18 on prime time), the oldest and largest pay-TV service (HBO), and the world's largest and most profitable record company.

Due to extraordinary charges the company showed a net loss of $256 million in 1989, but every division achieved record revenues and operating results. Hoping to cut costs, the company announced consolidation of its magazine and book publishing units in 1990.

NYSE symbol: TWX
Incorporated: Delaware, 1983
Fiscal year ends: December 31

WHO

Co-Chairman and Co-CEO: Steven J. Ross, age 62, $4,800,000 pay
Co-Chairman and Co-CEO: J. Richard Munro, age 59, $2,450,001 pay
VC: Gerald M. Levin, age 50, $1,774,039 pay
President and COO: N. J. Nicholas, Jr., age 50, $1,973,559 pay
EVP and CFO: Bert W. Wasserman, age 57
Auditors: Ernst & Young
Employees: 34,700

WHEN

Time Warner Inc. was created in 1990 when Time Inc. merged with Warner Communications Inc. Each has a fascinating history.

Time Inc. was founded by Henry R. Luce, the son of foreign missionaries, in 1922 when he and friend Briton Hadden created a news magazine, *Time*, that summarized a week's worth of news. The company added other magazines in the next decade, including *Fortune* (1930) and *Life* (1936). Luce, a controversial business manager and political philosopher, stepped down as editor-in-chief in 1964 and died in 1967. After 4 decades of Luce's powerful presence at Time, his influence on the company survived his death.

During the 1970s and 1980s Time Inc. explored new ventures. *People* was enormously successful; *Money* was a moderate success; *Discover*, its science magazine, was struggling; and *TV-Cable Weekly* was a disaster. The company established Home Box Office in 1972, entering the cable television market.

Warner Communications has had an equally rich history. Founded by brothers Harry, Albert, Jack, and Sam Warner, Warner Brothers was a member of Hollywood's Big Five movie studios (the others were Loew's, Paramount, Fox, and RKO). Although known best for its genre movies (westerns, musicals, crime stories) of the 1930s, Warner Brothers did poorly at the box office, but built a large number of movie theaters until they were sold for antitrust reasons. In the late 1940s the studio moved to 2nd place and to first place in the early 1950s. Brothers Harry (69) and Albert (66) retired in 1951; brother Jack remained until 1967 when Seven Arts Ltd. bought the studio. During its heyday in the 1930s through the early 1950s, the studio made such classics as *Little Caesar, Casablanca*, and *Rebel Without a Cause*. Warner Brothers-Seven Arts was bought in 1969 by Kinney National Services, owner of Famous Agency talent agency and National Periodical Publications, the publisher of *Superman* and *Batman* comic books and *Mad Magazine*.

After acquiring the company, Kinney sold the pre-1948 movies to United Artists and shared the studios with Columbia. The company changed its name to Warner Communications Inc.(WCI) in February 1972. During the 1970s and early 1980s WCI made most of its money with its game subsidiary, Atari (1976), but waning public enthusiasm and a flood of game companies brought great losses by 1983 and in 1984 Warner sold Atari.

In 1989 after an unsuccessful bid by Paramount to buy Time Inc., Time agreed to merge with Warner Communications Inc.

WHERE

HQ: Time & Life Building, Rockefeller Center, New York, NY 10020 and 75 Rockefeller Plaza, New York, NY 10019
Phone: 212-522-1212 and 212-484-8000
FAX: 212-522-0907

	1989 Sales		1989 Operating Income	
	$ mil	% of total	$ mil	% of total
US	6,828	89	774	91
Europe	504	7	42	5
Other	310	4	32	4
Adjustments	—	—	(85)	—
Total	**7,642**	**100**	**763**	**100**

WHAT

	1989 Sales		1989 Operating Income	
	$ mil	% of total	$ mil	% of total
Magazines	1,855	24	287	34
Books	1,063	14	(81)	(10)
Programming	1,177	15	154	18
Cable television	1,224	16	251	30
Films	1,315	17	91	11
Music	1,147	15	146	17
Adjustments	(139)	—	(85)	—
Total	**7,642**	**100**	**763**	**100**

Magazines
D.C. Comics
Entertainment Weekly
Fortune
Mad Magazine
Money
People
Sports Illustrated
Time

Filmed Entertainment
Movies (recent releases):
Batman
Driving Miss Daisy
Television:
"ALF"
"Growing Pains"

Cable Systems

Music
Major labels:
Atlantic Records
Elecktra
Nashville
Reprise
Warner Bros. Records

Television
HBO
Cinemax
The Comedy Channel
Turner Broadcasting (8.4%)

Books
Book-of-the-Month Club
Little, Brown & Company
Time-Life Book
Warner Books

HOW MUCH

Time, Inc. only	9 Yr. Growth	1980	1981	1982	1983	1984	1985	1986	1987	1988	1989
Sales ($ mil)	11.4%	2,882	3,296	3,564	2,717	3,067	3,404	3,762	4,193	4,507	7,642
Net income ($ mil)	—	141	185	156	143	216	200	376	250	289	(256)
Income as % of sales	—	4.9%	5.6%	4.4%	5.3%	7.1%	5.9%	10.0%	6.0%	6.4%	(3.4%)
Earnings per share ($)	—	2.51	3.02	2.50	2.25	3.37	3.15	5.95	4.18	5.01	(4.34)
Stock price – high ($)	—	31.56	41.38	52.38	78.38	62.75	65.25	91.38	116.88	122.50	182.75
Stock price – low ($)	—	19.00	26.63	25.50	44.50	33.75	42.50	57.50	65.75	78.75	103.63
Stock price – close ($)	16.2%	31.31	38.25	52.13	62.88	42.75	62.13	70.00	82.25	107.00	120.63
P/E – high	—	13	14	21	35	19	21	15	28	24	—
P/E – low	—	8	9	10	20	10	14	10	16	16	—
Dividends per share ($)	1.4%	0.88	0.95	1.00	1.00	0.82	1.00	1.00	1.00	1.00	1.00
Book value per share ($)	21.9%	19.75	21.64	23.96	14.81	16.99	19.28	21.60	21.60	23.97	117.60

1989 Year End:
Debt ratio: 61.6%
Return on equity: —
Cash (mil): $234
Current ratio: 1.17
Long-term debt (mil): $10,838
Number of shares (mil): $57
Dividends:
1989 average yield: 0.8%
1989 payout: —
Market value (mil): $6,924

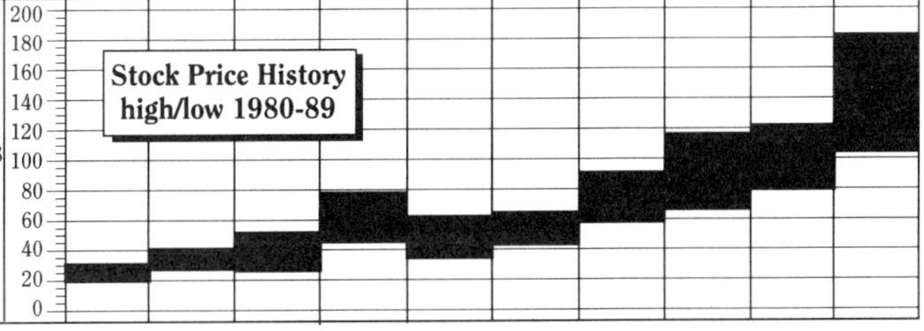

Stock Price History high/low 1980-89

200 180 160 140 120 100 80 60 40 20 0

RANKINGS

59th in *Fortune* 500 Industrial Cos.
167th in *Fortune* Global 500 Industrial Cos
102nd in *Forbes* 500
109th in *Business Week* 1000

COMPETITION

Capital Cities/ABC
CBS
General Electric
MCA
Paramount
Sony
Walt Disney
Other publishers
Other cable companies
Other entertainment companies

THE TIMES MIRROR COMPANY

OVERVIEW

Times Mirror is a 106-year-old multimedia conglomerate. Its largest paper, the *Los Angeles Times*, is the nation's 2nd largest metropolitan daily paper (after the *New York Daily News*), with a circulation of 1.1 million. *LA Times* revenues in 1989 exceeded $1 billion. The *LA Times* carries the 2nd largest amount of advertising space nationwide (after its competitor, the *Orange County Register*). Other Times Mirror newspapers include *Newsday* and the *Hartford Courant,* the oldest continually published paper in the US. Times Mirror's Los Angeles Times Syndicate includes columns by Art Buchwald, Henry Kissinger, Jesse Jackson, and Jacques Cousteau.

Times Mirror also owns 4 TV stations and is a major cable TV service provider. With over one million cable subscribers in 13 states, it is the 13th largest US multiple-system cable operator. Times Mirror magazines (*Field & Stream, Popular Science, Golf Magazine,* etc.) make it the 7th largest US magazine publisher.

The company's professional publishing division (law, medical, science, and technical books) is involved in a joint venture with Mir, a Soviet scientific and technical publisher. Descendants of the company's founder, Gray Otis, own a 49% voting interest in Times Mirror stock and 4 are members of the board.

WHEN

Union army general Gray Otis moved to California after the Civil War and became rich buying land during the spectacular growth of the 1880s. Among his acquisitions was the *Los Angeles Times.* Son-in-law Harry Chandler destroyed rival papers by controlling circulation routes. Otis and Chandler formed Times Mirror in 1884 to publish the *LA Times.* Chandler took over in 1917 and by the 1930s had amassed a fortune in shipping, road construction, oil, and California land (over 2 million acres).

The *LA Times* had a reputation for serving Chandler's political and economic interests in Southern California. The paper successfully prevented unionization long after unions had become strong in the East. Editors allegedly faked photos as part of the paper's campaign against a 1934 gubernatorial candidate. For years the paper was known for its right-wing slant, including support of Richard Nixon in the 1960s and early 1970s.

In 1960 the paper took on a more balanced character after Otis Chandler, grandson of Harry, took over. He hired the best journalists and transformed the paper into one of the nation's finest. During his tenure the paper was awarded 7 Pulitzer Prizes.

The 1960s also marked the beginning of Times Mirror diversification. The company acquired Jeppesen Sanderson (publisher of pilot information, 1961); Matthew Bender (legal publisher, 1963); C.V. Mosby (medical publisher, 1967); Long Island Cablevision (1970); KDFW-TV Dallas–Ft. Worth (1970); and *Newsday* (1970). Times Mirror entered the magazine field by purchasing *Popular Science* and *Outdoor Life* (1967) and *Ski* and *Golf* magazines (1972). The *LA Times* also improved; it was ranked 4th best in the US in a 1982 poll of publishers, editors, and journalism professors.

Gateway, an on-line videotex service in the mid-1980s, failed to generate much consumer interest. Times Mirror also sold businesses in the 1980s, including the New American Library (1984) and the *Denver Post* and the *Dallas Times Herald* (1987).

In the late 1980s Times Mirror spent $1.5 billion on acquisitions of TV stations, cable TV systems, newspapers (Baltimore Sun, 1986), magazines (*Yachting, Skiing, Field & Stream, Home Mechanix,* 1987), and publishers (CRC Press, 1986; Richard D. Irwin, 1988). New divisions included training systems Zenger-Miller and Kaset (1989).

HOW MUCH

	9 Yr. Growth	1980	1981	1982	1983	1984	1985	1986	1987	1988	1989
Sales ($ mil)	7.2%	1,857	2,131	2,200	2,479	2,771	2,947	2,920	3,080	3,259	3,475
Net income ($ mil)	8.8%	139	150	140	200	233	237	408	267	332	298
Income as % of sales	—	7.5%	7.1%	6.4%	8.1%	8.4%	8.0%	14.0%	8.7%	10.2%	8.6%
Earnings per share ($)	9.5%	1.02	1.10	1.02	1.45	1.69	1.75	3.16	2.06	2.58	2.30
Stock price – high ($)	—	11.41	14.63	17.13	22.00	22.81	29.50	36.94	52.94	40.25	45.00
Stock price – low ($)	—	7.19	9.94	8.88	14.75	14.13	19.00	25.06	30.19	29.00	32.38
Stock price – close ($)	14.7%	10.38	11.44	15.59	18.75	20.19	28.81	31.75	35.88	32.88	35.75
P/E – high	—	11	13	17	15	14	17	12	26	16	20
P/E – low	—	7	9	9	10	8	11	8	15	11	14
Dividends per share ($)	12.0%	0.36	0.43	0.50	0.50	0.60	0.68	0.75	0.82	0.92	1.00
Book value per share ($)	10.3%	6.03	6.70	7.23	8.16	9.25	7.56	10.09	11.31	13.12	14.54

1989 Year End:
Debt ratio: 32.2%
Return on equity: 16.6%
Cash (mil): $38
Current ratio: 1.19
Long-term debt (mil): $892
Number of shares (mil): 129
Dividends:
1989 average yield: 2.8%
1989 payout: 43.5%
Market value (mil): $4,617

Stock Price History high/low 1980-89

0 10 20 30 40 50 60

NYSE symbol: TMC
Incorporated: Delaware, 1986
Fiscal year ends: December 31

WHO

Chairman and CEO: Robert F. Erburu, age 59, $1,146,474 pay
President: David A. Laventhol, age 56, $758,857 pay
EVP and Principal Financial Officer: Charles R. Redmond, age 63, $494,322 pay
Auditors: Ernst & Young
Employees: 29,066

WHERE

HQ: Times Mirror Sq., Los Angeles, CA 90053
Phone: 213-237-3700
FAX: 213-237-3800

The Times Mirror does business throughout the US.

WHAT

	1989 Sales		1989 Operating Income	
	$ mil	% of total	$ mil	% of total
Newspaper publishing	2,067	59	309	56
Book, magazine & other publishing	960	27	144	27
Broadcast television	103	3	41	8
Cable television	332	9	58	11
Corporate & other	56	2	(13)	(2)
Adjustments	(43)	—	(42)	—
Total	**3,475**	**100**	**497**	**100**

Newspapers
The Advocate
Baltimore Sun newspapers
Greenwich Time
The Hartford Courant
LA Times Syndicate
LA Times - Washington Post News Service
Los Angeles Times
The Morning Call
New York Newsday
Newsday

Magazines
Field & Stream
Golf Magazine
Home Mechanix
Outdoor Life
Popular Science
Salt Water Sportsman
Ski Magazine
Skiing Magazine
Yachting

Other
Times Mirror Land & Timber Co.

Book Publishing
CRC Press (scientific and technical books)
Harry N. Abrams (art and illustrated books)
Jeppesen Sanderson (aeronautical charts)
Matthew Bender & Co. (legal, accounting, and other professional books)
Mosby-Year Book (medical books)
Richard D. Irwin (college textbooks)

TV & Cable
Dimension cable systems
KDFW-TV, Dallas–Ft. Worth
KTBC-TV, Austin
KTVI-TV, St. Louis
WVTM-TV, Birmingham

Professional Training
Learning International, Inc.

RANKINGS

131st in *Fortune* 500 Industrial Cos.
243rd in *Forbes* Sales 500
127th in *Business Week* 1000
441st in *Business Week* Global 1000

COMPETITION

Advance Publications
Commerce Clearing House
Dow Jones
New York Times
Tribune
Other publishers

TLC BEATRICE INTERNATIONAL HOLDINGS, INC.

OVERVIEW

TLC Beatrice International Holdings is a privately owned food company created by the 1987 spin-off of Beatrice's foreign operations. The company is engaged in 2 primary business segments: wholesale and retail food distribution and the manufacturing and marketing of grocery products. Although the company is based in New York and is the nation's largest black-owned enterprise, it sells no products in the US but rather is focused on the EC.

Food distribution includes wholesale distribution of grocery products to more than 450 independent grocers operating in the Paris area under the name Franprix. The company also provides marketing and other services to these grocers. In addition, TLC Beatrice owns and operates 40 Franprix stores around Paris through Minimarche.

The grocery products division makes and sells ice cream, dairy, and dessert products under the names La Menorquina (Spain), Interglas (Canary Islands), Sanson (Italy), Artic (Belgium), and Premier Is (Denmark). The Tayto subsidiary is the leader in the Irish potato chip market, and TLC Beatrice bottles soft drinks under several names.

Reginald Lewis, who completed the buyout of TLC Beatrice, remains as chairman, CEO, and principal stockholder.

WHEN

Reginald F. Lewis played quarterback for Virginia State in the mid 1960s and hoped for a pro career. After a shoulder injury ended his future in sports, Lewis concentrated on his studies and graduated from Harvard Law School in 1968. He worked briefly for the New York law firm of Paul, Weiss, Rifkind, Wharton & Garrison and left in 1970 to form Lewis and Clarkson, a firm specializing in providing venture capital to growing companies. Lewis then decided to move into the world of high finance. In 1983 he started TLC Group, Inc. (Lewis keeps the source of the name a secret) as a holding company.

The first move by TLC Group was the purchase of McCall Pattern Company for $24.5 million (only $1 million of which was Lewis's money; the rest was borrowed) in 1984. McCall, a Manhattan, Kansas–based sewing-pattern company founded in 1871, had stagnated, but under TLC sales increased from $6.5 million in 1984 to $14 million in 1986 (the 2 most profitable years of the company's history despite a declining market for home sewing products). Lewis raised the company's net worth by shuffling assets (he bought McCall's Manhattan factory through an affiliate and leased it back to the company) and was able to raise an additional $22 million through the bond market. At the end of 1986, TLC sold McCall to Britain's John Crowther Group for $95 million ($63 million cash and $32 million of assumed debt) — a return of 9,000%.

In 1987 the breakup of Beatrice by Donald Kelly and the buyout firm of Kohlberg Kravis Roberts & Company provided Lewis with another opportunity. Since first going overseas in 1961, Beatrice Foods had increased its international holdings to 64 food and consumer products companies in 31 countries, with a combined $2.5 billion in sales by 1987. Lewis arranged for a $495 million junk bond financing through Drexel Burnham Lambert's Michael Milken and purchased the international holdings of Beatrice (Beatrice International Companies) for $985 million. Lewis assumed the positions of chairman and CEO of Beatrice International. The acquisition increased TLC's sales from $63 million in 1986 to almost $1.5 billion in 1987.

Soon after the Beatrice purchase, TLC changed its name to TLC Beatrice International Holdings. Lewis retained his position as head of the company and began selling off numerous operations in Australia and Latin America to pay down the acquisition debt. He sold 80% of the company's Canadian interests to Toronto-based Onex Corporation.

In 1989, with the company's debt brought down, TLC Beatrice International Holdings made a public stock offering in an attempt to raise $180 million to buy privately owned shares from insiders and creditors. TLC Beatrice offered 18.5 million new shares at $9 to $10.50 apiece. The shares were not well received. Potential buyers were unhappy with the terms (each share cost nearly 30 times earnings), and skeptics argued that the company's cash flow was in question and that the offering was designed to enrich Lewis while leaving him with 93% of voting stock. In the wake of the cold public reception, the company rescinded the offer.

HOW MUCH

	2 Yr. Growth	1980	1981	1982	1983	1984	1985	1986	1987	1988	1989
Sales ($ mil)	—	—	—	—	—	—	—	—	1,446	1,639	1,141
Net income ($ mil)	—	—	—	—	—	—	—	—	39	(8)	16
Income as % of sales	—	—	—	—	—	—	—	—	2.7%	(0.5%)	1.4%

1989 Year End:
Debt ratio: 71.8%
Return on equity: 32.5%
Cash (mil): $149
Current ratio: 1.45
Long-term debt (mil): $163

Net Income ($ mil) 1987-89

Private company
Incorporated: Delaware, 1987
Fiscal year ends: December 31

WHO

Chairman and CEO: Reginald F. Lewis, age 47, no pay in 1989
President, European Grocery Products Division: John F. Sipple-Asher, age 66, $248,283 pay
VP and CFO: Mark J. Thorne, age 34
Auditors: Deloitte & Touche
Employees: 4,500

WHERE

HQ: 99 Wall St., New York, NY 10005
Phone: 212-269-4544
FAX: 212-269-4546

Most of the company's operations are in Europe, principally in France, but the company also has small operations in the US, Canada, and Thailand.

	1989 Sales		1989 Operating Income	
	$ mil	% of total	$ mil	% of total
France	766	67	31	41
Other EC countries	375	33	44	59
Adjustments	—	—	(14)	—
Total	**1,141**	**100**	**61**	**100**

WHAT

	1989 Sales		1989 Operating Income	
	$ mil	% of total	$ mil	% of total
Food distribution	757	66	32	43
Grocery products	384	34	43	57
Adjustments	—	—	(14)	—
Total	**1,141**	**100**	**61**	**100**

Food Distribution Operations
Choky (France) and Sodialim (France)
Distribute food and beverage mixes to restaurants and hospitals in France
Dairyworld S.A. (Switzerland), dairy products
Etablissements Baud S.A. (France)
Supplies 450 Franprix grocery stores
Maxime Delrue (France)
Distributes Tropicana juice in France
Minimarche (France)
Operates 40 Franprix grocery stores

Grocery Products Operations
Etablissements Biozet (France)
Specialty pork sausages and hams
Gelati Sanson (Italy)
Ice cream
Helados La Menorquina (Spain)
Ice cream and dessert items
Interglas (Canary Islands)
Kalise brand ice cream and yogurt
Tayto (Ireland)
Tayto and King brand snacks
Winters (Holland) and Sunco (Belgium)
Branded and private-label soft drinks

Affiliates
Onex Food Holdings, Inc. (20%)

COMPETITION

American Brands
Borden
BSN
Cadbury Schweppes
Coca-Cola
Grand Metropolitan
Nestlé
PepsiCo
Philip Morris
Sara Lee
Unilever

TOKIO MARINE & FIRE

OVERVIEW

Tokio Marine & Fire, part of the Mitsubishi Group enterprises, is Japan's largest nonlife insurance company. Japan's property and casualty insurance market is 2nd largest in the world, after the US.

Through a domestic network of 481 branches, the company provides marine, fire and casualty, and auto insurance. Assets at year-end 1989 totaled over $50 billion, including over $30 billion in stocks.

Tokio has subsidiaries and affiliates in 38 countries, serving Japanese businesses worldwide. In 1990 it announced plans to establish a subsidiary in London to oversee European operations that it expects will grow with the 1992 economic integration of European markets.

Tokio Asset Management (New York) and Tokio Marine Capital Research (London) provide investment consulting. Tokio also has a 10% interest in Delaware Management Holdings (Philadelphia), an investment advisory firm.

The 4 largest stockholders of Tokio (each owning less than 5%) are companies in the Mitsubishi Group. Tokio also owns stock of other Mitsubishi Group companies.

WHEN

Japan's first insurance company was founded in 1879 with 11 employees. The following year Tokio Marine & Fire began foreign operations in London, Paris, and New York. During the 1880s the company also worked through foreign insurance firms in Marseilles, Liverpool, Glasgow, and Brussels.

In the late 1800s and early 1900s the firm developed its foreign markets by appointing agents. Willis, Faber & Company, a London insurance broker, served as Tokio's agent in placing ship cargo and hull reinsurance. Tokio profited in marine insurance during the Russo-Japanese War (1904-1905) and became one of the world's leading marine insurers. Tokio selected Appleton & Cox (New York) as agent to develop its US operation.

The company began underwriting fire insurance in 1914 as a step toward becoming a full nonlife insurance company. In the period prior to WWII Tokio broadened its foreign operations through Cornhill Insurance of the UK and Assicurazioni Generali of Italy.

Tokio reorganized in 1944 by merging with Mitsubishi Marine & Fire and Meiji Fire & Marine. In 1956 Tokio resumed its overseas operation, disrupted by WWII, 4 years after the end of US occupation of Japan. The company became affiliated with Mitsubishi, one of the largest business groups in Japan. Other financial organizations in Mitsubishi are Mitsubishi Trust & Banking (Japan's largest trust company), Mitsubishi Bank (Japan's 4th largest), and Meiji Mutual Life.

In 1980 Tokio bought Houston General Insurance (Fort Worth), a commercial property and casualty insurer, and established a property and casualty company in Malaysia. The company formed Tokio Reinsurance in Switzerland in 1982.

Tokio registered 3 million ADRs, each representing 5 shares of common stock, with the SEC in 1987. The company undertook the public securities offering to increase ownership of its shares in the US and to increase operating funds.

In the late 1980s Tokio continued its foreign expansion by acquiring a 10% interest in Sark Sigorta T.A.S., a Turkish insurance company. It also opened offices in Madrid (1988), Istanbul (1990), Milan (1990), and Santiago (1990). In 1989 the company paid $42 million for a 10% interest in Delaware Management Holdings, a Philadelphia-based investment counseling firm that manages $24 billion of pension funds. Tokio further expanded its investment consulting business in 1990 by forming wholly owned subsidiaries in New York and London.

HOW MUCH

$=¥144 (Dec. 31, 1989)	9 Yr. Growth	1980	1981	1982	1983	1984	1985	1986	1987	1988	1989
Net premiums written (¥ bil)	6.5%	475.1	505.0	533.7	562.6	596.2	638.8	688.4	714.4	758.1	834.9
Net premiums earned (¥ bil)	7.0%	436.9	481.9	520.8	547.5	582.2	612.9	653.4	655.1	694.7	783.7
Combined loss & expense ratio	—	90.9%	91.7%	96.2%	99.2%	98.5%	98.2%	95.1%	93.4%	91.1%	89.5%
Net investmt. income (¥ mil)	8.4%	45,412	54,318	52,736	57,333	60,557	67,571	74,276	84,454	82,453	93,508
Net income (¥ mil)	9.6%	40,639	47,767	40,707	32,350	32,235	36,276	43,715	47,771	59,861	92,978
Assets (¥ bil)	18.8%	1,629	1,868	2,008	2,258	2,798	3,163	3,833	5,263	6,241	7,676
Stockholders' equity (¥ bil)	17.5%	642	736	793	876	1,080	1,209	1,441	1,921	2,285	2,748
Stock price – high (¥)	—	0	0	491	655	705	1,000	1,829	2,752	2,350	2,400
Stock price – low (¥)	—	0	0	380	438	489	714	781	1,590	1,476	1,960
Stock price – close (¥)	—	—	502	470	531	690	867	1,733	1,590	2,260	2,180

1989 Year End:
Debt ratio: 2.0%
Return on equity: 2.4%
Cash (bil): ¥268
Assets (bil): ¥7,676
Long-term debt (bil): ¥57.5
Number of shares (mil): 1,468
Market value (mil): US$22,218

Stock Price History high/low 1982-89

3,000
2,500
2,000
1,500
1,000
500
0

OTC symbol: TKIOY (ADR)
Incorporated: Japan, 1879
Fiscal year ends: March 31

WHO

President: Haruo Takeda
EVP: Shunji Kono
EVP: Haruo Kubota
Auditors: Peat Marwick Minato
Employees: 11,131

WHERE

HQ: The Tokio Marine & Fire Insurance Company, Limited, 2-1 Marunouchi 1-chome, Chiyoda-ku, Tokyo 100, Japan
Phone: 011-81-03-212-6211
FAX: 011-81-03-214-3944

Tokio operates 47 branches and 434 subbranches in Japan and offices in the US and 37 other countries.

WHAT

	1989 Net Premiums Written	
	$ mil	% of total
Hull	183	3
Cargo & transit	381	6
Fire & allied lines	881	14
Noncompulsory auto	2,571	41
Personal accident	902	14
Compulsory auto	734	11
Other	673	11
Total	**6,325**	**100**

Subsidiaries & Affiliates
América Latina Companhia de Seguros (São Paulo)
The Arab-Eastern Insurance Co. (Jeddah)
The Arab International Insurance Co. (Cairo)
First Insurance Co. of Hawaii
Houston General Insurance (Forth Worth)
Jerneh Insurance (Kuala Lumpur)
The Koryo Fire & Marine (Seoul)
La Rural del Paraguay S.A.
Pan-Malayan Insurance (Manila)
P.T. Asuransi Jayasraya (Jakarta)
Sri Muang Insurance (Bangkok)
Tokio Marine and Fire Insurance (Singapore)
Tokio Marine & Fire Insurance (UK)
Tokio Marine de Venezuela
Tokio Marine International Fund (Bahama)
Tokio Marine International Fund S.A. (Luxembourg)
Tokio Marine Internacional, S.A. (Mexico City)
Tokio Marine Management
Tokio Marine Management Pty. (Sydney)
Tokio Marine Realty
Tokio Re
Trans Pacific Insurance (New York)
The Wuphoon Insurance Co. (Hong Kong)

RANKINGS

81st in *Business Week* Global 1000

COMPETITION

AIG
CIGNA
General Re
ITT
Kemper
Lloyd's of London

TOYOTA MOTOR CORPORATION

OVERVIEW

With 40% of the domestic market, Toyota is the largest automobile manufacturer in Japan. Measured in revenue, Toyota is the 2nd largest non-US company and the world's 3rd largest maker of motor vehicles, behind General Motors and Ford. The company is racing against Honda to pass Chrysler and gain the #3 spot in US auto sales.

Toyota holds large stakes in a number of related companies, including Toyoda Automatic Loom Works, Daihatsu, Hino Motors (trucks), and Nippondenso (electronic auto parts).

Toyota plans to begin automobile assembly and engine production in England in 1992. Production there is expected to reach 200,000 vehicles by 1997, when anticipated EC limits on Japanese auto sales are expected to end. The company has announced plans to build another US plant and is considering a bid for full control of the New United Motors Manufacturing, Inc. (NUMMI) facility in Fremont, California.

Despite record-breaking sales, Toyota is trying to combat "big company disease," success-bred complacency and sluggishness.

OTC symbol: TOYOY (ADR)
Incorporated: 1937
Fiscal year ends: June 30

WHO

Chairman of the Board: Eiji Toyoda
President: Shoichiro Toyoda
Auditors: Itoh Audit Corporation
Employees: 91,790

WHERE

HQ: 1, Toyota-cho, Toyota City, Aichi Prefecture 471, Japan
Phone: 011-03-817-7111
FAX: 011-03-817-7924
US HQ (Toyota Motor Sales, U.S.A.): 19001 S. Western Ave., Torrance, CA 90509
US Phone: 213-618-4000
US FAX: 213-618-7800

Toyota operates 30 plants in more than 20 countries.

	1989 Motor Vehicle Sales	
	¥ bil	% of total
Japan	4,907	61
Foreign	3,114	39
Total	**8,021**	**100**

WHEN

In 1926 Sakichi Toyoda established the Toyoda Automatic Loom Works in central Japan to produce a loom he invented. Prior to his death in 1930, he sold the rights to his invention and gave the proceeds to his son, Kiichiro Toyoda, to begin an auto business. In 1933 Toyoda opened an automotive department within the loom works and began copying US engine designs. When protectionist legislation (1936) improved prospects for Japanese automakers, Toyoda split off the car department, took it public (1937) and, for clarity in spoken Japanese, changed its name to Toyota.

As Toyota began car production, the Japanese government forbade passenger vehicle manufacturing (1939) and forced the company to make trucks for the military.

The company suffered financial problems in the 5 years following WWII. In 1950 Toyota restructured by organizing Toyota Motor Sales, its marketing arm, as a separate company. Kiichiro Toyoda's resignation ended layoff-induced labor unrest.

Toyota's postwar commitment to R&D, modernization, quality, and the Kanban system of synchronized parts delivery paid off with the successful introductions of the 4-wheel-drive Land Cruiser (1951); full-sized Crown (1955), sold mostly as a taxi; and the small, mass-market Corona (1957). Toyota Motor Sales doubled the number of Toyota franchises in 1957 but kept rivalry low by forcing dealers to specialize in segments of the Toyota line. In 1961 the sales company opened driving schools to broaden its market in increasingly prosperous Japan.

Toyota Motor Sales, U.S.A. (Hollywood) launched the Toyopet Crown in the US in 1957. The small engine failed to bring the car up a hill to the showroom. After suspending auto exports to the US and studying the market, Toyota introduced the highly successful Corona (1965) and the Corolla subcompact (1968), now the best-selling car of all time. By 1970 Toyota had become the 4th largest automaker in the world.

With highly efficient manufacturing systems and very reliable products, Toyota continued to expand rapidly abroad through the 1970s and 1980s. In 1975 Toyota displaced Volkswagen as the #1 importer of autos into the US. After the oil crisis caused a sudden shift in demand toward fuel-efficient models, the company developed systems for quickly retooling factories.

Toyota recombined with Toyota Motor Sales in 1982. US auto production began in 1984 with NUMMI, a joint venture with General Motors, and was augmented by output from Toyota Motor Manufacturing (Georgetown, KY) in 1988. Toyota launched its new luxury line, Lexus, in the US in 1989.

WHAT

	1989 Sales	
	¥ bil	% of total
Motor vehicles	5,784	72
Parts & components	792	10
Industrial vehicles	130	2
Others	1,315	16
Total	**8,021**	**100**

US Motor Vehicles
Camry
Celica
Corolla
Cressida
4Runner
Land Cruiser
Lexus
MR2
Previa
Supra
Tercel

Industrial Vehicles
Forklifts

Other
Auto financing
Cellular telephone service
Prefabricated housing

HOW MUCH

$=¥144 (Dec. 31, 1989)	9 Yr. Growth	1980	1981	1982	1983	1984	1985	1986	1987	1988	1989
Sales (¥ bil)	10.3%	3,310	3,506	3,850	5,324	5,909	6,770	6,646	6,675	7,216	8,021
Net income (¥ bil)	10.2%	144	133	142	228	295	406	346	261	311	346
Income as % of sales	—	4.4%	3.8%	3.7%	4.3%	5.0%	6.0%	5.2%	3.9%	4.3%	4.3%
Earnings per share (¥)	7.8%	56	51	53	78	100	138	118	89	102	110
Stock price–high (¥)	—	608	1,122	912	1,242	1,258	1,192	2,132	2,222	2,748	2,940
Stock price–low (¥)	—	483	492	660	781	987	907	1,025	1,234	1,615	2,295
Stock price–close (¥)	19.5%	511	748	905	1,234	1,054	1,107	1,995	1,669	2,304	2,540
P/E–high	—	11	22	17	16	13	9	18	25	27	27
P/E–low	—	9	10	12	10	10	7	9	14	16	21
Dividends per share (¥)	8.1%	8.8	9.51	10	12.34	13.58	16.2	16.78	16.78	16.78	17.69
Book value per share (¥)	13.9%	382	424	488	643	763	898	972	1,036	1,117	1,236

1989 Year End:
Debt ratio: 24.7%
Return on equity: 9.3%
Cash (bil): ¥1,217
Long-term debt (bil): ¥1,219
Number of shares (mil): 2,857
Dividends:
1989 average yield: 7%
1989 Payout: 16.1%
Market value (mil): $50,394
Sales (mil): $55,701

Stock Price History high/low 1980-89

3,000
2,500
2,000
1,500
1,000
500
0

RANKINGS

6th in *Fortune* Global 500 Industrial Cos.
32nd in *Forbes* 100 Foreign Investments in the US
9th in *Business Week* Global 1000

COMPETITION

Caterpillar
Chrysler
Daimler-Benz
Fiat
Ford
General Motors
Honda
Hyundai
Mitsubishi
Navistar
PACCAR
Nissan
Renault
Volkswagen
Volvo

TOYS "R" US, INC.

OVERVIEW

New Jersey-based Toys "R" Us is a $4.8 billion chain of toy and children's clothing stores. The 33-year-old company, still run by its founder Charles Lazarus, is the largest and fastest growing children's specialty retail chain in the world. In 1989 the company opened a total of 46 toy stores in the US and 22 abroad, for a total of 478 stores. Plans call for opening an additional 70 to 75 in 1990.

The high-volume discount toy chain has captured 23% of the US toy market, giving it considerable influence in the toy industry. Toymakers listen closely to Toys "R" Us buyers when the buyers preview new offerings. The company's impressive growth comes in spite of its taking over and resuscitating its former parent company, Interstate Stores, which emerged from bankruptcy in 1978.

Toys "R" Us has also successfully applied its discount warehousing formula to the children's clothing market with its Kids "R" Us stores. The company plans to add 25 to 30 new Kids "R" Us clothing stores to its existing 137 stores in 1990.

Much of the growth of Toys "R" Us will come from its continued and highly successful expansion into foreign countries. One-third of the 70 to 75 planned toy stores for 1990 will be in foreign countries: Canada, France, Hong Kong, the UK, and Germany.

NYSE symbol: TOY
Incorporated: Delaware, 1978
Fiscal year ends: Sunday nearest January 31

WHO

Chairman and CEO: Charles Lazarus, age 66, $5,276,840 pay
VC; President, World Wide Toy Stores: Robert C. Nakasone, age 42, $725,662 pay
VC and Chief Financial and Administrative Officer: Michael Goldstein, age 48, $690,631 pay
VP; President, International Division: Joseph R. Baczko, age 44
EVP; General Merchandise Manager, USA Toy Stores: Roger V. Goddu, age 39, $369,881 pay
Auditors: Deloitte & Touche
Employees: 38,000

WHEN

Charles Lazarus entered retailing in 1948, adding his $2,000 savings to a $2,000 bank loan to convert his father's Washington, DC bicycle repair shop into a children's furniture store. Customer demand convinced him to add toys. He renamed the store Children's Supermart. Lazarus added a 2nd store, which he later converted to a cash-and-carry self service, but it was with his 3rd store that he established the pattern for his success. Opened in 1958, this 25,000-square-foot discount toy store offered a wider variety of toys than other retailers at 20% to 50% lower prices.

By 1966 sales had reached $12 million, but Lazarus had managed to add only one store and needed cash to expand, so he sold his company to discount store operator Interstate Stores for $7.5 million with the condition that he would retain control of the toys operation. Initially, the arrangement worked, but after a 1969 high of $11 million profit on $589 million in sales, Interstate began to feel the competition from stronger chains such as K mart. By 1974, although Lazarus had expanded to 47 stores and $130 million yearly sales, the parent showed a loss of $92 million and filed for bankruptcy.

Lazarus kept increasing sales in the toy division. His approach of selling toys year-round (not just during the Christmas season) was encouraged by toy manufacturers in the form of generous credit terms. By 1978 he had generated enough profit to pull Interstate Stores out of bankruptcy. Now under his control, the company adopted a new name: Toys "R" Us, with the R backwards to grab attention. With 72 toy stores (and 10 department stores remaining from Interstate) and a 5% share of the toy market, Toys "R" Us posted a $36 million pretax profit on $349 million in sales that year.

From 1978 to 1983 net earnings grew at an annual rate of 40%, market share climbed to 12.5%, and the number of toy stores grew to 169. The company diversified by opening 2 Kids "R" Us children's clothing stores in 1983, copying the toy stores' success formula of huge discount stores.

Toys "R" Us opened 4 stores in Canada and one in Singapore in 1984. It has since added 69 more stores in the UK, Hong Kong, Malaysia, Germany, France, and Taiwan, and has plans to enter Japan.

WHERE

HQ: 461 From Rd., Paramus, NJ 07652
Phone: 201-262-7800
FAX: 201-262-8919

	No. of Stores	
	Toys "R" Us	Kids "R" Us
California	52	17
Texas	32	0
New York	27	10
Florida	27	0
Illinois	27	16
Ohio	23	18
Pennsylvania	21	11
Michigan	19	16
New Jersey	18	13
Georgia	11	0
Maryland	11	6
Virginia	11	6
Other US	125	24
Total US	**404**	**137**

	No. of Stores
	Toys "R" US
Canada	27
UK	23
Germany	13
France	5
Malaysia	2
Singapore	2
Hong Kong	1
Taiwan	1
Total Foreign	**74**

	1989 Sales		1989 Operating Income	
	$ mil	% of total	$ mil	% of total
US	4,254	89	505	91
Foreign	534	11	48	9
Adjustments	—	—	(7)	—
Total	**4,788**	**100**	**546**	**100**

HOW MUCH

	9 Yr. Growth	1980	1981	1982	1983	1984	1985	1986	1987	1988	1989
Sales ($ mil)	26.0%	597	783	1,042	1,320	1,702	1,976	2,445	3,137	4,000	4,788
Net income ($ mil)	30.7%	29	49	64	92	111	120	152	204	268	321
Income as % of sales	—	4.8%	6.2%	6.2%	7.0%	6.5%	6.1%	6.2%	6.5%	6.7%	6.7%
Earnings per share ($)	28.7%	0.17	0.28	0.34	0.48	0.58	0.62	0.78	1.04	1.36	1.64
Stock price – high ($)	—	3.09	4.43	11.04	14.42	15.67	18.33	22.94	28.50	27.00	40.25
Stock price – low ($)	—	1.26	2.09	3.79	7.70	9.41	11.22	14.61	14.67	20.00	24.00
Stock price – close ($)	35.5%	2.33	3.90	8.05	10.67	11.44	15.61	19.17	21.00	24.75	35.88
P/E – high	—	18	16	32	30	27	30	29	27	20	25
P/E – low	—	7	8	11	16	16	18	19	14	15	15
Dividends per share ($)	0.0%	0.00	0.00	0.00	0.00	0.00	0.00	0.00	0.00	0.00	0.00
Book value per share ($)	27.5%	1.00	1.31	1.81	2.57	3.16	3.87	4.82	5.92	7.41	8.93

1989 Year End:
Debt ratio: 9.2%
Return on equity: 20.1%
Cash (mil): $41
Current ratio: 1.22
Long-term debt (mil): $173
Number of shares (mil): 191
Dividends:
1989 average yield: 0.0%
1989 payout: 0.0%
Market value (mil): $6,853

Stock Price History high/low 1980-89

WHAT

Toys "R" Us (toy stores)
Kids "R" Us (children's apparel stores)

RANKINGS

24th in *Fortune* 50 Retailing Cos.
185th in *Forbes* Sales 500
67th in *Business Week* 1000
191st in *Business Week* Global 1000

COMPETITION

Melville
Discount and department stores

TRAMMELL CROW COMPANY

OVERVIEW

Trammell Crow Company is the nation's largest real estate developer. While the numbers that spring from its $16 billion portfolio of owned and managed properties are staggering — 170 million square feet of commercial space, 50,000 apartment units, 32 hotels, and 75,000 acres of farmland — the company is also known as an incubator for developers.

Other operations include Trammell Crow Ventures (in-house investment banking) and Trammell Crow Realty Advisers (3rd-party property management). Trammell Crow Residential is the nation's largest residential developer, with many large apartment complexes. Holdings of the Crow family and its partners — organized under Trammell Crow Interests — include Wyndham Hotels, Trammell Crow Distribution public warehousing, and farmland.

Faced with difficulties in the real estate market in 1990, Trammell Crow refinanced 150 properties, mostly in the Southwest, through Equitable Life Assurance Society.

WHEN

Trammell Crow returned to his native Dallas after WWII. An accountant who earned his degree in night school, he tried the moving business, then went to work for the grain wholesaling firm of his wife's family. When Crow found tenants for vacant warehouse space in the firm's building, he took his first steps to becoming the US's largest landlord.

Another tenant, Ray-O-Vac, outgrew the grain firm's space in 1948, and Crow bought land and built a warehouse for the battery firm. Spurred by a booming postwar economy and the emergence of Dallas as a regional business center, Crow and his partners, the Stemmons brothers, would build more than 50 warehouses in one section of Dallas alone. Much of Crow's success sprang from his knack of anticipating the needs of his tenants and adding amenities to the workplace.

Crow's methods revolutionized real estate. Ebullient with sunny optimism, he broke with Depression-spawned conventional wisdom and built even when no tenants were signed. He avoided long leases so he could raise rents in an expanding economy. He formed partnerships, often with little more than a handshake and a smile, that shared incentives and rewards with what would otherwise be employees. Crow partners started at a low salary but earned sales commissions and equity participation in their projects.

Crow developed the Dallas Decorative Center (1955) to provide permanent showcasing for decorative furniture firms. Emboldened by the Decorative Center's success, Crow began to change the face of Dallas with his masterpiece, the Dallas Market Center, a complex of buildings along the Trinity River. Crow concentrated the furniture industry in the Dallas Homefurnishing Mart (1957) and housewares and fixtures in the Trade Mart (1960). The Trade Mart's design featured an atrium, a Trammell Crow signature feature. Crow next added Market Hall, the largest privately owned exhibition hall in the US, and combined the buildings' operations in 1963 as the Dallas Market Center Company.

In 1972 Crow planned to add the 1.5-million-square-foot World Trade Center to the Market Center, but longtime partner John Stemmons balked at the high interest rate, and Crow offered to buy out Stemmons. The 2 friends negotiated back and forth: Crow valued Stemmons's interests at $8 million, but Stemmons wouldn't take a penny more than $7 million. Finally Crow "lost" and paid the lower figure.

In the 1960s and 1970s Crow helped develop Atlanta's Peachtree Center and San Francisco's Embarcadero Center. With local partners, Crow delved into residential real estate, mostly apartment buildings.

Struggling with high interest rates and heavy debts, Crow's enterprises faltered in 1975. Crow and his partners sold off $100 million in properties to raise money. Crow installed lawyer Don Williams at the helm, and Trammell Crow Company was reorganized in 1977. The founder's wheeler-dealer instincts became more structured.

In the mid-1980s some longtime Crow partners defected as control became centralized in Dallas. Crow's company formally diversified into investment banking and properties management and put 13 properties into a publicly traded real estate investment trust, Trammell Crow Real Estate Investors.

HOW MUCH

	3 Yr. Growth	1980	1981	1982	1983	1984	1985	1986	1987	1988	1989
Estimated sales ($ mil)	—	—	—	—	—	—	—	1,000	1,074	1,400	1,628
No. of employees	68.1%	—	—	—	—	—	—	2,000	5,000	7,500	12,324
Total sq. ft. under construction (thou)	—	—	—	—	—	—	—	—	—	61,383	43,537

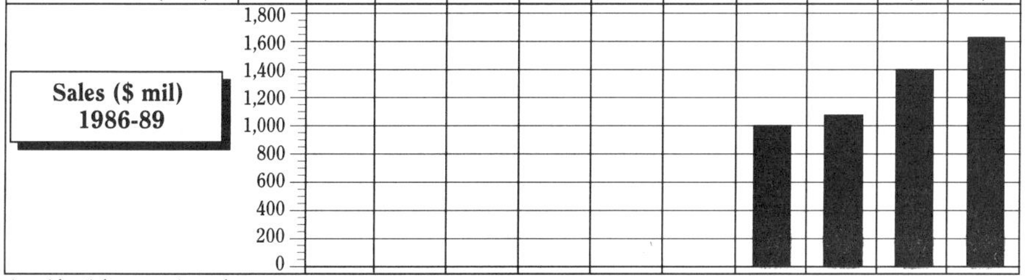

* residential companies only

Private company
Founded: Texas, 1946
Fiscal year ends: December 31

WHO

Chairman: Trammell Crow, age 76
Managing Partner (Commercial): J. McDonald (Don) Williams
Managing Partner (Residential): J. Ronald Terwilliger
Group Managing Partner: Cary Shafer
Group Managing Partner: Tom Simmons
Group Managing Partner: Tom Bailey
CFO: Robert A. Whitman
Employees: 12,324

WHERE

HQ: 2001 Ross Ave., Dallas, TX 75201
Phone: 214-979-5100
FAX: 214-979-6058

Trammell Crow has 62 offices throughout the US.

Top Markets	Los Angeles
Atlanta	Memphis
Chicago	San Francisco
Dallas	Seattle
Houston	Washington, DC

WHAT

Commercial Projects Under Construction 1989	% of Total
Office	19
Industrial	53
Retail	25
Mixed use	3
Total	**100**

Major Projects
Allen Center, Houston
Dallas Market Center, Dallas
Embarcadero Center, San Francisco
Hamilton Lakes, suburban Chicago
InfoMart, Dallas
Lincoln Tower, Portland
Market Square, Washington, DC
Milwaukee Center, Milwaukee
999 Peachtree, Atlanta
One Renaissance Center, Phoenix
Peachtree Center, Atlanta
Times Square redevelopment, New York

Subsidiaries/Affiliates
Trammell Crow Interests
- Trammell Crow Agriculture
- Trammell Crow Distribution Corp. (public warehousing)
- Trammell Crow International
- Trammell Crow Medical
- Wyndham Hotels

Trammell Crow Realty Advisers (portfolio management services)
Trammell Crow Residential (develops rental apartments)
Trammel Crow Ventures (investment banking)

RANKINGS

81st in *Forbes* 400 US Private Cos.

COMPETITION

Campeau
Edward J. DeBartolo
Helmsley Enterprises
Prudential
Sears
Other real estate developers

TRANS WORLD AIRLINES, INC.

OVERVIEW

TWA flies to destinations in the US, the Caribbean, Europe, and the Middle East, but Chairman Carl Icahn recently proposed selling all of the airline's domestic assets (including operations at its St. Louis hub) to America West, leaving its international routes intact. TWA served 23 European and Middle Eastern cities in 1989 and is awaiting DOT approval for service from St. Louis to Tokyo.

Unprofitable for 3 of the last 5 years, TWA has the added burden of long-term debt and capital leases exceeding $2.7 billion. Icahn is attempting to wrest $150 million in concessions from TWA's unions, including $80 million in wage and benefits reductions from its pilots. TWA's machinists have been at the bargaining table with Icahn since 1988, but no contract seems forthcoming.

Icahn has sold and leased back 19 of the airline's jets (1989-1990) but has made little progress toward modernizing TWA's fleet, one of the industry's oldest, with planes averaging 16 years. Some planes are more than 25 years old.

TWA Investment Plan, a TWA subsidiary, is a member of a limited partnership holding 10.6% of the USX Corporation.

WHEN

Los Angeles businessmen Harry Chandler and James Talbot founded Western Air Express (WAE) in 1925. WAE offered flights from Los Angeles to Salt Lake City in 1926, adding service to San Francisco in 1928 and Kansas City in 1929. In 1930 WAE merged with Transcontinental Air Transport (TAT) to form Transcontinental and Western Air (TWA), America's first coast-to-coast airline.

Airline magnate Clement Keys had established TAT in 1928, coordinating operations with the Pennsylvania and Santa Fe Railroads to establish air-rail service from New York to the West Coast. High fares ($350 per seat) caused steady losses, and the service was terminated after the WAE-TAT merger.

In 1939 Howard Hughes bought TWA. The company, then based in Kansas City, bought Marquette Airlines (St. Louis-Detroit) in 1941 and in the mid-1940s offered flights to Boston and Washington, DC. In 1946 TWA introduced transatlantic service (New York-Paris).

TWA moved to New York in 1947 and became Trans World Airlines in 1950, reflecting its expansion to over 21,000 international route miles. In 1953 TWA offered America's first nonstop flight from Los Angeles to New York.

In 1956 Hughes ordered 63 jets, with long-term financing through a New York investment banker. When Hughes was unable to meet the terms of the loan in 1960, the bank placed his TWA stock in a voting trust. Hughes sold his interest to the public in 1966.

TWA tried to stabilize earnings through several purchases that were consolidated under a holding company, Trans World Corporation, in 1979. These included Hilton International (hotels outside the US, 1967), the Canteen Corporation (food services and vending machines, 1973), Spartan Food Systems (Hardee's restaurants, 1979), and Century 21 (real estate, 1979). However, TWA's losses ($128 million between 1973 and 1980) led to a split from Trans World Corporation in 1984. Trans World Corporation became TW Services in 1986 after selling its hotels to United Air Lines.

In 1985 TWA became the stake in a takeover tug-of-war between Texas Air's Frank Lorenzo and raider Carl Icahn. Icahn won the fight, acquiring 40% of TWA by 1986. As CEO, Icahn purchased Ozark Air Lines (TWA's main competitor at its St. Louis hub) in 1987 and in 1988 took TWA private. By then Icahn owned 90% of TWA, with the other 10% owned by its employees.

In 1990, TWA, NWA (parent of Northwest Airlines), and Delta Airlines formed WORLDSPAN, a global computer reservations system.

HOW MUCH

	9 Yr. Growth	1980	1981	1982	1983	1984	1985	1986	1987	1988	1989
Sales ($ mil)	3.3%	3,374	3,509	3,320	3,354	3,657	3,725	3,145	4,056	4,361	4,507
Net income ($ mil)	—	22	(7)	(31)	(36)	30	(208)	(106)	45	250	(287)
Income as % of sales	—	0.7%	(0.2%)	(0.9%)	(1.1%)	0.8%	(5.6%)	(3.4%)	1.1%	5.7%	(6.4%)
Rev. passenger mi. (mil)	2.5%	28,108	25,727	25,531	27,261	28,297	32,047	27,334	32,861	34,700	35,046
Available seat miles (mil)	2.6%	45,532	41,252	40,426	42,501	45,510	49,178	46,880	51,811	56,102	57,230
Passenger load factor	—	61.7%	62.4%	63.2%	64.1%	62.2%	65.2%	58.3%	63.4%	61.9%	61.2%
Size of fleet	—	220	221	184	175	159	167	207	213	214	213
Employees	—	96,358*	94,400*	28,400	26,200	27,384	29,080	27,442	29,919	30,817	32,895

1989 Year End:
Debt ratio: 114.8%
Return on equity: —
Cash (mil): $465
Current ratio: 0.96
Long-term debt (mil): $2,672

Net Income ($ mil) 1980-89

300
200
100
0
-100
-200
-300

*for Trans World Corporation

Private company
Incorporated: Delaware, 1978
Fiscal year ends: December 31

WHO

Chairman and CEO: Carl C. Icahn, age 53
EVP Operations and COO: J. William Hoar, age 51, $179,275 pay (prior to promotion)
EVP Administration: Jerry Nichols, age 55, $323,302 pay (prior to promotion)
SVP External Affairs and General Counsel: Mark A. Buckstein, age 50, $331,287 pay
SVP Finance: Mark S. Mulvany, age 53, $200,306 pay
SVP Flight Operations: Ronald E. Reynolds, age 56, $190,650 pay
Auditors: Laventhol & Horwath
Employees: 32,395

WHERE

HQ: 100 S. Bedford Rd., Mt. Kisco, NY 10549
Phone: 914-242-3000
FAX: 914-242-3109 (Customer Relations)

TWA flies to cities in the US, Puerto Rico, the Bahamas, Europe, and the Middle East.

Hub Locations
New York
St. Louis
Paris

	1989 Sales		1989 Operating Income	
	$ mil	% of total	$ mil	% of total
US	2,917	65	10	41
Foreign	1,590	35	14	59
Total	**4,507**	**100**	**24**	**100**

WHAT

	1989 Sales	
	$ mil	% of total
Passenger service	3,836	85
Freight & mail operations	233	5
Other	438	10
Total	**4,507**	**100**

Trans World Airlines

Trans World Express (commuter services)

Operating Units/Affiliates
WORLDSPAN (20%; reservation system)

Flight Equipment	Owned	Leased	Total
Trans World Airlines			
Boeing 727	47	22	69
Boeing 747	12	7	19
Boeing 767	10	1	11
DC-9	2	46	48
Lockheed 1011	10	23	33
MD-80	4	29	33
Total	**85**	**128**	**213**

RANKINGS

13th in *Fortune* 50 Transportation Cos.
20th in *Forbes* 400 US Private Cos.

COMPETITION

Alaska Air	HAL	Pan Am
America West	KLM	Southwest
AMR	Midway	UAL
Continental	NWA	USAir
Delta		

TRANSAMERICA CORPORATION

OVERVIEW

One of America's largest financial services companies, Transamerica controls assets of almost $30 billion.

Transamerica Finance Group, the US's 3rd largest finance firm (after GE Capital and Household Finance), provides 44% of the parent's total income. The Finance Group is the US's 2nd largest financer of insurance premiums for companies (after Continental Insurance's AVCO); the group also leases (and lease-finances) the world's largest fleet of intermodal transportation equipment (*e.g.*, rail and over-the-road trailers).

The company's insurance operations include the US's largest life reinsurer and a leader in sports and leisure coverage (*e.g.*, pro sports). Transamerica also owns 39% of London-based Sedgwick Group (insurance broker) and operates a leading investment management firm.

The company has shed nonfinancial businesses to focus on financial services. Aging baby boomers, with increasing disposable income, should benefit the life insurance operations.

NYSE symbol: TA
Incorporated: Delaware, 1928
Fiscal year ends: December 31

WHO

Chairman and CEO: James R. Harvey, age 55, $1,385,650 pay
President: Frank C. Herringer, age 47, $983,520 pay
EVP: Arthur E. Van Leuven, age 64, $571,775 pay
EVP: Gary L. Depolo, age 54, $463,834 pay
SVP and Chief Investment Officer: Richard N. Latzer, age 52, $513,021 pay
Auditors: Ernst & Young
Employees: 17,400

WHEN

A. P. Giannini, the son of Italian immigrants to California, founded the Bank of Italy in San Francisco in 1904 to serve small businesses. The Bank of Italy soon expanded to a number of branches in California.

After Giannini acquired the powerful Bank of America (1920), he formed the Transamerica holding company (1928). Transamerica, under regulatory pressure as it diversified (Occidental Life, 1930) and strengthened, sold its Bank of America stock by the early 1950s. After the 1956 Bank Holding Company Act, Transamerica fully divested its banking group.

In the 3 decades following John Beckett's inception as president (1960), Transamerica embraced a wide range of businesses — mostly services — only to return to its old financial focus. Beckett handled the blooming; his successor, James Harvey (president in 1981), did the pruning.

The action included financial services (Pacific Financial, 1961), title insurance (City Title, 1962), manufacturing (Delaval Turbine, 1962; spun off to shareholders, 1986), entertainment (United Artists, 1967; sold to MGM, 1981), transportation (Budget Rent-a-Car, 1968, sold 1986; TransInternational Airlines, 1968, closed 1986), and leasing (Interway, 1979).

James Harvey's purchases, hewing closely to Transamerica's core strengths, included insurance brokers (Fred S. James, 1982; exchanged for 39% of Sedgwick Group, 1985), consumer financing (The Money Stores, 1983), commercial financing (BWAC, 1987; TIFCO, 1988), worker's compensation insurance (Fairmont Financial, 1987), and investment management (Criterion Group, 1989).

Harvey exchanged $1.5 billion worth of old businesses for $1.7 in new, to great effect: between 1985 and 1987 alone, net income tripled. In 1989 the company achieved further operating efficiencies and reduced borrowing costs by meshing its lending and leasing operations into a single unit with over $9 billion in assets.

Transamerica increasingly seeks to minimize its highly price-sensitive property/casualty operations, turning to specialty markets like sports and film and TV insurance.

The focus is now on high-return operations; areas of no competitive advantage are sold (*e.g.*, TA Title, 1990), and new purchases will complement the whole, as with Criterion's mutual fund marketing through Transamerica's life insurance network.

WHERE

HQ: 600 Montgomery St., San Francisco, CA 94111
Phone: 415-983-4000
FAX: 415-983-4234

Transamerica operates in all 50 states and in 48 other countries.

WHAT

	1989 Sales		1989 Operating Income	
	$ mil	% of total	$ mil	% of total
Lending	1,265	19	201	31
Leasing	432	6	83	13
Real estate services	397	6	71	11
Life insurance	2,765	40	218	33
Property-casualty insurance	1,921	28	62	9
Insurance brokerage	40	1	29	4
Other	14	—	(5)	(1)
Adjustments	—	—	598	—
Total	**6,834**	**100**	**1,257**	**100**

Transamerica Finance Group (consumer and commercial lending, leasing of freight containers and trailers; 981 offices)
Transamerica Real Estate Services (29% tax service offices; 70 investment properties)
Transamerica Life Companies, including Transamerica Occidental Life (life insurance and related products; 739 offices, 3,200 agents)
Transamerica Insurance Group (homeowners' insurance, commercial insurance, and specialty insurance; 43 offices)
Sedgwick Group (39%; 300 insurance brokerage offices)
Transamerica Criterion Group (mutual funds and investment management)

RANKINGS

16th in *Fortune* 50 Diversified Financial Cos.
31st in *Fortune* 50 Life Insurance Cos.
121st in *Forbes* Sales 500
211th in *Business Week* 1000
664th in *Business Week* Global 1000

COMPETITION

Household International
Primerica
Other insurance and financial firms

HOW MUCH

	9 Yr. Growth	1980	1981	1982	1983	1984	1985	1986	1987	1988	1989
Sales ($ mil)	5.1%	4,384	4,156	4,326	4,681	5,399	5,590	6,076	7,175	7,879	6,834*
Net income ($ mil)	3.4%	245	223	186	198	172	111	252	354	346	332
Income as % of sales	—	5.6%	5.4%	4.3%	4.2%	3.2%	2.0%	4.2%	4.9%	4.4%	4.9%
Earnings per share ($)	1.2%	3.75	3.45	2.95	3.12	2.64	1.62	3.36	4.51	4.42	4.18
Stock price – high ($)	—	20.13	26.25	24.38	33.00	30.75	36.25	40.13	51.50	36.75	48.00
Stock price – low ($)	—	14.63	17.50	16.50	21.13	20.88	26.00	31.75	22.63	29.75	32.75
Stock price – close ($)	10.0%	18.75	23.38	23.38	31.13	26.13	33.75	32.63	29.88	33.88	44.25
P/E – high	—	5	8	8	11	12	22	12	11	8	11
P/E – low	—	4	5	6	7	8	16	9	5	7	8
Dividends per share ($)	5.2%	1.20	1.34	1.45	1.53	1.60	1.66	1.28	2.24	1.86	1.90
Book value per share ($)	5.1%	22.78	24.93	26.71	28.21	28.57	29.12	28.61	31.84	34.63	35.63

1989 Year End:
Debt ratio: 70.4%
Return on equity: 11.9%
Cash (mil): $667
Assets (mil): $29,840
Long-term debt (mil): $6,960
Number of shares (mil): 76
Dividends:
1989 average yield: 4.3%
1989 payout: 45.5%
Market value (mil): $3,358

Stock Price History high/low 1980-89

* Decrease due to accounting rule change.

THE TRAVELERS CORPORATION

OVERVIEW

Travelers is the 8th largest US insurance company based on total assets, providing property and casualty, life, and health insurance. Only Aetna is a larger stock (publicly owned) life insurer. Hartford-based Travelers also offers managed health care and investment services.

Travelers's managed health care and employee benefits, with record 1989 sales of $1.3 billion, provides coverage to 8.8 million people through group health and life programs. Travelers also has one of the largest managed health care networks in the US, serving 130 major metropolitan areas.

Travelers expects its future product mix to be more concentrated on commercial customers and to offer more selective, profitable consumer insurance lines.

Noninsurance operations of Travelers include Dillon, Read, an international investment banking firm that represented RJR Nabisco in the $25 billion LBO of the company in 1989.

The Massachusetts Company is a banking subsidiary with more than $1.4 billion in assets in 1989.

NYSE symbol: TIC
Incorporated: Connecticut, 1965
Fiscal year ends: December 31

WHO

Chairman and CEO: Edward H. Budd, age 56, $950,000 pay
VC and CFO: Thomas O. Thorsen, age 58, $664,808 pay
VC and Chief Investment Officer: Richard J. Shima, age 50, $664,808 pay
VC and Chief Insurance Officer: Richard H. Booth, age 42
Auditors: Coopers & Lybrand
Employees: 36,000

WHEN

In 1864 James Batterson and 9 other Hartford businessmen founded Travelers as the first accident insurance company in the US. The company's red umbrella logo, used as a symbol of protection in ads as early as 1870, became a trademark in 1960.

Diversification was a principal reason the company, unlike other travel accident companies, survived. Travelers introduced life insurance (1865), annuities (1884), and liability insurance (1889). In 1897 the company issued the first automobile policy and in 1919 sold President Woodrow Wilson the industry's first air travel accident policy.

In 1903 Travelers opened the industry's first training school. In 1907 the school provided training in new services such as workers' compensation, 4 years before this coverage was declared constitutional. The company added group life insurance coverage in 1913, with the Victor Company (later part of RCA) as one of its first clients.

L. Edmund Zacher managed the company's investments in the 1920s and is credited with selling gold stocks and buying US government bonds prior to the stock market crash of 1929. Two days after the crash, Zacher was named president.

In 1940 the company agreed to insure all risks on projects (highways, roads, railroads) done by civilian defense contractors for government agencies (including the army and navy) during WWII. In many of these defense installations, Travelers engineers suggested safety procedures. This safety engineering corps, started in 1904, was the first in the nation.

The post-WWII boom in the US meant growth to Travelers in insuring people and property. In 1964 the company developed a standard homeowner's policy that became the industry model. Travelers issued the first space travel accident insurance, covering the Apollo 11 astronauts in their historic lunar landing.

The company bought Keystone (mutual funds, 1979) and Dillon, Read (investment banking, 1986). In 1989 Travelers sold Keystone and announced plans to sell Travelers Mortgage Services (home mortgage and relocation business) as part of a strategy to use capital for its core investment and insurance business. Travelers announced in 1990 it is withdrawing from the auto and homeowners markets in 9 states and, effective in 1991, agent compensation will be tied to the profitability of personal insurance policies written.

WHERE

HQ: One Tower Sq., Hartford, CT 06183
Phone: 203-277-0111
FAX: 203-277-7979

Travelers operates throughout the US and insures US businesses in over 100 countries.

WHAT

	1989 Sales		1989 Pretax Income	
	$ mil	% of total	$ mil	% of total
Life & health insurance	6,224	53	246	67
Property-casualty insurance	5,630	47	123	33
Adjustments	669	—	139	—
Total	**12,523**	**100**	**508**	**100**

Product Lines
Annuities
Consumer banking services
Investment banking
Life, health, and disability insurance
Managed health care
Pension and investment management services
Private placement loans
Property-casualty insurance

Subsidiaries
Dillon, Read Inc. (investment banking)
The Massachusetts Co. (bank)
The Travelers Investment Management Co.
The Travelers Mortgage Services, Inc.
The Travelers Realty Investment Co.

RANKINGS

8th in *Fortune* 50 Life Insurance Cos.
47th in *Forbes* Sales 500
183rd in *Business Week* 1000
636th in *Business Week* Global 1000

COMPETITION

Aetna
American Express
American Financial
AIG
Berkshire Hathaway
Blue Cross
CIGNA
Equitable
First Executive
GEICO
Goldman Sachs
ITT
John Hancock
Kemper
Lloyd's of London
Loews
Massachusetts Mutual
Merrill Lynch
Metropolitan
Morgan Stanley
New York Life
Northwestern Mutual
Primerica
Prudential
Sears
State Farm
Teachers Insurance
Transamerica
USF&G
Investment bankers

HOW MUCH

	9 Yr. Growth	1980	1981	1982	1983	1984	1985	1986	1987	1988	1989
Sales ($ mil)	4.1%	8,722	9,678	11,230	11,852	13,302	14,435	16,047	17,459	18,986	12,523*
Net income ($ mil)	1.7%	366	359	310	343	346	360	444	429	430	424
Income as % of sales	—	4.2%	3.7%	2.8%	2.9%	2.6%	2.5%	2.8%	2.5%	2.3%	3.4%
Earnings per share ($)	(0.9%)	4.32	4.23	3.67	4.08	4.11	4.00	4.45	4.10	4.14	3.99
Stock price – high ($)	—	22.44	27.00	28.88	34.25	38.25	49.25	59.50	52.63	40.00	45.00
Stock price – low ($)	—	17.44	18.81	16.50	22.38	25.50	36.88	42.50	30.75	33.00	34.50
Stock price – close ($)	7.4%	19.44	21.94	24.13	31.75	37.25	48.00	44.63	35.13	34.75	36.88
P/E – high	—	5	6	8	8	9	12	13	13	10	11
P/E – low	—	4	4	5	5	6	9	10	8	8	9
Dividends per share ($)	7.6%	1.24	1.44	1.64	1.80	1.92	2.04	2.16	2.28	2.40	2.40
Book value per share ($)	4.7%	31.21	33.12	35.37	36.53	38.89	41.16	45.17	45.28	44.85	47.02

1989 Year End:
Debt ratio: 17.9%
Return on equity: 8.7%
Cash (mil): $3,710
Assets (mil): $56,563
Long-term debt (mil): $1,055
Number of shares (mil): 103
Dividends:
1989 average yield: 6.5%
1989 payout: 60.2%
Market value (mil): $3,790

Stock Price History high/low 1980-89

60
50
40
30
20
10
0

* Decrease due to accounting rule change

TRIBUNE COMPANY

OVERVIEW

With its greatest strength in Chicago and New York, Tribune Company publishes 7 daily newspapers, owns 6 television and 4 radio stations, produces filmed entertainment, and runs 2 newsprint mills. On a daily basis, Tribune Company provides information and entertainment to 20% of US households.

Ranked the 5th largest US newspaper publisher, Tribune Company owns the *Chicago Tribune* (7th in daily, 5th in Sunday circulation) and the New York *Daily News* (3rd in daily, 2nd in Sunday circulation). Covering 18.7% of US households, the company is the 4th largest television broadcaster, with independent stations in New York, Los Angeles, Chicago, Atlanta, Denver, and New Orleans. In addition, Tribune Company owns the Chicago Cubs baseball team.

Net income rose in 1989 by 15% as all sectors of the business showed good growth with the exception of the newsprint operations, which suffered a modest decline owing to weak newsprint market conditions. The $13 million refurbishing of 75-year-old Wrigley Field improved facilities and added comfort for the record 2.5 million fans who visited it.

WHEN

Tribune Company had its beginnings as the *Chicago Tribune*, which produced just 400 newspapers on its first day in 1847. Joseph Medill, a major promoter of Lincoln for President, and who, some say, gave the Republican party its name, became part owner and editor in 1855 and spent the next 44 years building the *Chicago Tribune* into a conservative, Republican newspaper. One of the great legends about Medill involved his prophetic warning that Chicago was a fire hazard just a month before the great fire of 1871. He was able to rally his employees to publish the paper despite being burned out of their building and wrote his famous "Cheer Up" editorial to renew the spirit of the people. Joseph Medill died in 1899. In 1912 his grandsons Robert McCormick and Joseph Patterson took over the newspaper.

Patterson went to New York in 1919 to found the *Daily News*. McCormick, the great-nephew of the inventor of the harvest machine, carried on the Medill legacy, building the *Chicago Tribune* into the "World's Greatest Newspaper," a slogan that, though self-claimed, survives to this day.

During WWI the *Tribune* doubled in advertising and circulation. In 1924 the company began a radio station with call letters WGN. The station was the first to broadcast the World Series, the Indianapolis 500, and the Kentucky Derby. WGN began TV broadcasts in 1948.

After Patterson's death in 1946, McCormick became head of both newspapers, preferring to run the *Daily News* from headquarters in Chicago. He remained at that post until his death in 1955.

Tribune Company has expanded into other media since the 1950s. The company founded WPIX-TV in New York (1948) and bought stations in Denver (1965), New Orleans (1983), Atlanta (1984), and Los Angeles (1985). The company has also purchased other newspapers across the nation: Fort Lauderdale (1963), Orlando (1965), Los Angeles (1973), Escondido, California (1977), Northern California (1978), and Newport News, Virginia (1986).

Tribune Company has also moved into news and entertainment programming, beginning the Independent Network News (INN) in 1980 and the Tribune Broadcasting Company in 1981. Also that year the company acquired the Chicago Cubs baseball team from chewing gum manufacturer William Wrigley. The company went public in 1983. Since then net income has increased an average of 23% annually. Return on equity has grown from 10% to almost 23%, and the average total return to stockholders has been almost 24% per year.

HOW MUCH

	6 Yr. Growth	1980	1981	1982	1983	1984	1985	1986	1987	1988	1989
Sales ($ mil)	7.5%	—	—	—	1,587	1,794	1,938	2,030	2,160	2,335	2,455
Net income ($ mil)	23.3%	—	—	—	69	103	124	293	142	210	242
Income as % of sales	—	—	—	—	4.4%	5.7%	6.4%	14.4%	6.6%	9.0%	9.9%
Earnings per share ($)	21.1%	—	—	—	0.95	1.28	1.53	3.63	1.80	2.78	3.00
Stock price – high ($)	—	—	—	—	16.50	17.44	28.94	39.00	49.75	43.00	63.13
Stock price – low ($)	—	—	—	—	13.38	12.00	16.00	24.75	28.63	33.75	36.38
Stock price – close ($)	20.7%	—	—	—	15.31	17.25	27.88	28.50	41.00	38.88	47.38
P/E – high	—	—	—	—	17	14	19	11	28	15	21
P/E – low	—	—	—	—	14	9	10	7	16	12	12
Dividends per share ($)	46.2%	—	—	—	0.09	0.38	0.44	0.53	0.69	0.76	0.88
Book value per share ($)	1.8%	—	—	—	9.55	10.23	11.19	13.91	14.35	15.88	10.63

1989 Year End:
Debt ratio: 45.0%
Return on equity: 22.6%
Cash (mil): $28
Current ratio: 1.04
Long-term debt (mil): $881
Number of shares (mil): 69
Dividends:
1989 average yield: 1.9%
1989 payout: 29.3%
Market value (mil): $3,252

Stock Price History high/low 1983-89

70
60
50
40
30
20
10
0

NYSE symbol: TRB
Incorporated: Delaware, 1968
Fiscal year ends: December 31

WHO

Chairman and CEO; Publisher, *Chicago Tribune*: Stanton R. Cook, age 64, $1,157,670 pay
President and COO: Charles T. Brumback, age 61, $833,376 pay
President and CEO, Chicago Tribune Company: John W. Madigan, age 52, $763,293 pay
President and CEO, Tribune Broadcasting Company: James C. Dowdle, age 56, $550,035 pay
SVP and CFO: Scott C. Smith, age 39
Auditors: Price Waterhouse
Employees: 17,100

WHERE

HQ: 435 N. Michigan Ave., Chicago, IL 60611
Phone: 312-222-9100
FAX: 312-222-0449

	1989 Sales		1989 Operating Income	
	$ mil	% of total	$ mil	% of total
US	2,215	90	394	87
Canada	240	10	61	13
Adjustments	—	—	(12)	—
Total	**2,455**	**100**	**443**	**100**

WHAT

	1989 Sales		1989 Operating Income	
	$ mil	% of total	$ mil	% of total
Newspapers	1,631	66	297	66
Broadcasting & entertainment	584	24	97	21
Newsprint operations	240	10	61	13
Adjustments	—	—	(12)	—
Total	**2,455**	**100**	**443**	**100**

Newspapers
Chicago Tribune
Daily News, New York
Daily Press and *The Times-Herald*, Newport News, VA
News and *Sun-Sentinel*, Ft. Lauderdale
The Orlando Sentinel
Peninsula Times Tribune, Palo Alto, CA
Times-Advocate, Escondido, CA

Broadcasting & Entertainment

Television stations:
WPIX, New York
KTLA, Los Angeles
WGN, Chicago
WGNX, Atlanta
KWGN, Denver
WGNO, New Orleans

Radio stations:
WQCD, New York
WGN, Chicago
KYMX, Sacramento
KCTC, Sacramento

Chicago Cubs baseball team

Newsprint Operations
Quebec and Ontario Paper Company

RANKINGS

182nd in *Fortune* 500 Industrial Cos.
335th in *Forbes* Sales 500
174th in *Business Week* 1000
616th in *Business Week* Global 1000

COMPETITION

Cox
Gannett
Hearst
Knight-Ridder
New York Times
Times Mirror
Washington Post

TRW INC.

OVERVIEW

High-tech, futuristic TRW is a major conglomerate involved in space and defense projects and automotive products (now its largest business segment). It has one of the largest consumer and business credit reporting services in the world.

TRW's 43 divisions supply over 100 categories of products and services, principally automotive original and replacement equipment; spacecraft; software and systems engineering support services; electronic systems, equipment, and services; and information systems and services. Its credit reporting service will extend to Europe in the 1990s.

TRW played a major role in developing several technologies: microprocessors, computer-aided design and manufacturing, advanced composite materials, single-crystal turbine blades for large jet aircraft, fiber-optic communications, lasers, and satellites. Sales to the US government represented 42% of TRW's total sales in 1989.

In the future TRW will contribute to NASA's space station and Mission to Planet Earth program to collecting information for the world's largest environmental database by developing key instruments for 3 satellites in that program.

WHEN

TRW began as Cleveland Cap Screw Company, founded in 1901. In 1904 company welder Charles Thompson devised an improved method for assembling automobile valves, similar to the methods used to make cap screws. Within 3 years the firm was making most of the engine valves for the mushrooming automobile industry. Renamed the Steel Products Company in 1915, the company also made valves for American and French aircraft used in WWI. In 1921 the company produced the Silcrome metal valve that allowed aircraft to fly longer distances. A similar Thompson valve was used in Lindbergh's plane on the first transatlantic flight. Charles Thompson became president in 1915, and in 1926 the company name became Thompson Products.

Thompson suffered losses in the Great Depression years with the general slump in the automotive industry, but under the leadership of new president Frederick Crawford it avoided major plant closings and layoffs. Diversification began in the 1930s under Crawford, especially into products for the aviation industry (the company developed an improved fuel pump that prevented vapor lock at high altitudes). At the government-built Tapco plant (Thompson Aircraft Products Company) in Cleveland, the company hired up to 16,000 workers during WWII. By 1945 sales were 7 times those in 1939.

In 1953 the company provided financial support for the Ramo-Wooldridge Corporation, founded by former Hughes Aircraft engineers Simon Ramo and Dean Wooldridge to build the intercontinental ballistic missile. In one of the first uses of "systems engineering" to coordinate the work of 220 prime contractors, the Atlas ICBM was launched 5 years later. In 1958 the companies merged to form Thompson Ramo Wooldridge (name officially shortened to TRW in 1965).

In the 1960s TRW diversified and its current structure began to take shape. Internal development and acquisitions created the space and defense, automotive, and information systems segments. The company built rocket engines for the Apollo program, satellites, and missiles and was involved in many other important space and defense projects over the next 3 decades.

In response to takeover fears in the 1980s, TRW sold marginal businesses, focusing on automotive, space and defense, and information services. The company's credit reporting service grew significantly with the 1989 purchase of Chilton. TRW will make airbags for Ford in the 1990s under a $1 billion contract signed in 1989.

HOW MUCH

	9 Yr. Growth	1980	1981	1982	1983	1984	1985	1986	1987	1988	1989
Sales ($ mil)	4.4%	4,984	5,285	5,132	5,493	6,062	5,917	6,036	6,821	6,982	7,340
Net income ($ mil)	2.4%	212	229	196	205	267	134	218	243	261	263
Income as % of sales	—	4.3%	4.3%	3.8%	3.7%	4.4%	2.3%	3.6%	3.6%	3.7%	3.6%
Earnings per share ($)	4.6%	2.85	3.07	2.60	2.68	3.48	1.90	3.56	3.95	4.23	4.25
Stock price – high ($)	—	30.69	32.75	37.00	41.00	41.00	48.50	55.00	70.00	54.00	49.88
Stock price – low ($)	—	17.25	24.50	22.81	30.25	29.19	34.50	41.13	37.00	40.63	41.25
Stock price – close ($)	5.6%	30.31	27.38	33.81	39.81	36.25	44.00	42.25	47.63	41.63	49.38
P/E – high	—	11	11	14	15	12	26	15	18	13	12
P/E – low	—	6	8	9	11	8	18	12	9	10	10
Dividends per share ($)	5.4%	1.08	1.18	1.28	1.33	1.43	1.50	1.53	1.60	1.68	1.72
Book value per share ($)	4.1%	20.00	21.24	21.46	22.19	23.86	17.46	20.31	23.72	26.00	28.84

1989 Year End:
Debt ratio: 37.8%
Return on equity: 15.5%
Cash (mil): $114
Current ratio: 1.28
Long-term debt (mil): $1,063
Number of shares (mil): 61
Dividends:
1989 average yield: 3.5%
1989 payout: 40.5%
Market value (mil): $2,992

Stock Price History high/low 1980-89

NYSE symbol: TRW
Incorporated: Ohio, 1916
Fiscal year ends: December 31

WHO

Chairman, President, and CEO: Joseph T. Gordon, age 52, $1,060,000 pay
EVP and CFO: Stephen E. Frank, age 48, $550,749 pay
Auditors: Ernst & Young
Employees: 74,280

WHERE

HQ: 1900 Richmond Rd., Cleveland, OH 44124
Phone: 216-291-7000
FAX: 216-291-7629

TRW conducts operations at 114 facilities in 24 states and 95 facilities in 15 other countries.

	1989 Sales		1989 Operating Income	
	$ mil	% of total	$ mil	% of total
US	5,286	72	336	58
Europe	1,345	18	158	27
Other	709	10	87	15
Adjustments	—	—	(56)	—
Total	**7,340**	**100**	**525**	**100**

WHAT

	1989 Sales		1989 Operating Income	
	$ mil	% of total	$ mil	% of total
Automotive	3,436	47	287	49
Space & defense	3,185	43	231	40
Information systems	705	10	60	10
Other	14	—	3	1
Adjustments	—	—	(56)	—
Total	**7,340**	**100**	**525**	**100**

Automotive
Ceramic components
Passenger restraint systems
Steering systems
Suspension systems

Space & Defense Projects
Advanced X-Ray Astrophysics Facility
Earth Observing System
Gamma Ray Observatory satellite
Orbital Maneuvering Vehicle

Information Systems & Services
Credit reporting
Real estate services
Small Business Advisory Report
SuperChip

Other
Coal combustion systems
Environmental waste reduction

RANKINGS

62nd in *Fortune* 500 Industrial Cos.
174th in *Fortune* Global 500 Industrial Cos.
113th in *Forbes* Sales 500
207th in *Business Week* 1000
652nd in *Business Week* Global 1000

COMPETITION

Allied-Signal
Dun & Bradstreet
Electrolux
General Electric
Harris
ITT
Martin Marietta
Morton
Teledyne

TURNER BROADCASTING SYSTEM, INC.

OVERVIEW

Turner Broadcasting transmits news and entertainment programming by satellite from its headquarters in Atlanta to most local cable TV systems across the country. Turner broadcasts 4 basic cable channels: Cable News Network (CNN, the company's largest channel), Headline News, WTBS (TBS Superstation), and Turner Network Television (TNT).

Cable News Network, which revolutionized TV news with its 24-hour coverage, is now one of the big 4 national TV news networks. Governments around the world reportedly depend more on CNN for current information than their own intelligence services. Headline News is a 24-hour news channel using a fast-paced news format.

WTBS and TNT are 24-hour entertainment channels that offer a wide variety of programming. Turner also produces and telecasts the Goodwill Games (a multinational mini-Olympics) over WTBS.

The company also owns the Atlanta Braves and Atlanta Hawks sports teams (games are televised over the Turner network), the Turner Entertainment Company film library, and the Omni Coliseum in Atlanta. Founder Ted Turner, a champion yachtsman and America's Cup winner, owns 62% of the voting stock and is ranked among the world's billionaires.

WHEN

In 1970 Ted Turner bought Rice Broadcasting, a small Atlanta UHF TV station, with profits from his billboard advertising business and formed Turner Communications Corporation. In its first year Channel 17 lost $689,000, but its prospects were considered good enough to justify keeping it on the air. The following year, WTSG-TV (which stood for "watch this station grow" according to staffers) was the leading independent TV station in the South. Turner spun the billboard business off in 1975.

Discovering he could reach cable systems around the country by satellite, Turner created "superstation" WTBS, which broadcast older TV shows, movies, and Atlanta Braves and Hawks games (teams bought by Turner in 1976 and 1977, respectively). The station grew, reaching 5.8 million homes by 1979.

The first serious challenge to the major TV news networks, Turner's CNN (Cable News Network), launched in 1980, provided 24-hour, usually live news coverage and reached 1.7 million households its first year. Although criticized initially for its quality, CNN frequently "scooped" the major networks with its around-the-clock coverage, reporting first on the attempted assassination of President Reagan in 1981 and broadcasting live the explosion of the space shuttle in 1986. CNN2 (later Headline News) was introduced in 1982 in response to ABC-Westinghouse's Satellite News Channel, which offered news on an 18-minute cycle. Turner bought out SNC in 1983.

In 1986, after failing in an attempt to take over CBS, Turner bought a film library of 3,700 motion pictures from MGM/UA for $1.4 billion. The purchase nearly caused Turner to founder, but the company was bailed out the following year by 31 cable operators around the country who recognized Turner's importance to their operations. In 1988 Turner formed Turner Network Television (TNT), which broadcasts the film classics acquired in the MGM/UA purchase, many in a colorized version that has been criticized by purists.

CNN distribution to Europe began in 1985. Since then an increasing number of satellite dishes throughout the world receive and rebroadcast the 24-hour news program. Immediate availability of uncensored world news is considered to have influenced political events in Eastern Europe and Mexico. US officials and other governments monitored CNN to follow developments in China in 1989. A Spanish language version of Headline News appeared in 1988.

HOW MUCH

	9 Yr. Growth	1980	1981	1982	1983	1984	1985	1986	1987	1988	1989
Sales ($ mil)	39.2%	54	95	165	224	282	352	557	652	807	1,065
Net income ($ mil)	—	(4)	(13)	(3)	3	5	17	(187)	(131)	(95)	28
Income as % of sales	—	(6.9%)	(14.2%)	(2.0%)	1.5%	1.8%	4.9%	(33.6%)	(20.1%)	(11.7%)	2.6%
Earnings per share ($)	—	(0.10)	(0.33)	(0.08)	0.08	0.13	0.40	(5.49)	(4.40)	(3.18)	(0.38)
Stock price – high ($)	—	4.19	10.00	9.75	15.63	13.50	12.63	14.63	13.50	16.88	64.00
Stock price – low ($)	—	3.31	3.56	4.25	7.63	7.50	5.38	5.75	6.88	10.50	17.00
Stock price – close ($)	32.5%	4.06	5.50	9.50	11.88	8.75	7.06	6.94	10.88	16.88	51.00
P/E – high	—	—	—	—	195	108	32	—	—	—	—
P/E – low	—	—	—	—	95	60	14	—	—	—	—
Dividends per share ($)	0.0%	0.00	0.00	0.00	0.00	0.00	0.00	0.00	0.00	0.00	0.00
Book value per share ($)	—	(0.02)	(0.35)	(0.43)	(0.26)	0.65	0.68	(4.80)	(12.18)	(13.82)	(13.96)

1989 Year End:
Debt ratio: 134.3%
Return on equity: 2.7%
Cash (mil): $142
Current ratio: 1.54
Long-term debt (mil): $1,689
Number of shares (mil): 50
Dividends:
1989 average yield: 0.0%
1989 payout: 0.0%
Market value (mil): $2,528

Stock Price History high/low 1980-89

AMEX symbol: TBS
Incorporated: Georgia, 1965
Fiscal year ends: December 31

WHO

Chairman and President: R. E. "Ted" Turner, age 51, $676,952 pay
VC: Burton Reinhard, age 68, $379,040 pay (prior to promotion)
SVP Finance and Administration: Paul D. Beckham, age 46
President, CNN: W. Thomas Johnson, Jr., age 48
EVP, Cable Programming: Terence F. McGuirk, age 39, $392,221 pay
Auditors: Price Waterhouse
Employees: 3,466

WHERE

HQ: One CNN Center, 100 International Blvd., Atlanta, GA 30303
Phone: 404-827-1700
FAX: 404-827-1066

TBS and CNN reach over 50 million US households. CNN maintains 23 news bureaus worldwide and is available in 90 countries.

WHAT

	1989 Sales		1989 Operating Income	
	$ mil	% of total	$ mil	% of total
Entertainment	382	35	103	37
News	342	32	133	48
Syndication & licensing	266	25	51	18
Professional sports	27	3	(7)	(3)
Real estate	42	4	1	—
Other	6	1	—	—
Adjustments	—	—	(60)	—
Total	**1,065**	**100**	**221**	**100**

Entertainment Segment
Goodwill Games
Superstation TBS
"National Geographic Explorer"
"Portrait of the Soviet Union"
"TBS Sports"
"The New Leave It To Beaver"
Turner Network Television
Gone With the Wind
"The Muppet Show"
"Noticiero Telemundo-CNN"
"Science and Technology Week"
"Sports Tonight"
"World Today"
Headline News

News Segment
Cable News Network
"CNN Newsource"
"CNN Newsroom"
"CNN World Report"
"Crossfire"
"Larry King Live"
"Moneyline"

Professional Sports
Atlanta Braves (baseball)
Atlanta Hawks (basketball)

Real Estate
Omni Coliseum, Atlanta

Syndication & Licensing Segment
Home video
Pay and commercial television licensing
Turner Entertainment Company film library
Wrestling operations

RANKINGS

93rd in *Fortune* Diversified Service Cos.
271st in *Business Week* 1000

COMPETITION

Anheuser-Busch
Boston Celtics
Capital Cities/ABC
CBS
General Electric
MCA
News Corp.
Paramount
Tele-Communications
Time Warner
Viacom
Walt Disney

TW HOLDINGS, INC.

OVERVIEW

TW Holdings owns TW Services, the 4th largest food service company in the US. TW's restaurant business, primarily in the southeastern and western US, accounted for 61% of TW sales and 77% of operating income in 1989. It is the largest franchisee of Hardee's fast-food hamburger restaurants, and it owns and operates Denny's (the largest full-service family restaurant chain), Quincy's Family Steak Houses, and El Pollo Loco fast-food broiled chicken restaurants. TW's Proficient Foods and Portiontol Foods operations distribute and supply foods to these restaurants.

TW's Canteen division is one of the 3 largest contract food service companies in the US. Canteen's 10,000 vending accounts and more than 1,600 commercial food service accounts include many *Fortune* 500 companies. Canteen also serves factories, hospitals, offices, and other facilities. It provides contract concession services for sports events, concerts, and civic and convention centers. Canteen is responsible for food and beverages, gift shops, and lodging at national and state parks, including Yellowstone, Bryce Canyon, and Zion national parks and the North Rim of the Grand Canyon; it also provides services at the Kennedy Space Center.

The company owns 132,250 vending machines.

WHEN

As part of the reorganization of Trans World Airlines, the stockholders of TWA created a holding company called Trans World Corporation in 1979. In addition to the airlines, Trans World owned Canteen (food services, acquired by TWA in 1973) and Hilton International Hotels (acquired in 1967). Later in 1979 the company bought Spartan Food Systems and Century 21 Real Estate. Trans World spun off TWA in 1983 by distributing stock to its shareholders. After deciding that the potential for growth at Century 21 was in financial services, an area in which Trans World had little experience, the company sold Century 21 to Metropolitan Life for $251 million in 1985.

Of the 3 businesses remaining at the end of 1985, Canteen was the largest, providing 46% of revenue through food service contracts and vending machines in businesses, recreation areas, schools, and health care facilities. Hilton International ran 90 hotels in the US (under the Vista International name), Guam, Puerto Rico, and 43 foreign countries and provided 32% of revenues. Spartan operated 332 Hardee's restaurant franchises and 216 Quincy's Family Steak Houses in the southeastern US and provided 22% of revenues.

In 1986 Trans World bought American Medical Services (nursing homes) and sold Hilton International, which had an inconsistent earnings record, to UAL for $835 million and 2.5 million shares of UAL common stock. The same year Trans World changed its name to TW Services to reflect its new status.

In 1987 the company outbid Marriott for the purchase of privately owned Denny's for $843 million. With the purchase came El Pollo Loco, a Denny's subsidiary purchased in 1983. In 1988 TW Services was the 4th largest US restaurant company, with food sales of nearly $3.6 billion.

After a 9-month takeover fight, Coniston Partners, a New York investment firm, paid $1.7 billion to increase its ownership of TW Services stock from 19% to 80% in 1989; TW Services agreed to a merger and became a wholly owned subsidiary of TW Holdings, the name of Coniston's acquisition company. About 30% of TW Holdings is now publicly owned.

TW had a $56 million loss in 1989, mainly because of costs related to the buyout. The acquisition left TW Holdings with considerable debt ($1.9 billion at the end of 1989). In January 1990 TW agreed to sell American Medical Services to HostMasters, a California nursing home operator, for $30 million.

HOW MUCH

	9 Yr. Growth	1980	1981	1982	1983	1984	1985	1986	1987	1988	1989
Sales ($ mil)	(4.0%)	5,018	5,265	5,108	1,889	2,002	2,152	1,918	2,492	3,574	3,485
Net income ($ mil)	—	20	42	30	60	115	105	16	56	54	(56)
Income as % of sales	—	0.4%	0.8%	0.6%	3.2%	5.7%	4.9%	0.8%	2.3%	1.5%	(1.6%)
Earnings per share ($)	—	0.55	0.75	0.17	0.87	2.00	1.71	0.27	1.16	1.10	(1.74)
Stock price – high ($)	—	14.92	18.92	22.92	26.42	28.83	28.83	42.63	23.00	27.13	39.00
Stock price – low ($)	—	6.42	9.58	9.17	15.33	15.75	18.83	22.25	9.25	13.75	26.00
Stock price – close ($)	12.2%	12.33	10.00	19.00	26.17	20.67	26.42	32.38	14.25	26.25	34.63
P/E – high	—	27	25	138	30	14	17	158	20	25	—
P/E – low	—	12	13	55	18	8	11	82	8	13	—
Dividends per share ($)	—	0.00	0.00	0.00	0.00	0.20	0.31	0.38	0.10	0.10	0.06
Book value per share ($)	—	21.56	21.08	19.65	8.99	11.28	14.66	8.49	9.27	10.29	1.88

1989 Year End:
Debt ratio: 90.4%
Return on equity: —
Cash (mil): $8
Current ratio: 0.29
Long-term debt (mil): $1,948
Number of shares (mil): 110
Dividends:
1989 average yield: 0.2%
1989 payout: —
Market value (mil): $3,809

Stock Price History high/low 1980-89

45
40
35
30
25
20
15
10
5
0

OTC symbol: TWFS
Incorporated: Delaware, 1988
Fiscal year ends: December 31

WHO

Chairman: Paul E. Tierney, Jr., age 47
President and CEO: Jerome J. Richardson, age 53, $695,783 pay
VP and CFO: Walter M. Brice, III, age 56
VP: Keith R. Gollust, age 44
VP: Augustus K. Oliver, age 40
Auditors: Deloitte & Touche
Employees: 108,000

WHERE

HQ: PO Box 3168, 600 Shell Ln., Spartanburg, SC 29304
Phone: 803-596-8700
FAX: 803-596-8780 (Public Relations)

The company operates in 48 states, Washington, DC, and overseas.

US Restaurant Units by Region	
South	50%
West	29%
Elsewhere	21%
Total	**100%**

WHAT

	1989 Sales		1989 Operating Income	
	$ mil	% of total	$ mil	% of total
Restaurants	2,115	61	187	77
Contract food service	1,370	39	57	23
Adjustments	—	—	(11)	—
Total	**3,485**	**100**	**233**	**100**

Chain	No. of Restaurants
Hardee's	465
Quincy's	213
Denny's (owned)	1,001
Denny's (franchised/licensed)	341
El Pollo Loco (owned)	101
El Pollo Loco (franchised/licensed)	105
Total	**2,226**

1989 Contract Food Sales by Market	
Food business/industry	37%
Vending business/industry	37%
Volume services	12%
Recreational services	8%
Education/health care	6%
Total	**100%**

Other Operations
Contract Food Services (Canteen)
- Vending machines
- Commercial and institutional food service
- Concessions at ballparks and stadiums
- Lodging, food, and souvenirs at federal parks

Proficient Foods (food distribution service)

RANKINGS

31st in *Fortune* 50 Retailing Cos.
241st in *Forbes* Sales 500

COMPETITION

ARA
General Mills
Grand Metropolitan
Marriott
MCA
McDonald's
Ogden
PepsiCo
Wendy's

TYSON FOODS, INC.

OVERVIEW

Tyson Foods is the world's largest producer, processor, and marketer of poultry-based food products. Value-enhanced poultry products (including chicken patties, precooked and prepackaged chicken, and Rock Cornish game hens) account for 76% of revenues, while fresh and frozen poultry account for 13%. The company is the leader in both the food service (with over 500 value-enhanced products available to restaurants and fast-food operations) and retail poultry markets.

The company's vertically integrated poultry operations control every aspect of poultry production including genetic research, breeding, hatching, rearing, feed milling, veterinary and technical services, transportation, and delivery.

Tyson's 1989 acquisition of Holly Farms strengthened its lead in poultry and made the company a major supplier of beef and pork products. Other Tyson products include Mexican food (tortillas and chips) and protein by-products for pet food.

In 1989 Tyson was named *Institutional Distribution* magazine's #1 food service supplier for the 2nd year in a row. The company's decade average of 37.7% total return to investors has put Tyson among *Fortune's* top 10 US industrial companies by this key measure of success.

OTC symbol: TYSNA
Incorporated: Delaware, 1986
Fiscal year ends: September 30

WHO

Chairman and CEO: Don Tyson, age 59, $3,564,524 pay
President and COO: Leland Tollett, age 52, $1,129,601 pay
SVP Sales and Marketing: Donald Wray, age 52, $386,777 pay
EVP Finance: Gerald Johnston, age 47, $340,177 pay
VP Operations: David Purtle, age 45, $348,192 pay
Auditors: Ernst & Young
Employees: 42,000

WHEN

During the Great Depression, Arkansas poultry farmer John Tyson supported his family by buying, transporting, and selling vegetables and poultry. In 1935 he developed a method for transporting live poultry (he installed a food-and-water trough and nailed small feed cups on a trailer) and bought 500 Arkansas chickens (springers) that he sold for a profit of $235 in Chicago.

For the next decade Tyson bought, sold, and transported chickens exclusively. By 1947, the year Tyson incorporated his company as Tyson Feed & Hatchery, he was raising the chickens himself.

Tyson emphasized chicken production significantly more during the early 1950s by expanding the company's facilities and capabilities. In 1958 Tyson opened his first processing plant in Springdale, Arkansas, at which he implemented an ice-packing system that allowed the company to send its chicken products greater distances.

In 1960 Tyson's son Don took over as manager of the company. In 1962 the company began processing Rock Cornish game hens, and the following year went public and assumed the name Tyson Foods. The company introduced Tyson Country Fresh Chicken (packaged chicken that would become the company's mainstay) in 1967. In 1969 Tyson underwent an expansion and modification program that included the acquisition of Prospect Farms (precooked chicken for the food service industry).

During the early 1970s Tyson experienced rapid expansion that included a new egg building (1970), a new plant and computerized feed mill (1971), and the acquisition of Consolidated Food's (now Sara Lee) Ocoma Foods Division (poultry, 1972). This period of growth concluded with the acquisition of the Creswell, North Carolina, hog operation and Wilson Foods's Poultry Division.

During the 1980s health-conscious consumers increasingly turned away from red meats to poultry, causing phenomenal growth in the industry and at Tyson. In 1985 the company reached $1 billion in annual sales. Tyson became the industry leader with several key poultry operation acquisitions that included the Tastybird division of Valmac (1985), Lane Processing (1986), and Heritage Valley (1986).

In 1989 after a lengthy bidding struggle with ConAgra, Tyson purchased Holly Farms for $1.5 billion. The acquisition increased Tyson's poultry supply by 56% and greatly strengthened its lead in the poultry industry.

WHERE

HQ: 2210 W. Oaklawn, Springdale, AR 72764
Phone: 501-756-4000
FAX: 501-756-4061 (Public Relations)

The company owns processing plants in 13 states: Alabama, Arkansas, Georgia, Iowa, Maryland, Michigan, Missouri, North Carolina, Oklahoma, Pennsylvania, Tennessee, Texas, and Virginia. Foreign sales are primarily to the Far East, the Middle East, Canada, and the Caribbean.

WHAT

Brand Names
Canadian Gourmet Selection
Frozen dinners for Canadian market
Harker's
Beef
Henry House
Pork
Holly Farms
Processed chicken
Holly Oven Roasted
Microwaveable chicken
Holly Pak
Fresh chicken
Mexican Original Products
Tortillas
Quik-to-Fix
Beef
Tastybird
Military/commissary chicken
Tyson
Fresh, frozen, and processed chicken products
Tyson Cornish Game Hens
Tyson Gourmet Selection
Frozen dinners
Weaver
Processed chicken

HOW MUCH

	9 Yr. Growth	1980	1981	1982	1983	1984	1985	1986	1987	1988	1989
Sales ($ mil)	23.1%	390	502	559	604	750	1,136	1,504	1,786	1,936	2,538
Net income ($ mil)	64.1%	1	2	9	11	18	35	50	68	81	101
Income as % of sales	—	0.3%	0.4%	1.7%	1.8%	2.4%	3.1%	3.3%	3.8%	4.2%	4.0%
Earnings per share ($)	62.2%	0.02	0.04	0.16	0.19	0.31	0.59	0.79	1.06	1.27	1.55
Stock price – high ($)	—	1.12	1.18	1.57	2.33	4.80	9.50	25.50	24.00	20.38	26.25
Stock price – low ($)	—	0.48	0.75	0.82	1.40	1.97	3.67	8.42	10.88	11.00	14.75
Stock price – close ($)	41.8%	1.08	0.87	1.57	2.20	4.80	9.17	18.17	12.88	17.25	24.88
P/E – high	—	56	32	10	12	15	16	32	23	16	17
P/E – low	—	24	20	5	7	6	6	11	10	9	10
Dividends per share ($)	15.8%	0.01	0.01	0.01	0.01	0.01	0.02	0.02	0.04	0.04	0.04
Book value per share ($)	27.4%	0.78	0.81	0.96	1.14	1.44	2.43	3.19	4.20	5.35	6.92

1989 Year End:
Debt ratio: 74.7%
Return on equity: 25.3%
Cash (mil): $56
Current ratio: 1.6
Long-term debt (mil): $1,319
Number of shares (mil): 65
Dividends:
1989 average yield: 0.2%
1989 payout: 2.6%
Market value (mil): $1,608

Stock Price History high/low 1980-89

30 25 20 15 10 5 0

RANKINGS

174th in *Fortune* 500 Industrial Cos.
285th in *Forbes* Sales 500
347th in *Business Week* 1000

COMPETITION

Beatrice	Chiquita Brands	Occidental
Cargill	ConAgra	Sara Lee

UAL CORPORATION

OVERVIEW

UAL is the parent company of United Airlines, the world's 2nd largest airline (after American) in terms of 1989 sales. Every day, United handles more than 1,700 departures and 150,000 passengers at more than 154 cities in North America, Australia, the Far East, and Europe. United plans to expand European service late in 1990 with flights to Paris, Milan, and Rome. The airline has also received DOT recommendation, over rival American, to fly from Chicago to Tokyo, but a final decision will not be reached until late 1990.

Since 1987 United has been almost constantly subjected to external and internal buyout efforts from management, the unions, Coniston Partners, and Marvin Davis. During this period it was surpassed by American as the #1 airline and forced to shed its nonairline businesses. However, as the latest buyout offer (from its unions) begins to lose steam, there is some good news — it retook the #1 spot in passenger traffic for June, July, and August 1990.

NYSE symbol: UAL
Incorporated: Delaware, 1968
Fiscal year ends: December 31

WHO

Chairman, President, and CEO: Stephen M. Wolf, age 48, $1,150,000 pay
EVP, CFO, and Treasurer: John C. Pope, age 40, $642,500 pay
EVP: James M. Guyette, age 44, $467,500 pay
Auditors: Arthur Andersen & Co.
Employees: 72,300

WHEN

United Airlines first appeared in 1929, when aircraft designer Bill Boeing (Boeing Airplane and Transport) and engine designer Fred Rentschler (Pratt & Whitney) merged their companies to form United Aircraft and Transport. Renamed United Air Lines (1931), this New York–based combination offered one of America's first coast-to-coast airline services, with flights from New York to San Francisco. When United's manufacturing and transportation divisions split up (1934), ex-banker Bill Patterson became president of the transportation company (United Airlines) and moved its headquarters to Chicago. At that time, United was America's #1 airline.

In the years of Patterson's stewardship (1934-1963), United was slow to utilize new technology, offering jet service 8 months later than American, its leading competitor (1959). Still, in 1961 the airline regained its title as America's largest (lost to American in 1938) after buying Capital Airlines, adding points along the Great Lakes, Washington, DC, and Florida to United's network, which totaled 116 cities at the time of the acquisition.

United bought the Westin Hotel Company (1970) and named Westin president Eddie Carlson as United's CEO in 1971. Another hotelier, Richard Ferris, became CEO in 1979. Ferris spent $2.3 billion acquiring the Hertz Corporation (car rentals, 1985), Pan American's Pacific division (routes to Australia and the Orient , 1986), and Transworld Corporation's Hilton International Company (hotels, 1987). Ferris spent an additional $7.3 million changing United's name to Allegis Corporation (1987) but resigned when Coniston Partners, the company's largest shareholder, threatened to oust the board and liquidate the company in a 1987 proxy fight. Assuming its old name under the leadership of former Flying Tigers executive Stephen Wolf, United disposed of its hotels and car rental interests, and sold 50% of Covia Partnership (operates United's Apollo computer reservation system) to 5 other airlines, raising $3.7 billion. Wolf used the money to modernize the airline's fleet.

Another takeover bid in 1989 by Los Angeles billionaire Marvin Davis led to a proposed $6.6 billion management and union buyout plan, which collapsed in October. Coniston Partners resurfaced in support of a new $4.4 billion union buyout offer, approved by the UAL board in April 1990.

The buyout effort received a boost in June, when former Chrysler vice-chairman Gerald Greenwald (who is guaranteed over $9 million even if the offer fails) agreed to spearhead it. However, in September, the unions dissolved their alliance with Coniston, signalling that they were rethinking their offer. Speculation is that a new, lower offer will be made.

WHERE

HQ: 1200 Algonquin Rd., Elk Grove Township, IL 60007
Phone: 708-952-4000
FAX: 708-952-7680

United serves more than 154 cities in the US and 12 foreign countries.

Hub Locations

Chicago	San Francisco
Denver	Washington, DC

	1989 Sales	
	$ mil	% of total
US	7,615	78
Foreign	2,179	22
Total	**9,794**	**100**

WHAT

	1989 Sales	
	$ mil	% of total
Passenger service	8,536	87
Cargo operations	521	5
Other	737	8
Total	**9,794**	**100**

United Air Lines, Inc.

United Express (commuter services)
Air Wisconsin
Aspen
Atlantic Coast
WestAir

Operating Units/Affiliates
Covia (50%; reservation system)

Flight Equipment	Owned	Leased	Total
United Air Lines			
Boeing 727	115	25	140
Boeing 737	60	89	149
Boeing 747	24	10	34
Boeing 757	2	3	5
Boeing 767	19	—	19
DC-8	25	2	27
DC-10	34	21	55
Total	**279**	**150**	**429**

RANKINGS

3rd in *Fortune* 50 Transportation Cos.
77th in *Forbes* Sales 500
203rd in *Business Week* 1000
689th in *Business Week* Global 1000

COMPETITION

Alaska Air	Midway
America West	NWA
AMR	Pan Am
Continental	Southwest
Delta	TWA
HAL	USAir
KLM	

HOW MUCH

	9 Yr. Growth	1980	1981	1982	1983	1984	1985	1986	1987	1988	1989
Sales ($ mil)	7.7%	5,041	5,141	5,320	6,022	6,968	6,383	9,196	8,293	8,982	9,794
Net income ($ mil)	35.5%	21	(71)	11	142	261	(49)	12	(4)	600	324
Income as % of sales	—	0.4%	(1.4%)	0.2%	2.4%	3.7%	(0.8%)	0.1%	(0.1%)	6.7%	3.3%
Earnings per share ($)	40.2%	0.70	(2.40)	0.36	3.91	6.40	(1.20)	0.25	0.25	19.95	14.65
Stock price – high ($)	—	25.38	31.38	36.50	41.63	46.75	59.50	64.75	105.88	110.00	294.00
Stock price – low ($)	—	13.50	16.50	15.13	27.88	28.00	39.75	46.25	52.25	68.50	105.25
Stock price – close ($)	28.8%	17.50	16.50	33.25	36.75	44.00	49.75	52.25	71.50	109.50	171.25
P/E – high	—	36	—	101	11	7	—	259	424	6	20
P/E – low	—	19	—	42	7	4	—	185	209	3	7
Dividends per share ($)	(100%)	0.25	0.00	0.00	0.00	0.50	1.00	1.00	0.75	0.00	0.00
Book value per share ($)	6.9%	39.42	36.99	37.66	40.56	47.29	44.21	45.70	51.50	56.75	71.64

1989 Year End:
Debt ratio: 46.0%
Return on equity: 22.8%
Cash (mil): $1,423
Current ratio: 0.85
Long-term debt (mil): $1,334
Number of shares (mil): 22
Dividends:
1989 average yield: 0.0%
1989 payout: 0.0%
Market value (mil): $3,739

Stock Price History high/low 1980-89

UNILEVER GROUP

OVERVIEW

Unilever is one of the world's largest packaged consumer goods companies, with brands that are recognized internationally. The Anglo-Dutch giant recently expanded its presence in the cosmetics industry through acquisitions and lessened its European sales concentration. Major product groups include margarine and oils, soap and detergents, frozen foods, food and drinks, and personal care products.

In the US, Unilever is the leader in margarine sales and #2 after Procter & Gamble in household products. Unilever vies with L'Oreal for world leadership in personal product sales and is 4th in global food sales. Well-established US brands include Lipton, all, Dove, Vaseline, Q-Tips, and Imperial margarine. Unilever has always advertised heavily and ranks #1 in advertising spending outside the US.

The group is owned by 2 parent companies, Unilever PLC (UK) and Unilever NV (Netherlands), whose boards of directors are identical. An equalization agreement provides for shareholders of both firms to be treated as nearly the same as if they held shares in a single company.

NYSE symbols: UL (Unilever PLC [ADR]); UN (Unilever NV)
Incorporated: England, 1894 (Unilever PLC); The Netherlands, 1927 (Unilever NV)
Fiscal year ends: December 31

WHO

Chairmen: Sir Michael Angus, age 59, £408,980 pay (Unilever PLC); Floris A. Maljers, age 56 (Unilever NV)
Financial Director: C. Miller Smith, age 50
Auditors: Coopers & Lybrand Deloitte (Unilever PLC); Coopers & Lybrand Dijker Van Dien (Unilever NV)
Employees: 300,000

WHEN

After sharpening his sales skills in the family wholesale grocery business in England, William Hesketh Lever formed a new company in 1885 with his brother, James. Lever Brothers sold the world's first packaged, branded laundry soap, Sunlight. A proponent of large-scale advertising, Lever launched the product with a campaign that queried, "Why does a woman look old sooner than a man?" The answer: because she is aged by the "wash-day evil" of laundering without Sunlight soap. Sunlight was a success in Britain, and within 15 years Lever was selling soap in Europe, Australia, South Africa, and the US.

From 1906 through 1915 Lever acquired several soap companies in Britain, Australia, and South Africa, and dominated those markets. Needing vegetable oil to make soap, Lever established plantations and trading companies around the world. Lever's United Africa Company was Africa's largest enterprise in the 20 years following its formation in 1929. During WWI the company began using its vegetable oil to make margarine.

Dutch companies Jurgens and Van den Berghs were rivals in the butter trade and pioneers in margarine production. In 1927 they created the Margarine Union, a cartel that owned the European market. The Margarine Union and Lever Brothers merged in 1930 but for tax reasons formed 2 separate entities: Unilever PLC in London and Unilever NV in Rotterdam.

Despite the Depression, WWII, and efforts of archrival Procter & Gamble, Unilever continued to expand, acquiring American companies Thomas J. Lipton (1937) and Pepsodent (1944). However, Unilever's domination of the US market ended with P&G's 1946 introduction of the first synthetic detergent, Tide. Backed by massive advertising, Tide quickly became America's leading detergent in the first of many marketing battles lost by Unilever's Lever Brothers subsidiary to P&G in the US.

Outside America, Unilever was more successful. Its businesses benefited from the postwar boom in Europe, increasing acceptance of margarine, new detergent technologies, and the emergence of frozen foods and personal care products (toothpaste, shaving cream, shampoo, cosmetics, etc.).

Although internal product development fueled some of its growth, acquisitions have played a major role in shaping Unilever. Notable acquisitions included Birds Eye Foods of the UK (1957) and, in the US, National Starch (1978), Lawry's Foods (1979), Chesebrough-Pond's (1987), Calvin Klein Cosmetics (1989), and Fabergé/Elizabeth Arden (1989).

WHERE

HQ: Unilever House, Blackfriars, London EC4P 4BQ, England (Unilever PLC); Burgemeester s'Jacobplein 1, 3015 CA, Rotterdam, The Netherlands (Unilever NV)
US Phone: 212-888-1260
US HQ: Unilever United States, Inc., 390 Park Ave., New York, NY 10022
US FAX: 212-906-4411

	1989 Sales		1989 Operating Income	
	$ mil	% of total	$ mil	% of total
Europe	20,640	60	1,712	55
North America	7,426	22	741	23
Other	6,368	18	711	22
Total	**34,434**	**100**	**3,164**	**100**

WHAT

	1989 Sales		1989 Operating Income	
	$ mil	% of total	$ mil	% of total
Food products	17,220	50	1,555	50
Specialty chemicals	2,876	8	381	12
Detergents	7,343	21	538	17
Personal products	3,696	11	393	12
Other	3,299	10	297	9
Total	**34,434**	**100**	**3,164**	**100**

Brand Names

Personal Products
Aim
Close Up
Cutex
Pepsodent
Pond's
Q-Tips
Rexona (Europe)
Vaseline

Cosmetics/Perfume
Aziza
Calvin Klein
Elizabeth Arden
Fabergé

Soap/Laundry
all
Dove
Lever 2000
Lifebuoy
Lux
Omo (international)
Snuggle
Sunlight
Surf
Wisk

Foods
Becel (Europe)
Country Crock
Imperial
Lawry's
Lipton
Mrs. Butterworth's
Promise
Ragu
Unox (Europe)
Wishbone

HOW MUCH

	9 Yr. Growth	1980	1981	1982	1983	1984	1985	1986	1987	1988	1989
Sales ($ mil)	—	—	—	21,383	19,470	18,795	24,257	25,248	31,036	30,980	34,434
Net income ($ mil)	—	—	—	610	559	583	748	982	1,413	1,510	1,687
Income as % of sales	—	—	—	2.9%	2.9%	3.1%	3.1%	3.9%	4.6%	4.9%	4.9%
*Earnings per share ($)	7.4%	1.57	1.66	1.27	1.08	1.23	1.91	1.75	2.53	3.00	2.98
*Stock price – high ($)	—	10.00	9.80	10.80	10.40	11.10	16.10	26.40	47.50	38.00	47.75
*Stock price – low ($)	—	6.75	7.90	8.20	8.60	9.00	9.60	15.20	25.70	29.25	33.00
*Stock price – close ($)	21.3%	8.40	9.45	9.60	10.40	10.15	16.10	26.40	35.25	33.00	47.75
*P/E – high	—	6	6	9	10	9	8	15	19	13	16
*P/E – low	—	4	5	6	8	7	5	9	10	10	11
*Dividends per share ($)	15.0%	0.45	0.39	0.45	0.44	0.40	0.48	0.70	1.00	0.85	1.59
*Book value per share ($)	(2.5%)	13.01	11.96	11.16	10.83	9.75	12.19	12.96	12.10	12.53	10.33

1989 Year End:
Debt ratio: 35.1%
Return on equity: 22.1%
Cash (mil): $854
Long-term debt (mil): $2,384
Number of shares (mil): 160
Dividends:
1989 average yield: 2.5%
1989 payout: 30.4%
Market value (mil): $13,563

Stock Price History high/low 1980-89

50
45
40
35
30
25
20
15
10
5
0

* All share data is for Unilever PLC only

RANKINGS

18th in *Fortune* Global 500 Industrial Cos.
8th in *Forbes* 100 Foreign Investments in the US
44th in *Business Week* Global 1000

COMPETITION

Amway	Estée Lauder	Sara Lee
Avon	Grand Metropolitan	SmithKline Beecham
BSN	S. C. Johnson	TLC Beatrice
Campbell Soup	MacAndrews & Forbes	Other food and personal products companies
Clorox	Nestlé	
Colgate-Palmolive	Philip Morris	
ConAgra	Procter & Gamble	
CPC International	RJR Nabisco	

UNION CARBIDE CORPORATION

OVERVIEW

Danbury, Connecticut–based Union Carbide is the 3rd largest US chemical company (after Dow and Du Pont), 12th largest world chemical company, and 2nd largest US chemical exporter. It is the holding company for Union Carbide Chemicals and Plastics Company, the recently renamed operating company. It leads the world in production of ethylene glycol (for antifreeze and polyester) and graphite electrodes (for steel production). It is also the world's foremost supplier of carbon and graphite products. It leads North America in the production of industrial gases (air separated into its individual gases for use in industry and medicine).

Union Carbide has weathered the Bhopal, India, industrial accident, which killed more than 3,000 people and injured another 50,000, but still has had chemical leak problems, including 2 at its West Virginia plant in early 1990.

The company has developed the technology to use carbon dioxide rather than hydrocarbon solvents to dilute spray paints, thus reducing air pollution, and plans a plastic recycling plant in New Jersey.

WHEN

The beginnings of Union Carbide Corporation trace back to an 1886 company (National Carbon Company) which manufactured carbons for street lights and established the Eveready trademark, and an 1898 company (Union Carbide) which manufactured calcium carbide. In 1917 these 2 companies joined with 3 others, Linde Air Products (oxygen), Prest-O-Lite (calcium carbide), and Electro Metallurgical (metals), to form Union Carbide & Carbon Corporation (UCC).

In 1919 the company began forming subsidiaries in Canada and in 1925 expanded overseas with the purchase of a hydroelectric power plant in Norway. UCC expanded into chemical manufacturing and in 1920 established its own chemicals division, which developed ethylene glycol (antifreeze), eventually marketed under the name Prestone. The company bought vanadium interests in Colorado from U.S. Vanadium in 1926. UCC continued to grow with purchases including Acheson Graphite (graphite products, 1928) and Bakelite (an early developer of plastics, 1939). In the 1940s the company entered the atomic field and ran the US government's nuclear laboratories in Oak Ridge, Tennessee, and in Paducah, Kentucky, until 1984.

UCC bought Visking (food casings) in 1956. The company changed its name to Union Carbide Corporation in 1957. In the early 1960s the company introduced its Glad plastic household products (sold in 1985).

In 1975 the company built a pesticide plant in Bhopal, India, and kept 51% ownership (49% to Indian companies). In 1984, a tank at the Bhopal plant leaked 5 tons of poisonous methyl isocyanate gas, killing more than 3,000 people and permanently injuring 50,000, resulting in the worst recorded industrial accident. Legal action against Union Carbide stemming from the Bhopal disaster led to a $470 million settlement in India's Supreme Court in 1989. However, in 1990 the new Indian government indicated that it wished to change the settlement.

In 1985 GAF (chemicals and roofing materials) tried to take over Union Carbide, costing the company $3 billion in additional debt, which it used to buy back 55% of its stock to defeat the attempt. In 1986 Union Carbide sold its battery division (including Eveready) to Ralston Purina, its agricultural products business to Rhône-Poulenc, and its home and automotive products business to First Brands in order to concentrate on its 3 core businesses: chemicals and plastics, industrial gases, and carbon products. In 1989 Union Carbide agreed to sell its urethane polyols (urethane foams) and propylene glycols (personal care products) businesses to Arco Chemical. The sale was blocked by the FTC in 1990.

HOW MUCH

	9 Yr. Growth	1980	1981	1982	1983	1984	1985	1986	1987	1988	1989
Sales ($ mil)	(1.5%)	9,994	10,168	9,061	9,001	9,508	9,003	6,343	6,914	8,324	8,744
Net income ($ mil)	(1.8%)	673	649	310	79	341	(599)	130	232	662	573
Income as % of sales	—	6.7%	6.4%	3.4%	0.9%	3.6%	(6.7%)	2.1%	3.4%	8.0%	6.6%
Earnings per share ($)	1.7%	3.36	3.19	1.49	0.38	1.61	(2.86)	1.24	1.75	4.66	3.92
Stock price – high ($)	—	17.50	20.71	20.33	24.63	21.75	24.75	33.17	32.50	28.38	33.25
Stock price – low ($)	—	11.75	15.08	13.38	17.00	10.92	12.00	18.75	15.50	17.00	22.75
Stock price – close ($)	3.7%	16.75	17.13	17.63	20.92	12.25	23.63	22.50	21.75	25.63	23.25
P/E – high	—	5	7	14	65	13	—	27	19	6	8
P/E – low	—	4	5	9	45	7	—	15	9	4	6
Dividends per share ($)	(0.4%)	1.03	1.10	1.13	1.13	1.13	1.13	1.50	1.50	1.15	1.00
Book value per share ($)	(3.7%)	23.63	25.58	24.51	23.32	23.30	19.82	7.87	9.43	13.34	16.83

1989 Year End:
Debt ratio: 46.6%
Return on equity: 26.0%
Cash (mil): $142
Current ratio: 1.2
Long-term debt (mil): $2,080
Number of shares (mil): 142
Dividends:
1989 average yield: 4.3%
1989 payout: 25.5%
Market value (mil): $3,292

35 30 25 20 15 10 5 0

Stock Price History high/low 1980-89

NYSE symbol: UK
Incorporated: New York, 1989
Fiscal year ends: December 31

WHO

Chairman, President, and CEO: Robert D. Kennedy, age 57, $1,409,583 pay
VP; President, Union Carbide Chemicals and Plastics Company, Inc.: H. William Lichtenberger, age 54, $926,105 pay
VP; President, Union Carbide Industrial Gases, Inc.: John R. MacLean, age 59, $731,250 pay
VP; President, UCAR Carbon Company, Inc.: Robert P. Krass, age 53, $420,000 pay
VP, Treasurer, and Principal Financial Officer: John A. Clerico, age 48
Auditors: KPMG Peat Marwick
Employees: 45,987

WHERE

HQ: 39 Old Ridgebury Rd., Danbury, CT 06817
Phone: 203-794-2000
FAX: 203-794-4336

Union Carbide has manufacturing facilities in 18 US states, Puerto Rico, and 21 foreign countries.

	1989 Sales		1989 Operating Income	
	$ mil	% of total	$ mil	% of total
US & Puerto Rico	5,793	66	917	72
Europe	1,053	12	73	6
Latin America	961	11	144	11
Canada	463	11	106	11
Far East & other	474	—	29	—
Adjustments	—	—	(3)	—
Total	**8,744**	**100**	**1,266**	**100**

WHAT

	1989 Sales		1989 Operating Income	
	$ mil	% of total	$ mil	% of total
Carbon products	782	9	44	3
Chemicals & plastics	5,613	64	1,003	80
Industrial gases	2,349	27	222	17
Adjustments	—	—	(3)	—
Total	**8,744**	**100**	**1,266**	**100**

Chemicals & Plastics
Alkanolamines
Brake fluids
Glycol ethers
Ketones
Olefins
Photoresists
Polyethylene
Polypropylene
Silicones
Vinyl acetate

Industrial Gases
Coatings service
Helium
Hydrogen
Specialty gases

Carbon Products
Calcined coal
Graphite electrodes
Graphite tooling

RANKINGS

53rd in *Fortune* 500 Industrial Cos.
144th in *Fortune* Global 500 Industrial Cos.
20th in *Fortune* 50 Exporters
90th in *Forbes* Sales 500
202nd in *Business Week* 1000
701st in *Business Week* Global 1000

COMPETITION

BASF
British Petroleum
Chevron
Dow Chemical
Eastman Kodak
Exxon
Hoechst
Mobil
Occidental
Phillips
Royal Dutch/Shell
Texaco
Other chemical companies

UNION PACIFIC CORPORATION

OVERVIEW

Union Pacific Corporation controls a 22,000-mile rail network spanning the West, Midwest, and Gulf Coast regions. The familiar yellow locomotives of the nation's 2nd largest railroad system (after Burlington Northern) hauled nearly 4 million carloads in 1989, principally of coal, chemicals, grain, automotive products, machinery, forest products, and intermodal (truck-to-train) cargo.

UP's trucking subsidiary, Overnite Transportation, operates 139 terminals, mainly in the East, Southeast, and Midwest. Overnite specializes in less-than-truckload shipments (those weighing less than 10,000 pounds) of such products as textiles, paper goods, and foodstuffs.

The company's other businesses include UP Resources, which conducts oil and gas exploration and production in addition to the mining of coal, uranium, and trona (soda ash ore); USPCI, a comprehensive hazardous waste management company; and UP Technologies, which provides advanced computer systems and services to UP and other shippers. UP recently sold most of the assets of its realty subsidiary in order to concentrate on its transportation and resources concerns.

NYSE symbol: UNP
Incorporated: Utah, 1969
Fiscal year ends: December 31

WHO

Chairman, President, and CEO: Drew Lewis, age 58, $1,550,000 pay
Chairman and CEO, UP Railroad: Michael H. Walsh, age 47, $935,000 pay
Chairman and CEO, UP Resources: William L. Adams, age 60, $799,000 pay
President and CEO, USPCI, Inc.: John L. Messman, age 50, $587,500 pay
SVP Finance: L. White Matthews III, age 44
Auditors: Deloitte & Touche
Employees: 48,100

WHEN

The Union Pacific Railroad was chartered by Congress in 1862 to build a key part of the first transcontinental railway. Construction began at Omaha in 1865 and proceeded west under the direction of Major General Grenville Dodge. The driving of the Golden Spike at Promontory, Utah, in 1869 marked the linking of the East and West Coasts as the UP's rails met those of the Central Pacific (which had been built east from Sacramento).

In the Credit Mobilier scandal (revealed in 1872), the chief promoters of UP deceived other stockholders and the government by taking excess profits from the railroad's construction. The line continued to expand, but the lingering effects of the scandal, further mismanagement, and deepening debt forced the company into bankruptcy in 1893.

A syndicate headed by E. H. Harriman bought UP in 1897. Harriman instituted a program of physical and financial improvements, and within 3 years UP had tripled its earnings. The company reacquired branches lost in the bankruptcy (Oregon Railway & Navigation Company and Oregon Short Line, 1899) and gained control of the Southern Pacific (1901) and the Chicago & Alton (1904). Harriman died in 1909; the Supreme Court ordered UP to sell its Southern Pacific holdings in 1913.

The company bought control of 2 trucking operations in the 1930s: Union Pacific Stages and Interstate Transit Lines (ITL, sold in 1952). UP acquired Spokane International Railway in 1958 and 2 energy concerns, Champlin Petroleum and Pontiac Refining, in 1970.

In 1982 UP bought St. Louis–based Missouri Pacific (a 11,547-mile railroad stretching from Chicago to Omaha, New Orleans, El Paso, and Brownsville) and the Western Pacific (Salt Lake City to San Francisco). The company acquired Overnite Transportation, a trucking operation (1986), and in 1988 bought the 2,175-mile Missouri-Kansas-Texas Railroad and USPCI, Inc., a hazardous-waste disposal company. UP trimmed railroad employment substantially in the 1980s.

Under CEO Drew Lewis (former US transportation secretary under President Reagan), UP sold its refinery interests in 1988 and recently decided to sell its real estate assets. The railroad has invested heavily in equipment during the past 2 years, buying 412 new locomotives and building the $48 million Harriman Dispatching Center in Omaha. In 1989 UP invested $100 million in Blackstone Capital Partners, a limited partnership established to buy Chicago and Northwestern Transportation Company.

WHERE

HQ: Martin Tower, Eighth and Eaton Aves., Bethlehem, PA 18018
Phone: 215-861-3200
FAX: 215-861-3220

UP Railroad's 22,000-mile rail system links West Coast and Gulf Coast ports with the Midwest. The company conducts trucking operations in 39 states and part of Canada; oil, gas, and mining operations primarily in the US, the Gulf of Mexico, and offshore California and Canada; and hazardous-waste management services in 21 states.

WHAT

	1989 Sales		1989 Operating Income	
	$ mil	% of total	$ mil	% of total
Transportation	5,276	81	934	75
Natural resources	897	14	247	20
Land	177	3	59	5
Hazardous-waste management	142	2	3	—
Adjustments	—	—	(75)	—
Total	**6,492**	**100**	**1,168**	**100**

Transportation
Missouri Pacific Railroad Co.
Overnite Transportation Co.
Union Pacific Railroad Co.

Natural Resources
Union Pacific Resources Co.

Real Estate
Union Pacific Realty (real estate sales)

Hazardous-waste Management
USPCI (United States Pollution Control, Inc.)

Other Subsidiaries
Union Pacific Technologies (technological support)

RANKINGS

7th in *Fortune* 50 Transportation Cos.
130th in *Forbes* Sales 500
74th in *Business Week* 1000
216th in *Business Week* Global 1000

COMPETITION

Bechtel
Burlington Northern
Consolidated Freightways
Consolidated Rail
Federal Express
Ogden
Rio Grande Industries
Roadway
Santa Fe Pacific
UPS
Yellow Freight
Waste Management
Other trucking, oil, and mining companies

HOW MUCH

	9 Yr. Growth	1980	1981	1982	1983	1984	1985	1986	1987	1988	1989
Sales ($ mil)	3.3%	4,832	6,375	5,818	8,353	7,789	7,798	6,574	5,943	6,068	6,492
Net income ($ mil)	4.4%	405	411	327	441	494	501	(414)	560	559	595
Income as % of sales	—	8.4%	6.4%	5.6%	5.3%	6.3%	6.4%	(6.3%)	9.4%	9.2%	9.2%
Earnings per share ($)	3.2%	4.22	4.27	3.38	3.57	4.01	4.18	(4.13)	4.90	4.90	5.62
Stock price – high ($)	—	96.25	79.25	51.75	61.88	52.75	55.25	67.38	86.63	70.13	81.00
Stock price – low ($)	—	33.50	42.50	29.25	44.00	34.25	39.75	45.50	45.13	51.00	63.25
Stock price – close ($)	(0.3%)	78.75	52.00	47.00	50.75	40.88	53.88	62.25	54.00	64.25	76.63
P/E – high	—	23	19	15	17	13	13	—	18	14	14
P/E – low	—	8	10	9	12	9	10	—	9	10	11
Dividends per share ($)	4.9%	1.45	1.65	1.80	1.80	1.80	1.80	1.85	2.00	2.10	2.23
Book value per share ($)	3.1%	29.50	32.14	34.01	35.34	37.52	39.67	32.47	35.79	39.69	39.00

1989 Year End:
Debt ratio: 49.5%
Return on equity: 14.3%
Cash (mil): $187
Current ratio: 0.67
Long-term debt (mil): $3,837
Number of shares (mil): 100
Dividends:
1989 average yield: 2.9%
1989 payout: 39.7%
Market value (mil): $7,685

Stock Price History high/low 1980-89

UNION TEXAS PETROLEUM HOLDINGS, INC.

OVERVIEW

Union Texas is one of the largest independent oil and gas producers in the US, with proved reserves equivalent to almost 500 million barrels of oil. The company is involved in worldwide oil and gas exploration and production. Union Texas owns and operates 12 gas-processing plants and is one of the top 20 gas processors in the US. The company operates and owns 42% of a petrochemical plant producing ethylene. The company's domestic operations are located primarily offshore in the Gulf of Mexico and onshore in coastal Texas and Louisiana, West Texas, New Mexico, and parts of the Rocky Mountain region.

About 81% of Union Texas's oil and gas reserves are located overseas, where the company explores and produces through several joint ventures and partnerships. Union Texas has production operations in Pakistan, the UK's North Sea, Argentina, Egypt, and Indonesia and exploration activities in most of these countries and Spain. The company is a major supplier of liquefied natural gas to Japan and Taiwan.

WHEN

The Union Sulphur Company was founded to mine sulphur in southern Louisiana in 1896. In 1926 the company drilled its first oil well. During the 1920s and 1930s the company continued to explore for oil and gas reserves in Louisiana and Texas. In 1953 Union Sulphur discovered the Lake Arthur South field in Louisiana, which became the company's highest yielding property. In 1962 Union Sulphur merged with Texas Natural Gas and adopted the name Union Texas Natural Gas. The company now had production operations in Canada, Venezuela, and Argentina in addition to the US. In 1962 Union Texas was bought by Allied Chemical.

Between 1972 and 1974, Union Texas and partners discovered a major new gas field in Indonesia, and the Piper and Claymore oil fields in the North Sea. The company continued to explore and expand its production facilities during the 1980s, finding oil in the Indus basin of Pakistan and buying Supron in 1984 to increase the company's holdings in the western US. The company expanded its offshore drilling in the Gulf of Mexico in 1984 by winning bids at federal lease sales.

In 1985 Allied sold part of its interest in the company to Kohlberg Kravis Roberts in a leveraged buyout. Union Texas became a free-standing company once again but was burdened with $1.1 billion in debt. In 1986 crude oil prices dropped, and, after writing off $105 million of gas reserves, the company posted a net loss of over $57 million on sales of almost $1.3 billion. The company moved to strengthen its financial position by slashing payroll 1/3 and selling its Texgas subsidiary and related assets. Late in 1986 natural gas delivery began from the North Sea, and the company's domestic gas production was boosted 26% with the startup of production from wells in the Gulf of Mexico.

In 1987 Union Texas offered stock to the public, selling 22% of its equity. The 1/4 billion dollars of proceeds, together with cash from operations and sales of assets, allowed the company to reduce its debt burden to $524 million by the end of 1987.

In the summer of 1988 a disastrous explosion at the company's 20%-owned Piper platform in the North Sea cost Union Texas 50% of its production from that area. However, the company collected $228 million in business interruption insurance, netting more than it would have if production had continued.

During 1988 the company's exploration activities replaced 129% of its production worldwide, but this dropped to 86% in 1989. By 1989 earnings had recovered to $173 million on sales of just $981 million. In 1990 Union Texas was put up for sale by Allied-Signal and Kohlberg Kravis Roberts.

HOW MUCH

	4 Yr. Growth	1980	1981	1982	1983	1984	1985	1986	1987	1988	1989
Sales ($ mil)	(16.7%)	—	—	—	—	—	2,039	1,256	1,257	1,073	981
Net income ($ mil)	1.2%	—	—	—	—	—	165	(57)	56	109	173
Income as % of sales	—	—	—	—	—	—	8.1%	(4.6%)	4.4%	10.2%	17.6%
Earnings per share ($)	(9.3%)	—	—	—	—	—	2.20	(1.53)	0.05	0.73	1.49
Stock price – high ($)	—	—	—	—	—	—	—	—	14.63	13.25	18.75
Stock price – low ($)	—	—	—	—	—	—	—	—	5.75	8.13	10.38
Stock price – close ($)	—	—	—	—	—	—	—	—	8.00	10.38	18.13
P/E – high	—	—	—	—	—	—	—	—	293	18	13
P/E – low	—	—	—	—	—	—	—	—	115	11	7
Dividends per share ($)	—	—	—	—	—	—	—	—	0.00	0.15	0.20
Book value per share ($)	—	—	—	—	—	—	(4.20)	(5.70)	1.56	2.04	3.27

1989 Year End:
Debt ratio: 66.0%
Return on equity: 56.1%
Cash (mil): $61
Current ratio: 0.97
Long-term debt (mil): $534
Number of shares (mil): 84
Dividends:
1989 average yield: 1.1%
1989 payout: 13.4%
Market value (mil): $1,526

Stock Price History high/low 1987-89

20
18
16
14
12
10
8
6
4
2
0

NYSE symbol: UTH
Incorporated: Delaware, 1982
Fiscal year ends: December 31

WHO

Chairman and CEO: A. Clark Johnston, age 59, $679,800 pay
SVP, International Exploration and Production: A. C. Berman, age 53, $360,400 pay
SVP, US Exploration and Production: William M. Krips, age 50, $350,100 pay
SVP, Hydrocarbon Products Group: Arthur W. Peabody, age 46, $288,000 pay
VP Finance: Robert L. Ryan, age 46, $268,450 pay
Auditors: Price Waterhouse
Employees: 1,900

WHERE

HQ: 1330 Post Oak Blvd., Houston, TX 77056
Phone: 713-623-6544
FAX: 713-968-2771

Union Texas engages in oil and gas exploration in the Gulf of Mexico, Texas, Louisiana, New Mexico, the Rocky Mountains, and 6 foreign countries. The company owns interests in 13 processing plants in Texas, Oklahoma, and Louisiana.

	1989 Sales		1989 Operating Income	
	$ mil	% of total	$ mil	% of total
US	643	65	61	19
UK	67	7	122	39
Indonesia	235	24	122	39
Pakistan	26	3	11	3
Other	10	1	(1)	—
Adjustments	—	—	(204)	—
Total	**981**	**100**	**111**	**100**

WHAT

	1989 Sales		1989 Operating Income	
	$ mil	% of total	$ mil	% of total
Exploration & production	551	56	258	82
Hydrocarbon prods.	429	44	61	19
Other	—	—	(4)	(1)
Adjustments	1	—	(204)	—
Total	**981**	**100**	**111**	**100**

Products
Crude oil
Ethylene
Natural gas
Other petrochemical products

RANKINGS

318th in *Fortune* 500 Industrial Cos.
363rd in *Business Week* 1000

COMPETITION

Amoco
Ashland
Atlantic Richfield
British Petroleum
Chevron
Coastal
Du Pont
Exxon
Mobil
Occidental
Pennzoil
Phillips
Royal Dutch/Shell
Sun
Texaco
Unocal
USX

UNISYS CORPORATION

OVERVIEW

After IBM and DEC, Unisys is the 3rd largest information processing firm in the US and the 5th largest in the world (after NEC and Fujitsu). The company is a major worldwide systems integrator and a leader in on-line transaction-processing systems.

Unisys links its mainframe computers (the largest part of its revenues, at 30%), leading 4th-generation language applications, voice-data-image communications networks, and workstations and servers incorporating industry standards.

While 75% of the total workforce is US-based, foreign operations account for 49% of revenues and over 1/3 of Unisys's research, engineering, and manufacturing efforts. R&D expenditures were almost $1.5 billion in 1989. Unisys's defense-related revenues accounted for 23% of total 1989 revenues.

Problems in the defense sector and market shifts away from proprietary systems recently caused massive losses, layoffs, and corporate reorganizations.

WHEN

Unisys was formed in 1986 when struggling mainframe computer giant Burroughs swallowed fellow mainframe manufacturer Sperry Corporation. Burroughs traces its roots back to American Arithmometer (St. Louis, 1886), later Burroughs Adding Machine (Detroit, 1905) and Burroughs Corporation (1953). Burroughs entered data processing by purchasing Electrodata (1956) and many others, including Memorex (1982).

Sperry was the product of a 1955 merger of Sperry Gyroscope (an electronics company founded in 1910 by Elmer Sperry) and Remington Rand, an old-line typewriter manufacturer and maker of the first commercially viable computer, the UNIVAC. Sperry bought RCA's faltering computer business in 1971.

In 1986 Burroughs president Michael Blumenthal, a former treasury secretary to Carter, sought to achieve efficiencies in parts and development by merging Burroughs's small database managers with Sperry's defense-related number crunchers.

As Unisys's president, Blumenthal quickly disposed of $1.8 billion in assets (Sperry Aerospace and Marine divisions, Memorex), closed plants and cut the combined workforce of 120,000 by 24,000. He also promised continued support for Sperry's flagship 1100 line of mainframes and nourished Burroughs's prized A series of computers. The initial results were positive, with 1986's $43 million loss followed by 1987's $578 million profit.

Amidst an industry trend to stronger, smaller systems (where PCs could access mainframe power), Unisys in 1988 equipped its U line of servers with the open UNIX operating system, sponsored 4th-generation languages (4GLs) to connect its new 2200 and A mainframe series, and moved to networked smaller systems, spending $650 million to buy Timeplex (voice/data networks) and Convergent (UNIX-based workstations).

Plummeting mainframe demand in 1989 caught Unisys in mid-transition; company losses in 3rd quarter 1989 alone were $648 million, and its debt to equity ratio approached 50%. Further restructuring included elimination of some 8,000 jobs worldwide and in-house production of small systems (to boost margins, use excess capacity).

The networking/distributed computing focus emerged unscathed, signaled by the Micro A (1989) desktop mainframe, BTOS/CTOS workstations, and a forthcoming UNIX-based fault-tolerant computer (1991). Unisys's hottest growth area is imaging technologies that handle paper transactions, such as high-volume check processing, electronically.

HOW MUCH

	9 Yr. Growth	1980	1981	1982	1983	1984	1985	1986	1987	1988	1989
Sales ($ mil)	15.1%	2,857	3,319	4,095	4,297	4,808	5,038	7,432	9,713	9,902	10,097
Net income ($ mil)	—	82	130	110	197	245	248	(43)	578	681	(639)
Income as % of sales	—	2.9%	3.9%	2.7%	4.6%	5.1%	4.9%	(0.6%)	6.0%	6.9%	(6.3%)
Earnings per share ($)	—	0.66	1.04	0.87	1.53	1.80	1.82	(0.54)	2.93	3.27	(4.71)
Stock price – high ($)	—	29.17	18.46	16.38	19.21	19.96	22.67	28.83	48.38	39.00	30.50
Stock price – low ($)	—	15.42	9.04	9.88	13.42	14.79	17.33	19.17	24.00	25.00	12.38
Stock price – close ($)	(2.2%)	17.96	11.33	13.92	16.79	18.92	21.13	26.67	33.63	28.13	14.75
P/E – high	—	44	18	19	13	11	12	—	17	12	—
P/E – low	—	23	9	11	9	8	10	—	8	8	—
Dividends per share ($)	1.6%	0.87	0.87	0.87	0.87	0.87	0.87	0.87	0.91	0.98	1.00
Book value per share ($)	(1.1%)	17.06	17.14	16.12	16.37	16.88	18.24	17.31	20.90	22.24	15.49

1989 Year End:
Debt ratio: 45.6%
Return on equity: —
Cash (mil): $9
Current ratio: 1.44
Long-term debt (mil): $3,248
Number of shares (mil): 158
Dividends:
1989 average yield: 6.8%
1989 payout: —
Market value (mil): $2,336

Stock Price History high/low 1980-89

50 45 40 35 30 25 20 15 10 5 0

NYSE symbol: UIS
Incorporation: Delaware, 1984
Fiscal year ends: December 31

WHO

Chairman: W. Michael Blumenthal, age 64, $839,900 pay (before retiring as CEO)
President and CEO: James A. Unruh, age 48, $424,369 pay (before promotion)
VC: Curtis A. Hessler, age 46, $386,000 pay
VP and CFO: George T. Robson, age 42
Auditors: Ernst & Young
Employees: 82,300

WHERE

HQ: Township Line and Union Meeting Rds., Blue Bell, PA 19424
Phone: 215-986-4011
FAX: 215-986-6850

Unisys has operations in approximately 120 countries.

	1989 Sales		1989 Operating Income	
	$ mil	% of total	$ mil	% of total
US	5,137	51	(267)	—
Europe	2,935	29	(32)	—
Americas/Pacific	2,025	20	320	—
Adjustments	—	—	(231)	—
Total	**10,097**	**100**	**(210)**	**—**

WHAT

	1989 Sales	
	$ mil	% of total
Mainframes & peripherals	2,984	30
Distributed systems & workstations	1,496	15
Software & related services	1,827	18
Equipment maintenance	1,947	19
Custom products & services	1,636	16
Other	207	2
Total	**10,097**	**100**

Computer Systems
Mainframes
- 2200 Series
- 1100 Series
- A Series
- V Series
- Micro A (desktop)

Servers
- U Series

Workstations
- BTOS/CTOS

Personal computers
- Personal Workstation2

Disk subsystems
- M Series

Peripherals
- Printers, storage devices

Networking Systems
LINK/2
TIME/LAN
TX3/SuperHub

Software Systems
4th generation language
- LINC
- MAPPER
- Ally

Computer-aided software engineering (CASE)
InfoImage (imaging technology)

RANKINGS

43rd in *Fortune* 500 Industrial Cos.
115th in *Fortune* Global 500 Industrial Cos.
13th in *Fortune* 50 Exporters
70th in *Forbes* Sales 500
250th in *Business Week* 1000
878th in *Business Week* Global 1000

COMPETITION

Amdahl	Hitachi	Tandem
Control Data	IBM	Wang
Data General	NCR	Other computer and software companies
Digital Equipment	NEC	
Fujitsu	Storage Technology	
Hewlett-Packard		

THE UNITED NATIONS

OVERVIEW

The dream of an organization to promote peace among nations has been a persistent one in the 20th century. Woodrow Wilson's effort to realize the dream, the League of Nations, was a failure, but the dream persisted and was realized again as The United Nations, the largest representative organization in the world.

The UN has 159 member nations and 18 nonmember observer entities, representing virtually the entire world's population. Its 4 purposes are to maintain international peace, develop friendly relations among countries, resolve international problems, and harmonize the actions of nations.

To improve the social, medical, and educational welfare of the world's people, the UN operates 13 programs, the best known of which is probably the UN children's fund (UNICEF), and coordinates its activities with 16 specialized agencies.

The US has worked hard to make the UN dream a reality. John D. Rockefeller, Jr., provided the New York City riverfront site for the headquarters building; the US contributes the largest share of the UN's annual budget; and the US has appointed a number of its most distinguished citizens to represent it in the UN, including Henry Cabot Lodge, Adlai Stevenson, and George Bush.

Since WWII, the UN has reflected the major political and economic concerns of the day, playing a vital role in reducing world tensions, improving the health and welfare of the disadvantaged, protecting the common heritage of mankind, developing international law, and encouraging respect for basic human rights.

WHEN

Franklin Roosevelt described the nations allied against the Axis powers in WWII as the "United Nations." The Declaration of the United Nations signed in January 1942 affirmed the signatories' determination to win WWII. The structure of the UN was fixed by the US, the UK, the USSR, and China in a series of meetings at Dumbarton Oaks in Washington, DC, between August and October 1944. Issues of Security Council membership and voting procedures and the eligibility of some states for membership were settled at the Yalta Conference in 1945. At the end of WWII, the 26 original members, Poland (retroactively made an original member), and 24 other states signed the Charter of the United Nations in San Francisco on June 26, 1945. It went into effect on October 24, 1945.

The effects of one of the UN's early decisions, the partition of Palestine in 1947, continue today, resulting in instability and repeated UN military action in the region. During the 1950s the UN took armed action in Korea (which occurred due to Soviet absence from the Security Council when it voted to intervene) and Egypt (1956).

Also during the 1950s, under the leadership of Secretary General U Thant, the UN was an advocate for the end of colonialism, assisting in the movement to independence of many African nations. One of these, the Congo, erupted into tribal warfare, requiring military intervention (1960-1964).

During the 1960s, in addition to peacekeeping activities in Cyprus and the Middle East, the UN turned to prevention of nuclear proliferation and population control.

During the 1970s and 1980s focus shifted to differences between developed nations and the third world. Some UN agencies became politicized, resulting in withdrawal of US financial support to the UN Educational, Scientific and Cultural Organization (since resumed). Also during this time, attention turned to the environment, conservation, and apportionment of natural resources in extraterritorial areas, *e.g.*, sea floors.

Though for many years the world body seemed paralyzed by politics, it has recently begun to display some of its promise under the leadership of Secretary General Javier Pérez de Cuéllar. It oversaw the withdrawal of Soviet troops from Afghanistan and the elections in Nicaragua and has proven effective in mobilizing international action in the wake of the Iraqi invasion of Kuwait.

HOW MUCH

	9 Yr. Growth	1979	1980	1981	1982	1983	1984	1985	1986	1987	1988
Total contrib. ($ mil)	5.0%	3,504	3,932	3,865	4,011	3,873	3,847	3,666	4,168	4,691	5,443
Regular budget* ($ mil)	4.4%	488	510	565	632	592	683	618	722	662	720
Peace-keeping ($ mil)	1.5%	183	162	150	186	195	152	166	169	179	209
Food & health ($ mil)	1.6%	1,012	1,220	810	892	728	795	697	780	841	1,167
Econ. & social ($ mil)	6.3%	1,292	1,400	1,485	1,583	1,603	1,449	1,461	1,703	2,005	2,244
Technical coop. ($ mil)	10.5%	154	203	287	220	218	220	222	244	340	378
Refugee assistance ($ mil)	6.1%	326	364	510	410	462	436	443	477	553	556
Trust funds ($ mil)	14.7%	49	73	58	88	75	112	59	73	111	169

Total Contributions ($ mil) 1979-88

6,000
5,000
4,000
3,000
2,000
1,000
0

*This is devoted largely to adminstrative expenses and economic, social, and humanitarian activities.

Founded: 1945
Fiscal year ends: December 31

WHO

Secretary General: Javier Pérez de Cuéllar, age 70
Director General, UN Office at Geneva: Jan Martenson
Director General, UN Office at Vienna: Margaret Anstee
US Representative: Thomas R. Pickering
Auditors: UN Board of Auditors
Employees: 19,573

WHERE

HQ: United Nations, New York, NY 10017
Phone: 212-963-1234
FAX: 212-758-2718

The UN has offices in Geneva and Vienna.

	1988 Largest Contributors	
Country	**US$ mil**	**% of total**
US	934	17
Japan	537	10
Germany, West	388	7
Italy	366	7
Sweden	329	6
USSR	285	5
Netherlands	284	5
UK	265	5
Canada	244	5
Norway	244	5
France	228	4
Denmark	212	4
Finland	136	2
Others	991	18
Total	**5,443**	**100**

WHAT

Principal Organs
- General Assembly
- Security Council
- Economic and Social Council
- Trusteeship Council
- International Court of Justice
- Secretariat

Functions
- Dispute resolution
- Peacekeeping
- Development of international law
- Trusteeship of non–self-governing areas
- Trade agreements
- Economic and social development
- Food production and distribution
- Public health
- Children's welfare
- Refugee assistance
- Disaster relief
- Coordination of specialized agencies

Specialized Agencies
- Food and Agriculture Organization (FAO)
- General Agreement on Tariffs and Trade (GATT)
- International Atomic Energy Agency (IAEA)
- International Civil Aviation Organization (ICAO)
- International Fund for Agricultural Development (IFAD)
- International Labor Organization (ILO)
- International Maritime Organization (IMO)
- International Monetary Fund (IMF)
- International Telecommunication Union (ITU)
- United Nations Educational, Scientific and Cultural Organization (UNESCO)
- United Nations Industrial Development Organization (UNIDO)
- Universal Postal Union (UPU)
- World Bank
- World Health Organization (WHO)
- World Intellectual Property Organization (WIPO)
- World Meteorological Organization (WMO)

UNITED PARCEL SERVICE OF AMERICA, INC.

OVERVIEW

UPS delivers letters and packages to almost any address in more than 180 countries worldwide. Ranked #1 in the *Fortune* 50 Transportation Companies for the 2nd consecutive year, UPS continues to offer quality, reliable service to more than a million customers every day. In 1989 the company added 70,000 regular customers, including its one millionth daily pick-up customer.

In 1989 UPS expanded international service to include Moscow, Budapest, Warsaw, Seoul, Hong Kong, and 3 cities in Mexico. Global expansion has been costly, however, resulting in lowered profits over the past 2 years.

UPS offers truck leasing (UPS Truck Leasing), with a fleet of 3,094 lease and rental vehicles in the Southeast and Southwest. Martrac, a UPS subsidiary, delivers produce and other perishables in refrigerated rail containers. Another subsidiary, UPS Air Cargo, forwarded almost 20,000 air freight shipments in 1989, filling container positions on what would have been empty space on regularly scheduled UPS flights.

UPS actively supports the United Way and was awarded that organization's first Spirit of America Award in 1988. In 1989 the UPS Foundation approved $4.3 million in grants to improve adult literacy and support efforts to feed the poor.

WHEN

In 1907, 2 Seattle teenagers, Jim Casey and Claude Ryan, started a telephone-message service called the American Messenger Company. Soon thereafter the boys began making small-parcel deliveries for local department stores.

The company became Merchants Parcel Delivery in 1913 and by 1915 had a staff of 20 messengers, 5 motorcycles, and 4 automobiles to transport packages. By then Casey, who led the company for the next 47 years, had established a policy of manager-ownership, and Charlie Soderstrom, one of the company's 4 stockholders, had chosen the brown paint still used on the company's delivery vehicles.

Service expanded beyond Seattle in 1919 when Merchants Parcel bought Oakland-based Motor Parcel Delivery. Operating as United Parcel Service (UPS), the company continued to make home deliveries for local retailers and by 1930 served residents in New York City; Newark, New Jersey; and Greenwich, Connecticut (the company's new headquarters).

UPS expanded small-package delivery to include addresses within a 150-mile radius of certain metropolitan areas, starting with Los Angeles in 1952. Expanding westward from the East Coast and eastward from the West, the company slowly blanketed the US, operating between all of the 48 contiguous states by 1975.

Three years earlier the company had gained heightened public awareness when the US Postal Service, in an effort to improve its own public image, cited UPS as a competitor. Up to this time UPS had developed in relative obscurity, with most of its stock owned by managers, their families, heirs, or estates.

UPS expanded to Europe in 1976, with service to West Germany, and in the late 1970s established a base at Standiford Airfield in Louisville, Kentucky, spending $28 million on used aircraft to start an air express delivery service. By 1982 UPS Blue Label Air Service (renamed UPS 2nd Day Air) guaranteed delivery anywhere on the mainland US and Oahu, Hawaii, within 48 hours. Overnight service (UPS Next Day Air) began in 1982, expanding nationwide and to Puerto Rico by 1985.

In the late 1980s, when UPS adopted the slogan "We run the tightest ship in the shipping business," for its first television advertising campaign, the company was already one of America's most profitable transportation companies, earning $784 million on $9.7 billion in revenues (1987). By 1990 UPS was operating in more than 180 countries worldwide.

HOW MUCH

	9 Yr. Growth	1980	1981	1982	1983	1984	1985	1986	1987	1988	1989
Sales ($ mil)	12.9%	4,163	4,911	5,213	6,015	6,833	7,687	8,600	9,700	11,000	12,400
Net income ($ mil)	15.5%	189	328	332	490	477	568	669	784	759	693
Income as % of sales	—	4.5%	6.7%	6.4%	8.1%	7.0%	7.4%	7.8%	8.1%	6.9%	5.6%
Delivery volume (pkg., mil)	7.1%	1,495	1,588	1,625	1,800	1,900	2,061	2,261	2,492	2,685	2,778
Vehicles	7.7%	59,300	60,900	62,400	63,400	72,413	80,300	85,500	94,700	103,700	116,000
Customers (thou, daily pick-up)	7.2%	538	573	604	645	669	740	804	872	933	1,007
Employees (thou)	8.8%	111*	114*	118*	124	141	152	168	192	219	237

Sales ($ bil) 1980-89

*available to September 30 only

Private company
Incorporated: Delaware, 1930
Fiscal year ends: December 31

WHO

Chairman and CEO: Kent C. Nelson, age 52, $430,041 pay
SVP, Treasurer, and CFO: Edwin A. Jacoby, age 57
Auditors: Deloitte & Touche
Employees: 237,700

WHERE

HQ: Greenwich Office Park 5, Greenwich, CT 06831
Phone: 203-862-6000
FAX: 203-862-6593

UPS operates in 180 countries worldwide.

Hub Locations
Auckland, New Zealand
Cologne/Bonn, Germany
Hong Kong
Honolulu, HI
London, England
Louisville, KY
Manama, Bahrain
Miami, FL
Narita, Japan
Philadelphia, PA
Singapore
Sydney, Australia

WHAT

Flight Equipment			
Type	Owned (including those on order)	Chartered	Total
Boeing 727	47	—	47
Boeing 747	7	—	7
Boeing 757	30	—	30
DC-8	49	—	49
Other	—	240	240
Total	**133**	**240**	**373**

Subsidiaries
Martrac
Merchants Parcel Delivery
Minneagen Real Estate Co.
Red Arrow Bonded Messenger Corp.
UPS Air Cargo
UPS Air Forwarding, Inc.
UPS Air Leasing, Inc.
UPS Truck Leasing

Services
UPS Next Day Air (50 states and Puerto Rico)
UPS 2nd Day Air (50 states and Puerto Rico)
UPS Ground Service (48 contiguous states)
UPS Service to Canada (ground and air)
UPS International Air Service (between the US and 180 foreign countries)

Automotive Vehicle Fleet
116,000 vehicles

RANKINGS

1st in *Fortune* 50 Transportation Cos.
6th in *Forbes* 400 US Private Cos.

COMPETITION

Consolidated Freightways
Federal Express
Roadway
Ryder
Union Pacific
Airline companies

UNITED STATES OF AMERICA

OVERVIEW

The United States of America (US) is a North American federal republic consisting of 50 states, with a total area of 3,679,192 square miles, and several territories and possessions. The country's capital is Washington, DC.

The government of the US is divided between national (federal) and state levels established by the Constitution. The federal government is made up of 3 branches: the Executive, headed by the president; the Legislative, consisting of a 100-member Senate and a 435-member House of Representatives; and the Judiciary, encompassing the Supreme Court and federal court system. Most state governments closely resemble the national model.

A nation of immigrants, the US is a heterogeneous mixture of many ethnic groups blending into a culture that has created such quintessential American art forms as baseball, rock and roll, jazz, and the motion picture.

WHEN

The first successful English colonies in North America were established at Jamestown, Virginia (1607), and Plymouth, Massachusetts (1620). The English continued to expand their foothold in North America and by 1733 had established 13 colonies. England's victory in the French and Indian War (1754-1763) made it the dominant power in North America.

For the next several years, British rule became increasingly distasteful to many of the colonists. Following the Intolerable Acts of 1774, violence erupted at Lexington and Concord in 1775, starting the American Revolution. The 2nd Continental Congress declared American independence in 1776, and in 1781 General George Washington forced the British to surrender at Yorktown.

Government under the Articles of Confederation (established in 1776) proved inadequate for the new nation and resulted in the creation of the Constitution in 1787. The US defeated the British again during the War of 1812.

During the 1800s, following the acquisitions of large tracts of lands (notably the 1803 Louisiana purchase), a great westward migration began. Victory in the Mexican War brought more new territory to the US. The discovery of gold in California in 1848 caused another wave of settlers to flock to the West.

The new western territories intensified the debate over slavery, which was causing strain between the industrial North and the agricultural South. After Lincoln's election in 1860, the southern states seceded and plunged the nation into a civil war that ended with victory by the North in 1865.

After the Civil War, President Lincoln was assassinated and the North imposed a turbulent period of reconstruction on the South. Westward migration continued, and the North began a period of rapid industrialization characterized by the influx of a large number of mostly European immigrants.

After an 1898 war with Spain, the US became increasingly involved in international affairs. Despite strong isolationist sentiment, the US was unable to stay out of WWI and joined the Allied effort in 1917.

The post-WWI period was characterized by female suffrage (1920), Prohibition (1919-1933), bootlegging, and an optimism that was shattered by the stock market crash in 1929. The US did not fully emerge from the ensuing Great Depression until the economy was sparked by WWII (which the US entered in 1941 after the Japanese attacked Pearl Harbor).

After WWII ended in 1945, the US rose to its status as a great power and entered the Cold War with the USSR, becoming involved in wars against communism in Korea (1950-1953) and Vietnam (1961-1973). The 1960s brought a wave of civil rights struggles and internal strife. In 1969 the US put the first man on the moon.

During the 1970s the US weathered an energy crisis, soaring inflation, and the worst political scandal in its history (Watergate). The 1980s brought increasing globalization of the economy and the end of the Cold War.

HOW MUCH

	9 Yr. Growth	1980	1981	1982	1983	1984	1985	1986	1987	1988	1989
Population (mil)	1.0%	228	230	232	235	237	239	242	244	246	248
GNP ($ bil)	7.9%	2,632	2,958	3,069	3,305	3,772	4,015	4,240	4,524	4,881	5,234
GNP ($ bil, constant $)	3.2%	3,956	4,027	3,938	4,109	4,496	4,620	4,788	4,931	5,115	5,234
GNP per capita (const. $)	2.2%	17,371	17,507	16,946	17,499	18,972	19,305	19,818	20,218	20,767	21,037
Imports ($ bil)	7.5%	257	273	255	270	346	353	382	424	460	493
Exports ($ bil)	5.7%	221	234	212	206	224	219	227	254	322	364
Prime rate, average	—	15.3%	18.9%	14.9%	10.8%	12.0%	9.9%	8.4%	8.2%	9.3%	10.9%
Consumer price increase	—	13.5%	10.4%	6.1%	3.2%	4.3%	3.6%	1.9%	3.6%	4.0%	4.8%
Govt. deficit ($ bil)	7.2%	76.2	78.7	125.7	202.5	178.3	212.1	212.6	147.5	155.5	141.9

GNP per capita ($) 1980-89

25,000
20,000
15,000
10,000
5,000
0

Official name: United States of America

WHO

President: George Bush, age 66, $200,000 pay (plus $50,000 for expenses)
VP: Dan Quayle, age 43, $115,000 pay (plus $10,000 for expenses)
Secretary of the Treasury: Nicholas F. Brady, age 61, $99,500 pay
Auditors: General Accounting Office
Employees: 3,179,382

WHERE

HQ: The White House, 1600 Pennsylvania Ave. NW, Washington, DC 20510
Phone: 202-456-1414
FAX: 202-456-2883 (Executive Offices)

The United States borders 2 other countries (Canada and Mexico) and spans 6 time zones. It is made up of 50 states.

Geographic Region	Area (thou sq mi)	1989 Population (thou)
East North Central IL, IN, MI, OH, WI	302.4	41,997
East South Central AL, KY, MS, TN	181.9	15,505
Middle Atlantic NJ, NY, PA	106.5	37,432
Mountain AZ, CO, ID, MT, NM, NV, UT, WY	863.6	13,760
New England CT, MA, ME, NH RI, VT	66.7	12,992
Pacific AK, CA, HI, OR, WA	921.3	37,655
South Atlantic DC, DE, FL, GA, MD, NC, SC, VA, WV	279.0	43,045
West North Central IA, KS, MN, MO, ND, NE, SD	520.1	17,688
West South Central AR, LA, OK, TX	437.7	27,660
Total	**3,679.2**	**247,734**

Largest Metropolitan Areas	1989 Population (thou)
New York	18,054
Los Angeles	13,471
Chicago	8,147
San Francisco	5,953
Philadelphia	5,891
Detroit	4,629
Boston	4,093
Dallas–Ft. Worth	3,725
Houston	3,626
Miami	2,954

WHAT

GNP (1989): $4.9 trillion
Currency: 1 dollar = 100 cents
Total national debt: $2.8 trillion

Imports	Exports
Machinery and equipment	Machinery and equipment
Other manufactured goods	Chemicals
Mineral fuels	Food and animals
Food and animals	Crude materials
Chemicals	Other manufactured goods

RANKINGS

1st in GNP
4th in population (after China, India, and USSR)
4th in area (after USSR, Canada, and China)

THE UNITED STATES SHOE CORPORATION

OVERVIEW

US Shoe operates in 3 business segments: apparel retail, optical retail, and footwear. The apparel retail division sells women's apparel and accessories primarily in shopping malls through its Casual Corner, Petite Sophisticate, Ups 'N Downs, Caren Charles, August Max Woman, Career Image, Cabaret , and T.H. Mandy chains.

The optical retailing division sells eyewear through LensCrafters stores, which are located primarily in shopping malls and strip centers. LensCrafters stores contain lens grinding facilities and offer customers glasses made in about an hour.

The footwear division manufactures, wholesales, imports, and retails footwear. About 50% of the company's wholesale shoe volume is produced domestically. Retail shoe divisions include Hahn (women's and men's branded footwear); Cincinnati Shoe (leased departments in discount stores); Banister (factory outlet stores); and the Concept Stores division (women's shoes), which operates The Cobbie Shop, Joyce-Selby Shoes, and Shop for Pappagallo.

WHEN

US Shoe was incorporated in Ohio in 1923 to consolidate the business of 5 smaller shoe manufacturers: Holters, Krohn-Frechheimer, Val Duttenhofer Sons, Robert Wise, and Scheiffele Shoe Manufacturing. The company's Red Cross brand women's shoes have been advertised nationally since 1892. In 1928 the company's sales were almost $8 million. Reincorporation followed in 1931. In 1955 US Shoe bought Joyce, a maker of women's casual shoes. A series of acquisitions followed, including women's shoe maker Selby (1957), the maker of Jumping Jacks children's shoes (1961), importer of Italian women's shoes Marx and Newman (1962), and the Wm. Hahn chain of 21 family shoe stores (1963). By 1964 the company was the 5th largest US shoemaker, with sales of $108 million.

In 1966 the company merged with privately owned Freeman-Toor, maker of Freeman and Botany men's shoes. New chairman and CEO Harold O. Toor, whose family owned 16% of company stock after the merger, favored branching out into men's apparel. US Shoe company officials disagreed, and the merger was dissolved by both parties in 1967. Philip Barach was reinstated as CEO, a position he held until resigning in 1990 (although he remains as chairman).

The company bought Texas Boot (1966), Pappagallo shoe manufacturers and H. Scheft retail shoe stores (1968), the Casual Corner chain of 20 clothing stores (1970), the Capezio trademark (1974), and 171 Ups 'N Downs retail clothing stores (1982). The Casual Corner chain, which had undertaken an aggressive expansion program and merchandising shift beginning in 1977, showed a comparable store sale gain of 7% in 1979 and added 40 new stores in 1980, bringing the total to 419. Casual Corner's performance contributed to the company's specialty retailing division's 1980 32% earnings gain over the previous year on a sales gain of 15%.

In 1984, US Shoe bought the LensCrafters chain of optical stores with manufacturing facilities on-site, offering new eyeglasses "ready in about an hour." There were 240 LensCrafters locations by 1988, and in 1989 sales topped $500 million. US Shoe expanded Casual Corner to 756 stores by 1989, by which time its total enclosed mall store locations numbered more than 2,000.

After net profit decreased from $65 million in 1985 to $36 million in 1987, Barach put the company up for sale in 1988. In 1989, however, the company announced that it would sell only the shoe manufacturing division to an investment group led by Merrill Lynch, but the deal soured later that year. The company currently manufactures or imports more than 25 brands of shoes.

HOW MUCH

	9 Yr. Growth	1980	1981	1982	1983	1984	1985	1986	1987	1988	1989
Sales ($ mil)	11.3%	974	1,088	1,254	1,508	1,717	1,920	2,003	2,168	2,343	2,557
Net income ($ mil)	0.5%	47	59	60	75	53	65	25	36	13	49
Income as % of sales	—	4.8%	5.4%	4.8%	5.0%	3.1%	3.4%	1.3%	1.7%	0.6%	1.9%
Earnings per share ($)	0.2%	1.08	1.33	1.35	1.71	1.21	1.46	0.57	0.80	0.29	1.10
Stock price – high ($)	—	5.21	9.09	14.19	24.50	18.88	23.00	27.31	34.75	29.00	27.50
Stock price – low ($)	—	2.71	4.92	5.66	12.44	11.50	12.13	19.50	12.75	14.00	16.38
Stock price – close ($)	16.7%	5.00	8.34	13.72	18.81	13.31	21.38	20.75	13.88	24.75	20.13
P/E – high	—	5	7	11	14	16	16	48	43	100	25
P/E – low	—	3	4	4	7	10	8	34	16	48	15
Dividends per share ($)	6.2%	0.27	0.31	0.33	0.37	0.42	0.45	0.46	0.46	0.46	0.46
Book value per share ($)	8.9%	5.66	6.69	7.71	9.08	9.82	10.86	11.02	11.74	11.60	12.22

1989 Year End:
Debt ratio: 24.5%
Return on equity: 9.2%
Cash (mil): $21
Current ratio: 1.76
Long-term debt (mil): $178
Number of shares (mil): 45
Dividends:
1989 average yield: 2.3%
1989 payout: 41.8%
Market value (mil): $903

Stock Price History high/low 1980-89

NYSE symbol: USR
Incorporated: Ohio, 1931
Fiscal year ends: Saturday nearest January 31

WHO

Chairman: Philip G. Barach, age 60, $700,000 pay
President and CEO: Bannus B. Hudson, age 44, $487,500 pay
EVP; President, Footwear Wholesaling and Retailing: Howard Platt, age 63, $468,750 pay
SVP; CEO, Retail Development and Services Division: Martin Sherman, age 60, $318,750 pay
VP Finance: K. Brent Somers, age 41
Auditors: Arthur Andersen & Co.
Employees: approximately 49,000

WHERE

HQ: 1 Eastwood Dr., Cincinnati, OH 45227
Phone: 513-527-7000
FAX: 513-561-2007

US Shoe has 12 plants in 4 states. Its retailing segments operate throughout the United States.

WHAT

	1989 Sales		1989 Operating Income	
	$ mil	% of total	$ mil	% of total
Footwear	791	31	30	23
Specialty apparel & other retailing	1,234	48	53	40
Optical retailing	532	21	48	37
Adjustments	—	—	(18)	—
Total	**2,557**	**100**	**113**	**100**

Women's Wear—Store Chains	No. of stores
August Max Woman	93
Cabaret	16
Career Image	16
Caren Charles	198
Casual Corner	747
Petite Sophisticate	252
T. H. Mandy	21
Ups 'N Downs	378
Total	**1,721**

Optical Retailing
LensCrafters

Footwear—Brand Names
Abstrax
Amalfi
Bandolino
Capezio
Cobbie
Cobbie Cuddler
David Evins
Divertente
Easy Spirit
Evan-Picone (shoes only)
Innovations
Joyce
Leslie Fay
Liz Claiborne (shoes only)
Pappagallo
Red Cross
Selby
Vittorio Ricci Studio

RANKINGS

44th in *Fortune* 50 Retailing Cos.
331st in *Forbes* Sales 500
542nd in *Business Week* 1000

COMPETITION

General Cinema
Grand Metropolitan
INTERCO
The Limited
May Department Stores
Melville
NIKE
Nordstrom
Reebok
Woolworth
Department and discount stores

UNITED TECHNOLOGIES CORPORATION

OVERVIEW

Hartford, Connecticut–based United Technologies Corporation encompasses such well-known businesses as Pratt & Whitney (jet engines), Sikorsky (helicopters), Carrier (heating/air-conditioning systems), and Otis (elevators/escalators). The company also makes automotive components, rocket engines, space suits, and a host of other products.

UTC Chairman Bob Daniell is hailed as an innovator in managing the American corporation in the 1990s, and his efforts have produced results: Sikorsky, Carrier, and Otis are world leaders in their industries.

Pratt & Whitney (P&W), rejuvenated under Daniell, is the world's leading producer of small gas turbine engines and captured 60% of the US Air Force's 1989 fighter engine orders. The company is one of the world's leading suppliers of commercial jet engines, with P&W powerplants on all types of wide-body jetliners now in service. P&W owns part of International Aero Engines AG, a 5-nation consortium producing the V2500 jet engine for narrow-body planes. Approximately 24% of UTC's sales are defense-related.

NYSE symbol: UTX
Incorporated: Delaware, 1934
Fiscal year ends: December 31

WHO

Chairman, President, CEO, and COO: Robert F. Daniell, age 56, $1,280,000 pay
EVP; President, Aerospace/Defense: Arthur E. Wegner, age 52, $735,000 pay
EVP; President, Commercial/Industrial: George A. L. David, age 47, $645,800 pay
EVP and CFO: John A. Rolls, age 48, $620,000 pay
Auditors: Price Waterhouse
Employees: 201,400

WHEN

In 1925 Frederick Rentschler and engine designer George Mead founded Pratt & Whitney Aircraft, precursor of United Technologies, in Hartford, Connecticut, to develop aircraft engines. Rentschler merged P&W with William Boeing's Seattle-based Boeing Airplane Company and with Chance Vought Corporation in 1929 to form United Aircraft & Transport. United Aircraft soon acquired other aviation manufacturers, including Hamilton Aero, Standard Steel Propeller, and Sikorsky Aviation.

In 1934, after congressional investigations led to new antitrust laws, United Aircraft's management split the corporation into 3 independent companies: United Airlines in Chicago, Boeing Airplane Company in Seattle, and United Aircraft in Hartford. United Aircraft retained P&W and several of Rentschler's other manufacturing interests.

During WWII, United Aircraft produced half the engines used by US warplanes. Igor Sikorsky developed helicopters, and Vought produced the Corsair and Cutlass airplanes. After an initial postwar decline in sales, the company retooled for production of jet engines. United Aircraft spun off Chance Vought in 1954. In 1958 United purchased Norden-Ketay Corporation, a manufacturer of aeronautical electronics.

In the late 1960s engines produced for the Boeing 747 proved costly for P&W when a design flaw sparked an expensive return to the drawing boards. A concerned board of directors appointed Harry Gray, a 17-year Litton Industries executive, as president in 1971. Taking a page from the Litton script, Gray turned the company into a conglomerate, renaming it United Technologies Corporation (UTC) in 1975. To decrease UTC's dependence on government business, Gray diversified the company with numerous purchases, including Otis Elevator Company (1975) and Carrier Corporation, a large heating and air-conditioning company (1979). By 1986 Gray's acquisitions had expanded the company's sales to $15.7 billion. Gray, under pressure from his board to name a successor, tapped Bob Daniell in 1986. Gray retired a year later.

Daniell, a 25-year Sikorsky veteran, emphasized profitability rather than growth, selling many businesses (such as Mostek, a semiconductor firm) and implementing layoffs and management changes. To revamp UTC, Daniell flattened the organizational chart, gave workers more responsibility, and stressed customer contact and training for employees. P&W, crown jewel of the company, had lost market share in the mid-1980s, but by 1989 had regained the lead in commercial and military jet engines from General Electric.

WHERE

HQ: United Technologies Bldg., Hartford, CT 06101
Phone: 203-728-7000
FAX: 203-728-7979

UTC operates plants throughout the world.

	1989 Sales		1989 Operating Income	
	$ mil	% of total	$ mil	% of total
US	14,403	69	880	54
Europe	3,101	15	361	22
Other	3,406	16	391	24
Adjustments	(1,296)	—	(168)	—
Total	**19,614**	**100**	**1,464**	**100**

WHAT

	1989 Sales		1989 Operating Income	
	$ mil	% of total	$ mil	% of total
Jet engines	6,991	35	947	59
Flight systems	3,592	18	56	4
Building systems	7,261	36	481	30
Other industrial products	1,932	10	158	10
Other	217	1	(55)	(3)
Adjustments	(379)	—	(123)	—
Total	**19,614**	**100**	**1,464**	**100**

Brand Names
Carrier (heating, air conditioning)
Hamilton Standard (engine controls, flight systems)
Missile and Space Systems (rocket boosters)
Norden (radar and displays)
Otis (elevators, escalators)
Pratt & Whitney (engines and parts)
Sikorsky (helicopters and parts)

Jet Engines		**Helicopters**
F100	JT8D-200	Black Hawk
F117	JT9D	CH-53E Super Stallion
F404	PW2000	Jayhawk/Seahawk
IAE V2500	PW4000	MH-53E Sea Dragon
J52		S-76

HOW MUCH

	9 Yr. Growth	1980	1981	1982	1983	1984	1985	1986	1987	1988	1989
Sales ($ mil)	5.3%	12,324	13,668	13,577	14,669	16,332	14,992	15,669	17,170	18,088	19,614
Net income ($ mil)	6.6%	393	458	427	509	645	636	48	592	659	702
Income as % of sales	—	3.2%	3.3%	3.1%	3.5%	4.0%	4.2%	0.3%	3.4%	3.6%	3.6%
Earnings per share ($)	5.3%	3.26	3.53	3.21	3.74	4.70	4.58	0.36	4.52	5.05	5.20
Stock price – high ($)	—	31.56	32.88	29.44	38.38	41.63	46.50	56.25	60.50	42.63	57.38
Stock price – low ($)	—	18.56	20.00	15.63	26.94	28.50	34.50	39.25	30.00	33.00	39.88
Stock price – close ($)	6.6%	30.50	20.88	28.31	36.25	36.25	43.75	46.00	33.88	41.13	54.25
P/E – high	—	10	9	9	10	9	10	156	13	8	11
P/E – low	—	6	6	5	7	6	8	109	7	7	8
Dividends per share ($)	4.3%	1.10	1.20	1.20	1.28	1.38	1.40	1.40	1.40	1.55	1.60
Book value per share ($)	6.7%	21.80	23.72	25.64	27.19	30.01	31.29	29.14	32.90	36.88	39.14

1989 Year End:
Debt ratio: 29.2%
Return on equity: 13.7%
Cash (mil): $267
Current ratio: 1.33
Long-term debt (mil): $1,960
Number of shares (mil): 121
Dividends:
1989 average yield: 3.0%
1989 payout: 30.8%
Market value (mil): $6,569

Stock Price History high/low 1980-89

70 60 50 40 30 20 10 0

RANKINGS

17th in *Fortune* 500 Industrial Cos.
48th in *Fortune* Global 500 Industrial Cos.
8th in *Fortune* 50 Exporters
25th in *Forbes* Sales 500
79th in *Business Week* 1000
247th in *Business Week* Global 1000

COMPETITION

Allied-Signal	General Electric	Raytheon
American Standard	Lockheed	Rockwell International
Boeing	Martin Marietta	Textron
Daimler-Benz	McDonnell Douglas	Thiokol
Fiat	Mitsubishi	Westinghouse
General Dynamics	Northrop	

UNITED TELECOMMUNICATIONS, INC.

OVERVIEW

United Telecommunications is the nation's 9th largest telephone company, providing local phone services in 17 states to nearly 4 million lines. United is the 2nd largest non-Bell telephone company after GTE.

United owns 80.1% of US Sprint, the nation's 3rd largest long-distance provider, with 10% of the market, and has announced plans to purchase the remainder. When United completes the transaction, it will change its name to Sprint Corporation. Through Sprint the company owns Telenet, the largest data communications network in the world. Sprint provides service throughout the US and internationally and, through recently purchased subsidiary Private Transatlantic Telecommunications Systems Inc., owns 50% of a transatlantic fiber optic cable. Through a long-term government contract, Sprint provides phone services to the US government.

United publishes telephone directories and distributes telecommunications equipment through its North Supply subsidiary. United also provides operator services.

Sprint's unexpected 2nd quarter 1990 earnings drop caused United's stock to lose over 30% of its value and prompted several shareholder suits.

NYSE symbol: UT
Incorporated: Kansas, 1938
Fiscal year ends: December 31

WHO

Chairman: Paul H. Henson, age 64, $950,895 pay
President and CEO: William T. Esrey, age 50, $1,129,842 pay
President, Local Telecommunications Division: Curtis G. Fields, age 56, $487,206 pay
President, Long-Distance Division: Ronald T. LeMay, age 44, $417,257 pay
EVP and Chief Financial and Information Officer: Arthur B. Krause, age 48, $356,499 pay
Auditors: Ernst & Young
Employees: 41,359

WHEN

In 1899 Jacob and son Cleyson Brown received a franchise from the city of Abilene, Kansas, for one of the first non-Bell telephone companies in the West. Using poles from their electric utility, the men had their telephone company operational within 3 months. By 1903 they had 1,400 subscribers; their first long-distance circuit connected Abilene to Herington, Kansas.

Cleyson formed Union Electric Company to sell telephone equipment (1905), and a long-distance company, Home Telephone and Telegraph (1910). In 1911 he consolidated with other Kansas independents as United Telephone Company. That year he obtained capital from his fiercest competitor, Missouri and Kansas Telephone (later renamed Southwestern Bell), which bought 60% of United's stock. Missouri and Kansas could have seized control but feared antitrust regulation, and United continued to thrive.

WWI brought manpower and materials shortages that curtailed growth until its end, when Cleyson resumed acquisitions in Kansas. His electric utility was sold (1925) to finance telephony. Cleyson incorporated (1925) United Telephone and Electric and acquired more exchanges, even during the Great Depression while he was losing subscribers. By 1934 poor health had forced his retirement. WWII shortages also curtailed growth and created several years of order backlog, so acquisitions ceased until 1952, when United bought control of Investors Telephone, with operations in 8 states; further purchases followed.

In 1959 Carl Scupin took over the company. Concerned with United's antiquated equipment, Scupin offered dial service and person-to-person and collect calling. He installed the nation's first private electronic switch.

After Scupin's retirement (1964), president Paul Henson focused on satellite communications, nuclear power plants, and cable TV. He acquired North Electric (1965), the oldest independent telephone equipment manufacturer in the US; Automated Data Service (1967) to offer batch processing and time-sharing; and United Business Communications (1970) to sell telephone and data hardware (sold to Stromberg-Carlson in 1974). He renamed the company United Telecommunications (1971) and purchased Florida Telephone (1974).

United prospered through industry deregulation in the 1970s and the breakup of AT&T in 1983. In 1985 United acquired 50% of long-distance provider GTE Sprint, which was started in 1970 by Southern Pacific. GTE had acquired Sprint in 1983 but sold 1/2 due to Sprint's heavy losses.

WHERE

HQ: 2330 Shawnee Mission Pkwy., Westwood, KS 66205
Phone: 913-676-3000
FAX: 913-676-3281

United Telecom has nearly 4 million local customers in 17 states. US Sprint and North Supply operate throughout the US.

WHAT

	1989 Sales		1989 Operating Income	
	$ mil	% of total	$ mil	% of total
Local svcs.	2,637	34	635	70
Long-distance svcs.	4,324	56	227	25
Other	762	10	48	5
Adjustments	(174)	—	—	—
Total	**7,549**	**100**	**910**	**100**

Telephone Companies
Carolina Telephone and Telegraph Co.
Private Transatlantic Telecommunications Systems Inc.
Telenet
United Inter-Mountain Telephone Co.
United Telephone Co. of Arkansas
United Telephone Co. of the Carolinas
United Telephone Co. of Florida
United Telephone Co. of Indiana
United Telephone Co. of Iowa
United Telephone Co. of Kansas
United Telephone Co. of Minnesota
United Telephone Co. of Missouri
United Telephone Co. of New Jersey
United Telephone Co. of the Northwest
United Telephone Co. of Ohio
United Telephone Co. of Pennsylvania
United Telephone Co. of Texas
United Telephone Co. of the West
US Sprint (80.1%)

Other Companies
DirectoriesAmerica, Inc.
North Supply Co.

HOW MUCH

	9 Yr. Growth	1980	1981	1982	1983	1984	1985	1986	1987	1988	1989
Sales ($ mil)	16.5%	1,904	2,255	2,429	2,474	2,858	3,219	2,857	3,064	6,493	7,549
Net income ($ mil)	8.4%	175	206	202	233	216	21	187	(52)	142	363
Income as % of sales	—	9.2%	9.1%	8.3%	9.4%	7.6%	0.6%	6.6%	(1.7%)	2.2%	4.8%
Earnings per share ($)	4.3%	1.17	1.31	1.22	1.33	1.16	0.09	0.93	(0.28)	*0.68*	1.71
Stock price – high ($)	—	9.88	12.00	11.75	12.50	11.38	12.50	15.63	16.69	23.94	43.75
Stock price – low ($)	—	7.00	7.19	7.88	10.06	8.69	10.06	11.63	11.75	12.13	22.00
Stock price – close ($)	17.9%	8.63	10.88	10.44	10.56	11.13	11.88	12.75	12.31	23.19	38.00
P/E – high	—	8	9	10	9	10	139	17	—	35	26
P/E – low	—	6	5	6	8	7	112	13	—	18	13
Dividends per share ($)	2.7%	0.78	0.82	0.86	0.90	0.94	0.96	0.96	0.96	0.96	1.00
Book value per share ($)	2.0%	8.37	9.14	9.21	9.69	9.48	8.81	8.75	7.58	9.13	10.01

1989 Year End:
Debt ratio: 64.3%
Return on equity: 17.9%
Cash (mil): $115
Current ratio: 0.66
Long-term debt (mil): $3,747
Number of shares (mil): 207
Dividends:
1989 average yield: 2.6%
1989 payout: 58.2%
Market value (mil): $7,870

Stock Price History high/low 1980-89

RANKINGS

6th in *Fortune* 100 Diversified Service Cos.
106th in *Forbes* Sales 500
63rd in *Business Week* 1000
171st in *Business Week* Global 1000

COMPETITION

Ameritech	Dun & Bradstreet	Pacific Telesis
AT&T	GTE	Southwestern Bell
Bell Atlantic	MCI	U S West
BellSouth	NYNEX	

UNITED WAY OF AMERICA

OVERVIEW

United Way of America is a nonprofit service agency that provides assistance to local United Way chapters across the country. There are about 2,300 local United Way chapters, each of which is an independent, autonomous organization that coordinates its own fundraising campaigns to support numerous agencies and causes (such as the American Red Cross, Easter Seals, and YMCA). In addition to its headquarters in Alexandria, Virginia, United Way maintains 5 regional offices.

The national organization is directed by a voluntary board of governors and an executive committee. Funding comes primarily from member chapters, who pay 1% of total money raised to the United Way. Other sources of income include program services fees, conferences, sales of supplies, and private sources, such as NFL Charities, which has raised over $1.3 million for the United Way since 1975.

As part of its Second Century Initiative, the United Way is committing its prodigious resources to combating such crucial problems as drug abuse, homelessness, and illiteracy. In 1989 United Way chapters raised almost $3 billion.

WHEN

United Way traces its origins to the Charity Organizations Society, which was founded in Denver in 1887 to help coordinate the services of 22 local charitable agencies. The society raised $21,700 at its first fundraiser in 1888.

The Denver Society was followed by the first independent Jewish federation of agencies in Boston (1895) and Associated Charities in Pittsburgh (1908), which was organized to coordinate services for the urban poor. In 1910 a council was established in Columbus, Ohio, to better coordinate charitable services, and the following year the National Association of Societies for Organizing Charity was formed to provide a channel of communication between social agencies. In 1913 the Federation for Charity and Philanthropy was created in Cleveland; its practice of raising funds from all social classes and allocating them according to need would serve as a model for the present-day United Way.

In 1918 representatives from 12 fundraising organizations met in Chicago and established the American Association for Community Organizations (AACO), which changed its name to the Association of Community Chests and Councils (ACCC) in 1927 (shortened to CCC in 1933). By 1929 there were 353 Community Chest organizations in the US.

In 1943 the government introduced payroll deductions for charitable contributions, which allowed every worker to become a philanthropist. By 1948 there were more than 1,000 Community Chests, raising almost $182 million. Community Chests formed a cooperative relationship with the AFL and CIO in 1946, and in 1955 the AFL-CIO Services Committee was created. In 1949 the Detroit organization adopted the name United Fund.

In 1963 Los Angeles became the first city to adopt the United Way name when over 30 local Community Chests and United Funds merged. By 1967, 31,300 agencies serving 27.5 million families were affiliated with United Way. The CCC reorganized as United Way of America in 1970; established its headquarters in Alexandria, Virginia, in 1971; and in the early 1970s introduced the person/hand/rainbow logo.

United Way established a set of operating standards for community service agencies in 1973. The next year the organization launched the largest public service campaign in US history (which included its first public service announcements in conjunction with the National Football League) and established United Way International to facilitate the formation of United Way organizations worldwide. That same year United Way became the first single organization to raise over $1 billion in an annual fundraising campaign.

When Congress made its first emergency food and shelter grant to the private sector in 1983 ($50 million), United Way was selected as the fiscal agent. As a result of the grant, over 51 million meals and almost 7 million nights' shelter were provided to the needy. In 1985 United Way raised $2.33 billion and published *Rethinking Tomorrow and Beyond*, which outlined the organization's future visions. The US Postal Service recognized the organization's centennial by issuing a United Way postage stamp in 1987. As it enters its 2nd century of operation, United Way hopes to double its financial and human resources.

HOW MUCH

	9 Yr. Growth	1980	1981	1982	1983	1984	1985	1986	1987	1988	1989
National amount raised ($ mil)	7.7%	1,526	1,680	1,780	1,950	2,145	2,330	2,440	2,600	2,780	2,980
Increase over prev. yr.	—	7.2%	10.1%	6.0%	9.5%	10.0%	9.0%	5.7%	6.4%	6.9%	7.2%

1989 Year End:
Revenues ($ mil): $33
Assets (mil): $12

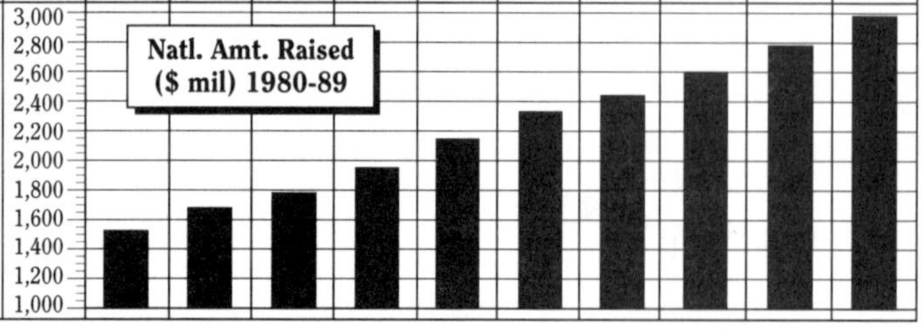

Natl. Amt. Raised ($ mil) 1980-89

Nonprofit organization
Incorporated: New York, 1932
Fiscal year ends: December 31

WHO

Chairman: Edward A. Brennan (Chairman and CEO, Sears, Roebuck & Co.)
VC: James D. Robinson III (Chairman, President, and CEO, American Express Co.)
VC: Morton Bahr (President, Communications Workers of America, AFL-CIO)
Chair-Elect (1990-1992): John F. Akers (Chairman, IBM Corp.)
President: William Aramony
Treasurer: Edward E. Phillips
Auditors: Arthur Andersen & Co.
Employees: 300

WHERE

HQ: 701 N. Fairfax St., Alexandria,VA 22314
Phone: 703-836-7100
FAX: 703-683-7840 (Public Relations)

UWA operates from its headquarters and 5 regional offices in the US. There are approximately 2,300 local chapters coast to coast.

WHAT

1989 Sources of income	% of total
Corporation and small-business employees	51
Corporations	23
Nonprofit and government employees	13
Other	6
Small businesses	3
Professionals	3
Noncorporate foundations	1
Total	**100**

1989 Distribution of funds

Recipient	% of total
Family service	22
Health	20
Youth and social development	18
Food/clothing/housing	9
Day care	7
Public safety	6
Community development	6
Income and jobs	5
Other	4
Education	3
Total	**100**

Representative recipients of United Way funds

Agencies for the Aged
American Red Cross
Association for Retarded Citizens
Big Brothers/Big Sisters
Boys Clubs
Boy Scouts
Camp Fire
Catholic Charities
Cerebral Palsy Associations
Child Welfare League
Easter Seal Societies
Girls Clubs
Girl Scouts
Goodwill Industries
Jewish Federations
Mental Health Associations
National Council on Alcoholism
National Recreation and Park Association
Salvation Army
Urban League
Visiting Nurse Associations
YMCA
YWCA

UNIVERSAL CORPORATION

OVERVIEW

Richmond, Virginia–based Universal, the world's largest tobacco dealer, purchases and processes leaf tobacco for sale to cigarette and other tobacco product companies. Additional operations include other agricultural products and title insurance.

Universal Leaf (the company's tobacco division) does not manufacture cigarettes or any other tobacco product. Rather, the company selects, buys, processes, packs, stores, and finances leaf tobacco on the account of, or for resale to, tobacco products manufacturers. The company has buyers in every domestic tobacco market and numerous foreign markets. The company also maintains a global sales force to serve foreign customers (mainly large firms or government monopolies). Philip Morris is the company's largest customer with 42% of US cigarette sales. In recent years the decline in US tobacco consumption has been offset by increases in developing nations.

Universal's agriproducts division (Deli) buys, ships, packs, stores, finances, and sells various agricultural products, including coffee, tea, rubber, and vegetable oil. The division also distributes and sells timber and other building products in the Netherlands and Belgium. The company's Blakely Peanut subsidiary buys and processes peanuts.

Universal's insurance division (Lawyers Title Insurance) issues both owner's and lender's title policies to protect customers against title defects on real property.

WHEN

In 1918 the American tobacco industry was booming because of increased cigarette demand resulting from WWI and the recent invention of a successful machine for making cigars. Universal Leaf was formed that year to consolidate and expand the J.P. Taylor Company (tobacco buyer, incorporated in North Carolina in 1904). Universal quickly acquired interests in a number of other competitors.

During the 1930s Universal was the 3rd largest buyer of burley (a type of leaf tobacco) 5 out of 9 years and also the 3rd largest buyer of flue-cured tobacco in 1938 and 1939. During this decade the company acquired Philip Morris as a customer. Universal financed the tobacco for Philip Morris, which was trying to win market share against more established names. Today industry leader Philip Morris remains a loyal customer from which Universal derives over 10% of its revenues.

By 1940 the company was purchasing as much leaf tobacco as any other domestic company. That year the US government filed charges of violation of the Sherman Antitrust Act against Universal and 7 other tobacco companies. Three of them (American, Liggett & Myers, and Reynolds) stood trial for the whole group, and, 4 years later, each of the 8 was fined $15,000.

Universal continued to grow during the next several decades by concentrating on its business of buying and selling tobacco. It diversified in 1968, buying Inta-Roto Machine (which manufactures packaging machinery and steel cylinders for printing fabrics) and Overton Container (tobacco containers). Shortly thereafter, Universal acquired a division of Usry Inc. (modular buildings).

The company attempted to diversify further in 1980 when it purchased Royster (fertilizer, sold in 1984 after poor returns). Universal entered the insurance industry in 1984 by buying Lawyers Title (Richmond, Virginia) and Continental Land Title (Universal City, California) together for $115 million. In 1986 the company acquired Netherlands-based Deli (timber and building products) for $48 million. Universal bought Thorpe and Ricks (a North Carolina tobacco processor) in 1988, and in 1990 announced its intention to buy Gebruder Kulenkamff, a $200 million sales German tobacco company that will give Universal a greater presence in the opening East European market.

HOW MUCH

	9 Yr. Growth	1980	1981	1982	1983	1984	1985	1986	1987	1988	1989
Sales ($ mil)	12.7%	992	1,040	1,253	1,082	1,019	1,079	1,145	2,116	2,420	2,920
Net income ($ mil)	7.4%	28	31	34	37	38	46	47	56	61	54
Income as % of sales	—	2.9%	3.0%	2.7%	3.4%	3.8%	4.3%	4.1%	2.6%	2.5%	1.9%
Earnings per share ($)	8.0%	1.60	1.78	1.97	2.11	2.21	2.66	2.74	3.25	3.56	3.19
Stock price – high ($)	—	17.13	17.44	17.00	21.13	22.00	24.50	31.00	36.75	33.75	39.00
Stock price – low ($)	—	7.75	10.88	11.25	13.25	15.25	18.75	23.25	25.63	27.88	33.00
Stock price – close ($)	9.1%	16.19	12.13	13.31	17.19	19.88	24.25	26.88	30.88	33.00	35.50
P/E – high	—	11	10	9	10	10	9	11	11	9	12
P/E – low	—	5	6	6	6	7	7	8	8	8	10
Dividends per share ($)	9.0%	0.63	0.71	0.79	0.85	0.90	0.96	1.04	1.12	1.25	1.37
Book value per share ($)	10.7%	9.10	10.16	11.32	12.35	13.48	15.17	17.08	18.94	21.04	22.82

1989 Year End:
Debt ratio: 18.1%
Return on equity: 14.5%
Cash (mil): $68
Current ratio: 1.46
Long-term debt (mil): $85
Number of shares (mil): 17
Dividends:
1989 average yield: 3.9%
1989 payout: 42.9%
Market value (mil): $601

Stock Price History high/low 1980-89

NYSE symbol: UVV
Incorporated: Virginia, 1918
Fiscal year ends: June 30

WHO

Chairman: Gordon L. Crenshaw, age 68, $258,873 pay
President and CEO: Henry H. Harrell, age 50, $481,492 pay
EVP: Allen B. King, age 44, $296,251 pay
VP and Treasurer: Houtwell H. Roper, age 42
Auditors: Ernst & Young
Employees: 20,000

WHERE

HQ: Hamilton St. at Broad, Richmond, VA 23230
Phone: 804-359-9311
FAX: 804-254-3584

The company is engaged in selecting, buying, shipping, processing, storing, financing, and selling tobacco in 26 countries. Its title insurance business is licensed in 49 states and in several Canadian provinces and Caribbean islands.

	1989 Sales		1989 Operating Income	
	$ mil	% of total	$ mil	% of total
US	1,863	64	53	47
South/Central America	97	3	21	18
Western Europe	828	28	34	30
Other	132	5	6	5
Adjustments	—	—	(9)	—
Total	**2,920**	**100**	**105**	**100**

WHAT

	1989 Sales		1989 Operating Income	
	$ mil	% of total	$ mil	% of total
Tobacco	1,526	52	93	82
Title insurance	458	16	(1)	(1)
Agriproducts	936	32	22	19
Adjustments	—	—	(9)	—
Total	**2,920**	**100**	**105**	**100**

Tobacco Products
Air-cured
Burley
Chewing
Cigar
Dark air-cured
Dark-fired
Flue-cured
Maryland

Title Insurance
Lawyers Title

Agricultural Products
Cocoa
Coffee
Oilseeds
Peanuts
Rubber
Sunflower seeds
Tea
Timber
Vegetable oils

RANKINGS

155th in *Fortune* 500 Industrial Cos.
292nd in *Forbes* Sales 500
756th in *Business Week* 1000

COMPETITION

Archer-Daniels-Midland
Cargill
ConAgra
Other agribusinesses

THE UNIVERSITY OF CHICAGO

OVERVIEW

Founded in 1891, the University of Chicago is among the youngest of America's major universities. It is a private, nonsectarian, coeducational institution devoted to research and teaching. Unlike many of America's colleges that in the 1960s and 1970s allowed students to select and even create their own courses, the university has been unwavering in its approach to undergraduate education. Its "common core" of courses ensures that every student receives exposure to the social, physical, and biological sciences and the humanities.

The university is known as the "teacher of teachers"; more than 81% of its undergraduate class of 1988 planned to go on to graduate studies. Many distinguished scholars have been associated with the university, including 57 Nobel laureates (among them, Milton Friedman and Saul Bellow), and more than 70 alumni serve as leaders of other colleges and universities. Among its strongest disciplines are sociology (in which it was a pioneer), archeology, economics, and the sciences. It is active in adult continuing education and operates the largest and most active university press in the country.

Despite the university's early reputation as a hotbed of radicalism, the "Chicago school" of thought, characterized by a free-market, conservative philosophy, is exemplified in the university's economics and law faculties.

WHEN

The first University of Chicago was a small Baptist school (1858-1886). The name was appropriated later, when a $600,000 gift from John D. Rockefeller, $400,000 in contributions from members of the American Baptist Education Society, and land donated by department store owner Marshall Field made possible the creation of the University of Chicago in 1891.

William Rainey Harper, a noted Bible scholar, was the university's first president. On October 1, 1892, the university opened with a faculty of 103, including 8 former college presidents, and 594 students.

While intellectual in outlook, the university organized its first football team, under famed coach Amos Alonzo Stagg, the day it opened. Its first games were against high school and YMCA teams, and at times the coach had to play in order to field enough men. The team won one game its first season. Improving in later seasons and earning the nickname "Monsters of the Midway," the team became a member of the Big 10. It later relapsed to its losing ways and withdrew from intercollegiate play in 1939.

So enthusiastic was the response to the new university that 4 years after its founding, its enrollment of 1,815 exceeded Harvard's. By 1907 enrollment was 5,038, with 43% women. Rockefeller continued to contribute to the university ($36 million by 1916), enabling the university to expand in size and intellectual influence under Harper and his successor, Harry Pratt Judson.

The university's greatest intellectual flowering came with Robert Maynard Hutchins's presidency (1929-1951), during which he revolutionized the university and American higher education by insisting on the study of original sources (the Great Books) and competency testing through comprehensive exams.

He organized the college and graduate divisions into their present structure, reaffirmed the role of the university as a place for intellectual exploration rather than vocational training. It was during his tenure, in 1942, that the nuclear age began when Enrico Fermi created the first self-sustaining nuclear chain reaction in the abandoned football stadium.

From the 1950s through the 1970s the university consolidated its position as one of the world's great centers of learning and successfully stemmed the tide of urban decay encroaching on its South-Side Chicago campus. During this time, it purchased and restored Frank Lloyd Wright's famed Robie House (now used by the Alumni Association), built the Joseph Regenstein Library (1970), and reinstated intercollegiate football (1969). Since 1978 the University has been led by Hanna Gray, until recently the only woman president of a major university. The University is currently preparing to celebrate its centennial with a series of academic and cultural events.

HOW MUCH

	9 Yr. Growth	1980	1981	1982	1983	1984	1985	1986	1987	1988	1989
Enrollment	1.6%	9,236	9,182	9,336	9,096	9,087	9,465	9,783	10,217	10,431	10,625
Faculty	0.5%	1,147	1,138	1,144	1,129	1,123	1,129	1,156	1,166	1,178	1,200
Student/faculty ratio	—	8.1	8.1	8.2	8.1	8.1	8.4	8.5	8.8	8.9	8.9
First-year tuition ($)	12.4%	4,500	5,100	6,000	7,050	7,920	8,670	9,600	11,352	12,120	12,930
Endowment market value ($ mil)	12.3%	343	397	394	541	517	641	801	914	898	974

First-Year Tuition ($) 1980-89

14,000
12,000
10,000
8,000
6,000
4,000
2,000
0

Private university
Founded: 1891
Fiscal year ends: June 30
Motto: Crescat Scientia Vita Excolatur

WHO

President: Hanna H. Gray, age 59, $208,000 pay in 1988
VP Business and Finance: Alexander E. Sharp
Auditors: KPMG Peat Marwick
Employees: 3,594

WHERE

HQ: 5801 S. Ellis Ave., Chicago, IL 60637
Phone: 312-702-1234
FAX: 312-702-8324

The university has a 175-acre campus in the Hyde Park neighborhood on Chicago's South Side, maintains a downtown Chicago campus, and owns Yerkes Observatory in Williams Bay, Wisconsin.

Geographic Distribution of Students	% of Total
Midwest	42
Mid-Atlantic	24
West	10
New England	10
South & Southwest	12
Foreign	2
Total	**100**

WHAT

	1989 Revenues	
	$ mil	% of total
Tuition & fees	129	36
Government grants	33	9
Private gifts	9	2
Endowment income	14	4
Educational activities	72	20
Auxiliary activities	81	22
Other	24	7
Total	**362**	**100**

Academic Unit	1989 Enrollment	% of Total
The College	3,332	31
Graduate Divisions		
Biological Sciences	282	3
Physical Sciences	482	5
Humanities	792	8
Social Sciences	1,219	11
Professional Schools		
Business	2,571	24
Divinity	294	3
Law	556	5
Library Science	38	—
Medicine	427	4
Public Policy	84	1
Social Service	255	2
Nondegree	293	3
Total	**10,625**	**100**

Affiliated Institutions

Argonne National Laboratory
Bergmann Gallery
Court Theatre
Enrico Fermi Institute
James Franck Institute
Laboratory School
Midway Studios
National Opinion Research Center
Office of Continuing Education
Oriental Institute
Smart Gallery
The University of Chicago Medical Center
The University of Chicago Press
Yerkes Observatory

COMPETITION

Harvard
Stanford
Ohio State
University of Texas

THE UNIVERSITY OF TEXAS AT AUSTIN

OVERVIEW

The University of Texas, #2 in enrollment size among US universities (after Ohio State), is funded by royalties earned on West Texas oil. UT has 21 science and engineering research labs and is a partner in several technology consortiums. Its new Texas Center for Writers is funded with over $4.5 million in gifts from writer James Michener. UT's privately funded faculty endowments numbered 1,022 at the end of 1989.

In 1989 UT faculty included 2 Nobel and 2 Pulitzer Prize winners, 17 scholars of the National Academy of Sciences, 28 of the National Academy of Engineering, 17 of the American Academy of Arts and Sciences, and 19 members of the American Law Institute among its almost 20,000 faculty and staff. Over 50,000 students enrolled in 6,500 courses, with UT ranked 2nd in enrollment of new National Merit scholars (217).

UT saw enrollment drop to 49,618 for fall 1990 due to long-term enrollment controls, including stricter admissions and transfer standards as part of the university's emphasis on undergraduate education.

Public university
Founded: 1883
Fiscal year ends: August 31

WHO

Chairman, Board of Regents: Louis A. Beecherl, Jr.
President: William H. Cunningham
EVP and Provost: Gerhard J. Fonken
VP Business Affairs: G. Charles Franklin
Auditors: Texas State Auditor
Employees: 19,117

WHERE

HQ: UT Station, Austin, TX 78713
Phone: 512-471-1506
FAX: 512-471-9241

The University of Texas at Austin has a main campus with 118 buildings on 357 acres in central Austin. Other facilities in or near Austin include a biological field lab and married student housing on a 445-acre tract and a research center and technology incubator on 94 acres.

	Geographic Distribution of Students	
	1989 enrollment	% of total
Texas	41,191	82
Other US	5,483	11
Foreign	3,571	7
Total	**50,245**	**100**

WHEN

In 1836 the Texas Declaration of Independence admonished Mexico for having failed to establish a public education system in Texas territory, yet over 40 more years passed before Texas had a university. In 1880 the statute creating the university was adopted, and in 1881 Texans voted to locate the main university in Austin. The first 2 departments, law and academic, were organized in 1882, and the first classes met in partitioned rooms of the capitol in 1883, with 8 professors teaching 218 students.

The school's first building, Old Main, opened in 1884, and in 1891 the school's medical branch opened. By 1894 UT had enrolled 534 students and hired its first football coach. The *Ranger*, a student newspaper first published in 1900, became the *Daily Texan* in 1916. In 1905 the College of Education opened, followed by the Graduate School (1910) and the College of Business Administration (1924).

UT's financial needs were met in 1923 when the Santa Rita, a well in the West Texas desert given to UT by the legislature, hit oil. The income from oil production became the Permanent University Fund (PUF), from which only interest on the revenues could be used, 2/3 by UT and 1/3 by Texas A&M University. By 1926 UT's oil royalties were over $4 million, twice as much as UT's state funding ($1.8 million). In 1928 Herman Joseph Muller won a Nobel Prize for genetic research he had done at UT. In 1933, 9 new buildings were dedicated. The Tower was built in 1937 to replace Old Main, and in 1938 the College of Fine Arts opened. By 1940 the PUF was over $100 million. In the 1940s and 1950s, the Graduate Schools of Library Science and Social Work opened, as did the School of Architecture.

In 1946 Heman Sweatt was denied admission to the law school because he was black, beginning a fight that ended with a Supreme Court order that UT admit him in 1950. UT hired its first black professor in 1964.

The College of Communication opened in 1965. Tragedy struck the school in 1966 when Charles Whitman shot 47 people from the Tower, killing 16, before he was killed by a policeman. The late 1960s and early 1970s brought student unrest to UT, related to the Vietnam War, environmental and race issues, and even the quality of food on campus. In 1969 the Longhorn football team became the national champions, and UT alumnus Alan Bean became the 4th man on the moon.

In 1970 and 1971 the Lyndon Baines Johnson School of Public Affairs and the LBJ Library opened. In 1978 UT bought one of only 5 Gutenberg Bibles in the US for $2.4 million.

UT celebrated its centennial in 1983, creating many new faculty endowments. By 1989 the Lady Longhorn teams had won 15 national team titles.

WHAT

	1989 Revenues	
	$ mil	% of total
General appropriations (taxes)	195	31
Sponsored research & services	127	21
Dormitories, athletics, student union	96	16
Permanent university fund income (oil)	76	12
Gifts, grants & designated funds	66	11
Tuition	33	5
Overhead for sponsored projects	20	3
Other & agency income	6	1
Total	**619**	**100**

Academic Unit	1989 Enrollment
Architecture	615
Business	10,235
Communication	4,209
Education	3,170
Engineering	6,422
Fine Arts	2,085
Law	1,589
Liberal Arts	12,376
Library/Info Science	288
Natural Sciences	7,304
Nursing	649
Pharmacy	599
Public Affairs	238
Social Work	466
Total	**50,245**

Affiliated Institutions

Archer M. Huntington Art Gallery
Balcones Research Center
Harry Ransom Humanities Research Center
Institute for Geophysics
LBJ Library and Museum
LBJ School of Public Affairs
Marine Science Institute
McDonald Observatory
Montopolis Research Center
Paisano Ranch
Texas Center for Writers
Texas Memorial Museum
Winedale Historical Center

HOW MUCH

	9 Yr. Growth	1980	1981	1982	1983	1984	1985	1986	1987	1988	1989
Enrollment	9.0%	46,148	48,145	48,039	47,631	47,973	47,838	46,140	47,743	50,107	50,245
Faculty	9.0%	2,090	2,105	2,188	2,191	2,278	2,189	2,215	2,215	2,245	2,273
Student/faculty ratio	—	22.4	22.2	22.2	21.5	21.4	21.1	20.5	21.7	22.3	21.9
Tuition & fees ($)	8.3%	396	396	396	406	419	621	731	739	742	811
% receiving financial aid	—	—	—	—	—	44.8%	46.7%	48.0%	47.7%	49.2%	—
Endowment market value ($ mil)*	14.0%	767	862	1,077	1,341	1,434	1,704	2,075	2,263	2,152	2,494

Tuition & Fees ($) 1980-89

*represents market value of endowment for entire University of Texas System

COMPETITION

Harvard
Ohio State
Stanford
University of Chicago

UNOCAL CORPORATION

OVERVIEW

Unocal, the 10th largest US petroleum company, styles itself as "an earth resources company," a California-esque description that embraces its alternative energy businesses as well as its oil activities.

It is the world's largest producer of geothermal energy. It owns 2 geothermal electricity plants in Southern California and is the major producer at a Northern California field. The company supplies geothermal steam in the Philippines. Unocal also produces synthetic crude from Colorado oil shale.

Unocal divides its North American oil drilling operations into 7 areas. The company also owns about 95% of a master limited partnership, Union Exploration Partners, that drills in the Gulf of Mexico.

It owns an interest in 5 US refineries, but, still recovering from its 1985 takeover defense, Unocal has shuttered one unprofitable facility. Unocal products are sold at more than 10,000 outlets in 45 states under the bright-orange-dot-and-blue-76 insignia.

WHEN

Not far from the 1859 Pennsylvania well that ushered in the modern oil industry, Lyman Stewart, just 19, hoped to finance Presbyterian evangelism by joining the boom. He plunked down $124 for a 1/8 interest in a Pennsylvania oil lease.

By the 1880s Stewart had put aside a religious career in favor of the oil business. He and partner Wallace Hardison headed for Southern California. When they united 3 oil companies in 1890, the result was Union Oil of California.

The fledgling company boasted a petroleum laboratory — the West's first — at its Santa Paula refinery. In 1901 one of its geologists discovered a trove of prehistoric bones in the La Brea tar pits. In 1903 Union Oil built the world's first oil tanker, a wooden ship outfitted with steel tanks.

As Union service stations multiplied in the 1930s, the company cast about for a new name for its gasoline. Lead in the gas added a reddish tinge and made the old brand name, White Magic, obsolete. An executive suggested 76 to conjure the spirit of America. The company recalled that spirit in a series of WWII advertisements that told the story of workers in all walks of life and declared: "America's fifth freedom is free enterprise."

In 1965 Union Oil of California acquired Pure Oil, formed in New Jersey in 1895 when independent refiners bristled at the dictates of the Standard Oil colossus. Pure Oil became the largest independent to challenge Standard. The merger with Pure Oil doubled Union's size.

Union operated the offshore well that produced the infamous 1969 Santa Barbara oil spill. The damage became a rallying point for the fledgling US environmental movement. During the 1970s Fred Hartley, named CEO in 1964, steered the company to develop alternative energy sources. Geothermal development proved profitable, but extracting oil from Colorado shale, underwritten by federal subsidies, has not lived up to company expectations.

The company adopted its Unocal nickname as the name for its corporate umbrella in 1983. In 1985 takeover artist T. Boone Pickens targeted Unocal, and the tenacious Hartley ran debt to more than $5.5 billion to repurchase almost 1/3 of Unocal's outstanding stock.

Unocal spent the rest of the 1980s coping with the debt. Hartley's successor, Richard Stegemeier, sold the Los Angeles headquarters complex (1988) and a Canadian coal mine (1989). Also in 1989 Unocal raised cash by transferring midwestern refining and marketing operations to UNO-VEN, a joint venture with a Petroleos de Venezuela subsidiary. In July 1990 the company purchased gas producing properties and processing plants from Placer Dome for $252 million.

HOW MUCH

	9 Yr. Growth	1980	1981	1982	1983	1984	1985	1986	1987	1988	1989
Sales ($ mil)	0.1%	9,984	10,746	10,390	10,066	10,838	10,738	7,482	8,466	8,853	10,056
Net income ($ mil)	(6.4%)	647	791	804	626	700	325	176	181	24	358
Income as % of sales	—	6.5%	7.4%	7.7%	6.2%	6.5%	3.0%	2.4%	2.1%	0.3%	3.6%
Earnings per share ($)	(2.1%)	1.86	2.28	2.32	1.80	2.02	1.18	0.76	0.78	0.11	1.53
Stock price – high ($)	—	28.25	23.00	18.94	18.81	21.63	25.50	14.13	22.50	20.19	31.25
Stock price – low ($)	—	10.47	14.13	10.63	13.50	15.00	12.81	7.81	10.50	14.25	18.69
Stock price – close ($)	3.2%	22.31	18.81	13.31	15.81	18.50	13.44	13.31	14.13	18.94	29.75
P/E – high	—	15	10	8	10	11	22	19	29	192	20
P/E – low	—	6	6	5	8	7	11	10	13	136	12
Dividends per share ($)	4.7%	0.36	0.43	0.50	0.50	0.50	0.58	0.55	0.50	0.50	0.55
Book value per share ($)	(0.2%)	10.02	11.85	13.66	14.91	16.39	7.01	7.23	7.58	9.26	9.83

1989 Year End:
Debt ratio: 62.8%
Return on equity: 16.0%
Cash (mil): $348
Current ratio: 1.35
Long-term debt (mil): $3,887
Number of shares (mil): 234
Dividends:
1989 average yield: 1.8%
1989 payout: 35.9%
Market value (mil): $6,961

Stock Price History high/low 1980-89

NYSE symbol: UCL
Incorporated: Delaware, 1983
Fiscal year ends: December 31

WHO

Chairman, President, and CEO: Richard J. Stegemeier, age 61, $1,064,769 pay
VC, EVP Administration, and CFO: Claude S. Brinegar, age 63, $652,107 pay
VP Corporate Human Resources: Wellman E. Branstrom, age 54
Auditors: Coopers & Lybrand
Employees: 17,286

WHERE

HQ: 1201 W. Fifth St., Los Angeles, CA 90017
Phone: 213-977-7600
FAX: 213-977-5362 (Personnel)

Most of Unocal's domestic oil and gas is produced in Alaska, California, Louisiana, Oklahoma, and Texas. The company also conducts exploration or production activities in 15 foreign countries.

	1989 Sales		1989 Operating Income	
	$ mil	% of total	$ mil	% of total
US	10,244	87	756	68
Foreign	1,532	13	351	32
Adjustments	(1,720)	—	(360)	—
Total	**10,056**	**100**	**747**	**100**

WHAT

	1989 Sales		1989 Operating Income	
	$ mil	% of total	$ mil	% of total
Chemicals	1,276	10	74	7
Exploration & production	2,853	22	744	67
Refining, mktg., & transportation	8,674	65	217	20
Metals	81	1	4	—
Geothermal	190	1	56	5
Other	122	1	12	1
Adjustments	(3,140)	—	(360)	—
Total	**10,056**	**100**	**747**	**100**

Principal Products & Activities
Crude oil and natural gas production
Fertilizers
Geothermal energy production
Graphite materials
Herbicides
Hydrocarbon solvents
Lanthanide mining
Molybdenum mining
Needle and sponge coke
Petroleum pipelining and refining
Real estate development
Service stations (Unocal 76)
Shale oil production
Vinyls and plastics
Wastewater treatment

RANKINGS

40th in *Fortune* 500 Industrial Cos.
109th in *Fortune* Global 500 Industrial Cos.
71st in *Forbes* Sales 500
73rd in *Business Week* 1000
260th in *Business Week* Global 1000

COMPETITION

Amoco
Ashland
Atlantic Richfield
British Petroleum
Chevron
Coastal
Du Pont
Exxon
Mobil
Occidental
Pennzoil
Phillips
Royal Dutch/Shell
Sun
Texaco
USX
Other oil, chemical, and mining companies

THE UPJOHN COMPANY

OVERVIEW

Upjohn of Kalamazoo, Michigan, is the maker of several well-known pharmaceuticals, including the pain-reliever Motrin (now sold nonprescription) and Rogaine (baldness treatment), one of the few prescription drugs advertised directly to the consumer. Besides pharmaceuticals, Upjohn produces animal health products, seeds, and chemicals and provides home health-care services. *Fortune* ranks Upjohn 10th in sales among US drug makers.

Like other companies, Upjohn markets foreign drug company products in the US and licenses its products to be sold overseas. Major alliances are the Japanese joint venture Chugai-Upjohn to sell Marogen (for treating a specific form of anemia) and an agreement with SmithKline Beecham to sell Eminase (for treating heart attacks). Foreign sales account for 33% of total sales.

Upjohn has 9 new investigational drug applications on file with the FDA as of January 1990. The company is developing new treatments for a specific type of anemia, viral and bacterial infections, cancers, head trauma, AIDS, and irregular heartbeat. The company conducts its own research at 3 labs, located in Kalamazoo, Japan, and the UK.

WHEN

Dr. William Upjohn formed the Upjohn Pill and Granule Company in partnership with his brothers in Kalamazoo, Michigan, in 1886. William's patented "friable" pill (which disintegrated readily after swallowing) was the basis for the company's success over early competitors. (Some pills of the day would not disintegrate when struck with a hammer.) Upjohn took its current name in 1902. Company stock was privately held, mostly by the Upjohn family, until the company went public in 1958. The company's most successful products at the beginning of the century were the antimalarial quinine and the Phenolax wafer, a candy-type laxative.

By 1912 annual sales had passed $1 million. Research initiated the following year led to the development of several new products, including Citrocarbonate, an effervescent antacid, which had sales of over $1 million in 1926. Other products included Cheracol cough syrup (1924), Kaopectate antidiarrheal (1936), and Unicap multivitamins (1940).

During WWII the company produced large amounts of penicillin and sulfanilamide. Research on steroids after the war eventually yielded important medicines for treating a variety of inflammatory conditions, including Medrol (methylprednisolone, 1956), which had fewer side effects than others.

Completion of a new manufacturing plant near Kalamazoo in 1951 at a cost of $33 million increased production by 1/3 and consolidated operations in one location. Increasing demand for the company's products overseas led to the formation of the Upjohn International Division in 1952. By 1955 annual sales had reached $100 million.

In 1957 Upjohn introduced Orinase, the first oral agent for diabetes. Introduced in 1959, Depo-Provera, a long-acting contraceptive, is sold by Upjohn throughout the world but has not been approved in the US because of fears over long-term effects. In the 1960s Upjohn combined its plant and animal health operations and acquired companies involved in agricultural products, home health care, and medical testing labs. A urethane plastics business acquired in 1962 was sold to Dow Chemical in 1985.

Motrin (generic name ibuprofen), an analgesic introduced in 1974, achieved greater first-year sales than any other drug and continued to be a top seller into the 1980s. The antidiabetic Micronase (1984) and the tranquilizers Xanax (1982) and Halcion (1983) have also sold well in the 1980s. In 1988 Upjohn marketed Rogaine, the first FDA-approved treatment for baldness.

HOW MUCH

	9 Yr. Growth	1980	1981	1982	1983	1984	1985	1986	1987	1988	1989
Sales ($ mil)	5.7%	1,768	1,903	1,836	1,993	2,188	2,017	2,291	2,530	2,754	2,916
Net income ($ mil)	6.9%	170	182	126	160	173	203	253	305	353	311
Income as % of sales	—	9.6%	9.6%	6.9%	8.0%	7.9%	10.1%	11.0%	12.1%	12.8%	10.7%
Earnings per share ($)	6.4%	0.95	1.01	0.70	0.88	0.95	1.10	1.35	1.63	1.90	1.67
Stock price – high ($)	—	11.33	11.50	9.90	11.46	12.02	23.58	35.42	53.75	35.25	42.13
Stock price – low ($)	—	6.92	7.60	6.33	7.71	7.50	11.13	20.58	22.63	26.88	27.63
Stock price – close ($)	14.6%	11.25	8.96	7.73	9.88	11.69	22.25	31.08	30.00	28.75	38.50
P/E – high	—	12	11	14	13	13	22	26	33	19	25
P/E – low	—	7	8	9	9	8	10	15	14	14	17
Dividends per share ($)	12.7%	0.31	0.33	0.38	0.38	0.43	0.44	0.50	0.58	0.76	0.91
Book value per share ($)	7.8%	4.82	5.34	5.37	5.79	6.17	6.96	7.85	8.95	9.83	9.44

1989 Year End:
Debt ratio: 12.9%
Return on equity: 17.3%
Cash (mil): $247
Current ratio: 1.78
Long-term debt (mil): $256
Number of shares (mil): 184
Dividends:
1989 average yield: 2.4%
1989 payout: 54.5%
Market value (mil): $7,081

Stock Price History high/low 1980-89

60
50
40
30
20
10
0

NYSE symbol: UPJ
Incorporated: Delaware, 1958
Fiscal year ends: December 31

WHO

Chairman, CEO, and President: Theodore Cooper, age 61, $1,187,071 pay
EVP: Mark Novitch, age 57, $340,615 pay
VP Finance and CFO: Robert C. Salisbury, age 46
Auditors: Coopers & Lybrand
Employees: 20,100

WHERE

HQ: 7000 Portage Rd., Kalamazoo, MI 49001
Phone: 616-323-4000
FAX: 616-323-7034

Upjohn has research, manufacturing, and marketing facilities in more than 200 locations worldwide.

	1989 Sales		1989 Operating Income	
	$ mil	% of total	$ mil	% of total
US	2,193	67	352	71
Europe	573	17	64	13
Japan & Pacific	327	10	52	10
Other foreign	213	6	31	6
Adjustments	(390)	—	12	—
Total	**2,916**	**100**	**511**	**100**

WHAT

	1989 Sales		1989 Operating Income	
	$ mil	% of total	$ mil	% of total
Human health care	2,333	80	462	94
Agriculture	574	20	28	6
Adjustments	9	—	21	—
Total	**2,916**	**100**	**511**	**100**

Brand Names

Prescription Drugs
Ansaid (arthritis drug)
Colestid (cholesterol-lowering drug)
Eminase (blood clot dissolver)
Halcion (sedative)
Marogen (red cell stimulant)
Micronase (diabetic drug)
Motrin (painkiller)
Provera (hormonal drug)
Rogaine (baldness treatment)
Xanax (tranquilizer)

Animal Drugs
Bovine somatotropin [BST] (lactation stimulant for cattle)

Consumer Products
Cheracol (cough syrup)
Cortaid (steroidal ointment)
Kaopectate (antidiarrheal drug)
Motrin IB (painkiller)
Unicap (vitamins)

RANKINGS

156th in *Fortune* 500 Industrial Cos.
420th in *Fortune* Global 500 Industrial Cos.
290th in *Forbes* Sales 500
78th in *Business Week* 1000
246th in *Business Week* Global 1000

COMPETITION

Abbott Labs
American Cyanamid
American Home Products
Baxter
Bayer
Bristol-Myers Squibb
Eli Lilly
Genentech
Glaxo
Hoechst
Johnson & Johnson
Merck
Monsanto
Pfizer
Procter & Gamble
Rhône-Poulenc
Roche Holding
Schering-Plough
SmithKline Beecham
Warner-Lambert

USAIR GROUP, INC.

OVERVIEW

With more departures per day than any other airline in the world except Aeroflot of the Soviet Union, USAir transported 61.2 million passengers in 1989 to more than 175 cities in 36 states, Puerto Rico, Canada, the Caribbean, and Western Europe. The company added nonstop flights from its 5 hubs to 16 US and 3 Caribbean destinations in 1989 and began service to West Germany in June 1990.

The airline is supported by USAir Express, a group of commuter airlines serving 115 airports in the US. With 1,500 daily departures, USAir Express carried about 6 million passengers in 1989, with 65% connecting to USAir flights. USAir also operates 6 nonairline subsidiaries that specialize in various aviation-related activities.

In February 1990 USAir and Piedmont Aviation completed one of the largest airline mergers in history. However, difficulties in integrating the 2 airlines' combined fleets (431 aircraft) and approximately 50,000 employees, coupled with the rising cost of jet fuel, contributed to USAir's $63 million loss in 1989, its only loss during the 1980s.

NYSE symbol: U
Incorporated: Delaware, 1983
Fiscal year ends: December 31

WHO

Chairman and President: Edwin I. Colodny, age 63, $570,673 pay
VC and EVP: Seth E. Schofield, age 50, $283,711 pay
VC and EVP: Randall Malin, age 52, $281,588 pay
VP Finance: William F. Loftus, age 51
Auditors: KPMG Peat Marwick
Employees: 53,700

WHEN

Pilot Richard C. du Pont (of the chemical dynasty) founded All American Aviation, a Washington, DC–based air mail service, in 1937. Serving small northeastern communities, All American picked up and delivered mail "on the fly," using a system of hooks and ropes. This service, begun in 1939, terminated in 1949, the year passenger service commenced.

The company changed its name to Allegheny Airlines in 1953, developing as a federally subsidized regional airline by serving communities too remote for major airline service in an area bounded by Boston, Washington, DC, Cleveland, and Detroit.

In 1959 Allegheny introduced no-reservations ticketing, allowing customers to receive discounts by purchasing time-stamped tickets immediately prior to flights, and in 1967 began its affiliation with Allegheny Commuters, which provided commuter service to Allegheny's system.

The company expanded to the Great Lakes area with its 1968 purchase of Indianapolis-based Lake Central Airlines, then in 1972 bought Mohawk Airlines, gaining routes in New York and along the East Coast. Allegheny was listed on the NYSE in 1978.

Edwin Colodny, formerly the airline's legal counsel and president, became chairman in 1978 when Henry Satterwhite retired after 25 years with the company. Colodny decided the best way to assure the airline's growth was to reemphasize its original purpose: shorter flights to smaller cities. He extended service to the South and in 1979 renamed the company USAir.

USAir augmented its commuter service by purchasing Pennsylvania Commuter Airlines (1985) and Suburban Airlines (1986). After rebuffing a takeover bid by TWA in 1987, USAir became America's 7th largest airline (in terms of passenger miles) by acquiring Piedmont Aviation, a major airline operating primarily in the Southeast, and Los Angeles–based PSA (Pacific Southwest Airlines). Piedmont's 2 commuters, Henson Aviation and Jetstream International Airlines, began operating as part of USAir Express in 1988.

In 1988 Colodny piloted the company through its 12th consecutive year of profitability and bought 11% of Covia Partnership, a joint venture established to operate United Airlines's Apollo computerized reservations system, for $113 million. In 1989 USAir offered its first transatlantic flight (Charlotte to London). However, further expansion plans are now on hold. The company has been losing money since mid-1989 and its on-time performance has been laggard. In August 1990 it furloughed about 3,600 employees and indicated that additional layoffs would follow.

WHERE

HQ: Crystal Park Four, 2345 Crystal Dr., Arlington, VA 22227
Phone: 703-418-5305
FAX: 703-418-5307 (Investor Relations)

USAir serves more than 175 cities and 135 airports in 36 states and 4 foreign countries.

Hub Locations

Baltimore, MD/ Washington, DC	Dayton, OH
Charlotte, NC/Douglas, NC	Philadelphia, PA
	Pittsburgh, PA

WHAT

	1989 Sales	
	$ mil	% of total
Passenger transportation	5,809	93
Other	443	7
Total	**6,252**	**100**

USAir, Inc.

USAir Express (Commuter Services)
Allegheny Commuter Airlines, Inc.
Henson Aviation, Inc.
Jetstream International Airlines, Inc.
Pennsylvania Commuter Airlines, Inc.

Support Services
Air Service, Inc.
Aviation Supply Corp.
Pacific Southwest Airmotive
Piedmont Aviation Services, Inc.
USAir Fuel Corp.
USAir Leasing and Services, Inc.
USAM Corp.

Flight Equipment	Owned	Leased	Total
USAir, Inc.			
BAe 146	4	17	21
Boeing 727	9	35	44
Boeing 737	115	97	212
Boeing 767	–	6	6
DC-9	60	14	74
Fokker 100	8	–	8
Fokker F-28	24	21	45
MD-80	15	16	31
Total	**235**	**206**	**441**

HOW MUCH

	9 Yr. Growth	1980	1981	1982	1983	1984	1985	1986	1987	1988	1989
Sales ($ mil)	23.0%	972	1,110	1,273	1,432	1,630	1,765	1,835	3,001	5,707	6,252
Net income ($ mil)	—	60	51	59	81	122	117	98	195	165	(63)
Income as % of sales	—	6.2%	4.6%	4.6%	5.6%	7.5%	6.6%	5.4%	6.5%	2.9%	(1.0%)
Earnings per share ($)	—	3.59	2.66	2.88	3.22	4.46	3.98	3.33	5.27	3.81	(1.36)
Stock price – high ($)	—	19.25	26.13	36.50	39.88	35.00	38.50	41.00	53.50	40.13	54.75
Stock price – low ($)	—	6.50	11.00	10.00	25.88	22.00	27.25	30.13	26.00	28.00	30.63
Stock price – close ($)	7.4%	17.50	11.88	33.25	31.75	33.25	34.38	36.25	33.75	34.50	33.38
P/E – high	—	5	10	13	12	8	10	12	10	11	—
P/E – low	—	2	4	3	8	5	7	9	5	7	—
Dividends per share ($)	3.2%	0.09	0.12	0.12	0.12	0.12	0.12	0.12	0.12	0.12	0.12
Book value per share ($)	9.6%	18.71	20.45	22.97	26.82	31.92	35.47	38.78	43.90	47.28	42.86

1989 Year End:
Debt ratio: 43.7%
Return on equity: —
Cash (mil): $15
Current ratio: 0.59
Long-term debt (mil): $1,468
Number of shares (mil): 44
Dividends:
1989 average yield: 0.4%
1989 payout: —
Market value (mil): $1,474

RANKINGS

9th in *Fortune* 50 Transportation Cos.
133rd in *Forbes* Sales 500
423rd in *Business Week* 1000

COMPETITION

America West	Midway	Southwest
AMR	NWA	TWA
Continental	Pan Am	UAL
Delta		

USF&G CORPORATION

OVERVIEW

USF&G, the 23rd largest diversified financial services company ($13.6 billion in 1989 assets), provides property/casualty insurance, life insurance, and investment management services. The company's largest subsidiary, United States Fidelity and Guaranty, is the 13th largest US property/casualty insurer based on premiums written.

The company's property/casualty insurance operations include underwriting, marketing, and claims services in 54 branch offices and 112 claim offices in the US. Property/casualty business represented almost 87% of USF&G's $4.7 billion total revenues in 1989.

Life insurance operations through Fidelity and Guaranty Life and Thomas Jefferson Life contributed 9%, or $410 million, of the company's revenues in 1989.

USF&G's Financial Services Corporation includes 20 companies providing investment management, real estate and leasing, and consulting services to businesses and institutions. The subsidiary had about $30 billion in assets under management at the end of 1989 and contributed $182 million in revenues (4% of USF&G's total revenues).

In recent years USF&G has tried to increase awareness through TV advertising.

WHEN

In 1896 Baltimore businessman John Bland had the idea of selling businesses a list of attorneys bonded by a surety company. He formed United States Fidelity and Guaranty Company to write surety bonds guaranteeing prompt remittance of money collected by attorneys for mercantile houses.

In 1900 the company added burglary insurance to operations that already had expanded to include the entire country. The company grew through a network of independent agents, many of whom were personally selected by Bland. By 1903 USF&G was also doing business in Alaska, Hawaii, and Canada. In 1906 the company moved to a larger facility.

Following the introduction of the automobile and enactment of workman's compensation laws, the company added casualty insurance in 1910. Within 5 years casualty insurance premiums equaled the combined total premiums of fidelity (bonds covering employee dishonesty), surety, and burglary insurance. In 1920 the company first offered fire and inland marine insurance.

In 1952, following the purchase of Fidelity and Guaranty Fire Insurance, the company was able to write all lines of property insurance. During the 1950s the company established new branches and further developed its agency force. In 1960 it formed F&G Life in response to requests from agents and branch offices, and in 1962 bought New York–based Merchants Fire Assurance and Merchants Indemnity. In 1969 USF&G purchased Thomas Jefferson Life Insurance from First Executive Corporation.

In the early 1970s the company centralized operations in Baltimore with a new building that anchored the project to revitalize the inner harbor area of the city. In 1975 the company experienced record losses of about $1 million per month but in 1978 was back on track with the highest underwriting profits of any stock insurance company.

In 1981 the life insurance business and property/casualty operation became part of USF&G, a holding company formed that year. In 1985 USF&G created USF&G Financial Services Corporation to provide investment management services to corporate and institutional clients worldwide. The company added to its financial services subsidiary in 1988 by purchasing Citicorp Investment Management (renamed Chancellor Capital Management) for $102.5 million; the Citicorp unit managed $18 billion in assets for pension funds and other institutional accounts. With the purchase USF&G became one of the top 20 US investment managers.

HOW MUCH

	9 Yr. Growth	1980	1981	1982	1983	1984	1985	1986	1987	1988	1989
Sales ($ mil)	8.5%	2,253	2,337	2,306	2,387	2,839	3,556	4,337	4,826	5,582	4,679
Net income ($ mil)	(7.2%)	229	169	114	172	93	(258)	243	373	306	117
Income as % of sales	—	10.1%	7.2%	5.0%	7.2%	3.3%	(7.3%)	5.6%	7.7%	5.5%	2.5%
Earnings per share ($)	(11.7%)	4.08	2.99	1.99	*3.02*	1.72	(4.30)	3.60	4.92	3.58	1.33
Stock price – high ($)	—	23.25	26.00	23.25	30.00	30.94	41.50	46.75	48.75	34.38	34.00
Stock price – low ($)	—	16.75	18.69	15.63	19.69	17.63	25.50	36.25	26.25	28.50	28.25
Stock price – close ($)	3.6%	21.19	20.69	22.69	27.69	27.50	39.00	39.75	28.38	28.50	29.00
P/E – high	—	6	9	12	10	18	—	13	10	10	26
P/E – low	—	4	6	8	7	10	—	10	5	8	21
Dividends per share ($)	8.0%	1.40	1.60	1.80	1.92	2.08	2.20	2.32	2.48	2.64	2.80
Book value per share ($)	(1.0%)	23.59	23.63	24.29	22.61	20.14	18.91	20.19	19.53	22.57	21.60

1989 Year End:
Debt ratio: 12.7%
Return on equity: 6.0%
Cash (mil): $105
Assets (mil): $13,604
Long-term debt (mil): $291
Number of shares (mil): 84
Dividends:
1989 average yield: 9.7%
1989 payout: 210.5%
Market value (mil): $2,426

Stock Price History high/low 1980-89

50 45 40 35 30 25 20 15 10 5 0

NYSE symbol: FG
Incorporated: Maryland, 1981
Fiscal year ends: December 31

WHO

Chairman, President, and CEO: Jack Moseley, age 58, $1,180,446 pay
EVP and CFO: James A. Flick, Jr., age 55, $674,014 pay
EVP: Paul J. Scheel, age 56, $636,674 pay
EVP: James M. Raley, Jr., age 39, $487,543 pay
Auditors: Ernst & Young
Employees: 12,600

WHERE

HQ: 100 Light St., Baltimore, MD 21202
Phone: 301-547-3000
FAX: 301-625-2829

USF&G property/casualty insurance is sold nationwide by 5,300 independent agencies; life insurance is sold by 6,100 independent agencies. USF&G Financial Services Corporation also has operations in 43 foreign countries.

WHAT

	1989 Sales		1989 Pretax Income	
	$ mil	% of total	$ mil	% of total
Property/casualty insurance	4,130	87	227	94
Life insurance	410	9	35	15
Financial services	182	4	(22)	(9)
Adjustments	(43)	—	(112)	—
Total	**4,679**	**100**	**128**	**100**

Property/Casualty Insurance
Auto
Business
Home
Reinsurance

Life Insurance
Annuities
Groups
Individuals
Universal life

Financial Services
Computer leasing
Investment management
Marketing
Planning
Real estate

Major Subsidiaries
Axe-Houghton Mgt. (investment mgt.)
Chancellor Capital Mgt. (investment mgt.)
Fidelity and Guaranty Life Insurance Co.
Kepner-Tregoe (human asset mgt.)
Lowry Associates (investment mgt.)
St. Andrews Insurance, Ltd.
St. George Reinsurance, Ltd.
Thomas Jefferson Life Insurance Co.
United States Fidelity and Guaranty

RANKINGS

23rd in *Fortune* 50 Diversified Financial Cos.
187th in *Forbes* Sales 500
249th in *Business Week* 1000
843rd in *Business Week* Global 1000

COMPETITION

Aetna
AIG
American Express
BankAmerica
CIGNA
GEICO
Kemper
Metropolitan Life
Prudential
Sears
State Farm
Travelers
Other insurance and investment management companies

USG CORPORATION

OVERVIEW

USG, headquartered in Chicago, is the largest manufacturer of gypsum products (34% of the 1989 market) and the largest caulk producer (almost 40%) in North America. The company also makes interior ceiling, wall, and floor systems, controlling about 30% of the domestic industry.

USG owns proven gypsum deposits sufficient for 37 years of operation and distributes its gypsum products through L&W Supply, a leading gypsum distributor. Through DAP, USG is the leading manufacturer of caulks and building repair and remodeling products.

USG is a former asbestos producer. As of December 31, 1989, the company was named a defendant in personal injury cases involving 33,647 persons and 139 property damage cases related to the asbestos health hazard pending before US courts.

The company expects the construction market to remain soft during the early 1990s but looks for strong performances from its remodeling and decorating businesses. Further expansion is planned in international sales, which are up 76% since 1986 and now constitute 16% of sales.

USG will continue to emphasize cost control and debt reduction and will explore joint ventures as a means of expansion.

NYSE symbol: USG
Incorporated: Delaware, 1984
Fiscal year ends: December 31

WHO

Chairman and CEO: Eugene B. Connolly, age 58, $334,568 pay (prior to promotion)
President and COO: Anthony J. Falvo, Jr., age 59, $332,686 pay (prior to promotion)
VC and CFO: Eugene Miller, age 64, $266,667 pay
VP Human Resources and Administration: Harold E. Pendexter, Jr., age 55
Auditors: Arthur Andersen & Co.
Employees: 14,200

WHERE

HQ: 101 S. Wacker Dr., Chicago, IL 60606
Phone: 312-606-4000
FAX: 312-606-4093

USG operates 57 plants in the US, 11 in Canada, 3 in Mexico, and 6 in other countries.

	1989 Sales		1989 Operating Income	
	$ mil	% of total	$ mil	% of total
US	1,843	84	249	74
Canada	204	9	53	16
Other foreign	144	7	33	10
Adjustments	—	—	(31)	—
Total	**2,191**	**100**	**304**	**100**

WHEN

In 1901, 35 gypsum-producing and -processing companies joined to form the largest company in the industry, headquartered in Chicago. Sewell Avery became CEO in 1905 and led the company until 1951.

U.S. Gypsum started lime production in 1915 and paint manufacturing in 1924. By 1931 the company had diversified into the metal lath business and insulating board production, and added 2 more lime companies and 2 gypsum concerns.

In 1931 Avery became chairman of Montgomery Ward, managing both companies simultaneously. USG continued making profits and paying dividends throughout the Great Depression. The company entered the asphalt roofing and mineral wool business in 1933, began making hardboard from highly compressed wood fibers in 1934, and entered the asbestos-cement siding field in 1937.

Beginning in the late 1960s USG diversified into the building materials and remodeling businesses, acquiring A.P. Green Refractories (1967; refractory brick, tile, and accessories), Wallace Manufacturing (1970; prefinished wood panels), Chicago Mastic (1971; mastics, cements, and adhesives), Kinkead Industries (1972; steel doors and frames), and various smaller businesses. In 1971 USG initiated the operations of L&W Supply, now the largest distributor of gypsum in the US.

Following the 1984 purchase of the Masonite Corporation for $380 million, the company adopted its present name (1985). USG acquired Donn (remodeling materials) in 1986 and DAP (caulk and sealants) in 1987 for a total of $260 million.

In 1987 USG engineered a $776 million buyback of 20% of its stock to ward off a takeover attempt. The following year Desert Partners of Midland, Texas, attempted another takeover, resolved 9 months later when shareholders approved a management plan to keep control of the company. The plan included taking on $2.5 billion of new debt, a $37-per-share payout, and a $5-per-share payment-in-kind debenture. Employees are now the largest stockholders, with 26% of the total.

After completing virtually all asset sales envisioned in the reorganization plan by the end of 1989, USG is now about 25% smaller. Proceeds from the sale of Masonite (to International Paper), Kinkead, and Marlite netted a total of $560 million, used to repay debt immediately.

WHAT

	1989 Sales		1989 Operating Income	
	$ mil	% of total	$ mil	% of total
Gypsum products	926	43	227	67
Building products distribution	485	22	7	2
Interior systems	594	27	89	27
Caulk	186	8	12	4
Adjustments	—	—	(31)	—
Total	**2,191**	**100**	**304**	**100**

Principal Subsidiaries

CGC Inc. (Canada, building products, 76%)
DAP Inc. (adhesives, caulks, paints, and sealants)
L&W Supply Corp. (building materials distribution)
United States Gypsum Co. (gypsum for construction and industrial markets)
USG Interiors, Inc. (ceiling, wall, and floor systems)

Brand Names

Acoustone	Kwik-Seal
Avanti	Linear Expressions
DAP	Sheetrock
Donn	Textone
Durock	Woodlife
Intersections	

HOW MUCH

	9 Yr. Growth	1980	1981	1982	1983	1984	1985	1986	1987	1988	1989
Sales ($ mil)	4.5%	1,474	1,491	1,325	1,611	2,319	2,526	2,724	2,898	2,248	2,191
Net income ($ mil)	(13.4%)	94	74	44	80	187	224	255	204	73	26
Income as % of sales	—	6.4%	5.0%	3.3%	5.0%	8.0%	8.9%	9.4%	7.1%	3.2%	1.2%
Earnings per share ($)	(11.3%)	1.41	1.11	0.65	1.18	2.78	3.32	3.98	3.93	1.38	0.48
Stock price – high ($)	—	9.34	9.69	13.50	14.94	16.31	25.31	46.50	55.88	49.50	7.38
Stock price – low ($)	—	6.44	7.56	6.50	10.00	11.25	14.69	22.25	23.50	4.75	2.88
Stock price – close ($)	(6.5%)	8.25	8.38	12.63	14.81	14.84	25.31	37.75	29.13	5.63	4.50
P/E – high	—	7	9	21	13	6	8	12	14	36	15
P/E – low	—	5	7	10	9	4	4	6	6	3	6
Dividends per share ($)	—	0.60	0.60	0.60	0.61	0.70	0.84	1.04	1.12	37.56	0.00
Book value per share ($)	—	10.48	10.75	10.61	11.13	13.01	15.18	11.15	11.81	(27.26)	(26.55)

1989 Year End:
Debt ratio: 274.7%
Return on equity: —
Cash (mil): $66
Current ratio: 0.9
Long-term debt (mil): $2,261
Number of shares (mil): 54
Dividends:
1989 average yield: 0.0%
1989 payout: 0.0%
Market value (mil): $244

Stock Price History high/low 1980-89

RANKINGS

198th in *Fortune* 500 Industrial Cos.
373rd in *Forbes* Sales 500

COMPETITION

Armstrong World	Hanson
Borden	3M
General Electric	PPG
Georgia-Pacific	Sherwin-Williams

U S WEST, INC.

OVERVIEW

Denver-based U S West provides local telephone services to more than 10 million customers in 14 states. To support U S West Communications, the company's telephone subsidiary, the company plans to spend $2 billion annually on network improvements.

U S West's New Vector Group has approximately 135,000 mobile telephone and 134,300 paging customers. The International division is a partner in cable TV franchises in Hong Kong, the UK, and France, with the potential to serve 6 million households, and is building the first Eastern European cellular system in Hungary. In the UK, U S West is a partner in developing the next generation of mobile communications, known as personal communications networks (PCNs).

The company is the nation's 2nd largest publisher of city directories, producing more than 900; subsidiary Marketing Resources Group is the nation's 2nd largest publisher of marketing reference guides.

As a provider of financial services, the company has focused on equipment leasing and asset-based lending but is now a dominant player in financial guaranty insurance. The company also develops commercial real estate through its BetaWest Properties subsidiary.

WHEN

U S West, incorporated in 1983 as one of 7 regional operating companies formed when AT&T was split, is rooted in AT&T's Mountain Bell, Northwestern Bell, and Pacific Northwest Bell companies. Chairman Jack MacAllister had earned a reputation as a maverick while CEO of Northwestern Bell; under MacAllister's leadership today, U S West enjoys the same reputation, moving into risky fields such as cable TV and equipment financing.

At the time of divestiture, U S West was composed of phone operations in 14 states; 1/7th interest in Bell Communications Research (R&D arm shared by the Bell companies); and New Vector, a cellular service provider. The company's primary business, local phone service, was growing only 3% to 5% annually. U S West, hoping to expand its ability to enter unregulated markets, sought changes in the divestiture agreement under which it was established in 1984 — the first Bell company to do so. While he has not yet received the total deregulation he advocates, MacAllister set a 1990 goal that 50% of revenues would come from unregulated businesses, up from 10% in 1985.

Within a few days of independence, MacAllister removed Yellow Pages operations to a new subsidiary, Landmark Communication (now part of U S West Marketing), which has added approximately 20 smaller directory publishers. In 1984 U S West established U S West Financial Services to provide diversified financial services and leasing, as well as 2 companies to sell and service communications equipment (FirstTel and Interline); within months the latter 2 companies were crossing paths. By 1985 FirstTel was dissolved. Other new subsidiaries include BetaWest Properties (1986), a developer of commercial real estate, and Applied Communications (1987), which provides software to the banking industry.

MacAllister stunned the industry in 1988 when he removed Bell's name, synonymous with telecommunications since the phone was invented, from local operations, consolidating operations as U S West Communications. That year U S West announced it would test-market a videotex system in its region, invested in a French cable TV company, made plans to offer cable billing and maintenance services domestically, and broke ground on a $45 million R&D facility in Boulder after expressing dissatisfaction with Bell Communications Research. The company is expanding internationally with projects in Hong Kong, the UK, France, Hungary, and the USSR. For the long term, MacAllister is eyeing insurance and brokerage businesses.

HOW MUCH

	5 Yr. Growth	1980	1981	1982	1983	1984	1985	1986	1987	1988	1989
Sales ($ mil)	5.9%	—	—	—	—	7,280	7,813	8,308	8,445	9,221	9,691
Net income ($ mil)	4.6%	—	—	—	—	887	926	924	1,006	1,132	1,111
Income as % of sales	—	—	—	—	—	12.2%	11.8%	11.1%	11.9%	12.3%	11.5%
Earnings per share ($)	5.4%	—	—	—	—	2.31	2.42	2.43	2.66	3.09	3.01
Stock price – high ($)	—	—	—	—	—	17.72	22.25	31.00	30.13	29.81	40.31
Stock price – low ($)	—	—	—	—	—	13.91	17.13	20.81	21.25	24.38	28.38
Stock price – close ($)	17.8%	—	—	—	—	17.63	22.25	27.00	25.56	28.88	40.06
P/E – high	—	—	—	—	—	8	9	13	11	10	13
P/E – low	—	—	—	—	—	6	7	9	8	8	9
Dividends per share ($)	6.5%	—	—	—	—	1.35	1.07	1.50	1.61	1.73	1.85
Book value per share ($)	4.6%	—	—	—	—	17.25	18.24	19.16	20.09	21.31	21.58

1989 Year End:
Debt ratio: 47.3%
Return on equity: 14.0%
Cash (mil): $291
Current ratio: 0.68
Long-term debt (mil): $7,248
Number of shares (mil): 374
Dividends:
1989 average yield: 4.6%
1989 payout: 61.5%
Market value (mil): $14,983

NYSE symbol: USW
Incorporated: Colorado, 1983
Fiscal year ends: December 31

WHO

Chairman and CEO: Jack A. MacAllister, age 62, $1,310,000 pay
President: Richard D. McCormick, age 49, $841,500 pay
EVP; President, U S West Communications: Thomas F. Madison, $513,700 pay
EVP and CFO: Howard P. Doerr, age 60, $479,500 pay
EVP, General Counsel, and Secretary: Laurence W. DeMuth, Jr., age 61, $472,500 pay
Auditors: Coopers & Lybrand
Employees: 70,587

WHERE

HQ: 7800 E. Orchard Rd., Englewood, CO 80111
Phone: 303-793-6500
FAX: 303-793-6654

U S West provides telephone exchange service in 14 states (Washington, Oregon, Idaho, Montana, Wyoming, North Dakota, South Dakota, Nebraska, Minnesota, Iowa, Colorado, Utah, Arizona, and New Mexico) and has international ventures in the UK, USSR, Hungary, France, and Hong Kong.

WHAT

	1989 Sales		1989 Operating Income	
	$ mil	% of total	$ mil	% of total
Communications & related services	9,226	95	1,906	98
Capital assets	512	5	40	2
Adjustments	(49)	—	247	—
Total	**9,691**	**100**	**2,193**	**100**

Operations

Bell Communications Research (14.3%)
Financial Security Assurance, Inc. (debt guarantees)
U S West Communications (telephone services)
U S West Financial Services (manages $3 billion portfolio)
U S West Marketing Resources Group (Yellow Pages and specialty directory publishing)
U S West New Vector Group (81% cellular and paging services)

RANKINGS

5th in *Fortune* 50 Utilities
79th in *Forbes* Sales 500
38th in *Business Week* 1000
97th in *Business Week* Global 1000

COMPETITION

Ameritech
AT&T
Bell Atlantic
BellSouth
Dun & Bradstreet
GTE
McCaw Cellular
MCI
NYNEX
Pacific Telesis
Southwestern Bell
United Telecommunications

USX CORPORATION

OVERVIEW

USX is the nation's largest steelmaker, but it's an oil company.

Sales by its energy operations in 1989 could have nudged it past Unocal as the 10th largest integrated petroleum company (production, refining, marketing).

Marathon Oil, USX's largest holding, conducts exploration and production worldwide. It owns 5 US refineries and wholesales 63% of its domestic output to private-brand marketers. Texas Oil & Gas, the 2nd part of USX's energy group, primarily gathers natural gas and processes it for pipelines or large industrial users.

USS, USX's steelmaker, manufactures at its own mills and participates in joint steelmaking ventures, sometimes with foreign competitors such as Pohang of South Korea (in Pittsburg, California) and Kobe of Japan (in Lorain, Ohio).

US Diversified Group covers a wide range of USX businesses, ranging from engineering consulting to mall development to Cyclone Fences.

WHEN

USX was born a billion-dollar baby in 1901. Its birthname was United States Steel, and its daddy was financier J. P. Morgan.

Morgan forged US Steel from the Federal Steel he controlled and from the steel holdings of Andrew Carnegie. Carnegie, a Scot who began as a Pennsylvania telegraph messenger, built a far-flung empire after the Civil War.

At the beginning of the 20th century, Carnegie's president, Charles Schwab, spoke at a New York dinner about the future of steel. An impressed Morgan told Schwab to get Carnegie to name a price for his mills. Carnegie did, and Morgan didn't haggle.

Carnegie received almost half a billion dollars for his interest in US Steel. He retired to pursue philanthropy, giving away 90% of his wealth. He poured $60 million into 2,811 free public libraries worldwide.

The Carnegie-Morgan combination created an enterprise with capitalization of $1.4 billion, the world's first billion-dollar company. In its first year it produced 67% of the US's steel output. But its weight also kept the company from changing its direction as foreign competition and aging plants ate into profits. When the 1980s began, US Steel began to change.

In 1982 US Steel purchased Marathon Oil, then the 17th largest US petroleum producer, and doubled its revenues.

Findlay, Ohio–based Marathon began in 1887 as Ohio Oil. Founded by 14 independents, Ohio Oil attracted the attention of Standard Oil, which purchased it in 1889. After the 1911 Standard Oil breakup, Ohio Oil drilled in the Rocky Mountains of Wyoming and into Kansas, Louisiana, and Texas. A major discovery came almost by accident. In 1924 Ohio Oil agreed to drill 3 wells on leases west of the Pecos River in Texas. By mistake, Ohio Oil drilled 3 dry holes on leases east of the river. Ohio Oil planned to abandon the properties when a frantic geologist reported the error. Drilled in the right place, the well flowed voluminously. Ohio Oil became Marathon in 1962.

In 1986 US Steel paid $3 billion in stock for Texas Oil & Gas, and US Steel became USX to reflect the decreasing role of steel. After Texas Oil & Gas proved a disappointment, USX decided in 1989 to put much of its reserves on the block, but offers were disappointing and they were not sold.

Investor Carl Icahn, USX's largest single shareholder with 13.3%, wanted the company to sell its steel operations but was rebuffed in a 1990 shareholder referendum. Management took the hint and opened discussions to sell some steel assets. Chairman Charles Corry was quoted as saying, "Energy is our future" — in effect putting J. P. Morgan's billion-dollar baby up for adoption.

HOW MUCH

	9 Yr. Growth	1980	1981	1982	1983	1984	1985	1986	1987	1988	1989
Sales ($ mil)	3.8%	12,492	13,941	18,375	16,869	18,274	18,429	14,000	13,898	15,792	17,533
Net income ($ mil)	8.6%	459	1,077	(361)	(1,161)	414	313	(1,593)	206	756	965
Income as % of sales	—	3.7%	7.7%	(2.0%)	(6.9%)	2.3%	1.7%	(11.4%)	1.5%	4.8%	5.5%
Earnings per share ($)	(4.0%)	5.05	11.47	*(3.99)*	(12.07)	2.79	1.81	(6.53)	0.52	2.62	3.49
Stock price – high ($)	—	25.88	35.25	30.13	31.00	33.25	33.00	28.75	39.38	34.38	39.50
Stock price – low ($)	—	16.25	23.38	16.00	19.63	22.00	24.38	14.50	21.00	26.00	28.88
Stock price – close ($)	4.2%	24.75	29.88	21.00	30.38	26.13	26.63	21.50	29.75	29.25	35.75
P/E – high	—	5	3	—	—	12	18	—	76	13	11
P/E – low	—	3	2	—	—	8	13	—	40	10	8
Dividends per share ($)	(1.5%)	1.60	2.00	1.75	1.00	1.00	1.10	1.20	1.20	1.25	1.40
Book value per share ($)	(11.0%)	59.98	69.11	58.11	43.67	45.36	43.80	18.26	17.77	18.91	20.95

1989 Year End:
Debt ratio: 51.0%
Return on equity: 17.5%
Cash (mil): $786
Current ratio: 1.08
Long-term debt (mil): $5,979
Number of shares (mil): 256
Dividends:
1989 average yield: 3.9%
1989 payout: 40.1%
Market value (mil): $9,137

Stock Price History high/low 1980-89

0 5 10 15 20 25 30 35 40

NYSE symbol: X
Incorporated: Delaware, 1965
Fiscal year ends: December 31

WHO

Chairman and CEO: Charles A. Corry, age 58, $1,346,599 pay
VC Energy: William E. Swales, age 64, $1,133,686 pay
VC Steel and Diversified Group: Thomas C. Graham, age 63, $998,621 pay
VC Administration and CFO: W. Bruce Thomas, age 63, $968,001 pay
Auditors: Price Waterhouse
Employees: 53,610

WHERE

HQ: 600 Grant St., Pittsburgh, PA 15219
Phone: 412-433-1121
FAX: 412-433-5733

USX produces steel and oil and sells gas in 13 states. It also produces oil and gas in Ireland, the UK, Norway, and Indonesia.

	1989 Sales		1989 Operating Income	
	$ mil	% of total	$ mil	% of total
US	17,864	96	1,460	92
Other North America	185	1	30	2
Europe	639	3	104	7
Middle East & Africa	—	—	(33)	(2)
Other foreign	29	—	9	1
Adjustments	(1,184)	—	—	—
Total	**17,533**	**100**	**1,570**	**100**

WHAT

	1989 Sales		1989 Operating Income	
	$ mil	% of total	$ mil	% of total
Energy	11,025	63	987	64
Steel	5,724	33	430	28
Diversified businesses	784	4	120	8
Adjustments	—	—	33	—
Total	**17,533**	**100**	**1,570**	**100**

Principal Products & Activities
Auto parts and precision fasteners
Coal mining
Crude oil and natural gas production
Engineering services
Fencing products (Cyclone)
Financial services
Land management
Petroleum pipelining, refining, and marketing
Real estate development
Steel production

Major Subsidiaries
Delhi Gas Pipeline Corp.
Emro Marketing Co.
FWA Drilling Co., Inc.
Marathon Oil Co.
Texas Oil & Gas Corp.
USS

RANKINGS

19th in *Fortune* 500 Industrial Cos.
52nd in *Fortune* Global 500 Industrial Cos.
30th in *Forbes* Sales 500
48th in *Business Week* 1000
195th in *Business Week* Global 1000

COMPETITION

USX competes with steel, oil, gas, coal mining, and other diversified companies

V. F. CORPORATION

OVERVIEW

The V. F. Corporation, the largest publicly owned clothing company in the world, is a holding company overseeing leading producers of jeans, sportswear, lingerie, and occupational clothing. The company's 10 divisions design, manufacture, and market such well-known brands as Wrangler and Lee jeans, Jantzen swimsuits, Vanity Fair lingerie, and Red Kap work clothes.

V. F.'s sales topped $2.5 billion in 1989, producing net income of $176 million.

Although they still commanded 25% of the 1989 US jeanswear market, V. F.'s jeans sales have declined 11% since 1987, largely due to losses by the Lee brand. Analysts point to V. F.'s 1986 decision to sell the brand in discount stores, which cut into sales from its essential department store customers. In the past year, earnings grew from other V. F. products, particularly its other jeans brands (Wrangler, Rustler, and Girbaud), its Bassett-Walker sportswear, and its occupational apparel.

WHEN

In 1899, 6 partners, including banker John Barbey, started the Reading Glove and Mitten Manufacturing Company. Barbey bought out his 5 partners in 1911 and changed the name of the Reading, Pennsylvania, company to Schuylkill Silk Mills in 1913.

Barbey expanded the mills' production to underwear and, in the 1920s, discontinued glove manufacturing. A company contest with a $25 prize produced the new name Vanity Fair, which was first used in the mills' advertisements in 1917. Barbey changed the mills' name to Vanity Fair Silk Mills in 1919.

Barbey and his son J. E. Barbey led their lingerie company (Barbey banned the word *underwear*) to national prominence. Until 1920 the mills produced only silk garments, but the development of synthetics such as rayon and acetate expanded their products' variety. WWII brought a national embargo on silk in 1941, and Vanity Fair converted to rayon. In 1948 it converted all production to the new wonder fabric, nylon tricot.

Vanity Fair opened its first Alabama production plant in Monroeville in 1937, with 5 other locations to follow: Jackson (1939), Demopolis (1950), Atmore (1951), Butler (1960), and Robertsdale (1962). It closed its Pennsylvania manufacturing plant in 1948, retaining its company offices there. By 1948 Vanity Fair manufactured all stages of its nylon products, from filament to finished garment. It expanded its color offerings and introduced permanent pleating and printed lingerie, including leopard and mermaid prints. Vanity Fair won the *American Fabrics Magazine* award for textile achievement in 1948 and the Coty award for design in 1950. Innovative advertising, considered daring at the time, brought awards for photographs of live models in Vanity Fair lingerie.

J. E. Barbey still owned all of Vanity Fair's stock in 1951, when he sold 1/3 of his holdings to the public. In 1966 the stock, previously traded OTC, was listed on the NYSE.

The company's name changed to V. F. Corporation in 1969. During the next 15 years, it expanded its lingerie business and began producing sportswear and blue jeans. It bought H.D. Lee (jeans, 1969), Kay Windsor (lingerie, 1971), Modern Globe (lingerie, 1984), and Bassett-Walker (fleecewear, 1984). In 1986 V. F. bought Blue Bell, a North Carolina maker of blue jeans (Wrangler and Rustler), sportswear (Jantzen and Jansport), and occupational clothing (Red Kap and Big Ben).

Most of V. F.'s products are sold in department stores or specialty shops. Its jeans brands are also sold in upscale discount stores (Lee), western specialty stores (Wrangler), and national discount chains (Rustler). Its JanSport gear is sold in outdoor and sporting good stores, and 75% of its Red Kap work clothes are sold to industrial laundries.

NYSE symbol: VFC
Incorporated: Pennsylvania, 1899
Fiscal year ends: Saturday nearest December 31

WHO

Chairman and CEO: Lawrence R. Pugh, age 57, $1,085,000 pay
President and Principal Operating Officer: Robert E. Gregory, Jr., age 47, $830,000 pay
VP Finance and CFO: Gerard G. Johnson, age 49, $410,000 pay
VP Human Resources and Administration: Harold E. Addis, age 59, $243,000 pay
Auditors: Ernst & Young
Employees: 44,500

WHERE

HQ: 1047 N. Park Rd., Wyomissing, PA 19610
Phone: 215-378-1151
FAX: 215-375-9371

	1989 Pretax Income	
	$ mil	% of total
US	266	94
Foreign	18	6
Total	**284**	**100**

WHAT

	1989 Sales		1989 Operating Income	
	$ mil	% of total	$ mil	% of total
Jeanswear	1,386	56	194	57
Sportswear/ activewear	517	20	36	11
Intimate apparel	316	12	50	15
Occupational apparel & other	314	12	56	17
Adjustments	—	—	(23)	—
Total	**2,533**	**100**	**313**	**100**

Principal Divisions
Bassett-Walker (Martinsville, VA)
Girbaud, Wrangler (Greensboro, NC)
JanSport (Appleton, WI)
Jantzen (Portland, OR)
Lee Apparel (Merriam, KS)
Modern Globe (North Wilkesboro, NC)
Red Kap (Nashville, TN)
Vanity Fair (New York, NY)

Brand Names

Jeanswear
Girbaud
Lee
Rustler
Wrangler

Intimate Apparel
Lollipop
Modern Globe
Vanity Fair
Vassarette

Sportswear/Activewear
Bassett-Walker
JanSport
Jantzen

Occupational Apparel
Big Ben
Red Kap

HOW MUCH

	9 Yr. Growth	1980	1981	1982	1983	1984	1985	1986	1987	1988	1989
Sales ($ mil)	16.6%	634	746	880	1,101	1,167	1,481	1,545	2,574	2,516	2,533
Net income ($ mil)	16.1%	46	52	92	119	125	139	129	180	174	176
Income as % of sales	—	7.2%	7.0%	10.4%	10.8%	10.7%	9.4%	8.4%	7.0%	6.9%	7.0%
Earnings per share ($)	17.3%	0.64	0.81	1.41	1.82	1.96	2.25	2.05	2.62	2.54	2.70
Stock price – high ($)	—	4.00	5.66	10.72	20.69	16.25	27.00	36.00	48.25	33.88	38.38
Stock price – low ($)	—	2.33	3.33	3.78	9.13	10.88	12.94	24.00	22.00	24.75	27.75
Stock price – close ($)	28.3%	3.39	5.09	9.91	15.06	13.31	25.94	30.88	24.50	28.75	31.88
P/E – high	—	6	7	8	11	8	12	18	18	13	14
P/E – low	—	4	4	3	5	6	6	12	8	10	10
Dividends per share ($)	17.5%	0.21	0.26	0.33	0.43	0.52	0.58	0.66	0.75	0.85	0.91
Book value per share ($)	17.5%	3.30	3.75	4.73	6.09	7.14	8.91	12.20	14.43	16.05	14.14

1989 Year End:
Debt ratio: 43.7%
Return on equity: 17.9%
Cash (mil): $36
Current ratio: 2.69
Long-term debt (mil): $638
Number of shares (mil): 58
Dividends:
1989 average yield: 2.9%
1989 payout: 33.7%
Market value (mil): $1,848

Stock Price History high/low 1980-89

RANKINGS

173rd in *Fortune* 500 Industrial Cos.
489th in *Fortune* Global 500 Industrial Cos.
326th in *Forbes Sales* 500
342nd in *Business Week* 1000

COMPETITION

Berkshire Hathaway
Hartmarx
Levi Strauss
Liz Claiborne
NIKE
Reebok
Riklis Family

VIACOM INC.

OVERVIEW

Viacom Inc. produces and distributes TV and cable programming, and owns and operates radio and TV stations and cable TV systems. Viacom is approximately 84% owned by Sumner Redstone's National Amusements.

Viacom is the 14th largest cable operator in the US, with more than a million subscribers in California, the East, and the Northwest. It also owns 5 TV and 12 radio stations in cities from Albany, New York, to Los Angeles.

Viacom operates MTV and VH-1, both 24-hour music video channels, and Nickelodeon, the self-styled "kid's channel." The company unveiled Ha!, a comedy network, in 1990. The company operates Showtime and The Movie Channel, with more than 10 million subscribers in 50 states. In partnership with Hearst/ABC Video, Viacom operates Lifetime, a cable channel aimed at women and medical professionals.

Viacom Entertainment syndicates TV programming ("Roseanne," "The Cosby Show") and produces TV series and programs for prime time ("Jake and the Fatman"). Viacom is investigating cable opportunities in Japan (with Sumitomo Corporation) and has agreements to provide cable consulting services in France, Sweden, and Hong Kong.

ASE symbol: VIA
Incorporated: Delaware, 1986
Fiscal year ends: December 31

WHO

Chairman: Sumner M. Redstone, age 66
President and CEO: Frank J. Biondi, Jr., age 45, $1,387,923 pay
SVP; President and CEO, Viacom Cable Television: John W. Goddard, age 48, $1,056,598 pay
SVP; Chairman, Viacom Pictures: Neil S. Braun, age 37, $515,000 pay
SVP and CFO: George S. Smith, Jr., age 41
Auditors: Price Waterhouse
Employees: 4,900

WHEN

Viacom International was formed by CBS in 1970. When the FCC ruled that TV networks could not own cable systems and TV stations in the same market, Viacom stock was issued to CBS shareholders, and the new company also took over CBS's program syndication division, selling programs for reruns after network airing.

In the early 1970s Viacom bought cable systems in California, Washington, Ohio, New York, and Indiana. In 1978 Viacom and Teleprompter formed Showtime, one of the first subscription TV services. Viacom bought out Teleprompter's interest in 1982.

Also in 1978 Viacom purchased WVIT-TV (Hartford) from Connecticut Television. From 1980 to 1983 the company bought TV and radio stations in Louisiana, Chicago, New York, and Houston. Viacom and Warner/Amex (a joint cable venture between Warner and American Express) combined Showtime with The Movie Channel to form Showtime Networks in 1983. As American Express bowed out of the scene in 1986, Viacom purchased the Warner Communications share of Showtime Networks and 2/3 of MTV Networks, including cable's first all-music video channel, started in 1981. Viacom also began producing series for network television and bought the remainder of MTV and a St. Louis TV station.

Carl Icahn attempted a hostile takeover of Viacom in 1986. A management group led by CEO Terrence Elkes in 1986 attempted an LBO and became enmeshed in a 6-month bidding war with Sumner Redstone's National Amusements, Inc., a movie theater chain. Viacom Inc. was formed as a merger vehicle to acquire Viacom International. When the cable untangled in 1987, Redstone bought 83% of Viacom for $3.4 billion. Redstone replaced Elkes with former HBO executive Frank Biondi. Also in 1987 MTV Europe began broadcasting, and MTV Networks licensed Australian, Latin American, and Japanese broadcasting companies to air MTV programming.

In 1988 Viacom sold the rerun syndication rights of "The Cosby Show" for more than $515 million, the highest gross in TV syndication history. The company also produced 5 network television shows in 1988 and, after a short-lived run at acquiring Orion Pictures, sold its Orion stock for an $18 million profit. The company sold its Long Island and Cleveland cable TV systems in 1989 for a record $545 million. Viacom agreed to sell 50% of Showtime Networks to Tele-Communications, Inc., the nation's largest cable operator. The FCC was reviewing the sale in 1990.

WHERE

HQ: 1515 Broadway, New York, NY 10036
Phone: 212-258-6000
FAX: 212-258-6627

Viacom has cable operations in 7 states, TV stations in 4 states, and radio stations in 7 states and the District of Columbia. Viacom also has international sales offices.

	1989 Sales	
	$ mil	% of total
US	1,424	99
Foreign	12	1
Total	**1,436**	**100**

WHAT

	1989 Sales		1989 Operating Income	
	$ mil	% of total	$ mil	% of total
Cable television	300	21	61	24
Entertainment	255	17	72	28
Networks	752	52	84	33
Broadcasting	146	10	35	14
Other	4	—	4	1
Adjustments	(21)	—	(112)	—
Total	**1,436**	**100**	**144**	**100**

Cable Programming
Lifetime (33%)
MTV Networks
- MTV
- MTV Europe (49.9%)
- Nickelodeon/Nick at Nite
- VH-1

Showtime Networks (50%)
- Showtime
- The Movie Channel

Television Stations
KMOV, St. Louis
KSLA, Shreveport
WHEC, Rochester
WNYT, Albany
WVIT, Hartford

Radio Stations
KBSG (AM/FM), Tacoma
KHOW (AM)/KSYY(FM), Denver
KIKK (AM/FM), Houston
KXEZ (FM), Los Angeles
WLIT (FM), Chicago
WLTI (FM), Detroit
WLTW (FM), New York
WMZQ (AM/FM), Washington, DC

HOW MUCH

	9 Yr. Growth	1980	1981	1982	1983	1984	1985	1986	1987	1988	1989
Sales ($ mil)	27.6%	160	210	275	316	320	444	919	1,011	1,259	1,436
Net income ($ mil)	26.5%	16	17	25	28	31	37	(10)	(123)	(123)	131
Income as % of sales	—	9.8%	8.1%	8.9%	8.9%	9.6%	8.3%	(1.1%)	(12.2%)	(9.8%)	9.1%
Earnings per share ($)	(6.1%)	1.88	1.69	2.44	2.56	2.78	2.71	(0.65)	(1.69)	(1.77)	1.07
Stock price – high ($)	—	36.88	42.19	43.91	51.09	43.44	82.81	112.19	138.75	15.69	32.63
Stock price – low ($)	—	19.14	27.50	21.56	33.44	29.69	40.47	63.13	5.00	8.88	15.25
Stock price – close ($)	(2.0%)	34.38	30.00	37.81	40.94	40.63	68.13	98.75	9.06	15.56	28.75
P/E – high	—	20	25	18	20	16	31	—	—	—	31
P/E – low	—	10	16	9	13	11	15	—	—	—	14
Dividends per share ($)	(100%)	0.23	0.28	0.34	0.52	0.50	0.58	0.68	21.78	0.00	0.00
Book value per share ($)	(13.1%)	15.16	16.85	18.98	19.91	22.47	36.55	29.61	4.98	3.21	4.27

1989 Year End:
Debt ratio: 83.4%
Return on equity: 28.5%
Cash (mil): $12
Current ratio: 0.83
Long-term debt (mil): $2,283
Number of shares (mil): 107
Dividends:
- 1989 average yield: 0.0%
- 1989 payout: 0.0%

Market value (mil): $3,069

Stock Price History high/low 1980-89

140 120 100 80 60 40 20 0

RANKINGS

71st in *Fortune* 100 Diversified Service Cos.
22nd in *Business Week* 1000
695th in *Business Week* Global 1000

COMPETITION

Advance Publications
Capital Cities/ABC
CBS
Cox
General Electric
Hearst
Knight-Ridder
New York Times
Paramount
E.W. Scripps
Tele-Communications
Time Warner
Times Mirror
Turner Broadcasting
Walt Disney
Washington Post
Other media companies

VOLKSWAGEN AG

OVERVIEW

Barely edged out by Fiat, Volkswagen is #2 in European auto sales. The VW Golf was the best-selling car in Europe for the 7th consecutive year in 1989. Vehicles are sold under the high-end Audi, mid-range Volkswagen, and lower-end SEAT (Sociedad Española de Automóviles de Turismo) nameplates.

Inefficient operations and Japanese competition have hurt Volkswagen's US sales in recent years. Audi sales in the US have stabilized after a sudden-acceleration scare caused volume to plunge 71% since 1985.

Volkswagen is taking a global approach to production, with factories in Belgium and in such low-cost countries as Brazil, Argentina, Mexico, Yugoslavia, and China. Autolatina, jointly-owned with Ford, is South America's largest automaker. Facing high West German labor costs, Volkswagen is moving VW Polo production to its SEAT subsidiary in Spain. In 1990 Volkswagen entered into a venture with East German automaker VEB IFA-KOMBINAT and is pursuing discussions concerning Czechoslovakian production.

Principal stock exchange: Frankfurt
Founded: Germany, 1937
Fiscal year ends: December 31

WHO

Chairman of the Supervisory Board: Klaus Liesen, age 59
Chairman of the Board of Management: Carl H. Hahn, age 63
Member of the Board of Management for Controlling and Finance: Dieter Ullsperger, age 44
Auditors: Treuarbeit Aktiengesellschaft; Wollert-Elmendorff Deutsche Industrie-Treuhand
Employees: 257,561

WHEN

Since the early 1920s automotive engineer Ferdinand Porsche, whose son founded the Porsche car company, wanted to make a small car for the masses. He found no financial backers for his idea until he met Adolph Hitler in 1934. Hitler formed the Gesellschaft zur Vorbereitung des Volkswagens (Company for the Development of People's Cars) in 1937 and built a factory and worker housing in Wolfsburg, Germany.

A German government agency instituted a savings plan in which workers regularly set aside small sums with the expectation of receiving a car in 3 years. During WWII, however, the plant produced military vehicles, and no cars were ever delivered.

Following WWII, British occupation forces oversaw the reconstruction of the bomb-damaged plant and initial production of the odd-looking "people's car" (1945). The British appointed Heinz Nordhoff, a tough but inspirational leader, to manage Volkswagen (1948) and turned the company over to the German government (1949).

In the 1950s Volkswagen launched the Microbus and built plants internationally. Although US sales began slowly, by the end of the decade acceptance of the unpretentious car had increased. Advertising carved VW's niche in the US, coining the name "Beetle" and featuring humorous slogans such as "ugly is only skin deep" and "think small."

In 1960 Volkswagen stock was sold to the German public. A year later the company settled with 87,000 participants in Hitler's savings plan. Volkswagen purchased Auto Union GmbH (Audi) in 1966 from Daimler-Benz. In the 1960s the Beetle became a counterculture symbol and US sales took off. By the time of Nordhoff's death in 1968, the VW Beetle had become the world's best-selling car.

In the 1970s the outdated Beetle was discontinued in every country except Mexico, where it is still sold as the "Sedan Clasico." Volkswagen lost heavily during the model changeover-period, although its Brazilian unit was highly profitable. New models sold well in the late 1970s. Volkswagen opened America's first foreign-owned auto plant in Westmoreland, Pennsylvania, in 1978.

Volkswagen agreed to several international deals in the 1980s, including a car production venture in China (1984), the purchase of 75% of SEAT (automaker, Spain, 1986), and the merger of its suddenly faltering Brazilian unit with Ford's ailing Argentinean operations to form Autolatina (1987). The company suffered costly in-house currency fraud in 1987 and closed its underutilized Westmoreland plant in 1988. In 1990 Volkswagen agreed to build China's largest automobile factory.

WHERE

HQ: Postfach, D-3180 Wolfsburg 1, Germany
Phone: 011-49-53-61-9-0
FAX: 011-49-53-61-9-2-82-82
US HQ (Volkswagen of America, Inc.): 888 W. Big Beaver Rd., Troy, MI 48084
US Phone: 313-362-6000
US FAX: 313-362-6047

The Volkswagen Group has manufacturing subsidiaries in 10 countries.

	1989 Sales	
	DM mil	% of total
West Germany	23,682	36
Other Europe	26,595	41
North America	5,383	8
Latin America	5,636	9
Africa	1,669	2
Asia/Oceania	2,387	4
Total	**65,352**	**100**

WHAT

1989 Sales	% of total
Vehicles	79
Parts	9
Other	12
Total	**100**

Vehicle Makes
Audi
SEAT
Volkswagen

Manufacturing Subsidiaries
AUDI AG (Germany, 99%)
Autolatina Argentina S.A. (51%)
Shanghai-Volkswagen Automotive Co. Ltd. (China, 50%)
Sociedad Española de Automóviles de Turismo, S.A. (SEAT) (Spain, 75%)
TAS Tvornica Automobila Sarajevo (Yugoslavia, 49%)
Volkswagen Bruxelles S.A. (Belgium, 100%)
Volkswagen de Mexico, S.A. de C.V. (100%)
Volkswagen do Brasil S.A. (80%)
Volkswagen of Nigeria Ltd. (40%)
Volkswagen of South Africa (Pty.) Ltd. (100%)

RANKINGS

21st in *Fortune* Global 500 Industrial Cos.
124th in *Business Week* Global 1000

COMPETITION

Chrysler
Daimler-Benz
Fiat
Ford
General Motors
Honda
Hyundai
Mitsubishi
Nissan
Renault
Toyota
Volvo

HOW MUCH

$= DM1.69 (Dec. 31, 1989)	9 Yr. Growth	1980	1981	1982	1983	1984	1985	1986*	1987	1988	1989
Sales (DM mil)	7.8%	33,288	37,878	37,434	40,089	45,671	52,502	52,794	54,635	59,221	65,352
Net income (DM mil)	—	311	224	(233)	(130)	245	665	621	598	738	984
Income as % of sales	—	0.9%	0.6%	(0.6%)	(0.3%)	0.5%	1.3%	1.2%	1.1%	1.2%	1.5%
Earnings per share (DM)**	—	13	9	(10)	(5)	10	28	26	25	31	41
Stock price – high (DM)	—	191	180	153	237	232	498	684	430	348	546
Stock price – low (DM)	—	148	120	126	141	163	189	424	218	202	308
Stock price – close (DM)	14.6%	159	132	150	228	205	498	427	225	348	540
P/E – high	—	15	20	—	—	23	18	26	17	11	13
P/E – low	—	11	13	—	—	16	7	16	9	7	8
Dividends per share (DM)	0.0%	10	8	5	0	0	5	10	10	10	10
Book value per share (DM)	—	248	258	255	268	265	297	468	509	542	589

1989 Year End:
Debt ratio: 30.0%
Return on equity: 7.3%
Cash (mil): DM12,289
Long-term debt (bil): DM5.0
Number of shares (mil): 24
Dividends:
1989 average yield: 1.9%
1989 payout: 24.4%
Market value (mil): $7,669
Sales (mil): $38,670

*accounting change **not fully diluted

VOLVO CORPORATION

OVERVIEW

Sweden's largest company has just become larger and less Swedish. Volvo's recent link-up with France's state-owned Renault was designed to give both companies the benefits of a merger without either giving up control. The deal calls for an exchange of stock and coordinated R&D, procurement, and production. The allied companies will operate the world's largest truck maker. Volvo and Renault anticipate substantial cost savings and the creation of a global scale automobile company. Volvo owns large minority stakes in many companies including Park Ridge, parent of Hertz Corporation, and is a partner with the Swedish government in Procordia, a holding company.

Volvo experiments with work methods to attract scarce Swedish labor. Its Uddevalla, Sweden, plant has no assembly lines and workers largely manage themselves. The plant has experienced low absenteeism and high morale, but lower productivity than a traditional assembly line.

WHEN

Swedish ball bearing manufacturer SKF formed Volvo as a subsidiary in 1915. Volvo began assembling cars (1926), trucks (1928), and bus chassis (1932) in Göteborg, Sweden. The 1931 purchase of an engine maker marked Volvo's move beyond assembly and into manufacturing. In 1935 Volvo became an independent company led by Assar Gabrielsson, a businessman, and Gustaf Larson, who attended to technical matters.

In the 1940s Volvo continued to acquire automotive component manufacturers and began farm tractor production. Truck sales were particularly strong, aided by the company's innovations in diesel engines and axles. Cumulative vehicle output exceeded 100,000 units in 1949, 80% of which were sold in Sweden.

Volvo's acquisition of Bolinder-Munktell (farm machinery, diesel engines; Sweden, 1950) gave the company a major position in the Swedish tractor market. Later in the 1950s Volvo introduced the first turbocharged diesel truck engines, windshield defrosters, and windshield washers. Sales of its PV444 automobile advanced to 100,000 in 1956 as car production outstripped truck and bus output. European and North American sales helped Volvo export nearly 50% of its output in 1959.

Exports soared in the 1960s as Volvo's reputation for durability spread and the highly acclaimed model 144 was launched (1966). The company began building production facilities internationally, the first in Belgium (1962).

In 1971 36-year-old Pehr Gyllenhammar took over as Volvo's CEO. Under his direction the company tried to provide more humane work conditions and opened an experimental plant in Kalmar (1974). Aware that Volvo was too small to compete for long in its global markets, Gyllenhammar diversified and enlarged the company's business.

In 1981 Volvo diversified by buying Beijerinvest (energy, industrial products, food, finance, trading; Sweden). Truck operations were bolstered by the purchase of White Motors's truck division (US, 1981) and formation of a North American truck venture with General Motors (US, 1986). A 1984 joint venture agreement with Clark Equipment (US) created the world's 3rd largest construction equipment company. Volvo acquired Leyland Bus (UK) in 1988. Throughout the 1980s Volvo steadily increased its holdings in Pharmacia (drugs, biotechnology; Sweden), Custos (investments; Sweden), and Park Ridge (Hertz, US), among others. In 1989 the company agreed to consolidate its food and drug businesses with state-controlled holding company Procordia.

In a 1990 transaction just short of a merger, Volvo and Renault (France) agreed to extensive cross-holdings of stock and the alliance of the companies' truck and car businesses.

HOW MUCH

	6 Yr. Growth	1980	1981	1982	1983	1984	1985	1986	1987	1988	1989
Sales ($ mil)	3.2%	—	—	—	12,160	9,689	11,378	12,474	15,965	15,762	14,656
Net income ($ mil)	79.1%	—	—	—	25	174	336	378	568	543	826
Income as % of sales	—	—	—	—	0.2%	1.8%	3.0%	3.0%	3.6%	3.4%	5.6%
Earnings per share ($)	78.4%	—	—	—	0.33	2.25	4.33	4.87	7.32	7.00	10.65
Stock price – high ($)	—	—	—	—	41.75	61.50	68.25	64.25	81.13	64.25	81.13
Stock price – low ($)	—	—	—	—	—	—	24.38	40.50	38.38	46.75	60.75
Stock price – close ($)	—	—	—	—	—	—	41.00	50.13	47.25	63.00	72.13
P/E – high	—	—	—	—	—	—	10	13	9	9	8
P/E – low	—	—	—	—	—	—	6	8	5	7	6
Dividends per share ($)	—	—	—	—	0.00	0.62	0.60	1.17	1.46	1.76	2.16
Book value per share ($)	23.5%	—	—	—	11.47	10.55	14.96	19.35	27.27	31.17	40.65

1989 Year End:
Debt ratio: 20.4%
Return on equity: 29.7%
Cash (mil): $2,976
Current ratio: 1.25
Long-term debt (mil): $806
Number of shares (mil): 78
Dividends:
1989 average yield: 3.0%
1989 payout: 20.3%
Market value (mil): $5,597

Stock Price History high/low 1985-89

OTC symbol: VOLVY (ADR)
Incorporated: Sweden, 1915
Fiscal year ends: December 31

WHO

Chairman and CEO: Pehr G. Gyllenhammar, age 55
President: Christer Zetterberg, age 49
EVP: Gösta Renell, age 57
EVP; President, Volvo Truck Corp.: Sten Langenius, age 56
EVP; President, Volvo Car Corp.: Roger Holtback, age 45
President, Volvo North America Corp.: Björn Ahlström
Auditors: Lars Elvstad and Nils Brehmer
Employees: 78,690

WHERE

HQ: S-405 08 Göteborg, Sweden
Phone: 011-46-31-59-00-00
US HQ (Volvo North America Corp.): 535 Madison Ave., New York, NY 10022
US Phone: 212-754-3300
US FAX: 212-418-7437

	1989 Sales	
	$ mil	% of total
Sweden	3,016	20
Nordic area, excl. Sweden	1,110	8
Europe, excl. Nordic area	4,658	32
North America	4,261	29
Other	1,611	11
Total	**14,656**	**100**

WHAT

	1989 Sales		1989 Operating Income	
	$ mil	% of total	$ mil	% of total
Cars	6,919	47	312	35
Marine & industrial engines	437	3	24	3
Aerospace	387	3	49	6
Food	1,498	10	49	6
Trucks	4,005	27	368	41
Buses	593	4	39	4
Other operations	817	6	47	5
Adjustments	—	—	(112)	—
Total	**14,656**	**100**	**776**	**100**

Model Names

Cars
200/700 series (large family cars and station wagons)
300/400 series (upper-medium-class cars)
900 Series (luxury cars)

Trucks
Volvo
WHITEGMC

Buses
Leyland Bus
Volvo

Marine Engines
Volvo Penta

RANKINGS

70th in *Fortune* Global 500 Industrial Cos.
35th in *Forbes* 100 Foreign Investments in the US
425th in *Business Week* Global 1000

COMPETITION

Brunswick
Chrysler
Cummins Engine
Daimler-Benz
Fiat
Ford
General Motors
Honda
Hyundai
Mitsubishi
Navistar
Nissan
Outboard Marine
PACCAR
Toyota
Volkswagen

THE VONS COMPANIES, INC.

OVERVIEW

Vons is the 9th largest US supermarket chain and the largest in Southern California. The company doubled its size through the acquisition of 162 Safeway stores in 1988.

Vons, recognized as a customer-oriented grocer, has a "three's a crowd" policy that another register is opened whenever lines exceed 3 people. Vons Express, a glass-enclosed convenience store within a Vons grocery store, has convenience store items at grocery store prices. Vons also is testing a Drive-Thru Express, where customers can choose from 1,400 items on a menu board.

Vons is known for its unique store formats, aimed at addressing Southern California's diverse cultural background. Its Pavilions store in Grove City has 3 times the normal produce selection, 1,500 wines, a coffee corner, a lobster tank, and fresh goods made on-site such as breads, sausage, and tortillas. Tianguis stores offer not only freshly made tortillas but also a wide selection of Latin American brands, a catfish tank, chorizo, carnitas, and Mexican baked goods, all in a festive and colorful atmosphere with strolling mariachis.

NYSE symbol: VON
Incorporated: Michigan, 1982
Fiscal year ends: Sunday closest to December 31

WHO

Chairman and CEO: Roger E. Stangeland, age 60, $645,846 pay
VC and COO: Dennis K. Eck, age 46
President: William S. Davila, age 58, $391,731 pay
EVP: Garrett R. Nelson, age 50, $309,423 pay
EVP and CFO: Michael F. Henn, age 41, $301,223 pay
Auditors: KPMG Peat Marwick
Employees: 35,000

WHEN

Charles Von der Ahe opened a small grocery market in Los Angeles in 1906 with $1,200. By 1929 he was operating a chain of 87 stores. Prior to the 1929 stock market crash, Von der Ahe sold his stores to McMarr Stores (eventually bought by Safeway), and he soon retired. His 2 sons, Ted and Wil, restarted Vons stores with their father's financing.

In 1948 Vons opened a 50,300-square-foot store (Los Angeles) that was the first US retail grocer to feature self-service produce, meat, and delicatessen sections. In 1960 Vons bought Shopping Bag Food Stores but, 7 years later, was forced by the US Supreme Court to divest. The company opened 10 stores in 1968, increasing to 80 locations spread over 7 counties. In 1969 Household Finance (now Household International) bought Vons.

During the 1970s Vons added stores in the San Diego area and also began selling products wholesale to retailers and fast-food restaurants. The company was the official supermarket and food supplier for the 1984 Olympics in Los Angeles, providing meat and produce for a million meals a day.

A management team led by Roger Stangeland, the current CEO, bought Vons supermarkets and other retail units, T. G. & Y. (discount), Ben Franklin (variety), and Coast to Coast (hardware) from Household International in a 1985 LBO. That year Vons opened its first Vons Pavilions, a huge store featuring a wide merchandise selection and specialty items such as fresh fish tanks, sushi, and espresso. In 1986 Stangeland sold T. G. & Y., Ben Franklin, and Coast to Coast and bought the 10-store Pantry Food Markets of California chain.

In 1987 Vons built its first Tianguis, a superstore with Spanish signage, Mexican food items, and a bilingual staff. Vons, a privately held company, that year completed a complicated merger and divestiture with publicly owned Allied Supermarkets. Allied, itself the result of a 1955 merger of Wrigley Stores, Big Bear Markets, and several smaller companies, operated Great Scott Supermarkets in the Detroit area. Under the merger terms Vons agreed to allow the management of Allied to buy out the Michigan operations of the newly formed company. Vons emerged as a public company with its Southern California locations intact and $100 million in cash.

Vons bought the 162 Southern California locations of Safeway in 1988, when Safeway sold assets in its own LBO, giving Vons the largest number of stores and an estimated 26% share of the Southern California market.

WHERE

HQ: 10150 Lower Azusa Rd., El Monte, CA 91731
Phone: 818-821-7000
FAX: 818-821-7933 (Corporate Communications)

Vons's stores are located in the Los Angeles, Orange, Ventura, Riverside, San Bernardino, San Diego, and Santa Barbara counties of Southern California and in the cities of Bakersfield and Fresno. The company also operates stores in the Las Vegas, Nevada, area.

WHAT

	1989 Store Formats	
	no. of stores	% of total
Vons Supermarkets	221	67
Vons Food & Drug	74	23
Pavilions	12	4
Pavilions Place	13	4
Tianguis	8	2
Total	**328**	**100**

Store Formats

Vons Supermarkets
Traditional grocery stores, some featuring in-store bakeries and delis

Vons Food & Drug
Combination stores generally including housewares and specialty departments

Pavilions
50,000- to 75,000-square-foot superstores featuring various specialty "shopping pavilions"

Pavilions Place
Scaled-down versions of Pavilions with less general merchandise

Tianguis
Stores designed to resemble a Mexican market, with bilingual employees and Spanish signs

RANKINGS

21st in *Fortune* 50 Retailing Cos.
169th in *Forbes* Sales 500
589th in *Business Week* 1000

COMPETITION

Albertson's
American Stores
Campeau

HOW MUCH

	2 Yr. Growth	1980	1981	1982	1983	1984	1985	1986	1987	1988	1989
Sales ($ mil)	—	—	—	—	—	—	—	—	—	3,917	5,221
Net income ($ mil)	—	—	—	—	—	—	—	—	—	(24)	(25)
Income as % of sales	—	—	—	—	—	—	—	—	—	(0.6%)	(0.5%)
Earnings per share ($)	—	—	—	—	—	—	—	—	—	(0.77)	(0.65)
Stock price – high ($)	—	—	—	—	—	—	—	—	13.75	13.50	23.75
Stock price – low ($)	—	—	—	—	—	—	—	—	6.00	6.75	11.38
Stock price – close ($)	62.6%	—	—	—	—	—	—	—	7.38	11.50	19.50
P/E – high	—	—	—	—	—	—	—	—	—	—	—
P/E – low	—	—	—	—	—	—	—	—	—	—	—
Dividends per share ($)	—	—	—	—	—	—	—	—	0.00	0.00	0.00
Book value per share ($)	(7.1%)	—	—	—	—	—	—	—	5.69	5.53	4.91

1989 Year End:
Debt ratio: 81.5%
Return on equity: —
Cash (mil): $7
Current ratio: 0.82
Long-term debt (mil): $839
Number of shares (mil): 39
Dividends:
1989 average yield: 0.0%
1989 payout: 0.0%
Market value (mil): $755

Stock Price History high/low 1987-89

25
20
15
10
5
0

VULCAN MATERIALS COMPANY

OVERVIEW

Vulcan Materials Company is the leading US producer of construction aggregates (gravel, sand, rock, and slag) as well as a major manufacturer of industrial chemicals and other construction materials.

The company's Construction Materials division (with sales of $646 million in 1989) produces crushed stone, sand, gravel, asphalt, crushed slag (a by-product of molten steel), asphalt paving materials, and ready-mixed concrete. Crushed stone accounts for almost 80% of sales revenue in the construction segment and 50% overall. Vulcan's total production of construction aggregates was 114 million tons in 1989.

Vulcan's Chemical division (1989 sales of $430 million) produces a wide range of industrial chemicals. The company's chemical trucking fleet is one of the largest in the nation.

To overcome the tremendous cost of transporting its construction materials (a trip of 30 miles can more than double the cost of the materials), Vulcan maintains a strategic distribution network, with facilities close to key marketing areas, and also operates 2 portable stone-crushing plants.

WHEN

In 1916 the Ireland family purchased a 75% interest in Birmingham Slag, a small Alabama company established in 1909 to process slag from a Birmingham steel plant. For the next several decades, under the leadership of brothers Glenn, Gene, and Barney Ireland, the small company prospered by selling its processed slag for use as a construction material.

Third-generation Charles Ireland became president of the company in 1951 and pursued his dream of transforming Birmingham Slag from a regional to a national operation. When the steel producers started using a purer grade of ore (which produced considerably less slag), Ireland turned the company's attention to other aggregates, chemicals, and detinning operations. In 1956 the company bought Vulcan Detinning (a small New Jersey company that reclaimed tin and steel scrap), changed its name to Vulcan Materials, and went public. During the late 1950s the company went through a period of rapid expansion, which included the purchases of Union Chemical and Materials (1957), Lambert Brothers (quarrying, 1957), and a number of other quarrying and materials companies. By 1959 the new giant was the largest producer of aggregates in the US, with sales of over $100 million.

In 1959 Bernard Monaghan, a Rhodes scholar who, at the age of 21, had turned down a clerkship for US Supreme Court justice Hugo Black, became the first non-Ireland president of Vulcan. Under Monaghan's strong management, the company continued to grow for the next 2 decades. During the 1960s and 1970s the company added Kolker Chemical (1962); Aluminum and Magnesium, Inc. (1967); Dolese and Shepard (limestone, 1967); Campbell Limestone (1968); Olmos Rock Products (1971); Madison Limestone (1973); the aggregate operations of Seminole Rock (1974); the aggregate operations of Blythe Brothers (1975); and United Materials (1976).

When Monaghan retired in 1981, Vulcan owned 90 quarries and claimed sales of $783 million. The company grew further during the 1980s by acquiring the Elizabeth, New Jersey, detinning operation of MRI (1981); Pontiac Stone (1981); Dixie Sand and Gravel (1982); Cen-Ken Stone (1982); 10 aggregate operations from Medusa (1982); 6 plants from Dalton Rock (1985); a crushed stone plant from Jasper Construction (1986); White's Mines (1987); Sanders Quarry (1987); an aggregate operation from Young Stone (1988); and 4 crushed stone, 1 limestone, and 2 asphalt plants in 1989. In 1987 the company entered a joint venture with a Mexican partner (Grupo ICA) to supply aggregates for Gulf Coast markets.

HOW MUCH

	9 Yr. Growth	1980	1981	1982	1983	1984	1985	1986	1987	1988	1989
Sales ($ mil)	4.0%	754	783	719	821	983	972	958	923	1,053	1,076
Net income ($ mil)	7.5%	70	78	55	54	78	80	93	114	136	133
Income as % of sales	—	9.3%	10.0%	7.6%	6.6%	8.0%	8.2%	9.7%	12.4%	12.9%	12.4%
Earnings per share ($)	9.1%	1.51	1.69	1.18	1.17	1.69	1.72	2.10	2.69	3.30	3.30
Stock price – high ($)	—	11.88	14.00	14.00	17.50	18.44	22.75	31.38	41.00	41.50	48.50
Stock price – low ($)	—	7.63	10.03	9.69	13.38	14.50	16.63	22.06	23.75	31.00	40.50
Stock price – close ($)	17.5%	10.44	13.50	13.50	16.97	17.34	22.75	31.13	32.75	41.50	44.50
P/E – high	—	8	8	12	15	11	13	15	15	13	15
P/E – low	—	5	6	8	11	9	10	11	9	9	12
Dividends per share ($)	9.4%	0.50	0.55	0.61	0.61	0.61	0.70	0.74	0.85	0.98	1.12
Book value per share ($)	9.1%	7.66	8.82	9.39	9.97	11.05	11.67	11.98	13.70	15.56	16.80

1989 Year End:
Debt ratio: 7.7%
Return on equity: 20.4%
Cash (mil): $84
Current ratio: 2.36
Long-term debt (mil): $55
Number of shares (mil): 40
Dividends:
1989 average yield: 2.5%
1989 payout: 33.9%
Market value (mil): $1,758

NYSE symbol: VMC
Incorporated: New Jersey, 1956
Fiscal year ends: December 31

WHO

President and CEO: Herbert A. Sklenar, age 59, $708,750 pay
EVP Construction Materials: William J. Grayson, Jr., age 59, $367,504 pay
SVP Finance: Peter J. Clemens, III, age 46, $303,630 pay
Auditors: Deloitte & Touche
Employees: 6,300

WHERE

HQ: One Metroplex Dr., Birmingham, AL 35209
Phone: 205-877-3000
FAX: 205-877-3094

The company operates 113 stone quarries, 3 chemical plants, 5 ready-mixed concrete plants, and over 90 production and distribution facilities.

WHAT

	1989 Sales		1989 Operating Income	
	$ mil	% of total	$ mil	% of total
Construction matls.	646	60	116	57
Chemicals	430	40	86	43
Adjustments	—	—	(1)	—
Total	**1,076**	**100**	**201**	**100**

Construction Materials
Crushed slag
Crushed stone
Expanded shale
Gravel
Other aggregates
Pulverized limestone
Ready-mixed concrete
Rock asphalt
Sand

Chemicals
Anhydrous hydrogen chloride
Caustic potash
Caustic soda
Chlorinated hydrocarbons
Chlorine
Hydrogen
Methyl chloride
Muriatic acid

RANKINGS

334th in *Fortune* 500 Industrial Cos.
349th in *Business Week* 1000

COMPETITION

American Cyanamid
Dow Chemical
Du Pont
FMC
W. R. Grace
General Dynamics
Hercules
Martin Marietta
Monsanto
Morton
Union Carbide

WALGREEN CO.

OVERVIEW

Walgreen's is the US's largest drugstore chain in terms of sales ($5.4 billion in 1989). The company operates 1,484 stores in over 650 cities, principally in the Midwest, Florida, and the Southwest. The stores are served by 7 regional distribution centers, with an 8th planned for 1990 and a 9th for 1991. Walgreen's also operates 5 regional photo finishing labs.

The chain serves over 1.7 million people per day. Based on its 5-year earnings growth (64%) and return on shareholder's equity (almost 20%), Walgreen's was named as one of the 6 great retailers in the US in 1989 by *Inside Retailing* magazine.

In mid-1989, 40% of Walgreen's stores were less than 5 years old, and the company had plans to open 600 more stores over the next 5 years. Walgreen's is in the process of installing price-scanning equipment throughout the chain, as well as linking all of its stores by a satellite communications system, a task it intends to complete by the end of 1990.

NYSE symbol: WAG
Incorporated: 1909, Illinois
Fiscal year ends: August 31

WHO

Chairman and CEO: Charles R. Walgreen III, age 53, $928,923 pay
President and COO: Daniel Jorndt, age 48
EVP and CFO: Charles D. Hunter, age 59, $517,126 pay
SVP: Glenn S. Kraiss, age 56, $386,651 pay
SVP: Vernon A. Bruner, age 49, $386,528 pay
SVP: John R. Brown, age 53
Auditors: Arthur Andersen & Co.
Employees: 46,500

WHEN

In 1901 Chicago pharmacist Charles Walgreen borrowed $2,000 from his father for a down payment on his first drug store. In 1909 Walgreen sold 1/2 interest in his first store and bought a 2nd, where he installed a large soda fountain and began serving lunches. In 1916, 9 stores consolidated under the corporate name Walgreen Co. By 1920 there were 20 stores in Chicago, with sales of $1.55 million. The firm was first listed on the NYSE in 1927. In 1929 the chain's 397 stores in 87 cities had sales of $47 million.

During the Great Depression Walgreen's did comparatively well. Although average sales per store dropped between 1931 and 1935, per-store earnings went up, thanks to a chain-wide emphasis on efficiency. In 1940 there were 489 Walgreen stores. In 1941 the company established a profit-sharing pension plan that the press called "a landmark in American industrial relations." During the WWII years the chain shrank as unprofitable stores were closed.

The 1950s saw a major change in the way retailers did business. Walgreen's was an early leader in self-service merchandising. The company opened its first self-service store in 1952 and had 22 by the end of 1953, leading the industry. Between 1950 and 1960, as small, older stores were replaced with larger, more efficient, self-service units, the total number of stores in the chain increased only about 10%, but sales grew by over 90%.

In 1960 there were 451 Walgreen's stores, 1/2 of which were self-service. In 1962 the company bought the 3 huge Globe discount department stores in Houston. By 1966 there were 13 Globes in the Southwest, doing over $120 million in annual sales. During the 1960s Walgreen's soda fountains proved unprofitable and were phased out.

The 1970s and 1980s saw rapid growth and modernization in the chain. In 1973 company management organized a planning committee to boost Walgreen's sagging return on investment. A customer survey characterized the stores as "junky, disorganized, and hard-to-shop." Walgreen's modernized the stores and emphasized health aid and pharmacy business. The company was among the first to computerize its planning and distribution systems. In 1977 it sold or closed all of the by then unprofitable Globe stores. By 1979, 45% of the 688 stores had been opened during the decade. Walgreen's began installing a central computer database linked to each pharmacy in 1981. The company opened its 1,000th store in 1984, and in 1985 sales topped $3 billion. In order to concentrate on its core business, Walgreen's sold its chain of 91 Wag's restaurants to Marriott in 1988 and in 1989 sold its private label manufacturing business.

WHERE

HQ: 200 Wilmot Rd., Deerfield IL 60015
Phone: 708-940-2500
FAX: 708-940-2804

Walgreen's operates drugstores in over 650 communities in 28 states and Puerto Rico.

	1989 Stores	
	no.	% of total
Illinois	261	18
Florida	249	17
Texas	176	12
Wisconsin	89	6
Arizona	82	6
Indiana	63	4
Tennessee	61	4
California	59	4
Missouri	50	3
Colorado	43	3
Minnesota	43	3
Other states & Puerto Rico	308	20
Total	**1,484**	**100**

1989 Sales by Geographic Area	%
Chicago and suburbs	17
Other Midwest locations	21
Southwest	18
South and Southeast	27
West	10
East	7
Total	**100**

HOW MUCH

	9 Yr. Growth	1980	1981	1982	1983	1984	1985	1986	1987	1988	1989
Sales ($ mil)	15.0%	1,531	1,743	2,040	2,361	2,745	3,162	3,661	4,282	4,884	5,380
Net income ($ mil)	18.0%	35	42	56	70	85	94	103	104	129	154
Income as % of sales	—	2.3%	2.4%	2.7%	3.0%	3.1%	3.0%	2.8%	2.4%	2.6%	2.9%
Earnings per share ($)	17.5%	0.59	0.69	0.92	1.14	1.39	1.53	1.67	1.68	2.10	2.50
Stock price – high ($)	—	5.16	6.84	14.59	20.19	22.63	30.25	39.50	44.88	37.38	50.25
Stock price – low ($)	—	3.30	4.80	5.56	13.00	14.31	21.50	24.25	24.75	27.13	30.00
Stock price – close ($)	28.7%	4.81	6.08	14.03	19.13	22.50	28.13	32.38	30.75	30.25	46.75
P/E – high	—	9	10	16	18	16	20	24	27	18	20
P/E – low	—	6	7	6	11	10	14	15	15	13	12
Dividends per share ($)	15.0%	0.19	0.22	0.25	0.30	0.36	0.44	0.50	0.54	0.60	0.68
Book value per share ($)	15.3%	3.72	4.24	4.90	5.74	6.76	7.83	9.00	10.12	11.59	13.39

1989 Year End:
Debt ratio: 16.9%
Return on equity: 20.0%
Cash (mil): $226
Current ratio: 1.99
Long-term debt (mil): $168
Number of shares (mil): 62
Dividends:
1989 average yield: 1.5%
1989 payout: 27.2%
Market value (mil): $2,876

Stock Price History high/low 1980-89

60
50
40
30
20
10
0

WHAT

Estimated Sales by Product Class	%
Prescription drugs	30
General merchandise	28
Proprietary drugs	14
Liquor, beverages	12
Cosmetics, toiletries	11
Tobacco products	5
Total	**100**

RANKINGS

19th in *Fortune* 50 Retailing Cos.
158th in *Forbes* Sales 500
242nd in *Business Week* 1000
710th in *Business Week* Global 1000

COMPETITION

American Stores
Jack Eckerd
K mart
Longs
Melville
Rite Aid

WAL-MART STORES, INC.

OVERVIEW

Bentonville, Arkansas–based Wal-Mart is the fastest growing chain of discount stores in the US. Located primarily in small towns and metropolitan suburbs in 32 states throughout the Sunbelt and Midwest, Wal-Mart is a $25.8 billion company selling brand name merchandise at low prices in spartan stores. The 1,470 stores have several formats — Wal-Mart Discount City, Wal-Mart SuperCenter, Sam's Wholesale Club, and Hypermart*USA.

Wal-Mart has a reputation as a shopper-friendly store touting "Everyday Low Prices," a pricing strategy based on frugal management practices, including a lean advertising budget, a mania for cost control, and hard bargains with suppliers. Wal-Mart's success also results from the 17 efficient distribution centers, state-of-the-art computer system, and good management-staff relations.

Ranking 3rd in 1989 (*Fortune*'s Service 500) behind Sears Roebuck and K mart, Wal-Mart's retail sales of $25.8 billion increased 25% from 1988 revenues. Due to its rapid growth, Wal-Mart is expected to become #1 in 1991.

WHEN

Sam Walton began his retail career as a J. C. Penney management trainee and later leased a Ben Franklin franchised dimestore in Newport, Arkansas (1945). In 1950 he relocated to Bentonville, Arkansas, and opened a Walton 5&10. By 1962, Walton owned 15 Ben Franklin stores under the Walton 5&10 name.

After Ben Franklin management rejected his suggestion to open discount stores in small towns, Walton, with his brother James (Bud) Walton, opened the first Wal-Mart Discount City in Rogers, Arkansas (1962). Growth was slow at first. Wal-Mart Stores, Inc., went public (1970) with only 18 stores and sales of $44 million.

During the 1970s growth accelerated due to 2 key developments in distribution and computerization. Each of the 17 highly automated distribution centers serves approximately 150 nearby stores, cutting shipping costs and time. Computerization tracks inventory and speeds checkout and reordering. By 1980 the 276 stores had sales of $1.2 billion.

Acquisitions included Mohr Value (1977), Hutchinson Wholesale Shoe (1978), Kuhn's Big-K Stores (1981), and Super Saver Warehouse Club (1987). Wal-Mart phased out Ben Franklin stores (1976) and sold the 15 dot Discount Drugstores (1989, opened 1983).

In 1983 Wal-Mart opened Sam's Wholesale Club, modeled on the successful format of cash-and-carry, membership-only warehouse retailing pioneered by the Price Company of California. This format, targeted at small businesses in metropolitan areas, has proven profitable — in 1989 the 123 stores (now 136) had sales of $4.8 billion, representing nearly 19% of revenues.

In 1987 Wal-Mart started Hypermart*USA, originally a joint venture with Cullum Companies, a Dallas-based supermarket chain (Wal-Mart bought out Cullum's interest in 1989). The hypermarket, a huge European hybrid of the discount store and supermarket, features over 200,000 square feet of shopping in a mall-like setting, including ancillary businesses and services (branch bank, fast food outlets, express photo developer, hair salon, supervised playroom for shoppers' children).

Wal-Mart is also experimenting with other formats. SuperCenters (90,000 to 120,000 square feet) are large Wal-Mart Discount Cities with supermarkets. Sam's has added meat and produce sections and bakeries. In 1989 the company also tested 6 convenience stores next to existing company units.

In 1990 Wal-Mart was named as one of the top 10 Most Admired Companies in America by *Fortune*. Sam Walton predicts that the company will have 3,000 stores by the year 2000, with revenues of $125 billion.

HOW MUCH

	9 Yr. Growth	1980	1981	1982	1983	1984	1985	1986	1987	1988	1989
Sales ($ mil)	35.8%	1,643	2,445	3,376	4,667	6,401	8,451	11,909	15,959	20,649	25,811
Net income ($ mil)	39.0%	56	83	124	196	271	327	450	628	837	1,076
Income as % of sales	—	3.4%	3.4%	3.7%	4.2%	4.2%	3.9%	3.8%	3.9%	4.1%	4.2%
Earnings per share ($)	37.5%	0.11	0.16	0.23	0.35	0.48	0.58	0.80	1.11	1.48	1.90
Stock price – high ($)	—	1.93	2.74	6.75	11.66	11.75	17.25	26.94	42.88	33.88	44.88
Stock price – low ($)	—	0.87	1.69	2.41	5.47	7.56	9.47	14.56	20.00	24.25	30.00
Stock price – close ($)	42.2%	1.89	2.66	6.23	9.75	9.47	15.94	23.25	26.00	31.38	44.88
P/E – high	—	18	18	30	33	25	30	34	39	23	24
P/E – low	—	8	11	11	16	16	16	18	18	16	16
Dividends per share ($)	37.5%	0.01	0.02	0.02	0.04	0.05	0.07	0.09	0.12	0.16	0.22
Book value per share ($)	34.7%	0.48	0.62	0.91	1.32	1.76	2.27	3.00	3.99	5.32	7.00

1989 Year End:
Debt ratio: 24.3%
Return on equity: 30.8%
Cash (mil): $13
Current ratio: 1.66
Long-term debt (mil): $1,273
Number of shares (mil): 566
Dividends:
1989 average yield: 0.5%
1989 payout: 11.6%
Market value (mil): $25,405

Stock Price History high/low 1980-89

NYSE symbol: WMT
Incorporated: Delaware, 1969
Fiscal year ends: January 31

WHO

Chairman: Sam M. Walton, age 72, $350,000 pay
President and CEO: David D. Glass, age 54, $630,000 pay
VC and COO: Donald G. Soderquist, age 56, $525,000 pay
VC; CEO, Sam's Wholesale Club: A. L. Johnson, age 55, $254,000 pay
VC: S. Robson Walton, age 45
EVP and CFO: Paul R. Carter, age 49
Auditors: Ernst & Young
Employees: 275,000

WHERE

HQ: 702 SW 8th St., Bentonville, AR 72716
Phone: 501-273-4000
FAX: 501-273-8650

Wal-Mart operates 1,470 Wal-Mart Discount Cities, SuperCenters, and Sam's Wholesale Clubs in 32 states and 4 Hypermart*USAs in Texas (2), Kansas, and Missouri.

State	Wal-Mart Discount City; SuperCenter	Sam's Wholesale Club
Alabama	70	5
Arkansas	77	4
Colorado	28	2
Florida	106	15
Georgia	77	7
Illinois	72	6
Indiana	41	2
Iowa	33	2
Kansas	41	2
Kentucky	62	3
Louisiana	75	9
Mississippi	55	2
Missouri	104	8
North Carolina	51	5
Ohio	23	4
Oklahoma	80	5
South Carolina	46	4
Tennessee	82	7
Texas	230	34
Wisconsin	29	3
Other states	88	7
Total	**1,470**	**136**

WHAT

Category	% of 1989 sales
Hard goods	28
Soft goods	27
Stationery & candy	11
Sporting goods & toys	9
Health & beauty aids	9
Gifts, records & electronics	6
Pharmaceuticals	5
Shoes	3
Jewelry	2
Total	**100**

RANKINGS

3rd in *Fortune* 50 Retailing Cos.
16th in *Forbes* Sales 500
11th in *Business Week* 1000
22nd in *Business Week* Global 1000

COMPETITION

Ames
Costco
Dayton Hudson
K mart
Price Co.
Riklis Family
Sears

THE WALT DISNEY COMPANY

OVERVIEW

With one of the world's best-known names, Disney is the purveyor of a Magic Kingdom, home to Mickey Mouse, Donald Duck, Goofy, and dozens of other characters. Disney operates theme parks and resorts in California and Florida; produces movies, television, and cable programming; owns a television station and record label; and markets Disney consumer products worldwide.

Disney World, Disneyland, and Tokyo Disneyland combined have attracted over 675 million people to the rides, shows, and characters of Walt Disney Imagineering, the company's creative development arm.

Animation, the original product of the Disney empire, still creates fans today. The re-release of its classic films every 7 years, a commitment to produce a new animated film each year, and the popularity of its other filmed entertainment brought Disney almost $1.6 billion in film revenues in 1989. The company also produces award-winning TV programs for all ages and leads the industry in home video sales. Through strong alliances with licensees, manufacturers, and retail outlets, Disney's consumer-products revenues increased 67% in 1989 to $411 million.

NYSE symbol: DIS
Incorporated: Delaware, 1986
Fiscal year ends: September 30

WHO

Chairman and CEO: Michael D. Eisner, age 47, $9,589,360 pay
President and COO: Frank G. Wells, age 57, $4,819,680 pay
EVP and CFO: Gary L. Wilson, age 49, $2,500,000 pay
Auditors: Price Waterhouse
Employees: 47,000

WHEN

After his first animated film business failed, artist Walt Disney and his brother Roy started a film studio in 1923 in Hollywood. Walt directed the first Mickey Mouse cartoon, "Plane Crazy," in 1928. Disney's studio created short animated cartoons like the "Three Little Pigs."

The studio produced its first animated feature film, *Snow White*, in 1937 and *Fantasia* and *Pinocchio* in the 1940s. Disney produced "The Mickey Mouse Club" (1955-1959) and "Disney's Wonderful World," the longest-running network series in television history, today in its 33rd season. Disneyland opened in 1955 in Anaheim, California, with over a million visitors in its first 6 months.

Disney died in 1966 of lung cancer, leaving his brother Roy as chairman of the company. Disney World opened in Florida in 1971 and Roy died the same year, leaving E. Cardon Walker as president. Roy's son, Roy E. Disney, VP of Disney's animation division, became the company's principal individual shareholder upon his father's death. Without Walt and Roy's leadership and creativity, Disney films went from producing over half the company's revenues in 1971 to only 20% in 1979.

In 1980 Walker became CEO and appointed Ron Miller, Walt's son-in-law, president and COO. Epcot Center opened in Florida in 1982, and in 1983 Miller became CEO. Miller started Touchstone Pictures in order to produce films like *Splash* (1984), Disney's first hit since *The Love Bug* (1969).

In 1984 Texas's wealthy Bass family, in alliance with Roy E. Disney, bought a controlling interest in the company. The old management was replaced by new CEO Michael Eisner (from Paramount) and President Frank Wells (from Warner Bros.), bringing a new era of innovation and prosperity to the company.

The company started The Disney Channel and opened Disney retail stores in the 1980s. Tokyo Disneyland opened in 1984, and the company began work on Euro Disneyland outside Paris, slated to open in 1992. As the 1980s ended, the company expanded its production of mainstream movies with hits such as *Dead Poets Society*, *Dick Tracy*, and *Who Framed Roger Rabbit*; opened the Disney-MGM Studios Theme Park in Florida; agreed to purchase Henson Associates (the Muppets); and continued expanding its retail outlets.

In 1988 Disney bought the Wrather Corporation, including the Disneyland Hotel and the Queen Mary and Spruce Goose in Long Beach, California. In 1989 Disney purchased a TV station in Los Angeles and started a record division. In 1990 Disney opened Mickey's Kitchen, its first mall restaurant, and earned its 60th Oscar.

WHERE

HQ: 500 S. Buena Vista St., Burbank, CA 91521
Phone: 818-560-1000
FAX: 818-840-1930

Disney locations are studios and corporate headquarters in Burbank, CA; theme parks are in California, Florida, and Japan; and 50 Disney Stores in 20 states. Disney distributes films and video internationally.

	1989 Pretax Income	
	$ mil	% of total
Domestic (including US exports)	1,103	96
Foreign subsidiaries	50	4
Total	**1,153**	**100**

WHAT

	1989 Sales		1989 Operating Income	
	$ mil	% of total	$ mil	% of total
Theme parks & resorts	2,595	56	785	64
Filmed entertainment	1,588	35	257	21
Consumer products	411	9	187	15
Adjustments	—	—	(120)	—
Total	**4,594**	**100**	**1,109**	**100**

Theme Parks & Resorts
Disneyland - CA
Euro Disneyland (scheduled to open in 1992)
Hotel Queen Mary
Spruce Goose
Tokyo Disneyland
Walt Disney World - FL
  Disney-MGM Studios Theme Park
  Epcot Center
  Magic Kingdom

Consumer Products
Childcraft catalog
Disney Stores
Walt Disney Records

Filmed Entertainment
Broadcast Television
  KCAL-TV Los Angeles
Movies
  Touchstone Pictures
  Walt Disney Pictures
Network Television
  Touchstone Television
  Walt Disney Television
Pay Television
  Buena Vista Home Video
  Buena Vista Television
  The Disney Channel

RANKINGS

19th in *Fortune* 100 Diversified Service Cos.
182nd in *Forbes* Sales 500
33rd in *Business Week* 1000
74th in *Business Week* Global 1000

COMPETITION

American Financial
Anheuser-Busch
Capital Cities/ABC
MCA
Paramount
Sony
Tele-Communications
Time Warner
Turner Broadcasting
Viacom
Other entertainment companies

HOW MUCH

	9 Yr. Growth	1980	1981	1982	1983	1984	1985	1986	1987	1988	1989
Sales ($ mil)	19.6%	915	1,005	1,030	1,307	1,656	2,015	2,471	2,877	3,438	4,594
Net income ($ mil)	20.1%	135	121	100	93	22	174	247	392	522	703
Income as % of sales	—	14.8%	12.1%	9.7%	7.1%	1.3%	8.6%	10.0%	13.6%	15.2%	15.3%
Earnings per share ($)	19.3%	1.04	0.93	0.75	0.68	0.15	1.29	1.82	2.85	3.80	5.10
Stock price – high ($)	—	13.47	16.78	17.88	21.19	17.13	29.38	54.88	82.50	68.38	136.25
Stock price – low ($)	—	10.13	10.84	11.75	11.81	11.31	14.81	28.06	41.25	54.00	64.88
Stock price – close ($)	27.2%	12.81	13.06	15.81	13.16	14.97	28.22	43.13	59.25	65.75	112.00
P/E – high	—	13	18	24	31	112	23	30	29	18	27
P/E – low	—	10	12	16	18	74	12	15	14	14	13
Dividends per share ($)	8.6%	0.21	0.25	0.30	0.23	0.38	0.30	0.32	0.32	0.28	0.44
Book value per share ($)	11.7%	8.31	9.00	9.56	10.15	8.56	9.16	10.85	14.01	17.71	22.50

1989 Year End:
Debt ratio: 22.0%
Return on equity: 25.4%
Cash (mil): $381
Current ratio: 1.73
Long-term debt (mil): $861
Number of shares (mil): 135
Dividends:
  1989 average yield: 0.4%
  1989 payout: 8.6%
Market value (mil): $15,154

Stock Price History high/low 1980-89
140
120
100
80
60
40
20
0

WANG LABORATORIES, INC.

OVERVIEW

Wang Laboratories, a 39-year-old company based in Lowell, Massachusetts, is a manufacturer of minicomputers, PCs, networking devices, and imaging products. In recent years sales have dropped, losses have mounted, and employment has declined from 31,000 to 20,000 as this struggling company has sought to find a place for itself in a changing computer market.

Wang's VS minicomputers range from the entry-level VS 5000 (6 to 128 users) to the superminicomputer VS 10000 (up to 255 users). Wang is an industry leader in imaging systems. The Wang Integrated Image System stores, sorts, and retrieves electronic images, including drawings, photos, and written documents input by scanner or FAX. Wang's Freestyle system allows users to attach written notes (with an electronic stylus) and voice messages (with a telephone-like handset) to documents displayed on the screen, prior to sending them to others on the network.

The company's marketing focus is on government, financial services, manufacturing, and professional and legal services. Combined, these markets account for 70% of Wang's revenues.

WHEN

In 1951, with $600 in savings, An Wang started Wang Laboratories in Boston. Wang had come to the US from China in 1945 to earn a PhD at Harvard. While working for Harvard's Computation Laboratory, he patented a magnetic pulse device that led to the development of memory cores. The small rings of iron were the central components of computer memory until replaced by microchips in the late 1960s. IBM bought Wang's patent in 1956 for $500,000.

Wang's initial success came from engineering custom digital devices (*e.g.*, the first digitally programmed scoreboard in New York's Shea Stadium). Another was the successful semiautomatic typesetter (Linasec) Wang developed in 1963 under contract, which increased sales to over $1 million in 1964.

Adhering to An Wang's philosophy of "Find a need and fill it," Wang entered the calculator business, introducing an innovative desktop calculator, the LOCI, in 1965. The subsequent demand for Wang calculators caused the company to go public in 1967 to finance its expansion.

In the mid-1970s Wang relinquished the calculator business to its competitors and entered the word processor market. Wang introduced the first screen-based (TV-like display) word processor in 1976, and by 1978 it had become the largest supplier of screen-based systems. In 1977 Wang introduced its VS minicomputer series — a product line built on compatibility among existing and future VS computers. The success of the VS series combined with strong sales of word processors caused Wang's revenues to rise from $543 million in 1980 to $2.4 billion in 1985.

In 1985 Wang's earnings declined 92% from the previous year, forcing layoffs and causing An Wang to return to active management of the company. The company has not fully recovered since. In 1986 Wang made his son Fred president, but his efforts to revitalize the company failed. Massive losses in 1989 caused Fred to resign as president that year. In 1990 An Wang died from cancer of the esophagus. His heirs and other Wang family members own almost 40% of the company.

Wang's sales have been hurt by the decreasing demand for minicomputers with proprietary architectures and by Wang's slowness in entering the desktop computer and local area network arenas. Wang's current market focus is on image processing — the storing and manipulating of graphics and digitized pictures — a technology whose anticipated demand has yet to be realized.

HOW MUCH

	9 Yr. Growth	1980	1981	1982	1983	1984	1985	1986	1987	1988	1989
Sales ($ mil)	20.3%	543	856	1,159	1,538	2,185	2,352	2,643	2,837	3,068	2,869
Net income ($ mil)	—	52	78	107	152	210	16	51	(71)	93	(321)
Income as % of sales	—	9.6%	9.1%	9.2%	9.9%	9.6%	0.7%	1.9%	(2.5%)	3.0%	(11.2%)
Earnings per share ($)	—	0.50	0.67	0.88	1.16	1.52	0.11	0.35	(0.44)	0.56	(1.96)
Stock price – high ($)	—	22.63	22.81	31.69	42.50	37.63	29.25	21.75	19.13	16.50	10.88
Stock price – low ($)	—	7.13	12.00	12.31	28.00	23.00	15.00	10.50	9.63	7.50	4.63
Stock price – close ($)	(14.3%)	20.50	16.63	29.50	35.63	25.88	19.63	11.63	11.50	8.75	5.13
P/E – high	—	45	34	36	37	25	266	62	—	29	—
P/E – low	—	14	18	14	24	15	136	30	—	13	—
Dividends per share ($)	16.7%	0.04	0.06	0.06	0.09	0.12	0.16	0.16	0.16	0.16	0.16
Book value per share($)	15.5%	1.88	3.91	4.81	7.09	9.01	8.93	9.59	9.15	9.67	6.90

1989 Year End:
Debt ratio: 35.5%
Return on equity: —
Cash (mil): $258
Current ratio: 1.37
Long-term debt (mil): $623
Number of shares (mil): 164
Dividends:
1989 average yield: 3.1%
1989 payout: —
Market value (mil): $840

Stock Price History high/low 1980-89

ASE symbol: WANB
Incorporated: Massachusetts, 1955
Fiscal year ends: June 30

WHO

Chairman, President, and CEO: Richard W. Miller, age 48
VC: Harry H. S. Chou, age 66, $383,195
EVP: Horace Tsiang, age 47, $277,604
EVP Operations: Joseph M. Tucci
EVP and CFO: Michael F. Mee, age 47
Auditors: Ernst & Young
Employees: 20,000

WHERE

HQ: One Industrial Ave., Lowell, MA 01851
Phone: 508-459-5000
FAX: 508-458-8969

Wang has offices in 25 countries and manufacturing locations in the US, Puerto Rico, Taiwan, Australia, and Ireland.

	1989 Sales		1989 Pretax Income	
	$ mil	% of total	$ mil	% of total
US	1,462	51	(185)	70
Europe	896	31	(160)	60
Asia/Pacific	389	14	84	(32)
Other Americas	122	4	(6)	2
Adjustments	—	—	4	—
Total	**2,869**	**100**	**(263)**	**100**

WHAT

	1989 Sales	
	$ mil	% of total
Product sales	1,864	65
Service & rental income	1,005	35
Total	**2,869**	**100**

Computers
VS 5000
VS 8200
VS 10000

Workstations
Wang PC 200/300 Series

Communications
Wang PC LAN
Wang Open Systems Networking (OSN)
WangNet

Software
Wang Integrated Image System (WIIS)
Wang Freestyle Personal Computing System
WP Plus — word processor
Wang OFFICE — office automation
Professional Application Creation Environment (PACE)
Speech and Telephony Environment for Programmers (STEP)

RANKINGS

147th in *Fortune* 500 Industrial Cos.
320th in *Forbes* Sales 500
563rd in *Business Week* 1000

COMPETITION

Apple
Compaq
Data General
Digital Equipment
IBM
NCR
Prime
Tandem
Unisys
Other computer and software companies

WARNER-LAMBERT COMPANY

OVERVIEW

While better known for its OTC health care products (Listerine, Rolaids, Halls) and confections (Trident, Dentyne, Certs), Warner-Lambert is the 7th largest pharmaceutical company in the US and a major drug maker worldwide. The company has leading nonprescription products for allergies, sinus problems, coughs and colds, and oral hygiene. It also sells more sugarless chewing gum in the US than any other company. In 1988, with $609 million spent on advertising, Warner-Lambert ranked 13th among all US advertisers.

Its 1989 advertising and promotional expenditures rose to $998 million.

Warner-Lambert's R&D spending increased 19% in 1989 to $309 million, with the company planning to invest over $2 billion in R&D through 1994. The company's "pipeline" of new drugs includes treatments for heart disease, cancer, Alzheimer's disease, epilepsy, and hypertension.

Other products include razors (Schick), aquarium products (Tetra), and gelatin capsules. The company is developing a biodegradable plastic-like material named Novon.

NYSE symbol: WLA
Incorporated: Delaware, 1920
Fiscal year ends: December 31

WHO

Chairman and CEO: Joseph D. Williams, age 63, $1,505,000 pay
President and COO: Melvin R. Goodes, age 54, $1,003,750 pay
EVP and CFO: Robert J. Dircks, age 62, $538,417 pay
Auditors: Price Waterhouse
Employees: 33,100

WHERE

HQ: 201 Tabor Rd., Morris Plains, NJ 07950
Phone: 201-540-2000
FAX: 201-540-3761

The company has 77 plants in over 40 countries.

	1989 Sales		1989 Operating Income	
	$ mil	% of total	$ mil	% of total
US	2,249	54	650	61
Americas & Asia	1,057	25	241	22
Other	890	21	181	17
Adjustments	—	—	(501)	—
Total	**4,196**	**100**	**571**	**100**

WHEN

Warner-Lambert's origins go back to a Philadelphia drugstore owned by William Warner, who established the drug manufacturing business of William Warner and Company in 1886. In 1908 the Pfeiffer Chemical Company of St. Louis bought Warner, adopting the name and moving it to New York City in 1916 to better serve Warner's growing market. By 1945 the company had acquired over 50 businesses, including Sloan's (liniment) and Corn Husker's (lotion); the largest was Hudnut (cosmetics) of New York.

After WWII Warner and Company began to take on its current structure under the leadership of Elmer Bobst, former president of Hoffman-LaRoche's US office. In 1950 Bobst changed the name to Warner-Hudnut (cosmetics then accounted for most of the company's sales), and the company went public. In 1952 Bobst bought Chilcott Labs (originally the Maltine Company, Brooklyn, 1874) and in 1955 changed the name to Warner-Lambert following the purchase of Lambert Pharmacal (founded by Jordan Lambert of St. Louis in 1884 upon acquiring the formula for the antiseptic Listerine).

In the late 1950s Bobst's major buys included Emerson Drugs (Bromo-Seltzer), Smith Brothers (cough drops), and Schick Shaving. American Chicle (Chiclets and Beeman's chewing gums) was bought in 1962.

The purchase of Parke-Davis in 1970 resulted in an antitrust investigation and the selling of certain product lines in 1976 (thyroid preparations, blood products, vaccines, and others). Founded in Detroit in 1866, Parke-Davis was the first company to make "biologicals" (vaccines). It later introduced Dilantin (anticonvulsant, 1938), Benadryl (antihistamine, 1946), and Chloromycetin (antibiotic, 1949), all still sold today.

In 1975 the FTC complained about Warner-Lambert ads for Listerine that claimed it prevented colds and the flu, forcing the company to run disclaimers. Slipping profits in the 1970s motivated the selling of unprofitable divisions and consolidation of others in the early 1980s. In 1985 the company's divestment of its ailing health technologies businesses, along with the costs associated with its restructuring and streamlining program, caused it to take a $553 million write-down. The restructuring, however, along with new robotic manufacturing methods for increased efficiency, resulted in annual savings of over $300 million and led to generally profitable results throughout the rest of the 1980s. Warner-Lambert's biggest drug product success has been Lopid (introduced in 1981), a cholesterol-lowering drug, which in 1989 accounted for $285 million in sales.

WHAT

	1989 Sales		1989 Operating Income	
	$ mil	% of total	$ mil	% of total
Ethical products	1,324	32	465	44
Nonprescription	1,370	32	311	29
Gum & mints	1,003	24	195	18
Other	499	12	101	9
Adjustments	—	—	(501)	—
Total	**4,196**	**100**	**571**	**100**

Ethical Products
Accupril (for hypertension)
Chloromycetin (antibiotic)
Comprecin (anti-infective)
Dilantin (anticonvulsant)
Doryx (anti-infective)
ERYC (erythromycin)
Loestrin (oral contraceptive)
Lopid (blood lipid regulator)
Lubriderm (skin lotion)
Mediquell (chewy cough squares)
Myadec (vitamins)
Remegel (antacid)
Rolaids (antacid)
Sinutab

Nonprescription Products
Anusol (hemorrhoidal preparation)
Benadryl (antihistamine)
Benylin (cough syrup)
Caladryl (anti-itch lotion)
E.P.T. (pregnancy test)
Efferdent (denture cleanser)
Gelusil (antacid)
Halls (cough tablets)
Listerine (mouthwash)

Confections
Beeman's
Bubblicious
Certs
Chiclets
Clorets
Dentyne
Junior Mints
Sugar Babies
Sugar Daddy
Trident

Other
Schick (razors)
Tetra (aquarium supplies)

HOW MUCH

	9 Yr. Growth	1980	1981	1982	1983	1984	1985	1986	1987	1988	1989
Sales ($ mil)	2.1%	3,479	3,380	3,246	3,108	3,167	3,200	3,103	3,485	3,908	4,196
Net income ($ mil)	8.8%	193	9	175	201	224	(316)	309	296	340	413
Income as % of sales	—	5.5%	0.3%	5.4%	6.5%	7.1%	(9.9%)	10.0%	8.5%	8.7%	9.8%
Earnings per share ($)	11.0%	1.20	0.06	1.10	1.26	1.41	(2.03)	2.09	2.08	2.50	3.05
Stock price – high ($)	—	11.63	12.50	15.06	17.50	18.06	24.69	31.56	43.75	39.75	59.38
Stock price – low ($)	—	8.50	8.50	9.81	12.88	14.38	16.69	21.69	24.13	29.94	37.25
Stock price – close ($)	21.4%	10.06	11.13	14.13	14.81	17.38	23.75	29.31	33.75	39.19	57.75
P/E – high	—	10	208	14	14	13	—	15	21	16	19
P/E – low	—	7	142	9	10	10	—	10	12	12	12
Dividends per share ($)	7.6%	0.66	0.67	0.70	0.71	0.74	0.75	0.80	0.89	1.08	1.28
Book value per share ($)	(1.2%)	9.34	8.69	8.64	8.88	9.09	5.89	6.32	6.37	7.36	8.38

1989 Year End:
Debt ratio: 21.2%
Return on equity: 38.7%
Cash (mil): $253
Current ratio: 1.33
Long-term debt (mil): $303
Number of shares (mil): 135
Dividends:
1989 average yield: 2.2%
1989 payout: 42.0%
Market value (mil): $7,787

RANKINGS

114th in *Fortune* 500 US Industrial Cos.
311th in *Fortune* Global 500 Industrial Cos.
203rd in *Forbes* Sales 500
77th in *Business Week* 1000
207th in *Business Week* Global 1000

COMPETITION

American Home Products
Bristol-Myers Squibb
Colgate-Palmolive
Eastman Kodak
Gillette
Procter & Gamble
RJR Nabisco
Unilever
Wrigley
Drug companies

THE WASHINGTON POST COMPANY

OVERVIEW

The Washington Post Company publishes the *Washington Post*, in its 113th year, with an average daily circulation of over 3/4 million (1.1 million on Sundays) in 1989. The company publishes *Newsweek* magazine (3.1 million average weekly circulation); *Newsweek International* (665,000 average weekly circulation), published in Atlantic, Pacific, and Latin American editions; and *Newsweek Japan* in Japanese. It also syndicates 31 features.

The company owns 4 TV stations and 51 cable systems with over 400,000 subscribers.

The company's 137 Stanley H. Kaplan Educational Centers prepare students for licensing exams and admission tests. Legi-Slate, Inc., is an on-line government information service subsidiary. The company also owns interests in paper companies in Nova Scotia and Virginia and timberland in Virginia. It is a partner in a news service and the *International Herald Tribune*, published in Europe and Asia, and owns 26% of Cowles Media Company, owners of the *Minneapolis Star and Tribune* and other publications.

NYSE symbol: WPO
Incorporated: Delaware, 1947
Fiscal year ends: December 31

WHO

Chairman and CEO: Katharine Graham, age 72, $739,874 pay
President and COO: Richard D. Simmons, age 55, $669,839 pay
VP Finance: John B. Morse, Jr., age 43
VP; Publisher, *The Washington Post*: Donald E. Graham, age 44
Auditors: Price Waterhouse
Employees: 6,200

WHEN

Stilson Hutchins, journalist and politician, published the first edition of the *Washington Post* in 1877. Strong reporting made the *Post* successful and Hutchins retired in 1889, selling the *Post* to Beriah Wilkins, a banker and politician, and Frank Hatton, a journalist. Hatton died in 1894, and the *Post* took on the conservative leanings of Wilkins and the Victorian perspective of the times. Wilkins died in 1905, and his heirs sold their interest in the *Post* to John R. McLean, active in Ohio Democratic party politics and inheritor of the *Cincinnati Enquirer*.

McLean changed the *Post*, focusing on society columns and features, adding color comics and the big headline style found in sensationalist papers. Hard news coverage suffered, while crime and scandal were emphasized. By the time McLean died in 1916, the *Post* had resorted to yellow journalism.

McLean's son Ned took over the *Post* and the *Enquirer*. Ned ruined the *Post*'s integrity by lying to a Senate committee (1924) about his involvement in the Teapot Dome oil scandal. He yielded the *Post*'s management in 1932 and died from alcoholism in 1941.

Wealthy, conservative banker Eugene Meyer bought the bankrupt *Post* for $825,000 in 1933. Meyer's credo of hard work, honesty, hands-on management, and personal funding saved the *Post*. Meyer spent the next 12 years building a first-class news staff. By 1946, when Meyer's son-in-law Philip Graham took over as publisher, the *Post* was in the black again. In 1948 Meyer transferred his stock to his daughter Katherine and Philip. In 1954 the *Post* bought the *Washington Times-Herald*, eliminating its morning competition.

Philip Graham bought radio and TV stations and established overseas bureaus. In 1961 he started a national news service with the *Los Angeles Times* and bought *Newsweek* magazine. In 1963, having struggled with manic depression since 1957, Philip Graham killed himself.

Katherine Graham became publisher of the *Post*, where she had worked as an editor since 1939. In 1971 the company went public. In 1972 reporters Bob Woodward and Carl Bernstein broke the Watergate story, which won a Pulitzer Prize in 1973 and led to Richard Nixon's resignation. In the 1970s and 1980s Katherine Graham bought TV and radio stations, databases, cable companies, newspapers, and newsprint mills. In 1979 her son Donald Graham, who had begun working at the *Post* in 1971, became publisher, and Katherine Graham remained as chairman and CEO.

In 1984 the company bought the Stanley H. Kaplan Educational Centers and in 1988 and 1989 expanded its cable TV system.

WHERE

HQ: 1150 15th St., NW, Washington, DC 20071
Phone: 202-334-6000
FAX: 202-334-4480

The company owns newspapers in Washington, DC, and Everett, WA; 4 TV stations in 3 states; and 51 cable TV systems in 15 states.

WHAT

	1989 Sales		1989 Operating Income	
	$ mil	% of total	$ mil	% of total
Newspaper publishing	727	50	177	57
Magazine publishing	334	23	28	9
Broadcasting	183	13	72	23
Cable television	129	9	26	8
Other	71	5	11	3
Total	**1,444**	**100**	**314**	**100**

Newspapers
The Washington Post
The Herald (Everett, WA)
Cowles Media Company (26%)
International Herald Tribune, S.A. (33 1/3%)

Magazines
Newsweek
Newsweek International
Newsweek Japan

TV Stations
WDIV-4, Detroit
WFSB-3, Hartford
WJXT-4, Jacksonville
WPLG-10, Miami

Other Businesses
51 cable TV systems
Stanley H. Kaplan Educational Centers
Legi-Slate, Inc. (on-line database)
Bowater Mersey Paper (newsprint, 49%)
Bear Island Paper (newsprint, 33 1/3%)
Bear Island Timberlands (timber, 33 1/3%)
L.A. Times–Washington Post News Service (50%)

RANKINGS

269th in *Fortune* 500 Industrial Cos.
498th in *Forbes* Sales 500
194th in *Business Week* 1000
623rd in *Business Week* Global 1000

COMPETITION

Dow Jones
Hearst
Knight-Rider
New York Times
E. W. Scripps
Tele-Communications
Time Warner
Tribune
Viacom
Other publishers, broadcasters, and cable operators

HOW MUCH

	9 Yr. Growth	1980	1981	1982	1983	1984	1985	1986	1987	1988	1989
Sales ($ mil)	9.1%	660	753	801	878	984	1,079	1,215	1,315	1,368	1,444
Net income ($ mil)	21.5%	34	33	52	68	86	114	100	187	269	198
Income as % of sales	—	5.2%	4.3%	6.5%	7.8%	8.7%	10.6%	8.2%	14.2%	19.7%	13.7%
Earnings per share ($)	22.8%	2.44	2.32	3.70	4.82	6.11	8.66	7.80	14.52	20.91	15.50
Stock price – high ($)	—	24.75	33.00	60.88	73.25	85.00	130.00	184.50	269.00	229.00	311.00
Stock price – low ($)	—	15.88	19.38	27.38	54.50	60.75	77.75	115.00	150.00	186.50	204.00
Stock price – close ($)	32.3%	22.63	31.38	55.25	73.25	80.25	118.75	156.00	187.00	210.75	281.50
P/E – high	—	10	14	16	15	14	15	24	19	11	20
P/E – low	—	7	8	7	11	10	9	15	10	9	13
Dividends per share ($)	17.2%	0.44	0.50	0.56	0.66	0.80	0.96	1.12	1.28	1.56	1.84
Book value per share ($)	21.1%	13.40	15.17	18.32	22.50	27.17	27.26	34.04	47.80	67.50	75.40

1989 Year End:
Debt ratio: 13.9%
Return on equity: 21.7%
Cash (mil): $365
Current ratio: 2.05
Long-term debt (mil): $152
Number of shares (mil): 12
Dividends:
1989 average yield: 0.7%
1989 payout: 11.9%
Market value (mil): $3,515

Stock Price History high/low 1980-89

WASTE MANAGEMENT, INC.

OVERVIEW

Waste Management is the largest waste collection, disposal, and recycling company in the world, with revenues of $4.5 billion in 1989, only 21 years after founding. It offers municipal, industrial, medical, and commercial waste pickup, transport, and disposal; owns and operates landfills in 35 states and Canada; and generates electricity from landfill-produced methane gas (equivalent to 1.6 million barrels of oil per year) or sells the gas directly to industrial end users.

It also offers waste-stream consulting services to industry and site-cleanup services for toxic wastes. The company disposed of 90% of the wastes produced during the cleanup of the Exxon *Valdez* oil spill (1988).

Waste is a growth industry. In the future, the company expects to add 60 new municipal sites and expand 40 existing sites. It has recently formed joint ventures with Du Pont and Stone Container to market the materials it collects for recycling, and plans to move into Europe more strongly in the coming years. The company has been cited for possible liability in Superfund sites, primarily through companies it acquired.

NYSE Symbol: WMX
Incorporated: Delaware, 1968
Fiscal year ends: December 31

WHO

Chairman and CEO: Dean L. Buntrock, age 58, $1,356,800 pay
President and COO: Phillip B. Rooney, age 45, $1,017,600 pay
SVP: Donald F. Flynn, age 50, $593,700 pay
SVP: Jerry E. Dempsey, age 57, $587,400 pay
VP, Treasurer, and CFO: James E. Koenig, age 42
Auditors: Arthur Andersen & Co.
Employees: 42,640

WHEN

In 1956 Dean L. Buntrock joined Ace Scavenger Service in Illinois, which had 12 collection trucks and $750,000 per year in revenues. Under Buntrock's leadership, the company expanded into Wisconsin.

In 1971 Waste Management, Inc., was formed when Buntrock joined forces with H. Wayne Huizenga, who had bought 2 waste routes in Broward County, Florida, in 1962. (Huizenga retired in 1983 and went on to control Blockbuster Video, the #1 video rental chain in the country.) Both companies had grown rapidly during the 1960s, as concern with air quality prompted bans on residential and industrial on-site waste burning. During 1969 and 1970 some of the company's future competitors began to form through acquisition. Waste Management reported earnings of $1.2 million on revenues of $16.8 million its first year, with customers in Florida, Illinois, Indiana, Minnesota, Ohio and Wisconsin. In the 1970s it made acquisitions in Michigan, New York, Ohio, Pennsylvania, and Canada.

In 1975 the company bid on and won a contract in Riyadh, Saudi Arabia (service started in 1978), and formed its international subsidiary. Other foreign contracts followed in Argentina (1980), Venezuela (1981), Australia (1984), and New Zealand (1986).

The company went into specialty areas, forming Chemical Waste Management (78% owned, 1975), which now offers site cleanup services (ENRAC, 1980) and low-level nuclear waste disposal (Chem-Nuclear Systems, 1982). Expansion in this period included companies in the Pacific Northwest and California and new contracts in Louisiana, Mississippi, and Texas. A great coup was acquisition of 60% of competitor SCA of Boston (1984).

Recent projects include joint ventures for sale of recyclable materials with Du Pont (1989) and Stone Container Corp. (1990), and a partnership with Henley Group in which the company ceded all its waste-to-energy operations to a new firm, Wheelabrator Technologies, in return for stock (22%, 1988; now 55%). In 1988 and 1989 it acquired operations in Germany, Italy, the Netherlands, and Sweden.

For many years the company has been the target of accusations, and in some cases has been fined, for violation of pollution ($12.5 million for the Vickery, Ohio, hazardous-waste facility, 1985) and antitrust laws ($2 million). It conducts local and national lobbying efforts on behalf of the waste management industry and supports many environmental legislation proposals.

In 1990 the company authorized the repurchase of up to 5% of its stock for possible use in future acquisitions.

WHERE

HQ: 3003 Butterfield Rd., Oak Brook, IL 60521
Phone: 708-572-8800
FAX: 708-572-3094

The company has customers in 48 states, Canada, and more than 12 other countries.

	1989 Sales		1989 Operating Income	
	$ mil	% of total	$ mil	% of total
US	3,961	89	904	93
Foreign	498	11	64	7
Total	**4,459**	**100**	**968**	**100**

WHAT

	1989 Sales		1989 Operating Income	
	$ mil	% of total	$ mil	% of total
Solid waste	3,539	79	736	76
Hazardous waste	920	21	232	24
Total	**4,459**	**100**	**968**	**100**

	1989 Sales	
	$ mil	% of total
Waste Management of North America	3,179	71
Chemical Waste Managment	892	20
Waste Management International	388	9
Total	**4,459**	**100**

Waste Management of North America
Modulaire (mobile offices)
Port-O-Let (portable sanitation)
TruGreen (lawn care services)
WMI Medical Services (medical refuse disposal)

Chemical Waste Management (78%)
Chem-Nuclear Systems (low-level radioactive material disposal)
ENRAC (site remediation)

Waste Management International (cleaning/waste services)

Wheelabrator Technologies (waste to energy, 55%)

RANKINGS

20th in *Fortune* 100 Diversified Service Cos.
194th in *Forbes* Sales 500
31st in *Business Week* 1000
63rd in *Business Week* Global 1000

COMPETITION

Bechtel
Browning-Ferris
Consolidated Rail
Ogden
Union Pacific

HOW MUCH

	9 Yr. Growth	1980	1981	1982	1983	1984	1985	1986	1987	1988	1989
Sales ($ mil)	25.9%	560	773	967	1,040	1,315	1,625	2,018	2,758	3,566	4,459
Net income ($ mil)	29.5%	55	84	107	120	143	172	371	327	464	562
Income as % of sales	—	9.8%	10.9%	11.0%	11.6%	10.8%	10.6%	18.4%	11.9%	13.0%	12.6%
Earnings per share ($)	23.7%	0.18	0.24	0.30	0.31	0.37	0.43	0.88	0.73	1.03	1.22
Stock price – high ($)	—	4.17	5.14	6.97	7.73	5.98	9.50	14.94	24.25	21.38	35.88
Stock price – low ($)	—	1.51	3.24	3.19	4.69	3.41	5.42	8.63	13.88	15.75	20.38
Stock price – close ($)	27.9%	3.81	4.23	6.69	5.80	5.48	8.88	13.91	18.81	20.69	35.00
P/E – high	—	23	21	23	25	16	22	17	33	21	29
P/E – low	—	8	13	11	15	9	13	10	19	15	17
Dividends per share ($)	26.3%	0.04	0.04	0.06	0.08	0.10	0.11	0.14	0.18	0.23	0.29
Book value per share ($)	22.3%	0.96	1.22	1.76	2.00	2.27	2.79	3.67	4.19	4.82	5.88

1989 Year End:
Debt ratio: 35.5%
Return on equity: 22.8%
Cash (mil): $107
Current ratio: 0.87
Long-term debt (mil): $1,504
Number of shares (mil): 466
Dividends:
1989 average yield: 0.8%
1989 payout: 23.8%
Market value (mil): $16,302

Stock Price History high/low 1980-89

40 35 30 25 20 15 10 5 0

WELLS FARGO & COMPANY

OVERVIEW

San Francisco–based Wells Fargo & Company is the holding company of Wells Fargo Bank, the 12th largest bank in the US (4th in California). The company's focus in recent years on expense control and efficiency of operations made it one of the industry leaders in return on assets and return on equity in 1989.

Over 98% of the company's 1989 revenues came from the bank. Wells Fargo's earnings come from 4 core businesses: consumer banking, corporate banking, real estate lending, and investment management. The 457-branch-office system contributes most of the $36.4 billion in deposits and a majority of the small business, consumer, and home mortgage loans that account for about 40% of the $41.7 billion loan portfolio.

Wells Fargo Investment Advisors, the investment management operation of the holding company, is the largest index fund (a mutual fund that mirrors stock market averages) manager in the US, with more than $80 billion in assets. Wells Fargo Ag Credit finances agricultural companies.

Wells Fargo is a California bank focused on serving that state. It is the state's largest bank in loans to agriculture and real estate construction, 3rd largest credit-card issuer, and 5th largest mortgage lender. The bank has the lowest exposure in foreign lending of any major US bank.

NYSE symbol: WFC
Incorporated: Delaware, 1987
Fiscal year ends: December 31

WHO

Chairman and CEO: Carl E. Reichardt, age 58, $1,522,500 pay
President and COO: Paul Hazen, age 48, $1,122,502 pay
VC: Robert L. Joss, age 48, $695,002 pay
VC: David M. Petrone, age 45, $717,500 pay
VC: William F. Zuendt, age 43, $717,500 pay
VC: Clyde W. Ostler, age 43
EVP and CFO: Rodney L. Jacobs, age 49
Auditors: KPMG Peat Marwick
Employees: 19,200

WHEN

Henry Wells and William G. Fargo started Wells Fargo & Company as an express delivery service and banking operation in San Francisco in 1852, 2 years after they had started American Express. The company separated its banking business from the express business in 1905.

That same year Wells Fargo & Company Bank merged with Nevada National Bank. The new institution, Wells Fargo Nevada National Bank, grew under the leadership of President Isaias W. Hellman, a pioneer in California banking. The express business later ran the western leg of the Pony Express and stagecoach lines in the western US. It became part of American Railway Express in 1918 when the US nationalized the express industry.

In 1923 Wells Fargo Nevada National Bank merged with Union Trust Company to form Wells Fargo Bank & Union Trust Company. The bank maintained this form until it merged with American Trust Company, one of the oldest western banks, in 1960. The present name was adopted in 1962.

The bank added branch operations in the 1960s. Much of its growth was from acquisitions of smaller banks in California. When it formed a bank holding company in 1969, Wells Fargo had more than 250 branches in the state, a total that would almost double to 452 by the end of 1988.

In 1970 Carl Reichardt and Paul Hazen joined the bank's real estate investment trust and in 1983 took over management of the bank. As CEO, Reichardt sold underperforming operations, cut costs, and made important acquisitions. He transformed the bank into a regional institution focused on basic banking and the middle market. The bank reorganized small loan operations to reduce costs and improve service, thus improving operations through its branch banking system.

The first major acquisition by Reichardt was Crocker National Bank (San Francisco, 1986), whose assets made Wells Fargo the 11th largest bank holding company in the US. This was followed by purchases of Bank of America's personal trust business (1987) and Barclays Bank of California (1988).

By 1989 the bank was 2nd only to Citicorp in leveraged buyout loans, loans that are attractive because they can yield at least 3% more in interest and fees than most corporate loans. Wells Fargo eliminated loans to developing countries in 1989, leaving the bank with only 1% in international loans.

WHERE

HQ: 420 Montgomery St., San Francisco, CA 94163
Phone: 415-477-1000
FAX: 415-396-7815

Wells Fargo operates 457 branch offices in California, Hong Kong, and Nassau.

	1989 Sales		1989 Net Income	
	$ mil	% of total	$ mil	% of total
US	5,624	100	713	118
Latin America	7	—	(110)	(18)
Asia & Pacific Basin	15	—	(3)	—
Europe	3	—	1	—
Total	**5,649**	**100**	**601**	**100**

WHAT

Consumer Banking
Consumer, small business, and home mortgage loans
Credit cards
Savings and checking

Corporate Banking
Cash management services
Commercial and residential construction loans
Commercial loans
Depository accounts
Project financing

Investment Management
High net worth individuals
Pension plans and institutions

HOW MUCH

	9 Yr. Growth	1980	1981	1982	1983	1984	1985	1986	1987	1988	1989
Sales ($ mil)	9.3%	2,546	3,302	3,284	2,993	3,392	3,450	3,988	4,568	4,860	5,649
Net income ($ mil)	19.4%	122	124	139	155	169	190	274	51	513	601
Income as % of sales	—	4.8%	3.8%	4.2%	5.2%	5.0%	5.5%	6.9%	1.1%	10.5%	10.6%
Earnings per share ($)	16.9%	2.67	2.67	2.91	3.02	3.43	4.15	4.93	0.51	9.06	10.84
Stock price – high ($)	—	14.50	18.06	17.13	20.88	24.88	32.50	57.50	60.13	71.25	87.50
Stock price – low ($)	—	10.81	12.44	9.13	13.00	15.44	22.75	30.50	37.50	43.13	59.00
Stock price – close ($)	20.1%	14.25	12.75	13.44	19.81	23.56	31.69	50.75	43.00	60.38	74.13
P/E – high	—	5	7	6	7	7	8	12	118	8	8
P/E – low	—	4	5	3	4	5	5	6	74	5	5
Dividends per share ($)	14.7%	0.96	0.96	0.96	0.99	1.08	1.24	1.41	1.67	2.45	3.30
Book value per share ($)	10.2%	19.97	21.19	23.31	25.08	28.11	30.94	36.11	34.93	41.38	48.08

1989 Year End:
Debt ratio: 47.0%
Return on equity: 24.2%
Cash (mil): $2,935
Assets (mil): $48,737
Long-term debt (mil): $2,541
Number of shares (mil): 51
Dividends:
1989 average yield: 4.5%
1989 payout: 30.4%
Market value (mil): $3,786

Stock Price History high/low 1980-89

90
80
70
60
50
40
30
20
10
0

RANKINGS

12th in *Fortune* 100 Commercial Banking Cos.
98th in *Fortune* World's 100 Commercial Banks
156th in *Forbes* Sales 500
163rd in *Business Week* 1000
475th in *Business Week* Global 1000

COMPETITION

H. F. Ahmanson
BankAmerica
First Interstate
Great Western
Security Pacific
Other investment managers
Other major banks

WENDY'S INTERNATIONAL, INC.

OVERVIEW

Wendy's is the world's 3rd largest chain of quick-service hamburger restaurants, with 3,755 locations worldwide. Wendy's advertising stresses the quality of its food, including the fact that its hamburgers are cooked to order and made from fresh, not frozen, meat. About 2/3 of all Wendy's restaurants are franchises and the remaining 1/3 company owned.

Under Wendy's franchising system, owners locate, purchase, and build on property approved by Wendy's and according to company standards. Franchisees pay a $25,000 technical assistance fee, which covers the cost of training in Wendy's operational techniques. Franchisees pay royalties of 4% of gross sales and in addition contribute 2% to national and 2% to local advertising. Wendy's does not sell fixtures, supplies, or food (with the exception of buns sold to 1,609 restaurants) to its franchisees.

The company is 7.7% owned by founder R. David Thomas, who, in 1989 and 1990, starred in a series of national TV advertisements.

NYSE symbol: WEN
Incorporated: Ohio, 1969
Fiscal year ends: December 31

WHO

Senior Chairman and Founder: R. David Thomas, age 57, $402,648 pay
Chairman: Robert L. Barney, age 53, $699,431 pay
CEO, President, and COO: James W. Near, age 51, $628,046 pay
EVP Finance and Administration: John K. Casey, age 57
Auditors: Coopers & Lybrand
Employees: approx. 39,000, of whom about 6,000 are full-time

WHEN

R. David Thomas, who had worked in restaurants from age 12, began his fast-food career in 1956 in a Knoxville, Tennessee, restaurant. According to a Harvard Business School study, it was Thomas who persuaded Colonel Harland Sanders to open a restaurant that sold only chicken. In 1962 Thomas moved to Columbus, Ohio, to revive 4 failing Kentucky Fried Chicken carryouts bought by his employer. Thomas's successful efforts were rewarded with a 45% interest in the 4 restaurants, which he sold back to Kentucky Fried Chicken for $1.5 million in 1968. Thomas traveled with and learned from Colonel Sanders while working as regional operations director for Kentucky Fried Chicken. Thomas left the chicken business and, after helping found the Arthur Treacher's Fish & Chips chain, opened his first Wendy's restaurant in 1969, naming it after his 8-year-old daughter. Thomas limited the menu to cooked-to-order hamburgers, chili, and shakes, at prices slightly higher than competitors Burger King and McDonald's. The restaurants were decorated with carpeting, wood paneling, and tiffany-style lamps to reinforce the upscale theme.

In 1972 the company began franchising to accelerate national expansion and founded its Management Institute to train owners and managers in Wendy's operational techniques.

In 1977, with 520 units across the US and in Canada, Wendy's started advertising on national TV. The number of Wendy's outlets had risen to 1,407 by the end of 1978. That year's $800 million in sales ranked Wendy's 3rd behind fast-burger giants McDonald's and Burger King. In 1979 Wendy's expanded its menu to include a salad bar, and opened its first restaurants in Puerto Rico, Switzerland, and West Germany. The company granted J. C. Penney the franchise rights to France, Belgium, Luxembourg, and the Netherlands, and in 1980 the first Wendy's in Belgium opened.

Thomas began competing with his old mentor Colonel Sanders with Sisters Chicken and Biscuit restaurants (1981) and had 49 outlets by 1984, mainly in the Midwest and South, but later sold this subsidiary (1987, $14 million). Wendy's added a baked potato to its menu (1983) and launched an $8 million television ad campaign featuring Clara Peller asking "Where's the Beef?" (1984), increasing market share to 12% (1985). Rivals McDonald's and Burger King responded with aggressive advertising of their Big Mac and Whopper hamburgers. Wendy's introduced a breakfast menu (1985), but it was not well received and the introduction of the Big Classic burger (1986) and SuperBar buffet (1987) did not reverse the erosion of Wendy's market share to 9% by 1987. A foundering 1987 ad campaign was canceled after only 7 weeks, and profits fell from a 1985 peak of $76 million to $24 million in 1989.

WHERE

HQ: PO Box 256, 4288 West Dublin-Granville Rd., Dublin, OH 43017
Phone: 614-764-3100
FAX: 614-764-3459

Wendy's and its franchisees operate restaurants in 49 states (Hawaii is the exception), the District of Columbia, and 22 foreign countries and territories.

Locations with the largest number of restaurants:

States	No.	Countries/Territories	No.
Ohio	293	US	3,490
Florida	265	Canada	131
California	223	Japan	26
Texas	223	Puerto Rico	20
Michigan	176	Spain	17
Illinois	172	South Korea	14
Georgia	162	Philippines	13
Pennsylvania	156	Taiwan	11
New York	130	Italy	8
Indiana	122	Israel	4
Tennessee	119	Switzerland	4
Others	1,327	Others	16
Total	**3,490**	**Total**	**3,755**

WHAT

Typical Menu
Sandwiches
- Hamburgers
- Cheeseburgers
- Chicken sandwiches

"SuperBar" hot-and-cold buffet
- "Garden Spot" salad bar
- Mexican food
- Italian pasta

Chili
Chicken "nuggets"
Stuffed baked potatoes
French fries
Soft drinks
Other nonalcoholic beverages
Separate breakfast menu items

HOW MUCH

	9 Yr. Growth	1980	1981	1982	1983	1984	1985	1986	1987	1988	1989
Sales ($ mil)	13.1%	347	487	604	715	939	1,100	1,103	1,051	1,046	1,051
Net income ($ mil)	(2.6%)	30	37	44	55	69	76	(5)	3	29	24
Income as % of sales	—	8.7%	7.6%	7.3%	7.7%	7.3%	6.9%	(0.4%)	0.3%	2.7%	2.3%
Earnings per share ($)	(4.7%)	0.40	0.46	0.51	0.61	0.75	0.82	(0.03)	0.05	0.31	0.26
Stock price – high ($)	—	3.95	5.81	7.54	9.90	12.30	15.30	17.80	13.25	8.00	7.00
Stock price – low ($)	—	1.68	3.10	3.68	5.85	7.88	9.98	10.00	4.13	5.13	4.50
Stock price – close ($)	5.5%	2.85	4.24	6.58	9.39	9.98	13.40	10.25	5.63	5.75	4.63
P/E – high	—	10	13	15	16	16	19	—	265	26	27
P/E – low	—	4	7	7	10	11	12	—	83	17	17
Dividends per share ($)	13.0%	0.08	0.08	0.09	0.12	0.15	0.17	0.21	0.24	0.24	0.24
Book value per share ($)	11.4%	1.68	2.37	2.92	3.40	3.98	4.65	4.45	4.29	4.36	4.45

1989 Year End:
Debt ratio: 29.4%
Return on equity: 5.9%
Cash (mil): $74
Current ratio: 0.95
Long-term debt (mil): $179
Number of shares (mil): 96
Dividends:
- 1989 average yield: 5.2%
- 1989 payout: 92.3%

Market value (mil): $446

Stock Price History high/low 1980-89

18
16
14
12
10
8
6
4
2
0

RANKINGS

894th in *Business Week* 1000

COMPETITION

General Mills
Grand Metropolitan
McDonald's
PepsiCo
TW Holdings

WESTINGHOUSE ELECTRIC CORPORATION

OVERVIEW

Westinghouse Electric is a diversified international company with 6 major operating groups: Broadcasting, Commercial, Electronics Systems, Energy and Utility Systems, Financial Services, and Industries. The US government is the company's largest single customer, accounting for 22% of consolidated sales and income in 1989.

Westinghouse Broadcasting Company, a wholly owned subsidiary, owns and operates 5 TV stations and 22 AM and FM radio stations.

The Commercial group includes Westinghouse Beverage, the largest 7Up bottler in the US, and Longines-Wittnauer Watch, which sells watches and clocks to jewelry and department stores in the US and Canada.

The company's Electronics Systems group is a world leader in advanced electronic systems for the DOD. Westinghouse Energy and Utility Systems sold its transmission and distribution business to Asea Brown Boveri in 1989, leaving Westinghouse to focus on nuclear energy and power generation.

Westinghouse Financial Services, a wholly owned subsidiary, provides a wide range of financial services, primarily through Westinghouse Credit.

The Industries Group includes 4 business units: Thermo King, Distribution and Control, Industries and Environmental Services, and Materials. All 4 of these operations focus on global markets, and about 1/3 of the group's $3.1 billion in 1989 sales came from overseas markets.

NYSE symbol: WX
Incorporated: Pennsylvania, 1872
Fiscal year ends: December 31

WHO

Chairman and CEO: John C. Marous, age 64, $1,808,326 pay
President and COO: Paul E. Lego, age 59, $1,404,167 pay
EVP Finance: Harry F. Murray, age 60
EVP Human Resources: George C. Dorman, age 60
Auditors: Price Waterhouse
Employees: 122,000

WHERE

HQ: Westinghouse Bldg., Gateway Center, Pittsburgh, PA 15222
Phone: 412-244-2000
FAX: 412-642-3404

Westinghouse has 187 manufacturing plants in 32 states and Puerto Rico and 15 foreign countries.

	1989 Sales		1989 Operating Income	
	$ mil	% of total	$ mil	% of total
US	11,305	88	846	85
Foreign	1,539	12	148	15
Adjustments	—	—	1,061	—
Total	**12,844**	**100**	**2,055**	**100**

WHEN

When George Westinghouse founded Westinghouse Electric in Pittsburgh in 1886, he had already established himself as the inventor of the train air brake, which had become the standard in the railroad industry.

Westinghouse entered the newly developing electric industry after having devised a system for transmitting electric current over long distances. The success of his system was due to his choice of using alternating current (AC) as opposed to the direct current (DC) favored by Thomas Edison. He paid Nikola Tesla, an eccentric Croatian inventor, $1 million for his AC patents and installed the first AC power system in Telluride, Colorado, in 1891. One of the company's early successes was powering the 1893 Chicago World's Fair. In 1896 Westinghouse and rival General Electric formed a patent pool that allowed the 2 companies to continue further development of electrical generation and distribution technology without the threat of being sued by the other for patent infringement.

Westinghouse expanded into manufacturing electrical products — from light bulbs (1890s) to radios (1920) to major appliances — as well as into building nuclear reactors for ship propulsion. In 1920 the company set up the first radio broadcasting station, KDKA, in East Pittsburgh.

Westinghouse, which concentrated on the market for huge turbines and generators, got a late start in the post–WWII home appliances market — and consequently was 2nd to GE.

During the 1970s, Westinghouse found itself in several more unrelated businesses, including 7Up bottling, watches, and low-income housing. In the mid-1970s, Westinghouse lost a large part of its main business (utility generators) to GE when its turbine generators were found defective. And after a series of costly lawsuits and heavy competition in most of its major consumer product lines, Westinghouse sold its appliance business to White Consolidated in 1975.

The 1980s was a period of restructuring for Westinghouse. It dropped its unprofitable businesses (sold 70 businesses between 1985 and 1987), acquired complementary ones, and entered into a series of joint ventures with foreign companies (Mitsubishi Electric, Siemens, Asea Brown Boveri, and AEG).

WHAT

	1989 Sales		1989 Operating Income	
	$ mil	% of total	$ mil	% of total
Broadcasting	646	5	121	12
Electronic systems	2,783	20	197	20
Energy & utility systems	2,139	16	209	21
Financial services	1,192	9	201	20
Industries Group	3,148	23	224	23
Commercial	2,419	18	83	8
Divested & other	1,274	9	(41)	(4)
Adjustments	(757)	—	1,061	—
Total	**12,844**	**100**	**2,055**	**100**

Major Subsidiaries
- Challenger Electrical Equipment Corp.
- Longines-Wittnauer Watch Co.
- Thermo King Corp. (refrigeration transport systems)
- WESCOR (telecommunications)
- Westinghouse Beverage Group, Inc. (soft drink bottling)
- Westinghouse Broadcasting Co. (Group W: 22 radio stations, 5 TV stations, and program production and distribution)

Other Activities
- Electricity generation plants
- Electronic systems for military applications and federal aerospace agencies
- Modular office furniture (Westinghouse Furniture Systems)
- Nuclear and fossil steam turbines and generators
- Toxic waste management
- Waste-to-energy projects

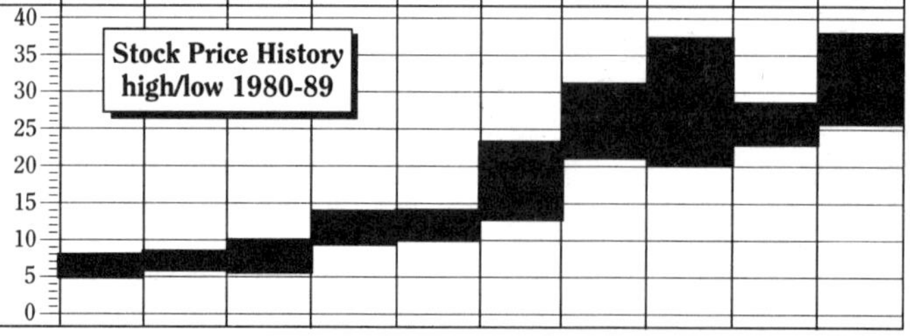

RANKINGS

28th in *Fortune* 500 Industrial Cos.
79th in *Fortune* Global 500 Industrial Cos.
45th in *Forbes* Sales 500
43rd in *Business Week* 1000
146th in *Business Week* Global 1000

COMPETITION

- Broadcasting companies
- Defense electronics contractors
- Power equipment companies
- Waste management companies

HOW MUCH

	9 Yr. Growth	1980	1981	1982	1983	1984	1985	1986	1987	1988	1989
Sales ($ mil)	4.7%	8,514	9,368	9,745	9,533	10,265	10,700	10,731	10,679	12,500	12,844
Net income ($ mil)	9.6%	403	438	449	449	536	605	671	739	823	922
Income as % of sales	—	4.7%	4.7%	4.6%	4.7%	5.2%	5.7%	6.3%	6.9%	6.6%	7.2%
Earnings per share ($)	11.4%	1.18	1.28	1.29	1.27	1.51	1.73	2.16	2.52	2.78	3.11
Stock price – high ($)	—	8.13	8.63	10.13	14.09	14.19	23.38	31.25	37.50	28.69	38.13
Stock price – low ($)	—	4.75	5.75	5.47	9.31	9.88	12.69	21.00	20.00	22.81	25.63
Stock price – close ($)	19.6%	7.41	6.38	9.72	13.69	13.06	22.25	27.88	24.88	26.31	37.00
P/E – high	—	7	7	8	11	9	14	15	15	10	12
P/E – low	—	4	5	4	7	7	7	10	8	8	8
Dividends per share ($)	14.1%	0.35	0.45	0.45	0.45	0.49	0.58	0.68	0.82	0.97	1.15
Book value per share ($)	8.2%	7.45	8.27	9.08	9.74	10.70	10.52	10.56	12.46	13.18	15.10

1989 Year End:
Debt ratio: 49.9%
Return on equity: 22.0%
Cash (mil): $1,516
Current ratio: 1.02
Long-term debt (mil): $4,365
Number of shares (mil): 290
Dividends:
1989 average yield: 3.1%
1989 payout: 37.0%
Market value (mil): $10,740

Stock Price History high/low 1980-89

WEYERHAEUSER COMPANY

OVERVIEW

Weyerhaeuser, the world's largest private owner of timberlands and one of the US's leading producers and exporters of forest products, is noted for innovations in forest management and recycling technology. Weyerhaeuser's products include lumber, plywood, pulp, paper, and packaging. The company also develops and owns real estate and has a financial services business, Weyerhaeuser Financial Services, Inc.

Weyerhaeuser's strong reforestation program now plants more than 51 million seedlings on 102,000 acres annually. Weyerhaeuser is a major newsprint and lumber supplier to Japan. In 1989 the company started a major restructuring that included selling its milk carton, gypsum and hardwood paneling, health and beauty aids, and nursery and garden supply businesses, for which Weyerhaeuser recorded a $497 million pretax restructuring charge against 1989 earnings. The company also announced a desire to sell Republic Federal Savings and Loan and continues to examine and restructure its businesses and product lines.

NYSE symbol: WY
Incorporated: Washington, 1900
Fiscal year ends: December 31

WHO

Chairman and CEO: George H. Weyerhaeuser, age 63, $1,060,000 pay
President and COO: John W. Creighton, Jr., age 57, $610,000 pay
EVP and CFO: Robert L. Schuyler, age 54, $450,000 pay
Auditors: Arthur Andersen & Co.
Employees: 45,214

WHEN

Frederick Weyerhaeuser, son of a German immigrant, purchased his first sawmill in Illinois in 1857. After joint logging ventures in Minnesota and Wisconsin, he and his financial backers, the Lair and Norton families, bought 900,000 acres of timberland in Washington and incorporated Weyerhaeuser in 1900.

Under family leadership Weyerhaeuser operated sawmills in Washington and Idaho during the company's early decades. In the 1930s, when forestry science developed uses for the entire tree, Weyerhaeuser built pulp mills and experimented to find uses for bark and shavings. By 1936 under J. P. Weyerhaeuser, brother of Frederick, the company reached the goal of replacing every tree it cut. As a big departure from the "cut and run" philosophy of the early logging industry, Weyerhaeuser adopted the slogan "Timber is a crop." The company also developed a reputation for being fiscally conservative by purchasing timberland from cash flow rather than borrowing heavily like some other timber companies.

Weyerhaeuser Real Estate Company, which began business in the 1920s, started building recreational homes in forestlands after WWII. Under Norton Clapp (president, 1960-1966), a member of the Norton founding family, Weyerhaeuser went public in 1963.

In 1963 Weyerhaeuser opened the company's first overseas marketing office in Tokyo, followed by an office in France in 1964. To compensate for the cyclical nature of the wood products industry, under CEO George Weyerhaeuser (1966-present), great-grandson of founder Frederick Weyerhaeuser, the company diversified, acquiring nursery and pet supply businesses as well as forestry-related businesses. Significant acquisitions included Centennial Homes (1971) and Hines Wholesale Nurseries (1976). In 1980 the volcanic eruption of the Mount St. Helens killed or vaporized 68,000 acres of Weyerhaeuser timberlands. The salvage effort took 3 years, with tree planters following logging crews. The company's earnings declined through 1982 because of a bad US lumber market in addition to the costs of the Mount St. Helens disaster. Weyerhaeuser cut its salaried work force by about 25%, eliminated some units, and cut expenses by 25%. In 1983 the company bought GNA Corporation, which sells annuities through financial institutions. The following year Weyerhaeuser opened an office in Beijing because the Chinese wood and paper products market was growing . It also continued to develop the Japan market and in 1987 became the first US forest products company to list its stock on the Tokyo Stock Exchange. By the end of that year Weyerhaeuser had its highest earnings since 1979 and was back on track until its recent restructuring began.

WHERE

HQ: Tacoma, WA 98477
Phone: 206-924-2345
FAX: 206-924-7407

	1989 Sales	
	$ mil	% of total
US	9,083	90
Foreign	1,023	10
Total	**10,106**	**100**

Owned or Leased Timberland	Acres
Washington	1,573,000
Oregon	1,289,000
Alabama, Arkansas, Mississippi, North Carolina, and Oklahoma	2,937,000
Canada	13,353,000
Total	**19,152,000**

WHAT

	1989 Sales		1989 Operating Income	
	$ mil	% of total	$ mil	% of total
Pulp & paper	3,723	36	617	94
Diversified businesses	675	7	(102)	(16)
Real estate	975	10	26	4
Financial services	851	8	(67)	(10)
Forest products	3,725	37	307	47
Corporate & other	158	2	(127)	(19)
Adjustments	(1)	—	694	—
Total	**10,106**	**100**	**1,348**	**100**

Paper Products
Coated and uncoated paper
Containerboard
Newsprint
Packaging, cartons
Recycling

Building Supplies
Architectural doors
Lumber, plywood
Veneer

Real Estate Development
Construction and sale of commercial and residential properties in 15 states

Financial Services
GNA Corp. (mutual funds, insurance, and investment services in 47 states)
Republic Federal Savings & Loan Association (California)

Other Businesses
Paper processing chemicals
Private-label personal care products (*e.g.*, diapers, suntan oil)

HOW MUCH

	9 Yr. Growth	1980	1981	1982	1983	1984	1985	1986	1987	1988	1989
Sales ($ mil)	9.3%	4,536	4,502	4,186	4,883	5,550	5,206	5,652	6,990	10,004	10,106
Net income ($ mil)	0.7%	321	234	140	205	226	200	277	447	564	341
Income as % of sales	—	7.1%	5.2%	3.3%	4.2%	4.1%	3.8%	4.9%	6.4%	5.6%	3.4%
Earnings per share ($)	(0.6%)	1.64	1.11	0.60	0.91	1.01	0.88	1.27	2.12	2.68	1.56
Stock price – high ($)	—	25.33	27.17	26.17	27.83	23.67	22.67	27.50	40.00	29.50	32.75
Stock price – low ($)	—	18.67	16.08	15.00	20.75	16.67	16.50	19.75	19.92	23.17	24.50
Stock price – close ($)	2.2%	22.75	19.33	24.00	22.50	19.42	20.50	25.17	25.83	25.13	27.63
P/E – high	—	15	24	44	31	23	26	22	19	11	21
P/E – low	—	11	14	25	23	16	19	16	9	9	16
Dividends per share ($)	3.7%	0.87	0.87	0.87	0.87	0.87	0.87	0.87	0.90	1.15	1.20
Book value per share ($)	3.3%	15.04	16.20	16.08	16.28	16.33	17.02	16.59	18.24	19.84	20.24

1989 Year End:
Debt ratio: 47.4%
Return on equity: 7.8%
Cash (mil): $261
Assets (mil): $15,976
Long-term debt (mil): $3,734
Number of shares (mil): 205
Dividends:
1989 average yield: 4.3%
1989 payout: 76.9%
Market value (mil): $5,656

Stock Price History high/low 1980-89

RANKINGS

42nd in *Fortune* 500 Industrial Cos.
114th in *Fortune* Global 500 Industrial Cos.
19th in *Fortune* 50 Exporters
69th in *Forbes* Sales 500
111th in *Business Week* 1000
319th in *Business Week* Global 1000

COMPETITION

Boise Cascade
Champion International
Georgia-Pacific
International Paper
James River
Kimberly-Clark
Manville
Mead
Scott

WHIRLPOOL CORPORATION

OVERVIEW

Whirlpool is the largest major appliance manufacturer and marketer in the world, with revenues of $6.3 billion in 1989. Whirlpool manufactures home laundry appliances; home refrigeration and room air conditioning equipment; and other appliances such as dishwashers, ranges, ovens, and food waste disposers.

Whirlpool is Sears's largest supplier of Kenmore brand major home appliances, with sales to Sears accounting for approximately 23% of Whirlpool's business in 1989. In addition to its manufacturing revenues, Whirlpool had $136 million in 1989 sales from Whirlpool Financial Corporation, which provides inventory financing services for dealers and distributors as well as other financial services.

Whirlpool manufactures in 10 countries and markets in more than 45 countries. Whirlpool International (53% owned), the company's European joint venture with Philips of the Netherlands, accounted for almost $2 billion in sales in 1989. Whirlpool's affiliates in Brazil (20-49% owned) and joint venture partners in India (33% owned) and Mexico (minority interest) have begun producing a "world washer" designed to sell in developing countries.

WHEN

The Upton Machine Company was founded in St. Joseph, Michigan, in 1911 by brothers Fred and Lou Upton and their uncle, Emory Upton. The company made hand-operated washing machines. In 1916 Sears, Roebuck began buying washing machines from the Uptons, and by 1925 the company was supplying all of Sears's washers. The Uptons combined their company with the Nineteen Hundred Washer Company in 1929 to form the Nineteen Hundred Corporation, the world's largest washing machine company. Sears and Nineteen Hundred continued to prosper through the Great Depression. During the WWII years Nineteen Hundred's factories produced products for the war effort. Sears was still Nineteen Hundred's principal customer in 1947 when the company decided to market a washing machine under the brand name Whirlpool. The new machine was a success, and the company adopted its current name in 1950.

During the 1950s and 1960s Whirlpool became a full-line appliance manufacturer while continuing as Sears's principal Kenmore appliance supplier. The company bought Seeger Refrigerator Company and the stove and air conditioning interests of RCA (1955); the gas refrigeration and ice-maker manufacturing facilities of Servel (1958); a majority interest in Heil-Quaker, makers of central heaters and space heaters (1964); Sears's major television set supplier, Warwick Electronics (1966); and 33% of Canadian appliance manufacturer/distributor John Inglis Company (1969). The company entered into an agreement with Sony in 1973 to distribute Whirlpool brand products in Japan. Whirlpool sold its television manufacturing business to Sanyo of Japan in 1976.

Between 1980 and 1989, in a static US market, Whirlpool net sales nearly tripled from $2.2 billion to $6.3 billion, while net income increased 83%. In 1986 Whirlpool bought top-end appliance manufacturer KitchenAid from Dart and Kraft, kitchen cabinet maker St. Charles Manufacturing, and 65% of Italian cooling compressor manufacturer Aspera. Also in 1986 it sold its Heil-Quaker central heating business for $156 million to Inter City Gas and closed much of its original St. Joseph, Michigan, manufacturing facility, moving production to other locations. The company increased its ownership of Inglis Ltd. to 70% in 1987 and to 100% in 1990. In 1989 Whirlpool focused on the worldwide appliance business, selling its kitchen cabinet interests and forming Whirlpool International with European giant Philips. The new joint venture, to which Whirlpool contributed $361 million, gives the company a projected market share of 25% in the US and 10% in Europe.

HOW MUCH

	9 Yr. Growth	1980	1981	1982	1983	1984	1985	1986	1987	1988	1989
Sales ($ mil)	12.1%	2,243	2,437	2,271	2,668	3,137	3,474	4,009	4,179	4,421	6,289
Net income ($ mil)	7.0%	102	135	136	163	190	182	200	181	161	187
Income as % of sales	—	4.5%	5.6%	6.0%	6.1%	6.0%	5.2%	5.0%	4.3%	3.6%	3.0%
Earnings per share ($)	7.5%	1.41	1.87	1.88	2.24	2.59	2.49	2.70	2.53	2.33	2.70
Stock price – high ($)	—	11.50	15.25	23.75	28.50	25.00	25.38	41.50	40.88	29.88	33.25
Stock price – low ($)	—	7.31	9.44	11.50	20.13	18.25	20.25	24.25	20.25	23.50	24.25
Stock price – close ($)	14.7%	9.63	12.69	21.88	24.25	23.25	24.69	33.88	24.38	24.75	33.00
P/E – high	—	8	8	13	13	10	10	15	16	13	12
P/E – low	—	5	5	6	9	7	8	9	8	10	9
Dividends per share ($)	5.2%	0.70	0.80	0.83	0.93	1.00	1.00	1.03	1.10	1.10	1.10
Book value per share ($)	8.3%	9.98	10.92	12.01	13.38	14.97	16.46	18.21	18.83	19.06	20.49

1989 Year End:
Debt ratio: 40.9%
Return on equity: 13.7%
Cash (mil): $141
Current ratio: 1.28
Long-term debt (mil): $982
Number of shares (mil): 69
Dividends:
1989 average yield: 3.3%
1989 payout: 40.7%
Market value (mil): $2,290

Stock Price History high/low 1980-89

NYSE symbol: WHR
Incorporated: Delaware, 1955
Fiscal year ends: December 31

WHO

Chairman, President, and CEO: David R. Whitwam, age 47, $1,030,000 pay
EVP; President and CEO, Whirlpool International: Jan Prising
EVP and CFO: James R. Samartini, age 54, $428,280 pay
EVP: William D. Marohn, age 49, $395,035 pay
Auditors: Ernst & Young
Employees: 39,411

WHERE

HQ: 2000 M-63, Benton Harbor, MI 49022
Phone: 616-926-5000
FAX: 616-926-3568

Whirlpool operates worldwide.

Principal manufacturing and service sites	
US	13
Italy	6
Canada	4
Germany	3
Sweden	1
Mexico	1
France	1
Total	**29**

	1989 Sales		1989 Operating Income	
	$ mil	% of total	$ mil	% of total
North America	4,132	66	300	75
Europe	2,169	34	102	25
Adjustments	(12)	—	72	—
Total	**6,289**	**100**	**474**	**100**

WHAT

	1989 Sales		1989 Operating Income	
	$ mil	% of total	$ mil	% of total
Major home apps.	6,153	97	368	94
Financial services	136	3	22	6
Adjustments	—	—	84	—
Total	**6,289**	**100**	**474**	**100**

	1989 Sales	
	$ mil	% of total
Home laundry appliances	2,113	34
Home refrigeration equipment	2,072	33
Other home appliances	1,968	31
Financial services	136	2
Total	**6,289**	**100**

Appliance Brands

US	Canada	Europe, Asia, Africa, South America
Capri	Admiral	Bauknecht
Kenmore	Inglis	Ignis
KitchenAid	Speed Queen	Laden
Roper		Philips
Whirlpool		Whirlpool

RANKINGS

73rd in *Fortune* 500 Industrial Cos.
208th in *Fortune* Global 500 Industrial Cos.
137th in *Forbes* Sales 500
270th in *Business Week* 1000
971st in *Business Week* Global 1000

COMPETITION

Raytheon
Appliance manufacturers

WHITMAN CORPORATION

OVERVIEW

Whitman Corporation, a food and consumer service company with sales close to $4 billion in 1989, manages 4 major food, drink, auto service, and refrigeration equipment businesses. Pet Inc. ($1.8 billion sales) sells leading brands in various specialty areas such as Mexican food (Old El Paso), frozen pie shells (Pet-Ritz), and Italian foods (Progresso).

Whitman's 80%-owned Pepsi-Cola General Bottlers, the nation's largest Pepsi bottler, shipped over 132 million cases in 1989 for sales of over $961 million. Pepsi General continues to outsell rival Coca-Cola in its midwestern 12-state region.

Midas International franchises more than 2,300 automotive shops that service exhaust systems, brakes, and steering and suspension systems. Midas shops are in 9 countries, and 1989 sales ($434 million) provided a high-margined $71 million operating income.

Hussman Corporation is a leading supplier of refrigeration equipment for the world's food industry. It manufactures produce and frozen food cases and refrigeration systems for supermarkets and convenience stores.

In 1990 Whitman will change from a holding company to an operating company.

NYSE symbol: WH
Incorporated: Delaware, 1962
Fiscal year ends: December 31

WHO

Chairman and CEO: James W. Cozad, age 63
President and COO: Miles L. Marsh, age 42
EVP Finance: John P. Fagan, age 59, $450,833 pay
Auditors: KPMG Peat Marwick
Employees: 25,188

WHEN

Whitman Corporation is a very different business from its grandparent company, the Illinois Central Railroad. Started in 1851 with a 3.6 million-acre land grant, Illinois Central became one of the nation's 10 largest rail systems. In 1901, its 50th year, it boasted 4,200 rail miles, a $32 million income, and freight and passenger service in 13 states. Its famous passenger trains included the Green Diamond (Chicago to St. Louis) and the Diamond Special and City of New Orleans (Chicago to New Orleans). Passenger service, no longer profitable, was sold to Amtrack in 1971. In 1972 the company (renamed Illinois Central Industries in 1962) acquired the Gulf, Mobile and Ohio Railroad (Chicago to Mobile) and the railroad was renamed Illinois Central Gulf (ICG).

The company maintained its focus on railroads until William Johnson, former president of Railway Express Agency, became president in 1966. Johnson served as president for 21 years and guided its transformation to a multinational conglomerate that was renamed IC Industries in 1975. IC bought numerous companies, including its current core businesses: Pepsi-Cola General Bottlers (1970); Midas International auto muffler shops (1972); and the venerable St. Louis company, Pet Inc. (for $406 million in 1978). Pet began in 1885 as an evaporated milk company and had made substantial diverse purchases of its own, including Hussmann Refrigeration, a leading producer of refrigeration systems for grocery stores; Downyflake Foods; Stuckey roadside candy stores; and the Philadelphia chocolate company, Stuart F. Whitman and Son. Pet is now the company's largest moneymaker.

By the late 1970s the ICG railroad provided only 1% of the company's pretax profits. IC was determined to sell it, but it wasn't until 1989 that IC spun off ICG to its stockholders. In the interim, IC sold many of its real estate holdings and its trackage had shrunk by 2/3. A private concern, Prospect Group, bought the railroad within a month of the spin-off.

The company changed its name in 1988 to Whitman Corporation (after Pet's well-known chocolate brand) to reflect its concentration on consumer goods and services. Since 1979 Whitman has sold 65 companies, including its Pneumo Abex aerospace operations, for $1.2 billion (1988). In the same time period, Whitman bought 98 companies, including Orval Kent refrigerated salad products (1988) and Van de Kamp's Frozen Seafoods (1989), which will be marketed by Pet. In 1989 Whitman announced plans to sell Hussmann but, lacking an acceptable offer, decided in 1990 to keep the unit.

WHERE

HQ: One Illinois Center, 111 E. Wacker Dr., Chicago, IL 60601
Phone: 312-565-3000
FAX: 312-565-3009 (Corporate Affairs)

Pet operates 53 manufacturing plants in the US and 5 foreign countries. Whitman's Pepsi bottling operations are located in 12 midwestern and southeastern states. Midas has 2,300 shops in 9 countries. Hussmann operates 21 plants in the US and abroad.

	1989 Sales		1989 Operating Income	
	$ mil	% of total	$ mil	% of total
US	3,337	83	464	88
Foreign	662	17	60	12
Adjustments	(13)	—	(67)	—
Total	**3,986**	**100**	**457**	**100**

WHAT

	1989 Sales		1989 Operating Income	
	$ mil	% of total	$ mil	% of total
Specialty foods	1,802	45	270	52
Automotive services	434	11	71	13
Soft drinks	961	24	121	23
Refrigeration prods.	789	20	62	12
Adjustments	—	—	(67)	—
Total	**3,986**	**100**	**457**	**100**

Brand Names (Pet Inc.)

Ac'cent
Downyflake
Hain
Heartland
Hollywood
La Creme
Old El Paso
Pet
Pet-Ritz
Progresso
Sego
Underwood
Van de Kamp's
Whitman's Sampler

Other Subsidiaries

Pepsi-Cola General Bottlers, Inc. (80%)
Midas International Corp. (auto service shops)
Hussmann Corp. (commercial refrigeration)

HOW MUCH

	9 Yr. Growth	1980	1981	1982	1983	1984	1985	1986	1987	1988	1989
Sales ($ mil)	(0.4%)	4,142	4,195	3,868	3,734	4,234	4,405	4,222	4,027	3,583	3,986
Net income ($ mil)	7.3%	121	134	68	95	133	154	(56)	249	177	228
Income as % of sales	—	2.9%	3.2%	1.8%	2.5%	3.1%	3.5%	(1.3%)	6.2%	4.9%	5.7%
Earnings per share ($)	4.6%	1.24	1.38	0.80	1.10	1.46	1.42	(0.51)	2.20	1.66	1.87
Stock price – high ($)	—	8.84	10.28	9.06	12.25	14.38	20.31	30.38	41.25	37.25	38.25
Stock price – low ($)	—	4.28	7.13	6.16	8.75	10.50	13.44	17.81	22.38	29.63	27.50
Stock price – close ($)	15.7%	7.72	8.75	8.75	11.94	14.38	19.19	23.00	32.88	35.75	28.75
P/E – high	—	7	7	11	11	10	14	—	19	22	20
P/E – low	—	3	5	8	8	7	9	—	10	18	15
Dividends per share ($)	8.3%	0.49	0.54	0.57	0.59	0.64	0.70	0.78	0.86	0.94	1.01
Book value per share ($)	(15.8%)	18.17	19.52	19.72	17.59	16.13	15.99	13.61	14.67	8.44	3.85

1989 Year End:
Debt ratio: 66.8%
Return on equity: 30.4%
Cash (mil): $102
Current ratio: 1.69
Long-term debt (mil): $1,796
Number of shares (mil): 102
Dividends:
1989 average yield: 3.5%
1989 payout: 53.7%
Market value (mil): $2,940

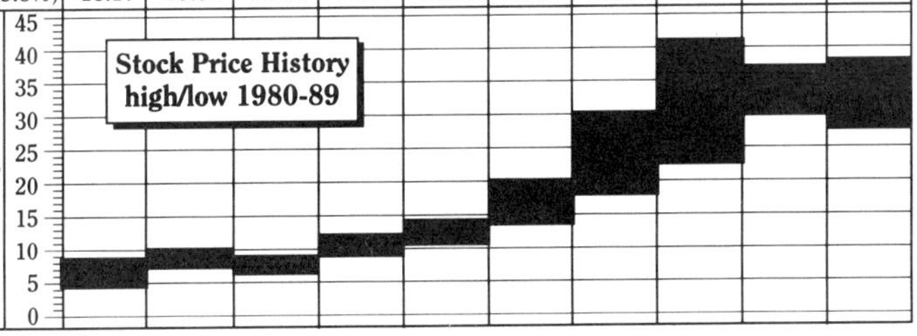

Stock Price History high/low 1980-89

RANKINGS

118th in *Fortune* 500 Industrial Cos.
329th in *Fortune* Global 500 Industrial Cos.
210th in *Forbes* Sales 500
232nd in *Business Week* 1000
692nd in *Business Week* Global 1000

COMPETITION

Anheuser Busch
Berkshire Hathaway
Beatrice
Borden
Campbell Soup
ConAgra
CPC International
General Mills
Grand Metropolitan
Hershey
Kellogg
Nestlé
Mars
Philip Morris
Quaker Oats
RJR Nabisco
Sara Lee

WINN-DIXIE STORES, INC.

OVERVIEW

Winn-Dixie operates over 1,200 supermarkets in 13 states in the southern US and in the Bahama Islands, making it the 5th largest supermarket operator in the US in 1989. The company operates 15 food distribution centers in 8 states and 21 plants for producing and processing dairy products, coffee and teas, grocery bags, etc.

Winn-Dixie has successfully resisted unionization. About half of the company's full-time employees participate in its employee stock-option plan, through which they purchased about $5.4 million worth of stock in 1989. Winn-Dixie also offers an employee profit-sharing retirement plan, to which it contributed almost $38 million in 1989.

Winn-Dixie has increased its stock dividend for 46 consecutive years — an NYSE record. With no long-term debt other than leases, the company is in good financial health.

Two sons and 3 grandsons of founder William Davis sit on the company's board of directors, and the Davis family still controls about 39% of the company's outstanding stock.

NYSE symbol: WIN
Incorporated: Florida, 1928
Fiscal year ends: Last Wednesday in June

WHO

Chairman and CEO: A. Dano Davis, age 44, $525,866 pay
VC: Robert D. Davis, age 57, $287,833 pay
President: James Kufeldt, age 51, $523,701 pay
EVP: Charles H. McKellar, age 51, $443,428 pay
EVP: Frank L. James, age 56, $385,323 pay
Auditors: KPMG Peat Marwick
Employees: 94,000 (42,500 full-time and 51,500 part-time)

WHEN

In 1925 William Davis borrowed $10,000 to open a new cash-and-carry grocery in Lemon City near Miami. After a slow start, Davis expanded his chain of Table Supply Stores and had opened 34 by the time of his death in 1934, when his 4 sons took over management of the company. From the 1930s through 1953, the Davis brothers fought successfully for the repeal of anti-chain-store legislation in Florida. In 1939 they purchased control of the Winn & Lovett Grocery Company, which operated 78 stores in Florida and Georgia. Winn & Lovett had been incorporated in 1928 and was a leader in the 1930s in the building of new "supermarket" type stores. In 1944 the company established headquarters in Jacksonville and assumed the Winn & Lovett name.

After WWII the company, still controlled by the Davis family, expanded by acquiring grocery chains throughout the South, including the Steiden Stores in Kentucky, Margaret Ann Stores in Florida, Wylie Company Stores in Alabama, Penney Stores in Mississippi, King Stores in Georgia, and the Eden and Ballentine Stores in South Carolina. In 1955 the company consolidated with Dixie Home Stores of the Carolinas and changed the name of the company to Winn-Dixie Stores, Inc. During the 1950s and early 1960s, Winn-Dixie continued to expand by acquisitions, adding the Ketner and Milner Stores in the Carolinas and the Hill Stores of Louisiana and Alabama.

By 1966 the company controlled so much of the grocery business in the South that, for antitrust reasons, the FTC imposed a 10-year moratorium on its buying stores. The company responded by buying 9 stores outside the US, in Nassau and Freeport in the Bahama Islands. At the end of the moratorium in 1976, the company bought Kimbell, Inc., of Texas, adding stores and extensive support facilities in Texas, Oklahoma, and New Mexico. Winn-Dixie refused to deal with the workers' union in New Mexico. When a pro-union boycott was organized in 1979, the company sold its 23 stores there.

The company continued to expand through most of the 1980s and by 1987 was operating 1,271 stores. During 1988 and 1989 the total number of stores declined to 1,229 as the company closed or sold stores that were not performing well. Despite operating fewer stores, the company increased total store square footage, and sales for 1989 rose 1.6% over 1988 to $9.15 billion, while net earnings rose by 15% to $135 million. In 1990 Winn-Dixie moved to everyday-low-price marketing. This approach lowers gross margins but raises sales per store and spreads corporate overhead across a larger sales base. Winn-Dixie has shown a 3% to 4% improvement in same-store sales growth since implementing this approach.

WHERE

HQ: 5050 Edgewood Ct., Jacksonville, FL 32203
Phone: 904-783-5000
FAX: 904-783-5294

Winn-Dixie operates primarily in the southern US.

	Number of Stores
Alabama	91
Florida	476
Georgia	120
Indiana	5
Kentucky	48
Louisiana	88
Mississippi	21
North Carolina	146
Oklahoma	7
South Carolina	89
Tennessee	22
Texas	80
Virginia	36
Total	**1,229**

WHAT

Subsidiaries

Astor Products
Crackin' Good Bakers
Deep South Products
Dixie Darling Bakers
Dixie Packers
Economy Wholesale Distrib.
  Ecoala Wholesalers
Fairway Food Stores Co.
First Northern Supply
Second Northern Supply
Third Northern Supply
Monterey Canning
Save Rite Foods
Sunbelt Products
Superbrand Dairy Products
Superior Food
Table Supply Food Stores
W-D (Bahamas)
  Bahamas Supermarkets
    The City Meat Markets
Winn-Dixie Atlanta
Winn-Dixie Charlotte
Winn-Dixie Greenville
Winn-Dixie Louisiana
Winn-Dixie Louisville
Winn-Dixie Montgomery
Winn-Dixie Raleigh
Winn-Dixie Texas

Winn-Dixie produces or processes its own:

Carbonated beverages
Cheese
Eggs
Frozen pizza
Ice cream
Jams and jellies
Mayonnaise
Meats
Milk
Paper bags
Peanut butter
Salad dressing

HOW MUCH

	9 Yr. Growth	1980	1981	1982	1983	1984	1985	1986	1987	1988	1989
Sales ($ mil)	6.1%	5,389	6,200	6,764	7,019	7,302	7,774	8,225	8,804	9,008	9,151
Net income ($ mil)	4.3%	92	95	104	113	116	108	116	112	117	135
Income as % of sales	—	1.7%	1.5%	1.5%	1.6%	1.6%	1.4%	1.4%	1.3%	1.3%	1.5%
Earnings per share ($)	5.8%	2.02	2.20	2.51	2.72	2.83	2.64	2.84	2.72	2.87	3.36
Stock price – high ($)	—	19.20	22.35	30.23	37.43	34.00	38.88	59.00	52.00	47.00	65.00
Stock price – low ($)	—	14.18	15.98	16.95	25.05	25.75	31.50	34.88	37.50	37.50	42.88
Stock price – close ($)	16.8%	16.13	18.38	26.85	28.88	31.88	38.38	45.88	44.25	44.00	65.00
P/E – high	—	10	10	12	14	12	15	21	19	16	19
P/E – low	—	7	7	7	9	9	12	12	14	13	13
Dividends per share ($)	7.4%	1.01	1.15	1.30	1.44	1.56	1.68	1.74	1.80	1.86	1.92
Book value per share ($)	6.8%	10.83	11.30	12.49	13.92	14.86	15.80	17.06	17.93	18.20	19.61

1989 Year End:
Debt ratio: 8.5%
Return on equity: 17.8%
Cash (mil): $128
Current ratio: 1.62
Long-term debt (mil): $72
Number of shares (mil): 40
Dividends:
  1989 average yield: 3.0%
  1989 payout: 57.1%
Market value (mil): $2,596

Stock Price History high/low 1980-89

70
60
50
40
30
20
10
0

RANKINGS

11th in *Fortune* 50 Retailing Cos.
83rd in *Forbes* Sales 500
262nd in *Business Week* 1000

COMPETITION

Albertson's
American Stores
Bruno's
Food Lion
Great A&P
Kroger
Publix
Safeway

WM. WRIGLEY JR. COMPANY

OVERVIEW

The Wm. Wrigley Jr. Company is the largest producer of chewing gum and gum base in the world and makes 47% of the gum chewed in the US. Wrigley's primary business since inception has been the production of chewing gum, which accounts for more than 90% of revenues. Wrigley's Doublemint, Spearmint, and Juicy Fruit brands have been popular for more than 75 years. Its Extra brand became the leading sugar-free gum in the US in 1989.

Wrigley has invested in operations that facilitate chewing gum production. Wrigley's L.A. Dreyfus subsidiary makes gum base for Wrigley and other gum manufacturers. Its Northwestern Chemical subsidiary processes mint and flavorings for Wrigley and other food producers. Wrigley's Wrico division makes the packaging for Wrigley's products.

Wrigley owns Amurol Products, best known for its Hubba Bubba brand, which makes bubble gum, suckers, baseball cards, and other products targeted for youth.

Wrigley is noted as a fiscally conservative company, one responding to market changes cautiously, understating assets, and holding no long-term debt.

WHEN

William Wrigley, Jr., a rebellious Philadelphia youth, got a start in sales at the age of 13. After being expelled from school, he was put to work by his father selling door to door. Wrigley was amazingly successful. In 1891 he moved to Chicago to sell soap and added baking powder to his product line. Wrigley began offering customers free chewing gum made of spruce gum and paraffin by Zeno Manufacturing (1892) and received numerous requests to buy the gum. Simultaneously, chicle (a naturally sweet gum base from Central America) was being imported for the rubber industry. Wrigley successfully gambled on the idea that chicle would work as a main ingredient for chewing gum.

By 1893 Wrigley had introduced Spearmint and Juicy Fruit and was selling only gum. He continued to use sales incentives, offering dealers counter scales, cash registers, and display cases for volume purchases. In 1898 he merged with Zeno to form Wm. Wrigley, Jr. & Co. By 1910 Spearmint gum was the leading US brand, and Wrigley began international expansion in Canada (1910), Australia (1915), and Great Britain (1927).

The Wrigley family bought real estate, including Catalina Island (1919) and the Arizona Biltmore Hotel (1931), and purchased the Chicago Cubs (1924; sold in 1981) as part of their estate. Another building, the Wrigley, constructed in Chicago in 1924, is owned by the company. Wrigley was keen on advertising; by the time of his death (1932), the company was the largest single-product advertiser. At that time son Philip took over.

For over 75 years the company made only 3 gums: Doublemint (introduced in 1914), Spearmint, and Juicy Fruit. During WWII Wrigley could not obtain the desired ingredients for his products; instead, the company produced inferior gum under a different label but kept the Wrigley brand alive with a picture of his former gum and the ad slogan "Remember this Wrapper." It worked; after the war Wrigley's popularity increased. The company did not raise its original $0.05 price until 1971, when management grudgingly went to $0.07.

By 1974 Wrigley faced severe competition from sugar-free gums. In spite of declining market share, management refused to bring out a sugar-free gum, instead introducing Freedent for denture wearers. Later the company introduced Big Red (1975); Orbit, a sugar-free gum that flopped because its sweetener was labeled a possible carcinogen (1977); and Hubba Bubba (1978). Philip died in 1977, and a 3rd-generation Wrigley (William III, president since 1961) took over. In 1984 Wrigley finally introduced a successful sugar-free gum, Extra, now the top sugar-free gum in the US.

HOW MUCH

	9 Yr. Growth	1980	1981	1982	1983	1984	1985	1986	1987	1988	1989
Sales ($ mil)	6.6%	558	608	581	582	591	620	699	781	891	993
Net income ($ mil)	14.8%	31	28	36	39	40	44	54	70	87	106
Income as % of sales	—	5.5%	4.7%	6.2%	6.7%	6.7%	7.0%	7.7%	9.0%	9.8%	10.7%
Earnings per share ($)	17.1%	0.65	0.60	0.76	0.85	0.93	1.03	1.28	1.69	2.18	2.70
Stock price – high ($)	—	6.67	7.21	7.67	9.38	10.00	15.83	26.00	35.50	41.00	53.75
Stock price – low ($)	—	4.83	5.29	4.85	6.54	7.50	9.58	13.75	19.50	32.00	35.50
Stock price – close ($)	29.5%	5.25	5.83	6.71	8.77	9.96	15.50	22.88	34.56	36.13	53.63
P/E – high	—	10	12	10	11	11	15	20	21	19	20
P/E – low	—	7	9	6	8	8	9	11	12	15	13
Dividends per share ($)	16.3%	0.35	0.37	0.39	0.42	0.47	0.52	0.62	0.85	1.09	1.36
Book value per share ($)	6.5%	4.95	5.18	5.27	5.38	5.43	6.13	6.93	7.18	7.77	8.73

1989 Year End:
Debt ratio: 0.0%
Return on equity: 32.7%
Cash (mil): $109
Current ratio: 2.08
Long-term debt (mil): —
Number of shares (mil): 39
Dividends:
1989 average yield: 2.5%
1989 payout: 50.4%
Market value (mil): $2,107

Stock Price History high/low 1980-89

60
50
40
30
20
10
0

NYSE symbol: WWY
Incorporated: Delaware, 1927
Fiscal year ends: December 31

WHO

President and CEO: William Wrigley III, age 56, $680,667 pay
EVP: R. Darrell Ewers, age 56, $441,250 pay
SVP: Paul W. Rogers, age 63, $246,704 pay
VP Finance: Edmund R. Meyer, age 60
Auditors: Ernst & Young
Employees: 5,380

WHERE

HQ: 410 N. Michigan Ave., Chicago, IL 60611
Phone: 312-644-2121
FAX: 312-345-4083 (Marketing)

Wrigley gum is produced in 13 company-owned factories worldwide and is sold in over 100 countries. The company's largest markets outside the US in 1989 were Australia, Canada, West Germany, the Philippines, Taiwan, and the UK.

	1989 Sales		1989 Operating Income	
	$ mil	% of total	$ mil	% of total
US	675	65	109	64
Europe	211	20	31	19
Other	159	15	29	17
Adjustments	(52)	—	(16)	—
Total	**993**	**100**	**153**	**100**

WHAT

US Brands (Gum)
Big Red
Doublemint
Extra
Freedent
Juicy Fruit
Spearmint
Winter Fresh

Foreign Brands (Gum)
Arrowmint
Big Boy
Big G
Freedent
Juicy Fruit
Orbit
P.K.

Amurol Products Brands
Big League Chew
Bubble Tape
Hubba Bubba
Reed's Candy

Real Estate
Wrigley Building, Chicago

RANKINGS

345th in *Fortune* 500 Industrial Cos.
324th in *Business Week* 1000
898th in *Business Week* Global 1000

COMPETITION

RJR Nabisco
Warner-Lambert

WOOLWORTH CORPORATION

OVERVIEW

Once the king of downtown dime stores, the Woolworth Corporation is now also a worldwide leader in specialty retailing, all operations generating $8.8 billion in sales in 1989. The 8,074 stores in the US, Canada, Australia, Germany, the Netherlands, and Belgium sell general merchandise, clothing, shoes, sporting goods, and accessories in more than 40 different store formats.

Although more than 1,400 Woolworth variety stores are still in business, recent expansion is focused on more than 6,400 specialty stores, such as Kinney Shoes and the Foot Locker stores (athletic shoes). In 1989 the company opened a net of 411 new specialty stores.

Perhaps more than any other US retailer, Woolworth has realized the potential of foreign markets, which in 1989 accounted for 42% of sales.

WHEN

With the idea of selling merchandise priced at no more than 5 cents (and later 10 cents), Frank W. Woolworth opened The Great Five Cent Store in Utica, New York, in 1879. It failed. That same year he moved to Lancaster, Pennsylvania, creating the first five-and-dime, and this time he succeeded.

Woolworth moved headquarters of the small chain to New York City (1886) and spent the rest of the century acquiring other dime store chains. The company also expanded into Canada (1897) and later England (1909), France (1922), and Germany (1926).

With $10 million in sales, the 120-store chain incorporated as F.W. Woolworth & Company, with Frank Woolworth as president (1905). In 1912 the company merged with 5 rival chains and went public with 596 stores, producing $52 million in sales the first year.

Woolworth's early success stemmed from a solid financial basis (competitive pricing and cash-only business practices) and effective management policies (internal promotion with managers paid on commission).

Frugal with his business, Frank Woolworth built lavish homes and corporate headquarters. From 1911 to 1913, paying $13.5 million in cash, he constructed the 50-story Woolworth Building, then the world's tallest skyscraper (792 feet). When Woolworth died in 1919, the chain had 1,081 stores with sales of $119 million.

In 1932 the company added a 20-cent line of merchandise and soon abolished price limits (1935). Woolworth became more competitive after WWII by advertising, establishing revolving credit and self-service, moving stores to the suburbs, and expanding merchandise selections. In 1962 Woolworth opened Woolco, a US and Canadian discount chain. The US stores were closed, but the Canadian Woolco stores remain.

Since the 1960s the company has become a specialty retail company, growing through acquisitions and expansions of US, Canadian, Australian, and European footwear, apparel, and sporting goods chains. Acquisitions have included G.R. Kinney (shoes, 1963); Richman Brothers (men's clothing, 1969); Holtzman's Little Folk Shop (1983); Champs (sporting goods, 1987); Moderna Shuh Center (shoes, Germany, 1988); Mathers (shoes, Australia, 1988); and Profoot (Netherlands and Belgium, 1990).

In 1974 the company developed Foot Locker, the athletic shoe chain, later spinning off Lady Foot Locker (1982) and Kids Foot Locker (1987). Woolworth Express (1987) is a smaller version of the original dime store.

Since 1980 specialty stores have increased from 2,936 to 6,438 while general merchandise stores have decreased from 1,851 to 1,636. Woolworth anticipates opening more dime stores in Germany, although over 90% of projected company-wide expansion (825 new stores planned) will be in specialty formats in 1990.

HOW MUCH

	9 Yr. Growth	1980	1981	1982	1983	1984	1985	1986	1987	1988	1989
Sales ($ mil)	2.3%	7,218	7,223	5,124	5,456	5,737	5,958	6,501	7,134	8,088	8,820
Net income ($ mil)	8.3%	161	82	82	118	141	177	214	251	288	329
Income as % of sales	—	2.2%	1.1%	1.6%	2.2%	2.5%	3.0%	3.3%	3.5%	3.6%	3.7%
Earnings per share ($)	7.8%	1.28	0.65	0.65	0.92	1.10	1.36	1.61	1.89	2.22	2.53
Stock price – high ($)	—	7.31	6.91	7.28	9.84	9.72	15.63	24.50	29.81	30.38	36.13
Stock price – low ($)	—	5.28	4.25	3.97	5.66	7.47	9.16	14.53	14.75	17.06	24.19
Stock price – close ($)	20.0%	6.19	4.50	6.47	8.78	9.25	15.00	19.31	17.25	25.88	31.94
P/E – high	—	6	11	11	11	9	11	15	16	14	14
P/E – low	—	4	7	6	6	7	7	9	8	8	10
Dividends per share ($)	8.5%	0.45	0.45	0.45	0.45	0.45	0.50	0.56	0.66	0.82	0.94
Book value per share ($)	3.6%	11.68	11.28	8.13	8.16	8.33	9.53	11.32	13.33	14.40	16.08

1989 Year End:
Debt ratio: 12.8%
Return on equity: 16.6%
Cash (mil): $56
Current ratio: 1.72
Long-term debt (mil): $306
Number of shares (mil): 129
Dividends:
 1989 average yield: 2.9%
 1989 payout: 37.2%
Market value (mil): $4,120

Stock Price History high/low 1980-89

40 35 30 25 20 15 10 5 0

NYSE symbol: Z
Incorporated: New York, 1989
Fiscal year ends: Last Saturday in January

WHO

Chairman and CEO: Harold E. Sells, age 61, $2,157,527 pay
President and COO: Frederick E. Hennig, age 57, $1,445,144 pay
EVP Administration: Arnold S. Anderson, age 55, $1,138,635
EVP Finance and CFO: William K. Lavin, age 45, $1,108,525
Auditors: Price Waterhouse
Employees: 77,000 full-time and 61,000 part-time

WHERE

HQ: 233 Broadway, New York, NY 10279
Phone: 212-553-2000
FAX: 212-553-2042 (Public Affairs)

The Woolworth Corporation is a multinational retail operation with 8,074 stores in the US, Canada, Australia, Germany, the Netherlands, and Belgium.

	1989 Sales		1989 Operating Income	
	$ mil	% of total	$ mil	% of total
US	5,151	58	399	61
Foreign	3,790	42	258	39
Adjustments	(121)	—	(42)	—
Total	**8,820**	**100**	**615**	**100**

WHAT

	1989 Sales		1989 Operating Income	
	$ mil	% of total	$ mil	% of total
General merchandise	5,164	58	307	47
Specialty stores	3,777	42	350	53
Adjustments	(121)	—	(42)	—
Total	**8,820**	**100**	**615**	**100**

Specialty Stores	No. of Stores 1/27/90
Kinney (shoes)	1,697
Foot Locker (athletic footwear)	1,309
Lady Foot Locker (athletic footwear)	596
Kids Foot Locker (athletic footwear)	23
Kids Mart (children's apparel)	430
Afterthoughts/Carimar (boutique)	314
Susie's (women's apparel)	224
Champs Sports (sporting goods)	199
Athletic X-Press (sporting goods)	196
Williams the Shoeman (shoes)	171
Mathers (shoes)	155
Richman (men's and women's apparel)	145
Other formats	979
Total	**6,438**

General Merchandise Stores	No. of Stores 1/27/90
Woolworth-US	1,024
Woolworth-Germany	222
Woolworth-Canada	159
Woolco	120
Other formats	111
Total	**1,636**

RANKINGS

12th in *Fortune* 50 Retailing Cos.
88th in *Forbes* Sales 500
153rd in *Business Week* 1000
442nd in *Business Week* Global 1000

COMPETITION

General merchandise and specialty retail companies

XEROX CORPORATION

OVERVIEW

Xerox is the world's leading manufacturer of high-end copiers and duplicating equipment, holding over 50% of the US market. Its name is synonymous with photocopying. In recent years it has all but ceded the low-end copier market to Japanese manufacturers.

At its world-renowned Palo Alto Research Center (PARC), Xerox pioneered a number of technical advances fundamental to the revolution in office automation. However, it failed to capitalize on such innovations as networking standards (Ethernet), the personal computer (Alto II), and the graphical user interface for personal computers, allowing others (most notably Apple) to profit from them. Xerox's foray into financial services has been distracting and, lately, unprofitable.

Xerox is again innovating. Its new multifunction device will have copying, laser printing, scanning, and FAX functions. What remains to be seen is whether a market will exist for these products.

WHEN

The Haloid Company was incorporated in 1906 to make and sell photographic paper. In 1935 it bought the Rectigraph Company (photocopiers), which led Haloid to take a license for a new process of electrophotography (later renamed xerography from the ancient Greek words for dry and writing) from the Battelle Memorial Institute in 1947. Battelle had backed inventor Chester Carlson, who had labored since 1937 to perfect a process of transferring electrostatic images from a photoconductive surface to paper.

Joseph C. Wilson, president of Haloid, poured money into commercializing the process. Haloid introduced the manually operated Model A copier in 1949 and the Xerox Copyflo, which made continuous copies on plain paper, in 1955. By 1956 xerographic products represented 40% of the company's sales. The company became Haloid Xerox in 1958 and, in 1959, introduced the Xerox 914, the first simplified office copier. The 914 took the world by storm, beating out competing mimeograph (A.B. Dick), thermal paper (3M), and damp copy (Kodak) technologies. Xerox's revenues soared from $37 million in 1960 to $268 million in 1965, along the way dropping Haloid from its name (1961) and entering the *Fortune* 500 (1962).

The company continued to grow in the 1960s and began to diversify. It bought into publishing (Wesleyan University Press, 1965; Learning Materials Inc., 1966; R.R. Bowker, 1967) and computers (Scientific Data Systems, 1969), all of which were subsequently sold or discontinued. It was during this time that the ideas for the personal computer were being conceived.

In the 1970s Xerox bought companies that made printers (Diablo, 1972), plotters (Versatec, 1975), and disk drives (Shugart, 1977; sold 1984); it also bought international record carrier Western Union International (1979, sold 1982). In 1974 the company lost its monopoly on xerographic patents when the FTC, believing Xerox was too dominant in the market, forced the company to license other manufacturers to use the technology.

The 1980s saw the company continue to buy image technology companies in optical character recognition (Kurzweill, 1980) and scanning and FAX (Datacopy, 1988); it also entered financial services, buying insurance companies (Crum & Forster, 1983) and investment banking companies (Van Kampen Merritt, 1984), among others.

The Xerox of the late 1980s was a conglomerate of increasingly troublesome financial units and an imaging technology unit that, despite past successes and great innovations, had failed to develop an identifiable strategy for its future. The company entered the 1990s planning the disposal of many of its financial units and sounding a new corporate theme, "Xerox. The Document Company."

HOW MUCH

	9 Yr. Growth	1980	1981	1982	1983	1984	1985	1986	1987	1988	1989
Sales ($ mil)	8.3%	8,197	8,691	8,456	8,464	8,792	8,732	9,355	10,320	15,994	16,806
Net income ($ mil)	1.4%	619	598	368	466	376	381	488	578	388	704
Income as % of sales	—	7.6%	6.9%	4.3%	5.5%	4.3%	4.4%	5.2%	5.6%	2.4%	4.2%
Earnings per share ($)	(1.3%)	7.18	6.94	4.29	4.36	3.38	3.40	4.44	5.25	3.49	6.41
Stock price – high ($)	—	71.75	64.00	41.75	52.13	51.13	60.50	72.25	85.00	63.00	69.00
Stock price – low ($)	—	48.63	37.38	27.13	35.00	33.25	37.25	48.63	50.00	50.25	54.38
Stock price – close ($)	(0.5%)	59.88	40.50	37.38	49.50	37.88	59.75	60.00	56.63	58.38	57.25
P/E – high	—	10	9	10	12	15	18	16	16	18	11
P/E – low	—	7	5	6	8	10	11	11	10	14	8
Dividends per share ($)	0.8%	2.80	3.00	3.00	3.00	3.00	3.00	3.00	3.00	3.00	3.00
Book value per share ($)	2.5%	42.90	44.11	43.96	44.40	42.77	45.47	48.00	51.00	52.22	53.61

1989 Year End:
Debt ratio: 56.3%
Return on equity: 12.1%
Cash (mil): $1,219
Current ratio: —
Long-term debt (mil): $7,511
Number of shares (mil): 94
Dividends:
1989 average yield: 5.2%
1989 payout: 46.8%
Market value (mil): $5,377

Stock Price History high/low 1980-89

NYSE symbol: XRX
Incorporated: New York, 1906
Fiscal year ends: December 31

WHO

Chairman: David T. Kearns, age 59, $1,347,918 pay
President and CEO: Paul A. Allaire, age 51, $929,288 pay (prior to promotion)
SVP and CFO: Stuart B. Ross, age 52
Auditors: KPMG Peat Marwick
Employees: 111,400

WHERE

HQ: PO Box 1600, 800 Long Ridge Rd., Stamford, CT 06904
Phone: 203-968-3000
FAX: 203-968-4312 (Public Relations)

Xerox has manufacturing and engineering facilities in the US and 6 foreign countries. It sells business products in over 130 countries.

	1989 Sales		1989 Net Income	
	$ mil	% of total	$ mil	% of total
US	11,542	65	530	69
Europe	4,225	24	74	10
Other	1,868	11	160	21
Adjustments	(829)	—	(60)	—
Total	**16,806**	**100**	**704**	**100**

WHAT

	1989 Sales		1989 Operating Income	
	$ mil	% of total	$ mil	% of total
Business equip.	11,720	67	875	57
Equip. financing	711	4	258	17
3rd-party financing	406	2	44	3
Insurance	4,591	26	331	21
Investment banking	207	1	39	3
Adjustments	(829)	—	(281)	—
Total	**16,806**	**100**	**1,266**	**100**

Business Products & Systems
Copiers
Duplicators
Networks
Printers
Scanners
Software and supplies
Typewriters
Workstations

Financial Services
Crum and Forster, Inc. (insurance)
Furman Selz (investment advice and services)
Van Kampen Merritt Inc. (trusts and funds)
Xerox Credit Corp. (purchase financing)
Xerox Life (insurance)

Other
Computer services
Medical systems
Realty
Technology ventures
Venture capital
Voice systems

RANKINGS

21st in *Fortune* 500 Industrial Cos.
54th in *Fortune* Global 500 Industrial Cos.
37th in *Fortune* 50 Exporters
28th in *Forbes* Sales 500
118th in *Business Week* 1000
428th in *Business Week* Global 1000

COMPETITION

Eastman Kodak
Harris
IBM
Matsushita
3M
Mitsubishi
Pitney Bowes
Insurance and financial services companies
Other imaging and office automation companies

YELLOW FREIGHT SYSTEM

OVERVIEW

Yellow Freight, unlike its main trucking competitors (Consolidated Freightways and Roadway), focuses almost exclusively on long-haul freight transportation, serving 35,000 destinations throughout the US, Puerto Rico, and 6 Canadian provinces. In 1989 Yellow transported 8.4 million tons of freight over more than 693 million route miles. Less-than-truckload shipments (those weighing less than 10,000 pounds) accounted for most of the freight carried.

Sales have been $2 billion strong for the last 2 years, but 1989 profits plunged 72% from 1988, primarily due to price cutting in the industry that year. As with other trucking companies, most of Yellow's expenses are labor related, and a 3% wage and employee benefits hike in 1989 (with another 3% planned in 1990) also contributed to the earnings slump. Rising fuel prices also affected earnings, and Overland Energy, Yellow's petroleum exploration unit, is seeking new reserves to help reduce energy costs.

Since 1952, 3 generations of the George Powell family have managed Yellow's day-to-day operations. The company's stock is 12% manager-owned, and another 17% is controlled by the Powells and the Powell Family Foundation.

OTC symbol: YELL
Incorporated: Delaware, 1983
Fiscal year ends: December 31

WHO

Chairman and CEO: George E. Powell, Jr., age 63, $662,786 pay
President: George E. Powell III, age 41, $450,728 pay
SVP Finance and Administration: David E. Loeffler, age 43, $285,750 pay
SVP Marketing: Robert W. Burdick, age 47, $275,875 pay
SVP Properties and Purchasing: Forrest H. Burm, age 60
SVP Operations: M. Reid Armstrong, age 52, $270, 825 pay
SVP and Secretary: Stephen P. Murphy, age 63
Auditors: Arthur Andersen & Co.
Employees: 29,200

WHEN

In 1924 A. J. Harrell established a trucking company in conjunction with his Oklahoma City Yellow Cab franchise. Operating as a part of the Yellow Cab Transit Company, Harrell's trucking operation hauled less-than-truckload (LTL) shipments between Oklahoma City and Tulsa. By 1944 the company was operating in Texas, Kansas, Missouri, Illinois, Indiana, and Kentucky, through 51 independent subsidiaries. However, its policy of high dividends inhibited growth, and by 1951 Yellow faced bankruptcy.

The company was losing about $75,000 a month when George Powell, formerly of Riss & Company (one of the leading trucking companies of the time), took over (1952). Within 5 months Yellow was profitable again.

Powell had decided to concentrate on long-haul interstate operations (for example, from Chicago to Los Angeles) rather than shorter hauls of a few hundred miles. To accomplish this Yellow needed a more extensive route network, so Powell established a central dispatch office in Kansas City and began to buy other trucking companies to extend Yellow's operations.

Renamed Yellow Freight System in 1968, the company expanded to the West Coast and Southeast in 1965 by purchasing Watson-Wilson Transportation System and gained routes in the Northeast in 1970 by acquiring a part of the Norwalk Truck Lines. Other purchases, including Adley Express (1973), connected Yellow's routes in the Northeast and the Southeast.

Yellow extended routes into the Pacific Northwest by purchasing Republic Freight Systems (1975). It bought Braswell Motor Freight, consolidating its routes in Texas, California, and the Southeast in 1977. Yellow's only deviation from route acquisitions was its $4 million investment in Overland Energy (oil and gas exploration company) in 1976.

The company was unprepared, however, when Congress passed the Motor Carrier Act of 1980, deregulating operating routes and shipping rates. Yellow began a belated effort to upgrade its aging depots and terminals, but still experienced a decline in earnings between 1980 and 1983. In 1982 the company established new centers at Denver and St. Paul, extending service to all 50 states in 1987, when a terminal opened in Alaska. Revenues exceeded $2 billion in 1988 and continued to grow, to $2.2 billion in 1989. However, profits were down due to discounting and rising fuel and labor costs.

WHERE

HQ: Yellow Freight System, Inc. of Delaware
10990 Roe Ave., PO Box 7563, Overland Park, KS 66207
Phone: 913-345-1020
FAX: 913-345-3433

Yellow Freight operates 25 hubs and 640 terminals throughout the US, Puerto Rico, and the Canadian provinces of Alberta, British Columbia, Manitoba, Ontario, Quebec, and Saskatchewan. The company owns 44,385 trucks, tractors, and trailers.

WHAT

	1989 Sales*	
	$ mil	% of total
Less-than-truckload	1,987	91
Truckload	203	9
Total	**2,190**	**100**

*Sales do not include Yellow Freight's Canadian subsidiaries.

Subsidiaries
Yellow Freight System of British Columbia, Inc.
Between British Columbia and the US
Yellow Freight System of Ontario, Inc.
Ontario and between Ontario and the US
Yellow Freight System, Inc.
50 states, Puerto Rico, Canadian provinces of Alberta, Manitoba, Quebec, and Saskatchewan

RANKINGS

21st in *Fortune* 50 Transportation Cos.
369th in *Forbes* Sales 500
639th in *Business Week* 1000

COMPETITION

Burlington Northern
Consolidated Freightways
Roadway
Union Pacific
Other railroads

HOW MUCH

	9 Yr. Growth	1980	1981	1982	1983	1984	1985	1986	1987	1988	1989
Sales ($ mil)	12.4%	776	936	936	1,089	1,380	1,530	1,714	1,760	2,016	2,220
Net income ($ mil)	(1.4%)	21	16	11	49	44	56	67	41	69	19
Income as % of sales	—	2.7%	1.8%	1.1%	4.5%	3.2%	3.6%	3.9%	2.3%	3.4%	0.8%
Earnings per share ($)	(1.4%)	0.74	0.58	0.38	1.73	1.55	1.95	2.35	1.44	2.40	0.65
Stock price – high ($)	—	9.50	10.63	10.75	24.25	22.81	29.88	41.50	42.50	34.00	32.88
Stock price – low ($)	—	6.00	7.38	5.44	9.25	11.63	15.81	27.50	20.88	23.88	23.88
Stock price – close ($)	14.8%	7.75	7.88	9.50	21.50	16.00	29.00	36.88	27.88	31.63	26.75
P/E – high	—	13	18	29	14	15	15	18	30	14	51
P/E – low	—	8	13	15	5	8	8	12	15	10	37
Dividends per share ($)	7.5%	0.38	0.40	0.42	0.44	0.48	0.52	0.58	0.62	0.66	0.73
Book value per share ($)	9.4%	6.76	7.53	7.48	8.77	9.84	11.27	13.14	13.82	14.21	15.24

1989 Year End:
Debt ratio: 29.9%
Return on equity: 4.4%
Cash (mil): $4
Current ratio: 0.99
Long-term debt (mil): $187
Number of shares (mil): 29
Dividends:
1989 average yield: 2.7%
1989 payout: 112.3%
Market value (mil): $770

Stock Price History
high/low 1980-89

45 40 35 30 25 20 15 10 5 0

YOUNG & RUBICAM INC.

OVERVIEW

Young & Rubicam is the largest independent advertising agency (measured by billings) in the US and the 3rd largest in the world after holding companies Dentsu (Japan) and Saatchi & Saatchi (UK).

Of the largest agencies in the US, it is one of only a few that are privately held. This has worked to its advantage with clients who are concerned about privacy and conflicts of interest. It promotes from within, distributes equity widely within the management ranks and, perhaps as a consequence, enjoys an unusually high degree of employee loyalty in an industry known for job hopping.

Y&R prides itself on creativity grounded in solid market research and, along with its competition, has in recent years been expanding its range of services beyond pure media advertising to provide clients with an integrated approach to marketing products and services. It now has 6 divisions providing advertising, public relations, sales promotion, corporate identity consulting, direct marketing, and health care communications.

Private company
Founded: Pennsylvania, 1923
Fiscal year ends: December 31

WHO

Chairman and CEO: Alexander S. Kroll
President: Peter A. Georgescu
EVP and CFO: Roger Craton
EVP, Secretary, and General Counsel: R. John Cooper
EVP and Executive Creative Director: Frazier Purdy
Auditors: Price Waterhouse
Employees: 10,473

WHEN

Raymond Rubicam and John Orr Young founded the advertising agency that bears their names in Philadelphia in 1923 quite literally on a shoestring — their first client was Presto Quick Tip Shoelaces. Y&R got its first major client, General Foods, when it asked for and received the account for the company's least successful product, a beverage. Its success in increasing sales of that product, Postum, led to more business with General Foods and to a move to New York in 1926 at that client's request. With its informal atmosphere and tolerance for eccentric behavior, the agency soon became a haven for the leading creative people in the industry.

In 1931 the firm opened its second office — in Chicago. In the early 1930s Rubicam, who by then dominated the firm, recruited George Gallup to create the first research department in the industry. In 1934 Young (who had a relaxed approach to business) was forced out of the agency, which despite its unconventional working environment had become an intensely hard-driving place.

Although the Great Depression put many agencies out of business, Y&R prospered. Billings grew from $6 million in 1927 to $22 million in 1937, making Y&R the 2nd largest agency (behind J. Walter Thompson).

WWII brought surprising prosperity to the advertising industry. By 1945 Y&R's billings had reached $53 million. Rubicam, suffering from professional ennui and indulging a desire to lead a less hectic life, retired to Arizona in 1944 at age 52.

During the 1950s the agency prospered; billings reached $212 million in 1960. During the 1960s, Y&R was a leading creative force in the field, producing the first color television commercials and fielding a series of notable advertising campaigns. The emphasis on creativity, teamwork, and group management instilled in the firm by Rubicam worked. However, it was also during this period that growth slowed, and expenses and staff grew.

In 1970 Edward Ney took over as CEO, cutting staff and installing Alex Kroll as creative director. Kroll required that creativity be controlled, disciplined, and quantifiable by sales results. Ney expanded the agency through acquisitions paid for with internally generated cash. Acquisitions included Wunderman Worldwide (direct marketing, 1973), Cato Johnson (sales promotion, 1976), and Burson-Marsteller (one of the largest public relations firms in the US, 1979).

In 1975, when Kroll became president of US operations, Y&R's billings of $477 million had made it the #1 agency in America. Since 1979 it has been the largest independent agency in the US. The 1980s saw challenges to Y&R's dominance from the growth of such huge holding company agencies as Saatchi & Saatchi and from other large agencies with higher rates of growth. Y&R's size and concomitant bureaucracy also threatened its reputation for creativity.

In 1985 Kroll became CEO and in 1987 began taking steps to reorganize the huge New York office into 3 smaller groups, each with a general manager and creative director. By 1990 Y&R had expanded its overseas operations to Zimbabwe and Kenya. Through its joint venture in the USSR, Y&R/Sovero, it will attempt to facilitate joint ventures for western companies that need Soviet operating partners.

WHERE

HQ: 285 Madison Ave., New York, NY 10017
Phone: 212-210-3000
FAX: 212-490-6397

Y&R has 322 offices in 45 countries and territories.

	Billings		Sales	
	$ mil	% of total	$ mil	% of total
US	3,115	50	409	47
Foreign	3,136	50	456	53
Total	**6,251**	**100**	**865**	**100**

WHAT

	1989 Billings	
	$ mil	% of total
Advertising & other	4,577	73
Public relations	827	13
Direct marketing	532	9
Health care communications	164	3
Sales promotion	151	2
Total	**6,251**	**100**

Divisions
Young & Rubicam Advertising
Burson-Marsteller (public relations)
Cato Johnson (sales promotion)
Landor Associates (corporate identity management)
Sudler & Hennessey (health care communications)
Wunderman Worldwide (direct marketing)

Subsidiaries
Young & Rubican Ventures (consumer marketing investment banking services)

Joint Ventures
HDM (with Dentsu and Eurocom)
Y&R/Sovero (with Sovero of Moscow)

Representative Clients
American Home Products
Arthur Andersen
AT&T
BSN
Chevron
Clorox
Colgate-Palmolive
Dr Pepper/Seven-Up
Du Pont
Eastman Kodak
Ford
Hartmarx
H. J. Heinz
Johnson & Johnson
Metropolitan Life
Monsanto
Motorola
Navistar
NYNEX
RJR Nabisco
Time Warner
TWA
Unisys
Warner-Lambert
Xerox

Notable Campaigns
"Nobody can eat just one" (Lay's potato chips)
"There's always room for Jell-O"
"Excedrin headache"

HOW MUCH

	9 Yr. Growth	1980	1981	1982	1983	1984	1985	1986	1987	1988	1989
Total billings ($ mil)	11.9%	2,273	2,334	2,512	2,761	3,202	3,575	4,191	4,905	5,390	6,251
Total sales ($ mil)	10.9%	341	350	377	414	480	536	628	736	758	865
US billings ($ mil)	9.9%	1,334	1,490	1,645	1,828	2,155	2,272	2,389	2,577	2,792	3,115
US sales ($ mil)	8.3%	200	223	247	274	323	341	358	386	373	410
Employees	11.9%	3,804	6,861	7,025	7,745	8,418	9,030	10,844	11,634	12,311	10,473

Total Sales ($ mil) 1980-89

900
800
700
600
500
400
300
200
100
0

RANKINGS

212th in *Forbes* 400 US Private Cos.

COMPETITION

Carlson
Dun & Bradstreet
Saatchi & Saatchi

ZENITH ELECTRONICS CORPORATION

OVERVIEW

Zenith has been responsible for much of the innovation in radio and TV technology for over 70 years. Zenith is the last remaining independent color television and picture tube manufacturer in the US. The company's consumer products also include videocassette recorders, computer monitors, cable TV products, and electronics parts and accessories. Zenith also manufactures electronic components, such as monochrome monitors, power supplies, and microcircuits, which are sold to other firms.

In an era of rising costs and intense competition in the consumer electronics field, with net losses in 4 of the past 5 years, Zenith's future may rest on the evolution of the market for high-definition television (HDTV) technology. Zenith planned to increase spending in 1990 on R&D in this area. Zenith is also developing new manufacturing technology for its patented flat-tension-mask, high-resolution picture tube, which has applications in the HDTV and computer-monitor fields.

WHEN

In 1915 Karl Hassel and R. H. G. Mathews, 2 ham radio operators, formed Chicago Radio Laboratory. In 1918 they began manufacturing radio equipment. In 1921 they were joined by Eugene F. McDonald, Jr., a wealthy investor who formed Zenith Radio Corporation in 1923 to act as the sales agent for Chicago Radio Laboratory. Zenith was an early innovator in radio, developing the first portable (1924), the first home receiver to run on alternating current (1926), and the first push-button radio (1927). The Great Depression caused sales to drop 80%, but the company survived. It started a radio station and a television station and began making hearing aids prior to WWII. During the war the company produced radar and communications equipment.

In 1948 Zenith bought the Rauland Corporation, which manufactured picture tubes, and produced its first black-and-white television sets. In 1957 Zenith's Robert Adler invented the first practical television remote control device. By 1959 the company was black-and-white sales leader. In 1961 Zenith introduced its first line of color televisions. In the same year the FCC adopted Zenith's system for broadcasting FM radio in stereo.

During the 1970s and 1980s Zenith had to face the challenge of low-priced Japanese imports. The company led the market in color television sales from 1972 to 1978, but prices were held down by the Japanese "dumping" of television sets in the US market (selling sets in America for less than their cost or home market price). Under the pressure of falling prices, the company moved some of its manufacturing operations to Mexico and Taiwan. Zenith chairman John Nevin lobbied Congress and filed suits against the Japanese TV manufacturers, eventually winning the battle but losing market share.

In 1979, in its first significant move away from the radio and television industry (Zenith had dabbled in hearing aids and watches but had sold these businesses by 1979), Zenith acquired The Heath Company, manufacturers of microcomputers and do-it-yourself electronics kits, for $61.5 million. The company's Zenith Data Systems subsidiary grew from sales of around $10 million in 1980 to over $1 billion in 1989, largely on the strength of government and university contracts for its IBM-compatible personal computers. In 1989 Zenith sold all computer operations, including the industry-leading laptop computer business, to Groupe Bull of France for $496 million. Zenith used the money to pay off all of its current and much of its long-term debt. In 1989 Zenith entered a joint venture with AT&T to develop an HDTV broadcast system which, if adopted, could provide Zenith with substantial royalties in the future.

HOW MUCH

	9 Yr. Growth	1980	1981	1982	1983	1984	1985	1986	1987	1988	1989
Sales ($ mil)	3.0%	1,186	1,275	1,239	1,361	1,716	1,624	1,892	2,363	2,686	1,549
Net income ($ mil)	—	26	16	(22)	46	64	(8)	(10)	(19)	5	(17)
Income as % of sales	—	2.2%	1.2%	(1.8%)	3.4%	3.7%	(0.5%)	(0.5%)	(0.8%)	0.2%	(1.1%)
Earnings per share ($)	—	1.40	0.82	(1.15)	2.11	2.88	(0.33)	(0.43)	(0.78)	0.20	(0.64)
Stock price – high ($)	—	21.25	21.50	16.63	36.00	38.63	25.00	29.88	33.63	30.00	21.50
Stock price – low ($)	—	7.88	10.25	9.75	13.38	19.50	16.25	17.88	10.00	13.50	11.50
Stock price – close ($)	(4.6%)	19.50	11.13	14.38	35.50	19.75	20.50	21.88	14.75	19.00	12.75
P/E – high	—	15	26	—	17	13	—	—	—	150	—
P/E – low	—	6	13	—	6	7	—	—	—	68	—
Dividends per share ($)	(100%)	0.60	0.53	0.15	0.00	0.00	0.00	0.00	0.00	0.00	0.00
Book value per share ($)	(0.4%)	15.43	15.73	14.42	17.08	20.00	18.90	18.49	18.45	18.84	14.90

1989 Year End:
Debt ratio: 27.5%
Return on equity: —
Cash (mil): $176
Current ratio: 1.89
Long-term debt (mil): $151
Number of shares (mil): 27
Dividends:
1989 average yield: 0.0%
1989 payout: —
Market value (mil): $341

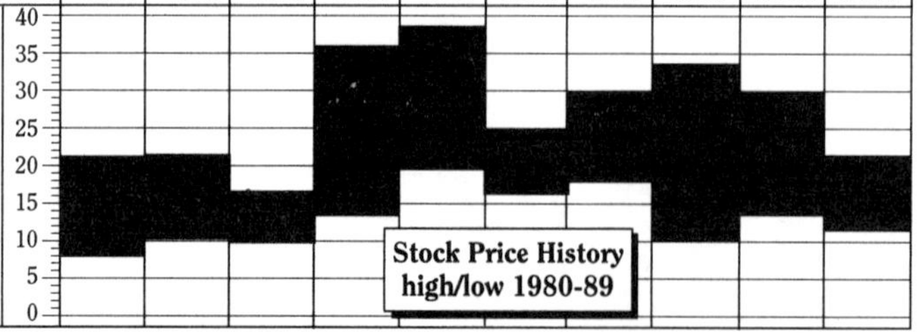

NYSE symbol: ZE
Incorporated: Delaware, 1958
Fiscal year ends: December 31

WHO

Chairman, President, and CEO: Jerry K. Pearlman, age 50, $462,500 pay
President, Consumer Products Group: Robert B. Hansen, age 59, $306,667 pay
President, Components Group: Otto M. Genutis, age 46, $188,433 pay
VP, General Counsel: John Borst, Jr., age 62, $144,800 pay
VP Finance and CFO: Kell B. Benson, age 42
Auditors: Arthur Andersen & Co.
Employees: 32,000

WHERE

HQ: 1000 Milwaukee Avenue, Glenview, IL 60025
Phone: 708-391-7000
FAX: 708-391-7253

Zenith sells its consumer products primarily in the US and Canada.

Factories and Warehouses	
Arizona	1
Canada	4
Chicago	6
Ireland	1
Mexico	14
Missouri	1
Taiwan	1
Texas	3

	1989 Sales		1989 Pretax Income	
	$ mil	% of total	$ mil	% of total
US	1,401	90	(24)	—
Foreign	148	10	7	—
Total	**1,549**	**100**	**(17)**	**—**

WHAT

	1989 Sales		1989 Operating Income	
	$ mil	% of total	$ mil	% of total
Consumer electronics	1,288	83	—	—
Components	261	17	6	—
Adjustments	—	—	(19)	—
Total	**1,549**	**100**	**(13)**	**—**

Products
Cable TV management software
Camcorders
Color television receivers
Hybrid circuits
Pay TV decoders
Power supplies
Television picture tubes
Videocassette recorders

RANKINGS

169th in *Fortune* 500 Industrial Cos.
476th in *Fortune* Global 500 Industrial Cos.
479th in *Forbes* Sales 500

COMPETITION

General Electric
Hitachi
Matsushita
Mitsubishi
NEC
Philips
Samsung
Sony
Tandy
Thomson

The Indexes

INDEX OF PROFILES BY INDUSTRY

INDEX OF PROFILES BY INDUSTRY

INDEX OF PROFILES BY HEADQUARTERS LOCATION

A

B

I

J

K

☐ I want to order _____ copies of *HOOVER'S HANDBOOK 1991* ($19.95 plus $1.95 shipping and handling).

☐ I want to order _____ copies of *HOOVER'S HANDBOOK 1992* (prepublication price $21.95 for orders placed prior to 5/31/91, plus $1.95 shipping and handling).

☐ Send me information about future *HOOVER'S HANDBOOKs*.

☐ I have the following suggestions for future editions:

____

____

____

Name ______________________ Telephone No. (   ) ____________

Street Address ______________________________

City ______________________ State _______ Zip _______

☐ American Express ☐ Visa ☐ MasterCard Account No. ______________

Signature ______________________ Expiration Date _______

THE REFERENCE PRESS, INC.
Phone: (512) 454-7778 Austin, Texas FAX: (512) 454-9401

☐ I want to order _____ copies of *HOOVER'S HANDBOOK 1991* ($19.95 plus $1.95 shipping and handling).

☐ I want to order _____ copies of *HOOVER'S HANDBOOK 1992* (prepublication price $21.95 for orders placed prior to 5/31/91, plus $1.95 shipping and handling).

☐ Send me information about future *HOOVER'S HANDBOOKs*.

☐ I have the following suggestions for future editions:

____

____

____

Name ______________________ Telephone No. (   ) ____________

Street Address ______________________________

City ______________________ State _______ Zip _______

☐ American Express ☐ Visa ☐ MasterCard Account No. ______________

Signature ______________________ Expiration Date _______

THE REFERENCE PRESS, INC.
Phone: (512) 454-7778 Austin, Texas FAX: (512) 454-9401

☐ I want to order _____ copies of *HOOVER'S HANDBOOK 1991* ($19.95 plus $1.95 shipping and handling).

☐ I want to order _____ copies of *HOOVER'S HANDBOOK 1992* (prepublication price $21.95 for orders placed prior to 5/31/91, plus $1.95 shipping and handling).

☐ Send me information about future *HOOVER'S HANDBOOKs*.

☐ I have the following suggestions for future editions:

____

____

____

Name ______________________ Telephone No. (   ) ____________

Street Address ______________________________

City ______________________ State _______ Zip _______

☐ American Express ☐ Visa ☐ MasterCard Account No. ______________

Signature ______________________ Expiration Date _______

THE REFERENCE PRESS, INC.
Phone: (512) 454-7778 Austin, Texas FAX: (512) 454-9401

BUSINESS REPLY MAIL

FIRST-CLASS MAIL PERMIT NO. 7641 AUSTIN, TEXAS

POSTAGE WILL BE PAID BY ADDRESSEE

THE REFERENCE PRESS INC
6448 HWY 290 E STE E 104
AUSTIN TX 78723-9828

BUSINESS REPLY MAIL

FIRST-CLASS MAIL PERMIT NO. 7641 AUSTIN, TEXAS

POSTAGE WILL BE PAID BY ADDRESSEE

THE REFERENCE PRESS INC
6448 HWY 290 E STE E 104
AUSTIN TX 78723-9828

BUSINESS REPLY MAIL

FIRST-CLASS MAIL PERMIT NO. 7641 AUSTIN, TEXAS

POSTAGE WILL BE PAID BY ADDRESSEE

THE REFERENCE PRESS INC
6448 HWY 290 E STE E 104
AUSTIN TX 78723-9828

L

M

N

O

P

Q

R

S

T

U

V

INDEX OF COMPANIES AND PRODUCTS NAMED IN THE PROFILES

Note: Page numbers in boldface indicate the company's profile. Lightface page numbers indicate references to other profiles.

A

B

C

D

E

G

H

K

L

N

O

P

Q

R

S

T

W

X

Y

Z

Notes

Notes